A2 ALTITUDE CORRECTION TABLES 10°-90°—SUN, STARS, PLANETS

SUN

OCT.—MAR. App. Alt.	Lower Limb	Upper Limb	APR.—SEPT. App. Alt.	Lower Limb	Upper Limb
° ′	′	′	° ′	′	′
9 33			9 39		
	+10·8	−21·5		+10·6	−21·2
9 45			9 50		
	+10·9	−21·4		+10·7	−21·1
9 56			10 02		
	+11·0	−21·3		+10·8	−21·0
10 08			10 14		
	+11·1	−21·2		+10·9	−20·9
10 20			10 27		
	+11·2	−21·1		+11·0	−20·8
10 33			10 40		
	+11·3	−21·0		+11·1	−20·7
10 46			10 53		
	+11·4	−20·9		+11·2	−20·6
11 00			11 07		
	+11·5	−20·8		+11·3	−20·5
11 15			11 22		
	+11·6	−20·7		+11·4	−20·4
11 30			11 37		
	+11·7	−20·6		+11·5	−20·3
11 45			11 53		
	+11·8	−20·5		+11·6	−20·2
12 01			12 10		
	+11·9	−20·4		+11·7	−20·1
12 18			12 27		
	+12·0	−20·3		+11·8	−20·0
12 36			12 45		
	+12·1	−20·2		+11·9	−19·9
12 54			13 04		
	+12·2	−20·1		+12·0	−19·8
13 14			13 24		
	+12·3	−20·0		+12·1	−19·7
13 34			13 44		
	+12·4	−19·9		+12·2	−19·6
13 55			14 06		
	+12·5	−19·8		+12·3	−19·5
14 17			14 29		
	+12·6	−19·7		+12·4	−19·4
14 41			14 53		
	+12·7	−19·6		+12·5	−19·3
15 05			15 18		
	+12·8	−19·5		+12·6	−19·2
15 31			15 45		
	+12·9	−19·4		+12·7	−19·1
15 59			16 13		
	+13·0	−19·3		+12·8	−19·0
16 27			16 43		
	+13·1	−19·2		+12·9	−18·9
16 58			17 14		
	+13·2	−19·1		+13·0	−18·8
17 30			17 47		
	+13·3	−19·0		+13·1	−18·7
18 05			18 23		
	+13·4	−18·9		+13·2	−18·6
18 41			19 00		
	+13·5	−18·8		+13·3	−18·5
19 20			19 41		
	+13·6	−18·7		+13·4	−18·4
20 02			20 24		
	+13·7	−18·6		+13·5	−18·3
20 46			21 10		
	+13·8	−18·5		+13·6	−18·2
21 34			21 59		
	+13·9	−18·4		+13·7	−18·1
22 25			22 52		
	+14·0	−18·3		+13·8	−18·0
23 20			23 49		
	+14·1	−18·2		+13·9	−17·9
24 20			24 51		
	+14·2	−18·1		+14·0	−17·8
25 24			25 58		
	+14·3	−18·0		+14·1	−17·7
26 34			27 11		
	+14·4	−17·9		+14·2	−17·6
27 50			28 31		
	+14·5	−17·8		+14·3	−17·5
29 13			29 58		
	+14·6	−17·7		+14·4	−17·4
30 44			31 33		
	+14·7	−17·6		+14·5	−17·3
32 24			33 18		
	+14·8	−17·5		+14·6	−17·2
34 15			35 15		
	+14·9	−17·4		+14·7	−17·1
36 17			37 24		
	+15·0	−17·3		+14·8	−17·0
38 34			39 48		
	+15·1	−17·2		+14·9	−16·9
41 06			42 28		
	+15·2	−17·1		+15·0	−16·8
43 56			45 29		
	+15·3	−17·0		+15·1	−16·7
47 07			48 52		
	+15·4	−16·9		+15·2	−16·6
50 43			52 41		
	+15·5	−16·8		+15·3	−16·5
54 46			56 59		
	+15·6	−16·7		+15·4	−16·4
59 21			61 50		
	+15·7	−16·6		+15·5	−16·3
64 28			67 15		
	+15·8	−16·5		+15·6	−16·2
70 10			73 14		
	+15·9	−16·4		+15·7	−16·1
76 24			79 42		
	+16·0	−16·3		+15·8	−16·0
83 05			86 31		
	+16·1	−16·2		+15·9	−15·9
90 00			90 00		

STARS AND PLANETS

App Alt.	Corr^n
° ′	′
9 55	
	−5·3
10 07	
	−5·2
10 20	
	−5·1
10 32	
	−5·0
10 46	
	−4·9
10 59	
	−4·8
11 14	
	−4·7
11 29	
	−4·6
11 44	
	−4·5
12 00	
	−4·4
12 17	
	−4·3
12 35	
	−4·2
12 53	
	−4·1
13 12	
	−4·0
13 32	
	−3·9
13 53	
	−3·8
14 16	
	−3·7
14 39	
	−3·6
15 03	
	−3·5
15 29	
	−3·4
15 56	
	−3·3
16 25	
	−3·2
16 55	
	−3·1
17 27	
	−3·0
18 01	
	−2·9
18 37	
	−2·8
19 16	
	−2·7
19 56	
	−2·6
20 40	
	−2·5
21 27	
	−2·4
22 17	
	−2·3
23 11	
	−2·2
24 09	
	−2·1
25 12	
	−2·0
26 20	
	−1·9
27 34	
	−1·8
28 54	
	−1·7
30 22	
	−1·6
31 58	
	−1·5
33 43	
	−1·4
35 38	
	−1·3
37 45	
	−1·2
40 06	
	−1·1
42 42	
	−1·0
45 34	
	−0·9
48 45	
	−0·8
52 16	
	−0·7
56 09	
	−0·6
60 26	
	−0·5
65 06	
	−0·4
70 09	
	−0·3
75 32	
	−0·2
81 12	
	−0·1
87 03	
	0·0
90 00	

App. Alt. — Additional Corr^n

2017

VENUS

Jan. 1–Jan. 25
May 21–July 8

°	′
0	
	+0·2
41	
	+0·1
76	

Jan. 26–Feb. 18
Apr. 28–May 20

°	′
0	
	+0·3
34	
	+0·2
60	
	+0·1
80	

Feb. 19–Mar. 6
Apr. 13–Apr. 27

°	′
0	
	+0·4
29	
	+0·3
51	
	+0·2
68	
	+0·1
83	

Mar. 7–Apr. 12

°	′
0	
	+0·5
26	
	+0·4
46	
	+0·3
60	
	+0·2
73	
	+0·1
84	

July 9–Dec. 31

°	′
0	
	+0·1
60	

MARS

Jan. 1–Dec. 31

°	′
0	
	+0·1
60	

DIP

Ht. of Eye	Corr^n	Ht. of Eye
m	′	ft.
2·4		8·0
	−2·8	
2·6		8·6
	−2·9	
2·8		9·2
	−3·0	
3·0		9·8
	−3·1	
3·2		10·5
	−3·2	
3·4		11·2
	−3·3	
3·6		11·9
	−3·4	
3·8		12·6
	−3·5	
4·0		13·3
	−3·6	
4·3		14·1
	−3·7	
4·5		14·9
	−3·8	
4·7		15·7
	−3·9	
5·0		16·5
	−4·0	
5·2		17·4
	−4·1	
5·5		18·3
	−4·2	
5·8		19·1
	−4·3	
6·1		20·1
	−4·4	
6·3		21·0
	−4·5	
6·6		22·0
	−4·6	
6·9		22·9
	−4·7	
7·2		23·9
	−4·8	
7·5		24·9
	−4·9	
7·9		26·0
	−5·0	
8·2		27·1
	−5·1	
8·5		28·1
	−5·2	
8·8		29·2
	−5·3	
9·2		30·4
	−5·4	
9·5		31·5
	−5·5	
9·9		32·7
	−5·6	
10·3		33·9
	−5·7	
10·6		35·1
	−5·8	
11·0		36·3
	−5·9	
11·4		37·6
	−6·0	
11·8		38·9
	−6·1	
12·2		40·1
	−6·2	
12·6		41·5
	−6·3	
13·0		42·8
	−6·4	
13·4		44·2
	−6·5	
13·8		45·5
	−6·6	
14·2		46·9
	−6·7	
14·7		48·4
	−6·8	
15·1		49·8
	−6·9	
15·5		51·3
	−7·0	
16·0		52·8
	−7·1	
16·5		54·3
	−7·2	
16·9		55·8
	−7·3	
17·4		57·4
	−7·4	
17·9		58·9
	−7·5	
18·4		60·5
	−7·6	
18·8		62·1
	−7·7	
19·3		63·8
	−7·8	
19·8		65·4
	−7·9	
20·4		67·1
	−8·0	
20·9		68·8
	−8·1	
21·4		70·5

Ht. of Eye	Corr^n
m	′
1·0	− 1·8
1·5	− 2·2
2·0	− 2·5
2·5	− 2·8
3·0	− 3·0
See table ←	
m	′
20	− 7·9
22	− 8·3
24	− 8·6
26	− 9·0
28	− 9·3
30	− 9·6
32	−10·0
34	−10·3
36	−10·6
38	−10·8
40	−11·1
42	−11·4
44	−11·7
46	−11·9
48	−12·2
ft.	′
2	− 1·4
4	− 1·9
6	− 2·4
8	− 2·7
10	− 3·1
See table ←	
ft.	′
70	− 8·1
75	− 8·4
80	− 8·7
85	− 8·9
90	− 9·2
95	− 9·5
100	− 9·7
105	− 9·9
110	−10·2
115	−10·4
120	−10·6
125	−10·8
130	−11·1
135	−11·3
140	−11·5
145	−11·7
150	−11·9
155	−12·1

App. Alt. = Apparent altitude = Sextant altitude corrected for index error and dip.

ALTITUDE CORRECTION TABLES 0°-10°—SUN, STARS, PLANETS A3

App. Alt.	SUN OCT.—MAR. Lower Limb	SUN OCT.—MAR. Upper Limb	SUN APR.—SEPT. Lower Limb	SUN APR.—SEPT. Upper Limb	STARS PLANETS
° ′	′	′	′	′	′
0 00	−17·5	−49·8	−17·8	−49·6	−33·8
0 03	16·9	49·2	17·2	49·0	33·2
0 06	16·3	48·6	16·6	48·4	32·6
0 09	15·7	48·0	16·0	47·8	32·0
0 12	15·2	47·5	15·4	47·2	31·5
0 15	14·6	46·9	14·8	46·6	30·9
0 18	−14·1	−46·4	−14·3	−46·1	−30·4
0 21	13·5	45·8	13·8	45·6	29·8
0 24	13·0	45·3	13·3	45·1	29·3
0 27	12·5	44·8	12·8	44·6	28·8
0 30	12·0	44·3	12·3	44·1	28·3
0 33	11·6	43·9	11·8	43·6	27·9
0 36	−11·1	−43·4	−11·3	−43·1	−27·4
0 39	10·6	42·9	10·9	42·7	26·9
0 42	10·2	42·5	10·5	42·3	26·5
0 45	9·8	42·1	10·0	41·8	26·1
0 48	9·4	41·7	9·6	41·4	25·7
0 51	9·0	41·3	9·2	41·0	25·3
0 54	− 8·6	−40·9	− 8·8	−40·6	−24·9
0 57	8·2	40·5	8·4	40·2	24·5
1 00	7·8	40·1	8·0	39·8	24·1
1 03	7·4	39·7	7·7	39·5	23·7
1 06	7·1	39·4	7·3	39·1	23·4
1 09	6·7	39·0	7·0	38·8	23·0
1 12	− 6·4	−38·7	− 6·6	−38·4	−22·7
1 15	6·0	38·3	6·3	38·1	22·3
1 18	5·7	38·0	6·0	37·8	22·0
1 21	5·4	37·7	5·7	37·5	21·7
1 24	5·1	37·4	5·3	37·1	21·4
1 27	4·8	37·1	5·0	36·8	21·1
1 30	− 4·5	36·8	− 4·7	−36·5	−20·8
1 35	4·0	36·3	4·3	36·1	20·3
1 40	3·6	35·9	3·8	35·6	19·9
1 45	3·1	35·4	3·4	35·2	19·4
1 50	2·7	35·0	2·9	34·7	19·0
1 55	2·3	34·6	2·5	34·3	18·6
2 00	− 1·9	−34·2	− 2·1	−33·9	−18·2
2 05	1·5	33·8	1·7	33·5	17·8
2 10	1·1	33·4	1·4	33·2	17·4
2 15	0·8	33·1	1·0	32·8	17·1
2 20	0·4	32·7	0·7	32·5	16·7
2 25	− 0·1	32·4	− 0·3	32·1	16·4
2 30	+ 0·2	−32·1	0·0	−31·8	−16·1
2 35	0·5	31·8	+ 0·3	31·5	15·8
2 40	0·8	31·5	0·6	31·2	15·4
2 45	1·1	31·2	0·9	30·9	15·2
2 50	1·4	30·9	1·2	30·6	14·9
2 55	1·7	30·6	1·4	30·4	14·6
3 00	+ 2·0	−30·3	+ 1·7	−30·1	−14·3
3 05	2·2	30·1	2·0	29·8	14·1
3 10	2·5	29·8	2·2	29·6	13·8
3 15	2·7	29·6	2·5	29·3	13·6
3 20	2·9	29·4	2·7	29·1	13·4
3 25	3·2	29·1	2·9	28·9	13·1
3 30	+ 3·4	−28·9	+ 3·1	−28·7	−12·9

App. Alt.	SUN OCT.—MAR. Lower Limb	SUN OCT.—MAR. Upper Limb	SUN APR.—SEPT. Lower Limb	SUN APR.—SEPT. Upper Limb	STARS PLANETS
° ′	′	′	′	′	′
3 30	+ 3·4	−28·9	+ 3·1	−28·7	−12·9
3 35	3·6	28·7	3·3	28·5	12·7
3 40	3·8	28·5	3·6	28·2	12·5
3 45	4·0	28·3	3·8	28·0	12·3
3 50	4·2	28·1	4·0	27·8	12·1
3 55	4·4	27·9	4·1	27·7	11·9
4 00	+ 4·6	−27·7	+ 4·3	−27·5	−11·7
4 05	4·8	27·5	4·5	27·3	11·5
4 10	4·9	27·4	4·7	27·1	11·4
4 15	5·1	27·2	4·9	26·9	11·2
4 20	5·3	27·0	5·0	26·8	11·0
4 25	5·4	26·9	5·2	26·6	10·9
4 30	+ 5·6	−26·7	+ 5·3	−26·5	−10·7
4 35	5·7	26·6	5·5	26·3	10·6
4 40	5·9	26·4	5·6	26·2	10·4
4 45	6·0	26·3	5·8	26·0	10·3
4 50	6·2	26·1	5·9	25·9	10·1
4 55	6·3	26·0	6·1	25·7	10·0
5 00	+ 6·4	−25·9	+ 6·2	−25·6	− 9·8
5 05	6·6	25·7	6·3	25·5	9·7
5 10	6·7	25·6	6·5	25·3	9·6
5 15	6·8	25·5	6·6	25·2	9·5
5 20	7·0	25·3	6·7	25·1	9·3
5 25	7·1	25·2	6·8	25·0	9·2
5 30	+ 7·2	−25·1	+ 6·9	−24·9	− 9·1
5 35	7·3	25·0	7·1	24·7	9·0
5 40	7·4	24·9	7·2	24·6	8·9
5 45	7·5	24·8	7·3	24·5	8·8
5 50	7·6	24·7	7·4	24·4	8·7
5 55	7·7	24·6	7·5	24·3	8·6
6 00	+ 7·8	−24·5	+ 7·6	−24·2	− 8·5
6 10	8·0	24·3	7·8	24·0	8·3
6 20	8·2	24·1	8·0	23·8	8·1
6 30	8·4	23·9	8·2	23·6	7·9
6 40	8·6	23·7	8·3	23·5	7·7
6 50	8·7	23·6	8·5	23·3	7·6
7 00	+ 8·9	−23·4	+ 8·7	−23·1	− 7·4
7 10	9·1	23·2	8·8	23·0	7·2
7 20	9·2	23·1	9·0	22·8	7·1
7 30	9·3	23·0	9·1	22·7	6·9
7 40	9·5	22·8	9·2	22·6	6·8
7 50	9·6	22·7	9·4	22·4	6·7
8 00	+ 9·7	−22·6	+ 9·5	−22·3	− 6·6
8 10	9·9	22·4	9·6	22·2	6·4
8 20	10·0	22·3	9·7	22·1	6·3
8 30	10·1	22·2	9·9	21·9	6·2
8 40	10·2	22·1	10·0	21·8	6·1
8 50	10·3	22·0	10·1	21·7	6·0
9 00	+10·4	−21·9	+10·2	−21·6	− 5·9
9 10	10·5	21·8	10·3	21·5	5·8
9 20	10·6	21·7	10·4	21·4	5·7
9 30	10·7	21·6	10·5	21·3	5·6
9 40	10·8	21·5	10·6	21·2	5·5
9 50	10·9	21·4	10·6	21·2	5·4
10 00	+11·0	−21·3	+10·7	−21·1	− 5·3

Additional corrections for temperature and pressure are given on the following page.

For bubble sextant observations ignore dip and use the star corrections for Sun, planets and stars.

A4 ALTITUDE CORRECTION TABLES—ADDITIONAL CORRECTIONS

ADDITIONAL REFRACTION CORRECTIONS FOR NON-STANDARD CONDITIONS

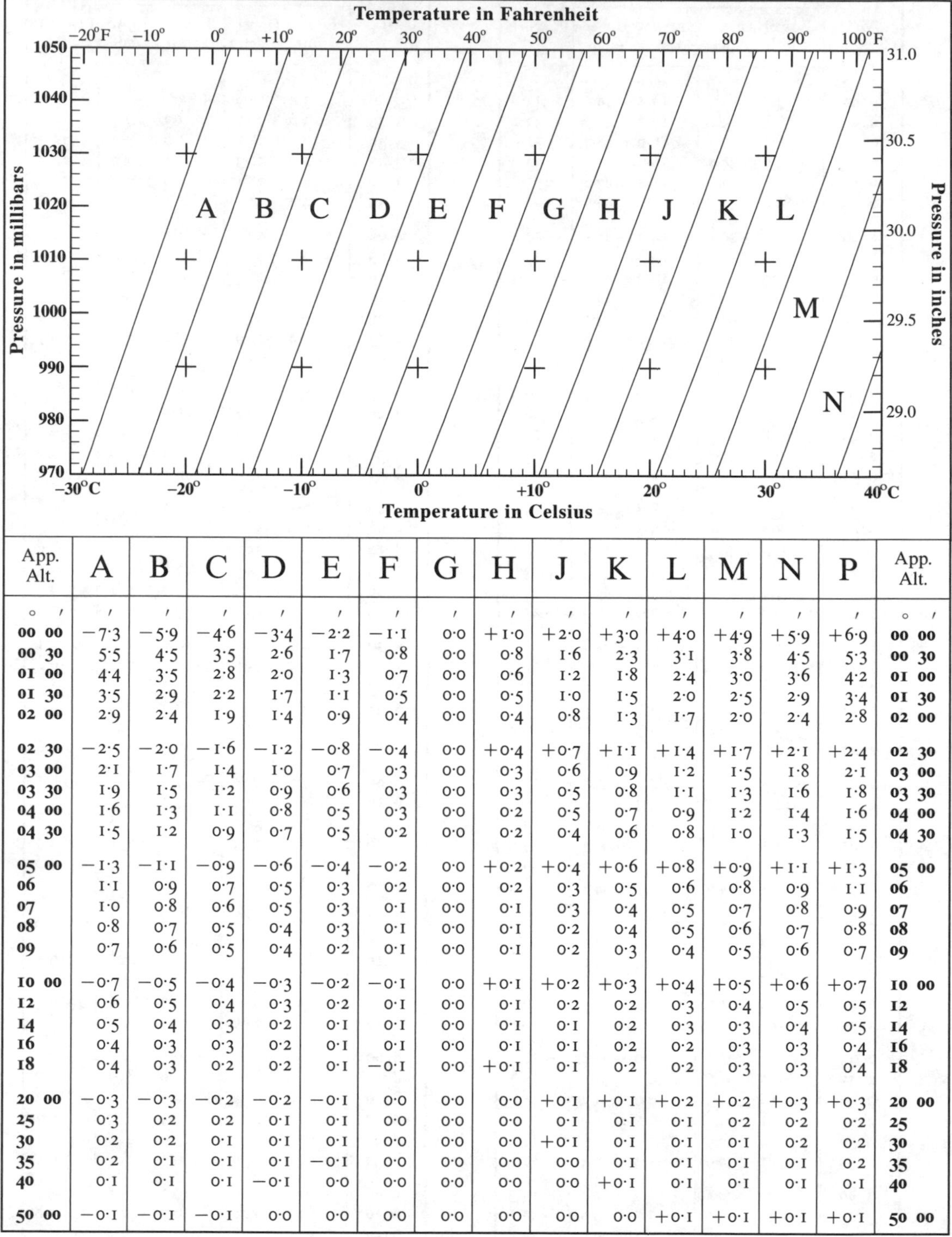

App. Alt.	A	B	C	D	E	F	G	H	J	K	L	M	N	P	App. Alt.
° ′	′	′	′	′	′	′	′	′	′	′	′	′	′	′	° ′
00 00	−7·3	−5·9	−4·6	−3·4	−2·2	−1·1	0·0	+1·0	+2·0	+3·0	+4·0	+4·9	+5·9	+6·9	**00 00**
00 30	5·5	4·5	3·5	2·6	1·7	0·8	0·0	0·8	1·6	2·3	3·1	3·8	4·5	5·3	**00 30**
01 00	4·4	3·5	2·8	2·0	1·3	0·7	0·0	0·6	1·2	1·8	2·4	3·0	3·6	4·2	**01 00**
01 30	3·5	2·9	2·2	1·7	1·1	0·5	0·0	0·5	1·0	1·5	2·0	2·5	2·9	3·4	**01 30**
02 00	2·9	2·4	1·9	1·4	0·9	0·4	0·0	0·4	0·8	1·3	1·7	2·0	2·4	2·8	**02 00**
02 30	−2·5	−2·0	−1·6	−1·2	−0·8	−0·4	0·0	+0·4	+0·7	+1·1	+1·4	+1·7	+2·1	+2·4	**02 30**
03 00	2·1	1·7	1·4	1·0	0·7	0·3	0·0	0·3	0·6	0·9	1·2	1·5	1·8	2·1	**03 00**
03 30	1·9	1·5	1·2	0·9	0·6	0·3	0·0	0·3	0·5	0·8	1·1	1·3	1·6	1·8	**03 30**
04 00	1·6	1·3	1·1	0·8	0·5	0·3	0·0	0·2	0·5	0·7	0·9	1·2	1·4	1·6	**04 00**
04 30	1·5	1·2	0·9	0·7	0·5	0·2	0·0	0·2	0·4	0·6	0·8	1·0	1·3	1·5	**04 30**
05 00	−1·3	−1·1	−0·9	−0·6	−0·4	−0·2	0·0	+0·2	+0·4	+0·6	+0·8	+0·9	+1·1	+1·3	**05 00**
06	1·1	0·9	0·7	0·5	0·3	0·2	0·0	0·2	0·3	0·5	0·6	0·8	0·9	1·1	**06**
07	1·0	0·8	0·6	0·5	0·3	0·1	0·0	0·1	0·3	0·4	0·5	0·7	0·8	0·9	**07**
08	0·8	0·7	0·5	0·4	0·3	0·1	0·0	0·1	0·2	0·4	0·5	0·6	0·7	0·8	**08**
09	0·7	0·6	0·5	0·4	0·2	0·1	0·0	0·1	0·2	0·3	0·4	0·5	0·6	0·7	**09**
10 00	−0·7	−0·5	−0·4	−0·3	−0·2	−0·1	0·0	+0·1	+0·2	+0·3	+0·4	+0·5	+0·6	+0·7	**10 00**
12	0·6	0·5	0·4	0·3	0·2	0·1	0·0	0·1	0·2	0·2	0·3	0·4	0·5	0·5	**12**
14	0·5	0·4	0·3	0·2	0·1	0·1	0·0	0·1	0·1	0·2	0·3	0·3	0·4	0·5	**14**
16	0·4	0·3	0·3	0·2	0·1	0·1	0·0	0·1	0·1	0·2	0·2	0·3	0·3	0·4	**16**
18	0·4	0·3	0·2	0·2	0·1	−0·1	0·0	+0·1	0·1	0·2	0·2	0·3	0·3	0·4	**18**
20 00	−0·3	−0·3	−0·2	−0·2	−0·1	0·0	0·0	0·0	+0·1	+0·1	+0·2	+0·2	+0·3	+0·3	**20 00**
25	0·3	0·2	0·2	0·1	0·1	0·0	0·0	0·0	0·1	0·1	0·1	0·2	0·2	0·2	**25**
30	0·2	0·2	0·1	0·1	0·1	0·0	0·0	0·0	+0·1	0·1	0·1	0·1	0·2	0·2	**30**
35	0·2	0·1	0·1	0·1	−0·1	0·0	0·0	0·0	0·0	0·1	0·1	0·1	0·1	0·2	**35**
40	0·1	0·1	0·1	−0·1	0·0	0·0	0·0	0·0	0·0	+0·1	0·1	0·1	0·1	0·1	**40**
50 00	−0·1	−0·1	−0·1	0·0	0·0	0·0	0·0	0·0	0·0	0·0	+0·1	+0·1	+0·1	+0·1	**50 00**

The graph is entered with arguments temperature and pressure to find a zone letter; using as arguments this zone letter and apparent altitude (sextant altitude corrected for index error and dip), a correction is taken from the table. This correction is to be applied to the sextant altitude in addition to the corrections for standard conditions (for the Sun, stars and planets from page A2-A3 and for the Moon from pages xxxiv and xxxv).

2017
Nautical Almanac
COMMERCIAL EDITION

PUBLISHED BY:

Paradise Cay Publications, Inc.
Post Office Box 29
Arcata, CA 95518-0029
Tel: 1-707-822-9063
Fax: 1-707-822-9163
www.paracay.com

ISBN: 978-1-937196-55-4

Printed and distributed with permission by Paradise Cay Publications, Inc.

NOTE

Every care is taken to prevent errors in the production of this publication. As a final precaution it is recommended that the sequence of pages in this copy be examined on receipt. If faulty, it should be returned for replacement.

PREFACE

The first three sections of this book are a complete and accurate duplication from *The Nautical Almanac* produced jointly by Her Majesty's Nautical Almanac Office, United Kingdom Hydrographic Office, Admiralty Way, Taunton, Somerset, TA1 2DN, United Kingdom and the Nautical Almanac Office of the US Naval Observatory.

We gratefully acknowledge the United Kingdom Hydrographic Office and the United States Naval Observatory for permission to use the material contained in the almanac sections of this publication.

The 2017 Nautical Almanac
Commercial Edition

Pages

RELIGIOUS CALENDARS

Epiphany	Jan. 6	Low Sunday	Apr. 23
Septuagesima Sunday	Feb. 12	Rogation Sunday	May 21
Quinquagesima Sunday	Feb. 26	Ascension Day—Holy Thursday	May 25
Ash Wednesday	Mar. 1	Whit Sunday—Pentecost	June 4
Quadragesima Sunday	Mar. 5	Trinity Sunday	June 11
Palm Sunday	Apr. 9	Corpus Christi	June 15
Good Friday	Apr. 14	First Sunday in Advent	Dec. 3
Easter Day	Apr. 16	Christmas Day (Monday)	Dec. 25

First Day of Passover (Pesach)	Apr. 11	Day of Atonement (Yom Kippur)	Sept. 30
Feast of Weeks (Shavuot)	May 31	First day of Tabernacles (Succoth)	Oct. 5
Jewish New Year 5778 (Rosh Hashanah)	Sept. 21		

Ramadân, First day of (tabular)	May 27	Islamic New Year (1439)	Sept. 22

The Jewish and Islamic dates above are tabular dates, which begin at sunset on the previous evening and end at sunset on the date tabulated. In practice, the dates of Islamic fasts and festivals are determined by an actual sighting of the appropriate new moon.

CIVIL CALENDAR—UNITED KINGDOM

Accession of Queen Elizabeth II	Feb. 6	The Queen's Official Birthday†	June 10
St David (Wales)	Mar. 1	Birthday of Prince Philip, Duke of Edinburgh	June 10
Commonwealth Day	Mar. 13	Remembrance Sunday	Nov. 12
St Patrick (Ireland)	Mar. 17	Birthday of the Prince of Wales	Nov. 14
Birthday of Queen Elizabeth II	Apr. 21	St Andrew (Scotland)	Nov. 30
St George (England)	Apr. 23		
Coronation Day	June 2		

PUBLIC HOLIDAYS

England and Wales—Jan. 2†, Apr. 14, Apr. 17, May 1†, May 29, Aug. 28, Dec. 25, Dec. 26
Northern Ireland—Jan. 2†, Mar. 17, Apr. 14, Apr. 17, May 1†, May 29, July 12†, Aug. 28, Dec. 25, Dec. 26
Scotland—Jan. 2, Jan. 3, Apr. 14, May 1, May 29†, Aug. 7, Dec. 25, Dec. 26†

CIVIL CALENDAR—UNITED STATES OF AMERICA

New Year's Day	Jan. 1	Labor Day	Sept. 4
Martin Luther King's Birthday	Jan. 16	Columbus Day	Oct. 9
Washington's Birthday	Feb. 20	Election Day (in certain States)	Nov. 7
Memorial Day	May 29	Veterans Day	Nov. 11
Independence Day	July 4	Thanksgiving Day	Nov. 23

†Dates subject to confirmation

PHASES OF THE MOON

New Moon	d	h	m	First Quarter	d	h	m	Full Moon	d	h	m	Last Quarter	d	h	m
				Jan.	5	19	47	Jan.	12	11	34	Jan.	19	22	13
Jan.	28	00	07	Feb.	4	04	19	Feb.	11	00	33	Feb.	18	19	33
Feb.	26	14	58	Mar.	5	11	32	Mar.	12	14	54	Mar.	20	15	58
Mar.	28	02	57	Apr.	3	18	39	Apr.	11	06	08	Apr.	19	09	57
Apr.	26	12	16	May	3	02	47	May	10	21	42	May	19	00	33
May	25	19	44	June	1	12	42	June	9	13	10	June	17	11	33
June	24	02	31	July	1	00	51	July	9	04	07	July	16	19	26
July	23	09	46	July	30	15	23	Aug.	7	18	11	Aug.	15	01	15
Aug.	21	18	30	Aug.	29	08	13	Sept.	6	07	03	Sept.	13	06	25
Sept.	20	05	30	Sept.	28	02	54	Oct.	5	18	40	Oct.	12	12	25
Oct.	19	19	12	Oct.	27	22	22	Nov.	4	05	23	Nov.	10	20	36
Nov.	18	11	42	Nov.	26	17	03	Dec.	3	15	47	Dec.	10	07	51
Dec.	18	06	30	Dec.	26	09	20								

DAYS OF THE WEEK AND DAYS OF THE YEAR

	JAN.		FEB.		MAR.		APR.		MAY		JUNE		JULY		AUG.		SEPT.		OCT.		NOV.		DEC.	
Day	Wk	Yr	Wk	Yr	Wk	Yr	Wk	Yr	Wk	Yr	Wk	Yr	Wk	Yr	Wk	Yr	Wk	Yr	Wk	Yr	Wk	Yr	Wk	Yr
1	Su.	1	W.	32	W.	60	Sa.	91	M.	121	Th.	152	Sa.	182	Tu.	213	F.	244	Su.	274	W.	305	F.	335
2	M.	2	Th.	33	Th.	61	Su.	92	Tu.	122	F.	153	Su.	183	W.	214	Sa.	245	M.	275	Th.	306	Sa.	336
3	Tu.	3	F.	34	F.	62	M.	93	W.	123	Sa.	154	M.	184	Th.	215	Su.	246	Tu.	276	F.	307	Su.	337
4	W.	4	Sa.	35	Sa.	63	Tu.	94	Th.	124	Su.	155	Tu.	185	F.	216	M.	247	W.	277	Sa.	308	M.	338
5	Th.	5	Su.	36	Su.	64	W.	95	F.	125	M.	156	W.	186	Sa.	217	Tu.	248	Th.	278	Su.	309	Tu.	339
6	F.	6	M.	37	M.	65	Th.	96	Sa.	126	Tu.	157	Th.	187	Su.	218	W.	249	F.	279	M.	310	W.	340
7	Sa.	7	Tu.	38	Tu.	66	F.	97	Su.	127	W.	158	F.	188	M.	219	Th.	250	Sa.	280	Tu.	311	Th.	341
8	Su.	8	W.	39	W.	67	Sa.	98	M.	128	Th.	159	Sa.	189	Tu.	220	F.	251	Su.	281	W.	312	F.	342
9	M.	9	Th.	40	Th.	68	Su.	99	Tu.	129	F.	160	Su.	190	W.	221	Sa.	252	M.	282	Th.	313	Sa.	343
10	Tu.	10	F.	41	F.	69	M.	100	W.	130	Sa.	161	M.	191	Th.	222	Su.	253	Tu.	283	F.	314	Su.	344
11	W.	11	Sa.	42	Sa.	70	Tu.	101	Th.	131	Su.	162	Tu.	192	F.	223	M.	254	W.	284	Sa.	315	M.	345
12	Th.	12	Su.	43	Su.	71	W.	102	F.	132	M.	163	W.	193	Sa.	224	Tu.	255	Th.	285	Su.	316	Tu.	346
13	F.	13	M.	44	M.	72	Th.	103	Sa.	133	Tu.	164	Th.	194	Su.	225	W.	256	F.	286	M.	317	W.	347
14	Sa.	14	Tu.	45	Tu.	73	F.	104	Su.	134	W.	165	F.	195	M.	226	Th.	257	Sa.	287	Tu.	318	Th.	348
15	Su.	15	W.	46	W.	74	Sa.	105	M.	135	Th.	166	Sa.	196	Tu.	227	F.	258	Su.	288	W.	319	F.	349
16	M.	16	Th.	47	Th.	75	Su.	106	Tu.	136	F.	167	Su.	197	W.	228	Sa.	259	M.	289	Th.	320	Sa.	350
17	Tu.	17	F.	48	F.	76	M.	107	W.	137	Sa.	168	M.	198	Th.	229	Su.	260	Tu.	290	F.	321	Su.	351
18	W.	18	Sa.	49	Sa.	77	Tu.	108	Th.	138	Su.	169	Tu.	199	F.	230	M.	261	W.	291	Sa.	322	M.	352
19	Th.	19	Su.	50	Su.	78	W.	109	F.	139	M.	170	W.	200	Sa.	231	Tu.	262	Th.	292	Su.	323	Tu.	353
20	F.	20	M.	51	M.	79	Th.	110	Sa.	140	Tu.	171	Th.	201	Su.	232	W.	263	F.	293	M.	324	W.	354
21	Sa.	21	Tu.	52	Tu.	80	F.	111	Su.	141	W.	172	F.	202	M.	233	Th.	264	Sa.	294	Tu.	325	Th.	355
22	Su.	22	W.	53	W.	81	Sa.	112	M.	142	Th.	173	Sa.	203	Tu.	234	F.	265	Su.	295	W.	326	F.	356
23	M.	23	Th.	54	Th.	82	Su.	113	Tu.	143	F.	174	Su.	204	W.	235	Sa.	266	M.	296	Th.	327	Sa.	357
24	Tu.	24	F.	55	F.	83	M.	114	W.	144	Sa.	175	M.	205	Th.	236	Su.	267	Tu.	297	F.	328	Su.	358
25	W.	25	Sa.	56	Sa.	84	Tu.	115	Th.	145	Su.	176	Tu.	206	F.	237	M.	268	W.	298	Sa.	329	M.	359
26	Th.	26	Su.	57	Su.	85	W.	116	F.	146	M.	177	W.	207	Sa.	238	Tu.	269	Th.	299	Su.	330	Tu.	360
27	F.	27	M.	58	M.	86	Th.	117	Sa.	147	Tu.	178	Th.	208	Su.	239	W.	270	F.	300	M.	331	W.	361
28	Sa.	28	Tu.	59	Tu.	87	F.	118	Su.	148	W.	179	F.	209	M.	240	Th.	271	Sa.	301	Tu.	332	Th.	362
29	Su.	29			W.	88	Sa.	119	M.	149	Th.	180	Sa.	210	Tu.	241	F.	272	Su.	302	W.	333	F.	363
30	M.	30			Th.	89	Su.	120	Tu.	150	F.	181	Su.	211	W.	242	Sa.	273	M.	303	Th.	334	Sa.	364
31	Tu.	31			F.	90			W.	151			M.	212	Th.	243			Tu.	304			Su.	365

ECLIPSES

There are two eclipses of the Sun and one of the Moon.

1. *An annular eclipse of the Sun,* February 26. See map on page 6. The eclipse begins at $12^h\ 11^m$ and ends at $17^h\ 36^m$; the annular phase begins at $13^h\ 16^m$ and ends at $16^h\ 31^m$. The maximum duration of annularity is $1^m\ 17^s$.

2. *A partial eclipse of the Moon,* August 7. The eclipse begins at $17^h\ 22^m$ and ends at $19^h\ 19^m$. The time of maximum eclipse is $18^h\ 20^m$ when 0·25 of the Moon's diameter is obscured. It is visible from the western Pacific Ocean, Australasia, Asia, Antarctica, Africa and most of Europe.

3. *A total eclipse of the Sun,* August 21. See map on page 7. The eclipse begins at $15^h\ 47^m$ and ends at $21^h\ 04^m$; the total phase begins at $16^h\ 49^m$ and ends at $20^h\ 02^m$. The maximum duration of totality is $2^m\ 45^s$.

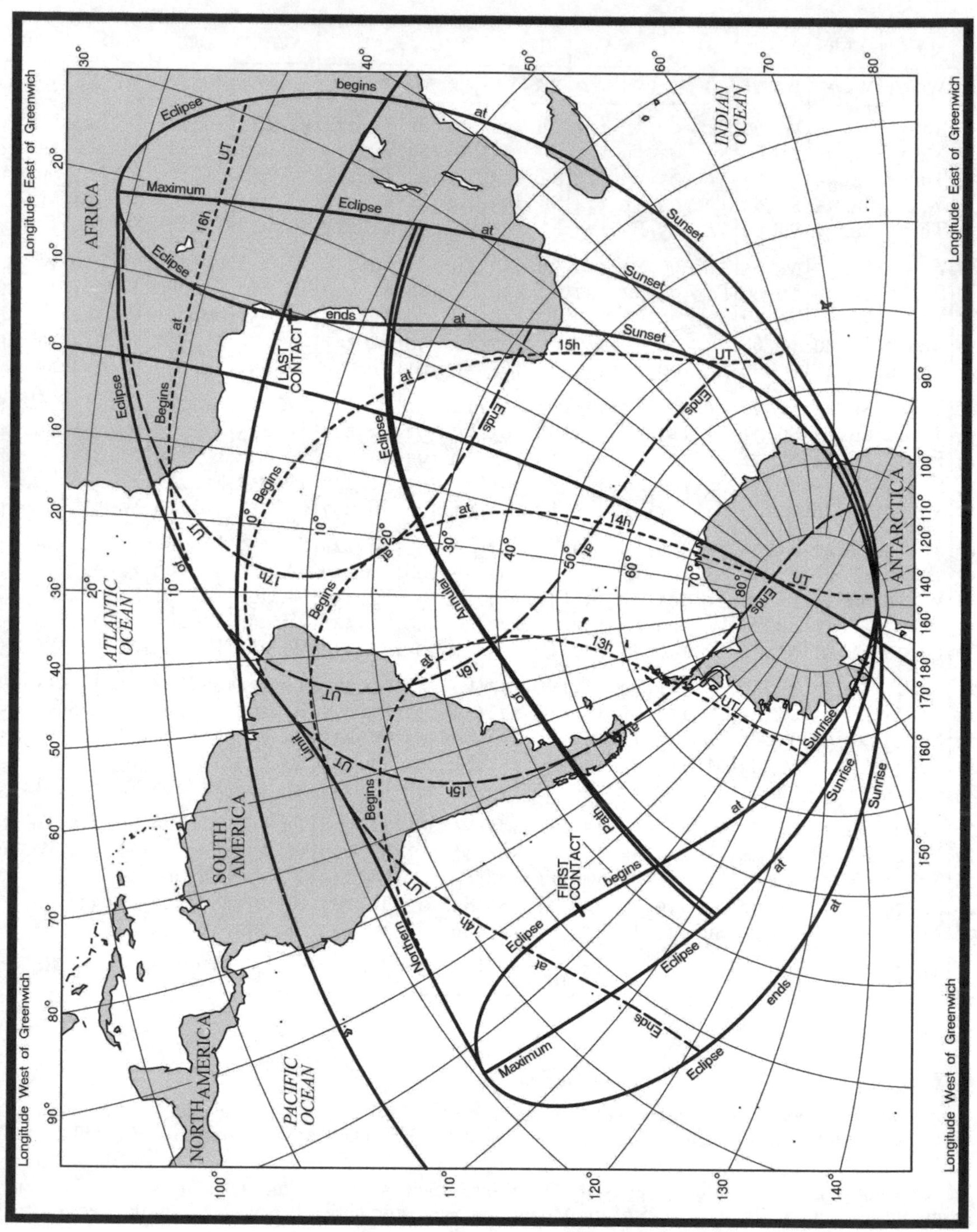

SOLAR ECLIPSE DIAGRAMS

The principal features shown on the above diagrams are: the paths of total and annular eclipses; the northern and southern limits of partial eclipse; the sunrise and sunset curves; dashed lines which show the times of beginning and end of partial eclipse at hourly intervals.

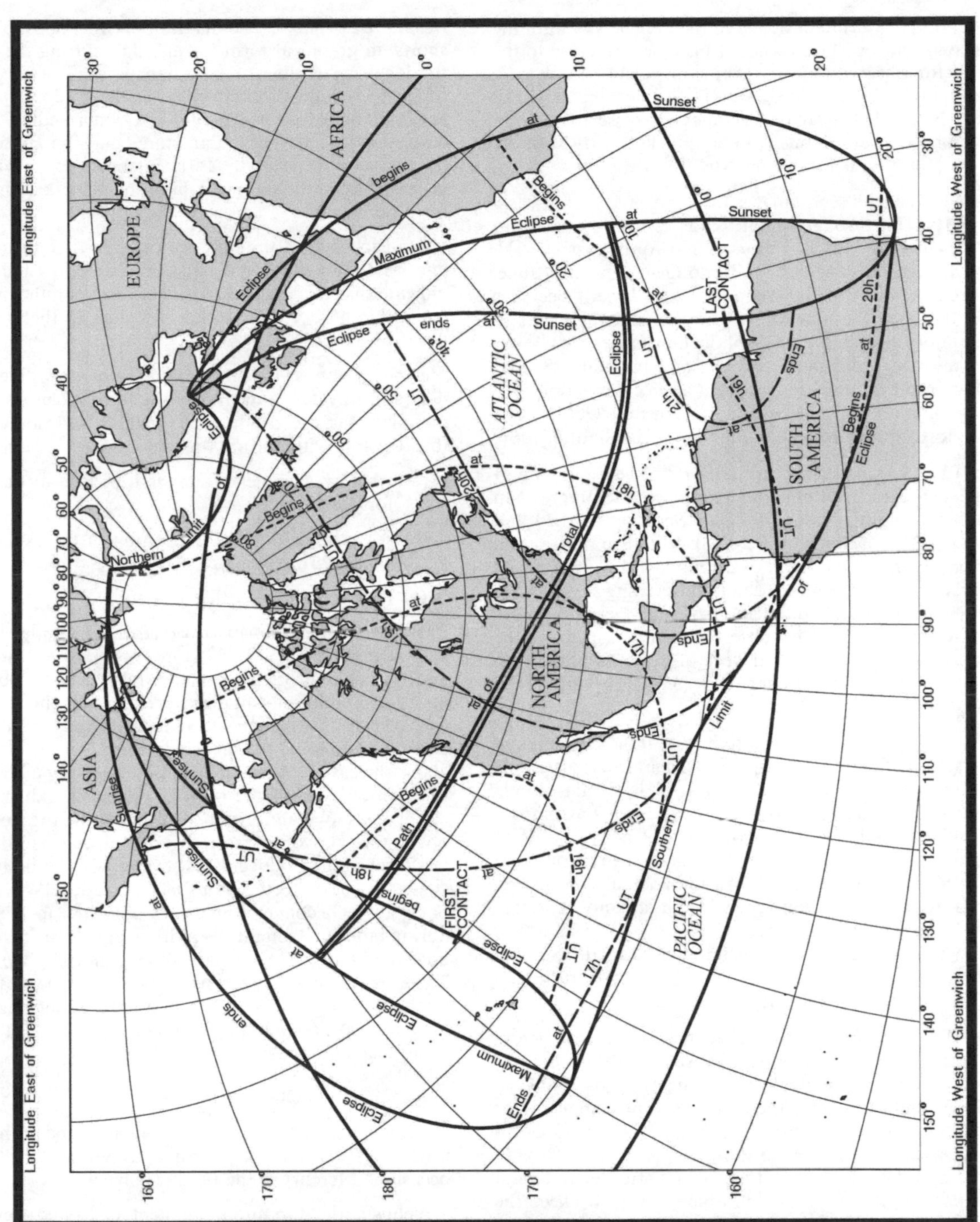

SOLAR ECLIPSE DIAGRAMS

Further details of the paths and times of central eclipse are given in *The Astronomical Almanac.*

VISIBILITY OF PLANETS

VENUS is a brilliant object in the evening sky until the second half of March when it becomes too close to the Sun for observation. It reappears in late March as a morning star and can be seen in the morning sky until late Nov. when it again becomes too close to the Sun for observation. Venus is in conjunction with Mars on Oct. 5 and with Jupiter on Nov. 13.

MARS can be seen only in the evening sky until early June passing through Aquarius, Pisces from late Jan., into Aries in early March, Taurus in mid-April (passing 6° N. of *Aldebaran* on May 7) and into Gemini in early June. From the start of the second week of June it becomes too close to the Sun for observation and reappears in the morning sky in mid-Sept. in Leo, moves into Virgo in mid-Oct. (passing 3° N. of *Spica* on Nov. 28) and then into Libra in late Dec. Mars is in conjunction with Mercury on Sept. 16 and with Venus on Oct. 5. The redddish tint of Mars should assist in its identification.

JUPITER can be seen in Virgo from the beginning of the year and from mid-Jan. can be seen for more than half the night (passing 4° N. of *Spica* on Jan. 20 and again 4° N. of *Spica* on Feb. 23). It is at opposition on April 7 when it can be seen throughout the night. From early July it can only be seen in the evening sky (passing 3° N. of *Spica* on Sept. 5) and from mid-Oct. it becomes too close to the Sun for observation. It reappears in the morning sky in the second week of Nov. and passes into Libra in mid-Nov. Jupiter is in conjuction with Venus on Nov. 13.

SATURN rises shortly before sunrise at the beginning of the year in Ophiucus, passing into Sagittarius in late Feb. and can only be seen in the morning sky until mid-March. Its westward elongation gradually increases, passing into Ophiucus again in the second half of May, and is at opposition on June 15, when it can be seen throughout the night. Its eastward elongation gradually decreases, and from mid-Sept. until early Dec. it can only be seen in the evening sky. It returns into Sagittarius in mid-Nov. and in early Dec. it becomes too close to the Sun for observation for the remainder of the year. Saturn is in conjunction with Mercury on Nov. 28.

MERCURY can only be seen low in the east before sunrise, or low in the west after sunset (about the time of beginning or end of civil twilight). It is visible in the mornings between the following approximate dates: Jan. 4 (+1·6) to Feb. 24 (−0·9), Apr. 29 (+3·1) to June 14 (−1·4), Sept. 4 (+1·9) to Sept. 28 (−1·3) and Dec. 19 (+1·6) to Dec. 31 (−0·3); the planet is brighter at the end of each period. It is visible in the evenings between the following approximate dates: Mar. 16 (−1·5) to Apr. 12 (+2·6), June 29 (−1·3) to Aug. 20 (+2·9) and Oct. 23 (−0·7) to Dec. 7 (+1·5); the planet is brighter at the beginning of each period. The figures in parentheses are the magnitudes.

PLANET DIAGRAM

General Description. The diagram on the opposite page shows, in graphical form for any date during the year, the local mean time of meridian passage of the Sun, of the five planets Mercury, Venus, Mars, Jupiter, and Saturn, and of each 30° of SHA; intermediate lines corresponding to particular stars, may be drawn in by the user if desired. It is intended to provide a general picture of the availability of planets and stars for observation.

On each side of the line marking the time of meridian passage of the Sun a band, 45^{m} wide, is shaded to indicate that planets and most stars crossing the meridian within 45^{m} of the Sun are too close to the Sun for observation.

Method of use and interpretation. For any date, the diagram provides immediately the local mean times of meridian passage of the Sun, planets and stars, and thus the following information:

(a) whether a planet or star is too close to the Sun for observation;

(b) some indication of its position in the sky, especially during twilight;

(c) the proximity of other planets.

When the meridian passage of an outer planet occurs at midnight, the body is in opposition to the Sun and is visible all night; a planet may then be observable during both morning and evening twilights. As the time of meridian passage decreases, the body eventually ceases to be observable in the morning, but its altitude above the eastern horizon at sunset gradually increases; this continues until the body is on the meridian during evening twilight. From then onwards, the body is observable above the western horizon and its altitude at sunset gradually decreases; eventually the body becomes too close to the Sun for observation. When the body again becomes visible it is seen low in the east during morning twilight; its altitude at sunrise increases until meridian passage occurs during morning twilight. Then, as the time of meridian passage decreases to 0^{h}, the body is observable in the west during morning twilight with a gradually decreasing altitude, until it once again reaches opposition.

DO NOT CONFUSE

Mercury with Mars in mid-September and with Saturn in late November to early December; on both occasions Mercury is the brighter object.

Venus with Mars in late September to mid-October and with Jupiter in mid-November; on both occasions Venus is the brighter object.

Mars with Jupiter in late December when Jupiter is the brighter object.

LOCAL MEAN TIME OF MERIDIAN PASSAGE

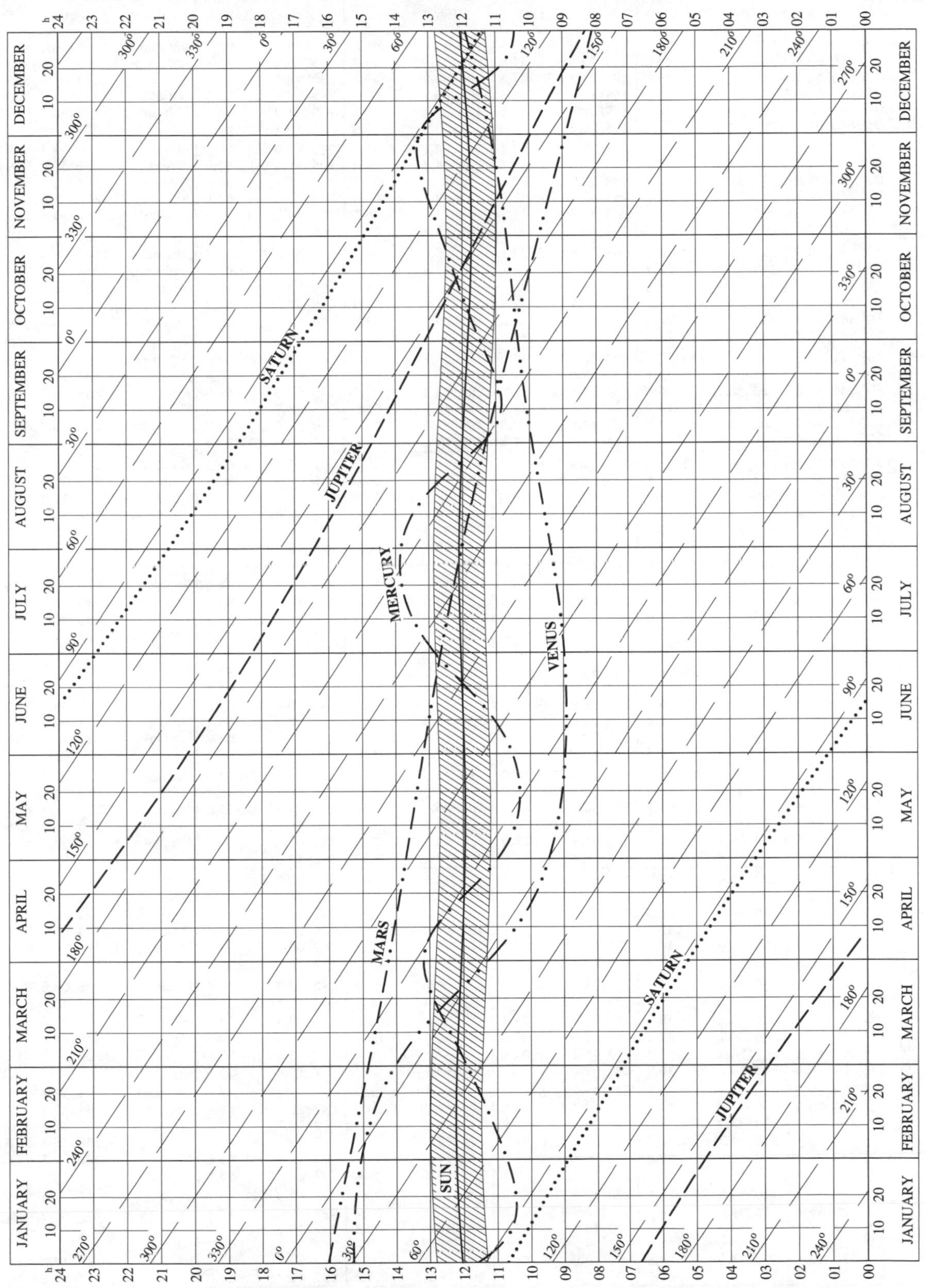

LOCAL MEAN TIME OF MERIDIAN PASSAGE

	UT	ARIES	VENUS −4·5		MARS +0·9		JUPITER −2·0		SATURN +0·5	
	d h	GHA ° ′	GHA ° ′	Dec ° ′	GHA ° ′	Dec ° ′	GHA ° ′	Dec ° ′	GHA ° ′	Dec ° ′
	1 00	100 50.2	130 38.5	S13 41.9	119 24.8	S 8 48.6	260 48.8	S 7 03.6	200 08.3	S21 52.4
	01	115 52.6	145 38.5	40.8	134 25.5	47.8	275 51.0	03.7	215 10.5	52.4
	02	130 55.1	160 38.4	39.7	149 26.2	47.1	290 53.2	03.8	230 12.7	52.5
	03	145 57.6	175 38.3	. . 38.6	164 27.0	. . 46.3	305 55.5	. . 03.9	245 14.8	. . 52.5
	04	161 00.0	190 38.2	37.5	179 27.7	45.6	320 57.7	04.0	260 17.0	52.5
	05	176 02.5	205 38.1	36.4	194 28.4	44.8	335 59.9	04.0	275 19.1	52.5
	06	191 05.0	220 38.0	S13 35.3	209 29.1	S 8 44.1	351 02.1	S 7 04.1	290 21.3	S21 52.5
	07	206 07.4	235 37.9	34.2	224 29.8	43.3	6 04.3	04.2	305 23.4	52.6
	08	221 09.9	250 37.8	33.1	239 30.5	42.6	21 06.5	04.3	320 25.6	52.6
S	09	236 12.4	265 37.7	. . 32.0	254 31.2	. . 41.8	36 08.7	. . 04.4	335 27.8	. . 52.6
U	10	251 14.8	280 37.6	30.9	269 31.9	41.1	51 11.0	04.5	350 29.9	52.6
N	11	266 17.3	295 37.5	29.8	284 32.7	40.3	66 13.2	04.6	5 32.1	52.6
D	12	281 19.7	310 37.5	S13 28.8	299 33.4	S 8 39.6	81 15.4	S 7 04.7	20 34.2	S21 52.7
A	13	296 22.2	325 37.4	27.7	314 34.1	38.8	96 17.6	04.8	35 36.4	52.7
Y	14	311 24.7	340 37.3	26.6	329 34.8	38.1	111 19.8	04.9	50 38.6	52.7
	15	326 27.1	355 37.2	. . 25.5	344 35.5	. . 37.3	126 22.0	. . 04.9	65 40.7	. . 52.7
	16	341 29.6	10 37.1	24.4	359 36.2	36.6	141 24.3	05.0	80 42.9	52.7
	17	356 32.1	25 37.0	23.3	14 36.9	35.8	156 26.5	05.1	95 45.0	52.8
	18	11 34.5	40 37.0	S13 22.2	29 37.6	S 8 35.0	171 28.7	S 7 05.2	110 47.2	S21 52.8
	19	26 37.0	55 36.9	21.1	44 38.4	34.3	186 30.9	05.3	125 49.3	52.8
	20	41 39.5	70 36.8	20.0	59 39.1	33.5	201 33.1	05.4	140 51.5	52.8
	21	56 41.9	85 36.7	. . 18.9	74 39.8	. . 32.8	216 35.4	. . 05.5	155 53.7	. . 52.8
	22	71 44.4	100 36.7	17.8	89 40.5	32.0	231 37.6	05.6	170 55.8	52.8
	23	86 46.9	115 36.6	16.7	104 41.2	31.3	246 39.8	05.6	185 58.0	52.9
	2 00	101 49.3	130 36.5	S13 15.6	119 41.9	S 8 30.5	261 42.0	S 7 05.7	201 00.1	S21 52.9
	01	116 51.8	145 36.4	14.5	134 42.6	29.8	276 44.2	05.8	216 02.3	52.9
	02	131 54.2	160 36.4	13.4	149 43.3	29.0	291 46.5	05.9	231 04.5	52.9
	03	146 56.7	175 36.3	. . 12.3	164 44.1	. . 28.3	306 48.7	. . 06.0	246 06.6	. . 52.9
	04	161 59.2	190 36.2	11.2	179 44.8	27.5	321 50.9	06.1	261 08.8	53.0
	05	177 01.6	205 36.1	10.1	194 45.5	26.8	336 53.1	06.2	276 10.9	53.0
	06	192 04.1	220 36.1	S13 08.9	209 46.2	S 8 26.0	351 55.3	S 7 06.3	291 13.1	S21 53.0
	07	207 06.6	235 36.0	07.8	224 46.9	25.2	6 57.6	06.3	306 15.3	53.0
	08	222 09.0	250 35.9	06.7	239 47.6	24.5	21 59.8	06.4	321 17.4	53.0
M	09	237 11.5	265 35.9	. . 05.6	254 48.3	. . 23.7	37 02.0	. . 06.5	336 19.6	. . 53.1
O	10	252 14.0	280 35.8	04.5	269 49.1	23.0	52 04.2	06.6	351 21.7	53.1
N	11	267 16.4	295 35.7	03.4	284 49.8	22.2	67 06.5	06.7	6 23.9	53.1
D	12	282 18.9	310 35.7	S13 02.3	299 50.5	S 8 21.5	82 08.7	S 7 06.8	21 26.1	S21 53.1
A	13	297 21.4	325 35.6	01.2	314 51.2	20.7	97 10.9	06.9	36 28.2	53.1
Y	14	312 23.8	340 35.6	13 00.1	329 51.9	20.0	112 13.1	07.0	51 30.4	53.1
	15	327 26.3	355 35.5	12 59.0	344 52.6	. . 19.2	127 15.3	. . 07.0	66 32.5	. . 53.2
	16	342 28.7	10 35.4	57.9	359 53.4	18.4	142 17.6	07.1	81 34.7	53.2
	17	357 31.2	25 35.4	56.8	14 54.1	17.7	157 19.8	07.2	96 36.9	53.2
	18	12 33.7	40 35.3	S12 55.7	29 54.8	S 8 16.9	172 22.0	S 7 07.3	111 39.0	S21 53.2
	19	27 36.1	55 35.3	54.6	44 55.5	16.2	187 24.2	07.4	126 41.2	53.2
	20	42 38.6	70 35.2	53.4	59 56.2	15.4	202 26.5	07.5	141 43.3	53.3
	21	57 41.1	85 35.1	. . 52.3	74 56.9	. . 14.7	217 28.7	. . 07.6	156 45.5	. . 53.3
	22	72 43.5	100 35.1	51.2	89 57.6	13.9	232 30.9	07.6	171 47.7	53.3
	23	87 46.0	115 35.0	50.1	104 58.4	13.2	247 33.1	07.7	186 49.8	53.3
	3 00	102 48.5	130 35.0	S12 49.0	119 59.1	S 8 12.4	262 35.4	S 7 07.8	201 52.0	S21 53.3
	01	117 50.9	145 34.9	47.9	134 59.8	11.6	277 37.6	07.9	216 54.1	53.3
	02	132 53.4	160 34.9	46.8	150 00.5	10.9	292 39.8	08.0	231 56.3	53.4
	03	147 55.8	175 34.8	. . 45.7	165 01.2	. . 10.1	307 42.0	. . 08.1	246 58.5	. . 53.4
	04	162 58.3	190 34.8	44.6	180 01.9	09.4	322 44.3	08.1	262 00.6	53.4
	05	178 00.8	205 34.7	43.4	195 02.7	08.6	337 46.5	08.2	277 02.8	53.4
	06	193 03.2	220 34.7	S12 42.3	210 03.4	S 8 07.9	352 48.7	S 7 08.3	292 04.9	S21 53.4
	07	208 05.7	235 34.6	41.2	225 04.1	07.1	7 50.9	08.4	307 07.1	53.5
T	08	223 08.2	250 34.6	40.1	240 04.8	06.3	22 53.2	08.5	322 09.3	53.5
U	09	238 10.6	265 34.6	. . 39.0	255 05.5	. . 05.6	37 55.4	. . 08.6	337 11.4	. . 53.5
E	10	253 13.1	280 34.5	37.9	270 06.3	04.8	52 57.6	08.7	352 13.6	53.5
S	11	268 15.6	295 34.5	36.8	285 07.0	04.1	67 59.9	08.7	7 15.8	53.5
D	12	283 18.0	310 34.4	S12 35.6	300 07.7	S 8 03.3	83 02.1	S 7 08.8	22 17.9	S21 53.6
A	13	298 20.5	325 34.4	34.5	315 08.4	02.6	98 04.3	08.9	37 20.1	53.6
Y	14	313 23.0	340 34.3	33.4	330 09.1	01.8	113 06.5	09.0	52 22.2	53.6
	15	328 25.4	355 34.3	. . 32.3	345 09.8	. . 01.0	128 08.8	. . 09.1	67 24.4	. . 53.6
	16	343 27.9	10 34.3	31.2	0 10.6	8 00.3	143 11.0	09.2	82 26.6	53.6
	17	358 30.3	25 34.2	30.0	15 11.3	7 59.5	158 13.2	09.2	97 28.7	53.6
	18	13 32.8	40 34.2	S12 28.9	30 12.0	S 7 58.8	173 15.5	S 7 09.3	112 30.9	S21 53.7
	19	28 35.3	55 34.2	27.8	45 12.7	58.0	188 17.7	09.4	127 33.0	53.7
	20	43 37.7	70 34.1	26.7	60 13.4	57.2	203 19.9	09.5	142 35.2	53.7
	21	58 40.2	85 34.1	. . 25.6	75 14.2	. . 56.5	218 22.2	. . 09.6	157 37.4	. . 53.7
	22	73 42.7	100 34.1	24.5	90 14.9	55.7	233 24.4	09.7	172 39.5	53.7
	23	88 45.1	115 34.0	23.3	105 15.6	55.0	248 26.6	09.7	187 41.7	53.8
	Mer. Pass.	h m 17 09.9	v −0.1	d 1.1	v 0.7	d 0.8	v 2.2	d 0.1	v 2.2	d 0.0

STARS

Name	SHA ° ′	Dec ° ′
Acamar	315 16.3	S40 14.6
Achernar	335 25.0	S57 09.4
Acrux	173 06.4	S63 11.2
Adhara	255 10.2	S28 59.9
Aldebaran	290 46.3	N16 32.4
Alioth	166 18.7	N55 51.8
Alkaid	152 57.2	N49 13.6
Al Na'ir	27 41.1	S46 52.9
Alnilam	275 43.6	S 1 11.7
Alphard	217 53.5	S 8 44.0
Alphecca	126 09.3	N26 39.5
Alpheratz	357 41.0	N29 11.1
Altair	62 06.2	N 8 55.0
Ankaa	353 13.4	S42 13.1
Antares	112 23.6	S26 27.9
Arcturus	145 53.7	N19 05.7
Atria	107 23.7	S69 03.1
Avior	234 16.3	S59 33.9
Bellatrix	278 29.1	N 6 21.7
Betelgeuse	270 58.4	N 7 24.4
Canopus	263 54.5	S52 42.5
Capella	280 30.4	N46 00.7
Deneb	49 30.2	N45 20.7
Denebola	182 31.2	N14 28.5
Diphda	348 53.5	S17 53.8
Dubhe	193 48.6	N61 39.3
Elnath	278 09.2	N28 37.1
Eltanin	90 45.6	N51 29.3
Enif	33 45.0	N 9 57.3
Fomalhaut	15 21.6	S29 32.1
Gacrux	171 58.1	S57 12.2
Gienah	175 49.8	S17 38.0
Hadar	148 44.6	S60 26.9
Hamal	327 57.9	N23 32.5
Kaus Aust.	83 41.1	S34 22.4
Kochab	137 21.0	N74 05.0
Markab	13 36.1	N15 17.9
Menkar	314 12.3	N 4 09.2
Menkent	148 04.8	S36 26.9
Miaplacidus	221 38.2	S69 47.1
Mirfak	308 36.5	N49 55.3
Nunki	75 55.7	S26 16.4
Peacock	53 16.1	S56 40.8
Pollux	243 24.5	N27 58.8
Procyon	244 56.9	N 5 10.7
Rasalhague	96 04.6	N12 33.0
Regulus	207 40.8	N11 52.9
Rigel	281 09.4	S 8 11.2
Rigil Kent.	139 48.7	S60 53.9
Sabik	102 10.1	S15 44.5
Schedar	349 37.7	N56 38.0
Shaula	96 19.1	S37 06.7
Sirius	258 31.2	S16 44.6
Spica	158 28.8	S11 14.8
Suhail	222 50.2	S43 30.1
Vega	80 37.8	N38 48.1
Zuben'ubi	137 02.9	S16 06.5

	SHA ° ′	Mer. Pass. h m
Venus	28 47.2	15 18
Mars	17 52.6	16 00
Jupiter	159 52.7	6 32
Saturn	99 10.8	10 34

UT d	h	SUN GHA ° ′	SUN Dec ° ′	MOON GHA ° ′	*v* ′	MOON Dec ° ′	*d* ′	HP ′
1	00	179 08.2	S22 59.9	147 06.1	11.1	S15 20.2	6.3	56.0
	01	194 07.9	59.7	161 36.2	11.1	15 13.9	6.3	56.1
	02	209 07.6	59.5	176 06.3	11.1	15 07.6	6.4	56.1
	03	224 07.3	. . 59.3	190 36.4	11.1	15 01.2	6.5	56.1
	04	239 07.1	59.1	205 06.5	11.2	14 54.7	6.6	56.1
	05	254 06.8	58.9	219 36.7	11.1	14 48.1	6.7	56.1
	06	269 06.5	S22 58.7	234 06.8	11.2	S14 41.4	6.7	56.2
	07	284 06.2	58.5	248 37.0	11.1	14 34.7	6.8	56.2
	08	299 05.9	58.3	263 07.1	11.2	14 27.9	6.9	56.2
S	09	314 05.6	. . 58.1	277 37.3	11.2	14 21.0	7.0	56.2
U	10	329 05.3	57.8	292 07.5	11.2	14 14.0	7.0	56.2
N	11	344 05.0	57.6	306 37.7	11.2	14 07.0	7.1	56.3
D	12	359 04.7	S22 57.4	321 07.9	11.3	S13 59.9	7.2	56.3
A	13	14 04.4	57.2	335 38.2	11.2	13 52.7	7.3	56.3
Y	14	29 04.1	57.0	350 08.4	11.3	13 45.4	7.4	56.3
	15	44 03.8	. . 56.8	4 38.7	11.2	13 38.0	7.4	56.3
	16	59 03.5	56.6	19 08.9	11.3	13 30.6	7.5	56.4
	17	74 03.2	56.3	33 39.2	11.3	13 23.1	7.5	56.4
	18	89 02.9	S22 56.1	48 09.5	11.3	S13 15.6	7.7	56.4
	19	104 02.6	55.9	62 39.8	11.3	13 07.9	7.7	56.4
	20	119 02.3	55.7	77 10.1	11.3	13 00.2	7.8	56.4
	21	134 02.1	. . 55.5	91 40.4	11.4	12 52.4	7.8	56.5
	22	149 01.8	55.2	106 10.8	11.3	12 44.6	7.9	56.5
	23	164 01.5	55.0	120 41.1	11.4	12 36.7	8.0	56.5
2	00	179 01.2	S22 54.8	135 11.5	11.4	S12 28.7	8.1	56.5
	01	194 00.9	54.6	149 41.9	11.4	12 20.6	8.1	56.6
	02	209 00.6	54.3	164 12.3	11.4	12 12.5	8.2	56.6
	03	224 00.3	. . 54.1	178 42.7	11.4	12 04.3	8.2	56.6
	04	239 00.0	53.9	193 13.1	11.4	11 56.1	8.4	56.6
	05	253 59.7	53.6	207 43.5	11.4	11 47.7	8.3	56.6
	06	268 59.4	S22 53.4	222 13.9	11.5	S11 39.4	8.5	56.7
	07	283 59.1	53.2	236 44.4	11.4	11 30.9	8.5	56.7
	08	298 58.8	53.0	251 14.8	11.5	11 22.4	8.6	56.7
M	09	313 58.6	. . 52.7	265 45.3	11.4	11 13.8	8.6	56.7
O	10	328 58.3	52.5	280 15.7	11.5	11 05.2	8.7	56.8
N	11	343 58.0	52.3	294 46.2	11.5	10 56.5	8.8	56.8
D	12	358 57.7	S22 52.0	309 16.7	11.5	S10 47.7	8.8	56.8
A	13	13 57.4	51.8	323 47.2	11.5	10 38.9	8.9	56.8
Y	14	28 57.1	51.6	338 17.7	11.5	10 30.0	9.0	56.8
	15	43 56.8	. . 51.3	352 48.2	11.6	10 21.0	9.0	56.9
	16	58 56.5	51.1	7 18.8	11.5	10 12.0	9.0	56.9
	17	73 56.2	50.9	21 49.3	11.5	10 03.0	9.1	56.9
	18	88 55.9	S22 50.6	36 19.8	11.6	S 9 53.9	9.2	56.9
	19	103 55.7	50.4	50 50.4	11.5	9 44.7	9.3	57.0
	20	118 55.4	50.1	65 20.9	11.6	9 35.4	9.2	57.0
	21	133 55.1	. . 49.9	79 51.5	11.5	9 26.2	9.4	57.0
	22	148 54.8	49.7	94 22.0	11.6	9 16.8	9.4	57.0
	23	163 54.5	49.4	108 52.6	11.6	9 07.4	9.4	57.0
3	00	178 54.2	S22 49.2	123 23.2	11.6	S 8 58.0	9.5	57.1
	01	193 53.9	48.9	137 53.8	11.5	8 48.5	9.6	57.1
	02	208 53.6	48.7	152 24.3	11.6	8 38.9	9.6	57.1
	03	223 53.3	. . 48.4	166 54.9	11.6	8 29.3	9.6	57.1
	04	238 53.1	48.2	181 25.5	11.6	8 19.7	9.7	57.2
	05	253 52.8	47.9	195 56.1	11.6	8 10.0	9.8	57.2
	06	268 52.5	S22 47.7	210 26.7	11.6	S 8 00.2	9.8	57.2
	07	283 52.2	47.4	224 57.3	11.6	7 50.4	9.8	57.2
T	08	298 51.9	47.2	239 27.9	11.6	7 40.6	9.9	57.3
U	09	313 51.6	. . 46.9	253 58.5	11.6	7 30.7	9.9	57.3
E	10	328 51.3	46.7	268 29.1	11.6	7 20.8	10.0	57.3
S	11	343 51.0	46.4	282 59.7	11.6	7 10.8	10.0	57.3
D	12	358 50.8	S22 46.2	297 30.3	11.6	S 7 00.8	10.1	57.3
A	13	13 50.5	45.9	312 00.9	11.6	6 50.7	10.1	57.4
Y	14	28 50.2	45.7	326 31.5	11.6	6 40.6	10.2	57.4
	15	43 49.9	. . 45.4	341 02.1	11.6	6 30.4	10.1	57.4
	16	58 49.6	45.2	355 32.7	11.6	6 20.3	10.3	57.4
	17	73 49.3	44.9	10 03.3	11.6	6 10.0	10.2	57.5
	18	88 49.0	S22 44.7	24 33.9	11.5	S 5 59.8	10.4	57.5
	19	103 48.8	44.4	39 04.4	11.6	5 49.4	10.3	57.5
	20	118 48.5	44.1	53 35.0	11.6	5 39.1	10.4	57.5
	21	133 48.2	. . 43.9	68 05.6	11.6	5 28.7	10.4	57.6
	22	148 47.9	43.6	82 36.2	11.5	5 18.3	10.5	57.6
	23	163 47.6	43.4	97 06.7	11.6	S 5 07.8	10.4	57.6
		SD 16.3	*d* 0.2	SD	15.3	15.5		15.6

Lat. °	Twilight Naut. h m	Twilight Civil h m	Sunrise h m	Moonrise 1 h m	Moonrise 2 h m	Moonrise 3 h m	Moonrise 4 h m
N 72	08 23	10 39	▬	11 58	11 49	11 41	11 34
N 70	08 04	09 47	▬	11 30	11 31	11 31	11 30
68	07 49	09 16	▬	11 09	11 17	11 22	11 26
66	07 37	08 52	10 25	10 52	11 05	11 15	11 24
64	07 26	08 33	09 48	10 39	10 56	11 09	11 21
62	07 17	08 18	09 22	10 27	10 47	11 04	11 19
60	07 09	08 05	09 02	10 17	10 40	10 59	11 17
N 58	07 02	07 54	08 45	10 08	10 34	10 55	11 16
56	06 55	07 44	08 31	10 01	10 28	10 52	11 14
54	06 50	07 35	08 19	09 54	10 23	10 49	11 13
52	06 44	07 27	08 08	09 48	10 18	10 46	11 12
50	06 39	07 20	07 58	09 42	10 14	10 43	11 11
45	06 28	07 05	07 38	09 30	10 05	10 37	11 08
N 40	06 18	06 52	07 22	09 20	09 57	10 32	11 06
35	06 09	06 40	07 08	09 12	09 51	10 28	11 04
30	06 00	06 30	06 56	09 04	09 45	10 24	11 03
20	05 44	06 12	06 36	08 51	09 35	10 18	11 00
N 10	05 28	05 55	06 17	08 40	09 26	10 12	10 58
0	05 12	05 38	06 00	08 29	09 18	10 07	10 56
S 10	04 53	05 20	05 43	08 18	09 10	10 01	10 53
20	04 31	05 00	05 25	08 07	09 01	09 56	10 51
30	04 03	04 36	05 03	07 54	08 51	09 49	10 48
35	03 45	04 21	04 51	07 46	08 45	09 45	10 47
40	03 22	04 03	04 36	07 37	08 38	09 41	10 45
45	02 52	03 41	04 18	07 27	08 31	09 36	10 43
S 50	02 09	03 13	03 57	07 15	08 21	09 30	10 41
52	01 43	02 58	03 46	07 09	08 17	09 27	10 40
54	01 04	02 41	03 34	07 03	08 12	09 24	10 38
56	////	02 20	03 20	06 56	08 07	09 21	10 37
58	////	01 52	03 04	06 48	08 01	09 17	10 36
S 60	////	01 10	02 45	06 38	07 54	09 13	10 34

Lat. °	Sunset h m	Twilight Civil h m	Twilight Naut. h m	Moonset 1 h m	Moonset 2 h m	Moonset 3 h m	Moonset 4 h m
N 72	▬	13 30	15 46	17 37	19 29	21 18	23 08
N 70	▬	14 21	16 05	18 04	19 45	21 27	23 09
68	▬	14 53	16 20	18 25	19 58	21 33	23 10
66	13 43	15 17	16 32	18 40	20 09	21 39	23 11
64	14 20	15 35	16 42	18 53	20 17	21 44	23 12
62	14 47	15 50	16 52	19 04	20 25	21 48	23 12
60	15 07	16 03	17 00	19 14	20 31	21 51	23 13
N 58	15 24	16 15	17 07	19 22	20 37	21 54	23 13
56	15 38	16 24	17 13	19 29	20 42	21 57	23 14
54	15 50	16 33	17 19	19 35	20 46	21 59	23 14
52	16 01	16 41	17 24	19 41	20 50	22 01	23 15
50	16 10	16 48	17 29	19 46	20 54	22 04	23 15
45	16 30	17 04	17 41	19 57	21 02	22 08	23 16
N 40	16 46	17 17	17 51	20 06	21 08	22 12	23 16
35	17 00	17 28	18 00	20 14	21 14	22 15	23 17
30	17 12	17 38	18 08	20 21	21 19	22 17	23 17
20	17 33	17 57	18 24	20 33	21 27	22 22	23 18
N 10	17 51	18 14	18 40	20 43	21 35	22 26	23 18
0	18 08	18 30	18 56	20 53	21 41	22 30	23 19
S 10	18 25	18 48	19 15	21 02	21 48	22 34	23 20
20	18 43	19 08	19 37	21 12	21 56	22 38	23 20
30	19 05	19 32	20 05	21 24	22 04	22 42	23 21
35	19 18	19 47	20 23	21 30	22 08	22 45	23 21
40	19 32	20 05	20 46	21 38	22 14	22 48	23 21
45	19 50	20 27	21 15	21 47	22 20	22 51	23 22
S 50	20 11	20 55	21 58	21 57	22 27	22 55	23 22
52	20 22	21 10	22 24	22 02	22 31	22 57	23 23
54	20 34	21 27	23 02	22 07	22 34	22 59	23 23
56	20 47	21 47	////	22 13	22 38	23 01	23 23
58	21 03	22 15	////	22 20	22 43	23 04	23 23
S 60	21 22	22 56	////	22 27	22 48	23 06	23 24

Day	SUN Eqn. of Time 00ʰ	SUN Eqn. of Time 12ʰ	SUN Mer. Pass.	MOON Mer. Pass. Upper	MOON Mer. Pass. Lower	MOON Age	MOON Phase
d	m s	m s	h m	h m	h m	d	%
1	03 26	03 41	12 04	14 41	02 16	03	10
2	03 55	04 09	12 04	15 30	03 05	04	17
3	04 23	04 36	12 05	16 18	03 54	05	26

UT d	h	ARIES GHA ° ′	VENUS −4·5 GHA ° ′	VENUS Dec ° ′	MARS +0·9 GHA ° ′	MARS Dec ° ′	JUPITER −2·0 GHA ° ′	JUPITER Dec ° ′	SATURN +0·5 GHA ° ′	SATURN Dec ° ′
4 WEDNESDAY	00	103 47.6	130 34.0	S12 22.2	120 16.3	S 7 54.2	263 28.9	S 7 09.8	202 43.8	S21 53.8
	01	118 50.1	145 34.0	21.1	135 17.0	53.4	278 31.1	09.9	217 46.0	53.8
	02	133 52.5	160 33.9	20.0	150 17.8	52.7	293 33.3	10.0	232 48.2	53.8
	03	148 55.0	175 33.9	. . 18.8	165 18.5	. . 51.9	308 35.5	. . 10.1	247 50.3	. . 53.8
	04	163 57.5	190 33.9	17.7	180 19.2	51.2	323 37.8	10.2	262 52.5	53.8
	05	178 59.9	205 33.9	16.6	195 19.9	50.4	338 40.0	10.2	277 54.7	53.9
	06	194 02.4	220 33.8	S12 15.5	210 20.6	S 7 49.7	353 42.2	S 7 10.3	292 56.8	S21 53.9
	07	209 04.8	235 33.8	14.4	225 21.3	48.9	8 44.5	10.4	307 59.0	53.9
	08	224 07.3	250 33.8	13.2	240 22.1	48.1	23 46.7	10.5	323 01.1	53.9
	09	239 09.8	265 33.8	. . 12.1	255 22.8	. . 47.4	38 48.9	. . 10.6	338 03.3	. . 53.9
	10	254 12.2	280 33.7	11.0	270 23.5	46.6	53 51.2	10.6	353 05.5	53.9
	11	269 14.7	295 33.7	09.9	285 24.2	45.9	68 53.4	10.7	8 07.6	54.0
	12	284 17.2	310 33.7	S12 08.7	300 25.0	S 7 45.1	83 55.6	S 7 10.8	23 09.8	S21 54.0
	13	299 19.6	325 33.7	07.6	315 25.7	44.3	98 57.9	10.9	38 12.0	54.0
	14	314 22.1	340 33.7	06.5	330 26.4	43.6	114 00.1	11.0	53 14.1	54.0
	15	329 24.6	355 33.7	. . 05.3	345 27.1	. . 42.8	129 02.4	. . 11.0	68 16.3	. . 54.0
	16	344 27.0	10 33.6	04.2	0 27.8	42.1	144 04.6	11.1	83 18.4	54.1
	17	359 29.5	25 33.6	03.1	15 28.6	41.3	159 06.8	11.2	98 20.6	54.1
	18	14 31.9	40 33.6	S12 02.0	30 29.3	S 7 40.5	174 09.1	S 7 11.3	113 22.8	S21 54.1
	19	29 34.4	55 33.6	12 00.8	45 30.0	39.8	189 11.3	11.4	128 24.9	54.1
	20	44 36.9	70 33.6	11 59.7	60 30.7	39.0	204 13.5	11.5	143 27.1	54.1
	21	59 39.3	85 33.6	. . 58.6	75 31.4	. . 38.2	219 15.8	. . 11.5	158 29.3	. . 54.1
	22	74 41.8	100 33.6	57.5	90 32.2	37.5	234 18.0	11.6	173 31.4	54.2
	23	89 44.3	115 33.6	56.3	105 32.9	36.7	249 20.2	11.7	188 33.6	54.2
5 THURSDAY	00	104 46.7	130 33.6	S11 55.2	120 33.6	S 7 36.0	264 22.5	S 7 11.8	203 35.7	S21 54.2
	01	119 49.2	145 33.5	54.1	135 34.3	35.2	279 24.7	11.9	218 37.9	54.2
	02	134 51.7	160 33.5	52.9	150 35.1	34.4	294 27.0	11.9	233 40.1	54.2
	03	149 54.1	175 33.5	. . 51.8	165 35.8	. . 33.7	309 29.2	. . 12.0	248 42.2	. . 54.2
	04	164 56.6	190 33.5	50.7	180 36.5	32.9	324 31.4	12.1	263 44.4	54.3
	05	179 59.1	205 33.5	49.5	195 37.2	32.2	339 33.7	12.2	278 46.6	54.3
	06	195 01.5	220 33.5	S11 48.4	210 37.9	S 7 31.4	354 35.9	S 7 12.3	293 48.7	S21 54.3
	07	210 04.0	235 33.5	47.3	225 38.7	30.6	9 38.2	12.3	308 50.9	54.3
	08	225 06.4	250 33.5	46.1	240 39.4	29.9	24 40.4	12.4	323 53.0	54.3
	09	240 08.9	265 33.5	. . 45.0	255 40.1	. . 29.1	39 42.6	. . 12.5	338 55.2	. . 54.4
	10	255 11.4	280 33.5	43.9	270 40.8	28.3	54 44.9	12.6	353 57.4	54.4
	11	270 13.8	295 33.5	42.7	285 41.6	27.6	69 47.1	12.6	8 59.5	54.4
	12	285 16.3	310 33.5	S11 41.6	300 42.3	S 7 26.8	84 49.4	S 7 12.7	24 01.7	S21 54.4
	13	300 18.8	325 33.5	40.5	315 43.0	26.1	99 51.6	12.8	39 03.9	54.4
	14	315 21.2	340 33.5	39.3	330 43.7	25.3	114 53.8	12.9	54 06.0	54.4
	15	330 23.7	355 33.5	. . 38.2	345 44.5	. . 24.5	129 56.1	. . 13.0	69 08.2	. . 54.5
	16	345 26.2	10 33.6	37.1	0 45.2	23.8	144 58.3	13.0	84 10.4	54.5
	17	0 28.6	25 33.6	35.9	15 45.9	23.0	160 00.6	13.1	99 12.5	54.5
	18	15 31.1	40 33.6	S11 34.8	30 46.6	S 7 22.2	175 02.8	S 7 13.2	114 14.7	S21 54.5
	19	30 33.5	55 33.6	33.7	45 47.3	21.5	190 05.0	13.3	129 16.9	54.5
	20	45 36.0	70 33.6	32.5	60 48.1	20.7	205 07.3	13.4	144 19.0	54.5
	21	60 38.5	85 33.6	. . 31.4	75 48.8	. . 20.0	220 09.5	. . 13.4	159 21.2	. . 54.6
	22	75 40.9	100 33.6	30.2	90 49.5	19.2	235 11.8	13.5	174 23.3	54.6
	23	90 43.4	115 33.6	29.1	105 50.2	18.4	250 14.0	13.6	189 25.5	54.6
6 FRIDAY	00	105 45.9	130 33.6	S11 28.0	120 51.0	S 7 17.7	265 16.3	S 7 13.7	204 27.7	S21 54.6
	01	120 48.3	145 33.7	26.8	135 51.7	16.9	280 18.5	13.7	219 29.8	54.6
	02	135 50.8	160 33.7	25.7	150 52.4	16.1	295 20.7	13.8	234 32.0	54.6
	03	150 53.3	175 33.7	. . 24.6	165 53.1	. . 15.4	310 23.0	. . 13.9	249 34.2	. . 54.7
	04	165 55.7	190 33.7	23.4	180 53.9	14.6	325 25.2	14.0	264 36.3	54.7
	05	180 58.2	205 33.7	22.3	195 54.6	13.9	340 27.5	14.1	279 38.5	54.7
	06	196 00.7	220 33.8	S11 21.1	210 55.3	S 7 13.1	355 29.7	S 7 14.1	294 40.7	S21 54.7
	07	211 03.1	235 33.8	20.0	225 56.0	12.3	10 32.0	14.2	309 42.8	54.7
	08	226 05.6	250 33.8	18.8	240 56.8	11.6	25 34.2	14.3	324 45.0	54.8
	09	241 08.0	265 33.8	. . 17.7	255 57.5	. . 10.8	40 36.5	. . 14.4	339 47.2	. . 54.8
	10	256 10.5	280 33.8	16.6	270 58.2	10.0	55 38.7	14.4	354 49.3	54.8
	11	271 13.0	295 33.9	15.4	285 58.9	09.3	70 41.0	14.5	9 51.5	54.8
	12	286 15.4	310 33.9	S11 14.3	300 59.7	S 7 08.5	85 43.2	S 7 14.6	24 53.6	S21 54.8
	13	301 17.9	325 33.9	13.1	316 00.4	07.7	100 45.4	14.7	39 55.8	54.8
	14	316 20.4	340 34.0	12.0	331 01.1	07.0	115 47.7	14.7	54 58.0	54.9
	15	331 22.8	355 34.0	. . 10.9	346 01.9	. . 06.2	130 49.9	. . 14.8	70 00.1	. . 54.9
	16	346 25.3	10 34.0	09.7	1 02.6	05.4	145 52.2	14.9	85 02.3	54.9
	17	1 27.8	25 34.0	08.6	16 03.3	04.7	160 54.4	15.0	100 04.5	54.9
	18	16 30.2	40 34.1	S11 07.4	31 04.0	S 7 03.9	175 56.7	S 7 15.0	115 06.6	S21 54.9
	19	31 32.7	55 34.1	06.3	46 04.8	03.2	190 58.9	15.1	130 08.8	54.9
	20	46 35.2	70 34.1	05.1	61 05.5	02.4	206 01.2	15.2	145 11.0	55.0
	21	61 37.6	85 34.2	. . 04.0	76 06.2	. . 01.6	221 03.4	. . 15.3	160 13.1	. . 55.0
	22	76 40.1	100 34.2	02.8	91 06.9	00.9	236 05.7	15.3	175 15.3	55.0
	23	91 42.5	115 34.2	01.7	106 07.7	00.1	251 07.9	15.4	190 17.5	55.0
Mer. Pass.		h m 16 58.1	*v* 0.0	*d* 1.1	*v* 0.7	*d* 0.8	*v* 2.2	*d* 0.1	*v* 2.2	*d* 0.0

STARS

Name	SHA ° ′	Dec ° ′
Acamar	315 16.3	S40 14.6
Achernar	335 25.0	S57 09.5
Acrux	173 06.3	S63 11.3
Adhara	255 10.2	S28 59.9
Aldebaran	290 46.3	N16 32.4
Alioth	166 18.7	N55 51.8
Alkaid	152 57.2	N49 13.6
Al Na'ir	27 41.1	S46 52.9
Alnilam	275 43.6	S 1 11.7
Alphard	217 53.5	S 8 44.0
Alphecca	126 09.2	N26 39.5
Alpheratz	357 41.0	N29 11.1
Altair	62 06.2	N 8 54.9
Ankaa	353 13.5	S42 13.1
Antares	112 23.6	S26 27.9
Arcturus	145 53.7	N19 05.6
Atria	107 23.7	S69 03.1
Avior	234 16.3	S59 33.9
Bellatrix	278 29.1	N 6 21.7
Betelgeuse	270 58.4	N 7 24.4
Canopus	263 54.5	S52 42.5
Capella	280 30.4	N46 00.7
Deneb	49 30.2	N45 20.7
Denebola	182 31.1	N14 28.5
Diphda	348 53.5	S17 53.8
Dubhe	193 48.6	N61 39.3
Elnath	278 09.2	N28 37.1
Eltanin	90 45.6	N51 29.3
Enif	33 45.0	N 9 57.3
Fomalhaut	15 21.6	S29 32.1
Gacrux	171 58.0	S57 12.2
Gienah	175 49.7	S17 38.1
Hadar	148 44.5	S60 26.9
Hamal	327 57.9	N23 32.5
Kaus Aust.	83 41.0	S34 22.4
Kochab	137 20.9	N74 05.0
Markab	13 36.1	N15 17.9
Menkar	314 12.4	N 4 09.2
Menkent	148 04.8	S36 26.9
Miaplacidus	221 38.2	S69 47.1
Mirfak	308 36.5	N49 55.3
Nunki	75 55.7	S26 16.3
Peacock	53 16.1	S56 40.8
Pollux	243 24.5	N27 58.8
Procyon	244 56.9	N 5 10.7
Rasalhague	96 04.6	N12 33.0
Regulus	207 40.8	N11 52.9
Rigel	281 09.4	S 8 11.2
Rigil Kent.	139 48.6	S60 53.9
Sabik	102 10.1	S15 44.5
Schedar	349 37.7	N56 38.0
Shaula	96 19.0	S37 06.7
Sirius	258 31.2	S16 44.6
Spica	158 28.7	S11 14.9
Suhail	222 50.2	S43 30.1
Vega	80 37.8	N38 48.1
Zuben'ubi	137 02.9	S16 06.5

	SHA ° ′	Mer. Pass. h m
Venus	25 46.8	15 18
Mars	15 46.9	15 57
Jupiter	159 35.8	6 22
Saturn	98 49.0	10 24

UT	SUN GHA	SUN Dec	MOON GHA	*v*	MOON Dec	*d*	HP
d h	° ′	° ′	° ′	′	° ′	′	′
WEDNESDAY							
4 00	178 47.3	S22 43.1	111 37.3	11.5	S 4 57.4	10.6	57.6
01	193 47.1	42.8	126 07.8	11.6	4 46.8	10.5	57.7
02	208 46.8	42.6	140 38.4	11.5	4 36.3	10.6	57.7
03	223 46.5	. . 42.3	155 08.9	11.5	4 25.7	10.6	57.7
04	238 46.2	42.0	169 39.4	11.5	4 15.1	10.7	57.7
05	253 45.9	41.8	184 09.9	11.5	4 04.4	10.7	57.7
06	268 45.6	S22 41.5	198 40.4	11.5	S 3 53.7	10.7	57.8
07	283 45.4	41.2	213 10.9	11.5	3 43.0	10.7	57.8
08	298 45.1	41.0	227 41.4	11.4	3 32.3	10.7	57.8
09	313 44.8	. . 40.7	242 11.8	11.5	3 21.6	10.8	57.8
10	328 44.5	40.4	256 42.3	11.4	3 10.8	10.8	57.9
11	343 44.2	40.2	271 12.7	11.4	3 00.0	10.9	57.9
12	358 43.9	S22 39.9	285 43.1	11.4	S 2 49.1	10.8	57.9
13	13 43.7	39.6	300 13.5	11.4	2 38.3	10.9	57.9
14	28 43.4	39.4	314 43.9	11.4	2 27.4	10.9	58.0
15	43 43.1	. . 39.1	329 14.3	11.3	2 16.5	10.9	58.0
16	58 42.8	38.8	343 44.6	11.3	2 05.6	11.0	58.0
17	73 42.5	38.5	358 14.9	11.4	1 54.6	10.9	58.0
18	88 42.3	S22 38.3	12 45.3	11.3	S 1 43.7	11.0	58.1
19	103 42.0	38.0	27 15.6	11.2	1 32.7	11.0	58.1
20	118 41.7	37.7	41 45.8	11.3	1 21.7	11.0	58.1
21	133 41.4	. . 37.4	56 16.1	11.2	1 10.7	11.0	58.1
22	148 41.1	37.1	70 46.3	11.2	0 59.7	11.1	58.2
23	163 40.9	36.9	85 16.5	11.2	0 48.6	11.0	58.2
THURSDAY							
5 00	178 40.6	S22 36.6	99 46.7	11.2	S 0 37.6	11.1	58.2
01	193 40.3	36.3	114 16.9	11.1	0 26.5	11.1	58.2
02	208 40.0	36.0	128 47.0	11.1	0 15.4	11.1	58.3
03	223 39.7	. . 35.7	143 17.1	11.1	S 0 04.3	11.1	58.3
04	238 39.5	35.5	157 47.2	11.0	N 0 06.8	11.1	58.3
05	253 39.2	35.2	172 17.2	11.1	0 17.9	11.1	58.3
06	268 38.9	S22 34.9	186 47.3	11.0	N 0 29.0	11.1	58.4
07	283 38.6	34.6	201 17.3	10.9	0 40.1	11.1	58.4
08	298 38.4	34.3	215 47.2	11.0	0 51.2	11.2	58.4
09	313 38.1	. . 34.0	230 17.2	10.9	1 02.4	11.1	58.4
10	328 37.8	33.7	244 47.1	10.9	1 13.5	11.1	58.5
11	343 37.5	33.4	259 17.0	10.8	1 24.6	11.2	58.5
12	358 37.2	S22 33.2	273 46.8	10.8	N 1 35.8	11.1	58.5
13	13 37.0	32.9	288 16.6	10.8	1 46.9	11.1	58.5
14	28 36.7	32.6	302 46.4	10.7	1 58.0	11.2	58.6
15	43 36.4	. . 32.3	317 16.1	10.7	2 09.2	11.1	58.6
16	58 36.1	32.0	331 45.8	10.7	2 20.3	11.1	58.6
17	73 35.9	31.7	346 15.5	10.7	2 31.4	11.2	58.6
18	88 35.6	S22 31.4	0 45.2	10.5	N 2 42.6	11.1	58.7
19	103 35.3	31.1	15 14.7	10.6	2 53.7	11.1	58.7
20	118 35.0	30.8	29 44.3	10.5	3 04.8	11.1	58.7
21	133 34.8	. . 30.5	44 13.8	10.5	3 15.9	11.1	58.7
22	148 34.5	30.2	58 43.3	10.5	3 27.0	11.1	58.8
23	163 34.2	29.9	73 12.8	10.4	3 38.1	11.1	58.8
FRIDAY							
6 00	178 33.9	S22 29.6	87 42.2	10.3	N 3 49.2	11.0	58.8
01	193 33.7	29.3	102 11.5	10.3	4 00.2	11.1	58.8
02	208 33.4	29.0	116 40.8	10.3	4 11.3	11.0	58.8
03	223 33.1	. . 28.7	131 10.1	10.2	4 22.3	11.0	58.9
04	238 32.8	28.4	145 39.3	10.2	4 33.3	11.0	58.9
05	253 32.6	28.1	160 08.5	10.2	4 44.3	11.0	58.9
06	268 32.3	S22 27.8	174 37.7	10.1	N 4 55.3	11.0	58.9
07	283 32.0	27.5	189 06.8	10.0	5 06.3	10.9	59.0
08	298 31.7	27.2	203 35.8	10.0	5 17.2	11.0	59.0
09	313 31.5	. . 26.9	218 04.8	10.0	5 28.2	10.9	59.0
10	328 31.2	26.6	232 33.8	9.9	5 39.1	10.9	59.0
11	343 30.9	26.3	247 02.7	9.8	5 50.0	10.8	59.1
12	358 30.7	S22 26.0	261 31.5	9.9	N 6 00.8	10.8	59.1
13	13 30.4	25.7	276 00.4	9.7	6 11.6	10.9	59.1
14	28 30.1	25.3	290 29.1	9.7	6 22.5	10.7	59.1
15	43 29.8	. . 25.0	304 57.8	9.7	6 33.2	10.8	59.2
16	58 29.6	24.7	319 26.5	9.6	6 44.0	10.7	59.2
17	73 29.3	24.4	333 55.1	9.5	6 54.7	10.7	59.2
18	88 29.0	S22 24.1	348 23.6	9.5	N 7 05.4	10.6	59.2
19	103 28.8	23.8	2 52.1	9.5	7 16.0	10.7	59.2
20	118 28.5	23.5	17 20.6	9.4	7 26.7	10.6	59.3
21	133 28.2	. . 23.2	31 49.0	9.3	7 37.3	10.5	59.3
22	148 27.9	22.8	46 17.3	9.3	7 47.8	10.5	59.3
23	163 27.7	22.5	60 45.6	9.2	N 7 58.3	10.5	59.3
	SD 16.3	*d* 0.3	SD 15.8		15.9		16.1

Lat.	Twilight Naut.	Twilight Civil	Sunrise	Moonrise 4	Moonrise 5	Moonrise 6	Moonrise 7
°	h m	h m	h m	h m	h m	h m	h m
N 72	08 19	10 29	▬	11 34	11 27	11 20	11 13
N 70	08 01	09 42	▬	11 30	11 29	11 28	11 29
68	07 47	09 12	11 27	11 26	11 31	11 35	11 41
66	07 35	08 49	10 19	11 24	11 32	11 41	11 51
64	07 25	08 31	09 44	11 21	11 33	11 45	12 00
62	07 16	08 16	09 19	11 19	11 34	11 49	12 07
60	07 08	08 04	08 59	11 17	11 35	11 53	12 14
N 58	07 01	07 53	08 43	11 16	11 35	11 56	12 20
56	06 55	07 43	08 30	11 14	11 36	11 59	12 25
54	06 49	07 35	08 18	11 13	11 37	12 02	12 29
52	06 44	07 27	08 07	11 12	11 37	12 04	12 33
50	06 39	07 20	07 58	11 11	11 38	12 06	12 37
45	06 28	07 05	07 38	11 08	11 39	12 11	12 45
N 40	06 18	06 52	07 22	11 06	11 40	12 15	12 52
35	06 09	06 41	07 09	11 04	11 41	12 18	12 58
30	06 01	06 31	06 57	11 03	11 41	12 21	13 04
20	05 45	06 12	06 36	11 00	11 43	12 27	13 13
N 10	05 30	05 56	06 19	10 58	11 44	12 31	13 21
0	05 13	05 39	06 02	10 56	11 45	12 36	13 29
S 10	04 55	05 22	05 45	10 53	11 46	12 40	13 36
20	04 33	05 02	05 27	10 51	11 47	12 45	13 45
30	04 05	04 38	05 05	10 48	11 49	12 51	13 54
35	03 47	04 24	04 53	10 47	11 50	12 54	14 00
40	03 25	04 06	04 39	10 45	11 51	12 58	14 06
45	02 56	03 45	04 21	10 43	11 52	13 02	14 13
S 50	02 14	03 16	04 00	10 41	11 53	13 07	14 22
52	01 49	03 02	03 50	10 40	11 54	13 09	14 27
54	01 13	02 46	03 38	10 38	11 54	13 12	14 31
56	////	02 25	03 25	10 37	11 55	13 15	14 36
58	////	01 59	03 09	10 36	11 56	13 18	14 42
S 60	////	01 20	02 50	10 34	11 57	13 22	14 48

Lat.	Sunset	Twilight Civil	Twilight Naut.	Moonset 4	Moonset 5	Moonset 6	Moonset 7
°	h m	h m	h m	h m	h m	h m	h m
N 72	▬	13 43	15 53	23 08	24 59	00 59	02 55
N 70	▬	14 29	16 10	23 09	24 53	00 53	02 41
68	12 44	15 00	16 25	23 10	24 49	00 49	02 30
66	13 52	15 22	16 37	23 11	24 45	00 45	02 21
64	14 27	15 40	16 47	23 12	24 42	00 42	02 14
62	14 52	15 55	16 56	23 12	24 39	00 39	02 08
60	15 12	16 08	17 03	23 13	24 37	00 37	02 02
N 58	15 28	16 19	17 10	23 13	24 34	00 34	01 57
56	15 42	16 28	17 17	23 14	24 33	00 33	01 53
54	15 54	16 37	17 22	23 14	24 31	00 31	01 49
52	16 04	16 44	17 28	23 15	24 29	00 29	01 46
50	16 13	16 51	17 32	23 15	24 28	00 28	01 42
45	16 33	17 07	17 43	23 16	24 25	00 25	01 36
N 40	16 49	17 19	17 53	23 16	24 22	00 22	01 30
35	17 03	17 31	18 02	23 17	24 20	00 20	01 25
30	17 14	17 41	18 10	23 17	24 18	00 18	01 21
20	17 35	17 59	18 26	23 18	24 15	00 15	01 13
N 10	17 53	18 15	18 41	23 18	24 12	00 12	01 07
0	18 09	18 32	18 58	23 19	24 09	00 09	01 01
S 10	18 26	18 49	19 16	23 20	24 06	00 06	00 54
20	18 44	19 09	19 38	23 20	24 03	00 03	00 48
30	19 05	19 33	20 05	23 21	24 00	00 00	00 41
35	19 18	19 47	20 23	23 21	23 58	24 36	00 36
40	19 32	20 04	20 45	23 21	23 55	24 31	00 31
45	19 49	20 26	21 14	23 22	23 53	24 26	00 26
S 50	20 11	20 54	21 56	23 22	23 50	24 19	00 19
52	20 21	21 08	22 20	23 23	23 48	24 16	00 16
54	20 32	21 25	22 55	23 23	23 47	24 13	00 13
56	20 46	21 45	////	23 23	23 45	24 09	00 09
58	21 01	22 11	////	23 23	23 43	24 05	00 05
S 60	21 20	22 48	////	23 24	23 41	24 00	00 00

Day	SUN Eqn. of Time 00^h	SUN Eqn. of Time 12^h	SUN Mer. Pass.	MOON Mer. Pass. Upper	MOON Mer. Pass. Lower	MOON Age	MOON Phase
d	m s	m s	h m	h m	h m	d %	
4	04 50	05 04	12 05	17 07	04 43	06 36	
5	05 17	05 30	12 06	17 57	05 32	07 47	◑
6	05 44	05 57	12 06	18 48	06 22	08 58	

	UT	ARIES	VENUS −4·5		MARS +0·9		JUPITER −2·0		SATURN +0·5	
		GHA	GHA	Dec	GHA	Dec	GHA	Dec	GHA	Dec
	d h	° ′	° ′	° ′	° ′	° ′	° ′	° ′	° ′	° ′
	7 00	106 45.0	130 34.3	S11 00.6	121 08.4	S 6 59.3	266 10.2	S 7 15.5	205 19.6	S21 55.0
	01	121 47.5	145 34.3	10 59.4	136 09.1	58.6	281 12.4	15.6	220 21.8	55.0
	02	136 49.9	160 34.4	58.3	151 09.9	57.8	296 14.7	15.6	235 24.0	55.1
	03	151 52.4	175 34.4	. . 57.1	166 10.6	. . 57.0	311 16.9	. . 15.7	250 26.1	. . 55.1
	04	166 54.9	190 34.4	56.0	181 11.3	56.3	326 19.2	15.8	265 28.3	55.1
	05	181 57.3	205 34.5	54.8	196 12.0	55.5	341 21.4	15.9	280 30.5	55.1
	06	196 59.8	220 34.5	S10 53.7	211 12.8	S 6 54.7	356 23.7	S 7 15.9	295 32.6	S21 55.1
	07	212 02.3	235 34.6	52.5	226 13.5	54.0	11 25.9	16.0	310 34.8	55.1
S	08	227 04.7	250 34.6	51.4	241 14.2	53.2	26 28.2	16.1	325 37.0	55.2
A	09	242 07.2	265 34.7	. . 50.2	256 14.9	. . 52.4	41 30.4	. . 16.2	340 39.1	. . 55.2
T	10	257 09.6	280 34.7	49.1	271 15.7	51.7	56 32.7	16.2	355 41.3	55.2
U	11	272 12.1	295 34.8	47.9	286 16.4	50.9	71 34.9	16.3	10 43.5	55.2
R	12	287 14.6	310 34.8	S10 46.8	301 17.1	S 6 50.1	86 37.2	S 7 16.4	25 45.6	S21 55.2
D	13	302 17.0	325 34.9	45.6	316 17.9	49.4	101 39.4	16.5	40 47.8	55.2
A	14	317 19.5	340 34.9	44.5	331 18.6	48.6	116 41.7	16.5	55 50.0	55.3
Y	15	332 22.0	355 35.0	. . 43.3	346 19.3	. . 47.8	131 44.0	. . 16.6	70 52.1	. . 55.3
	16	347 24.4	10 35.0	42.2	1 20.0	47.1	146 46.2	16.7	85 54.3	55.3
	17	2 26.9	25 35.1	41.0	16 20.8	46.3	161 48.5	16.8	100 56.5	55.3
	18	17 29.4	40 35.1	S10 39.9	31 21.5	S 6 45.5	176 50.7	S 7 16.8	115 58.6	S21 55.3
	19	32 31.8	55 35.2	38.7	46 22.2	44.8	191 53.0	16.9	131 00.8	55.3
	20	47 34.3	70 35.2	37.6	61 23.0	44.0	206 55.2	17.0	146 03.0	55.4
	21	62 36.8	85 35.3	. . 36.4	76 23.7	. . 43.2	221 57.5	. . 17.0	161 05.1	. . 55.4
	22	77 39.2	100 35.4	35.3	91 24.4	42.5	236 59.7	17.1	176 07.3	55.4
	23	92 41.7	115 35.4	34.1	106 25.2	41.7	252 02.0	17.2	191 09.5	55.4
	8 00	107 44.1	130 35.5	S10 33.0	121 25.9	S 6 40.9	267 04.2	S 7 17.3	206 11.6	S21 55.4
	01	122 46.6	145 35.5	31.8	136 26.6	40.2	282 06.5	17.3	221 13.8	55.4
	02	137 49.1	160 35.6	30.6	151 27.3	39.4	297 08.8	17.4	236 16.0	55.5
	03	152 51.5	175 35.7	. . 29.5	166 28.1	. . 38.6	312 11.0	. . 17.5	251 18.1	. . 55.5
	04	167 54.0	190 35.7	28.3	181 28.8	37.9	327 13.3	17.6	266 20.3	55.5
	05	182 56.5	205 35.8	27.2	196 29.5	37.1	342 15.5	17.6	281 22.5	55.5
	06	197 58.9	220 35.9	S10 26.0	211 30.3	S 6 36.3	357 17.8	S 7 17.7	296 24.6	S21 55.5
	07	213 01.4	235 35.9	24.9	226 31.0	35.6	12 20.0	17.8	311 26.8	55.5
	08	228 03.9	250 36.0	23.7	241 31.7	34.8	27 22.3	17.8	326 29.0	55.6
S	09	243 06.3	265 36.1	. . 22.6	256 32.5	. . 34.0	42 24.6	. . 17.9	341 31.1	. . 55.6
U	10	258 08.8	280 36.1	21.4	271 33.2	33.3	57 26.8	18.0	356 33.3	55.6
N	11	273 11.3	295 36.2	20.3	286 33.9	32.5	72 29.1	18.1	11 35.5	55.6
D	12	288 13.7	310 36.3	S10 19.1	301 34.7	S 6 31.7	87 31.3	S 7 18.1	26 37.6	S21 55.6
A	13	303 16.2	325 36.4	17.9	316 35.4	31.0	102 33.6	18.2	41 39.8	55.6
Y	14	318 18.6	340 36.4	16.8	331 36.1	30.2	117 35.9	18.3	56 42.0	55.7
	15	333 21.1	355 36.5	. . 15.6	346 36.8	. . 29.4	132 38.1	. . 18.3	71 44.1	. . 55.7
	16	348 23.6	10 36.6	14.5	1 37.6	28.7	147 40.4	18.4	86 46.3	55.7
	17	3 26.0	25 36.7	13.3	16 38.3	27.9	162 42.6	18.5	101 48.5	55.7
	18	18 28.5	40 36.7	S10 12.1	31 39.0	S 6 27.1	177 44.9	S 7 18.6	116 50.6	S21 55.7
	19	33 31.0	55 36.8	11.0	46 39.8	26.3	192 47.2	18.6	131 52.8	55.7
	20	48 33.4	70 36.9	09.8	61 40.5	25.6	207 49.4	18.7	146 55.0	55.7
	21	63 35.9	85 37.0	. . 08.7	76 41.2	. . 24.8	222 51.7	. . 18.8	161 57.1	. . 55.8
	22	78 38.4	100 37.1	07.5	91 42.0	24.0	237 53.9	18.8	176 59.3	55.8
	23	93 40.8	115 37.1	06.4	106 42.7	23.3	252 56.2	18.9	192 01.5	55.8
	9 00	108 43.3	130 37.2	S10 05.2	121 43.4	S 6 22.5	267 58.5	S 7 19.0	207 03.7	S21 55.8
	01	123 45.8	145 37.3	04.0	136 44.2	21.7	283 00.7	19.0	222 05.8	55.8
	02	138 48.2	160 37.4	02.9	151 44.9	21.0	298 03.0	19.1	237 08.0	55.8
	03	153 50.7	175 37.5	. . 01.7	166 45.6	. . 20.2	313 05.3	. . 19.2	252 10.2	. . 55.9
	04	168 53.1	190 37.6	10 00.6	181 46.4	19.4	328 07.5	19.3	267 12.3	55.9
	05	183 55.6	205 37.7	9 59.4	196 47.1	18.7	343 09.8	19.3	282 14.5	55.9
	06	198 58.1	220 37.7	S 9 58.2	211 47.8	S 6 17.9	358 12.0	S 7 19.4	297 16.7	S21 55.9
	07	214 00.5	235 37.8	57.1	226 48.6	17.1	13 14.3	19.5	312 18.8	55.9
	08	229 03.0	250 37.9	55.9	241 49.3	16.4	28 16.6	19.5	327 21.0	55.9
M	09	244 05.5	265 38.0	. . 54.7	256 50.0	. . 15.6	43 18.8	. . 19.6	342 23.2	. . 56.0
O	10	259 07.9	280 38.1	53.6	271 50.8	14.8	58 21.1	19.7	357 25.3	56.0
N	11	274 10.4	295 38.2	52.4	286 51.5	14.0	73 23.4	19.7	12 27.5	56.0
D	12	289 12.9	310 38.3	S 9 51.3	301 52.2	S 6 13.3	88 25.6	S 7 19.8	27 29.7	S21 56.0
A	13	304 15.3	325 38.4	50.1	316 53.0	12.5	103 27.9	19.9	42 31.8	56.0
Y	14	319 17.8	340 38.5	48.9	331 53.7	11.7	118 30.2	19.9	57 34.0	56.0
	15	334 20.2	355 38.6	. . 47.8	346 54.4	. . 11.0	133 32.4	. . 20.0	72 36.2	. . 56.1
	16	349 22.7	10 38.7	46.6	1 55.2	10.2	148 34.7	20.1	87 38.4	56.1
	17	4 25.2	25 38.8	45.4	16 55.9	09.4	163 37.0	20.1	102 40.5	56.1
	18	19 27.6	40 38.9	S 9 44.3	31 56.6	S 6 08.7	178 39.2	S 7 20.2	117 42.7	S21 56.1
	19	34 30.1	55 39.0	43.1	46 57.4	07.9	193 41.5	20.3	132 44.9	56.1
	20	49 32.6	70 39.1	41.9	61 58.1	07.1	208 43.8	20.3	147 47.0	56.1
	21	64 35.0	85 39.2	. . 40.8	76 58.8	. . 06.3	223 46.0	. . 20.4	162 49.2	. . 56.1
	22	79 37.5	100 39.3	39.6	91 59.6	05.6	238 48.3	20.5	177 51.4	56.2
	23	94 40.0	115 39.4	38.4	107 00.3	04.8	253 50.6	20.5	192 53.5	56.2
	Mer. Pass.	h m 16 46.3	v 0.1	d 1.2	v 0.7	d 0.8	v 2.3	d 0.1	v 2.2	d 0.0

STARS Name	SHA	Dec
	° ′	° ′
Acamar	315 16.4	S40 14.6
Achernar	335 25.0	S57 09.5
Acrux	173 06.3	S63 11.3
Adhara	255 10.2	S28 59.9
Aldebaran	290 46.3	N16 32.4
Alioth	166 18.7	N55 51.8
Alkaid	152 57.2	N49 13.5
Al Na'ir	27 41.1	S46 52.8
Alnilam	275 43.6	S 1 11.7
Alphard	217 53.4	S 8 44.1
Alphecca	126 09.2	N26 39.5
Alpheratz	357 41.1	N29 11.1
Altair	62 06.2	N 8 54.9
Ankaa	353 13.5	S42 13.1
Antares	112 23.6	S26 27.9
Arcturus	145 53.7	N19 05.6
Atria	107 23.7	S69 03.1
Avior	234 16.3	S59 33.9
Bellatrix	278 29.1	N 6 21.6
Betelgeuse	270 58.4	N 7 24.4
Canopus	263 54.5	S52 42.6
Capella	280 30.4	N46 00.7
Deneb	49 30.2	N45 20.7
Denebola	182 31.1	N14 28.5
Diphda	348 53.5	S17 53.8
Dubhe	193 48.6	N61 39.3
Elnath	278 09.2	N28 37.1
Eltanin	90 45.5	N51 29.3
Enif	33 45.0	N 9 57.3
Fomalhaut	15 21.6	S29 32.1
Gacrux	171 58.0	S57 12.2
Gienah	175 49.7	S17 38.1
Hadar	148 44.5	S60 26.9
Hamal	327 57.9	N23 32.5
Kaus Aust.	83 41.0	S34 22.4
Kochab	137 20.8	N74 05.0
Markab	13 36.1	N15 17.9
Menkar	314 12.4	N 4 09.2
Menkent	148 04.8	S36 26.9
Miaplacidus	221 38.2	S69 47.2
Mirfak	308 36.5	N49 55.3
Nunki	75 55.7	S26 16.3
Peacock	53 16.1	S56 40.8
Pollux	243 24.4	N27 58.8
Procyon	244 56.9	N 5 10.6
Rasalhague	96 04.5	N12 33.0
Regulus	207 40.7	N11 52.9
Rigel	281 09.4	S 8 11.2
Rigil Kent.	139 48.6	S60 53.9
Sabik	102 10.1	S15 44.5
Schedar	349 37.7	N56 38.0
Shaula	96 19.0	S37 06.7
Sirius	258 31.2	S16 44.6
Spica	158 28.7	S11 14.9
Suhail	222 50.2	S43 30.1
Vega	80 37.8	N38 48.1
Zuben'ubi	137 02.9	S16 06.5

	SHA	Mer. Pass.
	° ′	h m
Venus	22 51.3	15 18
Mars	13 41.7	15 53
Jupiter	159 20.1	6 11
Saturn	98 27.5	10 14

UT d h		SUN GHA ° ′	SUN Dec ° ′	MOON GHA ° ′	v ′	MOON Dec ° ′	d ′	HP ′
7 00		178 27.4	S22 22.2	75 13.8	9.2	N 8 08.8	10.4	59.4
01		193 27.1	21.9	89 42.0	9.1	8 19.2	10.4	59.4
02		208 26.9	21.6	104 10.1	9.0	8 29.6	10.4	59.4
03		223 26.6	. . 21.2	118 38.1	9.0	8 40.0	10.3	59.4
04		238 26.3	20.9	133 06.1	8.9	8 50.3	10.3	59.4
05		253 26.1	20.6	147 34.0	8.9	9 00.6	10.2	59.5
06		268 25.8	S22 20.3	162 01.9	8.8	N 9 10.8	10.2	59.5
07	S	283 25.5	20.0	176 29.7	8.8	9 21.0	10.1	59.5
08		298 25.3	19.6	190 57.5	8.7	9 31.1	10.1	59.5
09	A	313 25.0	. . 19.3	205 25.2	8.6	9 41.2	10.0	59.6
10	T	328 24.7	19.0	219 52.8	8.6	9 51.2	10.0	59.6
11	U	343 24.5	18.7	234 20.4	8.5	10 01.2	9.9	59.6
12	R	358 24.2	S22 18.3	248 47.9	8.5	N10 11.1	9.8	59.6
13	D	13 23.9	18.0	263 15.4	8.3	10 20.9	9.8	59.6
14	A	28 23.7	17.7	277 42.7	8.4	10 30.7	9.8	59.7
15	Y	43 23.4	. . 17.3	292 10.1	8.2	10 40.5	9.7	59.7
16		58 23.1	17.0	306 37.3	8.2	10 50.2	9.6	59.7
17		73 22.9	16.7	321 04.5	8.2	10 59.8	9.6	59.7
18		88 22.6	S22 16.4	335 31.7	8.1	N11 09.4	9.5	59.7
19		103 22.3	16.0	349 58.8	8.0	11 18.9	9.5	59.8
20		118 22.1	15.7	4 25.8	7.9	11 28.4	9.3	59.8
21		133 21.8	. . 15.4	18 52.7	7.9	11 37.7	9.3	59.8
22		148 21.5	15.0	33 19.6	7.8	11 47.0	9.3	59.8
23		163 21.3	14.7	47 46.4	7.8	11 56.3	9.2	59.8
8 00		178 21.0	S22 14.4	62 13.2	7.7	N12 05.5	9.1	59.8
01		193 20.7	14.0	76 39.9	7.6	12 14.6	9.0	59.9
02		208 20.5	13.7	91 06.5	7.6	12 23.6	9.0	59.9
03		223 20.2	. . 13.3	105 33.1	7.4	12 32.6	8.9	59.9
04		238 20.0	13.0	119 59.5	7.5	12 41.5	8.8	59.9
05		253 19.7	12.7	134 26.0	7.4	12 50.3	8.7	59.9
06		268 19.4	S22 12.3	148 52.4	7.3	N12 59.0	8.7	59.9
07		283 19.2	12.0	163 18.7	7.2	13 07.7	8.6	60.0
08		298 18.9	11.6	177 44.9	7.2	13 16.3	8.5	60.0
09	S	313 18.6	. . 11.3	192 11.1	7.1	13 24.8	8.4	60.0
10	U	328 18.4	11.0	206 37.2	7.0	13 33.2	8.4	60.0
11	N	343 18.1	10.6	221 03.2	7.0	13 41.6	8.2	60.0
12	D	358 17.9	S22 10.3	235 29.2	6.9	N13 49.8	8.2	60.0
13	A	13 17.6	09.9	249 55.1	6.9	13 58.0	8.1	60.1
14	Y	28 17.3	09.6	264 21.0	6.8	14 06.1	8.0	60.1
15		43 17.1	. . 09.2	278 46.8	6.7	14 14.1	7.9	60.1
16		58 16.8	08.9	293 12.5	6.7	14 22.0	7.8	60.1
17		73 16.6	08.5	307 38.2	6.6	14 29.8	7.7	60.1
18		88 16.3	S22 08.2	322 03.8	6.6	N14 37.5	7.7	60.1
19		103 16.0	07.8	336 29.4	6.4	14 45.2	7.5	60.1
20		118 15.8	07.5	350 54.8	6.5	14 52.7	7.4	60.1
21		133 15.5	. . 07.1	5 20.3	6.3	15 00.1	7.4	60.2
22		148 15.3	06.8	19 45.6	6.3	15 07.5	7.2	60.2
23		163 15.0	06.4	34 10.9	6.3	15 14.7	7.2	60.2
9 00		178 14.7	S22 06.1	48 36.2	6.2	N15 21.9	7.0	60.2
01		193 14.5	05.7	63 01.4	6.1	15 28.9	7.0	60.2
02		208 14.2	05.4	77 26.5	6.1	15 35.9	6.8	60.2
03		223 14.0	. . 05.0	91 51.6	6.0	15 42.7	6.8	60.2
04		238 13.7	04.6	106 16.6	5.9	15 49.5	6.6	60.2
05		253 13.5	04.3	120 41.5	5.9	15 56.1	6.6	60.2
06		268 13.2	S22 03.9	135 06.4	5.9	N16 02.7	6.4	60.3
07		283 12.9	03.6	149 31.3	5.8	16 09.1	6.3	60.3
08		298 12.7	03.2	163 56.1	5.7	16 15.4	6.2	60.3
09	M	313 12.4	. . 02.8	178 20.8	5.7	16 21.6	6.2	60.3
10	O	328 12.2	02.5	192 45.5	5.6	16 27.8	5.9	60.3
11	N	343 11.9	02.1	207 10.1	5.6	16 33.7	5.9	60.3
12	D	358 11.7	S22 01.8	221 34.7	5.6	N16 39.6	5.8	60.3
13	A	13 11.4	01.4	235 59.3	5.4	16 45.4	5.7	60.3
14	Y	28 11.2	01.0	250 23.7	5.5	16 51.1	5.5	60.3
15		43 10.9	. . 00.7	264 48.2	5.4	16 56.6	5.4	60.3
16		58 10.7	22 00.3	279 12.6	5.3	17 02.0	5.3	60.3
17		73 10.4	21 59.9	293 36.9	5.3	17 07.3	5.2	60.3
18		88 10.1	S21 59.6	308 01.2	5.3	N17 12.5	5.1	60.3
19		103 09.9	59.2	322 25.5	5.2	17 17.6	5.0	60.3
20		118 09.6	58.8	336 49.7	5.1	17 22.6	4.8	60.3
21		133 09.4	. . 58.5	351 13.8	5.2	17 27.4	4.7	60.4
22		148 09.1	58.1	5 38.0	5.1	17 32.1	4.6	60.4
23		163 08.9	57.7	20 02.1	5.0	N17 36.7	4.5	60.4
		SD 16.3	*d* 0.3	SD 16.2		16.4		16.4

Lat. °	Twilight Naut. h m	Twilight Civil h m	Sunrise h m	Moonrise 7 h m	Moonrise 8 h m	Moonrise 9 h m	Moonrise 10 h m
N 72	08 14	10 18	■	11 13	11 05	10 52	□
N 70	07 57	09 36	■	11 29	11 30	11 36	11 51
68	07 44	09 07	11 08	11 41	11 50	12 05	12 33
66	07 32	08 45	10 12	11 51	12 06	12 28	13 02
64	07 22	08 28	09 39	12 00	12 19	12 45	13 24
62	07 14	08 14	09 15	12 07	12 30	13 00	13 41
60	07 06	08 02	08 57	12 14	12 39	13 12	13 56
N 58	07 00	07 51	08 41	12 20	12 48	13 23	14 08
56	06 54	07 42	08 28	12 25	12 55	13 32	14 19
54	06 48	07 33	08 16	12 29	13 01	13 41	14 29
52	06 43	07 26	08 06	12 33	13 07	13 48	14 37
50	06 38	07 19	07 57	12 37	13 13	13 55	14 45
45	06 27	07 04	07 37	12 45	13 24	14 09	15 01
N 40	06 18	06 52	07 22	12 52	13 34	14 21	15 15
35	06 09	06 41	07 09	12 58	13 42	14 31	15 26
30	06 01	06 31	06 57	13 04	13 50	14 40	15 36
20	05 46	06 13	06 37	13 13	14 02	14 56	15 53
N 10	05 31	05 57	06 20	13 21	14 14	15 10	16 08
0	05 15	05 41	06 03	13 29	14 24	15 22	16 22
S 10	04 57	05 24	05 47	13 36	14 35	15 35	16 37
20	04 35	05 04	05 29	13 45	14 46	15 49	16 52
30	04 08	04 41	05 08	13 54	14 59	16 05	17 09
35	03 50	04 26	04 56	14 00	15 07	16 14	17 20
40	03 29	04 09	04 41	14 06	15 16	16 25	17 31
45	03 00	03 48	04 25	14 13	15 26	16 37	17 45
S 50	02 20	03 21	04 04	14 22	15 38	16 52	18 02
52	01 56	03 07	03 54	14 27	15 44	17 00	18 10
54	01 23	02 51	03 42	14 31	15 50	17 08	18 19
56	////	02 31	03 29	14 36	15 58	17 16	18 29
58	////	02 06	03 14	14 42	16 06	17 27	18 40
S 60	////	01 30	02 56	14 48	16 15	17 38	18 53

Lat. °	Sunset h m	Twilight Civil h m	Twilight Naut. h m	Moonset 7 h m	Moonset 8 h m	Moonset 9 h m	Moonset 10 h m
N 72	■	13 56	16 00	02 55	04 57	07 10	□
N 70	■	14 39	16 17	02 41	04 33	06 27	08 17
68	13 06	15 07	16 31	02 30	04 14	05 58	07 35
66	14 02	15 29	16 42	02 21	04 00	05 37	07 07
64	14 35	15 46	16 52	02 14	03 48	05 20	06 45
62	14 59	16 00	17 00	02 08	03 37	05 06	06 28
60	15 17	16 12	17 08	02 02	03 29	04 54	06 14
N 58	15 33	16 23	17 14	01 57	03 21	04 44	06 01
56	15 46	16 32	17 20	01 53	03 14	04 35	05 51
54	15 58	16 40	17 26	01 49	03 08	04 27	05 41
52	16 08	16 48	17 31	01 46	03 03	04 20	05 33
50	16 17	16 55	17 36	01 42	02 58	04 13	05 26
45	16 36	17 10	17 46	01 36	02 48	04 00	05 10
N 40	16 52	17 22	17 56	01 30	02 39	03 49	04 57
35	17 05	17 33	18 04	01 25	02 32	03 39	04 45
30	17 17	17 43	18 12	01 21	02 25	03 30	04 36
20	17 37	18 00	18 28	01 13	02 14	03 16	04 19
N 10	17 54	18 17	18 43	01 07	02 04	03 03	04 04
0	18 11	18 33	18 59	01 01	01 55	02 52	03 51
S 10	18 27	18 50	19 17	00 54	01 46	02 40	03 37
20	18 45	19 09	19 38	00 48	01 36	02 27	03 23
30	19 06	19 33	20 05	00 41	01 25	02 13	03 06
35	19 18	19 47	20 23	00 36	01 18	02 04	02 56
40	19 32	20 04	20 44	00 31	01 11	01 55	02 45
45	19 48	20 25	21 12	00 26	01 02	01 44	02 32
S 50	20 09	20 52	21 53	00 19	00 52	01 31	02 16
52	20 19	21 06	22 16	00 16	00 47	01 24	02 09
54	20 31	21 22	22 48	00 13	00 42	01 17	02 01
56	20 43	21 41	////	00 09	00 37	01 10	01 51
58	20 58	22 06	////	00 05	00 30	01 01	01 41
S 60	21 16	22 40	////	00 00	00 23	00 51	01 29

Day	SUN Eqn. of Time 00^h m s	SUN Eqn. of Time 12^h m s	SUN Mer. Pass. h m	MOON Mer. Pass. Upper h m	MOON Mer. Pass. Lower h m	Age d	%	Phase
7	06 10	06 23	12 06	19 42	07 15	09	69	
8	06 35	06 48	12 07	20 38	08 09	10	79	
9	07 00	07 13	12 07	21 37	09 07	11	88	

UT		ARIES	VENUS −4·5		MARS +1·0		JUPITER −2·0		SATURN +0·5	
	d h	GHA	GHA	Dec	GHA	Dec	GHA	Dec	GHA	Dec
		° ′	° ′	° ′	° ′	° ′	° ′	° ′	° ′	° ′
	10 00	109 42.4	130 39.5	S 9 37.3	122 01.1	S 6 04.0	268 52.8	S 7 20.6	207 55.7	S21 56.2
	01	124 44.9	145 39.6	36.1	137 01.8	03.3	283 55.1	20.7	222 57.9	56.2
	02	139 47.4	160 39.7	35.0	152 02.5	02.5	298 57.4	20.8	238 00.1	56.2
	03	154 49.8	175 39.9	. . 33.8	167 03.3	. . 01.7	313 59.6	. . 20.8	253 02.2	. . 56.2
	04	169 52.3	190 40.0	32.6	182 04.0	00.9	329 01.9	20.9	268 04.4	56.3
	05	184 54.7	205 40.1	31.5	197 04.7	6 00.2	344 04.2	21.0	283 06.6	56.3
	06	199 57.2	220 40.2	S 9 30.3	212 05.5	S 5 59.4	359 06.4	S 7 21.0	298 08.7	S21 56.3
	07	214 59.7	235 40.3	29.1	227 06.2	58.6	14 08.7	21.1	313 10.9	56.3
T	08	230 02.1	250 40.4	27.9	242 06.9	57.9	29 11.0	21.2	328 13.1	56.3
U	09	245 04.6	265 40.5	. . 26.8	257 07.7	. . 57.1	44 13.3	. . 21.2	343 15.2	. . 56.3
E	10	260 07.1	280 40.7	25.6	272 08.4	56.3	59 15.5	21.3	358 17.4	56.4
S	11	275 09.5	295 40.8	24.4	287 09.1	55.6	74 17.8	21.3	13 19.6	56.4
	12	290 12.0	310 40.9	S 9 23.3	302 09.9	S 5 54.8	89 20.1	S 7 21.4	28 21.8	S21 56.4
D	13	305 14.5	325 41.0	22.1	317 10.6	54.0	104 22.3	21.5	43 23.9	56.4
A	14	320 16.9	340 41.1	20.9	332 11.4	53.2	119 24.6	21.5	58 26.1	56.4
Y	15	335 19.4	355 41.3	. . 19.8	347 12.1	. . 52.5	134 26.9	. . 21.6	73 28.3	. . 56.4
	16	350 21.9	10 41.4	18.6	2 12.8	51.7	149 29.2	21.7	88 30.4	56.4
	17	5 24.3	25 41.5	17.4	17 13.6	50.9	164 31.4	21.7	103 32.6	56.5
	18	20 26.8	40 41.6	S 9 16.3	32 14.3	S 5 50.2	179 33.7	S 7 21.8	118 34.8	S21 56.5
	19	35 29.2	55 41.7	15.1	47 15.0	49.4	194 36.0	21.9	133 37.0	56.5
	20	50 31.7	70 41.9	13.9	62 15.8	48.6	209 38.3	21.9	148 39.1	56.5
	21	65 34.2	85 42.0	. . 12.8	77 16.5	. . 47.8	224 40.5	. . 22.0	163 41.3	. . 56.5
	22	80 36.6	100 42.1	11.6	92 17.2	47.1	239 42.8	22.1	178 43.5	56.5
	23	95 39.1	115 42.3	10.4	107 18.0	46.3	254 45.1	22.1	193 45.6	56.6
	11 00	110 41.6	130 42.4	S 9 09.2	122 18.7	S 5 45.5	269 47.4	S 7 22.2	208 47.8	S21 56.6
	01	125 44.0	145 42.5	08.1	137 19.5	44.8	284 49.6	22.3	223 50.0	56.6
	02	140 46.5	160 42.7	06.9	152 20.2	44.0	299 51.9	22.3	238 52.2	56.6
	03	155 49.0	175 42.8	. . 05.7	167 20.9	. . 43.2	314 54.2	. . 22.4	253 54.3	. . 56.6
	04	170 51.4	190 42.9	04.6	182 21.7	42.4	329 56.5	22.5	268 56.5	56.6
	05	185 53.9	205 43.1	03.4	197 22.4	41.7	344 58.7	22.5	283 58.7	56.6
	06	200 56.4	220 43.2	S 9 02.2	212 23.2	S 5 40.9	0 01.0	S 7 22.6	299 00.8	S21 56.7
W	07	215 58.8	235 43.3	9 01.0	227 23.9	40.1	15 03.3	22.6	314 03.0	56.7
E	08	231 01.3	250 43.5	8 59.9	242 24.6	39.3	30 05.6	22.7	329 05.2	56.7
D	09	246 03.7	265 43.6	. . 58.7	257 25.4	. . 38.6	45 07.8	. . 22.8	344 07.4	. . 56.7
N	10	261 06.2	280 43.8	57.5	272 26.1	37.8	60 10.1	22.8	359 09.5	56.7
E	11	276 08.7	295 43.9	56.3	287 26.8	37.0	75 12.4	22.9	14 11.7	56.7
S	12	291 11.1	310 44.0	S 8 55.2	302 27.6	S 5 36.3	90 14.7	S 7 23.0	29 13.9	S21 56.8
D	13	306 13.6	325 44.2	54.0	317 28.3	35.5	105 16.9	23.0	44 16.1	56.8
A	14	321 16.1	340 44.3	52.8	332 29.1	34.7	120 19.2	23.1	59 18.2	56.8
Y	15	336 18.5	355 44.5	. . 51.6	347 29.8	. . 33.9	135 21.5	. . 23.2	74 20.4	. . 56.8
	16	351 21.0	10 44.6	50.5	2 30.5	33.2	150 23.8	23.2	89 22.6	56.8
	17	6 23.5	25 44.8	49.3	17 31.3	32.4	165 26.1	23.3	104 24.7	56.8
	18	21 25.9	40 44.9	S 8 48.1	32 32.0	S 5 31.6	180 28.3	S 7 23.3	119 26.9	S21 56.8
	19	36 28.4	55 45.1	46.9	47 32.8	30.8	195 30.6	23.4	134 29.1	56.9
	20	51 30.9	70 45.2	45.8	62 33.5	30.1	210 32.9	23.5	149 31.3	56.9
	21	66 33.3	85 45.4	. . 44.6	77 34.2	. . 29.3	225 35.2	. . 23.5	164 33.4	. . 56.9
	22	81 35.8	100 45.5	43.4	92 35.0	28.5	240 37.5	23.6	179 35.6	56.9
	23	96 38.2	115 45.7	42.2	107 35.7	27.8	255 39.7	23.7	194 37.8	56.9
	12 00	111 40.7	130 45.8	S 8 41.1	122 36.5	S 5 27.0	270 42.0	S 7 23.7	209 40.0	S21 56.9
	01	126 43.2	145 46.0	39.9	137 37.2	26.2	285 44.3	23.8	224 42.1	57.0
	02	141 45.6	160 46.1	38.7	152 37.9	25.4	300 46.6	23.8	239 44.3	57.0
	03	156 48.1	175 46.3	. . 37.5	167 38.7	. . 24.7	315 48.9	. . 23.9	254 46.5	. . 57.0
	04	171 50.6	190 46.5	36.4	182 39.4	23.9	330 51.2	24.0	269 48.7	57.0
	05	186 53.0	205 46.6	35.2	197 40.2	23.1	345 53.4	24.0	284 50.8	57.0
	06	201 55.5	220 46.8	S 8 34.0	212 40.9	S 5 22.3	0 55.7	S 7 24.1	299 53.0	S21 57.0
	07	216 58.0	235 46.9	32.8	227 41.6	21.6	15 58.0	24.1	314 55.2	57.0
T	08	232 00.4	250 47.1	31.7	242 42.4	20.8	31 00.3	24.2	329 57.3	57.1
H	09	247 02.9	265 47.3	. . 30.5	257 43.1	. . 20.0	46 02.6	. . 24.3	344 59.5	. . 57.1
U	10	262 05.4	280 47.4	29.3	272 43.9	19.2	61 04.9	24.3	0 01.7	57.1
R	11	277 07.8	295 47.6	28.1	287 44.6	18.5	76 07.1	24.4	15 03.9	57.1
S	12	292 10.3	310 47.8	S 8 26.9	302 45.3	S 5 17.7	91 09.4	S 7 24.5	30 06.0	S21 57.1
D	13	307 12.7	325 47.9	25.8	317 46.1	16.9	106 11.7	24.5	45 08.2	57.1
A	14	322 15.2	340 48.1	24.6	332 46.8	16.2	121 14.0	24.6	60 10.4	57.1
Y	15	337 17.7	355 48.3	. . 23.4	347 47.6	. . 15.4	136 16.3	. . 24.6	75 12.6	. . 57.2
	16	352 20.1	10 48.4	22.2	2 48.3	14.6	151 18.6	24.7	90 14.7	57.2
	17	7 22.6	25 48.6	21.1	17 49.0	13.8	166 20.8	24.8	105 16.9	57.2
	18	22 25.1	40 48.8	S 8 19.9	32 49.8	S 5 13.1	181 23.1	S 7 24.8	120 19.1	S21 57.2
	19	37 27.5	55 48.9	18.7	47 50.5	12.3	196 25.4	24.9	135 21.3	57.2
	20	52 30.0	70 49.1	17.5	62 51.3	11.5	211 27.7	24.9	150 23.4	57.2
	21	67 32.5	85 49.3	. . 16.3	77 52.0	. . 10.7	226 30.0	. . 25.0	165 25.6	. . 57.2
	22	82 34.9	100 49.5	15.2	92 52.8	10.0	241 32.3	25.1	180 27.8	57.3
	23	97 37.4	115 49.7	14.0	107 53.5	09.2	256 34.6	25.1	195 30.0	57.3
	Mer. Pass.	h m 16 34.5	v 0.1	d 1.2	v 0.7	d 0.8	v 2.3	d 0.1	v 2.2	d 0.0

STARS		
Name	SHA	Dec
	° ′	° ′
Acamar	315 16.4	S40 14.6
Achernar	335 25.0	S57 09.5
Acrux	173 06.2	S63 11.3
Adhara	255 10.2	S29 00.0
Aldebaran	290 46.3	N16 32.4
Alioth	166 18.6	N55 51.8
Alkaid	152 57.1	N49 13.5
Al Na'ir	27 41.1	S46 52.8
Alnilam	275 43.6	S 1 11.7
Alphard	217 53.4	S 8 44.1
Alphecca	126 09.2	N26 39.5
Alpheratz	357 41.1	N29 11.1
Altair	62 06.2	N 8 54.9
Ankaa	353 13.5	S42 13.1
Antares	112 23.6	S26 27.9
Arcturus	145 53.6	N19 05.6
Atria	107 23.6	S69 03.1
Avior	234 16.3	S59 33.9
Bellatrix	278 29.1	N 6 21.6
Betelgeuse	270 58.4	N 7 24.4
Canopus	263 54.5	S52 42.6
Capella	280 30.4	N46 00.7
Deneb	49 30.2	N45 20.6
Denebola	182 31.1	N14 28.5
Diphda	348 53.5	S17 53.8
Dubhe	193 48.5	N61 39.3
Elnath	278 09.2	N28 37.1
Eltanin	90 45.5	N51 29.3
Enif	33 45.0	N 9 57.3
Fomalhaut	15 21.6	S29 32.1
Gacrux	171 57.9	S57 12.2
Gienah	175 49.7	S17 38.1
Hadar	148 44.4	S60 26.9
Hamal	327 57.9	N23 32.5
Kaus Aust.	83 41.0	S34 22.4
Kochab	137 20.8	N74 05.0
Markab	13 36.1	N15 17.9
Menkar	314 12.4	N 4 09.2
Menkent	148 04.8	S36 26.9
Miaplacidus	221 38.1	S69 47.2
Mirfak	308 36.5	N49 55.3
Nunki	75 55.7	S26 16.3
Peacock	53 16.1	S56 40.8
Pollux	243 24.4	N27 58.8
Procyon	244 56.9	N 5 10.6
Rasalhague	96 04.5	N12 33.0
Regulus	207 40.7	N11 52.9
Rigel	281 09.4	S 8 11.2
Rigil Kent.	139 48.5	S60 53.9
Sabik	102 10.1	S15 44.5
Schedar	349 37.7	N56 38.0
Shaula	96 19.0	S37 06.7
Sirius	258 31.2	S16 44.6
Spica	158 28.7	S11 14.9
Suhail	222 50.2	S43 30.1
Vega	80 37.7	N38 48.1
Zuben'ubi	137 02.9	S16 06.5

	SHA	Mer. Pass.
	° ′	h m
Venus	20 00.8	15 17
Mars	11 37.2	15 50
Jupiter	159 05.8	6 00
Saturn	98 06.2	10 03

UT		SUN GHA	SUN Dec	MOON GHA	v	MOON Dec	d	HP
d	h	° ′	° ′	° ′	′	° ′	′	′
10 TUESDAY	00	178 08.6	S21 57.3	34 26.1	5.0	N17 41.2	4.3	60.4
	01	193 08.4	57.0	48 50.1	5.0	17 45.5	4.2	60.4
	02	208 08.1	56.6	63 14.1	4.9	17 49.7	4.1	60.4
	03	223 07.9	. . 56.2	77 38.0	5.0	17 53.8	4.0	60.4
	04	238 07.6	55.9	92 02.0	4.8	17 57.8	3.8	60.4
	05	253 07.4	55.5	106 25.8	4.9	18 01.6	3.8	60.4
	06	268 07.1	S21 55.1	120 49.7	4.8	N18 05.4	3.5	60.4
	07	283 06.9	54.7	135 13.5	4.8	18 08.9	3.5	60.4
	08	298 06.6	54.3	149 37.3	4.7	18 12.4	3.3	60.4
	09	313 06.4	. . 54.0	164 01.0	4.8	18 15.7	3.2	60.4
	10	328 06.1	53.6	178 24.8	4.7	18 18.9	3.1	60.4
	11	343 05.9	53.2	192 48.5	4.7	18 22.0	3.0	60.4
	12	358 05.6	S21 52.8	207 12.2	4.7	N18 25.0	2.8	60.4
	13	13 05.4	52.4	221 35.9	4.6	18 27.8	2.6	60.4
	14	28 05.1	52.1	235 59.5	4.6	18 30.4	2.6	60.4
	15	43 04.9	. . 51.7	250 23.1	4.7	18 33.0	2.4	60.4
	16	58 04.6	51.3	264 46.8	4.6	18 35.4	2.3	60.3
	17	73 04.4	50.9	279 10.4	4.6	18 37.7	2.1	60.3
	18	88 04.1	S21 50.5	293 34.0	4.5	N18 39.8	2.1	60.3
	19	103 03.9	50.1	307 57.5	4.6	18 41.9	1.8	60.3
	20	118 03.6	49.8	322 21.1	4.6	18 43.7	1.8	60.3
	21	133 03.4	. . 49.4	336 44.7	4.5	18 45.5	1.6	60.3
	22	148 03.1	49.0	351 08.2	4.6	18 47.1	1.5	60.3
	23	163 02.9	48.6	5 31.8	4.5	18 48.6	1.3	60.3
11 WEDNESDAY	00	178 02.6	S21 48.2	19 55.3	4.5	N18 49.9	1.3	60.3
	01	193 02.4	47.8	34 18.8	4.6	18 51.2	1.0	60.3
	02	208 02.2	47.4	48 42.4	4.5	18 52.2	1.0	60.3
	03	223 01.9	. . 47.0	63 05.9	4.6	18 53.2	0.8	60.3
	04	238 01.7	46.6	77 29.5	4.5	18 54.0	0.7	60.3
	05	253 01.4	46.2	91 53.0	4.6	18 54.7	0.5	60.3
	06	268 01.2	S21 45.8	106 16.6	4.5	N18 55.2	0.4	60.2
	07	283 00.9	45.5	120 40.1	4.6	18 55.6	0.3	60.2
	08	298 00.7	45.1	135 03.7	4.6	18 55.9	0.1	60.2
	09	313 00.4	. . 44.7	149 27.3	4.6	18 56.0	0.0	60.2
	10	328 00.2	44.3	163 50.9	4.6	18 56.0	0.1	60.2
	11	343 00.0	43.9	178 14.5	4.6	18 55.9	0.3	60.2
	12	357 59.7	S21 43.5	192 38.1	4.7	N18 55.6	0.4	60.2
	13	12 59.5	43.1	207 01.8	4.6	18 55.2	0.5	60.2
	14	27 59.2	42.7	221 25.4	4.7	18 54.7	0.7	60.2
	15	42 59.0	. . 42.3	235 49.1	4.7	18 54.0	0.8	60.1
	16	57 58.7	41.9	250 12.8	4.8	18 53.2	0.9	60.1
	17	72 58.5	41.5	264 36.6	4.7	18 52.3	1.1	60.1
	18	87 58.3	S21 41.1	279 00.3	4.8	N18 51.2	1.2	60.1
	19	102 58.0	40.7	293 24.1	4.8	18 50.0	1.3	60.1
	20	117 57.8	40.3	307 47.9	4.9	18 48.7	1.5	60.1
	21	132 57.5	. . 39.8	322 11.8	4.8	18 47.2	1.6	60.0
	22	147 57.3	39.4	336 35.6	4.9	18 45.6	1.7	60.0
	23	162 57.1	39.0	350 59.5	5.0	18 43.9	1.9	60.0
12 THURSDAY	00	177 56.8	S21 38.6	5 23.5	5.0	N18 42.0	2.0	60.0
	01	192 56.6	38.2	19 47.5	5.0	18 40.0	2.1	60.0
	02	207 56.3	37.8	34 11.5	5.0	18 37.9	2.2	60.0
	03	222 56.1	. . 37.4	48 35.5	5.1	18 35.7	2.4	59.9
	04	237 55.9	37.0	62 59.6	5.2	18 33.3	2.5	59.9
	05	252 55.6	36.6	77 23.8	5.2	18 30.8	2.6	59.9
	06	267 55.4	S21 36.2	91 48.0	5.2	N18 28.2	2.8	59.9
	07	282 55.1	35.8	106 12.2	5.3	18 25.4	2.9	59.9
	08	297 54.9	35.3	120 36.5	5.3	18 22.5	3.0	59.8
	09	312 54.7	. . 34.9	135 00.8	5.4	18 19.5	3.1	59.8
	10	327 54.4	34.5	149 25.2	5.4	18 16.4	3.2	59.8
	11	342 54.2	34.1	163 49.6	5.5	18 13.2	3.4	59.8
	12	357 54.0	S21 33.7	178 14.1	5.5	N18 09.8	3.5	59.8
	13	12 53.7	33.3	192 38.6	5.6	18 06.3	3.6	59.7
	14	27 53.5	32.9	207 03.2	5.6	18 02.7	3.7	59.7
	15	42 53.2	. . 32.4	221 27.8	5.7	17 59.0	3.9	59.7
	16	57 53.0	32.0	235 52.5	5.7	17 55.1	3.9	59.7
	17	72 52.8	31.6	250 17.2	5.8	17 51.2	4.1	59.6
	18	87 52.5	S21 31.2	264 42.0	5.9	N17 47.1	4.2	59.6
	19	102 52.3	30.8	279 06.9	5.9	17 42.9	4.3	59.6
	20	117 52.1	30.3	293 31.8	6.0	17 38.6	4.5	59.6
	21	132 51.8	. . 29.9	307 56.8	6.1	17 34.1	4.5	59.5
	22	147 51.6	29.5	322 21.9	6.1	17 29.6	4.7	59.5
	23	162 51.4	29.1	336 47.0	6.2	N17 24.9	4.7	59.5
		SD 16.3	*d* 0.4	SD 16.4		16.4		16.3

Lat.	Twilight Naut.	Twilight Civil	Sunrise	Moonrise 10	Moonrise 11	Moonrise 12	Moonrise 13
°	h m	h m	h m	h m	h m	h m	h m
N 72	08 09	10 07	■	□	□	12 15	15 08
N 70	07 53	09 28	■	11 51	12 35	14 02	15 49
68	07 40	09 01	10 51	12 33	13 24	14 42	16 17
66	07 29	08 41	10 04	13 02	13 56	15 10	16 38
64	07 20	08 25	09 34	13 24	14 19	15 31	16 54
62	07 11	08 11	09 11	13 41	14 37	15 48	17 08
60	07 04	07 59	08 53	13 56	14 53	16 02	17 20
N 58	06 58	07 49	08 38	14 08	15 06	16 14	17 30
56	06 52	07 40	08 25	14 19	15 17	16 24	17 38
54	06 47	07 32	08 14	14 29	15 27	16 34	17 46
52	06 42	07 25	08 04	14 37	15 35	16 42	17 53
50	06 37	07 18	07 55	14 45	15 43	16 49	17 59
45	06 27	07 03	07 37	15 01	16 00	17 05	18 13
N 40	06 18	06 51	07 21	15 15	16 14	17 18	18 24
35	06 09	06 41	07 08	15 26	16 26	17 29	18 33
30	06 01	06 31	06 57	15 36	16 36	17 38	18 41
20	05 47	06 14	06 37	15 53	16 53	17 55	18 56
N 10	05 32	05 58	06 20	16 08	17 09	18 09	19 08
0	05 16	05 42	06 04	16 22	17 23	18 23	19 20
S 10	04 59	05 25	05 48	16 37	17 38	18 36	19 31
20	04 38	05 06	05 31	16 52	17 53	18 51	19 44
30	04 11	04 43	05 10	17 09	18 11	19 07	19 58
35	03 54	04 29	04 58	17 20	18 21	19 17	20 06
40	03 32	04 13	04 45	17 31	18 33	19 28	20 15
45	03 05	03 52	04 28	17 45	18 47	19 40	20 26
S 50	02 26	03 25	04 08	18 02	19 04	19 56	20 39
52	02 03	03 12	03 58	18 10	19 12	20 03	20 45
54	01 33	02 56	03 47	18 19	19 20	20 11	20 52
56	00 34	02 38	03 34	18 29	19 30	20 20	21 00
58	////	02 14	03 20	18 40	19 42	20 31	21 08
S 60	////	01 42	03 02	18 53	19 55	20 42	21 17

Lat.	Sunset	Twilight Civil	Twilight Naut.	Moonset 10	Moonset 11	Moonset 12	Moonset 13
°	h m	h m	h m	h m	h m	h m	h m
N 72	■	14 10	16 08	□	□	12 06	11 14
N 70	■	14 49	16 24	08 17	09 40	10 19	10 32
68	13 25	15 15	16 37	07 35	08 51	09 38	10 03
66	14 13	15 36	16 48	07 07	08 19	09 10	09 42
64	14 43	15 52	16 57	06 45	07 56	08 49	09 25
62	15 05	16 06	17 05	06 28	07 38	08 31	09 10
60	15 23	16 17	17 12	06 14	07 22	08 17	08 58
N 58	15 38	16 28	17 19	06 01	07 09	08 05	08 48
56	15 51	16 37	17 24	05 51	06 58	07 54	08 39
54	16 02	16 45	17 30	05 41	06 48	07 45	08 30
52	16 12	16 52	17 35	05 33	06 39	07 36	08 23
50	16 21	16 58	17 39	05 26	06 31	07 29	08 16
45	16 40	17 13	17 49	05 10	06 15	07 12	08 02
N 40	16 55	17 25	17 59	04 57	06 01	06 59	07 51
35	17 08	17 36	18 07	04 45	05 49	06 48	07 40
30	17 19	17 45	18 15	04 36	05 39	06 38	07 32
20	17 39	18 02	18 30	04 19	05 21	06 21	07 16
N 10	17 56	18 18	18 44	04 04	05 06	06 06	07 03
0	18 12	18 34	19 00	03 51	04 51	05 52	06 50
S 10	18 28	18 51	19 17	03 37	04 37	05 38	06 38
20	18 45	19 09	19 38	03 23	04 22	05 23	06 24
30	19 05	19 32	20 05	03 06	04 04	05 05	06 08
35	19 17	19 46	20 22	02 56	03 53	04 55	05 59
40	19 31	20 03	20 43	02 45	03 42	04 44	05 49
45	19 47	20 23	21 10	02 32	03 28	04 30	05 37
S 50	20 08	20 50	21 49	02 16	03 11	04 13	05 22
52	20 17	21 03	22 11	02 09	03 03	04 05	05 15
54	20 28	21 18	22 40	02 01	02 54	03 57	05 07
56	20 41	21 37	23 33	01 51	02 44	03 47	04 58
58	20 55	22 00	////	01 41	02 32	03 35	04 48
S 60	21 12	22 32	////	01 29	02 19	03 22	04 37

Day	SUN Eqn. of Time 00^h	SUN Eqn. of Time 12^h	SUN Mer. Pass.	MOON Mer. Pass. Upper	MOON Mer. Pass. Lower	MOON Age	MOON Phase
d	m s	m s	h m	h m	h m	d %	
10	07 25	07 37	12 08	22 37	10 07	12 94	
11	07 49	08 01	12 08	23 38	11 07	13 99	○
12	08 12	08 24	12 08	24 37	12 07	14 100	

UT	ARIES	VENUS −4·6		MARS +1·0		JUPITER −2·0		SATURN +0·5		STARS		
	GHA	GHA	Dec	GHA	Dec	GHA	Dec	GHA	Dec	Name	SHA	Dec
d h	° ′	° ′	° ′	° ′	° ′	° ′	° ′	° ′	° ′		° ′	° ′
13 00	112 39.8	130 49.8	S 8 12.8	122 54.2	S 5 08.4	271 36.9	S 7 25.2	210 32.1	S21 57.3	Acamar	315 16.4	S40 14.6
01	127 42.3	145 50.0	11.6	137 55.0	07.6	286 39.1	25.2	225 34.3	57.3	Achernar	335 25.1	S57 09.5
02	142 44.8	160 50.2	10.4	152 55.7	06.9	301 41.4	25.3	240 36.5	57.3	Acrux	173 06.2	S63 11.3
03	157 47.2	175 50.4	. . 09.3	167 56.5	. . 06.1	316 43.7	. . 25.3	255 38.7	. . 57.3	Adhara	255 10.2	S29 00.0
04	172 49.7	190 50.6	08.1	182 57.2	05.3	331 46.0	25.4	270 40.8	57.4	Aldebaran	290 46.3	N16 32.4
05	187 52.2	205 50.7	06.9	197 58.0	04.5	346 48.3	25.5	285 43.0	57.4			
06	202 54.6	220 50.9	S 8 05.7	212 58.7	S 5 03.8	1 50.6	S 7 25.5	300 45.2	S21 57.4	Alioth	166 18.6	N55 51.8
07	217 57.1	235 51.1	04.5	227 59.4	03.0	16 52.9	25.6	315 47.4	57.4	Alkaid	152 57.1	N49 13.5
08	232 59.6	250 51.3	03.4	243 00.2	02.2	31 55.2	25.6	330 49.5	57.4	Al Na'ir	27 41.1	S46 52.8
F 09	248 02.0	265 51.5	. . 02.2	258 00.9	. . 01.4	46 57.5	. . 25.7	345 51.7	. . 57.4	Alnilam	275 43.6	S 1 11.7
R 10	263 04.5	280 51.7	8 01.0	273 01.7	5 00.7	61 59.7	25.8	0 53.9	57.4	Alphard	217 53.4	S 8 44.1
I 11	278 07.0	295 51.9	7 59.8	288 02.4	4 59.9	77 02.0	25.8	15 56.1	57.5			
D 12	293 09.4	310 52.0	S 7 58.6	303 03.2	S 4 59.1	92 04.3	S 7 25.9	30 58.2	S21 57.5	Alphecca	126 09.2	N26 39.5
A 13	308 11.9	325 52.2	57.4	318 03.9	58.3	107 06.6	25.9	46 00.4	57.5	Alpheratz	357 41.1	N29 11.1
Y 14	323 14.3	340 52.4	56.3	333 04.6	57.6	122 08.9	26.0	61 02.6	57.5	Altair	62 06.2	N 8 54.9
15	338 16.8	355 52.6	. . 55.1	348 05.4	. . 56.8	137 11.2	. . 26.0	76 04.8	. . 57.5	Ankaa	353 13.5	S42 13.1
16	353 19.3	10 52.8	53.9	3 06.1	56.0	152 13.5	26.1	91 06.9	57.5	Antares	112 23.5	S26 27.9
17	8 21.7	25 53.0	52.7	18 06.9	55.2	167 15.8	26.2	106 09.1	57.5			
18	23 24.2	40 53.2	S 7 51.5	33 07.6	S 4 54.5	182 18.1	S 7 26.2	121 11.3	S21 57.6	Arcturus	145 53.6	N19 05.6
19	38 26.7	55 53.4	50.3	48 08.4	53.7	197 20.4	26.3	136 13.5	57.6	Atria	107 23.6	S69 03.1
20	53 29.1	70 53.6	49.2	63 09.1	52.9	212 22.7	26.3	151 15.6	57.6	Avior	234 16.3	S59 33.9
21	68 31.6	85 53.8	. . 48.0	78 09.9	. . 52.1	227 25.0	. . 26.4	166 17.8	. . 57.6	Bellatrix	278 29.1	N 6 21.6
22	83 34.1	100 54.0	46.8	93 10.6	51.4	242 27.2	26.4	181 20.0	57.6	Betelgeuse	270 58.4	N 7 24.3
23	98 36.5	115 54.2	45.6	108 11.3	50.6	257 29.5	26.5	196 22.2	57.6			
14 00	113 39.0	130 54.4	S 7 44.4	123 12.1	S 4 49.8	272 31.8	S 7 26.6	211 24.4	S21 57.6	Canopus	263 54.5	S52 42.6
01	128 41.5	145 54.6	43.2	138 12.8	49.0	287 34.1	26.6	226 26.5	57.7	Capella	280 30.4	N46 00.8
02	143 43.9	160 54.8	42.1	153 13.6	48.3	302 36.4	26.7	241 28.7	57.7	Deneb	49 30.2	N45 20.6
03	158 46.4	175 55.0	. . 40.9	168 14.3	. . 47.5	317 38.7	. . 26.7	256 30.9	. . 57.7	Denebola	182 31.1	N14 28.5
04	173 48.8	190 55.2	39.7	183 15.1	46.7	332 41.0	26.8	271 33.1	57.7	Diphda	348 53.5	S17 53.8
05	188 51.3	205 55.4	38.5	198 15.8	45.9	347 43.3	26.8	286 35.2	57.7			
06	203 53.8	220 55.6	S 7 37.3	213 16.6	S 4 45.2	2 45.6	S 7 26.9	301 37.4	S21 57.7	Dubhe	193 48.5	N61 39.3
S 07	218 56.2	235 55.9	36.1	228 17.3	44.4	17 47.9	27.0	316 39.6	57.7	Elnath	278 09.2	N28 37.1
08	233 58.7	250 56.1	35.0	243 18.0	43.6	32 50.2	27.0	331 41.8	57.8	Eltanin	90 45.5	N51 29.3
A 09	249 01.2	265 56.3	. . 33.8	258 18.8	. . 42.8	47 52.5	. . 27.1	346 43.9	. . 57.8	Enif	33 45.0	N 9 57.3
T 10	264 03.6	280 56.5	32.6	273 19.5	42.1	62 54.8	27.1	1 46.1	57.8	Fomalhaut	15 21.6	S29 32.1
U 11	279 06.1	295 56.7	31.4	288 20.3	41.3	77 57.1	27.2	16 48.3	57.8			
R 12	294 08.6	310 56.9	S 7 30.2	303 21.0	S 4 40.5	92 59.4	S 7 27.2	31 50.5	S21 57.8	Gacrux	171 57.9	S57 12.2
D 13	309 11.0	325 57.1	29.0	318 21.8	39.7	108 01.7	27.3	46 52.7	57.8	Gienah	175 49.7	S17 38.1
A 14	324 13.5	340 57.3	27.8	333 22.5	39.0	123 04.0	27.3	61 54.8	57.8	Hadar	148 44.4	S60 26.9
Y 15	339 16.0	355 57.6	. . 26.7	348 23.3	. . 38.2	138 06.3	. . 27.4	76 57.0	. . 57.9	Hamal	327 57.9	N23 32.5
16	354 18.4	10 57.8	25.5	3 24.0	37.4	153 08.6	27.5	91 59.2	57.9	Kaus Aust.	83 41.0	S34 22.4
17	9 20.9	25 58.0	24.3	18 24.8	36.6	168 10.9	27.5	107 01.4	57.9			
18	24 23.3	40 58.2	S 7 23.1	33 25.5	S 4 35.8	183 13.2	S 7 27.6	122 03.5	S21 57.9	Kochab	137 20.7	N74 05.0
19	39 25.8	55 58.4	21.9	48 26.2	35.1	198 15.5	27.6	137 05.7	57.9	Markab	13 36.1	N15 17.8
20	54 28.3	70 58.7	20.7	63 27.0	34.3	213 17.8	27.7	152 07.9	57.9	Menkar	314 12.4	N 4 09.2
21	69 30.7	85 58.9	. . 19.5	78 27.7	. . 33.5	228 20.1	. . 27.7	167 10.1	. . 57.9	Menkent	148 04.7	S36 26.9
22	84 33.2	100 59.1	18.4	93 28.5	32.7	243 22.4	27.8	182 12.3	58.0	Miaplacidus	221 38.1	S69 47.2
23	99 35.7	115 59.3	17.2	108 29.2	32.0	258 24.7	27.8	197 14.4	58.0			
15 00	114 38.1	130 59.6	S 7 16.0	123 30.0	S 4 31.2	273 27.0	S 7 27.9	212 16.6	S21 58.0	Mirfak	308 36.5	N49 55.3
01	129 40.6	145 59.8	14.8	138 30.7	30.4	288 29.3	27.9	227 18.8	58.0	Nunki	75 55.7	S26 16.3
02	144 43.1	161 00.0	13.6	153 31.5	29.6	303 31.6	28.0	242 21.0	58.0	Peacock	53 16.1	S56 40.7
03	159 45.5	176 00.3	. . 12.4	168 32.2	. . 28.9	318 33.9	. . 28.0	257 23.2	. . 58.0	Pollux	243 24.4	N27 58.8
04	174 48.0	191 00.5	11.2	183 33.0	28.1	333 36.2	28.1	272 25.3	58.0	Procyon	244 56.9	N 5 10.6
05	189 50.4	206 00.7	10.0	198 33.7	27.3	348 38.5	28.2	287 27.5	58.0			
06	204 52.9	221 00.9	S 7 08.9	213 34.5	S 4 26.5	3 40.8	S 7 28.2	302 29.7	S21 58.1	Rasalhague	96 04.5	N12 33.0
07	219 55.4	236 01.2	07.7	228 35.2	25.8	18 43.1	28.3	317 31.9	58.1	Regulus	207 40.7	N11 52.9
08	234 57.8	251 01.4	06.5	243 36.0	25.0	33 45.4	28.3	332 34.0	58.1	Rigel	281 09.4	S 8 11.2
S 09	250 00.3	266 01.7	. . 05.3	258 36.7	. . 24.2	48 47.7	. . 28.4	347 36.2	. . 58.1	Rigil Kent.	139 48.5	S60 53.9
U 10	265 02.8	281 01.9	04.1	273 37.4	23.4	63 50.0	28.4	2 38.4	58.1	Sabik	102 10.0	S15 44.5
N 11	280 05.2	296 02.1	02.9	288 38.2	22.6	78 52.3	28.5	17 40.6	58.1			
D 12	295 07.7	311 02.4	S 7 01.7	303 38.9	S 4 21.9	93 54.6	S 7 28.5	32 42.8	S21 58.1	Schedar	349 37.7	N56 38.0
A 13	310 10.2	326 02.6	7 00.5	318 39.7	21.1	108 56.9	28.6	47 44.9	58.2	Shaula	96 19.0	S37 06.7
Y 14	325 12.6	341 02.8	6 59.4	333 40.4	20.3	123 59.2	28.6	62 47.1	58.2	Sirius	258 31.2	S16 44.7
15	340 15.1	356 03.1	. . 58.2	348 41.2	. . 19.5	139 01.5	. . 28.7	77 49.3	. . 58.2	Spica	158 28.7	S11 14.9
16	355 17.6	11 03.3	57.0	3 41.9	18.8	154 03.8	28.7	92 51.5	58.2	Suhail	222 50.2	S43 30.1
17	10 20.0	26 03.6	55.8	18 42.7	18.0	169 06.1	28.8	107 53.7	58.2			
18	25 22.5	41 03.8	S 6 54.6	33 43.4	S 4 17.2	184 08.4	S 7 28.8	122 55.8	S21 58.2	Vega	80 37.7	N38 48.1
19	40 24.9	56 04.1	53.4	48 44.2	16.4	199 10.7	28.9	137 58.0	58.2	Zuben'ubi	137 02.8	S16 06.5
20	55 27.4	71 04.3	52.2	63 44.9	15.7	214 13.0	28.9	153 00.2	58.3		SHA	Mer. Pass.
21	70 29.9	86 04.6	. . 51.0	78 45.7	. . 14.9	229 15.4	. . 29.0	168 02.4	. . 58.3		° ′	h m
22	85 32.3	101 04.8	49.9	93 46.4	14.1	244 17.7	29.0	183 04.6	58.3	Venus	17 15.4	15 16
23	100 34.8	116 05.1	48.7	108 47.2	13.3	259 20.0	29.1	198 06.7	58.3	Mars	9 33.1	15 46
	h m									Jupiter	158 52.8	5 49
Mer. Pass.	16 22.7	*v* 0.2	*d* 1.2	*v* 0.7	*d* 0.8	*v* 2.3	*d* 0.1	*v* 2.2	*d* 0.0	Saturn	97 45.4	9 53

	UT	SUN GHA	SUN Dec	MOON GHA	*v*	MOON Dec	*d*	HP
	d h	° ′	° ′	° ′	′	° ′	′	′
	13 00	177 51.1	S21 28.6	351 12.2	6.2	N17 20.2	4.9	59.5
	01	192 50.9	28.2	5 37.4	6.4	17 15.3	5.0	59.4
	02	207 50.7	27.8	20 02.8	6.4	17 10.3	5.1	59.4
	03	222 50.4	. . 27.4	34 28.2	6.4	17 05.2	5.2	59.4
	04	237 50.2	26.9	48 53.6	6.5	17 00.0	5.3	59.4
	05	252 50.0	26.5	63 19.1	6.6	16 54.7	5.4	59.3
	06	267 49.7	S21 26.1	77 44.7	6.7	N16 49.3	5.5	59.3
	07	282 49.5	25.6	92 10.4	6.7	16 43.8	5.6	59.3
	08	297 49.3	25.2	106 36.1	6.8	16 38.2	5.8	59.2
F	09	312 49.1	. . 24.8	121 01.9	6.9	16 32.4	5.8	59.2
R	10	327 48.8	24.4	135 27.8	7.0	16 26.6	5.9	59.2
I	11	342 48.6	23.9	149 53.8	7.0	16 20.7	6.0	59.2
D	12	357 48.4	S21 23.5	164 19.8	7.1	N16 14.7	6.1	59.1
A	13	12 48.1	23.1	178 45.9	7.2	16 08.6	6.2	59.1
Y	14	27 47.9	22.6	193 12.1	7.2	16 02.4	6.3	59.1
	15	42 47.7	. . 22.2	207 38.3	7.4	15 56.1	6.4	59.0
	16	57 47.4	21.7	222 04.7	7.4	15 49.7	6.5	59.0
	17	72 47.2	21.3	236 31.1	7.5	15 43.2	6.6	59.0
	18	87 47.0	S21 20.9	250 57.6	7.6	N15 36.6	6.7	59.0
	19	102 46.8	20.4	265 24.2	7.6	15 29.9	6.7	58.9
	20	117 46.5	20.0	279 50.8	7.7	15 23.2	6.9	58.9
	21	132 46.3	. . 19.6	294 17.5	7.8	15 16.3	6.9	58.9
	22	147 46.1	19.1	308 44.3	7.9	15 09.4	7.0	58.8
	23	162 45.8	18.7	323 11.2	8.0	15 02.4	7.1	58.8
	14 00	177 45.6	S21 18.2	337 38.2	8.0	N14 55.3	7.2	58.8
	01	192 45.4	17.8	352 05.2	8.1	14 48.1	7.3	58.7
	02	207 45.2	17.3	6 32.3	8.2	14 40.8	7.3	58.7
	03	222 44.9	. . 16.9	20 59.5	8.3	14 33.5	7.4	58.7
	04	237 44.7	16.5	35 26.8	8.4	14 26.1	7.5	58.6
	05	252 44.5	16.0	49 54.2	8.4	14 18.6	7.6	58.6
	06	267 44.3	S21 15.6	64 21.6	8.6	N14 11.0	7.7	58.6
	07	282 44.0	15.1	78 49.2	8.6	14 03.3	7.7	58.5
S	08	297 43.8	14.7	93 16.8	8.7	13 55.6	7.8	58.5
A	09	312 43.6	. . 14.2	107 44.5	8.7	13 47.8	7.9	58.5
T	10	327 43.4	13.8	122 12.2	8.9	13 39.9	7.9	58.4
U	11	342 43.1	13.3	136 40.1	8.9	13 32.0	8.0	58.4
R	12	357 42.9	S21 12.9	151 08.0	9.0	N13 24.0	8.1	58.4
D	13	12 42.7	12.4	165 36.0	9.1	13 15.9	8.1	58.3
A	14	27 42.5	12.0	180 04.1	9.2	13 07.8	8.3	58.3
Y	15	42 42.3	. . 11.5	194 32.3	9.3	12 59.5	8.2	58.3
	16	57 42.0	11.1	209 00.6	9.3	12 51.3	8.4	58.2
	17	72 41.8	10.6	223 28.9	9.4	12 42.9	8.4	58.2
	18	87 41.6	S21 10.2	237 57.3	9.5	N12 34.5	8.4	58.2
	19	102 41.4	09.7	252 25.8	9.6	12 26.1	8.5	58.1
	20	117 41.1	09.3	266 54.4	9.6	12 17.6	8.6	58.1
	21	132 40.9	. . 08.8	281 23.0	9.8	12 09.0	8.6	58.0
	22	147 40.7	08.3	295 51.8	9.8	12 00.4	8.7	58.0
	23	162 40.5	07.9	310 20.6	9.9	11 51.7	8.8	58.0
	15 00	177 40.3	S21 07.4	324 49.5	10.0	N11 42.9	8.8	57.9
	01	192 40.0	07.0	339 18.5	10.0	11 34.1	8.8	57.9
	02	207 39.8	06.5	353 47.5	10.2	11 25.3	8.9	57.9
	03	222 39.6	. . 06.0	8 16.7	10.2	11 16.4	9.0	57.8
	04	237 39.4	05.6	22 45.9	10.3	11 07.4	9.0	57.8
	05	252 39.2	05.1	37 15.2	10.3	10 58.4	9.0	57.8
	06	267 38.9	S21 04.7	51 44.5	10.5	N10 49.4	9.1	57.7
	07	282 38.7	04.2	66 14.0	10.5	10 40.3	9.1	57.7
	08	297 38.5	03.7	80 43.5	10.6	10 31.2	9.2	57.7
S	09	312 38.3	. . 03.3	95 13.1	10.6	10 22.0	9.3	57.6
U	10	327 38.1	02.8	109 42.7	10.8	10 12.7	9.2	57.6
N	11	342 37.9	02.3	124 12.5	10.8	10 03.5	9.3	57.5
D	12	357 37.6	S21 01.9	138 42.3	10.9	N 9 54.2	9.4	57.5
A	13	12 37.4	01.4	153 12.2	11.0	9 44.8	9.4	57.5
Y	14	27 37.2	00.9	167 42.2	11.0	9 35.4	9.4	57.4
	15	42 37.0	. . 00.5	182 12.2	11.1	9 26.0	9.4	57.4
	16	57 36.8	21 00.0	196 42.3	11.2	9 16.6	9.5	57.4
	17	72 36.6	20 59.5	211 12.5	11.3	9 07.1	9.6	57.3
	18	87 36.3	S20 59.0	225 42.8	11.3	N 8 57.5	9.5	57.3
	19	102 36.1	58.6	240 13.1	11.4	8 48.0	9.6	57.3
	20	117 35.9	58.1	254 43.5	11.5	8 38.4	9.7	57.2
	21	132 35.7	. . 57.6	269 14.0	11.5	8 28.7	9.6	57.2
	22	147 35.5	57.2	283 44.5	11.6	8 19.1	9.7	57.2
	23	162 35.3	56.7	298 15.1	11.7	N 8 09.4	9.7	57.1
		SD 16.3	*d* 0.5	SD	16.1		15.9	15.7

Lat.	Twilight Naut.	Twilight Civil	Sunrise	Moonrise 13	Moonrise 14	Moonrise 15	Moonrise 16
°	h m	h m	h m	h m	h m	h m	h m
N 72	08 02	09 55	■	15 08	17 14	19 08	20 54
N 70	07 47	09 20	■	15 49	17 37	19 22	21 00
68	07 35	08 55	10 37	16 17	17 56	19 33	21 06
66	07 25	08 36	09 55	16 38	18 10	19 42	21 10
64	07 16	08 20	09 27	16 54	18 22	19 49	21 14
62	07 08	08 07	09 06	17 08	18 32	19 56	21 17
60	07 02	07 56	08 49	17 20	18 41	20 01	21 20
N 58	06 56	07 46	08 34	17 30	18 48	20 06	21 22
56	06 50	07 37	08 22	17 38	18 55	20 10	21 24
54	06 45	07 30	08 11	17 46	19 01	20 14	21 26
52	06 40	07 23	08 02	17 53	19 06	20 18	21 28
50	06 36	07 16	07 53	17 59	19 11	20 21	21 29
45	06 26	07 02	07 35	18 13	19 21	20 28	21 33
N 40	06 17	06 51	07 20	18 24	19 30	20 34	21 36
35	06 09	06 40	07 08	18 33	19 37	20 39	21 38
30	06 01	06 31	06 57	18 41	19 43	20 43	21 41
20	05 47	06 14	06 38	18 56	19 55	20 51	21 45
N 10	05 33	05 59	06 21	19 08	20 04	20 57	21 48
0	05 17	05 43	06 05	19 20	20 13	21 04	21 51
S 10	05 00	05 27	05 50	19 31	20 23	21 10	21 54
20	04 40	05 09	05 33	19 44	20 32	21 17	21 58
30	04 14	04 46	05 13	19 58	20 43	21 24	22 02
35	03 57	04 32	05 01	20 06	20 50	21 28	22 04
40	03 36	04 16	04 48	20 15	20 57	21 33	22 06
45	03 10	03 56	04 32	20 26	21 05	21 39	22 09
S 50	02 32	03 30	04 12	20 39	21 15	21 46	22 13
52	02 11	03 17	04 03	20 45	21 20	21 49	22 14
54	01 44	03 02	03 52	20 52	21 25	21 52	22 16
56	00 58	02 45	03 40	21 00	21 31	21 56	22 18
58	////	02 22	03 26	21 08	21 37	22 00	22 20
S 60	////	01 53	03 09	21 17	21 44	22 05	22 22

Lat.	Sunset	Twilight Civil	Twilight Naut.	Moonset 13	Moonset 14	Moonset 15	Moonset 16
°	h m	h m	h m	h m	h m	h m	h m
N 72	■	14 24	16 17	11 14	11 02	10 53	10 47
N 70	■	14 59	16 32	10 32	10 37	10 38	10 38
68	13 42	15 24	16 44	10 03	10 17	10 26	10 31
66	14 24	15 43	16 54	09 42	10 02	10 15	10 25
64	14 52	15 59	17 03	09 25	09 49	10 07	10 20
62	15 13	16 12	17 10	09 10	09 38	09 59	10 16
60	15 30	16 23	17 17	08 58	09 29	09 53	10 12
N 58	15 44	16 33	17 23	08 48	09 21	09 47	10 08
56	15 57	16 41	17 29	08 39	09 14	09 42	10 05
54	16 07	16 49	17 34	08 30	09 07	09 37	10 03
52	16 17	16 56	17 39	08 23	09 01	09 33	10 00
50	16 25	17 02	17 43	08 16	08 56	09 29	09 58
45	16 43	17 16	17 53	08 02	08 45	09 21	09 53
N 40	16 58	17 28	18 01	07 51	08 35	09 14	09 49
35	17 11	17 38	18 09	07 40	08 27	09 08	09 45
30	17 22	17 48	18 17	07 32	08 20	09 03	09 42
20	17 41	18 04	18 31	07 16	08 07	08 54	09 36
N 10	17 57	18 20	18 46	07 03	07 56	08 46	09 31
0	18 13	18 35	19 01	06 50	07 46	08 38	09 27
S 10	18 29	18 51	19 18	06 38	07 35	08 30	09 22
20	18 45	19 10	19 38	06 24	07 24	08 22	09 17
30	19 05	19 32	20 04	06 08	07 11	08 12	09 11
35	19 17	19 46	20 21	05 59	07 04	08 07	09 08
40	19 30	20 02	20 41	05 49	06 55	08 01	09 04
45	19 46	20 21	21 08	05 37	06 45	07 53	08 59
S 50	20 05	20 47	21 45	05 22	06 33	07 44	08 54
52	20 15	21 00	22 05	05 15	06 27	07 40	08 52
54	20 25	21 14	22 32	05 07	06 21	07 36	08 49
56	20 37	21 32	23 15	04 58	06 14	07 31	08 46
58	20 51	21 54	////	04 48	06 06	07 25	08 42
S 60	21 07	22 23	////	04 37	05 57	07 19	08 39

Day	SUN Eqn. of Time 00^h	SUN Eqn. of Time 12^h	SUN Mer. Pass.	MOON Mer. Pass. Upper	MOON Mer. Pass. Lower	MOON Age	MOON Phase
d	m s	m s	h m	h m	h m	d %	
13	08 35	08 46	12 09	00 37	13 05	15 99	○
14	08 57	09 08	12 09	01 33	14 00	16 95	
15	09 19	09 29	12 09	02 26	14 51	17 89	

UT	ARIES	VENUS −4·6		MARS +1·0		JUPITER −2·1		SATURN +0·5	
	GHA	GHA	Dec	GHA	Dec	GHA	Dec	GHA	Dec
d h	° ′	° ′	° ′	° ′	° ′	° ′	° ′	° ′	° ′
16 00	115 37.3	131 05.3	S 6 47.5	123 47.9	S 4 12.5	274 22.3	S 7 29.1	213 08.9	S21 58.3
01	130 39.7	146 05.6	46.3	138 48.7	11.8	289 24.6	29.2	228 11.1	58.3
02	145 42.2	161 05.8	45.1	153 49.4	11.0	304 26.9	29.2	243 13.3	58.3
03	160 44.7	176 06.1	43.9	168 50.2	10.2	319 29.2	29.3	258 15.5	58.3
04	175 47.1	191 06.3	42.7	183 50.9	09.4	334 31.5	29.4	273 17.6	58.4
05	190 49.6	206 06.6	41.5	198 51.7	08.7	349 33.8	29.4	288 19.8	58.4
06	205 52.1	221 06.8	S 6 40.3	213 52.4	S 4 07.9	4 36.1	S 7 29.5	303 22.0	S21 58.4
07	220 54.5	236 07.1	39.1	228 53.2	07.1	19 38.4	29.5	318 24.2	58.4
08	235 57.0	251 07.4	38.0	243 53.9	06.3	34 40.7	29.6	333 26.4	58.4
M 09	250 59.4	266 07.6	36.8	258 54.7	05.5	49 43.0	29.6	348 28.5	58.4
O 10	266 01.9	281 07.9	35.6	273 55.4	04.8	64 45.4	29.7	3 30.7	58.4
N 11	281 04.4	296 08.1	34.4	288 56.2	04.0	79 47.7	29.7	18 32.9	58.5
D 12	296 06.8	311 08.4	S 6 33.2	303 56.9	S 4 03.2	94 50.0	S 7 29.8	33 35.1	S21 58.5
A 13	311 09.3	326 08.7	32.0	318 57.7	02.4	109 52.3	29.8	48 37.3	58.5
Y 14	326 11.8	341 08.9	30.8	333 58.4	01.7	124 54.6	29.9	63 39.5	58.5
15	341 14.2	356 09.2	29.6	348 59.2	00.9	139 56.9	29.9	78 41.6	58.5
16	356 16.7	11 09.5	28.4	3 59.9	4 00.1	154 59.2	30.0	93 43.8	58.5
17	11 19.2	26 09.7	27.2	19 00.7	3 59.3	170 01.5	30.0	108 46.0	58.5
18	26 21.6	41 10.0	S 6 26.1	34 01.4	S 3 58.5	185 03.9	S 7 30.0	123 48.2	S21 58.5
19	41 24.1	56 10.3	24.9	49 02.2	57.8	200 06.2	30.1	138 50.4	58.6
20	56 26.5	71 10.6	23.7	64 02.9	57.0	215 08.5	30.1	153 52.5	58.6
21	71 29.0	86 10.8	22.5	79 03.7	56.2	230 10.8	30.2	168 54.7	58.6
22	86 31.5	101 11.1	21.3	94 04.4	55.4	245 13.1	30.2	183 56.9	58.6
23	101 33.9	116 11.4	20.1	109 05.2	54.7	260 15.4	30.3	198 59.1	58.6
17 00	116 36.4	131 11.6	S 6 18.9	124 05.9	S 3 53.9	275 17.7	S 7 30.3	214 01.3	S21 58.6
01	131 38.9	146 11.9	17.7	139 06.7	53.1	290 20.0	30.4	229 03.5	58.6
02	146 41.3	161 12.2	16.5	154 07.4	52.3	305 22.4	30.4	244 05.6	58.7
03	161 43.8	176 12.5	15.3	169 08.2	51.5	320 24.7	30.5	259 07.8	58.7
04	176 46.3	191 12.8	14.1	184 08.9	50.8	335 27.0	30.5	274 10.0	58.7
05	191 48.7	206 13.0	13.0	199 09.7	50.0	350 29.3	30.6	289 12.2	58.7
06	206 51.2	221 13.3	S 6 11.8	214 10.4	S 3 49.2	5 31.6	S 7 30.6	304 14.4	S21 58.7
07	221 53.7	236 13.6	10.6	229 11.2	48.4	20 33.9	30.7	319 16.5	58.7
T 08	236 56.1	251 13.9	09.4	244 11.9	47.7	35 36.3	30.7	334 18.7	58.7
U 09	251 58.6	266 14.2	08.2	259 12.7	46.9	50 38.6	30.8	349 20.9	58.7
E 10	267 01.0	281 14.5	07.0	274 13.4	46.1	65 40.9	30.8	4 23.1	58.8
S 11	282 03.5	296 14.8	05.8	289 14.2	45.3	80 43.2	30.9	19 25.3	58.8
D 12	297 06.0	311 15.0	S 6 04.6	304 14.9	S 3 44.5	95 45.5	S 7 30.9	34 27.5	S21 58.8
A 13	312 08.4	326 15.3	03.4	319 15.7	43.8	110 47.8	31.0	49 29.6	58.8
Y 14	327 10.9	341 15.6	02.2	334 16.4	43.0	125 50.2	31.0	64 31.8	58.8
15	342 13.4	356 15.9	6 01.0	349 17.2	42.2	140 52.5	31.1	79 34.0	58.8
16	357 15.8	11 16.2	5 59.8	4 17.9	41.4	155 54.8	31.1	94 36.2	58.8
17	12 18.3	26 16.5	58.7	19 18.7	40.7	170 57.1	31.1	109 38.4	58.9
18	27 20.8	41 16.8	S 5 57.5	34 19.4	S 3 39.9	185 59.4	S 7 31.2	124 40.6	S21 58.9
19	42 23.2	56 17.1	56.3	49 20.2	39.1	201 01.8	31.2	139 42.7	58.9
20	57 25.7	71 17.4	55.1	64 20.9	38.3	216 04.1	31.3	154 44.9	58.9
21	72 28.2	86 17.7	53.9	79 21.7	37.5	231 06.4	31.3	169 47.1	58.9
22	87 30.6	101 18.0	52.7	94 22.4	36.8	246 08.7	31.4	184 49.3	58.9
23	102 33.1	116 18.3	51.5	109 23.2	36.0	261 11.0	31.4	199 51.5	58.9
18 00	117 35.5	131 18.6	S 5 50.3	124 23.9	S 3 35.2	276 13.4	S 7 31.5	214 53.7	S21 58.9
01	132 38.0	146 18.9	49.1	139 24.7	34.4	291 15.7	31.5	229 55.8	59.0
02	147 40.5	161 19.2	47.9	154 25.4	33.6	306 18.0	31.6	244 58.0	59.0
03	162 42.9	176 19.5	46.7	169 26.2	32.9	321 20.3	31.6	260 00.2	59.0
04	177 45.4	191 19.8	45.5	184 26.9	32.1	336 22.6	31.7	275 02.4	59.0
05	192 47.9	206 20.1	44.3	199 27.7	31.3	351 25.0	31.7	290 04.6	59.0
06	207 50.3	221 20.4	S 5 43.2	214 28.5	S 3 30.5	6 27.3	S 7 31.7	305 06.8	S21 59.0
W 07	222 52.8	236 20.7	42.0	229 29.2	29.8	21 29.6	31.8	320 09.0	59.0
E 08	237 55.3	251 21.0	40.8	244 30.0	29.0	36 31.9	31.8	335 11.1	59.0
D 09	252 57.7	266 21.3	39.6	259 30.7	28.2	51 34.3	31.9	350 13.3	59.1
N 10	268 00.2	281 21.6	38.4	274 31.5	27.4	66 36.6	31.9	5 15.5	59.1
E 11	283 02.6	296 22.0	37.2	289 32.2	26.6	81 38.9	32.0	20 17.7	59.1
S 12	298 05.1	311 22.3	S 5 36.0	304 33.0	S 3 25.9	96 41.2	S 7 32.0	35 19.9	S21 59.1
D 13	313 07.6	326 22.6	34.8	319 33.7	25.1	111 43.5	32.1	50 22.1	59.1
A 14	328 10.0	341 22.9	33.6	334 34.5	24.3	126 45.9	32.1	65 24.2	59.1
Y 15	343 12.5	356 23.2	32.4	349 35.2	23.5	141 48.2	32.1	80 26.4	59.1
16	358 15.0	11 23.5	31.2	4 36.0	22.7	156 50.5	32.2	95 28.6	59.1
17	13 17.4	26 23.9	30.0	19 36.7	22.0	171 52.8	32.2	110 30.8	59.2
18	28 19.9	41 24.2	S 5 28.8	34 37.5	S 3 21.2	186 55.2	S 7 32.3	125 33.0	S21 59.2
19	43 22.4	56 24.5	27.6	49 38.2	20.4	201 57.5	32.3	140 35.2	59.2
20	58 24.8	71 24.8	26.5	64 39.0	19.6	216 59.8	32.4	155 37.4	59.2
21	73 27.3	86 25.1	25.3	79 39.8	18.8	232 02.2	32.4	170 39.5	59.2
22	88 29.8	101 25.5	24.1	94 40.5	18.1	247 04.5	32.4	185 41.7	59.2
23	103 32.2	116 25.8	22.9	109 41.3	17.3	262 06.8	32.5	200 43.9	59.2
Mer. Pass.	h m 16 10.9	*v* 0.3	*d* 1.2	*v* 0.8	*d* 0.8	*v* 2.3	*d* 0.0	*v* 2.2	*d* 0.0

STARS Name	SHA ° ′	Dec ° ′
Acamar	315 16.4	S40 14.6
Achernar	335 25.1	S57 09.5
Acrux	173 06.1	S63 11.3
Adhara	255 10.2	S29 00.0
Aldebaran	290 46.3	N16 32.4
Alioth	166 18.5	N55 51.8
Alkaid	152 57.1	N49 13.5
Al Na'ir	27 41.2	S46 52.8
Alnilam	275 43.6	S 1 11.8
Alphard	217 53.4	S 8 44.1
Alphecca	126 09.2	N26 39.4
Alpheratz	357 41.1	N29 11.1
Altair	62 06.2	N 8 54.9
Ankaa	353 13.5	S42 13.1
Antares	112 23.5	S26 27.9
Arcturus	145 53.6	N19 05.6
Atria	107 23.5	S69 03.1
Avior	234 16.3	S59 34.0
Bellatrix	278 29.1	N 6 21.6
Betelgeuse	270 58.4	N 7 24.3
Canopus	263 54.5	S52 42.6
Capella	280 30.4	N46 00.8
Deneb	49 30.2	N45 20.6
Denebola	182 31.0	N14 28.5
Diphda	348 53.6	S17 53.8
Dubhe	193 48.4	N61 39.3
Elnath	278 09.2	N28 37.1
Eltanin	90 45.5	N51 29.2
Enif	33 45.0	N 9 57.2
Fomalhaut	15 21.6	S29 32.1
Gacrux	171 57.9	S57 12.2
Gienah	175 49.6	S17 38.1
Hadar	148 44.4	S60 26.9
Hamal	327 57.9	N23 32.5
Kaus Aust.	83 41.0	S34 22.3
Kochab	137 20.7	N74 04.9
Markab	13 36.1	N15 17.8
Menkar	314 12.4	N 4 09.2
Menkent	148 04.7	S36 26.9
Miaplacidus	221 38.1	S69 47.2
Mirfak	308 36.6	N49 55.3
Nunki	75 55.7	S26 16.3
Peacock	53 16.1	S56 40.7
Pollux	243 24.4	N27 58.9
Procyon	244 56.9	N 5 10.6
Rasalhague	96 04.5	N12 33.0
Regulus	207 40.7	N11 52.9
Rigel	281 09.4	S 8 11.2
Rigil Kent.	139 48.5	S60 53.9
Sabik	102 10.0	S15 44.5
Schedar	349 37.8	N56 38.0
Shaula	96 19.0	S37 06.7
Sirius	258 31.2	S16 44.7
Spica	158 28.6	S11 14.9
Suhail	222 50.2	S43 30.1
Vega	80 37.7	N38 48.1
Zuben'ubi	137 02.8	S16 06.5

	SHA ° ′	Mer. Pass. h m
Venus	14 35.2	15 15
Mars	7 29.5	15 43
Jupiter	158 41.3	5 38
Saturn	97 24.9	9 43

	UT d h	SUN GHA ° ′	SUN Dec ° ′	MOON GHA ° ′	v ′	Dec ° ′	d ′	HP ′
	16 00	177 35.1	S20 56.2	312 45.8	11.7	N 7 59.7	9.8	57.1
	01	192 34.9	55.7	327 16.5	11.8	7 49.9	9.7	57.0
	02	207 34.6	55.2	341 47.3	11.9	7 40.2	9.8	57.0
	03	222 34.4	. . 54.8	356 18.2	11.9	7 30.4	9.9	57.0
	04	237 34.2	54.3	10 49.1	12.0	7 20.5	9.8	56.9
	05	252 34.0	53.8	25 20.1	12.1	7 10.7	9.9	56.9
	06	267 33.8	S20 53.3	39 51.2	12.1	N 7 00.8	9.8	56.9
	07	282 33.6	52.9	54 22.3	12.2	6 51.0	10.0	56.8
	08	297 33.4	52.4	68 53.5	12.3	6 41.0	9.9	56.8
M	09	312 33.2	. . 51.9	83 24.8	12.3	6 31.1	9.9	56.8
O	10	327 33.0	51.4	97 56.1	12.3	6 21.2	10.0	56.7
N	11	342 32.7	50.9	112 27.4	12.5	6 11.2	10.0	56.7
D	12	357 32.5	S20 50.4	126 58.9	12.5	N 6 01.2	10.0	56.7
A	13	12 32.3	50.0	141 30.4	12.5	5 51.2	10.0	56.6
Y	14	27 32.1	49.5	156 01.9	12.6	5 41.2	10.0	56.6
	15	42 31.9	. . 49.0	170 33.5	12.7	5 31.2	10.0	56.6
	16	57 31.7	48.5	185 05.2	12.7	5 21.2	10.1	56.5
	17	72 31.5	48.0	199 36.9	12.8	5 11.1	10.1	56.5
	18	87 31.3	S20 47.5	214 08.7	12.8	N 5 01.0	10.0	56.5
	19	102 31.1	47.0	228 40.5	12.9	4 51.0	10.1	56.4
	20	117 30.9	46.5	243 12.4	13.0	4 40.9	10.1	56.4
	21	132 30.7	. . 46.1	257 44.4	13.0	4 30.8	10.1	56.4
	22	147 30.5	45.6	272 16.4	13.0	4 20.7	10.1	56.3
	23	162 30.2	45.1	286 48.4	13.1	4 10.6	10.1	56.3
	17 00	177 30.0	S20 44.6	301 20.5	13.2	N 4 00.5	10.2	56.3
	01	192 29.8	44.1	315 52.7	13.2	3 50.3	10.1	56.2
	02	207 29.6	43.6	330 24.9	13.2	3 40.2	10.1	56.2
	03	222 29.4	. . 43.1	344 57.1	13.3	3 30.1	10.1	56.2
	04	237 29.2	42.6	359 29.4	13.3	3 20.0	10.2	56.1
	05	252 29.0	42.1	14 01.7	13.4	3 09.8	10.1	56.1
	06	267 28.8	S20 41.6	28 34.1	13.4	N 2 59.7	10.2	56.1
	07	282 28.6	41.1	43 06.5	13.5	2 49.5	10.1	56.0
T	08	297 28.4	40.6	57 39.0	13.5	2 39.4	10.2	56.0
U	09	312 28.2	. . 40.1	72 11.5	13.6	2 29.2	10.1	56.0
E	10	327 28.0	39.6	86 44.1	13.6	2 19.1	10.1	55.9
S	11	342 27.8	39.1	101 16.7	13.7	2 09.0	10.2	55.9
D	12	357 27.6	S20 38.6	115 49.4	13.6	N 1 58.8	10.1	55.9
A	13	12 27.4	38.1	130 22.0	13.8	1 48.7	10.1	55.9
Y	14	27 27.2	37.6	144 54.8	13.7	1 38.6	10.2	55.8
	15	42 27.0	. . 37.1	159 27.5	13.8	1 28.4	10.1	55.8
	16	57 26.8	36.6	174 00.3	13.9	1 18.3	10.1	55.8
	17	72 26.6	36.1	188 33.2	13.9	1 08.2	10.1	55.7
	18	87 26.4	S20 35.6	203 06.1	13.9	N 0 58.1	10.1	55.7
	19	102 26.2	35.1	217 39.0	13.9	0 48.0	10.1	55.7
	20	117 26.0	34.6	232 11.9	14.0	0 37.9	10.1	55.6
	21	132 25.8	. . 34.1	246 44.9	14.0	0 27.8	10.1	55.6
	22	147 25.6	33.6	261 17.9	14.1	0 17.7	10.0	55.6
	23	162 25.4	33.1	275 51.0	14.0	N 0 07.7	10.1	55.6
	18 00	177 25.2	S20 32.6	290 24.0	14.2	S 0 02.4	10.0	55.5
	01	192 25.0	32.1	304 57.2	14.1	0 12.4	10.1	55.5
	02	207 24.8	31.5	319 30.3	14.2	0 22.5	10.0	55.5
	03	222 24.6	. . 31.0	334 03.5	14.2	0 32.5	10.0	55.4
	04	237 24.4	30.5	348 36.7	14.2	0 42.5	10.0	55.4
	05	252 24.2	30.0	3 09.9	14.3	0 52.5	10.0	55.4
	06	267 24.0	S20 29.5	17 43.2	14.2	S 1 02.5	9.9	55.4
W	07	282 23.8	29.0	32 16.4	14.4	1 12.4	10.0	55.3
E	08	297 23.6	28.5	46 49.8	14.3	1 22.4	9.9	55.3
D	09	312 23.4	. . 28.0	61 23.1	14.3	1 32.3	9.9	55.3
N	10	327 23.2	27.4	75 56.4	14.4	1 42.2	9.9	55.3
E	11	342 23.0	26.9	90 29.8	14.4	1 52.1	9.9	55.2
S	12	357 22.8	S20 26.4	105 03.2	14.5	S 2 02.0	9.9	55.2
D	13	12 22.6	25.9	119 36.7	14.4	2 11.9	9.8	55.2
A	14	27 22.4	25.4	134 10.1	14.5	2 21.7	9.9	55.2
Y	15	42 22.2	. . 24.9	148 43.6	14.4	2 31.6	9.8	55.1
	16	57 22.0	24.3	163 17.0	14.6	2 41.4	9.8	55.1
	17	72 21.9	23.8	177 50.6	14.5	2 51.2	9.7	55.1
	18	87 21.7	S20 23.3	192 24.1	14.5	S 3 00.9	9.8	55.1
	19	102 21.5	22.8	206 57.6	14.6	3 10.7	9.7	55.0
	20	117 21.3	22.3	221 31.2	14.5	3 20.4	9.7	55.0
	21	132 21.1	. . 21.7	236 04.7	14.6	3 30.1	9.7	55.0
	22	147 20.9	21.2	250 38.3	14.6	3 39.8	9.6	55.0
	23	162 20.7	20.7	265 11.9	14.6	S 3 49.4	9.7	55.0
		SD 16.3	*d* 0.5	SD 15.4		15.2		15.0

Lat. °	Twilight Naut. h m	Twilight Civil h m	Sunrise h m	Moonrise 16 h m	Moonrise 17 h m	Moonrise 18 h m	Moonrise 19 h m
N 72	07 55	09 42	▬	20 54	22 35	24 13	00 13
N 70	07 41	09 11	11 37	21 00	22 35	24 07	00 07
68	07 30	08 48	10 22	21 06	22 35	24 02	00 02
66	07 20	08 30	09 46	21 10	22 35	23 58	25 19
64	07 12	08 15	09 20	21 14	22 35	23 54	25 12
62	07 05	08 03	09 00	21 17	22 35	23 52	25 06
60	06 58	07 52	08 44	21 20	22 35	23 49	25 01
N 58	06 53	07 43	08 30	21 22	22 35	23 47	24 56
56	06 47	07 34	08 19	21 24	22 35	23 45	24 52
54	06 43	07 27	08 08	21 26	22 36	23 43	24 49
52	06 38	07 20	07 59	21 28	22 36	23 41	24 45
50	06 34	07 14	07 51	21 29	22 36	23 40	24 42
45	06 25	07 01	07 33	21 33	22 36	23 37	24 36
N 40	06 16	06 49	07 19	21 36	22 36	23 34	24 31
35	06 09	06 40	07 07	21 38	22 36	23 32	24 26
30	06 01	06 31	06 56	21 41	22 36	23 30	24 22
20	05 47	06 14	06 38	21 45	22 36	23 26	24 15
N 10	05 33	05 59	06 22	21 48	22 36	23 23	24 09
0	05 19	05 44	06 07	21 51	22 36	23 20	24 04
S 10	05 02	05 29	05 51	21 54	22 36	23 17	23 58
20	04 42	05 11	05 35	21 58	22 37	23 14	23 52
30	04 17	04 49	05 15	22 02	22 37	23 11	23 45
35	04 00	04 35	05 04	22 04	22 37	23 09	23 41
40	03 40	04 20	04 51	22 06	22 37	23 07	23 37
45	03 15	04 00	04 36	22 09	22 37	23 05	23 32
S 50	02 39	03 35	04 17	22 13	22 38	23 02	23 26
52	02 19	03 23	04 08	22 14	22 38	23 00	23 23
54	01 54	03 09	03 57	22 16	22 38	22 59	23 20
56	01 16	02 52	03 46	22 18	22 38	22 57	23 17
58	////	02 31	03 33	22 20	22 38	22 55	23 13
S 60	////	02 04	03 17	22 22	22 38	22 53	23 09

Lat. °	Sunset h m	Twilight Civil h m	Twilight Naut. h m	Moonset 16 h m	Moonset 17 h m	Moonset 18 h m	Moonset 19 h m
N 72	▬	14 39	16 26	10 47	10 40	10 34	10 27
N 70	12 44	15 10	16 40	10 38	10 37	10 36	10 35
68	13 59	15 33	16 51	10 31	10 35	10 38	10 42
66	14 35	15 51	17 01	10 25	10 33	10 40	10 47
64	15 01	16 06	17 09	10 20	10 31	10 42	10 52
62	15 21	16 18	17 16	10 16	10 30	10 43	10 56
60	15 37	16 29	17 22	10 12	10 29	10 44	11 00
N 58	15 50	16 38	17 28	10 08	10 27	10 45	11 03
56	16 02	16 46	17 33	10 05	10 26	10 46	11 05
54	16 13	16 54	17 38	10 03	10 25	10 47	11 08
52	16 22	17 00	17 43	10 00	10 25	10 48	11 10
50	16 30	17 07	17 47	09 58	10 24	10 48	11 12
45	16 47	17 20	17 56	09 53	10 22	10 50	11 17
N 40	17 02	17 31	18 04	09 49	10 21	10 51	11 21
35	17 14	17 41	18 12	09 45	10 19	10 52	11 24
30	17 24	17 50	18 19	09 42	10 18	10 53	11 27
20	17 43	18 06	18 33	09 36	10 16	10 55	11 32
N 10	17 59	18 21	18 47	09 31	10 15	10 56	11 37
0	18 14	18 36	19 02	09 27	10 13	10 58	11 41
S 10	18 29	18 52	19 18	09 22	10 11	10 59	11 45
20	18 46	19 09	19 38	09 17	10 10	11 00	11 50
30	19 05	19 31	20 03	09 11	10 07	11 02	11 55
35	19 16	19 44	20 19	09 08	10 06	11 03	11 58
40	19 29	20 00	20 39	09 04	10 05	11 04	12 01
45	19 44	20 19	21 05	08 59	10 03	11 05	12 05
S 50	20 03	20 44	21 40	08 54	10 01	11 07	12 10
52	20 12	20 56	21 59	08 52	10 00	11 07	12 12
54	20 22	21 10	22 24	08 49	09 59	11 08	12 15
56	20 33	21 27	23 00	08 46	09 58	11 09	12 17
58	20 46	21 47	////	08 42	09 57	11 10	12 20
S 60	21 02	22 13	////	08 39	09 56	11 11	12 23

Day d	SUN Eqn. of Time 00^h m s	SUN Eqn. of Time 12^h m s	SUN Mer. Pass. h m	MOON Mer. Pass. Upper h m	MOON Mer. Pass. Lower h m	MOON Age d	MOON Phase %
16	09 39	09 49	12 10	03 15	15 39	18	81
17	09 59	10 09	12 10	04 02	16 25	19	73
18	10 19	10 28	12 10	04 47	17 09	20	64

Day	UT d h	ARIES GHA	VENUS −4·6 GHA	VENUS Dec	MARS +1·0 GHA	MARS Dec	JUPITER −2·1 GHA	JUPITER Dec	SATURN +0·5 GHA	SATURN Dec
		° ′	° ′	° ′	° ′	° ′	° ′	° ′	° ′	° ′
THURSDAY	19 00	118 34.7	131 26.1	S 5 21.7	124 42.0	S 3 16.5	277 09.1	S 7 32.5	215 46.1	S21 59.2
	01	133 37.1	146 26.4	20.5	139 42.8	15.7	292 11.5	32.6	230 48.3	59.3
	02	148 39.6	161 26.8	19.3	154 43.5	15.0	307 13.8	32.6	245 50.5	59.3
	03	163 42.1	176 27.1 . .	18.1	169 44.3 . .	14.2	322 16.1 . .	32.7	260 52.7 . .	59.3
	04	178 44.5	191 27.4	16.9	184 45.0	13.4	337 18.4	32.7	275 54.8	59.3
	05	193 47.0	206 27.8	15.7	199 45.8	12.6	352 20.8	32.7	290 57.0	59.3
	06	208 49.5	221 28.1	S 5 14.5	214 46.5	S 3 11.8	7 23.1	S 7 32.8	305 59.2	S21 59.3
	07	223 51.9	236 28.4	13.3	229 47.3	11.1	22 25.4	32.8	321 01.4	59.3
	08	238 54.4	251 28.8	12.1	244 48.0	10.3	37 27.8	32.9	336 03.6	59.3
	09	253 56.9	266 29.1 . .	10.9	259 48.8 . .	09.5	52 30.1 . .	32.9	351 05.8 . .	59.4
	10	268 59.3	281 29.4	09.7	274 49.6	08.7	67 32.4	33.0	6 08.0	59.4
	11	284 01.8	296 29.8	08.6	289 50.3	07.9	82 34.8	33.0	21 10.2	59.4
	12	299 04.2	311 30.1	S 5 07.4	304 51.1	S 3 07.2	97 37.1	S 7 33.0	36 12.3	S21 59.4
	13	314 06.7	326 30.5	06.2	319 51.8	06.4	112 39.4	33.1	51 14.5	59.4
	14	329 09.2	341 30.8	05.0	334 52.6	05.6	127 41.8	33.1	66 16.7	59.4
	15	344 11.6	356 31.1 . .	03.8	349 53.3 . .	04.8	142 44.1 . .	33.2	81 18.9 . .	59.4
	16	359 14.1	11 31.5	02.6	4 54.1	04.0	157 46.4	33.2	96 21.1	59.4
	17	14 16.6	26 31.8	01.4	19 54.8	03.3	172 48.7	33.2	111 23.3	59.5
	18	29 19.0	41 32.2	S 5 00.2	34 55.6	S 3 02.5	187 51.1	S 7 33.3	126 25.5	S21 59.5
	19	44 21.5	56 32.5	4 59.0	49 56.4	01.7	202 53.4	33.3	141 27.7	59.5
	20	59 24.0	71 32.9	57.8	64 57.1	00.9	217 55.7	33.4	156 29.8	59.5
	21	74 26.4	86 33.2 . .	56.6	79 57.9 . .	3 00.1	232 58.1 . .	33.4	171 32.0 . .	59.5
	22	89 28.9	101 33.6	55.4	94 58.6	2 59.4	248 00.4	33.4	186 34.2	59.5
	23	104 31.4	116 33.9	54.2	109 59.4	58.6	263 02.8	33.5	201 36.4	59.5
FRIDAY	20 00	119 33.8	131 34.3	S 4 53.0	125 00.1	S 2 57.8	278 05.1	S 7 33.5	216 38.6	S21 59.5
	01	134 36.3	146 34.6	51.9	140 00.9	57.0	293 07.4	33.6	231 40.8	59.6
	02	149 38.7	161 35.0	50.7	155 01.6	56.2	308 09.8	33.6	246 43.0	59.6
	03	164 41.2	176 35.3 . .	49.5	170 02.4 . .	55.5	323 12.1 . .	33.6	261 45.2 . .	59.6
	04	179 43.7	191 35.7	48.3	185 03.2	54.7	338 14.4	33.7	276 47.3	59.6
	05	194 46.1	206 36.0	47.1	200 03.9	53.9	353 16.8	33.7	291 49.5	59.6
	06	209 48.6	221 36.4	S 4 45.9	215 04.7	S 2 53.1	8 19.1	S 7 33.8	306 51.7	S21 59.6
	07	224 51.1	236 36.8	44.7	230 05.4	52.3	23 21.4	33.8	321 53.9	59.6
	08	239 53.5	251 37.1	43.5	245 06.2	51.6	38 23.8	33.8	336 56.1	59.6
	09	254 56.0	266 37.5 . .	42.3	260 06.9 . .	50.8	53 26.1 . .	33.9	351 58.3 . .	59.6
	10	269 58.5	281 37.8	41.1	275 07.7	50.0	68 28.4	33.9	7 00.5	59.7
	11	285 00.9	296 38.2	39.9	290 08.4	49.2	83 30.8	34.0	22 02.7	59.7
	12	300 03.4	311 38.6	S 4 38.7	305 09.2	S 2 48.4	98 33.1	S 7 34.0	37 04.9	S21 59.7
	13	315 05.9	326 38.9	37.5	320 10.0	47.7	113 35.5	34.0	52 07.0	59.7
	14	330 08.3	341 39.3	36.3	335 10.7	46.9	128 37.8	34.1	67 09.2	59.7
	15	345 10.8	356 39.7 . .	35.1	350 11.5 . .	46.1	143 40.1 . .	34.1	82 11.4 . .	59.7
	16	0 13.2	11 40.0	34.0	5 12.2	45.3	158 42.5	34.2	97 13.6	59.7
	17	15 15.7	26 40.4	32.8	20 13.0	44.6	173 44.8	34.2	112 15.8	59.7
	18	30 18.2	41 40.8	S 4 31.6	35 13.7	S 2 43.8	188 47.2	S 7 34.2	127 18.0	S21 59.8
	19	45 20.6	56 41.2	30.4	50 14.5	43.0	203 49.5	34.3	142 20.2	59.8
	20	60 23.1	71 41.5	29.2	65 15.3	42.2	218 51.8	34.3	157 22.4	59.8
	21	75 25.6	86 41.9 . .	28.0	80 16.0 . .	41.4	233 54.2 . .	34.3	172 24.6 . .	59.8
	22	90 28.0	101 42.3	26.8	95 16.8	40.7	248 56.5	34.4	187 26.8	59.8
	23	105 30.5	116 42.7	25.6	110 17.5	39.9	263 58.9	34.4	202 28.9	59.8
SATURDAY	21 00	120 33.0	131 43.0	S 4 24.4	125 18.3	S 2 39.1	279 01.2	S 7 34.5	217 31.1	S21 59.8
	01	135 35.4	146 43.4	23.2	140 19.0	38.3	294 03.5	34.5	232 33.3	59.8
	02	150 37.9	161 43.8	22.0	155 19.8	37.5	309 05.9	34.5	247 35.5	59.9
	03	165 40.3	176 44.2 . .	20.8	170 20.6 . .	36.8	324 08.2 . .	34.6	262 37.7 . .	59.9
	04	180 42.8	191 44.6	19.6	185 21.3	36.0	339 10.6	34.6	277 39.9	59.9
	05	195 45.3	206 44.9	18.5	200 22.1	35.2	354 12.9	34.6	292 42.1	59.9
	06	210 47.7	221 45.3	S 4 17.3	215 22.8	S 2 34.4	9 15.3	S 7 34.7	307 44.3	S21 59.9
	07	225 50.2	236 45.7	16.1	230 23.6	33.6	24 17.6	34.7	322 46.5	59.9
	08	240 52.7	251 46.1	14.9	245 24.3	32.9	39 19.9	34.8	337 48.7	59.9
	09	255 55.1	266 46.5 . .	13.7	260 25.1 . .	32.1	54 22.3 . .	34.8	352 50.8 . .	59.9
	10	270 57.6	281 46.9	12.5	275 25.9	31.3	69 24.6	34.8	7 53.0	21 59.9
	11	286 00.1	296 47.3	11.3	290 26.6	30.5	84 27.0	34.9	22 55.2	22 00.0
	12	301 02.5	311 47.7	S 4 10.1	305 27.4	S 2 29.7	99 29.3	S 7 34.9	37 57.4	S22 00.0
	13	316 05.0	326 48.0	08.9	320 28.1	29.0	114 31.7	34.9	52 59.6	00.0
	14	331 07.5	341 48.4	07.7	335 28.9	28.2	129 34.0	35.0	68 01.8	00.0
	15	346 09.9	356 48.8 . .	06.5	350 29.6 . .	27.4	144 36.4 . .	35.0	83 04.0 . .	00.0
	16	1 12.4	11 49.2	05.3	5 30.4	26.6	159 38.7	35.0	98 06.2	00.0
	17	16 14.8	26 49.6	04.1	20 31.2	25.8	174 41.1	35.1	113 08.4	00.0
	18	31 17.3	41 50.0	S 4 03.0	35 31.9	S 2 25.1	189 43.4	S 7 35.1	128 10.6	S22 00.0
	19	46 19.8	56 50.4	01.8	50 32.7	24.3	204 45.7	35.1	143 12.8	00.0
	20	61 22.2	71 50.8	4 00.6	65 33.4	23.5	219 48.1	35.2	158 15.0	00.1
	21	76 24.7	86 51.2 . .	3 59.4	80 34.2 . .	22.7	234 50.4 . .	35.2	173 17.1 . .	00.1
	22	91 27.2	101 51.6	58.2	95 35.0	21.9	249 52.8	35.2	188 19.3	00.1
	23	106 29.6	116 52.0	57.0	110 35.7	21.2	264 55.1	35.3	203 21.5	00.1
	Mer. Pass.	h m 15 59.1	v 0.4	d 1.2	v 0.8	d 0.8	v 2.3	d 0.0	v 2.2	d 0.0

STARS

Name	SHA	Dec
	° ′	° ′
Acamar	315 16.4	S40 14.6
Achernar	335 25.1	S57 09.5
Acrux	173 06.1	S63 11.3
Adhara	255 10.2	S29 00.0
Aldebaran	290 46.3	N16 32.4
Alioth	166 18.5	N55 51.8
Alkaid	152 57.0	N49 13.5
Al Na'ir	27 41.2	S46 52.8
Alnilam	275 43.6	S 1 11.8
Alphard	217 53.4	S 8 44.1
Alphecca	126 09.1	N26 39.4
Alpheratz	357 41.1	N29 11.1
Altair	62 06.2	N 8 54.9
Ankaa	353 13.5	S42 13.1
Antares	112 23.5	S26 27.9
Arcturus	145 53.6	N19 05.6
Atria	107 23.5	S69 03.0
Avior	234 16.3	S59 34.0
Bellatrix	278 29.1	N 6 21.6
Betelgeuse	270 58.4	N 7 24.3
Canopus	263 54.5	S52 42.6
Capella	280 30.5	N46 00.8
Deneb	49 30.2	N45 20.6
Denebola	182 31.0	N14 28.5
Diphda	348 53.6	S17 53.8
Dubhe	193 48.4	N61 39.3
Elnath	278 09.2	N28 37.1
Eltanin	90 45.5	N51 29.2
Enif	33 45.0	N 9 57.2
Fomalhaut	15 21.6	S29 32.1
Gacrux	171 57.8	S57 12.2
Gienah	175 49.6	S17 38.1
Hadar	148 44.3	S60 26.9
Hamal	327 57.9	N23 32.5
Kaus Aust.	83 41.0	S34 22.3
Kochab	137 20.6	N74 04.9
Markab	13 36.1	N15 17.8
Menkar	314 12.4	N 4 09.2
Menkent	148 04.7	S36 26.9
Miaplacidus	221 38.1	S69 47.2
Mirfak	308 36.6	N49 55.3
Nunki	75 55.7	S26 16.3
Peacock	53 16.1	S56 40.7
Pollux	243 24.4	N27 58.9
Procyon	244 56.9	N 5 10.6
Rasalhague	96 04.5	N12 33.0
Regulus	207 40.7	N11 52.9
Rigel	281 09.5	S 8 11.2
Rigil Kent.	139 48.4	S60 53.9
Sabik	102 10.0	S15 44.5
Schedar	349 37.8	N56 38.0
Shaula	96 18.9	S37 06.7
Sirius	258 31.2	S16 44.7
Spica	158 28.6	S11 14.9
Suhail	222 50.2	S43 30.2
Vega	80 37.7	N38 48.0
Zuben'ubi	137 02.8	S16 06.6

	SHA	Mer. Pass.
	° ′	h m
Venus	12 00.4	15 13
Mars	5 26.3	15 39
Jupiter	158 31.3	5 27
Saturn	97 04.8	9 32

UT	SUN GHA	SUN Dec	MOON GHA	v	MOON Dec	d	HP
d h	° ′	° ′	° ′	′	° ′	′	′
19 00	177 20.5	S20 20.2	279 45.5	14.6	S 3 59.1	9.6	54.9
01	192 20.3	19.6	294 19.1	14.7	4 08.7	9.6	54.9
02	207 20.1	19.1	308 52.8	14.6	4 18.3	9.5	54.9
03	222 19.9	. . 18.6	323 26.4	14.7	4 27.8	9.5	54.9
04	237 19.7	18.1	338 00.1	14.6	4 37.3	9.5	54.9
05	252 19.6	17.5	352 33.7	14.7	4 46.8	9.5	54.8
06	267 19.4	S20 17.0	7 07.4	14.7	S 4 56.3	9.5	54.8
T 07	282 19.2	16.5	21 41.1	14.7	5 05.8	9.4	54.8
H 08	297 19.0	15.9	36 14.8	14.7	5 15.2	9.4	54.8
U 09	312 18.8	. . 15.4	50 48.5	14.7	5 24.6	9.3	54.8
R 10	327 18.6	14.9	65 22.2	14.7	5 33.9	9.4	54.7
S 11	342 18.4	14.4	79 55.9	14.7	5 43.3	9.3	54.7
D 12	357 18.2	S20 13.8	94 29.6	14.7	S 5 52.6	9.2	54.7
A 13	12 18.0	13.3	109 03.3	14.7	6 01.8	9.3	54.7
Y 14	27 17.9	12.8	123 37.0	14.7	6 11.1	9.2	54.7
15	42 17.7	. . 12.2	138 10.7	14.8	6 20.3	9.1	54.6
16	57 17.5	11.7	152 44.5	14.7	6 29.4	9.2	54.6
17	72 17.3	11.1	167 18.2	14.7	6 38.6	9.1	54.6
18	87 17.1	S20 10.6	181 51.9	14.7	S 6 47.7	9.1	54.6
19	102 16.9	10.1	196 25.6	14.7	6 56.8	9.0	54.6
20	117 16.7	09.5	210 59.3	14.8	7 05.8	9.0	54.6
21	132 16.6	. . 09.0	225 33.1	14.7	7 14.8	9.0	54.5
22	147 16.4	08.5	240 06.8	14.7	7 23.8	8.9	54.5
23	162 16.2	07.9	254 40.5	14.7	7 32.7	8.9	54.5
20 00	177 16.0	S20 07.4	269 14.2	14.7	S 7 41.6	8.9	54.5
01	192 15.8	06.8	283 47.9	14.7	7 50.5	8.8	54.5
02	207 15.6	06.3	298 21.6	14.7	7 59.3	8.8	54.5
03	222 15.5	. . 05.8	312 55.3	14.7	8 08.1	8.7	54.5
04	237 15.3	05.2	327 29.0	14.6	8 16.8	8.7	54.4
05	252 15.1	04.7	342 02.6	14.7	8 25.5	8.7	54.4
06	267 14.9	S20 04.1	356 36.3	14.7	S 8 34.2	8.6	54.4
07	282 14.7	03.6	11 10.0	14.6	8 42.8	8.6	54.4
08	297 14.5	03.0	25 43.6	14.6	8 51.4	8.6	54.4
F 09	312 14.4	. . 02.5	40 17.2	14.7	9 00.0	8.5	54.4
R 10	327 14.2	01.9	54 50.9	14.6	9 08.5	8.5	54.4
I 11	342 14.0	01.4	69 24.5	14.6	9 17.0	8.4	54.4
D 12	357 13.8	S20 00.8	83 58.1	14.6	S 9 25.4	8.4	54.3
A 13	12 13.6	20 00.3	98 31.7	14.6	9 33.8	8.3	54.3
Y 14	27 13.5	19 59.7	113 05.3	14.5	9 42.1	8.3	54.3
15	42 13.3	. . 59.2	127 38.8	14.6	9 50.4	8.3	54.3
16	57 13.1	58.6	142 12.4	14.5	9 58.7	8.2	54.3
17	72 12.9	58.1	156 45.9	14.6	10 06.9	8.1	54.3
18	87 12.7	S19 57.5	171 19.5	14.5	S10 15.0	8.2	54.3
19	102 12.6	57.0	185 53.0	14.4	10 23.2	8.0	54.3
20	117 12.4	56.4	200 26.4	14.5	10 31.2	8.1	54.3
21	132 12.2	. . 55.9	214 59.9	14.5	10 39.3	8.0	54.3
22	147 12.0	55.3	229 33.4	14.4	10 47.3	7.9	54.3
23	162 11.9	54.8	244 06.8	14.4	10 55.2	7.9	54.2
21 00	177 11.7	S19 54.2	258 40.2	14.4	S11 03.1	7.8	54.2
01	192 11.5	53.7	273 13.6	14.4	11 10.9	7.8	54.2
02	207 11.3	53.1	287 47.0	14.4	11 18.7	7.8	54.2
03	222 11.2	. . 52.5	302 20.4	14.3	11 26.5	7.6	54.2
04	237 11.0	52.0	316 53.7	14.3	11 34.1	7.7	54.2
05	252 10.8	51.4	331 27.0	14.3	11 41.8	7.6	54.2
06	267 10.6	S19 50.9	346 00.3	14.3	S11 49.4	7.5	54.2
07	282 10.5	50.3	0 33.6	14.2	11 56.9	7.5	54.2
S 08	297 10.3	49.7	15 06.8	14.3	12 04.4	7.5	54.2
A 09	312 10.1	. . 49.2	29 40.1	14.2	12 11.9	7.3	54.2
T 10	327 09.9	48.6	44 13.3	14.1	12 19.2	7.4	54.2
U 11	342 09.8	48.1	58 46.4	14.2	12 26.6	7.3	54.2
R 12	357 09.6	S19 47.5	73 19.6	14.1	S12 33.9	7.2	54.2
D 13	12 09.4	46.9	87 52.7	14.1	12 41.1	7.2	54.2
A 14	27 09.3	46.4	102 25.8	14.1	12 48.3	7.1	54.2
Y 15	42 09.1	. . 45.8	116 58.9	14.0	12 55.4	7.0	54.2
16	57 08.9	45.2	131 31.9	14.1	13 02.4	7.1	54.2
17	72 08.7	44.7	146 05.0	14.0	13 09.5	6.9	54.2
18	87 08.6	S19 44.1	160 38.0	13.9	S13 16.4	6.9	54.2
19	102 08.4	43.5	175 10.9	14.0	13 23.3	6.8	54.2
20	117 08.2	43.0	189 43.9	13.9	13 30.1	6.8	54.2
21	132 08.1	. . 42.4	204 16.8	13.8	13 36.9	6.8	54.2
22	147 07.9	41.8	218 49.6	13.9	13 43.7	6.6	54.2
23	162 07.7	41.2	233 22.5	13.8	S13 50.3	6.6	54.2
	SD 16.3	*d* 0.5	SD 14.9		14.8		14.8

Lat.	Twilight Naut.	Twilight Civil	Sunrise	Moonrise 19	20	21	22
°	h m	h m	h m	h m	h m	h m	h m
N 72	07 47	09 30	▬	00 13	01 50	03 28	05 11
N 70	07 34	09 01	11 03	00 07	01 37	03 08	04 39
68	07 24	08 40	10 09	00 02	01 27	02 52	04 15
66	07 15	08 23	09 36	25 19	01 19	02 39	03 57
64	07 07	08 10	09 13	25 12	01 12	02 28	03 43
62	07 01	07 58	08 54	25 06	01 06	02 19	03 30
60	06 55	07 48	08 39	25 01	01 01	02 11	03 20
N 58	06 49	07 39	08 26	24 56	00 56	02 04	03 11
56	06 44	07 31	08 15	24 52	00 52	01 59	03 03
54	06 40	07 24	08 05	24 49	00 49	01 53	02 56
52	06 36	07 18	07 56	24 45	00 45	01 48	02 50
50	06 32	07 12	07 48	24 42	00 42	01 44	02 44
45	06 23	06 59	07 31	24 36	00 36	01 35	02 32
N 40	06 15	06 48	07 18	24 31	00 31	01 27	02 22
35	06 08	06 39	07 06	24 26	00 26	01 20	02 14
30	06 01	06 30	06 56	24 22	00 22	01 14	02 06
20	05 47	06 14	06 38	24 15	00 15	01 04	01 53
N 10	05 34	06 00	06 22	24 09	00 09	00 55	01 42
0	05 20	05 45	06 07	24 04	00 04	00 47	01 31
S 10	05 04	05 30	05 53	23 58	24 39	00 39	01 21
20	04 44	05 13	05 37	23 52	24 30	00 30	01 10
30	04 20	04 52	05 18	23 45	24 20	00 20	00 57
35	04 04	04 39	05 07	23 41	24 15	00 15	00 50
40	03 45	04 23	04 55	23 37	24 08	00 08	00 42
45	03 20	04 05	04 40	23 32	24 01	00 01	00 32
S 50	02 46	03 41	04 21	23 26	23 52	24 20	00 20
52	02 27	03 29	04 13	23 23	23 48	24 15	00 15
54	02 04	03 16	04 03	23 20	23 43	24 09	00 09
56	01 32	03 00	03 52	23 17	23 38	24 03	00 03
58	////	02 40	03 39	23 13	23 33	23 55	24 22
S 60	////	02 15	03 24	23 09	23 27	23 47	24 12

Lat.	Sunset	Twilight Civil	Twilight Naut.	Moonset 19	20	21	22
°	h m	h m	h m	h m	h m	h m	h m
N 72	▬	14 53	16 36	10 27	10 20	10 12	10 02
N 70	13 20	15 22	16 49	10 35	10 34	10 34	10 35
68	14 14	15 43	16 59	10 42	10 46	10 51	11 00
66	14 46	16 00	17 08	10 47	10 55	11 05	11 18
64	15 10	16 13	17 16	10 52	11 03	11 17	11 34
62	15 29	16 25	17 22	10 56	11 10	11 26	11 46
60	15 44	16 35	17 28	11 00	11 16	11 35	11 57
N 58	15 57	16 44	17 33	11 03	11 21	11 42	12 07
56	16 08	16 52	17 38	11 05	11 26	11 49	12 15
54	16 18	16 59	17 43	11 08	11 30	11 54	12 22
52	16 27	17 05	17 47	11 10	11 34	12 00	12 29
50	16 35	17 11	17 51	11 12	11 38	12 05	12 35
45	16 51	17 24	18 00	11 17	11 45	12 15	12 48
N 40	17 05	17 34	18 07	11 21	11 51	12 24	12 58
35	17 17	17 44	18 15	11 24	11 57	12 31	13 08
30	17 27	17 52	18 22	11 27	12 02	12 38	13 16
20	17 45	18 08	18 35	11 32	12 10	12 49	13 30
N 10	18 00	18 22	18 48	11 37	12 18	12 59	13 42
0	18 15	18 37	19 02	11 41	12 24	13 08	13 53
S 10	18 29	18 52	19 18	11 45	12 31	13 18	14 05
20	18 45	19 09	19 37	11 50	12 39	13 28	14 17
30	19 04	19 30	20 02	11 55	12 47	13 39	14 31
35	19 15	19 43	20 18	11 58	12 52	13 46	14 39
40	19 27	19 58	20 37	12 01	12 58	13 54	14 49
45	19 42	20 16	21 01	12 05	13 04	14 02	14 59
S 50	20 00	20 40	21 35	12 10	13 12	14 13	15 13
52	20 08	20 52	21 53	12 12	13 16	14 18	15 19
54	20 18	21 05	22 15	12 15	13 20	14 24	15 26
56	20 29	21 21	22 47	12 17	13 24	14 30	15 33
58	20 41	21 40	23 53	12 20	13 29	14 36	15 42
S 60	20 56	22 04	////	12 23	13 35	14 44	15 52

Day	SUN Eqn. of Time 00^h	SUN Eqn. of Time 12^h	SUN Mer. Pass.	MOON Mer. Pass. Upper	MOON Mer. Pass. Lower	Age	Phase
d	m s	m s	h m	h m	h m	d %	
19	10 38	10 47	12 11	05 31	17 52	21 54	◐
20	10 56	11 04	12 11	06 14	18 36	22 45	
21	11 13	11 21	12 11	06 58	19 20	23 35	

2017 JANUARY 22, 23, 24 (SUN., MON., TUES.)

UT d	h	ARIES GHA	VENUS −4·7 GHA	VENUS Dec	MARS +1·1 GHA	MARS Dec	JUPITER −2·1 GHA	JUPITER Dec	SATURN +0·5 GHA	SATURN Dec
		° ′	° ′	° ′	° ′	° ′	° ′	° ′	° ′	° ′
22	00	121 32.1	131 52.4	S 3 55.8	125 36.5	S 2 20.4	279 57.5	S 7 35.3	218 23.7	S22 00.1
	01	136 34.6	146 52.8	54.6	140 37.2	19.6	294 59.8	35.4	233 25.9	00.1
	02	151 37.0	161 53.2	53.4	155 38.0	18.8	310 02.2	35.4	248 28.1	00.1
	03	166 39.5	176 53.7	. . 52.2	170 38.7	. . 18.0	325 04.5	. . 35.4	263 30.3	. . 00.1
	04	181 42.0	191 54.1	51.0	185 39.5	17.3	340 06.9	35.5	278 32.5	00.2
	05	196 44.4	206 54.5	49.8	200 40.3	16.5	355 09.2	35.5	293 34.7	00.2
	06	211 46.9	221 54.9	S 3 48.7	215 41.0	S 2 15.7	10 11.6	S 7 35.5	308 36.9	S22 00.2
	07	226 49.3	236 55.3	47.5	230 41.8	14.9	25 13.9	35.6	323 39.1	00.2
	08	241 51.8	251 55.7	46.3	245 42.5	14.1	40 16.3	35.6	338 41.3	00.2
S	09	256 54.3	266 56.1	. . 45.1	260 43.3	. . 13.4	55 18.6	. . 35.6	353 43.5	. . 00.2
U	10	271 56.7	281 56.5	43.9	275 44.1	12.6	70 21.0	35.7	8 45.6	00.2
N	11	286 59.2	296 57.0	42.7	290 44.8	11.8	85 23.3	35.7	23 47.8	00.2
D	12	302 01.7	311 57.4	S 3 41.5	305 45.6	S 2 11.0	100 25.7	S 7 35.7	38 50.0	S22 00.2
A	13	317 04.1	326 57.8	40.3	320 46.3	10.2	115 28.0	35.8	53 52.2	00.3
Y	14	332 06.6	341 58.2	39.1	335 47.1	09.5	130 30.4	35.8	68 54.4	00.3
	15	347 09.1	356 58.6	. . 37.9	350 47.9	. . 08.7	145 32.7	. . 35.8	83 56.6	. . 00.3
	16	2 11.5	11 59.1	36.7	5 48.6	07.9	160 35.1	35.9	98 58.8	00.3
	17	17 14.0	26 59.5	35.6	20 49.4	07.1	175 37.5	35.9	114 01.0	00.3
	18	32 16.5	41 59.9	S 3 34.4	35 50.1	S 2 06.3	190 39.8	S 7 35.9	129 03.2	S22 00.3
	19	47 18.9	57 00.3	33.2	50 50.9	05.6	205 42.2	36.0	144 05.4	00.3
	20	62 21.4	72 00.8	32.0	65 51.7	04.8	220 44.5	36.0	159 07.6	00.3
	21	77 23.8	87 01.2	. . 30.8	80 52.4	. . 04.0	235 46.9	. . 36.0	174 09.8	. . 00.3
	22	92 26.3	102 01.6	29.6	95 53.2	03.2	250 49.2	36.0	189 12.0	00.4
	23	107 28.8	117 02.0	28.4	110 53.9	02.4	265 51.6	36.1	204 14.2	00.4
23	00	122 31.2	132 02.5	S 3 27.2	125 54.7	S 2 01.7	280 53.9	S 7 36.1	219 16.4	S22 00.4
	01	137 33.7	147 02.9	26.0	140 55.5	00.9	295 56.3	36.1	234 18.6	00.4
	02	152 36.2	162 03.3	24.8	155 56.2	2 00.1	310 58.6	36.2	249 20.7	00.4
	03	167 38.6	177 03.8	. . 23.7	170 57.0	1 59.3	326 01.0	. . 36.2	264 22.9	. . 00.4
	04	182 41.1	192 04.2	22.5	185 57.7	58.5	341 03.4	36.2	279 25.1	00.4
	05	197 43.6	207 04.6	21.3	200 58.5	57.8	356 05.7	36.3	294 27.3	00.4
	06	212 46.0	222 05.1	S 3 20.1	215 59.3	S 1 57.0	11 08.1	S 7 36.3	309 29.5	S22 00.4
	07	227 48.5	237 05.5	18.9	231 00.0	56.2	26 10.4	36.3	324 31.7	00.5
	08	242 50.9	252 06.0	17.7	246 00.8	55.4	41 12.8	36.4	339 33.9	00.5
M	09	257 53.4	267 06.4	. . 16.5	261 01.5	. . 54.6	56 15.1	. . 36.4	354 36.1	. . 00.5
O	10	272 55.9	282 06.8	15.3	276 02.3	53.9	71 17.5	36.4	9 38.3	00.5
N	11	287 58.3	297 07.3	14.1	291 03.1	53.1	86 19.9	36.5	24 40.5	00.5
D	12	303 00.8	312 07.7	S 3 13.0	306 03.8	S 1 52.3	101 22.2	S 7 36.5	39 42.7	S22 00.5
A	13	318 03.3	327 08.2	11.8	321 04.6	51.5	116 24.6	36.5	54 44.9	00.5
Y	14	333 05.7	342 08.6	10.6	336 05.3	50.7	131 26.9	36.5	69 47.1	00.5
	15	348 08.2	357 09.1	. . 09.4	351 06.1	. . 50.0	146 29.3	. . 36.6	84 49.3	. . 00.5
	16	3 10.7	12 09.5	08.2	6 06.9	49.2	161 31.7	36.6	99 51.5	00.5
	17	18 13.1	27 10.0	07.0	21 07.6	48.4	176 34.0	36.6	114 53.7	00.6
	18	33 15.6	42 10.4	S 3 05.8	36 08.4	S 1 47.6	191 36.4	S 7 36.7	129 55.9	S22 00.6
	19	48 18.1	57 10.9	04.6	51 09.1	46.8	206 38.7	36.7	144 58.1	00.6
	20	63 20.5	72 11.3	03.4	66 09.9	46.1	221 41.1	36.7	160 00.3	00.6
	21	78 23.0	87 11.8	. . 02.3	81 10.7	. . 45.3	236 43.5	. . 36.7	175 02.5	. . 00.6
	22	93 25.4	102 12.3	3 01.1	96 11.4	44.5	251 45.8	36.8	190 04.7	00.6
	23	108 27.9	117 12.7	2 59.9	111 12.2	43.7	266 48.2	36.8	205 06.9	00.6
24	00	123 30.4	132 13.2	S 2 58.7	126 13.0	S 1 42.9	281 50.6	S 7 36.8	220 09.1	S22 00.6
	01	138 32.8	147 13.6	57.5	141 13.7	42.2	296 52.9	36.9	235 11.2	00.6
	02	153 35.3	162 14.1	56.3	156 14.5	41.4	311 55.3	36.9	250 13.4	00.7
	03	168 37.8	177 14.6	. . 55.1	171 15.2	. . 40.6	326 57.6	. . 36.9	265 15.6	. . 00.7
	04	183 40.2	192 15.0	53.9	186 16.0	39.8	342 00.0	36.9	280 17.8	00.7
	05	198 42.7	207 15.5	52.8	201 16.8	39.0	357 02.4	37.0	295 20.0	00.7
	06	213 45.2	222 15.9	S 2 51.6	216 17.5	S 1 38.3	12 04.7	S 7 37.0	310 22.2	S22 00.7
	07	228 47.6	237 16.4	50.4	231 18.3	37.5	27 07.1	37.0	325 24.4	00.7
	08	243 50.1	252 16.9	49.2	246 19.0	36.7	42 09.5	37.1	340 26.6	00.7
T	09	258 52.6	267 17.4	. . 48.0	261 19.8	. . 35.9	57 11.8	. . 37.1	355 28.8	. . 00.7
U	10	273 55.0	282 17.8	46.8	276 20.6	35.1	72 14.2	37.1	10 31.0	00.7
E	11	288 57.5	297 18.3	45.6	291 21.3	34.4	87 16.6	37.1	25 33.2	00.8
S	12	303 59.9	312 18.8	S 2 44.4	306 22.1	S 1 33.6	102 18.9	S 7 37.2	40 35.4	S22 00.8
D	13	319 02.4	327 19.2	43.3	321 22.9	32.8	117 21.3	37.2	55 37.6	00.8
A	14	334 04.9	342 19.7	42.1	336 23.6	32.0	132 23.7	37.2	70 39.8	00.8
Y	15	349 07.3	357 20.2	. . 40.9	351 24.4	. . 31.2	147 26.0	. . 37.3	85 42.0	. . 00.8
	16	4 09.8	12 20.7	39.7	6 25.1	30.5	162 28.4	37.3	100 44.2	00.8
	17	19 12.3	27 21.1	38.5	21 25.9	29.7	177 30.8	37.3	115 46.4	00.8
	18	34 14.7	42 21.6	S 2 37.3	36 26.7	S 1 28.9	192 33.1	S 7 37.3	130 48.6	S22 00.8
	19	49 17.2	57 22.1	36.1	51 27.4	28.1	207 35.5	37.4	145 50.8	00.8
	20	64 19.7	72 22.6	35.0	66 28.2	27.3	222 37.9	37.4	160 53.0	00.8
	21	79 22.1	87 23.1	. . 33.8	81 28.9	. . 26.6	237 40.2	. . 37.4	175 55.2	. . 00.9
	22	94 24.6	102 23.6	32.6	96 29.7	25.8	252 42.6	37.4	190 57.4	00.9
	23	109 27.1	117 24.0	31.4	111 30.5	25.0	267 45.0	37.5	205 59.6	00.9
Mer. Pass.		h m 15 47.3	*v* 0.4	*d* 1.2	*v* 0.8	*d* 0.8	*v* 2.4	*d* 0.0	*v* 2.2	*d* 0.0

STARS

Name	SHA	Dec
	° ′	° ′
Acamar	315 16.4	S40 14.6
Achernar	335 25.1	S57 09.5
Acrux	173 06.1	S63 11.3
Adhara	255 10.2	S29 00.0
Aldebaran	290 46.3	N16 32.4
Alioth	166 18.5	N55 51.8
Alkaid	152 57.0	N49 13.5
Al Na'ir	27 41.2	S46 52.8
Alnilam	275 43.6	S 1 11.8
Alphard	217 53.4	S 8 44.1
Alphecca	126 09.1	N26 39.4
Alpheratz	357 41.1	N29 11.1
Altair	62 06.2	N 8 54.9
Ankaa	353 13.5	S42 13.1
Antares	112 23.5	S26 27.9
Arcturus	145 53.5	N19 05.6
Atria	107 23.4	S69 03.0
Avior	234 16.3	S59 34.0
Bellatrix	278 29.1	N 6 21.6
Betelgeuse	270 58.4	N 7 24.3
Canopus	263 54.6	S52 42.6
Capella	280 30.5	N46 00.8
Deneb	49 30.2	N45 20.6
Denebola	182 31.0	N14 28.5
Diphda	348 53.6	S17 53.8
Dubhe	193 48.4	N61 39.3
Elnath	278 09.2	N28 37.1
Eltanin	90 45.5	N51 29.2
Enif	33 45.0	N 9 57.2
Fomalhaut	15 21.6	S29 32.1
Gacrux	171 57.8	S57 12.2
Gienah	175 49.6	S17 38.1
Hadar	148 44.3	S60 26.9
Hamal	327 58.0	N23 32.5
Kaus Aust.	83 40.9	S34 22.3
Kochab	137 20.5	N74 04.9
Markab	13 36.1	N15 17.8
Menkar	314 12.4	N 4 09.2
Menkent	148 04.6	S36 26.9
Miaplacidus	221 38.1	S69 47.3
Mirfak	308 36.6	N49 55.3
Nunki	75 55.7	S26 16.3
Peacock	53 16.1	S56 40.7
Pollux	243 24.4	N27 58.9
Procyon	244 56.9	N 5 10.6
Rasalhague	96 04.5	N12 33.0
Regulus	207 40.6	N11 52.9
Rigel	281 09.5	S 8 11.2
Rigil Kent.	139 48.4	S60 53.9
Sabik	102 10.0	S15 44.5
Schedar	349 37.8	N56 38.0
Shaula	96 18.9	S37 06.7
Sirius	258 31.2	S16 44.7
Spica	158 28.6	S11 14.9
Suhail	222 50.2	S43 30.2
Vega	80 37.7	N38 48.0
Zuben'ubi	137 02.8	S16 06.6

	SHA	Mer. Pass.
	° ′	h m
Venus	9 31.2	15 11
Mars	3 23.5	15 36
Jupiter	158 22.7	5 16
Saturn	96 45.1	9 22

UT d h	SUN GHA ° ′	SUN Dec ° ′	MOON GHA ° ′	v ′	MOON Dec ° ′	d ′	HP ′
22 00 (SUNDAY)	177 07.6	S19 40.7	247 55.3	13.8	S13 56.9	6.6	54.2
01	192 07.4	40.1	262 28.1	13.8	14 03.5	6.5	54.2
02	207 07.2	39.5	277 00.9	13.7	14 10.0	6.4	54.2
03	222 07.0	. . 39.0	291 33.6	13.7	14 16.4	6.4	54.2
04	237 06.9	38.4	306 06.3	13.7	14 22.8	6.3	54.2
05	252 06.7	37.8	320 39.0	13.6	14 29.1	6.2	54.2
06	267 06.5	S19 37.2	335 11.6	13.6	S14 35.3	6.2	54.2
07	282 06.4	36.7	349 44.2	13.6	14 41.5	6.1	54.2
08	297 06.2	36.1	4 16.8	13.5	14 47.6	6.1	54.2
09	312 06.0	. . 35.5	18 49.3	13.5	14 53.7	5.9	54.2
10	327 05.9	34.9	33 21.8	13.5	14 59.6	6.0	54.2
11	342 05.7	34.3	47 54.3	13.4	15 05.6	5.8	54.2
12	357 05.6	S19 33.8	62 26.7	13.5	S15 11.4	5.8	54.2
13	12 05.4	33.2	76 59.2	13.3	15 17.2	5.8	54.2
14	27 05.2	32.6	91 31.5	13.4	15 23.0	5.6	54.2
15	42 05.1	. . 32.0	106 03.9	13.3	15 28.6	5.6	54.2
16	57 04.9	31.4	120 36.2	13.2	15 34.2	5.6	54.2
17	72 04.7	30.9	135 08.4	13.3	15 39.8	5.4	54.2
18	87 04.6	S19 30.3	149 40.7	13.2	S15 45.2	5.4	54.2
19	102 04.4	29.7	164 12.9	13.1	15 50.6	5.4	54.2
20	117 04.2	29.1	178 45.0	13.2	15 56.0	5.2	54.2
21	132 04.1	. . 28.5	193 17.2	13.1	16 01.2	5.2	54.2
22	147 03.9	27.9	207 49.3	13.0	16 06.4	5.1	54.2
23	162 03.8	27.4	222 21.3	13.0	16 11.5	5.1	54.2
23 00 (MONDAY)	177 03.6	S19 26.8	236 53.3	13.0	S16 16.6	5.0	54.2
01	192 03.4	26.2	251 25.3	13.0	16 21.6	4.9	54.2
02	207 03.3	25.6	265 57.3	12.9	16 26.5	4.8	54.2
03	222 03.1	. . 25.0	280 29.2	12.9	16 31.3	4.8	54.3
04	237 03.0	24.4	295 01.1	12.8	16 36.1	4.7	54.3
05	252 02.8	23.8	309 32.9	12.8	16 40.8	4.6	54.3
06	267 02.6	S19 23.2	324 04.7	12.8	S16 45.4	4.5	54.3
07	282 02.5	22.6	338 36.5	12.7	16 49.9	4.5	54.3
08	297 02.3	22.1	353 08.2	12.7	16 54.4	4.4	54.3
09	312 02.2	. . 21.5	7 39.9	12.7	16 58.8	4.3	54.3
10	327 02.0	20.9	22 11.6	12.6	17 03.1	4.3	54.3
11	342 01.9	20.3	36 43.2	12.6	17 07.4	4.1	54.3
12	357 01.7	S19 19.7	51 14.8	12.6	S17 11.5	4.1	54.3
13	12 01.5	19.1	65 46.4	12.5	17 15.6	4.0	54.3
14	27 01.4	18.5	80 17.9	12.4	17 19.6	4.0	54.3
15	42 01.2	. . 17.9	94 49.3	12.5	17 23.6	3.8	54.4
16	57 01.1	17.3	109 20.8	12.4	17 27.4	3.8	54.4
17	72 00.9	16.7	123 52.2	12.4	17 31.2	3.7	54.4
18	87 00.8	S19 16.1	138 23.6	12.3	S17 34.9	3.6	54.4
19	102 00.6	15.5	152 54.9	12.3	17 38.5	3.6	54.4
20	117 00.5	14.9	167 26.2	12.3	17 42.1	3.5	54.4
21	132 00.3	. . 14.3	181 57.5	12.2	17 45.6	3.3	54.4
22	147 00.2	13.7	196 28.7	12.2	17 48.9	3.3	54.4
23	162 00.0	13.1	210 59.9	12.1	17 52.2	3.3	54.4
24 00 (TUESDAY)	176 59.8	S19 12.5	225 31.0	12.1	S17 55.5	3.1	54.5
01	191 59.7	11.9	240 02.1	12.1	17 58.6	3.1	54.5
02	206 59.5	11.3	254 33.2	12.1	18 01.7	2.9	54.5
03	221 59.4	. . 10.7	269 04.3	12.0	18 04.6	2.9	54.5
04	236 59.2	10.1	283 35.3	11.9	18 07.5	2.8	54.5
05	251 59.1	09.5	298 06.2	12.0	18 10.3	2.8	54.5
06	266 58.9	S19 08.9	312 37.2	11.9	S18 13.1	2.6	54.5
07	281 58.8	08.3	327 08.1	11.9	18 15.7	2.6	54.5
08	296 58.6	07.7	341 39.0	11.8	18 18.3	2.4	54.6
09	311 58.5	. . 07.1	356 09.8	11.8	18 20.7	2.4	54.6
10	326 58.3	06.5	10 40.6	11.8	18 23.1	2.3	54.6
11	341 58.2	05.9	25 11.4	11.7	18 25.4	2.2	54.6
12	356 58.0	S19 05.2	39 42.1	11.7	S18 27.6	2.2	54.6
13	11 57.9	04.6	54 12.8	11.7	18 29.8	2.0	54.6
14	26 57.7	04.0	68 43.5	11.6	18 31.8	2.0	54.6
15	41 57.6	. . 03.4	83 14.1	11.6	18 33.8	1.8	54.7
16	56 57.5	02.8	97 44.7	11.6	18 35.6	1.8	54.7
17	71 57.3	02.2	112 15.3	11.6	18 37.4	1.7	54.7
18	86 57.2	S19 01.6	126 45.9	11.5	S18 39.1	1.6	54.7
19	101 57.0	01.0	141 16.4	11.4	18 40.7	1.5	54.7
20	116 56.9	19 00.4	155 46.8	11.5	18 42.2	1.5	54.7
21	131 56.7	18 59.7	170 17.3	11.4	18 43.7	1.3	54.8
22	146 56.6	59.1	184 47.7	11.4	18 45.0	1.2	54.8
23	161 56.4	58.5	199 18.1	11.4	S18 46.2	1.2	54.8
	SD 16.3	*d* 0.6	SD 14.8		14.8		14.9

Lat. °	Twilight Naut. h m	Twilight Civil h m	Sunrise h m	Moonrise 22 h m	Moonrise 23 h m	Moonrise 24 h m	Moonrise 25 h m
N 72	07 38	09 17	▬	05 11	07 04	▬	▬
N 70	07 27	08 51	10 39	04 39	06 10	07 36	08 46
68	07 17	08 32	09 55	04 15	05 37	06 52	07 54
66	07 09	08 16	09 27	03 57	05 13	06 23	07 22
64	07 02	08 03	09 05	03 43	04 54	06 01	06 58
62	06 56	07 52	08 47	03 30	04 39	05 43	06 39
60	06 51	07 43	08 33	03 20	04 26	05 28	06 24
N 58	06 46	07 35	08 21	03 11	04 15	05 16	06 11
56	06 41	07 27	08 10	03 03	04 06	05 05	05 59
54	06 37	07 21	08 01	02 56	03 57	04 56	05 49
52	06 33	07 15	07 52	02 50	03 50	04 47	05 41
50	06 29	07 09	07 45	02 44	03 43	04 40	05 33
45	06 21	06 57	07 29	02 32	03 29	04 24	05 16
N 40	06 14	06 46	07 16	02 22	03 17	04 10	05 02
35	06 07	06 37	07 04	02 14	03 07	03 59	04 50
30	06 00	06 29	06 55	02 06	02 58	03 49	04 40
20	05 47	06 14	06 37	01 53	02 43	03 33	04 22
N 10	05 35	06 00	06 22	01 42	02 29	03 18	04 07
0	05 21	05 46	06 08	01 31	02 17	03 04	03 53
S 10	05 05	05 32	05 54	01 21	02 05	02 51	03 39
20	04 47	05 15	05 39	01 10	01 52	02 36	03 23
30	04 23	04 54	05 21	00 57	01 37	02 20	03 06
35	04 08	04 42	05 10	00 50	01 28	02 10	02 56
40	03 49	04 27	04 58	00 42	01 18	01 59	02 44
45	03 25	04 09	04 44	00 32	01 07	01 46	02 31
S 50	02 53	03 47	04 26	00 20	00 53	01 30	02 14
52	02 36	03 35	04 18	00 15	00 46	01 23	02 06
54	02 14	03 22	04 09	00 09	00 39	01 15	01 58
56	01 46	03 07	03 58	00 03	00 31	01 06	01 48
58	00 57	02 49	03 46	24 22	00 22	00 55	01 37
S 60	////	02 26	03 32	24 12	00 12	00 44	01 24

Lat. °	Sunset h m	Twilight Civil h m	Twilight Naut. h m	Moonset 22 h m	Moonset 23 h m	Moonset 24 h m	Moonset 25 h m
N 72	▬	15 08	16 47	10 02	09 45	▬	▬
N 70	13 46	15 33	16 58	10 35	10 40	10 51	11 23
68	14 29	15 53	17 07	11 00	11 13	11 36	12 15
66	14 58	16 08	17 15	11 18	11 37	12 06	12 47
64	15 20	16 21	17 22	11 34	11 56	12 28	13 11
62	15 37	16 32	17 28	11 46	12 12	12 46	13 30
60	15 51	16 41	17 34	11 57	12 25	13 01	13 46
N 58	16 04	16 50	17 39	12 07	12 36	13 13	13 59
56	16 14	16 57	17 43	12 15	12 46	13 24	14 10
54	16 24	17 04	17 47	12 22	12 55	13 34	14 20
52	16 32	17 10	17 51	12 29	13 03	13 42	14 29
50	16 39	17 15	17 55	12 35	13 10	13 50	14 37
45	16 55	17 27	18 03	12 48	13 25	14 06	14 54
N 40	17 08	17 38	18 11	12 58	13 37	14 20	15 08
35	17 20	17 47	18 17	13 08	13 47	14 31	15 19
30	17 30	17 55	18 24	13 16	13 57	14 41	15 30
20	17 46	18 10	18 37	13 30	14 13	14 58	15 47
N 10	18 01	18 24	18 49	13 42	14 27	15 13	16 02
0	18 15	18 37	19 03	13 53	14 40	15 28	16 17
S 10	18 30	18 52	19 18	14 05	14 53	15 42	16 31
20	18 45	19 09	19 37	14 17	15 07	15 57	16 46
30	19 03	19 29	20 00	14 31	15 23	16 14	17 04
35	19 13	19 41	20 16	14 39	15 32	16 24	17 14
40	19 25	19 56	20 34	14 49	15 43	16 35	17 26
45	19 39	20 13	20 57	14 59	15 55	16 49	17 39
S 50	19 56	20 36	21 29	15 13	16 10	17 05	17 56
52	20 05	20 47	21 46	15 19	16 18	17 13	18 04
54	20 14	21 00	22 07	15 26	16 25	17 22	18 12
56	20 24	21 15	22 34	15 33	16 34	17 31	18 22
58	20 36	21 32	23 19	15 42	16 44	17 42	18 33
S 60	20 50	21 55	////	15 52	16 56	17 55	18 46

Day d	SUN Eqn. of Time 00^h m s	SUN Eqn. of Time 12^h m s	SUN Mer. Pass. h m	MOON Mer. Pass. Upper h m	MOON Mer. Pass. Lower h m	MOON Age d	MOON Phase %
22	11 29	11 37	12 12	07 42	20 05	24	27
23	11 45	11 53	12 12	08 28	20 52	25	19
24	12 00	12 08	12 12	09 16	21 40	26	12

UT d h		ARIES GHA ° ′	VENUS −4·7 GHA ° ′	Dec ° ′	MARS +1·1 GHA ° ′	Dec ° ′	JUPITER −2·1 GHA ° ′	Dec ° ′	SATURN +0·5 GHA ° ′	Dec ° ′
25	00	124 29.5	132 24.5	S 2 30.2	126 31.2	S 1 24.2	282 47.4	S 7 37.5	221 01.8	S22 00.9
	01	139 32.0	147 25.0	29.0	141 32.0	23.4	297 49.7	37.5	236 04.0	00.9
	02	154 34.4	162 25.5	27.9	156 32.8	22.7	312 52.1	37.5	251 06.2	00.9
	03	169 36.9	177 26.0	. . 26.7	171 33.5	. . 21.9	327 54.5	. . 37.6	266 08.4	. . 00.9
	04	184 39.4	192 26.5	25.5	186 34.3	21.1	342 56.8	37.6	281 10.6	00.9
	05	199 41.8	207 27.0	24.3	201 35.0	20.3	357 59.2	37.6	296 12.8	00.9
	06	214 44.3	222 27.5	S 2 23.1	216 35.8	S 1 19.5	13 01.6	S 7 37.6	311 15.0	S22 01.0
W	07	229 46.8	237 28.0	21.9	231 36.6	18.8	28 03.9	37.7	326 17.2	01.0
E	08	244 49.2	252 28.5	20.8	246 37.3	18.0	43 06.3	37.7	341 19.4	01.0
D	09	259 51.7	267 29.0	. . 19.6	261 38.1	. . 17.2	58 08.7	. . 37.7	356 21.6	. . 01.0
N	10	274 54.2	282 29.5	18.4	276 38.9	16.4	73 11.1	37.7	11 23.8	01.0
E	11	289 56.6	297 30.0	17.2	291 39.6	15.6	88 13.4	37.8	26 26.0	01.0
S	12	304 59.1	312 30.5	S 2 16.0	306 40.4	S 1 14.9	103 15.8	S 7 37.8	41 28.2	S22 01.0
D	13	320 01.5	327 31.0	14.8	321 41.2	14.1	118 18.2	37.8	56 30.4	01.0
A	14	335 04.0	342 31.5	13.7	336 41.9	13.3	133 20.6	37.8	71 32.6	01.0
Y	15	350 06.5	357 32.0	. . 12.5	351 42.7	. . 12.5	148 22.9	. . 37.9	86 34.8	. . 01.0
	16	5 08.9	12 32.5	11.3	6 43.4	11.7	163 25.3	37.9	101 37.0	01.1
	17	20 11.4	27 33.0	10.1	21 44.2	11.0	178 27.7	37.9	116 39.2	01.1
	18	35 13.9	42 33.5	S 2 08.9	36 45.0	S 1 10.2	193 30.1	S 7 37.9	131 41.4	S22 01.1
	19	50 16.3	57 34.0	07.7	51 45.7	09.4	208 32.4	38.0	146 43.6	01.1
	20	65 18.8	72 34.5	06.6	66 46.5	08.6	223 34.8	38.0	161 45.8	01.1
	21	80 21.3	87 35.0	. . 05.4	81 47.3	. . 07.8	238 37.2	. . 38.0	176 48.0	. . 01.1
	22	95 23.7	102 35.6	04.2	96 48.0	07.1	253 39.6	38.0	191 50.2	01.1
	23	110 26.2	117 36.1	03.0	111 48.8	06.3	268 41.9	38.1	206 52.4	01.1
26	00	125 28.7	132 36.6	S 2 01.8	126 49.5	S 1 05.5	283 44.3	S 7 38.1	221 54.6	S22 01.1
	01	140 31.1	147 37.1	2 00.7	141 50.3	04.7	298 46.7	38.1	236 56.8	01.1
	02	155 33.6	162 37.6	1 59.5	156 51.1	03.9	313 49.1	38.1	251 59.0	01.2
	03	170 36.0	177 38.1	. . 58.3	171 51.8	. . 03.2	328 51.5	. . 38.2	267 01.2	. . 01.2
	04	185 38.5	192 38.7	57.1	186 52.6	02.4	343 53.8	38.2	282 03.4	01.2
	05	200 41.0	207 39.2	55.9	201 53.4	01.6	358 56.2	38.2	297 05.6	01.2
	06	215 43.4	222 39.7	S 1 54.8	216 54.1	S 1 00.8	13 58.6	S 7 38.2	312 07.8	S22 01.2
T	07	230 45.9	237 40.2	53.6	231 54.9	1 00.0	29 01.0	38.2	327 10.0	01.2
H	08	245 48.4	252 40.8	52.4	246 55.7	0 59.3	44 03.3	38.3	342 12.2	01.2
U	09	260 50.8	267 41.3	. . 51.2	261 56.4	. . 58.5	59 05.7	. . 38.3	357 14.4	. . 01.2
R	10	275 53.3	282 41.8	50.0	276 57.2	57.7	74 08.1	38.3	12 16.6	01.2
	11	290 55.8	297 42.3	48.9	291 58.0	56.9	89 10.5	38.3	27 18.8	01.2
S	12	305 58.2	312 42.9	S 1 47.7	306 58.7	S 0 56.2	104 12.9	S 7 38.3	42 21.0	S22 01.3
D	13	321 00.7	327 43.4	46.5	321 59.5	55.4	119 15.2	38.4	57 23.2	01.3
A	14	336 03.2	342 43.9	45.3	337 00.2	54.6	134 17.6	38.4	72 25.4	01.3
Y	15	351 05.6	357 44.5	. . 44.1	352 01.0	. . 53.8	149 20.0	. . 38.4	87 27.6	. . 01.3
	16	6 08.1	12 45.0	43.0	7 01.8	53.0	164 22.4	38.4	102 29.8	01.3
	17	21 10.5	27 45.5	41.8	22 02.5	52.3	179 24.8	38.5	117 32.0	01.3
	18	36 13.0	42 46.1	S 1 40.6	37 03.3	S 0 51.5	194 27.2	S 7 38.5	132 34.2	S22 01.3
	19	51 15.5	57 46.6	39.4	52 04.1	50.7	209 29.5	38.5	147 36.4	01.3
	20	66 17.9	72 47.2	38.2	67 04.8	49.9	224 31.9	38.5	162 38.6	01.3
	21	81 20.4	87 47.7	. . 37.1	82 05.6	. . 49.1	239 34.3	. . 38.5	177 40.8	. . 01.3
	22	96 22.9	102 48.2	35.9	97 06.4	48.4	254 36.7	38.6	192 43.1	01.4
	23	111 25.3	117 48.8	34.7	112 07.1	47.6	269 39.1	38.6	207 45.3	01.4
27	00	126 27.8	132 49.3	S 1 33.5	127 07.9	S 0 46.8	284 41.5	S 7 38.6	222 47.5	S22 01.4
	01	141 30.3	147 49.9	32.4	142 08.7	46.0	299 43.8	38.6	237 49.7	01.4
	02	156 32.7	162 50.4	31.2	157 09.4	45.2	314 46.2	38.6	252 51.9	01.4
	03	171 35.2	177 51.0	. . 30.0	172 10.2	. . 44.5	329 48.6	. . 38.7	267 54.1	. . 01.4
	04	186 37.7	192 51.5	28.8	187 10.9	43.7	344 51.0	38.7	282 56.3	01.4
	05	201 40.1	207 52.1	27.7	202 11.7	42.9	359 53.4	38.7	297 58.5	01.4
	06	216 42.6	222 52.6	S 1 26.5	217 12.5	S 0 42.1	14 55.8	S 7 38.7	313 00.7	S22 01.4
	07	231 45.0	237 53.2	25.3	232 13.2	41.3	29 58.2	38.7	328 02.9	01.4
	08	246 47.5	252 53.7	24.1	247 14.0	40.6	45 00.5	38.8	343 05.1	01.5
F	09	261 50.0	267 54.3	. . 23.0	262 14.8	. . 39.8	60 02.9	. . 38.8	358 07.3	. . 01.5
R	10	276 52.4	282 54.8	21.8	277 15.5	39.0	75 05.3	38.8	13 09.5	01.5
I	11	291 54.9	297 55.4	20.6	292 16.3	38.2	90 07.7	38.8	28 11.7	01.5
D	12	306 57.4	312 56.0	S 1 19.4	307 17.1	S 0 37.5	105 10.1	S 7 38.8	43 13.9	S22 01.5
A	13	321 59.8	327 56.5	18.3	322 17.8	36.7	120 12.5	38.9	58 16.1	01.5
Y	14	337 02.3	342 57.1	17.1	337 18.6	35.9	135 14.9	38.9	73 18.3	01.5
	15	352 04.8	357 57.7	. . 15.9	352 19.4	. . 35.1	150 17.3	. . 38.9	88 20.5	. . 01.5
	16	7 07.2	12 58.2	14.7	7 20.1	34.3	165 19.6	38.9	103 22.7	01.5
	17	22 09.7	27 58.8	13.6	22 20.9	33.6	180 22.0	38.9	118 24.9	01.5
	18	37 12.1	42 59.4	S 1 12.4	37 21.7	S 0 32.8	195 24.4	S 7 38.9	133 27.1	S22 01.5
	19	52 14.6	57 59.9	11.2	52 22.4	32.0	210 26.8	39.0	148 29.3	01.6
	20	67 17.1	73 00.5	10.0	67 23.2	31.2	225 29.2	39.0	163 31.6	01.6
	21	82 19.5	88 01.1	. . 08.9	82 24.0	. . 30.4	240 31.6	. . 39.0	178 33.8	. . 01.6
	22	97 22.0	103 01.6	07.7	97 24.7	29.7	255 34.0	39.0	193 36.0	01.6
	23	112 24.5	118 02.2	06.5	112 25.5	28.9	270 36.4	39.0	208 38.2	01.6
Mer. Pass.		h m 15 35.5	*v* 0.5	*d* 1.2	*v* 0.8	*d* 0.8	*v* 2.4	*d* 0.0	*v* 2.2	*d* 0.0

STARS

Name	SHA ° ′	Dec ° ′
Acamar	315 16.4	S40 14.6
Achernar	335 25.2	S57 09.4
Acrux	173 06.0	S63 11.3
Adhara	255 10.2	S29 00.0
Aldebaran	290 46.4	N16 32.4
Alioth	166 18.4	N55 51.8
Alkaid	152 57.0	N49 13.5
Al Na'ir	27 41.2	S46 52.8
Alnilam	275 43.6	S 1 11.8
Alphard	217 53.4	S 8 44.1
Alphecca	126 09.1	N26 39.4
Alpheratz	357 41.1	N29 11.1
Altair	62 06.2	N 8 54.9
Ankaa	353 13.6	S42 13.1
Antares	112 23.4	S26 27.9
Arcturus	145 53.5	N19 05.6
Atria	107 23.4	S69 03.0
Avior	234 16.3	S59 34.0
Bellatrix	278 29.1	N 6 21.6
Betelgeuse	270 58.4	N 7 24.3
Canopus	263 54.6	S52 42.6
Capella	280 30.5	N46 00.8
Deneb	49 30.2	N45 20.6
Denebola	182 31.0	N14 28.5
Diphda	348 53.6	S17 53.8
Dubhe	193 48.3	N61 39.3
Elnath	278 09.2	N28 37.1
Eltanin	90 45.4	N51 29.2
Enif	33 45.0	N 9 57.2
Fomalhaut	15 21.6	S29 32.1
Gacrux	171 57.8	S57 12.2
Gienah	175 49.6	S17 38.1
Hadar	148 44.2	S60 26.9
Hamal	327 58.0	N23 32.5
Kaus Aust.	83 40.9	S34 22.3
Kochab	137 20.5	N74 04.9
Markab	13 36.1	N15 17.8
Menkar	314 12.4	N 4 09.2
Menkent	148 04.6	S36 26.9
Miaplacidus	221 38.1	S69 47.3
Mirfak	308 36.6	N49 55.3
Nunki	75 55.6	S26 16.3
Peacock	53 16.1	S56 40.7
Pollux	243 24.4	N27 58.9
Procyon	244 56.8	N 5 10.6
Rasalhague	96 04.4	N12 32.9
Regulus	207 40.6	N11 52.8
Rigel	281 09.5	S 8 11.2
Rigil Kent.	139 48.3	S60 53.9
Sabik	102 10.0	S15 44.5
Schedar	349 37.8	N56 38.0
Shaula	96 18.9	S37 06.7
Sirius	258 31.2	S16 44.7
Spica	158 28.6	S11 14.9
Suhail	222 50.1	S43 30.2
Vega	80 37.7	N38 48.0
Zuben'ubi	137 02.7	S16 06.6

	SHA ° ′	Mer. Pass. h m
Venus	7 07.9	15 09
Mars	1 20.9	15 32
Jupiter	158 15.7	5 04
Saturn	96 25.9	9 11

UT	SUN GHA	SUN Dec	MOON GHA	v	MOON Dec	d	HP
d h	° ′	° ′	° ′	′	° ′	′	′
WEDNESDAY							
25 00	176 56.3	S18 57.9	213 48.5	11.3	S18 47.4	1.0	54.8
01	191 56.1	57.3	228 18.8	11.3	18 48.4	1.0	54.8
02	206 56.0	56.7	242 49.1	11.3	18 49.4	0.9	54.8
03	221 55.9	. . 56.0	257 19.4	11.2	18 50.3	0.8	54.9
04	236 55.7	55.4	271 49.6	11.2	18 51.1	0.7	54.9
05	251 55.6	54.8	286 19.8	11.2	18 51.8	0.6	54.9
06	266 55.4	S18 54.2	300 50.0	11.2	S18 52.4	0.5	54.9
07	281 55.3	53.6	315 20.2	11.1	18 52.9	0.4	54.9
08	296 55.1	52.9	329 50.3	11.1	18 53.3	0.4	54.9
09	311 55.0	. . 52.3	344 20.4	11.1	18 53.7	0.2	55.0
10	326 54.9	51.7	358 50.5	11.1	18 53.9	0.1	55.0
11	341 54.7	51.1	13 20.6	11.0	18 54.0	0.1	55.0
12	356 54.6	S18 50.5	27 50.6	11.0	S18 54.1	0.1	55.0
13	11 54.4	49.8	42 20.6	11.0	18 54.0	0.1	55.0
14	26 54.3	49.2	56 50.6	10.9	18 53.9	0.2	55.1
15	41 54.2	. . 48.6	71 20.5	11.0	18 53.7	0.4	55.1
16	56 54.0	48.0	85 50.5	10.9	18 53.3	0.4	55.1
17	71 53.9	47.3	100 20.4	10.9	18 52.9	0.5	55.1
18	86 53.7	S18 46.7	114 50.3	10.9	S18 52.4	0.6	55.1
19	101 53.6	46.1	129 20.2	10.8	18 51.8	0.7	55.1
20	116 53.5	45.4	143 50.0	10.9	18 51.1	0.8	55.2
21	131 53.3	. . 44.8	158 19.9	10.8	18 50.3	0.9	55.2
22	146 53.2	44.2	172 49.7	10.8	18 49.4	1.0	55.2
23	161 53.1	43.6	187 19.5	10.7	18 48.4	1.1	55.2
THURSDAY							
26 00	176 52.9	S18 42.9	201 49.2	10.8	S18 47.3	1.2	55.2
01	191 52.8	42.3	216 19.0	10.7	18 46.1	1.2	55.3
02	206 52.7	41.7	230 48.7	10.7	18 44.9	1.4	55.3
03	221 52.5	. . 41.0	245 18.4	10.8	18 43.5	1.5	55.3
04	236 52.4	40.4	259 48.2	10.6	18 42.0	1.5	55.3
05	251 52.2	39.8	274 17.8	10.7	18 40.5	1.7	55.3
06	266 52.1	S18 39.1	288 47.5	10.7	S18 38.8	1.7	55.4
07	281 52.0	38.5	303 17.2	10.6	18 37.1	1.9	55.4
08	296 51.8	37.9	317 46.8	10.6	18 35.2	1.9	55.4
09	311 51.7	. . 37.2	332 16.4	10.7	18 33.3	2.1	55.4
10	326 51.6	36.6	346 46.1	10.6	18 31.2	2.1	55.5
11	341 51.4	36.0	1 15.7	10.5	18 29.1	2.3	55.5
12	356 51.3	S18 35.3	15 45.2	10.6	S18 26.8	2.3	55.5
13	11 51.2	34.7	30 14.8	10.6	18 24.5	2.4	55.5
14	26 51.1	34.0	44 44.4	10.5	18 22.1	2.6	55.5
15	41 50.9	. . 33.4	59 13.9	10.6	18 19.5	2.6	55.6
16	56 50.8	32.8	73 43.5	10.5	18 16.9	2.7	55.6
17	71 50.7	32.1	88 13.0	10.5	18 14.2	2.8	55.6
18	86 50.5	S18 31.5	102 42.5	10.6	S18 11.4	2.9	55.6
19	101 50.4	30.8	117 12.1	10.5	18 08.5	3.0	55.6
20	116 50.3	30.2	131 41.6	10.5	18 05.5	3.1	55.7
21	131 50.1	. . 29.6	146 11.1	10.5	18 02.4	3.2	55.7
22	146 50.0	28.9	160 40.6	10.4	17 59.2	3.3	55.7
23	161 49.9	28.3	175 10.0	10.5	17 55.9	3.4	55.7
FRIDAY							
27 00	176 49.8	S18 27.6	189 39.5	10.5	S17 52.5	3.5	55.7
01	191 49.6	27.0	204 09.0	10.5	17 49.0	3.5	55.8
02	206 49.5	26.3	218 38.5	10.4	17 45.5	3.7	55.8
03	221 49.4	. . 25.7	233 07.9	10.5	17 41.8	3.8	55.8
04	236 49.2	25.0	247 37.4	10.5	17 38.0	3.8	55.8
05	251 49.1	24.4	262 06.9	10.4	17 34.2	4.0	55.9
06	266 49.0	S18 23.7	276 36.3	10.5	S17 30.2	4.0	55.9
07	281 48.9	23.1	291 05.8	10.4	17 26.2	4.2	55.9
08	296 48.7	22.4	305 35.2	10.5	17 22.0	4.2	55.9
09	311 48.6	. . 21.8	320 04.7	10.4	17 17.8	4.3	55.9
10	326 48.5	21.1	334 34.1	10.5	17 13.5	4.4	56.0
11	341 48.4	20.5	349 03.6	10.4	17 09.1	4.6	56.0
12	356 48.2	S18 19.8	3 33.0	10.4	S17 04.5	4.6	56.0
13	11 48.1	19.2	18 02.4	10.5	16 59.9	4.7	56.0
14	26 48.0	18.5	32 31.9	10.4	16 55.2	4.7	56.1
15	41 47.9	. . 17.9	47 01.3	10.5	16 50.5	4.9	56.1
16	56 47.8	17.2	61 30.8	10.4	16 45.6	5.0	56.1
17	71 47.6	16.6	76 00.2	10.5	16 40.6	5.1	56.1
18	86 47.5	S18 15.9	90 29.7	10.5	S16 35.5	5.1	56.1
19	101 47.4	15.3	104 59.2	10.4	16 30.4	5.3	56.2
20	116 47.3	14.6	119 28.6	10.5	16 25.1	5.3	56.2
21	131 47.1	. . 14.0	133 58.1	10.4	16 19.8	5.4	56.2
22	146 47.0	13.3	148 27.5	10.5	16 14.4	5.5	56.2
23	161 46.9	12.6	162 57.0	10.5	S16 08.9	5.6	56.3
	SD 16.3	*d* 0.6	SD 15.0		15.1		15.3

Lat.	Twilight Naut.	Twilight Civil	Sunrise	Moonrise 25	26	27	28
°	h m	h m	h m	h m	h m	h m	h m
N 72	07 29	09 04	11 34	▬	▬	10 36	10 16
N 70	07 19	08 41	10 19	08 46	09 24	09 38	09 43
68	07 10	08 23	09 42	07 54	08 37	09 03	09 19
66	07 03	08 09	09 16	07 22	08 07	08 38	09 00
64	06 57	07 57	08 56	06 58	07 44	08 19	08 45
62	06 51	07 47	08 40	06 39	07 26	08 03	08 32
60	06 46	07 38	08 27	06 24	07 11	07 50	08 21
N 58	06 41	07 30	08 15	06 11	06 58	07 38	08 11
56	06 37	07 23	08 05	05 59	06 47	07 28	08 03
54	06 33	07 17	07 56	05 49	06 38	07 19	07 55
52	06 30	07 11	07 49	05 41	06 29	07 12	07 49
50	06 26	07 06	07 41	05 33	06 21	07 04	07 43
45	06 19	06 54	07 26	05 16	06 05	06 49	07 30
N 40	06 12	06 45	07 14	05 02	05 51	06 37	07 19
35	06 05	06 36	07 03	04 50	05 39	06 26	07 10
30	05 59	06 28	06 53	04 40	05 29	06 17	07 02
20	05 47	06 14	06 37	04 22	05 12	06 00	06 48
N 10	05 35	06 00	06 23	04 07	04 57	05 46	06 35
0	05 22	05 47	06 09	03 53	04 43	05 33	06 24
S 10	05 07	05 33	05 55	03 39	04 29	05 20	06 12
20	04 49	05 17	05 41	03 23	04 13	05 06	06 00
30	04 26	04 57	05 23	03 06	03 56	04 50	05 46
35	04 11	04 45	05 13	02 56	03 46	04 40	05 37
40	03 53	04 31	05 02	02 44	03 34	04 29	05 28
45	03 31	04 14	04 48	02 31	03 21	04 17	05 17
S 50	03 00	03 52	04 32	02 14	03 04	04 01	05 04
52	02 44	03 42	04 24	02 06	02 57	03 54	04 58
54	02 24	03 29	04 15	01 58	02 48	03 46	04 51
56	01 59	03 15	04 05	01 48	02 38	03 37	04 43
58	01 21	02 58	03 54	01 37	02 27	03 27	04 34
S 60	////	02 37	03 40	01 24	02 14	03 15	04 24

Lat.	Sunset	Twilight Civil	Twilight Naut.	Moonset 25	26	27	28
°	h m	h m	h m	h m	h m	h m	h m
N 72	12 53	15 22	16 57	▬	▬	13 03	15 08
N 70	14 07	15 45	17 08	11 23	12 30	14 01	15 40
68	14 44	16 03	17 16	12 15	13 16	14 34	16 04
66	15 10	16 17	17 23	12 47	13 46	14 59	16 22
64	15 30	16 29	17 30	13 11	14 08	15 18	16 37
62	15 46	16 39	17 35	13 30	14 26	15 33	16 49
60	15 59	16 48	17 40	13 46	14 41	15 46	16 59
N 58	16 11	16 56	17 44	13 59	14 54	15 58	17 08
56	16 21	17 03	17 49	14 10	15 05	16 07	17 16
54	16 29	17 09	17 52	14 20	15 14	16 16	17 23
52	16 37	17 15	17 56	14 29	15 23	16 23	17 29
50	16 44	17 20	17 59	14 37	15 30	16 30	17 35
45	17 00	17 31	18 07	14 54	15 47	16 45	17 47
N 40	17 12	17 41	18 14	15 08	16 00	16 57	17 57
35	17 23	17 50	18 20	15 19	16 11	17 07	18 06
30	17 32	17 57	18 26	15 30	16 21	17 16	18 13
20	17 48	18 12	18 38	15 47	16 38	17 32	18 26
N 10	18 03	18 25	18 50	16 02	16 53	17 45	18 37
0	18 16	18 38	19 03	16 17	17 07	17 57	18 48
S 10	18 30	18 52	19 18	16 31	17 21	18 10	18 58
20	18 44	19 08	19 36	16 46	17 35	18 23	19 09
30	19 01	19 27	19 59	17 04	17 52	18 38	19 22
35	19 11	19 39	20 13	17 14	18 02	18 47	19 29
40	19 23	19 53	20 31	17 26	18 13	18 57	19 37
45	19 36	20 10	20 53	17 39	18 26	19 09	19 47
S 50	19 53	20 32	21 23	17 56	18 42	19 23	19 59
52	20 00	20 42	21 39	18 04	18 49	19 29	20 04
54	20 09	20 54	21 58	18 12	18 57	19 36	20 10
56	20 19	21 08	22 23	18 22	19 07	19 44	20 16
58	20 30	21 25	22 59	18 33	19 17	19 53	20 23
S 60	20 43	21 45	////	18 46	19 29	20 04	20 32

Day	SUN Eqn. of Time 00^h	SUN Eqn. of Time 12^h	SUN Mer. Pass.	MOON Mer. Pass. Upper	MOON Mer. Pass. Lower	MOON Age	MOON Phase
d	m s	m s	h m	h m	h m	d	%
25	12 15	12 21	12 12	10 05	22 30	27	6
26	12 28	12 34	12 13	10 55	23 20	28	2
27	12 41	12 47	12 13	11 45	24 11	29	0

UT d	h	ARIES GHA	VENUS −4·7 GHA	VENUS Dec	MARS +1·1 GHA	MARS Dec	JUPITER −2·1 GHA	JUPITER Dec	SATURN +0·5 GHA	SATURN Dec
		° ′	° ′	° ′	° ′	° ′	° ′	° ′	° ′	° ′
28	00	127 26.9	133 02.8	S 1 05.4	127 26.3	S 0 28.1	285 38.8	S 7 39.1	223 40.4	S22 01.6
	01	142 29.4	148 03.4	04.2	142 27.0	27.3	300 41.2	39.1	238 42.6	01.6
	02	157 31.9	163 03.9	03.0	157 27.8	26.6	315 43.6	39.1	253 44.8	01.6
	03	172 34.3	178 04.5	. . 01.8	172 28.5	. . 25.8	330 45.9	. . 39.1	268 47.0	. . 01.6
	04	187 36.8	193 05.1	1 00.7	187 29.3	25.0	345 48.3	39.1	283 49.2	01.6
	05	202 39.3	208 05.7	0 59.5	202 30.1	24.2	0 50.7	39.1	298 51.4	01.7
	06	217 41.7	223 06.3	S 0 58.3	217 30.8	S 0 23.4	15 53.1	S 7 39.2	313 53.6	S22 01.7
	07	232 44.2	238 06.9	57.2	232 31.6	22.7	30 55.5	39.2	328 55.8	01.7
S	08	247 46.6	253 07.4	56.0	247 32.4	21.9	45 57.9	39.2	343 58.0	01.7
A	09	262 49.1	268 08.0	. . 54.8	262 33.1	. . 21.1	61 00.3	. . 39.2	359 00.2	. . 01.7
T	10	277 51.6	283 08.6	53.6	277 33.9	20.3	76 02.7	39.2	14 02.4	01.7
U	11	292 54.0	298 09.2	52.5	292 34.7	19.5	91 05.1	39.2	29 04.7	01.7
R	12	307 56.5	313 09.8	S 0 51.3	307 35.4	S 0 18.8	106 07.5	S 7 39.3	44 06.9	S22 01.7
D	13	322 59.0	328 10.4	50.1	322 36.2	18.0	121 09.9	39.3	59 09.1	01.7
A	14	338 01.4	343 11.0	49.0	337 37.0	17.2	136 12.3	39.3	74 11.3	01.7
Y	15	353 03.9	358 11.6	. . 47.8	352 37.7	. . 16.4	151 14.7	. . 39.3	89 13.5	. . 01.7
	16	8 06.4	13 12.2	46.6	7 38.5	15.7	166 17.1	39.3	104 15.7	01.8
	17	23 08.8	28 12.8	45.5	22 39.3	14.9	181 19.5	39.3	119 17.9	01.8
	18	38 11.3	43 13.4	S 0 44.3	37 40.0	S 0 14.1	196 21.9	S 7 39.3	134 20.1	S22 01.8
	19	53 13.8	58 14.0	43.1	52 40.8	13.3	211 24.3	39.4	149 22.3	01.8
	20	68 16.2	73 14.6	42.0	67 41.6	12.5	226 26.7	39.4	164 24.5	01.8
	21	83 18.7	88 15.2	. . 40.8	82 42.3	. . 11.8	241 29.1	. . 39.4	179 26.7	. . 01.8
	22	98 21.1	103 15.8	39.6	97 43.1	11.0	256 31.5	39.4	194 28.9	01.8
	23	113 23.6	118 16.4	38.5	112 43.9	10.2	271 33.9	39.4	209 31.1	01.8
29	00	128 26.1	133 17.0	S 0 37.3	127 44.6	S 0 09.4	286 36.3	S 7 39.4	224 33.4	S22 01.8
	01	143 28.5	148 17.6	36.1	142 45.4	08.7	301 38.7	39.4	239 35.6	01.8
	02	158 31.0	163 18.2	35.0	157 46.2	07.9	316 41.1	39.5	254 37.8	01.8
	03	173 33.5	178 18.8	. . 33.8	172 46.9	. . 07.1	331 43.5	. . 39.5	269 40.0	. . 01.9
	04	188 35.9	193 19.4	32.6	187 47.7	06.3	346 45.9	39.5	284 42.2	01.9
	05	203 38.4	208 20.0	31.5	202 48.5	05.5	1 48.3	39.5	299 44.4	01.9
	06	218 40.9	223 20.7	S 0 30.3	217 49.2	S 0 04.8	16 50.7	S 7 39.5	314 46.6	S22 01.9
	07	233 43.3	238 21.3	29.1	232 50.0	04.0	31 53.1	39.5	329 48.8	01.9
	08	248 45.8	253 21.9	28.0	247 50.8	03.2	46 55.5	39.5	344 51.0	01.9
S	09	263 48.2	268 22.5	. . 26.8	262 51.5	. . 02.4	61 57.9	. . 39.6	359 53.2	. . 01.9
U	10	278 50.7	283 23.1	25.6	277 52.3	01.7	77 00.3	39.6	14 55.4	01.9
N	11	293 53.2	298 23.7	24.5	292 53.1	00.9	92 02.7	39.6	29 57.7	01.9
D	12	308 55.6	313 24.4	S 0 23.3	307 53.8	S 0 00.1	107 05.1	S 7 39.6	44 59.9	S22 01.9
A	13	323 58.1	328 25.0	22.2	322 54.6	N 00.7	122 07.5	39.6	60 02.1	01.9
Y	14	339 00.6	343 25.6	21.0	337 55.4	01.5	137 09.9	39.6	75 04.3	02.0
	15	354 03.0	358 26.2	. . 19.8	352 56.1	. . 02.2	152 12.3	. . 39.6	90 06.5	. . 02.0
	16	9 05.5	13 26.9	18.7	7 56.9	03.0	167 14.7	39.6	105 08.7	02.0
	17	24 08.0	28 27.5	17.5	22 57.7	03.8	182 17.1	39.7	120 10.9	02.0
	18	39 10.4	43 28.1	S 0 16.3	37 58.4	N 0 04.6	197 19.5	S 7 39.7	135 13.1	S22 02.0
	19	54 12.9	58 28.8	15.2	52 59.2	05.3	212 21.9	39.7	150 15.3	02.0
	20	69 15.4	73 29.4	14.0	68 00.0	06.1	227 24.3	39.7	165 17.5	02.0
	21	84 17.8	88 30.0	. . 12.9	83 00.7	. . 06.9	242 26.7	. . 39.7	180 19.8	. . 02.0
	22	99 20.3	103 30.7	11.7	98 01.5	07.7	257 29.1	39.7	195 22.0	02.0
	23	114 22.7	118 31.3	10.5	113 02.3	08.5	272 31.5	39.7	210 24.2	02.0
30	00	129 25.2	133 31.9	S 0 09.4	128 03.0	N 0 09.2	287 33.9	S 7 39.7	225 26.4	S22 02.0
	01	144 27.7	148 32.6	08.2	143 03.8	10.0	302 36.3	39.8	240 28.6	02.0
	02	159 30.1	163 33.2	07.1	158 04.6	10.8	317 38.7	39.8	255 30.8	02.1
	03	174 32.6	178 33.9	. . 05.9	173 05.3	. . 11.6	332 41.1	. . 39.8	270 33.0	. . 02.1
	04	189 35.1	193 34.5	04.7	188 06.1	12.3	347 43.6	39.8	285 35.2	02.1
	05	204 37.5	208 35.2	03.6	203 06.9	13.1	2 46.0	39.8	300 37.5	02.1
	06	219 40.0	223 35.8	S 0 02.4	218 07.7	N 0 13.9	17 48.4	S 7 39.8	315 39.7	S22 02.1
	07	234 42.5	238 36.4	01.3	233 08.4	14.7	32 50.8	39.8	330 41.9	02.1
	08	249 44.9	253 37.1	S 00.1	248 09.2	15.4	47 53.2	39.8	345 44.1	02.1
M	09	264 47.4	268 37.7	N 01.1	263 10.0	. . 16.2	62 55.6	. . 39.8	0 46.3	. . 02.1
O	10	279 49.9	283 38.4	02.2	278 10.7	17.0	77 58.0	39.9	15 48.5	02.1
N	11	294 52.3	298 39.1	03.4	293 11.5	17.8	93 00.4	39.9	30 50.7	02.1
D	12	309 54.8	313 39.7	N 0 04.5	308 12.3	N 0 18.6	108 02.8	S 7 39.9	45 52.9	S22 02.1
A	13	324 57.2	328 40.4	05.7	323 13.0	19.3	123 05.2	39.9	60 55.1	02.2
Y	14	339 59.7	343 41.0	06.8	338 13.8	20.1	138 07.6	39.9	75 57.4	02.2
	15	355 02.2	358 41.7	. . 08.0	353 14.6	. . 20.9	153 10.1	. . 39.9	90 59.6	. . 02.2
	16	10 04.6	13 42.3	09.2	8 15.3	21.7	168 12.5	39.9	106 01.8	02.2
	17	25 07.1	28 43.0	10.3	23 16.1	22.4	183 14.9	39.9	121 04.0	02.2
	18	40 09.6	43 43.7	N 0 11.5	38 16.9	N 0 23.2	198 17.3	S 7 39.9	136 06.2	S22 02.2
	19	55 12.0	58 44.3	12.6	53 17.6	24.0	213 19.7	39.9	151 08.4	02.2
	20	70 14.5	73 45.0	13.8	68 18.4	24.8	228 22.1	39.9	166 10.6	02.2
	21	85 17.0	88 45.7	. . 14.9	83 19.2	. . 25.5	243 24.5	. . 40.0	181 12.9	. . 02.2
	22	100 19.4	103 46.3	16.1	98 19.9	26.3	258 26.9	40.0	196 15.1	02.2
	23	115 21.9	118 47.0	17.2	113 20.7	27.1	273 29.4	40.0	211 17.3	02.2
Mer. Pass.		h m 15 23.7	v 0.6	d 1.2	v 0.8	d 0.8	v 2.4	d 0.0	v 2.2	d 0.0

STARS Name	SHA	Dec
	° ′	° ′
Acamar	315 16.5	S40 14.6
Achernar	335 25.2	S57 09.4
Acrux	173 06.0	S63 11.3
Adhara	255 10.2	S29 00.0
Aldebaran	290 46.4	N16 32.4
Alioth	166 18.4	N55 51.8
Alkaid	152 56.9	N49 13.5
Al Na'ir	27 41.2	S46 52.8
Alnilam	275 43.6	S 1 11.8
Alphard	217 53.3	S 8 44.1
Alphecca	126 09.1	N26 39.4
Alpheratz	357 41.1	N29 11.1
Altair	62 06.2	N 8 54.9
Ankaa	353 13.6	S42 13.1
Antares	112 23.4	S26 27.9
Arcturus	145 53.5	N19 05.6
Atria	107 23.3	S69 03.0
Avior	234 16.3	S59 34.0
Bellatrix	278 29.1	N 6 21.6
Betelgeuse	270 58.4	N 7 24.3
Canopus	263 54.6	S52 42.7
Capella	280 30.5	N46 00.8
Deneb	49 30.2	N45 20.6
Denebola	182 31.0	N14 28.5
Diphda	348 53.6	S17 53.8
Dubhe	193 48.3	N61 39.3
Elnath	278 09.2	N28 37.1
Eltanin	90 45.4	N51 29.2
Enif	33 45.0	N 9 57.2
Fomalhaut	15 21.6	S29 32.1
Gacrux	171 57.7	S57 12.3
Gienah	175 49.6	S17 38.1
Hadar	148 44.2	S60 26.9
Hamal	327 58.0	N23 32.5
Kaus Aust.	83 40.9	S34 22.3
Kochab	137 20.4	N74 04.9
Markab	13 36.1	N15 17.8
Menkar	314 12.4	N 4 09.2
Menkent	148 04.6	S36 27.0
Miaplacidus	221 38.1	S69 47.3
Mirfak	308 36.6	N49 55.3
Nunki	75 55.6	S26 16.3
Peacock	53 16.1	S56 40.7
Pollux	243 24.4	N27 58.9
Procyon	244 56.8	N 5 10.6
Rasalhague	96 04.4	N12 32.9
Regulus	207 40.6	N11 52.8
Rigel	281 09.5	S 8 11.3
Rigil Kent.	139 48.3	S60 53.9
Sabik	102 09.9	S15 44.5
Schedar	349 37.9	N56 38.0
Shaula	96 18.9	S37 06.7
Sirius	258 31.2	S16 44.7
Spica	158 28.6	S11 14.9
Suhail	222 50.1	S43 30.2
Vega	80 37.7	N38 48.0
Zuben'ubi	137 02.7	S16 06.6

	SHA	Mer. Pass.
	° ′	h m
Venus	4 50.9	15 06
Mars	359 18.6	15 28
Jupiter	158 10.2	4 53
Saturn	96 07.3	9 00

UT	SUN GHA	SUN Dec	MOON GHA	v	MOON Dec	d	HP
d h	° ′	° ′	° ′	′	° ′	′	′
28 00 (SATURDAY)	176 46.8	S18 12.0	177 26.5	10.5	S16 03.3	5.7	56.3
01	191 46.7	11.3	191 56.0	10.5	15 57.6	5.8	56.3
02	206 46.6	10.7	206 25.5	10.5	15 51.8	5.9	56.3
03	221 46.4	. . 10.0	220 55.0	10.5	15 45.9	5.9	56.3
04	236 46.3	09.3	235 24.5	10.5	15 40.0	6.0	56.4
05	251 46.2	08.7	249 54.0	10.5	15 34.0	6.2	56.4
06	266 46.1	S18 08.0	264 23.5	10.5	S15 27.8	6.2	56.4
07	281 46.0	07.4	278 53.0	10.5	15 21.6	6.3	56.4
08	296 45.8	06.7	293 22.5	10.6	15 15.3	6.4	56.5
09	311 45.7	. . 06.0	307 52.1	10.5	15 08.9	6.4	56.5
10	326 45.6	05.4	322 21.6	10.6	15 02.5	6.6	56.5
11	341 45.5	04.7	336 51.2	10.5	14 55.9	6.6	56.5
12	356 45.4	S18 04.0	351 20.7	10.6	S14 49.3	6.7	56.5
13	11 45.3	03.4	5 50.3	10.6	14 42.6	6.8	56.6
14	26 45.2	02.7	20 19.9	10.5	14 35.8	6.9	56.6
15	41 45.0	. . 02.0	34 49.4	10.6	14 28.9	7.0	56.6
16	56 44.9	01.4	49 19.0	10.6	14 21.9	7.0	56.6
17	71 44.8	00.7	63 48.6	10.7	14 14.9	7.1	56.7
18	86 44.7	S18 00.0	78 18.3	10.6	S14 07.8	7.2	56.7
19	101 44.6	17 59.4	92 47.9	10.6	14 00.6	7.3	56.7
20	116 44.5	58.7	107 17.5	10.7	13 53.3	7.3	56.7
21	131 44.4	. . 58.0	121 47.2	10.6	13 46.0	7.5	56.7
22	146 44.2	57.4	136 16.8	10.7	13 38.5	7.5	56.8
23	161 44.1	56.7	150 46.5	10.7	13 31.0	7.6	56.8
29 00 (SUNDAY)	176 44.0	S17 56.0	165 16.2	10.7	S13 23.4	7.6	56.8
01	191 43.9	55.3	179 45.9	10.7	13 15.8	7.8	56.8
02	206 43.8	54.7	194 15.6	10.7	13 08.0	7.8	56.8
03	221 43.7	. . 54.0	208 45.3	10.7	13 00.2	7.9	56.9
04	236 43.6	53.3	223 15.0	10.7	12 52.3	7.9	56.9
05	251 43.5	52.6	237 44.7	10.8	12 44.4	8.1	56.9
06	266 43.4	S17 52.0	252 14.5	10.7	S12 36.3	8.1	56.9
07	281 43.3	51.3	266 44.2	10.8	12 28.2	8.1	57.0
08	296 43.2	50.6	281 14.0	10.8	12 20.1	8.3	57.0
09	311 43.0	. . 49.9	295 43.8	10.8	12 11.8	8.3	57.0
10	326 42.9	49.3	310 13.6	10.8	12 03.5	8.4	57.0
11	341 42.8	48.6	324 43.4	10.8	11 55.1	8.4	57.0
12	356 42.7	S17 47.9	339 13.2	10.8	S11 46.7	8.6	57.1
13	11 42.6	47.2	353 43.0	10.8	11 38.1	8.6	57.1
14	26 42.5	46.6	8 12.8	10.9	11 29.5	8.6	57.1
15	41 42.4	. . 45.9	22 42.7	10.8	11 20.9	8.7	57.1
16	56 42.3	45.2	37 12.5	10.9	11 12.2	8.8	57.1
17	71 42.2	44.5	51 42.4	10.9	11 03.4	8.9	57.2
18	86 42.1	S17 43.8	66 12.3	10.9	S10 54.5	8.9	57.2
19	101 42.0	43.1	80 42.2	10.8	10 45.6	8.9	57.2
20	116 41.9	42.5	95 12.0	11.0	10 36.7	9.1	57.2
21	131 41.8	. . 41.8	109 42.0	10.9	10 27.6	9.1	57.2
22	146 41.7	41.1	124 11.9	10.9	10 18.5	9.1	57.3
23	161 41.6	40.4	138 41.8	10.9	10 09.4	9.2	57.3
30 00 (MONDAY)	176 41.5	S17 39.7	153 11.7	11.0	S10 00.2	9.3	57.3
01	191 41.4	39.0	167 41.7	11.0	9 50.9	9.3	57.3
02	206 41.3	38.4	182 11.7	10.9	9 41.6	9.4	57.3
03	221 41.2	. . 37.7	196 41.6	11.0	9 32.2	9.5	57.4
04	236 41.1	37.0	211 11.6	11.0	9 22.7	9.5	57.4
05	251 41.0	36.3	225 41.6	11.0	9 13.2	9.5	57.4
06	266 40.9	S17 35.6	240 11.6	11.0	S 9 03.7	9.6	57.4
07	281 40.8	34.9	254 41.6	11.0	8 54.1	9.7	57.4
08	296 40.7	34.2	269 11.6	11.0	8 44.4	9.7	57.5
09	311 40.6	. . 33.5	283 41.6	11.1	8 34.7	9.7	57.5
10	326 40.5	32.8	298 11.7	11.0	8 25.0	9.9	57.5
11	341 40.4	32.2	312 41.7	11.0	8 15.1	9.8	57.5
12	356 40.3	S17 31.5	327 11.7	11.1	S 8 05.3	9.9	57.5
13	11 40.2	30.8	341 41.8	11.1	7 55.4	10.0	57.6
14	26 40.1	30.1	356 11.9	11.0	7 45.4	10.0	57.6
15	41 40.0	. . 29.4	10 41.9	11.1	7 35.4	10.0	57.6
16	56 39.9	28.7	25 12.0	11.1	7 25.4	10.1	57.6
17	71 39.8	28.0	39 42.1	11.1	7 15.3	10.2	57.6
18	86 39.7	S17 27.3	54 12.2	11.0	S 7 05.1	10.1	57.7
19	101 39.6	26.6	68 42.2	11.1	6 55.0	10.3	57.7
20	116 39.5	25.9	83 12.3	11.1	6 44.7	10.2	57.7
21	131 39.4	. . 25.2	97 42.4	11.1	6 34.5	10.3	57.7
22	146 39.3	24.5	112 12.5	11.1	6 24.2	10.4	57.7
23	161 39.2	23.8	126 42.6	11.1	S 6 13.8	10.4	57.7
	SD 16.3	*d* 0.7	SD	15.4	15.5		15.7

Lat.	Twilight Naut.	Twilight Civil	Sunrise	Moonrise 28	Moonrise 29	Moonrise 30	Moonrise 31
°	h m	h m	h m	h m	h m	h m	h m
N 72	07 19	08 51	10 53	10 16	10 06	09 57	09 50
N 70	07 10	08 30	10 01	09 43	09 45	09 45	09 44
68	07 03	08 14	09 29	09 19	09 28	09 35	09 39
66	06 56	08 01	09 06	09 00	09 15	09 26	09 35
64	06 50	07 50	08 48	08 45	09 04	09 19	09 32
62	06 45	07 40	08 33	08 32	08 54	09 12	09 28
60	06 41	07 32	08 20	08 21	08 46	09 07	09 26
N 58	06 37	07 25	08 10	08 11	08 39	09 02	09 23
56	06 33	07 18	08 00	08 03	08 32	08 58	09 21
54	06 30	07 13	07 52	07 55	08 27	08 54	09 19
52	06 26	07 07	07 44	07 49	08 21	08 50	09 17
50	06 23	07 02	07 38	07 43	08 17	08 47	09 16
45	06 16	06 52	07 23	07 30	08 06	08 40	09 12
N 40	06 10	06 42	07 11	07 19	07 58	08 34	09 09
35	06 04	06 34	07 01	07 10	07 51	08 29	09 06
30	05 58	06 27	06 52	07 02	07 44	08 25	09 04
20	05 47	06 13	06 36	06 48	07 33	08 17	09 00
N 10	05 35	06 01	06 23	06 35	07 23	08 10	08 57
0	05 23	05 48	06 10	06 24	07 14	08 04	08 53
S 10	05 08	05 34	05 57	06 12	07 05	07 57	08 50
20	04 51	05 19	05 42	06 00	06 55	07 51	08 47
30	04 29	05 00	05 26	05 46	06 44	07 43	08 43
35	04 15	04 49	05 16	05 37	06 37	07 38	08 40
40	03 58	04 35	05 06	05 28	06 30	07 33	08 38
45	03 36	04 19	04 53	05 17	06 21	07 27	08 35
S 50	03 07	03 58	04 37	05 04	06 11	07 20	08 31
52	02 52	03 48	04 29	04 58	06 06	07 17	08 30
54	02 34	03 37	04 21	04 51	06 00	07 13	08 28
56	02 11	03 23	04 12	04 43	05 54	07 09	08 26
58	01 40	03 07	04 01	04 34	05 48	07 04	08 23
S 60	00 30	02 48	03 49	04 24	05 40	06 59	08 21

Lat.	Sunset	Twilight Civil	Twilight Naut.	Moonset 28	Moonset 29	Moonset 30	Moonset 31
°	h m	h m	h m	h m	h m	h m	h m
N 72	13 35	15 37	17 09	15 08	17 03	18 55	20 46
N 70	14 26	15 57	17 17	15 40	17 23	19 06	20 49
68	14 58	16 13	17 25	16 04	17 38	19 15	20 52
66	15 21	16 26	17 31	16 22	17 51	19 22	20 55
64	15 39	16 37	17 37	16 37	18 01	19 28	20 57
62	15 54	16 47	17 42	16 49	18 09	19 33	20 58
60	16 07	16 55	17 46	16 59	18 17	19 38	21 00
N 58	16 18	17 02	17 50	17 08	18 23	19 42	21 01
56	16 27	17 09	17 54	17 16	18 29	19 45	21 02
54	16 35	17 14	17 57	17 23	18 34	19 48	21 04
52	16 43	17 20	18 01	17 29	18 39	19 51	21 05
50	16 49	17 25	18 04	17 35	18 43	19 54	21 05
45	17 04	17 35	18 11	17 47	18 52	19 59	21 07
N 40	17 16	17 44	18 17	17 57	19 00	20 04	21 09
35	17 26	17 53	18 23	18 06	19 06	20 08	21 10
30	17 35	18 00	18 29	18 13	19 12	20 11	21 12
20	17 50	18 13	18 40	18 26	19 22	20 17	21 14
N 10	18 04	18 26	18 51	18 37	19 30	20 23	21 15
0	18 17	18 38	19 04	18 48	19 38	20 28	21 17
S 10	18 30	18 52	19 18	18 58	19 46	20 32	21 19
20	18 44	19 07	19 35	19 09	19 54	20 38	21 20
30	19 00	19 26	19 57	19 22	20 04	20 43	21 22
35	19 09	19 37	20 11	19 29	20 09	20 47	21 23
40	19 20	19 50	20 27	19 37	20 15	20 50	21 25
45	19 33	20 06	20 49	19 47	20 22	20 55	21 26
S 50	19 49	20 27	21 17	19 59	20 31	21 00	21 28
52	19 56	20 37	21 32	20 04	20 35	21 02	21 28
54	20 04	20 48	21 50	20 10	20 39	21 05	21 29
56	20 13	21 01	22 12	20 16	20 44	21 08	21 30
58	20 24	21 17	22 42	20 23	20 49	21 11	21 31
S 60	20 36	21 35	23 38	20 32	20 55	21 14	21 32

Day	SUN Eqn. of Time 00^h	SUN Eqn. of Time 12^h	SUN Mer. Pass.	MOON Mer. Pass. Upper	MOON Mer. Pass. Lower	MOON Age	MOON Phase
d	m s	m s	h m	h m	h m	d	%
28	12 53	12 58	12 13	12 36	00 11	00	0
29	13 04	13 09	12 13	13 26	01 01	01	2
30	13 14	13 19	12 13	14 16	01 51	02	7

2017 JAN. 31, FEB. 1, 2 (TUES., WED., THURS.)

UT d	UT h	ARIES GHA	VENUS −4·7 GHA	VENUS Dec	MARS +1·1 GHA	MARS Dec	JUPITER −2·2 GHA	JUPITER Dec	SATURN +0·5 GHA	SATURN Dec
		° ′	° ′	° ′	° ′	° ′	° ′	° ′	° ′	° ′
31	00	130 24.3	133 47.7	N 0 18.4	128 21.5	N 0 27.9	288 31.8	S 7 40.0	226 19.5	S22 02.2
	01	145 26.8	148 48.3	19.5	143 22.2	28.6	303 34.2	40.0	241 21.7	02.3
	02	160 29.3	163 49.0	20.7	158 23.0	29.4	318 36.6	40.0	256 23.9	02.3
	03	175 31.7	178 49.7	. . 21.8	173 23.8	. . 30.2	333 39.0	. . 40.0	271 26.1	. . 02.3
	04	190 34.2	193 50.4	23.0	188 24.5	31.0	348 41.4	40.0	286 28.4	02.3
	05	205 36.7	208 51.0	24.1	203 25.3	31.8	3 43.8	40.0	301 30.6	02.3
	06	220 39.1	223 51.7	N 0 25.3	218 26.1	N 0 32.5	18 46.3	S 7 40.0	316 32.8	S22 02.3
	07	235 41.6	238 52.4	26.5	233 26.9	33.3	33 48.7	40.0	331 35.0	02.3
T	08	250 44.1	253 53.1	27.6	248 27.6	34.1	48 51.1	40.0	346 37.2	02.3
U	09	265 46.5	268 53.8	. . 28.8	263 28.4	. . 34.9	63 53.5	. . 40.1	1 39.4	. . 02.3
E	10	280 49.0	283 54.5	29.9	278 29.2	35.6	78 55.9	40.1	16 41.6	02.3
S	11	295 51.5	298 55.1	31.1	293 29.9	36.4	93 58.3	40.1	31 43.9	02.3
D	12	310 53.9	313 55.8	N 0 32.2	308 30.7	N 0 37.2	109 00.8	S 7 40.1	46 46.1	S22 02.3
A	13	325 56.4	328 56.5	33.4	323 31.5	38.0	124 03.2	40.1	61 48.3	02.4
Y	14	340 58.8	343 57.2	34.5	338 32.2	38.7	139 05.6	40.1	76 50.5	02.4
	15	356 01.3	358 57.9	. . 35.6	353 33.0	. . 39.5	154 08.0	. . 40.1	91 52.7	. . 02.4
	16	11 03.8	13 58.6	36.8	8 33.8	40.3	169 10.4	40.1	106 54.9	02.4
	17	26 06.2	28 59.3	37.9	23 34.5	41.1	184 12.9	40.1	121 57.1	02.4
	18	41 08.7	44 00.0	N 0 39.1	38 35.3	N 0 41.8	199 15.3	S 7 40.1	136 59.4	S22 02.4
	19	56 11.2	59 00.7	40.2	53 36.1	42.6	214 17.7	40.1	152 01.6	02.4
	20	71 13.6	74 01.4	41.4	68 36.8	43.4	229 20.1	40.1	167 03.8	02.4
	21	86 16.1	89 02.1	. . 42.5	83 37.6	. . 44.2	244 22.5	. . 40.1	182 06.0	. . 02.4
	22	101 18.6	104 02.8	43.7	98 38.4	44.9	259 24.9	40.1	197 08.2	02.4
	23	116 21.0	119 03.5	44.8	113 39.2	45.7	274 27.4	40.2	212 10.4	02.4
1	00	131 23.5	134 04.2	N 0 46.0	128 39.9	N 0 46.5	289 29.8	S 7 40.2	227 12.7	S22 02.4
	01	146 26.0	149 04.9	47.1	143 40.7	47.3	304 32.2	40.2	242 14.9	02.5
	02	161 28.4	164 05.6	48.3	158 41.5	48.0	319 34.6	40.2	257 17.1	02.5
	03	176 30.9	179 06.3	. . 49.4	173 42.2	. . 48.8	334 37.1	. . 40.2	272 19.3	. . 02.5
	04	191 33.3	194 07.0	50.6	188 43.0	49.6	349 39.5	40.2	287 21.5	02.5
	05	206 35.8	209 07.8	51.7	203 43.8	50.4	4 41.9	40.2	302 23.7	02.5
	06	221 38.3	224 08.5	N 0 52.8	218 44.5	N 0 51.1	19 44.3	S 7 40.2	317 26.0	S22 02.5
W	07	236 40.7	239 09.2	54.0	233 45.3	51.9	34 46.7	40.2	332 28.2	02.5
E	08	251 43.2	254 09.9	55.1	248 46.1	52.7	49 49.2	40.2	347 30.4	02.5
D	09	266 45.7	269 10.6	. . 56.3	263 46.8	. . 53.5	64 51.6	. . 40.2	2 32.6	. . 02.5
N	10	281 48.1	284 11.3	57.4	278 47.6	54.2	79 54.0	40.2	17 34.8	02.5
E	11	296 50.6	299 12.1	58.6	293 48.4	55.0	94 56.4	40.2	32 37.0	02.5
S	12	311 53.1	314 12.8	N 0 59.7	308 49.2	N 0 55.8	109 58.9	S 7 40.2	47 39.3	S22 02.5
D	13	326 55.5	329 13.5	1 00.8	323 49.9	56.6	125 01.3	40.2	62 41.5	02.6
A	14	341 58.0	344 14.2	02.0	338 50.7	57.3	140 03.7	40.2	77 43.7	02.6
Y	15	357 00.4	359 15.0	. . 03.1	353 51.5	. . 58.1	155 06.1	. . 40.2	92 45.9	. . 02.6
	16	12 02.9	14 15.7	04.3	8 52.2	58.9	170 08.6	40.2	107 48.1	02.6
	17	27 05.4	29 16.4	05.4	23 53.0	0 59.7	185 11.0	40.2	122 50.4	02.6
	18	42 07.8	44 17.1	N 1 06.5	38 53.8	N 1 00.4	200 13.4	S 7 40.2	137 52.6	S22 02.6
	19	57 10.3	59 17.9	07.7	53 54.5	01.2	215 15.8	40.2	152 54.8	02.6
	20	72 12.8	74 18.6	08.8	68 55.3	02.0	230 18.3	40.2	167 57.0	02.6
	21	87 15.2	89 19.4	. . 09.9	83 56.1	. . 02.8	245 20.7	. . 40.2	182 59.2	. . 02.6
	22	102 17.7	104 20.1	11.1	98 56.9	03.5	260 23.1	40.3	198 01.4	02.6
	23	117 20.2	119 20.8	12.2	113 57.6	04.3	275 25.6	40.3	213 03.7	02.6
2	00	132 22.6	134 21.6	N 1 13.4	128 58.4	N 1 05.1	290 28.0	S 7 40.3	228 05.9	S22 02.6
	01	147 25.1	149 22.3	14.5	143 59.2	05.9	305 30.4	40.3	243 08.1	02.6
	02	162 27.6	164 23.1	15.6	158 59.9	06.6	320 32.8	40.3	258 10.3	02.7
	03	177 30.0	179 23.8	. . 16.8	174 00.7	. . 07.4	335 35.3	. . 40.3	273 12.5	. . 02.7
	04	192 32.5	194 24.5	17.9	189 01.5	08.2	350 37.7	40.3	288 14.8	02.7
	05	207 34.9	209 25.3	19.0	204 02.2	08.9	5 40.1	40.3	303 17.0	02.7
	06	222 37.4	224 26.0	N 1 20.2	219 03.0	N 1 09.7	20 42.6	S 7 40.3	318 19.2	S22 02.7
	07	237 39.9	239 26.8	21.3	234 03.8	10.5	35 45.0	40.3	333 21.4	02.7
T	08	252 42.3	254 27.5	22.4	249 04.5	11.3	50 47.4	40.3	348 23.6	02.7
H	09	267 44.8	269 28.3	. . 23.6	264 05.3	. . 12.0	65 49.9	. . 40.3	3 25.9	. . 02.7
U	10	282 47.3	284 29.1	24.7	279 06.1	12.8	80 52.3	40.3	18 28.1	02.7
R	11	297 49.7	299 29.8	25.8	294 06.9	13.6	95 54.7	40.3	33 30.3	02.7
S	12	312 52.2	314 30.6	N 1 27.0	309 07.6	N 1 14.4	110 57.2	S 7 40.3	48 32.5	S22 02.7
D	13	327 54.7	329 31.3	28.1	324 08.4	15.1	125 59.6	40.3	63 34.7	02.7
A	14	342 57.1	344 32.1	29.2	339 09.2	15.9	141 02.0	40.3	78 37.0	02.7
Y	15	357 59.6	359 32.9	. . 30.4	354 09.9	. . 16.7	156 04.5	. . 40.3	93 39.2	. . 02.8
	16	13 02.0	14 33.6	31.5	9 10.7	17.5	171 06.9	40.3	108 41.4	02.8
	17	28 04.5	29 34.4	32.6	24 11.5	18.2	186 09.3	40.3	123 43.6	02.8
	18	43 07.0	44 35.2	N 1 33.8	39 12.3	N 1 19.0	201 11.8	S 7 40.3	138 45.9	S22 02.8
	19	58 09.4	59 35.9	34.9	54 13.0	19.8	216 14.2	40.3	153 48.1	02.8
	20	73 11.9	74 36.7	36.0	69 13.8	20.5	231 16.6	40.3	168 50.3	02.8
	21	88 14.4	89 37.5	. . 37.2	84 14.6	. . 21.3	246 19.1	. . 40.3	183 52.5	. . 02.8
	22	103 16.8	104 38.2	38.3	99 15.3	22.1	261 21.5	40.3	198 54.7	02.8
	23	118 19.3	119 39.0	39.4	114 16.1	22.9	276 23.9	40.3	213 57.0	02.8
Mer. Pass.		h m 15 11.9	*v* 0.7	*d* 1.1	*v* 0.8	*d* 0.8	*v* 2.4	*d* 0.0	*v* 2.2	*d* 0.0

STARS

Name	SHA	Dec
	° ′	° ′
Acamar	315 16.5	S40 14.6
Achernar	335 25.2	S57 09.4
Acrux	173 06.0	S63 11.4
Adhara	255 10.2	S29 00.1
Aldebaran	290 46.4	N16 32.4
Alioth	166 18.4	N55 51.8
Alkaid	152 56.9	N49 13.5
Al Na'ir	27 41.2	S46 52.8
Alnilam	275 43.6	S 1 11.8
Alphard	217 53.3	S 8 44.1
Alphecca	126 09.0	N26 39.4
Alpheratz	357 41.1	N29 11.1
Altair	62 06.2	N 8 54.9
Ankaa	353 13.6	S42 13.1
Antares	112 23.4	S26 27.9
Arcturus	145 53.5	N19 05.6
Atria	107 23.3	S69 03.0
Avior	234 16.3	S59 34.0
Bellatrix	278 29.1	N 6 21.6
Betelgeuse	270 58.4	N 7 24.3
Canopus	263 54.6	S52 42.7
Capella	280 30.5	N46 00.8
Deneb	49 30.2	N45 20.5
Denebola	182 30.9	N14 28.5
Diphda	348 53.6	S17 53.8
Dubhe	193 48.3	N61 39.3
Elnath	278 09.3	N28 37.1
Eltanin	90 45.4	N51 29.2
Enif	33 45.0	N 9 57.2
Fomalhaut	15 21.6	S29 32.1
Gacrux	171 57.7	S57 12.3
Gienah	175 49.5	S17 38.2
Hadar	148 44.2	S60 26.9
Hamal	327 58.0	N23 32.5
Kaus Aust.	83 40.9	S34 22.3
Kochab	137 20.3	N74 04.9
Markab	13 36.1	N15 17.8
Menkar	314 12.4	N 4 09.2
Menkent	148 04.6	S36 27.0
Miaplacidus	221 38.1	S69 47.3
Mirfak	308 36.7	N49 55.3
Nunki	75 55.6	S26 16.3
Peacock	53 16.0	S56 40.7
Pollux	243 24.4	N27 58.9
Procyon	244 56.8	N 5 10.6
Rasalhague	96 04.4	N12 32.9
Regulus	207 40.6	N11 52.8
Rigel	281 09.5	S 8 11.3
Rigil Kent.	139 48.3	S60 53.9
Sabik	102 09.9	S15 44.6
Schedar	349 37.9	N56 38.0
Shaula	96 18.9	S37 06.7
Sirius	258 31.3	S16 44.7
Spica	158 28.5	S11 14.9
Suhail	222 50.1	S43 30.2
Vega	80 37.6	N38 48.0
Zuben'ubi	137 02.7	S16 06.6

	SHA	Mer. Pass.
	° ′	h m
Venus	2 40.7	15 03
Mars	357 16.4	15 25
Jupiter	158 06.3	4 41
Saturn	95 49.2	8 50

UT (d h)	SUN GHA	SUN Dec	MOON GHA	v	MOON Dec	d	HP
	° ′	° ′	° ′	′	° ′	′	′
31 00 (TUESDAY)	176 39.1	S17 23.1	141 12.7	11.2	S 6 03.4	10.4	57.8
01	191 39.0	22.4	155 42.9	11.1	5 53.0	10.4	57.8
02	206 38.9	21.7	170 13.0	11.1	5 42.6	10.5	57.8
03	221 38.8	. . 21.0	184 43.1	11.1	5 32.1	10.5	57.8
04	236 38.7	20.3	199 13.2	11.1	5 21.6	10.6	57.8
05	251 38.7	19.6	213 43.3	11.1	5 11.0	10.6	57.9
06	266 38.6	S17 18.9	228 13.4	11.1	S 5 00.4	10.6	57.9
07	281 38.5	18.2	242 43.5	11.2	4 49.8	10.7	57.9
08	296 38.4	17.5	257 13.7	11.1	4 39.1	10.7	57.9
09	311 38.3	. . 16.8	271 43.8	11.1	4 28.4	10.7	57.9
10	326 38.2	16.1	286 13.9	11.1	4 17.7	10.7	57.9
11	341 38.1	15.4	300 44.0	11.1	4 07.0	10.8	58.0
12	356 38.0	S17 14.7	315 14.1	11.1	S 3 56.2	10.8	58.0
13	11 37.9	14.0	329 44.2	11.1	3 45.4	10.8	58.0
14	26 37.8	13.3	344 14.3	11.1	3 34.6	10.9	58.0
15	41 37.7	. . 12.6	358 44.4	11.1	3 23.7	10.8	58.0
16	56 37.7	11.9	13 14.5	11.1	3 12.9	10.9	58.0
17	71 37.6	11.2	27 44.6	11.1	3 02.0	10.9	58.1
18	86 37.5	S17 10.5	42 14.7	11.1	S 2 51.1	11.0	58.1
19	101 37.4	09.8	56 44.8	11.1	2 40.1	10.9	58.1
20	116 37.3	09.1	71 14.9	11.0	2 29.2	11.0	58.1
21	131 37.2	. . 08.3	85 44.9	11.1	2 18.2	11.0	58.1
22	146 37.1	07.6	100 15.0	11.1	2 07.2	11.0	58.1
23	161 37.1	06.9	114 45.1	11.0	1 56.2	11.0	58.2
1 00 (WEDNESDAY)	176 37.0	S17 06.2	129 15.1	11.0	S 1 45.2	11.0	58.2
01	191 36.9	05.5	143 45.1	11.1	1 34.2	11.1	58.2
02	206 36.8	04.8	158 15.2	11.0	1 23.1	11.1	58.2
03	221 36.7	. . 04.1	172 45.2	11.0	1 12.0	11.0	58.2
04	236 36.6	03.4	187 15.2	11.0	1 01.0	11.1	58.2
05	251 36.5	02.7	201 45.2	11.0	0 49.9	11.1	58.3
06	266 36.5	S17 01.9	216 15.2	10.9	S 0 38.8	11.1	58.3
07	281 36.4	01.2	230 45.1	11.0	0 27.7	11.1	58.3
08	296 36.3	17 00.5	245 15.1	10.9	0 16.6	11.1	58.3
09	311 36.2	16 59.8	259 45.0	10.9	S 0 05.5	11.1	58.3
10	326 36.1	59.1	274 14.9	11.0	N 0 05.6	11.2	58.3
11	341 36.1	58.4	288 44.9	10.9	0 16.8	11.1	58.4
12	356 36.0	S16 57.6	303 14.8	10.8	N 0 27.9	11.1	58.4
13	11 35.9	56.9	317 44.6	10.9	0 39.0	11.2	58.4
14	26 35.8	56.2	332 14.5	10.8	0 50.2	11.1	58.4
15	41 35.7	. . 55.5	346 44.3	10.9	1 01.3	11.1	58.4
16	56 35.7	54.8	1 14.2	10.8	1 12.4	11.2	58.4
17	71 35.6	54.1	15 44.0	10.8	1 23.6	11.1	58.4
18	86 35.5	S16 53.3	30 13.8	10.7	N 1 34.7	11.1	58.5
19	101 35.4	52.6	44 43.5	10.8	1 45.8	11.1	58.5
20	116 35.3	51.9	59 13.3	10.7	1 56.9	11.1	58.5
21	131 35.3	. . 51.2	73 43.0	10.7	2 08.0	11.2	58.5
22	146 35.2	50.5	88 12.7	10.7	2 19.2	11.1	58.5
23	161 35.1	49.7	102 42.4	10.7	2 30.3	11.0	58.5
2 00 (THURSDAY)	176 35.0	S16 49.0	117 12.1	10.6	N 2 41.3	11.1	58.5
01	191 35.0	48.3	131 41.7	10.6	2 52.4	11.1	58.6
02	206 34.9	47.6	146 11.3	10.6	3 03.5	11.0	58.6
03	221 34.8	. . 46.8	160 40.9	10.6	3 14.5	11.1	58.6
04	236 34.7	46.1	175 10.5	10.5	3 25.6	11.0	58.6
05	251 34.7	45.4	189 40.0	10.5	3 36.6	11.0	58.6
06	266 34.6	S16 44.7	204 09.5	10.5	N 3 47.6	11.0	58.6
07	281 34.5	43.9	218 39.0	10.4	3 58.6	11.0	58.6
08	296 34.4	43.2	233 08.4	10.5	4 09.6	11.0	58.7
09	311 34.4	. . 42.5	247 37.9	10.3	4 20.6	10.9	58.7
10	326 34.3	41.7	262 07.2	10.4	4 31.5	10.9	58.7
11	341 34.2	41.0	276 36.6	10.3	4 42.4	10.9	58.7
12	356 34.1	S16 40.3	291 05.9	10.4	N 4 53.3	10.9	58.7
13	11 34.1	39.6	305 35.3	10.2	5 04.2	10.8	58.7
14	26 34.0	38.8	320 04.5	10.3	5 15.0	10.9	58.7
15	41 33.9	. . 38.1	334 33.8	10.2	5 25.9	10.8	58.8
16	56 33.9	37.4	349 03.0	10.1	5 36.7	10.7	58.8
17	71 33.8	36.6	3 32.1	10.2	5 47.4	10.8	58.8
18	86 33.7	S16 35.9	18 01.3	10.1	N 5 58.2	10.7	58.8
19	101 33.6	35.2	32 30.4	10.1	6 08.9	10.7	58.8
20	116 33.6	34.4	46 59.5	10.0	6 19.6	10.6	58.8
21	131 33.5	. . 33.7	61 28.5	10.0	6 30.2	10.7	58.8
22	146 33.4	33.0	75 57.5	10.0	6 40.9	10.5	58.8
23	161 33.4	32.2	90 26.5	9.9	N 6 51.4	10.6	58.9
	SD 16.3	*d* 0.7	SD 15.8		15.9		16.0

Lat.	Twilight Naut.	Twilight Civil	Sunrise	Moonrise 31	Moonrise 1	Moonrise 2	Moonrise 3
°	h m	h m	h m	h m	h m	h m	h m
N 72	07 09	08 37	10 25	09 50	09 44	09 37	09 30
N 70	07 01	08 19	09 44	09 44	09 44	09 43	09 43
68	06 54	08 04	09 16	09 39	09 44	09 48	09 53
66	06 49	07 53	08 56	09 35	09 43	09 52	10 02
64	06 44	07 42	08 39	09 32	09 43	09 55	10 09
62	06 39	07 34	08 25	09 28	09 43	09 59	10 15
60	06 35	07 26	08 13	09 26	09 43	10 01	10 21
N 58	06 32	07 19	08 03	09 23	09 43	10 04	10 26
56	06 29	07 13	07 55	09 21	09 43	10 06	10 30
54	06 25	07 08	07 47	09 19	09 43	10 08	10 34
52	06 22	07 03	07 40	09 17	09 43	10 09	10 37
50	06 20	06 58	07 33	09 16	09 43	10 11	10 41
45	06 13	06 48	07 20	09 12	09 43	10 14	10 48
N 40	06 07	06 40	07 08	09 09	09 43	10 17	10 54
35	06 02	06 32	06 59	09 06	09 43	10 20	10 59
30	05 57	06 25	06 50	09 04	09 43	10 22	11 03
20	05 46	06 12	06 35	09 00	09 43	10 26	11 11
N 10	05 35	06 00	06 22	08 57	09 43	10 30	11 18
0	05 23	05 48	06 10	08 53	09 43	10 33	11 25
S 10	05 10	05 36	05 58	08 50	09 43	10 37	11 31
20	04 53	05 21	05 44	08 47	09 43	10 40	11 39
30	04 32	05 03	05 29	08 43	09 43	10 44	11 47
35	04 19	04 52	05 20	08 40	09 43	10 47	11 51
40	04 02	04 39	05 09	08 38	09 43	10 50	11 57
45	03 42	04 24	04 57	08 35	09 43	10 53	12 03
S 50	03 14	04 04	04 42	08 31	09 44	10 57	12 11
52	03 00	03 54	04 35	08 30	09 44	10 59	12 14
54	02 44	03 44	04 27	08 28	09 44	11 01	12 18
56	02 23	03 31	04 18	08 26	09 44	11 03	12 23
58	01 56	03 17	04 08	08 23	09 44	11 05	12 27
S 60	01 12	02 59	03 57	08 21	09 44	11 08	12 33

Lat.	Sunset	Twilight Civil	Twilight Naut.	Moonset 31	Moonset 1	Moonset 2	Moonset 3
°	h m	h m	h m	h m	h m	h m	h m
N 72	14 03	15 51	17 20	20 46	22 37	24 30	00 30
N 70	14 44	16 09	17 28	20 49	22 33	24 19	00 19
68	15 12	16 24	17 34	20 52	22 31	24 10	00 10
66	15 33	16 36	17 40	20 55	22 28	24 03	00 03
64	15 49	16 46	17 44	20 57	22 26	23 57	25 29
62	16 03	16 54	17 49	20 58	22 25	23 52	25 20
60	16 15	17 02	17 53	21 00	22 23	23 48	25 13
N 58	16 25	17 09	17 56	21 01	22 22	23 44	25 06
56	16 33	17 15	18 00	21 02	22 21	23 40	25 00
54	16 41	17 20	18 03	21 04	22 20	23 37	24 55
52	16 48	17 25	18 05	21 05	22 19	23 34	24 50
50	16 54	17 29	18 08	21 05	22 18	23 32	24 46
45	17 08	17 39	18 14	21 07	22 16	23 26	24 37
N 40	17 19	17 48	18 20	21 09	22 15	23 22	24 29
35	17 29	17 55	18 26	21 10	22 14	23 18	24 22
30	17 37	18 02	18 31	21 12	22 12	23 14	24 17
20	17 52	18 15	18 41	21 14	22 10	23 08	24 07
N 10	18 05	18 27	18 52	21 15	22 09	23 03	23 58
0	18 17	18 39	19 04	21 17	22 07	22 58	23 50
S 10	18 29	18 51	19 17	21 19	22 05	22 53	23 42
20	18 43	19 06	19 34	21 20	22 03	22 47	23 33
30	18 58	19 24	19 54	21 22	22 01	22 41	23 23
35	19 07	19 35	20 08	21 23	22 00	22 38	23 18
40	19 17	19 47	20 24	21 25	21 59	22 34	23 11
45	19 29	20 03	20 44	21 26	21 57	22 29	23 04
S 50	19 44	20 22	21 11	21 28	21 55	22 24	22 55
52	19 51	20 31	21 25	21 28	21 54	22 21	22 51
54	19 59	20 42	21 41	21 29	21 53	22 18	22 46
56	20 07	20 54	22 01	21 30	21 52	22 15	22 41
58	20 17	21 08	22 27	21 31	21 51	22 12	22 35
S 60	20 29	21 26	23 07	21 32	21 50	22 08	22 29

Day	SUN Eqn. of Time 00^h	SUN Eqn. of Time 12^h	SUN Mer. Pass.	MOON Mer. Pass. Upper	MOON Mer. Pass. Lower	MOON Age	MOON Phase
d	m s	m s	h m	h m	h m	d	%
31	13 23	13 28	12 13	15 05	02 40	03	13
1	13 32	13 36	12 14	15 55	03 30	04	22
2	13 40	13 43	12 14	16 45	04 20	05	32

	UT d h	ARIES GHA ° ′	VENUS −4·8 GHA ° ′	VENUS Dec ° ′	MARS +1·1 GHA ° ′	MARS Dec ° ′	JUPITER −2·2 GHA ° ′	JUPITER Dec ° ′	SATURN +0·5 GHA ° ′	SATURN Dec ° ′
	3 00	133 21.8	134 39.8	N 1 40.5	129 16.9	N 1 23.6	291 26.4	S 7 40.3	228 59.2	S22 02.8
	01	148 24.2	149 40.6	41.7	144 17.6	24.4	306 28.8	40.3	244 01.4	02.8
	02	163 26.7	164 41.3	42.8	159 18.4	25.2	321 31.2	40.3	259 03.6	02.8
	03	178 29.2	179 42.1	. . 43.9	174 19.2	. . 26.0	336 33.7	. . 40.3	274 05.8	. . 02.8
	04	193 31.6	194 42.9	45.0	189 20.0	26.7	351 36.1	40.3	289 08.1	02.9
	05	208 34.1	209 43.7	46.2	204 20.7	27.5	6 38.5	40.3	304 10.3	02.9
	06	223 36.5	224 44.5	N 1 47.3	219 21.5	N 1 28.3	21 41.0	S 7 40.3	319 12.5	S22 02.9
	07	238 39.0	239 45.3	48.4	234 22.3	29.0	36 43.4	40.3	334 14.7	02.9
	08	253 41.5	254 46.1	49.6	249 23.0	29.8	51 45.9	40.3	349 17.0	02.9
F	09	268 43.9	269 46.8	. . 50.7	264 23.8	. . 30.6	66 48.3	. . 40.3	4 19.2	. . 02.9
R	10	283 46.4	284 47.6	51.8	279 24.6	31.4	81 50.7	40.3	19 21.4	02.9
I	11	298 48.9	299 48.4	52.9	294 25.3	32.1	96 53.2	40.3	34 23.6	02.9
D	12	313 51.3	314 49.2	N 1 54.0	309 26.1	N 1 32.9	111 55.6	S 7 40.3	49 25.9	S22 02.9
A	13	328 53.8	329 50.0	55.2	324 26.9	33.7	126 58.1	40.3	64 28.1	02.9
Y	14	343 56.3	344 50.8	56.3	339 27.7	34.5	142 00.5	40.3	79 30.3	02.9
	15	358 58.7	359 51.6	. . 57.4	354 28.4	. . 35.2	157 02.9	. . 40.3	94 32.5	. . 02.9
	16	14 01.2	14 52.4	58.5	9 29.2	36.0	172 05.4	40.3	109 34.7	02.9
	17	29 03.7	29 53.2	1 59.7	24 30.0	36.8	187 07.8	40.3	124 37.0	02.9
	18	44 06.1	44 54.0	N 2 00.8	39 30.7	N 1 37.5	202 10.3	S 7 40.3	139 39.2	S22 03.0
	19	59 08.6	59 54.8	01.9	54 31.5	38.3	217 12.7	40.3	154 41.4	03.0
	20	74 11.0	74 55.6	03.0	69 32.3	39.1	232 15.1	40.3	169 43.6	03.0
	21	89 13.5	89 56.5	. . 04.1	84 33.1	. . 39.9	247 17.6	. . 40.3	184 45.9	. . 03.0
	22	104 16.0	104 57.3	05.3	99 33.8	40.6	262 20.0	40.3	199 48.1	03.0
	23	119 18.4	119 58.1	06.4	114 34.6	41.4	277 22.5	40.3	214 50.3	03.0
	4 00	134 20.9	134 58.9	N 2 07.5	129 35.4	N 1 42.2	292 24.9	S 7 40.3	229 52.5	S22 03.0
	01	149 23.4	149 59.7	08.6	144 36.1	42.9	307 27.4	40.2	244 54.8	03.0
	02	164 25.8	165 00.5	09.7	159 36.9	43.7	322 29.8	40.2	259 57.0	03.0
	03	179 28.3	180 01.3	. . 10.8	174 37.7	. . 44.5	337 32.2	. . 40.2	274 59.2	. . 03.0
	04	194 30.8	195 02.2	12.0	189 38.5	45.3	352 34.7	40.2	290 01.4	03.0
	05	209 33.2	210 03.0	13.1	204 39.2	46.0	7 37.1	40.2	305 03.7	03.0
	06	224 35.7	225 03.8	N 2 14.2	219 40.0	N 1 46.8	22 39.6	S 7 40.2	320 05.9	S22 03.0
S	07	239 38.1	240 04.6	15.3	234 40.8	47.6	37 42.0	40.2	335 08.1	03.0
	08	254 40.6	255 05.5	16.4	249 41.5	48.3	52 44.5	40.2	350 10.3	03.1
A	09	269 43.1	270 06.3	. . 17.5	264 42.3	. . 49.1	67 46.9	. . 40.2	5 12.6	. . 03.1
T	10	284 45.5	285 07.1	18.6	279 43.1	49.9	82 49.4	40.2	20 14.8	03.1
U	11	299 48.0	300 08.0	19.8	294 43.9	50.7	97 51.8	40.2	35 17.0	03.1
R	12	314 50.5	315 08.8	N 2 20.9	309 44.6	N 1 51.4	112 54.3	S 7 40.2	50 19.2	S22 03.1
D	13	329 52.9	330 09.6	22.0	324 45.4	52.2	127 56.7	40.2	65 21.5	03.1
A	14	344 55.4	345 10.5	23.1	339 46.2	53.0	142 59.2	40.2	80 23.7	03.1
Y	15	359 57.9	0 11.3	. . 24.2	354 46.9	. . 53.7	158 01.6	. . 40.2	95 25.9	. . 03.1
	16	15 00.3	15 12.1	25.3	9 47.7	54.5	173 04.0	40.2	110 28.2	03.1
	17	30 02.8	30 13.0	26.4	24 48.5	55.3	188 06.5	40.2	125 30.4	03.1
	18	45 05.3	45 13.8	N 2 27.5	39 49.3	N 1 56.0	203 08.9	S 7 40.2	140 32.6	S22 03.1
	19	60 07.7	60 14.7	28.7	54 50.0	56.8	218 11.4	40.2	155 34.8	03.1
	20	75 10.2	75 15.5	29.8	69 50.8	57.6	233 13.8	40.2	170 37.1	03.1
	21	90 12.6	90 16.4	. . 30.9	84 51.6	. . 58.4	248 16.3	. . 40.2	185 39.3	. . 03.1
	22	105 15.1	105 17.2	32.0	99 52.3	59.1	263 18.7	40.2	200 41.5	03.2
	23	120 17.6	120 18.1	33.1	114 53.1	1 59.9	278 21.2	40.1	215 43.7	03.2
	5 00	135 20.0	135 18.9	N 2 34.2	129 53.9	N 2 00.7	293 23.6	S 7 40.1	230 46.0	S22 03.2
	01	150 22.5	150 19.8	35.3	144 54.7	01.4	308 26.1	40.1	245 48.2	03.2
	02	165 25.0	165 20.6	36.4	159 55.4	02.2	323 28.5	40.1	260 50.4	03.2
	03	180 27.4	180 21.5	. . 37.5	174 56.2	. . 03.0	338 31.0	. . 40.1	275 52.7	. . 03.2
	04	195 29.9	195 22.3	38.6	189 57.0	03.8	353 33.5	40.1	290 54.9	03.2
	05	210 32.4	210 23.2	39.7	204 57.7	04.5	8 35.9	40.1	305 57.1	03.2
	06	225 34.8	225 24.1	N 2 40.8	219 58.5	N 2 05.3	23 38.4	S 7 40.1	320 59.3	S22 03.2
	07	240 37.3	240 24.9	41.9	234 59.3	06.1	38 40.8	40.1	336 01.6	03.2
	08	255 39.8	255 25.8	43.0	250 00.1	06.8	53 43.3	40.1	351 03.8	03.2
S	09	270 42.2	270 26.7	. . 44.1	265 00.8	. . 07.6	68 45.7	. . 40.1	6 06.0	. . 03.2
U	10	285 44.7	285 27.5	45.2	280 01.6	08.4	83 48.2	40.1	21 08.3	03.2
N	11	300 47.1	300 28.4	46.3	295 02.4	09.1	98 50.6	40.1	36 10.5	03.2
D	12	315 49.6	315 29.3	N 2 47.4	310 03.1	N 2 09.9	113 53.1	S 7 40.1	51 12.7	S22 03.2
A	13	330 52.1	330 30.2	48.5	325 03.9	10.7	128 55.5	40.1	66 14.9	03.3
Y	14	345 54.5	345 31.0	49.6	340 04.7	11.4	143 58.0	40.0	81 17.2	03.3
	15	0 57.0	0 31.9	. . 50.7	355 05.5	. . 12.2	159 00.4	. . 40.0	96 19.4	. . 03.3
	16	15 59.5	15 32.8	51.8	10 06.2	13.0	174 02.9	40.0	111 21.6	03.3
	17	31 01.9	30 33.7	52.9	25 07.0	13.8	189 05.4	40.0	126 23.9	03.3
	18	46 04.4	45 34.6	N 2 54.0	40 07.8	N 2 14.5	204 07.8	S 7 40.0	141 26.1	S22 03.3
	19	61 06.9	60 35.4	55.1	55 08.5	15.3	219 10.3	40.0	156 28.3	03.3
	20	76 09.3	75 36.3	56.2	70 09.3	16.1	234 12.7	40.0	171 30.5	03.3
	21	91 11.8	90 37.2	. . 57.3	85 10.1	. . 16.8	249 15.2	. . 40.0	186 32.8	. . 03.3
	22	106 14.2	105 38.1	58.4	100 10.9	17.6	264 17.6	40.0	201 35.0	03.3
	23	121 16.7	120 39.0	59.5	115 11.6	18.4	279 20.1	40.0	216 37.2	03.3
	Mer. Pass.	h m 15 00.1	*v* 0.8	*d* 1.1	*v* 0.8	*d* 0.8	*v* 2.4	*d* 0.0	*v* 2.2	*d* 0.0

STARS

Name	SHA ° ′	Dec ° ′
Acamar	315 16.5	S40 14.6
Achernar	335 25.2	S57 09.4
Acrux	173 05.9	S63 11.4
Adhara	255 10.2	S29 00.1
Aldebaran	290 46.4	N16 32.4
Alioth	166 18.3	N55 51.8
Alkaid	152 56.9	N49 13.5
Al Na'ir	27 41.2	S46 52.8
Alnilam	275 43.7	S 1 11.8
Alphard	217 53.3	S 8 44.1
Alphecca	126 09.0	N26 39.4
Alpheratz	357 41.1	N29 11.1
Altair	62 06.1	N 8 54.9
Ankaa	353 13.6	S42 13.1
Antares	112 23.4	S26 27.9
Arcturus	145 53.5	N19 05.6
Atria	107 23.2	S69 03.0
Avior	234 16.3	S59 34.1
Bellatrix	278 29.2	N 6 21.6
Betelgeuse	270 58.4	N 7 24.3
Canopus	263 54.6	S52 42.7
Capella	280 30.5	N46 00.8
Deneb	49 30.2	N45 20.5
Denebola	182 30.9	N14 28.5
Diphda	348 53.6	S17 53.8
Dubhe	193 48.3	N61 39.3
Elnath	278 09.3	N28 37.1
Eltanin	90 45.4	N51 29.1
Enif	33 45.0	N 9 57.2
Fomalhaut	15 21.6	S29 32.1
Gacrux	171 57.7	S57 12.3
Gienah	175 49.5	S17 38.2
Hadar	148 44.1	S60 26.9
Hamal	327 58.0	N23 32.5
Kaus Aust.	83 40.9	S34 22.3
Kochab	137 20.3	N74 04.9
Markab	13 36.1	N15 17.8
Menkar	314 12.5	N 4 09.1
Menkent	148 04.5	S36 27.0
Miaplacidus	221 38.1	S69 47.3
Mirfak	308 36.7	N49 55.3
Nunki	75 55.6	S26 16.3
Peacock	53 16.0	S56 40.7
Pollux	243 24.4	N27 58.9
Procyon	244 56.9	N 5 10.6
Rasalhague	96 04.4	N12 32.9
Regulus	207 40.6	N11 52.8
Rigel	281 09.5	S 8 11.3
Rigil Kent.	139 48.2	S60 53.9
Sabik	102 09.9	S15 44.6
Schedar	349 37.9	N56 38.0
Shaula	96 18.8	S37 06.7
Sirius	258 31.3	S16 44.7
Spica	158 28.5	S11 14.9
Suhail	222 50.1	S43 30.3
Vega	80 37.6	N38 48.0
Zuben'ubi	137 02.7	S16 06.6

	SHA ° ′	Mer. Pass. h m
Venus	0 38.0	14 59
Mars	355 14.5	15 21
Jupiter	158 04.0	4 30
Saturn	95 31.6	8 39

UT		SUN GHA	SUN Dec	MOON GHA	v	MOON Dec	d	HP
d	h	° ′	° ′	° ′	′	° ′	′	′
3 FRIDAY	00	176 33.3	S16 31.5	104 55.4	9.9	N 7 02.0	10.5	58.9
	01	191 33.2	30.8	119 24.3	9.8	7 12.5	10.5	58.9
	02	206 33.2	30.0	133 53.1	9.8	7 23.0	10.4	58.9
	03	221 33.1	. . 29.3	148 21.9	9.8	7 33.4	10.4	58.9
	04	236 33.0	28.6	162 50.7	9.7	7 43.8	10.4	58.9
	05	251 33.0	27.8	177 19.4	9.7	7 54.2	10.3	58.9
	06	266 32.9	S16 27.1	191 48.1	9.7	N 8 04.5	10.3	58.9
	07	281 32.8	26.3	206 16.8	9.6	8 14.8	10.2	58.9
	08	296 32.8	25.6	220 45.4	9.6	8 25.0	10.2	59.0
	09	311 32.7	. . 24.9	235 14.0	9.5	8 35.2	10.1	59.0
	10	326 32.6	24.1	249 42.5	9.5	8 45.3	10.1	59.0
	11	341 32.6	23.4	264 11.0	9.4	8 55.4	10.1	59.0
	12	356 32.5	S16 22.6	278 39.4	9.4	N 9 05.5	10.0	59.0
	13	11 32.5	21.9	293 07.8	9.3	9 15.5	9.9	59.0
	14	26 32.4	21.2	307 36.1	9.4	9 25.4	9.9	59.0
	15	41 32.3	. . 20.4	322 04.5	9.2	9 35.3	9.9	59.0
	16	56 32.3	19.7	336 32.7	9.2	9 45.2	9.8	59.0
	17	71 32.2	18.9	351 00.9	9.2	9 55.0	9.7	59.1
	18	86 32.1	S16 18.2	5 29.1	9.1	N10 04.7	9.7	59.1
	19	101 32.1	17.4	19 57.2	9.1	10 14.4	9.6	59.1
	20	116 32.0	16.7	34 25.3	9.0	10 24.0	9.6	59.1
	21	131 32.0	. . 16.0	48 53.3	9.0	10 33.6	9.5	59.1
	22	146 31.9	15.2	63 21.3	9.0	10 43.1	9.4	59.1
	23	161 31.8	14.5	77 49.3	8.9	10 52.5	9.4	59.1
4 SATURDAY	00	176 31.8	S16 13.7	92 17.2	8.8	N11 01.9	9.3	59.1
	01	191 31.7	13.0	106 45.0	8.8	11 11.2	9.3	59.1
	02	206 31.7	12.2	121 12.8	8.8	11 20.5	9.2	59.1
	03	221 31.6	. . 11.5	135 40.6	8.6	11 29.7	9.1	59.2
	04	236 31.6	10.7	150 08.2	8.7	11 38.8	9.0	59.2
	05	251 31.5	10.0	164 35.9	8.6	11 47.8	9.0	59.2
	06	266 31.4	S16 09.2	179 03.5	8.6	N11 56.8	9.0	59.2
	07	281 31.4	08.5	193 31.1	8.5	12 05.8	8.8	59.2
	08	296 31.3	07.7	207 58.6	8.4	12 14.6	8.8	59.2
	09	311 31.3	. . 07.0	222 26.0	8.4	12 23.4	8.7	59.2
	10	326 31.2	06.2	236 53.4	8.4	12 32.1	8.7	59.2
	11	341 31.2	05.5	251 20.8	8.3	12 40.8	8.5	59.2
	12	356 31.1	S16 04.7	265 48.1	8.2	N12 49.3	8.5	59.2
	13	11 31.0	04.0	280 15.3	8.2	12 57.8	8.4	59.2
	14	26 31.0	03.2	294 42.5	8.2	13 06.2	8.3	59.2
	15	41 30.9	. . 02.5	309 09.7	8.1	13 14.5	8.3	59.3
	16	56 30.9	01.7	323 36.8	8.0	13 22.8	8.2	59.3
	17	71 30.8	00.9	338 03.8	8.1	13 31.0	8.1	59.3
	18	86 30.8	S16 00.2	352 30.9	7.9	N13 39.1	8.0	59.3
	19	101 30.7	15 59.4	6 57.8	7.9	13 47.1	7.9	59.3
	20	116 30.7	58.7	21 24.7	7.9	13 55.0	7.9	59.3
	21	131 30.6	. . 57.9	35 51.6	7.8	14 02.9	7.7	59.3
	22	146 30.6	57.2	50 18.4	7.7	14 10.6	7.7	59.3
	23	161 30.5	56.4	64 45.1	7.7	14 18.3	7.6	59.3
5 SUNDAY	00	176 30.5	S15 55.6	79 11.8	7.7	N14 25.9	7.5	59.3
	01	191 30.4	54.9	93 38.5	7.6	14 33.4	7.4	59.3
	02	206 30.4	54.1	108 05.1	7.6	14 40.8	7.3	59.3
	03	221 30.3	. . 53.4	122 31.7	7.5	14 48.1	7.2	59.3
	04	236 30.3	52.6	136 58.2	7.4	14 55.3	7.2	59.3
	05	251 30.2	51.8	151 24.6	7.4	15 02.5	7.0	59.4
	06	266 30.2	S15 51.1	165 51.0	7.4	N15 09.5	7.0	59.4
	07	281 30.1	50.3	180 17.4	7.3	15 16.5	6.8	59.4
	08	296 30.1	49.6	194 43.7	7.3	15 23.3	6.8	59.4
	09	311 30.0	. . 48.8	209 10.0	7.2	15 30.1	6.7	59.4
	10	326 30.0	48.0	223 36.2	7.2	15 36.8	6.5	59.4
	11	341 29.9	47.3	238 02.4	7.1	15 43.3	6.5	59.4
	12	356 29.9	S15 46.5	252 28.5	7.1	N15 49.8	6.4	59.4
	13	11 29.8	45.7	266 54.6	7.0	15 56.2	6.2	59.4
	14	26 29.8	45.0	281 20.6	7.0	16 02.4	6.2	59.4
	15	41 29.8	. . 44.2	295 46.6	7.0	16 08.6	6.1	59.4
	16	56 29.7	43.4	310 12.6	6.9	16 14.7	5.9	59.4
	17	71 29.7	42.7	324 38.5	6.8	16 20.6	5.9	59.4
	18	86 29.6	S15 41.9	339 04.3	6.9	N16 26.5	5.7	59.4
	19	101 29.6	41.1	353 30.2	6.7	16 32.2	5.7	59.4
	20	116 29.5	40.4	7 55.9	6.8	16 37.9	5.5	59.4
	21	131 29.5	. . 39.6	22 21.7	6.6	16 43.4	5.4	59.4
	22	146 29.5	38.8	36 47.3	6.7	16 48.8	5.4	59.4
	23	161 29.4	38.1	51 13.0	6.6	N16 54.2	5.2	59.4
		SD 16.3	*d* 0.8	SD	16.1	16.1		16.2

Lat.	Twilight Naut.	Twilight Civil	Sunrise	Moonrise 3	Moonrise 4	Moonrise 5	Moonrise 6
°	h m	h m	h m	h m	h m	h m	h m
N 72	06 58	08 24	10 02	09 30	09 23	09 13	08 52
N 70	06 51	08 08	09 28	09 43	09 44	09 48	09 58
68	06 46	07 55	09 04	09 53	10 01	10 13	10 34
66	06 41	07 44	08 45	10 02	10 14	10 33	11 00
64	06 37	07 35	08 30	10 09	10 26	10 48	11 20
62	06 33	07 27	08 17	10 15	10 36	11 02	11 37
60	06 30	07 20	08 06	10 21	10 44	11 13	11 50
N 58	06 26	07 14	07 57	10 26	10 51	11 23	12 02
56	06 24	07 08	07 49	10 30	10 58	11 31	12 12
54	06 21	07 03	07 41	10 34	11 04	11 39	12 22
52	06 18	06 59	07 35	10 37	11 09	11 46	12 30
50	06 16	06 54	07 29	10 41	11 14	11 52	12 37
45	06 10	06 45	07 16	10 48	11 24	12 05	12 53
N 40	06 05	06 37	07 05	10 54	11 33	12 16	13 05
35	06 00	06 30	06 56	10 59	11 40	12 26	13 16
30	05 55	06 23	06 48	11 03	11 47	12 34	13 26
20	05 45	06 12	06 34	11 11	11 58	12 49	13 43
N 10	05 35	06 00	06 22	11 18	12 09	13 02	13 57
0	05 24	05 49	06 10	11 25	12 18	13 14	14 11
S 10	05 11	05 37	05 59	11 31	12 28	13 26	14 25
20	04 55	05 23	05 46	11 39	12 38	13 38	14 39
30	04 35	05 06	05 31	11 47	12 50	13 53	14 56
35	04 22	04 55	05 23	11 51	12 57	14 02	15 06
40	04 07	04 43	05 13	11 57	13 05	14 12	15 17
45	03 47	04 28	05 01	12 03	13 14	14 23	15 31
S 50	03 22	04 10	04 47	12 11	13 25	14 38	15 47
52	03 09	04 01	04 41	12 14	13 30	14 44	15 54
54	02 53	03 51	04 33	12 18	13 36	14 52	16 03
56	02 34	03 39	04 25	12 23	13 42	15 00	16 12
58	02 10	03 26	04 16	12 27	13 49	15 09	16 23
S 60	01 36	03 09	04 05	12 33	13 57	15 20	16 36

Lat.	Sunset	Twilight Civil	Twilight Naut.	Moonset 3	Moonset 4	Moonset 5	Moonset 6
°	h m	h m	h m	h m	h m	h m	h m
N 72	14 27	16 05	17 32	00 30	02 27	04 32	06 51
N 70	15 01	16 22	17 38	00 19	02 07	03 58	05 46
68	15 25	16 35	17 43	00 10	01 52	03 33	05 10
66	15 44	16 45	17 48	00 03	01 39	03 14	04 45
64	15 59	16 54	17 52	25 29	01 29	02 59	04 25
62	16 12	17 02	17 56	25 20	01 20	02 47	04 09
60	16 23	17 09	17 59	25 13	01 13	02 36	03 56
N 58	16 32	17 15	18 02	25 06	01 06	02 27	03 44
56	16 40	17 21	18 05	25 00	01 00	02 19	03 34
54	16 47	17 25	18 08	24 55	00 55	02 12	03 25
52	16 54	17 30	18 10	24 50	00 50	02 05	03 18
50	17 00	17 34	18 13	24 46	00 46	01 59	03 11
45	17 12	17 43	18 18	24 37	00 37	01 47	02 55
N 40	17 23	17 51	18 24	24 29	00 29	01 37	02 43
35	17 32	17 58	18 28	24 22	00 22	01 28	02 33
30	17 40	18 05	18 33	24 17	00 17	01 20	02 23
20	17 54	18 17	18 43	24 07	00 07	01 07	02 07
N 10	18 06	18 28	18 53	23 58	24 55	00 55	01 54
0	18 17	18 39	19 04	23 50	24 44	00 44	01 41
S 10	18 29	18 51	19 17	23 42	24 33	00 33	01 28
20	18 42	19 05	19 32	23 33	24 22	00 22	01 14
30	18 56	19 22	19 52	23 23	24 09	00 09	00 58
35	19 05	19 32	20 05	23 18	24 01	00 01	00 49
40	19 14	19 44	20 20	23 11	23 52	24 38	00 38
45	19 26	19 58	20 39	23 04	23 42	24 26	00 26
S 50	19 40	20 17	21 05	22 55	23 30	24 11	00 11
52	19 46	20 25	21 17	22 51	23 24	24 04	00 04
54	19 53	20 35	21 32	22 46	23 18	23 57	24 44
56	20 01	20 47	21 51	22 41	23 11	23 48	24 34
58	20 10	21 00	22 14	22 35	23 03	23 38	24 23
S 60	20 21	21 16	22 46	22 29	22 55	23 27	24 10

Day	SUN Eqn. of Time 00^h	SUN Eqn. of Time 12^h	SUN Mer. Pass.	MOON Mer. Pass. Upper	MOON Mer. Pass. Lower	MOON Age	MOON Phase
d	m s	m s	h m	h m	h m	d %	
3	13 47	13 50	12 14	17 37	05 11	06 42	
4	13 53	13 55	12 14	18 31	06 04	07 54	
5	13 58	14 00	12 14	19 27	06 59	08 65	

2017 FEBRUARY 6, 7, 8 (MON., TUES., WED.)

UT d h	ARIES GHA ° ′	VENUS −4·8 GHA ° ′	VENUS Dec ° ′	MARS +1·2 GHA ° ′	MARS Dec ° ′	JUPITER −2·2 GHA ° ′	JUPITER Dec ° ′	SATURN +0·5 GHA ° ′	SATURN Dec ° ′	STARS Name	SHA ° ′	Dec ° ′
6 00	136 19.2	135 39.9	N 3 00.6	130 12.4	N 2 19.1	294 22.6	S 7 40.0	231 39.5	S22 03.3	Acamar	315 16.5	S40 14.6
01	151 21.6	150 40.8	01.7	145 13.2	19.9	309 25.0	40.0	246 41.7	03.3	Achernar	335 25.3	S57 09.4
02	166 24.1	165 41.7	02.8	160 14.0	20.7	324 27.5	39.9	261 43.9	03.3	Acrux	173 05.9	S63 11.4
03	181 26.6	180 42.6	03.9	175 14.7	21.4	339 29.9	39.9	276 46.2	03.3	Adhara	255 10.3	S29 00.1
04	196 29.0	195 43.5	05.0	190 15.5	22.2	354 32.4	39.9	291 48.4	03.4	Aldebaran	290 46.4	N16 32.4
05	211 31.5	210 44.4	06.1	205 16.3	23.0	9 34.8	39.9	306 50.6	03.4			
06	226 34.0	225 45.3	N 3 07.2	220 17.0	N 2 23.7	24 37.3	S 7 39.9	321 52.9	S22 03.4	Alioth	166 18.3	N55 51.8
07	241 36.4	240 46.2	08.3	235 17.8	24.5	39 39.8	39.9	336 55.1	03.4	Alkaid	152 56.9	N49 13.5
08	256 38.9	255 47.1	09.4	250 18.6	25.3	54 42.2	39.9	351 57.3	03.4	Al Na'ir	27 41.2	S46 52.8
M 09	271 41.4	270 48.0	10.5	265 19.4	26.0	69 44.7	39.9	6 59.5	03.4	Alnilam	275 43.7	S 1 11.8
O 10	286 43.8	285 48.9	11.6	280 20.1	26.8	84 47.1	39.9	22 01.8	03.4	Alphard	217 53.3	S 8 44.2
N 11	301 46.3	300 49.8	12.6	295 20.9	27.6	99 49.6	39.9	37 04.0	03.4			
D 12	316 48.7	315 50.7	N 3 13.7	310 21.7	N 2 28.3	114 52.1	S 7 39.9	52 06.2	S22 03.4	Alphecca	126 09.0	N26 39.4
A 13	331 51.2	330 51.7	14.8	325 22.4	29.1	129 54.5	39.8	67 08.5	03.4	Alpheratz	357 41.1	N29 11.1
Y 14	346 53.7	345 52.6	15.9	340 23.2	29.9	144 57.0	39.8	82 10.7	03.4	Altair	62 06.1	N 8 54.9
15	1 56.1	0 53.5	17.0	355 24.0	30.6	159 59.5	39.8	97 12.9	03.4	Ankaa	353 13.6	S42 13.1
16	16 58.6	15 54.4	18.1	10 24.8	31.4	175 01.9	39.8	112 15.2	03.4	Antares	112 23.3	S26 27.9
17	32 01.1	30 55.3	19.2	25 25.5	32.2	190 04.4	39.8	127 17.4	03.4			
18	47 03.5	45 56.3	N 3 20.3	40 26.3	N 2 33.0	205 06.8	S 7 39.8	142 19.6	S22 03.4	Arcturus	145 53.4	N19 05.5
19	62 06.0	60 57.2	21.3	55 27.1	33.7	220 09.3	39.8	157 21.9	03.4	Atria	107 23.2	S69 03.0
20	77 08.5	75 58.1	22.4	70 27.9	34.5	235 11.8	39.8	172 24.1	03.5	Avior	234 16.3	S59 34.1
21	92 10.9	90 59.0	23.5	85 28.6	35.3	250 14.2	39.8	187 26.3	03.5	Bellatrix	278 29.2	N 6 21.6
22	107 13.4	106 00.0	24.6	100 29.4	36.0	265 16.7	39.7	202 28.6	03.5	Betelgeuse	270 58.4	N 7 24.3
23	122 15.9	121 00.9	25.7	115 30.2	36.8	280 19.2	39.7	217 30.8	03.5			
7 00	137 18.3	136 01.8	N 3 26.8	130 30.9	N 2 37.6	295 21.6	S 7 39.7	232 33.0	S22 03.5	Canopus	263 54.6	S52 42.7
01	152 20.8	151 02.8	27.8	145 31.7	38.3	310 24.1	39.7	247 35.3	03.5	Capella	280 30.5	N46 00.8
02	167 23.2	166 03.7	28.9	160 32.5	39.1	325 26.6	39.7	262 37.5	03.5	Deneb	49 30.2	N45 20.5
03	182 25.7	181 04.7	30.0	175 33.3	39.9	340 29.0	39.7	277 39.7	03.5	Denebola	182 30.9	N14 28.5
04	197 28.2	196 05.6	31.1	190 34.0	40.6	355 31.5	39.7	292 42.0	03.5	Diphda	348 53.6	S17 53.8
05	212 30.6	211 06.5	32.2	205 34.8	41.4	10 34.0	39.7	307 44.2	03.5			
06	227 33.1	226 07.5	N 3 33.3	220 35.6	N 2 42.2	25 36.4	S 7 39.6	322 46.4	S22 03.5	Dubhe	193 48.2	N61 39.3
07	242 35.6	241 08.4	34.3	235 36.4	42.9	40 38.9	39.6	337 48.7	03.5	Elnath	278 09.3	N28 37.1
T 08	257 38.0	256 09.4	35.4	250 37.1	43.7	55 41.4	39.6	352 50.9	03.5	Eltanin	90 45.4	N51 29.1
U 09	272 40.5	271 10.3	36.5	265 37.9	44.5	70 43.8	39.6	7 53.1	03.5	Enif	33 45.0	N 9 57.2
E 10	287 43.0	286 11.3	37.6	280 38.7	45.2	85 46.3	39.6	22 55.4	03.5	Fomalhaut	15 21.6	S29 32.0
S 11	302 45.4	301 12.2	38.6	295 39.4	46.0	100 48.8	39.6	37 57.6	03.5			
D 12	317 47.9	316 13.2	N 3 39.7	310 40.2	N 2 46.7	115 51.2	S 7 39.6	52 59.8	S22 03.6	Gacrux	171 57.6	S57 12.3
A 13	332 50.4	331 14.2	40.8	325 41.0	47.5	130 53.7	39.6	68 02.1	03.6	Gienah	175 49.5	S17 38.2
Y 14	347 52.8	346 15.1	41.9	340 41.8	48.3	145 56.2	39.5	83 04.3	03.6	Hadar	148 44.1	S60 26.9
15	2 55.3	1 16.1	42.9	355 42.5	49.0	160 58.7	39.5	98 06.6	03.6	Hamal	327 58.0	N23 32.5
16	17 57.7	16 17.0	44.0	10 43.3	49.8	176 01.1	39.5	113 08.8	03.6	Kaus Aust.	83 40.8	S34 22.3
17	33 00.2	31 18.0	45.1	25 44.1	50.6	191 03.6	39.5	128 11.0	03.6			
18	48 02.7	46 19.0	N 3 46.2	40 44.9	N 2 51.3	206 06.1	S 7 39.5	143 13.3	S22 03.6	Kochab	137 20.2	N74 04.9
19	63 05.1	61 19.9	47.2	55 45.6	52.1	221 08.5	39.5	158 15.5	03.6	Markab	13 36.1	N15 17.8
20	78 07.6	76 20.9	48.3	70 46.4	52.9	236 11.0	39.5	173 17.7	03.6	Menkar	314 12.5	N 4 09.1
21	93 10.1	91 21.9	49.4	85 47.2	53.6	251 13.5	39.5	188 20.0	03.6	Menkent	148 04.5	S36 27.0
22	108 12.5	106 22.9	50.5	100 47.9	54.4	266 16.0	39.4	203 22.2	03.6	Miaplacidus	221 38.1	S69 47.4
23	123 15.0	121 23.8	51.5	115 48.7	55.2	281 18.4	39.4	218 24.4	03.6			
8 00	138 17.5	136 24.8	N 3 52.6	130 49.5	N 2 55.9	296 20.9	S 7 39.4	233 26.7	S22 03.6	Mirfak	308 36.7	N49 55.3
01	153 19.9	151 25.8	53.7	145 50.3	56.7	311 23.4	39.4	248 28.9	03.6	Nunki	75 55.6	S26 16.3
02	168 22.4	166 26.8	54.7	160 51.0	57.5	326 25.8	39.4	263 31.1	03.6	Peacock	53 16.0	S56 40.7
03	183 24.9	181 27.8	55.8	175 51.8	58.2	341 28.3	39.4	278 33.4	03.6	Pollux	243 24.4	N27 58.9
04	198 27.3	196 28.7	56.9	190 52.6	59.0	356 30.8	39.3	293 35.6	03.7	Procyon	244 56.9	N 5 10.6
05	213 29.8	211 29.7	57.9	205 53.4	2 59.8	11 33.3	39.3	308 37.9	03.7			
06	228 32.2	226 30.7	N 3 59.0	220 54.1	N 3 00.5	26 35.7	S 7 39.3	323 40.1	S22 03.7	Rasalhague	96 04.4	N12 32.9
W 07	243 34.7	241 31.7	4 00.1	235 54.9	01.3	41 38.2	39.3	338 42.3	03.7	Regulus	207 40.6	N11 52.8
E 08	258 37.2	256 32.7	01.1	250 55.7	02.0	56 40.7	39.3	353 44.6	03.7	Rigel	281 09.5	S 8 11.3
D 09	273 39.6	271 33.7	02.2	265 56.4	02.8	71 43.2	39.3	8 46.8	03.7	Rigil Kent.	139 48.2	S60 53.9
N 10	288 42.1	286 34.7	03.3	280 57.2	03.6	86 45.6	39.3	23 49.0	03.7	Sabik	102 09.9	S15 44.6
E 11	303 44.6	301 35.7	04.3	295 58.0	04.3	101 48.1	39.2	38 51.3	03.7			
S 12	318 47.0	316 36.7	N 4 05.4	310 58.8	N 3 05.1	116 50.6	S 7 39.2	53 53.5	S22 03.7	Schedar	349 37.9	N56 38.0
D 13	333 49.5	331 37.7	06.5	325 59.5	05.9	131 53.1	39.2	68 55.8	03.7	Shaula	96 18.8	S37 06.7
A 14	348 52.0	346 38.7	07.5	341 00.3	06.6	146 55.6	39.2	83 58.0	03.7	Sirius	258 31.3	S16 44.7
Y 15	3 54.4	1 39.7	08.6	356 01.1	07.4	161 58.0	39.2	99 00.2	03.7	Spica	158 28.5	S11 15.0
16	18 56.9	16 40.7	09.6	11 01.9	08.2	177 00.5	39.2	114 02.5	03.7	Suhail	222 50.1	S43 30.3
17	33 59.3	31 41.7	10.7	26 02.6	08.9	192 03.0	39.1	129 04.7	03.7			
18	49 01.8	46 42.7	N 4 11.8	41 03.4	N 3 09.7	207 05.5	S 7 39.1	144 07.0	S22 03.7	Vega	80 37.6	N38 48.0
19	64 04.3	61 43.7	12.8	56 04.2	10.4	222 07.9	39.1	159 09.2	03.7	Zuben'ubi	137 02.6	S16 06.6
20	79 06.7	76 44.8	13.9	71 05.0	11.2	237 10.4	39.1	174 11.4	03.7			
21	94 09.2	91 45.8	14.9	86 05.7	12.0	252 12.9	39.1	189 13.7	03.8			
22	109 11.7	106 46.8	16.0	101 06.5	12.7	267 15.4	39.1	204 15.9	03.8			
23	124 14.1	121 47.8	17.0	116 07.3	13.5	282 17.9	39.0	219 18.1	03.8			
Mer. Pass. (h m)	14 48.3	v 1.0	d 1.1	v 0.8	d 0.8	v 2.5	d 0.0	v 2.2	d 0.0			

	SHA ° ′	Mer. Pass. h m
Venus	358 43.5	14 55
Mars	353 12.6	15 17
Jupiter	158 03.3	4 18
Saturn	95 14.7	8 29

UT	SUN GHA	SUN Dec	MOON GHA	v	MOON Dec	d	HP
d h	° ′	° ′	° ′	′	° ′	′	′
6 00	176 29.4	S15 37.3	65 38.6	6.6	N16 59.4	5.1	59.4
01	191 29.3	36.5	80 04.2	6.5	17 04.5	5.0	59.4
02	206 29.3	35.8	94 29.7	6.5	17 09.5	4.9	59.4
03	221 29.2	. . 35.0	108 55.2	6.5	17 14.4	4.7	59.4
04	236 29.2	34.2	123 20.7	6.4	17 19.1	4.7	59.4
05	251 29.2	33.4	137 46.1	6.4	17 23.8	4.5	59.4
06	266 29.1	S15 32.7	152 11.5	6.3	N17 28.3	4.5	59.4
07	281 29.1	31.9	166 36.8	6.3	17 32.8	4.3	59.4
08	296 29.0	31.1	181 02.1	6.3	17 37.1	4.2	59.5
M 09	311 29.0	. . 30.4	195 27.4	6.3	17 41.3	4.1	59.5
O 10	326 29.0	29.6	209 52.7	6.2	17 45.4	4.0	59.5
N 11	341 28.9	28.8	224 17.9	6.2	17 49.4	3.8	59.5
D 12	356 28.9	S15 28.0	238 43.1	6.1	N17 53.2	3.7	59.5
A 13	11 28.9	27.3	253 08.2	6.2	17 56.9	3.7	59.5
Y 14	26 28.8	26.5	267 33.4	6.1	18 00.6	3.5	59.5
15	41 28.8	. . 25.7	281 58.5	6.0	18 04.1	3.3	59.5
16	56 28.7	24.9	296 23.5	6.1	18 07.4	3.3	59.5
17	71 28.7	24.1	310 48.6	6.0	18 10.7	3.1	59.5
18	86 28.7	S15 23.4	325 13.6	6.0	N18 13.8	3.0	59.5
19	101 28.6	22.6	339 38.6	6.0	18 16.8	2.9	59.5
20	116 28.6	21.8	354 03.6	6.0	18 19.7	2.8	59.5
21	131 28.6	. . 21.0	8 28.6	5.9	18 22.5	2.7	59.4
22	146 28.5	20.2	22 53.5	5.9	18 25.2	2.5	59.4
23	161 28.5	19.5	37 18.4	5.9	18 27.7	2.4	59.4
7 00	176 28.5	S15 18.7	51 43.3	5.9	N18 30.1	2.3	59.4
01	191 28.4	17.9	66 08.2	5.9	18 32.4	2.1	59.4
02	206 28.4	17.1	80 33.1	5.8	18 34.5	2.1	59.4
03	221 28.4	. . 16.3	94 57.9	5.9	18 36.6	1.9	59.4
04	236 28.3	15.6	109 22.8	5.8	18 38.5	1.7	59.4
05	251 28.3	14.8	123 47.6	5.8	18 40.2	1.7	59.4
06	266 28.3	S15 14.0	138 12.4	5.8	N18 41.9	1.5	59.4
07	281 28.2	13.2	152 37.2	5.8	18 43.4	1.4	59.4
T 08	296 28.2	12.4	167 02.0	5.8	18 44.8	1.3	59.4
U 09	311 28.2	. . 11.6	181 26.8	5.8	18 46.1	1.2	59.4
E 10	326 28.2	10.9	195 51.6	5.7	18 47.3	1.0	59.4
S 11	341 28.1	10.1	210 16.3	5.8	18 48.3	0.9	59.4
D 12	356 28.1	S15 09.3	224 41.1	5.8	N18 49.2	0.8	59.4
A 13	11 28.1	08.5	239 05.9	5.7	18 50.0	0.6	59.4
Y 14	26 28.0	07.7	253 30.6	5.8	18 50.6	0.6	59.4
15	41 28.0	. . 06.9	267 55.4	5.8	18 51.2	0.4	59.4
16	56 28.0	06.1	282 20.2	5.7	18 51.6	0.2	59.4
17	71 28.0	05.4	296 44.9	5.8	18 51.8	0.2	59.4
18	86 27.9	S15 04.6	311 09.7	5.8	N18 52.0	0.0	59.4
19	101 27.9	03.8	325 34.5	5.8	18 52.0	0.1	59.4
20	116 27.9	03.0	339 59.3	5.8	18 51.9	0.2	59.4
21	131 27.8	. . 02.2	354 24.1	5.7	18 51.7	0.4	59.3
22	146 27.8	01.4	8 48.8	5.9	18 51.3	0.5	59.3
23	161 27.8	15 00.6	23 13.7	5.8	18 50.8	0.6	59.3
8 00	176 27.8	S14 59.8	37 38.5	5.8	N18 50.2	0.7	59.3
01	191 27.7	59.0	52 03.3	5.8	18 49.5	0.9	59.3
02	206 27.7	58.2	66 28.1	5.9	18 48.6	1.0	59.3
03	221 27.7	. . 57.4	80 53.0	5.9	18 47.6	1.1	59.3
04	236 27.7	56.7	95 17.9	5.9	18 46.5	1.2	59.3
05	251 27.7	55.9	109 42.8	5.9	18 45.3	1.4	59.3
06	266 27.6	S14 55.1	124 07.7	5.9	N18 43.9	1.5	59.3
W 07	281 27.6	54.3	138 32.6	6.0	18 42.4	1.6	59.3
E 08	296 27.6	53.5	152 57.6	5.9	18 40.8	1.7	59.3
D 09	311 27.6	. . 52.7	167 22.5	6.0	18 39.1	1.9	59.2
N 10	326 27.5	51.9	181 47.5	6.1	18 37.2	2.0	59.2
E 11	341 27.5	51.1	196 12.6	6.0	18 35.2	2.1	59.2
S 12	356 27.5	S14 50.3	210 37.6	6.1	N18 33.1	2.2	59.2
D 13	11 27.5	49.5	225 02.7	6.1	18 30.9	2.3	59.2
A 14	26 27.5	48.7	239 27.8	6.1	18 28.6	2.5	59.2
Y 15	41 27.4	. . 47.9	253 52.9	6.2	18 26.1	2.6	59.2
16	56 27.4	47.1	268 18.1	6.2	18 23.5	2.7	59.2
17	71 27.4	46.3	282 43.3	6.2	18 20.8	2.8	59.2
18	86 27.4	S14 45.5	297 08.5	6.2	N18 18.0	3.0	59.1
19	101 27.4	44.7	311 33.7	6.3	18 15.0	3.0	59.1
20	116 27.3	43.9	325 59.0	6.4	18 12.0	3.2	59.1
21	131 27.3	. . 43.1	340 24.4	6.3	18 08.8	3.3	59.1
22	146 27.3	42.3	354 49.7	6.5	18 05.5	3.4	59.1
23	161 27.3	41.5	9 15.2	6.4	N18 02.1	3.6	59.1
	SD 16.2	*d* 0.8	SD	16.2	16.2		16.1

Lat.	Twilight Naut.	Twilight Civil	Sunrise	Moonrise 6	7	8	9
°	h m	h m	h m	h m	h m	h m	h m
N 72	06 46	08 10	09 42	08 52	▭	▭	12 14
N 70	06 41	07 56	09 12	09 58	10 26	11 32	13 09
68	06 37	07 44	08 51	10 34	11 13	12 17	13 43
66	06 33	07 35	08 34	11 00	11 43	12 46	14 07
64	06 29	07 26	08 20	11 20	12 06	13 09	14 26
62	06 26	07 19	08 09	11 37	12 24	13 27	14 41
60	06 23	07 13	07 59	11 50	12 40	13 41	14 54
N 58	06 21	07 08	07 50	12 02	12 52	13 54	15 05
56	06 18	07 03	07 42	12 12	13 04	14 05	15 15
54	06 16	06 58	07 36	12 22	13 13	14 14	15 23
52	06 14	06 54	07 30	12 30	13 22	14 23	15 31
50	06 12	06 50	07 24	12 37	13 30	14 31	15 37
45	06 07	06 41	07 12	12 53	13 47	14 47	15 52
N 40	06 02	06 34	07 02	13 05	14 00	15 00	16 04
35	05 58	06 27	06 54	13 16	14 12	15 12	16 14
30	05 53	06 21	06 46	13 26	14 22	15 22	16 23
20	05 44	06 10	06 33	13 43	14 40	15 39	16 39
N 10	05 35	06 00	06 22	13 57	14 55	15 54	16 52
0	05 24	05 49	06 11	14 11	15 09	16 08	17 05
S 10	05 12	05 38	06 00	14 25	15 24	16 22	17 17
20	04 57	05 25	05 48	14 39	15 39	16 37	17 31
30	04 38	05 08	05 34	14 56	15 57	16 54	17 46
35	04 26	04 59	05 26	15 06	16 07	17 04	17 55
40	04 11	04 47	05 17	15 17	16 19	17 15	18 05
45	03 53	04 33	05 06	15 31	16 33	17 29	18 17
S 50	03 29	04 16	04 53	15 47	16 50	17 45	18 31
52	03 17	04 07	04 46	15 54	16 58	17 52	18 38
54	03 02	03 58	04 40	16 03	17 07	18 01	18 46
56	02 45	03 47	04 32	16 12	17 17	18 11	18 54
58	02 24	03 35	04 23	16 23	17 28	18 21	19 03
S 60	01 55	03 20	04 13	16 36	17 41	18 34	19 14

Lat.	Sunset	Twilight Civil	Twilight Naut.	Moonset 6	7	8	9
°	h m	h m	h m	h m	h m	h m	h m
N 72	14 48	16 19	17 44	06 51	▭	▭	09 35
N 70	15 17	16 34	17 49	05 46	07 20	08 17	08 39
68	15 39	16 45	17 53	05 10	06 33	07 31	08 05
66	15 55	16 55	17 57	04 45	06 03	07 02	07 41
64	16 09	17 03	18 00	04 25	05 40	06 39	07 21
62	16 21	17 10	18 03	04 09	05 22	06 21	07 05
60	16 30	17 16	18 06	03 56	05 07	06 06	06 52
N 58	16 39	17 22	18 08	03 44	04 54	05 53	06 41
56	16 47	17 27	18 11	03 34	04 43	05 42	06 31
54	16 53	17 31	18 13	03 25	04 33	05 33	06 22
52	16 59	17 35	18 15	03 18	04 25	05 24	06 14
50	17 05	17 39	18 17	03 11	04 17	05 16	06 07
45	17 17	17 47	18 22	02 55	04 00	05 00	05 52
N 40	17 26	17 55	18 27	02 43	03 47	04 46	05 39
35	17 35	18 01	18 31	02 33	03 35	04 34	05 28
30	17 42	18 07	18 36	02 23	03 25	04 24	05 19
20	17 55	18 18	18 44	02 07	03 08	04 07	05 03
N 10	18 07	18 28	18 54	01 54	02 53	03 52	04 49
0	18 18	18 39	19 04	01 41	02 39	03 37	04 35
S 10	18 29	18 50	19 16	01 28	02 24	03 23	04 22
20	18 40	19 03	19 30	01 14	02 09	03 08	04 07
30	18 54	19 19	19 49	00 58	01 52	02 50	03 51
35	19 02	19 29	20 01	00 49	01 42	02 40	03 41
40	19 11	19 40	20 16	00 38	01 30	02 28	03 30
45	19 22	19 54	20 34	00 26	01 17	02 14	03 17
S 50	19 35	20 11	20 58	00 11	01 00	01 57	03 01
52	19 41	20 19	21 10	00 04	00 52	01 49	02 54
54	19 47	20 29	21 24	24 44	00 44	01 40	02 46
56	19 55	20 39	21 40	24 34	00 34	01 30	02 36
58	20 03	20 52	22 01	24 23	00 23	01 19	02 26
S 60	20 13	21 06	22 28	24 10	00 10	01 06	02 13

Day	SUN Eqn. of Time 00^h	SUN Eqn. of Time 12^h	SUN Mer. Pass.	MOON Mer. Pass. Upper	MOON Mer. Pass. Lower	MOON Age	MOON Phase
d	m s	m s	h m	h m	h m	d %	
6	14 02	14 04	12 14	20 25	07 56	09 76	
7	14 06	14 08	12 14	21 23	08 54	10 85	
8	14 09	14 10	12 14	22 22	09 53	11 92	

UT d	h	ARIES GHA	VENUS −4·8 GHA	VENUS Dec	MARS +1·2 GHA	MARS Dec	JUPITER −2·2 GHA	JUPITER Dec	SATURN +0·5 GHA	SATURN Dec
		° ′	° ′	° ′	° ′	° ′	° ′	° ′	° ′	° ′
9 THURSDAY	00	139 16.6	136 48.8	N 4 18.1	131 08.0	N 3 14.3	297 20.3	S 7 39.0	234 20.4	S22 03.8
	01	154 19.1	151 49.9	19.2	146 08.8	15.0	312 22.8	39.0	249 22.6	03.8
	02	169 21.5	166 50.9	20.2	161 09.6	15.8	327 25.3	39.0	264 24.9	03.8
	03	184 24.0	181 51.9	. . 21.3	176 10.4	. . 16.6	342 27.8	. . 39.0	279 27.1	. . 03.8
	04	199 26.5	196 52.9	22.3	191 11.1	17.3	357 30.3	39.0	294 29.3	03.8
	05	214 28.9	211 54.0	23.4	206 11.9	18.1	12 32.7	38.9	309 31.6	03.8
	06	229 31.4	226 55.0	N 4 24.4	221 12.7	N 3 18.8	27 35.2	S 7 38.9	324 33.8	S22 03.8
	07	244 33.8	241 56.0	25.5	236 13.5	19.6	42 37.7	38.9	339 36.1	03.8
	08	259 36.3	256 57.1	26.5	251 14.2	20.4	57 40.2	38.9	354 38.3	03.8
	09	274 38.8	271 58.1	. . 27.6	266 15.0	. . 21.1	72 42.7	. . 38.9	9 40.5	. . 03.8
	10	289 41.2	286 59.2	28.6	281 15.8	21.9	87 45.2	38.8	24 42.8	03.8
	11	304 43.7	302 00.2	29.7	296 16.5	22.7	102 47.6	38.8	39 45.0	03.8
	12	319 46.2	317 01.3	N 4 30.7	311 17.3	N 3 23.4	117 50.1	S 7 38.8	54 47.3	S22 03.8
	13	334 48.6	332 02.3	31.8	326 18.1	24.2	132 52.6	38.8	69 49.5	03.8
	14	349 51.1	347 03.4	32.8	341 18.9	24.9	147 55.1	38.8	84 51.8	03.8
	15	4 53.6	2 04.4	. . 33.9	356 19.6	. . 25.7	162 57.6	. . 38.7	99 54.0	. . 03.9
	16	19 56.0	17 05.5	34.9	11 20.4	26.5	178 00.1	38.7	114 56.2	03.9
	17	34 58.5	32 06.5	36.0	26 21.2	27.2	193 02.6	38.7	129 58.5	03.9
	18	50 01.0	47 07.6	N 4 37.0	41 22.0	N 3 28.0	208 05.0	S 7 38.7	145 00.7	S22 03.9
	19	65 03.4	62 08.6	38.0	56 22.7	28.7	223 07.5	38.7	160 03.0	03.9
	20	80 05.9	77 09.7	39.1	71 23.5	29.5	238 10.0	38.7	175 05.2	03.9
	21	95 08.3	92 10.8	. . 40.1	86 24.3	. . 30.3	253 12.5	. . 38.6	190 07.4	. . 03.9
	22	110 10.8	107 11.8	41.2	101 25.1	31.0	268 15.0	38.6	205 09.7	03.9
	23	125 13.3	122 12.9	42.2	116 25.8	31.8	283 17.5	38.6	220 11.9	03.9
10 FRIDAY	00	140 15.7	137 14.0	N 4 43.2	131 26.6	N 3 32.6	298 20.0	S 7 38.6	235 14.2	S22 03.9
	01	155 18.2	152 15.0	44.3	146 27.4	33.3	313 22.4	38.6	250 16.4	03.9
	02	170 20.7	167 16.1	45.3	161 28.2	34.1	328 24.9	38.5	265 18.7	03.9
	03	185 23.1	182 17.2	. . 46.4	176 28.9	. . 34.8	343 27.4	. . 38.5	280 20.9	. . 03.9
	04	200 25.6	197 18.2	47.4	191 29.7	35.6	358 29.9	38.5	295 23.1	03.9
	05	215 28.1	212 19.3	48.4	206 30.5	36.4	13 32.4	38.5	310 25.4	03.9
	06	230 30.5	227 20.4	N 4 49.5	221 31.2	N 3 37.1	28 34.9	S 7 38.4	325 27.6	S22 03.9
	07	245 33.0	242 21.5	50.5	236 32.0	37.9	43 37.4	38.4	340 29.9	03.9
	08	260 35.5	257 22.6	51.6	251 32.8	38.6	58 39.9	38.4	355 32.1	03.9
	09	275 37.9	272 23.7	. . 52.6	266 33.6	. . 39.4	73 42.4	. . 38.4	10 34.4	. . 04.0
	10	290 40.4	287 24.7	53.6	281 34.3	40.2	88 44.9	38.4	25 36.6	04.0
	11	305 42.8	302 25.8	54.7	296 35.1	40.9	103 47.3	38.3	40 38.8	04.0
	12	320 45.3	317 26.9	N 4 55.7	311 35.9	N 3 41.7	118 49.8	S 7 38.3	55 41.1	S22 04.0
	13	335 47.8	332 28.0	56.7	326 36.7	42.4	133 52.3	38.3	70 43.3	04.0
	14	350 50.2	347 29.1	57.7	341 37.4	43.2	148 54.8	38.3	85 45.6	04.0
	15	5 52.7	2 30.2	. . 58.8	356 38.2	. . 44.0	163 57.3	. . 38.3	100 47.8	. . 04.0
	16	20 55.2	17 31.3	4 59.8	11 39.0	44.7	178 59.8	38.2	115 50.1	04.0
	17	35 57.6	32 32.4	5 00.8	26 39.8	45.5	194 02.3	38.2	130 52.3	04.0
	18	51 00.1	47 33.5	N 5 01.9	41 40.5	N 3 46.2	209 04.8	S 7 38.2	145 54.6	S22 04.0
	19	66 02.6	62 34.6	02.9	56 41.3	47.0	224 07.3	38.2	160 56.8	04.0
	20	81 05.0	77 35.7	03.9	71 42.1	47.8	239 09.8	38.1	175 59.0	04.0
	21	96 07.5	92 36.9	. . 04.9	86 42.8	. . 48.5	254 12.3	. . 38.1	191 01.3	. . 04.0
	22	111 09.9	107 38.0	06.0	101 43.6	49.3	269 14.8	38.1	206 03.5	04.0
	23	126 12.4	122 39.1	07.0	116 44.4	50.0	284 17.3	38.1	221 05.8	04.0
11 SATURDAY	00	141 14.9	137 40.2	N 5 08.0	131 45.2	N 3 50.8	299 19.8	S 7 38.0	236 08.0	S22 04.0
	01	156 17.3	152 41.3	09.0	146 45.9	51.5	314 22.3	38.0	251 10.3	04.0
	02	171 19.8	167 42.4	10.1	161 46.7	52.3	329 24.7	38.0	266 12.5	04.0
	03	186 22.3	182 43.6	. . 11.1	176 47.5	. . 53.1	344 27.2	. . 38.0	281 14.8	. . 04.0
	04	201 24.7	197 44.7	12.1	191 48.3	53.8	359 29.7	38.0	296 17.0	04.1
	05	216 27.2	212 45.8	13.1	206 49.0	54.6	14 32.2	37.9	311 19.3	04.1
	06	231 29.7	227 46.9	N 5 14.2	221 49.8	N 3 55.3	29 34.7	S 7 37.9	326 21.5	S22 04.1
	07	246 32.1	242 48.1	15.2	236 50.6	56.1	44 37.2	37.9	341 23.7	04.1
	08	261 34.6	257 49.2	16.2	251 51.4	56.9	59 39.7	37.9	356 26.0	04.1
	09	276 37.1	272 50.3	. . 17.2	266 52.1	. . 57.6	74 42.2	. . 37.8	11 28.2	. . 04.1
	10	291 39.5	287 51.5	18.2	281 52.9	58.4	89 44.7	37.8	26 30.5	04.1
	11	306 42.0	302 52.6	19.2	296 53.7	59.1	104 47.2	37.8	41 32.7	04.1
	12	321 44.4	317 53.8	N 5 20.3	311 54.4	N 3 59.9	119 49.7	S 7 37.8	56 35.0	S22 04.1
	13	336 46.9	332 54.9	21.3	326 55.2	4 00.6	134 52.2	37.7	71 37.2	04.1
	14	351 49.4	347 56.0	22.3	341 56.0	01.4	149 54.7	37.7	86 39.5	04.1
	15	6 51.8	2 57.2	. . 23.3	356 56.8	. . 02.2	164 57.2	. . 37.7	101 41.7	. . 04.1
	16	21 54.3	17 58.3	24.3	11 57.5	02.9	179 59.7	37.7	116 44.0	04.1
	17	36 56.8	32 59.5	25.3	26 58.3	03.7	195 02.2	37.6	131 46.2	04.1
	18	51 59.2	48 00.6	N 5 26.3	41 59.1	N 4 04.4	210 04.7	S 7 37.6	146 48.5	S22 04.1
	19	67 01.7	63 01.8	27.4	56 59.9	05.2	225 07.2	37.6	161 50.7	04.1
	20	82 04.2	78 03.0	28.4	72 00.6	05.9	240 09.7	37.6	176 53.0	04.1
	21	97 06.6	93 04.1	. . 29.4	87 01.4	. . 06.7	255 12.2	. . 37.5	191 55.2	. . 04.1
	22	112 09.1	108 05.3	30.4	102 02.2	07.5	270 14.7	37.5	206 57.5	04.1
	23	127 11.6	123 06.4	31.4	117 03.0	08.2	285 17.2	37.5	221 59.7	04.1
Mer. Pass.		h m 14 36.6	v 1.1	d 1.0	v 0.8	d 0.8	v 2.5	d 0.0	v 2.2	d 0.0

STARS Name	SHA	Dec
	° ′	° ′
Acamar	315 16.5	S40 14.6
Achernar	335 25.3	S57 09.4
Acrux	173 05.9	S63 11.4
Adhara	255 10.3	S29 00.1
Aldebaran	290 46.4	N16 32.4
Alioth	166 18.3	N55 51.8
Alkaid	152 56.8	N49 13.5
Al Na'ir	27 41.2	S46 52.7
Alnilam	275 43.7	S 1 11.8
Alphard	217 53.3	S 8 44.2
Alphecca	126 09.0	N26 39.4
Alpheratz	357 41.2	N29 11.1
Altair	62 06.1	N 8 54.9
Ankaa	353 13.6	S42 13.1
Antares	112 23.3	S26 27.9
Arcturus	145 53.4	N19 05.5
Atria	107 23.1	S69 03.0
Avior	234 16.3	S59 34.1
Bellatrix	278 29.2	N 6 21.6
Betelgeuse	270 58.4	N 7 24.3
Canopus	263 54.6	S52 42.7
Capella	280 30.5	N46 00.8
Deneb	49 30.2	N45 20.5
Denebola	182 30.9	N14 28.5
Diphda	348 53.6	S17 53.8
Dubhe	193 48.2	N61 39.3
Elnath	278 09.3	N28 37.1
Eltanin	90 45.3	N51 29.1
Enif	33 45.0	N 9 57.2
Fomalhaut	15 21.6	S29 32.0
Gacrux	171 57.6	S57 12.3
Gienah	175 49.5	S17 38.2
Hadar	148 44.0	S60 27.0
Hamal	327 58.0	N23 32.5
Kaus Aust.	83 40.8	S34 22.3
Kochab	137 20.1	N74 04.9
Markab	13 36.1	N15 17.8
Menkar	314 12.5	N 4 09.1
Menkent	148 04.5	S36 27.0
Miaplacidus	221 38.1	S69 47.4
Mirfak	308 36.7	N49 55.3
Nunki	75 55.5	S26 16.3
Peacock	53 16.0	S56 40.6
Pollux	243 24.4	N27 58.9
Procyon	244 56.9	N 5 10.6
Rasalhague	96 04.3	N12 32.9
Regulus	207 40.6	N11 52.8
Rigel	281 09.5	S 8 11.3
Rigil Kent.	139 48.1	S60 53.9
Sabik	102 09.8	S15 44.6
Schedar	349 37.9	N56 37.9
Shaula	96 18.8	S37 06.7
Sirius	258 31.3	S16 44.7
Spica	158 28.5	S11 15.0
Suhail	222 50.1	S43 30.3
Vega	80 37.6	N38 47.9
Zuben'ubi	137 02.6	S16 06.6

	SHA	Mer. Pass.
	° ′	h m
Venus	356 58.2	14 50
Mars	351 10.9	15 13
Jupiter	158 04.2	4 06
Saturn	94 58.4	8 18

Day	UT	SUN GHA	SUN Dec	MOON GHA	v	MOON Dec	d	HP
	d h	° ′	° ′	° ′	′	° ′	′	′
THURSDAY	9 00	176 27.3	S14 40.7	23 40.6	6.5	N17 58.5	3.6	59.1
	01	191 27.3	39.9	38 06.1	6.5	17 54.9	3.8	59.0
	02	206 27.2	39.1	52 31.6	6.6	17 51.1	3.8	59.0
	03	221 27.2	. . 38.3	66 57.2	6.6	17 47.3	4.0	59.0
	04	236 27.2	37.5	81 22.8	6.7	17 43.3	4.1	59.0
	05	251 27.2	36.7	95 48.5	6.7	17 39.2	4.2	59.0
	06	266 27.2	S14 35.9	110 14.2	6.7	N17 35.0	4.4	59.0
	07	281 27.2	35.1	124 39.9	6.8	17 30.6	4.4	59.0
	08	296 27.2	34.3	139 05.7	6.9	17 26.2	4.5	58.9
	09	311 27.1	. . 33.5	153 31.6	6.8	17 21.7	4.7	58.9
	10	326 27.1	32.7	167 57.4	7.0	17 17.0	4.8	58.9
	11	341 27.1	31.9	182 23.4	7.0	17 12.2	4.8	58.9
	12	356 27.1	S14 31.0	196 49.4	7.0	N17 07.4	5.0	58.9
	13	11 27.1	30.2	211 15.4	7.1	17 02.4	5.1	58.9
	14	26 27.1	29.4	225 41.5	7.2	16 57.3	5.2	58.8
	15	41 27.1	. . 28.6	240 07.7	7.2	16 52.1	5.2	58.8
	16	56 27.1	27.8	254 33.9	7.2	16 46.9	5.4	58.8
	17	71 27.0	27.0	269 00.1	7.4	16 41.5	5.5	58.8
	18	86 27.0	S14 26.2	283 26.5	7.3	N16 36.0	5.6	58.8
	19	101 27.0	25.4	297 52.8	7.5	16 30.4	5.7	58.7
	20	116 27.0	24.6	312 19.3	7.4	16 24.7	5.8	58.7
	21	131 27.0	. . 23.8	326 45.7	7.6	16 18.9	5.9	58.7
	22	146 27.0	23.0	341 12.3	7.6	16 13.0	6.0	58.7
	23	161 27.0	22.1	355 38.9	7.6	16 07.0	6.0	58.7
FRIDAY	10 00	176 27.0	S14 21.3	10 05.5	7.8	N16 01.0	6.2	58.7
	01	191 27.0	20.5	24 32.3	7.7	15 54.8	6.3	58.6
	02	206 27.0	19.7	38 59.0	7.9	15 48.5	6.3	58.6
	03	221 27.0	. . 18.9	53 25.9	7.9	15 42.2	6.5	58.6
	04	236 27.0	18.1	67 52.8	8.0	15 35.7	6.5	58.6
	05	251 26.9	17.3	82 19.8	8.0	15 29.2	6.7	58.5
	06	266 26.9	S14 16.5	96 46.8	8.1	N15 22.5	6.7	58.5
	07	281 26.9	15.6	111 13.9	8.1	15 15.8	6.8	58.5
	08	296 26.9	14.8	125 41.0	8.2	15 09.0	6.9	58.5
	09	311 26.9	. . 14.0	140 08.2	8.3	15 02.1	7.0	58.5
	10	326 26.9	13.2	154 35.5	8.4	14 55.1	7.0	58.4
	11	341 26.9	12.4	169 02.9	8.4	14 48.1	7.2	58.4
	12	356 26.9	S14 11.6	183 30.3	8.4	N14 40.9	7.2	58.4
	13	11 26.9	10.7	197 57.7	8.6	14 33.7	7.3	58.4
	14	26 26.9	09.9	212 25.3	8.6	14 26.4	7.4	58.4
	15	41 26.9	. . 09.1	226 52.9	8.6	14 19.0	7.5	58.3
	16	56 26.9	08.3	241 20.5	8.8	14 11.5	7.5	58.3
	17	71 26.9	07.5	255 48.3	8.8	14 04.0	7.6	58.3
	18	86 26.9	S14 06.7	270 16.1	8.8	N13 56.4	7.7	58.3
	19	101 26.9	05.8	284 43.9	9.0	13 48.7	7.8	58.2
	20	116 26.9	05.0	299 11.9	9.0	13 40.9	7.8	58.2
	21	131 26.9	. . 04.2	313 39.9	9.0	13 33.1	7.9	58.2
	22	146 26.9	03.4	328 07.9	9.2	13 25.2	8.0	58.2
	23	161 26.9	02.6	342 36.1	9.2	13 17.2	8.1	58.1
SATURDAY	11 00	176 26.9	S14 01.7	357 04.3	9.2	N13 09.1	8.1	58.1
	01	191 26.9	00.9	11 32.5	9.4	13 01.0	8.2	58.1
	02	206 26.9	14 00.1	26 00.9	9.4	12 52.8	8.3	58.1
	03	221 26.9	13 59.3	40 29.3	9.4	12 44.5	8.3	58.0
	04	236 26.9	58.4	54 57.7	9.6	12 36.2	8.4	58.0
	05	251 26.9	57.6	69 26.3	9.5	12 27.8	8.4	58.0
	06	266 26.9	S13 56.8	83 54.8	9.7	N12 19.4	8.5	58.0
	07	281 26.9	56.0	98 23.5	9.7	12 10.9	8.6	57.9
	08	296 26.9	55.1	112 52.2	9.8	12 02.3	8.6	57.9
	09	311 26.9	. . 54.3	127 21.0	9.9	11 53.7	8.7	57.9
	10	326 26.9	53.5	141 49.9	9.9	11 45.0	8.8	57.9
	11	341 26.9	52.7	156 18.8	10.0	11 36.2	8.8	57.8
	12	356 26.9	S13 51.8	170 47.8	10.1	N11 27.4	8.8	57.8
	13	11 26.9	51.0	185 16.9	10.1	11 18.6	9.0	57.8
	14	26 26.9	50.2	199 46.0	10.2	11 09.6	8.9	57.7
	15	41 26.9	. . 49.4	214 15.2	10.3	11 00.7	9.0	57.7
	16	56 26.9	48.5	228 44.5	10.3	10 51.7	9.1	57.7
	17	71 26.9	47.7	243 13.8	10.4	10 42.6	9.1	57.7
	18	86 26.9	S13 46.9	257 43.2	10.5	N10 33.5	9.2	57.6
	19	101 26.9	46.0	272 12.7	10.5	10 24.3	9.2	57.6
	20	116 26.9	45.2	286 42.2	10.6	10 15.1	9.3	57.6
	21	131 26.9	. . 44.4	301 11.8	10.6	10 05.8	9.3	57.6
	22	146 27.0	43.6	315 41.4	10.7	9 56.5	9.3	57.5
	23	161 27.0	42.7	330 11.1	10.8	N 9 47.2	9.4	57.5
		SD 16.2	*d* 0.8	SD	16.0		15.9	15.7

Lat.	Twilight Naut.	Twilight Civil	Sunrise	Moonrise 9	Moonrise 10	Moonrise 11	Moonrise 12
°	h m	h m	h m	h m	h m	h m	h m
N 72	06 34	07 57	09 22	12 14	14 26	16 24	18 15
N 70	06 31	07 44	08 57	13 09	14 56	16 42	18 24
68	06 27	07 34	08 38	13 43	15 19	16 57	18 32
66	06 24	07 25	08 23	14 07	15 36	17 08	18 39
64	06 22	07 18	08 11	14 26	15 51	17 18	18 45
62	06 19	07 12	08 00	14 41	16 03	17 26	18 49
60	06 17	07 06	07 51	14 54	16 13	17 33	18 54
N 58	06 15	07 01	07 43	15 05	16 21	17 40	18 57
56	06 13	06 57	07 36	15 15	16 29	17 45	19 01
54	06 11	06 53	07 30	15 23	16 36	17 50	19 03
52	06 09	06 49	07 24	15 31	16 42	17 55	19 06
50	06 07	06 45	07 19	15 37	16 48	17 59	19 09
45	06 03	06 38	07 08	15 52	17 00	18 07	19 14
N 40	05 59	06 31	06 59	16 04	17 09	18 14	19 18
35	05 55	06 25	06 51	16 14	17 18	18 21	19 22
30	05 51	06 19	06 44	16 23	17 25	18 26	19 25
20	05 43	06 09	06 32	16 39	17 38	18 35	19 31
N 10	05 34	05 59	06 21	16 52	17 49	18 44	19 36
0	05 25	05 49	06 11	17 05	17 59	18 51	19 41
S 10	05 13	05 39	06 00	17 17	18 10	18 59	19 45
20	04 59	05 26	05 49	17 31	18 21	19 07	19 50
30	04 41	05 11	05 36	17 46	18 34	19 17	19 56
35	04 30	05 02	05 29	17 55	18 41	19 22	19 59
40	04 16	04 51	05 20	18 05	18 49	19 28	20 03
45	03 58	04 38	05 10	18 17	18 59	19 35	20 07
S 50	03 36	04 22	04 58	18 31	19 10	19 43	20 12
52	03 24	04 14	04 52	18 38	19 16	19 47	20 15
54	03 11	04 05	04 46	18 46	19 22	19 52	20 17
56	02 56	03 55	04 39	18 54	19 28	19 56	20 20
58	02 36	03 43	04 31	19 03	19 36	20 02	20 23
S 60	02 12	03 30	04 22	19 14	19 44	20 07	20 27

Lat.	Sunset	Twilight Civil	Twilight Naut.	Moonset 9	Moonset 10	Moonset 11	Moonset 12
°	h m	h m	h m	h m	h m	h m	h m
N 72	15 08	16 33	17 56	09 35	09 19	09 10	09 03
N 70	15 32	16 46	18 00	08 39	08 47	08 50	08 51
68	15 51	16 56	18 03	08 05	08 24	08 34	08 41
66	16 07	17 04	18 06	07 41	08 05	08 22	08 33
64	16 19	17 12	18 08	07 21	07 50	08 11	08 26
62	16 29	17 18	18 11	07 05	07 38	08 02	08 20
60	16 38	17 23	18 13	06 52	07 27	07 54	08 15
N 58	16 46	17 28	18 15	06 41	07 18	07 47	08 11
56	16 53	17 33	18 17	06 31	07 10	07 41	08 07
54	16 59	17 37	18 19	06 22	07 02	07 35	08 03
52	17 05	17 40	18 20	06 14	06 56	07 30	08 00
50	17 10	17 44	18 22	06 07	06 50	07 26	07 57
45	17 21	17 51	18 26	05 52	06 37	07 16	07 50
N 40	17 30	17 58	18 30	05 39	06 26	07 08	07 45
35	17 38	18 04	18 34	05 28	06 17	07 01	07 40
30	17 45	18 09	18 38	05 19	06 09	06 54	07 35
20	17 57	18 20	18 46	05 03	05 55	06 43	07 28
N 10	18 08	18 29	18 54	04 49	05 43	06 34	07 21
0	18 18	18 39	19 04	04 35	05 31	06 25	07 15
S 10	18 28	18 50	19 15	04 22	05 20	06 16	07 09
20	18 39	19 02	19 29	04 07	05 07	06 06	07 02
30	18 52	19 17	19 47	03 51	04 53	05 54	06 55
35	18 59	19 26	19 58	03 41	04 45	05 48	06 50
40	19 07	19 36	20 12	03 30	04 35	05 41	06 45
45	19 17	19 49	20 29	03 17	04 24	05 32	06 39
S 50	19 29	20 05	20 51	03 01	04 10	05 21	06 32
52	19 35	20 13	21 02	02 54	04 04	05 16	06 29
54	19 41	20 22	21 15	02 46	03 57	05 11	06 25
56	19 48	20 32	21 30	02 36	03 49	05 05	06 21
58	19 56	20 43	21 49	02 26	03 40	04 58	06 17
S 60	20 05	20 56	22 12	02 13	03 30	04 51	06 12

Day	SUN Eqn. of Time 00^h	SUN Eqn. of Time 12^h	SUN Mer. Pass.	MOON Mer. Pass. Upper	MOON Mer. Pass. Lower	MOON Age	MOON Phase
d	m s	m s	h m	h m	h m	d	%
9	14 11	14 12	12 14	23 18	10 50	12	97
10	14 12	14 12	12 14	24 12	11 45	13	100
11	14 12	14 12	12 14	00 12	12 38	14	100

	UT d h	ARIES GHA ° ′	VENUS −4·8 GHA ° ′	VENUS Dec ° ′	MARS +1·2 GHA ° ′	MARS Dec ° ′	JUPITER −2·2 GHA ° ′	JUPITER Dec ° ′	SATURN +0·5 GHA ° ′	SATURN Dec ° ′
	12 00	142 14.0	138 07.6	N 5 32.4	132 03.7	N 4 09.0	300 19.7	S 7 37.5	237 02.0	S22 04.2
	01	157 16.5	153 08.8	33.4	147 04.5	09.7	315 22.2	37.4	252 04.2	04.2
	02	172 18.9	168 09.9	34.4	162 05.3	10.5	330 24.7	37.4	267 06.5	04.2
	03	187 21.4	183 11.1	. . 35.4	177 06.1	. . 11.2	345 27.2	. . 37.4	282 08.7	. . 04.2
	04	202 23.9	198 12.3	36.4	192 06.8	12.0	0 29.7	37.4	297 11.0	04.2
	05	217 26.3	213 13.5	37.4	207 07.6	12.7	15 32.2	37.3	312 13.2	04.2
	06	232 28.8	228 14.7	N 5 38.4	222 08.4	N 4 13.5	30 34.8	S 7 37.3	327 15.5	S22 04.2
	07	247 31.3	243 15.8	39.4	237 09.1	14.3	45 37.3	37.3	342 17.7	04.2
	08	262 33.7	258 17.0	40.4	252 09.9	15.0	60 39.8	37.2	357 20.0	04.2
S	09	277 36.2	273 18.2	. . 41.4	267 10.7	. . 15.8	75 42.3	. . 37.2	12 22.2	. . 04.2
U	10	292 38.7	288 19.4	42.4	282 11.5	16.5	90 44.8	37.2	27 24.5	04.2
N	11	307 41.1	303 20.6	43.4	297 12.2	17.3	105 47.3	37.2	42 26.7	04.2
D	12	322 43.6	318 21.8	N 5 44.4	312 13.0	N 4 18.0	120 49.8	S 7 37.1	57 29.0	S22 04.2
A	13	337 46.0	333 23.0	45.4	327 13.8	18.8	135 52.3	37.1	72 31.2	04.2
Y	14	352 48.5	348 24.2	46.4	342 14.6	19.5	150 54.8	37.1	87 33.5	04.2
	15	7 51.0	3 25.4	. . 47.4	357 15.3	. . 20.3	165 57.3	. . 37.1	102 35.7	. . 04.2
	16	22 53.4	18 26.6	48.4	12 16.1	21.1	180 59.8	37.0	117 38.0	04.2
	17	37 55.9	33 27.8	49.4	27 16.9	21.8	196 02.3	37.0	132 40.2	04.2
	18	52 58.4	48 29.0	N 5 50.4	42 17.7	N 4 22.6	211 04.8	S 7 37.0	147 42.5	S22 04.2
	19	68 00.8	63 30.2	51.4	57 18.4	23.3	226 07.3	36.9	162 44.7	04.2
	20	83 03.3	78 31.4	52.4	72 19.2	24.1	241 09.8	36.9	177 47.0	04.3
	21	98 05.8	93 32.6	. . 53.4	87 20.0	. . 24.8	256 12.4	. . 36.9	192 49.2	. . 04.3
	22	113 08.2	108 33.8	54.4	102 20.8	25.6	271 14.9	36.9	207 51.5	04.3
	23	128 10.7	123 35.0	55.4	117 21.5	26.3	286 17.4	36.8	222 53.7	04.3
	13 00	143 13.2	138 36.2	N 5 56.4	132 22.3	N 4 27.1	301 19.9	S 7 36.8	237 56.0	S22 04.3
	01	158 15.6	153 37.5	57.3	147 23.1	27.8	316 22.4	36.8	252 58.2	04.3
	02	173 18.1	168 38.7	58.3	162 23.8	28.6	331 24.9	36.7	268 00.5	04.3
	03	188 20.5	183 39.9	5 59.3	177 24.6	. . 29.4	346 27.4	. . 36.7	283 02.7	. . 04.3
	04	203 23.0	198 41.1	6 00.3	192 25.4	30.1	1 29.9	36.7	298 05.0	04.3
	05	218 25.5	213 42.4	01.3	207 26.2	30.9	16 32.4	36.7	313 07.2	04.3
	06	233 27.9	228 43.6	N 6 02.3	222 26.9	N 4 31.6	31 34.9	S 7 36.6	328 09.5	S22 04.3
	07	248 30.4	243 44.8	03.3	237 27.7	32.4	46 37.5	36.6	343 11.7	04.3
	08	263 32.9	258 46.1	04.2	252 28.5	33.1	61 40.0	36.6	358 14.0	04.3
M	09	278 35.3	273 47.3	. . 05.2	267 29.3	. . 33.9	76 42.5	. . 36.5	13 16.2	. . 04.3
O	10	293 37.8	288 48.5	06.2	282 30.0	34.6	91 45.0	36.5	28 18.5	04.3
N	11	308 40.3	303 49.8	07.2	297 30.8	35.4	106 47.5	36.5	43 20.7	04.3
D	12	323 42.7	318 51.0	N 6 08.2	312 31.6	N 4 36.1	121 50.0	S 7 36.4	58 23.0	S22 04.3
A	13	338 45.2	333 52.3	09.1	327 32.4	36.9	136 52.5	36.4	73 25.3	04.3
Y	14	353 47.6	348 53.5	10.1	342 33.1	37.6	151 55.1	36.4	88 27.5	04.3
	15	8 50.1	3 54.8	. . 11.1	357 33.9	. . 38.4	166 57.6	. . 36.4	103 29.8	. . 04.3
	16	23 52.6	18 56.0	12.1	12 34.7	39.1	182 00.1	36.3	118 32.0	04.3
	17	38 55.0	33 57.3	13.1	27 35.4	39.9	197 02.6	36.3	133 34.3	04.3
	18	53 57.5	48 58.5	N 6 14.0	42 36.2	N 4 40.7	212 05.1	S 7 36.3	148 36.5	S22 04.4
	19	69 00.0	63 59.8	15.0	57 37.0	41.4	227 07.6	36.2	163 38.8	04.4
	20	84 02.4	79 01.0	16.0	72 37.8	42.2	242 10.1	36.2	178 41.0	04.4
	21	99 04.9	94 02.3	. . 17.0	87 38.5	. . 42.9	257 12.7	. . 36.2	193 43.3	. . 04.4
	22	114 07.4	109 03.6	17.9	102 39.3	43.7	272 15.2	36.1	208 45.5	04.4
	23	129 09.8	124 04.8	18.9	117 40.1	44.4	287 17.7	36.1	223 47.8	04.4
	14 00	144 12.3	139 06.1	N 6 19.9	132 40.9	N 4 45.2	302 20.2	S 7 36.1	238 50.0	S22 04.4
	01	159 14.8	154 07.4	20.8	147 41.6	45.9	317 22.7	36.0	253 52.3	04.4
	02	174 17.2	169 08.7	21.8	162 42.4	46.7	332 25.2	36.0	268 54.6	04.4
	03	189 19.7	184 09.9	. . 22.8	177 43.2	. . 47.4	347 27.8	. . 36.0	283 56.8	. . 04.4
	04	204 22.1	199 11.2	23.7	192 44.0	48.2	2 30.3	35.9	298 59.1	04.4
	05	219 24.6	214 12.5	24.7	207 44.7	48.9	17 32.8	35.9	314 01.3	04.4
	06	234 27.1	229 13.8	N 6 25.7	222 45.5	N 4 49.7	32 35.3	S 7 35.9	329 03.6	S22 04.4
	07	249 29.5	244 15.1	26.6	237 46.3	50.4	47 37.8	35.8	344 05.8	04.4
T	08	264 32.0	259 16.4	27.6	252 47.0	51.2	62 40.4	35.8	359 08.1	04.4
U	09	279 34.5	274 17.6	. . 28.6	267 47.8	. . 51.9	77 42.9	. . 35.8	14 10.4	. . 04.4
E	10	294 36.9	289 18.9	29.5	282 48.6	52.7	92 45.4	35.7	29 12.6	04.4
S	11	309 39.4	304 20.2	30.5	297 49.4	53.4	107 47.9	35.7	44 14.9	04.4
D	12	324 41.9	319 21.5	N 6 31.4	312 50.1	N 4 54.2	122 50.4	S 7 35.7	59 17.1	S22 04.4
A	13	339 44.3	334 22.8	32.4	327 50.9	54.9	137 53.0	35.7	74 19.4	04.4
Y	14	354 46.8	349 24.1	33.4	342 51.7	55.7	152 55.5	35.6	89 21.6	04.4
	15	9 49.2	4 25.4	. . 34.3	357 52.5	. . 56.4	167 58.0	. . 35.6	104 23.9	. . 04.4
	16	24 51.7	19 26.7	35.3	12 53.2	57.2	183 00.5	35.6	119 26.1	04.4
	17	39 54.2	34 28.1	36.2	27 54.0	57.9	198 03.0	35.5	134 28.4	04.5
	18	54 56.6	49 29.4	N 6 37.2	42 54.8	N 4 58.7	213 05.6	S 7 35.5	149 30.7	S22 04.5
	19	69 59.1	64 30.7	38.1	57 55.6	4 59.4	228 08.1	35.4	164 32.9	04.5
	20	85 01.6	79 32.0	39.1	72 56.3	5 00.2	243 10.6	35.4	179 35.2	04.5
	21	100 04.0	94 33.3	. . 40.0	87 57.1	. . 00.9	258 13.1	. . 35.4	194 37.4	. . 04.5
	22	115 06.5	109 34.6	41.0	102 57.9	01.7	273 15.7	35.3	209 39.7	04.5
	23	130 09.0	124 36.0	42.0	117 58.6	02.4	288 18.2	35.3	224 42.0	04.5
	Mer. Pass. (h m)	14 24.8	v 1.2	d 1.0	v 0.8	d 0.8	v 2.5	d 0.0	v 2.3	d 0.0

STARS

Name	SHA ° ′	Dec ° ′
Acamar	315 16.6	S40 14.6
Achernar	335 25.3	S57 09.4
Acrux	173 05.8	S63 11.4
Adhara	255 10.3	S29 00.1
Aldebaran	290 46.4	N16 32.4
Alioth	166 18.2	N55 51.8
Alkaid	152 56.8	N49 13.5
Al Na'ir	27 41.2	S46 52.7
Alnilam	275 43.7	S 1 11.8
Alphard	217 53.3	S 8 44.2
Alphecca	126 08.9	N26 39.4
Alpheratz	357 41.2	N29 11.1
Altair	62 06.1	N 8 54.8
Ankaa	353 13.6	S42 13.1
Antares	112 23.3	S26 27.9
Arcturus	145 53.4	N19 05.5
Atria	107 23.0	S69 03.0
Avior	234 16.3	S59 34.1
Bellatrix	278 29.2	N 6 21.6
Betelgeuse	270 58.4	N 7 24.3
Canopus	263 54.7	S52 42.7
Capella	280 30.5	N46 00.8
Deneb	49 30.2	N45 20.5
Denebola	182 30.9	N14 28.5
Diphda	348 53.6	S17 53.8
Dubhe	193 48.2	N61 39.3
Elnath	278 09.3	N28 37.1
Eltanin	90 45.3	N51 29.1
Enif	33 45.0	N 9 57.2
Fomalhaut	15 21.6	S29 32.0
Gacrux	171 57.6	S57 12.3
Gienah	175 49.5	S17 38.2
Hadar	148 44.0	S60 27.0
Hamal	327 58.0	N23 32.5
Kaus Aust.	83 40.8	S34 22.3
Kochab	137 20.1	N74 04.9
Markab	13 36.1	N15 17.8
Menkar	314 12.5	N 4 09.1
Menkent	148 04.5	S36 27.0
Miaplacidus	221 38.1	S69 47.4
Mirfak	308 36.7	N49 55.3
Nunki	75 55.5	S26 16.3
Peacock	53 16.0	S56 40.6
Pollux	243 24.4	N27 58.9
Procyon	244 56.9	N 5 10.6
Rasalhague	96 04.3	N12 32.9
Regulus	207 40.6	N11 52.8
Rigel	281 09.5	S 8 11.3
Rigil Kent.	139 48.1	S60 53.9
Sabik	102 09.8	S15 44.6
Schedar	349 38.0	N56 37.9
Shaula	96 18.7	S37 06.7
Sirius	258 31.3	S16 44.7
Spica	158 28.4	S11 15.0
Suhail	222 50.1	S43 30.3
Vega	80 37.6	N38 47.9
Zuben'ubi	137 02.6	S16 06.6

	SHA ° ′	Mer. Pass. h m
Venus	355 23.1	14 44
Mars	349 09.1	15 10
Jupiter	158 06.7	3 54
Saturn	94 42.8	8 07

	UT	SUN GHA	SUN Dec	MOON GHA	*v*	MOON Dec	*d*	HP
	d h	° ′	° ′	° ′	′	° ′	′	′
	12 00	176 27.0	S13 41.9	344 40.9	10.9	N 9 37.8	9.4	57.5
	01	191 27.0	41.1	359 10.8	10.9	9 28.4	9.5	57.4
	02	206 27.0	40.2	13 40.7	10.9	9 18.9	9.5	57.4
	03	221 27.0	. . 39.4	28 10.6	11.1	9 09.4	9.6	57.4
	04	236 27.0	38.6	42 40.7	11.0	8 59.8	9.5	57.4
	05	251 27.0	37.7	57 10.7	11.2	8 50.3	9.7	57.3
	06	266 27.0	S13 36.9	71 40.9	11.2	N 8 40.6	9.6	57.3
	07	281 27.0	36.1	86 11.1	11.3	8 31.0	9.7	57.3
	08	296 27.0	35.2	100 41.4	11.3	8 21.3	9.7	57.2
S	09	311 27.0	. . 34.4	115 11.7	11.4	8 11.6	9.8	57.2
U	10	326 27.1	33.6	129 42.1	11.5	8 01.8	9.8	57.2
N	11	341 27.1	32.7	144 12.6	11.5	7 52.0	9.8	57.2
D	12	356 27.1	S13 31.9	158 43.1	11.5	N 7 42.2	9.8	57.1
A	13	11 27.1	31.1	173 13.6	11.7	7 32.4	9.9	57.1
Y	14	26 27.1	30.2	187 44.3	11.6	7 22.5	9.9	57.1
	15	41 27.1	. . 29.4	202 14.9	11.8	7 12.6	10.0	57.0
	16	56 27.1	28.5	216 45.7	11.8	7 02.6	9.9	57.0
	17	71 27.1	27.7	231 16.5	11.8	6 52.7	10.0	57.0
	18	86 27.2	S13 26.9	245 47.3	11.9	N 6 42.7	10.0	57.0
	19	101 27.2	26.0	260 18.2	12.0	6 32.7	10.0	56.9
	20	116 27.2	25.2	274 49.2	12.0	6 22.7	10.0	56.9
	21	131 27.2	. . 24.4	289 20.2	12.1	6 12.7	10.1	56.9
	22	146 27.2	23.5	303 51.3	12.1	6 02.6	10.1	56.8
	23	161 27.2	22.7	318 22.4	12.2	5 52.5	10.1	56.8
	13 00	176 27.2	S13 21.8	332 53.6	12.2	N 5 42.4	10.1	56.8
	01	191 27.3	21.0	347 24.8	12.3	5 32.3	10.1	56.8
	02	206 27.3	20.2	1 56.1	12.3	5 22.2	10.2	56.7
	03	221 27.3	. . 19.3	16 27.4	12.4	5 12.0	10.1	56.7
	04	236 27.3	18.5	30 58.8	12.5	5 01.9	10.2	56.7
	05	251 27.3	17.6	45 30.3	12.4	4 51.7	10.2	56.6
	06	266 27.3	S13 16.8	60 01.7	12.6	N 4 41.5	10.2	56.6
	07	281 27.4	15.9	74 33.3	12.5	4 31.3	10.2	56.6
	08	296 27.4	15.1	89 04.8	12.7	4 21.1	10.2	56.6
M	09	311 27.4	. . 14.3	103 36.5	12.6	4 10.9	10.3	56.5
O	10	326 27.4	13.4	118 08.1	12.8	4 00.6	10.2	56.5
N	11	341 27.4	12.6	132 39.9	12.7	3 50.4	10.2	56.5
D	12	356 27.5	S13 11.7	147 11.6	12.8	N 3 40.2	10.3	56.4
A	13	11 27.5	10.9	161 43.4	12.9	3 29.9	10.3	56.4
Y	14	26 27.5	10.0	176 15.3	12.9	3 19.6	10.2	56.4
	15	41 27.5	. . 09.2	190 47.2	12.9	3 09.4	10.3	56.4
	16	56 27.5	08.3	205 19.1	13.0	2 59.1	10.2	56.3
	17	71 27.6	07.5	219 51.1	13.1	2 48.9	10.3	56.3
	18	86 27.6	S13 06.6	234 23.2	13.0	N 2 38.6	10.3	56.3
	19	101 27.6	05.8	248 55.2	13.1	2 28.3	10.3	56.2
	20	116 27.6	04.9	263 27.3	13.2	2 18.0	10.2	56.2
	21	131 27.6	. . 04.1	277 59.5	13.2	2 07.8	10.3	56.2
	22	146 27.7	03.3	292 31.7	13.2	1 57.5	10.3	56.2
	23	161 27.7	02.4	307 03.9	13.3	1 47.2	10.2	56.1
	14 00	176 27.7	S13 01.6	321 36.2	13.3	N 1 37.0	10.3	56.1
	01	191 27.7	13 00.7	336 08.5	13.3	1 26.7	10.2	56.1
	02	206 27.8	12 59.9	350 40.8	13.4	1 16.5	10.3	56.0
	03	221 27.8	. . 59.0	5 13.2	13.4	1 06.2	10.2	56.0
	04	236 27.8	58.2	19 45.6	13.4	0 56.0	10.3	56.0
	05	251 27.8	57.3	34 18.0	13.5	0 45.7	10.2	56.0
	06	266 27.8	S12 56.5	48 50.5	13.5	N 0 35.5	10.2	55.9
	07	281 27.9	55.6	63 23.0	13.6	0 25.3	10.2	55.9
T	08	296 27.9	54.7	77 55.6	13.6	0 15.1	10.2	55.9
U	09	311 27.9	. . 53.9	92 28.2	13.6	N 0 04.9	10.2	55.9
E	10	326 28.0	53.0	107 00.8	13.6	S 0 05.3	10.2	55.8
S	11	341 28.0	52.2	121 33.4	13.7	0 15.5	10.2	55.8
	12	356 28.0	S12 51.3	136 06.1	13.7	S 0 25.7	10.2	55.8
D	13	11 28.0	50.5	150 38.8	13.7	0 35.9	10.1	55.8
A	14	26 28.1	49.6	165 11.5	13.8	0 46.0	10.1	55.7
Y	15	41 28.1	. . 48.8	179 44.3	13.7	0 56.1	10.1	55.7
	16	56 28.1	47.9	194 17.0	13.9	1 06.2	10.1	55.7
	17	71 28.1	47.1	208 49.9	13.8	1 16.3	10.1	55.6
	18	86 28.2	S12 46.2	223 22.7	13.9	S 1 26.4	10.1	55.6
	19	101 28.2	45.3	237 55.6	13.8	1 36.5	10.1	55.6
	20	116 28.2	44.5	252 28.4	14.0	1 46.6	10.0	55.6
	21	131 28.3	. . 43.6	267 01.4	13.9	1 56.6	10.0	55.5
	22	146 28.3	42.8	281 34.3	14.0	2 06.6	10.0	55.5
	23	161 28.3	41.9	296 07.3	13.9	S 2 16.6	10.0	55.5
		SD 16.2	*d* 0.8	SD 15.6		15.4		15.2

Lat.	Twilight Naut.	Twilight Civil	Sunrise	Moonrise 12	13	14	15
°	h m	h m	h m	h m	h m	h m	h m
N 72	06 22	07 43	09 04	18 15	19 59	21 40	23 19
N 70	06 20	07 32	08 42	18 24	20 02	21 37	23 09
68	06 17	07 23	08 26	18 32	20 05	21 34	23 02
66	06 15	07 16	08 12	18 39	20 07	21 32	22 55
64	06 13	07 09	08 01	18 45	20 09	21 30	22 50
62	06 12	07 04	07 51	18 49	20 10	21 29	22 45
60	06 10	06 59	07 43	18 54	20 12	21 28	22 41
N 58	06 08	06 54	07 36	18 57	20 13	21 26	22 38
56	06 07	06 50	07 29	19 01	20 14	21 25	22 35
54	06 05	06 47	07 24	19 03	20 15	21 24	22 32
52	06 04	06 43	07 19	19 06	20 16	21 24	22 30
50	06 02	06 40	07 14	19 09	20 17	21 23	22 27
45	05 59	06 33	07 04	19 14	20 18	21 21	22 22
N 40	05 56	06 27	06 55	19 18	20 20	21 20	22 18
35	05 52	06 22	06 48	19 22	20 21	21 19	22 15
30	05 49	06 17	06 41	19 25	20 22	21 18	22 11
20	05 42	06 08	06 30	19 31	20 24	21 16	22 06
N 10	05 34	05 59	06 20	19 36	20 26	21 14	22 01
0	05 25	05 50	06 11	19 41	20 27	21 13	21 57
S 10	05 14	05 40	06 01	19 45	20 29	21 11	21 53
20	05 01	05 28	05 51	19 50	20 31	21 10	21 48
30	04 44	05 14	05 39	19 56	20 33	21 08	21 43
35	04 33	05 05	05 32	19 59	20 34	21 07	21 40
40	04 20	04 55	05 24	20 03	20 35	21 06	21 36
45	04 04	04 43	05 15	20 07	20 37	21 05	21 33
S 50	03 43	04 28	05 03	20 12	20 39	21 03	21 28
52	03 32	04 20	04 58	20 15	20 39	21 03	21 26
54	03 20	04 12	04 52	20 17	20 40	21 02	21 24
56	03 06	04 03	04 46	20 20	20 41	21 01	21 21
58	02 48	03 52	04 38	20 23	20 42	21 00	21 18
S 60	02 27	03 40	04 30	20 27	20 44	20 59	21 15

Lat.	Sunset	Twilight Civil	Twilight Naut.	Moonset 12	13	14	15
°	h m	h m	h m	h m	h m	h m	h m
N 72	15 26	16 47	18 08	09 03	08 56	08 50	08 43
N 70	15 47	16 58	18 11	08 51	08 50	08 50	08 49
68	16 04	17 07	18 13	08 41	08 46	08 50	08 53
66	16 17	17 14	18 15	08 33	08 42	08 50	08 57
64	16 29	17 20	18 16	08 26	08 39	08 50	09 00
62	16 38	17 26	18 18	08 20	08 36	08 50	09 03
60	16 46	17 31	18 20	08 15	08 33	08 50	09 05
N 58	16 53	17 35	18 21	08 11	08 31	08 50	09 08
56	17 00	17 39	18 23	08 07	08 29	08 50	09 10
54	17 05	17 42	18 24	08 03	08 27	08 50	09 11
52	17 11	17 46	18 25	08 00	08 26	08 50	09 13
50	17 15	17 49	18 27	07 57	08 24	08 50	09 14
45	17 25	17 56	18 30	07 50	08 21	08 50	09 17
N 40	17 34	18 01	18 33	07 45	08 18	08 50	09 20
35	17 41	18 07	18 37	07 40	08 16	08 50	09 22
30	17 47	18 12	18 40	07 35	08 14	08 50	09 24
20	17 58	18 21	18 47	07 28	08 10	08 49	09 28
N 10	18 08	18 30	18 55	07 21	08 06	08 49	09 31
0	18 18	18 39	19 03	07 15	08 03	08 49	09 34
S 10	18 27	18 49	19 14	07 09	08 00	08 49	09 37
20	18 37	19 00	19 27	07 02	07 57	08 49	09 40
30	18 49	19 14	19 44	06 55	07 53	08 49	09 44
35	18 56	19 23	19 54	06 50	07 50	08 49	09 46
40	19 04	19 32	20 07	06 45	07 48	08 49	09 48
45	19 13	19 45	20 23	06 39	07 45	08 49	09 51
S 50	19 24	20 00	20 44	06 32	07 41	08 49	09 54
52	19 29	20 07	20 54	06 29	07 40	08 48	09 55
54	19 35	20 15	21 06	06 25	07 38	08 48	09 57
56	19 41	20 24	21 20	06 21	07 36	08 48	09 59
58	19 49	20 34	21 37	06 17	07 33	08 48	10 01
S 60	19 57	20 46	21 58	06 12	07 31	08 48	10 03

Day	SUN Eqn. of Time 00h	SUN Eqn. of Time 12h	SUN Mer. Pass.	MOON Mer. Pass. Upper	MOON Mer. Pass. Lower	Age	Phase
d	m s	m s	h m	h m	h m	d	%
12	14 12	14 12	12 14	01 03	13 28	15	97
13	14 11	14 10	12 14	01 52	14 15	16	93
14	14 09	14 08	12 14	02 38	15 01	17	87

	UT	ARIES	VENUS −4·8		MARS +1·2		JUPITER −2·3		SATURN +0·5	
		GHA	GHA	Dec	GHA	Dec	GHA	Dec	GHA	Dec
	d h	° ′	° ′	° ′	° ′	° ′	° ′	° ′	° ′	° ′
	15 00	145 11.4	139 37.3	N 6 42.9	132 59.4	N 5 03.2	303 20.7	S 7 35.3	239 44.2	S22 04.5
	01	160 13.9	154 38.6	43.9	148 00.2	03.9	318 23.2	35.2	254 46.5	04.5
	02	175 16.4	169 39.9	44.8	163 01.0	04.7	333 25.8	35.2	269 48.7	04.5
	03	190 18.8	184 41.3	. . 45.7	178 01.7	. . 05.4	348 28.3	. . 35.2	284 51.0	. . 04.5
	04	205 21.3	199 42.6	46.7	193 02.5	06.2	3 30.8	35.1	299 53.2	04.5
	05	220 23.7	214 43.9	47.6	208 03.3	06.9	18 33.3	35.1	314 55.5	04.5
	06	235 26.2	229 45.3	N 6 48.6	223 04.1	N 5 07.7	33 35.9	S 7 35.1	329 57.8	S22 04.5
W	07	250 28.7	244 46.6	49.5	238 04.8	08.4	48 38.4	35.0	345 00.0	04.5
E	08	265 31.1	259 48.0	50.5	253 05.6	09.2	63 40.9	35.0	0 02.3	04.5
D	09	280 33.6	274 49.3	. . 51.4	268 06.4	. . 09.9	78 43.4	. . 35.0	15 04.5	. . 04.5
	10	295 36.1	289 50.7	52.4	283 07.1	10.7	93 46.0	34.9	30 06.8	04.5
N	11	310 38.5	304 52.0	53.3	298 07.9	11.4	108 48.5	34.9	45 09.1	04.5
E	12	325 41.0	319 53.4	N 6 54.2	313 08.7	N 5 12.2	123 51.0	S 7 34.9	60 11.3	S22 04.5
S	13	340 43.5	334 54.7	55.2	328 09.5	12.9	138 53.6	34.8	75 13.6	04.5
D	14	355 45.9	349 56.1	56.1	343 10.2	13.7	153 56.1	34.8	90 15.8	04.5
A	15	10 48.4	4 57.4	. . 57.0	358 11.0	. . 14.4	168 58.6	. . 34.7	105 18.1	. . 04.5
Y	16	25 50.9	19 58.8	58.0	13 11.8	15.1	184 01.1	34.7	120 20.4	04.5
	17	40 53.3	35 00.2	58.9	28 12.6	15.9	199 03.7	34.7	135 22.6	04.5
	18	55 55.8	50 01.5	N 6 59.9	43 13.3	N 5 16.6	214 06.2	S 7 34.6	150 24.9	S22 04.6
	19	70 58.2	65 02.9	7 00.8	58 14.1	17.4	229 08.7	34.6	165 27.1	04.6
	20	86 00.7	80 04.3	01.7	73 14.9	18.1	244 11.3	34.6	180 29.4	04.6
	21	101 03.2	95 05.7	. . 02.7	88 15.6	. . 18.9	259 13.8	. . 34.5	195 31.7	. . 04.6
	22	116 05.6	110 07.0	03.6	103 16.4	19.6	274 16.3	34.5	210 33.9	04.6
	23	131 08.1	125 08.4	04.5	118 17.2	20.4	289 18.9	34.5	225 36.2	04.6
	16 00	146 10.6	140 09.8	N 7 05.4	133 18.0	N 5 21.1	304 21.4	S 7 34.4	240 38.5	S22 04.6
	01	161 13.0	155 11.2	06.4	148 18.7	21.9	319 23.9	34.4	255 40.7	04.6
	02	176 15.5	170 12.6	07.3	163 19.5	22.6	334 26.5	34.3	270 43.0	04.6
	03	191 18.0	185 14.0	. . 08.2	178 20.3	. . 23.4	349 29.0	. . 34.3	285 45.2	. . 04.6
	04	206 20.4	200 15.4	09.1	193 21.1	24.1	4 31.5	34.3	300 47.5	04.6
	05	221 22.9	215 16.8	10.1	208 21.8	24.9	19 34.1	34.2	315 49.8	04.6
	06	236 25.3	230 18.1	N 7 11.0	223 22.6	N 5 25.6	34 36.6	S 7 34.2	330 52.0	S22 04.6
	07	251 27.8	245 19.5	11.9	238 23.4	26.3	49 39.1	34.1	345 54.3	04.6
T	08	266 30.3	260 21.0	12.8	253 24.1	27.1	64 41.7	34.1	0 56.6	04.6
H	09	281 32.7	275 22.4	. . 13.8	268 24.9	. . 27.8	79 44.2	. . 34.1	15 58.8	. . 04.6
U	10	296 35.2	290 23.8	14.7	283 25.7	28.6	94 46.7	34.0	31 01.1	04.6
R	11	311 37.7	305 25.2	15.6	298 26.5	29.3	109 49.3	34.0	46 03.3	04.6
S	12	326 40.1	320 26.6	N 7 16.5	313 27.2	N 5 30.1	124 51.8	S 7 34.0	61 05.6	S22 04.6
D	13	341 42.6	335 28.0	17.4	328 28.0	30.8	139 54.3	33.9	76 07.9	04.6
A	14	356 45.1	350 29.4	18.3	343 28.8	31.6	154 56.9	33.9	91 10.1	04.6
Y	15	11 47.5	5 30.8	. . 19.3	358 29.6	. . 32.3	169 59.4	. . 33.8	106 12.4	. . 04.6
	16	26 50.0	20 32.3	20.2	13 30.3	33.0	185 01.9	33.8	121 14.7	04.6
	17	41 52.5	35 33.7	21.1	28 31.1	33.8	200 04.5	33.8	136 16.9	04.6
	18	56 54.9	50 35.1	N 7 22.0	43 31.9	N 5 34.5	215 07.0	S 7 33.7	151 19.2	S22 04.6
	19	71 57.4	65 36.5	22.9	58 32.6	35.3	230 09.6	33.7	166 21.4	04.6
	20	86 59.8	80 38.0	23.8	73 33.4	36.0	245 12.1	33.6	181 23.7	04.7
	21	102 02.3	95 39.4	. . 24.7	88 34.2	. . 36.8	260 14.6	. . 33.6	196 26.0	. . 04.7
	22	117 04.8	110 40.8	25.6	103 35.0	37.5	275 17.2	33.6	211 28.2	04.7
	23	132 07.2	125 42.3	26.5	118 35.7	38.3	290 19.7	33.5	226 30.5	04.7
	17 00	147 09.7	140 43.7	N 7 27.5	133 36.5	N 5 39.0	305 22.2	S 7 33.5	241 32.8	S22 04.7
	01	162 12.2	155 45.2	28.4	148 37.3	39.7	320 24.8	33.4	256 35.0	04.7
	02	177 14.6	170 46.6	29.3	163 38.1	40.5	335 27.3	33.4	271 37.3	04.7
	03	192 17.1	185 48.1	. . 30.2	178 38.8	. . 41.2	350 29.9	. . 33.4	286 39.6	. . 04.7
	04	207 19.6	200 49.5	31.1	193 39.6	42.0	5 32.4	33.3	301 41.8	04.7
	05	222 22.0	215 51.0	32.0	208 40.4	42.7	20 34.9	33.3	316 44.1	04.7
	06	237 24.5	230 52.4	N 7 32.9	223 41.1	N 5 43.5	35 37.5	S 7 33.2	331 46.4	S22 04.7
	07	252 26.9	245 53.9	33.8	238 41.9	44.2	50 40.0	33.2	346 48.6	04.7
	08	267 29.4	260 55.3	34.7	253 42.7	44.9	65 42.6	33.2	1 50.9	04.7
F	09	282 31.9	275 56.8	. . 35.6	268 43.5	. . 45.7	80 45.1	. . 33.1	16 53.2	. . 04.7
R	10	297 34.3	290 58.3	36.5	283 44.2	46.4	95 47.7	33.1	31 55.4	04.7
I	11	312 36.8	305 59.7	37.4	298 45.0	47.2	110 50.2	33.0	46 57.7	04.7
D	12	327 39.3	321 01.2	N 7 38.3	313 45.8	N 5 47.9	125 52.7	S 7 33.0	62 00.0	S22 04.7
A	13	342 41.7	336 02.7	39.2	328 46.5	48.7	140 55.3	33.0	77 02.2	04.7
Y	14	357 44.2	351 04.2	40.0	343 47.3	49.4	155 57.8	32.9	92 04.5	04.7
	15	12 46.7	6 05.6	. . 40.9	358 48.1	. . 50.1	171 00.4	. . 32.9	107 06.8	. . 04.7
	16	27 49.1	21 07.1	41.8	13 48.9	50.9	186 02.9	32.8	122 09.0	04.7
	17	42 51.6	36 08.6	42.7	28 49.6	51.6	201 05.5	32.8	137 11.3	04.7
	18	57 54.1	51 10.1	N 7 43.6	43 50.4	N 5 52.4	216 08.0	S 7 32.7	152 13.6	S22 04.7
	19	72 56.5	66 11.6	44.5	58 51.2	53.1	231 10.6	32.7	167 15.8	04.7
	20	87 59.0	81 13.1	45.4	73 51.9	53.9	246 13.1	32.7	182 18.1	04.7
	21	103 01.4	96 14.6	. . 46.3	88 52.7	. . 54.6	261 15.6	. . 32.6	197 20.4	. . 04.7
	22	118 03.9	111 16.1	47.1	103 53.5	55.3	276 18.2	32.6	212 22.6	04.7
	23	133 06.4	126 17.6	48.0	118 54.3	56.1	291 20.7	32.5	227 24.9	04.7
	Mer. Pass.	h m 14 13.0	v 1.4	d 0.9	v 0.8	d 0.7	v 2.5	d 0.0	v 2.3	d 0.0

STARS

Name	SHA	Dec
	° ′	° ′
Acamar	315 16.6	S40 14.6
Achernar	335 25.3	S57 09.4
Acrux	173 05.8	S63 11.4
Adhara	255 10.3	S29 00.1
Aldebaran	290 46.4	N16 32.4
Alioth	166 18.2	N55 51.8
Alkaid	152 56.8	N49 13.5
Al Na'ir	27 41.2	S46 52.7
Alnilam	275 43.7	S 1 11.8
Alphard	217 53.3	S 8 44.2
Alphecca	126 08.9	N26 39.4
Alpheratz	357 41.2	N29 11.0
Altair	62 06.1	N 8 54.8
Ankaa	353 13.6	S42 13.1
Antares	112 23.3	S26 27.9
Arcturus	145 53.4	N19 05.5
Atria	107 23.0	S69 03.0
Avior	234 16.3	S59 34.1
Bellatrix	278 29.2	N 6 21.6
Betelgeuse	270 58.4	N 7 24.3
Canopus	263 54.7	S52 42.7
Capella	280 30.6	N46 00.8
Deneb	49 30.2	N45 20.5
Denebola	182 30.9	N14 28.5
Diphda	348 53.7	S17 53.8
Dubhe	193 48.2	N61 39.4
Elnath	278 09.3	N28 37.1
Eltanin	90 45.3	N51 29.1
Enif	33 45.0	N 9 57.2
Fomalhaut	15 21.6	S29 32.0
Gacrux	171 57.6	S57 12.3
Gienah	175 49.5	S17 38.2
Hadar	148 44.0	S60 27.0
Hamal	327 58.1	N23 32.5
Kaus Aust.	83 40.8	S34 22.3
Kochab	137 20.0	N74 04.9
Markab	13 36.1	N15 17.8
Menkar	314 12.5	N 4 09.1
Menkent	148 04.4	S36 27.0
Miaplacidus	221 38.1	S69 47.4
Mirfak	308 36.8	N49 55.3
Nunki	75 55.5	S26 16.3
Peacock	53 16.0	S56 40.6
Pollux	243 24.4	N27 58.9
Procyon	244 56.9	N 5 10.6
Rasalhague	96 04.3	N12 32.9
Regulus	207 40.6	N11 52.8
Rigel	281 09.5	S 8 11.3
Rigil Kent.	139 48.1	S60 53.9
Sabik	102 09.8	S15 44.6
Schedar	349 38.0	N56 37.9
Shaula	96 18.7	S37 06.7
Sirius	258 31.3	S16 44.7
Spica	158 28.4	S11 15.0
Suhail	222 50.1	S43 30.3
Vega	80 37.6	N38 47.9
Zuben'ubi	137 02.6	S16 06.6

	SHA	Mer. Pass.
	° ′	h m
Venus	353 59.2	14 38
Mars	347 07.4	15 06
Jupiter	158 10.8	3 42
Saturn	94 27.9	7 56

Day	UT	SUN GHA	SUN Dec	MOON GHA	v	MOON Dec	d	HP
	d h	° ′	° ′	° ′	′	° ′	′	′
WEDNESDAY	15 00	176 28.3	S12 41.1	310 40.2	14.0	S 2 26.6	9.9	55.5
	01	191 28.4	40.2	325 13.2	14.1	2 36.5	10.0	55.4
	02	206 28.4	39.3	339 46.3	14.0	2 46.5	9.9	55.4
	03	221 28.4	. . 38.5	354 19.3	14.1	2 56.4	9.9	55.4
	04	236 28.5	37.6	8 52.4	14.0	3 06.3	9.8	55.4
	05	251 28.5	36.8	23 25.4	14.1	3 16.1	9.9	55.3
	06	266 28.5	S12 35.9	37 58.5	14.2	S 3 26.0	9.8	55.3
	07	281 28.6	35.0	52 31.7	14.1	3 35.8	9.8	55.3
	08	296 28.6	34.2	67 04.8	14.1	3 45.6	9.8	55.3
	09	311 28.6	. . 33.3	81 37.9	14.2	3 55.4	9.7	55.3
	10	326 28.7	32.5	96 11.1	14.2	4 05.1	9.7	55.2
	11	341 28.7	31.6	110 44.3	14.2	4 14.8	9.7	55.2
	12	356 28.7	S12 30.7	125 17.5	14.2	S 4 24.5	9.7	55.2
	13	11 28.8	29.9	139 50.7	14.2	4 34.2	9.6	55.2
	14	26 28.8	29.0	154 23.9	14.2	4 43.8	9.6	55.1
	15	41 28.8	. . 28.1	168 57.1	14.3	4 53.4	9.6	55.1
	16	56 28.9	27.3	183 30.4	14.2	5 03.0	9.5	55.1
	17	71 28.9	26.4	198 03.6	14.3	5 12.5	9.5	55.1
	18	86 28.9	S12 25.6	212 36.9	14.3	S 5 22.0	9.5	55.1
	19	101 29.0	24.7	227 10.2	14.3	5 31.5	9.5	55.0
	20	116 29.0	23.8	241 43.5	14.2	5 41.0	9.4	55.0
	21	131 29.1	. . 23.0	256 16.7	14.3	5 50.4	9.4	55.0
	22	146 29.1	22.1	270 50.0	14.4	5 59.8	9.3	55.0
	23	161 29.1	21.2	285 23.4	14.3	6 09.1	9.4	55.0
THURSDAY	16 00	176 29.2	S12 20.4	299 56.7	14.3	S 6 18.5	9.2	54.9
	01	191 29.2	19.5	314 30.0	14.3	6 27.7	9.3	54.9
	02	206 29.2	18.6	329 03.3	14.3	6 37.0	9.2	54.9
	03	221 29.3	. . 17.8	343 36.6	14.4	6 46.2	9.2	54.9
	04	236 29.3	16.9	358 10.0	14.3	6 55.4	9.1	54.9
	05	251 29.4	16.0	12 43.3	14.3	7 04.5	9.1	54.8
	06	266 29.4	S12 15.2	27 16.6	14.4	S 7 13.6	9.1	54.8
	07	281 29.4	14.3	41 50.0	14.3	7 22.7	9.0	54.8
	08	296 29.5	13.4	56 23.3	14.4	7 31.7	9.0	54.8
	09	311 29.5	. . 12.6	70 56.7	14.3	7 40.7	9.0	54.8
	10	326 29.6	11.7	85 30.0	14.3	7 49.7	8.9	54.8
	11	341 29.6	10.8	100 03.3	14.4	7 58.6	8.9	54.7
	12	356 29.6	S12 09.9	114 36.7	14.3	S 8 07.5	8.8	54.7
	13	11 29.7	09.1	129 10.0	14.4	8 16.3	8.8	54.7
	14	26 29.7	08.2	143 43.4	14.3	8 25.1	8.7	54.7
	15	41 29.8	. . 07.3	158 16.7	14.3	8 33.8	8.7	54.7
	16	56 29.8	06.5	172 50.0	14.3	8 42.5	8.7	54.7
	17	71 29.9	05.6	187 23.3	14.4	8 51.2	8.6	54.6
	18	86 29.9	S12 04.7	201 56.7	14.3	S 8 59.8	8.6	54.6
	19	101 29.9	03.8	216 30.0	14.3	9 08.4	8.5	54.6
	20	116 30.0	03.0	231 03.3	14.3	9 16.9	8.5	54.6
	21	131 30.0	. . 02.1	245 36.6	14.3	9 25.4	8.5	54.6
	22	146 30.1	01.2	260 09.9	14.3	9 33.9	8.4	54.6
	23	161 30.1	12 00.3	274 43.2	14.3	9 42.3	8.3	54.5
FRIDAY	17 00	176 30.2	S11 59.5	289 16.5	14.3	S 9 50.6	8.3	54.5
	01	191 30.2	58.6	303 49.8	14.2	9 58.9	8.3	54.5
	02	206 30.3	57.7	318 23.0	14.3	10 07.2	8.2	54.5
	03	221 30.3	. . 56.8	332 56.3	14.2	10 15.4	8.2	54.5
	04	236 30.3	56.0	347 29.5	14.3	10 23.6	8.1	54.5
	05	251 30.4	55.1	2 02.8	14.2	10 31.7	8.0	54.5
	06	266 30.4	S11 54.2	16 36.0	14.2	S10 39.7	8.1	54.5
	07	281 30.5	53.3	31 09.2	14.2	10 47.8	7.9	54.4
	08	296 30.5	52.5	45 42.4	14.2	10 55.7	7.9	54.4
	09	311 30.6	. . 51.6	60 15.6	14.2	11 03.6	7.9	54.4
	10	326 30.6	50.7	74 48.8	14.1	11 11.5	7.8	54.4
	11	341 30.7	49.8	89 21.9	14.2	11 19.3	7.8	54.4
	12	356 30.7	S11 48.9	103 55.1	14.1	S11 27.1	7.7	54.4
	13	11 30.8	48.1	118 28.2	14.1	11 34.8	7.7	54.4
	14	26 30.8	47.2	133 01.3	14.1	11 42.5	7.6	54.4
	15	41 30.9	. . 46.3	147 34.4	14.1	11 50.1	7.5	54.4
	16	56 30.9	45.4	162 07.5	14.1	11 57.6	7.5	54.4
	17	71 31.0	44.5	176 40.6	14.0	12 05.1	7.5	54.3
	18	86 31.0	S11 43.7	191 13.6	14.1	S12 12.6	7.4	54.3
	19	101 31.1	42.8	205 46.7	14.0	12 20.0	7.3	54.3
	20	116 31.1	41.9	220 19.7	14.0	12 27.3	7.3	54.3
	21	131 31.2	. . 41.0	234 52.7	14.0	12 34.6	7.2	54.3
	22	146 31.2	40.1	249 25.7	13.9	12 41.8	7.2	54.3
	23	161 31.3	39.3	263 58.6	14.0	S12 49.0	7.1	54.3
		SD 16.2	*d* 0.9	SD 15.0		14.9		14.8

Lat.	Twilight Naut.	Twilight Civil	Sunrise	Moonrise 15	Moonrise 16	Moonrise 17	Moonrise 18
°	h m	h m	h m	h m	h m	h m	h m
N 72	06 09	07 29	08 47	23 19	24 57	00 57	02 38
N 70	06 08	07 20	08 28	23 09	24 40	00 40	02 12
68	06 07	07 12	08 13	23 02	24 27	00 27	01 52
66	06 06	07 06	08 01	22 55	24 17	00 17	01 36
64	06 05	07 00	07 51	22 50	24 08	00 08	01 23
62	06 04	06 56	07 42	22 45	24 00	00 00	01 13
60	06 03	06 51	07 35	22 41	23 53	25 03	01 03
N 58	06 02	06 47	07 28	22 38	23 48	24 55	00 55
56	06 01	06 44	07 23	22 35	23 42	24 48	00 48
54	06 00	06 41	07 17	22 32	23 38	24 42	00 42
52	05 59	06 38	07 13	22 30	23 34	24 36	00 36
50	05 57	06 35	07 08	22 27	23 30	24 31	00 31
45	05 55	06 29	06 59	22 22	23 22	24 20	00 20
N 40	05 52	06 24	06 51	22 18	23 15	24 11	00 11
35	05 49	06 19	06 45	22 15	23 09	24 04	00 04
30	05 46	06 14	06 39	22 11	23 04	23 57	24 49
20	05 40	06 06	06 29	22 06	22 56	23 45	24 34
N 10	05 33	05 58	06 19	22 01	22 48	23 35	24 22
0	05 25	05 49	06 11	21 57	22 41	23 25	24 10
S 10	05 15	05 40	06 02	21 53	22 34	23 16	23 59
20	05 03	05 30	05 52	21 48	22 26	23 06	23 47
30	04 47	05 16	05 41	21 43	22 18	22 54	23 33
35	04 37	05 08	05 35	21 40	22 13	22 48	23 24
40	04 24	04 59	05 27	21 36	22 08	22 40	23 15
45	04 09	04 47	05 19	21 33	22 01	22 31	23 05
S 50	03 49	04 33	05 08	21 28	21 54	22 21	22 52
52	03 40	04 26	05 04	21 26	21 50	22 16	22 46
54	03 28	04 19	04 58	21 24	21 46	22 11	22 39
56	03 15	04 10	04 52	21 21	21 42	22 05	22 32
58	03 00	04 01	04 46	21 18	21 37	21 58	22 23
S 60	02 40	03 49	04 38	21 15	21 32	21 51	22 14

Lat.	Sunset	Twilight Civil	Twilight Naut.	Moonset 15	Moonset 16	Moonset 17	Moonset 18
°	h m	h m	h m	h m	h m	h m	h m
N 72	15 43	17 01	18 21	08 43	08 37	08 30	08 21
N 70	16 02	17 10	18 22	08 49	08 48	08 48	08 48
68	16 16	17 17	18 23	08 53	08 57	09 02	09 09
66	16 28	17 24	18 24	08 57	09 05	09 14	09 26
64	16 38	17 29	18 25	09 00	09 11	09 24	09 39
62	16 47	17 34	18 26	09 03	09 17	09 32	09 50
60	16 54	17 38	18 27	09 05	09 22	09 39	10 00
N 58	17 01	17 42	18 28	09 08	09 26	09 46	10 09
56	17 06	17 45	18 28	09 10	09 30	09 52	10 16
54	17 11	17 48	18 29	09 11	09 33	09 57	10 23
52	17 16	17 51	18 30	09 13	09 36	10 01	10 29
50	17 20	17 54	18 31	09 14	09 39	10 06	10 35
45	17 29	18 00	18 34	09 17	09 46	10 15	10 46
N 40	17 37	18 05	18 37	09 20	09 51	10 23	10 56
35	17 44	18 10	18 39	09 22	09 55	10 29	11 05
30	17 50	18 14	18 42	09 24	09 59	10 35	11 12
20	18 00	18 22	18 48	09 28	10 06	10 45	11 25
N 10	18 09	18 30	18 55	09 31	10 12	10 54	11 36
0	18 17	18 39	19 03	09 34	10 18	11 02	11 47
S 10	18 26	18 48	19 13	09 37	10 24	11 11	11 57
20	18 36	18 58	19 25	09 40	10 30	11 19	12 09
30	18 46	19 11	19 41	09 44	10 37	11 30	12 22
35	18 53	19 19	19 51	09 46	10 41	11 36	12 29
40	19 00	19 28	20 03	09 48	10 46	11 42	12 38
45	19 08	19 40	20 18	09 51	10 51	11 50	12 48
S 50	19 19	19 54	20 37	09 54	10 58	12 00	13 00
52	19 23	20 00	20 47	09 55	11 00	12 04	13 06
54	19 28	20 08	20 58	09 57	11 04	12 09	13 12
56	19 34	20 16	21 10	09 59	11 07	12 14	13 19
58	19 41	20 26	21 26	10 01	11 11	12 20	13 27
S 60	19 48	20 37	21 44	10 03	11 16	12 27	13 36

Day	SUN Eqn. of Time 00^h	SUN Eqn. of Time 12^h	SUN Mer. Pass.	MOON Mer. Pass. Upper	MOON Mer. Pass. Lower	MOON Age	MOON Phase
d	m s	m s	h m	h m	h m	d %	
15	14 07	14 05	12 14	03 23	15 46	18 80	
16	14 03	14 02	12 14	04 08	16 30	19 71	
17	13 59	13 57	12 14	04 52	17 14	20 62	

UT d h	ARIES GHA ° ′	VENUS −4·8 GHA ° ′	VENUS Dec ° ′	MARS +1·2 GHA ° ′	MARS Dec ° ′	JUPITER −2·3 GHA ° ′	JUPITER Dec ° ′	SATURN +0·5 GHA ° ′	SATURN Dec ° ′
18 00	148 08.8	141 19.1	N 7 48.9	133 55.0	N 5 56.8	306 23.3	S 7 32.5	242 27.2	S22 04.8
01	163 11.3	156 20.6	49.8	148 55.8	57.6	321 25.8	32.4	257 29.4	04.8
02	178 13.8	171 22.1	50.7	163 56.6	58.3	336 28.4	32.4	272 31.7	04.8
03	193 16.2	186 23.6 . .	51.6	178 57.4 . .	59.0	351 30.9 . .	32.4	287 34.0 . .	04.8
04	208 18.7	201 25.1	52.4	193 58.1	5 59.8	6 33.5	32.3	302 36.3	04.8
05	223 21.2	216 26.6	53.3	208 58.9	6 00.5	21 36.0	32.3	317 38.5	04.8
06	238 23.6	231 28.1	N 7 54.2	223 59.7	N 6 01.3	36 38.6	S 7 32.2	332 40.8	S22 04.8
07	253 26.1	246 29.7	55.1	239 00.4	02.0	51 41.1	32.2	347 43.1	04.8
S 08	268 28.6	261 31.2	55.9	254 01.2	02.7	66 43.7	32.1	2 45.3	04.8
A 09	283 31.0	276 32.7 . .	56.8	269 02.0 . .	03.5	81 46.2 . .	32.1	17 47.6 . .	04.8
T 10	298 33.5	291 34.2	57.7	284 02.8	04.2	96 48.8	32.1	32 49.9	04.8
U 11	313 35.9	306 35.8	58.6	299 03.5	05.0	111 51.3	32.0	47 52.1	04.8
R 12	328 38.4	321 37.3	N 7 59.4	314 04.3	N 6 05.7	126 53.9	S 7 32.0	62 54.4	S22 04.8
D 13	343 40.9	336 38.8	8 00.3	329 05.1	06.4	141 56.4	31.9	77 56.7	04.8
A 14	358 43.3	351 40.4	01.2	344 05.8	07.2	156 59.0	31.9	92 58.9	04.8
Y 15	13 45.8	6 41.9 . .	02.0	359 06.6 . .	07.9	172 01.5 . .	31.8	108 01.2 . .	04.8
16	28 48.3	21 43.5	02.9	14 07.4	08.7	187 04.1	31.8	123 03.5	04.8
17	43 50.7	36 45.0	03.8	29 08.2	09.4	202 06.6	31.7	138 05.8	04.8
18	58 53.2	51 46.6	N 8 04.6	44 08.9	N 6 10.1	217 09.2	S 7 31.7	153 08.0	S22 04.8
19	73 55.7	66 48.1	05.5	59 09.7	10.9	232 11.7	31.6	168 10.3	04.8
20	88 58.1	81 49.7	06.4	74 10.5	11.6	247 14.3	31.6	183 12.6	04.8
21	104 00.6	96 51.2 . .	07.2	89 11.2 . .	12.4	262 16.8 . .	31.6	198 14.8 . .	04.8
22	119 03.0	111 52.8	08.1	104 12.0	13.1	277 19.4	31.5	213 17.1	04.8
23	134 05.5	126 54.3	08.9	119 12.8	13.8	292 21.9	31.5	228 19.4	04.8
19 00	149 08.0	141 55.9	N 8 09.8	134 13.6	N 6 14.6	307 24.5	S 7 31.4	243 21.7	S22 04.8
01	164 10.4	156 57.5	10.6	149 14.3	15.3	322 27.0	31.4	258 23.9	04.8
02	179 12.9	171 59.1	11.5	164 15.1	16.0	337 29.6	31.3	273 26.2	04.8
03	194 15.4	187 00.6 . .	12.4	179 15.9 . .	16.8	352 32.1 . .	31.3	288 28.5 . .	04.8
04	209 17.8	202 02.2	13.2	194 16.6	17.5	7 34.7	31.2	303 30.7	04.8
05	224 20.3	217 03.8	14.1	209 17.4	18.3	22 37.3	31.2	318 33.0	04.8
06	239 22.8	232 05.4	N 8 14.9	224 18.2	N 6 19.0	37 39.8	S 7 31.1	333 35.3	S22 04.8
07	254 25.2	247 06.9	15.8	239 19.0	19.7	52 42.4	31.1	348 37.6	04.9
08	269 27.7	262 08.5	16.6	254 19.7	20.5	67 44.9	31.1	3 39.8	04.9
S 09	284 30.2	277 10.1 . .	17.5	269 20.5 . .	21.2	82 47.5 . .	31.0	18 42.1 . .	04.9
U 10	299 32.6	292 11.7	18.3	284 21.3	21.9	97 50.0	31.0	33 44.4	04.9
N 11	314 35.1	307 13.3	19.2	299 22.0	22.7	112 52.6	30.9	48 46.7	04.9
D 12	329 37.5	322 14.9	N 8 20.0	314 22.8	N 6 23.4	127 55.2	S 7 30.9	63 48.9	S22 04.9
A 13	344 40.0	337 16.5	20.8	329 23.6	24.2	142 57.7	30.8	78 51.2	04.9
Y 14	359 42.5	352 18.1	21.7	344 24.3	24.9	158 00.3	30.8	93 53.5	04.9
15	14 44.9	7 19.7 . .	22.5	359 25.1 . .	25.6	173 02.8 . .	30.7	108 55.8 . .	04.9
16	29 47.4	22 21.3	23.4	14 25.9	26.4	188 05.4	30.7	123 58.0	04.9
17	44 49.9	37 22.9	24.2	29 26.7	27.1	203 07.9	30.6	139 00.3	04.9
18	59 52.3	52 24.6	N 8 25.0	44 27.4	N 6 27.8	218 10.5	S 7 30.6	154 02.6	S22 04.9
19	74 54.8	67 26.2	25.9	59 28.2	28.6	233 13.1	30.5	169 04.9	04.9
20	89 57.3	82 27.8	26.7	74 29.0	29.3	248 15.6	30.5	184 07.1	04.9
21	104 59.7	97 29.4 . .	27.6	89 29.7 . .	30.0	263 18.2 . .	30.4	199 09.4 . .	04.9
22	120 02.2	112 31.0	28.4	104 30.5	30.8	278 20.7	30.4	214 11.7	04.9
23	135 04.7	127 32.7	29.2	119 31.3	31.5	293 23.3	30.3	229 14.0	04.9
20 00	150 07.1	142 34.3	N 8 30.1	134 32.1	N 6 32.2	308 25.9	S 7 30.3	244 16.2	S22 04.9
01	165 09.6	157 35.9	30.9	149 32.8	33.0	323 28.4	30.2	259 18.5	04.9
02	180 12.0	172 37.6	31.7	164 33.6	33.7	338 31.0	30.2	274 20.8	04.9
03	195 14.5	187 39.2 . .	32.5	179 34.4 . .	34.4	353 33.5 . .	30.1	289 23.1 . .	04.9
04	210 17.0	202 40.9	33.4	194 35.1	35.2	8 36.1	30.1	304 25.3	04.9
05	225 19.4	217 42.5	34.2	209 35.9	35.9	23 38.7	30.0	319 27.6	04.9
06	240 21.9	232 44.1	N 8 35.0	224 36.7	N 6 36.7	38 41.2	S 7 30.0	334 29.9	S22 04.9
07	255 24.4	247 45.8	35.8	239 37.4	37.4	53 43.8	30.0	349 32.2	04.9
08	270 26.8	262 47.5	36.7	254 38.2	38.1	68 46.4	29.9	4 34.4	04.9
M 09	285 29.3	277 49.1 . .	37.5	269 39.0 . .	38.9	83 48.9 . .	29.9	19 36.7 . .	04.9
O 10	300 31.8	292 50.8	38.3	284 39.8	39.6	98 51.5	29.8	34 39.0	04.9
N 11	315 34.2	307 52.4	39.1	299 40.5	40.3	113 54.1	29.8	49 41.3	04.9
D 12	330 36.7	322 54.1	N 8 39.9	314 41.3	N 6 41.1	128 56.6	S 7 29.7	64 43.5	S22 04.9
A 13	345 39.1	337 55.8	40.8	329 42.1	41.8	143 59.2	29.7	79 45.8	04.9
Y 14	0 41.6	352 57.4	41.6	344 42.8	42.5	159 01.7	29.6	94 48.1	04.9
15	15 44.1	7 59.1 . .	42.4	359 43.6 . .	43.3	174 04.3 . .	29.6	109 50.4 . .	04.9
16	30 46.5	23 00.8	43.2	14 44.4	44.0	189 06.9	29.5	124 52.7	04.9
17	45 49.0	38 02.5	44.0	29 45.1	44.7	204 09.4	29.5	139 54.9	05.0
18	60 51.5	53 04.1	N 8 44.8	44 45.9	N 6 45.5	219 12.0	S 7 29.4	154 57.2	S22 05.0
19	75 53.9	68 05.8	45.6	59 46.7	46.2	234 14.6	29.4	169 59.5	05.0
20	90 56.4	83 07.5	46.4	74 47.5	46.9	249 17.1	29.3	185 01.8	05.0
21	105 58.9	98 09.2 . .	47.3	89 48.2 . .	47.6	264 19.7 . .	29.2	200 04.0 . .	05.0
22	121 01.3	113 10.9	48.1	104 49.0	48.4	279 22.3	29.2	215 06.3	05.0
23	136 03.8	128 12.6	48.9	119 49.8	49.1	294 24.8	29.1	230 08.6	05.0
Mer. Pass. h m	14 01.2	*v* 1.6	*d* 0.8	*v* 0.8	*d* 0.7	*v* 2.6	*d* 0.0	*v* 2.3	*d* 0.0

STARS

Name	SHA ° ′	Dec ° ′
Acamar	315 16.6	S40 14.6
Achernar	335 25.3	S57 09.4
Acrux	173 05.8	S63 11.5
Adhara	255 10.3	S29 00.1
Aldebaran	290 46.4	N16 32.4
Alioth	166 18.2	N55 51.8
Alkaid	152 56.7	N49 13.5
Al Na'ir	27 41.1	S46 52.7
Alnilam	275 43.7	S 1 11.8
Alphard	217 53.3	S 8 44.2
Alphecca	126 08.9	N26 39.4
Alpheratz	357 41.2	N29 11.0
Altair	62 06.1	N 8 54.8
Ankaa	353 13.6	S42 13.1
Antares	112 23.2	S26 27.9
Arcturus	145 53.3	N19 05.5
Atria	107 22.9	S69 03.0
Avior	234 16.4	S59 34.2
Bellatrix	278 29.2	N 6 21.6
Betelgeuse	270 58.4	N 7 24.3
Canopus	263 54.7	S52 42.7
Capella	280 30.6	N46 00.8
Deneb	49 30.2	N45 20.5
Denebola	182 30.9	N14 28.5
Diphda	348 53.7	S17 53.8
Dubhe	193 48.1	N61 39.4
Elnath	278 09.3	N28 37.1
Eltanin	90 45.2	N51 29.1
Enif	33 45.0	N 9 57.2
Fomalhaut	15 21.6	S29 32.0
Gacrux	171 57.5	S57 12.4
Gienah	175 49.4	S17 38.2
Hadar	148 43.9	S60 27.0
Hamal	327 58.1	N23 32.5
Kaus Aust.	83 40.8	S34 22.3
Kochab	137 19.9	N74 04.9
Markab	13 36.1	N15 17.8
Menkar	314 12.5	N 4 09.1
Menkent	148 04.4	S36 27.0
Miaplacidus	221 38.1	S69 47.4
Mirfak	308 36.8	N49 55.3
Nunki	75 55.5	S26 16.3
Peacock	53 15.9	S56 40.6
Pollux	243 24.4	N27 58.9
Procyon	244 56.9	N 5 10.6
Rasalhague	96 04.3	N12 32.9
Regulus	207 40.6	N11 52.8
Rigel	281 09.6	S 8 11.3
Rigil Kent.	139 48.0	S60 53.9
Sabik	102 09.8	S15 44.6
Schedar	349 38.0	N56 37.9
Shaula	96 18.7	S37 06.7
Sirius	258 31.3	S16 44.8
Spica	158 28.4	S11 15.0
Suhail	222 50.1	S43 30.3
Vega	80 37.5	N38 47.9
Zuben'ubi	137 02.6	S16 06.6

	SHA ° ′	Mer. Pass. h m
Venus	352 47.9	14 31
Mars	345 05.6	15 02
Jupiter	158 16.5	3 30
Saturn	94 13.7	7 45

UT		SUN GHA	SUN Dec	MOON GHA	v	MOON Dec	d	HP
d	h	° ′	° ′	° ′	′	° ′	′	′
18	00	176 31.3	S11 38.4	278 31.6	13.9	S12 56.1	7.1	54.3
	01	191 31.4	37.5	293 04.5	13.9	13 03.2	7.0	54.3
	02	206 31.4	36.6	307 37.4	13.9	13 10.2	6.9	54.3
	03	221 31.5	. . 35.7	322 10.3	13.9	13 17.1	6.9	54.3
	04	236 31.5	34.8	336 43.2	13.8	13 24.0	6.8	54.3
	05	251 31.6	34.0	351 16.0	13.8	13 30.8	6.8	54.3
	06	266 31.6	S11 33.1	5 48.8	13.8	S13 37.6	6.7	54.3
	07	281 31.7	32.2	20 21.6	13.8	13 44.3	6.6	54.3
S	08	296 31.7	31.3	34 54.4	13.7	13 50.9	6.6	54.3
A	09	311 31.8	. . 30.4	49 27.1	13.7	13 57.5	6.5	54.2
T	10	326 31.9	29.5	63 59.8	13.7	14 04.0	6.5	54.2
U	11	341 31.9	28.7	78 32.5	13.7	14 10.5	6.4	54.2
R	12	356 32.0	S11 27.8	93 05.2	13.7	S14 16.9	6.3	54.2
D	13	11 32.0	26.9	107 37.9	13.6	14 23.2	6.3	54.2
A	14	26 32.1	26.0	122 10.5	13.6	14 29.5	6.2	54.2
Y	15	41 32.1	. . 25.1	136 43.1	13.6	14 35.7	6.1	54.2
	16	56 32.2	24.2	151 15.7	13.5	14 41.8	6.1	54.2
	17	71 32.2	23.3	165 48.2	13.6	14 47.9	6.0	54.2
	18	86 32.3	S11 22.4	180 20.8	13.4	S14 53.9	6.0	54.2
	19	101 32.4	21.6	194 53.2	13.5	14 59.9	5.9	54.2
	20	116 32.4	20.7	209 25.7	13.5	15 05.8	5.8	54.2
	21	131 32.5	. . 19.8	223 58.2	13.4	15 11.6	5.7	54.2
	22	146 32.5	18.9	238 30.6	13.4	15 17.3	5.7	54.2
	23	161 32.6	18.0	253 03.0	13.3	15 23.0	5.7	54.2
19	00	176 32.7	S11 17.1	267 35.3	13.4	S15 28.7	5.5	54.2
	01	191 32.7	16.2	282 07.7	13.3	15 34.2	5.5	54.2
	02	206 32.8	15.3	296 40.0	13.2	15 39.7	5.4	54.2
	03	221 32.8	. . 14.4	311 12.2	13.3	15 45.1	5.3	54.2
	04	236 32.9	13.5	325 44.5	13.2	15 50.4	5.3	54.2
	05	251 33.0	12.7	340 16.7	13.2	15 55.7	5.2	54.2
	06	266 33.0	S11 11.8	354 48.9	13.1	S16 00.9	5.2	54.2
	07	281 33.1	10.9	9 21.0	13.2	16 06.1	5.0	54.2
	08	296 33.1	10.0	23 53.2	13.1	16 11.1	5.0	54.2
S	09	311 33.2	. . 09.1	38 25.3	13.0	16 16.1	5.0	54.2
U	10	326 33.3	08.2	52 57.3	13.1	16 21.1	4.8	54.3
N	11	341 33.3	07.3	67 29.4	13.0	16 25.9	4.8	54.3
D	12	356 33.4	S11 06.4	82 01.4	12.9	S16 30.7	4.7	54.3
A	13	11 33.4	05.5	96 33.3	13.0	16 35.4	4.6	54.3
Y	14	26 33.5	04.6	111 05.3	12.9	16 40.0	4.6	54.3
	15	41 33.6	. . 03.7	125 37.2	12.9	16 44.6	4.5	54.3
	16	56 33.6	02.8	140 09.1	12.8	16 49.1	4.4	54.3
	17	71 33.7	01.9	154 40.9	12.9	16 53.5	4.3	54.3
	18	86 33.8	S11 01.0	169 12.8	12.7	S16 57.8	4.3	54.3
	19	101 33.8	11 00.1	183 44.5	12.8	17 02.1	4.2	54.3
	20	116 33.9	10 59.2	198 16.3	12.7	17 06.3	4.1	54.3
	21	131 34.0	. . 58.3	212 48.0	12.7	17 10.4	4.0	54.3
	22	146 34.0	57.4	227 19.7	12.7	17 14.4	4.0	54.3
	23	161 34.1	56.6	241 51.4	12.6	17 18.4	3.8	54.3
20	00	176 34.1	S10 55.7	256 23.0	12.6	S17 22.2	3.9	54.3
	01	191 34.2	54.8	270 54.6	12.6	17 26.1	3.7	54.3
	02	206 34.3	53.9	285 26.2	12.5	17 29.8	3.6	54.4
	03	221 34.3	. . 53.0	299 57.7	12.5	17 33.4	3.6	54.4
	04	236 34.4	52.1	314 29.2	12.5	17 37.0	3.5	54.4
	05	251 34.5	51.2	329 00.7	12.4	17 40.5	3.4	54.4
	06	266 34.5	S10 50.3	343 32.1	12.4	S17 43.9	3.3	54.4
	07	281 34.6	49.4	358 03.5	12.4	17 47.2	3.3	54.4
	08	296 34.7	48.5	12 34.9	12.3	17 50.5	3.1	54.4
M	09	311 34.7	. . 47.6	27 06.2	12.3	17 53.6	3.1	54.4
O	10	326 34.8	46.7	41 37.5	12.3	17 56.7	3.0	54.4
N	11	341 34.9	45.8	56 08.8	12.2	17 59.7	2.9	54.4
D	12	356 35.0	S10 44.9	70 40.0	12.2	S18 02.6	2.9	54.5
A	13	11 35.0	44.0	85 11.2	12.2	18 05.5	2.7	54.5
Y	14	26 35.1	43.1	99 42.4	12.2	18 08.2	2.7	54.5
	15	41 35.2	. . 42.2	114 13.6	12.1	18 10.9	2.6	54.5
	16	56 35.2	41.3	128 44.7	12.1	18 13.5	2.5	54.5
	17	71 35.3	40.4	143 15.8	12.0	18 16.0	2.4	54.5
	18	86 35.4	S10 39.5	157 46.8	12.0	S18 18.4	2.4	54.5
	19	101 35.4	38.6	172 17.8	12.0	18 20.8	2.2	54.5
	20	116 35.5	37.6	186 48.8	12.0	18 23.0	2.2	54.6
	21	131 35.6	. . 36.7	201 19.8	11.9	18 25.2	2.1	54.6
	22	146 35.7	35.8	215 50.7	11.9	18 27.3	2.0	54.6
	23	161 35.7	34.9	230 21.6	11.9	S18 29.3	1.9	54.6
		SD 16.2	*d* 0.9	SD 14.8		14.8		14.8

Lat.	Twilight Naut.	Twilight Civil	Sunrise	Moonrise 18	Moonrise 19	Moonrise 20	Moonrise 21
°	h m	h m	h m	h m	h m	h m	h m
N 72	05 56	07 15	08 30	02 38	04 25	06 38	■
N 70	05 56	07 07	08 13	02 12	03 43	05 11	06 30
68	05 56	07 01	08 01	01 52	03 14	04 33	05 41
66	05 56	06 56	07 50	01 36	02 53	04 06	05 09
64	05 56	06 51	07 41	01 23	02 36	03 45	04 46
62	05 56	06 47	07 33	01 13	02 23	03 28	04 28
60	05 55	06 44	07 27	01 03	02 11	03 15	04 13
N 58	05 55	06 40	07 21	00 55	02 01	03 03	04 00
56	05 54	06 37	07 16	00 48	01 52	02 53	03 49
54	05 54	06 35	07 11	00 42	01 44	02 44	03 39
52	05 53	06 32	07 07	00 36	01 37	02 35	03 30
50	05 52	06 30	07 03	00 31	01 31	02 28	03 22
45	05 50	06 25	06 55	00 20	01 17	02 13	03 06
N 40	05 48	06 20	06 48	00 11	01 06	02 00	02 52
35	05 46	06 16	06 41	00 04	00 57	01 49	02 41
30	05 44	06 12	06 36	24 49	00 49	01 40	02 31
20	05 38	06 04	06 27	24 34	00 34	01 24	02 13
N 10	05 32	05 57	06 18	24 22	00 22	01 10	01 58
0	05 25	05 49	06 10	24 10	00 10	00 57	01 44
S 10	05 16	05 41	06 02	23 59	24 44	00 44	01 30
20	05 05	05 31	05 54	23 47	24 30	00 30	01 15
30	04 50	05 19	05 44	23 33	24 14	00 14	00 58
35	04 40	05 11	05 38	23 24	24 04	00 04	00 48
40	04 29	05 03	05 31	23 15	23 54	24 37	00 37
45	04 14	04 52	05 23	23 05	23 42	24 24	00 24
S 50	03 56	04 39	05 14	22 52	23 27	24 07	00 07
52	03 47	04 33	05 09	22 46	23 20	24 00	00 00
54	03 36	04 26	05 04	22 39	23 12	23 51	24 38
56	03 24	04 18	04 59	22 32	23 03	23 42	24 28
58	03 10	04 09	04 53	22 23	22 54	23 31	24 17
S 60	02 53	03 58	04 46	22 14	22 42	23 18	24 04

Lat.	Sunset	Twilight Civil	Twilight Naut.	Moonset 18	Moonset 19	Moonset 20	Moonset 21
°	h m	h m	h m	h m	h m	h m	h m
N 72	15 59	17 15	18 34	08 21	08 08	07 32	■
N 70	16 16	17 22	18 33	08 48	08 51	08 59	09 20
68	16 28	17 28	18 33	09 09	09 20	09 38	10 09
66	16 39	17 33	18 33	09 26	09 42	10 06	10 41
64	16 48	17 38	18 33	09 39	09 59	10 26	11 04
62	16 55	17 42	18 33	09 50	10 13	10 43	11 23
60	17 02	17 45	18 34	10 00	10 26	10 57	11 38
N 58	17 08	17 48	18 34	10 09	10 36	11 09	11 51
56	17 13	17 51	18 34	10 16	10 45	11 20	12 02
54	17 17	17 54	18 35	10 23	10 53	11 29	12 12
52	17 22	17 56	18 36	10 29	11 01	11 37	12 21
50	17 25	17 59	18 36	10 35	11 07	11 45	12 28
45	17 34	18 04	18 38	10 46	11 21	12 01	12 45
N 40	17 41	18 08	18 40	10 56	11 33	12 14	12 59
35	17 47	18 12	18 42	11 05	11 43	12 25	13 11
30	17 52	18 16	18 44	11 12	11 52	12 35	13 21
20	18 01	18 23	18 49	11 25	12 07	12 51	13 38
N 10	18 09	18 31	18 55	11 36	12 20	13 06	13 53
0	18 17	18 38	19 03	11 47	12 33	13 19	14 08
S 10	18 25	18 47	19 12	11 57	12 45	13 33	14 22
20	18 34	18 56	19 23	12 09	12 58	13 48	14 37
30	18 43	19 08	19 37	12 22	13 13	14 04	14 55
35	18 49	19 15	19 47	12 29	13 22	14 14	15 05
40	18 56	19 24	19 58	12 38	13 32	14 25	15 16
45	19 03	19 34	20 12	12 48	13 44	14 38	15 30
S 50	19 13	19 47	20 30	13 00	13 59	14 54	15 47
52	19 17	19 53	20 39	13 06	14 05	15 02	15 54
54	19 22	20 00	20 49	13 12	14 13	15 10	16 03
56	19 27	20 08	21 01	13 19	14 21	15 20	16 13
58	19 33	20 17	21 15	13 27	14 31	15 30	16 24
S 60	19 40	20 27	21 31	13 36	14 41	15 42	16 37

Day	SUN Eqn. of Time 00^h	SUN Eqn. of Time 12^h	SUN Mer. Pass.	MOON Mer. Pass. Upper	MOON Mer. Pass. Lower	Age	Phase
d	m s	m s	h m	h m	h m	d	%
18	13 55	13 52	12 14	05 36	17 59	21	53
19	13 50	13 47	12 14	06 21	18 45	22	44
20	13 44	13 40	12 14	07 08	19 32	23	34

UT d	h	ARIES GHA	VENUS −4·8 GHA	VENUS Dec	MARS +1·3 GHA	MARS Dec	JUPITER −2·3 GHA	JUPITER Dec	SATURN +0·5 GHA	SATURN Dec
		° ′	° ′	° ′	° ′	° ′	° ′	° ′	° ′	° ′
21 TUESDAY	00	151 06.3	143 14.3	N 8 49.7	134 50.5	N 6 49.8	309 27.4	S 7 29.1	245 10.9	S22 05.0
	01	166 08.7	158 16.0	50.5	149 51.3	50.6	324 30.0	29.0	260 13.2	05.0
	02	181 11.2	173 17.7	51.3	164 52.1	51.3	339 32.6	29.0	275 15.4	05.0
	03	196 13.6	188 19.4	52.1	179 52.8	52.0	354 35.1	28.9	290 17.7	05.0
	04	211 16.1	203 21.1	52.9	194 53.6	52.8	9 37.7	28.9	305 20.0	05.0
	05	226 18.6	218 22.8	53.7	209 54.4	53.5	24 40.3	28.8	320 22.3	05.0
	06	241 21.0	233 24.5	N 8 54.5	224 55.2	N 6 54.2	39 42.8	S 7 28.8	335 24.6	S22 05.0
	07	256 23.5	248 26.3	55.3	239 55.9	55.0	54 45.4	28.7	350 26.8	05.0
	08	271 26.0	263 28.0	56.1	254 56.7	55.7	69 48.0	28.7	5 29.1	05.0
	09	286 28.4	278 29.7	56.8	269 57.5	56.4	84 50.5	28.6	20 31.4	05.0
	10	301 30.9	293 31.4	57.6	284 58.2	57.2	99 53.1	28.6	35 33.7	05.0
	11	316 33.4	308 33.2	58.4	299 59.0	57.9	114 55.7	28.5	50 36.0	05.0
	12	331 35.8	323 34.9	N 8 59.2	314 59.8	N 6 58.6	129 58.3	S 7 28.5	65 38.2	S22 05.0
	13	346 38.3	338 36.6	9 00.0	330 00.5	6 59.3	145 00.8	28.4	80 40.5	05.0
	14	1 40.8	353 38.4	00.8	345 01.3	7 00.1	160 03.4	28.4	95 42.8	05.0
	15	16 43.2	8 40.1	01.6	0 02.1	00.8	175 06.0	28.3	110 45.1	05.0
	16	31 45.7	23 41.9	02.4	15 02.8	01.5	190 08.5	28.3	125 47.4	05.0
	17	46 48.1	38 43.6	03.1	30 03.6	02.3	205 11.1	28.2	140 49.6	05.0
	18	61 50.6	53 45.4	N 9 03.9	45 04.4	N 7 03.0	220 13.7	S 7 28.2	155 51.9	S22 05.0
	19	76 53.1	68 47.1	04.7	60 05.2	03.7	235 16.3	28.1	170 54.2	05.0
	20	91 55.5	83 48.9	05.5	75 05.9	04.5	250 18.8	28.1	185 56.5	05.0
	21	106 58.0	98 50.6	06.3	90 06.7	05.2	265 21.4	28.0	200 58.8	05.0
	22	122 00.5	113 52.4	07.0	105 07.5	05.9	280 24.0	27.9	216 01.1	05.0
	23	137 02.9	128 54.2	07.8	120 08.2	06.6	295 26.6	27.9	231 03.3	05.0
22 WEDNESDAY	00	152 05.4	143 55.9	N 9 08.6	135 09.0	N 7 07.4	310 29.1	S 7 27.8	246 05.6	S22 05.0
	01	167 07.9	158 57.7	09.4	150 09.8	08.1	325 31.7	27.8	261 07.9	05.0
	02	182 10.3	173 59.5	10.1	165 10.5	08.8	340 34.3	27.7	276 10.2	05.0
	03	197 12.8	189 01.3	10.9	180 11.3	09.6	355 36.9	27.7	291 12.5	05.0
	04	212 15.3	204 03.0	11.7	195 12.1	10.3	10 39.4	27.6	306 14.7	05.0
	05	227 17.7	219 04.8	12.4	210 12.8	11.0	25 42.0	27.6	321 17.0	05.0
	06	242 20.2	234 06.6	N 9 13.2	225 13.6	N 7 11.7	40 44.6	S 7 27.5	336 19.3	S22 05.0
	07	257 22.6	249 08.4	14.0	240 14.4	12.5	55 47.2	27.5	351 21.6	05.1
	08	272 25.1	264 10.2	14.7	255 15.2	13.2	70 49.8	27.4	6 23.9	05.1
	09	287 27.6	279 12.0	15.5	270 15.9	13.9	85 52.3	27.3	21 26.2	05.1
	10	302 30.0	294 13.8	16.3	285 16.7	14.7	100 54.9	27.3	36 28.4	05.1
	11	317 32.5	309 15.6	17.0	300 17.5	15.4	115 57.5	27.2	51 30.7	05.1
	12	332 35.0	324 17.4	N 9 17.8	315 18.2	N 7 16.1	131 00.1	S 7 27.2	66 33.0	S22 05.1
	13	347 37.4	339 19.2	18.5	330 19.0	16.8	146 02.6	27.1	81 35.3	05.1
	14	2 39.9	354 21.0	19.3	345 19.8	17.6	161 05.2	27.1	96 37.6	05.1
	15	17 42.4	9 22.8	20.1	0 20.5	18.3	176 07.8	27.0	111 39.9	05.1
	16	32 44.8	24 24.6	20.8	15 21.3	19.0	191 10.4	27.0	126 42.2	05.1
	17	47 47.3	39 26.5	21.6	30 22.1	19.7	206 13.0	26.9	141 44.4	05.1
	18	62 49.7	54 28.3	N 9 22.3	45 22.8	N 7 20.5	221 15.5	S 7 26.8	156 46.7	S22 05.1
	19	77 52.2	69 30.1	23.1	60 23.6	21.2	236 18.1	26.8	171 49.0	05.1
	20	92 54.7	84 31.9	23.8	75 24.4	21.9	251 20.7	26.7	186 51.3	05.1
	21	107 57.1	99 33.8	24.6	90 25.1	22.6	266 23.3	26.7	201 53.6	05.1
	22	122 59.6	114 35.6	25.3	105 25.9	23.4	281 25.9	26.6	216 55.9	05.1
	23	138 02.1	129 37.4	26.1	120 26.7	24.1	296 28.4	26.6	231 58.2	05.1
23 THURSDAY	00	153 04.5	144 39.3	N 9 26.8	135 27.4	N 7 24.8	311 31.0	S 7 26.5	247 00.4	S22 05.1
	01	168 07.0	159 41.1	27.5	150 28.2	25.5	326 33.6	26.5	262 02.7	05.1
	02	183 09.5	174 43.0	28.3	165 29.0	26.3	341 36.2	26.4	277 05.0	05.1
	03	198 11.9	189 44.8	29.0	180 29.8	27.0	356 38.8	26.3	292 07.3	05.1
	04	213 14.4	204 46.7	29.8	195 30.5	27.7	11 41.4	26.3	307 09.6	05.1
	05	228 16.9	219 48.5	30.5	210 31.3	28.4	26 43.9	26.2	322 11.9	05.1
	06	243 19.3	234 50.4	N 9 31.2	225 32.1	N 7 29.2	41 46.5	S 7 26.2	337 14.2	S22 05.1
	07	258 21.8	249 52.3	32.0	240 32.8	29.9	56 49.1	26.1	352 16.4	05.1
	08	273 24.2	264 54.1	32.7	255 33.6	30.6	71 51.7	26.1	7 18.7	05.1
	09	288 26.7	279 56.0	33.4	270 34.4	31.3	86 54.3	26.0	22 21.0	05.1
	10	303 29.2	294 57.9	34.2	285 35.1	32.1	101 56.9	25.9	37 23.3	05.1
	11	318 31.6	309 59.7	34.9	300 35.9	32.8	116 59.5	25.9	52 25.6	05.1
	12	333 34.1	325 01.6	N 9 35.6	315 36.7	N 7 33.5	132 02.0	S 7 25.8	67 27.9	S22 05.1
	13	348 36.6	340 03.5	36.4	330 37.4	34.2	147 04.6	25.8	82 30.2	05.1
	14	3 39.0	355 05.4	37.1	345 38.2	35.0	162 07.2	25.7	97 32.5	05.1
	15	18 41.5	10 07.3	37.8	0 39.0	35.7	177 09.8	25.6	112 34.7	05.1
	16	33 44.0	25 09.2	38.5	15 39.7	36.4	192 12.4	25.6	127 37.0	05.1
	17	48 46.4	40 11.0	39.2	30 40.5	37.1	207 15.0	25.5	142 39.3	05.1
	18	63 48.9	55 12.9	N 9 40.0	45 41.3	N 7 37.9	222 17.6	S 7 25.5	157 41.6	S22 05.1
	19	78 51.4	70 14.8	40.7	60 42.0	38.6	237 20.2	25.4	172 43.9	05.1
	20	93 53.8	85 16.7	41.4	75 42.8	39.3	252 22.7	25.4	187 46.2	05.1
	21	108 56.3	100 18.7	42.1	90 43.6	40.0	267 25.3	25.3	202 48.5	05.1
	22	123 58.7	115 20.6	42.8	105 44.3	40.7	282 27.9	25.2	217 50.8	05.1
	23	139 01.2	130 22.5	43.5	120 45.1	41.5	297 30.5	25.2	232 53.1	05.1
Mer. Pass.		h m 13 49.4	*v* 1.8	*d* 0.8	*v* 0.8	*d* 0.7	*v* 2.6	*d* 0.1	*v* 2.3	*d* 0.0

STARS

Name	SHA	Dec
	° ′	° ′
Acamar	315 16.6	S40 14.6
Achernar	335 25.4	S57 09.4
Acrux	173 05.8	S63 11.5
Adhara	255 10.3	S29 00.1
Aldebaran	290 46.5	N16 32.4
Alioth	166 18.2	N55 51.8
Alkaid	152 56.7	N49 13.5
Al Na'ir	27 41.1	S46 52.7
Alnilam	275 43.7	S 1 11.8
Alphard	217 53.3	S 8 44.2
Alphecca	126 08.9	N26 39.4
Alpheratz	357 41.2	N29 11.0
Altair	62 06.1	N 8 54.8
Ankaa	353 13.6	S42 13.0
Antares	112 23.2	S26 27.9
Arcturus	145 53.3	N19 05.5
Atria	107 22.9	S69 03.0
Avior	234 16.4	S59 34.2
Bellatrix	278 29.2	N 6 21.6
Betelgeuse	270 58.4	N 7 24.3
Canopus	263 54.7	S52 42.7
Capella	280 30.6	N46 00.8
Deneb	49 30.2	N45 20.4
Denebola	182 30.8	N14 28.5
Diphda	348 53.7	S17 53.8
Dubhe	193 48.1	N61 39.4
Elnath	278 09.3	N28 37.1
Eltanin	90 45.2	N51 29.1
Enif	33 45.0	N 9 57.2
Fomalhaut	15 21.6	S29 32.0
Gacrux	171 57.5	S57 12.4
Gienah	175 49.4	S17 38.2
Hadar	148 43.9	S60 27.0
Hamal	327 58.1	N23 32.5
Kaus Aust.	83 40.7	S34 22.3
Kochab	137 19.9	N74 04.9
Markab	13 36.1	N15 17.8
Menkar	314 12.5	N 4 09.1
Menkent	148 04.4	S36 27.0
Miaplacidus	221 38.1	S69 47.4
Mirfak	308 36.8	N49 55.3
Nunki	75 55.5	S26 16.3
Peacock	53 15.9	S56 40.6
Pollux	243 24.4	N27 58.9
Procyon	244 56.9	N 5 10.6
Rasalhague	96 04.3	N12 32.9
Regulus	207 40.6	N11 52.8
Rigel	281 09.6	S 8 11.3
Rigil Kent.	139 48.0	S60 54.0
Sabik	102 09.8	S15 44.6
Schedar	349 38.0	N56 37.9
Shaula	96 18.7	S37 06.7
Sirius	258 31.3	S16 44.8
Spica	158 28.4	S11 15.0
Suhail	222 50.1	S43 30.3
Vega	80 37.5	N38 47.9
Zuben'ubi	137 02.5	S16 06.6

	SHA	Mer. Pass.
	° ′	h m
Venus	351 50.5	14 23
Mars	343 03.6	14 59
Jupiter	158 23.7	3 17
Saturn	94 00.2	7 34

INDEX TO SELECTED STARS, 2017

Name	No	Mag	SHA	Dec
			°	°
Acamar	**7**	3·2	315	S 40
Achernar	**5**	0·5	335	S 57
Acrux	**30**	1·3	173	S 63
Adhara	**19**	1·5	255	S 29
Aldebaran	**10**	0·9	291	N 17
Alioth	**32**	1·8	166	N 56
Alkaid	**34**	1·9	153	N 49
Al Na'ir	**55**	1·7	28	S 47
Alnilam	**15**	1·7	276	S 1
Alphard	**25**	2·0	218	S 9
Alphecca	**41**	2·2	126	N 27
Alpheratz	**1**	2·1	358	N 29
Altair	**51**	0·8	62	N 9
Ankaa	**2**	2·4	353	S 42
Antares	**42**	1·0	112	S 26
Arcturus	**37**	0·0	146	N 19
Atria	**43**	1·9	107	S 69
Avior	**22**	1·9	234	S 60
Bellatrix	**13**	1·6	278	N 6
Betelgeuse	**16**	Var.*	271	N 7
Canopus	**17**	−0·7	264	S 53
Capella	**12**	0·1	281	N 46
Deneb	**53**	1·3	49	N 45
Denebola	**28**	2·1	183	N 14
Diphda	**4**	2·0	349	S 18
Dubhe	**27**	1·8	194	N 62
Elnath	**14**	1·7	278	N 29
Eltanin	**47**	2·2	91	N 51
Enif	**54**	2·4	34	N 10
Fomalhaut	**56**	1·2	15	S 30
Gacrux	**31**	1·6	172	S 57
Gienah	**29**	2·6	176	S 18
Hadar	**35**	0·6	149	S 60
Hamal	**6**	2·0	328	N 24
Kaus Australis	**48**	1·9	84	S 34
Kochab	**40**	2·1	137	N 74
Markab	**57**	2·5	14	N 15
Menkar	**8**	2·5	314	N 4
Menkent	**36**	2·1	148	S 36
Miaplacidus	**24**	1·7	222	S 70
Mirfak	**9**	1·8	309	N 50
Nunki	**50**	2·0	76	S 26
Peacock	**52**	1·9	53	S 57
Pollux	**21**	1·1	243	N 28
Procyon	**20**	0·4	245	N 5
Rasalhague	**46**	2·1	96	N 13
Regulus	**26**	1·4	208	N 12
Rigel	**11**	0·1	281	S 8
Rigil Kentaurus	**38**	−0·3	140	S 61
Sabik	**44**	2·4	102	S 16
Schedar	**3**	2·2	350	N 57
Shaula	**45**	1·6	96	S 37
Sirius	**18**	−1·5	259	S 17
Spica	**33**	1·0	158	S 11
Suhail	**23**	2·2	223	S 44
Vega	**49**	0·0	81	N 39
Zubenelgenubi	**39**	2·8	137	S 16

No	Name	Mag	SHA	Dec
			°	°
1	*Alpheratz*	2·1	358	N 29
2	*Ankaa*	2·4	353	S 42
3	*Schedar*	2·2	350	N 57
4	*Diphda*	2·0	349	S 18
5	*Achernar*	0·5	335	S 57
6	*Hamal*	2·0	328	N 24
7	*Acamar*	3·2	315	S 40
8	*Menkar*	2·5	314	N 4
9	*Mirfak*	1·8	309	N 50
10	*Aldebaran*	0·9	291	N 17
11	*Rigel*	0·1	281	S 8
12	*Capella*	0·1	281	N 46
13	*Bellatrix*	1·6	278	N 6
14	*Elnath*	1·7	278	N 29
15	*Alnilam*	1·7	276	S 1
16	*Betelgeuse*	Var.*	271	N 7
17	*Canopus*	−0·7	264	S 53
18	*Sirius*	−1·5	259	S 17
19	*Adhara*	1·5	255	S 29
20	*Procyon*	0·4	245	N 5
21	*Pollux*	1·1	243	N 28
22	*Avior*	1·9	234	S 60
23	*Suhail*	2·2	223	S 44
24	*Miaplacidus*	1·7	222	S 70
25	*Alphard*	2·0	218	S 9
26	*Regulus*	1·4	208	N 12
27	*Dubhe*	1·8	194	N 62
28	*Denebola*	2·1	183	N 14
29	*Gienah*	2·6	176	S 18
30	*Acrux*	1·3	173	S 63
31	*Gacrux*	1·6	172	S 57
32	*Alioth*	1·8	166	N 56
33	*Spica*	1·0	158	S 11
34	*Alkaid*	1·9	153	N 49
35	*Hadar*	0·6	149	S 60
36	*Menkent*	2·1	148	S 36
37	*Arcturus*	0·0	146	N 19
38	*Rigil Kentaurus*	−0·3	140	S 61
39	*Zubenelgenubi*	2·8	137	S 16
40	*Kochab*	2·1	137	N 74
41	*Alphecca*	2·2	126	N 27
42	*Antares*	1·0	112	S 26
43	*Atria*	1·9	107	S 69
44	*Sabik*	2·4	102	S 16
45	*Shaula*	1·6	96	S 37
46	*Rasalhague*	2·1	96	N 13
47	*Eltanin*	2·2	91	N 51
48	*Kaus Australis*	1·9	84	S 34
49	*Vega*	0·0	81	N 39
50	*Nunki*	2·0	76	S 26
51	*Altair*	0·8	62	N 9
52	*Peacock*	1·9	53	S 57
53	*Deneb*	1·3	49	N 45
54	*Enif*	2·4	34	N 10
55	*Al Na'ir*	1·7	28	S 47
56	*Fomalhaut*	1·2	15	S 30
57	*Markab*	2·5	14	N 15

*0·1 — 1·2

OCT.—MAR. SUN			APR.—SEPT.		
App. Alt.	Lower Limb	Upper Limb	App. Alt.	Lower Limb	Upper Limb
° ′	′	′	° ′	′	′
9 33			9 39		
	+10.8	−21.5		+10.6	−21.2
9 45			9 50		
	+10.9	−21.4		+10.7	−21.1
9 56			10 02		
	+11.0	−21.3		+10.8	−21.0
10 08			10 14		
	+11.1	−21.2		+10.9	−20.9
10 20			10 27		
	+11.2	−21.1		+11.0	−20.8
10 33			10 40		
	+11.3	−21.0		+11.1	−20.7
10 46			10 53		
	+11.4	−20.9		+11.2	−20.6
11 00			11 07		
	+11.5	−20.8		+11.3	−20.5
11 15			11 22		
	+11.6	−20.7		+11.4	−20.4
11 30			11 37		
	+11.7	−20.6		+11.5	−20.3
11 45			11 53		
	+11.8	−20.5		+11.6	−20.2
12 01			12 10		
	+11.9	−20.4		+11.7	−20.1
12 18			12 27		
	+12.0	−20.3		+11.8	−20.0
12 36			12 45		
	+12.1	−20.2		+11.9	−19.9
12 54			13 04		
	+12.2	−20.1		+12.0	−19.8
13 14			13 24		
	+12.3	−20.0		+12.1	−19.7
13 34			13 44		
	+12.4	−19.9		+12.2	−19.6
13 55			14 06		
	+12.5	−19.8		+12.3	−19.5
14 17			14 29		
	+12.6	−19.7		+12.4	−19.4
14 41			14 53		
	+12.7	−19.6		+12.5	−19.3
15 05			15 18		
	+12.8	−19.5		+12.6	−19.2
15 31			15 45		
	+12.9	−19.4		+12.7	−19.1
15 59			16 13		
	+13.0	−19.3		+12.8	−19.0
16 27			16 43		
	+13.1	−19.2		+12.9	−18.9
16 58			17 14		
	+13.2	−19.1		+13.0	−18.8
17 30			17 47		
	+13.3	−19.0		+13.1	−18.7
18 05			18 23		
	+13.4	−18.9		+13.2	−18.6
18 41			19 00		
	+13.5	−18.8		+13.3	−18.5
19 20			19 41		
	+13.6	−18.7		+13.4	−18.4
20 02			20 24		
	+13.7	−18.6		+13.5	−18.3
20 46			21 10		
	+13.8	−18.5		+13.6	−18.2
21 34			21 59		
	+13.9	−18.4		+13.7	−18.1
22 25			22 52		
	+14.0	−18.3		+13.8	−18.0
23 20			23 49		
	+14.1	−18.2		+13.9	−17.9
24 20			24 51		
	+14.2	−18.1		+14.0	−17.8
25 24			25 58		
	+14.3	−18.0		+14.1	−17.7
26 34			27 11		
	+14.4	−17.9		+14.2	−17.6
27 50			28 31		
	+14.5	−17.8		+14.3	−17.5
29 13			29 58		
	+14.6	−17.7		+14.4	−17.4
30 44			31 33		
	+14.7	−17.6		+14.5	−17.3
32 24			33 18		
	+14.8	−17.5		+14.6	−17.2
34 15			35 15		
	+14.9	−17.4		+14.7	−17.1
36 17			37 24		
	+15.0	−17.3		+14.8	−17.0
38 34			39 48		
	+15.1	−17.2		+14.9	−16.9
41 06			42 28		
	+15.2	−17.1		+15.0	−16.8
43 56			45 29		
	+15.3	−17.0		+15.1	−16.7
47 07			48 52		
	+15.4	−16.9		+15.2	−16.6
50 43			52 41		
	+15.5	−16.8		+15.3	−16.5
54 46			56 59		
	+15.6	−16.7		+15.4	−16.4
59 21			61 50		
	+15.7	−16.6		+15.5	−16.3
64 28			67 15		
	+15.8	−16.5		+15.6	−16.2
70 10			73 14		
	+15.9	−16.4		+15.7	−16.1
76 24			79 42		
	+16.0	−16.3		+15.8	−16.0
83 05			86 31		
	+16.1	−16.2		+15.9	−15.9
90 00			90 00		

STARS AND PLANETS

App Alt.	Corr^n
° ′	′
9 55	
	−5.3
10 07	
	−5.2
10 20	
	−5.1
10 32	
	−5.0
10 46	
	−4.9
10 59	
	−4.8
11 14	
	−4.7
11 29	
	−4.6
11 44	
	−4.5
12 00	
	−4.4
12 17	
	−4.3
12 35	
	−4.2
12 53	
	−4.1
13 12	
	−4.0
13 32	
	−3.9
13 53	
	−3.8
14 16	
	−3.7
14 39	
	−3.6
15 03	
	−3.5
15 29	
	−3.4
15 56	
	−3.3
16 25	
	−3.2
16 55	
	−3.1
17 27	
	−3.0
18 01	
	−2.9
18 37	
	−2.8
19 16	
	−2.7
19 56	
	−2.6
20 40	
	−2.5
21 27	
	−2.4
22 17	
	−2.3
23 11	
	−2.2
24 09	
	−2.1
25 12	
	−2.0
26 20	
	−1.9
27 34	
	−1.8
28 54	
	−1.7
30 22	
	−1.6
31 58	
	−1.5
33 43	
	−1.4
35 38	
	−1.3
37 45	
	−1.2
40 06	
	−1.1
42 42	
	−1.0
45 34	
	−0.9
48 45	
	−0.8
52 16	
	−0.7
56 09	
	−0.6
60 26	
	−0.5
65 06	
	−0.4
70 09	
	−0.3
75 32	
	−0.2
81 12	
	−0.1
87 03	
	0.0
90 00	

App. Alt.	Additional Corr^n
2017	
VENUS	
Jan. 1–Jan. 25	
May 21–July 8	
°	′
0	
	+0.2
41	
	+0.1
76	
Jan. 26–Feb. 18	
Apr. 28–May 20	
°	′
0	
	+0.3
34	
	+0.2
60	
	+0.1
80	
Feb. 19–Mar. 6	
Apr. 13–Apr. 27	
°	′
0	
	+0.4
29	
	+0.3
51	
	+0.2
68	
	+0.1
83	
Mar. 7–Apr. 12	
°	′
0	
	+0.5
26	
	+0.4
46	
	+0.3
60	
	+0.2
73	
	+0.1
84	
July 9–Dec. 31	
°	′
0	
	+0.1
60	
MARS	
Jan. 1–Dec. 31	
°	′
0	
	+0.1
60	

DIP

Ht. of Eye	Corr^n	Ht. of Eye
m	′	ft.
2.4		8.0
	−2.8	
2.6		8.6
	−2.9	
2.8		9.2
	−3.0	
3.0		9.8
	−3.1	
3.2		10.5
	−3.2	
3.4		11.2
	−3.3	
3.6		11.9
	−3.4	
3.8		12.6
	−3.5	
4.0		13.3
	−3.6	
4.3		14.1
	−3.7	
4.5		14.9
	−3.8	
4.7		15.7
	−3.9	
5.0		16.5
	−4.0	
5.2		17.4
	−4.1	
5.5		18.3
	−4.2	
5.8		19.1
	−4.3	
6.1		20.1
	−4.4	
6.3		21.0
	−4.5	
6.6		22.0
	−4.6	
6.9		22.9
	−4.7	
7.2		23.9
	−4.8	
7.5		24.9
	−4.9	
7.9		26.0
	−5.0	
8.2		27.1
	−5.1	
8.5		28.1
	−5.2	
8.8		29.2
	−5.3	
9.2		30.4
	−5.4	
9.5		31.5
	−5.5	
9.9		32.7
	−5.6	
10.3		33.9
	−5.7	
10.6		35.1
	−5.8	
11.0		36.3
	−5.9	
11.4		37.6
	−6.0	
11.8		38.9
	−6.1	
12.2		40.1
	−6.2	
12.6		41.5
	−6.3	
13.0		42.8
	−6.4	
13.4		44.2
	−6.5	
13.8		45.5
	−6.6	
14.2		46.9
	−6.7	
14.7		48.4
	−6.8	
15.1		49.8
	−6.9	
15.5		51.3
	−7.0	
16.0		52.8
	−7.1	
16.5		54.3
	−7.2	
16.9		55.8
	−7.3	
17.4		57.4
	−7.4	
17.9		58.9
	−7.5	
18.4		60.5
	−7.6	
18.8		62.1
	−7.7	
19.3		63.8
	−7.8	
19.8		65.4
	−7.9	
20.4		67.1
	−8.0	
20.9		68.8
	−8.1	
21.4		70.5

Ht. of Eye	Corr^n
m	′
1.0	− 1.8
1.5	− 2.2
2.0	− 2.5
2.5	− 2.8
3.0	− 3.0
See table ←	
m	′
20	− 7.9
22	− 8.3
24	− 8.6
26	− 9.0
28	− 9.3
30	− 9.6
32	−10.0
34	−10.3
36	−10.6
38	−10.8
40	−11.1
42	−11.4
44	−11.7
46	−11.9
48	−12.2
ft.	′
2	− 1.4
4	− 1.9
6	− 2.4
8	− 2.7
10	− 3.1
See table ←	
ft.	′
70	− 8.1
75	− 8.4
80	− 8.7
85	− 8.9
90	− 9.2
95	− 9.5
100	− 9.7
105	− 9.9
110	−10.2
115	−10.4
120	−10.6
125	−10.8
130	−11.1
135	−11.3
140	−11.5
145	−11.7
150	−11.9
155	−12.1

App. Alt. = Apparent altitude = Sextant altitude corrected for index error and dip.

UT	SUN GHA	SUN Dec	MOON GHA	v	MOON Dec	d	HP
d h	° ′	° ′	° ′	′	° ′	′	′
21 00	176 35.8	S10 34.0	244 52.5	11.8	S18 31.2	1.8	54.6
01	191 35.9	33.1	259 23.3	11.8	18 33.0	1.8	54.6
02	206 35.9	32.2	273 54.1	11.8	18 34.8	1.6	54.6
03	221 36.0	. . 31.3	288 24.9	11.7	18 36.4	1.6	54.7
04	236 36.1	30.4	302 55.6	11.7	18 38.0	1.5	54.7
05	251 36.2	29.5	317 26.3	11.7	18 39.5	1.4	54.7
06	266 36.2	S10 28.6	331 57.0	11.6	S18 40.9	1.3	54.7
07	281 36.3	27.7	346 27.6	11.7	18 42.2	1.2	54.7
T 08	296 36.4	26.8	0 58.3	11.5	18 43.4	1.1	54.7
U 09	311 36.5	. . 25.9	15 28.8	11.6	18 44.5	1.0	54.8
E 10	326 36.5	25.0	29 59.4	11.5	18 45.5	1.0	54.8
S 11	341 36.6	24.1	44 29.9	11.5	18 46.5	0.8	54.8
D 12	356 36.7	S10 23.2	59 00.4	11.5	S18 47.3	0.8	54.8
A 13	11 36.8	22.3	73 30.9	11.5	18 48.1	0.7	54.8
Y 14	26 36.8	21.3	88 01.4	11.4	18 48.8	0.6	54.8
15	41 36.9	. . 20.4	102 31.8	11.4	18 49.4	0.5	54.9
16	56 37.0	19.5	117 02.2	11.3	18 49.9	0.4	54.9
17	71 37.1	18.6	131 32.5	11.4	18 50.3	0.3	54.9
18	86 37.1	S10 17.7	146 02.9	11.3	S18 50.6	0.2	54.9
19	101 37.2	16.8	160 33.2	11.2	18 50.8	0.1	54.9
20	116 37.3	15.9	175 03.4	11.3	18 50.9	0.0	55.0
21	131 37.4	. . 15.0	189 33.7	11.2	18 50.9	0.0	55.0
22	146 37.5	14.1	204 03.9	11.2	18 50.9	0.2	55.0
23	161 37.5	13.2	218 34.1	11.2	18 50.7	0.2	55.0
22 00	176 37.6	S10 12.2	233 04.3	11.2	S18 50.5	0.3	55.0
01	191 37.7	11.3	247 34.5	11.1	18 50.2	0.5	55.1
02	206 37.8	10.4	262 04.6	11.1	18 49.7	0.5	55.1
03	221 37.8	. . 09.5	276 34.7	11.1	18 49.2	0.6	55.1
04	236 37.9	08.6	291 04.8	11.0	18 48.6	0.7	55.1
05	251 38.0	07.7	305 34.8	11.1	18 47.9	0.8	55.2
06	266 38.1	S10 06.8	320 04.9	11.0	S18 47.1	0.9	55.2
W 07	281 38.2	05.9	334 34.9	10.9	18 46.2	1.0	55.2
E 08	296 38.2	04.9	349 04.8	11.0	18 45.2	1.1	55.2
D 09	311 38.3	. . 04.0	3 34.8	10.9	18 44.1	1.2	55.2
N 10	326 38.4	03.1	18 04.7	11.0	18 42.9	1.3	55.3
E 11	341 38.5	02.2	32 34.7	10.9	18 41.6	1.3	55.3
S 12	356 38.6	S10 01.3	47 04.6	10.8	S18 40.3	1.5	55.3
D 13	11 38.7	10 00.4	61 34.4	10.9	18 38.8	1.6	55.3
A 14	26 38.7	9 59.5	76 04.3	10.8	18 37.2	1.6	55.4
Y 15	41 38.8	. . 58.5	90 34.1	10.8	18 35.6	1.8	55.4
16	56 38.9	57.6	105 03.9	10.8	18 33.8	1.8	55.4
17	71 39.0	56.7	119 33.7	10.8	18 32.0	1.9	55.4
18	86 39.1	S 9 55.8	134 03.5	10.8	S18 30.1	2.1	55.5
19	101 39.2	54.9	148 33.3	10.7	18 28.0	2.1	55.5
20	116 39.2	54.0	163 03.0	10.7	18 25.9	2.2	55.5
21	131 39.3	. . 53.1	177 32.7	10.7	18 23.7	2.4	55.5
22	146 39.4	52.1	192 02.4	10.7	18 21.3	2.4	55.5
23	161 39.5	51.2	206 32.1	10.7	18 18.9	2.5	55.6
23 00	176 39.6	S 9 50.3	221 01.8	10.6	S18 16.4	2.6	55.6
01	191 39.7	49.4	235 31.4	10.7	18 13.8	2.7	55.6
02	206 39.7	48.5	250 01.1	10.6	18 11.1	2.8	55.7
03	221 39.8	. . 47.5	264 30.7	10.6	18 08.3	2.9	55.7
04	236 39.9	46.6	279 00.3	10.6	18 05.4	3.0	55.7
05	251 40.0	45.7	293 29.9	10.5	18 02.4	3.1	55.7
06	266 40.1	S 9 44.8	307 59.4	10.6	S17 59.3	3.2	55.8
07	281 40.2	43.9	322 29.0	10.6	17 56.1	3.3	55.8
T 08	296 40.3	43.0	336 58.6	10.5	17 52.8	3.4	55.8
H 09	311 40.3	. . 42.0	351 28.1	10.5	17 49.4	3.4	55.8
U 10	326 40.4	41.1	5 57.6	10.5	17 46.0	3.6	55.9
R 11	341 40.5	40.2	20 27.1	10.5	17 42.4	3.7	55.9
S 12	356 40.6	S 9 39.3	34 56.6	10.5	S17 38.7	3.7	55.9
D 13	11 40.7	38.4	49 26.1	10.5	17 35.0	3.9	55.9
A 14	26 40.8	37.4	63 55.6	10.4	17 31.1	3.9	56.0
Y 15	41 40.9	. . 36.5	78 25.0	10.5	17 27.2	4.1	56.0
16	56 41.0	35.6	92 54.5	10.4	17 23.1	4.1	56.0
17	71 41.1	34.7	107 23.9	10.5	17 19.0	4.2	56.0
18	86 41.1	S 9 33.7	121 53.4	10.4	S17 14.8	4.4	56.1
19	101 41.2	32.8	136 22.8	10.4	17 10.4	4.4	56.1
20	116 41.3	31.9	150 52.2	10.4	17 06.0	4.5	56.1
21	131 41.4	. . 31.0	165 21.6	10.4	17 01.5	4.6	56.2
22	146 41.5	30.1	179 51.0	10.4	16 56.9	4.7	56.2
23	161 41.6	29.1	194 20.4	10.4	S16 52.2	4.8	56.2
	SD 16.2	*d* 0.9	SD 14.9		15.1		15.2

Lat.	Twilight Naut.	Twilight Civil	Sunrise	Moonrise 21	22	23	24
°	h m	h m	h m	h m	h m	h m	h m
N 72	05 43	07 01	08 13	■	■	09 13	08 35
N 70	05 44	06 55	07 59	06 30	07 22	07 45	07 53
68	05 45	06 50	07 48	05 41	06 32	07 05	07 25
66	05 46	06 45	07 39	05 09	06 01	06 38	07 03
64	05 47	06 42	07 31	04 46	05 37	06 17	06 46
62	05 47	06 38	07 24	04 28	05 19	06 00	06 32
60	05 47	06 36	07 18	04 13	05 03	05 46	06 20
N 58	05 48	06 33	07 13	04 00	04 50	05 34	06 10
56	05 47	06 31	07 08	03 49	04 39	05 23	06 01
54	05 47	06 28	07 04	03 39	04 29	05 14	05 52
52	05 47	06 26	07 01	03 30	04 21	05 06	05 45
50	05 47	06 24	06 57	03 22	04 13	04 58	05 39
45	05 46	06 20	06 50	03 06	03 56	04 42	05 25
N 40	05 45	06 16	06 43	02 52	03 42	04 29	05 13
35	05 43	06 12	06 38	02 41	03 30	04 18	05 03
30	05 41	06 09	06 33	02 31	03 20	04 08	04 54
20	05 37	06 02	06 25	02 13	03 03	03 52	04 39
N 10	05 31	05 56	06 17	01 58	02 47	03 37	04 26
0	05 25	05 49	06 10	01 44	02 33	03 23	04 14
S 10	05 17	05 41	06 03	01 30	02 19	03 10	04 01
20	05 06	05 32	05 55	01 15	02 04	02 55	03 48
30	04 52	05 21	05 46	00 58	01 46	02 38	03 33
35	04 43	05 14	05 41	00 48	01 36	02 28	03 24
40	04 33	05 06	05 35	00 37	01 25	02 17	03 14
45	04 19	04 57	05 27	00 24	01 11	02 04	03 03
S 50	04 02	04 45	05 19	00 07	00 54	01 48	02 48
52	03 54	04 39	05 15	00 00	00 46	01 41	02 42
54	03 44	04 32	05 11	24 38	00 38	01 32	02 34
56	03 33	04 25	05 06	24 28	00 28	01 23	02 26
58	03 20	04 17	05 00	24 17	00 17	01 12	02 16
S 60	03 05	04 08	04 54	24 04	00 04	01 00	02 06

Lat.	Sunset	Twilight Civil	Twilight Naut.	Moonset 21	22	23	24
°	h m	h m	h m	h m	h m	h m	h m
N 72	16 15	17 28	18 47	■	■	10 05	12 28
N 70	16 29	17 34	18 45	09 20	10 10	11 32	13 09
68	16 40	17 39	18 43	10 09	11 00	12 11	13 37
66	16 50	17 43	18 42	10 41	11 31	12 38	13 57
64	16 57	17 47	18 42	11 04	11 55	12 59	14 14
62	17 04	17 50	18 41	11 23	12 13	13 15	14 28
60	17 10	17 53	18 41	11 38	12 28	13 29	14 39
N 58	17 15	17 55	18 41	11 51	12 41	13 41	14 49
56	17 19	17 57	18 41	12 02	12 52	13 51	14 58
54	17 23	18 00	18 41	12 12	13 02	14 00	15 06
52	17 27	18 02	18 41	12 21	13 11	14 08	15 12
50	17 31	18 03	18 41	12 28	13 19	14 16	15 19
45	17 38	18 08	18 42	12 45	13 35	14 31	15 32
N 40	17 44	18 11	18 43	12 59	13 49	14 44	15 43
35	17 49	18 15	18 44	13 11	14 01	14 55	15 52
30	17 54	18 18	18 46	13 21	14 11	15 04	16 00
20	18 02	18 25	18 50	13 38	14 28	15 20	16 15
N 10	18 10	18 31	18 56	13 53	14 43	15 34	16 27
0	18 17	18 38	19 02	14 08	14 57	15 47	16 38
S 10	18 24	18 45	19 10	14 22	15 11	16 01	16 50
20	18 32	18 54	19 20	14 37	15 26	16 14	17 02
30	18 41	19 05	19 34	14 55	15 43	16 30	17 15
35	18 46	19 12	19 43	15 05	15 53	16 40	17 23
40	18 52	19 20	19 53	15 16	16 05	16 50	17 32
45	18 59	19 29	20 06	15 30	16 18	17 02	17 43
S 50	19 07	19 41	20 23	15 47	16 34	17 17	17 56
52	19 11	19 47	20 31	15 54	16 42	17 24	18 01
54	19 15	19 53	20 41	16 03	16 51	17 32	18 08
56	19 20	20 00	20 51	16 13	17 00	17 41	18 15
58	19 25	20 08	21 04	16 24	17 11	17 50	18 23
S 60	19 31	20 17	21 19	16 37	17 23	18 01	18 32

Day	SUN Eqn. of Time 00h	SUN Eqn. of Time 12h	SUN Mer. Pass.	MOON Mer. Pass. Upper	MOON Mer. Pass. Lower	MOON Age	MOON Phase
d	m s	m s	h m	h m	h m	d %	
21	13 37	13 33	12 14	07 56	20 20	24 26	
22	13 30	13 26	12 13	08 45	21 10	25 18	
23	13 22	13 18	12 13	09 35	22 01	26 11	

	UT	ARIES	VENUS −4·8		MARS +1·3		JUPITER −2·3		SATURN +0·5	
		GHA	GHA	Dec	GHA	Dec	GHA	Dec	GHA	Dec
	d h	° ′	° ′	° ′	° ′	° ′	° ′	° ′	° ′	° ′
	24 00	154 03.7	145 24.4	N 9 44.3	135 45.9	N 7 42.2	312 33.1	S 7 25.1	247 55.4	S22 05.1
	01	169 06.1	160 26.3	45.0	150 46.6	42.9	327 35.7	25.1	262 57.6	05.1
	02	184 08.6	175 28.2	45.7	165 47.4	43.6	342 38.3	25.0	277 59.9	05.1
	03	199 11.1	190 30.2	. . 46.4	180 48.2	. . 44.4	357 40.9	. . 24.9	293 02.2	. . 05.2
	04	214 13.5	205 32.1	47.1	195 48.9	45.1	12 43.5	24.9	308 04.5	05.2
	05	229 16.0	220 34.0	47.8	210 49.7	45.8	27 46.0	24.8	323 06.8	05.2
	06	244 18.5	235 36.0	N 9 48.5	225 50.5	N 7 46.5	42 48.6	S 7 24.8	338 09.1	S22 05.2
	07	259 20.9	250 37.9	49.2	240 51.2	47.2	57 51.2	24.7	353 11.4	05.2
	08	274 23.4	265 39.8	49.9	255 52.0	48.0	72 53.8	24.6	8 13.7	05.2
F	09	289 25.8	280 41.8	. . 50.6	270 52.8	. . 48.7	87 56.4	. . 24.6	23 16.0	. . 05.2
R	10	304 28.3	295 43.7	51.3	285 53.5	49.4	102 59.0	24.5	38 18.3	05.2
I	11	319 30.8	310 45.7	52.0	300 54.3	50.1	118 01.6	24.5	53 20.5	05.2
D	12	334 33.2	325 47.6	N 9 52.7	315 55.1	N 7 50.8	133 04.2	S 7 24.4	68 22.8	S22 05.2
A	13	349 35.7	340 49.6	53.4	330 55.8	51.6	148 06.8	24.3	83 25.1	05.2
Y	14	4 38.2	355 51.5	54.1	345 56.6	52.3	163 09.4	24.3	98 27.4	05.2
	15	19 40.6	10 53.5	. . 54.8	0 57.4	. . 53.0	178 12.0	. . 24.2	113 29.7	. . 05.2
	16	34 43.1	25 55.5	55.4	15 58.1	53.7	193 14.6	24.2	128 32.0	05.2
	17	49 45.6	40 57.4	56.1	30 58.9	54.4	208 17.2	24.1	143 34.3	05.2
	18	64 48.0	55 59.4	N 9 56.8	45 59.7	N 7 55.2	223 19.7	S 7 24.0	158 36.6	S22 05.2
	19	79 50.5	71 01.4	57.5	61 00.4	55.9	238 22.3	24.0	173 38.9	05.2
	20	94 53.0	86 03.4	58.2	76 01.2	56.6	253 24.9	23.9	188 41.2	05.2
	21	109 55.4	101 05.4	. . 58.9	91 02.0	. . 57.3	268 27.5	. . 23.9	203 43.5	. . 05.2
	22	124 57.9	116 07.3	9 59.6	106 02.7	58.0	283 30.1	23.8	218 45.8	05.2
	23	140 00.3	131 09.3	10 00.2	121 03.5	58.8	298 32.7	23.7	233 48.1	05.2
	25 00	155 02.8	146 11.3	N10 00.9	136 04.3	N 7 59.5	313 35.3	S 7 23.7	248 50.4	S22 05.2
	01	170 05.3	161 13.3	01.6	151 05.0	8 00.2	328 37.9	23.6	263 52.6	05.2
	02	185 07.7	176 15.3	02.3	166 05.8	00.9	343 40.5	23.5	278 54.9	05.2
	03	200 10.2	191 17.3	. . 02.9	181 06.6	. . 01.6	358 43.1	. . 23.5	293 57.2	. . 05.2
	04	215 12.7	206 19.3	03.6	196 07.3	02.3	13 45.7	23.4	308 59.5	05.2
	05	230 15.1	221 21.3	04.3	211 08.1	03.1	28 48.3	23.4	324 01.8	05.2
	06	245 17.6	236 23.3	N10 04.9	226 08.9	N 8 03.8	43 50.9	S 7 23.3	339 04.1	S22 05.2
	07	260 20.1	251 25.4	05.6	241 09.6	04.5	58 53.5	23.2	354 06.4	05.2
S	08	275 22.5	266 27.4	06.3	256 10.4	05.2	73 56.1	23.2	9 08.7	05.2
A	09	290 25.0	281 29.4	. . 06.9	271 11.2	. . 05.9	88 58.7	. . 23.1	24 11.0	. . 05.2
T	10	305 27.5	296 31.4	07.6	286 11.9	06.6	104 01.3	23.0	39 13.3	05.2
U	11	320 29.9	311 33.5	08.3	301 12.7	07.4	119 03.9	23.0	54 15.6	05.2
R	12	335 32.4	326 35.5	N10 08.9	316 13.5	N 8 08.1	134 06.5	S 7 22.9	69 17.9	S22 05.2
D	13	350 34.8	341 37.5	09.6	331 14.2	08.8	149 09.1	22.9	84 20.2	05.2
A	14	5 37.3	356 39.6	10.2	346 15.0	09.5	164 11.7	22.8	99 22.5	05.2
Y	15	20 39.8	11 41.6	. . 10.9	1 15.8	. . 10.2	179 14.3	. . 22.7	114 24.8	. . 05.2
	16	35 42.2	26 43.6	11.6	16 16.5	10.9	194 16.9	22.7	129 27.1	05.2
	17	50 44.7	41 45.7	12.2	31 17.3	11.7	209 19.5	22.6	144 29.4	05.2
	18	65 47.2	56 47.7	N10 12.9	46 18.1	N 8 12.4	224 22.1	S 7 22.5	159 31.7	S22 05.2
	19	80 49.6	71 49.8	13.5	61 18.8	13.1	239 24.7	22.5	174 34.0	05.2
	20	95 52.1	86 51.9	14.2	76 19.6	13.8	254 27.3	22.4	189 36.3	05.2
	21	110 54.6	101 53.9	. . 14.8	91 20.3	. . 14.5	269 29.9	. . 22.3	204 38.5	. . 05.2
	22	125 57.0	116 56.0	15.4	106 21.1	15.2	284 32.5	22.3	219 40.8	05.2
	23	140 59.5	131 58.1	16.1	121 21.9	16.0	299 35.1	22.2	234 43.1	05.2
	26 00	156 01.9	147 00.1	N10 16.7	136 22.6	N 8 16.7	314 37.7	S 7 22.2	249 45.4	S22 05.2
	01	171 04.4	162 02.2	17.4	151 23.4	17.4	329 40.3	22.1	264 47.7	05.2
	02	186 06.9	177 04.3	18.0	166 24.2	18.1	344 42.9	22.0	279 50.0	05.2
	03	201 09.3	192 06.4	. . 18.6	181 24.9	. . 18.8	359 45.5	. . 22.0	294 52.3	. . 05.2
	04	216 11.8	207 08.4	19.3	196 25.7	19.5	14 48.1	21.9	309 54.6	05.2
	05	231 14.3	222 10.5	19.9	211 26.5	20.2	29 50.7	21.8	324 56.9	05.2
	06	246 16.7	237 12.6	N10 20.5	226 27.2	N 8 21.0	44 53.3	S 7 21.8	339 59.2	S22 05.2
	07	261 19.2	252 14.7	21.2	241 28.0	21.7	59 55.9	21.7	355 01.5	05.2
	08	276 21.7	267 16.8	21.8	256 28.8	22.4	74 58.6	21.6	10 03.8	05.3
S	09	291 24.1	282 18.9	. . 22.4	271 29.5	. . 23.1	90 01.2	. . 21.6	25 06.1	. . 05.3
U	10	306 26.6	297 21.0	23.1	286 30.3	23.8	105 03.8	21.5	40 08.4	05.3
N	11	321 29.1	312 23.1	23.7	301 31.1	24.5	120 06.4	21.4	55 10.7	05.3
D	12	336 31.5	327 25.2	N10 24.3	316 31.8	N 8 25.2	135 09.0	S 7 21.4	70 13.0	S22 05.3
A	13	351 34.0	342 27.4	24.9	331 32.6	26.0	150 11.6	21.3	85 15.3	05.3
Y	14	6 36.4	357 29.5	25.6	346 33.3	26.7	165 14.2	21.2	100 17.6	05.3
	15	21 38.9	12 31.6	. . 26.2	1 34.1	. . 27.4	180 16.8	. . 21.2	115 19.9	. . 05.3
	16	36 41.4	27 33.7	26.8	16 34.9	28.1	195 19.4	21.1	130 22.2	05.3
	17	51 43.8	42 35.9	27.4	31 35.6	28.8	210 22.0	21.0	145 24.5	05.3
	18	66 46.3	57 38.0	N10 28.0	46 36.4	N 8 29.5	225 24.6	S 7 21.0	160 26.8	S22 05.3
	19	81 48.8	72 40.1	28.6	61 37.2	30.2	240 27.2	20.9	175 29.1	05.3
	20	96 51.2	87 42.3	29.2	76 37.9	30.9	255 29.8	20.8	190 31.4	05.3
	21	111 53.7	102 44.4	. . 29.8	91 38.7	. . 31.6	270 32.4	. . 20.8	205 33.7	. . 05.3
	22	126 56.2	117 46.6	30.5	106 39.5	32.4	285 35.1	20.7	220 36.0	05.3
	23	141 58.6	132 48.7	31.1	121 40.2	33.1	300 37.7	20.6	235 38.3	05.3
	Mer. Pass.	h m 13 37.6	*v* 2.0	*d* 0.7	*v* 0.8	*d* 0.7	*v* 2.6	*d* 0.1	*v* 2.3	*d* 0.0

STARS

Name	SHA	Dec
	° ′	° ′
Acamar	315 16.6	S40 14.6
Achernar	335 25.4	S57 09.4
Acrux	173 05.7	S63 11.5
Adhara	255 10.3	S29 00.1
Aldebaran	290 46.5	N16 32.4
Alioth	166 18.1	N55 51.9
Alkaid	152 56.7	N49 13.5
Al Na'ir	27 41.1	S46 52.7
Alnilam	275 43.7	S 1 11.8
Alphard	217 53.3	S 8 44.2
Alphecca	126 08.8	N26 39.3
Alpheratz	357 41.2	N29 11.0
Altair	62 06.0	N 8 54.8
Ankaa	353 13.6	S42 13.0
Antares	112 23.2	S26 28.0
Arcturus	145 53.3	N19 05.5
Atria	107 22.8	S69 03.0
Avior	234 16.4	S59 34.2
Bellatrix	278 29.2	N 6 21.6
Betelgeuse	270 58.5	N 7 24.3
Canopus	263 54.8	S52 42.8
Capella	280 30.6	N46 00.8
Deneb	49 30.1	N45 20.4
Denebola	182 30.8	N14 28.5
Diphda	348 53.7	S17 53.8
Dubhe	193 48.1	N61 39.4
Elnath	278 09.3	N28 37.1
Eltanin	90 45.2	N51 29.1
Enif	33 45.0	N 9 57.2
Fomalhaut	15 21.6	S29 32.0
Gacrux	171 57.5	S57 12.4
Gienah	175 49.4	S17 38.2
Hadar	148 43.9	S60 27.0
Hamal	327 58.1	N23 32.5
Kaus Aust.	83 40.7	S34 22.3
Kochab	137 19.8	N74 04.9
Markab	13 36.1	N15 17.8
Menkar	314 12.5	N 4 09.1
Menkent	148 04.4	S36 27.0
Miaplacidus	221 38.1	S69 47.5
Mirfak	308 36.8	N49 55.3
Nunki	75 55.4	S26 16.3
Peacock	53 15.9	S56 40.6
Pollux	243 24.4	N27 58.9
Procyon	244 56.9	N 5 10.6
Rasalhague	96 04.2	N12 32.9
Regulus	207 40.5	N11 52.8
Rigel	281 09.6	S 8 11.3
Rigil Kent.	139 47.9	S60 54.0
Sabik	102 09.7	S15 44.6
Schedar	349 38.0	N56 37.9
Shaula	96 18.6	S37 06.7
Sirius	258 31.3	S16 44.8
Spica	158 28.4	S11 15.0
Suhail	222 50.1	S43 30.4
Vega	80 37.5	N38 47.9
Zuben'ubi	137 02.5	S16 06.6

	SHA	Mer. Pass.
	° ′	h m
Venus	351 08.5	14 13
Mars	341 01.5	14 55
Jupiter	158 32.5	3 05
Saturn	93 47.5	7 24

Day	UT (d h)	SUN GHA (° ′)	SUN Dec (° ′)	MOON GHA (° ′)	v (′)	MOON Dec (° ′)	d (′)	HP (′)
FRIDAY	24 00	176 41.7	S 9 28.2	208 49.8	10.3	S16 47.4	4.9	56.2
	01	191 41.8	27.3	223 19.1	10.4	16 42.5	5.0	56.3
	02	206 41.9	26.4	237 48.5	10.4	16 37.5	5.1	56.3
	03	221 42.0	. . 25.4	252 17.9	10.3	16 32.4	5.1	56.3
	04	236 42.1	24.5	266 47.2	10.4	16 27.3	5.3	56.4
	05	251 42.1	23.6	281 16.6	10.3	16 22.0	5.3	56.4
	06	266 42.2	S 9 22.7	295 45.9	10.4	S16 16.7	5.5	56.4
	07	281 42.3	21.7	310 15.3	10.3	16 11.2	5.5	56.4
	08	296 42.4	20.8	324 44.6	10.3	16 05.7	5.7	56.5
	09	311 42.5	. . 19.9	339 13.9	10.3	16 00.0	5.7	56.5
	10	326 42.6	19.0	353 43.2	10.4	15 54.3	5.8	56.5
	11	341 42.7	18.0	8 12.6	10.3	15 48.5	5.9	56.6
	12	356 42.8	S 9 17.1	22 41.9	10.3	S15 42.6	6.0	56.6
	13	11 42.9	16.2	37 11.2	10.3	15 36.6	6.0	56.6
	14	26 43.0	15.3	51 40.5	10.3	15 30.6	6.2	56.6
	15	41 43.1	. . 14.3	66 09.8	10.3	15 24.4	6.3	56.7
	16	56 43.2	13.4	80 39.1	10.3	15 18.1	6.3	56.7
	17	71 43.3	12.5	95 08.4	10.3	15 11.8	6.4	56.7
	18	86 43.4	S 9 11.5	109 37.7	10.3	S15 05.4	6.6	56.8
	19	101 43.5	10.6	124 07.0	10.3	14 58.8	6.6	56.8
	20	116 43.6	09.7	138 36.3	10.3	14 52.2	6.6	56.8
	21	131 43.7	. . 08.8	153 05.6	10.3	14 45.6	6.8	56.8
	22	146 43.8	07.8	167 34.9	10.3	14 38.8	6.9	56.9
	23	161 43.8	06.9	182 04.2	10.3	14 31.9	6.9	56.9
SATURDAY	25 00	176 43.9	S 9 06.0	196 33.5	10.3	S14 25.0	7.1	56.9
	01	191 44.0	05.0	211 02.8	10.3	14 17.9	7.1	56.9
	02	206 44.1	04.1	225 32.1	10.3	14 10.8	7.2	57.0
	03	221 44.2	. . 03.2	240 01.4	10.3	14 03.6	7.3	57.0
	04	236 44.3	02.2	254 30.7	10.3	13 56.3	7.3	57.0
	05	251 44.4	01.3	269 00.0	10.3	13 49.0	7.5	57.1
	06	266 44.5	S 9 00.4	283 29.3	10.3	S13 41.5	7.5	57.1
	07	281 44.6	8 59.5	297 58.6	10.3	13 34.0	7.6	57.1
	08	296 44.7	58.5	312 27.9	10.3	13 26.4	7.7	57.1
	09	311 44.8	. . 57.6	326 57.2	10.3	13 18.7	7.8	57.2
	10	326 44.9	56.7	341 26.5	10.3	13 10.9	7.8	57.2
	11	341 45.0	55.7	355 55.8	10.3	13 03.1	8.0	57.2
	12	356 45.1	S 8 54.8	10 25.1	10.3	S12 55.1	8.0	57.3
	13	11 45.2	53.9	24 54.4	10.3	12 47.1	8.0	57.3
	14	26 45.3	52.9	39 23.7	10.3	12 39.1	8.2	57.3
	15	41 45.4	. . 52.0	53 53.0	10.3	12 30.9	8.2	57.3
	16	56 45.5	51.1	68 22.3	10.3	12 22.7	8.3	57.4
	17	71 45.6	50.1	82 51.6	10.3	12 14.4	8.4	57.4
	18	86 45.7	S 8 49.2	97 20.9	10.3	S12 06.0	8.5	57.4
	19	101 45.8	48.3	111 50.2	10.3	11 57.5	8.5	57.5
	20	116 45.9	47.3	126 19.5	10.4	11 49.0	8.6	57.5
	21	131 46.0	. . 46.4	140 48.9	10.3	11 40.4	8.7	57.5
	22	146 46.1	45.5	155 18.2	10.3	11 31.7	8.7	57.5
	23	161 46.2	44.5	169 47.5	10.3	11 23.0	8.9	57.6
SUNDAY	26 00	176 46.3	S 8 43.6	184 16.8	10.4	S11 14.1	8.8	57.6
	01	191 46.4	42.7	198 46.2	10.3	11 05.3	9.0	57.6
	02	206 46.6	41.7	213 15.5	10.3	10 56.3	9.0	57.6
	03	221 46.7	. . 40.8	227 44.8	10.4	10 47.3	9.1	57.7
	04	236 46.8	39.9	242 14.2	10.3	10 38.2	9.2	57.7
	05	251 46.9	38.9	256 43.5	10.3	10 29.0	9.2	57.7
	06	266 47.0	S 8 38.0	271 12.8	10.4	S10 19.8	9.3	57.7
	07	281 47.1	37.0	285 42.2	10.3	10 10.5	9.3	57.8
	08	296 47.2	36.1	300 11.5	10.4	10 01.2	9.4	57.8
	09	311 47.3	. . 35.2	314 40.9	10.3	9 51.8	9.5	57.8
	10	326 47.4	34.2	329 10.2	10.4	9 42.3	9.6	57.9
	11	341 47.5	33.3	343 39.6	10.3	S 9 32.7	9.6	57.9
	12	356 47.6	S 8 32.4					
	13	11 47.7	31.4					
	14	26 47.8	30.5					
	15	41 47.9	. . 29.5					
	16	56 48.0	28.6					
	17	71 48.1	27.7					
	18	86 48.2	S 8 26.7	85 05.1	10.3	S 8 24.3	10.0	58.1
	19	101 48.3	25.8	99 34.4	10.4	8 14.3	10.0	58.1
	20	116 48.5	24.9	114 03.8	10.3	8 04.3	10.1	58.1
	21	131 48.6	. . 23.9	128 33.1	10.4	7 54.2	10.2	58.1
	22	146 48.7	23.0	143 02.5	10.4	7 44.0	10.2	58.2
	23	161 48.8	22.0	157 31.9	10.3	S 7 33.8	10.3	58.2
		SD 16.2	d 0.9	SD 15.4		15.6		15.8

An annular eclipse of the Sun occurs on this date. See page 5.

Lat. (°)	Twilight Naut. (h m)	Twilight Civil (h m)	Sunrise (h m)	Moonrise 24 (h m)	Moonrise 25 (h m)	Moonrise 26 (h m)	Moonrise 27 (h m)
N 72	05 29	06 46	07 57	08 35	08 22	08 13	08 06
N 70	05 32	06 42	07 45	07 53	07 56	07 57	07 57
68	05 34	06 38	07 35	07 25	07 37	07 44	07 50
66	05 36	06 35	07 27	07 03	07 21	07 34	07 44
64	05 37	06 32	07 21	06 46	07 08	07 25	07 39
62	05 39	06 30	07 15	06 32	06 57	07 18	07 35
60	05 39	06 27	07 10	06 20	06 48	07 11	07 31
N 58	05 40	06 25	07 05	06 10	06 40	07 05	07 28
56	05 41	06 23	07 01	06 01	06 32	07 00	07 25
54	05 41	06 22	06 57	05 52	06 26	06 55	07 22
52	05 41	06 20	06 54	05 45	06 20	06 51	07 19
50	05 41	06 19	06 51	05 39	06 15	06 47	07 17
45	05 41	06 15	06 45	05 25	06 03	06 39	07 12
N 40	05 40	06 12	06 39	05 13	05 54	06 32	07 08
35	05 39	06 09	06 34	05 03	05 46	06 26	07 04
30	05 38	06 06	06 30	04 54	05 38	06 21	07 01
20	05 35	06 00	06 23	04 39	05 26	06 11	06 56
N 10	05 30	05 55	06 16	04 26	05 15	06 03	06 51
0	05 24	05 49	06 10	04 14	05 05	05 56	06 46
S 10	05 17	05 42	06 03	04 01	04 54	05 48	06 42
20	05 08	05 34	05 56	03 48	04 43	05 40	06 37
30	04 55	05 24	05 48	03 33	04 31	05 30	06 31
35	04 47	05 17	05 43	03 24	04 24	05 25	06 28
40	04 37	05 10	05 38	03 14	04 15	05 19	06 25
45	04 24	05 01	05 32	03 03	04 05	05 12	06 20
S 50	04 09	04 50	05 24	02 48	03 54	05 03	06 15
52	04 01	04 45	05 21	02 42	03 48	04 59	06 13
54	03 52	04 39	05 17	02 34	03 42	04 55	06 10
56	03 42	04 32	05 12	02 26	03 35	04 50	06 08
58	03 30	04 25	05 08	02 16	03 28	04 44	06 04
S 60	03 16	04 16	05 02	02 06	03 19	04 38	06 01

Lat. (°)	Sunset (h m)	Twilight Civil (h m)	Twilight Naut. (h m)	Moonset 24 (h m)	Moonset 25 (h m)	Moonset 26 (h m)	Moonset 27 (h m)
N 72	16 31	17 42	19 00	12 28	14 27	16 22	18 16
N 70	16 43	17 46	18 57	13 09	14 52	16 36	18 22
68	16 52	17 50	18 54	13 37	15 10	16 48	18 27
66	17 00	17 53	18 52	13 57	15 25	16 57	18 31
64	17 07	17 55	18 50	14 14	15 37	17 05	18 35
62	17 12	17 58	18 49	14 28	15 47	17 11	18 38
60	17 17	18 00	18 48	14 39	15 56	17 17	18 41
N 58	17 22	18 02	18 47	14 49	16 03	17 22	18 43
56	17 26	18 04	18 47	14 58	16 10	17 26	18 45
54	17 29	18 05	18 46	15 06	16 16	17 30	18 47
52	17 33	18 07	18 46	15 12	16 21	17 34	18 49
50	17 36	18 08	18 46	15 19	16 26	17 37	18 50
45	17 42	18 12	18 46	15 32	16 37	17 44	18 54
N 40	17 47	18 15	18 46	15 43	16 45	17 50	18 56
35	17 52	18 18	18 47	15 52	16 53	17 55	18 59
30	17 56	18 20	18 48	16 00	16 59	17 59	19 01
20	18 04	18 26	18 52	16 15	17 10	18 07	19 04
N 10	18 10	18 31	18 56	16 27	17 20	18 14	19 08
0	18 16	18 37	19 02	16 38	17 29	18 20	19 11
S 10	18 23	18 44	19 09	16 50	17 38	18 26	19 13
20	18 29	18 52	19 18	17 02	17 48	18 32	19 16
30	18 37	19 02	19 31	17 15	17 58	18 40	19 20
35	18 42	19 08	19 39	17 23	18 05	18 44	19 22
40	18 47	19 15	19 48	17 32	18 12	18 49	19 24
45	18 53	19 24	20 00	17 43	18 20	18 54	19 27
S 50	19 01	19 35	20 16	17 56	18 30	19 01	19 30
52	19 04	19 40	20 24	18 01	18 34	19 04	19 31
54	19 08	19 45	20 32	18 08	18 39	19 07	19 32
56	19 12	19 52	20 42	18 15	18 45	19 10	19 34
58	19 17	19 59	20 53	18 23	18 51	19 14	19 36
S 60	19 22	20 07	21 07	18 32	18 58	19 19	19 38

Day	SUN Eqn. of Time 00^h (m s)	SUN Eqn. of Time 12^h (m s)	SUN Mer. Pass. (h m)	MOON Mer. Pass. Upper (h m)	MOON Mer. Pass. Lower (h m)	MOON Age (d)	MOON Phase (%)
24	13 13	13 09	12 13	10 26	22 51	27	5
25	13 04	13 00	12 13	11 17	23 42	28	1
26	12 55	12 50	12 13	12 08	24 33	29	0

Day	UT d h	ARIES GHA	VENUS −4·8 GHA	VENUS Dec	MARS +1·3 GHA	MARS Dec	JUPITER −2·3 GHA	JUPITER Dec	SATURN +0·5 GHA	SATURN Dec
		° ′	° ′	° ′	° ′	° ′	° ′	° ′	° ′	° ′
MONDAY	27 00	157 01.1	147 50.9	N10 31.7	136 41.0	N 8 33.8	315 40.3	S 7 20.6	250 40.6	S22 05.3
	01	172 03.6	162 53.0	32.3	151 41.8	34.5	330 42.9	20.5	265 42.9	05.3
	02	187 06.0	177 55.2	32.9	166 42.5	35.2	345 45.5	20.4	280 45.2	05.3
	03	202 08.5	192 57.3	33.5	181 43.3	35.9	0 48.1	20.4	295 47.5	05.3
	04	217 10.9	207 59.5	34.1	196 44.0	36.6	15 50.7	20.3	310 49.8	05.3
	05	232 13.4	223 01.7	34.7	211 44.8	37.3	30 53.3	20.2	325 52.1	05.3
	06	247 15.9	238 03.8	N10 35.3	226 45.6	N 8 38.0	45 55.9	S 7 20.2	340 54.4	S22 05.3
	07	262 18.3	253 06.0	35.9	241 46.3	38.8	60 58.6	20.1	355 56.7	05.3
	08	277 20.8	268 08.2	36.4	256 47.1	39.5	76 01.2	20.0	10 59.0	05.3
	09	292 23.3	283 10.4	37.0	271 47.9	40.2	91 03.8	20.0	26 01.3	05.3
	10	307 25.7	298 12.6	37.6	286 48.6	40.9	106 06.4	19.9	41 03.6	05.3
	11	322 28.2	313 14.8	38.2	301 49.4	41.6	121 09.0	19.8	56 05.9	05.3
	12	337 30.7	328 17.0	N10 38.8	316 50.2	N 8 42.3	136 11.6	S 7 19.8	71 08.2	S22 05.3
	13	352 33.1	343 19.2	39.4	331 50.9	43.0	151 14.2	19.7	86 10.5	05.3
	14	7 35.6	358 21.4	40.0	346 51.7	43.7	166 16.8	19.6	101 12.9	05.3
	15	22 38.0	13 23.6	40.5	1 52.4	44.4	181 19.5	19.6	116 15.2	05.3
	16	37 40.5	28 25.8	41.1	16 53.2	45.1	196 22.1	19.5	131 17.5	05.3
	17	52 43.0	43 28.0	41.7	31 54.0	45.8	211 24.7	19.4	146 19.8	05.3
	18	67 45.4	58 30.2	N10 42.3	46 54.7	N 8 46.6	226 27.3	S 7 19.4	161 22.1	S22 05.3
	19	82 47.9	73 32.4	42.8	61 55.5	47.3	241 29.9	19.3	176 24.4	05.3
	20	97 50.4	88 34.6	43.4	76 56.3	48.0	256 32.5	19.2	191 26.7	05.3
	21	112 52.8	103 36.9	44.0	91 57.0	48.7	271 35.1	19.1	206 29.0	05.3
	22	127 55.3	118 39.1	44.5	106 57.8	49.4	286 37.8	19.1	221 31.3	05.3
	23	142 57.8	133 41.3	45.1	121 58.5	50.1	301 40.4	19.0	236 33.6	05.3
TUESDAY	28 00	158 00.2	148 43.6	N10 45.7	136 59.3	N 8 50.8	316 43.0	S 7 18.9	251 35.9	S22 05.3
	01	173 02.7	163 45.8	46.2	152 00.1	51.5	331 45.6	18.9	266 38.2	05.3
	02	188 05.2	178 48.1	46.8	167 00.8	52.2	346 48.2	18.8	281 40.5	05.3
	03	203 07.6	193 50.3	47.4	182 01.6	52.9	1 50.8	18.7	296 42.8	05.3
	04	218 10.1	208 52.6	47.9	197 02.4	53.6	16 53.5	18.7	311 45.1	05.3
	05	233 12.5	223 54.8	48.5	212 03.1	54.3	31 56.1	18.6	326 47.4	05.3
	06	248 15.0	238 57.1	N10 49.0	227 03.9	N 8 55.0	46 58.7	S 7 18.5	341 49.7	S22 05.3
	07	263 17.5	253 59.3	49.6	242 04.6	55.7	62 01.3	18.4	356 52.0	05.3
	08	278 19.9	269 01.6	50.1	257 05.4	56.5	77 03.9	18.4	11 54.3	05.3
	09	293 22.4	284 03.9	50.7	272 06.2	57.2	92 06.6	18.3	26 56.6	05.3
	10	308 24.9	299 06.1	51.2	287 06.9	57.9	107 09.2	18.2	41 59.0	05.3
	11	323 27.3	314 08.4	51.8	302 07.7	58.6	122 11.8	18.2	57 01.3	05.3
	12	338 29.8	329 10.7	N10 52.3	317 08.5	N 8 59.3	137 14.4	S 7 18.1	72 03.6	S22 05.3
	13	353 32.3	344 13.0	52.9	332 09.2	9 00.0	152 17.0	18.0	87 05.9	05.3
	14	8 34.7	359 15.3	53.4	347 10.0	00.7	167 19.7	18.0	102 08.2	05.3
	15	23 37.2	14 17.5	53.9	2 10.7	01.4	182 22.3	17.9	117 10.5	05.3
	16	38 39.6	29 19.8	54.5	17 11.5	02.1	197 24.9	17.8	132 12.8	05.3
	17	53 42.1	44 22.1	55.0	32 12.3	02.8	212 27.5	17.7	147 15.1	05.3
	18	68 44.6	59 24.4	N10 55.6	47 13.0	N 9 03.5	227 30.1	S 7 17.7	162 17.4	S22 05.3
	19	83 47.0	74 26.7	56.1	62 13.8	04.2	242 32.8	17.6	177 19.7	05.3
	20	98 49.5	89 29.0	56.6	77 14.6	04.9	257 35.4	17.5	192 22.0	05.3
	21	113 52.0	104 31.4	57.1	92 15.3	05.6	272 38.0	17.5	207 24.3	05.3
	22	128 54.4	119 33.7	57.7	107 16.1	06.3	287 40.6	17.4	222 26.6	05.3
	23	143 56.9	134 36.0	58.2	122 16.8	07.0	302 43.2	17.3	237 28.9	05.3
WEDNESDAY	1 00	158 59.4	149 38.3	N10 58.7	137 17.6	N 9 07.7	317 45.9	S 7 17.2	252 31.3	S22 05.3
	01	174 01.8	164 40.6	59.2	152 18.4	08.4	332 48.5	17.2	267 33.6	05.3
	02	189 04.3	179 43.0	10 59.8	167 19.1	09.1	347 51.1	17.1	282 35.9	05.3
	03	204 06.8	194 45.3	11 00.3	182 19.9	09.8	2 53.7	17.0	297 38.2	05.3
	04	219 09.2	209 47.6	00.8	197 20.6	10.5	17 56.4	16.9	312 40.5	05.3
	05	234 11.7	224 50.0	01.3	212 21.4	11.2	32 59.0	16.9	327 42.8	05.3
	06	249 14.1	239 52.3	N11 01.8	227 22.2	N 9 11.9	48 01.6	S 7 16.8	342 45.1	S22 05.3
	07	264 16.6	254 54.7	02.3	242 22.9	12.6	63 04.2	16.7	357 47.4	05.3
	08	279 19.1	269 57.0	02.8	257 23.7	13.4	78 06.9	16.7	12 49.7	05.3
	09	294 21.5	284 59.4	03.3	272 24.5	14.1	93 09.5	16.6	27 52.0	05.3
	10	309 24.0	300 01.7	03.9	287 25.2	14.8	108 12.1	16.5	42 54.4	05.4
	11	324 26.5	315 04.1	04.4	302 26.0	15.5	123 14.7	16.4	57 56.7	05.4
	12	339 28.9	330 06.5	N11 04.9	317 26.7	N 9 16.2	138 17.4	S 7 16.4	72 59.0	S22 05.4
	13	354 31.4	345 08.8	05.4	332 27.5	16.9	153 20.0	16.3	88 01.3	05.4
	14	9 33.9	0 11.2	05.9	347 28.3	17.6	168 22.6	16.2	103 03.6	05.4
	15	24 36.3	15 13.6	06.4	2 29.0	18.3	183 25.2	16.1	118 05.9	05.4
	16	39 38.8	30 16.0	06.9	17 29.8	19.0	198 27.9	16.1	133 08.2	05.4
	17	54 41.2	45 18.3	07.3	32 30.5	19.7	213 30.5	16.0	148 10.5	05.4
	18	69 43.7	60 20.7	N11 07.8	47 31.3	N 9 20.4	228 33.1	S 7 15.9	163 12.8	S22 05.4
	19	84 46.2	75 23.1	08.3	62 32.1	21.1	243 35.8	15.8	178 15.2	05.4
	20	99 48.6	90 25.5	08.8	77 32.8	21.8	258 38.4	15.8	193 17.5	05.4
	21	114 51.1	105 27.9	09.3	92 33.6	22.5	273 41.0	15.7	208 19.8	05.4
	22	129 53.6	120 30.3	09.8	107 34.3	23.2	288 43.6	15.6	223 22.1	05.4
	23	144 56.0	135 32.7	10.3	122 35.1	23.9	303 46.3	15.6	238 24.4	05.4
	Mer. Pass.	h m 13 25.8	v 2.3	d 0.5	v 0.8	d 0.7	v 2.6	d 0.1	v 2.3	d 0.0

STARS

Name	SHA	Dec
	° ′	° ′
Acamar	315 16.6	S40 14.6
Achernar	335 25.4	S57 09.4
Acrux	173 05.7	S63 11.5
Adhara	255 10.3	S29 00.1
Aldebaran	290 46.5	N16 32.4
Alioth	166 18.1	N55 51.9
Alkaid	152 56.7	N49 13.5
Al Na'ir	27 41.1	S46 52.7
Alnilam	275 43.7	S 1 11.8
Alphard	217 53.3	S 8 44.2
Alphecca	126 08.8	N26 39.3
Alpheratz	357 41.2	N29 11.0
Altair	62 06.0	N 8 54.8
Ankaa	353 13.7	S42 13.0
Antares	112 23.2	S26 28.0
Arcturus	145 53.3	N19 05.5
Atria	107 22.8	S69 03.0
Avior	234 16.4	S59 34.2
Bellatrix	278 29.2	N 6 21.6
Betelgeuse	270 58.5	N 7 24.3
Canopus	263 54.8	S52 42.8
Capella	280 30.6	N46 00.8
Deneb	49 30.1	N45 20.4
Denebola	182 30.8	N14 28.5
Diphda	348 53.7	S17 53.8
Dubhe	193 48.1	N61 39.4
Elnath	278 09.4	N28 37.1
Eltanin	90 45.2	N51 29.1
Enif	33 45.0	N 9 57.2
Fomalhaut	15 21.6	S29 32.0
Gacrux	171 57.5	S57 12.4
Gienah	175 49.4	S17 38.3
Hadar	148 43.8	S60 27.0
Hamal	327 58.1	N23 32.4
Kaus Aust.	83 40.7	S34 22.3
Kochab	137 19.8	N74 04.9
Markab	13 36.1	N15 17.7
Menkar	314 12.5	N 4 09.1
Menkent	148 04.3	S36 27.1
Miaplacidus	221 38.2	S69 47.5
Mirfak	308 36.8	N49 55.3
Nunki	75 55.4	S26 16.3
Peacock	53 15.9	S56 40.6
Pollux	243 24.4	N27 58.9
Procyon	244 56.9	N 5 10.6
Rasalhague	96 04.2	N12 32.9
Regulus	207 40.5	N11 52.8
Rigel	281 09.6	S 8 11.3
Rigil Kent.	139 47.9	S60 54.0
Sabik	102 09.7	S15 44.6
Schedar	349 38.0	N56 37.9
Shaula	96 18.6	S37 06.7
Sirius	258 31.3	S16 44.8
Spica	158 28.4	S11 15.0
Suhail	222 50.2	S43 30.4
Vega	80 37.5	N38 47.9
Zuben'ubi	137 02.5	S16 06.7

	SHA	Mer. Pass.
	° ′	h m
Venus	350 43.3	14 03
Mars	338 59.1	14 51
Jupiter	158 42.8	2 53
Saturn	93 35.7	7 12

UT d	UT h	SUN GHA ° ′	SUN Dec ° ′	MOON GHA ° ′	MOON v ′	MOON Dec ° ′	MOON d ′	MOON HP ′
27	00	176 48.9	S 8 21.1	172 01.2	10.4	S 7 23.5	10.3	58.2
	01	191 49.0	20.2	186 30.6	10.3	7 13.2	10.3	58.2
	02	206 49.1	19.2	200 59.9	10.4	7 02.9	10.4	58.2
	03	221 49.2	. . 18.3	215 29.3	10.3	6 52.5	10.5	58.3
	04	236 49.3	17.3	229 58.6	10.4	6 42.0	10.5	58.3
	05	251 49.4	16.4	244 28.0	10.3	6 31.5	10.5	58.3
	06	266 49.5	S 8 15.4	258 57.3	10.4	S 6 21.0	10.6	58.3
	07	281 49.7	14.5	273 26.7	10.3	6 10.4	10.6	58.4
	08	296 49.8	13.6	287 56.0	10.4	5 59.8	10.7	58.4
M	09	311 49.9	. . 12.6	302 25.4	10.3	5 49.1	10.7	58.4
O	10	326 50.0	11.7	316 54.7	10.4	5 38.4	10.7	58.4
N	11	341 50.1	10.7	331 24.1	10.3	5 27.7	10.8	58.4
D	12	356 50.2	S 8 09.8	345 53.4	10.3	S 5 16.9	10.8	58.5
A	13	11 50.3	08.8	0 22.7	10.4	5 06.1	10.9	58.5
Y	14	26 50.4	07.9	14 52.1	10.3	4 55.2	10.8	58.5
	15	41 50.5	. . 07.0	29 21.4	10.3	4 44.4	11.0	58.5
	16	56 50.7	06.0	43 50.7	10.3	4 33.4	10.9	58.5
	17	71 50.8	05.1	58 20.0	10.3	4 22.5	11.0	58.6
	18	86 50.9	S 8 04.1	72 49.3	10.3	S 4 11.5	11.0	58.6
	19	101 51.0	03.2	87 18.6	10.3	4 00.5	11.1	58.6
	20	116 51.1	02.2	101 47.9	10.3	3 49.4	11.0	58.6
	21	131 51.2	. . 01.3	116 17.2	10.3	3 38.4	11.1	58.6
	22	146 51.3	8 00.4	130 46.5	10.3	3 27.3	11.2	58.7
	23	161 51.5	7 59.4	145 15.8	10.3	3 16.1	11.1	58.7
28	00	176 51.6	S 7 58.5	159 45.1	10.2	S 3 05.0	11.2	58.7
	01	191 51.7	57.5	174 14.3	10.3	2 53.8	11.2	58.7
	02	206 51.8	56.6	188 43.6	10.2	2 42.6	11.2	58.7
	03	221 51.9	. . 55.6	203 12.8	10.3	2 31.4	11.2	58.8
	04	236 52.0	54.7	217 42.1	10.2	2 20.2	11.3	58.8
	05	251 52.1	53.7	232 11.3	10.2	2 08.9	11.3	58.8
	06	266 52.3	S 7 52.8	246 40.5	10.2	S 1 57.6	11.3	58.8
	07	281 52.4	51.8	261 09.7	10.2	1 46.3	11.3	58.8
T	08	296 52.5	50.9	275 38.9	10.2	1 35.0	11.3	58.8
U	09	311 52.6	. . 49.9	290 08.1	10.2	1 23.7	11.3	58.9
E	10	326 52.7	49.0	304 37.3	10.2	1 12.4	11.4	58.9
S	11	341 52.8	48.1	319 06.5	10.1	1 01.0	11.3	58.9
D	12	356 53.0	S 7 47.1	333 35.6	10.2	S 0 49.7	11.4	58.9
A	13	11 53.1	46.2	348 04.8	10.1	0 38.3	11.4	58.9
Y	14	26 53.2	45.2	2 33.9	10.1	0 26.9	11.4	58.9
	15	41 53.3	. . 44.3	17 03.0	10.1	0 15.5	11.4	59.0
	16	56 53.4	43.3	31 32.1	10.1	S 0 04.1	11.4	59.0
	17	71 53.5	42.4	46 01.2	10.1	N 0 07.3	11.4	59.0
	18	86 53.7	S 7 41.4	60 30.3	10.0	N 0 18.7	11.4	59.0
	19	101 53.8	40.5	74 59.3	10.1	0 30.1	11.4	59.0
	20	116 53.9	39.5	89 28.4	10.0	0 41.5	11.4	59.0
	21	131 54.0	. . 38.6	103 57.4	10.0	0 52.9	11.4	59.0
	22	146 54.1	37.6	118 26.4	10.0	1 04.3	11.4	59.1
	23	161 54.3	36.7	132 55.4	10.0	1 15.7	11.4	59.1
1	00	176 54.4	S 7 35.7	147 24.4	9.9	N 1 27.1	11.4	59.1
	01	191 54.5	34.8	161 53.3	10.0	1 38.5	11.4	59.1
	02	206 54.6	33.8	176 22.3	9.9	1 49.9	11.4	59.1
	03	221 54.7	. . 32.9	190 51.2	9.9	2 01.3	11.4	59.1
	04	236 54.9	31.9	205 20.1	9.9	2 12.7	11.3	59.1
	05	251 55.0	31.0	219 49.0	9.8	2 24.0	11.4	59.1
	06	266 55.1	S 7 30.0	234 17.8	9.9	N 2 35.4	11.3	59.1
W	07	281 55.2	29.1	248 46.7	9.8	2 46.7	11.4	59.2
E	08	296 55.3	28.1	263 15.5	9.8	2 58.1	11.3	59.2
D	09	311 55.5	. . 27.2	277 44.3	9.8	3 09.4	11.3	59.2
N	10	326 55.6	26.2	292 13.1	9.7	3 20.7	11.3	59.2
E	11	341 55.7	25.3	306 41.8	9.7	3 32.0	11.3	59.2
S	12	356 55.8	S 7 24.3	321 10.5	9.8	N 3 43.3	11.2	59.2
D	13	11 56.0	23.4	335 39.3	9.6	3 54.5	11.3	59.2
A	14	26 56.1	22.4	350 07.9	9.7	4 05.8	11.2	59.2
Y	15	41 56.2	. . 21.5	4 36.6	9.6	4 17.0	11.2	59.2
	16	56 56.3	20.5	19 05.2	9.7	4 28.2	11.2	59.2
	17	71 56.4	19.5	33 33.9	9.6	4 39.4	11.1	59.3
	18	86 56.6	S 7 18.6	48 02.5	9.5	N 4 50.5	11.1	59.3
	19	101 56.7	17.6	62 31.0	9.6	5 01.6	11.1	59.3
	20	116 56.8	16.7	76 59.6	9.5	5 12.7	11.1	59.3
	21	131 56.9	. . 15.7	91 28.1	9.5	5 23.8	11.0	59.3
	22	146 57.1	14.8	105 56.6	9.4	5 34.8	11.0	59.3
	23	161 57.2	13.8	120 25.0	9.4	N 5 45.8	11.0	59.3
		SD 16.2	*d* 0.9	SD 15.9		16.1		16.1

Lat.	Twilight Naut.	Twilight Civil	Sunrise	Moonrise 27	Moonrise 28	Moonrise 1	Moonrise 2
°	h m	h m	h m	h m	h m	h m	h m
N 72	05 14	06 32	07 41	08 06	07 59	07 52	07 45
N 70	05 19	06 29	07 31	07 57	07 57	07 56	07 56
68	05 22	06 26	07 23	07 50	07 55	07 59	08 04
66	05 25	06 24	07 16	07 44	07 53	08 02	08 11
64	05 28	06 22	07 10	07 39	07 52	08 04	08 17
62	05 30	06 21	07 05	07 35	07 50	08 06	08 22
60	05 31	06 19	07 01	07 31	07 49	08 08	08 27
N 58	05 32	06 18	06 57	07 28	07 48	08 09	08 31
56	05 33	06 16	06 54	07 25	07 48	08 11	08 35
54	05 34	06 15	06 51	07 22	07 47	08 12	08 38
52	05 35	06 14	06 48	07 19	07 46	08 13	08 41
50	05 35	06 13	06 45	07 17	07 46	08 14	08 44
45	05 36	06 10	06 39	07 12	07 44	08 16	08 50
N 40	05 36	06 08	06 35	07 08	07 43	08 18	08 55
35	05 36	06 05	06 31	07 04	07 42	08 20	08 59
30	05 35	06 03	06 27	07 01	07 41	08 21	09 03
20	05 33	05 58	06 20	06 56	07 40	08 24	09 09
N 10	05 29	05 54	06 15	06 51	07 38	08 26	09 15
0	05 24	05 48	06 09	06 46	07 37	08 29	09 21
S 10	05 18	05 42	06 04	06 42	07 36	08 31	09 26
20	05 09	05 35	05 57	06 37	07 35	08 33	09 32
30	04 57	05 26	05 50	06 31	07 33	08 36	09 39
35	04 50	05 20	05 46	06 28	07 33	08 38	09 43
40	04 41	05 14	05 41	06 25	07 32	08 40	09 48
45	04 29	05 06	05 36	06 20	07 31	08 42	09 53
S 50	04 15	04 56	05 29	06 15	07 29	08 44	10 00
52	04 08	04 51	05 26	06 13	07 29	08 45	10 03
54	04 00	04 46	05 23	06 10	07 28	08 47	10 06
56	03 50	04 40	05 19	06 08	07 27	08 48	10 10
58	03 40	04 33	05 15	06 04	07 27	08 50	10 14
S 60	03 27	04 25	05 10	06 01	07 26	08 52	10 18

Lat.	Sunset	Twilight Civil	Twilight Naut.	Moonset 27	Moonset 28	Moonset 1	Moonset 2
°	h m	h m	h m	h m	h m	h m	h m
N 72	16 46	17 55	19 14	18 16	20 09	22 04	24 03
N 70	16 56	17 58	19 09	18 22	20 09	21 56	23 46
68	17 04	18 00	19 05	18 27	20 08	21 50	23 33
66	17 10	18 02	19 02	18 31	20 07	21 44	23 22
64	17 16	18 04	18 59	18 35	20 07	21 40	23 13
62	17 21	18 06	18 57	18 38	20 06	21 36	23 05
60	17 25	18 07	18 55	18 41	20 06	21 32	22 59
N 58	17 29	18 09	18 54	18 43	20 06	21 29	22 53
56	17 32	18 10	18 53	18 45	20 05	21 27	22 48
54	17 35	18 11	18 52	18 47	20 05	21 24	22 43
52	17 38	18 12	18 51	18 49	20 05	21 22	22 39
50	17 41	18 13	18 51	18 50	20 05	21 20	22 36
45	17 46	18 16	18 50	18 54	20 04	21 16	22 27
N 40	17 51	18 18	18 49	18 56	20 04	21 12	22 21
35	17 55	18 20	18 50	18 59	20 03	21 09	22 15
30	17 58	18 22	18 50	19 01	20 03	21 06	22 10
20	18 05	18 27	18 53	19 04	20 03	21 01	22 01
N 10	18 10	18 32	18 56	19 08	20 02	20 57	21 53
0	18 16	18 37	19 01	19 11	20 02	20 53	21 46
S 10	18 21	18 43	19 07	19 13	20 01	20 49	21 39
20	18 27	18 50	19 16	19 16	20 00	20 45	21 31
30	18 34	18 58	19 27	19 20	20 00	20 40	21 23
35	18 38	19 04	19 34	19 22	19 59	20 38	21 18
40	18 43	19 10	19 43	19 24	19 59	20 35	21 12
45	18 48	19 18	19 55	19 27	19 58	20 31	21 05
S 50	18 55	19 28	20 09	19 30	19 58	20 27	20 57
52	18 58	19 33	20 16	19 31	19 58	20 25	20 54
54	19 01	19 38	20 24	19 32	19 57	20 23	20 50
56	19 05	19 44	20 33	19 34	19 57	20 20	20 45
58	19 09	19 50	20 43	19 36	19 57	20 18	20 41
S 60	19 13	19 58	20 55	19 38	19 56	20 15	20 35

Day	SUN Eqn. of Time 00^h	SUN Eqn. of Time 12^h	SUN Mer. Pass.	MOON Mer. Pass. Upper	MOON Mer. Pass. Lower	MOON Age	MOON Phase
d	m s	m s	h m	h m	h m	d %	
27	12 45	12 39	12 13	12 58	00 33	01 1	●
28	12 34	12 28	12 12	13 49	01 24	02 4	
1	12 23	12 17	12 12	14 41	02 15	03 10	

Day	UT	ARIES	VENUS −4·8		MARS +1·3		JUPITER −2·3		SATURN +0·5	
		GHA	GHA	Dec	GHA	Dec	GHA	Dec	GHA	Dec
	d h	° ′	° ′	° ′	° ′	° ′	° ′	° ′	° ′	° ′
	2 00	159 58.5	150 35.1	N11 10.7	137 35.9	N 9 24.6	318 48.9	S 7 15.5	253 26.7	S22 05.4
	01	175 01.0	165 37.5	11.2	152 36.6	25.3	333 51.5	15.4	268 29.0	05.4
	02	190 03.4	180 40.0	11.7	167 37.4	26.0	348 54.2	15.3	283 31.3	05.4
	03	205 05.9	195 42.4	. . 12.2	182 38.1	. . 26.7	3 56.8	. . 15.3	298 33.7	. . 05.4
	04	220 08.4	210 44.8	12.6	197 38.9	27.4	18 59.4	15.2	313 36.0	05.4
	05	235 10.8	225 47.2	13.1	212 39.7	28.1	34 02.1	15.1	328 38.3	05.4
	06	250 13.3	240 49.7	N11 13.6	227 40.4	N 9 28.8	49 04.7	S 7 15.0	343 40.6	S22 05.4
	07	265 15.7	255 52.1	14.0	242 41.2	29.5	64 07.3	15.0	358 42.9	05.4
T	08	280 18.2	270 54.5	14.5	257 41.9	30.2	79 09.9	14.9	13 45.2	05.4
H	09	295 20.7	285 57.0	. . 15.0	272 42.7	. . 30.8	94 12.6	. . 14.8	28 47.5	. . 05.4
U	10	310 23.1	300 59.4	15.4	287 43.5	31.5	109 15.2	14.7	43 49.9	05.4
R	11	325 25.6	316 01.9	15.9	302 44.2	32.2	124 17.8	14.7	58 52.2	05.4
S	12	340 28.1	331 04.3	N11 16.4	317 45.0	N 9 32.9	139 20.5	S 7 14.6	73 54.5	S22 05.4
D	13	355 30.5	346 06.8	16.8	332 45.7	33.6	154 23.1	14.5	88 56.8	05.4
A	14	10 33.0	1 09.3	17.3	347 46.5	34.3	169 25.7	14.4	103 59.1	05.4
Y	15	25 35.5	16 11.7	. . 17.7	2 47.3	. . 35.0	184 28.4	. . 14.3	119 01.4	. . 05.4
	16	40 37.9	31 14.2	18.2	17 48.0	35.7	199 31.0	14.3	134 03.7	05.4
	17	55 40.4	46 16.7	18.6	32 48.8	36.4	214 33.6	14.2	149 06.1	05.4
	18	70 42.8	61 19.1	N11 19.1	47 49.5	N 9 37.1	229 36.3	S 7 14.1	164 08.4	S22 05.4
	19	85 45.3	76 21.6	19.5	62 50.3	37.8	244 38.9	14.0	179 10.7	05.4
	20	100 47.8	91 24.1	19.9	77 51.1	38.5	259 41.5	14.0	194 13.0	05.4
	21	115 50.2	106 26.6	. . 20.4	92 51.8	. . 39.2	274 44.2	. . 13.9	209 15.3	. . 05.4
	22	130 52.7	121 29.1	20.8	107 52.6	39.9	289 46.8	13.8	224 17.6	05.4
	23	145 55.2	136 31.6	21.3	122 53.3	40.6	304 49.5	13.7	239 20.0	05.4
	3 00	160 57.6	151 34.1	N11 21.7	137 54.1	N 9 41.3	319 52.1	S 7 13.7	254 22.3	S22 05.4
	01	176 00.1	166 36.6	22.1	152 54.9	42.0	334 54.7	13.6	269 24.6	05.4
	02	191 02.6	181 39.1	22.6	167 55.6	42.7	349 57.4	13.5	284 26.9	05.4
	03	206 05.0	196 41.6	. . 23.0	182 56.4	. . 43.4	5 00.0	. . 13.4	299 29.2	. . 05.4
	04	221 07.5	211 44.1	23.4	197 57.1	44.1	20 02.6	13.4	314 31.5	05.4
	05	236 10.0	226 46.6	23.8	212 57.9	44.8	35 05.3	13.3	329 33.9	05.4
	06	251 12.4	241 49.1	N11 24.3	227 58.7	N 9 45.5	50 07.9	S 7 13.2	344 36.2	S22 05.4
	07	266 14.9	256 51.7	24.7	242 59.4	46.2	65 10.6	13.1	359 38.5	05.4
	08	281 17.3	271 54.2	25.1	258 00.2	46.9	80 13.2	13.0	14 40.8	05.4
F	09	296 19.8	286 56.7	. . 25.5	273 00.9	. . 47.5	95 15.8	. . 13.0	29 43.1	. . 05.4
R	10	311 22.3	301 59.3	25.9	288 01.7	48.2	110 18.5	12.9	44 45.4	05.4
I	11	326 24.7	317 01.8	26.3	303 02.4	48.9	125 21.1	12.8	59 47.8	05.4
D	12	341 27.2	332 04.4	N11 26.8	318 03.2	N 9 49.6	140 23.7	S 7 12.7	74 50.1	S22 05.4
A	13	356 29.7	347 06.9	27.2	333 04.0	50.3	155 26.4	12.7	89 52.4	05.4
Y	14	11 32.1	2 09.5	27.6	348 04.7	51.0	170 29.0	12.6	104 54.7	05.4
	15	26 34.6	17 12.0	. . 28.0	3 05.5	. . 51.7	185 31.7	. . 12.5	119 57.0	. . 05.4
	16	41 37.1	32 14.6	28.4	18 06.2	52.4	200 34.3	12.4	134 59.4	05.4
	17	56 39.5	47 17.1	28.8	33 07.0	53.1	215 36.9	12.3	150 01.7	05.4
	18	71 42.0	62 19.7	N11 29.2	48 07.8	N 9 53.8	230 39.6	S 7 12.3	165 04.0	S22 05.4
	19	86 44.5	77 22.3	29.6	63 08.5	54.5	245 42.2	12.2	180 06.3	05.4
	20	101 46.9	92 24.8	30.0	78 09.3	55.2	260 44.9	12.1	195 08.6	05.4
	21	116 49.4	107 27.4	. . 30.4	93 10.0	. . 55.9	275 47.5	. . 12.0	210 11.0	. . 05.4
	22	131 51.8	122 30.0	30.8	108 10.8	56.5	290 50.1	11.9	225 13.3	05.4
	23	146 54.3	137 32.6	31.1	123 11.5	57.2	305 52.8	11.9	240 15.6	05.4
	4 00	161 56.8	152 35.2	N11 31.5	138 12.3	N 9 57.9	320 55.4	S 7 11.8	255 17.9	S22 05.4
	01	176 59.2	167 37.8	31.9	153 13.1	58.6	335 58.1	11.7	270 20.2	05.4
	02	192 01.7	182 40.4	32.3	168 13.8	9 59.3	351 00.7	11.6	285 22.6	05.4
	03	207 04.2	197 43.0	. . 32.7	183 14.6	10 00.0	6 03.4	. . 11.5	300 24.9	. . 05.4
	04	222 06.6	212 45.6	33.1	198 15.3	00.7	21 06.0	11.5	315 27.2	05.4
	05	237 09.1	227 48.2	33.4	213 16.1	01.4	36 08.6	11.4	330 29.5	05.4
	06	252 11.6	242 50.8	N11 33.8	228 16.8	N10 02.1	51 11.3	S 7 11.3	345 31.8	S22 05.4
	07	267 14.0	257 53.4	34.2	243 17.6	02.8	66 13.9	11.2	0 34.2	05.4
S	08	282 16.5	272 56.0	34.6	258 18.4	03.5	81 16.6	11.1	15 36.5	05.4
A	09	297 18.9	287 58.6	. . 34.9	273 19.1	. . 04.1	96 19.2	. . 11.1	30 38.8	. . 05.4
T	10	312 21.4	303 01.3	35.3	288 19.9	04.8	111 21.9	11.0	45 41.1	05.4
U	11	327 23.9	318 03.9	35.7	303 20.6	05.5	126 24.5	10.9	60 43.5	05.4
R	12	342 26.3	333 06.5	N11 36.0	318 21.4	N10 06.2	141 27.2	S 7 10.8	75 45.8	S22 05.4
D	13	357 28.8	348 09.2	36.4	333 22.1	06.9	156 29.8	10.7	90 48.1	05.4
A	14	12 31.3	3 11.8	36.7	348 22.9	07.6	171 32.4	10.7	105 50.4	05.4
Y	15	27 33.7	18 14.5	. . 37.1	3 23.7	. . 08.3	186 35.1	. . 10.6	120 52.7	. . 05.4
	16	42 36.2	33 17.1	37.4	18 24.4	09.0	201 37.7	10.5	135 55.1	05.4
	17	57 38.7	48 19.8	37.8	33 25.2	09.7	216 40.4	10.4	150 57.4	05.4
	18	72 41.1	63 22.4	N11 38.2	48 25.9	N10 10.3	231 43.0	S 7 10.3	165 59.7	S22 05.4
	19	87 43.6	78 25.1	38.5	63 26.7	11.0	246 45.7	10.3	181 02.0	05.4
	20	102 46.1	93 27.8	38.8	78 27.4	11.7	261 48.3	10.2	196 04.4	05.4
	21	117 48.5	108 30.4	. . 39.2	93 28.2	. . 12.4	276 51.0	. . 10.1	211 06.7	. . 05.4
	22	132 51.0	123 33.1	39.5	108 29.0	13.1	291 53.6	10.0	226 09.0	05.4
	23	147 53.4	138 35.8	39.9	123 29.7	13.8	306 56.3	09.9	241 11.3	05.4
	Mer. Pass.	h m 13 14.0	v 2.5	d 0.4	v 0.8	d 0.7	v 2.6	d 0.1	v 2.3	d 0.0

STARS

Name	SHA	Dec
	° ′	° ′
Acamar	315 16.7	S40 14.6
Achernar	335 25.4	S57 09.4
Acrux	173 05.7	S63 11.5
Adhara	255 10.3	S29 00.1
Aldebaran	290 46.5	N16 32.4
Alioth	166 18.1	N55 51.9
Alkaid	152 56.6	N49 13.5
Al Na'ir	27 41.1	S46 52.7
Alnilam	275 43.8	S 1 11.8
Alphard	217 53.3	S 8 44.2
Alphecca	126 08.8	N26 39.3
Alpheratz	357 41.2	N29 11.0
Altair	62 06.0	N 8 54.8
Ankaa	353 13.7	S42 13.0
Antares	112 23.1	S26 28.0
Arcturus	145 53.3	N19 05.5
Atria	107 22.7	S69 03.0
Avior	234 16.4	S59 34.2
Bellatrix	278 29.3	N 6 21.6
Betelgeuse	270 58.5	N 7 24.3
Canopus	263 54.8	S52 42.8
Capella	280 30.7	N46 00.8
Deneb	49 30.1	N45 20.4
Denebola	182 30.8	N14 28.5
Diphda	348 53.7	S17 53.8
Dubhe	193 48.1	N61 39.4
Elnath	278 09.4	N28 37.1
Eltanin	90 45.1	N51 29.1
Enif	33 45.0	N 9 57.2
Fomalhaut	15 21.6	S29 32.0
Gacrux	171 57.5	S57 12.4
Gienah	175 49.4	S17 38.3
Hadar	148 43.8	S60 27.0
Hamal	327 58.1	N23 32.4
Kaus Aust.	83 40.7	S34 22.3
Kochab	137 19.7	N74 04.9
Markab	13 36.1	N15 17.7
Menkar	314 12.6	N 4 09.1
Menkent	148 04.3	S36 27.1
Miaplacidus	221 38.2	S69 47.5
Mirfak	308 36.9	N49 55.3
Nunki	75 55.4	S26 16.3
Peacock	53 15.8	S56 40.6
Pollux	243 24.4	N27 58.9
Procyon	244 56.9	N 5 10.6
Rasalhague	96 04.2	N12 32.9
Regulus	207 40.6	N11 52.8
Rigel	281 09.6	S 8 11.3
Rigil Kent.	139 47.9	S60 54.0
Sabik	102 09.7	S15 44.6
Schedar	349 38.1	N56 37.9
Shaula	96 18.6	S37 06.7
Sirius	258 31.4	S16 44.8
Spica	158 28.3	S11 15.0
Suhail	222 50.2	S43 30.4
Vega	80 37.4	N38 47.9
Zuben'ubi	137 02.5	S16 06.7

	SHA	Mer. Pass.
	° ′	h m
Venus	350 36.4	13 51
Mars	336 56.5	14 48
Jupiter	158 54.5	2 40
Saturn	93 24.6	7 01

UT d h	SUN GHA	SUN Dec	MOON GHA	v	MOON Dec	d	HP
	° ′	° ′	° ′	′	° ′	′	′
2 00	176 57.3	S 7 12.9	134 53.4	9.4	N 5 56.8	10.9	59.3
01	191 57.4	11.9	149 21.8	9.4	6 07.7	10.9	59.3
02	206 57.6	11.0	163 50.2	9.4	6 18.6	10.9	59.3
03	221 57.7 . .	10.0	178 18.6	9.3	6 29.5	10.8	59.3
04	236 57.8	09.1	192 46.9	9.3	6 40.3	10.8	59.3
05	251 57.9	08.1	207 15.2	9.2	6 51.1	10.8	59.3
06	266 58.1	S 7 07.1	221 43.4	9.3	N 7 01.9	10.7	59.3
07	281 58.2	06.2	236 11.7	9.1	7 12.6	10.7	59.4
T 08	296 58.3	05.2	250 39.8	9.2	7 23.3	10.6	59.4
H 09	311 58.5 . .	04.3	265 08.0	9.2	7 33.9	10.6	59.4
U 10	326 58.6	03.3	279 36.2	9.1	7 44.5	10.5	59.4
R 11	341 58.7	02.4	294 04.3	9.0	7 55.0	10.5	59.4
S 12	356 58.8	S 7 01.4	308 32.3	9.1	N 8 05.5	10.5	59.4
D 13	11 59.0	7 00.4	323 00.4	9.0	8 16.0	10.4	59.4
A 14	26 59.1	6 59.5	337 28.4	9.0	8 26.4	10.3	59.4
Y 15	41 59.2 . .	58.5	351 56.4	8.9	8 36.7	10.4	59.4
16	56 59.3	57.6	6 24.3	8.9	8 47.1	10.2	59.4
17	71 59.5	56.6	20 52.2	8.9	8 57.3	10.2	59.4
18	86 59.6	S 6 55.7	35 20.1	8.8	N 9 07.5	10.1	59.4
19	101 59.7	54.7	49 47.9	8.8	9 17.6	10.1	59.4
20	116 59.9	53.7	64 15.7	8.8	9 27.7	10.1	59.4
21	132 00.0 . .	52.8	78 43.5	8.8	9 37.8	9.9	59.4
22	147 00.1	51.8	93 11.3	8.7	9 47.7	9.9	59.4
23	162 00.3	50.9	107 39.0	8.6	9 57.6	9.9	59.4
3 00	177 00.4	S 6 49.9	122 06.6	8.7	N10 07.5	9.8	59.4
01	192 00.5	49.0	136 34.3	8.6	10 17.3	9.7	59.4
02	207 00.6	48.0	151 01.9	8.5	10 27.0	9.7	59.4
03	222 00.8 . .	47.0	165 29.4	8.6	10 36.7	9.6	59.4
04	237 00.9	46.1	179 57.0	8.5	10 46.3	9.5	59.4
05	252 01.0	45.1	194 24.5	8.4	10 55.8	9.5	59.4
06	267 01.2	S 6 44.2	208 51.9	8.5	N11 05.3	9.4	59.4
07	282 01.3	43.2	223 19.4	8.3	11 14.7	9.3	59.4
08	297 01.4	42.2	237 46.7	8.4	11 24.0	9.3	59.4
F 09	312 01.6 . .	41.3	252 14.1	8.3	11 33.3	9.2	59.4
R 10	327 01.7	40.3	266 41.4	8.3	11 42.5	9.1	59.4
I 11	342 01.8	39.4	281 08.7	8.2	11 51.6	9.1	59.4
D 12	357 02.0	S 6 38.4	295 35.9	8.3	N12 00.7	8.9	59.4
A 13	12 02.1	37.4	310 03.2	8.1	12 09.6	8.9	59.4
Y 14	27 02.2	36.5	324 30.3	8.2	12 18.5	8.8	59.4
15	42 02.4 . .	35.5	338 57.5	8.1	12 27.3	8.8	59.4
16	57 02.5	34.6	353 24.6	8.0	12 36.1	8.7	59.4
17	72 02.6	33.6	7 51.6	8.1	12 44.8	8.5	59.4
18	87 02.8	S 6 32.6	22 18.7	7.9	N12 53.3	8.5	59.4
19	102 02.9	31.7	36 45.6	8.0	13 01.8	8.5	59.4
20	117 03.0	30.7	51 12.6	7.9	13 10.3	8.3	59.4
21	132 03.2 . .	29.8	65 39.5	7.9	13 18.6	8.3	59.4
22	147 03.3	28.8	80 06.4	7.9	13 26.9	8.1	59.4
23	162 03.4	27.8	94 33.3	7.8	13 35.0	8.1	59.4
4 00	177 03.6	S 6 26.9	109 00.1	7.7	N13 43.1	8.0	59.4
01	192 03.7	25.9	123 26.8	7.8	13 51.1	7.9	59.4
02	207 03.8	24.9	137 53.6	7.7	13 59.0	7.9	59.4
03	222 04.0 . .	24.0	152 20.3	7.7	14 06.9	7.7	59.4
04	237 04.1	23.0	166 47.0	7.6	14 14.6	7.6	59.4
05	252 04.2	22.1	181 13.6	7.6	14 22.2	7.6	59.4
06	267 04.4	S 6 21.1	195 40.2	7.6	N14 29.8	7.5	59.4
07	282 04.5	20.1	210 06.8	7.5	14 37.3	7.3	59.4
S 08	297 04.7	19.2	224 33.3	7.5	14 44.6	7.3	59.4
A 09	312 04.8 . .	18.2	238 59.8	7.5	14 51.9	7.2	59.4
T 10	327 04.9	17.2	253 26.3	7.4	14 59.1	7.1	59.4
U 11	342 05.1	16.3	267 52.7	7.4	15 06.2	7.0	59.3
R 12	357 05.2	S 6 15.3	282 19.1	7.4	N15 13.2	6.9	59.3
D 13	12 05.3	14.3	296 45.5	7.3	15 20.1	6.8	59.3
A 14	27 05.5	13.4	311 11.8	7.3	15 26.9	6.6	59.3
Y 15	42 05.6 . .	12.4	325 38.1	7.3	15 33.5	6.6	59.3
16	57 05.8	11.5	340 04.4	7.2	15 40.1	6.5	59.3
17	72 05.9	10.5	354 30.6	7.2	15 46.6	6.4	59.3
18	87 06.0	S 6 09.5	8 56.8	7.2	N15 53.0	6.3	59.3
19	102 06.2	08.6	23 23.0	7.2	15 59.3	6.2	59.3
20	117 06.3	07.6	37 49.2	7.1	16 05.5	6.1	59.3
21	132 06.5 . .	06.6	52 15.3	7.1	16 11.6	6.0	59.3
22	147 06.6	05.7	66 41.4	7.1	16 17.6	5.8	59.3
23	162 06.7	04.7	81 07.5	7.0	N16 23.4	5.8	59.3
	SD 16.2	*d* 1.0	SD 16.2		16.2		16.2

Lat.	Twilight Naut.	Twilight Civil	Sunrise	Moonrise 2	Moonrise 3	Moonrise 4	Moonrise 5
°	h m	h m	h m	h m	h m	h m	h m
N 72	04 59	06 17	07 25	07 45	07 38	07 29	07 14
N 70	05 05	06 16	07 17	07 56	07 56	07 59	08 07
68	05 10	06 14	07 10	08 04	08 11	08 22	08 39
66	05 14	06 13	07 05	08 11	08 23	08 39	09 03
64	05 18	06 12	07 00	08 17	08 33	08 54	09 22
62	05 20	06 11	06 56	08 22	08 42	09 06	09 38
60	05 23	06 11	06 52	08 27	08 49	09 16	09 51
N 58	05 24	06 10	06 49	08 31	08 56	09 25	10 02
56	05 26	06 09	06 46	08 35	09 02	09 33	10 12
54	05 27	06 08	06 44	08 38	09 07	09 40	10 20
52	05 28	06 07	06 41	08 41	09 12	09 47	10 28
50	05 29	06 07	06 39	08 44	09 16	09 53	10 35
45	05 31	06 05	06 34	08 50	09 25	10 05	10 50
N 40	05 32	06 03	06 30	08 55	09 33	10 16	11 03
35	05 32	06 01	06 27	08 59	09 40	10 25	11 13
30	05 32	06 00	06 24	09 03	09 46	10 32	11 23
20	05 31	05 56	06 18	09 09	09 56	10 46	11 39
N 10	05 28	05 52	06 13	09 15	10 06	10 58	11 53
0	05 24	05 48	06 09	09 21	10 14	11 09	12 06
S 10	05 18	05 43	06 04	09 26	10 23	11 21	12 19
20	05 10	05 36	05 58	09 32	10 33	11 33	12 33
30	05 00	05 28	05 52	09 39	10 43	11 47	12 50
35	04 53	05 23	05 49	09 43	10 50	11 55	12 59
40	04 44	05 17	05 45	09 48	10 57	12 05	13 10
45	04 34	05 10	05 40	09 53	11 05	12 16	13 23
S 50	04 21	05 01	05 34	10 00	11 15	12 29	13 39
52	04 14	04 57	05 32	10 03	11 20	12 35	13 46
54	04 07	04 52	05 29	10 06	11 25	12 42	13 54
56	03 58	04 47	05 25	10 10	11 31	12 50	14 04
58	03 49	04 41	05 22	10 14	11 37	12 58	14 14
S 60	03 37	04 34	05 18	10 18	11 45	13 08	14 26

Lat.	Sunset	Twilight Civil	Twilight Naut.	Moonset 2	Moonset 3	Moonset 4	Moonset 5
°	h m	h m	h m	h m	h m	h m	h m
N 72	17 00	18 09	19 28	24 03	00 03	02 06	04 18
N 70	17 08	18 10	19 21	23 46	25 37	01 37	03 27
68	17 15	18 11	19 16	23 33	25 16	01 16	02 55
66	17 21	18 12	19 12	23 22	24 59	00 59	02 31
64	17 25	18 13	19 08	23 13	24 45	00 45	02 13
62	17 29	18 14	19 05	23 05	24 34	00 34	01 58
60	17 33	18 15	19 03	22 59	24 24	00 24	01 45
N 58	17 36	18 15	19 01	22 53	24 16	00 16	01 34
56	17 39	18 16	18 59	22 48	24 08	00 08	01 25
54	17 41	18 17	18 58	22 43	24 01	00 01	01 16
52	17 44	18 17	18 56	22 39	23 56	25 09	01 09
50	17 46	18 18	18 55	22 36	23 50	25 02	01 02
45	17 50	18 20	18 54	22 27	23 39	24 48	00 48
N 40	17 54	18 21	18 53	22 21	23 29	24 36	00 36
35	17 57	18 23	18 52	22 15	23 21	24 26	00 26
30	18 01	18 25	18 52	22 10	23 14	24 17	00 17
20	18 06	18 28	18 54	22 01	23 01	24 02	00 02
N 10	18 11	18 32	18 56	21 53	22 51	23 49	24 47
0	18 15	18 36	19 00	21 46	22 40	23 36	24 33
S 10	18 20	18 41	19 06	21 39	22 30	23 24	24 19
20	18 25	18 47	19 13	21 31	22 20	23 11	24 04
30	18 31	18 55	19 23	21 23	22 07	22 55	23 47
35	18 34	19 00	19 30	21 18	22 00	22 47	23 38
40	18 38	19 06	19 38	21 12	21 52	22 37	23 26
45	18 43	19 13	19 49	21 05	21 43	22 25	23 13
S 50	18 48	19 22	20 02	20 57	21 32	22 11	22 57
52	18 51	19 26	20 08	20 54	21 26	22 04	22 49
54	18 54	19 30	20 15	20 50	21 21	21 57	22 41
56	18 57	19 36	20 23	20 45	21 14	21 49	22 31
58	19 00	19 41	20 33	20 41	21 07	21 40	22 21
S 60	19 04	19 48	20 44	20 35	20 59	21 29	22 08

Day	SUN Eqn. of Time 00^h	SUN Eqn. of Time 12^h	SUN Mer. Pass.	MOON Mer. Pass. Upper	MOON Mer. Pass. Lower	MOON Age	MOON Phase
d	m s	m s	h m	h m	h m	d	%
2	12 11	12 05	12 12	15 33	03 07	04	18
3	11 59	11 52	12 12	16 27	04 00	05	28
4	11 46	11 39	12 12	17 23	04 55	06	39

Day	UT d h	ARIES GHA ° ′	VENUS −4·7 GHA ° ′	VENUS Dec ° ′	MARS +1·3 GHA ° ′	MARS Dec ° ′	JUPITER −2·4 GHA ° ′	JUPITER Dec ° ′	SATURN +0·5 GHA ° ′	SATURN Dec ° ′
	5 00	162 55.9	153 38.5	N11 40.2	138 30.5	N10 14.5	321 58.9	S 7 09.9	256 13.7	S22 05.4
	01	177 58.4	168 41.1	40.5	153 31.2	15.2	337 01.6	09.8	271 16.0	05.4
	02	193 00.8	183 43.8	40.9	168 32.0	15.8	352 04.2	09.7	286 18.3	05.4
	03	208 03.3	198 46.5	. . 41.2	183 32.7	. . 16.5	7 06.9	. . 09.6	301 20.6	. . 05.4
	04	223 05.8	213 49.2	41.5	198 33.5	17.2	22 09.5	09.5	316 23.0	05.4
	05	238 08.2	228 51.9	41.9	213 34.3	17.9	37 12.2	09.4	331 25.3	05.4
	06	253 10.7	243 54.6	N11 42.2	228 35.0	N10 18.6	52 14.8	S 7 09.4	346 27.6	S22 05.4
	07	268 13.2	258 57.3	42.5	243 35.8	19.3	67 17.5	09.3	1 29.9	05.4
	08	283 15.6	274 00.0	42.8	258 36.5	20.0	82 20.1	09.2	16 32.3	05.4
S	09	298 18.1	289 02.8	. . 43.1	273 37.3	. . 20.6	97 22.8	. . 09.1	31 34.6	. . 05.4
U	10	313 20.6	304 05.5	43.5	288 38.0	21.3	112 25.4	09.0	46 36.9	05.4
N	11	328 23.0	319 08.2	43.8	303 38.8	22.0	127 28.1	09.0	61 39.2	05.4
D	12	343 25.5	334 10.9	N11 44.1	318 39.5	N10 22.7	142 30.7	S 7 08.9	76 41.6	S22 05.4
A	13	358 27.9	349 13.6	44.4	333 40.3	23.4	157 33.4	08.8	91 43.9	05.4
Y	14	13 30.4	4 16.4	44.7	348 41.1	24.1	172 36.0	08.7	106 46.2	05.4
	15	28 32.9	19 19.1	. . 45.0	3 41.8	. . 24.7	187 38.7	. . 08.6	121 48.5	. . 05.4
	16	43 35.3	34 21.9	45.3	18 42.6	25.4	202 41.3	08.5	136 50.9	05.4
	17	58 37.8	49 24.6	45.6	33 43.3	26.1	217 44.0	08.5	151 53.2	05.4
	18	73 40.3	64 27.4	N11 45.9	48 44.1	N10 26.8	232 46.6	S 7 08.4	166 55.5	S22 05.4
	19	88 42.7	79 30.1	46.2	63 44.8	27.5	247 49.3	08.3	181 57.9	05.4
	20	103 45.2	94 32.9	46.5	78 45.6	28.2	262 51.9	08.2	197 00.2	05.4
	21	118 47.7	109 35.6	. . 46.8	93 46.3	. . 28.8	277 54.6	. . 08.1	212 02.5	. . 05.4
	22	133 50.1	124 38.4	47.1	108 47.1	29.5	292 57.2	08.0	227 04.8	05.4
	23	148 52.6	139 41.2	47.4	123 47.9	30.2	307 59.9	08.0	242 07.2	05.4
	6 00	163 55.1	154 43.9	N11 47.7	138 48.6	N10 30.9	323 02.6	S 7 07.9	257 09.5	S22 05.4
	01	178 57.5	169 46.7	47.9	153 49.4	31.6	338 05.2	07.8	272 11.8	05.4
	02	194 00.0	184 49.5	48.2	168 50.1	32.3	353 07.9	07.7	287 14.2	05.4
	03	209 02.4	199 52.3	. . 48.5	183 50.9	. . 32.9	8 10.5	. . 07.6	302 16.5	. . 05.4
	04	224 04.9	214 55.1	48.8	198 51.6	33.6	23 13.2	07.5	317 18.8	05.4
	05	239 07.4	229 57.9	49.1	213 52.4	34.3	38 15.8	07.5	332 21.1	05.4
	06	254 09.8	245 00.7	N11 49.3	228 53.1	N10 35.0	53 18.5	S 7 07.4	347 23.5	S22 05.4
	07	269 12.3	260 03.5	49.6	243 53.9	35.7	68 21.1	07.3	2 25.8	05.4
	08	284 14.8	275 06.3	49.9	258 54.7	36.3	83 23.8	07.2	17 28.1	05.4
M	09	299 17.2	290 09.1	. . 50.1	273 55.4	. . 37.0	98 26.4	. . 07.1	32 30.5	. . 05.4
O	10	314 19.7	305 11.9	50.4	288 56.2	37.7	113 29.1	07.0	47 32.8	05.4
N	11	329 22.2	320 14.7	50.7	303 56.9	38.4	128 31.8	06.9	62 35.1	05.4
D	12	344 24.6	335 17.5	N11 50.9	318 57.7	N10 39.1	143 34.4	S 7 06.9	77 37.4	S22 05.4
A	13	359 27.1	350 20.3	51.2	333 58.4	39.7	158 37.1	06.8	92 39.8	05.4
Y	14	14 29.5	5 23.2	51.4	348 59.2	40.4	173 39.7	06.7	107 42.1	05.4
	15	29 32.0	20 26.0	. . 51.7	3 59.9	. . 41.1	188 42.4	. . 06.6	122 44.4	. . 05.4
	16	44 34.5	35 28.8	51.9	19 00.7	41.8	203 45.1	06.5	137 46.8	05.4
	17	59 36.9	50 31.7	52.2	34 01.4	42.5	218 47.7	06.4	152 49.1	05.4
	18	74 39.4	65 34.5	N11 52.4	49 02.2	N10 43.1	233 50.4	S 7 06.4	167 51.4	S22 05.4
	19	89 41.9	80 37.4	52.7	64 03.0	43.8	248 53.0	06.3	182 53.8	05.4
	20	104 44.3	95 40.2	52.9	79 03.7	44.5	263 55.7	06.2	197 56.1	05.4
	21	119 46.8	110 43.1	. . 53.2	94 04.5	. . 45.2	278 58.3	. . 06.1	212 58.4	. . 05.4
	22	134 49.3	125 45.9	53.4	109 05.2	45.9	294 01.0	06.0	228 00.8	05.4
	23	149 51.7	140 48.8	53.6	124 06.0	46.5	309 03.7	05.9	243 03.1	05.4
	7 00	164 54.2	155 51.6	N11 53.9	139 06.7	N10 47.2	324 06.3	S 7 05.8	258 05.4	S22 05.4
	01	179 56.7	170 54.5	54.1	154 07.5	47.9	339 09.0	05.8	273 07.8	05.4
	02	194 59.1	185 57.4	54.3	169 08.2	48.6	354 11.6	05.7	288 10.1	05.4
	03	210 01.6	201 00.3	. . 54.5	184 09.0	. . 49.2	9 14.3	. . 05.6	303 12.4	. . 05.4
	04	225 04.0	216 03.1	54.8	199 09.7	49.9	24 17.0	05.5	318 14.8	05.4
	05	240 06.5	231 06.0	55.0	214 10.5	50.6	39 19.6	05.4	333 17.1	05.4
	06	255 09.0	246 08.9	N11 55.2	229 11.2	N10 51.3	54 22.3	S 7 05.3	348 19.4	S22 05.4
	07	270 11.4	261 11.8	55.4	244 12.0	52.0	69 25.0	05.2	3 21.8	05.4
T	08	285 13.9	276 14.7	55.6	259 12.7	52.6	84 27.6	05.1	18 24.1	05.4
U	09	300 16.4	291 17.6	. . 55.8	274 13.5	. . 53.3	99 30.3	. . 05.1	33 26.4	. . 05.4
E	10	315 18.8	306 20.5	56.0	289 14.3	54.0	114 32.9	05.0	48 28.8	05.4
S	11	330 21.3	321 23.4	56.3	304 15.0	54.7	129 35.6	04.9	63 31.1	05.4
D	12	345 23.8	336 26.3	N11 56.5	319 15.8	N10 55.3	144 38.3	S 7 04.8	78 33.4	S22 05.4
A	13	0 26.2	351 29.2	56.7	334 16.5	56.0	159 40.9	04.7	93 35.8	05.4
Y	14	15 28.7	6 32.2	56.9	349 17.3	56.7	174 43.6	04.6	108 38.1	05.4
	15	30 31.2	21 35.1	. . 57.1	4 18.0	. . 57.4	189 46.3	. . 04.5	123 40.4	. . 05.4
	16	45 33.6	36 38.0	57.3	19 18.8	58.0	204 48.9	04.5	138 42.8	05.4
	17	60 36.1	51 40.9	57.4	34 19.5	58.7	219 51.6	04.4	153 45.1	05.4
	18	75 38.5	66 43.9	N11 57.6	49 20.3	N10 59.4	234 54.2	S 7 04.3	168 47.4	S22 05.4
	19	90 41.0	81 46.8	57.8	64 21.0	11 00.1	249 56.9	04.2	183 49.8	05.4
	20	105 43.5	96 49.7	58.0	79 21.8	00.7	264 59.6	04.1	198 52.1	05.4
	21	120 45.9	111 52.7	. . 58.2	94 22.5	. . 01.4	280 02.2	. . 04.0	213 54.4	. . 05.4
	22	135 48.4	126 55.6	58.4	109 23.3	02.1	295 04.9	03.9	228 56.8	05.4
	23	150 50.9	141 58.6	58.6	124 24.0	02.8	310 07.6	03.8	243 59.1	05.4
	Mer. Pass.	h m 13 02.2	*v* 2.8	*d* 0.3	*v* 0.8	*d* 0.7	*v* 2.7	*d* 0.1	*v* 2.3	*d* 0.0

STARS

Name	SHA ° ′	Dec ° ′
Acamar	315 16.7	S40 14.6
Achernar	335 25.4	S57 09.3
Acrux	173 05.7	S63 11.5
Adhara	255 10.4	S29 00.1
Aldebaran	290 46.5	N16 32.4
Alioth	166 18.1	N55 51.9
Alkaid	152 56.6	N49 13.5
Al Na'ir	27 41.1	S46 52.7
Alnilam	275 43.8	S 1 11.8
Alphard	217 53.3	S 8 44.2
Alphecca	126 08.8	N26 39.3
Alpheratz	357 41.2	N29 11.0
Altair	62 06.0	N 8 54.8
Ankaa	353 13.7	S42 13.0
Antares	112 23.1	S26 28.0
Arcturus	145 53.2	N19 05.5
Atria	107 22.6	S69 03.0
Avior	234 16.4	S59 34.2
Bellatrix	278 29.3	N 6 21.6
Betelgeuse	270 58.5	N 7 24.3
Canopus	263 54.8	S52 42.8
Capella	280 30.7	N46 00.8
Deneb	49 30.1	N45 20.4
Denebola	182 30.8	N14 28.5
Diphda	348 53.7	S17 53.8
Dubhe	193 48.1	N61 39.4
Elnath	278 09.4	N28 37.1
Eltanin	90 45.1	N51 29.1
Enif	33 45.0	N 9 57.2
Fomalhaut	15 21.6	S29 32.0
Gacrux	171 57.5	S57 12.4
Gienah	175 49.4	S17 38.3
Hadar	148 43.8	S60 27.1
Hamal	327 58.1	N23 32.4
Kaus Aust.	83 40.6	S34 22.3
Kochab	137 19.6	N74 04.9
Markab	13 36.1	N15 17.7
Menkar	314 12.6	N 4 09.1
Menkent	148 04.3	S36 27.1
Miaplacidus	221 38.2	S69 47.5
Mirfak	308 36.9	N49 55.3
Nunki	75 55.4	S26 16.3
Peacock	53 15.8	S56 40.5
Pollux	243 24.5	N27 58.9
Procyon	244 56.9	N 5 10.6
Rasalhague	96 04.2	N12 32.9
Regulus	207 40.5	N11 52.8
Rigel	281 09.6	S 8 11.3
Rigil Kent.	139 47.8	S60 54.0
Sabik	102 09.7	S15 44.6
Schedar	349 38.1	N56 37.9
Shaula	96 18.6	S37 06.7
Sirius	258 31.4	S16 44.8
Spica	158 28.3	S11 15.0
Suhail	222 50.2	S43 30.4
Vega	80 37.4	N38 47.9
Zuben'ubi	137 02.4	S16 06.7

	SHA ° ′	Mer. Pass. h m
Venus	350 48.9	13 39
Mars	334 53.6	14 44
Jupiter	159 07.5	2 27
Saturn	93 14.4	6 50

	UT	SUN GHA	SUN Dec	MOON GHA	*v*	MOON Dec	*d*	HP
d	h	° ′	° ′	° ′	′	° ′	′	′
5	00	177 06.9	S 6 03.7	95 33.5	7.0	N16 29.2	5.7	59.3
	01	192 07.0	02.8	109 59.5	7.0	16 34.9	5.5	59.3
	02	207 07.2	01.8	124 25.5	7.0	16 40.4	5.5	59.3
	03	222 07.3	6 00.8	138 51.5	6.9	16 45.9	5.3	59.3
	04	237 07.4	5 59.9	153 17.4	6.9	16 51.2	5.3	59.2
	05	252 07.6	58.9	167 43.3	6.9	16 56.5	5.1	59.2
	06	267 07.7	S 5 57.9	182 09.2	6.8	N17 01.6	5.0	59.2
	07	282 07.9	57.0	196 35.0	6.9	17 06.6	4.9	59.2
	08	297 08.0	56.0	211 00.9	6.8	17 11.5	4.8	59.2
S	09	312 08.1	. . 55.0	225 26.7	6.8	17 16.3	4.7	59.2
U	10	327 08.3	54.1	239 52.5	6.8	17 21.0	4.5	59.2
N	11	342 08.4	53.1	254 18.3	6.7	17 25.5	4.5	59.2
D	12	357 08.6	S 5 52.1	268 44.0	6.7	N17 30.0	4.3	59.2
A	13	12 08.7	51.2	283 09.7	6.8	17 34.3	4.2	59.2
Y	14	27 08.9	50.2	297 35.5	6.6	17 38.5	4.1	59.2
	15	42 09.0	. . 49.2	312 01.1	6.7	17 42.6	4.0	59.2
	16	57 09.1	48.3	326 26.8	6.7	17 46.6	3.9	59.2
	17	72 09.3	47.3	340 52.5	6.6	17 50.5	3.8	59.1
	18	87 09.4	S 5 46.3	355 18.1	6.7	N17 54.3	3.6	59.1
	19	102 09.6	45.4	9 43.8	6.6	17 57.9	3.5	59.1
	20	117 09.7	44.4	24 09.4	6.6	18 01.4	3.4	59.1
	21	132 09.9	. . 43.4	38 35.0	6.6	18 04.8	3.3	59.1
	22	147 10.0	42.4	53 00.6	6.5	18 08.1	3.2	59.1
	23	162 10.1	41.5	67 26.1	6.6	18 11.3	3.1	59.1
6	00	177 10.3	S 5 40.5	81 51.7	6.6	N18 14.4	2.9	59.1
	01	192 10.4	39.5	96 17.3	6.5	18 17.3	2.8	59.1
	02	207 10.6	38.6	110 42.8	6.6	18 20.1	2.7	59.1
	03	222 10.7	. . 37.6	125 08.4	6.5	18 22.8	2.6	59.1
	04	237 10.9	36.6	139 33.9	6.5	18 25.4	2.5	59.0
	05	252 11.0	35.7	153 59.4	6.5	18 27.9	2.3	59.0
	06	267 11.2	S 5 34.7	168 24.9	6.5	N18 30.2	2.2	59.0
	07	282 11.3	33.7	182 50.4	6.6	18 32.4	2.1	59.0
	08	297 11.5	32.8	197 16.0	6.5	18 34.5	2.0	59.0
M	09	312 11.6	. . 31.8	211 41.5	6.5	18 36.5	1.9	59.0
O	10	327 11.8	30.8	226 07.0	6.5	18 38.4	1.7	59.0
N	11	342 11.9	29.8	240 32.5	6.5	18 40.1	1.6	59.0
D	12	357 12.0	S 5 28.9	254 58.0	6.5	N18 41.7	1.5	59.0
A	13	12 12.2	27.9	269 23.5	6.5	18 43.2	1.4	58.9
Y	14	27 12.3	26.9	283 49.0	6.5	18 44.6	1.2	58.9
	15	42 12.5	. . 26.0	298 14.5	6.5	18 45.8	1.2	58.9
	16	57 12.6	25.0	312 40.0	6.5	18 47.0	1.0	58.9
	17	72 12.8	24.0	327 05.5	6.6	18 48.0	0.9	58.9
	18	87 12.9	S 5 23.0	341 31.1	6.5	N18 48.9	0.7	58.9
	19	102 13.1	22.1	355 56.6	6.5	18 49.6	0.7	58.9
	20	117 13.2	21.1	10 22.1	6.6	18 50.3	0.5	58.9
	21	132 13.4	. . 20.1	24 47.7	6.5	18 50.8	0.4	58.9
	22	147 13.5	19.2	39 13.2	6.6	18 51.2	0.3	58.8
	23	162 13.7	18.2	53 38.8	6.6	18 51.5	0.1	58.8
7	00	177 13.8	S 5 17.2	68 04.4	6.6	N18 51.6	0.1	58.8
	01	192 14.0	16.2	82 30.0	6.6	18 51.7	0.1	58.8
	02	207 14.1	15.3	96 55.6	6.6	18 51.6	0.2	58.8
	03	222 14.3	. . 14.3	111 21.2	6.6	18 51.4	0.3	58.8
	04	237 14.4	13.3	125 46.8	6.7	18 51.1	0.5	58.8
	05	252 14.6	12.4	140 12.5	6.7	18 50.6	0.5	58.8
	06	267 14.7	S 5 11.4	154 38.2	6.7	N18 50.1	0.7	58.7
	07	282 14.9	10.4	169 03.9	6.7	18 49.4	0.8	58.7
T	08	297 15.0	09.4	183 29.6	6.7	18 48.6	1.0	58.7
U	09	312 15.2	. . 08.5	197 55.3	6.7	18 47.6	1.0	58.7
E	10	327 15.3	07.5	212 21.0	6.8	18 46.6	1.2	58.7
S	11	342 15.5	06.5	226 46.8	6.8	18 45.4	1.2	58.7
D	12	357 15.6	S 5 05.5	241 12.6	6.8	N18 44.2	1.4	58.7
A	13	12 15.8	04.6	255 38.4	6.8	18 42.8	1.6	58.7
Y	14	27 15.9	03.6	270 04.2	6.9	18 41.2	1.6	58.6
	15	42 16.1	. . 02.6	284 30.1	6.9	18 39.6	1.8	58.6
	16	57 16.2	01.6	298 56.0	6.9	18 37.8	1.8	58.6
	17	72 16.4	5 00.7	313 21.9	7.0	18 36.0	2.0	58.6
	18	87 16.5	S 4 59.7	327 47.9	6.9	N18 34.0	2.1	58.6
	19	102 16.7	58.7	342 13.8	7.1	18 31.9	2.2	58.6
	20	117 16.8	57.7	356 39.9	7.0	18 29.7	2.4	58.6
	21	132 17.0	. . 56.8	11 05.9	7.1	18 27.3	2.4	58.5
	22	147 17.1	55.8	25 32.0	7.1	18 24.9	2.6	58.5
	23	162 17.3	54.8	39 58.1	7.1	N18 22.3	2.7	58.5
		SD 16.1	*d* 1.0	SD	16.1	16.1		16.0

Lat.	Twilight Naut.	Twilight Civil	Sunrise	Moonrise 5	Moonrise 6	Moonrise 7	Moonrise 8
°	h m	h m	h m	h m	h m	h m	h m
N 72	04 43	06 02	07 10	07 14	▭	▭	09 29
N 70	04 51	06 02	07 03	08 07	08 27	09 17	10 44
68	04 58	06 02	06 58	08 39	09 11	10 05	11 22
66	05 03	06 02	06 53	09 03	09 40	10 35	11 48
64	05 07	06 02	06 50	09 22	10 03	10 58	12 09
62	05 11	06 02	06 46	09 38	10 20	11 16	12 25
60	05 14	06 02	06 43	09 51	10 35	11 32	12 39
N 58	05 16	06 02	06 41	10 02	10 48	11 44	12 50
56	05 18	06 01	06 38	10 12	10 59	11 55	13 01
54	05 20	06 01	06 36	10 20	11 08	12 05	13 10
52	05 22	06 01	06 34	10 28	11 17	12 14	13 18
50	05 23	06 00	06 33	10 35	11 25	12 22	13 25
45	05 26	06 00	06 29	10 50	11 41	12 38	13 40
N 40	05 27	05 59	06 26	11 03	11 55	12 52	13 53
35	05 28	05 58	06 23	11 13	12 06	13 03	14 04
30	05 29	05 56	06 20	11 23	12 16	13 14	14 13
20	05 28	05 54	06 16	11 39	12 34	13 31	14 29
N 10	05 26	05 51	06 12	11 53	12 49	13 46	14 43
0	05 23	05 47	06 08	12 06	13 03	14 00	14 56
S 10	05 18	05 43	06 04	12 19	13 17	14 15	15 10
20	05 11	05 37	06 00	12 33	13 33	14 30	15 24
30	05 02	05 30	05 54	12 50	13 50	14 47	15 40
35	04 56	05 26	05 51	12 59	14 01	14 57	15 49
40	04 48	05 21	05 48	13 10	14 12	15 09	16 00
45	04 39	05 14	05 44	13 23	14 26	15 23	16 12
S 50	04 26	05 06	05 39	13 39	14 43	15 39	16 27
52	04 20	05 02	05 37	13 46	14 51	15 47	16 35
54	04 14	04 58	05 35	13 54	15 00	15 56	16 42
56	04 06	04 53	05 32	14 04	15 10	16 06	16 51
58	03 57	04 48	05 29	14 14	15 21	16 17	17 01
S 60	03 47	04 42	05 25	14 26	15 34	16 30	17 13

Lat.	Sunset	Twilight Civil	Twilight Naut.	Moonset 5	Moonset 6	Moonset 7	Moonset 8
°	h m	h m	h m	h m	h m	h m	h m
N 72	17 15	18 23	19 42	04 18	▭	▭	08 02
N 70	17 21	18 22	19 34	03 27	05 06	06 15	06 46
68	17 26	18 22	19 27	02 55	04 22	05 28	06 08
66	17 31	18 22	19 22	02 31	03 53	04 57	05 41
64	17 34	18 22	19 17	02 13	03 31	04 34	05 20
62	17 37	18 22	19 13	01 58	03 13	04 16	05 04
60	17 40	18 22	19 10	01 45	02 58	04 00	04 50
N 58	17 43	18 22	19 08	01 34	02 46	03 48	04 38
56	17 45	18 22	19 05	01 25	02 35	03 36	04 27
54	17 47	18 22	19 03	01 16	02 26	03 27	04 18
52	17 49	18 23	19 02	01 09	02 17	03 18	04 10
50	17 51	18 23	19 00	01 02	02 10	03 10	04 02
45	17 54	18 24	18 58	00 48	01 53	02 53	03 47
N 40	17 57	18 24	18 56	00 36	01 40	02 40	03 33
35	18 00	18 25	18 55	00 26	01 29	02 28	03 22
30	18 03	18 26	18 54	00 17	01 19	02 18	03 13
20	18 07	18 29	18 54	00 02	01 02	02 00	02 56
N 10	18 11	18 32	18 56	24 47	00 47	01 45	02 41
0	18 14	18 35	18 59	24 33	00 33	01 31	02 27
S 10	18 18	18 39	19 04	24 19	00 19	01 16	02 13
20	18 23	18 45	19 11	24 04	00 04	01 01	01 59
30	18 27	18 52	19 20	23 47	24 43	00 43	01 42
35	18 30	18 56	19 26	23 38	24 33	00 33	01 32
40	18 34	19 01	19 33	23 26	24 21	00 21	01 20
45	18 37	19 07	19 43	23 13	24 07	00 07	01 07
S 50	18 42	19 15	19 55	22 57	23 50	24 50	00 50
52	18 44	19 19	20 00	22 49	23 42	24 43	00 43
54	18 47	19 23	20 07	22 41	23 33	24 34	00 34
56	18 49	19 27	20 14	22 31	23 23	24 25	00 25
58	18 52	19 33	20 23	22 21	23 12	24 14	00 14
S 60	18 55	19 39	20 33	22 08	22 59	24 01	00 01

Day	SUN Eqn. of Time 00h	SUN Eqn. of Time 12h	SUN Mer. Pass.	MOON Mer. Pass. Upper	MOON Mer. Pass. Lower	MOON Age	MOON Phase
d	m s	m s	h m	h m	h m	d %	
5	11 33	11 26	12 11	18 20	05 51	07 50	
6	11 19	11 12	12 11	19 17	06 48	08 62	
7	11 05	10 58	12 11	20 14	07 45	09 72	

Day	UT	ARIES GHA	VENUS −4·6 GHA	VENUS Dec	MARS +1·4 GHA	MARS Dec	JUPITER −2·4 GHA	JUPITER Dec	SATURN +0·5 GHA	SATURN Dec
d h		° ′	° ′	° ′	° ′	° ′	° ′	° ′	° ′	° ′
WEDNESDAY	8 00	165 53.3	157 01.5	N11 58.7	139 24.8	N11 03.4	325 10.2	S 7 03.8	259 01.5	S22 05.4
	01	180 55.8	172 04.5	58.9	154 25.5	04.1	340 12.9	03.7	274 03.8	05.4
	02	195 58.3	187 07.5	59.1	169 26.3	04.8	355 15.6	03.6	289 06.1	05.4
	03	211 00.7	202 10.4	. . 59.2	184 27.1	. . 05.4	10 18.2	. . 03.5	304 08.5	. . 05.4
	04	226 03.2	217 13.4	59.4	199 27.8	06.1	25 20.9	03.4	319 10.8	05.4
	05	241 05.7	232 16.4	59.6	214 28.6	06.8	40 23.6	03.3	334 13.1	05.4
	06	256 08.1	247 19.4	N11 59.7	229 29.3	N11 07.5	55 26.2	S 7 03.2	349 15.5	S22 05.4
	07	271 10.6	262 22.4	11 59.9	244 30.1	08.1	70 28.9	03.1	4 17.8	05.4
	08	286 13.0	277 25.3	12 00.1	259 30.8	08.8	85 31.6	03.0	19 20.2	05.4
	09	301 15.5	292 28.3	. . 00.2	274 31.6	. . 09.5	100 34.2	. . 03.0	34 22.5	. . 05.4
	10	316 18.0	307 31.3	00.4	289 32.3	10.1	115 36.9	02.9	49 24.8	05.4
	11	331 20.4	322 34.3	00.5	304 33.1	10.8	130 39.6	02.8	64 27.2	05.4
	12	346 22.9	337 37.3	N12 00.7	319 33.8	N11 11.5	145 42.2	S 7 02.7	79 29.5	S22 05.4
	13	1 25.4	352 40.3	00.8	334 34.6	12.2	160 44.9	02.6	94 31.9	05.4
	14	16 27.8	7 43.3	01.0	349 35.3	12.8	175 47.6	02.5	109 34.2	05.4
	15	31 30.3	22 46.4	. . 01.1	4 36.1	. . 13.5	190 50.3	. . 02.4	124 36.5	. . 05.4
	16	46 32.8	37 49.4	01.2	19 36.8	14.2	205 52.9	02.3	139 38.9	05.4
	17	61 35.2	52 52.4	01.4	34 37.6	14.8	220 55.6	02.2	154 41.2	05.4
	18	76 37.7	67 55.4	N12 01.5	49 38.3	N11 15.5	235 58.3	S 7 02.2	169 43.5	S22 05.4
	19	91 40.1	82 58.5	01.6	64 39.1	16.2	251 00.9	02.1	184 45.9	05.4
	20	106 42.6	98 01.5	01.8	79 39.8	16.8	266 03.6	02.0	199 48.2	05.4
	21	121 45.1	113 04.5	. . 01.9	94 40.6	. . 17.5	281 06.3	. . 01.9	214 50.6	. . 05.4
	22	136 47.5	128 07.6	02.0	109 41.3	18.2	296 08.9	01.8	229 52.9	05.4
	23	151 50.0	143 10.6	02.1	124 42.1	18.9	311 11.6	01.7	244 55.2	05.4
THURSDAY	9 00	166 52.5	158 13.7	N12 02.3	139 42.8	N11 19.5	326 14.3	S 7 01.6	259 57.6	S22 05.4
	01	181 54.9	173 16.7	02.4	154 43.6	20.2	341 17.0	01.5	274 59.9	05.4
	02	196 57.4	188 19.8	02.5	169 44.3	20.9	356 19.6	01.4	290 02.3	05.4
	03	211 59.9	203 22.8	. . 02.6	184 45.1	. . 21.5	11 22.3	. . 01.3	305 04.6	. . 05.4
	04	227 02.3	218 25.9	02.7	199 45.8	22.2	26 25.0	01.2	320 07.0	05.4
	05	242 04.8	233 29.0	02.8	214 46.6	22.9	41 27.7	01.2	335 09.3	05.4
	06	257 07.3	248 32.0	N12 02.9	229 47.3	N11 23.5	56 30.3	S 7 01.1	350 11.6	S22 05.4
	07	272 09.7	263 35.1	03.0	244 48.1	24.2	71 33.0	01.0	5 14.0	05.4
	08	287 12.2	278 38.2	03.1	259 48.8	24.9	86 35.7	00.9	20 16.3	05.4
	09	302 14.6	293 41.3	. . 03.2	274 49.6	. . 25.5	101 38.3	. . 00.8	35 18.7	. . 05.4
	10	317 17.1	308 44.3	03.3	289 50.3	26.2	116 41.0	00.7	50 21.0	05.4
	11	332 19.6	323 47.4	03.4	304 51.1	26.9	131 43.7	00.6	65 23.3	05.4
	12	347 22.0	338 50.5	N12 03.5	319 51.8	N11 27.5	146 46.4	S 7 00.5	80 25.7	S22 05.4
	13	2 24.5	353 53.6	03.6	334 52.6	28.2	161 49.0	00.4	95 28.0	05.4
	14	17 27.0	8 56.7	03.7	349 53.3	28.9	176 51.7	00.3	110 30.4	05.4
	15	32 29.4	23 59.8	. . 03.7	4 54.1	. . 29.5	191 54.4	. . 00.2	125 32.7	. . 05.4
	16	47 31.9	39 02.9	03.8	19 54.8	30.2	206 57.1	00.2	140 35.1	05.4
	17	62 34.4	54 06.0	03.9	34 55.6	30.9	221 59.7	00.1	155 37.4	05.4
	18	77 36.8	69 09.2	N12 04.0	49 56.3	N11 31.5	237 02.4	S 7 00.0	170 39.8	S22 05.4
	19	92 39.3	84 12.3	04.0	64 57.1	32.2	252 05.1	6 59.9	185 42.1	05.4
	20	107 41.8	99 15.4	04.1	79 57.8	32.9	267 07.8	59.8	200 44.4	05.4
	21	122 44.2	114 18.5	. . 04.2	94 58.6	. . 33.5	282 10.4	. . 59.7	215 46.8	. . 05.4
	22	137 46.7	129 21.7	04.2	109 59.3	34.2	297 13.1	59.6	230 49.1	05.4
	23	152 49.1	144 24.8	04.3	125 00.1	34.8	312 15.8	59.5	245 51.5	05.4
FRIDAY	10 00	167 51.6	159 27.9	N12 04.4	140 00.8	N11 35.5	327 18.5	S 6 59.4	260 53.8	S22 05.4
	01	182 54.1	174 31.1	04.4	155 01.6	36.2	342 21.2	59.3	275 56.2	05.4
	02	197 56.5	189 34.2	04.5	170 02.3	36.8	357 23.8	59.2	290 58.5	05.4
	03	212 59.0	204 37.4	. . 04.5	185 03.1	. . 37.5	12 26.5	. . 59.1	306 00.9	. . 05.4
	04	228 01.5	219 40.5	04.6	200 03.8	38.2	27 29.2	59.1	321 03.2	05.4
	05	243 03.9	234 43.7	04.6	215 04.6	38.8	42 31.9	59.0	336 05.5	05.4
	06	258 06.4	249 46.8	N12 04.7	230 05.3	N11 39.5	57 34.5	S 6 58.9	351 07.9	S22 05.4
	07	273 08.9	264 50.0	04.7	245 06.1	40.2	72 37.2	58.8	6 10.2	05.4
	08	288 11.3	279 53.2	04.8	260 06.8	40.8	87 39.9	58.7	21 12.6	05.4
	09	303 13.8	294 56.3	. . 04.8	275 07.6	. . 41.5	102 42.6	. . 58.6	36 14.9	. . 05.4
	10	318 16.2	309 59.5	04.8	290 08.3	42.1	117 45.3	58.5	51 17.3	05.4
	11	333 18.7	325 02.7	04.9	305 09.1	42.8	132 47.9	58.4	66 19.6	05.4
	12	348 21.2	340 05.9	N12 04.9	320 09.8	N11 43.5	147 50.6	S 6 58.3	81 22.0	S22 05.4
	13	3 23.6	355 09.0	04.9	335 10.6	44.1	162 53.3	58.2	96 24.3	05.4
	14	18 26.1	10 12.2	04.9	350 11.3	44.8	177 56.0	58.1	111 26.7	05.4
	15	33 28.6	25 15.4	. . 05.0	5 12.1	. . 45.4	192 58.7	. . 58.0	126 29.0	. . 05.4
	16	48 31.0	40 18.6	05.0	20 12.8	46.1	208 01.3	57.9	141 31.4	05.4
	17	63 33.5	55 21.8	05.0	35 13.6	46.8	223 04.0	57.8	156 33.7	05.4
	18	78 36.0	70 25.0	N12 05.0	50 14.3	N11 47.4	238 06.7	S 6 57.7	171 36.1	S22 05.4
	19	93 38.4	85 28.2	05.0	65 15.1	48.1	253 09.4	57.7	186 38.4	05.4
	20	108 40.9	100 31.4	05.0	80 15.8	48.7	268 12.1	57.6	201 40.7	05.4
	21	123 43.4	115 34.7	. . 05.0	95 16.6	. . 49.4	283 14.7	. . 57.5	216 43.1	. . 05.4
	22	138 45.8	130 37.9	05.1	110 17.3	50.1	298 17.4	57.4	231 45.4	05.4
	23	153 48.3	145 41.1	05.1	125 18.1	50.7	313 20.1	57.3	246 47.8	05.4
	Mer. Pass.	h m 12 50.4	v 3.1	d 0.1	v 0.8	d 0.7	v 2.7	d 0.1	v 2.3	d 0.0

STARS

Name	SHA	Dec
	° ′	° ′
Acamar	315 16.7	S40 14.6
Achernar	335 25.4	S57 09.3
Acrux	173 05.7	S63 11.6
Adhara	255 10.4	S29 00.2
Aldebaran	290 46.5	N16 32.4
Alioth	166 18.1	N55 51.9
Alkaid	152 56.6	N49 13.5
Al Na'ir	27 41.1	S46 52.6
Alnilam	275 43.8	S 1 11.8
Alphard	217 53.3	S 8 44.2
Alphecca	126 08.7	N26 39.3
Alpheratz	357 41.2	N29 11.0
Altair	62 06.0	N 8 54.8
Ankaa	353 13.7	S42 13.0
Antares	112 23.1	S26 28.0
Arcturus	145 53.2	N19 05.5
Atria	107 22.6	S69 03.0
Avior	234 16.5	S59 34.2
Bellatrix	278 29.3	N 6 21.6
Betelgeuse	270 58.5	N 7 24.3
Canopus	263 54.9	S52 42.8
Capella	280 30.7	N46 00.8
Deneb	49 30.1	N45 20.4
Denebola	182 30.8	N14 28.5
Diphda	348 53.7	S17 53.8
Dubhe	193 48.1	N61 39.4
Elnath	278 09.4	N28 37.1
Eltanin	90 45.1	N51 29.1
Enif	33 44.9	N 9 57.1
Fomalhaut	15 21.6	S29 32.0
Gacrux	171 57.4	S57 12.5
Gienah	175 49.4	S17 38.3
Hadar	148 43.7	S60 27.1
Hamal	327 58.1	N23 32.4
Kaus Aust.	83 40.6	S34 22.3
Kochab	137 19.6	N74 04.9
Markab	13 36.1	N15 17.7
Menkar	314 12.6	N 4 09.1
Menkent	148 04.3	S36 27.1
Miaplacidus	221 38.2	S69 47.5
Mirfak	308 36.9	N49 55.3
Nunki	75 55.4	S26 16.3
Peacock	53 15.8	S56 40.5
Pollux	243 24.5	N27 58.9
Procyon	244 56.9	N 5 10.6
Rasalhague	96 04.1	N12 32.9
Regulus	207 40.5	N11 52.8
Rigel	281 09.6	S 8 11.3
Rigil Kent.	139 47.8	S60 54.0
Sabik	102 09.6	S15 44.6
Schedar	349 38.1	N56 37.8
Shaula	96 18.5	S37 06.7
Sirius	258 31.4	S16 44.8
Spica	158 28.3	S11 15.0
Suhail	222 50.2	S43 30.4
Vega	80 37.4	N38 47.9
Zuben'ubi	137 02.4	S16 06.7

	SHA	Mer. Pass.
	° ′	h m
Venus	351 21.2	13 24
Mars	332 50.4	14 40
Jupiter	159 21.8	2 15
Saturn	93 05.1	6 39

UT d	h	SUN GHA	SUN Dec	MOON GHA	v	MOON Dec	d	HP
d	h	° ′	° ′	° ′	′	° ′	′	′
8	00	177 17.5	S 4 53.9	54 24.2	7.2	N18 19.6	2.7	58.5
	01	192 17.6	52.9	68 50.4	7.2	18 16.9	2.9	58.5
	02	207 17.8	51.9	83 16.6	7.2	18 14.0	3.1	58.5
	03	222 17.9	. . 50.9	97 42.8	7.3	18 10.9	3.1	58.5
	04	237 18.1	50.0	112 09.1	7.3	18 07.8	3.2	58.4
	05	252 18.2	49.0	126 35.4	7.4	18 04.6	3.4	58.4
	06	267 18.4	S 4 48.0	141 01.8	7.4	N18 01.2	3.4	58.4
WEDNESDAY	07	282 18.5	47.0	155 28.2	7.4	17 57.8	3.6	58.4
	08	297 18.7	46.0	169 54.6	7.5	17 54.2	3.7	58.4
	09	312 18.8	. . 45.1	184 21.1	7.5	17 50.5	3.8	58.4
	10	327 19.0	44.1	198 47.6	7.5	17 46.7	3.9	58.4
	11	342 19.1	43.1	213 14.1	7.6	17 42.8	4.0	58.3
	12	357 19.3	S 4 42.1	227 40.7	7.7	N17 38.8	4.1	58.3
	13	12 19.5	41.2	242 07.4	7.7	17 34.7	4.2	58.3
	14	27 19.6	40.2	256 34.1	7.7	17 30.5	4.3	58.3
	15	42 19.8	. . 39.2	271 00.8	7.8	17 26.2	4.4	58.3
	16	57 19.9	38.2	285 27.6	7.8	17 21.8	4.6	58.3
	17	72 20.1	37.3	299 54.4	7.9	17 17.2	4.6	58.3
	18	87 20.2	S 4 36.3	314 21.3	7.9	N17 12.6	4.7	58.2
	19	102 20.4	35.3	328 48.2	7.9	17 07.9	4.8	58.2
	20	117 20.6	34.3	343 15.1	8.0	17 03.1	5.0	58.2
	21	132 20.7	. . 33.4	357 42.1	8.1	16 58.1	5.0	58.2
	22	147 20.9	32.4	12 09.2	8.1	16 53.1	5.1	58.2
	23	162 21.0	31.4	26 36.3	8.2	16 48.0	5.3	58.2
9	00	177 21.2	S 4 30.4	41 03.5	8.2	N16 42.7	5.3	58.1
	01	192 21.3	29.4	55 30.7	8.2	16 37.4	5.4	58.1
	02	207 21.5	28.5	69 57.9	8.3	16 32.0	5.5	58.1
	03	222 21.7	. . 27.5	84 25.2	8.4	16 26.5	5.6	58.1
	04	237 21.8	26.5	98 52.6	8.4	16 20.9	5.7	58.1
	05	252 22.0	25.5	113 20.0	8.4	16 15.2	5.8	58.1
	06	267 22.1	S 4 24.6	127 47.4	8.6	N16 09.4	5.9	58.0
THURSDAY	07	282 22.3	23.6	142 15.0	8.5	16 03.5	6.0	58.0
	08	297 22.4	22.6	156 42.5	8.6	15 57.5	6.1	58.0
	09	312 22.6	. . 21.6	171 10.1	8.7	15 51.4	6.1	58.0
	10	327 22.8	20.6	185 37.8	8.7	15 45.3	6.3	58.0
	11	342 22.9	19.7	200 05.5	8.8	15 39.0	6.3	57.9
	12	357 23.1	S 4 18.7	214 33.3	8.9	N15 32.7	6.5	57.9
	13	12 23.2	17.7	229 01.2	8.8	15 26.2	6.5	57.9
	14	27 23.4	16.7	243 29.0	9.0	15 19.7	6.6	57.9
	15	42 23.6	. . 15.8	257 57.0	9.0	15 13.1	6.6	57.9
	16	57 23.7	14.8	272 25.0	9.0	15 06.5	6.8	57.9
	17	72 23.9	13.8	286 53.0	9.2	14 59.7	6.9	57.8
	18	87 24.0	S 4 12.8	301 21.2	9.1	N14 52.8	6.9	57.8
	19	102 24.2	11.8	315 49.3	9.2	14 45.9	7.0	57.8
	20	117 24.4	10.9	330 17.5	9.3	14 38.9	7.1	57.8
	21	132 24.5	. . 09.9	344 45.8	9.4	14 31.8	7.1	57.8
	22	147 24.7	08.9	359 14.2	9.3	14 24.7	7.3	57.7
	23	162 24.8	07.9	13 42.5	9.5	14 17.4	7.3	57.7
10	00	177 25.0	S 4 06.9	28 11.0	9.5	N14 10.1	7.4	57.7
	01	192 25.2	06.0	42 39.5	9.6	14 02.7	7.5	57.7
	02	207 25.3	05.0	57 08.1	9.6	13 55.2	7.5	57.7
	03	222 25.5	. . 04.0	71 36.7	9.6	13 47.7	7.6	57.7
	04	237 25.6	03.0	86 05.3	9.8	13 40.1	7.7	57.6
	05	252 25.8	02.0	100 34.1	9.8	13 32.4	7.8	57.6
	06	267 26.0	S 4 01.1	115 02.9	9.8	N13 24.6	7.8	57.6
	07	282 26.1	4 00.1	129 31.7	9.9	13 16.8	7.9	57.6
	08	297 26.3	3 59.1	144 00.6	10.0	13 08.9	8.0	57.6
FRIDAY	09	312 26.5	. . 58.1	158 29.6	10.0	13 00.9	8.0	57.5
	10	327 26.6	57.1	172 58.6	10.0	12 52.9	8.1	57.5
	11	342 26.8	56.2	187 27.6	10.2	12 44.8	8.2	57.5
	12	357 26.9	S 3 55.2	201 56.8	10.1	N12 36.6	8.2	57.5
	13	12 27.1	54.2	216 25.9	10.3	12 28.4	8.3	57.5
	14	27 27.3	53.2	230 55.2	10.3	12 20.1	8.3	57.4
	15	42 27.4	. . 52.2	245 24.5	10.3	12 11.8	8.4	57.4
	16	57 27.6	51.3	259 53.8	10.4	12 03.4	8.5	57.4
	17	72 27.8	50.3	274 23.2	10.5	11 54.9	8.5	57.4
	18	87 27.9	S 3 49.3	288 52.7	10.5	N11 46.4	8.6	57.4
	19	102 28.1	48.3	303 22.2	10.6	11 37.8	8.7	57.3
	20	117 28.3	47.3	317 51.8	10.6	11 29.1	8.7	57.3
	21	132 28.4	. . 46.4	332 21.4	10.7	11 20.4	8.7	57.3
	22	147 28.6	45.4	346 51.1	10.8	11 11.7	8.8	57.3
	23	162 28.7	44.4	1 20.9	10.7	N11 02.9	8.9	57.3
		SD 16.1	*d* 1.0	SD 15.9		15.8		15.7

Lat.	Twilight Naut.	Twilight Civil	Sunrise	Moonrise 8	Moonrise 9	Moonrise 10	Moonrise 11
°	h m	h m	h m	h m	h m	h m	h m
N 72	04 27	05 47	06 54	09 29	11 49	13 49	15 40
N 70	04 37	05 49	06 49	10 44	12 27	14 11	15 53
68	04 45	05 50	06 45	11 22	12 53	14 29	16 04
66	04 51	05 51	06 42	11 48	13 13	14 43	16 13
64	04 57	05 52	06 39	12 09	13 29	14 54	16 20
62	05 01	05 53	06 37	12 25	13 42	15 04	16 26
60	05 05	05 53	06 34	12 39	13 54	15 12	16 32
N 58	05 08	05 53	06 32	12 50	14 03	15 19	16 36
56	05 11	05 54	06 31	13 01	14 12	15 26	16 40
54	05 13	05 54	06 29	13 10	14 19	15 32	16 44
52	05 15	05 54	06 28	13 18	14 26	15 37	16 48
50	05 17	05 54	06 26	13 25	14 32	15 41	16 51
45	05 20	05 54	06 23	13 40	14 45	15 51	16 57
N 40	05 23	05 54	06 21	13 53	14 56	16 00	17 03
35	05 24	05 54	06 19	14 04	15 05	16 07	17 08
30	05 25	05 53	06 17	14 13	15 13	16 13	17 12
20	05 26	05 51	06 13	14 29	15 27	16 24	17 19
N 10	05 25	05 49	06 10	14 43	15 39	16 34	17 26
0	05 22	05 46	06 07	14 56	15 51	16 42	17 32
S 10	05 18	05 43	06 04	15 10	16 02	16 51	17 38
20	05 13	05 38	06 01	15 24	16 14	17 01	17 44
30	05 04	05 32	05 56	15 40	16 28	17 11	17 52
35	04 59	05 29	05 54	15 49	16 36	17 18	17 56
40	04 52	05 24	05 51	16 00	16 45	17 25	18 00
45	04 43	05 18	05 48	16 12	16 55	17 33	18 06
S 50	04 32	05 11	05 44	16 27	17 08	17 42	18 12
52	04 27	05 08	05 42	16 35	17 14	17 47	18 15
54	04 21	05 04	05 40	16 42	17 21	17 52	18 19
56	04 14	05 00	05 38	16 51	17 28	17 57	18 22
58	04 06	04 55	05 36	17 01	17 36	18 04	18 26
S 60	03 57	04 50	05 33	17 13	17 45	18 10	18 31

Lat.	Sunset	Twilight Civil	Twilight Naut.	Moonset 8	Moonset 9	Moonset 10	Moonset 11
°	h m	h m	h m	h m	h m	h m	h m
N 72	17 29	18 36	19 57	08 02	07 36	07 26	07 18
N 70	17 34	18 34	19 47	06 46	06 57	07 01	07 03
68	17 37	18 33	19 39	06 08	06 30	06 43	06 51
66	17 41	18 32	19 32	05 41	06 09	06 28	06 41
64	17 43	18 31	19 26	05 20	05 53	06 16	06 32
62	17 46	18 30	19 22	05 04	05 39	06 05	06 25
60	17 48	18 29	19 18	04 50	05 27	05 56	06 19
N 58	17 50	18 29	19 14	04 38	05 17	05 48	06 13
56	17 51	18 28	19 12	04 27	05 08	05 41	06 08
54	17 53	18 28	19 09	04 18	05 00	05 35	06 04
52	17 54	18 28	19 07	04 10	04 53	05 29	06 00
50	17 55	18 28	19 05	04 02	04 47	05 24	05 56
45	17 58	18 28	19 02	03 47	04 33	05 13	05 48
N 40	18 01	18 28	18 59	03 33	04 21	05 04	05 42
35	18 03	18 28	18 57	03 22	04 12	04 56	05 36
30	18 05	18 28	18 56	03 13	04 03	04 49	05 31
20	18 08	18 30	18 55	02 56	03 48	04 37	05 22
N 10	18 11	18 32	18 56	02 41	03 35	04 26	05 14
0	18 14	18 34	18 59	02 27	03 23	04 16	05 06
S 10	18 17	18 38	19 02	02 13	03 10	04 05	04 59
20	18 20	18 42	19 08	01 59	02 57	03 55	04 51
30	18 24	18 48	19 16	01 42	02 42	03 42	04 42
35	18 26	18 52	19 22	01 32	02 33	03 35	04 36
40	18 29	18 56	19 28	01 20	02 23	03 26	04 30
45	18 32	19 02	19 37	01 07	02 11	03 17	04 23
S 50	18 36	19 08	19 48	00 50	01 56	03 05	04 14
52	18 37	19 12	19 53	00 43	01 49	02 59	04 10
54	18 39	19 15	19 59	00 34	01 42	02 53	04 06
56	18 41	19 19	20 05	00 25	01 33	02 46	04 01
58	18 44	19 24	20 13	00 14	01 24	02 39	03 56
S 60	18 46	19 29	20 22	00 01	01 13	02 30	03 50

Day	SUN Eqn. of Time 00^h	SUN Eqn. of Time 12^h	SUN Mer. Pass.	MOON Mer. Pass. Upper	MOON Mer. Pass. Lower	Age	Phase
d	m s	m s	h m	h m	h m	d %	
8	10 50	10 43	12 11	21 10	08 42	10 82	
9	10 36	10 28	12 10	22 03	09 37	11 89	
10	10 20	10 13	12 10	22 54	10 29	12 95	

UT d	h	ARIES GHA	VENUS −4·5 GHA	VENUS Dec	MARS +1·4 GHA	MARS Dec	JUPITER −2·4 GHA	JUPITER Dec	SATURN +0·5 GHA	SATURN Dec
		° ′	° ′	° ′	° ′	° ′	° ′	° ′	° ′	° ′
11	00	168 50.7	160 44.3	N12 05.1	140 18.8	N11 51.4	328 22.8	S 6 57.2	261 50.1	S22 05.4
	01	183 53.2	175 47.6	05.1	155 19.5	52.0	343 25.5	57.1	276 52.5	05.4
	02	198 55.7	190 50.8	05.0	170 20.3	52.7	358 28.2	57.0	291 54.8	05.4
	03	213 58.1	205 54.0	. . 05.0	185 21.0	. . 53.4	13 30.8	. . 56.9	306 57.2	. . 05.4
	04	229 00.6	220 57.3	05.0	200 21.8	54.0	28 33.5	56.8	321 59.5	05.4
	05	244 03.1	236 00.5	05.0	215 22.5	54.7	43 36.2	56.7	337 01.9	05.4
	06	259 05.5	251 03.7	N12 05.0	230 23.3	N11 55.3	58 38.9	S 6 56.6	352 04.2	S22 05.4
	07	274 08.0	266 07.0	05.0	245 24.0	56.0	73 41.6	56.5	7 06.6	05.4
S	08	289 10.5	281 10.2	05.0	260 24.8	56.6	88 44.3	56.4	22 08.9	05.4
A	09	304 12.9	296 13.5	. . 04.9	275 25.5	. . 57.3	103 46.9	. . 56.3	37 11.3	. . 05.4
T	10	319 15.4	311 16.8	04.9	290 26.3	58.0	118 49.6	56.2	52 13.6	05.4
U	11	334 17.8	326 20.0	04.9	305 27.0	58.6	133 52.3	56.1	67 16.0	05.4
R	12	349 20.3	341 23.3	N12 04.8	320 27.8	N11 59.3	148 55.0	S 6 56.0	82 18.3	S22 05.4
D	13	4 22.8	356 26.6	04.8	335 28.5	11 59.9	163 57.7	56.0	97 20.7	05.4
A	14	19 25.2	11 29.8	04.8	350 29.3	12 00.6	179 00.4	55.9	112 23.0	05.4
Y	15	34 27.7	26 33.1	. . 04.7	5 30.0	. . 01.2	194 03.1	. . 55.8	127 25.4	. . 05.4
	16	49 30.2	41 36.4	04.7	20 30.8	01.9	209 05.7	55.7	142 27.7	05.4
	17	64 32.6	56 39.7	04.7	35 31.5	02.6	224 08.4	55.6	157 30.1	05.4
	18	79 35.1	71 43.0	N12 04.6	50 32.2	N12 03.2	239 11.1	S 6 55.5	172 32.5	S22 05.4
	19	94 37.6	86 46.3	04.6	65 33.0	03.9	254 13.8	55.4	187 34.8	05.4
	20	109 40.0	101 49.6	04.5	80 33.7	04.5	269 16.5	55.3	202 37.2	05.4
	21	124 42.5	116 52.9	. . 04.5	95 34.5	. . 05.2	284 19.2	. . 55.2	217 39.5	. . 05.4
	22	139 45.0	131 56.2	04.4	110 35.2	05.8	299 21.9	55.1	232 41.9	05.4
	23	154 47.4	146 59.5	04.3	125 36.0	06.5	314 24.5	55.0	247 44.2	05.4
12	00	169 49.9	162 02.8	N12 04.3	140 36.7	N12 07.1	329 27.2	S 6 54.9	262 46.6	S22 05.4
	01	184 52.3	177 06.1	04.2	155 37.5	07.8	344 29.9	54.8	277 48.9	05.4
	02	199 54.8	192 09.4	04.1	170 38.2	08.4	359 32.6	54.7	292 51.3	05.4
	03	214 57.3	207 12.7	. . 04.1	185 39.0	. . 09.1	14 35.3	. . 54.6	307 53.6	. . 05.4
	04	229 59.7	222 16.0	04.0	200 39.7	09.7	29 38.0	54.5	322 56.0	05.4
	05	245 02.2	237 19.4	03.9	215 40.5	10.4	44 40.7	54.4	337 58.3	05.4
	06	260 04.7	252 22.7	N12 03.8	230 41.2	N12 11.1	59 43.4	S 6 54.3	353 00.7	S22 05.4
	07	275 07.1	267 26.0	03.8	245 41.9	11.7	74 46.0	54.2	8 03.0	05.4
	08	290 09.6	282 29.4	03.7	260 42.7	12.4	89 48.7	54.1	23 05.4	05.4
S	09	305 12.1	297 32.7	. . 03.6	275 43.4	. . 13.0	104 51.4	. . 54.0	38 07.8	. . 05.4
U	10	320 14.5	312 36.1	03.5	290 44.2	13.7	119 54.1	53.9	53 10.1	05.4
N	11	335 17.0	327 39.4	03.4	305 44.9	14.3	134 56.8	53.8	68 12.5	05.4
D	12	350 19.5	342 42.7	N12 03.3	320 45.7	N12 15.0	149 59.5	S 6 53.7	83 14.8	S22 05.4
A	13	5 21.9	357 46.1	03.2	335 46.4	15.6	165 02.2	53.6	98 17.2	05.4
Y	14	20 24.4	12 49.5	03.1	350 47.2	16.3	180 04.9	53.5	113 19.5	05.4
	15	35 26.8	27 52.8	. . 03.0	5 47.9	. . 16.9	195 07.6	. . 53.4	128 21.9	. . 05.4
	16	50 29.3	42 56.2	02.9	20 48.7	17.6	210 10.3	53.3	143 24.2	05.4
	17	65 31.8	57 59.5	02.8	35 49.4	18.2	225 13.0	53.3	158 26.6	05.4
	18	80 34.2	73 02.9	N12 02.7	50 50.1	N12 18.9	240 15.6	S 6 53.2	173 29.0	S22 05.4
	19	95 36.7	88 06.3	02.6	65 50.9	19.5	255 18.3	53.1	188 31.3	05.4
	20	110 39.2	103 09.7	02.5	80 51.6	20.2	270 21.0	53.0	203 33.7	05.4
	21	125 41.6	118 13.0	. . 02.4	95 52.4	. . 20.8	285 23.7	. . 52.9	218 36.0	. . 05.4
	22	140 44.1	133 16.4	02.2	110 53.1	21.5	300 26.4	52.8	233 38.4	05.4
	23	155 46.6	148 19.8	02.1	125 53.9	22.1	315 29.1	52.7	248 40.7	05.4
13	00	170 49.0	163 23.2	N12 02.0	140 54.6	N12 22.8	330 31.8	S 6 52.6	263 43.1	S22 05.4
	01	185 51.5	178 26.6	01.9	155 55.4	23.4	345 34.5	52.5	278 45.5	05.4
	02	200 53.9	193 30.0	01.7	170 56.1	24.1	0 37.2	52.4	293 47.8	05.4
	03	215 56.4	208 33.4	. . 01.6	185 56.8	. . 24.7	15 39.9	. . 52.3	308 50.2	. . 05.4
	04	230 58.9	223 36.8	01.5	200 57.6	25.4	30 42.6	52.2	323 52.5	05.4
	05	246 01.3	238 40.2	01.3	215 58.3	26.0	45 45.3	52.1	338 54.9	05.4
	06	261 03.8	253 43.6	N12 01.2	230 59.1	N12 26.7	60 48.0	S 6 52.0	353 57.2	S22 05.4
	07	276 06.3	268 47.0	01.1	245 59.8	27.3	75 50.7	51.9	8 59.6	05.4
	08	291 08.7	283 50.4	00.9	261 00.6	27.9	90 53.3	51.8	24 02.0	05.4
M	09	306 11.2	298 53.9	. . 00.8	276 01.3	. . 28.6	105 56.0	. . 51.7	39 04.3	. . 05.4
O	10	321 13.7	313 57.3	00.6	291 02.1	29.2	120 58.7	51.6	54 06.7	05.4
N	11	336 16.1	329 00.7	00.5	306 02.8	29.9	136 01.4	51.5	69 09.0	05.4
D	12	351 18.6	344 04.1	N12 00.3	321 03.5	N12 30.5	151 04.1	S 6 51.4	84 11.4	S22 05.4
A	13	6 21.1	359 07.6	00.1	336 04.3	31.2	166 06.8	51.3	99 13.8	05.4
Y	14	21 23.5	14 11.0	12 00.0	351 05.0	31.8	181 09.5	51.2	114 16.1	05.4
	15	36 26.0	29 14.4	11 59.8	6 05.8	. . 32.5	196 12.2	. . 51.1	129 18.5	. . 05.4
	16	51 28.4	44 17.9	59.6	21 06.5	33.1	211 14.9	51.0	144 20.8	05.4
	17	66 30.9	59 21.3	59.5	36 07.3	33.8	226 17.6	50.9	159 23.2	05.4
	18	81 33.4	74 24.8	N11 59.3	51 08.0	N12 34.4	241 20.3	S 6 50.8	174 25.6	S22 05.4
	19	96 35.8	89 28.2	59.1	66 08.7	35.1	256 23.0	50.7	189 27.9	05.4
	20	111 38.3	104 31.7	59.0	81 09.5	35.7	271 25.7	50.6	204 30.3	05.4
	21	126 40.8	119 35.1	. . 58.8	96 10.2	. . 36.3	286 28.4	. . 50.5	219 32.6	. . 05.4
	22	141 43.2	134 38.6	58.6	111 11.0	37.0	301 31.1	50.4	234 35.0	05.4
	23	156 45.7	149 42.1	58.4	126 11.7	37.6	316 33.8	50.3	249 37.4	05.4
Mer. Pass.		h m 12 38.6	*v* 3.4	*d* 0.1	*v* 0.7	*d* 0.7	*v* 2.7	*d* 0.1	*v* 2.4	*d* 0.0

STARS

Name	SHA	Dec
	° ′	° ′
Acamar	315 16.7	S40 14.6
Achernar	335 25.5	S57 09.3
Acrux	173 05.7	S63 11.6
Adhara	255 10.4	S29 00.2
Aldebaran	290 46.5	N16 32.4
Alioth	166 18.0	N55 51.9
Alkaid	152 56.6	N49 13.5
Al Na'ir	27 41.1	S46 52.6
Alnilam	275 43.8	S 1 11.8
Alphard	217 53.3	S 8 44.2
Alphecca	126 08.7	N26 39.3
Alpheratz	357 41.2	N29 11.0
Altair	62 06.0	N 8 54.8
Ankaa	353 13.7	S42 13.0
Antares	112 23.1	S26 28.0
Arcturus	145 53.2	N19 05.5
Atria	107 22.5	S69 03.0
Avior	234 16.5	S59 34.2
Bellatrix	278 29.3	N 6 21.6
Betelgeuse	270 58.5	N 7 24.3
Canopus	263 54.9	S52 42.8
Capella	280 30.7	N46 00.8
Deneb	49 30.1	N45 20.4
Denebola	182 30.8	N14 28.5
Diphda	348 53.7	S17 53.8
Dubhe	193 48.1	N61 39.5
Elnath	278 09.4	N28 37.1
Eltanin	90 45.0	N51 29.0
Enif	33 44.9	N 9 57.1
Fomalhaut	15 21.6	S29 32.0
Gacrux	171 57.4	S57 12.5
Gienah	175 49.4	S17 38.3
Hadar	148 43.7	S60 27.1
Hamal	327 58.1	N23 32.4
Kaus Aust.	83 40.6	S34 22.3
Kochab	137 19.5	N74 05.0
Markab	13 36.1	N15 17.7
Menkar	314 12.6	N 4 09.1
Menkent	148 04.3	S36 27.1
Miaplacidus	221 38.3	S69 47.5
Mirfak	308 36.9	N49 55.3
Nunki	75 55.3	S26 16.3
Peacock	53 15.7	S56 40.5
Pollux	243 24.5	N27 58.9
Procyon	244 56.9	N 5 10.6
Rasalhague	96 04.1	N12 32.9
Regulus	207 40.5	N11 52.8
Rigel	281 09.6	S 8 11.3
Rigil Kent.	139 47.8	S60 54.0
Sabik	102 09.6	S15 44.6
Schedar	349 38.1	N56 37.8
Shaula	96 18.5	S37 06.7
Sirius	258 31.4	S16 44.8
Spica	158 28.3	S11 15.0
Suhail	222 50.2	S43 30.4
Vega	80 37.4	N38 47.9
Zuben'ubi	137 02.4	S16 06.7

	SHA	Mer. Pass.
	° ′	h m
Venus	352 12.9	13 09
Mars	330 46.8	14 37
Jupiter	159 37.3	2 02
Saturn	92 56.7	6 28

UT		SUN GHA	SUN Dec	MOON GHA	v	MOON Dec	d	HP
d	h	° ′	° ′	° ′	′	° ′	′	′
11	00	177 28.9	S 3 43.4	15 50.6	10.9	N10 54.0	8.9	57.2
	01	192 29.1	42.4	30 20.5	10.9	10 45.1	9.0	57.2
	02	207 29.2	41.4	44 50.4	11.0	10 36.1	9.0	57.2
	03	222 29.4	. . 40.5	59 20.4	11.0	10 27.1	9.1	57.2
	04	237 29.6	39.5	73 50.4	11.0	10 18.0	9.1	57.2
	05	252 29.7	38.5	88 20.4	11.2	10 08.9	9.1	57.1
	06	267 29.9	S 3 37.5	102 50.6	11.1	N 9 59.8	9.2	57.1
	07	282 30.1	36.5	117 20.7	11.2	9 50.6	9.3	57.1
S	08	297 30.2	35.6	131 50.9	11.3	9 41.3	9.3	57.1
A	09	312 30.4	. . 34.6	146 21.2	11.4	9 32.0	9.3	57.0
T	10	327 30.6	33.6	160 51.6	11.3	9 22.7	9.4	57.0
U	11	342 30.7	32.6	175 21.9	11.5	9 13.3	9.4	57.0
R	12	357 30.9	S 3 31.6	189 52.4	11.4	N 9 03.9	9.4	57.0
D	13	12 31.1	30.6	204 22.8	11.6	8 54.5	9.5	57.0
A	14	27 31.2	29.7	218 53.4	11.6	8 45.0	9.6	56.9
Y	15	42 31.4	. . 28.7	233 24.0	11.6	8 35.4	9.5	56.9
	16	57 31.6	27.7	247 54.6	11.7	8 25.9	9.6	56.9
	17	72 31.7	26.7	262 25.3	11.7	8 16.3	9.7	56.9
	18	87 31.9	S 3 25.7	276 56.0	11.8	N 8 06.6	9.6	56.9
	19	102 32.1	24.8	291 26.8	11.8	7 57.0	9.8	56.8
	20	117 32.2	23.8	305 57.6	11.9	7 47.2	9.7	56.8
	21	132 32.4	. . 22.8	320 28.5	11.9	7 37.5	9.8	56.8
	22	147 32.6	21.8	334 59.4	12.0	7 27.7	9.8	56.8
	23	162 32.7	20.8	349 30.4	12.0	7 17.9	9.8	56.7
12	00	177 32.9	S 3 19.8	4 01.4	12.1	N 7 08.1	9.8	56.7
	01	192 33.1	18.9	18 32.5	12.1	6 58.3	9.9	56.7
	02	207 33.2	17.9	33 03.6	12.2	6 48.4	9.9	56.7
	03	222 33.4	. . 16.9	47 34.8	12.2	6 38.5	10.0	56.7
	04	237 33.6	15.9	62 06.0	12.2	6 28.5	9.9	56.6
	05	252 33.7	14.9	76 37.2	12.3	6 18.6	10.0	56.6
	06	267 33.9	S 3 13.9	91 08.5	12.3	N 6 08.6	10.0	56.6
	07	282 34.1	13.0	105 39.8	12.4	5 58.6	10.0	56.6
	08	297 34.2	12.0	120 11.2	12.4	5 48.6	10.1	56.5
S	09	312 34.4	. . 11.0	134 42.6	12.5	5 38.5	10.1	56.5
U	10	327 34.6	10.0	149 14.1	12.5	5 28.4	10.0	56.5
N	11	342 34.7	09.0	163 45.6	12.5	5 18.4	10.1	56.5
D	12	357 34.9	S 3 08.0	178 17.1	12.6	N 5 08.3	10.2	56.5
A	13	12 35.1	07.0	192 48.7	12.6	4 58.1	10.1	56.4
Y	14	27 35.3	06.1	207 20.3	12.7	4 48.0	10.2	56.4
	15	42 35.4	. . 05.1	221 52.0	12.7	4 37.8	10.1	56.4
	16	57 35.6	04.1	236 23.7	12.8	4 27.7	10.2	56.4
	17	72 35.8	03.1	250 55.5	12.7	4 17.5	10.2	56.3
	18	87 35.9	S 3 02.1	265 27.2	12.9	N 4 07.3	10.2	56.3
	19	102 36.1	01.1	279 59.1	12.8	3 57.1	10.2	56.3
	20	117 36.3	3 00.2	294 30.9	12.9	3 46.9	10.2	56.3
	21	132 36.4	2 59.2	309 02.8	12.9	3 36.7	10.3	56.3
	22	147 36.6	58.2	323 34.7	13.0	3 26.4	10.2	56.2
	23	162 36.8	57.2	338 06.7	13.0	3 16.2	10.2	56.2
13	00	177 37.0	S 2 56.2	352 38.7	13.0	N 3 06.0	10.3	56.2
	01	192 37.1	55.2	7 10.7	13.1	2 55.7	10.3	56.2
	02	207 37.3	54.3	21 42.8	13.1	2 45.4	10.2	56.1
	03	222 37.5	. . 53.3	36 14.9	13.2	2 35.2	10.3	56.1
	04	237 37.6	52.3	50 47.1	13.1	2 24.9	10.3	56.1
	05	252 37.8	51.3	65 19.2	13.2	2 14.6	10.2	56.1
	06	267 38.0	S 2 50.3	79 51.4	13.3	N 2 04.4	10.3	56.1
	07	282 38.2	49.3	94 23.7	13.2	1 54.1	10.3	56.0
	08	297 38.3	48.3	108 55.9	13.3	1 43.8	10.3	56.0
M	09	312 38.5	. . 47.4	123 28.2	13.3	1 33.5	10.2	56.0
O	10	327 38.7	46.4	138 00.5	13.4	1 23.3	10.3	56.0
N	11	342 38.8	45.4	152 32.9	13.4	1 13.0	10.3	55.9
D	12	357 39.0	S 2 44.4	167 05.3	13.4	N 1 02.7	10.2	55.9
A	13	12 39.2	43.4	181 37.7	13.4	0 52.5	10.3	55.9
Y	14	27 39.4	42.4	196 10.1	13.5	0 42.2	10.3	55.9
	15	42 39.5	. . 41.4	210 42.6	13.5	0 31.9	10.2	55.9
	16	57 39.7	40.5	225 15.1	13.5	0 21.7	10.3	55.8
	17	72 39.9	39.5	239 47.6	13.5	0 11.4	10.2	55.8
	18	87 40.0	S 2 38.5	254 20.1	13.6	N 0 01.2	10.2	55.8
	19	102 40.2	37.5	268 52.7	13.6	S 0 09.0	10.2	55.8
	20	117 40.4	36.5	283 25.3	13.6	0 19.2	10.3	55.7
	21	132 40.6	. . 35.5	297 57.9	13.6	0 29.5	10.2	55.7
	22	147 40.7	34.5	312 30.5	13.7	0 39.7	10.1	55.7
	23	162 40.9	33.6	327 03.2	13.7	S 0 49.8	10.2	55.7
		SD 16.1	d 1.0	SD	15.5		15.4	15.2

Lat.	Twilight Naut.	Twilight Civil	Sunrise	Moonrise 11	Moonrise 12	Moonrise 13	Moonrise 14
°	h m	h m	h m	h m	h m	h m	h m
N 72	04 10	05 32	06 39	15 40	17 26	19 08	20 48
N 70	04 22	05 35	06 35	15 53	17 32	19 08	20 42
68	04 32	05 38	06 33	16 04	17 37	19 08	20 36
66	04 39	05 40	06 31	16 13	17 41	19 07	20 32
64	04 46	05 42	06 29	16 20	17 44	19 07	20 28
62	04 51	05 43	06 27	16 26	17 47	19 07	20 25
60	04 56	05 44	06 25	16 32	17 50	19 07	20 22
N 58	04 59	05 45	06 24	16 36	17 52	19 07	20 19
56	05 03	05 46	06 23	16 40	17 54	19 06	20 17
54	05 06	05 47	06 22	16 44	17 56	19 06	20 15
52	05 08	05 47	06 21	16 48	17 58	19 06	20 13
50	05 10	05 48	06 20	16 51	17 59	19 06	20 12
45	05 15	05 49	06 18	16 57	18 02	19 06	20 08
N 40	05 18	05 49	06 16	17 03	18 05	19 06	20 05
35	05 20	05 50	06 15	17 08	18 07	19 06	20 03
30	05 22	05 49	06 13	17 12	18 10	19 06	20 00
20	05 23	05 49	06 11	17 19	18 13	19 05	19 56
N 10	05 23	05 48	06 09	17 26	18 16	19 05	19 53
0	05 22	05 46	06 06	17 32	18 19	19 05	19 50
S 10	05 19	05 43	06 04	17 38	18 22	19 05	19 47
20	05 14	05 39	06 01	17 44	18 25	19 05	19 43
30	05 06	05 34	05 58	17 52	18 29	19 05	19 40
35	05 01	05 31	05 57	17 56	18 31	19 05	19 38
40	04 55	05 27	05 55	18 00	18 33	19 05	19 35
45	04 47	05 23	05 52	18 06	18 36	19 05	19 32
S 50	04 38	05 16	05 49	18 12	18 39	19 05	19 29
52	04 33	05 14	05 48	18 15	18 41	19 05	19 28
54	04 27	05 10	05 46	18 19	18 42	19 04	19 26
56	04 21	05 07	05 45	18 22	18 44	19 04	19 24
58	04 14	05 03	05 43	18 26	18 46	19 04	19 22
S 60	04 06	04 58	05 41	18 31	18 48	19 04	19 20

Lat.	Sunset	Twilight Civil	Twilight Naut.	Moonset 11	Moonset 12	Moonset 13	Moonset 14
°	h m	h m	h m	h m	h m	h m	h m
N 72	17 43	18 50	20 13	07 18	07 11	07 04	06 58
N 70	17 46	18 47	20 00	07 03	07 03	07 02	07 01
68	17 48	18 44	19 50	06 51	06 56	07 00	07 04
66	17 50	18 41	19 42	06 41	06 50	06 58	07 06
64	17 52	18 40	19 36	06 32	06 46	06 57	07 07
62	17 54	18 38	19 30	06 25	06 42	06 56	07 09
60	17 55	18 37	19 26	06 19	06 38	06 55	07 10
N 58	17 56	18 36	19 22	06 13	06 35	06 54	07 12
56	17 58	18 35	19 18	06 08	06 32	06 53	07 13
54	17 59	18 34	19 15	06 04	06 29	06 52	07 14
52	17 59	18 33	19 12	06 00	06 27	06 51	07 15
50	18 00	18 33	19 10	05 56	06 25	06 51	07 16
45	18 02	18 31	19 06	05 48	06 20	06 49	07 17
N 40	18 04	18 31	19 02	05 42	06 16	06 48	07 19
35	18 05	18 30	19 00	05 36	06 12	06 47	07 20
30	18 06	18 30	18 58	05 31	06 09	06 46	07 21
20	18 09	18 31	18 56	05 22	06 04	06 44	07 23
N 10	18 11	18 32	18 56	05 14	05 59	06 43	07 25
0	18 13	18 34	18 58	05 06	05 55	06 41	07 27
S 10	18 15	18 36	19 01	04 59	05 50	06 40	07 28
20	18 18	18 40	19 05	04 51	05 45	06 38	07 30
30	18 20	18 44	19 12	04 42	05 40	06 37	07 32
35	18 22	18 48	19 17	04 36	05 37	06 36	07 33
40	18 24	18 51	19 23	04 30	05 33	06 34	07 34
45	18 26	18 56	19 31	04 23	05 29	06 33	07 36
S 50	18 29	19 02	19 41	04 14	05 24	06 31	07 38
52	18 31	19 05	19 45	04 10	05 21	06 31	07 39
54	18 32	19 08	19 51	04 06	05 19	06 30	07 39
56	18 34	19 11	19 57	04 01	05 16	06 29	07 40
58	18 35	19 15	20 03	03 56	05 12	06 28	07 41
S 60	18 37	19 20	20 11	03 50	05 09	06 27	07 43

Day	SUN Eqn. of Time 00^h	SUN Eqn. of Time 12^h	SUN Mer. Pass.	MOON Mer. Pass. Upper	MOON Mer. Pass. Lower	MOON Age	MOON Phase
d	m s	m s	h m	h m	h m	d %	
11	10 05	09 57	12 10	23 43	11 19	13 99	
12	09 49	09 41	12 10	24 30	12 07	14 100	○
13	09 33	09 24	12 09	00 30	12 53	15 99	

UT d	h	ARIES GHA ° ′	VENUS −4·4 GHA ° ′	VENUS Dec ° ′	MARS +1·4 GHA ° ′	MARS Dec ° ′	JUPITER −2·4 GHA ° ′	JUPITER Dec ° ′	SATURN +0·5 GHA ° ′	SATURN Dec ° ′
14 TUESDAY	00	171 48.2	164 45.5	N11 58.2	141 12.5	N12 38.3	331 36.5	S 6 50.2	264 39.7	S22 05.4
	01	186 50.6	179 49.0	58.0	156 13.2	38.9	346 39.2	50.1	279 42.1	05.4
	02	201 53.1	194 52.5	57.8	171 13.9	39.6	1 41.9	50.0	294 44.4	05.4
	03	216 55.5	209 55.9	. . 57.6	186 14.7	. . 40.2	16 44.6	. . 49.9	309 46.8	. . 05.4
	04	231 58.0	224 59.4	57.4	201 15.4	40.8	31 47.3	49.8	324 49.2	05.4
	05	247 00.5	240 02.9	57.2	216 16.2	41.5	46 50.0	49.7	339 51.5	05.4
	06	262 02.9	255 06.4	N11 57.0	231 16.9	N12 42.1	61 52.7	S 6 49.6	354 53.9	S22 05.4
	07	277 05.4	270 09.9	56.8	246 17.7	42.8	76 55.4	49.5	9 56.3	05.4
	08	292 07.9	285 13.4	56.6	261 18.4	43.4	91 58.1	49.4	24 58.6	05.4
	09	307 10.3	300 16.8	. . 56.4	276 19.1	. . 44.1	107 00.8	. . 49.3	40 01.0	. . 05.4
	10	322 12.8	315 20.3	56.2	291 19.9	44.7	122 03.5	49.2	55 03.3	05.4
	11	337 15.3	330 23.8	56.0	306 20.6	45.3	137 06.2	49.1	70 05.7	05.4
	12	352 17.7	345 27.3	N11 55.8	321 21.4	N12 46.0	152 08.9	S 6 49.0	85 08.1	S22 05.4
	13	7 20.2	0 30.8	55.5	336 22.1	46.6	167 11.6	48.9	100 10.4	05.4
	14	22 22.7	15 34.4	55.3	351 22.8	47.3	182 14.3	48.8	115 12.8	05.4
	15	37 25.1	30 37.9	. . 55.1	6 23.6	. . 47.9	197 17.0	. . 48.7	130 15.2	. . 05.4
	16	52 27.6	45 41.4	54.8	21 24.3	48.5	212 19.7	48.6	145 17.5	05.3
	17	67 30.0	60 44.9	54.6	36 25.1	49.2	227 22.4	48.5	160 19.9	05.3
	18	82 32.5	75 48.4	N11 54.4	51 25.8	N12 49.8	242 25.1	S 6 48.4	175 22.3	S22 05.3
	19	97 35.0	90 51.9	54.1	66 26.6	50.5	257 27.8	48.3	190 24.6	05.3
	20	112 37.4	105 55.5	53.9	81 27.3	51.1	272 30.5	48.2	205 27.0	05.3
	21	127 39.9	120 59.0	. . 53.7	96 28.0	. . 51.7	287 33.2	. . 48.1	220 29.4	. . 05.3
	22	142 42.4	136 02.5	53.4	111 28.8	52.4	302 35.9	48.0	235 31.7	05.3
	23	157 44.8	151 06.1	53.2	126 29.5	53.0	317 38.6	47.9	250 34.1	05.3
15 WEDNESDAY	00	172 47.3	166 09.6	N11 52.9	141 30.3	N12 53.7	332 41.3	S 6 47.8	265 36.5	S22 05.3
	01	187 49.8	181 13.1	52.7	156 31.0	54.3	347 44.0	47.7	280 38.8	05.3
	02	202 52.2	196 16.7	52.4	171 31.7	54.9	2 46.7	47.6	295 41.2	05.3
	03	217 54.7	211 20.2	. . 52.1	186 32.5	. . 55.6	17 49.4	. . 47.5	310 43.6	. . 05.3
	04	232 57.1	226 23.8	51.9	201 33.2	56.2	32 52.1	47.4	325 45.9	05.3
	05	247 59.6	241 27.3	51.6	216 34.0	56.8	47 54.8	47.3	340 48.3	05.3
	06	263 02.1	256 30.9	N11 51.4	231 34.7	N12 57.5	62 57.5	S 6 47.2	355 50.7	S22 05.3
	07	278 04.5	271 34.4	51.1	246 35.4	58.1	78 00.2	47.1	10 53.0	05.3
	08	293 07.0	286 38.0	50.8	261 36.2	58.8	93 02.9	47.0	25 55.4	05.3
	09	308 09.5	301 41.6	. . 50.5	276 36.9	12 59.4	108 05.6	. . 46.9	40 57.8	. . 05.3
	10	323 11.9	316 45.1	50.3	291 37.7	13 00.0	123 08.3	46.8	56 00.1	05.3
	11	338 14.4	331 48.7	50.0	306 38.4	00.7	138 11.0	46.7	71 02.5	05.3
	12	353 16.9	346 52.3	N11 49.7	321 39.1	N13 01.3	153 13.7	S 6 46.5	86 04.9	S22 05.3
	13	8 19.3	1 55.8	49.4	336 39.9	01.9	168 16.4	46.4	101 07.2	05.3
	14	23 21.8	16 59.4	49.1	351 40.6	02.6	183 19.1	46.3	116 09.6	05.3
	15	38 24.3	32 03.0	. . 48.8	6 41.4	. . 03.2	198 21.8	. . 46.2	131 12.0	. . 05.3
	16	53 26.7	47 06.6	48.5	21 42.1	03.8	213 24.5	46.1	146 14.3	05.3
	17	68 29.2	62 10.2	48.2	36 42.8	04.5	228 27.3	46.0	161 16.7	05.3
	18	83 31.6	77 13.7	N11 47.9	51 43.6	N13 05.1	243 30.0	S 6 45.9	176 19.1	S22 05.3
	19	98 34.1	92 17.3	47.6	66 44.3	05.7	258 32.7	45.8	191 21.4	05.3
	20	113 36.6	107 20.9	47.3	81 45.1	06.4	273 35.4	45.7	206 23.8	05.3
	21	128 39.0	122 24.5	. . 47.0	96 45.8	. . 07.0	288 38.1	. . 45.6	221 26.2	. . 05.3
	22	143 41.5	137 28.1	46.7	111 46.5	07.6	303 40.8	45.5	236 28.5	05.3
	23	158 44.0	152 31.7	46.4	126 47.3	08.3	318 43.5	45.4	251 30.9	05.3
16 THURSDAY	00	173 46.4	167 35.3	N11 46.1	141 48.0	N13 08.9	333 46.2	S 6 45.3	266 33.3	S22 05.3
	01	188 48.9	182 38.9	45.8	156 48.8	09.5	348 48.9	45.2	281 35.7	05.3
	02	203 51.4	197 42.5	45.5	171 49.5	10.2	3 51.6	45.1	296 38.0	05.3
	03	218 53.8	212 46.1	. . 45.1	186 50.2	. . 10.8	18 54.3	. . 45.0	311 40.4	. . 05.3
	04	233 56.3	227 49.7	44.8	201 51.0	11.4	33 57.0	44.9	326 42.8	05.3
	05	248 58.7	242 53.4	44.5	216 51.7	12.1	48 59.7	44.8	341 45.1	05.3
	06	264 01.2	257 57.0	N11 44.2	231 52.4	N13 12.7	64 02.4	S 6 44.7	356 47.5	S22 05.3
	07	279 03.7	273 00.6	43.8	246 53.2	13.3	79 05.2	44.6	11 49.9	05.3
	08	294 06.1	288 04.2	43.5	261 53.9	14.0	94 07.9	44.5	26 52.2	05.3
	09	309 08.6	303 07.8	. . 43.1	276 54.7	. . 14.6	109 10.6	. . 44.4	41 54.6	. . 05.3
	10	324 11.1	318 11.5	42.8	291 55.4	15.2	124 13.3	44.3	56 57.0	05.3
	11	339 13.5	333 15.1	42.5	306 56.1	15.9	139 16.0	44.2	71 59.4	05.3
	12	354 16.0	348 18.7	N11 42.1	321 56.9	N13 16.5	154 18.7	S 6 44.1	87 01.7	S22 05.3
	13	9 18.5	3 22.4	41.8	336 57.6	17.1	169 21.4	44.0	102 04.1	05.3
	14	24 20.9	18 26.0	41.4	351 58.4	17.8	184 24.1	43.9	117 06.5	05.3
	15	39 23.4	33 29.7	. . 41.1	6 59.1	. . 18.4	199 26.8	. . 43.8	132 08.9	. . 05.3
	16	54 25.9	48 33.3	40.7	21 59.8	19.0	214 29.5	43.7	147 11.2	05.3
	17	69 28.3	63 36.9	40.4	37 00.6	19.6	229 32.2	43.5	162 13.6	05.3
	18	84 30.8	78 40.6	N11 40.0	52 01.3	N13 20.3	244 35.0	S 6 43.4	177 16.0	S22 05.3
	19	99 33.2	93 44.2	39.6	67 02.0	20.9	259 37.7	43.3	192 18.3	05.3
	20	114 35.7	108 47.9	39.3	82 02.8	21.5	274 40.4	43.2	207 20.7	05.3
	21	129 38.2	123 51.5	. . 38.9	97 03.5	. . 22.2	289 43.1	. . 43.1	222 23.1	. . 05.3
	22	144 40.6	138 55.2	38.5	112 04.3	22.8	304 45.8	43.0	237 25.5	05.3
	23	159 43.1	153 58.9	38.1	127 05.0	23.4	319 48.5	42.9	252 27.8	05.3
Mer. Pass.		h m 12 26.8	v 3.6	d 0.3	v 0.7	d 0.6	v 2.7	d 0.1	v 2.4	d 0.0

STARS Name	SHA ° ′	Dec ° ′
Acamar	315 16.7	S40 14.6
Achernar	335 25.5	S57 09.3
Acrux	173 05.6	S63 11.6
Adhara	255 10.4	S29 00.2
Aldebaran	290 46.6	N16 32.4
Alioth	166 18.0	N55 51.9
Alkaid	152 56.6	N49 13.6
Al Na'ir	27 41.1	S46 52.6
Alnilam	275 43.8	S 1 11.8
Alphard	217 53.3	S 8 44.2
Alphecca	126 08.7	N26 39.3
Alpheratz	357 41.2	N29 11.0
Altair	62 05.9	N 8 54.8
Ankaa	353 13.7	S42 13.0
Antares	112 23.0	S26 28.0
Arcturus	145 53.2	N19 05.5
Atria	107 22.5	S69 03.0
Avior	234 16.5	S59 34.3
Bellatrix	278 29.3	N 6 21.6
Betelgeuse	270 58.5	N 7 24.3
Canopus	263 54.9	S52 42.8
Capella	280 30.7	N46 00.8
Deneb	49 30.0	N45 20.4
Denebola	182 30.8	N14 28.5
Diphda	348 53.7	S17 53.8
Dubhe	193 48.1	N61 39.5
Elnath	278 09.4	N28 37.1
Eltanin	90 45.0	N51 29.0
Enif	33 44.9	N 9 57.1
Fomalhaut	15 21.6	S29 32.0
Gacrux	171 57.4	S57 12.5
Gienah	175 49.4	S17 38.3
Hadar	148 43.7	S60 27.1
Hamal	327 58.2	N23 32.4
Kaus Aust.	83 40.6	S34 22.3
Kochab	137 19.5	N74 05.0
Markab	13 36.1	N15 17.7
Menkar	314 12.6	N 4 09.1
Menkent	148 04.2	S36 27.1
Miaplacidus	221 38.3	S69 47.6
Mirfak	308 36.9	N49 55.2
Nunki	75 55.3	S26 16.3
Peacock	53 15.7	S56 40.5
Pollux	243 24.5	N27 58.9
Procyon	244 56.9	N 5 10.6
Rasalhague	96 04.1	N12 32.9
Regulus	207 40.6	N11 52.8
Rigel	281 09.7	S 8 11.3
Rigil Kent.	139 47.8	S60 54.0
Sabik	102 09.6	S15 44.6
Schedar	349 38.1	N56 37.8
Shaula	96 18.5	S37 06.7
Sirius	258 31.4	S16 44.8
Spica	158 28.3	S11 15.0
Suhail	222 50.2	S43 30.4
Vega	80 37.3	N38 47.9
Zuben'ubi	137 02.4	S16 06.7

	SHA ° ′	Mer. Pass. h m
Venus	353 22.3	12 52
Mars	328 43.0	14 33
Jupiter	159 54.0	1 49
Saturn	92 49.2	6 17

UT		SUN GHA	SUN Dec	MOON GHA	v	MOON Dec	d	HP
d	h	° ′	° ′	° ′	′	° ′	′	′
14 TUESDAY	00	177 41.1	S 2 32.6	341 35.9	13.7	S 1 00.0	10.2	55.7
	01	192 41.3	31.6	356 08.6	13.7	1 10.2	10.1	55.6
	02	207 41.4	30.6	10 41.3	13.7	1 20.3	10.2	55.6
	03	222 41.6	. . 29.6	25 14.0	13.8	1 30.5	10.1	55.6
	04	237 41.8	28.6	39 46.8	13.8	1 40.6	10.1	55.6
	05	252 42.0	27.6	54 19.6	13.8	1 50.7	10.1	55.5
	06	267 42.1	S 2 26.7	68 52.4	13.8	S 2 00.8	10.1	55.5
	07	282 42.3	25.7	83 25.2	13.8	2 10.9	10.0	55.5
	08	297 42.5	24.7	97 58.0	13.9	2 20.9	10.0	55.5
	09	312 42.6	. . 23.7	112 30.9	13.8	2 30.9	10.1	55.5
	10	327 42.8	22.7	127 03.7	13.9	2 41.0	10.0	55.4
	11	342 43.0	21.7	141 36.6	13.9	2 51.0	9.9	55.4
	12	357 43.2	S 2 20.7	156 09.5	13.9	S 3 00.9	10.0	55.4
	13	12 43.3	19.8	170 42.4	14.0	3 10.9	9.9	55.4
	14	27 43.5	18.8	185 15.4	13.9	3 20.8	9.9	55.4
	15	42 43.7	. . 17.8	199 48.3	14.0	3 30.7	9.9	55.3
	16	57 43.9	16.8	214 21.3	13.9	3 40.6	9.9	55.3
	17	72 44.0	15.8	228 54.2	14.0	3 50.5	9.8	55.3
	18	87 44.2	S 2 14.8	243 27.2	14.0	S 4 00.3	9.8	55.3
	19	102 44.4	13.8	258 00.2	14.0	4 10.1	9.8	55.3
	20	117 44.6	12.8	272 33.2	14.0	4 19.9	9.8	55.2
	21	132 44.7	. . 11.9	287 06.2	14.0	4 29.7	9.7	55.2
	22	147 44.9	10.9	301 39.2	14.1	4 39.4	9.7	55.2
	23	162 45.1	09.9	316 12.3	14.0	4 49.1	9.7	55.2
15 WEDNESDAY	00	177 45.3	S 2 08.9	330 45.3	14.1	S 4 58.8	9.7	55.2
	01	192 45.4	07.9	345 18.4	14.0	5 08.5	9.6	55.1
	02	207 45.6	06.9	359 51.4	14.1	5 18.1	9.6	55.1
	03	222 45.8	. . 05.9	14 24.5	14.1	5 27.7	9.5	55.1
	04	237 46.0	05.0	28 57.6	14.0	5 37.2	9.6	55.1
	05	252 46.2	04.0	43 30.6	14.1	5 46.8	9.5	55.1
	06	267 46.3	S 2 03.0	58 03.7	14.1	S 5 56.3	9.4	55.0
	07	282 46.5	02.0	72 36.8	14.1	6 05.7	9.4	55.0
	08	297 46.7	01.0	87 09.9	14.1	6 15.1	9.4	55.0
	09	312 46.9	2 00.0	101 43.0	14.1	6 24.5	9.4	55.0
	10	327 47.0	1 59.0	116 16.1	14.1	6 33.9	9.3	55.0
	11	342 47.2	58.0	130 49.2	14.1	6 43.2	9.3	55.0
	12	357 47.4	S 1 57.1	145 22.3	14.1	S 6 52.5	9.3	54.9
	13	12 47.6	56.1	159 55.4	14.1	7 01.8	9.2	54.9
	14	27 47.7	55.1	174 28.5	14.2	7 11.0	9.2	54.9
	15	42 47.9	. . 54.1	189 01.7	14.1	7 20.2	9.1	54.9
	16	57 48.1	53.1	203 34.8	14.1	7 29.3	9.1	54.9
	17	72 48.3	52.1	218 07.9	14.1	7 38.4	9.1	54.9
	18	87 48.5	S 1 51.1	232 41.0	14.1	S 7 47.5	9.0	54.8
	19	102 48.6	50.1	247 14.1	14.1	7 56.5	9.0	54.8
	20	117 48.8	49.2	261 47.2	14.1	8 05.5	8.9	54.8
	21	132 49.0	. . 48.2	276 20.3	14.1	8 14.4	8.9	54.8
	22	147 49.2	47.2	290 53.4	14.1	8 23.3	8.9	54.8
	23	162 49.3	46.2	305 26.5	14.1	8 32.2	8.8	54.8
16 THURSDAY	00	177 49.5	S 1 45.2	319 59.6	14.1	S 8 41.0	8.7	54.7
	01	192 49.7	44.2	334 32.7	14.1	8 49.7	8.8	54.7
	02	207 49.9	43.2	349 05.8	14.1	8 58.5	8.7	54.7
	03	222 50.1	. . 42.2	3 38.9	14.1	9 07.2	8.6	54.7
	04	237 50.2	41.3	18 12.0	14.1	9 15.8	8.6	54.7
	05	252 50.4	40.3	32 45.1	14.1	9 24.4	8.5	54.7
	06	267 50.6	S 1 39.3	47 18.2	14.0	S 9 32.9	8.5	54.6
	07	282 50.8	38.3	61 51.2	14.1	9 41.4	8.5	54.6
	08	297 50.9	37.3	76 24.3	14.1	9 49.9	8.4	54.6
	09	312 51.1	. . 36.3	90 57.4	14.0	9 58.3	8.4	54.6
	10	327 51.3	35.3	105 30.4	14.0	10 06.7	8.3	54.6
	11	342 51.5	34.3	120 03.4	14.1	10 15.0	8.2	54.6
	12	357 51.7	S 1 33.4	134 36.5	14.0	S10 23.2	8.3	54.6
	13	12 51.8	32.4	149 09.5	14.0	10 31.5	8.1	54.6
	14	27 52.0	31.4	163 42.5	14.0	10 39.6	8.1	54.5
	15	42 52.2	. . 30.4	178 15.5	14.0	10 47.7	8.1	54.5
	16	57 52.4	29.4	192 48.5	14.0	10 55.8	8.0	54.5
	17	72 52.6	28.4	207 21.5	13.9	11 03.8	8.0	54.5
	18	87 52.7	S 1 27.4	221 54.4	14.0	S11 11.8	7.9	54.5
	19	102 52.9	26.4	236 27.4	14.0	11 19.7	7.8	54.5
	20	117 53.1	25.5	251 00.4	13.9	11 27.5	7.8	54.5
	21	132 53.3	. . 24.5	265 33.3	13.9	11 35.3	7.8	54.5
	22	147 53.5	23.5	280 06.2	13.9	11 43.1	7.7	54.4
	23	162 53.6	22.5	294 39.1	13.9	S11 50.8	7.6	54.4
		SD 16.1	*d* 1.0	SD 15.1		15.0		14.9

Lat.	Twilight Naut.	Twilight Civil	Sunrise	Moonrise 14	Moonrise 15	Moonrise 16	Moonrise 17
°	h m	h m	h m	h m	h m	h m	h m
N 72	03 52	05 16	06 23	20 48	22 28	24 08	00 08
N 70	04 07	05 21	06 22	20 42	22 14	23 46	25 18
68	04 18	05 25	06 20	20 36	22 03	23 29	24 54
66	04 27	05 28	06 19	20 32	21 55	23 16	24 35
64	04 35	05 31	06 18	20 28	21 47	23 04	24 19
62	04 41	05 33	06 17	20 25	21 41	22 55	24 07
60	04 46	05 35	06 16	20 22	21 35	22 47	23 56
N 58	04 51	05 37	06 16	20 19	21 30	22 40	23 47
56	04 55	05 38	06 15	20 17	21 26	22 33	23 38
54	04 58	05 39	06 15	20 15	21 22	22 28	23 31
52	05 01	05 40	06 14	20 13	21 19	22 23	23 25
50	05 04	05 41	06 13	20 12	21 16	22 18	23 19
45	05 09	05 43	06 12	20 08	21 09	22 08	23 06
N 40	05 13	05 44	06 11	20 05	21 03	22 00	22 56
35	05 16	05 45	06 11	20 03	20 58	21 53	22 47
30	05 18	05 46	06 10	20 00	20 54	21 47	22 39
20	05 21	05 46	06 08	19 56	20 47	21 37	22 26
N 10	05 22	05 46	06 07	19 53	20 40	21 27	22 15
0	05 21	05 45	06 06	19 50	20 34	21 19	22 04
S 10	05 19	05 43	06 04	19 47	20 28	21 10	21 53
20	05 15	05 40	06 02	19 43	20 22	21 01	21 41
30	05 08	05 36	06 00	19 40	20 15	20 51	21 28
35	05 04	05 34	05 59	19 38	20 11	20 45	21 21
40	04 59	05 31	05 58	19 35	20 06	20 38	21 12
45	04 52	05 27	05 56	19 32	20 01	20 30	21 02
S 50	04 43	05 21	05 54	19 29	19 54	20 21	20 50
52	04 39	05 19	05 53	19 28	19 51	20 17	20 45
54	04 34	05 16	05 52	19 26	19 48	20 12	20 39
56	04 28	05 13	05 51	19 24	19 45	20 07	20 32
58	04 22	05 10	05 49	19 22	19 41	20 01	20 24
S 60	04 14	05 06	05 48	19 20	19 36	19 55	20 16

Lat.	Sunset	Twilight Civil	Twilight Naut.	Moonset 14	Moonset 15	Moonset 16	Moonset 17
°	h m	h m	h m	h m	h m	h m	h m
N 72	17 57	19 04	20 29	06 58	06 51	06 44	06 36
N 70	17 58	18 59	20 14	07 01	07 00	06 59	06 59
68	17 59	18 55	20 03	07 04	07 07	07 11	07 17
66	18 00	18 51	19 53	07 06	07 13	07 21	07 32
64	18 01	18 49	19 45	07 07	07 18	07 30	07 44
62	18 02	18 46	19 39	07 09	07 23	07 37	07 54
60	18 03	18 44	19 33	07 10	07 26	07 43	08 03
N 58	18 03	18 42	19 29	07 12	07 30	07 49	08 11
56	18 04	18 41	19 25	07 13	07 33	07 54	08 17
54	18 04	18 39	19 21	07 14	07 36	07 58	08 24
52	18 05	18 38	19 18	07 15	07 38	08 03	08 29
50	18 05	18 37	19 15	07 16	07 40	08 06	08 34
45	18 06	18 35	19 10	07 17	07 45	08 14	08 45
N 40	18 07	18 34	19 05	07 19	07 49	08 21	08 54
35	18 08	18 33	19 02	07 20	07 53	08 27	09 02
30	18 08	18 32	19 00	07 21	07 56	08 32	09 08
20	18 10	18 32	18 57	07 23	08 02	08 41	09 20
N 10	18 11	18 32	18 56	07 25	08 07	08 48	09 31
0	18 12	18 33	18 57	07 27	08 11	08 56	09 40
S 10	18 13	18 34	18 59	07 28	08 16	09 03	09 50
20	18 15	18 37	19 03	07 30	08 21	09 11	10 01
30	18 17	18 41	19 09	07 32	08 26	09 20	10 12
35	18 18	18 43	19 13	07 33	08 30	09 25	10 19
40	18 19	18 46	19 18	07 34	08 33	09 31	10 27
45	18 21	18 50	19 25	07 36	08 37	09 38	10 36
S 50	18 23	18 55	19 34	07 38	08 43	09 46	10 48
52	18 24	18 57	19 38	07 39	08 45	09 50	10 53
54	18 25	19 00	19 43	07 39	08 47	09 54	10 58
56	18 26	19 03	19 48	07 40	08 50	09 59	11 05
58	18 27	19 06	19 54	07 41	08 53	10 04	11 12
S 60	18 28	19 10	20 01	07 43	08 57	10 10	11 20

Day	SUN Eqn. of Time 00^h	SUN Eqn. of Time 12^h	SUN Mer. Pass.	MOON Mer. Pass. Upper	MOON Mer. Pass. Lower	Age	Phase
d	m s	m s	h m	h m	h m	d %	
14	09 16	09 08	12 09	01 16	13 38	16 96	
15	08 59	08 51	12 09	02 01	14 23	17 92	
16	08 42	08 34	12 09	02 45	15 07	18 86	

	UT	ARIES	VENUS −4·2		MARS +1·4		JUPITER −2·4		SATURN +0·5	
	d h	GHA ° ′	GHA ° ′	Dec ° ′	GHA ° ′	Dec ° ′	GHA ° ′	Dec ° ′	GHA ° ′	Dec ° ′
	17 00	174 45.6	169 02.5	N11 37.8	142 05.7	N13 24.0	334 51.2	S 6 42.8	267 30.2	S22 05.3
	01	189 48.0	184 06.2	37.4	157 06.5	24.7	349 53.9	42.7	282 32.6	05.3
	02	204 50.5	199 09.8	37.0	172 07.2	25.3	4 56.7	42.6	297 35.0	05.3
	03	219 53.0	214 13.5	. . 36.6	187 07.9	. . 25.9	19 59.4	. . 42.5	312 37.3	. . 05.3
	04	234 55.4	229 17.2	36.2	202 08.7	26.6	35 02.1	42.4	327 39.7	05.3
	05	249 57.9	244 20.9	35.8	217 09.4	27.2	50 04.8	42.3	342 42.1	05.3
	06	265 00.4	259 24.5	N11 35.5	232 10.1	N13 27.8	65 07.5	S 6 42.2	357 44.5	S22 05.3
	07	280 02.8	274 28.2	35.1	247 10.9	28.4	80 10.2	42.1	12 46.8	05.3
	08	295 05.3	289 31.9	34.7	262 11.6	29.1	95 12.9	42.0	27 49.2	05.3
F	09	310 07.7	304 35.6	. . 34.3	277 12.4	. . 29.7	110 15.6	. . 41.9	42 51.6	. . 05.3
R	10	325 10.2	319 39.3	33.9	292 13.1	30.3	125 18.4	41.8	57 54.0	05.3
I	11	340 12.7	334 42.9	33.5	307 13.8	30.9	140 21.1	41.7	72 56.3	05.3
D	12	355 15.1	349 46.6	N11 33.0	322 14.6	N13 31.6	155 23.8	S 6 41.5	87 58.7	S22 05.3
A	13	10 17.6	4 50.3	32.6	337 15.3	32.2	170 26.5	41.4	103 01.1	05.3
Y	14	25 20.1	19 54.0	32.2	352 16.0	32.8	185 29.2	41.3	118 03.5	05.3
	15	40 22.5	34 57.7	. . 31.8	7 16.8	. . 33.4	200 31.9	. . 41.2	133 05.9	. . 05.3
	16	55 25.0	50 01.4	31.4	22 17.5	34.1	215 34.6	41.1	148 08.2	05.3
	17	70 27.5	65 05.1	31.0	37 18.2	34.7	230 37.4	41.0	163 10.6	05.3
	18	85 29.9	80 08.8	N11 30.6	52 19.0	N13 35.3	245 40.1	S 6 40.9	178 13.0	S22 05.3
	19	100 32.4	95 12.5	30.1	67 19.7	35.9	260 42.8	40.8	193 15.4	05.3
	20	115 34.8	110 16.2	29.7	82 20.4	36.6	275 45.5	40.7	208 17.7	05.3
	21	130 37.3	125 19.9	. . 29.3	97 21.2	. . 37.2	290 48.2	. . 40.6	223 20.1	. . 05.3
	22	145 39.8	140 23.6	28.8	112 21.9	37.8	305 50.9	40.5	238 22.5	05.3
	23	160 42.2	155 27.3	28.4	127 22.7	38.4	320 53.6	40.4	253 24.9	05.3
	18 00	175 44.7	170 31.0	N11 28.0	142 23.4	N13 39.0	335 56.4	S 6 40.3	268 27.3	S22 05.3
	01	190 47.2	185 34.8	27.5	157 24.1	39.7	350 59.1	40.2	283 29.6	05.3
	02	205 49.6	200 38.5	27.1	172 24.9	40.3	6 01.8	40.1	298 32.0	05.3
	03	220 52.1	215 42.2	. . 26.6	187 25.6	. . 40.9	21 04.5	. . 40.0	313 34.4	. . 05.3
	04	235 54.6	230 45.9	26.2	202 26.3	41.5	36 07.2	39.8	328 36.8	05.3
	05	250 57.0	245 49.6	25.7	217 27.1	42.2	51 09.9	39.7	343 39.1	05.3
	06	265 59.5	260 53.4	N11 25.3	232 27.8	N13 42.8	66 12.7	S 6 39.6	358 41.5	S22 05.3
	07	281 02.0	275 57.1	24.8	247 28.5	43.4	81 15.4	39.5	13 43.9	05.3
S	08	296 04.4	291 00.8	24.4	262 29.3	44.0	96 18.1	39.4	28 46.3	05.3
A	09	311 06.9	306 04.5	. . 23.9	277 30.0	. . 44.6	111 20.8	. . 39.3	43 48.7	. . 05.2
T	10	326 09.3	321 08.3	23.4	292 30.7	45.3	126 23.5	39.2	58 51.0	05.2
U	11	341 11.8	336 12.0	23.0	307 31.5	45.9	141 26.2	39.1	73 53.4	05.2
R	12	356 14.3	351 15.7	N11 22.5	322 32.2	N13 46.5	156 29.0	S 6 39.0	88 55.8	S22 05.2
D	13	11 16.7	6 19.5	22.0	337 32.9	47.1	171 31.7	38.9	103 58.2	05.2
A	14	26 19.2	21 23.2	21.6	352 33.7	47.7	186 34.4	38.8	119 00.6	05.2
Y	15	41 21.7	36 27.0	. . 21.1	7 34.4	. . 48.4	201 37.1	. . 38.7	134 03.0	. . 05.2
	16	56 24.1	51 30.7	20.6	22 35.1	49.0	216 39.8	38.6	149 05.3	05.2
	17	71 26.6	66 34.4	20.1	37 35.9	49.6	231 42.6	38.5	164 07.7	05.2
	18	86 29.1	81 38.2	N11 19.7	52 36.6	N13 50.2	246 45.3	S 6 38.3	179 10.1	S22 05.2
	19	101 31.5	96 41.9	19.2	67 37.3	50.8	261 48.0	38.2	194 12.5	05.2
	20	116 34.0	111 45.7	18.7	82 38.1	51.4	276 50.7	38.1	209 14.9	05.2
	21	131 36.5	126 49.4	. . 18.2	97 38.8	. . 52.1	291 53.4	. . 38.0	224 17.2	. . 05.2
	22	146 38.9	141 53.2	17.7	112 39.5	52.7	306 56.2	37.9	239 19.6	05.2
	23	161 41.4	156 57.0	17.2	127 40.3	53.3	321 58.9	37.8	254 22.0	05.2
	19 00	176 43.8	172 00.7	N11 16.7	142 41.0	N13 53.9	337 01.6	S 6 37.7	269 24.4	S22 05.2
	01	191 46.3	187 04.5	16.2	157 41.7	54.5	352 04.3	37.6	284 26.8	05.2
	02	206 48.8	202 08.2	15.7	172 42.5	55.1	7 07.0	37.5	299 29.2	05.2
	03	221 51.2	217 12.0	. . 15.2	187 43.2	. . 55.8	22 09.8	. . 37.4	314 31.5	. . 05.2
	04	236 53.7	232 15.8	14.7	202 43.9	56.4	37 12.5	37.3	329 33.9	05.2
	05	251 56.2	247 19.5	14.2	217 44.7	57.0	52 15.2	37.2	344 36.3	05.2
	06	266 58.6	262 23.3	N11 13.7	232 45.4	N13 57.6	67 17.9	S 6 37.1	359 38.7	S22 05.2
	07	282 01.1	277 27.0	13.2	247 46.1	58.2	82 20.6	36.9	14 41.1	05.2
	08	297 03.6	292 30.8	12.6	262 46.9	58.8	97 23.4	36.8	29 43.5	05.2
S	09	312 06.0	307 34.6	. . 12.1	277 47.6	13 59.5	112 26.1	. . 36.7	44 45.8	. . 05.2
U	10	327 08.5	322 38.4	11.6	292 48.3	14 00.1	127 28.8	36.6	59 48.2	05.2
N	11	342 10.9	337 42.1	11.1	307 49.1	00.7	142 31.5	36.5	74 50.6	05.2
D	12	357 13.4	352 45.9	N11 10.5	322 49.8	N14 01.3	157 34.2	S 6 36.4	89 53.0	S22 05.2
A	13	12 15.9	7 49.7	10.0	337 50.5	01.9	172 37.0	36.3	104 55.4	05.2
Y	14	27 18.3	22 53.5	09.5	352 51.3	02.5	187 39.7	36.2	119 57.8	05.2
	15	42 20.8	37 57.2	. . 09.0	7 52.0	. . 03.1	202 42.4	. . 36.1	135 00.2	. . 05.2
	16	57 23.3	53 01.0	08.4	22 52.7	03.8	217 45.1	36.0	150 02.5	05.2
	17	72 25.7	68 04.8	07.9	37 53.5	04.4	232 47.9	35.9	165 04.9	05.2
	18	87 28.2	83 08.6	N11 07.3	52 54.2	N14 05.0	247 50.6	S 6 35.7	180 07.3	S22 05.2
	19	102 30.7	98 12.4	06.8	67 54.9	05.6	262 53.3	35.6	195 09.7	05.2
	20	117 33.1	113 16.2	06.3	82 55.6	06.2	277 56.0	35.5	210 12.1	05.2
	21	132 35.6	128 20.0	. . 05.7	97 56.4	. . 06.8	292 58.8	. . 35.4	225 14.5	. . 05.2
	22	147 38.1	143 23.7	05.2	112 57.1	07.4	308 01.5	35.3	240 16.9	05.2
	23	162 40.5	158 27.5	04.6	127 57.8	08.0	323 04.2	35.2	255 19.2	05.2
	Mer. Pass.	h m 12 15.0	v 3.7	d 0.5	v 0.7	d 0.6	v 2.7	d 0.1	v 2.4	d 0.0

STARS

Name	SHA ° ′	Dec ° ′
Acamar	315 16.7	S40 14.6
Achernar	335 25.5	S57 09.3
Acrux	173 05.6	S63 11.6
Adhara	255 10.4	S29 00.2
Aldebaran	290 46.6	N16 32.4
Alioth	166 18.0	N55 51.9
Alkaid	152 56.6	N49 13.6
Al Na'ir	27 41.0	S46 52.6
Alnilam	275 43.8	S 1 11.8
Alphard	217 53.3	S 8 44.2
Alphecca	126 08.7	N26 39.4
Alpheratz	357 41.2	N29 11.0
Altair	62 05.9	N 8 54.8
Ankaa	353 13.7	S42 13.0
Antares	112 23.0	S26 28.0
Arcturus	145 53.2	N19 05.5
Atria	107 22.4	S69 03.0
Avior	234 16.5	S59 34.3
Bellatrix	278 29.3	N 6 21.6
Betelgeuse	270 58.6	N 7 24.3
Canopus	263 54.9	S52 42.8
Capella	280 30.8	N46 00.8
Deneb	49 30.0	N45 20.4
Denebola	182 30.8	N14 28.5
Diphda	348 53.7	S17 53.8
Dubhe	193 48.1	N61 39.5
Elnath	278 09.5	N28 37.1
Eltanin	90 45.0	N51 29.0
Enif	33 44.9	N 9 57.1
Fomalhaut	15 21.6	S29 31.9
Gacrux	171 57.4	S57 12.5
Gienah	175 49.4	S17 38.3
Hadar	148 43.7	S60 27.1
Hamal	327 58.2	N23 32.4
Kaus Aust.	83 40.5	S34 22.3
Kochab	137 19.4	N74 05.0
Markab	13 36.1	N15 17.7
Menkar	314 12.6	N 4 09.1
Menkent	148 04.2	S36 27.1
Miaplacidus	221 38.3	S69 47.6
Mirfak	308 37.0	N49 55.2
Nunki	75 55.3	S26 16.3
Peacock	53 15.7	S56 40.5
Pollux	243 24.5	N27 58.9
Procyon	244 57.0	N 5 10.6
Rasalhague	96 04.1	N12 32.9
Regulus	207 40.6	N11 52.8
Rigel	281 09.7	S 8 11.3
Rigil Kent.	139 47.7	S60 54.1
Sabik	102 09.6	S15 44.6
Schedar	349 38.1	N56 37.8
Shaula	96 18.5	S37 06.7
Sirius	258 31.4	S16 44.8
Spica	158 28.3	S11 15.1
Suhail	222 50.2	S43 30.4
Vega	80 37.3	N38 47.9
Zuben'ubi	137 02.4	S16 06.7

	SHA ° ′	Mer. Pass. h m
Venus	354 46.3	12 35
Mars	326 38.7	14 30
Jupiter	160 11.7	1 36
Saturn	92 42.5	6 05

UT		SUN GHA	SUN Dec	MOON GHA	*v*	MOON Dec	*d*	HP
d	h	° ′	° ′	° ′	′	° ′	′	′
17	00	177 53.8	S 1 21.5	309 12.0	13.9	S11 58.4	7.6	54.4
	01	192 54.0	20.5	323 44.9	13.9	12 06.0	7.5	54.4
	02	207 54.2	19.5	338 17.8	13.8	12 13.5	7.5	54.4
	03	222 54.4	. . 18.5	352 50.6	13.9	12 21.0	7.4	54.4
	04	237 54.5	17.5	7 23.5	13.8	12 28.4	7.4	54.4
	05	252 54.7	16.6	21 56.3	13.8	12 35.8	7.3	54.4
	06	267 54.9	S 1 15.6	36 29.1	13.8	S12 43.1	7.2	54.4
	07	282 55.1	14.6	51 01.9	13.8	12 50.3	7.2	54.4
	08	297 55.3	13.6	65 34.7	13.8	12 57.5	7.1	54.3
F	09	312 55.4	. . 12.6	80 07.5	13.7	13 04.6	7.1	54.3
R	10	327 55.6	11.6	94 40.2	13.7	13 11.7	7.0	54.3
I	11	342 55.8	10.6	109 12.9	13.8	13 18.7	6.9	54.3
D	12	357 56.0	S 1 09.6	123 45.7	13.7	S13 25.6	6.9	54.3
A	13	12 56.2	08.7	138 18.4	13.6	13 32.5	6.8	54.3
Y	14	27 56.3	07.7	152 51.0	13.7	13 39.3	6.8	54.3
	15	42 56.5	. . 06.7	167 23.7	13.6	13 46.1	6.7	54.3
	16	57 56.7	05.7	181 56.3	13.7	13 52.8	6.6	54.3
	17	72 56.9	04.7	196 29.0	13.6	13 59.4	6.6	54.3
	18	87 57.1	S 1 03.7	211 01.6	13.6	S14 06.0	6.5	54.3
	19	102 57.3	02.7	225 34.2	13.5	14 12.5	6.5	54.3
	20	117 57.4	01.7	240 06.7	13.6	14 19.0	6.4	54.3
	21	132 57.6	1 00.7	254 39.3	13.5	14 25.4	6.3	54.2
	22	147 57.8	0 59.8	269 11.8	13.5	14 31.7	6.2	54.2
	23	162 58.0	58.8	283 44.3	13.5	14 37.9	6.2	54.2
18	00	177 58.2	S 0 57.8	298 16.8	13.5	S14 44.1	6.1	54.2
	01	192 58.3	56.8	312 49.3	13.4	14 50.2	6.1	54.2
	02	207 58.5	55.8	327 21.7	13.4	14 56.3	6.0	54.2
	03	222 58.7	. . 54.8	341 54.1	13.5	15 02.3	5.9	54.2
	04	237 58.9	53.8	356 26.6	13.3	15 08.2	5.9	54.2
	05	252 59.1	52.8	10 58.9	13.4	15 14.1	5.8	54.2
	06	267 59.3	S 0 51.9	25 31.3	13.3	S15 19.9	5.7	54.2
	07	282 59.4	50.9	40 03.6	13.4	15 25.6	5.6	54.2
S	08	297 59.6	49.9	54 36.0	13.2	15 31.2	5.6	54.2
A	09	312 59.8	. . 48.9	69 08.2	13.3	15 36.8	5.5	54.2
T	10	328 00.0	47.9	83 40.5	13.3	15 42.3	5.5	54.2
U	11	343 00.2	46.9	98 12.8	13.2	15 47.8	5.3	54.2
R	12	358 00.3	S 0 45.9	112 45.0	13.2	S15 53.1	5.3	54.2
D	13	13 00.5	44.9	127 17.2	13.2	15 58.4	5.3	54.2
A	14	28 00.7	43.9	141 49.4	13.1	16 03.7	5.1	54.2
Y	15	43 00.9	. . 43.0	156 21.5	13.2	16 08.8	5.1	54.2
	16	58 01.1	42.0	170 53.7	13.1	16 13.9	5.0	54.2
	17	73 01.3	41.0	185 25.8	13.1	16 18.9	5.0	54.2
	18	88 01.4	S 0 40.0	199 57.9	13.0	S16 23.9	4.8	54.2
	19	103 01.6	39.0	214 29.9	13.1	16 28.7	4.8	54.2
	20	118 01.8	38.0	229 02.0	13.0	16 33.5	4.8	54.2
	21	133 02.0	. . 37.0	243 34.0	13.0	16 38.3	4.6	54.2
	22	148 02.2	36.0	258 06.0	12.9	16 42.9	4.6	54.2
	23	163 02.4	35.1	272 37.9	13.0	16 47.5	4.5	54.2
19	00	178 02.5	S 0 34.1	287 09.9	12.9	S16 52.0	4.4	54.2
	01	193 02.7	33.1	301 41.8	12.9	16 56.4	4.4	54.2
	02	208 02.9	32.1	316 13.7	12.9	17 00.8	4.2	54.2
	03	223 03.1	. . 31.1	330 45.6	12.8	17 05.0	4.2	54.2
	04	238 03.3	30.1	345 17.4	12.8	17 09.2	4.2	54.2
	05	253 03.5	29.1	359 49.2	12.8	17 13.4	4.0	54.2
	06	268 03.6	S 0 28.1	14 21.0	12.8	S17 17.4	4.0	54.2
	07	283 03.8	27.1	28 52.8	12.7	17 21.4	3.9	54.2
	08	298 04.0	26.2	43 24.5	12.7	17 25.3	3.8	54.2
S	09	313 04.2	. . 25.2	57 56.2	12.7	17 29.1	3.7	54.2
U	10	328 04.4	24.2	72 27.9	12.7	17 32.8	3.6	54.2
N	11	343 04.6	23.2	86 59.6	12.7	17 36.4	3.6	54.2
D	12	358 04.7	S 0 22.2	101 31.3	12.6	S17 40.0	3.5	54.2
A	13	13 04.9	21.2	116 02.9	12.6	17 43.5	3.4	54.2
Y	14	28 05.1	20.2	130 34.5	12.5	17 46.9	3.4	54.3
	15	43 05.3	. . 19.2	145 06.0	12.6	17 50.3	3.2	54.3
	16	58 05.5	18.3	159 37.6	12.5	17 53.5	3.2	54.3
	17	73 05.7	17.3	174 09.1	12.5	17 56.7	3.1	54.3
	18	88 05.8	S 0 16.3	188 40.6	12.4	S17 59.8	3.0	54.3
	19	103 06.0	15.3	203 12.0	12.5	18 02.8	2.9	54.3
	20	118 06.2	14.3	217 43.5	12.4	18 05.7	2.9	54.3
	21	133 06.4	. . 13.3	232 14.9	12.4	18 08.6	2.7	54.3
	22	148 06.6	12.3	246 46.3	12.4	18 11.3	2.7	54.3
	23	163 06.8	11.3	261 17.7	12.3	S18 14.0	2.6	54.3
		SD 16.1	*d* 1.0	SD	14.8	14.8		14.8

Lat.	Twilight Naut.	Twilight Civil	Sunrise	Moonrise 17	Moonrise 18	Moonrise 19	Moonrise 20
°	h m	h m	h m	h m	h m	h m	h m
N 72	03 34	05 00	06 08	00 08	01 53	03 49	▬
N 70	03 51	05 07	06 08	25 18	01 18	02 49	04 13
68	04 04	05 12	06 08	24 54	00 54	02 14	03 27
66	04 14	05 17	06 08	24 35	00 35	01 50	02 57
64	04 23	05 20	06 08	24 19	00 19	01 30	02 35
62	04 30	05 23	06 07	24 07	00 07	01 15	02 17
60	04 36	05 26	06 07	23 56	25 02	01 02	02 02
N 58	04 42	05 28	06 07	23 47	24 50	00 50	01 49
56	04 46	05 30	06 07	23 38	24 41	00 41	01 38
54	04 50	05 32	06 07	23 31	24 32	00 32	01 29
52	04 54	05 33	06 07	23 25	24 24	00 24	01 20
50	04 57	05 35	06 07	23 19	24 17	00 17	01 13
45	05 03	05 38	06 07	23 06	24 03	00 03	00 56
N 40	05 08	05 40	06 07	22 56	23 50	24 43	00 43
35	05 12	05 41	06 06	22 47	23 40	24 32	00 32
30	05 15	05 42	06 06	22 39	23 31	24 22	00 22
20	05 18	05 44	06 06	22 26	23 16	24 05	00 05
N 10	05 20	05 44	06 05	22 15	23 02	23 50	24 39
0	05 20	05 44	06 05	22 04	22 50	23 36	24 24
S 10	05 19	05 43	06 04	21 53	22 37	23 23	24 10
20	05 16	05 41	06 03	21 41	22 24	23 08	23 55
30	05 10	05 38	06 02	21 28	22 08	22 51	23 37
35	05 07	05 36	06 02	21 21	22 00	22 41	23 27
40	05 02	05 34	06 01	21 12	21 49	22 30	23 15
45	04 56	05 31	06 00	21 02	21 38	22 17	23 02
S 50	04 48	05 26	05 59	20 50	21 23	22 01	22 45
52	04 44	05 24	05 58	20 45	21 17	21 54	22 37
54	04 40	05 22	05 58	20 39	21 10	21 46	22 29
56	04 35	05 20	05 57	20 32	21 01	21 36	22 19
58	04 29	05 17	05 56	20 24	20 52	21 26	22 08
S 60	04 23	05 14	05 55	20 16	20 42	21 14	21 55

Lat.	Sunset	Twilight Civil	Twilight Naut.	Moonset 17	Moonset 18	Moonset 19	Moonset 20
°	h m	h m	h m	h m	h m	h m	h m
N 72	18 11	19 19	20 47	06 36	06 25	06 05	▬
N 70	18 10	19 12	20 29	06 59	07 01	07 06	07 19
68	18 10	19 06	20 15	07 17	07 26	07 41	08 05
66	18 10	19 01	20 04	07 32	07 46	08 06	08 35
64	18 10	18 58	19 55	07 44	08 02	08 26	08 58
62	18 10	18 54	19 48	07 54	08 15	08 42	09 16
60	18 10	18 52	19 41	08 03	08 26	08 55	09 31
N 58	18 10	18 49	19 36	08 11	08 36	09 06	09 44
56	18 10	18 47	19 31	08 17	08 44	09 17	09 55
54	18 10	18 45	19 27	08 24	08 52	09 25	10 05
52	18 10	18 44	19 23	08 29	08 59	09 33	10 13
50	18 10	18 42	19 20	08 34	09 05	09 40	10 21
45	18 10	18 39	19 14	08 45	09 18	09 56	10 38
N 40	18 10	18 37	19 09	08 54	09 29	10 08	10 51
35	18 10	18 35	19 05	09 02	09 39	10 19	11 03
30	18 10	18 34	19 02	09 08	09 47	10 28	11 13
20	18 10	18 32	18 58	09 20	10 01	10 45	11 30
N 10	18 11	18 32	18 56	09 31	10 14	10 59	11 45
0	18 11	18 32	18 56	09 40	10 26	11 12	11 59
S 10	18 12	18 33	18 57	09 50	10 37	11 25	12 14
20	18 12	18 34	19 00	10 01	10 50	11 39	12 29
30	18 13	18 37	19 05	10 12	11 04	11 56	12 46
35	18 14	18 39	19 09	10 19	11 13	12 05	12 56
40	18 14	18 41	19 13	10 27	11 22	12 16	13 07
45	18 15	18 45	19 19	10 36	11 34	12 29	13 21
S 50	18 16	18 48	19 27	10 48	11 47	12 44	13 38
52	18 17	18 50	19 30	10 53	11 54	12 51	13 45
54	18 17	18 53	19 35	10 58	12 01	12 59	13 54
56	18 18	18 55	19 39	11 05	12 08	13 08	14 04
58	18 18	18 58	19 45	11 12	12 17	13 19	14 15
S 60	18 19	19 01	19 51	11 20	12 27	13 31	14 28

Day	SUN Eqn. of Time 00^h	SUN Eqn. of Time 12^h	SUN Mer. Pass.	MOON Mer. Pass. Upper	MOON Mer. Pass. Lower	MOON Age	MOON Phase
d	m s	m s	h m	h m	h m	d %	
17	08 25	08 16	12 08	03 30	15 52	19 78	
18	08 08	07 59	12 08	04 15	16 38	20 70	◑
19	07 50	07 41	12 08	05 01	17 24	21 61	

Day	UT (d h)	ARIES GHA	VENUS −4·2 GHA	VENUS Dec	MARS +1·4 GHA	MARS Dec	JUPITER −2·4 GHA	JUPITER Dec	SATURN +0·5 GHA	SATURN Dec
		° ′	° ′	° ′	° ′	° ′	° ′	° ′	° ′	° ′
MONDAY	20 00	177 43.0	173 31.3	N11 04.0	142 58.6	N14 08.7	338 06.9	S 6 35.1	270 21.6	S22 05.2
	01	192 45.4	188 35.1	03.5	157 59.3	09.3	353 09.7	35.0	285 24.0	05.2
	02	207 47.9	203 38.9	02.9	173 00.0	09.9	8 12.4	34.9	300 26.4	05.2
	03	222 50.4	218 42.7	02.4	188 00.8	10.5	23 15.1	34.8	315 28.8	05.2
	04	237 52.8	233 46.5	01.8	203 01.5	11.1	38 17.8	34.7	330 31.2	05.2
	05	252 55.3	248 50.3	01.2	218 02.2	11.7	53 20.6	34.5	345 33.6	05.2
	06	267 57.8	263 54.1	N11 00.7	233 03.0	N14 12.3	68 23.3	S 6 34.4	0 36.0	S22 05.2
	07	283 00.2	278 57.9	11 00.1	248 03.7	12.9	83 26.0	34.3	15 38.4	05.2
	08	298 02.7	294 01.7	10 59.5	263 04.4	13.5	98 28.7	34.2	30 40.7	05.2
	09	313 05.2	309 05.5	59.0	278 05.1	14.1	113 31.5	34.1	45 43.1	05.2
	10	328 07.6	324 09.3	58.4	293 05.9	14.8	128 34.2	34.0	60 45.5	05.2
	11	343 10.1	339 13.1	57.8	308 06.6	15.4	143 36.9	33.9	75 47.9	05.2
	12	358 12.6	354 16.9	N10 57.2	323 07.3	N14 16.0	158 39.6	S 6 33.8	90 50.3	S22 05.2
	13	13 15.0	9 20.7	56.6	338 08.1	16.6	173 42.4	33.7	105 52.7	05.2
	14	28 17.5	24 24.5	56.0	353 08.8	17.2	188 45.1	33.6	120 55.1	05.2
	15	43 19.9	39 28.3	55.5	8 09.5	17.8	203 47.8	33.4	135 57.5	05.2
	16	58 22.4	54 32.2	54.9	23 10.3	18.4	218 50.5	33.3	150 59.9	05.2
	17	73 24.9	69 36.0	54.3	38 11.0	19.0	233 53.3	33.2	166 02.2	05.2
	18	88 27.3	84 39.8	N10 53.7	53 11.7	N14 19.6	248 56.0	S 6 33.1	181 04.6	S22 05.2
	19	103 29.8	99 43.6	53.1	68 12.4	20.2	263 58.7	33.0	196 07.0	05.2
	20	118 32.3	114 47.4	52.5	83 13.2	20.8	279 01.4	32.9	211 09.4	05.2
	21	133 34.7	129 51.2	51.9	98 13.9	21.4	294 04.2	32.8	226 11.8	05.2
	22	148 37.2	144 55.0	51.3	113 14.6	22.0	309 06.9	32.7	241 14.2	05.2
	23	163 39.7	159 58.9	50.7	128 15.4	22.6	324 09.6	32.6	256 16.6	05.2
TUESDAY	21 00	178 42.1	175 02.7	N10 50.0	143 16.1	N14 23.3	339 12.4	S 6 32.4	271 19.0	S22 05.2
	01	193 44.6	190 06.5	49.4	158 16.8	23.9	354 15.1	32.3	286 21.4	05.2
	02	208 47.0	205 10.3	48.8	173 17.5	24.5	9 17.8	32.2	301 23.8	05.2
	03	223 49.5	220 14.1	48.2	188 18.3	25.1	24 20.5	32.1	316 26.2	05.2
	04	238 52.0	235 18.0	47.6	203 19.0	25.7	39 23.3	32.0	331 28.6	05.2
	05	253 54.4	250 21.8	47.0	218 19.7	26.3	54 26.0	31.9	346 30.9	05.2
	06	268 56.9	265 25.6	N10 46.3	233 20.5	N14 26.9	69 28.7	S 6 31.8	1 33.3	S22 05.1
	07	283 59.4	280 29.4	45.7	248 21.2	27.5	84 31.5	31.7	16 35.7	05.1
	08	299 01.8	295 33.3	45.1	263 21.9	28.1	99 34.2	31.6	31 38.1	05.1
	09	314 04.3	310 37.1	44.5	278 22.6	28.7	114 36.9	31.4	46 40.5	05.1
	10	329 06.8	325 40.9	43.8	293 23.4	29.3	129 39.6	31.3	61 42.9	05.1
	11	344 09.2	340 44.7	43.2	308 24.1	29.9	144 42.4	31.2	76 45.3	05.1
	12	359 11.7	355 48.6	N10 42.6	323 24.8	N14 30.5	159 45.1	S 6 31.1	91 47.7	S22 05.1
	13	14 14.2	10 52.4	41.9	338 25.6	31.1	174 47.8	31.0	106 50.1	05.1
	14	29 16.6	25 56.2	41.3	353 26.3	31.7	189 50.6	30.9	121 52.5	05.1
	15	44 19.1	41 00.1	40.7	8 27.0	32.3	204 53.3	30.8	136 54.9	05.1
	16	59 21.5	56 03.9	40.0	23 27.7	32.9	219 56.0	30.7	151 57.3	05.1
	17	74 24.0	71 07.7	39.4	38 28.5	33.5	234 58.8	30.6	166 59.7	05.1
	18	89 26.5	86 11.5	N10 38.7	53 29.2	N14 34.1	250 01.5	S 6 30.4	182 02.1	S22 05.1
	19	104 28.9	101 15.4	38.1	68 29.9	34.7	265 04.2	30.3	197 04.5	05.1
	20	119 31.4	116 19.2	37.4	83 30.6	35.3	280 06.9	30.2	212 06.9	05.1
	21	134 33.9	131 23.1	36.8	98 31.4	35.9	295 09.7	30.1	227 09.2	05.1
	22	149 36.3	146 26.9	36.1	113 32.1	36.5	310 12.4	30.0	242 11.6	05.1
	23	164 38.8	161 30.7	35.4	128 32.8	37.1	325 15.1	29.9	257 14.0	05.1
WEDNESDAY	22 00	179 41.3	176 34.6	N10 34.8	143 33.6	N14 37.7	340 17.9	S 6 29.8	272 16.4	S22 05.1
	01	194 43.7	191 38.4	34.1	158 34.3	38.3	355 20.6	29.7	287 18.8	05.1
	02	209 46.2	206 42.2	33.5	173 35.0	38.9	10 23.3	29.5	302 21.2	05.1
	03	224 48.7	221 46.1	32.8	188 35.7	39.5	25 26.1	29.4	317 23.6	05.1
	04	239 51.1	236 49.9	32.1	203 36.5	40.1	40 28.8	29.3	332 26.0	05.1
	05	254 53.6	251 53.7	31.5	218 37.2	40.7	55 31.5	29.2	347 28.4	05.1
	06	269 56.0	266 57.6	N10 30.8	233 37.9	N14 41.3	70 34.3	S 6 29.1	2 30.8	S22 05.1
	07	284 58.5	282 01.4	30.1	248 38.6	41.9	85 37.0	29.0	17 33.2	05.1
	08	300 01.0	297 05.3	29.4	263 39.4	42.5	100 39.7	28.9	32 35.6	05.1
	09	315 03.4	312 09.1	28.7	278 40.1	43.1	115 42.5	28.8	47 38.0	05.1
	10	330 05.9	327 12.9	28.1	293 40.8	43.7	130 45.2	28.6	62 40.4	05.1
	11	345 08.4	342 16.8	27.4	308 41.5	44.3	145 47.9	28.5	77 42.8	05.1
	12	0 10.8	357 20.6	N10 26.7	323 42.3	N14 44.9	160 50.7	S 6 28.4	92 45.2	S22 05.1
	13	15 13.3	12 24.5	26.0	338 43.0	45.5	175 53.4	28.3	107 47.6	05.1
	14	30 15.8	27 28.3	25.3	353 43.7	46.1	190 56.1	28.2	122 50.0	05.1
	15	45 18.2	42 32.2	24.6	8 44.4	46.7	205 58.9	28.1	137 52.4	05.1
	16	60 20.7	57 36.0	23.9	23 45.2	47.3	221 01.6	28.0	152 54.8	05.1
	17	75 23.1	72 39.8	23.2	38 45.9	47.9	236 04.3	27.9	167 57.2	05.1
	18	90 25.6	87 43.7	N10 22.6	53 46.6	N14 48.5	251 07.1	S 6 27.7	182 59.6	S22 05.1
	19	105 28.1	102 47.5	21.9	68 47.3	49.1	266 09.8	27.6	198 02.0	05.1
	20	120 30.5	117 51.4	21.2	83 48.1	49.7	281 12.5	27.5	213 04.4	05.1
	21	135 33.0	132 55.2	20.5	98 48.8	50.3	296 15.3	27.4	228 06.8	05.1
	22	150 35.5	147 59.1	19.7	113 49.5	50.8	311 18.0	27.3	243 09.2	05.1
	23	165 37.9	163 02.9	19.0	128 50.2	51.4	326 20.7	27.2	258 11.6	05.1
	Mer. Pass.	h m 12 03.2	v 3.8	d 0.6	v 0.7	d 0.6	v 2.7	d 0.1	v 2.4	d 0.0

STARS

Name	SHA	Dec
	° ′	° ′
Acamar	315 16.8	S40 14.6
Achernar	335 25.5	S57 09.3
Acrux	173 05.6	S63 11.6
Adhara	255 10.4	S29 00.2
Aldebaran	290 46.6	N16 32.4
Alioth	166 18.0	N55 51.9
Alkaid	152 56.5	N49 13.6
Al Na'ir	27 41.0	S46 52.6
Alnilam	275 43.8	S 1 11.8
Alphard	217 53.4	S 8 44.2
Alphecca	126 08.7	N26 39.4
Alpheratz	357 41.2	N29 11.0
Altair	62 05.9	N 8 54.8
Ankaa	353 13.7	S42 12.9
Antares	112 23.0	S26 28.0
Arcturus	145 53.2	N19 05.5
Atria	107 22.4	S69 03.0
Avior	234 16.6	S59 34.3
Bellatrix	278 29.3	N 6 21.6
Betelgeuse	270 58.6	N 7 24.3
Canopus	263 55.0	S52 42.8
Capella	280 30.8	N46 00.8
Deneb	49 30.0	N45 20.3
Denebola	182 30.8	N14 28.5
Diphda	348 53.7	S17 53.8
Dubhe	193 48.1	N61 39.5
Elnath	278 09.5	N28 37.1
Eltanin	90 45.0	N51 29.0
Enif	33 44.9	N 9 57.1
Fomalhaut	15 21.6	S29 31.9
Gacrux	171 57.4	S57 12.5
Gienah	175 49.3	S17 38.3
Hadar	148 43.6	S60 27.1
Hamal	327 58.2	N23 32.4
Kaus Aust.	83 40.5	S34 22.3
Kochab	137 19.4	N74 05.0
Markab	13 36.1	N15 17.7
Menkar	314 12.6	N 4 09.1
Menkent	148 04.2	S36 27.1
Miaplacidus	221 38.4	S69 47.6
Mirfak	308 37.0	N49 55.2
Nunki	75 55.3	S26 16.3
Peacock	53 15.7	S56 40.5
Pollux	243 24.5	N27 58.9
Procyon	244 57.0	N 5 10.6
Rasalhague	96 04.1	N12 32.9
Regulus	207 40.6	N11 52.8
Rigel	281 09.7	S 8 11.3
Rigil Kent.	139 47.7	S60 54.1
Sabik	102 09.6	S15 44.6
Schedar	349 38.1	N56 37.8
Shaula	96 18.4	S37 06.7
Sirius	258 31.4	S16 44.8
Spica	158 28.3	S11 15.1
Suhail	222 50.2	S43 30.5
Vega	80 37.3	N38 47.9
Zuben'ubi	137 02.4	S16 06.7

	SHA	Mer. Pass.
	° ′	h m
Venus	356 20.6	12 17
Mars	324 34.0	14 26
Jupiter	160 30.2	1 23
Saturn	92 36.9	5 54

	UT	SUN GHA	SUN Dec	MOON GHA	v	MOON Dec	d	HP
	d h	° ′	° ′	° ′	′	° ′	′	′
	20 00	178 07.0	S 0 10.3	275 49.0	12.3	S18 16.6	2.5	54.3
	01	193 07.1	09.4	290 20.3	12.3	18 19.1	2.5	54.3
	02	208 07.3	08.4	304 51.6	12.3	18 21.6	2.3	54.3
	03	223 07.5	. . 07.4	319 22.9	12.2	18 23.9	2.3	54.4
	04	238 07.7	06.4	333 54.1	12.2	18 26.2	2.2	54.4
	05	253 07.9	05.4	348 25.3	12.2	18 28.4	2.1	54.4
	06	268 08.1	S 0 04.4	2 56.5	12.2	S18 30.5	2.0	54.4
	07	283 08.2	03.4	17 27.7	12.1	18 32.5	1.9	54.4
	08	298 08.4	02.4	31 58.8	12.2	18 34.4	1.9	54.4
M	09	313 08.6	. . 01.5	46 30.0	12.1	18 36.3	1.7	54.4
O	10	328 08.8	S 00.5	61 01.1	12.0	18 38.0	1.7	54.4
N	11	343 09.0	N 00.5	75 32.1	12.1	18 39.7	1.6	54.4
D	12	358 09.2	N 0 01.5	90 03.2	12.0	S18 41.3	1.5	54.5
A	13	13 09.4	02.5	104 34.2	12.0	18 42.8	1.4	54.5
Y	14	28 09.5	03.5	119 05.2	12.0	18 44.2	1.3	54.5
	15	43 09.7	. . 04.5	133 36.2	11.9	18 45.5	1.2	54.5
	16	58 09.9	05.5	148 07.1	11.9	18 46.7	1.2	54.5
	17	73 10.1	06.4	162 38.0	11.9	18 47.9	1.0	54.5
	18	88 10.3	N 0 07.4	177 08.9	11.9	S18 48.9	1.0	54.5
	19	103 10.5	08.4	191 39.8	11.9	18 49.9	0.9	54.6
	20	118 10.7	09.4	206 10.7	11.8	18 50.8	0.8	54.6
	21	133 10.8	. . 10.4	220 41.5	11.8	18 51.6	0.7	54.6
	22	148 11.0	11.4	235 12.3	11.8	18 52.3	0.6	54.6
	23	163 11.2	12.4	249 43.1	11.8	18 52.9	0.6	54.6
	21 00	178 11.4	N 0 13.4	264 13.9	11.7	S18 53.5	0.4	54.6
	01	193 11.6	14.3	278 44.6	11.8	18 53.9	0.3	54.6
	02	208 11.8	15.3	293 15.4	11.7	18 54.2	0.3	54.7
	03	223 12.0	. . 16.3	307 46.1	11.6	18 54.5	0.2	54.7
	04	238 12.1	17.3	322 16.7	11.7	18 54.7	0.1	54.7
	05	253 12.3	18.3	336 47.4	11.6	18 54.8	0.1	54.7
	06	268 12.5	N 0 19.3	351 18.0	11.6	S18 54.7	0.1	54.7
	07	283 12.7	20.3	5 48.6	11.6	18 54.6	0.1	54.8
T	08	298 12.9	21.3	20 19.2	11.6	18 54.5	0.3	54.8
U	09	313 13.1	. . 22.2	34 49.8	11.6	18 54.2	0.4	54.8
E	10	328 13.3	23.2	49 20.4	11.5	18 53.8	0.5	54.8
S	11	343 13.4	24.2	63 50.9	11.5	18 53.3	0.5	54.8
D	12	358 13.6	N 0 25.2	78 21.4	11.5	S18 52.8	0.7	54.8
	13	13 13.8	26.2	92 51.9	11.5	18 52.1	0.7	54.9
A	14	28 14.0	27.2	107 22.4	11.4	18 51.4	0.8	54.9
Y	15	43 14.2	. . 28.2	121 52.8	11.4	18 50.6	0.9	54.9
	16	58 14.4	29.2	136 23.2	11.5	18 49.7	1.1	54.9
	17	73 14.6	30.1	150 53.7	11.4	18 48.6	1.1	54.9
	18	88 14.7	N 0 31.1	165 24.1	11.3	S18 47.5	1.2	55.0
	19	103 14.9	32.1	179 54.4	11.4	18 46.3	1.3	55.0
	20	118 15.1	33.1	194 24.8	11.3	18 45.0	1.3	55.0
	21	133 15.3	. . 34.1	208 55.1	11.3	18 43.7	1.5	55.0
	22	148 15.5	35.1	223 25.4	11.3	18 42.2	1.6	55.1
	23	163 15.7	36.1	237 55.7	11.3	18 40.6	1.6	55.1
	22 00	178 15.9	N 0 37.1	252 26.0	11.3	S18 39.0	1.8	55.1
	01	193 16.1	38.0	266 56.3	11.2	18 37.2	1.8	55.1
	02	208 16.2	39.0	281 26.5	11.3	18 35.4	2.0	55.1
	03	223 16.4	. . 40.0	295 56.8	11.2	18 33.4	2.0	55.2
	04	238 16.6	41.0	310 27.0	11.2	18 31.4	2.1	55.2
	05	253 16.8	42.0	324 57.2	11.2	18 29.3	2.3	55.2
	06	268 17.0	N 0 43.0	339 27.4	11.1	S18 27.0	2.3	55.2
W	07	283 17.2	44.0	353 57.5	11.2	18 24.7	2.4	55.3
E	08	298 17.4	44.9	8 27.7	11.1	18 22.3	2.5	55.3
D	09	313 17.5	. . 45.9	22 57.8	11.1	18 19.8	2.6	55.3
N	10	328 17.7	46.9	37 27.9	11.2	18 17.2	2.7	55.3
	11	343 17.9	47.9	51 58.1	11.0	18 14.5	2.7	55.4
E	12	358 18.1	N 0 48.9	66 28.1	11.1	S18 11.8	2.9	55.4
S	13	13 18.3	49.9	80 58.2	11.1	18 08.9	3.0	55.4
D	14	28 18.5	50.9	95 28.3	11.0	18 05.9	3.0	55.5
A	15	43 18.7	. . 51.8	109 58.3	11.1	18 02.9	3.2	55.5
Y	16	58 18.9	52.8	124 28.4	11.0	17 59.7	3.2	55.5
	17	73 19.0	53.8	138 58.4	11.0	17 56.5	3.4	55.5
	18	88 19.2	N 0 54.8	153 28.4	11.0	S17 53.1	3.4	55.6
	19	103 19.4	55.8	167 58.4	10.9	17 49.7	3.5	55.6
	20	118 19.6	56.8	182 28.3	11.0	17 46.2	3.6	55.6
	21	133 19.8	. . 57.8	196 58.3	11.0	17 42.6	3.8	55.6
	22	148 20.0	58.7	211 28.3	10.9	17 38.8	3.8	55.7
	23	163 20.2	59.7	225 58.2	10.9	S17 35.0	3.9	55.7
		SD 16.1	*d* 1.0	SD	14.8	14.9		15.1

Lat.	Twilight Naut.	Twilight Civil	Sunrise	Moonrise 20	21	22	23
°	h m	h m	h m	h m	h m	h m	h m
N 72	03 13	04 44	05 52	■	■	■	06 59
N 70	03 34	04 52	05 54	04 13	05 18	05 51	06 03
68	03 49	04 59	05 55	03 27	04 26	05 06	05 30
66	04 01	05 05	05 56	02 57	03 53	04 36	05 06
64	04 11	05 09	05 57	02 35	03 30	04 13	04 47
62	04 20	05 13	05 58	02 17	03 11	03 56	04 31
60	04 27	05 17	05 58	02 02	02 55	03 41	04 18
N 58	04 33	05 20	05 59	01 49	02 42	03 28	04 06
56	04 38	05 22	05 59	01 38	02 31	03 17	03 57
54	04 43	05 24	06 00	01 29	02 21	03 07	03 48
52	04 47	05 26	06 00	01 20	02 12	02 59	03 40
50	04 50	05 28	06 00	01 13	02 04	02 51	03 33
45	04 58	05 32	06 01	00 56	01 47	02 35	03 18
N 40	05 03	05 35	06 02	00 43	01 33	02 21	03 06
35	05 07	05 37	06 02	00 32	01 22	02 10	02 55
30	05 11	05 39	06 03	00 22	01 11	02 00	02 46
20	05 16	05 41	06 03	00 05	00 54	01 42	02 30
N 10	05 18	05 43	06 04	24 39	00 39	01 27	02 16
0	05 19	05 43	06 04	24 24	00 24	01 13	02 03
S 10	05 19	05 43	06 04	24 10	00 10	00 59	01 50
20	05 17	05 42	06 04	23 55	24 44	00 44	01 36
30	05 12	05 40	06 04	23 37	24 27	00 27	01 20
35	05 09	05 39	06 04	23 27	24 17	00 17	01 10
40	05 05	05 37	06 04	23 15	24 05	00 05	01 00
45	05 00	05 34	06 04	23 02	23 52	24 47	00 47
S 50	04 53	05 31	06 04	22 45	23 35	24 32	00 32
52	04 50	05 30	06 03	22 37	23 27	24 25	00 25
54	04 46	05 28	06 03	22 29	23 19	24 17	00 17
56	04 42	05 26	06 03	22 19	23 09	24 08	00 08
58	04 37	05 24	06 03	22 08	22 58	23 58	25 05
S 60	04 31	05 21	06 03	21 55	22 45	23 46	24 55

Lat.	Sunset	Twilight Civil	Twilight Naut.	Moonset 20	21	22	23
°	h m	h m	h m	h m	h m	h m	h m
N 72	18 24	19 33	21 06	■	■	■	09 40
N 70	18 23	19 24	20 45	07 19	07 54	09 03	10 34
68	18 21	19 17	20 29	08 05	08 46	09 48	11 07
66	18 20	19 12	20 16	08 35	09 19	10 18	11 31
64	18 19	19 07	20 05	08 58	09 42	10 40	11 49
62	18 18	19 03	19 57	09 16	10 01	10 58	12 05
60	18 17	18 59	19 49	09 31	10 17	11 12	12 17
N 58	18 17	18 56	19 43	09 44	10 30	11 25	12 28
56	18 16	18 53	19 38	09 55	10 41	11 36	12 38
54	18 16	18 51	19 33	10 05	10 51	11 45	12 46
52	18 15	18 49	19 29	10 13	11 00	11 54	12 54
50	18 15	18 47	19 25	10 21	11 08	12 01	13 01
45	18 14	18 43	19 18	10 38	11 25	12 17	13 15
N 40	18 13	18 40	19 12	10 51	11 39	12 31	13 27
35	18 13	18 38	19 07	11 03	11 50	12 42	13 37
30	18 12	18 36	19 04	11 13	12 01	12 52	13 46
20	18 11	18 33	18 59	11 30	12 18	13 09	14 01
N 10	18 11	18 32	18 56	11 45	12 33	13 23	14 14
0	18 10	18 31	18 55	11 59	12 48	13 37	14 27
S 10	18 10	18 31	18 55	12 14	13 02	13 51	14 39
20	18 10	18 32	18 57	12 29	13 17	14 05	14 52
30	18 10	18 34	19 01	12 46	13 35	14 22	15 07
35	18 10	18 35	19 04	12 56	13 45	14 31	15 16
40	18 10	18 37	19 08	13 07	13 56	14 42	15 25
45	18 10	18 39	19 13	13 21	14 10	14 55	15 37
S 50	18 10	18 42	19 20	13 38	14 27	15 11	15 51
52	18 10	18 43	19 23	13 45	14 35	15 18	15 57
54	18 10	18 45	19 27	13 54	14 43	15 27	16 04
56	18 10	18 47	19 31	14 04	14 53	15 36	16 12
58	18 10	18 49	19 36	14 15	15 04	15 46	16 21
S 60	18 10	18 52	19 41	14 28	15 17	15 58	16 31

Day	SUN Eqn. of Time 00^h	SUN Eqn. of Time 12^h	SUN Mer. Pass.	MOON Mer. Pass. Upper	MOON Mer. Pass. Lower	MOON Age	MOON Phase
d	m s	m s	h m	h m	h m	d	%
20	07 33	07 24	12 07	05 48	18 12	22	52
21	07 15	07 06	12 07	06 36	19 00	23	42
22	06 57	06 48	12 07	07 25	19 50	24	33

UT		ARIES	VENUS −4·2		MARS +1·4		JUPITER −2·4		SATURN +0·4	
		GHA	GHA	Dec	GHA	Dec	GHA	Dec	GHA	Dec
d h		° ′	° ′	° ′	° ′	° ′	° ′	° ′	° ′	° ′
23 00		180 40.4	178 06.7	N10 18.3	143 51.0	N14 52.0	341 23.5	S 6 27.1	273 14.0	S22 05.1
01		195 42.9	193 10.6	17.6	158 51.7	52.6	356 26.2	27.0	288 16.4	05.1
02		210 45.3	208 14.4	16.9	173 52.4	53.2	11 28.9	26.8	303 18.8	05.1
03		225 47.8	223 18.3	. . 16.2	188 53.1	. . 53.8	26 31.7	. . 26.7	318 21.2	. . 05.1
04		240 50.3	238 22.1	15.5	203 53.9	54.4	41 34.4	26.6	333 23.6	05.1
05		255 52.7	253 26.0	14.8	218 54.6	55.0	56 37.2	26.5	348 26.0	05.1
06		270 55.2	268 29.8	N10 14.1	233 55.3	N14 55.6	71 39.9	S 6 26.4	3 28.4	S22 05.1
07		285 57.6	283 33.7	13.3	248 56.0	56.2	86 42.6	26.3	18 30.8	05.1
08	T	301 00.1	298 37.5	12.6	263 56.8	56.8	101 45.4	26.2	33 33.2	05.1
09	H	316 02.6	313 41.3	. . 11.9	278 57.5	. . 57.4	116 48.1	. . 26.0	48 35.6	. . 05.1
10	U	331 05.0	328 45.2	11.2	293 58.2	58.0	131 50.8	25.9	63 38.0	05.1
11	R	346 07.5	343 49.0	10.4	308 58.9	58.6	146 53.6	25.8	78 40.4	05.1
12	S	1 10.0	358 52.9	N10 09.7	323 59.7	N14 59.1	161 56.3	S 6 25.7	93 42.8	S22 05.1
13	D	16 12.4	13 56.7	09.0	339 00.4	14 59.7	176 59.0	25.6	108 45.2	05.1
14	A	31 14.9	29 00.6	08.2	354 01.1	15 00.3	192 01.8	25.5	123 47.6	05.1
15	Y	46 17.4	44 04.4	. . 07.5	9 01.8	. . 00.9	207 04.5	. . 25.4	138 50.0	. . 05.1
16		61 19.8	59 08.3	06.8	24 02.5	01.5	222 07.3	25.2	153 52.4	05.1
17		76 22.3	74 12.1	06.0	39 03.3	02.1	237 10.0	25.1	168 54.8	05.1
18		91 24.8	89 15.9	N10 05.3	54 04.0	N15 02.7	252 12.7	S 6 25.0	183 57.2	S22 05.0
19		106 27.2	104 19.8	04.5	69 04.7	03.3	267 15.5	24.9	198 59.6	05.0
20		121 29.7	119 23.6	03.8	84 05.4	03.9	282 18.2	24.8	214 02.0	05.0
21		136 32.1	134 27.5	. . 03.1	99 06.2	. . 04.5	297 20.9	. . 24.7	229 04.4	. . 05.0
22		151 34.6	149 31.3	02.3	114 06.9	05.0	312 23.7	24.6	244 06.9	05.0
23		166 37.1	164 35.2	01.6	129 07.6	05.6	327 26.4	24.4	259 09.3	05.0
24 00		181 39.5	179 39.0	N10 00.8	144 08.3	N15 06.2	342 29.2	S 6 24.3	274 11.7	S22 05.0
01		196 42.0	194 42.9	10 00.1	159 09.1	06.8	357 31.9	24.2	289 14.1	05.0
02		211 44.5	209 46.7	9 59.3	174 09.8	07.4	12 34.6	24.1	304 16.5	05.0
03		226 46.9	224 50.5	. . 58.5	189 10.5	. . 08.0	27 37.4	. . 24.0	319 18.9	. . 05.0
04		241 49.4	239 54.4	57.8	204 11.2	08.6	42 40.1	23.9	334 21.3	05.0
05		256 51.9	254 58.2	57.0	219 11.9	09.2	57 42.9	23.8	349 23.7	05.0
06		271 54.3	270 02.1	N 9 56.3	234 12.7	N15 09.7	72 45.6	S 6 23.6	4 26.1	S22 05.0
07		286 56.8	285 05.9	55.5	249 13.4	10.3	87 48.3	23.5	19 28.5	05.0
08		301 59.2	300 09.7	54.7	264 14.1	10.9	102 51.1	23.4	34 30.9	05.0
09	F	317 01.7	315 13.6	. . 54.0	279 14.8	. . 11.5	117 53.8	. . 23.3	49 33.3	. . 05.0
10	R	332 04.2	330 17.4	53.2	294 15.5	12.1	132 56.6	23.2	64 35.7	05.0
11	I	347 06.6	345 21.3	52.4	309 16.3	12.7	147 59.3	23.1	79 38.1	05.0
12	D	2 09.1	0 25.1	N 9 51.7	324 17.0	N15 13.3	163 02.0	S 6 23.0	94 40.5	S22 05.0
13	A	17 11.6	15 28.9	50.9	339 17.7	13.8	178 04.8	22.8	109 42.9	05.0
14	Y	32 14.0	30 32.8	50.1	354 18.4	14.4	193 07.5	22.7	124 45.3	05.0
15		47 16.5	45 36.6	. . 49.4	9 19.2	. . 15.0	208 10.3	. . 22.6	139 47.8	. . 05.0
16		62 19.0	60 40.5	48.6	24 19.9	15.6	223 13.0	22.5	154 50.2	05.0
17		77 21.4	75 44.3	47.8	39 20.6	16.2	238 15.7	22.4	169 52.6	05.0
18		92 23.9	90 48.1	N 9 47.0	54 21.3	N15 16.8	253 18.5	S 6 22.3	184 55.0	S22 05.0
19		107 26.4	105 52.0	46.2	69 22.0	17.3	268 21.2	22.1	199 57.4	05.0
20		122 28.8	120 55.8	45.5	84 22.8	17.9	283 24.0	22.0	214 59.8	05.0
21		137 31.3	135 59.6	. . 44.7	99 23.5	. . 18.5	298 26.7	. . 21.9	230 02.2	. . 05.0
22		152 33.7	151 03.5	43.9	114 24.2	19.1	313 29.4	21.8	245 04.6	05.0
23		167 36.2	166 07.3	43.1	129 24.9	19.7	328 32.2	21.7	260 07.0	05.0
25 00		182 38.7	181 11.1	N 9 42.3	144 25.6	N15 20.3	343 34.9	S 6 21.6	275 09.4	S22 05.0
01		197 41.1	196 15.0	41.5	159 26.4	20.8	358 37.7	21.5	290 11.8	05.0
02		212 43.6	211 18.8	40.7	174 27.1	21.4	13 40.4	21.3	305 14.3	05.0
03		227 46.1	226 22.6	. . 39.9	189 27.8	. . 22.0	28 43.1	. . 21.2	320 16.7	. . 05.0
04		242 48.5	241 26.5	39.1	204 28.5	22.6	43 45.9	21.1	335 19.1	05.0
05		257 51.0	256 30.3	38.3	219 29.2	23.2	58 48.6	21.0	350 21.5	05.0
06		272 53.5	271 34.1	N 9 37.5	234 30.0	N15 23.7	73 51.4	S 6 20.9	5 23.9	S22 05.0
07	S	287 55.9	286 38.0	36.7	249 30.7	24.3	88 54.1	20.8	20 26.3	05.0
08	A	302 58.4	301 41.8	35.9	264 31.4	24.9	103 56.9	20.6	35 28.7	05.0
09	T	318 00.9	316 45.6	. . 35.1	279 32.1	. . 25.5	118 59.6	. . 20.5	50 31.1	. . 05.0
10	U	333 03.3	331 49.4	34.3	294 32.8	26.1	134 02.3	20.4	65 33.5	05.0
11	R	348 05.8	346 53.3	33.5	309 33.6	26.6	149 05.1	20.3	80 35.9	05.0
12	D	3 08.2	1 57.1	N 9 32.7	324 34.3	N15 27.2	164 07.8	S 6 20.2	95 38.4	S22 05.0
13	A	18 10.7	17 00.9	31.9	339 35.0	27.8	179 10.6	20.1	110 40.8	05.0
14	Y	33 13.2	32 04.7	31.1	354 35.7	28.4	194 13.3	20.0	125 43.2	05.0
15		48 15.6	47 08.6	. . 30.3	9 36.4	. . 29.0	209 16.1	. . 19.8	140 45.6	. . 05.0
16		63 18.1	62 12.4	29.5	24 37.1	29.5	224 18.8	19.7	155 48.0	05.0
17		78 20.6	77 16.2	28.7	39 37.9	30.1	239 21.5	19.6	170 50.4	05.0
18		93 23.0	92 20.0	N 9 27.9	54 38.6	N15 30.7	254 24.3	S 6 19.5	185 52.8	S22 05.0
19		108 25.5	107 23.8	27.0	69 39.3	31.3	269 27.0	19.4	200 55.2	05.0
20		123 28.0	122 27.6	26.2	84 40.0	31.8	284 29.8	19.3	215 57.7	05.0
21		138 30.4	137 31.5	. . 25.4	99 40.7	. . 32.4	299 32.5	. . 19.1	231 00.1	. . 05.0
22		153 32.9	152 35.3	24.6	114 41.5	33.0	314 35.3	19.0	246 02.5	05.0
23		168 35.3	167 39.1	23.8	129 42.2	33.6	329 38.0	18.9	261 04.9	05.0
Mer. Pass.		h m 11 51.4	*v* 3.8	*d* 0.8	*v* 0.7	*d* 0.6	*v* 2.7	*d* 0.1	*v* 2.4	*d* 0.0

STARS

Name	SHA	Dec
	° ′	° ′
Acamar	315 16.8	S40 14.5
Achernar	335 25.5	S57 09.3
Acrux	173 05.6	S63 11.6
Adhara	255 10.5	S29 00.2
Aldebaran	290 46.6	N16 32.4
Alioth	166 18.0	N55 52.0
Alkaid	152 56.5	N49 13.6
Al Na'ir	27 41.0	S46 52.6
Alnilam	275 43.8	S 1 11.8
Alphard	217 53.4	S 8 44.2
Alphecca	126 08.7	N26 39.4
Alpheratz	357 41.2	N29 10.9
Altair	62 05.9	N 8 54.8
Ankaa	353 13.7	S42 12.9
Antares	112 23.0	S26 28.0
Arcturus	145 53.2	N19 05.5
Atria	107 22.3	S69 03.0
Avior	234 16.6	S59 34.3
Bellatrix	278 29.4	N 6 21.6
Betelgeuse	270 58.6	N 7 24.3
Canopus	263 55.0	S52 42.8
Capella	280 30.8	N46 00.8
Deneb	49 30.0	N45 20.3
Denebola	182 30.8	N14 28.5
Diphda	348 53.7	S17 53.8
Dubhe	193 48.1	N61 39.5
Elnath	278 09.5	N28 37.1
Eltanin	90 44.9	N51 29.0
Enif	33 44.9	N 9 57.1
Fomalhaut	15 21.6	S29 31.9
Gacrux	171 57.4	S57 12.5
Gienah	175 49.3	S17 38.3
Hadar	148 43.6	S60 27.1
Hamal	327 58.2	N23 32.4
Kaus Aust.	83 40.5	S34 22.3
Kochab	137 19.4	N74 05.0
Markab	13 36.1	N15 17.7
Menkar	314 12.6	N 4 09.1
Menkent	148 04.2	S36 27.1
Miaplacidus	221 38.4	S69 47.6
Mirfak	308 37.0	N49 55.2
Nunki	75 55.2	S26 16.3
Peacock	53 15.6	S56 40.5
Pollux	243 24.5	N27 58.9
Procyon	244 57.0	N 5 10.6
Rasalhague	96 04.0	N12 32.9
Regulus	207 40.6	N11 52.8
Rigel	281 09.7	S 8 11.3
Rigil Kent.	139 47.7	S60 54.1
Sabik	102 09.5	S15 44.6
Schedar	349 38.1	N56 37.8
Shaula	96 18.4	S37 06.7
Sirius	258 31.4	S16 44.8
Spica	158 28.3	S11 15.1
Suhail	222 50.2	S43 30.5
Vega	80 37.3	N38 47.8
Zuben'ubi	137 02.3	S16 06.7

	SHA	Mer. Pass.
	° ′	h m
Venus	357 59.5	11 58
Mars	322 28.8	14 23
Jupiter	160 49.6	1 10
Saturn	92 32.1	5 42

UT d h	SUN GHA ° ′	SUN Dec ° ′	MOON GHA ° ′	MOON v ′	MOON Dec ° ′	MOON d ′	MOON HP ′
THURSDAY							
23 00	178 20.4	N 1 00.7	240 28.1	10.9	S17 31.1	3.9	55.7
01	193 20.5	01.7	254 58.0	10.9	17 27.2	4.1	55.8
02	208 20.7	02.7	269 27.9	10.9	17 23.1	4.2	55.8
03	223 20.9	. . 03.7	283 57.8	10.9	17 18.9	4.3	55.8
04	238 21.1	04.7	298 27.7	10.9	17 14.6	4.3	55.8
05	253 21.3	05.6	312 57.6	10.8	17 10.3	4.5	55.9
06	268 21.5	N 1 06.6	327 27.4	10.9	S17 05.8	4.5	55.9
07	283 21.7	07.6	341 57.3	10.8	17 01.3	4.7	55.9
08	298 21.9	08.6	356 27.1	10.8	16 56.6	4.7	56.0
09	313 22.0	. . 09.6	10 56.9	10.8	16 51.9	4.8	56.0
10	328 22.2	10.6	25 26.7	10.8	16 47.1	4.9	56.0
11	343 22.4	11.6	39 56.5	10.8	16 42.2	5.0	56.1
12	358 22.6	N 1 12.5	54 26.3	10.8	S16 37.2	5.1	56.1
13	13 22.8	13.5	68 56.1	10.8	16 32.1	5.2	56.1
14	28 23.0	14.5	83 25.9	10.8	16 26.9	5.3	56.1
15	43 23.2	. . 15.5	97 55.7	10.7	16 21.6	5.4	56.2
16	58 23.4	16.5	112 25.4	10.8	16 16.2	5.4	56.2
17	73 23.5	17.5	126 55.2	10.7	16 10.8	5.6	56.2
18	88 23.7	N 1 18.5	141 24.9	10.7	S16 05.2	5.6	56.3
19	103 23.9	19.4	155 54.6	10.7	15 59.6	5.7	56.3
20	118 24.1	20.4	170 24.3	10.7	15 53.9	5.9	56.3
21	133 24.3	. . 21.4	184 54.0	10.7	15 48.0	5.9	56.4
22	148 24.5	22.4	199 23.7	10.7	15 42.1	6.0	56.4
23	163 24.7	23.4	213 53.4	10.7	15 36.1	6.1	56.4
FRIDAY							
24 00	178 24.9	N 1 24.4	228 23.1	10.7	S15 30.0	6.1	56.5
01	193 25.0	25.3	242 52.8	10.6	15 23.9	6.3	56.5
02	208 25.2	26.3	257 22.4	10.7	15 17.6	6.3	56.5
03	223 25.4	. . 27.3	271 52.1	10.7	15 11.3	6.5	56.6
04	238 25.6	28.3	286 21.8	10.6	15 04.8	6.5	56.6
05	253 25.8	29.3	300 51.4	10.6	14 58.3	6.6	56.6
06	268 26.0	N 1 30.3	315 21.0	10.7	S14 51.7	6.7	56.7
07	283 26.2	31.3	329 50.7	10.6	14 45.0	6.8	56.7
08	298 26.4	32.2	344 20.3	10.6	14 38.2	6.9	56.7
09	313 26.5	. . 33.2	358 49.9	10.6	14 31.3	6.9	56.8
10	328 26.7	34.2	13 19.5	10.6	14 24.4	7.0	56.8
11	343 26.9	35.2	27 49.1	10.6	14 17.4	7.2	56.8
12	358 27.1	N 1 36.2	42 18.7	10.5	S14 10.2	7.2	56.9
13	13 27.3	37.2	56 48.2	10.6	14 03.0	7.3	56.9
14	28 27.5	38.1	71 17.8	10.6	13 55.7	7.3	56.9
15	43 27.7	. . 39.1	85 47.4	10.5	13 48.4	7.5	57.0
16	58 27.9	40.1	100 16.9	10.6	13 40.9	7.5	57.0
17	73 28.0	41.1	114 46.5	10.5	13 33.4	7.6	57.0
18	88 28.2	N 1 42.1	129 16.0	10.6	S13 25.8	7.8	57.1
19	103 28.4	43.1	143 45.6	10.5	13 18.0	7.7	57.1
20	118 28.6	44.0	158 15.1	10.5	13 10.3	7.9	57.2
21	133 28.8	. . 45.0	172 44.6	10.5	13 02.4	7.9	57.2
22	148 29.0	46.0	187 14.1	10.5	12 54.5	8.1	57.2
23	163 29.2	47.0	201 43.6	10.5	12 46.4	8.1	57.3
SATURDAY							
25 00	178 29.4	N 1 48.0	216 13.1	10.5	S12 38.3	8.1	57.3
01	193 29.6	49.0	230 42.6	10.5	12 30.2	8.3	57.3
02	208 29.7	49.9	245 12.1	10.5	12 21.9	8.3	57.4
03	223 29.9	. . 50.9	259 41.6	10.4	12 13.6	8.4	57.4
04	238 30.1	51.9	274 11.0	10.5	12 05.2	8.5	57.4
05	253 30.3	52.9	288 40.5	10.4	11 56.7	8.6	57.5
06	268 30.5	N 1 53.9	303 09.9	10.5	S11 48.1	8.6	57.5
07	283 30.7	54.9	317 39.4	10.4	11 39.5	8.7	57.5
08	298 30.9	55.8	332 08.8	10.4	11 30.8	8.8	57.6
09	313 31.1	. . 56.8	346 38.2	10.4	11 22.0	8.9	57.6
10	328 31.2	57.8	1 07.6	10.5	11 13.1	8.9	57.6
11	343 31.4	58.8	15 37.1	10.4	11 04.2	9.0	57.7
12	358 31.6	N 1 59.8	30 06.5	10.3	S10 55.2	9.1	57.7
13	13 31.8	2 00.7	44 35.8	10.4	10 46.1	9.1	57.7
14	28 32.0	01.7	59 05.2	10.4	10 37.0	9.2	57.8
15	43 32.2	. . 02.7	73 34.6	10.4	10 27.8	9.3	57.8
16	58 32.4	03.7	88 04.0	10.3	10 18.5	9.3	57.8
17	73 32.6	04.7	102 33.3	10.4	10 09.2	9.5	57.9
18	88 32.7	N 2 05.7	117 02.7	10.3	S 9 59.7	9.4	57.9
19	103 32.9	06.6	131 32.0	10.3	9 50.3	9.6	57.9
20	118 33.1	07.6	146 01.3	10.3	9 40.7	9.6	58.0
21	133 33.3	. . 08.6	160 30.6	10.4	9 31.1	9.7	58.0
22	148 33.5	09.6	175 00.0	10.3	9 21.4	9.7	58.1
23	163 33.7	10.6	189 29.3	10.2	S 9 11.7	9.8	58.1
	SD 16.1	*d* 1.0	SD		15.3	15.5	15.7

Lat.	Twilight Naut.	Twilight Civil	Sunrise	Moonrise 23	Moonrise 24	Moonrise 25	Moonrise 26
°	h m	h m	h m	h m	h m	h m	h m
N 72	02 52	04 27	05 37	06 59	06 40	06 29	06 21
N 70	03 16	04 38	05 40	06 03	06 08	06 09	06 09
68	03 33	04 46	05 42	05 30	05 44	05 54	06 00
66	03 48	04 53	05 45	05 06	05 26	05 41	05 52
64	03 59	04 58	05 46	04 47	05 11	05 30	05 45
62	04 09	05 03	05 48	04 31	04 59	05 21	05 39
60	04 17	05 07	05 49	04 18	04 48	05 13	05 34
N 58	04 23	05 11	05 50	04 06	04 39	05 06	05 29
56	04 29	05 14	05 51	03 57	04 30	04 59	05 25
54	04 35	05 17	05 52	03 48	04 23	04 54	05 21
52	04 39	05 19	05 53	03 40	04 16	04 49	05 18
50	04 43	05 22	05 54	03 33	04 11	04 44	05 15
45	04 52	05 26	05 56	03 18	03 58	04 34	05 08
N 40	04 58	05 30	05 57	03 06	03 47	04 26	05 03
35	05 03	05 33	05 58	02 55	03 38	04 19	04 58
30	05 07	05 35	05 59	02 46	03 30	04 13	04 54
20	05 13	05 39	06 01	02 30	03 16	04 02	04 47
N 10	05 16	05 41	06 02	02 16	03 04	03 52	04 40
0	05 18	05 42	06 03	02 03	02 53	03 43	04 34
S 10	05 19	05 43	06 04	01 50	02 41	03 34	04 28
20	05 17	05 43	06 05	01 36	02 29	03 25	04 21
30	05 14	05 42	06 06	01 20	02 15	03 14	04 14
35	05 12	05 41	06 06	01 10	02 07	03 07	04 10
40	05 08	05 40	06 07	01 00	01 58	03 00	04 05
45	05 04	05 38	06 08	00 47	01 47	02 52	03 59
S 50	04 58	05 36	06 08	00 32	01 34	02 41	03 52
52	04 55	05 35	06 09	00 25	01 28	02 37	03 49
54	04 52	05 34	06 09	00 17	01 21	02 31	03 46
56	04 48	05 32	06 09	00 08	01 14	02 26	03 42
58	04 44	05 30	06 10	25 05	01 05	02 19	03 38
S 60	04 39	05 29	06 10	24 55	00 55	02 12	03 33

Lat.	Sunset	Twilight Civil	Twilight Naut.	Moonset 23	Moonset 24	Moonset 25	Moonset 26
°	h m	h m	h m	h m	h m	h m	h m
N 72	18 38	19 48	21 27	09 40	11 43	13 39	15 34
N 70	18 35	19 38	21 01	10 34	12 14	13 58	15 44
68	18 32	19 29	20 42	11 07	12 37	14 12	15 51
66	18 30	19 22	20 28	11 31	12 54	14 24	15 58
64	18 28	19 16	20 16	11 49	13 08	14 34	16 04
62	18 26	19 11	20 06	12 05	13 20	14 42	16 08
60	18 25	19 07	19 58	12 17	13 30	14 49	16 12
N 58	18 23	19 03	19 51	12 28	13 39	14 56	16 16
56	18 22	19 00	19 45	12 38	13 47	15 01	16 19
54	18 21	18 57	19 39	12 46	13 54	15 06	16 22
52	18 20	18 54	19 35	12 54	14 00	15 11	16 25
50	18 19	18 52	19 30	13 01	14 05	15 15	16 27
45	18 18	18 47	19 22	13 15	14 17	15 23	16 32
N 40	18 16	18 43	19 15	13 27	14 27	15 31	16 37
35	18 15	18 40	19 10	13 37	14 36	15 37	16 40
30	18 14	18 38	19 06	13 46	14 43	15 42	16 44
20	18 12	18 34	19 00	14 01	14 56	15 52	16 49
N 10	18 11	18 32	18 56	14 14	15 07	16 00	16 54
0	18 09	18 30	18 54	14 27	15 17	16 07	16 58
S 10	18 08	18 29	18 54	14 39	15 27	16 15	17 03
20	18 07	18 29	18 55	14 52	15 38	16 23	17 08
30	18 06	18 30	18 58	15 07	15 50	16 32	17 13
35	18 05	18 31	19 00	15 16	15 57	16 37	17 16
40	18 05	18 32	19 03	15 25	16 05	16 43	17 19
45	18 04	18 33	19 07	15 37	16 15	16 50	17 23
S 50	18 03	18 35	19 13	15 51	16 26	16 58	17 28
52	18 03	18 36	19 16	15 57	16 31	17 02	17 30
54	18 02	18 38	19 19	16 04	16 37	17 06	17 32
56	18 02	18 39	19 23	16 12	16 43	17 11	17 35
58	18 02	18 41	19 27	16 21	16 50	17 16	17 38
S 60	18 01	18 42	19 31	16 31	16 58	17 21	17 41

Day	SUN Eqn. of Time 00^h	SUN Eqn. of Time 12^h	SUN Mer. Pass.	MOON Mer. Pass. Upper	MOON Mer. Pass. Lower	MOON Age	MOON Phase
d	m s	m s	h m	h m	h m	d %	
23	06 39	06 30	12 06	08 15	20 40	25 24	
24	06 21	06 12	12 06	09 05	21 30	26 15	
25	06 03	05 54	12 06	09 55	22 21	27 9	

UT	ARIES	VENUS −4·2		MARS +1·4		JUPITER −2·4		SATURN +0·4		STARS		
d h	GHA	GHA	Dec	GHA	Dec	GHA	Dec	GHA	Dec	Name	SHA	Dec
	° ′	° ′	° ′	° ′	° ′	° ′	° ′	° ′	° ′		° ′	° ′
26 00	183 37.8	182 42.9	N 9 22.9	144 42.9	N15 34.2	344 40.8	S 6 18.8	276 07.3	S22 04.9	Acamar	315 16.8	S40 14.5
01	198 40.3	197 46.7	22.1	159 43.6	34.7	359 43.5	18.7	291 09.7	04.9	Achernar	335 25.5	S57 09.2
02	213 42.7	212 50.5	21.3	174 44.3	35.3	14 46.2	18.6	306 12.1	04.9	Acrux	173 05.6	S63 11.7
03	228 45.2	227 54.3	. . 20.5	189 45.0	. . 35.9	29 49.0	. . 18.4	321 14.6	. . 04.9	Adhara	255 10.5	S29 00.2
04	243 47.7	242 58.2	19.6	204 45.8	36.5	44 51.7	18.3	336 17.0	04.9	Aldebaran	290 46.6	N16 32.4
05	258 50.1	258 02.0	18.8	219 46.5	37.0	59 54.5	18.2	351 19.4	04.9			
06	273 52.6	273 05.8	N 9 18.0	234 47.2	N15 37.6	74 57.2	S 6 18.1	6 21.8	S22 04.9	Alioth	166 18.0	N55 52.0
07	288 55.1	288 09.6	17.2	249 47.9	38.2	90 00.0	18.0	21 24.2	04.9	Alkaid	152 56.5	N49 13.6
08	303 57.5	303 13.4	16.3	264 48.6	38.8	105 02.7	17.9	36 26.6	04.9	Al Na'ir	27 41.0	S46 52.6
S 09	319 00.0	318 17.2	. . 15.5	279 49.3	. . 39.3	120 05.5	. . 17.7	51 29.0	. . 04.9	Alnilam	275 43.9	S 1 11.8
U 10	334 02.5	333 21.0	14.7	294 50.1	39.9	135 08.2	17.6	66 31.5	04.9	Alphard	217 53.4	S 8 44.2
N 11	349 04.9	348 24.8	13.8	309 50.8	40.5	150 11.0	17.5	81 33.9	04.9			
D 12	4 07.4	3 28.6	N 9 13.0	324 51.5	N15 41.0	165 13.7	S 6 17.4	96 36.3	S22 04.9	Alphecca	126 08.6	N26 39.4
A 13	19 09.8	18 32.4	12.1	339 52.2	41.6	180 16.4	17.3	111 38.7	04.9	Alpheratz	357 41.2	N29 10.9
Y 14	34 12.3	33 36.2	11.3	354 52.9	42.2	195 19.2	17.2	126 41.1	04.9	Altair	62 05.9	N 8 54.8
15	49 14.8	48 40.0	. . 10.5	9 53.6	. . 42.8	210 21.9	. . 17.0	141 43.5	. . 04.9	Ankaa	353 13.7	S42 12.9
16	64 17.2	63 43.8	09.6	24 54.4	43.3	225 24.7	16.9	156 46.0	04.9	Antares	112 23.0	S26 28.0
17	79 19.7	78 47.6	08.8	39 55.1	43.9	240 27.4	16.8	171 48.4	04.9			
18	94 22.2	93 51.4	N 9 07.9	54 55.8	N15 44.5	255 30.2	S 6 16.7	186 50.8	S22 04.9	Arcturus	145 53.1	N19 05.5
19	109 24.6	108 55.2	07.1	69 56.5	45.0	270 32.9	16.6	201 53.2	04.9	Atria	107 22.3	S69 03.1
20	124 27.1	123 59.0	06.2	84 57.2	45.6	285 35.7	16.4	216 55.6	04.9	Avior	234 16.6	S59 34.3
21	139 29.6	139 02.8	. . 05.4	99 57.9	. . 46.2	300 38.4	. . 16.3	231 58.0	. . 04.9	Bellatrix	278 29.4	N 6 21.6
22	154 32.0	154 06.5	04.5	114 58.7	46.8	315 41.2	16.2	247 00.5	04.9	Betelgeuse	270 58.6	N 7 24.3
23	169 34.5	169 10.3	03.7	129 59.4	47.3	330 43.9	16.1	262 02.9	04.9			
27 00	184 36.9	184 14.1	N 9 02.8	145 00.1	N15 47.9	345 46.7	S 6 16.0	277 05.3	S22 04.9	Canopus	263 55.0	S52 42.8
01	199 39.4	199 17.9	02.0	160 00.8	48.5	0 49.4	15.9	292 07.7	04.9	Capella	280 30.8	N46 00.8
02	214 41.9	214 21.7	01.1	175 01.5	49.0	15 52.1	15.7	307 10.1	04.9	Deneb	49 30.0	N45 20.3
03	229 44.3	229 25.5	9 00.3	190 02.2	. . 49.6	30 54.9	. . 15.6	322 12.6	. . 04.9	Denebola	182 30.8	N14 28.5
04	244 46.8	244 29.3	8 59.4	205 03.0	50.2	45 57.6	15.5	337 15.0	04.9	Diphda	348 53.7	S17 53.8
05	259 49.3	259 33.0	58.6	220 03.7	50.7	61 00.4	15.4	352 17.4	04.9			
06	274 51.7	274 36.8	N 8 57.7	235 04.4	N15 51.3	76 03.1	S 6 15.3	7 19.8	S22 04.9	Dubhe	193 48.1	N61 39.5
07	289 54.2	289 40.6	56.9	250 05.1	51.9	91 05.9	15.2	22 22.2	04.9	Elnath	278 09.5	N28 37.1
08	304 56.7	304 44.4	56.0	265 05.8	52.5	106 08.6	15.0	37 24.6	04.9	Eltanin	90 44.9	N51 29.0
M 09	319 59.1	319 48.1	. . 55.1	280 06.5	. . 53.0	121 11.4	. . 14.9	52 27.1	. . 04.9	Enif	33 44.9	N 9 57.1
O 10	335 01.6	334 51.9	54.3	295 07.2	53.6	136 14.1	14.8	67 29.5	04.9	Fomalhaut	15 21.6	S29 31.9
N 11	350 04.1	349 55.7	53.4	310 08.0	54.2	151 16.9	14.7	82 31.9	04.9			
D 12	5 06.5	4 59.5	N 8 52.5	325 08.7	N15 54.7	166 19.6	S 6 14.6	97 34.3	S22 04.9	Gacrux	171 57.4	S57 12.6
A 13	20 09.0	20 03.2	51.7	340 09.4	55.3	181 22.4	14.4	112 36.8	04.9	Gienah	175 49.3	S17 38.3
Y 14	35 11.4	35 07.0	50.8	355 10.1	55.9	196 25.1	14.3	127 39.2	04.9	Hadar	148 43.6	S60 27.2
15	50 13.9	50 10.8	. . 50.0	10 10.8	. . 56.4	211 27.9	. . 14.2	142 41.6	. . 04.9	Hamal	327 58.2	N23 32.4
16	65 16.4	65 14.5	49.1	25 11.5	57.0	226 30.6	14.1	157 44.0	04.9	Kaus Aust.	83 40.4	S34 22.3
17	80 18.8	80 18.3	48.2	40 12.2	57.5	241 33.4	14.0	172 46.4	04.9			
18	95 21.3	95 22.0	N 8 47.3	55 13.0	N15 58.1	256 36.1	S 6 13.9	187 48.9	S22 04.9	Kochab	137 19.3	N74 05.0
19	110 23.8	110 25.8	46.5	70 13.7	58.7	271 38.9	13.7	202 51.3	04.9	Markab	13 36.1	N15 17.7
20	125 26.2	125 29.6	45.6	85 14.4	59.2	286 41.6	13.6	217 53.7	04.9	Menkar	314 12.6	N 4 09.1
21	140 28.7	140 33.3	. . 44.7	100 15.1	15 59.8	301 44.4	. . 13.5	232 56.1	. . 04.9	Menkent	148 04.2	S36 27.2
22	155 31.2	155 37.1	43.9	115 15.8	16 00.4	316 47.1	13.4	247 58.5	04.9	Miaplacidus	221 38.4	S69 47.6
23	170 33.6	170 40.8	43.0	130 16.5	00.9	331 49.9	13.3	263 01.0	04.9			
28 00	185 36.1	185 44.6	N 8 42.1	145 17.2	N16 01.5	346 52.6	S 6 13.2	278 03.4	S22 04.9	Mirfak	308 37.0	N49 55.2
01	200 38.5	200 48.3	41.2	160 18.0	02.1	1 55.4	13.0	293 05.8	04.9	Nunki	75 55.2	S26 16.3
02	215 41.0	215 52.1	40.4	175 18.7	02.6	16 58.1	12.9	308 08.2	04.8	Peacock	53 15.6	S56 40.5
03	230 43.5	230 55.8	. . 39.5	190 19.4	. . 03.2	32 00.9	. . 12.8	323 10.7	. . 04.8	Pollux	243 24.5	N27 58.9
04	245 45.9	245 59.5	38.6	205 20.1	03.8	47 03.6	12.7	338 13.1	04.8	Procyon	244 57.0	N 5 10.6
05	260 48.4	261 03.3	37.7	220 20.8	04.3	62 06.4	12.6	353 15.5	04.8			
06	275 50.9	276 07.0	N 8 36.8	235 21.5	N16 04.9	77 09.1	S 6 12.4	8 17.9	S22 04.8	Rasalhague	96 04.0	N12 32.9
07	290 53.3	291 10.8	36.0	250 22.2	05.4	92 11.9	12.3	23 20.4	04.8	Regulus	207 40.6	N11 52.8
T 08	305 55.8	306 14.5	35.1	265 22.9	06.0	107 14.6	12.2	38 22.8	04.8	Rigel	281 09.7	S 8 11.3
U 09	320 58.3	321 18.2	. . 34.2	280 23.7	. . 06.6	122 17.4	. . 12.1	53 25.2	. . 04.8	Rigil Kent.	139 47.6	S60 54.1
E 10	336 00.7	336 22.0	33.3	295 24.4	07.1	137 20.1	12.0	68 27.6	04.8	Sabik	102 09.5	S15 44.6
S 11	351 03.2	351 25.7	32.4	310 25.1	07.7	152 22.9	11.8	83 30.1	04.8			
12	6 05.7	6 29.4	N 8 31.6	325 25.8	N16 08.2	167 25.6	S 6 11.7	98 32.5	S22 04.8	Schedar	349 38.1	N56 37.8
D 13	21 08.1	21 33.2	30.7	340 26.5	08.8	182 28.4	11.6	113 34.9	04.8	Shaula	96 18.4	S37 06.7
A 14	36 10.6	36 36.9	29.8	355 27.2	09.4	197 31.1	11.5	128 37.3	04.8	Sirius	258 31.5	S16 44.8
Y 15	51 13.0	51 40.6	. . 28.9	10 27.9	. . 09.9	212 33.9	. . 11.4	143 39.8	. . 04.8	Spica	158 28.3	S11 15.1
16	66 15.5	66 44.3	28.0	25 28.6	10.5	227 36.6	11.3	158 42.2	04.8	Suhail	222 50.3	S43 30.5
17	81 18.0	81 48.1	27.1	40 29.4	11.0	242 39.4	11.1	173 44.6	04.8			
18	96 20.4	96 51.8	N 8 26.2	55 30.1	N16 11.6	257 42.1	S 6 11.0	188 47.0	S22 04.8	Vega	80 37.2	N38 47.8
19	111 22.9	111 55.5	25.3	70 30.8	12.2	272 44.9	10.9	203 49.5	04.8	Zuben'ubi	137 02.3	S16 06.7
20	126 25.4	126 59.2	24.5	85 31.5	12.7	287 47.6	10.8	218 51.9	04.8		SHA	Mer. Pass.
21	141 27.8	142 02.9	. . 23.6	100 32.2	. . 13.3	302 50.4	. . 10.7	233 54.3	. . 04.8		° ′	h m
22	156 30.3	157 06.6	22.7	115 32.9	13.8	317 53.1	10.5	248 56.7	04.8	Venus	359 37.2	11 40
23	171 32.8	172 10.3	21.8	130 33.6	14.4	332 55.9	10.4	263 59.2	04.8	Mars	320 23.1	14 19
Mer. Pass.	h m 11 39.6	*v* 3.8	*d* 0.9	*v* 0.7	*d* 0.6	*v* 2.7	*d* 0.1	*v* 2.4	*d* 0.0	Jupiter	161 09.7	0 57
										Saturn	92 28.3	5 31

UT		SUN GHA	SUN Dec	MOON GHA	v	MOON Dec	d	HP
d	h	° ′	° ′	° ′	′	° ′	′	′
26	00	178 33.9	N 2 11.5	203 58.5	10.3	S 9 01.9	9.9	58.1
	01	193 34.1	12.5	218 27.8	10.3	8 52.0	9.9	58.2
	02	208 34.3	13.5	232 57.1	10.2	8 42.1	10.0	58.2
	03	223 34.4	. . 14.5	247 26.3	10.3	8 32.1	10.1	58.2
	04	238 34.6	15.5	261 55.6	10.2	8 22.0	10.1	58.3
	05	253 34.8	16.4	276 24.8	10.2	8 11.9	10.1	58.3
	06	268 35.0	N 2 17.4	290 54.0	10.2	S 8 01.8	10.2	58.3
	07	283 35.2	18.4	305 23.2	10.2	7 51.6	10.3	58.4
	08	298 35.4	19.4	319 52.4	10.2	7 41.3	10.4	58.4
S	09	313 35.6	. . 20.4	334 21.6	10.2	7 30.9	10.3	58.4
U	10	328 35.8	21.3	348 50.8	10.1	7 20.6	10.5	58.5
N	11	343 35.9	22.3	3 19.9	10.2	7 10.1	10.5	58.5
D	12	358 36.1	N 2 23.3	17 49.1	10.1	S 6 59.6	10.5	58.5
A	13	13 36.3	24.3	32 18.2	10.1	6 49.1	10.6	58.6
Y	14	28 36.5	25.3	46 47.3	10.1	6 38.5	10.6	58.6
	15	43 36.7	. . 26.3	61 16.4	10.1	6 27.9	10.7	58.6
	16	58 36.9	27.2	75 45.5	10.1	6 17.2	10.8	58.6
	17	73 37.1	28.2	90 14.6	10.1	6 06.4	10.8	58.7
	18	88 37.3	N 2 29.2	104 43.7	10.0	S 5 55.6	10.8	58.7
	19	103 37.4	30.2	119 12.7	10.0	5 44.8	10.9	58.7
	20	118 37.6	31.1	133 41.7	10.0	5 33.9	10.9	58.8
	21	133 37.8	. . 32.1	148 10.7	10.0	5 23.0	11.0	58.8
	22	148 38.0	33.1	162 39.7	10.0	5 12.0	11.0	58.8
	23	163 38.2	34.1	177 08.7	10.0	5 01.0	11.0	58.9
27	00	178 38.4	N 2 35.1	191 37.7	9.9	S 4 50.0	11.1	58.9
	01	193 38.6	36.0	206 06.6	10.0	4 38.9	11.1	58.9
	02	208 38.8	37.0	220 35.6	9.9	4 27.8	11.2	59.0
	03	223 39.0	. . 38.0	235 04.5	9.9	4 16.6	11.2	59.0
	04	238 39.1	39.0	249 33.4	9.8	4 05.4	11.2	59.0
	05	253 39.3	40.0	264 02.2	9.9	3 54.2	11.3	59.0
	06	268 39.5	N 2 40.9	278 31.1	9.8	S 3 42.9	11.2	59.1
	07	283 39.7	41.9	292 59.9	9.8	3 31.7	11.4	59.1
	08	298 39.9	42.9	307 28.7	9.8	3 20.3	11.3	59.1
M	09	313 40.1	. . 43.9	321 57.5	9.8	3 09.0	11.4	59.2
O	10	328 40.3	44.9	336 26.3	9.8	2 57.6	11.4	59.2
N	11	343 40.5	45.8	350 55.1	9.7	2 46.2	11.5	59.2
D	12	358 40.6	N 2 46.8	5 23.8	9.7	S 2 34.7	11.5	59.2
A	13	13 40.8	47.8	19 52.5	9.7	2 23.2	11.4	59.3
Y	14	28 41.0	48.8	34 21.2	9.7	2 11.8	11.6	59.3
	15	43 41.2	. . 49.7	48 49.9	9.6	2 00.2	11.5	59.3
	16	58 41.4	50.7	63 18.5	9.6	1 48.7	11.6	59.3
	17	73 41.6	51.7	77 47.1	9.6	1 37.1	11.5	59.4
	18	88 41.8	N 2 52.7	92 15.7	9.6	S 1 25.6	11.6	59.4
	19	103 42.0	53.7	106 44.3	9.6	1 14.0	11.7	59.4
	20	118 42.1	54.6	121 12.9	9.5	1 02.3	11.6	59.4
	21	133 42.3	. . 55.6	135 41.4	9.5	0 50.7	11.6	59.5
	22	148 42.5	56.6	150 09.9	9.5	0 39.1	11.7	59.5
	23	163 42.7	57.6	164 38.4	9.5	0 27.4	11.7	59.5
28	00	178 42.9	N 2 58.5	179 06.9	9.4	S 0 15.7	11.7	59.5
	01	193 43.1	2 59.5	193 35.3	9.4	S 0 04.0	11.6	59.6
	02	208 43.3	3 00.5	208 03.7	9.4	N 0 07.6	11.7	59.6
	03	223 43.5	. . 01.5	222 32.1	9.3	0 19.3	11.8	59.6
	04	238 43.6	02.4	237 00.4	9.3	0 31.1	11.7	59.6
	05	253 43.8	03.4	251 28.7	9.3	0 42.8	11.7	59.7
	06	268 44.0	N 3 04.4	265 57.0	9.3	N 0 54.5	11.7	59.7
	07	283 44.2	05.4	280 25.3	9.2	1 06.2	11.7	59.7
T	08	298 44.4	06.3	294 53.5	9.3	1 17.9	11.8	59.7
U	09	313 44.6	. . 07.3	309 21.8	9.1	1 29.7	11.7	59.7
E	10	328 44.8	08.3	323 49.9	9.2	1 41.4	11.7	59.8
S	11	343 45.0	09.3	338 18.1	9.1	1 53.1	11.7	59.8
D	12	358 45.2	N 3 10.3	352 46.2	9.1	N 2 04.8	11.7	59.8
A	13	13 45.3	11.2	7 14.3	9.1	2 16.5	11.7	59.8
Y	14	28 45.5	12.2	21 42.4	9.0	2 28.2	11.7	59.8
	15	43 45.7	. . 13.2	36 10.4	9.0	2 39.9	11.7	59.9
	16	58 45.9	14.2	50 38.4	9.0	2 51.6	11.7	59.9
	17	73 46.1	15.1	65 06.4	8.9	3 03.3	11.7	59.9
	18	88 46.3	N 3 16.1	79 34.3	8.9	N 3 15.0	11.6	59.9
	19	103 46.5	17.1	94 02.2	8.9	3 26.6	11.7	59.9
	20	118 46.7	18.1	108 30.1	8.8	3 38.3	11.6	59.9
	21	133 46.8	. . 19.0	122 57.9	8.8	3 49.9	11.6	60.0
	22	148 47.0	20.0	137 25.7	8.8	4 01.5	11.6	60.0
	23	163 47.2	21.0	151 53.5	8.8	N 4 13.1	11.6	60.0
		SD 16.1	*d* 1.0	SD 15.9		16.1		16.3

Lat.	Twilight Naut.	Twilight Civil	Sunrise	Moonrise 26	Moonrise 27	Moonrise 28	Moonrise 29
°	h m	h m	h m	h m	h m	h m	h m
N 72	02 27	04 10	05 21	06 21	06 14	06 07	06 00
N 70	02 56	04 23	05 26	06 09	06 09	06 08	06 07
68	03 17	04 33	05 30	06 00	06 05	06 09	06 14
66	03 33	04 41	05 33	05 52	06 01	06 10	06 19
64	03 47	04 47	05 36	05 45	05 58	06 10	06 23
62	03 57	04 53	05 38	05 39	05 55	06 11	06 27
60	04 06	04 58	05 40	05 34	05 53	06 11	06 30
N 58	04 14	05 02	05 42	05 29	05 51	06 12	06 33
56	04 21	05 06	05 43	05 25	05 49	06 12	06 36
54	04 27	05 09	05 45	05 21	05 47	06 12	06 39
52	04 32	05 12	05 46	05 18	05 46	06 13	06 41
50	04 36	05 15	05 47	05 15	05 44	06 13	06 43
45	04 46	05 20	05 50	05 08	05 41	06 14	06 47
N 40	04 53	05 25	05 52	05 03	05 39	06 14	06 51
35	04 59	05 28	05 54	04 58	05 36	06 15	06 54
30	05 03	05 31	05 55	04 54	05 35	06 15	06 57
20	05 10	05 36	05 58	04 47	05 31	06 16	07 02
N 10	05 15	05 39	06 00	04 40	05 28	06 17	07 07
0	05 17	05 41	06 02	04 34	05 25	06 17	07 11
S 10	05 19	05 43	06 04	04 28	05 23	06 18	07 15
20	05 18	05 44	06 06	04 21	05 20	06 19	07 20
30	05 16	05 44	06 08	04 14	05 16	06 20	07 25
35	05 14	05 44	06 09	04 10	05 14	06 20	07 28
40	05 12	05 43	06 10	04 05	05 12	06 21	07 31
45	05 08	05 42	06 11	03 59	05 10	06 22	07 35
S 50	05 03	05 41	06 13	03 52	05 06	06 23	07 40
52	05 01	05 40	06 14	03 49	05 05	06 23	07 43
54	04 58	05 39	06 14	03 46	05 04	06 24	07 45
56	04 55	05 38	06 15	03 42	05 02	06 24	07 48
58	04 51	05 37	06 16	03 38	05 00	06 25	07 51
S 60	04 47	05 36	06 17	03 33	04 58	06 25	07 54

Lat.	Sunset	Twilight Civil	Twilight Naut.	Moonset 26	Moonset 27	Moonset 28	Moonset 29
°	h m	h m	h m	h m	h m	h m	h m
N 72	18 52	20 04	21 50	15 34	17 29	19 26	21 27
N 70	18 47	19 51	21 19	15 44	17 31	19 22	21 14
68	18 43	19 41	20 57	15 51	17 33	19 18	21 04
66	18 40	19 32	20 40	15 58	17 35	19 14	20 55
64	18 37	19 25	20 27	16 04	17 36	19 11	20 48
62	18 34	19 19	20 16	16 08	17 38	19 09	20 42
60	18 32	19 14	20 06	16 12	17 39	19 07	20 36
N 58	18 30	19 10	19 58	16 16	17 40	19 05	20 32
56	18 28	19 06	19 52	16 19	17 40	19 03	20 27
54	18 27	19 03	19 46	16 22	17 41	19 02	20 24
52	18 25	19 00	19 40	16 25	17 42	19 00	20 20
50	18 24	18 57	19 36	16 27	17 42	18 59	20 17
45	18 21	18 51	19 26	16 32	17 44	18 57	20 11
N 40	18 19	18 46	19 18	16 37	17 45	18 54	20 05
35	18 17	18 43	19 13	16 40	17 46	18 52	20 00
30	18 16	18 40	19 08	16 44	17 46	18 51	19 56
20	18 13	18 35	19 01	16 49	17 48	18 48	19 49
N 10	18 11	18 32	18 56	16 54	17 49	18 45	19 43
0	18 09	18 29	18 53	16 58	17 50	18 43	19 37
S 10	18 07	18 28	18 52	17 03	17 51	18 40	19 31
20	18 05	18 27	18 52	17 08	17 52	18 37	19 24
30	18 02	18 26	18 54	17 13	17 53	18 34	19 17
35	18 01	18 26	18 56	17 16	17 54	18 33	19 13
40	18 00	18 27	18 58	17 19	17 55	18 31	19 08
45	17 58	18 28	19 02	17 23	17 56	18 28	19 03
S 50	17 57	18 29	19 06	17 28	17 57	18 26	18 56
52	17 56	18 29	19 09	17 30	17 57	18 24	18 53
54	17 55	18 30	19 11	17 32	17 58	18 23	18 50
56	17 54	18 31	19 14	17 35	17 58	18 22	18 46
58	17 53	18 32	19 18	17 38	17 59	18 20	18 42
S 60	17 52	18 33	19 22	17 41	18 00	18 18	18 38

Day	SUN Eqn. of Time 00^h	SUN Eqn. of Time 12^h	SUN Mer. Pass.	MOON Mer. Pass. Upper	MOON Mer. Pass. Lower	MOON Age	MOON Phase
d	m s	m s	h m	h m	h m	d	%
26	05 45	05 36	12 06	10 46	23 12	28	3
27	05 27	05 18	12 05	11 38	24 04	29	1
28	05 09	05 00	12 05	12 30	00 04	00	0

2017 MARCH 29, 30, 31 (WED., THURS., FRI.)

UT	ARIES	VENUS −4·1		MARS +1·5		JUPITER −2·5		SATURN +0·4	
d h	GHA ° ′	GHA ° ′	Dec ° ′	GHA ° ′	Dec ° ′	GHA ° ′	Dec ° ′	GHA ° ′	Dec ° ′
29 00 (WEDNESDAY)	186 35.2	187 14.0	N 8 20.9	145 34.3	N16 14.9	347 58.6	S 6 10.3	279 01.6	S22 04.8
01	201 37.7	202 17.7	20.0	160 35.0	15.5	3 01.4	10.2	294 04.0	04.8
02	216 40.2	217 21.4	19.1	175 35.8	16.1	18 04.1	10.1	309 06.4	04.8
03	231 42.6	232 25.1	. . 18.2	190 36.5	. . 16.6	33 06.9	. . 09.9	324 08.9	. . 04.8
04	246 45.1	247 28.8	17.3	205 37.2	17.2	48 09.6	09.8	339 11.3	04.8
05	261 47.5	262 32.5	16.4	220 37.9	17.7	63 12.4	09.7	354 13.7	04.8
06	276 50.0	277 36.2	N 8 15.5	235 38.6	N16 18.3	78 15.2	S 6 09.6	9 16.2	S22 04.8
07	291 52.5	292 39.9	14.6	250 39.3	18.8	93 17.9	09.5	24 18.6	04.8
08	306 54.9	307 43.6	13.7	265 40.0	19.4	108 20.7	09.3	39 21.0	04.8
09	321 57.4	322 47.3	. . 12.8	280 40.7	. . 20.0	123 23.4	. . 09.2	54 23.4	. . 04.8
10	336 59.9	337 51.0	11.9	295 41.4	20.5	138 26.2	09.1	69 25.9	04.8
11	352 02.3	352 54.7	11.0	310 42.1	21.1	153 28.9	09.0	84 28.3	04.8
12	7 04.8	7 58.3	N 8 10.1	325 42.9	N16 21.6	168 31.7	S 6 08.9	99 30.7	S22 04.8
13	22 07.3	23 02.0	09.2	340 43.6	22.2	183 34.4	08.8	114 33.2	04.8
14	37 09.7	38 05.7	08.3	355 44.3	22.7	198 37.2	08.6	129 35.6	04.8
15	52 12.2	53 09.4	. . 07.4	10 45.0	. . 23.3	213 39.9	. . 08.5	144 38.0	. . 04.8
16	67 14.6	68 13.0	06.5	25 45.7	23.8	228 42.7	08.4	159 40.5	04.8
17	82 17.1	83 16.7	05.6	40 46.4	24.4	243 45.4	08.3	174 42.9	04.8
18	97 19.6	98 20.4	N 8 04.7	55 47.1	N16 24.9	258 48.2	S 6 08.2	189 45.3	S22 04.8
19	112 22.0	113 24.1	03.8	70 47.8	25.5	273 50.9	08.0	204 47.7	04.8
20	127 24.5	128 27.7	02.9	85 48.5	26.0	288 53.7	07.9	219 50.2	04.8
21	142 27.0	143 31.4	. . 02.0	100 49.2	. . 26.6	303 56.4	. . 07.8	234 52.6	. . 04.8
22	157 29.4	158 35.0	01.1	115 50.0	27.1	318 59.2	07.7	249 55.0	04.8
23	172 31.9	173 38.7	8 00.2	130 50.7	27.7	334 02.0	07.6	264 57.5	04.7
30 00 (THURSDAY)	187 34.4	188 42.3	N 7 59.3	145 51.4	N16 28.2	349 04.7	S 6 07.4	279 59.9	S22 04.7
01	202 36.8	203 46.0	58.4	160 52.1	28.8	4 07.5	07.3	295 02.3	04.7
02	217 39.3	218 49.6	57.5	175 52.8	29.3	19 10.2	07.2	310 04.8	04.7
03	232 41.8	233 53.3	. . 56.6	190 53.5	. . 29.9	34 13.0	. . 07.1	325 07.2	. . 04.7
04	247 44.2	248 56.9	55.7	205 54.2	30.4	49 15.7	07.0	340 09.6	04.7
05	262 46.7	264 00.6	54.8	220 54.9	31.0	64 18.5	06.8	355 12.1	04.7
06	277 49.1	279 04.2	N 7 53.8	235 55.6	N16 31.5	79 21.2	S 6 06.7	10 14.5	S22 04.7
07	292 51.6	294 07.9	52.9	250 56.3	32.1	94 24.0	06.6	25 16.9	04.7
08	307 54.1	309 11.5	52.0	265 57.0	32.6	109 26.7	06.5	40 19.4	04.7
09	322 56.5	324 15.1	. . 51.1	280 57.7	. . 33.2	124 29.5	. . 06.4	55 21.8	. . 04.7
10	337 59.0	339 18.8	50.2	295 58.5	33.7	139 32.3	06.2	70 24.2	04.7
11	353 01.5	354 22.4	49.3	310 59.2	34.3	154 35.0	06.1	85 26.7	04.7
12	8 03.9	9 26.0	N 7 48.4	325 59.9	N16 34.8	169 37.8	S 6 06.0	100 29.1	S22 04.7
13	23 06.4	24 29.6	47.5	341 00.6	35.4	184 40.5	05.9	115 31.5	04.7
14	38 08.9	39 33.2	46.6	356 01.3	35.9	199 43.3	05.8	130 34.0	04.7
15	53 11.3	54 36.9	. . 45.7	11 02.0	. . 36.5	214 46.0	. . 05.6	145 36.4	. . 04.7
16	68 13.8	69 40.5	44.7	26 02.7	37.0	229 48.8	05.5	160 38.8	04.7
17	83 16.2	84 44.1	43.8	41 03.4	37.6	244 51.5	05.4	175 41.3	04.7
18	98 18.7	99 47.7	N 7 42.9	56 04.1	N16 38.1	259 54.3	S 6 05.3	190 43.7	S22 04.7
19	113 21.2	114 51.3	42.0	71 04.8	38.7	274 57.0	05.2	205 46.1	04.7
20	128 23.6	129 54.9	41.1	86 05.5	39.2	289 59.8	05.0	220 48.6	04.7
21	143 26.1	144 58.5	. . 40.2	101 06.2	. . 39.7	305 02.6	. . 04.9	235 51.0	. . 04.7
22	158 28.6	160 02.1	39.3	116 06.9	40.3	320 05.3	04.8	250 53.4	04.7
23	173 31.0	175 05.7	38.4	131 07.6	40.8	335 08.1	04.7	265 55.9	04.7
31 00 (FRIDAY)	188 33.5	190 09.3	N 7 37.4	146 08.4	N16 41.4	350 10.8	S 6 04.6	280 58.3	S22 04.7
01	203 36.0	205 12.9	36.5	161 09.1	41.9	5 13.6	04.4	296 00.8	04.7
02	218 38.4	220 16.5	35.6	176 09.8	42.5	20 16.3	04.3	311 03.2	04.7
03	233 40.9	235 20.1	. . 34.7	191 10.5	. . 43.0	35 19.1	. . 04.2	326 05.6	. . 04.7
04	248 43.4	250 23.7	33.8	206 11.2	43.6	50 21.8	04.1	341 08.1	04.7
05	263 45.8	265 27.2	32.9	221 11.9	44.1	65 24.6	04.0	356 10.5	04.7
06	278 48.3	280 30.8	N 7 32.0	236 12.6	N16 44.6	80 27.4	S 6 03.8	11 12.9	S22 04.7
07	293 50.7	295 34.4	31.0	251 13.3	45.2	95 30.1	03.7	26 15.4	04.7
08	308 53.2	310 38.0	30.1	266 14.0	45.7	110 32.9	03.6	41 17.8	04.7
09	323 55.7	325 41.5	. . 29.2	281 14.7	. . 46.3	125 35.6	. . 03.5	56 20.3	. . 04.7
10	338 58.1	340 45.1	28.3	296 15.4	46.8	140 38.4	03.4	71 22.7	04.7
11	354 00.6	355 48.7	27.4	311 16.1	47.4	155 41.1	03.2	86 25.1	04.7
12	9 03.1	10 52.2	N 7 26.5	326 16.8	N16 47.9	170 43.9	S 6 03.1	101 27.6	S22 04.7
13	24 05.5	25 55.8	25.6	341 17.5	48.4	185 46.7	03.0	116 30.0	04.7
14	39 08.0	40 59.4	24.6	356 18.2	49.0	200 49.4	02.9	131 32.4	04.7
15	54 10.5	56 02.9	. . 23.7	11 18.9	. . 49.5	215 52.2	. . 02.8	146 34.9	. . 04.7
16	69 12.9	71 06.5	22.8	26 19.6	50.1	230 54.9	02.6	161 37.3	04.7
17	84 15.4	86 10.0	21.9	41 20.3	50.6	245 57.7	02.5	176 39.8	04.7
18	99 17.9	101 13.6	N 7 21.0	56 21.1	N16 51.1	261 00.4	S 6 02.4	191 42.2	S22 04.6
19	114 20.3	116 17.1	20.1	71 21.8	51.7	276 03.2	02.3	206 44.6	04.6
20	129 22.8	131 20.6	19.1	86 22.5	52.2	291 06.0	02.2	221 47.1	04.6
21	144 25.2	146 24.2	. . 18.2	101 23.2	. . 52.8	306 08.7	. . 02.0	236 49.5	. . 04.6
22	159 27.7	161 27.7	17.3	116 23.9	53.3	321 11.5	01.9	251 52.0	04.6
23	174 30.2	176 31.2	16.4	131 24.6	53.8	336 14.2	01.8	266 54.4	04.6
Mer. Pass.	h m 11 27.8	*v* 3.6	*d* 0.9	*v* 0.7	*d* 0.5	*v* 2.8	*d* 0.1	*v* 2.4	*d* 0.0

STARS

Name	SHA ° ′	Dec ° ′
Acamar	315 16.8	S40 14.5
Achernar	335 25.5	S57 09.2
Acrux	173 05.6	S63 11.7
Adhara	255 10.5	S29 00.2
Aldebaran	290 46.6	N16 32.4
Alioth	166 18.0	N55 52.0
Alkaid	152 56.5	N49 13.6
Al Na'ir	27 41.0	S46 52.6
Alnilam	275 43.9	S 1 11.8
Alphard	217 53.4	S 8 44.2
Alphecca	126 08.6	N26 39.4
Alpheratz	357 41.2	N29 10.9
Altair	62 05.9	N 8 54.8
Ankaa	353 13.7	S42 12.9
Antares	112 22.9	S26 28.0
Arcturus	145 53.1	N19 05.5
Atria	107 22.2	S69 03.1
Avior	234 16.7	S59 34.3
Bellatrix	278 29.4	N 6 21.6
Betelgeuse	270 58.6	N 7 24.3
Canopus	263 55.1	S52 42.8
Capella	280 30.8	N46 00.8
Deneb	49 29.9	N45 20.3
Denebola	182 30.8	N14 28.5
Diphda	348 53.7	S17 53.7
Dubhe	193 48.1	N61 39.5
Elnath	278 09.5	N28 37.1
Eltanin	90 44.9	N51 29.0
Enif	33 44.9	N 9 57.1
Fomalhaut	15 21.5	S29 31.9
Gacrux	171 57.4	S57 12.6
Gienah	175 49.3	S17 38.3
Hadar	148 43.6	S60 27.2
Hamal	327 58.2	N23 32.4
Kaus Aust.	83 40.4	S34 22.3
Kochab	137 19.3	N74 05.0
Markab	13 36.1	N15 17.7
Menkar	314 12.6	N 4 09.1
Menkent	148 04.2	S36 27.2
Miaplacidus	221 38.5	S69 47.6
Mirfak	308 37.0	N49 55.2
Nunki	75 55.2	S26 16.3
Peacock	53 15.6	S56 40.5
Pollux	243 24.6	N27 58.9
Procyon	244 57.0	N 5 10.6
Rasalhague	96 04.0	N12 32.9
Regulus	207 40.6	N11 52.8
Rigel	281 09.7	S 8 11.3
Rigil Kent.	139 47.6	S60 54.1
Sabik	102 09.5	S15 44.6
Schedar	349 38.1	N56 37.7
Shaula	96 18.3	S37 06.7
Sirius	258 31.5	S16 44.8
Spica	158 28.2	S11 15.1
Suhail	222 50.3	S43 30.5
Vega	80 37.2	N38 47.8
Zuben'ubi	137 02.3	S16 06.7

	SHA ° ′	Mer. Pass. h m
Venus	1 08.0	11 22
Mars	318 17.0	14 16
Jupiter	161 30.3	0 44
Saturn	92 25.5	5 19

UT		SUN GHA	SUN Dec	MOON GHA	*v*	MOON Dec	*d*	HP
d h		° ′	° ′	° ′	′	° ′	′	′
29 00		178 47.4	N 3 22.0	166 21.3	8.7	N 4 24.7	11.5	60.0
01		193 47.6	22.9	180 49.0	8.6	4 36.2	11.6	60.0
02		208 47.8	23.9	195 16.6	8.7	4 47.8	11.5	60.0
03		223 48.0	. . 24.9	209 44.3	8.6	4 59.3	11.4	60.0
04		238 48.1	25.8	224 11.9	8.6	5 10.7	11.5	60.1
05		253 48.3	26.8	238 39.5	8.5	5 22.2	11.4	60.1
06		268 48.5	N 3 27.8	253 07.0	8.5	N 5 33.6	11.4	60.1
07	W	283 48.7	28.8	267 34.5	8.5	5 45.0	11.4	60.1
08	E	298 48.9	29.7	282 02.0	8.4	5 56.4	11.3	60.1
09	D	313 49.1	. . 30.7	296 29.4	8.4	6 07.7	11.3	60.1
10	N	328 49.3	31.7	310 56.8	8.3	6 19.0	11.2	60.1
11	E	343 49.5	32.7	325 24.1	8.3	6 30.2	11.3	60.1
12	S	358 49.6	N 3 33.6	339 51.4	8.3	N 6 41.5	11.1	60.1
13	D	13 49.8	34.6	354 18.7	8.3	6 52.6	11.2	60.2
14	A	28 50.0	35.6	8 46.0	8.2	7 03.8	11.1	60.2
15	Y	43 50.2	. . 36.6	23 13.2	8.2	7 14.9	11.0	60.2
16		58 50.4	37.5	37 40.4	8.1	7 25.9	11.1	60.2
17		73 50.6	38.5	52 07.5	8.1	7 37.0	10.9	60.2
18		88 50.8	N 3 39.5	66 34.6	8.0	N 7 47.9	11.0	60.2
19		103 51.0	40.4	81 01.6	8.1	7 58.9	10.8	60.2
20		118 51.1	41.4	95 28.7	7.9	8 09.7	10.9	60.2
21		133 51.3	. . 42.4	109 55.6	8.0	8 20.6	10.7	60.2
22		148 51.5	43.4	124 22.6	7.9	8 31.3	10.8	60.2
23		163 51.7	44.3	138 49.5	7.9	8 42.1	10.6	60.2
30 00		178 51.9	N 3 45.3	153 16.4	7.8	N 8 52.7	10.6	60.2
01		193 52.1	46.3	167 43.2	7.8	9 03.3	10.6	60.2
02		208 52.3	47.2	182 10.0	7.7	9 13.9	10.5	60.2
03		223 52.5	. . 48.2	196 36.7	7.8	9 24.4	10.4	60.2
04		238 52.6	49.2	211 03.5	7.6	9 34.8	10.4	60.3
05		253 52.8	50.2	225 30.1	7.7	9 45.2	10.3	60.3
06		268 53.0	N 3 51.1	239 56.8	7.6	N 9 55.5	10.3	60.3
07		283 53.2	52.1	254 23.4	7.5	10 05.8	10.2	60.3
08	T	298 53.4	53.1	268 49.9	7.6	10 16.0	10.1	60.3
09	H	313 53.6	. . 54.0	283 16.5	7.4	10 26.1	10.1	60.3
10	U	328 53.8	55.0	297 42.9	7.5	10 36.2	10.0	60.3
11	R	343 53.9	56.0	312 09.4	7.4	10 46.2	9.9	60.3
12	S	358 54.1	N 3 56.9	326 35.8	7.4	N10 56.1	9.9	60.3
13	D	13 54.3	57.9	341 02.2	7.3	11 06.0	9.7	60.3
14	A	28 54.5	58.9	355 28.5	7.3	11 15.7	9.7	60.3
15	Y	43 54.7	3 59.9	9 54.8	7.3	11 25.4	9.7	60.3
16		58 54.9	4 00.8	24 21.1	7.2	11 35.1	9.5	60.3
17		73 55.1	01.8	38 47.3	7.2	11 44.6	9.5	60.3
18		88 55.2	N 4 02.8	53 13.5	7.1	N11 54.1	9.4	60.3
19		103 55.4	03.7	67 39.6	7.1	12 03.5	9.3	60.3
20		118 55.6	04.7	82 05.7	7.1	12 12.8	9.3	60.3
21		133 55.8	. . 05.7	96 31.8	7.0	12 22.1	9.1	60.3
22		148 56.0	06.6	110 57.8	7.0	12 31.2	9.1	60.2
23		163 56.2	07.6	125 23.8	7.0	12 40.3	9.0	60.2
31 00		178 56.4	N 4 08.6	139 49.8	6.9	N12 49.3	8.9	60.2
01		193 56.6	09.5	154 15.7	6.9	12 58.2	8.8	60.2
02		208 56.7	10.5	168 41.6	6.9	13 07.0	8.7	60.2
03		223 56.9	. . 11.5	183 07.5	6.8	13 15.7	8.7	60.2
04		238 57.1	12.5	197 33.3	6.8	13 24.4	8.5	60.2
05		253 57.3	13.4	211 59.1	6.8	13 32.9	8.5	60.2
06		268 57.5	N 4 14.4	226 24.9	6.7	N13 41.4	8.4	60.2
07		283 57.7	15.4	240 50.6	6.7	13 49.8	8.2	60.2
08		298 57.9	16.3	255 16.3	6.6	13 58.0	8.2	60.2
09	F	313 58.0	. . 17.3	269 41.9	6.7	14 06.2	8.1	60.2
10	R	328 58.2	18.3	284 07.6	6.6	14 14.3	8.0	60.2
11	I	343 58.4	19.2	298 33.2	6.5	14 22.3	7.9	60.2
12	D	358 58.6	N 4 20.2	312 58.7	6.6	N14 30.2	7.8	60.2
13	A	13 58.8	21.2	327 24.3	6.5	14 38.0	7.7	60.2
14	Y	28 59.0	22.1	341 49.8	6.4	14 45.7	7.5	60.1
15		43 59.2	. . 23.1	356 15.2	6.5	14 53.2	7.5	60.1
16		58 59.3	24.1	10 40.7	6.4	15 00.7	7.4	60.1
17		73 59.5	25.0	25 06.1	6.4	15 08.1	7.3	60.1
18		88 59.7	N 4 26.0	39 31.5	6.4	N15 15.4	7.2	60.1
19		103 59.9	27.0	53 56.9	6.3	15 22.6	7.1	60.1
20		119 00.1	27.9	68 22.2	6.3	15 29.7	6.9	60.1
21		134 00.3	. . 28.9	82 47.5	6.3	15 36.6	6.9	60.1
22		149 00.5	29.9	97 12.8	6.3	15 43.5	6.7	60.1
23		164 00.6	30.8	111 38.1	6.2	N15 50.2	6.7	60.1
		SD 16.0	*d* 1.0	SD	16.4		16.4	16.4

Lat.	Twilight Naut.	Twilight Civil	Sunrise	Moonrise 29	Moonrise 30	Moonrise 31	Moonrise 1
°	h m	h m	h m	h m	h m	h m	h m
N 72	01 59	03 53	05 06	06 00	05 52	05 43	05 30
N 70	02 35	04 07	05 12	06 07	06 07	06 09	06 14
68	03 00	04 19	05 17	06 14	06 20	06 28	06 43
66	03 19	04 28	05 21	06 19	06 30	06 44	07 05
64	03 34	04 36	05 25	06 23	06 38	06 57	07 23
62	03 46	04 43	05 28	06 27	06 45	07 08	07 38
60	03 56	04 48	05 31	06 30	06 52	07 17	07 50
N 58	04 04	04 53	05 33	06 33	06 57	07 26	08 01
56	04 12	04 58	05 36	06 36	07 02	07 33	08 10
54	04 18	05 02	05 38	06 39	07 07	07 40	08 18
52	04 24	05 05	05 39	06 41	07 11	07 45	08 26
50	04 29	05 08	05 41	06 43	07 15	07 51	08 32
45	04 40	05 15	05 44	06 47	07 23	08 02	08 47
N 40	04 48	05 20	05 47	06 51	07 30	08 12	08 59
35	04 54	05 24	05 50	06 54	07 36	08 20	09 09
30	05 00	05 28	05 52	06 57	07 41	08 28	09 18
20	05 07	05 33	05 55	07 02	07 50	08 40	09 33
N 10	05 13	05 37	05 58	07 07	07 58	08 51	09 47
0	05 16	05 40	06 01	07 11	08 06	09 02	10 00
S 10	05 18	05 43	06 04	07 15	08 13	09 13	10 13
20	05 19	05 45	06 07	07 20	08 21	09 24	10 26
30	05 18	05 46	06 10	07 25	08 31	09 37	10 42
35	05 17	05 46	06 11	07 28	08 36	09 45	10 51
40	05 15	05 46	06 13	07 31	08 43	09 53	11 02
45	05 12	05 46	06 15	07 35	08 50	10 03	11 14
S 50	05 08	05 45	06 18	07 40	08 59	10 16	11 30
52	05 06	05 45	06 19	07 43	09 03	10 22	11 37
54	05 04	05 45	06 20	07 45	09 07	10 28	11 45
56	05 01	05 44	06 21	07 48	09 12	10 35	11 53
58	04 58	05 44	06 23	07 51	09 18	10 43	12 04
S 60	04 54	05 43	06 25	07 54	09 24	10 52	12 15

Lat.	Sunset	Twilight Civil	Twilight Naut.	Moonset 29	Moonset 30	Moonset 31	Moonset 1
°	h m	h m	h m	h m	h m	h m	h m
N 72	19 06	20 20	22 19	21 27	23 33	25 47	01 47
N 70	18 59	20 05	21 39	21 14	23 09	25 04	01 04
68	18 54	19 53	21 13	21 04	22 51	24 36	00 36
66	18 49	19 43	20 54	20 55	22 36	24 14	00 14
64	18 45	19 35	20 38	20 48	22 24	23 57	25 21
62	18 42	19 28	20 26	20 42	22 14	23 43	25 04
60	18 39	19 22	20 15	20 36	22 05	23 31	24 50
N 58	18 37	19 17	20 06	20 32	21 58	23 21	24 38
56	18 34	19 12	19 59	20 27	21 51	23 12	24 27
54	18 32	19 08	19 52	20 24	21 45	23 04	24 18
52	18 31	19 05	19 46	20 20	21 40	22 57	24 09
50	18 29	19 02	19 41	20 17	21 35	22 51	24 02
45	18 25	18 55	19 30	20 11	21 25	22 37	23 46
N 40	18 22	18 50	19 22	20 05	21 16	22 26	23 33
35	18 20	18 45	19 15	20 00	21 09	22 17	23 22
30	18 18	18 42	19 10	19 56	21 02	22 08	23 12
20	18 14	18 36	19 02	19 49	20 51	21 54	22 56
N 10	18 11	18 32	18 56	19 43	20 41	21 41	22 41
0	18 08	18 28	18 52	19 37	20 32	21 29	22 27
S 10	18 05	18 26	18 50	19 31	20 23	21 18	22 14
20	18 02	18 24	18 50	19 24	20 13	21 05	21 59
30	17 59	18 23	18 50	19 17	20 02	20 51	21 43
35	17 57	18 22	18 52	19 13	19 56	20 42	21 33
40	17 55	18 22	18 53	19 08	19 49	20 33	21 22
45	17 53	18 22	18 56	19 03	19 40	20 22	21 09
S 50	17 50	18 22	19 00	18 56	19 30	20 08	20 53
52	17 49	18 23	19 02	18 53	19 25	20 02	20 46
54	17 48	18 23	19 04	18 50	19 20	19 55	20 38
56	17 46	18 23	19 06	18 46	19 15	19 48	20 28
58	17 45	18 24	19 09	18 42	19 08	19 39	20 18
S 60	17 43	18 24	19 13	18 38	19 01	19 30	20 06

Day	SUN Eqn. of Time 00^h	SUN Eqn. of Time 12^h	SUN Mer. Pass.	MOON Mer. Pass. Upper	MOON Mer. Pass. Lower	MOON Age	MOON Phase
d	m s	m s	h m	h m	h m	d	%
29	04 51	04 42	12 05	13 24	00 57	01	3
30	04 33	04 24	12 04	14 19	01 51	02	8
31	04 15	04 06	12 04	15 16	02 47	03	16

	UT	ARIES	VENUS −4·2		MARS +1·5		JUPITER −2·5		SATURN +0·4	
		GHA	GHA	Dec	GHA	Dec	GHA	Dec	GHA	Dec
	d h	° ′	° ′	° ′	° ′	° ′	° ′	° ′	° ′	° ′
	1 00	189 32.6	191 34.8	N 7 15.5	146 25.3	N16 54.4	351 17.0	S 6 01.7	281 56.8	S22 04.6
	01	204 35.1	206 38.3	14.6	161 26.0	54.9	6 19.7	01.5	296 59.3	04.6
	02	219 37.6	221 41.8	13.6	176 26.7	55.4	21 22.5	01.4	312 01.7	04.6
	03	234 40.0	236 45.3	. . 12.7	191 27.4	. . 56.0	36 25.3	. . 01.3	327 04.2	. . 04.6
	04	249 42.5	251 48.9	11.8	206 28.1	56.5	51 28.0	01.2	342 06.6	04.6
	05	264 45.0	266 52.4	10.9	221 28.8	57.1	66 30.8	01.1	357 09.0	04.6
	06	279 47.4	281 55.9	N 7 10.0	236 29.5	N16 57.6	81 33.5	S 6 00.9	12 11.5	S22 04.6
	07	294 49.9	296 59.4	09.1	251 30.2	58.1	96 36.3	00.8	27 13.9	04.6
S	08	309 52.3	312 02.9	08.2	266 30.9	58.7	111 39.0	00.7	42 16.4	04.6
A	09	324 54.8	327 06.4	. . 07.2	281 31.6	. . 59.2	126 41.8	. . 00.6	57 18.8	. . 04.6
T	10	339 57.3	342 09.9	06.3	296 32.3	16 59.7	141 44.6	00.5	72 21.3	04.6
U	11	354 59.7	357 13.4	05.4	311 33.0	17 00.3	156 47.3	00.3	87 23.7	04.6
R	12	10 02.2	12 16.9	N 7 04.5	326 33.7	N17 00.8	171 50.1	S 6 00.2	102 26.1	S22 04.6
D	13	25 04.7	27 20.4	03.6	341 34.4	01.3	186 52.8	00.1	117 28.6	04.6
A	14	40 07.1	42 23.9	02.7	356 35.1	01.9	201 55.6	6 00.0	132 31.0	04.6
Y	15	55 09.6	57 27.4	. . 01.8	11 35.8	. . 02.4	216 58.4	5 59.9	147 33.5	. . 04.6
	16	70 12.1	72 30.8	7 00.8	26 36.5	02.9	232 01.1	59.7	162 35.9	04.6
	17	85 14.5	87 34.3	6 59.9	41 37.2	03.5	247 03.9	59.6	177 38.4	04.6
	18	100 17.0	102 37.8	N 6 59.0	56 37.9	N17 04.0	262 06.6	S 5 59.5	192 40.8	S22 04.6
	19	115 19.5	117 41.3	58.1	71 38.6	04.5	277 09.4	59.4	207 43.2	04.6
	20	130 21.9	132 44.7	57.2	86 39.4	05.1	292 12.1	59.3	222 45.7	04.6
	21	145 24.4	147 48.2	. . 56.3	101 40.1	. . 05.6	307 14.9	. . 59.1	237 48.1	. . 04.6
	22	160 26.8	162 51.7	55.4	116 40.8	06.1	322 17.7	59.0	252 50.6	04.6
	23	175 29.3	177 55.1	54.4	131 41.5	06.7	337 20.4	58.9	267 53.0	04.6
	2 00	190 31.8	192 58.6	N 6 53.5	146 42.2	N17 07.2	352 23.2	S 5 58.8	282 55.5	S22 04.6
	01	205 34.2	208 02.0	52.6	161 42.9	07.7	7 25.9	58.6	297 57.9	04.6
	02	220 36.7	223 05.5	51.7	176 43.6	08.3	22 28.7	58.5	313 00.4	04.6
	03	235 39.2	238 08.9	. . 50.8	191 44.3	. . 08.8	37 31.5	. . 58.4	328 02.8	. . 04.6
	04	250 41.6	253 12.4	49.9	206 45.0	09.3	52 34.2	58.3	343 05.3	04.6
	05	265 44.1	268 15.8	49.0	221 45.7	09.8	67 37.0	58.2	358 07.7	04.6
	06	280 46.6	283 19.2	N 6 48.1	236 46.4	N17 10.4	82 39.7	S 5 58.0	13 10.1	S22 04.6
	07	295 49.0	298 22.7	47.1	251 47.1	10.9	97 42.5	57.9	28 12.6	04.6
	08	310 51.5	313 26.1	46.2	266 47.8	11.4	112 45.3	57.8	43 15.0	04.6
S	09	325 54.0	328 29.5	. . 45.3	281 48.5	. . 12.0	127 48.0	. . 57.7	58 17.5	. . 04.6
U	10	340 56.4	343 33.0	44.4	296 49.2	12.5	142 50.8	57.6	73 19.9	04.6
N	11	355 58.9	358 36.4	43.5	311 49.9	13.0	157 53.5	57.4	88 22.4	04.6
D	12	11 01.3	13 39.8	N 6 42.6	326 50.6	N17 13.5	172 56.3	S 5 57.3	103 24.8	S22 04.5
A	13	26 03.8	28 43.2	41.7	341 51.3	14.1	187 59.0	57.2	118 27.3	04.5
Y	14	41 06.3	43 46.6	40.8	356 52.0	14.6	203 01.8	57.1	133 29.7	04.5
	15	56 08.7	58 50.0	. . 39.9	11 52.7	. . 15.1	218 04.6	. . 57.0	148 32.2	. . 04.5
	16	71 11.2	73 53.5	39.0	26 53.4	15.7	233 07.3	56.8	163 34.6	04.5
	17	86 13.7	88 56.9	38.1	41 54.1	16.2	248 10.1	56.7	178 37.1	04.5
	18	101 16.1	104 00.3	N 6 37.1	56 54.8	N17 16.7	263 12.8	S 5 56.6	193 39.5	S22 04.5
	19	116 18.6	119 03.7	36.2	71 55.5	17.2	278 15.6	56.5	208 42.0	04.5
	20	131 21.1	134 07.0	35.3	86 56.2	17.8	293 18.4	56.3	223 44.4	04.5
	21	146 23.5	149 10.4	. . 34.4	101 56.9	. . 18.3	308 21.1	. . 56.2	238 46.9	. . 04.5
	22	161 26.0	164 13.8	33.5	116 57.6	18.8	323 23.9	56.1	253 49.3	04.5
	23	176 28.5	179 17.2	32.6	131 58.3	19.3	338 26.6	56.0	268 51.8	04.5
	3 00	191 30.9	194 20.6	N 6 31.7	146 59.0	N17 19.9	353 29.4	S 5 55.9	283 54.2	S22 04.5
	01	206 33.4	209 24.0	30.8	161 59.7	20.4	8 32.2	55.7	298 56.7	04.5
	02	221 35.8	224 27.3	29.9	177 00.4	20.9	23 34.9	55.6	313 59.1	04.5
	03	236 38.3	239 30.7	. . 29.0	192 01.1	. . 21.4	38 37.7	. . 55.5	329 01.6	. . 04.5
	04	251 40.8	254 34.1	28.1	207 01.8	22.0	53 40.4	55.4	344 04.0	04.5
	05	266 43.2	269 37.4	27.2	222 02.5	22.5	68 43.2	55.3	359 06.5	04.5
	06	281 45.7	284 40.8	N 6 26.3	237 03.2	N17 23.0	83 46.0	S 5 55.1	14 08.9	S22 04.5
	07	296 48.2	299 44.1	25.4	252 03.9	23.5	98 48.7	55.0	29 11.4	04.5
	08	311 50.6	314 47.5	24.5	267 04.6	24.0	113 51.5	54.9	44 13.8	04.5
M	09	326 53.1	329 50.8	. . 23.6	282 05.3	. . 24.6	128 54.2	. . 54.8	59 16.3	. . 04.5
O	10	341 55.6	344 54.2	22.7	297 06.0	25.1	143 57.0	54.6	74 18.7	04.5
N	11	356 58.0	359 57.5	21.8	312 06.7	25.6	158 59.8	54.5	89 21.2	04.5
D	12	12 00.5	15 00.9	N 6 20.9	327 07.4	N17 26.1	174 02.5	S 5 54.4	104 23.6	S22 04.5
A	13	27 02.9	30 04.2	20.0	342 08.1	26.7	189 05.3	54.3	119 26.1	04.5
Y	14	42 05.4	45 07.5	19.1	357 08.8	27.2	204 08.1	54.2	134 28.5	04.5
	15	57 07.9	60 10.9	. . 18.2	12 09.5	. . 27.7	219 10.8	. . 54.0	149 31.0	. . 04.5
	16	72 10.3	75 14.2	17.3	27 10.2	28.2	234 13.6	53.9	164 33.4	04.5
	17	87 12.8	90 17.5	16.4	42 10.9	28.7	249 16.3	53.8	179 35.9	04.5
	18	102 15.3	105 20.8	N 6 15.5	57 11.6	N17 29.3	264 19.1	S 5 53.7	194 38.3	S22 04.5
	19	117 17.7	120 24.2	14.6	72 12.3	29.8	279 21.9	53.6	209 40.8	04.5
	20	132 20.2	135 27.5	13.7	87 13.0	30.3	294 24.6	53.4	224 43.2	04.5
	21	147 22.7	150 30.8	. . 12.8	102 13.7	. . 30.8	309 27.4	. . 53.3	239 45.7	. . 04.5
	22	162 25.1	165 34.1	11.9	117 14.4	31.3	324 30.1	53.2	254 48.2	04.5
	23	177 27.6	180 37.4	11.0	132 15.1	31.8	339 32.9	53.1	269 50.6	04.5
	Mer. Pass.	h m 11 16.0	*v* 3.4	*d* 0.9	*v* 0.7	*d* 0.5	*v* 2.8	*d* 0.1	*v* 2.4	*d* 0.0

STARS Name	SHA	Dec
	° ′	° ′
Acamar	315 16.8	S40 14.5
Achernar	335 25.5	S57 09.2
Acrux	173 05.6	S63 11.7
Adhara	255 10.5	S29 00.2
Aldebaran	290 46.6	N16 32.4
Alioth	166 18.0	N55 52.0
Alkaid	152 56.5	N49 13.6
Al Na'ir	27 40.9	S46 52.5
Alnilam	275 43.9	S 1 11.8
Alphard	217 53.4	S 8 44.2
Alphecca	126 08.6	N26 39.4
Alpheratz	357 41.2	N29 10.9
Altair	62 05.8	N 8 54.8
Ankaa	353 13.7	S42 12.9
Antares	112 22.9	S26 28.0
Arcturus	145 53.1	N19 05.6
Atria	107 22.1	S69 03.1
Avior	234 16.7	S59 34.3
Bellatrix	278 29.4	N 6 21.6
Betelgeuse	270 58.6	N 7 24.3
Canopus	263 55.1	S52 42.8
Capella	280 30.9	N46 00.8
Deneb	49 29.9	N45 20.3
Denebola	182 30.8	N14 28.5
Diphda	348 53.7	S17 53.7
Dubhe	193 48.1	N61 39.5
Elnath	278 09.5	N28 37.1
Eltanin	90 44.8	N51 29.1
Enif	33 44.8	N 9 57.1
Fomalhaut	15 21.5	S29 31.9
Gacrux	171 57.4	S57 12.6
Gienah	175 49.3	S17 38.3
Hadar	148 43.6	S60 27.2
Hamal	327 58.2	N23 32.4
Kaus Aust.	83 40.4	S34 22.3
Kochab	137 19.2	N74 05.0
Markab	13 36.1	N15 17.7
Menkar	314 12.6	N 4 09.1
Menkent	148 04.2	S36 27.2
Miaplacidus	221 38.5	S69 47.6
Mirfak	308 37.0	N49 55.2
Nunki	75 55.2	S26 16.3
Peacock	53 15.5	S56 40.5
Pollux	243 24.6	N27 58.9
Procyon	244 57.0	N 5 10.6
Rasalhague	96 04.0	N12 32.9
Regulus	207 40.6	N11 52.8
Rigel	281 09.7	S 8 11.3
Rigil Kent.	139 47.6	S60 54.1
Sabik	102 09.5	S15 44.6
Schedar	349 38.1	N56 37.7
Shaula	96 18.3	S37 06.7
Sirius	258 31.5	S16 44.8
Spica	158 28.2	S11 15.1
Suhail	222 50.3	S43 30.5
Vega	80 37.2	N38 47.9
Zuben'ubi	137 02.3	S16 06.7

	SHA	Mer. Pass.
	° ′	h m
Venus	2 26.8	11 06
Mars	316 10.4	14 13
Jupiter	161 51.4	0 30
Saturn	92 23.7	5 07

UT (d h)	SUN GHA	SUN Dec	MOON GHA	v	MOON Dec	d	HP
	° ′	° ′	° ′	′	° ′	′	′
1 00 (SATURDAY)	179 00.8	N 4 31.8	126 03.3	6.2	N15 56.9	6.5	60.0
01	194 01.0	32.7	140 28.5	6.2	16 03.4	6.4	60.0
02	209 01.2	33.7	154 53.7	6.2	16 09.8	6.3	60.0
03	224 01.4	. . 34.7	169 18.9	6.1	16 16.1	6.2	60.0
04	239 01.6	35.6	183 44.0	6.2	16 22.3	6.1	60.0
05	254 01.7	36.6	198 09.2	6.1	16 28.4	6.0	60.0
06	269 01.9	N 4 37.6	212 34.3	6.1	N16 34.4	5.9	60.0
07	284 02.1	38.5	226 59.4	6.0	16 40.3	5.7	59.9
08	299 02.3	39.5	241 24.4	6.1	16 46.0	5.6	59.9
09	314 02.5	. . 40.5	255 49.5	6.0	16 51.6	5.6	59.9
10	329 02.7	41.4	270 14.5	6.1	16 57.2	5.4	59.9
11	344 02.9	42.4	284 39.6	6.0	17 02.6	5.2	59.9
12	359 03.0	N 4 43.4	299 04.6	6.0	N17 07.8	5.2	59.9
13	14 03.2	44.3	313 29.6	6.0	17 13.0	5.0	59.9
14	29 03.4	45.3	327 54.6	5.9	17 18.0	5.0	59.8
15	44 03.6	. . 46.2	342 19.5	6.0	17 23.0	4.8	59.8
16	59 03.8	47.2	356 44.5	6.0	17 27.8	4.7	59.8
17	74 04.0	48.2	11 09.5	5.9	17 32.5	4.5	59.8
18	89 04.2	N 4 49.1	25 34.4	5.9	N17 37.0	4.5	59.8
19	104 04.3	50.1	39 59.3	6.0	17 41.5	4.3	59.8
20	119 04.5	51.1	54 24.3	5.9	17 45.8	4.2	59.7
21	134 04.7	. . 52.0	68 49.2	5.9	17 50.0	4.1	59.7
22	149 04.9	53.0	83 14.1	5.9	17 54.1	3.9	59.7
23	164 05.1	53.9	97 39.0	5.9	17 58.0	3.9	59.7
2 00 (SUNDAY)	179 05.3	N 4 54.9	112 03.9	5.9	N18 01.9	3.7	59.7
01	194 05.4	55.9	126 28.8	5.9	18 05.6	3.6	59.7
02	209 05.6	56.8	140 53.7	5.9	18 09.2	3.5	59.6
03	224 05.8	. . 57.8	155 18.6	6.0	18 12.7	3.3	59.6
04	239 06.0	58.7	169 43.6	5.9	18 16.0	3.2	59.6
05	254 06.2	4 59.7	184 08.5	5.9	18 19.2	3.1	59.6
06	269 06.4	N 5 00.7	198 33.4	5.9	N18 22.3	3.0	59.6
07	284 06.5	01.6	212 58.3	5.9	18 25.3	2.8	59.5
08	299 06.7	02.6	227 23.2	5.9	18 28.1	2.7	59.5
09	314 06.9	. . 03.5	241 48.1	6.0	18 30.8	2.6	59.5
10	329 07.1	04.5	256 13.1	5.9	18 33.4	2.5	59.5
11	344 07.3	05.5	270 38.0	6.0	18 35.9	2.3	59.5
12	359 07.5	N 5 06.4	285 03.0	5.9	N18 38.2	2.3	59.4
13	14 07.6	07.4	299 27.9	6.0	18 40.5	2.0	59.4
14	29 07.8	08.3	313 52.9	6.0	18 42.5	2.0	59.4
15	44 08.0	. . 09.3	328 17.9	6.0	18 44.5	1.9	59.4
16	59 08.2	10.3	342 42.9	6.0	18 46.4	1.7	59.4
17	74 08.4	11.2	357 07.9	6.0	18 48.1	1.6	59.3
18	89 08.6	N 5 12.2	11 32.9	6.0	N18 49.7	1.4	59.3
19	104 08.7	13.1	25 57.9	6.1	18 51.1	1.4	59.3
20	119 08.9	14.1	40 23.0	6.1	18 52.5	1.2	59.3
21	134 09.1	. . 15.1	54 48.1	6.1	18 53.7	1.1	59.3
22	149 09.3	16.0	69 13.2	6.1	18 54.8	0.9	59.2
23	164 09.5	17.0	83 38.3	6.1	18 55.7	0.9	59.2
3 00 (MONDAY)	179 09.7	N 5 17.9	98 03.4	6.2	N18 56.6	0.7	59.2
01	194 09.8	18.9	112 28.6	6.2	18 57.3	0.6	59.2
02	209 10.0	19.8	126 53.8	6.2	18 57.9	0.4	59.2
03	224 10.2	. . 20.8	141 19.0	6.2	18 58.3	0.4	59.1
04	239 10.4	21.8	155 44.2	6.3	18 58.7	0.2	59.1
05	254 10.6	22.7	170 09.5	6.2	18 58.9	0.1	59.1
06	269 10.8	N 5 23.7	184 34.7	6.4	N18 59.0	0.1	59.1
07	284 10.9	24.6	199 00.1	6.3	18 58.9	0.1	59.0
08	299 11.1	25.6	213 25.4	6.4	18 58.8	0.3	59.0
09	314 11.3	. . 26.5	227 50.8	6.4	18 58.5	0.4	59.0
10	329 11.5	27.5	242 16.2	6.4	18 58.1	0.5	59.0
11	344 11.7	28.5	256 41.6	6.5	18 57.6	0.7	59.0
12	359 11.9	N 5 29.4	271 07.1	6.5	N18 56.9	0.7	58.9
13	14 12.0	30.4	285 32.6	6.5	18 56.2	0.9	58.9
14	29 12.2	31.3	299 58.1	6.6	18 55.3	1.0	58.9
15	44 12.4	. . 32.3	314 23.7	6.6	18 54.3	1.2	58.9
16	59 12.6	33.2	328 49.3	6.7	18 53.1	1.2	58.8
17	74 12.8	34.2	343 15.0	6.6	18 51.9	1.4	58.8
18	89 12.9	N 5 35.1	357 40.6	6.8	N18 50.5	1.5	58.8
19	104 13.1	36.1	12 06.4	6.7	18 49.0	1.6	58.8
20	119 13.3	37.1	26 32.1	6.8	18 47.4	1.7	58.7
21	134 13.5	. . 38.0	40 57.9	6.9	18 45.7	1.9	58.7
22	149 13.7	39.0	55 23.8	6.9	18 43.8	1.9	58.7
23	164 13.9	39.9	69 49.7	6.9	N18 41.9	2.1	58.7
	SD 16.0	d 1.0	SD 16.3		16.2		16.1

Lat.	Twilight Naut.	Twilight Civil	Sunrise	Moonrise 1	Moonrise 2	Moonrise 3	Moonrise 4
°	h m	h m	h m	h m	h m	h m	h m
N 72	01 23	03 34	04 50	05 30	▭	▭	▭
N 70	02 12	03 51	04 58	06 14	06 27	07 06	08 25
68	02 42	04 05	05 04	06 43	07 09	07 56	09 07
66	03 03	04 16	05 10	07 05	07 38	08 28	09 36
64	03 20	04 25	05 14	07 23	08 00	08 51	09 58
62	03 34	04 32	05 18	07 38	08 17	09 10	10 15
60	03 45	04 39	05 22	07 50	08 32	09 25	10 29
N 58	03 55	04 45	05 25	08 01	08 44	09 38	10 42
56	04 03	04 50	05 28	08 10	08 55	09 49	10 52
54	04 10	04 54	05 30	08 18	09 04	09 59	11 02
52	04 16	04 58	05 32	08 26	09 13	10 08	11 10
50	04 22	05 02	05 34	08 32	09 21	10 16	11 17
45	04 34	05 09	05 39	08 47	09 37	10 33	11 33
N 40	04 43	05 15	05 42	08 59	09 50	10 47	11 47
35	04 50	05 20	05 45	09 09	10 02	10 58	11 58
30	04 56	05 24	05 48	09 18	10 12	11 09	12 07
20	05 05	05 31	05 53	09 33	10 29	11 26	12 24
N 10	05 11	05 36	05 57	09 47	10 44	11 42	12 39
0	05 15	05 39	06 00	10 00	10 58	11 56	12 53
S 10	05 18	05 43	06 04	10 13	11 12	12 10	13 06
20	05 20	05 45	06 07	10 26	11 27	12 26	13 21
30	05 20	05 47	06 11	10 42	11 45	12 44	13 38
35	05 19	05 48	06 14	10 51	11 55	12 54	13 47
40	05 18	05 49	06 16	11 02	12 07	13 06	13 58
45	05 16	05 50	06 19	11 14	12 20	13 20	14 11
S 50	05 13	05 50	06 22	11 30	12 37	13 37	14 27
52	05 11	05 50	06 24	11 37	12 45	13 45	14 35
54	05 09	05 50	06 26	11 45	12 54	13 54	14 43
56	05 07	05 50	06 27	11 53	13 04	14 04	14 52
58	05 05	05 50	06 30	12 04	13 15	14 15	15 03
S 60	05 02	05 50	06 32	12 15	13 28	14 28	15 15

Lat.	Sunset	Twilight Civil	Twilight Naut.	Moonset 1	Moonset 2	Moonset 3	Moonset 4
°	h m	h m	h m	h m	h m	h m	h m
N 72	19 20	20 37	22 59	01 47	▭	▭	▭
N 70	19 12	20 19	22 02	01 04	02 53	04 16	04 56
68	19 05	20 05	21 30	00 36	02 11	03 26	04 13
66	18 59	19 54	21 08	00 14	01 43	02 54	03 44
64	18 54	19 45	20 50	25 21	01 21	02 31	03 22
62	18 50	19 37	20 36	25 04	01 04	02 12	03 05
60	18 47	19 30	20 24	24 50	00 50	01 57	02 50
N 58	18 43	19 24	20 14	24 38	00 38	01 44	02 38
56	18 41	19 19	20 06	24 27	00 27	01 33	02 27
54	18 38	19 14	19 58	24 18	00 18	01 23	02 17
52	18 36	19 10	19 52	24 09	00 09	01 14	02 09
50	18 34	19 07	19 46	24 02	00 02	01 06	02 01
45	18 29	18 59	19 34	23 46	24 49	00 49	01 45
N 40	18 25	18 53	19 25	23 33	24 35	00 35	01 31
35	18 22	18 48	19 18	23 22	24 24	00 24	01 20
30	18 19	18 43	19 12	23 12	24 13	00 13	01 10
20	18 15	18 37	19 03	22 56	23 56	24 52	00 52
N 10	18 11	18 32	18 56	22 41	23 40	24 37	00 37
0	18 07	18 28	18 52	22 27	23 26	24 23	00 23
S 10	18 03	18 24	18 49	22 14	23 11	24 09	00 09
20	17 59	18 21	18 47	21 59	22 56	23 54	24 52
30	17 55	18 19	18 47	21 43	22 38	23 36	24 36
35	17 53	18 18	18 47	21 33	22 28	23 26	24 27
40	17 50	18 17	18 49	21 22	22 16	23 14	24 16
45	17 47	18 17	18 50	21 09	22 02	23 01	24 03
S 50	17 44	18 16	18 53	20 53	21 45	22 44	23 48
52	17 42	18 16	18 55	20 46	21 37	22 36	23 41
54	17 40	18 16	18 56	20 38	21 28	22 27	23 33
56	17 38	18 15	18 58	20 28	21 18	22 17	23 24
58	17 36	18 15	19 01	20 18	21 07	22 06	23 14
S 60	17 34	18 15	19 04	20 06	20 54	21 53	23 02

Day	SUN Eqn. of Time 00^h	SUN Eqn. of Time 12^h	SUN Mer. Pass.	MOON Mer. Pass. Upper	MOON Mer. Pass. Lower	MOON Age	MOON Phase
d	m s	m s	h m	h m	h m	d %	
1	03 57	03 48	12 04	16 14	03 44	04 25	
2	03 39	03 31	12 04	17 12	04 43	05 36	
3	03 22	03 13	12 03	18 10	05 41	06 47	

Day	UT d h	ARIES GHA ° ′	VENUS −4·4 GHA ° ′	VENUS Dec ° ′	MARS +1·5 GHA ° ′	MARS Dec ° ′	JUPITER −2·5 GHA ° ′	JUPITER Dec ° ′	SATURN +0·4 GHA ° ′	SATURN Dec ° ′
TUESDAY	4 00	192 30.1	195 40.7	N 6 10.1	147 15.8	N17 32.4	354 35.7	S 5 52.9	284 53.1	S22 04.5
	01	207 32.5	210 44.0	09.3	162 16.5	32.9	9 38.4	52.8	299 55.5	04.5
	02	222 35.0	225 47.3	08.4	177 17.2	33.4	24 41.2	52.7	314 58.0	04.5
	03	237 37.4	240 50.6	. . 07.5	192 17.9	. . 33.9	39 43.9	. . 52.6	330 00.4	. . 04.5
	04	252 39.9	255 53.8	06.6	207 18.5	34.4	54 46.7	52.5	345 02.9	04.4
	05	267 42.4	270 57.1	05.7	222 19.2	34.9	69 49.5	52.3	0 05.3	04.4
	06	282 44.8	286 00.4	N 6 04.8	237 19.9	N17 35.5	84 52.2	S 5 52.2	15 07.8	S22 04.4
	07	297 47.3	301 03.7	03.9	252 20.6	36.0	99 55.0	52.1	30 10.2	04.4
	08	312 49.8	316 06.9	03.0	267 21.3	36.5	114 57.7	52.0	45 12.7	04.4
	09	327 52.2	331 10.2	. . 02.1	282 22.0	. . 37.0	130 00.5	. . 51.9	60 15.2	. . 04.4
	10	342 54.7	346 13.5	01.3	297 22.7	37.5	145 03.3	51.7	75 17.6	04.4
	11	357 57.2	1 16.7	6 00.4	312 23.4	38.0	160 06.0	51.6	90 20.1	04.4
	12	12 59.6	16 20.0	N 5 59.5	327 24.1	N17 38.6	175 08.8	S 5 51.5	105 22.5	S22 04.4
	13	28 02.1	31 23.2	58.6	342 24.8	39.1	190 11.6	51.4	120 25.0	04.4
	14	43 04.6	46 26.5	57.7	357 25.5	39.6	205 14.3	51.2	135 27.4	04.4
	15	58 07.0	61 29.7	. . 56.8	12 26.2	. . 40.1	220 17.1	. . 51.1	150 29.9	. . 04.4
	16	73 09.5	76 33.0	56.0	27 26.9	40.6	235 19.8	51.0	165 32.4	04.4
	17	88 11.9	91 36.2	55.1	42 27.6	41.1	250 22.6	50.9	180 34.8	04.4
	18	103 14.4	106 39.4	N 5 54.2	57 28.3	N17 41.6	265 25.4	S 5 50.8	195 37.3	S22 04.4
	19	118 16.9	121 42.7	53.3	72 29.0	42.1	280 28.1	50.6	210 39.7	04.4
	20	133 19.3	136 45.9	52.5	87 29.7	42.7	295 30.9	50.5	225 42.2	04.4
	21	148 21.8	151 49.1	. . 51.6	102 30.4	. . 43.2	310 33.6	. . 50.4	240 44.6	. . 04.4
	22	163 24.3	166 52.3	50.7	117 31.1	43.7	325 36.4	50.3	255 47.1	04.4
	23	178 26.7	181 55.6	49.8	132 31.8	44.2	340 39.2	50.2	270 49.6	04.4
WEDNESDAY	5 00	193 29.2	196 58.8	N 5 48.9	147 32.5	N17 44.7	355 41.9	S 5 50.0	285 52.0	S22 04.4
	01	208 31.7	212 02.0	48.1	162 33.2	45.2	10 44.7	49.9	300 54.5	04.4
	02	223 34.1	227 05.2	47.2	177 33.9	45.7	25 47.5	49.8	315 56.9	04.4
	03	238 36.6	242 08.4	. . 46.3	192 34.6	. . 46.2	40 50.2	. . 49.7	330 59.4	. . 04.4
	04	253 39.0	257 11.6	45.5	207 35.3	46.7	55 53.0	49.5	346 01.8	04.4
	05	268 41.5	272 14.8	44.6	222 36.0	47.3	70 55.7	49.4	1 04.3	04.4
	06	283 44.0	287 18.0	N 5 43.7	237 36.7	N17 47.8	85 58.5	S 5 49.3	16 06.8	S22 04.4
	07	298 46.4	302 21.2	42.8	252 37.3	48.3	101 01.3	49.2	31 09.2	04.4
	08	313 48.9	317 24.3	42.0	267 38.0	48.8	116 04.0	49.1	46 11.7	04.4
	09	328 51.4	332 27.5	. . 41.1	282 38.7	. . 49.3	131 06.8	. . 48.9	61 14.1	. . 04.4
	10	343 53.8	347 30.7	40.2	297 39.4	49.8	146 09.5	48.8	76 16.6	04.4
	11	358 56.3	2 33.9	39.4	312 40.1	50.3	161 12.3	48.7	91 19.1	04.4
	12	13 58.8	17 37.0	N 5 38.5	327 40.8	N17 50.8	176 15.1	S 5 48.6	106 21.5	S22 04.4
	13	29 01.2	32 40.2	37.7	342 41.5	51.3	191 17.8	48.5	121 24.0	04.4
	14	44 03.7	47 43.4	36.8	357 42.2	51.8	206 20.6	48.3	136 26.5	04.4
	15	59 06.2	62 46.5	. . 35.9	12 42.9	. . 52.3	221 23.4	. . 48.2	151 28.9	. . 04.4
	16	74 08.6	77 49.7	35.1	27 43.6	52.8	236 26.1	48.1	166 31.4	04.4
	17	89 11.1	92 52.8	34.2	42 44.3	53.3	251 28.9	48.0	181 33.8	04.4
	18	104 13.5	107 56.0	N 5 33.3	57 45.0	N17 53.9	266 31.6	S 5 47.8	196 36.3	S22 04.4
	19	119 16.0	122 59.1	32.5	72 45.7	54.4	281 34.4	47.7	211 38.8	04.4
	20	134 18.5	138 02.2	31.6	87 46.4	54.9	296 37.2	47.6	226 41.2	04.3
	21	149 20.9	153 05.4	. . 30.8	102 47.1	. . 55.4	311 39.9	. . 47.5	241 43.7	. . 04.3
	22	164 23.4	168 08.5	29.9	117 47.8	55.9	326 42.7	47.4	256 46.1	04.3
	23	179 25.9	183 11.6	29.1	132 48.5	56.4	341 45.5	47.2	271 48.6	04.3
THURSDAY	6 00	194 28.3	198 14.8	N 5 28.2	147 49.2	N17 56.9	356 48.2	S 5 47.1	286 51.1	S22 04.3
	01	209 30.8	213 17.9	27.4	162 49.8	57.4	11 51.0	47.0	301 53.5	04.3
	02	224 33.3	228 21.0	26.5	177 50.5	57.9	26 53.7	46.9	316 56.0	04.3
	03	239 35.7	243 24.1	. . 25.7	192 51.2	. . 58.4	41 56.5	. . 46.7	331 58.5	. . 04.3
	04	254 38.2	258 27.2	24.8	207 51.9	58.9	56 59.3	46.6	347 00.9	04.3
	05	269 40.7	273 30.3	24.0	222 52.6	59.4	72 02.0	46.5	2 03.4	04.3
	06	284 43.1	288 33.4	N 5 23.1	237 53.3	N17 59.9	87 04.8	S 5 46.4	17 05.9	S22 04.3
	07	299 45.6	303 36.5	22.3	252 54.0	18 00.4	102 07.6	46.3	32 08.3	04.3
	08	314 48.0	318 39.6	21.4	267 54.7	00.9	117 10.3	46.1	47 10.8	04.3
	09	329 50.5	333 42.7	. . 20.6	282 55.4	. . 01.4	132 13.1	. . 46.0	62 13.2	. . 04.3
	10	344 53.0	348 45.8	19.7	297 56.1	01.9	147 15.8	45.9	77 15.7	04.3
	11	359 55.4	3 48.9	18.9	312 56.8	02.4	162 18.6	45.8	92 18.2	04.3
	12	14 57.9	18 51.9	N 5 18.0	327 57.5	N18 02.9	177 21.4	S 5 45.7	107 20.6	S22 04.3
	13	30 00.4	33 55.0	17.2	342 58.2	03.4	192 24.1	45.5	122 23.1	04.3
	14	45 02.8	48 58.1	16.4	357 58.9	03.9	207 26.9	45.4	137 25.6	04.3
	15	60 05.3	64 01.2	. . 15.5	12 59.5	. . 04.4	222 29.7	. . 45.3	152 28.0	. . 04.3
	16	75 07.8	79 04.2	14.7	28 00.2	04.9	237 32.4	45.2	167 30.5	04.3
	17	90 10.2	94 07.3	13.9	43 00.9	05.4	252 35.2	45.0	182 33.0	04.3
	18	105 12.7	109 10.3	N 5 13.0	58 01.6	N18 05.9	267 37.9	S 5 44.9	197 35.4	S22 04.3
	19	120 15.1	124 13.4	12.2	73 02.3	06.4	282 40.7	44.8	212 37.9	04.3
	20	135 17.6	139 16.4	11.4	88 03.0	06.9	297 43.5	44.7	227 40.4	04.3
	21	150 20.1	154 19.5	. . 10.5	103 03.7	. . 07.4	312 46.2	. . 44.6	242 42.8	. . 04.3
	22	165 22.5	169 22.5	09.7	118 04.4	07.9	327 49.0	44.4	257 45.3	04.3
	23	180 25.0	184 25.6	08.9	133 05.1	08.4	342 51.8	44.3	272 47.8	04.3
	Mer. Pass.	h m 11 04.2	v 3.2	d 0.9	v 0.7	d 0.5	v 2.8	d 0.1	v 2.5	d 0.0

STARS

Name	SHA ° ′	Dec ° ′
Acamar	315 16.8	S40 14.5
Achernar	335 25.5	S57 09.2
Acrux	173 05.6	S63 11.7
Adhara	255 10.5	S29 00.2
Aldebaran	290 46.6	N16 32.4
Alioth	166 18.0	N55 52.0
Alkaid	152 56.5	N49 13.6
Al Na'ir	27 40.9	S46 52.5
Alnilam	275 43.9	S 1 11.8
Alphard	217 53.4	S 8 44.3
Alphecca	126 08.6	N26 39.4
Alpheratz	357 41.2	N29 10.9
Altair	62 05.8	N 8 54.8
Ankaa	353 13.7	S42 12.9
Antares	112 22.9	S26 28.0
Arcturus	145 53.1	N19 05.6
Atria	107 22.1	S69 03.1
Avior	234 16.7	S59 34.3
Bellatrix	278 29.4	N 6 21.6
Betelgeuse	270 58.6	N 7 24.3
Canopus	263 55.1	S52 42.8
Capella	280 30.9	N46 00.8
Deneb	49 29.9	N45 20.3
Denebola	182 30.8	N14 28.5
Diphda	348 53.7	S17 53.7
Dubhe	193 48.1	N61 39.6
Elnath	278 09.5	N28 37.1
Eltanin	90 44.8	N51 29.1
Enif	33 44.8	N 9 57.1
Fomalhaut	15 21.5	S29 31.9
Gacrux	171 57.4	S57 12.6
Gienah	175 49.3	S17 38.3
Hadar	148 43.5	S60 27.2
Hamal	327 58.2	N23 32.4
Kaus Aust.	83 40.4	S34 22.3
Kochab	137 19.2	N74 05.1
Markab	13 36.1	N15 17.7
Menkar	314 12.7	N 4 09.1
Menkent	148 04.1	S36 27.2
Miaplacidus	221 38.5	S69 47.6
Mirfak	308 37.0	N49 55.2
Nunki	75 55.1	S26 16.3
Peacock	53 15.5	S56 40.5
Pollux	243 24.6	N27 58.9
Procyon	244 57.0	N 5 10.6
Rasalhague	96 04.0	N12 32.9
Regulus	207 40.6	N11 52.8
Rigel	281 09.8	S 8 11.3
Rigil Kent.	139 47.6	S60 54.1
Sabik	102 09.4	S15 44.6
Schedar	349 38.1	N56 37.7
Shaula	96 18.3	S37 06.7
Sirius	258 31.5	S16 44.8
Spica	158 28.2	S11 15.1
Suhail	222 50.3	S43 30.5
Vega	80 37.2	N38 47.9
Zuben'ubi	137 02.3	S16 06.7

	SHA ° ′	Mer. Pass. h m
Venus	3 29.6	10 50
Mars	314 03.3	14 09
Jupiter	162 12.7	0 17
Saturn	92 22.8	4 56

Day	UT d h	SUN GHA ° ′	SUN Dec ° ′	MOON GHA ° ′	MOON v ′	MOON Dec ° ′	MOON d ′	MOON HP ′
TUESDAY	4 00	179 14.0	N 5 40.9	84 15.6	7.0	N18 39.8	2.2	58.7
	01	194 14.2	41.8	98 41.6	7.0	18 37.6	2.3	58.6
	02	209 14.4	42.8	113 07.6	7.1	18 35.3	2.4	58.6
	03	224 14.6	. . 43.7	127 33.7	7.1	18 32.9	2.5	58.6
	04	239 14.8	44.7	141 59.8	7.2	18 30.4	2.7	58.6
	05	254 14.9	45.6	156 26.0	7.2	18 27.7	2.8	58.5
	06	269 15.1	N 5 46.6	170 52.2	7.2	N18 24.9	2.8	58.5
	07	284 15.3	47.5	185 18.4	7.3	18 22.1	3.0	58.5
	08	299 15.5	48.5	199 44.7	7.4	18 19.1	3.1	58.5
	09	314 15.7	. . 49.4	214 11.1	7.4	18 16.0	3.2	58.4
	10	329 15.9	50.4	228 37.5	7.5	18 12.8	3.3	58.4
	11	344 16.0	51.3	243 04.0	7.5	18 09.5	3.5	58.4
	12	359 16.2	N 5 52.3	257 30.5	7.5	N18 06.0	3.5	58.4
	13	14 16.4	53.3	271 57.0	7.6	18 02.5	3.6	58.4
	14	29 16.6	54.2	286 23.6	7.7	17 58.9	3.8	58.3
	15	44 16.8	. . 55.2	300 50.3	7.7	17 55.1	3.8	58.3
	16	59 16.9	56.1	315 17.0	7.8	17 51.3	4.0	58.3
	17	74 17.1	57.1	329 43.8	7.8	17 47.3	4.1	58.3
	18	89 17.3	N 5 58.0	344 10.6	7.9	N17 43.2	4.1	58.2
	19	104 17.5	59.0	358 37.5	7.9	17 39.1	4.3	58.2
	20	119 17.7	5 59.9	13 04.4	8.0	17 34.8	4.4	58.2
	21	134 17.8	6 00.9	27 31.4	8.1	17 30.4	4.5	58.2
	22	149 18.0	01.8	41 58.5	8.1	17 25.9	4.5	58.1
	23	164 18.2	02.8	56 25.6	8.2	17 21.4	4.7	58.1
WEDNESDAY	5 00	179 18.4	N 6 03.7	70 52.8	8.2	N17 16.7	4.8	58.1
	01	194 18.6	04.7	85 20.0	8.3	17 11.9	4.9	58.1
	02	209 18.7	05.6	99 47.3	8.3	17 07.0	4.9	58.0
	03	224 18.9	. . 06.6	114 14.6	8.4	17 02.1	5.1	58.0
	04	239 19.1	07.5	128 42.0	8.4	16 57.0	5.2	58.0
	05	254 19.3	08.4	143 09.4	8.6	16 51.8	5.2	58.0
	06	269 19.5	N 6 09.4	157 37.0	8.5	N16 46.6	5.4	57.9
	07	284 19.6	10.3	172 04.5	8.7	16 41.2	5.4	57.9
	08	299 19.8	11.3	186 32.2	8.7	16 35.8	5.6	57.9
	09	314 20.0	. . 12.2	200 59.9	8.7	16 30.2	5.6	57.9
	10	329 20.2	13.2	215 27.6	8.8	16 24.6	5.7	57.9
	11	344 20.4	14.1	229 55.4	8.9	16 18.9	5.8	57.8
	12	359 20.5	N 6 15.1	244 23.3	8.9	N16 13.1	5.9	57.8
	13	14 20.7	16.0	258 51.2	9.0	16 07.2	6.0	57.8
	14	29 20.9	17.0	273 19.2	9.1	16 01.2	6.1	57.8
	15	44 21.1	. . 17.9	287 47.3	9.1	15 55.1	6.1	57.7
	16	59 21.2	18.9	302 15.4	9.2	15 49.0	6.3	57.7
	17	74 21.4	19.8	316 43.6	9.2	15 42.7	6.3	57.7
	18	89 21.6	N 6 20.8	331 11.8	9.3	N15 36.4	6.4	57.7
	19	104 21.8	21.7	345 40.1	9.4	15 30.0	6.5	57.6
	20	119 22.0	22.7	0 08.5	9.4	15 23.5	6.6	57.6
	21	134 22.1	. . 23.6	14 36.9	9.5	15 16.9	6.6	57.6
	22	149 22.3	24.5	29 05.4	9.5	15 10.3	6.8	57.6
	23	164 22.5	25.5	43 33.9	9.6	15 03.5	6.8	57.6
THURSDAY	6 00	179 22.7	N 6 26.4	58 02.5	9.7	N14 56.7	6.9	57.5
	01	194 22.9	27.4	72 31.2	9.7	14 49.8	7.0	57.5
	02	209 23.0	28.3	86 59.9	9.8	14 42.8	7.0	57.5
	03	224 23.2	. . 29.3	101 28.7	9.8	14 35.8	7.1	57.5
	04	239 23.4	30.2	115 57.5	9.9	14 28.7	7.2	57.4
	05	254 23.6	31.2	130 26.4	10.0	14 21.5	7.3	57.4
	06	269 23.7	N 6 32.1	144 55.4	10.0	N14 14.2	7.3	57.4
	07	284 23.9	33.0	159 24.4	10.1	14 06.9	7.5	57.4
	08	299 24.1	34.0	173 53.5	10.2	13 59.4	7.4	57.3
	09	314 24.3	. . 34.9	188 22.7	10.2	13 52.0	7.6	57.3
	10	329 24.5	35.9	202 51.9	10.3	13 44.4	7.6	57.3
	11	344 24.6	36.8	217 21.2	10.3	13 36.8	7.7	57.3
	12	359 24.8	N 6 37.8	231 50.5	10.4	N13 29.1	7.8	57.3
	13	14 25.0	38.7	246 19.9	10.4	13 21.3	7.8	57.2
	14	29 25.2	39.6	260 49.3	10.5	13 13.5	7.9	57.2
	15	44 25.3	. . 40.6	275 18.8	10.6	13 05.6	7.9	57.2
	16	59 25.5	41.5	289 48.4	10.6	12 57.7	8.1	57.2
	17	74 25.7	42.5	304 18.0	10.7	12 49.6	8.0	57.1
	18	89 25.9	N 6 43.4	318 47.7	10.8	N12 41.6	8.2	57.1
	19	104 26.0	44.3	333 17.5	10.8	12 33.4	8.2	57.1
	20	119 26.2	45.3	347 47.3	10.8	12 25.2	8.2	57.1
	21	134 26.4	. . 46.2	2 17.1	10.9	12 17.0	8.4	57.0
	22	149 26.6	47.2	16 47.0	11.0	12 08.6	8.3	57.0
	23	164 26.8	48.1	31 17.0	11.0	N12 00.3	8.5	57.0
		SD 16.0	d 0.9	SD 15.9		15.8		15.6

Lat. °	Twilight Naut. h m	Twilight Civil h m	Sunrise h m	Moonrise 4 h m	Moonrise 5 h m	Moonrise 6 h m	Moonrise 7 h m
N 72	////	03 15	04 34	▭	09 19	11 22	13 15
N 70	01 44	03 35	04 44	08 25	10 05	11 49	13 31
68	02 21	03 50	04 52	09 07	10 35	12 09	13 44
66	02 47	04 03	04 58	09 36	10 58	12 25	13 54
64	03 06	04 13	05 04	09 58	11 15	12 38	14 03
62	03 22	04 22	05 09	10 15	11 30	12 49	14 10
60	03 34	04 29	05 13	10 29	11 42	12 59	14 17
N 58	03 45	04 36	05 17	10 42	11 52	13 07	14 22
56	03 54	04 41	05 20	10 52	12 01	13 14	14 27
54	04 02	04 46	05 23	11 02	12 10	13 20	14 32
52	04 09	04 51	05 26	11 10	12 17	13 26	14 36
50	04 15	04 55	05 28	11 17	12 23	13 31	14 39
45	04 28	05 03	05 33	11 33	12 37	13 42	14 47
N 40	04 38	05 10	05 38	11 47	12 49	13 52	14 54
35	04 46	05 16	05 41	11 58	12 59	13 59	15 00
30	04 52	05 20	05 45	12 07	13 07	14 06	15 05
20	05 02	05 28	05 50	12 24	13 22	14 18	15 13
N 10	05 09	05 34	05 55	12 39	13 35	14 29	15 21
0	05 14	05 39	05 59	12 53	13 47	14 39	15 28
S 10	05 18	05 43	06 04	13 06	13 59	14 48	15 35
20	05 20	05 46	06 08	13 21	14 12	14 59	15 42
30	05 21	05 49	06 13	13 38	14 26	15 11	15 51
35	05 21	05 51	06 16	13 47	14 35	15 17	15 56
40	05 21	05 52	06 19	13 58	14 45	15 25	16 01
45	05 19	05 53	06 23	14 11	14 56	15 34	16 08
S 50	05 17	05 55	06 27	14 27	15 10	15 45	16 15
52	05 16	05 55	06 29	14 35	15 16	15 50	16 19
54	05 15	05 56	06 31	14 43	15 23	15 55	16 23
56	05 13	05 56	06 34	14 52	15 31	16 02	16 27
58	05 11	05 57	06 36	15 03	15 40	16 08	16 32
S 60	05 09	05 57	06 39	15 15	15 50	16 16	16 37

Lat. °	Sunset h m	Twilight Civil h m	Twilight Naut. h m	Moonset 4 h m	Moonset 5 h m	Moonset 6 h m	Moonset 7 h m
N 72	19 35	20 56	////	▭	05 57	05 43	05 34
N 70	19 24	20 34	22 31	04 56	05 10	05 15	05 16
68	19 16	20 18	21 50	04 13	04 39	04 54	05 02
66	19 09	20 05	21 23	03 44	04 16	04 37	04 50
64	19 03	19 54	21 02	03 22	03 58	04 23	04 41
62	18 58	19 45	20 47	03 05	03 43	04 11	04 32
60	18 54	19 38	20 34	02 50	03 31	04 01	04 25
N 58	18 50	19 31	20 23	02 38	03 20	03 53	04 19
56	18 47	19 25	20 13	02 27	03 10	03 45	04 13
54	18 44	19 20	20 05	02 17	03 02	03 38	04 08
52	18 41	19 16	19 58	02 09	02 54	03 32	04 03
50	18 38	19 12	19 52	02 01	02 47	03 26	03 59
45	18 33	19 03	19 39	01 45	02 33	03 14	03 50
N 40	18 28	18 56	19 29	01 31	02 21	03 04	03 42
35	18 25	18 50	19 20	01 20	02 10	02 55	03 36
30	18 21	18 45	19 14	01 10	02 01	02 48	03 30
20	18 15	18 38	19 04	00 52	01 45	02 34	03 20
N 10	18 10	18 32	18 56	00 37	01 32	02 23	03 11
0	18 06	18 27	18 51	00 23	01 19	02 12	03 02
S 10	18 01	18 23	18 47	00 09	01 06	02 01	02 54
20	17 57	18 19	18 45	24 52	00 52	01 49	02 45
30	17 52	18 16	18 43	24 36	00 36	01 36	02 34
35	17 49	18 14	18 43	24 27	00 27	01 28	02 28
40	17 46	18 13	18 44	24 16	00 16	01 19	02 21
45	17 42	18 11	18 45	24 03	00 03	01 08	02 13
S 50	17 37	18 10	18 47	23 48	24 55	00 55	02 04
52	17 35	18 09	18 48	23 41	24 49	00 49	01 59
54	17 33	18 08	18 49	23 33	24 43	00 43	01 54
56	17 31	18 08	18 51	23 24	24 35	00 35	01 49
58	17 28	18 07	18 53	23 14	24 27	00 27	01 42
S 60	17 25	18 07	18 55	23 02	24 17	00 17	01 35

Day d	SUN Eqn. of Time 00h m s	SUN Eqn. of Time 12h m s	SUN Mer. Pass. h m	MOON Mer. Pass. Upper h m	MOON Mer. Pass. Lower h m	MOON Age d	MOON %	MOON Phase
4	03 04	02 56	12 03	19 06	06 38	07	58	
5	02 47	02 38	12 03	19 59	07 33	08	69	
6	02 30	02 21	12 02	20 51	08 25	09	78	

	UT	ARIES	VENUS −4·5		MARS +1·5		JUPITER −2·5		SATURN +0·4	
		GHA	GHA	Dec	GHA	Dec	GHA	Dec	GHA	Dec
	d h	° ′	° ′	° ′	° ′	° ′	° ′	° ′	° ′	° ′
	7 00	195 27.5	199 28.6	N 5 08.0	148 05.8	N18 08.9	357 54.5	S 5 44.2	287 50.2	S22 04.3
	01	210 29.9	214 31.6	07.2	163 06.5	09.4	12 57.3	44.1	302 52.7	04.3
	02	225 32.4	229 34.6	06.4	178 07.2	09.9	28 00.0	44.0	317 55.2	04.3
	03	240 34.9	244 37.7	. . 05.6	193 07.8	. . 10.4	43 02.8	. . 43.8	332 57.6	. . 04.3
	04	255 37.3	259 40.7	04.7	208 08.5	10.9	58 05.6	43.7	348 00.1	04.3
	05	270 39.8	274 43.7	03.9	223 09.2	11.4	73 08.3	43.6	3 02.6	04.3
	06	285 42.3	289 46.7	N 5 03.1	238 09.9	N18 11.9	88 11.1	S 5 43.5	18 05.1	S22 04.3
	07	300 44.7	304 49.7	02.3	253 10.6	12.4	103 13.9	43.3	33 07.5	04.3
	08	315 47.2	319 52.7	01.4	268 11.3	12.9	118 16.6	43.2	48 10.0	04.3
F	09	330 49.6	334 55.7	5 00.6	283 12.0	. . 13.3	133 19.4	. . 43.1	63 12.5	. . 04.3
R	10	345 52.1	349 58.7	4 59.8	298 12.7	13.8	148 22.1	43.0	78 14.9	04.2
I	11	0 54.6	5 01.7	59.0	313 13.4	14.3	163 24.9	42.9	93 17.4	04.2
D	12	15 57.0	20 04.7	N 4 58.2	328 14.1	N18 14.8	178 27.7	S 5 42.7	108 19.9	S22 04.2
A	13	30 59.5	35 07.7	57.4	343 14.8	15.3	193 30.4	42.6	123 22.3	04.2
Y	14	46 02.0	50 10.6	56.6	358 15.4	15.8	208 33.2	42.5	138 24.8	04.2
	15	61 04.4	65 13.6	. . 55.7	13 16.1	. . 16.3	223 36.0	. . 42.4	153 27.3	. . 04.2
	16	76 06.9	80 16.6	54.9	28 16.8	16.8	238 38.7	42.2	168 29.7	04.2
	17	91 09.4	95 19.5	54.1	43 17.5	17.3	253 41.5	42.1	183 32.2	04.2
	18	106 11.8	110 22.5	N 4 53.3	58 18.2	N18 17.8	268 44.2	S 5 42.0	198 34.7	S22 04.2
	19	121 14.3	125 25.5	52.5	73 18.9	18.3	283 47.0	41.9	213 37.2	04.2
	20	136 16.8	140 28.4	51.7	88 19.6	18.8	298 49.8	41.8	228 39.6	04.2
	21	151 19.2	155 31.4	. . 50.9	103 20.3	. . 19.3	313 52.5	. . 41.6	243 42.1	. . 04.2
	22	166 21.7	170 34.3	50.1	118 21.0	19.7	328 55.3	41.5	258 44.6	04.2
	23	181 24.1	185 37.3	49.3	133 21.6	20.2	343 58.1	41.4	273 47.0	04.2
	8 00	196 26.6	200 40.2	N 4 48.5	148 22.3	N18 20.7	359 00.8	S 5 41.3	288 49.5	S22 04.2
	01	211 29.1	215 43.1	47.7	163 23.0	21.2	14 03.6	41.2	303 52.0	04.2
	02	226 31.5	230 46.1	46.9	178 23.7	21.7	29 06.3	41.0	318 54.5	04.2
	03	241 34.0	245 49.0	. . 46.1	193 24.4	. . 22.2	44 09.1	. . 40.9	333 56.9	. . 04.2
	04	256 36.5	260 51.9	45.3	208 25.1	22.7	59 11.9	40.8	348 59.4	04.2
	05	271 38.9	275 54.8	44.5	223 25.8	23.2	74 14.6	40.7	4 01.9	04.2
	06	286 41.4	290 57.7	N 4 43.7	238 26.5	N18 23.7	89 17.4	S 5 40.5	19 04.4	S22 04.2
	07	301 43.9	306 00.7	42.9	253 27.2	24.1	104 20.2	40.4	34 06.8	04.2
S	08	316 46.3	321 03.6	42.2	268 27.8	24.6	119 22.9	40.3	49 09.3	04.2
A	09	331 48.8	336 06.5	. . 41.4	283 28.5	. . 25.1	134 25.7	. . 40.2	64 11.8	. . 04.2
T	10	346 51.2	351 09.4	40.6	298 29.2	25.6	149 28.5	40.1	79 14.2	04.2
U	11	1 53.7	6 12.3	39.8	313 29.9	26.1	164 31.2	39.9	94 16.7	04.2
R	12	16 56.2	21 15.2	N 4 39.0	328 30.6	N18 26.6	179 34.0	S 5 39.8	109 19.2	S22 04.2
D	13	31 58.6	36 18.0	38.2	343 31.3	27.1	194 36.7	39.7	124 21.7	04.2
A	14	47 01.1	51 20.9	37.4	358 32.0	27.6	209 39.5	39.6	139 24.1	04.2
Y	15	62 03.6	66 23.8	. . 36.7	13 32.7	. . 28.0	224 42.3	. . 39.5	154 26.6	. . 04.2
	16	77 06.0	81 26.7	35.9	28 33.4	28.5	239 45.0	39.3	169 29.1	04.2
	17	92 08.5	96 29.6	35.1	43 34.0	29.0	254 47.8	39.2	184 31.6	04.2
	18	107 11.0	111 32.4	N 4 34.3	58 34.7	N18 29.5	269 50.6	S 5 39.1	199 34.0	S22 04.2
	19	122 13.4	126 35.3	33.6	73 35.4	30.0	284 53.3	39.0	214 36.5	04.2
	20	137 15.9	141 38.2	32.8	88 36.1	30.5	299 56.1	38.8	229 39.0	04.2
	21	152 18.4	156 41.0	. . 32.0	103 36.8	. . 30.9	314 58.8	. . 38.7	244 41.5	. . 04.2
	22	167 20.8	171 43.9	31.2	118 37.5	31.4	330 01.6	38.6	259 43.9	04.2
	23	182 23.3	186 46.7	30.5	133 38.2	31.9	345 04.4	38.5	274 46.4	04.1
	9 00	197 25.7	201 49.6	N 4 29.7	148 38.9	N18 32.4	0 07.1	S 5 38.4	289 48.9	S22 04.1
	01	212 28.2	216 52.4	28.9	163 39.5	32.9	15 09.9	38.2	304 51.4	04.1
	02	227 30.7	231 55.2	28.2	178 40.2	33.4	30 12.7	38.1	319 53.8	04.1
	03	242 33.1	246 58.1	. . 27.4	193 40.9	. . 33.8	45 15.4	. . 38.0	334 56.3	. . 04.1
	04	257 35.6	262 00.9	26.6	208 41.6	34.3	60 18.2	37.9	349 58.8	04.1
	05	272 38.1	277 03.7	25.9	223 42.3	34.8	75 20.9	37.8	5 01.3	04.1
	06	287 40.5	292 06.5	N 4 25.1	238 43.0	N18 35.3	90 23.7	S 5 37.6	20 03.8	S22 04.1
	07	302 43.0	307 09.4	24.4	253 43.7	35.8	105 26.5	37.5	35 06.2	04.1
	08	317 45.5	322 12.2	23.6	268 44.3	36.2	120 29.2	37.4	50 08.7	04.1
S	09	332 47.9	337 15.0	. . 22.8	283 45.0	. . 36.7	135 32.0	. . 37.3	65 11.2	. . 04.1
U	10	347 50.4	352 17.8	22.1	298 45.7	37.2	150 34.8	37.2	80 13.7	04.1
N	11	2 52.8	7 20.6	21.3	313 46.4	37.7	165 37.5	37.0	95 16.1	04.1
D	12	17 55.3	22 23.4	N 4 20.6	328 47.1	N18 38.2	180 40.3	S 5 36.9	110 18.6	S22 04.1
A	13	32 57.8	37 26.2	19.8	343 47.8	38.6	195 43.0	36.8	125 21.1	04.1
Y	14	48 00.2	52 29.0	19.1	358 48.5	39.1	210 45.8	36.7	140 23.6	04.1
	15	63 02.7	67 31.7	. . 18.3	13 49.2	. . 39.6	225 48.6	. . 36.5	155 26.1	. . 04.1
	16	78 05.2	82 34.5	17.6	28 49.8	40.1	240 51.3	36.4	170 28.5	04.1
	17	93 07.6	97 37.3	16.8	43 50.5	40.6	255 54.1	36.3	185 31.0	04.1
	18	108 10.1	112 40.1	N 4 16.1	58 51.2	N18 41.0	270 56.9	S 5 36.2	200 33.5	S22 04.1
	19	123 12.6	127 42.8	15.4	73 51.9	41.5	285 59.6	36.1	215 36.0	04.1
	20	138 15.0	142 45.6	14.6	88 52.6	42.0	301 02.4	35.9	230 38.5	04.1
	21	153 17.5	157 48.4	. . 13.9	103 53.3	. . 42.5	316 05.1	. . 35.8	245 40.9	. . 04.1
	22	168 20.0	172 51.1	13.1	118 54.0	42.9	331 07.9	35.7	260 43.4	04.1
	23	183 22.4	187 53.9	12.4	133 54.6	43.4	346 10.7	35.6	275 45.9	04.1
	Mer. Pass.	h m 10 52.4	v 2.9	d 0.8	v 0.7	d 0.5	v 2.8	d 0.1	v 2.5	d 0.0

STARS		
Name	SHA	Dec
	° ′	° ′
Acamar	315 16.8	S40 14.5
Achernar	335 25.5	S57 09.2
Acrux	173 05.6	S63 11.7
Adhara	255 10.5	S29 00.2
Aldebaran	290 46.7	N16 32.4
Alioth	166 18.0	N55 52.0
Alkaid	152 56.5	N49 13.6
Al Na'ir	27 40.9	S46 52.5
Alnilam	275 43.9	S 1 11.8
Alphard	217 53.4	S 8 44.2
Alphecca	126 08.6	N26 39.4
Alpheratz	357 41.2	N29 10.9
Altair	62 05.8	N 8 54.8
Ankaa	353 13.6	S42 12.9
Antares	112 22.9	S26 28.0
Arcturus	145 53.1	N19 05.6
Atria	107 22.0	S69 03.1
Avior	234 16.8	S59 34.3
Bellatrix	278 29.4	N 6 21.6
Betelgeuse	270 58.6	N 7 24.3
Canopus	263 55.1	S52 42.8
Capella	280 30.9	N46 00.8
Deneb	49 29.9	N45 20.3
Denebola	182 30.8	N14 28.5
Diphda	348 53.7	S17 53.7
Dubhe	193 48.1	N61 39.6
Elnath	278 09.6	N28 37.1
Eltanin	90 44.8	N51 29.1
Enif	33 44.8	N 9 57.1
Fomalhaut	15 21.5	S29 31.9
Gacrux	171 57.4	S57 12.6
Gienah	175 49.3	S17 38.3
Hadar	148 43.5	S60 27.2
Hamal	327 58.2	N23 32.4
Kaus Aust.	83 40.3	S34 22.3
Kochab	137 19.2	N74 05.1
Markab	13 36.0	N15 17.7
Menkar	314 12.7	N 4 09.1
Menkent	148 04.1	S36 27.2
Miaplacidus	221 38.6	S69 47.7
Mirfak	308 37.0	N49 55.2
Nunki	75 55.1	S26 16.3
Peacock	53 15.5	S56 40.4
Pollux	243 24.6	N27 58.9
Procyon	244 57.0	N 5 10.6
Rasalhague	96 03.9	N12 32.9
Regulus	207 40.6	N11 52.8
Rigel	281 09.8	S 8 11.3
Rigil Kent.	139 47.6	S60 54.1
Sabik	102 09.4	S15 44.6
Schedar	349 38.1	N56 37.7
Shaula	96 18.3	S37 06.7
Sirius	258 31.5	S16 44.8
Spica	158 28.2	S11 15.1
Suhail	222 50.3	S43 30.5
Vega	80 37.1	N38 47.9
Zuben'ubi	137 02.3	S16 06.7

	SHA	Mer. Pass.
	° ′	h m
Venus	4 13.6	10 35
Mars	311 55.7	14 06
Jupiter	162 34.2	0 04
Saturn	92 22.9	4 44

UT		SUN GHA	SUN Dec	MOON GHA	v	MOON Dec	d	HP
d	h	° ′	° ′	° ′	′	° ′	′	′
7	00	179 26.9	N 6 49.0	45 47.0	11.1	N11 51.8	8.5	57.0
	01	194 27.1	50.0	60 17.1	11.1	11 43.3	8.5	57.0
	02	209 27.3	50.9	74 47.2	11.2	11 34.8	8.6	56.9
	03	224 27.5	. . 51.9	89 17.4	11.3	11 26.2	8.6	56.9
	04	239 27.6	52.8	103 47.7	11.3	11 17.6	8.8	56.9
	05	254 27.8	53.7	118 18.0	11.4	11 08.8	8.7	56.9
	06	269 28.0	N 6 54.7	132 48.4	11.4	N11 00.1	8.8	56.9
	07	284 28.2	55.6	147 18.8	11.4	10 51.3	8.9	56.8
	08	299 28.3	56.6	161 49.2	11.6	10 42.4	8.9	56.8
FRIDAY	09	314 28.5	. . 57.5	176 19.8	11.5	10 33.5	8.9	56.8
	10	329 28.7	58.4	190 50.3	11.7	10 24.6	9.0	56.8
	11	344 28.9	6 59.4	205 21.0	11.7	10 15.6	9.0	56.7
	12	359 29.0	N 7 00.3	219 51.7	11.7	N10 06.6	9.1	56.7
	13	14 29.2	01.3	234 22.4	11.8	9 57.5	9.2	56.7
	14	29 29.4	02.2	248 53.2	11.8	9 48.3	9.1	56.7
	15	44 29.6	. . 03.1	263 24.0	11.9	9 39.2	9.3	56.7
	16	59 29.7	04.1	277 54.9	11.9	9 29.9	9.2	56.6
	17	74 29.9	05.0	292 25.8	12.0	9 20.7	9.3	56.6
	18	89 30.1	N 7 05.9	306 56.8	12.0	N 9 11.4	9.3	56.6
	19	104 30.3	06.9	321 27.8	12.1	9 02.1	9.4	56.6
	20	119 30.4	07.8	335 58.9	12.1	8 52.7	9.4	56.5
	21	134 30.6	. . 08.7	350 30.0	12.2	8 43.3	9.5	56.5
	22	149 30.8	09.7	5 01.2	12.2	8 33.8	9.5	56.5
	23	164 31.0	10.6	19 32.4	12.3	8 24.3	9.5	56.5
8	00	179 31.1	N 7 11.5	34 03.7	12.3	N 8 14.8	9.5	56.5
	01	194 31.3	12.5	48 35.0	12.4	8 05.3	9.6	56.4
	02	209 31.5	13.4	63 06.4	12.4	7 55.7	9.6	56.4
	03	224 31.6	. . 14.4	77 37.8	12.4	7 46.1	9.7	56.4
	04	239 31.8	15.3	92 09.2	12.5	7 36.4	9.7	56.4
	05	254 32.0	16.2	106 40.7	12.6	7 26.7	9.7	56.4
	06	269 32.2	N 7 17.2	121 12.3	12.5	N 7 17.0	9.7	56.3
	07	284 32.3	18.1	135 43.8	12.7	7 07.3	9.8	56.3
	08	299 32.5	19.0	150 15.5	12.6	6 57.5	9.8	56.3
SATURDAY	09	314 32.7	. . 20.0	164 47.1	12.7	6 47.7	9.8	56.3
	10	329 32.9	20.9	179 18.8	12.8	6 37.9	9.8	56.3
	11	344 33.0	21.8	193 50.6	12.8	6 28.1	9.9	56.2
	12	359 33.2	N 7 22.8	208 22.4	12.8	N 6 18.2	9.9	56.2
	13	14 33.4	23.7	222 54.2	12.9	6 08.3	9.9	56.2
	14	29 33.6	24.6	237 26.1	12.9	5 58.4	10.0	56.2
	15	44 33.7	. . 25.5	251 58.0	12.9	5 48.4	9.9	56.2
	16	59 33.9	26.5	266 29.9	13.0	5 38.5	10.0	56.1
	17	74 34.1	27.4	281 01.9	13.0	5 28.5	10.0	56.1
	18	89 34.2	N 7 28.3	295 33.9	13.1	N 5 18.5	10.0	56.1
	19	104 34.4	29.3	310 06.0	13.0	5 08.5	10.0	56.1
	20	119 34.6	30.2	324 38.0	13.2	4 58.5	10.1	56.1
	21	134 34.8	. . 31.1	339 10.2	13.1	4 48.4	10.1	56.0
	22	149 34.9	32.1	353 42.3	13.2	4 38.3	10.0	56.0
	23	164 35.1	33.0	8 14.5	13.2	4 28.3	10.1	56.0
9	00	179 35.3	N 7 33.9	22 46.7	13.3	N 4 18.2	10.2	56.0
	01	194 35.4	34.9	37 19.0	13.3	4 08.0	10.1	56.0
	02	209 35.6	35.8	51 51.3	13.3	3 57.9	10.1	55.9
	03	224 35.8	. . 36.7	66 23.6	13.4	3 47.8	10.2	55.9
	04	239 36.0	37.6	80 56.0	13.3	3 37.6	10.1	55.9
	05	254 36.1	38.6	95 28.3	13.5	3 27.5	10.2	55.9
	06	269 36.3	N 7 39.5	110 00.8	13.4	N 3 17.3	10.2	55.9
	07	284 36.5	40.4	124 33.2	13.5	3 07.1	10.1	55.8
	08	299 36.6	41.4	139 05.7	13.5	2 57.0	10.2	55.8
SUNDAY	09	314 36.8	. . 42.3	153 38.2	13.5	2 46.8	10.2	55.8
	10	329 37.0	43.2	168 10.7	13.6	2 36.6	10.2	55.8
	11	344 37.1	44.1	182 43.3	13.5	2 26.4	10.3	55.8
	12	359 37.3	N 7 45.1	197 15.8	13.7	N 2 16.1	10.2	55.7
	13	14 37.5	46.0	211 48.5	13.6	2 05.9	10.2	55.7
	14	29 37.7	46.9	226 21.1	13.6	1 55.7	10.2	55.7
	15	44 37.8	. . 47.8	240 53.7	13.7	1 45.5	10.2	55.7
	16	59 38.0	48.8	255 26.4	13.7	1 35.3	10.2	55.7
	17	74 38.2	49.7	269 59.1	13.8	1 25.1	10.3	55.6
	18	89 38.3	N 7 50.6	284 31.9	13.7	N 1 14.8	10.2	55.6
	19	104 38.5	51.5	299 04.6	13.8	1 04.6	10.2	55.6
	20	119 38.7	52.5	313 37.4	13.8	0 54.4	10.2	55.6
	21	134 38.8	. . 53.4	328 10.2	13.8	0 44.2	10.2	55.6
	22	149 39.0	54.3	342 43.0	13.8	0 34.0	10.2	55.6
	23	164 39.2	55.2	357 15.8	13.9	N 0 23.8	10.3	55.5
		SD 16.0	d 0.9	SD 15.5		15.3		15.2

Lat.	Twilight Naut.	Twilight Civil	Sunrise	Moonrise 7	Moonrise 8	Moonrise 9	Moonrise 10
°	h m	h m	h m	h m	h m	h m	h m
N 72	////	02 54	04 18	13 15	15 01	16 43	18 23
N 70	01 07	03 18	04 29	13 31	15 09	16 45	18 18
68	01 59	03 36	04 39	13 44	15 16	16 46	18 15
66	02 29	03 50	04 47	13 54	15 22	16 48	18 12
64	02 51	04 02	04 53	14 03	15 27	16 49	18 10
62	03 09	04 11	04 59	14 10	15 31	16 50	18 08
60	03 23	04 20	05 04	14 17	15 34	16 51	18 06
N 58	03 35	04 27	05 08	14 22	15 37	16 51	18 04
56	03 45	04 33	05 12	14 27	15 40	16 52	18 03
54	03 53	04 39	05 16	14 32	15 43	16 53	18 01
52	04 01	04 44	05 19	14 36	15 45	16 53	18 00
50	04 08	04 48	05 22	14 39	15 47	16 54	17 59
45	04 22	04 58	05 28	14 47	15 52	16 55	17 57
N 40	04 32	05 05	05 33	14 54	15 55	16 56	17 55
35	04 41	05 12	05 37	15 00	15 59	16 56	17 53
30	04 48	05 17	05 41	15 05	16 02	16 57	17 52
20	04 59	05 25	05 48	15 13	16 06	16 58	17 49
N 10	05 07	05 32	05 53	15 21	16 11	16 59	17 47
0	05 13	05 38	05 59	15 28	16 15	17 01	17 45
S 10	05 18	05 42	06 04	15 35	16 19	17 02	17 43
20	05 21	05 47	06 09	15 42	16 23	17 03	17 41
30	05 23	05 51	06 15	15 51	16 28	17 04	17 39
35	05 24	05 53	06 18	15 56	16 31	17 05	17 37
40	05 24	05 55	06 22	16 01	16 34	17 06	17 36
45	05 23	05 57	06 26	16 08	16 38	17 06	17 34
S 50	05 22	05 59	06 32	16 15	16 43	17 08	17 32
52	05 21	06 00	06 34	16 19	16 45	17 08	17 31
54	05 20	06 01	06 37	16 23	16 47	17 09	17 30
56	05 19	06 02	06 40	16 27	16 49	17 09	17 29
58	05 18	06 03	06 43	16 32	16 52	17 10	17 28
S 60	05 16	06 04	06 46	16 37	16 55	17 11	17 26

Lat.	Sunset	Twilight Civil	Twilight Naut.	Moonset 7	Moonset 8	Moonset 9	Moonset 10
°	h m	h m	h m	h m	h m	h m	h m
N 72	19 49	21 15	////	05 34	05 26	05 19	05 13
N 70	19 37	20 50	23 13	05 16	05 16	05 15	05 14
68	19 27	20 31	22 12	05 02	05 07	05 11	05 14
66	19 19	20 17	21 39	04 50	05 00	05 08	05 15
64	19 12	20 05	21 16	04 41	04 54	05 06	05 16
62	19 06	19 54	20 58	04 32	04 49	05 03	05 16
60	19 01	19 46	20 43	04 25	04 44	05 01	05 17
N 58	18 57	19 38	20 31	04 19	04 40	04 59	05 17
56	18 53	19 32	20 21	04 13	04 37	04 58	05 18
54	18 49	19 26	20 12	04 08	04 33	04 56	05 18
52	18 46	19 21	20 04	04 03	04 30	04 55	05 18
50	18 43	19 17	19 57	03 59	04 28	04 54	05 18
45	18 37	19 07	19 43	03 50	04 22	04 51	05 19
N 40	18 31	18 59	19 32	03 42	04 17	04 49	05 20
35	18 27	18 53	19 23	03 36	04 13	04 47	05 20
30	18 23	18 47	19 16	03 30	04 09	04 45	05 20
20	18 16	18 39	19 05	03 20	04 02	04 42	05 21
N 10	18 10	18 32	18 56	03 11	03 56	04 40	05 22
0	18 05	18 26	18 50	03 02	03 51	04 37	05 22
S 10	18 00	18 21	18 45	02 54	03 45	04 34	05 23
20	17 54	18 16	18 42	02 45	03 39	04 32	05 23
30	17 48	18 12	18 40	02 34	03 32	04 28	05 24
35	17 45	18 10	18 39	02 28	03 28	04 27	05 24
40	17 41	18 08	18 39	02 21	03 24	04 24	05 24
45	17 36	18 06	18 40	02 13	03 18	04 22	05 25
S 50	17 31	18 03	18 41	02 04	03 12	04 19	05 25
52	17 29	18 02	18 41	01 59	03 09	04 18	05 25
54	17 26	18 01	18 42	01 54	03 06	04 16	05 26
56	17 23	18 00	18 43	01 49	03 02	04 15	05 26
58	17 20	17 59	18 44	01 42	02 58	04 13	05 26
S 60	17 16	17 58	18 46	01 35	02 54	04 11	05 27

Day	SUN Eqn. of Time 00^h	SUN Eqn. of Time 12^h	SUN Mer. Pass.	MOON Mer. Pass. Upper	MOON Mer. Pass. Lower	MOON Age	MOON Phase
d	m s	m s	h m	h m	h m	d %	
7	02 13	02 04	12 02	21 39	09 15	10 86	
8	01 56	01 48	12 02	22 26	10 03	11 93	
9	01 39	01 31	12 02	23 11	10 49	12 97	

UT d h		ARIES GHA	VENUS −4·6 GHA	Dec	MARS +1·5 GHA	Dec	JUPITER −2·5 GHA	Dec	SATURN +0·4 GHA	Dec
		° ′	° ′	° ′	° ′	° ′	° ′	° ′	° ′	° ′
10 00		198 24.9	202 56.6	N 4 11.7	148 55.3	N18 43.9	1 13.4	S 5 35.5	290 48.4	S22 04.1
01		213 27.3	217 59.4	10.9	163 56.0	44.4	16 16.2	35.3	305 50.9	04.1
02		228 29.8	233 02.1	10.2	178 56.7	44.8	31 19.0	35.2	320 53.3	04.1
03		243 32.3	248 04.9	. . 09.5	193 57.4	. . 45.3	46 21.7	. . 35.1	335 55.8	. . 04.1
04		258 34.7	263 07.6	08.8	208 58.1	45.8	61 24.5	35.0	350 58.3	04.1
05		273 37.2	278 10.3	08.0	223 58.7	46.3	76 27.2	34.9	6 00.8	04.1
06		288 39.7	293 13.0	N 4 07.3	238 59.4	N18 46.7	91 30.0	S 5 34.7	21 03.3	S22 04.1
07		303 42.1	308 15.8	06.6	254 00.1	47.2	106 32.8	34.6	36 05.8	04.1
08		318 44.6	323 18.5	05.9	269 00.8	47.7	121 35.5	34.5	51 08.2	04.1
09	MONDAY	333 47.1	338 21.2	. . 05.1	284 01.5	. . 48.2	136 38.3	. . 34.4	66 10.7	. . 04.1
10		348 49.5	353 23.9	04.4	299 02.2	48.6	151 41.1	34.2	81 13.2	04.1
11		3 52.0	8 26.6	03.7	314 02.9	49.1	166 43.8	34.1	96 15.7	04.0
12		18 54.4	23 29.3	N 4 03.0	329 03.5	N18 49.6	181 46.6	S 5 34.0	111 18.2	S22 04.0
13		33 56.9	38 32.0	02.3	344 04.2	50.0	196 49.3	33.9	126 20.6	04.0
14		48 59.4	53 34.7	01.6	359 04.9	50.5	211 52.1	33.8	141 23.1	04.0
15		64 01.8	68 37.4	. . 00.8	14 05.6	. . 51.0	226 54.9	. . 33.6	156 25.6	. . 04.0
16		79 04.3	83 40.1	4 00.1	29 06.3	51.5	241 57.6	33.5	171 28.1	04.0
17		94 06.8	98 42.8	3 59.4	44 07.0	51.9	257 00.4	33.4	186 30.6	04.0
18		109 09.2	113 45.4	N 3 58.7	59 07.6	N18 52.4	272 03.2	S 5 33.3	201 33.1	S22 04.0
19		124 11.7	128 48.1	58.0	74 08.3	52.9	287 05.9	33.2	216 35.6	04.0
20		139 14.2	143 50.8	57.3	89 09.0	53.3	302 08.7	33.0	231 38.0	04.0
21		154 16.6	158 53.5	. . 56.6	104 09.7	. . 53.8	317 11.4	. . 32.9	246 40.5	. . 04.0
22		169 19.1	173 56.1	55.9	119 10.4	54.3	332 14.2	32.8	261 43.0	04.0
23		184 21.6	188 58.8	55.2	134 11.1	54.7	347 17.0	32.7	276 45.5	04.0
11 00		199 24.0	204 01.4	N 3 54.5	149 11.7	N18 55.2	2 19.7	S 5 32.6	291 48.0	S22 04.0
01		214 26.5	219 04.1	53.8	164 12.4	55.7	17 22.5	32.4	306 50.5	04.0
02		229 28.9	234 06.7	53.1	179 13.1	56.2	32 25.2	32.3	321 52.9	04.0
03		244 31.4	249 09.4	. . 52.4	194 13.8	. . 56.6	47 28.0	. . 32.2	336 55.4	. . 04.0
04		259 33.9	264 12.0	51.7	209 14.5	57.1	62 30.8	32.1	351 57.9	04.0
05		274 36.3	279 14.6	51.0	224 15.1	57.6	77 33.5	32.0	7 00.4	04.0
06		289 38.8	294 17.3	N 3 50.4	239 15.8	N18 58.0	92 36.3	S 5 31.8	22 02.9	S22 04.0
07		304 41.3	309 19.9	49.7	254 16.5	58.5	107 39.1	31.7	37 05.4	04.0
08	TUESDAY	319 43.7	324 22.5	49.0	269 17.2	59.0	122 41.8	31.6	52 07.9	04.0
09		334 46.2	339 25.1	. . 48.3	284 17.9	. . 59.4	137 44.6	. . 31.5	67 10.3	. . 04.0
10		349 48.7	354 27.7	47.6	299 18.6	18 59.9	152 47.3	31.4	82 12.8	04.0
11		4 51.1	9 30.4	46.9	314 19.2	19 00.3	167 50.1	31.2	97 15.3	04.0
12		19 53.6	24 33.0	N 3 46.3	329 19.9	N19 00.8	182 52.9	S 5 31.1	112 17.8	S22 04.0
13		34 56.1	39 35.6	45.6	344 20.6	01.3	197 55.6	31.0	127 20.3	04.0
14		49 58.5	54 38.2	44.9	359 21.3	01.7	212 58.4	30.9	142 22.8	04.0
15		65 01.0	69 40.8	. . 44.2	14 22.0	. . 02.2	228 01.2	. . 30.8	157 25.3	. . 04.0
16		80 03.4	84 43.4	43.6	29 22.6	02.7	243 03.9	30.6	172 27.8	04.0
17		95 05.9	99 45.9	42.9	44 23.3	03.1	258 06.7	30.5	187 30.2	04.0
18		110 08.4	114 48.5	N 3 42.2	59 24.0	N19 03.6	273 09.4	S 5 30.4	202 32.7	S22 04.0
19		125 10.8	129 51.1	41.6	74 24.7	04.1	288 12.2	30.3	217 35.2	04.0
20		140 13.3	144 53.7	40.9	89 25.4	04.5	303 15.0	30.2	232 37.7	04.0
21		155 15.8	159 56.2	. . 40.2	104 26.1	. . 05.0	318 17.7	. . 30.0	247 40.2	. . 04.0
22		170 18.2	174 58.8	39.6	119 26.7	05.4	333 20.5	29.9	262 42.7	03.9
23		185 20.7	190 01.4	38.9	134 27.4	05.9	348 23.2	29.8	277 45.2	03.9
12 00		200 23.2	205 03.9	N 3 38.2	149 28.1	N19 06.4	3 26.0	S 5 29.7	292 47.7	S22 03.9
01		215 25.6	220 06.5	37.6	164 28.8	06.8	18 28.8	29.5	307 50.2	03.9
02		230 28.1	235 09.0	36.9	179 29.5	07.3	33 31.5	29.4	322 52.7	03.9
03		245 30.5	250 11.6	. . 36.3	194 30.1	. . 07.7	48 34.3	. . 29.3	337 55.1	. . 03.9
04		260 33.0	265 14.1	35.6	209 30.8	08.2	63 37.0	29.2	352 57.6	03.9
05		275 35.5	280 16.7	35.0	224 31.5	08.7	78 39.8	29.1	8 00.1	03.9
06		290 37.9	295 19.2	N 3 34.3	239 32.2	N19 09.1	93 42.6	S 5 28.9	23 02.6	S22 03.9
07	WEDNESDAY	305 40.4	310 21.7	33.7	254 32.9	09.6	108 45.3	28.8	38 05.1	03.9
08		320 42.9	325 24.3	33.0	269 33.5	10.0	123 48.1	28.7	53 07.6	03.9
09		335 45.3	340 26.8	. . 32.4	284 34.2	. . 10.5	138 50.9	. . 28.6	68 10.1	. . 03.9
10		350 47.8	355 29.3	31.7	299 34.9	11.0	153 53.6	28.5	83 12.6	03.9
11		5 50.3	10 31.8	31.1	314 35.6	11.4	168 56.4	28.3	98 15.1	03.9
12		20 52.7	25 34.3	N 3 30.5	329 36.3	N19 11.9	183 59.1	S 5 28.2	113 17.6	S22 03.9
13		35 55.2	40 36.8	29.8	344 36.9	12.3	199 01.9	28.1	128 20.1	03.9
14		50 57.7	55 39.4	29.2	359 37.6	12.8	214 04.7	28.0	143 22.5	03.9
15		66 00.1	70 41.9	. . 28.5	14 38.3	. . 13.2	229 07.4	. . 27.9	158 25.0	. . 03.9
16		81 02.6	85 44.3	27.9	29 39.0	13.7	244 10.2	27.8	173 27.5	03.9
17		96 05.0	100 46.8	27.3	44 39.7	14.2	259 12.9	27.6	188 30.0	03.9
18		111 07.5	115 49.3	N 3 26.7	59 40.3	N19 14.6	274 15.7	S 5 27.5	203 32.5	S22 03.9
19		126 10.0	130 51.8	26.0	74 41.0	15.1	289 18.5	27.4	218 35.0	03.9
20		141 12.4	145 54.3	25.4	89 41.7	15.5	304 21.2	27.3	233 37.5	03.9
21		156 14.9	160 56.8	. . 24.8	104 42.4	. . 16.0	319 24.0	. . 27.2	248 40.0	. . 03.9
22		171 17.4	175 59.2	24.2	119 43.1	16.4	334 26.7	27.0	263 42.5	03.9
23		186 19.8	191 01.7	23.5	134 43.7	16.9	349 29.5	26.9	278 45.0	03.9
Mer. Pass.		h m 10 40.6	v 2.6	d 0.7	v 0.7	d 0.5	v 2.8	d 0.1	v 2.5	d 0.0

STARS

Name	SHA	Dec
	° ′	° ′
Acamar	315 16.8	S40 14.5
Achernar	335 25.5	S57 09.2
Acrux	173 05.6	S63 11.7
Adhara	255 10.6	S29 00.2
Aldebaran	290 46.7	N16 32.4
Alioth	166 18.0	N55 52.0
Alkaid	152 56.5	N49 13.7
Al Na'ir	27 40.9	S46 52.5
Alnilam	275 43.9	S 1 11.8
Alphard	217 53.4	S 8 44.2
Alphecca	126 08.6	N26 39.4
Alpheratz	357 41.2	N29 10.9
Altair	62 05.8	N 8 54.8
Ankaa	353 13.6	S42 12.8
Antares	112 22.9	S26 28.0
Arcturus	145 53.1	N19 05.6
Atria	107 22.0	S69 03.1
Avior	234 16.8	S59 34.3
Bellatrix	278 29.4	N 6 21.6
Betelgeuse	270 58.7	N 7 24.3
Canopus	263 55.2	S52 42.8
Capella	280 30.9	N46 00.8
Deneb	49 29.8	N45 20.3
Denebola	182 30.8	N14 28.5
Diphda	348 53.7	S17 53.7
Dubhe	193 48.2	N61 39.6
Elnath	278 09.6	N28 37.1
Eltanin	90 44.7	N51 29.1
Enif	33 44.8	N 9 57.1
Fomalhaut	15 21.5	S29 31.9
Gacrux	171 57.4	S57 12.6
Gienah	175 49.3	S17 38.3
Hadar	148 43.5	S60 27.2
Hamal	327 58.2	N23 32.4
Kaus Aust.	83 40.3	S34 22.3
Kochab	137 19.2	N74 05.1
Markab	13 36.0	N15 17.7
Menkar	314 12.7	N 4 09.1
Menkent	148 04.1	S36 27.2
Miaplacidus	221 38.6	S69 47.7
Mirfak	308 37.1	N49 55.2
Nunki	75 55.1	S26 16.3
Peacock	53 15.4	S56 40.4
Pollux	243 24.6	N27 58.9
Procyon	244 57.1	N 5 10.6
Rasalhague	96 03.9	N12 32.9
Regulus	207 40.6	N11 52.9
Rigel	281 09.8	S 8 11.3
Rigil Kent.	139 47.5	S60 54.2
Sabik	102 09.4	S15 44.6
Schedar	349 38.1	N56 37.7
Shaula	96 18.2	S37 06.7
Sirius	258 31.5	S16 44.8
Spica	158 28.2	S11 15.1
Suhail	222 50.3	S43 30.5
Vega	80 37.1	N38 47.9
Zuben'ubi	137 02.3	S16 06.7

	SHA	Mer. Pass.
	° ′	h m
Venus	4 37.4	10 22
Mars	309 47.7	14 03
Jupiter	162 55.7	23 46
Saturn	92 24.0	4 32

UT d h	SUN GHA	SUN Dec	MOON GHA	v	Dec	d	HP
	° ′	° ′	° ′	′	° ′	′	′
10 00	179 39.4	N 7 56.2	11 48.7	13.9	N 0 13.5	10.2	55.5
01	194 39.5	57.1	26 21.6	13.9	N 0 03.3	10.2	55.5
02	209 39.7	58.0	40 54.5	13.9	S 0 06.9	10.1	55.5
03	224 39.9	. . 58.9	55 27.4	13.9	0 17.0	10.2	55.5
04	239 40.0	7 59.9	70 00.3	14.0	0 27.2	10.2	55.4
05	254 40.2	8 00.8	84 33.3	13.9	0 37.4	10.2	55.4
06	269 40.4	N 8 01.7	99 06.2	14.0	S 0 47.6	10.1	55.4
07	284 40.5	02.6	113 39.2	14.0	0 57.7	10.2	55.4
08	299 40.7	03.6	128 12.2	14.0	1 07.9	10.1	55.4
M 09	314 40.9	. . 04.5	142 45.2	14.0	1 18.0	10.1	55.4
O 10	329 41.0	05.4	157 18.2	14.1	1 28.1	10.1	55.3
N 11	344 41.2	06.3	171 51.3	14.0	1 38.2	10.1	55.3
D 12	359 41.4	N 8 07.2	186 24.3	14.1	S 1 48.3	10.1	55.3
A 13	14 41.5	08.2	200 57.4	14.1	1 58.4	10.1	55.3
Y 14	29 41.7	09.1	215 30.5	14.0	2 08.5	10.1	55.3
15	44 41.9	. . 10.0	230 03.5	14.1	2 18.6	10.0	55.2
16	59 42.0	10.9	244 36.6	14.1	2 28.6	10.0	55.2
17	74 42.2	11.8	259 09.7	14.2	2 38.6	10.0	55.2
18	89 42.4	N 8 12.8	273 42.9	14.1	S 2 48.6	10.0	55.2
19	104 42.5	13.7	288 16.0	14.1	2 58.6	10.0	55.2
20	119 42.7	14.6	302 49.1	14.2	3 08.6	9.9	55.2
21	134 42.9	. . 15.5	317 22.3	14.1	3 18.5	10.0	55.1
22	149 43.0	16.4	331 55.4	14.2	3 28.5	9.9	55.1
23	164 43.2	17.4	346 28.6	14.1	3 38.4	9.9	55.1
11 00	179 43.4	N 8 18.3	1 01.7	14.2	S 3 48.3	9.8	55.1
01	194 43.5	19.2	15 34.9	14.2	3 58.1	9.9	55.1
02	209 43.7	20.1	30 08.1	14.2	4 08.0	9.8	55.1
03	224 43.9	. . 21.0	44 41.3	14.2	4 17.8	9.8	55.0
04	239 44.0	22.0	59 14.5	14.2	4 27.6	9.8	55.0
05	254 44.2	22.9	73 47.7	14.1	4 37.4	9.7	55.0
06	269 44.4	N 8 23.8	88 20.8	14.2	S 4 47.1	9.7	55.0
07	284 44.5	24.7	102 54.0	14.3	4 56.8	9.7	55.0
T 08	299 44.7	25.6	117 27.3	14.2	5 06.5	9.7	55.0
U 09	314 44.9	. . 26.5	132 00.5	14.2	5 16.2	9.6	54.9
E 10	329 45.0	27.5	146 33.7	14.2	5 25.8	9.6	54.9
S 11	344 45.2	28.4	161 06.9	14.2	5 35.4	9.6	54.9
D 12	359 45.3	N 8 29.3	175 40.1	14.2	S 5 45.0	9.6	54.9
A 13	14 45.5	30.2	190 13.3	14.2	5 54.6	9.5	54.9
Y 14	29 45.7	31.1	204 46.5	14.2	6 04.1	9.5	54.9
15	44 45.8	. . 32.0	219 19.7	14.2	6 13.6	9.4	54.9
16	59 46.0	32.9	233 52.9	14.2	6 23.0	9.5	54.8
17	74 46.2	33.9	248 26.1	14.2	6 32.5	9.3	54.8
18	89 46.3	N 8 34.8	262 59.3	14.2	S 6 41.8	9.4	54.8
19	104 46.5	35.7	277 32.5	14.2	6 51.2	9.3	54.8
20	119 46.7	36.6	292 05.7	14.2	7 00.5	9.3	54.8
21	134 46.8	. . 37.5	306 38.9	14.2	7 09.8	9.3	54.8
22	149 47.0	38.4	321 12.1	14.2	7 19.1	9.2	54.8
23	164 47.1	39.3	335 45.3	14.2	7 28.3	9.2	54.7
12 00	179 47.3	N 8 40.3	350 18.5	14.1	S 7 37.5	9.1	54.7
01	194 47.5	41.2	4 51.6	14.2	7 46.6	9.1	54.7
02	209 47.6	42.1	19 24.8	14.2	7 55.7	9.1	54.7
03	224 47.8	. . 43.0	33 58.0	14.1	8 04.8	9.0	54.7
04	239 48.0	43.9	48 31.1	14.2	8 13.8	9.0	54.7
05	254 48.1	44.8	63 04.3	14.1	8 22.8	8.9	54.7
06	269 48.3	N 8 45.7	77 37.4	14.2	S 8 31.7	8.9	54.6
W 07	284 48.4	46.6	92 10.6	14.1	8 40.6	8.9	54.6
E 08	299 48.6	47.5	106 43.7	14.1	8 49.5	8.8	54.6
D 09	314 48.8	. . 48.5	121 16.8	14.2	8 58.3	8.8	54.6
N 10	329 48.9	49.4	135 50.0	14.1	9 07.1	8.7	54.6
E 11	344 49.1	50.3	150 23.1	14.1	9 15.8	8.7	54.6
S 12	359 49.3	N 8 51.2	164 56.2	14.0	S 9 24.5	8.7	54.6
D 13	14 49.4	52.1	179 29.2	14.1	9 33.2	8.6	54.6
A 14	29 49.6	53.0	194 02.3	14.1	9 41.8	8.5	54.5
Y 15	44 49.7	. . 53.9	208 35.4	14.0	9 50.3	8.5	54.5
16	59 49.9	54.8	223 08.4	14.1	9 58.8	8.5	54.5
17	74 50.1	55.7	237 41.5	14.0	10 07.3	8.4	54.5
18	89 50.2	N 8 56.6	252 14.5	14.0	S10 15.7	8.4	54.5
19	104 50.4	57.5	266 47.5	14.1	10 24.1	8.3	54.5
20	119 50.5	58.5	281 20.6	14.0	10 32.4	8.3	54.5
21	134 50.7	8 59.4	295 53.6	13.9	10 40.7	8.2	54.5
22	149 50.9	9 00.3	310 26.5	14.0	10 48.9	8.2	54.4
23	164 51.0	N 9 01.2	324 59.5	14.0	S10 57.1	8.1	54.4
	SD 16.0	*d* 0.9	SD 15.1		15.0		14.9

Lat.	Twilight Naut.	Twilight Civil	Sunrise	Moonrise 10	Moonrise 11	Moonrise 12	Moonrise 13
°	h m	h m	h m	h m	h m	h m	h m
N 72	////	02 31	04 01	18 23	20 02	21 43	23 27
N 70	////	02 59	04 15	18 18	19 51	21 24	22 57
68	01 31	03 20	04 26	18 15	19 43	21 09	22 35
66	02 10	03 36	04 35	18 12	19 35	20 58	22 18
64	02 36	03 50	04 43	18 10	19 29	20 48	22 04
62	02 56	04 01	04 49	18 08	19 24	20 39	21 53
60	03 11	04 10	04 55	18 06	19 20	20 32	21 43
N 58	03 24	04 18	05 00	18 04	19 16	20 26	21 34
56	03 35	04 25	05 04	18 03	19 12	20 20	21 27
54	03 45	04 31	05 08	18 01	19 09	20 15	21 20
52	03 53	04 37	05 12	18 00	19 06	20 11	21 14
50	04 00	04 42	05 15	17 59	19 04	20 07	21 09
45	04 16	04 52	05 22	17 57	18 58	19 58	20 57
N 40	04 27	05 00	05 28	17 55	18 53	19 51	20 47
35	04 37	05 07	05 33	17 53	18 49	19 44	20 39
30	04 45	05 13	05 38	17 52	18 46	19 39	20 32
20	04 57	05 23	05 45	17 49	18 40	19 30	20 19
N 10	05 06	05 30	05 52	17 47	18 34	19 21	20 09
0	05 13	05 37	05 58	17 45	18 29	19 14	19 58
S 10	05 18	05 42	06 04	17 43	18 24	19 06	19 48
20	05 22	05 48	06 10	17 41	18 19	18 58	19 38
30	05 25	05 53	06 17	17 39	18 13	18 49	19 26
35	05 26	05 55	06 21	17 37	18 10	18 43	19 19
40	05 26	05 58	06 25	17 36	18 06	18 37	19 11
45	05 27	06 01	06 30	17 34	18 02	18 30	19 01
S 50	05 26	06 04	06 36	17 32	17 56	18 22	18 50
52	05 26	06 05	06 39	17 31	17 54	18 18	18 45
54	05 25	06 06	06 42	17 30	17 51	18 14	18 39
56	05 25	06 08	06 46	17 29	17 49	18 10	18 33
58	05 24	06 10	06 49	17 28	17 45	18 04	18 26
S 60	05 23	06 11	06 53	17 26	17 42	17 59	18 18

Lat.	Sunset	Twilight Civil	Twilight Naut.	Moonset 10	Moonset 11	Moonset 12	Moonset 13
°	h m	h m	h m	h m	h m	h m	h m
N 72	20 05	21 37	////	05 13	05 06	04 58	04 50
N 70	19 50	21 07	////	05 14	05 12	05 11	05 10
68	19 39	20 45	22 40	05 14	05 18	05 21	05 26
66	19 29	20 28	21 57	05 15	05 22	05 30	05 39
64	19 21	20 15	21 30	05 16	05 26	05 37	05 49
62	19 15	20 04	21 10	05 16	05 29	05 43	05 59
60	19 09	19 54	20 53	05 17	05 32	05 48	06 06
N 58	19 03	19 46	20 40	05 17	05 35	05 53	06 13
56	18 59	19 39	20 29	05 18	05 37	05 57	06 20
54	18 55	19 32	20 19	05 18	05 39	06 01	06 25
52	18 51	19 27	20 10	05 18	05 41	06 05	06 30
50	18 48	19 22	20 03	05 18	05 43	06 08	06 35
45	18 40	19 11	19 48	05 19	05 47	06 15	06 44
N 40	18 34	19 02	19 36	05 20	05 50	06 21	06 53
35	18 29	18 55	19 26	05 20	05 53	06 25	07 00
30	18 25	18 49	19 18	05 20	05 55	06 30	07 06
20	18 17	18 39	19 06	05 21	05 59	06 38	07 17
N 10	18 10	18 32	18 56	05 22	06 03	06 44	07 26
0	18 04	18 25	18 49	05 22	06 06	06 51	07 35
S 10	17 58	18 19	18 44	05 23	06 10	06 57	07 44
20	17 52	18 14	18 40	05 23	06 14	07 04	07 54
30	17 45	18 09	18 37	05 24	06 18	07 11	08 05
35	17 41	18 06	18 36	05 24	06 20	07 16	08 11
40	17 36	18 04	18 35	05 24	06 23	07 21	08 18
45	17 31	18 01	18 35	05 25	06 26	07 27	08 26
S 50	17 25	17 57	18 35	05 25	06 30	07 34	08 37
52	17 22	17 56	18 35	05 25	06 32	07 37	08 41
54	17 19	17 55	18 35	05 26	06 34	07 41	08 46
56	17 15	17 53	18 36	05 26	06 36	07 45	08 52
58	17 12	17 51	18 37	05 26	06 38	07 49	08 59
S 60	17 07	17 49	18 37	05 27	06 41	07 54	09 06

Day	SUN Eqn. of Time 00^h	SUN Eqn. of Time 12^h	SUN Mer. Pass.	MOON Mer. Pass. Upper	MOON Mer. Pass. Lower	Age	Phase
d	m s	m s	h m	h m	h m	d %	
10	01 23	01 15	12 01	23 56	11 34	13 99	○
11	01 07	00 59	12 01	24 40	12 18	14 100	
12	00 51	00 43	12 01	00 40	13 02	15 98	

UT d h	ARIES GHA ° ′	VENUS −4·6 GHA ° ′	VENUS Dec ° ′	MARS +1·5 GHA ° ′	MARS Dec ° ′	JUPITER −2·5 GHA ° ′	JUPITER Dec ° ′	SATURN +0·3 GHA ° ′	SATURN Dec ° ′
13 00	201 22.3	206 04.2	N 3 22.9	149 44.4	N19 17.3	4 32.3	S 5 26.8	293 47.5	S22 03.9
01	216 24.8	221 06.6	22.3	164 45.1	17.8	19 35.0	26.7	308 50.0	03.9
02	231 27.2	236 09.1	21.7	179 45.8	18.2	34 37.8	26.6	323 52.5	03.9
03	246 29.7	251 11.5	. . 21.1	194 46.4	. . 18.7	49 40.5	. . 26.4	338 55.0	. . 03.9
04	261 32.1	266 14.0	20.5	209 47.1	19.1	64 43.3	26.3	353 57.5	03.9
05	276 34.6	281 16.4	19.8	224 47.8	19.6	79 46.1	26.2	8 59.9	03.9
06	291 37.1	296 18.9	N 3 19.2	239 48.5	N19 20.0	94 48.8	S 5 26.1	24 02.4	S22 03.9
07	306 39.5	311 21.3	18.6	254 49.2	20.5	109 51.6	26.0	39 04.9	03.9
T 08	321 42.0	326 23.8	18.0	269 49.8	21.0	124 54.3	25.8	54 07.4	03.9
H 09	336 44.5	341 26.2	. . 17.4	284 50.5	. . 21.4	139 57.1	. . 25.7	69 09.9	. . 03.8
U 10	351 46.9	356 28.6	16.8	299 51.2	21.9	154 59.9	25.6	84 12.4	03.8
R 11	6 49.4	11 31.0	16.2	314 51.9	22.3	170 02.6	25.5	99 14.9	03.8
S 12	21 51.9	26 33.5	N 3 15.6	329 52.5	N19 22.8	185 05.4	S 5 25.4	114 17.4	S22 03.8
D 13	36 54.3	41 35.9	15.0	344 53.2	23.2	200 08.1	25.2	129 19.9	03.8
A 14	51 56.8	56 38.3	14.4	359 53.9	23.7	215 10.9	25.1	144 22.4	03.8
Y 15	66 59.3	71 40.7	. . 13.8	14 54.6	. . 24.1	230 13.7	. . 25.0	159 24.9	. . 03.8
16	82 01.7	86 43.1	13.2	29 55.3	24.5	245 16.4	24.9	174 27.4	03.8
17	97 04.2	101 45.5	12.6	44 55.9	25.0	260 19.2	24.8	189 29.9	03.8
18	112 06.6	116 47.9	N 3 12.1	59 56.6	N19 25.4	275 21.9	S 5 24.6	204 32.4	S22 03.8
19	127 09.1	131 50.3	11.5	74 57.3	25.9	290 24.7	24.5	219 34.9	03.8
20	142 11.6	146 52.7	10.9	89 58.0	26.3	305 27.5	24.4	234 37.4	03.8
21	157 14.0	161 55.0	. . 10.3	104 58.6	. . 26.8	320 30.2	. . 24.3	249 39.9	. . 03.8
22	172 16.5	176 57.4	09.7	119 59.3	27.2	335 33.0	24.2	264 42.4	03.8
23	187 19.0	191 59.8	09.1	135 00.0	27.7	350 35.7	24.1	279 44.9	03.8
14 00	202 21.4	207 02.2	N 3 08.6	150 00.7	N19 28.1	5 38.5	S 5 23.9	294 47.4	S22 03.8
01	217 23.9	222 04.5	08.0	165 01.3	28.6	20 41.3	23.8	309 49.9	03.8
02	232 26.4	237 06.9	07.4	180 02.0	29.0	35 44.0	23.7	324 52.4	03.8
03	247 28.8	252 09.3	. . 06.8	195 02.7	. . 29.5	50 46.8	. . 23.6	339 54.9	. . 03.8
04	262 31.3	267 11.6	06.3	210 03.4	29.9	65 49.5	23.5	354 57.4	03.8
05	277 33.8	282 14.0	05.7	225 04.0	30.4	80 52.3	23.3	9 59.9	03.8
06	292 36.2	297 16.3	N 3 05.1	240 04.7	N19 30.8	95 55.1	S 5 23.2	25 02.4	S22 03.8
07	307 38.7	312 18.7	04.6	255 05.4	31.2	110 57.8	23.1	40 04.9	03.8
08	322 41.1	327 21.0	04.0	270 06.1	31.7	126 00.6	23.0	55 07.4	03.8
F 09	337 43.6	342 23.3	. . 03.4	285 06.8	. . 32.1	141 03.3	. . 22.9	70 09.9	. . 03.8
R 10	352 46.1	357 25.7	02.9	300 07.4	32.6	156 06.1	22.7	85 12.4	03.8
I 11	7 48.5	12 28.0	02.3	315 08.1	33.0	171 08.9	22.6	100 14.9	03.8
D 12	22 51.0	27 30.3	N 3 01.7	330 08.8	N19 33.5	186 11.6	S 5 22.5	115 17.4	S22 03.8
A 13	37 53.5	42 32.7	01.2	345 09.5	33.9	201 14.4	22.4	130 19.9	03.8
Y 14	52 55.9	57 35.0	00.6	0 10.1	34.3	216 17.1	22.3	145 22.4	03.8
15	67 58.4	72 37.3	3 00.1	15 10.8	. . 34.8	231 19.9	. . 22.2	160 24.9	. . 03.8
16	83 00.9	87 39.6	2 59.5	30 11.5	35.2	246 22.7	22.0	175 27.4	03.8
17	98 03.3	102 41.9	59.0	45 12.2	35.7	261 25.4	21.9	190 29.9	03.8
18	113 05.8	117 44.2	N 2 58.4	60 12.8	N19 36.1	276 28.2	S 5 21.8	205 32.4	S22 03.8
19	128 08.2	132 46.5	57.9	75 13.5	36.5	291 30.9	21.7	220 34.9	03.7
20	143 10.7	147 48.8	57.4	90 14.2	37.0	306 33.7	21.6	235 37.4	03.7
21	158 13.2	162 51.1	. . 56.8	105 14.9	. . 37.4	321 36.4	. . 21.4	250 39.9	. . 03.7
22	173 15.6	177 53.4	56.3	120 15.5	37.9	336 39.2	21.3	265 42.4	03.7
23	188 18.1	192 55.7	55.7	135 16.2	38.3	351 42.0	21.2	280 44.9	03.7
15 00	203 20.6	207 58.0	N 2 55.2	150 16.9	N19 38.7	6 44.7	S 5 21.1	295 47.4	S22 03.7
01	218 23.0	223 00.2	54.7	165 17.6	39.2	21 47.5	21.0	310 49.9	03.7
02	233 25.5	238 02.5	54.1	180 18.2	39.6	36 50.2	20.9	325 52.4	03.7
03	248 28.0	253 04.8	. . 53.6	195 18.9	. . 40.1	51 53.0	. . 20.7	340 54.9	. . 03.7
04	263 30.4	268 07.0	53.1	210 19.6	40.5	66 55.7	20.6	355 57.4	03.7
05	278 32.9	283 09.3	52.5	225 20.2	40.9	81 58.5	20.5	10 59.9	03.7
06	293 35.4	298 11.6	N 2 52.0	240 20.9	N19 41.4	97 01.3	S 5 20.4	26 02.4	S22 03.7
07	308 37.8	313 13.8	51.5	255 21.6	41.8	112 04.0	20.3	41 04.9	03.7
S 08	323 40.3	328 16.1	51.0	270 22.3	42.2	127 06.8	20.1	56 07.4	03.7
A 09	338 42.7	343 18.3	. . 50.4	285 22.9	. . 42.7	142 09.5	. . 20.0	71 09.9	. . 03.7
T 10	353 45.2	358 20.6	49.9	300 23.6	43.1	157 12.3	19.9	86 12.4	03.7
U 11	8 47.7	13 22.8	49.4	315 24.3	43.5	172 15.1	19.8	101 14.9	03.7
R 12	23 50.1	28 25.0	N 2 48.9	330 25.0	N19 44.0	187 17.8	S 5 19.7	116 17.4	S22 03.7
D 13	38 52.6	43 27.3	48.4	345 25.6	44.4	202 20.6	19.6	131 19.9	03.7
A 14	53 55.1	58 29.5	47.9	0 26.3	44.9	217 23.3	19.4	146 22.4	03.7
Y 15	68 57.5	73 31.7	. . 47.4	15 27.0	. . 45.3	232 26.1	. . 19.3	161 24.9	. . 03.7
16	84 00.0	88 33.9	46.9	30 27.7	45.7	247 28.8	19.2	176 27.5	03.7
17	99 02.5	103 36.1	46.3	45 28.3	46.2	262 31.6	19.1	191 30.0	03.7
18	114 04.9	118 38.4	N 2 45.8	60 29.0	N19 46.6	277 34.4	S 5 19.0	206 32.5	S22 03.7
19	129 07.4	133 40.6	45.3	75 29.7	47.0	292 37.1	18.8	221 35.0	03.7
20	144 09.9	148 42.8	44.8	90 30.3	47.4	307 39.9	18.7	236 37.5	03.7
21	159 12.3	163 45.0	. . 44.3	105 31.0	. . 47.9	322 42.6	. . 18.6	251 40.0	. . 03.7
22	174 14.8	178 47.2	43.8	120 31.7	48.3	337 45.4	18.5	266 42.5	03.7
23	189 17.2	193 49.4	43.3	135 32.4	48.7	352 48.1	18.4	281 45.0	03.7
Mer. Pass. h m	10 28.8	*v* 2.3	*d* 0.6	*v* 0.7	*d* 0.4	*v* 2.8	*d* 0.1	*v* 2.5	*d* 0.0

STARS

Name	SHA ° ′	Dec ° ′
Acamar	315 16.8	S40 14.5
Achernar	335 25.5	S57 09.1
Acrux	173 05.6	S63 11.8
Adhara	255 10.6	S29 00.2
Aldebaran	290 46.7	N16 32.4
Alioth	166 18.0	N55 52.1
Alkaid	152 56.5	N49 13.7
Al Na'ir	27 40.9	S46 52.5
Alnilam	275 43.9	S 1 11.8
Alphard	217 53.4	S 8 44.3
Alphecca	126 08.5	N26 39.4
Alpheratz	357 41.1	N29 10.9
Altair	62 05.7	N 8 54.8
Ankaa	353 13.6	S42 12.8
Antares	112 22.8	S26 28.0
Arcturus	145 53.1	N19 05.6
Atria	107 22.0	S69 03.1
Avior	234 16.8	S59 34.3
Bellatrix	278 29.4	N 6 21.6
Betelgeuse	270 58.7	N 7 24.3
Canopus	263 55.2	S52 42.8
Capella	280 30.9	N46 00.8
Deneb	49 29.8	N45 20.3
Denebola	182 30.8	N14 28.5
Diphda	348 53.7	S17 53.7
Dubhe	193 48.2	N61 39.6
Elnath	278 09.6	N28 37.1
Eltanin	90 44.7	N51 29.1
Enif	33 44.8	N 9 57.1
Fomalhaut	15 21.5	S29 31.8
Gacrux	171 57.4	S57 12.7
Gienah	175 49.3	S17 38.3
Hadar	148 43.5	S60 27.2
Hamal	327 58.2	N23 32.4
Kaus Aust.	83 40.3	S34 22.3
Kochab	137 19.1	N74 05.1
Markab	13 36.0	N15 17.7
Menkar	314 12.7	N 4 09.1
Menkent	148 04.1	S36 27.2
Miaplacidus	221 38.7	S69 47.7
Mirfak	308 37.1	N49 55.2
Nunki	75 55.1	S26 16.3
Peacock	53 15.4	S56 40.4
Pollux	243 24.6	N27 58.9
Procyon	244 57.1	N 5 10.6
Rasalhague	96 03.9	N12 32.9
Regulus	207 40.6	N11 52.9
Rigel	281 09.8	S 8 11.3
Rigil Kent.	139 47.5	S60 54.2
Sabik	102 09.4	S15 44.6
Schedar	349 38.0	N56 37.7
Shaula	96 18.2	S37 06.7
Sirius	258 31.6	S16 44.8
Spica	158 28.2	S11 15.1
Suhail	222 50.4	S43 30.5
Vega	80 37.1	N38 47.9
Zuben'ubi	137 02.3	S16 06.7

	SHA ° ′	Mer. Pass. h m
Venus	4 40.7	10 10
Mars	307 39.2	13 59
Jupiter	163 17.1	23 33
Saturn	92 25.9	4 20

	UT	SUN GHA	SUN Dec	MOON GHA	v	MOON Dec	d	HP
	d h	° ′	° ′	° ′	′	° ′	′	′
	13 00	179 51.2	N 9 02.1	339 32.5	13.9	S11 05.2	8.0	54.4
	01	194 51.3	03.0	354 05.4	13.9	11 13.2	8.1	54.4
	02	209 51.5	03.9	8 38.3	14.0	11 21.3	7.9	54.4
	03	224 51.7	. . 04.8	23 11.3	13.9	11 29.2	7.9	54.4
	04	239 51.8	05.7	37 44.2	13.9	11 37.1	7.9	54.4
	05	254 52.0	06.6	52 17.1	13.8	11 45.0	7.8	54.4
	06	269 52.1	N 9 07.5	66 49.9	13.9	S11 52.8	7.7	54.4
	07	284 52.3	08.4	81 22.8	13.8	12 00.5	7.7	54.3
T	08	299 52.4	09.3	95 55.6	13.9	12 08.2	7.7	54.3
H	09	314 52.6	. . 10.2	110 28.5	13.8	12 15.9	7.6	54.3
U	10	329 52.8	11.1	125 01.3	13.8	12 23.5	7.5	54.3
R	11	344 52.9	12.0	139 34.1	13.7	12 31.0	7.5	54.3
S	12	359 53.1	N 9 12.9	154 06.8	13.8	S12 38.5	7.4	54.3
D	13	14 53.2	13.8	168 39.6	13.7	12 45.9	7.3	54.3
A	14	29 53.4	14.7	183 12.3	13.8	12 53.2	7.3	54.3
Y	15	44 53.6	. . 15.6	197 45.1	13.7	13 00.5	7.3	54.3
	16	59 53.7	16.6	212 17.8	13.7	13 07.8	7.1	54.3
	17	74 53.9	17.5	226 50.5	13.7	13 14.9	7.2	54.3
	18	89 54.0	N 9 18.4	241 23.2	13.6	S13 22.1	7.0	54.2
	19	104 54.2	19.3	255 55.8	13.6	13 29.1	7.0	54.2
	20	119 54.3	20.2	270 28.4	13.7	13 36.1	6.9	54.2
	21	134 54.5	. . 21.1	285 01.1	13.6	13 43.0	6.9	54.2
	22	149 54.6	22.0	299 33.7	13.5	13 49.9	6.8	54.2
	23	164 54.8	22.9	314 06.2	13.6	13 56.7	6.8	54.2
	14 00	179 55.0	N 9 23.8	328 38.8	13.6	S14 03.5	6.7	54.2
	01	194 55.1	24.7	343 11.4	13.5	14 10.2	6.6	54.2
	02	209 55.3	25.6	357 43.9	13.5	14 16.8	6.5	54.2
	03	224 55.4	. . 26.5	12 16.4	13.5	14 23.3	6.5	54.2
	04	239 55.6	27.4	26 48.9	13.4	14 29.8	6.5	54.2
	05	254 55.7	28.3	41 21.3	13.5	14 36.3	6.3	54.2
	06	269 55.9	N 9 29.2	55 53.8	13.4	S14 42.6	6.3	54.2
	07	284 56.0	30.1	70 26.2	13.4	14 48.9	6.2	54.2
	08	299 56.2	31.0	84 58.6	13.4	14 55.1	6.2	54.2
F	09	314 56.4	. . 31.8	99 31.0	13.4	15 01.3	6.1	54.1
R	10	329 56.5	32.7	114 03.4	13.3	15 07.4	6.0	54.1
I	11	344 56.7	33.6	128 35.7	13.3	15 13.4	6.0	54.1
D	12	359 56.8	N 9 34.5	143 08.0	13.3	S15 19.4	5.9	54.1
A	13	14 57.0	35.4	157 40.3	13.3	15 25.3	5.8	54.1
Y	14	29 57.1	36.3	172 12.6	13.3	15 31.1	5.7	54.1
	15	44 57.3	. . 37.2	186 44.9	13.2	15 36.8	5.7	54.1
	16	59 57.4	38.1	201 17.1	13.3	15 42.5	5.6	54.1
	17	74 57.6	39.0	215 49.4	13.2	15 48.1	5.6	54.1
	18	89 57.7	N 9 39.9	230 21.6	13.1	S15 53.7	5.5	54.1
	19	104 57.9	40.8	244 53.7	13.2	15 59.2	5.3	54.1
	20	119 58.0	41.7	259 25.9	13.1	16 04.5	5.4	54.1
	21	134 58.2	. . 42.6	273 58.0	13.2	16 09.9	5.2	54.1
	22	149 58.4	43.5	288 30.2	13.1	16 15.1	5.2	54.1
	23	164 58.5	44.4	303 02.3	13.0	16 20.3	5.1	54.1
	15 00	179 58.7	N 9 45.3	317 34.3	13.1	S16 25.4	5.1	54.1
	01	194 58.8	46.2	332 06.4	13.0	16 30.5	4.9	54.1
	02	209 59.0	47.1	346 38.4	13.0	16 35.4	4.9	54.1
	03	224 59.1	. . 48.0	1 10.4	13.0	16 40.3	4.8	54.1
	04	239 59.3	48.9	15 42.4	13.0	16 45.1	4.7	54.1
	05	254 59.4	49.7	30 14.4	12.9	16 49.8	4.7	54.1
	06	269 59.6	N 9 50.6	44 46.3	13.0	S16 54.5	4.6	54.1
	07	284 59.7	51.5	59 18.3	12.9	16 59.1	4.5	54.1
S	08	299 59.9	52.4	73 50.2	12.8	17 03.6	4.4	54.1
A	09	315 00.0	. . 53.3	88 22.0	12.9	17 08.0	4.4	54.1
T	10	330 00.2	54.2	102 53.9	12.8	17 12.4	4.3	54.1
U	11	345 00.3	55.1	117 25.7	12.9	17 16.7	4.2	54.1
R	12	0 00.5	N 9 56.0	131 57.6	12.8	S17 20.9	4.1	54.1
D	13	15 00.6	56.9	146 29.4	12.7	17 25.0	4.0	54.1
A	14	30 00.8	57.8	161 01.1	12.8	17 29.0	4.0	54.1
Y	15	45 00.9	. . 58.7	175 32.9	12.7	17 33.0	3.9	54.1
	16	60 01.1	9 59.5	190 04.6	12.8	17 36.9	3.8	54.1
	17	75 01.2	10 00.4	204 36.4	12.7	17 40.7	3.7	54.1
	18	90 01.4	N10 01.3	219 08.1	12.6	S17 44.4	3.7	54.1
	19	105 01.5	02.2	233 39.7	12.7	17 48.1	3.6	54.1
	20	120 01.7	03.1	248 11.4	12.6	17 51.7	3.4	54.1
	21	135 01.8	. . 04.0	262 43.0	12.6	17 55.1	3.5	54.1
	22	150 02.0	04.9	277 14.6	12.6	17 58.6	3.3	54.1
	23	165 02.1	05.8	291 46.2	12.6	S18 01.9	3.2	54.1
		SD 16.0	*d* 0.9	SD 14.8		14.7		14.7

Lat.	Twilight Naut.	Twilight Civil	Sunrise	Moonrise 13	14	15	16
°	h m	h m	h m	h m	h m	h m	h m
N 72	////	02 06	03 44	23 27	25 19	01 19	
N 70	////	02 40	04 00	22 57	24 30	00 30	01 59
68	00 54	03 04	04 13	22 35	23 58	25 16	01 16
66	01 48	03 23	04 23	22 18	23 36	24 47	00 47
64	02 19	03 38	04 32	22 04	23 18	24 25	00 25
62	02 42	03 50	04 40	21 53	23 03	24 08	00 08
60	03 00	04 00	04 46	21 43	22 50	23 53	24 49
N 58	03 14	04 09	04 52	21 34	22 40	23 41	24 36
56	03 26	04 17	04 57	21 27	22 30	23 30	24 25
54	03 36	04 24	05 01	21 20	22 22	23 21	24 15
52	03 45	04 30	05 05	21 14	22 15	23 13	24 06
50	03 53	04 35	05 09	21 09	22 08	23 05	23 58
45	04 10	04 46	05 17	20 57	21 54	22 49	23 41
N 40	04 22	04 56	05 24	20 47	21 42	22 36	23 27
35	04 32	05 03	05 29	20 39	21 33	22 25	23 15
30	04 41	05 10	05 34	20 32	21 24	22 15	23 05
20	04 54	05 20	05 43	20 19	21 09	21 59	22 47
N 10	05 04	05 29	05 50	20 09	20 56	21 44	22 32
0	05 12	05 36	05 57	19 58	20 44	21 30	22 18
S 10	05 18	05 42	06 04	19 48	20 32	21 17	22 03
20	05 23	05 48	06 11	19 38	20 19	21 03	21 48
30	05 26	05 54	06 19	19 26	20 05	20 46	21 31
35	05 28	05 57	06 23	19 19	19 56	20 37	21 21
40	05 29	06 01	06 28	19 11	19 46	20 26	21 09
45	05 30	06 04	06 34	19 01	19 35	20 13	20 55
S 50	05 31	06 08	06 41	18 50	19 22	19 57	20 39
52	05 31	06 10	06 44	18 45	19 15	19 50	20 31
54	05 31	06 12	06 48	18 39	19 08	19 42	20 22
56	05 31	06 14	06 52	18 33	19 01	19 33	20 12
58	05 30	06 16	06 56	18 26	18 52	19 23	20 01
S 60	05 30	06 18	07 01	18 18	18 42	19 11	19 48

Lat.	Sunset	Twilight Civil	Twilight Naut.	Moonset 13	14	15	16
°	h m	h m	h m	h m	h m	h m	h m
N 72	20 20	22 02	////	04 50	04 39	04 22	
N 70	20 03	21 25	////	05 10	05 10	05 12	05 19
68	19 50	21 00	23 25	05 26	05 33	05 44	06 03
66	19 39	20 41	22 19	05 39	05 51	06 08	06 32
64	19 30	20 25	21 46	05 49	06 05	06 26	06 54
62	19 23	20 13	21 22	05 59	06 17	06 41	07 12
60	19 16	20 02	21 04	06 06	06 28	06 54	07 27
N 58	19 10	19 53	20 49	06 13	06 37	07 05	07 39
56	19 05	19 45	20 37	06 20	06 45	07 15	07 50
54	19 00	19 38	20 26	06 25	06 52	07 23	08 00
52	18 56	19 32	20 17	06 30	06 58	07 31	08 08
50	18 52	19 27	20 09	06 35	07 04	07 38	08 16
45	18 44	19 15	19 52	06 44	07 17	07 52	08 32
N 40	18 38	19 06	19 39	06 53	07 27	08 05	08 46
35	18 32	18 58	19 29	07 00	07 36	08 15	08 57
30	18 27	18 51	19 20	07 06	07 44	08 24	09 07
20	18 18	18 40	19 07	07 17	07 57	08 40	09 24
N 10	18 10	18 32	18 57	07 26	08 09	08 53	09 39
0	18 04	18 24	18 49	07 35	08 20	09 06	09 53
S 10	17 57	18 18	18 43	07 44	08 31	09 19	10 07
20	17 50	18 12	18 38	07 54	08 43	09 33	10 22
30	17 42	18 06	18 34	08 05	08 57	09 49	10 39
35	17 37	18 02	18 32	08 11	09 05	09 58	10 49
40	17 32	17 59	18 31	08 18	09 14	10 08	11 01
45	17 26	17 55	18 30	08 26	09 25	10 21	11 14
S 50	17 19	17 51	18 29	08 37	09 37	10 36	11 31
52	17 15	17 50	18 29	08 41	09 43	10 43	11 38
54	17 12	17 48	18 29	08 46	09 50	10 51	11 47
56	17 08	17 46	18 29	08 52	09 57	10 59	11 57
58	17 04	17 44	18 29	08 59	10 06	11 09	12 08
S 60	16 59	17 41	18 29	09 06	10 15	11 21	12 20

Day	SUN Eqn. of Time 00^h	Eqn. of Time 12^h	Mer. Pass.	MOON Mer. Pass. Upper	Mer. Pass. Lower	Age	Phase
d	m s	m s	h m	h m	h m	d	%
13	00 36	00 28	12 00	01 24	13 47	16	95
14	00 20	00 13	12 00	02 09	14 32	17	90
15	00 06	00 02	12 00	02 55	15 18	18	84

UT		ARIES	VENUS −4·7		MARS +1·5		JUPITER −2·5		SATURN +0·3	
d	h	GHA ° ′	GHA ° ′	Dec ° ′	GHA ° ′	Dec ° ′	GHA ° ′	Dec ° ′	GHA ° ′	Dec ° ′
16	00	204 19.7	208 51.6	N 2 42.9	150 33.0	N19 49.2	7 50.9	S 5 18.3	296 47.5	S22 03.7
	01	219 22.2	223 53.7	42.4	165 33.7	49.6	22 53.7	18.1	311 50.0	03.7
	02	234 24.6	238 55.9	41.9	180 34.4	50.0	37 56.4	18.0	326 52.5	03.7
	03	249 27.1	253 58.1	. . 41.4	195 35.1	. . 50.5	52 59.2	. . 17.9	341 55.0	. . 03.7
	04	264 29.6	269 00.3	40.9	210 35.7	50.9	68 01.9	17.8	356 57.5	03.7
	05	279 32.0	284 02.5	40.4	225 36.4	51.3	83 04.7	17.7	12 00.0	03.6
	06	294 34.5	299 04.6	N 2 39.9	240 37.1	N19 51.8	98 07.4	S 5 17.6	27 02.5	S22 03.6
	07	309 37.0	314 06.8	39.4	255 37.7	52.2	113 10.2	17.4	42 05.1	03.6
	08	324 39.4	329 09.0	39.0	270 38.4	52.6	128 12.9	17.3	57 07.6	03.6
S	09	339 41.9	344 11.1	. . 38.5	285 39.1	. . 53.0	143 15.7	. . 17.2	72 10.1	. . 03.6
U	10	354 44.3	359 13.3	38.0	300 39.8	53.5	158 18.5	17.1	87 12.6	03.6
N	11	9 46.8	14 15.4	37.5	315 40.4	53.9	173 21.2	17.0	102 15.1	03.6
D	12	24 49.3	29 17.6	N 2 37.1	330 41.1	N19 54.3	188 24.0	S 5 16.9	117 17.6	S22 03.6
A	13	39 51.7	44 19.7	36.6	345 41.8	54.8	203 26.7	16.7	132 20.1	03.6
Y	14	54 54.2	59 21.8	36.1	0 42.4	55.2	218 29.5	16.6	147 22.6	03.6
	15	69 56.7	74 24.0	. . 35.7	15 43.1	. . 55.6	233 32.2	. . 16.5	162 25.1	. . 03.6
	16	84 59.1	89 26.1	35.2	30 43.8	56.0	248 35.0	16.4	177 27.6	03.6
	17	100 01.6	104 28.2	34.7	45 44.4	56.5	263 37.8	16.3	192 30.1	03.6
	18	115 04.1	119 30.4	N 2 34.3	60 45.1	N19 56.9	278 40.5	S 5 16.2	207 32.7	S22 03.6
	19	130 06.5	134 32.5	33.8	75 45.8	57.3	293 43.3	16.0	222 35.2	03.6
	20	145 09.0	149 34.6	33.4	90 46.5	57.7	308 46.0	15.9	237 37.7	03.6
	21	160 11.5	164 36.7	. . 32.9	105 47.1	. . 58.2	323 48.8	. . 15.8	252 40.2	. . 03.6
	22	175 13.9	179 38.8	32.4	120 47.8	58.6	338 51.5	15.7	267 42.7	03.6
	23	190 16.4	194 40.9	32.0	135 48.5	59.0	353 54.3	15.6	282 45.2	03.6
17	00	205 18.8	209 43.0	N 2 31.5	150 49.1	N19 59.4	8 57.0	S 5 15.5	297 47.7	S22 03.6
	01	220 21.3	224 45.1	31.1	165 49.8	19 59.9	23 59.8	15.3	312 50.2	03.6
	02	235 23.8	239 47.2	30.6	180 50.5	20 00.3	39 02.5	15.2	327 52.7	03.6
	03	250 26.2	254 49.3	. . 30.2	195 51.2	. . 00.7	54 05.3	. . 15.1	342 55.3	. . 03.6
	04	265 28.7	269 51.4	29.8	210 51.8	01.1	69 08.1	15.0	357 57.8	03.6
	05	280 31.2	284 53.5	29.3	225 52.5	01.5	84 10.8	14.9	13 00.3	03.6
	06	295 33.6	299 55.6	N 2 28.9	240 53.2	N20 02.0	99 13.6	S 5 14.8	28 02.8	S22 03.6
	07	310 36.1	314 57.7	28.4	255 53.8	02.4	114 16.3	14.6	43 05.3	03.6
	08	325 38.6	329 59.7	28.0	270 54.5	02.8	129 19.1	14.5	58 07.8	03.6
M	09	340 41.0	345 01.8	. . 27.6	285 55.2	. . 03.2	144 21.8	. . 14.4	73 10.3	. . 03.6
O	10	355 43.5	0 03.9	27.1	300 55.8	03.6	159 24.6	14.3	88 12.8	03.6
N	11	10 46.0	15 05.9	26.7	315 56.5	04.1	174 27.3	14.2	103 15.4	03.6
D	12	25 48.4	30 08.0	N 2 26.3	330 57.2	N20 04.5	189 30.1	S 5 14.1	118 17.9	S22 03.6
A	13	40 50.9	45 10.1	25.8	345 57.8	04.9	204 32.8	13.9	133 20.4	03.6
Y	14	55 53.3	60 12.1	25.4	0 58.5	05.3	219 35.6	13.8	148 22.9	03.5
	15	70 55.8	75 14.2	. . 25.0	15 59.2	. . 05.7	234 38.4	. . 13.7	163 25.4	. . 03.5
	16	85 58.3	90 16.2	24.6	30 59.9	06.2	249 41.1	13.6	178 27.9	03.5
	17	101 00.7	105 18.2	24.1	46 00.5	06.6	264 43.9	13.5	193 30.4	03.5
	18	116 03.2	120 20.3	N 2 23.7	61 01.2	N20 07.0	279 46.6	S 5 13.4	208 33.0	S22 03.5
	19	131 05.7	135 22.3	23.3	76 01.9	07.4	294 49.4	13.2	223 35.5	03.5
	20	146 08.1	150 24.4	22.9	91 02.5	07.8	309 52.1	13.1	238 38.0	03.5
	21	161 10.6	165 26.4	. . 22.5	106 03.2	. . 08.3	324 54.9	. . 13.0	253 40.5	. . 03.5
	22	176 13.1	180 28.4	22.1	121 03.9	08.7	339 57.6	12.9	268 43.0	03.5
	23	191 15.5	195 30.4	21.7	136 04.5	09.1	355 00.4	12.8	283 45.5	03.5
18	00	206 18.0	210 32.4	N 2 21.3	151 05.2	N20 09.5	10 03.1	S 5 12.7	298 48.0	S22 03.5
	01	221 20.5	225 34.5	20.9	166 05.9	09.9	25 05.9	12.6	313 50.6	03.5
	02	236 22.9	240 36.5	20.4	181 06.5	10.3	40 08.6	12.4	328 53.1	03.5
	03	251 25.4	255 38.5	. . 20.0	196 07.2	. . 10.7	55 11.4	. . 12.3	343 55.6	. . 03.5
	04	266 27.8	270 40.5	19.6	211 07.9	11.2	70 14.2	12.2	358 58.1	03.5
	05	281 30.3	285 42.5	19.2	226 08.5	11.6	85 16.9	12.1	14 00.6	03.5
	06	296 32.8	300 44.5	N 2 18.8	241 09.2	N20 12.0	100 19.7	S 5 12.0	29 03.1	S22 03.5
	07	311 35.2	315 46.5	18.5	256 09.9	12.4	115 22.4	11.9	44 05.7	03.5
T	08	326 37.7	330 48.5	18.1	271 10.5	12.8	130 25.2	11.7	59 08.2	03.5
U	09	341 40.2	345 50.4	. . 17.7	286 11.2	. . 13.2	145 27.9	. . 11.6	74 10.7	. . 03.5
E	10	356 42.6	0 52.4	17.3	301 11.9	13.6	160 30.7	11.5	89 13.2	03.5
S	11	11 45.1	15 54.4	16.9	316 12.5	14.1	175 33.4	11.4	104 15.7	03.5
D	12	26 47.6	30 56.4	N 2 16.5	331 13.2	N20 14.5	190 36.2	S 5 11.3	119 18.2	S22 03.5
A	13	41 50.0	45 58.4	16.1	346 13.9	14.9	205 38.9	11.2	134 20.8	03.5
Y	14	56 52.5	61 00.3	15.7	1 14.5	15.3	220 41.7	11.1	149 23.3	03.5
	15	71 54.9	76 02.3	. . 15.4	16 15.2	. . 15.7	235 44.4	. . 10.9	164 25.8	. . 03.5
	16	86 57.4	91 04.3	15.0	31 15.9	16.1	250 47.2	10.8	179 28.3	03.5
	17	101 59.9	106 06.2	14.6	46 16.5	16.5	265 49.9	10.7	194 30.8	03.5
	18	117 02.3	121 08.2	N 2 14.2	61 17.2	N20 16.9	280 52.7	S 5 10.6	209 33.4	S22 03.5
	19	132 04.8	136 10.1	13.9	76 17.9	17.3	295 55.4	10.5	224 35.9	03.5
	20	147 07.3	151 12.1	13.5	91 18.5	17.8	310 58.2	10.4	239 38.4	03.5
	21	162 09.7	166 14.0	. . 13.1	106 19.2	. . 18.2	326 00.9	. . 10.3	254 40.9	. . 03.5
	22	177 12.2	181 16.0	12.7	121 19.9	18.6	341 03.7	10.1	269 43.4	03.5
	23	192 14.7	196 17.9	12.4	136 20.5	19.0	356 06.4	10.0	284 45.9	03.4
Mer. Pass.		h m 10 17.1	*v* 2.1	*d* 0.4	*v* 0.7	*d* 0.4	*v* 2.8	*d* 0.1	*v* 2.5	*d* 0.0

STARS

Name	SHA ° ′	Dec ° ′
Acamar	315 16.8	S40 14.4
Achernar	335 25.5	S57 09.1
Acrux	173 05.6	S63 11.8
Adhara	255 10.6	S29 00.2
Aldebaran	290 46.7	N16 32.4
Alioth	166 18.0	N55 52.1
Alkaid	152 56.5	N49 13.7
Al Na'ir	27 40.8	S46 52.5
Alnilam	275 43.9	S 1 11.8
Alphard	217 53.4	S 8 44.3
Alphecca	126 08.5	N26 39.4
Alpheratz	357 41.1	N29 10.9
Altair	62 05.7	N 8 54.8
Ankaa	353 13.6	S42 12.8
Antares	112 22.8	S26 28.0
Arcturus	145 53.1	N19 05.6
Atria	107 21.9	S69 03.1
Avior	234 16.8	S59 34.3
Bellatrix	278 29.5	N 6 21.6
Betelgeuse	270 58.7	N 7 24.3
Canopus	263 55.2	S52 42.8
Capella	280 30.9	N46 00.8
Deneb	49 29.8	N45 20.3
Denebola	182 30.8	N14 28.5
Diphda	348 53.7	S17 53.7
Dubhe	193 48.2	N61 39.6
Elnath	278 09.6	N28 37.1
Eltanin	90 44.7	N51 29.1
Enif	33 44.7	N 9 57.1
Fomalhaut	15 21.5	S29 31.8
Gacrux	171 57.4	S57 12.7
Gienah	175 49.3	S17 38.4
Hadar	148 43.5	S60 27.3
Hamal	327 58.2	N23 32.4
Kaus Aust.	83 40.3	S34 22.3
Kochab	137 19.1	N74 05.1
Markab	13 36.0	N15 17.7
Menkar	314 12.7	N 4 09.1
Menkent	148 04.1	S36 27.2
Miaplacidus	221 38.7	S69 47.7
Mirfak	308 37.1	N49 55.2
Nunki	75 55.1	S26 16.3
Peacock	53 15.3	S56 40.4
Pollux	243 24.6	N27 58.9
Procyon	244 57.1	N 5 10.6
Rasalhague	96 03.9	N12 32.9
Regulus	207 40.6	N11 52.9
Rigel	281 09.8	S 8 11.3
Rigil Kent.	139 47.5	S60 54.2
Sabik	102 09.4	S15 44.6
Schedar	349 38.0	N56 37.7
Shaula	96 18.2	S37 06.7
Sirius	258 31.6	S16 44.8
Spica	158 28.2	S11 15.1
Suhail	222 50.4	S43 30.5
Vega	80 37.1	N38 47.9
Zuben'ubi	137 02.2	S16 06.7

	SHA ° ′	Mer. Pass. h m
Venus	4 24.2	10 00
Mars	305 30.3	13 56
Jupiter	163 38.2	23 20
Saturn	92 28.9	4 08

Day	UT (d h)	SUN GHA	SUN Dec	MOON GHA	v	MOON Dec	d	HP
		° ′	° ′	° ′	′	° ′	′	′
SUNDAY	16 00	180 02.3	N10 06.6	306 17.8	12.6	S18 05.1	3.2	54.1
	01	195 02.4	07.5	320 49.4	12.5	18 08.3	3.1	54.1
	02	210 02.6	08.4	335 20.9	12.5	18 11.4	3.0	54.1
	03	225 02.7	. . 09.3	349 52.4	12.5	18 14.4	2.9	54.1
	04	240 02.9	10.2	4 23.9	12.5	18 17.3	2.8	54.1
	05	255 03.0	11.1	18 55.4	12.4	18 20.1	2.8	54.1
	06	270 03.2	N10 12.0	33 26.8	12.5	S18 22.9	2.6	54.1
	07	285 03.3	12.8	47 58.3	12.4	18 25.5	2.6	54.1
	08	300 03.4	13.7	62 29.7	12.4	18 28.1	2.5	54.1
	09	315 03.6	. . 14.6	77 01.1	12.4	18 30.6	2.4	54.1
	10	330 03.7	15.5	91 32.5	12.3	18 33.0	2.4	54.1
	11	345 03.9	16.4	106 03.8	12.4	18 35.4	2.2	54.2
	12	0 04.0	N10 17.3	120 35.2	12.3	S18 37.6	2.2	54.2
	13	15 04.2	18.1	135 06.5	12.3	18 39.8	2.1	54.2
	14	30 04.3	19.0	149 37.8	12.3	18 41.9	2.0	54.2
	15	45 04.5	. . 19.9	164 09.1	12.2	18 43.9	1.9	54.2
	16	60 04.6	20.8	178 40.3	12.3	18 45.8	1.8	54.2
	17	75 04.8	21.7	193 11.6	12.2	18 47.6	1.7	54.2
	18	90 04.9	N10 22.6	207 42.8	12.2	S18 49.3	1.7	54.2
	19	105 05.1	23.4	222 14.0	12.2	18 51.0	1.5	54.2
	20	120 05.2	24.3	236 45.2	12.2	18 52.5	1.5	54.2
	21	135 05.3	. . 25.2	251 16.4	12.2	18 54.0	1.4	54.2
	22	150 05.5	26.1	265 47.6	12.1	18 55.4	1.3	54.2
	23	165 05.6	27.0	280 18.7	12.2	18 56.7	1.2	54.2
MONDAY	17 00	180 05.8	N10 27.8	294 49.9	12.1	S18 57.9	1.2	54.3
	01	195 05.9	28.7	309 21.0	12.1	18 59.1	1.0	54.3
	02	210 06.1	29.6	323 52.1	12.1	19 00.1	1.0	54.3
	03	225 06.2	. . 30.5	338 23.2	12.0	19 01.1	0.8	54.3
	04	240 06.4	31.4	352 54.2	12.1	19 01.9	0.8	54.3
	05	255 06.5	32.2	7 25.3	12.0	19 02.7	0.7	54.3
	06	270 06.6	N10 33.1	21 56.3	12.1	S19 03.4	0.6	54.3
	07	285 06.8	34.0	36 27.4	12.0	19 04.0	0.5	54.3
	08	300 06.9	34.9	50 58.4	12.0	19 04.5	0.4	54.3
	09	315 07.1	. . 35.7	65 29.4	11.9	19 04.9	0.4	54.4
	10	330 07.2	36.6	80 00.3	12.0	19 05.3	0.2	54.4
	11	345 07.4	37.5	94 31.3	12.0	19 05.5	0.2	54.4
	12	0 07.5	N10 38.4	109 02.3	11.9	S19 05.7	0.1	54.4
	13	15 07.6	39.3	123 33.2	11.9	19 05.8	0.1	54.4
	14	30 07.8	40.1	138 04.1	11.9	19 05.7	0.1	54.4
	15	45 07.9	. . 41.0	152 35.0	11.9	19 05.6	0.2	54.4
	16	60 08.1	41.9	167 05.9	11.9	19 05.4	0.3	54.4
	17	75 08.2	42.8	181 36.8	11.9	19 05.1	0.3	54.5
	18	90 08.3	N10 43.6	196 07.7	11.8	S19 04.8	0.5	54.5
	19	105 08.5	44.5	210 38.5	11.9	19 04.3	0.6	54.5
	20	120 08.6	45.4	225 09.4	11.8	19 03.7	0.6	54.5
	21	135 08.8	. . 46.2	239 40.2	11.8	19 03.1	0.8	54.5
	22	150 08.9	47.1	254 11.0	11.8	19 02.3	0.8	54.5
	23	165 09.0	48.0	268 41.8	11.8	19 01.5	0.9	54.6
TUESDAY	18 00	180 09.2	N10 48.9	283 12.6	11.8	S19 00.6	1.0	54.6
	01	195 09.3	49.7	297 43.4	11.8	18 59.6	1.1	54.6
	02	210 09.5	50.6	312 14.2	11.7	18 58.5	1.2	54.6
	03	225 09.6	. . 51.5	326 44.9	11.8	18 57.3	1.3	54.6
	04	240 09.7	52.4	341 15.7	11.7	18 56.0	1.4	54.6
	05	255 09.9	53.2	355 46.4	11.8	18 54.6	1.4	54.7
	06	270 10.0	N10 54.1	10 17.2	11.7	S18 53.2	1.6	54.7
	07	285 10.2	55.0	24 47.9	11.7	18 51.6	1.6	54.7
	08	300 10.3	55.8	39 18.6	11.7	18 50.0	1.7	54.7
	09	315 10.4	. . 56.7	53 49.3	11.7	18 48.3	1.9	54.7
	10	330 10.6	57.6	68 20.0	11.7	18 46.4	1.9	54.7
	11	345 10.7	58.4	82 50.7	11.6	18 44.5	2.0	54.8
	12	0 10.9	N10 59.3	97 21.3	11.7	S18 42.5	2.1	54.8
	13	15 11.0	11 00.2	111 52.0	11.7	18 40.4	2.2	54.8
	14	30 11.1	01.0	126 22.7	11.6	18 38.2	2.2	54.8
	15	45 11.3	. . 01.9	140 53.3	11.6	18 36.0	2.4	54.8
	16	60 11.4	02.8	155 23.9	11.7	18 33.6	2.5	54.9
	17	75 11.5	03.7	169 54.6	11.6	18 31.1	2.5	54.9
	18	90 11.7	N11 04.5	184 25.2	11.6	S18 28.6	2.7	54.9
	19	105 11.8	05.4	198 55.8	11.6	18 25.9	2.7	54.9
	20	120 12.0	06.3	213 26.4	11.6	18 23.2	2.8	55.0
	21	135 12.1	. . 07.1	227 57.0	11.6	18 20.4	2.9	55.0
	22	150 12.2	08.0	242 27.6	11.6	18 17.5	3.0	55.0
	23	165 12.4	08.8	256 58.2	11.5	S18 14.5	3.1	55.0
		SD 16.0	*d* 0.9	SD 14.8		14.8		14.9

Lat.	Twilight Naut.	Twilight Civil	Sunrise	Moonrise 16	Moonrise 17	Moonrise 18	Moonrise 19
°	h m	h m	h m	h m	h m	h m	h m
N 72	////	01 36	03 27	■	■	■	05 50
N 70	////	02 19	03 45	01 59	03 16	04 00	04 17
68	////	02 48	04 00	01 16	02 21	03 08	03 37
66	01 22	03 09	04 12	00 47	01 48	02 36	03 10
64	02 01	03 25	04 22	00 25	01 24	02 12	02 48
62	02 27	03 39	04 30	00 08	01 05	01 53	02 31
60	02 47	03 50	04 37	24 49	00 49	01 38	02 17
N 58	03 03	04 00	04 44	24 36	00 36	01 24	02 05
56	03 16	04 09	04 49	24 25	00 25	01 13	01 55
54	03 28	04 16	04 54	24 15	00 15	01 03	01 45
52	03 37	04 23	04 59	24 06	00 06	00 54	01 37
50	03 46	04 29	05 03	23 58	24 46	00 46	01 29
45	04 04	04 41	05 12	23 41	24 29	00 29	01 14
N 40	04 17	04 51	05 19	23 27	24 15	00 15	01 00
35	04 28	04 59	05 25	23 15	24 04	00 04	00 49
30	04 37	05 06	05 31	23 05	23 53	24 40	00 40
20	04 51	05 18	05 40	22 47	23 36	24 23	00 23
N 10	05 02	05 27	05 49	22 32	23 20	24 08	00 08
0	05 11	05 35	05 56	22 18	23 06	23 54	24 43
S 10	05 18	05 42	06 04	22 03	22 51	23 41	24 31
20	05 23	05 49	06 12	21 48	22 36	23 26	24 18
30	05 28	05 56	06 20	21 31	22 18	23 09	24 03
35	05 30	06 00	06 25	21 21	22 08	22 59	23 54
40	05 32	06 04	06 31	21 09	21 56	22 48	23 44
45	05 34	06 08	06 38	20 55	21 43	22 35	23 32
S 50	05 35	06 13	06 46	20 39	21 26	22 19	23 18
52	05 35	06 15	06 49	20 31	21 18	22 11	23 11
54	05 36	06 17	06 53	20 22	21 09	22 03	23 03
56	05 36	06 19	06 57	20 12	20 59	21 53	22 55
58	05 36	06 22	07 02	20 01	20 48	21 43	22 46
S 60	05 36	06 25	07 08	19 48	20 35	21 30	22 35

Lat.	Sunset	Twilight Civil	Twilight Naut.	Moonset 16	Moonset 17	Moonset 18	Moonset 19
°	h m	h m	h m	h m	h m	h m	h m
N 72	20 37	22 34	////	■	■	■	06 29
N 70	20 17	21 46	////	05 19	05 42	06 37	08 02
68	20 02	21 16	////	06 03	06 36	07 29	08 41
66	19 50	20 54	22 46	06 32	07 09	08 01	09 08
64	19 40	20 36	22 03	06 54	07 33	08 25	09 29
62	19 31	20 22	21 35	07 12	07 53	08 44	09 46
60	19 23	20 11	21 15	07 27	08 08	08 59	09 59
N 58	19 17	20 01	20 58	07 39	08 21	09 12	10 11
56	19 11	19 52	20 45	07 50	08 33	09 23	10 22
54	19 06	19 44	20 33	08 00	08 43	09 33	10 31
52	19 01	19 38	20 23	08 08	08 52	09 42	10 39
50	18 57	19 32	20 14	08 16	09 00	09 50	10 46
45	18 48	19 19	19 57	08 32	09 17	10 07	11 01
N 40	18 41	19 09	19 43	08 46	09 31	10 21	11 14
35	18 34	19 00	19 32	08 57	09 43	10 32	11 25
30	18 29	18 53	19 22	09 07	09 53	10 42	11 34
20	18 19	18 41	19 08	09 24	10 11	11 00	11 51
N 10	18 11	18 32	18 57	09 39	10 26	11 15	12 05
0	18 03	18 24	18 48	09 53	10 41	11 29	12 18
S 10	17 55	18 17	18 41	10 07	10 55	11 43	12 31
20	17 47	18 10	18 35	10 22	11 11	11 58	12 45
30	17 38	18 03	18 30	10 39	11 28	12 16	13 01
35	17 33	17 59	18 28	10 49	11 39	12 26	13 10
40	17 27	17 55	18 26	11 01	11 51	12 37	13 21
45	17 21	17 51	18 25	11 14	12 04	12 51	13 33
S 50	17 13	17 46	18 23	11 31	12 21	13 07	13 48
52	17 09	17 43	18 23	11 38	12 29	13 15	13 55
54	17 05	17 41	18 22	11 47	12 38	13 23	14 02
56	17 01	17 39	18 22	11 57	12 48	13 33	14 11
58	16 56	17 36	18 21	12 08	12 59	13 44	14 21
S 60	16 50	17 33	18 21	12 20	13 13	13 56	14 32

Day	SUN Eqn. of Time 00^h	SUN Eqn. of Time 12^h	SUN Mer. Pass.	MOON Mer. Pass. Upper	MOON Mer. Pass. Lower	MOON Age	MOON Phase
d	m s	m s	h m	h m	h m	d %	
16	00 09	00 16	12 00	03 42	16 05	19 77	
17	00 23	00 30	12 00	04 29	16 53	20 68	◑
18	00 36	00 43	11 59	05 17	17 42	21 59	

UT d h		ARIES GHA ° ′	VENUS −4·7 GHA ° ′	Dec ° ′	MARS +1·6 GHA ° ′	Dec ° ′	JUPITER −2·4 GHA ° ′	Dec ° ′	SATURN +0·3 GHA ° ′	Dec ° ′
19 00		207 17.1	211 19.8	N 2 12.0	151 21.2	N20 19.4	11 09.2	S 5 09.9	299 48.5	S22 03.4
01		222 19.6	226 21.8	11.7	166 21.9	19.8	26 11.9	09.8	314 51.0	03.4
02		237 22.1	241 23.7	11.3	181 22.5	20.2	41 14.7	09.7	329 53.5	03.4
03		252 24.5	256 25.6	. . 10.9	196 23.2	. . 20.6	56 17.4	. . 09.6	344 56.0	. . 03.4
04		267 27.0	271 27.5	10.6	211 23.9	21.0	71 20.2	09.5	359 58.5	03.4
05		282 29.4	286 29.5	10.2	226 24.5	21.4	86 22.9	09.3	15 01.1	03.4
06		297 31.9	301 31.4	N 2 09.9	241 25.2	N20 21.8	101 25.7	S 5 09.2	30 03.6	S22 03.4
07	W	312 34.4	316 33.3	09.5	256 25.9	22.2	116 28.5	09.1	45 06.1	03.4
08	E	327 36.8	331 35.2	09.2	271 26.5	22.6	131 31.2	09.0	60 08.6	03.4
09	D	342 39.3	346 37.1	. . 08.8	286 27.2	. . 23.0	146 34.0	. . 08.9	75 11.2	. . 03.4
10	N	357 41.8	1 39.0	08.5	301 27.9	23.5	161 36.7	08.8	90 13.7	03.4
11	E	12 44.2	16 40.9	08.1	316 28.5	23.9	176 39.5	08.7	105 16.2	03.4
12	S	27 46.7	31 42.8	N 2 07.8	331 29.2	N20 24.3	191 42.2	S 5 08.5	120 18.7	S22 03.4
13	D	42 49.2	46 44.7	07.4	346 29.9	24.7	206 45.0	08.4	135 21.2	03.4
14	A	57 51.6	61 46.6	07.1	1 30.5	25.1	221 47.7	08.3	150 23.8	03.4
15	Y	72 54.1	76 48.4	. . 06.8	16 31.2	. . 25.5	236 50.5	. . 08.2	165 26.3	. . 03.4
16		87 56.6	91 50.3	06.4	31 31.8	25.9	251 53.2	08.1	180 28.8	03.4
17		102 59.0	106 52.2	06.1	46 32.5	26.3	266 56.0	08.0	195 31.3	03.4
18		118 01.5	121 54.1	N 2 05.8	61 33.2	N20 26.7	281 58.7	S 5 07.9	210 33.9	S22 03.4
19		133 03.9	136 55.9	05.4	76 33.8	27.1	297 01.5	07.7	225 36.4	03.4
20		148 06.4	151 57.8	05.1	91 34.5	27.5	312 04.2	07.6	240 38.9	03.4
21		163 08.9	166 59.7	. . 04.8	106 35.2	. . 27.9	327 06.9	. . 07.5	255 41.4	. . 03.4
22		178 11.3	182 01.5	04.4	121 35.8	28.3	342 09.7	07.4	270 43.9	03.4
23		193 13.8	197 03.4	04.1	136 36.5	28.7	357 12.4	07.3	285 46.5	03.4
20 00		208 16.3	212 05.2	N 2 03.8	151 37.2	N20 29.1	12 15.2	S 5 07.2	300 49.0	S22 03.4
01		223 18.7	227 07.1	03.5	166 37.8	29.5	27 17.9	07.1	315 51.5	03.4
02		238 21.2	242 08.9	03.2	181 38.5	29.9	42 20.7	07.0	330 54.0	03.4
03		253 23.7	257 10.8	. . 02.9	196 39.2	. . 30.3	57 23.4	. . 06.8	345 56.6	. . 03.4
04		268 26.1	272 12.6	02.5	211 39.8	30.7	72 26.2	06.7	0 59.1	03.4
05		283 28.6	287 14.5	02.2	226 40.5	31.1	87 28.9	06.6	16 01.6	03.4
06		298 31.0	302 16.3	N 2 01.9	241 41.1	N20 31.5	102 31.7	S 5 06.5	31 04.1	S22 03.4
07		313 33.5	317 18.1	01.6	256 41.8	31.9	117 34.4	06.4	46 06.7	03.4
08	T	328 36.0	332 20.0	01.3	271 42.5	32.3	132 37.2	06.3	61 09.2	03.3
09	H	343 38.4	347 21.8	. . 01.0	286 43.1	. . 32.7	147 39.9	. . 06.2	76 11.7	. . 03.3
10	U	358 40.9	2 23.6	00.7	301 43.8	33.1	162 42.7	06.0	91 14.2	03.3
11	R	13 43.4	17 25.4	00.4	316 44.5	33.5	177 45.4	05.9	106 16.8	03.3
12	S	28 45.8	32 27.2	N 2 00.1	331 45.1	N20 33.9	192 48.2	S 5 05.8	121 19.3	S22 03.3
13	D	43 48.3	47 29.1	1 59.8	346 45.8	34.3	207 50.9	05.7	136 21.8	03.3
14	A	58 50.8	62 30.9	59.5	1 46.4	34.7	222 53.7	05.6	151 24.3	03.3
15	Y	73 53.2	77 32.7	. . 59.2	16 47.1	. . 35.1	237 56.4	. . 05.5	166 26.9	. . 03.3
16		88 55.7	92 34.5	58.9	31 47.8	35.5	252 59.2	05.4	181 29.4	03.3
17		103 58.2	107 36.3	58.6	46 48.4	35.8	268 01.9	05.3	196 31.9	03.3
18		119 00.6	122 38.1	N 1 58.3	61 49.1	N20 36.2	283 04.7	S 5 05.1	211 34.5	S22 03.3
19		134 03.1	137 39.9	58.0	76 49.8	36.6	298 07.4	05.0	226 37.0	03.3
20		149 05.5	152 41.6	57.7	91 50.4	37.0	313 10.2	04.9	241 39.5	03.3
21		164 08.0	167 43.4	. . 57.5	106 51.1	. . 37.4	328 12.9	. . 04.8	256 42.0	. . 03.3
22		179 10.5	182 45.2	57.2	121 51.7	37.8	343 15.7	04.7	271 44.6	03.3
23		194 12.9	197 47.0	56.9	136 52.4	38.2	358 18.4	04.6	286 47.1	03.3
21 00		209 15.4	212 48.8	N 1 56.6	151 53.1	N20 38.6	13 21.1	S 5 04.5	301 49.6	S22 03.3
01		224 17.9	227 50.5	56.3	166 53.7	39.0	28 23.9	04.4	316 52.1	03.3
02		239 20.3	242 52.3	56.1	181 54.4	39.4	43 26.6	04.2	331 54.7	03.3
03		254 22.8	257 54.1	. . 55.8	196 55.1	. . 39.8	58 29.4	. . 04.1	346 57.2	. . 03.3
04		269 25.3	272 55.8	55.5	211 55.7	40.2	73 32.1	04.0	1 59.7	03.3
05		284 27.7	287 57.6	55.3	226 56.4	40.6	88 34.9	03.9	17 02.3	03.3
06		299 30.2	302 59.4	N 1 55.0	241 57.0	N20 41.0	103 37.6	S 5 03.8	32 04.8	S22 03.3
07		314 32.7	318 01.1	54.7	256 57.7	41.3	118 40.4	03.7	47 07.3	03.3
08		329 35.1	333 02.9	54.5	271 58.4	41.7	133 43.1	03.6	62 09.9	03.3
09	F	344 37.6	348 04.6	. . 54.2	286 59.0	. . 42.1	148 45.9	. . 03.5	77 12.4	. . 03.3
10	R	359 40.0	3 06.4	53.9	301 59.7	42.5	163 48.6	03.4	92 14.9	03.3
11	I	14 42.5	18 08.1	53.7	317 00.3	42.9	178 51.3	03.2	107 17.4	03.3
12	D	29 45.0	33 09.8	N 1 53.4	332 01.0	N20 43.3	193 54.1	S 5 03.1	122 20.0	S22 03.3
13	A	44 47.4	48 11.6	53.2	347 01.7	43.7	208 56.8	03.0	137 22.5	03.3
14	Y	59 49.9	63 13.3	52.9	2 02.3	44.1	223 59.6	02.9	152 25.0	03.3
15		74 52.4	78 15.0	. . 52.7	17 03.0	. . 44.5	239 02.3	. . 02.8	167 27.6	. . 03.3
16		89 54.8	93 16.8	52.4	32 03.7	44.8	254 05.1	02.7	182 30.1	03.3
17		104 57.3	108 18.5	52.2	47 04.3	45.2	269 07.8	02.6	197 32.6	03.2
18		119 59.8	123 20.2	N 1 51.9	62 05.0	N20 45.6	284 10.6	S 5 02.5	212 35.2	S22 03.2
19		135 02.2	138 21.9	51.7	77 05.6	46.0	299 13.3	02.3	227 37.7	03.2
20		150 04.7	153 23.6	51.4	92 06.3	46.4	314 16.1	02.2	242 40.2	03.2
21		165 07.1	168 25.3	. . 51.2	107 07.0	. . 46.8	329 18.8	. . 02.1	257 42.8	. . 03.2
22		180 09.6	183 27.0	50.9	122 07.6	47.2	344 21.5	02.0	272 45.3	03.2
23		195 12.1	198 28.7	50.7	137 08.3	47.5	359 24.3	01.9	287 47.8	03.2
Mer. Pass.		h m 10 05.3	*v* 1.8	*d* 0.3	*v* 0.7	*d* 0.4	*v* 2.7	*d* 0.1	*v* 2.5	*d* 0.0

STARS Name	SHA ° ′	Dec ° ′
Acamar	315 16.8	S40 14.4
Achernar	335 25.5	S57 09.1
Acrux	173 05.6	S63 11.8
Adhara	255 10.6	S29 00.2
Aldebaran	290 46.7	N16 32.4
Alioth	166 18.0	N55 52.1
Alkaid	152 56.4	N49 13.7
Al Na'ir	27 40.8	S46 52.5
Alnilam	275 44.0	S 1 11.8
Alphard	217 53.5	S 8 44.3
Alphecca	126 08.5	N26 39.4
Alpheratz	357 41.1	N29 10.9
Altair	62 05.7	N 8 54.8
Ankaa	353 13.6	S42 12.8
Antares	112 22.8	S26 28.0
Arcturus	145 53.1	N19 05.6
Atria	107 21.9	S69 03.1
Avior	234 16.9	S59 34.3
Bellatrix	278 29.5	N 6 21.6
Betelgeuse	270 58.7	N 7 24.3
Canopus	263 55.2	S52 42.8
Capella	280 30.9	N46 00.8
Deneb	49 29.7	N45 20.3
Denebola	182 30.8	N14 28.5
Diphda	348 53.6	S17 53.7
Dubhe	193 48.2	N61 39.6
Elnath	278 09.6	N28 37.1
Eltanin	90 44.7	N51 29.1
Enif	33 44.7	N 9 57.2
Fomalhaut	15 21.4	S29 31.8
Gacrux	171 57.4	S57 12.7
Gienah	175 49.3	S17 38.4
Hadar	148 43.5	S60 27.3
Hamal	327 58.2	N23 32.4
Kaus Aust.	83 40.2	S34 22.3
Kochab	137 19.1	N74 05.1
Markab	13 36.0	N15 17.7
Menkar	314 12.7	N 4 09.1
Menkent	148 04.1	S36 27.2
Miaplacidus	221 38.8	S69 47.7
Mirfak	308 37.1	N49 55.1
Nunki	75 55.0	S26 16.3
Peacock	53 15.3	S56 40.4
Pollux	243 24.7	N27 58.9
Procyon	244 57.1	N 5 10.6
Rasalhague	96 03.9	N12 32.9
Regulus	207 40.6	N11 52.9
Rigel	281 09.8	S 8 11.3
Rigil Kent.	139 47.5	S60 54.2
Sabik	102 09.4	S15 44.6
Schedar	349 38.0	N56 37.7
Shaula	96 18.2	S37 06.7
Sirius	258 31.6	S16 44.8
Spica	158 28.2	S11 15.1
Suhail	222 50.4	S43 30.5
Vega	80 37.0	N38 47.9
Zuben'ubi	137 02.2	S16 06.7

	SHA ° ′	Mer. Pass. h m
Venus	3 49.0	9 50
Mars	303 20.9	13 53
Jupiter	163 58.9	23 07
Saturn	92 32.7	3 56

UT d	UT h	SUN GHA	SUN Dec	MOON GHA	MOON v	MOON Dec	MOON d	MOON HP
d	h	° ′	° ′	° ′	′	° ′	′	′
19	00	180 12.5	N11 09.7	271 28.7	11.6	S18 11.4	3.2	55.0
	01	195 12.6	10.6	285 59.3	11.6	18 08.2	3.3	55.1
	02	210 12.8	11.4	300 29.9	11.5	18 04.9	3.3	55.1
	03	225 12.9	. . 12.3	315 00.4	11.6	18 01.6	3.5	55.1
	04	240 13.0	13.2	329 31.0	11.5	17 58.1	3.5	55.1
	05	255 13.2	14.0	344 01.5	11.5	17 54.6	3.7	55.2
	06	270 13.3	N11 14.9	358 32.0	11.6	S17 50.9	3.7	55.2
W	07	285 13.4	15.8	13 02.6	11.5	17 47.2	3.8	55.2
E	08	300 13.6	16.6	27 33.1	11.5	17 43.4	3.9	55.2
D	09	315 13.7	. . 17.5	42 03.6	11.5	17 39.5	4.0	55.3
N	10	330 13.8	18.3	56 34.1	11.5	17 35.5	4.1	55.3
E	11	345 14.0	19.2	71 04.6	11.5	17 31.4	4.1	55.3
S	12	0 14.1	N11 20.1	85 35.1	11.5	S17 27.3	4.3	55.3
D	13	15 14.2	20.9	100 05.6	11.5	17 23.0	4.4	55.4
A	14	30 14.4	21.8	114 36.1	11.4	17 18.6	4.4	55.4
Y	15	45 14.5	. . 22.7	129 06.5	11.5	17 14.2	4.5	55.4
	16	60 14.6	23.5	143 37.0	11.5	17 09.7	4.6	55.4
	17	75 14.8	24.4	158 07.5	11.4	17 05.1	4.7	55.5
	18	90 14.9	N11 25.2	172 37.9	11.5	S17 00.4	4.8	55.5
	19	105 15.0	26.1	187 08.4	11.4	16 55.6	4.9	55.5
	20	120 15.2	26.9	201 38.8	11.5	16 50.7	5.0	55.6
	21	135 15.3	. . 27.8	216 09.3	11.4	16 45.7	5.0	55.6
	22	150 15.4	28.7	230 39.7	11.4	16 40.7	5.2	55.6
	23	165 15.6	29.5	245 10.1	11.5	16 35.5	5.2	55.6
20	00	180 15.7	N11 30.4	259 40.6	11.4	S16 30.3	5.3	55.7
	01	195 15.8	31.2	274 11.0	11.4	16 25.0	5.4	55.7
	02	210 16.0	32.1	288 41.4	11.4	16 19.6	5.5	55.7
	03	225 16.1	. . 32.9	303 11.8	11.4	16 14.1	5.6	55.8
	04	240 16.2	33.8	317 42.2	11.4	16 08.5	5.7	55.8
	05	255 16.4	34.7	332 12.6	11.4	16 02.8	5.7	55.8
	06	270 16.5	N11 35.5	346 43.0	11.4	S15 57.1	5.8	55.9
	07	285 16.6	36.4	1 13.4	11.4	15 51.3	6.0	55.9
T	08	300 16.7	37.2	15 43.8	11.3	15 45.3	6.0	55.9
H	09	315 16.9	. . 38.1	30 14.1	11.4	15 39.3	6.1	56.0
U	10	330 17.0	38.9	44 44.5	11.4	15 33.2	6.1	56.0
R	11	345 17.1	39.8	59 14.9	11.3	15 27.1	6.3	56.0
S	12	0 17.3	N11 40.6	73 45.2	11.4	S15 20.8	6.3	56.0
D	13	15 17.4	41.5	88 15.6	11.3	15 14.5	6.5	56.1
A	14	30 17.5	42.3	102 45.9	11.4	15 08.0	6.5	56.1
Y	15	45 17.6	. . 43.2	117 16.3	11.3	15 01.5	6.6	56.1
	16	60 17.8	44.0	131 46.6	11.3	14 54.9	6.6	56.2
	17	75 17.9	44.9	146 16.9	11.4	14 48.3	6.8	56.2
	18	90 18.0	N11 45.8	160 47.3	11.3	S14 41.5	6.8	56.2
	19	105 18.2	46.6	175 17.6	11.3	14 34.7	7.0	56.3
	20	120 18.3	47.5	189 47.9	11.3	14 27.7	7.0	56.3
	21	135 18.4	. . 48.3	204 18.2	11.3	14 20.7	7.1	56.3
	22	150 18.5	49.2	218 48.5	11.3	14 13.6	7.1	56.4
	23	165 18.7	50.0	233 18.8	11.2	14 06.5	7.3	56.4
21	00	180 18.8	N11 50.9	247 49.0	11.3	S13 59.2	7.3	56.5
	01	195 18.9	51.7	262 19.3	11.3	13 51.9	7.4	56.5
	02	210 19.0	52.6	276 49.6	11.2	13 44.5	7.5	56.5
	03	225 19.2	. . 53.4	291 19.8	11.3	13 37.0	7.6	56.6
	04	240 19.3	54.2	305 50.1	11.2	13 29.4	7.6	56.6
	05	255 19.4	55.1	320 20.3	11.3	13 21.8	7.7	56.6
	06	270 19.5	N11 55.9	334 50.6	11.2	S13 14.1	7.8	56.7
	07	285 19.7	56.8	349 20.8	11.2	13 06.3	7.9	56.7
	08	300 19.8	57.6	3 51.0	11.2	12 58.4	8.0	56.7
F	09	315 19.9	. . 58.5	18 21.2	11.2	12 50.4	8.0	56.8
R	10	330 20.0	11 59.3	32 51.4	11.2	12 42.4	8.1	56.8
I	11	345 20.2	12 00.2	47 21.6	11.2	12 34.3	8.2	56.8
D	12	0 20.3	N12 01.0	61 51.8	11.2	S12 26.1	8.2	56.9
A	13	15 20.4	01.9	76 22.0	11.1	12 17.9	8.4	56.9
Y	14	30 20.5	02.7	90 52.1	11.2	12 09.5	8.4	57.0
	15	45 20.7	. . 03.6	105 22.3	11.1	12 01.1	8.5	57.0
	16	60 20.8	04.4	119 52.4	11.2	11 52.6	8.5	57.0
	17	75 20.9	05.2	134 22.6	11.1	11 44.1	8.6	57.1
	18	90 21.0	N12 06.1	148 52.7	11.1	S11 35.5	8.7	57.1
	19	105 21.2	06.9	163 22.8	11.1	11 26.8	8.8	57.1
	20	120 21.3	07.8	177 52.9	11.1	11 18.0	8.8	57.2
	21	135 21.4	. . 08.6	192 23.0	11.1	11 09.2	9.0	57.2
	22	150 21.5	09.5	206 53.1	11.0	11 00.2	8.9	57.3
	23	165 21.6	10.3	221 23.1	11.1	S10 51.3	9.1	57.3
		SD 15.9	*d* 0.9	SD 15.1		15.3		15.5

Lat.	Twilight Naut.	Twilight Civil	Sunrise	Moonrise 19	Moonrise 20	Moonrise 21	Moonrise 22
°	h m	h m	h m	h m	h m	h m	h m
N 72	////	00 53	03 08	05 50	05 03	04 49	04 39
N 70	////	01 56	03 30	04 17	04 22	04 24	04 23
68	////	02 30	03 47	03 37	03 54	04 04	04 11
66	00 46	02 54	04 00	03 10	03 32	03 48	04 00
64	01 41	03 13	04 11	02 48	03 15	03 36	03 51
62	02 12	03 28	04 20	02 31	03 01	03 25	03 44
60	02 35	03 41	04 29	02 17	02 49	03 15	03 37
N 58	02 52	03 51	04 36	02 05	02 39	03 07	03 31
56	03 07	04 00	04 42	01 55	02 30	03 00	03 26
54	03 19	04 09	04 47	01 45	02 22	02 53	03 21
52	03 30	04 16	04 52	01 37	02 14	02 47	03 17
50	03 39	04 22	04 57	01 29	02 08	02 42	03 13
45	03 58	04 36	05 07	01 14	01 54	02 31	03 05
N 40	04 12	04 46	05 15	01 00	01 42	02 21	02 58
35	04 24	04 55	05 22	00 49	01 32	02 13	02 52
30	04 34	05 03	05 28	00 40	01 24	02 06	02 47
20	04 49	05 16	05 38	00 23	01 09	01 53	02 37
N 10	05 01	05 26	05 47	00 08	00 55	01 43	02 29
0	05 10	05 34	05 56	24 43	00 43	01 32	02 22
S 10	05 18	05 42	06 04	24 31	00 31	01 22	02 14
20	05 24	05 50	06 12	24 18	00 18	01 11	02 06
30	05 30	05 58	06 22	24 03	00 03	00 58	01 57
35	05 32	06 02	06 28	23 54	24 51	00 51	01 51
40	05 35	06 06	06 34	23 44	24 43	00 43	01 45
45	05 37	06 11	06 41	23 32	24 33	00 33	01 38
S 50	05 39	06 17	06 50	23 18	24 21	00 21	01 29
52	05 40	06 19	06 54	23 11	24 16	00 16	01 25
54	05 41	06 22	06 59	23 03	24 10	00 10	01 21
56	05 42	06 25	07 03	22 55	24 03	00 03	01 16
58	05 42	06 28	07 09	22 46	23 56	25 11	01 11
S 60	05 43	06 32	07 15	22 35	23 47	25 05	01 05

Lat.	Sunset	Twilight Civil	Twilight Naut.	Moonset 19	Moonset 20	Moonset 21	Moonset 22
°	h m	h m	h m	h m	h m	h m	h m
N 72	20 54	23 28	////	06 29	08 57	10 55	12 48
N 70	20 31	22 09	////	08 02	09 38	11 19	13 02
68	20 14	21 32	////	08 41	10 05	11 37	13 13
66	20 00	21 07	23 32	09 08	10 26	11 52	13 23
64	19 49	20 48	22 23	09 29	10 43	12 04	13 30
62	19 39	20 32	21 50	09 46	10 56	12 14	13 37
60	19 31	20 19	21 26	09 59	11 08	12 23	13 43
N 58	19 24	20 08	21 08	10 11	11 18	12 30	13 48
56	19 17	19 59	20 53	10 22	11 27	12 37	13 52
54	19 12	19 51	20 41	10 31	11 34	12 43	13 56
52	19 06	19 43	20 30	10 39	11 41	12 48	14 00
50	19 02	19 37	20 20	10 46	11 47	12 53	14 03
45	18 52	19 23	20 01	11 01	12 01	13 04	14 10
N 40	18 44	19 12	19 46	11 14	12 12	13 12	14 16
35	18 37	19 03	19 34	11 25	12 21	13 20	14 21
30	18 30	18 55	19 25	11 34	12 29	13 26	14 25
20	18 20	18 42	19 09	11 51	12 43	13 37	14 33
N 10	18 11	18 32	18 57	12 05	12 55	13 47	14 39
0	18 02	18 23	18 48	12 18	13 07	13 56	14 45
S 10	17 54	18 15	18 40	12 31	13 18	14 05	14 52
20	17 45	18 07	18 33	12 45	13 30	14 14	14 58
30	17 35	18 00	18 28	13 01	13 44	14 25	15 05
35	17 29	17 55	18 25	13 10	13 52	14 31	15 10
40	17 23	17 51	18 22	13 21	14 01	14 38	15 14
45	17 16	17 46	18 20	13 33	14 11	14 47	15 20
S 50	17 07	17 40	18 18	13 48	14 24	14 56	15 26
52	17 03	17 37	18 17	13 55	14 30	15 01	15 29
54	16 58	17 35	18 16	14 02	14 36	15 06	15 33
56	16 53	17 32	18 15	14 11	14 43	15 11	15 36
58	16 48	17 29	18 14	14 21	14 52	15 17	15 40
S 60	16 42	17 25	18 13	14 32	15 01	15 24	15 45

Day	SUN Eqn. of Time 00^h	SUN Eqn. of Time 12^h	SUN Mer. Pass.	MOON Mer. Pass. Upper	MOON Mer. Pass. Lower	MOON Age	MOON Phase
d	m s	m s	h m	h m	h m	d %	
19	00 50	00 56	11 59	06 06	18 30	22 49	
20	01 03	01 09	11 59	06 55	19 19	23 39	
21	01 15	01 21	11 59	07 44	20 09	24 30	

UT	ARIES	VENUS −4·7		MARS +1·6		JUPITER −2·4		SATURN +0·3	
	GHA	GHA	Dec	GHA	Dec	GHA	Dec	GHA	Dec
d h	° ′	° ′	° ′	° ′	° ′	° ′	° ′	° ′	° ′
22 00	210 14.5	213 30.4	N 1 50.5	152 08.9	N20 47.9	14 27.0	S 5 01.8	302 50.3	S22 03.2
01	225 17.0	228 32.1	50.2	167 09.6	48.3	29 29.8	01.7	317 52.9	03.2
02	240 19.5	243 33.8	50.0	182 10.3	48.7	44 32.5	01.6	332 55.4	03.2
03	255 21.9	258 35.5	. . 49.8	197 10.9	. . 49.1	59 35.3	. . 01.5	347 57.9	. . 03.2
04	270 24.4	273 37.2	49.5	212 11.6	49.5	74 38.0	01.3	3 00.5	03.2
05	285 26.9	288 38.9	49.3	227 12.2	49.8	89 40.7	01.2	18 03.0	03.2
06	300 29.3	303 40.6	N 1 49.1	242 12.9	N20 50.2	104 43.5	S 5 01.1	33 05.5	S22 03.2
07	315 31.8	318 42.3	48.8	257 13.5	50.6	119 46.2	01.0	48 08.1	03.2
SATURDAY 08	330 34.3	333 43.9	48.6	272 14.2	51.0	134 49.0	00.9	63 10.6	03.2
09	345 36.7	348 45.6	. . 48.4	287 14.9	. . 51.4	149 51.7	. . 00.8	78 13.1	. . 03.2
10	0 39.2	3 47.3	48.2	302 15.5	51.8	164 54.5	00.7	93 15.7	03.2
11	15 41.6	18 49.0	48.0	317 16.2	52.1	179 57.2	00.6	108 18.2	03.2
12	30 44.1	33 50.6	N 1 47.8	332 16.8	N20 52.5	194 59.9	S 5 00.5	123 20.7	S22 03.2
13	45 46.6	48 52.3	47.5	347 17.5	52.9	210 02.7	00.4	138 23.3	03.2
14	60 49.0	63 53.9	47.3	2 18.2	53.3	225 05.4	00.2	153 25.8	03.2
15	75 51.5	78 55.6	. . 47.1	17 18.8	. . 53.7	240 08.2	. . 00.1	168 28.4	. . 03.2
16	90 54.0	93 57.2	46.9	32 19.5	54.0	255 10.9	5 00.0	183 30.9	03.2
17	105 56.4	108 58.9	46.7	47 20.1	54.4	270 13.7	4 59.9	198 33.4	03.2
18	120 58.9	124 00.5	N 1 46.5	62 20.8	N20 54.8	285 16.4	S 4 59.8	213 36.0	S22 03.2
19	136 01.4	139 02.2	46.3	77 21.5	55.2	300 19.1	59.7	228 38.5	03.2
20	151 03.8	154 03.8	46.1	92 22.1	55.6	315 21.9	59.6	243 41.0	03.2
21	166 06.3	169 05.5	. . 45.9	107 22.8	. . 55.9	330 24.6	. . 59.5	258 43.6	. . 03.2
22	181 08.7	184 07.1	45.7	122 23.4	56.3	345 27.4	59.4	273 46.1	03.2
23	196 11.2	199 08.7	45.5	137 24.1	56.7	0 30.1	59.3	288 48.6	03.2
23 00	211 13.7	214 10.3	N 1 45.3	152 24.7	N20 57.1	15 32.9	S 4 59.1	303 51.2	S22 03.2
01	226 16.1	229 12.0	45.1	167 25.4	57.4	30 35.6	59.0	318 53.7	03.1
02	241 18.6	244 13.6	44.9	182 26.1	57.8	45 38.3	58.9	333 56.2	03.1
03	256 21.1	259 15.2	. . 44.7	197 26.7	. . 58.2	60 41.1	. . 58.8	348 58.8	. . 03.1
04	271 23.5	274 16.8	44.5	212 27.4	58.6	75 43.8	58.7	4 01.3	03.1
05	286 26.0	289 18.4	44.3	227 28.0	58.9	90 46.6	58.6	19 03.9	03.1
06	301 28.5	304 20.1	N 1 44.2	242 28.7	N20 59.3	105 49.3	S 4 58.5	34 06.4	S22 03.1
07	316 30.9	319 21.7	44.0	257 29.3	20 59.7	120 52.0	58.4	49 08.9	03.1
08	331 33.4	334 23.3	43.8	272 30.0	21 00.1	135 54.8	58.3	64 11.5	03.1
SUNDAY 09	346 35.9	349 24.9	. . 43.6	287 30.7	. . 00.4	150 57.5	. . 58.2	79 14.0	. . 03.1
10	1 38.3	4 26.5	43.4	302 31.3	00.8	166 00.3	58.1	94 16.5	03.1
11	16 40.8	19 28.1	43.3	317 32.0	01.2	181 03.0	57.9	109 19.1	03.1
12	31 43.2	34 29.7	N 1 43.1	332 32.6	N21 01.6	196 05.7	S 4 57.8	124 21.6	S22 03.1
13	46 45.7	49 31.2	42.9	347 33.3	01.9	211 08.5	57.7	139 24.2	03.1
14	61 48.2	64 32.8	42.7	2 33.9	02.3	226 11.2	57.6	154 26.7	03.1
15	76 50.6	79 34.4	. . 42.6	17 34.6	. . 02.7	241 14.0	. . 57.5	169 29.2	. . 03.1
16	91 53.1	94 36.0	42.4	32 35.3	03.1	256 16.7	57.4	184 31.8	03.1
17	106 55.6	109 37.6	42.2	47 35.9	03.4	271 19.4	57.3	199 34.3	03.1
18	121 58.0	124 39.1	N 1 42.1	62 36.6	N21 03.8	286 22.2	S 4 57.2	214 36.9	S22 03.1
19	137 00.5	139 40.7	41.9	77 37.2	04.2	301 24.9	57.1	229 39.4	03.1
20	152 03.0	154 42.3	41.7	92 37.9	04.5	316 27.7	57.0	244 41.9	03.1
21	167 05.4	169 43.9	. . 41.6	107 38.5	. . 04.9	331 30.4	. . 56.9	259 44.5	. . 03.1
22	182 07.9	184 45.4	41.4	122 39.2	05.3	346 33.1	56.8	274 47.0	03.1
23	197 10.4	199 47.0	41.3	137 39.9	05.6	1 35.9	56.6	289 49.6	03.1
24 00	212 12.8	214 48.5	N 1 41.1	152 40.5	N21 06.0	16 38.6	S 4 56.5	304 52.1	S22 03.1
01	227 15.3	229 50.1	41.0	167 41.2	06.4	31 41.3	56.4	319 54.6	03.1
02	242 17.7	244 51.6	40.8	182 41.8	06.8	46 44.1	56.3	334 57.2	03.1
03	257 20.2	259 53.2	. . 40.7	197 42.5	. . 07.1	61 46.8	. . 56.2	349 59.7	. . 03.1
04	272 22.7	274 54.7	40.5	212 43.1	07.5	76 49.6	56.1	5 02.3	03.1
05	287 25.1	289 56.3	40.4	227 43.8	07.9	91 52.3	56.0	20 04.8	03.1
06	302 27.6	304 57.8	N 1 40.2	242 44.4	N21 08.2	106 55.0	S 4 55.9	35 07.3	S22 03.1
07	317 30.1	319 59.4	40.1	257 45.1	08.6	121 57.8	55.8	50 09.9	03.1
08	332 32.5	335 00.9	39.9	272 45.8	09.0	137 00.5	55.7	65 12.4	03.0
MONDAY 09	347 35.0	350 02.4	. . 39.8	287 46.4	. . 09.3	152 03.2	. . 55.6	80 15.0	. . 03.0
10	2 37.5	5 04.0	39.7	302 47.1	09.7	167 06.0	55.5	95 17.5	03.0
11	17 39.9	20 05.5	39.5	317 47.7	10.1	182 08.7	55.3	110 20.1	03.0
12	32 42.4	35 07.0	N 1 39.4	332 48.4	N21 10.4	197 11.5	S 4 55.2	125 22.6	S22 03.0
13	47 44.8	50 08.5	39.3	347 49.0	10.8	212 14.2	55.1	140 25.1	03.0
14	62 47.3	65 10.1	39.1	2 49.7	11.1	227 16.9	55.0	155 27.7	03.0
15	77 49.8	80 11.6	. . 39.0	17 50.3	. . 11.5	242 19.7	. . 54.9	170 30.2	. . 03.0
16	92 52.2	95 13.1	38.9	32 51.0	11.9	257 22.4	54.8	185 32.8	03.0
17	107 54.7	110 14.6	38.8	47 51.7	12.2	272 25.1	54.7	200 35.3	03.0
18	122 57.2	125 16.1	N 1 38.6	62 52.3	N21 12.6	287 27.9	S 4 54.6	215 37.9	S22 03.0
19	137 59.6	140 17.6	38.5	77 53.0	13.0	302 30.6	54.5	230 40.4	03.0
20	153 02.1	155 19.1	38.4	92 53.6	13.3	317 33.3	54.4	245 42.9	03.0
21	168 04.6	170 20.6	. . 38.3	107 54.3	. . 13.7	332 36.1	. . 54.3	260 45.5	. . 03.0
22	183 07.0	185 22.1	38.1	122 54.9	14.0	347 38.8	54.2	275 48.0	03.0
23	198 09.5	200 23.6	38.0	137 55.6	14.4	2 41.5	54.1	290 50.6	03.0
Mer. Pass.	h m 9 53.5	v 1.6	d 0.2	v 0.7	d 0.4	v 2.7	d 0.1	v 2.5	d 0.0

STARS		
Name	SHA	Dec
	° ′	° ′
Acamar	315 16.8	S40 14.4
Achernar	335 25.5	S57 09.1
Acrux	173 05.6	S63 11.8
Adhara	255 10.6	S29 00.1
Aldebaran	290 46.7	N16 32.4
Alioth	166 18.0	N55 52.1
Alkaid	152 56.4	N49 13.7
Al Na'ir	27 40.8	S46 52.5
Alnilam	275 44.0	S 1 11.8
Alphard	217 53.5	S 8 44.2
Alphecca	126 08.5	N26 39.4
Alpheratz	357 41.1	N29 10.9
Altair	62 05.7	N 8 54.8
Ankaa	353 13.6	S42 12.8
Antares	112 22.8	S26 28.0
Arcturus	145 53.1	N19 05.6
Atria	107 21.8	S69 03.1
Avior	234 16.9	S59 34.3
Bellatrix	278 29.5	N 6 21.6
Betelgeuse	270 58.7	N 7 24.3
Canopus	263 55.3	S52 42.8
Capella	280 31.0	N46 00.8
Deneb	49 29.7	N45 20.3
Denebola	182 30.8	N14 28.5
Diphda	348 53.6	S17 53.7
Dubhe	193 48.2	N61 39.6
Elnath	278 09.6	N28 37.1
Eltanin	90 44.6	N51 29.1
Enif	33 44.7	N 9 57.2
Fomalhaut	15 21.4	S29 31.8
Gacrux	171 57.4	S57 12.7
Gienah	175 49.3	S17 38.4
Hadar	148 43.5	S60 27.3
Hamal	327 58.2	N23 32.4
Kaus Aust.	83 40.2	S34 22.3
Kochab	137 19.1	N74 05.1
Markab	13 36.0	N15 17.7
Menkar	314 12.7	N 4 09.2
Menkent	148 04.1	S36 27.2
Miaplacidus	221 38.8	S69 47.7
Mirfak	308 37.1	N49 55.1
Nunki	75 55.0	S26 16.3
Peacock	53 15.3	S56 40.4
Pollux	243 24.7	N27 58.9
Procyon	244 57.1	N 5 10.6
Rasalhague	96 03.8	N12 32.9
Regulus	207 40.7	N11 52.9
Rigel	281 09.8	S 8 11.3
Rigil Kent.	139 47.5	S60 54.2
Sabik	102 09.3	S15 44.6
Schedar	349 38.0	N56 37.7
Shaula	96 18.1	S37 06.7
Sirius	258 31.6	S16 44.8
Spica	158 28.2	S11 15.1
Suhail	222 50.4	S43 30.5
Vega	80 37.0	N38 47.9
Zuben'ubi	137 02.2	S16 06.7

	SHA	Mer. Pass.
	° ′	h m
Venus	2 56.7	9 42
Mars	301 11.1	13 50
Jupiter	164 19.2	22 54
Saturn	92 37.5	3 44

	UT d h	SUN GHA ° ′	SUN Dec ° ′	MOON GHA ° ′	v ′	MOON Dec ° ′	d ′	HP ′
	22 00	180 21.8	N12 11.1	235 53.2	11.0	S10 42.2	9.1	57.3
	01	195 21.9	12.0	250 23.2	11.0	10 33.1	9.2	57.4
	02	210 22.0	12.8	264 53.2	11.0	10 23.9	9.2	57.4
	03	225 22.1	. . 13.7	279 23.2	11.0	10 14.7	9.4	57.4
	04	240 22.3	14.5	293 53.2	11.0	10 05.3	9.4	57.5
	05	255 22.4	15.3	308 23.2	11.0	9 55.9	9.4	57.5
	06	270 22.5	N12 16.2	322 53.2	10.9	S 9 46.5	9.5	57.6
	07	285 22.6	17.0	337 23.1	11.0	9 37.0	9.6	57.6
S	08	300 22.7	17.9	351 53.1	10.9	9 27.4	9.7	57.6
A	09	315 22.9	. . 18.7	6 23.0	10.9	9 17.7	9.7	57.7
T	10	330 23.0	19.5	20 52.9	10.9	9 08.0	9.7	57.7
U	11	345 23.1	20.4	35 22.8	10.9	8 58.3	9.9	57.8
R	12	0 23.2	N12 21.2	49 52.7	10.8	S 8 48.4	9.9	57.8
D	13	15 23.3	22.0	64 22.5	10.8	8 38.5	9.9	57.8
A	14	30 23.5	22.9	78 52.3	10.9	8 28.6	10.0	57.9
Y	15	45 23.6	. . 23.7	93 22.2	10.8	8 18.6	10.1	57.9
	16	60 23.7	24.5	107 52.0	10.7	8 08.5	10.1	58.0
	17	75 23.8	25.4	122 21.7	10.8	7 58.4	10.2	58.0
	18	90 23.9	N12 26.2	136 51.5	10.7	S 7 48.2	10.3	58.0
	19	105 24.0	27.1	151 21.2	10.8	7 37.9	10.3	58.1
	20	120 24.2	27.9	165 51.0	10.7	7 27.6	10.3	58.1
	21	135 24.3	. . 28.7	180 20.7	10.6	7 17.3	10.5	58.2
	22	150 24.4	29.6	194 50.3	10.7	7 06.8	10.4	58.2
	23	165 24.5	30.4	209 20.0	10.6	6 56.4	10.5	58.2
	23 00	180 24.6	N12 31.2	223 49.6	10.6	S 6 45.9	10.6	58.3
	01	195 24.8	32.1	238 19.2	10.6	6 35.3	10.6	58.3
	02	210 24.9	32.9	252 48.8	10.6	6 24.7	10.7	58.3
	03	225 25.0	. . 33.7	267 18.4	10.5	6 14.0	10.7	58.4
	04	240 25.1	34.5	281 47.9	10.5	6 03.3	10.8	58.4
	05	255 25.2	35.4	296 17.4	10.5	5 52.5	10.8	58.5
	06	270 25.3	N12 36.2	310 46.9	10.5	S 5 41.7	10.9	58.5
	07	285 25.4	37.0	325 16.4	10.4	5 30.8	10.9	58.5
	08	300 25.6	37.9	339 45.8	10.5	5 19.9	10.9	58.6
S	09	315 25.7	. . 38.7	354 15.3	10.3	5 09.0	11.0	58.6
U	10	330 25.8	39.5	8 44.6	10.4	4 58.0	11.1	58.7
N	11	345 25.9	40.4	23 14.0	10.3	4 46.9	11.1	58.7
D	12	0 26.0	N12 41.2	37 43.3	10.3	S 4 35.8	11.1	58.7
A	13	15 26.1	42.0	52 12.6	10.3	4 24.7	11.1	58.8
Y	14	30 26.2	42.8	66 41.9	10.3	4 13.6	11.2	58.8
	15	45 26.4	. . 43.7	81 11.2	10.2	4 02.4	11.3	58.8
	16	60 26.5	44.5	95 40.4	10.2	3 51.1	11.3	58.9
	17	75 26.6	45.3	110 09.6	10.1	3 39.8	11.3	58.9
	18	90 26.7	N12 46.1	124 38.7	10.1	S 3 28.5	11.3	59.0
	19	105 26.8	47.0	139 07.8	10.1	3 17.2	11.4	59.0
	20	120 26.9	47.8	153 36.9	10.1	3 05.8	11.4	59.0
	21	135 27.0	. . 48.6	168 06.0	10.0	2 54.4	11.5	59.1
	22	150 27.2	49.5	182 35.0	10.0	2 42.9	11.5	59.1
	23	165 27.3	50.3	197 04.0	10.0	2 31.4	11.5	59.1
	24 00	180 27.4	N12 51.1	211 33.0	9.9	S 2 19.9	11.5	59.2
	01	195 27.5	51.9	226 01.9	9.9	2 08.4	11.6	59.2
	02	210 27.6	52.7	240 30.8	9.8	1 56.8	11.6	59.3
	03	225 27.7	. . 53.6	254 59.6	9.9	1 45.2	11.6	59.3
	04	240 27.8	54.4	269 28.5	9.8	1 33.6	11.6	59.3
	05	255 27.9	55.2	283 57.3	9.7	1 22.0	11.7	59.4
	06	270 28.0	N12 56.0	298 26.0	9.7	S 1 10.3	11.7	59.4
	07	285 28.2	56.9	312 54.7	9.7	0 58.6	11.7	59.4
	08	300 28.3	57.7	327 23.4	9.6	0 46.9	11.7	59.5
M	09	315 28.4	. . 58.5	341 52.0	9.6	0 35.2	11.7	59.5
O	10	330 28.5	12 59.3	356 20.6	9.6	0 23.5	11.8	59.5
N	11	345 28.6	13 00.1	10 49.2	9.5	S 0 11.7	11.8	59.6
D	12	0 28.7	N13 01.0	25 17.7	9.5	N 0 00.1	11.8	59.6
A	13	15 28.8	01.8	39 46.2	9.4	0 11.9	11.8	59.6
Y	14	30 28.9	02.6	54 14.6	9.4	0 23.7	11.8	59.7
	15	45 29.0	. . 03.4	68 43.0	9.3	0 35.5	11.8	59.7
	16	60 29.1	04.2	83 11.3	9.3	0 47.3	11.8	59.7
	17	75 29.2	05.1	97 39.6	9.3	0 59.1	11.9	59.8
	18	90 29.4	N13 05.9	112 07.9	9.2	N 1 11.0	11.8	59.8
	19	105 29.5	06.7	126 36.1	9.2	1 22.8	11.9	59.8
	20	120 29.6	07.5	141 04.3	9.1	1 34.7	11.8	59.9
	21	135 29.7	. . 08.3	155 32.4	9.1	1 46.5	11.9	59.9
	22	150 29.8	09.1	170 00.5	9.1	1 58.4	11.9	59.9
	23	165 29.9	10.0	184 28.6	9.0	N 2 10.3	11.8	60.0
		SD 15.9	*d* 0.8	SD	15.7	16.0		16.2

Lat. °	Twilight Naut. h m	Twilight Civil h m	Sunrise h m	Moonrise 22 h m	Moonrise 23 h m	Moonrise 24 h m	Moonrise 25 h m
N 72	////	////	02 49	04 39	04 31	04 23	04 16
N 70	////	01 28	03 14	04 23	04 22	04 21	04 20
68	////	02 11	03 33	04 11	04 15	04 19	04 23
66	////	02 39	03 48	04 00	04 09	04 18	04 26
64	01 17	03 00	04 01	03 51	04 04	04 16	04 29
62	01 55	03 17	04 11	03 44	04 00	04 15	04 31
60	02 21	03 31	04 20	03 37	03 56	04 14	04 33
N 58	02 41	03 42	04 28	03 31	03 53	04 13	04 34
56	02 57	03 52	04 35	03 26	03 50	04 13	04 36
54	03 10	04 01	04 41	03 21	03 47	04 12	04 37
52	03 22	04 09	04 46	03 17	03 45	04 11	04 38
50	03 32	04 16	04 51	03 13	03 42	04 11	04 39
45	03 52	04 30	05 02	03 05	03 37	04 09	04 42
N 40	04 07	04 42	05 11	02 58	03 33	04 08	04 44
35	04 20	04 52	05 18	02 52	03 30	04 07	04 46
30	04 30	05 00	05 25	02 47	03 27	04 07	04 48
20	04 47	05 13	05 36	02 37	03 21	04 05	04 50
N 10	04 59	05 24	05 46	02 29	03 16	04 04	04 53
0	05 09	05 34	05 55	02 22	03 12	04 03	04 55
S 10	05 18	05 42	06 04	02 14	03 07	04 02	04 58
20	05 25	05 51	06 13	02 06	03 02	04 00	05 01
30	05 31	06 00	06 24	01 57	02 57	03 59	05 04
35	05 35	06 04	06 30	01 51	02 54	03 58	05 05
40	05 38	06 09	06 37	01 45	02 50	03 58	05 07
45	05 40	06 15	06 45	01 38	02 46	03 57	05 10
S 50	05 43	06 21	06 55	01 29	02 41	03 55	05 13
52	05 45	06 24	06 59	01 25	02 39	03 55	05 14
54	05 46	06 27	07 04	01 21	02 36	03 54	05 15
56	05 47	06 31	07 09	01 16	02 33	03 54	05 17
58	05 48	06 34	07 15	01 11	02 30	03 53	05 19
S 60	05 49	06 38	07 22	01 05	02 26	03 52	05 21

Lat. °	Sunset h m	Twilight Civil h m	Twilight Naut. h m	Moonset 22 h m	Moonset 23 h m	Moonset 24 h m	Moonset 25 h m
N 72	21 12	////	////	12 48	14 42	16 38	18 38
N 70	20 46	22 38	////	13 02	14 48	16 37	18 29
68	20 26	21 51	////	13 13	14 53	16 36	18 22
66	20 11	21 21	////	13 23	14 57	16 35	18 16
64	19 58	20 59	22 48	13 30	15 01	16 34	18 11
62	19 47	20 42	22 06	13 37	15 04	16 34	18 07
60	19 38	20 28	21 39	13 43	15 06	16 33	18 03
N 58	19 30	20 16	21 18	13 48	15 09	16 33	18 00
56	19 23	20 06	21 02	13 52	15 11	16 33	17 57
54	19 17	19 57	20 48	13 56	15 13	16 32	17 54
52	19 12	19 49	20 37	14 00	15 14	16 32	17 52
50	19 07	19 42	20 26	14 03	15 16	16 32	17 50
45	18 56	19 27	20 06	14 10	15 19	16 31	17 45
N 40	18 47	19 15	19 50	14 16	15 22	16 30	17 41
35	18 39	19 06	19 37	14 21	15 24	16 30	17 38
30	18 32	18 57	19 27	14 25	15 26	16 30	17 35
20	18 21	18 44	19 10	14 33	15 30	16 29	17 30
N 10	18 11	18 32	18 58	14 39	15 33	16 28	17 25
0	18 02	18 23	18 47	14 45	15 36	16 28	17 21
S 10	17 53	18 14	18 39	14 52	15 39	16 27	17 17
20	17 43	18 05	18 31	14 58	15 42	16 26	17 12
30	17 32	17 57	18 25	15 05	15 45	16 25	17 07
35	17 26	17 52	18 22	15 10	15 47	16 25	17 04
40	17 19	17 47	18 18	15 14	15 49	16 24	17 01
45	17 11	17 41	18 15	15 20	15 52	16 24	16 57
S 50	17 01	17 35	18 12	15 26	15 55	16 23	16 52
52	16 57	17 32	18 11	15 29	15 56	16 23	16 50
54	16 52	17 28	18 10	15 33	15 58	16 22	16 48
56	16 46	17 25	18 09	15 36	15 59	16 22	16 45
58	16 40	17 21	18 07	15 40	16 01	16 21	16 43
S 60	16 33	17 17	18 06	15 45	16 03	16 21	16 40

Day	SUN Eqn. of Time 00^h	SUN Eqn. of Time 12^h	SUN Mer. Pass.	MOON Mer. Pass. Upper	MOON Mer. Pass. Lower	MOON Age	MOON Phase
d	m s	m s	h m	h m	h m	d %	
22	01 27	01 33	11 58	08 34	20 59	25 20	
23	01 38	01 44	11 58	09 24	21 49	26 12	
24	01 49	01 55	11 58	10 15	22 41	27 6	

UT		ARIES	VENUS −4·7		MARS +1·6		JUPITER −2·4		SATURN +0·3	
		GHA	GHA	Dec	GHA	Dec	GHA	Dec	GHA	Dec
d	h	° ′	° ′	° ′	° ′	° ′	° ′	° ′	° ′	° ′
25	00	213 12.0	215 25.1	N 1 37.9	152 56.2	N21 14.8	17 44.3	S 4 54.0	305 53.1	S22 03.0
	01	228 14.4	230 26.6	37.8	167 56.9	15.1	32 47.0	53.9	320 55.7	03.0
	02	243 16.9	245 28.1	37.7	182 57.5	15.5	47 49.8	53.7	335 58.2	03.0
	03	258 19.3	260 29.5	. . 37.6	197 58.2	. . 15.9	62 52.5	. . 53.6	351 00.8	. . 03.0
	04	273 21.8	275 31.0	37.5	212 58.9	16.2	77 55.2	53.5	6 03.3	03.0
	05	288 24.3	290 32.5	37.4	227 59.5	16.6	92 58.0	53.4	21 05.9	03.0
	06	303 26.7	305 34.0	N 1 37.3	243 00.2	N21 16.9	108 00.7	S 4 53.3	36 08.4	S22 03.0
	07	318 29.2	320 35.4	37.2	258 00.8	17.3	123 03.4	53.2	51 10.9	03.0
T	08	333 31.7	335 36.9	37.1	273 01.5	17.6	138 06.2	53.1	66 13.5	03.0
U	09	348 34.1	350 38.4	. . 37.0	288 02.1	. . 18.0	153 08.9	. . 53.0	81 16.0	. . 03.0
E	10	3 36.6	5 39.8	36.9	303 02.8	18.4	168 11.6	52.9	96 18.6	03.0
S	11	18 39.1	20 41.3	36.8	318 03.4	18.7	183 14.4	52.8	111 21.1	03.0
D	12	33 41.5	35 42.8	N 1 36.7	333 04.1	N21 19.1	198 17.1	S 4 52.7	126 23.7	S22 03.0
A	13	48 44.0	50 44.2	36.6	348 04.7	19.4	213 19.8	52.6	141 26.2	03.0
Y	14	63 46.4	65 45.7	36.5	3 05.4	19.8	228 22.6	52.5	156 28.8	03.0
	15	78 48.9	80 47.1	. . 36.4	18 06.0	. . 20.1	243 25.3	. . 52.4	171 31.3	. . 02.9
	16	93 51.4	95 48.6	36.3	33 06.7	20.5	258 28.0	52.3	186 33.9	02.9
	17	108 53.8	110 50.0	36.2	48 07.3	20.9	273 30.8	52.2	201 36.4	02.9
	18	123 56.3	125 51.5	N 1 36.1	63 08.0	N21 21.2	288 33.5	S 4 52.0	216 39.0	S22 02.9
	19	138 58.8	140 52.9	36.1	78 08.7	21.6	303 36.2	51.9	231 41.5	02.9
	20	154 01.2	155 54.3	36.0	93 09.3	21.9	318 39.0	51.8	246 44.1	02.9
	21	169 03.7	170 55.8	. . 35.9	108 10.0	. . 22.3	333 41.7	. . 51.7	261 46.6	. . 02.9
	22	184 06.2	185 57.2	35.8	123 10.6	22.6	348 44.4	51.6	276 49.2	02.9
	23	199 08.6	200 58.6	35.7	138 11.3	23.0	3 47.1	51.5	291 51.7	02.9
26	00	214 11.1	216 00.1	N 1 35.7	153 11.9	N21 23.3	18 49.9	S 4 51.4	306 54.3	S22 02.9
	01	229 13.6	231 01.5	35.6	168 12.6	23.7	33 52.6	51.3	321 56.8	02.9
	02	244 16.0	246 02.9	35.5	183 13.2	24.0	48 55.3	51.2	336 59.3	02.9
	03	259 18.5	261 04.3	. . 35.4	198 13.9	. . 24.4	63 58.1	. . 51.1	352 01.9	. . 02.9
	04	274 20.9	276 05.7	35.4	213 14.5	24.7	79 00.8	51.0	7 04.4	02.9
	05	289 23.4	291 07.1	35.3	228 15.2	25.1	94 03.5	50.9	22 07.0	02.9
	06	304 25.9	306 08.6	N 1 35.2	243 15.8	N21 25.4	109 06.3	S 4 50.8	37 09.5	S22 02.9
W	07	319 28.3	321 10.0	35.2	258 16.5	25.8	124 09.0	50.7	52 12.1	02.9
E	08	334 30.8	336 11.4	35.1	273 17.1	26.1	139 11.7	50.6	67 14.6	02.9
D	09	349 33.3	351 12.8	. . 35.1	288 17.8	. . 26.5	154 14.5	. . 50.5	82 17.2	. . 02.9
N	10	4 35.7	6 14.2	35.0	303 18.4	26.8	169 17.2	50.4	97 19.7	02.9
E	11	19 38.2	21 15.6	34.9	318 19.1	27.2	184 19.9	50.3	112 22.3	02.9
S	12	34 40.7	36 17.0	N 1 34.9	333 19.7	N21 27.5	199 22.6	S 4 50.2	127 24.8	S22 02.9
D	13	49 43.1	51 18.4	34.8	348 20.4	27.9	214 25.4	50.1	142 27.4	02.9
A	14	64 45.6	66 19.7	34.8	3 21.0	28.2	229 28.1	50.0	157 30.0	02.9
Y	15	79 48.1	81 21.1	. . 34.7	18 21.7	. . 28.6	244 30.8	. . 49.8	172 32.5	. . 02.9
	16	94 50.5	96 22.5	34.7	33 22.3	28.9	259 33.6	49.7	187 35.1	02.9
	17	109 53.0	111 23.9	34.6	48 23.0	29.3	274 36.3	49.6	202 37.6	02.9
	18	124 55.4	126 25.3	N 1 34.6	63 23.6	N21 29.6	289 39.0	S 4 49.5	217 40.2	S22 02.9
	19	139 57.9	141 26.7	34.5	78 24.3	30.0	304 41.8	49.4	232 42.7	02.9
	20	155 00.4	156 28.0	34.5	93 24.9	30.3	319 44.5	49.3	247 45.3	02.9
	21	170 02.8	171 29.4	. . 34.5	108 25.6	. . 30.7	334 47.2	. . 49.2	262 47.8	. . 02.9
	22	185 05.3	186 30.8	34.4	123 26.2	31.0	349 49.9	49.1	277 50.4	02.8
	23	200 07.8	201 32.1	34.4	138 26.9	31.4	4 52.7	49.0	292 52.9	02.8
27	00	215 10.2	216 33.5	N 1 34.3	153 27.5	N21 31.7	19 55.4	S 4 48.9	307 55.5	S22 02.8
	01	230 12.7	231 34.9	34.3	168 28.2	32.1	34 58.1	48.8	322 58.0	02.8
	02	245 15.2	246 36.2	34.3	183 28.9	32.4	50 00.8	48.7	338 00.6	02.8
	03	260 17.6	261 37.6	. . 34.2	198 29.5	. . 32.7	65 03.6	. . 48.6	353 03.1	. . 02.8
	04	275 20.1	276 38.9	34.2	213 30.2	33.1	80 06.3	48.5	8 05.7	02.8
	05	290 22.5	291 40.3	34.2	228 30.8	33.4	95 09.0	48.4	23 08.2	02.8
	06	305 25.0	306 41.6	N 1 34.1	243 31.5	N21 33.8	110 11.8	S 4 48.3	38 10.8	S22 02.8
	07	320 27.5	321 43.0	34.1	258 32.1	34.1	125 14.5	48.2	53 13.3	02.8
T	08	335 29.9	336 44.3	34.1	273 32.8	34.5	140 17.2	48.1	68 15.9	02.8
H	09	350 32.4	351 45.7	. . 34.1	288 33.4	. . 34.8	155 19.9	. . 48.0	83 18.5	. . 02.8
U	10	5 34.9	6 47.0	34.1	303 34.1	35.1	170 22.7	47.9	98 21.0	02.8
R	11	20 37.3	21 48.3	34.0	318 34.7	35.5	185 25.4	47.8	113 23.6	02.8
S	12	35 39.8	36 49.7	N 1 34.0	333 35.4	N21 35.8	200 28.1	S 4 47.7	128 26.1	S22 02.8
D	13	50 42.3	51 51.0	34.0	348 36.0	36.2	215 30.8	47.6	143 28.7	02.8
A	14	65 44.7	66 52.3	34.0	3 36.7	36.5	230 33.6	47.5	158 31.2	02.8
Y	15	80 47.2	81 53.7	. . 34.0	18 37.3	. . 36.8	245 36.3	. . 47.4	173 33.8	. . 02.8
	16	95 49.7	96 55.0	34.0	33 38.0	37.2	260 39.0	47.3	188 36.3	02.8
	17	110 52.1	111 56.3	33.9	48 38.6	37.5	275 41.7	47.2	203 38.9	02.8
	18	125 54.6	126 57.6	N 1 33.9	63 39.2	N21 37.9	290 44.5	S 4 47.1	218 41.4	S22 02.8
	19	140 57.0	141 58.9	33.9	78 39.9	38.2	305 47.2	47.0	233 44.0	02.8
	20	155 59.5	157 00.3	33.9	93 40.5	38.5	320 49.9	46.9	248 46.6	02.8
	21	171 02.0	172 01.6	. . 33.9	108 41.2	. . 38.9	335 52.6	. . 46.8	263 49.1	. . 02.8
	22	186 04.4	187 02.9	33.9	123 41.8	39.2	350 55.4	46.7	278 51.7	02.8
	23	201 06.9	202 04.2	33.9	138 42.5	39.5	5 58.1	46.6	293 54.2	02.8
Mer. Pass.		h m 9 41.7	*v* 1.4	*d* 0.1	*v* 0.7	*d* 0.3	*v* 2.7	*d* 0.1	*v* 2.6	*d* 0.0

STARS

Name	SHA	Dec
	° ′	° ′
Acamar	315 16.8	S40 14.4
Achernar	335 25.5	S57 09.1
Acrux	173 05.6	S63 11.8
Adhara	255 10.6	S29 00.1
Aldebaran	290 46.7	N16 32.4
Alioth	166 18.0	N55 52.1
Alkaid	152 56.4	N49 13.7
Al Na'ir	27 40.8	S46 52.4
Alnilam	275 44.0	S 1 11.8
Alphard	217 53.5	S 8 44.2
Alphecca	126 08.5	N26 39.4
Alpheratz	357 41.1	N29 10.9
Altair	62 05.7	N 8 54.8
Ankaa	353 13.6	S42 12.8
Antares	112 22.8	S26 28.0
Arcturus	145 53.1	N19 05.6
Atria	107 21.8	S69 03.1
Avior	234 16.9	S59 34.3
Bellatrix	278 29.5	N 6 21.6
Betelgeuse	270 58.7	N 7 24.3
Canopus	263 55.3	S52 42.7
Capella	280 31.0	N46 00.8
Deneb	49 29.7	N45 20.3
Denebola	182 30.8	N14 28.5
Diphda	348 53.6	S17 53.7
Dubhe	193 48.3	N61 39.6
Elnath	278 09.6	N28 37.1
Eltanin	90 44.6	N51 29.1
Enif	33 44.7	N 9 57.2
Fomalhaut	15 21.4	S29 31.8
Gacrux	171 57.4	S57 12.7
Gienah	175 49.3	S17 38.4
Hadar	148 43.5	S60 27.3
Hamal	327 58.2	N23 32.4
Kaus Aust.	83 40.2	S34 22.3
Kochab	137 19.1	N74 05.2
Markab	13 36.0	N15 17.7
Menkar	314 12.7	N 4 09.2
Menkent	148 04.1	S36 27.2
Miaplacidus	221 38.9	S69 47.7
Mirfak	308 37.1	N49 55.1
Nunki	75 55.0	S26 16.3
Peacock	53 15.2	S56 40.4
Pollux	243 24.7	N27 58.9
Procyon	244 57.1	N 5 10.6
Rasalhague	96 03.8	N12 32.9
Regulus	207 40.7	N11 52.9
Rigel	281 09.8	S 8 11.2
Rigil Kent.	139 47.5	S60 54.2
Sabik	102 09.3	S15 44.6
Schedar	349 38.0	N56 37.6
Shaula	96 18.1	S37 06.7
Sirius	258 31.6	S16 44.8
Spica	158 28.2	S11 15.1
Suhail	222 50.4	S43 30.5
Vega	80 37.0	N38 47.9
Zuben'ubi	137 02.2	S16 06.7

	SHA	Mer. Pass.
	° ′	h m
Venus	1 49.0	9 35
Mars	299 00.8	13 47
Jupiter	164 38.8	22 41
Saturn	92 43.2	3 32

UT d	UT h	SUN GHA	SUN Dec	MOON GHA	v	MOON Dec	d	HP
d	h	° ′	° ′	° ′	′	° ′	′	′
25	00	180 30.0	N13 10.8	198 56.6	8.9	N 2 22.1	11.9	60.0
	01	195 30.1	11.6	213 24.5	8.9	2 34.0	11.9	60.0
	02	210 30.2	12.4	227 52.4	8.9	2 45.9	11.8	60.0
	03	225 30.3	. . 13.2	242 20.3	8.8	2 57.7	11.9	60.1
	04	240 30.4	14.0	256 48.1	8.8	3 09.6	11.8	60.1
	05	255 30.5	14.8	271 15.9	8.7	3 21.4	11.8	60.1
	06	270 30.6	N13 15.7	285 43.6	8.6	N 3 33.2	11.9	60.2
	07	285 30.7	16.5	300 11.2	8.7	3 45.1	11.8	60.2
T	08	300 30.8	17.3	314 38.9	8.5	3 56.9	11.8	60.2
U	09	315 31.0	. . 18.1	329 06.4	8.5	4 08.7	11.7	60.2
E	10	330 31.1	18.9	343 33.9	8.5	4 20.4	11.8	60.3
S	11	345 31.2	19.7	358 01.4	8.4	4 32.2	11.8	60.3
D	12	0 31.3	N13 20.5	12 28.8	8.4	N 4 44.0	11.7	60.3
A	13	15 31.4	21.3	26 56.2	8.3	4 55.7	11.7	60.3
Y	14	30 31.5	22.1	41 23.5	8.3	5 07.4	11.7	60.4
	15	45 31.6	. . 23.0	55 50.8	8.2	5 19.1	11.7	60.4
	16	60 31.7	23.8	70 18.0	8.2	5 30.8	11.6	60.4
	17	75 31.8	24.6	84 45.2	8.1	5 42.4	11.6	60.4
	18	90 31.9	N13 25.4	99 12.3	8.0	N 5 54.0	11.6	60.5
	19	105 32.0	26.2	113 39.3	8.0	6 05.6	11.6	60.5
	20	120 32.1	27.0	128 06.3	8.0	6 17.2	11.5	60.5
	21	135 32.2	. . 27.8	142 33.3	7.9	6 28.7	11.5	60.5
	22	150 32.3	28.6	157 00.2	7.8	6 40.2	11.5	60.6
	23	165 32.4	29.4	171 27.0	7.8	6 51.7	11.4	60.6
26	00	180 32.5	N13 30.2	185 53.8	7.7	N 7 03.1	11.4	60.6
	01	195 32.6	31.0	200 20.5	7.7	7 14.5	11.4	60.6
	02	210 32.7	31.8	214 47.2	7.7	7 25.9	11.3	60.6
	03	225 32.8	. . 32.6	229 13.9	7.5	7 37.2	11.2	60.7
	04	240 32.9	33.4	243 40.4	7.5	7 48.4	11.3	60.7
	05	255 33.0	34.2	258 06.9	7.5	7 59.7	11.2	60.7
	06	270 33.1	N13 35.0	272 33.4	7.4	N 8 10.9	11.1	60.7
W	07	285 33.2	35.9	286 59.8	7.4	8 22.0	11.1	60.7
E	08	300 33.3	36.7	301 26.2	7.3	8 33.1	11.0	60.8
D	09	315 33.4	. . 37.5	315 52.5	7.2	8 44.1	11.0	60.8
N	10	330 33.5	38.3	330 18.7	7.2	8 55.1	11.0	60.8
E	11	345 33.6	39.1	344 44.9	7.1	9 06.1	10.8	60.8
S	12	0 33.7	N13 39.9	359 11.0	7.1	N 9 16.9	10.9	60.8
D	13	15 33.8	40.7	13 37.1	7.0	9 27.8	10.7	60.8
A	14	30 33.9	41.5	28 03.1	7.0	9 38.5	10.8	60.8
Y	15	45 34.0	. . 42.3	42 29.1	6.9	9 49.3	10.6	60.9
	16	60 34.1	43.1	56 55.0	6.9	9 59.9	10.6	60.9
	17	75 34.2	43.9	71 20.9	6.8	10 10.5	10.5	60.9
	18	90 34.3	N13 44.7	85 46.7	6.7	N10 21.0	10.5	60.9
	19	105 34.4	45.5	100 12.4	6.7	10 31.5	10.4	60.9
	20	120 34.5	46.3	114 38.1	6.7	10 41.9	10.3	60.9
	21	135 34.6	. . 47.1	129 03.8	6.6	10 52.2	10.3	60.9
	22	150 34.7	47.9	143 29.4	6.5	11 02.5	10.2	60.9
	23	165 34.8	48.7	157 54.9	6.5	11 12.7	10.1	60.9
27	00	180 34.9	N13 49.4	172 20.4	6.4	N11 22.8	10.0	61.0
	01	195 35.0	50.2	186 45.8	6.4	11 32.8	10.0	61.0
	02	210 35.1	51.0	201 11.2	6.3	11 42.8	9.9	61.0
	03	225 35.2	. . 51.8	215 36.5	6.3	11 52.7	9.8	61.0
	04	240 35.3	52.6	230 01.8	6.2	12 02.5	9.7	61.0
	05	255 35.4	53.4	244 27.0	6.2	12 12.2	9.7	61.0
	06	270 35.5	N13 54.2	258 52.2	6.1	N12 21.9	9.5	61.0
	07	285 35.5	55.0	273 17.3	6.0	12 31.4	9.5	61.0
T	08	300 35.6	55.8	287 42.3	6.0	12 40.9	9.4	61.0
H	09	315 35.7	. . 56.6	302 07.3	6.0	12 50.3	9.3	61.0
U	10	330 35.8	57.4	316 32.3	5.9	12 59.6	9.2	61.0
R	11	345 35.9	58.2	330 57.2	5.9	13 08.8	9.2	61.0
S	12	0 36.0	N13 59.0	345 22.1	5.8	N13 18.0	9.0	61.0
D	13	15 36.1	13 59.8	359 46.9	5.8	13 27.0	8.9	61.0
A	14	30 36.2	14 00.6	14 11.7	5.7	13 35.9	8.9	61.0
Y	15	45 36.3	. . 01.4	28 36.4	5.7	13 44.8	8.7	61.0
	16	60 36.4	02.1	43 01.1	5.6	13 53.5	8.7	61.0
	17	75 36.5	02.9	57 25.7	5.6	14 02.2	8.6	61.0
	18	90 36.6	N14 03.7	71 50.3	5.5	N14 10.8	8.4	61.0
	19	105 36.7	04.5	86 14.8	5.5	14 19.2	8.4	61.0
	20	120 36.8	05.3	100 39.3	5.4	14 27.6	8.2	61.0
	21	135 36.9	. . 06.1	115 03.7	5.5	14 35.8	8.2	61.0
	22	150 36.9	06.9	129 28.2	5.3	14 44.0	8.1	61.0
	23	165 37.0	07.7	143 52.5	5.3	N14 52.1	7.9	61.0
		SD 15.9	*d* 0.8	SD	16.4	16.6		16.6

Lat.	Twilight Naut.	Twilight Civil	Sunrise	Moonrise 25	Moonrise 26	Moonrise 27	Moonrise 28
°	h m	h m	h m	h m	h m	h m	h m
N 72	////	////	02 29	04 16	04 08	03 59	03 46
N 70	////	00 50	02 58	04 20	04 19	04 19	04 21
68	////	01 50	03 20	04 23	04 28	04 35	04 46
66	////	02 23	03 37	04 26	04 36	04 48	05 05
64	00 43	02 47	03 50	04 29	04 42	04 59	05 21
62	01 37	03 06	04 02	04 31	04 48	05 08	05 34
60	02 07	03 21	04 11	04 33	04 52	05 16	05 45
N 58	02 30	03 34	04 20	04 34	04 57	05 23	05 55
56	02 47	03 44	04 27	04 36	05 01	05 29	06 04
54	03 02	03 54	04 34	04 37	05 04	05 35	06 11
52	03 14	04 02	04 40	04 38	05 07	05 40	06 18
50	03 25	04 10	04 45	04 39	05 10	05 45	06 24
45	03 46	04 25	04 57	04 42	05 17	05 55	06 38
N 40	04 03	04 38	05 06	04 44	05 22	06 03	06 49
35	04 16	04 48	05 15	04 46	05 27	06 10	06 58
30	04 27	04 57	05 22	04 48	05 31	06 17	07 07
20	04 44	05 11	05 34	04 50	05 38	06 28	07 21
N 10	04 58	05 23	05 45	04 53	05 44	06 38	07 34
0	05 08	05 33	05 54	04 55	05 50	06 47	07 46
S 10	05 18	05 43	06 04	04 58	05 56	06 56	07 58
20	05 26	05 52	06 14	05 01	06 03	07 06	08 11
30	05 33	06 01	06 26	05 04	06 10	07 18	08 26
35	05 37	06 06	06 33	05 05	06 14	07 25	08 35
40	05 40	06 12	06 40	05 07	06 19	07 32	08 45
45	05 44	06 18	06 49	05 10	06 25	07 41	08 56
S 50	05 48	06 26	06 59	05 13	06 32	07 52	09 11
52	05 49	06 29	07 04	05 14	06 35	07 57	09 17
54	05 51	06 32	07 09	05 15	06 39	08 03	09 25
56	05 52	06 36	07 15	05 17	06 43	08 09	09 33
58	05 54	06 40	07 22	05 19	06 47	08 16	09 42
S 60	05 56	06 45	07 29	05 21	06 52	08 24	09 53

Lat.	Sunset	Twilight Civil	Twilight Naut.	Moonset 25	Moonset 26	Moonset 27	Moonset 28
°	h m	h m	h m	h m	h m	h m	h m
N 72	21 32	////	////	18 38	20 45	23 00	25 36
N 70	21 01	23 26	////	18 29	20 26	22 26	24 25
68	20 39	22 12	////	18 22	20 12	22 02	23 48
66	20 22	21 36	////	18 16	20 00	21 44	23 22
64	20 08	21 12	23 30	18 11	19 50	21 29	23 01
62	19 56	20 52	22 24	18 07	19 42	21 16	22 45
60	19 46	20 37	21 52	18 03	19 35	21 06	22 32
N 58	19 37	20 24	21 29	18 00	19 29	20 57	22 20
56	19 30	20 13	21 11	17 57	19 23	20 49	22 10
54	19 23	20 03	20 56	17 54	19 18	20 41	22 01
52	19 17	19 55	20 43	17 52	19 14	20 35	21 53
50	19 11	19 47	20 33	17 50	19 10	20 29	21 46
45	18 59	19 31	20 11	17 45	19 01	20 17	21 30
N 40	18 50	19 19	19 54	17 41	18 54	20 07	21 18
35	18 41	19 08	19 40	17 38	18 48	19 58	21 07
30	18 34	18 59	19 29	17 35	18 42	19 50	20 58
20	18 22	18 45	19 12	17 30	18 33	19 37	20 42
N 10	18 11	18 33	18 58	17 25	18 25	19 26	20 28
0	18 01	18 22	18 47	17 21	18 17	19 15	20 15
S 10	17 51	18 13	18 38	17 17	18 09	19 04	20 02
20	17 41	18 04	18 30	17 12	18 01	18 53	19 48
30	17 29	17 54	18 22	17 07	17 52	18 40	19 32
35	17 23	17 49	18 18	17 04	17 46	18 32	19 22
40	17 15	17 43	18 15	17 01	17 40	18 23	19 12
45	17 06	17 37	18 11	16 57	17 33	18 13	18 59
S 50	16 56	17 29	18 07	16 52	17 25	18 01	18 44
52	16 51	17 26	18 06	16 50	17 21	17 56	18 37
54	16 45	17 22	18 04	16 48	17 17	17 50	18 30
56	16 39	17 19	18 02	16 45	17 12	17 43	18 21
58	16 33	17 14	18 01	16 43	17 07	17 35	18 11
S 60	16 25	17 10	17 59	16 40	17 01	17 27	18 00

Day	SUN Eqn. of Time 00^h	SUN Eqn. of Time 12^h	SUN Mer. Pass.	MOON Mer. Pass. Upper	MOON Mer. Pass. Lower	MOON Age	MOON Phase
d	m s	m s	h m	h m	h m	d	%
25	02 00	02 05	11 58	11 08	23 36	28	2
26	02 10	02 15	11 58	12 03	24 32	29	0
27	02 19	02 24	11 58	13 01	00 32	01	2

2017 APRIL 28, 29, 30 (FRI., SAT., SUN.)

UT d	h	ARIES GHA	VENUS −4·7 GHA	VENUS Dec	MARS +1·6 GHA	MARS Dec	JUPITER −2·4 GHA	JUPITER Dec	SATURN +0·3 GHA	SATURN Dec
		° ′	° ′	° ′	° ′	° ′	° ′	° ′	° ′	° ′
28	00	216 09.4	217 05.5	N 1 33.9	153 43.1	N21 39.9	21 00.8	S 4 46.5	308 56.8	S22 02.8
	01	231 11.8	232 06.8	33.9	168 43.8	40.2	36 03.5	46.4	323 59.3	02.8
	02	246 14.3	247 08.1	33.9	183 44.4	40.6	51 06.3	46.3	339 01.9	02.8
	03	261 16.8	262 09.4	. . 33.9	198 45.1	. . 40.9	66 09.0	. . 46.2	354 04.5	. . 02.8
	04	276 19.2	277 10.7	33.9	213 45.7	41.2	81 11.7	46.1	9 07.0	02.7
	05	291 21.7	292 12.0	33.9	228 46.4	41.6	96 14.4	45.9	24 09.6	02.7
	06	306 24.2	307 13.3	N 1 34.0	243 47.0	N21 41.9	111 17.2	S 4 45.8	39 12.1	S22 02.7
	07	321 26.6	322 14.5	34.0	258 47.7	42.2	126 19.9	45.7	54 14.7	02.7
	08	336 29.1	337 15.8	34.0	273 48.3	42.6	141 22.6	45.6	69 17.2	02.7
F	09	351 31.5	352 17.1	. . 34.0	288 49.0	. . 42.9	156 25.3	. . 45.5	84 19.8	. . 02.7
R	10	6 34.0	7 18.4	34.0	303 49.6	43.2	171 28.1	45.4	99 22.4	02.7
I	11	21 36.5	22 19.7	34.0	318 50.3	43.6	186 30.8	45.3	114 24.9	02.7
D	12	36 38.9	37 20.9	N 1 34.0	333 50.9	N21 43.9	201 33.5	S 4 45.2	129 27.5	S22 02.7
A	13	51 41.4	52 22.2	34.1	348 51.6	44.2	216 36.2	45.1	144 30.0	02.7
Y	14	66 43.9	67 23.5	34.1	3 52.2	44.6	231 38.9	45.0	159 32.6	02.7
	15	81 46.3	82 24.8	. . 34.1	18 52.9	. . 44.9	246 41.7	. . 44.9	174 35.2	. . 02.7
	16	96 48.8	97 26.0	34.1	33 53.5	45.2	261 44.4	44.8	189 37.7	02.7
	17	111 51.3	112 27.3	34.2	48 54.2	45.6	276 47.1	44.7	204 40.3	02.7
	18	126 53.7	127 28.6	N 1 34.2	63 54.8	N21 45.9	291 49.8	S 4 44.6	219 42.8	S22 02.7
	19	141 56.2	142 29.8	34.2	78 55.5	46.2	306 52.6	44.5	234 45.4	02.7
	20	156 58.6	157 31.1	34.2	93 56.1	46.5	321 55.3	44.4	249 48.0	02.7
	21	172 01.1	172 32.3	. . 34.3	108 56.8	. . 46.9	336 58.0	. . 44.3	264 50.5	. . 02.7
	22	187 03.6	187 33.6	34.3	123 57.4	47.2	352 00.7	44.2	279 53.1	02.7
	23	202 06.0	202 34.8	34.3	138 58.1	47.5	7 03.4	44.1	294 55.6	02.7
29	00	217 08.5	217 36.1	N 1 34.4	153 58.7	N21 47.9	22 06.2	S 4 44.0	309 58.2	S22 02.7
	01	232 11.0	232 37.3	34.4	168 59.3	48.2	37 08.9	43.9	325 00.8	02.7
	02	247 13.4	247 38.6	34.5	184 00.0	48.5	52 11.6	43.8	340 03.3	02.7
	03	262 15.9	262 39.8	. . 34.5	199 00.6	. . 48.8	67 14.3	. . 43.7	355 05.9	. . 02.7
	04	277 18.4	277 41.0	34.5	214 01.3	49.2	82 17.0	43.6	10 08.4	02.7
	05	292 20.8	292 42.3	34.6	229 01.9	49.5	97 19.8	43.5	25 11.0	02.7
	06	307 23.3	307 43.5	N 1 34.6	244 02.6	N21 49.8	112 22.5	S 4 43.4	40 13.6	S22 02.7
S	07	322 25.8	322 44.7	34.7	259 03.2	50.2	127 25.2	43.3	55 16.1	02.7
A	08	337 28.2	337 46.0	34.7	274 03.9	50.5	142 27.9	43.2	70 18.7	02.7
T	09	352 30.7	352 47.2	. . 34.8	289 04.5	. . 50.8	157 30.6	. . 43.1	85 21.2	. . 02.7
U	10	7 33.1	7 48.4	34.8	304 05.2	51.1	172 33.3	43.0	100 23.8	02.6
R	11	22 35.6	22 49.6	34.9	319 05.8	51.5	187 36.1	42.9	115 26.4	02.6
D	12	37 38.1	37 50.9	N 1 34.9	334 06.5	N21 51.8	202 38.8	S 4 42.8	130 28.9	S22 02.6
A	13	52 40.5	52 52.1	35.0	349 07.1	52.1	217 41.5	42.7	145 31.5	02.6
Y	14	67 43.0	67 53.3	35.1	4 07.8	52.4	232 44.2	42.7	160 34.1	02.6
	15	82 45.5	82 54.5	. . 35.1	19 08.4	. . 52.8	247 46.9	. . 42.6	175 36.6	. . 02.6
	16	97 47.9	97 55.7	35.2	34 09.1	53.1	262 49.7	42.5	190 39.2	02.6
	17	112 50.4	112 56.9	35.2	49 09.7	53.4	277 52.4	42.4	205 41.7	02.6
	18	127 52.9	127 58.1	N 1 35.3	64 10.3	N21 53.7	292 55.1	S 4 42.3	220 44.3	S22 02.6
	19	142 55.3	142 59.3	35.4	79 11.0	54.0	307 57.8	42.2	235 46.9	02.6
	20	157 57.8	158 00.5	35.4	94 11.6	54.4	323 00.5	42.1	250 49.4	02.6
	21	173 00.3	173 01.7	. . 35.5	109 12.3	. . 54.7	338 03.2	. . 42.0	265 52.0	. . 02.6
	22	188 02.7	188 02.9	35.6	124 12.9	55.0	353 06.0	41.9	280 54.6	02.6
	23	203 05.2	203 04.1	35.6	139 13.6	55.3	8 08.7	41.8	295 57.1	02.6
30	00	218 07.6	218 05.3	N 1 35.7	154 14.2	N21 55.6	23 11.4	S 4 41.7	310 59.7	S22 02.6
	01	233 10.1	233 06.5	35.8	169 14.9	56.0	38 14.1	41.6	326 02.3	02.6
	02	248 12.6	248 07.7	35.9	184 15.5	56.3	53 16.8	41.5	341 04.8	02.6
	03	263 15.0	263 08.9	. . 35.9	199 16.2	. . 56.6	68 19.5	. . 41.4	356 07.4	. . 02.6
	04	278 17.5	278 10.1	36.0	214 16.8	56.9	83 22.3	41.3	11 10.0	02.6
	05	293 20.0	293 11.3	36.1	229 17.4	57.2	98 25.0	41.2	26 12.5	02.6
	06	308 22.4	308 12.4	N 1 36.2	244 18.1	N21 57.6	113 27.7	S 4 41.1	41 15.1	S22 02.6
	07	323 24.9	323 13.6	36.3	259 18.7	57.9	128 30.4	41.0	56 17.7	02.6
	08	338 27.4	338 14.8	36.3	274 19.4	58.2	143 33.1	40.9	71 20.2	02.6
S	09	353 29.8	353 16.0	. . 36.4	289 20.0	. . 58.5	158 35.8	. . 40.8	86 22.8	. . 02.6
U	10	8 32.3	8 17.1	36.5	304 20.7	58.8	173 38.5	40.7	101 25.3	02.6
N	11	23 34.8	23 18.3	36.6	319 21.3	59.1	188 41.3	40.6	116 27.9	02.6
D	12	38 37.2	38 19.5	N 1 36.7	334 22.0	N21 59.5	203 44.0	S 4 40.5	131 30.5	S22 02.6
A	13	53 39.7	53 20.6	36.8	349 22.6	21 59.8	218 46.7	40.4	146 33.0	02.6
Y	14	68 42.1	68 21.8	36.9	4 23.3	22 00.1	233 49.4	40.3	161 35.6	02.6
	15	83 44.6	83 22.9	. . 37.0	19 23.9	. . 00.4	248 52.1	. . 40.2	176 38.2	. . 02.5
	16	98 47.1	98 24.1	37.1	34 24.5	00.7	263 54.8	40.1	191 40.7	02.5
	17	113 49.5	113 25.3	37.2	49 25.2	01.0	278 57.5	40.0	206 43.3	02.5
	18	128 52.0	128 26.4	N 1 37.3	64 25.8	N22 01.4	294 00.3	S 4 39.9	221 45.9	S22 02.5
	19	143 54.5	143 27.6	37.4	79 26.5	01.7	309 03.0	39.8	236 48.5	02.5
	20	158 56.9	158 28.7	37.5	94 27.1	02.0	324 05.7	39.7	251 51.0	02.5
	21	173 59.4	173 29.9	. . 37.6	109 27.8	. . 02.3	339 08.4	. . 39.6	266 53.6	. . 02.5
	22	189 01.9	188 31.0	37.7	124 28.4	02.6	354 11.1	39.5	281 56.2	02.5
	23	204 04.3	203 32.1	37.8	139 29.1	02.9	9 13.8	39.4	296 58.7	02.5
Mer. Pass.		h m 9 29.9	v 1.2	d 0.1	v 0.6	d 0.3	v 2.7	d 0.1	v 2.6	d 0.0

STARS

Name	SHA	Dec
	° ′	° ′
Acamar	315 16.8	S40 14.4
Achernar	335 25.5	S57 09.0
Acrux	173 05.6	S63 11.8
Adhara	255 10.7	S29 00.1
Aldebaran	290 46.7	N16 32.4
Alioth	166 18.0	N55 52.1
Alkaid	152 56.5	N49 13.7
Al Na'ir	27 40.7	S46 52.4
Alnilam	275 44.0	S 1 11.8
Alphard	217 53.5	S 8 44.2
Alphecca	126 08.5	N26 39.5
Alpheratz	357 41.1	N29 10.9
Altair	62 05.6	N 8 54.8
Ankaa	353 13.6	S42 12.8
Antares	112 22.7	S26 28.0
Arcturus	145 53.1	N19 05.6
Atria	107 21.7	S69 03.2
Avior	234 17.0	S59 34.3
Bellatrix	278 29.5	N 6 21.6
Betelgeuse	270 58.7	N 7 24.3
Canopus	263 55.3	S52 42.7
Capella	280 31.0	N46 00.8
Deneb	49 29.7	N45 20.3
Denebola	182 30.8	N14 28.5
Diphda	348 53.6	S17 53.6
Dubhe	193 48.3	N61 39.7
Elnath	278 09.6	N28 37.1
Eltanin	90 44.6	N51 29.1
Enif	33 44.7	N 9 57.2
Fomalhaut	15 21.4	S29 31.8
Gacrux	171 57.4	S57 12.7
Gienah	175 49.3	S17 38.4
Hadar	148 43.5	S60 27.3
Hamal	327 58.2	N23 32.4
Kaus Aust.	83 40.2	S34 22.3
Kochab	137 19.1	N74 05.2
Markab	13 35.9	N15 17.7
Menkar	314 12.7	N 4 09.2
Menkent	148 04.1	S36 27.3
Miaplacidus	221 38.9	S69 47.7
Mirfak	308 37.1	N49 55.1
Nunki	75 55.0	S26 16.3
Peacock	53 15.2	S56 40.4
Pollux	243 24.7	N27 58.9
Procyon	244 57.1	N 5 10.6
Rasalhague	96 03.8	N12 32.9
Regulus	207 40.7	N11 52.9
Rigel	281 09.8	S 8 11.2
Rigil Kent.	139 47.5	S60 54.2
Sabik	102 09.3	S15 44.6
Schedar	349 38.0	N56 37.6
Shaula	96 18.1	S37 06.7
Sirius	258 31.6	S16 44.8
Spica	158 28.2	S11 15.1
Suhail	222 50.5	S43 30.5
Vega	80 37.0	N38 47.9
Zuben'ubi	137 02.2	S16 06.7

	SHA	Mer. Pass.
	° ′	h m
Venus	0 27.6	9 29
Mars	296 50.2	13 43
Jupiter	164 57.6	22 28
Saturn	92 49.7	3 20

UT d	UT h	SUN GHA	SUN Dec	MOON GHA	*v*	MOON Dec	*d*	HP
		° ′	° ′	° ′	′	° ′	′	′
28	00	180 37.1	N14 08.5	158 16.8	5.3	N15 00.0	7.8	61.0
	01	195 37.2	09.2	172 41.1	5.3	15 07.8	7.8	61.0
	02	210 37.3	10.0	187 05.4	5.2	15 15.6	7.6	61.0
	03	225 37.4	. . 10.8	201 29.6	5.2	15 23.2	7.5	61.0
	04	240 37.5	11.6	215 53.8	5.1	15 30.7	7.4	61.0
	05	255 37.6	12.4	230 17.9	5.1	15 38.1	7.3	61.0
	06	270 37.7	N14 13.2	244 42.0	5.0	N15 45.4	7.2	61.0
	07	285 37.8	14.0	259 06.0	5.1	15 52.6	7.0	61.0
	08	300 37.8	14.7	273 30.1	5.0	15 59.6	7.0	61.0
F	09	315 37.9	. . 15.5	287 54.1	4.9	16 06.6	6.8	61.0
R	10	330 38.0	16.3	302 18.0	5.0	16 13.4	6.7	60.9
I	11	345 38.1	17.1	316 42.0	4.9	16 20.1	6.6	60.9
D	12	0 38.2	N14 17.9	331 05.9	4.9	N16 26.7	6.5	60.9
A	13	15 38.3	18.6	345 29.8	4.8	16 33.2	6.3	60.9
Y	14	30 38.4	19.4	359 53.6	4.8	16 39.5	6.2	60.9
	15	45 38.5	. . 20.2	14 17.4	4.8	16 45.7	6.1	60.9
	16	60 38.6	21.0	28 41.2	4.8	16 51.8	6.0	60.9
	17	75 38.6	21.8	43 05.0	4.8	16 57.8	5.9	60.9
	18	90 38.7	N14 22.6	57 28.8	4.7	N17 03.7	5.7	60.9
	19	105 38.8	23.3	71 52.5	4.7	17 09.4	5.6	60.8
	20	120 38.9	24.1	86 16.2	4.7	17 15.0	5.5	60.8
	21	135 39.0	. . 24.9	100 39.9	4.7	17 20.5	5.3	60.8
	22	150 39.1	25.7	115 03.6	4.6	17 25.8	5.3	60.8
	23	165 39.2	26.4	129 27.2	4.7	17 31.1	5.1	60.8
29	00	180 39.3	N14 27.2	143 50.9	4.6	N17 36.2	4.9	60.8
	01	195 39.3	28.0	158 14.5	4.6	17 41.1	4.9	60.8
	02	210 39.4	28.8	172 38.1	4.6	17 46.0	4.7	60.7
	03	225 39.5	. . 29.6	187 01.7	4.6	17 50.7	4.6	60.7
	04	240 39.6	30.3	201 25.3	4.6	17 55.3	4.4	60.7
	05	255 39.7	31.1	215 48.9	4.6	17 59.7	4.3	60.7
	06	270 39.8	N14 31.9	230 12.5	4.6	N18 04.0	4.2	60.7
	07	285 39.8	32.7	244 36.1	4.5	18 08.2	4.1	60.7
S	08	300 39.9	33.4	258 59.6	4.6	18 12.3	3.9	60.6
A	09	315 40.0	. . 34.2	273 23.2	4.6	18 16.2	3.8	60.6
T	10	330 40.1	35.0	287 46.8	4.5	18 20.0	3.6	60.6
U	11	345 40.2	35.7	302 10.3	4.6	18 23.6	3.5	60.6
R	12	0 40.3	N14 36.5	316 33.9	4.6	N18 27.1	3.4	60.6
D	13	15 40.3	37.3	330 57.5	4.6	18 30.5	3.3	60.5
A	14	30 40.4	38.1	345 21.1	4.5	18 33.8	3.1	60.5
Y	15	45 40.5	. . 38.8	359 44.6	4.6	18 36.9	3.0	60.5
	16	60 40.6	39.6	14 08.2	4.6	18 39.9	2.8	60.5
	17	75 40.7	40.4	28 31.8	4.6	18 42.7	2.7	60.4
	18	90 40.8	N14 41.1	42 55.4	4.6	N18 45.4	2.6	60.4
	19	105 40.8	41.9	57 19.0	4.7	18 48.0	2.4	60.4
	20	120 40.9	42.7	71 42.7	4.6	18 50.4	2.3	60.4
	21	135 41.0	. . 43.4	86 06.3	4.7	18 52.7	2.2	60.4
	22	150 41.1	44.2	100 30.0	4.7	18 54.9	2.0	60.3
	23	165 41.2	45.0	114 53.7	4.7	18 56.9	1.9	60.3
30	00	180 41.2	N14 45.8	129 17.4	4.7	N18 58.8	1.8	60.3
	01	195 41.3	46.5	143 41.1	4.7	19 00.6	1.6	60.3
	02	210 41.4	47.3	158 04.8	4.8	19 02.2	1.5	60.2
	03	225 41.5	. . 48.1	172 28.6	4.7	19 03.7	1.3	60.2
	04	240 41.6	48.8	186 52.3	4.9	19 05.0	1.2	60.2
	05	255 41.6	49.6	201 16.2	4.8	19 06.2	1.1	60.2
	06	270 41.7	N14 50.3	215 40.0	4.9	N19 07.3	1.0	60.1
	07	285 41.8	51.1	230 03.9	4.8	19 08.3	0.8	60.1
	08	300 41.9	51.9	244 27.7	5.0	19 09.1	0.7	60.1
S	09	315 42.0	. . 52.6	258 51.7	4.9	19 09.8	0.5	60.1
U	10	330 42.0	53.4	273 15.6	5.0	19 10.3	0.4	60.0
N	11	345 42.1	54.2	287 39.6	5.0	19 10.7	0.3	60.0
D	12	0 42.2	N14 54.9	302 03.6	5.1	N19 11.0	0.1	60.0
A	13	15 42.3	55.7	316 27.7	5.1	19 11.1	0.0	59.9
Y	14	30 42.4	56.5	330 51.8	5.1	19 11.1	0.1	59.9
	15	45 42.4	. . 57.2	345 15.9	5.2	19 11.0	0.2	59.9
	16	60 42.5	58.0	359 40.1	5.2	19 10.8	0.4	59.9
	17	75 42.6	58.7	14 04.3	5.3	19 10.4	0.6	59.8
	18	90 42.7	N14 59.5	28 28.6	5.3	N19 09.8	0.6	59.8
	19	105 42.7	15 00.3	42 52.9	5.4	19 09.2	0.8	59.8
	20	120 42.8	01.0	57 17.3	5.4	19 08.4	0.9	59.7
	21	135 42.9	. . 01.8	71 41.7	5.4	19 07.5	1.0	59.7
	22	150 43.0	02.5	86 06.1	5.5	19 06.5	1.2	59.7
	23	165 43.0	03.3	100 30.6	5.5	N19 05.3	1.3	59.7
		SD 15.9	*d* 0.8	SD 16.6		16.5		16.3

Lat.	Twilight Naut.	Twilight Civil	Sunrise	Moonrise 28	Moonrise 29	Moonrise 30	Moonrise 1
°	h m	h m	h m	h m	h m	h m	h m
N 72	////	////	02 07	03 46	03 16	□	□
N 70	////	////	02 42	04 21	04 28	04 53	05 59
68	////	01 25	03 06	04 46	05 06	05 44	06 49
66	////	02 06	03 25	05 05	05 33	06 16	07 20
64	////	02 34	03 40	05 21	05 53	06 40	07 43
62	01 15	02 54	03 52	05 34	06 10	06 59	08 02
60	01 52	03 11	04 03	05 45	06 24	07 14	08 17
N 58	02 18	03 25	04 12	05 55	06 36	07 27	08 30
56	02 37	03 37	04 20	06 04	06 46	07 39	08 41
54	02 53	03 47	04 28	06 11	06 56	07 49	08 51
52	03 06	03 56	04 34	06 18	07 04	07 58	08 59
50	03 18	04 04	04 40	06 24	07 11	08 06	09 07
45	03 40	04 20	04 52	06 38	07 27	08 23	09 24
N 40	03 58	04 33	05 03	06 49	07 40	08 37	09 38
35	04 12	04 44	05 11	06 58	07 51	08 49	09 49
30	04 24	04 54	05 19	07 07	08 01	08 59	09 59
20	04 42	05 09	05 32	07 21	08 18	09 17	10 17
N 10	04 56	05 22	05 43	07 34	08 33	09 33	10 32
0	05 08	05 33	05 54	07 46	08 47	09 47	10 46
S 10	05 18	05 43	06 04	07 58	09 01	10 02	11 00
20	05 26	05 53	06 15	08 11	09 15	10 17	11 16
30	05 35	06 03	06 28	08 26	09 33	10 36	11 33
35	05 39	06 09	06 35	08 35	09 43	10 46	11 43
40	05 43	06 15	06 43	08 45	09 54	10 58	11 55
45	05 47	06 22	06 52	08 56	10 08	11 12	12 09
S 50	05 52	06 30	07 04	09 11	10 24	11 30	12 25
52	05 53	06 33	07 09	09 17	10 32	11 38	12 33
54	05 55	06 37	07 15	09 25	10 41	11 47	12 42
56	05 57	06 41	07 21	09 33	10 50	11 57	12 51
58	06 00	06 46	07 28	09 42	11 02	12 09	13 03
S 60	06 02	06 51	07 37	09 53	11 14	12 23	13 15

Lat.	Sunset	Twilight Civil	Twilight Naut.	Moonset 28	Moonset 29	Moonset 30	Moonset 1
°	h m	h m	h m	h m	h m	h m	h m
N 72	21 54	////	////	25 36	01 36	□	□
N 70	21 17	////	////	24 25	00 25	02 08	03 06
68	20 52	22 37	////	23 48	25 17	01 17	02 16
66	20 33	21 53	////	23 22	24 45	00 45	01 45
64	20 17	21 24	////	23 01	24 21	00 21	01 21
62	20 04	21 03	22 47	22 45	24 02	00 02	01 03
60	19 53	20 46	22 07	22 32	23 47	24 47	00 47
N 58	19 44	20 32	21 40	22 20	23 34	24 34	00 34
56	19 36	20 20	21 20	22 10	23 22	24 23	00 23
54	19 28	20 09	21 04	22 01	23 12	24 13	00 13
52	19 22	20 00	20 50	21 53	23 04	24 04	00 04
50	19 16	19 52	20 39	21 46	22 56	23 56	24 47
45	19 03	19 35	20 15	21 30	22 39	23 39	24 32
N 40	18 53	19 22	19 58	21 18	22 25	23 26	24 19
35	18 44	19 11	19 43	21 07	22 13	23 14	24 08
30	18 36	19 01	19 32	20 58	22 03	23 03	23 58
20	18 23	18 46	19 13	20 42	21 45	22 46	23 42
N 10	18 11	18 33	18 59	20 28	21 30	22 30	23 27
0	18 01	18 22	18 47	20 15	21 15	22 16	23 14
S 10	17 50	18 12	18 37	20 02	21 01	22 01	23 00
20	17 39	18 02	18 28	19 48	20 46	21 45	22 45
30	17 27	17 51	18 20	19 32	20 28	21 27	22 28
35	17 19	17 45	18 15	19 22	20 18	21 17	22 18
40	17 11	17 39	18 11	19 12	20 06	21 05	22 07
45	17 02	17 32	18 07	18 59	19 52	20 51	21 54
S 50	16 50	17 24	18 02	18 44	19 35	20 33	21 38
52	16 45	17 21	18 00	18 37	19 27	20 25	21 30
54	16 39	17 17	17 58	18 30	19 18	20 16	21 22
56	16 33	17 12	17 56	18 21	19 08	20 06	21 12
58	16 25	17 08	17 54	18 11	18 57	19 54	21 01
S 60	16 17	17 02	17 52	18 00	18 44	19 41	20 49

Day	SUN Eqn. of Time 00^h	SUN Eqn. of Time 12^h	SUN Mer. Pass.	MOON Mer. Pass. Upper	MOON Mer. Pass. Lower	MOON Age	MOON Phase
d	m s	m s	h m	h m	h m	d %	
28	02 28	02 33	11 57	14 00	01 30	02 6	
29	02 37	02 41	11 57	15 01	02 31	03 13	
30	02 45	02 49	11 57	16 01	03 31	04 22	

UT	ARIES	VENUS −4·7		MARS +1·6		JUPITER −2·4		SATURN +0·2	
d h	GHA ° ′	GHA ° ′	Dec ° ′	GHA ° ′	Dec ° ′	GHA ° ′	Dec ° ′	GHA ° ′	Dec ° ′
1 00 (MONDAY)	219 06.8	218 33.3	N 1 37.9	154 29.7	N22 03.2	24 16.5	S 4 39.3	312 01.3	S22 02.5
01	234 09.3	233 34.4	38.0	169 30.4	03.5	39 19.2	39.2	327 03.9	02.5
02	249 11.7	248 35.6	38.1	184 31.0	03.9	54 22.0	39.1	342 06.4	02.5
03	264 14.2	263 36.7	. . 38.2	199 31.6	. . 04.2	69 24.7	. . 39.1	357 09.0	. . 02.5
04	279 16.6	278 37.8	38.3	214 32.3	04.5	84 27.4	39.0	12 11.6	02.5
05	294 19.1	293 38.9	38.4	229 32.9	04.8	99 30.1	38.9	27 14.1	02.5
06	309 21.6	308 40.1	N 1 38.6	244 33.6	N22 05.1	114 32.8	S 4 38.8	42 16.7	S22 02.5
07	324 24.0	323 41.2	38.7	259 34.2	05.4	129 35.5	38.7	57 19.3	02.5
08	339 26.5	338 42.3	38.8	274 34.9	05.7	144 38.2	38.6	72 21.8	02.5
09	354 29.0	353 43.4	. . 38.9	289 35.5	. . 06.0	159 40.9	. . 38.5	87 24.4	. . 02.5
10	9 31.4	8 44.6	39.0	304 36.1	06.3	174 43.6	38.4	102 27.0	02.5
11	24 33.9	23 45.7	39.1	319 36.8	06.6	189 46.4	38.3	117 29.6	02.5
12	39 36.4	38 46.8	N 1 39.3	334 37.4	N22 07.0	204 49.1	S 4 38.2	132 32.1	S22 02.5
13	54 38.8	53 47.9	39.4	349 38.1	07.3	219 51.8	38.1	147 34.7	02.5
14	69 41.3	68 49.0	39.5	4 38.7	07.6	234 54.5	38.0	162 37.3	02.5
15	84 43.7	83 50.1	. . 39.7	19 39.4	. . 07.9	249 57.2	. . 37.9	177 39.8	. . 02.5
16	99 46.2	98 51.2	39.8	34 40.0	08.2	264 59.9	37.8	192 42.4	02.5
17	114 48.7	113 52.3	39.9	49 40.7	08.5	280 02.6	37.7	207 45.0	02.5
18	129 51.1	128 53.4	N 1 40.0	64 41.3	N22 08.8	295 05.3	S 4 37.6	222 47.5	S22 02.5
19	144 53.6	143 54.5	40.2	79 41.9	09.1	310 08.0	37.5	237 50.1	02.5
20	159 56.1	158 55.6	40.3	94 42.6	09.4	325 10.7	37.4	252 52.7	02.5
21	174 58.5	173 56.7	. . 40.4	109 43.2	. . 09.7	340 13.4	. . 37.3	267 55.3	. . 02.4
22	190 01.0	188 57.8	40.6	124 43.9	10.0	355 16.1	37.2	282 57.8	02.4
23	205 03.5	203 58.9	40.7	139 44.5	10.3	10 18.9	37.2	298 00.4	02.4
2 00 (TUESDAY)	220 05.9	219 00.0	N 1 40.9	154 45.2	N22 10.6	25 21.6	S 4 37.1	313 03.0	S22 02.4
01	235 08.4	234 01.1	41.0	169 45.8	10.9	40 24.3	37.0	328 05.5	02.4
02	250 10.9	249 02.2	41.1	184 46.4	11.2	55 27.0	36.9	343 08.1	02.4
03	265 13.3	264 03.3	. . 41.3	199 47.1	. . 11.5	70 29.7	. . 36.8	358 10.7	. . 02.4
04	280 15.8	279 04.3	41.4	214 47.7	11.8	85 32.4	36.7	13 13.3	02.4
05	295 18.2	294 05.4	41.6	229 48.4	12.1	100 35.1	36.6	28 15.8	02.4
06	310 20.7	309 06.5	N 1 41.7	244 49.0	N22 12.4	115 37.8	S 4 36.5	43 18.4	S22 02.4
07	325 23.2	324 07.6	41.9	259 49.7	12.7	130 40.5	36.4	58 21.0	02.4
08	340 25.6	339 08.6	42.0	274 50.3	13.0	145 43.2	36.3	73 23.6	02.4
09	355 28.1	354 09.7	. . 42.2	289 50.9	. . 13.3	160 45.9	. . 36.2	88 26.1	. . 02.4
10	10 30.6	9 10.8	42.3	304 51.6	13.6	175 48.6	36.1	103 28.7	02.4
11	25 33.0	24 11.9	42.5	319 52.2	13.9	190 51.3	36.0	118 31.3	02.4
12	40 35.5	39 12.9	N 1 42.7	334 52.9	N22 14.2	205 54.0	S 4 35.9	133 33.8	S22 02.4
13	55 38.0	54 14.0	42.8	349 53.5	14.5	220 56.7	35.8	148 36.4	02.4
14	70 40.4	69 15.0	43.0	4 54.2	14.8	235 59.5	35.8	163 39.0	02.4
15	85 42.9	84 16.1	. . 43.1	19 54.8	. . 15.1	251 02.2	. . 35.7	178 41.6	. . 02.4
16	100 45.4	99 17.2	43.3	34 55.4	15.4	266 04.9	35.6	193 44.1	02.4
17	115 47.8	114 18.2	43.5	49 56.1	15.7	281 07.6	35.5	208 46.7	02.4
18	130 50.3	129 19.3	N 1 43.6	64 56.7	N22 16.0	296 10.3	S 4 35.4	223 49.3	S22 02.4
19	145 52.7	144 20.3	43.8	79 57.4	16.3	311 13.0	35.3	238 51.9	02.4
20	160 55.2	159 21.4	44.0	94 58.0	16.6	326 15.7	35.2	253 54.4	02.4
21	175 57.7	174 22.4	. . 44.1	109 58.7	. . 16.9	341 18.4	. . 35.1	268 57.0	. . 02.4
22	191 00.1	189 23.5	44.3	124 59.3	17.2	356 21.1	35.0	283 59.6	02.4
23	206 02.6	204 24.5	44.5	139 59.9	17.5	11 23.8	34.9	299 02.2	02.4
3 00 (WEDNESDAY)	221 05.1	219 25.5	N 1 44.6	155 00.6	N22 17.8	26 26.5	S 4 34.8	314 04.7	S22 02.4
01	236 07.5	234 26.6	44.8	170 01.2	18.1	41 29.2	34.7	329 07.3	02.4
02	251 10.0	249 27.6	45.0	185 01.9	18.4	56 31.9	34.6	344 09.9	02.3
03	266 12.5	264 28.7	. . 45.2	200 02.5	. . 18.7	71 34.6	. . 34.6	359 12.5	. . 02.3
04	281 14.9	279 29.7	45.3	215 03.1	19.0	86 37.3	34.5	14 15.0	02.3
05	296 17.4	294 30.7	45.5	230 03.8	19.3	101 40.0	34.4	29 17.6	02.3
06	311 19.9	309 31.7	N 1 45.7	245 04.4	N22 19.6	116 42.7	S 4 34.3	44 20.2	S22 02.3
07	326 22.3	324 32.8	45.9	260 05.1	19.9	131 45.4	34.2	59 22.8	02.3
08	341 24.8	339 33.8	46.1	275 05.7	20.2	146 48.1	34.1	74 25.4	02.3
09	356 27.2	354 34.8	. . 46.3	290 06.4	. . 20.5	161 50.8	. . 34.0	89 27.9	. . 02.3
10	11 29.7	9 35.8	46.4	305 07.0	20.7	176 53.5	33.9	104 30.5	02.3
11	26 32.2	24 36.9	46.6	320 07.6	21.0	191 56.2	33.8	119 33.1	02.3
12	41 34.6	39 37.9	N 1 46.8	335 08.3	N22 21.3	206 58.9	S 4 33.7	134 35.7	S22 02.3
13	56 37.1	54 38.9	47.0	350 08.9	21.6	222 01.6	33.6	149 38.2	02.3
14	71 39.6	69 39.9	47.2	5 09.6	21.9	237 04.3	33.6	164 40.8	02.3
15	86 42.0	84 40.9	. . 47.4	20 10.2	. . 22.2	252 07.0	. . 33.5	179 43.4	. . 02.3
16	101 44.5	99 41.9	47.6	35 10.8	22.5	267 09.7	33.4	194 46.0	02.3
17	116 47.0	114 42.9	47.8	50 11.5	22.8	282 12.4	33.3	209 48.6	02.3
18	131 49.4	129 43.9	N 1 48.0	65 12.1	N22 23.1	297 15.1	S 4 33.2	224 51.1	S22 02.3
19	146 51.9	144 44.9	48.2	80 12.8	23.4	312 17.8	33.1	239 53.7	02.3
20	161 54.3	159 46.0	48.4	95 13.4	23.6	327 20.5	33.0	254 56.3	02.3
21	176 56.8	174 47.0	. . 48.6	110 14.1	. . 23.9	342 23.2	. . 32.9	269 58.9	. . 02.3
22	191 59.3	189 47.9	48.8	125 14.7	24.2	357 25.9	32.8	285 01.4	02.3
23	207 01.7	204 48.9	49.0	140 15.3	24.5	12 28.6	32.7	300 04.0	02.3
Mer. Pass.	h m 9 18.1	v 1.1	d 0.2	v 0.6	d 0.3	v 2.7	d 0.1	v 2.6	d 0.0

STARS

Name	SHA ° ′	Dec ° ′
Acamar	315 16.8	S40 14.4
Achernar	335 25.5	S57 09.0
Acrux	173 05.7	S63 11.8
Adhara	255 10.7	S29 00.1
Aldebaran	290 46.7	N16 32.4
Alioth	166 18.0	N55 52.1
Alkaid	152 56.4	N49 13.8
Al Na'ir	27 40.7	S46 52.4
Alnilam	275 44.0	S 1 11.8
Alphard	217 53.5	S 8 44.2
Alphecca	126 08.5	N26 39.5
Alpheratz	357 41.0	N29 10.9
Altair	62 05.6	N 8 54.9
Ankaa	353 13.5	S42 12.7
Antares	112 22.7	S26 28.0
Arcturus	145 53.1	N19 05.6
Atria	107 21.7	S69 03.2
Avior	234 17.0	S59 34.3
Bellatrix	278 29.5	N 6 21.6
Betelgeuse	270 58.7	N 7 24.3
Canopus	263 55.3	S52 42.7
Capella	280 31.0	N46 00.7
Deneb	49 29.6	N45 20.3
Denebola	182 30.8	N14 28.5
Diphda	348 53.6	S17 53.6
Dubhe	193 48.3	N61 39.7
Elnath	278 09.6	N28 37.1
Eltanin	90 44.6	N51 29.1
Enif	33 44.6	N 9 57.2
Fomalhaut	15 21.3	S29 31.8
Gacrux	171 57.4	S57 12.7
Gienah	175 49.3	S17 38.4
Hadar	148 43.4	S60 27.3
Hamal	327 58.1	N23 32.4
Kaus Aust.	83 40.1	S34 22.3
Kochab	137 19.1	N74 05.2
Markab	13 35.9	N15 17.7
Menkar	314 12.7	N 4 09.2
Menkent	148 04.1	S36 27.3
Miaplacidus	221 38.9	S69 47.7
Mirfak	308 37.1	N49 55.1
Nunki	75 54.9	S26 16.3
Peacock	53 15.2	S56 40.4
Pollux	243 24.7	N27 58.9
Procyon	244 57.1	N 5 10.6
Rasalhague	96 03.8	N12 32.9
Regulus	207 40.7	N11 52.9
Rigel	281 09.8	S 8 11.2
Rigil Kent.	139 47.4	S60 54.3
Sabik	102 09.3	S15 44.6
Schedar	349 37.9	N56 37.6
Shaula	96 18.1	S37 06.7
Sirius	258 31.6	S16 44.8
Spica	158 28.2	S11 15.1
Suhail	222 50.5	S43 30.5
Vega	80 37.0	N38 47.9
Zuben'ubi	137 02.2	S16 06.7

	SHA ° ′	Mer. Pass. h m
Venus	358 54.1	9 23
Mars	294 39.2	13 40
Jupiter	165 15.6	22 15
Saturn	92 57.0	3 07

UT (d h)	SUN GHA	SUN Dec	MOON GHA	v	MOON Dec	d	HP
	° ′	° ′	° ′	′	° ′	′	′
1 00	180 43.1	N15 04.0	114 55.1	5.6	N19 04.0	1.4	59.6
01	195 43.2	04.8	129 19.7	5.7	19 02.6	1.6	59.6
02	210 43.3	05.6	143 44.4	5.7	19 01.0	1.6	59.6
03	225 43.3	. . 06.3	158 09.1	5.7	18 59.4	1.8	59.5
04	240 43.4	07.1	172 33.8	5.9	18 57.6	2.0	59.5
05	255 43.5	07.8	186 58.7	5.8	18 55.6	2.0	59.5
06	270 43.6	N15 08.6	201 23.5	5.9	N18 53.6	2.2	59.4
07	285 43.6	09.3	215 48.4	6.0	18 51.4	2.3	59.4
08	300 43.7	10.1	230 13.4	6.1	18 49.1	2.4	59.4
M 09	315 43.8	. . 10.8	244 38.5	6.1	18 46.7	2.5	59.3
O 10	330 43.9	11.6	259 03.6	6.1	18 44.2	2.7	59.3
N 11	345 43.9	12.3	273 28.7	6.2	18 41.5	2.8	59.3
D 12	0 44.0	N15 13.1	287 53.9	6.3	N18 38.7	2.9	59.3
A 13	15 44.1	13.8	302 19.2	6.4	18 35.8	3.0	59.2
Y 14	30 44.1	14.6	316 44.6	6.4	18 32.8	3.1	59.2
15	45 44.2	. . 15.3	331 10.0	6.4	18 29.7	3.3	59.2
16	60 44.3	16.1	345 35.4	6.6	18 26.4	3.3	59.1
17	75 44.4	16.8	0 01.0	6.6	18 23.1	3.5	59.1
18	90 44.4	N15 17.6	14 26.6	6.7	N18 19.6	3.6	59.1
19	105 44.5	18.3	28 52.3	6.7	18 16.0	3.7	59.0
20	120 44.6	19.1	43 18.0	6.8	18 12.3	3.8	59.0
21	135 44.6	. . 19.8	57 43.8	6.9	18 08.5	3.9	59.0
22	150 44.7	20.6	72 09.7	6.9	18 04.6	4.1	58.9
23	165 44.8	21.3	86 35.6	7.1	18 00.5	4.1	58.9
2 00	180 44.9	N15 22.1	101 01.7	7.0	N17 56.4	4.3	58.9
01	195 44.9	22.8	115 27.7	7.2	17 52.1	4.3	58.8
02	210 45.0	23.6	129 53.9	7.2	17 47.8	4.5	58.8
03	225 45.1	. . 24.3	144 20.1	7.3	17 43.3	4.6	58.8
04	240 45.1	25.1	158 46.4	7.4	17 38.7	4.6	58.7
05	255 45.2	25.8	173 12.8	7.4	17 34.1	4.8	58.7
06	270 45.3	N15 26.5	187 39.2	7.6	N17 29.3	4.9	58.7
07	285 45.3	27.3	202 05.8	7.6	17 24.4	5.0	58.6
T 08	300 45.4	28.0	216 32.4	7.6	17 19.4	5.1	58.6
U 09	315 45.5	. . 28.8	230 59.0	7.8	17 14.3	5.1	58.6
E 10	330 45.5	29.5	245 25.8	7.8	17 09.2	5.3	58.5
S 11	345 45.6	30.3	259 52.6	7.9	17 03.9	5.4	58.5
D 12	0 45.7	N15 31.0	274 19.5	7.9	N16 58.5	5.5	58.5
A 13	15 45.7	31.7	288 46.4	8.1	16 53.0	5.5	58.4
Y 14	30 45.8	32.5	303 13.5	8.1	16 47.5	5.7	58.4
15	45 45.9	. . 33.2	317 40.6	8.2	16 41.8	5.8	58.4
16	60 45.9	34.0	332 07.8	8.3	16 36.0	5.8	58.3
17	75 46.0	34.7	346 35.1	8.3	16 30.2	6.0	58.3
18	90 46.1	N15 35.4	1 02.4	8.4	N16 24.2	6.0	58.3
19	105 46.1	36.2	15 29.8	8.5	16 18.2	6.1	58.2
20	120 46.2	36.9	29 57.3	8.6	16 12.1	6.2	58.2
21	135 46.3	. . 37.6	44 24.9	8.6	16 05.9	6.3	58.2
22	150 46.3	38.4	58 52.5	8.8	15 59.6	6.4	58.1
23	165 46.4	39.1	73 20.3	8.8	15 53.2	6.5	58.1
3 00	180 46.5	N15 39.9	87 48.1	8.8	N15 46.7	6.5	58.1
01	195 46.5	40.6	102 15.9	9.0	15 40.2	6.6	58.0
02	210 46.6	41.3	116 43.9	9.0	15 33.6	6.8	58.0
03	225 46.7	. . 42.1	131 11.9	9.1	15 26.8	6.7	58.0
04	240 46.7	42.8	145 40.0	9.2	15 20.1	6.9	57.9
05	255 46.8	43.5	160 08.2	9.2	15 13.2	7.0	57.9
06	270 46.9	N15 44.3	174 36.4	9.4	N15 06.2	7.0	57.9
W 07	285 46.9	45.0	189 04.8	9.4	14 59.2	7.1	57.9
E 08	300 47.0	45.7	203 33.2	9.5	14 52.1	7.2	57.8
D 09	315 47.0	. . 46.5	218 01.7	9.5	14 44.9	7.3	57.8
N 10	330 47.1	47.2	232 30.2	9.7	14 37.6	7.3	57.8
E 11	345 47.2	47.9	246 58.9	9.7	14 30.3	7.4	57.7
S 12	0 47.2	N15 48.6	261 27.6	9.7	N14 22.9	7.5	57.7
D 13	15 47.3	49.4	275 56.3	9.9	14 15.4	7.5	57.7
A 14	30 47.3	50.1	290 25.2	9.9	14 07.9	7.6	57.6
Y 15	45 47.4	. . 50.8	304 54.1	10.0	14 00.3	7.7	57.6
16	60 47.5	51.6	319 23.1	10.1	13 52.6	7.8	57.6
17	75 47.5	52.3	333 52.2	10.1	13 44.8	7.8	57.5
18	90 47.6	N15 53.0	348 21.3	10.3	N13 37.0	7.9	57.5
19	105 47.6	53.7	2 50.6	10.2	13 29.1	7.9	57.5
20	120 47.7	54.5	17 19.8	10.4	13 21.2	8.0	57.4
21	135 47.8	. . 55.2	31 49.2	10.4	13 13.2	8.1	57.4
22	150 47.8	55.9	46 18.6	10.6	13 05.1	8.1	57.4
23	165 47.9	56.7	60 48.2	10.5	N12 57.0	8.2	57.3
	SD 15.9	*d* 0.7	SD	16.1	15.9		15.7

Lat.	Twilight Naut.	Twilight Civil	Sunrise	Moonrise 1	Moonrise 2	Moonrise 3	Moonrise 4
°	h m	h m	h m	h m	h m	h m	h m
N 72	////	////	01 42	□	06 37	08 54	10 51
N 70	////	////	02 24	05 59	07 40	09 27	11 11
68	////	00 53	02 52	06 49	08 15	09 50	11 26
66	////	01 48	03 13	07 20	08 40	10 09	11 38
64	////	02 20	03 30	07 43	09 00	10 23	11 49
62	00 47	02 43	03 43	08 02	09 16	10 36	11 57
60	01 36	03 01	03 55	08 17	09 29	10 46	12 05
N 58	02 05	03 16	04 05	08 30	09 40	10 55	12 11
56	02 27	03 29	04 14	08 41	09 50	11 03	12 17
54	02 44	03 40	04 21	08 51	09 59	11 10	12 22
52	02 58	03 49	04 28	08 59	10 07	11 16	12 27
50	03 11	03 58	04 34	09 07	10 14	11 22	12 31
45	03 35	04 15	04 48	09 24	10 29	11 34	12 40
N 40	03 54	04 29	04 59	09 38	10 41	11 45	12 48
35	04 08	04 41	05 08	09 49	10 51	11 53	12 54
30	04 21	04 51	05 16	09 59	11 00	12 01	13 00
20	04 40	05 07	05 30	10 17	11 16	12 14	13 10
N 10	04 55	05 20	05 42	10 32	11 30	12 25	13 18
0	05 07	05 32	05 54	10 46	11 43	12 36	13 26
S 10	05 18	05 43	06 05	11 00	11 55	12 47	13 34
20	05 27	05 54	06 16	11 16	12 09	12 58	13 43
30	05 36	06 05	06 30	11 33	12 25	13 11	13 52
35	05 41	06 11	06 37	11 43	12 34	13 18	13 58
40	05 46	06 18	06 46	11 55	12 44	13 27	14 04
45	05 50	06 25	06 56	12 09	12 56	13 37	14 12
S 50	05 56	06 34	07 08	12 25	13 11	13 49	14 21
52	05 58	06 38	07 14	12 33	13 18	13 54	14 25
54	06 00	06 42	07 20	12 42	13 25	14 00	14 29
56	06 02	06 47	07 27	12 51	13 34	14 07	14 34
58	06 05	06 52	07 35	13 03	13 43	14 15	14 39
S 60	06 08	06 58	07 44	13 15	13 54	14 23	14 46

Lat.	Sunset	Twilight Civil	Twilight Naut.	Moonset 1	Moonset 2	Moonset 3	Moonset 4
°	h m	h m	h m	h m	h m	h m	h m
N 72	22 19	////	////	□	04 28	04 04	03 52
N 70	21 34	////	////	03 06	03 25	03 30	03 32
68	21 05	23 15	////	02 16	02 49	03 06	03 15
66	20 44	22 11	////	01 45	02 23	02 47	03 02
64	20 27	21 38	////	01 21	02 03	02 31	02 51
62	20 13	21 14	23 20	01 03	01 47	02 18	02 41
60	20 01	20 55	22 23	00 47	01 33	02 07	02 33
N 58	19 51	20 40	21 52	00 34	01 22	01 58	02 26
56	19 42	20 27	21 30	00 23	01 11	01 49	02 19
54	19 34	20 16	21 12	00 13	01 02	01 42	02 13
52	19 27	20 06	20 57	00 04	00 54	01 35	02 08
50	19 20	19 57	20 45	24 47	00 47	01 29	02 04
45	19 07	19 40	20 20	24 32	00 32	01 16	01 53
N 40	18 56	19 25	20 01	24 19	00 19	01 05	01 45
35	18 46	19 14	19 46	24 08	00 08	00 55	01 37
30	18 38	19 04	19 34	23 58	24 47	00 47	01 31
20	18 24	18 47	19 14	23 42	24 33	00 33	01 20
N 10	18 12	18 34	18 59	23 27	24 20	00 20	01 10
0	18 00	18 22	18 47	23 14	24 09	00 09	01 00
S 10	17 49	18 11	18 36	23 00	23 57	24 51	00 51
20	17 37	18 00	18 26	22 45	23 44	24 41	00 41
30	17 24	17 49	18 17	22 28	23 29	24 29	00 29
35	17 16	17 43	18 13	22 18	23 21	24 22	00 22
40	17 07	17 36	18 08	22 07	23 11	24 15	00 15
45	16 57	17 28	18 03	21 54	23 00	24 06	00 06
S 50	16 45	17 19	17 58	21 38	22 46	23 55	25 03
52	16 39	17 15	17 55	21 30	22 39	23 50	25 00
54	16 33	17 11	17 53	21 22	22 32	23 44	24 56
56	16 26	17 06	17 51	21 12	22 24	23 38	24 52
58	16 18	17 01	17 48	21 01	22 15	23 31	24 47
S 60	16 09	16 55	17 45	20 49	22 04	23 23	24 42

Day	SUN Eqn. of Time 00^h	SUN Eqn. of Time 12^h	SUN Mer. Pass.	MOON Mer. Pass. Upper	MOON Mer. Pass. Lower	MOON Age	MOON Phase
d	m s	m s	h m	h m	h m	d %	
1	02 52	02 56	11 57	17 00	04 31	05 32	
2	02 59	03 03	11 57	17 56	05 28	06 43	◑
3	03 06	03 09	11 57	18 48	06 22	07 54	

UT d h		ARIES GHA ° ′	VENUS −4·7 GHA ° ′	Dec ° ′	MARS +1·6 GHA ° ′	Dec ° ′	JUPITER −2·4 GHA ° ′	Dec ° ′	SATURN +0·2 GHA ° ′	Dec ° ′
4 00		222 04.2	219 49.9	N 1 49.2	155 16.0	N22 24.8	27 31.3	S 4 32.7	315 06.6	S22 02.3
01		237 06.7	234 50.9	49.4	170 16.6	25.1	42 34.0	32.6	330 09.2	02.3
02		252 09.1	249 51.9	49.6	185 17.3	25.4	57 36.7	32.5	345 11.8	02.3
03		267 11.6	264 52.9	. . 49.8	200 17.9	. . 25.7	72 39.4	. . 32.4	0 14.3	. . 02.3
04		282 14.1	279 53.9	50.0	215 18.5	25.9	87 42.1	32.3	15 16.9	02.3
05		297 16.5	294 54.9	50.2	230 19.2	26.2	102 44.8	32.2	30 19.5	02.3
06		312 19.0	309 55.9	N 1 50.4	245 19.8	N22 26.5	117 47.5	S 4 32.1	45 22.1	S22 02.3
07		327 21.5	324 56.8	50.6	260 20.5	26.8	132 50.2	32.0	60 24.7	02.2
08	T	342 23.9	339 57.8	50.9	275 21.1	27.1	147 52.9	31.9	75 27.2	02.2
09	H	357 26.4	354 58.8	. . 51.1	290 21.7	. . 27.4	162 55.6	. . 31.8	90 29.8	. . 02.2
10	U	12 28.8	9 59.8	51.3	305 22.4	27.6	177 58.3	31.8	105 32.4	02.2
11	R	27 31.3	25 00.8	51.5	320 23.0	27.9	193 01.0	31.7	120 35.0	02.2
12	S	42 33.8	40 01.7	N 1 51.7	335 23.7	N22 28.2	208 03.7	S 4 31.6	135 37.6	S22 02.2
13	D	57 36.2	55 02.7	52.0	350 24.3	28.5	223 06.4	31.5	150 40.2	02.2
14	A	72 38.7	70 03.7	52.2	5 24.9	28.8	238 09.1	31.4	165 42.7	02.2
15	Y	87 41.2	85 04.6	. . 52.4	20 25.6	. . 29.1	253 11.8	. . 31.3	180 45.3	. . 02.2
16		102 43.6	100 05.6	52.6	35 26.2	29.3	268 14.5	31.2	195 47.9	02.2
17		117 46.1	115 06.6	52.9	50 26.9	29.6	283 17.1	31.1	210 50.5	02.2
18		132 48.6	130 07.5	N 1 53.1	65 27.5	N22 29.9	298 19.8	S 4 31.0	225 53.1	S22 02.2
19		147 51.0	145 08.5	53.3	80 28.1	30.2	313 22.5	31.0	240 55.6	02.2
20		162 53.5	160 09.4	53.5	95 28.8	30.5	328 25.2	30.9	255 58.2	02.2
21		177 56.0	175 10.4	. . 53.8	110 29.4	. . 30.7	343 27.9	. . 30.8	271 00.8	. . 02.2
22		192 58.4	190 11.3	54.0	125 30.1	31.0	358 30.6	30.7	286 03.4	02.2
23		208 00.9	205 12.3	54.2	140 30.7	31.3	13 33.3	30.6	301 06.0	02.2
5 00		223 03.3	220 13.2	N 1 54.5	155 31.3	N22 31.6	28 36.0	S 4 30.5	316 08.6	S22 02.2
01		238 05.8	235 14.2	54.7	170 32.0	31.9	43 38.7	30.4	331 11.1	02.2
02		253 08.3	250 15.1	54.9	185 32.6	32.1	58 41.4	30.3	346 13.7	02.2
03		268 10.7	265 16.1	. . 55.2	200 33.3	. . 32.4	73 44.1	. . 30.3	1 16.3	. . 02.2
04		283 13.2	280 17.0	55.4	215 33.9	32.7	88 46.8	30.2	16 18.9	02.2
05		298 15.7	295 18.0	55.7	230 34.5	33.0	103 49.5	30.1	31 21.5	02.2
06		313 18.1	310 18.9	N 1 55.9	245 35.2	N22 33.2	118 52.2	S 4 30.0	46 24.1	S22 02.2
07		328 20.6	325 19.8	56.1	260 35.8	33.5	133 54.9	29.9	61 26.6	02.2
08		343 23.1	340 20.8	56.4	275 36.5	33.8	148 57.5	29.8	76 29.2	02.2
09	F	358 25.5	355 21.7	. . 56.6	290 37.1	. . 34.1	164 00.2	. . 29.7	91 31.8	. . 02.2
10	R	13 28.0	10 22.6	56.9	305 37.7	34.4	179 02.9	29.6	106 34.4	02.2
11	I	28 30.4	25 23.6	57.1	320 38.4	34.6	194 05.6	29.6	121 37.0	02.2
12	D	43 32.9	40 24.5	N 1 57.4	335 39.0	N22 34.9	209 08.3	S 4 29.5	136 39.6	S22 02.1
13	A	58 35.4	55 25.4	57.6	350 39.6	35.2	224 11.0	29.4	151 42.1	02.1
14	Y	73 37.8	70 26.3	57.9	5 40.3	35.4	239 13.7	29.3	166 44.7	02.1
15		88 40.3	85 27.3	. . 58.1	20 40.9	. . 35.7	254 16.4	. . 29.2	181 47.3	. . 02.1
16		103 42.8	100 28.2	58.4	35 41.6	36.0	269 19.1	29.1	196 49.9	02.1
17		118 45.2	115 29.1	58.7	50 42.2	36.3	284 21.8	29.0	211 52.5	02.1
18		133 47.7	130 30.0	N 1 58.9	65 42.8	N22 36.5	299 24.5	S 4 29.0	226 55.1	S22 02.1
19		148 50.2	145 30.9	59.2	80 43.5	36.8	314 27.1	28.9	241 57.7	02.1
20		163 52.6	160 31.9	59.4	95 44.1	37.1	329 29.8	28.8	257 00.2	02.1
21		178 55.1	175 32.8	1 59.7	110 44.8	. . 37.4	344 32.5	. . 28.7	272 02.8	. . 02.1
22		193 57.6	190 33.7	2 00.0	125 45.4	37.6	359 35.2	28.6	287 05.4	02.1
23		209 00.0	205 34.6	00.2	140 46.0	37.9	14 37.9	28.5	302 08.0	02.1
6 00		224 02.5	220 35.5	N 2 00.5	155 46.7	N22 38.2	29 40.6	S 4 28.4	317 10.6	S22 02.1
01		239 04.9	235 36.4	00.7	170 47.3	38.4	44 43.3	28.4	332 13.2	02.1
02		254 07.4	250 37.3	01.0	185 48.0	38.7	59 46.0	28.3	347 15.8	02.1
03		269 09.9	265 38.2	. . 01.3	200 48.6	. . 39.0	74 48.7	. . 28.2	2 18.3	. . 02.1
04		284 12.3	280 39.1	01.6	215 49.2	39.2	89 51.3	28.1	17 20.9	02.1
05		299 14.8	295 40.0	01.8	230 49.9	39.5	104 54.0	28.0	32 23.5	02.1
06		314 17.3	310 40.9	N 2 02.1	245 50.5	N22 39.8	119 56.7	S 4 27.9	47 26.1	S22 02.1
07		329 19.7	325 41.8	02.4	260 51.1	40.0	134 59.4	27.8	62 28.7	02.1
08	S	344 22.2	340 42.7	02.6	275 51.8	40.3	150 02.1	27.8	77 31.3	02.1
09	A	359 24.7	355 43.6	. . 02.9	290 52.4	. . 40.6	165 04.8	. . 27.7	92 33.9	. . 02.1
10	T	14 27.1	10 44.5	03.2	305 53.1	40.9	180 07.5	27.6	107 36.5	02.1
11	U	29 29.6	25 45.4	03.5	320 53.7	41.1	195 10.2	27.5	122 39.0	02.1
12	R	44 32.0	40 46.2	N 2 03.8	335 54.3	N22 41.4	210 12.8	S 4 27.4	137 41.6	S22 02.1
13	D	59 34.5	55 47.1	04.0	350 55.0	41.6	225 15.5	27.3	152 44.2	02.1
14	A	74 37.0	70 48.0	04.3	5 55.6	41.9	240 18.2	27.3	167 46.8	02.1
15	Y	89 39.4	85 48.9	. . 04.6	20 56.3	. . 42.2	255 20.9	. . 27.2	182 49.4	. . 02.1
16		104 41.9	100 49.8	04.9	35 56.9	42.4	270 23.6	27.1	197 52.0	02.0
17		119 44.4	115 50.6	05.2	50 57.5	42.7	285 26.3	27.0	212 54.6	02.0
18		134 46.8	130 51.5	N 2 05.4	65 58.2	N22 43.0	300 28.9	S 4 26.9	227 57.2	S22 02.0
19		149 49.3	145 52.4	05.7	80 58.8	43.2	315 31.6	26.8	242 59.8	02.0
20		164 51.8	160 53.3	06.0	95 59.4	43.5	330 34.3	26.8	258 02.3	02.0
21		179 54.2	175 54.1	. . 06.3	111 00.1	. . 43.8	345 37.0	. . 26.7	273 04.9	. . 02.0
22		194 56.7	190 55.0	06.6	126 00.7	44.0	0 39.7	26.6	288 07.5	02.0
23		209 59.2	205 55.9	06.9	141 01.4	44.3	15 42.4	26.5	303 10.1	02.0
Mer. Pass.		h m 9 06.3	*v* 0.9	*d* 0.3	*v* 0.6	*d* 0.3	*v* 2.7	*d* 0.1	*v* 2.6	*d* 0.0

STARS Name	SHA ° ′	Dec ° ′
Acamar	315 16.8	S40 14.4
Achernar	335 25.5	S57 09.0
Acrux	173 05.7	S63 11.9
Adhara	255 10.7	S29 00.1
Aldebaran	290 46.7	N16 32.4
Alioth	166 18.0	N55 52.1
Alkaid	152 56.4	N49 13.8
Al Na'ir	27 40.7	S46 52.4
Alnilam	275 44.0	S 1 11.8
Alphard	217 53.5	S 8 44.2
Alphecca	126 08.5	N26 39.5
Alpheratz	357 41.0	N29 10.9
Altair	62 05.6	N 8 54.9
Ankaa	353 13.5	S42 12.7
Antares	112 22.7	S26 28.0
Arcturus	145 53.1	N19 05.6
Atria	107 21.7	S69 03.2
Avior	234 17.0	S59 34.3
Bellatrix	278 29.5	N 6 21.6
Betelgeuse	270 58.7	N 7 24.3
Canopus	263 55.3	S52 42.7
Capella	280 31.0	N46 00.7
Deneb	49 29.6	N45 20.3
Denebola	182 30.8	N14 28.5
Diphda	348 53.6	S17 53.6
Dubhe	193 48.3	N61 39.7
Elnath	278 09.6	N28 37.1
Eltanin	90 44.5	N51 29.1
Enif	33 44.6	N 9 57.2
Fomalhaut	15 21.3	S29 31.8
Gacrux	171 57.4	S57 12.7
Gienah	175 49.4	S17 38.4
Hadar	148 43.4	S60 27.3
Hamal	327 58.1	N23 32.4
Kaus Aust.	83 40.1	S34 22.3
Kochab	137 19.1	N74 05.2
Markab	13 35.9	N15 17.7
Menkar	314 12.7	N 4 09.2
Menkent	148 04.1	S36 27.3
Miaplacidus	221 39.0	S69 47.7
Mirfak	308 37.1	N49 55.1
Nunki	75 54.9	S26 16.3
Peacock	53 15.1	S56 40.4
Pollux	243 24.7	N27 58.9
Procyon	244 57.2	N 5 10.6
Rasalhague	96 03.8	N12 32.9
Regulus	207 40.7	N11 52.9
Rigel	281 09.8	S 8 11.2
Rigil Kent.	139 47.4	S60 54.3
Sabik	102 09.3	S15 44.6
Schedar	349 37.9	N56 37.6
Shaula	96 18.1	S37 06.7
Sirius	258 31.6	S16 44.7
Spica	158 28.2	S11 15.1
Suhail	222 50.5	S43 30.5
Vega	80 36.9	N38 47.9
Zuben'ubi	137 02.2	S16 06.7

	SHA ° ′	Mer. Pass. h m
Venus	357 09.9	9 19
Mars	292 28.0	13 37
Jupiter	165 32.7	22 02
Saturn	93 05.2	2 55

UT	SUN GHA	SUN Dec	MOON GHA	v	MOON Dec	d	HP
d h	° ′	° ′	° ′	′	° ′	′	′
THURSDAY 4 00	180 47.9	N15 57.4	75 17.7	10.7	N12 48.8	8.3	57.3
01	195 48.0	58.1	89 47.4	10.7	12 40.5	8.3	57.3
02	210 48.1	58.8	104 17.1	10.8	12 32.2	8.4	57.3
03	225 48.1	15 59.5	118 46.9	10.8	12 23.8	8.4	57.2
04	240 48.2	16 00.3	133 16.7	10.9	12 15.4	8.5	57.2
05	255 48.2	01.0	147 46.6	11.0	12 06.9	8.5	57.2
06	270 48.3	N16 01.7	162 16.6	11.1	N11 58.4	8.6	57.1
07	285 48.4	02.4	176 46.7	11.1	11 49.8	8.7	57.1
08	300 48.4	03.2	191 16.8	11.2	11 41.1	8.6	57.1
09	315 48.5	. . 03.9	205 47.0	11.3	11 32.5	8.8	57.0
10	330 48.5	04.6	220 17.3	11.3	11 23.7	8.8	57.0
11	345 48.6	05.3	234 47.6	11.4	11 14.9	8.8	57.0
12	0 48.6	N16 06.0	249 18.0	11.4	N11 06.1	8.9	57.0
13	15 48.7	06.8	263 48.4	11.5	10 57.2	9.0	56.9
14	30 48.7	07.5	278 18.9	11.6	10 48.2	8.9	56.9
15	45 48.8	. . 08.2	292 49.5	11.6	10 39.3	9.1	56.9
16	60 48.9	08.9	307 20.1	11.7	10 30.2	9.0	56.8
17	75 48.9	09.6	321 50.8	11.8	10 21.2	9.2	56.8
18	90 49.0	N16 10.3	336 21.6	11.8	N10 12.0	9.1	56.8
19	105 49.0	11.1	350 52.4	11.9	10 02.9	9.2	56.8
20	120 49.1	11.8	5 23.3	11.9	9 53.7	9.3	56.7
21	135 49.1	. . 12.5	19 54.2	12.0	9 44.4	9.2	56.7
22	150 49.2	13.2	34 25.2	12.1	9 35.2	9.4	56.7
23	165 49.2	13.9	48 56.3	12.1	9 25.8	9.3	56.6
FRIDAY 5 00	180 49.3	N16 14.6	63 27.4	12.2	N 9 16.5	9.4	56.6
01	195 49.3	15.3	77 58.6	12.2	9 07.1	9.4	56.6
02	210 49.4	16.1	92 29.8	12.3	8 57.7	9.5	56.6
03	225 49.4	. . 16.8	107 01.1	12.3	8 48.2	9.5	56.5
04	240 49.5	17.5	121 32.4	12.4	8 38.7	9.5	56.5
05	255 49.6	18.2	136 03.8	12.5	8 29.2	9.6	56.5
06	270 49.6	N16 18.9	150 35.3	12.5	N 8 19.6	9.6	56.4
07	285 49.7	19.6	165 06.8	12.5	8 10.0	9.6	56.4
08	300 49.7	20.3	179 38.3	12.6	8 00.4	9.7	56.4
09	315 49.8	. . 21.0	194 09.9	12.7	7 50.7	9.7	56.4
10	330 49.8	21.7	208 41.6	12.7	7 41.0	9.7	56.3
11	345 49.9	22.4	223 13.3	12.8	7 31.3	9.7	56.3
12	0 49.9	N16 23.2	237 45.1	12.8	N 7 21.6	9.8	56.3
13	15 50.0	23.9	252 16.9	12.8	7 11.8	9.8	56.3
14	30 50.0	24.6	266 48.7	12.9	7 02.0	9.8	56.2
15	45 50.1	. . 25.3	281 20.6	13.0	6 52.2	9.9	56.2
16	60 50.1	26.0	295 52.6	13.0	6 42.3	9.8	56.2
17	75 50.2	26.7	310 24.6	13.0	6 32.5	9.9	56.2
18	90 50.2	N16 27.4	324 56.6	13.1	N 6 22.6	9.9	56.1
19	105 50.3	28.1	339 28.7	13.1	6 12.7	10.0	56.1
20	120 50.3	28.8	354 00.8	13.2	6 02.7	9.9	56.1
21	135 50.4	. . 29.5	8 33.0	13.2	5 52.8	10.0	56.1
22	150 50.4	30.2	23 05.2	13.2	5 42.8	10.0	56.0
23	165 50.5	30.9	37 37.4	13.3	5 32.8	10.0	56.0
SATURDAY 6 00	180 50.5	N16 31.6	52 09.7	13.4	N 5 22.8	10.0	56.0
01	195 50.5	32.3	66 42.1	13.3	5 12.8	10.1	56.0
02	210 50.6	33.0	81 14.4	13.5	5 02.7	10.0	55.9
03	225 50.6	. . 33.7	95 46.9	13.4	4 52.7	10.1	55.9
04	240 50.7	34.4	110 19.3	13.5	4 42.6	10.1	55.9
05	255 50.7	35.1	124 51.8	13.5	4 32.5	10.1	55.9
06	270 50.8	N16 35.8	139 24.3	13.6	N 4 22.4	10.1	55.8
07	285 50.8	36.5	153 56.9	13.6	4 12.3	10.1	55.8
08	300 50.9	37.2	168 29.5	13.6	4 02.2	10.1	55.8
09	315 50.9	. . 37.9	183 02.1	13.7	3 52.1	10.2	55.8
10	330 51.0	38.6	197 34.8	13.7	3 41.9	10.1	55.8
11	345 51.0	39.3	212 07.5	13.7	3 31.8	10.2	55.7
12	0 51.1	N16 40.0	226 40.2	13.8	N 3 21.6	10.2	55.7
13	15 51.1	40.7	241 13.0	13.8	3 11.4	10.1	55.7
14	30 51.1	41.4	255 45.8	13.8	3 01.3	10.2	55.7
15	45 51.2	. . 42.1	270 18.6	13.9	2 51.1	10.2	55.6
16	60 51.2	42.8	284 51.5	13.9	2 40.9	10.2	55.6
17	75 51.3	43.5	299 24.4	13.9	2 30.7	10.2	55.6
18	90 51.3	N16 44.2	313 57.3	13.9	N 2 20.5	10.2	55.6
19	105 51.4	44.9	328 30.2	14.0	2 10.3	10.2	55.6
20	120 51.4	45.6	343 03.2	14.0	2 00.1	10.2	55.5
21	135 51.4	. . 46.2	357 36.2	14.0	1 49.9	10.2	55.5
22	150 51.5	46.9	12 09.2	14.0	1 39.7	10.2	55.5
23	165 51.5	47.6	26 42.2	14.1	N 1 29.5	10.2	55.5
	SD 15.9	*d* 0.7	SD	15.5	15.3		15.2

Lat.	Twilight Naut.	Twilight Civil	Sunrise	Moonrise 4	Moonrise 5	Moonrise 6	Moonrise 7
°	h m	h m	h m	h m	h m	h m	h m
N 72	////	////	01 12	10 51	12 40	14 22	16 02
N 70	////	////	02 06	11 11	12 51	14 27	16 00
68	////	////	02 38	11 26	12 59	14 30	15 58
66	////	01 27	03 01	11 38	13 07	14 33	15 57
64	////	02 05	03 19	11 49	13 13	14 35	15 56
62	////	02 31	03 34	11 57	13 18	14 37	15 55
60	01 18	02 51	03 47	12 05	13 22	14 39	15 54
N 58	01 52	03 08	03 58	12 11	13 26	14 40	15 53
56	02 16	03 21	04 07	12 17	13 30	14 42	15 52
54	02 35	03 33	04 15	12 22	13 33	14 43	15 52
52	02 51	03 43	04 23	12 27	13 36	14 44	15 51
50	03 04	03 52	04 29	12 31	13 39	14 45	15 50
45	03 30	04 11	04 44	12 40	13 44	14 47	15 49
N 40	03 49	04 26	04 55	12 48	13 49	14 49	15 48
35	04 05	04 38	05 05	12 54	13 53	14 51	15 47
30	04 18	04 48	05 14	13 00	13 57	14 52	15 47
20	04 38	05 05	05 29	13 10	14 03	14 55	15 45
N 10	04 54	05 19	05 41	13 18	14 09	14 57	15 44
0	05 07	05 32	05 53	13 26	14 14	14 59	15 43
S 10	05 18	05 43	06 05	13 34	14 19	15 01	15 42
20	05 28	05 55	06 17	13 43	14 24	15 03	15 41
30	05 38	06 07	06 32	13 52	14 30	15 06	15 40
35	05 43	06 13	06 40	13 58	14 34	15 07	15 40
40	05 48	06 20	06 49	14 04	14 38	15 09	15 39
45	05 54	06 29	07 00	14 12	14 43	15 11	15 38
S 50	05 59	06 38	07 13	14 21	14 48	15 13	15 37
52	06 02	06 42	07 19	14 25	14 51	15 14	15 37
54	06 05	06 47	07 25	14 29	14 54	15 15	15 36
56	06 07	06 52	07 33	14 34	14 57	15 17	15 36
58	06 10	06 58	07 41	14 39	15 00	15 18	15 35
S 60	06 14	07 04	07 51	14 46	15 04	15 20	15 34

Lat.	Sunset	Twilight Civil	Twilight Naut.	Moonset 4	Moonset 5	Moonset 6	Moonset 7
°	h m	h m	h m	h m	h m	h m	h m
N 72	22 53	////	////	03 52	03 44	03 36	03 29
N 70	21 53	////	////	03 32	03 31	03 30	03 28
68	21 19	////	////	03 15	03 21	03 24	03 27
66	20 55	22 33	////	03 02	03 12	03 20	03 27
64	20 36	21 52	////	02 51	03 05	03 16	03 26
62	20 21	21 25	////	02 41	02 59	03 13	03 26
60	20 08	21 04	22 42	02 33	02 53	03 10	03 25
N 58	19 57	20 48	22 05	02 26	02 48	03 08	03 25
56	19 48	20 34	21 40	02 19	02 44	03 05	03 25
54	19 39	20 22	21 20	02 13	02 40	03 03	03 24
52	19 32	20 12	21 05	02 08	02 36	03 01	03 24
50	19 25	20 03	20 51	02 04	02 33	03 00	03 24
45	19 11	19 44	20 25	01 53	02 26	02 56	03 23
N 40	18 59	19 29	20 05	01 45	02 20	02 53	03 23
35	18 49	19 16	19 49	01 37	02 15	02 50	03 23
30	18 40	19 06	19 36	01 31	02 11	02 47	03 22
20	18 25	18 48	19 16	01 20	02 03	02 43	03 22
N 10	18 12	18 34	19 00	01 10	01 56	02 39	03 21
0	18 00	18 22	18 47	01 00	01 49	02 36	03 21
S 10	17 48	18 10	18 35	00 51	01 43	02 32	03 20
20	17 36	17 59	18 25	00 41	01 35	02 28	03 19
30	17 21	17 46	18 15	00 29	01 27	02 24	03 19
35	17 13	17 40	18 10	00 22	01 23	02 21	03 18
40	17 04	17 32	18 05	00 15	01 17	02 18	03 18
45	16 53	17 24	17 59	00 06	01 11	02 15	03 17
S 50	16 40	17 15	17 53	25 03	01 03	02 11	03 17
52	16 34	17 10	17 51	25 00	01 00	02 09	03 16
54	16 27	17 06	17 48	24 56	00 56	02 07	03 16
56	16 20	17 00	17 45	24 52	00 52	02 04	03 16
58	16 11	16 55	17 42	24 47	00 47	02 02	03 15
S 60	16 02	16 48	17 39	24 42	00 42	01 59	03 15

Day	SUN Eqn. of Time 00^h	SUN Eqn. of Time 12^h	SUN Mer. Pass.	MOON Mer. Pass. Upper	MOON Mer. Pass. Lower	MOON Age	MOON Phase
d	m s	m s	h m	h m	h m	d	%
4	03 12	03 14	11 57	19 38	07 13	08	65
5	03 17	03 20	11 57	20 25	08 01	09	74
6	03 22	03 24	11 57	21 10	08 47	10	83

2017 MAY 7, 8, 9 (SUN., MON., TUES.)

UT d	h	ARIES GHA	VENUS −4·7 GHA	VENUS Dec	MARS +1·6 GHA	MARS Dec	JUPITER −2·4 GHA	JUPITER Dec	SATURN +0·2 GHA	SATURN Dec
		° ′	° ′	° ′	° ′	° ′	° ′	° ′	° ′	° ′
7	00	225 01.6	220 56.7	N 2 07.2	156 02.0	N22 44.5	30 45.1	S 4 26.4	318 12.7	S22 02.0
	01	240 04.1	235 57.6	07.5	171 02.6	44.8	45 47.7	26.3	333 15.3	02.0
	02	255 06.5	250 58.5	07.8	186 03.3	45.1	60 50.4	26.3	348 17.9	02.0
	03	270 09.0	265 59.3	. . 08.1	201 03.9	. . 45.3	75 53.1	. . 26.2	3 20.5	. . 02.0
	04	285 11.5	281 00.2	08.4	216 04.5	45.6	90 55.8	26.1	18 23.1	02.0
	05	300 13.9	296 01.0	08.7	231 05.2	45.9	105 58.5	26.0	33 25.6	02.0
	06	315 16.4	311 01.9	N 2 09.0	246 05.8	N22 46.1	121 01.2	S 4 25.9	48 28.2	S22 02.0
	07	330 18.9	326 02.7	09.3	261 06.5	46.4	136 03.8	25.8	63 30.8	02.0
	08	345 21.3	341 03.6	09.6	276 07.1	46.6	151 06.5	25.8	78 33.4	02.0
S	09	0 23.8	356 04.4	. . 09.9	291 07.7	. . 46.9	166 09.2	. . 25.7	93 36.0	. . 02.0
U	10	15 26.3	11 05.3	10.2	306 08.4	47.1	181 11.9	25.6	108 38.6	02.0
N	11	30 28.7	26 06.1	10.5	321 09.0	47.4	196 14.6	25.5	123 41.2	02.0
D	12	45 31.2	41 07.0	N 2 10.8	336 09.6	N22 47.7	211 17.2	S 4 25.4	138 43.8	S22 02.0
A	13	60 33.6	56 07.8	11.1	351 10.3	47.9	226 19.9	25.3	153 46.4	02.0
Y	14	75 36.1	71 08.7	11.4	6 10.9	48.2	241 22.6	25.3	168 49.0	02.0
	15	90 38.6	86 09.5	. . 11.7	21 11.5	. . 48.4	256 25.3	. . 25.2	183 51.6	. . 02.0
	16	105 41.0	101 10.3	12.0	36 12.2	48.7	271 28.0	25.1	198 54.2	02.0
	17	120 43.5	116 11.2	12.4	51 12.8	48.9	286 30.6	25.0	213 56.7	02.0
	18	135 46.0	131 12.0	N 2 12.7	66 13.5	N22 49.2	301 33.3	S 4 24.9	228 59.3	S22 02.0
	19	150 48.4	146 12.9	13.0	81 14.1	49.5	316 36.0	24.9	244 01.9	02.0
	20	165 50.9	161 13.7	13.3	96 14.7	49.7	331 38.7	24.8	259 04.5	01.9
	21	180 53.4	176 14.5	. . 13.6	111 15.4	. . 50.0	346 41.4	. . 24.7	274 07.1	. . 01.9
	22	195 55.8	191 15.3	13.9	126 16.0	50.2	1 44.0	24.6	289 09.7	01.9
	23	210 58.3	206 16.2	14.3	141 16.6	50.5	16 46.7	24.5	304 12.3	01.9
8	00	226 00.8	221 17.0	N 2 14.6	156 17.3	N22 50.7	31 49.4	S 4 24.5	319 14.9	S22 01.9
	01	241 03.2	236 17.8	14.9	171 17.9	51.0	46 52.1	24.4	334 17.5	01.9
	02	256 05.7	251 18.6	15.2	186 18.6	51.2	61 54.8	24.3	349 20.1	01.9
	03	271 08.1	266 19.5	. . 15.6	201 19.2	. . 51.5	76 57.4	. . 24.2	4 22.7	. . 01.9
	04	286 10.6	281 20.3	15.9	216 19.8	51.7	92 00.1	24.1	19 25.3	01.9
	05	301 13.1	296 21.1	16.2	231 20.5	52.0	107 02.8	24.1	34 27.9	01.9
	06	316 15.5	311 21.9	N 2 16.5	246 21.1	N22 52.2	122 05.5	S 4 24.0	49 30.5	S22 01.9
	07	331 18.0	326 22.7	16.9	261 21.7	52.5	137 08.1	23.9	64 33.1	01.9
	08	346 20.5	341 23.5	17.2	276 22.4	52.7	152 10.8	23.8	79 35.6	01.9
M	09	1 22.9	356 24.4	. . 17.5	291 23.0	. . 53.0	167 13.5	. . 23.7	94 38.2	. . 01.9
O	10	16 25.4	11 25.2	17.9	306 23.6	53.2	182 16.2	23.7	109 40.8	01.9
N	11	31 27.9	26 26.0	18.2	321 24.3	53.5	197 18.8	23.6	124 43.4	01.9
D	12	46 30.3	41 26.8	N 2 18.5	336 24.9	N22 53.7	212 21.5	S 4 23.5	139 46.0	S22 01.9
A	13	61 32.8	56 27.6	18.9	351 25.6	54.0	227 24.2	23.4	154 48.6	01.9
Y	14	76 35.3	71 28.4	19.2	6 26.2	54.2	242 26.9	23.3	169 51.2	01.9
	15	91 37.7	86 29.2	. . 19.5	21 26.8	. . 54.5	257 29.5	. . 23.3	184 53.8	. . 01.9
	16	106 40.2	101 30.0	19.9	36 27.5	54.7	272 32.2	23.2	199 56.4	01.9
	17	121 42.6	116 30.8	20.2	51 28.1	55.0	287 34.9	23.1	214 59.0	01.9
	18	136 45.1	131 31.6	N 2 20.6	66 28.7	N22 55.2	302 37.6	S 4 23.0	230 01.6	S22 01.9
	19	151 47.6	146 32.4	20.9	81 29.4	55.5	317 40.2	22.9	245 04.2	01.9
	20	166 50.0	161 33.2	21.2	96 30.0	55.7	332 42.9	22.9	260 06.8	01.9
	21	181 52.5	176 34.0	. . 21.6	111 30.6	. . 56.0	347 45.6	. . 22.8	275 09.4	. . 01.9
	22	196 55.0	191 34.8	21.9	126 31.3	56.2	2 48.3	22.7	290 12.0	01.9
	23	211 57.4	206 35.5	22.3	141 31.9	56.5	17 50.9	22.6	305 14.6	01.9
9	00	226 59.9	221 36.3	N 2 22.6	156 32.5	N22 56.7	32 53.6	S 4 22.5	320 17.2	S22 01.8
	01	242 02.4	236 37.1	23.0	171 33.2	56.9	47 56.3	22.5	335 19.8	01.8
	02	257 04.8	251 37.9	23.3	186 33.8	57.2	62 59.0	22.4	350 22.4	01.8
	03	272 07.3	266 38.7	. . 23.7	201 34.5	. . 57.4	78 01.6	. . 22.3	5 25.0	. . 01.8
	04	287 09.7	281 39.5	24.0	216 35.1	57.7	93 04.3	22.2	20 27.6	01.8
	05	302 12.2	296 40.2	24.4	231 35.7	57.9	108 07.0	22.2	35 30.2	01.8
	06	317 14.7	311 41.0	N 2 24.7	246 36.4	N22 58.2	123 09.6	S 4 22.1	50 32.8	S22 01.8
	07	332 17.1	326 41.8	25.1	261 37.0	58.4	138 12.3	22.0	65 35.4	01.8
T	08	347 19.6	341 42.6	25.4	276 37.6	58.6	153 15.0	21.9	80 37.9	01.8
U	09	2 22.1	356 43.3	. . 25.8	291 38.3	. . 58.9	168 17.7	. . 21.8	95 40.5	. . 01.8
E	10	17 24.5	11 44.1	26.2	306 38.9	59.1	183 20.3	21.8	110 43.1	01.8
S	11	32 27.0	26 44.9	26.5	321 39.5	59.4	198 23.0	21.7	125 45.7	01.8
D	12	47 29.5	41 45.7	N 2 26.9	336 40.2	N22 59.6	213 25.7	S 4 21.6	140 48.3	S22 01.8
A	13	62 31.9	56 46.4	27.2	351 40.8	22 59.8	228 28.3	21.5	155 50.9	01.8
Y	14	77 34.4	71 47.2	27.6	6 41.4	23 00.1	243 31.0	21.5	170 53.5	01.8
	15	92 36.9	86 48.0	. . 28.0	21 42.1	. . 00.3	258 33.7	. . 21.4	185 56.1	. . 01.8
	16	107 39.3	101 48.7	28.3	36 42.7	00.6	273 36.3	21.3	200 58.7	01.8
	17	122 41.8	116 49.5	28.7	51 43.4	00.8	288 39.0	21.2	216 01.3	01.8
	18	137 44.2	131 50.2	N 2 29.1	66 44.0	N23 01.0	303 41.7	S 4 21.1	231 03.9	S22 01.8
	19	152 46.7	146 51.0	29.4	81 44.6	01.3	318 44.4	21.1	246 06.5	01.8
	20	167 49.2	161 51.8	29.8	96 45.3	01.5	333 47.0	21.0	261 09.1	01.8
	21	182 51.6	176 52.5	. . 30.2	111 45.9	. . 01.8	348 49.7	. . 20.9	276 11.7	. . 01.8
	22	197 54.1	191 53.3	30.6	126 46.5	02.0	3 52.4	20.8	291 14.3	01.8
	23	212 56.6	206 54.0	30.9	141 47.2	02.2	18 55.0	20.8	306 16.9	01.8
Mer. Pass.		h m 8 54.5	*v* 0.8	*d* 0.3	*v* 0.6	*d* 0.2	*v* 2.7	*d* 0.1	*v* 2.6	*d* 0.0

STARS

Name	SHA	Dec
	° ′	° ′
Acamar	315 16.8	S40 14.3
Achernar	335 25.5	S57 09.0
Acrux	173 05.7	S63 11.9
Adhara	255 10.7	S29 00.1
Aldebaran	290 46.7	N16 32.4
Alioth	166 18.0	N55 52.2
Alkaid	152 56.5	N49 13.8
Al Na'ir	27 40.6	S46 52.4
Alnilam	275 44.0	S 1 11.8
Alphard	217 53.5	S 8 44.2
Alphecca	126 08.5	N26 39.5
Alpheratz	357 41.0	N29 10.9
Altair	62 05.6	N 8 54.9
Ankaa	353 13.5	S42 12.7
Antares	112 22.7	S26 28.0
Arcturus	145 53.1	N19 05.6
Atria	107 21.6	S69 03.2
Avior	234 17.1	S59 34.3
Bellatrix	278 29.5	N 6 21.6
Betelgeuse	270 58.7	N 7 24.3
Canopus	263 55.4	S52 42.7
Capella	280 31.0	N46 00.7
Deneb	49 29.6	N45 20.3
Denebola	182 30.8	N14 28.5
Diphda	348 53.6	S17 53.6
Dubhe	193 48.4	N61 39.7
Elnath	278 09.6	N28 37.1
Eltanin	90 44.5	N51 29.2
Enif	33 44.6	N 9 57.2
Fomalhaut	15 21.3	S29 31.8
Gacrux	171 57.4	S57 12.8
Gienah	175 49.4	S17 38.4
Hadar	148 43.4	S60 27.4
Hamal	327 58.1	N23 32.4
Kaus Aust.	83 40.1	S34 22.3
Kochab	137 19.1	N74 05.2
Markab	13 35.9	N15 17.7
Menkar	314 12.7	N 4 09.2
Menkent	148 04.1	S36 27.3
Miaplacidus	221 39.0	S69 47.7
Mirfak	308 37.1	N49 55.1
Nunki	75 54.9	S26 16.3
Peacock	53 15.1	S56 40.4
Pollux	243 24.7	N27 58.9
Procyon	244 57.2	N 5 10.6
Rasalhague	96 03.8	N12 32.9
Regulus	207 40.7	N11 52.9
Rigel	281 09.8	S 8 11.2
Rigil Kent.	139 47.4	S60 54.3
Sabik	102 09.3	S15 44.6
Schedar	349 37.9	N56 37.6
Shaula	96 18.0	S37 06.7
Sirius	258 31.6	S16 44.7
Spica	158 28.2	S11 15.1
Suhail	222 50.5	S43 30.5
Vega	80 36.9	N38 47.9
Zuben'ubi	137 02.2	S16 06.7

	SHA	Mer. Pass.
	° ′	h m
Venus	355 16.2	9 14
Mars	290 16.5	13 34
Jupiter	165 48.6	21 49
Saturn	93 14.1	2 43

	UT	SUN GHA	SUN Dec	MOON GHA	v	MOON Dec	d	HP
	d h	° ′	° ′	° ′	′	° ′	′	′
	7 00	180 51.6	N16 48.3	41 15.3	14.1	N 1 19.3	10.3	55.4
	01	195 51.6	49.0	55 48.4	14.1	1 09.0	10.2	55.4
	02	210 51.7	49.7	70 21.5	14.2	0 58.8	10.2	55.4
	03	225 51.7	. . 50.4	84 54.7	14.1	0 48.6	10.2	55.4
	04	240 51.7	51.1	99 27.8	14.2	0 38.4	10.2	55.4
	05	255 51.8	51.8	114 01.0	14.2	0 28.2	10.2	55.3
	06	270 51.8	N16 52.4	128 34.2	14.2	N 0 18.0	10.2	55.3
	07	285 51.9	53.1	143 07.4	14.3	N 0 07.8	10.1	55.3
	08	300 51.9	53.8	157 40.7	14.2	S 0 02.3	10.2	55.3
S	09	315 51.9	. . 54.5	172 13.9	14.3	0 12.5	10.2	55.3
U	10	330 52.0	55.2	186 47.2	14.3	0 22.7	10.2	55.3
N	11	345 52.0	55.9	201 20.5	14.3	0 32.9	10.1	55.2
D	12	0 52.1	N16 56.6	215 53.8	14.3	S 0 43.0	10.2	55.2
A	13	15 52.1	57.2	230 27.1	14.4	0 53.2	10.1	55.2
Y	14	30 52.1	57.9	245 00.5	14.3	1 03.3	10.1	55.2
	15	45 52.2	. . 58.6	259 33.8	14.4	1 13.4	10.1	55.2
	16	60 52.2	16 59.3	274 07.2	14.4	1 23.5	10.1	55.1
	17	75 52.2	17 00.0	288 40.6	14.4	1 33.6	10.1	55.1
	18	90 52.3	N17 00.7	303 14.0	14.4	S 1 43.7	10.1	55.1
	19	105 52.3	01.3	317 47.4	14.4	1 53.8	10.1	55.1
	20	120 52.4	02.0	332 20.8	14.4	2 03.9	10.0	55.1
	21	135 52.4	. . 02.7	346 54.2	14.4	2 13.9	10.1	55.0
	22	150 52.4	03.4	1 27.6	14.5	2 24.0	10.0	55.0
	23	165 52.5	04.1	16 01.1	14.4	2 34.0	10.0	55.0
	8 00	180 52.5	N17 04.7	30 34.5	14.5	S 2 44.0	10.0	55.0
	01	195 52.5	05.4	45 08.0	14.4	2 54.0	10.0	55.0
	02	210 52.6	06.1	59 41.4	14.5	3 04.0	9.9	55.0
	03	225 52.6	. . 06.8	74 14.9	14.5	3 13.9	10.0	54.9
	04	240 52.6	07.4	88 48.4	14.5	3 23.9	9.9	54.9
	05	255 52.7	08.1	103 21.9	14.5	3 33.8	9.9	54.9
	06	270 52.7	N17 08.8	117 55.4	14.5	S 3 43.7	9.8	54.9
	07	285 52.7	09.5	132 28.9	14.5	3 53.5	9.9	54.9
	08	300 52.8	10.2	147 02.4	14.5	4 03.4	9.8	54.9
M	09	315 52.8	. . 10.8	161 35.9	14.5	4 13.2	9.8	54.9
O	10	330 52.8	11.5	176 09.4	14.5	4 23.0	9.8	54.8
N	11	345 52.9	12.2	190 42.9	14.5	4 32.8	9.8	54.8
D	12	0 52.9	N17 12.8	205 16.4	14.5	S 4 42.6	9.7	54.8
A	13	15 52.9	13.5	219 49.9	14.5	4 52.3	9.7	54.8
Y	14	30 53.0	14.2	234 23.4	14.5	5 02.0	9.7	54.8
	15	45 53.0	. . 14.9	248 56.9	14.5	5 11.7	9.7	54.8
	16	60 53.0	15.5	263 30.4	14.5	5 21.4	9.6	54.7
	17	75 53.1	16.2	278 03.9	14.5	5 31.0	9.6	54.7
	18	90 53.1	N17 16.9	292 37.4	14.5	S 5 40.6	9.6	54.7
	19	105 53.1	17.5	307 10.9	14.5	5 50.2	9.6	54.7
	20	120 53.2	18.2	321 44.4	14.5	5 59.8	9.5	54.7
	21	135 53.2	. . 18.9	336 17.9	14.5	6 09.3	9.5	54.7
	22	150 53.2	19.5	350 51.4	14.5	6 18.8	9.4	54.7
	23	165 53.3	20.2	5 24.9	14.5	6 28.2	9.5	54.6
	9 00	180 53.3	N17 20.9	19 58.4	14.4	S 6 37.7	9.4	54.6
	01	195 53.3	21.5	34 31.8	14.5	6 47.1	9.3	54.6
	02	210 53.4	22.2	49 05.3	14.5	6 56.4	9.4	54.6
	03	225 53.4	. . 22.9	63 38.8	14.4	7 05.8	9.3	54.6
	04	240 53.4	23.5	78 12.2	14.5	7 15.1	9.2	54.6
	05	255 53.4	24.2	92 45.7	14.4	7 24.3	9.3	54.6
	06	270 53.5	N17 24.9	107 19.1	14.5	S 7 33.6	9.1	54.6
	07	285 53.5	25.5	121 52.6	14.4	7 42.7	9.2	54.5
T	08	300 53.5	26.2	136 26.0	14.4	7 51.9	9.1	54.5
U	09	315 53.6	. . 26.9	150 59.4	14.4	8 01.0	9.1	54.5
E	10	330 53.6	27.5	165 32.8	14.4	8 10.1	9.1	54.5
S	11	345 53.6	28.2	180 06.2	14.4	8 19.2	9.0	54.5
D	12	0 53.6	N17 28.8	194 39.6	14.3	S 8 28.2	8.9	54.5
A	13	15 53.7	29.5	209 12.9	14.4	8 37.1	9.0	54.5
Y	14	30 53.7	30.2	223 46.3	14.4	8 46.1	8.8	54.5
	15	45 53.7	. . 30.8	238 19.7	14.3	8 54.9	8.9	54.4
	16	60 53.7	31.5	252 53.0	14.3	9 03.8	8.8	54.4
	17	75 53.8	32.1	267 26.3	14.3	9 12.6	8.8	54.4
	18	90 53.8	N17 32.8	281 59.6	14.3	S 9 21.4	8.7	54.4
	19	105 53.8	33.4	296 32.9	14.3	9 30.1	8.7	54.4
	20	120 53.8	34.1	311 06.2	14.3	9 38.8	8.6	54.4
	21	135 53.9	. . 34.8	325 39.5	14.2	9 47.4	8.6	54.4
	22	150 53.9	35.4	340 12.7	14.3	9 56.0	8.5	54.4
	23	165 53.9	36.1	354 46.0	14.2	S10 04.5	8.5	54.4
		SD 15.9	*d* 0.7	SD 15.0		14.9		14.8

Lat.	Twilight Naut.	Twilight Civil	Sunrise	Moonrise 7	Moonrise 8	Moonrise 9	Moonrise 10
°	h m	h m	h m	h m	h m	h m	h m
N 72	////	////	00 19	16 02	17 41	19 21	21 04
N 70	////	////	01 45	16 00	17 32	19 05	20 38
68	////	////	02 23	15 58	17 26	18 52	20 19
66	////	01 02	02 49	15 57	17 20	18 42	20 03
64	////	01 50	03 09	15 56	17 15	18 34	19 51
62	////	02 19	03 26	15 55	17 11	18 26	19 40
60	00 55	02 41	03 39	15 54	17 07	18 20	19 31
N 58	01 38	02 59	03 51	15 53	17 04	18 15	19 24
56	02 06	03 14	04 01	15 52	17 01	18 10	19 17
54	02 26	03 26	04 10	15 52	16 59	18 05	19 11
52	02 43	03 37	04 17	15 51	16 57	18 01	19 05
50	02 57	03 46	04 24	15 50	16 55	17 58	19 00
45	03 25	04 06	04 39	15 49	16 50	17 50	18 49
N 40	03 45	04 22	04 52	15 48	16 46	17 44	18 40
35	04 01	04 35	05 02	15 47	16 43	17 38	18 33
30	04 15	04 46	05 11	15 47	16 40	17 33	18 26
20	04 36	05 04	05 27	15 45	16 35	17 25	18 15
N 10	04 53	05 18	05 40	15 44	16 31	17 18	18 05
0	05 06	05 31	05 53	15 43	16 27	17 11	17 55
S 10	05 18	05 43	06 05	15 42	16 23	17 04	17 46
20	05 29	05 56	06 19	15 41	16 19	16 57	17 36
30	05 40	06 08	06 33	15 40	16 14	16 49	17 25
35	05 45	06 15	06 42	15 40	16 12	16 44	17 18
40	05 51	06 23	06 52	15 39	16 09	16 39	17 11
45	05 57	06 32	07 03	15 38	16 05	16 33	17 03
S 50	06 03	06 42	07 17	15 37	16 01	16 26	16 52
52	06 06	06 47	07 23	15 37	15 59	16 22	16 48
54	06 09	06 52	07 31	15 36	15 57	16 19	16 43
56	06 12	06 57	07 39	15 36	15 55	16 15	16 37
58	06 16	07 03	07 47	15 35	15 52	16 10	16 30
S 60	06 19	07 10	07 58	15 34	15 49	16 05	16 23

Lat.	Sunset	Twilight Civil	Twilight Naut.	Moonset 7	Moonset 8	Moonset 9	Moonset 10
°	h m	h m	h m	h m	h m	h m	h m
N 72	▭	▭	▭	03 29	03 22	03 14	03 05
N 70	22 14	////	////	03 28	03 26	03 24	03 22
68	21 34	////	////	03 27	03 30	03 33	03 36
66	21 07	23 01	////	03 27	03 33	03 40	03 48
64	20 46	22 08	////	03 26	03 36	03 46	03 57
62	20 29	21 37	////	03 26	03 38	03 51	04 05
60	20 15	21 14	23 07	03 25	03 40	03 55	04 12
N 58	20 04	20 56	22 19	03 25	03 42	03 59	04 18
56	19 54	20 41	21 50	03 25	03 44	04 03	04 24
54	19 45	20 28	21 29	03 24	03 45	04 06	04 29
52	19 37	20 17	21 12	03 24	03 46	04 09	04 33
50	19 29	20 08	20 57	03 24	03 48	04 12	04 38
45	19 14	19 48	20 30	03 23	03 50	04 18	04 46
N 40	19 02	19 32	20 09	03 23	03 53	04 23	04 54
35	18 51	19 19	19 52	03 23	03 55	04 27	05 00
30	18 42	19 08	19 39	03 22	03 56	04 31	05 06
20	18 26	18 50	19 17	03 22	03 59	04 37	05 16
N 10	18 13	18 35	19 01	03 21	04 02	04 43	05 24
0	18 00	18 22	18 47	03 21	04 05	04 48	05 32
S 10	17 47	18 09	18 35	03 20	04 07	04 54	05 40
20	17 34	17 57	18 24	03 19	04 10	04 59	05 49
30	17 19	17 44	18 13	03 19	04 13	05 06	05 59
35	17 11	17 37	18 07	03 18	04 14	05 10	06 05
40	17 01	17 29	18 02	03 18	04 16	05 14	06 11
45	16 49	17 21	17 56	03 17	04 19	05 19	06 19
S 50	16 35	17 10	17 49	03 17	04 21	05 25	06 28
52	16 29	17 06	17 46	03 16	04 23	05 28	06 32
54	16 22	17 01	17 43	03 16	04 24	05 31	06 37
56	16 14	16 55	17 40	03 16	04 25	05 34	06 42
58	16 05	16 49	17 37	03 15	04 27	05 38	06 48
S 60	15 54	16 42	17 33	03 15	04 29	05 42	06 54

	SUN			MOON			
Day	Eqn. of Time 00ʰ	Eqn. of Time 12ʰ	Mer. Pass.	Mer. Pass. Upper	Mer. Pass. Lower	Age	Phase
d	m s	m s	h m	h m	h m	d %	
7	03 26	03 28	11 57	21 54	09 32	11 89	
8	03 30	03 32	11 56	22 38	10 16	12 95	○
9	03 33	03 34	11 56	23 22	11 00	13 98	

UT (d h)	Day	ARIES GHA ° ′	VENUS −4·7 GHA ° ′	VENUS Dec ° ′	MARS +1·6 GHA ° ′	MARS Dec ° ′	JUPITER −2·4 GHA ° ′	JUPITER Dec ° ′	SATURN +0·2 GHA ° ′	SATURN Dec ° ′
10 00		227 59.0	221 54.8	N 2 31.3	156 47.8	N23 02.5	33 57.7	S 4 20.7	321 19.5	S22 01.8
01		243 01.5	236 55.5	31.7	171 48.4	02.7	49 00.4	20.6	336 22.1	01.8
02		258 04.0	251 56.3	32.1	186 49.1	02.9	64 03.0	20.5	351 24.7	01.8
03		273 06.4	266 57.0	. . 32.4	201 49.7	. . 03.2	79 05.7	. . 20.5	6 27.3	. . 01.7
04		288 08.9	281 57.8	32.8	216 50.3	03.4	94 08.4	20.4	21 29.9	01.7
05		303 11.4	296 58.5	33.2	231 51.0	03.6	109 11.0	20.3	36 32.5	01.7
06		318 13.8	311 59.2	N 2 33.6	246 51.6	N23 03.9	124 13.7	S 4 20.2	51 35.1	S22 01.7
07	W	333 16.3	327 00.0	33.9	261 52.2	04.1	139 16.4	20.2	66 37.7	01.7
08	E	348 18.7	342 00.7	34.3	276 52.9	04.3	154 19.0	20.1	81 40.3	01.7
09	D	3 21.2	357 01.5	. . 34.7	291 53.5	. . 04.6	169 21.7	. . 20.0	96 42.9	. . 01.7
10	N	18 23.7	12 02.2	35.1	306 54.1	04.8	184 24.4	19.9	111 45.5	01.7
11	E	33 26.1	27 02.9	35.5	321 54.8	05.0	199 27.0	19.9	126 48.1	01.7
12	S	48 28.6	42 03.7	N 2 35.9	336 55.4	N23 05.3	214 29.7	S 4 19.8	141 50.7	S22 01.7
13	D	63 31.1	57 04.4	36.3	351 56.0	05.5	229 32.4	19.7	156 53.3	01.7
14	A	78 33.5	72 05.1	36.6	6 56.7	05.7	244 35.0	19.6	171 55.9	01.7
15	Y	93 36.0	87 05.8	. . 37.0	21 57.3	. . 06.0	259 37.7	. . 19.6	186 58.5	. . 01.7
16		108 38.5	102 06.6	37.4	36 58.0	06.2	274 40.3	19.5	202 01.1	01.7
17		123 40.9	117 07.3	37.8	51 58.6	06.4	289 43.0	19.4	217 03.7	01.7
18		138 43.4	132 08.0	N 2 38.2	66 59.2	N23 06.7	304 45.7	S 4 19.3	232 06.3	S22 01.7
19		153 45.8	147 08.7	38.6	81 59.9	06.9	319 48.3	19.3	247 08.9	01.7
20		168 48.3	162 09.5	39.0	97 00.5	07.1	334 51.0	19.2	262 11.5	01.7
21		183 50.8	177 10.2	. . 39.4	112 01.1	. . 07.3	349 53.7	. . 19.1	277 14.2	. . 01.7
22		198 53.2	192 10.9	39.8	127 01.8	07.6	4 56.3	19.0	292 16.8	01.7
23		213 55.7	207 11.6	40.2	142 02.4	07.8	19 59.0	19.0	307 19.4	01.7
11 00		228 58.2	222 12.3	N 2 40.6	157 03.0	N23 08.0	35 01.7	S 4 18.9	322 22.0	S22 01.7
01		244 00.6	237 13.1	41.0	172 03.7	08.3	50 04.3	18.8	337 24.6	01.7
02		259 03.1	252 13.8	41.4	187 04.3	08.5	65 07.0	18.7	352 27.2	01.7
03		274 05.6	267 14.5	. . 41.8	202 04.9	. . 08.7	80 09.6	. . 18.7	7 29.8	. . 01.7
04		289 08.0	282 15.2	42.2	217 05.6	08.9	95 12.3	18.6	22 32.4	01.7
05		304 10.5	297 15.9	42.6	232 06.2	09.2	110 15.0	18.5	37 35.0	01.7
06		319 13.0	312 16.6	N 2 43.0	247 06.8	N23 09.4	125 17.6	S 4 18.5	52 37.6	S22 01.6
07	T	334 15.4	327 17.3	43.4	262 07.5	09.6	140 20.3	18.4	67 40.2	01.6
08	H	349 17.9	342 18.0	43.8	277 08.1	09.8	155 22.9	18.3	82 42.8	01.6
09	U	4 20.3	357 18.7	. . 44.2	292 08.7	. . 10.1	170 25.6	. . 18.2	97 45.4	. . 01.6
10	R	19 22.8	12 19.4	44.6	307 09.4	10.3	185 28.3	18.2	112 48.0	01.6
11	S	34 25.3	27 20.1	45.0	322 10.0	10.5	200 30.9	18.1	127 50.6	01.6
12	D	49 27.7	42 20.8	N 2 45.4	337 10.6	N23 10.7	215 33.6	S 4 18.0	142 53.2	S22 01.6
13	A	64 30.2	57 21.5	45.9	352 11.3	11.0	230 36.2	17.9	157 55.8	01.6
14	Y	79 32.7	72 22.2	46.3	7 11.9	11.2	245 38.9	17.9	172 58.4	01.6
15		94 35.1	87 22.9	. . 46.7	22 12.5	. . 11.4	260 41.6	. . 17.8	188 01.0	. . 01.6
16		109 37.6	102 23.6	47.1	37 13.2	11.6	275 44.2	17.7	203 03.6	01.6
17		124 40.1	117 24.3	47.5	52 13.8	11.8	290 46.9	17.7	218 06.2	01.6
18		139 42.5	132 25.0	N 2 47.9	67 14.4	N23 12.1	305 49.5	S 4 17.6	233 08.8	S22 01.6
19		154 45.0	147 25.7	48.4	82 15.1	12.3	320 52.2	17.5	248 11.4	01.6
20		169 47.5	162 26.3	48.8	97 15.7	12.5	335 54.8	17.4	263 14.0	01.6
21		184 49.9	177 27.0	. . 49.2	112 16.3	. . 12.7	350 57.5	. . 17.4	278 16.7	. . 01.6
22		199 52.4	192 27.7	49.6	127 17.0	12.9	6 00.2	17.3	293 19.3	01.6
23		214 54.8	207 28.4	50.0	142 17.6	13.2	21 02.8	17.2	308 21.9	01.6
12 00		229 57.3	222 29.1	N 2 50.5	157 18.2	N23 13.4	36 05.5	S 4 17.2	323 24.5	S22 01.6
01		244 59.8	237 29.8	50.9	172 18.9	13.6	51 08.1	17.1	338 27.1	01.6
02		260 02.2	252 30.4	51.3	187 19.5	13.8	66 10.8	17.0	353 29.7	01.6
03		275 04.7	267 31.1	. . 51.7	202 20.1	. . 14.0	81 13.4	. . 16.9	8 32.3	. . 01.6
04		290 07.2	282 31.8	52.2	217 20.8	14.3	96 16.1	16.9	23 34.9	01.6
05		305 09.6	297 32.5	52.6	232 21.4	14.5	111 18.8	16.8	38 37.5	01.6
06		320 12.1	312 33.1	N 2 53.0	247 22.0	N23 14.7	126 21.4	S 4 16.7	53 40.1	S22 01.6
07		335 14.6	327 33.8	53.4	262 22.7	14.9	141 24.1	16.7	68 42.7	01.6
08		350 17.0	342 34.5	53.9	277 23.3	15.1	156 26.7	16.6	83 45.3	01.6
09	F	5 19.5	357 35.2	. . 54.3	292 23.9	. . 15.3	171 29.4	. . 16.5	98 47.9	. . 01.5
10	R	20 21.9	12 35.8	54.7	307 24.6	15.6	186 32.0	16.5	113 50.5	01.5
11	I	35 24.4	27 36.5	55.2	322 25.2	15.8	201 34.7	16.4	128 53.1	01.5
12	D	50 26.9	42 37.1	N 2 55.6	337 25.8	N23 16.0	216 37.3	S 4 16.3	143 55.8	S22 01.5
13	A	65 29.3	57 37.8	56.0	352 26.5	16.2	231 40.0	16.2	158 58.4	01.5
14	Y	80 31.8	72 38.5	56.5	7 27.1	16.4	246 42.6	16.2	174 01.0	01.5
15		95 34.3	87 39.1	. . 56.9	22 27.7	. . 16.6	261 45.3	. . 16.1	189 03.6	. . 01.5
16		110 36.7	102 39.8	57.4	37 28.4	16.8	276 47.9	16.0	204 06.2	01.5
17		125 39.2	117 40.5	57.8	52 29.0	17.1	291 50.6	16.0	219 08.8	01.5
18		140 41.7	132 41.1	N 2 58.2	67 29.6	N23 17.3	306 53.2	S 4 15.9	234 11.4	S22 01.5
19		155 44.1	147 41.8	58.7	82 30.3	17.5	321 55.9	15.8	249 14.0	01.5
20		170 46.6	162 42.4	59.1	97 30.9	17.7	336 58.6	15.8	264 16.6	01.5
21		185 49.1	177 43.1	2 59.6	112 31.5	. . 17.9	352 01.2	. . 15.7	279 19.2	. . 01.5
22		200 51.5	192 43.7	3 00.0	127 32.2	18.1	7 03.9	15.6	294 21.8	01.5
23		215 54.0	207 44.4	N 3 00.5	142 32.8	18.3	22 06.5	15.5	309 24.4	01.5
Mer. Pass.		h m 8 42.7	v 0.7	d 0.4	v 0.6	d 0.2	v 2.7	d 0.1	v 2.6	d 0.0

STARS

Name	SHA ° ′	Dec ° ′
Acamar	315 16.8	S40 14.3
Achernar	335 25.5	S57 09.0
Acrux	173 05.7	S63 11.9
Adhara	255 10.7	S29 00.1
Aldebaran	290 46.7	N16 32.4
Alioth	166 18.1	N55 52.2
Alkaid	152 56.5	N49 13.8
Al Na'ir	27 40.6	S46 52.4
Alnilam	275 44.0	S 1 11.8
Alphard	217 53.5	S 8 44.2
Alphecca	126 08.5	N26 39.5
Alpheratz	357 41.0	N29 10.9
Altair	62 05.5	N 8 54.9
Ankaa	353 13.5	S42 12.7
Antares	112 22.7	S26 28.0
Arcturus	145 53.1	N19 05.6
Atria	107 21.6	S69 03.2
Avior	234 17.1	S59 34.3
Bellatrix	278 29.5	N 6 21.6
Betelgeuse	270 58.7	N 7 24.3
Canopus	263 55.4	S52 42.7
Capella	280 31.0	N46 00.7
Deneb	49 29.6	N45 20.4
Denebola	182 30.8	N14 28.5
Diphda	348 53.6	S17 53.6
Dubhe	193 48.4	N61 39.7
Elnath	278 09.6	N28 37.1
Eltanin	90 44.5	N51 29.2
Enif	33 44.6	N 9 57.2
Fomalhaut	15 21.3	S29 31.7
Gacrux	171 57.5	S57 12.8
Gienah	175 49.4	S17 38.4
Hadar	148 43.4	S60 27.4
Hamal	327 58.1	N23 32.4
Kaus Aust.	83 40.1	S34 22.3
Kochab	137 19.1	N74 05.2
Markab	13 35.9	N15 17.7
Menkar	314 12.6	N 4 09.2
Menkent	148 04.1	S36 27.3
Miaplacidus	221 39.1	S69 47.7
Mirfak	308 37.1	N49 55.1
Nunki	75 54.9	S26 16.3
Peacock	53 15.0	S56 40.4
Pollux	243 24.7	N27 58.9
Procyon	244 57.2	N 5 10.6
Rasalhague	96 03.7	N12 32.9
Regulus	207 40.7	N11 52.9
Rigel	281 09.9	S 8 11.2
Rigil Kent.	139 47.4	S60 54.3
Sabik	102 09.2	S15 44.6
Schedar	349 37.9	N56 37.6
Shaula	96 18.0	S37 06.7
Sirius	258 31.7	S16 44.7
Spica	158 28.2	S11 15.1
Suhail	222 50.5	S43 30.5
Vega	80 36.9	N38 47.9
Zuben'ubi	137 02.2	S16 06.7

	SHA ° ′	Mer. Pass. h m
Venus	353 14.2	9 11
Mars	288 04.9	13 31
Jupiter	166 03.5	21 36
Saturn	93 23.8	2 30

UT		SUN		MOON				
	d h	GHA ° ′	Dec ° ′	GHA ° ′	v ′	Dec ° ′	d ′	HP ′
WEDNESDAY	10 00	180 53.9	N17 36.7	9 19.2	14.2	S10 13.0	8.5	54.3
	01	195 54.0	37.4	23 52.4	14.2	10 21.5	8.4	54.3
	02	210 54.0	38.0	38 25.6	14.2	10 29.9	8.4	54.3
	03	225 54.0	. . 38.7	52 58.8	14.1	10 38.3	8.3	54.3
	04	240 54.0	39.3	67 31.9	14.2	10 46.6	8.3	54.3
	05	255 54.1	40.0	82 05.1	14.1	10 54.9	8.2	54.3
	06	270 54.1	N17 40.6	96 38.2	14.1	S11 03.1	8.1	54.3
	07	285 54.1	41.3	111 11.3	14.1	11 11.2	8.2	54.3
	08	300 54.1	41.9	125 44.4	14.1	11 19.4	8.0	54.3
	09	315 54.2	. . 42.6	140 17.5	14.0	11 27.4	8.0	54.3
	10	330 54.2	43.2	154 50.5	14.1	11 35.4	8.0	54.2
	11	345 54.2	43.9	169 23.6	14.0	11 43.4	7.9	54.2
	12	0 54.2	N17 44.5	183 56.6	14.0	S11 51.3	7.9	54.2
	13	15 54.2	45.2	198 29.6	14.0	11 59.2	7.8	54.2
	14	30 54.3	45.8	213 02.6	13.9	12 07.0	7.7	54.2
	15	45 54.3	. . 46.5	227 35.5	14.0	12 14.7	7.7	54.2
	16	60 54.3	47.1	242 08.5	13.9	12 22.4	7.7	54.2
	17	75 54.3	47.8	256 41.4	13.9	12 30.1	7.6	54.2
	18	90 54.3	N17 48.4	271 14.3	13.9	S12 37.7	7.5	54.2
	19	105 54.4	49.1	285 47.2	13.8	12 45.2	7.5	54.2
	20	120 54.4	49.7	300 20.0	13.8	12 52.7	7.4	54.2
	21	135 54.4	. . 50.3	314 52.8	13.9	13 00.1	7.3	54.2
	22	150 54.4	51.0	329 25.7	13.8	13 07.4	7.3	54.2
	23	165 54.4	51.6	343 58.5	13.7	13 14.7	7.3	54.1
THURSDAY	11 00	180 54.5	N17 52.3	358 31.2	13.8	S13 22.0	7.2	54.1
	01	195 54.5	52.9	13 04.0	13.7	13 29.2	7.1	54.1
	02	210 54.5	53.6	27 36.7	13.7	13 36.3	7.1	54.1
	03	225 54.5	. . 54.2	42 09.4	13.7	13 43.4	7.0	54.1
	04	240 54.5	54.8	56 42.1	13.6	13 50.4	6.9	54.1
	05	255 54.5	55.5	71 14.7	13.7	13 57.3	6.9	54.1
	06	270 54.6	N17 56.1	85 47.4	13.6	S14 04.2	6.8	54.1
	07	285 54.6	56.8	100 20.0	13.6	14 11.0	6.8	54.1
	08	300 54.6	57.4	114 52.6	13.6	14 17.8	6.7	54.1
	09	315 54.6	. . 58.0	129 25.2	13.5	14 24.5	6.6	54.1
	10	330 54.6	58.7	143 57.7	13.5	14 31.1	6.5	54.1
	11	345 54.6	59.3	158 30.2	13.5	14 37.6	6.5	54.1
	12	0 54.7	N17 59.9	173 02.7	13.5	S14 44.1	6.5	54.1
	13	15 54.7	18 00.6	187 35.2	13.4	14 50.6	6.3	54.1
	14	30 54.7	01.2	202 07.6	13.5	14 56.9	6.3	54.1
	15	45 54.7	. . 01.8	216 40.1	13.4	15 03.2	6.3	54.0
	16	60 54.7	02.5	231 12.5	13.4	15 09.5	6.2	54.0
	17	75 54.7	03.1	245 44.9	13.3	15 15.7	6.1	54.0
	18	90 54.7	N18 03.7	260 17.2	13.4	S15 21.8	6.0	54.0
	19	105 54.8	04.4	274 49.6	13.3	15 27.8	6.0	54.0
	20	120 54.8	05.0	289 21.9	13.3	15 33.8	5.8	54.0
	21	135 54.8	. . 05.6	303 54.2	13.2	15 39.6	5.9	54.0
	22	150 54.8	06.3	318 26.4	13.3	15 45.5	5.7	54.0
	23	165 54.8	06.9	332 58.7	13.2	15 51.2	5.7	54.0
FRIDAY	12 00	180 54.8	N18 07.5	347 30.9	13.2	S15 56.9	5.6	54.0
	01	195 54.8	08.2	2 03.1	13.1	16 02.5	5.6	54.0
	02	210 54.8	08.8	16 35.2	13.2	16 08.1	5.4	54.0
	03	225 54.9	. . 09.4	31 07.4	13.1	16 13.5	5.4	54.0
	04	240 54.9	10.0	45 39.5	13.1	16 18.9	5.4	54.0
	05	255 54.9	10.7	60 11.6	13.1	16 24.3	5.2	54.0
	06	270 54.9	N18 11.3	74 43.7	13.0	S16 29.5	5.2	54.0
	07	285 54.9	11.9	89 15.7	13.1	16 34.7	5.1	54.0
	08	300 54.9	12.5	103 47.8	13.0	16 39.8	5.0	54.0
	09	315 54.9	. . 13.2	118 19.8	13.0	16 44.8	5.0	54.0
	10	330 54.9	13.8	132 51.8	12.9	16 49.8	4.9	54.0
	11	345 54.9	14.4	147 23.7	13.0	16 54.7	4.8	54.0
	12	0 54.9	N18 15.0	161 55.7	12.9	S16 59.5	4.7	54.0
	13	15 55.0	15.7	176 27.6	12.9	17 04.2	4.7	54.0
	14	30 55.0	16.3	190 59.5	12.8	17 08.9	4.6	54.0
	15	45 55.0	. . 16.9	205 31.3	12.9	17 13.5	4.5	54.0
	16	60 55.0	17.5	220 03.2	12.8	17 18.0	4.4	54.0
	17	75 55.0	18.1	234 35.0	12.8	17 22.4	4.3	54.0
	18	90 55.0	N18 18.8	249 06.8	12.8	S17 26.7	4.3	54.0
	19	105 55.0	19.4	263 38.6	12.7	17 31.0	4.2	54.0
	20	120 55.0	20.0	278 10.3	12.8	17 35.2	4.1	54.0
	21	135 55.0	. . 20.6	292 42.1	12.7	17 39.3	4.0	54.0
	22	150 55.0	21.2	307 13.8	12.7	17 43.3	4.0	54.0
	23	165 55.0	21.9	321 45.5	12.7	S17 47.3	3.9	54.0
		SD 15.9	*d* 0.6	SD 14.8		14.7		14.7

Lat.	Twilight Naut.	Twilight Civil	Sunrise	Moonrise 10	Moonrise 11	Moonrise 12	Moonrise 13
°	h m	h m	h m	h m	h m	h m	h m
N 72	□	□	□	21 04	22 54	■	■
N 70	////	////	01 22	20 38	22 12	23 45	25 12
68	////	////	02 08	20 19	21 44	23 05	24 17
66	////	00 21	02 37	20 03	21 23	22 38	23 44
64	////	01 33	03 00	19 51	21 06	22 17	23 20
62	////	02 07	03 17	19 40	20 52	22 00	23 01
60	00 18	02 32	03 32	19 31	20 41	21 46	22 45
N 58	01 23	02 51	03 44	19 24	20 31	21 34	22 32
56	01 55	03 06	03 55	19 17	20 22	21 23	22 20
54	02 18	03 20	04 04	19 11	20 14	21 14	22 10
52	02 36	03 31	04 12	19 05	20 07	21 06	22 02
50	02 51	03 41	04 20	19 00	20 01	20 59	21 54
45	03 20	04 02	04 36	18 49	19 47	20 43	21 37
N 40	03 41	04 18	04 49	18 40	19 36	20 31	21 23
35	03 58	04 32	05 00	18 33	19 27	20 20	21 11
30	04 12	04 43	05 09	18 26	19 19	20 10	21 01
20	04 34	05 02	05 26	18 15	19 04	19 54	20 43
N 10	04 52	05 18	05 40	18 05	18 52	19 40	20 28
0	05 06	05 31	05 53	17 55	18 40	19 27	20 14
S 10	05 18	05 44	06 06	17 46	18 29	19 13	19 59
20	05 30	05 57	06 20	17 36	18 17	18 59	19 44
30	05 41	06 10	06 35	17 25	18 03	18 43	19 27
35	05 47	06 18	06 44	17 18	17 55	18 34	19 17
40	05 53	06 26	06 55	17 11	17 46	18 24	19 05
45	06 00	06 35	07 07	17 03	17 35	18 11	18 52
S 50	06 07	06 46	07 21	16 52	17 22	17 56	18 35
52	06 10	06 51	07 28	16 48	17 16	17 49	18 27
54	06 13	06 56	07 36	16 43	17 10	17 41	18 19
56	06 17	07 02	07 44	16 37	17 02	17 33	18 09
58	06 21	07 09	07 54	16 30	16 54	17 23	17 58
S 60	06 25	07 16	08 05	16 23	16 45	17 12	17 45

Lat.	Sunset	Twilight Civil	Twilight Naut.	Moonset 10	Moonset 11	Moonset 12	Moonset 13
°	h m	h m	h m	h m	h m	h m	h m
N 72	□	□	□	03 05	02 55	02 39	■
N 70	22 39	////	////	03 22	03 21	03 21	03 24
68	21 49	////	////	03 36	03 42	03 50	04 05
66	21 18	////	////	03 48	03 58	04 12	04 33
64	20 56	22 25	////	03 57	04 11	04 29	04 54
62	20 38	21 49	////	04 05	04 22	04 44	05 11
60	20 23	21 24	////	04 12	04 32	04 56	05 26
N 58	20 10	21 04	22 34	04 18	04 40	05 06	05 38
56	19 59	20 48	22 01	04 24	04 48	05 15	05 48
54	19 50	20 35	21 37	04 29	04 54	05 23	05 58
52	19 41	20 23	21 19	04 33	05 00	05 31	06 06
50	19 34	20 13	21 04	04 38	05 06	05 37	06 14
45	19 18	19 52	20 34	04 46	05 17	05 51	06 30
N 40	19 05	19 35	20 12	04 54	05 27	06 03	06 43
35	18 54	19 21	19 55	05 00	05 35	06 13	06 54
30	18 44	19 10	19 41	05 06	05 43	06 22	07 04
20	18 27	18 51	19 19	05 16	05 55	06 37	07 21
N 10	18 13	18 35	19 01	05 24	06 07	06 50	07 35
0	18 00	18 22	18 47	05 32	06 17	07 03	07 49
S 10	17 47	18 09	18 34	05 40	06 27	07 15	08 03
20	17 33	17 56	18 23	05 49	06 39	07 28	08 18
30	17 17	17 42	18 11	05 59	06 52	07 44	08 35
35	17 08	17 35	18 05	06 05	06 59	07 52	08 45
40	16 58	17 26	17 59	06 11	07 07	08 03	08 56
45	16 46	17 17	17 52	06 19	07 17	08 14	09 09
S 50	16 31	17 06	17 45	06 28	07 29	08 29	09 25
52	16 24	17 01	17 42	06 32	07 35	08 36	09 33
54	16 16	16 56	17 39	06 37	07 41	08 43	09 42
56	16 08	16 50	17 35	06 42	07 48	08 52	09 51
58	15 58	16 43	17 31	06 48	07 56	09 01	10 02
S 60	15 47	16 36	17 27	06 54	08 05	09 12	10 14

Day	SUN Eqn. of Time 00^h	SUN Eqn. of Time 12^h	SUN Mer. Pass.	MOON Mer. Pass. Upper	MOON Mer. Pass. Lower	MOON Age	MOON Phase
d	m s	m s	h m	h m	h m	d %	
10	03 36	03 37	11 56	24 06	11 44	14 100	○
11	03 38	03 39	11 56	00 06	12 29	15 99	
12	03 39	03 40	11 56	00 52	13 15	16 98	

2017 MAY 13, 14, 15 (SAT., SUN., MON.)

	UT d h	ARIES GHA ° ′	VENUS −4·6 GHA ° ′	Dec ° ′	MARS +1·6 GHA ° ′	Dec ° ′	JUPITER −2·4 GHA ° ′	Dec ° ′	SATURN +0·2 GHA ° ′	Dec ° ′
	13 00	230 56.4	222 45.0	N 3 00.9	157 33.4	N23 18.5	37 09.2	S 4 15.5	324 27.1	S22 01.5
	01	245 58.9	237 45.7	01.3	172 34.1	18.7	52 11.8	15.4	339 29.7	01.5
	02	261 01.4	252 46.3	01.8	187 34.7	19.0	67 14.5	15.3	354 32.3	01.5
	03	276 03.8	267 47.0	. . 02.2	202 35.3	. . 19.2	82 17.1	. . 15.3	9 34.9	. . 01.5
	04	291 06.3	282 47.6	02.7	217 36.0	19.4	97 19.8	15.2	24 37.5	01.5
	05	306 08.8	297 48.2	03.1	232 36.6	19.6	112 22.4	15.1	39 40.1	01.5
	06	321 11.2	312 48.9	N 3 03.6	247 37.2	N23 19.8	127 25.1	S 4 15.1	54 42.7	S22 01.5
	07	336 13.7	327 49.5	04.0	262 37.9	20.0	142 27.7	15.0	69 45.3	01.5
S	08	351 16.2	342 50.2	04.5	277 38.5	20.2	157 30.4	14.9	84 47.9	01.5
A	09	6 18.6	357 50.8	. . 05.0	292 39.1	. . 20.4	172 33.0	. . 14.9	99 50.5	. . 01.5
T	10	21 21.1	12 51.4	05.4	307 39.8	20.6	187 35.7	14.8	114 53.1	01.5
U	11	36 23.6	27 52.1	05.9	322 40.4	20.8	202 38.3	14.7	129 55.8	01.5
R	12	51 26.0	42 52.7	N 3 06.3	337 41.0	N23 21.0	217 40.9	S 4 14.7	144 58.4	S22 01.4
D	13	66 28.5	57 53.3	06.8	352 41.7	21.2	232 43.6	14.6	160 01.0	01.4
A	14	81 30.9	72 54.0	07.2	7 42.3	21.4	247 46.2	14.5	175 03.6	01.4
Y	15	96 33.4	87 54.6	. . 07.7	22 42.9	. . 21.6	262 48.9	. . 14.5	190 06.2	. . 01.4
	16	111 35.9	102 55.2	08.2	37 43.6	21.9	277 51.5	14.4	205 08.8	01.4
	17	126 38.3	117 55.8	08.6	52 44.2	22.1	292 54.2	14.3	220 11.4	01.4
	18	141 40.8	132 56.5	N 3 09.1	67 44.8	N23 22.3	307 56.8	S 4 14.3	235 14.0	S22 01.4
	19	156 43.3	147 57.1	09.6	82 45.4	22.5	322 59.5	14.2	250 16.6	01.4
	20	171 45.7	162 57.7	10.0	97 46.1	22.7	338 02.1	14.1	265 19.3	01.4
	21	186 48.2	177 58.3	. . 10.5	112 46.7	. . 22.9	353 04.8	. . 14.1	280 21.9	. . 01.4
	22	201 50.7	192 59.0	10.9	127 47.3	23.1	8 07.4	14.0	295 24.5	01.4
	23	216 53.1	207 59.6	11.4	142 48.0	23.3	23 10.1	13.9	310 27.1	01.4
	14 00	231 55.6	223 00.2	N 3 11.9	157 48.6	N23 23.5	38 12.7	S 4 13.9	325 29.7	S22 01.4
	01	246 58.1	238 00.8	12.4	172 49.2	23.7	53 15.4	13.8	340 32.3	01.4
	02	262 00.5	253 01.4	12.8	187 49.9	23.9	68 18.0	13.7	355 34.9	01.4
	03	277 03.0	268 02.0	. . 13.3	202 50.5	. . 24.1	83 20.6	. . 13.7	10 37.5	. . 01.4
	04	292 05.4	283 02.7	13.8	217 51.1	24.3	98 23.3	13.6	25 40.2	01.4
	05	307 07.9	298 03.3	14.2	232 51.8	24.5	113 25.9	13.5	40 42.8	01.4
	06	322 10.4	313 03.9	N 3 14.7	247 52.4	N23 24.7	128 28.6	S 4 13.5	55 45.4	S22 01.4
	07	337 12.8	328 04.5	15.2	262 53.0	24.9	143 31.2	13.4	70 48.0	01.4
	08	352 15.3	343 05.1	15.7	277 53.7	25.1	158 33.9	13.3	85 50.6	01.4
S	09	7 17.8	358 05.7	. . 16.1	292 54.3	. . 25.3	173 36.5	. . 13.3	100 53.2	. . 01.4
U	10	22 20.2	13 06.3	16.6	307 54.9	25.5	188 39.1	13.2	115 55.8	01.4
N	11	37 22.7	28 06.9	17.1	322 55.6	25.7	203 41.8	13.1	130 58.4	01.4
D	12	52 25.2	43 07.5	N 3 17.6	337 56.2	N23 25.9	218 44.4	S 4 13.1	146 01.1	S22 01.4
A	13	67 27.6	58 08.1	18.1	352 56.8	26.1	233 47.1	13.0	161 03.7	01.4
Y	14	82 30.1	73 08.7	18.5	7 57.5	26.3	248 49.7	13.0	176 06.3	01.4
	15	97 32.5	88 09.3	. . 19.0	22 58.1	. . 26.5	263 52.4	. . 12.9	191 08.9	. . 01.3
	16	112 35.0	103 09.9	19.5	37 58.7	26.7	278 55.0	12.8	206 11.5	01.3
	17	127 37.5	118 10.5	20.0	52 59.4	26.9	293 57.6	12.8	221 14.1	01.3
	18	142 39.9	133 11.1	N 3 20.5	68 00.0	N23 27.0	309 00.3	S 4 12.7	236 16.7	S22 01.3
	19	157 42.4	148 11.7	21.0	83 00.6	27.2	324 02.9	12.6	251 19.4	01.3
	20	172 44.9	163 12.3	21.4	98 01.3	27.4	339 05.6	12.6	266 22.0	01.3
	21	187 47.3	178 12.9	. . 21.9	113 01.9	. . 27.6	354 08.2	. . 12.5	281 24.6	. . 01.3
	22	202 49.8	193 13.5	22.4	128 02.5	27.8	9 10.8	12.4	296 27.2	01.3
	23	217 52.3	208 14.0	22.9	143 03.1	28.0	24 13.5	12.4	311 29.8	01.3
	15 00	232 54.7	223 14.6	N 3 23.4	158 03.8	N23 28.2	39 16.1	S 4 12.3	326 32.4	S22 01.3
	01	247 57.2	238 15.2	23.9	173 04.4	28.4	54 18.8	12.2	341 35.0	01.3
	02	262 59.7	253 15.8	24.4	188 05.0	28.6	69 21.4	12.2	356 37.7	01.3
	03	278 02.1	268 16.4	. . 24.9	203 05.7	. . 28.8	84 24.0	. . 12.1	11 40.3	. . 01.3
	04	293 04.6	283 17.0	25.4	218 06.3	29.0	99 26.7	12.1	26 42.9	01.3
	05	308 07.0	298 17.5	25.9	233 06.9	29.2	114 29.3	12.0	41 45.5	01.3
	06	323 09.5	313 18.1	N 3 26.3	248 07.6	N23 29.4	129 31.9	S 4 11.9	56 48.1	S22 01.3
	07	338 12.0	328 18.7	26.8	263 08.2	29.6	144 34.6	11.9	71 50.7	01.3
	08	353 14.4	343 19.3	27.3	278 08.8	29.7	159 37.2	11.8	86 53.4	01.3
M	09	8 16.9	358 19.9	. . 27.8	293 09.5	. . 29.9	174 39.9	. . 11.7	101 56.0	. . 01.3
O	10	23 19.4	13 20.4	28.3	308 10.1	30.1	189 42.5	11.7	116 58.6	01.3
N	11	38 21.8	28 21.0	28.8	323 10.7	30.3	204 45.1	11.6	132 01.2	01.3
D	12	53 24.3	43 21.6	N 3 29.3	338 11.4	N23 30.5	219 47.8	S 4 11.6	147 03.8	S22 01.3
A	13	68 26.8	58 22.1	29.8	353 12.0	30.7	234 50.4	11.5	162 06.4	01.3
Y	14	83 29.2	73 22.7	30.3	8 12.6	30.9	249 53.0	11.4	177 09.1	01.3
	15	98 31.7	88 23.3	. . 30.8	23 13.3	. . 31.1	264 55.7	. . 11.4	192 11.7	. . 01.3
	16	113 34.2	103 23.9	31.3	38 13.9	31.3	279 58.3	11.3	207 14.3	01.3
	17	128 36.6	118 24.4	31.8	53 14.5	31.4	295 00.9	11.3	222 16.9	01.2
	18	143 39.1	133 25.0	N 3 32.3	68 15.1	N23 31.6	310 03.6	S 4 11.2	237 19.5	S22 01.2
	19	158 41.5	148 25.5	32.9	83 15.8	31.8	325 06.2	11.1	252 22.1	01.2
	20	173 44.0	163 26.1	33.4	98 16.4	32.0	340 08.8	11.1	267 24.8	01.2
	21	188 46.5	178 26.7	. . 33.9	113 17.0	. . 32.2	355 11.5	. . 11.0	282 27.4	. . 01.2
	22	203 48.9	193 27.2	34.4	128 17.7	32.4	10 14.1	10.9	297 30.0	01.2
	23	218 51.4	208 27.8	34.9	143 18.3	32.6	25 16.7	10.9	312 32.6	01.2
	Mer. Pass.	h m 8 30.9	*v* 0.6	*d* 0.5	*v* 0.6	*d* 0.2	*v* 2.6	*d* 0.1	*v* 2.6	*d* 0.0

STARS

Name	SHA ° ′	Dec ° ′
Acamar	315 16.8	S40 14.3
Achernar	335 25.4	S57 09.0
Acrux	173 05.7	S63 11.9
Adhara	255 10.7	S29 00.1
Aldebaran	290 46.7	N16 32.4
Alioth	166 18.1	N55 52.2
Alkaid	152 56.5	N49 13.8
Al Na'ir	27 40.6	S46 52.4
Alnilam	275 44.0	S 1 11.8
Alphard	217 53.5	S 8 44.2
Alphecca	126 08.4	N26 39.5
Alpheratz	357 41.0	N29 10.9
Altair	62 05.5	N 8 54.9
Ankaa	353 13.5	S42 12.7
Antares	112 22.7	S26 28.0
Arcturus	145 53.1	N19 05.7
Atria	107 21.6	S69 03.2
Avior	234 17.1	S59 34.3
Bellatrix	278 29.5	N 6 21.6
Betelgeuse	270 58.8	N 7 24.3
Canopus	263 55.4	S52 42.7
Capella	280 31.0	N46 00.7
Deneb	49 29.5	N45 20.4
Denebola	182 30.8	N14 28.6
Diphda	348 53.5	S17 53.6
Dubhe	193 48.4	N61 39.7
Elnath	278 09.6	N28 37.1
Eltanin	90 44.5	N51 29.2
Enif	33 44.5	N 9 57.2
Fomalhaut	15 21.3	S29 31.7
Gacrux	171 57.5	S57 12.8
Gienah	175 49.4	S17 38.4
Hadar	148 43.4	S60 27.4
Hamal	327 58.1	N23 32.4
Kaus Aust.	83 40.0	S34 22.3
Kochab	137 19.1	N74 05.3
Markab	13 35.8	N15 17.7
Menkar	314 12.6	N 4 09.2
Menkent	148 04.1	S36 27.3
Miaplacidus	221 39.1	S69 47.7
Mirfak	308 37.1	N49 55.1
Nunki	75 54.8	S26 16.3
Peacock	53 15.0	S56 40.4
Pollux	243 24.8	N27 58.9
Procyon	244 57.2	N 5 10.6
Rasalhague	96 03.7	N12 32.9
Regulus	207 40.7	N11 52.9
Rigel	281 09.9	S 8 11.2
Rigil Kent.	139 47.4	S60 54.3
Sabik	102 09.2	S15 44.6
Schedar	349 37.8	N56 37.6
Shaula	96 18.0	S37 06.7
Sirius	258 31.7	S16 44.7
Spica	158 28.2	S11 15.1
Suhail	222 50.5	S43 30.5
Vega	80 36.9	N38 48.0
Zuben'ubi	137 02.2	S16 06.7

	SHA ° ′	Mer. Pass. h m
Venus	351 04.6	9 08
Mars	285 53.0	13 28
Jupiter	166 17.1	21 23
Saturn	93 34.1	2 18

Day	UT (d h)	SUN GHA (° ′)	SUN Dec (° ′)	MOON GHA (° ′)	*v* (′)	MOON Dec (° ′)	*d* (′)	HP (′)
SATURDAY	13 00	180 55.0	N18 22.5	336 17.2	12.6	S17 51.2	3.7	54.0
	01	195 55.0	23.1	350 48.8	12.6	17 54.9	3.8	54.0
	02	210 55.1	23.7	5 20.4	12.6	17 58.7	3.6	54.0
	03	225 55.1	. . 24.3	19 52.0	12.6	18 02.3	3.5	54.0
	04	240 55.1	24.9	34 23.6	12.6	18 05.8	3.5	54.0
	05	255 55.1	25.6	48 55.2	12.6	18 09.3	3.4	54.0
	06	270 55.1	N18 26.2	63 26.8	12.5	S18 12.7	3.3	54.0
	07	285 55.1	26.8	77 58.3	12.5	18 16.0	3.2	54.0
	08	300 55.1	27.4	92 29.8	12.5	18 19.2	3.1	54.0
	09	315 55.1	. . 28.0	107 01.3	12.5	18 22.3	3.1	54.0
	10	330 55.1	28.6	121 32.8	12.4	18 25.4	3.0	54.0
	11	345 55.1	29.2	136 04.2	12.4	18 28.4	2.9	54.0
	12	0 55.1	N18 29.8	150 35.6	12.5	S18 31.3	2.8	54.0
	13	15 55.1	30.4	165 07.1	12.4	18 34.1	2.7	54.0
	14	30 55.1	31.1	179 38.5	12.3	18 36.8	2.6	54.0
	15	45 55.1	. . 31.7	194 09.8	12.4	18 39.4	2.6	54.0
	16	60 55.1	32.3	208 41.2	12.3	18 42.0	2.4	54.0
	17	75 55.1	32.9	223 12.5	12.4	18 44.4	2.4	54.0
	18	90 55.1	N18 33.5	237 43.9	12.3	S18 46.8	2.3	54.0
	19	105 55.1	34.1	252 15.2	12.3	18 49.1	2.2	54.0
	20	120 55.1	34.7	266 46.5	12.3	18 51.3	2.1	54.0
	21	135 55.1	. . 35.3	281 17.8	12.2	18 53.4	2.1	54.0
	22	150 55.1	35.9	295 49.0	12.3	18 55.5	1.9	54.0
	23	165 55.1	36.5	310 20.3	12.2	18 57.4	1.9	54.0
SUNDAY	14 00	180 55.1	N18 37.1	324 51.5	12.2	S18 59.3	1.8	54.1
	01	195 55.1	37.7	339 22.7	12.2	19 01.1	1.7	54.1
	02	210 55.1	38.3	353 53.9	12.2	19 02.8	1.6	54.1
	03	225 55.1	. . 38.9	8 25.1	12.2	19 04.4	1.5	54.1
	04	240 55.1	39.5	22 56.3	12.1	19 05.9	1.4	54.1
	05	255 55.1	40.1	37 27.4	12.2	19 07.3	1.4	54.1
	06	270 55.1	N18 40.7	51 58.6	12.1	S19 08.7	1.2	54.1
	07	285 55.1	41.3	66 29.7	12.1	19 09.9	1.2	54.1
	08	300 55.1	41.9	81 00.8	12.2	19 11.1	1.1	54.1
	09	315 55.1	. . 42.5	95 32.0	12.1	19 12.2	0.9	54.1
	10	330 55.1	43.1	110 03.1	12.0	19 13.1	0.9	54.1
	11	345 55.1	43.7	124 34.1	12.1	19 14.0	0.9	54.1
	12	0 55.1	N18 44.3	139 05.2	12.1	S19 14.9	0.7	54.1
	13	15 55.1	44.9	153 36.3	12.0	19 15.6	0.6	54.1
	14	30 55.1	45.5	168 07.3	12.1	19 16.2	0.6	54.1
	15	45 55.1	. . 46.1	182 38.4	12.0	19 16.8	0.4	54.2
	16	60 55.1	46.7	197 09.4	12.0	19 17.2	0.4	54.2
	17	75 55.1	47.3	211 40.4	12.0	19 17.6	0.3	54.2
	18	90 55.1	N18 47.9	226 11.4	12.0	S19 17.9	0.1	54.2
	19	105 55.1	48.5	240 42.4	12.0	19 18.0	0.1	54.2
	20	120 55.1	49.1	255 13.4	12.0	19 18.1	0.0	54.2
	21	135 55.1	. . 49.7	269 44.4	12.0	19 18.1	0.0	54.2
	22	150 55.1	50.3	284 15.4	11.9	19 18.1	0.2	54.2
	23	165 55.1	50.8	298 46.3	12.0	19 17.9	0.3	54.2
MONDAY	15 00	180 55.1	N18 51.4	313 17.3	12.0	S19 17.6	0.3	54.2
	01	195 55.0	52.0	327 48.3	11.9	19 17.3	0.5	54.2
	02	210 55.0	52.6	342 19.2	11.9	19 16.8	0.5	54.3
	03	225 55.0	. . 53.2	356 50.1	12.0	19 16.3	0.6	54.3
	04	240 55.0	53.8	11 21.1	11.9	19 15.7	0.7	54.3
	05	255 55.0	54.4	25 52.0	11.9	19 15.0	0.8	54.3
	06	270 55.0	N18 55.0	40 22.9	11.9	S19 14.2	0.9	54.3
	07	285 55.0	55.6	54 53.8	11.9	19 13.3	1.0	54.3
	08	300 55.0	56.1	69 24.7	11.9	19 12.3	1.1	54.3
	09	315 55.0	. . 56.7	83 55.6	11.9	19 11.2	1.1	54.3
	10	330 55.0	57.3	98 26.5	11.9	19 10.1	1.3	54.4
	11	345 55.0	57.9	112 57.4	11.9	19 08.8	1.3	54.4
	12	0 55.0	N18 58.5	127 28.3	11.9	S19 07.5	1.4	54.4
	13	15 55.0	59.1	141 59.2	11.9	19 06.1	1.6	54.4
	14	30 54.9	18 59.6	156 30.1	11.9	19 04.5	1.6	54.4
	15	45 54.9	19 00.2	171 01.0	11.9	19 02.9	1.7	54.4
	16	60 54.9	00.8	185 31.9	11.8	19 01.2	1.8	54.4
	17	75 54.9	01.4	200 02.7	11.9	18 59.4	1.8	54.4
	18	90 54.9	N19 02.0	214 33.6	11.9	S18 57.6	2.0	54.5
	19	105 54.9	02.6	229 04.5	11.8	18 55.6	2.1	54.5
	20	120 54.9	03.1	243 35.3	11.9	18 53.5	2.1	54.5
	21	135 54.9	. . 03.7	258 06.2	11.9	18 51.4	2.3	54.5
	22	150 54.9	04.3	272 37.1	11.8	18 49.1	2.3	54.5
	23	165 54.9	04.9	287 07.9	11.9	S18 46.8	2.4	54.5
		SD 15.8	*d* 0.6	SD 14.7		14.7		14.8

Lat.	Twilight Naut.	Twilight Civil	Sunrise	Moonrise 13	Moonrise 14	Moonrise 15	Moonrise 16
°	h m	h m	h m	h m	h m	h m	h m
N 72	□	□	□	■	■	■	■
N 70	////	////	00 52	25 12	01 12	02 11	02 33
68	////	////	01 52	24 17	00 17	01 11	01 46
66	////	////	02 26	23 44	24 37	00 37	01 15
64	////	01 14	02 50	23 20	24 12	00 12	00 52
62	////	01 55	03 09	23 01	23 52	24 34	00 34
60	////	02 22	03 24	22 45	23 36	24 19	00 19
N 58	01 06	02 43	03 38	22 32	23 23	24 06	00 06
56	01 44	02 59	03 49	22 20	23 11	23 55	24 32
54	02 09	03 13	03 59	22 10	23 01	23 45	24 23
52	02 28	03 26	04 08	22 02	22 52	23 36	24 15
50	02 44	03 36	04 15	21 54	22 44	23 29	24 08
45	03 15	03 58	04 32	21 37	22 26	23 12	23 53
N 40	03 37	04 15	04 46	21 23	22 12	22 58	23 41
35	03 55	04 29	04 57	21 11	22 00	22 47	23 30
30	04 10	04 41	05 07	21 01	21 50	22 37	23 21
20	04 33	05 01	05 24	20 43	21 32	22 19	23 05
N 10	04 51	05 17	05 39	20 28	21 16	22 04	22 51
0	05 06	05 31	05 53	20 14	21 01	21 50	22 38
S 10	05 19	05 44	06 06	19 59	20 47	21 35	22 25
20	05 31	05 58	06 21	19 44	20 31	21 20	22 11
30	05 43	06 12	06 37	19 27	20 13	21 03	21 55
35	05 49	06 20	06 47	19 17	20 03	20 52	21 45
40	05 56	06 28	06 58	19 05	19 51	20 41	21 34
45	06 03	06 38	07 10	18 52	19 37	20 27	21 22
S 50	06 10	06 50	07 25	18 35	19 20	20 10	21 07
52	06 14	06 55	07 33	18 27	19 12	20 03	20 59
54	06 17	07 01	07 41	18 19	19 03	19 54	20 51
56	06 21	07 07	07 50	18 09	18 53	19 44	20 42
58	06 26	07 14	08 00	17 58	18 41	19 33	20 32
S 60	06 30	07 22	08 11	17 45	18 28	19 20	20 21

Lat.	Sunset	Twilight Civil	Twilight Naut.	Moonset 13	Moonset 14	Moonset 15	Moonset 16
°	h m	h m	h m	h m	h m	h m	h m
N 72	□	□	□	■	■	■	■
N 70	23 14	////	////	03 24	03 36	04 16	05 34
68	22 06	////	////	04 05	04 31	05 16	06 21
66	21 30	////	////	04 33	05 04	05 50	06 51
64	21 05	22 45	////	04 54	05 28	06 15	07 14
62	20 46	22 01	////	05 11	05 48	06 35	07 32
60	20 30	21 33	////	05 26	06 03	06 51	07 47
N 58	20 17	21 12	22 52	05 38	06 17	07 04	08 00
56	20 05	20 55	22 12	05 48	06 28	07 16	08 11
54	19 55	20 41	21 46	05 58	06 38	07 26	08 20
52	19 46	20 28	21 26	06 06	06 47	07 35	08 29
50	19 38	20 18	21 10	06 14	06 55	07 43	08 36
45	19 21	19 56	20 39	06 30	07 12	08 00	08 53
N 40	19 08	19 38	20 16	06 43	07 26	08 14	09 06
35	18 56	19 24	19 58	06 54	07 38	08 26	09 17
30	18 46	19 12	19 43	07 04	07 49	08 37	09 27
20	18 29	18 52	19 20	07 21	08 07	08 55	09 44
N 10	18 14	18 36	19 02	07 35	08 22	09 10	09 59
0	18 00	18 22	18 47	07 49	08 37	09 25	10 13
S 10	17 46	18 08	18 34	08 03	08 51	09 39	10 27
20	17 32	17 55	18 22	08 18	09 07	09 55	10 41
30	17 15	17 41	18 09	08 35	09 25	10 12	10 58
35	17 06	17 33	18 03	08 45	09 35	10 23	11 08
40	16 55	17 24	17 57	08 56	09 47	10 35	11 19
45	16 42	17 14	17 50	09 09	10 01	10 48	11 32
S 50	16 27	17 02	17 42	09 25	10 18	11 05	11 48
52	16 19	16 57	17 38	09 33	10 26	11 13	11 55
54	16 11	16 51	17 35	09 42	10 35	11 22	12 03
56	16 02	16 45	17 31	09 51	10 45	11 32	12 12
58	15 52	16 38	17 26	10 02	10 57	11 44	12 23
S 60	15 41	16 30	17 22	10 14	11 10	11 57	12 35

Day	SUN Eqn. of Time 00^h	SUN Eqn. of Time 12^h	SUN Mer. Pass.	MOON Mer. Pass. Upper	MOON Mer. Pass. Lower	MOON Age	MOON Phase
d	m s	m s	h m	h m	h m	d %	
13	03 40	03 40	11 56	01 38	14 01	17 94	
14	03 40	03 40	11 56	02 25	14 49	18 89	◑
15	03 40	03 40	11 56	03 13	15 37	19 82	

UT d	UT h	ARIES GHA	VENUS −4·6 GHA	VENUS Dec	MARS +1·6 GHA	MARS Dec	JUPITER −2·3 GHA	JUPITER Dec	SATURN +0·2 GHA	SATURN Dec
		° ′	° ′	° ′	° ′	° ′	° ′	° ′	° ′	° ′
16 TUESDAY	00	233 53.9	223 28.3	N 3 35.4	158 18.9	N23 32.7	40 19.4	S 4 10.8	327 35.2	S22 01.2
	01	248 56.3	238 28.9	35.9	173 19.6	32.9	55 22.0	10.8	342 37.8	01.2
	02	263 58.8	253 29.5	36.4	188 20.2	33.1	70 24.6	10.7	357 40.5	01.2
	03	279 01.3	268 30.0	36.9	203 20.8	33.3	85 27.3	10.6	12 43.1	01.2
	04	294 03.7	283 30.6	37.4	218 21.5	33.5	100 29.9	10.6	27 45.7	01.2
	05	309 06.2	298 31.1	38.0	233 22.1	33.7	115 32.5	10.5	42 48.3	01.2
	06	324 08.7	313 31.7	N 3 38.5	248 22.7	N23 33.8	130 35.2	S 4 10.5	57 50.9	S22 01.2
	07	339 11.1	328 32.2	39.0	263 23.3	34.0	145 37.8	10.4	72 53.6	01.2
	08	354 13.6	343 32.8	39.5	278 24.0	34.2	160 40.4	10.3	87 56.2	01.2
	09	9 16.0	358 33.3	40.0	293 24.6	34.4	175 43.1	10.3	102 58.8	01.2
	10	24 18.5	13 33.9	40.5	308 25.2	34.6	190 45.7	10.2	118 01.4	01.2
	11	39 21.0	28 34.4	41.1	323 25.9	34.8	205 48.3	10.2	133 04.0	01.2
	12	54 23.4	43 34.9	N 3 41.6	338 26.5	N23 34.9	220 51.0	S 4 10.1	148 06.7	S22 01.2
	13	69 25.9	58 35.5	42.1	353 27.1	35.1	235 53.6	10.0	163 09.3	01.2
	14	84 28.4	73 36.0	42.6	8 27.8	35.3	250 56.2	10.0	178 11.9	01.2
	15	99 30.8	88 36.6	43.1	23 28.4	35.5	265 58.8	09.9	193 14.5	01.2
	16	114 33.3	103 37.1	43.7	38 29.0	35.6	281 01.5	09.9	208 17.1	01.2
	17	129 35.8	118 37.6	44.2	53 29.7	35.8	296 04.1	09.8	223 19.8	01.2
	18	144 38.2	133 38.2	N 3 44.7	68 30.3	N23 36.0	311 06.7	S 4 09.7	238 22.4	S22 01.2
	19	159 40.7	148 38.7	45.2	83 30.9	36.2	326 09.4	09.7	253 25.0	01.1
	20	174 43.1	163 39.3	45.8	98 31.6	36.4	341 12.0	09.6	268 27.6	01.1
	21	189 45.6	178 39.8	46.3	113 32.2	36.5	356 14.6	09.6	283 30.2	01.1
	22	204 48.1	193 40.3	46.8	128 32.8	36.7	11 17.2	09.5	298 32.9	01.1
	23	219 50.5	208 40.8	47.4	143 33.4	36.9	26 19.9	09.5	313 35.5	01.1
17 WEDNESDAY	00	234 53.0	223 41.4	N 3 47.9	158 34.1	N23 37.1	41 22.5	S 4 09.4	328 38.1	S22 01.1
	01	249 55.5	238 41.9	48.4	173 34.7	37.2	56 25.1	09.3	343 40.7	01.1
	02	264 57.9	253 42.4	48.9	188 35.3	37.4	71 27.8	09.3	358 43.3	01.1
	03	280 00.4	268 43.0	49.5	203 36.0	37.6	86 30.4	09.2	13 46.0	01.1
	04	295 02.9	283 43.5	50.0	218 36.6	37.8	101 33.0	09.2	28 48.6	01.1
	05	310 05.3	298 44.0	50.5	233 37.2	37.9	116 35.6	09.1	43 51.2	01.1
	06	325 07.8	313 44.5	N 3 51.1	248 37.9	N23 38.1	131 38.3	S 4 09.1	58 53.8	S22 01.1
	07	340 10.3	328 45.1	51.6	263 38.5	38.3	146 40.9	09.0	73 56.4	01.1
	08	355 12.7	343 45.6	52.2	278 39.1	38.5	161 43.5	08.9	88 59.1	01.1
	09	10 15.2	358 46.1	52.7	293 39.8	38.6	176 46.1	08.9	104 01.7	01.1
	10	25 17.6	13 46.6	53.2	308 40.4	38.8	191 48.8	08.8	119 04.3	01.1
	11	40 20.1	28 47.1	53.8	323 41.0	39.0	206 51.4	08.8	134 06.9	01.1
	12	55 22.6	43 47.6	N 3 54.3	338 41.6	N23 39.1	221 54.0	S 4 08.7	149 09.6	S22 01.1
	13	70 25.0	58 48.2	54.8	353 42.3	39.3	236 56.6	08.7	164 12.2	01.1
	14	85 27.5	73 48.7	55.4	8 42.9	39.5	251 59.3	08.6	179 14.8	01.1
	15	100 30.0	88 49.2	55.9	23 43.5	39.7	267 01.9	08.5	194 17.4	01.1
	16	115 32.4	103 49.7	56.5	38 44.2	39.8	282 04.5	08.5	209 20.0	01.1
	17	130 34.9	118 50.2	57.0	53 44.8	40.0	297 07.1	08.4	224 22.7	01.1
	18	145 37.4	133 50.7	N 3 57.6	68 45.4	N23 40.2	312 09.7	S 4 08.4	239 25.3	S22 01.1
	19	160 39.8	148 51.2	58.1	83 46.1	40.3	327 12.4	08.3	254 27.9	01.1
	20	175 42.3	163 51.7	58.6	98 46.7	40.5	342 15.0	08.3	269 30.5	01.1
	21	190 44.8	178 52.2	59.2	113 47.3	40.7	357 17.6	08.2	284 33.2	01.0
	22	205 47.2	193 52.7	3 59.7	128 48.0	40.8	12 20.2	08.1	299 35.8	01.0
	23	220 49.7	208 53.2	4 00.3	143 48.6	41.0	27 22.9	08.1	314 38.4	01.0
18 THURSDAY	00	235 52.1	223 53.7	N 4 00.8	158 49.2	N23 41.2	42 25.5	S 4 08.0	329 41.0	S22 01.0
	01	250 54.6	238 54.2	01.4	173 49.8	41.3	57 28.1	08.0	344 43.6	01.0
	02	265 57.1	253 54.7	01.9	188 50.5	41.5	72 30.7	07.9	359 46.3	01.0
	03	280 59.5	268 55.2	02.5	203 51.1	41.7	87 33.3	07.9	14 48.9	01.0
	04	296 02.0	283 55.7	03.0	218 51.7	41.8	102 36.0	07.8	29 51.5	01.0
	05	311 04.5	298 56.2	03.6	233 52.4	42.0	117 38.6	07.8	44 54.1	01.0
	06	326 06.9	313 56.7	N 4 04.1	248 53.0	N23 42.2	132 41.2	S 4 07.7	59 56.8	S22 01.0
	07	341 09.4	328 57.2	04.7	263 53.6	42.3	147 43.8	07.7	74 59.4	01.0
	08	356 11.9	343 57.7	05.2	278 54.3	42.5	162 46.4	07.6	90 02.0	01.0
	09	11 14.3	358 58.2	05.8	293 54.9	42.7	177 49.0	07.5	105 04.6	01.0
	10	26 16.8	13 58.7	06.4	308 55.5	42.8	192 51.7	07.5	120 07.3	01.0
	11	41 19.2	28 59.2	06.9	323 56.1	43.0	207 54.3	07.4	135 09.9	01.0
	12	56 21.7	43 59.7	N 4 07.5	338 56.8	N23 43.2	222 56.9	S 4 07.4	150 12.5	S22 01.0
	13	71 24.2	59 00.2	08.0	353 57.4	43.3	237 59.5	07.3	165 15.1	01.0
	14	86 26.6	74 00.7	08.6	8 58.0	43.5	253 02.1	07.3	180 17.8	01.0
	15	101 29.1	89 01.2	09.1	23 58.7	43.6	268 04.8	07.2	195 20.4	01.0
	16	116 31.6	104 01.6	09.7	38 59.3	43.8	283 07.4	07.2	210 23.0	01.0
	17	131 34.0	119 02.1	10.3	53 59.9	44.0	298 10.0	07.1	225 25.6	01.0
	18	146 36.5	134 02.6	N 4 10.8	69 00.6	N23 44.1	313 12.6	S 4 07.1	240 28.3	S22 01.0
	19	161 39.0	149 03.1	11.4	84 01.2	44.3	328 15.2	07.0	255 30.9	01.0
	20	176 41.4	164 03.6	12.0	99 01.8	44.5	343 17.8	07.0	270 33.5	01.0
	21	191 43.9	179 04.0	12.5	114 02.4	44.6	358 20.5	06.9	285 36.1	01.0
	22	206 46.4	194 04.5	13.1	129 03.1	44.8	13 23.1	06.8	300 38.8	01.0
	23	221 48.8	209 05.0	13.7	144 03.7	44.9	28 25.7	06.8	315 41.4	00.9
Mer. Pass.		h m 8 19.1	v 0.5	d 0.5	v 0.6	d 0.2	v 2.6	d 0.1	v 2.6	d 0.0

STARS

Name	SHA	Dec
	° ′	° ′
Acamar	315 16.8	S40 14.3
Achernar	335 25.4	S57 08.9
Acrux	173 05.7	S63 11.9
Adhara	255 10.7	S29 00.1
Aldebaran	290 46.7	N16 32.4
Alioth	166 18.1	N55 52.2
Alkaid	152 56.5	N49 13.8
Al Na'ir	27 40.5	S46 52.4
Alnilam	275 44.0	S 1 11.7
Alphard	217 53.6	S 8 44.2
Alphecca	126 08.4	N26 39.5
Alpheratz	357 40.9	N29 10.9
Altair	62 05.5	N 8 54.9
Ankaa	353 13.4	S42 12.7
Antares	112 22.7	S26 28.0
Arcturus	145 53.0	N19 05.7
Atria	107 21.5	S69 03.2
Avior	234 17.1	S59 34.3
Bellatrix	278 29.5	N 6 21.6
Betelgeuse	270 58.8	N 7 24.3
Canopus	263 55.4	S52 42.7
Capella	280 31.0	N46 00.7
Deneb	49 29.5	N45 20.4
Denebola	182 30.9	N14 28.6
Diphda	348 53.5	S17 53.6
Dubhe	193 48.4	N61 39.7
Elnath	278 09.6	N28 37.1
Eltanin	90 44.5	N51 29.2
Enif	33 44.5	N 9 57.2
Fomalhaut	15 21.2	S29 31.7
Gacrux	171 57.5	S57 12.8
Gienah	175 49.4	S17 38.4
Hadar	148 43.4	S60 27.4
Hamal	327 58.1	N23 32.4
Kaus Aust.	83 40.0	S34 22.3
Kochab	137 19.1	N74 05.3
Markab	13 35.8	N15 17.8
Menkar	314 12.6	N 4 09.2
Menkent	148 04.1	S36 27.3
Miaplacidus	221 39.2	S69 47.7
Mirfak	308 37.0	N49 55.1
Nunki	75 54.8	S26 16.3
Peacock	53 15.0	S56 40.4
Pollux	243 24.8	N27 58.9
Procyon	244 57.2	N 5 10.6
Rasalhague	96 03.7	N12 33.0
Regulus	207 40.7	N11 52.9
Rigel	281 09.9	S 8 11.2
Rigil Kent.	139 47.4	S60 54.3
Sabik	102 09.2	S15 44.6
Schedar	349 37.8	N56 37.6
Shaula	96 18.0	S37 06.7
Sirius	258 31.7	S16 44.7
Spica	158 28.2	S11 15.1
Suhail	222 50.6	S43 30.5
Vega	80 36.9	N38 48.0
Zuben'ubi	137 02.2	S16 06.7

	SHA	Mer. Pass.
	° ′	h m
Venus	348 48.4	9 05
Mars	283 41.1	13 25
Jupiter	166 29.5	21 11
Saturn	93 45.1	2 05

UT	SUN GHA	SUN Dec	MOON GHA	v	MOON Dec	d	HP
d h	° ′	° ′	° ′	′	° ′	′	′
16 00	180 54.8	N19 05.4	301 38.8	11.9	S18 44.4	2.5	54.6
01	195 54.8	06.0	316 09.7	11.8	18 41.9	2.6	54.6
02	210 54.8	06.6	330 40.5	11.9	18 39.3	2.7	54.6
03	225 54.8	. . 07.2	345 11.4	11.9	18 36.6	2.8	54.6
04	240 54.8	07.7	359 42.3	11.8	18 33.8	2.8	54.6
05	255 54.8	08.3	14 13.1	11.9	18 31.0	3.0	54.6
06	270 54.8	N19 08.9	28 44.0	11.8	S18 28.0	3.0	54.7
07	285 54.8	09.5	43 14.8	11.9	18 25.0	3.2	54.7
T 08	300 54.7	10.0	57 45.7	11.9	18 21.8	3.2	54.7
U 09	315 54.7	. . 10.6	72 16.6	11.8	18 18.6	3.3	54.7
E 10	330 54.7	11.2	86 47.4	11.9	18 15.3	3.4	54.7
11	345 54.7	11.8	101 18.3	11.9	18 11.9	3.5	54.7
S 12	0 54.7	N19 12.3	115 49.2	11.8	S18 08.4	3.5	54.8
D 13	15 54.7	12.9	130 20.0	11.9	18 04.9	3.7	54.8
A 14	30 54.6	13.5	144 50.9	11.9	18 01.2	3.7	54.8
Y 15	45 54.6	. . 14.0	159 21.8	11.9	17 57.5	3.9	54.8
16	60 54.6	14.6	173 52.7	11.8	17 53.6	3.9	54.8
17	75 54.6	15.2	188 23.5	11.9	17 49.7	4.0	54.9
18	90 54.6	N19 15.7	202 54.4	11.9	S17 45.7	4.1	54.9
19	105 54.6	16.3	217 25.3	11.9	17 41.6	4.2	54.9
20	120 54.6	16.9	231 56.2	11.9	17 37.4	4.2	54.9
21	135 54.5	. . 17.4	246 27.1	11.9	17 33.2	4.4	54.9
22	150 54.5	18.0	260 58.0	11.9	17 28.8	4.4	55.0
23	165 54.5	18.6	275 28.9	11.9	17 24.4	4.6	55.0
17 00	180 54.5	N19 19.1	289 59.8	11.9	S17 19.8	4.6	55.0
01	195 54.5	19.7	304 30.7	11.9	17 15.2	4.7	55.0
02	210 54.4	20.3	319 01.6	11.9	17 10.5	4.8	55.1
03	225 54.4	. . 20.8	333 32.5	11.9	17 05.7	4.8	55.1
04	240 54.4	21.4	348 03.4	11.9	17 00.9	5.0	55.1
05	255 54.4	21.9	2 34.3	11.9	16 55.9	5.0	55.1
06	270 54.4	N19 22.5	17 05.2	11.9	S16 50.9	5.1	55.1
W 07	285 54.4	23.1	31 36.1	12.0	16 45.8	5.2	55.2
E 08	300 54.3	23.6	46 07.1	11.9	16 40.6	5.3	55.2
D 09	315 54.3	. . 24.2	60 38.0	11.9	16 35.3	5.4	55.2
N 10	330 54.3	24.7	75 08.9	11.9	16 29.9	5.4	55.2
E 11	345 54.3	25.3	89 39.8	12.0	16 24.5	5.6	55.3
12	0 54.3	N19 25.8	104 10.8	11.9	S16 18.9	5.6	55.3
S 13	15 54.2	26.4	118 41.7	12.0	16 13.3	5.7	55.3
D 14	30 54.2	27.0	133 12.7	11.9	16 07.6	5.8	55.3
A 15	45 54.2	. . 27.5	147 43.6	11.9	16 01.8	5.9	55.4
Y 16	60 54.2	28.1	162 14.5	12.0	15 55.9	5.9	55.4
17	75 54.1	28.6	176 45.5	11.9	15 50.0	6.0	55.4
18	90 54.1	N19 29.2	191 16.4	12.0	S15 44.0	6.1	55.4
19	105 54.1	29.7	205 47.4	12.0	15 37.9	6.2	55.5
20	120 54.1	30.3	220 18.4	11.9	15 31.7	6.3	55.5
21	135 54.1	. . 30.8	234 49.3	12.0	15 25.4	6.3	55.5
22	150 54.0	31.4	249 20.3	11.9	15 19.1	6.5	55.5
23	165 54.0	31.9	263 51.2	12.0	15 12.6	6.5	55.6
18 00	180 54.0	N19 32.5	278 22.2	12.0	S15 06.1	6.6	55.6
01	195 54.0	33.0	292 53.2	11.9	14 59.5	6.6	55.6
02	210 53.9	33.6	307 24.1	12.0	14 52.9	6.8	55.7
03	225 53.9	. . 34.1	321 55.1	12.0	14 46.1	6.8	55.7
04	240 53.9	34.7	336 26.1	12.0	14 39.3	6.9	55.7
05	255 53.9	35.2	350 57.1	11.9	14 32.4	7.0	55.7
06	270 53.8	N19 35.8	5 28.0	12.0	S14 25.4	7.0	55.8
07	285 53.8	36.3	19 59.0	12.0	14 18.4	7.2	55.8
T 08	300 53.8	36.9	34 30.0	12.0	14 11.2	7.2	55.8
H 09	315 53.8	. . 37.4	49 01.0	11.9	14 04.0	7.2	55.9
U 10	330 53.7	38.0	63 31.9	12.0	13 56.8	7.4	55.9
R 11	345 53.7	38.5	78 02.9	12.0	13 49.4	7.4	55.9
S 12	0 53.7	N19 39.0	92 33.9	12.0	S13 42.0	7.5	56.0
D 13	15 53.7	39.6	107 04.9	11.9	13 34.5	7.6	56.0
A 14	30 53.6	40.1	121 35.8	12.0	13 26.9	7.7	56.0
Y 15	45 53.6	. . 40.7	136 06.8	12.0	13 19.2	7.7	56.0
16	60 53.6	41.2	150 37.8	11.9	13 11.5	7.8	56.1
17	75 53.5	41.7	165 08.7	12.0	13 03.7	7.9	56.1
18	90 53.5	N19 42.3	179 39.7	12.0	S12 55.8	7.9	56.1
19	105 53.5	42.8	194 10.7	11.9	12 47.9	8.0	56.2
20	120 53.5	43.4	208 41.6	12.0	12 39.9	8.1	56.2
21	135 53.4	. . 43.9	223 12.6	12.0	12 31.8	8.2	56.2
22	150 53.4	44.4	237 43.6	11.9	12 23.6	8.2	56.3
23	165 53.4	45.0	252 14.5	12.0	S12 15.4	8.3	56.3
	SD 15.8	*d* 0.6	SD	14.9	15.1		15.2

Lat.	Twilight Naut.	Twilight Civil	Sunrise	Moonrise 16	17	18	19
°	h m	h m	h m	h m	h m	h m	h m
N 72	▭	▭	▭	■	03 34	03 12	02 59
N 70	▭	▭	▭	02 33	02 39	02 40	02 39
68	////	////	01 35	01 46	02 05	02 17	02 23
66	////	////	02 14	01 15	01 41	01 58	02 11
64	////	00 51	02 40	00 52	01 22	01 43	02 00
62	////	01 42	03 01	00 34	01 06	01 31	01 51
60	////	02 12	03 17	00 19	00 53	01 20	01 43
N 58	00 46	02 35	03 31	00 06	00 42	01 11	01 36
56	01 32	02 53	03 43	24 32	00 32	01 03	01 30
54	02 00	03 08	03 54	24 23	00 23	00 56	01 24
52	02 21	03 20	04 03	24 15	00 15	00 49	01 19
50	02 38	03 31	04 11	24 08	00 08	00 43	01 15
45	03 10	03 54	04 29	23 53	24 31	00 31	01 05
N 40	03 34	04 12	04 43	23 41	24 20	00 20	00 56
35	03 52	04 27	04 55	23 30	24 11	00 11	00 49
30	04 08	04 39	05 05	23 21	24 03	00 03	00 43
20	04 31	04 59	05 23	23 05	23 49	24 32	00 32
N 10	04 50	05 16	05 39	22 51	23 37	24 23	00 23
0	05 05	05 31	05 53	22 38	23 26	24 14	00 14
S 10	05 19	05 45	06 07	22 25	23 15	24 05	00 05
20	05 32	05 59	06 22	22 11	23 02	23 55	24 50
30	05 45	06 14	06 39	21 55	22 49	23 44	24 42
35	05 51	06 22	06 49	21 45	22 41	23 38	24 38
40	05 58	06 31	07 00	21 34	22 31	23 31	24 33
45	06 06	06 41	07 13	21 22	22 21	23 22	24 27
S 50	06 14	06 54	07 30	21 07	22 07	23 12	24 20
52	06 18	06 59	07 37	20 59	22 01	23 08	24 17
54	06 21	07 05	07 45	20 51	21 55	23 02	24 14
56	06 26	07 12	07 55	20 42	21 47	22 57	24 10
58	06 30	07 19	08 06	20 32	21 39	22 50	24 06
S 60	06 35	07 28	08 18	20 21	21 29	22 43	24 01

Lat.	Sunset	Twilight Civil	Twilight Naut.	Moonset 16	17	18	19
°	h m	h m	h m	h m	h m	h m	h m
N 72	▭	▭	▭	■	06 14	08 17	10 09
N 70	▭	▭	▭	05 34	07 08	08 47	10 28
68	22 23	////	////	06 21	07 41	09 10	10 42
66	21 43	////	////	06 51	08 05	09 27	10 54
64	21 15	23 11	////	07 14	08 24	09 41	11 04
62	20 54	22 15	////	07 32	08 39	09 53	11 12
60	20 37	21 43	////	07 47	08 52	10 03	11 19
N 58	20 23	21 20	23 15	08 00	09 03	10 12	11 25
56	20 11	21 02	22 24	08 11	09 12	10 19	11 31
54	20 00	20 47	21 55	08 20	09 21	10 26	11 36
52	19 51	20 34	21 34	08 29	09 28	10 32	11 40
50	19 42	20 22	21 16	08 36	09 35	10 38	11 44
45	19 25	19 59	20 44	08 53	09 49	10 50	11 53
N 40	19 10	19 41	20 20	09 06	10 01	11 00	12 00
35	18 58	19 27	20 01	09 17	10 11	11 08	12 06
30	18 48	19 14	19 46	09 27	10 20	11 15	12 12
20	18 30	18 54	19 22	09 44	10 35	11 28	12 21
N 10	18 14	18 37	19 03	09 59	10 49	11 39	12 29
0	18 00	18 22	18 47	10 13	11 01	11 49	12 37
S 10	17 46	18 08	18 34	10 27	11 13	11 59	12 44
20	17 31	17 54	18 21	10 41	11 26	12 10	12 52
30	17 13	17 39	18 08	10 58	11 41	12 22	13 02
35	17 03	17 31	18 01	11 08	11 50	12 29	13 07
40	16 52	17 21	17 54	11 19	12 00	12 37	13 13
45	16 39	17 11	17 47	11 32	12 11	12 47	13 19
S 50	16 23	16 59	17 38	11 48	12 25	12 58	13 28
52	16 15	16 53	17 35	11 55	12 31	13 03	13 31
54	16 07	16 47	17 31	12 03	12 38	13 09	13 35
56	15 57	16 40	17 26	12 12	12 46	13 15	13 40
58	15 47	16 33	17 22	12 23	12 55	13 22	13 45
S 60	15 34	16 24	17 17	12 35	13 05	13 30	13 51

Day	SUN Eqn. of Time 00^h	SUN Eqn. of Time 12^h	SUN Mer. Pass.	MOON Mer. Pass. Upper	MOON Mer. Pass. Lower	Age	Phase
d	m s	m s	h m	h m	h m	d	%
16	03 39	03 39	11 56	04 01	16 25	20	74
17	03 38	03 37	11 56	04 49	17 13	21	65
18	03 36	03 35	11 56	05 37	18 01	22	55

UT d	h	ARIES GHA	VENUS −4·6 GHA	VENUS Dec	MARS +1·6 GHA	MARS Dec	JUPITER −2·3 GHA	JUPITER Dec	SATURN +0·1 GHA	SATURN Dec
		° ′	° ′	° ′	° ′	° ′	° ′	° ′	° ′	° ′
19	00	236 51.3	224 05.5	N 4 14.2	159 04.3	N23 45.1	43 28.3	S 4 06.7	330 44.0	S22 00.9
	01	251 53.7	239 06.0	14.8	174 05.0	45.2	58 30.9	06.7	345 46.6	00.9
	02	266 56.2	254 06.4	15.4	189 05.6	45.4	73 33.5	06.6	0 49.3	00.9
	03	281 58.7	269 06.9	. . 15.9	204 06.2	. . 45.6	88 36.1	. . 06.6	15 51.9	. . 00.9
	04	297 01.1	284 07.4	16.5	219 06.9	45.7	103 38.8	06.5	30 54.5	00.9
	05	312 03.6	299 07.8	17.1	234 07.5	45.9	118 41.4	06.5	45 57.2	00.9
	06	327 06.1	314 08.3	N 4 17.6	249 08.1	N23 46.0	133 44.0	S 4 06.4	60 59.8	S22 00.9
	07	342 08.5	329 08.8	18.2	264 08.8	46.2	148 46.6	06.4	76 02.4	00.9
	08	357 11.0	344 09.3	18.8	279 09.4	46.3	163 49.2	06.3	91 05.0	00.9
F	09	12 13.5	359 09.7	. . 19.3	294 10.0	. . 46.5	178 51.8	. . 06.3	106 07.7	. . 00.9
R	10	27 15.9	14 10.2	19.9	309 10.6	46.7	193 54.4	06.2	121 10.3	00.9
I	11	42 18.4	29 10.6	20.5	324 11.3	46.8	208 57.0	06.2	136 12.9	00.9
D	12	57 20.9	44 11.1	N 4 21.1	339 11.9	N23 47.0	223 59.7	S 4 06.1	151 15.5	S22 00.9
A	13	72 23.3	59 11.6	21.6	354 12.5	47.1	239 02.3	06.1	166 18.2	00.9
Y	14	87 25.8	74 12.0	22.2	9 13.2	47.3	254 04.9	06.0	181 20.8	00.9
	15	102 28.2	89 12.5	. . 22.8	24 13.8	. . 47.4	269 07.5	. . 06.0	196 23.4	. . 00.9
	16	117 30.7	104 13.0	23.4	39 14.4	47.6	284 10.1	05.9	211 26.1	00.9
	17	132 33.2	119 13.4	24.0	54 15.1	47.7	299 12.7	05.9	226 28.7	00.9
	18	147 35.6	134 13.9	N 4 24.5	69 15.7	N23 47.9	314 15.3	S 4 05.8	241 31.3	S22 00.9
	19	162 38.1	149 14.3	25.1	84 16.3	48.0	329 17.9	05.8	256 33.9	00.9
	20	177 40.6	164 14.8	25.7	99 16.9	48.2	344 20.5	05.7	271 36.6	00.9
	21	192 43.0	179 15.2	. . 26.3	114 17.6	. . 48.3	359 23.1	. . 05.7	286 39.2	. . 00.9
	22	207 45.5	194 15.7	26.9	129 18.2	48.5	14 25.8	05.6	301 41.8	00.9
	23	222 48.0	209 16.1	27.4	144 18.8	48.6	29 28.4	05.6	316 44.4	00.9
20	00	237 50.4	224 16.6	N 4 28.0	159 19.5	N23 48.8	44 31.0	S 4 05.5	331 47.1	S22 00.9
	01	252 52.9	239 17.0	28.6	174 20.1	48.9	59 33.6	05.5	346 49.7	00.8
	02	267 55.3	254 17.5	29.2	189 20.7	49.1	74 36.2	05.4	1 52.3	00.8
	03	282 57.8	269 17.9	. . 29.8	204 21.4	. . 49.2	89 38.8	. . 05.4	16 55.0	. . 00.8
	04	298 00.3	284 18.4	30.4	219 22.0	49.4	104 41.4	05.3	31 57.6	00.8
	05	313 02.7	299 18.8	31.0	234 22.6	49.5	119 44.0	05.3	47 00.2	00.8
	06	328 05.2	314 19.3	N 4 31.5	249 23.2	N23 49.7	134 46.6	S 4 05.2	62 02.9	S22 00.8
	07	343 07.7	329 19.7	32.1	264 23.9	49.8	149 49.2	05.2	77 05.5	00.8
S	08	358 10.1	344 20.2	32.7	279 24.5	50.0	164 51.8	05.1	92 08.1	00.8
A	09	13 12.6	359 20.6	. . 33.3	294 25.1	. . 50.1	179 54.4	. . 05.1	107 10.7	. . 00.8
T	10	28 15.1	14 21.0	33.9	309 25.8	50.3	194 57.0	05.0	122 13.4	00.8
U	11	43 17.5	29 21.5	34.5	324 26.4	50.4	209 59.6	05.0	137 16.0	00.8
R	12	58 20.0	44 21.9	N 4 35.1	339 27.0	N23 50.6	225 02.3	S 4 04.9	152 18.6	S22 00.8
D	13	73 22.5	59 22.4	35.7	354 27.7	50.7	240 04.9	04.9	167 21.3	00.8
A	14	88 24.9	74 22.8	36.3	9 28.3	50.8	255 07.5	04.8	182 23.9	00.8
Y	15	103 27.4	89 23.2	. . 36.9	24 28.9	. . 51.0	270 10.1	. . 04.8	197 26.5	. . 00.8
	16	118 29.8	104 23.7	37.4	39 29.5	51.1	285 12.7	04.7	212 29.2	00.8
	17	133 32.3	119 24.1	38.0	54 30.2	51.3	300 15.3	04.7	227 31.8	00.8
	18	148 34.8	134 24.5	N 4 38.6	69 30.8	N23 51.4	315 17.9	S 4 04.6	242 34.4	S22 00.8
	19	163 37.2	149 25.0	39.2	84 31.4	51.6	330 20.5	04.6	257 37.0	00.8
	20	178 39.7	164 25.4	39.8	99 32.1	51.7	345 23.1	04.5	272 39.7	00.8
	21	193 42.2	179 25.8	. . 40.4	114 32.7	. . 51.9	0 25.7	. . 04.5	287 42.3	. . 00.8
	22	208 44.6	194 26.3	41.0	129 33.3	52.0	15 28.3	04.4	302 44.9	00.8
	23	223 47.1	209 26.7	41.6	144 34.0	52.1	30 30.9	04.4	317 47.6	00.8
21	00	238 49.6	224 27.1	N 4 42.2	159 34.6	N23 52.3	45 33.5	S 4 04.3	332 50.2	S22 00.8
	01	253 52.0	239 27.5	42.8	174 35.2	52.4	60 36.1	04.3	347 52.8	00.8
	02	268 54.5	254 28.0	43.4	189 35.8	52.6	75 38.7	04.2	2 55.5	00.7
	03	283 57.0	269 28.4	. . 44.0	204 36.5	. . 52.7	90 41.3	. . 04.2	17 58.1	. . 00.7
	04	298 59.4	284 28.8	44.6	219 37.1	52.8	105 43.9	04.2	33 00.7	00.7
	05	314 01.9	299 29.2	45.2	234 37.7	53.0	120 46.5	04.1	48 03.4	00.7
	06	329 04.3	314 29.6	N 4 45.8	249 38.4	N23 53.1	135 49.1	S 4 04.1	63 06.0	S22 00.7
	07	344 06.8	329 30.1	46.4	264 39.0	53.3	150 51.7	04.0	78 08.6	00.7
	08	359 09.3	344 30.5	47.0	279 39.6	53.4	165 54.3	04.0	93 11.2	00.7
S	09	14 11.7	359 30.9	. . 47.7	294 40.3	. . 53.5	180 56.9	. . 03.9	108 13.9	. . 00.7
U	10	29 14.2	14 31.3	48.3	309 40.9	53.7	195 59.5	03.9	123 16.5	00.7
N	11	44 16.7	29 31.7	48.9	324 41.5	53.8	211 02.1	03.8	138 19.1	00.7
D	12	59 19.1	44 32.2	N 4 49.5	339 42.1	N23 53.9	226 04.7	S 4 03.8	153 21.8	S22 00.7
A	13	74 21.6	59 32.6	50.1	354 42.8	54.1	241 07.3	03.7	168 24.4	00.7
Y	14	89 24.1	74 33.0	50.7	9 43.4	54.2	256 09.9	03.7	183 27.0	00.7
	15	104 26.5	89 33.4	. . 51.3	24 44.0	. . 54.4	271 12.5	. . 03.6	198 29.7	. . 00.7
	16	119 29.0	104 33.8	51.9	39 44.7	54.5	286 15.1	03.6	213 32.3	00.7
	17	134 31.4	119 34.2	52.5	54 45.3	54.6	301 17.7	03.6	228 34.9	00.7
	18	149 33.9	134 34.6	N 4 53.1	69 45.9	N23 54.8	316 20.3	S 4 03.5	243 37.6	S22 00.7
	19	164 36.4	149 35.0	53.7	84 46.6	54.9	331 22.9	03.5	258 40.2	00.7
	20	179 38.8	164 35.4	54.4	99 47.2	55.0	346 25.5	03.4	273 42.8	00.7
	21	194 41.3	179 35.8	. . 55.0	114 47.8	. . 55.2	1 28.1	. . 03.4	288 45.5	. . 00.7
	22	209 43.8	194 36.2	55.6	129 48.4	55.3	16 30.7	03.3	303 48.1	00.7
	23	224 46.2	209 36.7	56.2	144 49.1	55.4	31 33.3	03.3	318 50.7	00.7
Mer. Pass.		h m 8 07.3	*v* 0.4	*d* 0.6	*v* 0.6	*d* 0.1	*v* 2.6	*d* 0.0	*v* 2.6	*d* 0.0

STARS

Name	SHA	Dec
	° ′	° ′
Acamar	315 16.8	S40 14.3
Achernar	335 25.4	S57 08.9
Acrux	173 05.8	S63 11.9
Adhara	255 10.7	S29 00.1
Aldebaran	290 46.7	N16 32.4
Alioth	166 18.1	N55 52.2
Alkaid	152 56.5	N49 13.8
Al Na'ir	27 40.5	S46 52.4
Alnilam	275 44.0	S 1 11.7
Alphard	217 53.6	S 8 44.2
Alphecca	126 08.4	N26 39.5
Alpheratz	357 40.9	N29 10.9
Altair	62 05.5	N 8 54.9
Ankaa	353 13.4	S42 12.6
Antares	112 22.7	S26 28.0
Arcturus	145 53.1	N19 05.7
Atria	107 21.5	S69 03.2
Avior	234 17.2	S59 34.3
Bellatrix	278 29.5	N 6 21.6
Betelgeuse	270 58.8	N 7 24.4
Canopus	263 55.4	S52 42.7
Capella	280 31.0	N46 00.7
Deneb	49 29.5	N45 20.4
Denebola	182 30.9	N14 28.6
Diphda	348 53.5	S17 53.6
Dubhe	193 48.5	N61 39.7
Elnath	278 09.6	N28 37.1
Eltanin	90 44.4	N51 29.2
Enif	33 44.5	N 9 57.2
Fomalhaut	15 21.2	S29 31.7
Gacrux	171 57.5	S57 12.8
Gienah	175 49.4	S17 38.4
Hadar	148 43.5	S60 27.4
Hamal	327 58.1	N23 32.4
Kaus Aust.	83 40.0	S34 22.3
Kochab	137 19.1	N74 05.3
Markab	13 35.8	N15 17.8
Menkar	314 12.6	N 4 09.2
Menkent	148 04.1	S36 27.3
Miaplacidus	221 39.2	S69 47.7
Mirfak	308 37.0	N49 55.1
Nunki	75 54.8	S26 16.3
Peacock	53 14.9	S56 40.4
Pollux	243 24.8	N27 58.9
Procyon	244 57.2	N 5 10.6
Rasalhague	96 03.7	N12 33.0
Regulus	207 40.7	N11 52.9
Rigel	281 09.9	S 8 11.2
Rigil Kent.	139 47.4	S60 54.3
Sabik	102 09.2	S15 44.6
Schedar	349 37.8	N56 37.6
Shaula	96 18.0	S37 06.7
Sirius	258 31.7	S16 44.7
Spica	158 28.2	S11 15.1
Suhail	222 50.6	S43 30.5
Vega	80 36.8	N38 48.0
Zuben'ubi	137 02.2	S16 06.7

	SHA	Mer. Pass.
	° ′	h m
Venus	346 26.2	9 03
Mars	281 29.0	13 22
Jupiter	166 40.6	20 58
Saturn	93 56.7	1 53

UT	SUN GHA	SUN Dec	MOON GHA	v	MOON Dec	d	HP
d h	° ′	° ′	° ′	′	° ′	′	′
19 00 (FRIDAY)	180 53.3	N19 45.5	266 45.5	11.9	S12 07.1	8.3	56.3
01	195 53.3	46.0	281 16.4	11.9	11 58.8	8.5	56.4
02	210 53.3	46.6	295 47.3	12.0	11 50.3	8.5	56.4
03	225 53.2	. . 47.1	310 18.3	11.9	11 41.8	8.5	56.4
04	240 53.2	47.7	324 49.2	11.9	11 33.3	8.7	56.5
05	255 53.2	48.2	339 20.1	12.0	11 24.6	8.7	56.5
06	270 53.2	N19 48.7	353 51.1	11.9	S11 15.9	8.8	56.5
07	285 53.1	49.2	8 22.0	11.9	11 07.1	8.8	56.6
08	300 53.1	49.8	22 52.9	11.9	10 58.3	8.9	56.6
09	315 53.1	. . 50.3	37 23.8	11.8	10 49.4	9.0	56.6
10	330 53.0	50.8	51 54.6	11.9	10 40.4	9.0	56.7
11	345 53.0	51.4	66 25.5	11.9	10 31.4	9.1	56.7
12	0 53.0	N19 51.9	80 56.4	11.9	S10 22.3	9.1	56.8
13	15 52.9	52.4	95 27.3	11.8	10 13.2	9.2	56.8
14	30 52.9	53.0	109 58.1	11.8	10 04.0	9.3	56.8
15	45 52.9	. . 53.5	124 28.9	11.9	9 54.7	9.4	56.9
16	60 52.8	54.0	138 59.8	11.8	9 45.3	9.4	56.9
17	75 52.8	54.5	153 30.6	11.8	9 35.9	9.4	56.9
18	90 52.8	N19 55.1	168 01.4	11.8	S 9 26.5	9.5	57.0
19	105 52.7	55.6	182 32.2	11.8	9 17.0	9.6	57.0
20	120 52.7	56.1	197 03.0	11.7	9 07.4	9.7	57.0
21	135 52.7	. . 56.6	211 33.7	11.8	8 57.7	9.7	57.1
22	150 52.6	57.2	226 04.5	11.7	8 48.0	9.7	57.1
23	165 52.6	57.7	240 35.2	11.8	8 38.3	9.8	57.2
20 00 (SATURDAY)	180 52.6	N19 58.2	255 06.0	11.7	S 8 28.5	9.9	57.2
01	195 52.5	58.7	269 36.7	11.7	8 18.6	9.9	57.2
02	210 52.5	59.2	284 07.4	11.6	8 08.7	10.0	57.3
03	225 52.4	19 59.8	298 38.0	11.7	7 58.7	10.0	57.3
04	240 52.4	20 00.3	313 08.7	11.6	7 48.7	10.1	57.3
05	255 52.4	00.8	327 39.3	11.7	7 38.6	10.2	57.4
06	270 52.3	N20 01.3	342 10.0	11.6	S 7 28.4	10.1	57.4
07	285 52.3	01.8	356 40.6	11.5	7 18.3	10.3	57.5
08	300 52.3	02.4	11 11.1	11.6	7 08.0	10.3	57.5
09	315 52.2	. . 02.9	25 41.7	11.6	6 57.7	10.3	57.5
10	330 52.2	03.4	40 12.3	11.5	6 47.4	10.4	57.6
11	345 52.1	03.9	54 42.8	11.5	6 37.0	10.4	57.6
12	0 52.1	N20 04.4	69 13.3	11.5	S 6 26.6	10.5	57.7
13	15 52.1	04.9	83 43.8	11.4	6 16.1	10.6	57.7
14	30 52.0	05.4	98 14.2	11.4	6 05.5	10.6	57.7
15	45 52.0	. . 06.0	112 44.6	11.4	5 54.9	10.6	57.8
16	60 52.0	06.5	127 15.0	11.4	5 44.3	10.7	57.8
17	75 51.9	07.0	141 45.4	11.4	5 33.6	10.7	57.8
18	90 51.9	N20 07.5	156 15.8	11.3	S 5 22.9	10.7	57.9
19	105 51.8	08.0	170 46.1	11.3	5 12.2	10.8	57.9
20	120 51.8	08.5	185 16.4	11.3	5 01.4	10.9	58.0
21	135 51.8	. . 09.0	199 46.7	11.2	4 50.5	10.9	58.0
22	150 51.7	09.5	214 16.9	11.2	4 39.6	10.9	58.0
23	165 51.7	10.0	228 47.1	11.2	4 28.7	10.9	58.1
21 00 (SUNDAY)	180 51.6	N20 10.6	243 17.3	11.2	S 4 17.8	11.0	58.1
01	195 51.6	11.1	257 47.5	11.1	4 06.8	11.1	58.2
02	210 51.5	11.6	272 17.6	11.1	3 55.7	11.1	58.2
03	225 51.5	. . 12.1	286 47.7	11.1	3 44.6	11.1	58.2
04	240 51.5	12.6	301 17.8	11.0	3 33.5	11.1	58.3
05	255 51.4	13.1	315 47.8	11.0	3 22.4	11.2	58.3
06	270 51.4	N20 13.6	330 17.8	11.0	S 3 11.2	11.2	58.4
07	285 51.3	14.1	344 47.8	10.9	3 00.0	11.3	58.4
08	300 51.3	14.6	359 17.7	10.9	2 48.7	11.2	58.4
09	315 51.2	. . 15.1	13 47.6	10.8	2 37.5	11.4	58.5
10	330 51.2	15.6	28 17.4	10.8	2 26.1	11.3	58.5
11	345 51.2	16.1	42 47.2	10.8	2 14.8	11.4	58.6
12	0 51.1	N20 16.6	57 17.0	10.8	S 2 03.4	11.4	58.6
13	15 51.1	17.1	71 46.8	10.7	1 52.0	11.4	58.6
14	30 51.0	17.6	86 16.5	10.6	1 40.6	11.4	58.7
15	45 51.0	. . 18.1	100 46.1	10.6	1 29.2	11.5	58.7
16	60 50.9	18.6	115 15.7	10.6	1 17.7	11.5	58.8
17	75 50.9	19.1	129 45.3	10.5	1 06.2	11.5	58.8
18	90 50.8	N20 19.6	144 14.8	10.5	S 0 54.7	11.5	58.8
19	105 50.8	20.1	158 44.3	10.5	0 43.2	11.6	58.9
20	120 50.8	20.6	173 13.8	10.4	0 31.6	11.6	58.9
21	135 50.7	. . 21.1	187 43.2	10.3	0 20.0	11.6	59.0
22	150 50.7	21.6	202 12.5	10.4	S 0 08.4	11.6	59.0
23	165 50.6	22.1	216 41.9	10.2	N 0 03.2	11.6	59.0
	SD 15.8	d 0.5	SD	15.5	15.7		16.0

Lat.	Twilight Naut.	Twilight Civil	Sunrise	Moonrise 19	Moonrise 20	Moonrise 21	Moonrise 22
°	h m	h m	h m	h m	h m	h m	h m
N 72	▭	▭	▭	02 59	02 50	02 41	02 33
N 70	▭	▭	▭	02 39	02 38	02 36	02 34
68	////	////	01 15	02 23	02 28	02 32	02 35
66	////	////	02 01	02 11	02 20	02 28	02 35
64	////	00 08	02 31	02 00	02 13	02 25	02 36
62	////	01 28	02 53	01 51	02 07	02 22	02 36
60	////	02 03	03 11	01 43	02 02	02 19	02 37
N 58	00 07	02 27	03 26	01 36	01 57	02 17	02 37
56	01 20	02 46	03 38	01 30	01 53	02 15	02 37
54	01 51	03 02	03 49	01 24	01 50	02 14	02 37
52	02 14	03 15	03 59	01 19	01 46	02 12	02 38
50	02 32	03 27	04 07	01 15	01 43	02 11	02 38
45	03 06	03 51	04 26	01 05	01 37	02 08	02 38
N 40	03 31	04 09	04 40	00 56	01 31	02 05	02 39
35	03 50	04 24	04 53	00 49	01 26	02 03	02 39
30	04 05	04 37	05 04	00 43	01 22	02 01	02 40
20	04 30	04 58	05 22	00 32	01 15	01 57	02 40
N 10	04 49	05 16	05 38	00 23	01 08	01 54	02 41
0	05 05	05 31	05 53	00 14	01 02	01 51	02 41
S 10	05 20	05 45	06 08	00 05	00 56	01 48	02 42
20	05 33	06 00	06 23	24 50	00 50	01 45	02 43
30	05 46	06 15	06 41	24 42	00 42	01 42	02 43
35	05 53	06 24	06 51	24 38	00 38	01 40	02 44
40	06 00	06 33	07 03	24 33	00 33	01 37	02 44
45	06 08	06 44	07 17	24 27	00 27	01 35	02 45
S 50	06 17	06 57	07 33	24 20	00 20	01 32	02 46
52	06 21	07 03	07 41	24 17	00 17	01 30	02 46
54	06 25	07 09	07 50	24 14	00 14	01 29	02 46
56	06 30	07 16	08 00	24 10	00 10	01 27	02 47
58	06 35	07 24	08 11	24 06	00 06	01 25	02 47
S 60	06 40	07 33	08 24	24 01	00 01	01 23	02 48

Lat.	Sunset	Twilight Civil	Twilight Naut.	Moonset 19	Moonset 20	Moonset 21	Moonset 22
°	h m	h m	h m	h m	h m	h m	h m
N 72	▭	▭	▭	10 09	12 00	13 52	15 47
N 70	▭	▭	▭	10 28	12 10	13 54	15 43
68	22 44	////	////	10 42	12 18	13 56	15 39
66	21 55	////	////	10 54	12 24	13 58	15 36
64	21 24	////	////	11 04	12 30	14 00	15 33
62	21 02	22 29	////	11 12	12 35	14 01	15 31
60	20 44	21 53	////	11 19	12 39	14 02	15 29
N 58	20 29	21 28	////	11 25	12 43	14 03	15 27
56	20 16	21 09	22 37	11 31	12 46	14 04	15 26
54	20 05	20 52	22 04	11 36	12 49	14 05	15 24
52	19 55	20 39	21 41	11 40	12 51	14 06	15 23
50	19 46	20 27	21 22	11 44	12 54	14 06	15 22
45	19 28	20 03	20 48	11 53	12 59	14 08	15 19
N 40	19 13	19 44	20 23	12 00	13 03	14 09	15 17
35	19 01	19 29	20 04	12 06	13 07	14 10	15 15
30	18 50	19 16	19 48	12 12	13 10	14 11	15 14
20	18 31	18 55	19 23	12 21	13 16	14 12	15 11
N 10	18 15	18 37	19 04	12 29	13 21	14 14	15 08
0	18 00	18 22	18 48	12 37	13 25	14 15	15 06
S 10	17 45	18 08	18 33	12 44	13 30	14 16	15 04
20	17 30	17 53	18 20	12 52	13 35	14 17	15 01
30	17 12	17 37	18 07	13 02	13 40	14 19	14 58
35	17 02	17 29	18 00	13 07	13 43	14 19	14 57
40	16 50	17 19	17 52	13 13	13 47	14 20	14 55
45	16 36	17 08	17 44	13 19	13 51	14 21	14 53
S 50	16 19	16 55	17 35	13 28	13 55	14 22	14 50
52	16 11	16 50	17 31	13 31	13 58	14 23	14 49
54	16 02	16 43	17 27	13 35	14 00	14 24	14 48
56	15 53	16 36	17 23	13 40	14 03	14 24	14 46
58	15 41	16 28	17 18	13 45	14 05	14 25	14 45
S 60	15 28	16 19	17 12	13 51	14 09	14 26	14 43

Day	SUN Eqn. of Time 00^h	SUN Eqn. of Time 12^h	SUN Mer. Pass.	MOON Mer. Pass. Upper	MOON Mer. Pass. Lower	MOON Age	MOON Phase
d	m s	m s	h m	h m	h m	d	%
19	03 33	03 32	11 56	06 25	18 50	23	45
20	03 30	03 29	11 57	07 14	19 38	24	35
21	03 27	03 25	11 57	08 03	20 28	25	25

UT d h	ARIES GHA ° ′	VENUS −4·6 GHA ° ′	VENUS Dec ° ′	MARS +1·7 GHA ° ′	MARS Dec ° ′	JUPITER −2·3 GHA ° ′	JUPITER Dec ° ′	SATURN +0·1 GHA ° ′	SATURN Dec ° ′
22 00 MONDAY	239 48.7	224 37.1	N 4 56.8	159 49.7	N23 55.6	46 35.9	S 4 03.2	333 53.4	S22 00.7
01	254 51.2	239 37.5	57.4	174 50.3	55.7	61 38.5	03.2	348 56.0	00.7
02	269 53.6	254 37.9	58.0	189 51.0	55.8	76 41.1	03.2	3 58.6	00.7
03	284 56.1	269 38.3 . .	58.7	204 51.6 . .	56.0	91 43.6 . .	03.1	19 01.3 . .	00.6
04	299 58.6	284 38.7	59.3	219 52.2	56.1	106 46.2	03.1	34 03.9	00.6
05	315 01.0	299 39.1	4 59.9	234 52.9	56.2	121 48.8	03.0	49 06.5	00.6
06	330 03.5	314 39.5	N 5 00.5	249 53.5	N23 56.3	136 51.4	S 4 03.0	64 09.2	S22 00.6
07	345 05.9	329 39.8	01.1	264 54.1	56.5	151 54.0	02.9	79 11.8	00.6
08	0 08.4	344 40.2	01.7	279 54.7	56.6	166 56.6	02.9	94 14.4	00.6
09	15 10.9	359 40.6 . .	02.4	294 55.4 . .	56.7	181 59.2 . .	02.9	109 17.1 . .	00.6
10	30 13.3	14 41.0	03.0	309 56.0	56.9	197 01.8	02.8	124 19.7	00.6
11	45 15.8	29 41.4	03.6	324 56.6	57.0	212 04.4	02.8	139 22.3	00.6
12	60 18.3	44 41.8	N 5 04.2	339 57.3	N23 57.1	227 07.0	S 4 02.7	154 25.0	S22 00.6
13	75 20.7	59 42.2	04.9	354 57.9	57.2	242 09.6	02.7	169 27.6	00.6
14	90 23.2	74 42.6	05.5	9 58.5	57.4	257 12.2	02.6	184 30.3	00.6
15	105 25.7	89 43.0 . .	06.1	24 59.2 . .	57.5	272 14.8 . .	02.6	199 32.9 . .	00.6
16	120 28.1	104 43.4	06.7	39 59.8	57.6	287 17.4	02.6	214 35.5	00.6
17	135 30.6	119 43.8	07.4	55 00.4	57.8	302 19.9	02.5	229 38.2	00.6
18	150 33.1	134 44.1	N 5 08.0	70 01.0	N23 57.9	317 22.5	S 4 02.5	244 40.8	S22 00.6
19	165 35.5	149 44.5	08.6	85 01.7	58.0	332 25.1	02.4	259 43.4	00.6
20	180 38.0	164 44.9	09.2	100 02.3	58.1	347 27.7	02.4	274 46.1	00.6
21	195 40.4	179 45.3 . .	09.9	115 02.9 . .	58.3	2 30.3 . .	02.3	289 48.7 . .	00.6
22	210 42.9	194 45.7	10.5	130 03.6	58.4	17 32.9	02.3	304 51.3	00.6
23	225 45.4	209 46.1	11.1	145 04.2	58.5	32 35.5	02.3	319 54.0	00.6
23 00 TUESDAY	240 47.8	224 46.4	N 5 11.7	160 04.8	N23 58.6	47 38.1	S 4 02.2	334 56.6	S22 00.6
01	255 50.3	239 46.8	12.4	175 05.5	58.8	62 40.7	02.2	349 59.2	00.6
02	270 52.8	254 47.2	13.0	190 06.1	58.9	77 43.3	02.1	5 01.9	00.6
03	285 55.2	269 47.6 . .	13.6	205 06.7 . .	59.0	92 45.8 . .	02.1	20 04.5 . .	00.5
04	300 57.7	284 48.0	14.3	220 07.3	59.1	107 48.4	02.0	35 07.2	00.5
05	316 00.2	299 48.3	14.9	235 08.0	59.2	122 51.0	02.0	50 09.8	00.5
06	331 02.6	314 48.7	N 5 15.5	250 08.6	N23 59.4	137 53.6	S 4 02.0	65 12.4	S22 00.5
07	346 05.1	329 49.1	16.2	265 09.2	59.5	152 56.2	01.9	80 15.1	00.5
08	1 07.5	344 49.4	16.8	280 09.9	59.6	167 58.8	01.9	95 17.7	00.5
09	16 10.0	359 49.8 . .	17.4	295 10.5 . .	59.7	183 01.4 . .	01.8	110 20.3 . .	00.5
10	31 12.5	14 50.2	18.1	310 11.1	23 59.8	198 04.0	01.8	125 23.0	00.5
11	46 14.9	29 50.6	18.7	325 11.8	24 00.0	213 06.5	01.8	140 25.6	00.5
12	61 17.4	44 50.9	N 5 19.3	340 12.4	N24 00.1	228 09.1	S 4 01.7	155 28.2	S22 00.5
13	76 19.9	59 51.3	20.0	355 13.0	00.2	243 11.7	01.7	170 30.9	00.5
14	91 22.3	74 51.7	20.6	10 13.6	00.3	258 14.3	01.6	185 33.5	00.5
15	106 24.8	89 52.0 . .	21.3	25 14.3 . .	00.4	273 16.9 . .	01.6	200 36.2 . .	00.5
16	121 27.3	104 52.4	21.9	40 14.9	00.6	288 19.5	01.6	215 38.8	00.5
17	136 29.7	119 52.8	22.5	55 15.5	00.7	303 22.0	01.5	230 41.4	00.5
18	151 32.2	134 53.1	N 5 23.2	70 16.2	N24 00.8	318 24.6	S 4 01.5	245 44.1	S22 00.5
19	166 34.7	149 53.5	23.8	85 16.8	00.9	333 27.2	01.4	260 46.7	00.5
20	181 37.1	164 53.9	24.5	100 17.4	01.0	348 29.8	01.4	275 49.3	00.5
21	196 39.6	179 54.2 . .	25.1	115 18.1 . .	01.1	3 32.4 . .	01.4	290 52.0 . .	00.5
22	211 42.0	194 54.6	25.7	130 18.7	01.3	18 35.0	01.3	305 54.6	00.5
23	226 44.5	209 54.9	26.4	145 19.3	01.4	33 37.5	01.3	320 57.3	00.5
24 00 WEDNESDAY	241 47.0	224 55.3	N 5 27.0	160 19.9	N24 01.5	48 40.1	S 4 01.3	335 59.9	S22 00.5
01	256 49.4	239 55.6	27.7	175 20.6	01.6	63 42.7	01.2	351 02.5	00.5
02	271 51.9	254 56.0	28.3	190 21.2	01.7	78 45.3	01.2	6 05.2	00.5
03	286 54.4	269 56.4 . .	29.0	205 21.8 . .	01.8	93 47.9 . .	01.1	21 07.8 . .	00.5
04	301 56.8	284 56.7	29.6	220 22.5	01.9	108 50.5	01.1	36 10.5	00.4
05	316 59.3	299 57.1	30.2	235 23.1	02.1	123 53.0	01.1	51 13.1	00.4
06	332 01.8	314 57.4	N 5 30.9	250 23.7	N24 02.2	138 55.6	S 4 01.0	66 15.7	S22 00.4
07	347 04.2	329 57.8	31.5	265 24.4	02.3	153 58.2	01.0	81 18.4	00.4
08	2 06.7	344 58.1	32.2	280 25.0	02.4	169 00.8	00.9	96 21.0	00.4
09	17 09.1	359 58.5 . .	32.8	295 25.6 . .	02.5	184 03.4 . .	00.9	111 23.6 . .	00.4
10	32 11.6	14 58.8	33.5	310 26.2	02.6	199 05.9	00.9	126 26.3	00.4
11	47 14.1	29 59.2	34.1	325 26.9	02.7	214 08.5	00.8	141 28.9	00.4
12	62 16.5	44 59.5	N 5 34.8	340 27.5	N24 02.8	229 11.1	S 4 00.8	156 31.6	S22 00.4
13	77 19.0	59 59.9	35.4	355 28.1	03.0	244 13.7	00.8	171 34.2	00.4
14	92 21.5	75 00.2	36.1	10 28.8	03.1	259 16.3	00.7	186 36.8	00.4
15	107 23.9	90 00.6 . .	36.7	25 29.4 . .	03.2	274 18.8 . .	00.7	201 39.5 . .	00.4
16	122 26.4	105 00.9	37.4	40 30.0	03.3	289 21.4	00.6	216 42.1	00.4
17	137 28.9	120 01.2	38.0	55 30.7	03.4	304 24.0	00.6	231 44.8	00.4
18	152 31.3	135 01.6	N 5 38.7	70 31.3	N24 03.5	319 26.6	S 4 00.6	246 47.4	S22 00.4
19	167 33.8	150 01.9	39.3	85 31.9	03.6	334 29.1	00.5	261 50.0	00.4
20	182 36.3	165 02.3	40.0	100 32.5	03.7	349 31.7	00.5	276 52.7	00.4
21	197 38.7	180 02.6 . .	40.7	115 33.2 . .	03.8	4 34.3 . .	00.5	291 55.3 . .	00.4
22	212 41.2	195 02.9	41.3	130 33.8	03.9	19 36.9	00.4	306 58.0	00.4
23	227 43.6	210 03.3	42.0	145 34.4	04.0	34 39.5	00.4	322 00.6	00.4
Mer. Pass.	h m 7 55.5	*v* 0.4	*d* 0.6	*v* 0.6	*d* 0.1	*v* 2.6	*d* 0.0	*v* 2.6	*d* 0.0

STARS

Name	SHA ° ′	Dec ° ′
Acamar	315 16.8	S40 14.3
Achernar	335 25.4	S57 08.9
Acrux	173 05.8	S63 11.9
Adhara	255 10.7	S29 00.1
Aldebaran	290 46.7	N16 32.4
Alioth	166 18.1	N55 52.2
Alkaid	152 56.5	N49 13.8
Al Na'ir	27 40.5	S46 52.4
Alnilam	275 44.0	S 1 11.7
Alphard	217 53.6	S 8 44.2
Alphecca	126 08.4	N26 39.5
Alpheratz	357 40.9	N29 10.9
Altair	62 05.5	N 8 54.9
Ankaa	353 13.4	S42 12.6
Antares	112 22.6	S26 28.0
Arcturus	145 53.1	N19 05.7
Atria	107 21.5	S69 03.3
Avior	234 17.2	S59 34.3
Bellatrix	278 29.5	N 6 21.6
Betelgeuse	270 58.8	N 7 24.4
Canopus	263 55.4	S52 42.7
Capella	280 31.0	N46 00.7
Deneb	49 29.4	N45 20.4
Denebola	182 30.9	N14 28.6
Diphda	348 53.5	S17 53.6
Dubhe	193 48.5	N61 39.7
Elnath	278 09.7	N28 37.1
Eltanin	90 44.4	N51 29.2
Enif	33 44.5	N 9 57.2
Fomalhaut	15 21.2	S29 31.7
Gacrux	171 57.5	S57 12.8
Gienah	175 49.4	S17 38.4
Hadar	148 43.5	S60 27.4
Hamal	327 58.1	N23 32.4
Kaus Aust.	83 40.0	S34 22.3
Kochab	137 19.1	N74 05.3
Markab	13 35.8	N15 17.8
Menkar	314 12.6	N 4 09.2
Menkent	148 04.1	S36 27.3
Miaplacidus	221 39.3	S69 47.7
Mirfak	308 37.0	N49 55.1
Nunki	75 54.8	S26 16.3
Peacock	53 14.9	S56 40.4
Pollux	243 24.8	N27 58.9
Procyon	244 57.2	N 5 10.6
Rasalhague	96 03.7	N12 33.0
Regulus	207 40.8	N11 52.9
Rigel	281 09.9	S 8 11.2
Rigil Kent.	139 47.4	S60 54.3
Sabik	102 09.2	S15 44.6
Schedar	349 37.8	N56 37.6
Shaula	96 17.9	S37 06.7
Sirius	258 31.7	S16 44.7
Spica	158 28.2	S11 15.1
Suhail	222 50.6	S43 30.5
Vega	80 36.8	N38 48.0
Zuben'ubi	137 02.2	S16 06.7

	SHA ° ′	Mer. Pass. h m
Venus	343 58.6	9 01
Mars	279 17.0	13 19
Jupiter	166 50.2	20 46
Saturn	94 08.8	1 40

UT	SUN GHA	SUN Dec	MOON GHA	v	MOON Dec	d	HP
d h	° ′	° ′	° ′	′	° ′	′	′
22 00	180 50.6	N20 22.6	231 11.1	10.2	N 0 14.8	11.7	59.1
01	195 50.5	23.1	245 40.3	10.2	0 26.5	11.6	59.1
02	210 50.5	23.5	260 09.5	10.1	0 38.1	11.7	59.2
03	225 50.4	. . 24.0	274 38.6	10.1	0 49.8	11.7	59.2
04	240 50.4	24.5	289 07.7	10.0	1 01.5	11.7	59.2
05	255 50.3	25.0	303 36.7	10.0	1 13.2	11.7	59.3
06	270 50.3	N20 25.5	318 05.7	9.9	N 1 24.9	11.7	59.3
07	285 50.2	26.0	332 34.6	9.9	1 36.6	11.7	59.3
08	300 50.2	26.5	347 03.5	9.8	1 48.3	11.7	59.4
M 09	315 50.1	. . 27.0	1 32.3	9.8	2 00.0	11.8	59.4
O 10	330 50.1	27.5	16 01.1	9.7	2 11.8	11.7	59.5
N 11	345 50.0	27.9	30 29.8	9.7	2 23.5	11.7	59.5
D 12	0 50.0	N20 28.4	44 58.5	9.6	N 2 35.2	11.8	59.5
A 13	15 49.9	28.9	59 27.1	9.5	2 47.0	11.7	59.6
Y 14	30 49.9	29.4	73 55.6	9.5	2 58.7	11.7	59.6
15	45 49.8	. . 29.9	88 24.1	9.4	3 10.4	11.8	59.6
16	60 49.8	30.4	102 52.5	9.4	3 22.2	11.7	59.7
17	75 49.7	30.9	117 20.9	9.3	3 33.9	11.7	59.7
18	90 49.7	N20 31.3	131 49.2	9.3	N 3 45.6	11.7	59.8
19	105 49.6	31.8	146 17.5	9.2	3 57.3	11.7	59.8
20	120 49.6	32.3	160 45.7	9.1	4 09.0	11.7	59.8
21	135 49.5	. . 32.8	175 13.8	9.1	4 20.7	11.7	59.9
22	150 49.5	33.3	189 41.9	9.0	4 32.4	11.7	59.9
23	165 49.4	33.7	204 09.9	9.0	4 44.1	11.6	59.9
23 00	180 49.4	N20 34.2	218 37.9	8.9	N 4 55.7	11.7	60.0
01	195 49.3	34.7	233 05.8	8.8	5 07.4	11.6	60.0
02	210 49.3	35.2	247 33.6	8.8	5 19.0	11.6	60.0
03	225 49.2	. . 35.6	262 01.4	8.7	5 30.6	11.6	60.1
04	240 49.2	36.1	276 29.1	8.6	5 42.2	11.6	60.1
05	255 49.1	36.6	290 56.7	8.6	5 53.8	11.5	60.1
06	270 49.0	N20 37.1	305 24.3	8.5	N 6 05.3	11.5	60.2
07	285 49.0	37.5	319 51.8	8.4	6 16.8	11.5	60.2
T 08	300 48.9	38.0	334 19.2	8.4	6 28.3	11.5	60.2
U 09	315 48.9	. . 38.5	348 46.6	8.3	6 39.8	11.5	60.3
E 10	330 48.8	39.0	3 13.9	8.3	6 51.3	11.4	60.3
S 11	345 48.8	39.4	17 41.2	8.1	7 02.7	11.4	60.3
D 12	0 48.7	N20 39.9	32 08.3	8.2	N 7 14.1	11.3	60.4
A 13	15 48.7	40.4	46 35.5	8.0	7 25.4	11.3	60.4
Y 14	30 48.6	40.9	61 02.5	8.0	7 36.7	11.3	60.4
15	45 48.6	. . 41.3	75 29.5	7.9	7 48.0	11.2	60.5
16	60 48.5	41.8	89 56.4	7.8	7 59.2	11.2	60.5
17	75 48.4	42.3	104 23.2	7.8	8 10.4	11.2	60.5
18	90 48.4	N20 42.7	118 50.0	7.6	N 8 21.6	11.1	60.5
19	105 48.3	43.2	133 16.6	7.7	8 32.7	11.1	60.6
20	120 48.3	43.7	147 43.3	7.5	8 43.8	11.0	60.6
21	135 48.2	. . 44.1	162 09.8	7.5	8 54.8	11.0	60.6
22	150 48.2	44.6	176 36.3	7.4	9 05.8	11.0	60.7
23	165 48.1	45.1	191 02.7	7.4	9 16.8	10.8	60.7
24 00	180 48.0	N20 45.5	205 29.1	7.2	N 9 27.6	10.9	60.7
01	195 48.0	46.0	219 55.3	7.2	9 38.5	10.8	60.7
02	210 47.9	46.4	234 21.5	7.1	9 49.3	10.7	60.8
03	225 47.9	. . 46.9	248 47.6	7.1	10 00.0	10.7	60.8
04	240 47.8	47.4	263 13.7	7.0	10 10.7	10.6	60.8
05	255 47.7	47.8	277 39.7	6.9	10 21.3	10.5	60.8
06	270 47.7	N20 48.3	292 05.6	6.8	N10 31.8	10.5	60.9
W 07	285 47.6	48.8	306 31.4	6.8	10 42.3	10.5	60.9
E 08	300 47.6	49.2	320 57.2	6.7	10 52.8	10.3	60.9
D 09	315 47.5	. . 49.7	335 22.9	6.6	11 03.1	10.3	60.9
N 10	330 47.4	50.1	349 48.5	6.6	11 13.4	10.3	60.9
E 11	345 47.4	50.6	4 14.1	6.5	11 23.7	10.1	61.0
S 12	0 47.3	N20 51.0	18 39.6	6.4	N11 33.8	10.1	61.0
D 13	15 47.3	51.5	33 05.0	6.3	11 43.9	10.1	61.0
A 14	30 47.2	52.0	47 30.3	6.3	11 54.0	9.9	61.0
Y 15	45 47.1	. . 52.4	61 55.6	6.2	12 03.9	9.9	61.0
16	60 47.1	52.9	76 20.8	6.1	12 13.8	9.8	61.1
17	75 47.0	53.3	90 45.9	6.1	12 23.6	9.7	61.1
18	90 47.0	N20 53.8	105 11.0	5.9	N12 33.3	9.6	61.1
19	105 46.9	54.2	119 35.9	6.0	12 42.9	9.6	61.1
20	120 46.8	54.7	134 00.9	5.8	12 52.5	9.5	61.1
21	135 46.8	. . 55.1	148 25.7	5.8	13 02.0	9.4	61.2
22	150 46.7	55.6	162 50.5	5.7	13 11.4	9.3	61.2
23	165 46.6	56.0	177 15.2	5.6	N13 20.7	9.2	61.2
	SD 15.8	*d* 0.5	SD 16.2		16.4		16.6

Lat.	Twilight Naut.	Twilight Civil	Sunrise	Moonrise 22	Moonrise 23	Moonrise 24	Moonrise 25
°	h m	h m	h m	h m	h m	h m	h m
N 72	▭	▭	▭	02 33	02 25	02 16	02 05
N 70	▭	▭	▭	02 34	02 32	02 31	02 31
68	////	////	00 52	02 35	02 38	02 43	02 51
66	////	////	01 49	02 35	02 43	02 53	03 07
64	////	////	02 22	02 36	02 48	03 02	03 20
62	////	01 14	02 46	02 36	02 51	03 09	03 31
60	////	01 53	03 05	02 37	02 55	03 15	03 41
N 58	////	02 20	03 20	02 37	02 58	03 21	03 49
56	01 07	02 40	03 34	02 37	03 00	03 26	03 57
54	01 43	02 57	03 45	02 37	03 03	03 30	04 03
52	02 08	03 11	03 55	02 38	03 05	03 35	04 09
50	02 27	03 23	04 04	02 38	03 07	03 38	04 15
45	03 02	03 48	04 23	02 38	03 11	03 46	04 26
N 40	03 28	04 07	04 38	02 39	03 15	03 53	04 36
35	03 48	04 23	04 51	02 39	03 18	03 59	04 45
30	04 04	04 36	05 02	02 40	03 20	04 04	04 52
20	04 29	04 57	05 21	02 40	03 25	04 13	05 05
N 10	04 49	05 15	05 38	02 41	03 30	04 21	05 16
0	05 05	05 31	05 53	02 41	03 34	04 29	05 27
S 10	05 20	05 46	06 08	02 42	03 38	04 37	05 38
20	05 34	06 01	06 24	02 43	03 42	04 45	05 49
30	05 48	06 17	06 43	02 43	03 47	04 54	06 03
35	05 55	06 26	06 53	02 44	03 50	05 00	06 10
40	06 03	06 36	07 05	02 44	03 54	05 06	06 19
45	06 11	06 47	07 20	02 45	03 58	05 13	06 30
S 50	06 20	07 01	07 37	02 46	04 03	05 22	06 42
52	06 24	07 07	07 45	02 46	04 05	05 26	06 48
54	06 29	07 13	07 55	02 46	04 07	05 31	06 55
56	06 34	07 21	08 05	02 47	04 10	05 36	07 02
58	06 39	07 29	08 17	02 47	04 13	05 41	07 10
S 60	06 45	07 38	08 30	02 48	04 16	05 47	07 19

Lat.	Sunset	Twilight Civil	Twilight Naut.	Moonset 22	Moonset 23	Moonset 24	Moonset 25
°	h m	h m	h m	h m	h m	h m	h m
N 72	▭	▭	▭	15 47	17 49	19 59	22 25
N 70	▭	▭	▭	15 43	17 36	19 35	21 38
68	23 10	////	////	15 39	17 26	19 16	21 08
66	22 08	////	////	15 36	17 17	19 01	20 45
64	21 34	////	////	15 33	17 10	18 49	20 27
62	21 09	22 44	////	15 31	17 04	18 39	20 13
60	20 50	22 03	////	15 29	16 59	18 30	20 01
N 58	20 34	21 36	////	15 27	16 54	18 23	19 50
56	20 21	21 15	22 51	15 26	16 50	18 16	19 41
54	20 10	20 58	22 13	15 24	16 46	18 10	19 33
52	19 59	20 44	21 48	15 23	16 43	18 05	19 26
50	19 50	20 31	21 28	15 22	16 40	18 00	19 19
45	19 31	20 07	20 52	15 19	16 33	17 49	19 05
N 40	19 16	19 47	20 27	15 17	16 28	17 40	18 54
35	19 03	19 31	20 07	15 15	16 23	17 33	18 44
30	18 51	19 18	19 50	15 14	16 19	17 26	18 35
20	18 32	18 56	19 25	15 11	16 12	17 15	18 21
N 10	18 16	18 38	19 05	15 08	16 05	17 05	18 08
0	18 00	18 22	18 48	15 06	16 00	16 56	17 56
S 10	17 45	18 08	18 33	15 04	15 54	16 47	17 44
20	17 29	17 52	18 19	15 01	15 47	16 37	17 31
30	17 11	17 36	18 06	14 58	15 40	16 26	17 16
35	17 00	17 27	17 58	14 57	15 36	16 19	17 08
40	16 48	17 17	17 51	14 55	15 32	16 12	16 58
45	16 33	17 06	17 42	14 53	15 26	16 04	16 47
S 50	16 16	16 53	17 33	14 50	15 20	15 53	16 33
52	16 08	16 46	17 29	14 49	15 17	15 49	16 27
54	15 58	16 40	17 24	14 48	15 14	15 44	16 20
56	15 48	16 32	17 19	14 46	15 10	15 38	16 12
58	15 36	16 24	17 14	14 45	15 06	15 31	16 03
S 60	15 23	16 15	17 08	14 43	15 02	15 24	15 53

Day	SUN Eqn. of Time 00^h	SUN Eqn. of Time 12^h	SUN Mer. Pass.	MOON Mer. Pass. Upper	MOON Mer. Pass. Lower	MOON Age	MOON Phase
d	m s	m s	h m	h m	h m	d %	
22	03 22	03 20	11 57	08 54	21 20	26 16	
23	03 18	03 15	11 57	09 47	22 14	27 8	
24	03 12	03 09	11 57	10 42	23 11	28 3	

	UT	ARIES	VENUS −4·5		MARS +1·7		JUPITER −2·3		SATURN +0·1	
		GHA	GHA	Dec	GHA	Dec	GHA	Dec	GHA	Dec
	d h	° ′	° ′	° ′	° ′	° ′	° ′	° ′	° ′	° ′
	25 00	242 46.1	225 03.6	N 5 42.6	160 35.1	N24 04.1	49 42.0	S 4 00.4	337 03.2	S22 00.4
	01	257 48.6	240 04.0	43.3	175 35.7	04.3	64 44.6	00.3	352 05.9	00.4
	02	272 51.0	255 04.3	43.9	190 36.3	04.4	79 47.2	00.3	7 08.5	00.4
	03	287 53.5	270 04.6	. . 44.6	205 37.0	. . 04.5	94 49.8	. . 00.3	22 11.2	. . 00.4
	04	302 56.0	285 05.0	45.3	220 37.6	04.6	109 52.3	00.2	37 13.8	00.3
	05	317 58.4	300 05.3	45.9	235 38.2	04.7	124 54.9	00.2	52 16.4	00.3
	06	333 00.9	315 05.6	N 5 46.6	250 38.9	N24 04.8	139 57.5	S 4 00.1	67 19.1	S22 00.3
	07	348 03.4	330 06.0	47.2	265 39.5	04.9	155 00.0	00.1	82 21.7	00.3
T	08	3 05.8	345 06.3	47.9	280 40.1	05.0	170 02.6	00.1	97 24.4	00.3
H	09	18 08.3	0 06.6	. . 48.5	295 40.7	. . 05.1	185 05.2	. . 00.0	112 27.0	. . 00.3
U	10	33 10.8	15 06.9	49.2	310 41.4	05.2	200 07.8	00.0	127 29.6	00.3
R	11	48 13.2	30 07.3	49.9	325 42.0	05.3	215 10.3	4 00.0	142 32.3	00.3
S	12	63 15.7	45 07.6	N 5 50.5	340 42.6	N24 05.4	230 12.9	S 3 59.9	157 34.9	S22 00.3
D	13	78 18.1	60 07.9	51.2	355 43.3	05.5	245 15.5	59.9	172 37.6	00.3
A	14	93 20.6	75 08.2	51.9	10 43.9	05.6	260 18.1	59.9	187 40.2	00.3
Y	15	108 23.1	90 08.6	. . 52.5	25 44.5	. . 05.7	275 20.6	. . 59.8	202 42.9	. . 00.3
	16	123 25.5	105 08.9	53.2	40 45.2	05.8	290 23.2	59.8	217 45.5	00.3
	17	138 28.0	120 09.2	53.9	55 45.8	05.9	305 25.8	59.8	232 48.1	00.3
	18	153 30.5	135 09.5	N 5 54.5	70 46.4	N24 06.0	320 28.3	S 3 59.7	247 50.8	S22 00.3
	19	168 32.9	150 09.9	55.2	85 47.0	06.1	335 30.9	59.7	262 53.4	00.3
	20	183 35.4	165 10.2	55.9	100 47.7	06.2	350 33.5	59.7	277 56.1	00.3
	21	198 37.9	180 10.5	. . 56.5	115 48.3	. . 06.3	5 36.1	. . 59.6	292 58.7	. . 00.3
	22	213 40.3	195 10.8	57.2	130 48.9	06.4	20 38.6	59.6	308 01.3	00.3
	23	228 42.8	210 11.1	57.9	145 49.6	06.5	35 41.2	59.6	323 04.0	00.3
	26 00	243 45.3	225 11.4	N 5 58.5	160 50.2	N24 06.6	50 43.8	S 3 59.5	338 06.6	S22 00.3
	01	258 47.7	240 11.8	59.2	175 50.8	06.7	65 46.3	59.5	353 09.3	00.3
	02	273 50.2	255 12.1	5 59.9	190 51.5	06.8	80 48.9	59.5	8 11.9	00.3
	03	288 52.6	270 12.4	6 00.5	205 52.1	. . 06.9	95 51.5	. . 59.4	23 14.6	. . 00.3
	04	303 55.1	285 12.7	01.2	220 52.7	07.0	110 54.0	59.4	38 17.2	00.2
	05	318 57.6	300 13.0	01.9	235 53.4	07.1	125 56.6	59.4	53 19.8	00.2
	06	334 00.0	315 13.3	N 6 02.5	250 54.0	N24 07.2	140 59.2	S 3 59.3	68 22.5	S22 00.2
	07	349 02.5	330 13.6	03.2	265 54.6	07.3	156 01.7	59.3	83 25.1	00.2
	08	4 05.0	345 13.9	03.9	280 55.2	07.4	171 04.3	59.3	98 27.8	00.2
F	09	19 07.4	0 14.3	. . 04.6	295 55.9	. . 07.5	186 06.9	. . 59.2	113 30.4	. . 00.2
R	10	34 09.9	15 14.6	05.2	310 56.5	07.6	201 09.4	59.2	128 33.1	00.2
I	11	49 12.4	30 14.9	05.9	325 57.1	07.6	216 12.0	59.2	143 35.7	00.2
D	12	64 14.8	45 15.2	N 6 06.6	340 57.8	N24 07.7	231 14.6	S 3 59.2	158 38.3	S22 00.2
A	13	79 17.3	60 15.5	07.3	355 58.4	07.8	246 17.1	59.1	173 41.0	00.2
Y	14	94 19.8	75 15.8	07.9	10 59.0	07.9	261 19.7	59.1	188 43.6	00.2
	15	109 22.2	90 16.1	. . 08.6	25 59.7	. . 08.0	276 22.3	. . 59.1	203 46.3	. . 00.2
	16	124 24.7	105 16.4	09.3	41 00.3	08.1	291 24.8	59.0	218 48.9	00.2
	17	139 27.1	120 16.7	10.0	56 00.9	08.2	306 27.4	59.0	233 51.6	00.2
	18	154 29.6	135 17.0	N 6 10.6	71 01.6	N24 08.3	321 30.0	S 3 59.0	248 54.2	S22 00.2
	19	169 32.1	150 17.3	11.3	86 02.2	08.4	336 32.5	58.9	263 56.8	00.2
	20	184 34.5	165 17.6	12.0	101 02.8	08.5	351 35.1	58.9	278 59.5	00.2
	21	199 37.0	180 17.9	. . 12.7	116 03.5	. . 08.6	6 37.6	. . 58.9	294 02.1	. . 00.2
	22	214 39.5	195 18.2	13.3	131 04.1	08.7	21 40.2	58.8	309 04.8	00.2
	23	229 41.9	210 18.5	14.0	146 04.7	08.7	36 42.8	58.8	324 07.4	00.2
	27 00	244 44.4	225 18.8	N 6 14.7	161 05.3	N24 08.8	51 45.3	S 3 58.8	339 10.1	S22 00.2
	01	259 46.9	240 19.1	15.4	176 06.0	08.9	66 47.9	58.8	354 12.7	00.2
	02	274 49.3	255 19.4	16.1	191 06.6	09.0	81 50.5	58.7	9 15.4	00.2
	03	289 51.8	270 19.7	. . 16.7	206 07.2	. . 09.1	96 53.0	. . 58.7	24 18.0	. . 00.2
	04	304 54.2	285 20.0	17.4	221 07.9	09.2	111 55.6	58.7	39 20.6	00.1
	05	319 56.7	300 20.2	18.1	236 08.5	09.3	126 58.1	58.6	54 23.3	00.1
	06	334 59.2	315 20.5	N 6 18.8	251 09.1	N24 09.4	142 00.7	S 3 58.6	69 25.9	S22 00.1
	07	350 01.6	330 20.8	19.5	266 09.8	09.4	157 03.3	58.6	84 28.6	00.1
S	08	5 04.1	345 21.1	20.2	281 10.4	09.5	172 05.8	58.5	99 31.2	00.1
A	09	20 06.6	0 21.4	. . 20.8	296 11.0	. . 09.6	187 08.4	. . 58.5	114 33.9	. . 00.1
T	10	35 09.0	15 21.7	21.5	311 11.7	09.7	202 10.9	58.5	129 36.5	00.1
U	11	50 11.5	30 22.0	22.2	326 12.3	09.8	217 13.5	58.5	144 39.2	00.1
R	12	65 14.0	45 22.3	N 6 22.9	341 12.9	N24 09.9	232 16.1	S 3 58.4	159 41.8	S22 00.1
D	13	80 16.4	60 22.6	23.6	356 13.6	10.0	247 18.6	58.4	174 44.5	00.1
A	14	95 18.9	75 22.8	24.3	11 14.2	10.0	262 21.2	58.4	189 47.1	00.1
Y	15	110 21.4	90 23.1	. . 25.0	26 14.8	. . 10.1	277 23.7	. . 58.3	204 49.7	. . 00.1
	16	125 23.8	105 23.4	25.6	41 15.4	10.2	292 26.3	58.3	219 52.4	00.1
	17	140 26.3	120 23.7	26.3	56 16.1	10.3	307 28.9	58.3	234 55.0	00.1
	18	155 28.7	135 24.0	N 6 27.0	71 16.7	N24 10.4	322 31.4	S 3 58.3	249 57.7	S22 00.1
	19	170 31.2	150 24.3	27.7	86 17.3	10.5	337 34.0	58.2	265 00.3	00.1
	20	185 33.7	165 24.5	28.4	101 18.0	10.5	352 36.5	58.2	280 03.0	00.1
	21	200 36.1	180 24.8	. . 29.1	116 18.6	. . 10.6	7 39.1	. . 58.2	295 05.6	. . 00.1
	22	215 38.6	195 25.1	29.8	131 19.2	10.7	22 41.6	58.2	310 08.3	00.1
	23	230 41.1	210 25.4	30.5	146 19.9	10.8	37 44.2	58.1	325 10.9	00.1
	Mer. Pass.	h m 7 43.7	v 0.3	d 0.7	v 0.6	d 0.1	v 2.6	d 0.0	v 2.6	d 0.0

STARS

Name	SHA	Dec
	° ′	° ′
Acamar	315 16.8	S40 14.2
Achernar	335 25.4	S57 08.9
Acrux	173 05.8	S63 11.9
Adhara	255 10.7	S29 00.1
Aldebaran	290 46.7	N16 32.4
Alioth	166 18.1	N55 52.2
Alkaid	152 56.5	N49 13.9
Al Na'ir	27 40.5	S46 52.4
Alnilam	275 44.0	S 1 11.7
Alphard	217 53.6	S 8 44.2
Alphecca	126 08.4	N26 39.6
Alpheratz	357 40.9	N29 10.9
Altair	62 05.4	N 8 54.9
Ankaa	353 13.4	S42 12.6
Antares	112 22.6	S26 28.0
Arcturus	145 53.1	N19 05.7
Atria	107 21.5	S69 03.3
Avior	234 17.2	S59 34.3
Bellatrix	278 29.5	N 6 21.7
Betelgeuse	270 58.8	N 7 24.4
Canopus	263 55.5	S52 42.6
Capella	280 31.0	N46 00.7
Deneb	49 29.4	N45 20.4
Denebola	182 30.9	N14 28.6
Diphda	348 53.5	S17 53.5
Dubhe	193 48.5	N61 39.7
Elnath	278 09.6	N28 37.1
Eltanin	90 44.4	N51 29.3
Enif	33 44.5	N 9 57.2
Fomalhaut	15 21.2	S29 31.7
Gacrux	171 57.5	S57 12.8
Gienah	175 49.4	S17 38.4
Hadar	148 43.5	S60 27.4
Hamal	327 58.0	N23 32.4
Kaus Aust.	83 40.0	S34 22.3
Kochab	137 19.2	N74 05.3
Markab	13 35.7	N15 17.8
Menkar	314 12.6	N 4 09.2
Menkent	148 04.1	S36 27.3
Miaplacidus	221 39.3	S69 47.7
Mirfak	308 37.0	N49 55.0
Nunki	75 54.8	S26 16.3
Peacock	53 14.9	S56 40.4
Pollux	243 24.8	N27 58.9
Procyon	244 57.2	N 5 10.6
Rasalhague	96 03.7	N12 33.0
Regulus	207 40.8	N11 52.9
Rigel	281 09.9	S 8 11.2
Rigil Kent.	139 47.4	S60 54.4
Sabik	102 09.2	S15 44.6
Schedar	349 37.7	N56 37.6
Shaula	96 17.9	S37 06.7
Sirius	258 31.7	S16 44.7
Spica	158 28.2	S11 15.1
Suhail	222 50.6	S43 30.5
Vega	80 36.8	N38 48.0
Zuben'ubi	137 02.2	S16 06.7

	SHA	Mer. Pass.
	° ′	h m
Venus	341 26.2	8 59
Mars	277 04.9	13 16
Jupiter	166 58.5	20 34
Saturn	94 21.4	1 27

UT		SUN GHA	SUN Dec	MOON GHA	v	MOON Dec	d	HP
d h		° ′	° ′	° ′	′	° ′	′	′
25 00		180 46.6	N20 56.5	191 39.8	5.6	N13 29.9	9.1	61.2
01		195 46.5	56.9	206 04.4	5.5	13 39.0	9.0	61.2
02		210 46.5	57.4	220 28.9	5.5	13 48.0	9.0	61.2
03		225 46.4	. . 57.8	234 53.4	5.3	13 57.0	8.8	61.2
04		240 46.3	58.3	249 17.7	5.4	14 05.8	8.8	61.3
05		255 46.3	58.7	263 42.1	5.2	14 14.6	8.6	61.3
06		270 46.2	N20 59.1	278 06.3	5.2	N14 23.2	8.6	61.3
07		285 46.1	20 59.6	292 30.5	5.1	14 31.8	8.4	61.3
08	THURSDAY	300 46.1	21 00.0	306 54.6	5.1	14 40.2	8.4	61.3
09		315 46.0	. . 00.5	321 18.7	5.0	14 48.6	8.3	61.3
10		330 45.9	00.9	335 42.7	4.9	14 56.9	8.1	61.3
11		345 45.9	01.4	350 06.6	4.9	15 05.0	8.0	61.3
12		0 45.8	N21 01.8	4 30.5	4.8	N15 13.0	8.0	61.3
13		15 45.7	02.2	18 54.3	4.8	15 21.0	7.8	61.3
14		30 45.7	02.7	33 18.1	4.7	15 28.8	7.7	61.3
15		45 45.6	. . 03.1	47 41.8	4.6	15 36.5	7.6	61.4
16		60 45.5	03.6	62 05.4	4.6	15 44.1	7.5	61.4
17		75 45.5	04.0	76 29.0	4.5	15 51.6	7.4	61.4
18		90 45.4	N21 04.4	90 52.5	4.5	N15 59.0	7.2	61.4
19		105 45.3	04.9	105 16.0	4.5	16 06.2	7.2	61.4
20		120 45.3	05.3	119 39.5	4.3	16 13.4	7.0	61.4
21		135 45.2	. . 05.8	134 02.8	4.4	16 20.4	6.9	61.4
22		150 45.1	06.2	148 26.2	4.3	16 27.3	6.8	61.4
23		165 45.1	06.6	162 49.5	4.2	16 34.1	6.7	61.4
26 00		180 45.0	N21 07.1	177 12.7	4.2	N16 40.8	6.5	61.4
01		195 44.9	07.5	191 35.9	4.1	16 47.3	6.4	61.4
02		210 44.9	07.9	205 59.0	4.1	16 53.7	6.3	61.4
03		225 44.8	. . 08.4	220 22.1	4.1	17 00.0	6.2	61.4
04		240 44.7	08.8	234 45.2	4.0	17 06.2	6.0	61.4
05		255 44.7	09.2	249 08.2	4.0	17 12.2	5.9	61.4
06		270 44.6	N21 09.6	263 31.2	4.0	N17 18.1	5.8	61.4
07		285 44.5	10.1	277 54.2	3.9	17 23.9	5.7	61.4
08		300 44.4	10.5	292 17.1	3.8	17 29.6	5.5	61.4
09	FRIDAY	315 44.4	. . 10.9	306 39.9	3.9	17 35.1	5.4	61.4
10		330 44.3	11.4	321 02.8	3.8	17 40.5	5.2	61.4
11		345 44.2	11.8	335 25.6	3.8	17 45.7	5.2	61.4
12		0 44.2	N21 12.2	349 48.4	3.7	N17 50.9	5.0	61.4
13		15 44.1	12.6	4 11.1	3.7	17 55.9	4.8	61.3
14		30 44.0	13.1	18 33.8	3.7	18 00.7	4.7	61.3
15		45 43.9	. . 13.5	32 56.5	3.7	18 05.4	4.6	61.3
16		60 43.9	13.9	47 19.2	3.7	18 10.0	4.5	61.3
17		75 43.8	14.3	61 41.9	3.6	18 14.5	4.3	61.3
18		90 43.7	N21 14.8	76 04.5	3.6	N18 18.8	4.1	61.3
19		105 43.7	15.2	90 27.1	3.6	18 22.9	4.1	61.3
20		120 43.6	15.6	104 49.7	3.6	18 27.0	3.9	61.3
21		135 43.5	. . 16.0	119 12.3	3.5	18 30.9	3.7	61.3
22		150 43.4	16.4	133 34.8	3.6	18 34.6	3.6	61.3
23		165 43.4	16.9	147 57.4	3.5	18 38.2	3.5	61.3
27 00		180 43.3	N21 17.3	162 19.9	3.6	N18 41.7	3.3	61.2
01		195 43.2	17.7	176 42.5	3.5	18 45.0	3.2	61.2
02		210 43.1	18.1	191 05.0	3.5	18 48.2	3.0	61.2
03		225 43.1	. . 18.5	205 27.5	3.5	18 51.2	2.9	61.2
04		240 43.0	18.9	219 50.0	3.6	18 54.1	2.8	61.2
05		255 42.9	19.4	234 12.6	3.5	18 56.9	2.6	61.2
06		270 42.8	N21 19.8	248 35.1	3.5	N18 59.5	2.4	61.2
07		285 42.8	20.2	262 57.6	3.5	19 01.9	2.4	61.1
08	SATURDAY	300 42.7	20.6	277 20.1	3.6	19 04.3	2.1	61.1
09		315 42.6	. . 21.0	291 42.7	3.5	19 06.4	2.1	61.1
10		330 42.5	21.4	306 05.2	3.6	19 08.5	1.9	61.1
11		345 42.5	21.8	320 27.8	3.5	19 10.4	1.7	61.1
12		0 42.4	N21 22.3	334 50.3	3.6	N19 12.1	1.6	61.0
13		15 42.3	22.7	349 12.9	3.6	19 13.7	1.4	61.0
14		30 42.2	23.1	3 35.5	3.6	19 15.1	1.4	61.0
15		45 42.2	. . 23.5	17 58.1	3.6	19 16.5	1.1	61.0
16		60 42.1	23.9	32 20.7	3.7	19 17.6	1.0	61.0
17		75 42.0	24.3	46 43.4	3.6	19 18.6	0.9	60.9
18		90 41.9	N21 24.7	61 06.0	3.7	N19 19.5	0.8	60.9
19		105 41.9	25.1	75 28.7	3.8	19 20.3	0.5	60.9
20		120 41.8	25.5	89 51.5	3.7	19 20.8	0.5	60.9
21		135 41.7	. . 25.9	104 14.2	3.8	19 21.3	0.3	60.9
22		150 41.6	26.3	118 37.0	3.8	19 21.6	0.1	60.8
23		165 41.5	26.7	132 59.8	3.9	N19 21.7	0.1	60.8
		SD 15.8	d 0.4	SD 16.7		16.7		16.6

Lat.	Twilight Naut.	Twilight Civil	Sunrise	Moonrise 25	26	27	28
°	h m	h m	h m	h m	h m	h m	h m
N 72	▭	▭	▭	02 05	01 46	▭	▭
N 70	▭	▭	▭	02 31	02 34	02 45	03 28
68	////	////	00 13	02 51	03 05	03 32	04 24
66	////	////	01 37	03 07	03 28	04 02	04 58
64	////	////	02 13	03 20	03 46	04 25	05 22
62	////	00 58	02 39	03 31	04 02	04 44	05 42
60	////	01 44	02 59	03 41	04 14	04 59	05 57
N 58	////	02 13	03 15	03 49	04 25	05 12	06 11
56	00 52	02 34	03 29	03 57	04 35	05 23	06 23
54	01 34	02 52	03 41	04 03	04 43	05 33	06 33
52	02 01	03 07	03 52	04 09	04 51	05 42	06 42
50	02 22	03 19	04 01	04 15	04 58	05 50	06 50
45	02 59	03 45	04 20	04 26	05 13	06 07	07 07
N 40	03 25	04 05	04 36	04 36	05 25	06 20	07 21
35	03 45	04 21	04 50	04 45	05 36	06 32	07 33
30	04 02	04 34	05 01	04 52	05 45	06 42	07 44
20	04 28	04 57	05 21	05 05	06 01	07 00	08 02
N 10	04 48	05 15	05 38	05 16	06 15	07 16	08 18
0	05 05	05 31	05 53	05 27	06 28	07 30	08 32
S 10	05 21	05 47	06 09	05 38	06 41	07 45	08 47
20	05 35	06 02	06 26	05 49	06 55	08 00	09 03
30	05 49	06 19	06 44	06 03	07 11	08 18	09 21
35	05 57	06 28	06 55	06 10	07 21	08 29	09 31
40	06 05	06 38	07 08	06 19	07 32	08 41	09 44
45	06 14	06 50	07 23	06 30	07 45	08 55	09 58
S 50	06 23	07 04	07 41	06 42	08 00	09 13	10 15
52	06 28	07 10	07 49	06 48	08 08	09 21	10 23
54	06 32	07 17	07 59	06 55	08 16	09 30	10 33
56	06 37	07 25	08 10	07 02	08 25	09 40	10 43
58	06 43	07 33	08 22	07 10	08 36	09 52	10 55
S 60	06 49	07 43	08 36	07 19	08 48	10 06	11 08

Lat.	Sunset	Twilight Civil	Twilight Naut.	Moonset 25	26	27	28
°	h m	h m	h m	h m	h m	h m	h m
N 72	▭	▭	▭	22 25	▭	▭	▭
N 70	▭	▭	▭	21 38	23 37	25 05	01 05
68	▭	▭	▭	21 08	22 50	24 09	00 09
66	22 21	////	////	20 45	22 20	23 35	24 25
64	21 43	////	////	20 27	21 57	23 10	24 02
62	21 17	23 02	////	20 13	21 39	22 51	23 45
60	20 57	22 13	////	20 01	21 24	22 35	23 30
N 58	20 40	21 43	////	19 50	21 12	22 22	23 17
56	20 26	21 21	23 07	19 41	21 01	22 10	23 06
54	20 14	21 03	22 22	19 33	20 51	22 00	22 56
52	20 03	20 49	21 55	19 26	20 43	21 51	22 48
50	19 54	20 36	21 34	19 19	20 35	21 43	22 40
45	19 34	20 10	20 56	19 05	20 18	21 25	22 24
N 40	19 18	19 50	20 30	18 54	20 05	21 11	22 10
35	19 05	19 34	20 09	18 44	19 53	20 59	21 58
30	18 53	19 20	19 52	18 35	19 43	20 49	21 48
20	18 33	18 58	19 26	18 21	19 26	20 30	21 31
N 10	18 16	18 39	19 06	18 08	19 11	20 15	21 15
0	18 01	18 23	18 49	17 56	18 57	20 00	21 01
S 10	17 45	18 07	18 33	17 44	18 43	19 45	20 47
20	17 28	17 52	18 19	17 31	18 28	19 29	20 31
30	17 09	17 35	18 05	17 16	18 11	19 11	20 14
35	16 58	17 26	17 57	17 08	18 01	19 00	20 03
40	16 46	17 16	17 49	16 58	17 50	18 48	19 51
45	16 31	17 04	17 40	16 47	17 36	18 34	19 37
S 50	16 13	16 50	17 30	16 33	17 20	18 16	19 20
52	16 04	16 44	17 26	16 27	17 12	18 08	19 12
54	15 55	16 37	17 21	16 20	17 04	17 59	19 03
56	15 44	16 29	17 16	16 12	16 55	17 48	18 53
58	15 32	16 20	17 11	16 03	16 44	17 36	18 41
S 60	15 17	16 10	17 05	15 53	16 31	17 23	18 28

Day	SUN Eqn. of Time 00ʰ	12ʰ	Mer. Pass.	MOON Mer. Pass. Upper	Lower	Age	Phase
d	m s	m s	h m	h m	h m	d	%
25	03 06	03 03	11 57	11 41	24 12	29	0
26	03 00	02 57	11 57	12 43	00 12	01	1 ●
27	02 53	02 50	11 57	13 45	01 14	02	4

	UT	ARIES	VENUS −4·5		MARS +1·7		JUPITER −2·3		SATURN +0·1	
		GHA	GHA	Dec	GHA	Dec	GHA	Dec	GHA	Dec
	d h	° ′	° ′	° ′	° ′	° ′	° ′	° ′	° ′	° ′
	28 00	245 43.5	225 25.6	N 6 31.1	161 20.5	N24 10.9	52 46.7	S 3 58.1	340 13.6	S22 00.1
	01	260 46.0	240 25.9	31.8	176 21.1	10.9	67 49.3	58.1	355 16.2	00.1
	02	275 48.5	255 26.2	32.5	191 21.8	11.0	82 51.9	58.0	10 18.8	00.1
	03	290 50.9	270 26.5	. . 33.2	206 22.4	. . 11.1	97 54.4	. . 58.0	25 21.5	. . 00.0
	04	305 53.4	285 26.7	33.9	221 23.0	11.2	112 57.0	58.0	40 24.1	00.0
	05	320 55.9	300 27.0	34.6	236 23.7	11.3	127 59.5	58.0	55 26.8	00.0
	06	335 58.3	315 27.3	N 6 35.3	251 24.3	N24 11.3	143 02.1	S 3 57.9	70 29.4	S22 00.0
	07	351 00.8	330 27.6	36.0	266 24.9	11.4	158 04.6	57.9	85 32.1	00.0
	08	6 03.2	345 27.8	36.7	281 25.6	11.5	173 07.2	57.9	100 34.7	00.0
S	09	21 05.7	0 28.1	. . 37.4	296 26.2	. . 11.6	188 09.7	. . 57.9	115 37.4	. . 00.0
U	10	36 08.2	15 28.4	38.1	311 26.8	11.6	203 12.3	57.8	130 40.0	00.0
N	11	51 10.6	30 28.6	38.8	326 27.5	11.7	218 14.8	57.8	145 42.7	00.0
D	12	66 13.1	45 28.9	N 6 39.5	341 28.1	N24 11.8	233 17.4	S 3 57.8	160 45.3	S22 00.0
A	13	81 15.6	60 29.2	40.2	356 28.7	11.9	248 19.9	57.8	175 48.0	00.0
Y	14	96 18.0	75 29.4	40.9	11 29.4	11.9	263 22.5	57.7	190 50.6	00.0
	15	111 20.5	90 29.7	. . 41.6	26 30.0	. . 12.0	278 25.0	. . 57.7	205 53.3	. . 00.0
	16	126 23.0	105 30.0	42.2	41 30.6	12.1	293 27.6	57.7	220 55.9	00.0
	17	141 25.4	120 30.2	42.9	56 31.2	12.2	308 30.1	57.7	235 58.5	00.0
	18	156 27.9	135 30.5	N 6 43.6	71 31.9	N24 12.2	323 32.7	S 3 57.6	251 01.2	S22 00.0
	19	171 30.4	150 30.7	44.3	86 32.5	12.3	338 35.2	57.6	266 03.8	00.0
	20	186 32.8	165 31.0	45.0	101 33.1	12.4	353 37.8	57.6	281 06.5	00.0
	21	201 35.3	180 31.3	. . 45.7	116 33.8	. . 12.5	8 40.3	. . 57.6	296 09.1	. . 00.0
	22	216 37.7	195 31.5	46.4	131 34.4	12.5	23 42.9	57.5	311 11.8	00.0
	23	231 40.2	210 31.8	47.1	146 35.0	12.6	38 45.4	57.5	326 14.4	00.0
	29 00	246 42.7	225 32.0	N 6 47.8	161 35.7	N24 12.7	53 48.0	S 3 57.5	341 17.1	S22 00.0
	01	261 45.1	240 32.3	48.5	176 36.3	12.8	68 50.5	57.5	356 19.7	00.0
	02	276 47.6	255 32.5	49.2	191 36.9	12.8	83 53.1	57.4	11 22.4	22 00.0
	03	291 50.1	270 32.8	. . 49.9	206 37.6	. . 12.9	98 55.6	. . 57.4	26 25.0	21 59.9
	04	306 52.5	285 33.1	50.6	221 38.2	13.0	113 58.2	57.4	41 27.7	59.9
	05	321 55.0	300 33.3	51.3	236 38.8	13.0	129 00.7	57.4	56 30.3	59.9
	06	336 57.5	315 33.6	N 6 52.0	251 39.5	N24 13.1	144 03.3	S 3 57.3	71 33.0	S21 59.9
	07	351 59.9	330 33.8	52.8	266 40.1	13.2	159 05.8	57.3	86 35.6	59.9
	08	7 02.4	345 34.1	53.5	281 40.7	13.2	174 08.4	57.3	101 38.3	59.9
M	09	22 04.9	0 34.3	. . 54.2	296 41.4	. . 13.3	189 10.9	. . 57.3	116 40.9	. . 59.9
O	10	37 07.3	15 34.6	54.9	311 42.0	13.4	204 13.5	57.3	131 43.6	59.9
N	11	52 09.8	30 34.8	55.6	326 42.6	13.4	219 16.0	57.2	146 46.2	59.9
D	12	67 12.2	45 35.1	N 6 56.3	341 43.3	N24 13.5	234 18.6	S 3 57.2	161 48.9	S21 59.9
A	13	82 14.7	60 35.3	57.0	356 43.9	13.6	249 21.1	57.2	176 51.5	59.9
Y	14	97 17.2	75 35.6	57.7	11 44.5	13.6	264 23.6	57.2	191 54.2	59.9
	15	112 19.6	90 35.8	. . 58.4	26 45.2	. . 13.7	279 26.2	. . 57.1	206 56.8	. . 59.9
	16	127 22.1	105 36.0	59.1	41 45.8	13.8	294 28.7	57.1	221 59.5	59.9
	17	142 24.6	120 36.3	6 59.8	56 46.4	13.8	309 31.3	57.1	237 02.1	59.9
	18	157 27.0	135 36.5	N 7 00.5	71 47.1	N24 13.9	324 33.8	S 3 57.1	252 04.8	S21 59.9
	19	172 29.5	150 36.8	01.2	86 47.7	14.0	339 36.4	57.1	267 07.4	59.9
	20	187 32.0	165 37.0	01.9	101 48.3	14.0	354 38.9	57.0	282 10.1	59.9
	21	202 34.4	180 37.3	. . 02.6	116 49.0	. . 14.1	9 41.4	. . 57.0	297 12.7	. . 59.9
	22	217 36.9	195 37.5	03.3	131 49.6	14.2	24 44.0	57.0	312 15.4	59.9
	23	232 39.4	210 37.7	04.1	146 50.2	14.2	39 46.5	57.0	327 18.0	59.9
	30 00	247 41.8	225 38.0	N 7 04.8	161 50.9	N24 14.3	54 49.1	S 3 56.9	342 20.7	S21 59.9
	01	262 44.3	240 38.2	05.5	176 51.5	14.4	69 51.6	56.9	357 23.3	59.9
	02	277 46.7	255 38.5	06.2	191 52.1	14.4	84 54.2	56.9	12 26.0	59.9
	03	292 49.2	270 38.7	. . 06.9	206 52.8	. . 14.5	99 56.7	. . 56.9	27 28.6	. . 59.8
	04	307 51.7	285 38.9	07.6	221 53.4	14.5	114 59.2	56.9	42 31.3	59.8
	05	322 54.1	300 39.2	08.3	236 54.0	14.6	130 01.8	56.8	57 33.9	59.8
	06	337 56.6	315 39.4	N 7 09.0	251 54.7	N24 14.7	145 04.3	S 3 56.8	72 36.6	S21 59.8
	07	352 59.1	330 39.6	09.7	266 55.3	14.7	160 06.9	56.8	87 39.2	59.8
T	08	8 01.5	345 39.9	10.4	281 55.9	14.8	175 09.4	56.8	102 41.9	59.8
U	09	23 04.0	0 40.1	. . 11.2	296 56.6	. . 14.8	190 11.9	. . 56.8	117 44.5	. . 59.8
E	10	38 06.5	15 40.3	11.9	311 57.2	14.9	205 14.5	56.7	132 47.2	59.8
S	11	53 08.9	30 40.5	12.6	326 57.8	15.0	220 17.0	56.7	147 49.8	59.8
D	12	68 11.4	45 40.8	N 7 13.3	341 58.5	N24 15.0	235 19.6	S 3 56.7	162 52.5	S21 59.8
A	13	83 13.8	60 41.0	14.0	356 59.1	15.1	250 22.1	56.7	177 55.1	59.8
Y	14	98 16.3	75 41.2	14.7	11 59.7	15.1	265 24.6	56.7	192 57.8	59.8
	15	113 18.8	90 41.5	. . 15.4	27 00.4	. . 15.2	280 27.2	. . 56.6	208 00.4	. . 59.8
	16	128 21.2	105 41.7	16.2	42 01.0	15.3	295 29.7	56.6	223 03.1	59.8
	17	143 23.7	120 41.9	16.9	57 01.6	15.3	310 32.2	56.6	238 05.7	59.8
	18	158 26.2	135 42.1	N 7 17.6	72 02.3	N24 15.4	325 34.8	S 3 56.6	253 08.4	S21 59.8
	19	173 28.6	150 42.4	18.3	87 02.9	15.4	340 37.3	56.6	268 11.0	59.8
	20	188 31.1	165 42.6	19.0	102 03.5	15.5	355 39.8	56.6	283 13.7	59.8
	21	203 33.6	180 42.8	. . 19.7	117 04.2	. . 15.5	10 42.4	. . 56.5	298 16.3	. . 59.8
	22	218 36.0	195 43.0	20.5	132 04.8	15.6	25 44.9	56.5	313 19.0	59.8
	23	233 38.5	210 43.3	21.2	147 05.4	15.6	40 47.5	56.5	328 21.6	59.8
	Mer. Pass.	h m 7 31.9	*v* 0.2	*d* 0.7	*v* 0.6	*d* 0.1	*v* 2.5	*d* 0.0	*v* 2.6	*d* 0.0

STARS

Name	SHA	Dec
	° ′	° ′
Acamar	315 16.8	S40 14.2
Achernar	335 25.3	S57 08.9
Acrux	173 05.8	S63 11.9
Adhara	255 10.8	S29 00.1
Aldebaran	290 46.7	N16 32.4
Alioth	166 18.1	N55 52.2
Alkaid	152 56.5	N49 13.9
Al Na'ir	27 40.4	S46 52.3
Alnilam	275 44.0	S 1 11.7
Alphard	217 53.6	S 8 44.2
Alphecca	126 08.4	N26 39.6
Alpheratz	357 40.9	N29 10.9
Altair	62 05.4	N 8 54.9
Ankaa	353 13.4	S42 12.6
Antares	112 22.6	S26 28.0
Arcturus	145 53.1	N19 05.7
Atria	107 21.4	S69 03.3
Avior	234 17.2	S59 34.3
Bellatrix	278 29.5	N 6 21.7
Betelgeuse	270 58.8	N 7 24.4
Canopus	263 55.5	S52 42.6
Capella	280 31.0	N46 00.7
Deneb	49 29.4	N45 20.4
Denebola	182 30.9	N14 28.6
Diphda	348 53.4	S17 53.5
Dubhe	193 48.5	N61 39.7
Elnath	278 09.6	N28 37.1
Eltanin	90 44.4	N51 29.3
Enif	33 44.4	N 9 57.2
Fomalhaut	15 21.1	S29 31.7
Gacrux	171 57.5	S57 12.8
Gienah	175 49.4	S17 38.4
Hadar	148 43.5	S60 27.4
Hamal	327 58.0	N23 32.4
Kaus Aust.	83 39.9	S34 22.3
Kochab	137 19.2	N74 05.3
Markab	13 35.7	N15 17.8
Menkar	314 12.6	N 4 09.2
Menkent	148 04.1	S36 27.3
Miaplacidus	221 39.3	S69 47.7
Mirfak	308 37.0	N49 55.0
Nunki	75 54.7	S26 16.3
Peacock	53 14.8	S56 40.4
Pollux	243 24.8	N27 58.9
Procyon	244 57.2	N 5 10.6
Rasalhague	96 03.7	N12 33.0
Regulus	207 40.8	N11 52.9
Rigel	281 09.8	S 8 11.2
Rigil Kent.	139 47.4	S60 54.4
Sabik	102 09.2	S15 44.6
Schedar	349 37.7	N56 37.6
Shaula	96 17.9	S37 06.7
Sirius	258 31.7	S16 44.7
Spica	158 28.2	S11 15.1
Suhail	222 50.6	S43 30.5
Vega	80 36.8	N38 48.0
Zuben'ubi	137 02.2	S16 06.7

	SHA	Mer. Pass.
	° ′	h m
Venus	338 49.4	8 58
Mars	274 53.0	13 13
Jupiter	167 05.3	20 21
Saturn	94 34.4	1 15

UT (d h)	SUN GHA	SUN Dec	MOON GHA	v	MOON Dec	d	HP
	° ′	° ′	° ′	′	° ′	′	′
28 00	180 41.5	N21 27.1	147 22.7	3.8	N19 21.8	0.2	60.8
01	195 41.4	27.5	161 45.5	4.0	19 21.6	0.2	60.8
02	210 41.3	27.9	176 08.5	3.9	19 21.4	0.4	60.7
03	225 41.2	. . 28.3	190 31.4	4.0	19 21.0	0.6	60.7
04	240 41.2	28.7	204 54.4	4.0	19 20.4	0.7	60.7
05	255 41.1	29.1	219 17.4	4.1	19 19.7	0.8	60.7
06	270 41.0	N21 29.5	233 40.5	4.1	N19 18.9	1.0	60.6
07	285 40.9	29.9	248 03.6	4.2	19 17.9	1.1	60.6
08	300 40.8	30.3	262 26.8	4.2	19 16.8	1.2	60.6
S 09	315 40.8	. . 30.7	276 50.0	4.3	19 15.6	1.4	60.5
U 10	330 40.7	31.1	291 13.3	4.3	19 14.2	1.5	60.5
N 11	345 40.6	31.5	305 36.6	4.4	19 12.7	1.7	60.5
D 12	0 40.5	N21 31.9	320 00.0	4.4	N19 11.0	1.8	60.5
A 13	15 40.4	32.3	334 23.4	4.5	19 09.2	1.9	60.4
Y 14	30 40.4	32.7	348 46.9	4.5	19 07.3	2.1	60.4
15	45 40.3	. . 33.1	3 10.4	4.6	19 05.2	2.2	60.4
16	60 40.2	33.5	17 34.0	4.7	19 03.0	2.3	60.3
17	75 40.1	33.9	31 57.7	4.7	19 00.7	2.5	60.3
18	90 40.0	N21 34.3	46 21.4	4.8	N18 58.2	2.6	60.3
19	105 40.0	34.7	60 45.2	4.8	18 55.6	2.7	60.2
20	120 39.9	35.1	75 09.0	5.0	18 52.9	2.8	60.2
21	135 39.8	. . 35.5	89 33.0	4.9	18 50.1	3.0	60.2
22	150 39.7	35.8	103 56.9	5.1	18 47.1	3.1	60.1
23	165 39.6	36.2	118 21.0	5.1	18 44.0	3.3	60.1
29 00	180 39.5	N21 36.6	132 45.1	5.2	N18 40.7	3.3	60.1
01	195 39.5	37.0	147 09.3	5.2	18 37.4	3.5	60.0
02	210 39.4	37.4	161 33.5	5.3	18 33.9	3.6	60.0
03	225 39.3	. . 37.8	175 57.8	5.4	18 30.3	3.7	60.0
04	240 39.2	38.2	190 22.2	5.5	18 26.6	3.9	59.9
05	255 39.1	38.6	204 46.7	5.6	18 22.7	3.9	59.9
06	270 39.0	N21 38.9	219 11.3	5.6	N18 18.8	4.1	59.9
07	285 39.0	39.3	233 35.9	5.7	18 14.7	4.2	59.8
08	300 38.9	39.7	248 00.6	5.7	18 10.5	4.4	59.8
M 09	315 38.8	. . 40.1	262 25.3	5.9	18 06.1	4.4	59.8
O 10	330 38.7	40.5	276 50.2	5.9	18 01.7	4.6	59.7
N 11	345 38.6	40.8	291 15.1	6.0	17 57.1	4.6	59.7
D 12	0 38.5	N21 41.2	305 40.1	6.1	N17 52.5	4.8	59.7
A 13	15 38.4	41.6	320 05.2	6.2	17 47.7	4.9	59.6
Y 14	30 38.4	42.0	334 30.4	6.3	17 42.8	5.0	59.6
15	45 38.3	. . 42.4	348 55.7	6.3	17 37.8	5.1	59.6
16	60 38.2	42.7	3 21.0	6.4	17 32.7	5.3	59.5
17	75 38.1	43.1	17 46.4	6.5	17 27.4	5.3	59.5
18	90 38.0	N21 43.5	32 11.9	6.6	N17 22.1	5.4	59.4
19	105 37.9	43.9	46 37.5	6.7	17 16.7	5.6	59.4
20	120 37.8	44.2	61 03.2	6.8	17 11.1	5.6	59.4
21	135 37.8	. . 44.6	75 29.0	6.8	17 05.5	5.7	59.3
22	150 37.7	45.0	89 54.8	6.9	16 59.8	5.9	59.3
23	165 37.6	45.4	104 20.7	7.0	16 53.9	5.9	59.3
30 00	180 37.5	N21 45.7	118 46.7	7.2	N16 48.0	6.1	59.2
01	195 37.4	46.1	133 12.9	7.1	16 41.9	6.1	59.2
02	210 37.3	46.5	147 39.0	7.3	16 35.8	6.2	59.2
03	225 37.2	. . 46.8	162 05.3	7.4	16 29.6	6.4	59.1
04	240 37.2	47.2	176 31.7	7.4	16 23.2	6.4	59.1
05	255 37.1	47.6	190 58.1	7.6	16 16.8	6.5	59.0
06	270 37.0	N21 48.0	205 24.7	7.6	N16 10.3	6.6	59.0
07	285 36.9	48.3	219 51.3	7.7	16 03.7	6.7	59.0
T 08	300 36.8	48.7	234 18.0	7.8	15 57.0	6.8	58.9
U 09	315 36.7	. . 49.1	248 44.8	7.9	15 50.2	6.9	58.9
E 10	330 36.6	49.4	263 11.7	8.0	15 43.3	6.9	58.8
S 11	345 36.5	49.8	277 38.7	8.1	15 36.4	7.1	58.8
D 12	0 36.4	N21 50.1	292 05.8	8.2	N15 29.3	7.1	58.8
A 13	15 36.4	50.5	306 33.0	8.2	15 22.2	7.2	58.7
Y 14	30 36.3	50.9	321 00.2	8.4	15 15.0	7.3	58.7
15	45 36.2	. . 51.2	335 27.6	8.4	15 07.7	7.4	58.7
16	60 36.1	51.6	349 55.0	8.5	15 00.3	7.4	58.6
17	75 36.0	52.0	4 22.5	8.6	14 52.9	7.6	58.6
18	90 35.9	N21 52.3	18 50.1	8.7	N14 45.3	7.6	58.5
19	105 35.8	52.7	33 17.8	8.8	14 37.7	7.6	58.5
20	120 35.7	53.0	47 45.6	8.8	14 30.1	7.8	58.5
21	135 35.6	. . 53.4	62 13.4	9.0	14 22.3	7.8	58.4
22	150 35.5	53.8	76 41.4	9.0	14 14.5	7.9	58.4
23	165 35.5	54.1	91 09.4	9.2	N14 06.6	8.0	58.3
	SD 15.8	*d* 0.4	SD 16.5		16.3		16.0

Lat.	Twilight Naut.	Twilight Civil	Sunrise	Moonrise 28	Moonrise 29	Moonrise 30	Moonrise 31
°	h m	h m	h m	h m	h m	h m	h m
N 72	□	□	□	□	□	06 11	08 20
N 70	□	□	□	03 28	05 02	06 54	08 44
68	□	□	□	04 24	05 46	07 23	09 02
66	////	////	01 24	04 58	06 14	07 44	09 17
64	////	////	02 05	05 22	06 36	08 01	09 29
62	////	00 38	02 33	05 42	06 54	08 15	09 39
60	////	01 35	02 54	05 57	07 08	08 27	09 48
N 58	////	02 06	03 11	06 11	07 21	08 37	09 56
56	00 34	02 29	03 25	06 23	07 31	08 46	10 02
54	01 26	02 47	03 38	06 33	07 41	08 54	10 08
52	01 55	03 03	03 49	06 42	07 49	09 01	10 14
50	02 17	03 16	03 58	06 50	07 57	09 07	10 18
45	02 56	03 42	04 18	07 07	08 13	09 21	10 29
N 40	03 23	04 03	04 35	07 21	08 26	09 32	10 38
35	03 44	04 19	04 48	07 33	08 37	09 42	10 45
30	04 01	04 33	05 00	07 44	08 47	09 50	10 52
20	04 27	04 56	05 20	08 02	09 04	10 05	11 03
N 10	04 48	05 15	05 38	08 18	09 19	10 17	11 13
0	05 06	05 32	05 54	08 32	09 32	10 29	11 22
S 10	05 21	05 47	06 10	08 47	09 46	10 41	11 31
20	05 36	06 03	06 27	09 03	10 01	10 53	11 41
30	05 51	06 20	06 46	09 21	10 17	11 07	11 52
35	05 59	06 30	06 57	09 31	10 27	11 16	11 58
40	06 07	06 40	07 10	09 44	10 38	11 25	12 06
45	06 16	06 52	07 25	09 58	10 51	11 36	12 14
S 50	06 26	07 07	07 44	10 15	11 07	11 49	12 24
52	06 31	07 13	07 53	10 23	11 15	11 56	12 29
54	06 36	07 21	08 03	10 33	11 23	12 02	12 34
56	06 41	07 29	08 14	10 43	11 32	12 10	12 40
58	06 47	07 38	08 27	10 55	11 43	12 19	12 46
S 60	06 53	07 48	08 42	11 08	11 55	12 28	12 53

Lat.	Sunset	Twilight Civil	Twilight Naut.	Moonset 28	Moonset 29	Moonset 30	Moonset 31
°	h m	h m	h m	h m	h m	h m	h m
N 72	□	□	□	□	□	02 30	02 13
N 70	□	□	□	01 05	01 38	01 46	01 48
68	□	□	□	00 09	00 54	01 17	01 28
66	22 34	////	////	24 25	00 25	00 54	01 12
64	21 52	////	////	24 02	00 02	00 37	00 59
62	21 24	23 26	////	23 45	24 22	00 22	00 48
60	21 02	22 23	////	23 30	24 10	00 10	00 39
N 58	20 45	21 51	////	23 17	23 59	24 31	00 31
56	20 31	21 27	23 29	23 06	23 50	24 23	00 23
54	20 18	21 09	22 31	22 56	23 41	24 17	00 17
52	20 07	20 53	22 01	22 48	23 34	24 11	00 11
50	19 57	20 40	21 39	22 40	23 27	24 06	00 06
45	19 37	20 13	21 00	22 24	23 13	23 54	24 29
N 40	19 21	19 53	20 33	22 10	23 01	23 45	24 22
35	19 07	19 36	20 12	21 58	22 51	23 36	24 16
30	18 55	19 22	19 54	21 48	22 42	23 29	24 11
20	18 35	18 59	19 28	21 31	22 26	23 16	24 02
N 10	18 17	18 40	19 07	21 15	22 13	23 05	23 54
0	18 01	18 23	18 49	21 01	22 00	22 55	23 46
S 10	17 45	18 08	18 34	20 47	21 47	22 44	23 38
20	17 28	17 52	18 19	20 31	21 33	22 33	23 30
30	17 09	17 34	18 04	20 14	21 17	22 20	23 20
35	16 57	17 25	17 56	20 03	21 08	22 12	23 15
40	16 44	17 14	17 48	19 51	20 57	22 03	23 08
45	16 29	17 02	17 39	19 37	20 45	21 53	23 01
S 50	16 10	16 48	17 28	19 20	20 30	21 41	22 52
52	16 02	16 41	17 24	19 12	20 22	21 35	22 48
54	15 52	16 34	17 19	19 03	20 14	21 29	22 43
56	15 41	16 26	17 14	18 53	20 06	21 22	22 38
58	15 28	16 17	17 08	18 41	19 55	21 14	22 32
S 60	15 13	16 07	17 01	18 28	19 44	21 05	22 26

Day	SUN Eqn. of Time 00^h	SUN Eqn. of Time 12^h	SUN Mer. Pass.	MOON Mer. Pass. Upper	MOON Mer. Pass. Lower	MOON Age	MOON Phase
d	m s	m s	h m	h m	h m	d %	
28	02 46	02 42	11 57	14 47	02 16	03 11	
29	02 38	02 34	11 57	15 46	03 17	04 19	
30	02 30	02 26	11 58	16 42	04 14	05 29	

UT		ARIES	VENUS −4·5		MARS +1·7		JUPITER −2·2		SATURN +0·1	
		GHA	GHA	Dec	GHA	Dec	GHA	Dec	GHA	Dec
d	h	° ′	° ′	° ′	° ′	° ′	° ′	° ′	° ′	° ′
31	00	248 41.0	225 43.5	N 7 21.9	162 06.1	N24 15.7	55 50.0	S 3 56.5	343 24.3	S21 59.8
	01	263 43.4	240 43.7	22.6	177 06.7	15.8	70 52.5	56.5	358 26.9	59.8
	02	278 45.9	255 43.9	23.3	192 07.3	15.8	85 55.1	56.4	13 29.6	59.7
	03	293 48.3	270 44.1	24.0	207 08.0	15.9	100 57.6	56.4	28 32.2	59.7
	04	308 50.8	285 44.3	24.8	222 08.6	15.9	116 00.1	56.4	43 34.9	59.7
	05	323 53.3	300 44.6	25.5	237 09.3	16.0	131 02.7	56.4	58 37.5	59.7
	06	338 55.7	315 44.8	N 7 26.2	252 09.9	N24 16.0	146 05.2	S 3 56.4	73 40.2	S21 59.7
W	07	353 58.2	330 45.0	26.9	267 10.5	16.1	161 07.7	56.4	88 42.8	59.7
E	08	9 00.7	345 45.2	27.6	282 11.2	16.1	176 10.3	56.3	103 45.5	59.7
D	09	24 03.1	0 45.4	28.4	297 11.8	16.2	191 12.8	56.3	118 48.1	59.7
N	10	39 05.6	15 45.6	29.1	312 12.4	16.2	206 15.3	56.3	133 50.8	59.7
E	11	54 08.1	30 45.8	29.8	327 13.1	16.3	221 17.9	56.3	148 53.4	59.7
S	12	69 10.5	45 46.1	N 7 30.5	342 13.7	N24 16.3	236 20.4	S 3 56.3	163 56.1	S21 59.7
D	13	84 13.0	60 46.3	31.3	357 14.3	16.4	251 22.9	56.3	178 58.7	59.7
A	14	99 15.5	75 46.5	32.0	12 15.0	16.4	266 25.4	56.2	194 01.4	59.7
Y	15	114 17.9	90 46.7	32.7	27 15.6	16.5	281 28.0	56.2	209 04.0	59.7
	16	129 20.4	105 46.9	33.4	42 16.2	16.5	296 30.5	56.2	224 06.7	59.7
	17	144 22.8	120 47.1	34.1	57 16.9	16.6	311 33.0	56.2	239 09.3	59.7
	18	159 25.3	135 47.3	N 7 34.9	72 17.5	N24 16.6	326 35.6	S 3 56.2	254 12.0	S21 59.7
	19	174 27.8	150 47.5	35.6	87 18.1	16.7	341 38.1	56.2	269 14.6	59.7
	20	189 30.2	165 47.7	36.3	102 18.8	16.7	356 40.6	56.1	284 17.3	59.7
	21	204 32.7	180 47.9	37.0	117 19.4	16.8	11 43.2	56.1	299 19.9	59.7
	22	219 35.2	195 48.1	37.8	132 20.0	16.8	26 45.7	56.1	314 22.6	59.7
	23	234 37.6	210 48.3	38.5	147 20.7	16.9	41 48.2	56.1	329 25.3	59.7
1	00	249 40.1	225 48.5	N 7 39.2	162 21.3	N24 16.9	56 50.7	S 3 56.1	344 27.9	S21 59.7
	01	264 42.6	240 48.7	39.9	177 22.0	16.9	71 53.3	56.1	359 30.6	59.6
	02	279 45.0	255 48.9	40.7	192 22.6	17.0	86 55.8	56.0	14 33.2	59.6
	03	294 47.5	270 49.1	41.4	207 23.2	17.0	101 58.3	56.0	29 35.9	59.6
	04	309 49.9	285 49.3	42.1	222 23.9	17.1	117 00.9	56.0	44 38.5	59.6
	05	324 52.4	300 49.5	42.9	237 24.5	17.1	132 03.4	56.0	59 41.2	59.6
	06	339 54.9	315 49.7	N 7 43.6	252 25.1	N24 17.2	147 05.9	S 3 56.0	74 43.8	S21 59.6
	07	354 57.3	330 49.9	44.3	267 25.8	17.2	162 08.4	56.0	89 46.5	59.6
T	08	9 59.8	345 50.1	45.0	282 26.4	17.3	177 11.0	56.0	104 49.1	59.6
H	09	25 02.3	0 50.3	45.8	297 27.0	17.3	192 13.5	55.9	119 51.8	59.6
U	10	40 04.7	15 50.5	46.5	312 27.7	17.3	207 16.0	55.9	134 54.4	59.6
R	11	55 07.2	30 50.7	47.2	327 28.3	17.4	222 18.5	55.9	149 57.1	59.6
S	12	70 09.7	45 50.9	N 7 48.0	342 28.9	N24 17.4	237 21.1	S 3 55.9	164 59.7	S21 59.6
D	13	85 12.1	60 51.1	48.7	357 29.6	17.5	252 23.6	55.9	180 02.4	59.6
A	14	100 14.6	75 51.3	49.4	12 30.2	17.5	267 26.1	55.9	195 05.0	59.6
Y	15	115 17.1	90 51.5	50.1	27 30.9	17.5	282 28.6	55.9	210 07.7	59.6
	16	130 19.5	105 51.7	50.9	42 31.5	17.6	297 31.2	55.9	225 10.4	59.6
	17	145 22.0	120 51.8	51.6	57 32.1	17.6	312 33.7	55.8	240 13.0	59.6
	18	160 24.4	135 52.0	N 7 52.3	72 32.8	N24 17.7	327 36.2	S 3 55.8	255 15.7	S21 59.6
	19	175 26.9	150 52.2	53.1	87 33.4	17.7	342 38.7	55.8	270 18.3	59.6
	20	190 29.4	165 52.4	53.8	102 34.0	17.7	357 41.2	55.8	285 21.0	59.6
	21	205 31.8	180 52.6	54.5	117 34.7	17.8	12 43.8	55.8	300 23.6	59.6
	22	220 34.3	195 52.8	55.3	132 35.3	17.8	27 46.3	55.8	315 26.3	59.6
	23	235 36.8	210 53.0	56.0	147 35.9	17.9	42 48.8	55.8	330 28.9	59.6
2	00	250 39.2	225 53.2	N 7 56.7	162 36.6	N24 17.9	57 51.3	S 3 55.8	345 31.6	S21 59.6
	01	265 41.7	240 53.3	57.5	177 37.2	17.9	72 53.8	55.7	0 34.2	59.5
	02	280 44.2	255 53.5	58.2	192 37.9	18.0	87 56.4	55.7	15 36.9	59.5
	03	295 46.6	270 53.7	58.9	207 38.5	18.0	102 58.9	55.7	30 39.5	59.5
	04	310 49.1	285 53.9	7 59.7	222 39.1	18.0	118 01.4	55.7	45 42.2	59.5
	05	325 51.6	300 54.1	8 00.4	237 39.8	18.1	133 03.9	55.7	60 44.9	59.5
	06	340 54.0	315 54.2	N 8 01.1	252 40.4	N24 18.1	148 06.4	S 3 55.7	75 47.5	S21 59.5
	07	355 56.5	330 54.4	01.9	267 41.0	18.1	163 09.0	55.7	90 50.2	59.5
	08	10 58.9	345 54.6	02.6	282 41.7	18.2	178 11.5	55.7	105 52.8	59.5
F	09	26 01.4	0 54.8	03.3	297 42.3	18.2	193 14.0	55.6	120 55.5	59.5
R	10	41 03.9	15 55.0	04.1	312 42.9	18.2	208 16.5	55.6	135 58.1	59.5
I	11	56 06.3	30 55.1	04.8	327 43.6	18.3	223 19.0	55.6	151 00.8	59.5
D	12	71 08.8	45 55.3	N 8 05.5	342 44.2	N24 18.3	238 21.6	S 3 55.6	166 03.4	S21 59.5
A	13	86 11.3	60 55.5	06.3	357 44.9	18.3	253 24.1	55.6	181 06.1	59.5
Y	14	101 13.7	75 55.7	07.0	12 45.5	18.4	268 26.6	55.6	196 08.7	59.5
	15	116 16.2	90 55.8	07.8	27 46.1	18.4	283 29.1	55.6	211 11.4	59.5
	16	131 18.7	105 56.0	08.5	42 46.8	18.4	298 31.6	55.6	226 14.1	59.5
	17	146 21.1	120 56.2	09.2	57 47.4	18.5	313 34.1	55.6	241 16.7	59.5
	18	161 23.6	135 56.3	N 8 10.0	72 48.0	N24 18.5	328 36.7	S 3 55.5	256 19.4	S21 59.5
	19	176 26.0	150 56.5	10.7	87 48.7	18.5	343 39.2	55.5	271 22.0	59.5
	20	191 28.5	165 56.7	11.4	102 49.3	18.6	358 41.7	55.5	286 24.7	59.5
	21	206 31.0	180 56.9	12.2	117 50.0	18.6	13 44.2	55.5	301 27.3	59.5
	22	221 33.4	195 57.0	12.9	132 50.6	18.6	28 46.7	55.5	316 30.0	59.5
	23	236 35.9	210 57.2	13.7	147 51.2	18.6	43 49.2	55.5	331 32.6	59.4
Mer. Pass.		h m 7 20.1	v 0.2	d 0.7	v 0.6	d 0.0	v 2.5	d 0.0	v 2.7	d 0.0

STARS		
Name	SHA	Dec
	° ′	° ′
Acamar	315 16.8	S40 14.2
Achernar	335 25.3	S57 08.9
Acrux	173 05.8	S63 11.9
Adhara	255 10.8	S29 00.0
Aldebaran	290 46.7	N16 32.4
Alioth	166 18.2	N55 52.2
Alkaid	152 56.5	N49 13.9
Al Na'ir	27 40.4	S46 52.3
Alnilam	275 44.0	S 1 11.7
Alphard	217 53.6	S 8 44.2
Alphecca	126 08.4	N26 39.6
Alpheratz	357 40.8	N29 10.9
Altair	62 05.4	N 8 54.9
Ankaa	353 13.3	S42 12.6
Antares	112 22.6	S26 28.1
Arcturus	145 53.1	N19 05.7
Atria	107 21.4	S69 03.3
Avior	234 17.3	S59 34.3
Bellatrix	278 29.5	N 6 21.7
Betelgeuse	270 58.8	N 7 24.4
Canopus	263 55.5	S52 42.6
Capella	280 31.0	N46 00.7
Deneb	49 29.4	N45 20.4
Denebola	182 30.9	N14 28.6
Diphda	348 53.4	S17 53.5
Dubhe	193 48.6	N61 39.7
Elnath	278 09.6	N28 37.1
Eltanin	90 44.4	N51 29.3
Enif	33 44.4	N 9 57.3
Fomalhaut	15 21.1	S29 31.7
Gacrux	171 57.5	S57 12.8
Gienah	175 49.4	S17 38.4
Hadar	148 43.5	S60 27.5
Hamal	327 58.0	N23 32.4
Kaus Aust.	83 39.9	S34 22.3
Kochab	137 19.2	N74 05.3
Markab	13 35.7	N15 17.8
Menkar	314 12.6	N 4 09.2
Menkent	148 04.1	S36 27.3
Miaplacidus	221 39.4	S69 47.7
Mirfak	308 37.0	N49 55.0
Nunki	75 54.7	S26 16.3
Peacock	53 14.8	S56 40.4
Pollux	243 24.8	N27 58.9
Procyon	244 57.2	N 5 10.6
Rasalhague	96 03.7	N12 33.0
Regulus	207 40.8	N11 52.9
Rigel	281 09.8	S 8 11.2
Rigil Kent.	139 47.5	S60 54.4
Sabik	102 09.1	S15 44.6
Schedar	349 37.7	N56 37.6
Shaula	96 17.9	S37 06.7
Sirius	258 31.7	S16 44.7
Spica	158 28.2	S11 15.1
Suhail	222 50.6	S43 30.5
Vega	80 36.8	N38 48.0
Zuben'ubi	137 02.2	S16 06.7

	SHA	Mer. Pass.
	° ′	h m
Venus	336 08.4	8 57
Mars	272 41.2	13 10
Jupiter	167 10.6	20 09
Saturn	94 47.8	1 02

UT d	h	SUN GHA	SUN Dec	MOON GHA	v	MOON Dec	d	HP
		° ′	° ′	° ′	′	° ′	′	′
31	00	180 35.4	N21 54.5	105 37.6	9.2	N13 58.6	8.0	58.3
	01	195 35.3	54.8	120 05.8	9.3	13 50.6	8.1	58.3
	02	210 35.2	55.2	134 34.1	9.4	13 42.5	8.2	58.2
	03	225 35.1	. . 55.5	149 02.5	9.5	13 34.3	8.2	58.2
	04	240 35.0	55.9	163 31.0	9.5	13 26.1	8.3	58.2
	05	255 34.9	56.2	177 59.5	9.7	13 17.8	8.4	58.1
	06	270 34.8	N21 56.6	192 28.2	9.7	N13 09.4	8.4	58.1
W	07	285 34.7	56.9	206 56.9	9.8	13 01.0	8.5	58.0
E	08	300 34.6	57.3	221 25.7	9.9	12 52.5	8.6	58.0
D	09	315 34.5	. . 57.6	235 54.6	10.0	12 43.9	8.6	58.0
N	10	330 34.4	58.0	250 23.6	10.0	12 35.3	8.6	57.9
E	11	345 34.3	58.3	264 52.6	10.2	12 26.7	8.8	57.9
S	12	0 34.3	N21 58.7	279 21.8	10.2	N12 17.9	8.7	57.8
D	13	15 34.2	59.0	293 51.0	10.3	12 09.2	8.9	57.8
A	14	30 34.1	59.4	308 20.3	10.4	12 00.3	8.8	57.8
Y	15	45 34.0	21 59.7	322 49.7	10.5	11 51.5	9.0	57.7
	16	60 33.9	22 00.1	337 19.2	10.5	11 42.5	9.0	57.7
	17	75 33.8	00.4	351 48.7	10.6	11 33.5	9.0	57.7
	18	90 33.7	N22 00.8	6 18.3	10.7	N11 24.5	9.1	57.6
	19	105 33.6	01.1	20 48.0	10.8	11 15.4	9.1	57.6
	20	120 33.5	01.4	35 17.8	10.9	11 06.3	9.2	57.5
	21	135 33.4	. . 01.8	49 47.7	10.9	10 57.1	9.2	57.5
	22	150 33.3	02.1	64 17.6	11.0	10 47.9	9.3	57.5
	23	165 33.2	02.5	78 47.6	11.1	10 38.6	9.3	57.4
1	00	180 33.1	N22 02.8	93 17.7	11.2	N10 29.3	9.3	57.4
	01	195 33.0	03.2	107 47.9	11.2	10 20.0	9.4	57.4
	02	210 32.9	03.5	122 18.1	11.3	10 10.6	9.5	57.3
	03	225 32.8	. . 03.8	136 48.4	11.4	10 01.1	9.4	57.3
	04	240 32.7	04.2	151 18.8	11.4	9 51.7	9.5	57.3
	05	255 32.6	04.5	165 49.2	11.6	9 42.2	9.6	57.2
	06	270 32.5	N22 04.8	180 19.8	11.5	N 9 32.6	9.6	57.2
	07	285 32.5	05.2	194 50.3	11.7	9 23.0	9.6	57.1
T	08	300 32.4	05.5	209 21.0	11.7	9 13.4	9.7	57.1
H	09	315 32.3	. . 05.8	223 51.7	11.8	9 03.7	9.6	57.1
U	10	330 32.2	06.2	238 22.5	11.9	8 54.1	9.8	57.0
R	11	345 32.1	06.5	252 53.4	11.9	8 44.3	9.7	57.0
S	12	0 32.0	N22 06.8	267 24.3	12.0	N 8 34.6	9.8	57.0
D	13	15 31.9	07.2	281 55.3	12.1	8 24.8	9.8	56.9
A	14	30 31.8	07.5	296 26.4	12.1	8 15.0	9.9	56.9
Y	15	45 31.7	. . 07.8	310 57.5	12.2	8 05.1	9.8	56.9
	16	60 31.6	08.2	325 28.7	12.3	7 55.3	9.9	56.8
	17	75 31.5	08.5	340 00.0	12.3	7 45.4	9.9	56.8
	18	90 31.4	N22 08.8	354 31.3	12.3	N 7 35.5	10.0	56.8
	19	105 31.3	09.1	9 02.6	12.5	7 25.5	10.0	56.7
	20	120 31.2	09.5	23 34.1	12.5	7 15.5	10.0	56.7
	21	135 31.1	. . 09.8	38 05.6	12.5	7 05.5	10.0	56.7
	22	150 31.0	10.1	52 37.1	12.6	6 55.5	10.0	56.6
	23	165 30.9	10.5	67 08.7	12.7	6 45.5	10.1	56.6
2	00	180 30.8	N22 10.8	81 40.4	12.7	N 6 35.4	10.0	56.6
	01	195 30.7	11.1	96 12.1	12.8	6 25.4	10.1	56.5
	02	210 30.6	11.4	110 43.9	12.9	6 15.3	10.2	56.5
	03	225 30.5	. . 11.7	125 15.8	12.8	6 05.1	10.1	56.5
	04	240 30.4	12.1	139 47.6	13.0	5 55.0	10.1	56.4
	05	255 30.3	12.4	154 19.6	13.0	5 44.9	10.2	56.4
	06	270 30.2	N22 12.7	168 51.6	13.0	N 5 34.7	10.2	56.4
	07	285 30.1	13.0	183 23.6	13.1	5 24.5	10.2	56.3
	08	300 30.0	13.3	197 55.7	13.2	5 14.3	10.2	56.3
F	09	315 29.9	. . 13.7	212 27.9	13.2	5 04.1	10.2	56.3
R	10	330 29.8	14.0	227 00.1	13.2	4 53.9	10.2	56.2
I	11	345 29.7	14.3	241 32.3	13.3	4 43.7	10.3	56.2
D	12	0 29.6	N22 14.6	256 04.6	13.3	N 4 33.4	10.2	56.2
A	13	15 29.5	14.9	270 36.9	13.4	4 23.2	10.3	56.1
Y	14	30 29.4	15.2	285 09.3	13.4	4 12.9	10.3	56.1
	15	45 29.3	. . 15.6	299 41.7	13.5	4 02.6	10.3	56.1
	16	60 29.2	15.9	314 14.2	13.5	3 52.3	10.2	56.1
	17	75 29.1	16.2	328 46.7	13.6	3 42.1	10.3	56.0
	18	90 29.0	N22 16.5	343 19.3	13.5	N 3 31.8	10.3	56.0
	19	105 28.9	16.8	357 51.8	13.7	3 21.5	10.3	56.0
	20	120 28.8	17.1	12 24.5	13.7	3 11.2	10.3	55.9
	21	135 28.7	. . 17.4	26 57.2	13.7	3 00.9	10.4	55.9
	22	150 28.6	17.7	41 29.9	13.7	2 50.5	10.3	55.9
	23	165 28.5	18.0	56 02.6	13.8	N 2 40.2	10.3	55.9
		SD 15.8	*d* 0.3	SD	15.8	15.5		15.3

Lat.	Twilight Naut.	Twilight Civil	Sunrise	Moonrise 31	Moonrise 1	Moonrise 2	Moonrise 3
°	h m	h m	h m	h m	h m	h m	h m
N 72	▭	▭	▭	08 20	10 14	12 00	13 42
N 70	▭	▭	▭	08 44	10 28	12 07	13 42
68	▭	▭	▭	09 02	10 39	12 12	13 42
66	////	////	01 12	09 17	10 48	12 17	13 42
64	////	////	01 58	09 29	10 56	12 20	13 42
62	////	////	02 27	09 39	11 02	12 23	13 42
60	////	01 26	02 49	09 48	11 08	12 26	13 42
N 58	////	02 00	03 07	09 56	11 13	12 29	13 42
56	////	02 24	03 22	10 02	11 18	12 31	13 42
54	01 18	02 44	03 35	10 08	11 21	12 33	13 42
52	01 50	02 59	03 46	10 14	11 25	12 35	13 42
50	02 13	03 13	03 56	10 18	11 28	12 36	13 42
45	02 53	03 40	04 17	10 29	11 35	12 40	13 42
N 40	03 21	04 01	04 33	10 38	11 41	12 43	13 42
35	03 42	04 18	04 47	10 45	11 46	12 45	13 42
30	04 00	04 32	04 59	10 52	11 51	12 47	13 42
20	04 27	04 56	05 20	11 03	11 58	12 51	13 43
N 10	04 48	05 15	05 38	11 13	12 05	12 55	13 43
0	05 06	05 32	05 54	11 22	12 11	12 58	13 43
S 10	05 22	05 48	06 11	11 31	12 18	13 01	13 43
20	05 37	06 04	06 28	11 41	12 24	13 05	13 43
30	05 52	06 22	06 48	11 52	12 32	13 08	13 43
35	06 00	06 32	06 59	11 58	12 36	13 11	13 43
40	06 09	06 42	07 12	12 06	12 41	13 13	13 43
45	06 18	06 55	07 28	12 14	12 47	13 16	13 43
S 50	06 29	07 10	07 47	12 24	12 54	13 20	13 44
52	06 33	07 16	07 56	12 29	12 57	13 21	13 44
54	06 39	07 24	08 06	12 34	13 00	13 23	13 44
56	06 44	07 32	08 18	12 40	13 04	13 25	13 44
58	06 50	07 41	08 31	12 46	13 08	13 27	13 44
S 60	06 57	07 52	08 47	12 53	13 13	13 29	13 44

Lat.	Sunset	Twilight Civil	Twilight Naut.	Moonset 31	Moonset 1	Moonset 2	Moonset 3
°	h m	h m	h m	h m	h m	h m	h m
N 72	▭	▭	▭	02 13	02 03	01 54	01 46
N 70	▭	▭	▭	01 48	01 47	01 46	01 44
68	▭	▭	▭	01 28	01 35	01 39	01 41
66	22 48	////	////	01 12	01 24	01 33	01 39
64	22 00	////	////	00 59	01 15	01 28	01 38
62	21 30	////	////	00 48	01 08	01 23	01 36
60	21 08	22 33	////	00 39	01 01	01 19	01 35
N 58	20 50	21 57	////	00 31	00 56	01 16	01 34
56	20 35	21 33	////	00 23	00 50	01 13	01 33
54	20 22	21 13	22 40	00 17	00 46	01 10	01 32
52	20 11	20 57	22 08	00 11	00 42	01 08	01 31
50	20 01	20 43	21 44	00 06	00 38	01 05	01 30
45	19 40	20 16	21 04	24 29	00 29	01 00	01 29
N 40	19 23	19 55	20 36	24 22	00 22	00 56	01 27
35	19 09	19 38	20 14	24 16	00 16	00 53	01 26
30	18 57	19 24	19 56	24 11	00 11	00 49	01 25
20	18 36	19 00	19 29	24 02	00 02	00 44	01 23
N 10	18 18	18 41	19 08	23 54	24 39	00 39	01 21
0	18 02	18 24	18 50	23 46	24 34	00 34	01 20
S 10	17 45	18 08	18 34	23 38	24 29	00 29	01 18
20	17 28	17 51	18 19	23 30	24 24	00 24	01 16
30	17 08	17 34	18 03	23 20	24 18	00 18	01 14
35	16 56	17 24	17 55	23 15	24 15	00 15	01 13
40	16 43	17 13	17 47	23 08	24 11	00 11	01 12
45	16 27	17 01	17 37	23 01	24 06	00 06	01 10
S 50	16 08	16 46	17 27	22 52	24 01	00 01	01 08
52	15 59	16 39	17 22	22 48	23 58	25 07	01 07
54	15 49	16 32	17 17	22 43	23 56	25 06	01 06
56	15 38	16 23	17 11	22 38	23 53	25 05	01 05
58	15 24	16 14	17 05	22 32	23 49	25 04	01 04
S 60	15 09	16 03	16 59	22 26	23 45	25 03	01 03

Day	SUN Eqn. of Time 00^h	SUN Eqn. of Time 12^h	SUN Mer. Pass.	MOON Mer. Pass. Upper	MOON Mer. Pass. Lower	MOON Age	MOON Phase
d	m s	m s	h m	h m	h m	d %	
31	02 22	02 17	11 58	17 34	05 08	06 39	
1	02 13	02 08	11 58	18 23	05 59	07 50	
2	02 03	01 59	11 58	19 09	06 46	08 60	

UT	ARIES	VENUS −4·4		MARS +1·7		JUPITER −2·2		SATURN +0·1	
	GHA	GHA	Dec	GHA	Dec	GHA	Dec	GHA	Dec
d h	° ′	° ′	° ′	° ′	° ′	° ′	° ′	° ′	° ′
3 00	251 38.4	225 57.4	N 8 14.4	162 51.9	N24 18.7	58 51.7	S 3 55.5	346 35.3	S21 59.4
01	266 40.8	240 57.5	15.1	177 52.5	18.7	73 54.3	55.5	1 37.9	59.4
02	281 43.3	255 57.7	15.9	192 53.1	18.7	88 56.8	55.5	16 40.6	59.4
03	296 45.8	270 57.9	. . 16.6	207 53.8	. . 18.8	103 59.3	. . 55.5	31 43.3	. . 59.4
04	311 48.2	285 58.0	17.4	222 54.4	18.8	119 01.8	55.5	46 45.9	59.4
05	326 50.7	300 58.2	18.1	237 55.1	18.8	134 04.3	55.4	61 48.6	59.4
06	341 53.2	315 58.3	N 8 18.8	252 55.7	N24 18.8	149 06.8	S 3 55.4	76 51.2	S21 59.4
07	356 55.6	330 58.5	19.6	267 56.3	18.9	164 09.3	55.4	91 53.9	59.4
S 08	11 58.1	345 58.7	20.3	282 57.0	18.9	179 11.8	55.4	106 56.5	59.4
A 09	27 00.5	0 58.8	. . 21.1	297 57.6	. . 18.9	194 14.4	. . 55.4	121 59.2	. . 59.4
T 10	42 03.0	15 59.0	21.8	312 58.2	18.9	209 16.9	55.4	137 01.8	59.4
U 11	57 05.5	30 59.1	22.5	327 58.9	19.0	224 19.4	55.4	152 04.5	59.4
R 12	72 07.9	45 59.3	N 8 23.3	342 59.5	N24 19.0	239 21.9	S 3 55.4	167 07.2	S21 59.4
D 13	87 10.4	60 59.5	24.0	358 00.2	19.0	254 24.4	55.4	182 09.8	59.4
A 14	102 12.9	75 59.6	24.8	13 00.8	19.0	269 26.9	55.4	197 12.5	59.4
Y 15	117 15.3	90 59.8	. . 25.5	28 01.4	. . 19.1	284 29.4	. . 55.4	212 15.1	. . 59.4
16	132 17.8	105 59.9	26.3	43 02.1	19.1	299 31.9	55.4	227 17.8	59.4
17	147 20.3	121 00.1	27.0	58 02.7	19.1	314 34.4	55.4	242 20.4	59.4
18	162 22.7	136 00.2	N 8 27.7	73 03.4	N24 19.1	329 37.0	S 3 55.3	257 23.1	S21 59.4
19	177 25.2	151 00.4	28.5	88 04.0	19.1	344 39.5	55.3	272 25.7	59.4
20	192 27.7	166 00.5	29.2	103 04.6	19.2	359 42.0	55.3	287 28.4	59.4
21	207 30.1	181 00.7	. . 30.0	118 05.3	. . 19.2	14 44.5	. . 55.3	302 31.1	. . 59.4
22	222 32.6	196 00.8	30.7	133 05.9	19.2	29 47.0	55.3	317 33.7	59.3
23	237 35.0	211 01.0	31.5	148 06.5	19.2	44 49.5	55.3	332 36.4	59.3
4 00	252 37.5	226 01.1	N 8 32.2	163 07.2	N24 19.2	59 52.0	S 3 55.3	347 39.0	S21 59.3
01	267 40.0	241 01.3	33.0	178 07.8	19.3	74 54.5	55.3	2 41.7	59.3
02	282 42.4	256 01.4	33.7	193 08.5	19.3	89 57.0	55.3	17 44.3	59.3
03	297 44.9	271 01.6	. . 34.5	208 09.1	. . 19.3	104 59.5	. . 55.3	32 47.0	. . 59.3
04	312 47.4	286 01.7	35.2	223 09.7	19.3	120 02.0	55.3	47 49.7	59.3
05	327 49.8	301 01.9	35.9	238 10.4	19.3	135 04.5	55.3	62 52.3	59.3
06	342 52.3	316 02.0	N 8 36.7	253 11.0	N24 19.4	150 07.0	S 3 55.3	77 55.0	S21 59.3
07	357 54.8	331 02.2	37.4	268 11.7	19.4	165 09.5	55.3	92 57.6	59.3
08	12 57.2	346 02.3	38.2	283 12.3	19.4	180 12.0	55.3	108 00.3	59.3
S 09	27 59.7	1 02.5	. . 38.9	298 12.9	. . 19.4	195 14.6	. . 55.3	123 02.9	. . 59.3
U 10	43 02.1	16 02.6	39.7	313 13.6	19.4	210 17.1	55.2	138 05.6	59.3
N 11	58 04.6	31 02.7	40.4	328 14.2	19.4	225 19.6	55.2	153 08.3	59.3
D 12	73 07.1	46 02.9	N 8 41.2	343 14.9	N24 19.5	240 22.1	S 3 55.2	168 10.9	S21 59.3
A 13	88 09.5	61 03.0	41.9	358 15.5	19.5	255 24.6	55.2	183 13.6	59.3
Y 14	103 12.0	76 03.2	42.7	13 16.1	19.5	270 27.1	55.2	198 16.2	59.3
15	118 14.5	91 03.3	. . 43.4	28 16.8	. . 19.5	285 29.6	. . 55.2	213 18.9	. . 59.3
16	133 16.9	106 03.4	44.2	43 17.4	19.5	300 32.1	55.2	228 21.5	59.3
17	148 19.4	121 03.6	44.9	58 18.1	19.5	315 34.6	55.2	243 24.2	59.3
18	163 21.9	136 03.7	N 8 45.7	73 18.7	N24 19.5	330 37.1	S 3 55.2	258 26.9	S21 59.3
19	178 24.3	151 03.8	46.4	88 19.3	19.6	345 39.6	55.2	273 29.5	59.3
20	193 26.8	166 04.0	47.2	103 20.0	19.6	0 42.1	55.2	288 32.2	59.3
21	208 29.3	181 04.1	. . 47.9	118 20.6	. . 19.6	15 44.6	. . 55.2	303 34.8	. . 59.2
22	223 31.7	196 04.2	48.7	133 21.3	19.6	30 47.1	55.2	318 37.5	59.2
23	238 34.2	211 04.4	49.4	148 21.9	19.6	45 49.6	55.2	333 40.1	59.2
5 00	253 36.6	226 04.5	N 8 50.2	163 22.5	N24 19.6	60 52.1	S 3 55.2	348 42.8	S21 59.2
01	268 39.1	241 04.6	50.9	178 23.2	19.6	75 54.6	55.2	3 45.5	59.2
02	283 41.6	256 04.8	51.7	193 23.8	19.6	90 57.1	55.2	18 48.1	59.2
03	298 44.0	271 04.9	. . 52.4	208 24.5	. . 19.7	105 59.6	. . 55.2	33 50.8	. . 59.2
04	313 46.5	286 05.0	53.2	223 25.1	19.7	121 02.1	55.2	48 53.4	59.2
05	328 49.0	301 05.2	53.9	238 25.7	19.7	136 04.6	55.2	63 56.1	59.2
06	343 51.4	316 05.3	N 8 54.7	253 26.4	N24 19.7	151 07.1	S 3 55.2	78 58.7	S21 59.2
07	358 53.9	331 05.4	55.4	268 27.0	19.7	166 09.6	55.2	94 01.4	59.2
08	13 56.4	346 05.5	56.2	283 27.7	19.7	181 12.1	55.2	109 04.1	59.2
M 09	28 58.8	1 05.7	. . 56.9	298 28.3	. . 19.7	196 14.6	. . 55.2	124 06.7	. . 59.2
O 10	44 01.3	16 05.8	57.7	313 28.9	19.7	211 17.1	55.2	139 09.4	59.2
N 11	59 03.7	31 05.9	58.4	328 29.6	19.7	226 19.6	55.2	154 12.0	59.2
D 12	74 06.2	46 06.0	N 8 59.2	343 30.2	N24 19.7	241 22.1	S 3 55.2	169 14.7	S21 59.2
A 13	89 08.7	61 06.2	8 59.9	358 30.9	19.7	256 24.6	55.2	184 17.3	59.2
Y 14	104 11.1	76 06.3	9 00.7	13 31.5	19.7	271 27.1	55.2	199 20.0	59.2
15	119 13.6	91 06.4	. . 01.4	28 32.1	. . 19.7	286 29.6	. . 55.2	214 22.7	. . 59.2
16	134 16.1	106 06.5	02.2	43 32.8	19.8	301 32.1	55.2	229 25.3	59.2
17	149 18.5	121 06.6	02.9	58 33.4	19.8	316 34.5	55.1	244 28.0	59.2
18	164 21.0	136 06.8	N 9 03.7	73 34.1	N24 19.8	331 37.0	S 3 55.1	259 30.6	S21 59.2
19	179 23.5	151 06.9	04.5	88 34.7	19.8	346 39.5	55.1	274 33.3	59.2
20	194 25.9	166 07.0	05.2	103 35.4	19.8	1 42.0	55.1	289 36.0	59.1
21	209 28.4	181 07.1	. . 06.0	118 36.0	. . 19.8	16 44.5	. . 55.1	304 38.6	. . 59.1
22	224 30.9	196 07.2	06.7	133 36.6	19.8	31 47.0	55.1	319 41.3	59.1
23	239 33.3	211 07.4	07.5	148 37.3	19.8	46 49.5	55.1	334 43.9	59.1
Mer. Pass.	h m 7 08.3	*v* 0.1	*d* 0.7	*v* 0.6	*d* 0.0	*v* 2.5	*d* 0.0	*v* 2.7	*d* 0.0

STARS		
Name	SHA	Dec
	° ′	° ′
Acamar	315 16.7	S40 14.2
Achernar	335 25.3	S57 08.8
Acrux	173 05.9	S63 11.9
Adhara	255 10.8	S29 00.0
Aldebaran	290 46.7	N16 32.4
Alioth	166 18.2	N55 52.2
Alkaid	152 56.5	N49 13.9
Al Na'ir	27 40.4	S46 52.3
Alnilam	275 44.0	S 1 11.7
Alphard	217 53.6	S 8 44.2
Alphecca	126 08.4	N26 39.6
Alpheratz	357 40.8	N29 10.9
Altair	62 05.4	N 8 54.9
Ankaa	353 13.3	S42 12.6
Antares	112 22.6	S26 28.1
Arcturus	145 53.1	N19 05.7
Atria	107 21.4	S69 03.3
Avior	234 17.3	S59 34.3
Bellatrix	278 29.5	N 6 21.7
Betelgeuse	270 58.8	N 7 24.4
Canopus	263 55.5	S52 42.6
Capella	280 31.0	N46 00.7
Deneb	49 29.3	N45 20.4
Denebola	182 30.9	N14 28.6
Diphda	348 53.4	S17 53.5
Dubhe	193 48.6	N61 39.7
Elnath	278 09.6	N28 37.1
Eltanin	90 44.4	N51 29.3
Enif	33 44.4	N 9 57.3
Fomalhaut	15 21.1	S29 31.7
Gacrux	171 57.6	S57 12.8
Gienah	175 49.4	S17 38.4
Hadar	148 43.5	S60 27.5
Hamal	327 58.0	N23 32.4
Kaus Aust.	83 39.9	S34 22.3
Kochab	137 19.2	N74 05.4
Markab	13 35.7	N15 17.8
Menkar	314 12.6	N 4 09.2
Menkent	148 04.1	S36 27.3
Miaplacidus	221 39.4	S69 47.7
Mirfak	308 37.0	N49 55.0
Nunki	75 54.7	S26 16.3
Peacock	53 14.8	S56 40.4
Pollux	243 24.8	N27 58.9
Procyon	244 57.2	N 5 10.6
Rasalhague	96 03.6	N12 33.0
Regulus	207 40.8	N11 52.9
Rigel	281 09.8	S 8 11.2
Rigil Kent.	139 47.5	S60 54.4
Sabik	102 09.1	S15 44.6
Schedar	349 37.6	N56 37.6
Shaula	96 17.9	S37 06.7
Sirius	258 31.7	S16 44.7
Spica	158 28.2	S11 15.1
Suhail	222 50.7	S43 30.5
Vega	80 36.8	N38 48.1
Zuben'ubi	137 02.2	S16 06.7

	SHA	Mer. Pass.
	° ′	h m
Venus	333 23.6	8 56
Mars	270 29.7	13 07
Jupiter	167 14.5	19 57
Saturn	95 01.5	0 49

UT d	h	SUN GHA ° ′	SUN Dec ° ′	MOON GHA ° ′	v ′	MOON Dec ° ′	d ′	HP ′
3 SATURDAY	00	180 28.4	N22 18.4	70 35.4	13.8	N 2 29.9	10.3	55.8
	01	195 28.3	18.7	85 08.2	13.9	2 19.6	10.3	55.8
	02	210 28.2	19.0	99 41.1	13.9	2 09.3	10.3	55.8
	03	225 28.1	. . 19.3	114 14.0	13.9	1 59.0	10.4	55.7
	04	240 28.0	19.6	128 46.9	14.0	1 48.6	10.3	55.7
	05	255 27.9	19.9	143 19.9	14.0	1 38.3	10.3	55.7
	06	270 27.7	N22 20.2	157 52.9	14.0	N 1 28.0	10.3	55.7
	07	285 27.6	20.5	172 25.9	14.1	1 17.7	10.3	55.6
	08	300 27.5	20.8	186 59.0	14.0	1 07.4	10.3	55.6
	09	315 27.4	. . 21.1	201 32.0	14.2	0 57.1	10.3	55.6
	10	330 27.3	21.4	216 05.2	14.1	0 46.8	10.3	55.6
	11	345 27.2	21.7	230 38.3	14.2	0 36.5	10.3	55.5
	12	0 27.1	N22 22.0	245 11.5	14.2	N 0 26.2	10.3	55.5
	13	15 27.0	22.3	259 44.7	14.2	0 15.9	10.2	55.5
	14	30 26.9	22.6	274 17.9	14.2	N 0 05.7	10.3	55.5
	15	45 26.8	. . 22.9	288 51.1	14.3	S 0 04.6	10.3	55.4
	16	60 26.7	23.2	303 24.4	14.3	0 14.9	10.2	55.4
	17	75 26.6	23.5	317 57.7	14.3	0 25.1	10.2	55.4
	18	90 26.5	N22 23.8	332 31.0	14.4	S 0 35.3	10.3	55.4
	19	105 26.4	24.1	347 04.4	14.3	0 45.6	10.2	55.3
	20	120 26.3	24.4	1 37.7	14.4	0 55.8	10.2	55.3
	21	135 26.2	. . 24.7	16 11.1	14.4	1 06.0	10.2	55.3
	22	150 26.1	25.0	30 44.5	14.4	1 16.2	10.1	55.3
	23	165 26.0	25.2	45 17.9	14.5	1 26.3	10.2	55.2
4 SUNDAY	00	180 25.9	N22 25.5	59 51.4	14.4	S 1 36.5	10.2	55.2
	01	195 25.8	25.8	74 24.8	14.5	1 46.7	10.1	55.2
	02	210 25.6	26.1	88 58.3	14.5	1 56.8	10.1	55.2
	03	225 25.5	. . 26.4	103 31.8	14.5	2 06.9	10.1	55.1
	04	240 25.4	26.7	118 05.3	14.5	2 17.0	10.1	55.1
	05	255 25.3	27.0	132 38.8	14.5	2 27.1	10.1	55.1
	06	270 25.2	N22 27.3	147 12.3	14.5	S 2 37.2	10.0	55.1
	07	285 25.1	27.6	161 45.8	14.6	2 47.2	10.1	55.1
	08	300 25.0	27.8	176 19.4	14.6	2 57.3	10.0	55.0
	09	315 24.9	. . 28.1	190 53.0	14.5	3 07.3	10.0	55.0
	10	330 24.8	28.4	205 26.5	14.6	3 17.3	9.9	55.0
	11	345 24.7	28.7	220 00.1	14.6	3 27.2	10.0	55.0
	12	0 24.6	N22 29.0	234 33.7	14.6	S 3 37.2	9.9	55.0
	13	15 24.5	29.3	249 07.3	14.6	3 47.1	9.9	54.9
	14	30 24.4	29.5	263 40.9	14.6	3 57.0	9.9	54.9
	15	45 24.2	. . 29.8	278 14.5	14.7	4 06.9	9.9	54.9
	16	60 24.1	30.1	292 48.2	14.6	4 16.8	9.8	54.9
	17	75 24.0	30.4	307 21.8	14.6	4 26.6	9.8	54.9
	18	90 23.9	N22 30.7	321 55.4	14.7	S 4 36.4	9.8	54.8
	19	105 23.8	30.9	336 29.1	14.6	4 46.2	9.8	54.8
	20	120 23.7	31.2	351 02.7	14.7	4 56.0	9.7	54.8
	21	135 23.6	. . 31.5	5 36.4	14.6	5 05.7	9.7	54.8
	22	150 23.5	31.8	20 10.0	14.6	5 15.4	9.7	54.8
	23	165 23.4	32.1	34 43.6	14.7	5 25.1	9.7	54.7
5 MONDAY	00	180 23.3	N22 32.3	49 17.3	14.6	S 5 34.8	9.6	54.7
	01	195 23.2	32.6	63 50.9	14.7	5 44.4	9.6	54.7
	02	210 23.0	32.9	78 24.6	14.6	5 54.0	9.5	54.7
	03	225 22.9	. . 33.1	92 58.2	14.7	6 03.5	9.6	54.7
	04	240 22.8	33.4	107 31.9	14.6	6 13.1	9.5	54.7
	05	255 22.7	33.7	122 05.5	14.7	6 22.6	9.5	54.6
	06	270 22.6	N22 34.0	136 39.2	14.6	S 6 32.1	9.4	54.6
	07	285 22.5	34.2	151 12.8	14.6	6 41.5	9.4	54.6
	08	300 22.4	34.5	165 46.4	14.7	6 50.9	9.4	54.6
	09	315 22.3	. . 34.8	180 20.1	14.6	7 00.3	9.3	54.6
	10	330 22.2	35.0	194 53.7	14.6	7 09.6	9.4	54.6
	11	345 22.1	35.3	209 27.3	14.6	7 19.0	9.2	54.6
	12	0 21.9	N22 35.6	224 00.9	14.6	S 7 28.2	9.3	54.5
	13	15 21.8	35.8	238 34.5	14.6	7 37.5	9.2	54.5
	14	30 21.7	36.1	253 08.1	14.6	7 46.7	9.1	54.5
	15	45 21.6	. . 36.4	267 41.7	14.6	7 55.8	9.2	54.5
	16	60 21.5	36.6	282 15.3	14.6	8 05.0	9.1	54.5
	17	75 21.4	36.9	296 48.9	14.5	8 14.1	9.0	54.5
	18	90 21.3	N22 37.2	311 22.4	14.6	S 8 23.1	9.0	54.5
	19	105 21.2	37.4	325 56.0	14.5	8 32.1	9.0	54.4
	20	120 21.1	37.7	340 29.5	14.6	8 41.1	9.0	54.4
	21	135 20.9	. . 37.9	355 03.1	14.5	8 50.1	8.9	54.4
	22	150 20.8	38.2	9 36.6	14.5	8 59.0	8.8	54.4
	23	165 20.7	38.5	24 10.1	14.5	S 9 07.8	8.8	54.4
		SD 15.8	*d* 0.3	SD 15.1		15.0		14.9

Lat. °	Twilight Naut. h m	Twilight Civil h m	Sunrise h m	Moonrise 3 h m	Moonrise 4 h m	Moonrise 5 h m	Moonrise 6 h m
N 72	□	□	□	13 42	15 21	17 00	18 41
N 70	□	□	□	13 42	15 15	16 47	18 20
68	□	□	□	13 42	15 10	16 36	18 03
66	////	////	00 58	13 42	15 06	16 28	17 49
64	////	////	01 51	13 42	15 02	16 21	17 38
62	////	////	02 22	13 42	14 59	16 15	17 29
60	////	01 17	02 45	13 42	14 56	16 09	17 21
N 58	////	01 55	03 04	13 42	14 54	16 04	17 14
56	////	02 20	03 19	13 42	14 52	16 00	17 08
54	01 10	02 40	03 32	13 42	14 50	15 57	17 02
52	01 45	02 57	03 44	13 42	14 48	15 53	16 57
50	02 09	03 11	03 54	13 42	14 47	15 50	16 53
45	02 50	03 38	04 15	13 42	14 43	15 44	16 43
N 40	03 19	04 00	04 32	13 42	14 41	15 38	16 35
35	03 41	04 17	04 46	13 42	14 38	15 33	16 28
30	03 59	04 32	04 59	13 42	14 36	15 29	16 22
20	04 27	04 55	05 20	13 43	14 33	15 22	16 11
N 10	04 48	05 15	05 38	13 43	14 29	15 16	16 02
0	05 06	05 32	05 55	13 43	14 26	15 10	15 54
S 10	05 23	05 49	06 11	13 43	14 24	15 04	15 45
20	05 38	06 05	06 29	13 43	14 20	14 58	15 36
30	05 53	06 23	06 49	13 43	14 17	14 51	15 26
35	06 02	06 33	07 01	13 43	14 15	14 47	15 20
40	06 10	06 44	07 15	13 43	14 13	14 43	15 14
45	06 20	06 57	07 30	13 43	14 10	14 37	15 06
S 50	06 31	07 12	07 50	13 44	14 07	14 31	14 57
52	06 36	07 19	07 59	13 44	14 06	14 28	14 52
54	06 41	07 27	08 10	13 44	14 04	14 25	14 48
56	06 47	07 35	08 22	13 44	14 03	14 22	14 43
58	06 53	07 45	08 35	13 44	14 01	14 18	14 37
S 60	07 00	07 56	08 51	13 44	13 59	14 14	14 30

Lat. °	Sunset h m	Twilight Civil h m	Twilight Naut. h m	Moonset 3 h m	Moonset 4 h m	Moonset 5 h m	Moonset 6 h m
N 72	□	□	□	01 46	01 39	01 31	01 22
N 70	□	□	□	01 44	01 41	01 39	01 37
68	□	□	□	01 41	01 44	01 46	01 49
66	23 03	////	////	01 39	01 46	01 52	01 59
64	22 08	////	////	01 38	01 47	01 56	02 07
62	21 36	////	////	01 36	01 48	02 01	02 14
60	21 13	22 42	////	01 35	01 50	02 04	02 20
N 58	20 54	22 04	////	01 34	01 51	02 08	02 26
56	20 38	21 38	////	01 33	01 52	02 11	02 30
54	20 25	21 17	22 49	01 32	01 53	02 13	02 35
52	20 14	21 01	22 13	01 31	01 53	02 16	02 39
50	20 03	20 47	21 49	01 30	01 54	02 18	02 42
45	19 42	20 19	21 07	01 29	01 56	02 22	02 50
N 40	19 25	19 57	20 38	01 27	01 57	02 26	02 57
35	19 11	19 40	20 16	01 26	01 58	02 30	03 02
30	18 58	19 25	19 58	01 25	01 59	02 33	03 07
20	18 37	19 01	19 30	01 23	02 01	02 38	03 16
N 10	18 19	18 42	19 09	01 21	02 02	02 43	03 24
0	18 02	18 24	18 50	01 20	02 04	02 47	03 31
S 10	17 45	18 08	18 34	01 18	02 05	02 52	03 38
20	17 28	17 51	18 19	01 16	02 07	02 56	03 46
30	17 07	17 33	18 03	01 14	02 08	03 02	03 55
35	16 56	17 23	17 55	01 13	02 09	03 05	04 00
40	16 42	17 12	17 46	01 12	02 11	03 08	04 05
45	16 26	16 59	17 36	01 10	02 12	03 12	04 12
S 50	16 06	16 44	17 25	01 08	02 13	03 17	04 20
52	15 57	16 37	17 20	01 07	02 14	03 20	04 24
54	15 47	16 30	17 15	01 06	02 15	03 22	04 28
56	15 35	16 21	17 09	01 05	02 16	03 25	04 33
58	15 21	16 12	17 03	01 04	02 17	03 28	04 38
S 60	15 05	16 01	16 56	01 03	02 18	03 31	04 44

Day d	SUN Eqn. of Time 00^h m s	SUN Eqn. of Time 12^h m s	SUN Mer. Pass. h m	MOON Mer. Pass. Upper h m	MOON Mer. Pass. Lower h m	MOON Age d	MOON %	Phase
3	01 54	01 49	11 58	19 53	07 31	09	70	
4	01 44	01 39	11 58	20 37	08 15	10	78	◐
5	01 33	01 28	11 59	21 20	08 59	11	86	

	UT	ARIES	VENUS −4·4		MARS +1·7		JUPITER −2·2		SATURN +0·0	
		GHA	GHA	Dec	GHA	Dec	GHA	Dec	GHA	Dec
	d h	° ′	° ′	° ′	° ′	° ′	° ′	° ′	° ′	° ′
	6 00	254 35.8	226 07.5	N 9 08.2	163 37.9	N24 19.8	61 52.0	S 3 55.1	349 46.6	S21 59.1
	01	269 38.2	241 07.6	09.0	178 38.6	19.8	76 54.5	55.1	4 49.2	59.1
	02	284 40.7	256 07.7	09.7	193 39.2	19.8	91 57.0	55.1	19 51.9	59.1
	03	299 43.2	271 07.8	. . 10.5	208 39.8	. . 19.8	106 59.5	. . 55.1	34 54.6	. . 59.1
	04	314 45.6	286 07.9	11.2	223 40.5	19.8	122 02.0	55.1	49 57.2	59.1
	05	329 48.1	301 08.0	12.0	238 41.1	19.8	137 04.5	55.1	64 59.9	59.1
	06	344 50.6	316 08.1	N 9 12.8	253 41.8	N24 19.8	152 07.0	S 3 55.1	80 02.5	S21 59.1
	07	359 53.0	331 08.3	13.5	268 42.4	19.8	167 09.5	55.1	95 05.2	59.1
T	08	14 55.5	346 08.4	14.3	283 43.1	19.8	182 11.9	55.1	110 07.9	59.1
U	09	29 58.0	1 08.5	. . 15.0	298 43.7	. . 19.8	197 14.4	. . 55.1	125 10.5	. . 59.1
E	10	45 00.4	16 08.6	15.8	313 44.3	19.8	212 16.9	55.1	140 13.2	59.1
S	11	60 02.9	31 08.7	16.5	328 45.0	19.8	227 19.4	55.1	155 15.8	59.1
	12	75 05.4	46 08.8	N 9 17.3	343 45.6	N24 19.8	242 21.9	S 3 55.1	170 18.5	S21 59.1
D	13	90 07.8	61 08.9	18.1	358 46.3	19.8	257 24.4	55.1	185 21.1	59.1
A	14	105 10.3	76 09.0	18.8	13 46.9	19.8	272 26.9	55.2	200 23.8	59.1
Y	15	120 12.7	91 09.1	. . 19.6	28 47.6	. . 19.8	287 29.4	. . 55.2	215 26.5	. . 59.1
	16	135 15.2	106 09.2	20.3	43 48.2	19.8	302 31.9	55.2	230 29.1	59.1
	17	150 17.7	121 09.3	21.1	58 48.8	19.8	317 34.4	55.2	245 31.8	59.1
	18	165 20.1	136 09.4	N 9 21.8	73 49.5	N24 19.8	332 36.8	S 3 55.2	260 34.4	S21 59.0
	19	180 22.6	151 09.5	22.6	88 50.1	19.8	347 39.3	55.2	275 37.1	59.0
	20	195 25.1	166 09.6	23.4	103 50.8	19.8	2 41.8	55.2	290 39.8	59.0
	21	210 27.5	181 09.7	. . 24.1	118 51.4	. . 19.8	17 44.3	. . 55.2	305 42.4	. . 59.0
	22	225 30.0	196 09.8	24.9	133 52.1	19.8	32 46.8	55.2	320 45.1	59.0
	23	240 32.5	211 09.9	25.6	148 52.7	19.7	47 49.3	55.2	335 47.7	59.0
	7 00	255 34.9	226 10.0	N 9 26.4	163 53.3	N24 19.7	62 51.8	S 3 55.2	350 50.4	S21 59.0
	01	270 37.4	241 10.1	27.2	178 54.0	19.7	77 54.2	55.2	5 53.1	59.0
	02	285 39.8	256 10.2	27.9	193 54.6	19.7	92 56.7	55.2	20 55.7	59.0
	03	300 42.3	271 10.3	. . 28.7	208 55.3	. . 19.7	107 59.2	. . 55.2	35 58.4	. . 59.0
	04	315 44.8	286 10.4	29.4	223 55.9	19.7	123 01.7	55.2	51 01.0	59.0
	05	330 47.2	301 10.5	30.2	238 56.6	19.7	138 04.2	55.2	66 03.7	59.0
	06	345 49.7	316 10.6	N 9 30.9	253 57.2	N24 19.7	153 06.7	S 3 55.2	81 06.4	S21 59.0
W	07	0 52.2	331 10.7	31.7	268 57.8	19.7	168 09.2	55.2	96 09.0	59.0
E	08	15 54.6	346 10.8	32.5	283 58.5	19.7	183 11.6	55.2	111 11.7	59.0
D	09	30 57.1	1 10.9	. . 33.2	298 59.1	. . 19.7	198 14.1	. . 55.2	126 14.3	. . 59.0
N	10	45 59.6	16 11.0	34.0	313 59.8	19.7	213 16.6	55.2	141 17.0	59.0
E	11	61 02.0	31 11.1	34.7	329 00.4	19.7	228 19.1	55.2	156 19.7	59.0
S	12	76 04.5	46 11.1	N 9 35.5	344 01.1	N24 19.6	243 21.6	S 3 55.2	171 22.3	S21 59.0
D	13	91 07.0	61 11.2	36.3	359 01.7	19.6	258 24.1	55.2	186 25.0	59.0
A	14	106 09.4	76 11.3	37.0	14 02.4	19.6	273 26.5	55.2	201 27.6	59.0
Y	15	121 11.9	91 11.4	. . 37.8	29 03.0	. . 19.6	288 29.0	. . 55.2	216 30.3	. . 59.0
	16	136 14.3	106 11.5	38.6	44 03.6	19.6	303 31.5	55.2	231 33.0	59.0
	17	151 16.8	121 11.6	39.3	59 04.3	19.6	318 34.0	55.2	246 35.6	58.9
	18	166 19.3	136 11.7	N 9 40.1	74 04.9	N24 19.6	333 36.5	S 3 55.2	261 38.3	S21 58.9
	19	181 21.7	151 11.8	40.8	89 05.6	19.6	348 38.9	55.2	276 40.9	58.9
	20	196 24.2	166 11.8	41.6	104 06.2	19.5	3 41.4	55.2	291 43.6	58.9
	21	211 26.7	181 11.9	. . 42.4	119 06.9	. . 19.5	18 43.9	. . 55.3	306 46.3	. . 58.9
	22	226 29.1	196 12.0	43.1	134 07.5	19.5	33 46.4	55.3	321 48.9	58.9
	23	241 31.6	211 12.1	43.9	149 08.2	19.5	48 48.9	55.3	336 51.6	58.9
	8 00	256 34.1	226 12.2	N 9 44.6	164 08.8	N24 19.5	63 51.3	S 3 55.3	351 54.2	S21 58.9
	01	271 36.5	241 12.3	45.4	179 09.4	19.5	78 53.8	55.3	6 56.9	58.9
	02	286 39.0	256 12.3	46.2	194 10.1	19.5	93 56.3	55.3	21 59.6	58.9
	03	301 41.5	271 12.4	. . 46.9	209 10.7	. . 19.4	108 58.8	. . 55.3	37 02.2	. . 58.9
	04	316 43.9	286 12.5	47.7	224 11.4	19.4	124 01.3	55.3	52 04.9	58.9
	05	331 46.4	301 12.6	48.5	239 12.0	19.4	139 03.7	55.3	67 07.5	58.9
	06	346 48.8	316 12.6	N 9 49.2	254 12.7	N24 19.4	154 06.2	S 3 55.3	82 10.2	S21 58.9
	07	1 51.3	331 12.7	50.0	269 13.3	19.4	169 08.7	55.3	97 12.9	58.9
T	08	16 53.8	346 12.8	50.7	284 14.0	19.4	184 11.2	55.3	112 15.5	58.9
H	09	31 56.2	1 12.9	. . 51.5	299 14.6	. . 19.3	199 13.7	. . 55.3	127 18.2	. . 58.9
U	10	46 58.7	16 13.0	52.3	314 15.3	19.3	214 16.1	55.3	142 20.8	58.9
R	11	62 01.2	31 13.0	53.0	329 15.9	19.3	229 18.6	55.3	157 23.5	58.9
S	12	77 03.6	46 13.1	N 9 53.8	344 16.5	N24 19.3	244 21.1	S 3 55.3	172 26.2	S21 58.9
D	13	92 06.1	61 13.2	54.6	359 17.2	19.3	259 23.6	55.3	187 28.8	58.9
A	14	107 08.6	76 13.2	55.3	14 17.8	19.3	274 26.0	55.4	202 31.5	58.9
Y	15	122 11.0	91 13.3	. . 56.1	29 18.5	. . 19.2	289 28.5	. . 55.4	217 34.1	. . 58.8
	16	137 13.5	106 13.4	56.9	44 19.1	19.2	304 31.0	55.4	232 36.8	58.8
	17	152 16.0	121 13.5	57.6	59 19.8	19.2	319 33.5	55.4	247 39.5	58.8
	18	167 18.4	136 13.5	N 9 58.4	74 20.4	N24 19.2	334 35.9	S 3 55.4	262 42.1	S21 58.8
	19	182 20.9	151 13.6	59.1	89 21.1	19.2	349 38.4	55.4	277 44.8	58.8
	20	197 23.3	166 13.7	9 59.9	104 21.7	19.1	4 40.9	55.4	292 47.4	58.8
	21	212 25.8	181 13.7	. . 10 00.7	119 22.4	. . 19.1	19 43.4	. . 55.4	307 50.1	. . 58.8
	22	227 28.3	196 13.8	01.4	134 23.0	19.1	34 45.8	55.4	322 52.8	58.8
	23	242 30.7	211 13.9	02.2	149 23.6	19.1	49 48.3	55.4	337 55.4	58.8
	Mer. Pass.	h m 6 56.5	v 0.1	d 0.8	v 0.6	d 0.0	v 2.5	d 0.0	v 2.7	d 0.0

STARS		
Name	SHA	Dec
	° ′	° ′
Acamar	315 16.7	S40 14.2
Achernar	335 25.3	S57 08.8
Acrux	173 05.9	S63 12.0
Adhara	255 10.8	S29 00.0
Aldebaran	290 46.7	N16 32.4
Alioth	166 18.2	N55 52.3
Alkaid	152 56.5	N49 13.9
Al Na'ir	27 40.3	S46 52.3
Alnilam	275 44.0	S 1 11.7
Alphard	217 53.6	S 8 44.2
Alphecca	126 08.4	N26 39.6
Alpheratz	357 40.8	N29 10.9
Altair	62 05.4	N 8 55.0
Ankaa	353 13.3	S42 12.6
Antares	112 22.6	S26 28.1
Arcturus	145 53.1	N19 05.7
Atria	107 21.4	S69 03.3
Avior	234 17.3	S59 34.3
Bellatrix	278 29.5	N 6 21.7
Betelgeuse	270 58.8	N 7 24.4
Canopus	263 55.5	S52 42.6
Capella	280 31.0	N46 00.7
Deneb	49 29.3	N45 20.4
Denebola	182 30.9	N14 28.6
Diphda	348 53.4	S17 53.5
Dubhe	193 48.6	N61 39.7
Elnath	278 09.6	N28 37.1
Eltanin	90 44.4	N51 29.3
Enif	33 44.4	N 9 57.3
Fomalhaut	15 21.1	S29 31.7
Gacrux	171 57.6	S57 12.8
Gienah	175 49.4	S17 38.4
Hadar	148 43.5	S60 27.5
Hamal	327 58.0	N23 32.4
Kaus Aust.	83 39.9	S34 22.3
Kochab	137 19.3	N74 05.4
Markab	13 35.6	N15 17.8
Menkar	314 12.5	N 4 09.2
Menkent	148 04.1	S36 27.3
Miaplacidus	221 39.5	S69 47.7
Mirfak	308 36.9	N49 55.0
Nunki	75 54.7	S26 16.3
Peacock	53 14.7	S56 40.4
Pollux	243 24.8	N27 58.9
Procyon	244 57.2	N 5 10.6
Rasalhague	96 03.6	N12 33.0
Regulus	207 40.8	N11 52.9
Rigel	281 09.8	S 8 11.1
Rigil Kent.	139 47.5	S60 54.4
Sabik	102 09.1	S15 44.6
Schedar	349 37.6	N56 37.6
Shaula	96 17.9	S37 06.7
Sirius	258 31.7	S16 44.7
Spica	158 28.2	S11 15.1
Suhail	222 50.7	S43 30.5
Vega	80 36.7	N38 48.1
Zuben'ubi	137 02.2	S16 06.7

	SHA	Mer. Pass.
	° ′	h m
Venus	330 35.1	8 55
Mars	268 18.4	13 04
Jupiter	167 16.8	19 45
Saturn	95 15.5	0 37

UT		SUN GHA	SUN Dec	MOON GHA	v	MOON Dec	d	HP
d h		° ′	° ′	° ′	′	° ′	′	′
6 00	TUESDAY	180 20.6	N22 38.7	38 43.6	14.5	S 9 16.6	8.8	54.4
01		195 20.5	39.0	53 17.1	14.4	9 25.4	8.7	54.4
02		210 20.4	39.2	67 50.5	14.5	9 34.1	8.7	54.3
03		225 20.3	. . 39.5	82 24.0	14.4	9 42.8	8.7	54.3
04		240 20.1	39.7	96 57.4	14.4	9 51.5	8.6	54.3
05		255 20.0	40.0	111 30.8	14.4	10 00.1	8.5	54.3
06		270 19.9	N22 40.3	126 04.2	14.4	S10 08.6	8.5	54.3
07		285 19.8	40.5	140 37.6	14.4	10 17.1	8.5	54.3
08		300 19.7	40.8	155 11.0	14.4	10 25.6	8.4	54.3
09		315 19.6	. . 41.0	169 44.4	14.3	10 34.0	8.4	54.3
10		330 19.5	41.3	184 17.7	14.3	10 42.4	8.3	54.3
11		345 19.4	41.5	198 51.0	14.3	10 50.7	8.3	54.2
12		0 19.2	N22 41.8	213 24.3	14.3	S10 59.0	8.2	54.2
13		15 19.1	42.0	227 57.6	14.3	11 07.2	8.2	54.2
14		30 19.0	42.3	242 30.9	14.2	11 15.4	8.2	54.2
15		45 18.9	. . 42.5	257 04.1	14.3	11 23.6	8.0	54.2
16		60 18.8	42.8	271 37.4	14.2	11 31.6	8.1	54.2
17		75 18.7	43.0	286 10.6	14.2	11 39.7	7.9	54.2
18		90 18.6	N22 43.3	300 43.8	14.1	S11 47.6	8.0	54.2
19		105 18.4	43.5	315 16.9	14.2	11 55.6	7.8	54.2
20		120 18.3	43.7	329 50.1	14.1	12 03.4	7.9	54.2
21		135 18.2	. . 44.0	344 23.2	14.1	12 11.3	7.7	54.2
22		150 18.1	44.2	358 56.3	14.1	12 19.0	7.8	54.1
23		165 18.0	44.5	13 29.4	14.0	12 26.8	7.6	54.1
7 00	WEDNESDAY	180 17.9	N22 44.7	28 02.4	14.1	S12 34.4	7.6	54.1
01		195 17.7	45.0	42 35.5	14.0	12 42.0	7.6	54.1
02		210 17.6	45.2	57 08.5	14.0	12 49.6	7.5	54.1
03		225 17.5	. . 45.4	71 41.5	13.9	12 57.1	7.4	54.1
04		240 17.4	45.7	86 14.4	14.0	13 04.5	7.4	54.1
05		255 17.3	45.9	100 47.4	13.9	13 11.9	7.3	54.1
06		270 17.2	N22 46.2	115 20.3	13.9	S13 19.2	7.3	54.1
07		285 17.0	46.4	129 53.2	13.9	13 26.5	7.2	54.1
08		300 16.9	46.6	144 26.1	13.8	13 33.7	7.2	54.1
09		315 16.8	. . 46.9	158 58.9	13.8	13 40.9	7.0	54.1
10		330 16.7	47.1	173 31.7	13.8	13 47.9	7.1	54.1
11		345 16.6	47.3	188 04.5	13.8	13 55.0	6.9	54.1
12		0 16.5	N22 47.6	202 37.3	13.7	S14 01.9	7.0	54.1
13		15 16.3	47.8	217 10.0	13.8	14 08.9	6.8	54.0
14		30 16.2	48.0	231 42.8	13.7	14 15.7	6.8	54.0
15		45 16.1	. . 48.3	246 15.5	13.6	14 22.5	6.7	54.0
16		60 16.0	48.5	260 48.1	13.7	14 29.2	6.7	54.0
17		75 15.9	48.7	275 20.8	13.6	14 35.9	6.6	54.0
18		90 15.8	N22 49.0	289 53.4	13.6	S14 42.5	6.5	54.0
19		105 15.6	49.2	304 26.0	13.5	14 49.0	6.5	54.0
20		120 15.5	49.4	318 58.5	13.6	14 55.5	6.4	54.0
21		135 15.4	. . 49.6	333 31.1	13.5	15 01.9	6.3	54.0
22		150 15.3	49.9	348 03.6	13.5	15 08.2	6.3	54.0
23		165 15.2	50.1	2 36.1	13.4	15 14.5	6.2	54.0
8 00	THURSDAY	180 15.0	N22 50.3	17 08.5	13.4	S15 20.7	6.1	54.0
01		195 14.9	50.5	31 40.9	13.5	15 26.8	6.1	54.0
02		210 14.8	50.8	46 13.4	13.3	15 32.9	6.0	54.0
03		225 14.7	. . 51.0	60 45.7	13.4	15 38.9	5.9	54.0
04		240 14.6	51.2	75 18.1	13.3	15 44.8	5.9	54.0
05		255 14.5	51.4	89 50.4	13.3	15 50.7	5.8	54.0
06		270 14.3	N22 51.7	104 22.7	13.3	S15 56.5	5.7	54.0
07		285 14.2	51.9	118 55.0	13.2	16 02.2	5.7	54.0
08		300 14.1	52.1	133 27.2	13.2	16 07.9	5.5	54.0
09		315 14.0	. . 52.3	147 59.4	13.2	16 13.4	5.5	54.0
10		330 13.9	52.5	162 31.6	13.2	16 18.9	5.5	54.0
11		345 13.7	52.7	177 03.8	13.1	16 24.4	5.4	54.0
12		0 13.6	N22 53.0	191 35.9	13.1	S16 29.8	5.3	54.0
13		15 13.5	53.2	206 08.0	13.1	16 35.1	5.2	54.0
14		30 13.4	53.4	220 40.1	13.0	16 40.3	5.1	54.0
15		45 13.3	. . 53.6	235 12.1	13.0	16 45.4	5.1	54.0
16		60 13.1	53.8	249 44.1	13.0	16 50.5	5.0	54.0
17		75 13.0	54.0	264 16.1	13.0	16 55.5	4.9	54.0
18		90 12.9	N22 54.3	278 48.1	13.0	S17 00.4	4.9	54.0
19		105 12.8	54.5	293 20.1	12.9	17 05.3	4.7	54.0
20		120 12.7	54.7	307 52.0	12.9	17 10.0	4.7	54.0
21		135 12.5	. . 54.9	322 23.9	12.8	17 14.7	4.7	54.0
22		150 12.4	55.1	336 55.7	12.9	17 19.4	4.5	54.0
23		165 12.3	55.3	351 27.6	12.8	S17 23.9	4.5	54.0
		SD 15.8	*d* 0.2	SD	14.8	14.7		14.7

Lat.	Twilight Naut.	Twilight Civil	Sunrise	Moonrise 6	Moonrise 7	Moonrise 8	Moonrise 9
°	h m	h m	h m	h m	h m	h m	h m
N 72	▭	▭	▭	18 41	20 29	22 35	■
N 70	▭	▭	▭	18 20	19 54	21 28	23 01
68	▭	▭	▭	18 03	19 29	20 52	22 09
66	////	////	00 44	17 49	19 10	20 27	21 37
64	////	////	01 44	17 38	18 54	20 07	21 14
62	////	////	02 18	17 29	18 42	19 51	20 55
60	////	01 09	02 42	17 21	18 31	19 38	20 40
N 58	////	01 50	03 01	17 14	18 22	19 26	20 27
56	////	02 17	03 17	17 08	18 13	19 17	20 16
54	01 03	02 37	03 30	17 02	18 06	19 08	20 06
52	01 41	02 54	03 42	16 57	18 00	19 00	19 57
50	02 06	03 09	03 52	16 53	17 54	18 53	19 49
45	02 48	03 37	04 14	16 43	17 41	18 38	19 33
N 40	03 18	03 59	04 31	16 35	17 31	18 26	19 19
35	03 40	04 16	04 46	16 28	17 22	18 15	19 07
30	03 58	04 31	04 58	16 22	17 14	18 06	18 57
20	04 26	04 55	05 20	16 11	17 01	17 50	18 40
N 10	04 48	05 15	05 38	16 02	16 49	17 37	18 25
0	05 07	05 33	05 55	15 54	16 38	17 24	18 11
S 10	05 23	05 49	06 12	15 45	16 28	17 11	17 57
20	05 39	06 06	06 30	15 36	16 16	16 58	17 42
30	05 55	06 24	06 51	15 26	16 03	16 42	17 25
35	06 03	06 35	07 03	15 20	15 55	16 33	17 15
40	06 12	06 46	07 16	15 14	15 47	16 23	17 03
45	06 22	06 59	07 33	15 06	15 37	16 11	16 50
S 50	06 33	07 14	07 53	14 57	15 25	15 57	16 34
52	06 38	07 22	08 02	14 52	15 19	15 50	16 26
54	06 44	07 29	08 13	14 48	15 13	15 43	16 18
56	06 49	07 38	08 25	14 43	15 06	15 35	16 08
58	06 56	07 48	08 39	14 37	14 59	15 25	15 58
S 60	07 03	07 59	08 55	14 30	14 50	15 15	15 45

Lat.	Sunset	Twilight Civil	Twilight Naut.	Moonset 6	Moonset 7	Moonset 8	Moonset 9
°	h m	h m	h m	h m	h m	h m	h m
N 72	▭	▭	▭	01 22	01 12	00 58	00 27
N 70	▭	▭	▭	01 37	01 35	01 34	01 35
68	▭	▭	▭	01 49	01 53	02 00	02 11
66	23 19	////	////	01 59	02 07	02 19	02 37
64	22 15	////	////	02 07	02 19	02 35	02 57
62	21 41	////	////	02 14	02 29	02 49	03 14
60	21 17	22 51	////	02 20	02 38	03 00	03 27
N 58	20 58	22 09	////	02 26	02 46	03 10	03 39
56	20 42	21 42	////	02 30	02 53	03 18	03 49
54	20 28	21 21	22 57	02 35	02 59	03 26	03 58
52	20 16	21 04	22 18	02 39	03 04	03 33	04 06
50	20 06	20 50	21 53	02 42	03 09	03 39	04 14
45	19 44	20 21	21 10	02 50	03 20	03 53	04 29
N 40	19 27	19 59	20 40	02 57	03 29	04 04	04 42
35	19 12	19 42	20 18	03 02	03 37	04 13	04 53
30	19 00	19 27	20 00	03 07	03 43	04 21	05 02
20	18 38	19 03	19 32	03 16	03 55	04 36	05 19
N 10	18 20	18 43	19 10	03 24	04 05	04 48	05 33
0	18 03	18 25	18 51	03 31	04 15	05 00	05 47
S 10	17 46	18 08	18 35	03 38	04 25	05 12	06 00
20	17 28	17 52	18 19	03 46	04 35	05 25	06 14
30	17 07	17 33	18 03	03 55	04 47	05 39	06 31
35	16 55	17 23	17 55	04 00	04 54	05 48	06 41
40	16 41	17 12	17 46	04 05	05 02	05 57	06 52
45	16 25	16 59	17 36	04 12	05 11	06 09	07 05
S 50	16 05	16 43	17 24	04 20	05 22	06 22	07 20
52	15 56	16 36	17 19	04 24	05 27	06 29	07 28
54	15 45	16 28	17 14	04 28	05 33	06 36	07 36
56	15 33	16 19	17 08	04 33	05 39	06 44	07 45
58	15 19	16 10	17 02	04 38	05 46	06 53	07 56
S 60	15 02	15 59	16 55	04 44	05 54	07 03	08 08

Day	SUN Eqn. of Time 00^h	SUN Eqn. of Time 12^h	SUN Mer. Pass.	MOON Mer. Pass. Upper	MOON Mer. Pass. Lower	MOON Age	MOON Phase
d	m s	m s	h m	h m	h m	d %	
6	01 23	01 17	11 59	22 04	09 42	12 92	
7	01 12	01 06	11 59	22 49	10 27	13 96	○
8	01 00	00 55	11 59	23 35	11 12	14 99	

	UT	ARIES	VENUS −4·4		MARS +1·7		JUPITER −2·2		SATURN +0·0	
		GHA	GHA	Dec	GHA	Dec	GHA	Dec	GHA	Dec
	d h	° ′	° ′	° ′	° ′	° ′	° ′	° ′	° ′	° ′
	9 00	257 33.2	226 13.9	N10 03.0	164 24.3	N24 19.0	64 50.8	S 3 55.4	352 58.1	S21 58.8
	01	272 35.7	241 14.0	03.7	179 24.9	19.0	79 53.2	55.4	8 00.7	58.8
	02	287 38.1	256 14.1	04.5	194 25.6	19.0	94 55.7	55.5	23 03.4	58.8
	03	302 40.6	271 14.1	. . 05.3	209 26.2	. . 19.0	109 58.2	. . 55.5	38 06.1	. . 58.8
	04	317 43.1	286 14.2	06.0	224 26.9	18.9	125 00.7	55.5	53 08.7	58.8
	05	332 45.5	301 14.2	06.8	239 27.5	18.9	140 03.1	55.5	68 11.4	58.8
	06	347 48.0	316 14.3	N10 07.6	254 28.2	N24 18.9	155 05.6	S 3 55.5	83 14.0	S21 58.8
	07	2 50.4	331 14.4	08.3	269 28.8	18.9	170 08.1	55.5	98 16.7	58.8
	08	17 52.9	346 14.4	09.1	284 29.5	18.8	185 10.5	55.5	113 19.4	58.8
F	09	32 55.4	1 14.5	. . 09.9	299 30.1	. . 18.8	200 13.0	. . 55.5	128 22.0	. . 58.8
R	10	47 57.8	16 14.5	10.6	314 30.8	18.8	215 15.5	55.5	143 24.7	58.8
I	11	63 00.3	31 14.6	11.4	329 31.4	18.8	230 18.0	55.5	158 27.4	58.8
D	12	78 02.8	46 14.7	N10 12.2	344 32.1	N24 18.7	245 20.4	S 3 55.5	173 30.0	S21 58.8
A	13	93 05.2	61 14.7	12.9	359 32.7	18.7	260 22.9	55.6	188 32.7	58.7
Y	14	108 07.7	76 14.8	13.7	14 33.4	18.7	275 25.4	55.6	203 35.3	58.7
	15	123 10.2	91 14.8	. . 14.4	29 34.0	. . 18.7	290 27.8	. . 55.6	218 38.0	. . 58.7
	16	138 12.6	106 14.9	15.2	44 34.6	18.6	305 30.3	55.6	233 40.7	58.7
	17	153 15.1	121 14.9	16.0	59 35.3	18.6	320 32.8	55.6	248 43.3	58.7
	18	168 17.6	136 15.0	N10 16.7	74 35.9	N24 18.6	335 35.2	S 3 55.6	263 46.0	S21 58.7
	19	183 20.0	151 15.0	17.5	89 36.6	18.5	350 37.7	55.6	278 48.6	58.7
	20	198 22.5	166 15.1	18.3	104 37.2	18.5	5 40.2	55.6	293 51.3	58.7
	21	213 24.9	181 15.1	. . 19.0	119 37.9	. . 18.5	20 42.6	. . 55.6	308 54.0	. . 58.7
	22	228 27.4	196 15.2	19.8	134 38.5	18.4	35 45.1	55.6	323 56.6	58.7
	23	243 29.9	211 15.2	20.6	149 39.2	18.4	50 47.6	55.7	338 59.3	58.7
	10 00	258 32.3	226 15.3	N10 21.3	164 39.8	N24 18.4	65 50.0	S 3 55.7	354 01.9	S21 58.7
	01	273 34.8	241 15.3	22.1	179 40.5	18.4	80 52.5	55.7	9 04.6	58.7
	02	288 37.3	256 15.4	22.9	194 41.1	18.3	95 55.0	55.7	24 07.3	58.7
	03	303 39.7	271 15.4	. . 23.6	209 41.8	. . 18.3	110 57.4	. . 55.7	39 09.9	. . 58.7
	04	318 42.2	286 15.5	24.4	224 42.4	18.3	125 59.9	55.7	54 12.6	58.7
	05	333 44.7	301 15.5	25.2	239 43.1	18.2	141 02.4	55.7	69 15.3	58.7
	06	348 47.1	316 15.6	N10 25.9	254 43.7	N24 18.2	156 04.8	S 3 55.7	84 17.9	S21 58.7
	07	3 49.6	331 15.6	26.7	269 44.4	18.2	171 07.3	55.8	99 20.6	58.7
S	08	18 52.1	346 15.7	27.5	284 45.0	18.1	186 09.7	55.8	114 23.2	58.7
A	09	33 54.5	1 15.7	. . 28.2	299 45.7	. . 18.1	201 12.2	. . 55.8	129 25.9	. . 58.7
T	10	48 57.0	16 15.7	29.0	314 46.3	18.1	216 14.7	55.8	144 28.6	58.7
U	11	63 59.4	31 15.8	29.8	329 47.0	18.0	231 17.1	55.8	159 31.2	58.7
R	12	79 01.9	46 15.8	N10 30.6	344 47.6	N24 18.0	246 19.6	S 3 55.8	174 33.9	S21 58.6
D	13	94 04.4	61 15.9	31.3	359 48.3	17.9	261 22.1	55.8	189 36.5	58.6
A	14	109 06.8	76 15.9	32.1	14 48.9	17.9	276 24.5	55.8	204 39.2	58.6
Y	15	124 09.3	91 15.9	. . 32.9	29 49.6	. . 17.9	291 27.0	. . 55.9	219 41.9	. . 58.6
	16	139 11.8	106 16.0	33.6	44 50.2	17.8	306 29.4	55.9	234 44.5	58.6
	17	154 14.2	121 16.0	34.4	59 50.9	17.8	321 31.9	55.9	249 47.2	58.6
	18	169 16.7	136 16.0	N10 35.2	74 51.5	N24 17.8	336 34.4	S 3 55.9	264 49.9	S21 58.6
	19	184 19.2	151 16.1	35.9	89 52.2	17.7	351 36.8	55.9	279 52.5	58.6
	20	199 21.6	166 16.1	36.7	104 52.8	17.7	6 39.3	55.9	294 55.2	58.6
	21	214 24.1	181 16.2	. . 37.5	119 53.5	. . 17.6	21 41.7	. . 55.9	309 57.8	. . 58.6
	22	229 26.6	196 16.2	38.2	134 54.1	17.6	36 44.2	56.0	325 00.5	58.6
	23	244 29.0	211 16.2	39.0	149 54.8	17.6	51 46.7	56.0	340 03.2	58.6
	11 00	259 31.5	226 16.3	N10 39.8	164 55.4	N24 17.5	66 49.1	S 3 56.0	355 05.8	S21 58.6
	01	274 33.9	241 16.3	40.5	179 56.1	17.5	81 51.6	56.0	10 08.5	58.6
	02	289 36.4	256 16.3	41.3	194 56.7	17.4	96 54.0	56.0	25 11.2	58.6
	03	304 38.9	271 16.3	. . 42.1	209 57.4	. . 17.4	111 56.5	. . 56.0	40 13.8	. . 58.6
	04	319 41.3	286 16.4	42.8	224 58.0	17.4	126 59.0	56.0	55 16.5	58.6
	05	334 43.8	301 16.4	43.6	239 58.7	17.3	142 01.4	56.1	70 19.1	58.6
	06	349 46.3	316 16.4	N10 44.4	254 59.3	N24 17.3	157 03.9	S 3 56.1	85 21.8	S21 58.6
	07	4 48.7	331 16.5	45.1	270 00.0	17.2	172 06.3	56.1	100 24.5	58.6
	08	19 51.2	346 16.5	45.9	285 00.6	17.2	187 08.8	56.1	115 27.1	58.6
S	09	34 53.7	1 16.5	. . 46.7	300 01.3	. . 17.2	202 11.2	. . 56.1	130 29.8	. . 58.6
U	10	49 56.1	16 16.5	47.4	315 01.9	17.1	217 13.7	56.1	145 32.4	58.5
N	11	64 58.6	31 16.6	48.2	330 02.6	17.1	232 16.1	56.1	160 35.1	58.5
D	12	80 01.1	46 16.6	N10 49.0	345 03.2	N24 17.0	247 18.6	S 3 56.2	175 37.8	S21 58.5
A	13	95 03.5	61 16.6	49.8	0 03.9	17.0	262 21.1	56.2	190 40.4	58.5
Y	14	110 06.0	76 16.6	50.5	15 04.5	16.9	277 23.5	56.2	205 43.1	58.5
	15	125 08.4	91 16.7	. . 51.3	30 05.2	. . 16.9	292 26.0	. . 56.2	220 45.8	. . 58.5
	16	140 10.9	106 16.7	52.1	45 05.8	16.8	307 28.4	56.2	235 48.4	58.5
	17	155 13.4	121 16.7	52.8	60 06.5	16.8	322 30.9	56.2	250 51.1	58.5
	18	170 15.8	136 16.7	N10 53.6	75 07.1	N24 16.8	337 33.3	S 3 56.3	265 53.7	S21 58.5
	19	185 18.3	151 16.7	54.4	90 07.8	16.7	352 35.8	56.3	280 56.4	58.5
	20	200 20.8	166 16.8	55.1	105 08.4	16.7	7 38.2	56.3	295 59.1	58.5
	21	215 23.2	181 16.8	. . 55.9	120 09.1	. . 16.6	22 40.7	. . 56.3	311 01.7	. . 58.5
	22	230 25.7	196 16.8	56.7	135 09.7	16.6	37 43.1	56.3	326 04.4	58.5
	23	245 28.2	211 16.8	57.4	150 10.4	16.5	52 45.6	56.3	341 07.1	58.5
	Mer. Pass.	h m 6 44.7	*v* 0.0	*d* 0.8	*v* 0.6	*d* 0.0	*v* 2.5	*d* 0.0	*v* 2.7	*d* 0.0

STARS		
Name	SHA	Dec
	° ′	° ′
Acamar	315 16.7	S40 14.2
Achernar	335 25.2	S57 08.8
Acrux	173 05.9	S63 12.0
Adhara	255 10.8	S29 00.0
Aldebaran	290 46.6	N16 32.4
Alioth	166 18.2	N55 52.3
Alkaid	152 56.6	N49 13.9
Al Na'ir	27 40.3	S46 52.3
Alnilam	275 44.0	S 1 11.7
Alphard	217 53.6	S 8 44.2
Alphecca	126 08.4	N26 39.6
Alpheratz	357 40.8	N29 10.9
Altair	62 05.4	N 8 55.0
Ankaa	353 13.3	S42 12.6
Antares	112 22.6	S26 28.1
Arcturus	145 53.1	N19 05.7
Atria	107 21.4	S69 03.3
Avior	234 17.3	S59 34.3
Bellatrix	278 29.5	N 6 21.7
Betelgeuse	270 58.7	N 7 24.4
Canopus	263 55.5	S52 42.6
Capella	280 31.0	N46 00.7
Deneb	49 29.3	N45 20.5
Denebola	182 30.9	N14 28.6
Diphda	348 53.4	S17 53.5
Dubhe	193 48.6	N61 39.7
Elnath	278 09.6	N28 37.1
Eltanin	90 44.4	N51 29.3
Enif	33 44.3	N 9 57.3
Fomalhaut	15 21.0	S29 31.6
Gacrux	171 57.6	S57 12.8
Gienah	175 49.7	S17 38.4
Hadar	148 43.5	S60 27.5
Hamal	327 57.9	N23 32.4
Kaus Aust.	83 39.9	S34 22.3
Kochab	137 19.3	N74 05.4
Markab	13 35.6	N15 17.8
Menkar	314 12.5	N 4 09.2
Menkent	148 04.1	S36 27.3
Miaplacidus	221 39.5	S69 47.7
Mirfak	308 36.9	N49 55.0
Nunki	75 54.7	S26 16.3
Peacock	53 14.7	S56 40.4
Pollux	243 24.8	N27 58.9
Procyon	244 57.2	N 5 10.6
Rasalhague	96 03.6	N12 33.0
Regulus	207 40.8	N11 52.9
Rigel	281 09.8	S 8 11.1
Rigil Kent.	139 47.5	S60 54.4
Sabik	102 09.1	S15 44.6
Schedar	349 37.6	N56 37.6
Shaula	96 17.9	S37 06.8
Sirius	258 31.7	S16 44.7
Spica	158 28.2	S11 15.1
Suhail	222 50.7	S43 30.5
Vega	80 36.7	N38 48.1
Zuben'ubi	137 02.2	S16 06.7

	SHA	Mer. Pass.
	° ′	h m
Venus	327 42.9	8 55
Mars	266 07.5	13 01
Jupiter	167 17.7	19 33
Saturn	95 29.6	0 24

	UT	SUN GHA	SUN Dec	MOON GHA	*v*	MOON Dec	*d*	HP
	d h	° ′	° ′	° ′	′	° ′	′	′
	9 00	180 12.2	N22 55.5	5 59.4	12.8	S17 28.4	4.4	54.0
	01	195 12.0	55.7	20 31.2	12.7	17 32.8	4.3	54.0
	02	210 11.9	55.9	35 02.9	12.8	17 37.1	4.2	54.0
	03	225 11.8	. . 56.1	49 34.7	12.7	17 41.3	4.2	54.0
	04	240 11.7	56.3	64 06.4	12.7	17 45.5	4.0	54.0
	05	255 11.6	56.5	78 38.1	12.6	17 49.5	4.0	54.0
	06	270 11.4	N22 56.8	93 09.7	12.7	S17 53.5	3.9	54.0
	07	285 11.3	57.0	107 41.4	12.6	17 57.4	3.9	54.0
	08	300 11.2	57.2	122 13.0	12.6	18 01.3	3.7	54.0
F	09	315 11.1	. . 57.4	136 44.6	12.6	18 05.0	3.7	54.0
R	10	330 11.0	57.6	151 16.2	12.5	18 08.7	3.6	54.0
I	11	345 10.8	57.8	165 47.7	12.5	18 12.3	3.5	54.0
D	12	0 10.7	N22 58.0	180 19.2	12.5	S18 15.8	3.4	54.0
A	13	15 10.6	58.2	194 50.7	12.5	18 19.2	3.4	54.0
Y	14	30 10.5	58.4	209 22.2	12.4	18 22.6	3.2	54.0
	15	45 10.3	. . 58.6	223 53.6	12.5	18 25.8	3.2	54.0
	16	60 10.2	58.8	238 25.1	12.4	18 29.0	3.1	54.0
	17	75 10.1	59.0	252 56.5	12.4	18 32.1	3.0	54.0
	18	90 10.0	N22 59.1	267 27.9	12.3	S18 35.1	2.9	54.0
	19	105 09.8	59.3	281 59.2	12.4	18 38.0	2.9	54.0
	20	120 09.7	59.5	296 30.6	12.3	18 40.9	2.7	54.0
	21	135 09.6	. . 59.7	311 01.9	12.3	18 43.6	2.7	54.0
	22	150 09.5	22 59.9	325 33.2	12.3	18 46.3	2.6	54.0
	23	165 09.4	23 00.1	340 04.5	12.2	18 48.9	2.5	54.0
	10 00	180 09.2	N23 00.3	354 35.7	12.3	S18 51.4	2.4	54.0
	01	195 09.1	00.5	9 07.0	12.2	18 53.8	2.3	54.0
	02	210 09.0	00.7	23 38.2	12.2	18 56.1	2.3	54.0
	03	225 08.9	. . 00.9	38 09.4	12.2	18 58.4	2.1	54.0
	04	240 08.7	01.1	52 40.6	12.2	19 00.5	2.1	54.0
	05	255 08.6	01.3	67 11.8	12.1	19 02.6	2.0	54.0
	06	270 08.5	N23 01.4	81 42.9	12.2	S19 04.6	1.9	54.0
	07	285 08.4	01.6	96 14.1	12.1	19 06.5	1.8	54.0
S	08	300 08.2	01.8	110 45.2	12.1	19 08.3	1.7	54.0
A	09	315 08.1	. . 02.0	125 16.3	12.1	19 10.0	1.6	54.0
T	10	330 08.0	02.2	139 47.4	12.0	19 11.6	1.6	54.1
U	11	345 07.9	02.4	154 18.4	12.1	19 13.2	1.4	54.1
R	12	0 07.7	N23 02.6	168 49.5	12.0	S19 14.6	1.4	54.1
D	13	15 07.6	02.7	183 20.5	12.0	19 16.0	1.2	54.1
A	14	30 07.5	02.9	197 51.5	12.1	19 17.2	1.2	54.1
Y	15	45 07.4	. . 03.1	212 22.6	11.9	19 18.4	1.1	54.1
	16	60 07.2	03.3	226 53.5	12.0	19 19.5	1.0	54.1
	17	75 07.1	03.5	241 24.5	12.0	19 20.5	1.0	54.1
	18	90 07.0	N23 03.6	255 55.5	12.0	S19 21.5	0.8	54.1
	19	105 06.9	03.8	270 26.5	11.9	19 22.3	0.7	54.1
	20	120 06.7	04.0	284 57.4	11.9	19 23.0	0.7	54.1
	21	135 06.6	. . 04.2	299 28.3	12.0	19 23.7	0.5	54.1
	22	150 06.5	04.3	313 59.3	11.9	19 24.2	0.5	54.1
	23	165 06.4	04.5	328 30.2	11.9	19 24.7	0.4	54.1
	11 00	180 06.2	N23 04.7	343 01.1	11.9	S19 25.1	0.3	54.1
	01	195 06.1	04.9	357 32.0	11.9	19 25.4	0.2	54.2
	02	210 06.0	05.0	12 02.9	11.8	19 25.6	0.1	54.2
	03	225 05.9	. . 05.2	26 33.7	11.9	19 25.7	0.0	54.2
	04	240 05.7	05.4	41 04.6	11.9	19 25.7	0.1	54.2
	05	255 05.6	05.6	55 35.5	11.8	19 25.6	0.2	54.2
	06	270 05.5	N23 05.7	70 06.3	11.9	S19 25.4	0.2	54.2
	07	285 05.4	05.9	84 37.2	11.8	19 25.2	0.4	54.2
	08	300 05.2	06.1	99 08.0	11.8	19 24.8	0.4	54.2
S	09	315 05.1	. . 06.2	113 38.8	11.9	19 24.4	0.5	54.2
U	10	330 05.0	06.4	128 09.7	11.8	19 23.9	0.7	54.2
N	11	345 04.8	06.6	142 40.5	11.8	19 23.2	0.7	54.2
D	12	0 04.7	N23 06.7	157 11.3	11.8	S19 22.5	0.8	54.3
A	13	15 04.6	06.9	171 42.1	11.8	19 21.7	0.9	54.3
Y	14	30 04.5	07.1	186 12.9	11.8	19 20.8	0.9	54.3
	15	45 04.3	. . 07.2	200 43.7	11.8	19 19.9	1.1	54.3
	16	60 04.2	07.4	215 14.5	11.8	19 18.8	1.2	54.3
	17	75 04.1	07.6	229 45.3	11.8	19 17.6	1.2	54.3
	18	90 04.0	N23 07.7	244 16.1	11.8	S19 16.4	1.4	54.3
	19	105 03.8	07.9	258 46.9	11.8	19 15.0	1.4	54.3
	20	120 03.7	08.0	273 17.7	11.8	19 13.6	1.6	54.3
	21	135 03.6	. . 08.2	287 48.5	11.8	19 12.0	1.6	54.3
	22	150 03.4	08.4	302 19.3	11.8	19 10.4	1.7	54.4
	23	165 03.3	08.5	316 50.1	11.7	S19 08.7	1.8	54.4
		SD 15.8	*d* 0.2	SD 14.7		14.7		14.8

Lat.	Twilight Naut.	Twilight Civil	Sunrise	Moonrise 9	Moonrise 10	Moonrise 11	Moonrise 12
°	h m	h m	h m	h m	h m	h m	h m
N 72	▭	▭	▭	▬	▬	▬	▬
N 70	▭	▭	▭	23 01	24 15	00 15	00 48
68	▭	▭	▭	22 09	23 11	23 53	24 16
66	////	////	00 27	21 37	22 36	23 20	23 49
64	////	////	01 39	21 14	22 11	22 55	23 28
62	////	////	02 14	20 55	21 51	22 36	23 11
60	////	01 02	02 39	20 40	21 35	22 20	22 57
N 58	////	01 46	02 59	20 27	21 21	22 07	22 45
56	////	02 14	03 15	20 16	21 09	21 56	22 35
54	00 57	02 35	03 29	20 06	20 59	21 45	22 26
52	01 37	02 52	03 41	19 57	20 50	21 36	22 17
50	02 03	03 07	03 51	19 49	20 41	21 28	22 10
45	02 47	03 36	04 13	19 33	20 24	21 11	21 54
N 40	03 17	03 58	04 31	19 19	20 10	20 57	21 41
35	03 40	04 16	04 46	19 07	19 58	20 45	21 30
30	03 58	04 31	04 58	18 57	19 47	20 35	21 20
20	04 26	04 55	05 20	18 40	19 29	20 17	21 03
N 10	04 49	05 16	05 39	18 25	19 13	20 01	20 49
0	05 07	05 33	05 56	18 11	18 59	19 47	20 35
S 10	05 24	05 50	06 13	17 57	18 44	19 32	20 21
20	05 40	06 07	06 31	17 42	18 28	19 17	20 07
30	05 56	06 26	06 52	17 25	18 10	18 59	19 50
35	06 04	06 36	07 04	17 15	18 00	18 48	19 40
40	06 14	06 48	07 18	17 03	17 48	18 36	19 29
45	06 24	07 01	07 34	16 50	17 34	18 22	19 16
S 50	06 35	07 16	07 55	16 34	17 17	18 05	19 00
52	06 40	07 24	08 04	16 26	17 09	17 57	18 52
54	06 46	07 32	08 15	16 18	17 00	17 48	18 44
56	06 52	07 41	08 28	16 08	16 49	17 38	18 34
58	06 58	07 51	08 42	15 58	16 38	17 27	18 24
S 60	07 06	08 02	08 59	15 45	16 24	17 13	18 11

Lat.	Sunset	Twilight Civil	Twilight Naut.	Moonset 9	Moonset 10	Moonset 11	Moonset 12
°	h m	h m	h m	h m	h m	h m	h m
N 72	▭	▭	▭	00 27	▬	▬	▬
N 70	▭	▭	▭	01 35	01 40	02 05	03 13
68	▭	▭	▭	02 11	02 32	03 09	04 07
66	23 39	////	////	02 37	03 04	03 44	04 40
64	22 21	////	////	02 57	03 28	04 09	05 04
62	21 46	////	////	03 14	03 46	04 29	05 23
60	21 21	22 59	////	03 27	04 02	04 46	05 39
N 58	21 01	22 14	////	03 39	04 15	04 59	05 52
56	20 45	21 46	////	03 49	04 26	05 11	06 04
54	20 31	21 24	23 04	03 58	04 36	05 21	06 14
52	20 19	21 07	22 23	04 06	04 45	05 31	06 22
50	20 08	20 52	21 56	04 14	04 53	05 39	06 30
45	19 46	20 23	21 12	04 29	05 10	05 56	06 47
N 40	19 28	20 01	20 42	04 42	05 24	06 11	07 01
35	19 14	19 43	20 20	04 53	05 36	06 23	07 13
30	19 01	19 28	20 01	05 02	05 46	06 33	07 23
20	18 39	19 04	19 33	05 19	06 04	06 51	07 41
N 10	18 20	18 43	19 10	05 33	06 19	07 07	07 56
0	18 03	18 26	18 52	05 47	06 34	07 22	08 10
S 10	17 46	18 09	18 35	06 00	06 48	07 37	08 24
20	17 28	17 52	18 19	06 14	07 04	07 52	08 39
30	17 07	17 33	18 03	06 31	07 21	08 10	08 57
35	16 55	17 23	17 54	06 41	07 32	08 21	09 07
40	16 41	17 11	17 45	06 52	07 44	08 33	09 18
45	16 24	16 58	17 35	07 05	07 58	08 47	09 32
S 50	16 04	16 42	17 24	07 20	08 15	09 04	09 48
52	15 54	16 35	17 19	07 28	08 23	09 12	09 56
54	15 44	16 27	17 13	07 36	08 32	09 21	10 05
56	15 31	16 18	17 07	07 45	08 42	09 32	10 14
58	15 17	16 08	17 00	07 56	08 53	09 43	10 25
S 60	15 00	15 57	16 53	08 08	09 06	09 57	10 38

Day	SUN Eqn. of Time 00^h	SUN Eqn. of Time 12^h	SUN Mer. Pass.	MOON Mer. Pass. Upper	MOON Mer. Pass. Lower	MOON Age	MOON Phase
d	m s	m s	h m	h m	h m	d %	
9	00 49	00 43	11 59	24 22	11 59	15 100	○
10	00 37	00 31	11 59	00 22	12 46	16 99	
11	00 25	00 19	12 00	01 10	13 34	17 96	

d	h	ARIES GHA	VENUS −4·3 GHA	VENUS Dec	MARS +1·7 GHA	MARS Dec	JUPITER −2·2 GHA	JUPITER Dec	SATURN +0·0 GHA	SATURN Dec
		° ′	° ′	° ′	° ′	° ′	° ′	° ′	° ′	° ′
12	00	260 30.6	226 16.8	N10 58.2	165 11.0	N24 16.5	67 48.0	S 3 56.4	356 09.7	S21 58.5
	01	275 33.1	241 16.8	59.0	180 11.7	16.4	82 50.5	56.4	11 12.4	58.5
	02	290 35.5	256 16.9	10 59.7	195 12.3	16.4	97 53.0	56.4	26 15.0	58.5
	03	305 38.0	271 16.9	11 00.5	210 13.0	. . 16.3	112 55.4	. . 56.4	41 17.7	. . 58.5
	04	320 40.5	286 16.9	01.3	225 13.6	16.3	127 57.9	56.4	56 20.4	58.5
	05	335 42.9	301 16.9	02.1	240 14.3	16.2	143 00.3	56.4	71 23.0	58.5
	06	350 45.4	316 16.9	N11 02.8	255 14.9	N24 16.2	158 02.8	S 3 56.5	86 25.7	S21 58.5
	07	5 47.9	331 16.9	03.6	270 15.6	16.1	173 05.2	56.5	101 28.4	58.5
	08	20 50.3	346 16.9	04.4	285 16.3	16.1	188 07.7	56.5	116 31.0	58.5
M	09	35 52.8	1 16.9	. . 05.1	300 16.9	. . 16.0	203 10.1	. . 56.5	131 33.7	. . 58.4
O	10	50 55.3	16 17.0	05.9	315 17.6	16.0	218 12.6	56.5	146 36.3	58.4
N	11	65 57.7	31 17.0	06.7	330 18.2	15.9	233 15.0	56.6	161 39.0	58.4
D	12	81 00.2	46 17.0	N11 07.4	345 18.9	N24 15.9	248 17.4	S 3 56.6	176 41.7	S21 58.4
A	13	96 02.7	61 17.0	08.2	0 19.5	15.8	263 19.9	56.6	191 44.3	58.4
Y	14	111 05.1	76 17.0	09.0	15 20.2	15.8	278 22.3	56.6	206 47.0	58.4
	15	126 07.6	91 17.0	. . 09.7	30 20.8	. . 15.7	293 24.8	. . 56.6	221 49.7	. . 58.4
	16	141 10.0	106 17.0	10.5	45 21.5	15.7	308 27.2	56.6	236 52.3	58.4
	17	156 12.5	121 17.0	11.3	60 22.1	15.6	323 29.7	56.7	251 55.0	58.4
	18	171 15.0	136 17.0	N11 12.0	75 22.8	N24 15.5	338 32.1	S 3 56.7	266 57.6	S21 58.4
	19	186 17.4	151 17.0	12.8	90 23.4	15.5	353 34.6	56.7	282 00.3	58.4
	20	201 19.9	166 17.0	13.6	105 24.1	15.4	8 37.0	56.7	297 03.0	58.4
	21	216 22.4	181 17.0	. . 14.4	120 24.7	. . 15.4	23 39.5	. . 56.7	312 05.6	. . 58.4
	22	231 24.8	196 17.0	15.1	135 25.4	15.3	38 41.9	56.8	327 08.3	58.4
	23	246 27.3	211 17.0	15.9	150 26.0	15.3	53 44.4	56.8	342 11.0	58.4
13	00	261 29.8	226 17.0	N11 16.7	165 26.7	N24 15.2	68 46.8	S 3 56.8	357 13.6	S21 58.4
	01	276 32.2	241 17.0	17.4	180 27.4	15.2	83 49.3	56.8	12 16.3	58.4
	02	291 34.7	256 17.0	18.2	195 28.0	15.1	98 51.7	56.8	27 18.9	58.4
	03	306 37.2	271 17.0	. . 19.0	210 28.7	. . 15.0	113 54.1	. . 56.9	42 21.6	. . 58.4
	04	321 39.6	286 17.0	19.7	225 29.3	15.0	128 56.6	56.9	57 24.3	58.4
	05	336 42.1	301 17.0	20.5	240 30.0	14.9	143 59.0	56.9	72 26.9	58.4
	06	351 44.5	316 17.0	N11 21.3	255 30.6	N24 14.9	159 01.5	S 3 56.9	87 29.6	S21 58.4
	07	6 47.0	331 17.0	22.0	270 31.3	14.8	174 03.9	56.9	102 32.3	58.3
T	08	21 49.5	346 17.0	22.8	285 31.9	14.7	189 06.4	57.0	117 34.9	58.3
U	09	36 51.9	1 17.0	. . 23.6	300 32.6	. . 14.7	204 08.8	. . 57.0	132 37.6	. . 58.3
E	10	51 54.4	16 17.0	24.4	315 33.2	14.6	219 11.2	57.0	147 40.2	58.3
S	11	66 56.9	31 17.0	25.1	330 33.9	14.6	234 13.7	57.0	162 42.9	58.3
D	12	81 59.3	46 17.0	N11 25.9	345 34.6	N24 14.5	249 16.1	S 3 57.1	177 45.6	S21 58.3
A	13	97 01.8	61 17.0	26.7	0 35.2	14.4	264 18.6	57.1	192 48.2	58.3
Y	14	112 04.3	76 16.9	27.4	15 35.9	14.4	279 21.0	57.1	207 50.9	58.3
	15	127 06.7	91 16.9	. . 28.2	30 36.5	. . 14.3	294 23.5	. . 57.1	222 53.6	. . 58.3
	16	142 09.2	106 16.9	29.0	45 37.2	14.3	309 25.9	57.1	237 56.2	58.3
	17	157 11.7	121 16.9	29.7	60 37.8	14.2	324 28.3	57.2	252 58.9	58.3
	18	172 14.1	136 16.9	N11 30.5	75 38.5	N24 14.1	339 30.8	S 3 57.2	268 01.5	S21 58.3
	19	187 16.6	151 16.9	31.3	90 39.1	14.1	354 33.2	57.2	283 04.2	58.3
	20	202 19.0	166 16.9	32.0	105 39.8	14.0	9 35.7	57.2	298 06.9	58.3
	21	217 21.5	181 16.9	. . 32.8	120 40.5	. . 13.9	24 38.1	. . 57.3	313 09.5	. . 58.3
	22	232 24.0	196 16.9	33.6	135 41.1	13.9	39 40.5	57.3	328 12.2	58.3
	23	247 26.4	211 16.8	34.3	150 41.8	13.8	54 43.0	57.3	343 14.9	58.3
14	00	262 28.9	226 16.8	N11 35.1	165 42.4	N24 13.7	69 45.4	S 3 57.3	358 17.5	S21 58.3
	01	277 31.4	241 16.8	35.9	180 43.1	13.7	84 47.8	57.3	13 20.2	58.3
	02	292 33.8	256 16.8	36.7	195 43.7	13.6	99 50.3	57.4	28 22.8	58.3
	03	307 36.3	271 16.8	. . 37.4	210 44.4	. . 13.6	114 52.7	. . 57.4	43 25.5	. . 58.3
	04	322 38.8	286 16.7	38.2	225 45.0	13.5	129 55.2	57.4	58 28.2	58.3
	05	337 41.2	301 16.7	39.0	240 45.7	13.4	144 57.6	57.4	73 30.8	58.3
	06	352 43.7	316 16.7	N11 39.7	255 46.4	N24 13.4	160 00.0	S 3 57.5	88 33.5	S21 58.2
W	07	7 46.1	331 16.7	40.5	270 47.0	13.3	175 02.5	57.5	103 36.2	58.2
E	08	22 48.6	346 16.7	41.3	285 47.7	13.2	190 04.9	57.5	118 38.8	58.2
D	09	37 51.1	1 16.6	. . 42.0	300 48.3	. . 13.1	205 07.3	. . 57.5	133 41.5	. . 58.2
N	10	52 53.5	16 16.6	42.8	315 49.0	13.1	220 09.8	57.6	148 44.1	58.2
E	11	67 56.0	31 16.6	43.6	330 49.6	13.0	235 12.2	57.6	163 46.8	58.2
S	12	82 58.5	46 16.6	N11 44.3	345 50.3	N24 12.9	250 14.6	S 3 57.6	178 49.5	S21 58.2
D	13	98 00.9	61 16.6	45.1	0 51.0	12.9	265 17.1	57.6	193 52.1	58.2
A	14	113 03.4	76 16.5	45.9	15 51.6	12.8	280 19.5	57.7	208 54.8	58.2
Y	15	128 05.9	91 16.5	. . 46.6	30 52.3	. . 12.7	295 21.9	. . 57.7	223 57.5	. . 58.2
	16	143 08.3	106 16.5	47.4	45 52.9	12.7	310 24.4	57.7	239 00.1	58.2
	17	158 10.8	121 16.4	48.2	60 53.6	12.6	325 26.8	57.7	254 02.8	58.2
	18	173 13.3	136 16.4	N11 48.9	75 54.2	N24 12.5	340 29.2	S 3 57.8	269 05.5	S21 58.2
	19	188 15.7	151 16.4	49.7	90 54.9	12.5	355 31.7	57.8	284 08.1	58.2
	20	203 18.2	166 16.4	50.5	105 55.6	12.4	10 34.1	57.8	299 10.8	58.2
	21	218 20.6	181 16.3	. . 51.2	120 56.2	. . 12.3	25 36.5	. . 57.8	314 13.4	. . 58.2
	22	233 23.1	196 16.3	52.0	135 56.9	12.2	40 39.0	57.9	329 16.1	58.2
	23	248 25.6	211 16.3	52.8	150 57.5	12.2	55 41.4	57.9	344 18.8	58.2
Mer. Pass.		h m 6 32.9	*v* 0.0	*d* 0.8	*v* 0.7	*d* 0.1	*v* 2.4	*d* 0.0	*v* 2.7	*d* 0.0

STARS

Name	SHA	Dec
	° ′	° ′
Acamar	315 16.7	S40 14.1
Achernar	335 25.2	S57 08.8
Acrux	173 05.9	S63 12.0
Adhara	255 10.8	S29 00.0
Aldebaran	290 46.6	N16 32.4
Alioth	166 18.2	N55 52.3
Alkaid	152 56.6	N49 13.9
Al Na'ir	27 40.3	S46 52.3
Alnilam	275 44.0	S 1 11.7
Alphard	217 53.6	S 8 44.2
Alphecca	126 08.4	N26 39.6
Alpheratz	357 40.7	N29 11.0
Altair	62 05.3	N 8 55.0
Ankaa	353 13.2	S42 12.5
Antares	112 22.6	S26 28.1
Arcturus	145 53.1	N19 05.7
Atria	107 21.4	S69 03.3
Avior	234 17.3	S59 34.2
Bellatrix	278 29.5	N 6 21.7
Betelgeuse	270 58.7	N 7 24.4
Canopus	263 55.5	S52 42.5
Capella	280 31.0	N46 00.7
Deneb	49 29.3	N45 20.5
Denebola	182 30.9	N14 28.6
Diphda	348 53.3	S17 53.5
Dubhe	193 48.7	N61 39.7
Elnath	278 09.6	N28 37.1
Eltanin	90 44.4	N51 29.3
Enif	33 44.3	N 9 57.3
Fomalhaut	15 21.0	S29 31.6
Gacrux	171 57.6	S57 12.8
Gienah	175 49.4	S17 38.4
Hadar	148 43.5	S60 27.5
Hamal	327 57.9	N23 32.4
Kaus Aust.	83 39.9	S34 22.3
Kochab	137 19.3	N74 05.4
Markab	13 35.6	N15 17.8
Menkar	314 12.5	N 4 09.3
Menkent	148 04.1	S36 27.3
Miaplacidus	221 39.5	S69 47.7
Mirfak	308 36.9	N49 55.0
Nunki	75 54.7	S26 16.3
Peacock	53 14.7	S56 40.4
Pollux	243 24.8	N27 58.9
Procyon	244 57.2	N 5 10.6
Rasalhague	96 03.6	N12 33.0
Regulus	207 40.8	N11 52.9
Rigel	281 09.8	S 8 11.1
Rigil Kent.	139 47.5	S60 54.4
Sabik	102 09.1	S15 44.6
Schedar	349 37.5	N56 37.6
Shaula	96 17.8	S37 06.8
Sirius	258 31.7	S16 44.6
Spica	158 28.2	S11 15.1
Suhail	222 50.7	S43 30.5
Vega	80 36.7	N38 48.1
Zuben'ubi	137 02.2	S16 06.7

	SHA	Mer. Pass.
	° ′	h m
Venus	324 47.3	8 55
Mars	263 56.9	12 58
Jupiter	167 17.0	19 22
Saturn	95 43.9	0 11

UT d	h	SUN GHA ° ′	SUN Dec ° ′	MOON GHA ° ′	v ′	MOON Dec ° ′	d ′	HP ′
12	00	180 03.2	N23 08.7	331 20.8	11.8	S19 06.9	1.9	54.4
	01	195 03.1	08.8	345 51.6	11.8	19 05.0	2.0	54.4
	02	210 02.9	09.0	0 22.4	11.8	19 03.0	2.1	54.4
	03	225 02.8	. . 09.1	14 53.2	11.8	19 00.9	2.1	54.4
	04	240 02.7	09.3	29 24.0	11.8	18 58.8	2.3	54.4
	05	255 02.5	09.5	43 54.8	11.8	18 56.5	2.3	54.4
	06	270 02.4	N23 09.6	58 25.6	11.8	S18 54.2	2.5	54.5
	07	285 02.3	09.8	72 56.4	11.8	18 51.7	2.5	54.5
	08	300 02.2	09.9	87 27.2	11.8	18 49.2	2.6	54.5
MONDAY	09	315 02.0	. . 10.1	101 58.0	11.8	18 46.6	2.7	54.5
	10	330 01.9	10.2	116 28.8	11.8	18 43.9	2.8	54.5
	11	345 01.8	10.4	130 59.6	11.8	18 41.1	2.9	54.5
	12	0 01.6	N23 10.5	145 30.4	11.9	S18 38.2	3.0	54.5
	13	15 01.5	10.7	160 01.3	11.8	18 35.2	3.0	54.5
	14	30 01.4	10.8	174 32.1	11.8	18 32.2	3.2	54.6
	15	45 01.3	. . 11.0	189 02.9	11.9	18 29.0	3.2	54.6
	16	60 01.1	11.1	203 33.8	11.8	18 25.8	3.3	54.6
	17	75 01.0	11.3	218 04.6	11.8	18 22.5	3.4	54.6
	18	90 00.9	N23 11.4	232 35.4	11.9	S18 19.1	3.5	54.6
	19	105 00.7	11.5	247 06.3	11.9	18 15.6	3.6	54.6
	20	120 00.6	11.7	261 37.2	11.8	18 12.0	3.7	54.6
	21	135 00.5	. . 11.8	276 08.0	11.9	18 08.3	3.8	54.7
	22	150 00.4	12.0	290 38.9	11.9	18 04.5	3.8	54.7
	23	165 00.2	12.1	305 09.8	11.9	18 00.7	4.0	54.7
13	00	180 00.1	N23 12.3	319 40.7	11.9	S17 56.7	4.0	54.7
	01	195 00.0	12.4	334 11.6	11.9	17 52.7	4.1	54.7
	02	209 59.8	12.5	348 42.5	11.9	17 48.6	4.2	54.7
	03	224 59.7	. . 12.7	3 13.4	11.9	17 44.4	4.3	54.8
	04	239 59.6	12.8	17 44.3	12.0	17 40.1	4.4	54.8
	05	254 59.4	12.9	32 15.3	11.9	17 35.7	4.4	54.8
	06	269 59.3	N23 13.1	46 46.2	12.0	S17 31.3	4.6	54.8
	07	284 59.2	13.2	61 17.2	11.9	17 26.7	4.6	54.8
	08	299 59.1	13.4	75 48.1	12.0	17 22.1	4.7	54.8
TUESDAY	09	314 58.9	. . 13.5	90 19.1	12.0	17 17.4	4.8	54.9
	10	329 58.8	13.6	104 50.1	12.0	17 12.6	4.9	54.9
	11	344 58.7	13.8	119 21.1	12.0	17 07.7	4.9	54.9
	12	359 58.5	N23 13.9	133 52.1	12.0	S17 02.8	5.1	54.9
	13	14 58.4	14.0	148 23.1	12.0	16 57.7	5.1	54.9
	14	29 58.3	14.2	162 54.1	12.0	16 52.6	5.2	54.9
	15	44 58.1	. . 14.3	177 25.1	12.1	16 47.4	5.3	55.0
	16	59 58.0	14.4	191 56.2	12.0	16 42.1	5.4	55.0
	17	74 57.9	14.5	206 27.2	12.1	16 36.7	5.5	55.0
	18	89 57.7	N23 14.7	220 58.3	12.1	S16 31.2	5.5	55.0
	19	104 57.6	14.8	235 29.4	12.0	16 25.7	5.6	55.0
	20	119 57.5	14.9	250 00.4	12.1	16 20.1	5.7	55.1
	21	134 57.4	. . 15.0	264 31.5	12.1	16 14.4	5.8	55.1
	22	149 57.2	15.2	279 02.6	12.1	16 08.6	5.8	55.1
	23	164 57.1	15.3	293 33.7	12.2	16 02.8	6.0	55.1
14	00	179 57.0	N23 15.4	308 04.9	12.1	S15 56.8	6.0	55.1
	01	194 56.8	15.5	322 36.0	12.1	15 50.8	6.1	55.2
	02	209 56.7	15.7	337 07.1	12.2	15 44.7	6.2	55.2
	03	224 56.6	. . 15.8	351 38.3	12.2	15 38.5	6.2	55.2
	04	239 56.4	15.9	6 09.5	12.2	15 32.3	6.4	55.2
	05	254 56.3	16.0	20 40.7	12.1	15 25.9	6.4	55.2
	06	269 56.2	N23 16.1	35 11.8	12.2	S15 19.5	6.5	55.3
WEDNESDAY	07	284 56.0	16.3	49 43.0	12.2	15 13.0	6.5	55.3
	08	299 55.9	16.4	64 14.2	12.3	15 06.5	6.6	55.3
	09	314 55.8	. . 16.5	78 45.5	12.2	14 59.9	6.8	55.3
	10	329 55.6	16.6	93 16.7	12.2	14 53.1	6.7	55.4
	11	344 55.5	16.7	107 47.9	12.3	14 46.4	6.9	55.4
	12	359 55.4	N23 16.8	122 19.2	12.2	S14 39.5	6.9	55.4
	13	14 55.2	17.0	136 50.4	12.3	14 32.6	7.1	55.4
	14	29 55.1	17.1	151 21.7	12.3	14 25.5	7.0	55.4
	15	44 55.0	. . 17.2	165 53.0	12.3	14 18.5	7.2	55.5
	16	59 54.8	17.3	180 24.3	12.3	14 11.3	7.2	55.5
	17	74 54.7	17.4	194 55.6	12.3	14 04.1	7.3	55.5
	18	89 54.6	N23 17.5	209 26.9	12.3	S13 56.8	7.4	55.5
	19	104 54.5	17.6	223 58.2	12.3	13 49.4	7.4	55.6
	20	119 54.3	17.7	238 29.5	12.3	13 42.0	7.6	55.6
	21	134 54.2	. . 17.9	253 00.8	12.4	13 34.4	7.5	55.6
	22	149 54.1	18.0	267 32.2	12.3	13 26.9	7.7	55.6
	23	164 53.9	18.1	282 03.5	12.4	S13 19.2	7.7	55.7
		SD 15.8	d 0.1	SD 14.9		15.0		15.1

Lat. °	Twilight Naut. h m	Twilight Civil h m	Sunrise h m	Moonrise 12 h m	Moonrise 13 h m	Moonrise 14 h m	Moonrise 15 h m
N 72	□	□	□	■	02 19	01 35	01 20
N 70	□	□	□	00 48	00 55	00 57	00 56
68	□	□	□	24 16	00 16	00 30	00 37
66	□	□	□	23 49	24 09	00 09	00 22
64	////	////	01 35	23 28	23 52	24 10	00 10
62	////	////	02 11	23 11	23 38	23 59	24 16
60	////	00 56	02 37	22 57	23 27	23 50	24 10
N 58	////	01 43	02 57	22 45	23 17	23 42	24 04
56	////	02 12	03 14	22 35	23 08	23 35	23 59
54	00 51	02 34	03 28	22 26	23 00	23 29	23 55
52	01 34	02 51	03 40	22 17	22 53	23 24	23 51
50	02 01	03 06	03 50	22 10	22 46	23 18	23 47
45	02 46	03 35	04 13	21 54	22 33	23 07	23 39
N 40	03 16	03 58	04 31	21 41	22 21	22 58	23 33
35	03 39	04 16	04 45	21 30	22 11	22 50	23 27
30	03 58	04 31	04 58	21 20	22 03	22 43	23 22
20	04 27	04 56	05 20	21 03	21 48	22 31	23 13
N 10	04 49	05 16	05 39	20 49	21 35	22 21	23 05
0	05 08	05 34	05 56	20 35	21 23	22 11	22 58
S 10	05 25	05 51	06 14	20 21	21 11	22 01	22 51
20	05 41	06 08	06 32	20 07	20 58	21 50	22 43
30	05 57	06 27	06 53	19 50	20 43	21 38	22 34
35	06 06	06 37	07 05	19 40	20 34	21 31	22 29
40	06 15	06 49	07 19	19 29	20 25	21 23	22 23
45	06 25	07 02	07 36	19 16	20 13	21 13	22 16
S 50	06 37	07 18	07 57	19 00	19 59	21 02	22 08
52	06 42	07 26	08 06	18 52	19 52	20 57	22 04
54	06 48	07 34	08 17	18 44	19 45	20 51	22 00
56	06 54	07 43	08 30	18 34	19 37	20 44	21 55
58	07 00	07 53	08 44	18 24	19 28	20 37	21 50
S 60	07 08	08 04	09 02	18 11	19 17	20 28	21 44

Lat. °	Sunset h m	Twilight Civil h m	Twilight Naut. h m	Moonset 12 h m	Moonset 13 h m	Moonset 14 h m	Moonset 15 h m
N 72	□	□	□	■	03 22	05 45	07 40
N 70	□	□	□	03 13	04 45	06 23	08 03
68	□	□	□	04 07	05 24	06 50	08 20
66	□	□	□	04 40	05 50	07 10	08 34
64	22 26	////	////	05 04	06 11	07 26	08 46
62	21 50	////	////	05 23	06 27	07 39	08 55
60	21 24	23 06	////	05 39	06 41	07 50	09 04
N 58	21 04	22 18	////	05 52	06 53	08 00	09 11
56	20 47	21 49	////	06 04	07 03	08 08	09 17
54	20 33	21 27	23 10	06 14	07 12	08 16	09 23
52	20 21	21 09	22 26	06 22	07 20	08 22	09 28
50	20 10	20 54	21 59	06 30	07 27	08 28	09 33
45	19 48	20 25	21 14	06 47	07 43	08 41	09 43
N 40	19 30	20 03	20 44	07 01	07 55	08 52	09 51
35	19 15	19 44	20 21	07 13	08 06	09 01	09 58
30	19 02	19 29	20 03	07 23	08 15	09 09	10 05
20	18 40	19 05	19 34	07 41	08 31	09 23	10 15
N 10	18 21	18 44	19 11	07 56	08 45	09 35	10 25
0	18 04	18 26	18 52	08 10	08 58	09 46	10 33
S 10	17 46	18 09	18 36	08 24	09 11	09 57	10 42
20	17 28	17 52	18 20	08 39	09 25	10 09	10 51
30	17 07	17 33	18 03	08 57	09 41	10 22	11 02
35	16 55	17 23	17 55	09 07	09 50	10 30	11 08
40	16 41	17 11	17 45	09 18	10 00	10 39	11 14
45	16 24	16 58	17 35	09 32	10 13	10 49	11 22
S 50	16 04	16 42	17 23	09 48	10 27	11 01	11 32
52	15 54	16 35	17 18	09 56	10 34	11 07	11 36
54	15 43	16 26	17 13	10 05	10 42	11 13	11 41
56	15 30	16 17	17 06	10 14	10 50	11 20	11 46
58	15 16	16 07	17 00	10 25	11 00	11 28	11 52
S 60	14 59	15 56	16 52	10 38	11 11	11 37	11 59

Day	SUN Eqn. of Time 00ʰ	SUN Eqn. of Time 12ʰ	SUN Mer. Pass.	MOON Mer. Pass. Upper	MOON Mer. Pass. Lower	MOON Age	MOON Phase
d	m s	m s	h m	h m	h m	d %	
12	00 13	00 07	12 00	01 58	14 23	18 92	
13	00 01	00 06	12 00	02 47	15 11	19 86	◐
14	00 12	00 18	12 00	03 35	15 58	20 79	

2017 JUNE 15, 16, 17 (THURS., FRI., SAT.)

UT		ARIES	VENUS −4·3		MARS +1·7		JUPITER −2·1		SATURN +0·0		STARS		
		GHA	GHA	Dec	GHA	Dec	GHA	Dec	GHA	Dec	Name	SHA	Dec
d	h	° ′	° ′	° ′	° ′	° ′	° ′	° ′	° ′	° ′		° ′	° ′
15	00	263 28.0	226 16.2	N11 53.5	165 58.2	N24 12.1	70 43.8	S 3 57.9	359 21.4	S21 58.2	Acamar	315 16.7	S40 14.1
	01	278 30.5	241 16.2	54.3	180 58.8	12.0	85 46.3	57.9	14 24.1	58.2	Achernar	335 25.2	S57 08.8
	02	293 33.0	256 16.2	55.1	195 59.5	11.9	100 48.7	58.0	29 26.8	58.2	Acrux	173 06.0	S63 12.0
	03	308 35.4	271 16.1	. . 55.8	211 00.2	. . 11.9	115 51.1	. . 58.0	44 29.4	. . 58.2	Adhara	255 10.8	S29 00.0
	04	323 37.9	286 16.1	56.6	226 00.8	11.8	130 53.6	58.0	59 32.1	58.2	Aldebaran	290 46.6	N16 32.4
	05	338 40.4	301 16.1	57.4	241 01.5	11.7	145 56.0	58.0	74 34.7	58.1			
	06	353 42.8	316 16.0	N11 58.2	256 02.1	N24 11.6	160 58.4	S 3 58.1	89 37.4	S21 58.1	Alioth	166 18.2	N55 52.3
	07	8 45.3	331 16.0	58.9	271 02.8	11.6	176 00.9	58.1	104 40.1	58.1	Alkaid	152 56.6	N49 13.9
T	08	23 47.8	346 16.0	11 59.7	286 03.4	11.5	191 03.3	58.1	119 42.7	58.1	Al Na'ir	27 40.2	S46 52.3
H	09	38 50.2	1 15.9	12 00.5	301 04.1	. . 11.4	206 05.7	. . 58.1	134 45.4	. . 58.1	Alnilam	275 44.0	S 1 11.7
U	10	53 52.7	16 15.9	01.2	316 04.8	11.3	221 08.1	58.2	149 48.1	58.1	Alphard	217 53.6	S 8 44.2
R	11	68 55.1	31 15.8	02.0	331 05.4	11.3	236 10.6	58.2	164 50.7	58.1			
S	12	83 57.6	46 15.8	N12 02.8	346 06.1	N24 11.2	251 13.0	S 3 58.2	179 53.4	S21 58.1	Alphecca	126 08.4	N26 39.6
D	13	99 00.1	61 15.8	03.5	1 06.7	11.1	266 15.4	58.3	194 56.0	58.1	Alpheratz	357 40.7	N29 11.0
A	14	114 02.5	76 15.7	04.3	16 07.4	11.0	281 17.8	58.3	209 58.7	58.1	Altair	62 05.3	N 8 55.0
Y	15	129 05.0	91 15.7	. . 05.1	31 08.1	. . 10.9	296 20.3	. . 58.3	225 01.4	. . 58.1	Ankaa	353 13.2	S42 12.5
	16	144 07.5	106 15.6	05.8	46 08.7	10.9	311 22.7	58.3	240 04.0	58.1	Antares	112 22.6	S26 28.1
	17	159 09.9	121 15.6	06.6	61 09.4	10.8	326 25.1	58.4	255 06.7	58.1			
	18	174 12.4	136 15.6	N12 07.3	76 10.0	N24 10.7	341 27.6	S 3 58.4	270 09.4	S21 58.1	Arcturus	145 53.1	N19 05.7
	19	189 14.9	151 15.5	08.1	91 10.7	10.6	356 30.0	58.4	285 12.0	58.1	Atria	107 21.4	S69 03.4
	20	204 17.3	166 15.5	08.9	106 11.4	10.6	11 32.4	58.4	300 14.7	58.1	Avior	234 17.4	S59 34.2
	21	219 19.8	181 15.4	. . 09.6	121 12.0	. . 10.5	26 34.8	. . 58.5	315 17.4	. . 58.1	Bellatrix	278 29.5	N 6 21.7
	22	234 22.3	196 15.4	10.4	136 12.7	10.4	41 37.3	58.5	330 20.0	58.1	Betelgeuse	270 58.7	N 7 24.4
	23	249 24.7	211 15.3	11.2	151 13.3	10.3	56 39.7	58.5	345 22.7	58.1			
16	00	264 27.2	226 15.3	N12 11.9	166 14.0	N24 10.2	71 42.1	S 3 58.6	0 25.3	S21 58.1	Canopus	263 55.5	S52 42.5
	01	279 29.6	241 15.2	12.7	181 14.7	10.1	86 44.5	58.6	15 28.0	58.1	Capella	280 30.9	N46 00.7
	02	294 32.1	256 15.2	13.5	196 15.3	10.1	101 47.0	58.6	30 30.7	58.1	Deneb	49 29.3	N45 20.5
	03	309 34.6	271 15.1	. . 14.2	211 16.0	. . 10.0	116 49.4	. . 58.6	45 33.3	. . 58.0	Denebola	182 30.9	N14 28.6
	04	324 37.0	286 15.1	15.0	226 16.6	09.9	131 51.8	58.7	60 36.0	58.0	Diphda	348 53.3	S17 53.5
	05	339 39.5	301 15.0	15.8	241 17.3	09.8	146 54.2	58.7	75 38.7	58.0			
	06	354 42.0	316 15.0	N12 16.5	256 18.0	N24 09.7	161 56.7	S 3 58.7	90 41.3	S21 58.0	Dubhe	193 48.7	N61 39.7
	07	9 44.4	331 14.9	17.3	271 18.6	09.6	176 59.1	58.8	105 44.0	58.0	Elnath	278 09.6	N28 37.1
	08	24 46.9	346 14.9	18.1	286 19.3	09.6	192 01.5	58.8	120 46.6	58.0	Eltanin	90 44.3	N51 29.4
F	09	39 49.4	1 14.8	. . 18.8	301 19.9	. . 09.5	207 03.9	. . 58.8	135 49.3	. . 58.0	Enif	33 44.3	N 9 57.3
R	10	54 51.8	16 14.8	19.6	316 20.6	09.4	222 06.3	58.9	150 52.0	58.0	Fomalhaut	15 21.0	S29 31.6
I	11	69 54.3	31 14.7	20.4	331 21.3	09.3	237 08.8	58.9	165 54.6	58.0			
D	12	84 56.7	46 14.7	N12 21.1	346 21.9	N24 09.2	252 11.2	S 3 58.9	180 57.3	S21 58.0	Gacrux	171 57.6	S57 12.8
A	13	99 59.2	61 14.6	21.9	1 22.6	09.1	267 13.6	58.9	196 00.0	58.0	Gienah	175 49.5	S17 38.4
Y	14	115 01.7	76 14.5	22.7	16 23.2	09.1	282 16.0	59.0	211 02.6	58.0	Hadar	148 43.5	S60 27.5
	15	130 04.1	91 14.5	. . 23.4	31 23.9	. . 09.0	297 18.4	. . 59.0	226 05.3	. . 58.0	Hamal	327 57.9	N23 32.4
	16	145 06.6	106 14.4	24.2	46 24.6	08.9	312 20.9	59.0	241 07.9	58.0	Kaus Aust.	83 39.8	S34 22.3
	17	160 09.1	121 14.4	24.9	61 25.2	08.8	327 23.3	59.1	256 10.6	58.0			
	18	175 11.5	136 14.3	N12 25.7	76 25.9	N24 08.7	342 25.7	S 3 59.1	271 13.3	S21 58.0	Kochab	137 19.4	N74 05.4
	19	190 14.0	151 14.3	26.5	91 26.6	08.6	357 28.1	59.1	286 15.9	58.0	Markab	13 35.6	N15 17.8
	20	205 16.5	166 14.2	27.2	106 27.2	08.5	12 30.5	59.2	301 18.6	58.0	Menkar	314 12.5	N 4 09.3
	21	220 18.9	181 14.1	. . 28.0	121 27.9	. . 08.4	27 33.0	. . 59.2	316 21.3	. . 58.0	Menkent	148 04.1	S36 27.3
	22	235 21.4	196 14.1	28.8	136 28.5	08.3	42 35.4	59.2	331 23.9	58.0	Miaplacidus	221 39.6	S69 47.7
	23	250 23.9	211 14.0	29.5	151 29.2	08.3	57 37.8	59.3	346 26.6	58.0			
17	00	265 26.3	226 13.9	N12 30.3	166 29.9	N24 08.2	72 40.2	S 3 59.3	1 29.3	S21 58.0	Mirfak	308 36.9	N49 55.0
	01	280 28.8	241 13.9	31.1	181 30.5	08.1	87 42.6	59.3	16 31.9	58.0	Nunki	75 54.6	S26 16.3
	02	295 31.2	256 13.8	31.8	196 31.2	08.0	102 45.0	59.3	31 34.6	57.9	Peacock	53 14.6	S56 40.4
	03	310 33.7	271 13.7	. . 32.6	211 31.8	. . 07.9	117 47.5	. . 59.4	46 37.2	. . 57.9	Pollux	243 24.8	N27 58.9
	04	325 36.2	286 13.7	33.3	226 32.5	07.8	132 49.9	59.4	61 39.9	57.9	Procyon	244 57.2	N 5 10.6
	05	340 38.6	301 13.6	34.1	241 33.2	07.7	147 52.3	59.4	76 42.6	57.9			
	06	355 41.1	316 13.5	N12 34.9	256 33.8	N24 07.6	162 54.7	S 3 59.5	91 45.2	S21 57.9	Rasalhague	96 03.6	N12 33.0
	07	10 43.6	331 13.5	35.6	271 34.5	07.5	177 57.1	59.5	106 47.9	57.9	Regulus	207 40.8	N11 52.9
S	08	25 46.0	346 13.4	36.4	286 35.2	07.4	192 59.5	59.5	121 50.6	57.9	Rigel	281 09.8	S 8 11.1
A	09	40 48.5	1 13.3	. . 37.2	301 35.8	. . 07.3	208 02.0	. . 59.6	136 53.2	. . 57.9	Rigil Kent.	139 47.5	S60 54.4
T	10	55 51.0	16 13.3	37.9	316 36.5	07.3	223 04.4	59.6	151 55.9	57.9	Sabik	102 09.1	S15 44.6
U	11	70 53.4	31 13.2	38.7	331 37.2	07.2	238 06.8	59.6	166 58.5	57.9			
R	12	85 55.9	46 13.1	N12 39.4	346 37.8	N24 07.1	253 09.2	S 3 59.7	182 01.2	S21 57.9	Schedar	349 37.5	N56 37.6
D	13	100 58.3	61 13.1	40.2	1 38.5	07.0	268 11.6	59.7	197 03.9	57.9	Shaula	96 17.8	S37 06.8
A	14	116 00.8	76 13.0	41.0	16 39.1	06.9	283 14.0	59.7	212 06.5	57.9	Sirius	258 31.7	S16 44.6
Y	15	131 03.3	91 12.9	. . 41.7	31 39.8	. . 06.8	298 16.4	. . 59.8	227 09.2	. . 57.9	Spica	158 28.3	S11 15.1
	16	146 05.7	106 12.8	42.5	46 40.5	06.7	313 18.9	59.8	242 11.9	57.9	Suhail	222 50.7	S43 30.5
	17	161 08.2	121 12.8	43.3	61 41.1	06.6	328 21.3	59.8	257 14.5	57.9			
	18	176 10.7	136 12.7	N12 44.0	76 41.8	N24 06.5	343 23.7	S 3 59.9	272 17.2	S21 57.9	Vega	80 36.7	N38 48.1
	19	191 13.1	151 12.6	44.8	91 42.5	06.4	358 26.1	59.9	287 19.8	57.9	Zuben'ubi	137 02.2	S16 06.7
	20	206 15.6	166 12.5	45.5	106 43.1	06.3	13 28.5	3 59.9	302 22.5	57.9		SHA	Mer. Pass.
	21	221 18.1	181 12.5	. . 46.3	121 43.8	. . 06.2	28 30.9	4 00.0	317 25.2	. . 57.9		° ′	h m
	22	236 20.5	196 12.4	47.1	136 44.5	06.1	43 33.3	00.0	332 27.8	57.9	Venus	321 48.1	8 55
	23	251 23.0	211 12.3	47.8	151 45.1	06.0	58 35.7	00.0	347 30.5	57.9	Mars	261 46.8	12 54
		h m									Jupiter	167 14.9	19 10
Mer. Pass.		6 21.1	*v* −0.1	*d* 0.8	*v* 0.7	*d* 0.1	*v* 2.4	*d* 0.0	*v* 2.7	*d* 0.0	Saturn	95 58.2	23 54

UT		SUN GHA	SUN Dec	MOON GHA	*v*	MOON Dec	*d*	HP
d	h	° ′	° ′	° ′	′	° ′	′	′
15	00	179 53.8	N23 18.2	296 34.9	12.3	S13 11.5	7.8	55.7
	01	194 53.7	18.3	311 06.2	12.4	13 03.7	7.9	55.7
	02	209 53.5	18.4	325 37.6	12.4	12 55.8	7.9	55.7
	03	224 53.4	. . 18.5	340 09.0	12.4	12 47.9	8.0	55.8
	04	239 53.3	18.6	354 40.4	12.3	12 39.9	8.1	55.8
	05	254 53.1	18.7	9 11.7	12.4	12 31.8	8.1	55.8
	06	269 53.0	N23 18.8	23 43.1	12.4	S12 23.7	8.2	55.8
T	07	284 52.9	18.9	38 14.5	12.4	12 15.5	8.2	55.9
H	08	299 52.7	19.0	52 45.9	12.4	12 07.3	8.4	55.9
U	09	314 52.6	. . 19.1	67 17.3	12.5	11 58.9	8.3	55.9
R	10	329 52.5	19.2	81 48.8	12.4	11 50.6	8.5	55.9
S	11	344 52.3	19.3	96 20.2	12.4	11 42.1	8.5	56.0
D	12	359 52.2	N23 19.4	110 51.6	12.4	S11 33.6	8.6	56.0
A	13	14 52.1	19.5	125 23.0	12.4	11 25.0	8.6	56.0
Y	14	29 51.9	19.6	139 54.4	12.5	11 16.4	8.7	56.0
	15	44 51.8	. . 19.7	154 25.9	12.4	11 07.7	8.8	56.1
	16	59 51.7	19.8	168 57.3	12.4	10 58.9	8.8	56.1
	17	74 51.5	19.9	183 28.7	12.5	10 50.1	8.9	56.1
	18	89 51.4	N23 20.0	198 00.2	12.4	S10 41.2	8.9	56.2
	19	104 51.3	20.1	212 31.6	12.4	10 32.3	9.0	56.2
	20	119 51.1	20.2	227 03.0	12.5	10 23.3	9.1	56.2
	21	134 51.0	. . 20.3	241 34.5	12.4	10 14.2	9.1	56.2
	22	149 50.8	20.3	256 05.9	12.4	10 05.1	9.2	56.3
	23	164 50.7	20.4	270 37.3	12.5	9 55.9	9.2	56.3
16	00	179 50.6	N23 20.5	285 08.8	12.4	S 9 46.7	9.3	56.3
	01	194 50.4	20.6	299 40.2	12.4	9 37.4	9.4	56.4
	02	209 50.3	20.7	314 11.6	12.4	9 28.0	9.4	56.4
	03	224 50.2	. . 20.8	328 43.0	12.5	9 18.6	9.4	56.4
	04	239 50.0	20.9	343 14.5	12.4	9 09.2	9.5	56.4
	05	254 49.9	21.0	357 45.9	12.4	8 59.7	9.6	56.5
	06	269 49.8	N23 21.0	12 17.3	12.4	S 8 50.1	9.6	56.5
	07	284 49.6	21.1	26 48.7	12.4	8 40.5	9.6	56.5
	08	299 49.5	21.2	41 20.1	12.4	8 30.9	9.8	56.6
F	09	314 49.4	. . 21.3	55 51.5	12.4	8 21.1	9.7	56.6
R	10	329 49.2	21.4	70 22.9	12.3	8 11.4	9.8	56.6
I	11	344 49.1	21.5	84 54.2	12.4	8 01.6	9.9	56.7
D	12	359 49.0	N23 21.5	99 25.6	12.4	S 7 51.7	9.9	56.7
A	13	14 48.8	21.6	113 57.0	12.3	7 41.8	10.0	56.7
Y	14	29 48.7	21.7	128 28.3	12.4	7 31.8	10.0	56.8
	15	44 48.6	. . 21.8	142 59.7	12.3	7 21.8	10.0	56.8
	16	59 48.4	21.9	157 31.0	12.3	7 11.8	10.1	56.8
	17	74 48.3	21.9	172 02.3	12.3	7 01.7	10.2	56.9
	18	89 48.2	N23 22.0	186 33.6	12.3	S 6 51.5	10.2	56.9
	19	104 48.0	22.1	201 04.9	12.3	6 41.3	10.2	56.9
	20	119 47.9	22.2	215 36.2	12.3	6 31.1	10.3	57.0
	21	134 47.8	. . 22.2	230 07.5	12.2	6 20.8	10.3	57.0
	22	149 47.6	22.3	244 38.7	12.3	6 10.5	10.4	57.0
	23	164 47.5	22.4	259 10.0	12.2	6 00.1	10.4	57.0
17	00	179 47.3	N23 22.5	273 41.2	12.2	S 5 49.7	10.4	57.1
	01	194 47.2	22.5	288 12.4	12.2	5 39.3	10.5	57.1
	02	209 47.1	22.6	302 43.6	12.2	5 28.8	10.5	57.1
	03	224 46.9	. . 22.7	317 14.8	12.1	5 18.3	10.6	57.2
	04	239 46.8	22.7	331 45.9	12.1	5 07.7	10.6	57.2
	05	254 46.7	22.8	346 17.0	12.2	4 57.1	10.6	57.2
	06	269 46.5	N23 22.9	0 48.2	12.1	S 4 46.5	10.7	57.3
S	07	284 46.4	22.9	15 19.3	12.0	4 35.8	10.7	57.3
A	08	299 46.3	23.0	29 50.3	12.1	4 25.1	10.7	57.4
T	09	314 46.1	. . 23.1	44 21.4	12.0	4 14.4	10.8	57.4
U	10	329 46.0	23.1	58 52.4	12.0	4 03.6	10.8	57.4
R	11	344 45.9	23.2	73 23.4	12.0	3 52.8	10.9	57.5
D	12	359 45.7	N23 23.3	87 54.4	11.9	S 3 41.9	10.8	57.5
A	13	14 45.6	23.3	102 25.3	12.0	3 31.1	11.0	57.5
Y	14	29 45.4	23.4	116 56.3	11.9	3 20.1	10.9	57.6
	15	44 45.3	. . 23.5	131 27.2	11.8	3 09.2	11.0	57.6
	16	59 45.2	23.5	145 58.0	11.9	2 58.2	10.9	57.6
	17	74 45.0	23.6	160 28.9	11.8	2 47.3	11.1	57.7
	18	89 44.9	N23 23.6	174 59.7	11.8	S 2 36.2	11.0	57.7
	19	104 44.8	23.7	189 30.5	11.8	2 25.2	11.1	57.7
	20	119 44.6	23.8	204 01.3	11.7	2 14.1	11.1	57.8
	21	134 44.5	. . 23.8	218 32.0	11.7	2 03.0	11.1	57.8
	22	149 44.4	23.9	233 02.7	11.6	1 51.9	11.2	57.8
	23	164 44.2	23.9	247 33.3	11.7	S 1 40.7	11.1	57.9
		SD 15.8	*d* 0.1	SD		15.3	15.4	15.7

Lat.	Twilight Naut.	Twilight Civil	Sunrise	Moonrise 15	Moonrise 16	Moonrise 17	Moonrise 18
°	h m	h m	h m	h m	h m	h m	h m
N 72	▭	▭	▭	01 20	01 09	01 00	00 52
N 70	▭	▭	▭	00 56	00 54	00 52	00 50
68	▭	▭	▭	00 37	00 42	00 45	00 48
66	▭	▭	▭	00 22	00 32	00 40	00 47
64	////	////	01 32	00 10	00 24	00 35	00 46
62	////	////	02 10	24 16	00 16	00 31	00 45
60	////	00 52	02 36	24 10	00 10	00 27	00 44
N 58	////	01 41	02 56	24 04	00 04	00 24	00 43
56	////	02 11	03 13	23 59	24 21	00 21	00 42
54	00 47	02 33	03 27	23 55	24 19	00 19	00 42
52	01 33	02 51	03 39	23 51	24 16	00 16	00 41
50	02 00	03 06	03 50	23 47	24 14	00 14	00 40
45	02 46	03 35	04 13	23 39	24 10	00 10	00 39
N 40	03 16	03 58	04 31	23 33	24 06	00 06	00 38
35	03 39	04 16	04 46	23 27	24 02	00 02	00 37
30	03 58	04 31	04 59	23 22	23 59	24 37	00 37
20	04 27	04 56	05 21	23 13	23 54	24 35	00 35
N 10	04 49	05 16	05 40	23 05	23 50	24 34	00 34
0	05 08	05 35	05 57	22 58	23 45	24 33	00 33
S 10	05 25	05 52	06 14	22 51	23 41	24 32	00 32
20	05 41	06 09	06 33	22 43	23 36	24 31	00 31
30	05 58	06 28	06 54	22 34	23 31	24 30	00 30
35	06 07	06 38	07 06	22 29	23 28	24 29	00 29
40	06 16	06 50	07 21	22 23	23 25	24 29	00 29
45	06 26	07 04	07 37	22 16	23 21	24 28	00 28
S 50	06 38	07 20	07 58	22 08	23 16	24 27	00 27
52	06 43	07 27	08 08	22 04	23 14	24 26	00 26
54	06 49	07 35	08 19	22 00	23 11	24 26	00 26
56	06 55	07 44	08 32	21 55	23 09	24 25	00 25
58	07 02	07 54	08 46	21 50	23 06	24 24	00 24
S 60	07 09	08 06	09 04	21 44	23 03	24 24	00 24

Lat.	Sunset	Twilight Civil	Twilight Naut.	Moonset 15	Moonset 16	Moonset 17	Moonset 18
°	h m	h m	h m	h m	h m	h m	h m
N 72	▭	▭	▭	07 40	09 29	11 18	13 08
N 70	▭	▭	▭	08 03	09 43	11 23	13 07
68	▭	▭	▭	08 20	09 53	11 28	13 06
66	▭	▭	▭	08 34	10 02	11 32	13 05
64	22 30	////	////	08 46	10 09	11 35	13 04
62	21 52	////	////	08 55	10 15	11 38	13 04
60	21 26	23 11	////	09 04	10 21	11 41	13 03
N 58	21 06	22 21	////	09 11	10 26	11 43	13 03
56	20 49	21 51	////	09 17	10 30	11 45	13 02
54	20 35	21 29	23 15	09 23	10 34	11 46	13 02
52	20 22	21 11	22 29	09 28	10 37	11 48	13 01
50	20 11	20 56	22 01	09 33	10 40	11 49	13 01
45	19 49	20 26	21 16	09 43	10 47	11 52	13 00
N 40	19 31	20 04	20 45	09 51	10 52	11 55	13 00
35	19 16	19 46	20 22	09 58	10 57	11 57	12 59
30	19 03	19 30	20 04	10 05	11 01	11 59	12 59
20	18 41	19 05	19 35	10 15	11 08	12 03	12 58
N 10	18 22	18 45	19 12	10 25	11 15	12 05	12 57
0	18 04	18 27	18 53	10 33	11 21	12 08	12 57
S 10	17 47	18 10	18 36	10 42	11 26	12 11	12 56
20	17 28	17 53	18 20	10 51	11 33	12 14	12 55
30	17 07	17 34	18 04	11 02	11 39	12 17	12 54
35	16 55	17 23	17 55	11 08	11 43	12 19	12 54
40	16 41	17 11	17 45	11 14	11 48	12 21	12 53
45	16 24	16 58	17 35	11 22	11 53	12 23	12 53
S 50	16 03	16 42	17 23	11 32	11 59	12 26	12 52
52	15 54	16 34	17 18	11 36	12 02	12 27	12 51
54	15 42	16 26	17 12	11 41	12 05	12 28	12 51
56	15 30	16 17	17 06	11 46	12 09	12 30	12 51
58	15 15	16 07	17 00	11 52	12 13	12 32	12 50
S 60	14 58	15 55	16 52	11 59	12 17	12 33	12 50

Day	SUN Eqn. of Time 00^h	SUN Eqn. of Time 12^h	SUN Mer. Pass.	MOON Mer. Pass. Upper	MOON Mer. Pass. Lower	MOON Age	MOON Phase
d	m s	m s	h m	h m	h m	d %	
15	00 25	00 31	12 01	04 22	16 46	21 70	
16	00 37	00 44	12 01	05 09	17 33	22 60	◑
17	00 50	00 57	12 01	05 57	18 21	23 50	

UT	ARIES	VENUS −4·3		MARS +1·7		JUPITER −2·1		SATURN +0·0	
	GHA	GHA	Dec	GHA	Dec	GHA	Dec	GHA	Dec
d h	° ′	° ′	° ′	° ′	° ′	° ′	° ′	° ′	° ′
18 00	266 25.5	226 12.2	N12 48.6	166 45.8	N24 05.9	73 38.2	S 4 00.1	2 33.2	S21 57.9
01	281 27.9	241 12.1	49.3	181 46.4	05.8	88 40.6	00.1	17 35.8	57.8
02	296 30.4	256 12.1	50.1	196 47.1	05.7	103 43.0	00.1	32 38.5	57.8
03	311 32.8	271 12.0	. . 50.9	211 47.8	. . 05.6	118 45.4	. . 00.2	47 41.1	. . 57.8
04	326 35.3	286 11.9	51.6	226 48.4	05.5	133 47.8	00.2	62 43.8	57.8
05	341 37.8	301 11.8	52.4	241 49.1	05.4	148 50.2	00.2	77 46.5	57.8
06	356 40.2	316 11.7	N12 53.1	256 49.8	N24 05.3	163 52.6	S 4 00.3	92 49.1	S21 57.8
07	11 42.7	331 11.7	53.9	271 50.4	05.2	178 55.0	00.3	107 51.8	57.8
08	26 45.2	346 11.6	54.7	286 51.1	05.1	193 57.4	00.4	122 54.5	57.8
S 09	41 47.6	1 11.5	. . 55.4	301 51.8	. . 05.0	208 59.8	. . 00.4	137 57.1	. . 57.8
U 10	56 50.1	16 11.4	56.2	316 52.4	04.9	224 02.3	00.4	152 59.8	57.8
N 11	71 52.6	31 11.3	56.9	331 53.1	04.8	239 04.7	00.5	168 02.4	57.8
D 12	86 55.0	46 11.2	N12 57.7	346 53.8	N24 04.7	254 07.1	S 4 00.5	183 05.1	S21 57.8
A 13	101 57.5	61 11.1	58.5	1 54.4	04.6	269 09.5	00.5	198 07.8	57.8
Y 14	117 00.0	76 11.1	12 59.2	16 55.1	04.5	284 11.9	00.6	213 10.4	57.8
15	132 02.4	91 11.0	13 00.0	31 55.8	. . 04.4	299 14.3	. . 00.6	228 13.1	. . 57.8
16	147 04.9	106 10.9	00.7	46 56.4	04.3	314 16.7	00.6	243 15.8	57.8
17	162 07.3	121 10.8	01.5	61 57.1	04.2	329 19.1	00.7	258 18.4	57.8
18	177 09.8	136 10.7	N13 02.2	76 57.8	N24 04.1	344 21.5	S 4 00.7	273 21.1	S21 57.8
19	192 12.3	151 10.6	03.0	91 58.4	04.0	359 23.9	00.7	288 23.7	57.8
20	207 14.7	166 10.5	03.8	106 59.1	03.9	14 26.3	00.8	303 26.4	57.8
21	222 17.2	181 10.4	. . 04.5	121 59.8	. . 03.8	29 28.7	. . 00.8	318 29.1	. . 57.8
22	237 19.7	196 10.3	05.3	137 00.4	03.7	44 31.1	00.9	333 31.7	57.8
23	252 22.1	211 10.2	06.0	152 01.1	03.6	59 33.5	00.9	348 34.4	57.7
19 00	267 24.6	226 10.1	N13 06.8	167 01.8	N24 03.5	74 35.9	S 4 00.9	3 37.1	S21 57.7
01	282 27.1	241 10.0	07.6	182 02.4	03.4	89 38.3	01.0	18 39.7	57.7
02	297 29.5	256 09.9	08.3	197 03.1	03.2	104 40.7	01.0	33 42.4	57.7
03	312 32.0	271 09.8	. . 09.1	212 03.8	. . 03.1	119 43.1	. . 01.0	48 45.0	. . 57.7
04	327 34.4	286 09.8	09.8	227 04.4	03.0	134 45.6	01.1	63 47.7	57.7
05	342 36.9	301 09.7	10.6	242 05.1	02.9	149 48.0	01.1	78 50.4	57.7
06	357 39.4	316 09.6	N13 11.3	257 05.8	N24 02.8	164 50.4	S 4 01.2	93 53.0	S21 57.7
07	12 41.8	331 09.5	12.1	272 06.4	02.7	179 52.8	01.2	108 55.7	57.7
08	27 44.3	346 09.4	12.8	287 07.1	02.6	194 55.2	01.2	123 58.4	57.7
M 09	42 46.8	1 09.3	. . 13.6	302 07.8	. . 02.5	209 57.6	. . 01.3	139 01.0	. . 57.7
O 10	57 49.2	16 09.2	14.4	317 08.4	02.4	225 00.0	01.3	154 03.7	57.7
N 11	72 51.7	31 09.1	15.1	332 09.1	02.3	240 02.4	01.3	169 06.3	57.7
D 12	87 54.2	46 09.0	N13 15.9	347 09.8	N24 02.2	255 04.8	S 4 01.4	184 09.0	S21 57.7
A 13	102 56.6	61 08.8	16.6	2 10.4	02.1	270 07.2	01.4	199 11.7	57.7
Y 14	117 59.1	76 08.7	17.4	17 11.1	01.9	285 09.6	01.5	214 14.3	57.7
15	133 01.6	91 08.6	. . 18.1	32 11.8	. . 01.8	300 12.0	. . 01.5	229 17.0	. . 57.7
16	148 04.0	106 08.5	18.9	47 12.4	01.7	315 14.4	01.5	244 19.7	57.7
17	163 06.5	121 08.4	19.6	62 13.1	01.6	330 16.8	01.6	259 22.3	57.7
18	178 08.9	136 08.3	N13 20.4	77 13.8	N24 01.5	345 19.2	S 4 01.6	274 25.0	S21 57.7
19	193 11.4	151 08.2	21.1	92 14.4	01.4	0 21.6	01.7	289 27.6	57.7
20	208 13.9	166 08.1	21.9	107 15.1	01.3	15 24.0	01.7	304 30.3	57.7
21	223 16.3	181 08.0	. . 22.7	122 15.8	. . 01.2	30 26.4	. . 01.7	319 33.0	. . 57.7
22	238 18.8	196 07.9	23.4	137 16.4	01.0	45 28.8	01.8	334 35.6	57.6
23	253 21.3	211 07.8	24.2	152 17.1	00.9	60 31.2	01.8	349 38.3	57.6
20 00	268 23.7	226 07.7	N13 24.9	167 17.8	N24 00.8	75 33.6	S 4 01.9	4 41.0	S21 57.6
01	283 26.2	241 07.6	25.7	182 18.5	00.7	90 36.0	01.9	19 43.6	57.6
02	298 28.7	256 07.5	26.4	197 19.1	00.6	105 38.3	01.9	34 46.3	57.6
03	313 31.1	271 07.3	. . 27.2	212 19.8	. . 00.5	120 40.7	. . 02.0	49 48.9	. . 57.6
04	328 33.6	286 07.2	27.9	227 20.5	00.4	135 43.1	02.0	64 51.6	57.6
05	343 36.1	301 07.1	28.7	242 21.1	00.2	150 45.5	02.1	79 54.3	57.6
06	358 38.5	316 07.0	N13 29.4	257 21.8	N24 00.1	165 47.9	S 4 02.1	94 56.9	S21 57.6
07	13 41.0	331 06.9	30.2	272 22.5	24 00.0	180 50.3	02.1	109 59.6	57.6
T 08	28 43.4	346 06.8	30.9	287 23.1	23 59.9	195 52.7	02.2	125 02.2	57.6
U 09	43 45.9	1 06.7	. . 31.7	302 23.8	. . 59.8	210 55.1	. . 02.2	140 04.9	. . 57.6
E 10	58 48.4	16 06.5	32.4	317 24.5	59.7	225 57.5	02.3	155 07.6	57.6
S 11	73 50.8	31 06.4	33.2	332 25.2	59.5	240 59.9	02.3	170 10.2	57.6
D 12	88 53.3	46 06.3	N13 33.9	347 25.8	N23 59.4	256 02.3	S 4 02.3	185 12.9	S21 57.6
A 13	103 55.8	61 06.2	34.7	2 26.5	59.3	271 04.7	02.4	200 15.6	57.6
Y 14	118 58.2	76 06.1	35.4	17 27.2	59.2	286 07.1	02.4	215 18.2	57.6
15	134 00.7	91 05.9	. . 36.2	32 27.8	. . 59.1	301 09.5	. . 02.5	230 20.9	. . 57.6
16	149 03.2	106 05.8	36.9	47 28.5	58.9	316 11.9	02.5	245 23.5	57.6
17	164 05.6	121 05.7	37.7	62 29.2	58.8	331 14.3	02.6	260 26.2	57.6
18	179 08.1	136 05.6	N13 38.4	77 29.8	N23 58.7	346 16.7	S 4 02.6	275 28.9	S21 57.6
19	194 10.5	151 05.5	39.2	92 30.5	58.6	1 19.1	02.6	290 31.5	57.6
20	209 13.0	166 05.3	39.9	107 31.2	58.5	16 21.4	02.7	305 34.2	57.6
21	224 15.5	181 05.2	. . 40.7	122 31.9	. . 58.3	31 23.8	. . 02.7	320 36.9	. . 57.5
22	239 17.9	196 05.1	41.4	137 32.5	58.2	46 26.2	02.8	335 39.5	57.5
23	254 20.4	211 05.0	42.2	152 33.2	58.1	61 28.6	02.8	350 42.2	57.5
Mer. Pass.	h m 6 09.3	*v* −0.1	*d* 0.8	*v* 0.7	*d* 0.1	*v* 2.4	*d* 0.0	*v* 2.7	*d* 0.0

STARS

Name	SHA	Dec
	° ′	° ′
Acamar	315 16.7	S40 14.1
Achernar	335 25.1	S57 08.8
Acrux	173 06.0	S63 12.0
Adhara	255 10.8	S29 00.0
Aldebaran	290 46.6	N16 32.4
Alioth	166 18.3	N55 52.3
Alkaid	152 56.6	N49 13.9
Al Na'ir	27 40.2	S46 52.3
Alnilam	275 44.0	S 1 11.7
Alphard	217 53.6	S 8 44.2
Alphecca	126 08.4	N26 39.6
Alpheratz	357 40.7	N29 11.0
Altair	62 05.3	N 8 55.0
Ankaa	353 13.2	S42 12.5
Antares	112 22.6	S26 28.1
Arcturus	145 53.1	N19 05.7
Atria	107 21.4	S69 03.4
Avior	234 17.4	S59 34.2
Bellatrix	278 29.5	N 6 21.7
Betelgeuse	270 58.7	N 7 24.4
Canopus	263 55.5	S52 42.5
Capella	280 30.9	N46 00.6
Deneb	49 29.2	N45 20.5
Denebola	182 31.0	N14 28.6
Diphda	348 53.3	S17 53.5
Dubhe	193 48.7	N61 39.7
Elnath	278 09.6	N28 37.1
Eltanin	90 44.3	N51 29.4
Enif	33 44.3	N 9 57.3
Fomalhaut	15 21.0	S29 31.6
Gacrux	171 57.7	S57 12.8
Gienah	175 49.5	S17 38.4
Hadar	148 43.6	S60 27.5
Hamal	327 57.9	N23 32.4
Kaus Aust.	83 39.8	S34 22.3
Kochab	137 19.4	N74 05.4
Markab	13 35.6	N15 17.8
Menkar	314 12.5	N 4 09.3
Menkent	148 04.1	S36 27.3
Miaplacidus	221 39.6	S69 47.6
Mirfak	308 36.8	N49 55.0
Nunki	75 54.6	S26 16.3
Peacock	53 14.6	S56 40.4
Pollux	243 24.8	N27 58.9
Procyon	244 57.2	N 5 10.7
Rasalhague	96 03.6	N12 33.1
Regulus	207 40.8	N11 52.9
Rigel	281 09.8	S 8 11.1
Rigil Kent.	139 47.5	S60 54.4
Sabik	102 09.1	S15 44.6
Schedar	349 37.5	N56 37.6
Shaula	96 17.8	S37 06.8
Sirius	258 31.7	S16 44.6
Spica	158 28.3	S11 15.1
Suhail	222 50.7	S43 30.4
Vega	80 36.7	N38 48.1
Zuben'ubi	137 02.2	S16 06.7

	SHA	Mer. Pass.
	° ′	h m
Venus	318 45.5	8 55
Mars	259 37.2	12 51
Jupiter	167 11.3	18 59
Saturn	96 12.5	23 41

UT d	UT h	SUN GHA ° ′	SUN Dec ° ′	MOON GHA ° ′	v ′	MOON Dec ° ′	d ′	HP ′
18	00	179 44.1	N23 24.0	262 04.0	11.6	S 1 29.6	11.2	57.9
	01	194 44.0	24.0	276 34.6	11.5	1 18.4	11.2	57.9
	02	209 43.8	24.1	291 05.1	11.5	1 07.2	11.3	58.0
	03	224 43.7	. . 24.1	305 35.6	11.5	0 55.9	11.2	58.0
	04	239 43.5	24.2	320 06.1	11.5	0 44.7	11.3	58.1
	05	254 43.4	24.2	334 36.6	11.4	0 33.4	11.3	58.1
	06	269 43.3	N23 24.3	349 07.0	11.3	S 0 22.1	11.3	58.1
	07	284 43.1	24.3	3 37.3	11.4	S 0 10.8	11.3	58.2
	08	299 43.0	24.4	18 07.7	11.3	N 0 00.5	11.3	58.2
S	09	314 42.9	. . 24.4	32 38.0	11.2	0 11.8	11.4	58.2
U	10	329 42.7	24.5	47 08.2	11.2	0 23.2	11.3	58.3
N	11	344 42.6	24.5	61 38.4	11.2	0 34.5	11.4	58.3
D	12	359 42.5	N23 24.6	76 08.6	11.1	N 0 45.9	11.4	58.3
A	13	14 42.3	24.6	90 38.7	11.1	0 57.3	11.4	58.4
Y	14	29 42.2	24.7	105 08.8	11.0	1 08.7	11.4	58.4
	15	44 42.0	. . 24.7	119 38.8	11.0	1 20.1	11.4	58.5
	16	59 41.9	24.8	134 08.8	10.9	1 31.5	11.4	58.5
	17	74 41.8	24.8	148 38.7	10.9	1 42.9	11.4	58.5
	18	89 41.6	N23 24.8	163 08.6	10.8	N 1 54.3	11.4	58.6
	19	104 41.5	24.9	177 38.4	10.8	2 05.7	11.4	58.6
	20	119 41.4	24.9	192 08.2	10.7	2 17.1	11.5	58.6
	21	134 41.2	. . 25.0	206 37.9	10.7	2 28.6	11.4	58.7
	22	149 41.1	25.0	221 07.6	10.7	2 40.0	11.4	58.7
	23	164 41.0	25.0	235 37.3	10.5	2 51.4	11.5	58.7
19	00	179 40.8	N23 25.1	250 06.8	10.6	N 3 02.9	11.4	58.8
	01	194 40.7	25.1	264 36.4	10.4	3 14.3	11.4	58.8
	02	209 40.5	25.2	279 05.8	10.4	3 25.7	11.4	58.9
	03	224 40.4	. . 25.2	293 35.2	10.4	3 37.1	11.4	58.9
	04	239 40.3	25.2	308 04.6	10.3	3 48.5	11.4	58.9
	05	254 40.1	25.3	322 33.9	10.3	3 59.9	11.4	59.0
	06	269 40.0	N23 25.3	337 03.2	10.1	N 4 11.3	11.4	59.0
	07	284 39.9	25.3	351 32.3	10.2	4 22.7	11.4	59.0
	08	299 39.7	25.4	6 01.5	10.0	4 34.1	11.4	59.1
M	09	314 39.6	. . 25.4	20 30.5	10.1	4 45.5	11.3	59.1
O	10	329 39.5	25.4	34 59.6	9.9	4 56.8	11.4	59.1
N	11	344 39.3	25.5	49 28.5	9.9	5 08.2	11.3	59.2
D	12	359 39.2	N23 25.5	63 57.4	9.8	N 5 19.5	11.3	59.2
A	13	14 39.0	25.5	78 26.2	9.8	5 30.8	11.3	59.2
Y	14	29 38.9	25.5	92 55.0	9.7	5 42.1	11.3	59.3
	15	44 38.8	. . 25.6	107 23.7	9.6	5 53.4	11.3	59.3
	16	59 38.6	25.6	121 52.3	9.6	6 04.7	11.2	59.4
	17	74 38.5	25.6	136 20.9	9.5	6 15.9	11.2	59.4
	18	89 38.4	N23 25.6	150 49.4	9.4	N 6 27.1	11.2	59.4
	19	104 38.2	25.7	165 17.8	9.4	6 38.3	11.2	59.5
	20	119 38.1	25.7	179 46.2	9.3	6 49.5	11.1	59.5
	21	134 37.9	. . 25.7	194 14.5	9.2	7 00.6	11.1	59.5
	22	149 37.8	25.7	208 42.7	9.2	7 11.7	11.1	59.6
	23	164 37.7	25.8	223 10.9	9.0	7 22.8	11.0	59.6
20	00	179 37.5	N23 25.8	237 38.9	9.1	N 7 33.8	11.1	59.6
	01	194 37.4	25.8	252 07.0	8.9	7 44.9	10.9	59.7
	02	209 37.3	25.8	266 34.9	8.9	7 55.8	11.0	59.7
	03	224 37.1	. . 25.8	281 02.8	8.8	8 06.8	10.9	59.7
	04	239 37.0	25.9	295 30.6	8.7	8 17.7	10.9	59.8
	05	254 36.9	25.9	309 58.3	8.7	8 28.6	10.8	59.8
	06	269 36.7	N23 25.9	324 26.0	8.6	N 8 39.4	10.8	59.8
	07	284 36.6	25.9	338 53.6	8.5	8 50.2	10.8	59.9
T	08	299 36.4	25.9	353 21.1	8.4	9 01.0	10.7	59.9
U	09	314 36.3	. . 25.9	7 48.5	8.4	9 11.7	10.7	59.9
E	10	329 36.2	25.9	22 15.9	8.3	9 22.4	10.6	60.0
S	11	344 36.0	26.0	36 43.2	8.2	9 33.0	10.6	60.0
D	12	359 35.9	N23 26.0	51 10.4	8.1	N 9 43.6	10.5	60.0
A	13	14 35.8	26.0	65 37.5	8.1	9 54.1	10.5	60.0
Y	14	29 35.6	26.0	80 04.6	8.0	10 04.6	10.5	60.1
	15	44 35.5	. . 26.0	94 31.6	7.9	10 15.1	10.3	60.1
	16	59 35.3	26.0	108 58.5	7.8	10 25.4	10.4	60.1
	17	74 35.2	26.0	123 25.3	7.7	10 35.8	10.2	60.2
	18	89 35.1	N23 26.0	137 52.0	7.7	N10 46.0	10.2	60.2
	19	104 34.9	26.0	152 18.7	7.6	10 56.2	10.2	60.2
	20	119 34.8	26.0	166 45.3	7.5	11 06.4	10.1	60.3
	21	134 34.7	. . 26.0	181 11.8	7.5	11 16.5	10.0	60.3
	22	149 34.5	26.1	195 38.3	7.3	11 26.5	10.0	60.3
	23	164 34.4	26.1	210 04.6	7.3	N11 36.5	9.9	60.3
		SD 15.8	*d* 0.0	SD	15.9	16.1		16.4

Lat. °	Twilight Naut. h m	Twilight Civil h m	Sunrise h m	Moonrise 18 h m	Moonrise 19 h m	Moonrise 20 h m	Moonrise 21 h m
N 72	□	□	□	00 52	00 43	00 35	00 25
N 70	□	□	□	00 50	00 48	00 46	00 45
68	□	□	□	00 48	00 51	00 55	01 00
66	□	□	□	00 47	00 54	01 02	01 13
64	////	////	01 31	00 46	00 56	01 08	01 23
62	////	////	02 09	00 45	00 58	01 14	01 33
60	////	00 49	02 36	00 44	01 00	01 19	01 40
N 58	////	01 40	02 56	00 43	01 02	01 23	01 47
56	////	02 10	03 13	00 42	01 03	01 27	01 53
54	00 45	02 33	03 27	00 42	01 05	01 30	01 59
52	01 32	02 51	03 39	00 41	01 06	01 33	02 04
50	02 00	03 06	03 50	00 40	01 07	01 36	02 09
45	02 46	03 35	04 13	00 39	01 10	01 42	02 18
N 40	03 16	03 58	04 31	00 38	01 12	01 47	02 27
35	03 40	04 16	04 46	00 37	01 14	01 52	02 34
30	03 58	04 32	04 59	00 37	01 15	01 56	02 40
20	04 27	04 57	05 21	00 35	01 18	02 03	02 51
N 10	04 50	05 17	05 40	00 34	01 21	02 09	03 01
0	05 09	05 35	05 58	00 33	01 23	02 15	03 10
S 10	05 26	05 52	06 15	00 32	01 25	02 21	03 19
20	05 42	06 10	06 34	00 31	01 28	02 27	03 29
30	05 59	06 29	06 55	00 30	01 31	02 34	03 40
35	06 07	06 39	07 07	00 29	01 33	02 39	03 47
40	06 17	06 51	07 22	00 29	01 35	02 43	03 54
45	06 27	07 04	07 38	00 28	01 37	02 49	04 03
S 50	06 39	07 21	07 59	00 27	01 40	02 56	04 14
52	06 44	07 28	08 09	00 26	01 41	02 59	04 19
54	06 50	07 36	08 20	00 26	01 43	03 02	04 24
56	06 56	07 45	08 33	00 25	01 44	03 06	04 30
58	07 03	07 56	08 48	00 24	01 46	03 10	04 37
S 60	07 10	08 07	09 05	00 24	01 48	03 15	04 45

Lat. °	Sunset h m	Twilight Civil h m	Twilight Naut. h m	Moonset 18 h m	Moonset 19 h m	Moonset 20 h m	Moonset 21 h m
N 72	□	□	□	13 08	15 03	17 05	19 18
N 70	□	□	□	13 07	14 54	16 47	18 46
68	□	□	□	13 06	14 47	16 33	18 22
66	□	□	□	13 05	14 41	16 21	18 04
64	22 32	////	////	13 04	14 36	16 12	17 49
62	21 54	////	////	13 04	14 32	16 04	17 37
60	21 27	23 14	////	13 03	14 29	15 57	17 26
N 58	21 07	22 23	////	13 03	14 25	15 51	17 17
56	20 50	21 53	////	13 02	14 22	15 45	17 10
54	20 36	21 30	23 18	13 02	14 20	15 41	17 03
52	20 23	21 12	22 31	13 01	14 18	15 36	16 56
50	20 12	20 57	22 03	13 01	14 15	15 32	16 51
45	19 50	20 27	21 17	13 00	14 11	15 24	16 38
N 40	19 32	20 05	20 46	13 00	14 07	15 17	16 28
35	19 17	19 47	20 23	12 59	14 04	15 11	16 20
30	19 04	19 31	20 05	12 59	14 01	15 05	16 12
20	18 42	19 06	19 35	12 58	13 56	14 56	15 59
N 10	18 23	18 46	19 13	12 57	13 51	14 48	15 48
0	18 05	18 28	18 54	12 57	13 47	14 41	15 37
S 10	17 48	18 10	18 37	12 56	13 43	14 33	15 26
20	17 29	17 53	18 21	12 55	13 39	14 25	15 15
30	17 08	17 34	18 04	12 54	13 34	14 16	15 02
35	16 55	17 24	17 55	12 54	13 31	14 11	14 55
40	16 41	17 12	17 46	12 53	13 28	14 05	14 46
45	16 24	16 58	17 36	12 53	13 24	13 58	14 36
S 50	16 04	16 42	17 24	12 52	13 19	13 50	14 25
52	15 54	16 35	17 18	12 51	13 17	13 46	14 19
54	15 43	16 26	17 13	12 51	13 15	13 42	14 13
56	15 30	16 17	17 07	12 51	13 12	13 37	14 06
58	15 15	16 07	17 00	12 50	13 10	13 32	13 59
S 60	14 58	15 55	16 52	12 50	13 07	13 26	13 50

Day	SUN Eqn. of Time 00^h	SUN Eqn. of Time 12^h	SUN Mer. Pass.	MOON Mer. Pass. Upper	MOON Mer. Pass. Lower	MOON Age	MOON Phase
d	m s	m s	h m	h m	h m	d %	
18	01 03	01 10	12 01	06 45	19 10	24 39	
19	01 16	01 23	12 01	07 35	20 01	25 28	
20	01 30	01 36	12 02	08 28	20 55	26 19	

UT		ARIES	VENUS −4·3		MARS +1·7		JUPITER −2·1		SATURN +0·0	
d h		GHA ° ′	GHA ° ′	Dec ° ′	GHA ° ′	Dec ° ′	GHA ° ′	Dec ° ′	GHA ° ′	Dec ° ′
21 00		269 22.9	226 04.8	N13 42.9	167 33.9	N23 58.0	76 31.0	S 4 02.8	5 44.8	S21 57.5
01		284 25.3	241 04.7	43.7	182 34.5	57.8	91 33.4	02.9	20 47.5	57.5
02		299 27.8	256 04.6	44.4	197 35.2	57.7	106 35.8	02.9	35 50.2	57.5
03		314 30.3	271 04.5	. . 45.2	212 35.9	. . 57.6	121 38.2	. . 03.0	50 52.8	. . 57.5
04		329 32.7	286 04.3	45.9	227 36.6	57.5	136 40.6	03.0	65 55.5	57.5
05		344 35.2	301 04.2	46.7	242 37.2	57.4	151 43.0	03.1	80 58.1	57.5
06		359 37.7	316 04.1	N13 47.4	257 37.9	N23 57.2	166 45.3	S 4 03.1	96 00.8	S21 57.5
07	W	14 40.1	331 03.9	48.2	272 38.6	57.1	181 47.7	03.2	111 03.5	57.5
08	E	29 42.6	346 03.8	48.9	287 39.2	57.0	196 50.1	03.2	126 06.1	57.5
09	D	44 45.0	1 03.7	. . 49.6	302 39.9	. . 56.9	211 52.5	. . 03.2	141 08.8	. . 57.5
10	N	59 47.5	16 03.6	50.4	317 40.6	56.7	226 54.9	03.3	156 11.5	57.5
11	E	74 50.0	31 03.4	51.1	332 41.3	56.6	241 57.3	03.3	171 14.1	57.5
12	S	89 52.4	46 03.3	N13 51.9	347 41.9	N23 56.5	256 59.7	S 4 03.4	186 16.8	S21 57.5
13	D	104 54.9	61 03.2	52.6	2 42.6	56.3	272 02.1	03.4	201 19.4	57.5
14	A	119 57.4	76 03.0	53.4	17 43.3	56.2	287 04.4	03.5	216 22.1	57.5
15	Y	134 59.8	91 02.9	. . 54.1	32 44.0	. . 56.1	302 06.8	. . 03.5	231 24.8	. . 57.5
16		150 02.3	106 02.7	54.9	47 44.6	56.0	317 09.2	03.5	246 27.4	57.5
17		165 04.8	121 02.6	55.6	62 45.3	55.8	332 11.6	03.6	261 30.1	57.5
18		180 07.2	136 02.5	N13 56.4	77 46.0	N23 55.7	347 14.0	S 4 03.6	276 32.7	S21 57.5
19		195 09.7	151 02.3	57.1	92 46.7	55.6	2 16.4	03.7	291 35.4	57.5
20		210 12.2	166 02.2	57.8	107 47.3	55.5	17 18.8	03.7	306 38.1	57.4
21		225 14.6	181 02.1	. . 58.6	122 48.0	. . 55.3	32 21.1	. . 03.8	321 40.7	. . 57.4
22		240 17.1	196 01.9	13 59.3	137 48.7	55.2	47 23.5	03.8	336 43.4	57.4
23		255 19.5	211 01.8	14 00.1	152 49.3	55.1	62 25.9	03.9	351 46.0	57.4
22 00		270 22.0	226 01.6	N14 00.8	167 50.0	N23 54.9	77 28.3	S 4 03.9	6 48.7	S21 57.4
01		285 24.5	241 01.5	01.6	182 50.7	54.8	92 30.7	04.0	21 51.4	57.4
02		300 26.9	256 01.4	02.3	197 51.4	54.7	107 33.1	04.0	36 54.0	57.4
03		315 29.4	271 01.2	. . 03.0	212 52.0	. . 54.5	122 35.5	. . 04.0	51 56.7	. . 57.4
04		330 31.9	286 01.1	03.8	227 52.7	54.4	137 37.8	04.1	66 59.4	57.4
05		345 34.3	301 00.9	04.5	242 53.4	54.3	152 40.2	04.1	82 02.0	57.4
06		0 36.8	316 00.8	N14 05.3	257 54.1	N23 54.1	167 42.6	S 4 04.2	97 04.7	S21 57.4
07	T	15 39.3	331 00.6	06.0	272 54.7	54.0	182 45.0	04.2	112 07.3	57.4
08	H	30 41.7	346 00.5	06.8	287 55.4	53.9	197 47.4	04.3	127 10.0	57.4
09	U	45 44.2	1 00.3	. . 07.5	302 56.1	. . 53.7	212 49.7	. . 04.3	142 12.7	. . 57.4
10	R	60 46.7	16 00.2	08.2	317 56.8	53.6	227 52.1	04.4	157 15.3	57.4
11	S	75 49.1	31 00.1	09.0	332 57.4	53.5	242 54.5	04.4	172 18.0	57.4
12	D	90 51.6	45 59.9	N14 09.7	347 58.1	N23 53.3	257 56.9	S 4 04.5	187 20.6	S21 57.4
13	A	105 54.0	60 59.8	10.5	2 58.8	53.2	272 59.3	04.5	202 23.3	57.4
14	Y	120 56.5	75 59.6	11.2	17 59.5	53.1	288 01.7	04.6	217 26.0	57.4
15		135 59.0	90 59.5	. . 11.9	33 00.1	. . 52.9	303 04.0	. . 04.6	232 28.6	. . 57.4
16		151 01.4	105 59.3	12.7	48 00.8	52.8	318 06.4	04.7	247 31.3	57.4
17		166 03.9	120 59.2	13.4	63 01.5	52.7	333 08.8	04.7	262 33.9	57.4
18		181 06.4	135 59.0	N14 14.1	78 02.2	N23 52.5	348 11.2	S 4 04.8	277 36.6	S21 57.4
19		196 08.8	150 58.9	14.9	93 02.8	52.4	3 13.5	04.8	292 39.3	57.3
20		211 11.3	165 58.7	15.6	108 03.5	52.3	18 15.9	04.8	307 41.9	57.3
21		226 13.8	180 58.5	. . 16.4	123 04.2	. . 52.1	33 18.3	. . 04.9	322 44.6	. . 57.3
22		241 16.2	195 58.4	17.1	138 04.9	52.0	48 20.7	04.9	337 47.2	57.3
23		256 18.7	210 58.2	17.8	153 05.6	51.8	63 23.1	05.0	352 49.9	57.3
23 00		271 21.1	225 58.1	N14 18.6	168 06.2	N23 51.7	78 25.4	S 4 05.0	7 52.6	S21 57.3
01		286 23.6	240 57.9	19.3	183 06.9	51.6	93 27.8	05.1	22 55.2	57.3
02		301 26.1	255 57.8	20.0	198 07.6	51.4	108 30.2	05.1	37 57.9	57.3
03		316 28.5	270 57.6	. . 20.8	213 08.3	. . 51.3	123 32.6	. . 05.2	53 00.5	. . 57.3
04		331 31.0	285 57.4	21.5	228 08.9	51.1	138 34.9	05.2	68 03.2	57.3
05		346 33.5	300 57.3	22.3	243 09.6	51.0	153 37.3	05.3	83 05.9	57.3
06		1 35.9	315 57.1	N14 23.0	258 10.3	N23 50.9	168 39.7	S 4 05.3	98 08.5	S21 57.3
07		16 38.4	330 57.0	23.7	273 11.0	50.7	183 42.1	05.4	113 11.2	57.3
08		31 40.9	345 56.8	24.5	288 11.6	50.6	198 44.4	05.4	128 13.8	57.3
09	F	46 43.3	0 56.6	. . 25.2	303 12.3	. . 50.4	213 46.8	. . 05.5	143 16.5	. . 57.3
10	R	61 45.8	15 56.5	25.9	318 13.0	50.3	228 49.2	05.5	158 19.2	57.3
11	I	76 48.3	30 56.3	26.7	333 13.7	50.2	243 51.6	05.6	173 21.8	57.3
12	D	91 50.7	45 56.2	N14 27.4	348 14.4	N23 50.0	258 53.9	S 4 05.6	188 24.5	S21 57.3
13	A	106 53.2	60 56.0	28.1	3 15.0	49.9	273 56.3	05.7	203 27.1	57.3
14	Y	121 55.6	75 55.8	28.9	18 15.7	49.7	288 58.7	05.7	218 29.8	57.3
15		136 58.1	90 55.7	. . 29.6	33 16.4	. . 49.6	304 01.1	. . 05.8	233 32.5	. . 57.3
16		152 00.6	105 55.5	30.3	48 17.1	49.4	319 03.4	05.8	248 35.1	57.3
17		167 03.0	120 55.3	31.1	63 17.8	49.3	334 05.8	05.9	263 37.8	57.3
18		182 05.5	135 55.2	N14 31.8	78 18.4	N23 49.2	349 08.2	S 4 05.9	278 40.4	S21 57.3
19		197 08.0	150 55.0	32.5	93 19.1	49.0	4 10.6	06.0	293 43.1	57.2
20		212 10.4	165 54.8	33.3	108 19.8	48.9	19 12.9	06.0	308 45.8	57.2
21		227 12.9	180 54.7	. . 34.0	123 20.5	. . 48.7	34 15.3	. . 06.1	323 48.4	. . 57.2
22		242 15.4	195 54.5	34.7	138 21.1	48.6	49 17.7	06.1	338 51.1	57.2
23		257 17.8	210 54.3	35.5	153 21.8	48.4	64 20.0	06.2	353 53.7	57.2
Mer. Pass.		h m 5 57.6	v −0.1	d 0.7	v 0.7	d 0.1	v 2.4	d 0.0	v 2.7	d 0.0

STARS

Name	SHA ° ′	Dec ° ′
Acamar	315 16.6	S40 14.1
Achernar	335 25.1	S57 08.8
Acrux	173 06.0	S63 12.0
Adhara	255 10.8	S29 00.0
Aldebaran	290 46.6	N16 32.4
Alioth	166 18.3	N55 52.3
Alkaid	152 56.6	N49 13.9
Al Na'ir	27 40.2	S46 52.3
Alnilam	275 44.0	S 1 11.7
Alphard	217 53.6	S 8 44.2
Alphecca	126 08.4	N26 39.7
Alpheratz	357 40.7	N29 11.0
Altair	62 05.3	N 8 55.0
Ankaa	353 13.1	S42 12.5
Antares	112 22.6	S26 28.1
Arcturus	145 53.1	N19 05.8
Atria	107 21.4	S69 03.4
Avior	234 17.4	S59 34.2
Bellatrix	278 29.4	N 6 21.7
Betelgeuse	270 58.7	N 7 24.4
Canopus	263 55.5	S52 42.5
Capella	280 30.9	N46 00.6
Deneb	49 29.2	N45 20.5
Denebola	182 31.0	N14 28.6
Diphda	348 53.3	S17 53.4
Dubhe	193 48.7	N61 39.7
Elnath	278 09.6	N28 37.1
Eltanin	90 44.3	N51 29.4
Enif	33 44.3	N 9 57.3
Fomalhaut	15 20.9	S29 31.6
Gacrux	171 57.7	S57 12.8
Gienah	175 49.5	S17 38.4
Hadar	148 43.6	S60 27.5
Hamal	327 57.9	N23 32.4
Kaus Aust.	83 39.8	S34 22.3
Kochab	137 19.5	N74 05.4
Markab	13 35.5	N15 17.9
Menkar	314 12.5	N 4 09.3
Menkent	148 04.1	S36 27.3
Miaplacidus	221 39.6	S69 47.6
Mirfak	308 36.8	N49 55.0
Nunki	75 54.6	S26 16.3
Peacock	53 14.6	S56 40.4
Pollux	243 24.8	N27 58.9
Procyon	244 57.2	N 5 10.7
Rasalhague	96 03.6	N12 33.1
Regulus	207 40.8	N11 52.9
Rigel	281 09.8	S 8 11.1
Rigil Kent.	139 47.5	S60 54.4
Sabik	102 09.1	S15 44.6
Schedar	349 37.4	N56 37.6
Shaula	96 17.8	S37 06.8
Sirius	258 31.7	S16 44.6
Spica	158 28.3	S11 15.1
Suhail	222 50.7	S43 30.4
Vega	80 36.7	N38 48.2
Zuben'ubi	137 02.2	S16 06.7

	SHA ° ′	Mer. Pass. h m
Venus	315 39.6	8 56
Mars	257 28.0	12 48
Jupiter	167 06.3	18 47
Saturn	96 26.7	23 29

UT d h		SUN GHA ° ′	SUN Dec ° ′	MOON GHA ° ′	v ′	MOON Dec ° ′	d ′	HP ′
21 00		179 34.3	N23 26.1	224 30.9	7.2	N11 46.4	9.8	60.4
01		194 34.1	26.1	238 57.1	7.1	11 56.2	9.8	60.4
02		209 34.0	26.1	253 23.2	7.0	12 06.0	9.7	60.4
03		224 33.8	. . 26.1	267 49.2	7.0	12 15.7	9.6	60.5
04		239 33.7	26.1	282 15.2	6.9	12 25.3	9.6	60.5
05		254 33.6	26.1	296 41.1	6.8	12 34.9	9.5	60.5
06		269 33.4	N23 26.1	311 06.9	6.7	N12 44.4	9.4	60.5
07	W	284 33.3	26.1	325 32.6	6.7	12 53.8	9.3	60.6
08	E	299 33.2	26.1	339 58.3	6.5	13 03.1	9.3	60.6
09	D	314 33.0	. . 26.1	354 23.8	6.5	13 12.4	9.1	60.6
10	N	329 32.9	26.1	8 49.3	6.4	13 21.5	9.1	60.6
11	E	344 32.7	26.1	23 14.7	6.3	13 30.6	9.0	60.7
12	S	359 32.6	N23 26.0	37 40.0	6.3	N13 39.6	9.0	60.7
13	D	14 32.5	26.0	52 05.3	6.2	13 48.6	8.8	60.7
14	A	29 32.3	26.0	66 30.5	6.1	13 57.4	8.7	60.7
15	Y	44 32.2	. . 26.0	80 55.6	6.0	14 06.1	8.7	60.7
16		59 32.1	26.0	95 20.6	5.9	14 14.8	8.6	60.8
17		74 31.9	26.0	109 45.5	5.9	14 23.4	8.5	60.8
18		89 31.8	N23 26.0	124 10.4	5.8	N14 31.9	8.3	60.8
19		104 31.7	26.0	138 35.2	5.7	14 40.2	8.3	60.8
20		119 31.5	26.0	152 59.9	5.6	14 48.5	8.2	60.9
21		134 31.4	. . 26.0	167 24.5	5.6	14 56.7	8.1	60.9
22		149 31.2	26.0	181 49.1	5.5	15 04.8	8.0	60.9
23		164 31.1	25.9	196 13.6	5.4	15 12.8	7.9	60.9
22 00		179 31.0	N23 25.9	210 38.0	5.3	N15 20.7	7.8	60.9
01		194 30.8	25.9	225 02.3	5.3	15 28.5	7.7	60.9
02		209 30.7	25.9	239 26.6	5.2	15 36.2	7.6	61.0
03		224 30.6	. . 25.9	253 50.8	5.1	15 43.8	7.5	61.0
04		239 30.4	25.9	268 14.9	5.1	15 51.3	7.3	61.0
05		254 30.3	25.8	282 39.0	5.0	15 58.6	7.3	61.0
06		269 30.2	N23 25.8	297 03.0	4.9	N16 05.9	7.2	61.0
07		284 30.0	25.8	311 26.9	4.9	16 13.1	7.0	61.0
08	T	299 29.9	25.8	325 50.8	4.7	16 20.1	6.9	61.1
09	H	314 29.7	. . 25.8	340 14.5	4.8	16 27.0	6.8	61.1
10	U	329 29.6	25.8	354 38.3	4.6	16 33.8	6.7	61.1
11	R	344 29.5	25.7	9 01.9	4.6	16 40.5	6.6	61.1
12	S	359 29.3	N23 25.7	23 25.5	4.6	N16 47.1	6.5	61.1
13	D	14 29.2	25.7	37 49.1	4.4	16 53.6	6.3	61.1
14	A	29 29.1	25.7	52 12.5	4.4	16 59.9	6.2	61.1
15	Y	44 28.9	. . 25.6	66 35.9	4.4	17 06.1	6.1	61.2
16		59 28.8	25.6	80 59.3	4.3	17 12.2	6.0	61.2
17		74 28.7	25.6	95 22.6	4.2	17 18.2	5.8	61.2
18		89 28.5	N23 25.6	109 45.8	4.2	N17 24.0	5.8	61.2
19		104 28.4	25.5	124 09.0	4.2	17 29.8	5.6	61.2
20		119 28.2	25.5	138 32.2	4.0	17 35.4	5.4	61.2
21		134 28.1	. . 25.5	152 55.2	4.1	17 40.8	5.4	61.2
22		149 28.0	25.4	167 18.3	3.9	17 46.2	5.2	61.2
23		164 27.8	25.4	181 41.2	4.0	17 51.4	5.1	61.2
23 00		179 27.7	N23 25.4	196 04.2	3.9	N17 56.5	4.9	61.2
01		194 27.6	25.4	210 27.1	3.8	18 01.4	4.8	61.2
02		209 27.4	25.3	224 49.9	3.8	18 06.2	4.7	61.2
03		224 27.3	. . 25.3	239 12.7	3.7	18 10.9	4.6	61.2
04		239 27.2	25.3	253 35.4	3.8	18 15.5	4.4	61.2
05		254 27.0	25.2	267 58.2	3.6	18 19.9	4.3	61.3
06		269 26.9	N23 25.2	282 20.8	3.7	N18 24.2	4.1	61.3
07		284 26.7	25.1	296 43.5	3.6	18 28.3	4.0	61.3
08		299 26.6	25.1	311 06.1	3.5	18 32.3	3.9	61.3
09	F	314 26.5	. . 25.1	325 28.6	3.6	18 36.2	3.7	61.3
10	R	329 26.3	25.0	339 51.2	3.5	18 39.9	3.6	61.3
11	I	344 26.2	25.0	354 13.7	3.5	18 43.5	3.4	61.3
12	D	359 26.1	N23 25.0	8 36.2	3.4	N18 46.9	3.3	61.3
13	A	14 25.9	24.9	22 58.6	3.4	18 50.2	3.2	61.3
14	Y	29 25.8	24.9	37 21.0	3.5	18 53.4	3.0	61.3
15		44 25.7	. . 24.8	51 43.5	3.3	18 56.4	2.8	61.3
16		59 25.5	24.8	66 05.8	3.4	18 59.2	2.8	61.3
17		74 25.4	24.7	80 28.2	3.3	19 02.0	2.6	61.3
18		89 25.3	N23 24.7	94 50.5	3.4	N19 04.6	2.4	61.2
19		104 25.1	24.7	109 12.9	3.3	19 07.0	2.3	61.2
20		119 25.0	24.6	123 35.2	3.3	19 09.3	2.1	61.2
21		134 24.8	. . 24.6	137 57.5	3.3	19 11.4	2.0	61.2
22		149 24.7	24.5	152 19.8	3.3	19 13.4	1.9	61.2
23		164 24.6	24.5	166 42.1	3.3	N19 15.3	1.7	61.2
		SD 15.8	*d* 0.0	SD	16.5	16.7		16.7

Lat. °	Twilight Naut. h m	Twilight Civil h m	Sunrise h m	Moonrise 21 h m	Moonrise 22 h m	Moonrise 23 h m	Moonrise 24 h m
N 72	□	□	□	00 25	{00 23 / 11 36}	□	□
N 70	□	□	□	00 45	00 45	00 49	01 09
68	□	□	□	01 00	01 10	01 27	02 04
66	□	□	□	01 13	01 29	01 54	02 37
64	////	////	01 31	01 23	01 44	02 15	03 01
62	////	////	02 10	01 33	01 57	02 32	03 21
60	////	00 50	02 36	01 40	02 08	02 46	03 37
N 58	////	01 41	02 57	01 47	02 18	02 58	03 50
56	////	02 11	03 13	01 53	02 26	03 08	04 02
54	00 45	02 33	03 28	01 59	02 34	03 18	04 12
52	01 33	02 51	03 40	02 04	02 41	03 26	04 21
50	02 01	03 06	03 51	02 09	02 47	03 33	04 29
45	02 46	03 36	04 14	02 18	03 00	03 49	04 46
N 40	03 17	03 59	04 32	02 27	03 11	04 02	05 01
35	03 40	04 17	04 47	02 34	03 21	04 14	05 13
30	03 59	04 32	05 00	02 40	03 29	04 23	05 23
20	04 28	04 57	05 22	02 51	03 43	04 40	05 41
N 10	04 51	05 18	05 41	03 01	03 56	04 55	05 57
0	05 10	05 36	05 58	03 10	04 08	05 09	06 12
S 10	05 27	05 53	06 16	03 19	04 20	05 23	06 27
20	05 43	06 10	06 34	03 29	04 33	05 38	06 43
30	05 59	06 29	06 56	03 40	04 48	05 56	07 01
35	06 08	06 40	07 08	03 47	04 56	06 06	07 12
40	06 18	06 52	07 22	03 54	05 06	06 17	07 24
45	06 28	07 05	07 39	04 03	05 18	06 31	07 39
S 50	06 40	07 21	08 00	04 14	05 32	06 48	07 56
52	06 45	07 29	08 10	04 19	05 39	06 55	08 05
54	06 51	07 37	08 21	04 24	05 46	07 04	08 14
56	06 57	07 46	08 34	04 30	05 54	07 14	08 25
58	07 04	07 56	08 48	04 37	06 04	07 25	08 37
S 60	07 11	08 08	09 06	04 45	06 14	07 38	08 50

Lat. °	Sunset h m	Twilight Civil h m	Twilight Naut. h m	Moonset 21 h m	Moonset 22 h m	Moonset 23 h m	Moonset 24 h m
N 72	□	□	□	19 18	22 00	□	□
N 70	□	□	□	18 46	20 47	22 39	23 42
68	□	□	□	18 22	20 10	21 45	22 49
66	□	□	□	18 04	19 44	21 11	22 16
64	22 32	////	////	17 49	19 24	20 47	21 52
62	21 54	////	////	17 37	19 07	20 28	21 32
60	21 28	23 14	////	17 26	18 54	20 12	21 17
N 58	21 07	22 23	////	17 17	18 42	19 59	21 03
56	20 51	21 53	////	17 10	18 32	19 47	20 52
54	20 36	21 31	23 18	17 03	18 23	19 37	20 42
52	20 24	21 13	22 31	16 56	18 15	19 28	20 33
50	20 13	20 58	22 03	16 51	18 08	19 20	20 24
45	19 51	20 28	21 18	16 38	17 53	19 03	20 07
N 40	19 32	20 05	20 47	16 28	17 40	18 49	19 53
35	19 17	19 47	20 24	16 20	17 29	18 37	19 41
30	19 04	19 32	20 05	16 12	17 20	18 27	19 31
20	18 42	19 07	19 36	15 59	17 04	18 09	19 12
N 10	18 23	18 46	19 13	15 48	16 50	17 54	18 57
0	18 06	18 28	18 54	15 37	16 37	17 39	18 42
S 10	17 48	18 11	18 37	15 26	16 24	17 24	18 27
20	17 30	17 54	18 21	15 15	16 10	17 09	18 11
30	17 08	17 35	18 05	15 02	15 54	16 51	17 53
35	16 56	17 24	17 56	14 55	15 44	16 40	17 42
40	16 42	17 12	17 47	14 46	15 34	16 29	17 30
45	16 25	16 59	17 36	14 36	15 22	16 15	17 15
S 50	16 04	16 43	17 24	14 25	15 07	15 57	16 58
52	15 54	16 35	17 19	14 19	15 00	15 49	16 49
54	15 43	16 27	17 13	14 13	14 52	15 40	16 40
56	15 31	16 18	17 07	14 06	14 43	15 30	16 30
58	15 16	16 08	17 00	13 59	14 33	15 19	16 18
S 60	14 58	15 56	16 53	13 50	14 22	15 06	16 04

Day	SUN Eqn. of Time 00^h	SUN Eqn. of Time 12^h	SUN Mer. Pass.	MOON Mer. Pass. Upper	MOON Mer. Pass. Lower	MOON Age	MOON Phase
d	m s	m s	h m	h m	h m	d	%
21	01 43	01 49	12 02	09 23	21 52	27	10
22	01 56	02 02	12 02	10 22	22 53	28	4
23	02 09	02 15	12 02	11 24	23 56	29	1

UT		ARIES	VENUS −4·2		MARS +1·7		JUPITER −2·1		SATURN +0·0	
	d h	GHA ° ′	GHA ° ′	Dec ° ′	GHA ° ′	Dec ° ′	GHA ° ′	Dec ° ′	GHA ° ′	Dec ° ′
SATURDAY	24 00	272 20.3	225 54.2	N14 36.2	168 22.5	N23 48.3	79 22.4	S 4 06.2	8 56.4	S21 57.2
	01	287 22.8	240 54.0	36.9	183 23.2	48.1	94 24.8	06.3	23 59.1	57.2
	02	302 25.2	255 53.8	37.6	198 23.9	48.0	109 27.1	06.3	39 01.7	57.2
	03	317 27.7	270 53.6	. . 38.4	213 24.5	. . 47.8	124 29.5	. . 06.4	54 04.4	. . 57.2
	04	332 30.1	285 53.5	39.1	228 25.2	47.7	139 31.9	06.4	69 07.0	57.2
	05	347 32.6	300 53.3	39.8	243 25.9	47.5	154 34.3	06.5	84 09.7	57.2
	06	2 35.1	315 53.1	N14 40.6	258 26.6	N23 47.4	169 36.6	S 4 06.5	99 12.4	S21 57.2
	07	17 37.5	330 52.9	41.3	273 27.3	47.3	184 39.0	06.6	114 15.0	57.2
	08	32 40.0	345 52.8	42.0	288 27.9	47.1	199 41.4	06.6	129 17.7	57.2
	09	47 42.5	0 52.6	. . 42.7	303 28.6	. . 47.0	214 43.7	. . 06.7	144 20.3	. . 57.2
	10	62 44.9	15 52.4	43.5	318 29.3	46.8	229 46.1	06.8	159 23.0	57.2
	11	77 47.4	30 52.2	44.2	333 30.0	46.7	244 48.5	06.8	174 25.7	57.2
	12	92 49.9	45 52.1	N14 44.9	348 30.7	N23 46.5	259 50.8	S 4 06.9	189 28.3	S21 57.2
	13	107 52.3	60 51.9	45.7	3 31.3	46.4	274 53.2	06.9	204 31.0	57.2
	14	122 54.8	75 51.7	46.4	18 32.0	46.2	289 55.6	07.0	219 33.6	57.2
	15	137 57.3	90 51.5	. . 47.1	33 32.7	. . 46.1	304 57.9	. . 07.0	234 36.3	. . 57.2
	16	152 59.7	105 51.3	47.8	48 33.4	45.9	320 00.3	07.1	249 38.9	57.2
	17	168 02.2	120 51.2	48.6	63 34.1	45.7	335 02.7	07.1	264 41.6	57.2
	18	183 04.6	135 51.0	N14 49.3	78 34.8	N23 45.6	350 05.0	S 4 07.2	279 44.3	S21 57.2
	19	198 07.1	150 50.8	50.0	93 35.4	45.4	5 07.4	07.2	294 46.9	57.1
	20	213 09.6	165 50.6	50.7	108 36.1	45.3	20 09.8	07.3	309 49.6	57.1
	21	228 12.0	180 50.4	. . 51.5	123 36.8	. . 45.1	35 12.1	. . 07.3	324 52.2	. . 57.1
	22	243 14.5	195 50.2	52.2	138 37.5	45.0	50 14.5	07.4	339 54.9	57.1
	23	258 17.0	210 50.1	52.9	153 38.2	44.8	65 16.9	07.4	354 57.6	57.1
SUNDAY	25 00	273 19.4	225 49.9	N14 53.6	168 38.8	N23 44.7	80 19.2	S 4 07.5	10 00.2	S21 57.1
	01	288 21.9	240 49.7	54.4	183 39.5	44.5	95 21.6	07.5	25 02.9	57.1
	02	303 24.4	255 49.5	55.1	198 40.2	44.4	110 23.9	07.6	40 05.5	57.1
	03	318 26.8	270 49.3	. . 55.8	213 40.9	. . 44.2	125 26.3	. . 07.7	55 08.2	. . 57.1
	04	333 29.3	285 49.1	56.5	228 41.6	44.1	140 28.7	07.7	70 10.9	57.1
	05	348 31.8	300 48.9	57.2	243 42.3	43.9	155 31.0	07.8	85 13.5	57.1
	06	3 34.2	315 48.7	N14 58.0	258 42.9	N23 43.7	170 33.4	S 4 07.8	100 16.2	S21 57.1
	07	18 36.7	330 48.5	58.7	273 43.6	43.6	185 35.8	07.9	115 18.8	57.1
	08	33 39.1	345 48.4	14 59.4	288 44.3	43.4	200 38.1	07.9	130 21.5	57.1
	09	48 41.6	0 48.2	15 00.1	303 45.0	. . 43.3	215 40.5	. . 08.0	145 24.1	. . 57.1
	10	63 44.1	15 48.0	00.9	318 45.7	43.1	230 42.8	08.0	160 26.8	57.1
	11	78 46.5	30 47.8	01.6	333 46.4	43.0	245 45.2	08.1	175 29.5	57.1
	12	93 49.0	45 47.6	N15 02.3	348 47.0	N23 42.8	260 47.6	S 4 08.1	190 32.1	S21 57.1
	13	108 51.5	60 47.4	03.0	3 47.7	42.6	275 49.9	08.2	205 34.8	57.1
	14	123 53.9	75 47.2	03.7	18 48.4	42.5	290 52.3	08.3	220 37.4	57.1
	15	138 56.4	90 47.0	. . 04.5	33 49.1	. . 42.3	305 54.6	. . 08.3	235 40.1	. . 57.1
	16	153 58.9	105 46.8	05.2	48 49.8	42.2	320 57.0	08.4	250 42.7	57.1
	17	169 01.3	120 46.6	05.9	63 50.5	42.0	335 59.4	08.4	265 45.4	57.1
	18	184 03.8	135 46.4	N15 06.6	78 51.1	N23 41.8	351 01.7	S 4 08.5	280 48.1	S21 57.1
	19	199 06.3	150 46.2	07.3	93 51.8	41.7	6 04.1	08.5	295 50.7	57.0
	20	214 08.7	165 46.0	08.0	108 52.5	41.5	21 06.4	08.6	310 53.4	57.0
	21	229 11.2	180 45.8	. . 08.8	123 53.2	. . 41.4	36 08.8	. . 08.7	325 56.0	. . 57.0
	22	244 13.6	195 45.6	09.5	138 53.9	41.2	51 11.2	08.7	340 58.7	57.0
	23	259 16.1	210 45.4	10.2	153 54.6	41.0	66 13.5	08.8	356 01.4	57.0
MONDAY	26 00	274 18.6	225 45.2	N15 10.9	168 55.3	N23 40.9	81 15.9	S 4 08.8	11 04.0	S21 57.0
	01	289 21.0	240 45.0	11.6	183 55.9	40.7	96 18.2	08.9	26 06.7	57.0
	02	304 23.5	255 44.8	12.3	198 56.6	40.6	111 20.6	08.9	41 09.3	57.0
	03	319 26.0	270 44.6	. . 13.1	213 57.3	. . 40.4	126 22.9	. . 09.0	56 12.0	. . 57.0
	04	334 28.4	285 44.4	13.8	228 58.0	40.2	141 25.3	09.0	71 14.6	57.0
	05	349 30.9	300 44.2	14.5	243 58.7	40.1	156 27.7	09.1	86 17.3	57.0
	06	4 33.4	315 44.0	N15 15.2	258 59.4	N23 39.9	171 30.0	S 4 09.2	101 20.0	S21 57.0
	07	19 35.8	330 43.8	15.9	274 00.1	39.7	186 32.4	09.2	116 22.6	57.0
	08	34 38.3	345 43.6	16.6	289 00.7	39.6	201 34.7	09.3	131 25.3	57.0
	09	49 40.8	0 43.4	. . 17.3	304 01.4	. . 39.4	216 37.1	. . 09.3	146 27.9	. . 57.0
	10	64 43.2	15 43.2	18.0	319 02.1	39.2	231 39.4	09.4	161 30.6	57.0
	11	79 45.7	30 43.0	18.8	334 02.8	39.1	246 41.8	09.4	176 33.2	57.0
	12	94 48.1	45 42.8	N15 19.5	349 03.5	N23 38.9	261 44.1	S 4 09.5	191 35.9	S21 57.0
	13	109 50.6	60 42.6	20.2	4 04.2	38.7	276 46.5	09.6	206 38.6	57.0
	14	124 53.1	75 42.3	20.9	19 04.9	38.6	291 48.9	09.6	221 41.2	57.0
	15	139 55.5	90 42.1	. . 21.6	34 05.5	. . 38.4	306 51.2	. . 09.7	236 43.9	. . 57.0
	16	154 58.0	105 41.9	22.3	49 06.2	38.2	321 53.6	09.7	251 46.5	57.0
	17	170 00.5	120 41.7	23.0	64 06.9	38.1	336 55.9	09.8	266 49.2	57.0
	18	185 02.9	135 41.5	N15 23.7	79 07.6	N23 37.9	351 58.3	S 4 09.9	281 51.8	S21 57.0
	19	200 05.4	150 41.3	24.4	94 08.3	37.7	7 00.6	09.9	296 54.5	56.9
	20	215 07.9	165 41.1	25.2	109 09.0	37.6	22 03.0	10.0	311 57.2	56.9
	21	230 10.3	180 40.9	. . 25.9	124 09.7	. . 37.4	37 05.3	. . 10.0	326 59.8	. . 56.9
	22	245 12.8	195 40.7	26.6	139 10.4	37.2	52 07.7	10.1	342 02.5	56.9
	23	260 15.2	210 40.4	27.3	154 11.0	37.1	67 10.0	10.2	357 05.1	56.9
	Mer. Pass.	h m 5 45.8	*v* −0.2	*d* 0.7	*v* 0.7	*d* 0.2	*v* 2.4	*d* 0.1	*v* 2.7	*d* 0.0

STARS		
Name	SHA ° ′	Dec ° ′
Acamar	315 16.6	S40 14.1
Achernar	335 25.1	S57 08.7
Acrux	173 06.0	S63 12.0
Adhara	255 10.8	S29 00.0
Aldebaran	290 46.6	N16 32.4
Alioth	166 18.3	N55 52.3
Alkaid	152 56.6	N49 13.9
Al Na'ir	27 40.1	S46 52.3
Alnilam	275 44.0	S 1 11.7
Alphard	217 53.6	S 8 44.2
Alphecca	126 08.4	N26 39.7
Alpheratz	357 40.6	N29 11.0
Altair	62 05.3	N 8 55.0
Ankaa	353 13.1	S42 12.5
Antares	112 22.6	S26 28.1
Arcturus	145 53.1	N19 05.8
Atria	107 21.3	S69 03.4
Avior	234 17.4	S59 34.2
Bellatrix	278 29.4	N 6 21.7
Betelgeuse	270 58.7	N 7 24.4
Canopus	263 55.5	S52 42.5
Capella	280 30.9	N46 00.6
Deneb	49 29.2	N45 20.5
Denebola	182 31.0	N14 28.6
Diphda	348 53.2	S17 53.4
Dubhe	193 48.7	N61 39.7
Elnath	278 09.6	N28 37.1
Eltanin	90 44.3	N51 29.4
Enif	33 44.2	N 9 57.3
Fomalhaut	15 20.9	S29 31.6
Gacrux	171 57.7	S57 12.8
Gienah	175 49.5	S17 38.4
Hadar	148 43.6	S60 27.5
Hamal	327 57.8	N23 32.4
Kaus Aust.	83 39.8	S34 22.3
Kochab	137 19.5	N74 05.4
Markab	13 35.5	N15 17.9
Menkar	314 12.4	N 4 09.3
Menkent	148 04.1	S36 27.4
Miaplacidus	221 39.7	S69 47.6
Mirfak	308 36.8	N49 55.0
Nunki	75 54.6	S26 16.3
Peacock	53 14.5	S56 40.4
Pollux	243 24.8	N27 58.9
Procyon	244 57.2	N 5 10.7
Rasalhague	96 03.6	N12 33.1
Regulus	207 40.8	N11 52.9
Rigel	281 09.8	S 8 11.1
Rigil Kent.	139 47.5	S60 54.5
Sabik	102 09.1	S15 44.6
Schedar	349 37.4	N56 37.6
Shaula	96 17.8	S37 06.8
Sirius	258 31.7	S16 44.6
Spica	158 28.3	S11 15.1
Suhail	222 50.7	S43 30.4
Vega	80 36.7	N38 48.2
Zuben'ubi	137 02.2	S16 06.7

	SHA ° ′	Mer. Pass. h m
Venus	312 30.4	8 57
Mars	255 19.4	12 45
Jupiter	166 59.8	18 36
Saturn	96 40.8	23 16

	UT	SUN GHA	SUN Dec	MOON GHA	v	MOON Dec	d	HP
	d h	° ′	° ′	° ′	′	° ′	′	′
	24 00	179 24.4	N23 24.4	181 04.4	3.2	N19 17.0	1.6	61.2
	01	194 24.3	24.4	195 26.6	3.3	19 18.6	1.4	61.2
	02	209 24.2	24.3	209 48.9	3.3	19 20.0	1.3	61.2
	03	224 24.0	. . 24.3	224 11.2	3.3	19 21.3	1.1	61.2
	04	239 23.9	24.2	238 33.5	3.3	19 22.4	1.0	61.2
	05	254 23.8	24.2	252 55.8	3.3	19 23.4	0.8	61.2
	06	269 23.6	N23 24.1	267 18.1	3.3	N19 24.2	0.7	61.2
	07	284 23.5	24.1	281 40.4	3.3	19 24.9	0.5	61.1
S	08	299 23.4	24.0	296 02.7	3.3	19 25.4	0.4	61.1
A	09	314 23.2	. . 24.0	310 25.0	3.3	19 25.8	0.2	61.1
T	10	329 23.1	23.9	324 47.3	3.4	19 26.0	0.1	61.1
U	11	344 23.0	23.9	339 09.7	3.3	19 26.1	0.0	61.1
R	12	359 22.8	N23 23.8	353 32.0	3.4	N19 26.1	0.2	61.1
D	13	14 22.7	23.7	7 54.4	3.4	19 25.9	0.3	61.1
A	14	29 22.6	23.7	22 16.8	3.5	19 25.6	0.5	61.1
Y	15	44 22.4	. . 23.6	36 39.3	3.4	19 25.1	0.7	61.0
	16	59 22.3	23.6	51 01.7	3.5	19 24.4	0.8	61.0
	17	74 22.2	23.5	65 24.2	3.5	19 23.6	0.9	61.0
	18	89 22.0	N23 23.4	79 46.7	3.6	N19 22.7	1.0	61.0
	19	104 21.9	23.4	94 09.3	3.5	19 21.7	1.3	61.0
	20	119 21.7	23.3	108 31.8	3.7	19 20.4	1.3	61.0
	21	134 21.6	. . 23.3	122 54.5	3.6	19 19.1	1.5	60.9
	22	149 21.5	23.2	137 17.1	3.7	19 17.6	1.6	60.9
	23	164 21.3	23.1	151 39.8	3.7	19 16.0	1.8	60.9
	25 00	179 21.2	N23 23.1	166 02.5	3.8	N19 14.2	2.0	60.9
	01	194 21.1	23.0	180 25.3	3.8	19 12.2	2.0	60.9
	02	209 20.9	22.9	194 48.1	3.9	19 10.2	2.2	60.8
	03	224 20.8	. . 22.9	209 11.0	3.9	19 08.0	2.4	60.8
	04	239 20.7	22.8	223 33.9	4.0	19 05.6	2.4	60.8
	05	254 20.5	22.7	237 56.9	4.0	19 03.2	2.7	60.8
	06	269 20.4	N23 22.7	252 19.9	4.0	N19 00.5	2.7	60.7
	07	284 20.3	22.6	266 42.9	4.2	18 57.8	2.9	60.7
	08	299 20.1	22.5	281 06.1	4.1	18 54.9	3.0	60.7
S	09	314 20.0	. . 22.4	295 29.2	4.3	18 51.9	3.2	60.7
U	10	329 19.9	22.4	309 52.5	4.3	18 48.7	3.3	60.7
N	11	344 19.7	22.3	324 15.8	4.3	18 45.4	3.4	60.6
D	12	359 19.6	N23 22.2	338 39.1	4.4	N18 42.0	3.6	60.6
A	13	14 19.5	22.1	353 02.5	4.5	18 38.4	3.7	60.6
Y	14	29 19.3	22.1	7 26.0	4.5	18 34.7	3.8	60.6
	15	44 19.2	. . 22.0	21 49.5	4.6	18 30.9	3.9	60.5
	16	59 19.1	21.9	36 13.1	4.7	18 27.0	4.1	60.5
	17	74 18.9	21.8	50 36.8	4.7	18 22.9	4.2	60.5
	18	89 18.8	N23 21.8	65 00.5	4.8	N18 18.7	4.3	60.4
	19	104 18.7	21.7	79 24.3	4.9	18 14.4	4.5	60.4
	20	119 18.5	21.6	93 48.2	5.0	18 09.9	4.5	60.4
	21	134 18.4	. . 21.5	108 12.2	5.0	18 05.4	4.7	60.4
	22	149 18.3	21.4	122 36.2	5.1	18 00.7	4.9	60.3
	23	164 18.1	21.4	137 00.3	5.2	17 55.8	4.9	60.3
	26 00	179 18.0	N23 21.3	151 24.5	5.2	N17 50.9	5.0	60.3
	01	194 17.9	21.2	165 48.7	5.4	17 45.9	5.2	60.2
	02	209 17.7	21.1	180 13.1	5.4	17 40.7	5.3	60.2
	03	224 17.6	. . 21.0	194 37.5	5.4	17 35.4	5.4	60.2
	04	239 17.5	20.9	209 01.9	5.6	17 30.0	5.5	60.1
	05	254 17.4	20.9	223 26.5	5.7	17 24.5	5.7	60.1
	06	269 17.2	N23 20.8	237 51.2	5.7	N17 18.8	5.7	60.1
	07	284 17.1	20.7	252 15.9	5.8	17 13.1	5.8	60.0
	08	299 17.0	20.6	266 40.7	5.9	17 07.3	6.0	60.0
M	09	314 16.8	. . 20.5	281 05.6	6.0	17 01.3	6.1	60.0
O	10	329 16.7	20.4	295 30.6	6.0	16 55.2	6.1	59.9
N	11	344 16.6	20.3	309 55.6	6.2	16 49.1	6.3	59.9
D	12	359 16.4	N23 20.2	324 20.8	6.2	N16 42.8	6.4	59.9
A	13	14 16.3	20.1	338 46.0	6.3	16 36.4	6.5	59.8
Y	14	29 16.2	20.1	353 11.3	6.5	16 29.9	6.6	59.8
	15	44 16.0	. . 20.0	7 36.8	6.4	16 23.3	6.6	59.8
	16	59 15.9	19.9	22 02.2	6.6	16 16.7	6.8	59.7
	17	74 15.8	19.8	36 27.8	6.7	16 09.9	6.9	59.7
	18	89 15.6	N23 19.7	50 53.5	6.8	N16 03.0	7.0	59.7
	19	104 15.5	19.6	65 19.3	6.8	15 56.0	7.0	59.6
	20	119 15.4	19.5	79 45.1	7.0	15 49.0	7.2	59.6
	21	134 15.2	. . 19.4	94 11.1	7.0	15 41.8	7.3	59.6
	22	149 15.1	19.3	108 37.1	7.1	15 34.5	7.3	59.5
	23	164 15.0	19.2	123 03.2	7.2	N15 27.2	7.4	59.5
		SD 15.8	*d* 0.1	SD	16.6		16.5	16.3

Lat.	Twilight Naut.	Twilight Civil	Sunrise	Moonrise 24	Moonrise 25	Moonrise 26	Moonrise 27
°	h m	h m	h m	h m	h m	h m	h m
N 72	□	□	□	□	□	03 02	05 32
N 70	□	□	□	01 09	02 18	04 08	06 04
68	□	□	□	02 04	03 11	04 45	06 27
66	□	□	□	02 37	03 44	05 10	06 45
64	////	////	01 33	03 01	04 08	05 30	07 00
62	////	////	02 11	03 21	04 27	05 46	07 12
60	////	00 52	02 37	03 37	04 42	05 59	07 22
N 58	////	01 42	02 58	03 50	04 55	06 11	07 31
56	////	02 12	03 15	04 02	05 07	06 21	07 39
54	00 48	02 34	03 29	04 12	05 17	06 30	07 46
52	01 34	02 52	03 41	04 21	05 26	06 38	07 52
50	02 02	03 07	03 52	04 29	05 34	06 45	07 58
45	02 47	03 37	04 14	04 46	05 51	07 00	08 10
N 40	03 18	04 00	04 32	05 01	06 05	07 12	08 20
35	03 41	04 18	04 47	05 13	06 16	07 23	08 29
30	04 00	04 33	05 00	05 23	06 27	07 32	08 36
20	04 29	04 58	05 23	05 41	06 45	07 48	08 49
N 10	04 51	05 18	05 41	05 57	07 00	08 02	09 00
0	05 10	05 36	05 59	06 12	07 14	08 15	09 11
S 10	05 27	05 54	06 16	06 27	07 29	08 27	09 22
20	05 43	06 11	06 35	06 43	07 44	08 41	09 33
30	06 00	06 30	06 56	07 01	08 02	08 57	09 46
35	06 09	06 40	07 08	07 12	08 13	09 06	09 53
40	06 18	06 52	07 23	07 24	08 24	09 17	10 01
45	06 28	07 06	07 39	07 39	08 38	09 29	10 11
S 50	06 40	07 22	08 00	07 56	08 55	09 44	10 23
52	06 45	07 29	08 10	08 05	09 03	09 51	10 28
54	06 51	07 37	08 21	08 14	09 12	09 58	10 34
56	06 57	07 46	08 34	08 25	09 22	10 07	10 41
58	07 04	07 57	08 48	08 37	09 33	10 16	10 49
S 60	07 11	08 08	09 06	08 50	09 46	10 27	10 57

Lat.	Sunset	Twilight Civil	Twilight Naut.	Moonset 24	Moonset 25	Moonset 26	Moonset 27
°	h m	h m	h m	h m	h m	h m	h m
N 72	□	□	□	□	□	01 06	00 36
N 70	□	□	□	23 42	23 59	24 03	00 03
68	□	□	□	22 49	23 22	23 38	23 47
66	□	□	□	22 16	22 56	23 20	23 34
64	22 31	////	////	21 52	22 36	23 04	23 24
62	21 54	////	////	21 32	22 19	22 51	23 14
60	21 28	23 12	////	21 17	22 05	22 40	23 06
N 58	21 07	22 23	////	21 03	21 53	22 31	22 59
56	20 51	21 53	////	20 52	21 43	22 22	22 53
54	20 36	21 31	23 16	20 42	21 34	22 15	22 48
52	20 24	21 13	22 31	20 33	21 26	22 08	22 43
50	20 13	20 58	22 03	20 24	21 18	22 02	22 38
45	19 51	20 28	21 18	20 07	21 02	21 49	22 28
N 40	19 33	20 06	20 47	19 53	20 50	21 38	22 20
35	19 18	19 48	20 24	19 41	20 38	21 29	22 13
30	19 05	19 32	20 06	19 31	20 29	21 21	22 06
20	18 43	19 07	19 37	19 12	20 12	21 06	21 55
N 10	18 24	18 47	19 14	18 57	19 57	20 54	21 46
0	18 06	18 29	18 55	18 42	19 43	20 42	21 37
S 10	17 49	18 12	18 38	18 27	19 30	20 30	21 27
20	17 30	17 54	18 22	18 11	19 15	20 17	21 18
30	17 09	17 36	18 06	17 53	18 58	20 03	21 06
35	16 57	17 25	17 57	17 42	18 48	19 54	21 00
40	16 43	17 13	17 47	17 30	18 36	19 44	20 52
45	16 26	17 00	17 37	17 15	18 23	19 33	20 43
S 50	16 05	16 44	17 25	16 58	18 06	19 19	20 33
52	15 55	16 36	17 20	16 49	17 58	19 12	20 28
54	15 44	16 28	17 14	16 40	17 50	19 05	20 22
56	15 32	16 19	17 08	16 30	17 40	18 57	20 16
58	15 17	16 09	17 02	16 18	17 29	18 48	20 09
S 60	15 00	15 57	16 54	16 04	17 16	18 37	20 02

Day	SUN Eqn. of Time 00^h	SUN Eqn. of Time 12^h	SUN Mer. Pass.	MOON Mer. Pass. Upper	MOON Mer. Pass. Lower	MOON Age	MOON Phase
d	m s	m s	h m	h m	h m	d	%
24	02 22	02 28	12 02	12 27	24 58	00	0
25	02 35	02 41	12 03	13 29	00 58	01	3
26	02 48	02 54	12 03	14 28	01 59	02	8

Day	UT d h	ARIES GHA	VENUS −4·2 GHA	VENUS Dec	MARS +1·7 GHA	MARS Dec	JUPITER −2·1 GHA	JUPITER Dec	SATURN +0·1 GHA	SATURN Dec
		° ′	° ′	° ′	° ′	° ′	° ′	° ′	° ′	° ′
	27 00	275 17.7	225 40.2	N15 28.0	169 11.7	N23 36.9	82 12.4	S 4 10.2	12 07.8	S21 56.9
	01	290 20.2	240 40.0	28.7	184 12.4	36.7	97 14.7	10.3	27 10.4	56.9
	02	305 22.6	255 39.8	29.4	199 13.1	36.6	112 17.1	10.3	42 13.1	56.9
	03	320 25.1	270 39.6	. . 30.1	214 13.8	. . 36.4	127 19.4	. . 10.4	57 15.7	. . 56.9
	04	335 27.6	285 39.4	30.8	229 14.5	36.2	142 21.8	10.4	72 18.4	56.9
	05	350 30.0	300 39.1	31.5	244 15.2	36.0	157 24.1	10.5	87 21.1	56.9
	06	5 32.5	315 38.9	N15 32.2	259 15.9	N23 35.9	172 26.5	S 4 10.6	102 23.7	S21 56.9
	07	20 35.0	330 38.7	32.9	274 16.6	35.7	187 28.8	10.6	117 26.4	56.9
TUESDAY	08	35 37.4	345 38.5	33.6	289 17.2	35.5	202 31.2	10.7	132 29.0	56.9
	09	50 39.9	0 38.3	. . 34.3	304 17.9	. . 35.3	217 33.5	. . 10.7	147 31.7	. . 56.9
	10	65 42.4	15 38.0	35.0	319 18.6	35.2	232 35.9	10.8	162 34.3	56.9
	11	80 44.8	30 37.8	35.7	334 19.3	35.0	247 38.2	10.9	177 37.0	56.9
	12	95 47.3	45 37.6	N15 36.5	349 20.0	N23 34.8	262 40.6	S 4 10.9	192 39.7	S21 56.9
	13	110 49.7	60 37.4	37.2	4 20.7	34.7	277 42.9	11.0	207 42.3	56.9
	14	125 52.2	75 37.1	37.9	19 21.4	34.5	292 45.3	11.1	222 45.0	56.9
	15	140 54.7	90 36.9	. . 38.6	34 22.1	. . 34.3	307 47.6	. . 11.1	237 47.6	. . 56.9
	16	155 57.1	105 36.7	39.3	49 22.8	34.1	322 50.0	11.2	252 50.3	56.9
	17	170 59.6	120 36.5	40.0	64 23.5	34.0	337 52.3	11.2	267 52.9	56.9
	18	186 02.1	135 36.2	N15 40.7	79 24.1	N23 33.8	352 54.6	S 4 11.3	282 55.6	S21 56.9
	19	201 04.5	150 36.0	41.4	94 24.8	33.6	7 57.0	11.4	297 58.2	56.9
	20	216 07.0	165 35.8	42.1	109 25.5	33.4	22 59.3	11.4	313 00.9	56.8
	21	231 09.5	180 35.6	. . 42.8	124 26.2	. . 33.3	38 01.7	. . 11.5	328 03.6	. . 56.8
	22	246 11.9	195 35.3	43.5	139 26.9	33.1	53 04.0	11.5	343 06.2	56.8
	23	261 14.4	210 35.1	44.2	154 27.6	32.9	68 06.4	11.6	358 08.9	56.8
	28 00	276 16.9	225 34.9	N15 44.9	169 28.3	N23 32.7	83 08.7	S 4 11.7	13 11.5	S21 56.8
	01	291 19.3	240 34.6	45.6	184 29.0	32.5	98 11.1	11.7	28 14.2	56.8
	02	306 21.8	255 34.4	46.3	199 29.7	32.4	113 13.4	11.8	43 16.8	56.8
	03	321 24.2	270 34.2	. . 47.0	214 30.4	. . 32.2	128 15.7	. . 11.9	58 19.5	. . 56.8
	04	336 26.7	285 33.9	47.7	229 31.1	32.0	143 18.1	11.9	73 22.1	56.8
	05	351 29.2	300 33.7	48.4	244 31.7	31.8	158 20.4	12.0	88 24.8	56.8
	06	6 31.6	315 33.5	N15 49.0	259 32.4	N23 31.6	173 22.8	S 4 12.0	103 27.5	S21 56.8
WEDNESDAY	07	21 34.1	330 33.2	49.7	274 33.1	31.5	188 25.1	12.1	118 30.1	56.8
	08	36 36.6	345 33.0	50.4	289 33.8	31.3	203 27.5	12.2	133 32.8	56.8
	09	51 39.0	0 32.8	. . 51.1	304 34.5	. . 31.1	218 29.8	. . 12.2	148 35.4	. . 56.8
	10	66 41.5	15 32.5	51.8	319 35.2	30.9	233 32.1	12.3	163 38.1	56.8
	11	81 44.0	30 32.3	52.5	334 35.9	30.7	248 34.5	12.4	178 40.7	56.8
	12	96 46.4	45 32.1	N15 53.2	349 36.6	N23 30.6	263 36.8	S 4 12.4	193 43.4	S21 56.8
	13	111 48.9	60 31.8	53.9	4 37.3	30.4	278 39.2	12.5	208 46.0	56.8
	14	126 51.3	75 31.6	54.6	19 38.0	30.2	293 41.5	12.5	223 48.7	56.8
	15	141 53.8	90 31.3	. . 55.3	34 38.7	. . 30.0	308 43.8	. . 12.6	238 51.3	. . 56.8
	16	156 56.3	105 31.1	56.0	49 39.4	29.8	323 46.2	12.7	253 54.0	56.8
	17	171 58.7	120 30.9	56.7	64 40.1	29.7	338 48.5	12.7	268 56.7	56.8
	18	187 01.2	135 30.6	N15 57.4	79 40.8	N23 29.5	353 50.9	S 4 12.8	283 59.3	S21 56.8
	19	202 03.7	150 30.4	58.1	94 41.4	29.3	8 53.2	12.9	299 02.0	56.8
	20	217 06.1	165 30.1	58.8	109 42.1	29.1	23 55.5	12.9	314 04.6	56.8
	21	232 08.6	180 29.9	15 59.5	124 42.8	. . 28.9	38 57.9	. . 13.0	329 07.3	. . 56.8
	22	247 11.1	195 29.6	16 00.1	139 43.5	28.7	54 00.2	13.1	344 09.9	56.7
	23	262 13.5	210 29.4	00.8	154 44.2	28.5	69 02.6	13.1	359 12.6	56.7
	29 00	277 16.0	225 29.2	N16 01.5	169 44.9	N23 28.4	84 04.9	S 4 13.2	14 15.2	S21 56.7
	01	292 18.5	240 28.9	02.2	184 45.6	28.2	99 07.2	13.2	29 17.9	56.7
	02	307 20.9	255 28.7	02.9	199 46.3	28.0	114 09.6	13.3	44 20.5	56.7
	03	322 23.4	270 28.4	. . 03.6	214 47.0	. . 27.8	129 11.9	. . 13.4	59 23.2	. . 56.7
	04	337 25.8	285 28.2	04.3	229 47.7	27.6	144 14.3	13.4	74 25.8	56.7
	05	352 28.3	300 27.9	05.0	244 48.4	27.4	159 16.6	13.5	89 28.5	56.7
	06	7 30.8	315 27.7	N16 05.7	259 49.1	N23 27.2	174 18.9	S 4 13.6	104 31.2	S21 56.7
	07	22 33.2	330 27.4	06.3	274 49.8	27.1	189 21.3	13.6	119 33.8	56.7
THURSDAY	08	37 35.7	345 27.2	07.0	289 50.5	26.9	204 23.6	13.7	134 36.5	56.7
	09	52 38.2	0 26.9	. . 07.7	304 51.2	. . 26.7	219 25.9	. . 13.8	149 39.1	. . 56.7
	10	67 40.6	15 26.7	08.4	319 51.9	26.5	234 28.3	13.8	164 41.8	56.7
	11	82 43.1	30 26.4	09.1	334 52.6	26.3	249 30.6	13.9	179 44.4	56.7
	12	97 45.6	45 26.2	N16 09.8	349 53.3	N23 26.1	264 32.9	S 4 14.0	194 47.1	S21 56.7
	13	112 48.0	60 25.9	10.5	4 54.0	25.9	279 35.3	14.0	209 49.7	56.7
	14	127 50.5	75 25.7	11.1	19 54.7	25.7	294 37.6	14.1	224 52.4	56.7
	15	142 53.0	90 25.4	. . 11.8	34 55.3	. . 25.5	309 39.9	. . 14.2	239 55.0	. . 56.7
	16	157 55.4	105 25.2	12.5	49 56.0	25.4	324 42.3	14.2	254 57.7	56.7
	17	172 57.9	120 24.9	13.2	64 56.7	25.2	339 44.6	14.3	270 00.3	56.7
	18	188 00.3	135 24.6	N16 13.9	79 57.4	N23 25.0	354 46.9	S 4 14.4	285 03.0	S21 56.7
	19	203 02.8	150 24.4	14.6	94 58.1	24.8	9 49.3	14.4	300 05.6	56.7
	20	218 05.3	165 24.1	15.2	109 58.8	24.6	24 51.6	14.5	315 08.3	56.7
	21	233 07.7	180 23.9	. . 15.9	124 59.5	. . 24.4	39 53.9	. . 14.6	330 11.0	. . 56.7
	22	248 10.2	195 23.6	16.6	140 00.2	24.2	54 56.3	14.6	345 13.6	56.7
	23	263 12.7	210 23.4	17.3	155 00.9	24.0	69 58.6	14.7	0 16.3	56.6
	Mer. Pass.	h m 5 34.0	v −0.2	d 0.7	v 0.7	d 0.2	v 2.3	d 0.1	v 2.7	d 0.0

STARS Name	SHA ° ′	Dec ° ′
Acamar	315 16.6	S40 14.1
Achernar	335 25.0	S57 08.7
Acrux	173 06.1	S63 12.0
Adhara	255 10.8	S28 59.9
Aldebaran	290 46.6	N16 32.4
Alioth	166 18.3	N55 52.3
Alkaid	152 56.6	N49 13.9
Al Na'ir	27 40.1	S46 52.3
Alnilam	275 43.9	S 1 11.6
Alphard	217 53.7	S 8 44.2
Alphecca	126 08.4	N26 39.7
Alpheratz	357 40.6	N29 11.0
Altair	62 05.3	N 8 55.0
Ankaa	353 13.1	S42 12.5
Antares	112 22.6	S26 28.1
Arcturus	145 53.1	N19 05.8
Atria	107 21.4	S69 03.4
Avior	234 17.4	S59 34.2
Bellatrix	278 29.4	N 6 21.7
Betelgeuse	270 58.7	N 7 24.4
Canopus	263 55.5	S52 42.5
Capella	280 30.9	N46 00.6
Deneb	49 29.2	N45 20.6
Denebola	182 31.0	N14 28.6
Diphda	348 53.2	S17 53.4
Dubhe	193 48.8	N61 39.7
Elnath	278 09.5	N28 37.1
Eltanin	90 44.3	N51 29.4
Enif	33 44.2	N 9 57.4
Fomalhaut	15 20.9	S29 31.6
Gacrux	171 57.7	S57 12.9
Gienah	175 49.5	S17 38.4
Hadar	148 43.6	S60 27.5
Hamal	327 57.8	N23 32.4
Kaus Aust.	83 39.8	S34 22.3
Kochab	137 19.6	N74 05.4
Markab	13 35.5	N15 17.9
Menkar	314 12.4	N 4 09.3
Menkent	148 04.1	S36 27.4
Miaplacidus	221 39.7	S69 47.6
Mirfak	308 36.8	N49 55.0
Nunki	75 54.6	S26 16.3
Peacock	53 14.5	S56 40.4
Pollux	243 24.8	N27 58.9
Procyon	244 57.2	N 5 10.7
Rasalhague	96 03.6	N12 33.1
Regulus	207 40.8	N11 52.9
Rigel	281 09.8	S 8 11.1
Rigil Kent.	139 47.6	S60 54.5
Sabik	102 09.1	S15 44.6
Schedar	349 37.3	N56 37.6
Shaula	96 17.8	S37 06.8
Sirius	258 31.7	S16 44.6
Spica	158 28.3	S11 15.1
Suhail	222 50.7	S43 30.4
Vega	80 36.7	N38 48.2
Zuben'ubi	137 02.2	S16 06.7

	SHA ° ′	Mer. Pass. h m
Venus	309 18.0	8 58
Mars	253 11.4	12 42
Jupiter	166 51.9	18 25
Saturn	96 54.7	23 03

UT d h	SUN GHA ° ′	SUN Dec ° ′	MOON GHA ° ′	v ′	MOON Dec ° ′	d ′	HP ′
27 00 (TUESDAY)	179 14.9	N23 19.1	137 29.4	7.3	N15 19.8	7.5	59.5
01	194 14.7	19.0	151 55.7	7.4	15 12.3	7.6	59.4
02	209 14.6	18.9	166 22.1	7.5	15 04.7	7.7	59.4
03	224 14.5	. . 18.8	180 48.6	7.6	14 57.0	7.8	59.3
04	239 14.3	18.7	195 15.2	7.6	14 49.2	7.8	59.3
05	254 14.2	18.6	209 41.8	7.8	14 41.4	8.0	59.3
06	269 14.1	N23 18.5	224 08.6	7.9	N14 33.4	8.0	59.2
07	284 13.9	18.4	238 35.5	7.9	14 25.4	8.1	59.2
08	299 13.8	18.3	253 02.4	8.0	14 17.3	8.1	59.1
09	314 13.7	. . 18.2	267 29.4	8.1	14 09.2	8.3	59.1
10	329 13.5	18.1	281 56.5	8.3	14 00.9	8.3	59.1
11	344 13.4	17.9	296 23.8	8.3	13 52.6	8.4	59.0
12	359 13.3	N23 17.8	310 51.1	8.4	N13 44.2	8.4	59.0
13	14 13.2	17.7	325 18.5	8.4	13 35.8	8.6	59.0
14	29 13.0	17.6	339 45.9	8.6	13 27.2	8.5	58.9
15	44 12.9	. . 17.5	354 13.5	8.7	13 18.7	8.7	58.9
16	59 12.8	17.4	8 41.2	8.7	13 10.0	8.7	58.8
17	74 12.6	17.3	23 08.9	8.9	13 01.3	8.8	58.8
18	89 12.5	N23 17.2	37 36.8	8.9	N12 52.5	8.9	58.8
19	104 12.4	17.1	52 04.7	9.0	12 43.6	8.9	58.7
20	119 12.3	17.0	66 32.7	9.2	12 34.7	9.0	58.7
21	134 12.1	. . 16.8	81 00.9	9.2	12 25.7	9.0	58.6
22	149 12.0	16.7	95 29.1	9.2	12 16.7	9.1	58.6
23	164 11.9	16.6	109 57.3	9.4	12 07.6	9.1	58.6
28 00 (WEDNESDAY)	179 11.7	N23 16.5	124 25.7	9.5	N11 58.5	9.2	58.5
01	194 11.6	16.4	138 54.2	9.5	11 49.3	9.3	58.5
02	209 11.5	16.3	153 22.7	9.7	11 40.0	9.3	58.4
03	224 11.4	. . 16.1	167 51.4	9.7	11 30.7	9.4	58.4
04	239 11.2	16.0	182 20.1	9.8	11 21.3	9.4	58.4
05	254 11.1	15.9	196 48.9	9.9	11 11.9	9.4	58.3
06	269 11.0	N23 15.8	211 17.8	10.0	N11 02.5	9.5	58.3
07	284 10.8	15.7	225 46.8	10.0	10 53.0	9.6	58.2
08	299 10.7	15.5	240 15.8	10.2	10 43.4	9.6	58.2
09	314 10.6	. . 15.4	254 45.0	10.2	10 33.8	9.6	58.2
10	329 10.5	15.3	269 14.2	10.3	10 24.2	9.7	58.1
11	344 10.3	15.2	283 43.5	10.4	10 14.5	9.7	58.1
12	359 10.2	N23 15.0	298 12.9	10.5	N10 04.8	9.8	58.0
13	14 10.1	14.9	312 42.4	10.5	9 55.0	9.8	58.0
14	29 09.9	14.8	327 11.9	10.6	9 45.2	9.9	58.0
15	44 09.8	. . 14.7	341 41.5	10.7	9 35.3	9.8	57.9
16	59 09.7	14.5	356 11.2	10.8	9 25.5	10.0	57.9
17	74 09.6	14.4	10 41.0	10.9	9 15.5	9.9	57.8
18	89 09.4	N23 14.3	25 10.9	10.9	N 9 05.6	10.0	57.8
19	104 09.3	14.1	39 40.8	11.0	8 55.6	10.0	57.8
20	119 09.2	14.0	54 10.8	11.1	8 45.6	10.1	57.7
21	134 09.1	. . 13.9	68 40.9	11.2	8 35.5	10.1	57.7
22	149 08.9	13.7	83 11.1	11.2	8 25.4	10.1	57.6
23	164 08.8	13.6	97 41.3	11.3	8 15.3	10.1	57.6
29 00 (THURSDAY)	179 08.7	N23 13.5	112 11.6	11.4	N 8 05.2	10.2	57.6
01	194 08.6	13.3	126 42.0	11.5	7 55.0	10.2	57.5
02	209 08.4	13.2	141 12.5	11.5	7 44.8	10.2	57.5
03	224 08.3	. . 13.1	155 43.0	11.6	7 34.6	10.2	57.5
04	239 08.2	12.9	170 13.6	11.7	7 24.4	10.3	57.4
05	254 08.0	12.8	184 44.3	11.7	7 14.1	10.3	57.4
06	269 07.9	N23 12.7	199 15.0	11.8	N 7 03.8	10.3	57.3
07	284 07.8	12.5	213 45.8	11.9	6 53.5	10.3	57.3
08	299 07.7	12.4	228 16.7	11.9	6 43.2	10.4	57.3
09	314 07.5	. . 12.2	242 47.6	12.0	6 32.8	10.3	57.2
10	329 07.4	12.1	257 18.6	12.1	6 22.5	10.4	57.2
11	344 07.3	12.0	271 49.7	12.1	6 12.1	10.4	57.1
12	359 07.2	N23 11.8	286 20.8	12.2	N 6 01.7	10.4	57.1
13	14 07.0	11.7	300 52.0	12.3	5 51.3	10.5	57.1
14	29 06.9	11.5	315 23.3	12.3	5 40.8	10.4	57.0
15	44 06.8	. . 11.4	329 54.6	12.3	5 30.4	10.5	57.0
16	59 06.7	11.3	344 25.9	12.5	5 19.9	10.4	57.0
17	74 06.5	11.1	358 57.4	12.5	5 09.5	10.5	56.9
18	89 06.4	N23 11.0	13 28.9	12.5	N 4 59.0	10.5	56.9
19	104 06.3	10.8	28 00.4	12.6	4 48.5	10.5	56.8
20	119 06.2	10.7	42 32.0	12.7	4 38.0	10.5	56.8
21	134 06.0	. . 10.5	57 03.7	12.7	4 27.5	10.5	56.8
22	149 05.9	10.4	71 35.4	12.8	4 17.0	10.5	56.7
23	164 05.8	10.2	86 07.2	12.8	N 4 06.5	10.6	56.7
	SD 15.8	*d* 0.1	SD 16.1		15.8		15.6

Lat.	Twilight Naut. h m	Twilight Civil h m	Sunrise h m	Moonrise 27 h m	Moonrise 28 h m	Moonrise 29 h m	Moonrise 30 h m
N 72	▭	▭	▭	05 32	07 37	09 30	11 16
N 70	▭	▭	▭	06 04	07 55	09 39	11 18
68	▭	▭	▭	06 27	08 09	09 47	11 20
66	▭	▭	▭	06 45	08 21	09 54	11 22
64	////	////	01 37	07 00	08 31	09 59	11 24
62	////	////	02 14	07 12	08 39	10 04	11 25
60	////	00 57	02 39	07 22	08 46	10 08	11 26
N 58	////	01 45	03 00	07 31	08 52	10 11	11 27
56	////	02 14	03 16	07 39	08 58	10 14	11 28
54	00 52	02 36	03 30	07 46	09 03	10 17	11 29
52	01 37	02 54	03 43	07 52	09 07	10 20	11 30
50	02 04	03 09	03 53	07 58	09 11	10 22	11 30
45	02 49	03 38	04 16	08 10	09 20	10 27	11 32
N 40	03 19	04 01	04 34	08 20	09 27	10 31	11 33
35	03 42	04 19	04 49	08 29	09 33	10 35	11 34
30	04 01	04 34	05 01	08 36	09 38	10 38	11 35
20	04 30	04 59	05 23	08 49	09 48	10 44	11 37
N 10	04 52	05 19	05 42	09 00	09 56	10 48	11 38
0	05 11	05 37	06 00	09 11	10 04	10 53	11 40
S 10	05 28	05 54	06 17	09 22	10 11	10 58	11 41
20	05 44	06 11	06 35	09 33	10 20	11 02	11 42
30	06 00	06 30	06 56	09 46	10 29	11 08	11 44
35	06 09	06 41	07 09	09 53	10 34	11 11	11 45
40	06 18	06 52	07 23	10 01	10 40	11 15	11 46
45	06 28	07 06	07 39	10 11	10 47	11 19	11 47
S 50	06 40	07 22	08 00	10 23	10 56	11 24	11 49
52	06 45	07 29	08 10	10 28	11 00	11 26	11 50
54	06 51	07 37	08 21	10 34	11 04	11 28	11 50
56	06 57	07 46	08 33	10 41	11 08	11 31	11 51
58	07 04	07 56	08 48	10 49	11 14	11 34	11 52
S 60	07 11	08 08	09 05	10 57	11 19	11 38	11 53

Lat.	Sunset h m	Twilight Civil h m	Twilight Naut. h m	Moonset 27 h m	Moonset 28 h m	Moonset 29 h m	Moonset 30 h m
N 72	▭	▭	▭	00 36	00 23	00 13	{00 05 / 23 57}
N 70	▭	▭	▭	00 03	00 03	00 01	{00 00 / 23 57}
68	▭	▭	▭	23 47	23 52	23 55	23 58
66	▭	▭	▭	23 34	23 44	23 52	23 58
64	22 29	////	////	23 24	23 38	23 49	23 58
62	21 52	////	////	23 14	23 32	23 46	23 59
60	21 27	23 08	////	23 06	23 27	23 44	23 59
N 58	21 07	22 21	////	22 59	23 22	23 42	23 59
56	20 50	21 52	////	22 53	23 18	23 40	23 59
54	20 36	21 30	23 13	22 48	23 15	23 38	23 59
52	20 24	21 12	22 29	22 43	23 11	23 36	23 59
50	20 13	20 57	22 02	22 38	23 08	23 35	24 00
45	19 51	20 28	21 17	22 28	23 02	23 32	24 00
N 40	19 33	20 06	20 47	22 20	22 56	23 29	24 00
35	19 18	19 48	20 24	22 13	22 52	23 27	24 00
30	19 05	19 33	20 06	22 06	22 48	23 25	24 00
20	18 43	19 08	19 37	21 55	22 40	23 22	24 01
N 10	18 24	18 47	19 15	21 46	22 34	23 18	24 01
0	18 07	18 29	18 56	21 37	22 28	23 16	24 01
S 10	17 50	18 12	18 39	21 27	22 21	23 13	24 01
20	17 31	17 55	18 23	21 18	22 15	23 09	24 02
30	17 10	17 37	18 06	21 06	22 07	23 06	24 02
35	16 58	17 26	17 58	21 00	22 03	23 04	24 02
40	16 44	17 14	17 48	20 52	21 58	23 01	24 02
45	16 27	17 01	17 38	20 43	21 52	22 58	24 02
S 50	16 07	16 45	17 27	20 33	21 45	22 55	24 02
52	15 57	16 38	17 21	20 28	21 42	22 53	24 02
54	15 46	16 30	17 16	20 22	21 38	22 52	24 02
56	15 33	16 21	17 10	20 16	21 34	22 50	24 03
58	15 19	16 11	17 03	20 09	21 30	22 48	24 03
S 60	15 02	15 59	16 56	20 02	21 25	22 45	24 03

Day	SUN Eqn. of Time 00^h m s	SUN Eqn. of Time 12^h m s	SUN Mer. Pass. h m	MOON Mer. Pass. Upper h m	MOON Mer. Pass. Lower h m	MOON Age d	MOON Phase %
27	03 00	03 07	12 03	15 24	02 57	03	16
28	03 13	03 19	12 03	16 16	03 50	04	25
29	03 25	03 31	12 04	17 04	04 40	05	35

Day	UT d h	ARIES GHA ° ′	VENUS −4·2 GHA ° ′	VENUS Dec ° ′	MARS +1·7 GHA ° ′	MARS Dec ° ′	JUPITER −2·0 GHA ° ′	JUPITER Dec ° ′	SATURN +0·1 GHA ° ′	SATURN Dec ° ′
	30 00	278 15.1	225 23.1	N16 18.0	170 01.6	N23 23.8	85 00.9	S 4 14.8	15 18.9	S21 56.6
	01	293 17.6	240 22.8	18.6	185 02.3	23.6	100 03.3	14.8	30 21.6	56.6
	02	308 20.1	255 22.6	19.3	200 03.0	23.4	115 05.6	14.9	45 24.2	56.6
	03	323 22.5	270 22.3	20.0	215 03.7	23.2	130 07.9	15.0	60 26.9	56.6
	04	338 25.0	285 22.0	20.7	230 04.4	23.0	145 10.3	15.0	75 29.5	56.6
	05	353 27.4	300 21.8	21.3	245 05.1	22.9	160 12.6	15.1	90 32.2	56.6
	06	8 29.9	315 21.5	N16 22.0	260 05.8	N23 22.7	175 14.9	S 4 15.2	105 34.8	S21 56.6
	07	23 32.4	330 21.3	22.7	275 06.5	22.5	190 17.2	15.2	120 37.5	56.6
	08	38 34.8	345 21.0	23.4	290 07.2	22.3	205 19.6	15.3	135 40.1	56.6
FRIDAY	09	53 37.3	0 20.7	24.1	305 07.9	22.1	220 21.9	15.4	150 42.8	56.6
	10	68 39.8	15 20.5	24.7	320 08.6	21.9	235 24.2	15.4	165 45.4	56.6
	11	83 42.2	30 20.2	25.4	335 09.3	21.7	250 26.6	15.5	180 48.1	56.6
	12	98 44.7	45 19.9	N16 26.1	350 10.0	N23 21.5	265 28.9	S 4 15.6	195 50.7	S21 56.6
	13	113 47.2	60 19.7	26.8	5 10.7	21.3	280 31.2	15.6	210 53.4	56.6
	14	128 49.6	75 19.4	27.4	20 11.4	21.1	295 33.5	15.7	225 56.0	56.6
	15	143 52.1	90 19.1	28.1	35 12.1	20.9	310 35.9	15.8	240 58.7	56.6
	16	158 54.6	105 18.9	28.8	50 12.8	20.7	325 38.2	15.9	256 01.3	56.6
	17	173 57.0	120 18.6	29.4	65 13.5	20.5	340 40.5	15.9	271 04.0	56.6
	18	188 59.5	135 18.3	N16 30.1	80 14.2	N23 20.3	355 42.9	S 4 16.0	286 06.6	S21 56.6
	19	204 01.9	150 18.0	30.8	95 14.9	20.1	10 45.2	16.1	301 09.3	56.6
	20	219 04.4	165 17.8	31.5	110 15.6	19.9	25 47.5	16.1	316 11.9	56.6
	21	234 06.9	180 17.5	32.1	125 16.3	19.7	40 49.8	16.2	331 14.6	56.6
	22	249 09.3	195 17.2	32.8	140 17.0	19.5	55 52.2	16.3	346 17.2	56.6
	23	264 11.8	210 16.9	33.5	155 17.7	19.3	70 54.5	16.3	1 19.9	56.6
	1 00	279 14.3	225 16.7	N16 34.1	170 18.4	N23 19.1	85 56.8	S 4 16.4	16 22.6	S21 56.6
	01	294 16.7	240 16.4	34.8	185 19.1	18.9	100 59.1	16.5	31 25.2	56.6
	02	309 19.2	255 16.1	35.5	200 19.8	18.7	116 01.5	16.5	46 27.9	56.5
	03	324 21.7	270 15.8	36.1	215 20.5	18.5	131 03.8	16.6	61 30.5	56.5
	04	339 24.1	285 15.6	36.8	230 21.2	18.3	146 06.1	16.7	76 33.2	56.5
	05	354 26.6	300 15.3	37.5	245 21.9	18.1	161 08.4	16.8	91 35.8	56.5
	06	9 29.1	315 15.0	N16 38.2	260 22.6	N23 17.9	176 10.8	S 4 16.8	106 38.5	S21 56.5
	07	24 31.5	330 14.7	38.8	275 23.3	17.7	191 13.1	16.9	121 41.1	56.5
	08	39 34.0	345 14.5	39.5	290 24.0	17.5	206 15.4	17.0	136 43.8	56.5
SATURDAY	09	54 36.4	0 14.2	40.1	305 24.7	17.3	221 17.7	17.0	151 46.4	56.5
	10	69 38.9	15 13.9	40.8	320 25.4	17.1	236 20.0	17.1	166 49.1	56.5
	11	84 41.4	30 13.6	41.5	335 26.1	16.9	251 22.4	17.2	181 51.7	56.5
	12	99 43.8	45 13.3	N16 42.1	350 26.8	N23 16.7	266 24.7	S 4 17.3	196 54.4	S21 56.5
	13	114 46.3	60 13.1	42.8	5 27.5	16.5	281 27.0	17.3	211 57.0	56.5
	14	129 48.8	75 12.8	43.5	20 28.2	16.3	296 29.3	17.4	226 59.7	56.5
	15	144 51.2	90 12.5	44.1	35 28.9	16.1	311 31.7	17.5	242 02.3	56.5
	16	159 53.7	105 12.2	44.8	50 29.6	15.8	326 34.0	17.5	257 05.0	56.5
	17	174 56.2	120 11.9	45.5	65 30.3	15.6	341 36.3	17.6	272 07.6	56.5
	18	189 58.6	135 11.6	N16 46.1	80 31.0	N23 15.4	356 38.6	S 4 17.7	287 10.3	S21 56.5
	19	205 01.1	150 11.3	46.8	95 31.7	15.2	11 40.9	17.8	302 12.9	56.5
	20	220 03.5	165 11.1	47.4	110 32.5	15.0	26 43.3	17.8	317 15.6	56.5
	21	235 06.0	180 10.8	48.1	125 33.2	14.8	41 45.6	17.9	332 18.2	56.5
	22	250 08.5	195 10.5	48.8	140 33.9	14.6	56 47.9	18.0	347 20.9	56.5
	23	265 10.9	210 10.2	49.4	155 34.6	14.4	71 50.2	18.0	2 23.5	56.5
	2 00	280 13.4	225 09.9	N16 50.1	170 35.3	N23 14.2	86 52.5	S 4 18.1	17 26.2	S21 56.5
	01	295 15.9	240 09.6	50.7	185 36.0	14.0	101 54.9	18.2	32 28.8	56.5
	02	310 18.3	255 09.3	51.4	200 36.7	13.8	116 57.2	18.3	47 31.5	56.5
	03	325 20.8	270 09.0	52.0	215 37.4	13.6	131 59.5	18.3	62 34.1	56.5
	04	340 23.3	285 08.7	52.7	230 38.1	13.4	147 01.8	18.4	77 36.8	56.5
	05	355 25.7	300 08.4	53.4	245 38.8	13.1	162 04.1	18.5	92 39.4	56.4
	06	10 28.2	315 08.2	N16 54.0	260 39.5	N23 12.9	177 06.4	S 4 18.5	107 42.1	S21 56.4
	07	25 30.7	330 07.9	54.7	275 40.2	12.7	192 08.8	18.6	122 44.7	56.4
	08	40 33.1	345 07.6	55.3	290 40.9	12.5	207 11.1	18.7	137 47.4	56.4
SUNDAY	09	55 35.6	0 07.3	56.0	305 41.6	12.3	222 13.4	18.8	152 50.0	56.4
	10	70 38.0	15 07.0	56.6	320 42.3	12.1	237 15.7	18.8	167 52.6	56.4
	11	85 40.5	30 06.7	57.3	335 43.0	11.9	252 18.0	18.9	182 55.3	56.4
	12	100 43.0	45 06.4	N16 57.9	350 43.7	N23 11.7	267 20.3	S 4 19.0	197 57.9	S21 56.4
	13	115 45.4	60 06.1	58.6	5 44.4	11.5	282 22.7	19.1	213 00.6	56.4
	14	130 47.9	75 05.8	59.2	20 45.1	11.2	297 25.0	19.1	228 03.2	56.4
	15	145 50.4	90 05.5	16 59.9	35 45.8	11.0	312 27.3	19.2	243 05.9	56.4
	16	160 52.8	105 05.2	17 00.5	50 46.6	10.8	327 29.6	19.3	258 08.5	56.4
	17	175 55.3	120 04.9	01.2	65 47.3	10.6	342 31.9	19.4	273 11.2	56.4
	18	190 57.8	135 04.6	N17 01.8	80 48.0	N23 10.4	357 34.2	S 4 19.4	288 13.8	S21 56.4
	19	206 00.2	150 04.3	02.5	95 48.7	10.2	12 36.5	19.5	303 16.5	56.4
	20	221 02.7	165 04.0	03.1	110 49.4	10.0	27 38.9	19.6	318 19.1	56.4
	21	236 05.2	180 03.7	03.8	125 50.1	09.8	42 41.2	19.7	333 21.8	56.4
	22	251 07.6	195 03.4	04.4	140 50.8	09.5	57 43.5	19.7	348 24.4	56.4
	23	266 10.1	210 03.1	05.1	155 51.5	09.3	72 45.8	19.8	3 27.1	56.4
	Mer. Pass.	h m 5 22.2	v −0.3	d 0.7	v 0.7	d 0.2	v 2.3	d 0.1	v 2.7	d 0.0

STARS

Name	SHA ° ′	Dec ° ′
Acamar	315 16.6	S40 14.1
Achernar	335 25.0	S57 08.7
Acrux	173 06.1	S63 12.0
Adhara	255 10.8	S28 59.9
Aldebaran	290 46.5	N16 32.4
Alioth	166 18.4	N55 52.3
Alkaid	152 56.7	N49 14.0
Al Na'ir	27 40.1	S46 52.3
Alnilam	275 43.9	S 1 11.6
Alphard	217 53.7	S 8 44.2
Alphecca	126 08.5	N26 39.7
Alpheratz	357 40.6	N29 11.0
Altair	62 05.2	N 8 55.0
Ankaa	353 13.1	S42 12.5
Antares	112 22.6	S26 28.1
Arcturus	145 53.1	N19 05.8
Atria	107 21.4	S69 03.4
Avior	234 17.4	S59 34.2
Bellatrix	278 29.4	N 6 21.7
Betelgeuse	270 58.7	N 7 24.4
Canopus	263 55.5	S52 42.4
Capella	280 30.9	N46 00.6
Deneb	49 29.2	N45 20.6
Denebola	182 31.0	N14 28.6
Diphda	348 53.2	S17 53.4
Dubhe	193 48.8	N61 39.7
Elnath	278 09.5	N28 37.1
Eltanin	90 44.3	N51 29.4
Enif	33 44.2	N 9 57.4
Fomalhaut	15 20.9	S29 31.6
Gacrux	171 57.8	S57 12.8
Gienah	175 49.5	S17 38.3
Hadar	148 43.6	S60 27.5
Hamal	327 57.8	N23 32.4
Kaus Aust.	83 39.8	S34 22.3
Kochab	137 19.6	N74 05.4
Markab	13 35.5	N15 17.9
Menkar	314 12.4	N 4 09.3
Menkent	148 04.1	S36 27.4
Miaplacidus	221 39.7	S69 47.6
Mirfak	308 36.7	N49 55.0
Nunki	75 54.6	S26 16.3
Peacock	53 14.5	S56 40.4
Pollux	243 24.8	N27 58.9
Procyon	244 57.2	N 5 10.7
Rasalhague	96 03.6	N12 33.1
Regulus	207 40.8	N11 52.9
Rigel	281 09.8	S 8 11.1
Rigil Kent.	139 47.6	S60 54.5
Sabik	102 09.1	S15 44.6
Schedar	349 37.3	N56 37.6
Shaula	96 17.8	S37 06.8
Sirius	258 31.7	S16 44.6
Spica	158 28.3	S11 15.1
Suhail	222 50.8	S43 30.4
Vega	80 36.7	N38 48.2
Zuben'ubi	137 02.2	S16 06.7

	SHA ° ′	Mer. Pass. h m
Venus	306 02.4	8 59
Mars	251 04.1	12 38
Jupiter	166 42.5	18 13
Saturn	97 08.3	22 50

	UT (d h)	SUN GHA	SUN Dec	MOON GHA	v	MOON Dec	d	HP
		° ′	° ′	° ′	′	° ′	′	′
	30 00	179 05.7	N23 10.1	100 39.0	12.9	N 3 55.9	10.5	56.7
	01	194 05.6	09.9	115 10.9	12.9	3 45.4	10.5	56.6
	02	209 05.4	09.8	129 42.8	13.0	3 34.9	10.6	56.6
	03	224 05.3	. . 09.6	144 14.8	13.0	3 24.3	10.5	56.6
	04	239 05.2	09.5	158 46.8	13.1	3 13.8	10.6	56.5
	05	254 05.1	09.3	173 18.9	13.1	3 03.2	10.5	56.5
	06	269 04.9	N23 09.1	187 51.0	13.2	N 2 52.7	10.5	56.5
	07	284 04.8	09.0	202 23.2	13.2	2 42.2	10.6	56.4
	08	299 04.7	08.8	216 55.4	13.3	2 31.6	10.5	56.4
F	09	314 04.6	. . 08.7	231 27.7	13.3	2 21.1	10.6	56.4
R	10	329 04.4	08.5	246 00.0	13.4	2 10.5	10.5	56.3
I	11	344 04.3	08.4	260 32.4	13.4	2 00.0	10.5	56.3
D	12	359 04.2	N23 08.2	275 04.8	13.4	N 1 49.5	10.6	56.3
A	13	14 04.1	08.0	289 37.2	13.5	1 38.9	10.5	56.2
Y	14	29 04.0	07.9	304 09.7	13.5	1 28.4	10.5	56.2
	15	44 03.8	. . 07.7	318 42.2	13.6	1 17.9	10.5	56.2
	16	59 03.7	07.6	333 14.8	13.6	1 07.4	10.5	56.1
	17	74 03.6	07.4	347 47.4	13.6	0 56.9	10.5	56.1
	18	89 03.5	N23 07.2	2 20.0	13.7	N 0 46.4	10.5	56.1
	19	104 03.3	07.1	16 52.7	13.7	0 35.9	10.5	56.0
	20	119 03.2	06.9	31 25.4	13.7	0 25.4	10.5	56.0
	21	134 03.1	. . 06.7	45 58.1	13.8	0 14.9	10.4	56.0
	22	149 03.0	06.6	60 30.9	13.8	N 0 04.5	10.5	55.9
	23	164 02.9	06.4	75 03.7	13.9	S 0 06.0	10.4	55.9
	1 00	179 02.7	N23 06.2	89 36.6	13.9	S 0 16.4	10.4	55.9
	01	194 02.6	06.1	104 09.5	13.9	0 26.8	10.4	55.8
	02	209 02.5	05.9	118 42.4	13.9	0 37.2	10.4	55.8
	03	224 02.4	. . 05.7	133 15.3	14.0	0 47.6	10.4	55.8
	04	239 02.3	05.6	147 48.3	14.0	0 58.0	10.4	55.7
	05	254 02.1	05.4	162 21.3	14.0	1 08.4	10.3	55.7
	06	269 02.0	N23 05.2	176 54.3	14.1	S 1 18.7	10.4	55.7
	07	284 01.9	05.1	191 27.4	14.0	1 29.1	10.3	55.7
S	08	299 01.8	04.9	206 00.4	14.1	1 39.4	10.3	55.6
A	09	314 01.7	. . 04.7	220 33.5	14.2	1 49.7	10.2	55.6
T	10	329 01.5	04.5	235 06.7	14.1	1 59.9	10.3	55.6
U	11	344 01.4	04.4	249 39.8	14.2	2 10.2	10.2	55.5
R	12	359 01.3	N23 04.2	264 13.0	14.2	S 2 20.4	10.3	55.5
D	13	14 01.2	04.0	278 46.2	14.2	2 30.7	10.2	55.5
A	14	29 01.1	03.8	293 19.4	14.2	2 40.9	10.1	55.5
Y	15	44 00.9	. . 03.7	307 52.6	14.3	2 51.0	10.2	55.4
	16	59 00.8	03.5	322 25.9	14.2	3 01.2	10.1	55.4
	17	74 00.7	03.3	336 59.1	14.3	3 11.3	10.1	55.4
	18	89 00.6	N23 03.1	351 32.4	14.3	S 3 21.4	10.1	55.4
	19	104 00.5	02.9	6 05.7	14.4	3 31.5	10.1	55.3
	20	119 00.3	02.8	20 39.1	14.3	3 41.6	10.0	55.3
	21	134 00.2	. . 02.6	35 12.4	14.4	3 51.6	10.0	55.3
	22	149 00.1	02.4	49 45.8	14.3	4 01.6	10.0	55.2
	23	164 00.0	02.2	64 19.1	14.4	4 11.6	10.0	55.2
	2 00	178 59.9	N23 02.0	78 52.5	14.4	S 4 21.6	9.9	55.2
	01	193 59.8	01.8	93 25.9	14.4	4 31.5	9.9	55.2
	02	208 59.6	01.6	107 59.3	14.4	4 41.4	9.9	55.2
	03	223 59.5	. . 01.5	122 32.7	14.4	4 51.3	9.8	55.1
	04	238 59.4	01.3	137 06.1	14.5	5 01.1	9.9	55.1
	05	253 59.3	01.1	151 39.6	14.4	5 11.0	9.7	55.1
	06	268 59.2	N23 00.9	166 13.0	14.5	S 5 20.7	9.8	55.1
	07	283 59.0	00.7	180 46.5	14.4	5 30.5	9.7	55.0
	08	298 58.9	00.5	195 19.9	14.5	5 40.2	9.7	55.0
S	09	313 58.8	. . 00.3	209 53.4	14.5	5 49.9	9.7	55.0
U	10	328 58.7	23 00.1	224 26.9	14.4	5 59.6	9.6	55.0
N	11	343 58.6	22 59.9	239 00.3	14.5	6 09.2	9.6	54.9
D	12	358 58.5	N22 59.8	253 33.8	14.5	S 6 18.8	9.6	54.9
A	13	13 58.3	59.6	268 07.3	14.5	6 28.4	9.5	54.9
Y	14	28 58.2	59.4	282 40.8	14.5	6 37.9	9.5	54.9
	15	43 58.1	. . 59.2	297 14.3	14.5	6 47.4	9.4	54.9
	16	58 58.0	59.0	311 47.8	14.5	6 56.8	9.5	54.8
	17	73 57.9	58.8	326 21.3	14.4	7 06.3	9.4	54.8
	18	88 57.8	N22 58.6	340 54.7	14.5	S 7 15.7	9.3	54.8
	19	103 57.6	58.4	355 28.2	14.5	7 25.0	9.3	54.8
	20	118 57.5	58.2	10 01.7	14.5	7 34.3	9.3	54.8
	21	133 57.4	. . 58.0	24 35.2	14.5	7 43.6	9.2	54.7
	22	148 57.3	57.8	39 08.7	14.5	7 52.8	9.2	54.7
	23	163 57.2	57.6	53 42.2	14.5	S 8 02.0	9.2	54.7
		SD 15.8	*d* 0.2	SD	15.3		15.1	15.0

Lat.	Twilight Naut.	Twilight Civil	Sunrise	Moonrise 30	1	2	3
°	h m	h m	h m	h m	h m	h m	h m
N 72	▭	▭	▭	11 16	12 57	14 37	16 18
N 70	▭	▭	▭	11 18	12 53	14 27	15 59
68	▭	▭	▭	11 20	12 50	14 18	15 45
66	////	////	00 21	11 22	12 48	14 11	15 34
64	////	////	01 41	11 24	12 46	14 06	15 24
62	////	////	02 17	11 25	12 44	14 01	15 16
60	////	01 04	02 42	11 26	12 42	13 56	15 09
N 58	////	01 49	03 02	11 27	12 41	13 53	15 03
56	////	02 17	03 18	11 28	12 40	13 49	14 57
54	00 59	02 39	03 32	11 29	12 39	13 46	14 52
52	01 40	02 56	03 44	11 30	12 37	13 43	14 48
50	02 07	03 11	03 55	11 30	12 37	13 41	14 44
45	02 51	03 40	04 17	11 32	12 35	13 36	14 35
N 40	03 21	04 02	04 35	11 33	12 33	13 31	14 28
35	03 44	04 20	04 50	11 34	12 31	13 27	14 22
30	04 02	04 35	05 03	11 35	12 30	13 24	14 17
20	04 31	05 00	05 24	11 37	12 28	13 18	14 08
N 10	04 53	05 20	05 43	11 38	12 26	13 13	13 59
0	05 12	05 38	06 00	11 40	12 24	13 08	13 52
S 10	05 28	05 55	06 17	11 41	12 23	13 03	13 44
20	05 44	06 12	06 36	11 42	12 21	12 58	13 36
30	06 00	06 30	06 57	11 44	12 19	12 53	13 27
35	06 09	06 41	07 09	11 45	12 17	12 50	13 22
40	06 18	06 52	07 23	11 46	12 16	12 46	13 16
45	06 28	07 05	07 39	11 47	12 15	12 42	13 10
S 50	06 40	07 21	07 59	11 49	12 13	12 37	13 02
52	06 45	07 29	08 09	11 50	12 12	12 34	12 58
54	06 51	07 37	08 20	11 50	12 11	12 32	12 54
56	06 57	07 45	08 32	11 51	12 10	12 29	12 49
58	07 03	07 55	08 47	11 52	12 09	12 26	12 44
S 60	07 10	08 07	09 04	11 53	12 08	12 23	12 39

Lat.	Sunset	Twilight Civil	Twilight Naut.	Moonset 30	1	2	3
°	h m	h m	h m	h m	h m	h m	h m
N 72	▭	▭	▭	{00 05 / 23 57}	23 49	23 41	23 31
N 70	▭	▭	▭	{00 00 / 23 57}	23 55	23 53	23 51
68	▭	▭	▭	23 58	24 00	00 00	00 02
66	23 39	////	////	23 58	24 04	00 04	00 11
64	22 25	////	////	23 58	24 08	00 08	00 18
62	21 50	////	////	23 59	24 11	00 11	00 24
60	21 25	23 02	////	23 59	24 13	00 13	00 29
N 58	21 05	22 18	////	23 59	24 16	00 16	00 33
56	20 49	21 50	////	23 59	24 18	00 18	00 37
54	20 35	21 29	23 07	23 59	24 20	00 20	00 41
52	20 23	21 11	22 27	23 59	24 22	00 22	00 45
50	20 12	20 56	22 01	24 00	00 00	00 23	00 48
45	19 50	20 27	21 17	24 00	00 00	00 27	00 54
N 40	19 33	20 05	20 47	24 00	00 00	00 30	01 00
35	19 18	19 48	20 24	24 00	00 00	00 32	01 05
30	19 05	19 33	20 06	24 00	00 00	00 35	01 09
20	18 44	19 08	19 37	24 01	00 01	00 39	01 16
N 10	18 25	18 48	19 15	24 01	00 01	00 42	01 23
0	18 08	18 30	18 56	24 01	00 01	00 45	01 29
S 10	17 50	18 13	18 39	24 01	00 01	00 49	01 35
20	17 32	17 56	18 24	24 02	00 02	00 52	01 42
30	17 11	17 38	18 07	24 02	00 02	00 56	01 49
35	16 59	17 27	17 59	24 02	00 02	00 58	01 54
40	16 45	17 16	17 50	24 02	00 02	01 01	01 59
45	16 29	17 02	17 40	24 02	00 02	01 04	02 04
S 50	16 08	16 47	17 28	24 02	00 02	01 08	02 11
52	15 59	16 39	17 23	24 02	00 02	01 09	02 15
54	15 48	16 31	17 17	24 02	00 02	01 11	02 18
56	15 36	16 23	17 11	24 03	00 03	01 13	02 22
58	15 21	16 13	17 05	24 03	00 03	01 15	02 26
S 60	15 04	16 01	16 58	24 03	00 03	01 18	02 31

Day	SUN Eqn. of Time 00^h	SUN Eqn. of Time 12^h	SUN Mer. Pass.	MOON Mer. Pass. Upper	MOON Mer. Pass. Lower	MOON Age	MOON Phase
d	m s	m s	h m	h m	h m	d	%
30	03 37	03 43	12 04	17 50	05 28	06	45
1	03 49	03 55	12 04	18 35	06 13	07	55
2	04 00	04 06	12 04	19 19	06 57	08	64

d	h	ARIES GHA	VENUS −4·2 GHA	VENUS Dec	MARS +1·7 GHA	MARS Dec	JUPITER −2·0 GHA	JUPITER Dec	SATURN +0·1 GHA	SATURN Dec
		° ′	° ′	° ′	° ′	° ′	° ′	° ′	° ′	° ′
3 MONDAY	00	281 12.5	225 02.8	N17 05.7	170 52.2	N23 09.1	87 48.1	S 4 19.9	18 29.7	S21 56.4
	01	296 15.0	240 02.5	06.4	185 52.9	08.9	102 50.4	20.0	33 32.4	56.4
	02	311 17.5	255 02.2	07.0	200 53.6	08.7	117 52.7	20.0	48 35.0	56.4
	03	326 19.9	270 01.9	. . 07.7	215 54.3	. . 08.5	132 55.1	. . 20.1	63 37.7	. . 56.4
	04	341 22.4	285 01.6	08.3	230 55.0	08.2	147 57.4	20.2	78 40.3	56.4
	05	356 24.9	300 01.3	09.0	245 55.7	08.0	162 59.7	20.3	93 43.0	56.4
	06	11 27.3	315 00.9	N17 09.6	260 56.5	N23 07.8	178 02.0	S 4 20.3	108 45.6	S21 56.4
	07	26 29.8	330 00.6	10.3	275 57.2	07.6	193 04.3	20.4	123 48.3	56.4
	08	41 32.3	345 00.3	10.9	290 57.9	07.4	208 06.6	20.5	138 50.9	56.3
	09	56 34.7	0 00.0	. . 11.5	305 58.6	. . 07.2	223 08.9	. . 20.6	153 53.5	. . 56.3
	10	71 37.2	14 59.7	12.2	320 59.3	06.9	238 11.2	20.6	168 56.2	56.3
	11	86 39.6	29 59.4	12.8	336 00.0	06.7	253 13.5	20.7	183 58.8	56.3
	12	101 42.1	44 59.1	N17 13.5	351 00.7	N23 06.5	268 15.8	S 4 20.8	199 01.5	S21 56.3
	13	116 44.6	59 58.8	14.1	6 01.4	06.3	283 18.2	20.9	214 04.1	56.3
	14	131 47.0	74 58.5	14.7	21 02.1	06.1	298 20.5	20.9	229 06.8	56.3
	15	146 49.5	89 58.2	. . 15.4	36 02.8	. . 05.8	313 22.8	. . 21.0	244 09.4	. . 56.3
	16	161 52.0	104 57.8	16.0	51 03.5	05.6	328 25.1	21.1	259 12.1	56.3
	17	176 54.4	119 57.5	16.7	66 04.3	05.4	343 27.4	21.2	274 14.7	56.3
	18	191 56.9	134 57.2	N17 17.3	81 05.0	N23 05.2	358 29.7	S 4 21.2	289 17.4	S21 56.3
	19	206 59.4	149 56.9	17.9	96 05.7	05.0	13 32.0	21.3	304 20.0	56.3
	20	222 01.8	164 56.6	18.6	111 06.4	04.7	28 34.3	21.4	319 22.7	56.3
	21	237 04.3	179 56.3	. . 19.2	126 07.1	. . 04.5	43 36.6	. . 21.5	334 25.3	. . 56.3
	22	252 06.8	194 55.9	19.9	141 07.8	04.3	58 38.9	21.6	349 28.0	56.3
	23	267 09.2	209 55.6	20.5	156 08.5	04.1	73 41.2	21.6	4 30.6	56.3
4 TUESDAY	00	282 11.7	224 55.3	N17 21.1	171 09.2	N23 03.8	88 43.5	S 4 21.7	19 33.2	S21 56.3
	01	297 14.1	239 55.0	21.8	186 09.9	03.6	103 45.9	21.8	34 35.9	56.3
	02	312 16.6	254 54.7	22.4	201 10.7	03.4	118 48.2	21.9	49 38.5	56.3
	03	327 19.1	269 54.4	. . 23.0	216 11.4	. . 03.2	133 50.5	. . 21.9	64 41.2	. . 56.3
	04	342 21.5	284 54.0	23.7	231 12.1	02.9	148 52.8	22.0	79 43.8	56.3
	05	357 24.0	299 53.7	24.3	246 12.8	02.7	163 55.1	22.1	94 46.5	56.3
	06	12 26.5	314 53.4	N17 24.9	261 13.5	N23 02.5	178 57.4	S 4 22.2	109 49.1	S21 56.3
	07	27 28.9	329 53.1	25.6	276 14.2	02.3	193 59.7	22.2	124 51.8	56.3
	08	42 31.4	344 52.7	26.2	291 14.9	02.0	209 02.0	22.3	139 54.4	56.3
	09	57 33.9	359 52.4	. . 26.8	306 15.6	. . 01.8	224 04.3	. . 22.4	154 57.1	. . 56.3
	10	72 36.3	14 52.1	27.4	321 16.3	01.6	239 06.6	22.5	169 59.7	56.3
	11	87 38.8	29 51.8	28.1	336 17.1	01.4	254 08.9	22.6	185 02.3	56.3
	12	102 41.3	44 51.4	N17 28.7	351 17.8	N23 01.1	269 11.2	S 4 22.6	200 05.0	S21 56.3
	13	117 43.7	59 51.1	29.3	6 18.5	00.9	284 13.5	22.7	215 07.6	56.2
	14	132 46.2	74 50.8	30.0	21 19.2	00.7	299 15.8	22.8	230 10.3	56.2
	15	147 48.6	89 50.5	. . 30.6	36 19.9	. . 00.5	314 18.1	. . 22.9	245 12.9	. . 56.2
	16	162 51.1	104 50.1	31.2	51 20.6	00.2	329 20.4	23.0	260 15.6	56.2
	17	177 53.6	119 49.8	31.8	66 21.3	23 00.0	344 22.7	23.0	275 18.2	56.2
	18	192 56.0	134 49.5	N17 32.5	81 22.1	N22 59.8	359 25.0	S 4 23.1	290 20.9	S21 56.2
	19	207 58.5	149 49.1	33.1	96 22.8	59.5	14 27.3	23.2	305 23.5	56.2
	20	223 01.0	164 48.8	33.7	111 23.5	59.3	29 29.6	23.3	320 26.2	56.2
	21	238 03.4	179 48.5	. . 34.3	126 24.2	. . 59.1	44 31.9	. . 23.4	335 28.8	. . 56.2
	22	253 05.9	194 48.2	35.0	141 24.9	58.9	59 34.2	23.4	350 31.4	56.2
	23	268 08.4	209 47.8	35.6	156 25.6	58.6	74 36.5	23.5	5 34.1	56.2
5 WEDNESDAY	00	283 10.8	224 47.5	N17 36.2	171 26.3	N22 58.4	89 38.8	S 4 23.6	20 36.7	S21 56.2
	01	298 13.3	239 47.2	36.8	186 27.0	58.2	104 41.1	23.7	35 39.4	56.2
	02	313 15.7	254 46.8	37.5	201 27.8	57.9	119 43.4	23.8	50 42.0	56.2
	03	328 18.2	269 46.5	. . 38.1	216 28.5	. . 57.7	134 45.7	. . 23.8	65 44.7	. . 56.2
	04	343 20.7	284 46.2	38.7	231 29.2	57.5	149 48.0	23.9	80 47.3	56.2
	05	358 23.1	299 45.8	39.3	246 29.9	57.2	164 50.3	24.0	95 49.9	56.2
	06	13 25.6	314 45.5	N17 39.9	261 30.6	N22 57.0	179 52.6	S 4 24.1	110 52.6	S21 56.2
	07	28 28.1	329 45.1	40.6	276 31.3	56.8	194 54.9	24.2	125 55.2	56.2
	08	43 30.5	344 44.8	41.2	291 32.1	56.5	209 57.2	24.2	140 57.9	56.2
	09	58 33.0	359 44.5	. . 41.8	306 32.8	. . 56.3	224 59.5	. . 24.3	156 00.5	. . 56.2
	10	73 35.5	14 44.1	42.4	321 33.5	56.1	240 01.8	24.4	171 03.2	56.2
	11	88 37.9	29 43.8	43.0	336 34.2	55.8	255 04.1	24.5	186 05.8	56.2
	12	103 40.4	44 43.4	N17 43.6	351 34.9	N22 55.6	270 06.4	S 4 24.6	201 08.5	S21 56.2
	13	118 42.9	59 43.1	44.3	6 35.6	55.4	285 08.7	24.6	216 11.1	56.2
	14	133 45.3	74 42.8	44.9	21 36.4	55.1	300 11.0	24.7	231 13.7	56.2
	15	148 47.8	89 42.4	. . 45.5	36 37.1	. . 54.9	315 13.3	. . 24.8	246 16.4	. . 56.2
	16	163 50.2	104 42.1	46.1	51 37.8	54.7	330 15.6	24.9	261 19.0	56.2
	17	178 52.7	119 41.7	46.7	66 38.5	54.4	345 17.9	25.0	276 21.7	56.2
	18	193 55.2	134 41.4	N17 47.3	81 39.2	N22 54.2	0 20.2	S 4 25.0	291 24.3	S21 56.1
	19	208 57.6	149 41.1	47.9	96 39.9	54.0	15 22.5	25.1	306 27.0	56.1
	20	224 00.1	164 40.7	48.6	111 40.7	53.7	30 24.8	25.2	321 29.6	56.1
	21	239 02.6	179 40.4	. . 49.2	126 41.4	. . 53.5	45 27.1	. . 25.3	336 32.2	. . 56.1
	22	254 05.0	194 40.0	49.8	141 42.1	53.3	60 29.4	25.4	351 34.9	56.1
	23	269 07.5	209 39.7	50.4	156 42.8	53.0	75 31.7	25.5	6 37.5	56.1
Mer. Pass.		h m 5 10.4	v −0.3	d 0.6	v 0.7	d 0.2	v 2.3	d 0.1	v 2.6	d 0.0

STARS

Name	SHA	Dec
	° ′	° ′
Acamar	315 16.6	S40 14.0
Achernar	335 25.0	S57 08.7
Acrux	173 06.1	S63 12.0
Adhara	255 10.8	S28 59.9
Aldebaran	290 46.5	N16 32.4
Alioth	166 18.4	N55 52.3
Alkaid	152 56.7	N49 14.0
Al Na'ir	27 40.1	S46 52.3
Alnilam	275 43.9	S 1 11.6
Alphard	217 53.7	S 8 44.2
Alphecca	126 08.5	N26 39.7
Alpheratz	357 40.6	N29 11.0
Altair	62 05.2	N 8 55.0
Ankaa	353 13.0	S42 12.5
Antares	112 22.6	S26 28.1
Arcturus	145 53.1	N19 05.8
Atria	107 21.4	S69 03.4
Avior	234 17.4	S59 34.1
Bellatrix	278 29.4	N 6 21.7
Betelgeuse	270 58.7	N 7 24.4
Canopus	263 55.5	S52 42.4
Capella	280 30.8	N46 00.6
Deneb	49 29.1	N45 20.6
Denebola	182 31.0	N14 28.6
Diphda	348 53.2	S17 53.4
Dubhe	193 48.8	N61 39.7
Elnath	278 09.5	N28 37.1
Eltanin	90 44.3	N51 29.5
Enif	33 44.2	N 9 57.4
Fomalhaut	15 20.8	S29 31.6
Gacrux	171 57.8	S57 12.8
Gienah	175 49.5	S17 38.3
Hadar	148 43.7	S60 27.5
Hamal	327 57.8	N23 32.4
Kaus Aust.	83 39.8	S34 22.3
Kochab	137 19.6	N74 05.5
Markab	13 35.4	N15 17.9
Menkar	314 12.4	N 4 09.3
Menkent	148 04.2	S36 27.4
Miaplacidus	221 39.8	S69 47.6
Mirfak	308 36.7	N49 55.0
Nunki	75 54.6	S26 16.3
Peacock	53 14.5	S56 40.4
Pollux	243 24.8	N27 58.9
Procyon	244 57.2	N 5 10.7
Rasalhague	96 03.6	N12 33.1
Regulus	207 40.9	N11 52.9
Rigel	281 09.7	S 8 11.1
Rigil Kent.	139 47.6	S60 54.5
Sabik	102 09.1	S15 44.6
Schedar	349 37.3	N56 37.6
Shaula	96 17.8	S37 06.8
Sirius	258 31.7	S16 44.6
Spica	158 28.3	S11 15.1
Suhail	222 50.8	S43 30.4
Vega	80 36.7	N38 48.2
Zuben'ubi	137 02.2	S16 06.7

	SHA	Mer. Pass.
	° ′	h m
Venus	302 43.6	9 01
Mars	248 57.5	12 35
Jupiter	166 31.9	18 02
Saturn	97 21.6	22 38

Day	UT d h	SUN GHA ° ′	SUN Dec ° ′	MOON GHA ° ′	v ′	MOON Dec ° ′	d ′	HP ′
	3 00	178 57.1	N22 57.4	68 15.7	14.4	S 8 11.2	9.1	54.7
	01	193 57.0	57.2	82 49.1	14.5	8 20.3	9.1	54.7
	02	208 56.8	57.0	97 22.6	14.5	8 29.4	9.0	54.6
	03	223 56.7	. . 56.8	111 56.1	14.4	8 38.4	9.0	54.6
	04	238 56.6	56.6	126 29.5	14.5	8 47.4	9.0	54.6
	05	253 56.5	56.4	141 03.0	14.4	8 56.4	8.9	54.6
	06	268 56.4	N22 56.2	155 36.4	14.4	S 9 05.3	8.8	54.6
	07	283 56.3	56.0	170 09.8	14.5	9 14.1	8.9	54.6
	08	298 56.2	55.8	184 43.3	14.4	9 23.0	8.7	54.5
M	09	313 56.0	. . 55.6	199 16.7	14.4	9 31.7	8.8	54.5
O	10	328 55.9	55.3	213 50.1	14.4	9 40.5	8.7	54.5
N	11	343 55.8	55.1	228 23.5	14.4	9 49.2	8.6	54.5
D	12	358 55.7	N22 54.9	242 56.9	14.3	S 9 57.8	8.6	54.5
A	13	13 55.6	54.7	257 30.2	14.4	10 06.4	8.6	54.5
Y	14	28 55.5	54.5	272 03.6	14.3	10 15.0	8.5	54.5
	15	43 55.4	. . 54.3	286 36.9	14.4	10 23.5	8.4	54.4
	16	58 55.3	54.1	301 10.3	14.3	10 31.9	8.4	54.4
	17	73 55.1	53.9	315 43.6	14.3	10 40.3	8.4	54.4
	18	88 55.0	N22 53.7	330 16.9	14.3	S10 48.7	8.3	54.4
	19	103 54.9	53.4	344 50.2	14.3	10 57.0	8.3	54.4
	20	118 54.8	53.2	359 23.5	14.2	11 05.3	8.2	54.4
	21	133 54.7	. . 53.0	13 56.7	14.3	11 13.5	8.1	54.4
	22	148 54.6	52.8	28 30.0	14.2	11 21.6	8.2	54.3
	23	163 54.5	52.6	43 03.2	14.2	11 29.8	8.0	54.3
	4 00	178 54.4	N22 52.4	57 36.4	14.2	S11 37.8	8.0	54.3
	01	193 54.2	52.1	72 09.6	14.2	11 45.8	8.0	54.3
	02	208 54.1	51.9	86 42.8	14.2	11 53.8	7.9	54.3
	03	223 54.0	. . 51.7	101 16.0	14.1	12 01.7	7.8	54.3
	04	238 53.9	51.5	115 49.1	14.1	12 09.5	7.8	54.3
	05	253 53.8	51.3	130 22.2	14.1	12 17.3	7.8	54.3
	06	268 53.7	N22 51.0	144 55.3	14.1	S12 25.1	7.7	54.3
	07	283 53.6	50.8	159 28.4	14.1	12 32.8	7.6	54.2
T	08	298 53.5	50.6	174 01.5	14.0	12 40.4	7.6	54.2
U	09	313 53.4	. . 50.4	188 34.5	14.0	12 48.0	7.5	54.2
E	10	328 53.3	50.2	203 07.5	14.0	12 55.5	7.4	54.2
S	11	343 53.1	49.9	217 40.5	14.0	13 02.9	7.4	54.2
D	12	358 53.0	N22 49.7	232 13.5	14.0	S13 10.3	7.4	54.2
A	13	13 52.9	49.5	246 46.5	13.9	13 17.7	7.3	54.2
Y	14	28 52.8	49.2	261 19.4	13.9	13 25.0	7.2	54.2
	15	43 52.7	. . 49.0	275 52.3	13.9	13 32.2	7.2	54.2
	16	58 52.6	48.8	290 25.2	13.9	13 39.4	7.1	54.2
	17	73 52.5	48.6	304 58.1	13.8	13 46.5	7.0	54.2
	18	88 52.4	N22 48.3	319 30.9	13.8	S13 53.5	7.0	54.1
	19	103 52.3	48.1	334 03.7	13.8	14 00.5	7.0	54.1
	20	118 52.2	47.9	348 36.5	13.8	14 07.5	6.8	54.1
	21	133 52.1	. . 47.6	3 09.3	13.7	14 14.3	6.8	54.1
	22	148 51.9	47.4	17 42.0	13.7	14 21.1	6.8	54.1
	23	163 51.8	47.2	32 14.7	13.7	14 27.9	6.7	54.1
	5 00	178 51.7	N22 46.9	46 47.4	13.7	S14 34.6	6.6	54.1
	01	193 51.6	46.7	61 20.1	13.6	14 41.2	6.5	54.1
	02	208 51.5	46.5	75 52.7	13.6	14 47.7	6.5	54.1
	03	223 51.4	. . 46.2	90 25.3	13.6	14 54.2	6.4	54.1
	04	238 51.3	46.0	104 57.9	13.6	15 00.6	6.4	54.1
	05	253 51.2	45.8	119 30.5	13.5	15 07.0	6.3	54.1
	06	268 51.1	N22 45.5	134 03.0	13.5	S15 13.3	6.2	54.1
W	07	283 51.0	45.3	148 35.5	13.5	15 19.5	6.2	54.1
E	08	298 50.9	45.0	163 08.0	13.4	15 25.7	6.0	54.1
D	09	313 50.8	. . 44.8	177 40.4	13.5	15 31.7	6.1	54.1
N	10	328 50.7	44.6	192 12.9	13.4	15 37.8	5.9	54.1
E	11	343 50.6	44.3	206 45.3	13.3	15 43.7	5.9	54.0
S	12	358 50.4	N22 44.1	221 17.6	13.4	S15 49.6	5.8	54.0
D	13	13 50.3	43.8	235 50.0	13.3	15 55.4	5.8	54.0
A	14	28 50.2	43.6	250 22.3	13.3	16 01.2	5.6	54.0
Y	15	43 50.1	. . 43.3	264 54.6	13.2	16 06.8	5.6	54.0
	16	58 50.0	43.1	279 26.8	13.3	16 12.4	5.6	54.0
	17	73 49.9	42.9	293 59.1	13.2	16 18.0	5.4	54.0
	18	88 49.8	N22 42.6	308 31.3	13.1	S16 23.4	5.4	54.0
	19	103 49.7	42.4	323 03.4	13.2	16 28.8	5.3	54.0
	20	118 49.6	42.1	337 35.6	13.1	16 34.1	5.3	54.0
	21	133 49.5	. . 41.9	352 07.7	13.1	16 39.4	5.2	54.0
	22	148 49.4	41.6	6 39.8	13.1	16 44.6	5.1	54.0
	23	163 49.3	41.4	21 11.9	13.0	S16 49.7	5.0	54.0
		SD 15.8	*d* 0.2	SD 14.8		14.8		14.7

Lat. °	Twilight Naut. h m	Twilight Civil h m	Sunrise h m	Moonrise 3 h m	Moonrise 4 h m	Moonrise 5 h m	Moonrise 6 h m
N 72	□	□	□	16 18	18 02	19 58	■
N 70	□	□	□	15 59	17 33	19 08	20 42
68	□	□	□	15 45	17 11	18 36	19 56
66	////	////	00 43	15 34	16 55	18 13	19 27
64	////	////	01 47	15 24	16 41	17 55	19 04
62	////	////	02 21	15 16	16 29	17 40	18 47
60	////	01 12	02 46	15 09	16 20	17 28	18 32
N 58	////	01 53	03 05	15 03	16 11	17 17	18 20
56	////	02 21	03 21	14 57	16 04	17 08	18 09
54	01 06	02 42	03 35	14 52	15 57	17 00	17 59
52	01 44	02 59	03 47	14 48	15 51	16 52	17 51
50	02 10	03 13	03 57	14 44	15 46	16 46	17 43
45	02 53	03 42	04 19	14 35	15 34	16 32	17 27
N 40	03 23	04 04	04 36	14 28	15 25	16 20	17 14
35	03 45	04 22	04 51	14 22	15 16	16 10	17 03
30	04 03	04 36	05 04	14 17	15 09	16 01	16 53
20	04 32	05 01	05 25	14 08	14 57	15 46	16 36
N 10	04 54	05 21	05 44	13 59	14 46	15 33	16 21
0	05 12	05 38	06 01	13 52	14 36	15 21	16 08
S 10	05 29	05 55	06 18	13 44	14 26	15 09	15 54
20	05 45	06 12	06 36	13 36	14 16	14 57	15 40
30	06 00	06 30	06 56	13 27	14 04	14 42	15 23
35	06 09	06 40	07 08	13 22	13 57	14 33	15 13
40	06 18	06 52	07 22	13 16	13 49	14 24	15 02
45	06 28	07 05	07 38	13 10	13 40	14 13	14 50
S 50	06 39	07 20	07 59	13 02	13 29	13 59	14 34
52	06 44	07 28	08 08	12 58	13 24	13 53	14 27
54	06 50	07 35	08 19	12 54	13 18	13 46	14 19
56	06 56	07 44	08 31	12 49	13 12	13 38	14 10
58	07 02	07 54	08 45	12 44	13 05	13 29	13 59
S 60	07 09	08 05	09 01	12 39	12 57	13 19	13 47

Lat. °	Sunset h m	Twilight Civil h m	Twilight Naut. h m	Moonset 3 h m	Moonset 4 h m	Moonset 5 h m	Moonset 6 h m
N 72	□	□	□	23 31	23 19	22 58	■
N 70	□	□	□	23 51	23 49	23 48	23 51
68	□	□	□	00 02	00 06	00 11	00 20
66	23 21	////	////	00 11	00 19	00 29	00 44
64	22 20	////	////	00 18	00 29	00 43	01 03
62	21 46	////	////	00 24	00 38	00 56	01 18
60	21 22	22 55	////	00 29	00 46	01 06	01 31
N 58	21 03	22 14	////	00 33	00 53	01 15	01 42
56	20 47	21 47	////	00 37	00 59	01 23	01 52
54	20 34	21 26	23 01	00 41	01 04	01 30	02 00
52	20 22	21 09	22 23	00 45	01 09	01 36	02 08
50	20 11	20 55	21 58	00 48	01 14	01 42	02 15
45	19 50	20 27	21 15	00 54	01 23	01 55	02 29
N 40	19 32	20 05	20 46	01 00	01 31	02 05	02 42
35	19 18	19 47	20 23	01 05	01 38	02 14	02 52
30	19 05	19 32	20 05	01 09	01 44	02 22	03 01
20	18 44	19 08	19 37	01 16	01 55	02 35	03 17
N 10	18 25	18 48	19 15	01 23	02 04	02 47	03 31
0	18 08	18 31	18 57	01 29	02 13	02 58	03 44
S 10	17 51	18 14	18 40	01 35	02 22	03 09	03 57
20	17 33	17 57	18 24	01 42	02 31	03 21	04 10
30	17 13	17 39	18 09	01 49	02 42	03 34	04 26
35	17 01	17 29	18 00	01 54	02 48	03 42	04 36
40	16 47	17 17	17 51	01 59	02 55	03 51	04 46
45	16 31	17 04	17 41	02 04	03 04	04 02	04 58
S 50	16 11	16 49	17 30	02 11	03 14	04 15	05 14
52	16 01	16 42	17 25	02 15	03 18	04 21	05 21
54	15 50	16 34	17 20	02 18	03 23	04 27	05 28
56	15 38	16 25	17 14	02 22	03 29	04 35	05 37
58	15 24	16 15	17 07	02 26	03 36	04 43	05 47
S 60	15 08	16 04	17 00	02 31	03 43	04 52	05 59

Day	SUN Eqn. of Time 00^h	SUN Eqn. of Time 12^h	SUN Mer. Pass.	MOON Mer. Pass. Upper	MOON Mer. Pass. Lower	MOON Age	MOON Phase
d	m s	m s	h m	h m	h m	d %	
3	04 11	04 17	12 04	20 03	07 41	09 73	
4	04 22	04 28	12 04	20 47	08 25	10 81	
5	04 33	04 38	12 05	21 32	09 10	11 88	

	UT	ARIES	VENUS −4·1		MARS +1·7		JUPITER −2·0		SATURN +0·1	
	d h	GHA ° ′	GHA ° ′	Dec ° ′	GHA ° ′	Dec ° ′	GHA ° ′	Dec ° ′	GHA ° ′	Dec ° ′
	6 00	284 10.0	224 39.3	N17 51.0	171 43.5	N22 52.8	90 34.0	S 4 25.5	21 40.2	S21 56.1
	01	299 12.4	239 39.0	51.6	186 44.2	52.5	105 36.3	25.6	36 42.8	56.1
	02	314 14.9	254 38.6	52.2	201 45.0	52.3	120 38.5	25.7	51 45.4	56.1
	03	329 17.4	269 38.3	. . 52.8	216 45.7	. . 52.1	135 40.8	. . 25.8	66 48.1	. . 56.1
	04	344 19.8	284 37.9	53.4	231 46.4	51.8	150 43.1	25.9	81 50.7	56.1
	05	359 22.3	299 37.6	54.0	246 47.1	51.6	165 45.4	26.0	96 53.4	56.1
	06	14 24.7	314 37.2	N17 54.6	261 47.8	N22 51.3	180 47.7	S 4 26.0	111 56.0	S21 56.1
	07	29 27.2	329 36.9	55.3	276 48.6	51.1	195 50.0	26.1	126 58.7	56.1
T	08	44 29.7	344 36.5	55.9	291 49.3	50.9	210 52.3	26.2	142 01.3	56.1
H	09	59 32.1	359 36.2	. . 56.5	306 50.0	. . 50.6	225 54.6	. . 26.3	157 03.9	. . 56.1
U	10	74 34.6	14 35.8	57.1	321 50.7	50.4	240 56.9	26.4	172 06.6	56.1
R	11	89 37.1	29 35.5	57.7	336 51.4	50.1	255 59.2	26.4	187 09.2	56.1
S	12	104 39.5	44 35.1	N17 58.3	351 52.1	N22 49.9	271 01.5	S 4 26.5	202 11.9	S21 56.1
D	13	119 42.0	59 34.8	58.9	6 52.9	49.7	286 03.8	26.6	217 14.5	56.1
A	14	134 44.5	74 34.4	17 59.5	21 53.6	49.4	301 06.1	26.7	232 17.1	56.1
Y	15	149 46.9	89 34.0	18 00.1	36 54.3	. . 49.2	316 08.3	. . 26.8	247 19.8	. . 56.1
	16	164 49.4	104 33.7	00.7	51 55.0	48.9	331 10.6	26.9	262 22.4	56.1
	17	179 51.9	119 33.3	01.3	66 55.7	48.7	346 12.9	27.0	277 25.1	56.1
	18	194 54.3	134 33.0	N18 01.9	81 56.5	N22 48.4	1 15.2	S 4 27.0	292 27.7	S21 56.1
	19	209 56.8	149 32.6	02.5	96 57.2	48.2	16 17.5	27.1	307 30.4	56.1
	20	224 59.2	164 32.2	03.1	111 57.9	48.0	31 19.8	27.2	322 33.0	56.1
	21	240 01.7	179 31.9	. . 03.7	126 58.6	. . 47.7	46 22.1	. . 27.3	337 35.6	. . 56.1
	22	255 04.2	194 31.5	04.3	141 59.4	47.5	61 24.4	27.4	352 38.3	56.1
	23	270 06.6	209 31.2	04.9	157 00.1	47.2	76 26.7	27.5	7 40.9	56.1
	7 00	285 09.1	224 30.8	N18 05.5	172 00.8	N22 47.0	91 29.0	S 4 27.5	22 43.6	S21 56.1
	01	300 11.6	239 30.4	06.1	187 01.5	46.7	106 31.2	27.6	37 46.2	56.0
	02	315 14.0	254 30.1	06.7	202 02.2	46.5	121 33.5	27.7	52 48.8	56.0
	03	330 16.5	269 29.7	. . 07.3	217 03.0	. . 46.2	136 35.8	. . 27.8	67 51.5	. . 56.0
	04	345 19.0	284 29.4	07.8	232 03.7	46.0	151 38.1	27.9	82 54.1	56.0
	05	0 21.4	299 29.0	08.4	247 04.4	45.8	166 40.4	28.0	97 56.8	56.0
	06	15 23.9	314 28.6	N18 09.0	262 05.1	N22 45.5	181 42.7	S 4 28.1	112 59.4	S21 56.0
	07	30 26.3	329 28.3	09.6	277 05.8	45.3	196 45.0	28.1	128 02.0	56.0
	08	45 28.8	344 27.9	10.2	292 06.6	45.0	211 47.2	28.2	143 04.7	56.0
F	09	60 31.3	359 27.5	. . 10.8	307 07.3	. . 44.8	226 49.5	. . 28.3	158 07.3	. . 56.0
R	10	75 33.7	14 27.2	11.4	322 08.0	44.5	241 51.8	28.4	173 10.0	56.0
I	11	90 36.2	29 26.8	12.0	337 08.7	44.3	256 54.1	28.5	188 12.6	56.0
D	12	105 38.7	44 26.4	N18 12.6	352 09.5	N22 44.0	271 56.4	S 4 28.6	203 15.2	S21 56.0
A	13	120 41.1	59 26.0	13.2	7 10.2	43.8	286 58.7	28.7	218 17.9	56.0
Y	14	135 43.6	74 25.7	13.8	22 10.9	43.5	302 01.0	28.7	233 20.5	56.0
	15	150 46.1	89 25.3	. . 14.3	37 11.6	. . 43.3	317 03.2	. . 28.8	248 23.1	. . 56.0
	16	165 48.5	104 24.9	14.9	52 12.4	43.0	332 05.5	28.9	263 25.8	56.0
	17	180 51.0	119 24.6	15.5	67 13.1	42.8	347 07.8	29.0	278 28.4	56.0
	18	195 53.5	134 24.2	N18 16.1	82 13.8	N22 42.5	2 10.1	S 4 29.1	293 31.1	S21 56.0
	19	210 55.9	149 23.8	16.7	97 14.5	42.3	17 12.4	29.2	308 33.7	56.0
	20	225 58.4	164 23.4	17.3	112 15.3	42.0	32 14.7	29.3	323 36.3	56.0
	21	241 00.8	179 23.1	. . 17.9	127 16.0	. . 41.8	47 16.9	. . 29.3	338 39.0	. . 56.0
	22	256 03.3	194 22.7	18.4	142 16.7	41.5	62 19.2	29.4	353 41.6	56.0
	23	271 05.8	209 22.3	19.0	157 17.4	41.3	77 21.5	29.5	8 44.3	56.0
	8 00	286 08.2	224 21.9	N18 19.6	172 18.1	N22 41.0	92 23.8	S 4 29.6	23 46.9	S21 56.0
	01	301 10.7	239 21.6	20.2	187 18.9	40.8	107 26.1	29.7	38 49.5	56.0
	02	316 13.2	254 21.2	20.8	202 19.6	40.5	122 28.4	29.8	53 52.2	56.0
	03	331 15.6	269 20.8	. . 21.4	217 20.3	. . 40.3	137 30.6	. . 29.9	68 54.8	. . 56.0
	04	346 18.1	284 20.4	21.9	232 21.1	40.0	152 32.9	30.0	83 57.4	56.0
	05	1 20.6	299 20.1	22.5	247 21.8	39.7	167 35.2	30.0	99 00.1	56.0
	06	16 23.0	314 19.7	N18 23.1	262 22.5	N22 39.5	182 37.5	S 4 30.1	114 02.7	S21 56.0
	07	31 25.5	329 19.3	23.7	277 23.2	39.2	197 39.8	30.2	129 05.4	56.0
S	08	46 28.0	344 18.9	24.2	292 24.0	39.0	212 42.0	30.3	144 08.0	56.0
A	09	61 30.4	359 18.5	. . 24.8	307 24.7	. . 38.7	227 44.3	. . 30.4	159 10.6	. . 55.9
T	10	76 32.9	14 18.2	25.4	322 25.4	38.5	242 46.6	30.5	174 13.3	55.9
U	11	91 35.3	29 17.8	26.0	337 26.1	38.2	257 48.9	30.6	189 15.9	55.9
R	12	106 37.8	44 17.4	N18 26.5	352 26.9	N22 38.0	272 51.2	S 4 30.7	204 18.5	S21 55.9
D	13	121 40.3	59 17.0	27.1	7 27.6	37.7	287 53.4	30.7	219 21.2	55.9
A	14	136 42.7	74 16.6	27.7	22 28.3	37.5	302 55.7	30.8	234 23.8	55.9
Y	15	151 45.2	89 16.2	. . 28.3	37 29.0	. . 37.2	317 58.0	. . 30.9	249 26.5	. . 55.9
	16	166 47.7	104 15.9	28.8	52 29.8	36.9	333 00.3	31.0	264 29.1	55.9
	17	181 50.1	119 15.5	29.4	67 30.5	36.7	348 02.6	31.1	279 31.7	55.9
	18	196 52.6	134 15.1	N18 30.0	82 31.2	N22 36.4	3 04.8	S 4 31.2	294 34.4	S21 55.9
	19	211 55.1	149 14.7	30.6	97 32.0	36.2	18 07.1	31.3	309 37.0	55.9
	20	226 57.5	164 14.3	31.1	112 32.7	35.9	33 09.4	31.4	324 39.6	55.9
	21	242 00.0	179 13.9	. . 31.7	127 33.4	. . 35.7	48 11.7	. . 31.5	339 42.3	. . 55.9
	22	257 02.5	194 13.5	32.3	142 34.1	35.4	63 13.9	31.5	354 44.9	55.9
	23	272 04.9	209 13.1	32.8	157 34.9	35.1	78 16.2	31.6	9 47.5	55.9
	Mer. Pass.	h m 4 58.6	v −0.4	d 0.6	v 0.7	d 0.2	v 2.3	d 0.1	v 2.6	d 0.0

STARS Name	SHA ° ′	Dec ° ′
Acamar	315 16.5	S40 14.0
Achernar	335 24.9	S57 08.7
Acrux	173 06.2	S63 12.0
Adhara	255 10.8	S28 59.9
Aldebaran	290 46.5	N16 32.4
Alioth	166 18.4	N55 52.3
Alkaid	152 56.7	N49 14.0
Al Na'ir	27 40.0	S46 52.3
Alnilam	275 43.9	S 1 11.6
Alphard	217 53.7	S 8 44.1
Alphecca	126 08.5	N26 39.7
Alpheratz	357 40.5	N29 11.0
Altair	62 05.2	N 8 55.1
Ankaa	353 13.0	S42 12.5
Antares	112 22.6	S26 28.1
Arcturus	145 53.1	N19 05.8
Atria	107 21.4	S69 03.4
Avior	234 17.5	S59 34.1
Bellatrix	278 29.4	N 6 21.7
Betelgeuse	270 58.7	N 7 24.4
Canopus	263 55.5	S52 42.4
Capella	280 30.8	N46 00.6
Deneb	49 29.1	N45 20.6
Denebola	182 31.0	N14 28.6
Diphda	348 53.1	S17 53.4
Dubhe	193 48.8	N61 39.7
Elnath	278 09.5	N28 37.1
Eltanin	90 44.3	N51 29.5
Enif	33 44.2	N 9 57.4
Fomalhaut	15 20.8	S29 31.6
Gacrux	171 57.8	S57 12.8
Gienah	175 49.5	S17 38.3
Hadar	148 43.7	S60 27.5
Hamal	327 57.7	N23 32.4
Kaus Aust.	83 39.8	S34 22.3
Kochab	137 19.7	N74 05.5
Markab	13 35.4	N15 17.9
Menkar	314 12.4	N 4 09.3
Menkent	148 04.2	S36 27.4
Miaplacidus	221 39.8	S69 47.6
Mirfak	308 36.7	N49 55.0
Nunki	75 54.6	S26 16.3
Peacock	53 14.4	S56 40.4
Pollux	243 24.8	N27 58.9
Procyon	244 57.2	N 5 10.7
Rasalhague	96 03.6	N12 33.1
Regulus	207 40.9	N11 52.9
Rigel	281 09.7	S 8 11.0
Rigil Kent.	139 47.6	S60 54.5
Sabik	102 09.1	S15 44.6
Schedar	349 37.2	N56 37.6
Shaula	96 17.8	S37 06.8
Sirius	258 31.7	S16 44.6
Spica	158 28.3	S11 15.1
Suhail	222 50.8	S43 30.4
Vega	80 36.7	N38 48.2
Zuben'ubi	137 02.2	S16 06.7

	SHA ° ′	Mer. Pass. h m
Venus	299 21.7	9 02
Mars	246 51.7	12 31
Jupiter	166 19.9	17 51
Saturn	97 34.5	22 25

UT d h	SUN GHA ° ′	SUN Dec ° ′	MOON GHA ° ′	v ′	MOON Dec ° ′	d ′	HP ′
6 00 (THURSDAY)	178 49.2	N22 41.1	35 43.9	13.0	S16 54.7	4.9	54.0
01	193 49.1	40.9	50 15.9	13.0	16 59.6	4.9	54.0
02	208 49.0	40.6	64 47.9	12.9	17 04.5	4.8	54.0
03	223 48.9	. . 40.4	79 19.8	12.9	17 09.3	4.7	54.0
04	238 48.8	40.1	93 51.7	12.9	17 14.0	4.7	54.0
05	253 48.7	39.9	108 23.6	12.9	17 18.7	4.5	54.0
06	268 48.6	N22 39.6	122 55.5	12.8	S17 23.2	4.5	54.0
07	283 48.5	39.3	137 27.3	12.8	17 27.7	4.4	54.0
08	298 48.4	39.1	151 59.1	12.8	17 32.1	4.4	54.0
09	313 48.3	. . 38.8	166 30.9	12.8	17 36.5	4.2	54.0
10	328 48.2	38.6	181 02.7	12.7	17 40.7	4.2	54.0
11	343 48.0	38.3	195 34.4	12.7	17 44.9	4.1	54.0
12	358 47.9	N22 38.1	210 06.1	12.7	S17 49.0	4.0	54.0
13	13 47.8	37.8	224 37.8	12.6	17 53.0	4.0	54.0
14	28 47.7	37.5	239 09.4	12.6	17 57.0	3.9	54.0
15	43 47.6	. . 37.3	253 41.0	12.6	18 00.9	3.7	54.0
16	58 47.5	37.0	268 12.6	12.6	18 04.6	3.7	54.0
17	73 47.4	36.8	282 44.2	12.5	18 08.3	3.7	54.0
18	88 47.3	N22 36.5	297 15.7	12.5	S18 12.0	3.5	54.0
19	103 47.2	36.2	311 47.2	12.5	18 15.5	3.4	54.0
20	118 47.1	36.0	326 18.7	12.5	18 18.9	3.4	54.0
21	133 47.0	. . 35.7	340 50.2	12.4	18 22.3	3.3	54.0
22	148 46.9	35.4	355 21.6	12.4	18 25.6	3.2	54.0
23	163 46.8	35.2	9 53.0	12.4	18 28.8	3.1	54.1
7 00 (FRIDAY)	178 46.7	N22 34.9	24 24.4	12.4	S18 31.9	3.1	54.1
01	193 46.6	34.6	38 55.8	12.3	18 35.0	2.9	54.1
02	208 46.5	34.4	53 27.1	12.3	18 37.9	2.9	54.1
03	223 46.4	. . 34.1	67 58.4	12.3	18 40.8	2.8	54.1
04	238 46.3	33.8	82 29.7	12.3	18 43.6	2.7	54.1
05	253 46.2	33.6	97 01.0	12.2	18 46.3	2.6	54.1
06	268 46.1	N22 33.3	111 32.2	12.2	S18 48.9	2.5	54.1
07	283 46.0	33.0	126 03.4	12.2	18 51.4	2.5	54.1
08	298 45.9	32.7	140 34.6	12.2	18 53.9	2.3	54.1
09	313 45.8	. . 32.5	155 05.8	12.1	18 56.2	2.3	54.1
10	328 45.7	32.2	169 36.9	12.1	18 58.5	2.2	54.1
11	343 45.6	31.9	184 08.0	12.1	19 00.7	2.1	54.1
12	358 45.5	N22 31.6	198 39.1	12.1	S19 02.8	2.0	54.1
13	13 45.4	31.4	213 10.2	12.1	19 04.8	1.9	54.1
14	28 45.3	31.1	227 41.3	12.0	19 06.7	1.8	54.1
15	43 45.3	. . 30.8	242 12.3	12.1	19 08.5	1.8	54.1
16	58 45.2	30.5	256 43.4	12.0	19 10.3	1.6	54.1
17	73 45.1	30.3	271 14.4	11.9	19 11.9	1.6	54.1
18	88 45.0	N22 30.0	285 45.3	12.0	S19 13.5	1.5	54.1
19	103 44.9	29.7	300 16.3	12.0	19 15.0	1.4	54.2
20	118 44.8	29.4	314 47.3	11.9	19 16.4	1.3	54.2
21	133 44.7	. . 29.1	329 18.2	11.9	19 17.7	1.2	54.2
22	148 44.6	28.9	343 49.1	11.9	19 18.9	1.1	54.2
23	163 44.5	28.6	358 20.0	11.9	19 20.0	1.0	54.2
8 00 (SATURDAY)	178 44.4	N22 28.3	12 50.9	11.8	S19 21.0	1.0	54.2
01	193 44.3	28.0	27 21.7	11.9	19 22.0	0.8	54.2
02	208 44.2	27.7	41 52.6	11.8	19 22.8	0.8	54.2
03	223 44.1	. . 27.4	56 23.4	11.8	19 23.6	0.6	54.2
04	238 44.0	27.2	70 54.2	11.8	19 24.2	0.6	54.2
05	253 43.9	26.9	85 25.0	11.8	19 24.8	0.5	54.2
06	268 43.8	N22 26.6	99 55.8	11.8	S19 25.3	0.4	54.2
07	283 43.7	26.3	114 26.6	11.7	19 25.7	0.3	54.2
08	298 43.6	26.0	128 57.3	11.8	19 26.0	0.2	54.3
09	313 43.5	. . 25.7	143 28.1	11.7	19 26.2	0.1	54.3
10	328 43.4	25.4	157 58.8	11.7	19 26.3	0.0	54.3
11	343 43.3	25.1	172 29.5	11.7	19 26.3	0.0	54.3
12	358 43.2	N22 24.8	187 00.2	11.7	S19 26.3	0.2	54.3
13	13 43.1	24.6	201 30.9	11.7	19 26.1	0.2	54.3
14	28 43.1	24.3	216 01.6	11.7	19 25.9	0.4	54.3
15	43 43.0	. . 24.0	230 32.3	11.6	19 25.5	0.4	54.3
16	58 42.9	23.7	245 02.9	11.7	19 25.1	0.5	54.3
17	73 42.8	23.4	259 33.6	11.7	19 24.6	0.6	54.3
18	88 42.7	N22 23.1	274 04.3	11.6	S19 24.0	0.7	54.4
19	103 42.6	22.8	288 34.9	11.6	19 23.3	0.8	54.4
20	118 42.5	22.5	303 05.5	11.7	19 22.5	0.9	54.4
21	133 42.4	. . 22.2	317 36.2	11.6	19 21.6	1.0	54.4
22	148 42.3	21.9	332 06.8	11.6	19 20.6	1.1	54.4
23	163 42.2	21.6	346 37.4	11.6	S19 19.5	1.2	54.4
	SD 15.8	*d* 0.3	SD	14.7	14.7		14.8

Lat.	Twilight Naut.	Twilight Civil	Sunrise	Moonrise 6	Moonrise 7	Moonrise 8	Moonrise 9
°	h m	h m	h m	h m	h m	h m	h m
N 72	□	□	□	■	■	■	■
N 70	□	□	□	20 42	22 07	22 56	23 09
68	□	□	□	19 56	21 05	21 55	22 24
66	////	////	00 59	19 27	20 31	21 20	21 55
64	////	////	01 54	19 04	20 05	20 55	21 32
62	////	////	02 26	18 47	19 46	20 35	21 15
60	////	01 20	02 50	18 32	19 30	20 19	21 00
N 58	////	01 59	03 09	18 20	19 16	20 06	20 47
56	////	02 25	03 24	18 09	19 05	19 54	20 36
54	01 14	02 45	03 38	17 59	18 54	19 44	20 27
52	01 49	03 02	03 49	17 51	18 45	19 35	20 18
50	02 14	03 16	04 00	17 43	18 37	19 26	20 10
45	02 56	03 44	04 21	17 27	18 20	19 09	19 54
N 40	03 25	04 06	04 38	17 14	18 06	18 55	19 40
35	03 47	04 23	04 53	17 03	17 54	18 43	19 29
30	04 05	04 38	05 05	16 53	17 43	18 32	19 19
20	04 33	05 02	05 26	16 36	17 25	18 14	19 01
N 10	04 55	05 22	05 44	16 21	17 10	17 58	18 46
0	05 13	05 39	06 01	16 08	16 55	17 44	18 32
S 10	05 29	05 55	06 18	15 54	16 41	17 29	18 18
20	05 45	06 12	06 36	15 40	16 25	17 13	18 03
30	06 00	06 30	06 56	15 23	16 07	16 55	17 46
35	06 09	06 40	07 08	15 13	15 57	16 45	17 36
40	06 17	06 51	07 21	15 02	15 45	16 33	17 24
45	06 27	07 04	07 37	14 50	15 31	16 18	17 10
S 50	06 38	07 19	07 57	14 34	15 15	16 01	16 54
52	06 43	07 26	08 06	14 27	15 07	15 53	16 46
54	06 48	07 34	08 17	14 19	14 58	15 44	16 37
56	06 54	07 43	08 29	14 10	14 48	15 34	16 28
58	07 00	07 52	08 42	13 59	14 36	15 22	16 16
S 60	07 07	08 03	08 59	13 47	14 23	15 09	16 04

Lat.	Sunset	Twilight Civil	Twilight Naut.	Moonset 6	Moonset 7	Moonset 8	Moonset 9
°	h m	h m	h m	h m	h m	h m	h m
N 72	□	□	□	■	■	■	■
N 70	□	□	□	23 51	24 05	00 05	00 57
68	□	□	□	00 20	00 37	01 07	01 58
66	23 07	////	////	00 44	01 07	01 42	02 32
64	22 14	////	////	01 03	01 29	02 07	02 57
62	21 42	////	////	01 18	01 47	02 27	03 17
60	21 19	22 47	////	01 31	02 02	02 43	03 33
N 58	21 00	22 10	////	01 42	02 15	02 56	03 46
56	20 45	21 44	////	01 52	02 26	03 08	03 58
54	20 32	21 24	22 54	02 00	02 36	03 18	04 08
52	20 20	21 07	22 19	02 08	02 44	03 27	04 17
50	20 10	20 53	21 55	02 15	02 52	03 36	04 25
45	19 48	20 25	21 13	02 29	03 09	03 53	04 43
N 40	19 31	20 04	20 45	02 42	03 22	04 07	04 57
35	19 17	19 46	20 23	02 52	03 34	04 19	05 09
30	19 05	19 32	20 05	03 01	03 44	04 30	05 19
20	18 44	19 08	19 37	03 17	04 01	04 48	05 37
N 10	18 25	18 48	19 15	03 31	04 16	05 04	05 53
0	18 09	18 31	18 57	03 44	04 31	05 19	06 07
S 10	17 52	18 15	18 41	03 57	04 45	05 33	06 22
20	17 34	17 58	18 25	04 10	05 00	05 49	06 37
30	17 14	17 40	18 10	04 26	05 17	06 07	06 55
35	17 02	17 30	18 01	04 36	05 27	06 18	07 05
40	16 49	17 19	17 53	04 46	05 39	06 30	07 17
45	16 33	17 06	17 43	04 58	05 53	06 44	07 31
S 50	16 13	16 51	17 32	05 14	06 09	07 01	07 48
52	16 04	16 44	17 27	05 21	06 17	07 09	07 56
54	15 53	16 36	17 22	05 28	06 26	07 18	08 04
56	15 41	16 28	17 16	05 37	06 36	07 28	08 14
58	15 28	16 18	17 10	05 47	06 47	07 40	08 26
S 60	15 12	16 07	17 03	05 59	07 00	07 54	08 39

Day	SUN Eqn. of Time 00^h	SUN Eqn. of Time 12^h	SUN Mer. Pass.	MOON Mer. Pass. Upper	MOON Mer. Pass. Lower	MOON Age	MOON Phase
d	m s	m s	h m	h m	h m	d	%
6	04 43	04 48	12 05	22 19	09 56	12	93
7	04 53	04 58	12 05	23 07	10 43	13	97
8	05 02	05 07	12 05	23 55	11 31	14	99

	UT	ARIES	VENUS −4·1		MARS +1·7		JUPITER −2·0		SATURN +0·1	
		GHA	GHA	Dec	GHA	Dec	GHA	Dec	GHA	Dec
	d h	° ′	° ′	° ′	° ′	° ′	° ′	° ′	° ′	° ′
	9 00	287 07.4	224 12.7	N18 33.4	172 35.6	N22 34.9	93 18.5	S 4 31.7	24 50.2	S21 55.9
	01	302 09.8	239 12.4	34.0	187 36.3	34.6	108 20.8	31.8	39 52.8	55.9
	02	317 12.3	254 12.0	34.5	202 37.0	34.4	123 23.1	31.9	54 55.5	55.9
	03	332 14.8	269 11.6	. . 35.1	217 37.8	. . 34.1	138 25.3	. . 32.0	69 58.1	. . 55.9
	04	347 17.2	284 11.2	35.7	232 38.5	33.8	153 27.6	32.1	85 00.7	55.9
	05	2 19.7	299 10.8	36.2	247 39.2	33.6	168 29.9	32.2	100 03.4	55.9
	06	17 22.2	314 10.4	N18 36.8	262 40.0	N22 33.3	183 32.2	S 4 32.3	115 06.0	S21 55.9
	07	32 24.6	329 10.0	37.4	277 40.7	33.1	198 34.4	32.4	130 08.6	55.9
	08	47 27.1	344 09.6	37.9	292 41.4	32.8	213 36.7	32.4	145 11.3	55.9
S	09	62 29.6	359 09.2	. . 38.5	307 42.2	. . 32.5	228 39.0	. . 32.5	160 13.9	. . 55.9
U	10	77 32.0	14 08.8	39.1	322 42.9	32.3	243 41.3	32.6	175 16.5	55.9
N	11	92 34.5	29 08.4	39.6	337 43.6	32.0	258 43.5	32.7	190 19.2	55.9
D	12	107 37.0	44 08.0	N18 40.2	352 44.3	N22 31.7	273 45.8	S 4 32.8	205 21.8	S21 55.9
A	13	122 39.4	59 07.6	40.7	7 45.1	31.5	288 48.1	32.9	220 24.4	55.9
Y	14	137 41.9	74 07.2	41.3	22 45.8	31.2	303 50.3	33.0	235 27.1	55.9
	15	152 44.3	89 06.8	. . 41.9	37 46.5	. . 31.0	318 52.6	. . 33.1	250 29.7	. . 55.9
	16	167 46.8	104 06.4	42.4	52 47.3	30.7	333 54.9	33.2	265 32.3	55.9
	17	182 49.3	119 06.0	43.0	67 48.0	30.4	348 57.2	33.3	280 35.0	55.9
	18	197 51.7	134 05.6	N18 43.5	82 48.7	N22 30.2	3 59.4	S 4 33.4	295 37.6	S21 55.9
	19	212 54.2	149 05.2	44.1	97 49.5	29.9	19 01.7	33.4	310 40.2	55.9
	20	227 56.7	164 04.8	44.6	112 50.2	29.6	34 04.0	33.5	325 42.9	55.8
	21	242 59.1	179 04.4	. . 45.2	127 50.9	. . 29.4	49 06.3	. . 33.6	340 45.5	. . 55.8
	22	258 01.6	194 04.0	45.7	142 51.7	29.1	64 08.5	33.7	355 48.1	55.8
	23	273 04.1	209 03.6	46.3	157 52.4	28.8	79 10.8	33.8	10 50.8	55.8
	10 00	288 06.5	224 03.2	N18 46.8	172 53.1	N22 28.6	94 13.1	S 4 33.9	25 53.4	S21 55.8
	01	303 09.0	239 02.8	47.4	187 53.9	28.3	109 15.3	34.0	40 56.0	55.8
	02	318 11.4	254 02.4	48.0	202 54.6	28.0	124 17.6	34.1	55 58.7	55.8
	03	333 13.9	269 02.0	. . 48.5	217 55.3	. . 27.8	139 19.9	. . 34.2	71 01.3	. . 55.8
	04	348 16.4	284 01.6	49.1	232 56.0	27.5	154 22.1	34.3	86 03.9	55.8
	05	3 18.8	299 01.2	49.6	247 56.8	27.2	169 24.4	34.4	101 06.6	55.8
	06	18 21.3	314 00.8	N18 50.2	262 57.5	N22 27.0	184 26.7	S 4 34.5	116 09.2	S21 55.8
	07	33 23.8	329 00.4	50.7	277 58.2	26.7	199 29.0	34.5	131 11.8	55.8
	08	48 26.2	344 00.0	51.3	292 59.0	26.4	214 31.2	34.6	146 14.5	55.8
M	09	63 28.7	358 59.5	. . 51.8	307 59.7	. . 26.2	229 33.5	. . 34.7	161 17.1	. . 55.8
O	10	78 31.2	13 59.1	52.3	323 00.4	25.9	244 35.8	34.8	176 19.7	55.8
N	11	93 33.6	28 58.7	52.9	338 01.2	25.6	259 38.0	34.9	191 22.4	55.8
D	12	108 36.1	43 58.3	N18 53.4	353 01.9	N22 25.3	274 40.3	S 4 35.0	206 25.0	S21 55.8
A	13	123 38.6	58 57.9	54.0	8 02.6	25.1	289 42.6	35.1	221 27.6	55.8
Y	14	138 41.0	73 57.5	54.5	23 03.4	24.8	304 44.8	35.2	236 30.3	55.8
	15	153 43.5	88 57.1	. . 55.1	38 04.1	. . 24.5	319 47.1	. . 35.3	251 32.9	. . 55.8
	16	168 45.9	103 56.7	55.6	53 04.9	24.3	334 49.4	35.4	266 35.5	55.8
	17	183 48.4	118 56.2	56.2	68 05.6	24.0	349 51.6	35.5	281 38.2	55.8
	18	198 50.9	133 55.8	N18 56.7	83 06.3	N22 23.7	4 53.9	S 4 35.6	296 40.8	S21 55.8
	19	213 53.3	148 55.4	57.2	98 07.1	23.4	19 56.2	35.7	311 43.4	55.8
	20	228 55.8	163 55.0	57.8	113 07.8	23.2	34 58.4	35.8	326 46.1	55.8
	21	243 58.3	178 54.6	. . 58.3	128 08.5	. . 22.9	50 00.7	. . 35.9	341 48.7	. . 55.8
	22	259 00.7	193 54.2	58.9	143 09.3	22.6	65 03.0	35.9	356 51.3	55.8
	23	274 03.2	208 53.8	59.4	158 10.0	22.4	80 05.2	36.0	11 54.0	55.8
	11 00	289 05.7	223 53.3	N18 59.9	173 10.7	N22 22.1	95 07.5	S 4 36.1	26 56.6	S21 55.8
	01	304 08.1	238 52.9	19 00.5	188 11.5	21.8	110 09.8	36.2	41 59.2	55.8
	02	319 10.6	253 52.5	01.0	203 12.2	21.5	125 12.0	36.3	57 01.9	55.8
	03	334 13.1	268 52.1	. . 01.5	218 12.9	. . 21.3	140 14.3	. . 36.4	72 04.5	. . 55.8
	04	349 15.5	283 51.7	02.1	233 13.7	21.0	155 16.5	36.5	87 07.1	55.8
	05	4 18.0	298 51.2	02.6	248 14.4	20.7	170 18.8	36.6	102 09.7	55.8
	06	19 20.4	313 50.8	N19 03.1	263 15.1	N22 20.4	185 21.1	S 4 36.7	117 12.4	S21 55.8
	07	34 22.9	328 50.4	03.7	278 15.9	20.2	200 23.3	36.8	132 15.0	55.8
T	08	49 25.4	343 50.0	04.2	293 16.6	19.9	215 25.6	36.9	147 17.6	55.8
U	09	64 27.8	358 49.5	. . 04.7	308 17.4	. . 19.6	230 27.9	. . 37.0	162 20.3	. . 55.7
E	10	79 30.3	13 49.1	05.3	323 18.1	19.3	245 30.1	37.1	177 22.9	55.7
S	11	94 32.8	28 48.7	05.8	338 18.8	19.1	260 32.4	37.2	192 25.5	55.7
D	12	109 35.2	43 48.3	N19 06.3	353 19.6	N22 18.8	275 34.6	S 4 37.3	207 28.2	S21 55.7
A	13	124 37.7	58 47.8	06.9	8 20.3	18.5	290 36.9	37.4	222 30.8	55.7
Y	14	139 40.2	73 47.4	07.4	23 21.0	18.2	305 39.2	37.5	237 33.4	55.7
	15	154 42.6	88 47.0	. . 07.9	38 21.8	. . 18.0	320 41.4	. . 37.6	252 36.1	. . 55.7
	16	169 45.1	103 46.6	08.4	53 22.5	17.7	335 43.7	37.7	267 38.7	55.7
	17	184 47.6	118 46.1	09.0	68 23.3	17.4	350 46.0	37.8	282 41.3	55.7
	18	199 50.0	133 45.7	N19 09.5	83 24.0	N22 17.1	5 48.2	S 4 37.8	297 43.9	S21 55.7
	19	214 52.5	148 45.3	10.0	98 24.7	16.8	20 50.5	37.9	312 46.6	55.7
	20	229 54.9	163 44.9	10.5	113 25.5	16.6	35 52.7	38.0	327 49.2	55.7
	21	244 57.4	178 44.4	. . 11.1	128 26.2	. . 16.3	50 55.0	. . 38.1	342 51.8	. . 55.7
	22	259 59.9	193 44.0	11.6	143 27.0	16.0	65 57.3	38.2	357 54.5	55.7
	23	275 02.3	208 43.6	12.1	158 27.7	15.7	80 59.5	38.3	12 57.1	55.7
	Mer. Pass.	h m 4 46.8	v −0.4	d 0.5	v 0.7	d 0.3	v 2.3	d 0.1	v 2.6	d 0.0

STARS

Name	SHA	Dec
	° ′	° ′
Acamar	315 16.5	S40 14.0
Achernar	335 24.9	S57 08.7
Acrux	173 06.2	S63 12.0
Adhara	255 10.7	S28 59.9
Aldebaran	290 46.5	N16 32.4
Alioth	166 18.4	N55 52.3
Alkaid	152 56.7	N49 14.0
Al Na'ir	27 40.0	S46 52.3
Alnilam	275 43.9	S 1 11.6
Alphard	217 53.7	S 8 44.1
Alphecca	126 08.5	N26 39.7
Alpheratz	357 40.5	N29 11.0
Altair	62 05.2	N 8 55.1
Ankaa	353 13.0	S42 12.5
Antares	112 22.6	S26 28.1
Arcturus	145 53.1	N19 05.8
Atria	107 21.4	S69 03.5
Avior	234 17.5	S59 34.1
Bellatrix	278 29.4	N 6 21.7
Betelgeuse	270 58.6	N 7 24.4
Canopus	263 55.5	S52 42.4
Capella	280 30.8	N46 00.6
Deneb	49 29.1	N45 20.6
Denebola	182 31.0	N14 28.6
Diphda	348 53.1	S17 53.4
Dubhe	193 48.8	N61 39.7
Elnath	278 09.5	N28 37.1
Eltanin	90 44.4	N51 29.5
Enif	33 44.1	N 9 57.4
Fomalhaut	15 20.8	S29 31.6
Gacrux	171 57.8	S57 12.8
Gienah	175 49.5	S17 38.3
Hadar	148 43.7	S60 27.5
Hamal	327 57.7	N23 32.5
Kaus Aust.	83 39.8	S34 22.4
Kochab	137 19.8	N74 05.5
Markab	13 35.4	N15 17.9
Menkar	314 12.3	N 4 09.3
Menkent	148 04.2	S36 27.4
Miaplacidus	221 39.8	S69 47.6
Mirfak	308 36.6	N49 55.0
Nunki	75 54.5	S26 16.3
Peacock	53 14.4	S56 40.5
Pollux	243 24.8	N27 58.9
Procyon	244 57.2	N 5 10.7
Rasalhague	96 03.6	N12 33.1
Regulus	207 40.9	N11 52.9
Rigel	281 09.7	S 8 11.0
Rigil Kent.	139 47.6	S60 54.5
Sabik	102 09.1	S15 44.6
Schedar	349 37.2	N56 37.7
Shaula	96 17.8	S37 06.8
Sirius	258 31.6	S16 44.5
Spica	158 28.3	S11 15.1
Suhail	222 50.8	S43 30.4
Vega	80 36.7	N38 48.2
Zuben'ubi	137 02.2	S16 06.7

	SHA	Mer. Pass.
	° ′	h m
Venus	295 56.7	9 04
Mars	244 46.6	12 28
Jupiter	166 06.5	17 40
Saturn	97 46.9	22 13

UT (d h)	SUN GHA	SUN Dec	MOON GHA	*v*	MOON Dec	*d*	HP
	° ′	° ′	° ′	′	° ′	′	′
9 00	178 42.1	N22 21.3	1 08.0	11.6	S19 18.3	1.2	54.4
01	193 42.0	21.0	15 38.6	11.6	19 17.1	1.4	54.4
02	208 41.9	20.7	30 09.2	11.6	19 15.7	1.4	54.4
03	223 41.8	. . 20.4	44 39.8	11.6	19 14.3	1.6	54.4
04	238 41.8	20.1	59 10.4	11.6	19 12.7	1.6	54.5
05	253 41.7	19.8	73 41.0	11.6	19 11.1	1.7	54.5
06	268 41.6	N22 19.5	88 11.6	11.5	S19 09.4	1.8	54.5
07	283 41.5	19.2	102 42.1	11.6	19 07.6	1.9	54.5
08	298 41.4	18.9	117 12.7	11.6	19 05.7	2.0	54.5
S 09	313 41.3	. . 18.6	131 43.3	11.6	19 03.7	2.1	54.5
U 10	328 41.2	18.3	146 13.9	11.6	19 01.6	2.2	54.5
N 11	343 41.1	18.0	160 44.5	11.5	18 59.4	2.3	54.5
D 12	358 41.0	N22 17.7	175 15.0	11.6	S18 57.1	2.3	54.6
A 13	13 40.9	17.3	189 45.6	11.6	18 54.8	2.5	54.6
Y 14	28 40.9	17.0	204 16.2	11.6	18 52.3	2.6	54.6
15	43 40.8	. . 16.7	218 46.8	11.6	18 49.7	2.6	54.6
16	58 40.7	16.4	233 17.4	11.5	18 47.1	2.7	54.6
17	73 40.6	16.1	247 47.9	11.6	18 44.4	2.8	54.6
18	88 40.5	N22 15.8	262 18.5	11.6	S18 41.6	3.0	54.6
19	103 40.4	15.5	276 49.1	11.6	18 38.6	3.0	54.6
20	118 40.3	15.2	291 19.7	11.6	18 35.6	3.1	54.7
21	133 40.2	. . 14.9	305 50.3	11.6	18 32.5	3.1	54.7
22	148 40.1	14.5	320 20.9	11.6	18 29.4	3.3	54.7
23	163 40.1	14.2	334 51.5	11.6	18 26.1	3.4	54.7
10 00	178 40.0	N22 13.9	349 22.1	11.7	S18 22.7	3.4	54.7
01	193 39.9	13.6	3 52.8	11.6	18 19.3	3.6	54.7
02	208 39.8	13.3	18 23.4	11.6	18 15.7	3.6	54.7
03	223 39.7	. . 13.0	32 54.0	11.6	18 12.1	3.7	54.8
04	238 39.6	12.6	47 24.6	11.7	18 08.4	3.8	54.8
05	253 39.5	12.3	61 55.3	11.6	18 04.6	3.9	54.8
06	268 39.5	N22 12.0	76 25.9	11.7	S18 00.7	4.0	54.8
07	283 39.4	11.7	90 56.6	11.7	17 56.7	4.1	54.8
08	298 39.3	11.4	105 27.3	11.6	17 52.6	4.2	54.8
M 09	313 39.2	. . 11.1	119 57.9	11.7	17 48.4	4.2	54.8
O 10	328 39.1	10.7	134 28.6	11.7	17 44.2	4.4	54.9
N 11	343 39.0	10.4	148 59.3	11.7	17 39.8	4.4	54.9
D 12	358 38.9	N22 10.1	163 30.0	11.7	S17 35.4	4.5	54.9
A 13	13 38.9	09.8	178 00.7	11.7	17 30.9	4.6	54.9
Y 14	28 38.8	09.4	192 31.4	11.8	17 26.3	4.7	54.9
15	43 38.7	. . 09.1	207 02.2	11.7	17 21.6	4.7	54.9
16	58 38.6	08.8	221 32.9	11.8	17 16.9	4.9	55.0
17	73 38.5	08.5	236 03.7	11.7	17 12.0	4.9	55.0
18	88 38.4	N22 08.1	250 34.4	11.8	S17 07.1	5.1	55.0
19	103 38.3	07.8	265 05.2	11.8	17 02.0	5.1	55.0
20	118 38.3	07.5	279 36.0	11.8	16 56.9	5.2	55.0
21	133 38.2	. . 07.1	294 06.8	11.8	16 51.7	5.2	55.0
22	148 38.1	06.8	308 37.6	11.8	16 46.5	5.4	55.1
23	163 38.0	06.5	323 08.4	11.8	16 41.1	5.4	55.1
11 00	178 37.9	N22 06.2	337 39.2	11.9	S16 35.7	5.6	55.1
01	193 37.8	05.8	352 10.1	11.9	16 30.1	5.6	55.1
02	208 37.8	05.5	6 41.0	11.8	16 24.5	5.7	55.1
03	223 37.7	. . 05.2	21 11.8	11.9	16 18.8	5.7	55.1
04	238 37.6	04.8	35 42.7	11.9	16 13.1	5.9	55.2
05	253 37.5	04.5	50 13.6	11.9	16 07.2	5.9	55.2
06	268 37.4	N22 04.2	64 44.5	11.9	S16 01.3	6.0	55.2
07	283 37.4	03.8	79 15.4	12.0	15 55.3	6.1	55.2
T 08	298 37.3	03.5	93 46.4	11.9	15 49.2	6.2	55.2
U 09	313 37.2	. . 03.1	108 17.3	12.0	15 43.0	6.2	55.2
E 10	328 37.1	02.8	122 48.3	12.0	15 36.8	6.4	55.3
S 11	343 37.0	02.5	137 19.3	12.0	15 30.4	6.4	55.3
D 12	358 36.9	N22 02.1	151 50.3	12.0	S15 24.0	6.4	55.3
A 13	13 36.9	01.8	166 21.3	12.0	15 17.6	6.6	55.3
Y 14	28 36.8	01.5	180 52.3	12.0	15 11.0	6.6	55.3
15	43 36.7	. . 01.1	195 23.3	12.1	15 04.4	6.7	55.3
16	58 36.6	00.8	209 54.4	12.0	14 57.7	6.8	55.4
17	73 36.5	00.4	224 25.4	12.1	14 50.9	6.9	55.4
18	88 36.5	N22 00.1	238 56.5	12.1	S14 44.0	6.9	55.4
19	103 36.4	21 59.7	253 27.6	12.1	14 37.1	7.0	55.4
20	118 36.3	59.4	267 58.7	12.1	14 30.1	7.1	55.4
21	133 36.2	. . 59.1	282 29.8	12.2	14 23.0	7.2	55.5
22	148 36.2	58.7	297 01.0	12.1	14 15.8	7.2	55.5
23	163 36.1	58.4	311 32.1	12.2	S14 08.6	7.3	55.5
	SD 15.8	*d* 0.3	SD 14.9		15.0		15.1

Lat.	Twilight Naut.	Twilight Civil	Sunrise	Moonrise 9	Moonrise 10	Moonrise 11	Moonrise 12
°	h m	h m	h m	h m	h m	h m	h m
N 72	▭	▭	▭	■	23 59	23 39	23 27
N 70	▭	▭	▭	23 09	23 11	23 11	23 09
68	▭	▭	▭	22 24	22 41	22 50	22 55
66	////	////	01 13	21 55	22 18	22 33	22 44
64	////	////	02 02	21 32	21 59	22 19	22 34
62	////	////	02 32	21 15	21 44	22 07	22 25
60	////	01 29	02 55	21 00	21 32	21 57	22 18
N 58	////	02 05	03 13	20 47	21 21	21 49	22 12
56	////	02 30	03 28	20 36	21 11	21 41	22 06
54	01 22	02 50	03 41	20 27	21 03	21 34	22 01
52	01 55	03 06	03 52	20 18	20 55	21 28	21 57
50	02 18	03 19	04 02	20 10	20 49	21 22	21 52
45	02 59	03 47	04 23	19 54	20 34	21 10	21 43
N 40	03 27	04 08	04 40	19 40	20 22	21 00	21 36
35	03 49	04 25	04 54	19 29	20 12	20 52	21 29
30	04 07	04 39	05 07	19 19	20 03	20 44	21 23
20	04 34	05 03	05 27	19 01	19 47	20 31	21 13
N 10	04 56	05 22	05 45	18 46	19 34	20 20	21 05
0	05 13	05 39	06 02	18 32	19 21	20 09	20 56
S 10	05 29	05 56	06 18	18 18	19 08	19 58	20 48
20	05 45	06 12	06 36	18 03	18 54	19 46	20 39
30	06 00	06 30	06 56	17 46	18 39	19 33	20 29
35	06 08	06 39	07 07	17 36	18 29	19 26	20 23
40	06 17	06 50	07 20	17 24	18 19	19 17	20 17
45	06 26	07 03	07 36	17 10	18 07	19 07	20 09
S 50	06 37	07 18	07 55	16 54	17 52	18 54	19 59
52	06 42	07 25	08 04	16 46	17 45	18 48	19 55
54	06 47	07 32	08 15	16 37	17 37	18 42	19 50
56	06 52	07 40	08 26	16 28	17 29	18 35	19 45
58	06 58	07 50	08 40	16 16	17 19	18 27	19 39
S 60	07 05	08 00	08 55	16 04	17 07	18 18	19 32

Lat.	Sunset	Twilight Civil	Twilight Naut.	Moonset 9	Moonset 10	Moonset 11	Moonset 12
°	h m	h m	h m	h m	h m	h m	h m
N 72	▭	▭	▭	■	■	03 16	05 16
N 70	▭	▭	▭	00 57	02 25	04 03	05 43
68	▭	▭	▭	01 58	03 09	04 33	06 03
66	22 53	////	////	02 32	03 38	04 56	06 19
64	22 07	////	////	02 57	04 00	05 13	06 32
62	21 37	////	////	03 17	04 18	05 28	06 43
60	21 15	22 39	////	03 33	04 32	05 40	06 53
N 58	20 57	22 04	////	03 46	04 45	05 50	07 01
56	20 42	21 40	////	03 58	04 56	05 59	07 08
54	20 29	21 20	22 46	04 08	05 05	06 07	07 14
52	20 18	21 04	22 14	04 17	05 13	06 15	07 20
50	20 08	20 51	21 51	04 25	05 21	06 21	07 25
45	19 47	20 23	21 11	04 43	05 37	06 35	07 36
N 40	19 30	20 02	20 43	04 57	05 50	06 46	07 45
35	19 16	19 45	20 21	05 09	06 01	06 56	07 53
30	19 04	19 31	20 04	05 19	06 11	07 05	08 00
20	18 43	19 08	19 36	05 37	06 28	07 19	08 12
N 10	18 26	18 48	19 15	05 53	06 42	07 32	08 22
0	18 09	18 31	18 57	06 07	06 56	07 44	08 32
S 10	17 53	18 15	18 41	06 22	07 09	07 56	08 41
20	17 35	17 59	18 26	06 37	07 24	08 08	08 51
30	17 15	17 41	18 11	06 55	07 40	08 23	09 03
35	17 04	17 32	18 03	07 05	07 50	08 31	09 10
40	16 51	17 21	17 54	07 17	08 00	08 40	09 17
45	16 35	17 08	17 45	07 31	08 13	08 51	09 26
S 50	16 16	16 53	17 34	07 48	08 29	09 05	09 36
52	16 07	16 47	17 29	07 56	08 36	09 11	09 41
54	15 56	16 39	17 24	08 04	08 44	09 18	09 46
56	15 45	16 31	17 19	08 14	08 53	09 25	09 52
58	15 32	16 21	17 13	08 26	09 03	09 34	09 59
S 60	15 16	16 11	17 06	08 39	09 15	09 43	10 06

Day	SUN Eqn. of Time 00^h	SUN Eqn. of Time 12^h	SUN Mer. Pass.	MOON Mer. Pass. Upper	MOON Mer. Pass. Lower	MOON Age	MOON Phase
d	m s	m s	h m	h m	h m	d %	
9	05 11	05 16	12 05	24 44	12 20	15 100	○
10	05 20	05 24	12 05	00 44	13 08	16 98	
11	05 28	05 32	12 06	01 32	13 56	17 95	

	UT	ARIES	VENUS −4·1		MARS +1·7		JUPITER −2·0		SATURN +0·1	
		GHA	GHA	Dec	GHA	Dec	GHA	Dec	GHA	Dec
d	h	° ′	° ′	° ′	° ′	° ′	° ′	° ′	° ′	° ′
12	00	290 04.8	223 43.1	N19 12.6	173 28.4	N22 15.4	96 01.8	S 4 38.4	27 59.7	S21 55.7
	01	305 07.3	238 42.7	13.2	188 29.2	15.2	111 04.0	38.5	43 02.3	55.7
	02	320 09.7	253 42.3	13.7	203 29.9	14.9	126 06.3	38.6	58 05.0	55.7
	03	335 12.2	268 41.8	. . 14.2	218 30.7	. . 14.6	141 08.5	. . 38.7	73 07.6	. . 55.7
	04	350 14.7	283 41.4	14.7	233 31.4	14.3	156 10.8	38.8	88 10.2	55.7
	05	5 17.1	298 41.0	15.2	248 32.1	14.0	171 13.1	38.9	103 12.9	55.7
	06	20 19.6	313 40.5	N19 15.7	263 32.9	N22 13.8	186 15.3	S 4 39.0	118 15.5	S21 55.7
W	07	35 22.0	328 40.1	16.3	278 33.6	13.5	201 17.6	39.1	133 18.1	55.7
E	08	50 24.5	343 39.7	16.8	293 34.4	13.2	216 19.8	39.2	148 20.7	55.7
D	09	65 27.0	358 39.2	. . 17.3	308 35.1	. . 12.9	231 22.1	. . 39.3	163 23.4	. . 55.7
N	10	80 29.4	13 38.8	17.8	323 35.8	12.6	246 24.3	39.4	178 26.0	55.7
E	11	95 31.9	28 38.3	18.3	338 36.6	12.3	261 26.6	39.5	193 28.6	55.7
S	12	110 34.4	43 37.9	N19 18.8	353 37.3	N22 12.1	276 28.9	S 4 39.6	208 31.3	S21 55.7
D	13	125 36.8	58 37.5	19.4	8 38.1	11.8	291 31.1	39.7	223 33.9	55.7
A	14	140 39.3	73 37.0	19.9	23 38.8	11.5	306 33.4	39.8	238 36.5	55.7
Y	15	155 41.8	88 36.6	. . 20.4	38 39.5	. . 11.2	321 35.6	. . 39.9	253 39.1	. . 55.7
	16	170 44.2	103 36.1	20.9	53 40.3	10.9	336 37.9	40.0	268 41.8	55.7
	17	185 46.7	118 35.7	21.4	68 41.0	10.6	351 40.1	40.1	283 44.4	55.7
	18	200 49.2	133 35.3	N19 21.9	83 41.8	N22 10.3	6 42.4	S 4 40.2	298 47.0	S21 55.7
	19	215 51.6	148 34.8	22.4	98 42.5	10.1	21 44.6	40.3	313 49.6	55.7
	20	230 54.1	163 34.4	22.9	113 43.2	09.8	36 46.9	40.4	328 52.3	55.7
	21	245 56.5	178 33.9	. . 23.4	128 44.0	. . 09.5	51 49.2	. . 40.5	343 54.9	. . 55.7
	22	260 59.0	193 33.5	23.9	143 44.7	09.2	66 51.4	40.6	358 57.5	55.7
	23	276 01.5	208 33.0	24.4	158 45.5	08.9	81 53.7	40.7	14 00.2	55.7
13	00	291 03.9	223 32.6	N19 24.9	173 46.2	N22 08.6	96 55.9	S 4 40.8	29 02.8	S21 55.7
	01	306 06.4	238 32.1	25.5	188 47.0	08.3	111 58.2	40.9	44 05.4	55.6
	02	321 08.9	253 31.7	26.0	203 47.7	08.1	127 00.4	41.0	59 08.0	55.6
	03	336 11.3	268 31.3	. . 26.5	218 48.4	. . 07.8	142 02.7	. . 41.1	74 10.7	. . 55.6
	04	351 13.8	283 30.8	27.0	233 49.2	07.5	157 04.9	41.2	89 13.3	55.6
	05	6 16.3	298 30.4	27.5	248 49.9	07.2	172 07.2	41.3	104 15.9	55.6
	06	21 18.7	313 29.9	N19 28.0	263 50.7	N22 06.9	187 09.4	S 4 41.4	119 18.5	S21 55.6
	07	36 21.2	328 29.5	28.5	278 51.4	06.6	202 11.7	41.5	134 21.2	55.6
T	08	51 23.7	343 29.0	29.0	293 52.2	06.3	217 13.9	41.6	149 23.8	55.6
H	09	66 26.1	358 28.6	. . 29.5	308 52.9	. . 06.0	232 16.2	. . 41.7	164 26.4	. . 55.6
U	10	81 28.6	13 28.1	30.0	323 53.7	05.7	247 18.4	41.8	179 29.0	55.6
R	11	96 31.0	28 27.7	30.5	338 54.4	05.5	262 20.7	41.9	194 31.7	55.6
S	12	111 33.5	43 27.2	N19 31.0	353 55.1	N22 05.2	277 22.9	S 4 42.0	209 34.3	S21 55.6
D	13	126 36.0	58 26.8	31.5	8 55.9	04.9	292 25.2	42.1	224 36.9	55.6
A	14	141 38.4	73 26.3	31.9	23 56.6	04.6	307 27.4	42.2	239 39.5	55.6
Y	15	156 40.9	88 25.8	. . 32.4	38 57.4	. . 04.3	322 29.7	. . 42.3	254 42.2	. . 55.6
	16	171 43.4	103 25.4	32.9	53 58.1	04.0	337 31.9	42.4	269 44.8	55.6
	17	186 45.8	118 24.9	33.4	68 58.9	03.7	352 34.2	42.5	284 47.4	55.6
	18	201 48.3	133 24.5	N19 33.9	83 59.6	N22 03.4	7 36.4	S 4 42.6	299 50.0	S21 55.6
	19	216 50.8	148 24.0	34.4	99 00.4	03.1	22 38.7	42.7	314 52.7	55.6
	20	231 53.2	163 23.6	34.9	114 01.1	02.8	37 40.9	42.8	329 55.3	55.6
	21	246 55.7	178 23.1	. . 35.4	129 01.9	. . 02.5	52 43.2	. . 42.9	344 57.9	. . 55.6
	22	261 58.1	193 22.7	35.9	144 02.6	02.2	67 45.4	43.0	0 00.5	55.6
	23	277 00.6	208 22.2	36.4	159 03.3	01.9	82 47.7	43.1	15 03.2	55.6
14	00	292 03.1	223 21.7	N19 36.9	174 04.1	N22 01.7	97 49.9	S 4 43.2	30 05.8	S21 55.6
	01	307 05.5	238 21.3	37.4	189 04.8	01.4	112 52.2	43.3	45 08.4	55.6
	02	322 08.0	253 20.8	37.8	204 05.6	01.1	127 54.4	43.4	60 11.0	55.6
	03	337 10.5	268 20.4	. . 38.3	219 06.3	. . 00.8	142 56.7	. . 43.5	75 13.7	. . 55.6
	04	352 12.9	283 19.9	38.8	234 07.1	00.5	157 58.9	43.6	90 16.3	55.6
	05	7 15.4	298 19.4	39.3	249 07.8	22 00.2	173 01.2	43.7	105 18.9	55.6
	06	22 17.9	313 19.0	N19 39.8	264 08.6	N21 59.9	188 03.4	S 4 43.8	120 21.5	S21 55.6
	07	37 20.3	328 18.5	40.3	279 09.3	59.6	203 05.7	43.9	135 24.1	55.6
	08	52 22.8	343 18.1	40.7	294 10.1	59.3	218 07.9	44.0	150 26.8	55.6
F	09	67 25.3	358 17.6	. . 41.2	309 10.8	. . 59.0	233 10.1	. . 44.1	165 29.4	. . 55.6
R	10	82 27.7	13 17.1	41.7	324 11.6	58.7	248 12.4	44.2	180 32.0	55.6
I	11	97 30.2	28 16.7	42.2	339 12.3	58.4	263 14.6	44.3	195 34.6	55.6
D	12	112 32.6	43 16.2	N19 42.7	354 13.1	N21 58.1	278 16.9	S 4 44.4	210 37.3	S21 55.6
A	13	127 35.1	58 15.7	43.1	9 13.8	57.8	293 19.1	44.5	225 39.9	55.6
Y	14	142 37.6	73 15.3	43.6	24 14.6	57.5	308 21.4	44.6	240 42.5	55.6
	15	157 40.0	88 14.8	. . 44.1	39 15.3	. . 57.2	323 23.6	. . 44.7	255 45.1	. . 55.6
	16	172 42.5	103 14.3	44.6	54 16.1	56.9	338 25.9	44.8	270 47.8	55.6
	17	187 45.0	118 13.9	45.1	69 16.8	56.6	353 28.1	44.9	285 50.4	55.6
	18	202 47.4	133 13.4	N19 45.5	84 17.6	N21 56.3	8 30.3	S 4 45.0	300 53.0	S21 55.6
	19	217 49.9	148 12.9	46.0	99 18.3	56.0	23 32.6	45.1	315 55.6	55.6
	20	232 52.4	163 12.4	46.5	114 19.1	55.7	38 34.8	45.2	330 58.2	55.6
	21	247 54.8	178 12.0	. . 47.0	129 19.8	. . 55.4	53 37.1	. . 45.3	346 00.9	. . 55.6
	22	262 57.3	193 11.5	47.4	144 20.6	55.1	68 39.3	45.4	1 03.5	55.5
	23	277 59.7	208 11.0	47.9	159 21.3	54.8	83 41.6	45.5	16 06.1	55.5
Mer. Pass.		h m 4 35.0	*v* −0.5	*d* 0.5	*v* 0.7	*d* 0.3	*v* 2.3	*d* 0.1	*v* 2.6	*d* 0.0

STARS

Name	SHA	Dec
	° ′	° ′
Acamar	315 16.5	S40 14.0
Achernar	335 24.9	S57 08.7
Acrux	173 06.2	S63 12.0
Adhara	255 10.7	S28 59.9
Aldebaran	290 46.5	N16 32.4
Alioth	166 18.4	N55 52.3
Alkaid	152 56.7	N49 14.0
Al Na'ir	27 40.0	S46 52.3
Alnilam	275 43.9	S 1 11.6
Alphard	217 53.7	S 8 44.1
Alphecca	126 08.5	N26 39.7
Alpheratz	357 40.5	N29 11.1
Altair	62 05.2	N 8 55.1
Ankaa	353 12.9	S42 12.5
Antares	112 22.6	S26 28.1
Arcturus	145 53.2	N19 05.8
Atria	107 21.4	S69 03.5
Avior	234 17.5	S59 34.1
Bellatrix	278 29.3	N 6 21.7
Betelgeuse	270 58.6	N 7 24.4
Canopus	263 55.5	S52 42.4
Capella	280 30.8	N46 00.6
Deneb	49 29.1	N45 20.6
Denebola	182 31.0	N14 28.6
Diphda	348 53.1	S17 53.4
Dubhe	193 48.9	N61 39.7
Elnath	278 09.5	N28 37.1
Eltanin	90 44.4	N51 29.5
Enif	33 44.1	N 9 57.4
Fomalhaut	15 20.8	S29 31.6
Gacrux	171 57.8	S57 12.8
Gienah	175 49.5	S17 38.3
Hadar	148 43.7	S60 27.5
Hamal	327 57.7	N23 32.5
Kaus Aust.	83 39.8	S34 22.4
Kochab	137 19.8	N74 05.5
Markab	13 35.4	N15 17.9
Menkar	314 12.3	N 4 09.3
Menkent	148 04.2	S36 27.4
Miaplacidus	221 39.8	S69 47.6
Mirfak	308 36.6	N49 55.0
Nunki	75 54.5	S26 16.3
Peacock	53 14.4	S56 40.5
Pollux	243 24.8	N27 58.9
Procyon	244 57.2	N 5 10.7
Rasalhague	96 03.6	N12 33.1
Regulus	207 40.9	N11 52.9
Rigel	281 09.7	S 8 11.0
Rigil Kent.	139 47.7	S60 54.5
Sabik	102 09.1	S15 44.6
Schedar	349 37.2	N56 37.7
Shaula	96 17.8	S37 06.8
Sirius	258 31.6	S16 44.5
Spica	158 28.3	S11 15.1
Suhail	222 50.8	S43 30.4
Vega	80 36.7	N38 48.3
Zuben'ubi	137 02.2	S16 06.7

	SHA	Mer. Pass.
	° ′	h m
Venus	292 28.7	9 06
Mars	242 42.3	12 24
Jupiter	165 52.0	17 30
Saturn	97 58.8	22 00

UT d h	SUN GHA ° ′	SUN Dec ° ′	MOON GHA ° ′	v ′	MOON Dec ° ′	d ′	HP ′
12 00	178 36.0	N21 58.0	326 03.3	12.1	S14 01.3	7.4	55.5
01	193 35.9	57.7	340 34.4	12.2	13 53.9	7.4	55.5
02	208 35.8	57.3	355 05.6	12.2	13 46.5	7.5	55.6
03	223 35.8	. . 57.0	9 36.8	12.3	13 39.0	7.6	55.6
04	238 35.7	56.6	24 08.1	12.2	13 31.4	7.7	55.6
05	253 35.6	56.3	38 39.3	12.2	13 23.7	7.7	55.6
06	268 35.5	N21 55.9	53 10.5	12.3	S13 16.0	7.8	55.6
W 07	283 35.5	55.6	67 41.8	12.2	13 08.2	7.8	55.7
E 08	298 35.4	55.2	82 13.0	12.3	13 00.4	7.9	55.7
D 09	313 35.3	. . 54.9	96 44.3	12.3	12 52.5	8.0	55.7
N 10	328 35.2	54.5	111 15.6	12.3	12 44.5	8.1	55.7
E 11	343 35.1	54.2	125 46.9	12.3	12 36.4	8.1	55.7
S 12	358 35.1	N21 53.8	140 18.2	12.4	S12 28.3	8.2	55.8
D 13	13 35.0	53.4	154 49.6	12.3	12 20.1	8.2	55.8
A 14	28 34.9	53.1	169 20.9	12.4	12 11.9	8.3	55.8
Y 15	43 34.8	. . 52.7	183 52.3	12.3	12 03.6	8.4	55.8
16	58 34.8	52.4	198 23.6	12.4	11 55.2	8.5	55.8
17	73 34.7	52.0	212 55.0	12.4	11 46.7	8.5	55.9
18	88 34.6	N21 51.7	227 26.4	12.4	S11 38.2	8.5	55.9
19	103 34.5	51.3	241 57.8	12.4	11 29.7	8.6	55.9
20	118 34.5	50.9	256 29.2	12.4	11 21.1	8.7	55.9
21	133 34.4	. . 50.6	271 00.6	12.4	11 12.4	8.8	55.9
22	148 34.3	50.2	285 32.0	12.4	11 03.6	8.8	56.0
23	163 34.2	49.9	300 03.4	12.5	10 54.8	8.8	56.0
13 00	178 34.2	N21 49.5	314 34.9	12.4	S10 46.0	8.9	56.0
01	193 34.1	49.1	329 06.3	12.5	10 37.1	9.0	56.0
02	208 34.0	48.8	343 37.8	12.5	10 28.1	9.0	56.1
03	223 34.0	. . 48.4	358 09.3	12.4	10 19.1	9.1	56.1
04	238 33.9	48.0	12 40.7	12.5	10 10.0	9.2	56.1
05	253 33.8	47.7	27 12.2	12.5	10 00.8	9.1	56.1
06	268 33.7	N21 47.3	41 43.7	12.5	S 9 51.7	9.3	56.1
07	283 33.7	46.9	56 15.2	12.5	9 42.4	9.3	56.2
T 08	298 33.6	46.6	70 46.7	12.5	9 33.1	9.3	56.2
H 09	313 33.5	. . 46.2	85 18.2	12.5	9 23.8	9.4	56.2
U 10	328 33.4	45.8	99 49.7	12.5	9 14.4	9.5	56.2
R 11	343 33.4	45.5	114 21.2	12.5	9 04.9	9.5	56.3
S 12	358 33.3	N21 45.1	128 52.7	12.6	S 8 55.4	9.6	56.3
D 13	13 33.2	44.7	143 24.3	12.5	8 45.8	9.6	56.3
A 14	28 33.2	44.4	157 55.8	12.5	8 36.2	9.6	56.3
Y 15	43 33.1	. . 44.0	172 27.3	12.5	8 26.6	9.7	56.4
16	58 33.0	43.6	186 58.8	12.6	8 16.9	9.8	56.4
17	73 33.0	43.2	201 30.4	12.5	8 07.1	9.7	56.4
18	88 32.9	N21 42.9	216 01.9	12.5	S 7 57.4	9.9	56.4
19	103 32.8	42.5	230 33.4	12.6	7 47.5	9.9	56.5
20	118 32.7	42.1	245 05.0	12.5	7 37.6	9.9	56.5
21	133 32.7	. . 41.7	259 36.5	12.5	7 27.7	10.0	56.5
22	148 32.6	41.4	274 08.0	12.6	7 17.7	10.0	56.5
23	163 32.5	41.0	288 39.6	12.5	7 07.7	10.0	56.5
14 00	178 32.5	N21 40.6	303 11.1	12.5	S 6 57.7	10.1	56.6
01	193 32.4	40.2	317 42.6	12.6	6 47.6	10.2	56.6
02	208 32.3	39.8	332 14.2	12.5	6 37.4	10.1	56.6
03	223 32.3	. . 39.5	346 45.7	12.5	6 27.3	10.3	56.6
04	238 32.2	39.1	1 17.2	12.5	6 17.0	10.2	56.7
05	253 32.1	38.7	15 48.7	12.5	6 06.8	10.3	56.7
06	268 32.1	N21 38.3	30 20.2	12.5	S 5 56.5	10.3	56.7
07	283 32.0	37.9	44 51.7	12.5	5 46.2	10.4	56.7
08	298 31.9	37.6	59 23.2	12.5	5 35.8	10.4	56.8
F 09	313 31.9	. . 37.2	73 54.7	12.5	5 25.4	10.4	56.8
R 10	328 31.8	36.8	88 26.2	12.4	5 15.0	10.5	56.8
I 11	343 31.7	36.4	102 57.6	12.5	5 04.5	10.5	56.8
D 12	358 31.7	N21 36.0	117 29.1	12.5	S 4 54.0	10.6	56.9
A 13	13 31.6	35.6	132 00.6	12.4	4 43.4	10.5	56.9
Y 14	28 31.5	35.2	146 32.0	12.4	4 32.9	10.6	56.9
15	43 31.5	. . 34.9	161 03.4	12.4	4 22.3	10.6	57.0
16	58 31.4	34.5	175 34.8	12.4	4 11.7	10.7	57.0
17	73 31.3	34.1	190 06.2	12.4	4 01.0	10.7	57.0
18	88 31.3	N21 33.7	204 37.6	12.4	S 3 50.3	10.7	57.0
19	103 31.2	33.3	219 09.0	12.4	3 39.6	10.8	57.1
20	118 31.1	32.9	233 40.4	12.3	3 28.8	10.7	57.1
21	133 31.1	. . 32.5	248 11.7	12.4	3 18.1	10.8	57.1
22	148 31.0	32.1	262 43.1	12.3	3 07.3	10.8	57.1
23	163 30.9	31.7	277 14.4	12.3	S 2 56.5	10.9	57.2
	SD 15.8	*d* 0.4	SD	15.2		15.3	15.5

Lat.	Twilight Naut.	Twilight Civil	Sunrise	Moonrise 12	Moonrise 13	Moonrise 14	Moonrise 15
°	h m	h m	h m	h m	h m	h m	h m
N 72	▭	▭	▭	23 27	23 17	23 09	23 01
N 70	▭	▭	▭	23 09	23 07	23 05	23 03
68	▭	▭	▭	22 55	22 59	23 02	23 04
66	////	////	01 27	22 44	22 52	22 59	23 06
64	////	////	02 10	22 34	22 46	22 56	23 07
62	////	00 33	02 39	22 25	22 41	22 54	23 08
60	////	01 39	03 00	22 18	22 36	22 52	23 08
N 58	////	02 12	03 18	22 12	22 32	22 51	23 09
56	00 31	02 35	03 32	22 06	22 29	22 49	23 10
54	01 31	02 54	03 45	22 01	22 25	22 48	23 10
52	02 01	03 10	03 56	21 57	22 22	22 47	23 11
50	02 23	03 23	04 05	21 52	22 20	22 46	23 11
45	03 03	03 50	04 26	21 43	22 14	22 43	23 13
N 40	03 30	04 10	04 42	21 36	22 09	22 41	23 13
35	03 51	04 27	04 56	21 29	22 05	22 39	23 14
30	04 09	04 41	05 08	21 23	22 01	22 38	23 15
20	04 35	05 04	05 28	21 13	21 55	22 35	23 16
N 10	04 56	05 23	05 46	21 05	21 49	22 33	23 17
0	05 14	05 40	06 02	20 56	21 43	22 31	23 19
S 10	05 30	05 56	06 18	20 48	21 38	22 28	23 20
20	05 44	06 12	06 35	20 39	21 32	22 26	23 21
30	05 59	06 29	06 55	20 29	21 26	22 23	23 22
35	06 07	06 39	07 06	20 23	21 22	22 22	23 23
40	06 16	06 49	07 19	20 17	21 18	22 20	23 24
45	06 25	07 01	07 34	20 09	21 13	22 18	23 25
S 50	06 35	07 16	07 53	19 59	21 07	22 16	23 27
52	06 40	07 22	08 02	19 55	21 04	22 15	23 27
54	06 45	07 30	08 12	19 50	21 01	22 13	23 28
56	06 50	07 38	08 23	19 45	20 58	22 12	23 29
58	06 56	07 47	08 36	19 39	20 54	22 11	23 29
S 60	07 02	07 57	08 51	19 32	20 50	22 09	23 30

Lat.	Sunset	Twilight Civil	Twilight Naut.	Moonset 12	Moonset 13	Moonset 14	Moonset 15
°	h m	h m	h m	h m	h m	h m	h m
N 72	▭	▭	▭	05 16	07 07	08 54	10 42
N 70	▭	▭	▭	05 43	07 23	09 03	10 43
68	▭	▭	▭	06 03	07 36	09 09	10 44
66	22 41	////	////	06 19	07 46	09 15	10 45
64	21 59	////	////	06 32	07 55	09 19	10 46
62	21 31	23 29	////	06 43	08 02	09 23	10 47
60	21 10	22 30	////	06 53	08 09	09 27	10 47
N 58	20 53	21 58	////	07 01	08 14	09 30	10 48
56	20 38	21 35	23 33	07 08	08 19	09 33	10 48
54	20 26	21 16	22 38	07 14	08 24	09 35	10 49
52	20 15	21 01	22 09	07 20	08 28	09 37	10 49
50	20 05	20 48	21 47	07 25	08 31	09 39	10 49
45	19 45	20 21	21 08	07 36	08 39	09 44	10 50
N 40	19 29	20 01	20 41	07 45	08 46	09 47	10 50
35	19 15	19 44	20 20	07 53	08 51	09 51	10 51
30	19 03	19 30	20 03	08 00	08 56	09 53	10 51
20	18 43	19 07	19 36	08 12	09 05	09 58	10 52
N 10	18 26	18 48	19 15	08 22	09 12	10 02	10 53
0	18 09	18 32	18 58	08 32	09 19	10 06	10 53
S 10	17 53	18 16	18 42	08 41	09 26	10 10	10 54
20	17 36	18 00	18 27	08 51	09 33	10 14	10 54
30	17 17	17 43	18 12	09 03	09 41	10 18	10 55
35	17 06	17 33	18 05	09 10	09 46	10 21	10 55
40	16 53	17 23	17 56	09 17	09 51	10 24	10 56
45	16 37	17 10	17 47	09 26	09 57	10 27	10 56
S 50	16 19	16 56	17 37	09 36	10 05	10 31	10 57
52	16 10	16 49	17 32	09 41	10 08	10 33	10 57
54	16 00	16 42	17 27	09 46	10 12	10 35	10 57
56	15 49	16 34	17 22	09 52	10 16	10 37	10 58
58	15 36	16 25	17 16	09 59	10 20	10 40	10 58
S 60	15 21	16 15	17 10	10 06	10 25	10 42	10 58

Day	SUN Eqn. of Time 00^h	SUN Eqn. of Time 12^h	SUN Mer. Pass.	MOON Mer. Pass. Upper	MOON Mer. Pass. Lower	Age	Phase
d	m s	m s	h m	h m	h m	d %	
12	05 36	05 40	12 06	02 20	14 44	18 90	
13	05 43	05 47	12 06	03 08	15 31	19 83	
14	05 50	05 53	12 06	03 55	16 18	20 74	

UT		ARIES	VENUS −4·1		MARS +1·7		JUPITER −2·0		SATURN +0·2	
d h		GHA ° ′	GHA ° ′	Dec ° ′	GHA ° ′	Dec ° ′	GHA ° ′	Dec ° ′	GHA ° ′	Dec ° ′
15 00		293 02.2	223 10.6	N19 48.4	174 22.1	N21 54.5	98 43.8	S 4 45.6	31 08.7	S21 55.5
01		308 04.7	238 10.1	48.8	189 22.8	54.2	113 46.0	45.7	46 11.3	55.5
02		323 07.1	253 09.6	49.3	204 23.6	53.9	128 48.3	45.8	61 14.0	55.5
03		338 09.6	268 09.1	· · 49.8	219 24.3	· · 53.6	143 50.5	· · 45.9	76 16.6	· · 55.5
04		353 12.1	283 08.7	50.2	234 25.1	53.3	158 52.8	46.0	91 19.2	55.5
05		8 14.5	298 08.2	50.7	249 25.8	53.0	173 55.0	46.1	106 21.8	55.5
06		23 17.0	313 07.7	N19 51.2	264 26.6	N21 52.7	188 57.2	S 4 46.2	121 24.5	S21 55.5
07		38 19.5	328 07.2	51.6	279 27.3	52.4	203 59.5	46.3	136 27.1	55.5
08	S	53 21.9	343 06.8	52.1	294 28.1	52.1	219 01.7	46.4	151 29.7	55.5
09	A	68 24.4	358 06.3	· · 52.6	309 28.8	· · 51.8	234 04.0	· · 46.5	166 32.3	· · 55.5
10	T	83 26.9	13 05.8	53.0	324 29.6	51.5	249 06.2	46.7	181 34.9	55.5
11	U	98 29.3	28 05.3	53.5	339 30.3	51.2	264 08.4	46.8	196 37.6	55.5
12	R	113 31.8	43 04.9	N19 54.0	354 31.1	N21 50.9	279 10.7	S 4 46.9	211 40.2	S21 55.5
13	D	128 34.2	58 04.4	54.4	9 31.8	50.6	294 12.9	47.0	226 42.8	55.5
14	A	143 36.7	73 03.9	54.9	24 32.6	50.3	309 15.2	47.1	241 45.4	55.5
15	Y	158 39.2	88 03.4	· · 55.3	39 33.3	· · 50.0	324 17.4	· · 47.2	256 48.0	· · 55.5
16		173 41.6	103 02.9	55.8	54 34.1	49.7	339 19.6	47.3	271 50.7	55.5
17		188 44.1	118 02.5	56.3	69 34.8	49.4	354 21.9	47.4	286 53.3	55.5
18		203 46.6	133 02.0	N19 56.7	84 35.6	N21 49.0	9 24.1	S 4 47.5	301 55.9	S21 55.5
19		218 49.0	148 01.5	57.2	99 36.3	48.7	24 26.4	47.6	316 58.5	55.5
20		233 51.5	163 01.0	57.6	114 37.1	48.4	39 28.6	47.7	332 01.1	55.5
21		248 54.0	178 00.5	· · 58.1	129 37.8	· · 48.1	54 30.8	· · 47.8	347 03.7	· · 55.5
22		263 56.4	193 00.0	58.5	144 38.6	47.8	69 33.1	47.9	2 06.4	55.5
23		278 58.9	207 59.6	59.0	159 39.4	47.5	84 35.3	48.0	17 09.0	55.5
16 00		294 01.4	222 59.1	N19 59.5	174 40.1	N21 47.2	99 37.5	S 4 48.1	32 11.6	S21 55.5
01		309 03.8	237 58.6	19 59.9	189 40.9	46.9	114 39.8	48.2	47 14.2	55.5
02		324 06.3	252 58.1	20 00.4	204 41.6	46.6	129 42.0	48.3	62 16.8	55.5
03		339 08.7	267 57.6	· · 00.8	219 42.4	· · 46.3	144 44.3	· · 48.4	77 19.5	· · 55.5
04		354 11.2	282 57.1	01.3	234 43.1	46.0	159 46.5	48.5	92 22.1	55.5
05		9 13.7	297 56.6	01.7	249 43.9	45.7	174 48.7	48.6	107 24.7	55.5
06		24 16.1	312 56.2	N20 02.2	264 44.6	N21 45.4	189 51.0	S 4 48.8	122 27.3	S21 55.5
07		39 18.6	327 55.7	02.6	279 45.4	45.0	204 53.2	48.9	137 29.9	55.5
08		54 21.1	342 55.2	03.1	294 46.1	44.7	219 55.4	49.0	152 32.5	55.5
09	S	69 23.5	357 54.7	· · 03.5	309 46.9	· · 44.4	234 57.7	· · 49.1	167 35.2	· · 55.5
10	U	84 26.0	12 54.2	03.9	324 47.7	44.1	249 59.9	49.2	182 37.8	55.5
11	N	99 28.5	27 53.7	04.4	339 48.4	43.8	265 02.1	49.3	197 40.4	55.5
12	D	114 30.9	42 53.2	N20 04.8	354 49.2	N21 43.5	280 04.4	S 4 49.4	212 43.0	S21 55.5
13	A	129 33.4	57 52.7	05.3	9 49.9	43.2	295 06.6	49.5	227 45.6	55.5
14	Y	144 35.8	72 52.2	05.7	24 50.7	42.9	310 08.8	49.6	242 48.3	55.5
15		159 38.3	87 51.7	· · 06.2	39 51.4	· · 42.6	325 11.1	· · 49.7	257 50.9	· · 55.5
16		174 40.8	102 51.3	06.6	54 52.2	42.3	340 13.3	49.8	272 53.5	55.5
17		189 43.2	117 50.8	07.0	69 53.0	41.9	355 15.5	49.9	287 56.1	55.5
18		204 45.7	132 50.3	N20 07.5	84 53.7	N21 41.6	10 17.8	S 4 50.0	302 58.7	S21 55.5
19		219 48.2	147 49.8	07.9	99 54.5	41.3	25 20.0	50.1	318 01.3	55.5
20		234 50.6	162 49.3	08.4	114 55.2	41.0	40 22.2	50.2	333 04.0	55.5
21		249 53.1	177 48.8	· · 08.8	129 56.0	· · 40.7	55 24.5	· · 50.3	348 06.6	· · 55.5
22		264 55.6	192 48.3	09.2	144 56.7	40.4	70 26.7	50.5	3 09.2	55.5
23		279 58.0	207 47.8	09.7	159 57.5	40.1	85 28.9	50.6	18 11.8	55.5
17 00		295 00.5	222 47.3	N20 10.1	174 58.3	N21 39.7	100 31.1	S 4 50.7	33 14.4	S21 55.5
01		310 03.0	237 46.8	10.5	189 59.0	39.4	115 33.4	50.8	48 17.0	55.5
02		325 05.4	252 46.3	11.0	204 59.8	39.1	130 35.6	50.9	63 19.6	55.4
03		340 07.9	267 45.8	· · 11.4	220 00.5	· · 38.8	145 37.8	· · 51.0	78 22.3	· · 55.4
04		355 10.3	282 45.3	11.8	235 01.3	38.5	160 40.1	51.1	93 24.9	55.4
05		10 12.8	297 44.8	12.3	250 02.0	38.2	175 42.3	51.2	108 27.5	55.4
06		25 15.3	312 44.3	N20 12.7	265 02.8	N21 37.9	190 44.5	S 4 51.3	123 30.1	S21 55.4
07		40 17.7	327 43.8	13.1	280 03.6	37.5	205 46.8	51.4	138 32.7	55.4
08		55 20.2	342 43.3	13.6	295 04.3	37.2	220 49.0	51.5	153 35.3	55.4
09	M	70 22.7	357 42.8	· · 14.0	310 05.1	· · 36.9	235 51.2	· · 51.6	168 38.0	· · 55.4
10	O	85 25.1	12 42.3	14.4	325 05.8	36.6	250 53.4	51.8	183 40.6	55.4
11	N	100 27.6	27 41.8	14.8	340 06.6	36.3	265 55.7	51.9	198 43.2	55.4
12	D	115 30.1	42 41.3	N20 15.3	355 07.4	N21 36.0	280 57.9	S 4 52.0	213 45.8	S21 55.4
13	A	130 32.5	57 40.8	15.7	10 08.1	35.6	296 00.1	52.1	228 48.4	55.4
14	Y	145 35.0	72 40.3	16.1	25 08.9	35.3	311 02.4	52.2	243 51.0	55.4
15		160 37.5	87 39.8	· · 16.5	40 09.6	· · 35.0	326 04.6	· · 52.3	258 53.6	· · 55.4
16		175 39.9	102 39.3	17.0	55 10.4	34.7	341 06.8	52.4	273 56.3	55.4
17		190 42.4	117 38.8	17.4	70 11.2	34.4	356 09.0	52.5	288 58.9	55.4
18		205 44.8	132 38.2	N20 17.8	85 11.9	N21 34.0	11 11.3	S 4 52.6	304 01.5	S21 55.4
19		220 47.3	147 37.7	18.2	100 12.7	33.7	26 13.5	52.7	319 04.1	55.4
20		235 49.8	162 37.2	18.6	115 13.4	33.4	41 15.7	52.8	334 06.7	55.4
21		250 52.2	177 36.7	· · 19.1	130 14.2	· · 33.1	56 17.9	· · 52.9	349 09.3	· · 55.4
22		265 54.7	192 36.2	19.5	145 15.0	32.8	71 20.2	53.1	4 11.9	55.4
23		280 57.2	207 35.7	19.9	160 15.7	32.4	86 22.4	53.2	19 14.5	55.4
Mer. Pass.		h m 4 23.2	v −0.5	d 0.4	v 0.8	d 0.3	v 2.2	d 0.1	v 2.6	d 0.0

STARS

Name	SHA ° ′	Dec ° ′
Acamar	315 16.5	S40 14.0
Achernar	335 24.8	S57 08.7
Acrux	173 06.2	S63 12.0
Adhara	255 10.7	S28 59.9
Aldebaran	290 46.5	N16 32.4
Alioth	166 18.5	N55 52.3
Alkaid	152 56.8	N49 14.0
Al Na'ir	27 40.0	S46 52.3
Alnilam	275 43.9	S 1 11.6
Alphard	217 53.7	S 8 44.1
Alphecca	126 08.5	N26 39.7
Alpheratz	357 40.5	N29 11.1
Altair	62 05.2	N 8 55.1
Ankaa	353 12.9	S42 12.5
Antares	112 22.6	S26 28.1
Arcturus	145 53.2	N19 05.8
Atria	107 21.4	S69 03.5
Avior	234 17.5	S59 34.1
Bellatrix	278 29.3	N 6 21.7
Betelgeuse	270 58.6	N 7 24.4
Canopus	263 55.4	S52 42.4
Capella	280 30.8	N46 00.6
Deneb	49 29.1	N45 20.6
Denebola	182 31.0	N14 28.6
Diphda	348 53.1	S17 53.4
Dubhe	193 48.9	N61 39.7
Elnath	278 09.5	N28 37.1
Eltanin	90 44.4	N51 29.5
Enif	33 44.1	N 9 57.4
Fomalhaut	15 20.7	S29 31.6
Gacrux	171 57.9	S57 12.8
Gienah	175 49.5	S17 38.3
Hadar	148 43.7	S60 27.5
Hamal	327 57.7	N23 32.5
Kaus Aust.	83 39.8	S34 22.4
Kochab	137 19.9	N74 05.5
Markab	13 35.4	N15 18.0
Menkar	314 12.3	N 4 09.3
Menkent	148 04.2	S36 27.4
Miaplacidus	221 39.8	S69 47.5
Mirfak	308 36.6	N49 55.0
Nunki	75 54.5	S26 16.3
Peacock	53 14.4	S56 40.5
Pollux	243 24.8	N27 58.9
Procyon	244 57.2	N 5 10.7
Rasalhague	96 03.6	N12 33.1
Regulus	207 40.9	N11 52.9
Rigel	281 09.7	S 8 11.0
Rigil Kent.	139 47.7	S60 54.5
Sabik	102 09.1	S15 44.6
Schedar	349 37.1	N56 37.7
Shaula	96 17.8	S37 06.8
Sirius	258 31.6	S16 44.5
Spica	158 28.3	S11 15.0
Suhail	222 50.8	S43 30.3
Vega	80 36.7	N38 48.3
Zuben'ubi	137 02.2	S16 06.7

	SHA ° ′	Mer. Pass. h m
Venus	288 57.7	9 08
Mars	240 38.8	12 21
Jupiter	165 36.2	17 19
Saturn	98 10.3	21 47

UT (d h)	Day	SUN GHA (° ′)	SUN Dec (° ′)	MOON GHA (° ′)	v (′)	MOON Dec (° ′)	d (′)	HP (′)
15 00	SATURDAY	178 30.9	N21 31.3	291 45.7	12.2	S 2 45.6	10.8	57.2
01		193 30.8	30.9	306 16.9	12.3	2 34.8	10.9	57.2
02		208 30.8	30.5	320 48.2	12.2	2 23.9	10.9	57.2
03		223 30.7	. . 30.2	335 19.4	12.3	2 13.0	11.0	57.3
04		238 30.6	29.8	349 50.7	12.2	2 02.0	10.9	57.3
05		253 30.6	29.4	4 21.9	12.1	1 51.1	11.0	57.3
06		268 30.5	N21 29.0	18 53.0	12.2	S 1 40.1	11.0	57.4
07		283 30.4	28.6	33 24.2	12.1	1 29.1	11.0	57.4
08		298 30.4	28.2	47 55.3	12.1	1 18.1	11.0	57.4
09		313 30.3	. . 27.8	62 26.4	12.1	1 07.1	11.0	57.4
10		328 30.3	27.4	76 57.5	12.1	0 56.1	11.1	57.5
11		343 30.2	27.0	91 28.6	12.0	0 45.0	11.1	57.5
12		358 30.1	N21 26.6	105 59.6	12.0	S 0 33.9	11.0	57.5
13		13 30.1	26.2	120 30.6	12.0	0 22.9	11.1	57.5
14		28 30.0	25.8	135 01.6	11.9	0 11.8	11.1	57.6
15		43 29.9	. . 25.4	149 32.5	12.0	S 0 00.7	11.1	57.6
16		58 29.9	25.0	164 03.5	11.8	N 0 10.4	11.2	57.6
17		73 29.8	24.6	178 34.3	11.9	0 21.6	11.1	57.7
18		88 29.8	N21 24.2	193 05.2	11.8	N 0 32.7	11.1	57.7
19		103 29.7	23.7	207 36.0	11.8	0 43.8	11.2	57.7
20		118 29.6	23.3	222 06.8	11.8	0 55.0	11.1	57.7
21		133 29.6	. . 22.9	236 37.6	11.7	1 06.1	11.2	57.8
22		148 29.5	22.5	251 08.3	11.7	1 17.3	11.1	57.8
23		163 29.5	22.1	265 39.0	11.6	1 28.4	11.2	57.8
16 00	SUNDAY	178 29.4	N21 21.7	280 09.6	11.7	N 1 39.6	11.2	57.9
01		193 29.4	21.3	294 40.3	11.5	1 50.8	11.1	57.9
02		208 29.3	20.9	309 10.8	11.6	2 01.9	11.2	57.9
03		223 29.2	. . 20.5	323 41.4	11.5	2 13.1	11.2	57.9
04		238 29.2	20.1	338 11.9	11.5	2 24.3	11.1	58.0
05		253 29.1	19.7	352 42.4	11.4	2 35.4	11.2	58.0
06		268 29.1	N21 19.2	7 12.8	11.4	N 2 46.6	11.1	58.0
07		283 29.0	18.8	21 43.2	11.3	2 57.7	11.2	58.1
08		298 29.0	18.4	36 13.5	11.3	3 08.9	11.1	58.1
09		313 28.9	. . 18.0	50 43.8	11.3	3 20.0	11.2	58.1
10		328 28.8	17.6	65 14.1	11.2	3 31.2	11.1	58.1
11		343 28.8	17.2	79 44.3	11.1	3 42.3	11.1	58.2
12		358 28.7	N21 16.8	94 14.4	11.2	N 3 53.4	11.2	58.2
13		13 28.7	16.3	108 44.6	11.0	4 04.6	11.1	58.2
14		28 28.6	15.9	123 14.6	11.0	4 15.7	11.1	58.3
15		43 28.6	. . 15.5	137 44.6	11.0	4 26.8	11.0	58.3
16		58 28.5	15.1	152 14.6	11.0	4 37.8	11.1	58.3
17		73 28.4	14.7	166 44.6	10.8	4 48.9	11.1	58.3
18		88 28.4	N21 14.2	181 14.4	10.9	N 5 00.0	11.0	58.4
19		103 28.3	13.8	195 44.3	10.7	5 11.0	11.0	58.4
20		118 28.3	13.4	210 14.0	10.8	5 22.0	11.0	58.4
21		133 28.2	. . 13.0	224 43.8	10.6	5 33.0	11.0	58.5
22		148 28.2	12.6	239 13.4	10.6	5 44.0	10.9	58.5
23		163 28.1	12.1	253 43.0	10.6	5 54.9	11.0	58.5
17 00	MONDAY	178 28.1	N21 11.7	268 12.6	10.5	N 6 05.9	10.9	58.5
01		193 28.0	11.3	282 42.1	10.5	6 16.8	10.9	58.6
02		208 28.0	10.9	297 11.6	10.4	6 27.7	10.9	58.6
03		223 27.9	. . 10.4	311 41.0	10.3	6 38.6	10.8	58.6
04		238 27.9	10.0	326 10.3	10.3	6 49.4	10.8	58.7
05		253 27.8	09.6	340 39.6	10.2	7 00.2	10.8	58.7
06		268 27.8	N21 09.2	355 08.8	10.2	N 7 11.0	10.8	58.7
07		283 27.7	08.7	9 38.0	10.1	7 21.8	10.7	58.7
08		298 27.7	08.3	24 07.1	10.0	7 32.5	10.7	58.8
09		313 27.6	. . 07.9	38 36.1	10.0	7 43.2	10.6	58.8
10		328 27.5	07.4	53 05.1	9.9	7 53.8	10.7	58.8
11		343 27.5	07.0	67 34.0	9.9	8 04.5	10.6	58.9
12		358 27.4	N21 06.6	82 02.9	9.8	N 8 15.1	10.5	58.9
13		13 27.4	06.2	96 31.7	9.7	8 25.6	10.5	58.9
14		28 27.3	05.7	111 00.4	9.6	8 36.1	10.5	58.9
15		43 27.3	. . 05.3	125 29.0	9.6	8 46.6	10.5	59.0
16		58 27.2	04.9	139 57.6	9.6	8 57.1	10.4	59.0
17		73 27.2	04.4	154 26.2	9.5	9 07.5	10.3	59.0
18		88 27.1	N21 04.0	168 54.7	9.4	N 9 17.8	10.3	59.1
19		103 27.1	03.5	183 23.1	9.3	9 28.1	10.3	59.1
20		118 27.0	03.1	197 51.4	9.3	9 38.4	10.2	59.1
21		133 27.0	. . 02.7	212 19.7	9.1	9 48.6	10.2	59.1
22		148 27.0	02.2	226 47.8	9.2	9 58.8	10.1	59.2
23		163 26.9	01.8	241 16.0	9.0	N10 08.9	10.1	59.2
		SD 15.8	*d* 0.4	SD		15.7	15.9	16.0

Lat. (°)	Twilight Naut. (h m)	Twilight Civil (h m)	Sunrise (h m)	Moonrise 15 (h m)	Moonrise 16 (h m)	Moonrise 17 (h m)	Moonrise 18 (h m)
N 72	▭	▭	▭	23 01	22 53	22 44	22 32
N 70	▭	▭	▭	23 03	23 01	22 59	22 59
68	▭	▭	▭	23 04	23 07	23 12	23 19
66	////	////	01 40	23 06	23 13	23 22	23 35
64	////	////	02 19	23 07	23 18	23 31	23 48
62	////	00 58	02 45	23 08	23 22	23 38	23 59
60	////	01 49	03 06	23 08	23 25	23 45	24 09
N 58	////	02 19	03 22	23 09	23 28	23 50	24 17
56	00 53	02 41	03 37	23 10	23 31	23 55	24 24
54	01 40	02 59	03 49	23 10	23 34	24 00	00 00
52	02 08	03 14	03 59	23 11	23 36	24 04	00 04
50	02 28	03 27	04 09	23 11	23 38	24 08	00 08
45	03 06	03 53	04 29	23 13	23 43	24 16	00 16
N 40	03 33	04 13	04 45	23 13	23 47	24 23	00 23
35	03 54	04 29	04 58	23 14	23 50	24 29	00 29
30	04 10	04 43	05 10	23 15	23 54	24 35	00 35
20	04 37	05 05	05 30	23 16	23 59	24 44	00 44
N 10	04 57	05 24	05 47	23 17	24 04	00 04	00 52
0	05 14	05 40	06 02	23 19	24 08	00 08	01 00
S 10	05 30	05 56	06 18	23 20	24 13	00 13	01 08
20	05 44	06 11	06 35	23 21	24 17	00 17	01 16
30	05 59	06 28	06 54	23 22	24 23	00 23	01 26
35	06 06	06 37	07 05	23 23	24 26	00 26	01 31
40	06 14	06 48	07 18	23 24	24 30	00 30	01 37
45	06 23	07 00	07 32	23 25	24 34	00 34	01 45
S 50	06 33	07 14	07 51	23 27	24 39	00 39	01 54
52	06 38	07 20	07 59	23 27	24 42	00 42	01 58
54	06 42	07 27	08 09	23 28	24 44	00 44	02 03
56	06 47	07 35	08 20	23 29	24 47	00 47	02 08
58	06 53	07 44	08 32	23 29	24 50	00 50	02 13
S 60	06 59	07 53	08 46	23 30	24 54	00 54	02 20

Lat. (°)	Sunset (h m)	Twilight Civil (h m)	Twilight Naut. (h m)	Moonset 15 (h m)	Moonset 16 (h m)	Moonset 17 (h m)	Moonset 18 (h m)
N 72	▭	▭	▭	10 42	12 32	14 27	16 30
N 70	▭	▭	▭	10 43	12 26	14 13	16 05
68	▭	▭	▭	10 44	12 22	14 02	15 47
66	22 28	////	////	10 45	12 18	13 53	15 32
64	21 51	////	////	10 46	12 15	13 46	15 19
62	21 25	23 08	////	10 47	12 12	13 40	15 09
60	21 05	22 21	////	10 47	12 09	13 34	15 00
N 58	20 49	21 52	////	10 48	12 07	13 29	14 53
56	20 35	21 30	23 14	10 48	12 05	13 25	14 46
54	20 23	21 12	22 30	10 49	12 04	13 21	14 40
52	20 12	20 57	22 03	10 49	12 02	13 18	14 34
50	20 03	20 44	21 42	10 49	12 01	13 14	14 29
45	19 43	20 19	21 05	10 50	11 58	13 07	14 19
N 40	19 27	19 59	20 38	10 50	11 55	13 02	14 10
35	19 14	19 43	20 18	10 51	11 53	12 57	14 03
30	19 02	19 29	20 01	10 51	11 51	12 53	13 56
20	18 42	19 07	19 35	10 52	11 48	12 45	13 45
N 10	18 25	18 48	19 15	10 53	11 45	12 38	13 35
0	18 10	18 32	18 58	10 53	11 42	12 32	13 25
S 10	17 54	18 17	18 42	10 54	11 39	12 26	13 16
20	17 37	18 01	18 28	10 54	11 36	12 20	13 06
30	17 18	17 44	18 14	10 55	11 33	12 12	12 55
35	17 07	17 35	18 06	10 55	11 31	12 08	12 49
40	16 55	17 25	17 58	10 56	11 29	12 03	12 41
45	16 40	17 13	17 49	10 56	11 26	11 58	12 33
S 50	16 22	16 59	17 39	10 57	11 23	11 51	12 22
52	16 13	16 53	17 35	10 57	11 21	11 48	12 18
54	16 04	16 46	17 30	10 57	11 20	11 44	12 12
56	15 53	16 38	17 25	10 58	11 18	11 41	12 07
58	15 41	16 29	17 20	10 58	11 16	11 37	12 00
S 60	15 26	16 19	17 14	10 58	11 14	11 32	11 53

Day (d)	SUN Eqn. of Time 00^h (m s)	SUN Eqn. of Time 12^h (m s)	SUN Mer. Pass. (h m)	MOON Mer. Pass. Upper (h m)	MOON Mer. Pass. Lower (h m)	MOON Age (d)	MOON Phase (%)
15	05 56	05 59	12 06	04 42	17 06	21	64
16	06 02	06 05	12 06	05 30	17 55	22	54
17	06 08	06 10	12 06	06 20	18 46	23	42

UT d	h	ARIES GHA	VENUS −4·1 GHA	VENUS Dec	MARS +1·7 GHA	MARS Dec	JUPITER −1·9 GHA	JUPITER Dec	SATURN +0·2 GHA	SATURN Dec
		° ′	° ′	° ′	° ′	° ′	° ′	° ′	° ′	° ′
18 TUESDAY	00	295 59.6	222 35.2	N20 20.3	175 16.5	N21 32.1	101 24.6	S 4 53.3	34 17.2	S21 55.4
	01	311 02.1	237 34.7	20.7	190 17.2	31.8	116 26.9	53.4	49 19.8	55.4
	02	326 04.6	252 34.2	21.1	205 18.0	31.5	131 29.1	53.5	64 22.4	55.4
	03	341 07.0	267 33.7	. . 21.6	220 18.8	. . 31.2	146 31.3	. . 53.6	79 25.0	. . 55.4
	04	356 09.5	282 33.2	22.0	235 19.5	30.8	161 33.5	53.7	94 27.6	55.4
	05	11 11.9	297 32.6	22.4	250 20.3	30.5	176 35.7	53.8	109 30.2	55.4
	06	26 14.4	312 32.1	N20 22.8	265 21.1	N21 30.2	191 38.0	S 4 53.9	124 32.8	S21 55.4
	07	41 16.9	327 31.6	23.2	280 21.8	29.9	206 40.2	54.0	139 35.4	55.4
	08	56 19.3	342 31.1	23.6	295 22.6	29.5	221 42.4	54.2	154 38.1	55.4
	09	71 21.8	357 30.6	. . 24.0	310 23.3	. . 29.2	236 44.6	. . 54.3	169 40.7	. . 55.4
	10	86 24.3	12 30.1	24.4	325 24.1	28.9	251 46.9	54.4	184 43.3	55.4
	11	101 26.7	27 29.6	24.8	340 24.9	28.6	266 49.1	54.5	199 45.9	55.4
	12	116 29.2	42 29.0	N20 25.3	355 25.6	N21 28.3	281 51.3	S 4 54.6	214 48.5	S21 55.4
	13	131 31.7	57 28.5	25.7	10 26.4	27.9	296 53.5	54.7	229 51.1	55.4
	14	146 34.1	72 28.0	26.1	25 27.2	27.6	311 55.8	54.8	244 53.7	55.4
	15	161 36.6	87 27.5	. . 26.5	40 27.9	. . 27.3	326 58.0	. . 54.9	259 56.3	. . 55.4
	16	176 39.1	102 27.0	26.9	55 28.7	27.0	342 00.2	55.0	274 58.9	55.4
	17	191 41.5	117 26.5	27.3	70 29.4	26.6	357 02.4	55.2	290 01.6	55.4
	18	206 44.0	132 25.9	N20 27.7	85 30.2	N21 26.3	12 04.6	S 4 55.3	305 04.2	S21 55.4
	19	221 46.4	147 25.4	28.1	100 31.0	26.0	27 06.9	55.4	320 06.8	55.4
	20	236 48.9	162 24.9	28.5	115 31.7	25.7	42 09.1	55.5	335 09.4	55.4
	21	251 51.4	177 24.4	. . 28.9	130 32.5	. . 25.3	57 11.3	. . 55.6	350 12.0	. . 55.4
	22	266 53.8	192 23.9	29.3	145 33.3	25.0	72 13.5	55.7	5 14.6	55.4
	23	281 56.3	207 23.3	29.7	160 34.0	24.7	87 15.7	55.8	20 17.2	55.4
19 WEDNESDAY	00	296 58.8	222 22.8	N20 30.1	175 34.8	N21 24.3	102 18.0	S 4 55.9	35 19.8	S21 55.4
	01	312 01.2	237 22.3	30.5	190 35.6	24.0	117 20.2	56.0	50 22.4	55.4
	02	327 03.7	252 21.8	30.9	205 36.3	23.7	132 22.4	56.2	65 25.1	55.4
	03	342 06.2	267 21.2	. . 31.3	220 37.1	. . 23.4	147 24.6	. . 56.3	80 27.7	. . 55.4
	04	357 08.6	282 20.7	31.7	235 37.9	23.0	162 26.8	56.4	95 30.3	55.4
	05	12 11.1	297 20.2	32.0	250 38.6	22.7	177 29.1	56.5	110 32.9	55.4
	06	27 13.6	312 19.7	N20 32.4	265 39.4	N21 22.4	192 31.3	S 4 56.6	125 35.5	S21 55.4
	07	42 16.0	327 19.1	32.8	280 40.2	22.0	207 33.5	56.7	140 38.1	55.4
	08	57 18.5	342 18.6	33.2	295 40.9	21.7	222 35.7	56.8	155 40.7	55.4
	09	72 20.9	357 18.1	. . 33.6	310 41.7	. . 21.4	237 37.9	. . 56.9	170 43.3	. . 55.4
	10	87 23.4	12 17.6	34.0	325 42.5	21.1	252 40.2	57.1	185 45.9	55.4
	11	102 25.9	27 17.0	34.4	340 43.2	20.7	267 42.4	57.2	200 48.5	55.4
	12	117 28.3	42 16.5	N20 34.8	355 44.0	N21 20.4	282 44.6	S 4 57.3	215 51.1	S21 55.4
	13	132 30.8	57 16.0	35.2	10 44.8	20.1	297 46.8	57.4	230 53.8	55.4
	14	147 33.3	72 15.5	35.6	25 45.5	19.7	312 49.0	57.5	245 56.4	55.4
	15	162 35.7	87 14.9	. . 35.9	40 46.3	. . 19.4	327 51.2	. . 57.6	260 59.0	. . 55.4
	16	177 38.2	102 14.4	36.3	55 47.1	19.1	342 53.5	57.7	276 01.6	55.4
	17	192 40.7	117 13.9	36.7	70 47.8	18.7	357 55.7	57.9	291 04.2	55.4
	18	207 43.1	132 13.3	N20 37.1	85 48.6	N21 18.4	12 57.9	S 4 58.0	306 06.8	S21 55.3
	19	222 45.6	147 12.8	37.5	100 49.4	18.1	28 00.1	58.1	321 09.4	55.3
	20	237 48.0	162 12.3	37.9	115 50.1	17.7	43 02.3	58.2	336 12.0	55.3
	21	252 50.5	177 11.7	. . 38.2	130 50.9	. . 17.4	58 04.5	. . 58.3	351 14.6	. . 55.3
	22	267 53.0	192 11.2	38.6	145 51.7	17.1	73 06.8	58.4	6 17.2	55.3
	23	282 55.4	207 10.7	39.0	160 52.4	16.7	88 09.0	58.5	21 19.8	55.3
20 THURSDAY	00	297 57.9	222 10.1	N20 39.4	175 53.2	N21 16.4	103 11.2	S 4 58.6	36 22.4	S21 55.3
	01	313 00.4	237 09.6	39.7	190 54.0	16.1	118 13.4	58.8	51 25.0	55.3
	02	328 02.8	252 09.1	40.1	205 54.7	15.7	133 15.6	58.9	66 27.6	55.3
	03	343 05.3	267 08.5	. . 40.5	220 55.5	. . 15.4	148 17.8	. . 59.0	81 30.3	. . 55.3
	04	358 07.8	282 08.0	40.9	235 56.3	15.1	163 20.0	59.1	96 32.9	55.3
	05	13 10.2	297 07.5	41.2	250 57.1	14.7	178 22.3	59.2	111 35.5	55.3
	06	28 12.7	312 06.9	N20 41.6	265 57.8	N21 14.4	193 24.5	S 4 59.3	126 38.1	S21 55.3
	07	43 15.2	327 06.4	42.0	280 58.6	14.1	208 26.7	59.4	141 40.7	55.3
	08	58 17.6	342 05.9	42.4	295 59.4	13.7	223 28.9	59.6	156 43.3	55.3
	09	73 20.1	357 05.3	. . 42.7	311 00.1	. . 13.4	238 31.1	. . 59.7	171 45.9	. . 55.3
	10	88 22.5	12 04.8	43.1	326 00.9	13.1	253 33.3	59.8	186 48.5	55.3
	11	103 25.0	27 04.2	43.5	341 01.7	12.7	268 35.5	4 59.9	201 51.1	55.3
	12	118 27.5	42 03.7	N20 43.8	356 02.4	N21 12.4	283 37.7	S 5 00.0	216 53.7	S21 55.3
	13	133 29.9	57 03.2	44.2	11 03.2	12.0	298 40.0	00.1	231 56.3	55.3
	14	148 32.4	72 02.6	44.6	26 04.0	11.7	313 42.2	00.2	246 58.9	55.3
	15	163 34.9	87 02.1	. . 44.9	41 04.8	. . 11.4	328 44.4	. . 00.4	262 01.5	. . 55.3
	16	178 37.3	102 01.5	45.3	56 05.5	11.0	343 46.6	00.5	277 04.1	55.3
	17	193 39.8	117 01.0	45.7	71 06.3	10.7	358 48.8	00.6	292 06.7	55.3
	18	208 42.3	132 00.5	N20 46.0	86 07.1	N21 10.4	13 51.0	S 5 00.7	307 09.3	S21 55.3
	19	223 44.7	146 59.9	46.4	101 07.8	10.0	28 53.2	00.8	322 11.9	55.3
	20	238 47.2	161 59.4	46.8	116 08.6	09.7	43 55.4	00.9	337 14.5	55.3
	21	253 49.7	176 58.8	. . 47.1	131 09.4	. . 09.3	58 57.6	. . 01.1	352 17.2	. . 55.3
	22	268 52.1	191 58.3	47.5	146 10.2	09.0	73 59.9	01.2	7 19.8	55.3
	23	283 54.6	206 57.7	47.8	161 10.9	08.7	89 02.1	01.3	22 22.4	55.3
Mer. Pass.		h m 4 11.4	v −0.5	d 0.4	v 0.8	d 0.3	v 2.2	d 0.1	v 2.6	d 0.0

STARS

Name	SHA	Dec
	° ′	° ′
Acamar	315 16.4	S40 14.0
Achernar	335 24.8	S57 08.7
Acrux	173 06.3	S63 12.0
Adhara	255 10.7	S28 59.8
Aldebaran	290 46.4	N16 32.4
Alioth	166 18.5	N55 52.3
Alkaid	152 56.8	N49 14.0
Al Na'ir	27 39.9	S46 52.3
Alnilam	275 43.9	S 1 11.6
Alphard	217 53.7	S 8 44.1
Alphecca	126 08.5	N26 39.7
Alpheratz	357 40.4	N29 11.1
Altair	62 05.2	N 8 55.1
Ankaa	353 12.9	S42 12.5
Antares	112 22.6	S26 28.1
Arcturus	145 53.2	N19 05.8
Atria	107 21.4	S69 03.5
Avior	234 17.5	S59 34.1
Bellatrix	278 29.3	N 6 21.8
Betelgeuse	270 58.6	N 7 24.4
Canopus	263 55.4	S52 42.4
Capella	280 30.7	N46 00.6
Deneb	49 29.1	N45 20.7
Denebola	182 31.0	N14 28.6
Diphda	348 53.1	S17 53.4
Dubhe	193 48.9	N61 39.6
Elnath	278 09.4	N28 37.1
Eltanin	90 44.4	N51 29.5
Enif	33 44.1	N 9 57.4
Fomalhaut	15 20.7	S29 31.6
Gacrux	171 57.9	S57 12.8
Gienah	175 49.6	S17 38.3
Hadar	148 43.8	S60 27.5
Hamal	327 57.6	N23 32.5
Kaus Aust.	83 39.8	S34 22.4
Kochab	137 19.9	N74 05.5
Markab	13 35.3	N15 18.0
Menkar	314 12.3	N 4 09.4
Menkent	148 04.2	S36 27.4
Miaplacidus	221 39.9	S69 47.5
Mirfak	308 36.6	N49 55.0
Nunki	75 54.5	S26 16.3
Peacock	53 14.4	S56 40.5
Pollux	243 24.8	N27 58.9
Procyon	244 57.2	N 5 10.7
Rasalhague	96 03.6	N12 33.1
Regulus	207 40.9	N11 52.9
Rigel	281 09.7	S 8 11.0
Rigil Kent.	139 47.7	S60 54.5
Sabik	102 09.1	S15 44.6
Schedar	349 37.1	N56 37.7
Shaula	96 17.8	S37 06.8
Sirius	258 31.6	S16 44.5
Spica	158 28.3	S11 15.0
Suhail	222 50.8	S43 30.3
Vega	80 36.7	N38 48.3
Zuben'ubi	137 02.2	S16 06.7

	SHA	Mer. Pass.
	° ′	h m
Venus	285 24.0	9 11
Mars	238 36.0	12 17
Jupiter	165 19.2	17 08
Saturn	98 21.1	21 35

	UT	SUN GHA	SUN Dec	MOON GHA	*v*	MOON Dec	*d*	HP
	d h	° ′	° ′	° ′	′	° ′	′	′
	18 00	178 26.9	N21 01.4	255 44.0	9.0	N10 19.0	10.0	59.2
	01	193 26.8	00.9	270 12.0	8.9	10 29.0	10.0	59.3
	02	208 26.8	00.5	284 39.9	8.9	10 39.0	9.9	59.3
	03	223 26.7	21 00.0	299 07.8	8.8	10 48.9	9.9	59.3
	04	238 26.7	20 59.6	313 35.6	8.7	10 58.8	9.8	59.3
	05	253 26.6	59.2	328 03.3	8.6	11 08.6	9.8	59.4
	06	268 26.6	N20 58.7	342 30.9	8.6	N11 18.4	9.7	59.4
	07	283 26.5	58.3	356 58.5	8.5	11 28.1	9.6	59.4
T	08	298 26.5	57.8	11 26.0	8.4	11 37.7	9.6	59.4
U	09	313 26.4	. . 57.4	25 53.4	8.3	11 47.3	9.5	59.5
E	10	328 26.4	56.9	40 20.7	8.3	11 56.8	9.4	59.5
S	11	343 26.3	56.5	54 48.0	8.2	12 06.2	9.4	59.5
D	12	358 26.3	N20 56.1	69 15.2	8.1	N12 15.6	9.3	59.5
A	13	13 26.2	55.6	83 42.3	8.1	12 24.9	9.3	59.6
Y	14	28 26.2	55.2	98 09.4	7.9	12 34.2	9.1	59.6
	15	43 26.2	. . 54.7	112 36.3	7.9	12 43.3	9.2	59.6
	16	58 26.1	54.3	127 03.2	7.9	12 52.5	9.0	59.6
	17	73 26.1	53.8	141 30.1	7.7	13 01.5	8.9	59.7
	18	88 26.0	N20 53.4	155 56.8	7.7	N13 10.4	8.9	59.7
	19	103 26.0	52.9	170 23.5	7.6	13 19.3	8.8	59.7
	20	118 25.9	52.5	184 50.1	7.5	13 28.1	8.8	59.7
	21	133 25.9	. . 52.0	199 16.6	7.5	13 36.9	8.6	59.8
	22	148 25.9	51.6	213 43.1	7.3	13 45.5	8.6	59.8
	23	163 25.8	51.1	228 09.4	7.3	13 54.1	8.5	59.8
	19 00	178 25.8	N20 50.7	242 35.7	7.3	N14 02.6	8.4	59.8
	01	193 25.7	50.2	257 02.0	7.1	14 11.0	8.3	59.9
	02	208 25.7	49.7	271 28.1	7.1	14 19.3	8.3	59.9
	03	223 25.6	. . 49.3	285 54.2	7.0	14 27.6	8.1	59.9
	04	238 25.6	48.8	300 20.2	6.9	14 35.7	8.1	59.9
	05	253 25.6	48.4	314 46.1	6.8	14 43.8	8.0	60.0
	06	268 25.5	N20 47.9	329 11.9	6.8	N14 51.8	7.9	60.0
W	07	283 25.5	47.5	343 37.7	6.7	14 59.7	7.8	60.0
E	08	298 25.4	47.0	358 03.4	6.7	15 07.5	7.7	60.0
D	09	313 25.4	. . 46.5	12 29.1	6.5	15 15.2	7.6	60.0
N	10	328 25.4	46.1	26 54.6	6.5	15 22.8	7.5	60.1
E	11	343 25.3	45.6	41 20.1	6.4	15 30.3	7.4	60.1
S	12	358 25.3	N20 45.2	55 45.5	6.3	N15 37.7	7.3	60.1
D	13	13 25.2	44.7	70 10.8	6.3	15 45.0	7.3	60.1
A	14	28 25.2	44.2	84 36.1	6.2	15 52.3	7.1	60.1
Y	15	43 25.2	. . 43.8	99 01.3	6.1	15 59.4	7.0	60.2
	16	58 25.1	43.3	113 26.4	6.1	16 06.4	6.9	60.2
	17	73 25.1	42.9	127 51.5	5.9	16 13.3	6.8	60.2
	18	88 25.0	N20 42.4	142 16.4	6.0	N16 20.1	6.7	60.2
	19	103 25.0	41.9	156 41.4	5.8	16 26.8	6.6	60.2
	20	118 25.0	41.5	171 06.2	5.8	16 33.4	6.5	60.3
	21	133 24.9	. . 41.0	185 31.0	5.7	16 39.9	6.4	60.3
	22	148 24.9	40.5	199 55.7	5.6	16 46.3	6.3	60.3
	23	163 24.8	40.1	214 20.3	5.6	16 52.6	6.1	60.3
	20 00	178 24.8	N20 39.6	228 44.9	5.5	N16 58.7	6.1	60.3
	01	193 24.8	39.1	243 09.4	5.5	17 04.8	5.9	60.4
	02	208 24.7	38.7	257 33.9	5.4	17 10.7	5.8	60.4
	03	223 24.7	. . 38.2	271 58.3	5.3	17 16.5	5.7	60.4
	04	238 24.7	37.7	286 22.6	5.2	17 22.2	5.6	60.4
	05	253 24.6	37.2	300 46.8	5.2	17 27.8	5.4	60.4
	06	268 24.6	N20 36.8	315 11.0	5.2	N17 33.2	5.4	60.4
T	07	283 24.6	36.3	329 35.2	5.1	17 38.6	5.2	60.4
H	08	298 24.5	35.8	343 59.3	5.0	17 43.8	5.1	60.5
U	09	313 24.5	. . 35.4	358 23.3	5.0	17 48.9	5.0	60.5
R	10	328 24.5	34.9	12 47.3	4.9	17 53.9	4.8	60.5
S	11	343 24.4	34.4	27 11.2	4.8	17 58.7	4.8	60.5
D	12	358 24.4	N20 33.9	41 35.0	4.9	N18 03.5	4.6	60.5
A	13	13 24.4	33.5	55 58.9	4.7	18 08.1	4.5	60.5
Y	14	28 24.3	33.0	70 22.6	4.7	18 12.6	4.3	60.5
	15	43 24.3	. . 32.5	84 46.3	4.7	18 16.9	4.2	60.5
	16	58 24.3	32.0	99 10.0	4.6	18 21.1	4.1	60.6
	17	73 24.2	31.5	113 33.6	4.5	18 25.2	4.0	60.6
	18	88 24.2	N20 31.1	127 57.1	4.6	N18 29.2	3.8	60.6
	19	103 24.2	30.6	142 20.7	4.4	18 33.0	3.7	60.6
	20	118 24.1	30.1	156 44.1	4.5	18 36.7	3.6	60.6
	21	133 24.1	. . 29.6	171 07.6	4.4	18 40.3	3.4	60.6
	22	148 24.1	29.1	185 31.0	4.3	18 43.7	3.3	60.6
	23	163 24.0	28.7	199 54.3	4.3	N18 47.0	3.2	60.6
		SD 15.8	*d* 0.5	SD 16.2		16.4		16.5

Lat.	Twilight Naut.	Twilight Civil	Sunrise	Moonrise 18	Moonrise 19	Moonrise 20	Moonrise 21
°	h m	h m	h m	h m	h m	h m	h m
N 72	□	□	□	22 32	22 14	□	□
N 70	□	□	□	22 59	23 00	23 10	23 47
68	////	////	00 48	23 19	23 31	23 56	24 45
66	////	////	01 53	23 35	23 54	24 26	00 26
64	////	////	02 28	23 48	24 12	00 12	00 49
62	////	01 16	02 52	23 59	24 27	00 27	01 07
60	////	01 58	03 12	24 09	00 09	00 40	01 22
N 58	////	02 26	03 28	24 17	00 17	00 51	01 35
56	01 10	02 47	03 41	24 24	00 24	01 00	01 46
54	01 49	03 04	03 53	00 00	00 31	01 09	01 56
52	02 14	03 19	04 03	00 04	00 37	01 16	02 05
50	02 34	03 31	04 12	00 08	00 42	01 23	02 13
45	03 10	03 56	04 31	00 16	00 54	01 38	02 30
N 40	03 36	04 15	04 47	00 23	01 04	01 50	02 43
35	03 56	04 31	05 00	00 29	01 12	02 01	02 55
30	04 13	04 45	05 11	00 35	01 20	02 10	03 05
20	04 38	05 07	05 31	00 44	01 33	02 26	03 23
N 10	04 58	05 25	05 47	00 52	01 44	02 39	03 39
0	05 15	05 41	06 03	01 00	01 55	02 53	03 53
S 10	05 30	05 56	06 18	01 08	02 05	03 06	04 08
20	05 44	06 11	06 34	01 16	02 17	03 20	04 23
30	05 58	06 27	06 53	01 26	02 30	03 36	04 41
35	06 05	06 36	07 03	01 31	02 38	03 45	04 52
40	06 13	06 46	07 16	01 37	02 47	03 56	05 04
45	06 21	06 58	07 30	01 45	02 57	04 09	05 18
S 50	06 31	07 11	07 48	01 54	03 10	04 24	05 35
52	06 35	07 17	07 56	01 58	03 15	04 32	05 43
54	06 39	07 24	08 05	02 03	03 22	04 40	05 53
56	06 44	07 31	08 16	02 08	03 29	04 49	06 03
58	06 50	07 40	08 28	02 13	03 37	04 59	06 15
S 60	06 55	07 49	08 41	02 20	03 47	05 11	06 28

Lat.	Sunset	Twilight Civil	Twilight Naut.	Moonset 18	Moonset 19	Moonset 20	Moonset 21
°	h m	h m	h m	h m	h m	h m	h m
N 72	□	□	□	16 30	18 48	□	□
N 70	□	□	□	16 05	18 02	19 58	21 30
68	23 15	////	////	15 47	17 32	19 13	20 32
66	22 16	////	////	15 32	17 10	18 43	19 58
64	21 42	////	////	15 19	16 53	18 20	19 34
62	21 18	22 52	////	15 09	16 38	18 02	19 14
60	20 59	22 11	////	15 00	16 26	17 47	18 58
N 58	20 44	21 45	////	14 53	16 16	17 35	18 45
56	20 30	21 24	22 59	14 46	16 07	17 24	18 33
54	20 19	21 07	22 22	14 40	15 59	17 14	18 23
52	20 09	20 53	21 57	14 34	15 51	17 06	18 14
50	20 00	20 41	21 37	14 29	15 45	16 58	18 05
45	19 41	20 16	21 01	14 19	15 31	16 42	17 48
N 40	19 25	19 57	20 36	14 10	15 20	16 28	17 34
35	19 12	19 41	20 16	14 03	15 10	16 17	17 22
30	19 01	19 28	20 00	13 56	15 01	16 07	17 11
20	18 42	19 06	19 34	13 45	14 47	15 50	16 53
N 10	18 25	18 48	19 14	13 35	14 34	15 35	16 37
0	18 10	18 32	18 58	13 25	14 22	15 21	16 22
S 10	17 55	18 17	18 43	13 16	14 10	15 07	16 08
20	17 39	18 02	18 29	13 06	13 57	14 52	15 52
30	17 20	17 46	18 15	12 55	13 42	14 35	15 33
35	17 09	17 37	18 08	12 49	13 34	14 25	15 23
40	16 57	17 27	18 00	12 41	13 24	14 14	15 11
45	16 43	17 15	17 52	12 33	13 13	14 01	14 56
S 50	16 25	17 02	17 42	12 22	13 00	13 44	14 39
52	16 17	16 56	17 38	12 18	12 53	13 37	14 30
54	16 08	16 49	17 34	12 12	12 46	13 28	14 21
56	15 57	16 42	17 29	12 07	12 39	13 19	14 11
58	15 46	16 33	17 24	12 00	12 30	13 08	13 59
S 60	15 32	16 24	17 18	11 53	12 20	12 56	13 45

Day	SUN Eqn. of Time 00^h	SUN Eqn. of Time 12^h	SUN Mer. Pass.	MOON Mer. Pass. Upper	MOON Mer. Pass. Lower	MOON Age	MOON Phase
d	m s	m s	h m	h m	h m	d %	
18	06 12	06 15	12 06	07 13	19 40	24 31	
19	06 17	06 19	12 06	08 08	20 37	25 21	
20	06 21	06 22	12 06	09 07	21 37	26 12	

2017 JULY 21, 22, 23 (FRI., SAT., SUN.)

UT		ARIES	VENUS −4·1		MARS +1·7		JUPITER −1·9		SATURN +0·2		STARS		
d h		GHA	GHA	Dec	GHA	Dec	GHA	Dec	GHA	Dec	Name	SHA	Dec
		° ′	° ′	° ′	° ′	° ′	° ′	° ′	° ′	° ′		° ′	° ′
21 00		298 57.0	221 57.2	N20 48.2	176 11.7	N21 08.3	104 04.3	S 5 01.4	37 25.0	S21 55.3	Acamar	315 16.4	S40 14.0
01		313 59.5	236 56.7	48.5	191 12.5	08.0	119 06.5	01.5	52 27.6	55.3	Achernar	335 24.8	S57 08.7
02		329 02.0	251 56.1	48.9	206 13.3	07.6	134 08.7	01.6	67 30.2	55.3	Acrux	173 06.3	S63 12.0
03		344 04.4	266 55.6	. . 49.3	221 14.0	. . 07.3	149 10.9	. . 01.8	82 32.8	. . 55.3	Adhara	255 10.7	S28 59.8
04		359 06.9	281 55.0	49.6	236 14.8	07.0	164 13.1	01.9	97 35.4	55.3	Aldebaran	290 46.4	N16 32.4
05		14 09.4	296 54.5	50.0	251 15.6	06.6	179 15.3	02.0	112 38.0	55.3			
06		29 11.8	311 53.9	N20 50.3	266 16.3	N21 06.3	194 17.5	S 5 02.1	127 40.6	S21 55.3	Alioth	166 18.5	N55 52.3
07		44 14.3	326 53.4	50.7	281 17.1	05.9	209 19.7	02.2	142 43.2	55.3	Alkaid	152 56.8	N49 14.0
08		59 16.8	341 52.8	51.0	296 17.9	05.6	224 21.9	02.3	157 45.8	55.3	Al Na'ir	27 39.9	S46 52.3
09	F	74 19.2	356 52.3	. . 51.4	311 18.7	. . 05.2	239 24.1	. . 02.5	172 48.4	. . 55.3	Alnilam	275 43.8	S 1 11.6
10	R	89 21.7	11 51.7	51.7	326 19.4	04.9	254 26.4	02.6	187 51.0	55.3	Alphard	217 53.7	S 8 44.1
11	I	104 24.2	26 51.2	52.1	341 20.2	04.6	269 28.6	02.7	202 53.6	55.3			
12	D	119 26.6	41 50.6	N20 52.4	356 21.0	N21 04.2	284 30.8	S 5 02.8	217 56.2	S21 55.3	Alphecca	126 08.5	N26 39.7
13	A	134 29.1	56 50.1	52.8	11 21.8	03.9	299 33.0	02.9	232 58.8	55.3	Alpheratz	357 40.4	N29 11.1
14	Y	149 31.5	71 49.5	53.1	26 22.5	03.5	314 35.2	03.0	248 01.4	55.3	Altair	62 05.2	N 8 55.1
15		164 34.0	86 49.0	. . 53.5	41 23.3	. . 03.2	329 37.4	. . 03.2	263 04.0	. . 55.3	Ankaa	353 12.9	S42 12.5
16		179 36.5	101 48.4	53.8	56 24.1	02.8	344 39.6	03.3	278 06.6	55.3	Antares	112 22.6	S26 28.1
17		194 38.9	116 47.9	54.1	71 24.9	02.5	359 41.8	03.4	293 09.2	55.3			
18		209 41.4	131 47.3	N20 54.5	86 25.6	N21 02.2	14 44.0	S 5 03.5	308 11.8	S21 55.3	Arcturus	145 53.2	N19 05.8
19		224 43.9	146 46.8	54.8	101 26.4	01.8	29 46.2	03.6	323 14.4	55.3	Atria	107 21.5	S69 03.5
20		239 46.3	161 46.2	55.2	116 27.2	01.5	44 48.4	03.7	338 17.0	55.3	Avior	234 17.5	S59 34.1
21		254 48.8	176 45.7	. . 55.5	131 28.0	. . 01.1	59 50.6	. . 03.9	353 19.6	. . 55.3	Bellatrix	278 29.3	N 6 21.8
22		269 51.3	191 45.1	55.9	146 28.7	00.8	74 52.8	04.0	8 22.2	55.3	Betelgeuse	270 58.6	N 7 24.4
23		284 53.7	206 44.5	56.2	161 29.5	00.4	89 55.0	04.1	23 24.8	55.3			
22 00		299 56.2	221 44.0	N20 56.5	176 30.3	N21 00.1	104 57.2	S 5 04.2	38 27.4	S21 55.3	Canopus	263 55.4	S52 42.3
01		314 58.7	236 43.4	56.9	191 31.1	20 59.7	119 59.4	04.3	53 30.0	55.3	Capella	280 30.7	N46 00.6
02		330 01.1	251 42.9	57.2	206 31.9	59.4	135 01.6	04.4	68 32.6	55.3	Deneb	49 29.1	N45 20.7
03		345 03.6	266 42.3	. . 57.5	221 32.6	. . 59.0	150 03.8	. . 04.6	83 35.2	. . 55.3	Denebola	182 31.0	N14 28.6
04		0 06.0	281 41.8	57.9	236 33.4	58.7	165 06.0	04.7	98 37.8	55.3	Diphda	348 53.0	S17 53.4
05		15 08.5	296 41.2	58.2	251 34.2	58.3	180 08.2	04.8	113 40.4	55.3			
06		30 11.0	311 40.6	N20 58.5	266 35.0	N20 58.0	195 10.4	S 5 04.9	128 43.0	S21 55.3	Dubhe	193 48.9	N61 39.6
07		45 13.4	326 40.1	58.9	281 35.7	57.6	210 12.7	05.0	143 45.6	55.3	Elnath	278 09.4	N28 37.1
08	S	60 15.9	341 39.5	59.2	296 36.5	57.3	225 14.9	05.2	158 48.2	55.3	Eltanin	90 44.4	N51 29.5
09	A	75 18.4	356 39.0	. . 59.5	311 37.3	. . 57.0	240 17.1	. . 05.3	173 50.8	. . 55.3	Enif	33 44.1	N 9 57.4
10	T	90 20.8	11 38.4	20 59.9	326 38.1	56.6	255 19.3	05.4	188 53.4	55.3	Fomalhaut	15 20.7	S29 31.6
11	U	105 23.3	26 37.8	21 00.2	341 38.9	56.3	270 21.5	05.5	203 56.0	55.3			
12	R	120 25.8	41 37.3	N21 00.5	356 39.6	N20 55.9	285 23.7	S 5 05.6	218 58.6	S21 55.3	Gacrux	171 57.9	S57 12.8
13	D	135 28.2	56 36.7	00.8	11 40.4	55.6	300 25.9	05.8	234 01.2	55.3	Gienah	175 49.6	S17 38.3
14	A	150 30.7	71 36.2	01.2	26 41.2	55.2	315 28.1	05.9	249 03.8	55.3	Hadar	148 43.8	S60 27.5
15	Y	165 33.2	86 35.6	. . 01.5	41 42.0	. . 54.9	330 30.3	. . 06.0	264 06.4	. . 55.3	Hamal	327 57.6	N23 32.5
16		180 35.6	101 35.0	01.8	56 42.7	54.5	345 32.5	06.1	279 09.0	55.3	Kaus Aust.	83 39.8	S34 22.4
17		195 38.1	116 34.5	02.1	71 43.5	54.2	0 34.7	06.2	294 11.6	55.3			
18		210 40.5	131 33.9	N21 02.5	86 44.3	N20 53.8	15 36.9	S 5 06.4	309 14.2	S21 55.3	Kochab	137 20.0	N74 05.5
19		225 43.0	146 33.3	02.8	101 45.1	53.5	30 39.1	06.5	324 16.8	55.3	Markab	13 35.3	N15 18.0
20		240 45.5	161 32.8	03.1	116 45.9	53.1	45 41.3	06.6	339 19.4	55.3	Menkar	314 12.2	N 4 09.4
21		255 47.9	176 32.2	. . 03.4	131 46.6	. . 52.7	60 43.5	. . 06.7	354 22.0	. . 55.3	Menkent	148 04.2	S36 27.4
22		270 50.4	191 31.6	03.7	146 47.4	52.4	75 45.7	06.8	9 24.6	55.3	Miaplacidus	221 39.9	S69 47.5
23		285 52.9	206 31.1	04.1	161 48.2	52.0	90 47.9	07.0	24 27.2	55.3			
23 00		300 55.3	221 30.5	N21 04.4	176 49.0	N20 51.7	105 50.1	S 5 07.1	39 29.8	S21 55.3	Mirfak	308 36.5	N49 55.0
01		315 57.8	236 29.9	04.7	191 49.8	51.3	120 52.3	07.2	54 32.4	55.3	Nunki	75 54.5	S26 16.3
02		331 00.3	251 29.4	05.0	206 50.5	51.0	135 54.5	07.3	69 35.0	55.3	Peacock	53 14.3	S56 40.5
03		346 02.7	266 28.8	. . 05.3	221 51.3	. . 50.6	150 56.7	. . 07.4	84 37.6	. . 55.3	Pollux	243 24.7	N27 58.9
04		1 05.2	281 28.2	05.6	236 52.1	50.3	165 58.9	07.6	99 40.2	55.3	Procyon	244 57.2	N 5 10.7
05		16 07.6	296 27.7	06.0	251 52.9	49.9	181 01.1	07.7	114 42.8	55.3			
06		31 10.1	311 27.1	N21 06.3	266 53.7	N20 49.6	196 03.2	S 5 07.8	129 45.4	S21 55.3	Rasalhague	96 03.6	N12 33.2
07		46 12.6	326 26.5	06.6	281 54.4	49.2	211 05.4	07.9	144 48.0	55.3	Regulus	207 40.9	N11 52.9
08		61 15.0	341 26.0	06.9	296 55.2	48.9	226 07.6	08.0	159 50.6	55.3	Rigel	281 09.7	S 8 11.0
09	S	76 17.5	356 25.4	. . 07.2	311 56.0	. . 48.5	241 09.8	. . 08.2	174 53.2	. . 55.3	Rigil Kent.	139 47.7	S60 54.5
10	U	91 20.0	11 24.8	07.5	326 56.8	48.2	256 12.0	08.3	189 55.8	55.3	Sabik	102 09.1	S15 44.6
11	N	106 22.4	26 24.3	07.8	341 57.6	47.8	271 14.2	08.4	204 58.4	55.3			
12	D	121 24.9	41 23.7	N21 08.1	356 58.4	N20 47.4	286 16.4	S 5 08.5	220 01.0	S21 55.3	Schedar	349 37.1	N56 37.7
13	A	136 27.4	56 23.1	08.4	11 59.1	47.1	301 18.6	08.6	235 03.5	55.3	Shaula	96 17.8	S37 06.8
14	Y	151 29.8	71 22.5	08.7	26 59.9	46.7	316 20.8	08.8	250 06.1	55.3	Sirius	258 31.6	S16 44.5
15		166 32.3	86 22.0	. . 09.0	42 00.7	. . 46.4	331 23.0	. . 08.9	265 08.7	. . 55.3	Spica	158 28.3	S11 15.0
16		181 34.8	101 21.4	09.3	57 01.5	46.0	346 25.2	09.0	280 11.3	55.3	Suhail	222 50.8	S43 30.3
17		196 37.2	116 20.8	09.6	72 02.3	45.7	1 27.4	09.1	295 13.9	55.3			
18		211 39.7	131 20.2	N21 09.9	87 03.1	N20 45.3	16 29.6	S 5 09.2	310 16.5	S21 55.3	Vega	80 36.7	N38 48.3
19		226 42.1	146 19.7	10.2	102 03.8	44.9	31 31.8	09.4	325 19.1	55.3	Zuben'ubi	137 02.2	S16 06.7
20		241 44.6	161 19.1	10.5	117 04.6	44.6	46 34.0	09.5	340 21.7	55.3			
21		256 47.1	176 18.5	. . 10.8	132 05.4	. . 44.2	61 36.2	. . 09.6	355 24.3	. . 55.3			
22		271 49.5	191 18.0	11.1	147 06.2	43.9	76 38.4	09.7	10 26.9	55.3			
23		286 52.0	206 17.4	11.4	162 07.0	43.5	91 40.6	09.9	25 29.5	55.3			
Mer. Pass.		h m 3 59.6	v −0.6	d 0.3	v 0.8	d 0.3	v 2.2	d 0.1	v 2.6	d 0.0			

	SHA	Mer. Pass.
	° ′	h m
Venus	281 47.8	9 13
Mars	236 34.1	12 13
Jupiter	165 01.0	16 58
Saturn	98 31.2	21 22

UT d	UT h	SUN GHA	SUN Dec	MOON GHA	v	MOON Dec	d	HP
		° ′	° ′	° ′	′	° ′	′	′
21	00	178 24.0	N20 28.2	214 17.6	4.3	N18 50.2	3.0	60.6
	01	193 24.0	27.7	228 40.9	4.2	18 53.2	2.9	60.6
	02	208 23.9	27.2	243 04.1	4.3	18 56.1	2.8	60.6
	03	223 23.9	. . 26.7	257 27.4	4.1	18 58.9	2.6	60.7
	04	238 23.9	26.2	271 50.5	4.2	19 01.5	2.5	60.7
	05	253 23.8	25.8	286 13.7	4.1	19 04.0	2.3	60.7
	06	268 23.8	N20 25.3	300 36.8	4.1	N19 06.3	2.3	60.7
	07	283 23.8	24.8	314 59.9	4.0	19 08.6	2.0	60.7
	08	298 23.7	24.3	329 22.9	4.1	19 10.6	1.9	60.7
F	09	313 23.7	. . 23.8	343 46.0	4.0	19 12.5	1.8	60.7
R	10	328 23.7	23.3	358 09.0	4.0	19 14.3	1.7	60.7
I	11	343 23.7	22.8	12 32.0	4.0	19 16.0	1.5	60.7
D	12	358 23.6	N20 22.4	26 55.0	3.9	N19 17.5	1.4	60.7
A	13	13 23.6	21.9	41 17.9	4.0	19 18.9	1.2	60.7
Y	14	28 23.6	21.4	55 40.9	3.9	19 20.1	1.1	60.7
	15	43 23.5	. . 20.9	70 03.8	4.0	19 21.2	0.9	60.7
	16	58 23.5	20.4	84 26.8	3.9	19 22.1	0.8	60.7
	17	73 23.5	19.9	98 49.7	3.9	19 22.9	0.7	60.7
	18	88 23.5	N20 19.4	113 12.6	3.9	N19 23.6	0.5	60.7
	19	103 23.4	18.9	127 35.5	3.9	19 24.1	0.4	60.7
	20	118 23.4	18.4	141 58.4	3.9	19 24.5	0.2	60.7
	21	133 23.4	. . 17.9	156 21.3	3.9	19 24.7	0.1	60.7
	22	148 23.4	17.4	170 44.2	3.8	19 24.8	0.1	60.7
	23	163 23.3	16.9	185 07.0	3.9	19 24.7	0.2	60.7
22	00	178 23.3	N20 16.4	199 29.9	3.9	N19 24.5	0.3	60.7
	01	193 23.3	15.9	213 52.8	4.0	19 24.2	0.5	60.7
	02	208 23.3	15.4	228 15.8	3.9	19 23.7	0.6	60.7
	03	223 23.2	. . 14.9	242 38.7	3.9	19 23.1	0.8	60.7
	04	238 23.2	14.4	257 01.6	3.9	19 22.3	0.9	60.7
	05	253 23.2	13.9	271 24.5	4.0	19 21.4	1.0	60.7
	06	268 23.2	N20 13.4	285 47.5	3.9	N19 20.4	1.2	60.7
	07	283 23.1	12.9	300 10.4	4.0	19 19.2	1.4	60.7
S	08	298 23.1	12.4	314 33.4	4.0	19 17.8	1.4	60.6
A	09	313 23.1	. . 11.9	328 56.4	4.1	19 16.4	1.7	60.6
T	10	328 23.1	11.4	343 19.5	4.0	19 14.7	1.7	60.6
U	11	343 23.0	10.9	357 42.5	4.1	19 13.0	1.9	60.6
R	12	358 23.0	N20 10.4	12 05.6	4.1	N19 11.1	2.0	60.6
D	13	13 23.0	09.9	26 28.7	4.1	19 09.1	2.2	60.6
A	14	28 23.0	09.4	40 51.8	4.1	19 06.9	2.3	60.6
Y	15	43 23.0	. . 08.9	55 14.9	4.2	19 04.6	2.5	60.6
	16	58 22.9	08.4	69 38.1	4.2	19 02.1	2.6	60.6
	17	73 22.9	07.9	84 01.3	4.3	18 59.5	2.7	60.6
	18	88 22.9	N20 07.4	98 24.6	4.3	N18 56.8	2.8	60.6
	19	103 22.9	06.9	112 47.9	4.3	18 54.0	3.0	60.5
	20	118 22.9	06.4	127 11.2	4.4	18 51.0	3.2	60.5
	21	133 22.8	. . 05.9	141 34.6	4.4	18 47.8	3.2	60.5
	22	148 22.8	05.4	155 58.0	4.4	18 44.6	3.4	60.5
	23	163 22.8	04.9	170 21.4	4.5	18 41.2	3.5	60.5
23	00	178 22.8	N20 04.3	184 44.9	4.6	N18 37.7	3.7	60.5
	01	193 22.8	03.8	199 08.5	4.5	18 34.0	3.8	60.5
	02	208 22.7	03.3	213 32.0	4.7	18 30.2	3.9	60.4
	03	223 22.7	. . 02.8	227 55.7	4.7	18 26.3	4.1	60.4
	04	238 22.7	02.3	242 19.4	4.7	18 22.2	4.2	60.4
	05	253 22.7	01.8	256 43.1	4.8	18 18.0	4.3	60.4
	06	268 22.7	N20 01.3	271 06.9	4.8	N18 13.7	4.4	60.4
	07	283 22.6	00.8	285 30.7	4.9	18 09.3	4.5	60.4
	08	298 22.6	20 00.2	299 54.6	5.0	18 04.8	4.7	60.3
S	09	313 22.6	19 59.7	314 18.6	5.0	18 00.1	4.8	60.3
U	10	328 22.6	59.2	328 42.6	5.0	17 55.3	5.0	60.3
N	11	343 22.6	58.7	343 06.6	5.2	17 50.3	5.0	60.3
D	12	358 22.6	N19 58.2	357 30.8	5.2	N17 45.3	5.2	60.3
A	13	13 22.5	57.7	11 55.0	5.2	17 40.1	5.3	60.3
Y	14	28 22.5	57.1	26 19.2	5.3	17 34.8	5.4	60.2
	15	43 22.5	. . 56.6	40 43.5	5.4	17 29.4	5.5	60.2
	16	58 22.5	56.1	55 07.9	5.5	17 23.9	5.7	60.2
	17	73 22.5	55.6	69 32.4	5.5	17 18.2	5.7	60.2
	18	88 22.5	N19 55.1	83 56.9	5.6	N17 12.5	5.9	60.1
	19	103 22.4	54.5	98 21.5	5.6	17 06.6	6.0	60.1
	20	118 22.4	54.0	112 46.1	5.7	17 00.6	6.1	60.1
	21	133 22.4	. . 53.5	127 10.8	5.8	16 54.5	6.2	60.1
	22	148 22.4	53.0	141 35.6	5.9	16 48.3	6.3	60.1
	23	163 22.4	52.4	156 00.5	5.9	N16 42.0	6.4	60.0
		SD 15.8	*d* 0.5	SD	16.5	16.5		16.4

Lat.	Twilight Naut.	Twilight Civil	Sunrise	Moonrise 21	22	23	24
°	h m	h m	h m	h m	h m	h m	h m
N 72	▭	▭	▭	▭	▭	▭	02 32
N 70	▭	▭	▭	23 47	25 21	01 21	03 17
68	////	////	01 15	24 45	00 45	02 06	03 46
66	////	////	02 06	00 26	01 19	02 36	04 08
64	////	////	02 37	00 49	01 44	02 58	04 25
62	////	01 32	03 00	01 07	02 03	03 16	04 40
60	////	02 08	03 18	01 22	02 19	03 30	04 52
N 58	////	02 34	03 33	01 35	02 33	03 43	05 02
56	01 24	02 53	03 46	01 46	02 45	03 54	05 11
54	01 57	03 10	03 57	01 56	02 55	04 03	05 19
52	02 21	03 23	04 07	02 05	03 04	04 12	05 26
50	02 40	03 35	04 16	02 13	03 12	04 20	05 33
45	03 14	03 59	04 34	02 30	03 29	04 36	05 46
N 40	03 39	04 18	04 49	02 43	03 44	04 49	05 58
35	03 59	04 34	05 02	02 55	03 56	05 00	06 07
30	04 15	04 47	05 13	03 05	04 06	05 10	06 16
20	04 40	05 08	05 32	03 23	04 24	05 27	06 30
N 10	04 59	05 25	05 48	03 39	04 40	05 42	06 43
0	05 15	05 41	06 03	03 53	04 55	05 56	06 55
S 10	05 30	05 55	06 18	04 08	05 10	06 10	07 07
20	05 43	06 10	06 33	04 23	05 26	06 25	07 20
30	05 57	06 26	06 51	04 41	05 44	06 42	07 34
35	06 04	06 34	07 02	04 52	05 54	06 52	07 42
40	06 11	06 44	07 14	05 04	06 07	07 03	07 52
45	06 19	06 55	07 27	05 18	06 21	07 16	08 03
S 50	06 28	07 08	07 44	05 35	06 38	07 32	08 17
52	06 32	07 14	07 52	05 43	06 47	07 40	08 23
54	06 36	07 20	08 01	05 53	06 56	07 48	08 30
56	06 41	07 28	08 11	06 03	07 06	07 57	08 37
58	06 46	07 36	08 23	06 15	07 18	08 08	08 46
S 60	06 51	07 44	08 36	06 28	07 32	08 20	08 56

Lat.	Sunset	Twilight Civil	Twilight Naut.	Moonset 21	22	23	24
°	h m	h m	h m	h m	h m	h m	h m
N 72	▭	▭	▭	▭	▭	23 00	22 42
N 70	▭	▭	▭	21 30	22 06	22 15	22 16
68	22 51	////	////	20 32	21 20	21 44	21 56
66	22 04	////	////	19 58	20 50	21 22	21 41
64	21 33	////	////	19 34	20 28	21 04	21 28
62	21 11	22 37	////	19 14	20 09	20 49	21 17
60	20 53	22 02	////	18 58	19 54	20 36	21 07
N 58	20 38	21 37	////	18 45	19 42	20 25	20 59
56	20 26	21 18	22 45	18 33	19 30	20 16	20 51
54	20 15	21 02	22 13	18 23	19 21	20 07	20 45
52	20 05	20 48	21 50	18 14	19 12	20 00	20 39
50	19 56	20 37	21 32	18 05	19 04	19 53	20 34
45	19 38	20 13	20 58	17 48	18 47	19 38	20 22
N 40	19 23	19 54	20 33	17 34	18 34	19 26	20 12
35	19 10	19 39	20 14	17 22	18 22	19 16	20 04
30	19 00	19 26	19 58	17 11	18 12	19 07	19 57
20	18 41	19 05	19 33	16 53	17 54	18 51	19 44
N 10	18 25	18 47	19 14	16 37	17 39	18 37	19 33
0	18 10	18 32	18 58	16 22	17 24	18 24	19 22
S 10	17 55	18 18	18 43	16 08	17 10	18 11	19 11
20	17 40	18 03	18 30	15 52	16 54	17 57	19 00
30	17 22	17 47	18 17	15 33	16 36	17 41	18 47
35	17 11	17 39	18 10	15 23	16 26	17 32	18 39
40	17 00	17 29	18 02	15 11	16 14	17 21	18 30
45	16 46	17 18	17 54	14 56	16 00	17 09	18 20
S 50	16 29	17 05	17 45	14 39	15 42	16 53	18 08
52	16 21	16 59	17 41	14 30	15 34	16 46	18 02
54	16 12	16 53	17 37	14 21	15 25	16 38	17 55
56	16 02	16 46	17 33	14 11	15 15	16 29	17 48
58	15 51	16 38	17 28	13 59	15 03	16 19	17 40
S 60	15 38	16 29	17 22	13 45	14 50	16 07	17 31

Day	SUN Eqn. of Time 00ʰ	SUN Eqn. of Time 12ʰ	SUN Mer. Pass.	MOON Mer. Pass. Upper	MOON Mer. Pass. Lower	Age	Phase
d	m s	m s	h m	h m	h m	d	%
21	06 24	06 25	12 06	10 08	22 39	27	5
22	06 27	06 28	12 06	11 10	23 40	28	1
23	06 29	06 30	12 06	12 10	24 40	00	0 ●

2017 JULY 24, 25, 26 (MON., TUES., WED.)

UT		ARIES	VENUS −4·0		MARS +1·7		JUPITER −1·9		SATURN +0·2	
d	h	GHA ° ′	GHA ° ′	Dec ° ′	GHA ° ′	Dec ° ′	GHA ° ′	Dec ° ′	GHA ° ′	Dec ° ′
24	00	301 54.5	221 16.8	N21 11.7	177 07.8	N20 43.2	106 42.8	S 5 10.0	40 32.1	S21 55.3
	01	316 56.9	236 16.2	12.0	192 08.5	42.8	121 45.0	10.1	55 34.7	55.3
	02	331 59.4	251 15.6	12.3	207 09.3	42.4	136 47.2	10.2	70 37.3	55.3
	03	347 01.9	266 15.1	. . 12.6	222 10.1	. . 42.1	151 49.3	. . 10.3	85 39.9	. . 55.3
	04	2 04.3	281 14.5	12.9	237 10.9	41.7	166 51.5	10.5	100 42.5	55.3
	05	17 06.8	296 13.9	13.2	252 11.7	41.4	181 53.7	10.6	115 45.1	55.3
	06	32 09.3	311 13.3	N21 13.5	267 12.5	N20 41.0	196 55.9	S 5 10.7	130 47.7	S21 55.3
	07	47 11.7	326 12.8	13.8	282 13.3	40.6	211 58.1	10.8	145 50.2	55.3
M	08	62 14.2	341 12.2	14.1	297 14.0	40.3	227 00.3	11.0	160 52.8	55.3
O	09	77 16.6	356 11.6	. . 14.4	312 14.8	. . 39.9	242 02.5	. . 11.1	175 55.4	. . 55.3
N	10	92 19.1	11 11.0	14.6	327 15.6	39.6	257 04.7	11.2	190 58.0	55.3
D	11	107 21.6	26 10.4	14.9	342 16.4	39.2	272 06.9	11.3	206 00.6	55.3
A	12	122 24.0	41 09.8	N21 15.2	357 17.2	N20 38.8	287 09.1	S 5 11.4	221 03.2	S21 55.3
Y	13	137 26.5	56 09.3	15.5	12 18.0	38.5	302 11.3	11.6	236 05.8	55.3
	14	152 29.0	71 08.7	15.8	27 18.8	38.1	317 13.5	11.7	251 08.4	55.3
	15	167 31.4	86 08.1	. . 16.1	42 19.5	. . 37.7	332 15.6	. . 11.8	266 11.0	. . 55.3
	16	182 33.9	101 07.5	16.3	57 20.3	37.4	347 17.8	11.9	281 13.6	55.3
	17	197 36.4	116 06.9	16.6	72 21.1	37.0	2 20.0	12.1	296 16.2	55.3
	18	212 38.8	131 06.4	N21 16.9	87 21.9	N20 36.7	17 22.2	S 5 12.2	311 18.8	S21 55.3
	19	227 41.3	146 05.8	17.2	102 22.7	36.3	32 24.4	12.3	326 21.4	55.3
	20	242 43.8	161 05.2	17.5	117 23.5	35.9	47 26.6	12.4	341 23.9	55.3
	21	257 46.2	176 04.6	. . 17.7	132 24.3	. . 35.6	62 28.8	. . 12.6	356 26.5	. . 55.3
	22	272 48.7	191 04.0	18.0	147 25.1	35.2	77 31.0	12.7	11 29.1	55.3
	23	287 51.1	206 03.4	18.3	162 25.8	34.8	92 33.2	12.8	26 31.7	55.3
25	00	302 53.6	221 02.8	N21 18.6	177 26.6	N20 34.5	107 35.4	S 5 12.9	41 34.3	S21 55.3
	01	317 56.1	236 02.3	18.8	192 27.4	34.1	122 37.5	13.1	56 36.9	55.3
	02	332 58.5	251 01.7	19.1	207 28.2	33.7	137 39.7	13.2	71 39.5	55.3
	03	348 01.0	266 01.1	. . 19.4	222 29.0	. . 33.4	152 41.9	. . 13.3	86 42.1	. . 55.3
	04	3 03.5	281 00.5	19.7	237 29.8	33.0	167 44.1	13.4	101 44.7	55.3
	05	18 05.9	295 59.9	19.9	252 30.6	32.6	182 46.3	13.5	116 47.3	55.3
	06	33 08.4	310 59.3	N21 20.2	267 31.4	N20 32.3	197 48.5	S 5 13.7	131 49.9	S21 55.3
	07	48 10.9	325 58.7	20.5	282 32.2	31.9	212 50.7	13.8	146 52.4	55.3
T	08	63 13.3	340 58.1	20.7	297 32.9	31.5	227 52.9	13.9	161 55.0	55.3
U	09	78 15.8	355 57.5	. . 21.0	312 33.7	. . 31.2	242 55.0	. . 14.0	176 57.6	. . 55.3
E	10	93 18.2	10 57.0	21.3	327 34.5	30.8	257 57.2	14.2	192 00.2	55.3
S	11	108 20.7	25 56.4	21.5	342 35.3	30.4	272 59.4	14.3	207 02.8	55.3
D	12	123 23.2	40 55.8	N21 21.8	357 36.1	N20 30.1	288 01.6	S 5 14.4	222 05.4	S21 55.3
A	13	138 25.6	55 55.2	22.1	12 36.9	29.7	303 03.8	14.5	237 08.0	55.3
Y	14	153 28.1	70 54.6	22.3	27 37.7	29.3	318 06.0	14.7	252 10.6	55.3
	15	168 30.6	85 54.0	. . 22.6	42 38.5	. . 29.0	333 08.2	. . 14.8	267 13.2	. . 55.3
	16	183 33.0	100 53.4	22.8	57 39.3	28.6	348 10.3	14.9	282 15.7	55.2
	17	198 35.5	115 52.8	23.1	72 40.1	28.2	3 12.5	15.0	297 18.3	55.2
	18	213 38.0	130 52.2	N21 23.4	87 40.8	N20 27.9	18 14.7	S 5 15.2	312 20.9	S21 55.2
	19	228 40.4	145 51.6	23.6	102 41.6	27.5	33 16.9	15.3	327 23.5	55.2
	20	243 42.9	160 51.0	23.9	117 42.4	27.1	48 19.1	15.4	342 26.1	55.2
	21	258 45.4	175 50.4	. . 24.1	132 43.2	. . 26.7	63 21.3	. . 15.5	357 28.7	. . 55.2
	22	273 47.8	190 49.8	24.4	147 44.0	26.4	78 23.4	15.7	12 31.3	55.2
	23	288 50.3	205 49.3	24.6	162 44.8	26.0	93 25.6	15.8	27 33.9	55.2
26	00	303 52.7	220 48.7	N21 24.9	177 45.6	N20 25.6	108 27.8	S 5 15.9	42 36.4	S21 55.2
	01	318 55.2	235 48.1	25.1	192 46.4	25.3	123 30.0	16.1	57 39.0	55.2
	02	333 57.7	250 47.5	25.4	207 47.2	24.9	138 32.2	16.2	72 41.6	55.2
	03	349 00.1	265 46.9	. . 25.6	222 48.0	. . 24.5	153 34.4	. . 16.3	87 44.2	. . 55.2
	04	4 02.6	280 46.3	25.9	237 48.8	24.2	168 36.5	16.4	102 46.8	55.2
	05	19 05.1	295 45.7	26.1	252 49.6	23.8	183 38.7	16.6	117 49.4	55.2
	06	34 07.5	310 45.1	N21 26.4	267 50.4	N20 23.4	198 40.9	S 5 16.7	132 52.0	S21 55.2
W	07	49 10.0	325 44.5	26.6	282 51.1	23.0	213 43.1	16.8	147 54.6	55.2
E	08	64 12.5	340 43.9	26.9	297 51.9	22.7	228 45.3	16.9	162 57.1	55.2
D	09	79 14.9	355 43.3	. . 27.1	312 52.7	. . 22.3	243 47.5	. . 17.1	177 59.7	. . 55.2
N	10	94 17.4	10 42.7	27.4	327 53.5	21.9	258 49.6	17.2	193 02.3	55.2
E	11	109 19.9	25 42.1	27.6	342 54.3	21.5	273 51.8	17.3	208 04.9	55.2
S	12	124 22.3	40 41.5	N21 27.9	357 55.1	N20 21.2	288 54.0	S 5 17.4	223 07.5	S21 55.2
D	13	139 24.8	55 40.9	28.1	12 55.9	20.8	303 56.2	17.6	238 10.1	55.2
A	14	154 27.2	70 40.3	28.3	27 56.7	20.4	318 58.4	17.7	253 12.7	55.2
Y	15	169 29.7	85 39.7	. . 28.6	42 57.5	. . 20.0	334 00.5	. . 17.8	268 15.2	. . 55.3
	16	184 32.2	100 39.1	28.8	57 58.3	19.7	349 02.7	17.9	283 17.8	55.3
	17	199 34.6	115 38.5	29.1	72 59.1	19.3	4 04.9	18.1	298 20.4	55.3
	18	214 37.1	130 37.9	N21 29.3	87 59.9	N20 18.9	19 07.1	S 5 18.2	313 23.0	S21 55.3
	19	229 39.6	145 37.3	29.5	103 00.7	18.5	34 09.3	18.3	328 25.6	55.3
	20	244 42.0	160 36.7	29.8	118 01.5	18.2	49 11.4	18.5	343 28.2	55.3
	21	259 44.5	175 36.1	. . 30.0	133 02.3	. . 17.8	64 13.6	. . 18.6	358 30.8	. . 55.3
	22	274 47.0	190 35.5	30.2	148 03.1	17.4	79 15.8	18.7	13 33.3	55.3
	23	289 49.4	205 34.9	30.5	163 03.9	17.0	94 18.0	18.8	28 35.9	55.3
Mer. Pass.		h m 3 47.8	*v* −0.6	*d* 0.3	*v* 0.8	*d* 0.4	*v* 2.2	*d* 0.1	*v* 2.6	*d* 0.0

STARS

Name	SHA ° ′	Dec ° ′
Acamar	315 16.4	S40 14.0
Achernar	335 24.7	S57 08.7
Acrux	173 06.3	S63 11.9
Adhara	255 10.7	S28 59.8
Aldebaran	290 46.4	N16 32.4
Alioth	166 18.5	N55 52.3
Alkaid	152 56.8	N49 14.0
Al Na'ir	27 39.9	S46 52.3
Alnilam	275 43.8	S 1 11.6
Alphard	217 53.7	S 8 44.1
Alphecca	126 08.5	N26 39.7
Alpheratz	357 40.4	N29 11.1
Altair	62 05.2	N 8 55.1
Ankaa	353 12.8	S42 12.5
Antares	112 22.6	S26 28.1
Arcturus	145 53.2	N19 05.8
Atria	107 21.5	S69 03.5
Avior	234 17.5	S59 34.0
Bellatrix	278 29.3	N 6 21.8
Betelgeuse	270 58.6	N 7 24.5
Canopus	263 55.4	S52 42.3
Capella	280 30.7	N46 00.6
Deneb	49 29.1	N45 20.7
Denebola	182 31.0	N14 28.6
Diphda	348 53.0	S17 53.3
Dubhe	193 48.9	N61 39.6
Elnath	278 09.4	N28 37.1
Eltanin	90 44.4	N51 29.6
Enif	33 44.1	N 9 57.4
Fomalhaut	15 20.7	S29 31.6
Gacrux	171 57.9	S57 12.8
Gienah	175 49.6	S17 38.3
Hadar	148 43.8	S60 27.5
Hamal	327 57.6	N23 32.5
Kaus Aust.	83 39.8	S34 22.4
Kochab	137 20.0	N74 05.5
Markab	13 35.3	N15 18.0
Menkar	314 12.2	N 4 09.4
Menkent	148 04.2	S36 27.4
Miaplacidus	221 39.9	S69 47.5
Mirfak	308 36.5	N49 55.0
Nunki	75 54.5	S26 16.3
Peacock	53 14.3	S56 40.5
Pollux	243 24.7	N27 58.9
Procyon	244 57.2	N 5 10.7
Rasalhague	96 03.6	N12 33.2
Regulus	207 40.9	N11 52.9
Rigel	281 09.6	S 8 11.0
Rigil Kent.	139 47.8	S60 54.5
Sabik	102 09.1	S15 44.6
Schedar	349 37.0	N56 37.7
Shaula	96 17.8	S37 06.8
Sirius	258 31.6	S16 44.5
Spica	158 28.4	S11 15.0
Suhail	222 50.8	S43 30.3
Vega	80 36.7	N38 48.3
Zuben'ubi	137 02.2	S16 06.7

	SHA ° ′	Mer. Pass. h m
Venus	278 09.2	9 16
Mars	234 33.0	12 10
Jupiter	164 41.7	16 47
Saturn	98 40.7	21 10

UT d h	SUN GHA ° ′	SUN Dec ° ′	MOON GHA ° ′	v ′	MOON Dec ° ′	d ′	HP ′
24 00	178 22.4	N19 51.9	170 25.4	6.0	N16 35.6	6.5	60.0
01	193 22.4	51.4	184 50.4	6.1	16 29.1	6.6	60.0
02	208 22.3	50.9	199 15.5	6.2	16 22.5	6.8	60.0
03	223 22.3	. . 50.3	213 40.7	6.2	16 15.7	6.8	59.9
04	238 22.3	49.8	228 05.9	6.3	16 08.9	7.0	59.9
05	253 22.3	49.3	242 31.2	6.4	16 01.9	7.0	59.9
06	268 22.3	N19 48.8	256 56.6	6.5	N15 54.9	7.1	59.9
07	283 22.3	48.2	271 22.1	6.5	15 47.8	7.3	59.8
08	298 22.3	47.7	285 47.6	6.7	15 40.5	7.3	59.8
M 09	313 22.3	. . 47.2	300 13.3	6.7	15 33.2	7.4	59.8
O 10	328 22.3	46.6	314 39.0	6.7	15 25.8	7.5	59.7
N 11	343 22.2	46.1	329 04.7	6.9	15 18.3	7.7	59.7
D 12	358 22.2	N19 45.6	343 30.6	6.9	N15 10.6	7.7	59.7
A 13	13 22.2	45.0	357 56.5	7.1	15 02.9	7.7	59.7
Y 14	28 22.2	44.5	12 22.6	7.1	14 55.2	7.9	59.6
15	43 22.2	. . 44.0	26 48.7	7.2	14 47.3	8.0	59.6
16	58 22.2	43.4	41 14.9	7.2	14 39.3	8.0	59.6
17	73 22.2	42.9	55 41.1	7.4	14 31.3	8.2	59.5
18	88 22.2	N19 42.4	70 07.5	7.4	N14 23.1	8.2	59.5
19	103 22.2	41.8	84 33.9	7.5	14 14.9	8.3	59.5
20	118 22.2	41.3	99 00.4	7.6	14 06.6	8.4	59.5
21	133 22.2	. . 40.8	113 27.0	7.7	13 58.2	8.4	59.4
22	148 22.1	40.2	127 53.7	7.8	13 49.8	8.5	59.4
23	163 22.1	39.7	142 20.5	7.8	13 41.3	8.6	59.4
25 00	178 22.1	N19 39.2	156 47.3	7.9	N13 32.7	8.7	59.3
01	193 22.1	38.6	171 14.2	8.0	13 24.0	8.8	59.3
02	208 22.1	38.1	185 41.2	8.1	13 15.2	8.8	59.3
03	223 22.1	. . 37.5	200 08.3	8.2	13 06.4	8.9	59.2
04	238 22.1	37.0	214 35.5	8.3	12 57.5	8.9	59.2
05	253 22.1	36.5	229 02.8	8.3	12 48.6	9.1	59.2
06	268 22.1	N19 35.9	243 30.1	8.4	N12 39.5	9.1	59.1
07	283 22.1	35.4	257 57.5	8.6	12 30.4	9.1	59.1
T 08	298 22.1	34.8	272 25.1	8.5	12 21.3	9.2	59.1
U 09	313 22.1	. . 34.3	286 52.6	8.7	12 12.1	9.3	59.0
E 10	328 22.1	33.7	301 20.3	8.8	12 02.8	9.4	59.0
S 11	343 22.1	33.2	315 48.1	8.8	11 53.4	9.4	59.0
D 12	358 22.1	N19 32.7	330 15.9	8.9	N11 44.0	9.4	58.9
A 13	13 22.1	32.1	344 43.8	9.0	11 34.6	9.5	58.9
Y 14	28 22.1	31.6	359 11.8	9.1	11 25.1	9.6	58.9
15	43 22.1	. . 31.0	13 39.9	9.2	11 15.5	9.6	58.8
16	58 22.0	30.5	28 08.1	9.2	11 05.9	9.7	58.8
17	73 22.0	29.9	42 36.3	9.4	10 56.2	9.7	58.7
18	88 22.0	N19 29.4	57 04.7	9.4	N10 46.5	9.8	58.7
19	103 22.0	28.8	71 33.1	9.5	10 36.7	9.8	58.7
20	118 22.0	28.3	86 01.6	9.5	10 26.9	9.9	58.6
21	133 22.0	. . 27.7	100 30.1	9.7	10 17.0	9.9	58.6
22	148 22.0	27.2	114 58.8	9.7	10 07.1	10.0	58.6
23	163 22.0	26.6	129 27.5	9.8	9 57.1	10.0	58.5
26 00	178 22.0	N19 26.1	143 56.3	9.9	N 9 47.1	10.0	58.5
01	193 22.0	25.5	158 25.2	9.9	9 37.1	10.1	58.5
02	208 22.0	25.0	172 54.1	10.1	9 27.0	10.2	58.4
03	223 22.0	. . 24.4	187 23.2	10.1	9 16.8	10.1	58.4
04	238 22.0	23.9	201 52.3	10.2	9 06.7	10.2	58.4
05	253 22.0	23.3	216 21.5	10.2	8 56.5	10.3	58.3
06	268 22.0	N19 22.8	230 50.7	10.4	N 8 46.2	10.2	58.3
W 07	283 22.0	22.2	245 20.1	10.4	8 36.0	10.3	58.2
E 08	298 22.0	21.6	259 49.5	10.5	8 25.7	10.4	58.2
D 09	313 22.0	. . 21.1	274 19.0	10.5	8 15.3	10.3	58.2
N 10	328 22.0	20.5	288 48.5	10.7	8 05.0	10.4	58.1
E 11	343 22.0	20.0	303 18.2	10.7	7 54.6	10.5	58.1
S 12	358 22.0	N19 19.4	317 47.9	10.7	N 7 44.1	10.4	58.1
D 13	13 22.0	18.9	332 17.6	10.9	7 33.7	10.5	58.0
A 14	28 22.0	18.3	346 47.5	10.9	7 23.2	10.5	58.0
Y 15	43 22.0	. . 17.7	1 17.4	11.0	7 12.7	10.5	57.9
16	58 22.1	17.2	15 47.4	11.0	7 02.2	10.6	57.9
17	73 22.1	16.6	30 17.4	11.1	6 51.6	10.5	57.9
18	88 22.1	N19 16.1	44 47.5	11.2	N 6 41.1	10.6	57.8
19	103 22.1	15.5	59 17.7	11.3	6 30.5	10.6	57.8
20	118 22.1	14.9	73 48.0	11.3	6 19.9	10.7	57.8
21	133 22.1	. . 14.4	88 18.3	11.4	6 09.2	10.6	57.7
22	148 22.1	13.8	102 48.7	11.4	5 58.6	10.7	57.7
23	163 22.1	13.2	117 19.1	11.6	N 5 47.9	10.7	57.6
	SD 15.8	*d* 0.5	SD	16.3		16.1	15.8

Lat. °	Twilight Naut. h m	Twilight Civil h m	Sunrise h m	Moonrise 24 h m	Moonrise 25 h m	Moonrise 26 h m	Moonrise 27 h m
N 72	▭	▭	▭	02 32	04 48	06 49	08 41
N 70	▭	▭	▭	03 17	05 12	07 02	08 46
68	////	////	01 36	03 46	05 31	07 13	08 51
66	////	////	02 18	04 08	05 46	07 22	08 55
64	////	00 46	02 46	04 25	05 58	07 30	08 58
62	////	01 46	03 08	04 40	06 08	07 36	09 01
60	////	02 18	03 25	04 52	06 17	07 41	09 04
N 58	00 42	02 41	03 39	05 02	06 24	07 46	09 06
56	01 37	03 00	03 51	05 11	06 31	07 50	09 08
54	02 06	03 15	04 02	05 19	06 37	07 54	09 09
52	02 28	03 28	04 11	05 26	06 42	07 58	09 11
50	02 46	03 40	04 20	05 33	06 47	08 01	09 12
45	03 19	04 03	04 38	05 46	06 58	08 08	09 16
N 40	03 43	04 21	04 52	05 58	07 06	08 13	09 18
35	04 01	04 36	05 04	06 07	07 14	08 18	09 20
30	04 17	04 49	05 15	06 16	07 20	08 23	09 22
20	04 41	05 09	05 33	06 30	07 32	08 30	09 26
N 10	05 00	05 26	05 49	06 43	07 41	08 37	09 29
0	05 16	05 41	06 03	06 55	07 51	08 43	09 32
S 10	05 29	05 55	06 17	07 07	08 00	08 49	09 35
20	05 42	06 09	06 33	07 20	08 10	08 55	09 38
30	05 55	06 24	06 50	07 34	08 21	09 03	09 41
35	06 02	06 33	07 00	07 42	08 27	09 07	09 43
40	06 09	06 42	07 11	07 52	08 34	09 12	09 45
45	06 17	06 52	07 25	08 03	08 43	09 17	09 48
S 50	06 25	07 05	07 41	08 17	08 53	09 24	09 51
52	06 29	07 10	07 48	08 23	08 58	09 27	09 52
54	06 33	07 17	07 57	08 30	09 03	09 30	09 54
56	06 37	07 23	08 06	08 37	09 09	09 34	09 56
58	06 42	07 31	08 17	08 46	09 15	09 38	09 58
S 60	06 47	07 39	08 30	08 56	09 22	09 43	10 00

Lat. °	Sunset h m	Twilight Civil h m	Twilight Naut. h m	Moonset 24 h m	Moonset 25 h m	Moonset 26 h m	Moonset 27 h m
N 72	▭	▭	▭	22 42	22 31	22 22	22 14
N 70	▭	▭	▭	22 16	22 16	22 14	22 12
68	22 31	////	////	21 56	22 03	22 07	22 10
66	21 51	////	////	21 41	21 53	22 02	22 09
64	21 24	23 17	////	21 28	21 44	21 57	22 08
62	21 03	22 23	////	21 17	21 37	21 53	22 07
60	20 47	21 52	////	21 07	21 30	21 49	22 06
N 58	20 33	21 30	23 22	20 59	21 25	21 46	22 05
56	20 20	21 11	22 33	20 51	21 20	21 43	22 04
54	20 10	20 56	22 04	20 45	21 15	21 41	22 03
52	20 01	20 43	21 43	20 39	21 11	21 38	22 03
50	19 52	20 32	21 26	20 34	21 07	21 36	22 02
45	19 35	20 09	20 53	20 22	20 59	21 31	22 01
N 40	19 20	19 51	20 30	20 12	20 52	21 27	22 00
35	19 08	19 37	20 11	20 04	20 46	21 24	21 59
30	18 58	19 24	19 56	19 57	20 41	21 21	21 58
20	18 40	19 04	19 32	19 44	20 32	21 16	21 57
N 10	18 24	18 47	19 13	19 33	20 24	21 11	21 56
0	18 10	18 32	18 57	19 22	20 16	21 06	21 54
S 10	17 56	18 18	18 44	19 11	20 08	21 02	21 53
20	17 41	18 04	18 31	19 00	20 00	20 57	21 52
30	17 24	17 49	18 18	18 47	19 50	20 52	21 50
35	17 14	17 41	18 11	18 39	19 45	20 48	21 49
40	17 02	17 31	18 04	18 30	19 39	20 45	21 48
45	16 49	17 21	17 57	18 20	19 31	20 40	21 47
S 50	16 33	17 09	17 48	18 08	19 22	20 35	21 46
52	16 25	17 03	17 45	18 02	19 18	20 33	21 45
54	16 17	16 57	17 41	17 55	19 14	20 30	21 44
56	16 07	16 50	17 37	17 48	19 09	20 27	21 43
58	15 56	16 43	17 32	17 40	19 03	20 24	21 42
S 60	15 44	16 34	17 27	17 31	18 57	20 20	21 41

Day	SUN Eqn. of Time 00h	SUN Eqn. of Time 12h	SUN Mer. Pass.	MOON Mer. Pass. Upper	MOON Mer. Pass. Lower	MOON Age	MOON Phase
d	m s	m s	h m	h m	h m	d	%
24	06 30	06 31	12 07	13 09	00 40	01	2
25	06 31	06 32	12 07	14 03	01 36	02	6
26	06 32	06 32	12 07	14 55	02 29	03	12

UT	ARIES	VENUS −4·0		MARS +1·7		JUPITER −1·9		SATURN +0·2	
	GHA	GHA	Dec	GHA	Dec	GHA	Dec	GHA	Dec
d h	° ′	° ′	° ′	° ′	° ′	° ′	° ′	° ′	° ′
27 00	304 51.9	220 34.3	N21 30.7	178 04.7	N20 16.7	109 20.2	S 5 19.0	43 38.5	S21 55.3
01	319 54.3	235 33.6	30.9	193 05.5	16.3	124 22.3	19.1	58 41.1	55.3
02	334 56.8	250 33.0	31.2	208 06.3	15.9	139 24.5	19.2	73 43.7	55.3
03	349 59.3	265 32.4	. . 31.4	223 07.1	. . 15.5	154 26.7	. . 19.4	88 46.3	. . 55.3
04	5 01.7	280 31.8	31.6	238 07.8	15.2	169 28.9	19.5	103 48.8	55.3
05	20 04.2	295 31.2	31.8	253 08.6	14.8	184 31.0	19.6	118 51.4	55.3
06	35 06.7	310 30.6	N21 32.1	268 09.4	N20 14.4	199 33.2	S 5 19.7	133 54.0	S21 55.3
07	50 09.1	325 30.0	32.3	283 10.2	14.0	214 35.4	19.9	148 56.6	55.3
T 08	65 11.6	340 29.4	32.5	298 11.0	13.6	229 37.6	20.0	163 59.2	55.3
H 09	80 14.1	355 28.8	. . 32.7	313 11.8	. . 13.3	244 39.8	. . 20.1	179 01.8	. . 55.3
U 10	95 16.5	10 28.2	33.0	328 12.6	12.9	259 41.9	20.3	194 04.3	55.3
R 11	110 19.0	25 27.6	33.2	343 13.4	12.5	274 44.1	20.4	209 06.9	55.3
S 12	125 21.5	40 27.0	N21 33.4	358 14.2	N20 12.1	289 46.3	S 5 20.5	224 09.5	S21 55.3
D 13	140 23.9	55 26.4	33.6	13 15.0	11.7	304 48.5	20.6	239 12.1	55.3
A 14	155 26.4	70 25.8	33.8	28 15.8	11.4	319 50.6	20.8	254 14.7	55.3
Y 15	170 28.8	85 25.1	. . 34.0	43 16.6	. . 11.0	334 52.8	. . 20.9	269 17.2	. . 55.3
16	185 31.3	100 24.5	34.3	58 17.4	10.6	349 55.0	21.0	284 19.8	55.3
17	200 33.8	115 23.9	34.5	73 18.2	10.2	4 57.2	21.2	299 22.4	55.3
18	215 36.2	130 23.3	N21 34.7	88 19.0	N20 09.8	19 59.3	S 5 21.3	314 25.0	S21 55.3
19	230 38.7	145 22.7	34.9	103 19.8	09.5	35 01.5	21.4	329 27.6	55.3
20	245 41.2	160 22.1	35.1	118 20.6	09.1	50 03.7	21.5	344 30.2	55.3
21	260 43.6	175 21.5	. . 35.3	133 21.4	. . 08.7	65 05.9	. . 21.7	359 32.7	. . 55.3
22	275 46.1	190 20.9	35.5	148 22.2	08.3	80 08.0	21.8	14 35.3	55.3
23	290 48.6	205 20.2	35.8	163 23.0	07.9	95 10.2	21.9	29 37.9	55.3
28 00	305 51.0	220 19.6	N21 36.0	178 23.8	N20 07.5	110 12.4	S 5 22.1	44 40.5	S21 55.3
01	320 53.5	235 19.0	36.2	193 24.6	07.2	125 14.6	22.2	59 43.1	55.3
02	335 55.9	250 18.4	36.4	208 25.4	06.8	140 16.7	22.3	74 45.6	55.3
03	350 58.4	265 17.8	. . 36.6	223 26.2	. . 06.4	155 18.9	. . 22.4	89 48.2	. . 55.3
04	6 00.9	280 17.2	36.8	238 27.0	06.0	170 21.1	22.6	104 50.8	55.3
05	21 03.3	295 16.6	37.0	253 27.8	05.6	185 23.2	22.7	119 53.4	55.3
06	36 05.8	310 16.0	N21 37.2	268 28.6	N20 05.2	200 25.4	S 5 22.8	134 56.0	S21 55.3
07	51 08.3	325 15.3	37.4	283 29.4	04.9	215 27.6	23.0	149 58.5	55.3
08	66 10.7	340 14.7	37.6	298 30.2	04.5	230 29.8	23.1	165 01.1	55.3
F 09	81 13.2	355 14.1	. . 37.8	313 31.0	. . 04.1	245 31.9	. . 23.2	180 03.7	. . 55.3
R 10	96 15.7	10 13.5	38.0	328 31.8	03.7	260 34.1	23.4	195 06.3	55.3
I 11	111 18.1	25 12.9	38.2	343 32.6	03.3	275 36.3	23.5	210 08.8	55.3
D 12	126 20.6	40 12.3	N21 38.4	358 33.4	N20 02.9	290 38.4	S 5 23.6	225 11.4	S21 55.3
A 13	141 23.1	55 11.6	38.6	13 34.2	02.6	305 40.6	23.7	240 14.0	55.3
Y 14	156 25.5	70 11.0	38.8	28 35.0	02.2	320 42.8	23.9	255 16.6	55.3
15	171 28.0	85 10.4	. . 39.0	43 35.8	. . 01.8	335 45.0	. . 24.0	270 19.2	. . 55.3
16	186 30.4	100 09.8	39.2	58 36.6	01.4	350 47.1	24.1	285 21.7	55.3
17	201 32.9	115 09.2	39.4	73 37.5	01.0	5 49.3	24.3	300 24.3	55.3
18	216 35.4	130 08.5	N21 39.6	88 38.3	N20 00.6	20 51.5	S 5 24.4	315 26.9	S21 55.3
19	231 37.8	145 07.9	39.7	103 39.1	20 00.2	35 53.6	24.5	330 29.5	55.3
20	246 40.3	160 07.3	39.9	118 39.9	19 59.8	50 55.8	24.7	345 32.1	55.3
21	261 42.8	175 06.7	. . 40.1	133 40.7	. . 59.5	65 58.0	. . 24.8	0 34.6	. . 55.3
22	276 45.2	190 06.1	40.3	148 41.5	59.1	81 00.1	24.9	15 37.2	55.3
23	291 47.7	205 05.4	40.5	163 42.3	58.7	96 02.3	25.1	30 39.8	55.3
29 00	306 50.2	220 04.8	N21 40.7	178 43.1	N19 58.3	111 04.5	S 5 25.2	45 42.4	S21 55.3
01	321 52.6	235 04.2	40.9	193 43.9	57.9	126 06.7	25.3	60 44.9	55.3
02	336 55.1	250 03.6	41.1	208 44.7	57.5	141 08.8	25.5	75 47.5	55.3
03	351 57.6	265 03.0	. . 41.2	223 45.5	. . 57.1	156 11.0	. . 25.6	90 50.1	. . 55.3
04	7 00.0	280 02.3	41.4	238 46.3	56.7	171 13.2	25.7	105 52.7	55.3
05	22 02.5	295 01.7	41.6	253 47.1	56.3	186 15.3	25.8	120 55.2	55.3
06	37 04.9	310 01.1	N21 41.8	268 47.9	N19 56.0	201 17.5	S 5 26.0	135 57.8	S21 55.3
07	52 07.4	325 00.5	42.0	283 48.7	55.6	216 19.7	26.1	151 00.4	55.3
S 08	67 09.9	339 59.8	42.1	298 49.5	55.2	231 21.8	26.2	166 03.0	55.3
A 09	82 12.3	354 59.2	. . 42.3	313 50.3	. . 54.8	246 24.0	. . 26.4	181 05.5	. . 55.3
T 10	97 14.8	9 58.6	42.5	328 51.1	54.4	261 26.2	26.5	196 08.1	55.3
U 11	112 17.3	24 58.0	42.7	343 51.9	54.0	276 28.3	26.6	211 10.7	55.3
R 12	127 19.7	39 57.3	N21 42.8	358 52.7	N19 53.6	291 30.5	S 5 26.8	226 13.3	S21 55.3
D 13	142 22.2	54 56.7	43.0	13 53.5	53.2	306 32.7	26.9	241 15.8	55.3
A 14	157 24.7	69 56.1	43.2	28 54.4	52.8	321 34.8	27.0	256 18.4	55.3
Y 15	172 27.1	84 55.5	. . 43.4	43 55.2	. . 52.4	336 37.0	. . 27.2	271 21.0	. . 55.3
16	187 29.6	99 54.8	43.5	58 56.0	52.0	351 39.2	27.3	286 23.6	55.3
17	202 32.0	114 54.2	43.7	73 56.8	51.6	6 41.3	27.4	301 26.1	55.3
18	217 34.5	129 53.6	N21 43.9	88 57.6	N19 51.3	21 43.5	S 5 27.6	316 28.7	S21 55.3
19	232 37.0	144 53.0	44.0	103 58.4	50.9	36 45.7	27.7	331 31.3	55.3
20	247 39.4	159 52.3	44.2	118 59.2	50.5	51 47.8	27.8	346 33.9	55.3
21	262 41.9	174 51.7	. . 44.4	134 00.0	. . 50.1	66 50.0	. . 28.0	1 36.4	. . 55.3
22	277 44.4	189 51.1	44.5	149 00.8	49.7	81 52.1	28.1	16 39.0	55.3
23	292 46.8	204 50.4	44.7	164 01.6	49.3	96 54.3	28.2	31 41.6	55.3
Mer. Pass.	h m 3 36.0	v −0.6	d 0.2	v 0.8	d 0.4	v 2.2	d 0.1	v 2.6	d 0.0

STARS Name	SHA	Dec
	° ′	° ′
Acamar	315 16.3	S40 14.0
Achernar	335 24.7	S57 08.7
Acrux	173 06.3	S63 11.9
Adhara	255 10.7	S28 59.8
Aldebaran	290 46.4	N16 32.5
Alioth	166 18.5	N55 52.3
Alkaid	152 56.8	N49 14.0
Al Na'ir	27 39.9	S46 52.3
Alnilam	275 43.8	S 1 11.6
Alphard	217 53.7	S 8 44.1
Alphecca	126 08.5	N26 39.7
Alpheratz	357 40.4	N29 11.1
Altair	62 05.2	N 8 55.1
Ankaa	353 12.8	S42 12.5
Antares	112 22.6	S26 28.1
Arcturus	145 53.2	N19 05.8
Atria	107 21.5	S69 03.5
Avior	234 17.5	S59 34.0
Bellatrix	278 29.3	N 6 21.8
Betelgeuse	270 58.6	N 7 24.5
Canopus	263 55.4	S52 42.3
Capella	280 30.7	N46 00.6
Deneb	49 29.1	N45 20.7
Denebola	182 31.0	N14 28.6
Diphda	348 53.0	S17 53.3
Dubhe	193 48.9	N61 39.6
Elnath	278 09.4	N28 37.1
Eltanin	90 44.4	N51 29.6
Enif	33 44.1	N 9 57.5
Fomalhaut	15 20.7	S29 31.6
Gacrux	171 57.9	S57 12.8
Gienah	175 49.6	S17 38.3
Hadar	148 43.8	S60 27.5
Hamal	327 57.6	N23 32.5
Kaus Aust.	83 39.8	S34 22.4
Kochab	137 20.1	N74 05.5
Markab	13 35.3	N15 18.0
Menkar	314 12.2	N 4 09.4
Menkent	148 04.3	S36 27.4
Miaplacidus	221 39.9	S69 47.5
Mirfak	308 36.5	N49 55.0
Nunki	75 54.5	S26 16.3
Peacock	53 14.3	S56 40.5
Pollux	243 24.7	N27 58.9
Procyon	244 57.2	N 5 10.7
Rasalhague	96 03.6	N12 33.2
Regulus	207 40.9	N11 52.9
Rigel	281 09.6	S 8 11.0
Rigil Kent.	139 47.8	S60 54.5
Sabik	102 09.1	S15 44.6
Schedar	349 37.0	N56 37.7
Shaula	96 17.8	S37 06.8
Sirius	258 31.6	S16 44.5
Spica	158 28.4	S11 15.0
Suhail	222 50.8	S43 30.3
Vega	80 36.7	N38 48.3
Zuben'ubi	137 02.3	S16 06.7

	SHA	Mer. Pass.
	° ′	h m
Venus	274 28.6	9 19
Mars	232 32.8	12 06
Jupiter	164 21.4	16 37
Saturn	98 49.5	20 58

Day	UT (d h)	SUN GHA (° ′)	SUN Dec (° ′)	MOON GHA (° ′)	MOON v (′)	MOON Dec (° ′)	MOON d (′)	MOON HP (′)
THURSDAY	27 00	178 22.1	N19 12.7	131 49.7	11.5	N 5 37.2	10.7	57.6
	01	193 22.1	12.1	146 20.2	11.7	5 26.5	10.7	57.6
	02	208 22.1	11.5	160 50.9	11.7	5 15.8	10.7	57.5
	03	223 22.1	. . 11.0	175 21.6	11.7	5 05.1	10.7	57.5
	04	238 22.1	10.4	189 52.3	11.9	4 54.4	10.8	57.5
	05	253 22.1	09.8	204 23.2	11.8	4 43.6	10.7	57.4
	06	268 22.1	N19 09.3	218 54.0	12.0	N 4 32.9	10.8	57.4
	07	283 22.1	08.7	233 25.0	12.0	4 22.1	10.7	57.4
	08	298 22.1	08.1	247 56.0	12.0	4 11.4	10.8	57.3
	09	313 22.1	. . 07.6	262 27.0	12.1	4 00.6	10.8	57.3
	10	328 22.2	07.0	276 58.1	12.2	3 49.8	10.8	57.2
	11	343 22.2	06.4	291 29.3	12.2	3 39.0	10.7	57.2
	12	358 22.2	N19 05.9	306 00.5	12.3	N 3 28.3	10.8	57.2
	13	13 22.2	05.3	320 31.8	12.3	3 17.5	10.8	57.1
	14	28 22.2	04.7	335 03.1	12.4	3 06.7	10.8	57.1
	15	43 22.2	. . 04.1	349 34.5	12.5	2 55.9	10.8	57.1
	16	58 22.2	03.6	4 06.0	12.4	2 45.1	10.8	57.0
	17	73 22.2	03.0	18 37.4	12.6	2 34.3	10.8	57.0
	18	88 22.2	N19 02.4	33 09.0	12.6	N 2 23.5	10.7	57.0
	19	103 22.2	01.8	47 40.6	12.6	2 12.8	10.8	56.9
	20	118 22.3	01.3	62 12.2	12.7	2 02.0	10.8	56.9
	21	133 22.3	. . 00.7	76 43.9	12.7	1 51.2	10.8	56.8
	22	148 22.3	19 00.1	91 15.6	12.8	1 40.4	10.7	56.8
	23	163 22.3	18 59.5	105 47.4	12.8	1 29.7	10.8	56.8
FRIDAY	28 00	178 22.3	N18 59.0	120 19.2	12.8	N 1 18.9	10.7	56.7
	01	193 22.3	58.4	134 51.0	12.9	1 08.2	10.8	56.7
	02	208 22.3	57.8	149 22.9	13.0	0 57.4	10.7	56.7
	03	223 22.3	. . 57.2	163 54.9	13.0	0 46.7	10.7	56.6
	04	238 22.3	56.6	178 26.9	13.0	0 36.0	10.7	56.6
	05	253 22.4	56.1	192 58.9	13.1	0 25.3	10.7	56.6
	06	268 22.4	N18 55.5	207 31.0	13.1	N 0 14.6	10.7	56.5
	07	283 22.4	54.9	222 03.1	13.2	N 0 03.9	10.7	56.5
	08	298 22.4	54.3	236 35.3	13.1	S 0 06.8	10.6	56.5
	09	313 22.4	. . 53.7	251 07.4	13.3	0 17.4	10.7	56.4
	10	328 22.4	53.1	265 39.7	13.2	0 28.1	10.6	56.4
	11	343 22.4	52.6	280 11.9	13.3	0 38.7	10.6	56.4
	12	358 22.5	N18 52.0	294 44.2	13.4	S 0 49.3	10.6	56.3
	13	13 22.5	51.4	309 16.6	13.3	0 59.9	10.6	56.3
	14	28 22.5	50.8	323 48.9	13.4	1 10.5	10.5	56.3
	15	43 22.5	. . 50.2	338 21.3	13.5	1 21.0	10.6	56.2
	16	58 22.5	49.6	352 53.8	13.4	1 31.6	10.5	56.2
	17	73 22.5	49.0	7 26.2	13.5	1 42.1	10.5	56.2
	18	88 22.6	N18 48.5	21 58.7	13.6	S 1 52.6	10.4	56.1
	19	103 22.6	47.9	36 31.3	13.5	2 03.0	10.5	56.1
	20	118 22.6	47.3	51 03.8	13.6	2 13.5	10.4	56.1
	21	133 22.6	. . 46.7	65 36.4	13.6	2 23.9	10.4	56.0
	22	148 22.6	46.1	80 09.0	13.6	2 34.3	10.4	56.0
	23	163 22.6	45.5	94 41.6	13.7	2 44.7	10.4	56.0
SATURDAY	29 00	178 22.7	N18 44.9	109 14.3	13.7	S 2 55.1	10.3	55.9
	01	193 22.7	44.3	123 47.0	13.7	3 05.4	10.3	55.9
	02	208 22.7	43.7	138 19.7	13.7	3 15.7	10.3	55.9
	03	223 22.7	. . 43.1	152 52.4	13.8	3 26.0	10.3	55.8
	04	238 22.7	42.5	167 25.2	13.8	3 36.3	10.2	55.8
	05	253 22.8	42.0	181 58.0	13.8	3 46.5	10.2	55.8
	06	268 22.8	N18 41.4	196 30.8	13.8	S 3 56.7	10.2	55.8
	07	283 22.8	40.8	211 03.6	13.9	4 06.9	10.1	55.7
	08	298 22.8	40.2	225 36.5	13.8	4 17.0	10.1	55.7
	09	313 22.8	. . 39.6	240 09.3	13.9	4 27.1	10.1	55.7
	10	328 22.9	39.0	254 42.2	13.9	4 37.2	10.0	55.6
	11	343 22.9	38.4	269 15.1	13.9	4 47.2	10.1	55.6
	12	358 22.9	N18 37.8	283 48.0	13.9	S 4 57.3	9.9	55.6
	13	13 22.9	37.2	298 20.9	14.0	5 07.2	10.0	55.6
	14	28 22.9	36.6	312 53.9	14.0	5 17.2	9.9	55.5
	15	43 23.0	. . 36.0	327 26.9	13.9	5 27.1	9.9	55.5
	16	58 23.0	35.4	341 59.8	14.0	5 37.0	9.8	55.5
	17	73 23.0	34.8	356 32.8	14.0	5 46.8	9.9	55.4
	18	88 23.0	N18 34.2	11 05.8	14.0	S 5 56.7	9.7	55.4
	19	103 23.1	33.6	25 38.8	14.1	6 06.4	9.8	55.4
	20	118 23.1	33.0	40 11.9	14.0	6 16.2	9.7	55.4
	21	133 23.1	. . 32.4	54 44.9	14.0	6 25.9	9.6	55.3
	22	148 23.1	31.8	69 17.9	14.1	6 35.5	9.7	55.3
	23	163 23.2	31.2	83 51.0	14.0	S 6 45.2	9.6	55.3
		SD 15.8	*d* 0.6	SD		15.6	15.3	15.1

Lat.	Twilight Naut.	Twilight Civil	Sunrise	Moonrise 27	Moonrise 28	Moonrise 29	Moonrise 30
°	h m	h m	h m	h m	h m	h m	h m
N 72	▭	▭	▭	08 41	10 26	12 09	13 50
N 70	////	////	00 39	08 46	10 25	12 01	13 35
68	////	////	01 54	08 51	10 25	11 55	13 24
66	////	////	02 30	08 55	10 24	11 50	13 14
64	////	01 14	02 56	08 58	10 24	11 46	13 06
62	////	01 59	03 16	09 01	10 23	11 42	12 59
60	////	02 28	03 32	09 04	10 23	11 39	12 53
N 58	01 07	02 49	03 45	09 06	10 22	11 36	12 48
56	01 48	03 07	03 57	09 08	10 22	11 34	12 44
54	02 15	03 21	04 07	09 09	10 22	11 32	12 39
52	02 35	03 34	04 16	09 11	10 21	11 30	12 36
50	02 52	03 44	04 24	09 12	10 21	11 28	12 32
45	03 23	04 07	04 41	09 16	10 21	11 24	12 25
N 40	03 46	04 24	04 55	09 18	10 20	11 20	12 19
35	04 04	04 38	05 06	09 20	10 20	11 18	12 14
30	04 19	04 50	05 17	09 22	10 20	11 15	12 09
20	04 42	05 10	05 34	09 26	10 19	11 11	12 01
N 10	05 01	05 27	05 49	09 29	10 19	11 07	11 54
0	05 16	05 41	06 03	09 32	10 18	11 04	11 48
S 10	05 29	05 55	06 17	09 35	10 18	11 00	11 42
20	05 41	06 08	06 31	09 38	10 18	10 56	11 35
30	05 54	06 23	06 48	09 41	10 17	10 52	11 27
35	06 00	06 31	06 58	09 43	10 17	10 50	11 23
40	06 07	06 39	07 09	09 45	10 17	10 47	11 18
45	06 14	06 49	07 21	09 48	10 16	10 44	11 12
S 50	06 22	07 01	07 37	09 51	10 16	10 40	11 05
52	06 25	07 07	07 44	09 52	10 16	10 39	11 02
54	06 29	07 12	07 52	09 54	10 16	10 37	10 59
56	06 33	07 19	08 01	09 56	10 16	10 35	10 55
58	06 37	07 26	08 12	09 58	10 15	10 33	10 51
S 60	06 42	07 34	08 23	10 00	10 15	10 30	10 46

Lat.	Sunset	Twilight Civil	Twilight Naut.	Moonset 27	Moonset 28	Moonset 29	Moonset 30
°	h m	h m	h m	h m	h m	h m	h m
N 72	▭	▭	▭	22 14	22 06	21 58	21 49
N 70	23 18	////	////	22 12	22 10	22 07	22 05
68	22 14	////	////	22 10	22 13	22 15	22 18
66	21 39	////	////	22 09	22 15	22 22	22 29
64	21 15	22 52	////	22 08	22 17	22 27	22 38
62	20 55	22 10	////	22 07	22 19	22 32	22 46
60	20 40	21 43	////	22 06	22 21	22 36	22 53
N 58	20 26	21 22	23 00	22 05	22 22	22 40	22 59
56	20 15	21 05	22 21	22 04	22 24	22 43	23 04
54	20 05	20 50	21 56	22 03	22 25	22 46	23 09
52	19 56	20 38	21 36	22 03	22 26	22 49	23 13
50	19 48	20 27	21 20	22 02	22 27	22 51	23 17
45	19 31	20 06	20 49	22 01	22 29	22 57	23 25
N 40	19 18	19 48	20 26	22 00	22 31	23 01	23 32
35	19 06	19 34	20 08	21 59	22 32	23 05	23 39
30	18 56	19 22	19 53	21 58	22 34	23 09	23 44
20	18 39	19 02	19 30	21 57	22 36	23 15	23 53
N 10	18 24	18 46	19 12	21 56	22 38	23 20	24 02
0	18 10	18 32	18 57	21 54	22 40	23 25	24 09
S 10	17 56	18 18	18 44	21 53	22 42	23 30	24 17
20	17 42	18 05	18 32	21 52	22 44	23 35	24 25
30	17 25	17 51	18 20	21 50	22 47	23 41	24 35
35	17 16	17 43	18 13	21 49	22 48	23 45	24 40
40	17 05	17 34	18 07	21 48	22 49	23 49	24 47
45	16 52	17 24	18 00	21 47	22 51	23 53	24 54
S 50	16 37	17 12	17 52	21 46	22 53	23 59	25 03
52	16 29	17 07	17 48	21 45	22 54	24 01	00 01
54	16 21	17 01	17 45	21 44	22 55	24 04	00 04
56	16 12	16 55	17 41	21 43	22 57	24 07	00 07
58	16 02	16 48	17 36	21 42	22 58	24 11	00 11
S 60	15 50	16 40	17 32	21 41	22 59	24 15	00 15

Day	SUN Eqn. of Time 00^h	SUN Eqn. of Time 12^h	SUN Mer. Pass.	MOON Mer. Pass. Upper	MOON Mer. Pass. Lower	MOON Age	MOON Phase
d	m s	m s	h m	h m	h m	d %	
27	06 32	06 31	12 07	15 43	03 19	04 20	
28	06 31	06 30	12 07	16 29	04 06	05 29	
29	06 29	06 28	12 06	17 14	04 52	06 39	

UT		ARIES	VENUS −4·0		MARS +1·7		JUPITER −1·9		SATURN +0·3	
d h		GHA ° ′	GHA ° ′	Dec ° ′	GHA ° ′	Dec ° ′	GHA ° ′	Dec ° ′	GHA ° ′	Dec ° ′
30 00		307 49.3	219 49.8	N21 44.9	179 02.4	N19 48.9	111 56.5	S 5 28.4	46 44.2	S21 55.3
01		322 51.8	234 49.2	45.0	194 03.2	48.5	126 58.6	28.5	61 46.7	55.3
02		337 54.2	249 48.6	45.2	209 04.0	48.1	142 00.8	28.6	76 49.3	55.3
03		352 56.7	264 47.9	. . 45.4	224 04.9	. . 47.7	157 03.0	. . 28.8	91 51.9	. . 55.3
04		7 59.2	279 47.3	45.5	239 05.7	47.3	172 05.1	28.9	106 54.5	55.3
05		23 01.6	294 46.7	45.7	254 06.5	46.9	187 07.3	29.0	121 57.0	55.3
06		38 04.1	309 46.0	N21 45.8	269 07.3	N19 46.5	202 09.5	S 5 29.2	136 59.6	S21 55.3
07		53 06.5	324 45.4	46.0	284 08.1	46.1	217 11.6	29.3	152 02.2	55.3
08		68 09.0	339 44.8	46.1	299 08.9	45.7	232 13.8	29.4	167 04.7	55.3
09	S	83 11.5	354 44.1	. . 46.3	314 09.7	. . 45.3	247 15.9	. . 29.6	182 07.3	. . 55.3
10	U	98 13.9	9 43.5	46.5	329 10.5	44.9	262 18.1	29.7	197 09.9	55.3
11	N	113 16.4	24 42.9	46.6	344 11.3	44.5	277 20.3	29.8	212 12.5	55.3
12	D	128 18.9	39 42.2	N21 46.8	359 12.1	N19 44.1	292 22.4	S 5 30.0	227 15.0	S21 55.3
13	A	143 21.3	54 41.6	46.9	14 12.9	43.7	307 24.6	30.1	242 17.6	55.3
14	Y	158 23.8	69 41.0	47.1	29 13.8	43.3	322 26.7	30.2	257 20.2	55.3
15		173 26.3	84 40.3	. . 47.2	44 14.6	. . 43.0	337 28.9	. . 30.4	272 22.7	. . 55.3
16		188 28.7	99 39.7	47.4	59 15.4	42.6	352 31.1	30.5	287 25.3	55.3
17		203 31.2	114 39.1	47.5	74 16.2	42.2	7 33.2	30.6	302 27.9	55.3
18		218 33.7	129 38.4	N21 47.6	89 17.0	N19 41.8	22 35.4	S 5 30.8	317 30.5	S21 55.3
19		233 36.1	144 37.8	47.8	104 17.8	41.4	37 37.6	30.9	332 33.0	55.3
20		248 38.6	159 37.2	47.9	119 18.6	41.0	52 39.7	31.0	347 35.6	55.3
21		263 41.0	174 36.5	. . 48.1	134 19.4	. . 40.6	67 41.9	. . 31.2	2 38.2	. . 55.3
22		278 43.5	189 35.9	48.2	149 20.2	40.2	82 44.0	31.3	17 40.7	55.3
23		293 46.0	204 35.3	48.4	164 21.1	39.8	97 46.2	31.5	32 43.3	55.3
31 00		308 48.4	219 34.6	N21 48.5	179 21.9	N19 39.4	112 48.3	S 5 31.6	47 45.9	S21 55.3
01		323 50.9	234 34.0	48.6	194 22.7	39.0	127 50.5	31.7	62 48.4	55.3
02		338 53.4	249 33.4	48.8	209 23.5	38.6	142 52.7	31.9	77 51.0	55.3
03		353 55.8	264 32.7	. . 48.9	224 24.3	. . 38.2	157 54.8	. . 32.0	92 53.6	. . 55.3
04		8 58.3	279 32.1	49.1	239 25.1	37.8	172 57.0	32.1	107 56.1	55.3
05		24 00.8	294 31.4	49.2	254 25.9	37.4	187 59.1	32.3	122 58.7	55.3
06		39 03.2	309 30.8	N21 49.3	269 26.8	N19 37.0	203 01.3	S 5 32.4	138 01.3	S21 55.3
07		54 05.7	324 30.2	49.5	284 27.6	36.6	218 03.5	32.5	153 03.9	55.3
08		69 08.1	339 29.5	49.6	299 28.4	36.2	233 05.6	32.7	168 06.4	55.3
09	M	84 10.6	354 28.9	. . 49.7	314 29.2	. . 35.8	248 07.8	. . 32.8	183 09.0	. . 55.3
10	O	99 13.1	9 28.2	49.8	329 30.0	35.3	263 09.9	32.9	198 11.6	55.3
11	N	114 15.5	24 27.6	50.0	344 30.8	34.9	278 12.1	33.1	213 14.1	55.3
12	D	129 18.0	39 27.0	N21 50.1	359 31.6	N19 34.5	293 14.2	S 5 33.2	228 16.7	S21 55.3
13	A	144 20.5	54 26.3	50.2	14 32.4	34.1	308 16.4	33.3	243 19.3	55.3
14	Y	159 22.9	69 25.7	50.4	29 33.3	33.7	323 18.6	33.5	258 21.8	55.3
15		174 25.4	84 25.0	. . 50.5	44 34.1	. . 33.3	338 20.7	. . 33.6	273 24.4	. . 55.3
16		189 27.9	99 24.4	50.6	59 34.9	32.9	353 22.9	33.8	288 27.0	55.3
17		204 30.3	114 23.8	50.7	74 35.7	32.5	8 25.0	33.9	303 29.5	55.3
18		219 32.8	129 23.1	N21 50.9	89 36.5	N19 32.1	23 27.2	S 5 34.0	318 32.1	S21 55.3
19		234 35.3	144 22.5	51.0	104 37.3	31.7	38 29.3	34.2	333 34.7	55.3
20		249 37.7	159 21.8	51.1	119 38.2	31.3	53 31.5	34.3	348 37.2	55.3
21		264 40.2	174 21.2	. . 51.2	134 39.0	. . 30.9	68 33.6	. . 34.4	3 39.8	. . 55.3
22		279 42.6	189 20.6	51.3	149 39.8	30.5	83 35.8	34.6	18 42.4	55.3
23		294 45.1	204 19.9	51.5	164 40.6	30.1	98 38.0	34.7	33 44.9	55.3
1 00		309 47.6	219 19.3	N21 51.6	179 41.4	N19 29.7	113 40.1	S 5 34.8	48 47.5	S21 55.3
01		324 50.0	234 18.6	51.7	194 42.2	29.3	128 42.3	35.0	63 50.1	55.3
02		339 52.5	249 18.0	51.8	209 43.0	28.9	143 44.4	35.1	78 52.6	55.3
03		354 55.0	264 17.3	. . 51.9	224 43.9	. . 28.5	158 46.6	. . 35.3	93 55.2	. . 55.3
04		9 57.4	279 16.7	52.0	239 44.7	28.1	173 48.7	35.4	108 57.8	55.3
05		24 59.9	294 16.0	52.1	254 45.5	27.7	188 50.9	35.5	124 00.3	55.3
06		40 02.4	309 15.4	N21 52.3	269 46.3	N19 27.3	203 53.0	S 5 35.7	139 02.9	S21 55.3
07		55 04.8	324 14.8	52.4	284 47.1	26.8	218 55.2	35.8	154 05.4	55.3
08	T	70 07.3	339 14.1	52.5	299 48.0	26.4	233 57.3	35.9	169 08.0	55.3
09	U	85 09.8	354 13.5	. . 52.6	314 48.8	. . 26.0	248 59.5	. . 36.1	184 10.6	. . 55.4
10	E	100 12.2	9 12.8	52.7	329 49.6	25.6	264 01.6	36.2	199 13.1	55.4
11	S	115 14.7	24 12.2	52.8	344 50.4	25.2	279 03.8	36.4	214 15.7	55.4
12	D	130 17.1	39 11.5	N21 52.9	359 51.2	N19 24.8	294 06.0	S 5 36.5	229 18.3	S21 55.4
13	A	145 19.6	54 10.9	53.0	14 52.0	24.4	309 08.1	36.6	244 20.8	55.4
14	Y	160 22.1	69 10.2	53.1	29 52.9	24.0	324 10.3	36.8	259 23.4	55.4
15		175 24.5	84 09.6	. . 53.2	44 53.7	. . 23.6	339 12.4	. . 36.9	274 26.0	. . 55.4
16		190 27.0	99 08.9	53.3	59 54.5	23.2	354 14.6	37.0	289 28.5	55.4
17		205 29.5	114 08.3	53.4	74 55.3	22.8	9 16.7	37.2	304 31.1	55.4
18		220 31.9	129 07.6	N21 53.5	89 56.1	N19 22.4	24 18.9	S 5 37.3	319 33.6	S21 55.4
19		235 34.4	144 07.0	53.6	104 57.0	21.9	39 21.0	37.5	334 36.2	55.4
20		250 36.9	159 06.3	53.7	119 57.8	21.5	54 23.2	37.6	349 38.8	55.4
21		265 39.3	174 05.7	. . 53.8	134 58.6	. . 21.1	69 25.3	. . 37.7	4 41.3	. . 55.4
22		280 41.8	189 05.0	53.9	149 59.4	20.7	84 27.5	37.9	19 43.9	55.4
23		295 44.2	204 04.4	54.0	165 00.2	20.3	99 29.6	38.0	34 46.5	55.4
Mer. Pass.		h m 3 24.2	v −0.6	d 0.1	v 0.8	d 0.4	v 2.2	d 0.1	v 2.6	d 0.0

STARS

Name	SHA ° ′	Dec ° ′
Acamar	315 16.3	S40 14.0
Achernar	335 24.7	S57 08.7
Acrux	173 06.4	S63 11.9
Adhara	255 10.7	S28 59.8
Aldebaran	290 46.4	N16 32.5
Alioth	166 18.6	N55 52.3
Alkaid	152 56.8	N49 14.0
Al Na'ir	27 39.9	S46 52.3
Alnilam	275 43.8	S 1 11.6
Alphard	217 53.7	S 8 44.1
Alphecca	126 08.6	N26 39.7
Alpheratz	357 40.4	N29 11.1
Altair	62 05.2	N 8 55.1
Ankaa	353 12.8	S42 12.5
Antares	112 22.6	S26 28.1
Arcturus	145 53.2	N19 05.8
Atria	107 21.5	S69 03.5
Avior	234 17.5	S59 34.0
Bellatrix	278 29.2	N 6 21.8
Betelgeuse	270 58.5	N 7 24.5
Canopus	263 55.4	S52 42.3
Capella	280 30.6	N46 00.6
Deneb	49 29.1	N45 20.7
Denebola	182 31.1	N14 28.6
Diphda	348 53.0	S17 53.3
Dubhe	193 49.0	N61 39.6
Elnath	278 09.4	N28 37.1
Eltanin	90 44.4	N51 29.6
Enif	33 44.1	N 9 57.5
Fomalhaut	15 20.6	S29 31.6
Gacrux	171 58.0	S57 12.8
Gienah	175 49.6	S17 38.3
Hadar	148 43.9	S60 27.5
Hamal	327 57.5	N23 32.5
Kaus Aust.	83 39.8	S34 22.4
Kochab	137 20.1	N74 05.5
Markab	13 35.3	N15 18.0
Menkar	314 12.2	N 4 09.4
Menkent	148 04.3	S36 27.3
Miaplacidus	221 39.9	S69 47.5
Mirfak	308 36.4	N49 55.0
Nunki	75 54.5	S26 16.3
Peacock	53 14.3	S56 40.5
Pollux	243 24.7	N27 58.9
Procyon	244 57.1	N 5 10.7
Rasalhague	96 03.6	N12 33.2
Regulus	207 40.9	N11 52.9
Rigel	281 09.6	S 8 11.0
Rigil Kent.	139 47.8	S60 54.5
Sabik	102 09.1	S15 44.6
Schedar	349 37.0	N56 37.7
Shaula	96 17.8	S37 06.8
Sirius	258 31.6	S16 44.5
Spica	158 28.4	S11 15.0
Suhail	222 50.8	S43 30.3
Vega	80 36.7	N38 48.3
Zuben'ubi	137 02.3	S16 06.7

	SHA ° ′	Mer. Pass. h m
Venus	270 46.2	9 22
Mars	230 33.4	12 02
Jupiter	163 59.9	16 26
Saturn	98 57.4	20 45

UT d h	SUN GHA ° ′	SUN Dec ° ′	MOON GHA ° ′	v ′	MOON Dec ° ′	d ′	HP ′
SUNDAY 30 00	178 23.2	N18 30.6	98 24.0	14.1	S 6 54.8	9.5	55.3
01	193 23.2	30.0	112 57.1	14.1	7 04.3	9.5	55.2
02	208 23.2	29.4	127 30.2	14.1	7 13.8	9.5	55.2
03	223 23.3	. . 28.8	142 03.3	14.1	7 23.3	9.4	55.2
04	238 23.3	28.2	156 36.4	14.1	7 32.7	9.4	55.2
05	253 23.3	27.6	171 09.5	14.1	7 42.1	9.4	55.1
06	268 23.3	N18 26.9	185 42.6	14.1	S 7 51.5	9.3	55.1
07	283 23.4	26.3	200 15.7	14.1	8 00.8	9.3	55.1
08	298 23.4	25.7	214 48.8	14.1	8 10.1	9.2	55.1
09	313 23.4	. . 25.1	229 21.9	14.1	8 19.3	9.2	55.0
10	328 23.4	24.5	243 55.0	14.1	8 28.5	9.1	55.0
11	343 23.5	23.9	258 28.1	14.1	8 37.6	9.1	55.0
12	358 23.5	N18 23.3	273 01.2	14.1	S 8 46.7	9.0	55.0
13	13 23.5	22.7	287 34.3	14.1	8 55.7	9.0	55.0
14	28 23.6	22.1	302 07.4	14.1	9 04.7	9.0	54.9
15	43 23.6	. . 21.5	316 40.5	14.1	9 13.7	8.9	54.9
16	58 23.6	20.8	331 13.6	14.1	9 22.6	8.8	54.9
17	73 23.6	20.2	345 46.7	14.1	9 31.4	8.9	54.9
18	88 23.7	N18 19.6	0 19.8	14.1	S 9 40.3	8.7	54.9
19	103 23.7	19.0	14 52.9	14.1	9 49.0	8.7	54.8
20	118 23.7	18.4	29 26.0	14.1	9 57.7	8.7	54.8
21	133 23.8	. . 17.8	43 59.1	14.0	10 06.4	8.6	54.8
22	148 23.8	17.2	58 32.1	14.1	10 15.0	8.6	54.8
23	163 23.8	16.6	73 05.2	14.1	10 23.6	8.5	54.8
MONDAY 31 00	178 23.9	N18 15.9	87 38.3	14.0	S10 32.1	8.5	54.7
01	193 23.9	15.3	102 11.3	14.1	10 40.6	8.4	54.7
02	208 23.9	14.7	116 44.4	14.0	10 49.0	8.4	54.7
03	223 24.0	. . 14.1	131 17.4	14.0	10 57.4	8.3	54.7
04	238 24.0	13.5	145 50.4	14.1	11 05.7	8.2	54.7
05	253 24.0	12.8	160 23.5	14.0	11 13.9	8.2	54.6
06	268 24.1	N18 12.2	174 56.5	14.0	S11 22.1	8.2	54.6
07	283 24.1	11.6	189 29.5	14.0	11 30.3	8.1	54.6
08	298 24.1	11.0	204 02.5	13.9	11 38.4	8.0	54.6
09	313 24.2	. . 10.4	218 35.4	14.0	11 46.4	8.0	54.6
10	328 24.2	09.7	233 08.4	13.9	11 54.4	7.9	54.6
11	343 24.2	09.1	247 41.3	14.0	12 02.3	7.9	54.6
12	358 24.3	N18 08.5	262 14.3	13.9	S12 10.2	7.8	54.5
13	13 24.3	07.9	276 47.2	13.9	12 18.0	7.8	54.5
14	28 24.3	07.3	291 20.1	13.9	12 25.8	7.7	54.5
15	43 24.4	. . 06.6	305 53.0	13.9	12 33.5	7.6	54.5
16	58 24.4	06.0	320 25.9	13.9	12 41.1	7.6	54.5
17	73 24.4	05.4	334 58.8	13.8	12 48.7	7.6	54.5
18	88 24.5	N18 04.8	349 31.6	13.9	S12 56.3	7.4	54.5
19	103 24.5	04.1	4 04.5	13.8	13 03.7	7.5	54.4
20	118 24.5	03.5	18 37.3	13.8	13 11.2	7.3	54.4
21	133 24.6	. . 02.9	33 10.1	13.8	13 18.5	7.3	54.4
22	148 24.6	02.2	47 42.9	13.7	13 25.8	7.2	54.4
23	163 24.7	01.6	62 15.6	13.8	13 33.0	7.2	54.4
TUESDAY 1 00	178 24.7	N18 01.0	76 48.4	13.7	S13 40.2	7.1	54.4
01	193 24.7	18 00.4	91 21.1	13.7	13 47.3	7.1	54.4
02	208 24.8	17 59.7	105 53.8	13.7	13 54.4	6.9	54.4
03	223 24.8	. . 59.1	120 26.5	13.7	14 01.3	7.0	54.3
04	238 24.9	58.5	134 59.2	13.6	14 08.3	6.8	54.3
05	253 24.9	57.8	149 31.8	13.6	14 15.1	6.8	54.3
06	268 24.9	N17 57.2	164 04.4	13.7	S14 21.9	6.7	54.3
07	283 25.0	56.6	178 37.1	13.5	14 28.6	6.7	54.3
08	298 25.0	55.9	193 09.6	13.6	14 35.3	6.6	54.3
09	313 25.1	. . 55.3	207 42.2	13.5	14 41.9	6.5	54.3
10	328 25.1	54.7	222 14.7	13.6	14 48.4	6.5	54.3
11	343 25.1	54.0	236 47.3	13.5	14 54.9	6.4	54.3
12	358 25.2	N17 53.4	251 19.8	13.5	S15 01.3	6.3	54.3
13	13 25.2	52.8	265 52.3	13.4	15 07.6	6.3	54.2
14	28 25.3	52.1	280 24.7	13.4	15 13.9	6.2	54.2
15	43 25.3	. . 51.5	294 57.1	13.4	15 20.1	6.1	54.2
16	58 25.3	50.9	309 29.5	13.4	15 26.2	6.1	54.2
17	73 25.4	50.2	324 01.9	13.4	15 32.3	6.0	54.2
18	88 25.4	N17 49.6	338 34.3	13.3	S15 38.3	5.9	54.2
19	103 25.5	49.0	353 06.6	13.3	15 44.2	5.9	54.2
20	118 25.5	48.3	7 38.9	13.3	15 50.1	5.7	54.2
21	133 25.6	. . 47.7	22 11.2	13.3	15 55.8	5.8	54.2
22	148 25.6	47.0	36 43.5	13.2	16 01.6	5.6	54.2
23	163 25.6	46.4	51 15.7	13.3	S16 07.2	5.6	54.2
	SD 15.8	d 0.6	SD	15.0	14.9		14.8

Lat. °	Twilight Naut. h m	Twilight Civil h m	Sunrise h m	Moonrise 30 h m	Moonrise 31 h m	Moonrise 1 h m	Moonrise 2 h m
N 72	▭	▭	▭	13 50	15 34	17 23	19 47
N 70	////	////	01 19	13 35	15 09	16 44	18 18
68	////	////	02 11	13 24	14 51	16 17	17 39
66	////	////	02 42	13 14	14 36	15 56	17 12
64	////	01 34	03 05	13 06	14 24	15 40	16 52
62	////	02 12	03 24	12 59	14 14	15 27	16 35
60	////	02 37	03 39	12 53	14 06	15 15	16 21
N 58	01 26	02 57	03 51	12 48	13 58	15 05	16 09
56	02 00	03 13	04 02	12 44	13 51	14 57	15 59
54	02 24	03 27	04 12	12 39	13 45	14 49	15 50
52	02 42	03 39	04 20	12 36	13 40	14 42	15 42
50	02 58	03 49	04 28	12 32	13 35	14 36	15 35
45	03 28	04 10	04 44	12 25	13 25	14 23	15 19
N 40	03 50	04 27	04 58	12 19	13 16	14 12	15 07
35	04 07	04 41	05 09	12 14	13 09	14 03	14 56
30	04 21	04 52	05 18	12 09	13 02	13 55	14 47
20	04 44	05 12	05 35	12 01	12 51	13 41	14 31
N 10	05 01	05 27	05 50	11 54	12 41	13 29	14 16
0	05 16	05 41	06 03	11 48	12 32	13 17	14 03
S 10	05 29	05 54	06 16	11 42	12 23	13 06	13 50
20	05 40	06 07	06 30	11 35	12 14	12 54	13 36
30	05 52	06 21	06 46	11 27	12 03	12 41	13 21
35	05 58	06 28	06 55	11 23	11 57	12 33	13 11
40	06 04	06 37	07 06	11 18	11 50	12 24	13 01
45	06 11	06 46	07 18	11 12	11 41	12 13	12 49
S 50	06 18	06 57	07 33	11 05	11 32	12 01	12 34
52	06 21	07 02	07 40	11 02	11 27	11 55	12 27
54	06 25	07 08	07 47	10 59	11 22	11 48	12 19
56	06 28	07 14	07 56	10 55	11 17	11 41	12 11
58	06 32	07 21	08 06	10 51	11 10	11 33	12 01
S 60	06 37	07 28	08 17	10 46	11 03	11 24	11 50

Lat. °	Sunset h m	Twilight Civil h m	Twilight Naut. h m	Moonset 30 h m	Moonset 31 h m	Moonset 1 h m	Moonset 2 h m
N 72	▭	▭	▭	21 49	21 38	21 23	20 35
N 70	22 46	////	////	22 05	22 04	22 03	22 04
68	21 58	////	////	22 18	22 23	22 31	22 44
66	21 28	////	////	22 29	22 39	22 52	23 11
64	21 05	22 33	////	22 38	22 51	23 09	23 32
62	20 47	21 58	////	22 46	23 02	23 23	23 49
60	20 32	21 33	////	22 53	23 12	23 35	24 03
N 58	20 20	21 14	22 42	22 59	23 20	23 45	24 15
56	20 09	20 58	22 10	23 04	23 27	23 54	24 26
54	20 00	20 44	21 47	23 09	23 33	24 02	00 02
52	19 51	20 33	21 29	23 13	23 39	24 09	00 09
50	19 44	20 22	21 13	23 17	23 44	24 15	00 15
45	19 28	20 02	20 44	23 25	23 56	24 29	00 29
N 40	19 15	19 45	20 22	23 32	24 05	00 05	00 41
35	19 04	19 31	20 05	23 39	24 13	00 13	00 51
30	18 54	19 20	19 51	23 44	24 21	00 21	00 59
20	18 37	19 01	19 29	23 53	24 33	00 33	01 14
N 10	18 23	18 45	19 11	24 02	00 02	00 44	01 27
0	18 10	18 32	18 57	24 09	00 09	00 54	01 40
S 10	17 57	18 19	18 44	24 17	00 17	01 04	01 52
20	17 43	18 06	18 33	24 25	00 25	01 15	02 05
30	17 27	17 52	18 21	24 35	00 35	01 28	02 20
35	17 18	17 45	18 15	24 40	00 40	01 35	02 29
40	17 07	17 36	18 09	24 47	00 47	01 43	02 39
45	16 55	17 27	18 02	24 54	00 54	01 53	02 50
S 50	16 41	17 16	17 55	25 03	01 03	02 05	03 05
52	16 34	17 11	17 52	00 01	01 07	02 10	03 11
54	16 26	17 05	17 49	00 04	01 11	02 16	03 19
56	16 18	17 00	17 45	00 07	01 16	02 23	03 27
58	16 08	16 53	17 41	00 11	01 22	02 30	03 36
S 60	15 57	16 45	17 37	00 15	01 28	02 39	03 47

Day	SUN Eqn. of Time 00^h	SUN Eqn. of Time 12^h	SUN Mer. Pass.	MOON Mer. Pass. Upper	MOON Mer. Pass. Lower	Age	Phase
d	m s	m s	h m	h m	h m	d %	
30	06 27	06 26	12 06	17 59	05 36	07 49	
31	06 25	06 23	12 06	18 43	06 21	08 58	
1	06 21	06 19	12 06	19 28	07 06	09 68	

UT d h	ARIES GHA ° ′	VENUS −4·0 GHA ° ′	VENUS Dec ° ′	MARS +1·7 GHA ° ′	MARS Dec ° ′	JUPITER −1·9 GHA ° ′	JUPITER Dec ° ′	SATURN +0·3 GHA ° ′	SATURN Dec ° ′
2 00 (WEDNESDAY)	310 46.7	219 03.8	N21 54.1	180 01.1	N19 19.9	114 31.8	S 5 38.1	49 49.0	S21 55.4
01	325 49.2	234 03.1	54.2	195 01.9	19.5	129 33.9	38.3	64 51.6	55.4
02	340 51.6	249 02.5	54.3	210 02.7	19.1	144 36.1	38.4	79 54.1	55.4
03	355 54.1	264 01.8	. . 54.4	225 03.5	. . 18.7	159 38.2	. . 38.6	94 56.7	. . 55.4
04	10 56.6	279 01.1	54.4	240 04.3	18.2	174 40.4	38.7	109 59.3	55.4
05	25 59.0	294 00.5	54.5	255 05.2	17.8	189 42.5	38.8	125 01.8	55.4
06	41 01.5	308 59.8	N21 54.6	270 06.0	N19 17.4	204 44.7	S 5 39.0	140 04.4	S21 55.4
07	56 04.0	323 59.2	54.7	285 06.8	17.0	219 46.8	39.1	155 07.0	55.4
08	71 06.4	338 58.5	54.8	300 07.6	16.6	234 49.0	39.3	170 09.5	55.4
09	86 08.9	353 57.9	. . 54.9	315 08.4	. . 16.2	249 51.1	. . 39.4	185 12.1	. . 55.4
10	101 11.4	8 57.2	55.0	330 09.3	15.8	264 53.3	39.5	200 14.6	55.4
11	116 13.8	23 56.6	55.0	345 10.1	15.4	279 55.4	39.7	215 17.2	55.4
12	131 16.3	38 55.9	N21 55.1	0 10.9	N19 14.9	294 57.5	S 5 39.8	230 19.8	S21 55.4
13	146 18.7	53 55.3	55.2	15 11.7	14.5	309 59.7	40.0	245 22.3	55.4
14	161 21.2	68 54.6	55.3	30 12.6	14.1	325 01.8	40.1	260 24.9	55.4
15	176 23.7	83 54.0	. . 55.4	45 13.4	. . 13.7	340 04.0	. . 40.2	275 27.4	. . 55.4
16	191 26.1	98 53.3	55.4	60 14.2	13.3	355 06.1	40.4	290 30.0	55.4
17	206 28.6	113 52.7	55.5	75 15.0	12.9	10 08.3	40.5	305 32.6	55.4
18	221 31.1	128 52.0	N21 55.6	90 15.8	N19 12.5	25 10.4	S 5 40.7	320 35.1	S21 55.4
19	236 33.5	143 51.4	55.7	105 16.7	12.0	40 12.6	40.8	335 37.7	55.4
20	251 36.0	158 50.7	55.7	120 17.5	11.6	55 14.7	40.9	350 40.2	55.4
21	266 38.5	173 50.0	. . 55.8	135 18.3	. . 11.2	70 16.9	. . 41.1	5 42.8	. . 55.4
22	281 40.9	188 49.4	55.9	150 19.1	10.8	85 19.0	41.2	20 45.3	55.4
23	296 43.4	203 48.7	56.0	165 20.0	10.4	100 21.2	41.4	35 47.9	55.4
3 00 (THURSDAY)	311 45.9	218 48.1	N21 56.0	180 20.8	N19 10.0	115 23.3	S 5 41.5	50 50.5	S21 55.4
01	326 48.3	233 47.4	56.1	195 21.6	09.5	130 25.5	41.6	65 53.0	55.4
02	341 50.8	248 46.8	56.2	210 22.4	09.1	145 27.6	41.8	80 55.6	55.4
03	356 53.2	263 46.1	. . 56.2	225 23.3	. . 08.7	160 29.7	. . 41.9	95 58.1	. . 55.4
04	11 55.7	278 45.5	56.3	240 24.1	08.3	175 31.9	42.1	111 00.7	55.4
05	26 58.2	293 44.8	56.4	255 24.9	07.9	190 34.0	42.2	126 03.3	55.4
06	42 00.6	308 44.1	N21 56.4	270 25.7	N19 07.5	205 36.2	S 5 42.3	141 05.8	S21 55.4
07	57 03.1	323 43.5	56.5	285 26.6	07.0	220 38.3	42.5	156 08.4	55.4
08	72 05.6	338 42.8	56.5	300 27.4	06.6	235 40.5	42.6	171 10.9	55.4
09	87 08.0	353 42.2	. . 56.6	315 28.2	. . 06.2	250 42.6	. . 42.8	186 13.5	. . 55.4
10	102 10.5	8 41.5	56.7	330 29.0	05.8	265 44.7	42.9	201 16.0	55.4
11	117 13.0	23 40.9	56.7	345 29.9	05.4	280 46.9	43.0	216 18.6	55.4
12	132 15.4	38 40.2	N21 56.8	0 30.7	N19 04.9	295 49.0	S 5 43.2	231 21.1	S21 55.4
13	147 17.9	53 39.5	56.8	15 31.5	04.5	310 51.2	43.3	246 23.7	55.4
14	162 20.3	68 38.9	56.9	30 32.3	04.1	325 53.3	43.5	261 26.3	55.4
15	177 22.8	83 38.2	. . 56.9	45 33.2	. . 03.7	340 55.5	. . 43.6	276 28.8	. . 55.4
16	192 25.3	98 37.6	57.0	60 34.0	03.3	355 57.6	43.7	291 31.4	55.4
17	207 27.7	113 36.9	57.0	75 34.8	02.8	10 59.7	43.9	306 33.9	55.4
18	222 30.2	128 36.2	N21 57.1	90 35.7	N19 02.4	26 01.9	S 5 44.0	321 36.5	S21 55.4
19	237 32.7	143 35.6	57.2	105 36.5	02.0	41 04.0	44.2	336 39.0	55.4
20	252 35.1	158 34.9	57.2	120 37.3	01.6	56 06.2	44.3	351 41.6	55.5
21	267 37.6	173 34.3	. . 57.2	135 38.1	. . 01.2	71 08.3	. . 44.4	6 44.1	. . 55.5
22	282 40.1	188 33.6	57.3	150 39.0	00.7	86 10.5	44.6	21 46.7	55.5
23	297 42.5	203 32.9	57.3	165 39.8	19 00.3	101 12.6	44.7	36 49.3	55.5
4 00 (FRIDAY)	312 45.0	218 32.3	N21 57.4	180 40.6	N18 59.9	116 14.7	S 5 44.9	51 51.8	S21 55.5
01	327 47.5	233 31.6	57.4	195 41.4	59.5	131 16.9	45.0	66 54.4	55.5
02	342 49.9	248 31.0	57.5	210 42.3	59.0	146 19.0	45.2	81 56.9	55.5
03	357 52.4	263 30.3	. . 57.5	225 43.1	. . 58.6	161 21.2	. . 45.3	96 59.5	. . 55.5
04	12 54.8	278 29.6	57.6	240 43.9	58.2	176 23.3	45.4	112 02.0	55.5
05	27 57.3	293 29.0	57.6	255 44.8	57.8	191 25.4	45.6	127 04.6	55.5
06	42 59.8	308 28.3	N21 57.6	270 45.6	N18 57.4	206 27.6	S 5 45.7	142 07.1	S21 55.5
07	58 02.2	323 27.6	57.7	285 46.4	56.9	221 29.7	45.9	157 09.7	55.5
08	73 04.7	338 27.0	57.7	300 47.2	56.5	236 31.9	46.0	172 12.2	55.5
09	88 07.2	353 26.3	. . 57.8	315 48.1	. . 56.1	251 34.0	. . 46.2	187 14.8	. . 55.5
10	103 09.6	8 25.7	57.8	330 48.9	55.7	266 36.1	46.3	202 17.3	55.5
11	118 12.1	23 25.0	57.8	345 49.7	55.2	281 38.3	46.4	217 19.9	55.5
12	133 14.6	38 24.3	N21 57.9	0 50.6	N18 54.8	296 40.4	S 5 46.6	232 22.5	S21 55.5
13	148 17.0	53 23.7	57.9	15 51.4	54.4	311 42.6	46.7	247 25.0	55.5
14	163 19.5	68 23.0	57.9	30 52.2	54.0	326 44.7	46.9	262 27.6	55.5
15	178 22.0	83 22.3	. . 57.9	45 53.1	. . 53.5	341 46.8	. . 47.0	277 30.1	. . 55.5
16	193 24.4	98 21.7	58.0	60 53.9	53.1	356 49.0	47.2	292 32.7	55.5
17	208 26.9	113 21.0	58.0	75 54.7	52.7	11 51.1	47.3	307 35.2	55.5
18	223 29.3	128 20.3	N21 58.0	90 55.6	N18 52.3	26 53.2	S 5 47.4	322 37.8	S21 55.5
19	238 31.8	143 19.7	58.1	105 56.4	51.8	41 55.4	47.6	337 40.3	55.5
20	253 34.3	158 19.0	58.1	120 57.2	51.4	56 57.5	47.7	352 42.9	55.5
21	268 36.7	173 18.3	. . 58.1	135 58.0	. . 51.0	71 59.7	. . 47.9	7 45.4	. . 55.5
22	283 39.2	188 17.7	58.1	150 58.9	50.6	87 01.8	48.0	22 48.0	55.5
23	298 41.7	203 17.0	58.2	165 59.7	50.1	102 03.9	48.2	37 50.5	55.5
Mer. Pass.	h m 3 12.4	v −0.7	d 0.1	v 0.8	d 0.4	v 2.1	d 0.1	v 2.6	d 0.0

STARS

Name	SHA ° ′	Dec ° ′
Acamar	315 16.3	S40 13.9
Achernar	335 24.6	S57 08.7
Acrux	173 06.4	S63 11.9
Adhara	255 10.7	S28 59.8
Aldebaran	290 46.3	N16 32.5
Alioth	166 18.6	N55 52.3
Alkaid	152 56.9	N49 14.0
Al Na'ir	27 39.8	S46 52.3
Alnilam	275 43.8	S 1 11.6
Alphard	217 53.7	S 8 44.1
Alphecca	126 08.6	N26 39.7
Alpheratz	357 40.3	N29 11.1
Altair	62 05.2	N 8 55.1
Ankaa	353 12.8	S42 12.5
Antares	112 22.6	S26 28.1
Arcturus	145 53.2	N19 05.8
Atria	107 21.6	S69 03.5
Avior	234 17.5	S59 34.0
Bellatrix	278 29.2	N 6 21.8
Betelgeuse	270 58.5	N 7 24.5
Canopus	263 55.3	S52 42.3
Capella	280 30.6	N46 00.6
Deneb	49 29.1	N45 20.7
Denebola	182 31.1	N14 28.6
Diphda	348 52.9	S17 53.3
Dubhe	193 49.0	N61 39.6
Elnath	278 09.3	N28 37.1
Eltanin	90 44.4	N51 29.6
Enif	33 44.0	N 9 57.5
Fomalhaut	15 20.6	S29 31.6
Gacrux	171 58.0	S57 12.8
Gienah	175 49.6	S17 38.3
Hadar	148 43.9	S60 27.5
Hamal	327 57.5	N23 32.5
Kaus Aust.	83 39.8	S34 22.4
Kochab	137 20.2	N74 05.5
Markab	13 35.3	N15 18.0
Menkar	314 12.2	N 4 09.4
Menkent	148 04.3	S36 27.3
Miaplacidus	221 39.9	S69 47.4
Mirfak	308 36.4	N49 55.0
Nunki	75 54.5	S26 16.3
Peacock	53 14.3	S56 40.5
Pollux	243 24.7	N27 58.9
Procyon	244 57.1	N 5 10.7
Rasalhague	96 03.6	N12 33.2
Regulus	207 40.9	N11 52.9
Rigel	281 09.6	S 8 11.0
Rigil Kent.	139 47.9	S60 54.5
Sabik	102 09.1	S15 44.6
Schedar	349 36.9	N56 37.7
Shaula	96 17.8	S37 06.8
Sirius	258 31.6	S16 44.5
Spica	158 28.4	S11 15.0
Suhail	222 50.8	S43 30.3
Vega	80 36.7	N38 48.3
Zuben'ubi	137 02.3	S16 06.7

	SHA ° ′	Mer. Pass. h m
Venus	267 02.2	9 25
Mars	228 34.9	11 58
Jupiter	163 37.5	16 16
Saturn	99 04.6	20 33

UT (d h)		SUN GHA	SUN Dec	MOON GHA	v	MOON Dec	d	HP
		° ′	° ′	° ′	′	° ′	′	′
2 00		178 25.7	N17 45.8	65 48.0	13.1	S16 12.8	5.5	54.2
01		193 25.7	45.1	80 20.1	13.2	16 18.3	5.4	54.2
02		208 25.8	44.5	94 52.3	13.2	16 23.7	5.3	54.2
03		223 25.8	. . 43.8	109 24.5	13.1	16 29.0	5.3	54.2
04		238 25.9	43.2	123 56.6	13.1	16 34.3	5.2	54.2
05		253 25.9	42.5	138 28.7	13.0	16 39.5	5.2	54.2
06		268 26.0	N17 41.9	153 00.7	13.1	S16 44.7	5.0	54.2
07	WEDNESDAY	283 26.0	41.3	167 32.8	13.0	16 49.7	5.0	54.2
08		298 26.1	40.6	182 04.8	13.0	16 54.7	4.9	54.2
09		313 26.1	. . 40.0	196 36.8	12.9	16 59.6	4.8	54.1
10		328 26.1	39.3	211 08.7	12.9	17 04.4	4.8	54.1
11		343 26.2	38.7	225 40.6	13.0	17 09.2	4.7	54.1
12		358 26.2	N17 38.0	240 12.6	12.8	S17 13.9	4.6	54.1
13		13 26.3	37.4	254 44.4	12.9	17 18.5	4.5	54.1
14		28 26.3	36.7	269 16.3	12.8	17 23.0	4.4	54.1
15		43 26.4	. . 36.1	283 48.1	12.8	17 27.4	4.4	54.1
16		58 26.4	35.4	298 19.9	12.8	17 31.8	4.3	54.1
17		73 26.5	34.8	312 51.7	12.8	17 36.1	4.2	54.1
18		88 26.5	N17 34.1	327 23.5	12.7	S17 40.3	4.2	54.1
19		103 26.6	33.5	341 55.2	12.7	17 44.5	4.0	54.1
20		118 26.6	32.8	356 26.9	12.6	17 48.5	4.0	54.1
21		133 26.7	. . 32.2	10 58.5	12.7	17 52.5	3.9	54.1
22		148 26.7	31.5	25 30.2	12.6	17 56.4	3.8	54.1
23		163 26.8	30.9	40 01.8	12.6	18 00.2	3.7	54.1
3 00		178 26.8	N17 30.2	54 33.4	12.6	S18 03.9	3.7	54.1
01		193 26.9	29.6	69 05.0	12.5	18 07.6	3.5	54.1
02		208 26.9	28.9	83 36.5	12.5	18 11.1	3.5	54.1
03		223 27.0	. . 28.3	98 08.0	12.5	18 14.6	3.4	54.1
04		238 27.0	27.6	112 39.5	12.5	18 18.0	3.4	54.2
05		253 27.1	27.0	127 11.0	12.4	18 21.4	3.2	54.2
06		268 27.1	N17 26.3	141 42.4	12.4	S18 24.6	3.2	54.2
07		283 27.2	25.7	156 13.8	12.4	18 27.8	3.0	54.2
08	THURSDAY	298 27.3	25.0	170 45.2	12.4	18 30.8	3.0	54.2
09		313 27.3	. . 24.3	185 16.6	12.3	18 33.8	2.9	54.2
10		328 27.4	23.7	199 47.9	12.3	18 36.7	2.9	54.2
11		343 27.4	23.0	214 19.2	12.3	18 39.6	2.7	54.2
12		358 27.5	N17 22.4	228 50.5	12.3	S18 42.3	2.6	54.2
13		13 27.5	21.7	243 21.8	12.2	18 44.9	2.6	54.2
14		28 27.6	21.0	257 53.0	12.3	18 47.5	2.5	54.2
15		43 27.6	. . 20.4	272 24.3	12.1	18 50.0	2.4	54.2
16		58 27.7	19.7	286 55.4	12.2	18 52.4	2.3	54.2
17		73 27.7	19.1	301 26.6	12.2	18 54.7	2.2	54.2
18		88 27.8	N17 18.4	315 57.8	12.1	S18 56.9	2.1	54.2
19		103 27.9	17.7	330 28.9	12.1	18 59.0	2.1	54.2
20		118 27.9	17.1	345 00.0	12.1	19 01.1	1.9	54.2
21		133 28.0	. . 16.4	359 31.1	12.0	19 03.0	1.9	54.2
22		148 28.0	15.8	14 02.1	12.1	19 04.9	1.8	54.2
23		163 28.1	15.1	28 33.2	12.0	19 06.7	1.7	54.2
4 00		178 28.1	N17 14.4	43 04.2	12.0	S19 08.4	1.6	54.2
01		193 28.2	13.8	57 35.2	11.9	19 10.0	1.5	54.3
02		208 28.3	13.1	72 06.1	12.0	19 11.5	1.4	54.3
03		223 28.3	. . 12.4	86 37.1	11.9	19 12.9	1.4	54.3
04		238 28.4	11.8	101 08.0	11.9	19 14.3	1.2	54.3
05		253 28.4	11.1	115 38.9	11.9	19 15.5	1.2	54.3
06		268 28.5	N17 10.4	130 09.8	11.9	S19 16.7	1.1	54.3
07		283 28.5	09.8	144 40.7	11.8	19 17.8	0.9	54.3
08		298 28.6	09.1	159 11.5	11.9	19 18.7	0.9	54.3
09	FRIDAY	313 28.7	. . 08.4	173 42.4	11.8	19 19.6	0.8	54.3
10		328 28.7	07.8	188 13.2	11.8	19 20.4	0.7	54.3
11		343 28.8	07.1	202 44.0	11.8	19 21.1	0.7	54.3
12		358 28.8	N17 06.4	217 14.8	11.7	S19 21.8	0.5	54.3
13		13 28.9	05.7	231 45.5	11.8	19 22.3	0.4	54.4
14		28 29.0	05.1	246 16.3	11.7	19 22.7	0.4	54.4
15		43 29.0	. . 04.4	260 47.0	11.7	19 23.1	0.2	54.4
16		58 29.1	03.7	275 17.7	11.7	19 23.3	0.2	54.4
17		73 29.2	03.1	289 48.4	11.7	19 23.5	0.0	54.4
18		88 29.2	N17 02.4	304 19.1	11.6	S19 23.5	0.0	54.4
19		103 29.3	01.7	318 49.7	11.7	19 23.5	0.1	54.4
20		118 29.3	01.0	333 20.4	11.6	19 23.4	0.2	54.4
21		133 29.4	17 00.4	347 51.0	11.7	19 23.2	0.3	54.4
22		148 29.5	16 59.7	2 21.7	11.6	19 22.9	0.4	54.5
23		163 29.5	N16 59.0	16 52.3	11.6	S19 22.5	0.5	54.5
		SD 15.8	d 0.7	SD 14.8		14.8		14.8

Lat.	Twilight Naut.	Twilight Civil	Sunrise	Moonrise 2	Moonrise 3	Moonrise 4	Moonrise 5
°	h m	h m	h m	h m	h m	h m	h m
N 72	□	□	□	19 47	■	■	■
N 70	////	////	01 44	18 18	19 48	20 54	21 18
68	////	////	02 26	17 39	18 53	19 51	20 28
66	////	00 55	02 54	17 12	18 20	19 16	19 56
64	////	01 52	03 15	16 52	17 56	18 50	19 33
62	////	02 24	03 32	16 35	17 37	18 31	19 14
60	00 50	02 47	03 46	16 21	17 22	18 14	18 58
N 58	01 41	03 05	03 58	16 09	17 08	18 01	18 45
56	02 10	03 20	04 08	15 59	16 57	17 49	18 34
54	02 32	03 33	04 17	15 50	16 47	17 39	18 24
52	02 49	03 44	04 25	15 42	16 38	17 30	18 15
50	03 04	03 54	04 32	15 35	16 30	17 21	18 07
45	03 32	04 14	04 48	15 19	16 13	17 04	17 51
N 40	03 53	04 30	05 00	15 07	15 59	16 50	17 37
35	04 10	04 43	05 11	14 56	15 48	16 38	17 25
30	04 24	04 54	05 20	14 47	15 38	16 27	17 15
20	04 45	05 13	05 36	14 31	15 20	16 09	16 57
N 10	05 02	05 28	05 50	14 16	15 05	15 53	16 42
0	05 16	05 41	06 03	14 03	14 50	15 39	16 27
S 10	05 28	05 53	06 15	13 50	14 36	15 24	16 13
20	05 39	06 06	06 29	13 36	14 21	15 08	15 57
30	05 50	06 19	06 44	13 21	14 04	14 50	15 40
35	05 56	06 26	06 53	13 11	13 54	14 40	15 29
40	06 01	06 34	07 03	13 01	13 42	14 28	15 18
45	06 08	06 43	07 14	12 49	13 29	14 14	15 04
S 50	06 14	06 53	07 28	12 34	13 12	13 56	14 47
52	06 17	06 58	07 35	12 27	13 04	13 48	14 39
54	06 20	07 03	07 42	12 19	12 56	13 39	14 30
56	06 24	07 09	07 50	12 11	12 46	13 29	14 20
58	06 27	07 15	07 59	12 01	12 35	13 17	14 09
S 60	06 31	07 22	08 10	11 50	12 23	13 04	13 56

Lat.	Sunset	Twilight Civil	Twilight Naut.	Moonset 2	Moonset 3	Moonset 4	Moonset 5
°	h m	h m	h m	h m	h m	h m	h m
N 72	□	□	□	20 35	■	■	■
N 70	22 22	////	////	22 04	22 13	22 47	24 05
68	21 42	////	////	22 44	23 08	23 50	24 55
66	21 16	23 07	////	23 11	23 41	24 25	00 25
64	20 55	22 16	////	23 32	24 05	00 05	00 50
62	20 39	21 46	////	23 49	24 24	00 24	01 10
60	20 25	21 23	23 13	24 03	00 03	00 40	01 26
N 58	20 13	21 05	22 27	24 15	00 15	00 53	01 40
56	20 03	20 50	21 59	24 26	00 26	01 05	01 52
54	19 54	20 38	21 38	00 02	00 35	01 15	02 02
52	19 46	20 27	21 21	00 09	00 43	01 24	02 11
50	19 39	20 17	21 07	00 15	00 51	01 32	02 19
45	19 24	19 57	20 39	00 29	01 07	01 49	02 37
N 40	19 11	19 41	20 18	00 41	01 20	02 03	02 51
35	19 01	19 28	20 02	00 51	01 31	02 15	03 03
30	18 52	19 17	19 48	00 59	01 41	02 26	03 14
20	18 36	18 59	19 27	01 14	01 58	02 43	03 32
N 10	18 22	18 44	19 10	01 27	02 12	02 59	03 47
0	18 10	18 31	18 56	01 40	02 26	03 14	04 02
S 10	17 57	18 19	18 44	01 52	02 40	03 28	04 17
20	17 44	18 07	18 33	02 05	02 54	03 44	04 32
30	17 29	17 54	18 23	02 20	03 11	04 02	04 50
35	17 20	17 47	18 17	02 29	03 21	04 12	05 01
40	17 10	17 39	18 11	02 39	03 32	04 24	05 13
45	16 59	17 30	18 05	02 50	03 46	04 38	05 27
S 50	16 45	17 20	17 59	03 05	04 02	04 55	05 44
52	16 38	17 15	17 56	03 11	04 09	05 03	05 52
54	16 31	17 10	17 53	03 19	04 18	05 12	06 01
56	16 23	17 04	17 50	03 27	04 27	05 22	06 11
58	16 14	16 58	17 46	03 36	04 38	05 34	06 22
S 60	16 04	16 51	17 42	03 47	04 50	05 47	06 36

Day	SUN Eqn. of Time 00h	SUN Eqn. of Time 12h	SUN Mer. Pass.	MOON Mer. Pass. Upper	MOON Mer. Pass. Lower	MOON Age	MOON Phase
d	m s	m s	h m	h m	h m	d	%
2	06 17	06 15	12 06	20 15	07 51	10	76
3	06 13	06 10	12 06	21 02	08 38	11	84
4	06 08	06 05	12 06	21 50	09 26	12	90

Day	UT d h	ARIES GHA	VENUS −4·0 GHA	VENUS Dec	MARS +1·7 GHA	MARS Dec	JUPITER −1·8 GHA	JUPITER Dec	SATURN +0·3 GHA	SATURN Dec	STARS Name	SHA	Dec
		° ′	° ′	° ′	° ′	° ′	° ′	° ′	° ′	° ′		° ′	° ′
SATURDAY	5 00	313 44.1	218 16.3	N21 58.2	181 00.5	N18 49.7	117 06.1	S 5 48.3	52 53.1	S21 55.5	Acamar	315 16.3	S40 13.9
	01	328 46.6	233 15.7	58.2	196 01.4	49.3	132 08.2	48.4	67 55.6	55.5	Achernar	335 24.6	S57 08.7
	02	343 49.1	248 15.0	58.2	211 02.2	48.8	147 10.3	48.6	82 58.2	55.5	Acrux	173 06.4	S63 11.9
	03	358 51.5	263 14.3	. . 58.2	226 03.0	. . 48.4	162 12.5	. . 48.7	98 00.7	. . 55.5	Adhara	255 10.6	S28 59.8
	04	13 54.0	278 13.7	58.3	241 03.9	48.0	177 14.6	48.9	113 03.3	55.5	Aldebaran	290 46.3	N16 32.5
	05	28 56.5	293 13.0	58.3	256 04.7	47.6	192 16.7	49.0	128 05.8	55.5			
	06	43 58.9	308 12.3	N21 58.3	271 05.5	N18 47.1	207 18.9	S 5 49.2	143 08.4	S21 55.5	Alioth	166 18.6	N55 52.2
	07	59 01.4	323 11.7	58.3	286 06.4	46.7	222 21.0	49.3	158 10.9	55.5	Alkaid	152 56.9	N49 14.0
	08	74 03.8	338 11.0	58.3	301 07.2	46.3	237 23.1	49.4	173 13.5	55.5	Al Na'ir	27 39.8	S46 52.4
	09	89 06.3	353 10.3	. . 58.3	316 08.0	. . 45.8	252 25.3	. . 49.6	188 16.0	. . 55.5	Alnilam	275 43.7	S 1 11.6
	10	104 08.8	8 09.7	58.3	331 08.9	45.4	267 27.4	49.7	203 18.6	55.5	Alphard	217 53.7	S 8 44.1
	11	119 11.2	23 09.0	58.3	346 09.7	45.0	282 29.6	49.9	218 21.1	55.5			
	12	134 13.7	38 08.3	N21 58.4	1 10.5	N18 44.6	297 31.7	S 5 50.0	233 23.7	S21 55.5	Alphecca	126 08.6	N26 39.7
	13	149 16.2	53 07.7	58.4	16 11.4	44.1	312 33.8	50.2	248 26.2	55.5	Alpheratz	357 40.3	N29 11.1
	14	164 18.6	68 07.0	58.4	31 12.2	43.7	327 36.0	50.3	263 28.8	55.5	Altair	62 05.2	N 8 55.1
	15	179 21.1	83 06.3	. . 58.4	46 13.0	. . 43.3	342 38.1	. . 50.5	278 31.3	. . 55.5	Ankaa	353 12.7	S42 12.5
	16	194 23.6	98 05.7	58.4	61 13.9	42.8	357 40.2	50.6	293 33.9	55.6	Antares	112 22.6	S26 28.1
	17	209 26.0	113 05.0	58.4	76 14.7	42.4	12 42.4	50.7	308 36.4	55.6			
	18	224 28.5	128 04.3	N21 58.4	91 15.5	N18 42.0	27 44.5	S 5 50.9	323 38.9	S21 55.6	Arcturus	145 53.2	N19 05.8
	19	239 30.9	143 03.6	58.4	106 16.4	41.5	42 46.6	51.0	338 41.5	55.6	Atria	107 21.6	S69 03.5
	20	254 33.4	158 03.0	58.4	121 17.2	41.1	57 48.8	51.2	353 44.0	55.6	Avior	234 17.5	S59 34.0
	21	269 35.9	173 02.3	. . 58.4	136 18.1	. . 40.7	72 50.9	. . 51.3	8 46.6	. . 55.6	Bellatrix	278 29.2	N 6 21.8
	22	284 38.3	188 01.6	58.4	151 18.9	40.2	87 53.0	51.5	23 49.1	55.6	Betelgeuse	270 58.5	N 7 24.5
	23	299 40.8	203 01.0	58.4	166 19.7	39.8	102 55.2	51.6	38 51.7	55.6			
SUNDAY	6 00	314 43.3	218 00.3	N21 58.4	181 20.6	N18 39.4	117 57.3	S 5 51.8	53 54.2	S21 55.6	Canopus	263 55.3	S52 42.3
	01	329 45.7	232 59.6	58.4	196 21.4	38.9	132 59.4	51.9	68 56.8	55.6	Capella	280 30.6	N46 00.6
	02	344 48.2	247 58.9	58.4	211 22.2	38.5	148 01.5	52.0	83 59.3	55.6	Deneb	49 29.1	N45 20.8
	03	359 50.7	262 58.3	. . 58.4	226 23.1	. . 38.1	163 03.7	. . 52.2	99 01.9	. . 55.6	Denebola	182 31.1	N14 28.6
	04	14 53.1	277 57.6	58.4	241 23.9	37.6	178 05.8	52.3	114 04.4	55.6	Diphda	348 52.9	S17 53.3
	05	29 55.6	292 56.9	58.4	256 24.7	37.2	193 07.9	52.5	129 07.0	55.6			
	06	44 58.1	307 56.3	N21 58.3	271 25.6	N18 36.8	208 10.1	S 5 52.6	144 09.5	S21 55.6	Dubhe	193 49.0	N61 39.6
	07	60 00.5	322 55.6	58.3	286 26.4	36.3	223 12.2	52.8	159 12.1	55.6	Elnath	278 09.3	N28 37.1
	08	75 03.0	337 54.9	58.3	301 27.3	35.9	238 14.3	52.9	174 14.6	55.6	Eltanin	90 44.5	N51 29.6
	09	90 05.4	352 54.2	. . 58.3	316 28.1	. . 35.5	253 16.5	. . 53.1	189 17.1	. . 55.6	Enif	33 44.0	N 9 57.5
	10	105 07.9	7 53.6	58.3	331 28.9	35.0	268 18.6	53.2	204 19.7	55.6	Fomalhaut	15 20.6	S29 31.6
	11	120 10.4	22 52.9	58.3	346 29.8	34.6	283 20.7	53.4	219 22.2	55.6			
	12	135 12.8	37 52.2	N21 58.3	1 30.6	N18 34.2	298 22.9	S 5 53.5	234 24.8	S21 55.6	Gacrux	171 58.0	S57 12.8
	13	150 15.3	52 51.5	58.3	16 31.4	33.7	313 25.0	53.6	249 27.3	55.6	Gienah	175 49.6	S17 38.3
	14	165 17.8	67 50.9	58.2	31 32.3	33.3	328 27.1	53.8	264 29.9	55.6	Hadar	148 43.9	S60 27.5
	15	180 20.2	82 50.2	. . 58.2	46 33.1	. . 32.9	343 29.2	. . 53.9	279 32.4	. . 55.6	Hamal	327 57.5	N23 32.5
	16	195 22.7	97 49.5	58.2	61 34.0	32.4	358 31.4	54.1	294 35.0	55.6	Kaus Aust.	83 39.8	S34 22.4
	17	210 25.2	112 48.9	58.2	76 34.8	32.0	13 33.5	54.2	309 37.5	55.6			
	18	225 27.6	127 48.2	N21 58.2	91 35.6	N18 31.6	28 35.6	S 5 54.4	324 40.0	S21 55.6	Kochab	137 20.2	N74 05.5
	19	240 30.1	142 47.5	58.1	106 36.5	31.1	43 37.8	54.5	339 42.6	55.6	Markab	13 35.2	N15 18.0
	20	255 32.6	157 46.8	58.1	121 37.3	30.7	58 39.9	54.7	354 45.1	55.6	Menkar	314 12.1	N 4 09.4
	21	270 35.0	172 46.2	. . 58.1	136 38.2	. . 30.3	73 42.0	. . 54.8	9 47.7	. . 55.6	Menkent	148 04.3	S36 27.3
	22	285 37.5	187 45.5	58.1	151 39.0	29.8	88 44.1	55.0	24 50.2	55.6	Miaplacidus	221 39.9	S69 47.4
	23	300 39.9	202 44.8	58.0	166 39.8	29.4	103 46.3	55.1	39 52.8	55.6			
MONDAY	7 00	315 42.4	217 44.1	N21 58.0	181 40.7	N18 28.9	118 48.4	S 5 55.3	54 55.3	S21 55.6	Mirfak	308 36.4	N49 55.0
	01	330 44.9	232 43.5	58.0	196 41.5	28.5	133 50.5	55.4	69 57.8	55.6	Nunki	75 54.5	S26 16.3
	02	345 47.3	247 42.8	57.9	211 42.4	28.1	148 52.7	55.5	85 00.4	55.6	Peacock	53 14.3	S56 40.5
	03	0 49.8	262 42.1	. . 57.9	226 43.2	. . 27.6	163 54.8	. . 55.7	100 02.9	. . 55.6	Pollux	243 24.7	N27 58.9
	04	15 52.3	277 41.4	57.9	241 44.0	27.2	178 56.9	55.8	115 05.5	55.6	Procyon	244 57.1	N 5 10.7
	05	30 54.7	292 40.7	57.9	256 44.9	26.7	193 59.0	56.0	130 08.0	55.7			
	06	45 57.2	307 40.1	N21 57.8	271 45.7	N18 26.3	209 01.2	S 5 56.1	145 10.6	S21 55.7	Rasalhague	96 03.6	N12 33.2
	07	60 59.7	322 39.4	57.8	286 46.6	25.9	224 03.3	56.3	160 13.1	55.7	Regulus	207 40.9	N11 52.9
	08	76 02.1	337 38.7	57.7	301 47.4	25.4	239 05.4	56.4	175 15.6	55.7	Rigel	281 09.6	S 8 11.0
	09	91 04.6	352 38.0	. . 57.7	316 48.2	. . 25.0	254 07.5	. . 56.6	190 18.2	. . 55.7	Rigil Kent.	139 47.9	S60 54.5
	10	106 07.1	7 37.4	57.7	331 49.1	24.5	269 09.7	56.7	205 20.7	55.7	Sabik	102 09.1	S15 44.6
	11	121 09.5	22 36.7	57.6	346 49.9	24.1	284 11.8	56.9	220 23.3	55.7			
	12	136 12.0	37 36.0	N21 57.6	1 50.8	N18 23.7	299 13.9	S 5 57.0	235 25.8	S21 55.7	Schedar	349 36.9	N56 37.8
	13	151 14.4	52 35.3	57.6	16 51.6	23.2	314 16.0	57.2	250 28.3	55.7	Shaula	96 17.8	S37 06.8
	14	166 16.9	67 34.7	57.5	31 52.4	22.8	329 18.2	57.3	265 30.9	55.7	Sirius	258 31.5	S16 44.5
	15	181 19.4	82 34.0	. . 57.5	46 53.3	. . 22.3	344 20.3	. . 57.5	280 33.4	. . 55.7	Spica	158 28.4	S11 15.0
	16	196 21.8	97 33.3	57.4	61 54.1	21.9	359 22.4	57.6	295 36.0	55.7	Suhail	222 50.8	S43 30.2
	17	211 24.3	112 32.6	57.4	76 55.0	21.5	14 24.5	57.8	310 38.5	55.7			
	18	226 26.8	127 31.9	N21 57.3	91 55.8	N18 21.0	29 26.7	S 5 57.9	325 41.0	S21 55.7	Vega	80 36.7	N38 48.4
	19	241 29.2	142 31.3	57.3	106 56.7	20.6	44 28.8	58.1	340 43.6	55.7	Zuben'ubi	137 02.3	S16 06.7
	20	256 31.7	157 30.6	57.2	121 57.5	20.1	59 30.9	58.2	355 46.1	55.7			
	21	271 34.2	172 29.9	. . 57.2	136 58.3	. . 19.7	74 33.0	. . 58.3	10 48.7	. . 55.7			
	22	286 36.6	187 29.2	57.1	151 59.2	19.3	89 35.2	58.5	25 51.2	55.7			
	23	301 39.1	202 28.6	57.1	167 00.0	18.8	104 37.3	58.6	40 53.7	55.7			
	Mer. Pass.	h m 3 00.6	v −0.7	d 0.0	v 0.8	d 0.4	v 2.1	d 0.1	v 2.5	d 0.0			

	SHA	Mer. Pass.
	° ′	h m
Venus	263 17.0	9 28
Mars	226 37.3	11 54
Jupiter	163 14.0	16 06
Saturn	99 11.0	20 21

	UT	SUN GHA	SUN Dec	MOON GHA	v	MOON Dec	d	HP
	d h	° ′	° ′	° ′	′	° ′	′	′
	5 00	178 29.6	N16 58.3	31 22.9	11.5	S19 22.0	0.6	54.5
	01	193 29.7	57.7	45 53.4	11.6	19 21.4	0.6	54.5
	02	208 29.7	57.0	60 24.0	11.6	19 20.8	0.8	54.5
	03	223 29.8	. . 56.3	74 54.6	11.5	19 20.0	0.9	54.5
	04	238 29.8	55.6	89 25.1	11.6	19 19.1	0.9	54.5
	05	253 29.9	55.0	103 55.7	11.5	19 18.2	1.0	54.5
	06	268 30.0	N16 54.3	118 26.2	11.5	S19 17.2	1.2	54.5
	07	283 30.0	53.6	132 56.7	11.5	19 16.0	1.2	54.6
S	08	298 30.1	52.9	147 27.2	11.5	19 14.8	1.3	54.6
A	09	313 30.2	. . 52.2	161 57.7	11.5	19 13.5	1.4	54.6
T	10	328 30.2	51.6	176 28.2	11.5	19 12.1	1.6	54.6
U	11	343 30.3	50.9	190 58.7	11.4	19 10.5	1.6	54.6
R	12	358 30.4	N16 50.2	205 29.1	11.5	S19 08.9	1.6	54.6
D	13	13 30.4	49.5	219 59.6	11.5	19 07.3	1.8	54.6
A	14	28 30.5	48.8	234 30.1	11.4	19 05.5	1.9	54.7
Y	15	43 30.6	. . 48.1	249 00.5	11.5	19 03.6	2.0	54.7
	16	58 30.6	47.5	263 31.0	11.4	19 01.6	2.1	54.7
	17	73 30.7	46.8	278 01.4	11.4	18 59.5	2.1	54.7
	18	88 30.8	N16 46.1	292 31.8	11.5	S18 57.4	2.3	54.7
	19	103 30.9	45.4	307 02.3	11.4	18 55.1	2.3	54.7
	20	118 30.9	44.7	321 32.7	11.4	18 52.8	2.4	54.7
	21	133 31.0	. . 44.0	336 03.1	11.4	18 50.4	2.6	54.8
	22	148 31.1	43.4	350 33.5	11.4	18 47.8	2.6	54.8
	23	163 31.1	42.7	5 03.9	11.5	18 45.2	2.7	54.8
	6 00	178 31.2	N16 42.0	19 34.4	11.4	S18 42.5	2.8	54.8
	01	193 31.3	41.3	34 04.8	11.4	18 39.7	2.9	54.8
	02	208 31.3	40.6	48 35.2	11.4	18 36.8	3.0	54.8
	03	223 31.4	. . 39.9	63 05.6	11.4	18 33.8	3.1	54.8
	04	238 31.5	39.2	77 36.0	11.4	18 30.7	3.2	54.9
	05	253 31.6	38.5	92 06.4	11.4	18 27.5	3.2	54.9
	06	268 31.6	N16 37.9	106 36.8	11.4	S18 24.3	3.4	54.9
	07	283 31.7	37.2	121 07.2	11.4	18 20.9	3.5	54.9
	08	298 31.8	36.5	135 37.6	11.4	18 17.4	3.5	54.9
S	09	313 31.8	. . 35.8	150 08.0	11.4	18 13.9	3.6	54.9
U	10	328 31.9	35.1	164 38.4	11.4	18 10.3	3.8	55.0
N	11	343 32.0	34.4	179 08.8	11.4	18 06.5	3.8	55.0
D	12	358 32.1	N16 33.7	193 39.2	11.5	S18 02.7	3.9	55.0
A	13	13 32.1	33.0	208 09.7	11.4	17 58.8	4.0	55.0
Y	14	28 32.2	32.3	222 40.1	11.4	17 54.8	4.1	55.0
	15	43 32.3	. . 31.6	237 10.5	11.4	17 50.7	4.1	55.0
	16	58 32.4	30.9	251 40.9	11.5	17 46.6	4.3	55.1
	17	73 32.4	30.2	266 11.4	11.4	17 42.3	4.4	55.1
	18	88 32.5	N16 29.5	280 41.8	11.4	S17 37.9	4.4	55.1
	19	103 32.6	28.8	295 12.2	11.5	17 33.5	4.5	55.1
	20	118 32.7	28.1	309 42.7	11.4	17 29.0	4.7	55.1
	21	133 32.7	. . 27.4	324 13.1	11.5	17 24.3	4.7	55.1
	22	148 32.8	26.8	338 43.6	11.4	17 19.6	4.8	55.2
	23	163 32.9	26.1	353 14.0	11.5	17 14.8	4.8	55.2
	7 00	178 33.0	N16 25.4	7 44.5	11.5	S17 10.0	5.0	55.2
	01	193 33.0	24.7	22 15.0	11.5	17 05.0	5.1	55.2
	02	208 33.1	24.0	36 45.5	11.5	16 59.9	5.1	55.2
	03	223 33.2	. . 23.3	51 16.0	11.5	16 54.8	5.2	55.3
	04	238 33.3	22.6	65 46.5	11.5	16 49.6	5.4	55.3
	05	253 33.3	21.9	80 17.0	11.5	16 44.2	5.4	55.3
	06	268 33.4	N16 21.2	94 47.5	11.5	S16 38.8	5.4	55.3
	07	283 33.5	20.5	109 18.0	11.5	16 33.4	5.6	55.3
	08	298 33.6	19.8	123 48.5	11.6	16 27.8	5.7	55.3
M	09	313 33.7	. . 19.1	138 19.1	11.5	16 22.1	5.7	55.4
O	10	328 33.7	18.3	152 49.6	11.6	16 16.4	5.8	55.4
N	11	343 33.8	17.6	167 20.2	11.5	16 10.6	5.9	55.4
D	12	358 33.9	N16 16.9	181 50.7	11.6	S16 04.7	6.0	55.4
A	13	13 34.0	16.2	196 21.3	11.6	15 58.7	6.1	55.4
Y	14	28 34.0	15.5	210 51.9	11.6	15 52.6	6.2	55.5
	15	43 34.1	. . 14.8	225 22.5	11.6	15 46.4	6.2	55.5
	16	58 34.2	14.1	239 53.1	11.6	15 40.2	6.3	55.5
	17	73 34.3	13.4	254 23.7	11.7	15 33.9	6.4	55.5
	18	88 34.4	N16 12.7	268 54.4	11.6	S15 27.5	6.5	55.5
	19	103 34.5	12.0	283 25.0	11.6	15 21.0	6.5	55.6
	20	118 34.5	11.3	297 55.6	11.7	15 14.5	6.7	55.6
	21	133 34.6	. . 10.6	312 26.3	11.7	15 07.8	6.7	55.6
	22	148 34.7	09.9	326 57.0	11.7	15 01.1	6.8	55.6
	23	163 34.8	09.2	341 27.7	11.7	S14 54.3	6.9	55.6
		SD 15.8	*d* 0.7	SD 14.9		15.0		15.1

Lat.	Twilight Naut.	Twilight Civil	Sunrise	Moonrise 5	6	7	8
°	h m	h m	h m	h m	h m	h m	h m
N 72	////	////	01 00	■	22 25	21 57	21 44
N 70	////	////	02 05	21 18	21 24	21 24	21 23
68	////	////	02 40	20 28	20 48	21 00	21 07
66	////	01 25	03 05	19 56	20 23	20 41	20 53
64	////	02 07	03 24	19 33	20 03	20 26	20 42
62	////	02 35	03 40	19 14	19 47	20 13	20 33
60	01 16	02 56	03 53	18 58	19 34	20 02	20 25
N 58	01 55	03 13	04 04	18 45	19 22	19 52	20 18
56	02 21	03 27	04 14	18 34	19 12	19 44	20 11
54	02 40	03 39	04 22	18 24	19 03	19 37	20 05
52	02 56	03 50	04 30	18 15	18 55	19 30	20 00
50	03 10	03 59	04 37	18 07	18 48	19 24	19 56
45	03 37	04 18	04 51	17 51	18 33	19 11	19 45
N 40	03 57	04 33	05 03	17 37	18 20	19 00	19 37
35	04 13	04 46	05 13	17 25	18 09	18 51	19 30
30	04 26	04 56	05 22	17 15	18 00	18 43	19 23
20	04 46	05 14	05 37	16 57	17 44	18 29	19 12
N 10	05 03	05 28	05 50	16 42	17 30	18 17	19 02
0	05 16	05 41	06 02	16 27	17 16	18 05	18 53
S 10	05 27	05 53	06 14	16 13	17 03	17 53	18 44
20	05 38	06 04	06 27	15 57	16 49	17 41	18 34
30	05 48	06 17	06 42	15 40	16 32	17 27	18 23
35	05 53	06 23	06 50	15 29	16 23	17 19	18 17
40	05 58	06 31	06 59	15 18	16 12	17 09	18 09
45	06 04	06 39	07 10	15 04	15 59	16 58	18 01
S 50	06 10	06 49	07 23	14 47	15 43	16 45	17 50
52	06 13	06 53	07 30	14 39	15 36	16 39	17 45
54	06 15	06 58	07 36	14 30	15 28	16 32	17 40
56	06 18	07 03	07 44	14 20	15 19	16 24	17 34
58	06 22	07 09	07 53	14 09	15 09	16 15	17 27
S 60	06 25	07 15	08 02	13 56	14 57	16 05	17 20

Lat.	Sunset	Twilight Civil	Twilight Naut.	Moonset 5	6	7	8
°	h m	h m	h m	h m	h m	h m	h m
N 72	22 58	////	////	■	■	00 41	02 49
N 70	22 01	////	////	24 05	00 05	01 41	03 21
68	21 28	////	////	24 55	00 55	02 15	03 45
66	21 04	22 40	////	00 25	01 26	02 40	04 03
64	20 45	22 00	////	00 50	01 49	02 59	04 17
62	20 30	21 34	////	01 10	02 08	03 15	04 30
60	20 17	21 13	22 49	01 26	02 23	03 28	04 40
N 58	20 06	20 57	22 13	01 40	02 36	03 39	04 49
56	19 57	20 43	21 48	01 52	02 47	03 49	04 57
54	19 48	20 31	21 29	02 02	02 57	03 58	05 04
52	19 41	20 21	21 13	02 11	03 05	04 05	05 10
50	19 34	20 12	21 00	02 19	03 13	04 12	05 16
45	19 20	19 53	20 34	02 37	03 30	04 27	05 28
N 40	19 08	19 38	20 14	02 51	03 43	04 39	05 38
35	18 58	19 25	19 58	03 03	03 55	04 49	05 46
30	18 49	19 15	19 45	03 14	04 05	04 58	05 54
20	18 34	18 58	19 25	03 32	04 22	05 14	06 07
N 10	18 21	18 43	19 09	03 47	04 37	05 27	06 18
0	18 09	18 31	18 56	04 02	04 51	05 40	06 28
S 10	17 57	18 19	18 45	04 17	05 05	05 52	06 39
20	17 45	18 08	18 34	04 32	05 20	06 06	06 50
30	17 31	17 56	18 24	04 50	05 37	06 21	07 02
35	17 22	17 49	18 19	05 01	05 47	06 29	07 10
40	17 13	17 41	18 14	05 13	05 58	06 39	07 18
45	17 02	17 33	18 08	05 27	06 11	06 51	07 27
S 50	16 49	17 24	18 02	05 44	06 27	07 05	07 39
52	16 43	17 19	18 00	05 52	06 35	07 12	07 44
54	16 36	17 14	17 57	06 01	06 43	07 19	07 50
56	16 28	17 09	17 54	06 11	06 52	07 27	07 56
58	16 20	17 04	17 51	06 22	07 03	07 36	08 04
S 60	16 10	16 57	17 48	06 36	07 15	07 47	08 12

Day	SUN Eqn. of Time 00^h	12^h	Mer. Pass.	MOON Mer. Pass. Upper	Lower	Age	Phase
d	m s	m s	h m	h m	h m	d %	
5	06 02	05 59	12 06	22 39	10 15	13 95	○
6	05 55	05 52	12 06	23 28	11 04	14 98	
7	05 48	05 45	12 06	24 17	11 52	15 100	

2017 AUGUST 8, 9, 10 (TUES., WED., THURS.)

TUESDAY

UT (d h)	ARIES GHA	VENUS −4·0 GHA	VENUS Dec	MARS +1·7 GHA	MARS Dec	JUPITER −1·8 GHA	JUPITER Dec	SATURN +0·3 GHA	SATURN Dec
	° ′	° ′	° ′	° ′	° ′	° ′	° ′	° ′	° ′
8 00	316 41.5	217 27.9	N21 57.0	182 00.9	N18 18.4	119 39.4	S 5 58.8	55 56.3	S21 55.7
01	331 44.0	232 27.2	57.0	197 01.7	17.9	134 41.5	58.9	70 58.8	55.7
02	346 46.5	247 26.5	56.9	212 02.6	17.5	149 43.7	59.1	86 01.4	55.7
03	1 48.9	262 25.8	. . 56.9	227 03.4	. . 17.0	164 45.8	. . 59.2	101 03.9	. . 55.7
04	16 51.4	277 25.2	56.8	242 04.3	16.6	179 47.9	59.4	116 06.4	55.7
05	31 53.9	292 24.5	56.8	257 05.1	16.2	194 50.0	59.5	131 09.0	55.7
06	46 56.3	307 23.8	N21 56.7	272 05.9	N18 15.7	209 52.1	S 5 59.7	146 11.5	S21 55.7
07	61 58.8	322 23.1	56.6	287 06.8	15.3	224 54.3	5 59.8	161 14.0	55.7
08	77 01.3	337 22.4	56.6	302 07.6	14.8	239 56.4	6 00.0	176 16.6	55.7
09	92 03.7	352 21.8	. . 56.5	317 08.5	. . 14.4	254 58.5	. . 00.1	191 19.1	. . 55.7
10	107 06.2	7 21.1	56.5	332 09.3	13.9	270 00.6	00.3	206 21.7	55.7
11	122 08.7	22 20.4	56.4	347 10.2	13.5	285 02.8	00.4	221 24.2	55.7
12	137 11.1	37 19.7	N21 56.3	2 11.0	N18 13.0	300 04.9	S 6 00.6	236 26.7	S21 55.7
13	152 13.6	52 19.0	56.3	17 11.9	12.6	315 07.0	00.7	251 29.3	55.7
14	167 16.0	67 18.4	56.2	32 12.7	12.2	330 09.1	00.9	266 31.8	55.8
15	182 18.5	82 17.7	. . 56.1	47 13.5	. . 11.7	345 11.2	. . 01.0	281 34.3	. . 55.8
16	197 21.0	97 17.0	56.1	62 14.4	11.3	0 13.4	01.2	296 36.9	55.8
17	212 23.4	112 16.3	56.0	77 15.2	10.8	15 15.5	01.3	311 39.4	55.8
18	227 25.9	127 15.6	N21 55.9	92 16.1	N18 10.4	30 17.6	S 6 01.5	326 41.9	S21 55.8
19	242 28.4	142 14.9	55.9	107 16.9	09.9	45 19.7	01.6	341 44.5	55.8
20	257 30.8	157 14.3	55.8	122 17.8	09.5	60 21.8	01.8	356 47.0	55.8
21	272 33.3	172 13.6	. . 55.7	137 18.6	. . 09.0	75 24.0	. . 01.9	11 49.5	. . 55.8
22	287 35.8	187 12.9	55.6	152 19.5	08.6	90 26.1	02.1	26 52.1	55.8
23	302 38.2	202 12.2	55.6	167 20.3	08.1	105 28.2	02.2	41 54.6	55.8

WEDNESDAY

UT (d h)	ARIES GHA	VENUS GHA	VENUS Dec	MARS GHA	MARS Dec	JUPITER GHA	JUPITER Dec	SATURN GHA	SATURN Dec
9 00	317 40.7	217 11.5	N21 55.5	182 21.2	N18 07.7	120 30.3	S 6 02.4	56 57.2	S21 55.8
01	332 43.2	232 10.9	55.4	197 22.0	07.2	135 32.4	02.5	71 59.7	55.8
02	347 45.6	247 10.2	55.3	212 22.9	06.8	150 34.6	02.7	87 02.2	55.8
03	2 48.1	262 09.5	. . 55.2	227 23.7	. . 06.3	165 36.7	. . 02.8	102 04.8	. . 55.8
04	17 50.5	277 08.8	55.2	242 24.6	05.9	180 38.8	03.0	117 07.3	55.8
05	32 53.0	292 08.1	55.1	257 25.4	05.4	195 40.9	03.1	132 09.8	55.8
06	47 55.5	307 07.4	N21 55.0	272 26.3	N18 05.0	210 43.0	S 6 03.3	147 12.4	S21 55.8
07	62 57.9	322 06.8	54.9	287 27.1	04.5	225 45.2	03.4	162 14.9	55.8
08	78 00.4	337 06.1	54.8	302 28.0	04.1	240 47.3	03.6	177 17.4	55.8
09	93 02.9	352 05.4	. . 54.7	317 28.8	. . 03.6	255 49.4	. . 03.7	192 20.0	. . 55.8
10	108 05.3	7 04.7	54.7	332 29.7	03.2	270 51.5	03.9	207 22.5	55.8
11	123 07.8	22 04.0	54.6	347 30.5	02.7	285 53.6	04.0	222 25.0	55.8
12	138 10.3	37 03.3	N21 54.5	2 31.4	N18 02.3	300 55.7	S 6 04.2	237 27.6	S21 55.8
13	153 12.7	52 02.7	54.4	17 32.2	01.8	315 57.9	04.3	252 30.1	55.8
14	168 15.2	67 02.0	54.3	32 33.1	01.4	331 00.0	04.5	267 32.6	55.8
15	183 17.6	82 01.3	. . 54.2	47 33.9	. . 00.9	346 02.1	. . 04.6	282 35.2	. . 55.8
16	198 20.1	97 00.6	54.1	62 34.8	00.5	1 04.2	04.8	297 37.7	55.8
17	213 22.6	111 59.9	54.0	77 35.6	18 00.0	16 06.3	04.9	312 40.2	55.8
18	228 25.0	126 59.2	N21 53.9	92 36.5	N17 59.6	31 08.4	S 6 05.1	327 42.7	S21 55.8
19	243 27.5	141 58.6	53.8	107 37.3	59.1	46 10.6	05.2	342 45.3	55.9
20	258 30.0	156 57.9	53.7	122 38.2	58.7	61 12.7	05.4	357 47.8	55.9
21	273 32.4	171 57.2	. . 53.6	137 39.0	. . 58.2	76 14.8	. . 05.5	12 50.3	. . 55.9
22	288 34.9	186 56.5	53.5	152 39.9	57.8	91 16.9	05.7	27 52.9	55.9
23	303 37.4	201 55.8	53.4	167 40.7	57.3	106 19.0	05.8	42 55.4	55.9

THURSDAY

UT (d h)	ARIES GHA	VENUS GHA	VENUS Dec	MARS GHA	MARS Dec	JUPITER GHA	JUPITER Dec	SATURN GHA	SATURN Dec
10 00	318 39.8	216 55.1	N21 53.3	182 41.6	N17 56.9	121 21.1	S 6 06.0	57 57.9	S21 55.9
01	333 42.3	231 54.4	53.2	197 42.4	56.4	136 23.2	06.1	73 00.5	55.9
02	348 44.8	246 53.8	53.1	212 43.3	56.0	151 25.4	06.3	88 03.0	55.9
03	3 47.2	261 53.1	. . 53.0	227 44.1	. . 55.5	166 27.5	. . 06.4	103 05.5	. . 55.9
04	18 49.7	276 52.4	52.9	242 45.0	55.1	181 29.6	06.6	118 08.1	55.9
05	33 52.1	291 51.7	52.8	257 45.8	54.6	196 31.7	06.7	133 10.6	55.9
06	48 54.6	306 51.0	N21 52.7	272 46.7	N17 54.2	211 33.8	S 6 06.9	148 13.1	S21 55.9
07	63 57.1	321 50.3	52.6	287 47.5	53.7	226 35.9	07.0	163 15.6	55.9
08	78 59.5	336 49.6	52.5	302 48.4	53.2	241 38.0	07.2	178 18.2	55.9
09	94 02.0	351 49.0	. . 52.4	317 49.2	. . 52.8	256 40.2	. . 07.3	193 20.7	. . 55.9
10	109 04.5	6 48.3	52.3	332 50.1	52.3	271 42.3	07.5	208 23.2	55.9
11	124 06.9	21 47.6	52.1	347 50.9	51.9	286 44.4	07.6	223 25.8	55.9
12	139 09.4	36 46.9	N21 52.0	2 51.8	N17 51.4	301 46.5	S 6 07.8	238 28.3	S21 55.9
13	154 11.9	51 46.2	51.9	17 52.6	51.0	316 48.6	07.9	253 30.8	55.9
14	169 14.3	66 45.5	51.8	32 53.5	50.5	331 50.7	08.1	268 33.3	55.9
15	184 16.8	81 44.8	. . 51.7	47 54.3	. . 50.1	346 52.8	. . 08.2	283 35.9	. . 55.9
16	199 19.2	96 44.2	51.6	62 55.2	49.6	1 55.0	08.4	298 38.4	55.9
17	214 21.7	111 43.5	51.4	77 56.1	49.1	16 57.1	08.5	313 40.9	55.9
18	229 24.2	126 42.8	N21 51.3	92 56.9	N17 48.7	31 59.2	S 6 08.7	328 43.5	S21 55.9
19	244 26.6	141 42.1	51.2	107 57.8	48.2	47 01.3	08.8	343 46.0	55.9
20	259 29.1	156 41.4	51.1	122 58.6	47.8	62 03.4	09.0	358 48.5	55.9
21	274 31.6	171 40.7	. . 51.0	137 59.5	. . 47.3	77 05.5	. . 09.2	13 51.0	. . 55.9
22	289 34.0	186 40.0	50.8	153 00.3	46.9	92 07.6	09.3	28 53.6	56.0
23	304 36.5	201 39.3	50.7	168 01.2	46.4	107 09.7	09.5	43 56.1	56.0
Mer. Pass.	h m 2 48.8	v −0.7	d 0.1	v 0.8	d 0.5	v 2.1	d 0.2	v 2.5	d 0.0

STARS

Name	SHA	Dec
	° ′	° ′
Acamar	315 16.2	S40 13.9
Achernar	335 24.6	S57 08.7
Acrux	173 06.4	S63 11.9
Adhara	255 10.6	S28 59.8
Aldebaran	290 46.3	N16 32.5
Alioth	166 18.6	N55 52.2
Alkaid	152 56.9	N49 14.0
Al Na'ir	27 39.8	S46 52.4
Alnilam	275 43.7	S 1 11.5
Alphard	217 53.7	S 8 44.1
Alphecca	126 08.6	N26 39.7
Alpheratz	357 40.3	N29 11.2
Altair	62 05.2	N 8 55.2
Ankaa	353 12.7	S42 12.5
Antares	112 22.7	S26 28.1
Arcturus	145 53.3	N19 05.8
Atria	107 21.6	S69 03.5
Avior	234 17.5	S59 34.0
Bellatrix	278 29.2	N 6 21.8
Betelgeuse	270 58.5	N 7 24.5
Canopus	263 55.3	S52 42.2
Capella	280 30.5	N46 00.6
Deneb	49 29.1	N45 20.8
Denebola	182 31.1	N14 28.6
Diphda	348 52.9	S17 53.3
Dubhe	193 49.0	N61 39.6
Elnath	278 09.3	N28 37.1
Eltanin	90 44.5	N51 29.6
Enif	33 44.0	N 9 57.5
Fomalhaut	15 20.6	S29 31.6
Gacrux	171 58.0	S57 12.8
Gienah	175 49.6	S17 38.3
Hadar	148 43.9	S60 27.5
Hamal	327 57.5	N23 32.5
Kaus Aust.	83 39.8	S34 22.4
Kochab	137 20.3	N74 05.5
Markab	13 35.2	N15 18.0
Menkar	314 12.1	N 4 09.4
Menkent	148 04.3	S36 27.3
Miaplacidus	221 39.9	S69 47.4
Mirfak	308 36.3	N49 55.0
Nunki	75 54.5	S26 16.3
Peacock	53 14.3	S56 40.5
Pollux	243 24.7	N27 58.9
Procyon	244 57.1	N 5 10.7
Rasalhague	96 03.6	N12 33.2
Regulus	207 40.9	N11 52.9
Rigel	281 09.5	S 8 10.9
Rigil Kent.	139 47.9	S60 54.5
Sabik	102 09.1	S15 44.6
Schedar	349 36.9	N56 37.8
Shaula	96 17.8	S37 06.8
Sirius	258 31.5	S16 44.4
Spica	158 28.4	S11 15.0
Suhail	222 50.8	S43 30.2
Vega	80 36.7	N38 48.4
Zuben'ubi	137 02.3	S16 06.7

	SHA	Mer. Pass.
	° ′	h m
Venus	259 30.8	9 32
Mars	224 40.5	11 50
Jupiter	162 49.6	15 56
Saturn	99 16.5	20 09

UT d	h	SUN GHA ° ′	SUN Dec ° ′	MOON GHA ° ′	*v* ′	MOON Dec ° ′	*d* ′	HP ′
8 (TUESDAY)	00	178 34.9	N16 08.5	355 58.4	11.7	S14 47.4	6.9	55.7
	01	193 34.9	07.8	10 29.1	11.7	14 40.5	7.0	55.7
	02	208 35.0	07.0	24 59.8	11.7	14 33.5	7.1	55.7
	03	223 35.1	. . 06.3	39 30.5	11.8	14 26.4	7.2	55.7
	04	238 35.2	05.6	54 01.3	11.7	14 19.2	7.3	55.7
	05	253 35.3	04.9	68 32.0	11.8	14 11.9	7.3	55.8
	06	268 35.4	N16 04.2	83 02.8	11.8	S14 04.6	7.4	55.8
	07	283 35.4	03.5	97 33.6	11.8	13 57.2	7.5	55.8
	08	298 35.5	02.8	112 04.4	11.8	13 49.7	7.5	55.8
	09	313 35.6	. . 02.1	126 35.2	11.8	13 42.2	7.6	55.8
	10	328 35.7	01.3	141 06.0	11.8	13 34.6	7.7	55.9
	11	343 35.8	16 00.6	155 36.8	11.8	13 26.9	7.8	55.9
	12	358 35.9	N15 59.9	170 07.6	11.9	S13 19.1	7.8	55.9
	13	13 36.0	59.2	184 38.5	11.9	13 11.3	7.9	55.9
	14	28 36.0	58.5	199 09.4	11.8	13 03.4	8.0	55.9
	15	43 36.1	. . 57.8	213 40.2	11.9	12 55.4	8.0	56.0
	16	58 36.2	57.1	228 11.1	11.9	12 47.4	8.1	56.0
	17	73 36.3	56.3	242 42.0	11.9	12 39.3	8.2	56.0
	18	88 36.4	N15 55.6	257 12.9	12.0	S12 31.1	8.2	56.0
	19	103 36.5	54.9	271 43.9	11.9	12 22.9	8.3	56.0
	20	118 36.6	54.2	286 14.8	11.9	12 14.6	8.4	56.1
	21	133 36.6	. . 53.5	300 45.7	12.0	12 06.2	8.5	56.1
	22	148 36.7	52.8	315 16.7	12.0	11 57.7	8.5	56.1
	23	163 36.8	52.0	329 47.7	11.9	11 49.2	8.5	56.1
9 (WEDNESDAY)	00	178 36.9	N15 51.3	344 18.6	12.0	S11 40.7	8.7	56.1
	01	193 37.0	50.6	358 49.6	12.0	11 32.0	8.6	56.2
	02	208 37.1	49.9	13 20.6	12.0	11 23.4	8.8	56.2
	03	223 37.2	. . 49.2	27 51.6	12.0	11 14.6	8.8	56.2
	04	238 37.3	48.4	42 22.6	12.1	11 05.8	8.9	56.2
	05	253 37.4	47.7	56 53.7	12.0	10 56.9	8.9	56.2
	06	268 37.4	N15 47.0	71 24.7	12.1	S10 48.0	9.0	56.3
	07	283 37.5	46.3	85 55.8	12.0	10 39.0	9.1	56.3
	08	298 37.6	45.5	100 26.8	12.1	10 29.9	9.1	56.3
	09	313 37.7	. . 44.8	114 57.9	12.1	10 20.8	9.2	56.3
	10	328 37.8	44.1	129 29.0	12.0	10 11.6	9.2	56.3
	11	343 37.9	43.4	144 00.0	12.1	10 02.4	9.3	56.4
	12	358 38.0	N15 42.6	158 31.1	12.1	S 9 53.1	9.3	56.4
	13	13 38.1	41.9	173 02.2	12.2	9 43.8	9.4	56.4
	14	28 38.2	41.2	187 33.4	12.1	9 34.4	9.4	56.4
	15	43 38.3	. . 40.5	202 04.5	12.1	9 25.0	9.5	56.4
	16	58 38.4	39.7	216 35.6	12.1	9 15.5	9.6	56.5
	17	73 38.5	39.0	231 06.7	12.2	9 05.9	9.5	56.5
	18	88 38.5	N15 38.3	245 37.9	12.1	S 8 56.4	9.7	56.5
	19	103 38.6	37.6	260 09.0	12.2	8 46.7	9.7	56.5
	20	118 38.7	36.8	274 40.2	12.1	8 37.0	9.7	56.5
	21	133 38.8	. . 36.1	289 11.3	12.2	8 27.3	9.8	56.6
	22	148 38.9	35.4	303 42.5	12.1	8 17.5	9.9	56.6
	23	163 39.0	34.6	318 13.6	12.2	8 07.6	9.8	56.6
10 (THURSDAY)	00	178 39.1	N15 33.9	332 44.8	12.2	S 7 57.8	10.0	56.6
	01	193 39.2	33.2	347 16.0	12.2	7 47.8	10.0	56.7
	02	208 39.3	32.4	1 47.2	12.2	7 37.8	10.0	56.7
	03	223 39.4	. . 31.7	16 18.4	12.1	7 27.8	10.0	56.7
	04	238 39.5	31.0	30 49.5	12.2	7 17.8	10.1	56.7
	05	253 39.6	30.3	45 20.7	12.2	7 07.7	10.2	56.7
	06	268 39.7	N15 29.5	59 51.9	12.2	S 6 57.5	10.2	56.8
	07	283 39.8	28.8	74 23.1	12.2	6 47.3	10.2	56.8
	08	298 39.9	28.1	88 54.3	12.2	6 37.1	10.3	56.8
	09	313 40.0	. . 27.3	103 25.5	12.2	6 26.8	10.3	56.8
	10	328 40.1	26.6	117 56.7	12.2	6 16.5	10.3	56.8
	11	343 40.2	25.8	132 27.9	12.2	6 06.2	10.4	56.9
	12	358 40.3	N15 25.1	146 59.1	12.2	S 5 55.8	10.4	56.9
	13	13 40.4	24.4	161 30.3	12.2	5 45.4	10.5	56.9
	14	28 40.5	23.6	176 01.5	12.1	5 34.9	10.5	56.9
	15	43 40.6	. . 22.9	190 32.6	12.2	5 24.4	10.5	56.9
	16	58 40.7	22.2	205 03.8	12.2	5 13.9	10.6	57.0
	17	73 40.7	21.4	219 35.0	12.2	5 03.3	10.5	57.0
	18	88 40.8	N15 20.7	234 06.2	12.2	S 4 52.8	10.7	57.0
	19	103 40.9	20.0	248 37.4	12.1	4 42.1	10.6	57.0
	20	118 41.0	19.2	263 08.5	12.2	4 31.5	10.7	57.0
	21	133 41.1	. . 18.5	277 39.7	12.2	4 20.8	10.7	57.1
	22	148 41.2	17.7	292 10.9	12.1	4 10.1	10.7	57.1
	23	163 41.3	17.0	306 42.0	12.2	S 3 59.4	10.8	57.1
		SD 15.8	*d* 0.7	SD	15.2		15.4	15.5

Lat.	Twilight Naut. h m	Twilight Civil h m	Sunrise h m	Moonrise 8 h m	Moonrise 9 h m	Moonrise 10 h m	Moonrise 11 h m
N 72	////	////	01 37	21 44	21 34	21 25	21 17
N 70	////	////	02 24	21 23	21 21	21 19	21 17
68	////	00 33	02 54	21 07	21 11	21 14	21 17
66	////	01 47	03 16	20 53	21 03	21 10	21 17
64	////	02 22	03 34	20 42	20 55	21 06	21 17
62	00 30	02 46	03 48	20 33	20 49	21 03	21 17
60	01 36	03 05	04 00	20 25	20 44	21 01	21 17
N 58	02 08	03 21	04 10	20 18	20 39	20 58	21 17
56	02 30	03 34	04 19	20 11	20 35	20 56	21 17
54	02 48	03 45	04 27	20 05	20 31	20 54	21 17
52	03 03	03 55	04 35	20 00	20 27	20 52	21 17
50	03 16	04 04	04 41	19 56	20 24	20 51	21 17
45	03 41	04 22	04 55	19 45	20 17	20 47	21 17
N 40	04 00	04 36	05 06	19 37	20 11	20 44	21 17
35	04 15	04 48	05 16	19 30	20 06	20 42	21 17
30	04 28	04 58	05 24	19 23	20 02	20 39	21 17
20	04 48	05 15	05 38	19 12	19 54	20 36	21 17
N 10	05 03	05 29	05 51	19 02	19 48	20 32	21 17
0	05 16	05 41	06 02	18 53	19 41	20 29	21 17
S 10	05 26	05 52	06 13	18 44	19 35	20 26	21 17
20	05 36	06 03	06 25	18 34	19 28	20 22	21 17
30	05 46	06 14	06 39	18 23	19 20	20 18	21 17
35	05 50	06 20	06 47	18 17	19 16	20 16	21 17
40	05 55	06 27	06 56	18 09	19 11	20 13	21 17
45	06 00	06 35	07 06	18 01	19 05	20 10	21 17
S 50	06 06	06 44	07 18	17 50	18 58	20 07	21 17
52	06 08	06 48	07 24	17 45	18 54	20 05	21 18
54	06 10	06 53	07 31	17 40	18 51	20 03	21 18
56	06 13	06 57	07 38	17 34	18 47	20 01	21 18
58	06 16	07 03	07 46	17 27	18 42	19 59	21 18
S 60	06 19	07 09	07 55	17 20	18 37	19 57	21 18

Lat.	Sunset h m	Twilight Civil h m	Twilight Naut. h m	Moonset 8 h m	Moonset 9 h m	Moonset 10 h m	Moonset 11 h m
N 72	22 26	////	////	02 49	04 43	06 33	08 21
N 70	21 42	////	////	03 21	05 03	06 44	08 25
68	21 13	23 19	////	03 45	05 18	06 52	08 27
66	20 52	22 19	////	04 03	05 30	06 59	08 30
64	20 35	21 46	////	04 17	05 40	07 05	08 32
62	20 21	21 22	23 24	04 30	05 49	07 10	08 33
60	20 09	21 03	22 30	04 40	05 56	07 15	08 35
N 58	19 59	20 48	22 00	04 49	06 02	07 19	08 36
56	19 50	20 35	21 38	04 57	06 08	07 22	08 37
54	19 42	20 24	21 20	05 04	06 13	07 25	08 39
52	19 35	20 14	21 06	05 10	06 18	07 28	08 39
50	19 29	20 06	20 53	05 16	06 22	07 30	08 40
45	19 15	19 48	20 29	05 28	06 31	07 36	08 42
N 40	19 04	19 34	20 10	05 38	06 38	07 41	08 44
35	18 55	19 22	19 55	05 46	06 45	07 45	08 45
30	18 47	19 12	19 42	05 54	06 50	07 48	08 46
20	18 33	18 56	19 23	06 07	07 00	07 54	08 48
N 10	18 20	18 42	19 08	06 18	07 08	07 59	08 50
0	18 09	18 30	18 55	06 28	07 16	08 04	08 52
S 10	17 58	18 19	18 45	06 39	07 24	08 09	08 53
20	17 46	18 09	18 35	06 50	07 32	08 14	08 55
30	17 32	17 57	18 26	07 02	07 42	08 20	08 57
35	17 25	17 51	18 21	07 10	07 47	08 23	08 58
40	17 16	17 44	18 16	07 18	07 53	08 27	08 59
45	17 05	17 36	18 11	07 27	08 00	08 31	09 00
S 50	16 53	17 27	18 06	07 39	08 09	08 36	09 02
52	16 47	17 23	18 04	07 44	08 13	08 38	09 03
54	16 41	17 19	18 01	07 50	08 17	08 41	09 04
56	16 34	17 14	17 59	07 56	08 21	08 44	09 05
58	16 26	17 09	17 56	08 04	08 27	08 47	09 06
S 60	16 17	17 03	17 53	08 12	08 33	08 50	09 07

Day	SUN Eqn. of Time 00^h m s	SUN Eqn. of Time 12^h m s	SUN Mer. Pass. h m	MOON Mer. Pass. Upper h m	MOON Mer. Pass. Lower h m	MOON Age d	MOON %	Phase
8	05 41	05 37	12 06	00 17	12 41	16	99	○
9	05 33	05 28	12 05	01 05	13 29	17	97	
10	05 24	05 19	12 05	01 53	14 16	18	92	

UT d h	ARIES GHA ° ′	VENUS −4·0 GHA ° ′	VENUS Dec ° ′	MARS +1·7 GHA ° ′	MARS Dec ° ′	JUPITER −1·8 GHA ° ′	JUPITER Dec ° ′	SATURN +0·3 GHA ° ′	SATURN Dec ° ′
11 00	319 39.0	216 38.7	N21 50.6	183 02.0	N17 45.9	122 11.8	S 6 09.6	58 58.6	S21 56.0
01	334 41.4	231 38.0	50.5	198 02.9	45.5	137 14.0	09.8	74 01.1	56.0
02	349 43.9	246 37.3	50.3	213 03.7	45.0	152 16.1	09.9	89 03.7	56.0
03	4 46.4	261 36.6	. . 50.2	228 04.6	. . 44.6	167 18.2	. . 10.1	104 06.2	. . 56.0
04	19 48.8	276 35.9	50.1	243 05.5	44.1	182 20.3	10.2	119 08.7	56.0
05	34 51.3	291 35.2	49.9	258 06.3	43.7	197 22.4	10.4	134 11.2	56.0
06	49 53.7	306 34.5	N21 49.8	273 07.2	N17 43.2	212 24.5	S 6 10.5	149 13.8	S21 56.0
07	64 56.2	321 33.8	49.7	288 08.0	42.7	227 26.6	10.7	164 16.3	56.0
08	79 58.7	336 33.2	49.5	303 08.9	42.3	242 28.7	10.8	179 18.8	56.0
F 09	95 01.1	351 32.5	. . 49.4	318 09.7	. . 41.8	257 30.8	. . 11.0	194 21.3	. . 56.0
R 10	110 03.6	6 31.8	49.3	333 10.6	41.4	272 32.9	11.1	209 23.9	56.0
I 11	125 06.1	21 31.1	49.1	348 11.4	40.9	287 35.1	11.3	224 26.4	56.0
D 12	140 08.5	36 30.4	N21 49.0	3 12.3	N17 40.4	302 37.2	S 6 11.4	239 28.9	S21 56.0
A 13	155 11.0	51 29.7	48.8	18 13.2	40.0	317 39.3	11.6	254 31.4	56.0
Y 14	170 13.5	66 29.0	48.7	33 14.0	39.5	332 41.4	11.7	269 34.0	56.0
15	185 15.9	81 28.3	. . 48.6	48 14.9	. . 39.1	347 43.5	. . 11.9	284 36.5	. . 56.0
16	200 18.4	96 27.6	48.4	63 15.7	38.6	2 45.6	12.1	299 39.0	56.0
17	215 20.9	111 27.0	48.3	78 16.6	38.1	17 47.7	12.2	314 41.5	56.0
18	230 23.3	126 26.3	N21 48.1	93 17.5	N17 37.7	32 49.8	S 6 12.4	329 44.1	S21 56.0
19	245 25.8	141 25.6	48.0	108 18.3	37.2	47 51.9	12.5	344 46.6	56.0
20	260 28.2	156 24.9	47.8	123 19.2	36.7	62 54.0	12.7	359 49.1	56.0
21	275 30.7	171 24.2	. . 47.7	138 20.0	. . 36.3	77 56.1	. . 12.8	14 51.6	. . 56.0
22	290 33.2	186 23.5	47.5	153 20.9	35.8	92 58.2	13.0	29 54.2	56.0
23	305 35.6	201 22.8	47.4	168 21.7	35.4	108 00.3	13.1	44 56.7	56.0
12 00	320 38.1	216 22.1	N21 47.2	183 22.6	N17 34.9	123 02.5	S 6 13.3	59 59.2	S21 56.1
01	335 40.6	231 21.4	47.1	198 23.5	34.4	138 04.6	13.4	75 01.7	56.1
02	350 43.0	246 20.8	46.9	213 24.3	34.0	153 06.7	13.6	90 04.2	56.1
03	5 45.5	261 20.1	. . 46.8	228 25.2	. . 33.5	168 08.8	. . 13.7	105 06.8	. . 56.1
04	20 48.0	276 19.4	46.6	243 26.0	33.0	183 10.9	13.9	120 09.3	56.1
05	35 50.4	291 18.7	46.5	258 26.9	32.6	198 13.0	14.1	135 11.8	56.1
06	50 52.9	306 18.0	N21 46.3	273 27.8	N17 32.1	213 15.1	S 6 14.2	150 14.3	S21 56.1
07	65 55.3	321 17.3	46.1	288 28.6	31.7	228 17.2	14.4	165 16.9	56.1
S 08	80 57.8	336 16.6	46.0	303 29.5	31.2	243 19.3	14.5	180 19.4	56.1
A 09	96 00.3	351 15.9	. . 45.8	318 30.3	. . 30.7	258 21.4	. . 14.7	195 21.9	. . 56.1
T 10	111 02.7	6 15.2	45.7	333 31.2	30.3	273 23.5	14.8	210 24.4	56.1
U 11	126 05.2	21 14.6	45.5	348 32.1	29.8	288 25.6	15.0	225 26.9	56.1
R 12	141 07.7	36 13.9	N21 45.3	3 32.9	N17 29.3	303 27.7	S 6 15.1	240 29.5	S21 56.1
D 13	156 10.1	51 13.2	45.2	18 33.8	28.9	318 29.8	15.3	255 32.0	56.1
A 14	171 12.6	66 12.5	45.0	33 34.6	28.4	333 31.9	15.4	270 34.5	56.1
Y 15	186 15.1	81 11.8	. . 44.8	48 35.5	. . 27.9	348 34.0	. . 15.6	285 37.0	. . 56.1
16	201 17.5	96 11.1	44.7	63 36.4	27.5	3 36.1	15.8	300 39.5	56.1
17	216 20.0	111 10.4	44.5	78 37.2	27.0	18 38.2	15.9	315 42.1	56.1
18	231 22.5	126 09.7	N21 44.3	93 38.1	N17 26.5	33 40.4	S 6 16.1	330 44.6	S21 56.1
19	246 24.9	141 09.0	44.2	108 38.9	26.1	48 42.5	16.2	345 47.1	56.1
20	261 27.4	156 08.3	44.0	123 39.8	25.6	63 44.6	16.4	0 49.6	56.1
21	276 29.8	171 07.6	. . 43.8	138 40.7	. . 25.1	78 46.7	. . 16.5	15 52.1	. . 56.1
22	291 32.3	186 07.0	43.6	153 41.5	24.7	93 48.8	16.7	30 54.7	56.1
23	306 34.8	201 06.3	43.5	168 42.4	24.2	108 50.9	16.8	45 57.2	56.2
13 00	321 37.2	216 05.6	N21 43.3	183 43.3	N17 23.7	123 53.0	S 6 17.0	60 59.7	S21 56.2
01	336 39.7	231 04.9	43.1	198 44.1	23.3	138 55.1	17.1	76 02.2	56.2
02	351 42.2	246 04.2	42.9	213 45.0	22.8	153 57.2	17.3	91 04.7	56.2
03	6 44.6	261 03.5	. . 42.8	228 45.8	. . 22.3	168 59.3	. . 17.5	106 07.2	. . 56.2
04	21 47.1	276 02.8	42.6	243 46.7	21.9	184 01.4	17.6	121 09.8	56.2
05	36 49.6	291 02.1	42.4	258 47.6	21.4	199 03.5	17.8	136 12.3	56.2
06	51 52.0	306 01.4	N21 42.2	273 48.4	N17 20.9	214 05.6	S 6 17.9	151 14.8	S21 56.2
07	66 54.5	321 00.7	42.0	288 49.3	20.5	229 07.7	18.1	166 17.3	56.2
08	81 56.9	336 00.1	41.8	303 50.2	20.0	244 09.8	18.2	181 19.8	56.2
S 09	96 59.4	350 59.4	. . 41.7	318 51.0	. . 19.5	259 11.9	. . 18.4	196 22.3	. . 56.2
U 10	112 01.9	5 58.7	41.5	333 51.9	19.1	274 14.0	18.5	211 24.9	56.2
N 11	127 04.3	20 58.0	41.3	348 52.8	18.6	289 16.1	18.7	226 27.4	56.2
D 12	142 06.8	35 57.3	N21 41.1	3 53.6	N17 18.1	304 18.2	S 6 18.9	241 29.9	S21 56.2
A 13	157 09.3	50 56.6	40.9	18 54.5	17.6	319 20.3	19.0	256 32.4	56.2
Y 14	172 11.7	65 55.9	40.7	33 55.3	17.2	334 22.4	19.2	271 34.9	56.2
15	187 14.2	80 55.2	. . 40.5	48 56.2	. . 16.7	349 24.5	. . 19.3	286 37.4	. . 56.2
16	202 16.7	95 54.5	40.3	63 57.1	16.2	4 26.6	19.5	301 40.0	56.2
17	217 19.1	110 53.8	40.1	78 57.9	15.8	19 28.7	19.6	316 42.5	56.2
18	232 21.6	125 53.1	N21 39.9	93 58.8	N17 15.3	34 30.8	S 6 19.8	331 45.0	S21 56.2
19	247 24.1	140 52.5	39.7	108 59.7	14.8	49 32.9	20.0	346 47.5	56.2
20	262 26.5	155 51.8	39.5	124 00.5	14.4	64 35.0	20.1	1 50.0	56.2
21	277 29.0	170 51.1	. . 39.3	139 01.4	. . 13.9	79 37.1	. . 20.3	16 52.5	. . 56.2
22	292 31.4	185 50.4	39.1	154 02.3	13.4	94 39.2	20.4	31 55.0	56.3
23	307 33.9	200 49.7	38.9	169 03.1	12.9	109 41.3	20.6	46 57.6	56.3
Mer. Pass.	h m 2 37.0	v −0.7	d 0.2	v 0.9	d 0.5	v 2.1	d 0.2	v 2.5	d 0.0

STARS

Name	SHA ° ′	Dec ° ′
Acamar	315 16.2	S40 13.9
Achernar	335 24.5	S57 08.7
Acrux	173 06.5	S63 11.9
Adhara	255 10.6	S28 59.7
Aldebaran	290 46.3	N16 32.5
Alioth	166 18.6	N55 52.2
Alkaid	152 56.9	N49 14.0
Al Na'ir	27 39.8	S46 52.4
Alnilam	275 43.7	S 1 11.5
Alphard	217 53.7	S 8 44.1
Alphecca	126 08.6	N26 39.7
Alpheratz	357 40.3	N29 11.2
Altair	62 05.2	N 8 55.2
Ankaa	353 12.7	S42 12.5
Antares	112 22.7	S26 28.1
Arcturus	145 53.3	N19 05.8
Atria	107 21.7	S69 03.6
Avior	234 17.4	S59 33.9
Bellatrix	278 29.2	N 6 21.8
Betelgeuse	270 58.5	N 7 24.5
Canopus	263 55.3	S52 42.2
Capella	280 30.5	N46 00.6
Deneb	49 29.1	N45 20.8
Denebola	182 31.1	N14 28.6
Diphda	348 52.9	S17 53.3
Dubhe	193 49.0	N61 39.6
Elnath	278 09.3	N28 37.1
Eltanin	90 44.5	N51 29.6
Enif	33 44.0	N 9 57.5
Fomalhaut	15 20.6	S29 31.6
Gacrux	171 58.0	S57 12.8
Gienah	175 49.6	S17 38.3
Hadar	148 44.0	S60 27.5
Hamal	327 57.5	N23 32.6
Kaus Aust.	83 39.8	S34 22.4
Kochab	137 20.4	N74 05.5
Markab	13 35.2	N15 18.0
Menkar	314 12.1	N 4 09.4
Menkent	148 04.3	S36 27.3
Miaplacidus	221 39.9	S69 47.4
Mirfak	308 36.3	N49 55.0
Nunki	75 54.5	S26 16.3
Peacock	53 14.3	S56 40.6
Pollux	243 24.7	N27 58.9
Procyon	244 57.1	N 5 10.7
Rasalhague	96 03.7	N12 33.2
Regulus	207 40.9	N11 52.9
Rigel	281 09.5	S 8 10.9
Rigil Kent.	139 47.9	S60 54.5
Sabik	102 09.1	S15 44.6
Schedar	349 36.9	N56 37.8
Shaula	96 17.9	S37 06.8
Sirius	258 31.5	S16 44.4
Spica	158 28.4	S11 15.0
Suhail	222 50.8	S43 30.2
Vega	80 36.7	N38 48.4
Zuben'ubi	137 02.3	S16 06.7

	SHA ° ′	Mer. Pass. h m
Venus	255 44.0	9 35
Mars	222 44.5	11 46
Jupiter	162 24.4	15 46
Saturn	99 21.1	19 57

UT	SUN GHA	SUN Dec	MOON GHA	v	MOON Dec	d	HP
d h	° ′	° ′	° ′	′	° ′	′	′
11 00	178 41.4	N15 16.3	321 13.2	12.1	S 3 48.6	10.8	57.1
01	193 41.5	15.5	335 44.3	12.1	3 37.8	10.8	57.2
02	208 41.6	14.8	350 15.4	12.1	3 27.0	10.8	57.2
03	223 41.7	. . 14.0	4 46.5	12.2	3 16.2	10.9	57.2
04	238 41.8	13.3	19 17.7	12.1	3 05.3	10.8	57.2
05	253 41.9	12.5	33 48.8	12.1	2 54.5	11.0	57.2
06	268 42.1	N15 11.8	48 19.9	12.0	S 2 43.5	10.9	57.3
07	283 42.2	11.1	62 50.9	12.1	2 32.6	10.9	57.3
08	298 42.3	10.3	77 22.0	12.1	2 21.7	11.0	57.3
F 09	313 42.4	. . 09.6	91 53.1	12.0	2 10.7	11.0	57.3
R 10	328 42.5	08.8	106 24.1	12.0	1 59.7	11.0	57.3
I 11	343 42.6	08.1	120 55.1	12.1	1 48.7	11.0	57.4
D 12	358 42.7	N15 07.3	135 26.2	12.0	S 1 37.7	11.0	57.4
A 13	13 42.8	06.6	149 57.2	12.0	1 26.7	11.0	57.4
Y 14	28 42.9	05.8	164 28.2	11.9	1 15.7	11.1	57.4
15	43 43.0	. . 05.1	178 59.1	12.0	1 04.6	11.1	57.4
16	58 43.1	04.3	193 30.1	11.9	0 53.5	11.0	57.5
17	73 43.2	03.6	208 01.0	11.9	0 42.5	11.1	57.5
18	88 43.3	N15 02.9	222 31.9	11.9	S 0 31.4	11.1	57.5
19	103 43.4	02.1	237 02.8	11.9	0 20.3	11.1	57.5
20	118 43.5	01.4	251 33.7	11.9	S 0 09.2	11.2	57.5
21	133 43.6	15 00.6	266 04.6	11.8	N 0 02.0	11.1	57.6
22	148 43.7	14 59.9	280 35.4	11.9	0 13.1	11.1	57.6
23	163 43.8	59.1	295 06.3	11.8	0 24.2	11.1	57.6
12 00	178 43.9	N14 58.4	309 37.1	11.7	N 0 35.3	11.2	57.6
01	193 44.0	57.6	324 07.8	11.8	0 46.5	11.1	57.7
02	208 44.1	56.9	338 38.6	11.7	0 57.6	11.2	57.7
03	223 44.2	. . 56.1	353 09.3	11.7	1 08.8	11.1	57.7
04	238 44.3	55.3	7 40.0	11.7	1 19.9	11.2	57.7
05	253 44.5	54.6	22 10.7	11.7	1 31.1	11.1	57.7
06	268 44.6	N14 53.8	36 41.4	11.6	N 1 42.2	11.2	57.8
07	283 44.7	53.1	51 12.0	11.6	1 53.4	11.1	57.8
S 08	298 44.8	52.3	65 42.6	11.6	2 04.5	11.1	57.8
A 09	313 44.9	. . 51.6	80 13.2	11.5	2 15.6	11.2	57.8
T 10	328 45.0	50.8	94 43.7	11.5	2 26.8	11.1	57.8
U 11	343 45.1	50.1	109 14.2	11.5	2 37.9	11.1	57.9
R 12	358 45.2	N14 49.3	123 44.7	11.5	N 2 49.0	11.1	57.9
D 13	13 45.3	48.6	138 15.2	11.4	3 00.1	11.1	57.9
A 14	28 45.4	47.8	152 45.6	11.4	3 11.2	11.1	57.9
Y 15	43 45.5	. . 47.0	167 16.0	11.4	3 22.3	11.1	57.9
16	58 45.6	46.3	181 46.4	11.3	3 33.4	11.1	58.0
17	73 45.8	45.5	196 16.7	11.3	3 44.5	11.0	58.0
18	88 45.9	N14 44.8	210 47.0	11.3	N 3 55.5	11.1	58.0
19	103 46.0	44.0	225 17.3	11.2	4 06.6	11.0	58.0
20	118 46.1	43.3	239 47.5	11.2	4 17.6	11.0	58.0
21	133 46.2	. . 42.5	254 17.7	11.1	4 28.6	11.0	58.1
22	148 46.3	41.7	268 47.8	11.2	4 39.6	11.0	58.1
23	163 46.4	41.0	283 18.0	11.0	4 50.6	11.0	58.1
13 00	178 46.5	N14 40.2	297 48.0	11.1	N 5 01.6	10.9	58.1
01	193 46.6	39.5	312 18.1	11.0	5 12.5	10.9	58.1
02	208 46.8	38.7	326 48.1	10.9	5 23.4	10.9	58.2
03	223 46.9	. . 37.9	341 18.0	11.0	5 34.3	10.9	58.2
04	238 47.0	37.2	355 48.0	10.8	5 45.2	10.9	58.2
05	253 47.1	36.4	10 17.8	10.9	5 56.1	10.8	58.2
06	268 47.2	N14 35.6	24 47.7	10.8	N 6 06.9	10.8	58.2
07	283 47.3	34.9	39 17.5	10.7	6 17.7	10.8	58.3
08	298 47.4	34.1	53 47.2	10.7	6 28.5	10.7	58.3
S 09	313 47.5	. . 33.4	68 16.9	10.7	6 39.2	10.7	58.3
U 10	328 47.7	32.6	82 46.6	10.6	6 49.9	10.7	58.3
N 11	343 47.8	31.8	97 16.2	10.6	7 00.6	10.7	58.3
D 12	358 47.9	N14 31.1	111 45.8	10.5	N 7 11.3	10.6	58.4
A 13	13 48.0	30.3	126 15.3	10.5	7 21.9	10.6	58.4
Y 14	28 48.1	29.5	140 44.8	10.4	7 32.5	10.5	58.4
15	43 48.2	. . 28.8	155 14.2	10.4	7 43.0	10.6	58.4
16	58 48.3	28.0	169 43.6	10.3	7 53.6	10.5	58.4
17	73 48.5	27.2	184 12.9	10.3	8 04.1	10.4	58.5
18	88 48.6	N14 26.5	198 42.2	10.3	N 8 14.5	10.4	58.5
19	103 48.7	25.7	213 11.5	10.2	8 24.9	10.4	58.5
20	118 48.8	24.9	227 40.7	10.1	8 35.3	10.3	58.5
21	133 48.9	. . 24.2	242 09.8	10.1	8 45.6	10.3	58.5
22	148 49.0	23.4	256 38.9	10.0	8 55.9	10.2	58.5
23	163 49.2	22.6	271 07.9	10.0	N 9 06.1	10.2	58.6
	SD 15.8	*d* 0.8	SD	15.6	15.8		15.9

Lat.	Twilight Naut.	Twilight Civil	Sunrise	Moonrise 11	12	13	14
°	h m	h m	h m	h m	h m	h m	h m
N 72	////	////	02 03	21 17	21 09	21 00	20 50
N 70	////	////	02 41	21 17	21 15	21 13	21 12
68	////	01 18	03 07	21 17	21 20	21 23	21 29
66	////	02 05	03 27	21 17	21 24	21 32	21 43
64	////	02 35	03 43	21 17	21 27	21 39	21 55
62	01 09	02 57	03 56	21 17	21 30	21 46	22 04
60	01 52	03 14	04 07	21 17	21 33	21 51	22 13
N 58	02 19	03 29	04 17	21 17	21 36	21 56	22 20
56	02 40	03 41	04 25	21 17	21 38	22 01	22 27
54	02 56	03 51	04 33	21 17	21 40	22 05	22 33
52	03 10	04 01	04 39	21 17	21 41	22 08	22 38
50	03 22	04 09	04 45	21 17	21 43	22 11	22 43
45	03 46	04 26	04 58	21 17	21 47	22 18	22 54
N 40	04 04	04 39	05 09	21 17	21 50	22 24	23 03
35	04 18	04 51	05 18	21 17	21 52	22 30	23 10
30	04 30	05 00	05 26	21 17	21 55	22 34	23 17
20	04 49	05 16	05 39	21 17	21 59	22 42	23 29
N 10	05 03	05 29	05 51	21 17	22 02	22 49	23 39
0	05 15	05 40	06 02	21 17	22 06	22 56	23 48
S 10	05 26	05 51	06 12	21 17	22 09	23 03	23 58
20	05 35	06 01	06 24	21 17	22 13	23 10	24 09
30	05 43	06 12	06 36	21 17	22 17	23 18	24 21
35	05 48	06 17	06 44	21 17	22 19	23 23	24 28
40	05 52	06 24	06 52	21 17	22 22	23 28	24 36
45	05 56	06 31	07 02	21 17	22 25	23 35	24 45
S 50	06 01	06 39	07 13	21 17	22 29	23 42	24 56
52	06 03	06 43	07 19	21 18	22 31	23 46	25 02
54	06 05	06 47	07 25	21 18	22 33	23 50	25 07
56	06 07	06 51	07 31	21 18	22 35	23 54	25 14
58	06 10	06 56	07 39	21 18	22 38	23 59	25 21
S 60	06 12	07 02	07 47	21 18	22 41	24 05	00 05

Lat.	Sunset	Twilight Civil	Twilight Naut.	Moonset 11	12	13	14
°	h m	h m	h m	h m	h m	h m	h m
N 72	22 00	////	////	08 21	10 10	12 02	14 01
N 70	21 25	////	////	08 25	10 07	11 52	13 40
68	20 59	22 43	////	08 27	10 04	11 43	13 24
66	20 40	22 00	////	08 30	10 02	11 36	13 12
64	20 25	21 32	////	08 32	10 00	11 30	13 01
62	20 12	21 10	22 53	08 33	09 58	11 25	12 52
60	20 01	20 53	22 13	08 35	09 57	11 20	12 44
N 58	19 52	20 39	21 47	08 36	09 56	11 16	12 38
56	19 43	20 27	21 28	08 37	09 54	11 13	12 32
54	19 36	20 17	21 11	08 39	09 53	11 09	12 26
52	19 30	20 08	20 58	08 39	09 52	11 07	12 22
50	19 24	20 00	20 46	08 40	09 52	11 04	12 17
45	19 11	19 43	20 23	08 42	09 50	10 58	12 08
N 40	19 01	19 30	20 05	08 44	09 48	10 54	12 00
35	18 52	19 19	19 51	08 45	09 47	10 50	11 54
30	18 44	19 09	19 39	08 46	09 46	10 46	11 48
20	18 31	18 54	19 21	08 48	09 43	10 40	11 38
N 10	18 19	18 41	19 06	08 50	09 42	10 34	11 29
0	18 08	18 30	18 55	08 52	09 40	10 29	11 21
S 10	17 58	18 19	18 45	08 53	09 38	10 24	11 12
20	17 47	18 09	18 36	08 55	09 36	10 19	11 04
30	17 34	17 59	18 27	08 57	09 34	10 13	10 54
35	17 27	17 53	18 23	08 58	09 33	10 09	10 48
40	17 18	17 47	18 19	08 59	09 32	10 05	10 41
45	17 09	17 40	18 14	09 00	09 30	10 01	10 34
S 50	16 57	17 31	18 10	09 02	09 28	09 55	10 25
52	16 52	17 28	18 08	09 03	09 27	09 53	10 21
54	16 46	17 24	18 06	09 04	09 26	09 50	10 16
56	16 40	17 19	18 04	09 05	09 25	09 47	10 11
58	16 32	17 15	18 01	09 06	09 24	09 43	10 05
S 60	16 24	17 09	17 59	09 07	09 23	09 40	09 59

Day	SUN Eqn. of Time 00h	Eqn. of Time 12h	Mer. Pass.	MOON Mer. Pass. Upper	Lower	Age	Phase
d	m s	m s	h m	h m	h m	d %	
11	05 14	05 10	12 05	02 40	15 04	19 86	
12	05 05	04 59	12 05	03 28	15 53	20 77	
13	04 54	04 49	12 05	04 17	16 43	21 67	

UT	ARIES	VENUS −4·0		MARS +1·8		JUPITER −1·8		SATURN +0·3	
	GHA	GHA	Dec	GHA	Dec	GHA	Dec	GHA	Dec
d h	° ′	° ′	° ′	° ′	° ′	° ′	° ′	° ′	° ′
14 00	322 36.4	215 49.0	N21 38.7	184 04.0	N17 12.5	124 43.4	S 6 20.7	62 00.1	S21 56.3
01	337 38.8	230 48.3	38.5	199 04.9	12.0	139 45.5	20.9	77 02.6	56.3
02	352 41.3	245 47.6	38.3	214 05.7	11.5	154 47.6	21.0	92 05.1	56.3
03	7 43.8	260 46.9 . .	38.1	229 06.6 . .	11.0	169 49.7 . .	21.2	107 07.6 . .	56.3
04	22 46.2	275 46.2	37.9	244 07.5	10.6	184 51.8	21.4	122 10.1	56.3
05	37 48.7	290 45.5	37.7	259 08.3	10.1	199 53.9	21.5	137 12.6	56.3
06	52 51.2	305 44.8	N21 37.5	274 09.2	N17 09.6	214 56.0	S 6 21.7	152 15.2	S21 56.3
07	67 53.6	320 44.2	37.3	289 10.1	09.2	229 58.1	21.8	167 17.7	56.3
08	82 56.1	335 43.5	37.1	304 10.9	08.7	245 00.2	22.0	182 20.2	56.3
M 09	97 58.6	350 42.8 . .	36.9	319 11.8 . .	08.2	260 02.3 . .	22.1	197 22.7 . .	56.3
O 10	113 01.0	5 42.1	36.7	334 12.7	07.7	275 04.4	22.3	212 25.2	56.3
N 11	128 03.5	20 41.4	36.5	349 13.5	07.3	290 06.5	22.5	227 27.7	56.3
D 12	143 05.9	35 40.7	N21 36.2	4 14.4	N17 06.8	305 08.6	S 6 22.6	242 30.2	S21 56.3
A 13	158 08.4	50 40.0	36.0	19 15.3	06.3	320 10.7	22.8	257 32.7	56.3
Y 14	173 10.9	65 39.3	35.8	34 16.1	05.8	335 12.8	22.9	272 35.3	56.3
15	188 13.3	80 38.6 . .	35.6	49 17.0 . .	05.4	350 14.9 . .	23.1	287 37.8 . .	56.3
16	203 15.8	95 37.9	35.4	64 17.9	04.9	5 16.9	23.2	302 40.3	56.3
17	218 18.3	110 37.2	35.2	79 18.7	04.4	20 19.0	23.4	317 42.8	56.3
18	233 20.7	125 36.5	N21 34.9	94 19.6	N17 03.9	35 21.1	S 6 23.6	332 45.3	S21 56.3
19	248 23.2	140 35.9	34.7	109 20.5	03.5	50 23.2	23.7	347 47.8	56.4
20	263 25.7	155 35.2	34.5	124 21.4	03.0	65 25.3	23.9	2 50.3	56.4
21	278 28.1	170 34.5 . .	34.3	139 22.2 . .	02.5	80 27.4 . .	24.0	17 52.8 . .	56.4
22	293 30.6	185 33.8	34.1	154 23.1	02.0	95 29.5	24.2	32 55.3	56.4
23	308 33.0	200 33.1	33.8	169 24.0	01.6	110 31.6	24.4	47 57.9	56.4
15 00	323 35.5	215 32.4	N21 33.6	184 24.8	N17 01.1	125 33.7	S 6 24.5	63 00.4	S21 56.4
01	338 38.0	230 31.7	33.4	199 25.7	00.6	140 35.8	24.7	78 02.9	56.4
02	353 40.4	245 31.0	33.1	214 26.6	17 00.1	155 37.9	24.8	93 05.4	56.4
03	8 42.9	260 30.3 . .	32.9	229 27.4	16 59.6	170 40.0 . .	25.0	108 07.9 . .	56.4
04	23 45.4	275 29.6	32.7	244 28.3	59.2	185 42.1	25.1	123 10.4	56.4
05	38 47.8	290 28.9	32.5	259 29.2	58.7	200 44.2	25.3	138 12.9	56.4
06	53 50.3	305 28.2	N21 32.2	274 30.1	N16 58.2	215 46.3	S 6 25.5	153 15.4	S21 56.4
07	68 52.8	320 27.6	32.0	289 30.9	57.7	230 48.4	25.6	168 17.9	56.4
T 08	83 55.2	335 26.9	31.8	304 31.8	57.3	245 50.5	25.8	183 20.4	56.4
U 09	98 57.7	350 26.2 . .	31.5	319 32.7 . .	56.8	260 52.6 . .	25.9	198 22.9 . .	56.4
E 10	114 00.2	5 25.5	31.3	334 33.5	56.3	275 54.7	26.1	213 25.5	56.4
S 11	129 02.6	20 24.8	31.0	349 34.4	55.8	290 56.7	26.2	228 28.0	56.4
D 12	144 05.1	35 24.1	N21 30.8	4 35.3	N16 55.3	305 58.8	S 6 26.4	243 30.5	S21 56.4
13	159 07.5	50 23.4	30.6	19 36.1	54.9	321 00.9	26.6	258 33.0	56.4
A 14	174 10.0	65 22.7	30.3	34 37.0	54.4	336 03.0	26.7	273 35.5	56.4
Y 15	189 12.5	80 22.0 . .	30.1	49 37.9 . .	53.9	351 05.1 . .	26.9	288 38.0 . .	56.5
16	204 14.9	95 21.3	29.8	64 38.8	53.4	6 07.2	27.0	303 40.5	56.5
17	219 17.4	110 20.6	29.6	79 39.6	52.9	21 09.3	27.2	318 43.0	56.5
18	234 19.9	125 19.9	N21 29.4	94 40.5	N16 52.5	36 11.4	S 6 27.4	333 45.5	S21 56.5
19	249 22.3	140 19.3	29.1	109 41.4	52.0	51 13.5	27.5	348 48.0	56.5
20	264 24.8	155 18.6	28.9	124 42.3	51.5	66 15.6	27.7	3 50.5	56.5
21	279 27.3	170 17.9 . .	28.6	139 43.1 . .	51.0	81 17.7 . .	27.8	18 53.0 . .	56.5
22	294 29.7	185 17.2	28.4	154 44.0	50.5	96 19.8	28.0	33 55.5	56.5
23	309 32.2	200 16.5	28.1	169 44.9	50.1	111 21.9	28.2	48 58.0	56.5
16 00	324 34.7	215 15.8	N21 27.9	184 45.7	N16 49.6	126 23.9	S 6 28.3	64 00.6	S21 56.5
01	339 37.1	230 15.1	27.6	199 46.6	49.1	141 26.0	28.5	79 03.1	56.5
02	354 39.6	245 14.4	27.4	214 47.5	48.6	156 28.1	28.6	94 05.6	56.5
03	9 42.0	260 13.7 . .	27.1	229 48.4 . .	48.1	171 30.2 . .	28.8	109 08.1 . .	56.5
04	24 44.5	275 13.0	26.8	244 49.2	47.7	186 32.3	29.0	124 10.6	56.5
05	39 47.0	290 12.3	26.6	259 50.1	47.2	201 34.4	29.1	139 13.1	56.5
06	54 49.4	305 11.6	N21 26.3	274 51.0	N16 46.7	216 36.5	S 6 29.3	154 15.6	S21 56.5
W 07	69 51.9	320 11.0	26.1	289 51.9	46.2	231 38.6	29.4	169 18.1	56.5
E 08	84 54.4	335 10.3	25.8	304 52.7	45.7	246 40.7	29.6	184 20.6	56.5
D 09	99 56.8	350 09.6 . .	25.6	319 53.6 . .	45.2	261 42.8 . .	29.8	199 23.1 . .	56.5
N 10	114 59.3	5 08.9	25.3	334 54.5	44.8	276 44.8	29.9	214 25.6	56.5
E 11	130 01.8	20 08.2	25.0	349 55.4	44.3	291 46.9	30.1	229 28.1	56.6
S 12	145 04.2	35 07.5	N21 24.8	4 56.2	N16 43.8	306 49.0	S 6 30.2	244 30.6	S21 56.6
D 13	160 06.7	50 06.8	24.5	19 57.1	43.3	321 51.1	30.4	259 33.1	56.6
A 14	175 09.1	65 06.1	24.2	34 58.0	42.8	336 53.2	30.6	274 35.6	56.6
Y 15	190 11.6	80 05.4 . .	24.0	49 58.9 . .	42.3	351 55.3 . .	30.7	289 38.1 . .	56.6
16	205 14.1	95 04.7	23.7	64 59.7	41.9	6 57.4	30.9	304 40.6	56.6
17	220 16.5	110 04.0	23.4	80 00.6	41.4	21 59.5	31.0	319 43.1	56.6
18	235 19.0	125 03.4	N21 23.2	95 01.5	N16 40.9	37 01.6	S 6 31.2	334 45.6	S21 56.6
19	250 21.5	140 02.7	22.9	110 02.4	40.4	52 03.6	31.4	349 48.1	56.6
20	265 23.9	155 02.0	22.6	125 03.2	39.9	67 05.7	31.5	4 50.6	56.6
21	280 26.4	170 01.3 . .	22.4	140 04.1 . .	39.4	82 07.8 . .	31.7	19 53.1 . .	56.6
22	295 28.9	185 00.6	22.1	155 05.0	38.9	97 09.9	31.8	34 55.6	56.6
23	310 31.3	199 59.9	21.8	170 05.9	38.5	112 12.0	32.0	49 58.1	56.6
Mer. Pass.	h m 2 25.2	*v* −0.7	*d* 0.2	*v* 0.9	*d* 0.5	*v* 2.1	*d* 0.2	*v* 2.5	*d* 0.0

STARS

Name	SHA	Dec
	° ′	° ′
Acamar	315 16.2	S40 13.9
Achernar	335 24.5	S57 08.7
Acrux	173 06.5	S63 11.9
Adhara	255 10.6	S28 59.7
Aldebaran	290 46.2	N16 32.5
Alioth	166 18.6	N55 52.2
Alkaid	152 56.9	N49 13.9
Al Na'ir	27 39.8	S46 52.4
Alnilam	275 43.7	S 1 11.5
Alphard	217 53.6	S 8 44.1
Alphecca	126 08.6	N26 39.8
Alpheratz	357 40.3	N29 11.2
Altair	62 05.2	N 8 55.2
Ankaa	353 12.7	S42 12.5
Antares	112 22.7	S26 28.1
Arcturus	145 53.3	N19 05.8
Atria	107 21.7	S69 03.6
Avior	234 17.4	S59 33.9
Bellatrix	278 29.2	N 6 21.8
Betelgeuse	270 58.5	N 7 24.5
Canopus	263 55.3	S52 42.2
Capella	280 30.5	N46 00.6
Deneb	49 29.1	N45 20.8
Denebola	182 31.1	N14 28.6
Diphda	348 52.9	S17 53.3
Dubhe	193 49.0	N61 39.5
Elnath	278 09.2	N28 37.1
Eltanin	90 44.5	N51 29.6
Enif	33 44.0	N 9 57.5
Fomalhaut	15 20.6	S29 31.6
Gacrux	171 58.1	S57 12.8
Gienah	175 49.6	S17 38.3
Hadar	148 44.0	S60 27.5
Hamal	327 57.4	N23 32.6
Kaus Aust.	83 39.8	S34 22.4
Kochab	137 20.4	N74 05.5
Markab	13 35.2	N15 18.1
Menkar	314 12.1	N 4 09.4
Menkent	148 04.3	S36 27.3
Miaplacidus	221 39.9	S69 47.4
Mirfak	308 36.3	N49 55.0
Nunki	75 54.5	S26 16.3
Peacock	53 14.3	S56 40.6
Pollux	243 24.7	N27 58.9
Procyon	244 57.1	N 5 10.7
Rasalhague	96 03.7	N12 33.2
Regulus	207 40.9	N11 52.9
Rigel	281 09.5	S 8 10.9
Rigil Kent.	139 48.0	S60 54.5
Sabik	102 09.2	S15 44.6
Schedar	349 36.8	N56 37.8
Shaula	96 17.9	S37 06.8
Sirius	258 31.5	S16 44.4
Spica	158 28.4	S11 15.0
Suhail	222 50.8	S43 30.2
Vega	80 36.7	N38 48.4
Zuben'ubi	137 02.3	S16 06.7

	SHA	Mer. Pass.
	° ′	h m
Venus	251 56.9	9 38
Mars	220 49.3	11 42
Jupiter	161 58.2	15 36
Saturn	99 24.9	19 45

UT		SUN GHA	SUN Dec	MOON GHA	v	MOON Dec	d	HP
d	h	° ′	° ′	° ′	′	° ′	′	′
14	00	178 49.3	N14 21.8	285 36.9	9.9	N 9 16.3	10.2	58.6
	01	193 49.4	21.1	300 05.8	9.9	9 26.5	10.1	58.6
	02	208 49.5	20.3	314 34.7	9.8	9 36.6	10.0	58.6
	03	223 49.6	. . 19.5	329 03.5	9.8	9 46.6	10.0	58.6
	04	238 49.7	18.8	343 32.3	9.7	9 56.6	10.0	58.7
	05	253 49.9	18.0	358 01.0	9.6	10 06.6	9.9	58.7
	06	268 50.0	N14 17.2	12 29.6	9.6	N10 16.5	9.8	58.7
	07	283 50.1	16.4	26 58.2	9.6	10 26.3	9.8	58.7
	08	298 50.2	15.7	41 26.8	9.5	10 36.1	9.8	58.7
M	09	313 50.3	. . 14.9	55 55.3	9.4	10 45.9	9.6	58.8
O	10	328 50.5	14.1	70 23.7	9.4	10 55.5	9.7	58.8
N	11	343 50.6	13.3	84 52.1	9.3	11 05.2	9.5	58.8
D	12	358 50.7	N14 12.6	99 20.4	9.2	N11 14.7	9.6	58.8
A	13	13 50.8	11.8	113 48.6	9.2	11 24.3	9.4	58.8
Y	14	28 50.9	11.0	128 16.8	9.2	11 33.7	9.4	58.8
	15	43 51.1	. . 10.2	142 45.0	9.1	11 43.1	9.3	58.9
	16	58 51.2	09.5	157 13.1	9.0	11 52.4	9.3	58.9
	17	73 51.3	08.7	171 41.1	8.9	12 01.7	9.2	58.9
	18	88 51.4	N14 07.9	186 09.0	8.9	N12 10.9	9.1	58.9
	19	103 51.5	07.1	200 36.9	8.9	12 20.0	9.1	58.9
	20	118 51.7	06.4	215 04.8	8.8	12 29.1	9.0	59.0
	21	133 51.8	. . 05.6	229 32.6	8.7	12 38.1	8.9	59.0
	22	148 51.9	04.8	244 00.3	8.6	12 47.0	8.9	59.0
	23	163 52.0	04.0	258 27.9	8.6	12 55.9	8.7	59.0
15	00	178 52.2	N14 03.2	272 55.5	8.6	N13 04.6	8.8	59.0
	01	193 52.3	02.5	287 23.1	8.4	13 13.4	8.6	59.0
	02	208 52.4	01.7	301 50.5	8.4	13 22.0	8.6	59.1
	03	223 52.5	. . 00.9	316 17.9	8.4	13 30.6	8.4	59.1
	04	238 52.6	14 00.1	330 45.3	8.3	13 39.0	8.4	59.1
	05	253 52.8	13 59.3	345 12.6	8.2	13 47.4	8.4	59.1
	06	268 52.9	N13 58.6	359 39.8	8.2	N13 55.8	8.2	59.1
	07	283 53.0	57.8	14 07.0	8.1	14 04.0	8.2	59.1
T	08	298 53.1	57.0	28 34.1	8.0	14 12.2	8.1	59.2
U	09	313 53.3	. . 56.2	43 01.1	8.0	14 20.3	8.0	59.2
E	10	328 53.4	55.4	57 28.1	7.9	14 28.3	7.9	59.2
S	11	343 53.5	54.6	71 55.0	7.8	14 36.2	7.8	59.2
D	12	358 53.6	N13 53.9	86 21.8	7.8	N14 44.0	7.8	59.2
A	13	13 53.8	53.1	100 48.6	7.7	14 51.8	7.6	59.2
Y	14	28 53.9	52.3	115 15.3	7.7	14 59.4	7.6	59.3
	15	43 54.0	. . 51.5	129 42.0	7.6	15 07.0	7.5	59.3
	16	58 54.1	50.7	144 08.6	7.5	15 14.5	7.4	59.3
	17	73 54.3	49.9	158 35.1	7.5	15 21.9	7.3	59.3
	18	88 54.4	N13 49.1	173 01.6	7.4	N15 29.2	7.2	59.3
	19	103 54.5	48.4	187 28.0	7.4	15 36.4	7.1	59.3
	20	118 54.6	47.6	201 54.4	7.3	15 43.5	7.0	59.3
	21	133 54.8	. . 46.8	216 20.7	7.2	15 50.5	6.9	59.4
	22	148 54.9	46.0	230 46.9	7.2	15 57.4	6.8	59.4
	23	163 55.0	45.2	245 13.1	7.1	16 04.2	6.8	59.4
16	00	178 55.2	N13 44.4	259 39.2	7.1	N16 11.0	6.6	59.4
	01	193 55.3	43.6	274 05.3	7.0	16 17.6	6.5	59.4
	02	208 55.4	42.8	288 31.3	6.9	16 24.1	6.4	59.4
	03	223 55.5	. . 42.0	302 57.2	6.9	16 30.5	6.3	59.4
	04	238 55.7	41.3	317 23.1	6.8	16 36.8	6.2	59.5
	05	253 55.8	40.5	331 48.9	6.8	16 43.0	6.2	59.5
	06	268 55.9	N13 39.7	346 14.7	6.7	N16 49.2	6.0	59.5
W	07	283 56.1	38.9	0 40.4	6.6	16 55.2	5.9	59.5
E	08	298 56.2	38.1	15 06.0	6.6	17 01.1	5.7	59.5
D	09	313 56.3	. . 37.3	29 31.6	6.6	17 06.8	5.7	59.5
N	10	328 56.4	36.5	43 57.2	6.4	17 12.5	5.6	59.5
E	11	343 56.6	35.7	58 22.6	6.5	17 18.1	5.4	59.6
S	12	358 56.7	N13 34.9	72 48.1	6.3	N17 23.5	5.4	59.6
D	13	13 56.8	34.1	87 13.4	6.4	17 28.9	5.2	59.6
A	14	28 57.0	33.3	101 38.8	6.2	17 34.1	5.2	59.6
Y	15	43 57.1	. . 32.5	116 04.0	6.3	17 39.3	5.0	59.6
	16	58 57.2	31.7	130 29.3	6.1	17 44.3	4.9	59.6
	17	73 57.4	30.9	144 54.4	6.1	17 49.2	4.7	59.6
	18	88 57.5	N13 30.2	159 19.5	6.1	N17 53.9	4.7	59.6
	19	103 57.6	29.4	173 44.6	6.0	17 58.6	4.5	59.6
	20	118 57.7	28.6	188 09.6	6.0	18 03.1	4.5	59.7
	21	133 57.9	. . 27.8	202 34.6	5.9	18 07.6	4.3	59.7
	22	148 58.0	27.0	216 59.5	5.9	18 11.9	4.1	59.7
	23	163 58.1	26.2	231 24.4	5.9	N18 16.0	4.1	59.7
		SD 15.8	*d* 0.8	SD	16.0	16.1		16.2

Lat.	Twilight Naut.	Twilight Civil	Sunrise	Moonrise 14	15	16	17
°	h m	h m	h m	h m	h m	h m	h m
N 72	////	////	02 25	20 50	20 36	19 54	▭
N 70	////	////	02 57	21 12	21 13	21 18	21 39
68	////	01 45	03 20	21 29	21 39	21 57	22 33
66	////	02 22	03 38	21 43	21 59	22 25	23 07
64	////	02 47	03 52	21 55	22 15	22 46	23 31
62	01 33	03 07	04 04	22 04	22 29	23 03	23 50
60	02 07	03 23	04 14	22 13	22 40	23 17	24 06
N 58	02 30	03 36	04 23	22 20	22 50	23 29	24 19
56	02 49	03 48	04 31	22 27	22 59	23 40	24 31
54	03 04	03 57	04 38	22 33	23 07	23 49	24 41
52	03 17	04 06	04 44	22 38	23 14	23 57	24 50
50	03 28	04 14	04 50	22 43	23 20	24 05	00 05
45	03 50	04 30	05 02	22 54	23 34	24 21	00 21
N 40	04 07	04 43	05 12	23 03	23 45	24 34	00 34
35	04 21	04 53	05 20	23 10	23 55	24 45	00 45
30	04 32	05 02	05 27	23 17	24 04	00 04	00 55
20	04 50	05 17	05 40	23 29	24 18	00 18	01 12
N 10	05 04	05 29	05 51	23 39	24 31	00 31	01 27
0	05 15	05 40	06 01	23 48	24 44	00 44	01 41
S 10	05 24	05 49	06 11	23 58	24 56	00 56	01 55
20	05 33	05 59	06 22	24 09	00 09	01 09	02 10
30	05 41	06 09	06 33	24 21	00 21	01 24	02 28
35	05 44	06 14	06 40	24 28	00 28	01 33	02 38
40	05 48	06 20	06 48	24 36	00 36	01 43	02 50
45	05 52	06 27	06 57	24 45	00 45	01 55	03 03
S 50	05 56	06 34	07 08	24 56	00 56	02 10	03 20
52	05 58	06 37	07 13	25 02	01 02	02 16	03 28
54	05 59	06 41	07 18	25 07	01 07	02 24	03 37
56	06 01	06 45	07 24	25 14	01 14	02 32	03 46
58	06 03	06 49	07 31	25 21	01 21	02 42	03 58
S 60	06 05	06 54	07 39	00 05	01 30	02 53	04 11

Lat.	Sunset	Twilight Civil	Twilight Naut.	Moonset 14	15	16	17
°	h m	h m	h m	h m	h m	h m	h m
N 72	21 38	////	////	14 01	16 08	18 50	▭
N 70	21 08	23 27	////	13 40	15 32	17 26	19 09
68	20 46	22 18	////	13 24	15 07	16 48	18 15
66	20 28	21 43	////	13 12	14 48	16 21	17 42
64	20 14	21 18	23 32	13 01	14 32	16 00	17 17
62	20 03	20 59	22 30	12 52	14 19	15 43	16 58
60	19 53	20 44	21 58	12 44	14 09	15 29	16 43
N 58	19 44	20 31	21 35	12 38	13 59	15 18	16 29
56	19 36	20 20	21 17	12 32	13 51	15 07	16 18
54	19 30	20 10	21 03	12 26	13 43	14 58	16 08
52	19 24	20 01	20 50	12 22	13 37	14 50	15 59
50	19 18	19 54	20 39	12 17	13 31	14 43	15 51
45	19 06	19 38	20 17	12 08	13 18	14 28	15 34
N 40	18 57	19 25	20 01	12 00	13 08	14 15	15 20
35	18 48	19 15	19 47	11 54	12 59	14 04	15 08
30	18 41	19 06	19 36	11 48	12 51	13 55	14 57
20	18 29	18 51	19 18	11 38	12 37	13 38	14 40
N 10	18 18	18 39	19 05	11 29	12 26	13 24	14 24
0	18 08	18 29	18 54	11 21	12 14	13 11	14 10
S 10	17 58	18 19	18 44	11 12	12 03	12 58	13 55
20	17 47	18 10	18 36	11 04	11 52	12 43	13 39
30	17 36	18 00	18 29	10 54	11 38	12 27	13 22
35	17 29	17 55	18 25	10 48	11 30	12 18	13 11
40	17 21	17 49	18 21	10 41	11 22	12 07	12 59
45	17 12	17 43	18 17	10 34	11 11	11 55	12 45
S 50	17 02	17 35	18 14	10 25	10 59	11 39	12 28
52	16 57	17 32	18 12	10 21	10 53	11 32	12 20
54	16 51	17 29	18 10	10 16	10 47	11 24	12 11
56	16 45	17 25	18 09	10 11	10 40	11 16	12 01
58	16 39	17 20	18 07	10 05	10 32	11 06	11 50
S 60	16 31	17 16	18 05	09 59	10 23	10 54	11 36

Day	SUN Eqn. of Time 00^h	Eqn. of Time 12^h	Mer. Pass.	MOON Mer. Pass. Upper	Mer. Pass. Lower	Age	Phase
d	m s	m s	h m	h m	h m	d %	
14	04 43	04 37	12 05	05 08	17 34	22 56	
15	04 32	04 26	12 04	06 01	18 29	23 45	◑
16	04 20	04 13	12 04	06 57	19 26	24 34	

UT	ARIES	VENUS −3·9		MARS +1·8		JUPITER −1·8		SATURN +0·4	
d h	GHA ° ′	GHA ° ′	Dec ° ′	GHA ° ′	Dec ° ′	GHA ° ′	Dec ° ′	GHA ° ′	Dec ° ′
17 00	325 33.8	214 59.2	N21 21.5	185 06.7	N16 38.0	127 14.1	S 6 32.2	65 00.6	S21 56.6
01	340 36.3	229 58.5	21.2	200 07.6	37.5	142 16.2	32.3	80 03.1	56.6
02	355 38.7	244 57.8	21.0	215 08.5	37.0	157 18.3	32.5	95 05.6	56.6
03	10 41.2	259 57.1	. . 20.7	230 09.4	. . 36.5	172 20.3	. . 32.6	110 08.1	. . 56.6
04	25 43.6	274 56.4	20.4	245 10.3	36.0	187 22.4	32.8	125 10.6	56.6
05	40 46.1	289 55.8	20.1	260 11.1	35.5	202 24.5	33.0	140 13.1	56.7
06	55 48.6	304 55.1	N21 19.8	275 12.0	N16 35.1	217 26.6	S 6 33.1	155 15.6	S21 56.7
07	70 51.0	319 54.4	19.6	290 12.9	34.6	232 28.7	33.3	170 18.1	56.7
T 08	85 53.5	334 53.7	19.3	305 13.8	34.1	247 30.8	33.4	185 20.6	56.7
H 09	100 56.0	349 53.0	. . 19.0	320 14.6	. . 33.6	262 32.9	. . 33.6	200 23.1	. . 56.7
U 10	115 58.4	4 52.3	18.7	335 15.5	33.1	277 34.9	33.8	215 25.6	56.7
R 11	131 00.9	19 51.6	18.4	350 16.4	32.6	292 37.0	33.9	230 28.1	56.7
S 12	146 03.4	34 50.9	N21 18.1	5 17.3	N16 32.1	307 39.1	S 6 34.1	245 30.6	S21 56.7
D 13	161 05.8	49 50.2	17.8	20 18.2	31.6	322 41.2	34.2	260 33.1	56.7
A 14	176 08.3	64 49.5	17.6	35 19.0	31.2	337 43.3	34.4	275 35.6	56.7
Y 15	191 10.8	79 48.8	. . 17.3	50 19.9	. . 30.7	352 45.4	. . 34.6	290 38.1	. . 56.7
16	206 13.2	94 48.2	17.0	65 20.8	30.2	7 47.5	34.7	305 40.6	56.7
17	221 15.7	109 47.5	16.7	80 21.7	29.7	22 49.5	34.9	320 43.1	56.7
18	236 18.1	124 46.8	N21 16.4	95 22.6	N16 29.2	37 51.6	S 6 35.1	335 45.6	S21 56.7
19	251 20.6	139 46.1	16.1	110 23.4	28.7	52 53.7	35.2	350 48.1	56.7
20	266 23.1	154 45.4	15.8	125 24.3	28.2	67 55.8	35.4	5 50.6	56.7
21	281 25.5	169 44.7	. . 15.5	140 25.2	. . 27.7	82 57.9	. . 35.5	20 53.1	. . 56.7
22	296 28.0	184 44.0	15.2	155 26.1	27.2	98 00.0	35.7	35 55.6	56.7
23	311 30.5	199 43.3	14.9	170 27.0	26.8	113 02.0	35.9	50 58.1	56.8
18 00	326 32.9	214 42.6	N21 14.6	185 27.8	N16 26.3	128 04.1	S 6 36.0	66 00.6	S21 56.8
01	341 35.4	229 42.0	14.3	200 28.7	25.8	143 06.2	36.2	81 03.1	56.8
02	356 37.9	244 41.3	14.0	215 29.6	25.3	158 08.3	36.3	96 05.6	56.8
03	11 40.3	259 40.6	. . 13.7	230 30.5	. . 24.8	173 10.4	. . 36.5	111 08.1	. . 56.8
04	26 42.8	274 39.9	13.4	245 31.4	24.3	188 12.5	36.7	126 10.6	56.8
05	41 45.3	289 39.2	13.1	260 32.2	23.8	203 14.5	36.8	141 13.1	56.8
06	56 47.7	304 38.5	N21 12.8	275 33.1	N16 23.3	218 16.6	S 6 37.0	156 15.6	S21 56.8
07	71 50.2	319 37.8	12.5	290 34.0	22.8	233 18.7	37.2	171 18.1	56.8
08	86 52.6	334 37.1	12.1	305 34.9	22.3	248 20.8	37.3	186 20.6	56.8
F 09	101 55.1	349 36.4	. . 11.8	320 35.8	. . 21.8	263 22.9	. . 37.5	201 23.1	. . 56.8
R 10	116 57.6	4 35.7	11.5	335 36.6	21.3	278 24.9	37.6	216 25.6	56.8
I 11	132 00.0	19 35.1	11.2	350 37.5	20.9	293 27.0	37.8	231 28.1	56.8
D 12	147 02.5	34 34.4	N21 10.9	5 38.4	N16 20.4	308 29.1	S 6 38.0	246 30.6	S21 56.8
A 13	162 05.0	49 33.7	10.6	20 39.3	19.9	323 31.2	38.1	261 33.1	56.8
Y 14	177 07.4	64 33.0	10.3	35 40.2	19.4	338 33.3	38.3	276 35.6	56.8
15	192 09.9	79 32.3	. . 10.0	50 41.1	. . 18.9	353 35.4	. . 38.5	291 38.1	. . 56.8
16	207 12.4	94 31.6	09.6	65 41.9	18.4	8 37.4	38.6	306 40.6	56.9
17	222 14.8	109 30.9	09.3	80 42.8	17.9	23 39.5	38.8	321 43.0	56.9
18	237 17.3	124 30.2	N21 09.0	95 43.7	N16 17.4	38 41.6	S 6 38.9	336 45.5	S21 56.9
19	252 19.8	139 29.5	08.7	110 44.6	16.9	53 43.7	39.1	351 48.0	56.9
20	267 22.2	154 28.9	08.4	125 45.5	16.4	68 45.8	39.3	6 50.5	56.9
21	282 24.7	169 28.2	. . 08.0	140 46.4	. . 15.9	83 47.8	. . 39.4	21 53.0	. . 56.9
22	297 27.1	184 27.5	07.7	155 47.2	15.4	98 49.9	39.6	36 55.5	56.9
23	312 29.6	199 26.8	07.4	170 48.1	14.9	113 52.0	39.8	51 58.0	56.9
19 00	327 32.1	214 26.1	N21 07.1	185 49.0	N16 14.4	128 54.1	S 6 39.9	67 00.5	S21 56.9
01	342 34.5	229 25.4	06.7	200 49.9	13.9	143 56.2	40.1	82 03.0	56.9
02	357 37.0	244 24.7	06.4	215 50.8	13.5	158 58.2	40.3	97 05.5	56.9
03	12 39.5	259 24.0	. . 06.1	230 51.7	. . 13.0	174 00.3	. . 40.4	112 08.0	. . 56.9
04	27 41.9	274 23.4	05.8	245 52.5	12.5	189 02.4	40.6	127 10.5	56.9
05	42 44.4	289 22.7	05.4	260 53.4	12.0	204 04.5	40.7	142 13.0	56.9
06	57 46.9	304 22.0	N21 05.1	275 54.3	N16 11.5	219 06.5	S 6 40.9	157 15.5	S21 56.9
07	72 49.3	319 21.3	04.8	290 55.2	11.0	234 08.6	41.1	172 17.9	56.9
S 08	87 51.8	334 20.6	04.4	305 56.1	10.5	249 10.7	41.2	187 20.4	56.9
A 09	102 54.2	349 19.9	. . 04.1	320 57.0	. . 10.0	264 12.8	. . 41.4	202 22.9	. . 57.0
T 10	117 56.7	4 19.2	03.8	335 57.9	09.5	279 14.9	41.6	217 25.4	57.0
U 11	132 59.2	19 18.5	03.4	350 58.7	09.0	294 16.9	41.7	232 27.9	57.0
R 12	148 01.6	34 17.9	N21 03.1	5 59.6	N16 08.5	309 19.0	S 6 41.9	247 30.4	S21 57.0
D 13	163 04.1	49 17.2	02.7	21 00.5	08.0	324 21.1	42.0	262 32.9	57.0
A 14	178 06.6	64 16.5	02.4	36 01.4	07.5	339 23.2	42.2	277 35.4	57.0
Y 15	193 09.0	79 15.8	. . 02.1	51 02.3	. . 07.0	354 25.2	. . 42.4	292 37.9	. . 57.0
16	208 11.5	94 15.1	01.7	66 03.2	06.5	9 27.3	42.5	307 40.4	57.0
17	223 14.0	109 14.4	01.4	81 04.1	06.0	24 29.4	42.7	322 42.9	57.0
18	238 16.4	124 13.7	N21 01.0	96 04.9	N16 05.5	39 31.5	S 6 42.9	337 45.3	S21 57.0
19	253 18.9	139 13.0	00.7	111 05.8	05.0	54 33.6	43.0	352 47.8	57.0
20	268 21.4	154 12.4	00.3	126 06.7	04.5	69 35.6	43.2	7 50.3	57.0
21	283 23.8	169 11.7	21 00.0	141 07.6	. . 04.0	84 37.7	. . 43.4	22 52.8	. . 57.0
22	298 26.3	184 11.0	20 59.6	156 08.5	03.5	99 39.8	43.5	37 55.3	57.0
23	313 28.7	199 10.3	N20 59.3	171 09.4	03.0	114 41.9	43.7	52 57.8	57.0
Mer. Pass.	h m 2 13.4	v −0.7	d 0.3	v 0.9	d 0.5	v 2.1	d 0.2	v 2.5	d 0.0

STARS

Name	SHA ° ′	Dec ° ′
Acamar	315 16.2	S40 13.9
Achernar	335 24.5	S57 08.7
Acrux	173 06.5	S63 11.9
Adhara	255 10.6	S28 59.7
Aldebaran	290 46.2	N16 32.5
Alioth	166 18.7	N55 52.2
Alkaid	152 57.0	N49 13.9
Al Na'ir	27 39.8	S46 52.4
Alnilam	275 43.7	S 1 11.5
Alphard	217 53.6	S 8 44.1
Alphecca	126 08.6	N26 39.8
Alpheratz	357 40.2	N29 11.2
Altair	62 05.2	N 8 55.2
Ankaa	353 12.6	S42 12.5
Antares	112 22.7	S26 28.1
Arcturus	145 53.3	N19 05.8
Atria	107 21.7	S69 03.6
Avior	234 17.4	S59 33.9
Bellatrix	278 29.1	N 6 21.8
Betelgeuse	270 58.4	N 7 24.5
Canopus	263 55.2	S52 42.2
Capella	280 30.5	N46 00.6
Deneb	49 29.1	N45 20.8
Denebola	182 31.1	N14 28.6
Diphda	348 52.8	S17 53.3
Dubhe	193 49.0	N61 39.5
Elnath	278 09.2	N28 37.1
Eltanin	90 44.5	N51 29.6
Enif	33 44.0	N 9 57.5
Fomalhaut	15 20.6	S29 31.6
Gacrux	171 58.1	S57 12.8
Gienah	175 49.6	S17 38.3
Hadar	148 44.0	S60 27.5
Hamal	327 57.4	N23 32.6
Kaus Aust.	83 39.8	S34 22.4
Kochab	137 20.5	N74 05.5
Markab	13 35.2	N15 18.1
Menkar	314 12.0	N 4 09.4
Menkent	148 04.3	S36 27.3
Miaplacidus	221 39.9	S69 47.4
Mirfak	308 36.2	N49 55.0
Nunki	75 54.6	S26 16.3
Peacock	53 14.3	S56 40.6
Pollux	243 24.6	N27 58.9
Procyon	244 57.1	N 5 10.7
Rasalhague	96 03.7	N12 33.2
Regulus	207 40.9	N11 52.9
Rigel	281 09.5	S 8 10.9
Rigil Kent.	139 48.0	S60 54.5
Sabik	102 09.2	S15 44.6
Schedar	349 36.8	N56 37.8
Shaula	96 17.9	S37 06.8
Sirius	258 31.5	S16 44.4
Spica	158 28.4	S11 15.0
Suhail	222 50.8	S43 30.2
Vega	80 36.7	N38 48.4
Zuben'ubi	137 02.3	S16 06.7

	SHA ° ′	Mer. Pass. h m
Venus	248 09.7	9 42
Mars	218 54.9	11 37
Jupiter	161 31.2	15 26
Saturn	99 27.7	19 33

UT		SUN GHA	SUN Dec	MOON GHA	v	MOON Dec	d	HP
d	h	° ′	° ′	° ′	′	° ′	′	′
17 (THURSDAY)	00	178 58.3	N13 25.4	245 49.3	5.8	N18 20.1	3.9	59.7
	01	193 58.4	24.6	260 14.1	5.7	18 24.0	3.9	59.7
	02	208 58.5	23.8	274 38.8	5.7	18 27.9	3.7	59.7
	03	223 58.7	. . 23.0	289 03.5	5.7	18 31.6	3.5	59.7
	04	238 58.8	22.2	303 28.2	5.6	18 35.1	3.5	59.7
	05	253 58.9	21.4	317 52.8	5.6	18 38.6	3.3	59.7
	06	268 59.1	N13 20.6	332 17.4	5.6	N18 41.9	3.2	59.8
	07	283 59.2	19.8	346 42.0	5.5	18 45.1	3.1	59.8
	08	298 59.3	19.0	1 06.5	5.5	18 48.2	2.9	59.8
	09	313 59.5	. . 18.2	15 31.0	5.4	18 51.1	2.8	59.8
	10	328 59.6	17.4	29 55.4	5.4	18 53.9	2.7	59.8
	11	343 59.8	16.6	44 19.8	5.4	18 56.6	2.6	59.8
	12	358 59.9	N13 15.8	58 44.2	5.4	N18 59.2	2.4	59.8
	13	14 00.0	15.0	73 08.6	5.3	19 01.6	2.3	59.8
	14	29 00.2	14.2	87 32.9	5.3	19 03.9	2.2	59.8
	15	44 00.3	. . 13.4	101 57.2	5.3	19 06.1	2.0	59.8
	16	59 00.4	12.6	116 21.5	5.2	19 08.1	1.9	59.8
	17	74 00.6	11.7	130 45.7	5.2	19 10.0	1.8	59.8
	18	89 00.7	N13 10.9	145 09.9	5.2	N19 11.8	1.7	59.8
	19	104 00.8	10.1	159 34.1	5.2	19 13.5	1.5	59.8
	20	119 01.0	09.3	173 58.3	5.2	19 15.0	1.4	59.8
	21	134 01.1	. . 08.5	188 22.5	5.1	19 16.4	1.2	59.9
	22	149 01.3	07.7	202 46.6	5.1	19 17.6	1.1	59.9
	23	164 01.4	06.9	217 10.7	5.1	19 18.7	1.0	59.9
18 (FRIDAY)	00	179 01.5	N13 06.1	231 34.8	5.1	N19 19.7	0.9	59.9
	01	194 01.7	05.3	245 58.9	5.1	19 20.6	0.7	59.9
	02	209 01.8	04.5	260 23.0	5.1	19 21.3	0.6	59.9
	03	224 01.9	. . 03.7	274 47.1	5.0	19 21.9	0.4	59.9
	04	239 02.1	02.9	289 11.1	5.1	19 22.3	0.3	59.9
	05	254 02.2	02.1	303 35.2	5.0	19 22.6	0.2	59.9
	06	269 02.4	N13 01.3	317 59.2	5.0	N19 22.8	0.1	59.9
	07	284 02.5	13 00.5	332 23.2	5.0	19 22.9	0.1	59.9
	08	299 02.6	12 59.6	346 47.2	5.1	19 22.8	0.3	59.9
	09	314 02.8	. . 58.8	1 11.3	5.0	19 22.5	0.3	59.9
	10	329 02.9	58.0	15 35.3	5.0	19 22.2	0.5	59.9
	11	344 03.1	57.2	29 59.3	5.0	19 21.7	0.6	59.9
	12	359 03.2	N12 56.4	44 23.3	5.0	N19 21.1	0.8	59.9
	13	14 03.3	55.6	58 47.3	5.1	19 20.3	0.9	59.9
	14	29 03.5	54.8	73 11.4	5.0	19 19.4	1.0	59.9
	15	44 03.6	. . 54.0	87 35.4	5.0	19 18.4	1.2	59.9
	16	59 03.8	53.2	101 59.4	5.1	19 17.2	1.3	59.9
	17	74 03.9	52.3	116 23.5	5.0	19 15.9	1.4	59.9
	18	89 04.0	N12 51.5	130 47.5	5.1	N19 14.5	1.6	59.9
	19	104 04.2	50.7	145 11.6	5.1	19 12.9	1.7	59.9
	20	119 04.3	49.9	159 35.7	5.0	19 11.2	1.8	59.9
	21	134 04.5	. . 49.1	173 59.7	5.2	19 09.4	2.0	59.9
	22	149 04.6	48.3	188 23.9	5.1	19 07.4	2.1	59.9
	23	164 04.8	47.5	202 48.0	5.1	19 05.3	2.2	59.9
19 (SATURDAY)	00	179 04.9	N12 46.6	217 12.1	5.2	N19 03.1	2.4	59.9
	01	194 05.0	45.8	231 36.3	5.2	19 00.7	2.5	59.9
	02	209 05.2	45.0	246 00.5	5.2	18 58.2	2.6	59.9
	03	224 05.3	. . 44.2	260 24.7	5.2	18 55.6	2.8	59.9
	04	239 05.5	43.4	274 48.9	5.2	18 52.8	2.8	59.9
	05	254 05.6	42.6	289 13.1	5.3	18 50.0	3.1	59.9
	06	269 05.8	N12 41.7	303 37.4	5.3	N18 46.9	3.1	59.8
	07	284 05.9	40.9	318 01.7	5.3	18 43.8	3.3	59.8
	08	299 06.1	40.1	332 26.0	5.4	18 40.5	3.4	59.8
	09	314 06.2	. . 39.3	346 50.4	5.4	18 37.1	3.5	59.8
	10	329 06.3	38.5	1 14.8	5.4	18 33.6	3.7	59.8
	11	344 06.5	37.6	15 39.2	5.5	18 29.9	3.7	59.8
	12	359 06.6	N12 36.8	30 03.7	5.5	N18 26.2	3.9	59.8
	13	14 06.8	36.0	44 28.2	5.5	18 22.3	4.1	59.8
	14	29 06.9	35.2	58 52.7	5.6	18 18.2	4.1	59.8
	15	44 07.1	. . 34.4	73 17.3	5.6	18 14.1	4.3	59.8
	16	59 07.2	33.5	87 41.9	5.7	18 09.8	4.4	59.8
	17	74 07.4	32.7	102 06.6	5.6	18 05.4	4.5	59.8
	18	89 07.5	N12 31.9	116 31.2	5.8	N18 00.9	4.6	59.8
	19	104 07.7	31.1	130 56.0	5.8	17 56.3	4.8	59.7
	20	119 07.8	30.3	145 20.8	5.8	17 51.5	4.9	59.7
	21	134 07.9	. . 29.4	159 45.6	5.8	17 46.6	5.0	59.7
	22	149 08.1	28.6	174 10.4	6.0	17 41.6	5.1	59.7
	23	164 08.2	27.8	188 35.4	5.9	N17 36.5	5.2	59.7
		SD 15.8	*d* 0.8	SD 16.3		16.3		16.3

Lat.	Twilight Naut.	Twilight Civil	Sunrise	Moonrise 17	Moonrise 18	Moonrise 19	Moonrise 20
°	h m	h m	h m	h m	h m	h m	h m
N 72	////	////	02 45	▭	▭	23 27	25 57
N 70	////	01 15	03 12	21 39	22 46	24 34	00 34
68	////	02 06	03 32	22 33	23 39	25 10	01 10
66	////	02 37	03 48	23 07	24 11	00 11	01 35
64	01 06	03 00	04 01	23 31	24 35	00 35	01 55
62	01 52	03 17	04 12	23 50	24 54	00 54	02 11
60	02 20	03 32	04 22	24 06	00 06	01 09	02 25
N 58	02 41	03 44	04 30	24 19	00 19	01 22	02 36
56	02 58	03 54	04 37	24 31	00 31	01 34	02 46
54	03 12	04 03	04 43	24 41	00 41	01 44	02 55
52	03 24	04 12	04 49	24 50	00 50	01 52	03 03
50	03 34	04 19	04 54	00 05	00 58	02 00	03 10
45	03 55	04 34	05 05	00 21	01 15	02 17	03 25
N 40	04 11	04 46	05 14	00 34	01 30	02 31	03 37
35	04 24	04 56	05 22	00 45	01 42	02 43	03 48
30	04 34	05 04	05 29	00 55	01 52	02 53	03 57
20	04 51	05 18	05 41	01 12	02 10	03 11	04 13
N 10	05 04	05 29	05 51	01 27	02 26	03 26	04 27
0	05 15	05 39	06 00	01 41	02 41	03 41	04 39
S 10	05 23	05 48	06 10	01 55	02 56	03 55	04 52
20	05 31	05 57	06 19	02 10	03 11	04 10	05 06
30	05 38	06 06	06 31	02 28	03 30	04 28	05 22
35	05 41	06 11	06 37	02 38	03 40	04 38	05 31
40	05 44	06 16	06 44	02 50	03 53	04 50	05 42
45	05 48	06 22	06 52	03 03	04 07	05 04	05 54
S 50	05 51	06 29	07 02	03 20	04 25	05 21	06 08
52	05 52	06 32	07 07	03 28	04 33	05 29	06 15
54	05 54	06 35	07 12	03 37	04 42	05 38	06 23
56	05 55	06 39	07 17	03 46	04 52	05 48	06 32
58	05 56	06 42	07 24	03 58	05 04	05 59	06 41
S 60	05 58	06 47	07 31	04 11	05 18	06 12	06 52

Lat.	Sunset	Twilight Civil	Twilight Naut.	Moonset 17	Moonset 18	Moonset 19	Moonset 20
°	h m	h m	h m	h m	h m	h m	h m
N 72	21 17	////	////	▭	▭	21 31	21 01
N 70	20 52	22 42	////	19 09	20 07	20 24	20 28
68	20 32	21 56	////	18 15	19 15	19 47	20 04
66	20 17	21 27	////	17 42	18 42	19 21	19 45
64	20 04	21 05	22 52	17 17	18 18	19 01	19 29
62	19 53	20 48	22 11	16 58	17 59	18 44	19 16
60	19 44	20 34	21 44	16 43	17 43	18 30	19 05
N 58	19 36	20 22	21 24	16 29	17 30	18 18	18 56
56	19 29	20 12	21 07	16 18	17 19	18 08	18 47
54	19 23	20 03	20 54	16 08	17 08	17 59	18 40
52	19 17	19 55	20 42	15 59	16 59	17 51	18 33
50	19 12	19 48	20 32	15 51	16 51	17 43	18 27
45	19 01	19 33	20 12	15 34	16 34	17 28	18 14
N 40	18 52	19 21	19 56	15 20	16 20	17 15	18 03
35	18 45	19 11	19 43	15 08	16 08	17 04	17 54
30	18 38	19 03	19 33	14 57	15 58	16 54	17 45
20	18 26	18 49	19 16	14 40	15 40	16 37	17 31
N 10	18 16	18 38	19 03	14 24	15 24	16 23	17 19
0	18 07	18 28	18 53	14 10	15 09	16 09	17 07
S 10	17 58	18 19	18 44	13 55	14 55	15 55	16 55
20	17 48	18 11	18 37	13 39	14 39	15 40	16 42
30	17 37	18 02	18 30	13 22	14 21	15 23	16 27
35	17 31	17 57	18 27	13 11	14 10	15 13	16 19
40	17 24	17 52	18 24	12 59	13 58	15 02	16 09
45	17 16	17 46	18 21	12 45	13 43	14 48	15 58
S 50	17 06	17 40	18 17	12 28	13 26	14 32	15 44
52	17 02	17 37	18 16	12 20	13 18	14 24	15 37
54	16 57	17 33	18 15	12 11	13 08	14 16	15 30
56	16 51	17 30	18 14	12 01	12 58	14 06	15 22
58	16 45	17 26	18 12	11 50	12 46	13 55	15 13
S 60	16 38	17 22	18 11	11 36	12 32	13 42	15 02

Day	SUN Eqn. of Time 00^h	SUN Eqn. of Time 12^h	SUN Mer. Pass.	MOON Mer. Pass. Upper	MOON Mer. Pass. Lower	MOON Age	MOON Phase
d	m s	m s	h m	h m	h m	d	%
17	04 07	04 01	12 04	07 55	20 25	25	23
18	03 54	03 47	12 04	08 55	21 25	26	14
19	03 41	03 34	12 04	09 55	22 24	27	7

UT	ARIES	VENUS −3·9		MARS +1·8		JUPITER −1·8		SATURN +0·4	
	GHA	GHA	Dec	GHA	Dec	GHA	Dec	GHA	Dec
d h	° ′	° ′	° ′	° ′	° ′	° ′	° ′	° ′	° ′
20 00 (SUNDAY)	328 31.2	214 09.6	N20 58.9	186 10.3	N16 02.5	129 43.9	S 6 43.9	68 00.3	S21 57.0
01	343 33.7	229 08.9	58.6	201 11.2	02.0	144 46.0	44.0	83 02.8	57.1
02	358 36.1	244 08.2	58.2	216 12.0	01.5	159 48.1	44.2	98 05.3	57.1
03	13 38.6	259 07.6	. . 57.9	231 12.9	. . 01.0	174 50.2	. . 44.3	113 07.7	. . 57.1
04	28 41.1	274 06.9	57.5	246 13.8	00.5	189 52.2	44.5	128 10.2	57.1
05	43 43.5	289 06.2	57.2	261 14.7	16 00.0	204 54.3	44.7	143 12.7	57.1
06	58 46.0	304 05.5	N20 56.8	276 15.6	N15 59.5	219 56.4	S 6 44.8	158 15.2	S21 57.1
07	73 48.5	319 04.8	56.5	291 16.5	59.0	234 58.5	45.0	173 17.7	57.1
08	88 50.9	334 04.1	56.1	306 17.4	58.5	250 00.5	45.2	188 20.2	57.1
09	103 53.4	349 03.5	. . 55.7	321 18.3	. . 58.0	265 02.6	. . 45.3	203 22.7	. . 57.1
10	118 55.9	4 02.8	55.4	336 19.1	57.5	280 04.7	45.5	218 25.2	57.1
11	133 58.3	19 02.1	55.0	351 20.0	57.0	295 06.8	45.7	233 27.6	57.1
12	149 00.8	34 01.4	N20 54.7	6 20.9	N15 56.5	310 08.8	S 6 45.8	248 30.1	S21 57.1
13	164 03.2	49 00.7	54.3	21 21.8	56.0	325 10.9	46.0	263 32.6	57.1
14	179 05.7	64 00.0	53.9	36 22.7	55.5	340 13.0	46.2	278 35.1	57.1
15	194 08.2	78 59.3	. . 53.6	51 23.6	. . 55.0	355 15.1	. . 46.3	293 37.6	. . 57.1
16	209 10.6	93 58.7	53.2	66 24.5	54.5	10 17.1	46.5	308 40.1	57.1
17	224 13.1	108 58.0	52.8	81 25.4	54.0	25 19.2	46.7	323 42.6	57.2
18	239 15.6	123 57.3	N20 52.5	96 26.3	N15 53.5	40 21.3	S 6 46.8	338 45.0	S21 57.2
19	254 18.0	138 56.6	52.1	111 27.2	53.0	55 23.4	47.0	353 47.5	57.2
20	269 20.5	153 55.9	51.7	126 28.0	52.5	70 25.4	47.1	8 50.0	57.2
21	284 23.0	168 55.2	. . 51.4	141 28.9	. . 52.0	85 27.5	. . 47.3	23 52.5	. . 57.2
22	299 25.4	183 54.6	51.0	156 29.8	51.5	100 29.6	47.5	38 55.0	57.2
23	314 27.9	198 53.9	50.6	171 30.7	51.0	115 31.6	47.6	53 57.5	57.2
21 00 (MONDAY)	329 30.3	213 53.2	N20 50.2	186 31.6	N15 50.5	130 33.7	S 6 47.8	69 00.0	S21 57.2
01	344 32.8	228 52.5	49.9	201 32.5	50.0	145 35.8	48.0	84 02.4	57.2
02	359 35.3	243 51.8	49.5	216 33.4	49.5	160 37.9	48.1	99 04.9	57.2
03	14 37.7	258 51.1	. . 49.1	231 34.3	. . 49.0	175 39.9	. . 48.3	114 07.4	. . 57.2
04	29 40.2	273 50.5	48.7	246 35.2	48.5	190 42.0	48.5	129 09.9	57.2
05	44 42.7	288 49.8	48.3	261 36.1	48.0	205 44.1	48.6	144 12.4	57.2
06	59 45.1	303 49.1	N20 48.0	276 37.0	N15 47.5	220 46.1	S 6 48.8	159 14.9	S21 57.2
07	74 47.6	318 48.4	47.6	291 37.8	47.0	235 48.2	49.0	174 17.3	57.2
08	89 50.1	333 47.7	47.2	306 38.7	46.5	250 50.3	49.1	189 19.8	57.3
09	104 52.5	348 47.0	. . 46.8	321 39.6	. . 46.0	265 52.4	. . 49.3	204 22.3	. . 57.3
10	119 55.0	3 46.4	46.4	336 40.5	45.5	280 54.4	49.5	219 24.8	57.3
11	134 57.5	18 45.7	46.0	351 41.4	45.0	295 56.5	49.6	234 27.3	57.3
12	149 59.9	33 45.0	N20 45.7	6 42.3	N15 44.4	310 58.6	S 6 49.8	249 29.8	S21 57.3
13	165 02.4	48 44.3	45.3	21 43.2	43.9	326 00.6	50.0	264 32.2	57.3
14	180 04.8	63 43.6	44.9	36 44.1	43.4	341 02.7	50.1	279 34.7	57.3
15	195 07.3	78 43.0	. . 44.5	51 45.0	. . 42.9	356 04.8	. . 50.3	294 37.2	. . 57.3
16	210 09.8	93 42.3	44.1	66 45.9	42.4	11 06.8	50.5	309 39.7	57.3
17	225 12.2	108 41.6	43.7	81 46.8	41.9	26 08.9	50.6	324 42.2	57.3
18	240 14.7	123 40.9	N20 43.3	96 47.7	N15 41.4	41 11.0	S 6 50.8	339 44.6	S21 57.3
19	255 17.2	138 40.2	42.9	111 48.6	40.9	56 13.1	51.0	354 47.1	57.3
20	270 19.6	153 39.5	42.5	126 49.5	40.4	71 15.1	51.1	9 49.6	57.3
21	285 22.1	168 38.9	. . 42.1	141 50.4	. . 39.9	86 17.2	. . 51.3	24 52.1	. . 57.3
22	300 24.6	183 38.2	41.7	156 51.2	39.4	101 19.3	51.5	39 54.6	57.3
23	315 27.0	198 37.5	41.3	171 52.1	38.9	116 21.3	51.6	54 57.0	57.4
22 00 (TUESDAY)	330 29.5	213 36.8	N20 40.9	186 53.0	N15 38.4	131 23.4	S 6 51.8	69 59.5	S21 57.4
01	345 32.0	228 36.1	40.5	201 53.9	37.9	146 25.5	52.0	85 02.0	57.4
02	0 34.4	243 35.5	40.1	216 54.8	37.4	161 27.5	52.1	100 04.5	57.4
03	15 36.9	258 34.8	. . 39.7	231 55.7	. . 36.9	176 29.6	. . 52.3	115 07.0	. . 57.4
04	30 39.3	273 34.1	39.3	246 56.6	36.3	191 31.7	52.5	130 09.4	57.4
05	45 41.8	288 33.4	38.9	261 57.5	35.8	206 33.7	52.6	145 11.9	57.4
06	60 44.3	303 32.7	N20 38.5	276 58.4	N15 35.3	221 35.8	S 6 52.8	160 14.4	S21 57.4
07	75 46.7	318 32.1	38.1	291 59.3	34.8	236 37.9	53.0	175 16.9	57.4
08	90 49.2	333 31.4	37.7	307 00.2	34.3	251 39.9	53.1	190 19.4	57.4
09	105 51.7	348 30.7	. . 37.3	322 01.1	. . 33.8	266 42.0	. . 53.3	205 21.8	. . 57.4
10	120 54.1	3 30.0	36.9	337 02.0	33.3	281 44.1	53.5	220 24.3	57.4
11	135 56.6	18 29.4	36.5	352 02.9	32.8	296 46.1	53.6	235 26.8	57.4
12	150 59.1	33 28.7	N20 36.1	7 03.8	N15 32.3	311 48.2	S 6 53.8	250 29.3	S21 57.4
13	166 01.5	48 28.0	35.7	22 04.7	31.8	326 50.3	54.0	265 31.7	57.5
14	181 04.0	63 27.3	35.2	37 05.6	31.3	341 52.3	54.1	280 34.2	57.5
15	196 06.4	78 26.6	. . 34.8	52 06.5	. . 30.7	356 54.4	. . 54.3	295 36.7	. . 57.5
16	211 08.9	93 26.0	34.4	67 07.4	30.2	11 56.5	54.5	310 39.2	57.5
17	226 11.4	108 25.3	34.0	82 08.3	29.7	26 58.5	54.6	325 41.7	57.5
18	241 13.8	123 24.6	N20 33.6	97 09.2	N15 29.2	42 00.6	S 6 54.8	340 44.1	S21 57.5
19	256 16.3	138 23.9	33.2	112 10.1	28.7	57 02.7	55.0	355 46.6	57.5
20	271 18.8	153 23.3	32.7	127 11.0	28.2	72 04.7	55.1	10 49.1	57.5
21	286 21.2	168 22.6	. . 32.3	142 11.8	. . 27.7	87 06.8	. . 55.3	25 51.6	. . 57.5
22	301 23.7	183 21.9	31.9	157 12.7	27.2	102 08.9	55.5	40 54.0	57.5
23	316 26.2	198 21.2	31.5	172 13.6	26.7	117 10.9	55.6	55 56.5	57.5
Mer. Pass.	h m 2 01.6	*v* −0.7	*d* 0.4	*v* 0.9	*d* 0.5	*v* 2.1	*d* 0.2	*v* 2.5	*d* 0.0

STARS Name	SHA	Dec
	° ′	° ′
Acamar	315 16.1	S40 13.9
Achernar	335 24.4	S57 08.7
Acrux	173 06.5	S63 11.9
Adhara	255 10.6	S28 59.7
Aldebaran	290 46.2	N16 32.5
Alioth	166 18.7	N55 52.2
Alkaid	152 57.0	N49 13.9
Al Na'ir	27 39.8	S46 52.4
Alnilam	275 43.6	S 1 11.5
Alphard	217 53.6	S 8 44.1
Alphecca	126 08.6	N26 39.8
Alpheratz	357 40.2	N29 11.2
Altair	62 05.2	N 8 55.2
Ankaa	353 12.6	S42 12.5
Antares	112 22.7	S26 28.1
Arcturus	145 53.3	N19 05.8
Atria	107 21.7	S69 03.6
Avior	234 17.4	S59 33.9
Bellatrix	278 29.1	N 6 21.8
Betelgeuse	270 58.4	N 7 24.5
Canopus	263 55.2	S52 42.2
Capella	280 30.4	N46 00.6
Deneb	49 29.1	N45 20.8
Denebola	182 31.1	N14 28.6
Diphda	348 52.8	S17 53.3
Dubhe	193 49.0	N61 39.5
Elnath	278 09.2	N28 37.1
Eltanin	90 44.5	N51 29.6
Enif	33 44.0	N 9 57.5
Fomalhaut	15 20.5	S29 31.6
Gacrux	171 58.1	S57 12.7
Gienah	175 49.6	S17 38.3
Hadar	148 44.0	S60 27.5
Hamal	327 57.4	N23 32.6
Kaus Aust.	83 39.8	S34 22.4
Kochab	137 20.5	N74 05.5
Markab	13 35.2	N15 18.1
Menkar	314 12.0	N 4 09.4
Menkent	148 04.4	S36 27.3
Miaplacidus	221 39.9	S69 47.3
Mirfak	308 36.2	N49 55.1
Nunki	75 54.6	S26 16.3
Peacock	53 14.3	S56 40.6
Pollux	243 24.6	N27 58.9
Procyon	244 57.1	N 5 10.7
Rasalhague	96 03.7	N12 33.2
Regulus	207 40.8	N11 52.9
Rigel	281 09.5	S 8 10.9
Rigil Kent.	139 48.0	S60 54.5
Sabik	102 09.2	S15 44.6
Schedar	349 36.8	N56 37.8
Shaula	96 17.9	S37 06.9
Sirius	258 31.5	S16 44.4
Spica	158 28.4	S11 15.0
Suhail	222 50.8	S43 30.2
Vega	80 36.8	N38 48.4
Zuben'ubi	137 02.3	S16 06.7

	SHA	Mer. Pass.
	° ′	h m
Venus	244 22.8	9 45
Mars	217 01.3	11 33
Jupiter	161 03.4	15 16
Saturn	99 29.6	19 21

UT d h	SUN GHA ° ′	SUN Dec ° ′	MOON GHA ° ′	v ′	MOON Dec ° ′	d ′	HP ′
20 00	179 08.4	N12 27.0	203 00.3	6.0	N17 31.3	5.4	59.7
01	194 08.5	26.1	217 25.3	6.1	17 25.9	5.4	59.7
02	209 08.7	25.3	231 50.4	6.1	17 20.5	5.6	59.7
03	224 08.8	. . 24.5	246 15.5	6.2	17 14.9	5.7	59.7
04	239 09.0	23.7	260 40.7	6.2	17 09.2	5.8	59.6
05	254 09.1	22.8	275 05.9	6.2	17 03.4	5.9	59.6
06	269 09.3	N12 22.0	289 31.1	6.4	N16 57.5	6.0	59.6
07	284 09.4	21.2	303 56.5	6.3	16 51.5	6.2	59.6
08	299 09.6	20.4	318 21.8	6.5	16 45.3	6.2	59.6
S 09	314 09.7	. . 19.5	332 47.3	6.5	16 39.1	6.3	59.6
U 10	329 09.9	18.7	347 12.8	6.5	16 32.8	6.5	59.6
N 11	344 10.0	17.9	1 38.3	6.6	16 26.3	6.5	59.6
D 12	359 10.2	N12 17.1	16 03.9	6.7	N16 19.8	6.7	59.5
A 13	14 10.3	16.2	30 29.6	6.7	16 13.1	6.7	59.5
Y 14	29 10.5	15.4	44 55.3	6.8	16 06.4	6.9	59.5
15	44 10.6	. . 14.6	59 21.1	6.9	15 59.5	7.0	59.5
16	59 10.8	13.7	73 47.0	6.9	15 52.5	7.0	59.5
17	74 10.9	12.9	88 12.9	6.9	15 45.5	7.2	59.5
18	89 11.1	N12 12.1	102 38.8	7.1	N15 38.3	7.2	59.4
19	104 11.2	11.3	117 04.9	7.1	15 31.1	7.4	59.4
20	119 11.4	10.4	131 31.0	7.1	15 23.7	7.4	59.4
21	134 11.5	. . 09.6	145 57.1	7.2	15 16.3	7.6	59.4
22	149 11.7	08.8	160 23.3	7.3	15 08.7	7.6	59.4
23	164 11.8	07.9	174 49.6	7.4	15 01.1	7.7	59.3
21 00	179 12.0	N12 07.1	189 16.0	7.4	N14 53.4	7.8	59.3
01	194 12.2	06.3	203 42.4	7.5	14 45.6	7.9	59.3
02	209 12.3	05.4	218 08.9	7.5	14 37.7	8.0	59.3
03	224 12.5	. . 04.6	232 35.4	7.7	14 29.7	8.0	59.3
04	239 12.6	03.8	247 02.1	7.7	14 21.7	8.2	59.3
05	254 12.8	02.9	261 28.8	7.7	14 13.5	8.2	59.2
06	269 12.9	N12 02.1	275 55.5	7.8	N14 05.3	8.3	59.2
07	284 13.1	01.3	290 22.3	7.9	13 57.0	8.4	59.2
08	299 13.2	12 00.4	304 49.2	8.0	13 48.6	8.5	59.2
M 09	314 13.4	11 59.6	319 16.2	8.0	13 40.1	8.6	59.1
O 10	329 13.5	58.8	333 43.2	8.1	13 31.5	8.6	59.1
N 11	344 13.7	57.9	348 10.3	8.2	13 22.9	8.7	59.1
D 12	359 13.8	N11 57.1	2 37.5	8.2	N13 14.2	8.8	59.1
A 13	14 14.0	56.3	17 04.7	8.3	13 05.4	8.8	59.1
Y 14	29 14.2	55.4	31 32.0	8.4	12 56.6	9.0	59.0
15	44 14.3	. . 54.6	45 59.4	8.4	12 47.6	9.0	59.0
16	59 14.5	53.7	60 26.8	8.5	12 38.6	9.0	59.0
17	74 14.6	52.9	74 54.3	8.6	N12 29.6	9.1	59.0
18	89 14.8	N11 52.1					
19	104 14.9	51.2					
20	119 15.1	50.4					
21	134 15.2	. . 49.6					
22	149 15.4	48.7					
23	164 15.6	47.9					
22 00	179 15.7	N11 47.0	176 08.8	9.1	N11 24.3	9.5	58.8
01	194 15.9	46.2	190 36.9	9.1	11 14.8	9.7	58.8
02	209 16.0	45.4	205 05.0	9.2	11 05.1	9.6	58.7
03	224 16.2	. . 44.5	219 33.2	9.3	10 55.5	9.8	58.7
04	239 16.4	43.7	234 01.5	9.3	10 45.7	9.8	58.7
05	254 16.5	42.8	248 29.8	9.4	10 35.9	9.8	58.7
06	269 16.7	N11 42.0	262 58.2	9.5	N10 26.1	9.9	58.6
07	284 16.8	41.2	277 26.7	9.5	10 16.2	9.9	58.6
T 08	299 17.0	40.3	291 55.2	9.6	10 06.3	10.0	58.6
U 09	314 17.1	. . 39.5	306 23.8	9.7	9 56.3	10.1	58.6
E 10	329 17.3	38.6	320 52.5	9.7	9 46.2	10.0	58.5
S 11	344 17.5	37.8	335 21.2	9.8	9 36.2	10.2	58.5
D 12	359 17.6	N11 36.9	349 50.0	9.9	N 9 26.0	10.1	58.5
A 13	14 17.8	36.1	4 18.9	9.9	9 15.9	10.3	58.4
Y 14	29 17.9	35.3	18 47.8	10.0	9 05.6	10.2	58.4
15	44 18.1	. . 34.4	33 16.8	10.1	8 55.4	10.3	58.4
16	59 18.3	33.6	47 45.9	10.1	8 45.1	10.3	58.4
17	74 18.4	32.7	62 15.0	10.2	8 34.8	10.4	58.3
18	89 18.6	N11 31.9	76 44.2	10.3	N 8 24.4	10.4	58.3
19	104 18.7	31.0	91 13.5	10.3	8 14.0	10.4	58.3
20	119 18.9	30.2	105 42.8	10.4	8 03.6	10.5	58.2
21	134 19.1	. . 29.3	120 12.2	10.5	7 53.1	10.5	58.2
22	149 19.2	28.5	134 41.7	10.5	7 42.6	10.5	58.2
23	164 19.4	27.6	149 11.2	10.6	N 7 32.1	10.6	58.1
	SD 15.8	*d* 0.8	SD	16.2	16.1		15.9

A total eclipse of the Sun occurs on this date. See page 5.

Lat.	Twilight Naut.	Twilight Civil	Sunrise	Moonrise 20	Moonrise 21	Moonrise 22	Moonrise 23
°	h m	h m	h m	h m	h m	h m	h m
N 72	////	////	03 03	25 57	01 57	04 03	06 00
N 70	////	01 46	03 27	00 34	02 29	04 22	06 09
68	////	02 25	03 45	01 10	02 52	04 36	06 17
66	////	02 51	03 59	01 35	03 10	04 47	06 23
64	01 33	03 11	04 11	01 55	03 25	04 57	06 28
62	02 08	03 27	04 20	02 11	03 37	05 05	06 33
60	02 32	03 40	04 29	02 25	03 47	05 12	06 36
N 58	02 51	03 51	04 36	02 36	03 56	05 18	06 40
56	03 06	04 01	04 43	02 46	04 04	05 24	06 43
54	03 19	04 09	04 49	02 55	04 11	05 29	06 46
52	03 30	04 17	04 54	03 03	04 17	05 33	06 48
50	03 40	04 24	04 59	03 10	04 23	05 37	06 50
45	03 59	04 38	05 09	03 25	04 35	05 46	06 55
N 40	04 14	04 49	05 17	03 37	04 45	05 53	06 59
35	04 27	04 58	05 25	03 48	04 54	05 59	07 03
30	04 37	05 06	05 31	03 57	05 01	06 05	07 06
20	04 52	05 19	05 42	04 13	05 14	06 14	07 11
N 10	05 04	05 30	05 51	04 27	05 25	06 22	07 16
0	05 14	05 39	06 00	04 39	05 36	06 30	07 21
S 10	05 22	05 47	06 08	04 52	05 47	06 37	07 25
20	05 29	05 55	06 17	05 06	05 58	06 46	07 30
30	05 35	06 03	06 27	05 22	06 11	06 55	07 35
35	05 38	06 07	06 33	05 31	06 18	07 00	07 38
40	05 41	06 12	06 40	05 42	06 27	07 06	07 42
45	05 43	06 17	06 47	05 54	06 36	07 13	07 46
S 50	05 46	06 23	06 56	06 08	06 48	07 21	07 50
52	05 47	06 26	07 01	06 15	06 54	07 25	07 53
54	05 48	06 29	07 05	06 23	07 00	07 30	07 55
56	05 48	06 32	07 10	06 32	07 06	07 34	07 58
58	05 49	06 35	07 16	06 41	07 14	07 39	08 01
S 60	05 50	06 39	07 22	06 52	07 22	07 45	08 04

Lat.	Sunset	Twilight Civil	Twilight Naut.	Moonset 20	Moonset 21	Moonset 22	Moonset 23
°	h m	h m	h m	h m	h m	h m	h m
N 72	20 58	23 27	////	21 01	20 48	20 38	20 30
N 70	20 36	22 13	////	20 28	20 28	20 27	20 25
68	20 19	21 37	////	20 04	20 12	20 18	20 21
66	20 05	21 11	23 32	19 45	20 00	20 10	20 18
64	19 54	20 52	22 27	19 29	19 49	20 03	20 15
62	19 44	20 37	21 54	19 16	19 40	19 58	20 12
60	19 36	20 24	21 31	19 05	19 32	19 53	20 10
N 58	19 28	20 13	21 13	18 56	19 25	19 48	20 08
56	19 22	20 03	20 58	18 47	19 19	19 44	20 07
54	19 16	19 55	20 45	18 40	19 13	19 41	20 05
52	19 11	19 48	20 34	18 33	19 08	19 38	20 04
50	19 06	19 41	20 25	18 27	19 03	19 35	20 02
45	18 56	19 28	20 06	18 14	18 54	19 28	19 59
N 40	18 48	19 17	19 51	18 03	18 45	19 23	19 57
35	18 41	19 07	19 39	17 54	18 38	19 18	19 55
30	18 35	19 00	19 29	17 45	18 32	19 14	19 53
20	18 24	18 47	19 13	17 31	18 21	19 07	19 50
N 10	18 15	18 36	19 02	17 19	18 11	19 00	19 47
0	18 06	18 28	18 52	17 07	18 02	18 54	19 44
S 10	17 58	18 19	18 44	16 55	17 53	18 48	19 41
20	17 49	18 12	18 37	16 42	17 43	18 42	19 38
30	17 39	18 03	18 32	16 27	17 32	18 34	19 35
35	17 33	17 59	18 29	16 19	17 25	18 30	19 33
40	17 27	17 55	18 26	16 09	17 17	18 25	19 30
45	17 19	17 49	18 24	15 58	17 09	18 19	19 28
S 50	17 10	17 44	18 21	15 44	16 58	18 12	19 25
52	17 06	17 41	18 20	15 37	16 53	18 09	19 23
54	17 02	17 38	18 20	15 30	16 48	18 05	19 21
56	16 57	17 35	18 19	15 22	16 42	18 01	19 20
58	16 51	17 32	18 18	15 13	16 35	17 57	19 18
S 60	16 45	17 28	18 17	15 02	16 27	17 52	19 15

Day	SUN Eqn. of Time 00^h	SUN Eqn. of Time 12^h	SUN Mer. Pass.	MOON Mer. Pass. Upper	MOON Mer. Pass. Lower	Age	Phase
d	m s	m s	h m	h m	h m	d %	
20	03 27	03 20	12 03	10 53	23 21	28 2	
21	03 12	03 05	12 03	11 49	24 16	29 0	●
22	02 57	02 50	12 03	12 42	00 16	01 1	

UT d	UT h	ARIES GHA	VENUS −3·9 GHA	VENUS Dec	MARS +1·8 GHA	MARS Dec	JUPITER −1·8 GHA	JUPITER Dec	SATURN +0·4 GHA	SATURN Dec	STARS Name	SHA	Dec
		° ′	° ′	° ′	° ′	° ′	° ′	° ′	° ′	° ′		° ′	° ′
23	00	331 28.6	213 20.5	N20 31.1	187 14.5	N15 26.2	132 13.0	S 6 55.8	70 59.0	S21 57.5	Acamar	315 16.1	S40 13.9
	01	346 31.1	228 19.9	30.6	202 15.4	25.6	147 15.1	56.0	86 01.5	57.5	Achernar	335 24.4	S57 08.7
	02	1 33.6	243 19.2	30.2	217 16.3	25.1	162 17.1	56.1	101 03.9	57.5	Acrux	173 06.6	S63 11.9
	03	16 36.0	258 18.5	29.8	232 17.2	24.6	177 19.2	56.3	116 06.4	57.6	Adhara	255 10.6	S28 59.7
	04	31 38.5	273 17.8	29.3	247 18.1	24.1	192 21.3	56.5	131 08.9	57.6	Aldebaran	290 46.2	N16 32.5
	05	46 40.9	288 17.2	28.9	262 19.0	23.6	207 23.3	56.6	146 11.4	57.6			
	06	61 43.4	303 16.5	N20 28.5	277 19.9	N15 23.1	222 25.4	S 6 56.8	161 13.8	S21 57.6	Alioth	166 18.7	N55 52.2
W	07	76 45.9	318 15.8	28.1	292 20.8	22.6	237 27.5	57.0	176 16.3	57.6	Alkaid	152 57.0	N49 13.9
E	08	91 48.3	333 15.1	27.6	307 21.7	22.1	252 29.5	57.2	191 18.8	57.6	Al Na'ir	27 39.8	S46 52.4
D	09	106 50.8	348 14.5	27.2	322 22.6	21.5	267 31.6	57.3	206 21.3	57.6	Alnilam	275 43.6	S 1 11.5
N	10	121 53.3	3 13.8	26.8	337 23.5	21.0	282 33.6	57.5	221 23.7	57.6	Alphard	217 53.6	S 8 44.1
E	11	136 55.7	18 13.1	26.3	352 24.4	20.5	297 35.7	57.7	236 26.2	57.6			
S	12	151 58.2	33 12.4	N20 25.9	7 25.3	N15 20.0	312 37.8	S 6 57.8	251 28.7	S21 57.6	Alphecca	126 08.7	N26 39.8
D	13	167 00.7	48 11.8	25.5	22 26.2	19.5	327 39.8	58.0	266 31.2	57.6	Alpheratz	357 40.2	N29 11.2
A	14	182 03.1	63 11.1	25.0	37 27.1	19.0	342 41.9	58.2	281 33.6	57.6	Altair	62 05.2	N 8 55.2
Y	15	197 05.6	78 10.4	24.6	52 28.0	18.5	357 44.0	58.3	296 36.1	57.6	Ankaa	353 12.6	S42 12.5
	16	212 08.1	93 09.7	24.1	67 28.9	18.0	12 46.0	58.5	311 38.6	57.6	Antares	112 22.7	S26 28.1
	17	227 10.5	108 09.1	23.7	82 29.8	17.4	27 48.1	58.7	326 41.0	57.7			
	18	242 13.0	123 08.4	N20 23.3	97 30.7	N15 16.9	42 50.2	S 6 58.8	341 43.5	S21 57.7	Arcturus	145 53.3	N19 05.8
	19	257 15.4	138 07.7	22.8	112 31.6	16.4	57 52.2	59.0	356 46.0	57.7	Atria	107 21.8	S69 03.6
	20	272 17.9	153 07.0	22.4	127 32.5	15.9	72 54.3	59.2	11 48.5	57.7	Avior	234 17.4	S59 33.9
	21	287 20.4	168 06.4	21.9	142 33.4	15.4	87 56.3	59.3	26 50.9	57.7	Bellatrix	278 29.1	N 6 21.8
	22	302 22.8	183 05.7	21.5	157 34.3	14.9	102 58.4	59.5	41 53.4	57.7	Betelgeuse	270 58.4	N 7 24.5
	23	317 25.3	198 05.0	21.0	172 35.2	14.4	118 00.5	59.7	56 55.9	57.7			
24	00	332 27.8	213 04.4	N20 20.6	187 36.1	N15 13.8	133 02.5	S 6 59.8	71 58.3	S21 57.7	Canopus	263 55.2	S52 42.2
	01	347 30.2	228 03.7	20.1	202 37.0	13.3	148 04.6	7 00.0	87 00.8	57.7	Capella	280 30.4	N46 00.6
	02	2 32.7	243 03.0	19.7	217 37.9	12.8	163 06.6	00.2	102 03.3	57.7	Deneb	49 29.1	N45 20.9
	03	17 35.2	258 02.3	19.2	232 38.8	12.3	178 08.7	00.4	117 05.8	57.7	Denebola	182 31.1	N14 28.6
	04	32 37.6	273 01.7	18.8	247 39.7	11.8	193 10.8	00.5	132 08.2	57.7	Diphda	348 52.8	S17 53.3
	05	47 40.1	288 01.0	18.3	262 40.6	11.3	208 12.8	00.7	147 10.7	57.7			
	06	62 42.5	303 00.3	N20 17.9	277 41.5	N15 10.7	223 14.9	S 7 00.9	162 13.2	S21 57.7	Dubhe	193 49.0	N61 39.5
	07	77 45.0	317 59.6	17.4	292 42.4	10.2	238 17.0	01.0	177 15.6	57.8	Elnath	278 09.2	N28 37.1
T	08	92 47.5	332 59.0	17.0	307 43.4	09.7	253 19.0	01.2	192 18.1	57.8	Eltanin	90 44.6	N51 29.7
H	09	107 49.9	347 58.3	16.5	322 44.3	09.2	268 21.1	01.4	207 20.6	57.8	Enif	33 44.0	N 9 57.5
U	10	122 52.4	2 57.6	16.1	337 45.2	08.7	283 23.1	01.5	222 23.1	57.8	Fomalhaut	15 20.5	S29 31.6
R	11	137 54.9	17 57.0	15.6	352 46.1	08.2	298 25.2	01.7	237 25.5	57.8			
S	12	152 57.3	32 56.3	N20 15.1	7 47.0	N15 07.6	313 27.3	S 7 01.9	252 28.0	S21 57.8	Gacrux	171 58.1	S57 12.7
D	13	167 59.8	47 55.6	14.7	22 47.9	07.1	328 29.3	02.0	267 30.5	57.8	Gienah	175 49.6	S17 38.3
A	14	183 02.3	62 55.0	14.2	37 48.8	06.6	343 31.4	02.2	282 32.9	57.8	Hadar	148 44.1	S60 27.5
Y	15	198 04.7	77 54.3	13.8	52 49.7	06.1	358 33.4	02.4	297 35.4	57.8	Hamal	327 57.4	N23 32.6
	16	213 07.2	92 53.6	13.3	67 50.6	05.6	13 35.5	02.6	312 37.9	57.8	Kaus Aust.	83 39.8	S34 22.4
	17	228 09.7	107 52.9	12.8	82 51.5	05.1	28 37.6	02.7	327 40.3	57.8			
	18	243 12.1	122 52.3	N20 12.4	97 52.4	N15 04.5	43 39.6	S 7 02.9	342 42.8	S21 57.8	Kochab	137 20.6	N74 05.4
	19	258 14.6	137 51.6	11.9	112 53.3	04.0	58 41.7	03.1	357 45.3	57.8	Markab	13 35.2	N15 18.1
	20	273 17.0	152 50.9	11.4	127 54.2	03.5	73 43.7	03.2	12 47.7	57.9	Menkar	314 12.0	N 4 09.4
	21	288 19.5	167 50.3	11.0	142 55.1	03.0	88 45.8	03.4	27 50.2	57.9	Menkent	148 04.4	S36 27.3
	22	303 22.0	182 49.6	10.5	157 56.0	02.5	103 47.8	03.6	42 52.7	57.9	Miaplacidus	221 39.9	S69 47.3
	23	318 24.4	197 48.9	10.0	172 56.9	01.9	118 49.9	03.7	57 55.1	57.9			
25	00	333 26.9	212 48.3	N20 09.6	187 57.8	N15 01.4	133 52.0	S 7 03.9	72 57.6	S21 57.9	Mirfak	308 36.2	N49 55.1
	01	348 29.4	227 47.6	09.1	202 58.7	00.9	148 54.0	04.1	88 00.1	57.9	Nunki	75 54.6	S26 16.3
	02	3 31.8	242 46.9	08.6	217 59.6	15 00.4	163 56.1	04.3	103 02.5	57.9	Peacock	53 14.3	S56 40.6
	03	18 34.3	257 46.3	08.1	233 00.5	14 59.9	178 58.1	04.4	118 05.0	57.9	Pollux	243 24.6	N27 58.9
	04	33 36.8	272 45.6	07.7	248 01.4	59.3	194 00.2	04.6	133 07.5	57.9	Procyon	244 57.0	N 5 10.7
	05	48 39.2	287 44.9	07.2	263 02.3	58.8	209 02.2	04.8	148 09.9	57.9			
	06	63 41.7	302 44.2	N20 06.7	278 03.2	N14 58.3	224 04.3	S 7 04.9	163 12.4	S21 57.9	Rasalhague	96 03.7	N12 33.2
	07	78 44.1	317 43.6	06.2	293 04.1	57.8	239 06.4	05.1	178 14.9	57.9	Regulus	207 40.9	N11 52.9
	08	93 46.6	332 42.9	05.7	308 05.1	57.3	254 08.4	05.3	193 17.3	57.9	Rigel	281 09.4	S 8 10.9
F	09	108 49.1	347 42.2	05.3	323 06.0	56.7	269 10.5	05.4	208 19.8	58.0	Rigil Kent.	139 48.0	S60 54.5
R	10	123 51.5	2 41.6	04.8	338 06.9	56.2	284 12.5	05.6	223 22.3	58.0	Sabik	102 09.2	S15 44.6
I	11	138 54.0	17 40.9	04.3	353 07.8	55.7	299 14.6	05.8	238 24.7	58.0			
D	12	153 56.5	32 40.2	N20 03.8	8 08.7	N14 55.2	314 16.6	S 7 06.0	253 27.2	S21 58.0	Schedar	349 36.8	N56 37.8
A	13	168 58.9	47 39.6	03.3	23 09.6	54.7	329 18.7	06.1	268 29.7	58.0	Shaula	96 17.9	S37 06.9
Y	14	184 01.4	62 38.9	02.9	38 10.5	54.1	344 20.8	06.3	283 32.1	58.0	Sirius	258 31.4	S16 44.4
	15	199 03.9	77 38.3	02.4	53 11.4	53.6	359 22.8	06.5	298 34.6	58.0	Spica	158 28.5	S11 15.0
	16	214 06.3	92 37.6	01.9	68 12.3	53.1	14 24.9	06.6	313 37.1	58.0	Suhail	222 50.8	S43 30.2
	17	229 08.8	107 36.9	01.4	83 13.2	52.6	29 26.9	06.8	328 39.5	58.0			
	18	244 11.3	122 36.3	N20 00.9	98 14.1	N14 52.1	44 29.0	S 7 07.0	343 42.0	S21 58.0	Vega	80 36.8	N38 48.4
	19	259 13.7	137 35.6	20 00.4	113 15.0	51.5	59 31.0	07.1	358 44.4	58.0	Zuben'ubi	137 02.4	S16 06.7
	20	274 16.2	152 34.9	19 59.9	128 15.9	51.0	74 33.1	07.3	13 46.9	58.0		SHA	Mer. Pass.
	21	289 18.6	167 34.3	59.4	143 16.8	50.5	89 35.2	07.5	28 49.4	58.0		° ′	h m
	22	304 21.1	182 33.6	58.9	158 17.8	50.0	104 37.2	07.7	43 51.8	58.1	Venus	240 36.6	9 48
	23	319 23.6	197 32.9	58.4	173 18.7	49.4	119 39.3	07.8	58 54.3	58.1	Mars	215 08.4	11 29
Mer. Pass.	h m	1 49.8	*v* −0.7	*d* 0.5	*v* 0.9	*d* 0.5	*v* 2.1	*d* 0.2	*v* 2.5	*d* 0.0	Jupiter	160 34.8	15 06
											Saturn	99 30.6	19 09

UT d h	SUN GHA ° ′	SUN Dec ° ′	MOON GHA ° ′	v ′	MOON Dec ° ′	d ′	HP ′
23 00 (Wednesday)	179 19.6	N11 26.8	163 40.8	10.6	N 7 21.5	10.6	58.1
01	194 19.7	25.9	178 10.4	10.7	7 10.9	10.6	58.1
02	209 19.9	25.1	192 40.1	10.7	7 00.3	10.7	58.1
03	224 20.0	. . 24.2	207 09.8	10.9	6 49.6	10.6	58.0
04	239 20.2	23.4	221 39.7	10.8	6 39.0	10.7	58.0
05	254 20.4	22.6	236 09.5	11.0	6 28.3	10.7	58.0
06	269 20.5	N11 21.7	250 39.5	11.0	N 6 17.6	10.8	57.9
07	284 20.7	20.9	265 09.5	11.0	6 06.8	10.7	57.9
08	299 20.9	20.0	279 39.5	11.1	5 56.1	10.8	57.9
09	314 21.0	. . 19.2	294 09.6	11.2	5 45.3	10.8	57.8
10	329 21.2	18.3	308 39.8	11.2	5 34.5	10.8	57.8
11	344 21.4	17.5	323 10.0	11.3	5 23.7	10.9	57.8
12	359 21.5	N11 16.6	337 40.3	11.3	N 5 12.8	10.8	57.7
13	14 21.7	15.8	352 10.6	11.4	5 02.0	10.9	57.7
14	29 21.8	14.9	6 41.0	11.5	4 51.1	10.8	57.7
15	44 22.0	. . 14.0	21 11.5	11.5	4 40.3	10.9	57.7
16	59 22.2	13.2	35 42.0	11.5	4 29.4	10.9	57.6
17	74 22.3	12.3	50 12.5	11.6	4 18.5	10.9	57.6
18	89 22.5	N11 11.5	64 43.1	11.7	N 4 07.6	10.9	57.6
19	104 22.7	10.6	79 13.8	11.7	3 56.7	10.9	57.5
20	119 22.8	09.8	93 44.5	11.7	3 45.8	11.0	57.5
21	134 23.0	. . 08.9	108 15.2	11.8	3 34.8	10.9	57.5
22	149 23.2	08.1	122 46.0	11.9	3 23.9	10.9	57.4
23	164 23.3	07.2	137 16.9	11.9	3 13.0	11.0	57.4
24 00 (Thursday)	179 23.5	N11 06.4	151 47.8	11.9	N 3 02.0	10.9	57.4
01	194 23.7	05.5	166 18.7	12.0	2 51.1	11.0	57.3
02	209 23.8	04.7	180 49.7	12.1	2 40.1	10.9	57.3
03	224 24.0	. . 03.8	195 20.8	12.1	2 29.2	11.0	57.3
04	239 24.2	02.9	209 51.9	12.1	2 18.2	10.9	57.2
05	254 24.3	02.1	224 23.0	12.2	2 07.3	10.9	57.2
06	269 24.5	N11 01.2	238 54.2	12.2	N 1 56.4	11.0	57.2
07	284 24.7	11 00.4	253 25.4	12.3	1 45.4	10.9	57.1
08	299 24.8	10 59.5	267 56.7	12.3	1 34.5	10.9	57.1
09	314 25.0	. . 58.7	282 28.0	12.3	1 23.6	10.9	57.1
10	329 25.2	57.8	296 59.3	12.4	1 12.7	11.0	57.0
11	344 25.3	56.9	311 30.7	12.4	1 01.7	10.9	57.0
12	359 25.5	N10 56.1	326 02.1	12.5	N 0 50.8	10.9	57.0
13	14 25.7	55.2	340 33.6	12.5	0 39.9	10.8	57.0
14	29 25.9	54.4	355 05.1	12.6	0 29.1	10.9	56.9
15	44 26.0	. . 53.5	9 36.7	12.6	0 18.2	10.9	56.9
16	59 26.2	52.6	24 08.3	12.6	N 0 07.3	10.8	56.9
17	74 26.4	51.8	38 39.9	12.7	S 0 03.5	10.9	56.8
18	89 26.5	N10 50.9	53 11.6	12.7	S 0 14.4	10.8	56.8
19	104 26.7	50.1	67 43.3	12.7	0 25.2	10.8	56.8
20	119 26.9	49.2	82 15.0	12.8	0 36.0	10.8	56.7
21	134 27.0	. . 48.3	96 46.8	12.8	0 46.8	10.8	56.7
22	149 27.2	47.5	111 18.6	12.8	0 57.6	10.7	56.7
23	164 27.4	46.6	125 50.4	12.9	1 08.3	10.8	56.6
25 00 (Friday)	179 27.6	N10 45.8	140 22.3	12.9	S 1 19.1	10.7	56.6
01	194 27.7	44.9	154 54.2	12.9	1 29.8	10.7	56.6
02	209 27.9	44.0	169 26.1	12.9	1 40.5	10.7	56.5
03	224 28.1	. . 43.2	183 58.0	13.0	1 51.2	10.7	56.5
04	239 28.2	42.3	198 30.0	13.1	2 01.9	10.6	56.5
05	254 28.4	41.4	213 02.1	13.0	2 12.5	10.6	56.4
06	269 28.6	N10 40.6	227 34.1	13.1	S 2 23.1	10.6	56.4
07	284 28.8	39.7	242 06.2	13.1	2 33.7	10.6	56.4
08	299 28.9	38.9	256 38.3	13.1	2 44.3	10.5	56.4
09	314 29.1	. . 38.0	271 10.4	13.2	2 54.8	10.5	56.3
10	329 29.3	37.1	285 42.6	13.2	3 05.3	10.5	56.3
11	344 29.5	36.3	300 14.8	13.2	3 15.8	10.5	56.3
12	359 29.6	N10 35.4	314 47.0	13.2	S 3 26.3	10.4	56.2
13	14 29.8	34.5	329 19.2	13.2	3 36.7	10.5	56.2
14	29 30.0	33.7	343 51.4	13.3	3 47.2	10.3	56.2
15	44 30.1	. . 32.8	358 23.7	13.3	3 57.5	10.4	56.1
16	59 30.3	31.9	12 56.0	13.3	4 07.9	10.3	56.1
17	74 30.5	31.1	27 28.3	13.4	4 18.2	10.3	56.1
18	89 30.7	N10 30.2	42 00.7	13.3	S 4 28.5	10.2	56.1
19	104 30.8	29.3	56 33.0	13.4	4 38.7	10.3	56.0
20	119 31.0	28.5	71 05.4	13.4	4 49.0	10.1	56.0
21	134 31.2	. . 27.6	85 37.8	13.4	4 59.1	10.2	56.0
22	149 31.4	26.7	100 10.2	13.5	5 09.3	10.1	55.9
23	164 31.5	25.9	114 42.7	13.4	S 5 19.4	10.1	55.9
	SD 15.8	*d* 0.9	SD 15.7		15.5		15.3

Lat.	Twilight Naut. h m	Twilight Civil h m	Sunrise h m	Moonrise 23 h m	Moonrise 24 h m	Moonrise 25 h m	Moonrise 26 h m
N 72	////	01 17	03 20	06 00	07 50	09 35	11 19
N 70	////	02 10	03 41	06 09	07 52	09 31	11 07
68	////	02 42	03 56	06 17	07 54	09 27	10 58
66	01 07	03 04	04 09	06 23	07 55	09 24	10 51
64	01 54	03 22	04 20	06 28	07 56	09 22	10 44
62	02 22	03 37	04 28	06 33	07 57	09 19	10 39
60	02 44	03 49	04 36	06 36	07 58	09 17	10 34
N 58	03 01	03 59	04 43	06 40	07 59	09 16	10 30
56	03 15	04 08	04 49	06 43	08 00	09 14	10 26
54	03 26	04 15	04 54	06 46	08 00	09 13	10 23
52	03 37	04 22	04 59	06 48	08 01	09 12	10 20
50	03 46	04 29	05 03	06 50	08 02	09 10	10 17
45	04 04	04 41	05 13	06 55	08 03	09 08	10 11
N 40	04 18	04 52	05 20	06 59	08 04	09 06	10 06
35	04 29	05 01	05 27	07 03	08 05	09 04	10 02
30	04 39	05 08	05 33	07 06	08 05	09 03	09 58
20	04 53	05 20	05 42	07 11	08 07	09 00	09 52
N 10	05 05	05 30	05 51	07 16	08 08	08 58	09 46
0	05 13	05 38	05 59	07 21	08 09	08 56	09 41
S 10	05 21	05 45	06 07	07 25	08 10	08 54	09 36
20	05 27	05 53	06 15	07 30	08 11	08 51	09 31
30	05 32	06 00	06 24	07 35	08 13	08 49	09 24
35	05 34	06 04	06 30	07 38	08 14	08 47	09 21
40	05 36	06 08	06 35	07 42	08 14	08 46	09 17
45	05 38	06 12	06 42	07 46	08 16	08 44	09 12
S 50	05 40	06 18	06 51	07 50	08 17	08 42	09 07
52	05 41	06 20	06 54	07 53	08 17	08 41	09 04
54	05 41	06 22	06 58	07 55	08 18	08 40	09 01
56	05 42	06 25	07 03	07 58	08 19	08 39	08 58
58	05 42	06 28	07 08	08 01	08 19	08 37	08 55
S 60	05 43	06 31	07 14	08 04	08 20	08 36	08 51

Lat.	Sunset h m	Twilight Civil h m	Twilight Naut. h m	Moonset 23 h m	Moonset 24 h m	Moonset 25 h m	Moonset 26 h m
N 72	20 40	22 36	////	20 30	20 22	20 14	20 05
N 70	20 21	21 49	////	20 25	20 23	20 21	20 19
68	20 06	21 19	////	20 21	20 24	20 26	20 29
66	19 53	20 57	22 48	20 18	20 25	20 31	20 38
64	19 43	20 40	22 06	20 15	20 25	20 35	20 46
62	19 34	20 26	21 38	20 12	20 26	20 39	20 52
60	19 27	20 14	21 18	20 10	20 26	20 42	20 58
N 58	19 20	20 04	21 01	20 08	20 27	20 44	21 03
56	19 14	19 55	20 48	20 07	20 27	20 47	21 07
54	19 09	19 48	20 36	20 05	20 27	20 49	21 11
52	19 05	19 41	20 26	20 04	20 28	20 51	21 15
50	19 00	19 35	20 18	20 02	20 28	20 53	21 18
45	18 51	19 22	20 00	19 59	20 28	20 57	21 25
N 40	18 44	19 12	19 46	19 57	20 29	21 00	21 31
35	18 37	19 03	19 35	19 55	20 29	21 03	21 37
30	18 32	18 56	19 25	19 53	20 30	21 06	21 41
20	18 22	18 44	19 11	19 50	20 30	21 10	21 49
N 10	18 13	18 35	19 00	19 47	20 31	21 14	21 56
0	18 06	18 27	18 51	19 44	20 32	21 18	22 03
S 10	17 58	18 19	18 44	19 41	20 32	21 21	22 10
20	17 50	18 12	18 38	19 38	20 33	21 25	22 17
30	17 41	18 05	18 33	19 35	20 33	21 30	22 25
35	17 36	18 01	18 31	19 33	20 33	21 32	22 29
40	17 30	17 57	18 29	19 30	20 34	21 35	22 35
45	17 23	17 53	18 27	19 28	20 34	21 38	22 41
S 50	17 15	17 48	18 25	19 25	20 35	21 43	22 48
52	17 11	17 46	18 25	19 23	20 35	21 44	22 52
54	17 07	17 43	18 24	19 21	20 35	21 46	22 55
56	17 02	17 41	18 24	19 20	20 35	21 49	23 00
58	16 57	17 38	18 24	19 18	20 36	21 51	23 04
S 60	16 52	17 35	18 23	19 15	20 36	21 54	23 10

Day	SUN Eqn. of Time 00^h	SUN Eqn. of Time 12^h	SUN Mer. Pass.	MOON Mer. Pass. Upper	MOON Mer. Pass. Lower	Age	Phase
d	m s	m s	h m	h m	h m	d	%
23	02 42	02 34	12 03	13 32	01 08	02	4
24	02 26	02 18	12 02	14 20	01 57	03	9
25	02 10	02 02	12 02	15 07	02 44	04	16

2017 AUGUST 26, 27, 28 (SAT., SUN., MON.)

UT		ARIES	VENUS −3·9		MARS +1·8		JUPITER −1·8		SATURN +0·4	
d	h	GHA	GHA	Dec	GHA	Dec	GHA	Dec	GHA	Dec
		° ′	° ′	° ′	° ′	° ′	° ′	° ′	° ′	° ′
26	00	334 26.0	212 32.3	N19 57.9	188 19.6	N14 48.9	134 41.3	S 7 08.0	73 56.8	S21 58.1
	01	349 28.5	227 31.6	57.4	203 20.5	48.4	149 43.4	08.2	88 59.2	58.1
	02	4 31.0	242 30.9	57.0	218 21.4	47.9	164 45.4	08.3	104 01.7	58.1
	03	19 33.4	257 30.3	. . 56.5	233 22.3	. . 47.4	179 47.5	. . 08.5	119 04.1	. . 58.1
	04	34 35.9	272 29.6	56.0	248 23.2	46.8	194 49.5	08.7	134 06.6	58.1
	05	49 38.4	287 29.0	55.5	263 24.1	46.3	209 51.6	08.9	149 09.1	58.1
	06	64 40.8	302 28.3	N19 55.0	278 25.0	N14 45.8	224 53.6	S 7 09.0	164 11.5	S21 58.1
	07	79 43.3	317 27.6	54.5	293 25.9	45.3	239 55.7	09.2	179 14.0	58.1
S	08	94 45.7	332 27.0	53.9	308 26.8	44.7	254 57.7	09.4	194 16.4	58.1
A	09	109 48.2	347 26.3	. . 53.4	323 27.7	. . 44.2	269 59.8	. . 09.5	209 18.9	. . 58.1
T	10	124 50.7	2 25.6	52.9	338 28.7	43.7	285 01.9	09.7	224 21.4	58.1
U	11	139 53.1	17 25.0	52.4	353 29.6	43.2	300 03.9	09.9	239 23.8	58.2
R	12	154 55.6	32 24.3	N19 51.9	8 30.5	N14 42.6	315 06.0	S 7 10.1	254 26.3	S21 58.2
D	13	169 58.1	47 23.7	51.4	23 31.4	42.1	330 08.0	10.2	269 28.8	58.2
A	14	185 00.5	62 23.0	50.9	38 32.3	41.6	345 10.1	10.4	284 31.2	58.2
Y	15	200 03.0	77 22.3	. . 50.4	53 33.2	. . 41.1	0 12.1	. . 10.6	299 33.7	. . 58.2
	16	215 05.5	92 21.7	49.9	68 34.1	40.5	15 14.2	10.7	314 36.1	58.2
	17	230 07.9	107 21.0	49.4	83 35.0	40.0	30 16.2	10.9	329 38.6	58.2
	18	245 10.4	122 20.4	N19 48.9	98 35.9	N14 39.5	45 18.3	S 7 11.1	344 41.1	S21 58.2
	19	260 12.9	137 19.7	48.4	113 36.9	39.0	60 20.3	11.3	359 43.5	58.2
	20	275 15.3	152 19.0	47.8	128 37.8	38.4	75 22.4	11.4	14 46.0	58.2
	21	290 17.8	167 18.4	. . 47.3	143 38.7	. . 37.9	90 24.4	. . 11.6	29 48.4	. . 58.2
	22	305 20.2	182 17.7	46.8	158 39.6	37.4	105 26.5	11.8	44 50.9	58.2
	23	320 22.7	197 17.1	46.3	173 40.5	36.9	120 28.5	11.9	59 53.3	58.3
27	00	335 25.2	212 16.4	N19 45.8	188 41.4	N14 36.3	135 30.6	S 7 12.1	74 55.8	S21 58.3
	01	350 27.6	227 15.7	45.2	203 42.3	35.8	150 32.6	12.3	89 58.3	58.3
	02	5 30.1	242 15.1	44.7	218 43.2	35.3	165 34.7	12.5	105 00.7	58.3
	03	20 32.6	257 14.4	. . 44.2	233 44.1	. . 34.7	180 36.7	. . 12.6	120 03.2	. . 58.3
	04	35 35.0	272 13.8	43.7	248 45.1	34.2	195 38.8	12.8	135 05.6	58.3
	05	50 37.5	287 13.1	43.2	263 46.0	33.7	210 40.8	13.0	150 08.1	58.3
	06	65 40.0	302 12.4	N19 42.6	278 46.9	N14 33.2	225 42.9	S 7 13.2	165 10.5	S21 58.3
	07	80 42.4	317 11.8	42.1	293 47.8	32.6	240 44.9	13.3	180 13.0	58.3
	08	95 44.9	332 11.1	41.6	308 48.7	32.1	255 47.0	13.5	195 15.5	58.3
S	09	110 47.4	347 10.5	. . 41.1	323 49.6	. . 31.6	270 49.0	. . 13.7	210 17.9	. . 58.3
U	10	125 49.8	2 09.8	40.5	338 50.5	31.1	285 51.1	13.8	225 20.4	58.3
N	11	140 52.3	17 09.2	40.0	353 51.4	30.5	300 53.1	14.0	240 22.8	58.4
D	12	155 54.7	32 08.5	N19 39.5	8 52.4	N14 30.0	315 55.2	S 7 14.2	255 25.3	S21 58.4
A	13	170 57.2	47 07.9	38.9	23 53.3	29.5	330 57.2	14.4	270 27.7	58.4
Y	14	185 59.7	62 07.2	38.4	38 54.2	28.9	345 59.3	14.5	285 30.2	58.4
	15	201 02.1	77 06.5	. . 37.9	53 55.1	. . 28.4	1 01.3	. . 14.7	300 32.7	. . 58.4
	16	216 04.6	92 05.9	37.3	68 56.0	27.9	16 03.4	14.9	315 35.1	58.4
	17	231 07.1	107 05.2	36.8	83 56.9	27.4	31 05.4	15.0	330 37.6	58.4
	18	246 09.5	122 04.6	N19 36.3	98 57.8	N14 26.8	46 07.5	S 7 15.2	345 40.0	S21 58.4
	19	261 12.0	137 03.9	35.7	113 58.8	26.3	61 09.5	15.4	0 42.5	58.4
	20	276 14.5	152 03.3	35.2	128 59.7	25.8	76 11.6	15.6	15 44.9	58.4
	21	291 16.9	167 02.6	. . 34.7	144 00.6	. . 25.2	91 13.6	. . 15.7	30 47.4	. . 58.4
	22	306 19.4	182 02.0	34.1	159 01.5	24.7	106 15.7	15.9	45 49.8	58.4
	23	321 21.8	197 01.3	33.6	174 02.4	24.2	121 17.7	16.1	60 52.3	58.5
28	00	336 24.3	212 00.6	N19 33.0	189 03.3	N14 23.6	136 19.8	S 7 16.3	75 54.7	S21 58.5
	01	351 26.8	227 00.0	32.5	204 04.2	23.1	151 21.8	16.4	90 57.2	58.5
	02	6 29.2	241 59.3	31.9	219 05.2	22.6	166 23.9	16.6	105 59.6	58.5
	03	21 31.7	256 58.7	. . 31.4	234 06.1	. . 22.1	181 25.9	. . 16.8	121 02.1	. . 58.5
	04	36 34.2	271 58.0	30.9	249 07.0	21.5	196 28.0	16.9	136 04.6	58.5
	05	51 36.6	286 57.4	30.3	264 07.9	21.0	211 30.0	17.1	151 07.0	58.5
	06	66 39.1	301 56.7	N19 29.8	279 08.8	N14 20.5	226 32.1	S 7 17.3	166 09.5	S21 58.5
	07	81 41.6	316 56.1	29.2	294 09.7	19.9	241 34.1	17.5	181 11.9	58.5
	08	96 44.0	331 55.4	28.7	309 10.7	19.4	256 36.2	17.6	196 14.4	58.5
M	09	111 46.5	346 54.8	. . 28.1	324 11.6	. . 18.9	271 38.2	. . 17.8	211 16.8	. . 58.5
O	10	126 49.0	1 54.1	27.6	339 12.5	18.3	286 40.3	18.0	226 19.3	58.5
N	11	141 51.4	16 53.5	27.0	354 13.4	17.8	301 42.3	18.2	241 21.7	58.6
D	12	156 53.9	31 52.8	N19 26.5	9 14.3	N14 17.3	316 44.4	S 7 18.3	256 24.2	S21 58.6
A	13	171 56.3	46 52.2	25.9	24 15.2	16.7	331 46.4	18.5	271 26.6	58.6
Y	14	186 58.8	61 51.5	25.3	39 16.2	16.2	346 48.4	18.7	286 29.1	58.6
	15	202 01.3	76 50.9	. . 24.8	54 17.1	. . 15.7	1 50.5	. . 18.9	301 31.5	. . 58.6
	16	217 03.7	91 50.2	24.2	69 18.0	15.1	16 52.5	19.0	316 34.0	58.6
	17	232 06.2	106 49.6	23.7	84 18.9	14.6	31 54.6	19.2	331 36.4	58.6
	18	247 08.7	121 48.9	N19 23.1	99 19.8	N14 14.1	46 56.6	S 7 19.4	346 38.9	S21 58.6
	19	262 11.1	136 48.3	22.6	114 20.7	13.5	61 58.7	19.5	1 41.3	58.6
	20	277 13.6	151 47.6	22.0	129 21.7	13.0	77 00.7	19.7	16 43.8	58.6
	21	292 16.1	166 47.0	. . 21.4	144 22.6	. . 12.5	92 02.8	. . 19.9	31 46.2	. . 58.6
	22	307 18.5	181 46.3	20.9	159 23.5	11.9	107 04.8	20.1	46 48.7	58.6
	23	322 21.0	196 45.7	20.3	174 24.4	11.4	122 06.9	20.2	61 51.1	58.7
Mer. Pass.		h m 1 38.1	v −0.7	d 0.5	v 0.9	d 0.5	v 2.0	d 0.2	v 2.5	d 0.0

STARS		
Name	SHA	Dec
	° ′	° ′
Acamar	315 16.1	S40 13.9
Achernar	335 24.4	S57 08.7
Acrux	173 06.6	S63 11.8
Adhara	255 10.5	S28 59.7
Aldebaran	290 46.2	N16 32.5
Alioth	166 18.7	N55 52.2
Alkaid	152 57.0	N49 13.9
Al Na'ir	27 39.8	S46 52.4
Alnilam	275 43.6	S 1 11.5
Alphard	217 53.6	S 8 44.0
Alphecca	126 08.7	N26 39.8
Alpheratz	357 40.2	N29 11.2
Altair	62 05.2	N 8 55.2
Ankaa	353 12.6	S42 12.5
Antares	112 22.7	S26 28.1
Arcturus	145 53.3	N19 05.8
Atria	107 21.8	S69 03.6
Avior	234 17.4	S59 33.9
Bellatrix	278 29.1	N 6 21.8
Betelgeuse	270 58.4	N 7 24.5
Canopus	263 55.2	S52 42.2
Capella	280 30.4	N46 00.6
Deneb	49 29.1	N45 20.9
Denebola	182 31.1	N14 28.6
Diphda	348 52.8	S17 53.3
Dubhe	193 49.0	N61 39.5
Elnath	278 09.1	N28 37.1
Eltanin	90 44.6	N51 29.7
Enif	33 44.0	N 9 57.5
Fomalhaut	15 20.5	S29 31.6
Gacrux	171 58.1	S57 12.7
Gienah	175 49.6	S17 38.3
Hadar	148 44.1	S60 27.5
Hamal	327 57.4	N23 32.6
Kaus Aust.	83 39.8	S34 22.4
Kochab	137 20.6	N74 05.4
Markab	13 35.2	N15 18.1
Menkar	314 12.0	N 4 09.5
Menkent	148 04.4	S36 27.3
Miaplacidus	221 39.9	S69 47.3
Mirfak	308 36.1	N49 55.1
Nunki	75 54.6	S26 16.3
Peacock	53 14.3	S56 40.6
Pollux	243 24.6	N27 58.9
Procyon	244 57.0	N 5 10.7
Rasalhague	96 03.7	N12 33.2
Regulus	207 40.8	N11 52.9
Rigel	281 09.4	S 8 10.9
Rigil Kent.	139 48.1	S60 54.5
Sabik	102 09.2	S15 44.6
Schedar	349 36.7	N56 37.9
Shaula	96 17.9	S37 06.9
Sirius	258 31.4	S16 44.4
Spica	158 28.5	S11 15.0
Suhail	222 50.7	S43 30.2
Vega	80 36.8	N38 48.4
Zuben'ubi	137 02.4	S16 06.7

	SHA	Mer. Pass.
	° ′	h m
Venus	236 51.2	9 51
Mars	213 16.2	11 25
Jupiter	160 05.4	14 56
Saturn	99 30.6	18 57

	UT	SUN GHA	SUN Dec	MOON GHA	v	MOON Dec	d	HP
	d h	° ′	° ′	° ′	′	° ′	′	′
	26 00	179 31.7	N10 25.0	129 15.1	13.5	S 5 29.5	10.1	55.9
	01	194 31.9	24.1	143 47.6	13.4	5 39.6	10.0	55.9
	02	209 32.1	23.3	158 20.0	13.5	5 49.6	9.9	55.8
	03	224 32.2	. . 22.4	172 52.5	13.5	5 59.5	10.0	55.8
	04	239 32.4	21.5	187 25.0	13.6	6 09.5	9.9	55.8
	05	254 32.6	20.6	201 57.6	13.5	6 19.4	9.8	55.7
	06	269 32.8	N10 19.8	216 30.1	13.5	S 6 29.2	9.9	55.7
	07	284 33.0	18.9	231 02.6	13.6	6 39.1	9.7	55.7
S	08	299 33.1	18.0	245 35.2	13.6	6 48.8	9.8	55.7
A	09	314 33.3	. . 17.2	260 07.8	13.6	6 58.6	9.7	55.6
T	10	329 33.5	16.3	274 40.4	13.5	7 08.3	9.6	55.6
U	11	344 33.7	15.4	289 12.9	13.6	7 17.9	9.6	55.6
R	12	359 33.8	N10 14.5	303 45.5	13.6	S 7 27.5	9.6	55.6
D	13	14 34.0	13.7	318 18.1	13.7	7 37.1	9.5	55.5
A	14	29 34.2	12.8	332 50.8	13.6	7 46.6	9.5	55.5
Y	15	44 34.4	. . 11.9	347 23.4	13.6	7 56.1	9.5	55.5
	16	59 34.5	11.0	1 56.0	13.6	8 05.6	9.4	55.5
	17	74 34.7	10.2	16 28.6	13.7	8 15.0	9.3	55.4
	18	89 34.9	N10 09.3	31 01.3	13.6	S 8 24.3	9.3	55.4
	19	104 35.1	08.4	45 33.9	13.7	8 33.6	9.3	55.4
	20	119 35.3	07.6	60 06.6	13.6	8 42.9	9.2	55.4
	21	134 35.4	. . 06.7	74 39.2	13.7	8 52.1	9.1	55.3
	22	149 35.6	05.8	89 11.9	13.7	9 01.2	9.1	55.3
	23	164 35.8	04.9	103 44.6	13.6	9 10.3	9.1	55.3
	27 00	179 36.0	N10 04.1	118 17.2	13.7	S 9 19.4	9.0	55.3
	01	194 36.2	03.2	132 49.9	13.6	9 28.4	9.0	55.2
	02	209 36.3	02.3	147 22.5	13.7	9 37.4	8.9	55.2
	03	224 36.5	. . 01.4	161 55.2	13.7	9 46.3	8.8	55.2
	04	239 36.7	10 00.5	176 27.9	13.6	9 55.1	8.8	55.2
	05	254 36.9	9 59.7	191 00.5	13.7	10 03.9	8.8	55.1
	06	269 37.1	N 9 58.8	205 33.2	13.7	S10 12.7	8.7	55.1
	07	284 37.2	57.9	220 05.9	13.6	10 21.4	8.6	55.1
	08	299 37.4	57.0	234 38.5	13.7	10 30.0	8.6	55.1
S	09	314 37.6	. . 56.2	249 11.2	13.6	10 38.6	8.6	55.1
U	10	329 37.8	55.3	263 43.8	13.7	10 47.2	8.5	55.0
N	11	344 38.0	54.4	278 16.5	13.6	10 55.7	8.4	55.0
D	12	359 38.1	N 9 53.5	292 49.1	13.7	S11 04.1	8.4	55.0
A	13	14 38.3	52.6	307 21.8	13.6	11 12.5	8.3	55.0
Y	14	29 38.5	51.8	321 54.4	13.7	11 20.8	8.3	54.9
	15	44 38.7	. . 50.9	336 27.1	13.6	11 29.1	8.2	54.9
	16	59 38.9	50.0	350 59.7	13.6	11 37.3	8.1	54.9
	17	74 39.1	49.1	5 32.3	13.6	11 45.4	8.1	54.9
	18	89 39.2	N 9 48.2	20 04.9	13.6	S11 53.5	8.0	54.9
	19	104 39.4	47.4	34 37.5	13.6	12 01.5	8.0	54.9
	20	119 39.6	46.5	49 10.1	13.6	12 09.5	7.9	54.8
	21	134 39.8	. . 45.6	63 42.7	13.6	12 17.4	7.9	54.8
	22	149 40.0	44.7	78 15.3	13.6	12 25.3	7.8	54.8
	23	164 40.2	43.8	92 47.9	13.5	12 33.1	7.7	54.8
	28 00	179 40.3	N 9 43.0	107 20.4	13.6	S12 40.8	7.7	54.8
	01	194 40.5	42.1	121 53.0	13.5	12 48.5	7.6	54.7
	02	209 40.7	41.2	136 25.5	13.6	12 56.1	7.6	54.7
	03	224 40.9	. . 40.3	150 58.1	13.5	13 03.7	7.5	54.7
	04	239 41.1	39.4	165 30.6	13.5	13 11.2	7.4	54.7
	05	254 41.3	38.5	180 03.1	13.5	13 18.6	7.3	54.7
	06	269 41.4	N 9 37.7	194 35.6	13.5	S13 25.9	7.4	54.7
	07	284 41.6	36.8	209 08.1	13.5	13 33.3	7.2	54.6
	08	299 41.8	35.9	223 40.6	13.4	13 40.5	7.2	54.6
M	09	314 42.0	. . 35.0	238 13.0	13.5	13 47.7	7.1	54.6
O	10	329 42.2	34.1	252 45.5	13.4	13 54.8	7.0	54.6
N	11	344 42.4	33.2	267 17.9	13.4	14 01.8	7.0	54.6
D	12	359 42.6	N 9 32.4	281 50.3	13.4	S14 08.8	6.9	54.6
A	13	14 42.7	31.5	296 22.7	13.4	14 15.7	6.8	54.6
Y	14	29 42.9	30.6	310 55.1	13.4	14 22.5	6.8	54.5
	15	44 43.1	. . 29.7	325 27.5	13.4	14 29.3	6.7	54.5
	16	59 43.3	28.8	339 59.9	13.3	14 36.0	6.7	54.5
	17	74 43.5	27.9	354 32.2	13.4	14 42.7	6.5	54.5
	18	89 43.7	N 9 27.0	9 04.6	13.3	S14 49.2	6.5	54.5
	19	104 43.9	26.1	23 36.9	13.3	14 55.7	6.5	54.5
	20	119 44.0	25.3	38 09.2	13.3	15 02.2	6.4	54.5
	21	134 44.2	. . 24.4	52 41.5	13.2	15 08.6	6.3	54.5
	22	149 44.4	23.5	67 13.7	13.3	15 14.9	6.2	54.4
	23	164 44.6	22.6	81 46.0	13.2	S15 21.1	6.1	54.4
		SD 15.9	*d* 0.9	SD	15.1	15.0		14.9

Lat.	Twilight Naut.	Twilight Civil	Sunrise	Moonrise 26	27	28	29
°	h m	h m	h m	h m	h m	h m	h m
N 72	////	01 51	03 37	11 19	13 03	14 50	16 51
N 70	////	02 30	03 54	11 07	12 43	14 18	15 53
68	////	02 57	04 08	10 58	12 27	13 55	15 20
66	01 36	03 17	04 19	10 51	12 15	13 37	14 55
64	02 11	03 33	04 28	10 44	12 05	13 22	14 36
62	02 36	03 46	04 36	10 39	11 56	13 10	14 21
60	02 55	03 57	04 43	10 34	11 48	13 00	14 08
N 58	03 10	04 06	04 49	10 30	11 42	12 51	13 57
56	03 23	04 14	04 55	10 26	11 36	12 43	13 47
54	03 33	04 21	04 59	10 23	11 31	12 36	13 39
52	03 43	04 28	05 04	10 20	11 26	12 30	13 31
50	03 51	04 33	05 08	10 17	11 22	12 24	13 24
45	04 08	04 45	05 16	10 11	11 13	12 12	13 10
N 40	04 21	04 55	05 23	10 06	11 05	12 02	12 58
35	04 32	05 03	05 29	10 02	10 58	11 54	12 47
30	04 41	05 10	05 34	09 58	10 53	11 46	12 39
20	04 54	05 21	05 43	09 52	10 43	11 33	12 23
N 10	05 05	05 30	05 51	09 46	10 34	11 22	12 10
0	05 13	05 37	05 58	09 41	10 26	11 12	11 57
S 10	05 19	05 44	06 05	09 36	10 18	11 01	11 45
20	05 25	05 50	06 13	09 31	10 10	10 50	11 32
30	05 29	05 57	06 21	09 24	10 00	10 38	11 17
35	05 31	06 00	06 26	09 21	09 55	10 30	11 08
40	05 32	06 04	06 31	09 17	09 49	10 22	10 58
45	05 33	06 07	06 37	09 12	09 41	10 12	10 47
S 50	05 34	06 12	06 45	09 07	09 33	10 01	10 33
52	05 35	06 14	06 48	09 04	09 29	09 56	10 26
54	05 35	06 16	06 52	09 01	09 24	09 50	10 19
56	05 35	06 18	06 56	08 58	09 20	09 43	10 11
58	05 35	06 20	07 00	08 55	09 14	09 36	10 02
S 60	05 35	06 23	07 05	08 51	09 08	09 28	09 51

Lat.	Sunset	Twilight Civil	Twilight Naut.	Moonset 26	27	28	29
°	h m	h m	h m	h m	h m	h m	h m
N 72	20 23	22 04	////	20 05	19 55	19 42	19 18
N 70	20 06	21 27	////	20 19	20 17	20 15	20 16
68	19 52	21 02	23 25	20 29	20 33	20 40	20 50
66	19 42	20 43	22 20	20 38	20 47	20 58	21 15
64	19 32	20 27	21 47	20 46	20 58	21 14	21 34
62	19 25	20 15	21 24	20 52	21 08	21 26	21 50
60	19 18	20 04	21 06	20 58	21 16	21 37	22 03
N 58	19 12	19 55	20 51	21 03	21 23	21 47	22 15
56	19 07	19 47	20 38	21 07	21 29	21 55	22 25
54	19 02	19 40	20 28	21 11	21 35	22 02	22 34
52	18 58	19 34	20 18	21 15	21 40	22 09	22 42
50	18 54	19 28	20 10	21 18	21 45	22 15	22 49
45	18 46	19 17	19 54	21 25	21 55	22 28	23 04
N 40	18 39	19 07	19 41	21 31	22 04	22 39	23 16
35	18 33	18 59	19 30	21 37	22 11	22 48	23 27
30	18 28	18 53	19 22	21 41	22 18	22 56	23 36
20	18 19	18 42	19 08	21 49	22 29	23 10	23 53
N 10	18 12	18 33	18 58	21 56	22 39	23 22	24 07
0	18 05	18 26	18 50	22 03	22 48	23 34	24 20
S 10	17 58	18 19	18 44	22 10	22 57	23 45	24 33
20	17 51	18 13	18 39	22 17	23 07	23 57	24 47
30	17 42	18 07	18 34	22 25	23 19	24 11	00 11
35	17 38	18 03	18 33	22 29	23 25	24 20	00 20
40	17 32	18 00	18 31	22 35	23 33	24 29	00 29
45	17 26	17 56	18 30	22 41	23 41	24 40	00 40
S 50	17 19	17 52	18 30	22 48	23 52	24 53	00 53
52	17 16	17 50	18 29	22 52	23 57	24 59	00 59
54	17 12	17 48	18 29	22 55	24 02	00 02	01 06
56	17 08	17 46	18 29	23 00	24 08	00 08	01 14
58	17 04	17 44	18 29	23 04	24 15	00 15	01 23
S 60	16 59	17 41	18 30	23 10	24 23	00 23	01 33

Day	SUN Eqn. of Time 00^h	SUN Eqn. of Time 12^h	SUN Mer. Pass.	MOON Mer. Pass. Upper	MOON Mer. Pass. Lower	MOON Age	MOON Phase
d	m s	m s	h m	h m	h m	d	%
26	01 53	01 45	12 02	15 52	03 29	05	24
27	01 36	01 28	12 01	16 37	04 15	06	33
28	01 19	01 10	12 01	17 23	05 00	07	42

UT d h	ARIES GHA ° ′	VENUS −3·9 GHA ° ′	VENUS Dec ° ′	MARS +1·8 GHA ° ′	MARS Dec ° ′	JUPITER −1·7 GHA ° ′	JUPITER Dec ° ′	SATURN +0·4 GHA ° ′	SATURN Dec ° ′
29 00 (TUESDAY)	337 23.4	211 45.0	N19 19.7	189 25.3	N14 10.9	137 08.9	S 7 20.4	76 53.6	S21 58.7
01	352 25.9	226 44.4	19.2	204 26.2	10.3	152 11.0	20.6	91 56.0	58.7
02	7 28.4	241 43.7	18.6	219 27.2	09.8	167 13.0	20.8	106 58.5	58.7
03	22 30.8	256 43.1	. . 18.0	234 28.1	. . 09.3	182 15.0	. . 20.9	122 00.9	. . 58.7
04	37 33.3	271 42.4	17.5	249 29.0	08.7	197 17.1	21.1	137 03.4	58.7
05	52 35.8	286 41.8	16.9	264 29.9	08.2	212 19.1	21.3	152 05.8	58.7
06	67 38.2	301 41.1	N19 16.3	279 30.8	N14 07.7	227 21.2	S 7 21.5	167 08.3	S21 58.7
07	82 40.7	316 40.5	15.8	294 31.8	07.1	242 23.2	21.6	182 10.7	58.7
08	97 43.2	331 39.9	15.2	309 32.7	06.6	257 25.3	21.8	197 13.2	58.7
09	112 45.6	346 39.2	. . 14.6	324 33.6	. . 06.1	272 27.3	. . 22.0	212 15.6	. . 58.7
10	127 48.1	1 38.6	14.0	339 34.5	05.5	287 29.4	22.2	227 18.1	58.8
11	142 50.6	16 37.9	13.5	354 35.4	05.0	302 31.4	22.3	242 20.5	58.8
12	157 53.0	31 37.3	N19 12.9	9 36.4	N14 04.5	317 33.4	S 7 22.5	257 23.0	S21 58.8
13	172 55.5	46 36.6	12.3	24 37.3	03.9	332 35.5	22.7	272 25.4	58.8
14	187 57.9	61 36.0	11.7	39 38.2	03.4	347 37.5	22.9	287 27.8	58.8
15	203 00.4	76 35.3	. . 11.2	54 39.1	. . 02.8	2 39.6	. . 23.0	302 30.3	. . 58.8
16	218 02.9	91 34.7	10.6	69 40.0	02.3	17 41.6	23.2	317 32.7	58.8
17	233 05.3	106 34.0	10.0	84 41.0	01.8	32 43.7	23.4	332 35.2	58.8
18	248 07.8	121 33.4	N19 09.4	99 41.9	N14 01.2	47 45.7	S 7 23.6	347 37.6	S21 58.8
19	263 10.3	136 32.8	08.8	114 42.8	00.7	62 47.7	23.7	2 40.1	58.8
20	278 12.7	151 32.1	08.2	129 43.7	14 00.2	77 49.8	23.9	17 42.5	58.8
21	293 15.2	166 31.5	. . 07.7	144 44.6	13 59.6	92 51.8	. . 24.1	32 45.0	. . 58.9
22	308 17.7	181 30.8	07.1	159 45.6	59.1	107 53.9	24.3	47 47.4	58.9
23	323 20.1	196 30.2	06.5	174 46.5	58.5	122 55.9	24.4	62 49.9	58.9
30 00 (WEDNESDAY)	338 22.6	211 29.5	N19 05.9	189 47.4	N13 58.0	137 57.9	S 7 24.6	77 52.3	S21 58.9
01	353 25.1	226 28.9	05.3	204 48.3	57.5	153 00.0	24.8	92 54.8	58.9
02	8 27.5	241 28.3	04.7	219 49.2	56.9	168 02.0	25.0	107 57.2	58.9
03	23 30.0	256 27.6	. . 04.1	234 50.2	. . 56.4	183 04.1	. . 25.1	122 59.6	. . 58.9
04	38 32.4	271 27.0	03.5	249 51.1	55.9	198 06.1	25.3	138 02.1	58.9
05	53 34.9	286 26.3	02.9	264 52.0	55.3	213 08.2	25.5	153 04.5	58.9
06	68 37.4	301 25.7	N19 02.4	279 52.9	N13 54.8	228 10.2	S 7 25.7	168 07.0	S21 58.9
07	83 39.8	316 25.1	01.8	294 53.9	54.2	243 12.2	25.8	183 09.4	58.9
08	98 42.3	331 24.4	01.2	309 54.8	53.7	258 14.3	26.0	198 11.9	59.0
09	113 44.8	346 23.8	. . 00.6	324 55.7	. . 53.2	273 16.3	. . 26.2	213 14.3	. . 59.0
10	128 47.2	1 23.1	19 00.0	339 56.6	52.6	288 18.4	26.4	228 16.7	59.0
11	143 49.7	16 22.5	18 59.4	354 57.6	52.1	303 20.4	26.5	243 19.2	59.0
12	158 52.2	31 21.9	N18 58.8	9 58.5	N13 51.5	318 22.4	S 7 26.7	258 21.6	S21 59.0
13	173 54.6	46 21.2	58.2	24 59.4	51.0	333 24.5	26.9	273 24.1	59.0
14	188 57.1	61 20.6	57.6	40 00.3	50.5	348 26.5	27.1	288 26.5	59.0
15	203 59.6	76 19.9	. . 57.0	55 01.2	. . 49.9	3 28.6	. . 27.2	303 29.0	. . 59.0
16	219 02.0	91 19.3	56.4	70 02.2	49.4	18 30.6	27.4	318 31.4	59.0
17	234 04.5	106 18.7	55.8	85 03.1	48.9	33 32.6	27.6	333 33.8	59.0
18	249 06.9	121 18.0	N18 55.2	100 04.0	N13 48.3	48 34.7	S 7 27.8	348 36.3	S21 59.0
19	264 09.4	136 17.4	54.6	115 04.9	47.8	63 36.7	27.9	3 38.7	59.1
20	279 11.9	151 16.8	53.9	130 05.9	47.2	78 38.8	28.1	18 41.2	59.1
21	294 14.3	166 16.1	. . 53.3	145 06.8	. . 46.7	93 40.8	. . 28.3	33 43.6	. . 59.1
22	309 16.8	181 15.5	52.7	160 07.7	46.1	108 42.8	28.5	48 46.1	59.1
23	324 19.3	196 14.8	52.1	175 08.6	45.6	123 44.9	28.6	63 48.5	59.1
31 00 (THURSDAY)	339 21.7	211 14.2	N18 51.5	190 09.6	N13 45.1	138 46.9	S 7 28.8	78 50.9	S21 59.1
01	354 24.2	226 13.6	50.9	205 10.5	44.5	153 49.0	29.0	93 53.4	59.1
02	9 26.7	241 12.9	50.3	220 11.4	44.0	168 51.0	29.2	108 55.8	59.1
03	24 29.1	256 12.3	. . 49.7	235 12.3	. . 43.4	183 53.0	. . 29.3	123 58.3	. . 59.1
04	39 31.6	271 11.7	49.1	250 13.3	42.9	198 55.1	29.5	139 00.7	59.1
05	54 34.0	286 11.0	48.4	265 14.2	42.4	213 57.1	29.7	154 03.1	59.1
06	69 36.5	301 10.4	N18 47.8	280 15.1	N13 41.8	228 59.1	S 7 29.9	169 05.6	S21 59.2
07	84 39.0	316 09.8	47.2	295 16.0	41.3	244 01.2	30.0	184 08.0	59.2
08	99 41.4	331 09.1	46.6	310 17.0	40.7	259 03.2	30.2	199 10.5	59.2
09	114 43.9	346 08.5	. . 46.0	325 17.9	. . 40.2	274 05.3	. . 30.4	214 12.9	. . 59.2
10	129 46.4	1 07.9	45.4	340 18.8	39.6	289 07.3	30.6	229 15.3	59.2
11	144 48.8	16 07.2	44.7	355 19.7	39.1	304 09.3	30.7	244 17.8	59.2
12	159 51.3	31 06.6	N18 44.1	10 20.7	N13 38.6	319 11.4	S 7 30.9	259 20.2	S21 59.2
13	174 53.8	46 06.0	43.5	25 21.6	38.0	334 13.4	31.1	274 22.6	59.2
14	189 56.2	61 05.3	42.9	40 22.5	37.5	349 15.4	31.3	289 25.1	59.2
15	204 58.7	76 04.7	. . 42.2	55 23.4	. . 36.9	4 17.5	. . 31.4	304 27.5	. . 59.2
16	220 01.2	91 04.1	41.6	70 24.4	36.4	19 19.5	31.6	319 30.0	59.2
17	235 03.6	106 03.4	41.0	85 25.3	35.8	34 21.6	31.8	334 32.4	59.3
18	250 06.1	121 02.8	N18 40.4	100 26.2	N13 35.3	49 23.6	S 7 32.0	349 34.8	S21 59.3
19	265 08.5	136 02.2	39.7	115 27.2	34.8	64 25.6	32.2	4 37.3	59.3
20	280 11.0	151 01.5	39.1	130 28.1	34.2	79 27.7	32.3	19 39.7	59.3
21	295 13.5	166 00.9	. . 38.5	145 29.0	. . 33.7	94 29.7	. . 32.5	34 42.1	. . 59.3
22	310 15.9	181 00.3	37.9	160 29.9	33.1	109 31.7	32.7	49 44.6	59.3
23	325 18.4	195 59.7	37.2	175 30.9	32.6	124 33.8	32.9	64 47.0	59.3
Mer. Pass.	h m 1 26.3	v −0.6	d 0.6	v 0.9	d 0.5	v 2.0	d 0.2	v 2.4	d 0.0

STARS Name	SHA ° ′	Dec ° ′
Acamar	315 16.1	S40 13.9
Achernar	335 24.3	S57 08.7
Acrux	173 06.6	S63 11.8
Adhara	255 10.5	S28 59.7
Aldebaran	290 46.1	N16 32.5
Alioth	166 18.7	N55 52.2
Alkaid	152 57.0	N49 13.9
Al Na'ir	27 39.8	S46 52.4
Alnilam	275 43.6	S 1 11.5
Alphard	217 53.6	S 8 44.0
Alphecca	126 08.7	N26 39.8
Alpheratz	357 40.2	N29 11.2
Altair	62 05.2	N 8 55.2
Ankaa	353 12.6	S42 12.5
Antares	112 22.7	S26 28.1
Arcturus	145 53.3	N19 05.8
Atria	107 21.9	S69 03.6
Avior	234 17.4	S59 33.9
Bellatrix	278 29.0	N 6 21.8
Betelgeuse	270 58.4	N 7 24.5
Canopus	263 55.1	S52 42.2
Capella	280 30.3	N46 00.6
Deneb	49 29.1	N45 20.9
Denebola	182 31.1	N14 28.6
Diphda	348 52.8	S17 53.3
Dubhe	193 49.0	N61 39.5
Elnath	278 09.1	N28 37.1
Eltanin	90 44.6	N51 29.7
Enif	33 44.0	N 9 57.5
Fomalhaut	15 20.5	S29 31.6
Gacrux	171 58.1	S57 12.7
Gienah	175 49.7	S17 38.2
Hadar	148 44.1	S60 27.5
Hamal	327 57.3	N23 32.6
Kaus Aust.	83 39.9	S34 22.4
Kochab	137 20.7	N74 05.4
Markab	13 35.2	N15 18.1
Menkar	314 12.0	N 4 09.5
Menkent	148 04.4	S36 27.3
Miaplacidus	221 39.9	S69 47.3
Mirfak	308 36.1	N49 55.1
Nunki	75 54.6	S26 16.3
Peacock	53 14.3	S56 40.6
Pollux	243 24.6	N27 58.9
Procyon	244 57.0	N 5 10.7
Rasalhague	96 03.7	N12 33.2
Regulus	207 40.8	N11 52.9
Rigel	281 09.4	S 8 10.9
Rigil Kent.	139 48.1	S60 54.5
Sabik	102 09.2	S15 44.6
Schedar	349 36.7	N56 37.9
Shaula	96 17.9	S37 06.9
Sirius	258 31.4	S16 44.4
Spica	158 28.5	S11 15.0
Suhail	222 50.7	S43 30.1
Vega	80 36.8	N38 48.4
Zuben'ubi	137 02.4	S16 06.7
	SHA ° ′	**Mer. Pass.** h m
Venus	233 07.0	9 54
Mars	211 24.8	11 20
Jupiter	159 35.4	14 46
Saturn	99 29.7	18 45

UT d	UT h	SUN GHA ° ′	SUN Dec ° ′	MOON GHA ° ′	MOON *v* ′	MOON Dec ° ′	MOON *d* ′	MOON HP ′
29 TUESDAY	00	179 44.8	N 9 21.7	96 18.2	13.2	S15 27.2	6.1	54.4
	01	194 45.0	20.8	110 50.4	13.2	15 33.3	6.0	54.4
	02	209 45.2	19.9	125 22.6	13.2	15 39.3	6.0	54.4
	03	224 45.4	. . 19.0	139 54.8	13.1	15 45.3	5.9	54.4
	04	239 45.5	18.2	154 26.9	13.2	15 51.2	5.8	54.4
	05	254 45.7	17.3	168 59.1	13.1	15 57.0	5.7	54.4
	06	269 45.9	N 9 16.4	183 31.2	13.1	S16 02.7	5.6	54.4
	07	284 46.1	15.5	198 03.3	13.1	16 08.3	5.6	54.4
	08	299 46.3	14.6	212 35.4	13.1	16 13.9	5.5	54.3
	09	314 46.5	. . 13.7	227 07.5	13.0	16 19.4	5.5	54.3
	10	329 46.7	12.8	241 39.5	13.0	16 24.9	5.3	54.3
	11	344 46.9	11.9	256 11.5	13.0	16 30.2	5.3	54.3
	12	359 47.1	N 9 11.0	270 43.5	13.0	S16 35.5	5.2	54.3
	13	14 47.2	10.1	285 15.5	13.0	16 40.7	5.1	54.3
	14	29 47.4	09.2	299 47.5	12.9	16 45.8	5.1	54.3
	15	44 47.6	. . 08.4	314 19.4	12.9	16 50.9	5.0	54.3
	16	59 47.8	07.5	328 51.3	13.0	16 55.9	4.9	54.3
	17	74 48.0	06.6	343 23.3	12.8	17 00.8	4.8	54.3
	18	89 48.2	N 9 05.7	357 55.1	12.9	S17 05.6	4.8	54.3
	19	104 48.4	04.8	12 27.0	12.8	17 10.4	4.6	54.3
	20	119 48.6	03.9	26 58.8	12.9	17 15.0	4.6	54.3
	21	134 48.8	. . 03.0	41 30.7	12.8	17 19.6	4.5	54.3
	22	149 49.0	02.1	56 02.5	12.7	17 24.1	4.5	54.3
	23	164 49.2	01.2	70 34.2	12.8	17 28.6	4.3	54.3
30 WEDNESDAY	00	179 49.3	N 9 00.3	85 06.0	12.7	S17 32.9	4.3	54.3
	01	194 49.5	8 59.4	99 37.7	12.7	17 37.2	4.2	54.3
	02	209 49.7	58.5	114 09.4	12.7	17 41.4	4.1	54.2
	03	224 49.9	. . 57.6	128 41.1	12.7	17 45.5	4.1	54.2
	04	239 50.1	56.7	143 12.8	12.7	17 49.6	3.9	54.2
	05	254 50.3	55.8	157 44.5	12.6	17 53.5	3.9	54.2
	06	269 50.5	N 8 54.9	172 16.1	12.6	S17 57.4	3.8	54.2
	07	284 50.7	54.0	186 47.7	12.6	18 01.2	3.7	54.2
	08	299 50.9	53.1	201 19.3	12.5	18 04.9	3.7	54.2
	09	314 51.1	. . 52.2	215 50.8	12.6	18 08.6	3.5	54.2
	10	329 51.3	51.4	230 22.4	12.5	18 12.1	3.5	54.2
	11	344 51.5	50.5	244 53.9	12.5	18 15.6	3.4	54.2
	12	359 51.7	N 8 49.6	259 25.4	12.5	S18 19.0	3.3	54.2
	13	14 51.8	48.7	273 56.9	12.4	18 22.3	3.2	54.2
	14	29 52.0	47.8	288 28.3	12.5	18 25.5	3.1	54.2
	15	44 52.2	. . 46.9	302 59.8	12.4	18 28.6	3.1	54.2
	16	59 52.4	46.0	317 31.2	12.4	18 31.7	2.9	54.2
	17	74 52.6	45.1	332 02.6	12.4	18 34.6	2.9	54.2
	18	89 52.8	N 8 44.2	346 34.0	12.3	S18 37.5	2.8	54.2
	19	104 53.0	43.3	1 05.3	12.4	18 40.3	2.7	54.2
	20	119 53.2	42.4	15 36.7	12.3	18 43.0	2.6	54.2
	21	134 53.4	. . 41.5	30 08.0	12.3	18 45.6	2.6	54.2
	22	149 53.6	40.6	44 39.3	12.2	18 48.2	2.4	54.3
	23	164 53.8	39.7	59 10.5	12.3	18 50.6	2.4	54.3
31 THURSDAY	00	179 54.0	N 8 38.8	73 41.8	12.2	S18 53.0	2.3	54.3
	01	194 54.2	37.9	88 13.0	12.2	18 55.3	2.2	54.3
	02	209 54.4	37.0	102 44.2	12.2	18 57.5	2.1	54.3
	03	224 54.6	. . 36.1	117 15.4	12.2	18 59.6	2.0	54.3
	04	239 54.8	35.2	131 46.6	12.1	19 01.6	1.9	54.3
	05	254 55.0	34.3	146 17.7	12.2	19 03.5	1.9	54.3
	06	269 55.2	N 8 33.4	160 48.9	12.1	S19 05.4	1.7	54.3
	07	284 55.3	32.5	175 20.0	12.1	19 07.1	1.7	54.3
	08	299 55.5	31.6	189 51.1	12.0	19 08.8	1.6	54.3
	09	314 55.7	. . 30.7	204 22.1	12.1	19 10.4	1.5	54.3
	10	329 55.9	29.8	218 53.2	12.0	19 11.9	1.4	54.3
	11	344 56.1	28.9	233 24.2	12.0	19 13.3	1.3	54.3
	12	359 56.3	N 8 27.9	247 55.2	12.0	S19 14.6	1.2	54.3
	13	14 56.5	27.0	262 26.2	12.0	19 15.8	1.2	54.3
	14	29 56.7	26.1	276 57.2	12.0	19 17.0	1.0	54.3
	15	44 56.9	. . 25.2	291 28.2	11.9	19 18.0	1.0	54.3
	16	59 57.1	24.3	305 59.1	12.0	19 19.0	0.8	54.4
	17	74 57.3	23.4	320 30.1	11.9	19 19.8	0.8	54.4
	18	89 57.5	N 8 22.5	335 01.0	11.9	S19 20.6	0.7	54.4
	19	104 57.7	21.6	349 31.9	11.8	19 21.3	0.6	54.4
	20	119 57.9	20.7	4 02.7	11.9	19 21.9	0.5	54.4
	21	134 58.1	. . 19.8	18 33.6	11.8	19 22.4	0.4	54.4
	22	149 58.3	18.9	33 04.4	11.9	19 22.8	0.3	54.4
	23	164 58.5	18.0	47 35.3	11.8	S19 23.1	0.3	54.4
		SD 15.9	*d* 0.9	SD 14.8		14.8		14.8

Lat. °	Twilight Naut. h m	Twilight Civil h m	Sunrise h m	Moonrise 29 h m	Moonrise 30 h m	Moonrise 31 h m	Moonrise 1 h m
N 72	////	02 17	03 52	16 51	▬	▬	▬
N 70	////	02 49	04 07	15 53	17 26	18 45	19 24
68	01 11	03 12	04 19	15 20	16 38	17 43	18 28
66	01 58	03 29	04 29	14 55	16 07	17 08	17 54
64	02 27	03 43	04 37	14 36	15 44	16 43	17 29
62	02 48	03 55	04 44	14 21	15 26	16 23	17 10
60	03 05	04 05	04 50	14 08	15 11	16 07	16 54
N 58	03 19	04 13	04 56	13 57	14 58	15 53	16 41
56	03 30	04 21	05 01	13 47	14 47	15 41	16 29
54	03 40	04 27	05 05	13 39	14 37	15 31	16 19
52	03 49	04 33	05 09	13 31	14 29	15 22	16 10
50	03 57	04 38	05 12	13 24	14 21	15 14	16 02
45	04 12	04 49	05 20	13 10	14 05	14 57	15 45
N 40	04 25	04 58	05 26	12 58	13 51	14 42	15 31
35	04 35	05 05	05 31	12 47	13 40	14 30	15 19
30	04 43	05 11	05 36	12 39	13 30	14 20	15 08
20	04 55	05 22	05 44	12 23	13 13	14 02	14 50
N 10	05 05	05 30	05 51	12 10	12 58	13 46	14 35
0	05 12	05 36	05 57	11 57	12 44	13 32	14 20
S 10	05 18	05 42	06 04	11 45	12 30	13 17	14 05
20	05 22	05 48	06 10	11 32	12 16	13 01	13 50
30	05 26	05 53	06 18	11 17	11 59	12 44	13 32
35	05 27	05 56	06 22	11 08	11 49	12 33	13 21
40	05 28	05 59	06 26	10 58	11 38	12 21	13 09
45	05 28	06 02	06 32	10 47	11 25	12 07	12 55
S 50	05 28	06 06	06 38	10 33	11 09	11 50	12 38
52	05 28	06 07	06 41	10 26	11 01	11 42	12 30
54	05 28	06 09	06 45	10 19	10 53	11 33	12 21
56	05 28	06 11	06 48	10 11	10 44	11 23	12 11
58	05 27	06 12	06 52	10 02	10 33	11 12	11 59
S 60	05 26	06 14	06 57	09 51	10 21	10 59	11 46

Lat. °	Sunset h m	Twilight Civil h m	Twilight Naut. h m	Moonset 29 h m	Moonset 30 h m	Moonset 31 h m	Moonset 1 h m
N 72	20 05	21 38	////	19 18	▬	▬	▬
N 70	19 51	21 08	////	20 16	20 20	20 40	21 42
68	19 39	20 46	22 40	20 50	21 09	21 43	22 39
66	19 30	20 29	21 58	21 15	21 40	22 18	23 12
64	19 22	20 15	21 30	21 34	22 03	22 43	23 36
62	19 15	20 04	21 10	21 50	22 22	23 03	23 56
60	19 09	19 54	20 54	22 03	22 37	23 19	24 11
N 58	19 04	19 46	20 40	22 15	22 50	23 33	24 25
56	18 59	19 39	20 29	22 25	23 01	23 44	24 36
54	18 55	19 32	20 19	22 34	23 11	23 55	24 46
52	18 51	19 27	20 11	22 42	23 20	24 04	00 04
50	18 48	19 22	20 03	22 49	23 27	24 12	00 12
45	18 41	19 11	19 48	23 04	23 44	24 30	00 30
N 40	18 35	19 02	19 36	23 16	23 58	24 44	00 44
35	18 29	18 55	19 26	23 27	24 10	00 10	00 56
30	18 25	18 49	19 18	23 36	24 20	00 20	01 06
20	18 17	18 39	19 05	23 53	24 37	00 37	01 24
N 10	18 10	18 31	18 56	24 07	00 07	00 53	01 40
0	18 04	18 25	18 49	24 20	00 20	01 07	01 55
S 10	17 58	18 19	18 43	24 33	00 33	01 21	02 10
20	17 51	18 13	18 39	24 47	00 47	01 37	02 25
30	17 44	18 08	18 36	00 11	01 03	01 54	02 43
35	17 40	18 05	18 35	00 20	01 13	02 04	02 54
40	17 35	18 03	18 34	00 29	01 24	02 16	03 06
45	17 30	18 00	18 34	00 40	01 36	02 30	03 20
S 50	17 24	17 56	18 34	00 53	01 52	02 47	03 37
52	17 21	17 55	18 34	00 59	01 59	02 55	03 45
54	17 17	17 53	18 34	01 06	02 07	03 03	03 54
56	17 14	17 52	18 35	01 14	02 16	03 13	04 05
58	17 10	17 50	18 35	01 23	02 26	03 25	04 16
S 60	17 06	17 48	18 36	01 33	02 38	03 38	04 30

Day d	SUN Eqn. of Time 00^h m s	SUN Eqn. of Time 12^h m s	SUN Mer. Pass. h m	MOON Mer. Pass. Upper h m	MOON Mer. Pass. Lower h m	MOON Age d	MOON Phase %
29	01 01	00 52	12 01	18 09	05 45	08	52
30	00 43	00 34	12 01	18 56	06 32	09	61
31	00 24	00 15	12 00	19 43	07 19	10	70

	UT	ARIES	VENUS −3·9		MARS +1·8		JUPITER −1·7		SATURN +0·4	
	d h	GHA ° ′	GHA ° ′	Dec ° ′	GHA ° ′	Dec ° ′	GHA ° ′	Dec ° ′	GHA ° ′	Dec ° ′
	1 00	340 20.9	210 59.0	N18 36.6	190 31.8	N13 32.0	139 35.8	S 7 33.0	79 49.5	S21 59.3
	01	355 23.3	225 58.4	36.0	205 32.7	31.5	154 37.9	33.2	94 51.9	59.3
	02	10 25.8	240 57.8	35.3	220 33.6	31.0	169 39.9	33.4	109 54.3	59.3
	03	25 28.3	255 57.1	. . 34.7	235 34.6	. . 30.4	184 41.9	. . 33.6	124 56.8	. . 59.4
	04	40 30.7	270 56.5	34.1	250 35.5	29.9	199 44.0	33.7	139 59.2	59.4
	05	55 33.2	285 55.9	33.4	265 36.4	29.3	214 46.0	33.9	155 01.6	59.4
	06	70 35.7	300 55.2	N18 32.8	280 37.4	N13 28.8	229 48.0	S 7 34.1	170 04.1	S21 59.4
	07	85 38.1	315 54.6	32.1	295 38.3	28.2	244 50.1	34.3	185 06.5	59.4
	08	100 40.6	330 54.0	31.5	310 39.2	27.7	259 52.1	34.5	200 08.9	59.4
F	09	115 43.0	345 53.4	. . 30.9	325 40.1	. . 27.1	274 54.1	. . 34.6	215 11.4	. . 59.4
R	10	130 45.5	0 52.7	30.2	340 41.1	26.6	289 56.2	34.8	230 13.8	59.4
I	11	145 48.0	15 52.1	29.6	355 42.0	26.0	304 58.2	35.0	245 16.2	59.4
D	12	160 50.4	30 51.5	N18 28.9	10 42.9	N13 25.5	320 00.2	S 7 35.2	260 18.7	S21 59.4
A	13	175 52.9	45 50.9	28.3	25 43.9	25.0	335 02.3	35.3	275 21.1	59.4
Y	14	190 55.4	60 50.2	27.6	40 44.8	24.4	350 04.3	35.5	290 23.5	59.5
	15	205 57.8	75 49.6	. . 27.0	55 45.7	. . 23.9	5 06.3	. . 35.7	305 26.0	. . 59.5
	16	221 00.3	90 49.0	26.3	70 46.7	23.3	20 08.4	35.9	320 28.4	59.5
	17	236 02.8	105 48.4	25.7	85 47.6	22.8	35 10.4	36.0	335 30.8	59.5
	18	251 05.2	120 47.7	N18 25.1	100 48.5	N13 22.2	50 12.4	S 7 36.2	350 33.3	S21 59.5
	19	266 07.7	135 47.1	24.4	115 49.4	21.7	65 14.5	36.4	5 35.7	59.5
	20	281 10.1	150 46.5	23.7	130 50.4	21.1	80 16.5	36.6	20 38.1	59.5
	21	296 12.6	165 45.9	. . 23.1	145 51.3	. . 20.6	95 18.5	. . 36.8	35 40.6	. . 59.5
	22	311 15.1	180 45.2	22.4	160 52.2	20.0	110 20.6	36.9	50 43.0	59.5
	23	326 17.5	195 44.6	21.8	175 53.2	19.5	125 22.6	37.1	65 45.4	59.5
	2 00	341 20.0	210 44.0	N18 21.1	190 54.1	N13 18.9	140 24.6	S 7 37.3	80 47.9	S21 59.6
	01	356 22.5	225 43.4	20.5	205 55.0	18.4	155 26.7	37.5	95 50.3	59.6
	02	11 24.9	240 42.7	19.8	220 56.0	17.8	170 28.7	37.6	110 52.7	59.6
	03	26 27.4	255 42.1	. . 19.2	235 56.9	. . 17.3	185 30.7	. . 37.8	125 55.2	. . 59.6
	04	41 29.9	270 41.5	18.5	250 57.8	16.7	200 32.8	38.0	140 57.6	59.6
	05	56 32.3	285 40.9	17.9	265 58.8	16.2	215 34.8	38.2	156 00.0	59.6
	06	71 34.8	300 40.3	N18 17.2	280 59.7	N13 15.6	230 36.8	S 7 38.4	171 02.5	S21 59.6
	07	86 37.3	315 39.6	16.5	296 00.6	15.1	245 38.9	38.5	186 04.9	59.6
S	08	101 39.7	330 39.0	15.9	311 01.6	14.5	260 40.9	38.7	201 07.3	59.6
A	09	116 42.2	345 38.4	. . 15.2	326 02.5	. . 14.0	275 42.9	. . 38.9	216 09.7	. . 59.6
T	10	131 44.6	0 37.8	14.5	341 03.4	13.4	290 45.0	39.1	231 12.2	59.7
U	11	146 47.1	15 37.1	13.9	356 04.3	12.9	305 47.0	39.2	246 14.6	59.7
R	12	161 49.6	30 36.5	N18 13.2	11 05.3	N13 12.4	320 49.0	S 7 39.4	261 17.0	S21 59.7
D	13	176 52.0	45 35.9	12.5	26 06.2	11.8	335 51.1	39.6	276 19.5	59.7
A	14	191 54.5	60 35.3	11.9	41 07.1	11.3	350 53.1	39.8	291 21.9	59.7
Y	15	206 57.0	75 34.7	. . 11.2	56 08.1	. . 10.7	5 55.1	. . 40.0	306 24.3	. . 59.7
	16	221 59.4	90 34.1	10.5	71 09.0	10.2	20 57.1	40.1	321 26.8	59.7
	17	237 01.9	105 33.4	09.9	86 09.9	09.6	35 59.2	40.3	336 29.2	59.7
	18	252 04.4	120 32.8	N18 09.2	101 10.9	N13 09.1	51 01.2	S 7 40.5	351 31.6	S21 59.7
	19	267 06.8	135 32.2	08.5	116 11.8	08.5	66 03.2	40.7	6 34.0	59.7
	20	282 09.3	150 31.6	07.9	131 12.7	08.0	81 05.3	40.8	21 36.5	59.8
	21	297 11.8	165 31.0	. . 07.2	146 13.7	. . 07.4	96 07.3	. . 41.0	36 38.9	. . 59.8
	22	312 14.2	180 30.3	06.5	161 14.6	06.8	111 09.3	41.2	51 41.3	59.8
	23	327 16.7	195 29.7	05.8	176 15.5	06.3	126 11.4	41.4	66 43.8	59.8
	3 00	342 19.1	210 29.1	N18 05.2	191 16.5	N13 05.7	141 13.4	S 7 41.6	81 46.2	S21 59.8
	01	357 21.6	225 28.5	04.5	206 17.4	05.2	156 15.4	41.7	96 48.6	59.8
	02	12 24.1	240 27.9	03.8	221 18.3	04.6	171 17.5	41.9	111 51.0	59.8
	03	27 26.5	255 27.3	. . 03.1	236 19.3	. . 04.1	186 19.5	. . 42.1	126 53.5	. . 59.8
	04	42 29.0	270 26.6	02.4	251 20.2	03.5	201 21.5	42.3	141 55.9	59.8
	05	57 31.5	285 26.0	01.8	266 21.2	03.0	216 23.5	42.4	156 58.3	59.8
	06	72 33.9	300 25.4	N18 01.1	281 22.1	N13 02.4	231 25.6	S 7 42.6	172 00.7	S21 59.9
	07	87 36.4	315 24.8	18 00.4	296 23.0	01.9	246 27.6	42.8	187 03.2	59.9
	08	102 38.9	330 24.2	17 59.7	311 24.0	01.3	261 29.6	43.0	202 05.6	59.9
S	09	117 41.3	345 23.6	. . 59.0	326 24.9	. . 00.8	276 31.7	. . 43.2	217 08.0	. . 59.9
U	10	132 43.8	0 23.0	58.4	341 25.8	13 00.2	291 33.7	43.3	232 10.4	59.9
N	11	147 46.2	15 22.3	57.7	356 26.8	12 59.7	306 35.7	43.5	247 12.9	59.9
D	12	162 48.7	30 21.7	N17 57.0	11 27.7	N12 59.1	321 37.7	S 7 43.7	262 15.3	S21 59.9
A	13	177 51.2	45 21.1	56.3	26 28.6	58.6	336 39.8	43.9	277 17.7	59.9
Y	14	192 53.6	60 20.5	55.6	41 29.6	58.0	351 41.8	44.1	292 20.1	59.9
	15	207 56.1	75 19.9	. . 54.9	56 30.5	. . 57.5	6 43.8	. . 44.2	307 22.6	21 59.9
	16	222 58.6	90 19.3	54.2	71 31.4	56.9	21 45.9	44.4	322 25.0	22 00.0
	17	238 01.0	105 18.7	53.5	86 32.4	56.4	36 47.9	44.6	337 27.4	00.0
	18	253 03.5	120 18.1	N17 52.8	101 33.3	N12 55.8	51 49.9	S 7 44.8	352 29.8	S22 00.0
	19	268 06.0	135 17.5	52.1	116 34.3	55.3	66 51.9	44.9	7 32.3	00.0
	20	283 08.4	150 16.8	51.5	131 35.2	54.7	81 54.0	45.1	22 34.7	00.0
	21	298 10.9	165 16.2	. . 50.8	146 36.1	. . 54.1	96 56.0	. . 45.3	37 37.1	. . 00.0
	22	313 13.4	180 15.6	50.1	161 37.1	53.6	111 58.0	45.5	52 39.5	00.0
	23	328 15.8	195 15.0	49.4	176 38.0	53.0	127 00.0	45.7	67 42.0	00.0
	Mer. Pass.	h m 1 14.5	v −0.6	d 0.7	v 0.9	d 0.5	v 2.0	d 0.2	v 2.4	d 0.0

STARS Name	SHA ° ′	Dec ° ′
Acamar	315 16.0	S40 13.9
Achernar	335 24.3	S57 08.7
Acrux	173 06.6	S63 11.8
Adhara	255 10.5	S28 59.7
Aldebaran	290 46.1	N16 32.5
Alioth	166 18.7	N55 52.2
Alkaid	152 57.0	N49 13.9
Al Na'ir	27 39.8	S46 52.4
Alnilam	275 43.6	S 1 11.5
Alphard	217 53.6	S 8 44.0
Alphecca	126 08.7	N26 39.7
Alpheratz	357 40.2	N29 11.3
Altair	62 05.2	N 8 55.2
Ankaa	353 12.6	S42 12.5
Antares	112 22.8	S26 28.1
Arcturus	145 53.3	N19 05.8
Atria	107 21.9	S69 03.6
Avior	234 17.3	S59 33.8
Bellatrix	278 29.0	N 6 21.8
Betelgeuse	270 58.3	N 7 24.5
Canopus	263 55.1	S52 42.2
Capella	280 30.3	N46 00.6
Deneb	49 29.1	N45 20.9
Denebola	182 31.1	N14 28.6
Diphda	348 52.8	S17 53.3
Dubhe	193 49.0	N61 39.5
Elnath	278 09.1	N28 37.1
Eltanin	90 44.6	N51 29.7
Enif	33 44.0	N 9 57.6
Fomalhaut	15 20.5	S29 31.6
Gacrux	171 58.1	S57 12.7
Gienah	175 49.7	S17 38.2
Hadar	148 44.1	S60 27.5
Hamal	327 57.3	N23 32.6
Kaus Aust.	83 39.9	S34 22.4
Kochab	137 20.7	N74 05.4
Markab	13 35.2	N15 18.1
Menkar	314 11.9	N 4 09.5
Menkent	148 04.4	S36 27.3
Miaplacidus	221 39.8	S69 47.3
Mirfak	308 36.1	N49 55.1
Nunki	75 54.6	S26 16.3
Peacock	53 14.3	S56 40.6
Pollux	243 24.5	N27 58.9
Procyon	244 57.0	N 5 10.7
Rasalhague	96 03.7	N12 33.2
Regulus	207 40.8	N11 52.9
Rigel	281 09.4	S 8 10.9
Rigil Kent.	139 48.1	S60 54.4
Sabik	102 09.2	S15 44.6
Schedar	349 36.7	N56 37.9
Shaula	96 17.9	S37 06.9
Sirius	258 31.4	S16 44.4
Spica	158 28.5	S11 15.0
Suhail	222 50.7	S43 30.1
Vega	80 36.8	N38 48.4
Zuben'ubi	137 02.4	S16 06.7

	SHA ° ′	Mer. Pass. h m
Venus	229 24.0	9 57
Mars	209 34.1	11 16
Jupiter	159 04.6	14 36
Saturn	99 27.9	18 34

	UT (d h)	SUN GHA (° ′)	SUN Dec (° ′)	MOON GHA (° ′)	v (′)	MOON Dec (° ′)	d (′)	HP (′)
FRIDAY	1 00	179 58.7	N 8 17.1	62 06.1	11.8	S19 23.4	0.1	54.4
	01	194 58.9	16.2	76 36.9	11.8	19 23.5	0.1	54.4
	02	209 59.1	15.3	91 07.7	11.7	19 23.6	0.1	54.4
	03	224 59.3	. . 14.4	105 38.4	11.8	19 23.5	0.1	54.5
	04	239 59.5	13.5	120 09.2	11.7	19 23.4	0.2	54.5
	05	254 59.7	12.6	134 39.9	11.7	19 23.2	0.4	54.5
	06	269 59.9	N 8 11.7	149 10.6	11.8	S19 22.8	0.4	54.5
	07	285 00.1	10.7	163 41.4	11.6	19 22.4	0.5	54.5
	08	300 00.3	09.8	178 12.0	11.7	19 21.9	0.6	54.5
	09	315 00.5	. . 08.9	192 42.7	11.7	19 21.3	0.6	54.5
	10	330 00.7	08.0	207 13.4	11.7	19 20.7	0.8	54.5
	11	345 00.9	07.1	221 44.1	11.6	19 19.9	0.9	54.6
	12	0 01.1	N 8 06.2	236 14.7	11.6	S19 19.0	1.0	54.6
	13	15 01.3	05.3	250 45.3	11.7	19 18.0	1.0	54.6
	14	30 01.5	04.4	265 16.0	11.6	19 17.0	1.2	54.6
	15	45 01.7	. . 03.5	279 46.6	11.6	19 15.8	1.2	54.6
	16	60 01.9	02.6	294 17.2	11.6	19 14.6	1.3	54.6
	17	75 02.1	01.7	308 47.8	11.5	19 13.3	1.5	54.6
	18	90 02.3	N 8 00.7	323 18.3	11.6	S19 11.8	1.5	54.6
	19	105 02.5	7 59.8	337 48.9	11.6	19 10.3	1.6	54.7
	20	120 02.7	58.9	352 19.5	11.5	19 08.7	1.7	54.7
	21	135 02.9	. . 58.0	6 50.0	11.6	19 07.0	1.8	54.7
	22	150 03.1	57.1	21 20.6	11.5	19 05.2	1.9	54.7
	23	165 03.3	56.2	35 51.1	11.5	19 03.3	2.0	54.7
SATURDAY	2 00	180 03.5	N 7 55.3	50 21.6	11.5	S19 01.3	2.1	54.7
	01	195 03.7	54.4	64 52.1	11.5	18 59.2	2.1	54.8
	02	210 03.9	53.5	79 22.6	11.5	18 57.1	2.3	54.8
	03	225 04.1	. . 52.5	93 53.1	11.5	18 54.8	2.3	54.8
	04	240 04.3	51.6	108 23.6	11.5	18 52.5	2.5	54.8
	05	255 04.5	50.7	122 54.1	11.5	18 50.0	2.5	54.8
	06	270 04.7	N 7 49.8	137 24.6	11.5	S18 47.5	2.7	54.8
	07	285 04.9	48.9	151 55.1	11.4	18 44.8	2.7	54.9
	08	300 05.1	48.0	166 25.5	11.5	18 42.1	2.8	54.9
	09	315 05.3	. . 47.1	180 56.0	11.5	18 39.3	2.9	54.9
	10	330 05.5	46.2	195 26.5	11.4	18 36.4	3.0	54.9
	11	345 05.7	45.2	209 56.9	11.5	18 33.4	3.1	54.9
	12	0 05.9	N 7 44.3	224 27.4	11.4	S18 30.3	3.2	54.9
	13	15 06.1	43.4	238 57.8	11.4	18 27.1	3.3	55.0
	14	30 06.3	42.5	253 28.2	11.5	18 23.8	3.4	55.0
	15	45 06.5	. . 41.6	267 58.7	11.4	18 20.4	3.4	55.0
	16	60 06.7	40.7	282 29.1	11.4	18 17.0	3.6	55.0
	17	75 06.9	39.8	296 59.5	11.4	18 13.4	3.6	55.0
	18	90 07.1	N 7 38.8	311 29.9	11.5	S18 09.8	3.8	55.1
	19	105 07.3	37.9	326 00.4	11.4	18 06.0	3.8	55.1
	20	120 07.5	37.0	340 30.8	11.4	18 02.2	3.9	55.1
	21	135 07.7	. . 36.1	355 01.2	11.4	17 58.3	4.0	55.1
	22	150 08.0	35.2	9 31.6	11.4	17 54.3	4.1	55.1
	23	165 08.2	34.3	24 02.0	11.5	17 50.2	4.2	55.2
SUNDAY	3 00	180 08.4	N 7 33.3	38 32.5	11.4	S17 46.0	4.3	55.2
	01	195 08.6	32.4	53 02.9	11.4	17 41.7	4.4	55.2
	02	210 08.8	31.5	67 33.3	11.4	17 37.3	4.5	55.2
	03	225 09.0	. . 30.6	82 03.7	11.4	17 32.8	4.5	55.2
	04	240 09.2	29.7	96 34.1	11.4	17 28.3	4.7	55.3
	05	255 09.4	28.8	111 04.5	11.4	17 23.6	4.7	55.3
	06	270 09.6	N 7 27.8	125 34.9	11.4	S17 18.9	4.8	55.3
	07	285 09.8	26.9	140 05.3	11.5	17 14.1	4.9	55.3
	08	300 10.0	26.0	154 35.8	11.4	17 09.2	5.0	55.3
	09	315 10.2	. . 25.1	169 06.2	11.4	17 04.2	5.1	55.4
	10	330 10.4	24.2	183 36.6	11.4	16 59.1	5.2	55.4
	11	345 10.6	23.3	198 07.0	11.4	16 53.9	5.3	55.4
	12	0 10.8	N 7 22.3	212 37.4	11.4	S16 48.6	5.3	55.4
	13	15 11.0	21.4	227 07.8	11.5	16 43.3	5.4	55.5
	14	30 11.2	20.5	241 38.3	11.4	16 37.9	5.6	55.5
	15	45 11.4	. . 19.6	256 08.7	11.4	16 32.3	5.6	55.5
	16	60 11.6	18.7	270 39.1	11.5	16 26.7	5.7	55.5
	17	75 11.9	17.7	285 09.6	11.4	16 21.0	5.8	55.5
	18	90 12.1	N 7 16.8	299 40.0	11.4	S16 15.2	5.8	55.6
	19	105 12.3	15.9	314 10.4	11.5	16 09.4	6.0	55.6
	20	120 12.5	15.0	328 40.9	11.4	16 03.4	6.0	55.6
	21	135 12.7	. . 14.1	343 11.3	11.5	15 57.4	6.2	55.6
	22	150 12.9	13.1	357 41.8	11.4	15 51.2	6.2	55.7
	23	165 13.1	12.2	12 12.2	11.5	S15 45.0	6.2	55.7
		SD 15.9	*d* 0.9	SD 14.9		15.0		15.1

Lat. (°)	Twilight Naut. (h m)	Twilight Civil (h m)	Sunrise (h m)	Moonrise 1 (h m)	Moonrise 2 (h m)	Moonrise 3 (h m)	Moonrise 4 (h m)
N 72	////	02 39	04 07	▬	▬	20 18	20 01
N 70	00 21	03 06	04 20	19 24	19 35	19 36	19 36
68	01 41	03 25	04 30	18 28	18 54	19 08	19 17
66	02 16	03 41	04 39	17 54	18 26	18 47	19 01
64	02 41	03 53	04 46	17 29	18 04	18 30	18 49
62	03 00	04 04	04 52	17 10	17 47	18 16	18 38
60	03 15	04 13	04 58	16 54	17 33	18 04	18 29
N 58	03 27	04 20	05 02	16 41	17 21	17 53	18 20
56	03 38	04 27	05 06	16 29	17 10	17 44	18 13
54	03 47	04 33	05 10	16 19	17 01	17 36	18 07
52	03 55	04 38	05 14	16 10	16 52	17 29	18 01
50	04 02	04 43	05 17	16 02	16 45	17 23	17 56
45	04 17	04 53	05 23	15 45	16 29	17 08	17 45
N 40	04 28	05 01	05 29	15 31	16 15	16 57	17 35
35	04 37	05 08	05 33	15 19	16 04	16 47	17 27
30	04 45	05 13	05 38	15 08	15 54	16 38	17 20
20	04 56	05 22	05 45	14 50	15 37	16 23	17 08
N 10	05 05	05 29	05 51	14 35	15 23	16 10	16 57
0	05 11	05 35	05 56	14 20	15 09	15 58	16 47
S 10	05 16	05 41	06 02	14 05	14 55	15 45	16 36
20	05 20	05 45	06 08	13 50	14 40	15 32	16 26
30	05 22	05 50	06 14	13 32	14 23	15 17	16 13
35	05 23	05 52	06 18	13 21	14 13	15 08	16 06
40	05 23	05 55	06 22	13 09	14 02	14 58	15 58
45	05 23	05 57	06 26	12 55	13 49	14 46	15 48
S 50	05 22	06 00	06 32	12 38	13 32	14 32	15 36
52	05 22	06 01	06 35	12 30	13 25	14 25	15 31
54	05 21	06 02	06 37	12 21	13 16	14 18	15 25
56	05 20	06 03	06 41	12 11	13 07	14 10	15 18
58	05 19	06 04	06 44	11 59	12 56	14 00	15 11
S 60	05 18	06 06	06 48	11 46	12 43	13 49	15 02

Lat. (°)	Sunset (h m)	Twilight Civil (h m)	Twilight Naut. (h m)	Moonset 1 (h m)	Moonset 2 (h m)	Moonset 3 (h m)	Moonset 4 (h m)
N 72	19 49	21 14	////	▬	▬	▬	00 13
N 70	19 36	20 49	23 12	21 42	23 13	24 53	00 53
68	19 27	20 30	22 11	22 39	23 54	25 21	01 21
66	19 18	20 16	21 38	23 12	24 21	00 21	01 41
64	19 11	20 03	21 15	23 36	24 42	00 42	01 58
62	19 05	19 53	20 56	23 56	24 59	00 59	02 11
60	19 00	19 45	20 42	24 11	00 11	01 13	02 23
N 58	18 56	19 37	20 30	24 25	00 25	01 25	02 33
56	18 52	19 31	20 19	24 36	00 36	01 36	02 41
54	18 48	19 25	20 10	24 46	00 46	01 45	02 49
52	18 45	19 20	20 03	00 04	00 55	01 53	02 56
50	18 42	19 15	19 56	00 12	01 03	02 00	03 02
45	18 35	19 05	19 41	00 30	01 20	02 16	03 15
N 40	18 30	18 57	19 30	00 44	01 34	02 28	03 26
35	18 25	18 51	19 21	00 56	01 46	02 39	03 36
30	18 21	18 45	19 14	01 06	01 56	02 49	03 44
20	18 14	18 37	19 03	01 24	02 14	03 05	03 58
N 10	18 08	18 30	18 54	01 40	02 29	03 19	04 10
0	18 03	18 24	18 48	01 55	02 44	03 32	04 21
S 10	17 58	18 19	18 43	02 10	02 58	03 46	04 33
20	17 52	18 14	18 40	02 25	03 13	04 00	04 45
30	17 46	18 10	18 37	02 43	03 31	04 16	04 58
35	17 42	18 07	18 37	02 54	03 41	04 25	05 06
40	17 38	18 05	18 37	03 06	03 52	04 35	05 15
45	17 33	18 03	18 37	03 20	04 06	04 48	05 26
S 50	17 28	18 00	18 38	03 37	04 23	05 03	05 38
52	17 25	17 59	18 38	03 45	04 30	05 10	05 44
54	17 23	17 58	18 39	03 54	04 39	05 17	05 50
56	17 20	17 57	18 40	04 05	04 49	05 26	05 58
58	17 16	17 56	18 41	04 16	05 00	05 36	06 06
S 60	17 13	17 55	18 43	04 30	05 13	05 47	06 15

Day (d)	SUN Eqn. of Time 00ʰ (m s)	SUN Eqn. of Time 12ʰ (m s)	SUN Mer. Pass. (h m)	MOON Mer. Pass. Upper (h m)	MOON Mer. Pass. Lower (h m)	MOON Age (d)	MOON Phase (%)
1	00 06	00 04	12 00	20 32	08 07	11	78
2	00 14	00 23	12 00	21 21	08 56	12	86
3	00 33	00 43	11 59	22 10	09 45	13	92

	UT	ARIES	VENUS −3·9		MARS +1·8		JUPITER −1·7		SATURN +0·4	
		GHA	GHA	Dec	GHA	Dec	GHA	Dec	GHA	Dec
	d h	° ′	° ′	° ′	° ′	° ′	° ′	° ′	° ′	° ′
	4 00	343 18.3	210 14.4	N17 48.7	191 38.9	N12 52.5	142 02.1	S 7 45.8	82 44.4	S22 00.0
	01	358 20.7	225 13.8	48.0	206 39.9	51.9	157 04.1	46.0	97 46.8	00.0
	02	13 23.2	240 13.2	47.3	221 40.8	51.4	172 06.1	46.2	112 49.2	00.1
	03	28 25.7	255 12.6	. . 46.6	236 41.7	. . 50.8	187 08.2	. . 46.4	127 51.7	. . 00.1
	04	43 28.1	270 12.0	45.9	251 42.7	50.3	202 10.2	46.6	142 54.1	00.1
	05	58 30.6	285 11.4	45.2	266 43.6	49.7	217 12.2	46.7	157 56.5	00.1
	06	73 33.1	300 10.7	N17 44.5	281 44.6	N12 49.2	232 14.2	S 7 46.9	172 58.9	S22 00.1
	07	88 35.5	315 10.1	43.8	296 45.5	48.6	247 16.3	47.1	188 01.3	00.1
	08	103 38.0	330 09.5	43.1	311 46.4	48.0	262 18.3	47.3	203 03.8	00.1
M	09	118 40.5	345 08.9	. . 42.4	326 47.4	. . 47.5	277 20.3	. . 47.5	218 06.2	. . 00.1
O	10	133 42.9	0 08.3	41.7	341 48.3	46.9	292 22.3	47.6	233 08.6	00.1
N	11	148 45.4	15 07.7	40.9	356 49.2	46.4	307 24.4	47.8	248 11.0	00.1
D	12	163 47.9	30 07.1	N17 40.2	11 50.2	N12 45.8	322 26.4	S 7 48.0	263 13.5	S22 00.2
A	13	178 50.3	45 06.5	39.5	26 51.1	45.3	337 28.4	48.2	278 15.9	00.2
Y	14	193 52.8	60 05.9	38.8	41 52.1	44.7	352 30.4	48.3	293 18.3	00.2
	15	208 55.2	75 05.3	. . 38.1	56 53.0	. . 44.2	7 32.5	. . 48.5	308 20.7	. . 00.2
	16	223 57.7	90 04.7	37.4	71 53.9	43.6	22 34.5	48.7	323 23.1	00.2
	17	239 00.2	105 04.1	36.7	86 54.9	43.0	37 36.5	48.9	338 25.6	00.2
	18	254 02.6	120 03.5	N17 36.0	101 55.8	N12 42.5	52 38.5	S 7 49.1	353 28.0	S22 00.2
	19	269 05.1	135 02.9	35.3	116 56.8	41.9	67 40.6	49.2	8 30.4	00.2
	20	284 07.6	150 02.3	34.5	131 57.7	41.4	82 42.6	49.4	23 32.8	00.2
	21	299 10.0	165 01.7	. . 33.8	146 58.6	. . 40.8	97 44.6	. . 49.6	38 35.2	. . 00.3
	22	314 12.5	180 01.1	33.1	161 59.6	40.3	112 46.6	49.8	53 37.7	00.3
	23	329 15.0	195 00.5	32.4	177 00.5	39.7	127 48.7	50.0	68 40.1	00.3
	5 00	344 17.4	209 59.9	N17 31.7	192 01.5	N12 39.1	142 50.7	S 7 50.1	83 42.5	S22 00.3
	01	359 19.9	224 59.3	31.0	207 02.4	38.6	157 52.7	50.3	98 44.9	00.3
	02	14 22.3	239 58.6	30.2	222 03.3	38.0	172 54.7	50.5	113 47.3	00.3
	03	29 24.8	254 58.0	. . 29.5	237 04.3	. . 37.5	187 56.8	. . 50.7	128 49.7	. . 00.3
	04	44 27.3	269 57.4	28.8	252 05.2	36.9	202 58.8	50.9	143 52.2	00.3
	05	59 29.7	284 56.8	28.1	267 06.2	36.4	218 00.8	51.0	158 54.6	00.3
	06	74 32.2	299 56.2	N17 27.3	282 07.1	N12 35.8	233 02.8	S 7 51.2	173 57.0	S22 00.3
	07	89 34.7	314 55.6	26.6	297 08.0	35.2	248 04.9	51.4	188 59.4	00.4
T	08	104 37.1	329 55.0	25.9	312 09.0	34.7	263 06.9	51.6	204 01.8	00.4
U	09	119 39.6	344 54.4	. . 25.2	327 09.9	. . 34.1	278 08.9	. . 51.8	219 04.3	. . 00.4
E	10	134 42.1	359 53.8	24.4	342 10.9	33.6	293 10.9	51.9	234 06.7	00.4
S	11	149 44.5	14 53.2	23.7	357 11.8	33.0	308 12.9	52.1	249 09.1	00.4
D	12	164 47.0	29 52.6	N17 23.0	12 12.7	N12 32.4	323 15.0	S 7 52.3	264 11.5	S22 00.4
	13	179 49.5	44 52.0	22.3	27 13.7	31.9	338 17.0	52.5	279 13.9	00.4
A	14	194 51.9	59 51.4	21.5	42 14.6	31.3	353 19.0	52.7	294 16.3	00.4
Y	15	209 54.4	74 50.8	. . 20.8	57 15.6	. . 30.8	8 21.0	. . 52.8	309 18.8	. . 00.4
	16	224 56.8	89 50.3	20.1	72 16.5	30.2	23 23.1	53.0	324 21.2	00.5
	17	239 59.3	104 49.7	19.3	87 17.5	29.6	38 25.1	53.2	339 23.6	00.5
	18	255 01.8	119 49.1	N17 18.6	102 18.4	N12 29.1	53 27.1	S 7 53.4	354 26.0	S22 00.5
	19	270 04.2	134 48.5	17.9	117 19.3	28.5	68 29.1	53.6	9 28.4	00.5
	20	285 06.7	149 47.9	17.1	132 20.3	28.0	83 31.1	53.7	24 30.8	00.5
	21	300 09.2	164 47.3	. . 16.4	147 21.2	. . 27.4	98 33.2	. . 53.9	39 33.2	. . 00.5
	22	315 11.6	179 46.7	15.7	162 22.2	26.8	113 35.2	54.1	54 35.7	00.5
	23	330 14.1	194 46.1	14.9	177 23.1	26.3	128 37.2	54.3	69 38.1	00.5
	6 00	345 16.6	209 45.5	N17 14.2	192 24.1	N12 25.7	143 39.2	S 7 54.5	84 40.5	S22 00.5
	01	0 19.0	224 44.9	13.4	207 25.0	25.2	158 41.3	54.6	99 42.9	00.6
	02	15 21.5	239 44.3	12.7	222 25.9	24.6	173 43.3	54.8	114 45.3	00.6
	03	30 24.0	254 43.7	. . 12.0	237 26.9	. . 24.0	188 45.3	. . 55.0	129 47.7	. . 00.6
	04	45 26.4	269 43.1	11.2	252 27.8	23.5	203 47.3	55.2	144 50.1	00.6
	05	60 28.9	284 42.5	10.5	267 28.8	22.9	218 49.3	55.4	159 52.6	00.6
	06	75 31.3	299 41.9	N17 09.7	282 29.7	N12 22.4	233 51.4	S 7 55.6	174 55.0	S22 00.6
W	07	90 33.8	314 41.3	09.0	297 30.7	21.8	248 53.4	55.7	189 57.4	00.6
E	08	105 36.3	329 40.7	08.2	312 31.6	21.2	263 55.4	55.9	204 59.8	00.6
D	09	120 38.7	344 40.1	. . 07.5	327 32.5	. . 20.7	278 57.4	. . 56.1	220 02.2	. . 00.6
N	10	135 41.2	359 39.5	06.7	342 33.5	20.1	293 59.4	56.3	235 04.6	00.6
E	11	150 43.7	14 38.9	06.0	357 34.4	19.6	309 01.5	56.5	250 07.0	00.7
S	12	165 46.1	29 38.4	N17 05.2	12 35.4	N12 19.0	324 03.5	S 7 56.6	265 09.5	S22 00.7
	13	180 48.6	44 37.8	04.5	27 36.3	18.4	339 05.5	56.8	280 11.9	00.7
D	14	195 51.1	59 37.2	03.7	42 37.3	17.9	354 07.5	57.0	295 14.3	00.7
A	15	210 53.5	74 36.6	. . 03.0	57 38.2	. . 17.3	9 09.5	. . 57.2	310 16.7	. . 00.7
Y	16	225 56.0	89 36.0	02.2	72 39.2	16.7	24 11.6	57.4	325 19.1	00.7
	17	240 58.4	104 35.4	01.5	87 40.1	16.2	39 13.6	57.5	340 21.5	00.7
	18	256 00.9	119 34.8	N17 00.7	102 41.0	N12 15.6	54 15.6	S 7 57.7	355 23.9	S22 00.7
	19	271 03.4	134 34.2	17 00.0	117 42.0	15.1	69 17.6	57.9	10 26.3	00.7
	20	286 05.8	149 33.6	16 59.2	132 42.9	14.5	84 19.6	58.1	25 28.7	00.8
	21	301 08.3	164 33.0	. . 58.5	147 43.9	. . 13.9	99 21.7	. . 58.3	40 31.2	. . 00.8
	22	316 10.8	179 32.5	57.7	162 44.8	13.4	114 23.7	58.4	55 33.6	00.8
	23	331 13.2	194 31.9	56.9	177 45.8	12.8	129 25.7	58.6	70 36.0	00.8
	Mer. Pass.	h m 1 02.7	*v* −0.6	*d* 0.7	*v* 0.9	*d* 0.6	*v* 2.0	*d* 0.2	*v* 2.4	*d* 0.0

STARS

Name	SHA	Dec
	° ′	° ′
Acamar	315 16.0	S40 13.9
Achernar	335 24.3	S57 08.7
Acrux	173 06.6	S63 11.8
Adhara	255 10.5	S28 59.7
Aldebaran	290 46.1	N16 32.5
Alioth	166 18.7	N55 52.1
Alkaid	152 57.0	N49 13.9
Al Na'ir	27 39.8	S46 52.4
Alnilam	275 43.5	S 1 11.5
Alphard	217 53.6	S 8 44.0
Alphecca	126 08.7	N26 39.7
Alpheratz	357 40.2	N29 11.3
Altair	62 05.2	N 8 55.2
Ankaa	353 12.5	S42 12.5
Antares	112 22.8	S26 28.1
Arcturus	145 53.4	N19 05.8
Atria	107 21.9	S69 03.6
Avior	234 17.3	S59 33.8
Bellatrix	278 29.0	N 6 21.8
Betelgeuse	270 58.3	N 7 24.5
Canopus	263 55.1	S52 42.2
Capella	280 30.3	N46 00.6
Deneb	49 29.1	N45 20.9
Denebola	182 31.1	N14 28.6
Diphda	348 52.8	S17 53.3
Dubhe	193 49.0	N61 39.4
Elnath	278 09.1	N28 37.1
Eltanin	90 44.7	N51 29.7
Enif	33 44.0	N 9 57.6
Fomalhaut	15 20.5	S29 31.6
Gacrux	171 58.2	S57 12.7
Gienah	175 49.7	S17 38.2
Hadar	148 44.2	S60 27.5
Hamal	327 57.3	N23 32.6
Kaus Aust.	83 39.9	S34 22.4
Kochab	137 20.8	N74 05.4
Markab	13 35.2	N15 18.1
Menkar	314 11.9	N 4 09.5
Menkent	148 04.4	S36 27.3
Miaplacidus	221 39.8	S69 47.3
Mirfak	308 36.0	N49 55.1
Nunki	75 54.6	S26 16.3
Peacock	53 14.3	S56 40.6
Pollux	243 24.5	N27 58.9
Procyon	244 57.0	N 5 10.7
Rasalhague	96 03.7	N12 33.2
Regulus	207 40.8	N11 52.9
Rigel	281 09.4	S 8 10.9
Rigil Kent.	139 48.1	S60 54.4
Sabik	102 09.2	S15 44.6
Schedar	349 36.7	N56 37.9
Shaula	96 18.0	S37 06.9
Sirius	258 31.4	S16 44.4
Spica	158 28.5	S11 15.0
Suhail	222 50.7	S43 30.1
Vega	80 36.8	N38 48.4
Zuben'ubi	137 02.4	S16 06.7

	SHA	Mer. Pass.
	° ′	h m
Venus	225 42.4	10 00
Mars	207 44.0	11 11
Jupiter	158 33.3	14 27
Saturn	99 25.1	18 22

UT	SUN GHA	SUN Dec	MOON GHA	v	MOON Dec	d	HP
d h	° ′	° ′	° ′	′	° ′	′	′
4 00	180 13.3	N 7 11.3	26 42.7	11.4	S15 38.8	6.4	55.7
01	195 13.5	10.4	41 13.1	11.5	15 32.4	6.5	55.7
02	210 13.7	09.4	55 43.6	11.5	15 25.9	6.5	55.8
03	225 13.9	. . 08.5	70 14.1	11.4	15 19.4	6.6	55.8
04	240 14.1	07.6	84 44.5	11.5	15 12.8	6.7	55.8
05	255 14.3	06.7	99 15.0	11.5	15 06.1	6.8	55.8
06	270 14.5	N 7 05.8	113 45.5	11.5	S14 59.3	6.9	55.8
07	285 14.8	04.8	128 16.0	11.5	14 52.4	6.9	55.9
M 08	300 15.0	03.9	142 46.5	11.5	14 45.5	7.1	55.9
O 09	315 15.2	. . 03.0	157 17.0	11.5	14 38.4	7.1	55.9
N 10	330 15.4	02.1	171 47.5	11.5	14 31.3	7.1	55.9
D 11	345 15.6	01.1	186 18.0	11.5	14 24.2	7.3	56.0
A 12	0 15.8	N 7 00.2	200 48.5	11.5	S14 16.9	7.3	56.0
Y 13	15 16.0	6 59.3	215 19.0	11.5	14 09.6	7.5	56.0
14	30 16.2	58.4	229 49.5	11.6	14 02.1	7.5	56.0
15	45 16.4	. . 57.4	244 20.1	11.5	13 54.6	7.5	56.1
16	60 16.6	56.5	258 50.6	11.5	13 47.1	7.7	56.1
17	75 16.8	55.6	273 21.1	11.6	13 39.4	7.7	56.1
18	90 17.0	N 6 54.7	287 51.7	11.5	S13 31.7	7.8	56.1
19	105 17.3	53.7	302 22.2	11.6	13 23.9	7.9	56.2
20	120 17.5	52.8	316 52.8	11.6	13 16.0	7.9	56.2
21	135 17.7	. . 51.9	331 23.4	11.5	13 08.1	8.0	56.2
22	150 17.9	51.0	345 53.9	11.6	13 00.1	8.1	56.2
23	165 18.1	50.0	0 24.5	11.6	12 52.0	8.2	56.3
5 00	180 18.3	N 6 49.1	14 55.1	11.6	S12 43.8	8.2	56.3
01	195 18.5	48.2	29 25.7	11.5	12 35.6	8.3	56.3
02	210 18.7	47.3	43 56.2	11.6	12 27.3	8.4	56.3
03	225 18.9	. . 46.3	58 26.8	11.6	12 18.9	8.4	56.4
04	240 19.1	45.4	72 57.4	11.6	12 10.5	8.5	56.4
05	255 19.3	44.5	87 28.0	11.6	12 02.0	8.6	56.4
06	270 19.6	N 6 43.6	101 58.6	11.6	S11 53.4	8.6	56.4
07	285 19.8	42.6	116 29.2	11.7	11 44.8	8.8	56.5
T 08	300 20.0	41.7	130 59.9	11.6	11 36.0	8.7	56.5
U 09	315 20.2	. . 40.8	145 30.5	11.6	11 27.3	8.9	56.5
E 10	330 20.4	39.8	160 01.1	11.6	11 18.4	8.9	56.5
S 11	345 20.6	38.9	174 31.7	11.7	11 09.5	9.0	56.6
D 12	0 20.8	N 6 38.0	189 02.4	11.6	S11 00.5	9.0	56.6
A 13	15 21.0	37.1	203 33.0	11.6	10 51.5	9.1	56.6
Y 14	30 21.2	36.1	218 03.6	11.7	10 42.4	9.2	56.6
15	45 21.5	. . 35.2	232 34.3	11.6	10 33.2	9.2	56.7
16	60 21.7	34.3	247 04.9	11.7	10 24.0	9.3	56.7
17	75 21.9	33.3	261 35.6	11.6	10 14.7	9.3	56.7
18	90 22.1	N 6 32.4	276 06.2	11.7	S10 05.4	9.4	56.7
19	105 22.3	31.5	290 36.9	11.6	9 56.0	9.5	56.8
20	120 22.5	30.6	305 07.5	11.7	9 46.5	9.5	56.8
21	135 22.7	. . 29.6	319 38.2	11.7	9 37.0	9.6	56.8
22	150 22.9	28.7	334 08.9	11.6	9 27.4	9.6	56.8
23	165 23.1	27.8	348 39.5	11.7	9 17.8	9.7	56.9
6 00	180 23.4	N 6 26.8	3 10.2	11.7	S 9 08.1	9.7	56.9
01	195 23.6	25.9	17 40.9	11.6	8 58.4	9.8	56.9
02	210 23.8	25.0	32 11.5	11.7	8 48.6	9.9	56.9
03	225 24.0	. . 24.0	46 42.2	11.7	8 38.7	9.9	56.9
04	240 24.2	23.1	61 12.9	11.6	8 28.8	9.9	57.0
05	255 24.4	22.2	75 43.5	11.7	8 18.9	10.0	57.0
06	270 24.6	N 6 21.3	90 14.2	11.7	S 8 08.9	10.1	57.0
W 07	285 24.8	20.3	104 44.9	11.6	7 58.8	10.1	57.0
E 08	300 25.1	19.4	119 15.5	11.7	7 48.7	10.1	57.1
D 09	315 25.3	. . 18.5	133 46.2	11.7	7 38.6	10.2	57.1
N 10	330 25.5	17.5	148 16.9	11.6	7 28.4	10.3	57.1
E 11	345 25.7	16.6	162 47.5	11.7	7 18.1	10.3	57.1
S 12	0 25.9	N 6 15.7	177 18.2	11.7	S 7 07.8	10.3	57.2
D 13	15 26.1	14.7	191 48.9	11.6	6 57.5	10.4	57.2
A 14	30 26.3	13.8	206 19.5	11.7	6 47.1	10.4	57.2
Y 15	45 26.5	. . 12.9	220 50.2	11.6	6 36.7	10.5	57.2
16	60 26.8	11.9	235 20.8	11.7	6 26.2	10.5	57.3
17	75 27.0	11.0	249 51.5	11.6	6 15.7	10.5	57.3
18	90 27.2	N 6 10.1	264 22.1	11.7	S 6 05.2	10.6	57.3
19	105 27.4	09.1	278 52.8	11.6	5 54.6	10.6	57.3
20	120 27.6	08.2	293 23.4	11.6	5 44.0	10.7	57.4
21	135 27.8	. . 07.3	307 54.0	11.7	5 33.3	10.7	57.4
22	150 28.0	06.3	322 24.7	11.6	5 22.6	10.7	57.4
23	165 28.3	05.4	336 55.3	11.6	S 5 11.9	10.8	57.4
	SD 15.9	d 0.9	SD 15.3		15.4		15.6

Lat.	Twilight Naut.	Twilight Civil	Sunrise	Moonrise 4	Moonrise 5	Moonrise 6	Moonrise 7
°	h m	h m	h m	h m	h m	h m	h m
N 72	////	02 59	04 21	20 01	19 50	19 40	19 32
N 70	01 19	03 21	04 32	19 36	19 34	19 32	19 30
68	02 04	03 38	04 41	19 17	19 22	19 25	19 28
66	02 33	03 52	04 48	19 01	19 12	19 20	19 27
64	02 54	04 03	04 55	18 49	19 03	19 15	19 26
62	03 11	04 13	05 00	18 38	18 56	19 11	19 24
60	03 24	04 21	05 05	18 29	18 49	19 07	19 23
N 58	03 36	04 27	05 09	18 20	18 43	19 04	19 23
56	03 45	04 33	05 12	18 13	18 38	19 01	19 22
54	03 54	04 39	05 15	18 07	18 34	18 58	19 21
52	04 01	04 43	05 18	18 01	18 30	18 56	19 21
50	04 07	04 48	05 21	17 56	18 26	18 54	19 20
45	04 21	04 57	05 27	17 45	18 18	18 49	19 19
N 40	04 31	05 04	05 32	17 35	18 11	18 45	19 18
35	04 40	05 10	05 36	17 27	18 05	18 41	19 17
30	04 46	05 15	05 39	17 20	18 00	18 38	19 16
20	04 57	05 23	05 45	17 08	17 51	18 33	19 15
N 10	05 05	05 29	05 51	16 57	17 43	18 28	19 14
0	05 10	05 35	05 55	16 47	17 35	18 24	19 13
S 10	05 14	05 39	06 00	16 36	17 28	18 19	19 12
20	05 17	05 43	06 05	16 26	17 20	18 15	19 10
30	05 19	05 46	06 10	16 13	17 11	18 09	19 09
35	05 19	05 48	06 14	16 06	17 05	18 06	19 08
40	05 19	05 50	06 17	15 58	16 59	18 03	19 08
45	05 18	05 52	06 21	15 48	16 52	17 59	19 07
S 50	05 16	05 53	06 26	15 36	16 44	17 54	19 05
52	05 15	05 54	06 28	15 31	16 40	17 52	19 05
54	05 14	05 55	06 30	15 25	16 36	17 49	19 04
56	05 13	05 56	06 33	15 18	16 31	17 46	19 04
58	05 11	05 56	06 36	15 11	16 26	17 43	19 03
S 60	05 09	05 57	06 39	15 02	16 20	17 40	19 02

Lat.	Sunset	Twilight Civil	Twilight Naut.	Moonset 4	Moonset 5	Moonset 6	Moonset 7
°	h m	h m	h m	h m	h m	h m	h m
N 72	19 33	20 53	////	00 13	02 12	04 04	05 55
N 70	19 22	20 32	22 28	00 53	02 35	04 18	06 01
68	19 14	20 16	21 47	01 21	02 53	04 29	06 06
66	19 07	20 02	21 20	01 41	03 08	04 38	06 10
64	19 01	19 52	21 00	01 58	03 20	04 45	06 13
62	18 56	19 43	20 44	02 11	03 30	04 52	06 16
60	18 51	19 35	20 31	02 23	03 38	04 57	06 19
N 58	18 47	19 28	20 20	02 33	03 46	05 02	06 21
56	18 44	19 22	20 10	02 41	03 52	05 06	06 23
54	18 41	19 17	20 02	02 49	03 58	05 10	06 25
52	18 38	19 12	19 55	02 56	04 03	05 14	06 26
50	18 35	19 08	19 48	03 02	04 08	05 17	06 28
45	18 30	19 00	19 35	03 15	04 18	05 24	06 31
N 40	18 25	18 52	19 25	03 26	04 27	05 30	06 34
35	18 21	18 47	19 17	03 36	04 34	05 34	06 36
30	18 18	18 42	19 10	03 44	04 41	05 39	06 38
20	18 12	18 34	19 00	03 58	04 52	05 46	06 41
N 10	18 07	18 28	18 52	04 10	05 01	05 52	06 44
0	18 02	18 23	18 47	04 21	05 10	05 58	06 47
S 10	17 57	18 18	18 43	04 33	05 19	06 04	06 50
20	17 53	18 15	18 40	04 45	05 28	06 11	06 53
30	17 47	18 11	18 39	04 58	05 39	06 18	06 56
35	17 44	18 10	18 39	05 06	05 45	06 22	06 58
40	17 41	18 08	18 39	05 15	05 52	06 27	07 00
45	17 37	18 06	18 40	05 26	06 00	06 32	07 02
S 50	17 32	18 05	18 42	05 38	06 10	06 38	07 05
52	17 30	18 04	18 43	05 44	06 14	06 41	07 06
54	17 28	18 03	18 44	05 50	06 19	06 44	07 08
56	17 25	18 03	18 46	05 58	06 24	06 48	07 09
58	17 23	18 02	18 47	06 06	06 30	06 52	07 11
S 60	17 19	18 01	18 49	06 15	06 37	06 56	07 13

Day	SUN Eqn. of Time 00^h	SUN Eqn. of Time 12^h	SUN Mer. Pass.	MOON Mer. Pass. Upper	MOON Mer. Pass. Lower	MOON Age	MOON Phase
d	m s	m s	h m	h m	h m	d %	
4	00 53	01 03	11 59	22 58	10 34	14 97	○
5	01 13	01 23	11 59	23 47	11 23	15 99	
6	01 33	01 43	11 58	24 35	12 11	16 100	

UT d h	ARIES GHA	VENUS −3·9 GHA	VENUS Dec	MARS +1·8 GHA	MARS Dec	JUPITER −1·7 GHA	JUPITER Dec	SATURN +0·4 GHA	SATURN Dec
	° ′	° ′	° ′	° ′	° ′	° ′	° ′	° ′	° ′
7 00 (THURSDAY)	346 15.7	209 31.3	N16 56.2	192 46.7	N12 12.2	144 27.7	S 7 58.8	85 38.4	S22 00.8
01	1 18.2	224 30.7	55.4	207 47.7	11.7	159 29.7	59.0	100 40.8	00.8
02	16 20.6	239 30.1	54.7	222 48.6	11.1	174 31.8	59.2	115 43.2	00.8
03	31 23.1	254 29.5	. . 53.9	237 49.6	. . 10.6	189 33.8	. . 59.4	130 45.6	. . 00.8
04	46 25.6	269 28.9	53.1	252 50.5	10.0	204 35.8	59.5	145 48.0	00.8
05	61 28.0	284 28.3	52.4	267 51.4	09.4	219 37.8	59.7	160 50.4	00.9
06	76 30.5	299 27.8	N16 51.6	282 52.4	N12 08.9	234 39.8	S 7 59.9	175 52.8	S22 00.9
07	91 32.9	314 27.2	50.8	297 53.3	08.3	249 41.8	8 00.1	190 55.3	00.9
08	106 35.4	329 26.6	50.1	312 54.3	07.7	264 43.9	00.3	205 57.7	00.9
09	121 37.9	344 26.0	. . 49.3	327 55.2	. . 07.2	279 45.9	. . 00.4	221 00.1	. . 00.9
10	136 40.3	359 25.4	48.5	342 56.2	06.6	294 47.9	00.6	236 02.5	00.9
11	151 42.8	14 24.8	47.8	357 57.1	06.0	309 49.9	00.8	251 04.9	00.9
12	166 45.3	29 24.2	N16 47.0	12 58.1	N12 05.5	324 51.9	S 8 01.0	266 07.3	S22 00.9
13	181 47.7	44 23.7	46.2	27 59.0	04.9	339 53.9	01.2	281 09.7	00.9
14	196 50.2	59 23.1	45.5	43 00.0	04.3	354 56.0	01.3	296 12.1	01.0
15	211 52.7	74 22.5	. . 44.7	58 00.9	. . 03.8	9 58.0	. . 01.5	311 14.5	. . 01.0
16	226 55.1	89 21.9	43.9	73 01.9	03.2	25 00.0	01.7	326 16.9	01.0
17	241 57.6	104 21.3	43.1	88 02.8	02.6	40 02.0	01.9	341 19.3	01.0
18	257 00.0	119 20.7	N16 42.4	103 03.8	N12 02.1	55 04.0	S 8 02.1	356 21.7	S22 01.0
19	272 02.5	134 20.2	41.6	118 04.7	01.5	70 06.1	02.3	11 24.1	01.0
20	287 05.0	149 19.6	40.8	133 05.6	00.9	85 08.1	02.4	26 26.6	01.0
21	302 07.4	164 19.0	. . 40.0	148 06.6	12 00.4	100 10.1	. . 02.6	41 29.0	. . 01.0
22	317 09.9	179 18.4	39.3	163 07.5	11 59.8	115 12.1	02.8	56 31.4	01.0
23	332 12.4	194 17.8	38.5	178 08.5	59.2	130 14.1	03.0	71 33.8	01.1
8 00 (FRIDAY)	347 14.8	209 17.2	N16 37.7	193 09.4	N11 58.7	145 16.1	S 8 03.2	86 36.2	S22 01.1
01	2 17.3	224 16.7	36.9	208 10.4	58.1	160 18.1	03.3	101 38.6	01.1
02	17 19.8	239 16.1	36.1	223 11.3	57.5	175 20.2	03.5	116 41.0	01.1
03	32 22.2	254 15.5	. . 35.4	238 12.3	. . 57.0	190 22.2	. . 03.7	131 43.4	. . 01.1
04	47 24.7	269 14.9	34.6	253 13.2	56.4	205 24.2	03.9	146 45.8	01.1
05	62 27.2	284 14.3	33.8	268 14.2	55.8	220 26.2	04.1	161 48.2	01.1
06	77 29.6	299 13.8	N16 33.0	283 15.1	N11 55.3	235 28.2	S 8 04.3	176 50.6	S22 01.1
07	92 32.1	314 13.2	32.2	298 16.1	54.7	250 30.2	04.4	191 53.0	01.1
08	107 34.5	329 12.6	31.4	313 17.0	54.1	265 32.3	04.6	206 55.4	01.2
09	122 37.0	344 12.0	. . 30.7	328 18.0	. . 53.6	280 34.3	. . 04.8	221 57.8	. . 01.2
10	137 39.5	359 11.5	29.9	343 18.9	53.0	295 36.3	05.0	237 00.2	01.2
11	152 41.9	14 10.9	29.1	358 19.9	52.4	310 38.3	05.2	252 02.6	01.2
12	167 44.4	29 10.3	N16 28.3	13 20.8	N11 51.9	325 40.3	S 8 05.3	267 05.0	S22 01.2
13	182 46.9	44 09.7	27.5	28 21.8	51.3	340 42.3	05.5	282 07.4	01.2
14	197 49.3	59 09.1	26.7	43 22.7	50.7	355 44.3	05.7	297 09.8	01.2
15	212 51.8	74 08.6	. . 25.9	58 23.7	. . 50.2	10 46.4	. . 05.9	312 12.2	. . 01.2
16	227 54.3	89 08.0	25.1	73 24.6	49.6	25 48.4	06.1	327 14.7	01.2
17	242 56.7	104 07.4	24.3	88 25.6	49.0	40 50.4	06.3	342 17.1	01.3
18	257 59.2	119 06.8	N16 23.5	103 26.5	N11 48.5	55 52.4	S 8 06.4	357 19.5	S22 01.3
19	273 01.6	134 06.3	22.7	118 27.5	47.9	70 54.4	06.6	12 21.9	01.3
20	288 04.1	149 05.7	21.9	133 28.4	47.3	85 56.4	06.8	27 24.3	01.3
21	303 06.6	164 05.1	. . 21.2	148 29.4	. . 46.8	100 58.4	. . 07.0	42 26.7	. . 01.3
22	318 09.0	179 04.5	20.4	163 30.3	46.2	116 00.5	07.2	57 29.1	01.3
23	333 11.5	194 04.0	19.6	178 31.3	45.6	131 02.5	07.4	72 31.5	01.3
9 00 (SATURDAY)	348 14.0	209 03.4	N16 18.8	193 32.2	N11 45.1	146 04.5	S 8 07.5	87 33.9	S22 01.3
01	3 16.4	224 02.8	18.0	208 33.2	44.5	161 06.5	07.7	102 36.3	01.4
02	18 18.9	239 02.2	17.2	223 34.1	43.9	176 08.5	07.9	117 38.7	01.4
03	33 21.4	254 01.7	. . 16.4	238 35.1	. . 43.3	191 10.5	. . 08.1	132 41.1	. . 01.4
04	48 23.8	269 01.1	15.6	253 36.0	42.8	206 12.5	08.3	147 43.5	01.4
05	63 26.3	284 00.5	14.8	268 37.0	42.2	221 14.5	08.4	162 45.9	01.4
06	78 28.8	299 00.0	N16 13.9	283 37.9	N11 41.6	236 16.6	S 8 08.6	177 48.3	S22 01.4
07	93 31.2	313 59.4	13.1	298 38.9	41.1	251 18.6	08.8	192 50.7	01.4
08	108 33.7	328 58.8	12.3	313 39.8	40.5	266 20.6	09.0	207 53.1	01.4
09	123 36.1	343 58.2	. . 11.5	328 40.8	. . 39.9	281 22.6	. . 09.2	222 55.5	. . 01.4
10	138 38.6	358 57.7	10.7	343 41.8	39.4	296 24.6	09.4	237 57.9	01.5
11	153 41.1	13 57.1	09.9	358 42.7	38.8	311 26.6	09.5	253 00.3	01.5
12	168 43.5	28 56.5	N16 09.1	13 43.7	N11 38.2	326 28.6	S 8 09.7	268 02.7	S22 01.5
13	183 46.0	43 56.0	08.3	28 44.6	37.6	341 30.6	09.9	283 05.1	01.5
14	198 48.5	58 55.4	07.5	43 45.6	37.1	356 32.7	10.1	298 07.5	01.5
15	213 50.9	73 54.8	. . 06.7	58 46.5	. . 36.5	11 34.7	. . 10.3	313 09.9	. . 01.5
16	228 53.4	88 54.3	05.9	73 47.5	35.9	26 36.7	10.5	328 12.3	01.5
17	243 55.9	103 53.7	05.1	88 48.4	35.4	41 38.7	10.6	343 14.7	01.5
18	258 58.3	118 53.1	N16 04.2	103 49.4	N11 34.8	56 40.7	S 8 10.8	358 17.1	S22 01.5
19	274 00.8	133 52.6	03.4	118 50.3	34.2	71 42.7	11.0	13 19.5	01.6
20	289 03.2	148 52.0	02.6	133 51.3	33.6	86 44.7	11.2	28 21.9	01.6
21	304 05.7	163 51.4	. . 01.8	148 52.2	. . 33.1	101 46.7	. . 11.4	43 24.3	. . 01.6
22	319 08.2	178 50.9	01.0	163 53.2	32.5	116 48.7	11.6	58 26.7	01.6
23	334 10.6	193 50.3	00.2	178 54.1	31.9	131 50.8	11.7	73 29.1	01.6
Mer. Pass.	h m 0 50.9	*v* −0.6	*d* 0.8	*v* 0.9	*d* 0.6	*v* 2.0	*d* 0.2	*v* 2.4	*d* 0.0

STARS Name	SHA	Dec
	° ′	° ′
Acamar	315 16.0	S40 13.9
Achernar	335 24.3	S57 08.7
Acrux	173 06.6	S63 11.8
Adhara	255 10.5	S28 59.7
Aldebaran	290 46.1	N16 32.5
Alioth	166 18.7	N55 52.1
Alkaid	152 57.1	N49 13.9
Al Na'ir	27 39.8	S46 52.4
Alnilam	275 43.5	S 1 11.5
Alphard	217 53.6	S 8 44.0
Alphecca	126 08.7	N26 39.7
Alpheratz	357 40.2	N29 11.3
Altair	62 05.2	N 8 55.2
Ankaa	353 12.5	S42 12.5
Antares	112 22.8	S26 28.1
Arcturus	145 53.4	N19 05.8
Atria	107 22.0	S69 03.6
Avior	234 17.3	S59 33.8
Bellatrix	278 29.0	N 6 21.8
Betelgeuse	270 58.3	N 7 24.5
Canopus	263 55.1	S52 42.1
Capella	280 30.3	N46 00.6
Deneb	49 29.1	N45 20.9
Denebola	182 31.1	N14 28.6
Diphda	348 52.7	S17 53.3
Dubhe	193 49.0	N61 39.4
Elnath	278 09.0	N28 37.1
Eltanin	90 44.7	N51 29.7
Enif	33 44.0	N 9 57.6
Fomalhaut	15 20.5	S29 31.6
Gacrux	171 58.2	S57 12.7
Gienah	175 49.7	S17 38.2
Hadar	148 44.2	S60 27.5
Hamal	327 57.3	N23 32.6
Kaus Aust.	83 39.9	S34 22.4
Kochab	137 20.8	N74 05.4
Markab	13 35.2	N15 18.1
Menkar	314 11.9	N 4 09.5
Menkent	148 04.4	S36 27.3
Miaplacidus	221 39.8	S69 47.3
Mirfak	308 36.0	N49 55.1
Nunki	75 54.6	S26 16.3
Peacock	53 14.4	S56 40.7
Pollux	243 24.5	N27 58.9
Procyon	244 57.0	N 5 10.7
Rasalhague	96 03.8	N12 33.2
Regulus	207 40.8	N11 52.9
Rigel	281 09.3	S 8 10.9
Rigil Kent.	139 48.2	S60 54.4
Sabik	102 09.2	S15 44.6
Schedar	349 36.7	N56 37.9
Shaula	96 18.0	S37 06.9
Sirius	258 31.3	S16 44.4
Spica	158 28.5	S11 15.0
Suhail	222 50.7	S43 30.1
Vega	80 36.9	N38 48.4
Zuben'ubi	137 02.4	S16 06.7
	SHA	**Mer. Pass.**
	° ′	h m
Venus	222 02.4	10 03
Mars	205 54.6	11 07
Jupiter	158 01.3	14 17
Saturn	99 21.3	18 11

UT		SUN GHA	SUN Dec	MOON GHA	MOON v	MOON Dec	MOON d	MOON HP
d h		° ′	° ′	° ′	′	° ′	′	′
7 00		180 28.5	N 6 04.4	351 25.9	11.6	S 5 01.1	10.8	57.4
01		195 28.7	03.5	5 56.5	11.6	4 50.3	10.9	57.5
02		210 28.9	02.6	20 27.1	11.6	4 39.4	10.8	57.5
03		225 29.1	. . 01.6	34 57.7	11.6	4 28.6	10.9	57.5
04		240 29.3	6 00.7	49 28.3	11.5	4 17.7	11.0	57.5
05		255 29.5	5 59.8	63 58.8	11.6	4 06.7	10.9	57.6
06		270 29.8	N 5 58.8	78 29.4	11.6	S 3 55.8	11.0	57.6
07		285 30.0	57.9	93 00.0	11.5	3 44.8	11.0	57.6
08	T	300 30.2	57.0	107 30.5	11.5	3 33.8	11.1	57.6
09	H	315 30.4	. . 56.0	122 01.0	11.6	3 22.7	11.0	57.6
10	U	330 30.6	55.1	136 31.6	11.5	3 11.7	11.1	57.7
11	R	345 30.8	54.2	151 02.1	11.5	3 00.6	11.2	57.7
12	S	0 31.0	N 5 53.2	165 32.6	11.5	S 2 49.4	11.1	57.7
13	D	15 31.3	52.3	180 03.1	11.4	2 38.3	11.2	57.7
14	A	30 31.5	51.3	194 33.5	11.5	2 27.1	11.1	57.8
15	Y	45 31.7	. . 50.4	209 04.0	11.4	2 16.0	11.2	57.8
16		60 31.9	49.5	223 34.4	11.5	2 04.8	11.3	57.8
17		75 32.1	48.5	238 04.9	11.4	1 53.5	11.2	57.8
18		90 32.3	N 5 47.6	252 35.3	11.4	S 1 42.3	11.3	57.8
19		105 32.6	46.7	267 05.7	11.4	1 31.0	11.2	57.9
20		120 32.8	45.7	281 36.1	11.4	1 19.8	11.3	57.9
21		135 33.0	. . 44.8	296 06.5	11.3	1 08.5	11.3	57.9
22		150 33.2	43.8	310 36.8	11.4	0 57.2	11.3	57.9
23		165 33.4	42.9	325 07.2	11.3	0 45.9	11.4	57.9
8 00		180 33.6	N 5 42.0	339 37.5	11.3	S 0 34.5	11.3	58.0
01		195 33.8	41.0	354 07.8	11.3	0 23.2	11.3	58.0
02		210 34.1	40.1	8 38.1	11.2	0 11.9	11.4	58.0
03		225 34.3	. . 39.1	23 08.3	11.3	S 0 00.5	11.3	58.0
04		240 34.5	38.2	37 38.6	11.2	N 0 10.8	11.4	58.0
05		255 34.7	37.3	52 08.8	11.2	0 22.2	11.4	58.1
06		270 34.9	N 5 36.3	66 39.0	11.2	N 0 33.6	11.3	58.1
07		285 35.1	35.4	81 09.2	11.2	0 44.9	11.4	58.1
08		300 35.4	34.4	95 39.4	11.1	0 56.3	11.4	58.1
09	F	315 35.6	. . 33.5	110 09.5	11.1	1 07.7	11.4	58.1
10	R	330 35.8	32.6	124 39.6	11.1	1 19.1	11.4	58.1
11	I	345 36.0	31.6	139 09.7	11.1	1 30.5	11.3	58.2
12	D	0 36.2	N 5 30.7	153 39.8	11.0	N 1 41.8	11.4	58.2
13	A	15 36.4	29.7	168 09.8	11.0	1 53.2	11.4	58.2
14	Y	30 36.7	28.8	182 39.8	11.0	2 04.6	11.3	58.2
15		45 36.9	. . 27.9	197 09.8	11.0	2 15.9	11.4	58.2
16		60 37.1	26.9	211 39.8	10.9	2 27.3	11.4	58.3
17		75 37.3	26.0	226 09.7	10.9	2 38.7	11.3	58.3
18		90 37.5	N 5 25.0	240 39.6	10.9	N 2 50.0	11.3	58.3
19		105 37.7	24.1	255 09.5	10.9	3 01.3	11.4	58.3
20		120 38.0	23.1	269 39.4	10.8	3 12.7	11.3	58.3
21		135 38.2	. . 22.2	284 09.2	10.8	3 24.0	11.3	58.3
22		150 38.4	21.3	298 39.0	10.8	3 35.3	11.3	58.4
23		165 38.6	20.3	313 08.8	10.7	3 46.6	11.3	58.4
9 00		180 38.8	N 5 19.4	327 38.5	10.7	N 3 57.9	11.2	58.4
01		195 39.0	18.4	342 08.2	10.7	4 09.1	11.3	58.4
02		210 39.3	17.5	356 37.9	10.6	4 20.4	11.2	58.4
03		225 39.5	. . 16.5	11 07.5	10.7	4 31.6	11.2	58.4
04		240 39.7	15.6	25 37.2	10.5	4 42.8	11.2	58.5
05		255 39.9	14.7	40 06.7	10.6	4 54.0	11.1	58.5
06		270 40.1	N 5 13.7	54 36.3	10.5	N 5 05.1	11.2	58.5
07		285 40.4	12.8	69 05.8	10.5	5 16.3	11.1	58.5
08	S	300 40.6	11.8	83 35.3	10.4	5 27.4	11.1	58.5
09	A	315 40.8	. . 10.9	98 04.7	10.4	5 38.5	11.0	58.5
10	T	330 41.0	09.9	112 34.1	10.4	5 49.5	11.1	58.5
11	U	345 41.2	09.0	127 03.5	10.3	6 00.6	11.0	58.6
12	R	0 41.4	N 5 08.1	141 32.8	10.3	N 6 11.6	11.0	58.6
13	D	15 41.7	07.1	156 02.1	10.3	6 22.6	10.9	58.6
14	A	30 41.9	06.2	170 31.4	10.2	6 33.5	10.9	58.6
15	Y	45 42.1	. . 05.2	185 00.6	10.2	6 44.4	10.9	58.6
16		60 42.3	04.3	199 29.8	10.1	6 55.3	10.9	58.6
17		75 42.5	03.3	213 58.9	10.1	7 06.2	10.8	58.6
18		90 42.8	N 5 02.4	228 28.0	10.1	N 7 17.0	10.8	58.7
19		105 43.0	01.4	242 57.1	10.0	7 27.8	10.7	58.7
20		120 43.2	5 00.5	257 26.1	10.0	7 38.5	10.7	58.7
21		135 43.4	4 59.5	271 55.1	9.9	7 49.2	10.7	58.7
22		150 43.6	58.6	286 24.0	9.9	7 59.9	10.6	58.7
23		165 43.8	57.6	300 52.9	9.9	N 8 10.5	10.6	58.7
		SD 15.9	*d* 0.9	SD	15.7		15.9	16.0

Lat.	Twilight Naut.	Twilight Civil	Sunrise	Moonrise 7	Moonrise 8	Moonrise 9	Moonrise 10
°	h m	h m	h m	h m	h m	h m	h m
N 72	00 40	03 17	04 36	19 32	19 24	19 15	19 05
N 70	01 49	03 36	04 45	19 30	19 28	19 26	19 24
68	02 24	03 51	04 52	19 28	19 31	19 34	19 39
66	02 48	04 03	04 58	19 27	19 34	19 42	19 51
64	03 07	04 13	05 03	19 26	19 36	19 48	20 02
62	03 21	04 21	05 08	19 24	19 38	19 53	20 11
60	03 33	04 28	05 12	19 23	19 40	19 58	20 18
N 58	03 44	04 34	05 15	19 23	19 42	20 02	20 25
56	03 52	04 40	05 18	19 22	19 43	20 06	20 31
54	04 00	04 44	05 21	19 21	19 44	20 09	20 36
52	04 07	04 49	05 23	19 21	19 46	20 12	20 41
50	04 13	04 52	05 26	19 20	19 47	20 15	20 46
45	04 25	05 01	05 30	19 19	19 49	20 21	20 55
N 40	04 34	05 07	05 34	19 18	19 51	20 26	21 03
35	04 42	05 12	05 38	19 17	19 53	20 30	21 10
30	04 48	05 17	05 41	19 16	19 54	20 34	21 16
20	04 58	05 24	05 46	19 15	19 57	20 41	21 27
N 10	05 05	05 29	05 50	19 14	20 00	20 47	21 36
0	05 09	05 34	05 54	19 13	20 02	20 53	21 45
S 10	05 13	05 37	05 58	19 12	20 04	20 58	21 54
20	05 15	05 40	06 02	19 10	20 07	21 05	22 04
30	05 15	05 43	06 07	19 09	20 10	21 12	22 15
35	05 15	05 44	06 09	19 08	20 12	21 16	22 21
40	05 14	05 45	06 12	19 08	20 13	21 20	22 28
45	05 12	05 46	06 15	19 07	20 16	21 26	22 37
S 50	05 10	05 47	06 19	19 05	20 18	21 33	22 47
52	05 08	05 47	06 21	19 05	20 20	21 36	22 52
54	05 07	05 48	06 23	19 04	20 21	21 39	22 57
56	05 05	05 48	06 25	19 04	20 23	21 43	23 03
58	05 03	05 48	06 27	19 03	20 24	21 47	23 10
S 60	05 00	05 49	06 30	19 02	20 26	21 51	23 17

Lat.	Sunset	Twilight Civil	Twilight Naut.	Moonset 7	Moonset 8	Moonset 9	Moonset 10
°	h m	h m	h m	h m	h m	h m	h m
N 72	19 17	20 34	22 55	05 55	07 46	09 39	11 37
N 70	19 08	20 15	21 58	06 01	07 45	09 31	11 20
68	19 01	20 01	21 26	06 06	07 44	09 24	11 06
66	18 55	19 50	21 03	06 10	07 43	09 19	10 55
64	18 50	19 40	20 46	06 13	07 43	09 14	10 46
62	18 46	19 32	20 31	06 16	07 42	09 10	10 38
60	18 42	19 25	20 19	06 19	07 42	09 06	10 32
N 58	18 39	19 19	20 10	06 21	07 41	09 03	10 26
56	18 36	19 14	20 01	06 23	07 41	09 00	10 21
54	18 33	19 09	19 54	06 25	07 41	08 58	10 16
52	18 31	19 05	19 47	06 26	07 40	08 56	10 12
50	18 29	19 02	19 41	06 28	07 40	08 54	10 08
45	18 24	18 54	19 29	06 31	07 39	08 49	10 00
N 40	18 20	18 47	19 20	06 34	07 39	08 45	09 53
35	18 17	18 42	19 12	06 36	07 38	08 42	09 47
30	18 14	18 38	19 06	06 38	07 38	08 39	09 42
20	18 09	18 31	18 57	06 41	07 37	08 34	09 33
N 10	18 05	18 26	18 50	06 44	07 37	08 30	09 25
0	18 01	18 22	18 46	06 47	07 36	08 26	09 17
S 10	17 57	18 18	18 43	06 50	07 35	08 22	09 10
20	17 53	18 15	18 41	06 53	07 35	08 18	09 02
30	17 49	18 13	18 40	06 56	07 34	08 13	08 53
35	17 46	18 12	18 41	06 58	07 33	08 10	08 48
40	17 44	18 11	18 42	07 00	07 33	08 07	08 42
45	17 40	18 10	18 44	07 02	07 32	08 03	08 36
S 50	17 37	18 09	18 46	07 05	07 32	07 59	08 28
52	17 35	18 09	18 48	07 06	07 31	07 57	08 24
54	17 33	18 09	18 50	07 08	07 31	07 54	08 20
56	17 31	18 08	18 51	07 09	07 30	07 52	08 15
58	17 29	18 08	18 54	07 11	07 30	07 49	08 11
S 60	17 26	18 08	18 56	07 13	07 29	07 46	08 05

Day	SUN Eqn. of Time 00^h	SUN Eqn. of Time 12^h	SUN Mer. Pass.	MOON Mer. Pass. Upper	MOON Mer. Pass. Lower	MOON Age	MOON Phase
d	m s	m s	h m	h m	h m	d %	
7	01 53	02 04	11 58	00 35	13 00	17 98	
8	02 14	02 24	11 58	01 24	13 49	18 94	
9	02 35	02 45	11 57	02 14	14 39	19 88	

UT	ARIES	VENUS −3·9		MARS +1·8		JUPITER −1·7		SATURN +0·5	
	GHA	GHA	Dec	GHA	Dec	GHA	Dec	GHA	Dec
d h	° ′	° ′	° ′	° ′	° ′	° ′	° ′	° ′	° ′
10 00	349 13.1	208 49.7	N15 59.3	193 55.1	N11 31.4	146 52.8	S 8 11.9	88 31.5	S22 01.6
01	4 15.6	223 49.2	58.5	208 56.0	30.8	161 54.8	12.1	103 33.9	01.6
02	19 18.0	238 48.6	57.7	223 57.0	30.2	176 56.8	12.3	118 36.3	01.6
03	34 20.5	253 48.0	. . 56.9	238 58.0	. . 29.6	191 58.8	. . 12.5	133 38.6	. . 01.7
04	49 23.0	268 47.5	56.1	253 58.9	29.1	207 00.8	12.7	148 41.0	01.7
05	64 25.4	283 46.9	55.2	268 59.9	28.5	222 02.8	12.8	163 43.4	01.7
06	79 27.9	298 46.3	N15 54.4	284 00.8	N11 27.9	237 04.8	S 8 13.0	178 45.8	S22 01.7
07	94 30.4	313 45.8	53.6	299 01.8	27.3	252 06.8	13.2	193 48.2	01.7
08	109 32.8	328 45.2	52.8	314 02.7	26.8	267 08.9	13.4	208 50.6	01.7
S 09	124 35.3	343 44.6	. . 51.9	329 03.7	. . 26.2	282 10.9	. . 13.6	223 53.0	. . 01.7
U 10	139 37.7	358 44.1	51.1	344 04.6	25.6	297 12.9	13.8	238 55.4	01.7
N 11	154 40.2	13 43.5	50.3	359 05.6	25.1	312 14.9	13.9	253 57.8	01.7
D 12	169 42.7	28 42.9	N15 49.5	14 06.5	N11 24.5	327 16.9	S 8 14.1	269 00.2	S22 01.8
A 13	184 45.1	43 42.4	48.6	29 07.5	23.9	342 18.9	14.3	284 02.6	01.8
Y 14	199 47.6	58 41.8	47.8	44 08.5	23.3	357 20.9	14.5	299 05.0	01.8
15	214 50.1	73 41.3	. . 47.0	59 09.4	. . 22.8	12 22.9	. . 14.7	314 07.4	. . 01.8
16	229 52.5	88 40.7	46.1	74 10.4	22.2	27 24.9	14.9	329 09.8	01.8
17	244 55.0	103 40.1	45.3	89 11.3	21.6	42 26.9	15.0	344 12.2	01.8
18	259 57.5	118 39.6	N15 44.5	104 12.3	N11 21.0	57 28.9	S 8 15.2	359 14.6	S22 01.8
19	274 59.9	133 39.0	43.6	119 13.2	20.5	72 31.0	15.4	14 17.0	01.8
20	290 02.4	148 38.5	42.8	134 14.2	19.9	87 33.0	15.6	29 19.4	01.8
21	305 04.9	163 37.9	. . 42.0	149 15.1	. . 19.3	102 35.0	. . 15.8	44 21.8	. . 01.9
22	320 07.3	178 37.3	41.1	164 16.1	18.7	117 37.0	16.0	59 24.2	01.9
23	335 09.8	193 36.8	40.3	179 17.1	18.2	132 39.0	16.1	74 26.5	01.9
11 00	350 12.2	208 36.2	N15 39.5	194 18.0	N11 17.6	147 41.0	S 8 16.3	89 28.9	S22 01.9
01	5 14.7	223 35.7	38.6	209 19.0	17.0	162 43.0	16.5	104 31.3	01.9
02	20 17.2	238 35.1	37.8	224 19.9	16.4	177 45.0	16.7	119 33.7	01.9
03	35 19.6	253 34.5	. . 37.0	239 20.9	. . 15.9	192 47.0	. . 16.9	134 36.1	. . 01.9
04	50 22.1	268 34.0	36.1	254 21.8	15.3	207 49.0	17.1	149 38.5	01.9
05	65 24.6	283 33.4	35.3	269 22.8	14.7	222 51.0	17.2	164 40.9	02.0
06	80 27.0	298 32.9	N15 34.4	284 23.7	N11 14.1	237 53.0	S 8 17.4	179 43.3	S22 02.0
07	95 29.5	313 32.3	33.6	299 24.7	13.6	252 55.0	17.6	194 45.7	02.0
08	110 32.0	328 31.8	32.7	314 25.7	13.0	267 57.1	17.8	209 48.1	02.0
M 09	125 34.4	343 31.2	. . 31.9	329 26.6	. . 12.4	282 59.1	. . 18.0	224 50.5	. . 02.0
O 10	140 36.9	358 30.7	31.1	344 27.6	11.8	298 01.1	18.2	239 52.9	02.0
N 11	155 39.3	13 30.1	30.2	359 28.5	11.3	313 03.1	18.3	254 55.3	02.0
D 12	170 41.8	28 29.5	N15 29.4	14 29.5	N11 10.7	328 05.1	S 8 18.5	269 57.6	S22 02.0
A 13	185 44.3	43 29.0	28.5	29 30.4	10.1	343 07.1	18.7	285 00.0	02.1
Y 14	200 46.7	58 28.4	27.7	44 31.4	09.5	358 09.1	18.9	300 02.4	02.1
15	215 49.2	73 27.9	. . 26.8	59 32.4	. . 08.9	13 11.1	. . 19.1	315 04.8	. . 02.1
16	230 51.7	88 27.3	26.0	74 33.3	08.4	28 13.1	19.3	330 07.2	02.1
17	245 54.1	103 26.8	25.1	89 34.3	07.8	43 15.1	19.5	345 09.6	02.1
18	260 56.6	118 26.2	N15 24.3	104 35.2	N11 07.2	58 17.1	S 8 19.6	0 12.0	S22 02.1
19	275 59.1	133 25.7	23.4	119 36.2	06.6	73 19.1	19.8	15 14.4	02.1
20	291 01.5	148 25.1	22.6	134 37.2	06.1	88 21.1	20.0	30 16.8	02.1
21	306 04.0	163 24.6	. . 21.7	149 38.1	. . 05.5	103 23.1	. . 20.2	45 19.2	. . 02.1
22	321 06.5	178 24.0	20.9	164 39.1	04.9	118 25.1	20.4	60 21.5	02.2
23	336 08.9	193 23.5	20.0	179 40.0	04.3	133 27.2	20.6	75 23.9	02.2
12 00	351 11.4	208 22.9	N15 19.1	194 41.0	N11 03.8	148 29.2	S 8 20.7	90 26.3	S22 02.2
01	6 13.8	223 22.4	18.3	209 41.9	03.2	163 31.2	20.9	105 28.7	02.2
02	21 16.3	238 21.8	17.4	224 42.9	02.6	178 33.2	21.1	120 31.1	02.2
03	36 18.8	253 21.3	. . 16.6	239 43.9	. . 02.0	193 35.2	. . 21.3	135 33.5	. . 02.2
04	51 21.2	268 20.7	15.7	254 44.8	01.4	208 37.2	21.5	150 35.9	02.2
05	66 23.7	283 20.2	14.9	269 45.8	00.9	223 39.2	21.7	165 38.3	02.2
06	81 26.2	298 19.6	N15 14.0	284 46.7	N11 00.3	238 41.2	S 8 21.9	180 40.7	S22 02.3
07	96 28.6	313 19.1	13.1	299 47.7	10 59.7	253 43.2	22.0	195 43.0	02.3
T 08	111 31.1	328 18.5	12.3	314 48.7	59.1	268 45.2	22.2	210 45.4	02.3
U 09	126 33.6	343 18.0	. . 11.4	329 49.6	. . 58.5	283 47.2	. . 22.4	225 47.8	. . 02.3
E 10	141 36.0	358 17.4	10.5	344 50.6	58.0	298 49.2	22.6	240 50.2	02.3
S 11	156 38.5	13 16.9	09.7	359 51.5	57.4	313 51.2	22.8	255 52.6	02.3
D 12	171 41.0	28 16.3	N15 08.8	14 52.5	N10 56.8	328 53.2	S 8 23.0	270 55.0	S22 02.3
A 13	186 43.4	43 15.8	07.9	29 53.5	56.2	343 55.2	23.1	285 57.4	02.3
Y 14	201 45.9	58 15.2	07.1	44 54.4	55.7	358 57.2	23.3	300 59.7	02.4
15	216 48.3	73 14.7	. . 06.2	59 55.4	. . 55.1	13 59.2	. . 23.5	316 02.1	. . 02.4
16	231 50.8	88 14.1	05.3	74 56.3	54.5	29 01.2	23.7	331 04.5	02.4
17	246 53.3	103 13.6	04.5	89 57.3	53.9	44 03.2	23.9	346 06.9	02.4
18	261 55.7	118 13.0	N15 03.6	104 58.3	N10 53.3	59 05.2	S 8 24.1	1 09.3	S22 02.4
19	276 58.2	133 12.5	02.7	119 59.2	52.8	74 07.2	24.3	16 11.7	02.4
20	292 00.7	148 11.9	01.9	135 00.2	52.2	89 09.2	24.4	31 14.1	02.4
21	307 03.1	163 11.4	. . 01.0	150 01.1	. . 51.6	104 11.2	. . 24.6	46 16.4	. . 02.4
22	322 05.6	178 10.9	15 00.1	165 02.1	51.0	119 13.3	24.8	61 18.8	02.5
23	337 08.1	193 10.3	N14 59.3	180 03.1	50.4	134 15.3	25.0	76 21.2	02.5
Mer. Pass.	h m 0 39.1	v −0.6	d 0.8	v 1.0	d 0.6	v 2.0	d 0.2	v 2.4	d 0.0

STARS Name	SHA	Dec
	° ′	° ′
Acamar	315 16.0	S40 13.9
Achernar	335 24.2	S57 08.7
Acrux	173 06.6	S63 11.8
Adhara	255 10.4	S28 59.7
Aldebaran	290 46.0	N16 32.5
Alioth	166 18.8	N55 52.1
Alkaid	152 57.1	N49 13.9
Al Na'ir	27 39.8	S46 52.5
Alnilam	275 43.5	S 1 11.5
Alphard	217 53.6	S 8 44.0
Alphecca	126 08.8	N26 39.7
Alpheratz	357 40.2	N29 11.3
Altair	62 05.3	N 8 55.2
Ankaa	353 12.5	S42 12.5
Antares	112 22.8	S26 28.1
Arcturus	145 53.4	N19 05.8
Atria	107 22.0	S69 03.6
Avior	234 17.3	S59 33.8
Bellatrix	278 29.0	N 6 21.8
Betelgeuse	270 58.3	N 7 24.5
Canopus	263 55.0	S52 42.1
Capella	280 30.2	N46 00.6
Deneb	49 29.1	N45 20.9
Denebola	182 31.1	N14 28.6
Diphda	348 52.7	S17 53.3
Dubhe	193 49.0	N61 39.4
Elnath	278 09.0	N28 37.1
Eltanin	90 44.7	N51 29.7
Enif	33 44.0	N 9 57.6
Fomalhaut	15 20.5	S29 31.6
Gacrux	171 58.2	S57 12.7
Gienah	175 49.7	S17 38.2
Hadar	148 44.2	S60 27.4
Hamal	327 57.3	N23 32.6
Kaus Aust.	83 39.9	S34 22.4
Kochab	137 20.9	N74 05.4
Markab	13 35.1	N15 18.1
Menkar	314 11.9	N 4 09.5
Menkent	148 04.5	S36 27.3
Miaplacidus	221 39.8	S69 47.2
Mirfak	308 36.0	N49 55.1
Nunki	75 54.6	S26 16.3
Peacock	53 14.4	S56 40.7
Pollux	243 24.5	N27 58.9
Procyon	244 56.9	N 5 10.7
Rasalhague	96 03.8	N12 33.2
Regulus	207 40.8	N11 52.9
Rigel	281 09.3	S 8 10.9
Rigil Kent.	139 48.2	S60 54.4
Sabik	102 09.3	S15 44.6
Schedar	349 36.6	N56 37.9
Shaula	96 18.0	S37 06.9
Sirius	258 31.3	S16 44.4
Spica	158 28.5	S11 15.0
Suhail	222 50.7	S43 30.1
Vega	80 36.9	N38 48.5
Zuben'ubi	137 02.4	S16 06.7

	SHA	Mer. Pass.
	° ′	h m
Venus	218 24.0	10 06
Mars	204 05.8	11 02
Jupiter	157 28.8	14 07
Saturn	99 16.7	17 59

UT d h		SUN GHA ° ′	SUN Dec ° ′	MOON GHA ° ′	MOON v ′	MOON Dec ° ′	MOON d ′	MOON HP ′
10 00	SUNDAY	180 44.1	N 4 56.7	315 21.8	9.8	N 8 21.1	10.5	58.7
01		195 44.3	55.8	329 50.6	9.8	8 31.6	10.5	58.8
02		210 44.5	54.8	344 19.4	9.7	8 42.1	10.4	58.8
03		225 44.7	. . 53.9	358 48.1	9.7	8 52.5	10.4	58.8
04		240 44.9	52.9	13 16.8	9.7	9 02.9	10.4	58.8
05		255 45.2	52.0	27 45.5	9.6	9 13.3	10.3	58.8
06		270 45.4	N 4 51.0	42 14.1	9.5	N 9 23.6	10.2	58.8
07		285 45.6	50.1	56 42.6	9.5	9 33.8	10.2	58.8
08		300 45.8	49.1	71 11.1	9.5	9 44.0	10.2	58.8
09		315 46.0	. . 48.2	85 39.6	9.4	9 54.2	10.1	58.8
10		330 46.3	47.2	100 08.0	9.4	10 04.3	10.0	58.9
11		345 46.5	46.3	114 36.4	9.3	10 14.3	10.0	58.9
12		0 46.7	N 4 45.3	129 04.7	9.3	N10 24.3	9.9	58.9
13		15 46.9	44.4	143 33.0	9.2	10 34.2	9.9	58.9
14		30 47.1	43.4	158 01.2	9.2	10 44.1	9.8	58.9
15		45 47.4	. . 42.5	172 29.4	9.1	10 53.9	9.8	58.9
16		60 47.6	41.5	186 57.5	9.1	11 03.7	9.6	58.9
17		75 47.8	40.6	201 25.6	9.1	11 13.3	9.7	58.9
18		90 48.0	N 4 39.6	215 53.7	9.0	N11 23.0	9.5	58.9
19		105 48.2	38.7	230 21.7	8.9	11 32.5	9.5	59.0
20		120 48.5	37.7	244 49.6	8.9	11 42.0	9.4	59.0
21		135 48.7	. . 36.8	259 17.5	8.9	11 51.4	9.4	59.0
22		150 48.9	35.8	273 45.4	8.8	12 00.8	9.3	59.0
23		165 49.1	34.9	288 13.2	8.7	12 10.1	9.2	59.0
11 00	MONDAY	180 49.3	N 4 33.9	302 40.9	8.8	N12 19.3	9.2	59.0
01		195 49.6	33.0	317 08.7	8.6	12 28.5	9.0	59.0
02		210 49.8	32.0	331 36.3	8.6	12 37.5	9.0	59.0
03		225 50.0	. . 31.1	346 03.9	8.6	12 46.5	9.0	59.0
04		240 50.2	30.1	0 31.5	8.5	12 55.5	8.8	59.0
05		255 50.4	29.2	14 59.0	8.4	13 04.3	8.8	59.0
06		270 50.7	N 4 28.2	29 26.4	8.5	N13 13.1	8.7	59.1
07		285 50.9	27.3	43 53.9	8.3	13 21.8	8.6	59.1
08		300 51.1	26.3	58 21.2	8.3	13 30.4	8.6	59.1
09		315 51.3	. . 25.4	72 48.5	8.3	13 39.0	8.4	59.1
10		330 51.5	24.4	87 15.8	8.2	13 47.4	8.4	59.1
11		345 51.8	23.5	101 43.0	8.2	13 55.8	8.3	59.1
12		0 52.0	N 4 22.5	116 10.2	8.1	N14 04.1	8.2	59.1
13		15 52.2	21.6	130 37.3	8.1	14 12.3	8.1	59.1
14		30 52.4	20.6	145 04.4	8.0	14 20.4	8.1	59.1
15		45 52.6	. . 19.7	159 31.4	7.9	14 28.5	7.9	59.1
16		60 52.9	18.7	173 58.3	8.0	14 36.4	7.9	59.1
17		75 53.1	17.8	188 25.3	7.8	14 44.3	7.8	59.1
18		90 53.3	N 4 16.8	202 52.1	7.8	N14 52.1	7.7	59.1
19		105 53.5	15.9	217 18.9	7.8	14 59.8	7.6	59.1
20		120 53.7	14.9	231 45.7	7.7	15 07.4	7.5	59.2
21		135 54.0	. . 14.0	246 12.4	7.7	15 14.9	7.4	59.2
22		150 54.2	13.0	260 39.1	7.7	15 22.3	7.3	59.2
23		165 54.4	12.1	275 05.8	7.5	15 29.6	7.2	59.2
12 00	TUESDAY	180 54.6	N 4 11.1	289 32.3	7.6	N15 36.8	7.2	59.2
01		195 54.8	10.1	303 58.9	7.5	15 44.0	7.0	59.2
02		210 55.1	09.2	318 25.4	7.4	15 51.0	6.9	59.2
03		225 55.3	. . 08.2	332 51.8	7.4	15 57.9	6.9	59.2
04		240 55.5	07.3	347 18.2	7.3	16 04.8	6.7	59.2
05		255 55.7	06.3	1 44.5	7.3	16 11.5	6.6	59.2
06		270 56.0	N 4 05.4	16 10.8	7.3	N16 18.1	6.5	59.2
07		285 56.2	04.4	30 37.1	7.2	16 24.6	6.5	59.2
08		300 56.4	03.5	45 03.3	7.2	16 31.1	6.3	59.2
09		315 56.6	. . 02.5	59 29.5	7.1	16 37.4	6.2	59.2
10		330 56.8	01.6	73 55.6	7.1	16 43.6	6.1	59.2
11		345 57.1	4 00.6	88 21.7	7.0	16 49.7	6.0	59.2
12		0 57.3	N 3 59.7	102 47.7	7.0	N16 55.7	5.9	59.2
13		15 57.5	58.7	117 13.7	7.0	17 01.6	5.8	59.2
14		30 57.7	57.7	131 39.7	6.9	17 07.4	5.7	59.2
15		45 57.9	. . 56.8	146 05.6	6.9	17 13.1	5.6	59.2
16		60 58.2	55.8	160 31.5	6.8	17 18.7	5.5	59.2
17		75 58.4	54.9	174 57.3	6.8	17 24.2	5.3	59.2
18		90 58.6	N 3 53.9	189 23.1	6.8	N17 29.5	5.3	59.3
19		105 58.8	53.0	203 48.9	6.7	17 34.8	5.1	59.3
20		120 59.0	52.0	218 14.6	6.7	17 39.9	5.0	59.3
21		135 59.3	. . 51.1	232 40.3	6.6	17 44.9	4.9	59.3
22		150 59.5	50.1	247 05.9	6.6	17 49.8	4.8	59.3
23		165 59.7	49.1	261 31.5	6.6	N17 54.6	4.7	59.3
		SD 15.9	d 1.0	SD 16.0		16.1		16.1

Lat. °	Twilight Naut. h m	Twilight Civil h m	Sunrise h m	Moonrise 10 h m	Moonrise 11 h m	Moonrise 12 h m	Moonrise 13 h m
N 72	01 29	03 34	04 49	19 05	18 52	18 26	▭
N 70	02 13	03 51	04 57	19 24	19 24	19 27	19 39
68	02 41	04 03	05 03	19 39	19 47	20 02	20 30
66	03 02	04 14	05 08	19 51	20 05	20 27	21 02
64	03 18	04 22	05 12	20 02	20 20	20 47	21 26
62	03 31	04 29	05 16	20 11	20 33	21 03	21 45
60	03 42	04 36	05 19	20 18	20 44	21 17	22 00
N 58	03 51	04 41	05 21	20 25	20 53	21 28	22 14
56	03 59	04 46	05 24	20 31	21 01	21 38	22 25
54	04 06	04 50	05 26	20 36	21 08	21 47	22 35
52	04 12	04 54	05 28	20 41	21 15	21 55	22 44
50	04 18	04 57	05 30	20 46	21 21	22 03	22 52
45	04 29	05 04	05 34	20 55	21 34	22 18	23 09
N 40	04 38	05 10	05 37	21 03	21 44	22 31	23 23
35	04 45	05 14	05 40	21 10	21 54	22 42	23 35
30	04 50	05 18	05 42	21 16	22 02	22 51	23 46
20	04 59	05 24	05 47	21 27	22 16	23 08	24 03
N 10	05 04	05 29	05 50	21 36	22 28	23 22	24 19
0	05 08	05 33	05 53	21 45	22 39	23 36	24 34
S 10	05 11	05 35	05 56	21 54	22 51	23 50	24 49
20	05 12	05 38	06 00	22 04	23 04	24 04	00 04
30	05 12	05 39	06 03	22 15	23 18	24 21	00 21
35	05 11	05 40	06 05	22 21	23 26	24 31	00 31
40	05 09	05 40	06 07	22 28	23 36	24 42	00 42
45	05 07	05 41	06 10	22 37	23 47	24 55	00 55
S 50	05 03	05 41	06 13	22 47	24 01	00 01	01 12
52	05 01	05 41	06 14	22 52	24 07	00 07	01 19
54	04 59	05 40	06 16	22 57	24 14	00 14	01 28
56	04 57	05 40	06 17	23 03	24 22	00 22	01 37
58	04 54	05 40	06 19	23 10	24 31	00 31	01 48
S 60	04 51	05 40	06 21	23 17	24 41	00 41	02 01

Lat. °	Sunset h m	Twilight Civil h m	Twilight Naut. h m	Moonset 10 h m	Moonset 11 h m	Moonset 12 h m	Moonset 13 h m
N 72	19 01	20 15	22 14	11 37	13 43	16 06	▭
N 70	18 54	19 59	21 34	11 20	13 12	15 06	16 54
68	18 48	19 47	21 07	11 06	12 50	14 32	16 03
66	18 43	19 37	20 47	10 55	12 33	14 07	15 31
64	18 39	19 29	20 32	10 46	12 18	13 47	15 08
62	18 36	19 22	20 19	10 38	12 07	13 32	14 49
60	18 33	19 16	20 09	10 32	11 57	13 19	14 34
N 58	18 30	19 10	20 00	10 26	11 48	13 07	14 21
56	18 28	19 06	19 52	10 21	11 40	12 58	14 09
54	18 26	19 02	19 45	10 16	11 34	12 49	14 00
52	18 24	18 58	19 39	10 12	11 27	12 41	13 51
50	18 22	18 55	19 34	10 08	11 22	12 34	13 43
45	18 18	18 48	19 23	10 00	11 10	12 20	13 26
N 40	18 15	18 42	19 15	09 53	11 00	12 07	13 12
35	18 13	18 38	19 08	09 47	10 52	11 57	13 01
30	18 10	18 34	19 02	09 42	10 45	11 48	12 50
20	18 06	18 28	18 54	09 33	10 32	11 32	12 33
N 10	18 03	18 24	18 48	09 25	10 21	11 19	12 18
0	18 00	18 21	18 45	09 17	10 11	11 06	12 03
S 10	17 57	18 18	18 42	09 10	10 00	10 53	11 49
20	17 54	18 16	18 41	09 02	09 49	10 40	11 34
30	17 50	18 14	18 42	08 53	09 37	10 24	11 16
35	17 49	18 14	18 43	08 48	09 30	10 15	11 06
40	17 46	18 13	18 45	08 42	09 22	10 05	10 54
45	17 44	18 13	18 47	08 36	09 12	09 53	10 41
S 50	17 41	18 13	18 51	08 28	09 00	09 39	10 24
52	17 40	18 14	18 53	08 24	08 55	09 32	10 16
54	17 38	18 14	18 55	08 20	08 49	09 24	10 07
56	17 37	18 14	18 57	08 15	08 43	09 16	09 58
58	17 35	18 14	19 00	08 11	08 36	09 07	09 47
S 60	17 33	18 15	19 03	08 05	08 27	08 56	09 34

Day	SUN Eqn. of Time 00^h	SUN Eqn. of Time 12^h	SUN Mer. Pass.	MOON Mer. Pass. Upper	MOON Mer. Pass. Lower	MOON Age	MOON Phase
d	m s	m s	h m	h m	h m	d %	
10	02 56	03 06	11 57	03 05	15 31	20 80	
11	03 17	03 27	11 57	03 58	16 25	21 70	
12	03 38	03 49	11 56	04 53	17 21	22 59	

UT d	h	ARIES GHA	VENUS −3·9 GHA	VENUS Dec	MARS +1·8 GHA	MARS Dec	JUPITER −1·7 GHA	JUPITER Dec	SATURN +0·5 GHA	SATURN Dec
		° ′	° ′	° ′	° ′	° ′	° ′	° ′	° ′	° ′
13	00	352 10.5	208 09.8	N14 58.4	195 04.0	N10 49.9	149 17.3	S 8 25.2	91 23.6	S22 02.5
	01	7 13.0	223 09.2	57.5	210 05.0	49.3	164 19.3	25.4	106 26.0	02.5
	02	22 15.4	238 08.7	56.6	225 05.9	48.7	179 21.3	25.5	121 28.4	02.5
	03	37 17.9	253 08.1	. . 55.8	240 06.9	. . 48.1	194 23.3	. . 25.7	136 30.8	. . 02.5
	04	52 20.4	268 07.6	54.9	255 07.9	47.5	209 25.3	25.9	151 33.1	02.5
	05	67 22.8	283 07.1	54.0	270 08.8	47.0	224 27.3	26.1	166 35.5	02.5
	06	82 25.3	298 06.5	N14 53.1	285 09.8	N10 46.4	239 29.3	S 8 26.3	181 37.9	S22 02.6
WEDNESDAY	07	97 27.8	313 06.0	52.2	300 10.8	45.8	254 31.3	26.5	196 40.3	02.6
	08	112 30.2	328 05.4	51.4	315 11.7	45.2	269 33.3	26.7	211 42.7	02.6
	09	127 32.7	343 04.9	. . 50.5	330 12.7	. . 44.6	284 35.3	. . 26.8	226 45.1	. . 02.6
	10	142 35.2	358 04.3	49.6	345 13.6	44.0	299 37.3	27.0	241 47.4	02.6
	11	157 37.6	13 03.8	48.7	0 14.6	43.5	314 39.3	27.2	256 49.8	02.6
	12	172 40.1	28 03.3	N14 47.8	15 15.6	N10 42.9	329 41.3	S 8 27.4	271 52.2	S22 02.6
	13	187 42.6	43 02.7	47.0	30 16.5	42.3	344 43.3	27.6	286 54.6	02.6
	14	202 45.0	58 02.2	46.1	45 17.5	41.7	359 45.3	27.8	301 57.0	02.6
	15	217 47.5	73 01.6	. . 45.2	60 18.5	. . 41.1	14 47.3	. . 28.0	316 59.4	. . 02.7
	16	232 49.9	88 01.1	44.3	75 19.4	40.6	29 49.3	28.1	332 01.7	02.7
	17	247 52.4	103 00.6	43.4	90 20.4	40.0	44 51.3	28.3	347 04.1	02.7
	18	262 54.9	118 00.0	N14 42.5	105 21.3	N10 39.4	59 53.3	S 8 28.5	2 06.5	S22 02.7
	19	277 57.3	132 59.5	41.6	120 22.3	38.8	74 55.3	28.7	17 08.9	02.7
	20	292 59.8	147 59.0	40.7	135 23.3	38.2	89 57.3	28.9	32 11.3	02.7
	21	308 02.3	162 58.4	. . 39.9	150 24.2	. . 37.6	104 59.3	. . 29.1	47 13.6	. . 02.7
	22	323 04.7	177 57.9	39.0	165 25.2	37.1	120 01.3	29.3	62 16.0	02.7
	23	338 07.2	192 57.3	38.1	180 26.2	36.5	135 03.3	29.4	77 18.4	02.8
14	00	353 09.7	207 56.8	N14 37.2	195 27.1	N10 35.9	150 05.3	S 8 29.6	92 20.8	S22 02.8
	01	8 12.1	222 56.3	36.3	210 28.1	35.3	165 07.3	29.8	107 23.2	02.8
	02	23 14.6	237 55.7	35.4	225 29.0	34.7	180 09.3	30.0	122 25.5	02.8
	03	38 17.1	252 55.2	. . 34.5	240 30.0	. . 34.1	195 11.3	. . 30.2	137 27.9	. . 02.8
	04	53 19.5	267 54.7	33.6	255 31.0	33.6	210 13.3	30.4	152 30.3	02.8
	05	68 22.0	282 54.1	32.7	270 31.9	33.0	225 15.3	30.5	167 32.7	02.8
	06	83 24.4	297 53.6	N14 31.8	285 32.9	N10 32.4	240 17.3	S 8 30.7	182 35.1	S22 02.8
THURSDAY	07	98 26.9	312 53.1	30.9	300 33.9	31.8	255 19.3	30.9	197 37.4	02.9
	08	113 29.4	327 52.5	30.0	315 34.8	31.2	270 21.3	31.1	212 39.8	02.9
	09	128 31.8	342 52.0	. . 29.1	330 35.8	. . 30.6	285 23.3	. . 31.3	227 42.2	. . 02.9
	10	143 34.3	357 51.5	28.2	345 36.8	30.1	300 25.3	31.5	242 44.6	02.9
	11	158 36.8	12 50.9	27.3	0 37.7	29.5	315 27.3	31.7	257 47.0	02.9
	12	173 39.2	27 50.4	N14 26.4	15 38.7	N10 28.9	330 29.3	S 8 31.8	272 49.3	S22 02.9
	13	188 41.7	42 49.9	25.5	30 39.7	28.3	345 31.3	32.0	287 51.7	02.9
	14	203 44.2	57 49.3	24.6	45 40.6	27.7	0 33.3	32.2	302 54.1	03.0
	15	218 46.6	72 48.8	. . 23.7	60 41.6	. . 27.1	15 35.3	. . 32.4	317 56.5	. . 03.0
	16	233 49.1	87 48.3	22.8	75 42.5	26.6	30 37.3	32.6	332 58.8	03.0
	17	248 51.6	102 47.7	21.9	90 43.5	26.0	45 39.3	32.8	348 01.2	03.0
	18	263 54.0	117 47.2	N14 21.0	105 44.5	N10 25.4	60 41.3	S 8 33.0	3 03.6	S22 03.0
	19	278 56.5	132 46.7	20.1	120 45.4	24.8	75 43.3	33.2	18 06.0	03.0
	20	293 58.9	147 46.2	19.2	135 46.4	24.2	90 45.3	33.3	33 08.4	03.0
	21	309 01.4	162 45.6	. . 18.3	150 47.4	. . 23.6	105 47.3	. . 33.5	48 10.7	. . 03.0
	22	324 03.9	177 45.1	17.4	165 48.3	23.0	120 49.3	33.7	63 13.1	03.1
	23	339 06.3	192 44.6	16.5	180 49.3	22.5	135 51.3	33.9	78 15.5	03.1
15	00	354 08.8	207 44.0	N14 15.6	195 50.3	N10 21.9	150 53.3	S 8 34.1	93 17.9	S22 03.1
	01	9 11.3	222 43.5	14.7	210 51.2	21.3	165 55.3	34.3	108 20.2	03.1
	02	24 13.7	237 43.0	13.8	225 52.2	20.7	180 57.3	34.5	123 22.6	03.1
	03	39 16.2	252 42.4	. . 12.8	240 53.2	. . 20.1	195 59.3	. . 34.6	138 25.0	. . 03.1
	04	54 18.7	267 41.9	11.9	255 54.1	19.5	211 01.3	34.8	153 27.4	03.1
	05	69 21.1	282 41.4	11.0	270 55.1	18.9	226 03.3	35.0	168 29.7	03.1
	06	84 23.6	297 40.9	N14 10.1	285 56.1	N10 18.4	241 05.3	S 8 35.2	183 32.1	S22 03.2
	07	99 26.0	312 40.3	09.2	300 57.0	17.8	256 07.3	35.4	198 34.5	03.2
	08	114 28.5	327 39.8	08.3	315 58.0	17.2	271 09.3	35.6	213 36.9	03.2
FRIDAY	09	129 31.0	342 39.3	. . 07.4	330 59.0	. . 16.6	286 11.3	. . 35.8	228 39.2	. . 03.2
	10	144 33.4	357 38.8	06.5	345 59.9	16.0	301 13.3	35.9	243 41.6	03.2
	11	159 35.9	12 38.2	05.5	1 00.9	15.4	316 15.3	36.1	258 44.0	03.2
	12	174 38.4	27 37.7	N14 04.6	16 01.9	N10 14.8	331 17.3	S 8 36.3	273 46.4	S22 03.2
	13	189 40.8	42 37.2	03.7	31 02.8	14.3	346 19.3	36.5	288 48.7	03.2
	14	204 43.3	57 36.7	02.8	46 03.8	13.7	1 21.3	36.7	303 51.1	03.3
	15	219 45.8	72 36.1	. . 01.9	61 04.8	. . 13.1	16 23.2	. . 36.9	318 53.5	. . 03.3
	16	234 48.2	87 35.6	00.9	76 05.7	12.5	31 25.2	37.1	333 55.9	03.3
	17	249 50.7	102 35.1	14 00.0	91 06.7	11.9	46 27.2	37.2	348 58.2	03.3
	18	264 53.2	117 34.6	N13 59.1	106 07.7	N10 11.3	61 29.2	S 8 37.4	4 00.6	S22 03.3
	19	279 55.6	132 34.0	58.2	121 08.6	10.7	76 31.2	37.6	19 03.0	03.3
	20	294 58.1	147 33.5	57.3	136 09.6	10.1	91 33.2	37.8	34 05.3	03.3
	21	310 00.5	162 33.0	. . 56.3	151 10.6	. . 09.6	106 35.2	. . 38.0	49 07.7	. . 03.3
	22	325 03.0	177 32.5	55.4	166 11.5	09.0	121 37.2	38.2	64 10.1	03.4
	23	340 05.5	192 32.0	54.5	181 12.5	08.4	136 39.2	38.4	79 12.5	03.4
Mer. Pass.		h m 0 27.3	*v* −0.5	*d* 0.9	*v* 1.0	*d* 0.6	*v* 2.0	*d* 0.2	*v* 2.4	*d* 0.0

STARS

Name	SHA	Dec
	° ′	° ′
Acamar	315 16.0	S40 13.9
Achernar	335 24.2	S57 08.7
Acrux	173 06.6	S63 11.8
Adhara	255 10.4	S28 59.7
Aldebaran	290 46.0	N16 32.5
Alioth	166 18.8	N55 52.1
Alkaid	152 57.1	N49 13.9
Al Na'ir	27 39.8	S46 52.5
Alnilam	275 43.5	S 1 11.5
Alphard	217 53.6	S 8 44.0
Alphecca	126 08.8	N26 39.7
Alpheratz	357 40.1	N29 11.3
Altair	62 05.3	N 8 55.2
Ankaa	353 12.5	S42 12.5
Antares	112 22.8	S26 28.1
Arcturus	145 53.4	N19 05.8
Atria	107 22.1	S69 03.6
Avior	234 17.2	S59 33.8
Bellatrix	278 28.9	N 6 21.8
Betelgeuse	270 58.2	N 7 24.5
Canopus	263 55.0	S52 42.1
Capella	280 30.2	N46 00.6
Deneb	49 29.2	N45 20.9
Denebola	182 31.1	N14 28.6
Diphda	348 52.7	S17 53.3
Dubhe	193 49.0	N61 39.4
Elnath	278 09.0	N28 37.1
Eltanin	90 44.7	N51 29.7
Enif	33 44.0	N 9 57.6
Fomalhaut	15 20.5	S29 31.6
Gacrux	171 58.2	S57 12.6
Gienah	175 49.7	S17 38.2
Hadar	148 44.2	S60 27.4
Hamal	327 57.2	N23 32.6
Kaus Aust.	83 39.9	S34 22.4
Kochab	137 20.9	N74 05.4
Markab	13 35.1	N15 18.1
Menkar	314 11.9	N 4 09.5
Menkent	148 04.5	S36 27.3
Miaplacidus	221 39.7	S69 47.2
Mirfak	308 36.0	N49 55.1
Nunki	75 54.6	S26 16.3
Peacock	53 14.4	S56 40.7
Pollux	243 24.5	N27 58.8
Procyon	244 56.9	N 5 10.7
Rasalhague	96 03.8	N12 33.2
Regulus	207 40.8	N11 52.9
Rigel	281 09.3	S 8 10.9
Rigil Kent.	139 48.2	S60 54.4
Sabik	102 09.3	S15 44.6
Schedar	349 36.6	N56 38.0
Shaula	96 18.0	S37 06.9
Sirius	258 31.3	S16 44.4
Spica	158 28.5	S11 15.0
Suhail	222 50.7	S43 30.1
Vega	80 36.9	N38 48.5
Zuben'ubi	137 02.4	S16 06.7

	SHA	Mer. Pass.
	° ′	h m
Venus	214 47.2	10 09
Mars	202 17.5	10 57
Jupiter	156 55.6	13 58
Saturn	99 11.1	17 48

UT d h	SUN GHA	SUN Dec	MOON GHA	v	MOON Dec	d	HP
	° ′	° ′	° ′	′	° ′	′	′
13 00 (Wednesday)	180 59.9	N 3 48.2	275 57.1	6.5	N17 59.3	4.5	59.3
01	196 00.2	47.2	290 22.6	6.5	18 03.8	4.5	59.3
02	211 00.4	46.3	304 48.1	6.5	18 08.3	4.3	59.3
03	226 00.6	. . 45.3	319 13.6	6.5	18 12.6	4.2	59.3
04	241 00.8	44.4	333 39.1	6.4	18 16.8	4.1	59.3
05	256 01.0	43.4	348 04.5	6.3	18 20.9	3.9	59.3
06	271 01.3	N 3 42.4	2 29.8	6.4	N18 24.8	3.9	59.3
07	286 01.5	41.5	16 55.2	6.3	18 28.7	3.7	59.3
08	301 01.7	40.5	31 20.5	6.3	18 32.4	3.6	59.3
09	316 01.9	. . 39.6	45 45.8	6.3	18 36.0	3.5	59.3
10	331 02.2	38.6	60 11.1	6.2	18 39.5	3.4	59.3
11	346 02.4	37.7	74 36.3	6.2	18 42.9	3.2	59.3
12	1 02.6	N 3 36.7	89 01.5	6.2	N18 46.1	3.1	59.3
13	16 02.8	35.7	103 26.7	6.2	18 49.2	3.0	59.3
14	31 03.0	34.8	117 51.9	6.1	18 52.2	2.9	59.3
15	46 03.3	. . 33.8	132 17.0	6.1	18 55.1	2.7	59.3
16	61 03.5	32.9	146 42.1	6.1	18 57.8	2.6	59.3
17	76 03.7	31.9	161 07.2	6.1	19 00.4	2.5	59.3
18	91 03.9	N 3 31.0	175 32.3	6.1	N19 02.9	2.4	59.3
19	106 04.1	30.0	189 57.4	6.0	19 05.3	2.2	59.3
20	121 04.4	29.0	204 22.4	6.0	19 07.5	2.2	59.3
21	136 04.6	. . 28.1	218 47.4	6.0	19 09.7	1.9	59.3
22	151 04.8	27.1	233 12.4	6.0	19 11.6	1.9	59.3
23	166 05.0	26.2	247 37.4	6.0	19 13.5	1.7	59.3
14 00 (Thursday)	181 05.3	N 3 25.2	262 02.4	6.0	N19 15.2	1.7	59.3
01	196 05.5	24.2	276 27.4	6.0	19 16.9	1.4	59.3
02	211 05.7	23.3	290 52.4	5.9	19 18.3	1.4	59.3
03	226 05.9	. . 22.3	305 17.3	6.0	19 19.7	1.2	59.3
04	241 06.1	21.4	319 42.3	5.9	19 20.9	1.1	59.3
05	256 06.4	20.4	334 07.2	5.9	19 22.0	1.0	59.3
06	271 06.6	N 3 19.4	348 32.1	5.9	N19 23.0	0.8	59.3
07	286 06.8	18.5	2 57.0	6.0	19 23.8	0.7	59.3
08	301 07.0	17.5	17 22.0	5.9	19 24.5	0.6	59.3
09	316 07.3	. . 16.6	31 46.9	5.9	19 25.1	0.5	59.3
10	331 07.5	15.6	46 11.8	5.9	19 25.6	0.3	59.3
11	346 07.7	14.6	60 36.7	5.9	19 25.9	0.2	59.3
12	1 07.9	N 3 13.7	75 01.6	5.9	N19 26.1	0.1	59.3
13	16 08.1	12.7	89 26.5	5.9	19 26.2	0.1	59.3
14	31 08.4	11.8	103 51.4	5.9	19 26.1	0.2	59.3
15	46 08.6	. . 10.8	118 16.3	6.0	19 25.9	0.3	59.2
16	61 08.8	09.8	132 41.3	5.9	19 25.6	0.4	59.2
17	76 09.0	08.9	147 06.2	5.9	19 25.2	0.6	59.2
18	91 09.3	N 3 07.9	161 31.1	6.0	N19 24.6	0.7	59.2
19	106 09.5	07.0	175 56.1	5.9	19 23.9	0.8	59.2
20	121 09.7	06.0	190 21.0	6.0	19 23.1	1.0	59.2
21	136 09.9	. . 05.0	204 46.0	6.0	19 22.1	1.1	59.2
22	151 10.1	04.1	219 11.0	5.9	19 21.0	1.2	59.2
23	166 10.4	03.1	233 35.9	6.0	19 19.8	1.3	59.2
15 00 (Friday)	181 10.6	N 3 02.2	248 00.9	6.0	N19 18.5	1.5	59.2
01	196 10.8	01.2	262 25.9	6.1	19 17.0	1.6	59.2
02	211 11.0	3 00.2	276 51.0	6.0	19 15.4	1.7	59.2
03	226 11.3	2 59.3	291 16.0	6.1	19 13.7	1.9	59.2
04	241 11.5	58.3	305 41.1	6.1	19 11.8	2.0	59.2
05	256 11.7	57.3	320 06.2	6.1	19 09.8	2.1	59.2
06	271 11.9	N 2 56.4	334 31.3	6.1	N19 07.7	2.2	59.2
07	286 12.2	55.4	348 56.4	6.1	19 05.5	2.3	59.2
08	301 12.4	54.5	3 21.5	6.2	19 03.2	2.5	59.2
09	316 12.6	. . 53.5	17 46.7	6.2	19 00.7	2.6	59.2
10	331 12.8	52.5	32 11.9	6.2	18 58.1	2.7	59.2
11	346 13.0	51.6	46 37.1	6.3	18 55.4	2.9	59.2
12	1 13.3	N 2 50.6	61 02.4	6.3	N18 52.5	3.0	59.1
13	16 13.5	49.6	75 27.7	6.3	18 49.5	3.1	59.1
14	31 13.7	48.7	89 53.0	6.3	18 46.4	3.2	59.1
15	46 13.9	. . 47.7	104 18.3	6.4	18 43.2	3.3	59.1
16	61 14.2	46.8	118 43.7	6.3	18 39.9	3.5	59.1
17	76 14.4	45.8	133 09.0	6.5	18 36.4	3.5	59.1
18	91 14.6	N 2 44.8	147 34.5	6.4	N18 32.9	3.7	59.1
19	106 14.8	43.9	161 59.9	6.5	18 29.2	3.9	59.1
20	121 15.0	42.9	176 25.4	6.6	18 25.3	3.9	59.1
21	136 15.3	. . 41.9	190 51.0	6.5	18 21.4	4.1	59.1
22	151 15.5	41.0	205 16.5	6.6	18 17.3	4.1	59.1
23	166 15.7	40.0	219 42.1	6.7	N18 13.2	4.3	59.1
	SD 15.9	*d* 1.0	SD 16.2		16.1		16.1

Lat.	Twilight Naut.	Twilight Civil	Sunrise	Moonrise 13	Moonrise 14	Moonrise 15	Moonrise 16
°	h m	h m	h m	h m	h m	h m	h m
N 72	02 00	03 50	05 03	□	□	□	23 13
N 70	02 34	04 04	05 09	19 39	20 26	22 02	23 54
68	02 57	04 15	05 13	20 30	21 24	22 45	24 22
66	03 15	04 24	05 17	21 02	21 57	23 14	24 43
64	03 29	04 31	05 20	21 26	22 22	23 35	25 00
62	03 41	04 38	05 23	21 45	22 42	23 53	25 14
60	03 51	04 43	05 26	22 00	22 57	24 07	00 07
N 58	03 59	04 48	05 28	22 14	23 11	24 19	00 19
56	04 06	04 52	05 30	22 25	23 23	24 30	00 30
54	04 12	04 56	05 31	22 35	23 33	24 39	00 39
52	04 18	04 59	05 33	22 44	23 42	24 48	00 48
50	04 23	05 02	05 34	22 52	23 50	24 55	00 55
45	04 33	05 08	05 37	23 09	24 07	00 07	01 11
N 40	04 41	05 13	05 40	23 23	24 21	00 21	01 24
35	04 47	05 17	05 42	23 35	24 33	00 33	01 35
30	04 52	05 20	05 44	23 46	24 44	00 44	01 45
20	04 59	05 25	05 47	24 03	00 03	01 02	02 02
N 10	05 04	05 29	05 50	24 19	00 19	01 17	02 16
0	05 08	05 32	05 52	24 34	00 34	01 32	02 30
S 10	05 09	05 34	05 55	24 49	00 49	01 47	02 43
20	05 09	05 35	05 57	00 04	01 04	02 03	02 58
30	05 08	05 36	05 59	00 21	01 22	02 21	03 15
35	05 06	05 36	06 01	00 31	01 33	02 31	03 24
40	05 04	05 35	06 02	00 42	01 45	02 43	03 35
45	05 01	05 35	06 04	00 55	01 59	02 57	03 48
S 50	04 57	05 34	06 06	01 12	02 17	03 15	04 04
52	04 54	05 34	06 07	01 19	02 25	03 23	04 11
54	04 52	05 33	06 08	01 28	02 35	03 32	04 20
56	04 49	05 32	06 09	01 37	02 45	03 42	04 29
58	04 46	05 32	06 11	01 48	02 57	03 54	04 39
S 60	04 42	05 31	06 12	02 01	03 11	04 07	04 51

Lat.	Sunset	Twilight Civil	Twilight Naut.	Moonset 13	Moonset 14	Moonset 15	Moonset 16
°	h m	h m	h m	h m	h m	h m	h m
N 72	18 45	19 57	21 43	□	□	□	19 22
N 70	18 40	19 44	21 12	16 54	18 09	18 34	18 40
68	18 35	19 33	20 50	16 03	17 12	17 51	18 11
66	18 32	19 25	20 33	15 31	16 38	17 22	17 49
64	18 29	19 17	20 19	15 08	16 13	17 00	17 32
62	18 26	19 11	20 08	14 49	15 53	16 42	17 18
60	18 24	19 06	19 58	14 34	15 37	16 28	17 05
N 58	18 22	19 02	19 50	14 21	15 24	16 15	16 55
56	18 20	18 58	19 43	14 09	15 12	16 04	16 46
54	18 18	18 54	19 37	14 00	15 02	15 55	16 37
52	18 17	18 51	19 32	13 51	14 53	15 46	16 30
50	18 16	18 48	19 27	13 43	14 45	15 38	16 23
45	18 13	18 42	19 17	13 26	14 27	15 22	16 09
N 40	18 10	18 37	19 09	13 12	14 13	15 08	15 57
35	18 08	18 34	19 03	13 01	14 01	14 57	15 47
30	18 06	18 30	18 58	12 50	13 50	14 47	15 38
20	18 04	18 26	18 51	12 33	13 32	14 29	15 23
N 10	18 01	18 22	18 46	12 18	13 16	14 14	15 09
0	17 59	18 19	18 43	12 03	13 02	14 00	14 57
S 10	17 57	18 18	18 42	11 49	12 47	13 46	14 44
20	17 54	18 16	18 42	11 34	12 31	13 30	14 30
30	17 52	18 16	18 44	11 16	12 13	13 13	14 15
35	17 51	18 16	18 45	11 06	12 02	13 02	14 05
40	17 49	18 16	18 48	10 54	11 50	12 50	13 55
45	17 48	18 17	18 51	10 41	11 35	12 36	13 43
S 50	17 46	18 18	18 55	10 24	11 18	12 19	13 28
52	17 45	18 18	18 58	10 16	11 09	12 11	13 20
54	17 44	18 19	19 00	10 07	11 00	12 02	13 13
56	17 43	18 20	19 03	09 58	10 50	11 52	13 04
58	17 42	18 21	19 07	09 47	10 38	11 41	12 54
S 60	17 40	18 22	19 11	09 34	10 24	11 28	12 42

Day	SUN Eqn. of Time 00^h	SUN Eqn. of Time 12^h	SUN Mer. Pass.	MOON Mer. Pass. Upper	MOON Mer. Pass. Lower	MOON Age	MOON Phase
d	m s	m s	h m	h m	h m	d %	
13	03 59	04 10	11 56	05 50	18 19	23 47	
14	04 21	04 31	11 55	06 48	19 17	24 36	
15	04 42	04 53	11 55	07 46	20 15	25 26	

UT	ARIES	VENUS −3·9		MARS +1·8		JUPITER −1·7		SATURN +0·5	
	GHA	GHA	Dec	GHA	Dec	GHA	Dec	GHA	Dec
d h	° ′	° ′	° ′	° ′	° ′	° ′	° ′	° ′	° ′
16 00 SATURDAY	355 07.9	207 31.4	N13 53.6	196 13.5	N10 07.8	151 41.2	S 8 38.6	94 14.8	S22 03.4
01	10 10.4	222 30.9	52.6	211 14.4	07.2	166 43.2	38.7	109 17.2	03.4
02	25 12.9	237 30.4	51.7	226 15.4	06.6	181 45.2	38.9	124 19.6	03.4
03	40 15.3	252 29.9	. . 50.8	241 16.4	. . 06.0	196 47.2	. . 39.1	139 21.9	. . 03.4
04	55 17.8	267 29.4	49.8	256 17.4	05.4	211 49.2	39.3	154 24.3	03.4
05	70 20.3	282 28.8	48.9	271 18.3	04.9	226 51.2	39.5	169 26.7	03.5
06	85 22.7	297 28.3	N13 48.0	286 19.3	N10 04.3	241 53.2	S 8 39.7	184 29.1	S22 03.5
07	100 25.2	312 27.8	47.1	301 20.3	03.7	256 55.2	39.9	199 31.4	03.5
08	115 27.7	327 27.3	46.1	316 21.2	03.1	271 57.2	40.0	214 33.8	03.5
09	130 30.1	342 26.8	. . 45.2	331 22.2	. . 02.5	286 59.2	. . 40.2	229 36.2	. . 03.5
10	145 32.6	357 26.2	44.3	346 23.2	01.9	302 01.2	40.4	244 38.5	03.5
11	160 35.0	12 25.7	43.3	1 24.1	01.3	317 03.2	40.6	259 40.9	03.5
12	175 37.5	27 25.2	N13 42.4	16 25.1	N10 00.7	332 05.2	S 8 40.8	274 43.3	S22 03.5
13	190 40.0	42 24.7	41.5	31 26.1	10 00.1	347 07.1	41.0	289 45.7	03.6
14	205 42.4	57 24.2	40.5	46 27.0	9 59.6	2 09.1	41.2	304 48.0	03.6
15	220 44.9	72 23.7	. . 39.6	61 28.0	. . 59.0	17 11.1	. . 41.4	319 50.4	. . 03.6
16	235 47.4	87 23.1	38.7	76 29.0	58.4	32 13.1	41.5	334 52.8	03.6
17	250 49.8	102 22.6	37.7	91 30.0	57.8	47 15.1	41.7	349 55.1	03.6
18	265 52.3	117 22.1	N13 36.8	106 30.9	N 9 57.2	62 17.1	S 8 41.9	4 57.5	S22 03.6
19	280 54.8	132 21.6	35.8	121 31.9	56.6	77 19.1	42.1	19 59.9	03.6
20	295 57.2	147 21.1	34.9	136 32.9	56.0	92 21.1	42.3	35 02.2	03.6
21	310 59.7	162 20.6	. . 34.0	151 33.8	. . 55.4	107 23.1	. . 42.5	50 04.6	. . 03.7
22	326 02.2	177 20.0	33.0	166 34.8	54.8	122 25.1	42.7	65 07.0	03.7
23	341 04.6	192 19.5	32.1	181 35.8	54.3	137 27.1	42.8	80 09.3	03.7
17 00 SUNDAY	356 07.1	207 19.0	N13 31.1	196 36.7	N 9 53.7	152 29.1	S 8 43.0	95 11.7	S22 03.7
01	11 09.5	222 18.5	30.2	211 37.7	53.1	167 31.1	43.2	110 14.1	03.7
02	26 12.0	237 18.0	29.3	226 38.7	52.5	182 33.1	43.4	125 16.4	03.7
03	41 14.5	252 17.5	. . 28.3	241 39.7	. . 51.9	197 35.1	. . 43.6	140 18.8	. . 03.7
04	56 16.9	267 17.0	27.4	256 40.6	51.3	212 37.1	43.8	155 21.2	03.8
05	71 19.4	282 16.5	26.4	271 41.6	50.7	227 39.0	44.0	170 23.5	03.8
06	86 21.9	297 15.9	N13 25.5	286 42.6	N 9 50.1	242 41.0	S 8 44.2	185 25.9	S22 03.8
07	101 24.3	312 15.4	24.5	301 43.5	49.5	257 43.0	44.3	200 28.3	03.8
08	116 26.8	327 14.9	23.6	316 44.5	48.9	272 45.0	44.5	215 30.6	03.8
09	131 29.3	342 14.4	. . 22.6	331 45.5	. . 48.3	287 47.0	. . 44.7	230 33.0	. . 03.8
10	146 31.7	357 13.9	21.7	346 46.5	47.8	302 49.0	44.9	245 35.4	03.8
11	161 34.2	12 13.4	20.7	1 47.4	47.2	317 51.0	45.1	260 37.7	03.8
12	176 36.6	27 12.9	N13 19.8	16 48.4	N 9 46.6	332 53.0	S 8 45.3	275 40.1	S22 03.9
13	191 39.1	42 12.4	18.8	31 49.4	46.0	347 55.0	45.5	290 42.5	03.9
14	206 41.6	57 11.9	17.9	46 50.3	45.4	2 57.0	45.7	305 44.8	03.9
15	221 44.0	72 11.3	. . 16.9	61 51.3	. . 44.8	17 59.0	. . 45.8	320 47.2	. . 03.9
16	236 46.5	87 10.8	16.0	76 52.3	44.2	33 01.0	46.0	335 49.6	03.9
17	251 49.0	102 10.3	15.0	91 53.3	43.6	48 03.0	46.2	350 51.9	03.9
18	266 51.4	117 09.8	N13 14.1	106 54.2	N 9 43.0	63 04.9	S 8 46.4	5 54.3	S22 03.9
19	281 53.9	132 09.3	13.1	121 55.2	42.4	78 06.9	46.6	20 56.7	04.0
20	296 56.4	147 08.8	12.2	136 56.2	41.8	93 08.9	46.8	35 59.0	04.0
21	311 58.8	162 08.3	. . 11.2	151 57.1	. . 41.2	108 10.9	. . 47.0	51 01.4	. . 04.0
22	327 01.3	177 07.8	10.2	166 58.1	40.7	123 12.9	47.2	66 03.8	04.0
23	342 03.8	192 07.3	09.3	181 59.1	40.1	138 14.9	47.3	81 06.1	04.0
18 00 MONDAY	357 06.2	207 06.8	N13 08.3	197 00.1	N 9 39.5	153 16.9	S 8 47.5	96 08.5	S22 04.0
01	12 08.7	222 06.3	07.4	212 01.0	38.9	168 18.9	47.7	111 10.8	04.0
02	27 11.1	237 05.8	06.4	227 02.0	38.3	183 20.9	47.9	126 13.2	04.0
03	42 13.6	252 05.3	. . 05.5	242 03.0	. . 37.7	198 22.9	. . 48.1	141 15.6	. . 04.1
04	57 16.1	267 04.8	04.5	257 03.9	37.1	213 24.9	48.3	156 17.9	04.1
05	72 18.5	282 04.3	03.5	272 04.9	36.5	228 26.9	48.5	171 20.3	04.1
06	87 21.0	297 03.7	N13 02.6	287 05.9	N 9 35.9	243 28.8	S 8 48.7	186 22.7	S22 04.1
07	102 23.5	312 03.2	01.6	302 06.9	35.3	258 30.8	48.8	201 25.0	04.1
08	117 25.9	327 02.7	13 00.6	317 07.8	34.7	273 32.8	49.0	216 27.4	04.1
09	132 28.4	342 02.2	12 59.7	332 08.8	. . 34.1	288 34.8	. . 49.2	231 29.7	. . 04.1
10	147 30.9	357 01.7	58.7	347 09.8	33.5	303 36.8	49.4	246 32.1	04.2
11	162 33.3	12 01.2	57.8	2 10.8	32.9	318 38.8	49.6	261 34.5	04.2
12	177 35.8	27 00.7	N12 56.8	17 11.7	N 9 32.4	333 40.8	S 8 49.8	276 36.8	S22 04.2
13	192 38.2	42 00.2	55.8	32 12.7	31.8	348 42.8	50.0	291 39.2	04.2
14	207 40.7	56 59.7	54.9	47 13.7	31.2	3 44.8	50.2	306 41.6	04.2
15	222 43.2	71 59.2	. . 53.9	62 14.7	. . 30.6	18 46.8	. . 50.3	321 43.9	. . 04.2
16	237 45.6	86 58.7	52.9	77 15.6	30.0	33 48.7	50.5	336 46.3	04.2
17	252 48.1	101 58.2	51.9	92 16.6	29.4	48 50.7	50.7	351 48.6	04.2
18	267 50.6	116 57.7	N12 51.0	107 17.6	N 9 28.8	63 52.7	S 8 50.9	6 51.0	S22 04.3
19	282 53.0	131 57.2	50.0	122 18.6	28.2	78 54.7	51.1	21 53.4	04.3
20	297 55.5	146 56.7	49.0	137 19.5	27.6	93 56.7	51.3	36 55.7	04.3
21	312 58.0	161 56.2	. . 48.1	152 20.5	. . 27.0	108 58.7	. . 51.5	51 58.1	. . 04.3
22	328 00.4	176 55.7	47.1	167 21.5	26.4	124 00.7	51.7	67 00.4	04.3
23	343 02.9	191 55.2	46.1	182 22.5	25.8	139 02.7	51.8	82 02.8	04.3
Mer. Pass.	h m 0 15.5	v −0.5	d 1.0	v 1.0	d 0.6	v 2.0	d 0.2	v 2.4	d 0.0

STARS

Name	SHA	Dec
	° ′	° ′
Acamar	315 15.9	S40 13.9
Achernar	335 24.2	S57 08.7
Acrux	173 06.6	S63 11.7
Adhara	255 10.4	S28 59.7
Aldebaran	290 46.0	N16 32.5
Alioth	166 18.8	N55 52.1
Alkaid	152 57.1	N49 13.8
Al Na'ir	27 39.8	S46 52.5
Alnilam	275 43.5	S 1 11.5
Alphard	217 53.5	S 8 44.0
Alphecca	126 08.8	N26 39.7
Alpheratz	357 40.1	N29 11.3
Altair	62 05.3	N 8 55.2
Ankaa	353 12.5	S42 12.5
Antares	112 22.8	S26 28.1
Arcturus	145 53.4	N19 05.8
Atria	107 22.1	S69 03.6
Avior	234 17.2	S59 33.8
Bellatrix	278 28.9	N 6 21.8
Betelgeuse	270 58.2	N 7 24.5
Canopus	263 55.0	S52 42.1
Capella	280 30.2	N46 00.6
Deneb	49 29.2	N45 20.9
Denebola	182 31.1	N14 28.6
Diphda	348 52.7	S17 53.3
Dubhe	193 48.9	N61 39.4
Elnath	278 09.0	N28 37.1
Eltanin	90 44.8	N51 29.7
Enif	33 44.0	N 9 57.6
Fomalhaut	15 20.5	S29 31.6
Gacrux	171 58.2	S57 12.6
Gienah	175 49.7	S17 38.2
Hadar	148 44.2	S60 27.4
Hamal	327 57.2	N23 32.7
Kaus Aust.	83 39.9	S34 22.4
Kochab	137 21.0	N74 05.4
Markab	13 35.1	N15 18.2
Menkar	314 11.8	N 4 09.5
Menkent	148 04.5	S36 27.3
Miaplacidus	221 39.7	S69 47.2
Mirfak	308 35.9	N49 55.1
Nunki	75 54.7	S26 16.3
Peacock	53 14.4	S56 40.7
Pollux	243 24.4	N27 58.8
Procyon	244 56.9	N 5 10.7
Rasalhague	96 03.8	N12 33.2
Regulus	207 40.8	N11 52.9
Rigel	281 09.3	S 8 10.9
Rigil Kent.	139 48.2	S60 54.4
Sabik	102 09.3	S15 44.6
Schedar	349 36.6	N56 38.0
Shaula	96 18.0	S37 06.9
Sirius	258 31.3	S16 44.4
Spica	158 28.5	S11 15.0
Suhail	222 50.6	S43 30.1
Vega	80 36.9	N38 48.5
Zuben'ubi	137 02.4	S16 06.7

	SHA	Mer. Pass.
	° ′	h m
Venus	211 11.9	10 11
Mars	200 29.7	10 53
Jupiter	156 22.0	13 48
Saturn	99 04.6	17 36

	UT	SUN GHA	SUN Dec	MOON GHA	*v*	MOON Dec	*d*	HP
	d h	° ′	° ′	° ′	′	° ′	′	′
SATURDAY	16 00	181 15.9	N 2 39.0	234 07.8	6.7	N18 08.9	4.4	59.1
	01	196 16.2	38.1	248 33.5	6.7	18 04.5	4.5	59.0
	02	211 16.4	37.1	262 59.2	6.7	18 00.0	4.7	59.0
	03	226 16.6	. . 36.2	277 24.9	6.8	17 55.3	4.7	59.0
	04	241 16.8	35.2	291 50.7	6.9	17 50.6	4.9	59.0
	05	256 17.0	34.2	306 16.6	6.9	17 45.7	4.9	59.0
	06	271 17.3	N 2 33.3	320 42.5	6.9	N17 40.8	5.1	59.0
	07	286 17.5	32.3	335 08.4	7.0	17 35.7	5.2	59.0
	08	301 17.7	31.3	349 34.4	7.0	17 30.5	5.3	59.0
	09	316 17.9	. . 30.4	4 00.4	7.0	17 25.2	5.4	59.0
	10	331 18.2	29.4	18 26.4	7.2	17 19.8	5.5	59.0
	11	346 18.4	28.4	32 52.6	7.1	17 14.3	5.7	58.9
	12	1 18.6	N 2 27.5	47 18.7	7.2	N17 08.6	5.7	58.9
	13	16 18.8	26.5	61 44.9	7.3	17 02.9	5.8	58.9
	14	31 19.0	25.5	76 11.2	7.3	16 57.1	6.0	58.9
	15	46 19.3	. . 24.6	90 37.5	7.3	16 51.1	6.0	58.9
	16	61 19.5	23.6	105 03.8	7.4	16 45.1	6.2	58.9
	17	76 19.7	22.6	119 30.2	7.5	16 38.9	6.2	58.9
	18	91 19.9	N 2 21.7	133 56.7	7.5	N16 32.7	6.4	58.9
	19	106 20.2	20.7	148 23.2	7.5	16 26.3	6.4	58.9
	20	121 20.4	19.7	162 49.7	7.6	16 19.9	6.6	58.8
	21	136 20.6	. . 18.8	177 16.3	7.7	16 13.3	6.6	58.8
	22	151 20.8	17.8	191 43.0	7.7	16 06.7	6.8	58.8
	23	166 21.0	16.9	206 09.7	7.8	15 59.9	6.8	58.8
SUNDAY	17 00	181 21.3	N 2 15.9	220 36.5	7.8	N15 53.1	7.0	58.8
	01	196 21.5	14.9	235 03.3	7.9	15 46.1	7.0	58.8
	02	211 21.7	14.0	249 30.2	7.9	15 39.1	7.1	58.8
	03	226 21.9	. . 13.0	263 57.1	8.0	15 32.0	7.2	58.8
	04	241 22.2	12.0	278 24.1	8.0	15 24.8	7.3	58.7
	05	256 22.4	11.1	292 51.1	8.1	15 17.5	7.4	58.7
	06	271 22.6	N 2 10.1	307 18.2	8.2	N15 10.1	7.5	58.7
	07	286 22.8	09.1	321 45.4	8.2	15 02.6	7.6	58.7
	08	301 23.1	08.2	336 12.6	8.2	14 55.0	7.7	58.7
	09	316 23.3	. . 07.2	350 39.8	8.3	14 47.3	7.7	58.7
	10	331 23.5	06.2	5 07.1	8.4	14 39.6	7.8	58.7
	11	346 23.7	05.3	19 34.5	8.4	14 31.8	8.0	58.6
	12	1 23.9	N 2 04.3	34 01.9	8.5	N14 23.8	7.9	58.6
	13	16 24.2	03.3	48 29.4	8.6	14 15.9	8.1	58.6
	14	31 24.4	02.4	62 57.0	8.6	14 07.8	8.2	58.6
	15	46 24.6	. . 01.4	77 24.6	8.6	13 59.6	8.2	58.6
	16	61 24.8	2 00.4	91 52.2	8.8	13 51.4	8.3	58.6
	17	76 25.1	1 59.5	106 20.0	8.7	13 43.1	8.4	58.5
	18	91 25.3	N 1 58.5	120 47.7	8.9	N13 34.7	8.5	58.5
	19	106 25.5	57.5	135 15.6	8.9	13 26.2	8.6	58.5
	20	121 25.7	56.5	149 43.5	8.9	13 17.6	8.6	58.5
	21	136 25.9	. . 55.6	164 11.4	9.0	13 09.0	8.7	58.5
	22	151 26.2	54.6	178 39.4	9.1	13 00.3	8.7	58.5
	23	166 26.4	53.6	193 07.5	9.1	12 51.6	8.9	58.4
MONDAY	18 00	181 26.6	N 1 52.7	207 35.6	9.2	N12 42.7	8.9	58.4
	01	196 26.8	51.7	222 03.8	9.2	12 33.8	8.9	58.4
	02	211 27.1	50.7	236 32.0	9.3	12 24.9	9.1	58.4
	03	226 27.3	. . 49.8	251 00.3	9.4	12 15.8	9.1	58.4
	04	241 27.5	48.8	265 28.7	9.4	12 06.7	9.1	58.4
	05	256 27.7	47.8	279 57.1	9.5	11 57.6	9.3	58.3
	06	271 27.9	N 1 46.9	294 25.6	9.5	N11 48.3	9.2	58.3
	07	286 28.2	45.9	308 54.1	9.6	11 39.1	9.4	58.3
	08	301 28.4	44.9	323 22.7	9.7	11 29.7	9.4	58.3
	09	316 28.6	. . 44.0	337 51.4	9.7	11 20.3	9.5	58.3
	10	331 28.8	43.0	352 20.1	9.7	11 10.8	9.5	58.3
	11	346 29.1	42.0	6 48.8	9.8	11 01.3	9.6	58.2
	12	1 29.3	N 1 41.1	21 17.6	9.9	N10 51.7	9.6	58.2
	13	16 29.5	40.1	35 46.5	9.9	10 42.1	9.7	58.2
	14	31 29.7	39.1	50 15.4	10.0	10 32.4	9.8	58.2
	15	46 29.9	. . 38.2	64 44.4	10.1	10 22.6	9.8	58.2
	16	61 30.2	37.2	79 13.5	10.1	10 12.8	9.8	58.1
	17	76 30.4	36.2	93 42.6	10.1	10 03.0	9.9	58.1
	18	91 30.6	N 1 35.2	108 11.7	10.2	N 9 53.1	10.0	58.1
	19	106 30.8	34.3	122 40.9	10.3	9 43.1	10.0	58.1
	20	121 31.0	33.3	137 10.2	10.3	9 33.1	10.0	58.1
	21	136 31.3	. . 32.3	151 39.5	10.4	9 23.1	10.1	58.0
	22	151 31.5	31.4	166 08.9	10.4	9 13.0	10.1	58.0
	23	166 31.7	30.4	180 38.3	10.5	N 9 02.9	10.2	58.0
		SD 15.9	*d* 1.0	SD 16.1		16.0		15.9

Lat.	Twilight Naut.	Twilight Civil	Sunrise	Moonrise 16	Moonrise 17	Moonrise 18	Moonrise 19
°	h m	h m	h m	h m	h m	h m	h m
N 72	02 25	04 06	05 17	23 13	25 23	01 23	03 22
N 70	02 52	04 17	05 21	23 54	25 46	01 46	03 34
68	03 12	04 27	05 24	24 22	00 22	02 04	03 45
66	03 28	04 34	05 27	24 43	00 43	02 18	03 53
64	03 40	04 41	05 29	25 00	01 00	02 30	04 00
62	03 50	04 46	05 31	25 14	01 14	02 40	04 06
60	03 59	04 51	05 33	00 07	01 25	02 48	04 12
N 58	04 07	04 55	05 34	00 19	01 35	02 55	04 16
56	04 13	04 58	05 36	00 30	01 44	03 02	04 20
54	04 19	05 01	05 37	00 39	01 52	03 08	04 24
52	04 23	05 04	05 38	00 48	01 59	03 13	04 27
50	04 28	05 06	05 39	00 55	02 05	03 18	04 30
45	04 37	05 12	05 41	01 11	02 19	03 28	04 37
N 40	04 44	05 16	05 43	01 24	02 30	03 36	04 42
35	04 49	05 19	05 44	01 35	02 39	03 44	04 47
30	04 54	05 22	05 46	01 45	02 47	03 50	04 51
20	05 00	05 26	05 48	02 02	03 02	04 01	04 58
N 10	05 04	05 29	05 50	02 16	03 14	04 10	05 05
0	05 06	05 30	05 51	02 30	03 26	04 19	05 10
S 10	05 07	05 32	05 53	02 43	03 37	04 28	05 16
20	05 07	05 32	05 54	02 58	03 50	04 38	05 23
30	05 04	05 32	05 56	03 15	04 04	04 49	05 30
35	05 02	05 31	05 57	03 24	04 12	04 55	05 34
40	04 59	05 30	05 57	03 35	04 21	05 02	05 38
45	04 55	05 29	05 58	03 48	04 32	05 10	05 44
S 50	04 50	05 28	06 00	04 04	04 45	05 20	05 50
52	04 47	05 27	06 00	04 11	04 51	05 25	05 53
54	04 44	05 26	06 01	04 20	04 58	05 30	05 56
56	04 41	05 24	06 01	04 29	05 06	05 35	06 00
58	04 37	05 23	06 02	04 39	05 14	05 41	06 04
S 60	04 33	05 22	06 03	04 51	05 23	05 48	06 08

Lat.	Sunset	Twilight Civil	Twilight Naut.	Moonset 16	Moonset 17	Moonset 18	Moonset 19
°	h m	h m	h m	h m	h m	h m	h m
N 72	18 29	19 40	21 18	19 22	19 05	18 54	18 45
N 70	18 26	19 28	20 52	18 40	18 41	18 40	18 38
68	18 23	19 20	20 33	18 11	18 22	18 28	18 32
66	18 20	19 12	20 18	17 49	18 07	18 18	18 26
64	18 18	19 06	20 06	17 32	17 54	18 10	18 22
62	18 16	19 01	19 56	17 18	17 43	18 03	18 18
60	18 15	18 57	19 48	17 05	17 34	17 56	18 15
N 58	18 13	18 53	19 41	16 55	17 26	17 51	18 12
56	18 12	18 49	19 34	16 46	17 19	17 46	18 09
54	18 11	18 46	19 29	16 37	17 12	17 41	18 06
52	18 10	18 44	19 24	16 30	17 07	17 37	18 04
50	18 09	18 41	19 20	16 23	17 01	17 34	18 02
45	18 07	18 36	19 11	16 09	16 50	17 26	17 58
N 40	18 05	18 32	19 04	15 57	16 41	17 19	17 54
35	18 04	18 29	18 59	15 47	16 33	17 13	17 51
30	18 03	18 27	18 55	15 38	16 25	17 08	17 48
20	18 01	18 23	18 48	15 23	16 13	16 59	17 43
N 10	17 59	18 20	18 45	15 09	16 02	16 51	17 38
0	17 58	18 18	18 42	14 57	15 52	16 44	17 34
S 10	17 56	18 17	18 42	14 44	15 41	16 37	17 30
20	17 55	18 17	18 43	14 30	15 30	16 29	17 25
30	17 54	18 17	18 45	14 15	15 17	16 19	17 20
35	17 53	18 18	18 47	14 05	15 10	16 14	17 17
40	17 52	18 19	18 51	13 55	15 01	16 08	17 14
45	17 51	18 20	18 55	13 43	14 51	16 01	17 09
S 50	17 50	18 22	19 00	13 28	14 39	15 52	17 05
52	17 50	18 23	19 03	13 20	14 34	15 48	17 02
54	17 49	18 24	19 06	13 13	14 27	15 44	17 00
56	17 49	18 26	19 09	13 04	14 20	15 39	16 57
58	17 48	18 27	19 13	12 54	14 13	15 34	16 54
S 60	17 47	18 29	19 18	12 42	14 04	15 27	16 51

Day	SUN Eqn. of Time 00^h	SUN Eqn. of Time 12^h	SUN Mer. Pass.	MOON Mer. Pass. Upper	MOON Mer. Pass. Lower	MOON Age	MOON Phase
d	m s	m s	h m	h m	h m	d %	
16	05 03	05 14	11 55	08 43	21 11	26 16	
17	05 25	05 35	11 54	09 39	22 06	27 9	
18	05 46	05 57	11 54	10 32	22 57	28 4	

UT d h	ARIES GHA	VENUS −3·9 GHA	VENUS Dec	MARS +1·8 GHA	MARS Dec	JUPITER −1·7 GHA	JUPITER Dec	SATURN +0·5 GHA	SATURN Dec
	° ′	° ′	° ′	° ′	° ′	° ′	° ′	° ′	° ′
19 00	358 05.4	206 54.7	N12 45.1	197 23.4	N 9 25.2	154 04.7	S 8 52.0	97 05.2	S22 04.3
01	13 07.8	221 54.2	44.2	212 24.4	24.6	169 06.6	52.2	112 07.5	04.4
02	28 10.3	236 53.7	43.2	227 25.4	24.0	184 08.6	52.4	127 09.9	04.4
03	43 12.7	251 53.2	. . 42.2	242 26.4	. . 23.4	199 10.6	. . 52.6	142 12.2	. . 04.4
04	58 15.2	266 52.7	41.2	257 27.3	22.8	214 12.6	52.8	157 14.6	04.4
05	73 17.7	281 52.2	40.3	272 28.3	22.2	229 14.6	53.0	172 16.9	04.4
06	88 20.1	296 51.7	N12 39.3	287 29.3	N 9 21.7	244 16.6	S 8 53.2	187 19.3	S22 04.4
07	103 22.6	311 51.2	38.3	302 30.3	21.1	259 18.6	53.3	202 21.7	04.4
TUESDAY 08	118 25.1	326 50.7	37.3	317 31.2	20.5	274 20.6	53.5	217 24.0	04.4
09	133 27.5	341 50.2	. . 36.4	332 32.2	. . 19.9	289 22.6	. . 53.7	232 26.4	. . 04.5
10	148 30.0	356 49.7	35.4	347 33.2	19.3	304 24.5	53.9	247 28.7	04.5
11	163 32.5	11 49.2	34.4	2 34.2	18.7	319 26.5	54.1	262 31.1	04.5
12	178 34.9	26 48.7	N12 33.4	17 35.1	N 9 18.1	334 28.5	S 8 54.3	277 33.5	S22 04.5
13	193 37.4	41 48.3	32.4	32 36.1	17.5	349 30.5	54.5	292 35.8	04.5
14	208 39.9	56 47.8	31.5	47 37.1	16.9	4 32.5	54.7	307 38.2	04.5
15	223 42.3	71 47.3	. . 30.5	62 38.1	. . 16.3	19 34.5	. . 54.8	322 40.5	. . 04.5
16	238 44.8	86 46.8	29.5	77 39.0	15.7	34 36.5	55.0	337 42.9	04.6
17	253 47.2	101 46.3	28.5	92 40.0	15.1	49 38.5	55.2	352 45.2	04.6
18	268 49.7	116 45.8	N12 27.5	107 41.0	N 9 14.5	64 40.4	S 8 55.4	7 47.6	S22 04.6
19	283 52.2	131 45.3	26.5	122 42.0	13.9	79 42.4	55.6	22 50.0	04.6
20	298 54.6	146 44.8	25.5	137 42.9	13.3	94 44.4	55.8	37 52.3	04.6
21	313 57.1	161 44.3	. . 24.6	152 43.9	. . 12.7	109 46.4	. . 56.0	52 54.7	. . 04.6
22	328 59.6	176 43.8	23.6	167 44.9	12.1	124 48.4	56.2	67 57.0	04.6
23	344 02.0	191 43.3	22.6	182 45.9	11.5	139 50.4	56.4	82 59.4	04.7
20 00	359 04.5	206 42.8	N12 21.6	197 46.8	N 9 10.9	154 52.4	S 8 56.5	98 01.7	S22 04.7
01	14 07.0	221 42.3	20.6	212 47.8	10.3	169 54.4	56.7	113 04.1	04.7
02	29 09.4	236 41.8	19.6	227 48.8	09.7	184 56.3	56.9	128 06.4	04.7
03	44 11.9	251 41.4	. . 18.6	242 49.8	. . 09.1	199 58.3	. . 57.1	143 08.8	. . 04.7
04	59 14.3	266 40.9	17.6	257 50.8	08.5	215 00.3	57.3	158 11.1	04.7
05	74 16.8	281 40.4	16.6	272 51.7	07.9	230 02.3	57.5	173 13.5	04.7
06	89 19.3	296 39.9	N12 15.7	287 52.7	N 9 07.3	245 04.3	S 8 57.7	188 15.9	S22 04.7
WEDNESDAY 07	104 21.7	311 39.4	14.7	302 53.7	06.7	260 06.3	57.9	203 18.2	04.8
08	119 24.2	326 38.9	13.7	317 54.7	06.1	275 08.3	58.0	218 20.6	04.8
09	134 26.7	341 38.4	. . 12.7	332 55.6	. . 05.5	290 10.2	. . 58.2	233 22.9	. . 04.8
10	149 29.1	356 37.9	11.7	347 56.6	05.0	305 12.2	58.4	248 25.3	04.8
11	164 31.6	11 37.4	10.7	2 57.6	04.4	320 14.2	58.6	263 27.6	04.8
12	179 34.1	26 36.9	N12 09.7	17 58.6	N 9 03.8	335 16.2	S 8 58.8	278 30.0	S22 04.8
13	194 36.5	41 36.5	08.7	32 59.6	03.2	350 18.2	59.0	293 32.3	04.8
14	209 39.0	56 36.0	07.7	48 00.5	02.6	5 20.2	59.2	308 34.7	04.9
15	224 41.5	71 35.5	. . 06.7	63 01.5	. . 02.0	20 22.2	. . 59.4	323 37.0	. . 04.9
16	239 43.9	86 35.0	05.7	78 02.5	01.4	35 24.1	59.6	338 39.4	04.9
17	254 46.4	101 34.5	04.7	93 03.5	00.8	50 26.1	59.7	353 41.7	04.9
18	269 48.8	116 34.0	N12 03.7	108 04.5	N 9 00.2	65 28.1	S 8 59.9	8 44.1	S22 04.9
19	284 51.3	131 33.5	02.7	123 05.4	8 59.6	80 30.1	9 00.1	23 46.4	04.9
20	299 53.8	146 33.0	01.7	138 06.4	59.0	95 32.1	00.3	38 48.8	04.9
21	314 56.2	161 32.6	12 00.7	153 07.4	. . 58.4	110 34.1	. . 00.5	53 51.2	. . 05.0
22	329 58.7	176 32.1	11 59.7	168 08.4	57.8	125 36.1	00.7	68 53.5	05.0
23	345 01.2	191 31.6	58.7	183 09.3	57.2	140 38.0	00.9	83 55.9	05.0
21 00	0 03.6	206 31.1	N11 57.7	198 10.3	N 8 56.6	155 40.0	S 9 01.1	98 58.2	S22 05.0
01	15 06.1	221 30.6	56.7	213 11.3	56.0	170 42.0	01.3	114 00.6	05.0
02	30 08.6	236 30.1	55.7	228 12.3	55.4	185 44.0	01.4	129 02.9	05.0
03	45 11.0	251 29.7	. . 54.7	243 13.3	. . 54.8	200 46.0	. . 01.6	144 05.3	. . 05.0
04	60 13.5	266 29.2	53.7	258 14.2	54.2	215 48.0	01.8	159 07.6	05.1
05	75 15.9	281 28.7	52.7	273 15.2	53.6	230 49.9	02.0	174 10.0	05.1
06	90 18.4	296 28.2	N11 51.7	288 16.2	N 8 53.0	245 51.9	S 9 02.2	189 12.3	S22 05.1
THURSDAY 07	105 20.9	311 27.7	50.6	303 17.2	52.4	260 53.9	02.4	204 14.7	05.1
08	120 23.3	326 27.2	49.6	318 18.2	51.8	275 55.9	02.6	219 17.0	05.1
09	135 25.8	341 26.8	. . 48.6	333 19.1	. . 51.2	290 57.9	. . 02.8	234 19.4	. . 05.1
10	150 28.3	356 26.3	47.6	348 20.1	50.6	305 59.9	03.0	249 21.7	05.1
11	165 30.7	11 25.8	46.6	3 21.1	50.0	321 01.8	03.1	264 24.1	05.1
12	180 33.2	26 25.3	N11 45.6	18 22.1	N 8 49.4	336 03.8	S 9 03.3	279 26.4	S22 05.2
13	195 35.7	41 24.8	44.6	33 23.1	48.8	351 05.8	03.5	294 28.8	05.2
14	210 38.1	56 24.4	43.6	48 24.0	48.2	6 07.8	03.7	309 31.1	05.2
15	225 40.6	71 23.9	. . 42.6	63 25.0	. . 47.6	21 09.8	. . 03.9	324 33.5	. . 05.2
16	240 43.1	86 23.4	41.6	78 26.0	47.0	36 11.8	04.1	339 35.8	05.2
17	255 45.5	101 22.9	40.5	93 27.0	46.4	51 13.7	04.3	354 38.1	05.2
18	270 48.0	116 22.4	N11 39.5	108 28.0	N 8 45.8	66 15.7	S 9 04.5	9 40.5	S22 05.2
19	285 50.4	131 22.0	38.5	123 28.9	45.2	81 17.7	04.6	24 42.8	05.3
20	300 52.9	146 21.5	37.5	138 29.9	44.6	96 19.7	04.8	39 45.2	05.3
21	315 55.4	161 21.0	. . 36.5	153 30.9	. . 44.0	111 21.7	. . 05.0	54 47.5	. . 05.3
22	330 57.8	176 20.5	35.5	168 31.9	43.4	126 23.7	05.2	69 49.9	05.3
23	346 00.3	191 20.0	34.5	183 32.9	42.8	141 25.6	05.4	84 52.2	05.3
Mer. Pass.	h m 0 03.7	v −0.5	d 1.0	v 1.0	d 0.6	v 2.0	d 0.2	v 2.4	d 0.0

STARS Name	SHA	Dec
	° ′	° ′
Acamar	315 15.9	S40 13.9
Achernar	335 24.2	S57 08.8
Acrux	173 06.6	S63 11.7
Adhara	255 10.4	S28 59.7
Aldebaran	290 46.0	N16 32.5
Alioth	166 18.8	N55 52.1
Alkaid	152 57.1	N49 13.8
Al Na'ir	27 39.8	S46 52.5
Alnilam	275 43.4	S 1 11.5
Alphard	217 53.5	S 8 44.0
Alphecca	126 08.8	N26 39.7
Alpheratz	357 40.1	N29 11.3
Altair	62 05.3	N 8 55.2
Ankaa	353 12.5	S42 12.5
Antares	112 22.8	S26 28.1
Arcturus	145 53.4	N19 05.8
Atria	107 22.2	S69 03.6
Avior	234 17.2	S59 33.8
Bellatrix	278 28.9	N 6 21.8
Betelgeuse	270 58.2	N 7 24.5
Canopus	263 54.9	S52 42.1
Capella	280 30.1	N46 00.6
Deneb	49 29.2	N45 21.0
Denebola	182 31.1	N14 28.6
Diphda	348 52.7	S17 53.3
Dubhe	193 48.9	N61 39.4
Elnath	278 08.9	N28 37.1
Eltanin	90 44.8	N51 29.7
Enif	33 44.0	N 9 57.6
Fomalhaut	15 20.5	S29 31.6
Gacrux	171 58.2	S57 12.6
Gienah	175 49.7	S17 38.2
Hadar	148 44.3	S60 27.4
Hamal	327 57.2	N23 32.7
Kaus Aust.	83 40.0	S34 22.4
Kochab	137 21.0	N74 05.4
Markab	13 35.1	N15 18.2
Menkar	314 11.8	N 4 09.5
Menkent	148 04.5	S36 27.3
Miaplacidus	221 39.7	S69 47.2
Mirfak	308 35.9	N49 55.1
Nunki	75 54.7	S26 16.3
Peacock	53 14.4	S56 40.7
Pollux	243 24.4	N27 58.8
Procyon	244 56.9	N 5 10.7
Rasalhague	96 03.8	N12 33.2
Regulus	207 40.8	N11 52.9
Rigel	281 09.2	S 8 10.9
Rigil Kent.	139 48.3	S60 54.4
Sabik	102 09.3	S15 44.6
Schedar	349 36.6	N56 38.0
Shaula	96 18.0	S37 06.9
Sirius	258 31.3	S16 44.4
Spica	158 28.5	S11 15.0
Suhail	222 50.6	S43 30.1
Vega	80 36.9	N38 48.5
Zuben'ubi	137 02.5	S16 06.7

	SHA	Mer. Pass.
	° ′	h m
Venus	207 38.3	10 13
Mars	198 42.4	10 48
Jupiter	155 47.9	13 39
Saturn	98 57.2	17 25

	UT	SUN GHA	SUN Dec	MOON GHA	v	MOON Dec	d	HP
	d h	° ′	° ′	° ′	′	° ′	′	′
	19 00	181 31.9	N 1 29.4	195 07.8	10.5	N 8 52.7	10.2	58.0
	01	196 32.2	28.5	209 37.3	10.6	8 42.5	10.2	57.9
	02	211 32.4	27.5	224 06.9	10.6	8 32.3	10.3	57.9
	03	226 32.6	. . 26.5	238 36.5	10.7	8 22.0	10.4	57.9
	04	241 32.8	25.6	253 06.2	10.8	8 11.6	10.3	57.9
	05	256 33.0	24.6	267 36.0	10.8	8 01.3	10.4	57.9
	06	271 33.3	N 1 23.6	282 05.8	10.8	N 7 50.9	10.5	57.8
	07	286 33.5	22.6	296 35.6	10.9	7 40.4	10.4	57.8
T	08	301 33.7	21.7	311 05.5	11.0	7 30.0	10.5	57.8
U	09	316 33.9	. . 20.7	325 35.5	11.0	7 19.5	10.6	57.8
E	10	331 34.2	19.7	340 05.5	11.0	7 08.9	10.5	57.8
S	11	346 34.4	18.8	354 35.5	11.1	6 58.4	10.6	57.7
D	12	1 34.6	N 1 17.8	9 05.6	11.2	N 6 47.8	10.6	57.7
A	13	16 34.8	16.8	23 35.8	11.1	6 37.2	10.7	57.7
Y	14	31 35.0	15.9	38 05.9	11.3	6 26.5	10.7	57.7
	15	46 35.3	. . 14.9	52 36.2	11.3	6 15.8	10.7	57.6
	16	61 35.5	13.9	67 06.5	11.3	6 05.1	10.7	57.6
	17	76 35.7	12.9	81 36.8	11.4	5 54.4	10.7	57.6
	18	91 35.9	N 1 12.0	96 07.2	11.4	N 5 43.7	10.8	57.6
	19	106 36.1	11.0	110 37.6	11.5	5 32.9	10.8	57.5
	20	121 36.4	10.0	125 08.1	11.5	5 22.1	10.8	57.5
	21	136 36.6	. . 09.1	139 38.6	11.6	5 11.3	10.8	57.5
	22	151 36.8	08.1	154 09.2	11.6	5 00.5	10.8	57.5
	23	166 37.0	07.1	168 39.8	11.6	4 49.7	10.9	57.4
	20 00	181 37.3	N 1 06.1	183 10.4	11.7	N 4 38.8	10.9	57.4
	01	196 37.5	05.2	197 41.1	11.7	4 27.9	10.9	57.4
	02	211 37.7	04.2	212 11.8	11.8	4 17.0	10.9	57.4
	03	226 37.9	. . 03.2	226 42.6	11.8	4 06.1	10.9	57.4
	04	241 38.1	02.3	241 13.4	11.9	3 55.2	10.9	57.3
	05	256 38.4	01.3	255 44.3	11.9	3 44.3	10.9	57.3
	06	271 38.6	N 1 00.3	270 15.2	11.9	N 3 33.4	10.9	57.3
W	07	286 38.8	0 59.4	284 46.1	12.0	3 22.5	11.0	57.3
E	08	301 39.0	58.4	299 17.1	12.0	3 11.5	10.9	57.2
D	09	316 39.2	. . 57.4	313 48.1	12.1	3 00.6	11.0	57.2
N	10	331 39.5	56.4	328 19.2	12.0	2 49.6	11.0	57.2
E	11	346 39.7	55.5	342 50.2	12.2	2 38.6	10.9	57.2
S	12	1 39.9	N 0 54.5	357 21.4	12.1	N 2 27.7	11.0	57.1
D	13	16 40.1	53.5	11 52.5	12.2	2 16.7	11.0	57.1
A	14	31 40.3	52.6	26 23.7	12.3	2 05.7	10.9	57.1
Y	15	46 40.6	. . 51.6	40 55.0	12.2	1 54.8	11.0	57.1
	16	61 40.8	50.6	55 26.2	12.4	1 43.8	11.0	57.0
	17	76 41.0	49.6	69 57.6	12.3	1 32.8	11.0	57.0
	18	91 41.2	N 0 48.7	84 28.9	12.4	N 1 21.8	10.9	57.0
	19	106 41.5	47.7	99 00.3	12.4	1 10.9	11.0	57.0
	20	121 41.7	46.7	113 31.7	12.4	0 59.9	10.9	56.9
	21	136 41.9	. . 45.8	128 03.1	12.5	0 49.0	11.0	56.9
	22	151 42.1	44.8	142 34.6	12.5	0 38.0	10.9	56.9
	23	166 42.3	43.8	157 06.1	12.5	0 27.1	11.0	56.9
	21 00	181 42.6	N 0 42.8	171 37.6	12.6	N 0 16.1	10.9	56.8
	01	196 42.8	41.9	186 09.2	12.5	N 0 05.2	10.9	56.8
	02	211 43.0	40.9	200 40.7	12.7	S 0 05.7	10.9	56.8
	03	226 43.2	. . 39.9	215 12.4	12.6	0 16.6	10.9	56.7
	04	241 43.4	38.9	229 44.0	12.7	0 27.5	10.9	56.7
	05	256 43.7	38.0	244 15.7	12.7	0 38.4	10.9	56.7
	06	271 43.9	N 0 37.0	258 47.4	12.7	S 0 49.3	10.8	56.7
	07	286 44.1	36.0	273 19.1	12.7	1 00.1	10.9	56.6
T	08	301 44.3	35.1	287 50.8	12.8	1 11.0	10.8	56.6
H	09	316 44.5	. . 34.1	302 22.6	12.8	1 21.8	10.8	56.6
U	10	331 44.8	33.1	316 54.4	12.8	1 32.6	10.8	56.6
R	11	346 45.0	32.1	331 26.2	12.9	1 43.4	10.8	56.5
S	12	1 45.2	N 0 31.2	345 58.1	12.9	S 1 54.2	10.7	56.5
D	13	16 45.4	30.2	0 30.0	12.9	2 04.9	10.8	56.5
A	14	31 45.6	29.2	15 01.9	12.9	2 15.7	10.7	56.5
Y	15	46 45.9	. . 28.3	29 33.8	12.9	2 26.4	10.7	56.4
	16	61 46.1	27.3	44 05.7	13.0	2 37.1	10.7	56.4
	17	76 46.3	26.3	58 37.7	12.9	2 47.8	10.6	56.4
	18	91 46.5	N 0 25.3	73 09.6	13.0	S 2 58.4	10.6	56.4
	19	106 46.7	24.4	87 41.6	13.1	3 09.0	10.6	56.3
	20	121 47.0	23.4	102 13.7	13.0	3 19.6	10.6	56.3
	21	136 47.2	. . 22.4	116 45.7	13.0	3 30.2	10.5	56.3
	22	151 47.4	21.4	131 17.7	13.1	3 40.7	10.6	56.3
	23	166 47.6	20.5	145 49.8	13.1	S 3 51.3	10.5	56.2
		SD 16.0	*d* 1.0	SD		15.7	15.6	15.4

Lat.	Twilight Naut.	Twilight Civil	Sunrise	Moonrise 19	20	21	22
°	h m	h m	h m	h m	h m	h m	h m
N 72	02 46	04 21	05 30	03 22	05 13	07 01	08 46
N 70	03 09	04 30	05 33	03 34	05 18	06 59	08 37
68	03 26	04 38	05 34	03 45	05 23	06 58	08 31
66	03 39	04 44	05 36	03 53	05 26	06 57	08 25
64	03 50	04 50	05 38	04 00	05 29	06 56	08 20
62	04 00	04 54	05 39	04 06	05 32	06 55	08 16
60	04 07	04 58	05 40	04 12	05 34	06 54	08 13
N 58	04 14	05 01	05 41	04 16	05 36	06 54	08 10
56	04 20	05 04	05 41	04 20	05 38	06 53	08 07
54	04 24	05 07	05 42	04 24	05 39	06 53	08 04
52	04 29	05 09	05 43	04 27	05 41	06 52	08 02
50	04 33	05 11	05 43	04 30	05 42	06 52	08 00
45	04 41	05 15	05 45	04 37	05 45	06 51	07 56
N 40	04 47	05 19	05 46	04 42	05 47	06 50	07 52
35	04 52	05 21	05 47	04 47	05 49	06 50	07 49
30	04 55	05 23	05 47	04 51	05 51	06 49	07 46
20	05 01	05 26	05 48	04 58	05 54	06 48	07 41
N 10	05 04	05 28	05 49	05 05	05 57	06 48	07 37
0	05 05	05 29	05 50	05 10	05 59	06 47	07 33
S 10	05 05	05 30	05 51	05 16	06 02	06 46	07 29
20	05 04	05 29	05 51	05 23	06 05	06 45	07 25
30	05 00	05 28	05 52	05 30	06 08	06 45	07 20
35	04 58	05 27	05 52	05 34	06 10	06 44	07 18
40	04 54	05 26	05 52	05 38	06 12	06 44	07 15
45	04 49	05 24	05 53	05 44	06 14	06 43	07 11
S 50	04 43	05 21	05 53	05 50	06 17	06 42	07 07
52	04 40	05 20	05 53	05 53	06 18	06 42	07 05
54	04 37	05 18	05 53	05 56	06 20	06 42	07 03
56	04 33	05 16	05 53	06 00	06 21	06 41	07 01
58	04 28	05 15	05 54	06 04	06 23	06 41	06 59
S 60	04 23	05 12	05 54	06 08	06 25	06 41	06 56

Lat.	Sunset	Twilight Civil	Twilight Naut.	Moonset 19	20	21	22
°	h m	h m	h m	h m	h m	h m	h m
N 72	18 14	19 23	20 55	18 45	18 37	18 29	18 20
N 70	18 12	19 14	20 34	18 38	18 36	18 33	18 31
68	18 10	19 06	20 17	18 32	18 34	18 37	18 39
66	18 09	19 00	20 04	18 26	18 33	18 40	18 46
64	18 08	18 55	19 54	18 22	18 32	18 42	18 52
62	18 06	18 51	19 45	18 18	18 32	18 44	18 57
60	18 06	18 47	19 38	18 15	18 31	18 46	19 02
N 58	18 05	18 44	19 31	18 12	18 30	18 48	19 06
56	18 04	18 41	19 26	18 09	18 30	18 50	19 10
54	18 03	18 39	19 21	18 06	18 29	18 51	19 13
52	18 03	18 37	19 17	18 04	18 29	18 52	19 16
50	18 02	18 35	19 13	18 02	18 28	18 53	19 19
45	18 01	18 31	19 05	17 58	18 27	18 56	19 24
N 40	18 00	18 27	18 59	17 54	18 27	18 58	19 29
35	18 00	18 25	18 54	17 51	18 26	19 00	19 34
30	17 59	18 23	18 51	17 48	18 25	19 01	19 37
20	17 58	18 20	18 46	17 43	18 24	19 04	19 44
N 10	17 57	18 18	18 43	17 38	18 23	19 07	19 50
0	17 57	18 17	18 41	17 34	18 22	19 09	19 55
S 10	17 56	18 17	18 41	17 30	18 21	19 11	20 00
20	17 56	18 18	18 43	17 25	18 20	19 14	20 06
30	17 55	18 19	18 47	17 20	18 19	19 17	20 13
35	17 55	18 20	18 50	17 17	18 18	19 18	20 17
40	17 55	18 22	18 53	17 14	18 18	19 20	20 21
45	17 55	18 24	18 58	17 09	18 17	19 22	20 26
S 50	17 55	18 27	19 05	17 05	18 16	19 25	20 32
52	17 55	18 28	19 08	17 02	18 15	19 26	20 35
54	17 54	18 30	19 11	17 00	18 14	19 27	20 38
56	17 54	18 32	19 16	16 57	18 14	19 28	20 41
58	17 54	18 34	19 20	16 54	18 13	19 30	20 45
S 60	17 54	18 36	19 26	16 51	18 12	19 32	20 49

Day	SUN Eqn. of Time 00^h	SUN Eqn. of Time 12^h	SUN Mer. Pass.	MOON Mer. Pass. Upper	MOON Mer. Pass. Lower	Age	Phase
d	m s	m s	h m	h m	h m	d	%
19	06 07	06 18	11 54	11 22	23 47	29	1
20	06 29	06 39	11 53	12 11	24 35	00	0
21	06 50	07 00	11 53	12 58	00 35	01	2

Day	UT d h	ARIES GHA ° ′	VENUS −3·9 GHA ° ′	VENUS Dec ° ′	MARS +1·8 GHA ° ′	MARS Dec ° ′	JUPITER −1·7 GHA ° ′	JUPITER Dec ° ′	SATURN +0·5 GHA ° ′	SATURN Dec ° ′
	22 00	1 02.8	206 19.6	N11 33.4	198 33.8	N 8 42.2	156 27.6	S 9 05.6	99 54.6	S22 05.3
	01	16 05.2	221 19.1	32.4	213 34.8	41.6	171 29.6	05.8	114 56.9	05.3
	02	31 07.7	236 18.6	31.4	228 35.8	41.0	186 31.6	06.0	129 59.3	05.4
	03	46 10.2	251 18.1 . .	30.4	243 36.8 . .	40.4	201 33.6 . .	06.2	145 01.6 . .	05.4
	04	61 12.6	266 17.7	29.4	258 37.8	39.8	216 35.6	06.3	160 04.0	05.4
	05	76 15.1	281 17.2	28.3	273 38.8	39.2	231 37.5	06.5	175 06.3	05.4
	06	91 17.5	296 16.7	N11 27.3	288 39.7	N 8 38.6	246 39.5	S 9 06.7	190 08.7	S22 05.4
	07	106 20.0	311 16.2	26.3	303 40.7	38.0	261 41.5	06.9	205 11.0	05.4
	08	121 22.5	326 15.7	25.3	318 41.7	37.4	276 43.5	07.1	220 13.4	05.4
F	09	136 24.9	341 15.3 . .	24.3	333 42.7 . .	36.8	291 45.5 . .	07.3	235 15.7 . .	05.5
R	10	151 27.4	356 14.8	23.2	348 43.7	36.2	306 47.4	07.5	250 18.0	05.5
I	11	166 29.9	11 14.3	22.2	3 44.6	35.6	321 49.4	07.7	265 20.4	05.5
D	12	181 32.3	26 13.8	N11 21.2	18 45.6	N 8 35.0	336 51.4	S 9 07.9	280 22.7	S22 05.5
A	13	196 34.8	41 13.4	20.2	33 46.6	34.4	351 53.4	08.1	295 25.1	05.5
Y	14	211 37.3	56 12.9	19.1	48 47.6	33.8	6 55.4	08.2	310 27.4	05.5
	15	226 39.7	71 12.4 . .	18.1	63 48.6 . .	33.2	21 57.4 . .	08.4	325 29.8 . .	05.5
	16	241 42.2	86 12.0	17.1	78 49.6	32.6	36 59.3	08.6	340 32.1	05.6
	17	256 44.7	101 11.5	16.1	93 50.5	32.0	52 01.3	08.8	355 34.5	05.6
	18	271 47.1	116 11.0	N11 15.0	108 51.5	N 8 31.3	67 03.3	S 9 09.0	10 36.8	S22 05.6
	19	286 49.6	131 10.5	14.0	123 52.5	30.7	82 05.3	09.2	25 39.1	05.6
	20	301 52.0	146 10.1	13.0	138 53.5	30.1	97 07.3	09.4	40 41.5	05.6
	21	316 54.5	161 09.6 . .	11.9	153 54.5 . .	29.5	112 09.2 . .	09.6	55 43.8 . .	05.6
	22	331 57.0	176 09.1	10.9	168 55.5	28.9	127 11.2	09.8	70 46.2	05.6
	23	346 59.4	191 08.6	09.9	183 56.4	28.3	142 13.2	09.9	85 48.5	05.7
	23 00	2 01.9	206 08.2	N11 08.8	198 57.4	N 8 27.7	157 15.2	S 9 10.1	100 50.9	S22 05.7
	01	17 04.4	221 07.7	07.8	213 58.4	27.1	172 17.2	10.3	115 53.2	05.7
	02	32 06.8	236 07.2	06.8	228 59.4	26.5	187 19.1	10.5	130 55.5	05.7
	03	47 09.3	251 06.8 . .	05.7	244 00.4 . .	25.9	202 21.1 . .	10.7	145 57.9 . .	05.7
	04	62 11.8	266 06.3	04.7	259 01.4	25.3	217 23.1	10.9	161 00.2	05.7
	05	77 14.2	281 05.8	03.7	274 02.3	24.7	232 25.1	11.1	176 02.6	05.7
	06	92 16.7	296 05.4	N11 02.6	289 03.3	N 8 24.1	247 27.1	S 9 11.3	191 04.9	S22 05.8
S	07	107 19.1	311 04.9	01.6	304 04.3	23.5	262 29.0	11.5	206 07.3	05.8
A	08	122 21.6	326 04.4	11 00.6	319 05.3	22.9	277 31.0	11.6	221 09.6	05.8
T	09	137 24.1	341 03.9	10 59.5	334 06.3 . .	22.3	292 33.0 . .	11.8	236 11.9 . .	05.8
U	10	152 26.5	356 03.5	58.5	349 07.3	21.7	307 35.0	12.0	251 14.3	05.8
R	11	167 29.0	11 03.0	57.5	4 08.2	21.1	322 37.0	12.2	266 16.6	05.8
D	12	182 31.5	26 02.5	N10 56.4	19 09.2	N 8 20.5	337 38.9	S 9 12.4	281 19.0	S22 05.8
A	13	197 33.9	41 02.1	55.4	34 10.2	19.9	352 40.9	12.6	296 21.3	05.9
Y	14	212 36.4	56 01.6	54.4	49 11.2	19.3	7 42.9	12.8	311 23.6	05.9
	15	227 38.9	71 01.1 . .	53.3	64 12.2 . .	18.7	22 44.9 . .	13.0	326 26.0 . .	05.9
	16	242 41.3	86 00.7	52.3	79 13.2	18.1	37 46.9	13.2	341 28.3	05.9
	17	257 43.8	101 00.2	51.2	94 14.1	17.5	52 48.8	13.4	356 30.7	05.9
	18	272 46.3	115 59.7	N10 50.2	109 15.1	N 8 16.9	67 50.8	S 9 13.5	11 33.0	S22 05.9
	19	287 48.7	130 59.3	49.2	124 16.1	16.3	82 52.8	13.7	26 35.3	05.9
	20	302 51.2	145 58.8	48.1	139 17.1	15.7	97 54.8	13.9	41 37.7	06.0
	21	317 53.6	160 58.3 . .	47.1	154 18.1 . .	15.1	112 56.8 . .	14.1	56 40.0 . .	06.0
	22	332 56.1	175 57.9	46.0	169 19.1	14.5	127 58.7	14.3	71 42.4	06.0
	23	347 58.6	190 57.4	45.0	184 20.1	13.8	143 00.7	14.5	86 44.7	06.0
	24 00	3 01.0	205 57.0	N10 43.9	199 21.0	N 8 13.2	158 02.7	S 9 14.7	101 47.0	S22 06.0
	01	18 03.5	220 56.5	42.9	214 22.0	12.6	173 04.7	14.9	116 49.4	06.0
	02	33 06.0	235 56.0	41.8	229 23.0	12.0	188 06.7	15.1	131 51.7	06.0
	03	48 08.4	250 55.6 . .	40.8	244 24.0 . .	11.4	203 08.6 . .	15.2	146 54.1 . .	06.1
	04	63 10.9	265 55.1	39.8	259 25.0	10.8	218 10.6	15.4	161 56.4	06.1
	05	78 13.4	280 54.6	38.7	274 26.0	10.2	233 12.6	15.6	176 58.7	06.1
	06	93 15.8	295 54.2	N10 37.7	289 27.0	N 8 09.6	248 14.6	S 9 15.8	192 01.1	S22 06.1
	07	108 18.3	310 53.7	36.6	304 27.9	09.0	263 16.5	16.0	207 03.4	06.1
	08	123 20.8	325 53.2	35.6	319 28.9	08.4	278 18.5	16.2	222 05.7	06.1
S	09	138 23.2	340 52.8 . .	34.5	334 29.9 . .	07.8	293 20.5 . .	16.4	237 08.1 . .	06.1
U	10	153 25.7	355 52.3	33.5	349 30.9	07.2	308 22.5	16.6	252 10.4	06.2
N	11	168 28.1	10 51.9	32.4	4 31.9	06.6	323 24.5	16.8	267 12.8	06.2
D	12	183 30.6	25 51.4	N10 31.4	19 32.9	N 8 06.0	338 26.4	S 9 17.0	282 15.1	S22 06.2
A	13	198 33.1	40 50.9	30.3	34 33.9	05.4	353 28.4	17.1	297 17.4	06.2
Y	14	213 35.5	55 50.5	29.3	49 34.8	04.8	8 30.4	17.3	312 19.8	06.2
	15	228 38.0	70 50.0 . .	28.2	64 35.8 . .	04.2	23 32.4 . .	17.5	327 22.1 . .	06.2
	16	243 40.5	85 49.6	27.2	79 36.8	03.6	38 34.3	17.7	342 24.4	06.2
	17	258 42.9	100 49.1	26.1	94 37.8	02.9	53 36.3	17.9	357 26.8	06.3
	18	273 45.4	115 48.6	N10 25.0	109 38.8	N 8 02.3	68 38.3	S 9 18.1	12 29.1	S22 06.3
	19	288 47.9	130 48.2	24.0	124 39.8	01.7	83 40.3	18.3	27 31.5	06.3
	20	303 50.3	145 47.7	22.9	139 40.8	01.1	98 42.3	18.5	42 33.8	06.3
	21	318 52.8	160 47.3 . .	21.9	154 41.8	8 00.5	113 44.2 . .	18.7	57 36.1 . .	06.3
	22	333 55.2	175 46.8	20.8	169 42.7	7 59.9	128 46.2	18.8	72 38.5	06.3
	23	348 57.7	190 46.3	19.8	184 43.7	N 7 59.3	143 48.2	19.0	87 40.8	06.3
	Mer. Pass.	h m 23 48.0	v −0.5	d 1.0	v 1.0	d 0.6	v 2.0	d 0.2	v 2.3	d 0.0

STARS

Name	SHA ° ′	Dec ° ′
Acamar	315 15.9	S40 14.0
Achernar	335 24.2	S57 08.8
Acrux	173 06.7	S63 11.7
Adhara	255 10.4	S28 59.7
Aldebaran	290 46.0	N16 32.5
Alioth	166 18.8	N55 52.1
Alkaid	152 57.1	N49 13.8
Al Na'ir	27 39.8	S46 52.5
Alnilam	275 43.4	S 1 11.5
Alphard	217 53.5	S 8 44.0
Alphecca	126 08.8	N26 39.7
Alpheratz	357 40.1	N29 11.3
Altair	62 05.3	N 8 55.2
Ankaa	353 12.5	S42 12.6
Antares	112 22.9	S26 28.1
Arcturus	145 53.4	N19 05.8
Atria	107 22.2	S69 03.6
Avior	234 17.2	S59 33.8
Bellatrix	278 28.9	N 6 21.8
Betelgeuse	270 58.2	N 7 24.5
Canopus	263 54.9	S52 42.1
Capella	280 30.1	N46 00.6
Deneb	49 29.2	N45 21.0
Denebola	182 31.1	N14 28.6
Diphda	348 52.7	S17 53.3
Dubhe	193 48.9	N61 39.3
Elnath	278 08.9	N28 37.1
Eltanin	90 44.8	N51 29.7
Enif	33 44.0	N 9 57.6
Fomalhaut	15 20.5	S29 31.6
Gacrux	171 58.2	S57 12.6
Gienah	175 49.7	S17 38.2
Hadar	148 44.3	S60 27.4
Hamal	327 57.2	N23 32.7
Kaus Aust.	83 40.0	S34 22.4
Kochab	137 21.1	N74 05.3
Markab	13 35.1	N15 18.2
Menkar	314 11.8	N 4 09.5
Menkent	148 04.5	S36 27.2
Miaplacidus	221 39.7	S69 47.2
Mirfak	308 35.9	N49 55.1
Nunki	75 54.7	S26 16.3
Peacock	53 14.4	S56 40.7
Pollux	243 24.4	N27 58.8
Procyon	244 56.9	N 5 10.7
Rasalhague	96 03.8	N12 33.2
Regulus	207 40.8	N11 52.9
Rigel	281 09.2	S 8 10.9
Rigil Kent.	139 48.3	S60 54.4
Sabik	102 09.3	S15 44.6
Schedar	349 36.6	N56 38.0
Shaula	96 18.1	S37 06.9
Sirius	258 31.2	S16 44.4
Spica	158 28.5	S11 15.0
Suhail	222 50.6	S43 30.1
Vega	80 37.0	N38 48.5
Zuben'ubi	137 02.5	S16 06.7

	SHA ° ′	Mer. Pass. h m
Venus	204 06.3	10 16
Mars	196 55.5	10 43
Jupiter	155 13.3	13 29
Saturn	98 49.0	17 14

UT d h	SUN GHA ° ′	SUN Dec ° ′	MOON GHA ° ′	v ′	MOON Dec ° ′	d ′	HP ′
22 00 (FRIDAY)	181 47.8	N 0 19.5	160 21.9	13.1	S 4 01.8	10.4	56.2
01	196 48.1	18.5	174 54.0	13.1	4 12.2	10.5	56.2
02	211 48.3	17.6	189 26.1	13.2	4 22.7	10.4	56.2
03	226 48.5	. . 16.6	203 58.3	13.1	4 33.1	10.3	56.1
04	241 48.7	15.6	218 30.4	13.2	4 43.4	10.4	56.1
05	256 48.9	14.6	233 02.6	13.2	4 53.8	10.3	56.1
06	271 49.2	N 0 13.7	247 34.8	13.1	S 5 04.1	10.3	56.1
07	286 49.4	12.7	262 06.9	13.2	5 14.4	10.2	56.0
08	301 49.6	11.7	276 39.1	13.3	5 24.6	10.2	56.0
09	316 49.8	. . 10.7	291 11.4	13.2	5 34.8	10.2	56.0
10	331 50.0	09.8	305 43.6	13.2	5 45.0	10.1	56.0
11	346 50.2	08.8	320 15.8	13.3	5 55.1	10.1	55.9
12	1 50.5	N 0 07.8	334 48.1	13.2	S 6 05.2	10.1	55.9
13	16 50.7	06.9	349 20.3	13.3	6 15.3	10.0	55.9
14	31 50.9	05.9	3 52.6	13.3	6 25.3	10.0	55.9
15	46 51.1	. . 04.9	18 24.9	13.3	6 35.3	9.9	55.8
16	61 51.3	03.9	32 57.2	13.3	6 45.2	9.9	55.8
17	76 51.6	03.0	47 29.5	13.3	6 55.1	9.9	55.8
18	91 51.8	N 0 02.0	62 01.8	13.3	S 7 05.0	9.8	55.8
19	106 52.0	N 01.0	76 34.1	13.3	7 14.8	9.8	55.7
20	121 52.2	00.0	91 06.4	13.3	7 24.6	9.7	55.7
21	136 52.4	S 00.9	105 38.7	13.3	7 34.3	9.7	55.7
22	151 52.7	01.9	120 11.0	13.4	7 44.0	9.7	55.7
23	166 52.9	02.9	134 43.4	13.3	7 53.7	9.6	55.6
23 00 (SATURDAY)	181 53.1	S 0 03.9	149 15.7	13.3	S 8 03.3	9.6	55.6
01	196 53.3	04.8	163 48.0	13.4	8 12.9	9.5	55.6
02	211 53.5	05.8	178 20.4	13.3	8 22.4	9.4	55.6
03	226 53.7	. . 06.8	192 52.7	13.4	8 31.8	9.5	55.5
04	241 54.0	07.7	207 25.1	13.3	8 41.3	9.3	55.5
05	256 54.2	08.7	221 57.4	13.4	8 50.6	9.4	55.5
06	271 54.4	S 0 09.7	236 29.8	13.4	S 9 00.0	9.2	55.5
07	286 54.6	10.7	251 02.2	13.3	9 09.2	9.3	55.4
08	301 54.8	11.6	265 34.5	13.4	9 18.5	9.1	55.4
09	316 55.1	. . 12.6	280 06.9	13.3	9 27.6	9.2	55.4
10	331 55.3	13.6	294 39.2	13.4	9 36.8	9.0	55.4
11	346 55.5	14.6	309 11.6	13.4	9 45.8	9.1	55.4
12	1 55.7	S 0 15.5	323 44.0	13.3	S 9 54.9	8.9	55.3
13	16 55.9	16.5	338 16.3	13.4	10 03.8	8.9	55.3
14	31 56.1	17.5	352 48.7	13.3	10 12.7	8.9	55.3
15	46 56.4	. . 18.5	7 21.0	13.4	10 21.6	8.8	55.3
16	61 56.6	19.4	21 53.4	13.3	10 30.4	8.8	55.3
17	76 56.8	20.4	36 25.7	13.4	10 39.2	8.7	55.2
18	91 57.0	S 0 21.4	50 58.1	13.3	S10 47.9	8.6	55.2
19	106 57.2	22.3	65 30.4	13.4	10 56.5	8.6	55.2
20	121 57.5	23.3	80 02.8	13.3	11 05.1	8.5	55.2
21	136 57.7	. . 24.3	94 35.1	13.3	11 13.6	8.5	55.1
22	151 57.9	25.3	109 07.4	13.4	11 22.1	8.4	55.1
23	166 58.1	26.2	123 39.8	13.3	11 30.5	8.4	55.1
24 00 (SUNDAY)	181 58.3	S 0 27.2	138 12.1	13.3	S11 38.9	8.3	55.1
01	196 58.5	28.2	152 44.4	13.3	11 47.2	8.2	55.1
02	211 58.8	29.2	167 16.7	13.3	11 55.4	8.2	55.0
03	226 59.0	. . 30.1	181 49.0	13.3	12 03.6	8.1	55.0
04	241 59.2	31.1	196 21.3	13.3	12 11.7	8.1	55.0
05	256 59.4	32.1	210 53.6	13.3	12 19.8	8.0	55.0
06	271 59.6	S 0 33.1	225 25.9	13.3	S12 27.8	7.9	55.0
07	286 59.8	34.0	239 58.2	13.2	12 35.7	7.9	54.9
08	302 00.1	35.0	254 30.4	13.3	12 43.6	7.8	54.9
09	317 00.3	. . 36.0	269 02.7	13.2	12 51.4	7.7	54.9
10	332 00.5	37.0	283 34.9	13.3	12 59.1	7.7	54.9
11	347 00.7	37.9	298 07.2	13.2	13 06.8	7.6	54.9
12	2 00.9	S 0 38.9	312 39.4	13.2	S13 14.4	7.6	54.9
13	17 01.1	39.9	327 11.6	13.3	13 22.0	7.5	54.8
14	32 01.4	40.8	341 43.9	13.2	13 29.5	7.4	54.8
15	47 01.6	. . 41.8	356 16.1	13.2	13 36.9	7.4	54.8
16	62 01.8	42.8	10 48.3	13.2	13 44.3	7.3	54.8
17	77 02.0	43.8	25 20.5	13.1	13 51.6	7.2	54.8
18	92 02.2	S 0 44.7	39 52.6	13.2	S13 58.8	7.1	54.8
19	107 02.4	45.7	54 24.8	13.1	14 05.9	7.1	54.7
20	122 02.7	46.7	68 56.9	13.2	14 13.0	7.0	54.7
21	137 02.9	. . 47.7	83 29.1	13.1	14 20.0	7.0	54.7
22	152 03.1	48.6	98 01.2	13.1	14 27.0	6.9	54.7
23	167 03.3	49.6	112 33.3	13.1	S14 33.9	6.8	54.7
	SD 16.0	*d* 1.0	SD 15.2		15.1		14.9

Lat. °	Twilight Naut. h m	Twilight Civil h m	Sunrise h m	Moonrise 22 h m	Moonrise 23 h m	Moonrise 24 h m	Moonrise 25 h m
N 72	03 05	04 35	05 44	08 46	10 31	12 18	14 14
N 70	03 24	04 43	05 44	08 37	10 15	11 51	13 28
68	03 39	04 49	05 45	08 31	10 02	11 32	12 59
66	03 51	04 54	05 46	08 25	09 51	11 16	12 37
64	04 00	04 58	05 46	08 20	09 43	11 03	12 20
62	04 08	05 02	05 46	08 16	09 35	10 52	12 05
60	04 15	05 05	05 47	08 13	09 29	10 43	11 53
N 58	04 21	05 08	05 47	08 10	09 23	10 35	11 43
56	04 26	05 10	05 47	08 07	09 18	10 28	11 34
54	04 30	05 12	05 48	08 04	09 14	10 21	11 26
52	04 34	05 14	05 48	08 02	09 10	10 16	11 19
50	04 38	05 16	05 48	08 00	09 06	10 11	11 12
45	04 45	05 19	05 48	07 56	08 58	10 00	10 59
N 40	04 50	05 22	05 49	07 52	08 52	09 50	10 47
35	04 54	05 23	05 49	07 49	08 46	09 43	10 38
30	04 57	05 25	05 49	07 46	08 41	09 36	10 29
20	05 01	05 27	05 49	07 41	08 33	09 24	10 15
N 10	05 04	05 28	05 49	07 37	08 26	09 14	10 02
0	05 04	05 28	05 49	07 33	08 19	09 04	09 50
S 10	05 04	05 28	05 49	07 29	08 12	08 55	09 39
20	05 01	05 27	05 49	07 25	08 05	08 45	09 26
30	04 56	05 24	05 48	07 20	07 56	08 33	09 12
35	04 53	05 23	05 48	07 18	07 52	08 27	09 04
40	04 49	05 21	05 48	07 15	07 46	08 19	08 54
45	04 43	05 18	05 47	07 11	07 40	08 11	08 44
S 50	04 36	05 14	05 46	07 07	07 33	08 00	08 30
52	04 33	05 13	05 46	07 05	07 29	07 55	08 24
54	04 29	05 11	05 46	07 03	07 26	07 50	08 18
56	04 24	05 08	05 45	07 01	07 22	07 44	08 10
58	04 19	05 06	05 45	06 59	07 17	07 38	08 02
S 60	04 13	05 03	05 45	06 56	07 12	07 30	07 52

Lat. °	Sunset h m	Twilight Civil h m	Twilight Naut. h m	Moonset 22 h m	Moonset 23 h m	Moonset 24 h m	Moonset 25 h m
N 72	17 59	19 06	20 35	18 20	18 11	17 58	17 39
N 70	17 58	18 59	20 17	18 31	18 28	18 26	18 25
68	17 58	18 53	20 02	18 39	18 42	18 47	18 55
66	17 57	18 48	19 51	18 46	18 54	19 04	19 18
64	17 57	18 44	19 42	18 52	19 04	19 17	19 36
62	17 57	18 41	19 34	18 57	19 12	19 29	19 50
60	17 56	18 38	19 28	19 02	19 19	19 39	20 03
N 58	17 56	18 35	19 22	19 06	19 25	19 48	20 14
56	17 56	18 33	19 17	19 10	19 31	19 55	20 23
54	17 56	18 31	19 13	19 13	19 36	20 02	20 31
52	17 56	18 29	19 09	19 16	19 41	20 08	20 39
50	17 56	18 28	19 06	19 19	19 45	20 14	20 46
45	17 56	18 25	18 59	19 24	19 54	20 25	21 00
N 40	17 55	18 22	18 54	19 29	20 01	20 35	21 12
35	17 55	18 21	18 50	19 34	20 08	20 44	21 22
30	17 55	18 19	18 47	19 37	20 14	20 51	21 31
20	17 55	18 17	18 43	19 44	20 24	21 04	21 47
N 10	17 55	18 16	18 41	19 50	20 32	21 16	22 00
0	17 56	18 16	18 40	19 55	20 41	21 26	22 13
S 10	17 56	18 17	18 41	20 00	20 49	21 37	22 25
20	17 56	18 18	18 44	20 06	20 58	21 49	22 39
30	17 57	18 21	18 49	20 13	21 08	22 02	22 55
35	17 57	18 23	18 52	20 17	21 14	22 09	23 04
40	17 58	18 25	18 56	20 21	21 20	22 18	23 14
45	17 58	18 28	19 02	20 26	21 28	22 28	23 26
S 50	17 59	18 31	19 10	20 32	21 37	22 40	23 41
52	17 59	18 33	19 13	20 35	21 42	22 46	23 48
54	18 00	18 35	19 17	20 38	21 46	22 53	23 55
56	18 00	18 38	19 22	20 41	21 52	23 00	24 04
58	18 01	18 40	19 27	20 45	21 58	23 08	24 14
S 60	18 01	18 43	19 33	20 49	22 04	23 17	24 25

Day d	SUN Eqn. of Time 00h m s	SUN Eqn. of Time 12h m s	SUN Mer. Pass. h m	MOON Mer. Pass. Upper h m	MOON Mer. Pass. Lower h m	MOON Age d	MOON Phase %
22	07 11	07 21	11 53	13 44	01 21	02	6
23	07 32	07 42	11 52	14 30	02 07	03	11
24	07 53	08 03	11 52	15 15	02 52	04	18

	UT	ARIES	VENUS −3·9		MARS +1·8		JUPITER −1·7		SATURN +0·5	
	d h	GHA ° ′	GHA ° ′	Dec ° ′	GHA ° ′	Dec ° ′	GHA ° ′	Dec ° ′	GHA ° ′	Dec ° ′
	25 00	4 00.2	205 45.9	N10 18.7	199 44.7	N 7 58.7	158 50.2	S 9 19.2	102 43.1	S22 06.4
	01	19 02.6	220 45.4	17.7	214 45.7	58.1	173 52.1	19.4	117 45.5	06.4
	02	34 05.1	235 45.0	16.6	229 46.7	57.5	188 54.1	19.6	132 47.8	06.4
	03	49 07.6	250 44.5	. . 15.5	244 47.7	. . 56.9	203 56.1	. . 19.8	147 50.1	. . 06.4
	04	64 10.0	265 44.1	14.5	259 48.7	56.3	218 58.1	20.0	162 52.5	06.4
	05	79 12.5	280 43.6	13.4	274 49.6	55.7	234 00.0	20.2	177 54.8	06.4
	06	94 15.0	295 43.1	N10 12.4	289 50.6	N 7 55.1	249 02.0	S 9 20.4	192 57.1	S22 06.4
	07	109 17.4	310 42.7	11.3	304 51.6	54.5	264 04.0	20.6	207 59.5	06.5
	08	124 19.9	325 42.2	10.2	319 52.6	53.9	279 06.0	20.7	223 01.8	06.5
M	09	139 22.4	340 41.8	. . 09.2	334 53.6	. . 53.2	294 07.9	. . 20.9	238 04.1	. . 06.5
O	10	154 24.8	355 41.3	08.1	349 54.6	52.6	309 09.9	21.1	253 06.5	06.5
N	11	169 27.3	10 40.9	07.0	4 55.6	52.0	324 11.9	21.3	268 08.8	06.5
D	12	184 29.7	25 40.4	N10 06.0	19 56.6	N 7 51.4	339 13.9	S 9 21.5	283 11.1	S22 06.5
A	13	199 32.2	40 40.0	04.9	34 57.6	50.8	354 15.8	21.7	298 13.5	06.5
Y	14	214 34.7	55 39.5	03.9	49 58.5	50.2	9 17.8	21.9	313 15.8	06.6
	15	229 37.1	70 39.1	. . 02.8	64 59.5	. . 49.6	24 19.8	. . 22.1	328 18.1	. . 06.6
	16	244 39.6	85 38.6	01.7	80 00.5	49.0	39 21.8	22.3	343 20.5	06.6
	17	259 42.1	100 38.1	10 00.7	95 01.5	48.4	54 23.8	22.5	358 22.8	06.6
	18	274 44.5	115 37.7	N 9 59.6	110 02.5	N 7 47.8	69 25.7	S 9 22.6	13 25.1	S22 06.6
	19	289 47.0	130 37.2	58.5	125 03.5	47.2	84 27.7	22.8	28 27.5	06.6
	20	304 49.5	145 36.8	57.5	140 04.5	46.6	99 29.7	23.0	43 29.8	06.6
	21	319 51.9	160 36.3	. . 56.4	155 05.5	. . 46.0	114 31.7	. . 23.2	58 32.1	. . 06.7
	22	334 54.4	175 35.9	55.3	170 06.4	45.3	129 33.6	23.4	73 34.5	06.7
	23	349 56.9	190 35.4	54.3	185 07.4	44.7	144 35.6	23.6	88 36.8	06.7
	26 00	4 59.3	205 35.0	N 9 53.2	200 08.4	N 7 44.1	159 37.6	S 9 23.8	103 39.1	S22 06.7
	01	20 01.8	220 34.5	52.1	215 09.4	43.5	174 39.6	24.0	118 41.4	06.7
	02	35 04.2	235 34.1	51.0	230 10.4	42.9	189 41.5	24.2	133 43.8	06.7
	03	50 06.7	250 33.6	. . 50.0	245 11.4	. . 42.3	204 43.5	. . 24.4	148 46.1	. . 06.7
	04	65 09.2	265 33.2	48.9	260 12.4	41.7	219 45.5	24.5	163 48.4	06.8
	05	80 11.6	280 32.7	47.8	275 13.4	41.1	234 47.4	24.7	178 50.8	06.8
	06	95 14.1	295 32.3	N 9 46.8	290 14.4	N 7 40.5	249 49.4	S 9 24.9	193 53.1	S22 06.8
	07	110 16.6	310 31.8	45.7	305 15.4	39.9	264 51.4	25.1	208 55.4	06.8
T	08	125 19.0	325 31.4	44.6	320 16.3	39.3	279 53.4	25.3	223 57.8	06.8
U	09	140 21.5	340 30.9	. . 43.5	335 17.3	. . 38.7	294 55.3	. . 25.5	239 00.1	. . 06.8
E	10	155 24.0	355 30.5	42.5	350 18.3	38.0	309 57.3	25.7	254 02.4	06.8
S	11	170 26.4	10 30.0	41.4	5 19.3	37.4	324 59.3	25.9	269 04.7	06.9
D	12	185 28.9	25 29.6	N 9 40.3	20 20.3	N 7 36.8	340 01.3	S 9 26.1	284 07.1	S22 06.9
A	13	200 31.3	40 29.1	39.2	35 21.3	36.2	355 03.2	26.3	299 09.4	06.9
Y	14	215 33.8	55 28.7	38.2	50 22.3	35.6	10 05.2	26.4	314 11.7	06.9
	15	230 36.3	70 28.2	. . 37.1	65 23.3	. . 35.0	25 07.2	. . 26.6	329 14.1	. . 06.9
	16	245 38.7	85 27.8	36.0	80 24.3	34.4	40 09.2	26.8	344 16.4	06.9
	17	260 41.2	100 27.3	34.9	95 25.3	33.8	55 11.1	27.0	359 18.7	07.0
	18	275 43.7	115 26.9	N 9 33.8	110 26.2	N 7 33.2	70 13.1	S 9 27.2	14 21.0	S22 07.0
	19	290 46.1	130 26.4	32.8	125 27.2	32.6	85 15.1	27.4	29 23.4	07.0
	20	305 48.6	145 26.0	31.7	140 28.2	31.9	100 17.1	27.6	44 25.7	07.0
	21	320 51.1	160 25.6	. . 30.6	155 29.2	. . 31.3	115 19.0	. . 27.8	59 28.0	. . 07.0
	22	335 53.5	175 25.1	29.5	170 30.2	30.7	130 21.0	28.0	74 30.4	07.0
	23	350 56.0	190 24.7	28.4	185 31.2	30.1	145 23.0	28.2	89 32.7	07.0
	27 00	5 58.5	205 24.2	N 9 27.4	200 32.2	N 7 29.5	160 25.0	S 9 28.4	104 35.0	S22 07.1
	01	21 00.9	220 23.8	26.3	215 33.2	28.9	175 26.9	28.5	119 37.3	07.1
	02	36 03.4	235 23.3	25.2	230 34.2	28.3	190 28.9	28.7	134 39.7	07.1
	03	51 05.8	250 22.9	. . 24.1	245 35.2	. . 27.7	205 30.9	. . 28.9	149 42.0	. . 07.1
	04	66 08.3	265 22.4	23.0	260 36.2	27.1	220 32.8	29.1	164 44.3	07.1
	05	81 10.8	280 22.0	22.0	275 37.1	26.5	235 34.8	29.3	179 46.6	07.1
	06	96 13.2	295 21.5	N 9 20.9	290 38.1	N 7 25.8	250 36.8	S 9 29.5	194 49.0	S22 07.1
W	07	111 15.7	310 21.1	19.8	305 39.1	25.2	265 38.8	29.7	209 51.3	07.2
E	08	126 18.2	325 20.7	18.7	320 40.1	24.6	280 40.7	29.9	224 53.6	07.2
D	09	141 20.6	340 20.2	. . 17.6	335 41.1	. . 24.0	295 42.7	. . 30.1	239 55.9	. . 07.2
N	10	156 23.1	355 19.8	16.5	350 42.1	23.4	310 44.7	30.3	254 58.3	07.2
E	11	171 25.6	10 19.3	15.4	5 43.1	22.8	325 46.6	30.4	270 00.6	07.2
S	12	186 28.0	25 18.9	N 9 14.4	20 44.1	N 7 22.2	340 48.6	S 9 30.6	285 02.9	S22 07.2
D	13	201 30.5	40 18.4	13.3	35 45.1	21.6	355 50.6	30.8	300 05.2	07.2
A	14	216 33.0	55 18.0	12.2	50 46.1	21.0	10 52.6	31.0	315 07.6	07.3
Y	15	231 35.4	70 17.6	. . 11.1	65 47.1	. . 20.4	25 54.5	. . 31.2	330 09.9	. . 07.3
	16	246 37.9	85 17.1	10.0	80 48.1	19.7	40 56.5	31.4	345 12.2	07.3
	17	261 40.3	100 16.7	08.9	95 49.0	19.1	55 58.5	31.6	0 14.5	07.3
	18	276 42.8	115 16.2	N 9 07.8	110 50.0	N 7 18.5	71 00.5	S 9 31.8	15 16.9	S22 07.3
	19	291 45.3	130 15.8	06.7	125 51.0	17.9	86 02.4	32.0	30 19.2	07.3
	20	306 47.7	145 15.4	05.6	140 52.0	17.3	101 04.4	32.2	45 21.5	07.4
	21	321 50.2	160 14.9	. . 04.5	155 53.0	. . 16.7	116 06.4	. . 32.3	60 23.8	. . 07.4
	22	336 52.7	175 14.5	03.5	170 54.0	16.1	131 08.3	32.5	75 26.2	07.4
	23	351 55.1	190 14.0	02.4	185 55.0	15.5	146 10.3	32.7	90 28.5	07.4
	Mer. Pass.	h m 23 36.2	*v* −0.4	*d* 1.1	*v* 1.0	*d* 0.6	*v* 2.0	*d* 0.2	*v* 2.3	*d* 0.0

STARS

Name	SHA ° ′	Dec ° ′
Acamar	315 15.9	S40 14.0
Achernar	335 24.2	S57 08.8
Acrux	173 06.6	S63 11.7
Adhara	255 10.3	S28 59.7
Aldebaran	290 45.9	N16 32.5
Alioth	166 18.8	N55 52.0
Alkaid	152 57.1	N49 13.8
Al Na'ir	27 39.8	S46 52.5
Alnilam	275 43.4	S 1 11.5
Alphard	217 53.5	S 8 44.0
Alphecca	126 08.8	N26 39.7
Alpheratz	357 40.1	N29 11.3
Altair	62 05.3	N 8 55.2
Ankaa	353 12.5	S42 12.6
Antares	112 22.9	S26 28.1
Arcturus	145 53.4	N19 05.7
Atria	107 22.2	S69 03.6
Avior	234 17.1	S59 33.8
Bellatrix	278 28.9	N 6 21.8
Betelgeuse	270 58.2	N 7 24.5
Canopus	263 54.9	S52 42.1
Capella	280 30.1	N46 00.6
Deneb	49 29.2	N45 21.0
Denebola	182 31.1	N14 28.6
Diphda	348 52.7	S17 53.3
Dubhe	193 48.9	N61 39.3
Elnath	278 08.9	N28 37.1
Eltanin	90 44.9	N51 29.7
Enif	33 44.0	N 9 57.6
Fomalhaut	15 20.5	S29 31.7
Gacrux	171 58.2	S57 12.6
Gienah	175 49.7	S17 38.2
Hadar	148 44.3	S60 27.4
Hamal	327 57.2	N23 32.7
Kaus Aust.	83 40.0	S34 22.4
Kochab	137 21.1	N74 05.3
Markab	13 35.1	N15 18.2
Menkar	314 11.8	N 4 09.5
Menkent	148 04.5	S36 27.2
Miaplacidus	221 39.6	S69 47.2
Mirfak	308 35.9	N49 55.2
Nunki	75 54.7	S26 16.3
Peacock	53 14.5	S56 40.7
Pollux	243 24.4	N27 58.8
Procyon	244 56.8	N 5 10.7
Rasalhague	96 03.8	N12 33.2
Regulus	207 40.7	N11 52.9
Rigel	281 09.2	S 8 10.9
Rigil Kent.	139 48.3	S60 54.4
Sabik	102 09.3	S15 44.6
Schedar	349 36.6	N56 38.0
Shaula	96 18.1	S37 06.9
Sirius	258 31.2	S16 44.4
Spica	158 28.5	S11 15.0
Suhail	222 50.6	S43 30.1
Vega	80 37.0	N38 48.5
Zuben'ubi	137 02.5	S16 06.7

	SHA ° ′	Mer. Pass. h m
Venus	200 35.7	10 18
Mars	195 09.1	10 39
Jupiter	154 38.3	13 20
Saturn	98 39.8	17 03

UT	SUN GHA	SUN Dec	MOON GHA	*v*	MOON Dec	*d*	HP
d h	° ′	° ′	° ′	′	° ′	′	′
25 00	182 03.5	S 0 50.6	127 05.4	13.1	S14 40.7	6.7	54.7
01	197 03.7	51.6	141 37.5	13.1	14 47.4	6.7	54.6
02	212 03.9	52.5	156 09.6	13.1	14 54.1	6.6	54.6
03	227 04.2	. . 53.5	170 41.7	13.1	15 00.7	6.5	54.6
04	242 04.4	54.5	185 13.8	13.0	15 07.2	6.5	54.6
05	257 04.6	55.5	199 45.8	13.0	15 13.7	6.4	54.6
06	272 04.8	S 0 56.4	214 17.8	13.0	S15 20.1	6.3	54.6
07	287 05.0	57.4	228 49.8	13.1	15 26.4	6.3	54.6
08	302 05.2	58.4	243 21.9	12.9	15 32.7	6.1	54.5
M 09	317 05.5	0 59.4	257 53.8	13.0	15 38.8	6.1	54.5
O 10	332 05.7	1 00.3	272 25.8	13.0	15 44.9	6.0	54.5
N 11	347 05.9	01.3	286 57.8	12.9	15 50.9	6.0	54.5
D 12	2 06.1	S 1 02.3	301 29.7	13.0	S15 56.9	5.9	54.5
A 13	17 06.3	03.2	316 01.7	12.9	16 02.8	5.8	54.5
Y 14	32 06.5	04.2	330 33.6	12.9	16 08.6	5.7	54.5
15	47 06.7	. . 05.2	345 05.5	12.9	16 14.3	5.6	54.5
16	62 07.0	06.2	359 37.4	12.9	16 19.9	5.6	54.4
17	77 07.2	07.1	14 09.3	12.8	16 25.5	5.5	54.4
18	92 07.4	S 1 08.1	28 41.1	12.9	S16 31.0	5.4	54.4
19	107 07.6	09.1	43 13.0	12.8	16 36.4	5.4	54.4
20	122 07.8	10.1	57 44.8	12.8	16 41.8	5.2	54.4
21	137 08.0	. . 11.0	72 16.6	12.8	16 47.0	5.2	54.4
22	152 08.2	12.0	86 48.4	12.8	16 52.2	5.1	54.4
23	167 08.5	13.0	101 20.2	12.8	16 57.3	5.1	54.4
26 00	182 08.7	S 1 14.0	115 52.0	12.8	S17 02.4	4.9	54.4
01	197 08.9	14.9	130 23.8	12.7	17 07.3	4.9	54.4
02	212 09.1	15.9	144 55.5	12.7	17 12.2	4.8	54.4
03	227 09.3	. . 16.9	159 27.2	12.7	17 17.0	4.7	54.3
04	242 09.5	17.9	173 58.9	12.7	17 21.7	4.6	54.3
05	257 09.7	18.8	188 30.6	12.7	17 26.3	4.6	54.3
06	272 10.0	S 1 19.8	203 02.3	12.7	S17 30.9	4.5	54.3
07	287 10.2	20.8	217 34.0	12.6	17 35.4	4.4	54.3
T 08	302 10.4	21.7	232 05.6	12.7	17 39.8	4.3	54.3
U 09	317 10.6	. . 22.7	246 37.3	12.6	17 44.1	4.2	54.3
E 10	332 10.8	23.7	261 08.9	12.6	17 48.3	4.2	54.3
S 11	347 11.0	24.7	275 40.5	12.6	17 52.5	4.0	54.3
D 12	2 11.2	S 1 25.6	290 12.1	12.6	S17 56.5	4.0	54.3
A 13	17 11.4	26.6	304 43.7	12.5	18 00.5	3.9	54.3
Y 14	32 11.7	27.6	319 15.2	12.5	18 04.4	3.8	54.3
15	47 11.9	. . 28.6	333 46.7	12.6	18 08.2	3.8	54.3
16	62 12.1	29.5	348 18.3	12.5	18 12.0	3.6	54.3
17	77 12.3	30.5	2 49.8	12.5	18 15.6	3.6	54.3
18	92 12.5	S 1 31.5	17 21.3	12.5	S18 19.2	3.5	54.3
19	107 12.7	32.5	31 52.8	12.4	18 22.7	3.4	54.2
20	122 12.9	33.4	46 24.2	12.5	18 26.1	3.3	54.2
21	137 13.2	. . 34.4	60 55.7	12.4	18 29.4	3.2	54.2
22	152 13.4	35.4	75 27.1	12.4	18 32.6	3.2	54.2
23	167 13.6	36.3	89 58.5	12.4	18 35.8	3.0	54.2
27 00	182 13.8	S 1 37.3	104 29.9	12.4	S18 38.8	3.0	54.2
01	197 14.0	38.3	119 01.3	12.4	18 41.8	2.9	54.2
02	212 14.2	39.3	133 32.7	12.4	18 44.7	2.8	54.2
03	227 14.4	. . 40.2	148 04.1	12.3	18 47.5	2.7	54.2
04	242 14.6	41.2	162 35.4	12.3	18 50.2	2.7	54.2
05	257 14.8	42.2	177 06.7	12.3	18 52.9	2.5	54.2
06	272 15.1	S 1 43.2	191 38.0	12.3	S18 55.4	2.5	54.2
W 07	287 15.3	44.1	206 09.3	12.3	18 57.9	2.4	54.2
E 08	302 15.5	45.1	220 40.6	12.3	19 00.3	2.2	54.2
D 09	317 15.7	. . 46.1	235 11.9	12.3	19 02.5	2.2	54.2
N 10	332 15.9	47.1	249 43.2	12.2	19 04.7	2.2	54.2
E 11	347 16.1	48.0	264 14.4	12.2	19 06.9	2.0	54.2
S 12	2 16.3	S 1 49.0	278 45.6	12.3	S19 08.9	1.9	54.2
D 13	17 16.5	50.0	293 16.9	12.2	19 10.8	1.9	54.2
A 14	32 16.7	50.9	307 48.1	12.2	19 12.7	1.7	54.2
Y 15	47 17.0	. . 51.9	322 19.3	12.1	19 14.4	1.7	54.2
16	62 17.2	52.9	336 50.4	12.2	19 16.1	1.6	54.2
17	77 17.4	53.9	351 21.6	12.1	19 17.7	1.5	54.2
18	92 17.6	S 1 54.8	5 52.7	12.2	S19 19.2	1.4	54.2
19	107 17.8	55.8	20 23.9	12.1	19 20.6	1.3	54.3
20	122 18.0	56.8	34 55.0	12.1	19 21.9	1.2	54.3
21	137 18.2	. . 57.8	49 26.1	12.1	19 23.1	1.2	54.3
22	152 18.4	58.7	63 57.2	12.1	19 24.3	1.0	54.3
23	167 18.6	59.7	78 28.3	12.1	S19 25.3	1.0	54.3
	SD 16.0	*d* 1.0	SD 14.8		14.8		14.8

Lat.	Twilight Naut.	Twilight Civil	Sunrise	Moonrise 25	Moonrise 26	Moonrise 27	Moonrise 28
°	h m	h m	h m	h m	h m	h m	h m
N 72	03 23	04 49	05 57	14 14	▬	▬	▬
N 70	03 39	04 55	05 56	13 28	15 04	16 34	17 32
68	03 52	05 00	05 56	12 59	14 21	15 33	16 27
66	04 02	05 04	05 55	12 37	13 53	14 59	15 51
64	04 10	05 07	05 55	12 20	13 31	14 34	15 25
62	04 17	05 10	05 54	12 05	13 13	14 14	15 05
60	04 23	05 12	05 54	11 53	12 59	13 58	14 49
N 58	04 28	05 14	05 54	11 43	12 47	13 45	14 35
56	04 32	05 16	05 53	11 34	12 36	13 33	14 23
54	04 36	05 18	05 53	11 26	12 27	13 23	14 13
52	04 39	05 19	05 53	11 19	12 19	13 14	14 04
50	04 42	05 20	05 52	11 12	12 11	13 06	13 56
45	04 48	05 23	05 52	10 59	11 55	12 48	13 38
N 40	04 53	05 24	05 51	10 47	11 42	12 34	13 24
35	04 56	05 26	05 51	10 38	11 31	12 22	13 11
30	04 59	05 27	05 51	10 29	11 21	12 12	13 01
20	05 02	05 28	05 50	10 15	11 05	11 54	12 43
N 10	05 04	05 28	05 49	10 02	10 50	11 39	12 27
0	05 03	05 27	05 48	09 50	10 37	11 24	12 12
S 10	05 02	05 26	05 47	09 39	10 24	11 10	11 57
20	04 58	05 24	05 46	09 26	10 09	10 54	11 41
30	04 53	05 21	05 44	09 12	09 53	10 37	11 23
35	04 49	05 18	05 44	09 04	09 43	10 26	11 13
40	04 44	05 16	05 43	08 54	09 33	10 15	11 01
45	04 37	05 12	05 41	08 44	09 20	10 01	10 46
S 50	04 29	05 08	05 40	08 30	09 05	09 44	10 29
52	04 25	05 05	05 39	08 24	08 57	09 36	10 21
54	04 21	05 03	05 38	08 18	08 50	09 27	10 12
56	04 16	05 00	05 38	08 10	08 41	09 17	10 01
58	04 10	04 57	05 37	08 02	08 31	09 06	09 50
S 60	04 03	04 54	05 35	07 52	08 19	08 53	09 36

Lat.	Sunset	Twilight Civil	Twilight Naut.	Moonset 25	Moonset 26	Moonset 27	Moonset 28
°	h m	h m	h m	h m	h m	h m	h m
N 72	17 43	18 50	20 16	17 39	▬	▬	▬
N 70	17 44	18 45	20 00	18 25	18 26	18 35	19 16
68	17 45	18 40	19 48	18 55	19 10	19 36	20 22
66	17 46	18 37	19 38	19 18	19 39	20 11	20 57
64	17 46	18 33	19 30	19 36	20 01	20 36	21 23
62	17 47	18 31	19 24	19 50	20 18	20 55	21 43
60	17 47	18 29	19 18	20 03	20 33	21 11	21 59
N 58	17 48	18 27	19 13	20 14	20 46	21 25	22 13
56	17 48	18 25	19 09	20 23	20 57	21 37	22 25
54	17 48	18 24	19 05	20 31	21 06	21 47	22 35
52	17 49	18 22	19 02	20 39	21 15	21 56	22 44
50	17 49	18 21	18 59	20 46	21 22	22 04	22 52
45	17 50	18 19	18 53	21 00	21 39	22 22	23 10
N 40	17 50	18 17	18 49	21 12	21 52	22 36	23 24
35	17 51	18 16	18 46	21 22	22 03	22 48	23 36
30	17 52	18 15	18 43	21 31	22 13	22 59	23 47
20	17 53	18 14	18 40	21 47	22 31	23 17	24 05
N 10	17 53	18 14	18 39	22 00	22 46	23 32	24 21
0	17 55	18 15	18 39	22 13	23 00	23 47	24 35
S 10	17 56	18 17	18 41	22 25	23 14	24 02	00 02
20	17 57	18 19	18 45	22 39	23 29	24 18	00 18
30	17 59	18 22	18 50	22 55	23 46	24 36	00 36
35	18 00	18 25	18 54	23 04	23 56	24 46	00 46
40	18 01	18 28	19 00	23 14	24 08	00 08	00 58
45	18 02	18 31	19 06	23 26	24 21	00 21	01 13
S 50	18 04	18 36	19 15	23 41	24 38	00 38	01 30
52	18 04	18 38	19 19	23 48	24 45	00 45	01 38
54	18 05	18 41	19 23	23 55	24 54	00 54	01 47
56	18 06	18 44	19 28	24 04	00 04	01 04	01 57
58	18 07	18 47	19 34	24 14	00 14	01 15	02 09
S 60	18 08	18 50	19 41	24 25	00 25	01 28	02 23

Day	SUN Eqn. of Time 00^h	SUN Eqn. of Time 12^h	SUN Mer. Pass.	MOON Mer. Pass. Upper	MOON Mer. Pass. Lower	MOON Age	MOON Phase
d	m s	m s	h m	h m	h m	d	%
25	08 14	08 24	11 52	16 02	03 38	05	26
26	08 34	08 45	11 51	16 48	04 25	06	35
27	08 55	09 05	11 51	17 36	05 12	07	44

UT d h	ARIES GHA	VENUS −3·9 GHA	VENUS Dec	MARS +1·8 GHA	MARS Dec	JUPITER −1·7 GHA	JUPITER Dec	SATURN +0·5 GHA	SATURN Dec
	° ′	° ′	° ′	° ′	° ′	° ′	° ′	° ′	° ′
28 00	6 57.6	205 13.6	N 9 01.3	200 56.0	N 7 14.9	161 12.3	S 9 32.9	105 30.8	S22 07.4
01	22 00.1	220 13.2	9 00.2	215 57.0	14.2	176 14.3	33.1	120 33.1	07.4
02	37 02.5	235 12.7	8 59.1	230 58.0	13.6	191 16.2	33.3	135 35.5	07.4
03	52 05.0	250 12.3	. . 58.0	245 59.0	. . 13.0	206 18.2	. . 33.5	150 37.8	. . 07.5
04	67 07.4	265 11.8	56.9	261 00.0	12.4	221 20.2	33.7	165 40.1	07.5
05	82 09.9	280 11.4	55.8	276 01.0	11.8	236 22.1	33.9	180 42.4	07.5
06	97 12.4	295 11.0	N 8 54.7	291 01.9	N 7 11.2	251 24.1	S 9 34.1	195 44.7	S22 07.5
T 07	112 14.8	310 10.5	53.6	306 02.9	10.6	266 26.1	34.3	210 47.1	07.5
H 08	127 17.3	325 10.1	52.5	321 03.9	10.0	281 28.0	34.4	225 49.4	07.5
U 09	142 19.8	340 09.6	. . 51.4	336 04.9	. . 09.3	296 30.0	. . 34.6	240 51.7	. . 07.5
R 10	157 22.2	355 09.2	50.3	351 05.9	08.7	311 32.0	34.8	255 54.0	07.6
S 11	172 24.7	10 08.8	49.2	6 06.9	08.1	326 34.0	35.0	270 56.4	07.6
D 12	187 27.2	25 08.3	N 8 48.1	21 07.9	N 7 07.5	341 35.9	S 9 35.2	285 58.7	S22 07.6
A 13	202 29.6	40 07.9	47.0	36 08.9	06.9	356 37.9	35.4	301 01.0	07.6
Y 14	217 32.1	55 07.5	45.9	51 09.9	06.3	11 39.9	35.6	316 03.3	07.6
15	232 34.6	70 07.0	. . 44.8	66 10.9	. . 05.7	26 41.8	. . 35.8	331 05.6	. . 07.6
16	247 37.0	85 06.6	43.7	81 11.9	05.1	41 43.8	36.0	346 08.0	07.6
17	262 39.5	100 06.1	42.6	96 12.9	04.4	56 45.8	36.2	1 10.3	07.7
18	277 41.9	115 05.7	N 8 41.5	111 13.9	N 7 03.8	71 47.8	S 9 36.3	16 12.6	S22 07.7
19	292 44.4	130 05.3	40.4	126 14.9	03.2	86 49.7	36.5	31 14.9	07.7
20	307 46.9	145 04.8	39.3	141 15.9	02.6	101 51.7	36.7	46 17.2	07.7
21	322 49.3	160 04.4	. . 38.2	156 16.9	. . 02.0	116 53.7	. . 36.9	61 19.6	. . 07.7
22	337 51.8	175 04.0	37.1	171 17.8	01.4	131 55.6	37.1	76 21.9	07.7
23	352 54.3	190 03.5	36.0	186 18.8	00.8	146 57.6	37.3	91 24.2	07.8
29 00	7 56.7	205 03.1	N 8 34.9	201 19.8	N 7 00.2	161 59.6	S 9 37.5	106 26.5	S22 07.8
01	22 59.2	220 02.7	33.8	216 20.8	6 59.5	177 01.5	37.7	121 28.8	07.8
02	38 01.7	235 02.2	32.7	231 21.8	58.9	192 03.5	37.9	136 31.2	07.8
03	53 04.1	250 01.8	. . 31.6	246 22.8	. . 58.3	207 05.5	. . 38.1	151 33.5	. . 07.8
04	68 06.6	265 01.4	30.5	261 23.8	57.7	222 07.4	38.3	166 35.8	07.8
05	83 09.1	280 00.9	29.4	276 24.8	57.1	237 09.4	38.4	181 38.1	07.8
06	98 11.5	295 00.5	N 8 28.3	291 25.8	N 6 56.5	252 11.4	S 9 38.6	196 40.4	S22 07.9
07	113 14.0	310 00.1	27.2	306 26.8	55.9	267 13.4	38.8	211 42.7	07.9
08	128 16.4	324 59.6	26.1	321 27.8	55.2	282 15.3	39.0	226 45.1	07.9
F 09	143 18.9	339 59.2	. . 25.0	336 28.8	. . 54.6	297 17.3	. . 39.2	241 47.4	. . 07.9
R 10	158 21.4	354 58.8	23.8	351 29.8	54.0	312 19.3	39.4	256 49.7	07.9
I 11	173 23.8	9 58.3	22.7	6 30.8	53.4	327 21.2	39.6	271 52.0	07.9
D 12	188 26.3	24 57.9	N 8 21.6	21 31.8	N 6 52.8	342 23.2	S 9 39.8	286 54.3	S22 07.9
A 13	203 28.8	39 57.5	20.5	36 32.8	52.2	357 25.2	40.0	301 56.7	08.0
Y 14	218 31.2	54 57.0	19.4	51 33.8	51.6	12 27.1	40.2	316 59.0	08.0
15	233 33.7	69 56.6	. . 18.3	66 34.8	. . 51.0	27 29.1	. . 40.4	332 01.3	. . 08.0
16	248 36.2	84 56.2	17.2	81 35.8	50.3	42 31.1	40.5	347 03.6	08.0
17	263 38.6	99 55.8	16.1	96 36.8	49.7	57 33.0	40.7	2 05.9	08.0
18	278 41.1	114 55.3	N 8 15.0	111 37.7	N 6 49.1	72 35.0	S 9 40.9	17 08.2	S22 08.0
19	293 43.5	129 54.9	13.9	126 38.7	48.5	87 37.0	41.1	32 10.6	08.1
20	308 46.0	144 54.5	12.7	141 39.7	47.9	102 38.9	41.3	47 12.9	08.1
21	323 48.5	159 54.0	. . 11.6	156 40.7	. . 47.3	117 40.9	. . 41.5	62 15.2	. . 08.1
22	338 50.9	174 53.6	10.5	171 41.7	46.7	132 42.9	41.7	77 17.5	08.1
23	353 53.4	189 53.2	09.4	186 42.7	46.0	147 44.9	41.9	92 19.8	08.1
30 00	8 55.9	204 52.7	N 8 08.3	201 43.7	N 6 45.4	162 46.8	S 9 42.1	107 22.1	S22 08.1
01	23 58.3	219 52.3	07.2	216 44.7	44.8	177 48.8	42.3	122 24.4	08.1
02	39 00.8	234 51.9	06.1	231 45.7	44.2	192 50.8	42.4	137 26.8	08.2
03	54 03.3	249 51.5	. . 04.9	246 46.7	. . 43.6	207 52.7	. . 42.6	152 29.1	. . 08.2
04	69 05.7	264 51.0	03.8	261 47.7	43.0	222 54.7	42.8	167 31.4	08.2
05	84 08.2	279 50.6	02.7	276 48.7	42.3	237 56.7	43.0	182 33.7	08.2
06	99 10.7	294 50.2	N 8 01.6	291 49.7	N 6 41.7	252 58.6	S 9 43.2	197 36.0	S22 08.2
07	114 13.1	309 49.7	8 00.5	306 50.7	41.1	268 00.6	43.4	212 38.3	08.2
S 08	129 15.6	324 49.3	7 59.4	321 51.7	40.5	283 02.6	43.6	227 40.6	08.3
A 09	144 18.0	339 48.9	. . 58.2	336 52.7	. . 39.9	298 04.5	. . 43.8	242 43.0	. . 08.3
T 10	159 20.5	354 48.5	57.1	351 53.7	39.3	313 06.5	44.0	257 45.3	08.3
U 11	174 23.0	9 48.0	56.0	6 54.7	38.7	328 08.5	44.2	272 47.6	08.3
R 12	189 25.4	24 47.6	N 7 54.9	21 55.7	N 6 38.0	343 10.4	S 9 44.4	287 49.9	S22 08.3
D 13	204 27.9	39 47.2	53.8	36 56.7	37.4	358 12.4	44.5	302 52.2	08.3
A 14	219 30.4	54 46.8	52.6	51 57.7	36.8	13 14.4	44.7	317 54.5	08.3
Y 15	234 32.8	69 46.3	. . 51.5	66 58.7	. . 36.2	28 16.3	. . 44.9	332 56.8	. . 08.4
16	249 35.3	84 45.9	50.4	81 59.7	35.6	43 18.3	45.1	347 59.2	08.4
17	264 37.8	99 45.5	49.3	97 00.7	35.0	58 20.3	45.3	3 01.5	08.4
18	279 40.2	114 45.1	N 7 48.2	112 01.7	N 6 34.4	73 22.2	S 9 45.5	18 03.8	S22 08.4
19	294 42.7	129 44.6	47.0	127 02.7	33.7	88 24.2	45.7	33 06.1	08.4
20	309 45.2	144 44.2	45.9	142 03.7	33.1	103 26.2	45.9	48 08.4	08.4
21	324 47.6	159 43.8	. . 44.8	157 04.7	. . 32.5	118 28.1	. . 46.1	63 10.7	. . 08.4
22	339 50.1	174 43.4	43.7	172 05.7	31.9	133 30.1	46.3	78 13.0	08.5
23	354 52.5	189 42.9	42.6	187 06.6	31.3	148 32.1	46.5	93 15.3	08.5
Mer. Pass.	h m 23 24.4	*v* −0.4	*d* 1.1	*v* 1.0	*d* 0.6	*v* 2.0	*d* 0.2	*v* 2.3	*d* 0.0

STARS

Name	SHA	Dec
	° ′	° ′
Acamar	315 15.9	S40 14.0
Achernar	335 24.1	S57 08.8
Acrux	173 06.6	S63 11.7
Adhara	255 10.3	S28 59.7
Aldebaran	290 45.9	N16 32.5
Alioth	166 18.8	N55 52.0
Alkaid	152 57.1	N49 13.8
Al Na'ir	27 39.8	S46 52.5
Alnilam	275 43.4	S 1 11.5
Alphard	217 53.5	S 8 44.0
Alphecca	126 08.8	N26 39.7
Alpheratz	357 40.1	N29 11.4
Altair	62 05.3	N 8 55.2
Ankaa	353 12.5	S42 12.6
Antares	112 22.9	S26 28.1
Arcturus	145 53.4	N19 05.7
Atria	107 22.3	S69 03.6
Avior	234 17.1	S59 33.8
Bellatrix	278 28.8	N 6 21.8
Betelgeuse	270 58.1	N 7 24.5
Canopus	263 54.8	S52 42.1
Capella	280 30.0	N46 00.6
Deneb	49 29.2	N45 21.0
Denebola	182 31.1	N14 28.6
Diphda	348 52.7	S17 53.3
Dubhe	193 48.9	N61 39.3
Elnath	278 08.9	N28 37.1
Eltanin	90 44.9	N51 29.7
Enif	33 44.0	N 9 57.6
Fomalhaut	15 20.5	S29 31.7
Gacrux	171 58.2	S57 12.6
Gienah	175 49.6	S17 38.2
Hadar	148 44.3	S60 27.4
Hamal	327 57.2	N23 32.7
Kaus Aust.	83 40.0	S34 22.4
Kochab	137 21.2	N74 05.3
Markab	13 35.1	N15 18.2
Menkar	314 11.8	N 4 09.5
Menkent	148 04.5	S36 27.2
Miaplacidus	221 39.6	S69 47.2
Mirfak	308 35.8	N49 55.2
Nunki	75 54.7	S26 16.3
Peacock	53 14.5	S56 40.7
Pollux	243 24.4	N27 58.8
Procyon	244 56.8	N 5 10.7
Rasalhague	96 03.9	N12 33.2
Regulus	207 40.7	N11 52.9
Rigel	281 09.2	S 8 10.9
Rigil Kent.	139 48.3	S60 54.4
Sabik	102 09.3	S15 44.6
Schedar	349 36.6	N56 38.0
Shaula	96 18.1	S37 06.9
Sirius	258 31.2	S16 44.4
Spica	158 28.5	S11 15.0
Suhail	222 50.6	S43 30.0
Vega	80 37.0	N38 48.5
Zuben'ubi	137 02.5	S16 06.7

	SHA	Mer. Pass.
	° ′	h m
Venus	197 06.4	10 20
Mars	193 23.1	10 34
Jupiter	154 02.8	13 10
Saturn	98 29.8	16 52

Day	UT d h	SUN GHA ° ′	SUN Dec ° ′	MOON GHA ° ′	v ′	MOON Dec ° ′	d ′	HP ′
	28 00	182 18.9	S 2 00.7	92 59.4	12.1	S19 26.3	0.8	54.3
	01	197 19.1	01.6	107 30.5	12.0	19 27.1	0.8	54.3
	02	212 19.3	02.6	122 01.5	12.0	19 27.9	0.7	54.3
	03	227 19.5	. . 03.6	136 32.5	12.1	19 28.6	0.6	54.3
	04	242 19.7	04.6	151 03.6	12.0	19 29.2	0.5	54.3
	05	257 19.9	05.5	165 34.6	12.0	19 29.7	0.4	54.3
	06	272 20.1	S 2 06.5	180 05.6	12.0	S19 30.1	0.4	54.3
	07	287 20.3	07.5	194 36.6	12.0	19 30.5	0.2	54.3
T	08	302 20.5	08.5	209 07.6	12.0	19 30.7	0.1	54.3
H	09	317 20.7	. . 09.4	223 38.6	11.9	19 30.8	0.1	54.3
U	10	332 21.0	10.4	238 09.5	12.0	19 30.9	0.0	54.3
R	11	347 21.2	11.4	252 40.5	11.9	19 30.9	0.2	54.3
S	12	2 21.4	S 2 12.3	267 11.4	12.0	S19 30.7	0.2	54.4
D	13	17 21.6	13.3	281 42.4	11.9	19 30.5	0.3	54.4
A	14	32 21.8	14.3	296 13.3	11.9	19 30.2	0.4	54.4
Y	15	47 22.0	. . 15.3	310 44.2	11.9	19 29.8	0.5	54.4
	16	62 22.2	16.2	325 15.1	11.9	19 29.3	0.6	54.4
	17	77 22.4	17.2	339 46.0	11.9	19 28.7	0.6	54.4
	18	92 22.6	S 2 18.2	354 16.9	11.9	S19 28.1	0.8	54.4
	19	107 22.8	19.1	8 47.8	11.9	19 27.3	0.8	54.4
	20	122 23.0	20.1	23 18.7	11.9	19 26.5	1.0	54.4
	21	137 23.2	. . 21.1	37 49.6	11.8	19 25.5	1.0	54.4
	22	152 23.5	22.1	52 20.4	11.9	19 24.5	1.2	54.5
	23	167 23.7	23.0	66 51.3	11.8	19 23.3	1.2	54.5
	29 00	182 23.9	S 2 24.0	81 22.1	11.9	S19 22.1	1.3	54.5
	01	197 24.1	25.0	95 53.0	11.8	19 20.8	1.4	54.5
	02	212 24.3	26.0	110 23.8	11.8	19 19.4	1.5	54.5
	03	227 24.5	. . 26.9	124 54.6	11.8	19 17.9	1.6	54.5
	04	242 24.7	27.9	139 25.4	11.9	19 16.3	1.7	54.5
	05	257 24.9	28.9	153 56.3	11.8	19 14.6	1.8	54.6
	06	272 25.1	S 2 29.8	168 27.1	11.8	S19 12.8	1.8	54.6
	07	287 25.3	30.8	182 57.9	11.8	19 11.0	2.0	54.6
	08	302 25.5	31.8	197 28.7	11.7	19 09.0	2.0	54.6
F	09	317 25.7	. . 32.8	211 59.4	11.8	19 07.0	2.2	54.6
R	10	332 25.9	33.7	226 30.2	11.8	19 04.8	2.2	54.6
I	11	347 26.2	34.7	241 01.0	11.8	19 02.6	2.3	54.6
D	12	2 26.4	S 2 35.7	255 31.8	11.8	S19 00.3	2.4	54.7
A	13	17 26.6	36.6	270 02.6	11.7	18 57.9	2.5	54.7
Y	14	32 26.8	37.6	284 33.3	11.8	18 55.4	2.6	54.7
	15	47 27.0	. . 38.6	299 04.1	11.7	18 52.8	2.7	54.7
	16	62 27.2	39.6	313 34.8	11.8	18 50.1	2.8	54.7
	17	77 27.4	40.5	328 05.6	11.7	18 47.3	2.9	54.7
	18	92 27.6	S 2 41.5	342 36.3	11.8	S18 44.4	2.9	54.8
	19	107 27.8	42.5	357 07.1	11.7	18 41.5	3.1	54.8
	20	122 28.0	43.4	11 37.8	11.8	18 38.4	3.1	54.8
	21	137 28.2	. . 44.4	26 08.6	11.7	18 35.3	3.3	54.8
	22	152 28.4	45.4	40 39.3	11.7	18 32.0	3.3	54.8
	23	167 28.6	46.3	55 10.0	11.8	18 28.7	3.4	54.8
	30 00	182 28.8	S 2 47.3	69 40.8	11.7	S18 25.3	3.5	54.9
	01	197 29.0	48.3	84 11.5	11.7	18 21.8	3.6	54.9
	02	212 29.2	49.3	98 42.2	11.7	18 18.2	3.7	54.9
	03	227 29.4	. . 50.2	113 12.9	11.8	18 14.5	3.8	54.9
	04	242 29.6	51.2	127 43.7	11.7	18 10.7	3.9	54.9
	05	257 29.9	52.2	142 14.4	11.7	18 06.8	3.9	55.0
	06	272 30.1	S 2 53.1	156 45.1	11.7	S18 02.9	4.1	55.0
S	07	287 30.3	54.1	171 15.8	11.7	17 58.8	4.1	55.0
A	08	302 30.5	55.1	185 46.5	11.7	17 54.7	4.2	55.0
T	09	317 30.7	. . 56.1	200 17.2	11.7	17 50.5	4.3	55.0
U	10	332 30.9	57.0	214 47.9	11.8	17 46.2	4.4	55.1
R	11	347 31.1	58.0	229 18.7	11.7	17 41.8	4.5	55.1
D	12	2 31.3	S 2 59.0	243 49.4	11.7	S17 37.3	4.6	55.1
A	13	17 31.5	2 59.9	258 20.1	11.7	17 32.7	4.7	55.1
Y	14	32 31.7	3 00.9	272 50.8	11.7	17 28.0	4.8	55.2
	15	47 31.9	. . 01.9	287 21.5	11.7	17 23.2	4.8	55.2
	16	62 32.1	02.8	301 52.2	11.7	17 18.4	4.9	55.2
	17	77 32.3	03.8	316 22.9	11.7	17 13.5	5.1	55.2
	18	92 32.5	S 3 04.8	330 53.6	11.7	S17 08.4	5.1	55.2
	19	107 32.7	05.8	345 24.3	11.7	17 03.3	5.2	55.3
	20	122 32.9	06.7	359 55.0	11.7	16 58.1	5.3	55.3
	21	137 33.1	. . 07.7	14 25.7	11.7	16 52.8	5.3	55.3
	22	152 33.3	08.7	28 56.4	11.7	16 47.5	5.5	55.3
	23	167 33.5	09.6	43 27.1	11.7	S16 42.0	5.5	55.4
		SD 16.0	d 1.0	SD	14.8	14.9		15.0

Lat.	Twilight Naut.	Twilight Civil	Sunrise	Moonrise 28	Moonrise 29	Moonrise 30	Moonrise 1
°	h m	h m	h m	h m	h m	h m	h m
N 72	03 39	05 03	06 10	■	■	18 46	18 21
N 70	03 53	05 07	06 08	17 32	17 48	17 51	17 50
68	04 04	05 11	06 06	16 27	16 59	17 17	17 27
66	04 12	05 14	06 05	15 51	16 28	16 52	17 09
64	04 19	05 16	06 03	15 25	16 05	16 33	16 54
62	04 25	05 18	06 02	15 05	15 46	16 17	16 42
60	04 31	05 20	06 01	14 49	15 31	16 04	16 31
N 58	04 35	05 21	06 00	14 35	15 18	15 53	16 22
56	04 39	05 22	05 59	14 23	15 07	15 43	16 14
54	04 42	05 23	05 58	14 13	14 57	15 34	16 07
52	04 45	05 24	05 58	14 04	14 48	15 26	16 00
50	04 47	05 25	05 57	13 56	14 40	15 19	15 54
45	04 52	05 26	05 56	13 38	14 23	15 04	15 42
N 40	04 56	05 27	05 54	13 24	14 09	14 52	15 31
35	04 59	05 28	05 53	13 11	13 58	14 41	15 22
30	05 01	05 28	05 52	13 01	13 48	14 32	15 14
20	05 03	05 28	05 50	12 43	13 30	14 16	15 00
N 10	05 03	05 28	05 49	12 27	13 15	14 02	14 48
0	05 02	05 26	05 47	12 12	13 00	13 49	14 37
S 10	05 00	05 24	05 45	11 57	12 46	13 36	14 26
20	04 55	05 21	05 43	11 41	12 31	13 21	14 14
30	04 49	05 17	05 41	11 23	12 13	13 05	14 00
35	04 44	05 14	05 39	11 13	12 03	12 56	13 52
40	04 39	05 10	05 38	11 01	11 51	12 45	13 43
45	04 31	05 06	05 36	10 46	11 37	12 33	13 32
S 50	04 22	05 01	05 33	10 29	11 20	12 17	13 19
52	04 18	04 58	05 32	10 21	11 12	12 10	13 13
54	04 13	04 55	05 31	10 12	11 03	12 02	13 06
56	04 07	04 52	05 30	10 01	10 53	11 53	12 59
58	04 00	04 48	05 28	09 50	10 42	11 43	12 50
S 60	03 53	04 44	05 26	09 36	10 29	11 31	12 41

Lat.	Sunset	Twilight Civil	Twilight Naut.	Moonset 28	Moonset 29	Moonset 30	Moonset 1
°	h m	h m	h m	h m	h m	h m	h m
N 72	17 28	18 35	19 57	■	■	21 24	23 31
N 70	17 30	18 31	19 44	19 16	20 41	22 19	24 01
68	17 32	18 28	19 34	20 22	21 30	22 52	24 23
66	17 34	18 25	19 26	20 57	22 00	23 16	24 40
64	17 36	18 23	19 19	21 23	22 23	23 35	24 54
62	17 37	18 21	19 13	21 43	22 42	23 50	25 06
60	17 38	18 20	19 08	21 59	22 57	24 03	00 03
N 58	17 39	18 18	19 04	22 13	23 09	24 14	00 14
56	17 40	18 17	19 00	22 25	23 20	24 23	00 23
54	17 41	18 16	18 57	22 35	23 30	24 32	00 32
52	17 42	18 15	18 55	22 44	23 39	24 39	00 39
50	17 43	18 15	18 52	22 52	23 47	24 46	00 46
45	17 44	18 13	18 47	23 10	24 03	00 03	01 00
N 40	17 45	18 12	18 44	23 24	24 16	00 16	01 12
35	17 47	18 12	18 41	23 36	24 28	00 28	01 22
30	17 48	18 12	18 39	23 47	24 38	00 38	01 31
20	17 50	18 12	18 37	24 05	00 05	00 55	01 46
N 10	17 52	18 13	18 37	24 21	00 21	01 10	02 00
0	17 54	18 14	18 38	24 35	00 35	01 24	02 12
S 10	17 55	18 16	18 41	00 02	00 50	01 37	02 24
20	17 58	18 20	18 45	00 18	01 06	01 52	02 37
30	18 00	18 24	18 52	00 36	01 24	02 09	02 52
35	18 02	18 27	18 57	00 46	01 34	02 19	03 01
40	18 04	18 31	19 03	00 58	01 46	02 30	03 11
45	18 06	18 35	19 10	01 13	02 00	02 43	03 22
S 50	18 08	18 41	19 20	01 30	02 17	02 59	03 36
52	18 09	18 43	19 24	01 38	02 25	03 06	03 42
54	18 11	18 46	19 29	01 47	02 34	03 15	03 49
56	18 12	18 50	19 35	01 57	02 44	03 24	03 57
58	18 14	18 54	19 42	02 09	02 56	03 34	04 06
S 60	18 16	18 58	19 50	02 23	03 09	03 46	04 16

Day	SUN Eqn. of Time 00^h	SUN Eqn. of Time 12^h	SUN Mer. Pass.	MOON Mer. Pass. Upper	MOON Mer. Pass. Lower	MOON Age	MOON Phase
d	m s	m s	h m	h m	h m	d	%
28	09 15	09 25	11 51	18 24	06 00	08	54
29	09 35	09 45	11 50	19 12	06 48	09	63
30	09 55	10 05	11 50	20 00	07 36	10	72

2017 OCTOBER 1, 2, 3 (SUN., MON., TUES.)

UT d	h	ARIES GHA	VENUS −3·9 GHA	VENUS Dec	MARS +1·8 GHA	MARS Dec	JUPITER −1·7 GHA	JUPITER Dec	SATURN +0·5 GHA	SATURN Dec
		° ′	° ′	° ′	° ′	° ′	° ′	° ′	° ′	° ′
1	00	9 55.0	204 42.5	N 7 41.4	202 07.6	N 6 30.7	163 34.0	S 9 46.6	108 17.7	S22 08.5
	01	24 57.5	219 42.1	40.3	217 08.6	30.0	178 36.0	46.8	123 20.0	08.5
	02	39 59.9	234 41.7	39.2	232 09.6	29.4	193 38.0	47.0	138 22.3	08.5
	03	55 02.4	249 41.2	. . 38.1	247 10.6	. . 28.8	208 39.9	. . 47.2	153 24.6	. . 08.5
	04	70 04.9	264 40.8	36.9	262 11.6	28.2	223 41.9	47.4	168 26.9	08.6
	05	85 07.3	279 40.4	35.8	277 12.6	27.6	238 43.9	47.6	183 29.2	08.6
	06	100 09.8	294 40.0	N 7 34.7	292 13.6	N 6 27.0	253 45.8	S 9 47.8	198 31.5	S22 08.6
	07	115 12.3	309 39.5	33.5	307 14.6	26.3	268 47.8	48.0	213 33.8	08.6
	08	130 14.7	324 39.1	32.4	322 15.6	25.7	283 49.8	48.2	228 36.1	08.6
S	09	145 17.2	339 38.7	. . 31.3	337 16.6	. . 25.1	298 51.7	. . 48.4	243 38.5	. . 08.6
U	10	160 19.6	354 38.3	30.2	352 17.6	24.5	313 53.7	48.6	258 40.8	08.6
N	11	175 22.1	9 37.9	29.0	7 18.6	23.9	328 55.7	48.7	273 43.1	08.7
D	12	190 24.6	24 37.4	N 7 27.9	22 19.6	N 6 23.3	343 57.6	S 9 48.9	288 45.4	S22 08.7
A	13	205 27.0	39 37.0	26.8	37 20.6	22.6	358 59.6	49.1	303 47.7	08.7
Y	14	220 29.5	54 36.6	25.6	52 21.6	22.0	14 01.6	49.3	318 50.0	08.7
	15	235 32.0	69 36.2	. . 24.5	67 22.6	. . 21.4	29 03.5	. . 49.5	333 52.3	. . 08.7
	16	250 34.4	84 35.7	23.4	82 23.6	20.8	44 05.5	49.7	348 54.6	08.7
	17	265 36.9	99 35.3	22.3	97 24.6	20.2	59 07.4	49.9	3 56.9	08.8
	18	280 39.4	114 34.9	N 7 21.1	112 25.6	N 6 19.6	74 09.4	S 9 50.1	18 59.2	S22 08.8
	19	295 41.8	129 34.5	20.0	127 26.6	18.9	89 11.4	50.3	34 01.5	08.8
	20	310 44.3	144 34.1	18.9	142 27.6	18.3	104 13.3	50.5	49 03.9	08.8
	21	325 46.8	159 33.6	. . 17.7	157 28.6	. . 17.7	119 15.3	. . 50.7	64 06.2	. . 08.8
	22	340 49.2	174 33.2	16.6	172 29.6	17.1	134 17.3	50.8	79 08.5	08.8
	23	355 51.7	189 32.8	15.5	187 30.6	16.5	149 19.2	51.0	94 10.8	08.8
2	00	10 54.1	204 32.4	N 7 14.3	202 31.6	N 6 15.9	164 21.2	S 9 51.2	109 13.1	S22 08.9
	01	25 56.6	219 32.0	13.2	217 32.6	15.2	179 23.2	51.4	124 15.4	08.9
	02	40 59.1	234 31.5	12.1	232 33.6	14.6	194 25.1	51.6	139 17.7	08.9
	03	56 01.5	249 31.1	. . 10.9	247 34.6	. . 14.0	209 27.1	. . 51.8	154 20.0	. . 08.9
	04	71 04.0	264 30.7	09.8	262 35.6	13.4	224 29.1	52.0	169 22.3	08.9
	05	86 06.5	279 30.3	08.7	277 36.6	12.8	239 31.0	52.2	184 24.6	08.9
	06	101 08.9	294 29.9	N 7 07.5	292 37.6	N 6 12.2	254 33.0	S 9 52.4	199 26.9	S22 09.0
	07	116 11.4	309 29.5	06.4	307 38.6	11.5	269 35.0	52.6	214 29.2	09.0
	08	131 13.9	324 29.0	05.2	322 39.6	10.9	284 36.9	52.8	229 31.5	09.0
M	09	146 16.3	339 28.6	. . 04.1	337 40.6	. . 10.3	299 38.9	. . 52.9	244 33.8	. . 09.0
O	10	161 18.8	354 28.2	03.0	352 41.6	09.7	314 40.8	53.1	259 36.2	09.0
N	11	176 21.3	9 27.8	01.8	7 42.6	09.1	329 42.8	53.3	274 38.5	09.0
D	12	191 23.7	24 27.4	N 7 00.7	22 43.6	N 6 08.4	344 44.8	S 9 53.5	289 40.8	S22 09.0
A	13	206 26.2	39 26.9	6 59.6	37 44.6	07.8	359 46.7	53.7	304 43.1	09.1
Y	14	221 28.6	54 26.5	58.4	52 45.6	07.2	14 48.7	53.9	319 45.4	09.1
	15	236 31.1	69 26.1	. . 57.3	67 46.6	. . 06.6	29 50.7	. . 54.1	334 47.7	. . 09.1
	16	251 33.6	84 25.7	56.1	82 47.6	06.0	44 52.6	54.3	349 50.0	09.1
	17	266 36.0	99 25.3	55.0	97 48.6	05.4	59 54.6	54.5	4 52.3	09.1
	18	281 38.5	114 24.9	N 6 53.9	112 49.6	N 6 04.7	74 56.6	S 9 54.7	19 54.6	S22 09.1
	19	296 41.0	129 24.5	52.7	127 50.6	04.1	89 58.5	54.9	34 56.9	09.2
	20	311 43.4	144 24.0	51.6	142 51.6	03.5	105 00.5	55.0	49 59.2	09.2
	21	326 45.9	159 23.6	. . 50.4	157 52.6	. . 02.9	120 02.5	. . 55.2	65 01.5	. . 09.2
	22	341 48.4	174 23.2	49.3	172 53.6	02.3	135 04.4	55.4	80 03.8	09.2
	23	356 50.8	189 22.8	48.2	187 54.6	01.6	150 06.4	55.6	95 06.1	09.2
3	00	11 53.3	204 22.4	N 6 47.0	202 55.6	N 6 01.0	165 08.3	S 9 55.8	110 08.4	S22 09.2
	01	26 55.7	219 22.0	45.9	217 56.6	6 00.4	180 10.3	56.0	125 10.7	09.2
	02	41 58.2	234 21.5	44.7	232 57.6	5 59.8	195 12.3	56.2	140 13.0	09.3
	03	57 00.7	249 21.1	. . 43.6	247 58.6	. . 59.2	210 14.2	. . 56.4	155 15.3	. . 09.3
	04	72 03.1	264 20.7	42.4	262 59.6	58.6	225 16.2	56.6	170 17.6	09.3
	05	87 05.6	279 20.3	41.3	278 00.6	57.9	240 18.2	56.8	185 19.9	09.3
	06	102 08.1	294 19.9	N 6 40.1	293 01.6	N 5 57.3	255 20.1	S 9 57.0	200 22.2	S22 09.3
	07	117 10.5	309 19.5	39.0	308 02.6	56.7	270 22.1	57.1	215 24.6	09.3
T	08	132 13.0	324 19.1	37.9	323 03.6	56.1	285 24.0	57.3	230 26.9	09.4
U	09	147 15.5	339 18.6	. . 36.7	338 04.6	55.5	300 26.0	. . 57.5	245 29.2	. . 09.4
E	10	162 17.9	354 18.2	35.6	353 05.6	54.8	315 28.0	57.7	260 31.5	09.4
S	11	177 20.4	9 17.8	34.4	8 06.6	54.2	330 29.9	57.9	275 33.8	09.4
D	12	192 22.9	24 17.4	N 6 33.3	23 07.6	N 5 53.6	345 31.9	S 9 58.1	290 36.1	S22 09.4
A	13	207 25.3	39 17.0	32.1	38 08.6	53.0	0 33.9	58.3	305 38.4	09.4
Y	14	222 27.8	54 16.6	31.0	53 09.6	52.4	15 35.8	58.5	320 40.7	09.4
	15	237 30.2	69 16.2	. . 29.8	68 10.6	. . 51.7	30 37.8	. . 58.7	335 43.0	. . 09.5
	16	252 32.7	84 15.8	28.7	83 11.6	51.1	45 39.7	58.9	350 45.3	09.5
	17	267 35.2	99 15.3	27.5	98 12.6	50.5	60 41.7	59.1	5 47.6	09.5
	18	282 37.6	114 14.9	N 6 26.4	113 13.6	N 5 49.9	75 43.7	S 9 59.2	20 49.9	S22 09.5
	19	297 40.1	129 14.5	25.2	128 14.6	49.3	90 45.6	59.4	35 52.2	09.5
	20	312 42.6	144 14.1	24.1	143 15.6	48.6	105 47.6	59.6	50 54.5	09.5
	21	327 45.0	159 13.7	. . 22.9	158 16.6	. . 48.0	120 49.6	9 59.8	65 56.8	. . 09.6
	22	342 47.5	174 13.3	21.8	173 17.6	47.4	135 51.5	10 00.0	80 59.1	09.6
	23	357 50.0	189 12.9	20.6	188 18.6	46.8	150 53.5	S10 00.2	96 01.4	09.6
Mer. Pass.		h m 23 12.6	*v* −0.4	*d* 1.1	*v* 1.0	*d* 0.6	*v* 2.0	*d* 0.2	*v* 2.3	*d* 0.0

STARS

Name	SHA	Dec
	° ′	° ′
Acamar	315 15.8	S40 14.0
Achernar	335 24.1	S57 08.8
Acrux	173 06.6	S63 11.7
Adhara	255 10.3	S28 59.7
Aldebaran	290 45.9	N16 32.5
Alioth	166 18.8	N55 52.0
Alkaid	152 57.1	N49 13.8
Al Na'ir	27 39.8	S46 52.5
Alnilam	275 43.4	S 1 11.5
Alphard	217 53.5	S 8 44.0
Alphecca	126 08.8	N26 39.7
Alpheratz	357 40.1	N29 11.4
Altair	62 05.3	N 8 55.2
Ankaa	353 12.5	S42 12.6
Antares	112 22.9	S26 28.1
Arcturus	145 53.4	N19 05.7
Atria	107 22.3	S69 03.5
Avior	234 17.1	S59 33.8
Bellatrix	278 28.8	N 6 21.8
Betelgeuse	270 58.1	N 7 24.5
Canopus	263 54.8	S52 42.1
Capella	280 30.0	N46 00.6
Deneb	49 29.3	N45 21.0
Denebola	182 31.1	N14 28.5
Diphda	348 52.7	S17 53.3
Dubhe	193 48.9	N61 39.3
Elnath	278 08.9	N28 37.1
Eltanin	90 44.9	N51 29.7
Enif	33 44.1	N 9 57.6
Fomalhaut	15 20.5	S29 31.7
Gacrux	171 58.2	S57 12.6
Gienah	175 49.6	S17 38.2
Hadar	148 44.3	S60 27.4
Hamal	327 57.2	N23 32.7
Kaus Aust.	83 40.0	S34 22.4
Kochab	137 21.2	N74 05.3
Markab	13 35.1	N15 18.2
Menkar	314 11.8	N 4 09.5
Menkent	148 04.5	S36 27.2
Miaplacidus	221 39.5	S69 47.2
Mirfak	308 35.8	N49 55.2
Nunki	75 54.7	S26 16.3
Peacock	53 14.5	S56 40.7
Pollux	243 24.3	N27 58.8
Procyon	244 56.8	N 5 10.7
Rasalhague	96 03.9	N12 33.2
Regulus	207 40.7	N11 52.9
Rigel	281 09.2	S 8 10.9
Rigil Kent.	139 48.3	S60 54.4
Sabik	102 09.4	S15 44.6
Schedar	349 36.6	N56 38.0
Shaula	96 18.1	S37 06.9
Sirius	258 31.2	S16 44.4
Spica	158 28.5	S11 15.0
Suhail	222 50.6	S43 30.0
Vega	80 37.0	N38 48.5
Zuben'ubi	137 02.5	S16 06.7

	SHA	Mer. Pass.
	° ′	h m
Venus	193 38.2	10 22
Mars	191 37.5	10 29
Jupiter	153 27.1	13 01
Saturn	98 18.9	16 41

UT d h	SUN GHA ° ′	SUN Dec ° ′	MOON GHA ° ′	v ′	MOON Dec ° ′	d ′	HP ′
1 00	182 33.7	S 3 10.6	57 57.8	11.7	S16 36.5	5.7	55.4
01	197 33.9	11.6	72 28.5	11.7	16 30.8	5.7	55.4
02	212 34.1	12.5	86 59.2	11.7	16 25.1	5.8	55.4
03	227 34.3	. . 13.5	101 29.9	11.7	16 19.3	5.9	55.5
04	242 34.5	14.5	116 00.6	11.7	16 13.4	5.9	55.5
05	257 34.7	15.4	130 31.3	11.7	16 07.5	6.1	55.5
06	272 34.9	S 3 16.4	145 02.0	11.8	S16 01.4	6.1	55.5
07	287 35.1	17.4	159 32.8	11.7	15 55.3	6.3	55.6
S 08	302 35.3	18.4	174 03.5	11.7	15 49.0	6.3	55.6
U 09	317 35.5	. . 19.3	188 34.2	11.7	15 42.7	6.4	55.6
N 10	332 35.7	20.3	203 04.9	11.7	15 36.3	6.4	55.7
D 11	347 35.9	21.3	217 35.6	11.7	15 29.9	6.6	55.7
A 12	2 36.1	S 3 22.2	232 06.3	11.7	S15 23.3	6.6	55.7
Y 13	17 36.3	23.2	246 37.0	11.7	15 16.7	6.7	55.7
14	32 36.5	24.2	261 07.7	11.7	15 10.0	6.8	55.8
15	47 36.7	. . 25.1	275 38.4	11.7	15 03.2	6.9	55.8
16	62 36.9	26.1	290 09.1	11.7	14 56.3	7.0	55.8
17	77 37.1	27.1	304 39.8	11.7	14 49.3	7.0	55.8
18	92 37.3	S 3 28.0	319 10.5	11.7	S14 42.3	7.2	55.9
19	107 37.6	29.0	333 41.2	11.7	14 35.1	7.2	55.9
20	122 37.8	30.0	348 11.9	11.7	14 27.9	7.2	55.9
21	137 38.0	. . 30.9	2 42.6	11.7	14 20.7	7.4	56.0
22	152 38.2	31.9	17 13.3	11.7	14 13.3	7.4	56.0
23	167 38.4	32.9	31 44.0	11.7	14 05.9	7.6	56.0
2 00	182 38.5	S 3 33.8	46 14.7	11.7	S13 58.3	7.6	56.0
01	197 38.7	34.8	60 45.4	11.7	13 50.7	7.6	56.1
02	212 38.9	35.8	75 16.1	11.7	13 43.1	7.8	56.1
03	227 39.1	. . 36.7	89 46.8	11.8	13 35.3	7.8	56.1
04	242 39.3	37.7	104 17.6	11.7	13 27.5	7.9	56.2
05	257 39.5	38.7	118 48.3	11.6	13 19.6	8.0	56.2
06	272 39.7	S 3 39.6	133 18.9	11.7	S13 11.6	8.0	56.2
07	287 39.9	40.6	147 49.6	11.7	13 03.6	8.2	56.2
08	302 40.1	41.6	162 20.3	11.7	12 55.4	8.1	56.3
M 09	317 40.3	. . 42.5	176 51.0	11.7	12 47.3	8.3	56.3
O 10	332 40.5	43.5	191 21.7	11.7	12 39.0	8.4	56.3
N 11	347 40.7	44.5	205 52.4	11.7	12 30.6	8.4	56.4
D 12	2 40.9	S 3 45.5	220 23.1	11.7	S12 22.2	8.5	56.4
A 13	17 41.1	46.4	234 53.8	11.7	12 13.7	8.5	56.4
Y 14	32 41.3	47.4	249 24.5	11.7	12 05.2	8.6	56.5
15	47 41.5	. . 48.4	263 55.2	11.6	11 56.6	8.7	56.5
16	62 41.7	49.3	278 25.8	11.7	11 47.9	8.8	56.5
17	77 41.9	50.3	292 56.5	11.7	11 39.1	8.8	56.5
18	92 42.1	S 3 51.3	307 27.2	11.7	S11 30.3	9.0	56.6
19	107 42.3	52.2	321 57.9	11.6	11 21.3	8.9	56.6
20	122 42.5	53.2	336 28.5	11.7	11 12.4	9.1	56.6
21	137 42.7	. . 54.1	350 59.2	11.6	11 03.3	9.1	56.7
22	152 42.9	55.1	5 29.8	11.7	10 54.2	9.1	56.7
23	167 43.1	56.1	20 00.5	11.6	10 45.1	9.3	56.7
3 00	182 43.3	S 3 57.0	34 31.1	11.7	S10 35.8	9.3	56.8
01	197 43.5	58.0	49 01.8	11.6	10 26.5	9.3	56.8
02	212 43.7	59.0	63 32.4	11.6	10 17.2	9.5	56.8
03	227 43.9	3 59.9	78 03.0	11.7	10 07.7	9.4	56.9
04	242 44.1	4 00.9	92 33.7	11.6	9 58.3	9.6	56.9
05	257 44.3	01.9	107 04.3	11.6	9 48.7	9.6	56.9
06	272 44.5	S 4 02.8	121 34.9	11.6	S 9 39.1	9.7	57.0
07	287 44.7	03.8	136 05.5	11.6	9 29.4	9.7	57.0
T 08	302 44.9	04.8	150 36.1	11.6	9 19.7	9.8	57.0
U 09	317 45.1	. . 05.7	165 06.7	11.6	9 09.9	9.8	57.0
E 10	332 45.3	06.7	179 37.3	11.5	9 00.1	9.9	57.1
S 11	347 45.5	07.7	194 07.8	11.6	8 50.2	10.0	57.1
D 12	2 45.6	S 4 08.6	208 38.4	11.6	S 8 40.2	10.0	57.1
A 13	17 45.8	09.6	223 09.0	11.5	8 30.2	10.1	57.2
Y 14	32 46.0	10.6	237 39.5	11.5	8 20.1	10.1	57.2
15	47 46.2	. . 11.5	252 10.0	11.6	8 10.0	10.2	57.2
16	62 46.4	12.5	266 40.6	11.5	7 59.8	10.2	57.3
17	77 46.6	13.5	281 11.1	11.5	7 49.6	10.3	57.3
18	92 46.8	S 4 14.4	295 41.6	11.5	S 7 39.3	10.4	57.3
19	107 47.0	15.4	310 12.1	11.5	7 28.9	10.4	57.4
20	122 47.2	16.3	324 42.6	11.5	7 18.5	10.4	57.4
21	137 47.4	. . 17.3	339 13.1	11.4	7 08.1	10.5	57.4
22	152 47.6	18.3	353 43.5	11.5	6 57.6	10.5	57.5
23	167 47.8	19.2	8 14.0	11.4	S 6 47.1	10.6	57.5
	SD 16.0	d 1.0	SD	15.2	15.4		15.6

Lat. °	Twilight Naut. h m	Twilight Civil h m	Sunrise h m	Moonrise 1 h m	Moonrise 2 h m	Moonrise 3 h m	Moonrise 4 h m
N 72	03 55	05 17	06 24	18 21	18 07	17 57	17 48
N 70	04 06	05 19	06 20	17 50	17 48	17 46	17 43
68	04 15	05 21	06 17	17 27	17 33	17 36	17 39
66	04 23	05 23	06 14	17 09	17 20	17 29	17 36
64	04 29	05 25	06 12	16 54	17 10	17 22	17 33
62	04 34	05 26	06 10	16 42	17 01	17 17	17 31
60	04 38	05 27	06 08	16 31	16 53	17 12	17 28
N 58	04 42	05 27	06 07	16 22	16 46	17 07	17 27
56	04 45	05 28	06 05	16 14	16 40	17 03	17 25
54	04 47	05 29	06 04	16 07	16 35	17 00	17 23
52	04 50	05 29	06 03	16 00	16 30	16 57	17 22
50	04 52	05 29	06 02	15 54	16 25	16 54	17 21
45	04 56	05 30	05 59	15 42	16 16	16 47	17 18
N 40	04 59	05 30	05 57	15 31	16 07	16 42	17 16
35	05 01	05 30	05 56	15 22	16 01	16 37	17 14
30	05 02	05 30	05 54	15 14	15 54	16 33	17 12
20	05 04	05 29	05 51	15 00	15 44	16 26	17 09
N 10	05 03	05 28	05 49	14 48	15 34	16 20	17 06
0	05 01	05 25	05 46	14 37	15 26	16 14	17 03
S 10	04 58	05 22	05 43	14 26	15 17	16 08	17 01
20	04 53	05 18	05 40	14 14	15 07	16 02	16 58
30	04 45	05 13	05 37	14 00	14 57	15 55	16 55
35	04 40	05 10	05 35	13 52	14 50	15 51	16 53
40	04 33	05 06	05 33	13 43	14 43	15 46	16 51
45	04 25	05 00	05 30	13 32	14 35	15 41	16 49
S 50	04 15	04 54	05 27	13 19	14 25	15 34	16 46
52	04 10	04 51	05 25	13 13	14 20	15 31	16 45
54	04 05	04 48	05 23	13 06	14 15	15 28	16 43
56	03 58	04 44	05 22	12 59	14 10	15 24	16 42
58	03 51	04 40	05 20	12 50	14 03	15 20	16 40
S 60	03 42	04 35	05 17	12 41	13 56	15 16	16 38

Lat. °	Sunset h m	Twilight Civil h m	Twilight Naut. h m	Moonset 1 h m	Moonset 2 h m	Moonset 3 h m	Moonset 4 h m
N 72	17 13	18 19	19 40	23 31	25 26	01 26	03 18
N 70	17 17	18 17	19 29	24 01	00 01	01 43	03 27
68	17 20	18 15	19 21	24 23	00 23	01 57	03 35
66	17 23	18 14	19 14	24 40	00 40	02 09	03 41
64	17 25	18 12	19 08	24 54	00 54	02 18	03 46
62	17 27	18 11	19 03	25 06	01 06	02 26	03 50
60	17 29	18 10	18 59	00 03	01 16	02 33	03 54
N 58	17 31	18 10	18 55	00 14	01 24	02 39	03 58
56	17 32	18 09	18 52	00 23	01 32	02 45	04 01
54	17 34	18 09	18 50	00 32	01 39	02 49	04 04
52	17 35	18 08	18 48	00 39	01 45	02 54	04 06
50	17 36	18 08	18 46	00 46	01 50	02 58	04 08
45	17 39	18 08	18 42	01 00	02 02	03 06	04 13
N 40	17 41	18 08	18 39	01 12	02 11	03 13	04 17
35	17 42	18 08	18 37	01 22	02 20	03 19	04 21
30	17 44	18 08	18 36	01 31	02 27	03 24	04 24
20	17 47	18 09	18 35	01 46	02 39	03 34	04 29
N 10	17 50	18 11	18 35	02 00	02 50	03 42	04 33
0	17 53	18 13	18 37	02 12	03 00	03 49	04 38
S 10	17 55	18 16	18 41	02 24	03 10	03 56	04 42
20	17 58	18 20	18 46	02 37	03 21	04 04	04 46
30	18 02	18 26	18 54	02 52	03 33	04 13	04 51
35	18 04	18 30	18 59	03 01	03 40	04 18	04 54
40	18 07	18 34	19 06	03 11	03 48	04 24	04 57
45	18 09	18 39	19 14	03 22	03 57	04 30	05 01
S 50	18 13	18 46	19 25	03 36	04 09	04 38	05 06
52	18 14	18 49	19 30	03 42	04 14	04 42	05 08
54	18 16	18 52	19 36	03 49	04 19	04 46	05 10
56	18 18	18 56	19 42	03 57	04 26	04 50	05 12
58	18 20	19 00	19 50	04 06	04 32	04 55	05 15
S 60	18 23	19 05	19 58	04 16	04 40	05 00	05 18

Day d	SUN Eqn. of Time 00^h m s	SUN Eqn. of Time 12^h m s	SUN Mer. Pass. h m	MOON Mer. Pass. Upper h m	MOON Mer. Pass. Lower h m	MOON Age d	MOON %	Phase
1	10 14	10 24	11 50	20 49	08 25	11	81	
2	10 34	10 43	11 49	21 37	09 13	12	88	
3	10 53	11 02	11 49	22 26	10 02	13	94	

UT		ARIES	VENUS −3·9		MARS +1·8		JUPITER −1·7		SATURN +0·5	
		GHA	GHA	Dec	GHA	Dec	GHA	Dec	GHA	Dec
d	h	° ′	° ′	° ′	° ′	° ′	° ′	° ′	° ′	° ′
4	00	12 52.4	204 12.5	N 6 19.5	203 19.6	N 5 46.2	165 55.4	S10 00.4	111 03.7	S22 09.6
	01	27 54.9	219 12.0	18.3	218 20.6	45.5	180 57.4	00.6	126 06.0	09.6
	02	42 57.3	234 11.6	17.2	233 21.6	44.9	195 59.4	00.8	141 08.3	09.6
	03	57 59.8	249 11.2	. . 16.0	248 22.6	. . 44.3	211 01.3	. . 01.0	156 10.6	. . 09.7
	04	73 02.3	264 10.8	14.9	263 23.6	43.7	226 03.3	01.2	171 12.9	09.7
	05	88 04.7	279 10.4	13.7	278 24.6	43.1	241 05.2	01.3	186 15.2	09.7
WEDNESDAY	06	103 07.2	294 10.0	N 6 12.6	293 25.7	N 5 42.4	256 07.2	S10 01.5	201 17.5	S22 09.7
	07	118 09.7	309 09.6	11.4	308 26.7	41.8	271 09.2	01.7	216 19.8	09.7
	08	133 12.1	324 09.2	10.3	323 27.7	41.2	286 11.1	01.9	231 22.1	09.7
	09	148 14.6	339 08.8	. . 09.1	338 28.7	. . 40.6	301 13.1	. . 02.1	246 24.4	. . 09.7
	10	163 17.1	354 08.4	08.0	353 29.7	40.0	316 15.1	02.3	261 26.7	09.8
	11	178 19.5	9 07.9	06.8	8 30.7	39.3	331 17.0	02.5	276 29.0	09.8
	12	193 22.0	24 07.5	N 6 05.6	23 31.7	N 5 38.7	346 19.0	S10 02.7	291 31.3	S22 09.8
	13	208 24.5	39 07.1	04.5	38 32.7	38.1	1 20.9	02.9	306 33.6	09.8
	14	223 26.9	54 06.7	03.3	53 33.7	37.5	16 22.9	03.1	321 35.9	09.8
	15	238 29.4	69 06.3	. . 02.2	68 34.7	. . 36.9	31 24.9	. . 03.3	336 38.2	. . 09.8
	16	253 31.8	84 05.9	6 01.0	83 35.7	36.2	46 26.8	03.4	351 40.5	09.9
	17	268 34.3	99 05.5	5 59.9	98 36.7	35.6	61 28.8	03.6	6 42.8	09.9
	18	283 36.8	114 05.1	N 5 58.7	113 37.7	N 5 35.0	76 30.7	S10 03.8	21 45.1	S22 09.9
	19	298 39.2	129 04.7	57.5	128 38.7	34.4	91 32.7	04.0	36 47.4	09.9
	20	313 41.7	144 04.3	56.4	143 39.7	33.8	106 34.7	04.2	51 49.7	09.9
	21	328 44.2	159 03.9	. . 55.2	158 40.7	. . 33.1	121 36.6	. . 04.4	66 52.0	. . 09.9
	22	343 46.6	174 03.5	54.1	173 41.7	32.5	136 38.6	04.6	81 54.3	09.9
	23	358 49.1	189 03.0	52.9	188 42.7	31.9	151 40.5	04.8	96 56.5	10.0
5	00	13 51.6	204 02.6	N 5 51.8	203 43.7	N 5 31.3	166 42.5	S10 05.0	111 58.8	S22 10.0
	01	28 54.0	219 02.2	50.6	218 44.7	30.7	181 44.5	05.2	127 01.1	10.0
	02	43 56.5	234 01.8	49.4	233 45.7	30.0	196 46.4	05.4	142 03.4	10.0
	03	58 58.9	249 01.4	. . 48.3	248 46.7	. . 29.4	211 48.4	. . 05.6	157 05.7	. . 10.0
	04	74 01.4	264 01.0	47.1	263 47.7	28.8	226 50.3	05.7	172 08.0	10.0
	05	89 03.9	279 00.6	46.0	278 48.7	28.2	241 52.3	05.9	187 10.3	10.1
THURSDAY	06	104 06.3	294 00.2	N 5 44.8	293 49.7	N 5 27.5	256 54.3	S10 06.1	202 12.6	S22 10.1
	07	119 08.8	308 59.8	43.6	308 50.7	26.9	271 56.2	06.3	217 14.9	10.1
	08	134 11.3	323 59.4	42.5	323 51.7	26.3	286 58.2	06.5	232 17.2	10.1
	09	149 13.7	338 59.0	. . 41.3	338 52.7	. . 25.7	302 00.1	. . 06.7	247 19.5	. . 10.1
	10	164 16.2	353 58.6	40.1	353 53.7	25.1	317 02.1	06.9	262 21.8	10.1
	11	179 18.7	8 58.2	39.0	8 54.7	24.4	332 04.1	07.1	277 24.1	10.1
	12	194 21.1	23 57.8	N 5 37.8	23 55.7	N 5 23.8	347 06.0	S10 07.3	292 26.4	S22 10.2
	13	209 23.6	38 57.4	36.7	38 56.7	23.2	2 08.0	07.5	307 28.7	10.2
	14	224 26.1	53 56.9	35.5	53 57.8	22.6	17 09.9	07.7	322 31.0	10.2
	15	239 28.5	68 56.5	. . 34.3	68 58.8	. . 22.0	32 11.9	. . 07.8	337 33.3	. . 10.2
	16	254 31.0	83 56.1	33.2	83 59.8	21.3	47 13.9	08.0	352 35.6	10.2
	17	269 33.4	98 55.7	32.0	99 00.8	20.7	62 15.8	08.2	7 37.9	10.2
	18	284 35.9	113 55.3	N 5 30.8	114 01.8	N 5 20.1	77 17.8	S10 08.4	22 40.2	S22 10.3
	19	299 38.4	128 54.9	29.7	129 02.8	19.5	92 19.7	08.6	37 42.5	10.3
	20	314 40.8	143 54.5	28.5	144 03.8	18.8	107 21.7	08.8	52 44.7	10.3
	21	329 43.3	158 54.1	. . 27.3	159 04.8	. . 18.2	122 23.7	. . 09.0	67 47.0	. . 10.3
	22	344 45.8	173 53.7	26.2	174 05.8	17.6	137 25.6	09.2	82 49.3	10.3
	23	359 48.2	188 53.3	25.0	189 06.8	17.0	152 27.6	09.4	97 51.6	10.3
6	00	14 50.7	203 52.9	N 5 23.8	204 07.8	N 5 16.4	167 29.5	S10 09.6	112 53.9	S22 10.4
	01	29 53.2	218 52.5	22.7	219 08.8	15.7	182 31.5	09.8	127 56.2	10.4
	02	44 55.6	233 52.1	21.5	234 09.8	15.1	197 33.5	09.9	142 58.5	10.4
	03	59 58.1	248 51.7	. . 20.3	249 10.8	. . 14.5	212 35.4	. . 10.1	158 00.8	. . 10.4
	04	75 00.6	263 51.3	19.2	264 11.8	13.9	227 37.4	10.3	173 03.1	10.4
	05	90 03.0	278 50.9	18.0	279 12.8	13.2	242 39.3	10.5	188 05.4	10.4
	06	105 05.5	293 50.5	N 5 16.8	294 13.8	N 5 12.6	257 41.3	S10 10.7	203 07.7	S22 10.4
	07	120 07.9	308 50.1	15.7	309 14.8	12.0	272 43.2	10.9	218 10.0	10.5
	08	135 10.4	323 49.7	14.5	324 15.8	11.4	287 45.2	11.1	233 12.3	10.5
FRIDAY	09	150 12.9	338 49.3	. . 13.3	339 16.8	. . 10.8	302 47.2	. . 11.3	248 14.6	. . 10.5
	10	165 15.3	353 48.9	12.2	354 17.8	10.1	317 49.1	11.5	263 16.8	10.5
	11	180 17.8	8 48.5	11.0	9 18.8	09.5	332 51.1	11.7	278 19.1	10.5
	12	195 20.3	23 48.1	N 5 09.8	24 19.9	N 5 08.9	347 53.0	S10 11.9	293 21.4	S22 10.5
	13	210 22.7	38 47.7	08.6	39 20.9	08.3	2 55.0	12.0	308 23.7	10.6
	14	225 25.2	53 47.3	07.5	54 21.9	07.6	17 57.0	12.2	323 26.0	10.6
	15	240 27.7	68 46.9	. . 06.3	69 22.9	. . 07.0	32 58.9	. . 12.4	338 28.3	. . 10.6
	16	255 30.1	83 46.5	05.1	84 23.9	06.4	48 00.9	12.6	353 30.6	10.6
	17	270 32.6	98 46.0	04.0	99 24.9	05.8	63 02.8	12.8	8 32.9	10.6
	18	285 35.0	113 45.6	N 5 02.8	114 25.9	N 5 05.2	78 04.8	S10 13.0	23 35.2	S22 10.6
	19	300 37.5	128 45.2	01.6	129 26.9	04.5	93 06.7	13.2	38 37.5	10.6
	20	315 40.0	143 44.8	5 00.4	144 27.9	03.9	108 08.7	13.4	53 39.8	10.7
	21	330 42.4	158 44.4	4 59.3	159 28.9	. . 03.3	123 10.7	. . 13.6	68 42.0	. . 10.7
	22	345 44.9	173 44.0	58.1	174 29.9	02.7	138 12.6	13.8	83 44.3	10.7
	23	0 47.4	188 43.6	56.9	189 30.9	02.0	153 14.6	14.0	98 46.6	10.7
Mer. Pass.		h m 23 00.8	*v* −0.4	*d* 1.2	*v* 1.0	*d* 0.6	*v* 2.0	*d* 0.2	*v* 2.3	*d* 0.0

STARS

Name	SHA	Dec
	° ′	° ′
Acamar	315 15.8	S40 14.0
Achernar	335 24.1	S57 08.8
Acrux	173 06.6	S63 11.7
Adhara	255 10.3	S28 59.7
Aldebaran	290 45.9	N16 32.5
Alioth	166 18.8	N55 52.0
Alkaid	152 57.1	N49 13.8
Al Na'ir	27 39.8	S46 52.5
Alnilam	275 43.3	S 1 11.5
Alphard	217 53.5	S 8 44.0
Alphecca	126 08.8	N26 39.7
Alpheratz	357 40.1	N29 11.4
Altair	62 05.3	N 8 55.2
Ankaa	353 12.5	S42 12.6
Antares	112 22.9	S26 28.1
Arcturus	145 53.4	N19 05.7
Atria	107 22.3	S69 03.5
Avior	234 17.0	S59 33.7
Bellatrix	278 28.8	N 6 21.8
Betelgeuse	270 58.1	N 7 24.5
Canopus	263 54.8	S52 42.1
Capella	280 30.0	N46 00.6
Deneb	49 29.3	N45 21.0
Denebola	182 31.1	N14 28.5
Diphda	348 52.7	S17 53.3
Dubhe	193 48.9	N61 39.3
Elnath	278 08.8	N28 37.1
Eltanin	90 44.9	N51 29.7
Enif	33 44.1	N 9 57.6
Fomalhaut	15 20.5	S29 31.7
Gacrux	171 58.2	S57 12.6
Gienah	175 49.6	S17 38.2
Hadar	148 44.3	S60 27.4
Hamal	327 57.1	N23 32.7
Kaus Aust.	83 40.0	S34 22.4
Kochab	137 21.2	N74 05.3
Markab	13 35.2	N15 18.2
Menkar	314 11.8	N 4 09.5
Menkent	148 04.5	S36 27.2
Miaplacidus	221 39.5	S69 47.2
Mirfak	308 35.8	N49 55.2
Nunki	75 54.8	S26 16.3
Peacock	53 14.5	S56 40.7
Pollux	243 24.3	N27 58.8
Procyon	244 56.8	N 5 10.7
Rasalhague	96 03.9	N12 33.2
Regulus	207 40.7	N11 52.9
Rigel	281 09.1	S 8 10.9
Rigil Kent.	139 48.3	S60 54.3
Sabik	102 09.4	S15 44.6
Schedar	349 36.6	N56 38.1
Shaula	96 18.1	S37 06.9
Sirius	258 31.2	S16 44.4
Spica	158 28.5	S11 15.0
Suhail	222 50.5	S43 30.0
Vega	80 37.0	N38 48.5
Zuben'ubi	137 02.5	S16 06.7

	SHA	Mer. Pass.
	° ′	h m
Venus	190 11.1	10 24
Mars	189 52.1	10 24
Jupiter	152 50.9	12 51
Saturn	98 07.3	16 30

	UT	SUN GHA	SUN Dec	MOON GHA	*v*	MOON Dec	*d*	HP
	d h	° ′	° ′	° ′	′	° ′	′	′
WEDNESDAY	4 00	182 48.0	S 4 20.2	22 44.4	11.4	S 6 36.5	10.6	57.5
	01	197 48.2	21.2	37 14.8	11.5	6 25.9	10.7	57.5
	02	212 48.4	22.1	51 45.3	11.4	6 15.2	10.7	57.6
	03	227 48.6	. . 23.1	66 15.7	11.3	6 04.5	10.8	57.6
	04	242 48.7	24.1	80 46.0	11.4	5 53.7	10.8	57.6
	05	257 48.9	25.0	95 16.4	11.4	5 42.9	10.8	57.7
	06	272 49.1	S 4 26.0	109 46.8	11.3	S 5 32.1	10.9	57.7
	07	287 49.3	26.9	124 17.1	11.3	5 21.2	11.0	57.7
	08	302 49.5	27.9	138 47.4	11.3	5 10.2	10.9	57.8
	09	317 49.7	. . 28.9	153 17.7	11.3	4 59.3	11.0	57.8
	10	332 49.9	29.8	167 48.0	11.3	4 48.3	11.1	57.8
	11	347 50.1	30.8	182 18.3	11.2	4 37.2	11.1	57.8
	12	2 50.3	S 4 31.8	196 48.5	11.3	S 4 26.1	11.1	57.9
	13	17 50.5	32.7	211 18.8	11.2	4 15.0	11.1	57.9
	14	32 50.7	33.7	225 49.0	11.2	4 03.9	11.2	57.9
	15	47 50.9	. . 34.6	240 19.2	11.1	3 52.7	11.2	58.0
	16	62 51.0	35.6	254 49.3	11.2	3 41.5	11.3	58.0
	17	77 51.2	36.6	269 19.5	11.1	3 30.2	11.3	58.0
	18	92 51.4	S 4 37.5	283 49.6	11.2	S 3 18.9	11.3	58.1
	19	107 51.6	38.5	298 19.8	11.0	3 07.6	11.3	58.1
	20	122 51.8	39.5	312 49.8	11.1	2 56.3	11.4	58.1
	21	137 52.0	. . 40.4	327 19.9	11.1	2 44.9	11.4	58.1
	22	152 52.2	41.4	341 50.0	11.0	2 33.5	11.4	58.2
	23	167 52.4	42.3	356 20.0	11.0	2 22.1	11.4	58.2
THURSDAY	5 00	182 52.6	S 4 43.3	10 50.0	11.0	S 2 10.7	11.5	58.2
	01	197 52.8	44.3	25 20.0	10.9	1 59.2	11.5	58.3
	02	212 52.9	45.2	39 49.9	11.0	1 47.7	11.5	58.3
	03	227 53.1	. . 46.2	54 19.9	10.9	1 36.2	11.5	58.3
	04	242 53.3	47.1	68 49.8	10.8	1 24.7	11.6	58.3
	05	257 53.5	48.1	83 19.6	10.9	1 13.1	11.5	58.4
	06	272 53.7	S 4 49.1	97 49.5	10.8	S 1 01.6	11.6	58.4
	07	287 53.9	50.0	112 19.3	10.8	0 50.0	11.6	58.4
	08	302 54.1	51.0	126 49.1	10.8	0 38.4	11.6	58.4
	09	317 54.3	. . 52.0	141 18.9	10.7	0 26.8	11.6	58.5
	10	332 54.4	52.9	155 48.6	10.7	0 15.2	11.7	58.5
	11	347 54.6	53.9	170 18.3	10.7	S 0 03.5	11.6	58.5
	12	2 54.8	S 4 54.8	184 48.0	10.7	N 0 08.1	11.7	58.6
	13	17 55.0	55.8	199 17.7	10.6	0 19.8	11.7	58.6
	14	32 55.2	56.8	213 47.3	10.6	0 31.5	11.6	58.6
	15	47 55.4	. . 57.7	228 16.9	10.5	0 43.1	11.7	58.6
	16	62 55.6	58.7	242 46.4	10.6	0 54.8	11.7	58.7
	17	77 55.8	4 59.6	257 16.0	10.5	1 06.5	11.7	58.7
	18	92 55.9	S 5 00.6	271 45.5	10.4	N 1 18.2	11.7	58.7
	19	107 56.1	01.6	286 14.9	10.5	1 29.9	11.7	58.7
	20	122 56.3	02.5	300 44.4	10.4	1 41.6	11.7	58.8
	21	137 56.5	. . 03.5	315 13.8	10.3	1 53.3	11.7	58.8
	22	152 56.7	04.4	329 43.1	10.3	2 05.0	11.7	58.8
	23	167 56.9	05.4	344 12.4	10.3	2 16.7	11.7	58.8
FRIDAY	6 00	182 57.1	S 5 06.3	358 41.7	10.3	N 2 28.4	11.7	58.8
	01	197 57.2	07.3	13 11.0	10.2	2 40.1	11.6	58.9
	02	212 57.4	08.3	27 40.2	10.2	2 51.7	11.7	58.9
	03	227 57.6	. . 09.2	42 09.4	10.1	3 03.4	11.7	58.9
	04	242 57.8	10.2	56 38.5	10.2	3 15.1	11.6	58.9
	05	257 58.0	11.1	71 07.7	10.0	3 26.7	11.7	59.0
	06	272 58.2	S 5 12.1	85 36.7	10.1	N 3 38.4	11.6	59.0
	07	287 58.4	13.1	100 05.8	10.0	3 50.0	11.6	59.0
	08	302 58.5	14.0	114 34.8	9.9	4 01.6	11.7	59.0
	09	317 58.7	. . 15.0	129 03.7	9.9	4 13.3	11.5	59.0
	10	332 58.9	15.9	143 32.6	9.9	4 24.8	11.6	59.1
	11	347 59.1	16.9	158 01.5	9.8	4 36.4	11.6	59.1
	12	2 59.3	S 5 17.8	172 30.3	9.8	N 4 48.0	11.5	59.1
	13	17 59.5	18.8	186 59.1	9.8	4 59.5	11.5	59.1
	14	32 59.6	19.8	201 27.9	9.7	5 11.0	11.5	59.1
	15	47 59.8	. . 20.7	215 56.6	9.7	5 22.5	11.5	59.2
	16	63 00.0	21.7	230 25.3	9.6	5 34.0	11.4	59.2
	17	78 00.2	22.6	244 53.9	9.6	5 45.4	11.5	59.2
	18	93 00.4	S 5 23.6	259 22.5	9.5	N 5 56.9	11.4	59.2
	19	108 00.6	24.5	273 51.0	9.5	6 08.3	11.3	59.2
	20	123 00.7	25.5	288 19.5	9.5	6 19.6	11.4	59.3
	21	138 00.9	. . 26.5	302 48.0	9.4	6 31.0	11.3	59.3
	22	153 01.1	27.4	317 16.4	9.4	6 42.3	11.2	59.3
	23	168 01.3	28.4	331 44.8	9.3	N 6 53.5	11.3	59.3
		SD 16.0	*d* 1.0	SD	15.8	16.0		16.1

Lat.	Twilight Naut.	Twilight Civil	Sunrise	Moonrise 4	Moonrise 5	Moonrise 6	Moonrise 7
°	h m	h m	h m	h m	h m	h m	h m
N 72	04 10	05 30	06 38	17 48	17 39	17 30	17 20
N 70	04 19	05 31	06 32	17 43	17 40	17 38	17 36
68	04 27	05 32	06 28	17 39	17 42	17 44	17 48
66	04 33	05 33	06 24	17 36	17 43	17 50	17 59
64	04 38	05 33	06 21	17 33	17 44	17 55	18 08
62	04 42	05 33	06 18	17 31	17 44	17 59	18 15
60	04 45	05 34	06 15	17 28	17 45	18 02	18 22
N 58	04 48	05 34	06 13	17 27	17 46	18 05	18 28
56	04 51	05 34	06 11	17 25	17 46	18 08	18 33
54	04 53	05 34	06 09	17 23	17 47	18 11	18 37
52	04 55	05 34	06 08	17 22	17 47	18 13	18 42
50	04 57	05 34	06 06	17 21	17 47	18 15	18 46
45	05 00	05 34	06 03	17 18	17 48	18 20	18 54
N 40	05 02	05 33	06 00	17 16	17 49	18 24	19 01
35	05 03	05 33	05 58	17 14	17 50	18 27	19 07
30	05 04	05 32	05 56	17 12	17 50	18 30	19 12
20	05 04	05 30	05 52	17 09	17 51	18 36	19 22
N 10	05 03	05 27	05 48	17 06	17 52	18 40	19 30
0	05 00	05 24	05 45	17 03	17 53	18 45	19 38
S 10	04 56	05 21	05 42	17 01	17 54	18 49	19 46
20	04 50	05 16	05 38	16 58	17 55	18 54	19 54
30	04 41	05 09	05 33	16 55	17 57	19 00	20 04
35	04 35	05 05	05 31	16 53	17 57	19 03	20 10
40	04 28	05 01	05 28	16 51	17 58	19 06	20 16
45	04 19	04 55	05 24	16 49	17 59	19 11	20 24
S 50	04 08	04 47	05 20	16 46	18 00	19 16	20 33
52	04 02	04 44	05 18	16 45	18 01	19 18	20 37
54	03 56	04 40	05 16	16 43	18 01	19 21	20 41
56	03 49	04 36	05 14	16 42	18 02	19 24	20 47
58	03 41	04 31	05 11	16 40	18 03	19 27	20 52
S 60	03 32	04 25	05 08	16 38	18 03	19 31	20 59

Lat.	Sunset	Twilight Civil	Twilight Naut.	Moonset 4	Moonset 5	Moonset 6	Moonset 7
°	h m	h m	h m	h m	h m	h m	h m
N 72	16 57	18 04	19 24	03 18	05 11	07 06	09 05
N 70	17 03	18 03	19 15	03 27	05 13	07 00	08 52
68	17 07	18 03	19 08	03 35	05 14	06 56	08 41
66	17 11	18 02	19 02	03 41	05 15	06 52	08 32
64	17 15	18 02	18 57	03 46	05 16	06 49	08 24
62	17 18	18 02	18 53	03 50	05 17	06 47	08 18
60	17 20	18 02	18 50	03 54	05 18	06 44	08 12
N 58	17 22	18 02	18 47	03 58	05 19	06 42	08 07
56	17 24	18 01	18 45	04 01	05 19	06 40	08 03
54	17 26	18 02	18 42	04 04	05 20	06 39	07 59
52	17 28	18 02	18 41	04 06	05 21	06 37	07 55
50	17 30	18 02	18 39	04 08	05 21	06 36	07 52
45	17 33	18 02	18 36	04 13	05 22	06 33	07 45
N 40	17 36	18 03	18 34	04 17	05 23	06 30	07 39
35	17 38	18 04	18 33	04 21	05 24	06 28	07 34
30	17 41	18 04	18 32	04 24	05 24	06 26	07 30
20	17 45	18 07	18 32	04 29	05 25	06 23	07 23
N 10	17 48	18 09	18 34	04 33	05 26	06 20	07 16
0	17 52	18 12	18 36	04 38	05 27	06 18	07 10
S 10	17 55	18 16	18 41	04 42	05 28	06 15	07 04
20	17 59	18 21	18 47	04 46	05 29	06 12	06 57
30	18 04	18 28	18 56	04 51	05 30	06 09	06 49
35	18 06	18 32	19 02	04 54	05 30	06 07	06 45
40	18 10	18 37	19 09	04 57	05 31	06 05	06 40
45	18 13	18 43	19 18	05 01	05 31	06 02	06 35
S 50	18 18	18 50	19 30	05 06	05 32	05 59	06 28
52	18 20	18 54	19 36	05 08	05 33	05 58	06 25
54	18 22	18 58	19 42	05 10	05 33	05 56	06 21
56	18 24	19 02	19 49	05 12	05 33	05 55	06 18
58	18 27	19 07	19 58	05 15	05 34	05 53	06 14
S 60	18 30	19 13	20 07	05 18	05 34	05 51	06 09

Day	SUN Eqn. of Time 00^h	SUN Eqn. of Time 12^h	SUN Mer. Pass.	MOON Mer. Pass. Upper	MOON Mer. Pass. Lower	MOON Age	MOON Phase
d	m s	m s	h m	h m	h m	d %	
4	11 12	11 21	11 49	23 15	10 50	14 98	
5	11 30	11 39	11 48	24 05	11 40	15 100	○
6	11 48	11 57	11 48	00 05	12 31	16 99	

UT	ARIES	VENUS −3·9		MARS +1·8		JUPITER −1·7		SATURN +0·5	
	GHA	GHA	Dec	GHA	Dec	GHA	Dec	GHA	Dec
d h	° ′	° ′	° ′	° ′	° ′	° ′	° ′	° ′	° ′
7 00	15 49.8	203 43.2	N 4 55.7	204 31.9	N 5 01.4	168 16.5	S10 14.1	113 48.9	S22 10.7
01	30 52.3	218 42.8	54.6	219 32.9	00.8	183 18.5	14.3	128 51.2	10.7
02	45 54.8	233 42.4	53.4	234 33.9	5 00.2	198 20.4	14.5	143 53.5	10.8
03	60 57.2	248 42.0	. . 52.2	249 34.9	4 59.5	213 22.4	. . 14.7	158 55.8	. . 10.8
04	75 59.7	263 41.6	51.0	264 35.9	58.9	228 24.4	14.9	173 58.1	10.8
05	91 02.2	278 41.2	49.9	279 36.9	58.3	243 26.3	15.1	189 00.4	10.8
06	106 04.6	293 40.8	N 4 48.7	294 38.0	N 4 57.7	258 28.3	S10 15.3	204 02.6	S22 10.8
07	121 07.1	308 40.4	47.5	309 39.0	57.1	273 30.2	15.5	219 04.9	10.8
S 08	136 09.5	323 40.0	46.3	324 40.0	56.4	288 32.2	15.7	234 07.2	10.9
A 09	151 12.0	338 39.6	. . 45.2	339 41.0	. . 55.8	303 34.1	. . 15.9	249 09.5	. . 10.9
T 10	166 14.5	353 39.2	44.0	354 42.0	55.2	318 36.1	16.1	264 11.8	10.9
U 11	181 16.9	8 38.8	42.8	9 43.0	54.6	333 38.1	16.2	279 14.1	10.9
R 12	196 19.4	23 38.4	N 4 41.6	24 44.0	N 4 53.9	348 40.0	S10 16.4	294 16.4	S22 10.9
D 13	211 21.9	38 38.0	40.5	39 45.0	53.3	3 42.0	16.6	309 18.7	10.9
A 14	226 24.3	53 37.6	39.3	54 46.0	52.7	18 43.9	16.8	324 21.0	10.9
Y 15	241 26.8	68 37.2	. . 38.1	69 47.0	. . 52.1	33 45.9	. . 17.0	339 23.2	. . 11.0
16	256 29.3	83 36.8	36.9	84 48.0	51.4	48 47.8	17.2	354 25.5	11.0
17	271 31.7	98 36.4	35.7	99 49.0	50.8	63 49.8	17.4	9 27.8	11.0
18	286 34.2	113 36.0	N 4 34.6	114 50.0	N 4 50.2	78 51.8	S10 17.6	24 30.1	S22 11.0
19	301 36.6	128 35.6	33.4	129 51.0	49.6	93 53.7	17.8	39 32.4	11.0
20	316 39.1	143 35.2	32.2	144 52.0	48.9	108 55.7	18.0	54 34.7	11.0
21	331 41.6	158 34.8	. . 31.0	159 53.0	. . 48.3	123 57.6	. . 18.2	69 37.0	. . 11.1
22	346 44.0	173 34.4	29.8	174 54.1	47.7	138 59.6	18.3	84 39.2	11.1
23	1 46.5	188 34.0	28.7	189 55.1	47.1	154 01.5	18.5	99 41.5	11.1
8 00	16 49.0	203 33.6	N 4 27.5	204 56.1	N 4 46.4	169 03.5	S10 18.7	114 43.8	S22 11.1
01	31 51.4	218 33.2	26.3	219 57.1	45.8	184 05.5	18.9	129 46.1	11.1
02	46 53.9	233 32.8	25.1	234 58.1	45.2	199 07.4	19.1	144 48.4	11.1
03	61 56.4	248 32.4	. . 23.9	249 59.1	. . 44.6	214 09.4	. . 19.3	159 50.7	. . 11.2
04	76 58.8	263 32.0	22.8	265 00.1	43.9	229 11.3	19.5	174 53.0	11.2
05	92 01.3	278 31.7	21.6	280 01.1	43.3	244 13.3	19.7	189 55.2	11.2
06	107 03.8	293 31.3	N 4 20.4	295 02.1	N 4 42.7	259 15.2	S10 19.9	204 57.5	S22 11.2
07	122 06.2	308 30.9	19.2	310 03.1	42.1	274 17.2	20.1	219 59.8	11.2
08	137 08.7	323 30.5	18.0	325 04.1	41.5	289 19.1	20.3	235 02.1	11.2
S 09	152 11.1	338 30.1	. . 16.9	340 05.1	. . 40.8	304 21.1	. . 20.4	250 04.4	. . 11.2
U 10	167 13.6	353 29.7	15.7	355 06.1	40.2	319 23.1	20.6	265 06.7	11.3
N 11	182 16.1	8 29.3	14.5	10 07.1	39.6	334 25.0	20.8	280 09.0	11.3
D 12	197 18.5	23 28.9	N 4 13.3	25 08.1	N 4 39.0	349 27.0	S10 21.0	295 11.2	S22 11.3
A 13	212 21.0	38 28.5	12.1	40 09.2	38.3	4 28.9	21.2	310 13.5	11.3
Y 14	227 23.5	53 28.1	10.9	55 10.2	37.7	19 30.9	21.4	325 15.8	11.3
15	242 25.9	68 27.7	. . 09.7	70 11.2	. . 37.1	34 32.8	. . 21.6	340 18.1	. . 11.3
16	257 28.4	83 27.3	08.6	85 12.2	36.5	49 34.8	21.8	355 20.4	11.4
17	272 30.9	98 26.9	07.4	100 13.2	35.8	64 36.7	22.0	10 22.7	11.4
18	287 33.3	113 26.5	N 4 06.2	115 14.2	N 4 35.2	79 38.7	S10 22.2	25 24.9	S22 11.4
19	302 35.8	128 26.1	05.0	130 15.2	34.6	94 40.7	22.4	40 27.2	11.4
20	317 38.3	143 25.7	03.8	145 16.2	34.0	109 42.6	22.5	55 29.5	11.4
21	332 40.7	158 25.3	. . 02.6	160 17.2	. . 33.3	124 44.6	. . 22.7	70 31.8	. . 11.4
22	347 43.2	173 24.9	01.5	175 18.2	32.7	139 46.5	22.9	85 34.1	11.5
23	2 45.6	188 24.5	4 00.3	190 19.2	32.1	154 48.5	23.1	100 36.4	11.5
9 00	17 48.1	203 24.1	N 3 59.1	205 20.2	N 4 31.5	169 50.4	S10 23.3	115 38.6	S22 11.5
01	32 50.6	218 23.7	57.9	220 21.2	30.8	184 52.4	23.5	130 40.9	11.5
02	47 53.0	233 23.3	56.7	235 22.3	30.2	199 54.3	23.7	145 43.2	11.5
03	62 55.5	248 22.9	. . 55.5	250 23.3	. . 29.6	214 56.3	. . 23.9	160 45.5	. . 11.5
04	77 58.0	263 22.5	54.3	265 24.3	29.0	229 58.3	24.1	175 47.8	11.5
05	93 00.4	278 22.1	53.1	280 25.3	28.3	245 00.2	24.3	190 50.0	11.6
06	108 02.9	293 21.7	N 3 52.0	295 26.3	N 4 27.7	260 02.2	S10 24.5	205 52.3	S22 11.6
07	123 05.4	308 21.3	50.8	310 27.3	27.1	275 04.1	24.6	220 54.6	11.6
08	138 07.8	323 20.9	49.6	325 28.3	26.5	290 06.1	24.8	235 56.9	11.6
M 09	153 10.3	338 20.5	. . 48.4	340 29.3	. . 25.8	305 08.0	. . 25.0	250 59.2	. . 11.6
O 10	168 12.7	353 20.1	47.2	355 30.3	25.2	320 10.0	25.2	266 01.5	11.6
N 11	183 15.2	8 19.7	46.0	10 31.3	24.6	335 11.9	25.4	281 03.7	11.7
D 12	198 17.7	23 19.4	N 3 44.8	25 32.3	N 4 23.9	350 13.9	S10 25.6	296 06.0	S22 11.7
A 13	213 20.1	38 19.0	43.6	40 33.3	23.3	5 15.8	25.8	311 08.3	11.7
Y 14	228 22.6	53 18.6	42.4	55 34.4	22.7	20 17.8	26.0	326 10.6	11.7
15	243 25.1	68 18.2	. . 41.2	70 35.4	. . 22.1	35 19.7	. . 26.2	341 12.9	. . 11.7
16	258 27.5	83 17.8	40.1	85 36.4	21.4	50 21.7	26.4	356 15.1	11.7
17	273 30.0	98 17.4	38.9	100 37.4	20.8	65 23.7	26.6	11 17.4	11.8
18	288 32.5	113 17.0	N 3 37.7	115 38.4	N 4 20.2	80 25.6	S10 26.7	26 19.7	S22 11.8
19	303 34.9	128 16.6	36.5	130 39.4	19.6	95 27.6	26.9	41 22.0	11.8
20	318 37.4	143 16.2	35.3	145 40.4	18.9	110 29.5	27.1	56 24.3	11.8
21	333 39.9	158 15.8	. . 34.1	160 41.4	. . 18.3	125 31.5	. . 27.3	71 26.5	. . 11.8
22	348 42.3	173 15.4	32.9	175 42.4	17.7	140 33.4	27.5	86 28.8	11.8
23	3 44.8	188 15.0	31.7	190 43.4	17.1	155 35.4	27.7	101 31.1	11.8
	h m								
Mer. Pass.	22 49.0	*v* −0.4	*d* 1.2	*v* 1.0	*d* 0.6	*v* 2.0	*d* 0.2	*v* 2.3	*d* 0.0

STARS Name	SHA	Dec
	° ′	° ′
Acamar	315 15.8	S40 14.0
Achernar	335 24.1	S57 08.8
Acrux	173 06.6	S63 11.6
Adhara	255 10.2	S28 59.7
Aldebaran	290 45.9	N16 32.5
Alioth	166 18.8	N55 52.0
Alkaid	152 57.1	N49 13.7
Al Na'ir	27 39.8	S46 52.5
Alnilam	275 43.3	S 1 11.5
Alphard	217 53.4	S 8 44.0
Alphecca	126 08.9	N26 39.7
Alpheratz	357 40.1	N29 11.4
Altair	62 05.4	N 8 55.2
Ankaa	353 12.5	S42 12.6
Antares	112 22.9	S26 28.1
Arcturus	145 53.4	N19 05.7
Atria	107 22.4	S69 03.5
Avior	234 17.0	S59 33.7
Bellatrix	278 28.8	N 6 21.8
Betelgeuse	270 58.1	N 7 24.5
Canopus	263 54.8	S52 42.1
Capella	280 30.0	N46 00.6
Deneb	49 29.3	N45 21.0
Denebola	182 31.0	N14 28.5
Diphda	348 52.7	S17 53.3
Dubhe	193 48.8	N61 39.3
Elnath	278 08.8	N28 37.1
Eltanin	90 45.0	N51 29.7
Enif	33 44.1	N 9 57.6
Fomalhaut	15 20.5	S29 31.7
Gacrux	171 58.2	S57 12.5
Gienah	175 49.6	S17 38.2
Hadar	148 44.3	S60 27.3
Hamal	327 57.1	N23 32.7
Kaus Aust.	83 40.1	S34 22.4
Kochab	137 21.3	N74 05.3
Markab	13 35.2	N15 18.2
Menkar	314 11.7	N 4 09.5
Menkent	148 04.5	S36 27.2
Miaplacidus	221 39.5	S69 47.1
Mirfak	308 35.8	N49 55.2
Nunki	75 54.8	S26 16.3
Peacock	53 14.6	S56 40.7
Pollux	243 24.3	N27 58.8
Procyon	244 56.8	N 5 10.7
Rasalhague	96 03.9	N12 33.2
Regulus	207 40.7	N11 52.9
Rigel	281 09.1	S 8 10.9
Rigil Kent.	139 48.4	S60 54.3
Sabik	102 09.4	S15 44.5
Schedar	349 36.6	N56 38.1
Shaula	96 18.1	S37 06.9
Sirius	258 31.1	S16 44.4
Spica	158 28.5	S11 15.0
Suhail	222 50.5	S43 30.0
Vega	80 37.1	N38 48.5
Zuben'ubi	137 02.5	S16 06.7

	SHA	Mer. Pass.
	° ′	h m
Venus	186 44.7	10 26
Mars	188 07.1	10 20
Jupiter	152 14.5	12 42
Saturn	97 54.8	16 19

Day	UT (d h)	SUN GHA (° ′)	SUN Dec (° ′)	MOON GHA (° ′)	v (′)	MOON Dec (° ′)	d (′)	HP (′)
	7 00	183 01.5	S 5 29.3	346 13.1	9.2	N 7 04.8	11.2	59.3
	01	198 01.6	30.3	0 41.3	9.3	7 16.0	11.1	59.3
	02	213 01.8	31.2	15 09.6	9.2	7 27.1	11.2	59.4
	03	228 02.0	. . 32.2	29 37.8	9.1	7 38.3	11.0	59.4
	04	243 02.2	33.2	44 05.9	9.1	7 49.3	11.1	59.4
	05	258 02.4	34.1	58 34.0	9.0	8 00.4	11.0	59.4
	06	273 02.5	S 5 35.1	73 02.0	9.0	N 8 11.4	10.9	59.4
	07	288 02.7	36.0	87 30.0	9.0	8 22.3	11.0	59.4
SATURDAY	08	303 02.9	37.0	101 58.0	8.9	8 33.3	10.8	59.5
	09	318 03.1	. . 37.9	116 25.9	8.8	8 44.1	10.9	59.5
	10	333 03.3	38.9	130 53.7	8.8	8 55.0	10.7	59.5
	11	348 03.4	39.8	145 21.5	8.8	9 05.7	10.7	59.5
	12	3 03.6	S 5 40.8	159 49.3	8.7	N 9 16.4	10.7	59.5
	13	18 03.8	41.7	174 17.0	8.7	9 27.1	10.6	59.5
	14	33 04.0	42.7	188 44.7	8.6	9 37.7	10.6	59.5
	15	48 04.2	. . 43.7	203 12.3	8.5	9 48.3	10.5	59.5
	16	63 04.3	44.6	217 39.8	8.6	9 58.8	10.5	59.6
	17	78 04.5	45.6	232 07.4	8.4	10 09.3	10.4	59.6
	18	93 04.7	S 5 46.5	246 34.8	8.4	N10 19.7	10.3	59.6
	19	108 04.9	47.5	261 02.2	8.4	10 30.0	10.3	59.6
	20	123 05.0	48.4	275 29.6	8.3	10 40.3	10.2	59.6
	21	138 05.2	. . 49.4	289 56.9	8.3	10 50.5	10.1	59.6
	22	153 05.4	50.3	304 24.2	8.2	11 00.6	10.1	59.6
	23	168 05.6	51.3	318 51.4	8.2	11 10.7	10.0	59.6
	8 00	183 05.8	S 5 52.2	333 18.6	8.1	N11 20.7	10.0	59.6
	01	198 05.9	53.2	347 45.7	8.1	11 30.7	9.9	59.6
	02	213 06.1	54.1	2 12.8	8.0	11 40.6	9.8	59.7
	03	228 06.3	. . 55.1	16 39.8	7.9	11 50.4	9.7	59.7
	04	243 06.5	56.1	31 06.7	8.0	12 00.1	9.7	59.7
	05	258 06.6	57.0	45 33.7	7.8	12 09.8	9.6	59.7
	06	273 06.8	S 5 58.0	60 00.5	7.9	N12 19.4	9.5	59.7
	07	288 07.0	58.9	74 27.4	7.7	12 28.9	9.4	59.7
	08	303 07.2	5 59.9	88 54.1	7.8	12 38.3	9.4	59.7
SUNDAY	09	318 07.3	6 00.8	103 20.9	7.6	12 47.7	9.3	59.7
	10	333 07.5	01.8	117 47.5	7.7	12 57.0	9.2	59.7
	11	348 07.7	02.7	132 14.2	7.5	13 06.2	9.1	59.7
	12	3 07.9	S 6 03.7	146 40.7	7.6	N13 15.3	9.1	59.7
	13	18 08.0	04.6	161 07.3	7.4	13 24.4	8.9	59.7
	14	33 08.2	05.6	175 33.7	7.5	13 33.3	8.9	59.7
	15	48 08.4	. . 06.5	190 00.2	7.4	13 42.2	8.8	59.7
	16	63 08.6	07.5	204 26.6	7.3	13 51.0	8.7	59.7
	17	78 08.7	08.4	218 52.9	7.3	13 59.7	8.6	59.7
	18	93 08.9	S 6 09.4	233 19.2	7.2	N14 08.3	8.5	59.8
	19	108 09.1	10.3	247 45.4	7.2	14 16.8	8.5	59.8
	20	123 09.3	11.3	262 11.6	7.2	14 25.3	8.3	59.8
	21	138 09.4	. . 12.2	276 37.8	7.1	14 33.6	8.3	59.8
	22	153 09.6	13.2	291 03.9	7.0	14 41.9	8.1	59.8
	23	168 09.8	14.1	305 29.9	7.0	14 50.0	8.1	59.8
	9 00	183 09.9	S 6 15.1	319 55.9	7.0	N14 58.1	7.9	59.8
	01	198 10.1	16.0	334 21.9	6.9	15 06.0	7.9	59.8
	02	213 10.3	17.0	348 47.8	6.9	15 13.9	7.8	59.8
	03	228 10.5	. . 17.9	3 13.7	6.8	15 21.7	7.6	59.8
	04	243 10.6	18.9	17 39.5	6.8	15 29.3	7.6	59.8
	05	258 10.8	19.8	32 05.3	6.8	15 36.9	7.5	59.8
	06	273 11.0	S 6 20.8	46 31.1	6.7	N15 44.4	7.3	59.8
	07	288 11.1	21.7	60 56.8	6.7	15 51.7	7.3	59.8
	08	303 11.3	22.7	75 22.5	6.6	15 59.0	7.1	59.8
MONDAY	09	318 11.5	. . 23.6	89 48.1	6.6	16 06.1	7.1	59.8
	10	333 11.7	24.6	104 13.7	6.5	16 13.2	6.9	59.8
	11	348 11.8	25.5	118 39.2	6.5	16 20.1	6.9	59.8
	12	3 12.0	S 6 26.5	133 04.7	6.5	N16 27.0	6.7	59.8
	13	18 12.2	27.4	147 30.2	6.4	16 33.7	6.6	59.8
	14	33 12.3	28.4	161 55.6	6.4	16 40.3	6.5	59.8
	15	48 12.5	. . 29.3	176 21.0	6.4	16 46.8	6.4	59.8
	16	63 12.7	30.3	190 46.4	6.3	16 53.2	6.3	59.8
	17	78 12.8	31.2	205 11.7	6.3	16 59.5	6.1	59.8
	18	93 13.0	S 6 32.1	219 37.0	6.2	N17 05.6	6.1	59.8
	19	108 13.2	33.1	234 02.2	6.3	17 11.7	5.9	59.7
	20	123 13.3	34.0	248 27.5	6.1	17 17.6	5.9	59.7
	21	138 13.5	. . 35.0	262 52.6	6.2	17 23.5	5.7	59.7
	22	153 13.7	35.9	277 17.8	6.1	17 29.2	5.6	59.7
	23	168 13.8	36.9	291 42.9	6.1	N17 34.8	5.4	59.7
		SD 16.0	*d* 1.0	SD	16.2	16.3		16.3

Lat. (°)	Twilight Naut. (h m)	Twilight Civil (h m)	Sunrise (h m)	Moonrise 7 (h m)	Moonrise 8 (h m)	Moonrise 9 (h m)	Moonrise 10 (h m)
N 72	04 24	05 43	06 51	17 20	17 07	16 45	▭
N 70	04 32	05 43	06 44	17 36	17 34	17 34	17 40
68	04 38	05 42	06 38	17 48	17 55	18 06	18 28
66	04 43	05 42	06 33	17 59	18 11	18 30	19 00
64	04 47	05 42	06 29	18 08	18 24	18 48	19 23
62	04 50	05 41	06 26	18 15	18 36	19 03	19 41
60	04 53	05 41	06 23	18 22	18 46	19 16	19 57
N 58	04 55	05 40	06 20	18 28	18 54	19 27	20 10
56	04 57	05 40	06 17	18 33	19 02	19 37	20 21
54	04 59	05 40	06 15	18 37	19 08	19 46	20 31
52	05 00	05 39	06 13	18 42	19 14	19 53	20 40
50	05 01	05 39	06 11	18 46	19 20	20 00	20 48
45	05 03	05 37	06 07	18 54	19 32	20 15	21 05
N 40	05 05	05 36	06 03	19 01	19 42	20 27	21 19
35	05 06	05 35	06 00	19 07	19 50	20 38	21 30
30	05 06	05 34	05 58	19 12	19 58	20 47	21 41
20	05 05	05 31	05 53	19 22	20 11	21 03	21 59
N 10	05 03	05 27	05 48	19 30	20 22	21 17	22 14
0	04 59	05 23	05 44	19 38	20 33	21 30	22 29
S 10	04 54	05 19	05 40	19 46	20 44	21 44	22 43
20	04 47	05 13	05 35	19 54	20 56	21 58	22 59
30	04 37	05 06	05 30	20 04	21 09	22 14	23 17
35	04 31	05 01	05 27	20 10	21 17	22 24	23 28
40	04 23	04 56	05 23	20 16	21 26	22 35	23 40
45	04 13	04 49	05 19	20 24	21 36	22 47	23 54
S 50	04 01	04 41	05 14	20 33	21 49	23 03	24 12
52	03 55	04 37	05 11	20 37	21 55	23 11	24 20
54	03 48	04 32	05 09	20 41	22 02	23 19	24 29
56	03 40	04 28	05 06	20 47	22 09	23 28	24 40
58	03 31	04 22	05 03	20 52	22 17	23 38	24 51
S 60	03 21	04 16	04 59	20 59	22 27	23 51	25 05

Lat. (°)	Sunset (h m)	Twilight Civil (h m)	Twilight Naut. (h m)	Moonset 7 (h m)	Moonset 8 (h m)	Moonset 9 (h m)	Moonset 10 (h m)
N 72	16 42	17 49	19 08	09 05	11 12	13 33	▭
N 70	16 49	17 50	19 01	08 52	10 47	12 45	14 41
68	16 55	17 51	18 55	08 41	10 27	12 14	13 53
66	17 00	17 51	18 50	08 32	10 12	11 51	13 22
64	17 04	17 52	18 47	08 24	10 00	11 33	12 59
62	17 08	17 52	18 43	08 18	09 49	11 19	12 41
60	17 11	17 53	18 41	08 12	09 40	11 06	12 26
N 58	17 14	17 53	18 39	08 07	09 32	10 56	12 13
56	17 17	17 54	18 37	08 03	09 25	10 46	12 02
54	17 19	17 54	18 35	07 59	09 19	10 38	11 52
52	17 21	17 55	18 34	07 55	09 14	10 31	11 44
50	17 23	17 55	18 33	07 52	09 09	10 24	11 36
45	17 27	17 57	18 31	07 45	08 58	10 10	11 19
N 40	17 31	17 58	18 29	07 39	08 49	09 59	11 06
35	17 34	18 00	18 29	07 34	08 42	09 49	10 54
30	17 37	18 01	18 29	07 30	08 35	09 40	10 44
20	17 42	18 04	18 30	07 23	08 23	09 25	10 27
N 10	17 46	18 08	18 32	07 16	08 13	09 12	10 12
0	17 51	18 12	18 36	07 10	08 04	09 00	09 58
S 10	17 55	18 16	18 41	07 04	07 54	08 48	09 44
20	18 00	18 22	18 48	06 57	07 44	08 35	09 29
30	18 06	18 30	18 58	06 49	07 33	08 20	09 12
35	18 09	18 34	19 05	06 45	07 26	08 12	09 02
40	18 13	18 40	19 13	06 40	07 19	08 02	08 50
45	18 17	18 47	19 23	06 35	07 10	07 51	08 37
S 50	18 22	18 55	19 36	06 28	07 00	07 37	08 21
52	18 25	18 59	19 42	06 25	06 55	07 31	08 13
54	18 27	19 04	19 49	06 21	06 50	07 23	08 05
56	18 30	19 09	19 57	06 18	06 44	07 16	07 55
58	18 34	19 15	20 06	06 14	06 37	07 07	07 44
S 60	18 37	19 21	20 17	06 09	06 30	06 57	07 32

Day	SUN Eqn. of Time 00^h	SUN Eqn. of Time 12^h	SUN Mer. Pass.	MOON Mer. Pass. Upper	MOON Mer. Pass. Lower	MOON Age	MOON Phase
d	m s	m s	h m	h m	h m	d	%
7	12 05	12 14	11 48	00 57	13 24	17	96
8	12 23	12 31	11 47	01 51	14 18	18	90
9	12 39	12 48	11 47	02 47	15 15	19	82

UT	ARIES	VENUS −3·9		MARS +1·8		JUPITER −1·7		SATURN +0·5	
	GHA	GHA	Dec	GHA	Dec	GHA	Dec	GHA	Dec
d h	° ′	° ′	° ′	° ′	° ′	° ′	° ′	° ′	° ′
10 00 (TUESDAY)	18 47.2	203 14.6	N 3 30.5	205 44.4	N 4 16.4	170 37.3	S10 27.9	116 33.4	S22 11.9
01	33 49.7	218 14.2	29.3	220 45.4	15.8	185 39.3	28.1	131 35.7	11.9
02	48 52.2	233 13.8	28.1	235 46.5	15.2	200 41.2	28.3	146 37.9	11.9
03	63 54.6	248 13.4	26.9	250 47.5	14.6	215 43.2	28.5	161 40.2	11.9
04	78 57.1	263 13.0	25.8	265 48.5	13.9	230 45.1	28.7	176 42.5	11.9
05	93 59.6	278 12.6	24.6	280 49.5	13.3	245 47.1	28.8	191 44.8	11.9
06	109 02.0	293 12.2	N 3 23.4	295 50.5	N 4 12.7	260 49.1	S10 29.0	206 47.0	S22 12.0
07	124 04.5	308 11.9	22.2	310 51.5	12.1	275 51.0	29.2	221 49.3	12.0
08	139 07.0	323 11.5	21.0	325 52.5	11.4	290 53.0	29.4	236 51.6	12.0
09	154 09.4	338 11.1	19.8	340 53.5	10.8	305 54.9	29.6	251 53.9	12.0
10	169 11.9	353 10.7	18.6	355 54.5	10.2	320 56.9	29.8	266 56.2	12.0
11	184 14.4	8 10.3	17.4	10 55.5	09.6	335 58.8	30.0	281 58.4	12.0
12	199 16.8	23 09.9	N 3 16.2	25 56.5	N 4 08.9	351 00.8	S10 30.2	297 00.7	S22 12.1
13	214 19.3	38 09.5	15.0	40 57.6	08.3	6 02.7	30.4	312 03.0	12.1
14	229 21.7	53 09.1	13.8	55 58.6	07.7	21 04.7	30.6	327 05.3	12.1
15	244 24.2	68 08.7	12.6	70 59.6	07.0	36 06.6	30.8	342 07.5	12.1
16	259 26.7	83 08.3	11.4	86 00.6	06.4	51 08.6	30.9	357 09.8	12.1
17	274 29.1	98 07.9	10.2	101 01.6	05.8	66 10.5	31.1	12 12.1	12.1
18	289 31.6	113 07.5	N 3 09.0	116 02.6	N 4 05.2	81 12.5	S10 31.3	27 14.4	S22 12.1
19	304 34.1	128 07.1	07.8	131 03.6	04.5	96 14.4	31.5	42 16.6	12.2
20	319 36.5	143 06.7	06.6	146 04.6	03.9	111 16.4	31.7	57 18.9	12.2
21	334 39.0	158 06.3	05.4	161 05.6	03.3	126 18.4	31.9	72 21.2	12.2
22	349 41.5	173 06.0	04.2	176 06.6	02.7	141 20.3	32.1	87 23.5	12.2
23	4 43.9	188 05.6	03.0	191 07.6	02.0	156 22.3	32.3	102 25.7	12.2
11 00 (WEDNESDAY)	19 46.4	203 05.2	N 3 01.8	206 08.7	N 4 01.4	171 24.2	S10 32.5	117 28.0	S22 12.2
01	34 48.9	218 04.8	3 00.6	221 09.7	00.8	186 26.2	32.7	132 30.3	12.3
02	49 51.3	233 04.4	2 59.4	236 10.7	4 00.1	201 28.1	32.8	147 32.6	12.3
03	64 53.8	248 04.0	58.2	251 11.7	3 59.5	216 30.1	33.0	162 34.8	12.3
04	79 56.2	263 03.6	57.1	266 12.7	58.9	231 32.0	33.2	177 37.1	12.3
05	94 58.7	278 03.2	55.9	281 13.7	58.3	246 34.0	33.4	192 39.4	12.3
06	110 01.2	293 02.8	N 2 54.7	296 14.7	N 3 57.6	261 35.9	S10 33.6	207 41.7	S22 12.3
07	125 03.6	308 02.4	53.5	311 15.7	57.0	276 37.9	33.8	222 43.9	12.4
08	140 06.1	323 02.0	52.3	326 16.7	56.4	291 39.8	34.0	237 46.2	12.4
09	155 08.6	338 01.6	51.1	341 17.7	55.8	306 41.8	34.2	252 48.5	12.4
10	170 11.0	353 01.2	49.9	356 18.8	55.1	321 43.7	34.4	267 50.8	12.4
11	185 13.5	8 00.8	48.7	11 19.8	54.5	336 45.7	34.6	282 53.0	12.4
12	200 16.0	23 00.5	N 2 47.5	26 20.8	N 3 53.9	351 47.6	S10 34.8	297 55.3	S22 12.4
13	215 18.4	38 00.1	46.3	41 21.8	53.3	6 49.6	34.9	312 57.6	12.4
14	230 20.9	52 59.7	45.1	56 22.8	52.6	21 51.5	35.1	327 59.9	12.5
15	245 23.3	67 59.3	43.9	71 23.8	52.0	36 53.5	35.3	343 02.1	12.5
16	260 25.8	82 58.9	42.7	86 24.8	51.4	51 55.4	35.5	358 04.4	12.5
17	275 28.3	97 58.5	41.5	101 25.8	50.7	66 57.4	35.7	13 06.7	12.5
18	290 30.7	112 58.1	N 2 40.3	116 26.8	N 3 50.1	81 59.3	S10 35.9	28 09.0	S22 12.5
19	305 33.2	127 57.7	39.1	131 27.8	49.5	97 01.3	36.1	43 11.2	12.5
20	320 35.7	142 57.3	37.8	146 28.9	48.9	112 03.2	36.3	58 13.5	12.6
21	335 38.1	157 56.9	36.6	161 29.9	48.2	127 05.2	36.5	73 15.8	12.6
22	350 40.6	172 56.5	35.4	176 30.9	47.6	142 07.2	36.7	88 18.0	12.6
23	5 43.1	187 56.1	34.2	191 31.9	47.0	157 09.1	36.9	103 20.3	12.6
12 00 (THURSDAY)	20 45.5	202 55.8	N 2 33.0	206 32.9	N 3 46.3	172 11.1	S10 37.0	118 22.6	S22 12.6
01	35 48.0	217 55.4	31.8	221 33.9	45.7	187 13.0	37.2	133 24.9	12.6
02	50 50.5	232 55.0	30.6	236 34.9	45.1	202 15.0	37.4	148 27.1	12.7
03	65 52.9	247 54.6	29.4	251 35.9	44.5	217 16.9	37.6	163 29.4	12.7
04	80 55.4	262 54.2	28.2	266 36.9	43.8	232 18.9	37.8	178 31.7	12.7
05	95 57.8	277 53.8	27.0	281 37.9	43.2	247 20.8	38.0	193 33.9	12.7
06	111 00.3	292 53.4	N 2 25.8	296 39.0	N 3 42.6	262 22.8	S10 38.2	208 36.2	S22 12.7
07	126 02.8	307 53.0	24.6	311 40.0	42.0	277 24.7	38.4	223 38.5	12.7
08	141 05.2	322 52.6	23.4	326 41.0	41.3	292 26.7	38.6	238 40.8	12.8
09	156 07.7	337 52.2	22.2	341 42.0	40.7	307 28.6	38.8	253 43.0	12.8
10	171 10.2	352 51.8	21.0	356 43.0	40.1	322 30.6	38.9	268 45.3	12.8
11	186 12.6	7 51.4	19.8	11 44.0	39.4	337 32.5	39.1	283 47.6	12.8
12	201 15.1	22 51.1	N 2 18.6	26 45.0	N 3 38.8	352 34.5	S10 39.3	298 49.8	S22 12.8
13	216 17.6	37 50.7	17.4	41 46.0	38.2	7 36.4	39.5	313 52.1	12.8
14	231 20.0	52 50.3	16.2	56 47.0	37.6	22 38.4	39.7	328 54.4	12.8
15	246 22.5	67 49.9	15.0	71 48.1	36.9	37 40.3	39.9	343 56.7	12.9
16	261 25.0	82 49.5	13.8	86 49.1	36.3	52 42.3	40.1	358 58.9	12.9
17	276 27.4	97 49.1	12.6	101 50.1	35.7	67 44.2	40.3	14 01.2	12.9
18	291 29.9	112 48.7	N 2 11.4	116 51.1	N 3 35.0	82 46.2	S10 40.5	29 03.5	S22 12.9
19	306 32.3	127 48.3	10.2	131 52.1	34.4	97 48.1	40.7	44 05.7	12.9
20	321 34.8	142 47.9	09.0	146 53.1	33.8	112 50.1	40.9	59 08.0	12.9
21	336 37.3	157 47.5	07.8	161 54.1	33.2	127 52.0	41.0	74 10.3	13.0
22	351 39.7	172 47.1	06.5	176 55.1	32.5	142 54.0	41.2	89 12.5	13.0
23	6 42.2	187 46.7	05.3	191 56.1	31.9	157 55.9	41.4	104 14.8	13.0
Mer. Pass. (h m)	22 37.2	v −0.4	d 1.2	v 1.0	d 0.6	v 2.0	d 0.2	v 2.3	d 0.0

STARS

Name	SHA	Dec
	° ′	° ′
Acamar	315 15.8	S40 14.0
Achernar	335 24.1	S57 08.8
Acrux	173 06.6	S63 11.6
Adhara	255 10.2	S28 59.7
Aldebaran	290 45.8	N16 32.5
Alioth	166 18.8	N55 52.0
Alkaid	152 57.1	N49 13.7
Al Na'ir	27 39.8	S46 52.6
Alnilam	275 43.3	S 1 11.5
Alphard	217 53.4	S 8 44.0
Alphecca	126 08.9	N26 39.7
Alpheratz	357 40.1	N29 11.4
Altair	62 05.4	N 8 55.2
Ankaa	353 12.5	S42 12.6
Antares	112 22.9	S26 28.1
Arcturus	145 53.4	N19 05.7
Atria	107 22.4	S69 03.5
Avior	234 17.0	S59 33.7
Bellatrix	278 28.7	N 6 21.8
Betelgeuse	270 58.1	N 7 24.5
Canopus	263 54.7	S52 42.1
Capella	280 29.9	N46 00.6
Deneb	49 29.3	N45 21.0
Denebola	182 31.0	N14 28.5
Diphda	348 52.7	S17 53.4
Dubhe	193 48.8	N61 39.2
Elnath	278 08.8	N28 37.1
Eltanin	90 45.0	N51 29.7
Enif	33 44.1	N 9 57.6
Fomalhaut	15 20.5	S29 31.7
Gacrux	171 58.2	S57 12.5
Gienah	175 49.6	S17 38.2
Hadar	148 44.3	S60 27.3
Hamal	327 57.1	N23 32.7
Kaus Aust.	83 40.1	S34 22.4
Kochab	137 21.3	N74 05.3
Markab	13 35.2	N15 18.2
Menkar	314 11.7	N 4 09.5
Menkent	148 04.5	S36 27.2
Miaplacidus	221 39.4	S69 47.1
Mirfak	308 35.7	N49 55.2
Nunki	75 54.8	S26 16.3
Peacock	53 14.6	S56 40.7
Pollux	243 24.3	N27 58.8
Procyon	244 56.7	N 5 10.7
Rasalhague	96 03.9	N12 33.2
Regulus	207 40.7	N11 52.9
Rigel	281 09.1	S 8 10.9
Rigil Kent.	139 48.4	S60 54.3
Sabik	102 09.4	S15 44.5
Schedar	349 36.6	N56 38.1
Shaula	96 18.2	S37 06.9
Sirius	258 31.1	S16 44.4
Spica	158 28.5	S11 15.0
Suhail	222 50.5	S43 30.0
Vega	80 37.1	N38 48.5
Zuben'ubi	137 02.5	S16 06.7

	SHA	Mer. Pass.
	° ′	h m
Venus	183 18.8	10 28
Mars	186 22.3	10 15
Jupiter	151 37.8	12 33
Saturn	97 41.6	16 08

UT (d h)		SUN GHA	SUN Dec	MOON GHA	v	MOON Dec	d	HP
		° ′	° ′	° ′	′	° ′	′	′
10 00		183 14.0	S 6 37.8	306 08.0	6.1	N17 40.2	5.4	59.7
01		198 14.2	38.8	320 33.1	6.0	17 45.6	5.2	59.7
02		213 14.3	39.7	334 58.1	6.0	17 50.8	5.1	59.7
03		228 14.5	. . 40.7	349 23.1	6.0	17 55.9	5.0	59.7
04		243 14.7	41.6	3 48.1	6.0	18 00.9	4.9	59.7
05		258 14.8	42.6	18 13.1	5.9	18 05.8	4.7	59.7
06		273 15.0	S 6 43.5	32 38.0	5.9	N18 10.5	4.7	59.7
07		288 15.2	44.4	47 02.9	5.9	18 15.2	4.5	59.7
08	TUESDAY	303 15.3	45.4	61 27.8	5.9	18 19.7	4.4	59.7
09		318 15.5	. . 46.3	75 52.7	5.9	18 24.1	4.2	59.7
10		333 15.7	47.3	90 17.6	5.8	18 28.3	4.1	59.7
11		348 15.8	48.2	104 42.4	5.8	18 32.4	4.0	59.7
12		3 16.0	S 6 49.2	119 07.2	5.8	N18 36.4	3.9	59.7
13		18 16.2	50.1	133 32.0	5.8	18 40.3	3.8	59.6
14		33 16.3	51.1	147 56.8	5.7	18 44.1	3.6	59.6
15		48 16.5	. . 52.0	162 21.5	5.8	18 47.7	3.5	59.6
16		63 16.7	52.9	176 46.3	5.7	18 51.2	3.4	59.6
17		78 16.8	53.9	191 11.0	5.7	18 54.6	3.2	59.6
18		93 17.0	S 6 54.8	205 35.7	5.7	N18 57.8	3.1	59.6
19		108 17.2	55.8	220 00.4	5.7	19 00.9	3.0	59.6
20		123 17.3	56.7	234 25.1	5.7	19 03.9	2.9	59.6
21		138 17.5	. . 57.7	248 49.8	5.7	19 06.8	2.7	59.6
22		153 17.6	58.6	263 14.5	5.7	19 09.5	2.6	59.6
23		168 17.8	6 59.6	277 39.2	5.7	19 12.1	2.5	59.6
11 00		183 18.0	S 7 00.5	292 03.9	5.7	N19 14.6	2.3	59.5
01		198 18.1	01.4	306 28.6	5.6	19 16.9	2.2	59.5
02		213 18.3	02.4	320 53.2	5.7	19 19.1	2.1	59.5
03		228 18.4	. . 03.3	335 17.9	5.7	19 21.2	2.0	59.5
04		243 18.6	04.3	349 42.6	5.6	19 23.2	1.8	59.5
05		258 18.8	05.2	4 07.2	5.7	19 25.0	1.7	59.5
06		273 18.9	S 7 06.1	18 31.9	5.7	N19 26.7	1.5	59.5
07	WEDNESDAY	288 19.1	07.1	32 56.6	5.6	19 28.2	1.4	59.5
08		303 19.3	08.0	47 21.2	5.7	19 29.6	1.3	59.5
09		318 19.4	. . 09.0	61 45.9	5.7	19 30.9	1.2	59.5
10		333 19.6	09.9	76 10.6	5.7	19 32.1	1.0	59.4
11		348 19.7	10.9	90 35.3	5.7	19 33.1	0.9	59.4
12		3 19.9	S 7 11.8	105 00.0	5.7	N19 34.0	0.8	59.4
13		18 20.1	12.7	119 24.7	5.8	19 34.8	0.6	59.4
14		33 20.2	13.7	133 49.4	5.8	19 35.4	0.5	59.4
15		48 20.4	. . 14.6	148 14.2	5.7	19 35.9	0.4	59.4
16		63 20.5	15.6	162 38.9	5.8	19 36.3	0.3	59.4
17		78 20.7	16.5	177 03.7	5.8	19 36.6	0.1	59.4
18		93 20.8	S 7 17.4	191 28.5	5.8	N19 36.7	0.0	59.3
19		108 21.0	18.4	205 53.3	5.8	19 36.7	0.2	59.3
20		123 21.2	19.3	220 18.1	5.8	19 36.5	0.3	59.3
21		138 21.3	. . 20.3	234 42.9	5.9	19 36.2	0.4	59.3
22		153 21.5	21.2	249 07.8	5.8	19 35.8	0.5	59.3
23		168 21.6	22.1	263 32.6	5.9	19 35.3	0.7	59.3
12 00		183 21.8	S 7 23.1	277 57.5	6.0	N19 34.6	0.8	59.3
01		198 21.9	24.0	292 22.5	5.9	19 33.8	0.9	59.2
02		213 22.1	24.9	306 47.4	6.0	19 32.9	1.0	59.2
03		228 22.3	. . 25.9	321 12.4	6.0	19 31.9	1.2	59.2
04		243 22.4	26.8	335 37.4	6.0	19 30.7	1.3	59.2
05		258 22.6	27.8	350 02.4	6.1	19 29.4	1.5	59.2
06		273 22.7	S 7 28.7	4 27.5	6.1	N19 27.9	1.5	59.2
07	THURSDAY	288 22.9	29.6	18 52.6	6.1	19 26.4	1.7	59.2
08		303 23.0	30.6	33 17.7	6.1	19 24.7	1.8	59.1
09		318 23.2	. . 31.5	47 42.8	6.2	19 22.9	2.0	59.1
10		333 23.3	32.4	62 08.0	6.2	19 20.9	2.0	59.1
11		348 23.5	33.4	76 33.2	6.3	19 18.9	2.2	59.1
12		3 23.7	S 7 34.3	90 58.5	6.3	N19 16.7	2.3	59.1
13		18 23.8	35.3	105 23.8	6.3	19 14.4	2.5	59.1
14		33 24.0	36.2	119 49.1	6.3	19 11.9	2.5	59.1
15		48 24.1	. . 37.1	134 14.4	6.5	19 09.4	2.7	59.0
16		63 24.3	38.1	148 39.9	6.4	19 06.7	2.8	59.0
17		78 24.4	39.0	163 05.3	6.5	19 03.9	3.0	59.0
18		93 24.6	S 7 39.9	177 30.8	6.5	N19 00.9	3.0	59.0
19		108 24.7	40.9	191 56.3	6.6	18 57.9	3.2	59.0
20		123 24.9	41.8	206 21.9	6.6	18 54.7	3.3	59.0
21		138 25.0	. . 42.7	220 47.5	6.6	18 51.4	3.4	59.0
22		153 25.2	43.7	235 13.1	6.7	18 48.0	3.5	58.9
23		168 25.3	44.6	249 38.8	6.8	N18 44.5	3.6	58.9
		SD 16.0	d 0.9	SD	16.3	16.2		16.1

Lat.	Twilight Naut.	Twilight Civil	Sunrise	Moonrise 10	Moonrise 11	Moonrise 12	Moonrise 13
°	h m	h m	h m	h m	h m	h m	h m
N 72	04 38	05 56	07 06	□	□	□	20 34
N 70	04 44	05 55	06 57	17 40	18 10	19 37	21 28
68	04 48	05 53	06 49	18 28	19 13	20 27	22 01
66	04 52	05 52	06 43	19 00	19 48	20 59	22 25
64	04 55	05 50	06 38	19 23	20 14	21 22	22 43
62	04 58	05 49	06 34	19 41	20 34	21 41	22 59
60	05 00	05 48	06 30	19 57	20 50	21 56	23 11
N 58	05 01	05 47	06 26	20 10	21 04	22 09	23 22
56	05 03	05 46	06 23	20 21	21 16	22 20	23 32
54	05 04	05 45	06 20	20 31	21 26	22 30	23 40
52	05 05	05 44	06 18	20 40	21 35	22 39	23 48
50	05 06	05 43	06 16	20 48	21 44	22 46	23 55
45	05 07	05 41	06 11	21 05	22 01	23 03	24 09
N 40	05 08	05 39	06 06	21 19	22 15	23 17	24 21
35	05 08	05 37	06 03	21 30	22 28	23 28	24 31
30	05 08	05 35	05 59	21 41	22 38	23 39	24 40
20	05 06	05 31	05 54	21 59	22 57	23 56	24 55
N 10	05 03	05 27	05 48	22 14	23 13	24 11	00 11
0	04 58	05 23	05 43	22 29	23 28	24 25	00 25
S 10	04 52	05 17	05 38	22 43	23 43	24 39	00 39
20	04 45	05 11	05 33	22 59	23 59	24 55	00 55
30	04 34	05 02	05 26	23 17	24 17	00 17	01 12
35	04 27	04 57	05 23	23 28	24 28	00 28	01 22
40	04 18	04 51	05 18	23 40	24 40	00 40	01 34
45	04 07	04 43	05 13	23 54	24 55	00 55	01 47
S 50	03 54	04 34	05 07	24 12	00 12	01 12	02 04
52	03 47	04 30	05 05	24 20	00 20	01 21	02 11
54	03 40	04 25	05 02	24 29	00 29	01 30	02 20
56	03 31	04 19	04 58	24 40	00 40	01 41	02 30
58	03 21	04 13	04 54	24 51	00 51	01 53	02 41
S 60	03 10	04 06	04 50	25 05	01 05	02 07	02 53

Lat.	Sunset	Twilight Civil	Twilight Naut.	Moonset 10	Moonset 11	Moonset 12	Moonset 13
°	h m	h m	h m	h m	h m	h m	h m
N 72	16 26	17 35	18 53	□	□	□	17 50
N 70	16 35	17 37	18 47	14 41	16 14	16 49	16 55
68	16 42	17 39	18 43	13 53	15 11	15 58	16 22
66	16 49	17 40	18 39	13 22	14 36	15 26	15 57
64	16 54	17 42	18 36	12 59	14 10	15 03	15 38
62	16 58	17 43	18 34	12 41	13 51	14 44	15 22
60	17 02	17 44	18 32	12 26	13 34	14 28	15 09
N 58	17 06	17 45	18 31	12 13	13 20	14 15	14 58
56	17 09	17 46	18 29	12 02	13 09	14 04	14 48
54	17 12	17 47	18 28	11 52	12 58	13 54	14 39
52	17 15	17 48	18 27	11 44	12 49	13 45	14 31
50	17 17	17 49	18 27	11 36	12 41	13 37	14 24
45	17 22	17 51	18 25	11 19	12 23	13 20	14 09
N 40	17 26	17 54	18 25	11 06	12 09	13 06	13 56
35	17 30	17 56	18 25	10 54	11 57	12 54	13 46
30	17 34	17 58	18 25	10 44	11 46	12 44	13 36
20	17 40	18 02	18 27	10 27	11 28	12 26	13 20
N 10	17 45	18 06	18 30	10 12	11 12	12 10	13 06
0	17 50	18 11	18 35	09 58	10 57	11 55	12 52
S 10	17 55	18 16	18 41	09 44	10 42	11 41	12 39
20	18 01	18 23	18 49	09 29	10 26	11 25	12 24
30	18 07	18 32	19 00	09 12	10 08	11 07	12 08
35	18 11	18 37	19 07	09 02	09 57	10 56	11 58
40	18 16	18 43	19 16	08 50	09 45	10 44	11 47
45	18 21	18 51	19 27	08 37	09 30	10 29	11 34
S 50	18 27	19 00	19 41	08 21	09 12	10 12	11 18
52	18 30	19 05	19 48	08 13	09 04	10 04	11 10
54	18 33	19 10	19 56	08 05	08 55	09 54	11 02
56	18 37	19 16	20 04	07 55	08 44	09 44	10 53
58	18 40	19 22	20 14	07 44	08 32	09 32	10 42
S 60	18 45	19 29	20 26	07 32	08 18	09 18	10 30

Day	SUN Eqn. of Time 00^h	SUN Eqn. of Time 12^h	SUN Mer. Pass.	MOON Mer. Pass. Upper	MOON Mer. Pass. Lower	Age	Phase
d	m s	m s	h m	h m	h m	d %	
10	12 56	13 04	11 47	03 44	16 13	20 73	
11	13 12	13 19	11 47	04 43	17 12	21 62	◑
12	13 27	13 34	11 46	05 41	18 10	22 50	

	UT	ARIES	VENUS −3·9		MARS +1·8		JUPITER −1·7		SATURN +0·5	
	d h	GHA ° ′	GHA ° ′	Dec ° ′	GHA ° ′	Dec ° ′	GHA ° ′	Dec ° ′	GHA ° ′	Dec ° ′
	13 00	21 44.7	202 46.4	N 2 04.1	206 57.2	N 3 31.3	172 57.9	S10 41.6	119 17.1	S22 13.0
	01	36 47.1	217 46.0	02.9	221 58.2	30.6	187 59.8	41.8	134 19.3	13.0
	02	51 49.6	232 45.6	01.7	236 59.2	30.0	203 01.8	42.0	149 21.6	13.0
	03	66 52.1	247 45.2	2 00.5	252 00.2	29.4	218 03.7	42.2	164 23.9	13.1
	04	81 54.5	262 44.8	1 59.3	267 01.2	28.8	233 05.7	42.4	179 26.2	13.1
	05	96 57.0	277 44.4	58.1	282 02.2	28.1	248 07.6	42.6	194 28.4	13.1
	06	111 59.5	292 44.0	N 1 56.9	297 03.2	N 3 27.5	263 09.6	S10 42.8	209 30.7	S22 13.1
	07	127 01.9	307 43.6	55.7	312 04.2	26.9	278 11.5	42.9	224 33.0	13.1
	08	142 04.4	322 43.2	54.5	327 05.2	26.3	293 13.5	43.1	239 35.2	13.1
F	09	157 06.8	337 42.8	53.3	342 06.3	25.6	308 15.4	43.3	254 37.5	13.2
R	10	172 09.3	352 42.4	52.1	357 07.3	25.0	323 17.4	43.5	269 39.8	13.2
I	11	187 11.8	7 42.1	50.9	12 08.3	24.4	338 19.3	43.7	284 42.0	13.2
D	12	202 14.2	22 41.7	N 1 49.6	27 09.3	N 3 23.7	353 21.3	S10 43.9	299 44.3	S22 13.2
A	13	217 16.7	37 41.3	48.4	42 10.3	23.1	8 23.2	44.1	314 46.6	13.2
Y	14	232 19.2	52 40.9	47.2	57 11.3	22.5	23 25.2	44.3	329 48.8	13.2
	15	247 21.6	67 40.5	46.0	72 12.3	21.9	38 27.1	44.5	344 51.1	13.2
	16	262 24.1	82 40.1	44.8	87 13.3	21.2	53 29.1	44.7	359 53.4	13.3
	17	277 26.6	97 39.7	43.6	102 14.3	20.6	68 31.0	44.9	14 55.6	13.3
	18	292 29.0	112 39.3	N 1 42.4	117 15.4	N 3 20.0	83 33.0	S10 45.0	29 57.9	S22 13.3
	19	307 31.5	127 38.9	41.2	132 16.4	19.3	98 34.9	45.2	45 00.2	13.3
	20	322 33.9	142 38.5	40.0	147 17.4	18.7	113 36.9	45.4	60 02.4	13.3
	21	337 36.4	157 38.2	38.8	162 18.4	18.1	128 38.8	45.6	75 04.7	13.3
	22	352 38.9	172 37.8	37.6	177 19.4	17.4	143 40.8	45.8	90 07.0	13.4
	23	7 41.3	187 37.4	36.3	192 20.4	16.8	158 42.7	46.0	105 09.2	13.4
	14 00	22 43.8	202 37.0	N 1 35.1	207 21.4	N 3 16.2	173 44.7	S10 46.2	120 11.5	S22 13.4
	01	37 46.3	217 36.6	33.9	222 22.4	15.6	188 46.6	46.4	135 13.7	13.4
	02	52 48.7	232 36.2	32.7	237 23.5	14.9	203 48.6	46.6	150 16.0	13.4
	03	67 51.2	247 35.8	31.5	252 24.5	14.3	218 50.5	46.8	165 18.3	13.4
	04	82 53.7	262 35.4	30.3	267 25.5	13.7	233 52.5	46.9	180 20.5	13.5
	05	97 56.1	277 35.0	29.1	282 26.5	13.0	248 54.4	47.1	195 22.8	13.5
	06	112 58.6	292 34.6	N 1 27.9	297 27.5	N 3 12.4	263 56.4	S10 47.3	210 25.1	S22 13.5
S	07	128 01.1	307 34.2	26.7	312 28.5	11.8	278 58.3	47.5	225 27.3	13.5
	08	143 03.5	322 33.9	25.5	327 29.5	11.2	294 00.3	47.7	240 29.6	13.5
A	09	158 06.0	337 33.5	24.2	342 30.5	10.5	309 02.2	47.9	255 31.9	13.5
T	10	173 08.4	352 33.1	23.0	357 31.5	09.9	324 04.2	48.1	270 34.1	13.6
U	11	188 10.9	7 32.7	21.8	12 32.6	09.3	339 06.1	48.3	285 36.4	13.6
R	12	203 13.4	22 32.3	N 1 20.6	27 33.6	N 3 08.6	354 08.1	S10 48.5	300 38.7	S22 13.6
D	13	218 15.8	37 31.9	19.4	42 34.6	08.0	9 10.0	48.7	315 40.9	13.6
A	14	233 18.3	52 31.5	18.2	57 35.6	07.4	24 11.9	48.8	330 43.2	13.6
Y	15	248 20.8	67 31.1	17.0	72 36.6	06.8	39 13.9	49.0	345 45.4	13.6
	16	263 23.2	82 30.7	15.8	87 37.6	06.1	54 15.8	49.2	0 47.7	13.6
	17	278 25.7	97 30.3	14.5	102 38.6	05.5	69 17.8	49.4	15 50.0	13.7
	18	293 28.2	112 29.9	N 1 13.3	117 39.6	N 3 04.9	84 19.7	S10 49.6	30 52.2	S22 13.7
	19	308 30.6	127 29.6	12.1	132 40.7	04.2	99 21.7	49.8	45 54.5	13.7
	20	323 33.1	142 29.2	10.9	147 41.7	03.6	114 23.6	50.0	60 56.8	13.7
	21	338 35.6	157 28.8	09.7	162 42.7	03.0	129 25.6	50.2	75 59.0	13.7
	22	353 38.0	172 28.4	08.5	177 43.7	02.3	144 27.5	50.4	91 01.3	13.7
	23	8 40.5	187 28.0	07.3	192 44.7	01.7	159 29.5	50.6	106 03.5	13.8
	15 00	23 42.9	202 27.6	N 1 06.1	207 45.7	N 3 01.1	174 31.4	S10 50.7	121 05.8	S22 13.8
	01	38 45.4	217 27.2	04.8	222 46.7	3 00.5	189 33.4	50.9	136 08.1	13.8
	02	53 47.9	232 26.8	03.6	237 47.7	2 59.8	204 35.3	51.1	151 10.3	13.8
	03	68 50.3	247 26.4	02.4	252 48.8	59.2	219 37.3	51.3	166 12.6	13.8
	04	83 52.8	262 26.0	01.2	267 49.8	58.6	234 39.2	51.5	181 14.9	13.8
	05	98 55.3	277 25.7	1 00.0	282 50.8	57.9	249 41.2	51.7	196 17.1	13.9
	06	113 57.7	292 25.3	N 0 58.8	297 51.8	N 2 57.3	264 43.1	S10 51.9	211 19.4	S22 13.9
	07	129 00.2	307 24.9	57.6	312 52.8	56.7	279 45.1	52.1	226 21.6	13.9
	08	144 02.7	322 24.5	56.3	327 53.8	56.1	294 47.0	52.3	241 23.9	13.9
S	09	159 05.1	337 24.1	55.1	342 54.8	55.4	309 49.0	52.5	256 26.2	13.9
U	10	174 07.6	352 23.7	53.9	357 55.8	54.8	324 50.9	52.6	271 28.4	13.9
N	11	189 10.0	7 23.3	52.7	12 56.9	54.2	339 52.9	52.8	286 30.7	14.0
D	12	204 12.5	22 22.9	N 0 51.5	27 57.9	N 2 53.5	354 54.8	S10 53.0	301 32.9	S22 14.0
A	13	219 15.0	37 22.5	50.3	42 58.9	52.9	9 56.8	53.2	316 35.2	14.0
Y	14	234 17.4	52 22.1	49.1	57 59.9	52.3	24 58.7	53.4	331 37.5	14.0
	15	249 19.9	67 21.7	47.8	73 00.9	51.6	40 00.6	53.6	346 39.7	14.0
	16	264 22.4	82 21.4	46.6	88 01.9	51.0	55 02.6	53.8	1 42.0	14.0
	17	279 24.8	97 21.0	45.4	103 02.9	50.4	70 04.5	54.0	16 44.2	14.0
	18	294 27.3	112 20.6	N 0 44.2	118 03.9	N 2 49.8	85 06.5	S10 54.2	31 46.5	S22 14.1
	19	309 29.8	127 20.2	43.0	133 05.0	49.1	100 08.4	54.4	46 48.8	14.1
	20	324 32.2	142 19.8	41.8	148 06.0	48.5	115 10.4	54.5	61 51.0	14.1
	21	339 34.7	157 19.4	40.6	163 07.0	47.9	130 12.3	54.7	76 53.3	14.1
	22	354 37.2	172 19.0	39.3	178 08.0	47.2	145 14.3	54.9	91 55.5	14.1
	23	9 39.6	187 18.6	38.1	193 09.0	46.6	160 16.2	55.1	106 57.8	14.1
	Mer. Pass.	h m 22 25.4	v −0.4	d 1.2	v 1.0	d 0.6	v 1.9	d 0.2	v 2.3	d 0.0

STARS

Name	SHA ° ′	Dec ° ′
Acamar	315 15.8	S40 14.0
Achernar	335 24.1	S57 08.9
Acrux	173 06.6	S63 11.6
Adhara	255 10.2	S28 59.7
Aldebaran	290 45.8	N16 32.5
Alioth	166 18.8	N55 51.9
Alkaid	152 57.1	N49 13.7
Al Na'ir	27 39.9	S46 52.6
Alnilam	275 43.3	S 1 11.5
Alphard	217 53.4	S 8 44.0
Alphecca	126 08.9	N26 39.7
Alpheratz	357 40.1	N29 11.4
Altair	62 05.4	N 8 55.2
Ankaa	353 12.5	S42 12.6
Antares	112 22.9	S26 28.1
Arcturus	145 53.4	N19 05.7
Atria	107 22.4	S69 03.5
Avior	234 16.9	S59 33.7
Bellatrix	278 28.7	N 6 21.8
Betelgeuse	270 58.0	N 7 24.5
Canopus	263 54.7	S52 42.1
Capella	280 29.9	N46 00.6
Deneb	49 29.3	N45 21.0
Denebola	182 31.0	N14 28.5
Diphda	348 52.7	S17 53.4
Dubhe	193 48.8	N61 39.2
Elnath	278 08.8	N28 37.1
Eltanin	90 45.0	N51 29.7
Enif	33 44.1	N 9 57.6
Fomalhaut	15 20.5	S29 31.7
Gacrux	171 58.1	S57 12.5
Gienah	175 49.6	S17 38.2
Hadar	148 44.3	S60 27.3
Hamal	327 57.1	N23 32.7
Kaus Aust.	83 40.1	S34 22.4
Kochab	137 21.3	N74 05.2
Markab	13 35.2	N15 18.2
Menkar	314 11.7	N 4 09.5
Menkent	148 04.5	S36 27.2
Miaplacidus	221 39.4	S69 47.1
Mirfak	308 35.7	N49 55.2
Nunki	75 54.8	S26 16.3
Peacock	53 14.6	S56 40.7
Pollux	243 24.2	N27 58.8
Procyon	244 56.7	N 5 10.7
Rasalhague	96 03.9	N12 33.2
Regulus	207 40.7	N11 52.9
Rigel	281 09.1	S 8 10.9
Rigil Kent.	139 48.4	S60 54.3
Sabik	102 09.4	S15 44.6
Schedar	349 36.6	N56 38.1
Shaula	96 18.2	S37 06.8
Sirius	258 31.1	S16 44.4
Spica	158 28.5	S11 15.0
Suhail	222 50.5	S43 30.0
Vega	80 37.1	N38 48.5
Zuben'ubi	137 02.5	S16 06.7

	SHA ° ′	Mer. Pass. h m
Venus	179 53.2	10 30
Mars	184 37.6	10 10
Jupiter	151 00.9	12 23
Saturn	97 27.7	15 57

Day	UT	SUN GHA	SUN Dec	MOON GHA	v	MOON Dec	d	HP
	d h	° ′	° ′	° ′	′	° ′	′	′
	13 00	183 25.5	S 7 45.5	264 04.6	6.7	N18 40.9	3.8	58.9
	01	198 25.6	46.5	278 30.3	6.9	18 37.1	3.9	58.9
	02	213 25.8	47.4	292 56.2	6.9	18 33.2	4.0	58.9
	03	228 25.9	. . 48.3	307 22.1	6.9	18 29.2	4.1	58.9
	04	243 26.1	49.3	321 48.0	7.0	18 25.1	4.2	58.8
	05	258 26.2	50.2	336 14.0	7.0	18 20.9	4.3	58.8
	06	273 26.4	S 7 51.1	350 40.0	7.1	N18 16.6	4.5	58.8
	07	288 26.5	52.1	5 06.1	7.1	18 12.1	4.6	58.8
	08	303 26.7	53.0	19 32.2	7.2	18 07.5	4.6	58.8
F	09	318 26.8	. . 53.9	33 58.4	7.2	18 02.9	4.8	58.8
R	10	333 27.0	54.9	48 24.6	7.3	17 58.1	4.9	58.7
I	11	348 27.1	55.8	62 50.9	7.4	17 53.2	5.0	58.7
D	12	3 27.3	S 7 56.7	77 17.3	7.4	N17 48.2	5.1	58.7
A	13	18 27.4	57.7	91 43.7	7.4	17 43.1	5.2	58.7
Y	14	33 27.6	58.6	106 10.1	7.5	17 37.9	5.3	58.7
	15	48 27.7	7 59.5	120 36.6	7.6	17 32.6	5.4	58.7
	16	63 27.9	8 00.5	135 03.2	7.6	17 27.2	5.6	58.6
	17	78 28.0	01.4	149 29.8	7.7	17 21.6	5.6	58.6
	18	93 28.2	S 8 02.3	163 56.5	7.7	N17 16.0	5.7	58.6
	19	108 28.3	03.3	178 23.2	7.8	17 10.3	5.9	58.6
	20	123 28.5	04.2	192 50.0	7.8	17 04.4	5.9	58.6
	21	138 28.6	. . 05.1	207 16.8	7.9	16 58.5	6.0	58.5
	22	153 28.7	06.1	221 43.7	8.0	16 52.5	6.2	58.5
	23	168 28.9	07.0	236 10.7	8.0	16 46.3	6.2	58.5
	14 00	183 29.0	S 8 07.9	250 37.7	8.1	N16 40.1	6.3	58.5
	01	198 29.2	08.8	265 04.8	8.1	16 33.8	6.5	58.5
	02	213 29.3	09.8	279 31.9	8.2	16 27.3	6.5	58.5
	03	228 29.5	. . 10.7	293 59.1	8.3	16 20.8	6.6	58.4
	04	243 29.6	11.6	308 26.4	8.3	16 14.2	6.7	58.4
	05	258 29.8	12.6	322 53.7	8.3	16 07.5	6.8	58.4
	06	273 29.9	S 8 13.5	337 21.0	8.5	N16 00.7	6.9	58.4
	07	288 30.1	14.4	351 48.5	8.5	15 53.8	7.0	58.4
S	08	303 30.2	15.3	6 16.0	8.5	15 46.8	7.0	58.4
A	09	318 30.3	. . 16.3	20 43.5	8.6	15 39.8	7.2	58.3
T	10	333 30.5	17.2	35 11.1	8.7	15 32.6	7.2	58.3
U	11	348 30.6	18.1	49 38.8	8.7	15 25.4	7.4	58.3
R	12	3 30.8	S 8 19.1	64 06.5	8.8	N15 18.0	7.4	58.3
D	13	18 30.9	20.0	78 34.3	8.9	15 10.6	7.5	58.3
A	14	33 31.1	20.9	93 02.2	8.9	15 03.1	7.6	58.2
Y	15	48 31.2	. . 21.8	107 30.1	9.0	14 55.5	7.6	58.2
	16	63 31.3	22.8	121 58.1	9.0	14 47.9	7.8	58.2
	17	78 31.5	23.7	136 26.1	9.1	14 40.1	7.8	58.2
	18	93 31.6	S 8 24.6	150 54.2	9.2	N14 32.3	7.9	58.2
	19	108 31.8	25.5	165 22.4	9.2	14 24.4	8.0	58.1
	20	123 31.9	26.5	179 50.6	9.3	14 16.4	8.1	58.1
	21	138 32.0	. . 27.4	194 18.9	9.3	14 08.3	8.1	58.1
	22	153 32.2	28.3	208 47.2	9.4	14 00.2	8.2	58.1
	23	168 32.3	29.2	223 15.6	9.4	13 52.0	8.3	58.1
	15 00	183 32.5	S 8 30.2	237 44.0	9.6	N13 43.7	8.3	58.1
	01	198 32.6	31.1	252 12.6	9.5	13 35.4	8.5	58.0
	02	213 32.7	32.0	266 41.1	9.7	13 26.9	8.5	58.0
	03	228 32.9	. . 32.9	281 09.8	9.7	13 18.4	8.5	58.0
	04	243 33.0	33.9	295 38.5	9.7	13 09.9	8.7	58.0
	05	258 33.2	34.8	310 07.2	9.8	13 01.2	8.7	58.0
	06	273 33.3	S 8 35.7	324 36.0	9.9	N12 52.5	8.8	57.9
	07	288 33.4	36.6	339 04.9	10.0	12 43.7	8.8	57.9
	08	303 33.6	37.6	353 33.9	9.9	12 34.9	8.9	57.9
S	09	318 33.7	. . 38.5	8 02.8	10.1	12 26.0	9.0	57.9
U	10	333 33.8	39.4	22 31.9	10.1	12 17.0	9.0	57.9
N	11	348 34.0	40.3	37 01.0	10.2	12 08.0	9.1	57.8
D	12	3 34.1	S 8 41.3	51 30.2	10.2	N11 58.9	9.1	57.8
A	13	18 34.3	42.2	65 59.4	10.3	11 49.8	9.2	57.8
Y	14	33 34.4	43.1	80 28.7	10.3	11 40.6	9.3	57.8
	15	48 34.5	. . 44.0	94 58.0	10.4	11 31.3	9.3	57.8
	16	63 34.7	44.9	109 27.4	10.4	11 22.0	9.4	57.7
	17	78 34.8	45.9	123 56.8	10.5	11 12.6	9.4	57.7
	18	93 34.9	S 8 46.8	138 26.3	10.6	N11 03.2	9.5	57.7
	19	108 35.1	47.7	152 55.9	10.6	10 53.7	9.6	57.7
	20	123 35.2	48.6	167 25.5	10.7	10 44.1	9.6	57.7
	21	138 35.3	. . 49.6	181 55.2	10.7	10 34.5	9.6	57.7
	22	153 35.5	50.5	196 24.9	10.8	10 24.9	9.7	57.6
	23	168 35.6	51.4	210 54.7	10.8	N10 15.2	9.7	57.6
		SD 16.1	*d* 0.9	SD 16.0		15.9		15.8

Lat.	Twilight Naut.	Twilight Civil	Sunrise	Moonrise 13	Moonrise 14	Moonrise 15	Moonrise 16
°	h m	h m	h m	h m	h m	h m	h m
N 72	04 51	06 10	07 20	20 34	22 51	24 51	00 51
N 70	04 56	06 06	07 09	21 28	23 20	25 08	01 08
68	04 59	06 03	07 00	22 01	23 41	25 21	01 21
66	05 02	06 01	06 53	22 25	23 57	25 31	01 31
64	05 04	05 59	06 47	22 43	24 11	00 11	01 40
62	05 05	05 57	06 42	22 59	24 22	00 22	01 47
60	05 07	05 55	06 37	23 11	24 32	00 32	01 54
N 58	05 08	05 53	06 33	23 22	24 40	00 40	01 59
56	05 09	05 52	06 29	23 32	24 48	00 48	02 04
54	05 09	05 50	06 26	23 40	24 54	00 54	02 09
52	05 10	05 49	06 23	23 48	25 00	01 00	02 13
50	05 10	05 48	06 20	23 55	25 05	01 05	02 17
45	05 11	05 45	06 14	24 09	00 09	01 17	02 25
N 40	05 11	05 42	06 09	24 21	00 21	01 26	02 31
35	05 10	05 40	06 05	24 31	00 31	01 34	02 37
30	05 09	05 37	06 01	24 40	00 40	01 41	02 42
20	05 07	05 32	05 54	24 55	00 55	01 54	02 50
N 10	05 03	05 27	05 48	00 11	01 09	02 04	02 58
0	04 58	05 22	05 43	00 25	01 21	02 14	03 05
S 10	04 51	05 16	05 37	00 39	01 33	02 24	03 12
20	04 42	05 08	05 30	00 55	01 47	02 35	03 20
30	04 30	04 59	05 23	01 12	02 02	02 47	03 28
35	04 22	04 53	05 19	01 22	02 11	02 54	03 33
40	04 13	04 46	05 14	01 34	02 21	03 02	03 39
45	04 01	04 38	05 08	01 47	02 32	03 11	03 45
S 50	03 46	04 27	05 01	02 04	02 47	03 22	03 53
52	03 39	04 23	04 58	02 11	02 53	03 27	03 56
54	03 31	04 17	04 54	02 20	03 00	03 33	04 00
56	03 22	04 11	04 50	02 30	03 09	03 39	04 04
58	03 11	04 04	04 46	02 41	03 18	03 46	04 09
S 60	02 58	03 56	04 41	02 53	03 28	03 54	04 15

Lat.	Sunset	Twilight Civil	Twilight Naut.	Moonset 13	Moonset 14	Moonset 15	Moonset 16
°	h m	h m	h m	h m	h m	h m	h m
N 72	16 10	17 20	18 38	17 50	17 26	17 12	17 02
N 70	16 21	17 24	18 34	16 55	16 56	16 54	16 52
68	16 30	17 27	18 31	16 22	16 34	16 40	16 44
66	16 37	17 29	18 28	15 57	16 16	16 28	16 37
64	16 44	17 32	18 26	15 38	16 02	16 18	16 31
62	16 49	17 34	18 25	15 22	15 50	16 10	16 26
60	16 54	17 36	18 24	15 09	15 39	16 03	16 21
N 58	16 58	17 37	18 23	14 58	15 30	15 56	16 17
56	17 02	17 39	18 22	14 48	15 22	15 50	16 14
54	17 05	17 40	18 21	14 39	15 15	15 45	16 11
52	17 08	17 42	18 21	14 31	15 09	15 41	16 08
50	17 11	17 43	18 21	14 24	15 03	15 36	16 05
45	17 17	17 46	18 20	14 09	14 51	15 27	15 59
N 40	17 22	17 49	18 20	13 56	14 40	15 19	15 54
35	17 26	17 52	18 21	13 46	14 31	15 13	15 50
30	17 30	17 54	18 22	13 36	14 24	15 07	15 46
20	17 37	17 59	18 25	13 20	14 10	14 56	15 40
N 10	17 43	18 05	18 29	13 06	13 58	14 47	15 34
0	17 49	18 10	18 34	12 52	13 47	14 39	15 29
S 10	17 55	18 17	18 41	12 39	13 35	14 30	15 23
20	18 02	18 24	18 50	12 24	13 23	14 21	15 17
30	18 09	18 34	19 03	12 08	13 09	14 10	15 10
35	18 14	18 40	19 10	11 58	13 01	14 04	15 06
40	18 19	18 47	19 20	11 47	12 52	13 57	15 02
45	18 25	18 55	19 32	11 34	12 41	13 49	14 57
S 50	18 32	19 06	19 47	11 18	12 28	13 39	14 50
52	18 35	19 11	19 54	11 10	12 22	13 35	14 48
54	18 39	19 16	20 03	11 02	12 15	13 30	14 44
56	18 43	19 22	20 12	10 53	12 07	13 24	14 41
58	18 47	19 29	20 23	10 42	11 58	13 18	14 37
S 60	18 52	19 38	20 37	10 30	11 48	13 10	14 32

Day	SUN Eqn. of Time 00^h	SUN Eqn. of Time 12^h	SUN Mer. Pass.	MOON Mer. Pass. Upper	MOON Mer. Pass. Lower	MOON Age	MOON Phase
d	m s	m s	h m	h m	h m	d	%
13	13 42	13 49	11 46	06 39	19 07	23	39
14	13 56	14 03	11 46	07 34	20 01	24	29
15	14 10	14 16	11 46	08 27	20 52	25	19

UT d	UT h	ARIES GHA	VENUS −3·9 GHA	VENUS Dec	MARS +1·8 GHA	MARS Dec	JUPITER −1·7 GHA	JUPITER Dec	SATURN +0·5 GHA	SATURN Dec
		° ′	° ′	° ′	° ′	° ′	° ′	° ′	° ′	° ′
16	00	24 42.1	202 18.2	N 0 36.9	208 10.0	N 2 46.0	175 18.2	S10 55.3	122 00.1	S22 14.2
	01	39 44.5	217 17.8	35.7	223 11.0	45.3	190 20.1	55.5	137 02.3	14.2
	02	54 47.0	232 17.5	34.5	238 12.1	44.7	205 22.1	55.7	152 04.6	14.2
	03	69 49.5	247 17.1	. . 33.3	253 13.1	. . 44.1	220 24.0	. . 55.9	167 06.8	. . 14.2
	04	84 51.9	262 16.7	32.0	268 14.1	43.5	235 26.0	56.1	182 09.1	14.2
	05	99 54.4	277 16.3	30.8	283 15.1	42.8	250 27.9	56.3	197 11.3	14.2
	06	114 56.9	292 15.9	N 0 29.6	298 16.1	N 2 42.2	265 29.9	S10 56.4	212 13.6	S22 14.3
	07	129 59.3	307 15.5	28.4	313 17.1	41.6	280 31.8	56.6	227 15.9	14.3
	08	145 01.8	322 15.1	27.2	328 18.1	40.9	295 33.8	56.8	242 18.1	14.3
M	09	160 04.3	337 14.7	. . 26.0	343 19.1	. . 40.3	310 35.7	. . 57.0	257 20.4	. . 14.3
O	10	175 06.7	352 14.3	24.7	358 20.2	39.7	325 37.6	57.2	272 22.6	14.3
N	11	190 09.2	7 13.9	23.5	13 21.2	39.0	340 39.6	57.4	287 24.9	14.3
D	12	205 11.6	22 13.5	N 0 22.3	28 22.2	N 2 38.4	355 41.5	S10 57.6	302 27.1	S22 14.3
A	13	220 14.1	37 13.1	21.1	43 23.2	37.8	10 43.5	57.8	317 29.4	14.4
Y	14	235 16.6	52 12.8	19.9	58 24.2	37.2	25 45.4	58.0	332 31.7	14.4
	15	250 19.0	67 12.4	. . 18.7	73 25.2	. . 36.5	40 47.4	. . 58.2	347 33.9	. . 14.4
	16	265 21.5	82 12.0	17.4	88 26.2	35.9	55 49.3	58.3	2 36.2	14.4
	17	280 24.0	97 11.6	16.2	103 27.3	35.3	70 51.3	58.5	17 38.4	14.4
	18	295 26.4	112 11.2	N 0 15.0	118 28.3	N 2 34.6	85 53.2	S10 58.7	32 40.7	S22 14.4
	19	310 28.9	127 10.8	13.8	133 29.3	34.0	100 55.2	58.9	47 42.9	14.5
	20	325 31.4	142 10.4	12.6	148 30.3	33.4	115 57.1	59.1	62 45.2	14.5
	21	340 33.8	157 10.0	. . 11.4	163 31.3	. . 32.7	130 59.1	. . 59.3	77 47.5	. . 14.5
	22	355 36.3	172 09.6	10.1	178 32.3	32.1	146 01.0	59.5	92 49.7	14.5
	23	10 38.8	187 09.2	08.9	193 33.3	31.5	161 02.9	59.7	107 52.0	14.5
17	00	25 41.2	202 08.8	N 0 07.7	208 34.4	N 2 30.9	176 04.9	S10 59.9	122 54.2	S22 14.5
	01	40 43.7	217 08.5	06.5	223 35.4	30.2	191 06.8	11 00.1	137 56.5	14.6
	02	55 46.1	232 08.1	05.3	238 36.4	29.6	206 08.8	00.2	152 58.7	14.6
	03	70 48.6	247 07.7	. . 04.0	253 37.4	. . 29.0	221 10.7	. . 00.4	168 01.0	. . 14.6
	04	85 51.1	262 07.3	02.8	268 38.4	28.3	236 12.7	00.6	183 03.2	14.6
	05	100 53.5	277 06.9	01.6	283 39.4	27.7	251 14.6	00.8	198 05.5	14.6
	06	115 56.0	292 06.5	N 0 00.4	298 40.4	N 2 27.1	266 16.6	S11 01.0	213 07.7	S22 14.6
	07	130 58.5	307 06.1	S 00.8	313 41.4	26.4	281 18.5	01.2	228 10.0	14.7
T	08	146 00.9	322 05.7	02.0	328 42.5	25.8	296 20.5	01.4	243 12.3	14.7
U	09	161 03.4	337 05.3	. . 03.3	343 43.5	. . 25.2	311 22.4	. . 01.6	258 14.5	. . 14.7
E	10	176 05.9	352 04.9	04.5	358 44.5	24.5	326 24.4	01.8	273 16.8	14.7
S	11	191 08.3	7 04.5	05.7	13 45.5	23.9	341 26.3	01.9	288 19.0	14.7
D	12	206 10.8	22 04.1	S 0 06.9	28 46.5	N 2 23.3	356 28.2	S11 02.1	303 21.3	S22 14.7
A	13	221 13.2	37 03.8	08.1	43 47.5	22.7	11 30.2	02.3	318 23.5	14.7
Y	14	236 15.7	52 03.4	09.4	58 48.5	22.0	26 32.1	02.5	333 25.8	14.8
	15	251 18.2	67 03.0	. . 10.6	73 49.6	. . 21.4	41 34.1	. . 02.7	348 28.0	. . 14.8
	16	266 20.6	82 02.6	11.8	88 50.6	20.8	56 36.0	02.9	3 30.3	14.8
	17	281 23.1	97 02.2	13.0	103 51.6	20.1	71 38.0	03.1	18 32.5	14.8
	18	296 25.6	112 01.8	S 0 14.2	118 52.6	N 2 19.5	86 39.9	S11 03.3	33 34.8	S22 14.8
	19	311 28.0	127 01.4	15.5	133 53.6	18.9	101 41.9	03.5	48 37.0	14.8
	20	326 30.5	142 01.0	16.7	148 54.6	18.2	116 43.8	03.7	63 39.3	14.9
	21	341 33.0	157 00.6	. . 17.9	163 55.6	. . 17.6	131 45.8	. . 03.8	78 41.5	. . 14.9
	22	356 35.4	172 00.2	19.1	178 56.7	17.0	146 47.7	04.0	93 43.8	14.9
	23	11 37.9	186 59.8	20.3	193 57.7	16.4	161 49.6	04.2	108 46.1	14.9
18	00	26 40.4	201 59.4	S 0 21.5	208 58.7	N 2 15.7	176 51.6	S11 04.4	123 48.3	S22 14.9
	01	41 42.8	216 59.0	22.8	223 59.7	15.1	191 53.5	04.6	138 50.6	14.9
	02	56 45.3	231 58.7	24.0	239 00.7	14.5	206 55.5	04.8	153 52.8	15.0
	03	71 47.7	246 58.3	. . 25.2	254 01.7	. . 13.8	221 57.4	. . 05.0	168 55.1	. . 15.0
	04	86 50.2	261 57.9	26.4	269 02.7	13.2	236 59.4	05.2	183 57.3	15.0
	05	101 52.7	276 57.5	27.6	284 03.8	12.6	252 01.3	05.4	198 59.6	15.0
	06	116 55.1	291 57.1	S 0 28.9	299 04.8	N 2 11.9	267 03.3	S11 05.5	214 01.8	S22 15.0
W	07	131 57.6	306 56.7	30.1	314 05.8	11.3	282 05.2	05.7	229 04.1	15.0
E	08	147 00.1	321 56.3	31.3	329 06.8	10.7	297 07.2	05.9	244 06.3	15.1
D	09	162 02.5	336 55.9	. . 32.5	344 07.8	. . 10.0	312 09.1	. . 06.1	259 08.6	. . 15.1
N	10	177 05.0	351 55.5	33.7	359 08.8	09.4	327 11.0	06.3	274 10.8	15.1
E	11	192 07.5	6 55.1	35.0	14 09.8	08.8	342 13.0	06.5	289 13.1	15.1
S	12	207 09.9	21 54.7	S 0 36.2	29 10.9	N 2 08.2	357 14.9	S11 06.7	304 15.3	S22 15.1
D	13	222 12.4	36 54.3	37.4	44 11.9	07.5	12 16.9	06.9	319 17.6	15.1
A	14	237 14.9	51 53.9	38.6	59 12.9	06.9	27 18.8	07.1	334 19.8	15.1
Y	15	252 17.3	66 53.5	. . 39.8	74 13.9	. . 06.3	42 20.8	. . 07.2	349 22.1	. . 15.2
	16	267 19.8	81 53.2	41.1	89 14.9	05.6	57 22.7	07.4	4 24.3	15.2
	17	282 22.2	96 52.8	42.3	104 15.9	05.0	72 24.7	07.6	19 26.6	15.2
	18	297 24.7	111 52.4	S 0 43.5	119 16.9	N 2 04.4	87 26.6	S11 07.8	34 28.8	S22 15.2
	19	312 27.2	126 52.0	44.7	134 18.0	03.7	102 28.5	08.0	49 31.1	15.2
	20	327 29.6	141 51.6	45.9	149 19.0	03.1	117 30.5	08.2	64 33.3	15.2
	21	342 32.1	156 51.2	. . 47.2	164 20.0	. . 02.5	132 32.4	. . 08.4	79 35.6	. . 15.3
	22	357 34.6	171 50.8	48.4	179 21.0	01.8	147 34.4	08.6	94 37.8	15.3
	23	12 37.0	186 50.4	49.6	194 22.0	01.2	162 36.3	08.8	109 40.1	15.3
Mer. Pass.		h m 22 13.6	v −0.4	d 1.2	v 1.0	d 0.6	v 1.9	d 0.2	v 2.3	d 0.0

STARS

Name	SHA	Dec
	° ′	° ′
Acamar	315 15.8	S40 14.0
Achernar	335 24.1	S57 08.9
Acrux	173 06.6	S63 11.6
Adhara	255 10.2	S28 59.7
Aldebaran	290 45.8	N16 32.5
Alioth	166 18.8	N55 51.9
Alkaid	152 57.1	N49 13.7
Al Na'ir	27 39.9	S46 52.6
Alnilam	275 43.3	S 1 11.5
Alphard	217 53.4	S 8 44.0
Alphecca	126 08.9	N26 39.7
Alpheratz	357 40.1	N29 11.4
Altair	62 05.4	N 8 55.2
Ankaa	353 12.5	S42 12.6
Antares	112 23.0	S26 28.1
Arcturus	145 53.4	N19 05.7
Atria	107 22.5	S69 03.5
Avior	234 16.9	S59 33.7
Bellatrix	278 28.7	N 6 21.8
Betelgeuse	270 58.0	N 7 24.5
Canopus	263 54.7	S52 42.1
Capella	280 29.9	N46 00.6
Deneb	49 29.4	N45 21.0
Denebola	182 31.0	N14 28.5
Diphda	348 52.7	S17 53.4
Dubhe	193 48.8	N61 39.2
Elnath	278 08.7	N28 37.1
Eltanin	90 45.0	N51 29.7
Enif	33 44.1	N 9 57.6
Fomalhaut	15 20.5	S29 31.7
Gacrux	171 58.1	S57 12.5
Gienah	175 49.6	S17 38.2
Hadar	148 44.3	S60 27.3
Hamal	327 57.1	N23 32.7
Kaus Aust.	83 40.1	S34 22.4
Kochab	137 21.3	N74 05.2
Markab	13 35.2	N15 18.2
Menkar	314 11.7	N 4 09.5
Menkent	148 04.5	S36 27.2
Miaplacidus	221 39.3	S69 47.1
Mirfak	308 35.7	N49 55.2
Nunki	75 54.8	S26 16.3
Peacock	53 14.6	S56 40.7
Pollux	243 24.2	N27 58.8
Procyon	244 56.7	N 5 10.7
Rasalhague	96 03.9	N12 33.2
Regulus	207 40.6	N11 52.9
Rigel	281 09.1	S 8 10.9
Rigil Kent.	139 48.4	S60 54.3
Sabik	102 09.4	S15 44.6
Schedar	349 36.6	N56 38.1
Shaula	96 18.2	S37 06.8
Sirius	258 31.1	S16 44.4
Spica	158 28.5	S11 15.0
Suhail	222 50.4	S43 30.0
Vega	80 37.1	N38 48.5
Zuben'ubi	137 02.5	S16 06.7

	SHA	Mer. Pass.
	° ′	h m
Venus	176 27.6	10 32
Mars	182 53.1	10 05
Jupiter	150 23.7	12 14
Saturn	97 13.0	15 46

Day	UT d h	SUN GHA ° ′	SUN Dec ° ′	MOON GHA ° ′	MOON v ′	MOON Dec ° ′	MOON d ′	MOON HP ′
16	00	183 35.7	S 8 52.3	225 24.5	10.9	N10 05.5	9.8	57.6
	01	198 35.9	53.2	239 54.4	10.9	9 55.7	9.9	57.6
	02	213 36.0	54.2	254 24.3	11.0	9 45.8	9.9	57.6
	03	228 36.1	. . 55.1	268 54.3	11.0	9 35.9	9.9	57.5
	04	243 36.3	56.0	283 24.3	11.1	9 26.0	10.0	57.5
	05	258 36.4	56.9	297 54.4	11.2	9 16.0	10.0	57.5
	06	273 36.5	S 8 57.8	312 24.6	11.2	N 9 06.0	10.0	57.5
	07	288 36.7	58.7	326 54.8	11.2	8 56.0	10.1	57.5
	08	303 36.8	8 59.7	341 25.0	11.3	8 45.9	10.2	57.4
M	09	318 36.9	9 00.6	355 55.3	11.3	8 35.7	10.1	57.4
O	10	333 37.1	01.5	10 25.6	11.4	8 25.6	10.2	57.4
N	11	348 37.2	02.4	24 56.0	11.4	8 15.4	10.3	57.4
D	12	3 37.3	S 9 03.3	39 26.4	11.5	N 8 05.1	10.3	57.4
A	13	18 37.4	04.3	53 56.9	11.5	7 54.8	10.3	57.3
Y	14	33 37.6	05.2	68 27.4	11.6	7 44.5	10.3	57.3
	15	48 37.7	. . 06.1	82 58.0	11.6	7 34.2	10.4	57.3
	16	63 37.8	07.0	97 28.6	11.7	7 23.8	10.4	57.3
	17	78 38.0	07.9	111 59.3	11.7	7 13.4	10.5	57.3
	18	93 38.1	S 9 08.8	126 30.0	11.7	N 7 02.9	10.5	57.2
	19	108 38.2	09.8	141 00.7	11.8	6 52.4	10.5	57.2
	20	123 38.4	10.7	155 31.5	11.9	6 41.9	10.5	57.2
	21	138 38.5	. . 11.6	170 02.4	11.8	6 31.4	10.6	57.2
	22	153 38.6	12.5	184 33.2	12.0	6 20.8	10.5	57.2
	23	168 38.7	13.4	199 04.2	11.9	6 10.3	10.6	57.1
17	00	183 38.9	S 9 14.3	213 35.1	12.0	N 5 59.7	10.7	57.1
	01	198 39.0	15.2	228 06.1	12.1	5 49.0	10.6	57.1
	02	213 39.1	16.2	242 37.2	12.1	5 38.4	10.7	57.1
	03	228 39.2	. . 17.1	257 08.3	12.1	5 27.7	10.7	57.0
	04	243 39.4	18.0	271 39.4	12.1	5 17.0	10.7	57.0
	05	258 39.5	18.9	286 10.5	12.2	5 06.3	10.7	57.0
	06	273 39.6	S 9 19.8	300 41.7	12.3	N 4 55.6	10.8	57.0
	07	288 39.7	20.7	315 13.0	12.2	4 44.8	10.8	57.0
T	08	303 39.9	21.6	329 44.2	12.3	4 34.0	10.7	56.9
U	09	318 40.0	. . 22.5	344 15.5	12.4	4 23.3	10.8	56.9
E	10	333 40.1	23.5	358 46.9	12.4	4 12.5	10.9	56.9
S	11	348 40.2	24.4	13 18.3	12.4	4 01.6	10.8	56.9
D	12	3 40.4	S 9 25.3	27 49.7	12.4	N 3 50.8	10.8	56.9
A	13	18 40.5	26.2	42 21.1	12.5	3 40.0	10.9	56.8
Y	14	33 40.6	27.1	56 52.6	12.5	3 29.1	10.8	56.8
	15	48 40.7	. . 28.0	71 24.1	12.6	3 18.3	10.9	56.8
	16	63 40.9	28.9	85 55.7	12.5	3 07.4	10.9	56.8
	17	78 41.0	29.8	100 27.2	12.6	2 56.5	10.9	56.8
	18	93 41.1	S 9 30.8	114 58.8	12.7	N 2 45.6	10.8	56.7
	19	108 41.2	31.7	129 30.5	12.6	2 34.8	10.9	56.7
	20	123 41.4	32.6	144 02.1	12.7	2 23.9	10.9	56.7
	21	138 41.5	. . 33.5	158 33.8	12.8	2 13.0	10.9	56.7
	22	153 41.6	34.4	173 05.6	12.7	2 02.1	10.9	56.7
	23	168 41.7	35.3	187 37.3	12.8	1 51.2	10.9	56.6
18	00	183 41.8	S 9 36.2	202 09.1	12.8	N 1 40.3	11.0	56.6
	01	198 42.0	37.1	216 40.9	12.8	1 29.3	10.9	56.6
	02	213 42.1	38.0	231 12.7	12.9	1 18.4	10.9	56.6
	03	228 42.2	. . 38.9	245 44.6	12.9	1 07.5	10.9	56.6
	04	243 42.3	39.8	260 16.5	12.9	0 56.6	10.9	56.5
	05	258 42.4	40.8	274 48.4	12.9	0 45.7	10.9	56.5
	06	273 42.6	S 9 41.7	289 20.3	12.9	N 0 34.8	10.9	56.5
W	07	288 42.7	42.6	303 52.2	13.0	0 23.9	10.9	56.5
E	08	303 42.8	43.5	318 24.2	13.0	0 13.0	10.9	56.4
D	09	318 42.9	. . 44.4	332 56.2	13.0	N 0 02.1	10.8	56.4
N	10	333 43.0	45.3	347 28.2	13.1	S 0 08.7	10.9	56.4
E	11	348 43.2	46.2	2 00.3	13.0	0 19.6	10.9	56.4
S	12	3 43.3	S 9 47.1	16 32.3	13.1	S 0 30.5	10.8	56.4
D	13	18 43.4	48.0	31 04.4	13.1	0 41.3	10.8	56.3
A	14	33 43.5	48.9	45 36.5	13.1	0 52.1	10.9	56.3
Y	15	48 43.6	. . 49.8	60 08.6	13.2	1 03.0	10.8	56.3
	16	63 43.7	50.7	74 40.8	13.1	1 13.8	10.8	56.3
	17	78 43.9	51.6	89 12.9	13.2	1 24.6	10.8	56.3
	18	93 44.0	S 9 52.5	103 45.1	13.2	S 1 35.4	10.8	56.2
	19	108 44.1	53.4	118 17.3	13.2	1 46.2	10.7	56.2
	20	123 44.2	54.3	132 49.5	13.2	1 56.9	10.8	56.2
	21	138 44.3	. . 55.2	147 21.7	13.2	2 07.7	10.7	56.2
	22	153 44.4	56.1	161 53.9	13.2	2 18.4	10.7	56.2
	23	168 44.5	57.1	176 26.1	13.3	S 2 29.1	10.7	56.1
		SD 16.1	*d* 0.9	SD 15.6		15.5		15.4

Lat.	Twilight Naut.	Twilight Civil	Sunrise	Moonrise 16	Moonrise 17	Moonrise 18	Moonrise 19
°	h m	h m	h m	h m	h m	h m	h m
N 72	05 05	06 23	07 35	00 51	02 44	04 31	06 16
N 70	05 07	06 18	07 22	01 08	02 52	04 32	06 10
68	05 09	06 14	07 12	01 21	02 58	04 33	06 06
66	05 11	06 10	07 03	01 31	03 03	04 34	06 02
64	05 12	06 07	06 56	01 40	03 08	04 34	05 59
62	05 13	06 04	06 50	01 47	03 12	04 35	05 56
60	05 14	06 02	06 45	01 54	03 15	04 35	05 54
N 58	05 14	06 00	06 40	01 59	03 18	04 36	05 52
56	05 15	05 58	06 36	02 04	03 21	04 36	05 50
54	05 15	05 56	06 32	02 09	03 23	04 36	05 48
52	05 15	05 54	06 28	02 13	03 25	04 37	05 46
50	05 15	05 52	06 25	02 17	03 27	04 37	05 45
45	05 15	05 49	06 18	02 25	03 32	04 37	05 42
N 40	05 14	05 45	06 13	02 31	03 35	04 38	05 39
35	05 13	05 42	06 08	02 37	03 38	04 38	05 37
30	05 11	05 39	06 03	02 42	03 41	04 39	05 35
20	05 07	05 33	05 55	02 50	03 46	04 39	05 32
N 10	05 03	05 27	05 49	02 58	03 50	04 40	05 29
0	04 57	05 21	05 42	03 05	03 54	04 41	05 27
S 10	04 49	05 14	05 35	03 12	03 58	04 41	05 24
20	04 39	05 06	05 28	03 20	04 02	04 42	05 21
30	04 26	04 55	05 20	03 28	04 06	04 43	05 18
35	04 18	04 49	05 15	03 33	04 09	04 43	05 16
40	04 08	04 41	05 09	03 39	04 12	04 44	05 14
45	03 55	04 32	05 03	03 45	04 16	04 44	05 12
S 50	03 39	04 21	04 55	03 53	04 20	04 45	05 09
52	03 31	04 16	04 51	03 56	04 22	04 45	05 08
54	03 23	04 10	04 47	04 00	04 24	04 46	05 07
56	03 12	04 03	04 43	04 04	04 26	04 46	05 05
58	03 00	03 55	04 38	04 09	04 29	04 46	05 03
S 60	02 46	03 47	04 32	04 15	04 32	04 47	05 02

Lat.	Sunset	Twilight Civil	Twilight Naut.	Moonset 16	Moonset 17	Moonset 18	Moonset 19
°	h m	h m	h m	h m	h m	h m	h m
N 72	15 54	17 06	18 24	17 02	16 53	16 44	16 35
N 70	16 07	17 11	18 21	16 52	16 49	16 46	16 43
68	16 17	17 15	18 19	16 44	16 46	16 48	16 50
66	16 26	17 19	18 18	16 37	16 43	16 49	16 55
64	16 33	17 22	18 17	16 31	16 41	16 50	17 00
62	16 40	17 25	18 16	16 26	16 39	16 51	17 04
60	16 45	17 27	18 15	16 21	16 37	16 52	17 07
N 58	16 50	17 30	18 15	16 17	16 36	16 53	17 10
56	16 54	17 32	18 15	16 14	16 34	16 54	17 13
54	16 58	17 34	18 15	16 11	16 33	16 55	17 16
52	17 01	17 36	18 15	16 08	16 32	16 55	17 18
50	17 05	17 37	18 15	16 05	16 31	16 56	17 20
45	17 12	17 41	18 15	15 59	16 29	16 57	17 25
N 40	17 17	17 45	18 16	15 54	16 27	16 58	17 28
35	17 22	17 48	18 17	15 50	16 25	16 59	17 32
30	17 27	17 51	18 19	15 46	16 24	16 59	17 35
20	17 35	17 57	18 23	15 40	16 21	17 01	17 40
N 10	17 42	18 03	18 28	15 34	16 19	17 02	17 44
0	17 49	18 10	18 34	15 29	16 16	17 03	17 48
S 10	17 55	18 17	18 42	15 23	16 14	17 04	17 53
20	18 03	18 25	18 52	15 17	16 12	17 05	17 57
30	18 11	18 36	19 05	15 10	16 09	17 06	18 02
35	18 16	18 42	19 13	15 06	16 07	17 07	18 05
40	18 22	18 50	19 24	15 02	16 05	17 08	18 09
45	18 29	18 59	19 36	14 57	16 03	17 08	18 13
S 50	18 37	19 11	19 53	14 50	16 01	17 10	18 17
52	18 40	19 16	20 01	14 48	15 59	17 10	18 19
54	18 45	19 22	20 10	14 44	15 58	17 11	18 22
56	18 49	19 29	20 20	14 41	15 57	17 11	18 24
58	18 54	19 37	20 33	14 37	15 55	17 12	18 27
S 60	19 00	19 46	20 47	14 32	15 53	17 13	18 30

Day	SUN Eqn. of Time 00^h	SUN Eqn. of Time 12^h	SUN Mer. Pass.	MOON Mer. Pass. Upper	MOON Mer. Pass. Lower	MOON Age	MOON Phase
d	m s	m s	h m	h m	h m	d	%
16	14 23	14 29	11 46	09 17	21 41	26	12
17	14 35	14 41	11 45	10 05	22 29	27	6
18	14 47	14 53	11 45	10 52	23 15	28	2

UT (d h)	ARIES GHA	VENUS −3·9 GHA	VENUS Dec	MARS +1·8 GHA	MARS Dec	JUPITER −1·7 GHA	JUPITER Dec	SATURN +0·5 GHA	SATURN Dec
	° ′	° ′	° ′	° ′	° ′	° ′	° ′	° ′	° ′
19 00 THURSDAY	27 39.5	201 50.0	S 0 50.8	209 23.0	N 2 00.6	177 38.3	S11 08.9	124 42.3	S22 15.3
01	42 42.0	216 49.6	52.1	224 24.1	1 59.9	192 40.2	09.1	139 44.6	15.3
02	57 44.4	231 49.2	53.3	239 25.1	59.3	207 42.2	09.3	154 46.8	15.3
03	72 46.9	246 48.8	. . 54.5	254 26.1	. . 58.7	222 44.1	. . 09.5	169 49.1	. . 15.4
04	87 49.3	261 48.4	55.7	269 27.1	58.1	237 46.1	09.7	184 51.3	15.4
05	102 51.8	276 48.0	56.9	284 28.1	57.4	252 48.0	09.9	199 53.6	15.4
06	117 54.3	291 47.6	S 0 58.2	299 29.1	N 1 56.8	267 49.9	S11 10.1	214 55.8	S22 15.4
07	132 56.7	306 47.2	0 59.4	314 30.1	56.2	282 51.9	10.3	229 58.1	15.4
08	147 59.2	321 46.9	1 00.6	329 31.2	55.5	297 53.8	10.5	245 00.3	15.4
09	163 01.7	336 46.5	. . 01.8	344 32.2	. . 54.9	312 55.8	. . 10.6	260 02.6	. . 15.4
10	178 04.1	351 46.1	03.0	359 33.2	54.3	327 57.7	10.8	275 04.8	15.5
11	193 06.6	6 45.7	04.3	14 34.2	53.6	342 59.7	11.0	290 07.0	15.5
12	208 09.1	21 45.3	S 1 05.5	29 35.2	N 1 53.0	358 01.6	S11 11.2	305 09.3	S22 15.5
13	223 11.5	36 44.9	06.7	44 36.2	52.4	13 03.5	11.4	320 11.5	15.5
14	238 14.0	51 44.5	07.9	59 37.2	51.7	28 05.5	11.6	335 13.8	15.5
15	253 16.5	66 44.1	. . 09.1	74 38.3	. . 51.1	43 07.4	. . 11.8	350 16.0	. . 15.5
16	268 18.9	81 43.7	10.4	89 39.3	50.5	58 09.4	12.0	5 18.3	15.6
17	283 21.4	96 43.3	11.6	104 40.3	49.9	73 11.3	12.2	20 20.5	15.6
18	298 23.8	111 42.9	S 1 12.8	119 41.3	N 1 49.2	88 13.3	S11 12.3	35 22.8	S22 15.6
19	313 26.3	126 42.5	14.0	134 42.3	48.6	103 15.2	12.5	50 25.0	15.6
20	328 28.8	141 42.1	15.2	149 43.3	48.0	118 17.2	12.7	65 27.3	15.6
21	343 31.2	156 41.7	. . 16.5	164 44.4	. . 47.3	133 19.1	. . 12.9	80 29.5	. . 15.6
22	358 33.7	171 41.3	17.7	179 45.4	46.7	148 21.0	13.1	95 31.8	15.7
23	13 36.2	186 40.9	18.9	194 46.4	46.1	163 23.0	13.3	110 34.0	15.7
20 00 FRIDAY	28 38.6	201 40.5	S 1 20.1	209 47.4	N 1 45.4	178 24.9	S11 13.5	125 36.3	S22 15.7
01	43 41.1	216 40.1	21.4	224 48.4	44.8	193 26.9	13.7	140 38.5	15.7
02	58 43.6	231 39.7	22.6	239 49.4	44.2	208 28.8	13.9	155 40.7	15.7
03	73 46.0	246 39.3	. . 23.8	254 50.4	. . 43.5	223 30.8	. . 14.0	170 43.0	. . 15.7
04	88 48.5	261 38.9	25.0	269 51.5	42.9	238 32.7	14.2	185 45.2	15.8
05	103 50.9	276 38.6	26.2	284 52.5	42.3	253 34.7	14.4	200 47.5	15.8
06	118 53.4	291 38.2	S 1 27.5	299 53.5	N 1 41.6	268 36.6	S11 14.6	215 49.7	S22 15.8
07	133 55.9	306 37.8	28.7	314 54.5	41.0	283 38.5	14.8	230 52.0	15.8
08	148 58.3	321 37.4	29.9	329 55.5	40.4	298 40.5	15.0	245 54.2	15.8
09	164 00.8	336 37.0	. . 31.1	344 56.5	. . 39.8	313 42.4	. . 15.2	260 56.5	. . 15.8
10	179 03.3	351 36.6	32.3	359 57.6	39.1	328 44.4	15.4	275 58.7	15.8
11	194 05.7	6 36.2	33.6	14 58.6	38.5	343 46.3	15.6	291 00.9	15.9
12	209 08.2	21 35.8	S 1 34.8	29 59.6	N 1 37.9	358 48.3	S11 15.7	306 03.2	S22 15.9
13	224 10.7	36 35.4	36.0	45 00.6	37.2	13 50.2	15.9	321 05.4	15.9
14	239 13.1	51 35.0	37.2	60 01.6	36.6	28 52.1	16.1	336 07.7	15.9
15	254 15.6	66 34.6	. . 38.5	75 02.6	. . 36.0	43 54.1	. . 16.3	351 09.9	. . 15.9
16	269 18.1	81 34.2	39.7	90 03.6	35.3	58 56.0	16.5	6 12.2	15.9
17	284 20.5	96 33.8	40.9	105 04.7	34.7	73 58.0	16.7	21 14.4	16.0
18	299 23.0	111 33.4	S 1 42.1	120 05.7	N 1 34.1	88 59.9	S11 16.9	36 16.7	S22 16.0
19	314 25.4	126 33.0	43.3	135 06.7	33.4	104 01.9	17.1	51 18.9	16.0
20	329 27.9	141 32.6	44.6	150 07.7	32.8	119 03.8	17.3	66 21.1	16.0
21	344 30.4	156 32.2	. . 45.8	165 08.7	. . 32.2	134 05.7	. . 17.4	81 23.4	. . 16.0
22	359 32.8	171 31.8	47.0	180 09.7	31.5	149 07.7	17.6	96 25.6	16.0
23	14 35.3	186 31.4	48.2	195 10.8	30.9	164 09.6	17.8	111 27.9	16.1
21 00 SATURDAY	29 37.8	201 31.0	S 1 49.4	210 11.8	N 1 30.3	179 11.6	S11 18.0	126 30.1	S22 16.1
01	44 40.2	216 30.6	50.7	225 12.8	29.6	194 13.5	18.2	141 32.4	16.1
02	59 42.7	231 30.2	51.9	240 13.8	29.0	209 15.5	18.4	156 34.6	16.1
03	74 45.2	246 29.8	. . 53.1	255 14.8	. . 28.4	224 17.4	. . 18.6	171 36.8	. . 16.1
04	89 47.6	261 29.4	54.3	270 15.8	27.8	239 19.3	18.8	186 39.1	16.1
05	104 50.1	276 29.0	55.5	285 16.9	27.1	254 21.3	18.9	201 41.3	16.1
06	119 52.6	291 28.6	S 1 56.8	300 17.9	N 1 26.5	269 23.2	S11 19.1	216 43.6	S22 16.2
07	134 55.0	306 28.2	58.0	315 18.9	25.9	284 25.2	19.3	231 45.8	16.2
08	149 57.5	321 27.8	1 59.2	330 19.9	25.2	299 27.1	19.5	246 48.1	16.2
09	164 59.9	336 27.4	2 00.4	345 20.9	. . 24.6	314 29.1	. . 19.7	261 50.3	. . 16.2
10	180 02.4	351 27.0	01.7	0 21.9	24.0	329 31.0	19.9	276 52.5	16.2
11	195 04.9	6 26.6	02.9	15 22.9	23.3	344 32.9	20.1	291 54.8	16.2
12	210 07.3	21 26.2	S 2 04.1	30 24.0	N 1 22.7	359 34.9	S11 20.3	306 57.0	S22 16.3
13	225 09.8	36 25.8	05.3	45 25.0	22.1	14 36.8	20.5	321 59.3	16.3
14	240 12.3	51 25.4	06.5	60 26.0	21.4	29 38.8	20.6	337 01.5	16.3
15	255 14.7	66 25.0	. . 07.8	75 27.0	. . 20.8	44 40.7	. . 20.8	352 03.7	. . 16.3
16	270 17.2	81 24.6	09.0	90 28.0	20.2	59 42.7	21.0	7 06.0	16.3
17	285 19.7	96 24.2	10.2	105 29.0	19.5	74 44.6	21.2	22 08.2	16.3
18	300 22.1	111 23.8	S 2 11.4	120 30.1	N 1 18.9	89 46.5	S11 21.4	37 10.5	S22 16.4
19	315 24.6	126 23.4	12.6	135 31.1	18.3	104 48.5	21.6	52 12.7	16.4
20	330 27.0	141 23.0	13.9	150 32.1	17.7	119 50.4	21.8	67 14.9	16.4
21	345 29.5	156 22.6	. . 15.1	165 33.1	. . 17.0	134 52.4	. . 22.0	82 17.2	. . 16.4
22	0 32.0	171 22.2	16.3	180 34.1	16.4	149 54.3	22.1	97 19.4	16.4
23	15 34.4	186 21.8	17.5	195 35.1	15.8	164 56.3	22.3	112 21.7	16.4
Mer. Pass. (h m)	22 01.8	v −0.4	d 1.2	v 1.0	d 0.6	v 1.9	d 0.2	v 2.2	d 0.0

STARS Name	SHA	Dec
	° ′	° ′
Acamar	315 15.8	S40 14.0
Achernar	335 24.1	S57 08.9
Acrux	173 06.6	S63 11.6
Adhara	255 10.1	S28 59.7
Aldebaran	290 45.8	N16 32.5
Alioth	166 18.8	N55 51.9
Alkaid	152 57.1	N49 13.7
Al Na'ir	27 39.9	S46 52.6
Alnilam	275 43.2	S 1 11.5
Alphard	217 53.4	S 8 44.0
Alphecca	126 08.9	N26 39.6
Alpheratz	357 40.1	N29 11.4
Altair	62 05.4	N 8 55.2
Ankaa	353 12.5	S42 12.7
Antares	112 23.0	S26 28.0
Arcturus	145 53.4	N19 05.7
Atria	107 22.5	S69 03.5
Avior	234 16.9	S59 33.7
Bellatrix	278 28.7	N 6 21.8
Betelgeuse	270 58.0	N 7 24.5
Canopus	263 54.6	S52 42.2
Capella	280 29.8	N46 00.6
Deneb	49 29.4	N45 21.0
Denebola	182 31.0	N14 28.5
Diphda	348 52.7	S17 53.4
Dubhe	193 48.7	N61 39.2
Elnath	278 08.7	N28 37.1
Eltanin	90 45.1	N51 29.6
Enif	33 44.1	N 9 57.6
Fomalhaut	15 20.5	S29 31.7
Gacrux	171 58.1	S57 12.5
Gienah	175 49.6	S17 38.2
Hadar	148 44.3	S60 27.3
Hamal	327 57.1	N23 32.7
Kaus Aust.	83 40.1	S34 22.4
Kochab	137 21.4	N74 05.2
Markab	13 35.2	N15 18.2
Menkar	314 11.7	N 4 09.5
Menkent	148 04.5	S36 27.2
Miaplacidus	221 39.3	S69 47.1
Mirfak	308 35.7	N49 55.2
Nunki	75 54.8	S26 16.3
Peacock	53 14.7	S56 40.7
Pollux	243 24.2	N27 58.8
Procyon	244 56.7	N 5 10.7
Rasalhague	96 04.0	N12 33.2
Regulus	207 40.6	N11 52.9
Rigel	281 09.1	S 8 10.9
Rigil Kent.	139 48.4	S60 54.3
Sabik	102 09.4	S15 44.6
Schedar	349 36.6	N56 38.1
Shaula	96 18.2	S37 06.8
Sirius	258 31.1	S16 44.4
Spica	158 28.5	S11 15.0
Suhail	222 50.4	S43 30.0
Vega	80 37.1	N38 48.4
Zuben'ubi	137 02.5	S16 06.7

	SHA	Mer. Pass.
	° ′	h m
Venus	173 01.9	10 34
Mars	181 08.8	10 00
Jupiter	149 46.3	12 05
Saturn	96 57.6	15 35

UT	SUN GHA	SUN Dec	MOON GHA	v	MOON Dec	d	HP
d h	° ′	° ′	° ′	′	° ′	′	′
19 00	183 44.7	S 9 58.0	190 58.4	13.3	S 2 39.8	10.7	56.1
01	198 44.8	58.9	205 30.7	13.2	2 50.5	10.6	56.1
02	213 44.9	9 59.8	220 02.9	13.3	3 01.1	10.6	56.1
03	228 45.0	10 00.7	234 35.2	13.3	3 11.7	10.7	56.1
04	243 45.1	01.6	249 07.5	13.4	3 22.4	10.5	56.0
05	258 45.2	02.5	263 39.9	13.3	3 32.9	10.6	56.0
06	273 45.3	S10 03.4	278 12.2	13.3	S 3 43.5	10.5	56.0
T 07	288 45.5	04.3	292 44.5	13.4	3 54.0	10.5	56.0
H 08	303 45.6	05.2	307 16.9	13.3	4 04.5	10.5	56.0
U 09	318 45.7	. . 06.1	321 49.2	13.4	4 15.0	10.5	55.9
R 10	333 45.8	07.0	336 21.6	13.4	4 25.5	10.4	55.9
S 11	348 45.9	07.9	350 54.0	13.3	4 35.9	10.4	55.9
D 12	3 46.0	S10 08.8	5 26.3	13.4	S 4 46.3	10.4	55.9
A 13	18 46.1	09.7	19 58.7	13.4	4 56.7	10.3	55.8
Y 14	33 46.2	10.6	34 31.1	13.4	5 07.0	10.4	55.8
15	48 46.3	. . 11.5	49 03.5	13.4	5 17.4	10.2	55.8
16	63 46.5	12.4	63 35.9	13.4	5 27.6	10.3	55.8
17	78 46.6	13.3	78 08.3	13.4	5 37.9	10.2	55.8
18	93 46.7	S10 14.2	92 40.7	13.4	S 5 48.1	10.2	55.7
19	108 46.8	15.1	107 13.1	13.4	5 58.3	10.2	55.7
20	123 46.9	16.0	121 45.5	13.5	6 08.5	10.1	55.7
21	138 47.0	. . 16.9	136 18.0	13.4	6 18.6	10.1	55.7
22	153 47.1	17.8	150 50.4	13.4	6 28.7	10.0	55.7
23	168 47.2	18.7	165 22.8	13.4	6 38.7	10.0	55.6
20 00	183 47.3	S10 19.6	179 55.2	13.5	S 6 48.7	10.0	55.6
01	198 47.4	20.5	194 27.7	13.4	6 58.7	9.9	55.6
02	213 47.5	21.3	209 00.1	13.4	7 08.6	9.9	55.6
03	228 47.6	. . 22.2	223 32.5	13.4	7 18.5	9.9	55.6
04	243 47.8	23.1	238 04.9	13.5	7 28.4	9.8	55.5
05	258 47.9	24.0	252 37.4	13.4	7 38.2	9.7	55.5
06	273 48.0	S10 24.9	267 09.8	13.4	S 7 47.9	9.8	55.5
07	288 48.1	25.8	281 42.2	13.4	7 57.7	9.6	55.5
08	303 48.2	26.7	296 14.6	13.5	8 07.3	9.7	55.5
F 09	318 48.3	. . 27.6	310 47.1	13.4	8 17.0	9.6	55.4
R 10	333 48.4	28.5	325 19.5	13.4	8 26.6	9.5	55.4
I 11	348 48.5	29.4	339 51.9	13.4	8 36.1	9.6	55.4
D 12	3 48.6	S10 30.3	354 24.3	13.4	S 8 45.7	9.4	55.4
A 13	18 48.7	31.2	8 56.7	13.4	8 55.1	9.4	55.4
Y 14	33 48.8	32.1	23 29.1	13.4	9 04.5	9.4	55.4
15	48 48.9	. . 33.0	38 01.5	13.4	9 13.9	9.3	55.3
16	63 49.0	33.9	52 33.9	13.4	9 23.2	9.3	55.3
17	78 49.1	34.8	67 06.3	13.4	9 32.5	9.2	55.3
18	93 49.2	S10 35.7	81 38.7	13.3	S 9 41.7	9.2	55.3
19	108 49.3	36.5	96 11.0	13.4	9 50.9	9.1	55.3
20	123 49.4	37.4	110 43.4	13.4	10 00.0	9.1	55.2
21	138 49.5	. . 38.3	125 15.8	13.3	10 09.1	9.0	55.2
22	153 49.6	39.2	139 48.1	13.4	10 18.1	9.0	55.2
23	168 49.7	40.1	154 20.5	13.3	10 27.1	8.9	55.2
21 00	183 49.8	S10 41.0	168 52.8	13.4	S10 36.0	8.8	55.2
01	198 49.9	41.9	183 25.2	13.3	10 44.8	8.9	55.1
02	213 50.0	42.8	197 57.5	13.3	10 53.7	8.7	55.1
03	228 50.1	. . 43.7	212 29.8	13.3	11 02.4	8.7	55.1
04	243 50.2	44.6	227 02.1	13.3	11 11.1	8.6	55.1
05	258 50.3	45.5	241 34.4	13.3	11 19.7	8.6	55.1
06	273 50.4	S10 46.3	256 06.7	13.3	S11 28.3	8.6	55.1
S 07	288 50.5	47.2	270 39.0	13.3	11 36.9	8.4	55.0
A 08	303 50.6	48.1	285 11.3	13.2	11 45.3	8.4	55.0
T 09	318 50.7	. . 49.0	299 43.5	13.3	11 53.7	8.4	55.0
U 10	333 50.8	49.9	314 15.8	13.2	12 02.1	8.3	55.0
R 11	348 50.9	50.8	328 48.0	13.2	12 10.4	8.2	55.0
D 12	3 51.0	S10 51.7	343 20.2	13.3	S12 18.6	8.2	55.0
A 13	18 51.1	52.6	357 52.5	13.2	12 26.8	8.1	54.9
Y 14	33 51.2	53.4	12 24.7	13.2	12 34.9	8.0	54.9
15	48 51.3	. . 54.3	26 56.9	13.1	12 42.9	8.0	54.9
16	63 51.4	55.2	41 29.0	13.2	12 50.9	8.0	54.9
17	78 51.5	56.1	56 01.2	13.2	12 58.9	7.8	54.9
18	93 51.6	S10 57.0	70 33.4	13.1	S13 06.7	7.8	54.9
19	108 51.7	57.9	85 05.5	13.2	13 14.5	7.7	54.8
20	123 51.8	58.8	99 37.7	13.1	13 22.2	7.7	54.8
21	138 51.9	10 59.6	114 09.8	13.1	13 29.9	7.6	54.8
22	153 52.0	11 00.5	128 41.9	13.1	13 37.5	7.6	54.8
23	168 52.1	S11 01.4	143 14.0	13.1	S13 45.1	7.4	54.8
	SD 16.1	*d* 0.9	SD 15.2		15.1		15.0

Lat.	Twilight Naut.	Twilight Civil	Sunrise	Moonrise 19	Moonrise 20	Moonrise 21	Moonrise 22
°	h m	h m	h m	h m	h m	h m	h m
N 72	05 17	06 36	07 50	06 16	08 01	09 48	11 41
N 70	05 19	06 30	07 35	06 10	07 48	09 26	11 04
68	05 20	06 24	07 23	06 06	07 38	09 09	10 38
66	05 20	06 20	07 13	06 02	07 29	08 55	10 19
64	05 21	06 16	07 05	05 59	07 22	08 44	10 03
62	05 21	06 12	06 58	05 56	07 16	08 34	09 50
60	05 21	06 09	06 52	05 54	07 11	08 26	09 39
N 58	05 21	06 06	06 47	05 52	07 06	08 19	09 29
56	05 21	06 04	06 42	05 50	07 02	08 12	09 21
54	05 20	06 01	06 38	05 48	06 58	08 07	09 13
52	05 20	05 59	06 34	05 46	06 55	08 02	09 07
50	05 20	05 57	06 30	05 45	06 52	07 57	09 01
45	05 18	05 52	06 22	05 42	06 45	07 47	08 48
N 40	05 17	05 48	06 16	05 39	06 40	07 39	08 37
35	05 15	05 45	06 10	05 37	06 35	07 32	08 28
30	05 13	05 41	06 05	05 35	06 31	07 26	08 20
20	05 08	05 34	05 57	05 32	06 24	07 16	08 07
N 10	05 03	05 27	05 49	05 29	06 18	07 06	07 55
0	04 56	05 20	05 41	05 27	06 12	06 58	07 44
S 10	04 48	05 13	05 34	05 24	06 06	06 49	07 33
20	04 37	05 03	05 26	05 21	06 00	06 40	07 21
30	04 23	04 52	05 17	05 18	05 54	06 30	07 08
35	04 14	04 45	05 11	05 16	05 50	06 24	07 00
40	04 03	04 37	05 05	05 14	05 45	06 17	06 51
45	03 50	04 27	04 58	05 12	05 40	06 10	06 41
S 50	03 32	04 15	04 49	05 09	05 34	06 00	06 29
52	03 24	04 09	04 45	05 08	05 31	05 56	06 23
54	03 14	04 02	04 40	05 07	05 28	05 51	06 17
56	03 03	03 55	04 35	05 05	05 25	05 46	06 10
58	02 50	03 46	04 30	05 03	05 21	05 40	06 02
S 60	02 34	03 37	04 24	05 02	05 17	05 34	05 54

Lat.	Sunset	Twilight Civil	Twilight Naut.	Moonset 19	Moonset 20	Moonset 21	Moonset 22
°	h m	h m	h m	h m	h m	h m	h m
N 72	15 38	16 51	18 10	16 35	16 26	16 14	15 56
N 70	15 53	16 58	18 09	16 43	16 40	16 37	16 35
68	16 05	17 04	18 08	16 50	16 52	16 55	17 01
66	16 15	17 08	18 08	16 55	17 02	17 10	17 22
64	16 23	17 12	18 07	17 00	17 10	17 22	17 38
62	16 30	17 16	18 07	17 04	17 17	17 33	17 52
60	16 36	17 19	18 07	17 07	17 23	17 41	18 03
N 58	16 42	17 22	18 08	17 10	17 29	17 49	18 13
56	16 47	17 25	18 08	17 13	17 34	17 56	18 22
54	16 51	17 27	18 08	17 16	17 38	18 02	18 30
52	16 55	17 29	18 09	17 18	17 42	18 08	18 37
50	16 59	17 32	18 09	17 20	17 46	18 13	18 43
45	17 07	17 36	18 10	17 25	17 53	18 24	18 57
N 40	17 13	17 41	18 12	17 28	18 00	18 33	19 08
35	17 19	17 44	18 14	17 32	18 06	18 41	19 18
30	17 24	17 48	18 16	17 35	18 11	18 48	19 27
20	17 33	17 55	18 21	17 40	18 19	19 00	19 41
N 10	17 41	18 02	18 27	17 44	18 27	19 10	19 54
0	17 48	18 09	18 34	17 48	18 34	19 20	20 06
S 10	17 56	18 17	18 42	17 53	18 41	19 30	20 18
20	18 04	18 26	18 53	17 57	18 49	19 40	20 31
30	18 13	18 38	19 07	18 02	18 58	19 52	20 46
35	18 19	18 45	19 16	18 05	19 03	19 59	20 55
40	18 25	18 54	19 27	18 09	19 09	20 07	21 04
45	18 33	19 04	19 41	18 13	19 15	20 17	21 16
S 50	18 42	19 16	19 59	18 17	19 23	20 28	21 30
52	18 46	19 22	20 08	18 19	19 27	20 33	21 36
54	18 50	19 29	20 17	18 22	19 31	20 39	21 44
56	18 56	19 36	20 29	18 24	19 36	20 45	21 52
58	19 01	19 45	20 42	18 27	19 41	20 53	22 01
S 60	19 08	19 55	20 59	18 30	19 47	21 01	22 12

Day	SUN Eqn. of Time 00^h	SUN Eqn. of Time 12^h	SUN Mer. Pass.	MOON Mer. Pass. Upper	MOON Mer. Pass. Lower	MOON Age	MOON Phase
d	m s	m s	h m	h m	h m	d %	
19	14 58	15 04	11 45	11 38	24 00	29 0	●
20	15 09	15 14	11 45	12 23	00 00	01 1	
21	15 19	15 24	11 45	13 09	00 46	02 3	

UT	ARIES	VENUS −3·9		MARS +1·8		JUPITER −1·7		SATURN +0·5	
	GHA	GHA	Dec	GHA	Dec	GHA	Dec	GHA	Dec
d h	° ′	° ′	° ′	° ′	° ′	° ′	° ′	° ′	° ′
22 00	30 36.9	201 21.4	S 2 18.7	210 36.2	N 1 15.1	179 58.2	S11 22.5	127 23.9	S22 16.4
01	45 39.4	216 21.0	20.0	225 37.2	14.5	195 00.1	22.7	142 26.1	16.5
02	60 41.8	231 20.6	21.2	240 38.2	13.9	210 02.1	22.9	157 28.4	16.5
03	75 44.3	246 20.2	22.4	255 39.2	13.2	225 04.0	23.1	172 30.6	16.5
04	90 46.8	261 19.8	23.6	270 40.2	12.6	240 06.0	23.3	187 32.9	16.5
05	105 49.2	276 19.4	24.9	285 41.2	12.0	255 07.9	23.5	202 35.1	16.5
06	120 51.7	291 19.0	S 2 26.1	300 42.3	N 1 11.3	270 09.9	S11 23.7	217 37.3	S22 16.5
07	135 54.2	306 18.6	27.3	315 43.3	10.7	285 11.8	23.8	232 39.6	16.6
08	150 56.6	321 18.2	28.5	330 44.3	10.1	300 13.7	24.0	247 41.8	16.6
S 09	165 59.1	336 17.8	29.7	345 45.3	09.4	315 15.7	24.2	262 44.1	16.6
U 10	181 01.5	351 17.4	31.0	0 46.3	08.8	330 17.6	24.4	277 46.3	16.6
N 11	196 04.0	6 17.0	32.2	15 47.3	08.2	345 19.6	24.6	292 48.5	16.6
D 12	211 06.5	21 16.6	S 2 33.4	30 48.3	N 1 07.5	0 21.5	S11 24.8	307 50.8	S22 16.6
A 13	226 08.9	36 16.2	34.6	45 49.4	06.9	15 23.5	25.0	322 53.0	16.7
Y 14	241 11.4	51 15.8	35.8	60 50.4	06.3	30 25.4	25.2	337 55.2	16.7
15	256 13.9	66 15.4	37.1	75 51.4	05.7	45 27.3	25.3	352 57.5	16.7
16	271 16.3	81 15.0	38.3	90 52.4	05.0	60 29.3	25.5	7 59.7	16.7
17	286 18.8	96 14.6	39.5	105 53.4	04.4	75 31.2	25.7	23 02.0	16.7
18	301 21.3	111 14.2	S 2 40.7	120 54.4	N 1 03.8	90 33.2	S11 25.9	38 04.2	S22 16.7
19	316 23.7	126 13.8	41.9	135 55.5	03.1	105 35.1	26.1	53 06.4	16.7
20	331 26.2	141 13.4	43.2	150 56.5	02.5	120 37.0	26.3	68 08.7	16.8
21	346 28.7	156 13.0	44.4	165 57.5	01.9	135 39.0	26.5	83 10.9	16.8
22	1 31.1	171 12.6	45.6	180 58.5	01.2	150 40.9	26.7	98 13.1	16.8
23	16 33.6	186 12.2	46.8	195 59.5	00.6	165 42.9	26.8	113 15.4	16.8
23 00	31 36.0	201 11.8	S 2 48.0	211 00.5	N 1 00.0	180 44.8	S11 27.0	128 17.6	S22 16.8
01	46 38.5	216 11.4	49.3	226 01.6	0 59.3	195 46.8	27.2	143 19.9	16.8
02	61 41.0	231 11.0	50.5	241 02.6	58.7	210 48.7	27.4	158 22.1	16.9
03	76 43.4	246 10.6	51.7	256 03.6	58.1	225 50.6	27.6	173 24.3	16.9
04	91 45.9	261 10.2	52.9	271 04.6	57.4	240 52.6	27.8	188 26.6	16.9
05	106 48.4	276 09.8	54.1	286 05.6	56.8	255 54.5	28.0	203 28.8	16.9
06	121 50.8	291 09.4	S 2 55.4	301 06.6	N 0 56.2	270 56.5	S11 28.2	218 31.0	S22 16.9
07	136 53.3	306 09.0	56.6	316 07.7	55.6	285 58.4	28.3	233 33.3	16.9
08	151 55.8	321 08.6	57.8	331 08.7	54.9	301 00.3	28.5	248 35.5	17.0
M 09	166 58.2	336 08.2	2 59.0	346 09.7	54.3	316 02.3	28.7	263 37.7	17.0
O 10	182 00.7	351 07.8	3 00.2	1 10.7	53.7	331 04.2	28.9	278 40.0	17.0
N 11	197 03.1	6 07.4	01.4	16 11.7	53.0	346 06.2	29.1	293 42.2	17.0
D 12	212 05.6	21 07.0	S 3 02.7	31 12.7	N 0 52.4	1 08.1	S11 29.3	308 44.4	S22 17.0
A 13	227 08.1	36 06.5	03.9	46 13.8	51.8	16 10.1	29.5	323 46.7	17.0
Y 14	242 10.5	51 06.1	05.1	61 14.8	51.1	31 12.0	29.7	338 48.9	17.0
15	257 13.0	66 05.7	06.3	76 15.8	50.5	46 13.9	29.8	353 51.2	17.1
16	272 15.5	81 05.3	07.5	91 16.8	49.9	61 15.9	30.0	8 53.4	17.1
17	287 17.9	96 04.9	08.8	106 17.8	49.2	76 17.8	30.2	23 55.6	17.1
18	302 20.4	111 04.5	S 3 10.0	121 18.8	N 0 48.6	91 19.8	S11 30.4	38 57.9	S22 17.1
19	317 22.9	126 04.1	11.2	136 19.9	48.0	106 21.7	30.6	54 00.1	17.1
20	332 25.3	141 03.7	12.4	151 20.9	47.3	121 23.6	30.8	69 02.3	17.1
21	347 27.8	156 03.3	13.6	166 21.9	46.7	136 25.6	31.0	84 04.6	17.2
22	2 30.3	171 02.9	14.9	181 22.9	46.1	151 27.5	31.2	99 06.8	17.2
23	17 32.7	186 02.5	16.1	196 23.9	45.4	166 29.5	31.3	114 09.0	17.2
24 00	32 35.2	201 02.1	S 3 17.3	211 24.9	N 0 44.8	181 31.4	S11 31.5	129 11.3	S22 17.2
01	47 37.6	216 01.7	18.5	226 26.0	44.2	196 33.4	31.7	144 13.5	17.2
02	62 40.1	231 01.3	19.7	241 27.0	43.6	211 35.3	31.9	159 15.7	17.2
03	77 42.6	246 00.9	20.9	256 28.0	42.9	226 37.2	32.1	174 18.0	17.2
04	92 45.0	261 00.5	22.2	271 29.0	42.3	241 39.2	32.3	189 20.2	17.3
05	107 47.5	276 00.1	23.4	286 30.0	41.7	256 41.1	32.5	204 22.4	17.3
06	122 50.0	290 59.6	S 3 24.6	301 31.0	N 0 41.0	271 43.1	S11 32.7	219 24.7	S22 17.3
07	137 52.4	305 59.2	25.8	316 32.1	40.4	286 45.0	32.8	234 26.9	17.3
T 08	152 54.9	320 58.8	27.0	331 33.1	39.8	301 46.9	33.0	249 29.1	17.3
U 09	167 57.4	335 58.4	28.3	346 34.1	39.1	316 48.9	33.2	264 31.4	17.3
E 10	182 59.8	350 58.0	29.5	1 35.1	38.5	331 50.8	33.4	279 33.6	17.4
S 11	198 02.3	5 57.6	30.7	16 36.1	37.9	346 52.8	33.6	294 35.8	17.4
D 12	213 04.8	20 57.2	S 3 31.9	31 37.1	N 0 37.2	1 54.7	S11 33.8	309 38.1	S22 17.4
A 13	228 07.2	35 56.8	33.1	46 38.2	36.6	16 56.6	34.0	324 40.3	17.4
Y 14	243 09.7	50 56.4	34.3	61 39.2	36.0	31 58.6	34.2	339 42.5	17.4
15	258 12.1	65 56.0	35.6	76 40.2	35.3	47 00.5	34.3	354 44.7	17.4
16	273 14.6	80 55.6	36.8	91 41.2	34.7	62 02.5	34.5	9 47.0	17.5
17	288 17.1	95 55.2	38.0	106 42.2	34.1	77 04.4	34.7	24 49.2	17.5
18	303 19.5	110 54.7	S 3 39.2	121 43.2	N 0 33.5	92 06.4	S11 34.9	39 51.4	S22 17.5
19	318 22.0	125 54.3	40.4	136 44.3	32.8	107 08.3	35.1	54 53.7	17.5
20	333 24.5	140 53.9	41.6	151 45.3	32.2	122 10.2	35.3	69 55.9	17.5
21	348 26.9	155 53.5	42.9	166 46.3	31.6	137 12.2	35.5	84 58.1	17.5
22	3 29.4	170 53.1	44.1	181 47.3	30.9	152 14.1	35.6	100 00.4	17.5
23	18 31.9	185 52.7	45.3	196 48.3	30.3	167 16.1	35.8	115 02.6	17.6
Mer. Pass.	h m 21 50.0	v −0.4	d 1.2	v 1.0	d 0.6	v 1.9	d 0.2	v 2.2	d 0.0

STARS

Name	SHA	Dec
	° ′	° ′
Acamar	315 15.7	S40 14.1
Achernar	335 24.1	S57 08.9
Acrux	173 06.5	S63 11.6
Adhara	255 10.1	S28 59.7
Aldebaran	290 45.8	N16 32.5
Alioth	166 18.7	N55 51.9
Alkaid	152 57.1	N49 13.7
Al Na'ir	27 39.9	S46 52.6
Alnilam	275 43.2	S 1 11.5
Alphard	217 53.3	S 8 44.0
Alphecca	126 08.9	N26 39.6
Alpheratz	357 40.1	N29 11.4
Altair	62 05.4	N 8 55.2
Ankaa	353 12.5	S42 12.7
Antares	112 23.0	S26 28.0
Arcturus	145 53.4	N19 05.7
Atria	107 22.5	S69 03.5
Avior	234 16.8	S59 33.7
Bellatrix	278 28.7	N 6 21.8
Betelgeuse	270 58.0	N 7 24.5
Canopus	263 54.6	S52 42.2
Capella	280 29.8	N46 00.6
Deneb	49 29.4	N45 21.0
Denebola	182 31.0	N14 28.5
Diphda	348 52.7	S17 53.4
Dubhe	193 48.7	N61 39.2
Elnath	278 08.7	N28 37.1
Eltanin	90 45.1	N51 29.6
Enif	33 44.1	N 9 57.6
Fomalhaut	15 20.6	S29 31.7
Gacrux	171 58.1	S57 12.5
Gienah	175 49.6	S17 38.2
Hadar	148 44.3	S60 27.3
Hamal	327 57.1	N23 32.7
Kaus Aust.	83 40.1	S34 22.4
Kochab	137 21.4	N74 05.2
Markab	13 35.2	N15 18.2
Menkar	314 11.7	N 4 09.5
Menkent	148 04.5	S36 27.2
Miaplacidus	221 39.2	S69 47.1
Mirfak	308 35.7	N49 55.2
Nunki	75 54.8	S26 16.3
Peacock	53 14.7	S56 40.7
Pollux	243 24.2	N27 58.8
Procyon	244 56.7	N 5 10.7
Rasalhague	96 04.0	N12 33.2
Regulus	207 40.6	N11 52.8
Rigel	281 09.0	S 8 10.9
Rigil Kent.	139 48.4	S60 54.3
Sabik	102 09.4	S15 44.5
Schedar	349 36.6	N56 38.2
Shaula	96 18.2	S37 06.8
Sirius	258 31.0	S16 44.4
Spica	158 28.5	S11 15.0
Suhail	222 50.4	S43 30.0
Vega	80 37.1	N38 48.4
Zuben'ubi	137 02.5	S16 06.7

	SHA	Mer. Pass.
	° ′	h m
Venus	169 35.8	10 35
Mars	179 24.5	9 55
Jupiter	149 08.8	11 55
Saturn	96 41.6	15 25

UT d	UT h	SUN GHA ° ′	SUN Dec ° ′	MOON GHA ° ′	v ′	MOON Dec ° ′	d ′	HP ′
22	00	183 52.2	S11 02.3	157 46.1	13.0	S13 52.5	7.4	54.8
	01	198 52.3	03.2	172 18.1	13.1	13 59.9	7.4	54.7
	02	213 52.4	04.1	186 50.2	13.1	14 07.3	7.2	54.7
	03	228 52.5	. . 04.9	201 22.3	13.0	14 14.5	7.2	54.7
	04	243 52.5	05.8	215 54.3	13.0	14 21.7	7.2	54.7
	05	258 52.6	06.7	230 26.3	13.0	14 28.9	7.0	54.7
	06	273 52.7	S11 07.6	244 58.3	13.0	S14 35.9	7.0	54.7
	07	288 52.8	08.5	259 30.3	13.0	14 42.9	6.9	54.7
	08	303 52.9	09.4	274 02.3	12.9	14 49.8	6.9	54.6
SUNDAY	09	318 53.0	. . 10.2	288 34.2	13.0	14 56.7	6.8	54.6
	10	333 53.1	11.1	303 06.2	12.9	15 03.5	6.7	54.6
	11	348 53.2	12.0	317 38.1	12.9	15 10.2	6.6	54.6
	12	3 53.3	S11 12.9	332 10.0	13.0	S15 16.8	6.6	54.6
	13	18 53.4	13.8	346 42.0	12.8	15 23.4	6.5	54.6
	14	33 53.5	14.6	1 13.8	12.9	15 29.9	6.4	54.6
	15	48 53.6	. . 15.5	15 45.7	12.9	15 36.3	6.3	54.5
	16	63 53.6	16.4	30 17.6	12.8	15 42.6	6.3	54.5
	17	78 53.7	17.3	44 49.4	12.9	15 48.9	6.2	54.5
	18	93 53.8	S11 18.2	59 21.3	12.8	S15 55.1	6.1	54.5
	19	108 53.9	19.0	73 53.1	12.8	16 01.2	6.1	54.5
	20	123 54.0	19.9	88 24.9	12.8	16 07.3	5.9	54.5
	21	138 54.1	. . 20.8	102 56.7	12.8	16 13.2	5.9	54.5
	22	153 54.2	21.7	117 28.5	12.7	16 19.1	5.8	54.5
	23	168 54.3	22.5	132 00.2	12.8	16 24.9	5.8	54.4
23	00	183 54.3	S11 23.4	146 32.0	12.7	S16 30.7	5.6	54.4
	01	198 54.4	24.3	161 03.7	12.7	16 36.3	5.6	54.4
	02	213 54.5	25.2	175 35.4	12.7	16 41.9	5.5	54.4
	03	228 54.6	. . 26.0	190 07.1	12.7	16 47.4	5.5	54.4
	04	243 54.7	26.9	204 38.8	12.7	16 52.9	5.3	54.4
	05	258 54.8	27.8	219 10.5	12.7	16 58.2	5.3	54.4
	06	273 54.9	S11 28.7	233 42.2	12.6	S17 03.5	5.2	54.4
	07	288 55.0	29.5	248 13.8	12.6	17 08.7	5.1	54.4
	08	303 55.0	30.4	262 45.4	12.7	17 13.8	5.0	54.3
MONDAY	09	318 55.1	. . 31.3	277 17.1	12.6	17 18.8	5.0	54.3
	10	333 55.2	32.2	291 48.7	12.6	17 23.8	4.8	54.3
	11	348 55.3	33.0	306 20.3	12.5	17 28.6	4.8	54.3
	12	3 55.4	S11 33.9	320 51.8	12.6	S17 33.4	4.7	54.3
	13	18 55.5	34.8	335 23.4	12.6	17 38.1	4.6	54.3
	14	33 55.5	35.7	349 55.0	12.5	17 42.7	4.6	54.3
	15	48 55.6	. . 36.5	4 26.5	12.5	17 47.3	4.4	54.3
	16	63 55.7	37.4	18 58.0	12.5	17 51.7	4.4	54.3
	17	78 55.8	38.3	33 29.5	12.5	17 56.1	4.3	54.3
	18	93 55.9	S11 39.1	48 01.0	12.5	S18 00.4	4.2	54.3
	19	108 56.0	40.0	62 32.5	12.5	18 04.6	4.1	54.2
	20	123 56.0	40.9	77 04.0	12.4	18 08.7	4.1	54.2
	21	138 56.1	. . 41.8	91 35.4	12.5	18 12.8	3.9	54.2
	22	153 56.2	42.6	106 06.9	12.4	18 16.7	3.9	54.2
	23	168 56.3	43.5	120 38.3	12.4	18 20.6	3.8	54.2
24	00	183 56.4	S11 44.4	135 09.7	12.5	S18 24.4	3.7	54.2
	01	198 56.4	45.2	149 41.2	12.3	18 28.1	3.6	54.2
	02	213 56.5	46.1	164 12.5	12.4	18 31.7	3.6	54.2
	03	228 56.6	. . 47.0	178 43.9	12.4	18 35.3	3.4	54.2
	04	243 56.7	47.8	193 15.3	12.4	18 38.7	3.4	54.2
	05	258 56.8	48.7	207 46.7	12.3	18 42.1	3.2	54.2
	06	273 56.8	S11 49.6	222 18.0	12.4	S18 45.3	3.2	54.2
	07	288 56.9	50.4	236 49.4	12.3	18 48.5	3.1	54.2
TUESDAY	08	303 57.0	51.3	251 20.7	12.3	18 51.6	3.0	54.2
	09	318 57.1	. . 52.2	265 52.0	12.3	18 54.6	3.0	54.2
	10	333 57.1	53.0	280 23.3	12.3	18 57.6	2.8	54.2
	11	348 57.2	53.9	294 54.6	12.3	19 00.4	2.8	54.2
	12	3 57.3	S11 54.8	309 25.9	12.3	S19 03.2	2.6	54.1
	13	18 57.4	55.6	323 57.2	12.3	19 05.8	2.6	54.1
	14	33 57.4	56.5	338 28.5	12.2	19 08.4	2.5	54.1
	15	48 57.5	. . 57.4	352 59.7	12.3	19 10.9	2.4	54.1
	16	63 57.6	58.2	7 31.0	12.2	19 13.3	2.3	54.1
	17	78 57.7	11 59.1	22 02.2	12.2	19 15.6	2.2	54.1
	18	93 57.7	S12 00.0	36 33.4	12.3	S19 17.8	2.2	54.1
	19	108 57.8	00.8	51 04.7	12.2	19 20.0	2.0	54.1
	20	123 57.9	01.7	65 35.9	12.2	19 22.0	2.0	54.1
	21	138 58.0	. . 02.6	80 07.1	12.2	19 24.0	1.9	54.1
	22	153 58.0	03.4	94 38.3	12.2	19 25.9	1.7	54.1
	23	168 58.1	04.3	109 09.5	12.1	S19 27.6	1.7	54.1
		SD 16.1	*d* 0.9	SD 14.9		14.8		14.8

Lat. °	Twilight Naut. h m	Twilight Civil h m	Sunrise h m	Moonrise 22 h m	Moonrise 23 h m	Moonrise 24 h m	Moonrise 25 h m
N 72	05 30	06 49	08 06	11 41	14 06	▬	▬
N 70	05 30	06 41	07 49	11 04	12 43	14 21	15 44
68	05 30	06 35	07 35	10 38	12 05	13 23	14 26
66	05 29	06 29	07 24	10 19	11 38	12 49	13 48
64	05 29	06 24	07 14	10 03	11 17	12 25	13 22
62	05 28	06 20	07 06	09 50	11 01	12 06	13 01
60	05 28	06 16	07 00	09 39	10 47	11 50	12 44
N 58	05 27	06 13	06 54	09 29	10 35	11 36	12 30
56	05 26	06 10	06 48	09 21	10 25	11 25	12 18
54	05 26	06 07	06 43	09 13	10 16	11 15	12 08
52	05 25	06 04	06 39	09 07	10 08	11 06	11 58
50	05 24	06 02	06 35	09 01	10 01	10 58	11 50
45	05 22	05 56	06 26	08 48	09 46	10 41	11 32
N 40	05 20	05 51	06 19	08 37	09 33	10 27	11 17
35	05 17	05 47	06 13	08 28	09 23	10 15	11 05
30	05 15	05 43	06 07	08 20	09 13	10 05	10 54
20	05 09	05 35	05 58	08 07	08 57	09 47	10 36
N 10	05 03	05 28	05 49	07 55	08 43	09 32	10 20
0	04 55	05 20	05 41	07 44	08 30	09 17	10 05
S 10	04 46	05 11	05 33	07 33	08 17	09 03	09 50
20	04 35	05 01	05 24	07 21	08 04	08 48	09 34
30	04 19	04 49	05 13	07 08	07 48	08 30	09 16
35	04 10	04 41	05 07	07 00	07 39	08 20	09 05
40	03 58	04 32	05 01	06 51	07 28	08 09	08 53
45	03 44	04 22	04 53	06 41	07 16	07 55	08 39
S 50	03 25	04 08	04 43	06 29	07 01	07 39	08 21
52	03 16	04 02	04 38	06 23	06 55	07 31	08 13
54	03 05	03 55	04 34	06 17	06 47	07 22	08 04
56	02 53	03 47	04 28	06 10	06 39	07 12	07 53
58	02 39	03 38	04 22	06 02	06 29	07 01	07 42
S 60	02 21	03 27	04 15	05 54	06 18	06 49	07 28

Lat. °	Sunset h m	Twilight Civil h m	Twilight Naut. h m	Moonset 22 h m	Moonset 23 h m	Moonset 24 h m	Moonset 25 h m
N 72	15 21	16 37	17 56	15 56	15 09	▬	▬
N 70	15 39	16 46	17 57	16 35	16 32	16 33	16 49
68	15 52	16 52	17 57	17 01	17 11	17 31	18 07
66	16 04	16 58	17 58	17 22	17 39	18 05	18 45
64	16 13	17 03	17 58	17 38	18 00	18 30	19 11
62	16 21	17 07	17 59	17 52	18 16	18 49	19 32
60	16 28	17 11	18 00	18 03	18 31	19 05	19 49
N 58	16 34	17 15	18 00	18 13	18 43	19 19	20 03
56	16 40	17 18	18 01	18 22	18 53	19 30	20 15
54	16 44	17 21	18 02	18 30	19 02	19 41	20 26
52	16 49	17 24	18 03	18 37	19 11	19 50	20 35
50	16 53	17 26	18 04	18 43	19 18	19 58	20 43
45	17 02	17 32	18 06	18 57	19 34	20 15	21 01
N 40	17 09	17 37	18 08	19 08	19 47	20 29	21 16
35	17 15	17 41	18 11	19 18	19 58	20 41	21 28
30	17 21	17 45	18 13	19 27	20 08	20 52	21 39
20	17 31	17 53	18 19	19 41	20 25	21 10	21 57
N 10	17 39	18 01	18 26	19 54	20 39	21 26	22 13
0	17 48	18 09	18 33	20 06	20 53	21 40	22 28
S 10	17 56	18 18	18 43	20 18	21 07	21 55	22 43
20	18 05	18 28	18 54	20 31	21 21	22 11	22 59
30	18 16	18 40	19 10	20 46	21 38	22 29	23 17
35	18 22	18 48	19 20	20 55	21 48	22 39	23 28
40	18 29	18 57	19 31	21 04	21 59	22 52	23 40
45	18 37	19 08	19 46	21 16	22 13	23 06	23 55
S 50	18 47	19 22	20 05	21 30	22 29	23 23	24 12
52	18 51	19 28	20 14	21 36	22 36	23 31	24 21
54	18 56	19 35	20 25	21 44	22 45	23 40	24 30
56	19 02	19 44	20 38	21 52	22 54	23 51	24 40
58	19 08	19 53	20 52	22 01	23 05	24 02	00 02
S 60	19 15	20 04	21 11	22 12	23 17	24 16	00 16

Day	SUN Eqn. of Time 00^h	SUN Eqn. of Time 12^h	SUN Mer. Pass.	MOON Mer. Pass. Upper	MOON Mer. Pass. Lower	MOON Age	MOON Phase
d	m s	m s	h m	h m	h m	d %	
22	15 29	15 33	11 44	13 55	01 32	03 7	
23	15 37	15 41	11 44	14 42	02 18	04 13	◐
24	15 45	15 49	11 44	15 29	03 05	05 20	

UT d h	ARIES GHA ° ′	VENUS −3·9 GHA ° ′	VENUS Dec ° ′	MARS +1·8 GHA ° ′	MARS Dec ° ′	JUPITER −1·7 GHA ° ′	JUPITER Dec ° ′	SATURN +0·5 GHA ° ′	SATURN Dec ° ′
25 00 (WEDNESDAY)	33 34.3	200 52.3	S 3 46.5	211 49.4	N 0 29.7	182 18.0	S11 36.0	130 04.8	S22 17.6
01	48 36.8	215 51.9	47.7	226 50.4	29.0	197 19.9	36.2	145 07.1	17.6
02	63 39.2	230 51.5	48.9	241 51.4	28.4	212 21.9	36.4	160 09.3	17.6
03	78 41.7	245 51.1	. . 50.2	256 52.4	. . 27.8	227 23.8	. . 36.6	175 11.5	. . 17.6
04	93 44.2	260 50.6	51.4	271 53.4	27.1	242 25.8	36.8	190 13.8	17.6
05	108 46.6	275 50.2	52.6	286 54.4	26.5	257 27.7	37.0	205 16.0	17.7
06	123 49.1	290 49.8	S 3 53.8	301 55.5	N 0 25.9	272 29.6	S11 37.1	220 18.2	S22 17.7
07	138 51.6	305 49.4	55.0	316 56.5	25.2	287 31.6	37.3	235 20.4	17.7
08	153 54.0	320 49.0	56.2	331 57.5	24.6	302 33.5	37.5	250 22.7	17.7
09	168 56.5	335 48.6	. . 57.4	346 58.5	. . 24.0	317 35.5	. . 37.7	265 24.9	. . 17.7
10	183 59.0	350 48.2	58.7	1 59.5	23.4	332 37.4	37.9	280 27.1	17.7
11	199 01.4	5 47.8	3 59.9	17 00.5	22.7	347 39.3	38.1	295 29.4	17.8
12	214 03.9	20 47.4	S 4 01.1	32 01.6	N 0 22.1	2 41.3	S11 38.3	310 31.6	S22 17.8
13	229 06.4	35 46.9	02.3	47 02.6	21.5	17 43.2	38.4	325 33.8	17.8
14	244 08.8	50 46.5	03.5	62 03.6	20.8	32 45.2	38.6	340 36.0	17.8
15	259 11.3	65 46.1	. . 04.7	77 04.6	. . 20.2	47 47.1	. . 38.8	355 38.3	. . 17.8
16	274 13.7	80 45.7	05.9	92 05.6	19.6	62 49.0	39.0	10 40.5	17.8
17	289 16.2	95 45.3	07.2	107 06.6	18.9	77 51.0	39.2	25 42.7	17.8
18	304 18.7	110 44.9	S 4 08.4	122 07.7	N 0 18.3	92 52.9	S11 39.4	40 45.0	S22 17.9
19	319 21.1	125 44.5	09.6	137 08.7	17.7	107 54.9	39.6	55 47.2	17.9
20	334 23.6	140 44.1	10.8	152 09.7	17.0	122 56.8	39.8	70 49.4	17.9
21	349 26.1	155 43.6	. . 12.0	167 10.7	. . 16.4	137 58.8	. . 39.9	85 51.6	. . 17.9
22	4 28.5	170 43.2	13.2	182 11.7	15.8	153 00.7	40.1	100 53.9	17.9
23	19 31.0	185 42.8	14.4	197 12.7	15.1	168 02.6	40.3	115 56.1	17.9
26 00 (THURSDAY)	34 33.5	200 42.4	S 4 15.7	212 13.8	N 0 14.5	183 04.6	S11 40.5	130 58.3	S22 18.0
01	49 35.9	215 42.0	16.9	227 14.8	13.9	198 06.5	40.7	146 00.6	18.0
02	64 38.4	230 41.6	18.1	242 15.8	13.3	213 08.5	40.9	161 02.8	18.0
03	79 40.9	245 41.2	. . 19.3	257 16.8	. . 12.6	228 10.4	. . 41.1	176 05.0	. . 18.0
04	94 43.3	260 40.7	20.5	272 17.8	12.0	243 12.3	41.2	191 07.2	18.0
05	109 45.8	275 40.3	21.7	287 18.8	11.4	258 14.3	41.4	206 09.5	18.0
06	124 48.2	290 39.9	S 4 22.9	302 19.9	N 0 10.7	273 16.2	S11 41.6	221 11.7	S22 18.0
07	139 50.7	305 39.5	24.2	317 20.9	10.1	288 18.2	41.8	236 13.9	18.1
08	154 53.2	320 39.1	25.4	332 21.9	09.5	303 20.1	42.0	251 16.2	18.1
09	169 55.6	335 38.7	. . 26.6	347 22.9	. . 08.8	318 22.0	. . 42.2	266 18.4	. . 18.1
10	184 58.1	350 38.2	27.8	2 23.9	08.2	333 24.0	42.4	281 20.6	18.1
11	200 00.6	5 37.8	29.0	17 25.0	07.6	348 25.9	42.5	296 22.8	18.1
12	215 03.0	20 37.4	S 4 30.2	32 26.0	N 0 06.9	3 27.9	S11 42.7	311 25.1	S22 18.1
13	230 05.5	35 37.0	31.4	47 27.0	06.3	18 29.8	42.9	326 27.3	18.2
14	245 08.0	50 36.6	32.6	62 28.0	05.7	33 31.7	43.1	341 29.5	18.2
15	260 10.4	65 36.2	. . 33.9	77 29.0	. . 05.0	48 33.7	. . 43.3	356 31.7	. . 18.2
16	275 12.9	80 35.7	35.1	92 30.0	04.4	63 35.6	43.5	11 34.0	18.2
17	290 15.4	95 35.3	36.3	107 31.1	03.8	78 37.6	43.7	26 36.2	18.2
18	305 17.8	110 34.9	S 4 37.5	122 32.1	N 0 03.2	93 39.5	S11 43.8	41 38.4	S22 18.2
19	320 20.3	125 34.5	38.7	137 33.1	02.5	108 41.4	44.0	56 40.6	18.2
20	335 22.7	140 34.1	39.9	152 34.1	01.9	123 43.4	44.2	71 42.9	18.3
21	350 25.2	155 33.7	. . 41.1	167 35.1	. . 01.3	138 45.3	. . 44.4	86 45.1	. . 18.3
22	5 27.7	170 33.2	42.3	182 36.1	N 00.6	153 47.3	44.6	101 47.3	18.3
23	20 30.1	185 32.8	43.5	197 37.2	00.0	168 49.2	44.8	116 49.5	18.3
27 00 (FRIDAY)	35 32.6	200 32.4	S 4 44.8	212 38.2	S 0 00.6	183 51.1	S11 45.0	131 51.8	S22 18.3
01	50 35.1	215 32.0	46.0	227 39.2	01.3	198 53.1	45.2	146 54.0	18.3
02	65 37.5	230 31.6	47.2	242 40.2	01.9	213 55.0	45.3	161 56.2	18.4
03	80 40.0	245 31.2	. . 48.4	257 41.2	. . 02.5	228 57.0	. . 45.5	176 58.4	. . 18.4
04	95 42.5	260 30.7	49.6	272 42.2	03.2	243 58.9	45.7	192 00.7	18.4
05	110 44.9	275 30.3	50.8	287 43.3	03.8	259 00.8	45.9	207 02.9	18.4
06	125 47.4	290 29.9	S 4 52.0	302 44.3	S 0 04.4	274 02.8	S11 46.1	222 05.1	S22 18.4
07	140 49.8	305 29.5	53.2	317 45.3	05.0	289 04.7	46.3	237 07.3	18.4
08	155 52.3	320 29.1	54.4	332 46.3	05.7	304 06.7	46.5	252 09.6	18.4
09	170 54.8	335 28.6	. . 55.6	347 47.3	. . 06.3	319 08.6	. . 46.6	267 11.8	. . 18.5
10	185 57.2	350 28.2	56.8	2 48.4	06.9	334 10.5	46.8	282 14.0	18.5
11	200 59.7	5 27.8	58.1	17 49.4	07.6	349 12.5	47.0	297 16.2	18.5
12	216 02.2	20 27.4	S 4 59.3	32 50.4	S 0 08.2	4 14.4	S11 47.2	312 18.5	S22 18.5
13	231 04.6	35 26.9	5 00.5	47 51.4	08.8	19 16.4	47.4	327 20.7	18.5
14	246 07.1	50 26.5	01.7	62 52.4	09.5	34 18.3	47.6	342 22.9	18.5
15	261 09.6	65 26.1	. . 02.9	77 53.4	. . 10.1	49 20.2	. . 47.8	357 25.1	. . 18.6
16	276 12.0	80 25.7	04.1	92 54.5	10.7	64 22.2	47.9	12 27.4	18.6
17	291 14.5	95 25.3	05.3	107 55.5	11.4	79 24.1	48.1	27 29.6	18.6
18	306 17.0	110 24.8	S 5 06.5	122 56.5	S 0 12.0	94 26.1	S11 48.3	42 31.8	S22 18.6
19	321 19.4	125 24.4	07.7	137 57.5	12.6	109 28.0	48.5	57 34.0	18.6
20	336 21.9	140 24.0	08.9	152 58.5	13.2	124 29.9	48.7	72 36.2	18.6
21	351 24.3	155 23.6	. . 10.1	167 59.5	. . 13.9	139 31.9	. . 48.9	87 38.5	. . 18.6
22	6 26.8	170 23.1	11.3	183 00.6	14.5	154 33.8	49.1	102 40.7	18.7
23	21 29.3	185 22.7	12.6	198 01.6	15.1	169 35.8	49.2	117 42.9	18.7
Mer. Pass. (h m)	21 38.2	*v* −0.4	*d* 1.2	*v* 1.0	*d* 0.6	*v* 1.9	*d* 0.2	*v* 2.2	*d* 0.0

STARS

Name	SHA ° ′	Dec ° ′
Acamar	315 15.7	S40 14.1
Achernar	335 24.1	S57 08.9
Acrux	173 06.5	S63 11.6
Adhara	255 10.1	S28 59.7
Aldebaran	290 45.7	N16 32.5
Alioth	166 18.7	N55 51.9
Alkaid	152 57.1	N49 13.6
Al Na'ir	27 39.9	S46 52.6
Alnilam	275 43.2	S 1 11.5
Alphard	217 53.3	S 8 44.0
Alphecca	126 08.9	N26 39.6
Alpheratz	357 40.1	N29 11.4
Altair	62 05.4	N 8 55.2
Ankaa	353 12.5	S42 12.7
Antares	112 23.0	S26 28.0
Arcturus	145 53.4	N19 05.7
Atria	107 22.5	S69 03.5
Avior	234 16.8	S59 33.7
Bellatrix	278 28.7	N 6 21.8
Betelgeuse	270 57.9	N 7 24.5
Canopus	263 54.6	S52 42.2
Capella	280 29.8	N46 00.6
Deneb	49 29.4	N45 21.0
Denebola	182 31.0	N14 28.5
Diphda	348 52.7	S17 53.4
Dubhe	193 48.7	N61 39.2
Elnath	278 08.7	N28 37.1
Eltanin	90 45.1	N51 29.6
Enif	33 44.1	N 9 57.6
Fomalhaut	15 20.6	S29 31.7
Gacrux	171 58.1	S57 12.5
Gienah	175 49.6	S17 38.2
Hadar	148 44.3	S60 27.3
Hamal	327 57.1	N23 32.7
Kaus Aust.	83 40.1	S34 22.4
Kochab	137 21.4	N74 05.2
Markab	13 35.2	N15 18.2
Menkar	314 11.7	N 4 09.5
Menkent	148 04.5	S36 27.2
Miaplacidus	221 39.2	S69 47.1
Mirfak	308 35.6	N49 55.3
Nunki	75 54.8	S26 16.3
Peacock	53 14.7	S56 40.7
Pollux	243 24.1	N27 58.8
Procyon	244 56.6	N 5 10.7
Rasalhague	96 04.0	N12 33.2
Regulus	207 40.6	N11 52.8
Rigel	281 09.0	S 8 10.9
Rigil Kent.	139 48.4	S60 54.3
Sabik	102 09.4	S15 44.5
Schedar	349 36.6	N56 38.2
Shaula	96 18.2	S37 06.8
Sirius	258 31.0	S16 44.4
Spica	158 28.5	S11 15.0
Suhail	222 50.4	S43 30.0
Vega	80 37.2	N38 48.4
Zuben'ubi	137 02.5	S16 06.7

	SHA ° ′	Mer. Pass. h m
Venus	166 08.9	10 37
Mars	177 40.3	9 50
Jupiter	148 31.1	11 46
Saturn	96 24.9	15 14

Day	UT (d h)	SUN GHA (° ′)	SUN Dec (° ′)	MOON GHA (° ′)	v (′)	MOON Dec (° ′)	d (′)	HP (′)
	25 00	183 58.2	S12 05.1	123 40.6	12.2	S19 29.3	1.6	54.1
	01	198 58.3	06.0	138 11.8	12.2	19 30.9	1.5	54.1
	02	213 58.3	06.9	152 43.0	12.2	19 32.4	1.5	54.1
	03	228 58.4	. . 07.7	167 14.2	12.1	19 33.9	1.3	54.1
	04	243 58.5	08.6	181 45.3	12.2	19 35.2	1.2	54.1
	05	258 58.5	09.4	196 16.5	12.1	19 36.4	1.2	54.1
	06	273 58.6	S12 10.3	210 47.6	12.1	S19 37.6	1.1	54.1
WEDNESDAY	07	288 58.7	11.2	225 18.7	12.2	19 38.7	0.9	54.1
	08	303 58.8	12.0	239 49.9	12.1	19 39.6	0.9	54.1
	09	318 58.8	. . 12.9	254 21.0	12.1	19 40.5	0.8	54.1
	10	333 58.9	13.7	268 52.1	12.1	19 41.3	0.7	54.1
	11	348 59.0	14.6	283 23.2	12.1	19 42.0	0.6	54.1
	12	3 59.0	S12 15.5	297 54.3	12.1	S19 42.6	0.5	54.1
	13	18 59.1	16.3	312 25.4	12.1	19 43.1	0.5	54.1
	14	33 59.2	17.2	326 56.5	12.1	19 43.6	0.3	54.1
	15	48 59.2	. . 18.0	341 27.6	12.1	19 43.9	0.3	54.1
	16	63 59.3	18.9	355 58.7	12.1	19 44.2	0.1	54.1
	17	78 59.4	19.7	10 29.8	12.1	19 44.3	0.1	54.1
	18	93 59.4	S12 20.6	25 00.9	12.1	S19 44.4	0.0	54.2
	19	108 59.5	21.5	39 32.0	12.1	19 44.4	0.2	54.2
	20	123 59.6	22.3	54 03.1	12.1	19 44.2	0.2	54.2
	21	138 59.6	. . 23.2	68 34.2	12.0	19 44.0	0.3	54.2
	22	153 59.7	24.0	83 05.2	12.1	19 43.7	0.4	54.2
	23	168 59.8	24.9	97 36.3	12.1	19 43.3	0.4	54.2
	26 00	183 59.8	S12 25.7	112 07.4	12.1	S19 42.9	0.6	54.2
	01	198 59.9	26.6	126 38.5	12.0	19 42.3	0.7	54.2
	02	214 00.0	27.4	141 09.5	12.1	19 41.6	0.7	54.2
	03	229 00.0	. . 28.3	155 40.6	12.1	19 40.9	0.9	54.2
	04	244 00.1	29.1	170 11.7	12.0	19 40.0	0.9	54.2
	05	259 00.2	30.0	184 42.7	12.1	19 39.1	1.0	54.2
	06	274 00.2	S12 30.8	199 13.8	12.1	S19 38.1	1.1	54.2
	07	289 00.3	31.7	213 44.9	12.0	19 37.0	1.2	54.2
THURSDAY	08	304 00.4	32.6	228 15.9	12.1	19 35.8	1.3	54.2
	09	319 00.4	. . 33.4	242 47.0	12.1	19 34.5	1.4	54.3
	10	334 00.5	34.3	257 18.1	12.0	19 33.1	1.5	54.3
	11	349 00.5	35.1	271 49.1	12.1	19 31.6	1.6	54.3
	12	4 00.6	S12 36.0	286 20.2	12.1	S19 30.0	1.6	54.3
	13	19 00.7	36.8	300 51.3	12.0	19 28.4	1.8	54.3
	14	34 00.7	37.7	315 22.3	12.1	19 26.6	1.8	54.3
	15	49 00.8	. . 38.5	329 53.4	12.1	19 24.8	2.0	54.3
	16	64 00.8	39.4	344 24.5	12.1	19 22.8	2.0	54.3
	17	79 00.9	40.2	358 55.6	12.0	19 20.8	2.1	54.3
	18	94 01.0	S12 41.0	13 26.6	12.1	S19 18.7	2.2	54.3
	19	109 01.0	41.9	27 57.7	12.1	19 16.5	2.3	54.4
	20	124 01.1	42.7	42 28.8	12.1	19 14.2	2.4	54.4
	21	139 01.1	. . 43.6	56 59.9	12.1	19 11.8	2.4	54.4
	22	154 01.2	44.4	71 31.0	12.0	19 09.4	2.6	54.4
	23	169 01.3	45.3	86 02.0	12.1	19 06.8	2.6	54.4
	27 00	184 01.3	S12 46.1	100 33.1	12.1	S19 04.2	2.8	54.4
	01	199 01.4	47.0	115 04.2	12.1	19 01.4	2.8	54.4
	02	214 01.4	47.8	129 35.3	12.1	18 58.6	2.9	54.4
	03	229 01.5	. . 48.7	144 06.4	12.1	18 55.7	3.0	54.5
	04	244 01.6	49.5	158 37.5	12.1	18 52.7	3.1	54.5
	05	259 01.6	50.4	173 08.6	12.1	18 49.6	3.2	54.5
	06	274 01.7	S12 51.2	187 39.7	12.1	S18 46.4	3.3	54.5
	07	289 01.7	52.0	202 10.8	12.2	18 43.1	3.4	54.5
	08	304 01.8	52.9	216 42.0	12.1	18 39.7	3.4	54.5
FRIDAY	09	319 01.8	. . 53.7	231 13.1	12.1	18 36.3	3.6	54.5
	10	334 01.9	54.6	245 44.2	12.1	18 32.7	3.6	54.6
	11	349 01.9	55.4	260 15.3	12.2	18 29.1	3.7	54.6
	12	4 02.0	S12 56.3	274 46.5	12.1	S18 25.4	3.8	54.6
	13	19 02.0	57.1	289 17.6	12.1	18 21.6	3.9	54.6
	14	34 02.1	57.9	303 48.7	12.2	18 17.7	4.0	54.6
	15	49 02.2	. . 58.8	318 19.9	12.1	18 13.7	4.1	54.6
	16	64 02.2	12 59.6	332 51.0	12.2	18 09.6	4.1	54.7
	17	79 02.3	13 00.5	347 22.2	12.1	18 05.5	4.3	54.7
	18	94 02.3	S13 01.3	1 53.3	12.2	S18 01.2	4.3	54.7
	19	109 02.4	02.1	16 24.5	12.2	17 56.9	4.4	54.7
	20	124 02.4	03.0	30 55.7	12.1	17 52.5	4.5	54.7
	21	139 02.5	. . 03.8	45 26.8	12.2	17 48.0	4.6	54.8
	22	154 02.5	04.6	59 58.0	12.2	17 43.4	4.7	54.8
	23	169 02.6	05.5	74 29.2	12.2	S17 38.7	4.7	54.8
		SD 16.1	*d* 0.8	SD 14.7		14.8		14.9

Lat. (°)	Twilight Naut. (h m)	Twilight Civil (h m)	Sunrise (h m)	Moonrise 25 (h m)	Moonrise 26 (h m)	Moonrise 27 (h m)	Moonrise 28 (h m)
N 72	05 43	07 03	08 22	■	■	■	16 48
N 70	05 41	06 53	08 02	15 44	16 08	16 09	16 07
68	05 40	06 45	07 47	14 26	15 06	15 27	15 39
66	05 38	06 39	07 34	13 48	14 31	14 59	15 17
64	05 37	06 33	07 24	13 22	14 05	14 37	15 00
62	05 36	06 28	07 15	13 01	13 46	14 20	14 46
60	05 34	06 23	07 07	12 44	13 29	14 06	14 34
N 58	05 33	06 19	07 00	12 30	13 16	13 53	14 24
56	05 32	06 16	06 54	12 18	13 04	13 43	14 15
54	05 31	06 12	06 49	12 08	12 54	13 33	14 07
52	05 30	06 09	06 44	11 58	12 44	13 25	14 00
50	05 29	06 06	06 40	11 50	12 36	13 17	13 53
45	05 26	06 00	06 30	11 32	12 19	13 01	13 39
N 40	05 23	05 55	06 22	11 17	12 04	12 48	13 27
35	05 20	05 50	06 16	11 05	11 52	12 36	13 18
30	05 17	05 45	06 09	10 54	11 42	12 27	13 09
20	05 10	05 36	05 59	10 36	11 24	12 09	12 54
N 10	05 03	05 28	05 49	10 20	11 08	11 55	12 41
0	04 55	05 19	05 41	10 05	10 53	11 41	12 28
S 10	04 45	05 10	05 32	09 50	10 38	11 27	12 16
20	04 32	04 59	05 22	09 34	10 22	11 12	12 03
30	04 16	04 46	05 11	09 16	10 04	10 55	11 48
35	04 06	04 38	05 04	09 05	09 53	10 45	11 39
40	03 53	04 28	04 57	08 53	09 41	10 33	11 29
45	03 38	04 16	04 48	08 39	09 27	10 20	11 17
S 50	03 18	04 02	04 37	08 21	09 10	10 04	11 03
52	03 08	03 55	04 32	08 13	09 01	09 56	10 56
54	02 57	03 47	04 27	08 04	08 52	09 47	10 48
56	02 44	03 39	04 21	07 53	08 42	09 38	10 40
58	02 28	03 29	04 14	07 42	08 30	09 27	10 31
S 60	02 08	03 17	04 06	07 28	08 16	09 14	10 20

Lat. (°)	Sunset (h m)	Twilight Civil (h m)	Twilight Naut. (h m)	Moonset 25 (h m)	Moonset 26 (h m)	Moonset 27 (h m)	Moonset 28 (h m)
N 72	15 04	16 23	17 43	■	■	■	20 44
N 70	15 24	16 33	17 45	16 49	18 05	19 43	21 24
68	15 40	16 41	17 47	18 07	19 07	20 24	21 51
66	15 52	16 48	17 48	18 45	19 41	20 52	22 12
64	16 03	16 54	17 50	19 11	20 06	21 13	22 28
62	16 12	16 59	17 51	19 32	20 26	21 30	22 42
60	16 20	17 04	17 52	19 49	20 42	21 44	22 53
N 58	16 27	17 08	17 54	20 03	20 55	21 56	23 03
56	16 33	17 11	17 55	20 15	21 07	22 06	23 12
54	16 38	17 15	17 56	20 26	21 17	22 16	23 19
52	16 43	17 18	17 57	20 35	21 26	22 24	23 26
50	16 47	17 21	17 58	20 43	21 35	22 31	23 32
45	16 57	17 27	18 01	21 01	21 52	22 47	23 46
N 40	17 05	17 33	18 04	21 16	22 06	23 00	23 56
35	17 12	17 38	18 07	21 28	22 18	23 10	24 06
30	17 18	17 43	18 11	21 39	22 28	23 20	24 14
20	17 29	17 51	18 17	21 57	22 46	23 36	24 28
N 10	17 38	18 00	18 25	22 13	23 01	23 50	24 40
0	17 47	18 09	18 33	22 28	23 16	24 04	00 04
S 10	17 57	18 18	18 43	22 43	23 30	24 17	00 17
20	18 06	18 29	18 56	22 59	23 46	24 31	00 31
30	18 18	18 43	19 12	23 17	24 03	00 03	00 47
35	18 24	18 51	19 23	23 28	24 14	00 14	00 56
40	18 32	19 01	19 35	23 40	24 25	00 25	01 07
45	18 41	19 13	19 51	23 55	24 39	00 39	01 19
S 50	18 52	19 27	20 12	24 12	00 12	00 56	01 34
52	18 57	19 34	20 22	24 21	00 21	01 04	01 41
54	19 02	19 42	20 33	24 30	00 30	01 13	01 49
56	19 09	19 51	20 47	24 40	00 40	01 22	01 58
58	19 15	20 01	21 03	00 02	00 52	01 34	02 07
S 60	19 23	20 13	21 23	00 16	01 06	01 47	02 19

	SUN			MOON				
Day	Eqn. of Time 00^h	Eqn. of Time 12^h	Mer. Pass.	Mer. Pass. Upper	Mer. Pass. Lower	Age		Phase
d	m s	m s	h m	h m	h m	d	%	
25	15 53	15 56	11 44	16 17	03 53	06	28	
26	15 59	16 02	11 44	17 04	04 41	07	37	
27	16 05	16 08	11 44	17 52	05 28	08	46	

	UT	ARIES	VENUS −3·9		MARS +1·8		JUPITER −1·7		SATURN +0·5	
	d h	GHA ° ′	GHA ° ′	Dec ° ′	GHA ° ′	Dec ° ′	GHA ° ′	Dec ° ′	GHA ° ′	Dec ° ′
	28 00	36 31.7	200 22.3	S 5 13.8	213 02.6	S 0 15.8	184 37.7	S11 49.4	132 45.1	S22 18.7
	01	51 34.2	215 21.9	15.0	228 03.6	16.4	199 39.6	49.6	147 47.4	18.7
	02	66 36.7	230 21.5	16.2	243 04.6	17.0	214 41.6	49.8	162 49.6	18.7
	03	81 39.1	245 21.0	. . 17.4	258 05.6	. . 17.7	229 43.5	. . 50.0	177 51.8	. . 18.7
	04	96 41.6	260 20.6	18.6	273 06.7	18.3	244 45.5	50.2	192 54.0	18.8
	05	111 44.1	275 20.2	19.8	288 07.7	18.9	259 47.4	50.4	207 56.2	18.8
	06	126 46.5	290 19.8	S 5 21.0	303 08.7	S 0 19.5	274 49.3	S11 50.5	222 58.5	S22 18.8
	07	141 49.0	305 19.3	22.2	318 09.7	20.2	289 51.3	50.7	238 00.7	18.8
S	08	156 51.5	320 18.9	23.4	333 10.7	20.8	304 53.2	50.9	253 02.9	18.8
A	09	171 53.9	335 18.5	. . 24.6	348 11.8	. . 21.4	319 55.2	. . 51.1	268 05.1	. . 18.8
T	10	186 56.4	350 18.1	25.8	3 12.8	22.1	334 57.1	51.3	283 07.4	18.9
U	11	201 58.8	5 17.6	27.0	18 13.8	22.7	349 59.0	51.5	298 09.6	18.9
R	12	217 01.3	20 17.2	S 5 28.2	33 14.8	S 0 23.3	5 01.0	S11 51.6	313 11.8	S22 18.9
D	13	232 03.8	35 16.8	29.4	48 15.8	24.0	20 02.9	51.8	328 14.0	18.9
A	14	247 06.2	50 16.4	30.6	63 16.8	24.6	35 04.9	52.0	343 16.2	18.9
Y	15	262 08.7	65 15.9	. . 31.8	78 17.9	. . 25.2	50 06.8	. . 52.2	358 18.5	. . 18.9
	16	277 11.2	80 15.5	33.0	93 18.9	25.9	65 08.7	52.4	13 20.7	18.9
	17	292 13.6	95 15.1	34.3	108 19.9	26.5	80 10.7	52.6	28 22.9	19.0
	18	307 16.1	110 14.6	S 5 35.5	123 20.9	S 0 27.1	95 12.6	S11 52.8	43 25.1	S22 19.0
	19	322 18.6	125 14.2	36.7	138 21.9	27.7	110 14.6	52.9	58 27.3	19.0
	20	337 21.0	140 13.8	37.9	153 22.9	28.4	125 16.5	53.1	73 29.6	19.0
	21	352 23.5	155 13.4	. . 39.1	168 24.0	. . 29.0	140 18.4	. . 53.3	88 31.8	. . 19.0
	22	7 25.9	170 12.9	40.3	183 25.0	29.6	155 20.4	53.5	103 34.0	19.0
	23	22 28.4	185 12.5	41.5	198 26.0	30.3	170 22.3	53.7	118 36.2	19.0
	29 00	37 30.9	200 12.1	S 5 42.7	213 27.0	S 0 30.9	185 24.3	S11 53.9	133 38.4	S22 19.1
	01	52 33.3	215 11.6	43.9	228 28.0	31.5	200 26.2	54.1	148 40.7	19.1
	02	67 35.8	230 11.2	45.1	243 29.0	32.2	215 28.1	54.2	163 42.9	19.1
	03	82 38.3	245 10.8	. . 46.3	258 30.1	. . 32.8	230 30.1	. . 54.4	178 45.1	. . 19.1
	04	97 40.7	260 10.4	47.5	273 31.1	33.4	245 32.0	54.6	193 47.3	19.1
	05	112 43.2	275 09.9	48.7	288 32.1	34.0	260 34.0	54.8	208 49.5	19.1
	06	127 45.7	290 09.5	S 5 49.9	303 33.1	S 0 34.7	275 35.9	S11 55.0	223 51.8	S22 19.2
	07	142 48.1	305 09.1	51.1	318 34.1	35.3	290 37.8	55.2	238 54.0	19.2
	08	157 50.6	320 08.6	52.3	333 35.2	35.9	305 39.8	55.3	253 56.2	19.2
S	09	172 53.1	335 08.2	. . 53.5	348 36.2	. . 36.6	320 41.7	. . 55.5	268 58.4	. . 19.2
U	10	187 55.5	350 07.8	54.7	3 37.2	37.2	335 43.6	55.7	284 00.6	19.2
N	11	202 58.0	5 07.3	55.9	18 38.2	37.8	350 45.6	55.9	299 02.8	19.2
D	12	218 00.4	20 06.9	S 5 57.1	33 39.2	S 0 38.5	5 47.5	S11 56.1	314 05.1	S22 19.2
A	13	233 02.9	35 06.5	58.3	48 40.2	39.1	20 49.5	56.3	329 07.3	19.3
Y	14	248 05.4	50 06.1	5 59.5	63 41.3	39.7	35 51.4	56.5	344 09.5	19.3
	15	263 07.8	65 05.6	6 00.7	78 42.3	. . 40.3	50 53.3	. . 56.6	359 11.7	. . 19.3
	16	278 10.3	80 05.2	01.9	93 43.3	41.0	65 55.3	56.8	14 13.9	19.3
	17	293 12.8	95 04.8	03.1	108 44.3	41.6	80 57.2	57.0	29 16.2	19.3
	18	308 15.2	110 04.3	S 6 04.3	123 45.3	S 0 42.2	95 59.2	S11 57.2	44 18.4	S22 19.3
	19	323 17.7	125 03.9	05.5	138 46.3	42.9	111 01.1	57.4	59 20.6	19.4
	20	338 20.2	140 03.5	06.7	153 47.4	43.5	126 03.0	57.6	74 22.8	19.4
	21	353 22.6	155 03.0	. . 07.9	168 48.4	. . 44.1	141 05.0	. . 57.7	89 25.0	. . 19.4
	22	8 25.1	170 02.6	09.1	183 49.4	44.8	156 06.9	57.9	104 27.2	19.4
	23	23 27.6	185 02.2	10.3	198 50.4	45.4	171 08.9	58.1	119 29.5	19.4
	30 00	38 30.0	200 01.7	S 6 11.5	213 51.4	S 0 46.0	186 10.8	S11 58.3	134 31.7	S22 19.4
	01	53 32.5	215 01.3	12.7	228 52.4	46.6	201 12.7	58.5	149 33.9	19.4
	02	68 34.9	230 00.9	13.9	243 53.5	47.3	216 14.7	58.7	164 36.1	19.5
	03	83 37.4	245 00.4	. . 15.1	258 54.5	. . 47.9	231 16.6	. . 58.9	179 38.3	. . 19.5
	04	98 39.9	260 00.0	16.3	273 55.5	48.5	246 18.6	59.0	194 40.5	19.5
	05	113 42.3	274 59.5	17.5	288 56.5	49.2	261 20.5	59.2	209 42.8	19.5
	06	128 44.8	289 59.1	S 6 18.7	303 57.5	S 0 49.8	276 22.4	S11 59.4	224 45.0	S22 19.5
	07	143 47.3	304 58.7	19.9	318 58.5	50.4	291 24.4	59.6	239 47.2	19.5
	08	158 49.7	319 58.2	21.1	333 59.6	51.1	306 26.3	11 59.8	254 49.4	19.6
M	09	173 52.2	334 57.8	. . 22.3	349 00.6	. . 51.7	321 28.3	12 00.0	269 51.6	. . 19.6
O	10	188 54.7	349 57.4	23.5	4 01.6	52.3	336 30.2	00.1	284 53.8	19.6
N	11	203 57.1	4 56.9	24.6	19 02.6	52.9	351 32.1	00.3	299 56.1	19.6
D	12	218 59.6	19 56.5	S 6 25.8	34 03.6	S 0 53.6	6 34.1	S12 00.5	314 58.3	S22 19.6
A	13	234 02.0	34 56.1	27.0	49 04.7	54.2	21 36.0	00.7	330 00.5	19.6
Y	14	249 04.5	49 55.6	28.2	64 05.7	54.8	36 37.9	00.9	345 02.7	19.6
	15	264 07.0	64 55.2	. . 29.4	79 06.7	. . 55.5	51 39.9	. . 01.1	0 04.9	. . 19.7
	16	279 09.4	79 54.7	30.6	94 07.7	56.1	66 41.8	01.2	15 07.1	19.7
	17	294 11.9	94 54.3	31.8	109 08.7	56.7	81 43.8	01.4	30 09.4	19.7
	18	309 14.4	109 53.9	S 6 33.0	124 09.7	S 0 57.3	96 45.7	S12 01.6	45 11.6	S22 19.7
	19	324 16.8	124 53.4	34.2	139 10.8	58.0	111 47.6	01.8	60 13.8	19.7
	20	339 19.3	139 53.0	35.4	154 11.8	58.6	126 49.6	02.0	75 16.0	19.7
	21	354 21.8	154 52.5	. . 36.6	169 12.8	. . 59.2	141 51.5	. . 02.2	90 18.2	. . 19.7
	22	9 24.2	169 52.1	37.8	184 13.8	0 59.9	156 53.5	02.4	105 20.4	19.8
	23	24 26.7	184 51.7	39.0	199 14.8	S 1 00.5	171 55.4	02.5	120 22.6	19.8
	Mer. Pass.	h m 21 26.4	v −0.4	d 1.2	v 1.0	d 0.6	v 1.9	d 0.2	v 2.2	d 0.0

STARS		
Name	SHA ° ′	Dec ° ′
Acamar	315 15.7	S40 14.1
Achernar	335 24.1	S57 08.9
Acrux	173 06.5	S63 11.6
Adhara	255 10.1	S28 59.7
Aldebaran	290 45.7	N16 32.5
Alioth	166 18.7	N55 51.9
Alkaid	152 57.1	N49 13.6
Al Na'ir	27 39.9	S46 52.6
Alnilam	275 43.2	S 1 11.5
Alphard	217 53.3	S 8 44.0
Alphecca	126 08.9	N26 39.6
Alpheratz	357 40.1	N29 11.4
Altair	62 05.5	N 8 55.2
Ankaa	353 12.5	S42 12.7
Antares	112 23.0	S26 28.0
Arcturus	145 53.4	N19 05.6
Atria	107 22.6	S69 03.5
Avior	234 16.7	S59 33.7
Bellatrix	278 28.6	N 6 21.8
Betelgeuse	270 57.9	N 7 24.5
Canopus	263 54.6	S52 42.2
Capella	280 29.8	N46 00.7
Deneb	49 29.4	N45 21.0
Denebola	182 31.0	N14 28.5
Diphda	348 52.7	S17 53.4
Dubhe	193 48.6	N61 39.1
Elnath	278 08.6	N28 37.1
Eltanin	90 45.1	N51 29.6
Enif	33 44.1	N 9 57.6
Fomalhaut	15 20.6	S29 31.7
Gacrux	171 58.1	S57 12.5
Gienah	175 49.6	S17 38.2
Hadar	148 44.3	S60 27.3
Hamal	327 57.1	N23 32.7
Kaus Aust.	83 40.2	S34 22.4
Kochab	137 21.4	N74 05.1
Markab	13 35.2	N15 18.2
Menkar	314 11.7	N 4 09.5
Menkent	148 04.5	S36 27.2
Miaplacidus	221 39.1	S69 47.1
Mirfak	308 35.6	N49 55.3
Nunki	75 54.9	S26 16.3
Peacock	53 14.7	S56 40.8
Pollux	243 24.1	N27 58.8
Procyon	244 56.6	N 5 10.7
Rasalhague	96 04.0	N12 33.2
Regulus	207 40.6	N11 52.8
Rigel	281 09.0	S 8 10.9
Rigil Kent.	139 48.4	S60 54.2
Sabik	102 09.4	S15 44.6
Schedar	349 36.6	N56 38.2
Shaula	96 18.2	S37 06.8
Sirius	258 31.0	S16 44.4
Spica	158 28.5	S11 15.0
Suhail	222 50.3	S43 30.0
Vega	80 37.2	N38 48.4
Zuben'ubi	137 02.5	S16 06.7

	SHA ° ′	Mer. Pass. h m
Venus	162 41.2	10 40
Mars	175 56.1	9 46
Jupiter	147 53.4	11 37
Saturn	96 07.6	15 03

UT		SUN GHA	SUN Dec	MOON GHA	v	MOON Dec	d	HP
d	h	° ′	° ′	° ′	′	° ′	′	′
28 SATURDAY	00	184 02.6	S13 06.3	89 00.4	12.2	S17 34.0	4.9	54.8
	01	199 02.7	07.2	103 31.6	12.1	17 29.1	4.9	54.8
	02	214 02.7	08.0	118 02.7	12.2	17 24.2	5.0	54.9
	03	229 02.8	. . 08.8	132 33.9	12.2	17 19.2	5.1	54.9
	04	244 02.8	09.7	147 05.1	12.3	17 14.1	5.2	54.9
	05	259 02.9	10.5	161 36.4	12.2	17 08.9	5.2	54.9
	06	274 02.9	S13 11.3	176 07.6	12.2	S17 03.7	5.4	54.9
	07	289 03.0	12.2	190 38.8	12.2	16 58.3	5.4	55.0
	08	304 03.0	13.0	205 10.0	12.2	16 52.9	5.6	55.0
	09	319 03.1	. . 13.8	219 41.2	12.2	16 47.3	5.6	55.0
	10	334 03.1	14.7	234 12.4	12.3	16 41.7	5.6	55.0
	11	349 03.2	15.5	248 43.7	12.2	16 36.1	5.8	55.1
	12	4 03.2	S13 16.3	263 14.9	12.3	S16 30.3	5.9	55.1
	13	19 03.2	17.2	277 46.2	12.2	16 24.4	5.9	55.1
	14	34 03.3	18.0	292 17.4	12.2	16 18.5	6.0	55.1
	15	49 03.3	. . 18.8	306 48.6	12.3	16 12.5	6.1	55.2
	16	64 03.4	19.7	321 19.9	12.2	16 06.4	6.2	55.2
	17	79 03.4	20.5	335 51.1	12.3	16 00.2	6.2	55.2
	18	94 03.5	S13 21.3	350 22.4	12.3	S15 54.0	6.4	55.2
	19	109 03.5	22.2	4 53.7	12.2	15 47.6	6.4	55.3
	20	124 03.6	23.0	19 24.9	12.3	15 41.2	6.5	55.3
	21	139 03.6	. . 23.8	33 56.2	12.3	15 34.7	6.6	55.3
	22	154 03.6	24.7	48 27.5	12.2	15 28.1	6.6	55.3
	23	169 03.7	25.5	62 58.7	12.3	15 21.5	6.8	55.4
29 SUNDAY	00	184 03.7	S13 26.3	77 30.0	12.3	S15 14.7	6.8	55.4
	01	199 03.8	27.1	92 01.3	12.3	15 07.9	6.9	55.4
	02	214 03.8	28.0	106 32.6	12.2	15 01.0	7.0	55.4
	03	229 03.9	. . 28.8	121 03.8	12.3	14 54.0	7.0	55.5
	04	244 03.9	29.6	135 35.1	12.3	14 47.0	7.1	55.5
	05	259 03.9	30.5	150 06.4	12.3	14 39.9	7.2	55.5
	06	274 04.0	S13 31.3	164 37.7	12.3	S14 32.7	7.3	55.5
	07	289 04.0	32.1	179 09.0	12.2	14 25.4	7.4	55.6
	08	304 04.1	32.9	193 40.2	12.3	14 18.0	7.4	55.6
	09	319 04.1	. . 33.8	208 11.5	12.3	14 10.6	7.5	55.6
	10	334 04.1	34.6	222 42.8	12.3	14 03.1	7.6	55.7
	11	349 04.2	35.4	237 14.1	12.3	13 55.5	7.7	55.7
	12	4 04.2	S13 36.2	251 45.4	12.3	S13 47.8	7.7	55.7
	13	19 04.3	37.1	266 16.7	12.2	13 40.1	7.8	55.8
	14	34 04.3	37.9	280 47.9	12.3	13 32.3	7.9	55.8
	15	49 04.3	. . 38.7	295 19.2	12.3	13 24.4	7.9	55.8
	16	64 04.4	39.5	309 50.5	12.3	13 16.5	8.0	55.8
	17	79 04.4	40.3	324 21.8	12.3	13 08.5	8.1	55.9
	18	94 04.4	S13 41.2	338 53.1	12.2	S13 00.4	8.2	55.9
	19	109 04.5	42.0	353 24.3	12.3	12 52.2	8.3	55.9
	20	124 04.5	42.8	7 55.6	12.3	12 43.9	8.3	56.0
	21	139 04.6	. . 43.6	22 26.9	12.2	12 35.6	8.3	56.0
	22	154 04.6	44.5	36 58.1	12.3	12 27.3	8.5	56.0
	23	169 04.6	45.3	51 29.4	12.3	12 18.8	8.5	56.1
30 MONDAY	00	184 04.7	S13 46.1	66 00.7	12.2	S12 10.3	8.6	56.1
	01	199 04.7	46.9	80 31.9	12.3	12 01.7	8.7	56.1
	02	214 04.7	47.7	95 03.2	12.2	11 53.0	8.7	56.2
	03	229 04.8	. . 48.5	109 34.4	12.2	11 44.3	8.8	56.2
	04	244 04.8	49.4	124 05.6	12.3	11 35.5	8.9	56.2
	05	259 04.8	50.2	138 36.9	12.2	11 26.6	8.9	56.3
	06	274 04.9	S13 51.0	153 08.1	12.2	S11 17.7	9.0	56.3
	07	289 04.9	51.8	167 39.3	12.2	11 08.7	9.0	56.3
	08	304 04.9	52.6	182 10.5	12.2	10 59.7	9.2	56.4
	09	319 05.0	. . 53.5	196 41.7	12.2	10 50.5	9.1	56.4
	10	334 05.0	54.3	211 12.9	12.2	10 41.4	9.3	56.4
	11	349 05.0	55.1	225 44.1	12.2	10 32.1	9.3	56.5
	12	4 05.0	S13 55.9	240 15.3	12.2	S10 22.8	9.4	56.5
	13	19 05.1	56.7	254 46.5	12.1	10 13.4	9.4	56.5
	14	34 05.1	57.5	269 17.6	12.2	10 04.0	9.5	56.6
	15	49 05.1	. . 58.3	283 48.8	12.1	9 54.5	9.6	56.6
	16	64 05.2	13 59.2	298 19.9	12.1	9 44.9	9.6	56.6
	17	79 05.2	14 00.0	312 51.0	12.1	9 35.3	9.7	56.7
	18	94 05.2	S14 00.8	327 22.1	12.1	S 9 25.6	9.7	56.7
	19	109 05.3	01.6	341 53.2	12.1	9 15.9	9.9	56.7
	20	124 05.3	02.4	356 24.3	12.1	9 06.0	9.8	56.8
	21	139 05.3	. . 03.2	10 55.4	12.1	8 56.2	9.9	56.8
	22	154 05.3	04.0	25 26.5	12.0	8 46.3	10.0	56.9
	23	169 05.4	04.8	39 57.5	12.1	S 8 36.3	10.0	56.9
		SD 16.1	*d* 0.8	SD 15.0		15.2		15.4

Lat.	Twilight Naut.	Twilight Civil	Sunrise	Moonrise 28	Moonrise 29	Moonrise 30	Moonrise 31
°	h m	h m	h m	h m	h m	h m	h m
N 72	05 55	07 16	08 39	16 48	16 29	16 16	16 06
N 70	05 52	07 05	08 17	16 07	16 04	16 01	15 58
68	05 49	06 56	07 59	15 39	15 45	15 49	15 51
66	05 47	06 48	07 45	15 17	15 30	15 39	15 46
64	05 45	06 41	07 33	15 00	15 17	15 30	15 41
62	05 43	06 35	07 23	14 46	15 06	15 23	15 37
60	05 41	06 30	07 15	14 34	14 57	15 16	15 33
N 58	05 39	06 26	07 07	14 24	14 49	15 11	15 30
56	05 38	06 22	07 01	14 15	14 42	15 06	15 27
54	05 36	06 18	06 55	14 07	14 36	15 01	15 25
52	05 35	06 14	06 50	14 00	14 30	14 57	15 22
50	05 33	06 11	06 45	13 53	14 25	14 53	15 20
45	05 30	06 04	06 34	13 39	14 14	14 45	15 16
N 40	05 26	05 58	06 26	13 27	14 04	14 39	15 12
35	05 22	05 52	06 18	13 18	13 56	14 33	15 08
30	05 19	05 47	06 12	13 09	13 49	14 28	15 05
20	05 12	05 38	06 00	12 54	13 37	14 19	15 00
N 10	05 03	05 28	05 50	12 41	13 26	14 11	14 56
0	04 54	05 19	05 40	12 28	13 16	14 03	14 51
S 10	04 44	05 09	05 31	12 16	13 06	13 56	14 47
20	04 30	04 57	05 20	12 03	12 55	13 48	14 43
30	04 13	04 43	05 08	11 48	12 42	13 39	14 37
35	04 02	04 34	05 01	11 39	12 35	13 34	14 34
40	03 49	04 24	04 53	11 29	12 27	13 28	14 31
45	03 32	04 11	04 43	11 17	12 17	13 21	14 27
S 50	03 11	03 56	04 32	11 03	12 06	13 13	14 22
52	03 00	03 49	04 26	10 56	12 00	13 09	14 20
54	02 48	03 40	04 20	10 48	11 55	13 04	14 18
56	02 34	03 31	04 14	10 40	11 48	13 00	14 15
58	02 16	03 20	04 06	10 31	11 40	12 54	14 12
S 60	01 54	03 07	03 58	10 20	11 32	12 49	14 09

Lat.	Sunset	Twilight Civil	Twilight Naut.	Moonset 28	Moonset 29	Moonset 30	Moonset 31
°	h m	h m	h m	h m	h m	h m	h m
N 72	14 46	16 09	17 31	20 44	22 42	24 34	00 34
N 70	15 09	16 21	17 34	21 24	23 05	24 47	00 47
68	15 27	16 30	17 37	21 51	23 23	24 58	00 58
66	15 41	16 38	17 39	22 12	23 37	25 07	01 07
64	15 53	16 45	17 41	22 28	23 49	25 14	01 14
62	16 03	16 51	17 43	22 42	23 59	25 21	01 21
60	16 12	16 56	17 45	22 53	24 08	00 08	01 26
N 58	16 19	17 01	17 47	23 03	24 15	00 15	01 31
56	16 26	17 05	17 49	23 12	24 22	00 22	01 35
54	16 32	17 09	17 50	23 19	24 27	00 27	01 39
52	16 37	17 12	17 52	23 26	24 33	00 33	01 42
50	16 42	17 16	17 53	23 32	24 37	00 37	01 45
45	16 52	17 23	17 57	23 46	24 47	00 47	01 52
N 40	17 01	17 29	18 01	23 56	24 56	00 56	01 58
35	17 09	17 35	18 05	24 06	00 06	01 03	02 03
30	17 15	17 40	18 08	24 14	00 14	01 09	02 07
20	17 27	17 50	18 16	24 28	00 28	01 20	02 14
N 10	17 37	17 59	18 24	24 40	00 40	01 30	02 20
0	17 47	18 08	18 33	00 04	00 51	01 39	02 26
S 10	17 57	18 19	18 44	00 17	01 02	01 47	02 32
20	18 08	18 31	18 57	00 31	01 14	01 57	02 38
30	18 20	18 45	19 15	00 47	01 28	02 07	02 45
35	18 27	18 54	19 26	00 56	01 36	02 13	02 49
40	18 35	19 04	19 40	01 07	01 45	02 20	02 54
45	18 45	19 17	19 56	01 19	01 55	02 28	02 59
S 50	18 57	19 33	20 18	01 34	02 08	02 38	03 05
52	19 02	19 40	20 29	01 41	02 14	02 42	03 08
54	19 08	19 49	20 41	01 49	02 20	02 47	03 11
56	19 15	19 58	20 56	01 58	02 27	02 52	03 15
58	19 23	20 09	21 14	02 07	02 35	02 58	03 19
S 60	19 31	20 22	21 37	02 19	02 44	03 05	03 23

Day	SUN Eqn. of Time 00^h	SUN Eqn. of Time 12^h	SUN Mer. Pass.	MOON Mer. Pass. Upper	MOON Mer. Pass. Lower	MOON Age	MOON Phase
d	m s	m s	h m	h m	h m	d	%
28	16 10	16 13	11 44	18 40	06 16	09	56
29	16 15	16 17	11 44	19 27	07 04	10	65
30	16 19	16 20	11 44	20 15	07 51	11	75

UT	ARIES	VENUS −3·9		MARS +1·8		JUPITER −1·7		SATURN +0·5	
d h	GHA ° ′	GHA ° ′	Dec ° ′	GHA ° ′	Dec ° ′	GHA ° ′	Dec ° ′	GHA ° ′	Dec ° ′
31 00	39 29.2	199 51.2	S 6 40.2	214 15.8	S 1 01.1	186 57.3	S12 02.7	135 24.9	S22 19.8
01	54 31.6	214 50.8	41.4	229 16.9	01.8	201 59.3	02.9	150 27.1	19.8
02	69 34.1	229 50.3	42.6	244 17.9	02.4	217 01.2	03.1	165 29.3	19.8
03	84 36.5	244 49.9	. . 43.8	259 18.9	. . 03.0	232 03.2	. . 03.3	180 31.5	. . 19.8
04	99 39.0	259 49.5	44.9	274 19.9	03.6	247 05.1	03.5	195 33.7	19.9
05	114 41.5	274 49.0	46.1	289 20.9	04.3	262 07.0	03.6	210 35.9	19.9
06	129 43.9	289 48.6	S 6 47.3	304 21.9	S 1 04.9	277 09.0	S12 03.8	225 38.1	S22 19.9
T 07	144 46.4	304 48.1	48.5	319 23.0	05.5	292 10.9	04.0	240 40.4	19.9
U 08	159 48.9	319 47.7	49.7	334 24.0	06.2	307 12.9	04.2	255 42.6	19.9
E 09	174 51.3	334 47.3	. . 50.9	349 25.0	. . 06.8	322 14.8	. . 04.4	270 44.8	. . 19.9
S 10	189 53.8	349 46.8	52.1	4 26.0	07.4	337 16.7	04.6	285 47.0	19.9
D 11	204 56.3	4 46.4	53.3	19 27.0	08.0	352 18.7	04.7	300 49.2	20.0
A 12	219 58.7	19 45.9	S 6 54.5	34 28.0	S 1 08.7	7 20.6	S12 04.9	315 51.4	S22 20.0
Y 13	235 01.2	34 45.5	55.7	49 29.1	09.3	22 22.5	05.1	330 53.6	20.0
14	250 03.6	49 45.0	56.8	64 30.1	09.9	37 24.5	05.3	345 55.8	20.0
15	265 06.1	64 44.6	. . 58.0	79 31.1	. . 10.6	52 26.4	. . 05.5	0 58.1	. . 20.0
16	280 08.6	79 44.1	6 59.2	94 32.1	11.2	67 28.4	05.7	16 00.3	20.0
17	295 11.0	94 43.7	7 00.4	109 33.1	11.8	82 30.3	05.8	31 02.5	20.1
18	310 13.5	109 43.3	S 7 01.6	124 34.2	S 1 12.4	97 32.2	S12 06.0	46 04.7	S22 20.1
19	325 16.0	124 42.8	02.8	139 35.2	13.1	112 34.2	06.2	61 06.9	20.1
20	340 18.4	139 42.4	04.0	154 36.2	13.7	127 36.1	06.4	76 09.1	20.1
21	355 20.9	154 41.9	. . 05.2	169 37.2	. . 14.3	142 38.1	. . 06.6	91 11.3	. . 20.1
22	10 23.4	169 41.5	06.4	184 38.2	15.0	157 40.0	06.8	106 13.5	20.1
23	25 25.8	184 41.0	07.5	199 39.2	15.6	172 41.9	06.9	121 15.8	20.1
1 00	40 28.3	199 40.6	S 7 08.7	214 40.3	S 1 16.2	187 43.9	S12 07.1	136 18.0	S22 20.2
01	55 30.8	214 40.1	09.9	229 41.3	16.8	202 45.8	07.3	151 20.2	20.2
02	70 33.2	229 39.7	11.1	244 42.3	17.5	217 47.8	07.5	166 22.4	20.2
03	85 35.7	244 39.2	. . 12.3	259 43.3	. . 18.1	232 49.7	. . 07.7	181 24.6	. . 20.2
04	100 38.1	259 38.8	13.5	274 44.3	18.7	247 51.6	07.9	196 26.8	20.2
05	115 40.6	274 38.3	14.7	289 45.3	19.4	262 53.6	08.0	211 29.0	20.2
06	130 43.1	289 37.9	S 7 15.8	304 46.4	S 1 20.0	277 55.5	S12 08.2	226 31.2	S22 20.2
W 07	145 45.5	304 37.4	17.0	319 47.4	20.6	292 57.4	08.4	241 33.4	20.3
E 08	160 48.0	319 37.0	18.2	334 48.4	21.2	307 59.4	08.6	256 35.7	20.3
D 09	175 50.5	334 36.5	. . 19.4	349 49.4	. . 21.9	323 01.3	. . 08.8	271 37.9	. . 20.3
N 10	190 52.9	349 36.1	20.6	4 50.4	22.5	338 03.3	09.0	286 40.1	20.3
E 11	205 55.4	4 35.6	21.8	19 51.4	23.1	353 05.2	09.1	301 42.3	20.3
S 12	220 57.9	19 35.2	S 7 23.0	34 52.5	S 1 23.8	8 07.1	S12 09.3	316 44.5	S22 20.3
D 13	236 00.3	34 34.7	24.1	49 53.5	24.4	23 09.1	09.5	331 46.7	20.3
A 14	251 02.8	49 34.3	25.3	64 54.5	25.0	38 11.0	09.7	346 48.9	20.4
Y 15	266 05.3	64 33.8	. . 26.5	79 55.5	. . 25.6	53 13.0	. . 09.9	1 51.1	. . 20.4
16	281 07.7	79 33.4	27.7	94 56.5	26.3	68 14.9	10.1	16 53.3	20.4
17	296 10.2	94 32.9	28.9	109 57.5	26.9	83 16.8	10.2	31 55.6	20.4
18	311 12.6	109 32.5	S 7 30.1	124 58.6	S 1 27.5	98 18.8	S12 10.4	46 57.8	S22 20.4
19	326 15.1	124 32.0	31.2	139 59.6	28.2	113 20.7	10.6	62 00.0	20.4
20	341 17.6	139 31.6	32.4	155 00.6	28.8	128 22.7	10.8	77 02.2	20.5
21	356 20.0	154 31.1	. . 33.6	170 01.6	. . 29.4	143 24.6	. . 11.0	92 04.4	. . 20.5
22	11 22.5	169 30.7	34.8	185 02.6	30.0	158 26.5	11.2	107 06.6	20.5
23	26 25.0	184 30.2	36.0	200 03.6	30.7	173 28.5	11.3	122 08.8	20.5
2 00	41 27.4	199 29.8	S 7 37.1	215 04.7	S 1 31.3	188 30.4	S12 11.5	137 11.0	S22 20.5
01	56 29.9	214 29.3	38.3	230 05.7	31.9	203 32.3	11.7	152 13.2	20.5
02	71 32.4	229 28.9	39.5	245 06.7	32.6	218 34.3	11.9	167 15.4	20.5
03	86 34.8	244 28.4	. . 40.7	260 07.7	. . 33.2	233 36.2	. . 12.1	182 17.6	. . 20.6
04	101 37.3	259 28.0	41.9	275 08.7	33.8	248 38.2	12.2	197 19.9	20.6
05	116 39.7	274 27.5	43.0	290 09.7	34.4	263 40.1	12.4	212 22.1	20.6
06	131 42.2	289 27.0	S 7 44.2	305 10.8	S 1 35.1	278 42.0	S12 12.6	227 24.3	S22 20.6
07	146 44.7	304 26.6	45.4	320 11.8	35.7	293 44.0	12.8	242 26.5	20.6
T 08	161 47.1	319 26.1	46.6	335 12.8	36.3	308 45.9	13.0	257 28.7	20.6
H 09	176 49.6	334 25.7	. . 47.8	350 13.8	. . 36.9	323 47.9	. . 13.2	272 30.9	. . 20.6
U 10	191 52.1	349 25.2	48.9	5 14.8	37.6	338 49.8	13.3	287 33.1	20.7
R 11	206 54.5	4 24.8	50.1	20 15.8	38.2	353 51.7	13.5	302 35.3	20.7
S 12	221 57.0	19 24.3	S 7 51.3	35 16.9	S 1 38.8	8 53.7	S12 13.7	317 37.5	S22 20.7
D 13	236 59.5	34 23.9	52.5	50 17.9	39.5	23 55.6	13.9	332 39.7	20.7
A 14	252 01.9	49 23.4	53.6	65 18.9	40.1	38 57.6	14.1	347 41.9	20.7
Y 15	267 04.4	64 22.9	. . 54.8	80 19.9	. . 40.7	53 59.5	. . 14.3	2 44.1	. . 20.7
16	282 06.9	79 22.5	56.0	95 20.9	41.3	69 01.4	14.4	17 46.4	20.7
17	297 09.3	94 22.0	57.2	110 21.9	42.0	84 03.4	14.6	32 48.6	20.8
18	312 11.8	109 21.6	S 7 58.3	125 23.0	S 1 42.6	99 05.3	S12 14.8	47 50.8	S22 20.8
19	327 14.2	124 21.1	7 59.5	140 24.0	43.2	114 07.2	15.0	62 53.0	20.8
20	342 16.7	139 20.6	8 00.7	155 25.0	43.9	129 09.2	15.2	77 55.2	20.8
21	357 19.2	154 20.2	. . 01.9	170 26.0	. . 44.5	144 11.1	. . 15.3	92 57.4	. . 20.8
22	12 21.6	169 19.7	03.0	185 27.0	45.1	159 13.1	15.5	107 59.6	20.8
23	27 24.1	184 19.3	04.2	200 28.0	45.7	174 15.0	15.7	123 01.8	20.9
Mer. Pass.	h m 21 14.6	v −0.5	d 1.2	v 1.0	d 0.6	v 1.9	d 0.2	v 2.2	d 0.0

STARS

Name	SHA ° ′	Dec ° ′
Acamar	315 15.7	S40 14.1
Achernar	335 24.1	S57 09.0
Acrux	173 06.5	S63 11.6
Adhara	255 10.1	S28 59.7
Aldebaran	290 45.7	N16 32.5
Alioth	166 18.7	N55 51.8
Alkaid	152 57.1	N49 13.6
Al Na'ir	27 40.0	S46 52.6
Alnilam	275 43.2	S 1 11.5
Alphard	217 53.3	S 8 44.1
Alphecca	126 08.9	N26 39.6
Alpheratz	357 40.1	N29 11.4
Altair	62 05.5	N 8 55.2
Ankaa	353 12.5	S42 12.7
Antares	112 23.0	S26 28.0
Arcturus	145 53.4	N19 05.6
Atria	107 22.6	S69 03.5
Avior	234 16.7	S59 33.7
Bellatrix	278 28.6	N 6 21.8
Betelgeuse	270 57.9	N 7 24.5
Canopus	263 54.5	S52 42.2
Capella	280 29.7	N46 00.7
Deneb	49 29.5	N45 21.0
Denebola	182 30.9	N14 28.5
Diphda	348 52.7	S17 53.4
Dubhe	193 48.6	N61 39.1
Elnath	278 08.6	N28 37.1
Eltanin	90 45.1	N51 29.6
Enif	33 44.2	N 9 57.6
Fomalhaut	15 20.6	S29 31.7
Gacrux	171 58.0	S57 12.5
Gienah	175 49.5	S17 38.2
Hadar	148 44.3	S60 27.3
Hamal	327 57.1	N23 32.7
Kaus Aust.	83 40.2	S34 22.4
Kochab	137 21.4	N74 05.1
Markab	13 35.2	N15 18.2
Menkar	314 11.7	N 4 09.5
Menkent	148 04.5	S36 27.2
Miaplacidus	221 39.1	S69 47.1
Mirfak	308 35.6	N49 55.3
Nunki	75 54.9	S26 16.3
Peacock	53 14.8	S56 40.8
Pollux	243 24.1	N27 58.8
Procyon	244 56.6	N 5 10.7
Rasalhague	96 04.0	N12 33.2
Regulus	207 40.5	N11 52.8
Rigel	281 09.0	S 8 10.9
Rigil Kent.	139 48.4	S60 54.2
Sabik	102 09.5	S15 44.6
Schedar	349 36.6	N56 38.2
Shaula	96 18.2	S37 06.8
Sirius	258 31.0	S16 44.4
Spica	158 28.5	S11 15.0
Suhail	222 50.3	S43 30.0
Vega	80 37.2	N38 48.4
Zuben'ubi	137 02.5	S16 06.7

	SHA ° ′	Mer. Pass. h m
Venus	159 12.3	10 42
Mars	174 12.0	9 41
Jupiter	147 15.6	11 28
Saturn	95 49.7	14 53

UT d	h	SUN GHA	SUN Dec	MOON GHA	*v*	MOON Dec	*d*	HP
		° ′	° ′	° ′	′	° ′	′	′
31	00	184 05.4	S14 05.7	54 28.6	12.0	S 8 26.3	10.1	56.9
	01	199 05.4	06.5	68 59.6	12.0	8 16.2	10.2	57.0
	02	214 05.4	07.3	83 30.6	12.0	8 06.0	10.2	57.0
	03	229 05.5	. . 08.1	98 01.6	11.9	7 55.8	10.2	57.0
	04	244 05.5	08.9	112 32.5	12.0	7 45.6	10.3	57.1
	05	259 05.5	09.7	127 03.5	11.9	7 35.3	10.4	57.1
	06	274 05.5	S14 10.5	141 34.4	11.9	S 7 24.9	10.4	57.1
	07	289 05.6	11.3	156 05.3	11.9	7 14.5	10.4	57.2
T	08	304 05.6	12.1	170 36.2	11.9	7 04.1	10.5	57.2
U	09	319 05.6	. . 12.9	185 07.1	11.9	6 53.6	10.6	57.3
E	10	334 05.6	13.7	199 38.0	11.8	6 43.0	10.6	57.3
S	11	349 05.7	14.5	214 08.8	11.8	6 32.4	10.6	57.3
D	12	4 05.7	S14 15.3	228 39.6	11.8	S 6 21.8	10.7	57.4
A	13	19 05.7	16.1	243 10.4	11.8	6 11.1	10.8	57.4
Y	14	34 05.7	17.0	257 41.2	11.8	6 00.3	10.8	57.4
	15	49 05.8	. . 17.8	272 12.0	11.7	5 49.5	10.8	57.5
	16	64 05.8	18.6	286 42.7	11.7	5 38.7	10.9	57.5
	17	79 05.8	19.4	301 13.4	11.7	5 27.8	10.9	57.6
	18	94 05.8	S14 20.2	315 44.1	11.6	S 5 16.9	11.0	57.6
	19	109 05.8	21.0	330 14.7	11.7	5 05.9	11.0	57.6
	20	124 05.9	21.8	344 45.4	11.6	4 54.9	11.0	57.7
	21	139 05.9	. . 22.6	359 16.0	11.6	4 43.9	11.1	57.7
	22	154 05.9	23.4	13 46.6	11.5	4 32.8	11.2	57.7
	23	169 05.9	24.2	28 17.1	11.5	4 21.6	11.1	57.8
1	00	184 05.9	S14 25.0	42 47.6	11.5	S 4 10.5	11.2	57.8
	01	199 06.0	25.8	57 18.1	11.5	3 59.3	11.3	57.9
	02	214 06.0	26.6	71 48.6	11.4	3 48.0	11.2	57.9
	03	229 06.0	. . 27.4	86 19.0	11.4	3 36.8	11.3	57.9
	04	244 06.0	28.2	100 49.4	11.4	3 25.5	11.4	58.0
	05	259 06.0	29.0	115 19.8	11.3	3 14.1	11.4	58.0
	06	274 06.0	S14 29.8	129 50.1	11.3	S 3 02.7	11.4	58.0
W	07	289 06.1	30.6	144 20.4	11.3	2 51.3	11.4	58.1
E	08	304 06.1	31.4	158 50.7	11.3	2 39.9	11.5	58.1
D	09	319 06.1	. . 32.2	173 21.0	11.2	2 28.4	11.5	58.2
N	10	334 06.1	33.0	187 51.2	11.1	2 16.9	11.5	58.2
E	11	349 06.1	33.8	202 21.3	11.2	2 05.4	11.5	58.2
S	12	4 06.1	S14 34.6	216 51.5	11.1	S 1 53.9	11.6	58.3
D	13	19 06.1	35.4	231 21.6	11.0	1 42.3	11.6	58.3
A	14	34 06.2	36.1	245 51.6	11.1	1 30.7	11.6	58.3
Y	15	49 06.2	. . 36.9	260 21.7	11.0	1 19.1	11.7	58.4
	16	64 06.2	37.7	274 51.7	10.9	1 07.4	11.7	58.4
	17	79 06.2	38.5	289 21.6	10.9	0 55.7	11.7	58.4
	18	94 06.2	S14 39.3	303 51.5	10.9	S 0 44.0	11.7	58.5
	19	109 06.2	40.1	318 21.4	10.8	0 32.3	11.7	58.5
	20	124 06.2	40.9	332 51.2	10.8	0 20.6	11.7	58.6
	21	139 06.2	. . 41.7	347 21.0	10.8	S 0 08.9	11.8	58.6
	22	154 06.3	42.5	1 50.8	10.7	N 0 02.9	11.8	58.6
	23	169 06.3	43.3	16 20.5	10.6	0 14.7	11.8	58.7
2	00	184 06.3	S14 44.1	30 50.1	10.6	N 0 26.5	11.8	58.7
	01	199 06.3	44.9	45 19.7	10.6	0 38.3	11.8	58.7
	02	214 06.3	45.7	59 49.3	10.6	0 50.1	11.8	58.8
	03	229 06.3	. . 46.4	74 18.9	10.4	1 01.9	11.9	58.8
	04	244 06.3	47.2	88 48.3	10.5	1 13.8	11.8	58.8
	05	259 06.3	48.0	103 17.8	10.4	1 25.6	11.9	58.9
	06	274 06.3	S14 48.8	117 47.2	10.3	N 1 37.5	11.8	58.9
T	07	289 06.3	49.6	132 16.5	10.3	1 49.3	11.9	58.9
H	08	304 06.4	50.4	146 45.8	10.3	2 01.2	11.9	59.0
U	09	319 06.4	. . 51.2	161 15.1	10.2	2 13.1	11.8	59.0
R	10	334 06.4	52.0	175 44.3	10.1	2 24.9	11.9	59.0
S	11	349 06.4	52.8	190 13.4	10.1	2 36.8	11.9	59.1
D	12	4 06.4	S14 53.5	204 42.5	10.1	N 2 48.7	11.8	59.1
A	13	19 06.4	54.3	219 11.6	10.0	3 00.5	11.9	59.1
Y	14	34 06.4	55.1	233 40.6	9.9	3 12.4	11.9	59.2
	15	49 06.4	. . 55.9	248 09.5	9.9	3 24.3	11.8	59.2
	16	64 06.4	56.7	262 38.4	9.8	3 36.1	11.9	59.2
	17	79 06.4	57.5	277 07.2	9.8	3 48.0	11.8	59.3
	18	94 06.4	S14 58.2	291 36.0	9.8	N 3 59.8	11.9	59.3
	19	109 06.4	59.0	306 04.8	9.6	4 11.7	11.8	59.3
	20	124 06.4	14 59.8	320 33.4	9.7	4 23.5	11.8	59.4
	21	139 06.4	15 00.6	335 02.1	9.5	4 35.3	11.8	59.4
	22	154 06.4	01.4	349 30.6	9.5	4 47.1	11.8	59.4
	23	169 06.4	02.2	3 59.1	9.5	N 4 58.9	11.8	59.5
		SD 16.1	*d* 0.8	SD 15.6		15.9		16.1

Lat.	Twilight Naut.	Twilight Civil	Sunrise	Moonrise 31	Moonrise 1	Moonrise 2	Moonrise 3
°	h m	h m	h m	h m	h m	h m	h m
N 72	06 07	07 30	08 58	16 06	15 56	15 47	15 37
N 70	06 03	07 17	08 31	15 58	15 55	15 51	15 48
68	05 59	07 06	08 11	15 51	15 53	15 55	15 58
66	05 56	06 57	07 56	15 46	15 52	15 58	16 06
64	05 53	06 50	07 43	15 41	15 51	16 01	16 13
62	05 50	06 43	07 32	15 37	15 50	16 04	16 19
60	05 48	06 37	07 23	15 33	15 49	16 06	16 24
N 58	05 46	06 32	07 14	15 30	15 49	16 08	16 28
56	05 43	06 28	07 07	15 27	15 48	16 09	16 32
54	05 41	06 23	07 01	15 25	15 48	16 11	16 36
52	05 39	06 19	06 55	15 22	15 47	16 12	16 39
50	05 38	06 16	06 50	15 20	15 47	16 13	16 42
45	05 33	06 08	06 39	15 16	15 46	16 16	16 49
N 40	05 29	06 01	06 29	15 12	15 45	16 19	16 55
35	05 25	05 55	06 21	15 08	15 44	16 21	16 59
30	05 21	05 49	06 14	15 05	15 43	16 22	17 04
20	05 13	05 39	06 02	15 00	15 42	16 26	17 11
N 10	05 04	05 29	05 51	14 56	15 41	16 28	17 18
0	04 54	05 19	05 40	14 51	15 40	16 31	17 24
S 10	04 42	05 08	05 30	14 47	15 40	16 34	17 30
20	04 28	04 55	05 18	14 43	15 39	16 37	17 37
30	04 10	04 40	05 05	14 37	15 38	16 40	17 45
35	03 58	04 31	04 58	14 34	15 37	16 42	17 49
40	03 44	04 20	04 49	14 31	15 36	16 44	17 55
45	03 27	04 07	04 39	14 27	15 36	16 47	18 01
S 50	03 04	03 50	04 26	14 22	15 35	16 50	18 08
52	02 53	03 42	04 20	14 20	15 34	16 52	18 11
54	02 39	03 33	04 14	14 18	15 34	16 53	18 15
56	02 24	03 23	04 07	14 15	15 34	16 55	18 19
58	02 04	03 11	03 59	14 12	15 33	16 57	18 24
S 60	01 39	02 58	03 50	14 09	15 32	16 59	18 29

Lat.	Sunset	Twilight Civil	Twilight Naut.	Moonset 31	Moonset 1	Moonset 2	Moonset 3
°	h m	h m	h m	h m	h m	h m	h m
N 72	14 28	15 56	17 19	00 34	02 26	04 19	06 18
N 70	14 55	16 09	17 23	00 47	02 31	04 18	06 09
68	15 15	16 20	17 27	00 58	02 36	04 17	06 01
66	15 30	16 29	17 30	01 07	02 40	04 15	05 55
64	15 43	16 36	17 33	01 14	02 43	04 14	05 49
62	15 54	16 43	17 36	01 21	02 45	04 14	05 45
60	16 04	16 49	17 38	01 26	02 48	04 13	05 41
N 58	16 12	16 54	17 41	01 31	02 50	04 12	05 37
56	16 19	16 59	17 43	01 35	02 52	04 12	05 34
54	16 26	17 03	17 45	01 39	02 54	04 11	05 31
52	16 31	17 07	17 47	01 42	02 55	04 11	05 29
50	16 37	17 11	17 49	01 45	02 56	04 10	05 27
45	16 48	17 19	17 53	01 52	02 59	04 09	05 22
N 40	16 58	17 26	17 58	01 58	03 02	04 09	05 17
35	17 06	17 32	18 02	02 03	03 04	04 08	05 14
30	17 13	17 38	18 06	02 07	03 06	04 07	05 11
20	17 25	17 48	18 14	02 14	03 09	04 06	05 05
N 10	17 37	17 58	18 23	02 20	03 12	04 05	05 00
0	17 47	18 08	18 33	02 26	03 15	04 04	04 56
S 10	17 58	18 19	18 45	02 32	03 17	04 03	04 51
20	18 09	18 32	18 59	02 38	03 20	04 02	04 47
30	18 22	18 48	19 18	02 45	03 23	04 01	04 41
35	18 30	18 57	19 29	02 49	03 25	04 01	04 38
40	18 39	19 08	19 44	02 54	03 27	04 00	04 35
45	18 49	19 22	20 01	02 59	03 29	03 59	04 30
S 50	19 02	19 38	20 25	03 05	03 32	03 58	04 26
52	19 08	19 46	20 36	03 08	03 33	03 57	04 23
54	19 14	19 56	20 50	03 11	03 34	03 57	04 21
56	19 22	20 06	21 06	03 15	03 36	03 56	04 18
58	19 30	20 18	21 26	03 19	03 37	03 56	04 15
S 60	19 39	20 32	21 52	03 23	03 39	03 55	04 12

Day	SUN Eqn. of Time 00^h	SUN Eqn. of Time 12^h	SUN Mer. Pass.	MOON Mer. Pass. Upper	MOON Mer. Pass. Lower	MOON Age	MOON Phase
d	m s	m s	h m	h m	h m	d	%
31	16 22	16 23	11 44	21 03	08 39	12	83
1	16 24	16 25	11 44	21 52	09 28	13	90
2	16 25	16 26	11 44	22 43	10 18	14	96

2017 NOVEMBER 3, 4, 5 (FRI., SAT., SUN.)

	UT	ARIES	VENUS −3·9		MARS +1·8		JUPITER −1·7		SATURN +0·5		STARS		
	d h	GHA	GHA	Dec	GHA	Dec	GHA	Dec	GHA	Dec	Name	SHA	Dec
		° ′	° ′	° ′	° ′	° ′	° ′	° ′	° ′	° ′		° ′	° ′
	3 00	42 26.6	199 18.8	S 8 05.4	215 29.1	S 1 46.4	189 16.9	S12 15.9	138 04.0	S22 20.9	Acamar	315 15.7	S40 14.1
	01	57 29.0	214 18.3	06.6	230 30.1	47.0	204 18.9	16.1	153 06.2	20.9	Achernar	335 24.1	S57 09.0
	02	72 31.5	229 17.9	07.7	245 31.1	47.6	219 20.8	16.3	168 08.4	20.9	Acrux	173 06.5	S63 11.5
	03	87 34.0	244 17.4	. . 08.9	260 32.1	. . 48.2	234 22.8	. . 16.4	183 10.6	. . 20.9	Adhara	255 10.0	S28 59.7
	04	102 36.4	259 17.0	10.1	275 33.1	48.9	249 24.7	16.6	198 12.8	20.9	Aldebaran	290 45.7	N16 32.5
	05	117 38.9	274 16.5	11.3	290 34.1	49.5	264 26.6	16.8	213 15.0	20.9			
	06	132 41.3	289 16.0	S 8 12.4	305 35.2	S 1 50.1	279 28.6	S12 17.0	228 17.2	S22 21.0	Alioth	166 18.7	N55 51.8
	07	147 43.8	304 15.6	13.6	320 36.2	50.8	294 30.5	17.2	243 19.5	21.0	Alkaid	152 57.1	N49 13.6
	08	162 46.3	319 15.1	14.8	335 37.2	51.4	309 32.5	17.3	258 21.7	21.0	Al Na'ir	27 40.0	S46 52.6
F	09	177 48.7	334 14.6	. . 16.0	350 38.2	. . 52.0	324 34.4	. . 17.5	273 23.9	. . 21.0	Alnilam	275 43.1	S 1 11.5
R	10	192 51.2	349 14.2	17.1	5 39.2	52.6	339 36.3	17.7	288 26.1	21.0	Alphard	217 53.3	S 8 44.1
I	11	207 53.7	4 13.7	18.3	20 40.2	53.3	354 38.3	17.9	303 28.3	21.0			
D	12	222 56.1	19 13.2	S 8 19.5	35 41.3	S 1 53.9	9 40.2	S12 18.1	318 30.5	S22 21.0	Alphecca	126 08.9	N26 39.6
A	13	237 58.6	34 12.8	20.6	50 42.3	54.5	24 42.1	18.3	333 32.7	21.1	Alpheratz	357 40.2	N29 11.4
Y	14	253 01.1	49 12.3	21.8	65 43.3	55.1	39 44.1	18.4	348 34.9	21.1	Altair	62 05.5	N 8 55.2
	15	268 03.5	64 11.9	. . 23.0	80 44.3	. . 55.8	54 46.0	. . 18.6	3 37.1	. . 21.1	Ankaa	353 12.5	S42 12.7
	16	283 06.0	79 11.4	24.1	95 45.3	56.4	69 48.0	18.8	18 39.3	21.1	Antares	112 23.0	S26 28.0
	17	298 08.5	94 10.9	25.3	110 46.3	57.0	84 49.9	19.0	33 41.5	21.1			
	18	313 10.9	109 10.5	S 8 26.5	125 47.4	S 1 57.7	99 51.8	S12 19.2	48 43.7	S22 21.1	Arcturus	145 53.4	N19 05.6
	19	328 13.4	124 10.0	27.6	140 48.4	58.3	114 53.8	19.3	63 45.9	21.1	Atria	107 22.6	S69 03.4
	20	343 15.8	139 09.5	28.8	155 49.4	58.9	129 55.7	19.5	78 48.1	21.2	Avior	234 16.7	S59 33.8
	21	358 18.3	154 09.1	. . 30.0	170 50.4	1 59.5	144 57.7	. . 19.7	93 50.3	. . 21.2	Bellatrix	278 28.6	N 6 21.8
	22	13 20.8	169 08.6	31.1	185 51.4	2 00.2	159 59.6	19.9	108 52.5	21.2	Betelgeuse	270 57.9	N 7 24.5
	23	28 23.2	184 08.1	32.3	200 52.4	00.8	175 01.5	20.1	123 54.7	21.2			
	4 00	43 25.7	199 07.6	S 8 33.5	215 53.4	S 2 01.4	190 03.5	S12 20.3	138 56.9	S22 21.2	Canopus	263 54.5	S52 42.2
	01	58 28.2	214 07.2	34.6	230 54.5	02.0	205 05.4	20.4	153 59.1	21.2	Capella	280 29.7	N46 00.7
	02	73 30.6	229 06.7	35.8	245 55.5	02.7	220 07.4	20.6	169 01.4	21.2	Deneb	49 29.5	N45 21.0
	03	88 33.1	244 06.2	. . 37.0	260 56.5	. . 03.3	235 09.3	. . 20.8	184 03.6	. . 21.3	Denebola	182 30.9	N14 28.5
	04	103 35.6	259 05.8	38.1	275 57.5	03.9	250 11.2	21.0	199 05.8	21.3	Diphda	348 52.7	S17 53.4
	05	118 38.0	274 05.3	39.3	290 58.5	04.5	265 13.2	21.2	214 08.0	21.3			
	06	133 40.5	289 04.8	S 8 40.5	305 59.5	S 2 05.2	280 15.1	S12 21.3	229 10.2	S22 21.3	Dubhe	193 48.6	N61 39.1
	07	148 43.0	304 04.4	41.6	321 00.6	05.8	295 17.0	21.5	244 12.4	21.3	Elnath	278 08.6	N28 37.1
S	08	163 45.4	319 03.9	42.8	336 01.6	06.4	310 19.0	21.7	259 14.6	21.3	Eltanin	90 45.2	N51 29.6
A	09	178 47.9	334 03.4	. . 44.0	351 02.6	. . 07.1	325 20.9	. . 21.9	274 16.8	. . 21.3	Enif	33 44.2	N 9 57.6
T	10	193 50.3	349 02.9	45.1	6 03.6	07.7	340 22.9	22.1	289 19.0	21.4	Fomalhaut	15 20.6	S29 31.7
U	11	208 52.8	4 02.5	46.3	21 04.6	08.3	355 24.8	22.2	304 21.2	21.4			
R	12	223 55.3	19 02.0	S 8 47.5	36 05.6	S 2 08.9	10 26.7	S12 22.4	319 23.4	S22 21.4	Gacrux	171 58.0	S57 12.4
D	13	238 57.7	34 01.5	48.6	51 06.7	09.6	25 28.7	22.6	334 25.6	21.4	Gienah	175 49.5	S17 38.2
A	14	254 00.2	49 01.1	49.8	66 07.7	10.2	40 30.6	22.8	349 27.8	21.4	Hadar	148 44.3	S60 27.2
Y	15	269 02.7	64 00.6	. . 50.9	81 08.7	. . 10.8	55 32.6	. . 23.0	4 30.0	. . 21.4	Hamal	327 57.1	N23 32.7
	16	284 05.1	79 00.1	52.1	96 09.7	11.4	70 34.5	23.2	19 32.2	21.4	Kaus Aust.	83 40.2	S34 22.4
	17	299 07.6	93 59.6	53.3	111 10.7	12.1	85 36.4	23.3	34 34.4	21.5			
	18	314 10.1	108 59.2	S 8 54.4	126 11.7	S 2 12.7	100 38.4	S12 23.5	49 36.6	S22 21.5	Kochab	137 21.4	N74 05.1
	19	329 12.5	123 58.7	55.6	141 12.7	13.3	115 40.3	23.7	64 38.8	21.5	Markab	13 35.2	N15 18.2
	20	344 15.0	138 58.2	56.7	156 13.8	13.9	130 42.3	23.9	79 41.0	21.5	Menkar	314 11.7	N 4 09.5
	21	359 17.4	153 57.7	. . 57.9	171 14.8	. . 14.6	145 44.2	. . 24.1	94 43.2	. . 21.5	Menkent	148 04.5	S36 27.2
	22	14 19.9	168 57.3	8 59.1	186 15.8	15.2	160 46.1	24.2	109 45.4	21.5	Miaplacidus	221 39.0	S69 47.1
	23	29 22.4	183 56.8	9 00.2	201 16.8	15.8	175 48.1	24.4	124 47.6	21.5			
	5 00	44 24.8	198 56.3	S 9 01.4	216 17.8	S 2 16.4	190 50.0	S12 24.6	139 49.8	S22 21.6	Mirfak	308 35.6	N49 55.3
	01	59 27.3	213 55.8	02.5	231 18.8	17.1	205 51.9	24.8	154 52.0	21.6	Nunki	75 54.9	S26 16.3
	02	74 29.8	228 55.4	03.7	246 19.9	17.7	220 53.9	25.0	169 54.2	21.6	Peacock	53 14.8	S56 40.8
	03	89 32.2	243 54.9	. . 04.9	261 20.9	. . 18.3	235 55.8	. . 25.1	184 56.4	. . 21.6	Pollux	243 24.1	N27 58.8
	04	104 34.7	258 54.4	06.0	276 21.9	18.9	250 57.8	25.3	199 58.6	21.6	Procyon	244 56.6	N 5 10.7
	05	119 37.2	273 53.9	07.2	291 22.9	19.6	265 59.7	25.5	215 00.8	21.6			
	06	134 39.6	288 53.4	S 9 08.3	306 23.9	S 2 20.2	281 01.6	S12 25.7	230 03.0	S22 21.6	Rasalhague	96 04.0	N12 33.2
	07	149 42.1	303 53.0	09.5	321 24.9	20.8	296 03.6	25.9	245 05.2	21.7	Regulus	207 40.5	N11 52.8
	08	164 44.6	318 52.5	10.6	336 25.9	21.4	311 05.5	26.0	260 07.4	21.7	Rigel	281 09.0	S 8 10.9
S	09	179 47.0	333 52.0	. . 11.8	351 27.0	. . 22.1	326 07.5	. . 26.2	275 09.6	. . 21.7	Rigil Kent.	139 48.4	S60 54.2
U	10	194 49.5	348 51.5	13.0	6 28.0	22.7	341 09.4	26.4	290 11.8	21.7	Sabik	102 09.5	S15 44.6
N	11	209 51.9	3 51.0	14.1	21 29.0	23.3	356 11.3	26.6	305 14.0	21.7			
D	12	224 54.4	18 50.6	S 9 15.3	36 30.0	S 2 24.0	11 13.3	S12 26.8	320 16.2	S22 21.7	Schedar	349 36.6	N56 38.2
A	13	239 56.9	33 50.1	16.4	51 31.0	24.6	26 15.2	26.9	335 18.4	21.7	Shaula	96 18.3	S37 06.8
Y	14	254 59.3	48 49.6	17.6	66 32.0	25.2	41 17.2	27.1	350 20.6	21.8	Sirius	258 30.9	S16 44.4
	15	270 01.8	63 49.1	. . 18.7	81 33.1	. . 25.8	56 19.1	. . 27.3	5 22.8	. . 21.8	Spica	158 28.5	S11 15.0
	16	285 04.3	78 48.6	19.9	96 34.1	26.5	71 21.0	27.5	20 25.0	21.8	Suhail	222 50.3	S43 30.0
	17	300 06.7	93 48.2	21.0	111 35.1	27.1	86 23.0	27.7	35 27.2	21.8			
	18	315 09.2	108 47.7	S 9 22.2	126 36.1	S 2 27.7	101 24.9	S12 27.8	50 29.4	S22 21.8	Vega	80 37.2	N38 48.4
	19	330 11.7	123 47.2	23.3	141 37.1	28.3	116 26.8	28.0	65 31.6	21.8	Zuben'ubi	137 02.5	S16 06.7
	20	345 14.1	138 46.7	24.5	156 38.1	29.0	131 28.8	28.2	80 33.8	21.8			
	21	0 16.6	153 46.2	. . 25.6	171 39.1	. . 29.6	146 30.7	. . 28.4	95 36.0	. . 21.9			
	22	15 19.1	168 45.7	26.8	186 40.2	30.2	161 32.7	28.6	110 38.2	21.9			
	23	30 21.5	183 45.3	27.9	201 41.2	30.8	176 34.6	28.7	125 40.4	21.9			
	Mer. Pass.	h m 21 02.8	v −0.5	d 1.2	v 1.0	d 0.6	v 1.9	d 0.2	v 2.2	d 0.0			

	SHA	Mer. Pass.
	° ′	h m
Venus	155 41.9	10 44
Mars	172 27.7	9 36
Jupiter	146 37.8	11 18
Saturn	95 31.2	14 42

UT d h	SUN GHA ° ′	SUN Dec ° ′	MOON GHA ° ′	v ′	MOON Dec ° ′	d ′	HP ′
3 00	184 06.4	S15 02.9	18 27.6	9.4	N 5 10.7	11.7	59.5
01	199 06.4	03.7	32 56.0	9.3	5 22.4	11.7	59.5
02	214 06.4	04.5	47 24.3	9.3	5 34.1	11.7	59.6
03	229 06.4	. . 05.3	61 52.6	9.2	5 45.8	11.7	59.6
04	244 06.4	06.1	76 20.8	9.2	5 57.5	11.7	59.6
05	259 06.4	06.8	90 49.0	9.1	6 09.2	11.6	59.6
06	274 06.4	S15 07.6	105 17.1	9.1	N 6 20.8	11.7	59.7
07	289 06.4	08.4	119 45.2	9.0	6 32.5	11.6	59.7
08	304 06.4	09.2	134 13.2	8.9	6 44.1	11.5	59.7
F 09	319 06.4	. . 09.9	148 41.1	8.9	6 55.6	11.5	59.8
R 10	334 06.4	10.7	163 09.0	8.8	7 07.1	11.5	59.8
I 11	349 06.4	11.5	177 36.8	8.7	7 18.6	11.5	59.8
D 12	4 06.4	S15 12.3	192 04.5	8.7	N 7 30.1	11.4	59.8
A 13	19 06.4	13.0	206 32.2	8.6	7 41.5	11.4	59.9
Y 14	34 06.4	13.8	220 59.8	8.6	7 52.9	11.4	59.9
15	49 06.4	. . 14.6	235 27.4	8.4	8 04.3	11.3	59.9
16	64 06.4	15.4	249 54.8	8.5	8 15.6	11.3	59.9
17	79 06.4	16.1	264 22.3	8.3	8 26.9	11.2	60.0
18	94 06.4	S15 16.9	278 49.6	8.4	N 8 38.1	11.2	60.0
19	109 06.4	17.7	293 17.0	8.2	8 49.3	11.2	60.0
20	124 06.4	18.5	307 44.2	8.2	9 00.5	11.1	60.0
21	139 06.4	. . 19.2	322 11.4	8.1	9 11.6	11.0	60.1
22	154 06.4	20.0	336 38.5	8.0	9 22.6	11.0	60.1
23	169 06.4	20.8	351 05.5	8.0	9 33.6	11.0	60.1
4 00	184 06.4	S15 21.5	5 32.5	7.9	N 9 44.6	10.9	60.1
01	199 06.4	22.3	19 59.4	7.9	9 55.5	10.8	60.1
02	214 06.4	23.1	34 26.3	7.8	10 06.3	10.8	60.2
03	229 06.4	. . 23.9	48 53.1	7.7	10 17.1	10.7	60.2
04	244 06.3	24.6	63 19.8	7.6	10 27.8	10.7	60.2
05	259 06.3	25.4	77 46.4	7.6	10 38.5	10.6	60.2
06	274 06.3	S15 26.2	92 13.0	7.6	N10 49.1	10.6	60.3
07	289 06.3	26.9	106 39.6	7.4	10 59.7	10.4	60.3
S 08	304 06.3	27.7	121 06.0	7.4	11 10.1	10.5	60.3
A 09	319 06.3	. . 28.5	135 32.4	7.4	11 20.6	10.3	60.3
T 10	334 06.3	29.2	149 58.8	7.2	11 30.9	10.3	60.3
U 11	349 06.3	30.0	164 25.0	7.2	11 41.2	10.2	60.3
R 12	4 06.3	S15 30.8	178 51.2	7.2	N11 51.4	10.2	60.4
D 13	19 06.3	31.5	193 17.4	7.0	12 01.6	10.0	60.4
A 14	34 06.2	32.3	207 43.4	7.0	12 11.6	10.0	60.4
Y 15	49 06.2	. . 33.1	222 09.4	7.0	12 21.6	10.0	60.4
16	64 06.2	33.8	236 35.4	6.9	12 31.6	9.8	60.4
17	79 06.2	34.6	251 01.3	6.8	12 41.4	9.8	60.4
18	94 06.2	S15 35.3	265 27.1	6.7	N12 51.2	9.7	60.5
19	109 06.2	36.1	279 52.8	6.7	13 00.9	9.6	60.5
20	124 06.2	36.9	294 18.5	6.6	13 10.5	9.5	60.5
21	139 06.2	. . 37.6	308 44.1	6.6	13 20.0	9.4	60.5
22	154 06.1	38.4	323 09.7	6.5	13 29.4	9.4	60.5
23	169 06.1	39.1	337 35.2	6.4	13 38.8	9.3	60.5
5 00	184 06.1	S15 39.9	352 00.6	6.4	N13 48.1	9.1	60.5
01	199 06.1	40.7	6 26.0	6.3	13 57.2	9.1	60.5
02	214 06.1	41.4	20 51.3	6.3	14 06.3	9.0	60.6
03	229 06.1	. . 42.2	35 16.6	6.2	14 15.3	8.9	60.6
04	244 06.0	42.9	49 41.8	6.1	14 24.2	8.8	60.6
05	259 06.0	43.7	64 06.9	6.1	14 33.0	8.7	60.6
06	274 06.0	S15 44.5	78 32.0	6.0	N14 41.7	8.7	60.6
07	289 06.0	45.2	92 57.0	5.9	14 50.4	8.5	60.6
08	304 06.0	46.0	107 21.9	5.9	14 58.9	8.4	60.6
S 09	319 06.0	. . 46.7	121 46.8	5.9	15 07.3	8.3	60.6
U 10	334 05.9	47.5	136 11.7	5.8	15 15.6	8.2	60.6
N 11	349 05.9	48.2	150 36.5	5.7	15 23.8	8.1	60.6
D 12	4 05.9	S15 49.0	165 01.2	5.7	N15 31.9	8.0	60.6
A 13	19 05.9	. 49.7	179 25.9	5.6	15 39.9	7.9	60.6
Y 14	34 05.9	50.5	193 50.5	5.6	15 47.8	7.8	60.6
15	49 05.8	. . 51.3	208 15.1	5.5	15 55.6	7.7	60.6
16	64 05.8	52.0	222 39.6	5.5	16 03.3	7.5	60.7
17	79 05.8	52.8	237 04.1	5.4	16 10.8	7.5	60.7
18	94 05.8	S15 53.5	251 28.5	5.4	N16 18.3	7.3	60.7
19	109 05.8	54.3	265 52.9	5.3	16 25.6	7.3	60.7
20	124 05.7	55.0	280 17.2	5.2	16 32.9	7.1	60.7
21	139 05.7	. . 55.8	294 41.4	5.3	16 40.0	7.0	60.7
22	154 05.7	56.5	309 05.7	5.1	16 47.0	6.9	60.7
23	169 05.7	57.3	323 29.8	5.2	N16 53.9	6.7	60.7
	SD 16.2	*d* 0.8	SD 16.3		16.4		16.5

Lat. °	Twilight Naut. h m	Twilight Civil h m	Sunrise h m	Moonrise 3 h m	Moonrise 4 h m	Moonrise 5 h m	Moonrise 6 h m
N 72	06 19	07 44	09 17	15 37	15 24	15 06	▭
N 70	06 13	07 29	08 47	15 48	15 46	15 44	15 44
68	06 08	07 17	08 24	15 58	16 02	16 10	16 27
66	06 04	07 07	08 07	16 06	16 16	16 31	16 55
64	06 01	06 58	07 52	16 13	16 27	16 47	17 17
62	05 57	06 51	07 40	16 19	16 37	17 01	17 35
60	05 54	06 44	07 30	16 24	16 45	17 13	17 50
N 58	05 52	06 39	07 21	16 28	16 53	17 23	18 02
56	05 49	06 33	07 14	16 32	16 59	17 32	18 13
54	05 47	06 29	07 07	16 36	17 05	17 40	18 23
52	05 44	06 24	07 00	16 39	17 10	17 47	18 32
50	05 42	06 21	06 55	16 42	17 15	17 53	18 39
45	05 37	06 12	06 43	16 49	17 26	18 07	18 56
N 40	05 32	06 04	06 33	16 55	17 34	18 19	19 09
35	05 28	05 58	06 24	16 59	17 42	18 29	19 21
30	05 23	05 51	06 16	17 04	17 48	18 37	19 31
20	05 14	05 40	06 03	17 11	18 00	18 52	19 49
N 10	05 04	05 29	05 51	17 18	18 10	19 05	20 04
0	04 54	05 19	05 40	17 24	18 20	19 18	20 18
S 10	04 41	05 07	05 29	17 30	18 29	19 30	20 33
20	04 27	04 54	05 17	17 37	18 40	19 44	20 48
30	04 07	04 37	05 03	17 45	18 52	19 59	21 06
35	03 55	04 28	04 55	17 49	18 59	20 08	21 16
40	03 40	04 16	04 45	17 55	19 06	20 18	21 28
45	03 22	04 02	04 34	18 01	19 16	20 31	21 42
S 50	02 57	03 44	04 21	18 08	19 27	20 45	21 59
52	02 45	03 36	04 15	18 11	19 32	20 52	22 08
54	02 31	03 26	04 08	18 15	19 38	21 00	22 17
56	02 13	03 15	04 00	18 19	19 44	21 08	22 27
58	01 52	03 03	03 52	18 24	19 52	21 18	22 38
S 60	01 23	02 48	03 42	18 29	20 00	21 29	22 52

Lat. °	Sunset h m	Twilight Civil h m	Twilight Naut. h m	Moonset 3 h m	Moonset 4 h m	Moonset 5 h m	Moonset 6 h m
N 72	14 08	15 42	17 07	06 18	08 25	10 44	▭
N 70	14 39	15 57	17 13	06 09	08 05	10 07	12 12
68	15 02	16 09	17 17	06 01	07 50	09 41	11 30
66	15 19	16 19	17 22	05 55	07 38	09 22	11 02
64	15 34	16 28	17 25	05 49	07 27	09 06	10 40
62	15 46	16 35	17 29	05 45	07 19	08 53	10 23
60	15 56	16 42	17 32	05 41	07 11	08 42	10 08
N 58	16 05	16 48	17 35	05 37	07 05	08 32	09 56
56	16 13	16 53	17 37	05 34	06 59	08 24	09 46
54	16 20	16 58	17 40	05 31	06 54	08 17	09 36
52	16 26	17 02	17 42	05 29	06 49	08 10	09 28
50	16 32	17 06	17 44	05 27	06 45	08 04	09 21
45	16 44	17 15	17 50	05 22	06 36	07 51	09 05
N 40	16 54	17 22	17 55	05 17	06 29	07 41	08 52
35	17 03	17 29	17 59	05 14	06 22	07 32	08 41
30	17 11	17 35	18 04	05 11	06 16	07 24	08 31
20	17 24	17 47	18 13	05 05	06 07	07 10	08 14
N 10	17 36	17 58	18 23	05 00	05 58	06 58	08 00
0	17 47	18 09	18 33	04 56	05 50	06 47	07 46
S 10	17 58	18 20	18 46	04 51	05 42	06 36	07 33
20	18 11	18 34	19 01	04 47	05 34	06 24	07 18
30	18 25	18 50	19 21	04 41	05 24	06 11	07 02
35	18 33	19 00	19 33	04 38	05 18	06 03	06 52
40	18 42	19 12	19 48	04 35	05 12	05 54	06 41
45	18 54	19 26	20 07	04 30	05 05	05 44	06 28
S 50	19 07	19 44	20 32	04 26	04 56	05 31	06 13
52	19 13	19 53	20 44	04 23	04 52	05 25	06 06
54	19 20	20 02	20 59	04 21	04 48	05 19	05 58
56	19 28	20 14	21 16	04 18	04 43	05 12	05 49
58	19 37	20 26	21 39	04 15	04 37	05 04	05 38
S 60	19 47	20 42	22 09	04 12	04 31	04 55	05 27

Day d	SUN Eqn. of Time 00^h m s	SUN Eqn. of Time 12^h m s	SUN Mer. Pass. h m	MOON Mer. Pass. Upper h m	MOON Mer. Pass. Lower h m	MOON Age d	MOON Phase %
3	16 26	16 26	11 44	23 37	11 10	15	99
4	16 26	16 25	11 44	24 33	12 05	16	100 ○
5	16 24	16 24	11 44	00 33	13 02	17	97

UT d	h	ARIES GHA	VENUS −3·9 GHA	VENUS Dec	MARS +1·8 GHA	MARS Dec	JUPITER −1·7 GHA	JUPITER Dec	SATURN +0·5 GHA	SATURN Dec
		° ′	° ′	° ′	° ′	° ′	° ′	° ′	° ′	° ′
6	00	45 24.0	198 44.8	S 9 29.1	216 42.2	S 2 31.5	191 36.5	S12 28.9	140 42.6	S22 21.9
	01	60 26.4	213 44.3	30.2	231 43.2	32.1	206 38.5	29.1	155 44.8	21.9
	02	75 28.9	228 43.8	31.4	246 44.2	32.7	221 40.4	29.3	170 47.0	21.9
	03	90 31.4	243 43.3	32.5	261 45.2	33.3	236 42.4	29.5	185 49.2	21.9
	04	105 33.8	258 42.8	33.7	276 46.3	34.0	251 44.3	29.6	200 51.4	22.0
	05	120 36.3	273 42.3	34.8	291 47.3	34.6	266 46.2	29.8	215 53.6	22.0
	06	135 38.8	288 41.9	S 9 36.0	306 48.3	S 2 35.2	281 48.2	S12 30.0	230 55.8	S22 22.0
	07	150 41.2	303 41.4	37.1	321 49.3	35.8	296 50.1	30.2	245 58.0	22.0
	08	165 43.7	318 40.9	38.3	336 50.3	36.5	311 52.1	30.4	261 00.2	22.0
M	09	180 46.2	333 40.4	39.4	351 51.3	37.1	326 54.0	30.5	276 02.4	22.0
O	10	195 48.6	348 39.9	40.6	6 52.3	37.7	341 55.9	30.7	291 04.6	22.0
N	11	210 51.1	3 39.4	41.7	21 53.4	38.3	356 57.9	30.9	306 06.8	22.1
D	12	225 53.6	18 38.9	S 9 42.9	36 54.4	S 2 39.0	11 59.8	S12 31.1	321 09.0	S22 22.1
A	13	240 56.0	33 38.4	44.0	51 55.4	39.6	27 01.8	31.3	336 11.2	22.1
Y	14	255 58.5	48 38.0	45.2	66 56.4	40.2	42 03.7	31.4	351 13.4	22.1
	15	271 00.9	63 37.5	46.3	81 57.4	40.8	57 05.6	31.6	6 15.6	22.1
	16	286 03.4	78 37.0	47.4	96 58.4	41.5	72 07.6	31.8	21 17.8	22.1
	17	301 05.9	93 36.5	48.6	111 59.4	42.1	87 09.5	32.0	36 20.0	22.1
	18	316 08.3	108 36.0	S 9 49.7	127 00.5	S 2 42.7	102 11.4	S12 32.2	51 22.2	S22 22.2
	19	331 10.8	123 35.5	50.9	142 01.5	43.3	117 13.4	32.3	66 24.4	22.2
	20	346 13.3	138 35.0	52.0	157 02.5	44.0	132 15.3	32.5	81 26.6	22.2
	21	1 15.7	153 34.5	53.2	172 03.5	44.6	147 17.3	32.7	96 28.8	22.2
	22	16 18.2	168 34.0	54.3	187 04.5	45.2	162 19.2	32.9	111 31.0	22.2
	23	31 20.7	183 33.5	55.5	202 05.5	45.8	177 21.1	33.1	126 33.2	22.2
7	00	46 23.1	198 33.0	S 9 56.6	217 06.5	S 2 46.4	192 23.1	S12 33.2	141 35.4	S22 22.2
	01	61 25.6	213 32.5	57.7	232 07.6	47.1	207 25.0	33.4	156 37.6	22.3
	02	76 28.0	228 32.0	9 58.9	247 08.6	47.7	222 27.0	33.6	171 39.8	22.3
	03	91 30.5	243 31.5	10 00.0	262 09.6	48.3	237 28.9	33.8	186 42.0	22.3
	04	106 33.0	258 31.1	01.2	277 10.6	48.9	252 30.8	34.0	201 44.2	22.3
	05	121 35.4	273 30.6	02.3	292 11.6	49.6	267 32.8	34.1	216 46.4	22.3
	06	136 37.9	288 30.1	S10 03.4	307 12.6	S 2 50.2	282 34.7	S12 34.3	231 48.6	S22 22.3
	07	151 40.4	303 29.6	04.6	322 13.6	50.8	297 36.7	34.5	246 50.8	22.3
T	08	166 42.8	318 29.1	05.7	337 14.7	51.4	312 38.6	34.7	261 53.0	22.4
U	09	181 45.3	333 28.6	06.8	352 15.7	52.1	327 40.5	34.9	276 55.2	22.4
E	10	196 47.8	348 28.1	08.0	7 16.7	52.7	342 42.5	35.0	291 57.4	22.4
S	11	211 50.2	3 27.6	09.1	22 17.7	53.3	357 44.4	35.2	306 59.6	22.4
D	12	226 52.7	18 27.1	S10 10.3	37 18.7	S 2 53.9	12 46.4	S12 35.4	322 01.8	S22 22.4
A	13	241 55.2	33 26.6	11.4	52 19.7	54.6	27 48.3	35.6	337 04.0	22.4
Y	14	256 57.6	48 26.1	12.5	67 20.7	55.2	42 50.2	35.8	352 06.1	22.4
	15	272 00.1	63 25.6	13.7	82 21.8	55.8	57 52.2	35.9	7 08.3	22.5
	16	287 02.5	78 25.1	14.8	97 22.8	56.4	72 54.1	36.1	22 10.5	22.5
	17	302 05.0	93 24.6	15.9	112 23.8	57.1	87 56.0	36.3	37 12.7	22.5
	18	317 07.5	108 24.1	S10 17.1	127 24.8	S 2 57.7	102 58.0	S12 36.5	52 14.9	S22 22.5
	19	332 09.9	123 23.6	18.2	142 25.8	58.3	117 59.9	36.6	67 17.1	22.5
	20	347 12.4	138 23.1	19.3	157 26.8	58.9	133 01.9	36.8	82 19.3	22.5
	21	2 14.9	153 22.6	20.5	172 27.8	2 59.5	148 03.8	37.0	97 21.5	22.5
	22	17 17.3	168 22.1	21.6	187 28.9	3 00.2	163 05.7	37.2	112 23.7	22.6
	23	32 19.8	183 21.6	22.7	202 29.9	00.8	178 07.7	37.4	127 25.9	22.6
8	00	47 22.3	198 21.1	S10 23.9	217 30.9	S 3 01.4	193 09.6	S12 37.5	142 28.1	S22 22.6
	01	62 24.7	213 20.6	25.0	232 31.9	02.0	208 11.6	37.7	157 30.3	22.6
	02	77 27.2	228 20.1	26.1	247 32.9	02.7	223 13.5	37.9	172 32.5	22.6
	03	92 29.7	243 19.6	27.3	262 33.9	03.3	238 15.4	38.1	187 34.7	22.6
	04	107 32.1	258 19.1	28.4	277 34.9	03.9	253 17.4	38.3	202 36.9	22.6
	05	122 34.6	273 18.6	29.5	292 35.9	04.5	268 19.3	38.4	217 39.1	22.7
	06	137 37.0	288 18.1	S10 30.7	307 37.0	S 3 05.2	283 21.3	S12 38.6	232 41.3	S22 22.7
W	07	152 39.5	303 17.5	31.8	322 38.0	05.8	298 23.2	38.8	247 43.5	22.7
E	08	167 42.0	318 17.0	32.9	337 39.0	06.4	313 25.1	39.0	262 45.7	22.7
D	09	182 44.4	333 16.5	34.0	352 40.0	07.0	328 27.1	39.2	277 47.9	22.7
N	10	197 46.9	348 16.0	35.2	7 41.0	07.6	343 29.0	39.3	292 50.0	22.7
E	11	212 49.4	3 15.5	36.3	22 42.0	08.3	358 31.0	39.5	307 52.2	22.7
S	12	227 51.8	18 15.0	S10 37.4	37 43.0	S 3 08.9	13 32.9	S12 39.7	322 54.4	S22 22.7
D	13	242 54.3	33 14.5	38.5	52 44.1	09.5	28 34.8	39.9	337 56.6	22.8
A	14	257 56.8	48 14.0	39.7	67 45.1	10.1	43 36.8	40.0	352 58.8	22.8
Y	15	272 59.2	63 13.5	40.8	82 46.1	10.8	58 38.7	40.2	8 01.0	22.8
	16	288 01.7	78 13.0	41.9	97 47.1	11.4	73 40.7	40.4	23 03.2	22.8
	17	303 04.2	93 12.5	43.1	112 48.1	12.0	88 42.6	40.6	38 05.4	22.8
	18	318 06.6	108 12.0	S10 44.2	127 49.1	S 3 12.6	103 44.5	S12 40.8	53 07.6	S22 22.8
	19	333 09.1	123 11.5	45.3	142 50.1	13.3	118 46.5	40.9	68 09.8	22.8
	20	348 11.5	138 10.9	46.4	157 51.1	13.9	133 48.4	41.1	83 12.0	22.9
	21	3 14.0	153 10.4	47.5	172 52.2	14.5	148 50.4	41.3	98 14.2	22.9
	22	18 16.5	168 09.9	48.7	187 53.2	15.1	163 52.3	41.5	113 16.4	22.9
	23	33 18.9	183 09.4	49.8	202 54.2	15.7	178 54.2	41.6	128 18.6	22.9
Mer. Pass.		h m 20 51.0	*v* −0.5	*d* 1.1	*v* 1.0	*d* 0.6	*v* 1.9	*d* 0.2	*v* 2.2	*d* 0.0

STARS

Name	SHA	Dec
	° ′	° ′
Acamar	315 15.7	S40 14.1
Achernar	335 24.1	S57 09.0
Acrux	173 06.4	S63 11.5
Adhara	255 10.0	S28 59.7
Aldebaran	290 45.7	N16 32.5
Alioth	166 18.7	N55 51.8
Alkaid	152 57.1	N49 13.6
Al Na'ir	27 40.0	S46 52.6
Alnilam	275 43.1	S 1 11.5
Alphard	217 53.2	S 8 44.1
Alphecca	126 08.9	N26 39.6
Alpheratz	357 40.2	N29 11.4
Altair	62 05.5	N 8 55.2
Ankaa	353 12.5	S42 12.7
Antares	112 23.0	S26 28.0
Arcturus	145 53.4	N19 05.6
Atria	107 22.6	S69 03.4
Avior	234 16.6	S59 33.8
Bellatrix	278 28.6	N 6 21.8
Betelgeuse	270 57.9	N 7 24.5
Canopus	263 54.5	S52 42.2
Capella	280 29.7	N46 00.7
Deneb	49 29.5	N45 21.0
Denebola	182 30.9	N14 28.4
Diphda	348 52.7	S17 53.4
Dubhe	193 48.6	N61 39.1
Elnath	278 08.6	N28 37.1
Eltanin	90 45.2	N51 29.6
Enif	33 44.2	N 9 57.6
Fomalhaut	15 20.6	S29 31.8
Gacrux	171 58.0	S57 12.4
Gienah	175 49.5	S17 38.2
Hadar	148 44.3	S60 27.2
Hamal	327 57.1	N23 32.8
Kaus Aust.	83 40.2	S34 22.4
Kochab	137 21.4	N74 05.1
Markab	13 35.2	N15 18.2
Menkar	314 11.6	N 4 09.5
Menkent	148 04.5	S36 27.2
Miaplacidus	221 39.0	S69 47.1
Mirfak	308 35.6	N49 55.3
Nunki	75 54.9	S26 16.3
Peacock	53 14.8	S56 40.8
Pollux	243 24.0	N27 58.8
Procyon	244 56.5	N 5 10.7
Rasalhague	96 04.0	N12 33.2
Regulus	207 40.5	N11 52.8
Rigel	281 08.9	S 8 11.0
Rigil Kent.	139 48.3	S60 54.2
Sabik	102 09.5	S15 44.6
Schedar	349 36.6	N56 38.2
Shaula	96 18.3	S37 06.8
Sirius	258 30.9	S16 44.4
Spica	158 28.4	S11 15.0
Suhail	222 50.2	S43 30.0
Vega	80 37.2	N38 48.4
Zuben'ubi	137 02.5	S16 06.6

	SHA	Mer. Pass.
	° ′	h m
Venus	152 09.9	10 46
Mars	170 43.4	9 31
Jupiter	146 00.0	11 09
Saturn	95 12.3	14 32

UT		SUN GHA	SUN Dec	MOON GHA	*v*	MOON Dec	*d*	HP
d	h	° ′	° ′	° ′	′	° ′	′	′
6	00	184 05.6	S15 58.0	337 54.0	5.1	N17 00.6	6.7	60.7
	01	199 05.6	58.8	352 18.1	5.0	17 07.3	6.5	60.7
	02	214 05.6	15 59.5	6 42.1	5.0	17 13.8	6.4	60.7
	03	229 05.6	16 00.3	21 06.1	5.0	17 20.2	6.3	60.7
	04	244 05.5	01.0	35 30.1	4.9	17 26.5	6.1	60.7
	05	259 05.5	01.7	49 54.0	4.9	17 32.6	6.0	60.7
	06	274 05.5	S16 02.5	64 17.9	4.8	N17 38.6	6.0	60.7
	07	289 05.5	03.2	78 41.7	4.9	17 44.6	5.7	60.7
	08	304 05.4	04.0	93 05.6	4.7	17 50.3	5.7	60.7
MONDAY	09	319 05.4	. . 04.7	107 29.3	4.8	17 56.0	5.5	60.6
	10	334 05.4	05.5	121 53.1	4.7	18 01.5	5.4	60.6
	11	349 05.4	06.2	136 16.8	4.7	18 06.9	5.2	60.6
	12	4 05.3	S16 07.0	150 40.5	4.6	N18 12.1	5.2	60.6
	13	19 05.3	07.7	165 04.1	4.7	18 17.3	5.0	60.6
	14	34 05.3	08.4	179 27.8	4.6	18 22.3	4.8	60.6
	15	49 05.2	. . 09.2	193 51.4	4.6	18 27.1	4.8	60.6
	16	64 05.2	09.9	208 15.0	4.5	18 31.9	4.6	60.6
	17	79 05.2	10.7	222 38.5	4.5	18 36.5	4.4	60.6
	18	94 05.2	S16 11.4	237 02.0	4.6	N18 40.9	4.4	60.6
	19	109 05.1	12.2	251 25.6	4.4	18 45.3	4.2	60.6
	20	124 05.1	12.9	265 49.0	4.5	18 49.5	4.0	60.6
	21	139 05.1	. . 13.6	280 12.5	4.5	18 53.5	3.9	60.6
	22	154 05.0	14.4	294 36.0	4.4	18 57.4	3.8	60.6
	23	169 05.0	15.1	308 59.4	4.4	19 01.2	3.7	60.6
7	00	184 05.0	S16 15.8	323 22.8	4.5	N19 04.9	3.5	60.5
	01	199 04.9	16.6	337 46.3	4.4	19 08.4	3.4	60.5
	02	214 04.9	17.3	352 09.7	4.4	19 11.8	3.2	60.5
	03	229 04.9	. . 18.1	6 33.1	4.4	19 15.0	3.1	60.5
	04	244 04.8	18.8	20 56.5	4.3	19 18.1	2.9	60.5
	05	259 04.8	19.5	35 19.8	4.4	19 21.0	2.9	60.5
	06	274 04.8	S16 20.3	49 43.2	4.4	N19 23.9	2.6	60.5
	07	289 04.7	21.0	64 06.6	4.4	19 26.5	2.6	60.5
	08	304 04.7	21.7	78 30.0	4.3	19 29.1	2.4	60.4
TUESDAY	09	319 04.7	. . 22.5	92 53.3	4.4	19 31.5	2.2	60.4
	10	334 04.6	23.2	107 16.7	4.4	19 33.7	2.1	60.4
	11	349 04.6	23.9	121 40.1	4.4	19 35.8	2.0	60.4
	12	4 04.5	S16 24.7	136 03.5	4.4	N19 37.8	1.8	60.4
	13	19 04.5	25.4	150 26.9	4.4	19 39.6	1.7	60.4
	14	34 04.5	26.1	164 50.3	4.4	19 41.3	1.5	60.4
	15	49 04.4	. . 26.9	179 13.7	4.4	19 42.8	1.4	60.3
	16	64 04.4	27.6	193 37.1	4.5	19 44.2	1.3	60.3
	17	79 04.4	28.3	208 00.6	4.4	19 45.5	1.1	60.3
	18	94 04.3	S16 29.0	222 24.0	4.5	N19 46.6	1.0	60.3
	19	109 04.3	29.8	236 47.5	4.5	19 47.6	0.8	60.3
	20	124 04.2	30.5	251 11.0	4.5	19 48.4	0.7	60.3
	21	139 04.2	. . 31.2	265 34.5	4.5	19 49.1	0.6	60.2
	22	154 04.2	32.0	279 58.0	4.5	19 49.7	0.4	60.2
	23	169 04.1	32.7	294 21.5	4.6	19 50.1	0.3	60.2
8	00	184 04.1	S16 33.4	308 45.1	4.6	N19 50.4	0.1	60.2
	01	199 04.0	34.1	323 08.7	4.6	19 50.5	0.0	60.2
	02	214 04.0	34.9	337 32.3	4.7	19 50.5	0.1	60.1
	03	229 03.9	. . 35.6	351 56.0	4.7	19 50.4	0.3	60.1
	04	244 03.9	36.3	6 19.7	4.7	19 50.1	0.4	60.1
	05	259 03.9	37.0	20 43.4	4.7	19 49.7	0.6	60.1
	06	274 03.8	S16 37.8	35 07.1	4.8	N19 49.1	0.7	60.1
WEDNESDAY	07	289 03.8	38.5	49 30.9	4.8	19 48.4	0.8	60.0
	08	304 03.7	39.2	63 54.7	4.9	19 47.6	1.0	60.0
	09	319 03.7	. . 39.9	78 18.6	4.9	19 46.6	1.1	60.0
	10	334 03.6	40.6	92 42.5	4.9	19 45.5	1.3	60.0
	11	349 03.6	41.4	107 06.4	5.0	19 44.2	1.4	60.0
	12	4 03.5	S16 42.1	121 30.4	5.0	N19 42.8	1.5	59.9
	13	19 03.5	42.8	135 54.4	5.0	19 41.3	1.6	59.9
	14	34 03.5	43.5	150 18.4	5.1	19 39.7	1.8	59.9
	15	49 03.4	. . 44.2	164 42.5	5.2	19 37.9	1.9	59.9
	16	64 03.4	45.0	179 06.7	5.2	19 36.0	2.1	59.9
	17	79 03.3	45.7	193 30.9	5.2	19 33.9	2.2	59.8
	18	94 03.3	S16 46.4	207 55.1	5.3	N19 31.7	2.3	59.8
	19	109 03.2	47.1	222 19.4	5.4	19 29.4	2.4	59.8
	20	124 03.2	47.8	236 43.8	5.4	19 27.0	2.6	59.8
	21	139 03.1	. . 48.6	251 08.2	5.4	19 24.4	2.7	59.7
	22	154 03.1	49.3	265 32.6	5.5	19 21.7	2.9	59.7
	23	169 03.0	50.0	279 57.1	5.6	N19 18.8	2.9	59.7
		SD 16.2	*d* 0.7	SD 16.5		16.5		16.3

Lat.	Twilight Naut.	Twilight Civil	Sunrise	Moonrise 6	Moonrise 7	Moonrise 8	Moonrise 9
°	h m	h m	h m	h m	h m	h m	h m
N 72	06 30	07 57	09 39	□	□	□	17 24
N 70	06 23	07 41	09 03	15 44	15 55	17 04	18 59
68	06 18	07 27	08 37	16 27	17 01	18 07	19 39
66	06 13	07 16	08 18	16 55	17 37	18 42	20 06
64	06 08	07 06	08 02	17 17	18 03	19 07	20 27
62	06 04	06 58	07 49	17 35	18 23	19 27	20 44
60	06 01	06 51	07 38	17 50	18 40	19 43	20 58
N 58	05 57	06 45	07 28	18 02	18 54	19 57	21 10
56	05 54	06 39	07 20	18 13	19 06	20 09	21 20
54	05 52	06 34	07 13	18 23	19 16	20 19	21 29
52	05 49	06 29	07 06	18 32	19 25	20 28	21 37
50	05 46	06 25	07 00	18 39	19 34	20 36	21 45
45	05 41	06 16	06 47	18 56	19 52	20 54	22 00
N 40	05 35	06 08	06 36	19 09	20 06	21 08	22 13
35	05 30	06 00	06 27	19 21	20 18	21 20	22 24
30	05 25	05 54	06 19	19 31	20 29	21 31	22 33
20	05 15	05 42	06 04	19 49	20 48	21 49	22 50
N 10	05 05	05 30	05 52	20 04	21 04	22 04	23 04
0	04 54	05 19	05 40	20 18	21 19	22 19	23 17
S 10	04 41	05 06	05 28	20 33	21 34	22 34	23 30
20	04 25	04 52	05 15	20 48	21 51	22 50	23 44
30	04 05	04 35	05 01	21 06	22 09	23 08	24 01
35	03 52	04 25	04 52	21 16	22 20	23 19	24 10
40	03 36	04 12	04 42	21 28	22 33	23 31	24 21
45	03 17	03 58	04 30	21 42	22 48	23 45	24 33
S 50	02 51	03 39	04 16	21 59	23 06	24 02	00 02
52	02 37	03 30	04 10	22 08	23 14	24 10	00 10
54	02 22	03 20	04 02	22 17	23 24	24 20	00 20
56	02 03	03 08	03 54	22 27	23 35	24 30	00 30
58	01 39	02 54	03 45	22 38	23 47	24 41	00 41
S 60	01 04	02 38	03 34	22 52	24 02	00 02	00 55

Lat.	Sunset	Twilight Civil	Twilight Naut.	Moonset 6	Moonset 7	Moonset 8	Moonset 9
°	h m	h m	h m	h m	h m	h m	h m
N 72	13 47	15 29	16 56	□	□	□	16 50
N 70	14 24	15 46	17 03	12 12	14 09	15 06	15 14
68	14 49	15 59	17 08	11 30	13 03	14 04	14 34
66	15 09	16 10	17 14	11 02	12 27	13 28	14 06
64	15 24	16 20	17 18	10 40	12 01	13 03	13 44
62	15 38	16 28	17 22	10 23	11 41	12 43	13 27
60	15 49	16 35	17 26	10 08	11 25	12 27	13 13
N 58	15 58	16 42	17 29	09 56	11 11	12 13	13 00
56	16 07	16 47	17 32	09 46	10 59	12 01	12 50
54	16 14	16 53	17 35	09 36	10 49	11 50	12 40
52	16 21	16 57	17 38	09 28	10 40	11 41	12 32
50	16 27	17 02	17 40	09 21	10 31	11 33	12 24
45	16 40	17 11	17 46	09 05	10 14	11 15	12 08
N 40	16 51	17 19	17 52	08 52	09 59	11 01	11 55
35	17 00	17 27	17 57	08 41	09 47	10 48	11 43
30	17 08	17 33	18 02	08 31	09 36	10 38	11 33
20	17 23	17 46	18 12	08 14	09 18	10 19	11 16
N 10	17 35	17 57	18 22	08 00	09 02	10 03	11 01
0	17 47	18 09	18 34	07 46	08 47	09 48	10 47
S 10	17 59	18 21	18 47	07 33	08 32	09 33	10 33
20	18 12	18 35	19 03	07 18	08 16	09 17	10 18
30	18 27	18 53	19 23	07 02	07 58	08 58	10 00
35	18 36	19 03	19 36	06 52	07 47	08 47	09 50
40	18 46	19 16	19 52	06 41	07 35	08 35	09 38
45	18 58	19 31	20 12	06 28	07 21	08 20	09 24
S 50	19 12	19 50	20 38	06 13	07 03	08 02	09 08
52	19 19	19 59	20 52	06 06	06 55	07 53	09 00
54	19 26	20 09	21 08	05 58	06 45	07 44	08 51
56	19 35	20 21	21 27	05 49	06 35	07 33	08 41
58	19 44	20 35	21 52	05 38	06 23	07 20	08 29
S 60	19 55	20 52	22 30	05 27	06 09	07 06	08 16

Day	SUN Eqn. of Time 00^h	SUN Eqn. of Time 12^h	SUN Mer. Pass.	MOON Mer. Pass. Upper	MOON Mer. Pass. Lower	MOON Age	MOON Phase
d	m s	m s	h m	h m	h m	d %	
6	16 23	16 21	11 44	01 32	14 02	18 92	
7	16 20	16 18	11 44	02 33	15 03	19 85	◑
8	16 16	16 14	11 44	03 34	16 04	20 76	

UT	ARIES	VENUS −3·9		MARS +1·8		JUPITER −1·7		SATURN +0·5	
	GHA	GHA	Dec	GHA	Dec	GHA	Dec	GHA	Dec
d h	° ′	° ′	° ′	° ′	° ′	° ′	° ′	° ′	° ′
9 00	48 21.4	198 08.9	S10 50.9	217 55.2	S 3 16.4	193 56.2	S12 41.8	143 20.8	S22 22.9
01	63 23.9	213 08.4	52.0	232 56.2	17.0	208 58.1	42.0	158 22.9	22.9
02	78 26.3	228 07.9	53.2	247 57.2	17.6	224 00.0	42.2	173 25.1	22.9
03	93 28.8	243 07.4	. . 54.3	262 58.2	. . 18.2	239 02.0	. . 42.4	188 27.3	. . 23.0
04	108 31.3	258 06.8	55.4	277 59.3	18.9	254 03.9	42.5	203 29.5	23.0
05	123 33.7	273 06.3	56.5	293 00.3	19.5	269 05.9	42.7	218 31.7	23.0
06	138 36.2	288 05.8	S10 57.6	308 01.3	S 3 20.1	284 07.8	S12 42.9	233 33.9	S22 23.0
07	153 38.7	303 05.3	58.8	323 02.3	20.7	299 09.7	43.1	248 36.1	23.0
T 08	168 41.1	318 04.8	10 59.9	338 03.3	21.3	314 11.7	43.2	263 38.3	23.0
H 09	183 43.6	333 04.3	11 01.0	353 04.3	. . 22.0	329 13.6	. . 43.4	278 40.5	. . 23.0
U 10	198 46.0	348 03.8	02.1	8 05.3	22.6	344 15.6	43.6	293 42.7	23.1
R 11	213 48.5	3 03.2	03.2	23 06.3	23.2	359 17.5	43.8	308 44.9	23.1
S 12	228 51.0	18 02.7	S11 04.3	38 07.4	S 3 23.8	14 19.4	S12 44.0	323 47.1	S22 23.1
D 13	243 53.4	33 02.2	05.5	53 08.4	24.5	29 21.4	44.1	338 49.3	23.1
A 14	258 55.9	48 01.7	06.6	68 09.4	25.1	44 23.3	44.3	353 51.4	23.1
Y 15	273 58.4	63 01.2	. . 07.7	83 10.4	. . 25.7	59 25.3	. . 44.5	8 53.6	. . 23.1
16	289 00.8	78 00.7	08.8	98 11.4	26.3	74 27.2	44.7	23 55.8	23.1
17	304 03.3	93 00.1	09.9	113 12.4	26.9	89 29.1	44.8	38 58.0	23.1
18	319 05.8	107 59.6	S11 11.0	128 13.4	S 3 27.6	104 31.1	S12 45.0	54 00.2	S22 23.2
19	334 08.2	122 59.1	12.1	143 14.4	28.2	119 33.0	45.2	69 02.4	23.2
20	349 10.7	137 58.6	13.3	158 15.5	28.8	134 35.0	45.4	84 04.6	23.2
21	4 13.1	152 58.1	. . 14.4	173 16.5	. . 29.4	149 36.9	. . 45.6	99 06.8	. . 23.2
22	19 15.6	167 57.5	15.5	188 17.5	30.0	164 38.8	45.7	114 09.0	23.2
23	34 18.1	182 57.0	16.6	203 18.5	30.7	179 40.8	45.9	129 11.2	23.2
10 00	49 20.5	197 56.5	S11 17.7	218 19.5	S 3 31.3	194 42.7	S12 46.1	144 13.4	S22 23.2
01	64 23.0	212 56.0	18.8	233 20.5	31.9	209 44.7	46.3	159 15.5	23.3
02	79 25.5	227 55.4	19.9	248 21.5	32.5	224 46.6	46.4	174 17.7	23.3
03	94 27.9	242 54.9	. . 21.0	263 22.5	. . 33.1	239 48.5	. . 46.6	189 19.9	. . 23.3
04	109 30.4	257 54.4	22.1	278 23.5	33.8	254 50.5	46.8	204 22.1	23.3
05	124 32.9	272 53.9	23.3	293 24.6	34.4	269 52.4	47.0	219 24.3	23.3
06	139 35.3	287 53.4	S11 24.4	308 25.6	S 3 35.0	284 54.4	S12 47.2	234 26.5	S22 23.3
07	154 37.8	302 52.8	25.5	323 26.6	35.6	299 56.3	47.3	249 28.7	23.3
08	169 40.3	317 52.3	26.6	338 27.6	36.3	314 58.2	47.5	264 30.9	23.4
F 09	184 42.7	332 51.8	. . 27.7	353 28.6	. . 36.9	330 00.2	. . 47.7	279 33.1	. . 23.4
R 10	199 45.2	347 51.2	28.8	8 29.6	37.5	345 02.1	47.9	294 35.3	23.4
I 11	214 47.6	2 50.7	29.9	23 30.6	38.1	0 04.1	48.0	309 37.4	23.4
D 12	229 50.1	17 50.2	S11 31.0	38 31.6	S 3 38.7	15 06.0	S12 48.2	324 39.6	S22 23.4
A 13	244 52.6	32 49.7	32.1	53 32.7	39.4	30 07.9	48.4	339 41.8	23.4
Y 14	259 55.0	47 49.1	33.2	68 33.7	40.0	45 09.9	48.6	354 44.0	23.4
15	274 57.5	62 48.6	. . 34.3	83 34.7	. . 40.6	60 11.8	. . 48.7	9 46.2	. . 23.4
16	290 00.0	77 48.1	35.4	98 35.7	41.2	75 13.8	48.9	24 48.4	23.5
17	305 02.4	92 47.6	36.5	113 36.7	41.8	90 15.7	49.1	39 50.6	23.5
18	320 04.9	107 47.0	S11 37.6	128 37.7	S 3 42.5	105 17.6	S12 49.3	54 52.8	S22 23.5
19	335 07.4	122 46.5	38.7	143 38.7	43.1	120 19.6	49.5	69 55.0	23.5
20	350 09.8	137 46.0	39.8	158 39.7	43.7	135 21.5	49.6	84 57.1	23.5
21	5 12.3	152 45.4	. . 40.9	173 40.7	. . 44.3	150 23.5	. . 49.8	99 59.3	. . 23.5
22	20 14.8	167 44.9	42.0	188 41.8	44.9	165 25.4	50.0	115 01.5	23.5
23	35 17.2	182 44.4	43.1	203 42.8	45.6	180 27.3	50.2	130 03.7	23.6
11 00	50 19.7	197 43.8	S11 44.2	218 43.8	S 3 46.2	195 29.3	S12 50.3	145 05.9	S22 23.6
01	65 22.1	212 43.3	45.3	233 44.8	46.8	210 31.2	50.5	160 08.1	23.6
02	80 24.6	227 42.8	46.4	248 45.8	47.4	225 33.2	50.7	175 10.3	23.6
03	95 27.1	242 42.2	. . 47.5	263 46.8	. . 48.0	240 35.1	. . 50.9	190 12.5	. . 23.6
04	110 29.5	257 41.7	48.6	278 47.8	48.7	255 37.0	51.0	205 14.7	23.6
05	125 32.0	272 41.2	49.7	293 48.8	49.3	270 39.0	51.2	220 16.8	23.6
06	140 34.5	287 40.6	S11 50.8	308 49.8	S 3 49.9	285 40.9	S12 51.4	235 19.0	S22 23.6
07	155 36.9	302 40.1	51.9	323 50.9	50.5	300 42.9	51.6	250 21.2	23.7
S 08	170 39.4	317 39.6	53.0	338 51.9	51.1	315 44.8	51.7	265 23.4	23.7
A 09	185 41.9	332 39.0	. . 54.1	353 52.9	. . 51.8	330 46.7	. . 51.9	280 25.6	. . 23.7
T 10	200 44.3	347 38.5	55.2	8 53.9	52.4	345 48.7	52.1	295 27.8	23.7
U 11	215 46.8	2 38.0	56.3	23 54.9	53.0	0 50.6	52.3	310 30.0	23.7
R 12	230 49.3	17 37.4	S11 57.4	38 55.9	S 3 53.6	15 52.6	S12 52.5	325 32.2	S22 23.7
D 13	245 51.7	32 36.9	58.5	53 56.9	54.2	30 54.5	52.6	340 34.3	23.7
A 14	260 54.2	47 36.4	11 59.6	68 57.9	54.9	45 56.4	52.8	355 36.5	23.8
Y 15	275 56.6	62 35.8	12 00.7	83 58.9	. . 55.5	60 58.4	. . 53.0	10 38.7	. . 23.8
16	290 59.1	77 35.3	01.8	99 00.0	56.1	76 00.3	53.2	25 40.9	23.8
17	306 01.6	92 34.7	02.9	114 01.0	56.7	91 02.3	53.3	40 43.1	23.8
18	321 04.0	107 34.2	S12 04.0	129 02.0	S 3 57.3	106 04.2	S12 53.5	55 45.3	S22 23.8
19	336 06.5	122 33.7	05.1	144 03.0	58.0	121 06.2	53.7	70 47.5	23.8
20	351 09.0	137 33.1	06.1	159 04.0	58.6	136 08.1	53.9	85 49.7	23.8
21	6 11.4	152 32.6	. . 07.2	174 05.0	. . 59.2	151 10.0	. . 54.0	100 51.8	. . 23.8
22	21 13.9	167 32.0	08.3	189 06.0	3 59.8	166 12.0	54.2	115 54.0	23.9
23	36 16.4	182 31.5	09.4	204 07.0	S 4 00.4	181 13.9	54.4	130 56.2	23.9
Mer. Pass. (h m)	20 39.2	*v* −0.5	*d* 1.1	*v* 1.0	*d* 0.6	*v* 1.9	*d* 0.2	*v* 2.2	*d* 0.0

STARS Name	SHA	Dec
	° ′	° ′
Acamar	315 15.7	S40 14.1
Achernar	335 24.1	S57 09.0
Acrux	173 06.4	S63 11.5
Adhara	255 10.0	S28 59.7
Aldebaran	290 45.7	N16 32.5
Alioth	166 18.6	N55 51.8
Alkaid	152 57.1	N49 13.6
Al Na'ir	27 40.0	S46 52.6
Alnilam	275 43.1	S 1 11.5
Alphard	217 53.2	S 8 44.1
Alphecca	126 08.9	N26 39.6
Alpheratz	357 40.2	N29 11.5
Altair	62 05.5	N 8 55.2
Ankaa	353 12.5	S42 12.7
Antares	112 23.0	S26 28.0
Arcturus	145 53.4	N19 05.6
Atria	107 22.6	S69 03.4
Avior	234 16.6	S59 33.8
Bellatrix	278 28.6	N 6 21.8
Betelgeuse	270 57.8	N 7 24.5
Canopus	263 54.4	S52 42.2
Capella	280 29.7	N46 00.7
Deneb	49 29.5	N45 21.0
Denebola	182 30.9	N14 28.4
Diphda	348 52.7	S17 53.4
Dubhe	193 48.5	N61 39.1
Elnath	278 08.6	N28 37.1
Eltanin	90 45.2	N51 29.6
Enif	33 44.2	N 9 57.6
Fomalhaut	15 20.6	S29 31.8
Gacrux	171 58.0	S57 12.4
Gienah	175 49.5	S17 38.2
Hadar	148 44.2	S60 27.2
Hamal	327 57.1	N23 32.8
Kaus Aust.	83 40.2	S34 22.4
Kochab	137 21.4	N74 05.1
Markab	13 35.2	N15 18.2
Menkar	314 11.6	N 4 09.5
Menkent	148 04.4	S36 27.1
Miaplacidus	221 38.9	S69 47.1
Mirfak	308 35.6	N49 55.3
Nunki	75 54.9	S26 16.3
Peacock	53 14.8	S56 40.8
Pollux	243 24.0	N27 58.8
Procyon	244 56.5	N 5 10.7
Rasalhague	96 04.0	N12 33.1
Regulus	207 40.5	N11 52.8
Rigel	281 08.9	S 8 11.0
Rigil Kent.	139 48.3	S60 54.2
Sabik	102 09.5	S15 44.6
Schedar	349 36.6	N56 38.2
Shaula	96 18.3	S37 06.8
Sirius	258 30.9	S16 44.5
Spica	158 28.4	S11 15.0
Suhail	222 50.2	S43 30.0
Vega	80 37.2	N38 48.4
Zuben'ubi	137 02.5	S16 06.7

	SHA	Mer. Pass.
	° ′	h m
Venus	148 35.9	10 49
Mars	168 59.0	9 26
Jupiter	145 22.2	11 00
Saturn	94 52.8	14 21

UT		SUN GHA	SUN Dec	MOON GHA	v	MOON Dec	d	HP
d	h	° ′	° ′	° ′	′	° ′	′	′
9	00	184 03.0	S16 50.7	294 21.7	5.6	N19 15.9	3.1	59.7
	01	199 02.9	51.4	308 46.3	5.7	19 12.8	3.3	59.6
	02	214 02.9	52.1	323 11.0	5.7	19 09.5	3.3	59.6
	03	229 02.8	. . 52.8	337 35.7	5.8	19 06.2	3.5	59.6
	04	244 02.8	53.6	352 00.5	5.9	19 02.7	3.6	59.6
	05	259 02.7	54.3	6 25.4	5.9	18 59.1	3.7	59.5
	06	274 02.7	S16 55.0	20 50.3	5.9	N18 55.4	3.8	59.5
	07	289 02.6	55.7	35 15.2	6.1	18 51.6	4.0	59.5
T	08	304 02.5	56.4	49 40.3	6.1	18 47.6	4.1	59.5
H	09	319 02.5	. . 57.1	64 05.4	6.2	18 43.5	4.2	59.4
U	10	334 02.4	57.8	78 30.6	6.2	18 39.3	4.3	59.4
R	11	349 02.4	58.5	92 55.8	6.3	18 35.0	4.4	59.4
S	12	4 02.3	S16 59.2	107 21.1	6.4	N18 30.6	4.6	59.4
D	13	19 02.3	16 59.9	121 46.5	6.4	18 26.0	4.6	59.3
A	14	34 02.2	17 00.7	136 11.9	6.5	18 21.4	4.8	59.3
Y	15	49 02.2	. . 01.4	150 37.4	6.6	18 16.6	4.9	59.3
	16	64 02.1	02.1	165 03.0	6.6	18 11.7	5.0	59.3
	17	79 02.0	02.8	179 28.6	6.7	18 06.7	5.1	59.2
	18	94 02.0	S17 03.5	193 54.3	6.8	N18 01.6	5.2	59.2
	19	109 01.9	04.2	208 20.1	6.9	17 56.4	5.4	59.2
	20	124 01.9	04.9	222 46.0	6.9	17 51.0	5.4	59.1
	21	139 01.8	. . 05.6	237 11.9	7.0	17 45.6	5.6	59.1
	22	154 01.8	06.3	251 37.9	7.1	17 40.0	5.6	59.1
	23	169 01.7	07.0	266 04.0	7.1	17 34.4	5.8	59.1
10	00	184 01.6	S17 07.7	280 30.1	7.2	N17 28.6	5.9	59.0
	01	199 01.6	08.4	294 56.3	7.3	17 22.7	5.9	59.0
	02	214 01.5	09.1	309 22.6	7.4	17 16.8	6.1	59.0
	03	229 01.5	. . 09.8	323 49.0	7.4	17 10.7	6.2	59.0
	04	244 01.4	10.5	338 15.4	7.5	17 04.5	6.3	58.9
	05	259 01.3	11.2	352 41.9	7.6	16 58.2	6.3	58.9
	06	274 01.3	S17 11.9	7 08.5	7.7	N16 51.9	6.5	58.9
	07	289 01.2	12.6	21 35.2	7.7	16 45.4	6.6	58.8
	08	304 01.1	13.3	36 01.9	7.8	16 38.8	6.6	58.8
F	09	319 01.1	. . 14.0	50 28.7	7.9	16 32.2	6.8	58.8
R	10	334 01.0	14.7	64 55.6	8.0	16 25.4	6.8	58.8
I	11	349 01.0	15.4	79 22.6	8.0	16 18.6	7.0	58.7
D	12	4 00.9	S17 16.1	93 49.6	8.2	N16 11.6	7.0	58.7
A	13	19 00.8	16.8	108 16.8	8.2	16 04.6	7.1	58.7
Y	14	34 00.8	17.5	122 44.0	8.2	15 57.5	7.2	58.6
	15	49 00.7	. . 18.2	137 11.2	8.4	15 50.3	7.3	58.6
	16	64 00.6	18.9	151 38.6	8.4	15 43.0	7.4	58.6
	17	79 00.6	19.6	166 06.0	8.5	15 35.6	7.5	58.6
	18	94 00.5	S17 20.3	180 33.5	8.6	N15 28.1	7.5	58.5
	19	109 00.4	21.0	195 01.1	8.6	15 20.6	7.7	58.5
	20	124 00.4	21.6	209 28.7	8.8	15 12.9	7.7	58.5
	21	139 00.3	. . 22.3	223 56.5	8.8	15 05.2	7.8	58.4
	22	154 00.2	23.0	238 24.3	8.9	14 57.4	7.9	58.4
	23	169 00.2	23.7	252 52.2	8.9	14 49.5	7.9	58.4
11	00	184 00.1	S17 24.4	267 20.1	9.0	N14 41.6	8.0	58.4
	01	199 00.0	25.1	281 48.1	9.1	14 33.6	8.1	58.3
	02	214 00.0	25.8	296 16.2	9.2	14 25.5	8.2	58.3
	03	228 59.9	. . 26.5	310 44.4	9.3	14 17.3	8.3	58.3
	04	243 59.8	27.2	325 12.7	9.3	14 09.0	8.3	58.2
	05	258 59.7	27.9	339 41.0	9.4	14 00.7	8.4	58.2
	06	273 59.7	S17 28.5	354 09.4	9.5	N13 52.3	8.5	58.2
S	07	288 59.6	29.2	8 37.9	9.5	13 43.8	8.5	58.2
A	08	303 59.5	29.9	23 06.4	9.7	13 35.3	8.6	58.1
T	09	318 59.5	. . 30.6	37 35.1	9.7	13 26.7	8.7	58.1
U	10	333 59.4	31.3	52 03.8	9.7	13 18.0	8.7	58.1
R	11	348 59.3	32.0	66 32.5	9.9	13 09.3	8.8	58.1
D	12	3 59.2	S17 32.7	81 01.4	9.9	N13 00.5	8.9	58.0
A	13	18 59.2	33.3	95 30.3	10.0	12 51.6	8.9	58.0
Y	14	33 59.1	34.0	109 59.3	10.0	12 42.7	9.0	58.0
	15	48 59.0	. . 34.7	124 28.3	10.1	12 33.7	9.1	57.9
	16	63 58.9	35.4	138 57.4	10.2	12 24.6	9.1	57.9
	17	78 58.9	36.1	153 26.6	10.3	12 15.5	9.2	57.9
	18	93 58.8	S17 36.8	167 55.9	10.3	N12 06.3	9.2	57.9
	19	108 58.7	37.4	182 25.2	10.4	11 57.1	9.3	57.8
	20	123 58.6	38.1	196 54.6	10.5	11 47.8	9.3	57.8
	21	138 58.6	. . 38.8	211 24.1	10.5	11 38.5	9.4	57.8
	22	153 58.5	39.5	225 53.6	10.6	11 29.1	9.5	57.7
	23	168 58.4	40.2	240 23.2	10.7	N11 19.6	9.5	57.7
		SD 16.2	*d* 0.7	SD 16.2		16.0		15.8

Lat.	Twilight Naut.	Twilight Civil	Sunrise	Moonrise 9	Moonrise 10	Moonrise 11	Moonrise 12
°	h m	h m	h m	h m	h m	h m	h m
N 72	06 42	08 11	10 04	17 24	20 20	22 26	24 20
N 70	06 33	07 52	09 19	18 59	20 55	22 46	24 31
68	06 27	07 37	08 50	19 39	21 20	23 01	24 39
66	06 21	07 25	08 29	20 06	21 39	23 14	24 46
64	06 16	07 15	08 12	20 27	21 55	23 24	24 52
62	06 11	07 06	07 58	20 44	22 08	23 33	24 57
60	06 07	06 58	07 46	20 58	22 18	23 41	25 02
N 58	06 03	06 51	07 35	21 10	22 28	23 47	25 06
56	06 00	06 45	07 26	21 20	22 36	23 53	25 09
54	05 57	06 39	07 18	21 29	22 43	23 58	25 12
52	05 54	06 34	07 11	21 37	22 50	24 03	00 03
50	05 51	06 30	07 05	21 45	22 56	24 07	00 07
45	05 44	06 20	06 51	22 00	23 08	24 16	00 16
N 40	05 38	06 11	06 39	22 13	23 19	24 24	00 24
35	05 33	06 03	06 30	22 24	23 28	24 31	00 31
30	05 27	05 56	06 21	22 33	23 36	24 36	00 36
20	05 17	05 43	06 06	22 50	23 49	24 46	00 46
N 10	05 06	05 31	05 53	23 04	24 01	00 01	00 55
0	04 54	05 19	05 40	23 17	24 12	00 12	01 03
S 10	04 40	05 06	05 28	23 30	24 23	00 23	01 11
20	04 23	04 51	05 14	23 44	24 34	00 34	01 20
30	04 02	04 33	04 59	24 01	00 01	00 48	01 30
35	03 49	04 22	04 50	24 10	00 10	00 55	01 35
40	03 32	04 09	04 39	24 21	00 21	01 04	01 42
45	03 12	03 53	04 27	24 33	00 33	01 14	01 49
S 50	02 44	03 34	04 12	00 02	00 49	01 26	01 58
52	02 30	03 24	04 04	00 10	00 56	01 32	02 02
54	02 13	03 13	03 57	00 20	01 04	01 38	02 07
56	01 53	03 01	03 48	00 30	01 12	01 45	02 12
58	01 25	02 46	03 38	00 41	01 22	01 53	02 17
S 60	00 41	02 28	03 26	00 55	01 34	02 02	02 23

Lat.	Sunset	Twilight Civil	Twilight Naut.	Moonset 9	Moonset 10	Moonset 11	Moonset 12
°	h m	h m	h m	h m	h m	h m	h m
N 72	13 23	15 15	16 45	16 50	15 50	15 33	15 21
N 70	14 07	15 34	16 53	15 14	15 13	15 11	15 08
68	14 36	15 49	17 00	14 34	14 47	14 54	14 58
66	14 58	16 02	17 06	14 06	14 27	14 41	14 49
64	15 15	16 12	17 11	13 44	14 11	14 29	14 42
62	15 29	16 21	17 16	13 27	13 58	14 19	14 36
60	15 41	16 29	17 20	13 13	13 46	14 11	14 30
N 58	15 52	16 36	17 24	13 00	13 36	14 04	14 26
56	16 01	16 42	17 27	12 50	13 27	13 57	14 21
54	16 09	16 48	17 30	12 40	13 20	13 51	14 17
52	16 16	16 53	17 33	12 32	13 13	13 46	14 14
50	16 23	16 57	17 36	12 24	13 06	13 41	14 11
45	16 36	17 08	17 43	12 08	12 53	13 31	14 04
N 40	16 48	17 17	17 49	11 55	12 42	13 22	13 58
35	16 58	17 24	17 55	11 43	12 32	13 14	13 53
30	17 07	17 32	18 00	11 33	12 23	13 08	13 48
20	17 22	17 45	18 11	11 16	12 09	12 56	13 40
N 10	17 35	17 57	18 22	11 01	11 56	12 46	13 33
0	17 47	18 09	18 34	10 47	11 43	12 37	13 27
S 10	18 00	18 22	18 48	10 33	11 31	12 27	13 20
20	18 14	18 37	19 05	10 18	11 18	12 17	13 13
30	18 30	18 55	19 26	10 00	11 03	12 05	13 05
35	18 39	19 07	19 40	09 50	10 54	11 58	13 00
40	18 49	19 20	19 57	09 38	10 44	11 50	12 55
45	19 02	19 35	20 17	09 24	10 32	11 41	12 48
S 50	19 17	19 56	20 45	09 08	10 18	11 30	12 41
52	19 25	20 05	21 00	09 00	10 11	11 24	12 37
54	19 33	20 16	21 17	08 51	10 04	11 19	12 34
56	19 42	20 29	21 38	08 41	09 55	11 12	12 29
58	19 52	20 44	22 07	08 29	09 46	11 05	12 25
S 60	20 04	21 02	22 56	08 16	09 35	10 57	12 19

Day	SUN Eqn. of Time 00^h	SUN Eqn. of Time 12^h	SUN Mer. Pass.	MOON Mer. Pass. Upper	MOON Mer. Pass. Lower	MOON Age	MOON Phase
d	m s	m s	h m	h m	h m	d %	
9	16 12	16 09	11 44	04 33	17 02	21 65	
10	16 07	16 04	11 44	05 30	17 58	22 54	
11	16 01	15 57	11 44	06 24	18 50	23 43	

UT d h		ARIES GHA	VENUS −3·9 GHA	VENUS Dec	MARS +1·8 GHA	MARS Dec	JUPITER −1·7 GHA	JUPITER Dec	SATURN +0·5 GHA	SATURN Dec
		° ′	° ′	° ′	° ′	° ′	° ′	° ′	° ′	° ′
12 00		51 18.8	197 31.0	S12 10.5	219 08.0	S 4 01.0	196 15.9	S12 54.6	145 58.4	S22 23.9
01		66 21.3	212 30.4	11.6	234 09.1	01.7	211 17.8	54.7	161 00.6	23.9
02		81 23.7	227 29.9	12.7	249 10.1	02.3	226 19.7	54.9	176 02.8	23.9
03		96 26.2	242 29.3 . .	13.8	264 11.1 . .	02.9	241 21.7 . .	55.1	191 05.0 . .	23.9
04		111 28.7	257 28.8	14.8	279 12.1	03.5	256 23.6	55.3	206 07.1	23.9
05		126 31.1	272 28.2	15.9	294 13.1	04.1	271 25.6	55.4	221 09.3	24.0
06		141 33.6	287 27.7	S12 17.0	309 14.1	S 4 04.8	286 27.5	S12 55.6	236 11.5	S22 24.0
07		156 36.1	302 27.1	18.1	324 15.1	05.4	301 29.4	55.8	251 13.7	24.0
08		171 38.5	317 26.6	19.2	339 16.1	06.0	316 31.4	56.0	266 15.9	24.0
09	S	186 41.0	332 26.1 . .	20.3	354 17.1 . .	06.6	331 33.3 . .	56.1	281 18.1 . .	24.0
10	U	201 43.5	347 25.5	21.4	9 18.1	07.2	346 35.3	56.3	296 20.3	24.0
11	N	216 45.9	2 25.0	22.4	24 19.2	07.9	1 37.2	56.5	311 22.4	24.0
12	D	231 48.4	17 24.4	S12 23.5	39 20.2	S 4 08.5	16 39.1	S12 56.7	326 24.6	S22 24.0
13	A	246 50.9	32 23.9	24.6	54 21.2	09.1	31 41.1	56.8	341 26.8	24.1
14	Y	261 53.3	47 23.3	25.7	69 22.2	09.7	46 43.0	57.0	356 29.0	24.1
15		276 55.8	62 22.8 . .	26.8	84 23.2 . .	10.3	61 45.0 . .	57.2	11 31.2 . .	24.1
16		291 58.2	77 22.2	27.8	99 24.2	10.9	76 46.9	57.4	26 33.4	24.1
17		307 00.7	92 21.7	28.9	114 25.2	11.6	91 48.8	57.5	41 35.6	24.1
18		322 03.2	107 21.1	S12 30.0	129 26.2	S 4 12.2	106 50.8	S12 57.7	56 37.7	S22 24.1
19		337 05.6	122 20.6	31.1	144 27.2	12.8	121 52.7	57.9	71 39.9	24.1
20		352 08.1	137 20.0	32.2	159 28.2	13.4	136 54.7	58.1	86 42.1	24.1
21		7 10.6	152 19.5 . .	33.2	174 29.3 . .	14.0	151 56.6 . .	58.2	101 44.3 . .	24.2
22		22 13.0	167 18.9	34.3	189 30.3	14.6	166 58.6	58.4	116 46.5	24.2
23		37 15.5	182 18.4	35.4	204 31.3	15.3	182 00.5	58.6	131 48.7	24.2
13 00		52 18.0	197 17.8	S12 36.5	219 32.3	S 4 15.9	197 02.4	S12 58.8	146 50.8	S22 24.2
01		67 20.4	212 17.3	37.5	234 33.3	16.5	212 04.4	58.9	161 53.0	24.2
02		82 22.9	227 16.7	38.6	249 34.3	17.1	227 06.3	59.1	176 55.2	24.2
03		97 25.3	242 16.2 . .	39.7	264 35.3 . .	17.7	242 08.3 . .	59.3	191 57.4 . .	24.2
04		112 27.8	257 15.6	40.8	279 36.3	18.4	257 10.2	59.5	206 59.6	24.3
05		127 30.3	272 15.0	41.8	294 37.3	19.0	272 12.1	59.6	222 01.8	24.3
06		142 32.7	287 14.5	S12 42.9	309 38.3	S 4 19.6	287 14.1	S12 59.8	237 03.9	S22 24.3
07		157 35.2	302 13.9	44.0	324 39.4	20.2	302 16.0	13 00.0	252 06.1	24.3
08		172 37.7	317 13.4	45.1	339 40.4	20.8	317 18.0	00.2	267 08.3	24.3
09	M	187 40.1	332 12.8 . .	46.1	354 41.4 . .	21.4	332 19.9 . .	00.3	282 10.5 . .	24.3
10	O	202 42.6	347 12.3	47.2	9 42.4	22.1	347 21.8	00.5	297 12.7	24.3
11	N	217 45.1	2 11.7	48.3	24 43.4	22.7	2 23.8	00.7	312 14.9	24.3
12	D	232 47.5	17 11.1	S12 49.3	39 44.4	S 4 23.3	17 25.7	S13 00.9	327 17.1	S22 24.4
13	A	247 50.0	32 10.6	50.4	54 45.4	23.9	32 27.7	01.0	342 19.2	24.4
14	Y	262 52.5	47 10.0	51.5	69 46.4	24.5	47 29.6	01.2	357 21.4	24.4
15		277 54.9	62 09.5 . .	52.5	84 47.4 . .	25.1	62 31.6 . .	01.4	12 23.6 . .	24.4
16		292 57.4	77 08.9	53.6	99 48.4	25.8	77 33.5	01.6	27 25.8	24.4
17		307 59.8	92 08.3	54.7	114 49.4	26.4	92 35.4	01.7	42 28.0	24.4
18		323 02.3	107 07.8	S12 55.8	129 50.5	S 4 27.0	107 37.4	S13 01.9	57 30.1	S22 24.4
19		338 04.8	122 07.2	56.8	144 51.5	27.6	122 39.3	02.1	72 32.3	24.4
20		353 07.2	137 06.7	57.9	159 52.5	28.2	137 41.3	02.3	87 34.5	24.5
21		8 09.7	152 06.1 . .	12 58.9	174 53.5 . .	28.8	152 43.2 . .	02.4	102 36.7 . .	24.5
22		23 12.2	167 05.5	13 00.0	189 54.5	29.5	167 45.1	02.6	117 38.9	24.5
23		38 14.6	182 05.0	01.1	204 55.5	30.1	182 47.1	02.8	132 41.1	24.5
14 00		53 17.1	197 04.4	S13 02.1	219 56.5	S 4 30.7	197 49.0	S13 03.0	147 43.2	S22 24.5
01		68 19.6	212 03.9	03.2	234 57.5	31.3	212 51.0	03.1	162 45.4	24.5
02		83 22.0	227 03.3	04.3	249 58.5	31.9	227 52.9	03.3	177 47.6	24.5
03		98 24.5	242 02.7 . .	05.3	264 59.5 . .	32.5	242 54.9 . .	03.5	192 49.8 . .	24.5
04		113 27.0	257 02.2	06.4	280 00.5	33.2	257 56.8	03.7	207 52.0	24.6
05		128 29.4	272 01.6	07.4	295 01.5	33.8	272 58.7	03.8	222 54.2	24.6
06		143 31.9	287 01.0	S13 08.5	310 02.6	S 4 34.4	288 00.7	S13 04.0	237 56.3	S22 24.6
07		158 34.3	302 00.5	09.6	325 03.6	35.0	303 02.6	04.2	252 58.5	24.6
08	T	173 36.8	316 59.9	10.6	340 04.6	35.6	318 04.6	04.4	268 00.7	24.6
09	U	188 39.3	331 59.3 . .	11.7	355 05.6 . .	36.2	333 06.5 . .	04.5	283 02.9 . .	24.6
10	E	203 41.7	346 58.8	12.7	10 06.6	36.8	348 08.4	04.7	298 05.1	24.6
11	S	218 44.2	1 58.2	13.8	25 07.6	37.5	3 10.4	04.9	313 07.2	24.7
12	D	233 46.7	16 57.6	S13 14.9	40 08.6	S 4 38.1	18 12.3	S13 05.0	328 09.4	S22 24.7
13	A	248 49.1	31 57.0	15.9	55 09.6	38.7	33 14.3	05.2	343 11.6	24.7
14	Y	263 51.6	46 56.5	17.0	70 10.6	39.3	48 16.2	05.4	358 13.8	24.7
15		278 54.1	61 55.9 . .	18.0	85 11.6 . .	39.9	63 18.2 . .	05.6	13 16.0 . .	24.7
16		293 56.5	76 55.3	19.1	100 12.6	40.5	78 20.1	05.7	28 18.1	24.7
17		308 59.0	91 54.8	20.1	115 13.6	41.2	93 22.0	05.9	43 20.3	24.7
18		324 01.4	106 54.2	S13 21.2	130 14.7	S 4 41.8	108 24.0	S13 06.1	58 22.5	S22 24.7
19		339 03.9	121 53.6	22.2	145 15.7	42.4	123 25.9	06.3	73 24.7	24.8
20		354 06.4	136 53.0	23.3	160 16.7	43.0	138 27.9	06.4	88 26.9	24.8
21		9 08.8	151 52.5 . .	24.3	175 17.7 . .	43.6	153 29.8 . .	06.6	103 29.1 . .	24.8
22		24 11.3	166 51.9	25.4	190 18.7	44.2	168 31.7	06.8	118 31.2	24.8
23		39 13.8	181 51.3	26.4	205 19.7	44.8	183 33.7	07.0	133 33.4	24.8
Mer. Pass.		h m 20 27.4	v −0.6	d 1.1	v 1.0	d 0.6	v 1.9	d 0.2	v 2.2	d 0.0

STARS Name	SHA	Dec
	° ′	° ′
Acamar	315 15.7	S40 14.1
Achernar	335 24.1	S57 09.0
Acrux	173 06.4	S63 11.5
Adhara	255 10.0	S28 59.7
Aldebaran	290 45.6	N16 32.5
Alioth	166 18.6	N55 51.8
Alkaid	152 57.1	N49 13.5
Al Na'ir	27 40.0	S46 52.6
Alnilam	275 43.1	S 1 11.5
Alphard	217 53.2	S 8 44.1
Alphecca	126 08.9	N26 39.5
Alpheratz	357 40.2	N29 11.5
Altair	62 05.5	N 8 55.2
Ankaa	353 12.5	S42 12.7
Antares	112 23.0	S26 28.0
Arcturus	145 53.4	N19 05.6
Atria	107 22.6	S69 03.4
Avior	234 16.6	S59 33.8
Bellatrix	278 28.5	N 6 21.8
Betelgeuse	270 57.8	N 7 24.5
Canopus	263 54.4	S52 42.2
Capella	280 29.6	N46 00.7
Deneb	49 29.5	N45 21.0
Denebola	182 30.9	N14 28.4
Diphda	348 52.7	S17 53.4
Dubhe	193 48.5	N61 39.1
Elnath	278 08.5	N28 37.1
Eltanin	90 45.2	N51 29.6
Enif	33 44.2	N 9 57.6
Fomalhaut	15 20.6	S29 31.8
Gacrux	171 57.9	S57 12.4
Gienah	175 49.5	S17 38.2
Hadar	148 44.2	S60 27.2
Hamal	327 57.1	N23 32.8
Kaus Aust.	83 40.2	S34 22.4
Kochab	137 21.4	N74 05.0
Markab	13 35.2	N15 18.2
Menkar	314 11.6	N 4 09.5
Menkent	148 04.4	S36 27.1
Miaplacidus	221 38.9	S69 47.1
Mirfak	308 35.6	N49 55.3
Nunki	75 54.9	S26 16.3
Peacock	53 14.8	S56 40.8
Pollux	243 24.0	N27 58.8
Procyon	244 56.5	N 5 10.7
Rasalhague	96 04.0	N12 33.1
Regulus	207 40.4	N11 52.8
Rigel	281 08.9	S 8 11.0
Rigil Kent.	139 48.3	S60 54.2
Sabik	102 09.5	S15 44.6
Schedar	349 36.6	N56 38.2
Shaula	96 18.3	S37 06.8
Sirius	258 30.9	S16 44.5
Spica	158 28.4	S11 15.0
Suhail	222 50.2	S43 30.0
Vega	80 37.3	N38 48.4
Zuben'ubi	137 02.5	S16 06.7

	SHA	Mer. Pass.
	° ′	h m
Venus	144 59.9	10 51
Mars	167 14.3	9 21
Jupiter	144 44.5	10 50
Saturn	94 32.9	14 11

Day	UT (d h)	SUN GHA (° ′)	SUN Dec (° ′)	MOON GHA (° ′)	v (′)	MOON Dec (° ′)	d (′)	HP (′)
SUNDAY	12 00	183 58.3	S17 40.8	254 52.9	10.7	N11 10.1	9.5	57.7
	01	198 58.3	41.5	269 22.6	10.8	11 00.6	9.6	57.7
	02	213 58.2	42.2	283 52.4	10.9	10 51.0	9.7	57.6
	03	228 58.1	. . 42.9	298 22.3	10.9	10 41.3	9.7	57.6
	04	243 58.0	43.5	312 52.2	11.0	10 31.6	9.7	57.6
	05	258 57.9	44.2	327 22.2	11.1	10 21.9	9.8	57.6
	06	273 57.9	S17 44.9	341 52.3	11.1	N10 12.1	9.8	57.5
	07	288 57.8	45.6	356 22.4	11.2	10 02.3	9.9	57.5
	08	303 57.7	46.2	10 52.6	11.2	9 52.4	9.9	57.5
	09	318 57.6	. . 46.9	25 22.8	11.3	9 42.5	10.0	57.4
	10	333 57.5	47.6	39 53.1	11.4	9 32.5	10.0	57.4
	11	348 57.5	48.3	54 23.5	11.4	9 22.5	10.0	57.4
	12	3 57.4	S17 48.9	68 53.9	11.5	N 9 12.5	10.1	57.4
	13	18 57.3	49.6	83 24.4	11.5	9 02.4	10.1	57.3
	14	33 57.2	50.3	97 54.9	11.6	8 52.3	10.1	57.3
	15	48 57.1	. . 50.9	112 25.5	11.7	8 42.2	10.2	57.3
	16	63 57.0	51.6	126 56.2	11.7	8 32.0	10.3	57.3
	17	78 57.0	52.3	141 26.9	11.7	8 21.7	10.2	57.2
	18	93 56.9	S17 52.9	155 57.6	11.8	N 8 11.5	10.3	57.2
	19	108 56.8	53.6	170 28.4	11.9	8 01.2	10.3	57.2
	20	123 56.7	54.3	184 59.3	11.9	7 50.9	10.4	57.2
	21	138 56.6	. . 54.9	199 30.2	12.0	7 40.5	10.3	57.1
	22	153 56.5	55.6	214 01.2	12.0	7 30.2	10.4	57.1
	23	168 56.5	56.3	228 32.2	12.1	7 19.8	10.5	57.1
MONDAY	13 00	183 56.4	S17 56.9	243 03.3	12.1	N 7 09.3	10.4	57.1
	01	198 56.3	57.6	257 34.4	12.2	6 58.9	10.5	57.0
	02	213 56.2	58.3	272 05.6	12.2	6 48.4	10.6	57.0
	03	228 56.1	. . 58.9	286 36.8	12.3	6 37.8	10.5	57.0
	04	243 56.0	17 59.6	301 08.1	12.3	6 27.3	10.5	57.0
	05	258 55.9	18 00.3	315 39.4	12.4	6 16.8	10.6	56.9
	06	273 55.8	S18 00.9	330 10.8	12.4	N 6 06.2	10.6	56.9
	07	288 55.7	01.6	344 42.2	12.4	5 55.6	10.7	56.9
	08	303 55.7	02.2	359 13.6	12.5	5 44.9	10.6	56.9
	09	318 55.6	. . 02.9	13 45.1	12.6	5 34.3	10.7	56.8
	10	333 55.5	03.6	28 16.7	12.5	5 23.6	10.7	56.8
	11	348 55.4	04.2	42 48.2	12.7	5 12.9	10.6	56.8
	12	3 55.3	S18 04.9	57 19.9	12.6	N 5 02.3	10.8	56.8
	13	18 55.2	05.5	71 51.5	12.8	4 51.5	10.7	56.7
	14	33 55.1	06.2	86 23.3	12.7	4 40.8	10.7	56.7
	15	48 55.0	. . 06.8	100 55.0	12.8	4 30.1	10.8	56.7
	16	63 54.9	07.5	115 26.8	12.8	4 19.3	10.8	56.7
	17	78 54.8	08.2	129 58.6	12.9	4 08.5	10.7	56.6
	18	93 54.7	S18 08.8	144 30.5	12.9	N 3 57.8	10.8	56.6
	19	108 54.6	09.5	159 02.4	12.9	3 47.0	10.8	56.6
	20	123 54.6	10.1	173 34.3	13.0	3 36.2	10.8	56.6
	21	138 54.5	. . 10.8	188 06.3	13.0	3 25.4	10.9	56.5
	22	153 54.4	11.4	202 38.3	13.0	3 14.5	10.8	56.5
	23	168 54.3	12.1	217 10.3	13.1	3 03.7	10.8	56.5
TUESDAY	14 00	183 54.2	S18 12.7	231 42.4	13.1	N 2 52.9	10.9	56.5
	01	198 54.1	13.4	246 14.5	13.1	2 42.0	10.8	56.4
	02	213 54.0	14.0	260 46.6	13.2	2 31.2	10.8	56.4
	03	228 53.9	. . 14.7	275 18.8	13.2	2 20.4	10.9	56.4
	04	243 53.8	15.3	289 51.0	13.2	2 09.5	10.9	56.4
	05	258 53.7	16.0	304 23.2	13.3	1 58.6	10.8	56.3
	06	273 53.6	S18 16.6	318 55.5	13.3	N 1 47.8	10.9	56.3
	07	288 53.5	17.3	333 27.8	13.3	1 36.9	10.8	56.3
	08	303 53.4	17.9	348 00.1	13.3	1 26.1	10.9	56.3
	09	318 53.3	. . 18.6	2 32.4	13.4	1 15.2	10.8	56.3
	10	333 53.2	19.2	17 04.8	13.4	1 04.4	10.9	56.2
	11	348 53.1	19.9	31 37.2	13.4	0 53.5	10.8	56.2
	12	3 53.0	S18 20.5	46 09.6	13.4	N 0 42.7	10.9	56.2
	13	18 52.9	21.2	60 42.0	13.5	0 31.8	10.8	56.2
	14	33 52.8	21.8	75 14.5	13.5	0 21.0	10.8	56.1
	15	48 52.7	. . 22.4	89 47.0	13.5	N 0 10.2	10.9	56.1
	16	63 52.6	23.1	104 19.5	13.5	S 0 00.7	10.8	56.1
	17	78 52.5	23.7	118 52.0	13.5	0 11.5	10.8	56.1
	18	93 52.4	S18 24.4	133 24.5	13.6	S 0 22.3	10.8	56.1
	19	108 52.3	25.0	147 57.1	13.6	0 33.1	10.8	56.0
	20	123 52.2	25.7	162 29.7	13.6	0 43.9	10.8	56.0
	21	138 52.1	. . 26.3	177 02.3	13.6	0 54.7	10.7	56.0
	22	153 52.0	26.9	191 34.9	13.6	1 05.4	10.8	56.0
	23	168 51.9	27.6	206 07.5	13.7	S 1 16.2	10.7	56.0
		SD 16.2	*d* 0.7	SD 15.6		15.5		15.3

Lat. (°)	Twilight Naut. (h m)	Twilight Civil (h m)	Sunrise (h m)	Moonrise 12 (h m)	Moonrise 13 (h m)	Moonrise 14 (h m)	Moonrise 15 (h m)
N 72	06 53	08 25	10 35	24 20	00 20	02 08	03 52
N 70	06 43	08 04	09 38	24 31	00 31	02 11	03 49
68	06 35	07 48	09 04	24 39	00 39	02 14	03 46
66	06 29	07 34	08 40	24 46	00 46	02 16	03 44
64	06 23	07 23	08 21	24 52	00 52	02 18	03 42
62	06 18	07 13	08 06	24 57	00 57	02 20	03 41
60	06 13	07 05	07 53	25 02	01 02	02 21	03 39
N 58	06 09	06 57	07 42	25 06	01 06	02 23	03 38
56	06 05	06 51	07 33	25 09	01 09	02 24	03 37
54	06 02	06 45	07 24	25 12	01 12	02 25	03 36
52	05 58	06 39	07 17	00 03	01 15	02 26	03 35
50	05 55	06 34	07 10	00 07	01 18	02 27	03 34
45	05 48	06 23	06 55	00 16	01 23	02 29	03 33
N 40	05 41	06 14	06 43	00 24	01 28	02 30	03 31
35	05 35	06 06	06 33	00 31	01 32	02 32	03 30
30	05 29	05 58	06 23	00 36	01 35	02 33	03 29
20	05 18	05 45	06 08	00 46	01 42	02 35	03 27
N 10	05 06	05 32	05 54	00 55	01 47	02 37	03 25
0	04 54	05 19	05 41	01 03	01 52	02 39	03 24
S 10	04 39	05 05	05 28	01 11	01 57	02 40	03 22
20	04 22	04 50	05 13	01 20	02 02	02 42	03 21
30	04 00	04 31	04 57	01 30	02 08	02 44	03 19
35	03 46	04 19	04 47	01 35	02 12	02 46	03 18
40	03 29	04 06	04 36	01 42	02 16	02 47	03 17
45	03 07	03 49	04 23	01 49	02 20	02 49	03 16
S 50	02 38	03 29	04 07	01 58	02 26	02 50	03 14
52	02 23	03 18	04 00	02 02	02 28	02 51	03 14
54	02 05	03 07	03 51	02 07	02 31	02 52	03 13
56	01 42	02 54	03 42	02 12	02 34	02 53	03 12
58	01 10	02 38	03 31	02 17	02 37	02 55	03 11
S 60	////	02 19	03 19	02 23	02 41	02 56	03 10

Lat. (°)	Sunset (h m)	Twilight Civil (h m)	Twilight Naut. (h m)	Moonset 12 (h m)	Moonset 13 (h m)	Moonset 14 (h m)	Moonset 15 (h m)
N 72	12 53	15 02	16 35	15 21	15 11	15 01	14 52
N 70	13 50	15 23	16 44	15 08	15 05	15 01	14 58
68	14 23	15 40	16 52	14 58	15 00	15 01	15 03
66	14 48	15 54	16 59	14 49	14 56	15 01	15 06
64	15 06	16 05	17 05	14 42	14 52	15 01	15 10
62	15 22	16 15	17 10	14 36	14 49	15 01	15 13
60	15 35	16 23	17 14	14 30	14 47	15 01	15 15
N 58	15 46	16 31	17 19	14 26	14 44	15 01	15 18
56	15 55	16 37	17 23	14 21	14 42	15 01	15 20
54	16 04	16 43	17 26	14 17	14 40	15 01	15 21
52	16 11	16 49	17 30	14 14	14 38	15 01	15 23
50	16 18	16 54	17 33	14 11	14 37	15 01	15 25
45	16 33	17 05	17 40	14 04	14 33	15 01	15 28
N 40	16 45	17 14	17 47	13 58	14 30	15 01	15 31
35	16 56	17 23	17 53	13 53	14 28	15 01	15 33
30	17 05	17 30	17 59	13 48	14 25	15 01	15 35
20	17 21	17 44	18 10	13 40	14 21	15 01	15 39
N 10	17 35	17 57	18 22	13 33	14 18	15 01	15 42
0	17 48	18 10	18 35	13 27	14 14	15 00	15 46
S 10	18 01	18 23	18 49	13 20	14 11	15 00	15 49
20	18 16	18 39	19 07	13 13	14 07	15 00	15 52
30	18 32	18 58	19 29	13 05	14 03	15 00	15 56
35	18 42	19 10	19 44	13 00	14 01	15 00	15 58
40	18 53	19 23	20 01	12 55	13 58	15 00	16 00
45	19 06	19 40	20 23	12 48	13 55	15 00	16 03
S 50	19 22	20 01	20 53	12 41	13 51	14 59	16 06
52	19 30	20 11	21 08	12 37	13 49	14 59	16 08
54	19 38	20 23	21 26	12 34	13 47	14 59	16 10
56	19 48	20 37	21 50	12 29	13 45	14 59	16 12
58	19 59	20 53	22 24	12 25	13 43	14 59	16 14
S 60	20 12	21 13	////	12 19	13 40	14 59	16 16

Day	SUN Eqn. of Time 00^h	SUN Eqn. of Time 12^h	SUN Mer. Pass.	MOON Mer. Pass. Upper	MOON Mer. Pass. Lower	MOON Age	MOON Phase
d	m s	m s	h m	h m	h m	d	%
12	15 54	15 50	11 44	07 15	19 39	24	33
13	15 46	15 41	11 44	08 03	20 27	25	23
14	15 37	15 32	11 44	08 50	21 12	26	15

UT d h	ARIES GHA	VENUS −3·9 GHA	VENUS Dec	MARS +1·7 GHA	MARS Dec	JUPITER −1·7 GHA	JUPITER Dec	SATURN +0·5 GHA	SATURN Dec
	° ′	° ′	° ′	° ′	° ′	° ′	° ′	° ′	° ′
15 00	54 16.2	196 50.8	S13 27.5	220 20.7	S 4 45.5	198 35.6	S13 07.1	148 35.6	S22 24.8
01	69 18.7	211 50.2	28.5	235 21.7	46.1	213 37.6	07.3	163 37.8	24.8
02	84 21.2	226 49.6	29.6	250 22.7	46.7	228 39.5	07.5	178 40.0	24.8
03	99 23.6	241 49.0	. . 30.6	265 23.7	. . 47.3	243 41.5	. . 07.6	193 42.1	. . 24.9
04	114 26.1	256 48.5	31.7	280 24.7	47.9	258 43.4	07.8	208 44.3	24.9
05	129 28.6	271 47.9	32.7	295 25.7	48.5	273 45.3	08.0	223 46.5	24.9
W 06	144 31.0	286 47.3	S13 33.8	310 26.7	S 4 49.1	288 47.3	S13 08.2	238 48.7	S22 24.9
E 07	159 33.5	301 46.7	34.8	325 27.8	49.8	303 49.2	08.3	253 50.9	24.9
D 08	174 35.9	316 46.1	35.9	340 28.8	50.4	318 51.2	08.5	268 53.0	24.9
N 09	189 38.4	331 45.6	. . 36.9	355 29.8	. . 51.0	333 53.1	. . 08.7	283 55.2	. . 24.9
E 10	204 40.9	346 45.0	38.0	10 30.8	51.6	348 55.1	08.9	298 57.4	24.9
S 11	219 43.3	1 44.4	39.0	25 31.8	52.2	3 57.0	09.0	313 59.6	25.0
D 12	234 45.8	16 43.8	S13 40.0	40 32.8	S 4 52.8	18 58.9	S13 09.2	329 01.8	S22 25.0
A 13	249 48.3	31 43.2	41.1	55 33.8	53.4	34 00.9	09.4	344 03.9	25.0
Y 14	264 50.7	46 42.7	42.1	70 34.8	54.1	49 02.8	09.6	359 06.1	25.0
15	279 53.2	61 42.1	. . 43.2	85 35.8	. . 54.7	64 04.8	. . 09.7	14 08.3	. . 25.0
16	294 55.7	76 41.5	44.2	100 36.8	55.3	79 06.7	09.9	29 10.5	25.0
17	309 58.1	91 40.9	45.3	115 37.8	55.9	94 08.7	10.1	44 12.6	25.0
18	325 00.6	106 40.3	S13 46.3	130 38.8	S 4 56.5	109 10.6	S13 10.2	59 14.8	S22 25.0
19	340 03.0	121 39.8	47.3	145 39.8	57.1	124 12.5	10.4	74 17.0	25.1
20	355 05.5	136 39.2	48.4	160 40.8	57.7	139 14.5	10.6	89 19.2	25.1
21	10 08.0	151 38.6	. . 49.4	175 41.9	. . 58.4	154 16.4	. . 10.8	104 21.4	. . 25.1
22	25 10.4	166 38.0	50.4	190 42.9	59.0	169 18.4	10.9	119 23.5	25.1
23	40 12.9	181 37.4	51.5	205 43.9	4 59.6	184 20.3	11.1	134 25.7	25.1
16 00	55 15.4	196 36.8	S13 52.5	220 44.9	S 5 00.2	199 22.3	S13 11.3	149 27.9	S22 25.1
01	70 17.8	211 36.2	53.6	235 45.9	00.8	214 24.2	11.4	164 30.1	25.1
02	85 20.3	226 35.7	54.6	250 46.9	01.4	229 26.1	11.6	179 32.3	25.1
03	100 22.8	241 35.1	. . 55.6	265 47.9	. . 02.0	244 28.1	. . 11.8	194 34.4	. . 25.2
04	115 25.2	256 34.5	56.7	280 48.9	02.6	259 30.0	12.0	209 36.6	25.2
05	130 27.7	271 33.9	57.7	295 49.9	03.3	274 32.0	12.1	224 38.8	25.2
06	145 30.2	286 33.3	S13 58.7	310 50.9	S 5 03.9	289 33.9	S13 12.3	239 41.0	S22 25.2
T 07	160 32.6	301 32.7	13 59.8	325 51.9	04.5	304 35.9	12.5	254 43.1	25.2
H 08	175 35.1	316 32.1	14 00.8	340 52.9	05.1	319 37.8	12.7	269 45.3	25.2
U 09	190 37.5	331 31.5	. . 01.8	355 53.9	. . 05.7	334 39.7	. . 12.8	284 47.5	. . 25.2
R 10	205 40.0	346 30.9	02.8	10 54.9	06.3	349 41.7	13.0	299 49.7	25.2
S 11	220 42.5	1 30.4	03.9	25 55.9	06.9	4 43.6	13.2	314 51.9	25.3
D 12	235 44.9	16 29.8	S14 04.9	40 57.0	S 5 07.5	19 45.6	S13 13.3	329 54.0	S22 25.3
A 13	250 47.4	31 29.2	05.9	55 58.0	08.2	34 47.5	13.5	344 56.2	25.3
Y 14	265 49.9	46 28.6	07.0	70 59.0	08.8	49 49.5	13.7	359 58.4	25.3
15	280 52.3	61 28.0	. . 08.0	86 00.0	. . 09.4	64 51.4	. . 13.9	15 00.6	. . 25.3
16	295 54.8	76 27.4	09.0	101 01.0	10.0	79 53.3	14.0	30 02.7	25.3
17	310 57.3	91 26.8	10.0	116 02.0	10.6	94 55.3	14.2	45 04.9	25.3
18	325 59.7	106 26.2	S14 11.1	131 03.0	S 5 11.2	109 57.2	S13 14.4	60 07.1	S22 25.3
19	341 02.2	121 25.6	12.1	146 04.0	11.8	124 59.2	14.5	75 09.3	25.3
20	356 04.7	136 25.0	13.1	161 05.0	12.4	140 01.1	14.7	90 11.5	25.4
21	11 07.1	151 24.4	. . 14.1	176 06.0	. . 13.1	155 03.1	. . 14.9	105 13.6	. . 25.4
22	26 09.6	166 23.8	15.2	191 07.0	13.7	170 05.0	15.1	120 15.8	25.4
23	41 12.0	181 23.2	16.2	206 08.0	14.3	185 06.9	15.2	135 18.0	25.4
17 00	56 14.5	196 22.6	S14 17.2	221 09.0	S 5 14.9	200 08.9	S13 15.4	150 20.2	S22 25.4
01	71 17.0	211 22.0	18.2	236 10.0	15.5	215 10.8	15.6	165 22.3	25.4
02	86 19.4	226 21.4	19.2	251 11.0	16.1	230 12.8	15.7	180 24.5	25.4
03	101 21.9	241 20.8	. . 20.3	266 12.0	. . 16.7	245 14.7	. . 15.9	195 26.7	. . 25.4
04	116 24.4	256 20.2	21.3	281 13.0	17.3	260 16.7	16.1	210 28.9	25.5
05	131 26.8	271 19.6	22.3	296 14.1	18.0	275 18.6	16.3	225 31.0	25.5
06	146 29.3	286 19.0	S14 23.3	311 15.1	S 5 18.6	290 20.6	S13 16.4	240 33.2	S22 25.5
07	161 31.8	301 18.4	24.3	326 16.1	19.2	305 22.5	16.6	255 35.4	25.5
08	176 34.2	316 17.8	25.3	341 17.1	19.8	320 24.4	16.8	270 37.6	25.5
F 09	191 36.7	331 17.2	. . 26.4	356 18.1	. . 20.4	335 26.4	. . 16.9	285 39.7	. . 25.5
R 10	206 39.1	346 16.6	27.4	11 19.1	21.0	350 28.3	17.1	300 41.9	25.5
I 11	221 41.6	1 16.0	28.4	26 20.1	21.6	5 30.3	17.3	315 44.1	25.5
D 12	236 44.1	16 15.4	S14 29.4	41 21.1	S 5 22.2	20 32.2	S13 17.5	330 46.3	S22 25.6
A 13	251 46.5	31 14.8	30.4	56 22.1	22.8	35 34.2	17.6	345 48.4	25.6
Y 14	266 49.0	46 14.2	31.4	71 23.1	23.5	50 36.1	17.8	0 50.6	25.6
15	281 51.5	61 13.6	. . 32.4	86 24.1	. . 24.1	65 38.0	. . 18.0	15 52.8	. . 25.6
16	296 53.9	76 13.0	33.5	101 25.1	24.7	80 40.0	18.1	30 55.0	25.6
17	311 56.4	91 12.4	34.5	116 26.1	25.3	95 41.9	18.3	45 57.1	25.6
18	326 58.9	106 11.8	S14 35.5	131 27.1	S 5 25.9	110 43.9	S13 18.5	60 59.3	S22 25.6
19	342 01.3	121 11.2	36.5	146 28.1	26.5	125 45.8	18.7	76 01.5	25.6
20	357 03.8	136 10.6	37.5	161 29.1	27.1	140 47.8	18.8	91 03.7	25.7
21	12 06.3	151 10.0	. . 38.5	176 30.1	. . 27.7	155 49.7	. . 19.0	106 05.8	. . 25.7
22	27 08.7	166 09.4	39.5	191 31.1	28.3	170 51.7	19.2	121 08.0	25.7
23	42 11.2	181 08.8	40.5	206 32.1	28.9	185 53.6	19.3	136 10.2	25.7
Mer. Pass.	h m 20 15.6	*v* −0.6	*d* 1.0	*v* 1.0	*d* 0.6	*v* 1.9	*d* 0.2	*v* 2.2	*d* 0.0

STARS Name	SHA	Dec
	° ′	° ′
Acamar	315 15.7	S40 14.2
Achernar	335 24.1	S57 09.0
Acrux	173 06.3	S63 11.5
Adhara	255 09.9	S28 59.7
Aldebaran	290 45.6	N16 32.5
Alioth	166 18.6	N55 51.7
Alkaid	152 57.1	N49 13.5
Al Na'ir	27 40.0	S46 52.6
Alnilam	275 43.1	S 1 11.6
Alphard	217 53.2	S 8 44.1
Alphecca	126 08.9	N26 39.5
Alpheratz	357 40.2	N29 11.5
Altair	62 05.5	N 8 55.2
Ankaa	353 12.5	S42 12.8
Antares	112 23.0	S26 28.0
Arcturus	145 53.4	N19 05.6
Atria	107 22.6	S69 03.4
Avior	234 16.5	S59 33.8
Bellatrix	278 28.5	N 6 21.8
Betelgeuse	270 57.8	N 7 24.5
Canopus	263 54.4	S52 42.3
Capella	280 29.6	N46 00.7
Deneb	49 29.6	N45 21.0
Denebola	182 30.8	N14 28.4
Diphda	348 52.7	S17 53.4
Dubhe	193 48.4	N61 39.1
Elnath	278 08.5	N28 37.1
Eltanin	90 45.2	N51 29.6
Enif	33 44.2	N 9 57.6
Fomalhaut	15 20.6	S29 31.8
Gacrux	171 57.9	S57 12.4
Gienah	175 49.5	S17 38.2
Hadar	148 44.2	S60 27.2
Hamal	327 57.1	N23 32.8
Kaus Aust.	83 40.2	S34 22.4
Kochab	137 21.4	N74 05.0
Markab	13 35.3	N15 18.2
Menkar	314 11.6	N 4 09.5
Menkent	148 04.4	S36 27.1
Miaplacidus	221 38.8	S69 47.1
Mirfak	308 35.5	N49 55.3
Nunki	75 54.9	S26 16.3
Peacock	53 14.9	S56 40.7
Pollux	243 24.0	N27 58.8
Procyon	244 56.5	N 5 10.7
Rasalhague	96 04.0	N12 33.1
Regulus	207 40.4	N11 52.8
Rigel	281 08.9	S 8 11.0
Rigil Kent.	139 48.3	S60 54.2
Sabik	102 09.5	S15 44.6
Schedar	349 36.6	N56 38.2
Shaula	96 18.3	S37 06.8
Sirius	258 30.9	S16 44.5
Spica	158 28.4	S11 15.0
Suhail	222 50.2	S43 30.1
Vega	80 37.3	N38 48.4
Zuben'ubi	137 02.5	S16 06.7

	SHA	Mer. Pass.
	° ′	h m
Venus	141 21.5	10 54
Mars	165 29.5	9 16
Jupiter	144 06.9	10 41
Saturn	94 12.5	14 00

UT	SUN GHA	SUN Dec	MOON GHA	*v*	MOON Dec	*d*	HP
d h	° ′	° ′	° ′	′	° ′	′	′
15 00 WEDNESDAY	183 51.8	S18 28.2	220 40.2	13.6	S 1 26.9	10.8	55.9
01	198 51.7	28.9	235 12.8	13.7	1 37.7	10.7	55.9
02	213 51.6	29.5	249 45.5	13.7	1 48.4	10.7	55.9
03	228 51.4	. . 30.1	264 18.2	13.7	1 59.1	10.7	55.9
04	243 51.3	30.8	278 50.9	13.7	2 09.8	10.7	55.9
05	258 51.2	31.4	293 23.6	13.8	2 20.5	10.6	55.8
06	273 51.1	S18 32.0	307 56.4	13.7	S 2 31.1	10.7	55.8
07	288 51.0	32.7	322 29.1	13.8	2 41.8	10.6	55.8
08	303 50.9	33.3	337 01.9	13.7	2 52.4	10.6	55.8
09	318 50.8	. . 33.9	351 34.6	13.8	3 03.0	10.6	55.7
10	333 50.7	34.6	6 07.4	13.8	3 13.6	10.5	55.7
11	348 50.6	35.2	20 40.2	13.8	3 24.1	10.5	55.7
12	3 50.5	S18 35.8	35 13.0	13.8	S 3 34.6	10.6	55.7
13	18 50.4	36.5	49 45.8	13.8	3 45.2	10.5	55.7
14	33 50.3	37.1	64 18.6	13.8	3 55.7	10.4	55.7
15	48 50.1	. . 37.7	78 51.4	13.8	4 06.1	10.5	55.6
16	63 50.0	38.4	93 24.2	13.8	4 16.6	10.4	55.6
17	78 49.9	39.0	107 57.0	13.8	4 27.0	10.4	55.6
18	93 49.8	S18 39.6	122 29.8	13.9	S 4 37.4	10.4	55.6
19	108 49.7	40.2	137 02.7	13.8	4 47.8	10.3	55.6
20	123 49.6	40.9	151 35.5	13.8	4 58.1	10.3	55.5
21	138 49.5	. . 41.5	166 08.3	13.9	5 08.4	10.3	55.5
22	153 49.4	42.1	180 41.2	13.8	5 18.7	10.2	55.5
23	168 49.3	42.7	195 14.0	13.8	5 28.9	10.3	55.5
16 00 THURSDAY	183 49.1	S18 43.4	209 46.8	13.9	S 5 39.2	10.2	55.5
01	198 49.0	44.0	224 19.7	13.8	5 49.4	10.1	55.4
02	213 48.9	44.6	238 52.5	13.8	5 59.5	10.1	55.4
03	228 48.8	. . 45.2	253 25.3	13.9	6 09.6	10.1	55.4
04	243 48.7	45.9	267 58.2	13.8	6 19.7	10.1	55.4
05	258 48.6	46.5	282 31.0	13.8	6 29.8	10.0	55.4
06	273 48.5	S18 47.1	297 03.8	13.9	S 6 39.8	10.0	55.4
07	288 48.3	47.7	311 36.7	13.8	6 49.8	10.0	55.3
08	303 48.2	48.4	326 09.5	13.8	6 59.8	9.9	55.3
09	318 48.1	. . 49.0	340 42.3	13.8	7 09.7	9.9	55.3
10	333 48.0	49.6	355 15.1	13.9	7 19.6	9.8	55.3
11	348 47.9	50.2	9 48.0	13.8	7 29.4	9.9	55.3
12	3 47.8	S18 50.8	24 20.8	13.8	S 7 39.3	9.7	55.2
13	18 47.6	51.4	38 53.6	13.8	7 49.0	9.8	55.2
14	33 47.5	52.1	53 26.4	13.7	7 58.8	9.7	55.2
15	48 47.4	. . 52.7	67 59.1	13.8	8 08.5	9.6	55.2
16	63 47.3	53.3	82 31.9	13.8	8 18.1	9.6	55.2
17	78 47.2	53.9	97 04.7	13.8	8 27.7	9.6	55.2
18	93 47.0	S18 54.5	111 37.5	13.7	S 8 37.3	9.5	55.1
19	108 46.9	55.1	126 10.2	13.8	8 46.8	9.5	55.1
20	123 46.8	55.8	140 43.0	13.7	8 56.3	9.4	55.1
21	138 46.7	. . 56.4	155 15.7	13.7	9 05.7	9.4	55.1
22	153 46.6	57.0	169 48.4	13.8	9 15.1	9.4	55.1
23	168 46.4	57.6	184 21.2	13.7	9 24.5	9.3	55.1
17 00 FRIDAY	183 46.3	S18 58.2	198 53.9	13.7	S 9 33.8	9.2	55.0
01	198 46.2	58.8	213 26.6	13.7	9 43.0	9.2	55.0
02	213 46.1	18 59.4	227 59.3	13.6	9 52.2	9.2	55.0
03	228 45.9	19 00.0	242 31.9	13.7	10 01.4	9.1	55.0
04	243 45.8	00.6	257 04.6	13.7	10 10.5	9.0	55.0
05	258 45.7	01.2	271 37.3	13.6	10 19.5	9.0	55.0
06	273 45.6	S19 01.9	286 09.9	13.6	S10 28.5	9.0	54.9
07	288 45.4	02.5	300 42.5	13.6	10 37.5	8.9	54.9
08	303 45.3	03.1	315 15.1	13.6	10 46.4	8.9	54.9
09	318 45.2	. . 03.7	329 47.7	13.6	10 55.3	8.8	54.9
10	333 45.1	04.3	344 20.3	13.6	11 04.1	8.7	54.9
11	348 44.9	04.9	358 52.9	13.5	11 12.8	8.7	54.9
12	3 44.8	S19 05.5	13 25.4	13.6	S11 21.5	8.7	54.9
13	18 44.7	06.1	27 58.0	13.5	11 30.2	8.5	54.8
14	33 44.6	06.7	42 30.5	13.5	11 38.7	8.6	54.8
15	48 44.4	. . 07.3	57 03.0	13.5	11 47.3	8.5	54.8
16	63 44.3	07.9	71 35.5	13.5	11 55.8	8.4	54.8
17	78 44.2	08.5	86 08.0	13.5	12 04.2	8.3	54.8
18	93 44.0	S19 09.1	100 40.5	13.4	S12 12.5	8.3	54.8
19	108 43.9	09.7	115 12.9	13.4	12 20.8	8.3	54.8
20	123 43.8	10.3	129 45.3	13.5	12 29.1	8.2	54.7
21	138 43.7	. . 10.9	144 17.8	13.4	12 37.3	8.1	54.7
22	153 43.5	11.5	158 50.2	13.3	12 45.4	8.1	54.7
23	168 43.4	12.1	173 22.5	13.4	S12 53.5	8.0	54.7
	SD 16.2	*d* 0.6	SD 15.2		15.1		14.9

Lat.	Twilight Naut.	Twilight Civil	Sunrise	Moonrise 15	Moonrise 16	Moonrise 17	Moonrise 18
°	h m	h m	h m	h m	h m	h m	h m
N 72	07 03	08 40	▬	03 52	05 36	07 21	09 12
N 70	06 53	08 16	09 57	03 49	05 26	07 03	08 41
68	06 44	07 58	09 18	03 46	05 18	06 48	08 19
66	06 37	07 43	08 51	03 44	05 11	06 37	08 01
64	06 30	07 31	08 31	03 42	05 05	06 27	07 47
62	06 24	07 20	08 15	03 41	05 00	06 19	07 35
60	06 19	07 11	08 01	03 39	04 56	06 11	07 25
N 58	06 15	07 03	07 49	03 38	04 52	06 05	07 16
56	06 10	06 56	07 39	03 37	04 49	06 00	07 09
54	06 06	06 50	07 30	03 36	04 46	05 55	07 02
52	06 03	06 44	07 22	03 35	04 43	05 50	06 56
50	05 59	06 39	07 15	03 34	04 41	05 46	06 50
45	05 52	06 27	06 59	03 33	04 36	05 38	06 38
N 40	05 44	06 17	06 46	03 31	04 31	05 30	06 29
35	05 38	06 09	06 35	03 30	04 28	05 24	06 20
30	05 32	06 01	06 26	03 29	04 24	05 19	06 13
20	05 20	05 46	06 09	03 27	04 18	05 09	06 00
N 10	05 07	05 33	05 55	03 25	04 13	05 01	05 49
0	04 54	05 19	05 41	03 24	04 09	04 54	05 39
S 10	04 39	05 05	05 27	03 22	04 04	04 46	05 29
20	04 21	04 49	05 13	03 21	03 59	04 38	05 18
30	03 58	04 29	04 55	03 19	03 54	04 29	05 06
35	03 43	04 17	04 45	03 18	03 51	04 24	04 59
40	03 25	04 03	04 34	03 17	03 47	04 18	04 51
45	03 03	03 46	04 20	03 16	03 43	04 11	04 41
S 50	02 32	03 24	04 03	03 14	03 38	04 03	04 30
52	02 16	03 13	03 55	03 14	03 36	03 59	04 25
54	01 56	03 01	03 46	03 13	03 33	03 55	04 19
56	01 30	02 47	03 36	03 12	03 31	03 51	04 13
58	00 52	02 30	03 25	03 11	03 28	03 46	04 06
S 60	////	02 09	03 12	03 10	03 24	03 40	03 58

Lat.	Sunset	Twilight Civil	Twilight Naut.	Moonset 15	Moonset 16	Moonset 17	Moonset 18
°	h m	h m	h m	h m	h m	h m	h m
N 72	▬	14 49	16 25	14 52	14 42	14 31	14 15
N 70	13 31	15 13	16 36	14 58	14 54	14 50	14 47
68	14 10	15 31	16 44	15 03	15 04	15 06	15 10
66	14 37	15 46	16 52	15 06	15 12	15 19	15 28
64	14 58	15 58	16 59	15 10	15 19	15 30	15 43
62	15 14	16 08	17 04	15 13	15 25	15 39	15 56
60	15 28	16 18	17 10	15 15	15 30	15 47	16 06
N 58	15 40	16 26	17 14	15 18	15 35	15 54	16 16
56	15 50	16 33	17 19	15 20	15 39	16 00	16 24
54	15 59	16 39	17 22	15 21	15 43	16 05	16 31
52	16 07	16 45	17 26	15 23	15 46	16 10	16 38
50	16 15	16 50	17 30	15 25	15 49	16 15	16 44
45	16 30	17 02	17 38	15 28	15 56	16 25	16 56
N 40	16 43	17 12	17 45	15 31	16 01	16 33	17 07
35	16 54	17 21	17 51	15 33	16 06	16 40	17 16
30	17 03	17 29	17 58	15 35	16 10	16 46	17 24
20	17 20	17 43	18 10	15 39	16 18	16 57	17 38
N 10	17 35	17 57	18 22	15 42	16 24	17 07	17 50
0	17 48	18 10	18 36	15 46	16 30	17 16	18 01
S 10	18 02	18 25	18 51	15 49	16 37	17 24	18 13
20	18 17	18 41	19 09	15 52	16 43	17 34	18 25
30	18 35	19 01	19 32	15 56	16 51	17 45	18 39
35	18 45	19 13	19 47	15 58	16 55	17 51	18 47
40	18 57	19 27	20 05	16 00	17 00	17 59	18 56
45	19 10	19 45	20 28	16 03	17 06	18 07	19 07
S 50	19 27	20 07	21 00	16 06	17 12	18 17	19 20
52	19 35	20 18	21 16	16 08	17 16	18 22	19 26
54	19 44	20 30	21 36	16 10	17 19	18 27	19 33
56	19 54	20 45	22 03	16 12	17 23	18 33	19 41
58	20 06	21 02	22 44	16 14	17 27	18 39	19 49
S 60	20 20	21 23	////	16 16	17 32	18 47	19 59

Day	SUN Eqn. of Time 00^h	SUN Eqn. of Time 12^h	SUN Mer. Pass.	MOON Mer. Pass. Upper	MOON Mer. Pass. Lower	MOON Age	MOON Phase
d	m s	m s	h m	h m	h m	d	%
15	15 27	15 22	11 45	09 35	21 57	27	9
16	15 17	15 11	11 45	10 20	22 42	28	4
17	15 05	14 59	11 45	11 05	23 27	29	1

	UT	ARIES	VENUS −3·9		MARS +1·7		JUPITER −1·7		SATURN +0·5		STARS		
		GHA	GHA	Dec	GHA	Dec	GHA	Dec	GHA	Dec	Name	SHA	Dec
	d h	° ′	° ′	° ′	° ′	° ′	° ′	° ′	° ′	° ′		° ′	° ′
	18 00	57 13.6	196 08.1	S14 41.5	221 33.2	S 5 29.6	200 55.5	S13 19.5	151 12.4	S22 25.7	Acamar	315 15.7	S40 14.2
	01	72 16.1	211 07.5	42.5	236 34.2	30.2	215 57.5	19.7	166 14.5	25.7	Achernar	335 24.1	S57 09.0
	02	87 18.6	226 06.9	43.5	251 35.2	30.8	230 59.4	19.9	181 16.7	25.7	Acrux	173 06.3	S63 11.5
	03	102 21.0	241 06.3	44.5	266 36.2	31.4	246 01.4	20.0	196 18.9	25.7	Adhara	255 09.9	S28 59.8
	04	117 23.5	256 05.7	45.5	281 37.2	32.0	261 03.3	20.2	211 21.1	25.7	Aldebaran	290 45.6	N16 32.5
	05	132 26.0	271 05.1	46.5	296 38.2	32.6	276 05.3	20.4	226 23.2	25.8			
	06	147 28.4	286 04.5	S14 47.6	311 39.2	S 5 33.2	291 07.2	S13 20.5	241 25.4	S22 25.8	Alioth	166 18.6	N55 51.7
	07	162 30.9	301 03.9	48.6	326 40.2	33.8	306 09.2	20.7	256 27.6	25.8	Alkaid	152 57.1	N49 13.5
S	08	177 33.4	316 03.3	49.6	341 41.2	34.4	321 11.1	20.9	271 29.8	25.8	Al Na'ir	27 40.1	S46 52.6
A	09	192 35.8	331 02.6	50.6	356 42.2	35.0	336 13.0	21.0	286 31.9	25.8	Alnilam	275 43.1	S 1 11.6
T	10	207 38.3	346 02.0	51.6	11 43.2	35.7	351 15.0	21.2	301 34.1	25.8	Alphard	217 53.1	S 8 44.1
U	11	222 40.8	1 01.4	52.6	26 44.2	36.3	6 16.9	21.4	316 36.3	25.8			
R	12	237 43.2	16 00.8	S14 53.6	41 45.2	S 5 36.9	21 18.9	S13 21.6	331 38.5	S22 25.8	Alphecca	126 08.9	N26 39.5
D	13	252 45.7	31 00.2	54.5	56 46.2	37.5	36 20.8	21.7	346 40.6	25.9	Alpheratz	357 40.2	N29 11.5
A	14	267 48.1	45 59.6	55.5	71 47.2	38.1	51 22.8	21.9	1 42.8	25.9	Altair	62 05.5	N 8 55.2
Y	15	282 50.6	60 59.0	56.5	86 48.2	38.7	66 24.7	22.1	16 45.0	25.9	Ankaa	353 12.6	S42 12.8
	16	297 53.1	75 58.3	57.5	101 49.2	39.3	81 26.7	22.2	31 47.2	25.9	Antares	112 23.0	S26 28.0
	17	312 55.5	90 57.7	58.5	116 50.2	39.9	96 28.6	22.4	46 49.3	25.9			
	18	327 58.0	105 57.1	S14 59.5	131 51.2	S 5 40.5	111 30.5	S13 22.6	61 51.5	S22 25.9	Arcturus	145 53.4	N19 05.6
	19	343 00.5	120 56.5	15 00.5	146 52.2	41.1	126 32.5	22.7	76 53.7	25.9	Atria	107 22.6	S69 03.4
	20	358 02.9	135 55.9	01.5	161 53.2	41.7	141 34.4	22.9	91 55.9	25.9	Avior	234 16.5	S59 33.8
	21	13 05.4	150 55.2	02.5	176 54.2	42.4	156 36.4	23.1	106 58.0	25.9	Bellatrix	278 28.5	N 6 21.8
	22	28 07.9	165 54.6	03.5	191 55.2	43.0	171 38.3	23.3	122 00.2	26.0	Betelgeuse	270 57.8	N 7 24.5
	23	43 10.3	180 54.0	04.5	206 56.3	43.6	186 40.3	23.4	137 02.4	26.0			
	19 00	58 12.8	195 53.4	S15 05.5	221 57.3	S 5 44.2	201 42.2	S13 23.6	152 04.5	S22 26.0	Canopus	263 54.4	S52 42.3
	01	73 15.2	210 52.8	06.5	236 58.3	44.8	216 44.2	23.8	167 06.7	26.0	Capella	280 29.6	N46 00.7
	02	88 17.7	225 52.1	07.5	251 59.3	45.4	231 46.1	23.9	182 08.9	26.0	Deneb	49 29.6	N45 21.0
	03	103 20.2	240 51.5	08.5	267 00.3	46.0	246 48.1	24.1	197 11.1	26.0	Denebola	182 30.8	N14 28.4
	04	118 22.6	255 50.9	09.4	282 01.3	46.6	261 50.0	24.3	212 13.2	26.0	Diphda	348 52.7	S17 53.4
	05	133 25.1	270 50.3	10.4	297 02.3	47.2	276 51.9	24.4	227 15.4	26.0			
	06	148 27.6	285 49.7	S15 11.4	312 03.3	S 5 47.8	291 53.9	S13 24.6	242 17.6	S22 26.1	Dubhe	193 48.4	N61 39.1
	07	163 30.0	300 49.0	12.4	327 04.3	48.4	306 55.8	24.8	257 19.8	26.1	Elnath	278 08.5	N28 37.1
	08	178 32.5	315 48.4	13.4	342 05.3	49.0	321 57.8	25.0	272 21.9	26.1	Eltanin	90 45.2	N51 29.5
S	09	193 35.0	330 47.8	14.4	357 06.3	49.6	336 59.7	25.1	287 24.1	26.1	Enif	33 44.2	N 9 57.6
U	10	208 37.4	345 47.2	15.4	12 07.3	50.3	352 01.7	25.3	302 26.3	26.1	Fomalhaut	15 20.7	S29 31.8
N	11	223 39.9	0 46.5	16.3	27 08.3	50.9	7 03.6	25.5	317 28.4	26.1			
D	12	238 42.4	15 45.9	S15 17.3	42 09.3	S 5 51.5	22 05.6	S13 25.6	332 30.6	S22 26.1	Gacrux	171 57.9	S57 12.4
A	13	253 44.8	30 45.3	18.3	57 10.3	52.1	37 07.5	25.8	347 32.8	26.1	Gienah	175 49.4	S17 38.2
Y	14	268 47.3	45 44.6	19.3	72 11.3	52.7	52 09.5	26.0	2 35.0	26.1	Hadar	148 44.2	S60 27.2
	15	283 49.7	60 44.0	20.3	87 12.3	53.3	67 11.4	26.1	17 37.1	26.2	Hamal	327 57.1	N23 32.8
	16	298 52.2	75 43.4	21.2	102 13.3	53.9	82 13.3	26.3	32 39.3	26.2	Kaus Aust.	83 40.2	S34 22.4
	17	313 54.7	90 42.8	22.2	117 14.3	54.5	97 15.3	26.5	47 41.5	26.2			
	18	328 57.1	105 42.1	S15 23.2	132 15.3	S 5 55.1	112 17.2	S13 26.6	62 43.6	S22 26.2	Kochab	137 21.4	N74 05.0
	19	343 59.6	120 41.5	24.2	147 16.3	55.7	127 19.2	26.8	77 45.8	26.2	Markab	13 35.3	N15 18.2
	20	359 02.1	135 40.9	25.2	162 17.3	56.3	142 21.1	27.0	92 48.0	26.2	Menkar	314 11.6	N 4 09.5
	21	14 04.5	150 40.2	26.1	177 18.3	56.9	157 23.1	27.2	107 50.2	26.2	Menkent	148 04.4	S36 27.1
	22	29 07.0	165 39.6	27.1	192 19.3	57.5	172 25.0	27.3	122 52.3	26.2	Miaplacidus	221 38.8	S69 47.1
	23	44 09.5	180 39.0	28.1	207 20.3	58.2	187 27.0	27.5	137 54.5	26.2			
	20 00	59 11.9	195 38.3	S15 29.1	222 21.3	S 5 58.8	202 28.9	S13 27.7	152 56.7	S22 26.3	Mirfak	308 35.5	N49 55.3
	01	74 14.4	210 37.7	30.0	237 22.3	5 59.4	217 30.9	27.8	167 58.8	26.3	Nunki	75 54.9	S26 16.3
	02	89 16.9	225 37.1	31.0	252 23.3	6 00.0	232 32.8	28.0	183 01.0	26.3	Peacock	53 14.9	S56 40.7
	03	104 19.3	240 36.4	32.0	267 24.3	00.6	247 34.8	28.2	198 03.2	26.3	Pollux	243 23.9	N27 58.8
	04	119 21.8	255 35.8	32.9	282 25.3	01.2	262 36.7	28.3	213 05.4	26.3	Procyon	244 56.5	N 5 10.6
	05	134 24.2	270 35.2	33.9	297 26.3	01.8	277 38.6	28.5	228 07.5	26.3			
	06	149 26.7	285 34.5	S15 34.9	312 27.3	S 6 02.4	292 40.6	S13 28.7	243 09.7	S22 26.3	Rasalhague	96 04.0	N12 33.1
	07	164 29.2	300 33.9	35.9	327 28.3	03.0	307 42.5	28.8	258 11.9	26.3	Regulus	207 40.4	N11 52.8
	08	179 31.6	315 33.3	36.8	342 29.3	03.6	322 44.5	29.0	273 14.0	26.4	Rigel	281 08.9	S 8 11.0
M	09	194 34.1	330 32.6	37.8	357 30.3	04.2	337 46.4	29.2	288 16.2	26.4	Rigil Kent.	139 48.3	S60 54.2
O	10	209 36.6	345 32.0	38.8	12 31.4	04.8	352 48.4	29.3	303 18.4	26.4	Sabik	102 09.5	S15 44.6
N	11	224 39.0	0 31.3	39.7	27 32.4	05.4	7 50.3	29.5	318 20.6	26.4			
D	12	239 41.5	15 30.7	S15 40.7	42 33.4	S 6 06.0	22 52.3	S13 29.7	333 22.7	S22 26.4	Schedar	349 36.6	N56 38.3
A	13	254 44.0	30 30.1	41.7	57 34.4	06.6	37 54.2	29.9	348 24.9	26.4	Shaula	96 18.3	S37 06.8
Y	14	269 46.4	45 29.4	42.6	72 35.4	07.2	52 56.2	30.0	3 27.1	26.4	Sirius	258 30.8	S16 44.5
	15	284 48.9	60 28.8	43.6	87 36.4	07.8	67 58.1	30.2	18 29.2	26.4	Spica	158 28.4	S11 15.0
	16	299 51.4	75 28.1	44.6	102 37.4	08.5	83 00.1	30.4	33 31.4	26.4	Suhail	222 50.1	S43 30.1
	17	314 53.8	90 27.5	45.5	117 38.4	09.1	98 02.0	30.5	48 33.6	26.5			
	18	329 56.3	105 26.9	S15 46.5	132 39.4	S 6 09.7	113 03.9	S13 30.7	63 35.8	S22 26.5	Vega	80 37.3	N38 48.4
	19	344 58.7	120 26.2	47.4	147 40.4	10.3	128 05.9	30.9	78 37.9	26.5	Zuben'ubi	137 02.5	S16 06.7
	20	0 01.2	135 25.6	48.4	162 41.4	10.9	143 07.8	31.0	93 40.1	26.5			
	21	15 03.7	150 24.9	49.4	177 42.4	11.5	158 09.8	31.2	108 42.3	26.5			
	22	30 06.1	165 24.3	50.3	192 43.4	12.1	173 11.7	31.4	123 44.4	26.5			
	23	45 08.6	180 23.7	51.3	207 44.4	12.7	188 13.7	31.5	138 46.6	26.5			
	Mer. Pass.	h m 20 03.9	*v* −0.6	*d* 1.0	*v* 1.0	*d* 0.6	*v* 1.9	*d* 0.2	*v* 2.2	*d* 0.0			

	SHA	Mer. Pass.
	° ′	h m
Venus	137 40.6	10 57
Mars	163 44.5	9 12
Jupiter	143 29.4	10 32
Saturn	93 51.8	13 50

UT d	UT h	SUN GHA	SUN Dec	MOON GHA	MOON v	MOON Dec	MOON d	MOON HP
d	h	° ′	° ′	° ′	′	° ′	′	′
18	00	183 43.3	S19 12.7	187 54.9	13.3	S13 01.5	7.9	54.7
	01	198 43.1	13.3	202 27.2	13.4	13 09.4	7.9	54.7
	02	213 43.0	13.9	216 59.6	13.3	13 17.3	7.8	54.7
	03	228 42.9	. . 14.5	231 31.9	13.3	13 25.1	7.8	54.6
	04	243 42.7	15.1	246 04.2	13.2	13 32.9	7.7	54.6
	05	258 42.6	15.7	260 36.4	13.3	13 40.6	7.6	54.6
SATURDAY	06	273 42.5	S19 16.3	275 08.7	13.2	S13 48.2	7.6	54.6
	07	288 42.3	16.8	289 40.9	13.2	13 55.8	7.5	54.6
	08	303 42.2	17.4	304 13.1	13.2	14 03.3	7.4	54.6
	09	318 42.1	. . 18.0	318 45.3	13.2	14 10.7	7.4	54.6
	10	333 41.9	18.6	333 17.5	13.2	14 18.1	7.3	54.6
	11	348 41.8	19.2	347 49.7	13.1	14 25.4	7.2	54.5
	12	3 41.7	S19 19.8	2 21.8	13.1	S14 32.6	7.2	54.5
	13	18 41.5	20.4	16 53.9	13.1	14 39.8	7.1	54.5
	14	33 41.4	21.0	31 26.0	13.1	14 46.9	7.0	54.5
	15	48 41.3	. . 21.6	45 58.1	13.1	14 53.9	7.0	54.5
	16	63 41.1	22.2	60 30.2	13.0	15 00.9	6.8	54.5
	17	78 41.0	22.7	75 02.2	13.1	15 07.7	6.9	54.5
	18	93 40.8	S19 23.3	89 34.3	13.0	S15 14.6	6.7	54.5
	19	108 40.7	23.9	104 06.3	13.0	15 21.3	6.7	54.4
	20	123 40.6	24.5	118 38.3	12.9	15 28.0	6.6	54.4
	21	138 40.4	. . 25.1	133 10.2	13.0	15 34.6	6.5	54.4
	22	153 40.3	25.7	147 42.2	12.9	15 41.1	6.5	54.4
	23	168 40.2	26.2	162 14.1	12.9	15 47.6	6.4	54.4
19	00	183 40.0	S19 26.8	176 46.0	12.9	S15 54.0	6.3	54.4
	01	198 39.9	27.4	191 17.9	12.9	16 00.3	6.2	54.4
	02	213 39.7	28.0	205 49.8	12.8	16 06.5	6.2	54.4
	03	228 39.6	. . 28.6	220 21.6	12.9	16 12.7	6.1	54.4
	04	243 39.4	29.2	234 53.5	12.8	16 18.8	6.0	54.3
	05	258 39.3	29.7	249 25.3	12.8	16 24.8	5.9	54.3
SUNDAY	06	273 39.2	S19 30.3	263 57.1	12.8	S16 30.7	5.9	54.3
	07	288 39.0	30.9	278 28.9	12.7	16 36.6	5.8	54.3
	08	303 38.9	31.5	293 00.6	12.8	16 42.4	5.7	54.3
	09	318 38.7	. . 32.0	307 32.4	12.7	16 48.1	5.6	54.3
	10	333 38.6	32.6	322 04.1	12.7	16 53.7	5.6	54.3
	11	348 38.5	33.2	336 35.8	12.7	16 59.3	5.4	54.3
	12	3 38.3	S19 33.8	351 07.5	12.6	S17 04.7	5.4	54.3
	13	18 38.2	34.3	5 39.1	12.7	17 10.1	5.3	54.3
	14	33 38.0	34.9	20 10.8	12.6	17 15.4	5.3	54.2
	15	48 37.9	. . 35.5	34 42.4	12.6	17 20.7	5.1	54.2
	16	63 37.7	36.1	49 14.0	12.6	17 25.8	5.1	54.2
	17	78 37.6	36.6	63 45.6	12.6	17 30.9	5.0	54.2
	18	93 37.4	S19 37.2	78 17.2	12.6	S17 35.9	4.9	54.2
	19	108 37.3	37.8	92 48.8	12.5	17 40.8	4.8	54.2
	20	123 37.1	38.4	107 20.3	12.5	17 45.6	4.8	54.2
	21	138 37.0	. . 38.9	121 51.8	12.5	17 50.4	4.6	54.2
	22	153 36.8	39.5	136 23.3	12.5	17 55.0	4.6	54.2
	23	168 36.7	40.1	150 54.8	12.5	17 59.6	4.5	54.2
20	00	183 36.6	S19 40.6	165 26.3	12.5	S18 04.1	4.4	54.2
	01	198 36.4	41.2	179 57.8	12.4	18 08.5	4.4	54.2
	02	213 36.3	41.8	194 29.2	12.4	18 12.9	4.2	54.1
	03	228 36.1	. . 42.3	209 00.6	12.5	18 17.1	4.2	54.1
	04	243 36.0	42.9	223 32.1	12.4	18 21.3	4.0	54.1
	05	258 35.8	43.5	238 03.5	12.4	18 25.3	4.0	54.1
MONDAY	06	273 35.7	S19 44.0	252 34.9	12.3	S18 29.3	3.9	54.1
	07	288 35.5	44.6	267 06.2	12.4	18 33.2	3.9	54.1
	08	303 35.4	45.1	281 37.6	12.3	18 37.1	3.7	54.1
	09	318 35.2	. . 45.7	296 08.9	12.4	18 40.8	3.6	54.1
	10	333 35.1	46.3	310 40.3	12.3	18 44.4	3.6	54.1
	11	348 34.9	46.8	325 11.6	12.3	18 48.0	3.5	54.1
	12	3 34.7	S19 47.4	339 42.9	12.3	S18 51.5	3.4	54.1
	13	18 34.6	47.9	354 14.2	12.3	18 54.9	3.3	54.1
	14	33 34.4	48.5	8 45.5	12.2	18 58.2	3.2	54.1
	15	48 34.3	. . 49.1	23 16.7	12.3	19 01.4	3.1	54.1
	16	63 34.1	49.6	37 48.0	12.2	19 04.5	3.1	54.1
	17	78 34.0	50.2	52 19.2	12.3	19 07.6	2.9	54.1
	18	93 33.8	S19 50.7	66 50.5	12.2	S19 10.5	2.9	54.1
	19	108 33.7	51.3	81 21.7	12.2	19 13.4	2.7	54.0
	20	123 33.5	51.8	95 52.9	12.2	19 16.1	2.7	54.0
	21	138 33.4	. . 52.4	110 24.1	12.2	19 18.8	2.6	54.0
	22	153 33.2	53.0	124 55.3	12.2	19 21.4	2.5	54.0
	23	168 33.1	53.5	139 26.5	12.1	S19 23.9	2.5	54.0
		SD 16.2	*d* 0.6	SD	14.9	14.8		14.7

Lat.	Twilight Naut.	Twilight Civil	Sunrise	Moonrise 18	Moonrise 19	Moonrise 20	Moonrise 21
°	h m	h m	h m	h m	h m	h m	h m
N 72	07 14	08 54	▬	09 12	11 20	▬	▬
N 70	07 02	08 28	10 19	08 41	10 21	12 04	13 51
68	06 52	08 08	09 33	08 19	09 48	11 11	12 23
66	06 44	07 52	09 03	08 01	09 23	10 39	11 44
64	06 37	07 39	08 41	07 47	09 04	10 16	11 17
62	06 31	07 27	08 23	07 35	08 49	09 57	10 57
60	06 25	07 18	08 08	07 25	08 36	09 41	10 40
N 58	06 20	07 09	07 56	07 16	08 25	09 28	10 26
56	06 15	07 02	07 45	07 09	08 15	09 17	10 13
54	06 11	06 55	07 35	07 02	08 07	09 07	10 03
52	06 07	06 49	07 27	06 56	07 59	08 59	09 53
50	06 04	06 43	07 19	06 50	07 52	08 51	09 45
45	05 55	06 31	07 03	06 38	07 38	08 34	09 27
N 40	05 48	06 20	06 50	06 29	07 26	08 20	09 12
35	05 41	06 11	06 38	06 20	07 15	08 09	09 00
30	05 34	06 03	06 28	06 13	07 06	07 59	08 49
20	05 21	05 48	06 11	06 00	06 51	07 41	08 31
N 10	05 08	05 34	05 56	05 49	06 38	07 26	08 15
0	04 54	05 20	05 42	05 39	06 25	07 12	08 00
S 10	04 39	05 05	05 27	05 29	06 13	06 58	07 45
20	04 20	04 48	05 12	05 18	06 00	06 43	07 29
30	03 56	04 28	04 54	05 06	05 45	06 26	07 11
35	03 41	04 15	04 44	04 59	05 36	06 16	07 00
40	03 22	04 01	04 31	04 51	05 26	06 05	06 48
45	02 58	03 43	04 17	04 41	05 15	05 52	06 34
S 50	02 26	03 20	03 59	04 30	05 01	05 36	06 16
52	02 09	03 08	03 51	04 25	04 54	05 28	06 08
54	01 47	02 55	03 42	04 19	04 47	05 20	05 59
56	01 19	02 40	03 31	04 13	04 39	05 10	05 48
58	00 30	02 22	03 19	04 06	04 30	05 00	05 37
S 60	////	01 59	03 05	03 58	04 20	04 47	05 23

Lat.	Sunset	Twilight Civil	Twilight Naut.	Moonset 18	Moonset 19	Moonset 20	Moonset 21
°	h m	h m	h m	h m	h m	h m	h m
N 72	▬	14 36	16 16	14 15	13 44	▬	▬
N 70	13 11	15 02	16 28	14 47	14 43	14 38	14 30
68	13 57	15 22	16 37	15 10	15 17	15 31	15 59
66	14 27	15 38	16 46	15 28	15 42	16 04	16 37
64	14 50	15 52	16 53	15 43	16 02	16 28	17 04
62	15 07	16 03	16 59	15 56	16 18	16 47	17 25
60	15 22	16 12	17 05	16 06	16 31	17 02	17 42
N 58	15 35	16 21	17 10	16 16	16 42	17 15	17 56
56	15 45	16 28	17 15	16 24	16 52	17 27	18 08
54	15 55	16 35	17 19	16 31	17 01	17 37	18 19
52	16 03	16 41	17 23	16 38	17 09	17 46	18 29
50	16 11	16 47	17 27	16 44	17 16	17 54	18 37
45	16 27	16 59	17 35	16 56	17 32	18 11	18 55
N 40	16 41	17 10	17 43	17 07	17 44	18 25	19 10
35	16 52	17 19	17 50	17 16	17 55	18 37	19 22
30	17 02	17 28	17 57	17 24	18 04	18 47	19 33
20	17 19	17 43	18 10	17 38	18 21	19 05	19 52
N 10	17 35	17 57	18 23	17 50	18 35	19 21	20 08
0	17 49	18 11	18 37	18 01	18 48	19 35	20 23
S 10	18 04	18 26	18 52	18 13	19 01	19 50	20 38
20	18 19	18 43	19 11	18 25	19 16	20 05	20 54
30	18 37	19 04	19 35	18 39	19 32	20 23	21 13
35	18 48	19 16	19 51	18 47	19 41	20 34	21 24
40	19 00	19 31	20 09	18 56	19 52	20 46	21 36
45	19 14	19 49	20 34	19 07	20 05	21 00	21 51
S 50	19 32	20 12	21 07	19 20	20 21	21 17	22 09
52	19 41	20 24	21 24	19 26	20 28	21 25	22 17
54	19 50	20 37	21 46	19 33	20 36	21 34	22 27
56	20 01	20 52	22 16	19 41	20 45	21 44	22 37
58	20 13	21 11	23 11	19 49	20 56	21 56	22 49
S 60	20 27	21 34	////	19 59	21 07	22 10	23 03

Day	SUN Eqn. of Time 00^h	SUN Eqn. of Time 12^h	SUN Mer. Pass.	MOON Mer. Pass. Upper	MOON Mer. Pass. Lower	MOON Age	MOON Phase
d	m s	m s	h m	h m	h m	d	%
18	14 53	14 47	11 45	11 50	24 13	00	0
19	14 40	14 34	11 45	12 37	00 13	01	1
20	14 27	14 19	11 46	13 24	01 00	02	4

UT d h	ARIES GHA ° ′	VENUS −3·9 GHA ° ′	VENUS Dec ° ′	MARS +1·7 GHA ° ′	MARS Dec ° ′	JUPITER −1·7 GHA ° ′	JUPITER Dec ° ′	SATURN +0·5 GHA ° ′	SATURN Dec ° ′
21 00	60 11.1	195 23.0	S15 52.2	222 45.4	S 6 13.3	203 15.6	S13 31.7	153 48.8	S22 26.5
01	75 13.5	210 22.4	53.2	237 46.4	13.9	218 17.6	31.9	168 50.9	26.5
02	90 16.0	225 21.7	54.2	252 47.4	14.5	233 19.5	32.0	183 53.1	26.6
03	105 18.5	240 21.1	. . 55.1	267 48.4	. . 15.1	248 21.5	. . 32.2	198 55.3	. . 26.6
04	120 20.9	255 20.4	56.1	282 49.4	15.7	263 23.4	32.4	213 57.4	26.6
05	135 23.4	270 19.8	57.0	297 50.4	16.3	278 25.4	32.5	228 59.6	26.6
06	150 25.9	285 19.1	S15 58.0	312 51.4	S 6 16.9	293 27.3	S13 32.7	244 01.8	S22 26.6
07	165 28.3	300 18.5	58.9	327 52.4	17.5	308 29.3	32.9	259 04.0	26.6
08	180 30.8	315 17.8	15 59.9	342 53.4	18.1	323 31.2	33.0	274 06.1	26.6
09	195 33.2	330 17.2	16 00.8	357 54.4	. . 18.7	338 33.2	. . 33.2	289 08.3	. . 26.6
10	210 35.7	345 16.5	01.8	12 55.4	19.3	353 35.1	33.4	304 10.5	26.6
11	225 38.2	0 15.9	02.7	27 56.4	19.9	8 37.1	33.5	319 12.6	26.7
12	240 40.6	15 15.2	S16 03.7	42 57.4	S 6 20.5	23 39.0	S13 33.7	334 14.8	S22 26.7
13	255 43.1	30 14.6	04.6	57 58.4	21.2	38 40.9	33.9	349 17.0	26.7
14	270 45.6	45 13.9	05.6	72 59.4	21.8	53 42.9	34.0	4 19.1	26.7
15	285 48.0	60 13.3	. . 06.5	88 00.4	. . 22.4	68 44.8	. . 34.2	19 21.3	. . 26.7
16	300 50.5	75 12.6	07.5	103 01.4	23.0	83 46.8	34.4	34 23.5	26.7
17	315 53.0	90 12.0	08.4	118 02.4	23.6	98 48.7	34.5	49 25.6	26.7
18	330 55.4	105 11.3	S16 09.4	133 03.4	S 6 24.2	113 50.7	S13 34.7	64 27.8	S22 26.7
19	345 57.9	120 10.7	10.3	148 04.4	24.8	128 52.6	34.9	79 30.0	26.7
20	1 00.3	135 10.0	11.2	163 05.4	25.4	143 54.6	35.1	94 32.1	26.8
21	16 02.8	150 09.3	. . 12.2	178 06.4	. . 26.0	158 56.5	. . 35.2	109 34.3	. . 26.8
22	31 05.3	165 08.7	13.1	193 07.4	26.6	173 58.5	35.4	124 36.5	26.8
23	46 07.7	180 08.0	14.1	208 08.4	27.2	189 00.4	35.6	139 38.7	26.8
22 00	61 10.2	195 07.4	S16 15.0	223 09.4	S 6 27.8	204 02.4	S13 35.7	154 40.8	S22 26.8
01	76 12.7	210 06.7	15.9	238 10.4	28.4	219 04.3	35.9	169 43.0	26.8
02	91 15.1	225 06.1	16.9	253 11.4	29.0	234 06.3	36.1	184 45.2	26.8
03	106 17.6	240 05.4	. . 17.8	268 12.4	. . 29.6	249 08.2	. . 36.2	199 47.3	. . 26.8
04	121 20.1	255 04.7	18.8	283 13.4	30.2	264 10.2	36.4	214 49.5	26.8
05	136 22.5	270 04.1	19.7	298 14.4	30.8	279 12.1	36.6	229 51.7	26.9
06	151 25.0	285 03.4	S16 20.6	313 15.4	S 6 31.4	294 14.1	S13 36.7	244 53.8	S22 26.9
07	166 27.5	300 02.8	21.6	328 16.4	32.0	309 16.0	36.9	259 56.0	26.9
08	181 29.9	315 02.1	22.5	343 17.4	32.6	324 18.0	37.1	274 58.2	26.9
09	196 32.4	330 01.4	. . 23.4	358 18.4	. . 33.2	339 19.9	. . 37.2	290 00.3	. . 26.9
10	211 34.8	345 00.8	24.4	13 19.4	33.8	354 21.9	37.4	305 02.5	26.9
11	226 37.3	0 00.1	25.3	28 20.4	34.4	9 23.8	37.6	320 04.7	26.9
12	241 39.8	14 59.5	S16 26.2	43 21.4	S 6 35.0	24 25.8	S13 37.7	335 06.8	S22 26.9
13	256 42.2	29 58.8	27.2	58 22.4	35.6	39 27.7	37.9	350 09.0	26.9
14	271 44.7	44 58.1	28.1	73 23.4	36.2	54 29.6	38.1	5 11.2	27.0
15	286 47.2	59 57.5	. . 29.0	88 24.4	. . 36.8	69 31.6	. . 38.2	20 13.3	. . 27.0
16	301 49.6	74 56.8	30.0	103 25.4	37.4	84 33.5	38.4	35 15.5	27.0
17	316 52.1	89 56.1	30.9	118 26.4	38.0	99 35.5	38.6	50 17.7	27.0
18	331 54.6	104 55.5	S16 31.8	133 27.4	S 6 38.6	114 37.4	S13 38.7	65 19.8	S22 27.0
19	346 57.0	119 54.8	32.7	148 28.4	39.2	129 39.4	38.9	80 22.0	27.0
20	1 59.5	134 54.1	33.7	163 29.4	39.8	144 41.3	39.0	95 24.2	27.0
21	17 02.0	149 53.5	. . 34.6	178 30.4	. . 40.4	159 43.3	. . 39.2	110 26.3	. . 27.0
22	32 04.4	164 52.8	35.5	193 31.4	41.0	174 45.2	39.4	125 28.5	27.0
23	47 06.9	179 52.1	36.4	208 32.4	41.6	189 47.2	39.5	140 30.7	27.1
23 00	62 09.3	194 51.5	S16 37.4	223 33.4	S 6 42.2	204 49.1	S13 39.7	155 32.8	S22 27.1
01	77 11.8	209 50.8	38.3	238 34.4	42.8	219 51.1	39.9	170 35.0	27.1
02	92 14.3	224 50.1	39.2	253 35.4	43.4	234 53.0	40.0	185 37.2	27.1
03	107 16.7	239 49.4	. . 40.1	268 36.4	. . 44.0	249 55.0	. . 40.2	200 39.3	. . 27.1
04	122 19.2	254 48.8	41.0	283 37.4	44.6	264 56.9	40.4	215 41.5	27.1
05	137 21.7	269 48.1	42.0	298 38.4	45.2	279 58.9	40.5	230 43.7	27.1
06	152 24.1	284 47.4	S16 42.9	313 39.4	S 6 45.8	295 00.8	S13 40.7	245 45.8	S22 27.1
07	167 26.6	299 46.8	43.8	328 40.4	46.4	310 02.8	40.9	260 48.0	27.1
08	182 29.1	314 46.1	44.7	343 41.4	47.0	325 04.7	41.0	275 50.2	27.1
09	197 31.5	329 45.4	. . 45.6	358 42.4	. . 47.6	340 06.7	. . 41.2	290 52.3	. . 27.2
10	212 34.0	344 44.7	46.5	13 43.4	48.2	355 08.6	41.4	305 54.5	27.2
11	227 36.5	359 44.1	47.5	28 44.4	48.8	10 10.6	41.5	320 56.7	27.2
12	242 38.9	14 43.4	S16 48.4	43 45.4	S 6 49.4	25 12.5	S13 41.7	335 58.8	S22 27.2
13	257 41.4	29 42.7	49.3	58 46.4	50.0	40 14.5	41.9	351 01.0	27.2
14	272 43.8	44 42.0	50.2	73 47.4	50.6	55 16.4	42.0	6 03.2	27.2
15	287 46.3	59 41.4	. . 51.1	88 48.4	. . 51.2	70 18.4	. . 42.2	21 05.3	. . 27.2
16	302 48.8	74 40.7	52.0	103 49.4	51.8	85 20.3	42.4	36 07.5	27.2
17	317 51.2	89 40.0	52.9	118 50.4	52.4	100 22.3	42.5	51 09.7	27.2
18	332 53.7	104 39.3	S16 53.8	133 51.4	S 6 53.0	115 24.2	S13 42.7	66 11.8	S22 27.3
19	347 56.2	119 38.6	54.7	148 52.4	53.6	130 26.2	42.9	81 14.0	27.3
20	2 58.6	134 38.0	55.6	163 53.4	54.2	145 28.1	43.0	96 16.2	27.3
21	18 01.1	149 37.3	. . 56.6	178 54.4	. . 54.8	160 30.1	. . 43.2	111 18.3	. . 27.3
22	33 03.6	164 36.6	57.5	193 55.4	55.4	175 32.0	43.4	126 20.5	27.3
23	48 06.0	179 35.9	58.4	208 56.4	56.0	190 34.0	43.5	141 22.7	27.3
Mer. Pass. (h m)	19 52.1	*v* −0.7	*d* 0.9	*v* 1.0	*d* 0.6	*v* 1.9	*d* 0.2	*v* 2.2	*d* 0.0

STARS

Name	SHA ° ′	Dec ° ′
Acamar	315 15.7	S40 14.2
Achernar	335 24.2	S57 09.0
Acrux	173 06.2	S63 11.5
Adhara	255 09.9	S28 59.8
Aldebaran	290 45.6	N16 32.5
Alioth	166 18.6	N55 51.7
Alkaid	152 57.0	N49 13.5
Al Na'ir	27 40.1	S46 52.6
Alnilam	275 43.0	S 1 11.6
Alphard	217 53.1	S 8 44.1
Alphecca	126 08.9	N26 39.5
Alpheratz	357 40.2	N29 11.5
Altair	62 05.5	N 8 55.2
Ankaa	353 12.6	S42 12.8
Antares	112 23.0	S26 28.0
Arcturus	145 53.4	N19 05.5
Atria	107 22.6	S69 03.4
Avior	234 16.5	S59 33.8
Bellatrix	278 28.5	N 6 21.8
Betelgeuse	270 57.8	N 7 24.5
Canopus	263 54.4	S52 42.3
Capella	280 29.6	N46 00.7
Deneb	49 29.6	N45 21.0
Denebola	182 30.8	N14 28.4
Diphda	348 52.7	S17 53.4
Dubhe	193 48.4	N61 39.0
Elnath	278 08.5	N28 37.1
Eltanin	90 45.2	N51 29.5
Enif	33 44.2	N 9 57.6
Fomalhaut	15 20.7	S29 31.8
Gacrux	171 57.8	S57 12.4
Gienah	175 49.4	S17 38.2
Hadar	148 44.1	S60 27.2
Hamal	327 57.1	N23 32.8
Kaus Aust.	83 40.2	S34 22.4
Kochab	137 21.4	N74 05.0
Markab	13 35.3	N15 18.2
Menkar	314 11.6	N 4 09.5
Menkent	148 04.4	S36 27.1
Miaplacidus	221 38.7	S69 47.2
Mirfak	308 35.5	N49 55.4
Nunki	75 54.9	S26 16.3
Peacock	53 14.9	S56 40.7
Pollux	243 23.9	N27 58.8
Procyon	244 56.4	N 5 10.6
Rasalhague	96 04.0	N12 33.1
Regulus	207 40.4	N11 52.8
Rigel	281 08.9	S 8 11.0
Rigil Kent.	139 48.3	S60 54.2
Sabik	102 09.5	S15 44.6
Schedar	349 36.7	N56 38.3
Shaula	96 18.3	S37 06.8
Sirius	258 30.8	S16 44.5
Spica	158 28.4	S11 15.0
Suhail	222 50.1	S43 30.1
Vega	80 37.3	N38 48.4
Zuben'ubi	137 02.4	S16 06.7

	SHA ° ′	Mer. Pass. h m
Venus	133 57.2	11 00
Mars	161 59.2	9 07
Jupiter	142 52.2	10 22
Saturn	93 30.6	13 39

2017 NOVEMBER 21, 22, 23 (TUES., WED., THURS.)

UT	SUN GHA	SUN Dec	MOON GHA	v	MOON Dec	d	HP
d h	° ′	° ′	° ′	′	° ′	′	′
21 00	183 32.9	S19 54.1	153 57.6	12.2	S19 26.4	2.3	54.0
01	198 32.7	54.6	168 28.8	12.2	19 28.7	2.2	54.0
02	213 32.6	55.2	183 00.0	12.1	19 30.9	2.2	54.0
03	228 32.4	. . 55.7	197 31.1	12.2	19 33.1	2.0	54.0
04	243 32.3	56.3	212 02.3	12.1	19 35.1	2.0	54.0
05	258 32.1	56.8	226 33.4	12.1	19 37.1	1.9	54.0
06	273 31.9	S19 57.4	241 04.5	12.1	S19 39.0	1.8	54.0
T 07	288 31.8	57.9	255 35.6	12.2	19 40.8	1.7	54.0
U 08	303 31.6	58.5	270 06.8	12.1	19 42.5	1.6	54.0
E 09	318 31.5	. . 59.0	284 37.9	12.1	19 44.1	1.5	54.0
S 10	333 31.3	19 59.6	299 09.0	12.1	19 45.6	1.4	54.0
D 11	348 31.2	20 00.1	313 40.1	12.1	19 47.0	1.4	54.0
A 12	3 31.0	S20 00.6	328 11.2	12.1	S19 48.4	1.2	54.0
Y 13	18 30.8	01.2	342 42.3	12.1	19 49.6	1.2	54.0
14	33 30.7	01.7	357 13.4	12.0	19 50.8	1.0	54.0
15	48 30.5	. . 02.3	11 44.4	12.1	19 51.8	1.0	54.0
16	63 30.3	02.8	26 15.5	12.1	19 52.8	0.9	54.0
17	78 30.2	03.4	40 46.6	12.1	19 53.7	0.8	54.0
18	93 30.0	S20 03.9	55 17.7	12.0	S19 54.5	0.6	54.0
19	108 29.9	04.4	69 48.7	12.1	19 55.1	0.7	54.0
20	123 29.7	05.0	84 19.8	12.1	19 55.8	0.5	54.0
21	138 29.5	. . 05.5	98 50.9	12.1	19 56.3	0.4	54.0
22	153 29.4	06.1	113 22.0	12.0	19 56.7	0.3	54.0
23	168 29.2	06.6	127 53.0	12.1	19 57.0	0.3	54.0
22 00	183 29.0	S20 07.1	142 24.1	12.1	S19 57.3	0.1	54.0
01	198 28.9	07.7	156 55.2	12.0	19 57.4	0.1	54.0
02	213 28.7	08.2	171 26.2	12.1	19 57.5	0.1	54.0
03	228 28.5	. . 08.7	185 57.3	12.1	19 57.4	0.1	54.0
04	243 28.4	09.3	200 28.4	12.1	19 57.3	0.2	54.0
05	258 28.2	09.8	214 59.5	12.0	19 57.1	0.3	54.0
06	273 28.0	S20 10.4	229 30.5	12.1	S19 56.8	0.4	54.0
W 07	288 27.9	10.9	244 01.6	12.1	19 56.4	0.5	54.0
E 08	303 27.7	11.4	258 32.7	12.1	19 55.9	0.6	54.0
D 09	318 27.5	. . 11.9	273 03.8	12.1	19 55.3	0.7	54.0
N 10	333 27.4	12.5	287 34.9	12.1	19 54.6	0.8	54.0
E 11	348 27.2	13.0	302 06.0	12.1	19 53.8	0.8	54.0
S 12	3 27.0	S20 13.5	316 37.1	12.1	S19 53.0	1.0	54.0
D 13	18 26.9	14.1	331 08.2	12.1	19 52.0	1.0	54.0
A 14	33 26.7	14.6	345 39.3	12.1	19 51.0	1.1	54.0
Y 15	48 26.5	. . 15.1	0 10.4	12.1	19 49.9	1.3	54.0
16	63 26.4	15.7	14 41.5	12.1	19 48.6	1.3	54.0
17	78 26.2	16.2	29 12.6	12.2	19 47.3	1.4	54.0
18	93 26.0	S20 16.7	43 43.8	12.1	S19 45.9	1.5	54.0
19	108 25.8	17.2	58 14.9	12.1	19 44.4	1.6	54.1
20	123 25.7	17.8	72 46.0	12.2	19 42.8	1.7	54.1
21	138 25.5	. . 18.3	87 17.2	12.1	19 41.1	1.7	54.1
22	153 25.3	18.8	101 48.3	12.2	19 39.4	1.9	54.1
23	168 25.2	19.3	116 19.5	12.2	19 37.5	1.9	54.1
23 00	183 25.0	S20 19.8	130 50.7	12.2	S19 35.6	2.1	54.1
01	198 24.8	20.4	145 21.9	12.2	19 33.5	2.1	54.1
02	213 24.6	20.9	159 53.1	12.2	19 31.4	2.2	54.1
03	228 24.5	. . 21.4	174 24.3	12.2	19 29.2	2.3	54.1
04	243 24.3	21.9	188 55.5	12.2	19 26.9	2.4	54.1
05	258 24.1	22.4	203 26.7	12.2	19 24.5	2.5	54.1
06	273 23.9	S20 23.0	217 57.9	12.2	S19 22.0	2.6	54.1
T 07	288 23.8	23.5	232 29.1	12.3	19 19.4	2.6	54.1
H 08	303 23.6	24.0	247 00.4	12.2	19 16.8	2.8	54.1
U 09	318 23.4	. . 24.5	261 31.6	12.3	19 14.0	2.8	54.2
R 10	333 23.2	25.0	276 02.9	12.3	19 11.2	3.0	54.2
S 11	348 23.1	25.5	290 34.2	12.3	19 08.2	3.0	54.2
D 12	3 22.9	S20 26.1	305 05.5	12.3	S19 05.2	3.1	54.2
A 13	18 22.7	26.6	319 36.8	12.3	19 02.1	3.2	54.2
Y 14	33 22.5	27.1	334 08.1	12.3	18 58.9	3.3	54.2
15	48 22.4	. . 27.6	348 39.4	12.3	18 55.6	3.3	54.2
16	63 22.2	28.1	3 10.7	12.4	18 52.3	3.5	54.2
17	78 22.0	28.6	17 42.1	12.3	18 48.8	3.5	54.2
18	93 21.8	S20 29.1	32 13.4	12.4	S18 45.3	3.6	54.2
19	108 21.6	29.6	46 44.8	12.4	18 41.7	3.8	54.3
20	123 21.5	30.1	61 16.2	12.4	18 37.9	3.8	54.3
21	138 21.3	. . 30.7	75 47.6	12.4	18 34.1	3.8	54.3
22	153 21.1	31.2	90 19.0	12.4	18 30.3	4.0	54.3
23	168 20.9	31.7	104 50.4	12.4	S18 26.3	4.1	54.3
	SD 16.2	*d* 0.5	SD 14.7		14.7		14.8

Lat.	Twilight Naut.	Twilight Civil	Sunrise	Moonrise 21	Moonrise 22	Moonrise 23	Moonrise 24
°	h m	h m	h m	h m	h m	h m	h m
N 72	07 24	09 08	■	■	■	■	15 23
N 70	07 11	08 39	10 47	13 51	14 38	14 31	14 26
68	07 00	08 17	09 48	12 23	13 12	13 39	13 52
66	06 51	08 00	09 14	11 44	12 33	13 06	13 27
64	06 44	07 46	08 50	11 17	12 06	12 43	13 08
62	06 37	07 34	08 31	10 57	11 46	12 24	12 52
60	06 31	07 24	08 15	10 40	11 29	12 08	12 39
N 58	06 25	07 15	08 02	10 26	11 14	11 55	12 28
56	06 20	07 07	07 51	10 13	11 02	11 43	12 18
54	06 16	07 00	07 41	10 03	10 52	11 33	12 09
52	06 12	06 53	07 32	09 53	10 42	11 25	12 01
50	06 08	06 48	07 24	09 45	10 34	11 17	11 54
45	05 59	06 35	07 07	09 27	10 16	11 00	11 39
N 40	05 51	06 24	06 53	09 12	10 01	10 46	11 26
35	05 43	06 14	06 41	09 00	09 49	10 34	11 15
30	05 36	06 05	06 31	08 49	09 38	10 23	11 06
20	05 23	05 50	06 13	08 31	09 19	10 05	10 50
N 10	05 09	05 35	05 57	08 15	09 03	09 50	10 36
0	04 55	05 21	05 43	08 00	08 48	09 35	10 23
S 10	04 39	05 05	05 28	07 45	08 33	09 21	10 09
20	04 19	04 48	05 12	07 29	08 16	09 05	09 55
30	03 55	04 26	04 53	07 11	07 58	08 47	09 39
35	03 39	04 14	04 42	07 00	07 47	08 37	09 30
40	03 19	03 58	04 29	06 48	07 35	08 25	09 19
45	02 55	03 40	04 15	06 34	07 20	08 11	09 06
S 50	02 20	03 16	03 56	06 16	07 02	07 54	08 51
52	02 02	03 04	03 47	06 08	06 54	07 46	08 43
54	01 39	02 50	03 38	05 59	06 44	07 37	08 35
56	01 06	02 34	03 27	05 48	06 34	07 27	08 26
58	////	02 15	03 14	05 37	06 22	07 15	08 16
S 60	////	01 50	02 59	05 23	06 07	07 01	08 04

Lat.	Sunset	Twilight Civil	Twilight Naut.	Moonset 21	Moonset 22	Moonset 23	Moonset 24
°	h m	h m	h m	h m	h m	h m	h m
N 72	■	14 23	16 07	■	■	■	17 55
N 70	12 45	14 52	16 20	14 30	15 22	17 09	18 51
68	13 44	15 14	16 31	15 59	16 49	18 00	19 25
66	14 17	15 31	16 40	16 37	17 27	18 32	19 49
64	14 42	15 46	16 48	17 04	17 54	18 56	20 08
62	15 01	15 57	16 55	17 25	18 14	19 14	20 23
60	15 16	16 08	17 01	17 42	18 31	19 30	20 36
N 58	15 30	16 17	17 06	17 56	18 45	19 43	20 47
56	15 41	16 25	17 11	18 08	18 58	19 54	20 56
54	15 51	16 32	17 16	18 19	19 08	20 04	21 05
52	16 00	16 38	17 20	18 29	19 18	20 12	21 12
50	16 08	16 44	17 24	18 37	19 26	20 20	21 19
45	16 25	16 57	17 33	18 55	19 44	20 37	21 34
N 40	16 39	17 08	17 42	19 10	19 58	20 50	21 45
35	16 51	17 18	17 49	19 22	20 11	21 02	21 56
30	17 01	17 27	17 56	19 33	20 21	21 12	22 04
20	17 19	17 43	18 10	19 52	20 40	21 29	22 20
N 10	17 35	17 57	18 23	20 08	20 56	21 44	22 33
0	17 50	18 12	18 37	20 23	21 11	21 58	22 45
S 10	18 05	18 27	18 54	20 38	21 26	22 12	22 58
20	18 21	18 45	19 13	20 54	21 42	22 27	23 11
30	18 40	19 06	19 38	21 13	22 00	22 44	23 26
35	18 51	19 19	19 54	21 24	22 11	22 54	23 34
40	19 03	19 35	20 14	21 36	22 23	23 05	23 44
45	19 19	19 54	20 39	21 51	22 37	23 18	23 55
S 50	19 37	20 18	21 14	22 09	22 54	23 35	24 09
52	19 46	20 30	21 32	22 17	23 03	23 42	24 16
54	19 56	20 44	21 56	22 27	23 12	23 50	24 23
56	20 07	21 00	22 30	22 37	23 22	24 00	00 00
58	20 20	21 20	////	22 49	23 34	24 10	00 10
S 60	20 35	21 45	////	23 03	23 48	24 23	00 23

Day	SUN Eqn. of Time 00^h	SUN Eqn. of Time 12^h	SUN Mer. Pass.	MOON Mer. Pass. Upper	MOON Mer. Pass. Lower	MOON Age	MOON Phase
d	m s	m s	h m	h m	h m	d	%
21	14 12	14 04	11 46	14 11	01 48	03	8
22	13 56	13 48	11 46	14 59	02 35	04	14
23	13 40	13 32	11 46	15 47	03 23	05	21

2017 NOVEMBER 24, 25, 26 (FRI., SAT., SUN.)

UT d	h	ARIES GHA	VENUS −3·9 GHA	VENUS Dec	MARS +1·7 GHA	MARS Dec	JUPITER −1·7 GHA	JUPITER Dec	SATURN +0·5 GHA	SATURN Dec
		° ′	° ′	° ′	° ′	° ′	° ′	° ′	° ′	° ′
24	00	63 08.5	194 35.2	S16 59.3	223 57.4	S 6 56.6	205 35.9	S13 43.7	156 24.8	S22 27.3
	01	78 10.9	209 34.6	17 00.2	238 58.3	57.2	220 37.9	43.8	171 27.0	27.3
	02	93 13.4	224 33.9	01.1	253 59.3	57.8	235 39.8	44.0	186 29.1	27.3
	03	108 15.9	239 33.2	. . 02.0	269 00.3	. . 58.4	250 41.8	. . 44.2	201 31.3	. . 27.3
	04	123 18.3	254 32.5	02.9	284 01.3	59.0	265 43.7	44.3	216 33.5	27.4
	05	138 20.8	269 31.8	03.8	299 02.3	6 59.6	280 45.7	44.5	231 35.6	27.4
	06	153 23.3	284 31.1	S17 04.7	314 03.3	S 7 00.2	295 47.6	S13 44.7	246 37.8	S22 27.4
	07	168 25.7	299 30.5	05.6	329 04.3	00.8	310 49.6	44.8	261 40.0	27.4
	08	183 28.2	314 29.8	06.5	344 05.3	01.4	325 51.5	45.0	276 42.1	27.4
F	09	198 30.7	329 29.1	. . 07.4	359 06.3	. . 02.0	340 53.5	. . 45.2	291 44.3	. . 27.4
R	10	213 33.1	344 28.4	08.3	14 07.3	02.6	355 55.4	45.3	306 46.5	27.4
I	11	228 35.6	359 27.7	09.2	29 08.3	03.2	10 57.4	45.5	321 48.6	27.4
D	12	243 38.1	14 27.0	S17 10.1	44 09.3	S 7 03.8	25 59.3	S13 45.7	336 50.8	S22 27.4
A	13	258 40.5	29 26.3	10.9	59 10.3	04.4	41 01.3	45.8	351 53.0	27.5
Y	14	273 43.0	44 25.6	11.8	74 11.3	05.0	56 03.2	46.0	6 55.1	27.5
	15	288 45.4	59 25.0	. . 12.7	89 12.3	. . 05.6	71 05.2	. . 46.2	21 57.3	. . 27.5
	16	303 47.9	74 24.3	13.6	104 13.3	06.2	86 07.1	46.3	36 59.5	27.5
	17	318 50.4	89 23.6	14.5	119 14.3	06.8	101 09.1	46.5	52 01.6	27.5
	18	333 52.8	104 22.9	S17 15.4	134 15.3	S 7 07.4	116 11.0	S13 46.6	67 03.8	S22 27.5
	19	348 55.3	119 22.2	16.3	149 16.3	08.0	131 13.0	46.8	82 05.9	27.5
	20	3 57.8	134 21.5	17.2	164 17.3	08.6	146 14.9	47.0	97 08.1	27.5
	21	19 00.2	149 20.8	. . 18.1	179 18.3	. . 09.2	161 16.9	. . 47.1	112 10.3	. . 27.5
	22	34 02.7	164 20.1	19.0	194 19.3	09.8	176 18.9	47.3	127 12.4	27.5
	23	49 05.2	179 19.4	19.8	209 20.3	10.4	191 20.8	47.5	142 14.6	27.6
25	00	64 07.6	194 18.7	S17 20.7	224 21.3	S 7 11.0	206 22.8	S13 47.6	157 16.8	S22 27.6
	01	79 10.1	209 18.0	21.6	239 22.3	11.6	221 24.7	47.8	172 18.9	27.6
	02	94 12.6	224 17.3	22.5	254 23.3	12.2	236 26.7	48.0	187 21.1	27.6
	03	109 15.0	239 16.6	. . 23.4	269 24.3	. . 12.8	251 28.6	. . 48.1	202 23.3	. . 27.6
	04	124 17.5	254 16.0	24.3	284 25.3	13.4	266 30.6	48.3	217 25.4	27.6
	05	139 19.9	269 15.3	25.1	299 26.3	14.0	281 32.5	48.4	232 27.6	27.6
	06	154 22.4	284 14.6	S17 26.0	314 27.3	S 7 14.6	296 34.5	S13 48.6	247 29.7	S22 27.6
	07	169 24.9	299 13.9	26.9	329 28.3	15.2	311 36.4	48.8	262 31.9	27.6
S	08	184 27.3	314 13.2	27.8	344 29.3	15.8	326 38.4	48.9	277 34.1	27.7
A	09	199 29.8	329 12.5	. . 28.7	359 30.2	. . 16.4	341 40.3	. . 49.1	292 36.2	. . 27.7
T	10	214 32.3	344 11.8	29.5	14 31.2	16.9	356 42.3	49.3	307 38.4	27.7
U	11	229 34.7	359 11.1	30.4	29 32.2	17.5	11 44.2	49.4	322 40.6	27.7
R	12	244 37.2	14 10.4	S17 31.3	44 33.2	S 7 18.1	26 46.2	S13 49.6	337 42.7	S22 27.7
D	13	259 39.7	29 09.7	32.2	59 34.2	18.7	41 48.1	49.8	352 44.9	27.7
A	14	274 42.1	44 09.0	33.0	74 35.2	19.3	56 50.1	49.9	7 47.0	27.7
Y	15	289 44.6	59 08.3	. . 33.9	89 36.2	. . 19.9	71 52.0	. . 50.1	22 49.2	. . 27.7
	16	304 47.1	74 07.6	34.8	104 37.2	20.5	86 54.0	50.2	37 51.4	27.7
	17	319 49.5	89 06.9	35.6	119 38.2	21.1	101 55.9	50.4	52 53.5	27.7
	18	334 52.0	104 06.2	S17 36.5	134 39.2	S 7 21.7	116 57.9	S13 50.6	67 55.7	S22 27.8
	19	349 54.4	119 05.4	37.4	149 40.2	22.3	131 59.8	50.7	82 57.9	27.8
	20	4 56.9	134 04.7	38.3	164 41.2	22.9	147 01.8	50.9	98 00.0	27.8
	21	19 59.4	149 04.0	. . 39.1	179 42.2	. . 23.5	162 03.8	. . 51.1	113 02.2	. . 27.8
	22	35 01.8	164 03.3	40.0	194 43.2	24.1	177 05.7	51.2	128 04.3	27.8
	23	50 04.3	179 02.6	40.9	209 44.2	24.7	192 07.7	51.4	143 06.5	27.8
26	00	65 06.8	194 01.9	S17 41.7	224 45.2	S 7 25.3	207 09.6	S13 51.5	158 08.7	S22 27.8
	01	80 09.2	209 01.2	42.6	239 46.2	25.9	222 11.6	51.7	173 10.8	27.8
	02	95 11.7	224 00.5	43.5	254 47.2	26.5	237 13.5	51.9	188 13.0	27.8
	03	110 14.2	238 59.8	. . 44.3	269 48.2	. . 27.1	252 15.5	. . 52.0	203 15.2	. . 27.8
	04	125 16.6	253 59.1	45.2	284 49.2	27.7	267 17.4	52.2	218 17.3	27.9
	05	140 19.1	268 58.4	46.0	299 50.2	28.3	282 19.4	52.4	233 19.5	27.9
	06	155 21.5	283 57.7	S17 46.9	314 51.2	S 7 28.8	297 21.3	S13 52.5	248 21.6	S22 27.9
	07	170 24.0	298 57.0	47.8	329 52.1	29.4	312 23.3	52.7	263 23.8	27.9
	08	185 26.5	313 56.3	48.6	344 53.1	30.0	327 25.2	52.9	278 26.0	27.9
S	09	200 28.9	328 55.5	. . 49.5	359 54.1	. . 30.6	342 27.2	. . 53.0	293 28.1	. . 27.9
U	10	215 31.4	343 54.8	50.3	14 55.1	31.2	357 29.1	53.2	308 30.3	27.9
N	11	230 33.9	358 54.1	51.2	29 56.1	31.8	12 31.1	53.3	323 32.5	27.9
D	12	245 36.3	13 53.4	S17 52.0	44 57.1	S 7 32.4	27 33.0	S13 53.5	338 34.6	S22 27.9
A	13	260 38.8	28 52.7	52.9	59 58.1	33.0	42 35.0	53.7	353 36.8	27.9
Y	14	275 41.3	43 52.0	53.8	74 59.1	33.6	57 37.0	53.8	8 38.9	28.0
	15	290 43.7	58 51.3	. . 54.6	90 00.1	. . 34.2	72 38.9	. . 54.0	23 41.1	. . 28.0
	16	305 46.2	73 50.5	55.5	105 01.1	34.8	87 40.9	54.1	38 43.3	28.0
	17	320 48.7	88 49.8	56.3	120 02.1	35.4	102 42.8	54.3	53 45.4	28.0
	18	335 51.1	103 49.1	S17 57.2	135 03.1	S 7 36.0	117 44.8	S13 54.5	68 47.6	S22 28.0
	19	350 53.6	118 48.4	58.0	150 04.1	36.6	132 46.7	54.6	83 49.7	28.0
	20	5 56.0	133 47.7	58.9	165 05.1	37.2	147 48.7	54.8	98 51.9	28.0
	21	20 58.5	148 47.0	17 59.7	180 06.1	. . 37.7	162 50.6	. . 55.0	113 54.1	. . 28.0
	22	36 01.0	163 46.2	18 00.6	195 07.1	38.3	177 52.6	55.1	128 56.2	28.0
	23	51 03.4	178 45.5	S18 01.4	210 08.1	38.9	192 54.5	55.3	143 58.4	28.0
Mer. Pass.		h m 19 40.3	v −0.7	d 0.9	v 1.0	d 0.6	v 2.0	d 0.2	v 2.2	d 0.0

STARS Name	SHA	Dec
	° ′	° ′
Acamar	315 15.7	S40 14.2
Achernar	335 24.2	S57 09.1
Acrux	173 06.2	S63 11.5
Adhara	255 09.9	S28 59.8
Aldebaran	290 45.6	N16 32.5
Alioth	166 18.5	N55 51.7
Alkaid	152 57.0	N49 13.5
Al Na'ir	27 40.1	S46 52.6
Alnilam	275 43.0	S 1 11.6
Alphard	217 53.1	S 8 44.1
Alphecca	126 08.9	N26 39.5
Alpheratz	357 40.2	N29 11.5
Altair	62 05.5	N 8 55.2
Ankaa	353 12.6	S42 12.8
Antares	112 23.0	S26 28.0
Arcturus	145 53.3	N19 05.5
Atria	107 22.6	S69 03.4
Avior	234 16.4	S59 33.8
Bellatrix	278 28.5	N 6 21.8
Betelgeuse	270 57.8	N 7 24.5
Canopus	263 54.3	S52 42.3
Capella	280 29.6	N46 00.7
Deneb	49 29.6	N45 21.0
Denebola	182 30.8	N14 28.4
Diphda	348 52.7	S17 53.5
Dubhe	193 48.3	N61 39.0
Elnath	278 08.5	N28 37.1
Eltanin	90 45.3	N51 29.5
Enif	33 44.2	N 9 57.6
Fomalhaut	15 20.7	S29 31.8
Gacrux	171 57.8	S57 12.4
Gienah	175 49.4	S17 38.2
Hadar	148 44.1	S60 27.2
Hamal	327 57.1	N23 32.8
Kaus Aust.	83 40.2	S34 22.4
Kochab	137 21.4	N74 05.0
Markab	13 35.3	N15 18.2
Menkar	314 11.6	N 4 09.5
Menkent	148 04.4	S36 27.1
Miaplacidus	221 38.7	S69 47.2
Mirfak	308 35.5	N49 55.4
Nunki	75 54.9	S26 16.3
Peacock	53 14.9	S56 40.7
Pollux	243 23.9	N27 58.8
Procyon	244 56.4	N 5 10.6
Rasalhague	96 04.0	N12 33.1
Regulus	207 40.3	N11 52.8
Rigel	281 08.9	S 8 11.0
Rigil Kent.	139 48.2	S60 54.2
Sabik	102 09.5	S15 44.6
Schedar	349 36.7	N56 38.3
Shaula	96 18.3	S37 06.8
Sirius	258 30.8	S16 44.5
Spica	158 28.3	S11 15.0
Suhail	222 50.1	S43 30.1
Vega	80 37.3	N38 48.3
Zuben'ubi	137 02.4	S16 06.7

	SHA	Mer. Pass.
	° ′	h m
Venus	130 11.1	11 03
Mars	160 13.7	9 02
Jupiter	142 15.1	10 13
Saturn	93 09.1	13 29

UT		SUN GHA	SUN Dec	MOON GHA	v	MOON Dec	d	HP
d	h	° ′	° ′	° ′	′	° ′	′	′
24	00	183 20.7	S20 32.2	119 21.8	12.4	S18 22.2	4.1	54.3
	01	198 20.6	32.7	133 53.2	12.5	18 18.1	4.2	54.3
	02	213 20.4	33.2	148 24.7	12.5	18 13.9	4.3	54.3
	03	228 20.2	. . 33.7	162 56.2	12.4	18 09.6	4.4	54.4
	04	243 20.0	34.2	177 27.6	12.5	18 05.2	4.5	54.4
	05	258 19.8	34.7	191 59.1	12.5	18 00.7	4.6	54.4
	06	273 19.6	S20 35.2	206 30.6	12.6	S17 56.1	4.6	54.4
	07	288 19.5	35.7	221 02.2	12.5	17 51.5	4.8	54.4
	08	303 19.3	36.2	235 33.7	12.5	17 46.7	4.8	54.4
F	09	318 19.1	. . 36.7	250 05.2	12.6	17 41.9	4.9	54.4
R	10	333 18.9	37.2	264 36.8	12.6	17 37.0	5.0	54.5
I	11	348 18.7	37.7	279 08.4	12.5	17 32.0	5.0	54.5
D	12	3 18.5	S20 38.2	293 39.9	12.6	S17 27.0	5.2	54.5
A	13	18 18.4	38.7	308 11.5	12.6	17 21.8	5.2	54.5
Y	14	33 18.2	39.2	322 43.1	12.7	17 16.6	5.3	54.5
	15	48 18.0	. . 39.7	337 14.8	12.6	17 11.3	5.4	54.5
	16	63 17.8	40.2	351 46.4	12.6	17 05.9	5.4	54.6
	17	78 17.6	40.7	6 18.0	12.7	17 00.5	5.6	54.6
	18	93 17.4	S20 41.2	20 49.7	12.7	S16 54.9	5.6	54.6
	19	108 17.2	41.7	35 21.4	12.6	16 49.3	5.7	54.6
	20	123 17.1	42.2	49 53.0	12.7	16 43.6	5.8	54.6
	21	138 16.9	. . 42.7	64 24.7	12.7	16 37.8	5.9	54.6
	22	153 16.7	43.1	78 56.4	12.8	16 31.9	5.9	54.7
	23	168 16.5	43.6	93 28.2	12.7	16 26.0	6.0	54.7
25	00	183 16.3	S20 44.1	107 59.9	12.7	S16 20.0	6.1	54.7
	01	198 16.1	44.6	122 31.6	12.8	16 13.9	6.2	54.7
	02	213 15.9	45.1	137 03.4	12.8	16 07.7	6.3	54.7
	03	228 15.7	. . 45.6	151 35.2	12.7	16 01.4	6.3	54.8
	04	243 15.5	46.1	166 06.9	12.8	15 55.1	6.4	54.8
	05	258 15.4	46.6	180 38.7	12.8	15 48.7	6.5	54.8
	06	273 15.2	S20 47.1	195 10.5	12.8	S15 42.2	6.5	54.8
	07	288 15.0	47.5	209 42.3	12.8	15 35.7	6.7	54.8
S	08	303 14.8	48.0	224 14.1	12.9	15 29.0	6.7	54.9
A	09	318 14.6	. . 48.5	238 46.0	12.8	15 22.3	6.8	54.9
T	10	333 14.4	49.0	253 17.8	12.9	15 15.5	6.8	54.9
U	11	348 14.2	49.5	267 49.7	12.8	15 08.7	7.0	54.9
R	12	3 14.0	S20 50.0	282 21.5	12.9	S15 01.7	7.0	54.9
D	13	18 13.8	50.4	296 53.4	12.9	14 54.7	7.0	55.0
A	14	33 13.6	50.9	311 25.3	12.9	14 47.7	7.2	55.0
Y	15	48 13.4	. . 51.4	325 57.2	12.9	14 40.5	7.2	55.0
	16	63 13.2	51.9	340 29.1	12.9	14 33.3	7.3	55.0
	17	78 13.1	52.4	355 01.0	12.9	14 26.0	7.4	55.1
	18	93 12.9	S20 52.8	9 32.9	12.9	S14 18.6	7.4	55.1
	19	108 12.7	53.3	24 04.8	12.9	14 11.2	7.5	55.1
	20	123 12.5	53.8	38 36.7	13.0	14 03.7	7.6	55.1
	21	138 12.3	. . 54.3	53 08.7	12.9	13 56.1	7.7	55.2
	22	153 12.1	54.7	67 40.6	13.0	13 48.4	7.7	55.2
	23	168 11.9	55.2	82 12.6	12.9	13 40.7	7.8	55.2
26	00	183 11.7	S20 55.7	96 44.5	13.0	S13 32.9	7.8	55.2
	01	198 11.5	56.2	111 16.5	12.9	13 25.1	8.0	55.3
	02	213 11.3	56.6	125 48.4	13.0	13 17.1	7.9	55.3
	03	228 11.1	. . 57.1	140 20.4	13.0	13 09.2	8.1	55.3
	04	243 10.9	57.6	154 52.4	12.9	13 01.1	8.1	55.3
	05	258 10.7	58.0	169 24.3	13.0	12 53.0	8.2	55.4
	06	273 10.5	S20 58.5	183 56.3	13.0	S12 44.8	8.3	55.4
	07	288 10.3	59.0	198 28.3	13.0	12 36.5	8.3	55.4
	08	303 10.1	59.5	213 00.3	13.0	12 28.2	8.4	55.5
S	09	318 09.9	20 59.9	227 32.3	13.0	12 19.8	8.5	55.5
U	10	333 09.7	21 00.4	242 04.3	13.0	12 11.3	8.5	55.5
N	11	348 09.5	00.9	256 36.3	13.0	12 02.8	8.6	55.5
D	12	3 09.3	S21 01.3	271 08.3	13.0	S11 54.2	8.6	55.6
A	13	18 09.1	01.8	285 40.3	12.9	11 45.6	8.7	55.6
Y	14	33 08.9	02.3	300 12.2	13.0	11 36.9	8.8	55.6
	15	48 08.7	. . 02.7	314 44.2	13.0	11 28.1	8.8	55.7
	16	63 08.5	03.2	329 16.2	13.0	11 19.3	8.9	55.7
	17	78 08.3	03.6	343 48.2	13.0	11 10.4	9.0	55.7
	18	93 08.1	S21 04.1	358 20.2	13.0	S11 01.4	9.0	55.7
	19	108 07.9	04.6	12 52.2	13.0	10 52.4	9.1	55.8
	20	123 07.7	05.0	27 24.2	13.0	10 43.3	9.1	55.8
	21	138 07.5	. . 05.5	41 56.2	12.9	10 34.2	9.2	55.8
	22	153 07.3	05.9	56 28.1	13.0	10 25.0	9.3	55.9
	23	168 07.1	06.4	71 00.1	13.0	S10 15.7	9.3	55.9
		SD 16.2	*d* 0.5	SD	14.8	15.0		15.1

Lat.	Twilight Naut.	Twilight Civil	Sunrise	Moonrise 24	25	26	27
°	h m	h m	h m	h m	h m	h m	h m
N 72	07 34	09 23	■	15 23	14 53	14 38	14 26
N 70	07 20	08 50	11 43	14 26	14 22	14 18	14 14
68	07 08	08 27	10 03	13 52	13 59	14 03	14 05
66	06 58	08 08	09 26	13 27	13 41	13 50	13 57
64	06 50	07 53	08 59	13 08	13 26	13 40	13 51
62	06 43	07 41	08 39	12 52	13 14	13 31	13 45
60	06 36	07 30	08 22	12 39	13 03	13 23	13 40
N 58	06 30	07 21	08 08	12 28	12 54	13 16	13 36
56	06 25	07 12	07 56	12 18	12 46	13 10	13 32
54	06 20	07 05	07 46	12 09	12 39	13 05	13 28
52	06 16	06 58	07 37	12 01	12 32	13 00	13 25
50	06 11	06 52	07 28	11 54	12 26	12 55	13 22
45	06 02	06 38	07 11	11 39	12 14	12 46	13 16
N 40	05 53	06 27	06 56	11 26	12 03	12 38	13 10
35	05 46	06 17	06 44	11 15	11 54	12 31	13 06
30	05 38	06 08	06 33	11 06	11 46	12 25	13 01
20	05 24	05 51	06 15	10 50	11 33	12 14	12 54
N 10	05 10	05 36	05 59	10 36	11 21	12 05	12 48
0	04 56	05 21	05 43	10 23	11 09	11 56	12 42
S 10	04 39	05 05	05 28	10 09	10 58	11 47	12 36
20	04 19	04 47	05 11	09 55	10 46	11 38	12 30
30	03 53	04 25	04 52	09 39	10 32	11 27	12 23
35	03 37	04 12	04 41	09 30	10 24	11 21	12 19
40	03 17	03 56	04 28	09 19	10 15	11 13	12 14
45	02 51	03 37	04 12	09 06	10 04	11 05	12 08
S 50	02 15	03 12	03 53	08 51	09 51	10 55	12 02
52	01 56	03 00	03 44	08 43	09 45	10 50	11 59
54	01 30	02 45	03 34	08 35	09 38	10 45	11 55
56	00 53	02 28	03 22	08 26	09 31	10 40	11 52
58	////	02 08	03 09	08 16	09 22	10 33	11 47
S 60	////	01 40	02 53	08 04	09 13	10 26	11 43

Lat.	Sunset	Twilight Civil	Twilight Naut.	Moonset 24	25	26	27
°	h m	h m	h m	h m	h m	h m	h m
N 72	■	14 11	15 59	17 55	20 02	21 54	23 43
N 70	11 50	14 43	16 14	18 51	20 32	22 12	23 52
68	13 30	15 07	16 25	19 25	20 54	22 26	24 00
66	14 08	15 25	16 35	19 49	21 11	22 38	24 06
64	14 34	15 40	16 43	20 08	21 25	22 47	24 12
62	14 55	15 53	16 51	20 23	21 37	22 55	24 16
60	15 11	16 04	16 57	20 36	21 47	23 02	24 20
N 58	15 25	16 13	17 03	20 47	21 56	23 08	24 24
56	15 37	16 21	17 09	20 56	22 03	23 14	24 27
54	15 48	16 29	17 13	21 05	22 10	23 18	24 30
52	15 57	16 36	17 18	21 12	22 16	23 23	24 32
50	16 05	16 42	17 22	21 19	22 21	23 27	24 34
45	16 23	16 56	17 32	21 34	22 33	23 35	24 39
N 40	16 37	17 07	17 40	21 45	22 43	23 42	24 43
35	16 50	17 17	17 48	21 56	22 51	23 48	24 47
30	17 00	17 26	17 56	22 04	22 58	23 53	24 50
20	17 19	17 43	18 10	22 20	23 11	24 03	00 03
N 10	17 35	17 58	18 24	22 33	23 22	24 11	00 11
0	17 51	18 13	18 39	22 45	23 32	24 18	00 18
S 10	18 06	18 29	18 55	22 58	23 42	24 25	00 25
20	18 23	18 47	19 15	23 11	23 52	24 33	00 33
30	18 42	19 09	19 41	23 26	24 05	00 05	00 42
35	18 54	19 22	19 58	23 34	24 12	00 12	00 47
40	19 07	19 38	20 18	23 44	24 20	00 20	00 53
45	19 22	19 58	20 44	23 55	24 29	00 29	00 59
S 50	19 42	20 23	21 20	24 09	00 09	00 40	01 07
52	19 51	20 36	21 40	24 16	00 16	00 45	01 11
54	20 01	20 50	22 06	24 23	00 23	00 51	01 15
56	20 13	21 07	22 46	00 00	00 31	00 57	01 19
58	20 26	21 29	////	00 10	00 40	01 04	01 24
S 60	20 43	21 56	////	00 23	00 50	01 12	01 30

Day	SUN Eqn. of Time 00^h	SUN Eqn. of Time 12^h	SUN Mer. Pass.	MOON Mer. Pass. Upper	MOON Mer. Pass. Lower	MOON Age	MOON Phase
d	m s	m s	h m	h m	h m	d	%
24	13 23	13 15	11 47	16 34	04 10	06	29
25	13 06	12 56	11 47	17 21	04 57	07	38
26	12 47	12 38	11 47	18 07	05 44	08	48

UT	ARIES	VENUS −3·9		MARS +1·7		JUPITER −1·7		SATURN +0·5	
d h	GHA	GHA	Dec	GHA	Dec	GHA	Dec	GHA	Dec
	° ′	° ′	° ′	° ′	° ′	° ′	° ′	° ′	° ′
27 00 MONDAY	66 05.9	193 44.8	S18 02.2	225 09.0	S 7 39.5	207 56.5	S13 55.4	159 00.6	S22 28.0
01	81 08.4	208 44.1	03.1	240 10.0	40.1	222 58.4	55.6	174 02.7	28.1
02	96 10.8	223 43.4	03.9	255 11.0	40.7	238 00.4	55.8	189 04.9	28.1
03	111 13.3	238 42.7	. . 04.8	270 12.0	. . 41.3	253 02.4	. . 55.9	204 07.0	. . 28.1
04	126 15.8	253 41.9	05.6	285 13.0	41.9	268 04.3	56.1	219 09.2	28.1
05	141 18.2	268 41.2	06.5	300 14.0	42.5	283 06.3	56.3	234 11.4	28.1
06	156 20.7	283 40.5	S18 07.3	315 15.0	S 7 43.1	298 08.2	S13 56.4	249 13.5	S22 28.1
07	171 23.2	298 39.8	08.1	330 16.0	43.7	313 10.2	56.6	264 15.7	28.1
08	186 25.6	313 39.0	09.0	345 17.0	44.3	328 12.1	56.7	279 17.8	28.1
09	201 28.1	328 38.3	. . 09.8	0 18.0	. . 44.9	343 14.1	. . 56.9	294 20.0	. . 28.1
10	216 30.5	343 37.6	10.7	15 19.0	45.4	358 16.0	57.1	309 22.2	28.1
11	231 33.0	358 36.9	11.5	30 20.0	46.0	13 18.0	57.2	324 24.3	28.2
12	246 35.5	13 36.1	S18 12.3	45 21.0	S 7 46.6	28 19.9	S13 57.4	339 26.5	S22 28.2
13	261 37.9	28 35.4	13.2	60 22.0	47.2	43 21.9	57.5	354 28.6	28.2
14	276 40.4	43 34.7	14.0	75 23.0	47.8	58 23.9	57.7	9 30.8	28.2
15	291 42.9	58 34.0	. . 14.8	90 23.9	. . 48.4	73 25.8	. . 57.9	24 33.0	. . 28.2
16	306 45.3	73 33.2	15.7	105 24.9	49.0	88 27.8	58.0	39 35.1	28.2
17	321 47.8	88 32.5	16.5	120 25.9	49.6	103 29.7	58.2	54 37.3	28.2
18	336 50.3	103 31.8	S18 17.3	135 26.9	S 7 50.2	118 31.7	S13 58.3	69 39.4	S22 28.2
19	351 52.7	118 31.1	18.2	150 27.9	50.8	133 33.6	58.5	84 41.6	28.2
20	6 55.2	133 30.3	19.0	165 28.9	51.4	148 35.6	58.7	99 43.8	28.2
21	21 57.6	148 29.6	. . 19.8	180 29.9	. . 51.9	163 37.5	. . 58.8	114 45.9	. . 28.3
22	37 00.1	163 28.9	20.6	195 30.9	52.5	178 39.5	59.0	129 48.1	28.3
23	52 02.6	178 28.1	21.5	210 31.9	53.1	193 41.5	59.2	144 50.2	28.3
28 00 TUESDAY	67 05.0	193 27.4	S18 22.3	225 32.9	S 7 53.7	208 43.4	S13 59.3	159 52.4	S22 28.3
01	82 07.5	208 26.7	23.1	240 33.9	54.3	223 45.4	59.5	174 54.6	28.3
02	97 10.0	223 25.9	23.9	255 34.9	54.9	238 47.3	59.6	189 56.7	28.3
03	112 12.4	238 25.2	. . 24.8	270 35.9	. . 55.5	253 49.3	13 59.8	204 58.9	. . 28.3
04	127 14.9	253 24.5	25.6	285 36.9	56.1	268 51.2	14 00.0	220 01.0	28.3
05	142 17.4	268 23.7	26.4	300 37.8	56.7	283 53.2	00.1	235 03.2	28.3
06	157 19.8	283 23.0	S18 27.2	315 38.8	S 7 57.3	298 55.1	S14 00.3	250 05.4	S22 28.3
07	172 22.3	298 22.3	28.0	330 39.8	57.8	313 57.1	00.4	265 07.5	28.3
08	187 24.8	313 21.5	28.9	345 40.8	58.4	328 59.1	00.6	280 09.7	28.4
09	202 27.2	328 20.8	. . 29.7	0 41.8	. . 59.0	344 01.0	. . 00.8	295 11.8	. . 28.4
10	217 29.7	343 20.1	30.5	15 42.8	7 59.6	359 03.0	00.9	310 14.0	28.4
11	232 32.1	358 19.3	31.3	30 43.8	8 00.2	14 04.9	01.1	325 16.2	28.4
12	247 34.6	13 18.6	S18 32.1	45 44.8	S 8 00.8	29 06.9	S14 01.2	340 18.3	S22 28.4
13	262 37.1	28 17.8	32.9	60 45.8	01.4	44 08.8	01.4	355 20.5	28.4
14	277 39.5	43 17.1	33.7	75 46.8	02.0	59 10.8	01.6	10 22.6	28.4
15	292 42.0	58 16.4	. . 34.6	90 47.8	. . 02.6	74 12.8	. . 01.7	25 24.8	. . 28.4
16	307 44.5	73 15.6	35.4	105 48.8	03.1	89 14.7	01.9	40 27.0	28.4
17	322 46.9	88 14.9	36.2	120 49.7	03.7	104 16.7	02.0	55 29.1	28.4
18	337 49.4	103 14.1	S18 37.0	135 50.7	S 8 04.3	119 18.6	S14 02.2	70 31.3	S22 28.4
19	352 51.9	118 13.4	37.8	150 51.7	04.9	134 20.6	02.4	85 33.4	28.5
20	7 54.3	133 12.7	38.6	165 52.7	05.5	149 22.5	02.5	100 35.6	28.5
21	22 56.8	148 11.9	. . 39.4	180 53.7	. . 06.1	164 24.5	. . 02.7	115 37.7	. . 28.5
22	37 59.2	163 11.2	40.2	195 54.7	06.7	179 26.4	02.8	130 39.9	28.5
23	53 01.7	178 10.4	41.0	210 55.7	07.3	194 28.4	03.0	145 42.1	28.5
29 00 WEDNESDAY	68 04.2	193 09.7	S18 41.8	225 56.7	S 8 07.9	209 30.4	S14 03.2	160 44.2	S22 28.5
01	83 06.6	208 08.9	42.6	240 57.7	08.4	224 32.3	03.3	175 46.4	28.5
02	98 09.1	223 08.2	43.4	255 58.7	09.0	239 34.3	03.5	190 48.5	28.5
03	113 11.6	238 07.5	. . 44.2	270 59.7	. . 09.6	254 36.2	. . 03.6	205 50.7	. . 28.5
04	128 14.0	253 06.7	45.0	286 00.6	10.2	269 38.2	03.8	220 52.9	28.5
05	143 16.5	268 06.0	45.8	301 01.6	10.8	284 40.1	04.0	235 55.0	28.5
06	158 19.0	283 05.2	S18 46.6	316 02.6	S 8 11.4	299 42.1	S14 04.1	250 57.2	S22 28.6
07	173 21.4	298 04.5	47.4	331 03.6	12.0	314 44.1	04.3	265 59.3	28.6
08	188 23.9	313 03.7	48.2	346 04.6	12.6	329 46.0	04.4	281 01.5	28.6
09	203 26.4	328 03.0	. . 49.0	1 05.6	. . 13.1	344 48.0	. . 04.6	296 03.6	. . 28.6
10	218 28.8	343 02.2	49.8	16 06.6	13.7	359 49.9	04.8	311 05.8	28.6
11	233 31.3	358 01.5	50.6	31 07.6	14.3	14 51.9	04.9	326 08.0	28.6
12	248 33.7	13 00.7	S18 51.4	46 08.6	S 8 14.9	29 53.9	S14 05.1	341 10.1	S22 28.6
13	263 36.2	28 00.0	52.2	61 09.6	15.5	44 55.8	05.2	356 12.3	28.6
14	278 38.7	42 59.2	53.0	76 10.5	16.1	59 57.8	05.4	11 14.4	28.6
15	293 41.1	57 58.5	. . 53.8	91 11.5	. . 16.7	74 59.7	. . 05.5	26 16.6	. . 28.6
16	308 43.6	72 57.7	54.6	106 12.5	17.2	90 01.7	05.7	41 18.8	28.6
17	323 46.1	87 57.0	55.3	121 13.5	17.8	105 03.6	05.9	56 20.9	28.7
18	338 48.5	102 56.2	S18 56.1	136 14.5	S 8 18.4	120 05.6	S14 06.0	71 23.1	S22 28.7
19	353 51.0	117 55.5	56.9	151 15.5	19.0	135 07.6	06.2	86 25.2	28.7
20	8 53.5	132 54.7	57.7	166 16.5	19.6	150 09.5	06.3	101 27.4	28.7
21	23 55.9	147 54.0	. . 58.5	181 17.5	. . 20.2	165 11.5	. . 06.5	116 29.5	. . 28.7
22	38 58.4	162 53.2	18 59.3	196 18.5	20.8	180 13.4	06.7	131 31.7	28.7
23	54 00.9	177 52.4	S19 00.1	211 19.5	21.3	195 15.4	06.8	146 33.9	28.7
Mer. Pass.	h m 19 28.5	v −0.7	d 0.8	v 1.0	d 0.6	v 2.0	d 0.2	v 2.2	d 0.0

STARS

Name	SHA	Dec
	° ′	° ′
Acamar	315 15.7	S40 14.2
Achernar	335 24.2	S57 09.1
Acrux	173 06.2	S63 11.5
Adhara	255 09.9	S28 59.8
Aldebaran	290 45.6	N16 32.5
Alioth	166 18.5	N55 51.7
Alkaid	152 57.0	N49 13.5
Al Na'ir	27 40.1	S46 52.6
Alnilam	275 43.0	S 1 11.6
Alphard	217 53.1	S 8 44.1
Alphecca	126 08.9	N26 39.5
Alpheratz	357 40.2	N29 11.5
Altair	62 05.6	N 8 55.2
Ankaa	353 12.6	S42 12.8
Antares	112 23.0	S26 28.0
Arcturus	145 53.3	N19 05.5
Atria	107 22.6	S69 03.3
Avior	234 16.4	S59 33.8
Bellatrix	278 28.5	N 6 21.8
Betelgeuse	270 57.8	N 7 24.5
Canopus	263 54.3	S52 42.3
Capella	280 29.5	N46 00.7
Deneb	49 29.6	N45 21.0
Denebola	182 30.8	N14 28.4
Diphda	348 52.7	S17 53.5
Dubhe	193 48.3	N61 39.0
Elnath	278 08.5	N28 37.1
Eltanin	90 45.3	N51 29.5
Enif	33 44.3	N 9 57.6
Fomalhaut	15 20.7	S29 31.8
Gacrux	171 57.8	S57 12.4
Gienah	175 49.4	S17 38.2
Hadar	148 44.1	S60 27.2
Hamal	327 57.1	N23 32.8
Kaus Aust.	83 40.2	S34 22.4
Kochab	137 21.4	N74 04.9
Markab	13 35.3	N15 18.2
Menkar	314 11.6	N 4 09.5
Menkent	148 04.4	S36 27.1
Miaplacidus	221 38.6	S69 47.2
Mirfak	308 35.5	N49 55.4
Nunki	75 54.9	S26 16.3
Peacock	53 14.9	S56 40.7
Pollux	243 23.9	N27 58.8
Procyon	244 56.4	N 5 10.6
Rasalhague	96 04.0	N12 33.1
Regulus	207 40.3	N11 52.7
Rigel	281 08.9	S 8 11.0
Rigil Kent.	139 48.2	S60 54.1
Sabik	102 09.5	S15 44.6
Schedar	349 36.7	N56 38.3
Shaula	96 18.3	S37 06.8
Sirius	258 30.8	S16 44.5
Spica	158 28.3	S11 15.0
Suhail	222 50.0	S43 30.1
Vega	80 37.3	N38 48.3
Zuben'ubi	137 02.4	S16 06.7

	SHA	Mer. Pass.
	° ′	h m
Venus	126 22.4	11 07
Mars	158 27.8	8 57
Jupiter	141 38.4	10 04
Saturn	92 47.4	13 19

UT d	h	SUN GHA	SUN Dec	MOON GHA	v	MOON Dec	d	HP
		° ′	° ′	° ′	′	° ′	′	′
27	00	183 06.9	S21 06.9	85 32.1	12.9	S10 06.4	9.4	55.9
	01	198 06.7	07.3	100 04.0	13.0	9 57.0	9.4	56.0
	02	213 06.5	07.8	114 36.0	12.9	9 47.6	9.5	56.0
	03	228 06.3	. . 08.2	129 07.9	13.0	9 38.1	9.5	56.0
	04	243 06.1	08.7	143 39.9	12.9	9 28.6	9.6	56.1
	05	258 05.9	09.1	158 11.8	12.9	9 19.0	9.7	56.1
	06	273 05.7	S21 09.6	172 43.7	12.9	S 9 09.3	9.7	56.1
	07	288 05.5	10.0	187 15.6	12.9	8 59.6	9.8	56.2
	08	303 05.3	10.5	201 47.5	12.9	8 49.8	9.8	56.2
MONDAY	09	318 05.0	. . 10.9	216 19.4	12.9	8 40.0	9.8	56.2
	10	333 04.8	11.4	230 51.3	12.9	8 30.2	10.0	56.3
	11	348 04.6	11.8	245 23.2	12.8	8 20.2	9.9	56.3
	12	3 04.4	S21 12.3	259 55.0	12.9	S 8 10.3	10.1	56.3
	13	18 04.2	12.7	274 26.9	12.8	8 00.2	10.0	56.4
	14	33 04.0	13.2	288 58.7	12.8	7 50.2	10.2	56.4
	15	48 03.8	. . 13.6	303 30.5	12.8	7 40.0	10.1	56.4
	16	63 03.6	14.1	318 02.3	12.8	7 29.9	10.3	56.5
	17	78 03.4	14.5	332 34.1	12.8	7 19.6	10.2	56.5
	18	93 03.2	S21 15.0	347 05.9	12.7	S 7 09.4	10.3	56.6
	19	108 03.0	15.4	1 37.6	12.7	6 59.1	10.4	56.6
	20	123 02.8	15.9	16 09.3	12.8	6 48.7	10.4	56.6
	21	138 02.6	. . 16.3	30 41.1	12.7	6 38.3	10.5	56.7
	22	153 02.3	16.7	45 12.8	12.6	6 27.8	10.5	56.7
	23	168 02.1	17.2	59 44.4	12.7	6 17.3	10.5	56.7
28	00	183 01.9	S21 17.6	74 16.1	12.6	S 6 06.8	10.6	56.8
	01	198 01.7	18.1	88 47.7	12.6	5 56.2	10.6	56.8
	02	213 01.5	18.5	103 19.3	12.6	5 45.6	10.7	56.8
	03	228 01.3	. . 19.0	117 50.9	12.6	5 34.9	10.7	56.9
	04	243 01.1	19.4	132 22.5	12.5	5 24.2	10.8	56.9
	05	258 00.9	19.8	146 54.0	12.5	5 13.4	10.8	57.0
	06	273 00.6	S21 20.3	161 25.5	12.5	S 5 02.6	10.8	57.0
	07	288 00.4	20.7	175 57.0	12.5	4 51.8	10.9	57.0
	08	303 00.2	21.1	190 28.5	12.4	4 40.9	10.9	57.1
TUESDAY	09	318 00.0	. . 21.6	204 59.9	12.4	4 30.0	11.0	57.1
	10	332 59.8	22.0	219 31.3	12.4	4 19.0	10.9	57.2
	11	347 59.6	22.4	234 02.7	12.3	4 08.1	11.1	57.2
	12	2 59.4	S21 22.9	248 34.0	12.4	S 3 57.0	11.0	57.2
	13	17 59.2	23.3	263 05.4	12.2	3 46.0	11.1	57.3
	14	32 58.9	23.7	277 36.6	12.3	3 34.9	11.1	57.3
	15	47 58.7	. . 24.2	292 07.9	12.2	3 23.8	11.2	57.4
	16	62 58.5	24.6	306 39.1	12.2	3 12.6	11.2	57.4
	17	77 58.3	25.0	321 10.3	12.2	3 01.4	11.2	57.4
	18	92 58.1	S21 25.4	335 41.5	12.1	S 2 50.2	11.3	57.5
	19	107 57.9	25.9	350 12.6	12.0	2 38.9	11.3	57.5
	20	122 57.6	26.3	4 43.6	12.1	2 27.6	11.3	57.5
	21	137 57.4	. . 26.7	19 14.7	12.0	2 16.3	11.3	57.6
	22	152 57.2	27.2	33 45.7	12.0	2 05.0	11.4	57.6
	23	167 57.0	27.6	48 16.7	11.9	1 53.6	11.4	57.7
29	00	182 56.8	S21 28.0	62 47.6	11.9	S 1 42.2	11.4	57.7
	01	197 56.6	28.4	77 18.5	11.8	1 30.8	11.4	57.8
	02	212 56.3	28.8	91 49.3	11.8	1 19.4	11.5	57.8
	03	227 56.1	. . 29.3	106 20.1	11.8	1 07.9	11.5	57.8
	04	242 55.9	29.7	120 50.9	11.7	0 56.4	11.5	57.9
	05	257 55.7	30.1	135 21.6	11.7	0 44.9	11.6	57.9
	06	272 55.5	S21 30.5	149 52.3	11.6	S 0 33.3	11.5	58.0
WEDNESDAY	07	287 55.2	30.9	164 22.9	11.6	0 21.8	11.6	58.0
	08	302 55.0	31.4	178 53.5	11.6	S 0 10.2	11.6	58.0
	09	317 54.8	. . 31.8	193 24.1	11.5	N 0 01.4	11.6	58.1
	10	332 54.6	32.2	207 54.6	11.4	0 13.0	11.6	58.1
	11	347 54.4	32.6	222 25.0	11.4	0 24.6	11.7	58.2
	12	2 54.1	S21 33.0	236 55.4	11.3	N 0 36.3	11.6	58.2
	13	17 53.9	33.4	251 25.7	11.3	0 47.9	11.7	58.2
	14	32 53.7	33.9	265 56.0	11.3	0 59.6	11.7	58.3
	15	47 53.5	. . 34.3	280 26.3	11.2	1 11.3	11.7	58.3
	16	62 53.3	34.7	294 56.5	11.1	1 23.0	11.7	58.4
	17	77 53.0	35.1	309 26.6	11.1	1 34.7	11.7	58.4
	18	92 52.8	S21 35.5	323 56.7	11.0	N 1 46.4	11.7	58.4
	19	107 52.6	35.9	338 26.7	11.0	1 58.1	11.7	58.5
	20	122 52.4	36.3	352 56.7	10.9	2 09.8	11.7	58.5
	21	137 52.1	. . 36.7	7 26.6	10.9	2 21.5	11.8	58.6
	22	152 51.9	37.1	21 56.5	10.8	2 33.3	11.7	58.6
	23	167 51.7	37.6	36 26.3	10.7	N 2 45.0	11.8	58.6
		SD 16.2	*d* 0.4	SD	15.4		15.6	15.9

Lat.	Twilight Naut.	Twilight Civil	Sunrise	Moonrise 27	Moonrise 28	Moonrise 29	Moonrise 30
°	h m	h m	h m	h m	h m	h m	h m
N 72	07 43	09 37	▬	14 26	14 16	14 06	13 56
N 70	07 28	09 01	▬	14 14	14 11	14 07	14 03
68	07 15	08 36	10 20	14 05	14 07	14 08	14 10
66	07 05	08 16	09 37	13 57	14 03	14 09	14 15
64	06 56	08 00	09 08	13 51	14 00	14 09	14 19
62	06 48	07 47	08 46	13 45	13 58	14 10	14 23
60	06 41	07 36	08 29	13 40	13 55	14 11	14 27
N 58	06 35	07 26	08 14	13 36	13 53	14 11	14 30
56	06 29	07 17	08 02	13 32	13 52	14 12	14 33
54	06 24	07 09	07 51	13 28	13 50	14 12	14 35
52	06 20	07 02	07 41	13 25	13 49	14 12	14 37
50	06 15	06 56	07 33	13 22	13 47	14 13	14 39
45	06 05	06 42	07 15	13 16	13 44	14 13	14 44
N 40	05 56	06 30	07 00	13 10	13 42	14 14	14 48
35	05 48	06 19	06 47	13 06	13 40	14 15	14 51
30	05 41	06 10	06 36	13 01	13 38	14 15	14 54
20	05 26	05 53	06 17	12 54	13 35	14 16	14 59
N 10	05 12	05 38	06 00	12 48	13 32	14 17	15 04
0	04 56	05 22	05 44	12 42	13 29	14 17	15 08
S 10	04 39	05 06	05 29	12 36	13 26	14 18	15 12
20	04 19	04 47	05 11	12 30	13 24	14 19	15 17
30	03 52	04 25	04 52	12 23	13 20	14 20	15 22
35	03 36	04 11	04 40	12 19	13 18	14 21	15 25
40	03 15	03 55	04 26	12 14	13 16	14 21	15 29
45	02 48	03 35	04 10	12 08	13 14	14 22	15 33
S 50	02 11	03 09	03 51	12 02	13 11	14 23	15 38
52	01 50	02 56	03 41	11 59	13 10	14 23	15 40
54	01 22	02 41	03 31	11 55	13 08	14 24	15 43
56	00 37	02 23	03 19	11 52	13 06	14 24	15 46
58	////	02 01	03 05	11 47	13 05	14 25	15 49
S 60	////	01 31	02 48	11 43	13 03	14 26	15 52

Lat.	Sunset	Twilight Civil	Twilight Naut.	Moonset 27	Moonset 28	Moonset 29	Moonset 30
°	h m	h m	h m	h m	h m	h m	h m
N 72	▬	13 58	15 52	23 43	25 33	01 33	03 26
N 70	▬	14 34	16 08	23 52	25 35	01 35	03 21
68	13 16	15 00	16 20	24 00	00 00	01 37	03 17
66	13 59	15 19	16 31	24 06	00 06	01 38	03 14
64	14 27	15 35	16 40	24 12	00 12	01 39	03 11
62	14 49	15 49	16 47	24 16	00 16	01 41	03 08
60	15 07	16 00	16 54	24 20	00 20	01 41	03 06
N 58	15 21	16 10	17 00	24 24	00 24	01 42	03 04
56	15 34	16 19	17 06	24 27	00 27	01 43	03 02
54	15 45	16 26	17 11	24 30	00 30	01 44	03 01
52	15 54	16 34	17 16	24 32	00 32	01 44	02 59
50	16 03	16 40	17 21	24 34	00 34	01 45	02 58
45	16 21	16 54	17 31	24 39	00 39	01 46	02 55
N 40	16 36	17 06	17 39	24 43	00 43	01 47	02 53
35	16 49	17 16	17 48	24 47	00 47	01 48	02 51
30	17 00	17 26	17 55	24 50	00 50	01 49	02 49
20	17 19	17 43	18 10	00 03	00 55	01 50	02 46
N 10	17 36	17 58	18 24	00 11	01 00	01 51	02 44
0	17 52	18 14	18 40	00 18	01 04	01 52	02 41
S 10	18 08	18 30	18 57	00 25	01 09	01 53	02 39
20	18 25	18 49	19 18	00 33	01 13	01 54	02 36
30	18 45	19 12	19 44	00 42	01 18	01 55	02 33
35	18 57	19 25	20 01	00 47	01 21	01 56	02 31
40	19 10	19 42	20 22	00 53	01 25	01 56	02 29
45	19 26	20 02	20 49	00 59	01 29	01 57	02 27
S 50	19 46	20 28	21 27	01 07	01 33	01 58	02 24
52	19 56	20 41	21 48	01 11	01 35	01 59	02 23
54	20 06	20 56	22 16	01 15	01 37	01 59	02 21
56	20 19	21 14	23 05	01 19	01 40	02 00	02 20
58	20 33	21 37	////	01 24	01 43	02 00	02 18
S 60	20 50	22 08	////	01 30	01 46	02 01	02 16

Day	SUN Eqn. of Time 00^h	SUN Eqn. of Time 12^h	SUN Mer. Pass.	MOON Mer. Pass. Upper	MOON Mer. Pass. Lower	MOON Age	MOON Phase
d	m s	m s	h m	h m	h m	d %	
27	12 28	12 18	11 48	18 53	06 30	09 58	◐
28	12 08	11 58	11 48	19 40	07 17	10 68	
29	11 48	11 37	11 48	20 29	08 05	11 78	

	UT (d h)	ARIES GHA	VENUS −3·9 GHA	VENUS Dec	MARS +1·7 GHA	MARS Dec	JUPITER −1·7 GHA	JUPITER Dec	SATURN +0·5 GHA	SATURN Dec
		° ′	° ′	° ′	° ′	° ′	° ′	° ′	° ′	° ′
	30 00	69 03.3	192 51.7	S19 00.8	226 20.4	S 8 21.9	210 17.3	S14 07.0	161 36.0	S22 28.7
	01	84 05.8	207 50.9	01.6	241 21.4	22.5	225 19.3	07.1	176 38.2	28.7
	02	99 08.2	222 50.2	02.4	256 22.4	23.1	240 21.3	07.3	191 40.3	28.7
	03	114 10.7	237 49.4	. . 03.2	271 23.4	. . 23.7	255 23.2	. . 07.4	206 42.5	. . 28.7
	04	129 13.2	252 48.7	04.0	286 24.4	24.3	270 25.2	07.6	221 44.6	28.8
	05	144 15.6	267 47.9	04.7	301 25.4	24.9	285 27.1	07.8	236 46.8	28.8
	06	159 18.1	282 47.1	S19 05.5	316 26.4	S 8 25.4	300 29.1	S14 07.9	251 49.0	S22 28.8
	07	174 20.6	297 46.4	06.3	331 27.4	26.0	315 31.1	08.1	266 51.1	28.8
T	08	189 23.0	312 45.6	07.1	346 28.4	26.6	330 33.0	08.2	281 53.3	28.8
H	09	204 25.5	327 44.9	. . 07.8	1 29.3	. . 27.2	345 35.0	. . 08.4	296 55.4	. . 28.8
U	10	219 28.0	342 44.1	08.6	16 30.3	27.8	0 36.9	08.6	311 57.6	28.8
R	11	234 30.4	357 43.3	09.4	31 31.3	28.4	15 38.9	08.7	326 59.7	28.8
S	12	249 32.9	12 42.6	S19 10.2	46 32.3	S 8 28.9	30 40.9	S14 08.9	342 01.9	S22 28.8
D	13	264 35.3	27 41.8	10.9	61 33.3	29.5	45 42.8	09.0	357 04.1	28.8
A	14	279 37.8	42 41.0	11.7	76 34.3	30.1	60 44.8	09.2	12 06.2	28.8
Y	15	294 40.3	57 40.3	. . 12.5	91 35.3	. . 30.7	75 46.7	. . 09.3	27 08.4	. . 28.9
	16	309 42.7	72 39.5	13.2	106 36.3	31.3	90 48.7	09.5	42 10.5	28.9
	17	324 45.2	87 38.8	14.0	121 37.3	31.9	105 50.7	09.7	57 12.7	28.9
	18	339 47.7	102 38.0	S19 14.8	136 38.2	S 8 32.5	120 52.6	S14 09.8	72 14.8	S22 28.9
	19	354 50.1	117 37.2	15.5	151 39.2	33.0	135 54.6	10.0	87 17.0	28.9
	20	9 52.6	132 36.5	16.3	166 40.2	33.6	150 56.5	10.1	102 19.1	28.9
	21	24 55.1	147 35.7	. . 17.0	181 41.2	. . 34.2	165 58.5	. . 10.3	117 21.3	. . 28.9
	22	39 57.5	162 34.9	17.8	196 42.2	34.8	181 00.5	10.4	132 23.5	28.9
	23	55 00.0	177 34.2	18.6	211 43.2	35.4	196 02.4	10.6	147 25.6	28.9
	1 00	70 02.5	192 33.4	S19 19.3	226 44.2	S 8 36.0	211 04.4	S14 10.8	162 27.8	S22 28.9
	01	85 04.9	207 32.6	20.1	241 45.2	36.5	226 06.3	10.9	177 29.9	28.9
	02	100 07.4	222 31.8	20.8	256 46.1	37.1	241 08.3	11.1	192 32.1	28.9
	03	115 09.8	237 31.1	. . 21.6	271 47.1	. . 37.7	256 10.3	. . 11.2	207 34.2	. . 29.0
	04	130 12.3	252 30.3	22.4	286 48.1	38.3	271 12.2	11.4	222 36.4	29.0
	05	145 14.8	267 29.5	23.1	301 49.1	38.9	286 14.2	11.5	237 38.6	29.0
	06	160 17.2	282 28.8	S19 23.9	316 50.1	S 8 39.4	301 16.1	S14 11.7	252 40.7	S22 29.0
	07	175 19.7	297 28.0	24.6	331 51.1	40.0	316 18.1	11.9	267 42.9	29.0
	08	190 22.2	312 27.2	25.4	346 52.1	40.6	331 20.1	12.0	282 45.0	29.0
F	09	205 24.6	327 26.4	. . 26.1	1 53.1	. . 41.2	346 22.0	. . 12.2	297 47.2	. . 29.0
R	10	220 27.1	342 25.7	26.9	16 54.0	41.8	1 24.0	12.3	312 49.3	29.0
I	11	235 29.6	357 24.9	27.6	31 55.0	42.4	16 25.9	12.5	327 51.5	29.0
D	12	250 32.0	12 24.1	S19 28.4	46 56.0	S 8 42.9	31 27.9	S14 12.6	342 53.6	S22 29.0
A	13	265 34.5	27 23.4	29.1	61 57.0	43.5	46 29.9	12.8	357 55.8	29.0
Y	14	280 37.0	42 22.6	29.9	76 58.0	44.1	61 31.8	13.0	12 58.0	29.1
	15	295 39.4	57 21.8	. . 30.6	91 59.0	. . 44.7	76 33.8	. . 13.1	28 00.1	. . 29.1
	16	310 41.9	72 21.0	31.4	107 00.0	45.3	91 35.7	13.3	43 02.3	29.1
	17	325 44.3	87 20.2	32.1	122 00.9	45.8	106 37.7	13.4	58 04.4	29.1
	18	340 46.8	102 19.5	S19 32.8	137 01.9	S 8 46.4	121 39.7	S14 13.6	73 06.6	S22 29.1
	19	355 49.3	117 18.7	33.6	152 02.9	47.0	136 41.6	13.7	88 08.7	29.1
	20	10 51.7	132 17.9	34.3	167 03.9	47.6	151 43.6	13.9	103 10.9	29.1
	21	25 54.2	147 17.1	. . 35.1	182 04.9	. . 48.2	166 45.6	. . 14.1	118 13.0	. . 29.1
	22	40 56.7	162 16.4	35.8	197 05.9	48.8	181 47.5	14.2	133 15.2	29.1
	23	55 59.1	177 15.6	36.6	212 06.9	49.3	196 49.5	14.4	148 17.4	29.1
	2 00	71 01.6	192 14.8	S19 37.3	227 07.9	S 8 49.9	211 51.4	S14 14.5	163 19.5	S22 29.1
	01	86 04.1	207 14.0	38.0	242 08.8	50.5	226 53.4	14.7	178 21.7	29.1
	02	101 06.5	222 13.2	38.8	257 09.8	51.1	241 55.4	14.8	193 23.8	29.2
	03	116 09.0	237 12.4	. . 39.5	272 10.8	. . 51.7	256 57.3	. . 15.0	208 26.0	. . 29.2
	04	131 11.4	252 11.7	40.2	287 11.8	52.2	271 59.3	15.1	223 28.1	29.2
	05	146 13.9	267 10.9	41.0	302 12.8	52.8	287 01.2	15.3	238 30.3	29.2
	06	161 16.4	282 10.1	S19 41.7	317 13.8	S 8 53.4	302 03.2	S14 15.5	253 32.4	S22 29.2
	07	176 18.8	297 09.3	42.4	332 14.8	54.0	317 05.2	15.6	268 34.6	29.2
S	08	191 21.3	312 08.5	43.2	347 15.7	54.6	332 07.1	15.8	283 36.8	29.2
A	09	206 23.8	327 07.7	. . 43.9	2 16.7	. . 55.1	347 09.1	. . 15.9	298 38.9	. . 29.2
T	10	221 26.2	342 07.0	44.6	17 17.7	55.7	2 11.1	16.1	313 41.1	29.2
U	11	236 28.7	357 06.2	45.3	32 18.7	56.3	17 13.0	16.2	328 43.2	29.2
R	12	251 31.2	12 05.4	S19 46.1	47 19.7	S 8 56.9	32 15.0	S14 16.4	343 45.4	S22 29.2
D	13	266 33.6	27 04.6	46.8	62 20.7	57.4	47 16.9	16.6	358 47.5	29.2
A	14	281 36.1	42 03.8	47.5	77 21.6	58.0	62 18.9	16.7	13 49.7	29.2
Y	15	296 38.6	57 03.0	. . 48.2	92 22.6	. . 58.6	77 20.9	. . 16.9	28 51.8	. . 29.3
	16	311 41.0	72 02.2	49.0	107 23.6	59.2	92 22.8	17.0	43 54.0	29.3
	17	326 43.5	87 01.4	49.7	122 24.6	8 59.8	107 24.8	17.2	58 56.1	29.3
	18	341 45.9	102 00.7	S19 50.4	137 25.6	S 9 00.3	122 26.8	S14 17.3	73 58.3	S22 29.3
	19	356 48.4	116 59.9	51.1	152 26.6	00.9	137 28.7	17.5	89 00.5	29.3
	20	11 50.9	131 59.1	51.8	167 27.6	01.5	152 30.7	17.6	104 02.6	29.3
	21	26 53.3	146 58.3	. . 52.5	182 28.5	. . 02.1	167 32.6	. . 17.8	119 04.8	. . 29.3
	22	41 55.8	161 57.5	53.3	197 29.5	02.7	182 34.6	17.9	134 06.9	29.3
	23	56 58.3	176 56.7	54.0	212 30.5	03.2	197 36.6	18.1	149 09.1	29.3
	Mer. Pass.	h m 19 16.7	v −0.8	d 0.7	v 1.0	d 0.6	v 2.0	d 0.2	v 2.2	d 0.0

STARS

Name	SHA	Dec
	° ′	° ′
Acamar	315 15.7	S40 14.2
Achernar	335 24.2	S57 09.1
Acrux	173 06.1	S63 11.5
Adhara	255 09.8	S28 59.8
Aldebaran	290 45.6	N16 32.5
Alioth	166 18.5	N55 51.7
Alkaid	152 57.0	N49 13.4
Al Na'ir	27 40.1	S46 52.6
Alnilam	275 43.0	S 1 11.6
Alphard	217 53.0	S 8 44.1
Alphecca	126 08.9	N26 39.5
Alpheratz	357 40.2	N29 11.5
Altair	62 05.6	N 8 55.2
Ankaa	353 12.6	S42 12.8
Antares	112 23.0	S26 28.0
Arcturus	145 53.3	N19 05.5
Atria	107 22.6	S69 03.3
Avior	234 16.4	S59 33.8
Bellatrix	278 28.5	N 6 21.8
Betelgeuse	270 57.7	N 7 24.5
Canopus	263 54.3	S52 42.3
Capella	280 29.5	N46 00.7
Deneb	49 29.7	N45 21.0
Denebola	182 30.7	N14 28.4
Diphda	348 52.7	S17 53.5
Dubhe	193 48.2	N61 39.0
Elnath	278 08.5	N28 37.1
Eltanin	90 45.3	N51 29.5
Enif	33 44.3	N 9 57.6
Fomalhaut	15 20.7	S29 31.8
Gacrux	171 57.8	S57 12.4
Gienah	175 49.3	S17 38.2
Hadar	148 44.1	S60 27.2
Hamal	327 57.1	N23 32.8
Kaus Aust.	83 40.2	S34 22.4
Kochab	137 21.3	N74 04.9
Markab	13 35.3	N15 18.2
Menkar	314 11.6	N 4 09.5
Menkent	148 04.3	S36 27.1
Miaplacidus	221 38.6	S69 47.2
Mirfak	308 35.5	N49 55.4
Nunki	75 54.9	S26 16.3
Peacock	53 15.0	S56 40.7
Pollux	243 23.8	N27 58.7
Procyon	244 56.4	N 5 10.6
Rasalhague	96 04.0	N12 33.1
Regulus	207 40.3	N11 52.7
Rigel	281 08.8	S 8 11.0
Rigil Kent.	139 48.2	S60 54.1
Sabik	102 09.5	S15 44.6
Schedar	349 36.7	N56 38.3
Shaula	96 18.3	S37 06.8
Sirius	258 30.8	S16 44.5
Spica	158 28.3	S11 15.0
Suhail	222 50.0	S43 30.1
Vega	80 37.3	N38 48.3
Zuben'ubi	137 02.4	S16 06.7

	SHA	Mer. Pass.
	° ′	h m
Venus	122 30.9	11 10
Mars	156 41.7	8 52
Jupiter	141 01.9	9 54
Saturn	92 25.3	13 08

Day	UT (d h)	SUN GHA (° ′)	SUN Dec (° ′)	MOON GHA (° ′)	v (′)	MOON Dec (° ′)	d (′)	HP (′)
THURSDAY	30 00	182 51.5	S21 38.0	50 56.0	10.7	N 2 56.8	11.7	58.7
	01	197 51.2	38.4	65 25.7	10.7	3 08.5	11.8	58.7
	02	212 51.0	38.8	79 55.4	10.5	3 20.3	11.7	58.8
	03	227 50.8	. . 39.2	94 24.9	10.5	3 32.0	11.8	58.8
	04	242 50.6	39.6	108 54.4	10.5	3 43.8	11.7	58.9
	05	257 50.3	40.0	123 23.9	10.4	3 55.5	11.7	58.9
	06	272 50.1	S21 40.4	137 53.3	10.3	N 4 07.2	11.8	58.9
	07	287 49.9	40.8	152 22.6	10.2	4 19.0	11.7	59.0
	08	302 49.7	41.2	166 51.8	10.2	4 30.7	11.7	59.0
	09	317 49.4	. . 41.6	181 21.0	10.1	4 42.4	11.7	59.1
	10	332 49.2	42.0	195 50.1	10.1	4 54.1	11.7	59.1
	11	347 49.0	42.4	210 19.2	10.0	5 05.8	11.7	59.1
	12	2 48.7	S21 42.8	224 48.2	9.9	N 5 17.5	11.6	59.2
	13	17 48.5	43.2	239 17.1	9.8	5 29.1	11.7	59.2
	14	32 48.3	43.6	253 45.9	9.8	5 40.8	11.6	59.2
	15	47 48.1	. . 44.0	268 14.7	9.7	5 52.4	11.7	59.3
	16	62 47.8	44.4	282 43.4	9.6	6 04.1	11.6	59.3
	17	77 47.6	44.8	297 12.0	9.6	6 15.7	11.5	59.4
	18	92 47.4	S21 45.2	311 40.6	9.5	N 6 27.2	11.6	59.4
	19	107 47.1	45.6	326 09.1	9.4	6 38.8	11.5	59.4
	20	122 46.9	45.9	340 37.5	9.4	6 50.3	11.6	59.5
	21	137 46.7	. . 46.3	355 05.9	9.2	7 01.9	11.5	59.5
	22	152 46.5	46.7	9 34.1	9.2	7 13.4	11.4	59.6
	23	167 46.2	47.1	24 02.3	9.2	7 24.8	11.4	59.6
FRIDAY	1 00	182 46.0	S21 47.5	38 30.5	9.0	N 7 36.2	11.5	59.6
	01	197 45.8	47.9	52 58.5	9.0	7 47.7	11.3	59.7
	02	212 45.5	48.3	67 26.5	8.9	7 59.0	11.4	59.7
	03	227 45.3	. . 48.7	81 54.4	8.8	8 10.4	11.3	59.7
	04	242 45.1	49.1	96 22.2	8.7	8 21.7	11.2	59.8
	05	257 44.8	49.4	110 49.9	8.7	8 32.9	11.3	59.8
	06	272 44.6	S21 49.8	125 17.6	8.6	N 8 44.2	11.2	59.9
	07	287 44.4	50.2	139 45.2	8.5	8 55.4	11.1	59.9
	08	302 44.1	50.6	154 12.7	8.4	9 06.5	11.2	59.9
	09	317 43.9	. . 51.0	168 40.1	8.3	9 17.7	11.0	60.0
	10	332 43.7	51.4	183 07.4	8.3	9 28.7	11.0	60.0
	11	347 43.4	51.7	197 34.7	8.2	9 39.7	11.0	60.0
	12	2 43.2	S21 52.1	212 01.9	8.1	N 9 50.7	11.0	60.1
	13	17 43.0	52.5	226 29.0	8.0	10 01.7	10.8	60.1
	14	32 42.7	52.9	240 56.0	7.9	10 12.5	10.9	60.1
	15	47 42.5	. . 53.3	255 22.9	7.9	10 23.4	10.8	60.2
	16	62 42.3	53.6	269 49.8	7.8	10 34.2	10.7	60.2
	17	77 42.0	54.0	284 16.6	7.7	10 44.9	10.7	60.2
	18	92 41.8	S21 54.4	298 43.3	7.6	N10 55.6	10.6	60.3
	19	107 41.5	54.8	313 09.9	7.5	11 06.2	10.5	60.3
	20	122 41.3	55.1	327 36.4	7.4	11 16.7	10.5	60.3
	21	137 41.1	. . 55.5	342 02.8	7.4	11 27.2	10.5	60.4
	22	152 40.8	55.9	356 29.2	7.3	11 37.7	10.3	60.4
	23	167 40.6	56.3	10 55.5	7.2	11 48.0	10.3	60.4
SATURDAY	2 00	182 40.4	S21 56.6	25 21.7	7.1	N11 58.3	10.3	60.4
	01	197 40.1	57.0	39 47.8	7.0	12 08.6	10.1	60.5
	02	212 39.9	57.4	54 13.8	6.9	12 18.7	10.1	60.5
	03	227 39.6	. . 57.8	68 39.7	6.9	12 28.8	10.1	60.5
	04	242 39.4	58.1	83 05.6	6.8	12 38.9	9.9	60.6
	05	257 39.2	58.5	97 31.4	6.7	12 48.8	9.9	60.6
	06	272 38.9	S21 58.9	111 57.1	6.6	N12 58.7	9.8	60.6
	07	287 38.7	59.2	126 22.7	6.5	13 08.5	9.7	60.6
	08	302 38.4	21 59.6	140 48.2	6.4	13 18.2	9.7	60.7
	09	317 38.2	22 00.0	155 13.6	6.4	13 27.9	9.5	60.7
	10	332 38.0	00.3	169 39.0	6.3	13 37.4	9.5	60.7
	11	347 37.7	00.7	184 04.3	6.2	13 46.9	9.4	60.7
	12	2 37.5	S22 01.0	198 29.5	6.1	N13 56.3	9.3	60.8
	13	17 37.2	01.4	212 54.6	6.0	14 05.6	9.2	60.8
	14	32 37.0	01.8	227 19.6	5.9	14 14.8	9.2	60.8
	15	47 36.8	. . 02.1	241 44.5	5.9	14 24.0	9.0	60.8
	16	62 36.5	02.5	256 09.4	5.8	14 33.0	9.0	60.9
	17	77 36.3	02.9	270 34.2	5.7	14 42.0	8.8	60.9
	18	92 36.0	S22 03.2	284 58.9	5.6	N14 50.8	8.8	60.9
	19	107 35.8	03.6	299 23.5	5.6	14 59.6	8.6	60.9
	20	122 35.5	03.9	313 48.1	5.5	15 08.2	8.6	60.9
	21	137 35.3	. . 04.3	328 12.6	5.3	15 16.8	8.4	61.0
	22	152 35.1	04.6	342 36.9	5.4	15 25.2	8.4	61.0
	23	167 34.8	05.0	357 01.3	5.2	N15 33.6	8.3	61.0
		SD 16.2	*d* 0.4	SD 16.1		16.4		16.6

Lat. (°)	Twilight Naut. (h m)	Twilight Civil (h m)	Sunrise (h m)	Moonrise 30 (h m)	Moonrise 1 (h m)	Moonrise 2 (h m)	Moonrise 3 (h m)
N 72	07 51	09 51	▬	13 56	13 44	13 29	12 59
N 70	07 35	09 11	▬	14 03	14 00	13 57	13 54
68	07 22	08 44	10 37	14 10	14 12	14 17	14 28
66	07 11	08 23	09 47	14 15	14 23	14 34	14 52
64	07 01	08 07	09 16	14 19	14 32	14 48	15 12
62	06 53	07 53	08 54	14 23	14 39	14 59	15 27
60	06 46	07 41	08 35	14 27	14 46	15 09	15 41
N 58	06 40	07 31	08 20	14 30	14 51	15 18	15 52
56	06 34	07 22	08 07	14 33	14 57	15 25	16 02
54	06 28	07 13	07 56	14 35	15 01	15 32	16 11
52	06 23	07 06	07 46	14 37	15 05	15 38	16 19
50	06 19	06 59	07 37	14 39	15 09	15 44	16 26
45	06 08	06 45	07 18	14 44	15 18	15 56	16 41
N 40	05 59	06 33	07 03	14 48	15 25	16 06	16 54
35	05 51	06 22	06 50	14 51	15 31	16 15	17 05
30	05 43	06 12	06 38	14 54	15 36	16 22	17 14
20	05 28	05 55	06 19	14 59	15 45	16 36	17 31
N 10	05 13	05 39	06 02	15 04	15 54	16 47	17 45
0	04 57	05 23	05 45	15 08	16 01	16 58	17 59
S 10	04 40	05 06	05 29	15 12	16 09	17 09	18 12
20	04 19	04 47	05 12	15 17	16 18	17 21	18 27
30	03 52	04 24	04 51	15 22	16 27	17 35	18 44
35	03 35	04 10	04 39	15 25	16 33	17 43	18 54
40	03 13	03 53	04 25	15 29	16 39	17 52	19 05
45	02 46	03 33	04 09	15 33	16 47	18 03	19 18
S 50	02 07	03 06	03 49	15 38	16 56	18 16	19 34
52	01 44	02 53	03 39	15 40	17 00	18 22	19 42
54	01 14	02 37	03 28	15 43	17 05	18 29	19 50
56	00 16	02 19	03 15	15 46	17 10	18 36	20 00
58	////	01 55	03 01	15 49	17 16	18 45	20 11
S 60	////	01 22	02 43	15 52	17 22	18 54	20 23

Lat. (°)	Sunset (h m)	Twilight Civil (h m)	Twilight Naut. (h m)	Moonset 30 (h m)	Moonset 1 (h m)	Moonset 2 (h m)	Moonset 3 (h m)
N 72	▬	13 47	15 46	03 26	05 27	07 38	10 13
N 70	▬	14 26	16 02	03 21	05 13	07 12	09 19
68	13 01	14 53	16 16	03 17	05 02	06 53	08 46
66	13 50	15 14	16 27	03 14	04 54	06 38	08 23
64	14 21	15 31	16 36	03 11	04 46	06 25	08 04
62	14 44	15 45	16 44	03 08	04 40	06 14	07 49
60	15 03	15 57	16 52	03 06	04 34	06 05	07 36
N 58	15 18	16 07	16 58	03 04	04 29	05 57	07 25
56	15 31	16 16	17 04	03 02	04 25	05 50	07 16
54	15 42	16 24	17 10	03 01	04 21	05 44	07 07
52	15 52	16 32	17 15	02 59	04 18	05 39	07 00
50	16 01	16 38	17 19	02 58	04 15	05 33	06 53
45	16 20	16 53	17 30	02 55	04 08	05 23	06 38
N 40	16 35	17 05	17 39	02 53	04 02	05 14	06 27
35	16 48	17 16	17 47	02 51	03 57	05 06	06 16
30	17 00	17 26	17 55	02 49	03 53	04 59	06 08
20	17 19	17 43	18 10	02 46	03 46	04 48	05 52
N 10	17 37	17 59	18 25	02 44	03 39	04 38	05 39
0	17 53	18 15	18 41	02 41	03 33	04 28	05 27
S 10	18 09	18 32	18 59	02 39	03 27	04 19	05 14
20	18 27	18 51	19 20	02 36	03 20	04 08	05 01
30	18 47	19 14	19 47	02 33	03 13	03 57	04 46
35	18 59	19 28	20 04	02 31	03 09	03 50	04 37
40	19 13	19 45	20 26	02 29	03 04	03 43	04 27
45	19 30	20 06	20 53	02 27	02 58	03 34	04 16
S 50	19 50	20 33	21 33	02 24	02 52	03 24	04 02
52	20 00	20 46	21 56	02 23	02 49	03 19	03 55
54	20 11	21 02	22 27	02 21	02 45	03 13	03 48
56	20 24	21 21	23 35	02 20	02 42	03 08	03 40
58	20 39	21 45	////	02 18	02 38	03 01	03 31
S 60	20 56	22 19	////	02 16	02 33	02 54	03 20

Day (d)	SUN Eqn. of Time 00^h (m s)	SUN Eqn. of Time 12^h (m s)	SUN Mer. Pass. (h m)	MOON Mer. Pass. Upper (h m)	MOON Mer. Pass. Lower (h m)	MOON Age (d)	MOON Phase (%)
30	11 26	11 15	11 49	21 20	08 54	12	86
1	11 04	10 53	11 49	22 15	09 47	13	93
2	10 42	10 30	11 49	23 12	10 43	14	98

UT	ARIES	VENUS −3·9		MARS +1·7		JUPITER −1·7		SATURN +0·5		STARS		
	GHA	GHA	Dec	GHA	Dec	GHA	Dec	GHA	Dec	Name	SHA	Dec
d h	° ′	° ′	° ′	° ′	° ′	° ′	° ′	° ′	° ′		° ′	° ′
3 00	72 00.7	191 55.9	S19 54.7	227 31.5	S 9 03.8	212 38.5	S14 18.3	164 11.2	S22 29.3	Acamar	315 15.7	S40 14.2
01	87 03.2	206 55.1	55.4	242 32.5	04.4	227 40.5	18.4	179 13.4	29.3	Achernar	335 24.2	S57 09.1
02	102 05.7	221 54.3	56.1	257 33.5	05.0	242 42.5	18.6	194 15.5	29.3	Acrux	173 06.1	S63 11.5
03	117 08.1	236 53.5	. . 56.8	272 34.4	. . 05.5	257 44.4	. . 18.7	209 17.7	. . 29.4	Adhara	255 09.8	S28 59.8
04	132 10.6	251 52.7	57.5	287 35.4	06.1	272 46.4	18.9	224 19.8	29.4	Aldebaran	290 45.6	N16 32.5
05	147 13.1	266 51.9	58.3	302 36.4	06.7	287 48.4	19.0	239 22.0	29.4			
06	162 15.5	281 51.1	S19 59.0	317 37.4	S 9 07.3	302 50.3	S14 19.2	254 24.1	S22 29.4	Alioth	166 18.4	N55 51.7
07	177 18.0	296 50.3	19 59.7	332 38.4	07.9	317 52.3	19.3	269 26.3	29.4	Alkaid	152 57.0	N49 13.4
08	192 20.4	311 49.5	20 00.4	347 39.4	08.4	332 54.2	19.5	284 28.5	29.4	Al Na'ir	27 40.1	S46 52.6
S 09	207 22.9	326 48.7	. . 01.1	2 40.4	. . 09.0	347 56.2	. . 19.7	299 30.6	. . 29.4	Alnilam	275 43.0	S 1 11.6
U 10	222 25.4	341 47.9	01.8	17 41.3	09.6	2 58.2	19.8	314 32.8	29.4	Alphard	217 53.0	S 8 44.1
N 11	237 27.8	356 47.1	02.5	32 42.3	10.2	18 00.1	20.0	329 34.9	29.4			
D 12	252 30.3	11 46.4	S20 03.2	47 43.3	S 9 10.7	33 02.1	S14 20.1	344 37.1	S22 29.4	Alphecca	126 08.8	N26 39.4
A 13	267 32.8	26 45.6	03.9	62 44.3	11.3	48 04.1	20.3	359 39.2	29.4	Alpheratz	357 40.2	N29 11.5
Y 14	282 35.2	41 44.8	04.6	77 45.3	11.9	63 06.0	20.4	14 41.4	29.4	Altair	62 05.6	N 8 55.2
15	297 37.7	56 44.0	. . 05.3	92 46.3	. . 12.5	78 08.0	. . 20.6	29 43.5	. . 29.4	Ankaa	353 12.6	S42 12.8
16	312 40.2	71 43.2	06.0	107 47.2	13.0	93 10.0	20.7	44 45.7	29.5	Antares	112 22.9	S26 28.0
17	327 42.6	86 42.3	06.7	122 48.2	13.6	108 11.9	20.9	59 47.8	29.5			
18	342 45.1	101 41.5	S20 07.4	137 49.2	S 9 14.2	123 13.9	S14 21.0	74 50.0	S22 29.5	Arcturus	145 53.3	N19 05.5
19	357 47.6	116 40.7	08.1	152 50.2	14.8	138 15.9	21.2	89 52.1	29.5	Atria	107 22.6	S69 03.3
20	12 50.0	131 39.9	08.8	167 51.2	15.3	153 17.8	21.4	104 54.3	29.5	Avior	234 16.3	S59 33.9
21	27 52.5	146 39.1	. . 09.5	182 52.1	. . 15.9	168 19.8	. . 21.5	119 56.5	. . 29.5	Bellatrix	278 28.5	N 6 21.8
22	42 54.9	161 38.3	10.2	197 53.1	16.5	183 21.8	21.7	134 58.6	29.5	Betelgeuse	270 57.7	N 7 24.4
23	57 57.4	176 37.5	10.9	212 54.1	17.1	198 23.7	21.8	150 00.8	29.5			
4 00	72 59.9	191 36.7	S20 11.5	227 55.1	S 9 17.7	213 25.7	S14 22.0	165 02.9	S22 29.5	Canopus	263 54.3	S52 42.4
01	88 02.3	206 35.9	12.2	242 56.1	18.2	228 27.6	22.1	180 05.1	29.5	Capella	280 29.5	N46 00.7
02	103 04.8	221 35.1	12.9	257 57.1	18.8	243 29.6	22.3	195 07.2	29.5	Deneb	49 29.7	N45 21.0
03	118 07.3	236 34.3	. . 13.6	272 58.0	. . 19.4	258 31.6	. . 22.4	210 09.4	. . 29.5	Denebola	182 30.7	N14 28.3
04	133 09.7	251 33.5	14.3	287 59.0	20.0	273 33.5	22.6	225 11.5	29.6	Diphda	348 52.7	S17 53.5
05	148 12.2	266 32.7	15.0	303 00.0	20.5	288 35.5	22.7	240 13.7	29.6			
06	163 14.7	281 31.9	S20 15.7	318 01.0	S 9 21.1	303 37.5	S14 22.9	255 15.8	S22 29.6	Dubhe	193 48.2	N61 39.0
07	178 17.1	296 31.1	16.3	333 02.0	21.7	318 39.4	23.0	270 18.0	29.6	Elnath	278 08.4	N28 37.1
08	193 19.6	311 30.3	17.0	348 03.0	22.3	333 41.4	23.2	285 20.1	29.6	Eltanin	90 45.3	N51 29.5
M 09	208 22.1	326 29.5	. . 17.7	3 03.9	. . 22.8	348 43.4	. . 23.4	300 22.3	. . 29.6	Enif	33 44.3	N 9 57.6
O 10	223 24.5	341 28.7	18.4	18 04.9	23.4	3 45.3	23.5	315 24.4	29.6	Fomalhaut	15 20.7	S29 31.8
N 11	238 27.0	356 27.8	19.1	33 05.9	24.0	18 47.3	23.7	330 26.6	29.6			
D 12	253 29.4	11 27.0	S20 19.7	48 06.9	S 9 24.5	33 49.3	S14 23.8	345 28.7	S22 29.6	Gacrux	171 57.7	S57 12.4
A 13	268 31.9	26 26.2	20.4	63 07.9	25.1	48 51.2	24.0	0 30.9	29.6	Gienah	175 49.3	S17 38.3
Y 14	283 34.4	41 25.4	21.1	78 08.8	25.7	63 53.2	24.1	15 33.1	29.6	Hadar	148 44.0	S60 27.2
15	298 36.8	56 24.6	. . 21.8	93 09.8	. . 26.3	78 55.2	. . 24.3	30 35.2	. . 29.6	Hamal	327 57.1	N23 32.8
16	313 39.3	71 23.8	22.5	108 10.8	26.8	93 57.1	24.4	45 37.4	29.6	Kaus Aust.	83 40.2	S34 22.4
17	328 41.8	86 23.0	23.1	123 11.8	27.4	108 59.1	24.6	60 39.5	29.6			
18	343 44.2	101 22.2	S20 23.8	138 12.8	S 9 28.0	124 01.1	S14 24.7	75 41.7	S22 29.7	Kochab	137 21.3	N74 04.9
19	358 46.7	116 21.3	24.5	153 13.8	28.6	139 03.0	24.9	90 43.8	29.7	Markab	13 35.3	N15 18.2
20	13 49.2	131 20.5	25.1	168 14.7	29.1	154 05.0	25.0	105 46.0	29.7	Menkar	314 11.6	N 4 09.4
21	28 51.6	146 19.7	. . 25.8	183 15.7	. . 29.7	169 07.0	. . 25.2	120 48.1	. . 29.7	Menkent	148 04.3	S36 27.1
22	43 54.1	161 18.9	26.5	198 16.7	30.3	184 08.9	25.3	135 50.3	29.7	Miaplacidus	221 38.5	S69 47.2
23	58 56.6	176 18.1	27.1	213 17.7	30.9	199 10.9	25.5	150 52.4	29.7			
5 00	73 59.0	191 17.3	S20 27.8	228 18.7	S 9 31.4	214 12.9	S14 25.6	165 54.6	S22 29.7	Mirfak	308 35.5	N49 55.4
01	89 01.5	206 16.4	28.5	243 19.6	32.0	229 14.8	25.8	180 56.7	29.7	Nunki	75 54.9	S26 16.3
02	104 03.9	221 15.6	29.1	258 20.6	32.6	244 16.8	26.0	195 58.9	29.7	Peacock	53 15.0	S56 40.7
03	119 06.4	236 14.8	. . 29.8	273 21.6	. . 33.1	259 18.8	. . 26.1	211 01.0	. . 29.7	Pollux	243 23.8	N27 58.7
04	134 08.9	251 14.0	30.5	288 22.6	33.7	274 20.7	26.3	226 03.2	29.7	Procyon	244 56.4	N 5 10.6
05	149 11.3	266 13.2	31.1	303 23.6	34.3	289 22.7	26.4	241 05.3	29.7			
06	164 13.8	281 12.4	S20 31.8	318 24.5	S 9 34.9	304 24.7	S14 26.6	256 07.5	S22 29.7	Rasalhague	96 04.0	N12 33.1
07	179 16.3	296 11.5	32.5	333 25.5	35.4	319 26.6	26.7	271 09.6	29.8	Regulus	207 40.3	N11 52.7
T 08	194 18.7	311 10.7	33.1	348 26.5	36.0	334 28.6	26.9	286 11.8	29.8	Rigel	281 08.8	S 8 11.0
U 09	209 21.2	326 09.9	. . 33.8	3 27.5	. . 36.6	349 30.6	. . 27.0	301 13.9	. . 29.8	Rigil Kent.	139 48.2	S60 54.1
E 10	224 23.7	341 09.1	34.4	18 28.5	37.1	4 32.5	27.2	316 16.1	29.8	Sabik	102 09.5	S15 44.6
S 11	239 26.1	356 08.3	35.1	33 29.4	37.7	19 34.5	27.3	331 18.3	29.8			
D 12	254 28.6	11 07.4	S20 35.7	48 30.4	S 9 38.3	34 36.5	S14 27.5	346 20.4	S22 29.8	Schedar	349 36.7	N56 38.3
13	269 31.0	26 06.6	36.4	63 31.4	38.9	49 38.4	27.6	1 22.6	29.8	Shaula	96 18.3	S37 06.8
A 14	284 33.5	41 05.8	37.0	78 32.4	39.4	64 40.4	27.8	16 24.7	29.8	Sirius	258 30.8	S16 44.5
Y 15	299 36.0	56 05.0	. . 37.7	93 33.4	. . 40.0	79 42.4	. . 27.9	31 26.9	. . 29.8	Spica	158 28.3	S11 15.0
16	314 38.4	71 04.1	38.3	108 34.3	40.6	94 44.3	28.1	46 29.0	29.8	Suhail	222 50.0	S43 30.1
17	329 40.9	86 03.3	39.0	123 35.3	41.1	109 46.3	28.2	61 31.2	29.8			
18	344 43.4	101 02.5	S20 39.6	138 36.3	S 9 41.7	124 48.3	S14 28.4	76 33.3	S22 29.8	Vega	80 37.3	N38 48.3
19	359 45.8	116 01.7	40.3	153 37.3	42.3	139 50.3	28.5	91 35.5	29.8	Zuben'ubi	137 02.4	S16 06.7
20	14 48.3	131 00.8	40.9	168 38.3	42.9	154 52.2	28.7	106 37.6	29.8			
21	29 50.8	146 00.0	. . 41.6	183 39.2	. . 43.4	169 54.2	. . 28.8	121 39.8	. . 29.9			
22	44 53.2	160 59.2	42.2	198 40.2	44.0	184 56.2	29.0	136 41.9	29.9			
23	59 55.7	175 58.4	42.9	213 41.2	44.6	199 58.1	29.1	151 44.1	29.9			
Mer. Pass.	h m 19 04.9	*v* −0.8	*d* 0.7	*v* 1.0	*d* 0.6	*v* 2.0	*d* 0.2	*v* 2.2	*d* 0.0			

	SHA	Mer. Pass.
	° ′	h m
Venus	118 36.9	11 14
Mars	154 55.2	8 48
Jupiter	140 25.8	9 45
Saturn	92 03.0	12 58

UT	SUN GHA	SUN Dec	MOON GHA	v	MOON Dec	d	HP
d h	° ′	° ′	° ′	′	° ′	′	′
3 00	182 34.6	S22 05.4	11 25.5	5.2	N15 41.9	8.1	61.0
01	197 34.3	05.7	25 49.7	5.1	15 50.0	8.0	61.0
02	212 34.1	06.1	40 13.8	5.0	15 58.0	8.0	61.1
03	227 33.8	. . 06.4	54 37.8	4.9	16 06.0	7.8	61.1
04	242 33.6	06.8	69 01.7	4.9	16 13.8	7.7	61.1
05	257 33.3	07.1	83 25.6	4.8	16 21.5	7.6	61.1
06	272 33.1	S22 07.5	97 49.4	4.7	N16 29.1	7.5	61.1
07	287 32.9	07.8	112 13.1	4.7	16 36.6	7.4	61.1
S 08	302 32.6	08.2	126 36.8	4.6	16 44.0	7.2	61.2
U 09	317 32.4	. . 08.5	141 00.4	4.5	16 51.2	7.2	61.2
N 10	332 32.1	08.9	155 23.9	4.5	16 58.4	7.0	61.2
D 11	347 31.9	09.2	169 47.4	4.4	17 05.4	6.9	61.2
A 12	2 31.6	S22 09.5	184 10.8	4.3	N17 12.3	6.7	61.2
Y 13	17 31.4	09.9	198 34.1	4.3	17 19.0	6.7	61.2
14	32 31.1	10.2	212 57.4	4.2	17 25.7	6.5	61.2
15	47 30.9	. . 10.6	227 20.6	4.1	17 32.2	6.4	61.2
16	62 30.6	10.9	241 43.7	4.1	17 38.6	6.3	61.3
17	77 30.4	11.3	256 06.8	4.1	17 44.9	6.1	61.3
18	92 30.1	S22 11.6	270 29.9	3.9	N17 51.0	6.0	61.3
19	107 29.9	11.9	284 52.8	4.0	17 57.0	5.9	61.3
20	122 29.6	12.3	299 15.8	3.8	18 02.9	5.7	61.3
21	137 29.4	. . 12.6	313 38.6	3.8	18 08.6	5.7	61.3
22	152 29.1	13.0	328 01.4	3.8	18 14.3	5.4	61.3
23	167 28.9	13.3	342 24.2	3.7	18 19.7	5.4	61.3
4 00	182 28.6	S22 13.6	356 46.9	3.7	N18 25.1	5.2	61.3
01	197 28.4	14.0	11 09.6	3.6	18 30.3	5.0	61.3
02	212 28.1	14.3	25 32.2	3.6	18 35.3	5.0	61.3
03	227 27.9	. . 14.6	39 54.8	3.6	18 40.3	4.8	61.3
04	242 27.6	15.0	54 17.4	3.5	18 45.1	4.6	61.3
05	257 27.4	15.3	68 39.9	3.4	18 49.7	4.5	61.3
06	272 27.1	S22 15.6	83 02.3	3.5	N18 54.2	4.4	61.3
07	287 26.9	16.0	97 24.8	3.4	18 58.6	4.2	61.3
08	302 26.6	16.3	111 47.2	3.3	19 02.8	4.1	61.3
M 09	317 26.4	. . 16.6	126 09.5	3.3	19 06.9	3.9	61.3
O 10	332 26.1	17.0	140 31.8	3.3	19 10.8	3.8	61.3
N 11	347 25.9	17.3	154 54.1	3.3	19 14.6	3.6	61.3
D 12	2 25.6	S22 17.6	169 16.4	3.3	N19 18.2	3.5	61.3
A 13	17 25.4	17.9	183 38.7	3.2	19 21.7	3.4	61.3
Y 14	32 25.1	18.3	198 00.9	3.2	19 25.1	3.2	61.3
15	47 24.9	. . 18.6	212 23.1	3.2	19 28.3	3.0	61.3
16	62 24.6	18.9	226 45.3	3.1	19 31.3	3.0	61.3
17	77 24.3	19.2	241 07.4	3.2	19 34.3	2.7	61.3
18	92 24.1	S22 19.6	255 29.6	3.1	N19 37.0	2.6	61.3
19	107 23.8	19.9	269 51.7	3.1	19 39.6	2.5	61.3
20	122 23.6	20.2	284 13.8	3.2	19 42.1	2.3	61.3
21	137 23.3	. . 20.5	298 36.0	3.1	19 44.4	2.1	61.3
22	152 23.1	20.8	312 58.1	3.1	19 46.5	2.0	61.3
23	167 22.8	21.2	327 20.2	3.1	19 48.5	1.9	61.3
5 00	182 22.6	S22 21.5	341 42.3	3.0	N19 50.4	1.7	61.3
01	197 22.3	21.8	356 04.3	3.1	19 52.1	1.5	61.3
02	212 22.0	22.1	10 26.4	3.1	19 53.6	1.4	61.3
03	227 21.8	. . 22.4	24 48.5	3.1	19 55.0	1.3	61.2
04	242 21.5	22.8	39 10.6	3.1	19 56.3	1.1	61.2
05	257 21.3	23.1	53 32.7	3.2	19 57.4	0.9	61.2
06	272 21.0	S22 23.4	67 54.9	3.1	N19 58.3	0.8	61.2
07	287 20.8	23.7	82 17.0	3.1	19 59.1	0.6	61.2
T 08	302 20.5	24.0	96 39.1	3.2	19 59.7	0.5	61.2
U 09	317 20.2	. . 24.3	111 01.3	3.1	20 00.2	0.3	61.2
E 10	332 20.0	24.6	125 23.4	3.2	20 00.5	0.2	61.2
S 11	347 19.7	24.9	139 45.6	3.2	20 00.7	0.1	61.1
D 12	2 19.5	S22 25.2	154 07.8	3.3	N20 00.8	0.2	61.1
A 13	17 19.2	25.6	168 30.1	3.2	20 00.6	0.2	61.1
Y 14	32 18.9	25.9	182 52.3	3.3	20 00.4	0.5	61.1
15	47 18.7	. . 26.2	197 14.6	3.3	19 59.9	0.5	61.1
16	62 18.4	26.5	211 36.9	3.4	19 59.4	0.8	61.1
17	77 18.2	26.8	225 59.3	3.3	19 58.6	0.8	61.0
18	92 17.9	S22 27.1	240 21.6	3.4	N19 57.8	1.0	61.0
19	107 17.6	27.4	254 44.0	3.5	19 56.8	1.2	61.0
20	122 17.4	27.7	269 06.5	3.5	19 55.6	1.3	61.0
21	137 17.1	. . 28.0	283 29.0	3.5	19 54.3	1.5	61.0
22	152 16.9	28.3	297 51.5	3.6	19 52.8	1.6	61.0
23	167 16.6	28.6	312 14.1	3.6	N19 51.2	1.8	60.9
	SD 16.3	d 0.3	SD 16.7		16.7		16.7

Lat.	Twilight Naut.	Twilight Civil	Sunrise	Moonrise 3	Moonrise 4	Moonrise 5	Moonrise 6
°	h m	h m	h m	h m	h m	h m	h m
N 72	07 59	10 05	■	12 59	□	□	□
N 70	07 42	09 21	■	13 54	13 54	14 20	16 15
68	07 28	08 52	10 56	14 28	14 50	15 40	17 06
66	07 16	08 30	09 58	14 52	15 24	16 18	17 38
64	07 07	08 13	09 24	15 12	15 49	16 45	18 02
62	06 58	07 58	09 00	15 27	16 08	17 06	18 21
60	06 50	07 46	08 41	15 41	16 24	17 23	18 36
N 58	06 44	07 35	08 25	15 52	16 38	17 37	18 49
56	06 38	07 26	08 12	16 02	16 49	17 49	19 00
54	06 32	07 17	08 00	16 11	17 00	18 00	19 10
52	06 27	07 10	07 50	16 19	17 09	18 09	19 19
50	06 22	07 03	07 41	16 26	17 17	18 18	19 27
45	06 11	06 48	07 21	16 41	17 35	18 36	19 44
N 40	06 02	06 35	07 06	16 54	17 49	18 51	19 57
35	05 53	06 24	06 52	17 05	18 01	19 03	20 09
30	05 45	06 15	06 41	17 14	18 12	19 14	20 19
20	05 29	05 57	06 21	17 31	18 30	19 33	20 37
N 10	05 14	05 40	06 03	17 45	18 46	19 49	20 52
0	04 58	05 24	05 47	17 59	19 01	20 04	21 06
S 10	04 40	05 07	05 30	18 12	19 16	20 20	21 20
20	04 19	04 48	05 12	18 27	19 33	20 36	21 35
30	03 51	04 24	04 51	18 44	19 51	20 55	21 53
35	03 34	04 10	04 39	18 54	20 02	21 06	22 03
40	03 12	03 53	04 25	19 05	20 15	21 19	22 14
45	02 44	03 31	04 08	19 18	20 29	21 33	22 28
S 50	02 03	03 04	03 47	19 34	20 48	21 52	22 45
52	01 40	02 50	03 37	19 42	20 56	22 00	22 52
54	01 07	02 34	03 26	19 50	21 06	22 10	23 01
56	////	02 14	03 13	20 00	21 17	22 21	23 11
58	////	01 49	02 57	20 11	21 29	22 33	23 22
S 60	////	01 14	02 39	20 23	21 43	22 47	23 34

Lat.	Sunset	Twilight Civil	Twilight Naut.	Moonset 3	Moonset 4	Moonset 5	Moonset 6
°	h m	h m	h m	h m	h m	h m	h m
N 72	■	13 35	15 41	10 13	□	□	□
N 70	■	14 19	15 58	09 19	11 30	13 16	13 32
68	12 44	14 48	16 12	08 46	10 34	11 56	12 40
66	13 42	15 10	16 24	08 23	10 01	11 18	12 08
64	14 16	15 28	16 34	08 04	09 36	10 51	11 44
62	14 40	15 42	16 42	07 49	09 17	10 30	11 25
60	14 59	15 54	16 50	07 36	09 01	10 14	11 09
N 58	15 15	16 05	16 56	07 25	08 48	09 59	10 56
56	15 28	16 14	17 03	07 16	08 36	09 47	10 44
54	15 40	16 23	17 08	07 07	08 26	09 36	10 34
52	15 50	16 30	17 13	07 00	08 17	09 27	10 25
50	16 00	16 37	17 18	06 53	08 09	09 18	10 17
45	16 19	16 52	17 29	06 38	07 52	09 00	10 00
N 40	16 35	17 05	17 39	06 27	07 38	08 45	09 46
35	16 48	17 16	17 47	06 16	07 26	08 33	09 33
30	17 00	17 26	17 56	06 08	07 16	08 22	09 23
20	17 20	17 44	18 11	05 52	06 58	08 03	09 05
N 10	17 37	18 00	18 26	05 39	06 43	07 47	08 49
0	17 54	18 16	18 42	05 27	06 28	07 31	08 34
S 10	18 11	18 34	19 00	05 14	06 14	07 16	08 19
20	18 29	18 53	19 22	05 01	05 58	07 00	08 03
30	18 50	19 17	19 50	04 46	05 41	06 41	07 45
35	19 02	19 31	20 07	04 37	05 30	06 30	07 34
40	19 16	19 48	20 29	04 27	05 19	06 17	07 22
45	19 33	20 10	20 58	04 16	05 05	06 02	07 07
S 50	19 54	20 37	21 39	04 02	04 48	05 44	06 49
52	20 04	20 51	22 03	03 55	04 40	05 35	06 41
54	20 16	21 08	22 36	03 48	04 31	05 25	06 31
56	20 29	21 27	////	03 40	04 21	05 15	06 20
58	20 44	21 53	////	03 31	04 10	05 02	06 08
S 60	21 02	22 29	////	03 20	03 57	04 48	05 54

Day	SUN Eqn. of Time 00^h	SUN Eqn. of Time 12^h	SUN Mer. Pass.	MOON Mer. Pass. Upper	MOON Mer. Pass. Lower	MOON Age	MOON Phase
d	m s	m s	h m	h m	h m	d	%
3	10 19	10 07	11 50	24 13	11 43	15	100
4	09 55	09 43	11 50	00 13	12 45	16	99
5	09 31	09 18	11 51	01 16	13 48	17	95

UT (d h)	ARIES GHA	VENUS −3·9 GHA	VENUS Dec	MARS +1·6 GHA	MARS Dec	JUPITER −1·7 GHA	JUPITER Dec	SATURN +0·5 GHA	SATURN Dec
	° ′	° ′	° ′	° ′	° ′	° ′	° ′	° ′	° ′
6 00	74 58.2	190 57.5	S20 43.5	228 42.2	S 9 45.1	215 00.1	S14 29.3	166 46.2	S22 29.9
01	90 00.6	205 56.7	44.1	243 43.1	45.7	230 02.1	29.5	181 48.4	29.9
02	105 03.1	220 55.9	44.8	258 44.1	46.3	245 04.0	29.6	196 50.5	29.9
03	120 05.5	235 55.0	. . 45.4	273 45.1	. . 46.8	260 06.0	. . 29.8	211 52.7	. . 29.9
04	135 08.0	250 54.2	46.1	288 46.1	47.4	275 08.0	29.9	226 54.8	29.9
05	150 10.5	265 53.4	46.7	303 47.1	48.0	290 09.9	30.1	241 57.0	29.9
06	165 12.9	280 52.5	S20 47.3	318 48.0	S 9 48.6	305 11.9	S14 30.2	256 59.1	S22 29.9
WEDNESDAY 07	180 15.4	295 51.7	48.0	333 49.0	49.1	320 13.9	30.4	272 01.3	29.9
08	195 17.9	310 50.9	48.6	348 50.0	49.7	335 15.8	30.5	287 03.4	29.9
09	210 20.3	325 50.0	. . 49.2	3 51.0	. . 50.3	350 17.8	. . 30.7	302 05.6	. . 29.9
10	225 22.8	340 49.2	49.9	18 52.0	50.8	5 19.8	30.8	317 07.7	29.9
11	240 25.3	355 48.4	50.5	33 52.9	51.4	20 21.8	31.0	332 09.9	30.0
12	255 27.7	10 47.5	S20 51.1	48 53.9	S 9 52.0	35 23.7	S14 31.1	347 12.0	S22 30.0
13	270 30.2	25 46.7	51.8	63 54.9	52.5	50 25.7	31.3	2 14.2	30.0
14	285 32.7	40 45.9	52.4	78 55.9	53.1	65 27.7	31.4	17 16.3	30.0
15	300 35.1	55 45.0	. . 53.0	93 56.8	. . 53.7	80 29.6	. . 31.6	32 18.5	. . 30.0
16	315 37.6	70 44.2	53.6	108 57.8	54.2	95 31.6	31.7	47 20.6	30.0
17	330 40.0	85 43.4	54.3	123 58.8	54.8	110 33.6	31.9	62 22.8	30.0
18	345 42.5	100 42.5	S20 54.9	138 59.8	S 9 55.4	125 35.5	S14 32.0	77 24.9	S22 30.0
19	0 45.0	115 41.7	55.5	154 00.8	55.9	140 37.5	32.2	92 27.1	30.0
20	15 47.4	130 40.9	56.1	169 01.7	56.5	155 39.5	32.3	107 29.2	30.0
21	30 49.9	145 40.0	. . 56.7	184 02.7	. . 57.1	170 41.5	. . 32.5	122 31.4	. . 30.0
22	45 52.4	160 39.2	57.4	199 03.7	57.6	185 43.4	32.6	137 33.5	30.0
23	60 54.8	175 38.3	58.0	214 04.7	58.2	200 45.4	32.8	152 35.7	30.0
7 00	75 57.3	190 37.5	S20 58.6	229 05.6	S 9 58.8	215 47.4	S14 32.9	167 37.8	S22 30.0
01	90 59.8	205 36.7	59.2	244 06.6	59.3	230 49.3	33.1	182 40.0	30.1
02	106 02.2	220 35.8	20 59.8	259 07.6	9 59.9	245 51.3	33.2	197 42.1	30.1
03	121 04.7	235 35.0	21 00.4	274 08.6	10 00.5	260 53.3	. . 33.4	212 44.3	. . 30.1
04	136 07.2	250 34.1	01.1	289 09.5	01.0	275 55.3	33.5	227 46.4	30.1
05	151 09.6	265 33.3	01.7	304 10.5	01.6	290 57.2	33.7	242 48.6	30.1
06	166 12.1	280 32.5	S21 02.3	319 11.5	S10 02.2	305 59.2	S14 33.8	257 50.7	S22 30.1
THURSDAY 07	181 14.5	295 31.6	02.9	334 12.5	02.7	321 01.2	34.0	272 52.9	30.1
08	196 17.0	310 30.8	03.5	349 13.4	03.3	336 03.1	34.1	287 55.1	30.1
09	211 19.5	325 29.9	. . 04.1	4 14.4	. . 03.9	351 05.1	. . 34.3	302 57.2	. . 30.1
10	226 21.9	340 29.1	04.7	19 15.4	04.4	6 07.1	34.4	317 59.4	30.1
11	241 24.4	355 28.2	05.3	34 16.4	05.0	21 09.1	34.6	333 01.5	30.1
12	256 26.9	10 27.4	S21 05.9	49 17.4	S10 05.6	36 11.0	S14 34.7	348 03.7	S22 30.1
13	271 29.3	25 26.5	06.5	64 18.3	06.1	51 13.0	34.9	3 05.8	30.1
14	286 31.8	40 25.7	07.1	79 19.3	06.7	66 15.0	35.0	18 08.0	30.1
15	301 34.3	55 24.9	. . 07.7	94 20.3	. . 07.3	81 16.9	. . 35.2	33 10.1	. . 30.1
16	316 36.7	70 24.0	08.3	109 21.3	07.8	96 18.9	35.3	48 12.3	30.2
17	331 39.2	85 23.2	08.9	124 22.2	08.4	111 20.9	35.5	63 14.4	30.2
18	346 41.7	100 22.3	S21 09.5	139 23.2	S10 09.0	126 22.9	S14 35.6	78 16.6	S22 30.2
19	1 44.1	115 21.5	10.1	154 24.2	09.5	141 24.8	35.8	93 18.7	30.2
20	16 46.6	130 20.6	10.7	169 25.2	10.1	156 26.8	35.9	108 20.9	30.2
21	31 49.0	145 19.8	. . 11.3	184 26.1	. . 10.7	171 28.8	. . 36.1	123 23.0	. . 30.2
22	46 51.5	160 18.9	11.9	199 27.1	11.2	186 30.7	36.2	138 25.2	30.2
23	61 54.0	175 18.1	12.5	214 28.1	11.8	201 32.7	36.4	153 27.3	30.2
8 00	76 56.4	190 17.2	S21 13.1	229 29.1	S10 12.4	216 34.7	S14 36.5	168 29.5	S22 30.2
01	91 58.9	205 16.4	13.7	244 30.0	12.9	231 36.7	36.7	183 31.6	30.2
02	107 01.4	220 15.5	14.3	259 31.0	13.5	246 38.6	36.8	198 33.8	30.2
03	122 03.8	235 14.7	. . 14.9	274 32.0	. . 14.1	261 40.6	. . 37.0	213 35.9	. . 30.2
04	137 06.3	250 13.8	15.4	289 33.0	14.6	276 42.6	37.1	228 38.1	30.2
05	152 08.8	265 13.0	16.0	304 33.9	15.2	291 44.6	37.3	243 40.2	30.2
06	167 11.2	280 12.1	S21 16.6	319 34.9	S10 15.7	306 46.5	S14 37.4	258 42.3	S22 30.2
07	182 13.7	295 11.2	17.2	334 35.9	16.3	321 48.5	37.6	273 44.5	30.3
08	197 16.1	310 10.4	17.8	349 36.9	16.9	336 50.5	37.7	288 46.6	30.3
FRIDAY 09	212 18.6	325 09.5	. . 18.4	4 37.8	. . 17.4	351 52.4	. . 37.9	303 48.8	. . 30.3
10	227 21.1	340 08.7	18.9	19 38.8	18.0	6 54.4	38.0	318 50.9	30.3
11	242 23.5	355 07.8	19.5	34 39.8	18.6	21 56.4	38.2	333 53.1	30.3
12	257 26.0	10 07.0	S21 20.1	49 40.8	S10 19.1	36 58.4	S14 38.3	348 55.2	S22 30.3
13	272 28.5	25 06.1	20.7	64 41.7	19.7	52 00.3	38.4	3 57.4	30.3
14	287 30.9	40 05.3	21.3	79 42.7	20.2	67 02.3	38.6	18 59.5	30.3
15	302 33.4	55 04.4	. . 21.8	94 43.7	. . 20.8	82 04.3	. . 38.7	34 01.7	. . 30.3
16	317 35.9	70 03.5	22.4	109 44.6	21.4	97 06.3	38.9	49 03.8	30.3
17	332 38.3	85 02.7	23.0	124 45.6	21.9	112 08.2	39.0	64 06.0	30.3
18	347 40.8	100 01.8	S21 23.6	139 46.6	S10 22.5	127 10.2	S14 39.2	79 08.1	S22 30.3
19	2 43.3	115 01.0	24.1	154 47.6	23.1	142 12.2	39.3	94 10.3	30.3
20	17 45.7	130 00.1	24.7	169 48.5	23.6	157 14.2	39.5	109 12.4	30.3
21	32 48.2	144 59.2	. . 25.3	184 49.5	. . 24.2	172 16.1	. . 39.6	124 14.6	. . 30.3
22	47 50.6	159 58.4	25.8	199 50.5	24.7	187 18.1	39.8	139 16.7	30.4
23	62 53.1	174 57.5	26.4	214 51.5	25.3	202 20.1	39.9	154 18.9	30.4
Mer. Pass.	h m 18 53.1	*v* −0.8	*d* 0.6	*v* 1.0	*d* 0.6	*v* 2.0	*d* 0.1	*v* 2.2	*d* 0.0

STARS Name	SHA	Dec
	° ′	° ′
Acamar	315 15.7	S40 14.2
Achernar	335 24.2	S57 09.1
Acrux	173 06.0	S63 11.5
Adhara	255 09.8	S28 59.8
Aldebaran	290 45.6	N16 32.5
Alioth	166 18.4	N55 51.6
Alkaid	152 56.9	N49 13.4
Al Na'ir	27 40.1	S46 52.6
Alnilam	275 43.0	S 1 11.6
Alphard	217 53.0	S 8 44.2
Alphecca	126 08.8	N26 39.4
Alpheratz	357 40.2	N29 11.5
Altair	62 05.6	N 8 55.1
Ankaa	353 12.6	S42 12.8
Antares	112 22.9	S26 28.0
Arcturus	145 53.3	N19 05.5
Atria	107 22.6	S69 03.3
Avior	234 16.3	S59 33.9
Bellatrix	278 28.4	N 6 21.8
Betelgeuse	270 57.7	N 7 24.4
Canopus	263 54.3	S52 42.4
Capella	280 29.5	N46 00.7
Deneb	49 29.7	N45 21.0
Denebola	182 30.7	N14 28.3
Diphda	348 52.7	S17 53.5
Dubhe	193 48.1	N61 39.0
Elnath	278 08.4	N28 37.1
Eltanin	90 45.3	N51 29.4
Enif	33 44.3	N 9 57.6
Fomalhaut	15 20.7	S29 31.8
Gacrux	171 57.7	S57 12.4
Gienah	175 49.3	S17 38.3
Hadar	148 44.0	S60 27.2
Hamal	327 57.1	N23 32.8
Kaus Aust.	83 40.2	S34 22.4
Kochab	137 21.3	N74 04.9
Markab	13 35.3	N15 18.2
Menkar	314 11.6	N 4 09.4
Menkent	148 04.3	S36 27.1
Miaplacidus	221 38.5	S69 47.2
Mirfak	308 35.5	N49 55.4
Nunki	75 54.9	S26 16.3
Peacock	53 15.0	S56 40.7
Pollux	243 23.8	N27 58.7
Procyon	244 56.3	N 5 10.6
Rasalhague	96 04.0	N12 33.1
Regulus	207 40.2	N11 52.7
Rigel	281 08.8	S 8 11.0
Rigil Kent.	139 48.1	S60 54.1
Sabik	102 09.4	S15 44.6
Schedar	349 36.7	N56 38.3
Shaula	96 18.2	S37 06.8
Sirius	258 30.7	S16 44.6
Spica	158 28.3	S11 15.1
Suhail	222 50.0	S43 30.1
Vega	80 37.3	N38 48.3
Zuben'ubi	137 02.4	S16 06.7

	SHA	Mer. Pass.
	° ′	h m
Venus	114 40.2	11 18
Mars	153 08.3	8 43
Jupiter	139 50.1	9 36
Saturn	91 40.6	12 48

UT	SUN GHA	SUN Dec	MOON GHA	*v*	MOON Dec	*d*	HP
d h	° ′	° ′	° ′	′	° ′	′	′
6 00	182 16.3	S22 28.9	326 36.7	3.6	N19 49.4	1.9	60.9
01	197 16.1	29.2	340 59.3	3.7	19 47.5	2.0	60.9
02	212 15.8	29.5	355 22.0	3.8	19 45.5	2.2	60.9
03	227 15.5	. . 29.8	9 44.8	3.8	19 43.3	2.3	60.8
04	242 15.3	30.1	24 07.6	3.8	19 41.0	2.5	60.8
05	257 15.0	30.4	38 30.4	3.9	19 38.5	2.6	60.8
06	272 14.8	S22 30.7	52 53.3	4.0	N19 35.9	2.8	60.8
W 07	287 14.5	31.0	67 16.3	4.0	19 33.1	2.9	60.8
E 08	302 14.2	31.3	81 39.3	4.1	19 30.2	3.0	60.7
D 09	317 14.0	. . 31.6	96 02.4	4.1	19 27.2	3.2	60.7
N 10	332 13.7	31.9	110 25.5	4.2	19 24.0	3.3	60.7
E 11	347 13.4	32.2	124 48.7	4.2	19 20.7	3.5	60.7
S 12	2 13.2	S22 32.5	139 11.9	4.4	N19 17.2	3.6	60.6
D 13	17 12.9	32.7	153 35.3	4.4	19 13.6	3.7	60.6
A 14	32 12.6	33.0	167 58.7	4.4	19 09.9	3.9	60.6
Y 15	47 12.4	. . 33.3	182 22.1	4.5	19 06.0	3.9	60.5
16	62 12.1	33.6	196 45.6	4.6	19 02.1	4.2	60.5
17	77 11.8	33.9	211 09.2	4.7	18 57.9	4.2	60.5
18	92 11.6	S22 34.2	225 32.9	4.7	N18 53.7	4.4	60.5
19	107 11.3	34.5	239 56.6	4.8	18 49.3	4.5	60.4
20	122 11.0	34.8	254 20.4	4.9	18 44.8	4.6	60.4
21	137 10.8	. . 35.0	268 44.3	5.0	18 40.2	4.8	60.4
22	152 10.5	35.3	283 08.3	5.0	18 35.4	4.9	60.4
23	167 10.2	35.6	297 32.3	5.1	18 30.5	5.0	60.3
7 00	182 10.0	S22 35.9	311 56.4	5.2	N18 25.5	5.1	60.3
01	197 09.7	36.2	326 20.6	5.3	18 20.4	5.3	60.3
02	212 09.4	36.4	340 44.9	5.4	18 15.1	5.4	60.2
03	227 09.2	. . 36.7	355 09.3	5.4	18 09.7	5.4	60.2
04	242 08.9	37.0	9 33.7	5.5	18 04.3	5.6	60.2
05	257 08.6	37.3	23 58.2	5.6	17 58.7	5.8	60.1
06	272 08.4	S22 37.6	38 22.8	5.7	N17 52.9	5.8	60.1
T 07	287 08.1	37.8	52 47.5	5.8	17 47.1	6.0	60.1
H 08	302 07.8	38.1	67 12.3	5.8	17 41.1	6.0	60.0
U 09	317 07.6	. . 38.4	81 37.1	5.9	17 35.1	6.2	60.0
R 10	332 07.3	38.7	96 02.0	6.1	17 28.9	6.3	60.0
S 11	347 07.0	38.9	110 27.1	6.1	17 22.6	6.4	59.9
D 12	2 06.8	S22 39.2	124 52.2	6.2	N17 16.2	6.5	59.9
A 13	17 06.5	39.5	139 17.4	6.3	17 09.7	6.6	59.9
Y 14	32 06.2	39.8	153 42.7	6.3	17 03.1	6.7	59.8
15	47 05.9	. . 40.0	168 08.0	6.5	16 56.4	6.8	59.8
16	62 05.7	40.3	182 33.5	6.5	16 49.6	6.9	59.8
17	77 05.4	40.6	196 59.0	6.7	16 42.7	7.1	59.7
18	92 05.1	S22 40.8	211 24.7	6.7	N16 35.6	7.1	59.7
19	107 04.9	41.1	225 50.4	6.8	16 28.5	7.2	59.7
20	122 04.6	41.4	240 16.2	6.9	16 21.3	7.3	59.6
21	137 04.3	. . 41.6	254 42.1	7.0	16 14.0	7.4	59.6
22	152 04.0	41.9	269 08.1	7.1	16 06.6	7.5	59.6
23	167 03.8	42.2	283 34.2	7.2	15 59.1	7.6	59.5
8 00	182 03.5	S22 42.4	298 00.4	7.3	N15 51.5	7.7	59.5
01	197 03.2	42.7	312 26.7	7.4	15 43.8	7.7	59.5
02	212 02.9	43.0	326 53.1	7.4	15 36.1	7.9	59.4
03	227 02.7	. . 43.2	341 19.5	7.6	15 28.2	7.9	59.4
04	242 02.4	43.5	355 46.1	7.6	15 20.3	8.0	59.4
05	257 02.1	43.7	10 12.7	7.7	15 12.3	8.2	59.3
06	272 01.9	S22 44.0	24 39.4	7.8	N15 04.1	8.2	59.3
07	287 01.6	44.3	39 06.2	8.0	14 55.9	8.2	59.3
08	302 01.3	44.5	53 33.2	8.0	14 47.7	8.4	59.2
F 09	317 01.0	. . 44.8	68 00.2	8.0	14 39.3	8.4	59.2
R 10	332 00.8	45.0	82 27.2	8.2	14 30.9	8.5	59.1
I 11	347 00.5	45.3	96 54.4	8.3	14 22.4	8.6	59.1
D 12	2 00.2	S22 45.5	111 21.7	8.4	N14 13.8	8.7	59.1
A 13	16 59.9	45.8	125 49.1	8.4	14 05.1	8.7	59.0
Y 14	31 59.7	46.0	140 16.5	8.6	13 56.4	8.8	59.0
15	46 59.4	. . 46.3	154 44.1	8.6	13 47.6	8.9	59.0
16	61 59.1	46.5	169 11.7	8.7	13 38.7	8.9	58.9
17	76 58.8	46.8	183 39.4	8.8	13 29.8	9.0	58.9
18	91 58.5	S22 47.0	198 07.2	8.9	N13 20.8	9.1	58.9
19	106 58.3	47.3	212 35.1	9.0	13 11.7	9.2	58.8
20	121 58.0	47.5	227 03.1	9.1	13 02.5	9.2	58.8
21	136 57.7	. . 47.8	241 31.2	9.1	12 53.3	9.2	58.7
22	151 57.4	48.0	255 59.3	9.3	12 44.1	9.4	58.7
23	166 57.2	48.3	270 27.6	9.3	N12 34.7	9.4	58.7
	SD 16.3	*d* 0.3	SD	16.5	16.3		16.1

Lat.	Twilight Naut.	Twilight Civil	Sunrise	Moonrise 6	Moonrise 7	Moonrise 8	Moonrise 9
°	h m	h m	h m	h m	h m	h m	h m
N 72	08 06	10 18	■	□	17 30	19 52	21 53
N 70	07 48	09 30	■	16 15	18 19	20 17	22 07
68	07 33	08 59	11 20	17 06	18 50	20 36	22 18
66	07 21	08 36	10 07	17 38	19 13	20 51	22 27
64	07 11	08 18	09 32	18 02	19 31	21 04	22 35
62	07 02	08 03	09 06	18 21	19 46	21 14	22 41
60	06 54	07 50	08 46	18 36	19 58	21 23	22 47
N 58	06 47	07 39	08 30	18 49	20 09	21 31	22 52
56	06 41	07 30	08 16	19 00	20 18	21 38	22 56
54	06 35	07 21	08 04	19 10	20 26	21 44	23 00
52	06 30	07 13	07 54	19 19	20 33	21 49	23 04
50	06 25	07 06	07 44	19 27	20 40	21 54	23 07
45	06 14	06 51	07 24	19 44	20 54	22 05	23 14
N 40	06 04	06 38	07 08	19 57	21 06	22 14	23 20
35	05 55	06 27	06 55	20 09	21 16	22 21	23 25
30	05 47	06 17	06 43	20 19	21 24	22 28	23 29
20	05 31	05 59	06 22	20 37	21 39	22 39	23 37
N 10	05 16	05 42	06 05	20 52	21 52	22 49	23 43
0	04 59	05 25	05 48	21 06	22 04	22 59	23 50
S 10	04 41	05 08	05 31	21 20	22 16	23 08	23 56
20	04 19	04 48	05 13	21 35	22 29	23 18	24 02
30	03 51	04 24	04 51	21 53	22 44	23 29	24 10
35	03 33	04 10	04 39	22 03	22 53	23 36	24 14
40	03 11	03 52	04 24	22 14	23 02	23 43	24 19
45	02 42	03 31	04 07	22 28	23 14	23 52	24 25
S 50	02 00	03 02	03 46	22 45	23 27	24 02	00 02
52	01 35	02 48	03 36	22 52	23 34	24 07	00 07
54	00 59	02 31	03 24	23 01	23 41	24 12	00 12
56	////	02 11	03 11	23 11	23 49	24 18	00 18
58	////	01 45	02 55	23 22	23 57	24 24	00 24
S 60	////	01 06	02 36	23 34	24 07	00 07	00 32

Lat.	Sunset	Twilight Civil	Twilight Naut.	Moonset 6	Moonset 7	Moonset 8	Moonset 9
°	h m	h m	h m	h m	h m	h m	h m
N 72	■	13 25	15 36	□	14 21	13 55	13 41
N 70	■	14 13	15 55	13 32	13 31	13 29	13 25
68	12 22	14 44	16 09	12 40	13 00	13 08	13 13
66	13 35	15 07	16 21	12 08	12 36	12 52	13 02
64	14 11	15 25	16 31	11 44	12 17	12 39	12 53
62	14 37	15 40	16 40	11 25	12 02	12 27	12 46
60	14 56	15 52	16 48	11 09	11 49	12 18	12 39
N 58	15 13	16 03	16 55	10 56	11 38	12 09	12 33
56	15 27	16 13	17 02	10 44	11 28	12 02	12 28
54	15 39	16 22	17 07	10 34	11 20	11 55	12 24
52	15 49	16 29	17 13	10 25	11 12	11 49	12 19
50	15 59	16 37	17 18	10 17	11 05	11 44	12 15
45	16 18	16 52	17 29	10 00	10 50	11 32	12 07
N 40	16 35	17 05	17 39	09 46	10 37	11 22	12 00
35	16 48	17 16	17 48	09 33	10 27	11 13	11 54
30	17 00	17 26	17 56	09 23	10 18	11 06	11 49
20	17 21	17 44	18 12	09 05	10 02	10 53	11 39
N 10	17 38	18 01	18 27	08 49	09 47	10 41	11 31
0	17 55	18 18	18 44	08 34	09 34	10 31	11 23
S 10	18 12	18 35	19 02	08 19	09 21	10 20	11 16
20	18 31	18 55	19 24	08 03	09 07	10 08	11 07
30	18 52	19 19	19 52	07 45	08 50	09 55	10 57
35	19 04	19 34	20 10	07 34	08 41	09 47	10 52
40	19 19	19 51	20 32	07 22	08 30	09 38	10 45
45	19 36	20 13	21 02	07 07	08 17	09 28	10 38
S 50	19 58	20 41	21 44	06 49	08 01	09 15	10 29
52	20 08	20 56	22 09	06 41	07 53	09 09	10 25
54	20 20	21 13	22 46	06 31	07 45	09 03	10 20
56	20 33	21 33	////	06 20	07 36	08 55	10 15
58	20 49	22 00	////	06 08	07 25	08 47	10 09
S 60	21 08	22 40	////	05 54	07 13	08 38	10 03

Day	SUN Eqn. of Time 00^h	SUN Eqn. of Time 12^h	SUN Mer. Pass.	MOON Mer. Pass. Upper	MOON Mer. Pass. Lower	Age	%	Phase
d	m s	m s	h m	h m	h m	d	%	
6	09 06	08 53	11 51	02 19	14 50	18	88	
7	08 40	08 28	11 52	03 20	15 49	19	80	
8	08 15	08 01	11 52	04 18	16 45	20	70	

	UT d h	ARIES GHA ° ′	VENUS −3·9 GHA ° ′	VENUS Dec ° ′	MARS +1·6 GHA ° ′	MARS Dec ° ′	JUPITER −1·7 GHA ° ′	JUPITER Dec ° ′	SATURN +0·5 GHA ° ′	SATURN Dec ° ′
	9 00	77 55.6	189 56.7	S21 27.0	229 52.4	S10 25.9	217 22.1	S14 40.1	169 21.0	S22 30.4
	01	92 58.0	204 55.8	27.5	244 53.4	26.4	232 24.0	40.2	184 23.2	30.4
	02	108 00.5	219 54.9	28.1	259 54.4	27.0	247 26.0	40.4	199 25.3	30.4
	03	123 03.0	234 54.1	. . 28.7	274 55.4	. . 27.5	262 28.0	. . 40.5	214 27.5	. . 30.4
	04	138 05.4	249 53.2	29.2	289 56.3	28.1	277 30.0	40.7	229 29.6	30.4
	05	153 07.9	264 52.4	29.8	304 57.3	28.7	292 31.9	40.8	244 31.8	30.4
	06	168 10.4	279 51.5	S21 30.3	319 58.3	S10 29.2	307 33.9	S14 41.0	259 33.9	S22 30.4
	07	183 12.8	294 50.6	30.9	334 59.2	29.8	322 35.9	41.1	274 36.1	30.4
S	08	198 15.3	309 49.8	31.5	350 00.2	30.4	337 37.9	41.3	289 38.2	30.4
A	09	213 17.8	324 48.9	. . 32.0	5 01.2	. . 30.9	352 39.8	. . 41.4	304 40.4	. . 30.4
T	10	228 20.2	339 48.0	32.6	20 02.2	31.5	7 41.8	41.6	319 42.5	30.4
U	11	243 22.7	354 47.2	33.1	35 03.1	32.0	22 43.8	41.7	334 44.7	30.4
R	12	258 25.1	9 46.3	S21 33.7	50 04.1	S10 32.6	37 45.8	S14 41.9	349 46.8	S22 30.4
D	13	273 27.6	24 45.4	34.2	65 05.1	33.2	52 47.7	42.0	4 49.0	30.4
A	14	288 30.1	39 44.6	34.8	80 06.0	33.7	67 49.7	42.1	19 51.1	30.5
Y	15	303 32.5	54 43.7	. . 35.3	95 07.0	. . 34.3	82 51.7	. . 42.3	34 53.3	. . 30.5
	16	318 35.0	69 42.8	35.9	110 08.0	34.8	97 53.7	42.4	49 55.4	30.5
	17	333 37.5	84 42.0	36.4	125 09.0	35.4	112 55.6	42.6	64 57.6	30.5
	18	348 39.9	99 41.1	S21 37.0	140 09.9	S10 35.9	127 57.6	S14 42.7	79 59.7	S22 30.5
	19	3 42.4	114 40.2	37.5	155 10.9	36.5	142 59.6	42.9	95 01.9	30.5
	20	18 44.9	129 39.3	38.0	170 11.9	37.1	158 01.6	43.0	110 04.0	30.5
	21	33 47.3	144 38.5	. . 38.6	185 12.8	. . 37.6	173 03.5	. . 43.2	125 06.2	. . 30.5
	22	48 49.8	159 37.6	39.1	200 13.8	38.2	188 05.5	43.3	140 08.3	30.5
	23	63 52.3	174 36.7	39.7	215 14.8	38.7	203 07.5	43.5	155 10.5	30.5
	10 00	78 54.7	189 35.9	S21 40.2	230 15.8	S10 39.3	218 09.5	S14 43.6	170 12.6	S22 30.5
	01	93 57.2	204 35.0	40.8	245 16.7	39.9	233 11.5	43.8	185 14.8	30.5
	02	108 59.6	219 34.1	41.3	260 17.7	40.4	248 13.4	43.9	200 16.9	30.5
	03	124 02.1	234 33.2	. . 41.8	275 18.7	. . 41.0	263 15.4	. . 44.1	215 19.1	. . 30.5
	04	139 04.6	249 32.4	42.4	290 19.6	41.5	278 17.4	44.2	230 21.2	30.5
	05	154 07.0	264 31.5	42.9	305 20.6	42.1	293 19.4	44.3	245 23.3	30.5
	06	169 09.5	279 30.6	S21 43.4	320 21.6	S10 42.6	308 21.3	S14 44.5	260 25.5	S22 30.5
	07	184 12.0	294 29.7	44.0	335 22.6	43.2	323 23.3	44.6	275 27.6	30.6
	08	199 14.4	309 28.9	44.5	350 23.5	43.8	338 25.3	44.8	290 29.8	30.6
S	09	214 16.9	324 28.0	. . 45.0	5 24.5	. . 44.3	353 27.3	. . 44.9	305 31.9	. . 30.6
U	10	229 19.4	339 27.1	45.5	20 25.5	44.9	8 29.2	45.1	320 34.1	30.6
N	11	244 21.8	354 26.2	46.1	35 26.4	45.4	23 31.2	45.2	335 36.2	30.6
D	12	259 24.3	9 25.4	S21 46.6	50 27.4	S10 46.0	38 33.2	S14 45.4	350 38.4	S22 30.6
A	13	274 26.7	24 24.5	47.1	65 28.4	46.5	53 35.2	45.5	5 40.5	30.6
Y	14	289 29.2	39 23.6	47.6	80 29.3	47.1	68 37.2	45.7	20 42.7	30.6
	15	304 31.7	54 22.7	. . 48.2	95 30.3	. . 47.7	83 39.1	. . 45.8	35 44.8	. . 30.6
	16	319 34.1	69 21.9	48.7	110 31.3	48.2	98 41.1	46.0	50 47.0	30.6
	17	334 36.6	84 21.0	49.2	125 32.3	48.8	113 43.1	46.1	65 49.1	30.6
	18	349 39.1	99 20.1	S21 49.7	140 33.2	S10 49.3	128 45.1	S14 46.2	80 51.3	S22 30.6
	19	4 41.5	114 19.2	50.3	155 34.2	49.9	143 47.1	46.4	95 53.4	30.6
	20	19 44.0	129 18.3	50.8	170 35.2	50.4	158 49.0	46.5	110 55.6	30.6
	21	34 46.5	144 17.5	. . 51.3	185 36.1	. . 51.0	173 51.0	. . 46.7	125 57.7	. . 30.6
	22	49 48.9	159 16.6	51.8	200 37.1	51.6	188 53.0	46.8	140 59.9	30.6
	23	64 51.4	174 15.7	52.3	215 38.1	52.1	203 55.0	47.0	156 02.0	30.6
	11 00	79 53.9	189 14.8	S21 52.8	230 39.0	S10 52.7	218 56.9	S14 47.1	171 04.2	S22 30.7
	01	94 56.3	204 13.9	53.3	245 40.0	53.2	233 58.9	47.3	186 06.3	30.7
	02	109 58.8	219 13.0	53.8	260 41.0	53.8	249 00.9	47.4	201 08.5	30.7
	03	125 01.2	234 12.2	. . 54.4	275 42.0	. . 54.3	264 02.9	. . 47.6	216 10.6	. . 30.7
	04	140 03.7	249 11.3	54.9	290 42.9	54.9	279 04.9	47.7	231 12.8	30.7
	05	155 06.2	264 10.4	55.4	305 43.9	55.4	294 06.8	47.8	246 14.9	30.7
	06	170 08.6	279 09.5	S21 55.9	320 44.9	S10 56.0	309 08.8	S14 48.0	261 17.0	S22 30.7
	07	185 11.1	294 08.6	56.4	335 45.8	56.5	324 10.8	48.1	276 19.2	30.7
	08	200 13.6	309 07.7	56.9	350 46.8	57.1	339 12.8	48.3	291 21.3	30.7
M	09	215 16.0	324 06.9	. . 57.4	5 47.8	. . 57.7	354 14.8	. . 48.4	306 23.5	. . 30.7
O	10	230 18.5	339 06.0	57.9	20 48.7	58.2	9 16.7	48.6	321 25.6	30.7
N	11	245 21.0	354 05.1	58.4	35 49.7	58.8	24 18.7	48.7	336 27.8	30.7
D	12	260 23.4	9 04.2	S21 58.9	50 50.7	S10 59.3	39 20.7	S14 48.9	351 29.9	S22 30.7
A	13	275 25.9	24 03.3	59.4	65 51.6	10 59.9	54 22.7	49.0	6 32.1	30.7
Y	14	290 28.3	39 02.4	21 59.9	80 52.6	11 00.4	69 24.7	49.1	21 34.2	30.7
	15	305 30.8	54 01.5	22 00.4	95 53.6	. . 01.0	84 26.6	. . 49.3	36 36.4	. . 30.7
	16	320 33.3	69 00.6	00.9	110 54.5	01.5	99 28.6	49.4	51 38.5	30.7
	17	335 35.7	83 59.7	01.4	125 55.5	02.1	114 30.6	49.6	66 40.7	30.7
	18	350 38.2	98 58.9	S22 01.9	140 56.5	S11 02.6	129 32.6	S14 49.7	81 42.8	S22 30.8
	19	5 40.7	113 58.0	02.4	155 57.4	03.2	144 34.6	49.9	96 45.0	30.8
	20	20 43.1	128 57.1	02.8	170 58.4	03.7	159 36.5	50.0	111 47.1	30.8
	21	35 45.6	143 56.2	. . 03.3	185 59.4	. . 04.3	174 38.5	. . 50.2	126 49.3	. . 30.8
	22	50 48.1	158 55.3	03.8	201 00.3	04.8	189 40.5	50.3	141 51.4	30.8
	23	65 50.5	173 54.4	04.3	216 01.3	05.4	204 42.5	50.4	156 53.6	30.8
	Mer. Pass.	h m 18 41.3	*v* −0.9	*d* 0.5	*v* 1.0	*d* 0.6	*v* 2.0	*d* 0.1	*v* 2.1	*d* 0.0

STARS

Name	SHA ° ′	Dec ° ′
Acamar	315 15.7	S40 14.3
Achernar	335 24.2	S57 09.1
Acrux	173 06.0	S63 11.5
Adhara	255 09.8	S28 59.9
Aldebaran	290 45.6	N16 32.5
Alioth	166 18.4	N55 51.6
Alkaid	152 56.9	N49 13.4
Al Na'ir	27 40.2	S46 52.6
Alnilam	275 43.0	S 1 11.6
Alphard	217 53.0	S 8 44.2
Alphecca	126 08.8	N26 39.4
Alpheratz	357 40.3	N29 11.5
Altair	62 05.6	N 8 55.1
Ankaa	353 12.6	S42 12.8
Antares	112 22.9	S26 28.0
Arcturus	145 53.3	N19 05.5
Atria	107 22.6	S69 03.3
Avior	234 16.3	S59 33.9
Bellatrix	278 28.4	N 6 21.8
Betelgeuse	270 57.7	N 7 24.4
Canopus	263 54.3	S52 42.4
Capella	280 29.5	N46 00.7
Deneb	49 29.7	N45 21.0
Denebola	182 30.7	N14 28.3
Diphda	348 52.7	S17 53.5
Dubhe	193 48.1	N61 39.0
Elnath	278 08.4	N28 37.1
Eltanin	90 45.3	N51 29.4
Enif	33 44.3	N 9 57.6
Fomalhaut	15 20.7	S29 31.8
Gacrux	171 57.6	S57 12.4
Gienah	175 49.3	S17 38.3
Hadar	148 44.0	S60 27.1
Hamal	327 57.1	N23 32.8
Kaus Aust.	83 40.2	S34 22.4
Kochab	137 21.3	N74 04.9
Markab	13 35.3	N15 18.2
Menkar	314 11.6	N 4 09.4
Menkent	148 04.3	S36 27.1
Miaplacidus	221 38.4	S69 47.2
Mirfak	308 35.5	N49 55.4
Nunki	75 54.9	S26 16.3
Peacock	53 15.0	S56 40.7
Pollux	243 23.8	N27 58.7
Procyon	244 56.3	N 5 10.6
Rasalhague	96 04.0	N12 33.1
Regulus	207 40.2	N11 52.7
Rigel	281 08.8	S 8 11.0
Rigil Kent.	139 48.1	S60 54.1
Sabik	102 09.4	S15 44.6
Schedar	349 36.8	N56 38.3
Shaula	96 18.2	S37 06.8
Sirius	258 30.7	S16 44.6
Spica	158 28.2	S11 15.1
Suhail	222 49.9	S43 30.1
Vega	80 37.3	N38 48.3
Zuben'ubi	137 02.4	S16 06.7

	SHA ° ′	Mer. Pass. h m
Venus	110 41.1	11 22
Mars	151 21.0	8 38
Jupiter	139 14.8	9 26
Saturn	91 17.9	12 37

UT		SUN GHA	SUN Dec	MOON GHA	*v*	MOON Dec	*d*	HP
	d h	° ′	° ′	° ′	′	° ′	′	′
	9 00	181 56.9	S22 48.5	284 55.9	9.4	N12 25.3	9.4	58.6
	01	196 56.6	48.8	299 24.3	9.5	12 15.9	9.5	58.6
	02	211 56.3	49.0	313 52.8	9.6	12 06.4	9.6	58.6
	03	226 56.0	. . 49.3	328 21.4	9.7	11 56.8	9.6	58.5
	04	241 55.8	49.5	342 50.1	9.8	11 47.2	9.7	58.5
	05	256 55.5	49.7	357 18.9	9.8	11 37.5	9.7	58.4
	06	271 55.2	S22 50.0	11 47.7	9.9	N11 27.8	9.8	58.4
	07	286 54.9	50.2	26 16.6	10.0	11 18.0	9.8	58.4
S	08	301 54.7	50.5	40 45.6	10.1	11 08.2	9.9	58.3
A	09	316 54.4	. . 50.7	55 14.7	10.2	10 58.3	9.9	58.3
T	10	331 54.1	50.9	69 43.9	10.2	10 48.4	10.0	58.3
U	11	346 53.8	51.2	84 13.1	10.3	10 38.4	10.0	58.2
R	12	1 53.5	S22 51.4	98 42.4	10.4	N10 28.4	10.0	58.2
D	13	16 53.3	51.6	113 11.8	10.5	10 18.4	10.1	58.2
A	14	31 53.0	51.9	127 41.3	10.6	10 08.3	10.2	58.1
Y	15	46 52.7	. . 52.1	142 10.9	10.6	9 58.1	10.1	58.1
	16	61 52.4	52.3	156 40.5	10.7	9 48.0	10.3	58.0
	17	76 52.1	52.6	171 10.2	10.8	9 37.7	10.2	58.0
	18	91 51.8	S22 52.8	185 40.0	10.8	N 9 27.5	10.3	58.0
	19	106 51.6	53.0	200 09.8	11.0	9 17.2	10.3	57.9
	20	121 51.3	53.3	214 39.8	11.0	9 06.9	10.4	57.9
	21	136 51.0	. . 53.5	229 09.8	11.0	8 56.5	10.4	57.9
	22	151 50.7	53.7	243 39.8	11.2	8 46.1	10.4	57.8
	23	166 50.4	53.9	258 10.0	11.2	8 35.7	10.5	57.8
	10 00	181 50.2	S22 54.2	272 40.2	11.3	N 8 25.2	10.5	57.8
	01	196 49.9	54.4	287 10.5	11.3	8 14.7	10.5	57.7
	02	211 49.6	54.6	301 40.8	11.5	8 04.2	10.6	57.7
	03	226 49.3	. . 54.8	316 11.3	11.4	7 53.6	10.6	57.6
	04	241 49.0	55.1	330 41.7	11.6	7 43.0	10.6	57.6
	05	256 48.7	55.3	345 12.3	11.6	7 32.4	10.6	57.6
	06	271 48.5	S22 55.5	359 42.9	11.7	N 7 21.8	10.7	57.5
	07	286 48.2	55.7	14 13.6	11.7	7 11.1	10.6	57.5
	08	301 47.9	56.0	28 44.3	11.9	7 00.5	10.7	57.5
S	09	316 47.6	. . 56.2	43 15.2	11.8	6 49.8	10.8	57.4
U	10	331 47.3	56.4	57 46.0	12.0	6 39.0	10.7	57.4
N	11	346 47.0	56.6	72 17.0	12.0	6 28.3	10.8	57.4
D	12	1 46.8	S22 56.8	86 48.0	12.0	N 6 17.5	10.8	57.3
A	13	16 46.5	57.0	101 19.0	12.1	6 06.7	10.8	57.3
Y	14	31 46.2	57.3	115 50.1	12.2	5 55.9	10.8	57.3
	15	46 45.9	. . 57.5	130 21.3	12.2	5 45.1	10.8	57.2
	16	61 45.6	57.7	144 52.5	12.3	5 34.3	10.9	57.2
	17	76 45.3	57.9	159 23.8	12.3	5 23.4	10.8	57.2
	18	91 45.0	S22 58.1	173 55.1	12.4	N 5 12.6	10.9	57.1
	19	106 44.8	58.3	188 26.5	12.5	5 01.7	10.9	57.1
	20	121 44.5	58.5	202 58.0	12.5	4 50.8	10.9	57.1
	21	136 44.2	. . 58.7	217 29.5	12.5	4 39.9	10.9	57.0
	22	151 43.9	58.9	232 01.0	12.6	4 29.0	10.9	57.0
	23	166 43.6	59.2	246 32.6	12.7	4 18.1	10.9	57.0
	11 00	181 43.3	S22 59.4	261 04.3	12.6	N 4 07.2	10.9	56.9
	01	196 43.0	59.6	275 35.9	12.8	3 56.3	11.0	56.9
	02	211 42.7	22 59.8	290 07.7	12.8	3 45.3	10.9	56.9
	03	226 42.5	23 00.0	304 39.5	12.8	3 34.4	11.0	56.8
	04	241 42.2	00.2	319 11.3	12.9	3 23.4	10.9	56.8
	05	256 41.9	00.4	333 43.2	12.9	3 12.5	11.0	56.8
	06	271 41.6	S23 00.6	348 15.1	13.0	N 3 01.5	10.9	56.7
	07	286 41.3	00.8	2 47.1	13.0	2 50.6	11.0	56.7
	08	301 41.0	01.0	17 19.1	13.1	2 39.6	11.0	56.7
M	09	316 40.7	. . 01.2	31 51.2	13.1	2 28.6	10.9	56.6
O	10	331 40.4	01.4	46 23.3	13.1	2 17.7	11.0	56.6
N	11	346 40.2	01.6	60 55.4	13.2	2 06.7	10.9	56.6
D	12	1 39.9	S23 01.8	75 27.6	13.2	N 1 55.8	11.0	56.5
A	13	16 39.6	02.0	89 59.8	13.2	1 44.8	11.0	56.5
Y	14	31 39.3	02.2	104 32.0	13.3	1 33.8	10.9	56.5
	15	46 39.0	. . 02.4	119 04.3	13.4	1 22.9	10.9	56.5
	16	61 38.7	02.6	133 36.7	13.3	1 12.0	11.0	56.4
	17	76 38.4	02.8	148 09.0	13.4	1 01.0	10.9	56.4
	18	91 38.1	S23 03.0	162 41.4	13.4	N 0 50.1	10.9	56.4
	19	106 37.8	03.2	177 13.8	13.5	0 39.2	11.0	56.3
	20	121 37.5	03.3	191 46.3	13.5	0 28.2	10.9	56.3
	21	136 37.3	. . 03.5	206 18.8	13.5	0 17.3	10.9	56.3
	22	151 37.0	03.7	220 51.3	13.5	N 0 06.4	10.9	56.2
	23	166 36.7	03.9	235 23.8	13.6	S 0 04.5	10.8	56.2
		SD 16.3	*d* 0.2	SD	15.9		15.6	15.4

Lat.	Twilight Naut.	Twilight Civil	Sunrise	Moonrise 9	Moonrise 10	Moonrise 11	Moonrise 12
°	h m	h m	h m	h m	h m	h m	h m
N 72	08 12	10 30	▬	21 53	23 45	25 31	01 31
N 70	07 53	09 38	▬	22 07	23 51	25 30	01 30
68	07 38	09 05	▬	22 18	23 56	25 29	01 29
66	07 26	08 41	10 16	22 27	24 00	00 00	01 29
64	07 15	08 23	09 38	22 35	24 03	00 03	01 28
62	07 06	08 07	09 11	22 41	24 06	00 06	01 28
60	06 58	07 54	08 51	22 47	24 08	00 08	01 27
N 58	06 51	07 43	08 34	22 52	24 11	00 11	01 27
56	06 44	07 33	08 20	22 56	24 13	00 13	01 27
54	06 38	07 24	08 08	23 00	24 15	00 15	01 26
52	06 33	07 16	07 57	23 04	24 16	00 16	01 26
50	06 28	07 09	07 47	23 07	24 18	00 18	01 26
45	06 17	06 54	07 27	23 14	24 21	00 21	01 26
N 40	06 07	06 41	07 11	23 20	24 23	00 23	01 25
35	05 57	06 29	06 57	23 25	24 26	00 26	01 25
30	05 49	06 19	06 45	23 29	24 28	00 28	01 25
20	05 33	06 00	06 24	23 37	24 31	00 31	01 24
N 10	05 17	05 43	06 06	23 43	24 34	00 34	01 24
0	05 01	05 27	05 49	23 50	24 37	00 37	01 23
S 10	04 42	05 09	05 32	23 56	24 40	00 40	01 23
20	04 20	04 49	05 13	24 02	00 02	00 43	01 22
30	03 51	04 25	04 52	24 10	00 10	00 47	01 22
35	03 33	04 10	04 39	24 14	00 14	00 49	01 22
40	03 11	03 52	04 25	24 19	00 19	00 51	01 22
45	02 41	03 30	04 07	24 25	00 25	00 54	01 21
S 50	01 58	03 01	03 45	00 02	00 31	00 57	01 21
52	01 32	02 47	03 35	00 07	00 34	00 59	01 21
54	00 53	02 30	03 23	00 12	00 38	01 00	01 21
56	////	02 08	03 09	00 18	00 42	01 02	01 21
58	////	01 41	02 53	00 24	00 46	01 04	01 20
S 60	////	00 59	02 34	00 32	00 50	01 06	01 20

Lat.	Sunset	Twilight Civil	Twilight Naut.	Moonset 9	Moonset 10	Moonset 11	Moonset 12
°	h m	h m	h m	h m	h m	h m	h m
N 72	▬	13 15	15 33	13 41	13 30	13 20	13 10
N 70	▬	14 08	15 52	13 25	13 22	13 18	13 14
68	▬	14 40	16 07	13 13	13 15	13 16	13 17
66	13 30	15 04	16 20	13 02	13 09	13 15	13 19
64	14 08	15 23	16 30	12 53	13 04	13 13	13 22
62	14 34	15 38	16 39	12 46	13 00	13 12	13 24
60	14 55	15 51	16 47	12 39	12 56	13 11	13 25
N 58	15 11	16 02	16 55	12 33	12 53	13 10	13 27
56	15 26	16 12	17 01	12 28	12 50	13 10	13 28
54	15 38	16 21	17 07	12 24	12 48	13 09	13 29
52	15 49	16 29	17 13	12 19	12 45	13 08	13 30
50	15 58	16 36	17 18	12 15	12 43	13 08	13 31
45	16 18	16 52	17 29	12 07	12 38	13 06	13 33
N 40	16 35	17 05	17 39	12 00	12 34	13 05	13 35
35	16 49	17 17	17 48	11 54	12 31	13 04	13 37
30	17 01	17 27	17 57	11 49	12 27	13 04	13 38
20	17 21	17 45	18 13	11 39	12 22	13 02	13 41
N 10	17 40	18 02	18 29	11 31	12 17	13 01	13 43
0	17 57	18 19	18 45	11 23	12 13	13 00	13 45
S 10	18 14	18 37	19 04	11 16	12 08	12 58	13 47
20	18 32	18 57	19 26	11 07	12 03	12 57	13 49
30	18 54	19 21	19 54	10 57	11 58	12 55	13 51
35	19 07	19 36	20 13	10 52	11 54	12 54	13 53
40	19 21	19 54	20 35	10 45	11 50	12 53	13 54
45	19 39	20 16	21 05	10 38	11 46	12 52	13 56
S 50	20 01	20 45	21 49	10 29	11 41	12 51	13 58
52	20 12	21 00	22 15	10 25	11 38	12 50	13 59
54	20 24	21 17	22 55	10 20	11 36	12 49	14 00
56	20 37	21 38	////	10 15	11 33	12 48	14 01
58	20 53	22 06	////	10 09	11 30	12 47	14 03
S 60	21 13	22 50	////	10 03	11 26	12 46	14 04

Day	SUN Eqn. of Time 00^h	SUN Eqn. of Time 12^h	SUN Mer. Pass.	MOON Mer. Pass. Upper	MOON Mer. Pass. Lower	MOON Age	MOON Phase
d	m s	m s	h m	h m	h m	d	%
9	07 48	07 35	11 52	05 11	17 37	21	59
10	07 21	07 08	11 53	06 01	18 25	22	48
11	06 54	06 40	11 53	06 48	19 11	23	38

UT d	h	ARIES GHA	VENUS −3·9 GHA	VENUS Dec	MARS +1·6 GHA	MARS Dec	JUPITER −1·7 GHA	JUPITER Dec	SATURN +0·5 GHA	SATURN Dec
		° ′	° ′	° ′	° ′	° ′	° ′	° ′	° ′	° ′
12	00	80 53.0	188 53.5	S22 04.8	231 02.3	S11 06.0	219 44.5	S14 50.6	171 55.7	S22 30.8
	01	95 55.5	203 52.6	05.3	246 03.2	06.5	234 46.5	50.7	186 57.8	30.8
	02	110 57.9	218 51.7	05.8	261 04.2	07.1	249 48.4	50.9	202 00.0	30.8
	03	126 00.4	233 50.8	. . 06.2	276 05.2	. . 07.6	264 50.4	. . 51.0	217 02.1	. . 30.8
	04	141 02.8	248 49.9	06.7	291 06.1	08.2	279 52.4	51.2	232 04.3	30.8
	05	156 05.3	263 49.1	07.2	306 07.1	08.7	294 54.4	51.3	247 06.4	30.8
	06	171 07.8	278 48.2	S22 07.7	321 08.1	S11 09.3	309 56.4	S14 51.5	262 08.6	S22 30.8
	07	186 10.2	293 47.3	08.2	336 09.0	09.8	324 58.3	51.6	277 10.7	30.8
T	08	201 12.7	308 46.4	08.6	351 10.0	10.4	340 00.3	51.7	292 12.9	30.8
U	09	216 15.2	323 45.5	. . 09.1	6 11.0	. . 10.9	355 02.3	. . 51.9	307 15.0	. . 30.8
E	10	231 17.6	338 44.6	09.6	21 11.9	11.5	10 04.3	52.0	322 17.2	30.8
S	11	246 20.1	353 43.7	10.1	36 12.9	12.0	25 06.3	52.2	337 19.3	30.8
D	12	261 22.6	8 42.8	S22 10.5	51 13.9	S11 12.6	40 08.3	S14 52.3	352 21.5	S22 30.8
	13	276 25.0	23 41.9	11.0	66 14.8	13.1	55 10.2	52.5	7 23.6	30.9
A	14	291 27.5	38 41.0	11.5	81 15.8	13.7	70 12.2	52.6	22 25.8	30.9
Y	15	306 30.0	53 40.1	. . 11.9	96 16.8	. . 14.2	85 14.2	. . 52.7	37 27.9	. . 30.9
	16	321 32.4	68 39.2	12.4	111 17.7	14.8	100 16.2	52.9	52 30.1	30.9
	17	336 34.9	83 38.3	12.9	126 18.7	15.3	115 18.2	53.0	67 32.2	30.9
	18	351 37.3	98 37.4	S22 13.3	141 19.7	S11 15.9	130 20.2	S14 53.2	82 34.3	S22 30.9
	19	6 39.8	113 36.5	13.8	156 20.6	16.4	145 22.1	53.3	97 36.5	30.9
	20	21 42.3	128 35.6	14.3	171 21.6	17.0	160 24.1	53.5	112 38.6	30.9
	21	36 44.7	143 34.7	. . 14.7	186 22.6	. . 17.5	175 26.1	. . 53.6	127 40.8	. . 30.9
	22	51 47.2	158 33.8	15.2	201 23.5	18.1	190 28.1	53.7	142 42.9	30.9
	23	66 49.7	173 32.9	15.6	216 24.5	18.6	205 30.1	53.9	157 45.1	30.9
13	00	81 52.1	188 32.0	S22 16.1	231 25.5	S11 19.2	220 32.1	S14 54.0	172 47.2	S22 30.9
	01	96 54.6	203 31.1	16.6	246 26.4	19.7	235 34.0	54.2	187 49.4	30.9
	02	111 57.1	218 30.2	17.0	261 27.4	20.3	250 36.0	54.3	202 51.5	30.9
	03	126 59.5	233 29.3	. . 17.5	276 28.4	. . 20.8	265 38.0	. . 54.5	217 53.7	. . 30.9
	04	142 02.0	248 28.4	17.9	291 29.3	21.4	280 40.0	54.6	232 55.8	30.9
	05	157 04.4	263 27.5	18.4	306 30.3	21.9	295 42.0	54.7	247 58.0	30.9
	06	172 06.9	278 26.6	S22 18.8	321 31.3	S11 22.5	310 44.0	S14 54.9	263 00.1	S22 30.9
W	07	187 09.4	293 25.7	19.3	336 32.2	23.0	325 45.9	55.0	278 02.3	30.9
E	08	202 11.8	308 24.8	19.7	351 33.2	23.6	340 47.9	55.2	293 04.4	30.9
D	09	217 14.3	323 23.9	. . 20.2	6 34.1	. . 24.1	355 49.9	. . 55.3	308 06.5	. . 31.0
N	10	232 16.8	338 23.0	20.6	21 35.1	24.6	10 51.9	55.5	323 08.7	31.0
E	11	247 19.2	353 22.1	21.1	36 36.1	25.2	25 53.9	55.6	338 10.8	31.0
S	12	262 21.7	8 21.2	S22 21.5	51 37.0	S11 25.7	40 55.9	S14 55.7	353 13.0	S22 31.0
D	13	277 24.2	23 20.3	22.0	66 38.0	26.3	55 57.8	55.9	8 15.1	31.0
A	14	292 26.6	38 19.3	22.4	81 39.0	26.8	70 59.8	56.0	23 17.3	31.0
Y	15	307 29.1	53 18.4	. . 22.8	96 39.9	. . 27.4	86 01.8	. . 56.2	38 19.4	. . 31.0
	16	322 31.6	68 17.5	23.3	111 40.9	27.9	101 03.8	56.3	53 21.6	31.0
	17	337 34.0	83 16.6	23.7	126 41.9	28.5	116 05.8	56.4	68 23.7	31.0
	18	352 36.5	98 15.7	S22 24.2	141 42.8	S11 29.0	131 07.8	S14 56.6	83 25.9	S22 31.0
	19	7 38.9	113 14.8	24.6	156 43.8	29.6	146 09.8	56.7	98 28.0	31.0
	20	22 41.4	128 13.9	25.0	171 44.7	30.1	161 11.7	56.9	113 30.2	31.0
	21	37 43.9	143 13.0	. . 25.5	186 45.7	. . 30.7	176 13.7	. . 57.0	128 32.3	. . 31.0
	22	52 46.3	158 12.1	25.9	201 46.7	31.2	191 15.7	57.2	143 34.4	31.0
	23	67 48.8	173 11.2	26.3	216 47.6	31.8	206 17.7	57.3	158 36.6	31.0
14	00	82 51.3	188 10.3	S22 26.8	231 48.6	S11 32.3	221 19.7	S14 57.4	173 38.7	S22 31.0
	01	97 53.7	203 09.4	27.2	246 49.6	32.8	236 21.7	57.6	188 40.9	31.0
	02	112 56.2	218 08.4	27.6	261 50.5	33.4	251 23.7	57.7	203 43.0	31.0
	03	127 58.7	233 07.5	. . 28.0	276 51.5	. . 33.9	266 25.6	. . 57.9	218 45.2	. . 31.0
	04	143 01.1	248 06.6	28.5	291 52.5	34.5	281 27.6	58.0	233 47.3	31.0
	05	158 03.6	263 05.7	28.9	306 53.4	35.0	296 29.6	58.1	248 49.5	31.0
	06	173 06.1	278 04.8	S22 29.3	321 54.4	S11 35.6	311 31.6	S14 58.3	263 51.6	S22 31.1
	07	188 08.5	293 03.9	29.7	336 55.3	36.1	326 33.6	58.4	278 53.8	31.1
T	08	203 11.0	308 03.0	30.2	351 56.3	36.7	341 35.6	58.6	293 55.9	31.1
H	09	218 13.4	323 02.1	. . 30.6	6 57.3	. . 37.2	356 37.6	. . 58.7	308 58.1	. . 31.1
U	10	233 15.9	338 01.1	31.0	21 58.2	37.8	11 39.6	58.9	324 00.2	31.1
R	11	248 18.4	353 00.2	31.4	36 59.2	38.3	26 41.5	59.0	339 02.3	31.1
S	12	263 20.8	7 59.3	S22 31.8	52 00.1	S11 38.8	41 43.5	S14 59.1	354 04.5	S22 31.1
D	13	278 23.3	22 58.4	32.2	67 01.1	39.4	56 45.5	59.3	9 06.6	31.1
A	14	293 25.8	37 57.5	32.7	82 02.1	39.9	71 47.5	59.4	24 08.8	31.1
Y	15	308 28.2	52 56.6	. . 33.1	97 03.0	. . 40.5	86 49.5	. . 59.6	39 10.9	. . 31.1
	16	323 30.7	67 55.7	33.5	112 04.0	41.0	101 51.5	59.7	54 13.1	31.1
	17	338 33.2	82 54.7	33.9	127 05.0	41.6	116 53.5	14 59.8	69 15.2	31.1
	18	353 35.6	97 53.8	S22 34.3	142 05.9	S11 42.1	131 55.5	S15 00.0	84 17.4	S22 31.1
	19	8 38.1	112 52.9	34.7	157 06.9	42.6	146 57.4	00.1	99 19.5	31.1
	20	23 40.5	127 52.0	35.1	172 07.8	43.2	161 59.4	00.3	114 21.7	31.1
	21	38 43.0	142 51.1	. . 35.5	187 08.8	. . 43.7	177 01.4	. . 00.4	129 23.8	. . 31.1
	22	53 45.5	157 50.2	35.9	202 09.8	44.3	192 03.4	00.5	144 26.0	31.1
	23	68 47.9	172 49.2	36.3	217 10.7	44.8	207 05.4	00.7	159 28.1	31.1
Mer. Pass.		h m 18 29.5	v −0.9	d 0.4	v 1.0	d 0.5	v 2.0	d 0.1	v 2.1	d 0.0

STARS

Name	SHA	Dec
	° ′	° ′
Acamar	315 15.7	S40 14.3
Achernar	335 24.3	S57 09.1
Acrux	173 06.0	S63 11.5
Adhara	255 09.8	S28 59.9
Aldebaran	290 45.6	N16 32.5
Alioth	166 18.3	N55 51.6
Alkaid	152 56.9	N49 13.4
Al Na'ir	27 40.2	S46 52.6
Alnilam	275 43.0	S 1 11.6
Alphard	217 52.9	S 8 44.2
Alphecca	126 08.8	N26 39.4
Alpheratz	357 40.3	N29 11.5
Altair	62 05.6	N 8 55.1
Ankaa	353 12.7	S42 12.8
Antares	112 22.9	S26 28.0
Arcturus	145 53.2	N19 05.4
Atria	107 22.5	S69 03.3
Avior	234 16.2	S59 33.9
Bellatrix	278 28.4	N 6 21.8
Betelgeuse	270 57.7	N 7 24.4
Canopus	263 54.2	S52 42.4
Capella	280 29.5	N46 00.8
Deneb	49 29.7	N45 20.9
Denebola	182 30.6	N14 28.3
Diphda	348 52.8	S17 53.5
Dubhe	193 48.1	N61 39.0
Elnath	278 08.4	N28 37.1
Eltanin	90 45.3	N51 29.4
Enif	33 44.3	N 9 57.6
Fomalhaut	15 20.7	S29 31.8
Gacrux	171 57.6	S57 12.4
Gienah	175 49.2	S17 38.3
Hadar	148 43.9	S60 27.1
Hamal	327 57.1	N23 32.8
Kaus Aust.	83 40.2	S34 22.4
Kochab	137 21.2	N74 04.9
Markab	13 35.3	N15 18.2
Menkar	314 11.6	N 4 09.4
Menkent	148 04.2	S36 27.1
Miaplacidus	221 38.4	S69 47.2
Mirfak	308 35.5	N49 55.4
Nunki	75 54.9	S26 16.3
Peacock	53 15.0	S56 40.7
Pollux	243 23.8	N27 58.7
Procyon	244 56.3	N 5 10.6
Rasalhague	96 04.0	N12 33.0
Regulus	207 40.2	N11 52.7
Rigel	281 08.8	S 8 11.0
Rigil Kent.	139 48.1	S60 54.1
Sabik	102 09.4	S15 44.6
Schedar	349 36.8	N56 38.3
Shaula	96 18.2	S37 06.8
Sirius	258 30.7	S16 44.6
Spica	158 28.2	S11 15.1
Suhail	222 49.9	S43 30.2
Vega	80 37.3	N38 48.3
Zuben'ubi	137 02.3	S16 06.7

	SHA	Mer. Pass.
	° ′	h m
Venus	106 39.9	11 27
Mars	149 33.3	8 34
Jupiter	138 39.9	9 17
Saturn	90 55.1	12 27

Day	UT (d h)	SUN GHA (° ′)	SUN Dec (° ′)	MOON GHA (° ′)	v (′)	MOON Dec (° ′)	d (′)	HP (′)
TUESDAY	12 00	181 36.4	S23 04.1	249 56.4	13.6	S 0 15.3	10.9	56.2
	01	196 36.1	04.3	264 29.0	13.7	0 26.2	10.9	56.2
	02	211 35.8	04.5	279 01.7	13.6	0 37.1	10.8	56.1
	03	226 35.5	. . 04.7	293 34.3	13.7	0 47.9	10.8	56.1
	04	241 35.2	04.9	308 07.0	13.7	0 58.7	10.8	56.1
	05	256 34.9	05.0	322 39.7	13.7	1 09.5	10.8	56.0
	06	271 34.6	S23 05.2	337 12.4	13.8	S 1 20.3	10.8	56.0
	07	286 34.3	05.4	351 45.2	13.8	1 31.1	10.8	56.0
	08	301 34.1	05.6	6 18.0	13.8	1 41.9	10.7	56.0
	09	316 33.8	. . 05.8	20 50.8	13.8	1 52.6	10.8	55.9
	10	331 33.5	05.9	35 23.6	13.8	2 03.4	10.7	55.9
	11	346 33.2	06.1	49 56.4	13.9	2 14.1	10.7	55.9
	12	1 32.9	S23 06.3	64 29.3	13.8	S 2 24.8	10.7	55.9
	13	16 32.6	06.5	79 02.1	13.9	2 35.5	10.6	55.8
	14	31 32.3	06.7	93 35.0	14.0	2 46.1	10.6	55.8
	15	46 32.0	. . 06.8	108 08.0	13.9	2 56.7	10.7	55.8
	16	61 31.7	07.0	122 40.9	13.9	3 07.4	10.5	55.8
	17	76 31.4	07.2	137 13.8	14.0	3 17.9	10.6	55.7
	18	91 31.1	S23 07.4	151 46.8	13.9	S 3 28.5	10.6	55.7
	19	106 30.8	07.5	166 19.7	14.0	3 39.1	10.5	55.7
	20	121 30.5	07.7	180 52.7	14.0	3 49.6	10.5	55.7
	21	136 30.2	. . 07.9	195 25.7	14.0	4 00.1	10.4	55.6
	22	151 29.9	08.1	209 58.7	14.0	4 10.5	10.5	55.6
	23	166 29.7	08.2	224 31.7	14.0	4 21.0	10.4	55.6
WEDNESDAY	13 00	181 29.4	S23 08.4	239 04.7	14.1	S 4 31.4	10.4	55.6
	01	196 29.1	08.6	253 37.8	14.0	4 41.8	10.3	55.5
	02	211 28.8	08.7	268 10.8	14.1	4 52.1	10.3	55.5
	03	226 28.5	. . 08.9	282 43.9	14.0	5 02.4	10.3	55.5
	04	241 28.2	09.1	297 16.9	14.1	5 12.7	10.3	55.5
	05	256 27.9	09.2	311 50.0	14.0	5 23.0	10.2	55.4
	06	271 27.6	S23 09.4	326 23.0	14.1	S 5 33.2	10.3	55.4
	07	286 27.3	09.6	340 56.1	14.1	5 43.5	10.1	55.4
	08	301 27.0	09.7	355 29.2	14.1	5 53.6	10.2	55.4
	09	316 26.7	. . 09.9	10 02.3	14.1	6 03.8	10.1	55.4
	10	331 26.4	10.0	24 35.4	14.0	6 13.9	10.0	55.3
	11	346 26.1	10.2	39 08.4	14.1	6 23.9	10.1	55.3
	12	1 25.8	S23 10.4	53 41.5	14.1	S 6 34.0	10.0	55.3
	13	16 25.5	10.5	68 14.6	14.1	6 44.0	10.0	55.3
	14	31 25.2	10.7	82 47.7	14.1	6 54.0	9.9	55.2
	15	46 24.9	. . 10.8	97 20.8	14.1	7 03.9	9.9	55.2
	16	61 24.6	11.0	111 53.9	14.0	7 13.8	9.8	55.2
	17	76 24.3	11.1	126 26.9	14.1	7 23.6	9.8	55.2
	18	91 24.0	S23 11.3	141 00.0	14.1	S 7 33.4	9.8	55.2
	19	106 23.7	11.5	155 33.1	14.1	7 43.2	9.8	55.1
	20	121 23.4	11.6	170 06.2	14.0	7 53.0	9.7	55.1
	21	136 23.1	. . 11.8	184 39.2	14.1	8 02.7	9.6	55.1
	22	151 22.8	11.9	199 12.3	14.1	8 12.3	9.6	55.1
	23	166 22.5	12.1	213 45.4	14.0	8 21.9	9.6	55.1
THURSDAY	14 00	181 22.2	S23 12.2	228 18.4	14.1	S 8 31.5	9.5	55.0
	01	196 21.9	12.4	242 51.5	14.0	8 41.0	9.5	55.0
	02	211 21.6	12.5	257 24.5	14.0	8 50.5	9.5	55.0
	03	226 21.3	. . 12.7	271 57.5	14.1	9 00.0	9.4	55.0
	04	241 21.0	12.8	286 30.6	14.0	9 09.4	9.3	55.0
	05	256 20.7	13.0	301 03.6	14.0	9 18.7	9.4	54.9
	06	271 20.5	S23 13.1	315 36.6	14.0	S 9 28.1	9.2	54.9
	07	286 20.2	13.2	330 09.6	14.0	9 37.3	9.2	54.9
	08	301 19.9	13.4	344 42.6	13.9	9 46.5	9.2	54.9
	09	316 19.6	. . 13.5	359 15.5	14.0	9 55.7	9.1	54.9
	10	331 19.3	13.7	13 48.5	14.0	10 04.8	9.1	54.9
	11	346 19.0	13.8	28 21.5	13.9	10 13.9	9.0	54.8
	12	1 18.7	S23 14.0	42 54.4	13.9	S10 22.9	9.0	54.8
	13	16 18.4	14.1	57 27.3	13.9	10 31.9	8.9	54.8
	14	31 18.1	14.2	72 00.2	13.9	10 40.8	8.9	54.8
	15	46 17.8	. . 14.4	86 33.1	13.9	10 49.7	8.8	54.8
	16	61 17.5	14.5	101 06.0	13.9	10 58.5	8.8	54.8
	17	76 17.2	14.6	115 38.9	13.9	11 07.3	8.7	54.7
	18	91 16.9	S23 14.8	130 11.8	13.8	S11 16.0	8.7	54.7
	19	106 16.6	14.9	144 44.6	13.8	11 24.7	8.6	54.7
	20	121 16.3	15.1	159 17.4	13.8	11 33.3	8.6	54.7
	21	136 16.0	. . 15.2	173 50.2	13.8	11 41.9	8.5	54.7
	22	151 15.7	15.3	188 23.0	13.8	11 50.4	8.4	54.7
	23	166 15.4	15.4	202 55.8	13.8	S11 58.8	8.4	54.6
		SD 16.3	d 0.2	SD	15.2	15.1		14.9

Lat. (°)	Twilight Naut. (h m)	Twilight Civil (h m)	Sunrise (h m)	Moonrise 12 (h m)	Moonrise 13 (h m)	Moonrise 14 (h m)	Moonrise 15 (h m)
N 72	08 17	10 41	▬	01 31	03 14	04 58	06 46
N 70	07 58	09 44	▬	01 30	03 07	04 43	06 20
68	07 42	09 11	▬	01 29	03 01	04 31	06 01
66	07 30	08 46	10 23	01 29	02 56	04 21	05 46
64	07 19	08 27	09 43	01 28	02 51	04 13	05 33
62	07 10	08 11	09 16	01 28	02 48	04 06	05 22
60	07 01	07 58	08 55	01 27	02 44	04 00	05 13
N 58	06 54	07 46	08 38	01 27	02 41	03 54	05 06
56	06 47	07 36	08 23	01 27	02 39	03 50	04 59
54	06 41	07 27	08 11	01 26	02 37	03 45	04 52
52	06 36	07 19	08 00	01 26	02 35	03 41	04 47
50	06 31	07 12	07 50	01 26	02 33	03 38	04 42
45	06 19	06 56	07 30	01 26	02 29	03 30	04 31
N 40	06 09	06 43	07 13	01 25	02 25	03 24	04 22
35	06 00	06 31	06 59	01 25	02 22	03 19	04 15
30	05 51	06 21	06 47	01 25	02 20	03 14	04 08
20	05 35	06 02	06 26	01 24	02 15	03 06	03 56
N 10	05 19	05 45	06 08	01 24	02 12	02 59	03 46
0	05 02	05 28	05 51	01 23	02 08	02 52	03 37
S 10	04 43	05 10	05 33	01 23	02 04	02 46	03 28
20	04 21	04 50	05 14	01 22	02 01	02 39	03 18
30	03 52	04 25	04 53	01 22	01 56	02 31	03 07
35	03 34	04 10	04 40	01 22	01 54	02 26	03 00
40	03 11	03 52	04 25	01 22	01 51	02 21	02 53
45	02 41	03 30	04 07	01 21	01 48	02 15	02 44
S 50	01 56	03 01	03 45	01 21	01 44	02 08	02 34
52	01 30	02 46	03 34	01 21	01 43	02 05	02 30
54	00 47	02 28	03 22	01 21	01 41	02 02	02 24
56	////	02 07	03 08	01 21	01 39	01 58	02 19
58	////	01 38	02 52	01 20	01 36	01 53	02 12
S 60	////	00 53	02 32	01 20	01 34	01 49	02 05

Lat. (°)	Sunset (h m)	Twilight Civil (h m)	Twilight Naut. (h m)	Moonset 12 (h m)	Moonset 13 (h m)	Moonset 14 (h m)	Moonset 15 (h m)
N 72	▬	13 07	15 31	13 10	13 00	12 49	12 35
N 70	▬	14 04	15 50	13 14	13 10	13 06	13 02
68	▬	14 38	16 06	13 17	13 18	13 19	13 22
66	13 25	15 02	16 19	13 19	13 25	13 31	13 38
64	14 05	15 21	16 29	13 22	13 30	13 40	13 52
62	14 32	15 37	16 39	13 24	13 35	13 48	14 03
60	14 53	15 51	16 47	13 25	13 39	13 55	14 13
N 58	15 11	16 02	16 54	13 27	13 43	14 01	14 21
56	15 25	16 12	17 01	13 28	13 47	14 06	14 29
54	15 37	16 21	17 07	13 29	13 50	14 11	14 35
52	15 48	16 29	17 13	13 30	13 52	14 16	14 41
50	15 58	16 36	17 18	13 31	13 55	14 20	14 47
45	16 19	16 52	17 29	13 33	14 00	14 28	14 59
N 40	16 35	17 06	17 40	13 35	14 05	14 36	15 08
35	16 49	17 17	17 49	13 37	14 09	14 42	15 17
30	17 01	17 28	17 58	13 38	14 13	14 48	15 24
20	17 22	17 46	18 14	13 41	14 19	14 57	15 37
N 10	17 41	18 04	18 30	13 43	14 24	15 06	15 48
0	17 58	18 21	18 47	13 45	14 29	15 14	15 59
S 10	18 15	18 38	19 05	13 47	14 34	15 22	16 09
20	18 34	18 59	19 28	13 49	14 40	15 30	16 21
30	18 56	19 23	19 57	13 51	14 46	15 40	16 34
35	19 09	19 39	20 15	13 53	14 50	15 46	16 41
40	19 24	19 57	20 38	13 54	14 54	15 52	16 50
45	19 42	20 19	21 08	13 56	14 58	16 00	17 00
S 50	20 04	20 48	21 53	13 58	15 04	16 09	17 12
52	20 15	21 03	22 20	13 59	15 07	16 13	17 18
54	20 27	21 21	23 03	14 00	15 10	16 18	17 24
56	20 41	21 42	////	14 01	15 13	16 23	17 31
58	20 57	22 11	////	14 03	15 16	16 28	17 39
S 60	21 17	22 58	////	14 04	15 20	16 35	17 48

	SUN			MOON			
Day (d)	Eqn. of Time 00^h (m s)	Eqn. of Time 12^h (m s)	Mer. Pass. (h m)	Mer. Pass. Upper (h m)	Mer. Pass. Lower (h m)	Age (d)	Phase (%)
12	06 26	06 12	11 54	07 34	19 56	24	28
13	05 58	05 44	11 54	08 19	20 41	25	20
14	05 30	05 15	11 55	09 03	21 25	26	13

UT	ARIES	VENUS −3·9		MARS +1·6		JUPITER −1·7		SATURN +0·5	
d h	GHA ° ′	GHA ° ′	Dec ° ′	GHA ° ′	Dec ° ′	GHA ° ′	Dec ° ′	GHA ° ′	Dec ° ′
15 00	83 50.4	187 48.3	S22 36.7	232 11.7	S11 45.4	222 07.4	S15 00.8	174 30.2	S22 31.1
01	98 52.9	202 47.4	37.1	247 12.6	45.9	237 09.4	01.0	189 32.4	31.1
02	113 55.3	217 46.5	37.5	262 13.6	46.4	252 11.4	01.1	204 34.5	31.1
03	128 57.8	232 45.6	37.9	277 14.6	47.0	267 13.3	01.2	219 36.7	31.1
04	144 00.3	247 44.6	38.3	292 15.5	47.5	282 15.3	01.4	234 38.8	31.2
05	159 02.7	262 43.7	38.7	307 16.5	48.1	297 17.3	01.5	249 41.0	31.2
06	174 05.2	277 42.8	S22 39.1	322 17.5	S11 48.6	312 19.3	S15 01.7	264 43.1	S22 31.2
07	189 07.7	292 41.9	39.5	337 18.4	49.2	327 21.3	01.8	279 45.3	31.2
08	204 10.1	307 41.0	39.9	352 19.4	49.7	342 23.3	01.9	294 47.4	31.2
F 09	219 12.6	322 40.0	40.3	7 20.3	50.2	357 25.3	02.1	309 49.6	31.2
R 10	234 15.0	337 39.1	40.7	22 21.3	50.8	12 27.3	02.2	324 51.7	31.2
I 11	249 17.5	352 38.2	41.1	37 22.3	51.3	27 29.3	02.4	339 53.8	31.2
D 12	264 20.0	7 37.3	S22 41.5	52 23.2	S11 51.9	42 31.3	S15 02.5	354 56.0	S22 31.2
A 13	279 22.4	22 36.4	41.8	67 24.2	52.4	57 33.2	02.6	9 58.1	31.2
Y 14	294 24.9	37 35.4	42.2	82 25.1	52.9	72 35.2	02.8	25 00.3	31.2
15	309 27.4	52 34.5	42.6	97 26.1	53.5	87 37.2	02.9	40 02.4	31.2
16	324 29.8	67 33.6	43.0	112 27.1	54.0	102 39.2	03.1	55 04.6	31.2
17	339 32.3	82 32.7	43.4	127 28.0	54.6	117 41.2	03.2	70 06.7	31.2
18	354 34.8	97 31.7	S22 43.8	142 29.0	S11 55.1	132 43.2	S15 03.3	85 08.9	S22 31.2
19	9 37.2	112 30.8	44.1	157 29.9	55.6	147 45.2	03.5	100 11.0	31.2
20	24 39.7	127 29.9	44.5	172 30.9	56.2	162 47.2	03.6	115 13.2	31.2
21	39 42.2	142 29.0	44.9	187 31.9	56.7	177 49.2	03.7	130 15.3	31.2
22	54 44.6	157 28.0	45.3	202 32.8	57.3	192 51.2	03.9	145 17.4	31.2
23	69 47.1	172 27.1	45.7	217 33.8	57.8	207 53.1	04.0	160 19.6	31.2
16 00	84 49.5	187 26.2	S22 46.0	232 34.7	S11 58.3	222 55.1	S15 04.2	175 21.7	S22 31.2
01	99 52.0	202 25.3	46.4	247 35.7	58.9	237 57.1	04.3	190 23.9	31.2
02	114 54.5	217 24.3	46.8	262 36.6	59.4	252 59.1	04.4	205 26.0	31.2
03	129 56.9	232 23.4	47.1	277 37.6	11 59.9	268 01.1	04.6	220 28.2	31.3
04	144 59.4	247 22.5	47.5	292 38.6	12 00.5	283 03.1	04.7	235 30.3	31.3
05	160 01.9	262 21.6	47.9	307 39.5	01.0	298 05.1	04.9	250 32.5	31.3
06	175 04.3	277 20.6	S22 48.2	322 40.5	S12 01.6	313 07.1	S15 05.0	265 34.6	S22 31.3
07	190 06.8	292 19.7	48.6	337 41.4	02.1	328 09.1	05.1	280 36.8	31.3
S 08	205 09.3	307 18.8	49.0	352 42.4	02.6	343 11.1	05.3	295 38.9	31.3
A 09	220 11.7	322 17.8	49.3	7 43.4	03.2	358 13.1	05.4	310 41.0	31.3
T 10	235 14.2	337 16.9	49.7	22 44.3	03.7	13 15.1	05.6	325 43.2	31.3
U 11	250 16.7	352 16.0	50.1	37 45.3	04.3	28 17.0	05.7	340 45.3	31.3
R 12	265 19.1	7 15.0	S22 50.4	52 46.2	S12 04.8	43 19.0	S15 05.8	355 47.5	S22 31.3
D 13	280 21.6	22 14.1	50.8	67 47.2	05.3	58 21.0	06.0	10 49.6	31.3
A 14	295 24.0	37 13.2	51.1	82 48.1	05.9	73 23.0	06.1	25 51.8	31.3
Y 15	310 26.5	52 12.3	51.5	97 49.1	06.4	88 25.0	06.2	40 53.9	31.3
16	325 29.0	67 11.3	51.8	112 50.1	06.9	103 27.0	06.4	55 56.1	31.3
17	340 31.4	82 10.4	52.2	127 51.0	07.5	118 29.0	06.5	70 58.2	31.3
18	355 33.9	97 09.5	S22 52.5	142 52.0	S12 08.0	133 31.0	S15 06.7	86 00.4	S22 31.3
19	10 36.4	112 08.5	52.9	157 52.9	08.5	148 33.0	06.8	101 02.5	31.3
20	25 38.8	127 07.6	53.2	172 53.9	09.1	163 35.0	06.9	116 04.6	31.3
21	40 41.3	142 06.7	53.6	187 54.9	09.6	178 37.0	07.1	131 06.8	31.3
22	55 43.8	157 05.7	53.9	202 55.8	10.2	193 39.0	07.2	146 08.9	31.3
23	70 46.2	172 04.8	54.3	217 56.8	10.7	208 41.0	07.3	161 11.1	31.3
17 00	85 48.7	187 03.9	S22 54.6	232 57.7	S12 11.2	223 43.0	S15 07.5	176 13.2	S22 31.3
01	100 51.1	202 02.9	55.0	247 58.7	11.8	238 44.9	07.6	191 15.4	31.3
02	115 53.6	217 02.0	55.3	262 59.6	12.3	253 46.9	07.8	206 17.5	31.3
03	130 56.1	232 01.1	55.7	278 00.6	12.8	268 48.9	07.9	221 19.7	31.3
04	145 58.5	247 00.1	56.0	293 01.5	13.4	283 50.9	08.0	236 21.8	31.3
05	161 01.0	261 59.2	56.3	308 02.5	13.9	298 52.9	08.2	251 23.9	31.4
06	176 03.5	276 58.3	S22 56.7	323 03.5	S12 14.4	313 54.9	S15 08.3	266 26.1	S22 31.4
07	191 05.9	291 57.3	57.0	338 04.4	15.0	328 56.9	08.4	281 28.2	31.4
08	206 08.4	306 56.4	57.4	353 05.4	15.5	343 58.9	08.6	296 30.4	31.4
S 09	221 10.9	321 55.5	57.7	8 06.3	16.0	359 00.9	08.7	311 32.5	31.4
U 10	236 13.3	336 54.5	58.0	23 07.3	16.6	14 02.9	08.9	326 34.7	31.4
N 11	251 15.8	351 53.6	58.3	38 08.2	17.1	29 04.9	09.0	341 36.8	31.4
D 12	266 18.3	6 52.6	S22 58.7	53 09.2	S12 17.6	44 06.9	S15 09.1	356 39.0	S22 31.4
A 13	281 20.7	21 51.7	59.0	68 10.2	18.2	59 08.9	09.3	11 41.1	31.4
Y 14	296 23.2	36 50.8	59.3	83 11.1	18.7	74 10.9	09.4	26 43.3	31.4
15	311 25.6	51 49.8	22 59.7	98 12.1	19.2	89 12.9	09.5	41 45.4	31.4
16	326 28.1	66 48.9	23 00.0	113 13.0	19.8	104 14.9	09.7	56 47.5	31.4
17	341 30.6	81 48.0	00.3	128 14.0	20.3	119 16.9	09.8	71 49.7	31.4
18	356 33.0	96 47.0	S23 00.6	143 14.9	S12 20.8	134 18.9	S15 09.9	86 51.8	S22 31.4
19	11 35.5	111 46.1	01.0	158 15.9	21.4	149 20.9	10.1	101 54.0	31.4
20	26 38.0	126 45.1	01.3	173 16.8	21.9	164 22.9	10.2	116 56.1	31.4
21	41 40.4	141 44.2	01.6	188 17.8	22.4	179 24.8	10.4	131 58.3	31.4
22	56 42.9	156 43.3	01.9	203 18.8	23.0	194 26.8	10.5	147 00.4	31.4
23	71 45.4	171 42.3	02.2	218 19.7	23.5	209 28.8	10.6	162 02.6	31.4
Mer. Pass.	h m 18 17.7	v −0.9	d 0.4	v 1.0	d 0.5	v 2.0	d 0.1	v 2.1	d 0.0

STARS		
Name	SHA ° ′	Dec ° ′
Acamar	315 15.7	S40 14.3
Achernar	335 24.3	S57 09.1
Acrux	173 05.9	S63 11.5
Adhara	255 09.8	S28 59.9
Aldebaran	290 45.6	N16 32.5
Alioth	166 18.3	N55 51.6
Alkaid	152 56.9	N49 13.4
Al Na'ir	27 40.2	S46 52.6
Alnilam	275 43.0	S 1 11.6
Alphard	217 52.9	S 8 44.2
Alphecca	126 08.8	N26 39.4
Alpheratz	357 40.3	N29 11.5
Altair	62 05.6	N 8 55.1
Ankaa	353 12.7	S42 12.8
Antares	112 22.9	S26 28.0
Arcturus	145 53.2	N19 05.4
Atria	107 22.5	S69 03.3
Avior	234 16.2	S59 33.9
Bellatrix	278 28.4	N 6 21.8
Betelgeuse	270 57.7	N 7 24.4
Canopus	263 54.2	S52 42.4
Capella	280 29.5	N46 00.8
Deneb	49 29.7	N45 20.9
Denebola	182 30.6	N14 28.3
Diphda	348 52.8	S17 53.5
Dubhe	193 48.0	N61 39.0
Elnath	278 08.4	N28 37.1
Eltanin	90 45.3	N51 29.4
Enif	33 44.3	N 9 57.5
Fomalhaut	15 20.8	S29 31.8
Gacrux	171 57.6	S57 12.4
Gienah	175 49.2	S17 38.3
Hadar	148 43.9	S60 27.1
Hamal	327 57.1	N23 32.8
Kaus Aust.	83 40.2	S34 22.4
Kochab	137 21.2	N74 04.8
Markab	13 35.4	N15 18.2
Menkar	314 11.6	N 4 09.4
Menkent	148 04.2	S36 27.1
Miaplacidus	221 38.3	S69 47.2
Mirfak	308 35.5	N49 55.4
Nunki	75 54.9	S26 16.3
Peacock	53 15.0	S56 40.7
Pollux	243 23.7	N27 58.7
Procyon	244 56.3	N 5 10.6
Rasalhague	96 04.0	N12 33.0
Regulus	207 40.2	N11 52.7
Rigel	281 08.8	S 8 11.1
Rigil Kent.	139 48.0	S60 54.1
Sabik	102 09.4	S15 44.6
Schedar	349 36.8	N56 38.3
Shaula	96 18.2	S37 06.8
Sirius	258 30.7	S16 44.6
Spica	158 28.2	S11 15.1
Suhail	222 49.9	S43 30.2
Vega	80 37.3	N38 48.2
Zuben'ubi	137 02.3	S16 06.7

	SHA ° ′	Mer. Pass. h m
Venus	102 36.6	11 31
Mars	147 45.2	8 29
Jupiter	138 05.6	9 07
Saturn	90 32.2	12 17

UT d	UT h	SUN GHA	SUN Dec	MOON GHA	v	MOON Dec	d	HP
d	h	° ′	° ′	° ′	′	° ′	′	′
15	00	181 15.0	S23 15.6	217 28.6	13.7	S12 07.2	8.4	54.6
	01	196 14.7	15.7	232 01.3	13.7	12 15.6	8.3	54.6
	02	211 14.4	15.8	246 34.0	13.8	12 23.9	8.2	54.6
	03	226 14.1	. . 16.0	261 06.8	13.6	12 32.1	8.2	54.6
	04	241 13.8	16.1	275 39.4	13.7	12 40.3	8.1	54.6
	05	256 13.5	16.2	290 12.1	13.7	12 48.4	8.0	54.6
	06	271 13.2	S23 16.3	304 44.8	13.6	S12 56.4	8.0	54.5
	07	286 12.9	16.5	319 17.4	13.6	13 04.4	7.9	54.5
	08	301 12.6	16.6	333 50.0	13.6	13 12.3	7.9	54.5
F	09	316 12.3	. . 16.7	348 22.6	13.6	13 20.2	7.8	54.5
R	10	331 12.0	16.8	2 55.2	13.5	13 28.0	7.8	54.5
I	11	346 11.7	17.0	17 27.7	13.6	13 35.8	7.6	54.5
D	12	1 11.4	S23 17.1	32 00.3	13.5	S13 43.4	7.7	54.5
A	13	16 11.1	17.2	46 32.8	13.5	13 51.1	7.5	54.5
Y	14	31 10.8	17.3	61 05.3	13.4	13 58.6	7.5	54.4
	15	46 10.5	. . 17.4	75 37.7	13.5	14 06.1	7.5	54.4
	16	61 10.2	17.6	90 10.2	13.4	14 13.6	7.3	54.4
	17	76 09.9	17.7	104 42.6	13.4	14 20.9	7.3	54.4
	18	91 09.6	S23 17.8	119 15.0	13.4	S14 28.2	7.3	54.4
	19	106 09.3	17.9	133 47.4	13.4	14 35.5	7.1	54.4
	20	121 09.0	18.0	148 19.8	13.3	14 42.6	7.1	54.4
	21	136 08.7	. . 18.1	162 52.1	13.3	14 49.7	7.1	54.4
	22	151 08.4	18.3	177 24.4	13.3	14 56.8	6.9	54.3
	23	166 08.1	18.4	191 56.7	13.3	15 03.7	6.9	54.3
16	00	181 07.8	S23 18.5	206 29.0	13.2	S15 10.6	6.8	54.3
	01	196 07.5	18.6	221 01.2	13.3	15 17.4	6.8	54.3
	02	211 07.2	18.7	235 33.5	13.2	15 24.2	6.7	54.3
	03	226 06.9	. . 18.8	250 05.7	13.2	15 30.9	6.6	54.3
	04	241 06.6	18.9	264 37.9	13.1	15 37.5	6.6	54.3
	05	256 06.3	19.0	279 10.0	13.2	15 44.1	6.4	54.3
	06	271 06.0	S23 19.1	293 42.2	13.1	S15 50.5	6.4	54.3
S	07	286 05.7	19.2	308 14.3	13.1	15 56.9	6.4	54.3
A	08	301 05.4	19.3	322 46.4	13.0	16 03.3	6.2	54.2
T	09	316 05.1	. . 19.4	337 18.4	13.1	16 09.5	6.2	54.2
U	10	331 04.7	19.6	351 50.5	13.0	16 15.7	6.1	54.2
R	11	346 04.4	19.7	6 22.5	13.0	16 21.8	6.1	54.2
D	12	1 04.1	S23 19.8	20 54.5	13.0	S16 27.9	5.9	54.2
A	13	16 03.8	19.9	35 26.5	12.9	16 33.8	5.9	54.2
Y	14	31 03.5	20.0	49 58.4	12.9	16 39.7	5.8	54.2
	15	46 03.2	. . 20.1	64 30.3	12.9	16 45.5	5.8	54.2
	16	61 02.9	20.2	79 02.2	12.9	16 51.3	5.6	54.2
	17	76 02.6	20.3	93 34.1	12.9	16 56.9	5.6	54.2
	18	91 02.3	S23 20.3	108 06.0	12.8	S17 02.5	5.5	54.2
	19	106 02.0	20.4	122 37.8	12.8	17 08.0	5.4	54.1
	20	121 01.7	20.5	137 09.6	12.8	17 13.4	5.4	54.1
	21	136 01.4	. . 20.6	151 41.4	12.8	17 18.8	5.2	54.1
	22	151 01.1	20.7	166 13.2	12.7	17 24.0	5.2	54.1
	23	166 00.8	20.8	180 44.9	12.8	17 29.2	5.1	54.1
17	00	181 00.5	S23 20.9	195 16.7	12.7	S17 34.3	5.1	54.1
	01	196 00.2	21.0	209 48.4	12.7	17 39.4	4.9	54.1
	02	210 59.9	21.1	224 20.1	12.6	17 44.3	4.9	54.1
	03	225 59.6	. . 21.2	238 51.7	12.7	17 49.2	4.8	54.1
	04	240 59.2	21.3	253 23.4	12.6	17 54.0	4.7	54.1
	05	255 58.9	21.4	267 55.0	12.6	17 58.7	4.6	54.1
	06	270 58.6	S23 21.5	282 26.6	12.6	S18 03.3	4.6	54.1
	07	285 58.3	21.5	296 58.2	12.5	18 07.9	4.4	54.1
	08	300 58.0	21.6	311 29.7	12.6	18 12.3	4.4	54.1
S	09	315 57.7	. . 21.7	326 01.3	12.5	18 16.7	4.3	54.0
U	10	330 57.4	21.8	340 32.8	12.5	18 21.0	4.2	54.0
N	11	345 57.1	21.9	355 04.3	12.4	18 25.2	4.1	54.0
D	12	0 56.8	S23 22.0	9 35.7	12.5	S18 29.3	4.1	54.0
A	13	15 56.5	22.0	24 07.2	12.4	18 33.4	3.9	54.0
Y	14	30 56.2	22.1	38 38.6	12.5	18 37.3	3.9	54.0
	15	45 55.9	. . 22.2	53 10.1	12.4	18 41.2	3.8	54.0
	16	60 55.6	22.3	67 41.5	12.4	18 45.0	3.7	54.0
	17	75 55.3	22.4	82 12.9	12.3	18 48.7	3.6	54.0
	18	90 54.9	S23 22.4	96 44.2	12.4	S18 52.3	3.5	54.0
	19	105 54.6	22.5	111 15.6	12.3	18 55.8	3.5	54.0
	20	120 54.3	22.6	125 46.9	12.3	18 59.3	3.3	54.0
	21	135 54.0	. . 22.7	140 18.2	12.3	19 02.6	3.3	54.0
	22	150 53.7	22.7	154 49.5	12.3	19 05.9	3.2	54.0
	23	165 53.4	22.8	169 20.8	12.3	S19 09.1	3.1	54.0
		SD 16.3	*d* 0.1	SD 14.8		14.8		14.7

Lat.	Twilight Naut.	Twilight Civil	Sunrise	Moonrise 15	Moonrise 16	Moonrise 17	Moonrise 18
°	h m	h m	h m	h m	h m	h m	h m
N 72	08 21	10 50	▬	06 46	08 45	▬	▬
N 70	08 02	09 49	▬	06 20	08 00	09 42	11 31
68	07 46	09 15	▬	06 01	07 30	08 57	10 15
66	07 33	08 50	10 29	05 46	07 08	08 27	09 37
64	07 22	08 30	09 48	05 33	06 51	08 05	09 11
62	07 12	08 14	09 20	05 22	06 37	07 47	08 51
60	07 04	08 01	08 58	05 13	06 25	07 33	08 34
N 58	06 57	07 49	08 41	05 06	06 15	07 20	08 20
56	06 50	07 39	08 26	04 59	06 06	07 09	08 08
54	06 44	07 30	08 14	04 52	05 58	07 00	07 58
52	06 38	07 22	08 03	04 47	05 51	06 52	07 48
50	06 33	07 14	07 53	04 42	05 44	06 44	07 40
45	06 21	06 58	07 32	04 31	05 31	06 28	07 22
N 40	06 11	06 45	07 15	04 22	05 19	06 15	07 08
35	06 01	06 33	07 01	04 15	05 10	06 04	06 56
30	05 53	06 23	06 49	04 08	05 01	05 54	06 45
20	05 36	06 04	06 28	03 56	04 47	05 37	06 27
N 10	05 20	05 47	06 09	03 46	04 34	05 23	06 11
0	05 03	05 29	05 52	03 37	04 23	05 09	05 56
S 10	04 44	05 11	05 34	03 28	04 11	04 55	05 42
20	04 22	04 51	05 16	03 18	03 58	04 41	05 26
30	03 53	04 26	04 54	03 07	03 44	04 25	05 08
35	03 34	04 11	04 41	03 00	03 36	04 15	04 57
40	03 11	03 53	04 26	02 53	03 27	04 04	04 45
45	02 41	03 30	04 08	02 44	03 16	03 51	04 31
S 50	01 56	03 01	03 45	02 34	03 03	03 36	04 14
52	01 28	02 46	03 34	02 30	02 57	03 29	04 06
54	00 43	02 28	03 22	02 24	02 50	03 21	03 57
56	////	02 06	03 08	02 19	02 43	03 12	03 47
58	////	01 37	02 51	02 12	02 34	03 02	03 35
S 60	////	00 48	02 31	02 05	02 25	02 50	03 22

Lat.	Sunset	Twilight Civil	Twilight Naut.	Moonset 15	Moonset 16	Moonset 17	Moonset 18
°	h m	h m	h m	h m	h m	h m	h m
N 72	▬	13 02	15 30	12 35	12 11	▬	▬
N 70	▬	14 02	15 50	13 02	12 57	12 52	12 41
68	▬	14 37	16 05	13 22	13 27	13 37	13 58
66	13 22	15 02	16 18	13 38	13 50	14 07	14 35
64	14 04	15 21	16 29	13 52	14 08	14 30	15 02
62	14 32	15 37	16 39	14 03	14 22	14 48	15 22
60	14 53	15 51	16 47	14 13	14 35	15 03	15 39
N 58	15 10	16 02	16 55	14 21	14 46	15 16	15 53
56	15 25	16 12	17 02	14 29	14 55	15 27	16 05
54	15 38	16 21	17 08	14 35	15 03	15 37	16 16
52	15 49	16 30	17 13	14 41	15 11	15 45	16 25
50	15 59	16 37	17 19	14 47	15 18	15 53	16 34
45	16 19	16 53	17 30	14 59	15 32	16 10	16 52
N 40	16 36	17 07	17 41	15 08	15 44	16 23	17 06
35	16 50	17 18	17 50	15 17	15 54	16 35	17 19
30	17 02	17 29	17 59	15 24	16 03	16 45	17 30
20	17 24	17 48	18 15	15 37	16 19	17 02	17 48
N 10	17 42	18 05	18 31	15 48	16 32	17 18	18 04
0	17 59	18 22	18 48	15 59	16 45	17 32	18 19
S 10	18 17	18 40	19 07	16 09	16 58	17 46	18 35
20	18 36	19 00	19 30	16 21	17 11	18 01	18 51
30	18 58	19 25	19 59	16 34	17 27	18 19	19 09
35	19 11	19 41	20 17	16 41	17 36	18 29	19 20
40	19 26	19 59	20 40	16 50	17 46	18 41	19 32
45	19 44	20 21	21 11	17 00	17 58	18 54	19 47
S 50	20 06	20 51	21 56	17 12	18 13	19 11	20 05
52	20 17	21 06	22 24	17 18	18 20	19 19	20 13
54	20 29	21 24	23 09	17 24	18 28	19 28	20 23
56	20 44	21 46	////	17 31	18 37	19 38	20 33
58	21 00	22 16	////	17 39	18 46	19 49	20 46
S 60	21 21	23 05	////	17 48	18 58	20 02	21 00

Day	SUN Eqn. of Time 00^h	SUN Eqn. of Time 12^h	SUN Mer. Pass.	MOON Mer. Pass. Upper	MOON Mer. Pass. Lower	MOON Age	MOON Phase
d	m s	m s	h m	h m	h m	d %	
15	05 01	04 46	11 55	09 48	22 11	27 7	
16	04 32	04 17	11 56	10 34	22 57	28 3	
17	04 02	03 48	11 56	11 20	23 44	29 1	

UT	ARIES	VENUS −3·9		MARS +1·6		JUPITER −1·8		SATURN +0·4	
	GHA	GHA	Dec	GHA	Dec	GHA	Dec	GHA	Dec
d h	° ′	° ′	° ′	° ′	° ′	° ′	° ′	° ′	° ′
18 00	86 47.8	186 41.4	S23 02.6	233 20.7	S12 24.0	224 30.8	S15 10.8	177 04.7	S22 31.4
01	101 50.3	201 40.4	02.9	248 21.6	24.6	239 32.8	10.9	192 06.8	31.4
02	116 52.8	216 39.5	03.2	263 22.6	25.1	254 34.8	11.0	207 09.0	31.4
03	131 55.2	231 38.6	. . 03.5	278 23.5	. . 25.6	269 36.8	. . 11.2	222 11.1	. . 31.4
04	146 57.7	246 37.6	03.8	293 24.5	26.2	284 38.8	11.3	237 13.3	31.4
05	162 00.1	261 36.7	04.1	308 25.4	26.7	299 40.8	11.4	252 15.4	31.4
06	177 02.6	276 35.7	S23 04.4	323 26.4	S12 27.2	314 42.8	S15 11.6	267 17.6	S22 31.4
07	192 05.1	291 34.8	04.7	338 27.3	27.8	329 44.8	11.7	282 19.7	31.4
08	207 07.5	306 33.9	05.0	353 28.3	28.3	344 46.8	11.8	297 21.9	31.4
M 09	222 10.0	321 32.9	. . 05.3	8 29.3	. . 28.8	359 48.8	. . 12.0	312 24.0	. . 31.5
O 10	237 12.5	336 32.0	05.6	23 30.2	29.3	14 50.8	12.1	327 26.2	31.5
N 11	252 14.9	351 31.0	05.9	38 31.2	29.9	29 52.8	12.3	342 28.3	31.5
D 12	267 17.4	6 30.1	S23 06.2	53 32.1	S12 30.4	44 54.8	S15 12.4	357 30.4	S22 31.5
A 13	282 19.9	21 29.1	06.5	68 33.1	30.9	59 56.8	12.5	12 32.6	31.5
Y 14	297 22.3	36 28.2	06.8	83 34.0	31.5	74 58.8	12.7	27 34.7	31.5
15	312 24.8	51 27.3	. . 07.1	98 35.0	. . 32.0	90 00.8	. . 12.8	42 36.9	. . 31.5
16	327 27.3	66 26.3	07.4	113 35.9	32.5	105 02.8	12.9	57 39.0	31.5
17	342 29.7	81 25.4	07.7	128 36.9	33.1	120 04.8	13.1	72 41.2	31.5
18	357 32.2	96 24.4	S23 08.0	143 37.8	S12 33.6	135 06.8	S15 13.2	87 43.3	S22 31.5
19	12 34.6	111 23.5	08.3	158 38.8	34.1	150 08.8	13.3	102 45.5	31.5
20	27 37.1	126 22.5	08.6	173 39.7	34.6	165 10.8	13.5	117 47.6	31.5
21	42 39.6	141 21.6	. . 08.9	188 40.7	. . 35.2	180 12.8	. . 13.6	132 49.7	. . 31.5
22	57 42.0	156 20.6	09.2	203 41.7	35.7	195 14.8	13.7	147 51.9	31.5
23	72 44.5	171 19.7	09.5	218 42.6	36.2	210 16.8	13.9	162 54.0	31.5
19 00	87 47.0	186 18.7	S23 09.8	233 43.6	S12 36.8	225 18.8	S15 14.0	177 56.2	S22 31.5
01	102 49.4	201 17.8	10.1	248 44.5	37.3	240 20.8	14.1	192 58.3	31.5
02	117 51.9	216 16.9	10.3	263 45.5	37.8	255 22.8	14.3	208 00.5	31.5
03	132 54.4	231 15.9	. . 10.6	278 46.4	. . 38.3	270 24.8	. . 14.4	223 02.6	. . 31.5
04	147 56.8	246 15.0	10.9	293 47.4	38.9	285 26.8	14.5	238 04.8	31.5
05	162 59.3	261 14.0	11.2	308 48.3	39.4	300 28.8	14.7	253 06.9	31.5
06	178 01.8	276 13.1	S23 11.5	323 49.3	S12 39.9	315 30.8	S15 14.8	268 09.0	S22 31.5
07	193 04.2	291 12.1	11.7	338 50.2	40.5	330 32.8	15.0	283 11.2	31.5
T 08	208 06.7	306 11.2	12.0	353 51.2	41.0	345 34.8	15.1	298 13.3	31.5
U 09	223 09.1	321 10.2	. . 12.3	8 52.1	. . 41.5	0 36.8	. . 15.2	313 15.5	. . 31.5
E 10	238 11.6	336 09.3	12.6	23 53.1	42.0	15 38.8	15.4	328 17.6	31.5
S 11	253 14.1	351 08.3	12.8	38 54.0	42.6	30 40.8	15.5	343 19.8	31.5
D 12	268 16.5	6 07.4	S23 13.1	53 55.0	S12 43.1	45 42.8	S15 15.6	358 21.9	S22 31.5
A 13	283 19.0	21 06.4	13.4	68 55.9	43.6	60 44.8	15.8	13 24.1	31.5
Y 14	298 21.5	36 05.5	13.6	83 56.9	44.1	75 46.8	15.9	28 26.2	31.5
15	313 23.9	51 04.5	. . 13.9	98 57.8	. . 44.7	90 48.8	. . 16.0	43 28.3	. . 31.5
16	328 26.4	66 03.6	14.2	113 58.8	45.2	105 50.8	16.2	58 30.5	31.5
17	343 28.9	81 02.6	14.5	128 59.8	45.7	120 52.8	16.3	73 32.6	31.6
18	358 31.3	96 01.7	S23 14.7	144 00.7	S12 46.2	135 54.8	S15 16.4	88 34.8	S22 31.6
19	13 33.8	111 00.7	15.0	159 01.7	46.8	150 56.8	16.6	103 36.9	31.6
20	28 36.2	125 59.8	15.2	174 02.6	47.3	165 58.8	16.7	118 39.1	31.6
21	43 38.7	140 58.8	. . 15.5	189 03.6	. . 47.8	181 00.8	. . 16.8	133 41.2	. . 31.6
22	58 41.2	155 57.9	15.8	204 04.5	48.3	196 02.8	17.0	148 43.4	31.6
23	73 43.6	170 56.9	16.0	219 05.5	48.9	211 04.8	17.1	163 45.5	31.6
20 00	88 46.1	185 56.0	S23 16.3	234 06.4	S12 49.4	226 06.8	S15 17.2	178 47.6	S22 31.6
01	103 48.6	200 55.0	16.5	249 07.4	49.9	241 08.8	17.4	193 49.8	31.6
02	118 51.0	215 54.1	16.8	264 08.3	50.4	256 10.8	17.5	208 51.9	31.6
03	133 53.5	230 53.1	. . 17.0	279 09.3	. . 51.0	271 12.8	. . 17.6	223 54.1	. . 31.6
04	148 56.0	245 52.2	17.3	294 10.2	51.5	286 14.8	17.8	238 56.2	31.6
05	163 58.4	260 51.2	17.5	309 11.2	52.0	301 16.8	17.9	253 58.4	31.6
06	179 00.9	275 50.2	S23 17.8	324 12.1	S12 52.5	316 18.8	S15 18.0	269 00.5	S22 31.6
W 07	194 03.4	290 49.3	18.0	339 13.1	53.1	331 20.8	18.2	284 02.7	31.6
E 08	209 05.8	305 48.3	18.3	354 14.0	53.6	346 22.8	18.3	299 04.8	31.6
D 09	224 08.3	320 47.4	. . 18.5	9 15.0	. . 54.1	1 24.8	. . 18.4	314 06.9	. . 31.6
N 10	239 10.7	335 46.4	18.8	24 15.9	54.6	16 26.8	18.6	329 09.1	31.6
E 11	254 13.2	350 45.5	19.0	39 16.9	55.2	31 28.8	18.7	344 11.2	31.6
S 12	269 15.7	5 44.5	S23 19.3	54 17.8	S12 55.7	46 30.8	S15 18.8	359 13.4	S22 31.6
D 13	284 18.1	20 43.6	19.5	69 18.8	56.2	61 32.8	19.0	14 15.5	31.6
A 14	299 20.6	35 42.6	19.7	84 19.7	56.7	76 34.8	19.1	29 17.7	31.6
Y 15	314 23.1	50 41.7	. . 20.0	99 20.7	. . 57.3	91 36.8	. . 19.2	44 19.8	. . 31.6
16	329 25.5	65 40.7	20.2	114 21.6	57.8	106 38.9	19.3	59 22.0	31.6
17	344 28.0	80 39.7	20.5	129 22.6	58.3	121 40.9	19.5	74 24.1	31.6
18	359 30.5	95 38.8	S23 20.7	144 23.5	S12 58.8	136 42.9	S15 19.6	89 26.2	S22 31.6
19	14 32.9	110 37.8	20.9	159 24.5	59.3	151 44.9	19.7	104 28.4	31.6
20	29 35.4	125 36.9	21.2	174 25.4	12 59.9	166 46.9	19.9	119 30.5	31.6
21	44 37.9	140 35.9	. . 21.4	189 26.4	13 00.4	181 48.9	. . 20.0	134 32.7	. . 31.6
22	59 40.3	155 35.0	21.6	204 27.3	00.9	196 50.9	20.1	149 34.8	31.6
23	74 42.8	170 34.0	21.8	219 28.3	01.4	211 52.9	20.3	164 37.0	31.6
Mer. Pass.	h m 18 05.9	*v* −0.9	*d* 0.3	*v* 1.0	*d* 0.5	*v* 2.0	*d* 0.1	*v* 2.1	*d* 0.0

STARS		
Name	SHA	Dec
	° ′	° ′
Acamar	315 15.7	S40 14.3
Achernar	335 24.3	S57 09.1
Acrux	173 05.9	S63 11.5
Adhara	255 09.8	S28 59.9
Aldebaran	290 45.5	N16 32.5
Alioth	166 18.3	N55 51.6
Alkaid	152 56.8	N49 13.3
Al Na'ir	27 40.2	S46 52.6
Alnilam	275 42.9	S 1 11.6
Alphard	217 52.9	S 8 44.2
Alphecca	126 08.8	N26 39.4
Alpheratz	357 40.3	N29 11.5
Altair	62 05.6	N 8 55.1
Ankaa	353 12.7	S42 12.8
Antares	112 22.9	S26 28.0
Arcturus	145 53.2	N19 05.4
Atria	107 22.5	S69 03.3
Avior	234 16.2	S59 33.9
Bellatrix	278 28.4	N 6 21.7
Betelgeuse	270 57.7	N 7 24.4
Canopus	263 54.2	S52 42.4
Capella	280 29.5	N46 00.8
Deneb	49 29.7	N45 20.9
Denebola	182 30.6	N14 28.3
Diphda	348 52.8	S17 53.5
Dubhe	193 48.0	N61 39.0
Elnath	278 08.4	N28 37.1
Eltanin	90 45.3	N51 29.4
Enif	33 44.3	N 9 57.5
Fomalhaut	15 20.8	S29 31.8
Gacrux	171 57.5	S57 12.4
Gienah	175 49.2	S17 38.3
Hadar	148 43.8	S60 27.1
Hamal	327 57.1	N23 32.8
Kaus Aust.	83 40.2	S34 22.4
Kochab	137 21.1	N74 04.8
Markab	13 35.4	N15 18.2
Menkar	314 11.6	N 4 09.4
Menkent	148 04.2	S36 27.1
Miaplacidus	221 38.3	S69 47.3
Mirfak	308 35.5	N49 55.4
Nunki	75 54.9	S26 16.3
Peacock	53 15.0	S56 40.7
Pollux	243 23.7	N27 58.7
Procyon	244 56.3	N 5 10.6
Rasalhague	96 04.0	N12 33.0
Regulus	207 40.2	N11 52.7
Rigel	281 08.8	S 8 11.1
Rigil Kent.	139 48.0	S60 54.1
Sabik	102 09.4	S15 44.6
Schedar	349 36.8	N56 38.3
Shaula	96 18.2	S37 06.8
Sirius	258 30.7	S16 44.6
Spica	158 28.2	S11 15.1
Suhail	222 49.9	S43 30.2
Vega	80 37.3	N38 48.2
Zuben'ubi	137 02.3	S16 06.7

	SHA	Mer. Pass.
	° ′	h m
Venus	98 31.8	11 35
Mars	145 56.6	8 25
Jupiter	137 31.8	8 58
Saturn	90 09.2	12 07

UT	SUN GHA	SUN Dec	MOON GHA	v	MOON Dec	d	HP
d h	° ′	° ′	° ′	′	° ′	′	′
18 00 (MONDAY)	180 53.1	S23 22.9	183 52.1	12.2	S19 12.2	3.0	54.0
01	195 52.8	23.0	198 23.3	12.3	19 15.2	2.9	54.0
02	210 52.5	23.0	212 54.6	12.2	19 18.1	2.8	54.0
03	225 52.2	. . 23.1	227 25.8	12.2	19 20.9	2.8	54.0
04	240 51.9	23.2	241 57.0	12.2	19 23.7	2.6	54.0
05	255 51.6	23.2	256 28.2	12.2	19 26.3	2.6	54.0
06	270 51.3	S23 23.3	270 59.4	12.1	S19 28.9	2.5	54.0
07	285 50.9	23.4	285 30.5	12.2	19 31.4	2.3	54.0
08	300 50.6	23.4	300 01.7	12.1	19 33.7	2.3	54.0
09	315 50.3	. . 23.5	314 32.8	12.2	19 36.0	2.2	53.9
10	330 50.0	23.6	329 04.0	12.1	19 38.2	2.2	53.9
11	345 49.7	23.6	343 35.1	12.1	19 40.4	2.0	53.9
12	0 49.4	S23 23.7	358 06.2	12.1	S19 42.4	1.9	53.9
13	15 49.1	23.8	12 37.3	12.1	19 44.3	1.8	53.9
14	30 48.8	23.8	27 08.4	12.1	19 46.1	1.8	53.9
15	45 48.5	. . 23.9	41 39.5	12.1	19 47.9	1.7	53.9
16	60 48.2	23.9	56 10.6	12.0	19 49.6	1.5	53.9
17	75 47.9	24.0	70 41.6	12.1	19 51.1	1.5	53.9
18	90 47.5	S23 24.1	85 12.7	12.0	S19 52.6	1.4	53.9
19	105 47.2	24.1	99 43.7	12.1	19 54.0	1.3	53.9
20	120 46.9	24.2	114 14.8	12.0	19 55.3	1.2	53.9
21	135 46.6	. . 24.2	128 45.8	12.0	19 56.5	1.1	53.9
22	150 46.3	24.3	143 16.8	12.1	19 57.6	1.0	53.9
23	165 46.0	24.3	157 47.9	12.0	19 58.6	0.9	53.9
19 00 (TUESDAY)	180 45.7	S23 24.4	172 18.9	12.0	S19 59.5	0.9	53.9
01	195 45.4	24.4	186 49.9	12.0	20 00.4	0.7	53.9
02	210 45.1	24.5	201 20.9	12.0	20 01.1	0.7	53.9
03	225 44.8	. . 24.5	215 51.9	12.0	20 01.8	0.5	53.9
04	240 44.5	24.6	230 22.9	12.0	20 02.3	0.5	53.9
05	255 44.1	24.6	244 53.9	12.0	20 02.8	0.4	53.9
06	270 43.8	S23 24.7	259 24.9	12.0	S20 03.2	0.2	53.9
07	285 43.5	24.7	273 55.9	12.0	20 03.4	0.2	53.9
08	300 43.2	24.8	288 26.9	12.0	20 03.6	0.1	53.9
09	315 42.9	. . 24.8	302 57.9	12.0	20 03.7	0.0	53.9
10	330 42.6	24.9	317 28.9	11.9	20 03.7	0.1	53.9
11	345 42.3	24.9	331 59.8	12.0	20 03.6	0.2	53.9
12	0 42.0	S23 25.0	346 30.8	12.0	S20 03.4	0.2	53.9
13	15 41.7	25.0	1 01.8	12.0	20 03.2	0.4	53.9
14	30 41.4	25.0	15 32.8	12.0	20 02.8	0.5	53.9
15	45 41.0	. . 25.1	30 03.8	12.0	20 02.3	0.5	53.9
16	60 40.7	25.1	44 34.8	12.0	20 01.8	0.7	53.9
17	75 40.4	25.2	59 05.8	12.0	20 01.1	0.7	53.9
18	90 40.1	S23 25.2	73 36.8	12.0	S20 00.4	0.8	53.9
19	105 39.8	25.2	88 07.8	12.0	19 59.6	0.9	54.0
20	120 39.5	25.3	102 38.8	12.1	19 58.7	1.1	54.0
21	135 39.2	. . 25.3	117 09.9	12.0	19 57.6	1.1	54.0
22	150 38.9	25.3	131 40.9	12.0	19 56.5	1.2	54.0
23	165 38.6	25.4	146 11.9	12.0	19 55.3	1.2	54.0
20 00 (WEDNESDAY)	180 38.3	S23 25.4	160 42.9	12.1	S19 54.1	1.4	54.0
01	195 37.9	25.4	175 14.0	12.0	19 52.7	1.5	54.0
02	210 37.6	25.5	189 45.0	12.1	19 51.2	1.6	54.0
03	225 37.3	. . 25.5	204 16.1	12.0	19 49.6	1.6	54.0
04	240 37.0	25.5	218 47.1	12.1	19 48.0	1.8	54.0
05	255 36.7	25.6	233 18.2	12.1	19 46.2	1.8	54.0
06	270 36.4	S23 25.6	247 49.3	12.1	S19 44.4	1.9	54.0
07	285 36.1	25.6	262 20.4	12.1	19 42.5	2.1	54.0
08	300 35.8	25.7	276 51.5	12.1	19 40.4	2.1	54.0
09	315 35.5	. . 25.7	291 22.6	12.1	19 38.3	2.2	54.0
10	330 35.1	25.7	305 53.7	12.1	19 36.1	2.3	54.0
11	345 34.8	25.7	320 24.8	12.2	19 33.8	2.3	54.0
12	0 34.5	S23 25.8	334 56.0	12.1	S19 31.5	2.5	54.0
13	15 34.2	25.8	349 27.1	12.2	19 29.0	2.6	54.0
14	30 33.9	25.8	3 58.3	12.2	19 26.4	2.6	54.0
15	45 33.6	. . 25.8	18 29.5	12.1	19 23.8	2.8	54.0
16	60 33.3	25.8	33 00.6	12.2	19 21.0	2.8	54.0
17	75 33.0	25.9	47 31.8	12.3	19 18.2	2.9	54.1
18	90 32.7	S23 25.9	62 03.1	12.2	S19 15.3	3.0	54.1
19	105 32.3	25.9	76 34.3	12.2	19 12.3	3.1	54.1
20	120 32.0	25.9	91 05.5	12.3	19 09.2	3.2	54.1
21	135 31.7	. . 25.9	105 36.8	12.2	19 06.0	3.2	54.1
22	150 31.4	25.9	120 08.0	12.3	19 02.8	3.4	54.1
23	165 31.1	26.0	134 39.3	12.3	S18 59.4	3.4	54.1
	SD 16.3	*d* 0.0	SD	14.7	14.7		14.7

Lat.	Twilight Naut.	Twilight Civil	Sunrise	Moonrise 18	Moonrise 19	Moonrise 20	Moonrise 21
°	h m	h m	h m	h m	h m	h m	h m
N 72	08 24	10 56	■	■	■	■	■
N 70	08 04	09 53	■	11 31	■	12 53	12 45
68	07 48	09 18	■	10 15	11 13	11 48	12 05
66	07 35	08 52	10 33	09 37	10 33	11 12	11 37
64	07 24	08 33	09 51	09 11	10 05	10 46	11 15
62	07 15	08 17	09 22	08 51	09 44	10 26	10 58
60	07 06	08 03	09 01	08 34	09 27	10 10	10 44
N 58	06 59	07 51	08 43	08 20	09 12	09 56	10 32
56	06 52	07 41	08 29	08 08	09 00	09 44	10 21
54	06 46	07 32	08 16	07 58	08 49	09 34	10 12
52	06 40	07 24	08 05	07 48	08 40	09 25	10 03
50	06 35	07 16	07 55	07 40	08 31	09 16	09 56
45	06 23	07 00	07 34	07 22	08 13	08 59	09 40
N 40	06 13	06 47	07 17	07 08	07 58	08 44	09 26
35	06 03	06 35	07 03	06 56	07 45	08 32	09 15
30	05 54	06 24	06 51	06 45	07 35	08 21	09 05
20	05 38	06 05	06 29	06 27	07 16	08 03	08 48
N 10	05 22	05 48	06 11	06 11	06 59	07 47	08 33
0	05 05	05 31	05 53	05 56	06 44	07 32	08 20
S 10	04 46	05 13	05 36	05 42	06 29	07 17	08 06
20	04 23	04 52	05 17	05 26	06 13	07 01	07 51
30	03 54	04 27	04 55	05 08	05 54	06 43	07 34
35	03 35	04 12	04 42	04 57	05 43	06 32	07 24
40	03 12	03 54	04 27	04 45	05 31	06 20	07 12
45	02 41	03 31	04 09	04 31	05 16	06 05	06 59
S 50	01 56	03 01	03 46	04 14	04 58	05 48	06 43
52	01 28	02 46	03 35	04 06	04 49	05 39	06 35
54	00 41	02 28	03 23	03 57	04 40	05 30	06 26
56	////	02 06	03 09	03 47	04 29	05 19	06 17
58	////	01 36	02 52	03 35	04 17	05 07	06 06
S 60	////	00 46	02 31	03 22	04 03	04 53	05 53

Lat.	Sunset	Twilight Civil	Twilight Naut.	Moonset 18	Moonset 19	Moonset 20	Moonset 21
°	h m	h m	h m	h m	h m	h m	h m
N 72	■	12 59	15 30	■	■	■	■
N 70	■	14 01	15 50	12 41	■	14 39	16 25
68	■	14 37	16 06	13 58	14 39	15 44	17 05
66	13 21	15 02	16 19	14 35	15 19	16 19	17 32
64	14 04	15 22	16 30	15 02	15 46	16 44	17 53
62	14 32	15 38	16 40	15 22	16 08	17 04	18 10
60	14 54	15 51	16 48	15 39	16 25	17 20	18 24
N 58	15 11	16 03	16 56	15 53	16 39	17 34	18 36
56	15 26	16 13	17 02	16 05	16 52	17 46	18 46
54	15 38	16 22	17 09	16 16	17 03	17 56	18 55
52	15 50	16 31	17 14	16 25	17 12	18 05	19 03
50	16 00	16 38	17 20	16 34	17 21	18 13	19 11
45	16 20	16 54	17 31	16 52	17 39	18 31	19 26
N 40	16 37	17 08	17 42	17 06	17 54	18 45	19 39
35	16 51	17 19	17 51	17 19	18 06	18 57	19 49
30	17 04	17 30	18 00	17 30	18 17	19 07	19 59
20	17 25	17 49	18 16	17 48	18 36	19 25	20 15
N 10	17 43	18 06	18 33	18 04	18 52	19 41	20 29
0	18 01	18 23	18 50	18 19	19 07	19 55	20 42
S 10	18 19	18 42	19 09	18 35	19 23	20 10	20 55
20	18 38	19 02	19 31	18 51	19 39	20 25	21 09
30	19 00	19 27	20 00	19 09	19 57	20 43	21 25
35	19 13	19 42	20 19	19 20	20 08	20 53	21 34
40	19 28	20 01	20 42	19 32	20 21	21 05	21 45
45	19 46	20 23	21 13	19 47	20 35	21 19	21 57
S 50	20 08	20 53	21 59	20 05	20 53	21 35	22 12
52	20 19	21 08	22 27	20 13	21 02	21 43	22 19
54	20 32	21 26	23 14	20 23	21 11	21 52	22 27
56	20 46	21 48	////	20 33	21 22	22 02	22 35
58	21 03	22 18	////	20 46	21 34	22 13	22 45
S 60	21 23	23 09	////	21 00	21 48	22 26	22 56

Day	SUN Eqn. of Time 00^h	SUN Eqn. of Time 12^h	SUN Mer. Pass.	MOON Mer. Pass. Upper	MOON Mer. Pass. Lower	Age	Phase
d	m s	m s	h m	h m	h m	d %	
18	03 33	03 18	11 57	12 08	24 32	00 0	●
19	03 03	02 49	11 57	12 56	00 32	01 1	
20	02 34	02 19	11 58	13 44	01 20	02 4	

2017 DECEMBER 21, 22, 23 (THURS., FRI., SAT.)

UT d	h	ARIES GHA	VENUS −3·9 GHA	VENUS Dec	MARS +1·6 GHA	MARS Dec	JUPITER −1·8 GHA	JUPITER Dec	SATURN +0·4 GHA	SATURN Dec
		° ′	° ′	° ′	° ′	° ′	° ′	° ′	° ′	° ′
21 THURSDAY	00	89 45.2	185 33.1	S23 22.1	234 29.2	S13 01.9	226 54.9	S15 20.4	179 39.1	S22 31.6
	01	104 47.7	200 32.1	22.3	249 30.2	02.5	241 56.9	20.5	194 41.3	31.6
	02	119 50.2	215 31.1	22.5	264 31.1	03.0	256 58.9	20.7	209 43.4	31.6
	03	134 52.6	230 30.2	. . 22.7	279 32.1	. . 03.5	272 00.9	. . 20.8	224 45.5	. . 31.6
	04	149 55.1	245 29.2	23.0	294 33.0	04.0	287 02.9	20.9	239 47.7	31.6
	05	164 57.6	260 28.3	23.2	309 34.0	04.6	302 04.9	21.1	254 49.8	31.6
	06	180 00.0	275 27.3	S23 23.4	324 34.9	S13 05.1	317 06.9	S15 21.2	269 52.0	S22 31.6
	07	195 02.5	290 26.4	23.6	339 35.8	05.6	332 08.9	21.3	284 54.1	31.7
	08	210 05.0	305 25.4	23.8	354 36.8	06.1	347 10.9	21.5	299 56.3	31.7
	09	225 07.4	320 24.4	. . 24.1	9 37.7	. . 06.6	2 12.9	. . 21.6	314 58.4	. . 31.7
	10	240 09.9	335 23.5	24.3	24 38.7	07.2	17 14.9	21.7	330 00.6	31.7
	11	255 12.4	350 22.5	24.5	39 39.6	07.7	32 17.0	21.9	345 02.7	31.7
	12	270 14.8	5 21.6	S23 24.7	54 40.6	S13 08.2	47 19.0	S15 22.0	0 04.8	S22 31.7
	13	285 17.3	20 20.6	24.9	69 41.5	08.7	62 21.0	22.1	15 07.0	31.7
	14	300 19.7	35 19.6	25.1	84 42.5	09.2	77 23.0	22.2	30 09.1	31.7
	15	315 22.2	50 18.7	. . 25.3	99 43.4	. . 09.7	92 25.0	. . 22.4	45 11.3	. . 31.7
	16	330 24.7	65 17.7	25.5	114 44.4	10.3	107 27.0	22.5	60 13.4	31.7
	17	345 27.1	80 16.8	25.7	129 45.3	10.8	122 29.0	22.6	75 15.6	31.7
	18	0 29.6	95 15.8	S23 26.0	144 46.3	S13 11.3	137 31.0	S15 22.8	90 17.7	S22 31.7
	19	15 32.1	110 14.8	26.2	159 47.2	11.8	152 33.0	22.9	105 19.9	31.7
	20	30 34.5	125 13.9	26.4	174 48.2	12.3	167 35.0	23.0	120 22.0	31.7
	21	45 37.0	140 12.9	. . 26.6	189 49.1	. . 12.9	182 37.0	. . 23.2	135 24.1	. . 31.7
	22	60 39.5	155 12.0	26.8	204 50.1	13.4	197 39.0	23.3	150 26.3	31.7
	23	75 41.9	170 11.0	27.0	219 51.0	13.9	212 41.0	23.4	165 28.4	31.7
22 FRIDAY	00	90 44.4	185 10.0	S23 27.2	234 52.0	S13 14.4	227 43.0	S15 23.6	180 30.6	S22 31.7
	01	105 46.9	200 09.1	27.4	249 52.9	14.9	242 45.1	23.7	195 32.7	31.7
	02	120 49.3	215 08.1	27.5	264 53.9	15.4	257 47.1	23.8	210 34.9	31.7
	03	135 51.8	230 07.2	. . 27.7	279 54.8	. . 16.0	272 49.1	. . 23.9	225 37.0	. . 31.7
	04	150 54.2	245 06.2	27.9	294 55.7	16.5	287 51.1	24.1	240 39.2	31.7
	05	165 56.7	260 05.2	28.1	309 56.7	17.0	302 53.1	24.2	255 41.3	31.7
	06	180 59.2	275 04.3	S23 28.3	324 57.6	S13 17.5	317 55.1	S15 24.3	270 43.5	S22 31.7
	07	196 01.6	290 03.3	28.5	339 58.6	18.0	332 57.1	24.5	285 45.6	31.7
	08	211 04.1	305 02.3	28.7	354 59.5	18.5	347 59.1	24.6	300 47.7	31.7
	09	226 06.6	320 01.4	. . 28.9	10 00.5	. . 19.1	3 01.1	. . 24.7	315 49.9	. . 31.7
	10	241 09.0	335 00.4	29.1	25 01.4	19.6	18 03.1	24.9	330 52.0	31.7
	11	256 11.5	349 59.5	29.2	40 02.4	20.1	33 05.1	25.0	345 54.2	31.7
	12	271 14.0	4 58.5	S23 29.4	55 03.3	S13 20.6	48 07.2	S15 25.1	0 56.3	S22 31.7
	13	286 16.4	19 57.5	29.6	70 04.3	21.1	63 09.2	25.2	15 58.5	31.7
	14	301 18.9	34 56.6	29.8	85 05.2	21.6	78 11.2	25.4	31 00.6	31.7
	15	316 21.3	49 55.6	. . 30.0	100 06.2	. . 22.1	93 13.2	. . 25.5	46 02.8	. . 31.7
	16	331 23.8	64 54.6	30.1	115 07.1	22.7	108 15.2	25.6	61 04.9	31.7
	17	346 26.3	79 53.7	30.3	130 08.0	23.2	123 17.2	25.8	76 07.0	31.7
	18	1 28.7	94 52.7	S23 30.5	145 09.0	S13 23.7	138 19.2	S15 25.9	91 09.2	S22 31.7
	19	16 31.2	109 51.7	30.7	160 09.9	24.2	153 21.2	26.0	106 11.3	31.7
	20	31 33.7	124 50.8	30.8	175 10.9	24.7	168 23.2	26.1	121 13.5	31.7
	21	46 36.1	139 49.8	. . 31.0	190 11.8	. . 25.2	183 25.2	. . 26.3	136 15.6	. . 31.7
	22	61 38.6	154 48.9	31.2	205 12.8	25.7	198 27.3	26.4	151 17.8	31.7
	23	76 41.1	169 47.9	31.3	220 13.7	26.3	213 29.3	26.5	166 19.9	31.7
23 SATURDAY	00	91 43.5	184 46.9	S23 31.5	235 14.7	S13 26.8	228 31.3	S15 26.7	181 22.1	S22 31.7
	01	106 46.0	199 46.0	31.7	250 15.6	27.3	243 33.3	26.8	196 24.2	31.7
	02	121 48.5	214 45.0	31.8	265 16.5	27.8	258 35.3	26.9	211 26.3	31.7
	03	136 50.9	229 44.0	. . 32.0	280 17.5	. . 28.3	273 37.3	. . 27.1	226 28.5	. . 31.8
	04	151 53.4	244 43.1	32.2	295 18.4	28.8	288 39.3	27.2	241 30.6	31.8
	05	166 55.8	259 42.1	32.3	310 19.4	29.3	303 41.3	27.3	256 32.8	31.8
	06	181 58.3	274 41.1	S23 32.5	325 20.3	S13 29.9	318 43.3	S15 27.4	271 34.9	S22 31.8
	07	197 00.8	289 40.2	32.7	340 21.3	30.4	333 45.4	27.6	286 37.1	31.8
	08	212 03.2	304 39.2	32.8	355 22.2	30.9	348 47.4	27.7	301 39.2	31.8
	09	227 05.7	319 38.2	. . 33.0	10 23.2	. . 31.4	3 49.4	. . 27.8	316 41.4	. . 31.8
	10	242 08.2	334 37.3	33.1	25 24.1	31.9	18 51.4	28.0	331 43.5	31.8
	11	257 10.6	349 36.3	33.3	40 25.0	32.4	33 53.4	28.1	346 45.6	31.8
	12	272 13.1	4 35.3	S23 33.4	55 26.0	S13 32.9	48 55.4	S15 28.2	1 47.8	S22 31.8
	13	287 15.6	19 34.4	33.6	70 26.9	33.4	63 57.4	28.3	16 49.9	31.8
	14	302 18.0	34 33.4	33.7	85 27.9	33.9	78 59.5	28.5	31 52.1	31.8
	15	317 20.5	49 32.4	. . 33.9	100 28.8	. . 34.5	94 01.5	. . 28.6	46 54.2	. . 31.8
	16	332 23.0	64 31.5	34.0	115 29.8	35.0	109 03.5	28.7	61 56.4	31.8
	17	347 25.4	79 30.5	34.2	130 30.7	35.5	124 05.5	28.8	76 58.5	31.8
	18	2 27.9	94 29.5	S23 34.3	145 31.7	S13 36.0	139 07.5	S15 29.0	92 00.7	S22 31.8
	19	17 30.3	109 28.6	34.5	160 32.6	36.5	154 09.5	29.1	107 02.8	31.8
	20	32 32.8	124 27.6	34.6	175 33.5	37.0	169 11.5	29.2	122 04.9	31.8
	21	47 35.3	139 26.6	. . 34.7	190 34.5	. . 37.5	184 13.5	. . 29.4	137 07.1	. . 31.8
	22	62 37.7	154 25.7	34.9	205 35.4	38.0	199 15.6	29.5	152 09.2	31.8
	23	77 40.2	169 24.7	35.0	220 36.4	38.5	214 17.6	29.6	167 11.4	31.8
Mer. Pass.		h m 17 54.1	v −1.0	d 0.2	v 0.9	d 0.5	v 2.0	d 0.1	v 2.1	d 0.0

STARS

Name	SHA	Dec
	° ′	° ′
Acamar	315 15.8	S40 14.3
Achernar	335 24.3	S57 09.1
Acrux	173 05.8	S63 11.5
Adhara	255 09.7	S28 59.9
Aldebaran	290 45.5	N16 32.5
Alioth	166 18.2	N55 51.6
Alkaid	152 56.8	N49 13.3
Al Na'ir	27 40.2	S46 52.6
Alnilam	275 42.9	S 1 11.6
Alphard	217 52.9	S 8 44.2
Alphecca	126 08.8	N26 39.4
Alpheratz	357 40.3	N29 11.5
Altair	62 05.6	N 8 55.1
Ankaa	353 12.7	S42 12.8
Antares	112 22.9	S26 28.0
Arcturus	145 53.2	N19 05.4
Atria	107 22.5	S69 03.2
Avior	234 16.2	S59 33.9
Bellatrix	278 28.4	N 6 21.7
Betelgeuse	270 57.7	N 7 24.4
Canopus	263 54.2	S52 42.5
Capella	280 29.4	N46 00.8
Deneb	49 29.7	N45 20.9
Denebola	182 30.6	N14 28.3
Diphda	348 52.8	S17 53.5
Dubhe	193 47.9	N61 39.0
Elnath	278 08.4	N28 37.2
Eltanin	90 45.3	N51 29.4
Enif	33 44.3	N 9 57.5
Fomalhaut	15 20.8	S29 31.8
Gacrux	171 57.5	S57 12.4
Gienah	175 49.2	S17 38.3
Hadar	148 43.8	S60 27.1
Hamal	327 57.1	N23 32.8
Kaus Aust.	83 40.2	S34 22.4
Kochab	137 21.1	N74 04.8
Markab	13 35.4	N15 18.2
Menkar	314 11.6	N 4 09.4
Menkent	148 04.2	S36 27.1
Miaplacidus	221 38.3	S69 47.3
Mirfak	308 35.5	N49 55.4
Nunki	75 54.9	S26 16.3
Peacock	53 15.0	S56 40.7
Pollux	243 23.7	N27 58.7
Procyon	244 56.2	N 5 10.6
Rasalhague	96 04.0	N12 33.0
Regulus	207 40.1	N11 52.7
Rigel	281 08.8	S 8 11.1
Rigil Kent.	139 47.9	S60 54.1
Sabik	102 09.4	S15 44.6
Schedar	349 36.8	N56 38.3
Shaula	96 18.2	S37 06.8
Sirius	258 30.7	S16 44.6
Spica	158 28.2	S11 15.1
Suhail	222 49.8	S43 30.2
Vega	80 37.3	N38 48.2
Zuben'ubi	137 02.3	S16 06.7

	SHA	Mer. Pass.
	° ′	h m
Venus	94 25.7	11 40
Mars	144 07.6	8 20
Jupiter	136 58.7	8 48
Saturn	89 46.2	11 56

UT (d h)	SUN GHA	SUN Dec	MOON GHA	v	MOON Dec	d	HP
d h	° ′	° ′	° ′	′	° ′	′	′
21 00	180 30.8	S23 26.0	149 10.6	12.3	S18 56.0	3.6	54.1
01	195 30.5	26.0	163 41.9	12.4	18 52.4	3.6	54.1
02	210 30.2	26.0	178 13.3	12.3	18 48.8	3.7	54.1
03	225 29.9	. . 26.0	192 44.6	12.4	18 45.1	3.8	54.1
04	240 29.5	26.0	207 16.0	12.4	18 41.3	3.9	54.1
05	255 29.2	26.0	221 47.4	12.4	18 37.4	3.9	54.1
06	270 28.9	S23 26.0	236 18.8	12.4	S18 33.5	4.1	54.1
07	285 28.6	26.0	250 50.2	12.4	18 29.4	4.1	54.2
T 08	300 28.3	26.1	265 21.6	12.4	18 25.3	4.2	54.2
H 09	315 28.0	. . 26.1	279 53.0	12.5	18 21.1	4.3	54.2
U 10	330 27.7	26.1	294 24.5	12.5	18 16.8	4.4	54.2
R 11	345 27.4	26.1	308 56.0	12.5	18 12.4	4.5	54.2
S 12	0 27.1	S23 26.1	323 27.5	12.5	S18 07.9	4.5	54.2
D 13	15 26.7	26.1	337 59.0	12.5	18 03.4	4.7	54.2
A 14	30 26.4	26.1	352 30.5	12.6	17 58.7	4.7	54.2
Y 15	45 26.1	. . 26.1	7 02.1	12.6	17 54.0	4.8	54.2
16	60 25.8	26.1	21 33.7	12.6	17 49.2	4.9	54.2
17	75 25.5	26.1	36 05.3	12.6	17 44.3	4.9	54.3
18	90 25.2	S23 26.1	50 36.9	12.6	S17 39.4	5.1	54.3
19	105 24.9	26.1	65 08.5	12.6	17 34.3	5.1	54.3
20	120 24.6	26.1	79 40.1	12.7	17 29.2	5.2	54.3
21	135 24.3	. . 26.1	94 11.8	12.7	17 24.0	5.3	54.3
22	150 23.9	26.1	108 43.5	12.7	17 18.7	5.4	54.3
23	165 23.6	26.1	123 15.2	12.7	17 13.3	5.4	54.3
22 00	180 23.3	S23 26.1	137 46.9	12.7	S17 07.9	5.6	54.3
01	195 23.0	26.1	152 18.6	12.8	17 02.3	5.6	54.4
02	210 22.7	26.1	166 50.4	12.8	16 56.7	5.6	54.4
03	225 22.4	. . 26.0	181 22.2	12.8	16 51.1	5.8	54.4
04	240 22.1	26.0	195 54.0	12.8	16 45.3	5.8	54.4
05	255 21.8	26.0	210 25.8	12.8	16 39.5	6.0	54.4
06	270 21.5	S23 26.0	224 57.6	12.9	S16 33.5	6.0	54.4
07	285 21.1	26.0	239 29.5	12.9	16 27.5	6.0	54.4
08	300 20.8	26.0	254 01.4	12.9	16 21.5	6.2	54.4
F 09	315 20.5	. . 26.0	268 33.3	12.9	16 15.3	6.2	54.5
R 10	330 20.2	26.0	283 05.2	12.9	16 09.1	6.3	54.5
I 11	345 19.9	25.9	297 37.1	13.0	16 02.8	6.4	54.5
D 12	0 19.6	S23 25.9	312 09.1	12.9	S15 56.4	6.4	54.5
A 13	15 19.3	25.9	326 41.0	13.0	15 50.0	6.5	54.5
Y 14	30 19.0	25.9	341 13.0	13.0	15 43.5	6.6	54.5
15	45 18.6	. . 25.9	355 45.0	13.0	15 36.9	6.7	54.5
16	60 18.3	25.9	10 17.0	13.1	15 30.2	6.7	54.6
17	75 18.0	25.8	24 49.1	13.1	15 23.5	6.8	54.6
18	90 17.7	S23 25.8	39 21.2	13.0	S15 16.7	6.9	54.6
19	105 17.4	25.8	53 53.2	13.1	15 09.8	6.9	54.6
20	120 17.1	25.8	68 25.3	13.1	15 02.9	7.1	54.6
21	135 16.8	. . 25.8	82 57.4	13.2	14 55.8	7.1	54.6
22	150 16.5	25.7	97 29.6	13.1	14 48.7	7.1	54.7
23	165 16.2	25.7	112 01.7	13.2	14 41.6	7.2	54.7
23 00	180 15.8	S23 25.7	126 33.9	13.2	S14 34.4	7.3	54.7
01	195 15.5	25.7	141 06.1	13.2	14 27.1	7.4	54.7
02	210 15.2	25.6	155 38.3	13.2	14 19.7	7.4	54.7
03	225 14.9	. . 25.6	170 10.5	13.2	14 12.3	7.5	54.7
04	240 14.6	25.6	184 42.7	13.3	14 04.8	7.6	54.8
05	255 14.3	25.5	199 15.0	13.2	13 57.2	7.6	54.8
06	270 14.0	S23 25.5	213 47.2	13.3	S13 49.6	7.7	54.8
07	285 13.7	25.5	228 19.5	13.3	13 41.9	7.8	54.8
S 08	300 13.4	25.5	242 51.8	13.3	13 34.1	7.8	54.8
A 09	315 13.0	. . 25.4	257 24.1	13.3	13 26.3	7.9	54.9
T 10	330 12.7	25.4	271 56.4	13.3	13 18.4	8.0	54.9
U 11	345 12.4	25.4	286 28.7	13.4	13 10.4	8.0	54.9
R 12	0 12.1	S23 25.3	301 01.1	13.4	S13 02.4	8.1	54.9
D 13	15 11.8	25.3	315 33.5	13.3	12 54.3	8.2	54.9
A 14	30 11.5	25.2	330 05.8	13.4	12 46.1	8.2	55.0
Y 15	45 11.2	. . 25.2	344 38.2	13.4	12 37.9	8.2	55.0
16	60 10.9	25.2	359 10.6	13.4	12 29.7	8.4	55.0
17	75 10.6	25.1	13 43.0	13.4	12 21.3	8.4	55.0
18	90 10.2	S23 25.1	28 15.4	13.5	S12 12.9	8.4	55.0
19	105 09.9	25.0	42 47.9	13.4	12 04.5	8.5	55.1
20	120 09.6	25.0	57 20.3	13.5	11 56.0	8.6	55.1
21	135 09.3	. . 25.0	71 52.8	13.4	11 47.4	8.6	55.1
22	150 09.0	24.9	86 25.2	13.5	11 38.8	8.7	55.1
23	165 08.7	24.9	100 57.7	13.5	S11 30.1	8.8	55.2
	SD 16.3	*d* 0.0	SD 14.8		14.8		15.0

Lat.	Twilight Naut.	Twilight Civil	Sunrise	Moonrise 21	Moonrise 22	Moonrise 23	Moonrise 24
°	h m	h m	h m	h m	h m	h m	h m
N 72	08 26	10 58	▬	▬	13 19	12 59	12 46
N 70	08 06	09 55	▬	12 45	12 40	12 35	12 31
68	07 50	09 20	▬	12 05	12 13	12 17	12 20
66	07 37	08 54	10 35	11 37	11 52	12 02	12 10
64	07 26	08 34	09 53	11 15	11 36	11 50	12 02
62	07 16	08 18	09 24	10 58	11 22	11 40	11 55
60	07 08	08 05	09 03	10 44	11 10	11 31	11 48
N 58	07 00	07 53	08 45	10 32	11 00	11 23	11 43
56	06 54	07 43	08 30	10 21	10 51	11 16	11 38
54	06 47	07 34	08 17	10 12	10 43	11 10	11 34
52	06 42	07 25	08 06	10 03	10 36	11 05	11 30
50	06 36	07 18	07 56	09 56	10 30	11 00	11 26
45	06 25	07 02	07 36	09 40	10 16	10 49	11 18
N 40	06 14	06 48	07 19	09 26	10 05	10 39	11 12
35	06 05	06 36	07 05	09 15	09 55	10 32	11 06
30	05 56	06 26	06 52	09 05	09 46	10 25	11 01
20	05 39	06 07	06 31	08 48	09 31	10 13	10 53
N 10	05 23	05 50	06 12	08 33	09 19	10 02	10 45
0	05 06	05 32	05 55	08 20	09 06	09 52	10 38
S 10	04 47	05 14	05 37	08 06	08 54	09 43	10 31
20	04 24	04 54	05 18	07 51	08 41	09 32	10 23
30	03 55	04 29	04 56	07 34	08 26	09 20	10 14
35	03 37	04 13	04 43	07 24	08 18	09 13	10 09
40	03 13	03 55	04 28	07 12	08 08	09 05	10 04
45	02 43	03 33	04 10	06 59	07 56	08 56	09 57
S 50	01 57	03 03	03 47	06 43	07 42	08 44	09 49
52	01 29	02 48	03 37	06 35	07 35	08 39	09 45
54	00 42	02 30	03 24	06 26	07 28	08 33	09 41
56	////	02 07	03 10	06 17	07 20	08 27	09 36
58	////	01 37	02 53	06 06	07 10	08 19	09 31
S 60	////	00 46	02 33	05 53	07 00	08 11	09 26

Lat.	Sunset	Twilight Civil	Twilight Naut.	Moonset 21	Moonset 22	Moonset 23	Moonset 24
°	h m	h m	h m	h m	h m	h m	h m
N 72	▬	12 59	15 31	▬	17 29	19 24	21 12
N 70	▬	14 03	15 51	16 25	18 07	19 46	21 25
68	▬	14 38	16 07	17 05	18 33	20 03	21 35
66	13 22	15 03	16 20	17 32	18 53	20 17	21 43
64	14 05	15 23	16 32	17 53	19 09	20 28	21 50
62	14 33	15 39	16 41	18 10	19 22	20 38	21 56
60	14 55	15 53	16 50	18 24	19 33	20 46	22 02
N 58	15 12	16 04	16 57	18 36	19 43	20 53	22 06
56	15 27	16 15	17 04	18 46	19 51	21 00	22 10
54	15 40	16 24	17 10	18 55	19 59	21 05	22 14
52	15 51	16 32	17 16	19 03	20 05	21 10	22 17
50	16 01	16 39	17 21	19 11	20 11	21 15	22 20
45	16 22	16 56	17 33	19 26	20 24	21 25	22 27
N 40	16 39	17 09	17 43	19 39	20 35	21 33	22 32
35	16 53	17 21	17 53	19 49	20 44	21 40	22 37
30	17 05	17 32	18 01	19 59	20 52	21 46	22 41
20	17 26	17 50	18 18	20 15	21 06	21 57	22 48
N 10	17 45	18 08	18 34	20 29	21 18	22 06	22 54
0	18 02	18 25	18 51	20 42	21 29	22 14	23 00
S 10	18 20	18 43	19 10	20 55	21 40	22 23	23 05
20	18 39	19 04	19 33	21 09	21 51	22 32	23 11
30	19 01	19 29	20 02	21 25	22 05	22 42	23 18
35	19 14	19 44	20 21	21 34	22 13	22 48	23 22
40	19 29	20 02	20 44	21 45	22 21	22 55	23 26
45	19 47	20 25	21 15	21 57	22 31	23 03	23 31
S 50	20 10	20 55	22 00	22 12	22 44	23 12	23 37
52	20 21	21 10	22 28	22 19	22 49	23 16	23 40
54	20 33	21 28	23 15	22 27	22 56	23 21	23 43
56	20 47	21 50	////	22 35	23 03	23 26	23 47
58	21 04	22 20	////	22 45	23 10	23 32	23 50
S 60	21 25	23 11	////	22 56	23 19	23 38	23 54

Day	SUN Eqn. of Time 00^h	SUN Eqn. of Time 12^h	SUN Mer. Pass.	MOON Mer. Pass. Upper	MOON Mer. Pass. Lower	MOON Age	MOON Phase
d	m s	m s	h m	h m	h m	d %	
21	02 04	01 49	11 58	14 31	02 07	03 9	
22	01 34	01 19	11 59	15 18	02 54	04 15	
23	01 04	00 49	11 59	16 03	03 41	05 23	

UT		ARIES	VENUS −4·0		MARS +1·5		JUPITER −1·8		SATURN +0·5	
d	h	GHA	GHA	Dec	GHA	Dec	GHA	Dec	GHA	Dec
		° ′	° ′	° ′	° ′	° ′	° ′	° ′	° ′	° ′
24	00	92 42.7	184 23.7	S23 35.2	235 37.3	S13 39.0	229 19.6	S15 29.7	182 13.5	S22 31.8
	01	107 45.1	199 22.8	35.3	250 38.3	39.6	244 21.6	29.9	197 15.7	31.8
	02	122 47.6	214 21.8	35.4	265 39.2	40.1	259 23.6	30.0	212 17.8	31.8
	03	137 50.1	229 20.8	. . 35.6	280 40.1	. . 40.6	274 25.6	. . 30.1	227 20.0	. . 31.8
	04	152 52.5	244 19.9	35.7	295 41.1	41.1	289 27.6	30.3	242 22.1	31.8
	05	167 55.0	259 18.9	35.8	310 42.0	41.6	304 29.7	30.4	257 24.2	31.8
	06	182 57.4	274 17.9	S23 35.9	325 43.0	S13 42.1	319 31.7	S15 30.5	272 26.4	S22 31.8
	07	197 59.9	289 16.9	36.1	340 43.9	42.6	334 33.7	30.6	287 28.5	31.8
	08	213 02.4	304 16.0	36.2	355 44.8	43.1	349 35.7	30.8	302 30.7	31.8
S	09	228 04.8	319 15.0	. . 36.3	10 45.8	. . 43.6	4 37.7	. . 30.9	317 32.8	. . 31.8
U	10	243 07.3	334 14.0	36.5	25 46.7	44.1	19 39.7	31.0	332 35.0	31.8
N	11	258 09.8	349 13.1	36.6	40 47.7	44.6	34 41.8	31.1	347 37.1	31.8
D	12	273 12.2	4 12.1	S23 36.7	55 48.6	S13 45.1	49 43.8	S15 31.3	2 39.3	S22 31.8
A	13	288 14.7	19 11.1	36.8	70 49.6	45.7	64 45.8	31.4	17 41.4	31.8
Y	14	303 17.2	34 10.2	36.9	85 50.5	46.2	79 47.8	31.5	32 43.5	31.8
	15	318 19.6	49 09.2	. . 37.1	100 51.4	. . 46.7	94 49.8	. . 31.6	47 45.7	. . 31.8
	16	333 22.1	64 08.2	37.2	115 52.4	47.2	109 51.8	31.8	62 47.8	31.8
	17	348 24.6	79 07.3	37.3	130 53.3	47.7	124 53.9	31.9	77 50.0	31.8
	18	3 27.0	94 06.3	S23 37.4	145 54.3	S13 48.2	139 55.9	S15 32.0	92 52.1	S22 31.8
	19	18 29.5	109 05.3	37.5	160 55.2	48.7	154 57.9	32.2	107 54.3	31.8
	20	33 31.9	124 04.3	37.6	175 56.1	49.2	169 59.9	32.3	122 56.4	31.8
	21	48 34.4	139 03.4	. . 37.7	190 57.1	. . 49.7	185 01.9	. . 32.4	137 58.6	. . 31.8
	22	63 36.9	154 02.4	37.8	205 58.0	50.2	200 03.9	32.5	153 00.7	31.8
	23	78 39.3	169 01.4	38.0	220 59.0	50.7	215 06.0	32.7	168 02.8	31.8
25	00	93 41.8	184 00.5	S23 38.1	235 59.9	S13 51.2	230 08.0	S15 32.8	183 05.0	S22 31.8
	01	108 44.3	198 59.5	38.2	251 00.9	51.7	245 10.0	32.9	198 07.1	31.8
	02	123 46.7	213 58.5	38.3	266 01.8	52.2	260 12.0	33.0	213 09.3	31.8
	03	138 49.2	228 57.6	. . 38.4	281 02.7	. . 52.7	275 14.0	. . 33.2	228 11.4	. . 31.8
	04	153 51.7	243 56.6	38.5	296 03.7	53.2	290 16.0	33.3	243 13.6	31.8
	05	168 54.1	258 55.6	38.6	311 04.6	53.8	305 18.1	33.4	258 15.7	31.8
	06	183 56.6	273 54.6	S23 38.7	326 05.6	S13 54.3	320 20.1	S15 33.5	273 17.9	S22 31.8
	07	198 59.1	288 53.7	38.8	341 06.5	54.8	335 22.1	33.7	288 20.0	31.8
	08	214 01.5	303 52.7	38.9	356 07.4	55.3	350 24.1	33.8	303 22.1	31.8
M	09	229 04.0	318 51.7	. . 39.0	11 08.4	. . 55.8	5 26.1	. . 33.9	318 24.3	. . 31.8
O	10	244 06.4	333 50.8	39.1	26 09.3	56.3	20 28.2	34.0	333 26.4	31.8
N	11	259 08.9	348 49.8	39.1	41 10.3	56.8	35 30.2	34.2	348 28.6	31.8
D	12	274 11.4	3 48.8	S23 39.2	56 11.2	S13 57.3	50 32.2	S15 34.3	3 30.7	S22 31.8
A	13	289 13.8	18 47.8	39.3	71 12.1	57.8	65 34.2	34.4	18 32.9	31.8
Y	14	304 16.3	33 46.9	39.4	86 13.1	58.3	80 36.2	34.5	33 35.0	31.8
	15	319 18.8	48 45.9	. . 39.5	101 14.0	. . 58.8	95 38.3	. . 34.7	48 37.2	. . 31.8
	16	334 21.2	63 44.9	39.6	116 15.0	59.3	110 40.3	34.8	63 39.3	31.8
	17	349 23.7	78 44.0	39.7	131 15.9	13 59.8	125 42.3	34.9	78 41.5	31.8
	18	4 26.2	93 43.0	S23 39.8	146 16.8	S14 00.3	140 44.3	S15 35.0	93 43.6	S22 31.8
	19	19 28.6	108 42.0	39.8	161 17.8	00.8	155 46.3	35.2	108 45.7	31.8
	20	34 31.1	123 41.0	39.9	176 18.7	01.3	170 48.4	35.3	123 47.9	31.8
	21	49 33.5	138 40.1	. . 40.0	191 19.6	. . 01.8	185 50.4	. . 35.4	138 50.0	. . 31.9
	22	64 36.0	153 39.1	40.1	206 20.6	02.3	200 52.4	35.5	153 52.2	31.9
	23	79 38.5	168 38.1	40.2	221 21.5	02.8	215 54.4	35.7	168 54.3	31.9
26	00	94 40.9	183 37.2	S23 40.2	236 22.5	S14 03.3	230 56.4	S15 35.8	183 56.5	S22 31.9
	01	109 43.4	198 36.2	40.3	251 23.4	03.8	245 58.5	35.9	198 58.6	31.9
	02	124 45.9	213 35.2	40.4	266 24.3	04.3	261 00.5	36.0	214 00.8	31.9
	03	139 48.3	228 34.2	. . 40.5	281 25.3	. . 04.8	276 02.5	. . 36.2	229 02.9	. . 31.9
	04	154 50.8	243 33.3	40.5	296 26.2	05.3	291 04.5	36.3	244 05.0	31.9
	05	169 53.3	258 32.3	40.6	311 27.2	05.8	306 06.5	36.4	259 07.2	31.9
	06	184 55.7	273 31.3	S23 40.7	326 28.1	S14 06.3	321 08.6	S15 36.5	274 09.3	S22 31.9
	07	199 58.2	288 30.3	40.7	341 29.0	06.8	336 10.6	36.7	289 11.5	31.9
T	08	215 00.7	303 29.4	40.8	356 30.0	07.3	351 12.6	36.8	304 13.6	31.9
U	09	230 03.1	318 28.4	. . 40.9	11 30.9	. . 07.8	6 14.6	. . 36.9	319 15.8	. . 31.9
E	10	245 05.6	333 27.4	40.9	26 31.8	08.3	21 16.7	37.0	334 17.9	31.9
S	11	260 08.0	348 26.5	41.0	41 32.8	08.8	36 18.7	37.2	349 20.1	31.9
D	12	275 10.5	3 25.5	S23 41.0	56 33.7	S14 09.3	51 20.7	S15 37.3	4 22.2	S22 31.9
A	13	290 13.0	18 24.5	41.1	71 34.7	09.8	66 22.7	37.4	19 24.4	31.9
Y	14	305 15.4	33 23.5	41.2	86 35.6	10.3	81 24.7	37.5	34 26.5	31.9
	15	320 17.9	48 22.6	. . 41.2	101 36.5	. . 10.8	96 26.8	. . 37.6	49 28.6	. . 31.9
	16	335 20.4	63 21.6	41.3	116 37.5	11.3	111 28.8	37.8	64 30.8	31.9
	17	350 22.8	78 20.6	41.3	131 38.4	11.8	126 30.8	37.9	79 32.9	31.9
	18	5 25.3	93 19.6	S23 41.4	146 39.3	S14 12.3	141 32.8	S15 38.0	94 35.1	S22 31.9
	19	20 27.8	108 18.7	41.4	161 40.3	12.8	156 34.9	38.1	109 37.2	31.9
	20	35 30.2	123 17.7	41.5	176 41.2	13.3	171 36.9	38.3	124 39.4	31.9
	21	50 32.7	138 16.7	. . 41.5	191 42.2	. . 13.8	186 38.9	. . 38.4	139 41.5	. . 31.9
	22	65 35.2	153 15.8	41.6	206 43.1	14.3	201 40.9	38.5	154 43.7	31.9
	23	80 37.6	168 14.8	41.6	221 44.0	14.8	216 43.0	38.6	169 45.8	31.9
Mer. Pass.		h m 17 42.3	v −1.0	d 0.1	v 0.9	d 0.5	v 2.0	d 0.1	v 2.1	d 0.0

STARS Name	SHA	Dec
	° ′	° ′
Acamar	315 15.8	S40 14.3
Achernar	335 24.4	S57 09.2
Acrux	173 05.8	S63 11.5
Adhara	255 09.7	S28 59.9
Aldebaran	290 45.5	N16 32.5
Alioth	166 18.2	N55 51.6
Alkaid	152 56.8	N49 13.3
Al Na'ir	27 40.2	S46 52.6
Alnilam	275 42.9	S 1 11.6
Alphard	217 52.9	S 8 44.2
Alphecca	126 08.7	N26 39.3
Alpheratz	357 40.3	N29 11.5
Altair	62 05.6	N 8 55.1
Ankaa	353 12.7	S42 12.8
Antares	112 22.8	S26 28.0
Arcturus	145 53.2	N19 05.4
Atria	107 22.4	S69 03.2
Avior	234 16.1	S59 34.0
Bellatrix	278 28.4	N 6 21.7
Betelgeuse	270 57.7	N 7 24.4
Canopus	263 54.2	S52 42.5
Capella	280 29.4	N46 00.8
Deneb	49 29.8	N45 20.9
Denebola	182 30.5	N14 28.3
Diphda	348 52.8	S17 53.5
Dubhe	193 47.9	N61 39.0
Elnath	278 08.4	N28 37.2
Eltanin	90 45.3	N51 29.3
Enif	33 44.3	N 9 57.5
Fomalhaut	15 20.8	S29 31.8
Gacrux	171 57.4	S57 12.4
Gienah	175 49.1	S17 38.3
Hadar	148 43.8	S60 27.1
Hamal	327 57.1	N23 32.8
Kaus Aust.	83 40.2	S34 22.4
Kochab	137 21.0	N74 04.8
Markab	13 35.4	N15 18.2
Menkar	314 11.6	N 4 09.4
Menkent	148 04.1	S36 27.2
Miaplacidus	221 38.2	S69 47.3
Mirfak	308 35.5	N49 55.5
Nunki	75 54.9	S26 16.3
Peacock	53 15.0	S56 40.7
Pollux	243 23.7	N27 58.7
Procyon	244 56.2	N 5 10.6
Rasalhague	96 04.0	N12 33.0
Regulus	207 40.1	N11 52.7
Rigel	281 08.8	S 8 11.1
Rigil Kent.	139 47.9	S60 54.1
Sabik	102 09.4	S15 44.6
Schedar	349 36.9	N56 38.3
Shaula	96 18.2	S37 06.8
Sirius	258 30.7	S16 44.6
Spica	158 28.1	S11 15.1
Suhail	222 49.8	S43 30.2
Vega	80 37.3	N38 48.2
Zuben'ubi	137 02.3	S16 06.7

	SHA	Mer. Pass.
	° ′	h m
Venus	90 18.7	11 45
Mars	142 18.1	8 15
Jupiter	136 26.2	8 38
Saturn	89 23.2	11 46

UT d h		SUN GHA ° ′	SUN Dec ° ′	MOON GHA ° ′	v ′	MOON Dec ° ′	d ′	HP ′
24 00		180 08.4	S23 24.8	115 30.2	13.4	S11 21.3	8.8	55.2
01		195 08.1	24.8	130 02.6	13.5	11 12.5	8.8	55.2
02		210 07.8	24.7	144 35.1	13.5	11 03.7	9.0	55.2
03		225 07.4	. . 24.7	159 07.6	13.5	10 54.7	8.9	55.2
04		240 07.1	24.6	173 40.1	13.6	10 45.8	9.1	55.3
05		255 06.8	24.6	188 12.7	13.5	10 36.7	9.0	55.3
06		270 06.5	S23 24.5	202 45.2	13.5	S10 27.7	9.2	55.3
07		285 06.2	24.5	217 17.7	13.5	10 18.5	9.2	55.3
08		300 05.9	24.4	231 50.2	13.6	10 09.3	9.2	55.4
09	SUNDAY	315 05.6	. . 24.4	246 22.8	13.5	10 00.1	9.3	55.4
10		330 05.3	24.3	260 55.3	13.5	9 50.8	9.3	55.4
11		345 05.0	24.3	275 27.8	13.6	9 41.5	9.4	55.4
12		0 04.6	S23 24.2	290 00.4	13.5	S 9 32.1	9.5	55.5
13		15 04.3	24.2	304 32.9	13.6	9 22.6	9.5	55.5
14		30 04.0	24.1	319 05.5	13.5	9 13.1	9.5	55.5
15		45 03.7	. . 24.1	333 38.0	13.5	9 03.6	9.6	55.5
16		60 03.4	24.0	348 10.5	13.6	8 54.0	9.7	55.6
17		75 03.1	23.9	2 43.1	13.5	8 44.3	9.6	55.6
18		90 02.8	S23 23.9	17 15.6	13.6	S 8 34.7	9.8	55.6
19		105 02.5	23.8	31 48.2	13.5	8 24.9	9.8	55.7
20		120 02.2	23.8	46 20.7	13.5	8 15.1	9.8	55.7
21		135 01.8	. . 23.7	60 53.2	13.6	8 05.3	9.9	55.7
22		150 01.5	23.6	75 25.8	13.5	7 55.4	9.9	55.7
23		165 01.2	23.6	89 58.3	13.5	7 45.5	10.0	55.8
25 00		180 00.9	S23 23.5	104 30.8	13.5	S 7 35.5	10.0	55.8
01		195 00.6	23.4	119 03.3	13.5	7 25.5	10.0	55.8
02		210 00.3	23.4	133 35.8	13.5	7 15.5	10.1	55.9
03		225 00.0	. . 23.3	148 08.3	13.5	7 05.4	10.2	55.9
04		239 59.7	23.2	162 40.8	13.5	6 55.2	10.1	55.9
05		254 59.4	23.2	177 13.3	13.5	6 45.1	10.3	55.9
06		269 59.1	S23 23.1	191 45.8	13.4	S 6 34.8	10.2	56.0
07		284 58.7	23.0	206 18.2	13.5	6 24.6	10.3	56.0
08		299 58.4	23.0	220 50.7	13.4	6 14.3	10.4	56.0
09	MONDAY	314 58.1	. . 22.9	235 23.1	13.4	6 03.9	10.3	56.1
10		329 57.8	22.8	249 55.5	13.4	5 53.6	10.4	56.1
11		344 57.5	22.7	264 27.9	13.4	5 43.2	10.5	56.1
12		359 57.2	S23 22.7	279 00.3	13.4	S 5 32.7	10.5	56.2
13		14 56.9	22.6	293 32.7	13.4	5 22.2	10.5	56.2
14		29 56.6	22.5	308 05.1	13.4	5 11.7	10.6	56.2
15		44 56.3	. . 22.4	322 37.5	13.3	5 01.1	10.6	56.2
16		59 56.0	22.4	337 09.8	13.3	4 50.5	10.6	56.3
17		74 55.7	22.3	351 42.1	13.3	4 39.9	10.7	56.3
18		89 55.3	S23 22.2	6 14.4	13.3	S 4 29.2	10.7	56.3
19		104 55.0	22.1	20 46.7	13.2	4 18.5	10.7	56.4
20		119 54.7	22.0	35 18.9	13.3	4 07.8	10.7	56.4
21		134 54.4	. . 22.0	49 51.2	13.2	3 57.1	10.8	56.4
22		149 54.1	21.9	64 23.4	13.2	3 46.3	10.8	56.5
23		164 53.8	21.8	78 55.6	13.2	3 35.5	10.9	56.5
26 00		179 53.5	S23 21.7	93 27.8	13.1	S 3 24.6	10.9	56.5
01		194 53.2	21.6	107 59.9	13.1	3 13.7	10.9	56.6
02		209 52.9	21.5	122 32.0	13.1	3 02.8	10.9	56.6
03		224 52.6	. . 21.5	137 04.1	13.1	2 51.9	11.0	56.6
04		239 52.3	21.4	151 36.2	13.0	2 40.9	10.9	56.7
05		254 51.9	21.3	166 08.2	13.1	2 30.0	11.1	56.7
06		269 51.6	S23 21.2	180 40.3	12.9	S 2 18.9	11.0	56.7
07		284 51.3	21.1	195 12.2	13.0	2 07.9	11.0	56.8
08		299 51.0	21.0	209 44.2	12.9	1 56.9	11.1	56.8
09		314 50.7	. . 20.9	224 16.1	12.9	1 45.8	11.1	56.9
10		329 50.4	20.8	238 48.0	12.9	1 34.7	11.1	56.9
11		344 50.1	20.7	253 19.9	12.8	1 23.6	11.2	56.9
12	TUESDAY	359 49.8	S23 20.6	267 51.7	12.8	S 1 12.4	11.2	57.0
13		14 49.5	20.6	282 23.5	12.7	1 01.2	11.1	57.0
14		29 49.2	20.5	296 55.2	12.8	0 50.1	11.2	57.0
15		44 48.9	. . 20.4	311 27.0	12.6	0 38.9	11.3	57.1
16		59 48.6	20.3	325 58.6	12.7	0 27.6	11.2	57.1
17		74 48.2	20.2	340 30.3	12.6	0 16.4	11.2	57.1
18		89 47.9	S23 20.1	355 01.9	12.5	S 0 05.2	11.3	57.2
19		104 47.6	20.0	9 33.4	12.6	N 0 06.1	11.3	57.2
20		119 47.3	19.9	24 05.0	12.5	0 17.4	11.3	57.3
21		134 47.0	. . 19.8	38 36.5	12.4	0 28.7	11.3	57.3
22		149 46.7	19.7	53 07.9	12.4	0 40.0	11.3	57.3
23		164 46.4	19.6	67 39.3	12.3	N 0 51.3	11.3	57.4
		SD 16.3	*d* 0.1	SD 15.1		15.3		15.5

Lat.	Twilight Naut.	Twilight Civil	Sunrise	Moonrise 24	Moonrise 25	Moonrise 26	Moonrise 27
°	h m	h m	h m	h m	h m	h m	h m
N 72	08 27	10 57	▬	12 46	12 35	12 25	12 15
N 70	08 07	09 55	▬	12 31	12 27	12 23	12 19
68	07 51	09 20	▬	12 20	12 21	12 22	12 23
66	07 38	08 55	10 35	12 10	12 16	12 21	12 26
64	07 27	08 35	09 53	12 02	12 11	12 20	12 29
62	07 17	08 19	09 25	11 55	12 07	12 19	12 31
60	07 09	08 06	09 03	11 48	12 04	12 18	12 33
N 58	07 01	07 54	08 46	11 43	12 01	12 17	12 35
56	06 55	07 44	08 31	11 38	11 58	12 17	12 36
54	06 49	07 35	08 19	11 34	11 55	12 16	12 38
52	06 43	07 27	08 07	11 30	11 53	12 16	12 39
50	06 38	07 19	07 58	11 26	11 51	12 15	12 40
45	06 26	07 03	07 37	11 18	11 47	12 14	12 43
N 40	06 15	06 50	07 20	11 12	11 43	12 14	12 45
35	06 06	06 38	07 06	11 06	11 40	12 13	12 47
30	05 57	06 27	06 54	11 01	11 37	12 12	12 49
20	05 41	06 08	06 32	10 53	11 32	12 11	12 52
N 10	05 25	05 51	06 14	10 45	11 27	12 10	12 54
0	05 08	05 34	05 56	10 38	11 23	12 09	12 57
S 10	04 49	05 16	05 39	10 31	11 19	12 08	12 59
20	04 26	04 55	05 20	10 23	11 15	12 08	13 02
30	03 57	04 30	04 58	10 14	11 10	12 07	13 05
35	03 38	04 15	04 45	10 09	11 07	12 06	13 07
40	03 15	03 57	04 30	10 04	11 04	12 05	13 09
45	02 45	03 34	04 12	09 57	11 00	12 05	13 12
S 50	01 59	03 05	03 49	09 49	10 55	12 04	13 15
52	01 31	02 50	03 38	09 45	10 53	12 03	13 16
54	00 45	02 32	03 26	09 41	10 51	12 03	13 18
56	////	02 09	03 12	09 36	10 48	12 02	13 19
58	////	01 40	02 55	09 31	10 45	12 02	13 21
S 60	////	00 49	02 35	09 26	10 42	12 01	13 23

Lat.	Sunset	Twilight Civil	Twilight Naut.	Moonset 24	Moonset 25	Moonset 26	Moonset 27
°	h m	h m	h m	h m	h m	h m	h m
N 72	▬	13 04	15 34	21 12	22 58	24 46	00 46
N 70	▬	14 05	15 54	21 25	23 03	24 44	00 44
68	▬	14 40	16 09	21 35	23 08	24 43	00 43
66	13 25	15 05	16 22	21 43	23 11	24 42	00 42
64	14 07	15 25	16 34	21 50	23 14	24 41	00 41
62	14 36	15 41	16 43	21 56	23 17	24 40	00 40
60	14 57	15 55	16 52	22 02	23 19	24 40	00 40
N 58	15 15	16 06	16 59	22 06	23 21	24 39	00 39
56	15 29	16 17	17 06	22 10	23 23	24 39	00 39
54	15 42	16 26	17 12	22 14	23 25	24 38	00 38
52	15 53	16 34	17 18	22 17	23 26	24 38	00 38
50	16 03	16 41	17 23	22 20	23 28	24 37	00 37
45	16 24	16 57	17 35	22 27	23 31	24 36	00 36
N 40	16 40	17 11	17 45	22 32	23 33	24 36	00 36
35	16 54	17 23	17 54	22 37	23 35	24 35	00 35
30	17 07	17 33	18 03	22 41	23 37	24 34	00 34
20	17 28	17 52	18 20	22 48	23 40	24 33	00 33
N 10	17 47	18 09	18 36	22 54	23 43	24 33	00 33
0	18 04	18 26	18 53	23 00	23 45	24 32	00 32
S 10	18 21	18 45	19 12	23 05	23 48	24 31	00 31
20	18 40	19 05	19 34	23 11	23 50	24 30	00 30
30	19 02	19 30	20 03	23 18	23 53	24 29	00 29
35	19 15	19 45	20 22	23 22	23 55	24 28	00 28
40	19 30	20 03	20 45	23 26	23 57	24 28	00 28
45	19 48	20 26	21 16	23 31	23 59	24 27	00 27
S 50	20 11	20 56	22 01	23 37	24 02	00 02	00 26
52	20 22	21 11	22 29	23 40	24 03	00 03	00 26
54	20 34	21 28	23 14	23 43	24 04	00 04	00 25
56	20 48	21 51	////	23 47	24 06	00 06	00 24
58	21 05	22 20	////	23 50	24 07	00 07	00 24
S 60	21 25	23 10	////	23 54	24 09	00 09	00 23

Day	SUN Eqn. of Time 00^h	SUN Eqn. of Time 12^h	SUN Mer. Pass.	MOON Mer. Pass. Upper	MOON Mer. Pass. Lower	MOON Age	MOON Phase
d	m s	m s	h m	h m	h m	d	%
24	00 34	00 19	12 00	16 49	04 26	06	31
25	00 04	00 11	12 00	17 34	05 11	07	41
26	00 25	00 40	12 01	18 21	05 57	08	51

	UT	ARIES	VENUS −4·0		MARS +1·5		JUPITER −1·8		SATURN +0·5	
		GHA	GHA	Dec	GHA	Dec	GHA	Dec	GHA	Dec
	d h	° ′	° ′	° ′	° ′	° ′	° ′	° ′	° ′	° ′
	27 00	95 40.1	183 13.8	S23 41.7	236 45.0	S14 15.3	231 45.0	S15 38.8	184 47.9	S22 31.9
	01	110 42.5	198 12.8	41.7	251 45.9	15.8	246 47.0	38.9	199 50.1	31.9
	02	125 45.0	213 11.9	41.8	266 46.8	16.3	261 49.0	39.0	214 52.2	31.9
	03	140 47.5	228 10.9	. . 41.8	281 47.8	. . 16.8	276 51.1	. . 39.1	229 54.4	. . 31.9
	04	155 49.9	243 09.9	41.8	296 48.7	17.3	291 53.1	39.2	244 56.5	31.9
	05	170 52.4	258 08.9	41.9	311 49.6	17.8	306 55.1	39.4	259 58.7	31.9
WEDNESDAY	06	185 54.9	273 08.0	S23 41.9	326 50.6	S14 18.3	321 57.1	S15 39.5	275 00.8	S22 31.9
	07	200 57.3	288 07.0	42.0	341 51.5	18.8	336 59.2	39.6	290 03.0	31.9
	08	215 59.8	303 06.0	42.0	356 52.5	19.3	352 01.2	39.7	305 05.1	31.9
	09	231 02.3	318 05.1	. . 42.0	11 53.4	. . 19.8	7 03.2	. . 39.9	320 07.3	. . 31.9
	10	246 04.7	333 04.1	42.1	26 54.3	20.3	22 05.2	40.0	335 09.4	31.9
	11	261 07.2	348 03.1	42.1	41 55.3	20.8	37 07.3	40.1	350 11.5	31.9
	12	276 09.6	3 02.1	S23 42.1	56 56.2	S14 21.2	52 09.3	S15 40.2	5 13.7	S22 31.9
	13	291 12.1	18 01.2	42.2	71 57.1	21.7	67 11.3	40.4	20 15.8	31.9
	14	306 14.6	33 00.2	42.2	86 58.1	22.2	82 13.3	40.5	35 18.0	31.9
	15	321 17.0	47 59.2	. . 42.2	101 59.0	. . 22.7	97 15.4	. . 40.6	50 20.1	. . 31.9
	16	336 19.5	62 58.2	42.2	116 59.9	23.2	112 17.4	40.7	65 22.3	31.9
	17	351 22.0	77 57.3	42.3	132 00.9	23.7	127 19.4	40.8	80 24.4	31.9
	18	6 24.4	92 56.3	S23 42.3	147 01.8	S14 24.2	142 21.4	S15 41.0	95 26.6	S22 31.9
	19	21 26.9	107 55.3	42.3	162 02.7	24.7	157 23.5	41.1	110 28.7	31.9
	20	36 29.4	122 54.3	42.3	177 03.7	25.2	172 25.5	41.2	125 30.9	31.9
	21	51 31.8	137 53.4	. . 42.3	192 04.6	. . 25.7	187 27.5	. . 41.3	140 33.0	. . 31.9
	22	66 34.3	152 52.4	42.4	207 05.5	26.2	202 29.6	41.4	155 35.1	31.9
	23	81 36.8	167 51.4	42.4	222 06.5	26.7	217 31.6	41.6	170 37.3	31.9
	28 00	96 39.2	182 50.4	S23 42.4	237 07.4	S14 27.2	232 33.6	S15 41.7	185 39.4	S22 31.9
	01	111 41.7	197 49.5	42.4	252 08.3	27.7	247 35.6	41.8	200 41.6	31.9
	02	126 44.1	212 48.5	42.4	267 09.3	28.2	262 37.7	41.9	215 43.7	31.9
	03	141 46.6	227 47.5	. . 42.4	282 10.2	. . 28.7	277 39.7	. . 42.1	230 45.9	. . 31.9
	04	156 49.1	242 46.6	42.4	297 11.2	29.2	292 41.7	42.2	245 48.0	31.9
	05	171 51.5	257 45.6	42.4	312 12.1	29.6	307 43.7	42.3	260 50.2	31.9
THURSDAY	06	186 54.0	272 44.6	S23 42.4	327 13.0	S14 30.1	322 45.8	S15 42.4	275 52.3	S22 31.9
	07	201 56.5	287 43.6	42.5	342 14.0	30.6	337 47.8	42.5	290 54.5	31.9
	08	216 58.9	302 42.7	42.5	357 14.9	31.1	352 49.8	42.7	305 56.6	31.9
	09	232 01.4	317 41.7	. . 42.5	12 15.8	. . 31.6	7 51.9	. . 42.8	320 58.7	. . 31.9
	10	247 03.9	332 40.7	42.5	27 16.8	32.1	22 53.9	42.9	336 00.9	31.9
	11	262 06.3	347 39.7	42.5	42 17.7	32.6	37 55.9	43.0	351 03.0	31.9
	12	277 08.8	2 38.8	S23 42.5	57 18.6	S14 33.1	52 58.0	S15 43.1	6 05.2	S22 31.9
	13	292 11.3	17 37.8	42.5	72 19.6	33.6	68 00.0	43.3	21 07.3	31.9
	14	307 13.7	32 36.8	42.5	87 20.5	34.1	83 02.0	43.4	36 09.5	31.9
	15	322 16.2	47 35.8	. . 42.5	102 21.4	. . 34.6	98 04.0	. . 43.5	51 11.6	. . 31.9
	16	337 18.6	62 34.9	42.4	117 22.4	35.0	113 06.1	43.6	66 13.8	31.9
	17	352 21.1	77 33.9	42.4	132 23.3	35.5	128 08.1	43.7	81 15.9	31.9
	18	7 23.6	92 32.9	S23 42.4	147 24.2	S14 36.0	143 10.1	S15 43.9	96 18.1	S22 31.9
	19	22 26.0	107 31.9	42.4	162 25.2	36.5	158 12.2	44.0	111 20.2	31.9
	20	37 28.5	122 31.0	42.4	177 26.1	37.0	173 14.2	44.1	126 22.3	31.9
	21	52 31.0	137 30.0	. . 42.4	192 27.0	. . 37.5	188 16.2	. . 44.2	141 24.5	. . 31.9
	22	67 33.4	152 29.0	42.4	207 27.9	38.0	203 18.3	44.3	156 26.6	31.9
	23	82 35.9	167 28.1	42.4	222 28.9	38.5	218 20.3	44.5	171 28.8	31.9
	29 00	97 38.4	182 27.1	S23 42.4	237 29.8	S14 39.0	233 22.3	S15 44.6	186 30.9	S22 31.9
	01	112 40.8	197 26.1	42.3	252 30.7	39.5	248 24.3	44.7	201 33.1	31.9
	02	127 43.3	212 25.1	42.3	267 31.7	39.9	263 26.4	44.8	216 35.2	31.9
	03	142 45.7	227 24.2	. . 42.3	282 32.6	. . 40.4	278 28.4	. . 44.9	231 37.4	. . 31.9
	04	157 48.2	242 23.2	42.3	297 33.5	40.9	293 30.4	45.1	246 39.5	31.9
	05	172 50.7	257 22.2	42.3	312 34.5	41.4	308 32.5	45.2	261 41.7	31.9
FRIDAY	06	187 53.1	272 21.2	S23 42.2	327 35.4	S14 41.9	323 34.5	S15 45.3	276 43.8	S22 31.9
	07	202 55.6	287 20.3	42.2	342 36.3	42.4	338 36.5	45.4	291 46.0	31.9
	08	217 58.1	302 19.3	42.2	357 37.3	42.9	353 38.6	45.5	306 48.1	31.9
	09	233 00.5	317 18.3	. . 42.2	12 38.2	. . 43.4	8 40.6	. . 45.7	321 50.2	. . 31.9
	10	248 03.0	332 17.4	42.1	27 39.1	43.8	23 42.6	45.8	336 52.4	31.9
	11	263 05.5	347 16.4	42.1	42 40.1	44.3	38 44.7	45.9	351 54.5	31.9
	12	278 07.9	2 15.4	S23 42.1	57 41.0	S14 44.8	53 46.7	S15 46.0	6 56.7	S22 31.9
	13	293 10.4	17 14.4	42.0	72 41.9	45.3	68 48.7	46.1	21 58.8	31.9
	14	308 12.9	32 13.5	42.0	87 42.9	45.8	83 50.8	46.3	37 01.0	31.9
	15	323 15.3	47 12.5	. . 42.0	102 43.8	. . 46.3	98 52.8	. . 46.4	52 03.1	. . 31.9
	16	338 17.8	62 11.5	41.9	117 44.7	46.8	113 54.8	46.5	67 05.3	31.9
	17	353 20.2	77 10.5	41.9	132 45.6	47.3	128 56.9	46.6	82 07.4	31.9
	18	8 22.7	92 09.6	S23 41.9	147 46.6	S14 47.7	143 58.9	S15 46.7	97 09.6	S22 31.9
	19	23 25.2	107 08.6	41.8	162 47.5	48.2	159 00.9	46.9	112 11.7	31.9
	20	38 27.6	122 07.6	41.8	177 48.4	48.7	174 03.0	47.0	127 13.9	31.9
	21	53 30.1	137 06.6	. . 41.7	192 49.4	. . 49.2	189 05.0	. . 47.1	142 16.0	. . 31.9
	22	68 32.6	152 05.7	41.7	207 50.3	49.7	204 07.0	47.2	157 18.1	31.9
	23	83 35.0	167 04.7	41.6	222 51.2	50.2	219 09.1	47.3	172 20.3	31.9
	Mer. Pass.	h m 17 30.5	*v* −1.0	*d* 0.0	*v* 0.9	*d* 0.5	*v* 2.0	*d* 0.1	*v* 2.1	*d* 0.0

STARS

Name	SHA	Dec
	° ′	° ′
Acamar	315 15.8	S40 14.3
Achernar	335 24.4	S57 09.2
Acrux	173 05.7	S63 11.5
Adhara	255 09.7	S28 59.9
Aldebaran	290 45.5	N16 32.5
Alioth	166 18.2	N55 51.6
Alkaid	152 56.7	N49 13.3
Al Na'ir	27 40.2	S46 52.6
Alnilam	275 42.9	S 1 11.7
Alphard	217 52.8	S 8 44.2
Alphecca	126 08.7	N26 39.3
Alpheratz	357 40.3	N29 11.5
Altair	62 05.6	N 8 55.1
Ankaa	353 12.7	S42 12.8
Antares	112 22.8	S26 28.0
Arcturus	145 53.1	N19 05.4
Atria	107 22.4	S69 03.2
Avior	234 16.1	S59 34.0
Bellatrix	278 28.4	N 6 21.7
Betelgeuse	270 57.6	N 7 24.4
Canopus	263 54.2	S52 42.5
Capella	280 29.4	N46 00.8
Deneb	49 29.8	N45 20.9
Denebola	182 30.5	N14 28.3
Diphda	348 52.8	S17 53.5
Dubhe	193 47.8	N61 39.0
Elnath	278 08.4	N28 37.2
Eltanin	90 45.3	N51 29.3
Enif	33 44.3	N 9 57.5
Fomalhaut	15 20.8	S29 31.8
Gacrux	171 57.4	S57 12.4
Gienah	175 49.1	S17 38.3
Hadar	148 43.7	S60 27.1
Hamal	327 57.1	N23 32.8
Kaus Aust.	83 40.2	S34 22.4
Kochab	137 21.0	N74 04.8
Markab	13 35.4	N15 18.2
Menkar	314 11.6	N 4 09.4
Menkent	148 04.1	S36 27.2
Miaplacidus	221 38.2	S69 47.3
Mirfak	308 35.5	N49 55.5
Nunki	75 54.9	S26 16.3
Peacock	53 15.0	S56 40.7
Pollux	243 23.7	N27 58.7
Procyon	244 56.2	N 5 10.6
Rasalhague	96 04.0	N12 33.0
Regulus	207 40.1	N11 52.7
Rigel	281 08.8	S 8 11.1
Rigil Kent.	139 47.9	S60 54.1
Sabik	102 09.4	S15 44.6
Schedar	349 36.9	N56 38.3
Shaula	96 18.2	S37 06.8
Sirius	258 30.7	S16 44.6
Spica	158 28.1	S11 15.1
Suhail	222 49.8	S43 30.2
Vega	80 37.3	N38 48.2
Zuben'ubi	137 02.2	S16 06.7

	SHA	Mer. Pass.
	° ′	h m
Venus	86 11.2	11 49
Mars	140 28.2	8 11
Jupiter	135 54.4	8 29
Saturn	89 00.2	11 36

Day	UT d h	SUN GHA ° ′	SUN Dec ° ′	MOON GHA ° ′	v ′	MOON Dec ° ′	d ′	HP ′
WEDNESDAY	27 00	179 46.1	S23 19.5	82 10.6	12.3	N 1 02.6	11.4	57.4
	01	194 45.8	19.4	96 41.9	12.3	1 14.0	11.3	57.4
	02	209 45.5	19.2	111 13.2	12.2	1 25.3	11.4	57.5
	03	224 45.2	. . 19.1	125 44.4	12.2	1 36.7	11.3	57.5
	04	239 44.9	19.0	140 15.6	12.1	1 48.0	11.4	57.6
	05	254 44.6	18.9	154 46.7	12.1	1 59.4	11.4	57.6
	06	269 44.3	S23 18.8	169 17.8	12.0	N 2 10.8	11.4	57.6
	07	284 43.9	18.7	183 48.8	11.9	2 22.2	11.4	57.7
	08	299 43.6	18.6	198 19.7	12.0	2 33.6	11.3	57.7
	09	314 43.3	. . 18.5	212 50.7	11.8	2 44.9	11.4	57.7
	10	329 43.0	18.4	227 21.5	11.8	2 56.3	11.4	57.8
	11	344 42.7	18.3	241 52.3	11.8	3 07.7	11.4	57.8
	12	359 42.4	S23 18.1	256 23.1	11.7	N 3 19.1	11.4	57.9
	13	14 42.1	18.0	270 53.8	11.6	3 30.5	11.4	57.9
	14	29 41.8	17.9	285 24.4	11.6	3 41.9	11.4	57.9
	15	44 41.5	. . 17.8	299 55.0	11.5	3 53.3	11.3	58.0
	16	59 41.2	17.7	314 25.5	11.4	4 04.6	11.4	58.0
	17	74 40.9	17.6	328 55.9	11.4	4 16.0	11.4	58.1
	18	89 40.6	S23 17.5	343 26.3	11.4	N 4 27.4	11.3	58.1
	19	104 40.3	17.3	357 56.7	11.2	4 38.7	11.4	58.1
	20	119 40.0	17.2	12 26.9	11.3	4 50.1	11.3	58.2
	21	134 39.7	. . 17.1	26 57.2	11.1	5 01.4	11.4	58.2
	22	149 39.4	17.0	41 27.3	11.1	5 12.8	11.3	58.3
	23	164 39.0	16.8	55 57.4	11.0	5 24.1	11.3	58.3
THURSDAY	28 00	179 38.7	S23 16.7	70 27.4	10.9	N 5 35.4	11.3	58.3
	01	194 38.4	16.6	84 57.3	10.9	5 46.7	11.3	58.4
	02	209 38.1	16.5	99 27.2	10.8	5 58.0	11.2	58.4
	03	224 37.8	. . 16.4	113 57.0	10.8	6 09.2	11.3	58.5
	04	239 37.5	16.2	128 26.8	10.7	6 20.5	11.2	58.5
	05	254 37.2	16.1	142 56.5	10.6	6 31.7	11.2	58.5
	06	269 36.9	S23 16.0	157 26.1	10.5	N 6 42.9	11.2	58.6
	07	284 36.6	15.8	171 55.6	10.4	6 54.1	11.2	58.6
	08	299 36.3	15.7	186 25.0	10.4	7 05.3	11.1	58.7
	09	314 36.0	. . 15.6	200 54.4	10.3	7 16.4	11.2	58.7
	10	329 35.7	15.4	215 23.7	10.3	7 27.6	11.0	58.7
	11	344 35.4	15.3	229 53.0	10.1	7 38.6	11.1	58.8
	12	359 35.1	S23 15.2	244 22.1	10.1	N 7 49.7	11.1	58.8
	13	14 34.8	15.1	258 51.2	10.0	8 00.8	11.0	58.9
	14	29 34.5	14.9	273 20.2	9.9	8 11.8	11.0	58.9
	15	44 34.2	. . 14.8	287 49.1	9.9	8 22.8	10.9	58.9
	16	59 33.9	14.6	302 18.0	9.8	8 33.7	10.9	59.0
	17	74 33.6	14.5	316 46.8	9.7	8 44.6	10.9	59.0
	18	89 33.3	S23 14.4	331 15.5	9.6	N 8 55.5	10.8	59.0
	19	104 33.0	14.2	345 44.1	9.5	9 06.3	10.9	59.1
	20	119 32.7	14.1	0 12.6	9.4	9 17.2	10.7	59.1
	21	134 32.3	. . 14.0	14 41.0	9.4	9 27.9	10.8	59.2
	22	149 32.0	13.8	29 09.4	9.3	9 38.7	10.6	59.2
	23	164 31.7	13.7	43 37.7	9.2	9 49.3	10.7	59.2
FRIDAY	29 00	179 31.4	S23 13.5	58 05.9	9.1	N10 00.0	10.6	59.3
	01	194 31.1	13.4	72 34.0	9.0	10 10.6	10.6	59.3
	02	209 30.8	13.2	87 02.0	8.9	10 21.2	10.5	59.4
	03	224 30.5	. . 13.1	101 29.9	8.9	10 31.7	10.4	59.4
	04	239 30.2	12.9	115 57.8	8.7	10 42.1	10.4	59.4
	05	254 29.9	12.8	130 25.5	8.7	10 52.5	10.4	59.5
	06	269 29.6	S23 12.7	144 53.2	8.6	N11 02.9	10.3	59.5
	07	284 29.3	12.5	159 20.8	8.5	11 13.2	10.3	59.6
	08	299 29.0	12.4	173 48.3	8.4	11 23.5	10.2	59.6
	09	314 28.7	. . 12.2	188 15.7	8.3	11 33.7	10.1	59.6
	10	329 28.4	12.1	202 43.0	8.3	11 43.8	10.1	59.7
	11	344 28.1	11.9	217 10.3	8.1	11 53.9	10.0	59.7
	12	359 27.8	S23 11.8	231 37.4	8.1	N12 03.9	10.0	59.7
	13	14 27.5	11.6	246 04.5	7.9	12 13.9	9.9	59.8
	14	29 27.2	11.4	260 31.4	7.9	12 23.8	9.9	59.8
	15	44 26.9	. . 11.3	274 58.3	7.8	12 33.7	9.7	59.8
	16	59 26.6	11.1	289 25.1	7.7	12 43.4	9.7	59.9
	17	74 26.3	11.0	303 51.8	7.6	12 53.1	9.7	59.9
	18	89 26.0	S23 10.8	318 18.4	7.5	N13 02.8	9.6	60.0
	19	104 25.7	10.7	332 44.9	7.4	13 12.4	9.5	60.0
	20	119 25.4	10.5	347 11.3	7.3	13 21.9	9.4	60.0
	21	134 25.1	. . 10.3	1 37.6	7.2	13 31.3	9.3	60.1
	22	149 24.8	10.2	16 03.8	7.2	13 40.6	9.3	60.1
	23	164 24.5	10.0	30 30.0	7.0	N13 49.9	9.2	60.1
		SD 16.3	*d* 0.1	SD 15.8		16.0		16.3

Lat. °	Twilight Naut. h m	Twilight Civil h m	Sunrise h m	Moonrise 27 h m	Moonrise 28 h m	Moonrise 29 h m	Moonrise 30 h m
N 72	08 26	10 52	▬	12 15	12 04	11 52	11 33
N 70	08 07	09 54	▬	12 19	12 16	12 12	12 09
68	07 51	09 19	▬	12 23	12 25	12 28	12 34
66	07 38	08 55	10 33	12 26	12 32	12 41	12 54
64	07 27	08 35	09 52	12 29	12 39	12 52	13 10
62	07 18	08 19	09 25	12 31	12 44	13 01	13 23
60	07 09	08 06	09 03	12 33	12 49	13 09	13 35
N 58	07 02	07 55	08 46	12 35	12 54	13 16	13 45
56	06 55	07 44	08 32	12 36	12 57	13 22	13 53
54	06 49	07 35	08 19	12 38	13 01	13 28	14 01
52	06 44	07 27	08 08	12 39	13 04	13 33	14 08
50	06 38	07 20	07 58	12 40	13 07	13 38	14 14
45	06 27	07 04	07 38	12 43	13 13	13 48	14 28
N 40	06 17	06 51	07 21	12 45	13 19	13 56	14 39
35	06 07	06 39	07 07	12 47	13 23	14 03	14 49
30	05 59	06 28	06 55	12 49	13 27	14 10	14 57
20	05 42	06 10	06 34	12 52	13 35	14 21	15 12
N 10	05 26	05 52	06 15	12 54	13 41	14 31	15 25
0	05 09	05 35	05 58	12 57	13 47	14 40	15 37
S 10	04 50	05 17	05 40	12 59	13 53	14 49	15 49
20	04 28	04 57	05 22	13 02	13 59	14 59	16 03
30	03 59	04 32	05 00	13 05	14 07	15 11	16 18
35	03 40	04 17	04 47	13 07	14 11	15 18	16 26
40	03 17	03 59	04 32	13 09	14 16	15 25	16 37
45	02 47	03 37	04 14	13 12	14 22	15 34	16 48
S 50	02 02	03 07	03 52	13 15	14 29	15 45	17 03
52	01 35	02 52	03 41	13 16	14 32	15 50	17 10
54	00 50	02 34	03 29	13 18	14 35	15 56	17 17
56	////	02 12	03 14	13 19	14 39	16 02	17 26
58	////	01 43	02 58	13 21	14 44	16 09	17 35
S 60	////	00 55	02 38	13 23	14 48	16 17	17 46

Lat. °	Sunset h m	Twilight Civil h m	Twilight Naut. h m	Moonset 27 h m	Moonset 28 h m	Moonset 29 h m	Moonset 30 h m
N 72	▬	13 11	15 37	00 46	02 38	04 39	06 55
N 70	▬	14 10	15 57	00 44	02 29	04 21	06 20
68	▬	14 44	16 12	00 43	02 22	04 06	05 56
66	13 30	15 09	16 25	00 42	02 16	03 55	05 37
64	14 11	15 28	16 36	00 41	02 11	03 45	05 22
62	14 39	15 44	16 46	00 40	02 07	03 37	05 09
60	15 00	15 57	16 54	00 40	02 03	03 30	04 58
N 58	15 17	16 09	17 01	00 39	02 00	03 23	04 49
56	15 32	16 19	17 08	00 39	01 57	03 18	04 41
54	15 44	16 28	17 14	00 38	01 54	03 13	04 34
52	15 55	16 36	17 20	00 38	01 52	03 08	04 27
50	16 05	16 43	17 25	00 37	01 49	03 04	04 22
45	16 26	16 59	17 37	00 36	01 45	02 56	04 09
N 40	16 42	17 13	17 47	00 36	01 41	02 49	03 59
35	16 56	17 25	17 56	00 35	01 37	02 42	03 50
30	17 09	17 35	18 05	00 34	01 34	02 37	03 42
20	17 30	17 54	18 21	00 33	01 29	02 28	03 29
N 10	17 48	18 11	18 37	00 33	01 25	02 19	03 18
0	18 05	18 28	18 54	00 32	01 20	02 12	03 07
S 10	18 23	18 46	19 13	00 31	01 16	02 04	02 56
20	18 42	19 06	19 35	00 30	01 11	01 56	02 44
30	19 04	19 31	20 04	00 29	01 06	01 47	02 31
35	19 16	19 46	20 23	00 28	01 03	01 41	02 24
40	19 31	20 04	20 46	00 28	01 00	01 35	02 15
45	19 49	20 26	21 16	00 27	00 56	01 28	02 05
S 50	20 12	20 56	22 01	00 26	00 51	01 20	01 53
52	20 22	21 11	22 28	00 26	00 49	01 16	01 47
54	20 34	21 28	23 11	00 25	00 47	01 12	01 41
56	20 48	21 50	////	00 24	00 44	01 07	01 34
58	21 05	22 19	////	00 24	00 42	01 02	01 27
S 60	21 25	23 06	////	00 23	00 38	00 56	01 18

Day	SUN Eqn. of Time 00^h	SUN Eqn. of Time 12^h	SUN Mer. Pass.	MOON Mer. Pass. Upper	MOON Mer. Pass. Lower	MOON Age	MOON Phase
d	m s	m s	h m	h m	h m	d %	
27	00 55	01 10	12 01	19 09	06 44	09 62	
28	01 24	01 39	12 02	19 59	07 33	10 72	◐
29	01 54	02 08	12 02	20 53	08 26	11 82	

UT		ARIES	VENUS −4·0		MARS +1·5		JUPITER −1·8		SATURN +0·5	
d	h	GHA ° ′	GHA ° ′	Dec ° ′	GHA ° ′	Dec ° ′	GHA ° ′	Dec ° ′	GHA ° ′	Dec ° ′
30	00	98 37.5	182 03.7	S23 41.6	237 52.2	S14 50.7	234 11.1	S15 47.4	187 22.4	S22 31.9
	01	113 40.0	197 02.8	41.5	252 53.1	51.1	249 13.1	47.6	202 24.6	31.9
	02	128 42.4	212 01.8	41.5	267 54.0	51.6	264 15.2	47.7	217 26.7	31.9
	03	143 44.9	227 00.8	. . 41.4	282 54.9	. . 52.1	279 17.2	. . 47.8	232 28.9	. . 31.9
	04	158 47.4	241 59.8	41.4	297 55.9	52.6	294 19.3	47.9	247 31.0	31.9
	05	173 49.8	256 58.9	41.3	312 56.8	53.1	309 21.3	48.0	262 33.2	31.9
	06	188 52.3	271 57.9	S23 41.3	327 57.7	S14 53.6	324 23.3	S15 48.2	277 35.3	S22 31.9
	07	203 54.7	286 56.9	41.2	342 58.7	54.0	339 25.4	48.3	292 37.5	31.9
S	08	218 57.2	301 56.0	41.2	357 59.6	54.5	354 27.4	48.4	307 39.6	31.9
A	09	233 59.7	316 55.0	. . 41.1	13 00.5	. . 55.0	9 29.4	. . 48.5	322 41.8	. . 31.9
T	10	249 02.1	331 54.0	41.1	28 01.5	55.5	24 31.5	48.6	337 43.9	31.9
U	11	264 04.6	346 53.0	41.0	43 02.4	56.0	39 33.5	48.7	352 46.0	31.9
R	12	279 07.1	1 52.1	S23 40.9	58 03.3	S14 56.5	54 35.5	S15 48.9	7 48.2	S22 31.9
D	13	294 09.5	16 51.1	40.9	73 04.2	56.9	69 37.6	49.0	22 50.3	31.9
A	14	309 12.0	31 50.1	40.8	88 05.2	57.4	84 39.6	49.1	37 52.5	31.9
Y	15	324 14.5	46 49.2	. . 40.7	103 06.1	. . 57.9	99 41.7	. . 49.2	52 54.6	. . 31.9
	16	339 16.9	61 48.2	40.7	118 07.0	58.4	114 43.7	49.3	67 56.8	31.9
	17	354 19.4	76 47.2	40.6	133 08.0	58.9	129 45.7	49.5	82 58.9	31.9
	18	9 21.9	91 46.2	S23 40.5	148 08.9	S14 59.3	144 47.8	S15 49.6	98 01.1	S22 31.9
	19	24 24.3	106 45.3	40.5	163 09.8	14 59.8	159 49.8	49.7	113 03.2	31.9
	20	39 26.8	121 44.3	40.4	178 10.7	15 00.3	174 51.8	49.8	128 05.4	31.9
	21	54 29.2	136 43.3	. . 40.3	193 11.7	. . 00.8	189 53.9	. . 49.9	143 07.5	. . 31.9
	22	69 31.7	151 42.4	40.2	208 12.6	01.3	204 55.9	50.0	158 09.7	31.9
	23	84 34.2	166 41.4	40.2	223 13.5	01.8	219 58.0	50.2	173 11.8	31.9
31	00	99 36.6	181 40.4	S23 40.1	238 14.5	S15 02.2	235 00.0	S15 50.3	188 14.0	S22 31.9
	01	114 39.1	196 39.4	40.0	253 15.4	02.7	250 02.0	50.4	203 16.1	31.9
	02	129 41.6	211 38.5	39.9	268 16.3	03.2	265 04.1	50.5	218 18.2	31.9
	03	144 44.0	226 37.5	. . 39.9	283 17.2	. . 03.7	280 06.1	. . 50.6	233 20.4	. . 31.9
	04	159 46.5	241 36.5	39.8	298 18.2	04.2	295 08.1	50.7	248 22.5	31.9
	05	174 49.0	256 35.6	39.7	313 19.1	04.6	310 10.2	50.9	263 24.7	31.9
	06	189 51.4	271 34.6	S23 39.6	328 20.0	S15 05.1	325 12.2	S15 51.0	278 26.8	S22 31.9
	07	204 53.9	286 33.6	39.5	343 20.9	05.6	340 14.3	51.1	293 29.0	31.9
	08	219 56.3	301 32.6	39.4	358 21.9	06.1	355 16.3	51.2	308 31.1	31.9
S	09	234 58.8	316 31.7	. . 39.3	13 22.8	. . 06.6	10 18.3	. . 51.3	323 33.3	. . 31.9
U	10	250 01.3	331 30.7	39.2	28 23.7	07.0	25 20.4	51.4	338 35.4	31.9
N	11	265 03.7	346 29.7	39.2	43 24.7	07.5	40 22.4	51.6	353 37.6	31.9
D	12	280 06.2	1 28.8	S23 39.1	58 25.6	S15 08.0	55 24.5	S15 51.7	8 39.7	S22 31.9
A	13	295 08.7	16 27.8	39.0	73 26.5	08.5	70 26.5	51.8	23 41.9	31.9
Y	14	310 11.1	31 26.8	38.9	88 27.4	08.9	85 28.5	51.9	38 44.0	31.9
	15	325 13.6	46 25.9	. . 38.8	103 28.4	. . 09.4	100 30.6	. . 52.0	53 46.2	. . 31.9
	16	340 16.1	61 24.9	38.7	118 29.3	09.9	115 32.6	52.1	68 48.3	31.9
	17	355 18.5	76 23.9	38.6	133 30.2	10.4	130 34.7	52.3	83 50.4	31.9
	18	10 21.0	91 22.9	S23 38.5	148 31.1	S15 10.9	145 36.7	S15 52.4	98 52.6	S22 31.9
	19	25 23.5	106 22.0	38.4	163 32.1	11.3	160 38.8	52.5	113 54.7	31.9
	20	40 25.9	121 21.0	38.3	178 33.0	11.8	175 40.8	52.6	128 56.9	31.9
	21	55 28.4	136 20.0	. . 38.2	193 33.9	. . 12.3	190 42.8	. . 52.7	143 59.0	. . 31.9
	22	70 30.8	151 19.1	38.1	208 34.8	12.8	205 44.9	52.8	159 01.2	31.9
	23	85 33.3	166 18.1	38.0	223 35.8	13.2	220 46.9	52.9	174 03.3	31.9
1	00	100 35.8	181 17.1	S23 37.9	238 36.7	S15 13.7	235 49.0	S15 53.1	189 05.5	S22 31.9
	01	115 38.2	196 16.2	37.7	253 37.6	14.2	250 51.0	53.2	204 07.6	31.9
	02	130 40.7	211 15.2	37.6	268 38.5	14.7	265 53.0	53.3	219 09.8	31.9
	03	145 43.2	226 14.2	. . 37.5	283 39.5	. . 15.1	280 55.1	. . 53.4	234 11.9	. . 31.9
	04	160 45.6	241 13.3	37.4	298 40.4	15.6	295 57.1	53.5	249 14.1	31.9
	05	175 48.1	256 12.3	37.3	313 41.3	16.1	310 59.2	53.6	264 16.2	31.9
	06	190 50.6	271 11.3	S23 37.2	328 42.2	S15 16.6	326 01.2	S15 53.8	279 18.4	S22 31.9
	07	205 53.0	286 10.4	37.1	343 43.2	17.0	341 03.3	53.9	294 20.5	31.9
	08	220 55.5	301 09.4	36.9	358 44.1	17.5	356 05.3	54.0	309 22.7	31.9
M	09	235 58.0	316 08.4	. . 36.8	13 45.0	. . 18.0	11 07.4	. . 54.1	324 24.8	. . 31.9
O	10	251 00.4	331 07.4	36.7	28 45.9	18.5	26 09.4	54.2	339 27.0	31.9
N	11	266 02.9	346 06.5	36.6	43 46.9	18.9	41 11.4	54.3	354 29.1	31.8
D	12	281 05.3	1 05.5	S23 36.5	58 47.8	S15 19.4	56 13.5	S15 54.4	9 31.2	S22 31.8
A	13	296 07.8	16 04.5	36.3	73 48.7	19.9	71 15.5	54.6	24 33.4	31.8
Y	14	311 10.3	31 03.6	36.2	88 49.6	20.4	86 17.6	54.7	39 35.5	31.8
	15	326 12.7	46 02.6	. . 36.1	103 50.6	. . 20.8	101 19.6	. . 54.8	54 37.7	. . 31.8
	16	341 15.2	61 01.6	36.0	118 51.5	21.3	116 21.7	54.9	69 39.8	31.8
	17	356 17.7	76 00.7	35.8	133 52.4	21.8	131 23.7	55.0	84 42.0	31.8
	18	11 20.1	90 59.7	S23 35.7	148 53.3	S15 22.3	146 25.8	S15 55.1	99 44.1	S22 31.8
	19	26 22.6	105 58.7	35.6	163 54.3	22.7	161 27.8	55.2	114 46.3	31.8
	20	41 25.1	120 57.8	35.4	178 55.2	23.2	176 29.8	55.4	129 48.4	31.8
	21	56 27.5	135 56.8	. . 35.3	193 56.1	. . 23.7	191 31.9	. . 55.5	144 50.6	. . 31.8
	22	71 30.0	150 55.8	35.2	208 57.0	24.1	206 33.9	55.6	159 52.7	31.8
	23	86 32.5	165 54.9	35.0	223 58.0	24.6	221 36.0	55.7	174 54.9	31.8
Mer. Pass.		h m 17 18.7	*v* −1.0	*d* 0.1	*v* 0.9	*d* 0.5	*v* 2.0	*d* 0.1	*v* 2.1	*d* 0.0

STARS

Name	SHA ° ′	Dec ° ′
Acamar	315 15.8	S40 14.3
Achernar	335 24.4	S57 09.2
Acrux	173 05.7	S63 11.5
Adhara	255 09.7	S29 00.0
Aldebaran	290 45.5	N16 32.5
Alioth	166 18.1	N55 51.5
Alkaid	152 56.7	N49 13.3
Al Na'ir	27 40.3	S46 52.6
Alnilam	275 42.9	S 1 11.7
Alphard	217 52.8	S 8 44.2
Alphecca	126 08.7	N26 39.3
Alpheratz	357 40.3	N29 11.4
Altair	62 05.6	N 8 55.1
Ankaa	353 12.7	S42 12.8
Antares	112 22.8	S26 28.0
Arcturus	145 53.1	N19 05.4
Atria	107 22.4	S69 03.2
Avior	234 16.1	S59 34.0
Bellatrix	278 28.4	N 6 21.7
Betelgeuse	270 57.6	N 7 24.4
Canopus	263 54.2	S52 42.5
Capella	280 29.4	N46 00.8
Deneb	49 29.8	N45 20.9
Denebola	182 30.5	N14 28.2
Diphda	348 52.8	S17 53.5
Dubhe	193 47.8	N61 39.0
Elnath	278 08.4	N28 37.2
Eltanin	90 45.3	N51 29.3
Enif	33 44.3	N 9 57.5
Fomalhaut	15 20.8	S29 31.8
Gacrux	171 57.4	S57 12.5
Gienah	175 49.1	S17 38.3
Hadar	148 43.7	S60 27.1
Hamal	327 57.1	N23 32.8
Kaus Aust.	83 40.2	S34 22.4
Kochab	137 20.9	N74 04.8
Markab	13 35.4	N15 18.2
Menkar	314 11.6	N 4 09.4
Menkent	148 04.1	S36 27.2
Miaplacidus	221 38.2	S69 47.3
Mirfak	308 35.5	N49 55.5
Nunki	75 54.9	S26 16.3
Peacock	53 15.0	S56 40.6
Pollux	243 23.6	N27 58.7
Procyon	244 56.2	N 5 10.5
Rasalhague	96 03.9	N12 33.0
Regulus	207 40.1	N11 52.6
Rigel	281 08.8	S 8 11.1
Rigil Kent.	139 47.8	S60 54.1
Sabik	102 09.4	S15 44.6
Schedar	349 36.9	N56 38.3
Shaula	96 18.2	S37 06.7
Sirius	258 30.7	S16 44.6
Spica	158 28.1	S11 15.1
Suhail	222 49.8	S43 30.3
Vega	80 37.3	N38 48.2
Zuben'ubi	137 02.2	S16 06.7

	SHA ° ′	Mer. Pass. h m
Venus	82 03.8	11 54
Mars	138 37.8	8 07
Jupiter	135 23.4	8 19
Saturn	88 37.3	11 25

UT	SUN GHA	SUN Dec	MOON GHA	v	MOON Dec	d	HP
d h	° ′	° ′	° ′	′	° ′	′	′
30 00	179 24.2	S23 09.9	44 56.0	7.0	N13 59.1	9.1	60.2
01	194 23.9	09.7	59 22.0	6.8	14 08.2	9.1	60.2
02	209 23.6	09.5	73 47.8	6.8	14 17.3	8.9	60.2
03	224 23.3	. . 09.4	88 13.6	6.7	14 26.2	8.9	60.3
04	239 23.0	09.2	102 39.3	6.6	14 35.1	8.8	60.3
05	254 22.7	09.0	117 04.9	6.5	14 43.9	8.7	60.3
06	269 22.4	S23 08.9	131 30.4	6.4	N14 52.6	8.6	60.4
07	284 22.1	08.7	145 55.8	6.3	15 01.2	8.5	60.4
S 08	299 21.8	08.5	160 21.1	6.2	15 09.7	8.4	60.4
A 09	314 21.5	. . 08.4	174 46.3	6.1	15 18.1	8.3	60.5
T 10	329 21.2	08.2	189 11.4	6.0	15 26.4	8.3	60.5
U 11	344 20.9	08.0	203 36.4	6.0	15 34.7	8.1	60.5
R 12	359 20.6	S23 07.9	218 01.4	5.8	N15 42.8	8.0	60.6
D 13	14 20.3	07.7	232 26.2	5.8	15 50.8	8.0	60.6
A 14	29 20.0	07.5	246 51.0	5.7	15 58.8	7.8	60.6
Y 15	44 19.7	. . 07.3	261 15.7	5.6	16 06.6	7.8	60.6
16	59 19.4	07.2	275 40.3	5.5	16 14.4	7.6	60.7
17	74 19.1	07.0	290 04.8	5.4	16 22.0	7.5	60.7
18	89 18.8	S23 06.8	304 29.2	5.3	N16 29.5	7.5	60.7
19	104 18.5	06.6	318 53.5	5.2	16 37.0	7.3	60.8
20	119 18.2	06.5	333 17.7	5.2	16 44.3	7.2	60.8
21	134 17.9	. . 06.3	347 41.9	5.1	16 51.5	7.1	60.8
22	149 17.6	06.1	2 06.0	5.0	16 58.6	6.9	60.8
23	164 17.3	05.9	16 30.0	4.9	17 05.5	6.9	60.9
31 00	179 17.0	S23 05.7	30 53.9	4.8	N17 12.4	6.7	60.9
01	194 16.7	05.6	45 17.7	4.7	17 19.1	6.7	60.9
02	209 16.4	05.4	59 41.4	4.7	17 25.8	6.5	60.9
03	224 16.1	. . 05.2	74 05.1	4.6	17 32.3	6.4	61.0
04	239 15.8	05.0	88 28.7	4.5	17 38.7	6.2	61.0
05	254 15.5	04.8	102 52.2	4.4	17 44.9	6.2	61.0
06	269 15.2	S23 04.6	117 15.6	4.4	N17 51.1	6.0	61.0
07	284 14.9	04.4	131 39.0	4.2	17 57.1	5.9	61.1
08	299 14.6	04.3	146 02.2	4.2	18 03.0	5.8	61.1
S 09	314 14.3	. . 04.1	160 25.4	4.2	18 08.8	5.6	61.1
U 10	329 14.0	03.9	174 48.6	4.0	18 14.4	5.5	61.1
N 11	344 13.7	03.7	189 11.6	4.0	18 19.9	5.4	61.1
D 12	359 13.4	S23 03.5	203 34.6	3.9	N18 25.3	5.2	61.2
A 13	14 13.2	03.3	217 57.5	3.9	18 30.5	5.1	61.2
Y 14	29 12.9	03.1	232 20.4	3.8	18 35.6	5.0	61.2
15	44 12.6	. . 02.9	246 43.2	3.7	18 40.6	4.9	61.2
16	59 12.3	02.7	261 05.9	3.7	18 45.5	4.7	61.2
17	74 12.0	02.5	275 28.6	3.6	18 50.2	4.5	61.2
18	89 11.7	S23 02.3	289 51.2	3.6	N18 54.7	4.5	61.3
19	104 11.4	02.1	304 13.8	3.4	18 59.2	4.2	61.3
20	119 11.1	01.9	318 36.2	3.5	19 03.4	4.2	61.3
21	134 10.8	. . 01.7	332 58.7	3.4	19 07.6	4.0	61.3
22	149 10.5	01.5	347 21.1	3.3	19 11.6	3.9	61.3
23	164 10.2	01.3	1 43.4	3.3	19 15.5	3.7	61.3
1 00	179 09.9	S23 01.1	16 05.7	3.2	N19 19.2	3.5	61.4
01	194 09.6	00.9	30 27.9	3.2	19 22.7	3.5	61.4
02	209 09.3	00.7	44 50.1	3.1	19 26.2	3.2	61.4
03	224 09.0	. . 00.5	59 12.2	3.1	19 29.4	3.2	61.4
04	239 08.7	00.3	73 34.3	3.1	19 32.6	3.0	61.4
05	254 08.4	23 00.1	87 56.4	3.0	19 35.6	2.8	61.4
06	269 08.1	S22 59.9	102 18.4	3.0	N19 38.4	2.7	61.4
07	284 07.8	59.7	116 40.4	2.9	19 41.1	2.5	61.4
08	299 07.6	59.5	131 02.3	2.9	19 43.6	2.4	61.4
M 09	314 07.3	. . 59.3	145 24.2	2.9	19 46.0	2.2	61.4
O 10	329 07.0	59.1	159 46.1	2.9	19 48.2	2.1	61.5
N 11	344 06.7	58.9	174 08.0	2.8	19 50.3	2.0	61.5
D 12	359 06.4	S22 58.7	188 29.8	2.8	N19 52.3	1.7	61.5
A 13	14 06.1	58.5	202 51.6	2.8	19 54.0	1.7	61.5
Y 14	29 05.8	58.3	217 13.4	2.7	19 55.7	1.4	61.5
15	44 05.5	. . 58.0	231 35.1	2.8	19 57.1	1.3	61.5
16	59 05.2	57.8	245 56.9	2.7	19 58.4	1.2	61.5
17	74 04.9	57.6	260 18.6	2.7	19 59.6	1.0	61.5
18	89 04.6	S22 57.4	274 40.3	2.7	N20 00.6	0.9	61.5
19	104 04.3	57.2	289 02.0	2.7	20 01.5	0.7	61.5
20	119 04.0	57.0	303 23.7	2.7	20 02.2	0.5	61.5
21	134 03.7	. . 56.8	317 45.4	2.7	20 02.7	0.4	61.5
22	149 03.5	56.5	332 07.1	2.6	20 03.1	0.2	61.5
23	164 03.2	56.3	346 28.7	2.7	N20 03.3	0.1	61.5
	SD 16.3	*d* 0.2	SD 16.5		16.7		16.7

Lat.	Twilight Naut.	Twilight Civil	Sunrise	Moonrise 30	Moonrise 31	Moonrise 1	Moonrise 2
°	h m	h m	h m	h m	h m	h m	h m
N 72	08 25	10 45	■	11 33	□	□	□
N 70	08 06	09 51	■	12 09	12 06	12 08	13 15
68	07 50	09 18	■	12 34	12 48	13 19	14 26
66	07 38	08 54	10 29	12 54	13 16	13 56	15 03
64	07 27	08 35	09 50	13 10	13 38	14 22	15 29
62	07 18	08 19	09 23	13 23	13 56	14 43	15 49
60	07 09	08 06	09 03	13 35	14 10	15 00	16 06
N 58	07 02	07 54	08 46	13 45	14 23	15 14	16 20
56	06 56	07 44	08 31	13 53	14 34	15 26	16 32
54	06 50	07 36	08 19	14 01	14 43	15 37	16 43
52	06 44	07 28	08 08	14 08	14 52	15 46	16 52
50	06 39	07 20	07 59	14 14	14 59	15 55	17 00
45	06 27	07 05	07 38	14 28	15 16	16 13	17 18
N 40	06 17	06 51	07 22	14 39	15 29	16 27	17 33
35	06 08	06 40	07 08	14 49	15 41	16 40	17 45
30	06 00	06 29	06 56	14 57	15 51	16 51	17 56
20	05 43	06 11	06 35	15 12	16 08	17 10	18 14
N 10	05 27	05 54	06 17	15 25	16 24	17 26	18 30
0	05 11	05 37	05 59	15 37	16 38	17 41	18 45
S 10	04 52	05 19	05 42	15 49	16 52	17 57	19 00
20	04 30	04 59	05 23	16 03	17 08	18 13	19 16
30	04 01	04 34	05 02	16 18	17 26	18 32	19 35
35	03 43	04 19	04 49	16 26	17 36	18 43	19 45
40	03 20	04 01	04 34	16 37	17 48	18 56	19 58
45	02 50	03 39	04 16	16 48	18 02	19 11	20 12
S 50	02 06	03 10	03 54	17 03	18 19	19 29	20 30
52	01 39	02 55	03 44	17 10	18 27	19 38	20 38
54	00 58	02 38	03 32	17 17	18 36	19 48	20 48
56	////	02 16	03 18	17 26	18 47	19 59	20 58
58	////	01 48	03 01	17 35	18 58	20 11	21 10
S 60	////	01 03	02 42	17 46	19 12	20 26	21 24

Lat.	Sunset	Twilight Civil	Twilight Naut.	Moonset 30	Moonset 31	Moonset 1	Moonset 2
°	h m	h m	h m	h m	h m	h m	h m
N 72	■	13 21	15 42	06 55	□	□	□
N 70	■	14 16	16 01	06 20	08 28	10 38	11 45
68	■	14 49	16 16	05 56	07 47	09 27	10 34
66	13 37	15 13	16 29	05 37	07 19	08 50	09 57
64	14 16	15 32	16 40	05 22	06 58	08 24	09 31
62	14 43	15 47	16 49	05 09	06 41	08 03	09 10
60	15 04	16 01	16 57	04 58	06 26	07 47	08 53
N 58	15 21	16 12	17 04	04 49	06 14	07 33	08 39
56	15 35	16 22	17 11	04 41	06 04	07 21	08 27
54	15 47	16 31	17 17	04 34	05 55	07 10	08 16
52	15 58	16 39	17 22	04 27	05 46	07 01	08 07
50	16 08	16 46	17 27	04 22	05 39	06 53	07 58
45	16 28	17 02	17 39	04 09	05 23	06 35	07 40
N 40	16 45	17 15	17 49	03 59	05 10	06 20	07 26
35	16 58	17 27	17 58	03 50	04 59	06 08	07 13
30	17 11	17 37	18 07	03 42	04 50	05 57	07 02
20	17 31	17 55	18 23	03 29	04 33	05 39	06 43
N 10	17 50	18 12	18 39	03 18	04 19	05 23	06 27
0	18 07	18 29	18 55	03 07	04 06	05 08	06 12
S 10	18 24	18 47	19 14	02 56	03 52	04 53	05 56
20	18 43	19 07	19 36	02 44	03 38	04 37	05 40
30	19 04	19 32	20 05	02 31	03 22	04 18	05 21
35	19 17	19 47	20 23	02 24	03 12	04 08	05 10
40	19 32	20 05	20 46	02 15	03 01	03 55	04 57
45	19 50	20 27	21 16	02 05	02 49	03 41	04 42
S 50	20 12	20 56	22 00	01 53	02 33	03 23	04 24
52	20 22	21 10	22 26	01 47	02 26	03 15	04 15
54	20 34	21 28	23 06	01 41	02 18	03 05	04 05
56	20 48	21 49	////	01 34	02 09	02 55	03 54
58	21 04	22 17	////	01 27	01 59	02 43	03 41
S 60	21 24	23 01	////	01 18	01 47	02 29	03 27

Day	SUN Eqn. of Time 00^h	SUN Eqn. of Time 12^h	SUN Mer. Pass.	MOON Mer. Pass. Upper	MOON Mer. Pass. Lower	Age	Phase
d	m s	m s	h m	h m	h m	d %	
30	02 23	02 37	12 03	21 51	09 22	12 90	○
31	02 51	03 06	12 03	22 53	10 22	13 96	
1	03 20	03 34	12 04	23 56	11 25	14 99	

EXPLANATION

PRINCIPLE AND ARRANGEMENT

1. *Object.* The object of this Almanac is to provide, in a convenient form, the data required for the practice of astronomical navigation at sea.

2. *Principle.* The main contents of the Almanac consist of data from which the *Greenwich Hour Angle* (GHA) and the *Declination* (Dec) of all the bodies used for navigation can be obtained for any instant of *Universal Time* (UT, specifically UT1, or previously Greenwich Mean Time (GMT)).

The *Local Hour Angle* (LHA) can then be obtained by means of the formula:

$$\text{LHA} = \text{GHA} \begin{smallmatrix} -\text{ west} \\ +\text{ east} \end{smallmatrix} \text{ longitude}$$

The remaining data consist of: times of rising and setting of the Sun and Moon, and times of twilight; miscellaneous calendarial and planning data and auxiliary tables, including a list of Standard Times; corrections to be applied to observed altitude.

For the Sun, Moon, and planets the GHA and Dec are tabulated directly for each hour of UT throughout the year. For the stars the *Sidereal Hour Angle* (SHA) is given, and the GHA is obtained from:

$$\text{GHA Star} = \text{GHA Aries} + \text{SHA Star}$$

The SHA and Dec of the stars change slowly and may be regarded as constant over periods of several days. GHA Aries, or the Greenwich Hour Angle of the first point of Aries (the Vernal Equinox), is tabulated for each hour. Permanent tables give the appropriate increments and corrections to the tabulated hourly values of GHA and Dec for the minutes and seconds of UT.

The six-volume series of *Sight Reduction Tables for Marine Navigation* (published in U.S.A. as Pub. No. 229) has been designed for the solution of the navigational triangle and is intended for use with *The Nautical Almanac*.

Two alternative procedures for sight reduction are described on pages 277–318. The first requires the use of programmable calculators or computers, while the second uses a set of concise tables that is given on pages 286–317.

The tabular accuracy is 0′.1 throughout. The time argument on the daily pages of this Almanac is UT1 denoted throughout by UT. This scale may differ from the broadcast time signals (UTC) by an amount which, if ignored, will introduce an error of up to 0′.2 in longitude determined from astronomical observations. The difference arises because the time argument depends on the variable rate of rotation of the Earth while the broadcast time signals are based on an atomic time-scale. Step adjustments of exactly one second are made to the time signals as required (normally at 24^h on December 31 and June 30) so that the difference between the time signals and UT, as used in this Almanac, may not exceed $0^s.9$. Those who require to reduce observations to a precision of better than 1^s must therefore obtain the correction (DUT1) to the time signals from coding in the signal, or from other sources; the required time is given by UT1=UTC+DUT1 to a precision of $0^s.1$. Alternatively, the longitude, when determined from astronomical observations, may be corrected by the corresponding amount shown in the following table:

Correction to time signals	Correction to longitude
$-0^s.9$ to $-0^s.7$	0′.2 to east
$-0^s.6$ to $-0^s.3$	0′.1 to east
$-0^s.2$ to $+0^s.2$	no correction
$+0^s.3$ to $+0^s.6$	0′.1 to west
$+0^s.7$ to $+0^s.9$	0′.2 to west

3. *Lay-out.* The ephemeral data for three days are presented on an opening of two pages: the left-hand page contains the data for the planets and stars; the right-hand page contains the data for the Sun and Moon, together with times of twilight, sunrise, sunset, moonrise and moonset.

The remaining contents are arranged as follows: for ease of reference the altitude-correction tables are given on pages A2, A3, A4, xxxiv and xxxv; calendar, Moon's phases, eclipses, and planet notes (i.e. data of general interest) precede the main tabulations. The Explanation is followed by information on standard times, star charts and list of star positions, sight reduction procedures and concise sight reduction tables, polar phenomena information and graphs, tables of increments and corrections and other auxiliary tables that are frequently used.

MAIN DATA

4. *Daily pages.* The daily pages give the GHA of Aries, the GHA and Dec of the Sun, Moon, and the four navigational planets, for each hour of UT. For the Moon, values of v and d are also tabulated for each hour to facilitate the correction of GHA and Dec to intermediate times; v and d for the Sun and planets change so slowly that they are given, at the foot of the appropriate columns, once only on the page; v is zero for Aries and negligible for the Sun, and is omitted. The SHA and Dec of the 57 selected stars, arranged in alphabetical order of proper name, are also given.

5. *Stars.* The SHA and Dec of 173 stars, including the 57 selected stars, are tabulated for each month on pages 268–273; no interpolation is required and the data can be used in precisely the same way as those for the selected stars on the daily pages. The stars are arranged in order of SHA.

The list of 173 includes all stars down to magnitude 3·0, together with a few fainter ones to fill the larger gaps. The 57 selected stars have been chosen from amongst these on account of brightness and distribution in the sky; they will suffice for the majority of observations.

The 57 selected stars are known by their proper names, but they are also numbered in descending order of SHA. In the list of 173 stars, the constellation names are always given on the left-hand page; on the facing page proper names are given where well-known names exist. Numbers for the selected stars are given in both columns.

An index to the selected stars, containing lists in both alphabetical and numerical order, is given on page xxxiii and is also reprinted on the bookmark.

6. *Increments and corrections.* The tables printed on tinted paper (pages ii–xxxi) at the back of the Almanac provide the increments and corrections for minutes and seconds to be applied to the hourly values of GHA and Dec. They consist of sixty tables, one for each minute, separated into two parts: increments to GHA for Sun and planets, Aries, and Moon for every minute and second; and, for each minute, corrections to be applied to GHA and Dec corresponding to the values of v and d given on the daily pages.

The increments are based on the following adopted hourly rates of increase of the GHA: Sun and planets, 15° precisely; Aries, 15° 02′·46; Moon, 14° 19′·0. The values of v on the daily pages are the excesses of the actual hourly motions over the adopted values; they are generally positive, except for Venus. The tabulated hourly values of the Sun's GHA have been adjusted to reduce to a minimum the error caused by treating v as negligible. The values of d on the daily pages are the hourly differences of the Dec. For the Moon, the true values of v and d are given for each hour; otherwise mean values are given for the three days on the page.

7. *Method of entry.* The UT of an observation is expressed as a day and hour, followed by a number of minutes and seconds. The tabular values of GHA and Dec, and, where necessary, the corresponding values of v and d, are taken directly from the daily pages for the day and hour of UT; this hour is always *before* the time of observation. SHA and Dec of the selected stars are also taken from the daily pages.

The table of Increments and Corrections for the minute of UT is then selected. For the GHA, the increment for minutes and seconds is taken from the appropriate column opposite the seconds of UT; the *v*-correction is taken from the second part of the same table opposite the value of *v* as given on the daily pages. Both increment and *v*-correction are to be added to the GHA, except for Venus when *v* is prefixed by a minus sign and the *v*-correction is to be subtracted. For the Dec there is no increment, but a *d*-correction is applied in the same way as the *v*-correction; *d* is given without sign on the daily pages and the sign of the correction is to be supplied by inspection of the Dec column. In many cases the correction may be applied mentally.

8. *Examples.* (a) Sun and Moon. Required the GHA and Dec of the Sun and Moon on 2017 July 31 at $15^h\ 47^m\ 13^s$ UT.

		SUN			MOON			
		GHA	Dec	*d*	GHA	*v*	Dec	*d*
		° ′	° ′	′	° ′	′	° ′	′
Daily page, July $31^d\ 15^h$		43 24·4	N 18 06·6	0·6	305 53·0	13·9	S 12 33·5	7·6
Increments for	$47^m\ 13^s$	11 48·3			11 16·0			
v or *d* corrections for	47^m		−0·5		+11·0		+6·0	
Sum for	July $31^d\ 15^h\ 47^m\ 13^s$	55 12·7	N 18 06·1		317 20·0		S 12 39·5	

(b) Planets. Required the LHA and Dec of (i) Venus on 2017 July 31 at $10^h\ 21^m\ 41^s$ UT in longitude W 83° 14′; (ii) Jupiter on 2017 July 31 at $13^h\ 59^m\ 27^s$ UT in longitude E 69° 57′.

		VENUS					JUPITER			
		GHA	*v*	Dec	*d*		GHA	*v*	Dec	*d*
		° ′	′	° ′	′		° ′	′	° ′	′
Daily page, July 31^d	(10^h)	9 28·2	−0·6	N21 49·8	0·1	(13^h)	308 16·4	2·2	S5 33·3	0·1
Increments (planets)	$(21^m\ 41^s)$	5 25·3				$(59^m\ 27^s)$	14 51·8			
v or *d* corrections	(21^m)	−0·2		+0·0		(59^m)	+2·2		+0·1	
Sum = GHA and Dec.		14 53·3		N21 49·8			323 10·4		S5 33·4	
Longitude	(west)	− 83 14·0				(east)	+ 69 57·0			
Multiples of 360°		+360					−360			
LHA planet		291 39·3					33 07·4			

(c) Stars. Required the GHA and Dec of (i) *Aldebaran* on 2017 July 31 at $9^h\ 21^m\ 35^s$ UT; (ii) *Vega* on 2017 July 31 at $23^h\ 56^m\ 28^s$ UT.

		Aldebaran			*Vega*	
		GHA	Dec		GHA	Dec
		° ′	° ′		° ′	° ′
Daily page (SHA and Dec)		290 46·4	N 16 32.5		80 36·7	N 38 48.3
Daily page (GHA Aries)	(9^h)	84 10·6		(23^h)	294 45·1	
Increments (Aries)	$(21^m\ 35^s)$	5 24·6		$(56^m\ 28^s)$	14 09·3	
Sum = GHA star		380 21·6			389 31·1	
Multiples of 360°		−360			−360	
GHA star		20 21·6			29 31·1	

9. *Polaris (Pole Star) tables.* The tables on pages 274–276 provide means by which the latitude can be deduced from an observed altitude of *Polaris*, and they also give its azimuth; their use is explained and illustrated on those pages. They are based on the following formula:

$$\text{Latitude} - H_O = -p\cos h + \tfrac{1}{2}p\,\sin p\,\sin^2 h\,\tan(\text{latitude})$$

where
H_O = Apparent altitude (corrected for refraction)
p = polar distance of *Polaris* = 90° − Dec
h = local hour angle of *Polaris* = LHA Aries + SHA

a_0, which is a function of LHA Aries only, is the value of both terms of the above formula calculated for mean values of the SHA (316° 30′) and Dec (N 89° 20′.2) of *Polaris*, for a mean latitude of 50°, and adjusted by the addition of a constant (58′.8).

a_1, which is a function of LHA Aries and latitude, is the excess of the value of the second term over its mean value for latitude 50°, increased by a constant (0′.6) to make it always positive. a_2, which is a function of LHA Aries and date, is the correction to the first term for the variation of *Polaris* from its adopted mean position; it is increased by a constant (0′.6) to make it positive. The sum of the added constants is 1°, so that:

$$\text{Latitude} = \text{Apparent altitude (corrected for refraction)} - 1° + a_0 + a_1 + a_2$$

RISING AND SETTING PHENOMENA

10. *General.* On the right-hand daily pages are given the times of sunrise and sunset, of the beginning and end of civil and nautical twilights, and of moonrise and moonset for a range of latitudes from N 72° to S 60°. These times, which are given to the nearest minute, are strictly the UT of the phenomena on the Greenwich meridian; they are given for every day for moonrise and moonset, but only for the middle day of the three on each page for the solar phenomena.

They are approximately the Local Mean Times (LMT) of the corresponding phenomena on other meridians; they can be formally interpolated if desired. The UT of a phenomenon is obtained from the LMT by:

$$\text{UT} = \text{LMT} \begin{matrix} + \text{ west} \\ - \text{ east} \end{matrix} \text{ longitude}$$

in which the longitude must first be converted to time by the table on page i or otherwise. Interpolation for latitude can be done mentally or with the aid of Table I on page xxxii.

The following symbols are used to indicate the conditions under which, in high latitudes, some of the phenomena do not occur:

□ Sun or Moon remains continuously above the horizon;

■ Sun or Moon remains continuously below the horizon;

//// twilight lasts all night.

Basis of the tabulations. At sunrise and sunset 16′ is allowed for semi-diameter and 34′ for horizontal refraction, so that at the times given the Sun's upper limb is on the visible horizon; all times refer to phenomena as seen from sea level with a clear horizon.

At the times given for the beginning and end of twilight, the Sun's zenith distance is 96° for civil, and 102° for nautical twilight. The degree of illumination at the times given for civil twilight (in good conditions and in the absence of other illumination) is such that the brightest stars are visible and the horizon is clearly defined. At the times given for nautical twilight the horizon is in general not visible, and it is too dark for observation with a marine sextant.

Times corresponding to other depressions of the Sun may be obtained by interpolation or, for depressions of more than 12°, less reliably, by extrapolation; times so obtained will be subject to considerable uncertainty near extreme conditions.

At moonrise and moonset, allowance is made for semi-diameter, parallax, and refraction (34′), so that at the times given the Moon's upper limb is on the visible horizon as seen from sea level.

Polar phenomena. Information and graphs concerning the rising and setting of the Sun and Moon and the duration of civil twilight for high latitudes are given on pages 320–325.

11. *Sunrise, sunset, twilight.* The tabulated times may be regarded, without serious error, as the LMT of the phenomena on any of the three days on the page and in any longitude. Precise times may normally be obtained by interpolating the tabular values for latitude and to the correct day and longitude, the latter being expressed as a fraction of a day by dividing it by 360°, positive for west and negative for east longitudes. In the extreme conditions near □, ■ or //// interpolation may not be possible in one direction, but accurate times are of little value in these circumstances.

Examples. Required the UT of (a) the beginning of morning twilights and sunrise on 2017 January 13 for latitude S 48° 55′, longitude E 75° 18′; (b) sunset and the end of evening twilights on 2017 January 15 for latitude N 67° 10′, longitude W 168° 05′.

	(a)	Twilight Nautical	Civil	Sunrise	(b)	Sunset	Twilight Civil	Nautical
From p. 19		d h m	d h m	d h m		d h m	d h m	d h m
LMT for Lat	S 45°	13 03 10	13 03 56	13 04 32	N 66°	15 14 24	15 15 43	15 16 54
Corr. to (p. xxxii, Table I)	S 48° 55′	−30	−20	−16	N 67° 10′	−22	−12	−6
Long (p. i)	E 75° 18′	−5 01	−5 01	−5 01	W 168° 05′	+11 12	+11 12	+11 12
UT		12 21 39	12 22 35	12 23 15		16 01 14	16 02 43	16 04 00

The LMT are strictly for January 14 (middle date on page) and 0° longitude; for more precise times it is necessary to interpolate, but rounding errors may accumulate to about 2^m.

(a) to January $13^d - 75°/360° =$ Jan. $12^d\!\cdot\!8$, i.e. $\frac{1}{3}(1{\cdot}2) = 0{\cdot}4$ backwards towards the data for the same latitude interpolated similarly from page 17; the corrections are -2^m to nautical twilight, -2^m to civil twilight and -2^m to sunrise.

(b) to January $15^d + 168°/360° =$ Jan. $15^d\!\cdot\!5$, i.e. $\frac{1}{3}(1{\cdot}5) = 0{\cdot}5$ forwards towards the data for the same latitude interpolated similarly from page 21; the corrections are $+7^m$ to sunset, $+4^m$ to civil twilight, and $+4^m$ to nautical twilight.

12. *Moonrise, moonset.* Precise times of moonrise and moonset are rarely needed; a glance at the tables will generally give sufficient indication of whether the Moon is available for observation and of the hours of rising and setting. If needed, precise times may be obtained as follows. Interpolate for latitude, using Table I on page xxxii, on the day wanted and also on the preceding day in east longitudes or the following day in west longitudes; take the difference between these times and interpolate for longitude by applying to the time for the day wanted the correction from Table II on page xxxii, so that the resulting time is between the two times used. In extreme conditions near ▭ or ■ interpolation for latitude or longitude may be possible only in one direction; accurate times are of little value in these circumstances.

To facilitate this interpolation, the times of moonrise and moonset are given for four days on each page; where no phenomenon occurs during a particular day (as happens once a month) the time of the phenomenon on the following day, increased by 24^h, is given; extra care must be taken when interpolating between two values, when one of those values exceeds 24^h. In practice it suffices to use the daily difference between the times for the nearest tabular latitude, and generally, to enter Table II with the nearest tabular arguments as in the examples below.

Examples. Required the UT of moonrise and moonset in latitude S 47° 10′, longitudes E 124° 00′ and W 78° 31′ on 2017 January 14.

	Longitude E 124° 00′ Moonrise	Moonset	Longitude W 78° 31′ Moonrise	Moonset
	d h m	d h m	d h m	d h m
LMT for Lat. S 45°	14 21 05	14 06 45	14 21 05	14 06 45
Lat correction (p. xxxii, Table I)	+04	−04	+04	−04
Long correction (p. xxxii, Table II)	−13	−23	+07	+16
Correct LMT	14 20 56	14 06 18	14 21 16	14 06 57
Longitude (p. i)	−8 16	−8 16	+5 14	+5 14
UT	14 12 40	13 22 02	15 02 30	14 12 11

ALTITUDE CORRECTION TABLES

13. *General.* In general, two corrections are given for application to altitudes observed with a marine sextant; additional corrections are required for Venus and Mars and also for very low altitudes.

Tables of the correction for dip of the horizon, due to height of eye above sea level, are given on pages A2 and xxxiv. Strictly this correction should be applied first and subtracted from the sextant altitude to give apparent altitude, which is the correct argument for the other tables.

Separate tables are given of the second correction for the Sun, for stars and planets (on pages A2 and A3), and for the Moon (on pages xxxiv and xxxv). For the Sun, values are given for both lower and upper limbs, for two periods of the year. The star tables are used for the planets, but additional corrections for parallax (page A2) are required for Venus and Mars. The Moon tables are in two parts: the main correction is a function of apparent altitude only and is tabulated for the lower limb (30′ must be subtracted to obtain the correction for the upper limb); the other, which is given for both lower and upper limbs, depends also on the horizontal parallax, which has to be taken from the daily pages.

An additional correction, given on page A4, is required for the change in the refraction, due to variations of pressure and temperature from the adopted standard conditions; it may generally be ignored for altitudes greater than 10°, except possibly in extreme conditions. The correction tables for the Sun, stars, and planets are in two parts; only those for altitudes greater than 10° are reprinted on the bookmark.

14. *Critical tables.* Some of the altitude correction tables are arranged as critical tables. In these, an interval of apparent altitude (or height of eye) corresponds to a single value of the correction; no interpolation is required. At a "critical" entry the upper of the two possible values of the correction is to be taken. For example, in the table of dip, a correction of −4′.1 corresponds to all values of the height of eye from 5·3 to 5·5 metres (17·5 to 18·3 feet) inclusive.

15. *Examples.* The following examples illustrate the use of the altitude correction tables; the sextant altitudes given are assumed to be taken on 2017 August 9 with a marine sextant at height 5·4 metres (18 feet), temperature −3°C and pressure 982 mb, the Moon sights being taken at about 10^{h} UT.

	SUN lower limb	SUN upper limb	MOON lower limb	MOON upper limb	VENUS	*Polaris*
	° ′	° ′	° ′	° ′	° ′	° ′
Sextant altitude	21 19·7	3 20·2	33 27·6	26 06·7	4 32·6	49 36·5
Dip, height 5·4 metres (18 feet)	−4·1	−4·1	−4·1	−4·1	−4·1	−4·1
Main correction	+13·6	−29·3	+57·4	+60·5	−10·8	−0·8
−30′ for upper limb (Moon)	—	—	—	−30·0	—	—
L, U correction for Moon	—	—	+3·4	+2·7	—	—
Additional correction for Venus	—	—	—	—	+0·1	—
Additional refraction correction	−0·1	−0·6	−0·1	−0·1	−0·5	0·0
Corrected sextant altitude	21 29·1	2 46·2	34 24·2	26 35·7	4 17·3	49 31·6

The main corrections have been taken out with apparent altitude (sextant altitude corrected for index error and dip) as argument, interpolating where possible. These refinements are rarely necessary.

16. *Composition of the Corrections.* The table for the dip of the sea horizon is based on the formula:

$$\text{Correction for dip} = -1'.76\sqrt{\text{(height of eye in metres)}} = -0'.97\sqrt{\text{(height of eye in feet)}}$$

The correction table for the Sun includes the effects of semi-diameter, parallax and mean refraction.

The correction tables for the stars and planets allow for the effect of mean refraction.

The phase correction for Venus has been incorporated in the tabulations for GHA and Dec, and no correction for phase is required. The additional corrections for Venus and Mars allow for parallax. Alternatively, the correction for parallax may be calculated from $p \cos H$, where p is the parallax and H is the altitude. In 2017 the values for p are:

	Jan. 1		Jan. 25		Feb. 18		Mar. 6		Apr. 12		Apr. 27		May 20		July 8		Dec. 31
Venus		0′.2		0′.3		0′.4		0′.5		0′.4		0′.3		0′.2		0′.1	

	Jan. 1		Dec. 31
Mars		0′.1	

The correction table for the Moon includes the effect of semi-diameter, parallax, augmentation and mean refraction.

Mean refraction is calculated for a temperature of 10°C (50°F), a pressure of 1010 mb (29·83 inches), humidity of 80% and wavelength 0·50169 μm.

17. *Bubble sextant observations.* When observing with a bubble sextant, no correction is necessary for dip, semi-diameter, or augmentation. The altitude corrections for the stars and planets on page A2 and on the bookmark should be used for the Sun as well as for the stars and planets; for the Moon, it is easiest to take the mean of the corrections for lower and upper limbs and subtract 15′ from the altitude; the correction for dip must not be applied.

AUXILIARY AND PLANNING DATA

18. *Sun and Moon.* On the daily pages are given: hourly values of the horizontal parallax of the Moon; the semi-diameters and the times of meridian passage of both Sun and Moon over the Greenwich meridian; the equation of time; the age of the Moon, the percent (%) illuminated and a symbol indicating the phase. The times of the phases of the Moon are given in UT on page 4. For the Moon, the semi-diameters for each of the three days are given at the foot of the column; for the Sun a single value is sufficient. Table II on page xxxii may be used for interpolating the time of the Moon's meridian passage for longitude. The equation of time is given daily at 00^h and 12^h UT. The sign is *positive* for unshaded values and *negative* for shaded values. To obtain apparent time add the equation of time to mean time when the sign is *positive*. Subtract the equation of time from mean time when the sign is *negative*. At 12^h UT, when the sign is *positive*, meridian passage of the Sun occurs *before* 12^h UT, otherwise it occurs *after* 12^h UT.

19. *Planets.* The magnitudes of the planets are given immediately following their names in the headings on the daily pages; also given, for the middle day of the three on the page, are their SHA at 00^h UT and their times of meridian passage.

The planet notes and diagram on pages 8 and 9 provide descriptive information as to the suitability of the planets for observation during the year, and of their positions and movements.

20. *Stars.* The time of meridian passage of the first point of Aries over the Greenwich meridian is given on the daily pages, for the middle day of the three on the page, to $0^m\!.1$. The interval between successive meridian passages is $23^h\ 56^m\!.1$ (24^h less $3^m\!.9$), so that times for intermediate days and other meridians can readily be derived. If a precise time is required, it may be obtained by finding the UT at which LHA Aries is zero.

The meridian passage of a star occurs when its LHA is zero, that is when LHA Aries + SHA = 360°. An approximate time can be obtained from the planet diagram on page 9.

The star charts on pages 266 and 267 are intended to assist identification. They show the relative positions of the stars in the sky as seen from the Earth and include all 173 stars used in the Almanac, together with a few others to complete the main constellation configurations. The local meridian at any time may be located on the chart by means of its SHA which is 360° − LHA Aries, or west longitude − GHA Aries.

21. *Star globe.* To set a star globe on which is printed a scale of LHA Aries, first set the globe for latitude and then rotate about the polar axis until the scale under the edge of the meridian circle reads LHA Aries.

To mark the positions of the Sun, Moon, and planets on the star globe, take the difference GHA Aries − GHA body and use this along the LHA Aries scale, in conjunction with the declination, to plot the position. GHA Aries − GHA body is most conveniently found by taking the difference when the GHA of the body is small (less than 15°), which happens once a day.

22. *Calendar.* On page 4 are given lists of ecclesiastical festivals, and of the principal anniversaries and holidays in the United Kingdom and the United States of America. The calendar on page 5 includes the day of the year as well as the day of the week.

Brief particulars are given, at the foot of page 5, of the solar and lunar eclipses occurring during the year; the times given are in UT. The principal features of the more important solar eclipses are shown on the maps on pages 6 and 7.

23. *Standard times.* The lists on pages 262–265 give the standard times used in most countries. In general no attempt is made to give details of the beginning and end of summer time, since they are liable to frequent changes at short notice. For the latest information consult Admiralty List of Radio Signals Volume 2 (NP 282) corrected by Section VI of the weekly edition of Admiralty Notices to Mariners.

The Date or Calendar Line is an arbitrary line, on either side of which the date differs by one day; when crossing this line on a westerly course, the date must be advanced one day; when crossing it on an easterly course, the date must be put back one day. The line is a modification of the line of the 180th meridian, and is drawn so as to include, as far as possible, islands of any one group, etc., on the same side of the line. It may be traced by starting at the South Pole and joining up to the following positions:

	°	°	°	°	°	°	°
Lat	S 51·0	S 45·0	S 15·0	S 5·0	N 48·0	N 53·0	N 65·5
Long	180·0	W 172·5	W 172·5	180·0	180·0	E 170·0	W 169·0

thence through the middle of the Diomede Islands to Lat N 68°·0, Long W 169°·0, passing east of Ostrov Vrangelya (Wrangel Island) to Lat N 75°·0, Long 180°·0, and thence to the North Pole.

ACCURACY

24. *Main data.* The quantities tabulated in this Almanac are generally correct to the nearest 0′·1; the exception is the Sun's GHA which is deliberately adjusted by up to 0′·15 to reduce the error due to ignoring the *v*-correction. The GHA and Dec at intermediate times cannot be obtained to this precision, since at least two quantities must be added; moreover, the *v*- and *d*-corrections are based on mean values of *v* and *d* and are taken from tables for the whole minute only. The largest error that can occur in the GHA or Dec of any body other than the Sun or Moon is less than 0′·2; it may reach 0′·25 for the GHA of the Sun and 0′·3 for that of the Moon.

In practice, it may be expected that only one third of the values of GHA and Dec taken out will have errors larger than 0′·05 and less than one tenth will have errors larger than 0′·1.

25. *Altitude corrections.* The errors in the altitude corrections are nominally of the same order as those in GHA and Dec, as they result from the addition of several quantities each correctly rounded off to 0′·1. But the actual values of the dip and of the refraction at low altitudes may, in extreme atmospheric conditions, differ considerably from the mean values used in the tables.

USE OF THIS ALMANAC IN 2018

This Almanac may be used for the Sun and stars in 2018 in the following manner.

For the Sun, take out the GHA and Dec for the same date but for a time 5^h 48^m 00^s *earlier* than the UT of observation; add 87° 00′ to the GHA so obtained. The error, mainly due to planetary perturbations of the Earth, is unlikely to exceed 0′·4.

For the stars, calculate the GHA and Dec for the same date and the same time, but *subtract* 15′·1 from the GHA so found. The error due to incomplete correction for precession and nutation is unlikely to exceed 0′·4. If preferred, the same result can be obtained by using a time 5^h 48^m 00^s earlier than the UT of observation (as for the Sun) and adding 86° 59′·2 to the GHA (or adding 87° as for the Sun and subtracting 0′·8, for precession, from the SHA of the star).

The Almanac cannot be so used for the Moon or planets.

LIST I — PLACES FAST ON UTC (mainly those EAST OF GREENWICH)

The times given below should be *added* to UTC to give Standard Time / *subtracted* from Standard Time to give UTC.

Place	h	m
Admiralty Islands	10	
Afghanistan	04	30
Albania*	01	
Algeria	01	
Amirante Islands	04	
Andaman Islands	05	30
Angola	01	
Armenia	04	
Australia		
Australian Capital Territory*	10	
New South Wales*[1]	10	
Northern Territory	09	30
Queensland	10	
South Australia*	09	30
Tasmania*	10	
Victoria*	10	
Western Australia	08	
Whitsunday Islands	10	
Austria*†	01	
Azerbaijan*	04	
Bahrain	03	
Balearic Islands*†	01	
Bangladesh	06	
Belarus	03	
Belgium*†	01	
Benin	01	
Bosnia and Herzegovina*	01	
Botswana, Republic of	02	
Brunei	08	
Bulgaria*†	02	
Burma (Myanmar)	06	30
Burundi	02	
Cambodia	07	
Cameroon Republic	01	
Caroline Islands[2]	10	
Central African Republic	01	
Chad	01	
Chagos Archipelago & Diego Garcia	06	
Chatham Islands*	12	45
China, People's Republic of	08	
Christmas Island, Indian Ocean	07	
Cocos (Keeling) Islands	06	30
Comoro Islands (Comoros)	03	
Congo, Democratic Republic		
West: Kinshasa, Equateur	01	
East: Orientale, Kasai, Kivu, Shaba	02	
Congo Republic	01	
Corsica*†	01	
Crete*†	02	
Croatia*†	01	
Cyprus†: Ercan*, Larnaca*	02	
Czech Republic*†	01	
Denmark*†	01	
Djibouti	03	
Egypt, Arab Republic of	02	
Equatorial Guinea, Republic of	01	
Bioko	01	
Eritrea	03	
Estonia*†	02	
Ethiopia	03	
Fiji*	12	
Finland*†	02	
France*†	01	
Gabon	01	
Georgia	04	
Germany*†	01	
Gibraltar*	01	
Greece*†	02	
Guam	10	
Hong Kong	08	
Hungary*†	01	
India	05	30
Indonesia, Republic of		
Bangka, Billiton, Java, West and Central Kalimantan, Madura, Sumatra	07	
Bali, Flores, South, North and East Kalimantan, Lombok, Sulawesi, Sumba, Sumbawa, West Timor	08	
Aru, Irian Jaya, Kai, Moluccas Tanimbar	09	
Iran*	03	30
Iraq	03	
Israel*	02	
Italy*†	01	
Jan Mayen Island*	01	
Japan	09	
Jordan	02	
Kazakhstan		
Western: Aktau, Uralsk, Atyrau	05	
Eastern & Central: Kzyl-Orda, Astana	06	
Kenya	03	
Kerguelen Islands	05	
Kiribati Republic		
Gilbert Islands	12	
Phoenix Islands[3]	13	
Line Islands[3]	14	
Korea, North	08	30
Korea, South	09	
Kuwait	03	
Kyrgyzstan	06	
Laccadive Islands	05	30
Laos	07	

* Daylight-saving time may be kept in these places. † For Summer time dates see List II footnotes.

1 Except Broken Hill Area* which keeps $09^h\ 30^m$.

2 Except Pohnpei, Pingelap and Kosrae which keep 11^h and Palau which keeps 09^h.

3 The Line and Phoenix Is. not part of the Kiribati Republic may keep other time zones.

LIST I — *(continued)*

	h	m
Latvia*†	02	
Lebanon*	02	
Lesotho	02	
Libya	02	
Liechtenstein*	01	
Lithuania*†	02	
Lord Howe Island*	10	30
Luxembourg*†	01	
Macau	08	
Macedonia*, former Yugoslav Republic	01	
Madagascar, Democratic Republic of	03	
Malawi	02	
Malaysia, Malaya, Sabah, Sarawak	08	
Maldives, Republic of The	05	
Malta*†	01	
Mariana Islands	10	
Marshall Islands	12	
Mauritius	04	
Moldova*	02	
Monaco*	01	
Mongolia*	08	
Montenegro*	01	
Mozambique	02	
Namibia*	01	
Nauru	12	
Nepal	05	45
Netherlands, The*†	01	
New Caledonia	11	
New Zealand*	12	
Nicobar Islands	05	30
Niger	01	
Nigeria, Republic of	01	
Norfolk Island	11	
Norway*	01	
Novaya Zemlya	03	
Okinawa	09	
Oman	04	
Pagalu (Annobon Islands)	01	
Pakistan	05	
Palau Islands	09	
Papua New Guinea[1]	10	
Pescadores Islands	08	
Philippine Republic	08	
Poland*†	01	
Qatar	03	
Reunion	04	
Romania*†	02	
Russia[2]		
Kaliningrad	02	
Moscow, St. Petersburg, Volgograd, Arkhangelsk, Astrakhan	03	
Samara	04	
Ekaterinburg, Ufa, Perm, Novyy Port	05	
Omsk, Novosibirsk, Tomsk	06	

	h	m
Norilsk, Krasnoyarsk, Dikson	07	
Irkutsk, Bratsk, Ulan-Ude, Chita	08	
Tiksi, Yakutsk	09	
Vladivostok, Khabarovsk, Okhotsk, Magadan, Sakhalin Island	10	
Severo-Kurilsk	11	
Petropavlovsk-K., Anadyr	12	
Rwanda	02	
Ryukyu Islands	09	
Samoa*	13	
Santa Cruz Islands	11	
Sardinia*†	01	
Saudi Arabia	03	
Schouten Islands	09	
Serbia*	01	
Seychelles	04	
Sicily*†	01	
Singapore	08	
Slovakia*†	01	
Slovenia*†	01	
Socotra	03	
Solomon Islands	11	
Somalia Republic	03	
South Africa, Republic of	02	
Spain*†	01	
Spanish Possessions in North Africa*	01	
Spitsbergen (Svalbard)*	01	
Sri Lanka	05	30
Sudan, Republic of	03	
Swaziland	02	
Sweden*†	01	
Switzerland*	01	
Syria (Syrian Arab Republic)*	02	
Taiwan	08	
Tajikistan	05	
Tanzania	03	
Thailand	07	
Timor-Leste	09	
Tonga	13	
Tunisia	01	
Turkey*	02	
Turkmenistan	05	
Tuvalu	12	
Uganda	03	
Ukraine*	02	
United Arab Emirates	04	
Uzbekistan	05	
Vanuatu, Republic of	11	
Vietnam, Socialist Republic of	07	
Yemen	03	
Zambia, Republic of	02	
Zimbabwe	02	

* Daylight-saving time may be kept in these places. † For Summer time dates see List II footnotes.

1 Excluding the Autonomous Region of Bougainville which keeps 11^{h}.

2 The boundaries between the zones are irregular; listed are chief towns in each zone.

LIST II — PLACES NORMALLY KEEPING UTC

Ascension Island	Ghana	Irish Republic*†	Morocco*	Sierra Leone
Burkina-Faso	Great Britain†	Ivory Coast	Portugal*†	Togo Republic
Canary Islands*†	Guinea-Bissau	Liberia	Principe	Tristan da Cunha
Channel Islands†	Guinea Republic	Madeira*†	St. Helena	
Faeroes*, The	Iceland	Mali	São Tomé	
Gambia, The	Ireland, Northern†	Mauritania	Senegal	

* Daylight-saving time may be kept in these places.

† Summer time (daylight-saving time), one hour in advance of UTC, will be kept from 2017 March 26^{d} 01^{h} to October 29^{d} 01^{h} UTC (Ninth Summer Time Directive of the European Union). Ratification by member countries has not been verified.

LIST III — PLACES SLOW ON UTC (WEST OF GREENWICH)

The times given below should be *subtracted* from UTC to give Standard Time / *added* to Standard Time to give UTC.

Place	h	m
American Samoa	11	
Argentina	03	
Austral (Tubuai) Islands[1]	10	
Azores*†	01	
Bahamas*	05	
Barbados	04	
Belize	06	
Bermuda*	04	
Bolivia	04	
Brazil		
Fernando de Noronha I., Trindade I., Oceanic Is.	02	
N and NE coastal states, Tocantins, Minas Gerais*, Goiás*, Brasilia*, S and E coastal states*	03	
Amazonas[2], Mato Grosso do Sul*, Mato Grosso*, Rondônia, Roraima	04	
Acre	05	
British Antarctic Territory[3,4]	03	
Canada[4]‡		
Alberta*	07	
British Columbia*	08	
Labrador*	04	
Manitoba*	06	
New Brunswick*	04	
Newfoundland*	03	30
Nunavut*		
east of long. W. 85°	05	
long. W. 85° to W. 102°	06	
west of long. W. 102°	07	
Northwest Territories*	07	
Nova Scotia*	04	
Ontario, east of long. W. 90°*	05	
Ontario, west of long. W. 90°*	06	
Canada (*continued*)		
Prince Edward Island*	04	
Quebec, east of long. W. 63°	04	
west of long. W. 63°*	05	
Saskatchewan	06	
Yukon*	08	
Cape Verde Islands	01	
Cayman Islands	05	
Chile	03	
Colombia	05	
Cook Islands	10	
Costa Rica	06	
Cuba*	05	
Curaçao Island	04	
Dominican Republic	04	
Easter Island (I. de Pascua)	05	
Ecuador	05	
El Salvador	06	
Falkland Islands	03	
Fernando de Noronha Island	02	
French Guiana	03	
Galápagos Islands	06	
Greenland		
Danmarkshavn, Mesters Vig	00	
General*	03	
Scoresby Sound*	01	
Thule*, Pituffik*	04	
Grenada	04	
Guadeloupe	04	
Guatemala	06	
Guyana, Republic of	04	

* Daylight-saving time may be kept in these places. ‡ Dates for DST are given at the end of List III.

1 This is the legal standard time, but local mean time is generally used.

2 Except the cities of Eirunepe, Benjamin Constant and Tabatinga which keep 05^{h}.

3 Stations may use UTC.

4 Some areas may keep another time zone.

LIST III — (*continued*)

	h	m
Haiti*	05	
Honduras	06	
Jamaica	05	
Johnston Island	10	
Juan Fernandez Islands	03	
Leeward Islands	04	
Marquesas Islands	09	30
Martinique	04	
Mexico		
General*	06	
Quintana Roo	05	
Baja California Sur*, Chihuahua* Nayarit*, Sinaloa* and Sonara	07	
Baja California Norte*	08	
Midway Islands	11	
Nicaragua	06	
Niue	11	
Panama, Republic of	05	
Paraguay*	04	
Peru	05	
Pitcairn Island	08	
Puerto Rico	04	
St. Pierre and Miquelon*	03	
Society Islands	10	
South Georgia	02	
Suriname	03	
Trindade Island, South Atlantic	02	
Trinidad and Tobago	04	
Tuamotu Archipelago	10	
Tubuai (Austral) Islands	10	
Turks and Caicos Islands	04	
United States of America‡		
Alabama	06	
Alaska	09	
Aleutian Islands, east of W. 169° 30′	09	
Aleutian Islands, west of W. 169° 30′	10	
Arizona[1]	07	
Arkansas	06	
California	08	
Colorado	07	
Connecticut	05	
Delaware	05	
District of Columbia	05	
Florida[2]	05	
Georgia	05	
Hawaii[1]	10	

	h	m
United States of America‡(*continued*)		
Idaho, southern part	07	
northern part	08	
Illinois	06	
Indiana[2]	05	
Iowa	06	
Kansas[2]	06	
Kentucky, eastern part	05	
western part	06	
Louisiana	06	
Maine	05	
Maryland	05	
Massachusetts	05	
Michigan[2]	05	
Minnesota	06	
Mississippi	06	
Missouri	06	
Montana	07	
Nebraska, eastern part	06	
western part	07	
Nevada	08	
New Hampshire	05	
New Jersey	05	
New Mexico	07	
New York	05	
North Carolina	05	
North Dakota, eastern part	06	
western part	07	
Ohio	05	
Oklahoma	06	
Oregon[2]	08	
Pennsylvania	05	
Rhode Island	05	
South Carolina	05	
South Dakota, eastern part	06	
western part	07	
Tennessee, eastern part	05	
western part	06	
Texas[2]	06	
Utah	07	
Vermont	05	
Virginia	05	
Washington D.C.	05	
Washington	08	
West Virginia	05	
Wisconsin	06	
Wyoming	07	
Uruguay	03	
Venezuela	04	30
Virgin Islands	04	
Windward Islands	04	

* Daylight-saving time may be kept in these places.

‡ Daylight-saving (Summer) time, one hour fast on the time given, is kept during 2017 from March 12 (second Sunday) to November 5 (first Sunday), changing at $02^h\ 00^m$ local clock time.

1 Exempt from keeping daylight-saving time, except for a portion of Arizona.

2 A small portion of the state is in another time zone.

NORTHERN STARS

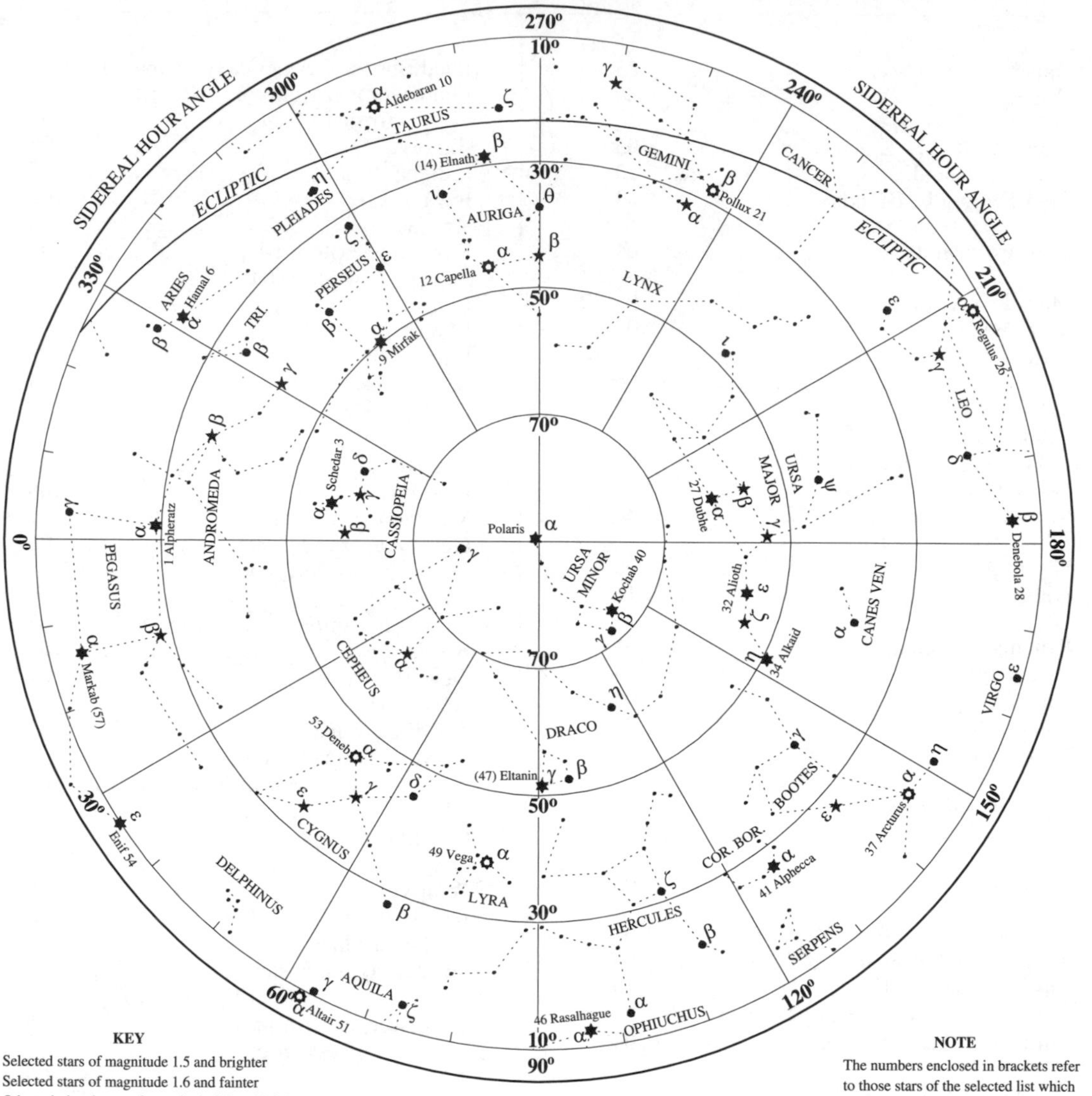

KEY

- Selected stars of magnitude 1.5 and brighter
- Selected stars of magnitude 1.6 and fainter
- Other tabulated stars of magnitude 2.5 and brighter
- Other tabulated stars of magnitude 2.6 and fainter
- Untabulated stars

NOTE

The numbers enclosed in brackets refer to those stars of the selected list which are not used in Sight Reduction Tables A.P. 3270, N.P. 303.

EQUATORIAL STARS (SHA 0° to 180°)

SIDEREAL HOUR ANGLE

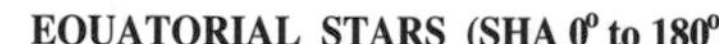

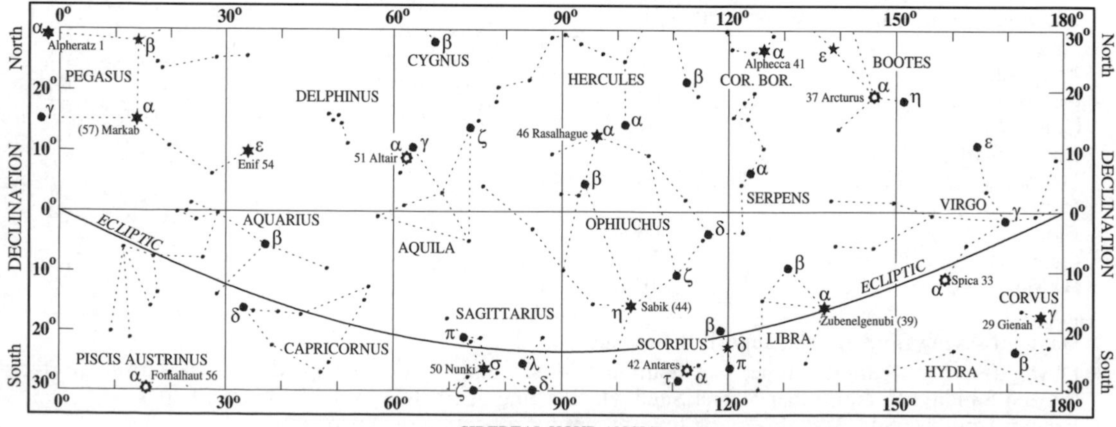

SOUTHERN STARS

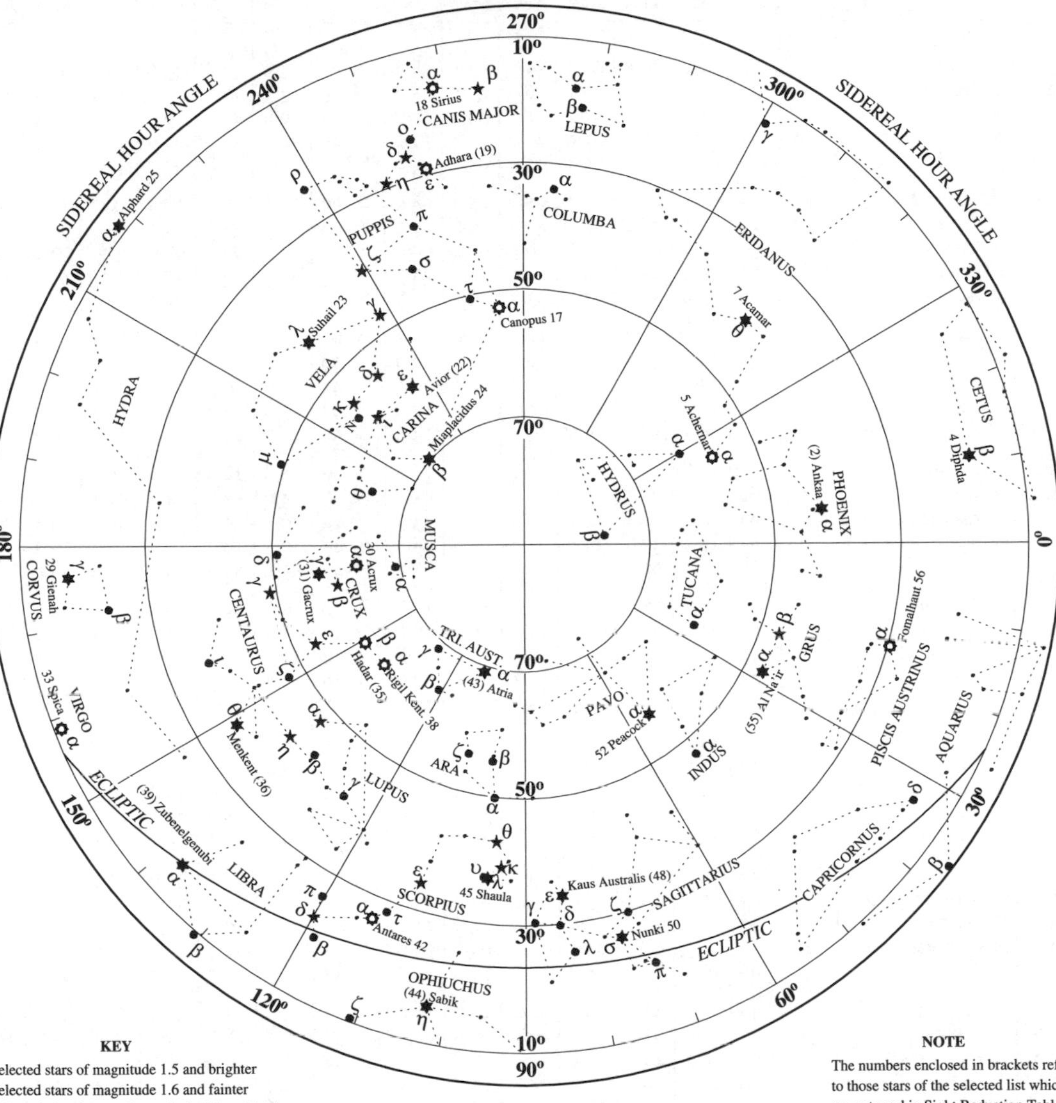

KEY

- ✪ Selected stars of magnitude 1.5 and brighter
- ✸ Selected stars of magnitude 1.6 and fainter
- ★ Other tabulated stars of magnitude 2.5 and brighter
- ● Other tabulated stars of magnitude 2.6 and fainter
- • Untabulated stars

NOTE

The numbers enclosed in brackets refer to those stars of the selected list which are not used in Sight Reduction Tables A.P. 3270, N.P. 303.

EQUATORIAL STARS (SHA 180° to 360°)

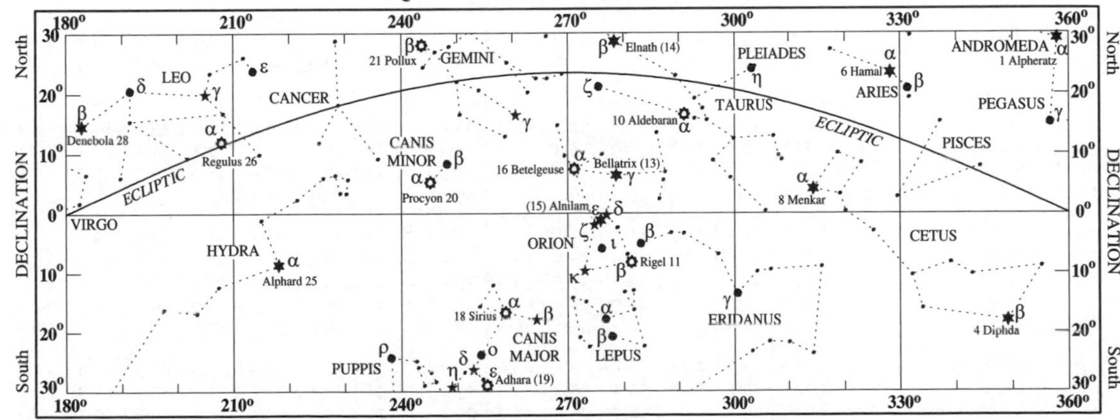

Mag.	Name and Number		SHA							Declination						
				JAN.	FEB.	MAR.	APR.	MAY	JUNE		JAN.	FEB.	MAR.	APR.	MAY	JUNE
			°	′	′	′	′	′	′	°	′	′	′	′	′	′
3·2	γ Cephei		**4**	59·2	59·8	60·0	59·7	59·1	58·3	N **77**	43·9	43·8	43·6	43·5	43·4	43·4
2·5	α Pegasi	57	**13**	36·1	36·1	36·1	36·0	35·8	35·6	N **15**	17·8	17·8	17·7	17·7	17·7	17·8
2·4	β Pegasi		**13**	51·2	51·3	51·2	51·1	50·9	50·7	N **28**	10·6	10·5	10·4	10·4	10·4	10·5
1·2	α Piscis Aust.	56	**15**	21·6	21·6	21·6	21·5	21·3	21·0	S **29**	32·1	32·0	32·0	31·8	31·7	31·6
2·1	β Gruis		**19**	05·4	05·5	05·4	05·2	05·0	04·7	S **46**	47·9	47·8	47·7	47·6	47·4	47·4
2·9	α Tucanæ		**25**	06·0	06·1	06·0	05·7	05·4	04·9	S **60**	10·6	10·5	10·4	10·2	10·1	10·0
1·7	α Gruis	55	**27**	41·1	41·2	41·1	40·9	40·6	40·2	S **46**	52·8	52·7	52·6	52·5	52·4	52·3
2·9	δ Capricorni		**33**	00·7	00·7	00·6	00·5	00·2	00·0	S **16**	03·0	03·0	03·0	02·9	02·8	02·7
2·4	ε Pegasi	54	**33**	45·0	45·0	44·9	44·8	44·5	44·3	N **9**	57·3	57·2	57·1	57·1	57·2	57·3
2·9	β Aquarii		**36**	53·6	53·6	53·5	53·3	53·1	52·8	S **5**	29·7	29·8	29·8	29·7	29·7	29·6
2·4	α Cephei		**40**	15·7	15·8	15·6	15·3	14·9	14·5	N **62**	39·7	39·5	39·4	39·3	39·3	39·4
2·5	ε Cygni		**48**	16·9	16·8	16·7	16·5	16·2	16·0	N **34**	02·2	02·1	02·0	01·9	02·0	02·1
1·3	α Cygni	53	**49**	30·2	30·2	30·0	29·8	29·5	29·3	N **45**	20·6	20·5	20·4	20·3	20·4	20·5
3·1	α Indi		**50**	19·3	19·2	19·0	18·8	18·4	18·1	S **47**	13·9	13·8	13·7	13·6	13·5	13·5
1·9	α Pavonis	52	**53**	16·1	16·0	15·7	15·4	15·0	14·6	S **56**	40·7	40·6	40·5	40·4	40·4	40·4
2·2	γ Cygni		**54**	17·8	17·8	17·6	17·4	17·1	16·9	N **40**	18·8	18·7	18·6	18·5	18·6	18·7
0·8	α Aquilæ	51	**62**	06·2	06·1	05·9	05·7	05·5	05·3	N **8**	54·9	54·8	54·8	54·8	54·9	55·0
2·7	γ Aquilæ		**63**	14·4	14·3	14·1	13·9	13·7	13·5	N **10**	39·4	39·3	39·3	39·3	39·4	39·5
2·9	δ Cygni		**63**	37·9	37·8	37·6	37·3	37·0	36·8	N **45**	10·5	10·3	10·2	10·2	10·3	10·4
3·1	β Cygni		**67**	09·3	09·2	09·0	08·8	08·6	08·4	N **27**	59·8	59·7	59·7	59·7	59·7	59·9
2·9	π Sagittarii		**72**	18·8	18·7	18·5	18·3	18·0	17·8	S **20**	59·6	59·6	59·6	59·6	59·5	59·5
3·0	ζ Aquilæ		**73**	27·5	27·4	27·2	27·0	26·8	26·6	N **13**	53·5	53·4	53·3	53·3	53·4	53·5
2·6	ζ Sagittarii		**74**	05·1	04·9	04·7	04·5	04·2	04·0	S **29**	51·2	51·1	51·1	51·1	51·1	51·1
2·0	σ Sagittarii	50	**75**	55·7	55·5	55·3	55·1	54·8	54·6	S **26**	16·3	16·3	16·3	16·3	16·3	16·3
0·0	α Lyræ	49	**80**	37·7	37·6	37·3	37·1	36·9	36·7	N **38**	48·1	47·9	47·9	47·9	48·0	48·1
2·8	λ Sagittarii		**82**	45·2	45·0	44·8	44·5	44·3	44·1	S **25**	24·5	24·5	24·5	24·5	24·5	24·5
1·9	ε Sagittarii	48	**83**	41·0	40·8	40·6	40·3	40·0	39·9	S **34**	22·4	22·3	22·3	22·3	22·3	22·3
2·7	δ Sagittarii		**84**	29·2	29·0	28·8	28·6	28·3	28·1	S **29**	49·0	49·0	49·0	49·0	49·0	49·0
3·0	γ Sagittarii		**88**	16·9	16·7	16·5	16·3	16·0	15·9	S **30**	25·2	25·2	25·2	25·2	25·2	25·2
2·2	γ Draconis	47	**90**	45·5	45·3	45·0	44·7	44·5	44·4	N **51**	29·3	29·1	29·0	29·1	29·2	29·4
2·8	β Ophiuchi		**93**	55·7	55·5	55·3	55·1	54·9	54·8	N **4**	33·8	33·7	33·6	33·7	33·7	33·8
2·4	κ Scorpii		**94**	05·5	05·3	05·0	04·7	04·5	04·3	S **39**	02·0	02·0	02·0	02·0	02·1	02·1
1·9	θ Scorpii		**95**	22·4	22·1	21·8	21·5	21·3	21·1	S **43**	00·2	00·2	00·2	00·2	00·2	00·3
2·1	α Ophiuchi	46	**96**	04·5	04·3	04·1	03·9	03·7	03·6	N **12**	33·0	32·9	32·9	32·9	32·9	33·0
1·6	λ Scorpii	45	**96**	19·0	18·7	18·5	18·2	18·0	17·8	S **37**	06·7	06·7	06·7	06·7	06·7	06·8
3·0	α Aræ		**96**	43·2	42·9	42·6	42·2	42·0	41·8	S **49**	53·0	53·0	53·0	53·0	53·1	53·2
2·7	υ Scorpii		**97**	01·6	01·4	01·1	00·9	00·6	00·5	S **37**	18·3	18·3	18·3	18·3	18·3	18·4
2·8	β Draconis		**97**	18·3	18·0	17·7	17·4	17·2	17·1	N **52**	17·3	17·2	17·2	17·2	17·3	17·5
2·8	β Aræ		**98**	19·8	19·5	19·2	18·8	18·5	18·3	S **55**	32·4	32·3	32·3	32·4	32·4	32·5
Var.‡	α Herculis		**101**	09·0	08·8	08·6	08·4	08·2	08·1	N **14**	22·4	22·3	22·2	22·3	22·3	22·4
2·4	η Ophiuchi	44	**102**	10·0	09·8	09·6	09·4	09·2	09·1	S **15**	44·5	44·6	44·6	44·6	44·6	44·6
3·1	ζ Aræ		**104**	60·0	59·7	59·3	59·0	58·7	58·5	S **56**	00·6	00·6	00·6	00·7	00·7	00·8
2·3	ε Scorpii		**107**	11·4	11·1	10·9	10·6	10·4	10·3	S **34**	19·1	19·1	19·2	19·2	19·3	19·3
1·9	α Triang. Aust.	43	**107**	23·6	23·0	22·5	22·0	21·6	21·4	S **69**	03·1	03·0	03·0	03·1	03·2	03·4
2·8	ζ Herculis		**109**	31·5	31·2	31·0	30·8	30·6	30·6	N **31**	34·3	34·2	34·2	34·2	34·4	34·5
2·6	ζ Ophiuchi		**110**	28·9	28·6	28·4	28·2	28·1	28·0	S **10**	35·9	35·9	36·0	36·0	36·0	35·9
2·8	τ Scorpii		**110**	46·2	45·9	45·7	45·5	45·3	45·2	S **28**	14·8	14·8	14·9	14·9	14·9	14·9
2·8	β Herculis		**112**	16·1	15·8	15·6	15·4	15·3	15·2	N **21**	27·2	27·1	27·1	27·1	27·2	27·3
1·0	α Scorpii	42	**112**	23·5	23·3	23·1	22·8	22·7	22·6	S **26**	27·9	27·9	28·0	28·0	28·0	28·1
2·7	η Draconis		**113**	57·2	56·9	56·5	56·2	56·0	56·0	N **61**	28·5	28·4	28·3	28·4	28·6	28·7
2·7	δ Ophiuchi		**116**	11·7	11·5	11·3	11·1	11·0	10·9	S **3**	44·1	44·2	44·2	44·2	44·2	44·2
2·6	β Scorpii		**118**	23·8	23·6	23·4	23·2	23·1	23·0	S **19**	50·9	50·9	51·0	51·0	51·0	51·0
2·3	δ Scorpii		**119**	40·1	39·9	39·7	39·5	39·3	39·3	S **22**	39·9	40·0	40·0	40·1	40·1	40·1
2·9	π Scorpii		**120**	02·0	01·8	01·5	01·3	01·2	01·1	S **26**	09·5	09·5	09·6	09·6	09·7	09·7
2·8	β Trianguli Aust.		**120**	50·6	50·1	49·7	49·3	49·1	49·0	S **63**	28·5	28·5	28·6	28·7	28·8	28·9
2·6	α Serpentis		**123**	43·7	43·4	43·2	43·1	43·0	42·9	N **6**	22·4	22·4	22·3	22·3	22·4	22·5
2·8	γ Lupi		**125**	56·1	55·8	55·5	55·3	55·2	55·1	S **41**	13·1	13·1	13·2	13·3	13·3	13·4
2·2	α Coronæ Bor.	41	**126**	09·2	08·9	08·7	08·5	08·4	08·4	N **26**	39·4	39·4	39·3	39·4	39·5	39·6

‡ 2·9 — 3·6

Mag.	Name and Number		SHA							Declination						
				JULY	AUG.	SEPT.	OCT.	NOV.	DEC.		JULY	AUG.	SEPT.	OCT.	NOV.	DEC.
			°	′	′	′	′	′	′	°	′	′	′	′	′	′
3·2	γ Cephei		**4**	57·6	57·0	56·8	56·9	57·4	58·0	**N 77**	43·5	43·6	43·8	44·0	44·2	44·2
2·5	*Markab*	57	**13**	35·4	35·2	35·1	35·2	35·3	35·4	**N 15**	17·9	18·1	18·1	18·2	18·2	18·2
2·4	*Scheat*		**13**	50·4	50·3	50·2	50·2	50·3	50·5	**N 28**	10·6	10·7	10·8	10·9	11·0	11·0
1·2	*Fomalhaut*	56	**15**	20·8	20·6	20·5	20·5	20·6	20·8	**S 29**	31·6	31·6	31·6	31·7	31·8	31·8
2·1	β Gruis		**19**	04·4	04·2	04·1	04·2	04·3	04·5	**S 46**	47·3	47·4	47·5	47·6	47·7	47·7
2·9	α Tucanæ		**25**	04·6	04·4	04·3	04·4	04·7	04·9	**S 60**	10·1	10·1	10·3	10·4	10·5	10·5
1·7	*Al Na'ir*	55	**27**	40·0	39·8	39·8	39·9	40·0	40·2	**S 46**	52·3	52·4	52·5	52·6	52·6	52·6
2·9	δ Capricorni		**32**	59·8	59·7	59·7	59·7	59·9	60·0	**S 16**	02·7	02·7	02·7	02·7	02·7	02·8
2·4	*Enif*	54	**33**	44·1	44·0	44·0	44·1	44·2	44·3	**N 9**	57·4	57·5	57·6	57·6	57·6	57·6
2·9	β Aquarii		**36**	52·7	52·6	52·6	52·6	52·7	52·8	**S 5**	29·5	29·4	29·4	29·4	29·5	29·5
2·4	*Alderamin*		**40**	14·3	14·2	14·3	14·6	14·9	15·2	**N 62**	39·5	39·7	39·9	40·0	40·0	40·0
2·5	ε Cygni		**48**	15·8	15·8	15·9	16·0	16·2	16·3	**N 34**	02·2	02·4	02·5	02·6	02·6	02·5
1·3	*Deneb*	53	**49**	29·1	29·1	29·2	29·3	29·6	29·7	**N 45**	20·6	20·8	20·9	21·0	21·0	20·9
3·1	α Indi		**50**	17·9	17·8	17·9	18·0	18·2	18·4	**S 47**	13·6	13·6	13·7	13·8	13·8	13·8
1·9	*Peacock*	52	**53**	14·4	14·3	14·4	14·6	14·9	15·0	**S 56**	40·5	40·6	40·7	40·7	40·7	40·7
2·2	γ Cygni		**54**	16·7	16·7	16·8	17·0	17·2	17·3	**N 40**	18·9	19·0	19·1	19·2	19·2	19·1
0·8	*Altair*	51	**62**	05·2	05·2	05·3	05·4	05·5	05·6	**N 8**	55·1	55·2	55·2	55·2	55·2	55·1
2·7	γ Aquilæ		**63**	13·4	13·4	13·4	13·6	13·7	13·8	**N 10**	39·6	39·6	39·7	39·7	39·7	39·6
2·9	δ Cygni		**63**	36·7	36·7	36·9	37·1	37·3	37·4	**N 45**	10·6	10·7	10·8	10·9	10·8	10·7
3·1	*Albireo*		**67**	08·3	08·3	08·4	08·5	08·7	08·8	**N 28**	00·0	00·1	00·2	00·2	00·2	00·1
2·9	π Sagittarii		**72**	17·7	17·7	17·8	18·0	18·1	18·1	**S 20**	59·5	59·5	59·5	59·5	59·6	59·6
3·0	ζ Aquilæ		**73**	26·5	26·5	26·6	26·8	26·9	27·0	**N 13**	53·6	53·7	53·7	53·7	53·7	53·6
2·6	ζ Sagittarii		**74**	03·9	03·9	04·0	04·2	04·3	04·3	**S 29**	51·1	51·1	51·1	51·1	51·1	51·1
2·0	*Nunki*	50	**75**	54·5	54·5	54·6	54·8	54·9	54·9	**S 26**	16·3	16·3	16·3	16·3	16·3	16·3
0·0	*Vega*	49	**80**	36·7	36·7	36·9	37·1	37·3	37·3	**N 38**	48·3	48·4	48·5	48·5	48·4	48·3
2·8	λ Sagittarii		**82**	44·0	44·1	44·2	44·3	44·4	44·4	**S 25**	24·5	24·5	24·5	24·5	24·5	24·5
1·9	*Kaus Australis*	48	**83**	39·8	39·8	39·9	40·1	40·2	40·2	**S 34**	22·4	22·4	22·4	22·4	22·4	22·4
2·7	δ Sagittarii		**84**	28·1	28·1	28·2	28·4	28·5	28·5	**S 29**	49·0	49·0	49·1	49·1	49·1	49·0
3·0	γ Sagittarii		**88**	15·8	15·8	16·0	16·1	16·2	16·2	**S 30**	25·2	25·2	25·3	25·3	25·2	25·2
2·2	*Eltanin*	47	**90**	44·4	44·5	44·7	45·0	45·2	45·3	**N 51**	29·5	29·6	29·7	29·7	29·6	29·4
2·8	β Ophiuchi		**93**	54·7	54·8	54·9	55·1	55·1	55·1	**N 4**	33·9	33·9	33·9	33·9	33·9	33·8
2·4	κ Scorpii		**94**	04·3	04·3	04·5	04·6	04·8	04·7	**S 39**	02·1	02·2	02·2	02·2	02·2	02·1
1·9	θ Scorpii		**95**	21·1	21·2	21·3	21·5	21·6	21·6	**S 43**	00·4	00·4	00·4	00·4	00·4	00·3
2·1	*Rasalhague*	46	**96**	03·6	03·7	03·8	03·9	04·0	04·0	**N 12**	33·1	33·2	33·2	33·2	33·1	33·0
1·6	*Shaula*	45	**96**	17·8	17·9	18·0	18·2	18·3	18·2	**S 37**	06·8	06·8	06·9	06·8	06·8	06·8
3·0	α Aræ		**96**	41·7	41·8	42·0	42·2	42·4	42·3	**S 49**	53·2	53·3	53·3	53·3	53·2	53·2
2·7	υ Scorpii		**97**	00·4	00·5	00·7	00·8	00·9	00·9	**S 37**	18·4	18·4	18·5	18·4	18·4	18·4
2·8	β Draconis		**97**	17·2	17·3	17·6	17·8	18·0	18·1	**N 52**	17·6	17·7	17·8	17·7	17·6	17·5
2·8	β Aræ		**98**	18·3	18·4	18·6	18·8	19·0	19·0	**S 55**	32·6	32·7	32·7	32·7	32·6	32·5
Var.‡	α Herculis		**101**	08·1	08·2	08·3	08·5	08·5	08·5	**N 14**	22·5	22·6	22·6	22·6	22·5	22·4
2·4	*Sabik*	44	**102**	09·1	09·2	09·3	09·4	09·5	09·4	**S 15**	44·6	44·6	44·6	44·6	44·6	44·6
3·1	ζ Aræ		**104**	58·5	58·7	58·9	59·1	59·3	59·2	**S 56**	00·9	01·0	01·0	01·0	00·9	00·8
2·3	ε Scorpii		**107**	10·3	10·4	10·5	10·7	10·8	10·7	**S 34**	19·3	19·4	19·4	19·3	19·3	19·3
1·9	*Atria*	43	**107**	21·4	21·7	22·1	22·4	22·6	22·5	**S 69**	03·5	03·6	03·6	03·5	03·4	03·3
2·8	ζ Herculis		**109**	30·6	30·7	30·9	31·1	31·1	31·1	**N 31**	34·6	34·7	34·7	34·6	34·5	34·4
2·6	ζ Ophiuchi		**110**	28·0	28·1	28·2	28·3	28·4	28·3	**S 10**	35·9	35·9	35·9	35·9	35·9	36·0
2·8	τ Scorpii		**110**	45·2	45·3	45·4	45·6	45·6	45·5	**S 28**	15·0	15·0	15·0	14·9	14·9	14·9
2·8	β Herculis		**112**	15·3	15·4	15·5	15·6	15·7	15·6	**N 21**	27·4	27·5	27·5	27·4	27·3	27·2
1·0	*Antares*	42	**112**	22·6	22·7	22·8	22·9	23·0	22·9	**S 26**	28·1	28·1	28·1	28·1	28·0	28·0
2·7	η Draconis		**113**	56·2	56·4	56·8	57·1	57·3	57·3	**N 61**	28·9	28·9	28·9	28·8	28·7	28·5
2·7	δ Ophiuchi		**116**	10·9	11·0	11·1	11·2	11·3	11·2	**S 3**	44·1	44·1	44·1	44·1	44·1	44·2
2·6	β Scorpii		**118**	23·0	23·1	23·2	23·3	23·4	23·3	**S 19**	51·0	51·0	51·0	51·0	51·0	51·0
2·3	*Dschubba*		**119**	39·3	39·4	39·5	39·6	39·7	39·6	**S 22**	40·1	40·1	40·1	40·1	40·1	40·1
2·9	π Scorpii		**120**	01·2	01·3	01·4	01·5	01·5	01·4	**S 26**	09·7	09·7	09·7	09·7	09·6	09·6
2·8	β Trianguli Aust.		**120**	49·1	49·4	49·7	49·9	50·0	49·8	**S 63**	29·0	29·1	29·1	29·0	28·9	28·8
2·6	α Serpentis		**123**	43·0	43·1	43·2	43·3	43·3	43·2	**N 6**	22·5	22·6	22·6	22·5	22·5	22·4
2·8	γ Lupi		**125**	55·2	55·3	55·5	55·6	55·6	55·4	**S 41**	13·5	13·5	13·4	13·4	13·3	13·3
2·2	*Alphecca*	41	**126**	08·5	08·6	08·8	08·9	08·9	08·8	**N 26**	39·7	39·8	39·7	39·7	39·5	39·4

‡ 2·9 — 3·6

Mag.	Name and Number			SHA							Declination						
					JAN.	FEB.	MAR.	APR.	MAY	JUNE		JAN.	FEB.	MAR.	APR.	MAY	JUNE
				°	′	′	′	′	′	′	°	′	′	′	′	′	′
3·1	γ	Ursæ Minoris		**129**	50·1	49·5	49·0	48·6	48·5	48·7	**N 71**	46·2	46·2	46·2	46·3	46·5	46·6
2·9	γ	Trianguli Aust.		**129**	52·5	51·9	51·4	51·0	50·8	50·8	**S 68**	44·0	44·1	44·2	44·3	44·4	44·6
2·6	β	Libræ		**130**	31·3	31·1	30·9	30·8	30·7	30·6	**S 9**	26·6	26·6	26·7	26·7	26·7	26·7
2·7	β	Lupi		**135**	05·4	05·1	04·8	04·6	04·5	04·5	**S 43**	11·8	11·8	11·9	12·0	12·1	12·2
2·8	α	Libræ	39	**137**	02·8	02·6	02·4	02·3	02·2	02·2	**S 16**	06·5	06·6	06·7	06·7	06·7	06·7
2·1	β	Ursæ Minoris	40	**137**	20·7	20·1	19·5	19·1	19·1	19·4	**N 74**	05·0	04·9	05·0	05·1	05·3	05·4
2·4	ε	Bootis		**138**	34·3	34·1	33·9	33·7	33·7	33·7	**N 27**	00·2	00·1	00·1	00·2	00·3	00·4
2·3	α	Lupi		**139**	14·1	13·8	13·5	13·3	13·2	13·2	**S 47**	27·3	27·4	27·5	27·6	27·7	27·8
−0·3	α	Centauri	38	**139**	48·5	48·1	47·8	47·5	47·4	47·5	**S 60**	53·9	53·9	54·0	54·2	54·3	54·4
2·3	η	Centauri		**140**	51·2	50·9	50·7	50·5	50·4	50·4	**S 42**	13·6	13·7	13·8	13·9	14·0	14·0
3·0	γ	Bootis		**141**	48·8	48·6	48·3	48·2	48·2	48·2	**N 38**	13·9	13·9	13·9	14·0	14·1	14·2
0·0	α	Bootis	37	**145**	53·6	53·4	53·2	53·1	53·1	53·1	**N 19**	05·6	05·5	05·5	05·6	05·7	05·7
2·1	θ	Centauri	36	**148**	04·7	04·4	04·2	04·1	04·1	04·1	**S 36**	26·9	27·0	27·1	27·2	27·3	27·3
0·6	β	Centauri	35	**148**	44·4	44·0	43·7	43·5	43·4	43·5	**S 60**	26·9	27·0	27·1	27·2	27·4	27·5
2·6	ζ	Centauri		**150**	50·9	50·6	50·3	50·2	50·2	50·2	**S 47**	22·0	22·1	22·2	22·3	22·4	22·5
2·7	η	Bootis		**151**	07·7	07·5	07·3	07·2	07·2	07·2	**N 18**	18·7	18·6	18·6	18·7	18·8	18·8
1·9	η	Ursæ Majoris	34	**152**	57·1	56·8	56·6	56·5	56·5	56·6	**N 49**	13·5	13·5	13·6	13·7	13·8	13·9
2·3	ε	Centauri		**154**	45·3	45·0	44·7	44·6	44·6	44·7	**S 53**	32·8	32·9	33·0	33·2	33·3	33·4
1·0	α	Virginis	33	**158**	28·7	28·4	28·3	28·2	28·2	28·2	**S 11**	14·9	15·0	15·0	15·1	15·1	15·1
2·3	ζ	Ursæ Majoris		**158**	51·1	50·8	50·5	50·5	50·5	50·7	**N 54**	50·0	50·0	50·0	50·2	50·3	50·4
2·8	ι	Centauri		**159**	36·6	36·3	36·2	36·1	36·1	36·1	**S 36**	47·9	48·0	48·1	48·2	48·3	48·3
2·8	ε	Virginis		**164**	14·7	14·5	14·4	14·3	14·3	14·4	**N 10**	52·0	52·0	52·0	52·0	52·0	52·1
2·9	α	Canum Venat.		**165**	47·8	47·5	47·4	47·3	47·4	47·5	**N 38**	13·4	13·4	13·5	13·6	13·7	13·7
1·8	ε	Ursæ Majoris	32	**166**	18·6	18·2	18·0	18·0	18·1	18·2	**N 55**	51·8	51·8	51·9	52·1	52·2	52·3
1·3	β	Crucis		**167**	48·8	48·5	48·3	48·2	48·3	48·4	**S 59**	46·6	46·7	46·8	47·0	47·1	47·2
2·9	γ	Virginis		**169**	22·2	22·0	21·8	21·8	21·8	21·9	**S 1**	32·6	32·6	32·7	32·7	32·7	32·6
2·2	γ	Centauri		**169**	22·9	22·6	22·4	22·4	22·4	22·5	**S 49**	02·9	03·0	03·2	03·3	03·4	03·5
2·7	α	Muscæ		**170**	26·2	25·8	25·5	25·5	25·6	25·9	**S 69**	13·4	13·5	13·7	13·9	14·0	14·1
2·7	β	Corvi		**171**	10·7	10·4	10·3	10·3	10·3	10·4	**S 23**	29·3	29·4	29·5	29·6	29·6	29·6
1·6	γ	Crucis	31	**171**	57·9	57·6	57·4	57·4	57·5	57·6	**S 57**	12·2	12·3	12·5	12·7	12·8	12·8
1·3	α	Crucis	30	**173**	06·2	05·8	05·6	05·6	05·7	05·9	**S 63**	11·3	11·4	11·6	11·8	11·9	12·0
2·6	γ	Corvi	29	**175**	49·7	49·5	49·4	49·3	49·4	49·5	**S 17**	38·1	38·2	38·3	38·3	38·4	38·4
2·6	δ	Centauri		**177**	41·0	40·8	40·6	40·6	40·7	40·9	**S 50**	48·8	48·9	49·1	49·2	49·3	49·4
2·4	γ	Ursæ Majoris		**181**	19·2	19·0	18·8	18·9	19·0	19·2	**N 53**	35·8	35·8	35·9	36·0	36·1	36·2
2·1	β	Leonis	28	**182**	31·1	30·9	30·8	30·8	30·8	30·9	**N 14**	28·5	28·5	28·5	28·5	28·6	28·6
2·6	δ	Leonis		**191**	14·8	14·6	14·5	14·5	14·6	14·7	**N 20**	25·7	25·6	25·7	25·7	25·8	25·8
3·0	ψ	Ursæ Majoris		**192**	20·7	20·5	20·4	20·5	20·6	20·8	**N 44**	24·1	24·2	24·2	24·3	24·4	24·5
1·8	α	Ursæ Majoris	27	**193**	48·5	48·2	48·1	48·2	48·4	48·7	**N 61**	39·3	39·3	39·5	39·6	39·7	39·7
2·4	β	Ursæ Majoris		**194**	17·1	16·8	16·7	16·8	17·0	17·2	**N 56**	17·2	17·3	17·4	17·5	17·6	17·6
2·7	μ	Velorum		**198**	07·0	06·8	06·8	06·9	07·0	07·2	**S 49**	30·5	30·7	30·8	30·9	31·0	31·0
2·8	θ	Carinæ		**199**	05·7	05·5	05·5	05·7	05·9	06·3	**S 64**	28·8	29·0	29·2	29·4	29·4	29·5
2·3	γ	Leonis		**204**	46·2	46·1	46·1	46·1	46·2	46·3	**N 19**	45·1	45·1	45·1	45·2	45·2	45·2
1·4	α	Leonis	26	**207**	40·7	40·6	40·6	40·6	40·7	40·8	**N 11**	52·9	52·8	52·8	52·9	52·9	52·9
3·0	ε	Leonis		**213**	17·6	17·5	17·5	17·6	17·7	17·8	**N 23**	41·5	41·5	41·6	41·6	41·7	41·7
3·1	N	Velorum		**217**	03·2	03·1	03·2	03·4	03·7	03·9	**S 57**	06·5	06·7	06·9	07·0	07·0	07·0
2·0	α	Hydræ	25	**217**	53·4	53·3	53·3	53·4	53·5	53·6	**S 8**	44·1	44·2	44·2	44·3	44·2	44·2
2·5	κ	Velorum		**219**	19·7	19·7	19·8	20·0	20·2	20·4	**S 55**	05·0	05·2	05·3	05·4	05·5	05·4
2·2	ι	Carinæ		**220**	36·1	36·0	36·1	36·4	36·7	36·9	**S 59**	20·8	21·0	21·1	21·2	21·3	21·2
1·7	β	Carinæ	24	**221**	38·1	38·1	38·3	38·7	39·1	39·6	**S 69**	47·2	47·4	47·6	47·7	47·7	47·7
2·2	λ	Velorum	23	**222**	50·2	50·1	50·2	50·4	50·5	50·7	**S 43**	30·1	30·3	30·4	30·5	30·5	30·5
3·1	ι	Ursæ Majoris		**224**	54·3	54·2	54·2	54·4	54·6	54·7	**N 47**	58·2	58·3	58·4	58·5	58·5	58·5
2·0	δ	Velorum		**228**	41·7	41·7	41·9	42·1	42·3	42·6	**S 54**	46·3	46·5	46·7	46·7	46·7	46·7
1·9	ε	Carinæ	22	**234**	16·3	16·3	16·5	16·8	17·1	17·4	**S 59**	33·9	34·1	34·3	34·3	34·3	34·2
1·8	γ	Velorum		**237**	28·6	28·6	28·8	29·0	29·2	29·3	**S 47**	23·3	23·5	23·6	23·7	23·7	23·6
2·8	ρ	Puppis		**237**	55·6	55·6	55·7	55·8	56·0	56·1	**S 24**	21·4	21·5	21·6	21·6	21·6	21·5
2·3	ζ	Puppis		**238**	56·8	56·8	56·9	57·1	57·3	57·4	**S 40**	03·2	03·4	03·5	03·5	03·5	03·4
1·1	β	Geminorum	21	**243**	24·4	24·4	24·5	24·6	24·8	24·8	**N 27**	58·8	58·9	58·9	58·9	58·9	58·9
0·4	α	Canis Minoris	20	**244**	56·9	56·9	56·9	57·1	57·2	57·2	**N 5**	10·6	10·6	10·6	10·6	10·6	10·6

Mag.	Name and Number		SHA °	JULY ′	AUG. ′	SEPT. ′	OCT. ′	NOV. ′	DEC. ′	Declination °	JULY ′	AUG. ′	SEPT. ′	OCT. ′	NOV. ′	DEC. ′
3·1	γ Ursæ Minoris		**129**	49·0	49·5	50·1	50·4	50·6	50·5	N **71**	46·7	46·7	46·7	46·5	46·4	46·2
2·9	γ Trianguli Aust.		**129**	51·0	51·4	51·8	52·0	52·0	51·8	S **68**	44·7	44·7	44·7	44·6	44·4	44·3
2·6	β Libræ		**130**	30·7	30·8	30·9	31·0	31·0	30·8	S **9**	26·7	26·6	26·6	26·6	26·6	26·7
2·7	β Lupi		**135**	04·6	04·7	04·9	05·0	05·0	04·8	S **43**	12·2	12·2	12·2	12·1	12·0	12·0
2·8	*Zubenelgenubi*	39	**137**	02·2	02·3	02·4	02·5	02·5	02·3	S **16**	06·7	06·7	06·7	06·7	06·7	06·7
2·1	*Kochab*	40	**137**	19·8	20·4	21·0	21·3	21·4	21·2	N **74**	05·5	05·5	05·4	05·2	05·0	04·9
2·4	ε Bootis		**138**	33·8	33·9	34·0	34·1	34·1	33·9	N **27**	00·4	00·5	00·4	00·3	00·2	00·1
2·3	α Lupi		**139**	13·3	13·5	13·7	13·8	13·7	13·5	S **47**	27·8	27·8	27·7	27·7	27·6	27·5
−0·3	*Rigil Kent.*	38	**139**	47·7	48·0	48·2	48·4	48·3	48·0	S **60**	54·5	54·5	54·4	54·3	54·2	54·1
2·3	η Centauri		**140**	50·5	50·7	50·8	50·9	50·9	50·7	S **42**	14·1	14·1	14·0	13·9	13·9	13·8
3·0	γ Bootis		**141**	48·3	48·5	48·6	48·7	48·7	48·5	N **38**	14·3	14·3	14·3	14·1	14·0	13·8
0·0	*Arcturus*	37	**145**	53·2	53·3	53·4	53·4	53·4	53·2	N **19**	05·8	05·8	05·8	05·7	05·6	05·4
2·1	*Menkent*	36	**148**	04·2	04·3	04·5	04·5	04·4	04·2	S **36**	27·4	27·3	27·3	27·2	27·1	27·1
0·6	*Hadar*	35	**148**	43·7	44·0	44·2	44·3	44·2	43·9	S **60**	27·5	27·5	27·4	27·3	27·2	27·1
2·6	ζ Centauri		**150**	50·3	50·5	50·7	50·7	50·6	50·4	S **47**	22·5	22·5	22·4	22·3	22·2	22·2
2·7	η Bootis		**151**	07·3	07·4	07·5	07·6	07·5	07·3	N **18**	18·9	18·9	18·9	18·8	18·7	18·6
1·9	*Alkaid*	34	**152**	56·7	56·9	57·1	57·1	57·1	56·9	N **49**	14·0	13·9	13·9	13·7	13·5	13·4
2·3	ε Centauri		**154**	44·8	45·0	45·2	45·2	45·1	44·8	S **53**	33·4	33·4	33·3	33·2	33·1	33·0
1·0	*Spica*	33	**158**	28·3	28·4	28·5	28·5	28·4	28·2	S **11**	15·1	15·0	15·0	15·0	15·0	15·1
2·3	*Mizar*		**158**	50·9	51·1	51·2	51·3	51·2	50·9	N **54**	50·5	50·4	50·3	50·1	50·0	49·8
2·8	ι Centauri		**159**	36·2	36·4	36·5	36·5	36·4	36·1	S **36**	48·3	48·3	48·2	48·1	48·1	48·1
2·8	ε Virginis		**164**	14·4	14·5	14·6	14·6	14·5	14·3	N **10**	52·1	52·1	52·1	52·1	52·0	51·8
2·9	*Cor Caroli*		**165**	47·6	47·7	47·8	47·8	47·7	47·4	N **38**	13·8	13·7	13·7	13·5	13·4	13·2
1·8	*Alioth*	32	**166**	18·4	18·6	18·8	18·8	18·6	18·3	N **55**	52·3	52·2	52·1	51·9	51·8	51·6
1·3	*Mimosa*		**167**	48·7	48·9	49·1	49·1	48·8	48·5	S **59**	47·2	47·2	47·0	46·9	46·8	46·8
2·9	γ Virginis		**169**	22·0	22·0	22·1	22·1	21·9	21·7	S **1**	32·6	32·6	32·6	32·6	32·7	32·7
2·2	*Muhlifain*		**169**	22·7	22·9	23·0	22·9	22·8	22·5	S **49**	03·5	03·4	03·3	03·2	03·1	03·1
2·7	α Muscæ		**170**	26·3	26·6	26·9	26·8	26·5	26·1	S **69**	14·1	14·0	13·9	13·8	13·7	13·6
2·7	β Corvi		**171**	10·5	10·6	10·6	10·6	10·5	10·2	S **23**	29·6	29·6	29·5	29·4	29·4	29·5
1·6	*Gacrux*	31	**171**	57·9	58·1	58·2	58·1	57·9	57·6	S **57**	12·8	12·8	12·6	12·5	12·4	12·4
1·3	*Acrux*	30	**173**	06·2	06·5	06·6	06·6	06·3	05·9	S **63**	12·0	11·9	11·8	11·6	11·5	11·5
2·6	*Gienah*	29	**175**	49·5	49·6	49·7	49·6	49·5	49·2	S **17**	38·3	38·3	38·2	38·2	38·2	38·3
2·6	δ Centauri		**177**	41·0	41·2	41·3	41·2	41·0	40·7	S **50**	49·3	49·3	49·1	49·0	49·0	49·0
2·4	*Phecda*		**181**	19·3	19·5	19·5	19·4	19·2	18·9	N **53**	36·2	36·1	35·9	35·8	35·6	35·5
2·1	*Denebola*	28	**182**	31·0	31·1	31·1	31·0	30·9	30·6	N **14**	28·6	28·6	28·6	28·5	28·4	28·3
2·6	δ Leonis		**191**	14·8	14·8	14·8	14·7	14·5	14·3	N **20**	25·8	25·8	25·8	25·7	25·6	25·5
3·0	ψ Ursæ Majoris		**192**	20·9	21·0	20·9	20·8	20·6	20·3	N **44**	24·4	24·4	24·2	24·1	24·0	23·9
1·8	*Dubhe*	27	**193**	48·9	49·0	49·0	48·8	48·5	48·0	N **61**	39·7	39·5	39·4	39·2	39·1	39·0
2·4	*Merak*		**194**	17·4	17·5	17·4	17·3	17·0	16·6	N **56**	17·6	17·5	17·3	17·2	17·0	16·9
2·7	μ Velorum		**198**	07·4	07·5	07·5	07·3	07·0	06·7	S **49**	30·9	30·8	30·7	30·6	30·6	30·6
2·8	θ Carinæ		**199**	06·5	06·7	06·7	06·5	06·1	05·7	S **64**	29·4	29·3	29·1	29·0	28·9	29·0
2·3	*Algeiba*		**204**	46·4	46·4	46·3	46·2	46·0	45·7	N **19**	45·3	45·2	45·2	45·1	45·0	44·9
1·4	*Regulus*	26	**207**	40·9	40·9	40·8	40·6	40·4	40·2	N **11**	52·9	52·9	52·9	52·9	52·8	52·7
3·0	ε Leonis		**213**	17·8	17·8	17·7	17·6	17·3	17·1	N **23**	41·7	41·6	41·6	41·5	41·4	41·3
3·1	N Velorum		**217**	04·1	04·1	04·0	03·8	03·5	03·1	S **57**	06·9	06·7	06·6	06·5	06·5	06·6
2·0	*Alphard*	25	**217**	53·7	53·6	53·6	53·4	53·2	52·9	S **8**	44·1	44·1	44·0	44·0	44·1	44·2
2·5	κ Velorum		**219**	20·6	20·6	20·5	20·3	19·9	19·6	S **55**	05·3	05·2	05·0	04·9	04·9	05·0
2·2	ι Carinæ		**220**	37·1	37·1	37·0	36·7	36·4	36·0	S **59**	21·1	20·9	20·8	20·7	20·7	20·8
1·7	*Miaplacidus*	24	**221**	39·8	39·9	39·7	39·4	38·8	38·4	S **69**	47·5	47·4	47·2	47·1	47·1	47·2
2·2	*Suhail*	23	**222**	50·8	50·8	50·7	50·5	50·2	49·9	S **43**	30·3	30·2	30·1	30·0	30·1	30·2
3·1	ι Ursæ Majoris		**224**	54·7	54·7	54·5	54·2	53·9	53·6	N **47**	58·4	58·3	58·2	58·1	58·0	58·0
2·0	δ Velorum		**228**	42·7	42·7	42·5	42·2	41·9	41·6	S **54**	46·5	46·4	46·3	46·2	46·2	46·3
1·9	*Avior*	22	**234**	17·5	17·4	17·2	16·9	16·5	16·2	S **59**	34·1	33·9	33·8	33·7	33·8	33·9
1·8	γ Velorum		**237**	29·4	29·3	29·1	28·9	28·6	28·3	S **47**	23·4	23·3	23·2	23·1	23·2	23·3
2·8	ρ Puppis		**237**	56·1	56·0	55·8	55·6	55·4	55·2	S **24**	21·4	21·3	21·2	21·2	21·3	21·4
2·3	ζ Puppis		**238**	57·5	57·4	57·2	57·0	56·7	56·5	S **40**	03·3	03·1	03·0	03·0	03·1	03·2
1·1	*Pollux*	21	**243**	24·8	24·7	24·5	24·2	24·0	23·7	N **27**	58·9	58·9	58·8	58·8	58·8	58·7
0·4	*Procyon*	20	**244**	57·2	57·1	56·9	56·7	56·5	56·3	N **5**	10·7	10·7	10·7	10·7	10·7	10·6

Mag.	Name and Number		SHA	JAN.	FEB.	MAR.	APR.	MAY	JUNE	Declination	JAN.	FEB.	MAR.	APR.	MAY	JUNE
			°	′	′	′	′	′	′	°	′	′	′	′	′	′
1·6	α Geminorum		**246**	04·5	04·5	04·6	04·8	04·9	04·9	**N 31**	50·8	50·8	50·9	50·9	50·9	50·9
3·3	σ Puppis		**247**	33·0	33·0	33·2	33·4	33·6	33·7	**S 43**	20·4	20·5	20·6	20·6	20·6	20·5
2·9	β Canis Minoris		**247**	58·6	58·6	58·7	58·9	59·0	59·0	**N 8**	15·0	15·0	15·0	15·0	15·0	15·1
2·4	η Canis Majoris		**248**	48·1	48·1	48·3	48·4	48·6	48·6	**S 29**	20·4	20·5	20·6	20·6	20·6	20·5
2·7	π Puppis		**250**	33·4	33·5	33·6	33·8	34·0	34·1	**S 37**	07·9	08·1	08·1	08·1	08·1	08·0
1·8	δ Canis Majoris		**252**	43·4	43·4	43·6	43·7	43·9	43·9	**S 26**	25·5	25·6	25·6	25·7	25·6	25·5
3·0	ο Canis Majoris		**254**	03·6	03·7	03·8	04·0	04·1	04·1	**S 23**	51·8	51·9	51·9	51·9	51·9	51·8
1·5	ε Canis Majoris	19	**255**	10·2	10·3	10·4	10·6	10·7	10·8	**S 29**	00·0	00·1	00·2	00·2	00·1	00·0
2·9	τ Puppis		**257**	24·1	24·2	24·4	24·7	24·9	25·0	**S 50**	38·3	38·5	38·6	38·6	38·5	38·4
−1·5	α Canis Majoris	18	**258**	31·2	31·3	31·4	31·6	31·7	31·7	**S 16**	44·7	44·7	44·8	44·8	44·7	44·6
1·9	γ Geminorum		**260**	19·3	19·4	19·5	19·6	19·7	19·7	**N 16**	22·8	22·8	22·8	22·8	22·8	22·9
−0·7	α Carinæ	17	**263**	54·5	54·7	54·9	55·2	55·4	55·5	**S 52**	42·6	42·7	42·8	42·8	42·7	42·5
2·0	β Canis Majoris		**264**	08·0	08·0	08·2	08·3	08·4	08·4	**S 17**	58·2	58·2	58·3	58·3	58·2	58·1
2·6	θ Aurigæ		**269**	46·5	46·5	46·7	46·9	47·0	46·9	**N 37**	12·6	12·7	12·7	12·7	12·6	12·6
1·9	β Aurigæ		**269**	48·0	48·1	48·3	48·4	48·6	48·5	**N 44**	56·7	56·8	56·8	56·8	56·8	56·7
Var.‡	α Orionis	16	**270**	58·4	58·4	58·5	58·7	58·8	58·7	**N 7**	24·3	24·3	24·3	24·3	24·3	24·4
2·1	κ Orionis		**272**	51·3	51·4	51·5	51·6	51·7	51·7	**S 9**	40·1	40·2	40·2	40·2	40·1	40·0
1·9	ζ Orionis		**274**	35·5	35·6	35·7	35·8	35·9	35·9	**S 1**	56·3	56·3	56·4	56·3	56·3	56·2
2·6	α Columbæ		**274**	55·7	55·8	56·0	56·2	56·3	56·3	**S 34**	04·2	04·3	04·4	04·3	04·2	04·1
3·0	ζ Tauri		**275**	19·8	19·9	20·0	20·2	20·2	20·2	**N 21**	08·9	08·9	09·0	08·9	08·9	08·9
1·7	ε Orionis	15	**275**	43·6	43·7	43·8	43·9	44·0	44·0	**S 1**	11·7	11·8	11·8	11·8	11·8	11·7
2·8	ι Orionis		**275**	55·8	55·9	56·0	56·1	56·2	56·2	**S 5**	54·2	54·3	54·3	54·3	54·2	54·1
2·6	α Leporis		**276**	37·5	37·6	37·8	37·9	38·0	38·0	**S 17**	48·9	49·0	49·0	49·0	48·9	48·8
2·2	δ Orionis		**276**	46·6	46·7	46·8	47·0	47·0	47·0	**S 0**	17·5	17·5	17·5	17·5	17·5	17·4
2·8	β Leporis		**277**	45·1	45·2	45·4	45·5	45·6	45·6	**S 20**	45·1	45·2	45·2	45·1	45·1	45·0
1·7	β Tauri	14	**278**	09·2	09·3	09·4	09·6	09·6	09·6	**N 28**	37·1	37·1	37·1	37·1	37·1	37·1
1·6	γ Orionis	13	**278**	29·1	29·2	29·3	29·4	29·5	29·5	**N 6**	21·6	21·6	21·6	21·6	21·6	21·7
0·1	α Aurigæ	12	**280**	30·4	30·5	30·7	30·9	31·0	30·9	**N 46**	00·8	00·8	00·8	00·8	00·7	00·7
0·1	β Orionis	11	**281**	09·4	09·5	09·7	09·8	09·9	09·8	**S 8**	11·2	11·3	11·3	11·3	11·2	11·1
2·8	β Eridani		**282**	49·5	49·6	49·7	49·8	49·9	49·8	**S 5**	04·2	04·2	04·2	04·2	04·1	04·1
2·7	ι Aurigæ		**285**	28·2	28·3	28·4	28·6	28·6	28·6	**N 33**	11·4	11·4	11·4	11·4	11·4	11·3
0·9	α Tauri	10	**290**	46·3	46·4	46·6	46·7	46·7	46·6	**N 16**	32·4	32·4	32·4	32·4	32·4	32·4
2·9	ε Persei		**300**	14·8	14·9	15·1	15·2	15·2	15·1	**N 40**	03·5	03·5	03·5	03·4	03·3	03·3
3·0	γ Eridani		**300**	17·5	17·6	17·8	17·9	17·9	17·8	**S 13**	27·9	28·0	28·0	27·9	27·8	27·7
2·9	ζ Persei		**301**	11·7	11·8	12·0	12·1	12·1	12·0	**N 31**	55·9	55·9	55·9	55·9	55·8	55·8
2·9	η Tauri		**302**	52·3	52·5	52·6	52·7	52·7	52·6	**N 24**	09·3	09·3	09·3	09·3	09·2	09·2
1·8	α Persei	9	**308**	36·5	36·7	36·9	37·1	37·0	36·9	**N 49**	55·3	55·3	55·2	55·2	55·1	55·0
Var.§	β Persei		**312**	40·6	40·7	40·9	41·0	41·0	40·8	**N 41**	01·2	01·2	01·2	01·1	01·0	01·0
2·5	α Ceti	8	**314**	12·4	12·5	12·6	12·7	12·6	12·5	**N 4**	09·2	09·1	09·1	09·1	09·2	09·3
3·2	θ Eridani	7	**315**	16·4	16·6	16·7	16·8	16·8	16·7	**S 40**	14·6	14·6	14·6	14·5	14·3	14·1
2·0	α Ursæ Minoris		**316**	29·5	42·7	54·5	61·4	60·5	52·8	**N 89**	20·3	20·4	20·3	20·2	20·0	19·9
3·0	β Trianguli		**327**	21·5	21·6	21·8	21·8	21·7	21·5	**N 35**	04·1	04·0	04·0	03·9	03·8	03·9
2·0	α Arietis	6	**327**	57·9	58·0	58·1	58·2	58·1	57·9	**N 23**	32·5	32·5	32·4	32·4	32·4	32·4
2·3	γ Andromedæ		**328**	45·6	45·8	45·9	46·0	45·9	45·7	**N 42**	24·7	24·7	24·6	24·5	24·5	24·4
2·9	α Hydri		**330**	10·6	10·9	11·1	11·2	11·2	10·9	**S 61**	29·7	29·6	29·5	29·4	29·2	29·0
2·6	β Arietis		**331**	06·2	06·4	06·5	06·5	06·4	06·2	**N 20**	53·4	53·4	53·3	53·3	53·3	53·3
0·5	α Eridani	5	**335**	25·1	25·3	25·5	25·5	25·4	25·2	**S 57**	09·5	09·4	09·3	09·1	09·0	08·8
2·7	δ Cassiopeiæ		**338**	15·7	16·0	16·2	16·2	16·0	15·7	**N 60**	19·6	19·5	19·4	19·3	19·2	19·1
2·1	β Andromedæ		**342**	19·7	19·8	19·9	19·9	19·7	19·5	**N 35**	42·7	42·6	42·6	42·5	42·4	42·5
Var.||	γ Cassiopeiæ		**345**	33·7	34·0	34·1	34·1	33·9	33·5	**N 60**	48·7	48·6	48·5	48·4	48·3	48·3
2·0	β Ceti	4	**348**	53·6	53·6	53·7	53·7	53·5	53·3	**S 17**	53·8	53·8	53·8	53·7	53·6	53·5
2·2	α Cassiopeiæ	3	**349**	37·7	38·0	38·1	38·0	37·8	37·5	**N 56**	38·0	37·9	37·8	37·7	37·6	37·6
2·4	α Phœnicis	2	**353**	13·5	13·6	13·7	13·6	13·5	13·2	**S 42**	13·1	13·1	13·0	12·8	12·7	12·5
2·8	β Hydri		**353**	21·8	22·3	22·5	22·5	22·1	21·4	**S 77**	09·9	09·8	09·6	09·4	09·3	09·1
2·8	γ Pegasi		**356**	28·4	28·5	28·6	28·5	28·3	28·1	**N 15**	16·7	16·6	16·6	16·6	16·6	16·7
2·3	β Cassiopeiæ		**357**	28·6	28·8	28·9	28·8	28·6	28·2	**N 59**	14·8	14·7	14·6	14·5	14·4	14·4
2·1	α Andromedæ	1	**357**	41·1	41·2	41·2	41·1	41·0	40·7	**N 29**	11·1	11·1	11·0	10·9	10·9	11·0

‡ 0·1 — 1·2 § 2·1 — 3·4 || Irregular variable; 2015 mag. 2·1

Mag.	Name and Number		SHA							Declination						
				JULY	AUG.	SEPT.	OCT.	NOV.	DEC.		JULY	AUG.	SEPT.	OCT.	NOV.	DEC.
			°	′	′	′	′	′	′	°	′	′	′	′	′	′
1·6	*Castor*		**246**	04·9	04·8	04·5	04·3	04·0	03·8	N **31**	50·8	50·8	50·8	50·7	50·7	50·7
3·3	σ Puppis		**247**	33·7	33·6	33·4	33·1	32·9	32·6	S **43**	20·3	20·2	20·1	20·1	20·1	20·3
2·9	β Canis Minoris		**247**	59·0	58·9	58·7	58·5	58·2	58·0	N **8**	15·1	15·1	15·2	15·1	15·1	15·0
2·4	η Canis Majoris		**248**	48·6	48·5	48·3	48·1	47·9	47·7	S **29**	20·4	20·2	20·1	20·1	20·2	20·3
2·7	π Puppis		**250**	34·0	33·9	33·7	33·5	33·2	33·0	S **37**	07·8	07·7	07·6	07·6	07·7	07·8
1·8	*Wezen*		**252**	43·9	43·8	43·6	43·4	43·1	42·9	S **26**	25·4	25·3	25·2	25·2	25·3	25·4
3·0	ο Canis Majoris		**254**	04·1	04·0	03·8	03·6	03·3	03·2	S **23**	51·6	51·5	51·5	51·5	51·5	51·7
1·5	*Adhara*	19	**255**	10·7	10·6	10·4	10·2	10·0	09·8	S **28**	59·9	59·7	59·7	59·7	59·7	59·9
2·9	τ Puppis		**257**	25·0	24·8	24·6	24·3	24·0	23·8	S **50**	38·2	38·1	38·0	38·0	38·0	38·2
−1·5	*Sirius*	18	**258**	31·6	31·5	31·3	31·1	30·9	30·7	S **16**	44·5	44·4	44·4	44·4	44·5	44·6
1·9	*Alhena*		**260**	19·6	19·5	19·3	19·1	18·8	18·7	N **16**	22·9	22·9	22·9	22·9	22·9	22·8
−0·7	*Canopus*	17	**263**	55·4	55·3	55·0	54·7	54·4	54·2	S **52**	42·4	42·2	42·1	42·1	42·2	42·4
2·0	*Mirzam*		**264**	08·4	08·2	08·0	07·8	07·6	07·4	S **17**	58·0	57·9	57·8	57·8	57·9	58·0
2·6	θ Aurigæ		**269**	46·8	46·6	46·3	46·1	45·8	45·6	N **37**	12·6	12·5	12·5	12·5	12·6	12·6
1·9	*Menkalinan*		**269**	48·4	48·2	47·9	47·6	47·3	47·1	N **44**	56·7	56·6	56·6	56·6	56·6	56·7
Var.‡	*Betelgeuse*	16	**270**	58·6	58·5	58·2	58·0	57·8	57·7	N **7**	24·4	24·5	24·5	24·5	24·5	24·4
2·1	κ Orionis		**272**	51·6	51·4	51·2	51·0	50·8	50·7	S **9**	39·9	39·9	39·8	39·8	39·9	40·0
1·9	*Alnitak*		**274**	35·8	35·6	35·4	35·2	35·0	34·9	S **1**	56·2	56·1	56·0	56·1	56·1	56·2
2·6	*Phact*		**274**	56·2	56·0	55·8	55·5	55·3	55·2	S **34**	04·0	03·8	03·8	03·8	03·9	04·0
3·0	ζ Tauri		**275**	20·1	19·9	19·6	19·4	19·2	19·1	N **21**	09·0	09·0	09·0	09·0	09·0	09·0
1·7	*Alnilam*	15	**275**	43·9	43·7	43·5	43·3	43·1	43·0	S **1**	11·6	11·5	11·5	11·5	11·5	11·6
2·8	ι Orionis		**275**	56·1	55·9	55·7	55·5	55·3	55·2	S **5**	54·1	54·0	53·9	53·9	54·0	54·1
2·6	α Leporis		**276**	37·9	37·7	37·5	37·3	37·1	37·0	S **17**	48·7	48·6	48·5	48·6	48·6	48·8
2·2	δ Orionis		**276**	46·9	46·7	46·5	46·3	46·1	46·0	S **0**	17·3	17·3	17·2	17·2	17·3	17·3
2·8	β Leporis		**277**	45·5	45·3	45·1	44·9	44·7	44·6	S **20**	44·8	44·7	44·7	44·7	44·8	44·9
1·7	*Elnath*	14	**278**	09·5	09·2	09·0	08·8	08·5	08·4	N **28**	37·1	37·1	37·1	37·1	37·1	37·1
1·6	*Bellatrix*	13	**278**	29·3	29·2	28·9	28·7	28·5	28·4	N **6**	21·7	21·8	21·8	21·8	21·8	21·8
0·1	*Capella*	12	**280**	30·8	30·5	30·2	29·9	29·6	29·5	N **46**	00·6	00·6	00·6	00·6	00·7	00·8
0·1	*Rigel*	11	**281**	09·7	09·5	09·3	09·1	08·9	08·8	S **8**	11·0	10·9	10·9	10·9	11·0	11·1
2·8	β Eridani		**282**	49·7	49·5	49·3	49·1	48·9	48·8	S **5**	04·0	03·9	03·9	03·9	03·9	04·0
2·7	ι Aurigæ		**285**	28·4	28·2	27·9	27·6	27·4	27·3	N **33**	11·3	11·3	11·4	11·4	11·4	11·5
0·9	*Aldebaran*	10	**290**	46·5	46·2	46·0	45·8	45·6	45·6	N **16**	32·4	32·5	32·5	32·5	32·5	32·5
2·9	ε Persei		**300**	14·9	14·6	14·3	14·1	13·9	13·8	N **40**	03·3	03·3	03·4	03·5	03·5	03·6
3·0	γ Eridani		**300**	17·6	17·4	17·2	17·0	16·9	16·8	S **13**	27·6	27·5	27·5	27·5	27·6	27·7
2·9	ζ Persei		**301**	11·8	11·5	11·3	11·1	10·9	10·8	N **31**	55·8	55·9	55·9	56·0	56·0	56·1
2·9	*Alcyone*		**302**	52·4	52·1	51·9	51·7	51·6	51·5	N **24**	09·3	09·3	09·4	09·4	09·5	09·5
1·8	*Mirfak*	9	**308**	36·6	36·3	35·9	35·7	35·5	35·5	N **49**	55·0	55·0	55·1	55·2	55·3	55·4
Var.§	*Algol*		**312**	40·5	40·3	40·0	39·8	39·7	39·6	N **41**	01·0	01·1	01·2	01·3	01·3	01·4
2·5	*Menkar*	8	**314**	12·3	12·1	11·9	11·7	11·6	11·6	N **4**	09·3	09·4	09·5	09·5	09·5	09·4
3·2	*Acamar*	7	**315**	16·5	16·2	15·9	15·8	15·7	15·7	S **40**	14·0	13·9	13·9	14·0	14·1	14·3
2·0	*Polaris*		**315**	100·2	85·4	71·8	62·2	58·0	62·0	N **89**	19·9	19·9	20·0	20·1	20·3	20·5
3·0	β Trianguli		**327**	21·3	21·0	20·8	20·6	20·6	20·6	N **35**	03·9	04·0	04·1	04·2	04·3	04·3
2·0	*Hamal*	6	**327**	57·7	57·4	57·2	57·1	57·1	57·1	N **23**	32·5	32·6	32·6	32·7	32·8	32·8
2·3	*Almak*		**328**	45·4	45·1	44·9	44·7	44·7	44·7	N **42**	24·5	24·6	24·7	24·8	24·9	25·0
2·9	α Hydri		**330**	10·6	10·2	09·8	09·7	09·7	09·9	S **61**	28·9	28·9	28·9	29·1	29·2	29·4
2·6	*Sheratan*		**331**	06·0	05·7	05·5	05·4	05·4	05·4	N **20**	53·4	53·5	53·6	53·6	53·7	53·7
0·5	*Achernar*	5	**335**	24·9	24·5	24·2	24·1	24·1	24·3	S **57**	08·7	08·7	08·7	08·9	09·0	09·1
2·7	*Ruchbah*		**338**	15·3	14·9	14·6	14·5	14·5	14·6	N **60**	19·2	19·3	19·4	19·6	19·7	19·8
2·1	*Mirach*		**342**	19·2	19·0	18·8	18·7	18·7	18·8	N **35**	42·5	42·6	42·8	42·9	43·0	43·0
Var.‖	γ Cassiopeiæ		**345**	33·1	32·8	32·5	32·4	32·5	32·7	N **60**	48·3	48·4	48·6	48·8	48·9	49·0
2·0	*Diphda*	4	**348**	53·1	52·9	52·7	52·7	52·7	52·8	S **17**	53·4	53·3	53·3	53·4	53·4	53·5
2·2	*Schedar*	3	**349**	37·1	36·8	36·6	36·6	36·6	36·8	N **56**	37·7	37·8	38·0	38·1	38·2	38·3
2·4	*Ankaa*	2	**353**	12·9	12·7	12·5	12·5	12·5	12·7	S **42**	12·5	12·5	12·5	12·6	12·7	12·8
2·8	β Hydri		**353**	20·6	19·8	19·4	19·3	19·7	20·3	S **77**	09·1	09·1	09·3	09·4	09·6	09·6
2·8	*Algenib*		**356**	27·9	27·7	27·6	27·5	27·6	27·7	N **15**	16·8	16·9	17·0	17·0	17·0	17·0
2·3	*Caph*		**357**	27·8	27·5	27·4	27·4	27·5	27·7	N **59**	14·5	14·6	14·8	15·0	15·1	15·1
2·1	*Alpheratz*	1	**357**	40·5	40·3	40·1	40·1	40·2	40·3	N **29**	11·1	11·2	11·3	11·4	11·5	11·5

‡ 0·1 — 1·2 § 2·1 — 3·4 ‖ Irregular variable; 2015 mag. 2·1

POLARIS (POLE STAR) TABLES, 2017

FOR DETERMINING LATITUDE FROM SEXTANT ALTITUDE AND FOR AZIMUTH

LHA ARIES	0° – 9°	10° – 19°	20° – 29°	30° – 39°	40° – 49°	50° – 59°	60° – 69°	70° – 79°	80° – 89°	90° – 99°	100° – 109°	110° – 119°
	a_0	a_0	a_0	a_0	a_0	a_0	a_0	a_0	a_0	a_0	a_0	a_0
°	° ′	° ′	° ′	° ′	° ′	° ′	° ′	° ′	° ′	° ′	° ′	° ′
0	0 30·1	0 25·7	0 22·3	0 20·1	0 19·1	0 19·3	0 20·7	0 23·2	0 26·9	0 31·5	0 37·0	0 43·2
1	29·6	25·3	22·1	20·0	19·0	19·3	20·9	23·6	27·3	32·1	37·6	43·8
2	29·1	24·9	21·8	19·8	19·0	19·4	21·1	23·9	27·8	32·6	38·2	44·5
3	28·7	24·6	21·6	19·7	19·0	19·6	21·3	24·2	28·2	33·1	38·8	45·1
4	28·2	24·2	21·3	19·6	19·0	19·7	21·6	24·6	28·7	33·6	39·4	45·8
5	0 27·8	0 23·9	0 21·1	0 19·4	0 19·0	0 19·8	0 21·8	0 24·9	0 29·1	0 34·2	0 40·0	0 46·4
6	27·3	23·6	20·9	19·3	19·0	20·0	22·1	25·3	29·6	34·7	40·6	47·1
7	26·9	23·2	20·7	19·3	19·1	20·1	22·3	25·7	30·1	35·3	41·3	47·7
8	26·5	22·9	20·5	19·2	19·1	20·3	22·6	26·1	30·5	35·9	41·9	48·4
9	26·1	22·6	20·3	19·1	19·2	20·5	22·9	26·5	31·0	36·4	42·5	49·1
10	0 25·7	0 22·3	0 20·1	0 19·1	0 19·3	0 20·7	0 23·2	0 26·9	0 31·5	0 37·0	0 43·2	0 49·8
Lat.	a_1	a_1	a_1	a_1	a_1	a_1	a_1	a_1	a_1	a_1	a_1	a_1
°	′	′	′	′	′	′	′	′	′	′	′	′
0	0·5	0·5	0·6	0·6	0·6	0·6	0·6	0·5	0·5	0·4	0·4	0·4
10	·5	·5	·6	·6	·6	·6	·6	·5	·5	·5	·4	·4
20	·5	·6	·6	·6	·6	·6	·6	·5	·5	·5	·5	·4
30	·5	·6	·6	·6	·6	·6	·6	·6	·5	·5	·5	·5
40	0·6	0·6	0·6	0·6	0·6	0·6	0·6	0·6	0·6	0·6	0·5	0·5
45	·6	·6	·6	·6	·6	·6	·6	·6	·6	·6	·6	·6
50	·6	·6	·6	·6	·6	·6	·6	·6	·6	·6	·6	·6
55	·6	·6	·6	·6	·6	·6	·6	·6	·6	·6	·6	·6
60	·6	·6	·6	·6	·6	·6	·6	·6	·7	·7	·7	·7
62	0·7	0·6	0·6	0·6	0·6	0·6	0·6	0·6	0·7	0·7	0·7	0·7
64	·7	·6	·6	·6	·6	·6	·6	·7	·7	·7	·8	·8
66	·7	·7	·6	·6	·6	·6	·6	·7	·7	·7	·8	·8
68	0·7	0·7	0·6	0·6	0·6	0·6	0·6	0·7	0·7	0·8	0·8	0·9
Month	a_2	a_2	a_2	a_2	a_2	a_2	a_2	a_2	a_2	a_2	a_2	a_2
	′	′	′	′	′	′	′	′	′	′	′	′
Jan.	0·7	0·7	0·7	0·7	0·7	0·7	0·7	0·7	0·7	0·7	0·7	0·6
Feb.	·6	·7	·7	·8	·8	·8	·8	·8	·8	·8	·8	·8
Mar.	·5	·6	·6	·7	·7	·8	·8	·8	·9	·9	·9	·9
Apr.	0·4	0·4	0·5	0·5	0·6	0·6	0·7	0·8	0·8	0·9	0·9	0·9
May	·2	·3	·3	·4	·4	·5	·6	·6	·7	·8	·8	·9
June	·2	·2	·2	·3	·3	·4	·4	·5	·6	·6	·7	·8
July	0·3	0·2	0·2	0·2	0·3	0·3	0·3	0·4	0·4	0·5	0·5	0·6
Aug.	·4	·3	·3	·3	·3	·3	·3	·3	·3	·4	·4	·4
Sept.	·6	·5	·5	·4	·4	·3	·3	·3	·3	·3	·3	·3
Oct.	0·7	0·7	0·6	0·6	0·5	0·5	0·4	0·4	0·3	0·3	0·3	0·3
Nov.	0·9	0·9	0·8	·8	·7	·6	·6	·5	·4	·4	·3	·3
Dec.	1·0	1·0	1·0	0·9	0·9	0·8	0·7	0·7	0·6	0·5	0·4	0·4
Lat.	AZIMUTH											
°	°	°	°	°	°	°	°	°	°	°	°	°
0	0·4	0·3	0·2	0·1	0·0	359·9	359·8	359·7	359·6	359·5	359·4	359·4
20	0·4	0·3	0·2	0·1	0·0	359·9	359·7	359·6	359·5	359·4	359·4	359·3
40	0·5	0·4	0·3	0·1	0·0	359·8	359·7	359·5	359·4	359·3	359·2	359·2
50	0·6	0·5	0·3	0·2	0·0	359·8	359·6	359·5	359·3	359·2	359·1	359·0
55	0·7	0·6	0·4	0·2	0·0	359·8	359·6	359·4	359·2	359·1	359·0	358·9
60	0·8	0·6	0·4	0·2	0·0	359·7	359·5	359·3	359·1	358·9	358·8	358·7
65	1·0	0·8	0·5	0·2	0·0	359·7	359·4	359·2	358·9	358·8	358·6	358·5

Latitude = Apparent altitude (corrected for refraction) $-1° + a_0 + a_1 + a_2$

The table is entered with LHA Aries to determine the column to be used; each column refers to a range of 10°. a_0 is taken, with mental interpolation, from the upper table with the units of LHA Aries in degrees as argument; a_1, a_2 are taken, without interpolation, from the second and third tables with arguments latitude and month respectively. a_0, a_1, a_2, are always positive. The final table gives the azimuth of *Polaris.*

FOR DETERMINING LATITUDE FROM SEXTANT ALTITUDE AND FOR AZIMUTH

LHA ARIES	120° – 129°	130° – 139°	140° – 149°	150° – 159°	160° – 169°	170° – 179°	180° – 189°	190° – 199°	200° – 209°	210° – 219°	220° – 229°	230° – 239°
	a_0	a_0	a_0	a_0	a_0	a_0	a_0	a_0	a_0	a_0	a_0	a_0
°	° ′	° ′	° ′	° ′	° ′	° ′	° ′	° ′	° ′	° ′	° ′	° ′
0	0 49·8	0 56·6	1 03·6	1 10·4	1 16·8	1 22·7	1 27·8	1 32·1	1 35·3	1 37·5	1 38·5	1 38·3
1	50·4	57·3	04·3	11·0	17·4	23·2	28·3	32·4	35·6	37·7	38·6	38·3
2	51·1	58·0	05·0	11·7	18·0	23·7	28·7	32·8	35·9	37·8	38·6	38·2
3	51·8	58·7	05·6	12·3	18·6	24·3	29·2	33·2	36·1	37·9	38·6	38·1
4	52·5	0 59·4	06·3	13·0	19·2	24·8	29·6	33·5	36·3	38·1	38·6	37·9
5	0 53·2	1 00·1	1 07·0	1 13·6	1 19·8	1 25·3	1 30·1	1 33·8	1 36·6	1 38·2	1 38·6	1 37·8
6	53·9	00·8	07·7	14·3	20·4	25·8	30·5	34·2	36·8	38·3	38·6	37·7
7	54·6	01·5	08·4	14·9	21·0	26·3	30·9	34·5	37·0	38·3	38·5	37·5
8	55·3	02·2	09·0	15·5	21·5	26·8	31·3	34·8	37·2	38·4	38·5	37·3
9	56·0	02·9	09·7	16·2	22·1	27·3	31·7	35·1	37·3	38·5	38·4	37·2
10	0 56·6	1 03·6	1 10·4	1 16·8	1 22·7	1 27·8	1 32·1	1 35·3	1 37·5	1 38·5	1 38·3	1 37·0
Lat.	a_1	a_1	a_1	a_1	a_1	a_1	a_1	a_1	a_1	a_1	a_1	a_1
°	′	′	′	′	′	′	′	′	′	′	′	′
0	0·3	0·3	0·3	0·4	0·4	0·4	0·5	0·5	0·6	0·6	0·6	0·6
10	·4	·4	·4	·4	·4	·5	·5	·5	·6	·6	·6	·6
20	·4	·4	·4	·4	·5	·5	·5	·6	·6	·6	·6	·6
30	·5	·5	·5	·5	·5	·5	·5	·6	·6	·6	·6	·6
40	0·5	0·5	0·5	0·5	0·5	0·6	0·6	0·6	0·6	0·6	0·6	0·6
45	·6	·6	·6	·6	·6	·6	·6	·6	·6	·6	·6	·6
50	·6	·6	·6	·6	·6	·6	·6	·6	·6	·6	·6	·6
55	·7	·7	·7	·6	·6	·6	·6	·6	·6	·6	·6	·6
60	·7	·7	·7	·7	·7	·7	·6	·6	·6	·6	·6	·6
62	0·8	0·8	0·8	0·7	0·7	0·7	0·7	0·6	0·6	0·6	0·6	0·6
64	·8	·8	·8	·8	·7	·7	·7	·6	·6	·6	·6	·6
66	·8	·8	·8	·8	·8	·7	·7	·7	·6	·6	·6	·6
68	0·9	0·9	0·9	0·9	0·8	0·8	0·7	0·7	0·6	0·6	0·6	0·6
Month	a_2	a_2	a_2	a_2	a_2	a_2	a_2	a_2	a_2	a_2	a_2	a_2
	′	′	′	′	′	′	′	′	′	′	′	′
Jan.	0·6	0·6	0·6	0·5	0·5	0·5	0·5	0·5	0·5	0·5	0·5	0·5
Feb.	·8	·7	·7	·7	·6	·6	·6	·5	·5	·4	·4	·4
Mar.	0·9	0·9	0·9	·8	·8	·7	·7	·6	·6	·5	·5	·4
Apr.	1·0	1·0	1·0	0·9	0·9	0·9	0·8	0·8	0·7	0·7	0·6	0·6
May	0·9	1·0	1·0	1·0	1·0	1·0	1·0	0·9	0·9	·8	·8	·7
June	·8	0·9	0·9	1·0	1·0	1·0	1·0	1·0	1·0	0·9	·9	·8
July	0·7	0·7	0·8	0·8	0·9	0·9	0·9	1·0	1·0	1·0	0·9	0·9
Aug.	·5	·6	·6	·7	·7	·8	·8	0·9	0·9	0·9	·9	·9
Sept.	·4	·4	·4	·5	·5	·6	·6	·7	·7	·8	·8	·9
Oct.	0·3	0·3	0·3	0·3	0·4	0·4	0·5	0·5	0·6	0·6	0·7	0·7
Nov.	·3	·2	·2	·2	·2	·3	·3	·3	·4	·4	·5	·6
Dec.	0·3	0·3	0·2	0·2	0·2	0·2	0·2	0·2	0·2	0·3	0·3	0·4
Lat.	AZIMUTH											
°	°	°	°	°	°	°	°	°	°	°	°	°
0	359·3	359·3	359·3	359·4	359·4	359·5	359·6	359·7	359·8	359·9	0·0	0·1
20	359·3	359·3	359·3	359·3	359·4	359·5	359·6	359·7	359·8	359·9	0·0	0·1
40	359·1	359·1	359·2	359·2	359·3	359·4	359·5	359·6	359·7	359·9	0·0	0·2
50	359·0	359·0	359·0	359·0	359·1	359·2	359·4	359·5	359·7	359·8	0·0	0·2
55	358·9	358·8	358·9	358·9	359·0	359·1	359·3	359·5	359·6	359·8	0·0	0·2
60	358·7	358·7	358·7	358·8	358·9	359·0	359·2	359·4	359·6	359·8	0·0	0·3
65	358·4	358·4	358·5	358·6	358·7	358·8	359·0	359·3	359·5	359·8	0·0	0·3

ILLUSTRATION

On 2017 April 21 at $23^h\ 18^m\ 56^s$ UT in longitude W 37° 14′ the apparent altitude (corrected for refraction), *Ho*, of *Polaris* was 49° 31′·6

From the daily pages:	° ′		° ′
GHA Aries (23^h)	195 12·1	*Ho*	49 31·6
Increment ($18^m\ 56^s$)	4 44·8	a_0 (argument 162° 43′)	1 18·4
Longitude (west)	−37 14	a_1 (Lat 50° approx.)	0·6
		a_2 (April)	0·9
LHA Aries	162 43	Sum − 1° = Lat =	49 51·5

POLARIS (POLE STAR) TABLES, 2017

FOR DETERMINING LATITUDE FROM SEXTANT ALTITUDE AND FOR AZIMUTH

LHA ARIES	240° – 249°	250° – 259°	260° – 269°	270° – 279°	280° – 289°	290° – 299°	300° – 309°	310° – 319°	320° – 329°	330° – 339°	340° – 349°	350° – 359°
	a_0	a_0	a_0	a_0	a_0	a_0	a_0	a_0	a_0	a_0	a_0	a_0
°	° ′	° ′	° ′	° ′	° ′	° ′	° ′	° ′	° ′	° ′	° ′	° ′
0	1 37·0	1 34·5	1 30·9	1 26·3	1 21·0	1 14·9	1 08·4	1 01·5	0 54·6	0 47·7	0 41·3	0 35·3
1	36·8	34·2	30·5	25·8	20·4	14·3	07·7	00·8	53·9	47·1	40·6	34·7
2	36·6	33·8	30·1	25·3	19·8	13·6	07·0	1 00·1	53·2	46·4	40·0	34·2
3	36·3	33·5	29·6	24·8	19·2	13·0	06·3	0 59·4	52·5	45·8	39·4	33·6
4	36·1	33·2	29·2	24·3	18·6	12·3	05·6	58·7	51·8	45·1	38·8	33·1
5	1 35·9	1 32·8	1 28·7	1 23·7	1 18·0	1 11·7	1 05·0	0 58·0	0 51·1	0 44·5	0 38·2	0 32·6
6	35·6	32·4	28·3	23·2	17·4	11·0	04·3	57·3	50·4	43·8	37·6	32·1
7	35·3	32·1	27·8	22·7	16·8	10·4	03·6	56·6	49·8	43·2	37·0	31·5
8	35·1	31·7	27·3	22·1	16·2	09·7	02·9	56·0	49·1	42·5	36·4	31·0
9	34·8	31·3	26·8	21·5	15·5	09·0	02·2	55·3	48·4	41·9	35·9	30·5
10	1 34·5	1 30·9	1 26·3	1 21·0	1 14·9	1 08·4	1 01·5	0 54·6	0 47·7	0 41·3	0 35·3	0 30·1
Lat.	a_1	a_1	a_1	a_1	a_1	a_1	a_1	a_1	a_1	a_1	a_1	a_1
°	′	′	′	′	′	′	′	′	′	′	′	′
0	0·6	0·5	0·5	0·4	0·4	0·4	0·3	0·3	0·3	0·4	0·4	0·4
10	·6	·5	·5	·5	·4	·4	·4	·4	·4	·4	·4	·5
20	·6	·5	·5	·5	·5	·4	·4	·4	·4	·4	·5	·5
30	·6	·6	·5	·5	·5	·5	·5	·5	·5	·5	·5	·5
40	0·6	0·6	0·6	0·6	0·5	0·5	0·5	0·5	0·5	0·5	0·5	0·6
45	·6	·6	·6	·6	·6	·6	·6	·6	·6	·6	·6	·6
50	·6	·6	·6	·6	·6	·6	·6	·6	·6	·6	·6	·6
55	·6	·6	·6	·6	·6	·6	·7	·7	·7	·6	·6	·6
60	·6	·6	·7	·7	·7	·7	·7	·7	·7	·7	·7	·7
62	0·6	0·6	0·7	0·7	0·7	0·7	0·8	0·8	0·8	0·7	0·7	0·7
64	·6	·7	·7	·7	·8	·8	·8	·8	·8	·8	·7	·7
66	·6	·7	·7	·7	·8	·8	·8	·8	·8	·8	·8	·7
68	0·6	0·7	0·7	0·8	0·8	0·9	0·9	0·9	0·9	0·9	0·8	0·8
Month	a_2	a_2	a_2	a_2	a_2	a_2	a_2	a_2	a_2	a_2	a_2	a_2
	′	′	′	′	′	′	′	′	′	′	′	′
Jan.	0·5	0·5	0·5	0·5	0·5	0·6	0·6	0·6	0·6	0·7	0·7	0·7
Feb.	·4	·4	·4	·4	·4	·4	·4	·5	·5	·5	·6	·6
Mar.	·4	·4	·3	·3	·3	·3	·3	·3	·3	·4	·4	·5
Apr.	0·5	0·4	0·4	0·3	0·3	0·3	0·2	0·2	0·2	0·3	0·3	0·3
May	·6	·6	·5	·4	·4	·3	·3	·2	·2	·2	·2	·2
June	·8	·7	·6	·6	·5	·4	·4	·3	·3	·2	·2	·2
July	0·9	0·8	0·8	0·7	0·7	0·6	0·5	0·5	0·4	0·4	0·3	0·3
Aug.	·9	·9	·9	·8	·8	·8	·7	·6	·6	·5	·5	·4
Sept.	·9	·9	·9	·9	·9	·9	·8	·8	·8	·7	·7	·6
Oct.	0·8	0·8	0·9	0·9	0·9	0·9	0·9	0·9	0·9	0·9	0·8	0·8
Nov.	·6	·7	·8	·8	·9	·9	·9	1·0	1·0	1·0	1·0	0·9
Dec.	0·5	0·5	0·6	0·7	0·8	0·8	0·9	0·9	1·0	1·0	1·0	1·0
Lat.	AZIMUTH											
°	°	°	°	°	°	°	°	°	°	°	°	°
0	0·2	0·3	0·4	0·5	0·6	0·6	0·7	0·7	0·7	0·6	0·6	0·5
20	0·3	0·4	0·5	0·6	0·6	0·7	0·7	0·7	0·7	0·7	0·6	0·5
40	0·3	0·4	0·6	0·7	0·8	0·8	0·9	0·9	0·9	0·8	0·7	0·7
50	0·4	0·5	0·7	0·8	0·9	1·0	1·0	1·0	1·0	1·0	0·9	0·8
55	0·4	0·6	0·8	0·9	1·0	1·1	1·1	1·2	1·1	1·1	1·0	0·9
60	0·5	0·7	0·9	1·0	1·2	1·3	1·3	1·3	1·3	1·2	1·1	1·0
65	0·6	0·8	1·0	1·2	1·4	1·5	1·5	1·6	1·5	1·5	1·4	1·2

$$\text{Latitude} = \text{Apparent altitude (corrected for refraction)} - 1^\circ + a_0 + a_1 + a_2$$

The table is entered with LHA Aries to determine the column to be used; each column refers to a range of 10°. a_0 is taken, with mental interpolation, from the upper table with the units of LHA Aries in degrees as argument; a_1, a_2 are taken, without interpolation, from the second and third tables with arguments latitude and month respectively. a_0, a_1, a_2, are always positive. The final table gives the azimuth of *Polaris.*

SIGHT REDUCTION PROCEDURES

METHODS AND FORMULAE FOR DIRECT COMPUTATION

1. *Introduction.* In this section formulae and methods are provided for *calculating* position at sea from observed altitudes taken with a marine sextant using a computer or programmable calculator.

The method uses analogous concepts and similar terminology as that used in *manual* methods of astro-navigation, where position is found by plotting position lines from their intercept and azimuth on a marine chart.

The algorithms are presented in standard algebra suitable for translating into the programming language of the user's computer. The basic ephemeris data may be taken directly from the main tabular pages of a current version of *The Nautical Almanac.* Formulae are given for calculating altitude and azimuth from the *GHA* and *Dec* of a body, and the estimated position of the observer. Formulae are also given for reducing sextant observations to observed altitudes by applying the corrections for dip, refraction, parallax and semi-diameter.

The intercept and azimuth obtained from each observation determine a position line, and the observer should lie on or close to each position line. The method of least squares is used to calculate the fix by finding the position where the sum of the squares of the distances from the position lines is a minimum. The use of least squares has other advantages. For example, it is possible to improve the estimated position at the time of fix by repeating the calculation. It is also possible to include more observations in the solution and to reject doubtful ones.

2. *Notation.*

GHA = Greenwich hour angle. The range of *GHA* is from 0° to 360° starting at 0° on the Greenwich meridian increasing to the west, back to 360° on the Greenwich meridian.

SHA = sidereal hour angle. The range is 0° to 360°.

Dec = declination. The sign convention for declination is north is positive, south is negative. The range is from −90° at the south celestial pole to +90° at the north celestial pole.

Long = longitude. The sign convention is east is positive, west is negative. The range is −180° to +180°.

Lat = latitude. The sign convention is north is positive, south is negative. The range is from −90° to +90°.

LHA = $GHA + Long$ = local hour angle. The *LHA* increases to the west from 0° on the local meridian to 360°.

H_C = calculated altitude. Above the horizon is positive, below the horizon is negative. The range is from −90° in the nadir to +90° in the zenith.

H_S = sextant altitude.

H = apparent altitude = sextant altitude corrected for instrumental error and dip.

H_O = observed altitude = apparent altitude corrected for refraction and, in appropriate cases, corrected for parallax and semi-diameter.

Z = Z_n= true azimuth. *Z* is measured from true north through east, south, west and back to north. The range is from 0° to 360°.

I = sextant index error.

D = dip of horizon.

R = atmospheric refraction.

HP = horizontal parallax of the Sun, Moon, Venus or Mars.
PA = parallax in altitude of the Sun, Moon, Venus or Mars.
SD = semi-diameter of the Sun or Moon.
p = intercept = $H_O - H_C$. Towards is positive, away is negative.
T = course or track, measured as for azimuth from the north.
V = speed in knots.

3. *Entering Basic Data.* When quantities such as *GHA* are entered, which in *The Nautical Almanac* are given in degrees and minutes, convert them to degrees and decimals of a degree by dividing the minutes by 60 and adding to the degrees; for example, if *GHA* = 123° 45′.6, enter the two numbers 123 and 45·6 into the memory and set $GHA = 123 + 45{\cdot}6/60 = 123^{\circ}.7600$. Although four decimal places of a degree are shown in the examples, it is assumed that full precision is maintained in the calculations.

When using a computer or programmable calculator, write a subroutine to convert degrees and minutes to degrees and decimals. Scientific calculators usually have a special key for this purpose. For quantities like *Dec* which require a minus sign for southern declination, change the sign from plus to minus after the value has been converted to degrees and decimals, *e.g.* $Dec = \text{S}\,0^{\circ}\ 12'.3 = \text{S}\,0^{\circ}.2050 = -0^{\circ}.2050$. Other quantities which require conversion are semi-diameter, horizontal parallax, longitude and latitude.

4. *Interpolation of GHA and Dec* The *GHA* and *Dec* of the Sun, Moon and planets are interpolated to the time of observation by direct calculation as follows: If the universal time is $a^{h}\ b^{m}\ c^{s}$, form the interpolation factor $x = b/60 + c/3600$. Enter the tabular value GHA_0 for the preceding hour (a) and the tabular value GHA_1 for the following hour ($a + 1$) then the interpolated value *GHA* is given by

$$GHA = GHA_0 + x(GHA_1 - GHA_0)$$

If the *GHA* passes through 360° between tabular values, add 360° to GHA_1 before interpolation. If the interpolated value exceeds 360°, subtract 360° from *GHA*.

Similarly for declination, enter the tabular value Dec_0 for the preceding hour (a) and the tabular value Dec_1 for the following hour ($a + 1$), then the interpolated value *Dec* is given by

$$Dec = Dec_0 + x(Dec_1 - Dec_0)$$

5. *Example.* (a) Find the *GHA* and *Dec* of the Sun on 2017 November 16 at $20^{h}\ 47^{m}\ 13^{s}$ UT.

The interpolation factor $x = 47/60 + 13/3600 = 0^{h}.7869$

page 223 $20^{h}\ GHA_0 = 123^{\circ}\ 46'.8 = 123^{\circ}.7800$

$21^{h}\ GHA_1 = 138^{\circ}\ 46'.7 = 138^{\circ}.7783$

$20^{h}.7869\ GHA = 123{\cdot}7800 + 0{\cdot}7869(138{\cdot}7783 - 123{\cdot}7800) = 135^{\circ}.5829$

$20^{h}\ Dec_0 = \text{S}\,18^{\circ}\ 55'.8 = -18^{\circ}.9300$

$21^{h}\ Dec_1 = \text{S}\,18^{\circ}\ 56'.4 = -18^{\circ}.9400$

$20^{h}.7869\ Dec = -18{\cdot}9300 + 0{\cdot}7869(-18{\cdot}9400 + 18{\cdot}9300) = -18^{\circ}.9379$

GHA Aries is interpolated in the same way as *GHA* of a body. For a star the *SHA* and *Dec* are taken from the tabular page and do not require interpolation, then

$$GHA = GHA \text{ Aries} + SHA$$

where *GHA* Aries is interpolated to the time of observation.

(b) Find the *GHA* and *Dec* of *Vega* on 2017 November 16 at $20^h\ 47^m\ 13^s$ UT.

The interpolation factor $x = 0^h.7869$ as in the previous example

page 222 $\quad 20^h\ GHA\ \text{Aries}_0 = 356°\ 04'.7 = 356°.0783$

$$21^h\ GHA\ \text{Aries}_1 = 11°\ 07'.1 = 371°.1183 \quad (360° \text{ added})$$

$$20^h.7869\ GHA\ \text{Aries} = 356{\cdot}0783 + 0{\cdot}7869(371{\cdot}1183 - 356{\cdot}0783) = 367°.9140$$

$$SHA = 80°\ 37'.3 = 80°.6217$$

$$GHA = GHA\ \text{Aries} + SHA = 88°.5356 \quad (\text{multiple of } 360° \text{ removed})$$

$$Dec = \text{N}\,38°\ 48'.4 = +38°.8067$$

6. *The calculated altitude and azimuth.* The calculated altitude H_C and true azimuth Z are determined from the *GHA* and *Dec* interpolated to the time of observation and from the *Long* and *Lat* estimated at the time of observation as follows:

Step 1. Calculate the local hour angle

$$LHA = GHA + Long$$

Add or subtract multiples of 360° to set *LHA* in the range 0° to 360°.

Step 2. Calculate S, C and the altitude H_C from

$$S = \sin Dec$$
$$C = \cos Dec \cos LHA$$
$$H_C = \sin^{-1}(S \sin Lat + C \cos Lat)$$

where $\sin^{-1}$ is the inverse function of sine.

Step 3. Calculate X and A from

$$X = (S \cos Lat - C \sin Lat)/\cos H_C$$
$$\text{If } X > +1 \quad \text{set} \quad X = +1$$
$$\text{If } X < -1 \quad \text{set} \quad X = -1$$
$$A = \cos^{-1} X$$

where $\cos^{-1}$ is the inverse function of cosine.

Step 4. Determine the azimuth Z

$$\text{If } LHA > 180° \quad \text{then} \quad Z = A$$
$$\text{Otherwise} \quad Z = 360° - A$$

7. *Example.* Find the calculated altitude H_C and azimuth Z when

$$GHA = 53° \quad Dec = \text{S}\,15° \quad Lat = \text{N}\,32° \quad Long = \text{W}\,16°$$

For the calculation

$$GHA = 53°.0000 \quad Dec = -15°.0000 \quad Lat = +32°.0000 \quad Long = -16°.0000$$

Step 1. $\quad LHA = 53{\cdot}0000 - 16{\cdot}0000 = 37{\cdot}0000$

Step 2. $\quad S = -0{\cdot}2588$

$$C = +0{\cdot}9659 \times 0{\cdot}7986 = 0{\cdot}7714$$
$$\sin H_C = -0{\cdot}2588 \times 0{\cdot}5299 + 0{\cdot}7714 \times 0{\cdot}8480 = 0{\cdot}5171$$
$$H_C = 31°.1346$$

Step 3. $X = (-0{\cdot}2588 \times 0{\cdot}8480 - 0{\cdot}7714 \times 0{\cdot}5299)/0{\cdot}8560 = -0{\cdot}7340$

$A = 137^{\circ}\!.2239$

Step 4. Since $LHA \leq 180^{\circ}$ then $Z = 360^{\circ} - A = 222^{\circ}\!.7761$

8. *Reduction from sextant altitude to observed altitude.* The sextant altitude H_S is corrected for both dip and index error to produce the apparent altitude. The observed altitude H_O is calculated by applying a correction for refraction. For the Sun, Moon, Venus and Mars a correction for parallax is also applied to H, and for the Sun and Moon a further correction for semi-diameter is required. The corrections are calculated as follows:

Step 1. Calculate dip

$$D = 0^{\circ}\!.0293\sqrt{h}$$

where h is the height of eye above the horizon in metres.

Step 2. Calculate apparent altitude

$$H = H_S + I - D$$

where I is the sextant index error.

Step 3. Calculate refraction (R) at a standard temperature of 10° Celsius (C) and pressure of 1010 millibars (mb)

$$R_0 = 0^{\circ}\!.0167/\tan(H + 7{\cdot}32/(H + 4{\cdot}32))$$

If the temperature $T°$ C and pressure P mb are known calculate the refraction from

$$R = fR_0 \qquad \text{where} \qquad f = 0{\cdot}28P/(T + 273)$$

otherwise set $R = R_0$

Step 4. Calculate the parallax in altitude (PA) from the horizontal parallax (HP) and the apparent altitude (H) for the Sun, Moon, Venus and Mars as follows:

$$PA = HP\cos H$$

For the Sun $HP = 0^{\circ}\!.0024$. This correction is very small and could be ignored.

For the Moon HP is taken for the nearest hour from the main tabular page and converted to degrees.

For Venus and Mars the HP is taken from the critical table at the bottom of page 259 and converted to degrees.

For the navigational stars and the remaining planets, Jupiter and Saturn set $PA = 0$.

If an error of $0'\!.2$ is significant the expression for the parallax in altitude for the Moon should include a small correction OB for the oblateness of the Earth as follows:

$$PA = HP\cos H + OB$$

where $OB = -0^{\circ}\!.0032\sin^2 Lat\cos H + 0^{\circ}\!.0032\sin(2Lat)\cos Z\sin H$

At mid-latitudes and for altitudes of the Moon below 60° a simple approximation to OB is

$$OB = -0^{\circ}\!.0017\cos H$$

Step 5. Calculate the semi-diameter for the Sun and Moon as follows:

Sun: SD is taken from the main tabular page and converted to degrees.

Moon: $SD = 0\overset{\circ}{.}2724HP$ where HP is taken for the nearest hour from the main tabular page and converted to degrees.

Step 6. Calculate the observed altitude

$$H_O = H - R + PA \pm SD$$

where the plus sign is used if the lower limb of the Sun or Moon was observed and the minus sign if the upper limb was observed.

9. *Example.* The following example illustrates how to use a calculator to reduce the sextant altitude (H_S) to observed altitude (H_O); the sextant altitudes given are assumed to be taken on 2017 August 9 with a marine sextant, zero index error, at height 5·4 m, temperature −3° C and pressure 982 mb, the Moon sights are assumed to be taken at 10^h UT.

Body limb	Sun lower	Sun upper	Moon lower	Moon upper	Venus –	*Polaris* –
Sextant altitude:						
H_S	21·3283	3·3367	33·4600	26·1117	4·5433	49·6083
Step 1. Dip:						
$D = 0{\cdot}0293\sqrt{h}$	0·0681	0·0681	0·0681	0·0681	0·0681	0·0681
Step 2. Apparent altitude:						
$H = H_S + I - D$	21·2602	3·2686	33·3919	26·0436	4·4752	49·5402
Step 3. Refraction:						
R_0	0·0423	0·2256	0·0251	0·0338	0·1798	0·0142
f	1·0184	1·0184	1·0184	1·0184	1·0184	1·0184
$R = fR_0$	0·0431	0·2298	0·0256	0·0344	0·1831	0·0144
Step 4. Parallax:			(56′.3)	(56′.3)	(0′.1)	
HP	0·0024	0·0024	0·9383	0·9383	0·0017	–
Parallax in altitude:						
$PA = HP \cos H$	0·0022	0·0024	0·7834	0·8431	0·0017	–
Step 5. Semi-diameter:						
Sun : $SD = 15{\cdot}8/60$	0·2633	0·2633	–	–	–	–
Moon : $SD = 0{\cdot}2724HP$	–	–	0·2556	0·2556	–	–
Step 6. Observed altitude:						
$H_O = H - R + PA \pm SD$	21·4827	2·7779	34·4053	26·5966	4·2938	49·5258

Note that for the Moon the correction for the oblateness of the Earth of about $-0\overset{\circ}{.}0017 \cos H$, which equals $-0\overset{\circ}{.}0014$ for the lower limb and $-0\overset{\circ}{.}0015$ for the upper limb, has been ignored in the above calculation.

10. *Position from intercept and azimuth using a chart.* An estimate is made of the position at the adopted time of fix. The position at the time of observation is then calculated by dead reckoning from the time of fix. For example, if the course (track) T and the speed V (in knots) of the observer are constant, then *Long* and *Lat* at the time of observation are calculated from

$$Long = L_F + t\,(V/60)\sin T/\cos B_F$$
$$Lat = B_F + t\,(V/60)\cos T$$

where L_F and B_F are the estimated longitude and latitude at the time of fix and t is the time interval in hours from the time of fix to the time of observation, t is positive if the time of observation is after the time of fix and negative if it was before.

The position line of an observation is plotted on a chart using the intercept

$$p = H_O - H_C$$

and azimuth Z with origin at the calculated position (*Long*, *Lat*) at the time of observation, where H_C and Z are calculated using the method in section 6, page 279. Starting from this calculated position a line is drawn on the chart along the direction of the azimuth to the body. Convert p to nautical miles by multiplying by 60. The position line is drawn at right angles to the azimuth line, distance p from (*Long*, *Lat*) towards the body if p is positive and distance p away from the body if p is negative. Provided there are no gross errors the navigator should be somewhere on or near the position line at the time of observation. Two or more position lines are required to determine a fix.

11. *Position from intercept and azimuth by calculation.* The position of the fix may be calculated from two or more sextant observations as follows.

If p_1, Z_1, are the intercept and azimuth of the first observation, p_2, Z_2, of the second observation and so on, form the summations

$$A = \cos^2 Z_1 + \cos^2 Z_2 + \cdots$$
$$B = \cos Z_1 \sin Z_1 + \cos Z_2 \sin Z_2 + \cdots$$
$$C = \sin^2 Z_1 + \sin^2 Z_2 + \cdots$$
$$D = p_1 \cos Z_1 + p_2 \cos Z_2 + \cdots$$
$$E = p_1 \sin Z_1 + p_2 \sin Z_2 + \cdots$$

where the number of terms in each summation is equal to the number of observations.

With $G = A\,C - B^2$, an improved estimate of the position at the time of fix (L_I, B_I) is given by

$$L_I = L_F + (A\,E - B\,D)/(G\cos B_F), \qquad B_I = B_F + (C\,D - B\,E)/G$$

Calculate the distance d between the initial estimated position (L_F, B_F) at the time of fix and the improved estimated position (L_I, B_I) in nautical miles from

$$d = 60\sqrt{((L_I - L_F)^2\cos^2 B_F + (B_I - B_F)^2)}$$

If d exceeds about 20 nautical miles set $L_F = L_I$, $B_F = B_I$ and repeat the calculation until d, the distance between the position at the previous estimate and the improved estimate, is less than about 20 nautical miles.

12. *Example of direct computation.* Using the method described above, calculate the position of a ship on 2017 July 4 at $21^h\,00^m\,00^s$ UT from the marine sextant observations of the three stars *Regulus* (No. 26) at $20^h\,39^m\,23^s$ UT, *Antares* (No. 42) at $20^h\,45^m\,47^s$ UT and *Kochab* (No. 40) at $21^h\,10^m\,34^s$ UT, where the observed altitudes of the three stars corrected for the effects of refraction, dip and instrumental error, are 26°8543, 26°0611 and 47°5292 respectively. The ship was travelling at a constant speed of 20 knots on a course of 325° during the period of observation, and the position of the ship at the time of fix $21^h\,00^m\,00^s$ UT is only known to the nearest whole degree W 15°, N 32°.

Intermediate values for the first iteration are shown in the table. *GHA* Aries was interpolated from the nearest tabular values on page 132. For the first iteration set $L_F = -15^\circ\!.0000$, $B_F = +32^\circ\!.0000$ at the time of fix at $21^h\ 00^m\ 00^s$ UT.

First Iteration

Body	*Regulus*	*Antares*	*Kochab*
No.	26	42	40
time of observation	$20^h\ 39^m\ 23^s$	$20^h\ 45^m\ 47^s$	$21^h\ 10^m\ 34^s$
H_O	26·8543	26·0611	47·5292
interpolation factor	0·6564	0·7631	0·1761
GHA Aries	232·8888	234·4930	240·7057
SHA (page 132)	207·6817	112·3767	137·3267
GHA	80·5704	346·8697	18·0323
Dec (page 132)	+11·8817	−26·4683	+74·0917
t	−0·3436	−0·2369	+0·1761
Long	−14·9225	−14·9466	−15·0397
Lat	+31·9062	+31·9353	+32·0481
Z	267·5283	152·1088	358·7763
H_C	26·8312	25·7553	47·9293
p	+0·0231	+0·3058	−0·4001

$$A = 1{\cdot}7826 \quad B = -0{\cdot}3917 \quad C = 1{\cdot}2174 \quad D = -0{\cdot}6713 \quad E = 0{\cdot}1285 \quad G = 2{\cdot}0167$$

$$(A\,E - B\,D)/(G \cos B_F) = -0{\cdot}0198, \qquad (C\,D - B\,E)/G = -0{\cdot}3803$$

An improved estimate of the position at the time of fix is

$$L_I = L_F - 0{\cdot}0198 = -15{\cdot}0198 \quad \text{and} \quad B_I = B_F - 0{\cdot}3803 = +31{\cdot}6197$$

Since the distance between the previous estimated position and the improved estimate $d = 22{\cdot}8$ nautical miles set $L_F = -15{\cdot}0198$, and $B_F = +31{\cdot}6197$ and repeat the calculation. The table shows the intermediate values of the calculation for the second iteration. In each iteration the quantities H_O, *GHA*, *Dec* and *t* do not change.

Second Iteration

Body	*Regulus*	*Antares*	*Kochab*
No.	26	42	40
Long	−14·9427	−14·9666	−15·0593
Lat	+31·5259	+31·5550	+31·6678
Z	267·7097	152·0044	358·7931
H_C	26·8641	26·0833	47·5495
p	−0·0098	−0·0222	−0·0203

$$A = 1{\cdot}7808 \quad B = -0{\cdot}3956 \quad C = 1{\cdot}2192 \quad D = -0{\cdot}0003 \quad E = -0{\cdot}0002 \quad G = 2{\cdot}0146$$

$$(A\,E - B\,D)/(G \cos B_F) = -0{\cdot}0003, \qquad (C\,D - B\,E)/G = -0{\cdot}0002$$

An improved estimate of the position at the time of fix is

$$L_I = L_F - 0{\cdot}0003 = -15{\cdot}0201 \quad \text{and} \quad B_I = B_F - 0{\cdot}0002 = +31{\cdot}6195$$

The distance between the previous estimated position and the improved estimated position $d = 0{\cdot}02$ nautical miles is so small that a third iteration would produce a negligible improvement to the estimate of the position.

USE OF CONCISE SIGHT REDUCTION TABLES

1. *Introduction.* The concise sight reduction tables given on pages 286 to 317 are intended for use when neither more extensive tables nor electronic computing aids are available. These "NAO sight reduction tables" provide for the reduction of the local hour angle and declination of a celestial object to azimuth and altitude, referred to an assumed position on the Earth, for use in the intercept method of celestial navigation which is now standard practice.

2. *Form of tables.* Entries in the reduction table are at a fixed interval of one degree for all latitudes and hour angles. A compact arrangement results from division of the navigational triangle into two right spherical triangles, so that the table has to be entered twice. Assumed latitude and local hour angle are the arguments for the first entry. The reduction table responds with the intermediate arguments A, B, and Z_1, where A is used as one of the arguments for the second entry to the table, B has to be incremented by the declination to produce the quantity F, and Z_1 is a component of the azimuth angle. The reduction table is then reentered with A and F and yields H, P, and Z_2 where H is the altitude, P is the complement of the parallactic angle, and Z_2 is the second component of the azimuth angle. It is usually necessary to adjust the tabular altitude for the fractional parts of the intermediate entering arguments to derive computed altitude, and an auxiliary table is provided for the purpose. Rules governing signs of the quantities which must be added or subtracted are given in the instructions and summarized on each tabular page. Azimuth angle is the sum of two components and is converted to true azimuth by familiar rules, repeated at the bottom of the tabular pages.

Tabular altitude and intermediate quantities are given to the nearest minute of arc, although errors of $2'$ in computed altitude may accrue during adjustment for the minutes parts of entering arguments. Components of azimuth angle are stated to $0.^\circ1$; for derived true azimuth, only whole degrees are warranted. Since objects near the zenith are difficult to observe with a marine sextant, they should be avoided; altitudes greater than about 80° are not suited to reduction by this method.

In many circumstances, the accuracy provided by these tables is sufficient. However, to maintain the full accuracy ($0.'1$) of the ephemeral data in the almanac throughout their reduction to altitude and azimuth, more extensive tables or a calculator should be used.

3. *Use of Tables.*

Step 1. Determine the Greenwich hour angle (*GHA*) and Declination (*Dec*) of the body from the almanac. Select an assumed latitude (*Lat*) of integral degrees nearest to the estimated latitude. Choose an assumed longitude nearest to the estimated longitude such that the local hour angle

$$LHA = GHA \begin{array}{c} - \text{ west} \\ + \text{ east} \end{array} \text{longitude}$$

has integral degrees.

Step 2. Enter the reduction table with *Lat* and *LHA* as arguments. Record the quantities A, B and Z_1. Apply the rules for the sign of B and Z_1: B is minus if $90^\circ < LHA < 270^\circ$: Z_1 has the same sign as B. Set A° = nearest whole degree of A and A' = minutes part of A. This step may be repeated for all reductions before leaving the latitude opening of the table.

Step 3. Record the declination *Dec*. Apply the rules for the sign of *Dec*: *Dec* is minus if the name of *Dec* (*i.e.* N or S) is contrary to latitude. Add B and *Dec* algebraically to produce F. If F is negative, the object is below the horizon (in sight reduction, this can occur when the objects are close to the horizon). Regard F as positive until step 7. Set F° = nearest whole degree of F and F' = minutes part of F.

Step 4. Enter the reduction table a second time with $A°$ and $F°$ as arguments and record H, P, and Z_2. Set $P° =$ nearest whole degree of P and $Z_2° =$ nearest whole degree of Z_2.

Step 5. Enter the auxiliary table with F' and $P°$ as arguments to obtain $corr_1$ to H for F'. Apply the rule for the sign of $corr_1$: $corr_1$ is minus if $F < 90°$ and $F' > 29'$ or if $F > 90°$ and $F' < 30'$, otherwise $corr_1$ is plus.

Step 6. Enter the auxiliary table with A' and $Z_2°$ as arguments to obtain $corr_2$ to H for A'. Apply the rule for the sign of $corr_2$: $corr_2$ is minus if $A' < 30'$, otherwise $corr_2$ is plus.

Step 7. Calculate the computed altitude H_C as the sum of H, $corr_1$ and $corr_2$. Apply the rule for the sign of H_C: H_C is minus if F is negative.

Step 8. Apply the rule for the sign of Z_2: Z_2 is minus if $F > 90°$. If F is negative, replace Z_2 by $180° - Z_2$. Set the azimuth angle Z equal to the algebraic sum of Z_1 and Z_2 and ignore the resulting sign. Obtain the true azimuth Z_n from the rules

For N latitude, if	$LHA > 180°$	$Z_n = Z$
if	$LHA < 180°$	$Z_n = 360° - Z$
For S latitude, if	$LHA > 180°$	$Z_n = 180° - Z$
if	$LHA < 180°$	$Z_n = 180° + Z$

Observed altitude H_O is compared with H_C to obtain the altitude difference, which, with Z_n, is used to plot the position line.

4. *Example.* (a) Required the altitude and azimuth of *Schedar* on 2017 February 4 at UT $06^h\ 32^m$ from the estimated position 5° east, 53° north.

1. Assumed latitude	$Lat =$	53° N		
From the almanac	$GHA =$	222° 15′		
Assumed longitude		4° 45′ E		
Local hour angle	$LHA =$	227		
2. Reduction table, 1st entry $(Lat, LHA) = (53, 227)$	$A =$	26 07	$A° = 26$, $A' = 7$	
	$B =$	−27 12	$Z_1 = -49{\cdot}4$,	$90° < LHA < 270°$
3. From the almanac	$Dec =$	+56 38		*Lat* and *Dec* same
Sum $= B + Dec$	$F =$	+29 26	$F° = 29$, $F' = 26$	
4. Reduction table, 2nd entry $(A°, F°) = (26, 29)$	$H =$	25 50	$P° = 61$	
			$Z_2 = 76{\cdot}3, Z_2° = 76$	
5. Auxiliary table, 1st entry $(F', P°) = (26, 61)$	$corr_1 =$	+23		$F < 90°$, $F' < 29'$
Sum		26 13		
6. Auxiliary table, 2nd entry $(A', Z_2°) = (7, 76)$	$corr_2 =$	−2		$A' < 30'$
7. Sum = computed altitude	$H_C =$	+26° 11′		$F > 0°$
8. Azimuth, first component	$Z_1 =$	−49·4		same sign as B
second component	$Z_2 =$	+76·3		$F < 90°$, $F > 0°$
Sum = azimuth angle	$Z =$	26·9		
True azimuth	$Z_n =$	027°		N *Lat*, $LHA > 180°$

continued on page 318

SIGHT REDUCTION TABLE

B: (–) for 90° < LHA < 270°
Dec:(–) for Lat. contrary name

Z_1: same sign as B
Z_2: (–) for F > 90°

Lat. / A		0°			1°			2°			3°			4°			5°			Lat. / A	
LHA/F		A/H	B/P	Z_1/Z_2	A/H	B/P	Z_1/Z_2	A/H	B/P	Z_1/Z_2	A/H	B/P	Z_1/Z_2	A/H	B/P	Z_1/Z_2	A/H	B/P	Z_1/Z_2	LHA	
°	°	° ′	° ′	°	° ′	° ′	°	° ′	° ′	°	° ′	° ′	°	° ′	° ′	°	° ′	° ′	°	°	°
0	180	0 00	90 00	90·0	0 00	89 00	90·0	0 00	88 00	90·0	0 00	87 00	90·0	0 00	86 00	90·0	0 00	85 00	90·0	180	360
1	179	1 00	90 00	90·0	1 00	89 00	90·0	1 00	88 00	90·0	1 00	87 00	89·9	1 00	86 00	89·9	1 00	85 00	89·9	181	359
2	178	2 00	90 00	90·0	2 00	89 00	90·0	2 00	88 00	89·9	2 00	87 00	89·9	2 00	86 00	89·9	2 00	85 00	89·8	182	358
3	177	3 00	90 00	90·0	3 00	89 00	89·9	3 00	88 00	89·9	3 00	87 00	89·8	3 00	86 00	89·8	2 59	85 00	89·7	183	357
4	176	4 00	90 00	90·0	4 00	89 00	89·9	4 00	88 00	89·9	4 00	87 00	89·8	3 59	85 59	89·7	3 59	84 59	89·7	184	356
5	175	5 00	90 00	90·0	5 00	89 00	89·9	5 00	88 00	89·8	5 00	86 59	89·7	4 59	85 59	89·7	4 59	84 59	89·6	185	355
6	174	6 00	90 00	90·0	6 00	89 00	89·9	6 00	87 59	89·8	6 00	86 59	89·7	5 59	85 59	89·6	5 59	84 58	89·5	186	354
7	173	7 00	90 00	90·0	7 00	89 00	89·9	7 00	87 59	89·8	6 59	86 59	89·6	6 59	85 58	89·5	6 58	84 58	89·4	187	353
8	172	8 00	90 00	90·0	8 00	88 59	89·9	8 00	87 59	89·7	7 59	86 58	89·6	7 59	85 58	89·4	7 58	84 57	89·3	188	352
9	171	9 00	90 00	90·0	9 00	88 59	89·8	9 00	87 59	89·7	8 59	86 58	89·5	8 59	85 57	89·4	8 58	84 56	89·2	189	351
10	170	10 00	90 00	90·0	10 00	88 59	89·8	10 00	87 58	89·6	9 59	86 57	89·5	9 59	85 56	89·3	9 58	84 55	89·1	190	350
11	169	11 00	90 00	90·0	11 00	88 59	89·8	11 00	87 58	89·6	10 59	86 57	89·4	10 58	85 56	89·2	10 57	84 54	89·0	191	349
12	168	12 00	90 00	90·0	12 00	88 59	89·8	12 00	87 57	89·6	11 59	86 56	89·4	11 58	85 55	89·2	11 57	84 53	88·9	192	348
13	167	13 00	90 00	90·0	13 00	88 58	89·8	13 00	87 57	89·5	12 59	86 55	89·3	12 58	85 54	89·1	12 57	84 52	88·8	193	347
14	166	14 00	90 00	90·0	14 00	88 58	89·8	13 59	87 56	89·5	13 59	86 55	89·3	13 58	85 53	89·0	13 57	84 51	88·8	194	346
15	165	15 00	90 00	90·0	15 00	88 58	89·7	14 59	87 56	89·5	14 59	86 54	89·2	14 58	85 52	88·9	14 56	84 49	88·7	195	345
16	164	16 00	90 00	90·0	16 00	88 58	89·7	15 59	87 55	89·4	15 59	86 53	89·1	15 58	85 50	88·9	15 56	84 48	88·6	196	344
17	163	17 00	90 00	90·0	17 00	88 57	89·7	16 59	87 55	89·4	16 59	86 52	89·1	16 57	85 49	88·8	16 56	84 46	88·5	197	343
18	162	18 00	90 00	90·0	18 00	88 57	89·7	17 59	87 54	89·4	17 58	86 51	89·0	17 57	85 48	88·7	17 56	84 45	88·4	198	342
19	161	19 00	90 00	90·0	19 00	88 57	89·7	18 59	87 53	89·3	18 58	86 50	89·0	18 57	85 46	88·6	18 55	84 43	88·3	199	341
20	160	20 00	90 00	90·0	20 00	88 56	89·6	19 59	87 52	89·3	19 58	86 48	88·9	19 57	85 45	88·5	19 55	84 41	88·2	200	340
21	159	21 00	90 00	90·0	21 00	88 56	89·6	20 59	87 51	89·2	20 58	86 47	88·8	20 57	85 43	88·5	20 55	84 39	88·1	201	339
22	158	22 00	90 00	90·0	22 00	88 55	89·6	21 59	87 51	89·2	21 58	86 46	88·8	21 57	85 41	88·4	21 55	84 37	88·0	202	338
23	157	23 00	90 00	90·0	23 00	88 55	89·6	22 59	87 50	89·2	22 58	86 44	88·7	22 56	85 39	88·3	22 54	84 34	87·9	203	337
24	156	24 00	90 00	90·0	24 00	88 54	89·6	23 59	87 49	89·1	23 58	86 43	88·7	23 56	85 37	88·2	23 54	84 32	87·8	204	336
25	155	25 00	90 00	90·0	25 00	88 54	89·5	24 59	87 48	89·1	24 58	86 41	88·6	24 56	85 35	88·1	24 54	84 29	87·7	205	335
26	154	26 00	90 00	90·0	26 00	88 53	89·5	25 59	87 47	89·0	25 58	86 40	88·5	25 56	85 33	88·1	25 54	84 26	87·6	206	334
27	153	27 00	90 00	90·0	27 00	88 53	89·5	26 59	87 45	89·0	26 58	86 38	88·5	26 56	85 31	88·0	26 53	84 24	87·5	207	333
28	152	28 00	90 00	90·0	28 00	88 52	89·5	27 59	87 44	88·9	27 57	86 36	88·4	27 56	85 28	87·9	27 53	84 20	87·3	208	332
29	151	29 00	90 00	90·0	29 00	88 51	89·4	28 59	87 43	88·9	28 57	86 34	88·3	28 55	85 26	87·8	28 53	84 17	87·2	209	331
30	150	30 00	90 00	90·0	30 00	88 51	89·4	29 59	87 41	88·8	29 57	86 32	88·3	29 55	85 23	87·7	29 52	84 14	87·1	210	330
31	149	31 00	90 00	90·0	31 00	88 50	89·4	30 59	87 40	88·8	30 57	86 30	88·2	30 55	85 20	87·6	30 52	84 10	87·0	211	329
32	148	32 00	90 00	90·0	32 00	88 49	89·4	31 59	87 39	88·8	31 57	86 28	88·1	31 55	85 17	87·5	31 52	84 07	86·9	212	328
33	147	33 00	90 00	90·0	33 00	88 48	89·4	32 59	87 37	88·7	32 57	86 25	88·1	32 55	85 14	87·4	32 52	84 03	86·8	213	327
34	146	34 00	90 00	90·0	34 00	88 48	89·3	33 59	87 35	88·7	33 57	86 23	88·0	33 54	85 11	87·3	33 51	83 59	86·6	214	326
35	145	35 00	90 00	90·0	35 00	88 47	89·3	34 59	87 34	88·6	34 57	86 20	87·9	34 54	85 07	87·2	34 51	83 54	86·5	215	325
36	144	36 00	90 00	90·0	36 00	88 46	89·3	35 58	87 32	88·5	35 57	86 18	87·8	35 54	85 04	87·1	35 51	83 50	86·4	216	324
37	143	37 00	90 00	90·0	37 00	88 45	89·2	36 58	87 30	88·5	36 56	86 15	87·7	36 54	85 00	87·0	36 50	83 45	86·2	217	323
38	142	38 00	90 00	90·0	38 00	88 44	89·2	37 58	87 28	88·4	37 56	86 12	87·7	37 53	84 56	86·9	37 50	83 40	86·1	218	322
39	141	39 00	90 00	90·0	39 00	88 43	89·2	38 58	87 26	88·4	38 56	86 09	87·6	38 53	84 52	86·8	38 49	83 35	86·0	219	321
40	140	40 00	90 00	90·0	40 00	88 42	89·2	39 58	87 23	88·3	39 56	86 05	87·5	39 53	84 47	86·7	39 49	83 29	85·8	220	320
41	139	41 00	90 00	90·0	41 00	88 41	89·1	40 58	87 21	88·3	40 56	86 02	87·4	40 53	84 42	86·5	40 49	83 23	85·7	221	319
42	138	42 00	90 00	90·0	42 00	88 39	89·1	41 58	87 19	88·2	41 56	85 58	87·3	41 52	84 37	86·4	41 48	83 17	85·5	222	318
43	137	43 00	90 00	90·0	43 00	88 38	89·1	42 58	87 16	88·1	42 56	85 54	87·2	42 52	84 32	86·3	42 48	83 11	85·4	223	317
44	136	44 00	90 00	90·0	43 59	88 37	89·0	43 58	87 13	88·1	43 55	85 50	87·1	43 52	84 27	86·1	43 47	83 04	85·2	224	316
45	135	45 00	90 00	90·0	44 59	88 35	89·0	44 58	87 10	88·0	44 55	85 46	87·0	44 52	84 21	86·0	44 47	82 57	85·0	225	315

Lat. / A		0°			1°			2°			3°			4°			5°			Lat. / A	
LHA/F		A/H	B/P	Z_1/Z_2	A/H	B/P	Z_1/Z_2	A/H	B/P	Z_1/Z_2	A/H	B/P	Z_1/Z_2	A/H	B/P	Z_1/Z_2	A/H	B/P	Z_1/Z_2	LHA	
°	°	° ′	° ′	°	° ′	° ′	°	° ′	° ′	°	° ′	° ′	°	° ′	° ′	°	° ′	° ′	°	°	°
45	135	45 00	90 00	90·0	44 59	88 35	89·0	44 58	87 10	88·0	44 55	85 46	87·0	44 52	84 21	86·0	44 47	82 57	85·0	225	315
46	134	46 00	90 00	90·0	45 59	88 34	89·0	45 58	87 07	87·9	45 55	85 41	86·9	45 51	84 15	85·9	45 46	82 49	84·8	226	314
47	133	47 00	90 00	90·0	46 59	88 32	88·9	46 58	87 04	87·9	46 55	85 36	86·8	46 51	84 09	85·7	46 46	82 41	84·7	227	313
48	132	48 00	90 00	90·0	47 59	88 30	88·9	47 58	87 01	87·8	47 55	85 31	86·7	47 51	84 02	85·6	47 46	82 33	84·5	228	312
49	131	49 00	90 00	90·0	48 59	88 29	88·8	48 58	86 57	87·7	48 55	85 25	86·6	48 50	83 55	85·4	48 45	82 24	84·3	229	311
50	130	50 00	90 00	90·0	49 59	88 27	88·8	49 58	86 53	87·6	49 54	85 20	86·4	49 50	83 47	85·2	49 44	82 15	84·1	230	310
51	129	51 00	90 00	90·0	50 59	88 25	88·8	50 57	86 49	87·5	50 54	85 14	86·3	50 50	83 40	85·1	50 44	82 05	83·9	231	309
52	128	52 00	90 00	90·0	51 59	88 23	88·7	51 57	86 45	87·4	51 54	85 08	86·2	51 49	83 31	84·9	51 43	81 55	83·6	232	308
53	127	53 00	90 00	90·0	52 59	88 20	88·7	52 57	86 41	87·3	52 54	85 01	86·0	52 49	83 22	84·7	52 43	81 44	83·4	233	307
54	126	54 00	90 00	90·0	53 59	88 18	88·6	53 57	86 36	87·2	53 54	84 54	85·9	53 49	83 13	84·5	53 42	81 32	83·2	234	306
55	125	55 00	90 00	90·0	54 59	88 15	88·6	54 57	86 31	87·1	54 53	84 47	85·7	54 48	83 03	84·3	54 41	81 20	82·9	235	305
56	124	56 00	90 00	90·0	55 59	88 13	88·5	55 57	86 26	87·0	55 53	84 39	85·6	55 48	82 52	84·1	55 41	81 06	82·6	236	304
57	123	57 00	90 00	90·0	56 59	88 10	88·5	56 57	86 20	86·9	56 53	84 30	85·4	56 47	82 41	83·9	56 40	80 52	82·4	237	303
58	122	58 00	90 00	90·0	57 59	88 07	88·4	57 57	86 14	86·8	57 52	84 21	85·2	57 47	82 29	83·6	57 39	80 38	82·1	238	302
59	121	59 00	90 00	90·0	58 59	88 04	88·3	58 57	86 07	86·7	58 52	84 11	85·0	58 46	82 16	83·4	58 38	80 22	81·7	239	301
60	120	60 00	90 00	90·0	59 59	88 00	88·3	59 56	86 00	86·5	59 52	84 01	84·8	59 46	82 02	83·1	59 37	80 05	81·4	240	300
61	119	61 00	90 00	90·0	60 59	87 56	88·2	60 56	85 53	86·4	60 52	83 50	84·6	60 45	81 48	82·8	60 37	79 46	81·1	241	299
62	118	62 00	90 00	90·0	61 59	87 52	88·1	61 56	85 45	86·2	61 51	83 38	84·4	61 44	81 32	82·5	61 36	79 27	80·7	242	298
63	117	63 00	90 00	90·0	62 59	87 48	88·0	62 56	85 36	86·1	62 51	83 25	84·1	62 44	81 15	82·2	62 35	79 06	80·3	243	297
64	116	64 00	90 00	90·0	63 59	87 43	88·0	63 56	85 27	85·9	63 50	83 11	83·9	63 43	80 56	81·9	63 33	78 43	79·9	244	296
65	115	65 00	90 00	90·0	64 59	87 38	87·9	64 56	85 17	85·7	64 50	82 56	83·6	64 42	80 36	81·5	64 32	78 18	79·4	245	295
66	114	66 00	90 00	90·0	65 59	87 33	87·8	65 55	85 06	85·5	65 49	82 39	83·3	65 41	80 15	81·1	65 31	77 52	78·9	246	294
67	113	67 00	90 00	90·0	66 59	87 27	87·6	66 55	84 54	85·3	66 49	82 22	83·0	66 40	79 51	80·7	66 29	77 23	78·4	247	293
68	112	68 00	90 00	90·0	67 59	87 20	87·5	67 55	84 40	85·1	67 48	82 02	82·6	67 39	79 26	80·2	67 28	76 51	77·8	248	292
69	111	69 00	90 00	90·0	68 59	87 13	87·4	68 55	84 26	84·8	68 48	81 41	82·2	68 38	78 58	79·7	68 26	76 17	77·2	249	291
70	110	70 00	90 00	90·0	69 59	87 05	87·3	69 54	84 10	84·5	69 47	81 17	81·8	69 37	78 27	79·2	69 25	75 39	76·5	250	290
71	109	71 00	90 00	90·0	70 58	86 56	87·1	70 54	83 53	84·2	70 46	80 51	81·4	70 36	77 53	78·5	70 23	74 58	75·8	251	289
72	108	72 00	90 00	90·0	71 58	86 46	86·9	71 54	83 33	83·9	71 46	80 22	80·8	71 35	77 15	77·9	71 20	74 12	75·0	252	288
73	107	73 00	90 00	90·0	72 58	86 35	86·7	72 53	83 11	83·5	72 45	79 50	80·3	72 33	76 33	77·1	72 18	73 20	74·1	253	287
74	106	74 00	90 00	90·0	73 58	86 23	86·5	73 53	82 47	83·1	73 44	79 14	79·7	73 31	75 46	76·3	73 15	72 23	73·1	254	286
75	105	75 00	90 00	90·0	74 58	86 09	86·3	74 52	82 19	82·6	74 43	78 33	78·9	74 29	74 53	75·4	74 12	71 19	72·0	255	285
76	104	76 00	90 00	90·0	75 58	85 52	86·0	75 52	81 47	82·0	75 41	77 47	78·1	75 27	73 53	74·4	75 09	70 07	70·7	256	284
77	103	77 00	90 00	90·0	76 58	85 34	85·7	76 51	81 11	81·4	76 40	76 53	77·2	76 25	72 44	73·2	76 05	68 45	69·3	257	283
78	102	78 00	90 00	90·0	77 58	85 12	85·3	77 50	80 28	80·7	77 38	75 51	76·2	77 22	71 25	71·8	77 01	67 11	67·7	258	282
79	101	79 00	90 00	90·0	78 57	84 46	84·9	78 49	79 38	79·8	78 36	74 39	74·9	78 18	69 52	70·3	77 56	65 22	65·8	259	281
80	100	80 00	90 00	90·0	79 57	84 16	84·3	79 48	78 38	78·8	79 34	73 12	73·5	79 14	68 04	68·4	78 50	63 16	63·7	260	280
81	99	81 00	90 00	90·0	80 57	83 38	83·7	80 47	77 25	77·6	80 31	71 29	71·7	80 09	65 55	66·2	79 43	60 47	61·2	261	279
82	98	82 00	90 00	90·0	81 56	82 51	82·9	81 45	75 55	76·1	81 28	69 22	69·6	81 04	63 19	63·6	80 34	57 51	58·2	262	278
83	97	83 00	90 00	90·0	82 56	81 51	81·9	82 43	74 01	74·1	82 23	66 44	66·9	81 57	60 09	60·4	81 24	54 20	54·6	263	277
84	96	84 00	90 00	90·0	83 55	80 31	80·6	83 41	71 32	71·6	83 18	63 22	63·5	82 48	56 13	56·4	82 12	50 04	50·3	264	276
85	95	85 00	90 00	90·0	84 54	78 40	78·7	84 37	68 10	68·3	84 10	58 59	59·1	83 36	51 16	51·4	82 56	44 53	45·1	265	275
86	94	86 00	90 00	90·0	85 53	75 57	76·0	85 32	63 24	63·5	85 00	53 05	53·2	84 21	44 56	45·1	83 36	38 34	38·7	266	274
87	93	87 00	90 00	90·0	86 50	71 33	71·6	86 24	56 17	56·3	85 45	44 58	45·0	85 00	36 49	36·9	84 10	30 53	31·0	267	273
88	92	88 00	90 00	90·0	87 46	63 26	63·4	87 10	44 59	45·0	86 24	33 40	33·7	85 32	26 31	26·6	84 37	21 45	21·8	268	272
89	91	89 00	90 00	90·0	88 35	45 00	45·0	87 46	26 33	26·6	86 50	18 25	18·4	85 53	14 01	14·0	84 54	11 17	11·3	269	271
90	90	90 00	0 00	0·0	89 00	0 00	0·0	88 00	0 00	0·0	87 00	0 00	0·0	86 00	0 00	0·0	85 00	0 00	0·0	270	270

N. Lat: for LHA > 180° … $Z_n = Z$
for LHA < 180° … $Z_n = 360° - Z$

S. Lat.: for LHA > 180° … $Z_n = 180° - Z$
for LHA < 180° … $Z_n = 180° + Z$

SIGHT REDUCTION TABLE

B: (−) for 90° < LHA < 270°
Dec:(−) for Lat. contrary name

Z_1: same sign as B
Z_2: (−) for F > 90°

Lat. / A		6°			7°			8°			9°			10°			11°			Lat. / A	
LHA/F		A/H	B/P	Z_1/Z_2	A/H	B/P	Z_1/Z_2	A/H	B/P	Z_1/Z_2	A/H	B/P	Z_1/Z_2	A/H	B/P	Z_1/Z_2	A/H	B/P	Z_1/Z_2	LHA	
°	°	° ′	° ′	°	° ′	° ′	°	° ′	° ′	°	° ′	° ′	°	° ′	° ′	°	° ′	° ′	°	°	°
0	180	0 00	84 00	90·0	0 00	83 00	90·0	0 00	82 00	90·0	0 00	81 00	90·0	0 00	80 00	90·0	0 00	79 00	90·0	180	360
1	179	1 00	84 00	89·9	1 00	83 00	89·9	0 59	82 00	89·9	0 59	81 00	89·8	0 59	80 00	89·8	0 59	79 00	89·8	181	359
2	178	1 59	84 00	89·8	1 59	83 00	89·8	1 59	82 00	89·7	1 59	81 00	89·7	1 58	80 00	89·7	1 58	79 00	89·6	182	358
3	177	2 59	84 00	89·7	2 59	82 59	89·6	2 58	81 59	89·6	2 58	80 59	89·5	2 57	79 59	89·5	2 57	78 59	89·4	183	357
4	176	3 59	83 59	89·6	3 58	82 59	89·5	3 58	81 59	89·4	3 57	80 59	89·4	3 56	79 59	89·3	3 56	78 58	89·2	184	356
5	175	4 58	83 59	89·5	4 58	82 58	89·4	4 57	81 58	89·3	4 56	80 58	89·2	4 55	79 58	89·1	4 54	78 58	89·0	185	355
6	174	5 58	83 58	89·4	5 57	82 58	89·3	5 56	81 57	89·2	5 56	80 57	89·1	5 55	79 57	89·0	5 53	78 56	88·9	186	354
7	173	6 58	83 57	89·3	6 57	82 57	89·1	6 56	81 56	89·0	6 55	80 56	88·9	6 54	79 56	88·8	6 52	78 55	88·7	187	353
8	172	7 57	83 56	89·2	7 56	82 56	89·0	7 55	81 55	88·9	7 54	80 55	88·7	7 53	79 54	88·6	7 51	78 54	88·5	188	352
9	171	8 57	83 56	89·1	8 56	82 55	88·9	8 55	81 54	88·7	8 53	80 53	88·6	8 52	79 53	88·4	8 50	78 52	88·3	189	351
10	170	9 57	83 54	88·9	9 55	82 54	88·8	9 54	81 53	88·6	9 53	80 52	88·4	9 51	79 51	88·2	9 49	78 50	88·1	190	350
11	169	10 56	83 53	88·8	10 55	82 52	88·6	10 53	81 51	88·5	10 52	80 50	88·3	10 50	79 49	88·1	10 48	78 48	87·9	191	349
12	168	11 56	83 52	88·7	11 55	82 51	88·5	11 53	81 49	88·3	11 51	80 48	88·1	11 49	79 47	87·9	11 47	78 46	87·7	192	348
13	167	12 56	83 51	88·6	12 54	82 49	88·4	12 52	81 48	88·2	12 50	80 46	87·9	12 48	79 45	87·7	12 45	78 43	87·5	193	347
14	166	13 55	83 49	88·5	13 54	82 47	88·3	13 52	81 46	88·0	13 49	80 44	87·8	13 47	79 42	87·5	13 44	78 40	87·3	194	346
15	165	14 55	83 47	88·4	14 53	82 45	88·1	14 51	81 43	87·9	14 49	80 41	87·6	14 46	79 39	87·3	14 43	78 37	87·1	195	345
16	164	15 55	83 46	88·3	15 53	82 43	88·0	15 50	81 41	87·7	15 48	80 39	87·4	15 45	79 36	87·1	15 42	78 34	86·9	196	344
17	163	16 54	83 44	88·2	16 52	82 41	87·9	16 50	81 38	87·6	16 47	80 36	87·3	16 44	79 33	87·0	16 41	78 31	86·7	197	343
18	162	17 54	83 42	88·1	17 52	82 39	87·7	17 49	81 36	87·4	17 46	80 33	87·1	17 43	79 30	86·8	17 39	78 27	86·5	198	342
19	161	18 54	83 39	87·9	18 51	82 36	87·6	18 48	81 33	87·3	18 45	80 29	86·9	18 42	79 26	86·6	18 38	78 23	86·2	199	341
20	160	19 53	83 37	87·8	19 51	82 33	87·5	19 48	81 30	87·1	19 45	80 26	86·7	19 41	79 22	86·4	19 37	78 19	86·0	200	340
21	159	20 53	83 35	87·7	20 50	82 30	87·3	20 47	81 26	86·9	20 44	80 22	86·6	20 40	79 18	86·2	20 36	78 14	85·8	201	339
22	158	21 52	83 32	87·6	21 50	82 27	87·2	21 46	81 23	86·8	21 43	80 18	86·4	21 39	79 14	86·0	21 35	78 10	85·6	202	338
23	157	22 52	83 29	87·5	22 49	82 24	87·0	22 46	81 19	86·6	22 42	80 14	86·2	22 38	79 09	85·8	22 33	78 05	85·4	203	337
24	156	23 52	83 26	87·3	23 49	82 21	86·9	23 45	81 15	86·5	23 41	80 10	86·0	23 37	79 05	85·6	23 32	77 59	85·1	204	336
25	155	24 51	83 23	87·2	24 48	82 17	86·7	24 44	81 11	86·3	24 40	80 05	85·8	24 36	78 59	85·4	24 31	77 54	84·9	205	335
26	154	25 51	83 20	87·1	25 48	82 13	86·6	25 44	81 07	86·1	25 39	80 00	85·6	25 35	78 54	85·2	25 29	77 48	84·7	206	334
27	153	26 50	83 16	87·0	26 47	82 09	86·4	26 43	81 02	85·9	26 38	79 55	85·4	26 33	78 48	84·9	26 28	77 42	84·4	207	333
28	152	27 50	83 13	86·8	27 46	82 05	86·3	27 42	80 57	85·8	27 38	79 50	85·2	27 32	78 42	84·7	27 27	77 35	84·2	208	332
29	151	28 50	83 09	86·7	28 46	82 01	86·1	28 41	80 52	85·6	28 37	79 44	85·0	28 31	78 36	84·5	28 25	77 28	84·0	209	331
30	150	29 49	83 05	86·5	29 45	81 56	86·0	29 41	80 47	85·4	29 36	79 38	84·8	29 30	78 29	84·3	29 24	77 21	83·7	210	330
31	149	30 49	83 01	86·4	30 45	81 51	85·8	30 40	80 41	85·2	30 35	79 32	84·6	30 29	78 23	84·0	30 22	77 13	83·5	211	329
32	148	31 48	82 56	86·3	31 44	81 46	85·6	31 39	80 35	85·0	31 34	79 25	84·4	31 27	78 15	83·8	31 21	77 05	83·2	212	328
33	147	32 48	82 51	86·1	32 43	81 40	85·5	32 38	80 29	84·8	32 33	79 18	84·2	32 26	78 08	83·6	32 19	76 57	82·9	213	327
34	146	33 47	82 46	86·0	33 43	81 35	85·3	33 37	80 23	84·6	33 32	79 11	84·0	33 25	78 00	83·3	33 18	76 48	82·7	214	326
35	145	34 47	82 41	85·8	34 42	81 29	85·1	34 37	80 16	84·4	34 30	79 03	83·7	34 24	77 51	83·1	34 16	76 39	82·4	215	325
36	144	35 46	82 36	85·7	35 41	81 22	84·9	35 36	80 09	84·2	35 29	78 55	83·5	35 22	77 42	82·8	35 14	76 29	82·1	216	324
37	143	36 46	82 30	85·5	36 41	81 16	84·8	36 35	80 01	84·0	36 28	78 47	83·3	36 21	77 33	82·5	36 13	76 19	81·8	217	323
38	142	37 45	82 24	85·3	37 40	81 09	84·6	37 34	79 53	83·8	37 27	78 38	83·0	37 19	77 23	82·3	37 11	76 09	81·5	218	322
39	141	38 45	82 18	85·2	38 39	81 01	84·4	38 33	79 45	83·6	38 26	78 29	82·8	38 18	77 13	82·0	38 09	75 57	81·2	219	321
40	140	39 44	82 11	85·0	39 39	80 54	84·2	39 32	79 36	83·3	39 25	78 19	82·5	39 16	77 02	81·7	39 07	75 46	80·9	220	320
41	139	40 44	82 04	84·8	40 38	80 46	84·0	40 31	79 27	83·1	40 23	78 09	82·3	40 15	76 51	81·4	40 05	75 33	80·6	221	319
42	138	41 43	81 57	84·6	41 37	80 37	83·7	41 30	79 17	82·9	41 22	77 58	82·0	41 13	76 39	81·1	41 04	75 21	80·3	222	318
43	137	42 42	81 49	84·4	42 36	80 28	83·5	42 29	79 07	82·6	42 21	77 47	81·7	42 12	76 27	80·8	42 02	75 07	79·9	223	317
44	136	43 42	81 41	84·2	43 35	80 19	83·3	43 28	78 57	82·3	43 19	77 35	81·4	43 10	76 14	80·5	43 00	74 53	79·6	224	316
45	135	44 41	81 33	84·0	44 34	80 09	83·1	44 27	78 46	82·1	44 18	77 22	81·1	44 08	76 00	80·1	43 57	74 38	79·2	225	315

Lat. / A		6°			7°			8°			9°			10°			11°			Lat. / A	
LHA/F		A/H	B/P	Z_1/Z_2	A/H	B/P	Z_1/Z_2	A/H	B/P	Z_1/Z_2	A/H	B/P	Z_1/Z_2	A/H	B/P	Z_1/Z_2	A/H	B/P	Z_1/Z_2	LHA	
°	°	° ′	° ′	°	° ′	° ′	°	° ′	° ′	°	° ′	° ′	°	° ′	° ′	°	° ′	° ′	°	°	°
45	135	44 41	81 33	84·0	44 34	80 09	83·1	44 27	78 46	82·1	44 18	77 22	81·1	44 08	76 00	80·1	43 57	74 38	79·2	225	315
46	134	45 41	81 24	83·8	45 34	79 59	82·8	45 26	78 34	81·8	45 16	77 09	80·8	45 06	75 45	79·8	44 55	74 22	78·8	226	314
47	133	46 40	81 14	83·6	46 33	79 48	82·6	46 24	78 21	81·5	46 15	76 56	80·5	46 04	75 30	79·5	45 53	74 05	78·4	227	313
48	132	47 39	81 04	83·4	47 32	79 36	82·3	47 23	78 08	81·2	47 13	76 41	80·1	47 03	75 14	79·1	46 51	73 48	78·0	228	312
49	131	48 38	80 54	83·1	48 31	79 24	82·0	48 22	77 55	80·9	48 12	76 26	79·8	48 01	74 57	78·7	47 48	73 30	77·6	229	311
50	130	49 38	80 43	82·9	49 30	79 11	81·7	49 20	77 40	80·6	49 10	76 09	79·4	48 58	74 40	78·3	48 46	73 10	77·2	230	310
51	129	50 37	80 31	82·6	50 29	78 58	81·4	50 19	77 25	80·2	50 08	75 52	79·1	49 56	74 21	77·9	49 43	72 50	76·7	231	309
52	128	51 36	80 19	82·4	51 27	78 43	81·1	51 18	77 08	79·9	51 06	75 34	78·7	50 54	74 01	77·5	50 40	72 29	76·3	232	308
53	127	52 35	80 06	82·1	52 26	78 28	80·8	52 16	76 51	79·5	52 04	75 15	78·3	51 52	73 40	77·0	51 37	72 06	75·8	233	307
54	126	53 34	79 52	81·8	53 25	78 12	80·5	53 14	76 33	79·2	53 02	74 55	77·8	52 49	73 18	76·6	52 35	71 42	75·3	234	306
55	125	54 33	79 37	81·5	54 24	77 55	80·1	54 13	76 14	78·8	54 00	74 34	77·4	53 47	72 55	76·1	53 31	71 17	74·8	235	305
56	124	55 32	79 21	81·2	55 22	77 37	79·8	55 11	75 54	78·3	54 58	74 11	76·9	54 44	72 30	75·6	54 28	70 50	74·2	236	304
57	123	56 31	79 05	80·9	56 21	77 18	79·4	56 09	75 32	77·9	55 56	73 47	76·5	55 41	72 04	75·0	55 25	70 22	73·6	237	303
58	122	57 30	78 47	80·5	57 19	76 57	79·0	57 07	75 09	77·4	56 53	73 22	75·9	56 38	71 36	74·5	56 21	69 51	73·0	238	302
59	121	58 29	78 28	80·1	58 18	76 35	78·5	58 05	74 44	77·0	57 51	72 54	75·4	57 35	71 06	73·9	57 17	69 19	72·4	239	301
60	120	59 28	78 08	79·7	59 16	76 12	78·1	59 03	74 18	76·4	58 48	72 25	74·8	58 32	70 34	73·3	58 13	68 45	71·7	240	300
61	119	60 26	77 46	79·3	60 14	75 47	77·6	60 01	73 50	75·9	59 45	71 54	74·2	59 28	70 01	72·6	59 09	68 09	71·0	241	299
62	118	61 25	77 23	78·9	61 12	75 21	77·1	60 58	73 20	75·3	60 42	71 21	73·6	60 24	69 25	71·9	60 05	67 31	70·3	242	298
63	117	62 23	76 58	78·4	62 10	74 52	76·5	61 56	72 48	74·7	61 39	70 46	72·9	61 20	68 46	71·2	61 00	66 49	69·5	243	297
64	116	63 22	76 31	77·9	63 08	74 21	76·0	62 53	72 13	74·1	62 35	70 08	72·2	62 16	68 05	70·4	61 55	66 05	68·6	244	296
65	115	64 20	76 02	77·4	64 06	73 48	75·4	63 50	71 36	73·4	63 32	69 27	71·5	63 12	67 21	69·6	62 50	65 18	67·7	245	295
66	114	65 18	75 31	76·8	65 03	73 12	74·7	64 47	70 56	72·6	64 28	68 43	70·6	64 07	66 34	68·7	63 44	64 27	66·8	246	294
67	113	66 16	74 57	76·2	66 01	72 33	74·0	65 43	70 13	71·8	65 23	67 56	69·8	65 02	65 43	67·8	64 38	63 33	65·8	247	293
68	112	67 14	74 20	75·5	66 58	71 51	73·2	66 40	69 26	71·0	66 19	67 05	68·8	65 56	64 48	66·7	65 32	62 35	64·7	248	292
69	111	68 12	73 39	74·8	67 55	71 05	72·4	67 36	68 35	70·1	67 14	66 09	67·8	66 50	63 48	65·7	66 25	61 31	63·6	249	291
70	110	69 09	72 55	74·0	68 51	70 15	71·5	68 31	67 40	69·1	68 09	65 09	66·7	67 44	62 44	64·5	67 17	60 23	62·3	250	290
71	109	70 07	72 06	73·1	69 48	69 20	70·5	69 27	66 39	68·0	69 03	64 03	65·6	68 37	61 34	63·2	68 09	59 10	61·0	251	289
72	108	71 03	71 13	72·2	70 44	68 20	69·4	70 21	65 33	66·8	69 57	62 52	64·3	69 29	60 17	61·9	69 00	57 50	59·6	252	288
73	107	72 00	70 14	71·1	71 39	67 13	68·3	71 16	64 20	65·5	70 50	61 33	62·9	70 21	58 54	60·4	69 50	56 23	58·0	253	287
74	106	72 56	69 08	70·0	72 34	65 59	67·0	72 09	62 59	64·1	71 42	60 07	61·4	71 12	57 24	58·8	70 40	54 49	56·4	254	286
75	105	73 52	67 54	68·7	73 29	64 37	65·5	73 03	61 30	62·6	72 34	58 32	59·7	72 02	55 44	57·1	71 28	53 06	54·5	255	285
76	104	74 48	66 31	67·3	74 23	63 05	64·0	73 55	59 51	60·8	73 24	56 47	57·9	72 51	53 55	55·1	72 16	51 13	52·6	256	284
77	103	75 42	64 57	65·6	75 16	61 22	62·2	74 46	58 00	58·9	74 14	54 51	55·9	73 39	51 55	53·1	73 02	49 10	50·4	257	283
78	102	76 36	63 11	63·8	76 08	59 26	60·2	75 37	55 57	56·8	75 02	52 42	53·6	74 26	49 42	50·8	73 47	46 56	48·1	258	282
79	101	77 29	61 09	61·7	76 59	57 14	57·9	76 26	53 38	54·4	75 49	50 18	51·2	75 11	47 16	48·2	74 30	44 28	45·5	259	281
80	100	78 21	58 49	59·3	77 49	54 44	55·3	77 13	51 01	51·7	76 35	47 38	48·4	75 54	44 34	45·4	75 11	41 47	42·7	260	280
81	99	79 12	56 06	56·6	78 37	51 52	52·4	77 59	48 04	48·7	77 18	44 39	45·4	76 35	41 35	42·4	75 49	38 50	39·7	261	279
82	98	80 01	52 56	53·4	79 23	48 35	49·1	78 42	44 43	45·3	77 59	41 18	41·9	77 13	38 17	39·0	76 26	35 36	36·4	262	278
83	97	80 47	49 13	49·6	80 07	44 47	45·2	79 23	40 56	41·4	78 37	37 35	38·1	77 49	34 39	35·3	76 59	32 05	32·8	263	277
84	96	81 31	44 51	45·2	80 47	40 24	40·8	80 01	36 38	37·1	79 12	33 25	33·9	78 21	30 40	31·2	77 29	28 16	28·8	264	276
85	95	82 12	39 40	39·9	81 24	35 22	35·7	80 34	31 48	32·2	79 43	28 49	29·2	78 50	26 18	26·7	77 56	24 09	24·6	265	275
86	94	82 48	33 34	33·8	81 57	29 36	29·8	81 04	26 24	26·7	80 09	23 46	24·1	79 14	21 35	21·9	78 18	19 44	20·1	266	274
87	93	83 18	26 28	26·6	82 23	23 05	23·3	81 28	20 25	20·6	80 31	18 17	18·5	79 34	16 32	16·8	78 36	15 04	15·4	267	273
88	92	83 41	18 22	18·5	82 43	15 52	16·0	81 45	13 57	14·1	80 47	12 26	12·6	79 48	11 12	11·4	78 49	10 11	10·4	268	272
89	91	83 55	9 26	9·5	82 56	8 05	8·2	81 56	7 05	7·1	80 57	6 17	6·4	79 57	5 39	5·7	78 57	5 08	5·2	269	271
90	90	84 00	0 00	0·0	83 00	0 00	0·0	82 00	0 00	0·0	81 00	0 00	0·0	80 00	0 00	0·0	79 00	0 00	0·0	270	270

N. Lat: for LHA > 180° … $Z_n = Z$
for LHA < 180° … $Z_n = 360° - Z$

S. Lat.: for LHA > 180° … $Z_n = 180° - Z$
for LHA < 180° … $Z_n = 180° + Z$

SIGHT REDUCTION TABLE

B: (−) for 90° < LHA < 270°
Dec:(−) for Lat. contrary name

Z_1: same sign as B
Z_2: (−) for F > 90°

Lat. / A		12°			13°			14°			15°			16°			17°			Lat. / A	
LHA/F		A/H	B/P	Z_1/Z_2	A/H	B/P	Z_1/Z_2	A/H	B/P	Z_1/Z_2	A/H	B/P	Z_1/Z_2	A/H	B/P	Z_1/Z_2	A/H	B/P	Z_1/Z_2	LHA	
°	°	° ′	° ′	°	° ′	° ′	°	° ′	° ′	°	° ′	° ′	°	° ′	° ′	°	° ′	° ′	°	°	°
0	180	0 00	78 00	90·0	0 00	77 00	90·0	0 00	76 00	90·0	0 00	75 00	90·0	0 00	74 00	90·0	0 00	73 00	90·0	180	360
1	179	0 59	78 00	89·8	0 58	77 00	89·8	0 58	76 00	89·8	0 58	75 00	89·7	0 58	74 00	89·7	0 57	73 00	89·7	181	359
2	178	1 57	78 00	89·6	1 57	77 00	89·5	1 56	76 00	89·5	1 56	74 59	89·5	1 55	73 59	89·4	1 55	72 59	89·4	182	358
3	177	2 56	77 59	89·4	2 55	76 59	89·3	2 55	75 59	89·3	2 54	74 59	89·2	2 53	73 59	89·2	2 52	72 59	89·1	183	357
4	176	3 55	77 58	89·2	3 54	76 58	89·1	3 53	75 58	89·0	3 52	74 58	89·0	3 51	73 58	88·9	3 49	72 58	88·8	184	356
5	175	4 53	77 57	89·0	4 52	76 57	88·9	4 51	75 57	88·8	4 50	74 57	88·7	4 48	73 57	88·6	4 47	72 56	88·5	185	355
6	174	5 52	77 56	88·7	5 51	76 56	88·6	5 49	75 56	88·5	5 48	74 55	88·4	5 46	73 55	88·3	5 44	72 55	88·2	186	354
7	173	6 51	77 55	88·5	6 49	76 54	88·4	6 47	75 54	88·3	6 46	74 54	88·2	6 44	73 53	88·1	6 42	72 53	87·9	187	353
8	172	7 49	77 53	88·3	7 48	76 53	88·2	7 46	75 52	88·1	7 44	74 52	87·9	7 41	73 51	87·8	7 39	72 51	87·6	188	352
9	171	8 48	77 51	88·1	8 46	76 51	88·0	8 44	75 50	87·8	8 41	74 49	87·7	8 39	73 49	87·5	8 36	72 48	87·3	189	351
10	170	9 47	77 49	87·9	9 44	76 48	87·7	9 42	75 48	87·6	9 39	74 47	87·4	9 37	73 46	87·2	9 34	72 45	87·0	190	350
11	169	10 45	77 47	87·7	10 43	76 46	87·5	10 40	75 45	87·3	10 37	74 44	87·1	10 34	73 43	86·9	10 31	72 42	86·7	191	349
12	168	11 44	77 44	87·5	11 41	76 43	87·3	11 38	75 42	87·1	11 35	74 41	86·9	11 32	73 40	86·6	11 28	72 39	86·4	192	348
13	167	12 43	77 42	87·3	12 40	76 40	87·0	12 36	75 39	86·8	12 33	74 37	86·6	12 29	73 36	86·4	12 25	72 35	86·1	193	347
14	166	13 41	77 39	87·0	13 38	76 37	86·8	13 35	75 35	86·5	13 31	74 34	86·3	13 27	73 32	86·1	13 23	72 31	85·8	194	346
15	165	14 40	77 35	86·8	14 36	76 33	86·6	14 33	75 32	86·3	14 29	74 30	86·0	14 24	73 28	85·8	14 20	72 26	85·5	195	345
16	164	15 38	77 32	86·6	15 35	76 30	86·3	15 31	75 28	86·0	15 26	74 25	85·8	15 22	73 23	85·5	15 17	72 21	85·2	196	344
17	163	16 37	77 28	86·4	16 33	76 26	86·1	16 29	75 23	85·8	16 24	74 21	85·5	16 19	73 19	85·2	16 14	72 16	84·9	197	343
18	162	17 36	77 24	86·1	17 31	76 21	85·8	17 27	75 19	85·5	17 22	74 16	85·2	17 17	73 13	84·9	17 11	72 11	84·6	198	342
19	161	18 34	77 20	85·9	18 30	76 17	85·6	18 25	75 14	85·2	18 20	74 11	84·9	18 14	73 08	84·6	18 08	72 05	84·3	199	341
20	160	19 33	77 15	85·7	19 28	76 12	85·3	19 23	75 08	85·0	19 17	74 05	84·6	19 12	73 02	84·3	19 05	71 59	83·9	200	340
21	159	20 31	77 10	85·4	20 26	76 07	85·1	20 21	75 03	84·7	20 15	73 59	84·3	20 09	72 56	84·0	20 03	71 52	83·6	201	339
22	158	21 30	77 05	85·2	21 24	76 01	84·8	21 19	74 57	84·4	21 13	73 53	84·0	21 06	72 49	83·6	21 00	71 45	83·3	202	338
23	157	22 28	77 00	85·0	22 23	75 55	84·5	22 17	74 51	84·1	22 10	73 46	83·7	22 04	72 42	83·3	21 56	71 38	82·9	203	337
24	156	23 27	76 54	84·7	23 21	75 49	84·3	23 15	74 44	83·9	23 08	73 39	83·4	23 01	72 34	83·0	22 53	71 30	82·6	204	336
25	155	24 25	76 48	84·5	24 19	75 43	84·0	24 13	74 37	83·6	24 06	73 32	83·1	23 58	72 27	82·7	23 50	71 22	82·2	205	335
26	154	25 23	76 42	84·2	25 17	75 36	83·7	25 10	74 30	83·3	25 03	73 24	82·8	24 55	72 18	82·3	24 47	71 13	81·9	206	334
27	153	26 22	76 35	84·0	26 15	75 28	83·5	26 08	74 22	83·0	26 01	73 16	82·5	25 52	72 10	82·0	25 44	71 04	81·5	207	333
28	152	27 20	76 28	83·7	27 13	75 21	83·2	27 06	74 14	82·7	26 58	73 07	82·2	26 50	72 00	81·7	26 41	70 54	81·2	208	332
29	151	28 18	76 20	83·4	28 11	75 13	82·9	28 04	74 05	82·4	27 55	72 58	81·8	27 47	71 51	81·3	27 37	70 44	80·8	209	331
30	150	29 17	76 13	83·2	29 09	75 04	82·6	29 01	73 56	82·0	28 53	72 48	81·5	28 44	71 41	81·0	28 34	70 33	80·4	210	330
31	149	30 15	76 04	82·9	30 07	74 56	82·3	29 59	73 47	81·7	29 50	72 38	81·2	29 41	71 30	80·6	29 30	70 22	80·0	211	329
32	148	31 13	75 56	82·6	31 05	74 46	82·0	30 57	73 37	81·4	30 47	72 28	80·8	30 37	71 19	80·2	30 27	70 11	79·6	212	328
33	147	32 11	75 47	82·3	32 03	74 37	81·7	31 54	73 27	81·1	31 44	72 17	80·5	31 34	71 07	79·9	31 23	69 58	79·2	213	327
34	146	33 10	75 37	82·0	33 01	74 26	81·4	32 52	73 16	80·7	32 42	72 05	80·1	32 31	70 55	79·5	32 20	69 45	78·8	214	326
35	145	34 08	75 27	81·7	33 59	74 16	81·0	33 49	73 04	80·4	33 39	71 53	79·7	33 28	70 42	79·1	33 16	69 32	78·4	215	325
36	144	35 06	75 17	81·4	34 56	74 04	80·7	34 46	72 52	80·0	34 36	71 40	79·4	34 24	70 29	78·7	34 12	69 18	78·0	216	324
37	143	36 04	75 06	81·1	35 54	73 53	80·4	35 44	72 40	79·7	35 33	71 27	79·0	35 21	70 15	78·3	35 08	69 03	77·6	217	323
38	142	37 02	74 54	80·8	36 52	73 40	80·0	36 41	72 27	79·3	36 29	71 13	78·6	36 17	70 00	77·8	36 04	68 48	77·1	218	322
39	141	38 00	74 42	80·4	37 49	73 27	79·7	37 38	72 13	78·9	37 26	70 59	78·2	37 13	69 45	77·4	37 00	68 32	76·7	219	321
40	140	38 57	74 30	80·1	38 47	73 14	79·3	38 35	71 58	78·5	38 23	70 43	77·7	38 10	69 29	77·0	37 56	68 15	76·2	220	320
41	139	39 55	74 16	79·8	39 44	72 59	78·9	39 32	71 43	78·1	39 19	70 27	77·3	39 06	69 12	76·5	38 51	67 57	75·7	221	319
42	138	40 53	74 02	79·4	40 41	72 45	78·5	40 29	71 27	77·7	40 16	70 10	76·9	40 02	68 54	76·1	39 47	67 38	75·3	222	318
43	137	41 51	73 48	79·0	41 39	72 29	78·2	41 26	71 11	77·3	41 12	69 53	76·4	40 58	68 35	75·6	40 42	67 19	74·7	223	317
44	136	42 48	73 32	78·6	42 36	72 12	77·7	42 23	70 53	76·9	42 09	69 34	76·0	41 54	68 16	75·1	41 38	66 58	74·2	224	316
45	135	43 46	73 16	78·3	43 33	71 55	77·3	43 19	70 35	76·4	43 05	69 15	75·5	42 49	67 56	74·6	42 33	66 37	73·7	225	315

Lat. / A		12°			13°			14°			15°			16°			17°			Lat. / A	
LHA/F		A/H	B/P	Z_1/Z_2	A/H	B/P	Z_1/Z_2	A/H	B/P	Z_1/Z_2	A/H	B/P	Z_1/Z_2	A/H	B/P	Z_1/Z_2	A/H	B/P	Z_1/Z_2	LHA	
°	°	° ′	° ′	°	° ′	° ′	°	° ′	° ′	°	° ′	° ′	°	° ′	° ′	°	° ′	° ′	°	°	°
45	135	43 46	73 16	78·3	43 33	71 55	77·3	43 19	70 35	76·4	43 05	69 15	75·5	42 49	67 56	74·6	42 33	66 37	73·7	225	315
46	134	44 43	72 59	77·8	44 30	71 37	76·9	44 16	70 15	75·9	44 01	68 54	75·0	43 45	67 34	74·1	43 28	66 15	73·2	226	314
47	133	45 40	72 41	77·4	45 27	71 18	76·4	45 12	69 55	75·5	44 57	68 33	74·5	44 40	67 12	73·5	44 23	65 51	72·6	227	313
48	132	46 38	72 23	77·0	46 24	70 58	76·0	46 09	69 34	75·0	45 53	68 11	74·0	45 35	66 48	73·0	45 17	65 27	72·0	228	312
49	131	47 35	72 03	76·5	47 20	70 37	75·5	47 05	69 11	74·4	46 48	67 47	73·4	46 30	66 23	72·4	46 12	65 01	71·4	229	311
50	130	48 32	71 42	76·1	48 17	70 15	75·0	48 01	68 48	73·9	47 44	67 22	72·9	47 25	65 58	71·8	47 06	64 34	70·8	230	310
51	129	49 29	71 20	75·6	49 13	69 51	74·5	48 57	68 23	73·4	48 39	66 56	72·3	48 20	65 30	71·2	48 00	64 05	70·1	231	309
52	128	50 25	70 57	75·1	50 09	69 27	73·9	49 52	67 57	72·8	49 34	66 29	71·7	49 15	65 02	70·6	48 54	63 35	69·5	232	308
53	127	51 22	70 33	74·6	51 06	69 01	73·4	50 48	67 30	72·2	50 29	66 00	71·0	50 09	64 31	69·9	49 48	63 04	68·8	233	307
54	126	52 19	70 07	74·0	52 02	68 33	72·8	51 43	67 01	71·6	51 24	65 30	70·4	51 03	64 00	69·2	50 41	62 31	68·1	234	306
55	125	53 15	69 40	73·5	52 57	68 04	72·2	52 38	66 30	70·9	52 18	64 58	69·7	51 57	63 26	68·5	51 34	61 56	67·3	235	305
56	124	54 11	69 11	72·9	53 53	67 34	71·6	53 33	65 58	70·3	53 12	64 24	69·0	52 50	62 51	67·8	52 27	61 20	66·6	236	304
57	123	55 07	68 41	72·2	54 48	67 02	70·9	54 28	65 24	69·6	54 06	63 48	68·3	53 43	62 14	67·0	53 19	60 42	65·8	237	303
58	122	56 03	68 09	71·6	55 43	66 28	70·2	55 22	64 48	68·8	55 00	63 11	67·5	54 36	61 35	66·2	54 12	60 01	64·9	238	302
59	121	56 59	67 34	70·9	56 38	65 51	69·5	56 16	64 10	68·1	55 53	62 31	66·7	55 29	60 54	65·4	55 03	59 18	64·1	239	301
60	120	57 54	66 58	70·2	57 33	65 13	68·7	57 10	63 30	67·3	56 46	61 49	65·9	56 21	60 10	64·5	55 55	58 33	63·1	240	300
61	119	58 49	66 20	69·4	58 27	64 32	67·9	58 04	62 47	66·4	57 39	61 04	65·0	57 13	59 24	63·6	56 46	57 46	62·2	241	299
62	118	59 44	65 38	68·6	59 21	63 49	67·1	58 57	62 02	65·5	58 31	60 17	64·0	58 05	58 35	62·6	57 36	56 56	61·2	242	298
63	117	60 38	64 55	67·8	60 15	63 03	66·2	59 50	61 13	64·6	59 23	59 27	63·1	58 55	57 43	61·6	58 26	56 03	60·2	243	297
64	116	61 32	64 08	66·9	61 08	62 14	65·2	60 42	60 22	63·6	60 15	58 34	62·0	59 46	56 49	60·5	59 16	55 06	59·1	244	296
65	115	62 26	63 18	66·0	62 01	61 21	64·2	61 34	59 28	62·6	61 06	57 37	61·0	60 36	55 51	59·4	60 05	54 07	57·9	245	295
66	114	63 20	62 25	65·0	62 53	60 25	63·2	62 26	58 30	61·5	61 56	56 37	59·8	61 25	54 49	58·2	60 53	53 04	56·7	246	294
67	113	64 13	61 27	63·9	63 45	59 25	62·1	63 16	57 27	60·3	62 46	55 34	58·6	62 14	53 44	57·0	61 41	51 57	55·4	247	293
68	112	65 05	60 26	62·8	64 37	58 21	60·9	64 07	56 21	59·1	63 35	54 25	57·4	63 02	52 34	55·7	62 27	50 47	54·1	248	292
69	111	65 57	59 20	61·6	65 27	57 13	59·6	64 56	55 10	57·8	64 23	53 13	56·0	63 49	51 20	54·3	63 14	49 32	52·7	249	291
70	110	66 48	58 08	60·3	66 18	55 59	58·3	65 45	53 55	56·4	65 11	51 55	54·6	64 36	50 01	52·9	63 59	48 12	51·2	250	290
71	109	67 39	56 52	58·9	67 07	54 40	56·8	66 33	52 33	54·9	65 58	50 33	53·1	65 21	48 38	51·3	64 43	46 48	49·7	251	289
72	108	68 29	55 29	57·4	67 55	53 14	55·3	67 20	51 06	53·3	66 44	49 04	51·5	66 06	47 08	49·7	65 26	45 18	48·0	252	288
73	107	69 18	53 59	55·8	68 43	51 42	53·7	68 07	49 33	51·6	67 29	47 30	49·8	66 49	45 33	48·0	66 08	43 43	46·3	253	287
74	106	70 06	52 22	54·1	69 30	50 03	51·9	68 52	47 52	49·8	68 12	45 49	47·9	67 31	43 52	46·1	66 49	42 02	44·4	254	286
75	105	70 53	50 36	52·2	70 15	48 16	50·0	69 36	46 04	47·9	68 55	44 00	46·0	68 12	42 04	44·2	67 29	40 15	42·5	255	285
76	104	71 38	48 42	50·2	70 59	46 20	47·9	70 18	44 08	45·9	69 36	42 05	43·9	68 52	40 09	42·1	68 07	38 21	40·5	256	284
77	103	72 23	46 37	48·0	71 42	44 15	45·7	70 59	42 03	43·7	70 15	40 01	41·7	69 30	38 07	39·9	68 43	36 21	38·3	257	283
78	102	73 06	44 22	45·6	72 23	42 00	43·4	71 38	39 49	41·3	70 53	37 49	39·4	70 06	35 57	37·6	69 18	34 13	36·0	258	282
79	101	73 47	41 55	43·1	73 02	39 34	40·8	72 16	37 26	38·8	71 28	35 27	36·9	70 40	33 38	35·2	69 50	31 58	33·6	259	281
80	100	74 26	39 15	40·3	73 39	36 57	38·1	72 51	34 51	36·1	72 02	32 57	34·3	71 12	31 12	32·6	70 21	29 36	31·1	260	280
81	99	75 02	36 21	37·3	74 14	34 07	35·1	73 24	32 06	33·2	72 34	30 17	31·5	71 42	28 37	29·9	70 50	27 06	28·4	261	279
82	98	75 37	33 13	34·1	74 46	31 05	32·0	73 55	29 10	30·2	73 03	27 27	28·5	72 09	25 53	27·0	71 16	24 29	25·7	262	278
83	97	76 08	29 50	30·6	75 16	27 50	28·6	74 23	26 03	26·9	73 29	24 27	25·4	72 34	23 02	24·0	71 39	21 44	22·8	263	277
84	96	76 36	26 11	26·8	75 42	24 22	25·0	74 48	22 45	23·5	73 52	21 19	22·1	72 56	20 02	20·9	72 00	18 53	19·8	264	276
85	95	77 01	22 18	22·8	76 05	20 41	21·3	75 09	19 16	19·9	74 12	18 01	18·7	73 15	16 54	17·6	72 18	15 55	16·7	265	275
86	94	77 22	18 10	18·6	76 25	16 49	17·3	75 27	15 38	16·1	74 29	14 36	15·1	73 31	13 40	14·2	72 33	12 51	13·5	266	274
87	93	77 38	13 50	14·1	76 40	12 46	13·1	75 41	11 51	12·2	74 43	11 03	11·4	73 44	10 21	10·8	72 45	9 43	10·2	267	273
88	92	77 50	9 19	9·5	76 51	8 36	8·8	75 52	7 58	8·2	74 52	7 25	7·7	73 53	6 56	7·2	72 53	6 31	6·8	268	272
89	91	77 58	4 42	4·8	76 58	4 19	4·4	75 58	4 00	4·1	74 58	3 44	3·9	73 58	3 29	3·6	72 58	3 16	3·4	269	271
90	90	78 00	0 00	0·0	77 00	0 00	0·0	76 00	0 00	0·0	75 00	0 00	0·0	74 00	0 00	0·0	73 00	0 00	0·0	270	270

N. Lat: for LHA > 180° … $Z_n = Z$
for LHA < 180° … $Z_n = 360° - Z$

S. Lat.: for LHA > 180° … $Z_n = 180° - Z$
for LHA < 180° … $Z_n = 180° + Z$

SIGHT REDUCTION TABLE

B: (−) for 90° < LHA < 270°
Dec:(−) for Lat. contrary name

Z_1: same sign as B
Z_2: (−) for F > 90°

Lat. / A		18°			19°			20°			21°			22°			23°			Lat. / A	
LHA/F		A/H	B/P	Z_1/Z_2	A/H	B/P	Z_1/Z_2	A/H	B/P	Z_1/Z_2	A/H	B/P	Z_1/Z_2	A/H	B/P	Z_1/Z_2	A/H	B/P	Z_1/Z_2	LHA	
°	°	° ′	° ′	°	° ′	° ′	°	° ′	° ′	°	° ′	° ′	°	° ′	° ′	°	° ′	° ′	°	°	°
0	180	0 00	72 00	90·0	0 00	71 00	90·0	0 00	70 00	90·0	0 00	69 00	90·0	0 00	68 00	90·0	0 00	67 00	90·0	180	360
1	179	0 57	72 00	89·7	0 57	71 00	89·7	0 56	70 00	89·7	0 56	69 00	89·6	0 56	68 00	89·6	0 55	67 00	89·6	181	359
2	178	1 54	71 59	89·4	1 53	70 59	89·3	1 53	69 59	89·3	1 52	68 59	89·3	1 51	67 59	89·3	1 50	66 59	89·2	182	358
3	177	2 51	71 59	89·1	2 50	70 59	89·0	2 49	69 58	89·0	2 48	68 58	88·9	2 47	67 58	88·9	2 46	66 58	88·8	183	357
4	176	3 48	71 58	88·8	3 47	70 57	88·7	3 46	69 57	88·6	3 44	68 57	88·6	3 42	67 57	88·5	3 41	66 57	88·4	184	356
5	175	4 45	71 56	88·5	4 44	70 56	88·4	4 42	69 56	88·3	4 40	68 56	88·2	4 38	67 55	88·1	4 36	66 55	88·0	185	355
6	174	5 42	71 54	88·1	5 40	70 54	88·0	5 38	69 54	87·9	5 36	68 54	87·8	5 34	67 53	87·7	5 31	66 53	87·6	186	354
7	173	6 39	71 52	87·8	6 37	70 52	87·7	6 35	69 52	87·6	6 32	68 51	87·5	6 29	67 51	87·4	6 26	66 51	87·3	187	353
8	172	7 36	71 50	87·5	7 34	70 50	87·4	7 31	69 49	87·2	7 28	68 49	87·1	7 25	67 48	87·0	7 22	66 48	86·9	188	352
9	171	8 33	71 47	87·2	8 30	70 47	87·0	8 27	69 46	86·9	8 24	68 46	86·8	8 20	67 45	86·6	8 17	66 45	86·5	189	351
10	170	9 30	71 44	86·9	9 27	70 44	86·7	9 23	69 43	86·5	9 20	68 42	86·4	9 16	67 42	86·2	9 12	66 41	86·1	190	350
11	169	10 27	71 41	86·6	10 24	70 40	86·4	10 20	69 39	86·2	10 16	68 39	86·0	10 11	67 38	85·8	10 07	66 37	85·7	191	349
12	168	11 24	71 37	86·2	11 20	70 36	86·0	11 16	69 35	85·8	11 12	68 34	85·6	11 07	67 33	85·4	11 02	66 32	85·3	192	348
13	167	12 21	71 33	85·9	12 17	70 32	85·7	12 12	69 31	85·5	12 07	68 30	85·3	12 02	67 29	85·1	11 57	66 28	84·8	193	347
14	166	13 18	71 29	85·6	13 13	70 28	85·4	13 08	69 26	85·1	13 03	68 25	84·9	12 58	67 24	84·7	12 52	66 22	84·4	194	346
15	165	14 15	71 24	85·3	14 10	70 23	85·0	14 05	69 21	84·8	13 59	68 20	84·5	13 53	67 18	84·3	13 47	66 17	84·0	195	345
16	164	15 12	71 19	84·9	15 06	70 18	84·7	15 01	69 16	84·4	14 55	68 14	84·1	14 48	67 12	83·9	14 42	66 10	83·6	196	344
17	163	16 09	71 14	84·6	16 03	70 12	84·3	15 57	69 10	84·0	15 50	68 08	83·7	15 44	67 06	83·5	15 37	66 04	83·2	197	343
18	162	17 05	71 08	84·3	16 59	70 06	84·0	16 53	69 03	83·7	16 46	68 01	83·4	16 39	66 59	83·1	16 32	65 57	82·8	198	342
19	161	18 02	71 02	83·9	17 56	69 59	83·6	17 49	68 57	83·3	17 42	67 54	83·0	17 34	66 52	82·7	17 26	65 49	82·3	199	341
20	160	18 59	70 56	83·6	18 52	69 53	83·2	18 45	68 50	82·9	18 37	67 47	82·6	18 29	66 44	82·2	18 21	65 41	81·9	200	340
21	159	19 56	70 49	83·2	19 48	69 45	82·9	19 41	68 42	82·5	19 33	67 39	82·2	19 24	66 36	81·8	19 16	65 33	81·5	201	339
22	158	20 52	70 41	82·9	20 45	69 38	82·5	20 37	68 34	82·1	20 28	67 31	81·8	20 19	66 27	81·4	20 10	65 24	81·0	202	338
23	157	21 49	70 33	82·5	21 41	69 29	82·1	21 32	68 26	81·7	21 24	67 22	81·4	21 14	66 18	81·0	21 05	65 15	80·6	203	337
24	156	22 45	70 25	82·2	22 37	69 21	81·8	22 28	68 17	81·3	22 19	67 12	80·9	22 09	66 09	80·5	21 59	65 05	80·1	204	336
25	155	23 42	70 17	81·8	23 33	69 12	81·4	23 24	68 07	80·9	23 14	67 03	80·5	23 04	65 58	80·1	22 54	64 54	79·7	205	335
26	154	24 38	70 07	81·4	24 29	69 02	81·0	24 20	67 57	80·5	24 09	66 52	80·1	23 59	65 48	79·6	23 48	64 43	79·2	206	334
27	153	25 35	69 58	81·1	25 25	68 52	80·6	25 15	67 47	80·1	25 05	66 42	79·7	24 54	65 36	79·2	24 42	64 32	78·7	207	333
28	152	26 31	69 48	80·7	26 21	68 42	80·2	26 11	67 36	79·7	26 00	66 30	79·2	25 48	65 25	78·7	25 36	64 19	78·3	208	332
29	151	27 27	69 37	80·3	27 17	68 31	79·8	27 06	67 24	79·3	26 55	66 18	78·8	26 43	65 12	78·3	26 30	64 07	77·8	209	331
30	150	28 24	69 26	79·9	28 13	68 19	79·4	28 01	67 12	78·8	27 50	66 06	78·3	27 37	64 59	77·8	27 24	63 53	77·3	210	330
31	149	29 20	69 14	79·5	29 09	68 07	78·9	28 57	67 00	78·4	28 44	65 53	77·8	28 31	64 46	77·3	28 18	63 39	76·8	211	329
32	148	30 16	69 02	79·1	30 04	67 54	78·5	29 52	66 46	77·9	29 39	65 39	77·4	29 26	64 32	76·8	29 12	63 25	76·3	212	328
33	147	31 12	68 49	78·7	31 00	67 41	78·1	30 47	66 32	77·5	30 34	65 24	76·9	30 20	64 17	76·3	30 05	63 09	75·8	213	327
34	146	32 08	68 36	78·2	31 55	67 27	77·6	31 42	66 18	77·0	31 28	65 09	76·4	31 14	64 01	75·8	30 59	62 53	75·2	214	326
35	145	33 04	68 22	77·8	32 51	67 12	77·2	32 37	66 03	76·5	32 23	64 54	75·9	32 08	63 45	75·3	31 52	62 36	74·7	215	325
36	144	33 59	68 07	77·3	33 46	66 57	76·7	33 32	65 47	76·0	33 17	64 37	75·4	33 01	63 28	74·8	32 45	62 19	74·2	216	324
37	143	34 55	67 52	76·9	34 41	66 41	76·2	34 26	65 30	75·5	34 11	64 20	74·9	33 55	63 10	74·2	33 38	62 01	73·6	217	323
38	142	35 50	67 36	76·4	35 36	66 24	75·7	35 21	65 13	75·0	35 05	64 02	74·4	34 48	62 51	73·7	34 31	61 41	73·0	218	322
39	141	36 46	67 19	76·0	36 31	66 06	75·2	36 15	64 54	74·5	35 59	63 43	73·8	35 42	62 32	73·1	35 24	61 21	72·4	219	321
40	140	37 41	67 01	75·5	37 26	65 48	74·7	37 10	64 35	74·0	36 53	63 23	73·3	36 35	62 12	72·6	36 17	61 01	71·8	220	320
41	139	38 36	66 42	75·0	38 20	65 29	74·2	38 04	64 15	73·4	37 46	63 02	72·7	37 28	61 50	72·0	37 09	60 39	71·2	221	319
42	138	39 31	66 23	74·5	39 15	65 08	73·7	38 58	63 54	72·9	38 40	62 41	72·1	38 21	61 28	71·4	38 01	60 16	70·6	222	318
43	137	40 26	66 03	73·9	40 09	64 47	73·1	39 51	63 33	72·3	39 33	62 18	71·5	39 13	61 05	70·7	38 53	59 52	70·0	223	317
44	136	41 21	65 42	73·4	41 03	64 25	72·5	40 45	63 10	71·7	40 26	61 55	70·9	40 06	60 41	70·1	39 45	59 27	69·3	224	316
45	135	42 16	65 19	72·8	41 57	64 02	72·0	41 38	62 46	71·1	41 19	61 30	70·3	40 58	60 15	69·5	40 37	59 01	68·7	225	315

Lat. / A		18°			19°			20°			21°			22°			23°			Lat. / A	
LHA/F		A/H	B/P	Z_1/Z_2	A/H	B/P	Z_1/Z_2	A/H	B/P	Z_1/Z_2	A/H	B/P	Z_1/Z_2	A/H	B/P	Z_1/Z_2	A/H	B/P	Z_1/Z_2	LHA	
°	°	° ′	° ′	°	° ′	° ′	°	° ′	° ′	°	° ′	° ′	°	° ′	° ′	°	° ′	° ′	°	°	°
45	135	42 16	65 19	72·8	41 57	64 02	72·0	41 38	62 46	71·1	41 19	61 30	70·3	40 58	60 15	69·5	40 37	59 01	68·7	225	315
46	134	43 10	64 56	72·3	42 51	63 38	71·4	42 32	62 21	70·5	42 11	61 05	69·6	41 50	59 49	68·8	41 28	58 34	68·0	226	314
47	133	44 04	64 32	71·7	43 45	63 13	70·8	43 25	61 55	69·9	43 04	60 38	69·0	42 42	59 21	68·1	42 19	58 06	67·3	227	313
48	132	44 58	64 06	71·1	44 38	62 46	70·1	44 18	61 27	69·2	43 56	60 09	68·3	43 33	58 53	67·4	43 10	57 37	66·5	228	312
49	131	45 52	63 39	70·4	45 32	62 18	69·5	45 10	60 59	68·5	44 48	59 40	67·6	44 24	58 22	66·7	44 00	57 06	65·8	229	311
50	130	46 46	63 11	69·8	46 25	61 49	68·8	46 03	60 29	67·8	45 39	59 09	66·9	45 15	57 51	65·9	44 50	56 34	65·0	230	310
51	129	47 39	62 42	69·1	47 17	61 19	68·1	46 55	59 57	67·1	46 31	58 37	66·1	46 06	57 18	65·2	45 40	56 00	64·2	231	309
52	128	48 33	62 11	68·4	48 10	60 47	67·4	47 46	59 25	66·4	47 22	58 03	65·4	46 56	56 44	64·4	46 30	55 25	63·4	232	308
53	127	49 25	61 38	67·7	49 02	60 13	66·6	48 38	58 50	65·6	48 13	57 28	64·6	47 46	56 07	63·6	47 19	54 48	62·6	233	307
54	126	50 18	61 04	67·0	49 54	59 38	65·9	49 29	58 14	64·8	49 03	56 51	63·7	48 36	55 30	62·7	48 08	54 10	61·7	234	306
55	125	51 10	60 28	66·2	50 46	59 01	65·1	50 20	57 36	64·0	49 53	56 12	62·9	49 25	54 50	61·9	48 56	53 30	60·8	235	305
56	124	52 03	59 50	65·4	51 37	58 23	64·2	51 10	56 56	63·1	50 43	55 32	62·0	50 14	54 09	61·0	49 44	52 48	59·9	236	304
57	123	52 54	59 11	64·6	52 28	57 42	63·4	52 00	56 15	62·2	51 32	54 49	61·1	51 02	53 26	60·0	50 32	52 04	59·0	237	303
58	122	53 46	58 29	63·7	53 18	56 59	62·5	52 50	55 31	61·3	52 21	54 05	60·2	51 50	52 41	59·1	51 19	51 18	58·0	238	302
59	121	54 37	57 45	62·8	54 08	56 14	61·5	53 39	54 45	60·4	53 09	53 18	59·2	52 38	51 53	58·1	52 06	50 30	57·0	239	301
60	120	55 27	56 59	61·8	54 58	55 27	60·6	54 28	53 57	59·4	53 57	52 29	58·2	53 25	51 04	57·0	52 52	49 40	55·9	240	300
61	119	56 17	56 10	60·9	55 47	54 37	59·6	55 16	53 06	58·3	54 44	51 38	57·1	54 11	50 12	55·9	53 37	48 48	54·8	241	299
62	118	57 07	55 19	59·8	56 36	53 45	58·5	56 04	52 13	57·2	55 31	50 44	56·0	54 57	49 17	54·8	54 22	47 53	53·7	242	298
63	117	57 56	54 25	58·8	57 24	52 49	57·4	56 51	51 17	56·1	56 17	49 47	54·9	55 42	48 20	53·7	55 06	46 55	52·5	243	297
64	116	58 44	53 27	57·6	58 12	51 51	56·3	57 38	50 18	55·0	57 03	48 48	53·7	56 27	47 20	52·5	55 50	45 55	51·3	244	296
65	115	59 32	52 27	56·5	58 58	50 50	55·1	58 24	49 16	53·7	57 47	47 45	52·5	57 10	46 17	51·2	56 32	44 52	50·0	245	295
66	114	60 19	51 23	55·2	59 45	49 45	53·8	59 09	48 11	52·5	58 32	46 39	51·2	57 53	45 11	49·9	57 14	43 47	48·7	246	294
67	113	61 06	50 15	53·9	60 30	48 37	52·5	59 53	47 02	51·1	59 15	45 30	49·8	58 36	44 02	48·6	57 55	42 38	47·4	247	293
68	112	61 52	49 04	52·6	61 15	47 25	51·1	60 36	45 50	49·8	59 57	44 18	48·4	59 17	42 50	47·2	58 36	41 26	46·0	248	292
69	111	62 37	47 48	51·2	61 58	46 09	49·7	61 19	44 33	48·3	60 39	43 02	47·0	59 57	41 34	45·7	59 15	40 10	44·5	249	291
70	110	63 21	46 28	49·7	62 41	44 48	48·2	62 01	43 13	46·8	61 19	41 42	45·4	60 36	40 15	44·2	59 53	38 52	43·0	250	290
71	109	64 04	45 03	48·1	63 23	43 24	46·6	62 41	41 49	45·2	61 58	40 18	43·9	61 15	38 52	42·6	60 30	37 29	41·4	251	289
72	108	64 45	43 34	46·4	64 04	41 54	44·9	63 21	40 20	43·5	62 37	38 50	42·2	61 52	37 25	40·9	61 06	36 03	39·7	252	288
73	107	65 26	41 59	44·7	64 43	40 20	43·2	63 59	38 46	41·8	63 14	37 18	40·5	62 27	35 53	39·2	61 41	34 34	38·0	253	287
74	106	66 06	40 19	42·9	65 21	38 41	41·4	64 36	37 08	40·0	63 49	35 41	38·7	63 02	34 18	37·4	62 14	33 00	36·3	254	286
75	105	66 44	38 32	40·9	65 58	36 56	39·5	65 11	35 25	38·1	64 23	33 59	36·8	63 35	32 39	35·6	62 46	31 22	34·4	255	285
76	104	67 20	36 40	38·9	66 33	35 05	37·4	65 45	33 37	36·1	64 56	32 13	34·8	64 07	30 55	33·6	63 16	29 41	32·5	256	284
77	103	67 55	34 42	36·8	67 07	33 09	35·3	66 18	31 43	34·0	65 27	30 22	32·8	64 37	29 06	31·6	63 45	27 55	30·6	257	283
78	102	68 29	32 37	34·5	67 39	31 07	33·1	66 48	29 44	31·9	65 57	28 26	30·7	65 05	27 14	29·6	64 13	26 06	28·5	258	282
79	101	69 00	30 25	32·2	68 09	29 00	30·8	67 17	27 40	29·6	66 25	26 26	28·5	65 32	25 17	27·4	64 38	24 12	26·4	259	281
80	100	69 29	28 07	29·7	68 37	26 46	28·4	67 44	25 30	27·3	66 50	24 20	26·2	65 56	23 15	25·2	65 02	22 15	24·3	260	280
81	99	69 57	25 43	27·1	69 03	24 26	25·9	68 09	23 15	24·8	67 14	22 10	23·8	66 19	21 10	22·9	65 23	20 14	22·1	261	279
82	98	70 21	23 11	24·5	69 27	22 00	23·3	68 31	20 56	22·3	67 36	19 56	21·4	66 40	19 00	20·6	65 43	18 09	19·8	262	278
83	97	70 44	20 34	21·7	69 48	19 29	20·7	68 51	18 31	19·7	67 55	17 37	18·9	66 58	16 47	18·1	66 01	16 01	17·4	263	277
84	96	71 03	17 50	18·8	70 07	16 53	17·9	69 09	16 01	17·1	68 12	15 14	16·3	67 14	14 30	15·7	66 16	13 50	15·1	264	276
85	95	71 20	15 01	15·8	70 23	14 12	15·0	69 25	13 28	14·3	68 26	12 48	13·7	67 28	12 10	13·1	66 29	11 36	12·6	265	275
86	94	71 35	12 07	12·8	70 36	11 27	12·1	69 37	10 51	11·6	68 38	10 18	11·0	67 39	9 48	10·6	66 40	9 20	10·1	266	274
87	93	71 46	9 09	9·6	70 46	8 39	9·1	69 47	8 11	8·7	68 48	7 46	8·3	67 48	7 23	8·0	66 49	7 02	7·6	267	273
88	92	71 54	6 08	6·4	70 54	5 47	6·1	69 54	5 29	5·8	68 55	5 12	5·6	67 55	4 56	5·3	66 55	4 42	5·1	268	272
89	91	71 58	3 04	3·2	70 58	2 54	3·1	69 59	2 45	2·9	68 59	2 36	2·8	67 59	2 28	2·7	66 59	2 21	2·6	269	271
90	90	72 00	0 00	0·0	71 00	0 00	0·0	70 00	0 00	0·0	69 00	0 00	0·0	68 00	0 00	0·0	67 00	0 00	0·0	270	270

N. Lat: for LHA > 180° … $Z_n = Z$
for LHA < 180° … $Z_n = 360° - Z$

S. Lat.: for LHA > 180° … $Z_n = 180° - Z$
for LHA < 180° … $Z_n = 180° + Z$

SIGHT REDUCTION TABLE

B: (–) for 90° < LHA < 270°
Dec:(–) for Lat. contrary name

Z_1: same sign as B
Z_2: (–) for F > 90°

Lat. / A		24°			25°			26°			27°			28°			29°			Lat. / A	
LHA/F		A/H	B/P	Z_1/Z_2	A/H	B/P	Z_1/Z_2	A/H	B/P	Z_1/Z_2	A/H	B/P	Z_1/Z_2	A/H	B/P	Z_1/Z_2	A/H	B/P	Z_1/Z_2	LHA	
°	°	° ′	° ′	°	° ′	° ′	°	° ′	° ′	°	° ′	° ′	°	° ′	° ′	°	° ′	° ′	°	°	°
0	180	0 00	66 00	90·0	0 00	65 00	90·0	0 00	64 00	90·0	0 00	63 00	90·0	0 00	62 00	90·0	0 00	61 00	90·0	180	360
1	179	0 55	66 00	89·6	0 54	65 00	89·6	0 54	64 00	89·6	0 53	63 00	89·5	0 53	62 00	89·5	0 52	61 00	89·5	181	359
2	178	1 50	65 59	89·2	1 49	64 59	89·2	1 48	63 59	89·1	1 47	62 59	89·1	1 46	61 59	89·1	1 45	60 59	89·0	182	358
3	177	2 44	65 58	88·8	2 43	64 58	88·7	2 42	63 58	88·7	2 40	62 58	88·6	2 39	61 58	88·6	2 37	60 58	88·5	183	357
4	176	3 39	65 57	88·4	3 37	64 57	88·3	3 36	63 57	88·2	3 34	62 57	88·2	3 32	61 57	88·1	3 30	60 56	88·1	184	356
5	175	4 34	65 55	88·0	4 32	64 55	87·9	4 30	63 55	87·8	4 27	62 55	87·7	4 25	61 55	87·6	4 22	60 54	87·6	185	355
6	174	5 29	65 53	87·6	5 26	64 53	87·5	5 23	63 53	87·4	5 21	62 52	87·3	5 18	61 52	87·2	5 15	60 52	87·1	186	354
7	173	6 24	65 50	87·1	6 20	64 50	87·0	6 17	63 50	86·9	6 14	62 50	86·8	6 11	61 49	86·7	6 07	60 49	86·6	187	353
8	172	7 18	65 47	86·7	7 15	64 47	86·6	7 11	63 47	86·5	7 07	62 46	86·3	7 04	61 46	86·2	6 59	60 46	86·1	188	352
9	171	8 13	65 44	86·3	8 09	64 44	86·2	8 05	63 43	86·0	8 01	62 43	85·9	7 56	61 42	85·7	7 52	60 42	85·6	189	351
10	170	9 08	65 40	85·9	9 03	64 40	85·7	8 59	63 39	85·6	8 54	62 39	85·4	8 49	61 38	85·3	8 44	60 38	85·1	190	350
11	169	10 02	65 36	85·5	9 57	64 35	85·3	9 52	63 35	85·1	9 47	62 34	85·0	9 42	61 33	84·8	9 36	60 33	84·6	191	349
12	168	10 57	65 32	85·1	10 52	64 31	84·9	10 46	63 30	84·7	10 41	62 29	84·5	10 35	61 28	84·3	10 29	60 28	84·1	192	348
13	167	11 52	65 27	84·6	11 46	64 26	84·4	11 40	63 25	84·2	11 34	62 24	84·0	11 27	61 23	83·8	11 21	60 22	83·6	193	347
14	166	12 46	65 21	84·2	12 40	64 20	84·0	12 34	63 19	83·8	12 27	62 18	83·5	12 20	61 17	83·3	12 13	60 16	83·1	194	346
15	165	13 41	65 15	83·8	13 34	64 14	83·5	13 27	63 13	83·3	13 20	62 11	83·1	13 13	61 10	82·8	13 05	60 09	82·6	195	345
16	164	14 35	65 09	83·3	14 28	64 07	83·1	14 21	63 06	82·8	14 13	62 04	82·6	14 05	61 03	82·3	13 57	60 02	82·1	196	344
17	163	15 29	65 02	82·9	15 22	64 00	82·6	15 14	62 59	82·4	15 06	61 57	82·1	14 58	60 56	81·8	14 49	59 54	81·6	197	343
18	162	16 24	64 55	82·5	16 16	63 53	82·2	16 08	62 51	81·9	15 59	61 49	81·6	15 50	60 47	81·3	15 41	59 46	81·0	198	342
19	161	17 18	64 47	82·0	17 10	63 45	81·7	17 01	62 43	81·4	16 52	61 41	81·1	16 42	60 39	80·8	16 33	59 37	80·5	199	341
20	160	18 12	64 39	81·6	18 03	63 36	81·3	17 54	62 34	80·9	17 45	61 32	80·6	17 35	60 30	80·3	17 24	59 28	80·0	200	340
21	159	19 07	64 30	81·1	18 57	63 28	80·8	18 47	62 25	80·4	18 37	61 23	80·1	18 27	60 20	79·8	18 16	59 18	79·5	201	339
22	158	20 01	64 21	80·7	19 51	63 18	80·3	19 41	62 15	80·0	19 30	61 13	79·6	19 19	60 10	79·3	19 08	59 08	78·9	202	338
23	157	20 55	64 11	80·2	20 44	63 08	79·8	20 34	62 05	79·5	20 22	61 02	79·1	20 11	59 59	78·7	19 59	58 57	78·4	203	337
24	156	21 49	64 01	79·7	21 38	62 58	79·3	21 27	61 54	79·0	21 15	60 51	78·6	21 03	59 48	78·2	20 50	58 45	77·8	204	336
25	155	22 43	63 50	79·3	22 31	62 46	78·9	22 19	61 43	78·4	22 07	60 39	78·0	21 55	59 36	77·7	21 42	58 33	77·3	205	335
26	154	23 36	63 39	78·8	23 25	62 35	78·4	23 12	61 31	77·9	22 59	60 27	77·5	22 46	59 24	77·1	22 33	58 20	76·7	206	334
27	153	24 30	63 27	78·3	24 18	62 22	77·8	24 05	61 18	77·4	23 52	60 14	77·0	23 38	59 10	76·5	23 24	58 07	76·1	207	333
28	152	25 24	63 14	77·8	25 11	62 10	77·3	24 57	61 05	76·9	24 44	60 01	76·4	24 29	58 57	76·0	24 15	57 53	75·5	208	332
29	151	26 17	63 01	77·3	26 04	61 56	76·8	25 50	60 51	76·3	25 36	59 47	75·9	25 21	58 42	75·4	25 05	57 38	75·0	209	331
30	150	27 11	62 48	76·8	26 57	61 42	76·3	26 42	60 37	75·8	26 27	59 32	75·3	26 12	58 27	74·8	25 56	57 23	74·4	210	330
31	149	28 04	62 33	76·3	27 50	61 27	75·8	27 35	60 22	75·2	27 19	59 16	74·7	27 03	58 11	74·2	26 46	57 07	73·8	211	329
32	148	28 57	62 18	75·7	28 42	61 12	75·2	28 27	60 06	74·7	28 10	59 00	74·2	27 54	57 55	73·7	27 37	56 50	73·1	212	328
33	147	29 50	62 02	75·2	29 35	60 56	74·7	29 19	59 49	74·1	29 02	58 43	73·6	28 45	57 38	73·0	28 27	56 32	72·5	213	327
34	146	30 43	61 46	74·7	30 27	60 39	74·1	30 10	59 32	73·5	29 53	58 26	73·0	29 35	57 20	72·4	29 17	56 14	71·9	214	326
35	145	31 36	61 28	74·1	31 19	60 21	73·5	31 02	59 14	72·9	30 44	58 07	72·4	30 26	57 01	71·8	30 07	55 55	71·2	215	325
36	144	32 29	61 10	73·5	32 11	60 02	72·9	31 53	58 55	72·3	31 35	57 48	71·7	31 16	56 41	71·2	30 56	55 35	70·6	216	324
37	143	33 21	60 52	73·0	33 03	59 43	72·3	32 45	58 35	71·7	32 26	57 28	71·1	32 06	56 21	70·5	31 46	55 14	69·9	217	323
38	142	34 13	60 32	72·4	33 55	59 23	71·7	33 36	58 15	71·1	33 16	57 07	70·5	32 56	55 59	69·9	32 35	54 53	69·3	218	322
39	141	35 06	60 11	71·8	34 47	59 02	71·1	34 27	57 53	70·5	34 06	56 45	69·8	33 45	55 37	69·2	33 24	54 30	68·6	219	321
40	140	35 58	59 50	71·2	35 38	58 40	70·5	35 17	57 31	69·8	34 56	56 22	69·1	34 35	55 14	68·5	34 12	54 07	67·9	220	320
41	139	36 49	59 28	70·5	36 29	58 17	69·8	36 08	57 08	69·1	35 46	55 59	68·5	35 24	54 50	67·8	35 01	53 42	67·1	221	319
42	138	37 41	59 04	69·9	37 20	57 54	69·2	36 58	56 43	68·5	36 36	55 34	67·8	36 13	54 25	67·1	35 49	53 17	66·4	222	318
43	137	38 32	58 40	69·2	38 11	57 29	68·5	37 48	56 18	67·8	37 25	55 08	67·1	37 02	53 59	66·4	36 37	52 50	65·7	223	317
44	136	39 23	58 15	68·6	39 01	57 03	67·8	38 38	55 52	67·1	38 14	54 41	66·3	37 50	53 32	65·6	37 25	52 23	64·9	224	316
45	135	40 14	57 48	67·9	39 51	56 36	67·1	39 28	55 24	66·3	39 03	54 13	65·6	38 38	53 04	64·9	38 12	51 54	64·1	225	315

Lat. / A		24°			25°			26°			27°			28°			29°			Lat. / A	
LHA/F		A/H	B/P	Z_1/Z_2	A/H	B/P	Z_1/Z_2	A/H	B/P	Z_1/Z_2	A/H	B/P	Z_1/Z_2	A/H	B/P	Z_1/Z_2	A/H	B/P	Z_1/Z_2	LHA	
°	°	° ′	° ′	°	° ′	° ′	°	° ′	° ′	°	° ′	° ′	°	° ′	° ′	°	° ′	° ′	°	°	°
45	135	40 14	57 48	67·9	39 51	56 36	67·1	39 28	55 24	66·3	39 03	54 13	65·6	38 38	53 04	64·9	38 12	51 54	64·1	225	315
46	134	41 05	57 21	67·2	40 41	56 08	66·4	40 17	54 56	65·6	39 52	53 44	64·8	39 26	52 34	64·1	38 59	51 25	63·3	226	314
47	133	41 55	56 52	66·4	41 31	55 38	65·6	41 06	54 26	64·8	40 40	53 14	64·0	40 13	52 04	63·3	39 46	50 54	62·5	227	313
48	132	42 45	56 22	65·7	42 20	55 08	64·9	41 54	53 55	64·0	41 28	52 43	63·2	41 00	51 32	62·5	40 32	50 22	61·7	228	312
49	131	43 35	55 50	64·9	43 09	54 36	64·1	42 43	53 22	63·2	42 15	52 10	62·4	41 47	50 59	61·6	41 18	49 48	60·9	229	311
50	130	44 25	55 17	64·1	43 58	54 02	63·3	43 31	52 49	62·4	43 03	51 36	61·6	42 34	50 24	60·8	42 04	49 14	60·0	230	310
51	129	45 14	54 43	63·3	44 47	53 28	62·4	44 18	52 13	61·6	43 49	51 00	60·7	43 20	49 48	59·9	42 49	48 38	59·1	231	309
52	128	46 03	54 08	62·5	45 35	52 52	61·6	45 06	51 37	60·7	44 36	50 23	59·8	44 05	49 11	59·0	43 34	48 00	58·2	232	308
53	127	46 51	53 30	61·6	46 22	52 14	60·7	45 52	50 59	59·8	45 22	49 45	58·9	44 51	48 32	58·1	44 18	47 21	57·2	233	307
54	126	47 39	52 51	60·8	47 09	51 34	59·8	46 39	50 19	58·9	46 07	49 05	58·0	45 35	47 52	57·1	45 02	46 41	56·3	234	306
55	125	48 27	52 11	59·8	47 56	50 53	58·9	47 25	49 37	58·0	46 53	48 23	57·0	46 19	47 10	56·2	45 46	45 59	55·3	235	305
56	124	49 14	51 28	58·9	48 43	50 11	57·9	48 10	48 54	57·0	47 37	47 40	56·1	47 03	46 27	55·2	46 29	45 15	54·3	236	304
57	123	50 01	50 44	57·9	49 28	49 26	56·9	48 55	48 09	56·0	48 21	46 54	55·0	47 46	45 41	54·1	47 11	44 30	53·3	237	303
58	122	50 47	49 58	56·9	50 14	48 39	55·9	49 40	47 22	54·9	49 05	46 07	54·0	48 29	44 54	53·1	47 53	43 43	52·2	238	302
59	121	51 33	49 09	55·9	50 58	47 51	54·9	50 23	46 34	53·9	49 48	45 18	52·9	49 11	44 05	52·0	48 34	42 54	51·1	239	301
60	120	52 18	48 19	54·8	51 43	47 00	53·8	51 07	45 43	52·8	50 30	44 28	51·8	49 53	43 14	50·9	49 14	42 03	50·0	240	300
61	119	53 02	47 26	53·7	52 26	46 07	52·7	51 49	44 50	51·7	51 12	43 35	50·7	50 33	42 22	49·7	49 54	41 10	48·8	241	299
62	118	53 46	46 31	52·6	53 09	45 12	51·5	52 31	43 54	50·5	51 53	42 39	49·5	51 13	41 27	48·6	50 33	40 16	47·6	242	298
63	117	54 29	45 33	51·4	53 51	44 14	50·3	53 13	42 57	49·3	52 33	41 42	48·3	51 53	40 30	47·3	51 12	39 19	46·4	243	297
64	116	55 12	44 33	50·2	54 33	43 14	49·1	53 53	41 57	48·1	53 13	40 42	47·1	52 31	39 30	46·1	51 49	38 20	45·2	244	296
65	115	55 53	43 30	48·9	55 13	42 11	47·8	54 33	40 55	46·8	53 51	39 40	45·8	53 09	38 29	44·8	52 26	37 19	43·9	245	295
66	114	56 34	42 25	47·6	55 53	41 06	46·5	55 12	39 50	45·4	54 29	38 36	44·4	53 46	37 25	43·5	53 02	36 16	42·6	246	294
67	113	57 14	41 16	46·2	56 32	39 58	45·1	55 50	38 42	44·1	55 06	37 29	43·1	54 22	36 19	42·1	53 37	35 11	41·2	247	293
68	112	57 53	40 05	44·8	57 10	38 47	43·7	56 27	37 32	42·7	55 42	36 19	41·7	54 57	35 10	40·7	54 11	34 03	39·8	248	292
69	111	58 32	38 50	43·3	57 47	37 33	42·2	57 03	36 18	41·2	56 17	35 07	40·2	55 31	33 59	39·3	54 44	32 53	38·4	249	291
70	110	59 09	37 32	41·8	58 24	36 16	40·7	57 38	35 02	39·7	56 51	33 52	38·7	56 04	32 45	37·8	55 16	31 41	36·9	250	290
71	109	59 45	36 11	40·2	58 58	34 55	39·2	58 12	33 43	38·1	57 24	32 35	37·2	56 36	31 29	36·3	55 47	30 26	35·4	251	289
72	108	60 19	34 46	38·6	59 32	33 32	37·6	58 44	32 21	36·5	57 56	31 14	35·6	57 07	30 10	34·7	56 17	29 08	33·8	252	288
73	107	60 53	33 18	36·9	60 05	32 05	35·9	59 16	30 56	34·9	58 26	29 51	34·0	57 36	28 48	33·1	56 46	27 49	32·2	253	287
74	106	61 25	31 46	35·2	60 36	30 35	34·2	59 46	29 28	33·2	58 55	28 25	32·3	58 05	27 24	31·4	57 13	26 26	30·6	254	286
75	105	61 56	30 10	33·4	61 06	29 02	32·4	60 15	27 57	31·4	59 23	26 56	30·5	58 31	25 57	29·7	57 39	25 02	28·9	255	285
76	104	62 26	28 31	31·5	61 34	27 25	30·5	60 42	26 23	29·6	59 50	25 24	28·8	58 57	24 28	28·0	58 04	23 35	27·2	256	284
77	103	62 53	26 48	29·6	62 01	25 45	28·6	61 08	24 46	27·8	60 15	23 49	27·0	59 21	22 56	26·2	58 27	22 05	25·5	257	283
78	102	63 20	25 02	27·6	62 26	24 02	26·7	61 32	23 05	25·9	60 38	22 12	25·1	59 44	21 21	24·4	58 49	20 34	23·7	258	282
79	101	63 44	23 12	25·5	62 50	22 15	24·7	61 55	21 22	23·9	61 00	20 32	23·2	60 05	19 44	22·5	59 09	19 00	21·8	259	281
80	100	64 07	21 18	23·4	63 12	20 25	22·6	62 16	19 36	21·9	61 20	18 49	21·2	60 24	18 05	20·6	59 28	17 24	20·0	260	280
81	99	64 28	19 22	21·3	63 32	18 33	20·5	62 35	17 47	19·9	61 39	17 04	19·2	60 42	16 24	18·6	59 45	15 46	18·1	261	279
82	98	64 47	17 22	19·1	63 50	16 37	18·4	62 53	15 56	17·8	61 56	15 17	17·2	60 58	14 40	16·7	60 01	14 06	16·2	262	278
83	97	65 03	15 18	16·8	64 06	14 39	16·2	63 08	14 02	15·6	62 10	13 27	15·1	61 12	12 55	14·7	60 14	12 24	14·2	263	277
84	96	65 18	13 13	14·5	64 20	12 38	14·0	63 22	12 06	13·5	62 23	11 36	13·0	61 25	11 07	12·6	60 26	10 41	12·2	264	276
85	95	65 31	11 05	12·1	64 32	10 35	11·7	63 33	10 08	11·3	62 35	9 42	10·9	61 36	9 19	10·6	60 37	8 56	10·2	265	275
86	94	65 41	8 54	9·8	64 42	8 30	9·4	63 43	8 08	9·1	62 44	7 48	8·8	61 44	7 28	8·5	60 45	7 10	8·2	266	274
87	93	65 49	6 42	7·3	64 50	6 24	7·1	63 50	6 07	6·8	62 51	5 52	6·6	61 51	5 37	6·4	60 52	5 24	6·2	267	273
88	92	65 55	4 29	4·9	64 56	4 17	4·7	63 56	4 06	4·6	62 56	3 55	4·4	61 56	3 45	4·3	60 56	3 36	4·1	268	272
89	91	65 59	2 15	2·5	64 59	2 09	2·4	63 59	2 03	2·3	62 59	1 58	2·2	61 59	1 53	2·1	60 59	1 48	2·1	269	271
90	90	66 00	0 00	0·0	65 00	0 00	0·0	64 00	0 00	0·0	63 00	0 00	0·0	62 00	0 00	0·0	61 00	0 00	0·0	270	270

N. Lat: for LHA > 180° … $Z_n = Z$
for LHA < 180° … $Z_n = 360° - Z$

S. Lat.: for LHA > 180° … $Z_n = 180° - Z$
for LHA < 180° … $Z_n = 180° + Z$

SIGHT REDUCTION TABLE

B: (−) for 90° < LHA < 270°
Dec: (−) for Lat. contrary name

Z_1: same sign as B
Z_2: (−) for F > 90°

Lat. / A		30°			31°			32°			33°			34°			35°			Lat. / A	
LHA/F		A/H	B/P	Z_1/Z_2	A/H	B/P	Z_1/Z_2	A/H	B/P	Z_1/Z_2	A/H	B/P	Z_1/Z_2	A/H	B/P	Z_1/Z_2	A/H	B/P	Z_1/Z_2	LHA	
°	°	° ′	° ′	°	° ′	° ′	°	° ′	° ′	°	° ′	° ′	°	° ′	° ′	°	° ′	° ′	°	°	°
0	180	0 00	60 00	90·0	0 00	59 00	90·0	0 00	58 00	90·0	0 00	57 00	90·0	0 00	56 00	90·0	0 00	55 00	90·0	180	360
1	179	0 52	60 00	89·5	0 51	59 00	89·5	0 51	58 00	89·5	0 50	57 00	89·5	0 50	56 00	89·4	0 49	55 00	89·4	181	359
2	178	1 44	59 59	89·0	1 43	58 59	89·0	1 42	57 59	88·9	1 41	56 59	88·9	1 39	55 59	88·9	1 38	54 59	88·9	182	358
3	177	2 36	59 58	88·5	2 34	58 58	88·5	2 33	57 58	88·4	2 31	56 58	88·4	2 29	55 58	88·3	2 27	54 58	88·3	183	357
4	176	3 28	59 56	88·0	3 26	58 56	87·9	3 23	57 56	87·9	3 21	56 56	87·8	3 19	55 56	87·8	3 17	54 56	87·7	184	356
5	175	4 20	59 54	87·5	4 17	58 54	87·4	4 14	57 54	87·3	4 12	56 54	87·3	4 09	55 54	87·2	4 06	54 54	87·1	185	355
6	174	5 12	59 52	87·0	5 08	58 52	86·9	5 05	57 52	86·8	5 02	56 51	86·7	4 58	55 51	86·6	4 55	54 51	86·6	186	354
7	173	6 04	59 49	86·5	6 00	58 49	86·4	5 56	57 48	86·3	5 52	56 48	86·2	5 48	55 48	86·1	5 44	54 48	86·0	187	353
8	172	6 55	59 45	86·0	6 51	58 45	85·9	6 47	57 45	85·7	6 42	56 45	85·6	6 38	55 44	85·5	6 33	54 44	85·4	188	352
9	171	7 47	59 42	85·5	7 42	58 41	85·3	7 37	57 41	85·2	7 32	56 40	85·1	7 27	55 40	84·9	7 22	54 40	84·8	189	351
10	170	8 39	59 37	85·0	8 34	58 37	84·8	8 28	57 36	84·7	8 22	56 36	84·5	8 17	55 36	84·4	8 11	54 35	84·2	190	350
11	169	9 31	59 32	84·4	9 25	58 32	84·3	9 19	57 31	84·1	9 13	56 31	84·0	9 06	55 30	83·8	9 00	54 30	83·6	191	349
12	168	10 22	59 27	83·9	10 16	58 26	83·8	10 09	57 26	83·6	10 03	56 25	83·4	9 56	55 25	83·2	9 48	54 24	83·0	192	348
13	167	11 14	59 21	83·4	11 07	58 20	83·2	11 00	57 20	83·0	10 52	56 19	82·8	10 45	55 18	82·6	10 37	54 18	82·5	193	347
14	166	12 06	59 15	82·9	11 58	58 14	82·7	11 50	57 13	82·5	11 42	56 12	82·3	11 34	55 12	82·1	11 26	54 11	81·9	194	346
15	165	12 57	59 08	82·4	12 49	58 07	82·1	12 41	57 06	81·9	12 32	56 05	81·7	12 23	55 04	81·5	12 14	54 04	81·3	195	345
16	164	13 49	59 01	81·8	13 40	57 59	81·6	13 31	56 58	81·4	13 22	55 57	81·1	13 13	54 57	80·9	13 03	53 56	80·7	196	344
17	163	14 40	58 53	81·3	14 31	57 51	81·1	14 21	56 50	80·8	14 12	55 49	80·5	14 02	54 48	80·3	13 51	53 47	80·1	197	343
18	162	15 31	58 44	80·8	15 22	57 43	80·5	15 12	56 42	80·2	15 01	55 40	80·0	14 51	54 39	79·7	14 40	53 38	79·4	198	342
19	161	16 23	58 35	80·2	16 12	57 34	79·9	16 02	56 32	79·7	15 51	55 31	79·4	15 40	54 30	79·1	15 28	53 29	78·8	199	341
20	160	17 14	58 26	79·7	17 03	57 24	79·4	16 52	56 23	79·1	16 40	55 21	78·8	16 28	54 20	78·5	16 16	53 19	78·2	200	340
21	159	18 05	58 16	79·1	17 53	57 14	78·8	17 42	56 12	78·5	17 29	55 11	78·2	17 17	54 09	77·9	17 04	53 08	77·6	201	339
22	158	18 56	58 05	78·6	18 44	57 03	78·2	18 31	56 01	77·9	18 19	55 00	77·6	18 06	53 58	77·3	17 52	52 56	77·0	202	338
23	157	19 47	57 54	78·0	19 34	56 52	77·7	19 21	55 50	77·3	19 08	54 48	77·0	18 54	53 46	76·6	18 40	52 44	76·3	203	337
24	156	20 37	57 42	77·4	20 24	56 40	77·1	20 11	55 38	76·7	19 57	54 36	76·4	19 42	53 34	76·0	19 28	52 32	75·7	204	336
25	155	21 28	57 30	76·9	21 14	56 27	76·5	21 00	55 25	76·1	20 46	54 23	75·7	20 31	53 21	75·4	20 15	52 19	75·0	205	335
26	154	22 19	57 17	76·3	22 04	56 14	75·9	21 49	55 12	75·5	21 34	54 09	75·1	21 19	53 07	74·7	21 03	52 05	74·4	206	334
27	153	23 09	57 03	75·7	22 54	56 00	75·3	22 39	54 57	74·9	22 23	53 55	74·5	22 07	52 52	74·1	21 50	51 50	73·7	207	333
28	152	23 59	56 49	75·1	23 44	55 46	74·7	23 28	54 43	74·3	23 11	53 40	73·8	22 54	52 37	73·4	22 37	51 35	73·0	208	332
29	151	24 50	56 34	74·5	24 33	55 31	74·1	24 17	54 27	73·6	23 59	53 24	73·2	23 42	52 22	72·8	23 24	51 19	72·4	209	331
30	150	25 40	56 19	73·9	25 23	55 15	73·4	25 05	54 11	73·0	24 48	53 08	72·5	24 29	52 05	72·1	24 11	51 03	71·7	210	330
31	149	26 29	56 02	73·3	26 12	54 58	72·8	25 54	53 54	72·3	25 35	52 51	71·9	25 17	51 48	71·4	24 57	50 45	71·0	211	329
32	148	27 19	55 45	72·6	27 01	54 41	72·2	26 42	53 37	71·7	26 23	52 33	71·2	26 04	51 30	70·7	25 44	50 27	70·3	212	328
33	147	28 09	55 27	72·0	27 50	54 23	71·5	27 31	53 19	71·0	27 11	52 15	70·5	26 50	51 12	70·0	26 30	50 08	69·6	213	327
34	146	28 58	55 09	71·4	28 38	54 04	70·8	28 19	53 00	70·3	27 58	51 56	69·8	27 37	50 52	69·3	27 16	49 49	68·8	214	326
35	145	29 47	54 49	70·7	29 27	53 44	70·2	29 06	52 40	69·6	28 45	51 36	69·1	28 24	50 32	68·6	28 01	49 29	68·1	215	325
36	144	30 36	54 29	70·0	30 15	53 24	69·5	29 54	52 19	68·9	29 32	51 15	68·4	29 10	50 11	67·9	28 47	49 07	67·4	216	324
37	143	31 25	54 08	69·4	31 03	53 03	68·8	30 41	51 58	68·2	30 19	50 53	67·7	29 56	49 49	67·2	29 32	48 45	66·6	217	323
38	142	32 13	53 46	68·7	31 51	52 40	68·1	31 28	51 35	67·5	31 05	50 30	66·9	30 41	49 26	66·4	30 17	48 23	65·9	218	322
39	141	33 02	53 23	68·0	32 39	52 17	67·4	32 15	51 12	66·8	31 51	50 07	66·2	31 27	49 03	65·6	31 02	47 59	65·1	219	321
40	140	33 50	53 00	67·2	33 26	51 53	66·6	33 02	50 48	66·0	32 37	49 43	65·4	32 12	48 38	64·9	31 46	47 34	64·3	220	320
41	139	34 37	52 35	66·5	34 13	51 29	65·9	33 48	50 23	65·3	33 23	49 17	64·7	32 57	48 13	64·1	32 30	47 09	63·5	221	319
42	138	35 25	52 09	65·8	35 00	51 03	65·1	34 34	49 56	64·5	34 08	48 51	63·9	33 42	47 46	63·3	33 14	46 42	62·7	222	318
43	137	36 12	51 43	65·0	35 46	50 36	64·3	35 20	49 29	63·7	34 53	48 24	63·1	34 26	47 19	62·5	33 58	46 15	61·9	223	317
44	136	36 59	51 15	64·2	36 33	50 08	63·6	36 06	49 01	62·9	35 38	47 55	62·3	35 10	46 51	61·6	34 41	45 46	61·0	224	316
45	135	37 46	50 46	63·4	37 19	49 39	62·7	36 51	48 32	62·1	36 22	47 26	61·4	35 53	46 21	60·8	35 24	45 17	60·2	225	315

Lat. / A		30°			31°			32°			33°			34°			35°			Lat. / A	
LHA/F		A/H	B/P	Z₁/Z₂	A/H	B/P	Z₁/Z₂	A/H	B/P	Z₁/Z₂	A/H	B/P	Z₁/Z₂	A/H	B/P	Z₁/Z₂	A/H	B/P	Z₁/Z₂	LHA	
°	°	° ′	° ′	°	° ′	° ′	°	° ′	° ′	°	° ′	° ′	°	° ′	° ′	°	° ′	° ′	°	°	°
45	135	37 46	50 46	63·4	37 19	49 39	62·7	36 51	48 32	62·1	36 22	47 26	61·4	35 53	46 21	60·8	35 24	45 17	60·2	225	315
46	134	38 32	50 16	62·6	38 04	49 08	61·9	37 36	48 02	61·2	37 06	46 56	60·6	36 37	45 51	59·9	36 06	44 46	59·3	226	314
47	133	39 18	49 45	61·8	38 49	48 37	61·1	38 20	47 30	60·4	37 50	46 24	59·7	37 19	45 19	59·1	36 48	44 15	58·4	227	313
48	132	40 04	49 13	61·0	39 34	48 05	60·2	39 04	46 58	59·5	38 33	45 51	58·8	38 02	44 46	58·2	37 30	43 42	57·5	228	312
49	131	40 49	48 39	60·1	40 19	47 31	59·4	39 48	46 24	58·6	39 16	45 18	57·9	38 44	44 12	57·2	38 11	43 08	56·6	229	311
50	130	41 34	48 04	59·2	41 03	46 56	58·5	40 31	45 49	57·7	39 59	44 42	57·0	39 26	43 37	56·3	38 52	42 33	55·6	230	310
51	129	42 18	47 28	58·3	41 46	46 20	57·5	41 14	45 12	56·8	40 41	44 06	56·1	40 07	43 01	55·4	39 32	41 57	54·7	231	309
52	128	43 02	46 50	57·4	42 29	45 42	56·6	41 56	44 34	55·9	41 22	43 28	55·1	40 47	42 23	54·4	40 12	41 19	53·7	232	308
53	127	43 46	46 11	56·4	43 12	45 03	55·6	42 38	43 55	54·9	42 03	42 49	54·1	41 28	41 44	53·4	40 52	40 41	52·7	233	307
54	126	44 29	45 31	55·5	43 54	44 22	54·7	43 19	43 15	53·9	42 44	42 09	53·1	42 07	41 04	52·4	41 30	40 01	51·7	234	306
55	125	45 11	44 49	54·5	44 36	43 40	53·7	44 00	42 33	52·9	43 24	41 27	52·1	42 46	40 23	51·4	42 09	39 19	50·7	235	305
56	124	45 53	44 05	53·5	45 17	42 57	52·6	44 40	41 50	51·8	44 03	40 44	51·1	43 25	39 40	50·3	42 46	38 37	49·6	236	304
57	123	46 35	43 20	52·4	45 58	42 11	51·6	45 20	41 05	50·8	44 42	39 59	50·0	44 03	38 55	49·3	43 24	37 53	48·5	237	303
58	122	47 16	42 33	51·3	46 38	41 25	50·5	45 59	40 18	49·7	45 20	39 13	48·9	44 40	38 09	48·2	44 00	37 07	47·5	238	302
59	121	47 56	41 44	50·2	47 17	40 36	49·4	46 38	39 30	48·6	45 58	38 25	47·8	45 17	37 22	47·1	44 36	36 20	46·3	239	301
60	120	48 35	40 54	49·1	47 56	39 46	48·3	47 16	38 40	47·5	46 35	37 36	46·7	45 53	36 33	45·9	45 11	35 32	45·2	240	300
61	119	49 14	40 01	47·9	48 34	38 54	47·1	47 53	37 48	46·3	47 11	36 45	45·5	46 29	35 42	44·7	45 46	34 42	44·0	241	299
62	118	49 53	39 07	46·8	49 11	38 00	45·9	48 29	36 55	45·1	47 46	35 52	44·3	47 03	34 50	43·6	46 19	33 50	42·8	242	298
63	117	50 30	38 11	45·5	49 48	37 04	44·7	49 05	36 00	43·9	48 21	34 57	43·1	47 37	33 57	42·3	46 53	32 57	41·6	243	297
64	116	51 07	37 13	44·3	50 23	36 07	43·4	49 40	35 03	42·6	48 55	34 01	41·8	48 10	33 01	41·1	47 25	32 03	40·4	244	296
65	115	51 43	36 12	43·0	50 58	35 07	42·2	50 14	34 04	41·3	49 28	33 03	40·6	48 43	32 04	39·8	47 56	31 07	39·1	245	295
66	114	52 18	35 10	41·7	51 33	34 06	40·8	50 47	33 04	40·0	50 01	32 04	39·3	49 14	31 05	38·5	48 27	30 09	37·8	246	294
67	113	52 52	34 05	40·3	52 06	33 02	39·5	51 19	32 01	38·7	50 32	31 02	37·9	49 44	30 05	37·2	48 56	29 10	36·5	247	293
68	112	53 25	32 59	38·9	52 38	31 56	38·1	51 50	30 57	37·3	51 02	29 59	36·6	50 14	29 03	35·8	49 25	28 09	35·2	248	292
69	111	53 57	31 50	37·5	53 09	30 49	36·7	52 21	29 50	35·9	51 32	28 53	35·2	50 43	27 59	34·5	49 53	27 06	33·8	249	291
70	110	54 28	30 39	36·1	53 39	29 39	35·2	52 50	28 42	34·5	52 00	27 46	33·8	51 10	26 53	33·1	50 20	26 02	32·4	250	290
71	109	54 58	29 25	34·6	54 08	28 27	33·8	53 18	27 31	33·0	52 28	26 38	32·3	51 37	25 46	31·6	50 46	24 56	31·0	251	289
72	108	55 27	28 09	33·0	54 37	27 13	32·2	53 46	26 19	31·5	52 54	25 27	30·8	52 03	24 37	30·2	51 10	23 49	29·5	252	288
73	107	55 55	26 51	31·4	55 03	25 57	30·7	54 12	25 04	30·0	53 19	24 14	29·3	52 27	23 26	28·7	51 34	22 40	28·1	253	287
74	106	56 21	25 31	29·8	55 29	24 39	29·1	54 36	23 48	28·4	53 43	23 00	27·8	52 50	22 14	27·1	51 57	21 29	26·6	254	286
75	105	56 46	24 09	28·2	55 53	23 18	27·5	55 00	22 30	26·8	54 06	21 44	26·2	53 12	21 00	25·6	52 18	20 17	25·0	255	285
76	104	57 10	22 44	26·5	56 16	21 56	25·8	55 22	21 10	25·2	54 28	20 26	24·6	53 33	19 44	24·0	52 38	19 04	23·5	256	284
77	103	57 33	21 17	24·8	56 38	20 31	24·1	55 43	19 48	23·5	54 48	19 06	23·0	53 53	18 27	22·4	52 57	17 49	21·9	257	283
78	102	57 54	19 48	23·0	56 59	19 05	22·4	56 03	18 24	21·9	55 07	17 45	21·3	54 11	17 08	20·8	53 15	16 32	20·3	258	282
79	101	58 13	18 17	21·2	57 17	17 37	20·7	56 21	16 59	20·1	55 25	16 22	19·6	54 28	15 48	19·2	53 31	15 15	18·7	259	281
80	100	58 32	16 44	19·4	57 35	16 07	18·9	56 38	15 32	18·4	55 41	14 58	17·9	54 44	14 26	17·5	53 47	13 56	17·1	260	280
81	99	58 48	15 10	17·6	57 51	14 36	17·1	56 53	14 03	16·6	55 56	13 33	16·2	54 58	13 03	15·8	54 00	12 36	15·4	261	279
82	98	59 03	13 33	15·7	58 05	13 02	15·3	57 07	12 33	14·9	56 09	12 06	14·5	55 11	11 40	14·1	54 13	11 14	13·8	262	278
83	97	59 16	11 55	13·8	58 18	11 28	13·4	57 19	11 02	13·0	56 21	10 38	12·7	55 22	10 14	12·4	54 24	9 52	12·1	263	277
84	96	59 28	10 16	11·9	58 29	9 52	11·5	57 30	9 30	11·2	56 31	9 09	10·9	55 32	8 49	10·6	54 33	8 29	10·4	264	276
85	95	59 37	8 35	9·9	58 38	8 15	9·6	57 39	7 56	9·4	56 40	7 39	9·1	55 41	7 22	8·9	54 41	7 06	8·7	265	275
86	94	59 46	6 53	8·0	58 46	6 37	7·7	57 47	6 22	7·5	56 47	6 08	7·3	55 48	5 54	7·1	54 48	5 41	7·0	266	274
87	93	59 52	5 11	6·0	58 52	4 59	5·8	57 52	4 47	5·6	56 53	4 36	5·5	55 53	4 26	5·4	54 53	4 16	5·2	267	273
88	92	59 56	3 28	4·0	58 57	3 19	3·9	57 57	3 12	3·8	56 57	3 05	3·7	55 57	2 58	3·6	54 57	2 51	3·5	268	272
89	91	59 59	1 44	2·0	58 59	1 40	1·9	57 59	1 36	1·9	56 59	1 32	1·8	55 59	1 29	1·8	54 59	1 26	1·7	269	271
90	90	60 00	0 00	0·0	59 00	0 00	0·0	58 00	0 00	0·0	57 00	0 00	0·0	56 00	0 00	0·0	55 00	0 00	0·0	270	270

N. Lat: for LHA > 180° … $Z_n = Z$
for LHA < 180° … $Z_n = 360° - Z$

S. Lat.: for LHA > 180° … $Z_n = 180° - Z$
for LHA < 180° … $Z_n = 180° + Z$

SIGHT REDUCTION TABLE

B: (–) for 90° < LHA < 270°
Dec:(–) for Lat. contrary name

Z_1: same sign as B
Z_2: (–) for F > 90°

Lat. / A		36°			37°			38°			39°			40°			41°			Lat. / A	
LHA/F		A/H	B/P	Z_1/Z_2	A/H	B/P	Z_1/Z_2	A/H	B/P	Z_1/Z_2	A/H	B/P	Z_1/Z_2	A/H	B/P	Z_1/Z_2	A/H	B/P	Z_1/Z_2	LHA	
°	°	° ′	° ′	°	° ′	° ′	°	° ′	° ′	°	° ′	° ′	°	° ′	° ′	°	° ′	° ′	°	°	°
0	180	0 00	54 00	90·0	0 00	53 00	90·0	0 00	52 00	90·0	0 00	51 00	90·0	0 00	50 00	90·0	0 00	49 00	90·0	180	360
1	179	0 49	54 00	89·4	0 48	53 00	89·4	0 47	52 00	89·4	0 47	51 00	89·4	0 46	50 00	89·4	0 45	49 00	89·3	181	359
2	178	1 37	53 59	88·8	1 36	52 59	88·8	1 35	51 59	88·8	1 33	50 59	88·7	1 32	49 59	88·7	1 31	48 59	88·7	182	358
3	177	2 26	53 58	88·2	2 24	52 58	88·2	2 22	51 58	88·2	2 20	50 58	88·1	2 18	49 58	88·1	2 16	48 58	88·0	183	357
4	176	3 14	53 56	87·6	3 12	52 56	87·6	3 09	51 56	87·5	3 06	50 56	87·5	3 04	49 56	87·4	3 01	48 56	87·4	184	356
5	175	4 03	53 54	87·1	3 59	52 54	87·0	3 56	51 54	86·9	3 53	50 54	86·8	3 50	49 54	86·8	3 46	48 54	86·7	185	355
6	174	4 51	53 51	86·5	4 47	52 51	86·4	4 43	51 51	86·3	4 40	50 51	86·2	4 36	49 51	86·1	4 31	48 51	86·1	186	354
7	173	5 39	53 48	85·9	5 35	52 48	85·8	5 31	51 48	85·7	5 26	50 47	85·6	5 21	49 47	85·5	5 17	48 47	85·4	187	353
8	172	6 28	53 44	85·3	6 23	52 44	85·2	6 18	51 44	85·1	6 13	50 44	84·9	6 07	49 43	84·8	6 02	48 43	84·7	188	352
9	171	7 16	53 40	84·7	7 11	52 39	84·6	7 05	51 39	84·4	6 59	50 39	84·3	6 53	49 39	84·2	6 47	48 39	84·1	189	351
10	170	8 05	53 35	84·1	7 58	52 35	83·9	7 52	51 34	83·8	7 45	50 34	83·7	7 39	49 34	83·5	7 32	48 34	83·4	190	350
11	169	8 53	53 30	83·5	8 46	52 29	83·3	8 39	51 29	83·2	8 32	50 29	83·0	8 24	49 29	82·9	8 17	48 28	82·7	191	349
12	168	9 41	53 24	82·9	9 33	52 23	82·7	9 26	51 23	82·5	9 18	50 23	82·4	9 10	49 23	82·2	9 02	48 22	82·1	192	348
13	167	10 29	53 17	82·3	10 21	52 17	82·1	10 13	51 17	81·9	10 04	50 16	81·7	9 55	49 16	81·6	9 46	48 16	81·4	193	347
14	166	11 17	53 10	81·7	11 08	52 10	81·5	10 59	51 10	81·3	10 50	50 09	81·1	10 41	49 09	80·9	10 31	48 09	80·7	194	346
15	165	12 05	53 03	81·0	11 56	52 02	80·8	11 46	51 02	80·6	11 36	50 02	80·4	11 26	49 01	80·2	11 16	48 01	80·0	195	345
16	164	12 53	52 55	80·4	12 43	51 54	80·2	12 33	50 54	80·0	12 22	49 53	79·8	12 11	48 53	79·6	12 00	47 53	79·3	196	344
17	163	13 41	52 46	79·8	13 30	51 46	79·6	13 19	50 45	79·3	13 08	49 45	79·1	12 57	48 44	78·9	12 45	47 44	78·7	197	343
18	162	14 29	52 37	79·2	14 17	51 37	78·9	14 06	50 36	78·7	13 54	49 35	78·4	13 42	48 35	78·2	13 29	47 34	78·0	198	342
19	161	15 16	52 28	78·6	15 04	51 27	78·3	14 52	50 26	78·0	14 39	49 25	77·8	14 27	48 25	77·5	14 13	47 24	77·3	199	341
20	160	16 04	52 17	77·9	15 51	51 16	77·6	15 38	50 16	77·4	15 25	49 15	77·1	15 11	48 14	76·8	14 58	47 14	76·6	200	340
21	159	16 51	52 07	77·3	16 38	51 05	77·0	16 24	50 05	76·7	16 10	49 04	76·4	15 56	48 03	76·1	15 42	47 03	75·9	201	339
22	158	17 39	51 55	76·6	17 24	50 54	76·3	17 10	49 53	76·0	16 56	48 52	75·7	16 41	47 51	75·4	16 25	46 51	75·2	202	338
23	157	18 26	51 43	76·0	18 11	50 42	75·7	17 56	49 41	75·4	17 41	48 40	75·0	17 25	47 39	74·7	17 09	46 38	74·4	203	337
24	156	19 13	51 30	75·3	18 57	50 29	75·0	18 42	49 28	74·7	18 26	48 27	74·3	18 09	47 26	74·0	17 53	46 25	73·7	204	336
25	155	20 00	51 17	74·7	19 44	50 15	74·3	19 27	49 14	74·0	19 10	48 13	73·6	18 53	47 12	73·3	18 36	46 12	73·0	205	335
26	154	20 46	51 03	74·0	20 30	50 01	73·6	20 13	49 00	73·3	19 55	47 59	72·9	19 37	46 58	72·6	19 19	45 57	72·3	206	334
27	153	21 33	50 48	73·3	21 15	49 47	73·0	20 58	48 45	72·6	20 40	47 44	72·2	20 21	46 43	71·9	20 02	45 42	71·5	207	333
28	152	22 19	50 33	72·6	22 01	49 31	72·3	21 43	48 30	71·9	21 24	47 28	71·5	21 05	46 28	71·1	20 45	45 27	70·8	208	332
29	151	23 06	50 17	72·0	22 47	49 15	71·6	22 28	48 14	71·2	22 08	47 12	70·8	21 48	46 11	70·4	21 28	45 11	70·0	209	331
30	150	23 52	50 00	71·3	23 32	48 58	70·8	23 12	47 57	70·4	22 52	46 55	70·0	22 31	45 54	69·6	22 10	44 54	69·3	210	330
31	149	24 37	49 43	70·5	24 17	48 41	70·1	23 57	47 39	69·7	23 36	46 38	69·3	23 14	45 37	68·9	22 52	44 36	68·5	211	329
32	148	25 23	49 25	69·8	25 02	48 23	69·4	24 41	47 21	69·0	24 19	46 19	68·5	23 57	45 18	68·1	23 34	44 17	67·7	212	328
33	147	26 09	49 06	69·1	25 47	48 04	68·7	25 25	47 02	68·2	25 02	46 00	67·8	24 40	44 59	67·3	24 16	43 58	66·9	213	327
34	146	26 54	48 46	68·4	26 32	47 44	67·9	26 09	46 42	67·4	25 45	45 40	67·0	25 22	44 39	66·6	24 58	43 39	66·1	214	326
35	145	27 39	48 26	67·6	27 16	47 23	67·1	26 52	46 21	66·7	26 28	45 20	66·2	26 04	44 19	65·8	25 39	43 18	65·3	215	325
36	144	28 24	48 04	66·9	28 00	47 02	66·4	27 36	46 00	65·9	27 11	44 58	65·4	26 46	43 57	65·0	26 20	42 57	64·5	216	324
37	143	29 08	47 42	66·1	28 44	46 40	65·6	28 19	45 38	65·1	27 53	44 36	64·6	27 27	43 35	64·2	27 01	42 34	63·7	217	323
38	142	29 52	47 19	65·3	29 27	46 17	64·8	29 01	45 15	64·3	28 35	44 13	63·8	28 08	43 12	63·3	27 41	42 12	62·9	218	322
39	141	30 36	46 56	64·5	30 10	45 53	64·0	29 44	44 51	63·5	29 17	43 49	63·0	28 49	42 48	62·5	28 21	41 48	62·0	219	321
40	140	31 20	46 31	63·7	30 53	45 28	63·2	30 26	44 26	62·7	29 58	43 25	62·2	29 30	42 24	61·7	29 01	41 23	61·2	220	320
41	139	32 03	46 05	62·9	31 36	45 03	62·4	31 08	44 01	61·8	30 39	42 59	61·3	30 10	41 58	60·8	29 41	40 58	60·3	221	319
42	138	32 46	45 39	62·1	32 18	44 36	61·5	31 49	43 34	61·0	31 20	42 33	60·5	30 50	41 32	59·9	30 20	40 32	59·4	222	318
43	137	33 29	45 11	61·3	33 00	44 09	60·7	32 30	43 07	60·1	32 00	42 05	59·6	31 30	41 05	59·1	30 59	40 04	58·5	223	317
44	136	34 12	44 43	60·4	33 42	43 40	59·8	33 11	42 38	59·3	32 40	41 37	58·7	32 09	40 36	58·2	31 37	39 36	57·6	224	316
45	135	34 54	44 13	59·6	34 23	43 11	59·0	33 52	42 09	58·4	33 20	41 08	57·8	32 48	40 07	57·3	32 15	39 08	56·7	225	315

Lat. / A		36°			37°			38°			39°			40°			41°			Lat. / A	
LHA/F		A/H	B/P	Z_1/Z_2	A/H	B/P	Z_1/Z_2	A/H	B/P	Z_1/Z_2	A/H	B/P	Z_1/Z_2	A/H	B/P	Z_1/Z_2	A/H	B/P	Z_1/Z_2	LHA	
°	°	° ′	° ′	°	° ′	° ′	°	° ′	° ′	°	° ′	° ′	°	° ′	° ′	°	° ′	° ′	°	°	°
45	135	34 54	44 13	59·6	34 23	43 11	59·0	33 52	42 09	58·4	33 20	41 08	57·8	32 48	40 07	57·3	32 15	39 08	56·7	225	315
46	134	35 35	43 43	58·7	35 04	42 40	58·1	34 32	41 38	57·5	33 59	40 37	56·9	33 26	39 37	56·4	32 53	38 38	55·8	226	314
47	133	36 17	43 11	57·8	35 44	42 09	57·2	35 12	41 07	56·6	34 38	40 06	56·0	34 04	39 06	55·4	33 30	38 07	54·9	227	313
48	132	36 57	42 39	56·9	36 24	41 36	56·2	35 51	40 35	55·6	35 17	39 34	55·0	34 42	38 34	54·5	34 07	37 35	53·9	228	312
49	131	37 38	42 05	55·9	37 04	41 03	55·3	36 30	40 01	54·7	35 55	39 01	54·1	35 19	38 01	53·5	34 43	37 03	53·0	229	311
50	130	38 18	41 30	55·0	37 43	40 28	54·4	37 08	39 27	53·7	36 32	38 27	53·1	35 56	37 27	52·5	35 19	36 29	52·0	230	310
51	129	38 57	40 54	54·0	38 22	39 52	53·4	37 46	38 51	52·8	37 09	37 51	52·1	36 32	36 52	51·6	35 55	35 54	51·0	231	309
52	128	39 36	40 17	53·0	39 00	39 15	52·4	38 23	38 14	51·8	37 46	37 15	51·1	37 08	36 16	50·6	36 30	35 18	50·0	232	308
53	127	40 15	39 38	52·0	39 38	38 37	51·4	39 00	37 36	50·8	38 22	36 37	50·1	37 43	35 39	49·5	37 04	34 42	49·0	233	307
54	126	40 53	38 58	51·0	40 15	37 57	50·4	39 36	36 57	49·7	38 57	35 58	49·1	38 18	35 01	48·5	37 38	34 04	47·9	234	306
55	125	41 30	38 17	50·0	40 52	37 17	49·3	40 12	36 17	48·7	39 32	35 19	48·1	38 52	34 21	47·4	38 11	33 25	46·9	235	305
56	124	42 07	37 35	48·9	41 28	36 35	48·3	40 47	35 36	47·6	40 07	34 38	47·0	39 26	33 41	46·4	38 44	32 45	45·8	236	304
57	123	42 44	36 51	47·9	42 03	35 51	47·2	41 22	34 53	46·5	40 41	33 55	45·9	39 59	32 59	45·3	39 16	32 04	44·7	237	303
58	122	43 19	36 06	46·8	42 38	35 07	46·1	41 56	34 09	45·4	41 14	33 12	44·8	40 31	32 16	44·2	39 48	31 22	43·6	238	302
59	121	43 54	35 20	45·6	43 12	34 21	45·0	42 29	33 24	44·3	41 46	32 27	43·7	41 03	31 32	43·1	40 19	30 39	42·5	239	301
60	120	44 29	34 32	44·5	43 46	33 34	43·8	43 02	32 37	43·2	42 18	31 42	42·5	41 34	30 47	41·9	40 49	29 54	41·3	240	300
61	119	45 02	33 43	43·3	44 18	32 45	42·6	43 34	31 49	42·0	42 49	30 55	41·4	42 04	30 01	40·8	41 18	29 09	40·2	241	299
62	118	45 35	32 52	42·1	44 51	31 55	41·5	44 05	31 00	40·8	43 20	30 06	40·2	42 34	29 14	39·6	41 47	28 22	39·0	242	298
63	117	46 07	32 00	40·9	45 22	31 04	40·3	44 36	30 10	39·6	43 49	29 17	39·0	43 03	28 25	38·4	42 15	27 35	37·8	243	297
64	116	46 39	31 06	39·7	45 52	30 11	39·0	45 06	29 18	38·4	44 18	28 26	37·8	43 31	27 35	37·2	42 43	26 46	36·6	244	296
65	115	47 09	30 11	38·4	46 22	29 17	37·8	45 35	28 25	37·1	44 47	27 34	36·5	43 58	26 44	36·0	43 09	25 56	35·4	245	295
66	114	47 39	29 14	37·1	46 51	28 21	36·5	46 03	27 30	35·9	45 14	26 40	35·3	44 25	25 52	34·7	43 35	25 04	34·2	246	294
67	113	48 08	28 16	35·8	47 19	27 24	35·2	46 30	26 34	34·6	45 40	25 45	34·0	44 50	24 58	33·4	44 00	24 12	32·9	247	293
68	112	48 36	27 17	34·5	47 46	26 26	33·9	46 56	25 37	33·3	46 06	24 50	32·7	45 15	24 03	32·2	44 24	23 19	31·6	248	292
69	111	49 03	26 15	33·1	48 13	25 26	32·5	47 22	24 38	31·9	46 31	23 52	31·4	45 39	23 08	30·8	44 48	22 24	30·3	249	291
70	110	49 29	25 13	31·8	48 38	24 25	31·2	47 46	23 39	30·6	46 55	22 54	30·0	46 03	22 11	29·5	45 10	21 29	29·0	250	290
71	109	49 54	24 08	30·4	49 02	23 22	29·8	48 10	22 37	29·2	47 17	21 54	28·7	46 25	21 12	28·2	45 32	20 32	27·7	251	289
72	108	50 18	23 02	28·9	49 25	22 18	28·4	48 33	21 35	27·8	47 39	20 53	27·3	46 46	20 13	26·8	45 52	19 34	26·3	252	288
73	107	50 41	21 55	27·5	49 48	21 12	26·9	48 54	20 31	26·4	48 00	19 51	25·9	47 06	19 13	25·4	46 12	18 35	25·0	253	287
74	106	51 03	20 47	26·0	50 09	20 06	25·5	49 15	19 26	25·0	48 20	18 48	24·5	47 25	18 11	24·0	46 30	17 36	23·6	254	286
75	105	51 24	19 36	24·5	50 29	18 57	24·0	49 34	18 20	23·5	48 39	17 43	23·1	47 44	17 09	22·6	46 48	16 35	22·2	255	285
76	104	51 43	18 25	23·0	50 48	17 48	22·5	49 52	17 12	22·0	48 57	16 38	21·6	48 01	16 05	21·2	47 05	15 33	20·8	256	284
77	103	52 02	17 12	21·4	51 06	16 37	21·0	50 09	16 04	20·6	49 13	15 31	20·1	48 17	15 00	19·8	47 20	14 31	19·4	257	283
78	102	52 19	15 58	19·9	51 22	15 25	19·5	50 25	14 54	19·0	49 29	14 24	18·7	48 32	13 55	18·3	47 35	13 27	18·0	258	282
79	101	52 35	14 43	18·3	51 37	14 13	17·9	50 40	13 43	17·5	49 43	13 16	17·2	48 46	12 49	16·8	47 48	12 23	16·5	259	281
80	100	52 49	13 27	16·7	51 52	12 59	16·3	50 54	12 32	16·0	49 56	12 06	15·7	48 58	11 42	15·3	48 01	11 18	15·0	260	280
81	99	53 02	12 09	15·1	52 04	11 44	14·7	51 06	11 19	14·4	50 08	10 56	14·1	49 10	10 34	13·8	48 12	10 12	13·6	261	279
82	98	53 14	10 51	13·4	52 16	10 28	13·1	51 18	10 06	12·9	50 19	9 45	12·6	49 20	9 25	12·3	48 22	9 06	12·1	262	278
83	97	53 25	9 31	11·8	52 26	9 11	11·5	51 27	8 52	11·3	50 29	8 34	11·0	49 30	8 16	10·8	48 31	7 59	10·6	263	277
84	96	53 34	8 11	10·1	52 35	7 54	9·9	51 36	7 37	9·7	50 37	7 21	9·5	49 38	7 06	9·3	48 38	6 51	9·1	264	276
85	95	53 42	6 50	8·5	52 43	6 36	8·3	51 43	6 22	8·1	50 44	6 09	7·9	49 44	5 56	7·8	48 45	5 44	7·6	265	275
86	94	53 49	5 29	6·8	52 49	5 17	6·6	51 49	5 06	6·5	50 50	4 55	6·3	49 50	4 45	6·2	48 50	4 35	6·1	266	274
87	93	53 54	4 07	5·1	52 54	3 58	5·0	51 54	3 50	4·9	50 54	3 42	4·8	49 54	3 34	4·7	48 55	3 27	4·6	267	273
88	92	53 57	2 45	3·4	52 57	2 39	3·3	51 57	2 33	3·2	50 57	2 28	3·2	49 58	2 23	3·1	48 58	2 18	3·0	268	272
89	91	53 59	1 23	1·7	52 59	1 20	1·7	51 59	1 17	1·6	50 59	1 14	1·6	49 59	1 11	1·6	48 59	1 09	1·5	269	271
90	90	54 00	0 00	0·0	53 00	0 00	0·0	52 00	0 00	0·0	51 00	0 00	0·0	50 00	0 00	0·0	49 00	0 00	0·0	270	270

N. Lat: for LHA > 180° … $Z_n = Z$
for LHA < 180° … $Z_n = 360° - Z$

S. Lat.: for LHA > 180° … $Z_n = 180° - Z$
for LHA < 180° … $Z_n = 180° + Z$

SIGHT REDUCTION TABLE

B: (–) for 90° < LHA < 270°
Dec: (–) for Lat. contrary name

Z_1: same sign as B
Z_2: (–) for F > 90°

Lat. / A		42°			43°			44°			45°			46°			47°			Lat. / A	
LHA/F		A/H	B/P	Z_1/Z_2	A/H	B/P	Z_1/Z_2	A/H	B/P	Z_1/Z_2	A/H	B/P	Z_1/Z_2	A/H	B/P	Z_1/Z_2	A/H	B/P	Z_1/Z_2	LHA	
°	°	° ′	° ′	°	° ′	° ′	°	° ′	° ′	°	° ′	° ′	°	° ′	° ′	°	° ′	° ′	°	°	°
0	180	0 00	48 00	90·0	0 00	47 00	90·0	0 00	46 00	90·0	0 00	45 00	90·0	0 00	44 00	90·0	0 00	43 00	90·0	180	360
1	179	0 45	48 00	89·3	0 44	47 00	89·3	0 43	46 00	89·3	0 42	45 00	89·3	0 42	44 00	89·3	0 41	43 00	89·3	181	359
2	178	1 29	47 59	88·7	1 28	46 59	88·6	1 26	45 59	88·6	1 25	44 59	88·6	1 23	43 59	88·6	1 22	42 59	88·5	182	358
3	177	2 14	47 58	88·0	2 12	46 58	88·0	2 09	45 58	87·9	2 07	44 58	87·9	2 05	43 58	87·8	2 03	42 58	87·8	183	357
4	176	2 58	47 56	87·3	2 55	46 56	87·3	2 53	45 56	87·2	2 50	44 56	87·2	2 47	43 56	87·1	2 44	42 56	87·1	184	356
5	175	3 43	47 53	86·6	3 39	46 53	86·6	3 36	45 53	86·5	3 32	44 53	86·5	3 28	43 53	86·4	3 24	42 53	86·3	185	355
6	174	4 27	47 51	86·0	4 23	46 51	85·9	4 19	45 51	85·8	4 14	44 51	85·7	4 10	43 51	85·7	4 05	42 51	85·6	186	354
7	173	5 12	47 47	85·3	5 07	46 47	85·2	5 02	45 47	85·1	4 57	44 47	85·0	4 51	43 47	85·0	4 46	42 47	84·9	187	353
8	172	5 56	47 43	84·6	5 51	46 43	84·5	5 45	45 43	84·4	5 39	44 43	84·3	5 33	43 43	84·2	5 27	42 43	84·1	188	352
9	171	6 41	47 39	84·0	6 34	46 39	83·8	6 28	45 39	83·7	6 21	44 39	83·6	6 14	43 39	83·5	6 07	42 39	83·4	189	351
10	170	7 25	47 34	83·3	7 18	46 34	83·1	7 11	45 34	83·0	7 03	44 34	82·9	6 56	43 34	82·8	6 48	42 34	82·7	190	350
11	169	8 09	47 28	82·6	8 01	46 28	82·4	7 53	45 28	82·3	7 45	44 28	82·2	7 37	43 28	82·0	7 29	42 28	81·9	191	349
12	168	8 53	47 22	81·9	8 45	46 22	81·8	8 36	45 22	81·6	8 27	44 22	81·5	8 18	43 22	81·3	8 09	42 22	81·2	192	348
13	167	9 37	47 16	81·2	9 28	46 15	81·1	9 19	45 15	80·9	9 09	44 15	80·7	8 59	43 15	80·6	8 49	42 16	80·4	193	347
14	166	10 21	47 08	80·5	10 11	46 08	80·3	10 01	45 08	80·2	9 51	44 08	80·0	9 40	43 08	79·8	9 30	42 08	79·7	194	346
15	165	11 05	47 01	79·8	10 55	46 00	79·6	10 44	45 00	79·5	10 33	44 00	79·3	10 21	43 00	79·1	10 10	42 01	78·9	195	345
16	164	11 49	46 52	79·1	11 38	45 52	78·9	11 26	44 52	78·7	11 14	43 52	78·5	11 02	42 52	78·3	10 50	41 52	78·2	196	344
17	163	12 33	46 43	78·4	12 21	45 43	78·2	12 08	44 43	78·0	11 56	43 43	77·8	11 43	42 43	77·6	11 30	41 44	77·4	197	343
18	162	13 17	46 34	77·7	13 04	45 34	77·5	12 51	44 34	77·3	12 37	43 34	77·1	12 24	42 34	76·8	12 10	41 34	76·6	198	342
19	161	14 00	46 24	77·0	13 46	45 24	76·8	13 33	44 24	76·5	13 19	43 24	76·3	13 04	42 24	76·1	12 50	41 24	75·9	199	341
20	160	14 43	46 13	76·3	14 29	45 13	76·1	14 15	44 13	75·8	14 00	43 13	75·6	13 45	42 13	75·3	13 29	41 14	75·1	200	340
21	159	15 27	46 02	75·6	15 12	45 02	75·3	14 56	44 02	75·1	14 41	43 02	74·8	14 25	42 02	74·6	14 09	41 03	74·3	201	339
22	158	16 10	45 50	74·9	15 54	44 50	74·6	15 38	43 50	74·3	15 22	42 50	74·1	15 05	41 50	73·8	14 48	40 51	73·5	202	338
23	157	16 53	45 38	74·1	16 36	44 38	73·9	16 19	43 38	73·6	16 02	42 38	73·3	15 45	41 38	73·0	15 27	40 39	72·8	203	337
24	156	17 36	45 25	73·4	17 18	44 25	73·1	17 01	43 25	72·8	16 43	42 25	72·5	16 25	41 25	72·2	16 06	40 26	72·0	204	336
25	155	18 18	45 11	72·7	18 00	44 11	72·4	17 42	43 11	72·1	17 23	42 11	71·8	17 04	41 12	71·5	16 45	40 12	71·2	205	335
26	154	19 01	44 57	71·9	18 42	43 57	71·6	18 23	42 57	71·3	18 03	41 57	71·0	17 44	40 57	70·7	17 24	39 58	70·4	206	334
27	153	19 43	44 42	71·2	19 24	43 42	70·8	19 04	42 42	70·5	18 43	41 42	70·2	18 23	40 43	69·9	18 02	39 43	69·6	207	333
28	152	20 25	44 26	70·4	20 05	43 26	70·1	19 44	42 26	69·7	19 23	41 27	69·4	19 02	40 27	69·1	18 40	39 28	68·8	208	332
29	151	21 07	44 10	69·6	20 46	43 10	69·3	20 25	42 10	68·9	20 03	41 10	68·6	19 41	40 11	68·3	19 18	39 12	67·9	209	331
30	150	21 49	43 53	68·9	21 27	42 53	68·5	21 05	41 53	68·1	20 42	40 54	67·8	20 19	39 54	67·4	19 56	38 55	67·1	210	330
31	149	22 30	43 35	68·1	22 08	42 35	67·7	21 45	41 36	67·3	21 21	40 36	67·0	20 58	39 37	66·6	20 34	38 38	66·3	211	329
32	148	23 11	43 17	67·3	22 48	42 17	66·9	22 24	41 17	66·5	22 00	40 18	66·2	21 36	39 19	65·8	21 11	38 20	65·4	212	328
33	147	23 53	42 58	66·5	23 28	41 58	66·1	23 04	40 58	65·7	22 39	39 59	65·3	22 14	39 00	65·0	21 48	38 02	64·6	213	327
34	146	24 33	42 38	65·7	24 08	41 38	65·3	23 43	40 39	64·9	23 17	39 40	64·5	22 51	38 41	64·1	22 25	37 42	63·7	214	326
35	145	25 14	42 18	64·9	24 48	41 18	64·5	24 22	40 18	64·1	23 56	39 19	63·7	23 29	38 21	63·3	23 02	37 23	62·9	215	325
36	144	25 54	41 56	64·1	25 28	40 57	63·6	25 01	39 57	63·2	24 34	38 58	62·8	24 06	38 00	62·4	23 38	37 02	62·0	216	324
37	143	26 34	41 34	63·2	26 07	40 35	62·8	25 39	39 35	62·4	25 11	38 37	61·9	24 43	37 38	61·5	24 14	36 41	61·1	217	323
38	142	27 14	41 11	62·4	26 46	40 12	61·9	26 17	39 13	61·5	25 48	38 14	61·1	25 19	37 16	60·7	24 50	36 19	60·3	218	322
39	141	27 53	40 48	61·5	27 24	39 48	61·1	26 55	38 50	60·6	26 25	37 51	60·2	25 55	36 53	59·8	25 25	35 56	59·4	219	321
40	140	28 32	40 23	60·7	28 02	39 24	60·2	27 32	38 25	59·8	27 02	37 27	59·3	26 31	36 30	58·9	26 00	35 32	58·5	220	320
41	139	29 11	39 58	59·8	28 40	38 59	59·3	28 10	38 01	58·9	27 38	37 03	58·4	27 07	36 05	58·0	26 35	35 08	57·6	221	319
42	138	29 49	39 32	58·9	29 18	38 33	58·4	28 46	37 35	58·0	28 14	36 37	57·5	27 42	35 40	57·1	27 09	34 43	56·6	222	318
43	137	30 27	39 05	58·0	29 55	38 06	57·5	29 23	37 08	57·1	28 50	36 11	56·6	28 17	35 14	56·1	27 43	34 18	55·7	223	317
44	136	31 05	38 37	57·1	30 32	37 39	56·6	29 59	36 41	56·1	29 25	35 44	55·7	28 51	34 47	55·2	28 17	33 51	54·8	224	316
45	135	31 42	38 09	56·2	31 08	37 10	55·7	30 34	36 13	55·2	30 00	35 16	54·7	29 25	34 20	54·3	28 50	33 24	53·8	225	315

Lat. / A		42°			43°			44°			45°			46°			47°			Lat. / A	
LHA	F	A/H	B/P	Z_1/Z_2	A/H	B/P	Z_1/Z_2	A/H	B/P	Z_1/Z_2	A/H	B/P	Z_1/Z_2	A/H	B/P	Z_1/Z_2	A/H	B/P	Z_1/Z_2	LHA	
°	°	° ′	° ′	°	° ′	° ′	°	° ′	° ′	°	° ′	° ′	°	° ′	° ′	°	° ′	° ′	°	°	°
45	135	31 42	38 09	56·2	31 08	37 10	55·7	30 34	36 13	55·2	30 00	35 16	54·7	29 25	34 20	54·3	28 50	33 24	53·8	225	315
46	134	32 19	37 39	55·3	31 45	36 41	54·8	31 10	35 44	54·3	30 34	34 47	53·8	29 59	33 51	53·3	29 23	32 56	52·9	226	314
47	133	32 55	37 08	54·3	32 20	36 11	53·8	31 45	35 14	53·3	31 08	34 18	52·8	30 32	33 22	52·4	29 55	32 27	51·9	227	313
48	132	33 31	36 37	53·4	32 55	35 40	52·9	32 19	34 43	52·3	31 42	33 47	51·9	31 05	32 52	51·4	30 27	31 58	50·9	228	312
49	131	34 07	36 05	52·4	33 30	35 08	51·9	32 53	34 11	51·4	32 15	33 16	50·9	31 37	32 21	50·4	30 59	31 27	49·9	229	311
50	130	34 42	35 31	51·4	34 04	34 35	50·9	33 26	33 39	50·4	32 48	32 44	49·9	32 09	31 50	49·4	31 30	30 56	48·9	230	310
51	129	35 17	34 57	50·4	34 38	34 01	49·9	33 59	33 05	49·4	33 20	32 11	48·9	32 40	31 17	48·4	32 00	30 24	47·9	231	309
52	128	35 51	34 22	49·4	35 12	33 26	48·9	34 32	32 31	48·4	33 52	31 37	47·9	33 11	30 44	47·4	32 30	29 52	46·9	232	308
53	127	36 24	33 45	48·4	35 44	32 50	47·9	35 04	31 56	47·3	34 23	31 02	46·8	33 42	30 10	46·3	33 00	29 18	45·9	233	307
54	126	36 57	33 08	47·4	36 17	32 13	46·8	35 35	31 20	46·3	34 54	30 27	45·8	34 12	29 35	45·3	33 29	28 44	44·8	234	306
55	125	37 30	32 30	46·3	36 48	31 36	45·8	36 06	30 43	45·2	35 24	29 50	44·7	34 41	28 59	44·2	33 58	28 08	43·8	235	305
56	124	38 02	31 51	45·2	37 19	30 57	44·7	36 37	30 04	44·2	35 53	29 13	43·6	35 10	28 22	43·2	34 26	27 32	42·7	236	304
57	123	38 33	31 10	44·1	37 50	30 17	43·6	37 06	29 25	43·1	36 22	28 34	42·6	35 38	27 45	42·1	34 53	26 56	41·6	237	303
58	122	39 04	30 29	43·0	38 20	29 36	42·5	37 36	28 45	42·0	36 51	27 55	41·5	36 06	27 06	41·0	35 20	26 18	40·5	238	302
59	121	39 34	29 46	41·9	38 49	28 55	41·4	38 04	28 04	40·9	37 19	27 15	40·4	36 33	26 27	39·9	35 46	25 39	39·4	239	301
60	120	40 04	29 03	40·8	39 18	28 12	40·2	38 32	27 22	39·7	37 46	26 34	39·2	36 59	25 46	38·8	36 12	25 00	38·3	240	300
61	119	40 32	28 18	39·6	39 46	27 28	39·1	38 59	26 39	38·6	38 12	25 52	38·1	37 25	25 05	37·6	36 37	24 20	37·2	241	299
62	118	41 00	27 32	38·5	40 13	26 43	37·9	39 26	25 56	37·4	38 38	25 09	36·9	37 50	24 23	36·5	37 02	23 39	36·0	242	298
63	117	41 28	26 45	37·3	40 40	25 58	36·8	39 52	25 11	36·3	39 03	24 25	35·8	38 14	23 40	35·3	37 25	22 57	34·9	243	297
64	116	41 54	25 58	36·1	41 06	25 11	35·6	40 17	24 25	35·1	39 28	23 40	34·6	38 38	22 57	34·1	37 48	22 14	33·7	244	296
65	115	42 20	25 09	34·9	41 31	24 23	34·4	40 41	23 38	33·9	39 51	22 55	33·4	39 01	22 12	33·0	38 11	21 31	32·5	245	295
66	114	42 45	24 19	33·6	41 55	23 34	33·1	41 05	22 50	32·7	40 14	22 08	32·2	39 23	21 27	31·8	38 32	20 46	31·3	246	294
67	113	43 10	23 28	32·4	42 19	22 44	31·9	41 28	22 02	31·4	40 37	21 21	31·0	39 45	20 40	30·5	38 53	20 01	30·1	247	293
68	112	43 33	22 35	31·1	42 42	21 53	30·6	41 50	21 12	30·2	40 58	20 32	29·7	40 06	19 53	29·3	39 13	19 15	28·9	248	292
69	111	43 56	21 42	29·8	43 04	21 01	29·4	42 11	20 22	28·9	41 19	19 43	28·5	40 26	19 05	28·1	39 33	18 29	27·7	249	291
70	110	44 18	20 48	28·5	43 25	20 08	28·1	42 32	19 30	27·7	41 38	18 53	27·2	40 45	18 17	26·8	39 51	17 41	26·5	250	290
71	109	44 38	19 53	27·2	43 45	19 15	26·8	42 51	18 38	26·4	41 57	18 02	26·0	41 03	17 27	25·6	40 09	16 53	25·2	251	289
72	108	44 58	18 57	25·9	44 04	18 20	25·5	43 10	17 45	25·1	42 16	17 10	24·7	41 21	16 37	24·3	40 26	16 05	24·0	252	288
73	107	45 17	17 59	24·6	44 23	17 24	24·1	43 28	16 51	23·8	42 33	16 18	23·4	41 38	15 46	23·0	40 42	15 15	22·7	253	287
74	106	45 35	17 01	23·2	44 40	16 28	22·8	43 45	15 56	22·4	42 49	15 25	22·1	41 54	14 54	21·7	40 58	14 25	21·4	254	286
75	105	45 53	16 02	21·8	44 57	15 31	21·4	44 01	15 00	21·1	43 05	14 31	20·8	42 09	14 02	20·4	41 12	13 34	20·1	255	285
76	104	46 09	15 02	20·4	45 12	14 33	20·1	44 16	14 04	19·7	43 19	13 36	19·4	42 23	13 09	19·1	41 26	12 43	18·8	256	284
77	103	46 24	14 02	19·0	45 27	13 34	18·7	44 30	13 07	18·4	43 33	12 41	18·1	42 36	12 15	17·8	41 39	11 51	17·5	257	283
78	102	46 38	13 00	17·6	45 40	12 34	17·3	44 43	12 09	17·0	43 46	11 45	16·7	42 48	11 21	16·5	41 51	10 58	16·2	258	282
79	101	46 51	11 58	16·2	45 53	11 34	15·9	44 55	11 11	15·6	43 57	10 48	15·4	43 00	10 26	15·1	42 02	10 05	14·9	259	281
80	100	47 03	10 55	14·8	46 04	10 33	14·5	45 06	10 12	14·2	44 08	9 51	14·0	43 10	9 31	13·8	42 12	9 12	13·6	260	280
81	99	47 13	9 51	13·3	46 15	9 31	13·1	45 16	9 12	12·8	44 18	8 53	12·6	43 19	8 35	12·4	42 21	8 18	12·2	261	279
82	98	47 23	8 47	11·9	46 24	8 29	11·6	45 26	8 12	11·4	44 27	7 55	11·2	43 28	7 39	11·1	42 29	7 24	10·9	262	278
83	97	47 32	7 42	10·4	46 33	7 27	10·2	45 34	7 12	10·0	44 34	6 57	9·9	43 35	6 43	9·7	42 36	6 29	9·5	263	277
84	96	47 39	6 37	8·9	46 40	6 24	8·8	45 41	6 11	8·6	44 41	5 58	8·5	43 42	5 46	8·3	42 42	5 34	8·2	264	276
85	95	47 46	5 32	7·4	46 46	5 20	7·3	45 46	5 09	7·2	44 47	4 59	7·1	43 47	4 49	6·9	42 48	4 39	6·8	265	275
86	94	47 51	4 26	6·0	46 51	4 17	5·9	45 51	4 08	5·7	44 52	3 59	5·6	43 52	3 51	5·6	42 52	3 43	5·5	266	274
87	93	47 55	3 20	4·5	46 55	3 13	4·4	45 55	3 06	4·3	44 55	3 00	4·2	43 55	2 54	4·2	42 56	2 48	4·1	267	273
88	92	47 58	2 13	3·0	46 58	2 09	2·9	45 58	2 04	2·9	44 58	2 00	2·8	43 58	1 56	2·8	42 58	1 52	2·7	268	272
89	91	47 59	1 07	1·5	46 59	1 04	1·5	45 59	1 02	1·4	44 59	1 00	1·4	43 59	0 58	1·4	43 00	0 56	1·4	269	271
90	90	48 00	0 00	0·0	47 00	0 00	0·0	46 00	0 00	0·0	45 00	0 00	0·0	44 00	0 00	0·0	43 00	0 00	0·0	270	270

N. Lat: for LHA > 180° … $Z_n = Z$
for LHA < 180° … $Z_n = 360° - Z$

S. Lat.: for LHA > 180° … $Z_n = 180° - Z$
for LHA < 180° … $Z_n = 180° + Z$

SIGHT REDUCTION TABLE

B: (−) for 90° < LHA < 270°
Dec:(−) for Lat. contrary name

Z_1: same sign as B
Z_2: (−) for F > 90°

Lat. / A		48°			49°			50°			51°			52°			53°			Lat. / A	
LHA/F		A/H	B/P	Z_1/Z_2	A/H	B/P	Z_1/Z_2	A/H	B/P	Z_1/Z_2	A/H	B/P	Z_1/Z_2	A/H	B/P	Z_1/Z_2	A/H	B/P	Z_1/Z_2	LHA	
°	°	° ′	° ′	°	° ′	° ′	°	° ′	° ′	°	° ′	° ′	°	° ′	° ′	°	° ′	° ′	°	°	°
0	180	0 00	42 00	90·0	0 00	41 00	90·0	0 00	40 00	90·0	0 00	39 00	90·0	0 00	38 00	90·0	0 00	37 00	90·0	180	360
1	179	0 40	42 00	89·3	0 39	41 00	89·2	0 39	40 00	89·2	0 38	39 00	89·2	0 37	38 00	89·2	0 36	37 00	89·2	181	359
2	178	1 20	41 59	88·5	1 19	40 59	88·5	1 17	39 59	88·5	1 16	38 59	88·4	1 14	37 59	88·4	1 12	36 59	88·4	182	358
3	177	2 00	41 58	87·8	1 58	40 58	87·7	1 56	39 58	87·7	1 53	38 58	87·7	1 51	37 58	87·6	1 48	36 58	87·6	183	357
4	176	2 41	41 56	87·0	2 37	40 56	87·0	2 34	39 56	86·9	2 31	38 56	86·9	2 28	37 56	86·8	2 24	36 56	86·8	184	356
5	175	3 21	41 53	86·3	3 17	40 54	86·2	3 13	39 54	86·2	3 09	38 54	86·1	3 05	37 54	86·1	3 00	36 54	86·0	185	355
6	174	4 01	41 51	85·5	3 56	40 51	85·5	3 51	39 51	85·4	3 46	38 51	85·3	3 41	37 51	85·3	3 36	36 51	85·2	186	354
7	173	4 41	41 47	84·8	4 35	40 47	84·7	4 30	39 47	84·6	4 24	38 47	84·5	4 18	37 48	84·5	4 12	36 48	84·4	187	353
8	172	5 21	41 43	84·0	5 14	40 43	83·9	5 08	39 43	83·9	5 01	38 44	83·8	4 55	37 44	83·7	4 48	36 44	83·6	188	352
9	171	6 01	41 39	83·3	5 53	40 39	83·2	5 46	39 39	83·1	5 39	38 39	83·0	5 32	37 39	82·9	5 24	36 40	82·8	189	351
10	170	6 40	41 34	82·5	6 32	40 34	82·4	6 25	39 34	82·3	6 16	38 34	82·2	6 08	37 35	82·1	6 00	36 35	82·0	190	350
11	169	7 20	41 28	81·8	7 11	40 28	81·7	7 03	39 29	81·5	6 54	38 29	81·4	6 45	37 29	81·3	6 36	36 29	81·2	191	349
12	168	8 00	41 22	81·0	7 50	40 22	80·9	7 41	39 23	80·8	7 31	38 23	80·6	7 21	37 23	80·5	7 11	36 24	80·4	192	348
13	167	8 39	41 16	80·3	8 29	40 16	80·1	8 19	39 16	80·0	8 08	38 16	79·8	7 58	37 17	79·7	7 47	36 17	79·6	193	347
14	166	9 19	41 09	79·5	9 08	40 09	79·3	8 57	39 09	79·2	8 45	38 09	79·0	8 34	37 10	78·9	8 22	36 10	78·7	194	346
15	165	9 58	41 01	78·7	9 47	40 01	78·6	9 35	39 02	78·4	9 22	38 02	78·2	9 10	37 02	78·1	8 58	36 03	77·9	195	345
16	164	10 38	40 53	78·0	10 25	39 53	77·8	10 12	38 53	77·6	9 59	37 54	77·4	9 46	36 54	77·3	9 33	35 55	77·1	196	344
17	163	11 17	40 44	77·2	11 04	39 44	77·0	10 50	38 45	76·8	10 36	37 45	76·6	10 22	36 46	76·5	10 08	35 47	76·3	197	343
18	162	11 56	40 34	76·4	11 42	39 35	76·2	11 27	38 35	76·0	11 13	37 36	75·8	10 58	36 37	75·6	10 43	35 38	75·5	198	342
19	161	12 35	40 25	75·6	12 20	39 25	75·4	12 05	38 26	75·2	11 49	37 26	75·0	11 34	36 27	74·8	11 18	35 28	74·6	199	341
20	160	13 14	40 14	74·9	12 58	39 15	74·6	12 42	38 15	74·4	12 26	37 16	74·2	12 09	36 17	74·0	11 53	35 18	73·8	200	340
21	159	13 52	40 03	74·1	13 36	39 04	73·8	13 19	38 04	73·6	13 02	37 05	73·4	12 45	36 06	73·2	12 27	35 08	73·0	201	339
22	158	14 31	39 51	73·3	14 14	38 52	73·0	13 56	37 53	72·8	13 38	36 54	72·6	13 20	35 55	72·3	13 02	34 56	72·1	202	338
23	157	15 09	39 39	72·5	14 51	38 40	72·2	14 33	37 41	72·0	14 14	36 42	71·7	13 55	35 43	71·5	13 36	34 45	71·3	203	337
24	156	15 48	39 26	71·7	15 29	38 27	71·4	15 09	37 28	71·2	14 50	36 30	70·9	14 30	35 31	70·7	14 10	34 33	70·4	204	336
25	155	16 26	39 13	70·9	16 06	38 14	70·6	15 46	37 15	70·3	15 25	36 17	70·1	15 05	35 18	69·8	14 44	34 20	69·6	205	335
26	154	17 03	38 59	70·1	16 43	38 00	69·8	16 22	37 01	69·5	16 01	36 03	69·2	15 39	35 05	69·0	15 18	34 07	68·7	206	334
27	153	17 41	38 44	69·3	17 20	37 46	69·0	16 58	36 47	68·7	16 36	35 49	68·4	16 14	34 51	68·1	15 51	33 53	67·9	207	333
28	152	18 19	38 29	68·4	17 56	37 30	68·1	17 34	36 32	67·8	17 11	35 34	67·5	16 48	34 36	67·3	16 25	33 38	67·0	208	332
29	151	18 56	38 13	67·6	18 33	37 15	67·3	18 09	36 16	67·0	17 46	35 18	66·7	17 22	34 21	66·4	16 58	33 23	66·1	209	331
30	150	19 33	37 57	66·8	19 09	36 58	66·5	18 45	36 00	66·1	18 20	35 03	65·8	17 56	34 05	65·5	17 31	33 08	65·2	210	330
31	149	20 10	37 40	65·9	19 45	36 41	65·6	19 20	35 44	65·3	18 55	34 46	65·0	18 29	33 49	64·7	18 03	32 52	64·4	211	329
32	148	20 46	37 22	65·1	20 21	36 24	64·8	19 55	35 26	64·4	19 29	34 29	64·1	19 02	33 32	63·8	18 36	32 35	63·5	212	328
33	147	21 22	37 03	64·2	20 56	36 06	63·9	20 30	35 08	63·6	20 03	34 11	63·2	19 35	33 14	62·9	19 08	32 18	62·6	213	327
34	146	21 58	36 44	63·4	21 31	35 47	63·0	21 04	34 49	62·7	20 36	33 53	62·3	20 08	32 56	62·0	19 40	32 00	61·7	214	326
35	145	22 34	36 25	62·5	22 06	35 27	62·1	21 38	34 30	61·8	21 10	33 33	61·4	20 41	32 37	61·1	20 12	31 41	60·8	215	325
36	144	23 10	36 04	61·6	22 41	35 07	61·3	22 12	34 10	60·9	21 43	33 14	60·5	21 13	32 18	60·2	20 43	31 22	59·9	216	324
37	143	23 45	35 43	60·8	23 15	34 46	60·4	22 45	33 50	60·0	22 15	32 53	59·6	21 45	31 58	59·3	21 14	31 02	59·0	217	323
38	142	24 20	35 21	59·9	23 49	34 25	59·5	23 19	33 28	59·1	22 48	32 33	58·7	22 16	31 37	58·4	21 45	30 42	58·0	218	322
39	141	24 54	34 59	59·0	24 23	34 02	58·6	23 52	33 07	58·2	23 20	32 11	57·8	22 48	31 16	57·5	22 15	30 21	57·1	219	321
40	140	25 28	34 36	58·1	24 57	33 40	57·7	24 24	32 44	57·3	23 52	31 49	56·9	23 19	30 54	56·5	22 45	30 00	56·2	220	320
41	139	26 02	34 12	57·1	25 30	33 16	56·7	24 57	32 21	56·3	24 23	31 26	56·0	23 49	30 32	55·6	23 15	29 38	55·2	221	319
42	138	26 36	33 47	56·2	26 02	32 52	55·8	25 28	31 57	55·4	24 54	31 02	55·0	24 20	30 08	54·6	23 45	29 15	54·3	222	318
43	137	27 09	33 22	55·3	26 35	32 27	54·9	26 00	31 32	54·5	25 25	30 38	54·1	24 50	29 45	53·7	24 14	28 52	53·3	223	317
44	136	27 42	32 56	54·3	27 07	32 01	53·9	26 31	31 07	53·5	25 55	30 13	53·1	25 19	29 20	52·7	24 43	28 28	52·4	224	316
45	135	28 14	32 29	53·4	27 38	31 35	53·0	27 02	30 41	52·5	26 25	29 48	52·1	25 48	28 55	51·8	25 11	28 03	51·4	225	315

Lat. / A		48°			49°			50°			51°			52°			53°			Lat. / A	
LHA/F		A/H	B/P	Z_1/Z_2	A/H	B/P	Z_1/Z_2	A/H	B/P	Z_1/Z_2	A/H	B/P	Z_1/Z_2	A/H	B/P	Z_1/Z_2	A/H	B/P	Z_1/Z_2	LHA	
°	°	° ′	° ′	°	° ′	° ′	°	° ′	° ′	°	° ′	° ′	°	° ′	° ′	°	° ′	° ′	°	°	°
45	135	28 14	32 29	53·4	27 38	31 35	53·0	27 02	30 41	52·5	26 25	29 48	52·1	25 48	28 55	51·8	25 11	28 03	51·4	225	315
46	134	28 46	32 01	52·4	28 10	31 08	52·0	27 32	30 14	51·6	26 55	29 22	51·2	26 17	28 29	50·8	25 39	27 38	50·4	226	314
47	133	29 18	31 33	51·4	28 40	30 40	51·0	28 02	29 47	50·6	27 24	28 55	50·2	26 46	28 03	49·8	26 07	27 12	49·4	227	313
48	132	29 49	31 04	50·5	29 11	30 11	50·0	28 32	29 19	49·6	27 53	28 27	49·2	27 14	27 36	48·8	26 34	26 46	48·4	228	312
49	131	30 20	30 34	49·5	29 41	29 42	49·0	29 01	28 50	48·6	28 21	27 59	48·2	27 41	27 08	47·8	27 01	26 18	47·4	229	311
50	130	30 50	30 04	48·5	30 10	29 12	48·0	29 30	28 20	47·6	28 49	27 30	47·2	28 08	26 40	46·8	27 27	25 51	46·4	230	310
51	129	31 20	29 32	47·5	30 39	28 41	47·0	29 58	27 50	46·6	29 17	27 00	46·2	28 35	26 11	45·8	27 53	25 22	45·4	231	309
52	128	31 49	29 00	46·4	31 08	28 09	46·0	30 26	27 19	45·6	29 44	26 30	45·2	29 01	25 41	44·8	28 19	24 53	44·4	232	308
53	127	32 18	28 27	45·4	31 36	27 37	45·0	30 53	26 48	44·5	30 10	25 59	44·1	29 27	25 11	43·7	28 44	24 24	43·3	233	307
54	126	32 46	27 53	44·4	32 03	27 04	43·9	31 20	26 15	43·5	30 36	25 27	43·1	29 52	24 40	42·7	29 08	23 53	42·3	234	306
55	125	33 14	27 19	43·3	32 30	26 30	42·9	31 46	25 42	42·4	31 02	24 55	42·0	30 17	24 08	41·6	29 32	23 23	41·2	235	305
56	124	33 42	26 44	42·2	32 57	25 55	41·8	32 12	25 08	41·4	31 27	24 22	41·0	30 41	23 36	40·6	29 56	22 51	40·2	236	304
57	123	34 08	26 07	41·1	33 23	25 20	40·7	32 37	24 34	40·3	31 51	23 48	39·9	31 05	23 03	39·5	30 19	22 19	39·1	237	303
58	122	34 34	25 30	40·1	33 48	24 44	39·6	33 02	23 58	39·2	32 15	23 14	38·8	31 28	22 29	38·4	30 41	21 46	38·0	238	302
59	121	35 00	24 53	39·0	34 13	24 07	38·5	33 26	23 22	38·1	32 39	22 38	37·7	31 51	21 55	37·3	31 03	21 13	37·0	239	301
60	120	35 25	24 14	37·8	34 37	23 30	37·4	33 50	22 46	37·0	33 02	22 03	36·6	32 13	21 20	36·2	31 25	20 39	35·9	240	300
61	119	35 49	23 35	36·7	35 01	22 51	36·3	34 12	22 08	35·9	33 24	21 26	35·5	32 35	20 45	35·1	31 46	20 04	34·8	241	299
62	118	36 13	22 55	35·6	35 24	22 12	35·2	34 35	21 30	34·8	33 45	20 49	34·4	32 56	20 09	34·0	32 06	19 29	33·7	242	298
63	117	36 36	22 14	34·4	35 46	21 32	34·0	34 56	20 51	33·6	34 06	20 11	33·3	33 16	19 32	32·9	32 26	18 53	32·5	243	297
64	116	36 58	21 32	33·3	36 08	20 52	32·9	35 17	20 12	32·5	34 27	19 33	32·1	33 36	18 54	31·8	32 45	18 17	31·4	244	296
65	115	37 20	20 50	32·1	36 29	20 10	31·7	35 38	19 32	31·3	34 47	18 54	31·0	33 55	18 16	30·6	33 03	17 40	30·3	245	295
66	114	37 41	20 07	30·9	36 49	19 28	30·5	35 58	18 51	30·2	35 06	18 14	29·8	34 13	17 38	29·5	33 21	17 02	29·1	246	294
67	113	38 01	19 23	29·7	37 09	18 46	29·4	36 17	18 09	29·0	35 24	17 33	28·6	34 31	16 59	28·3	33 38	16 24	28·0	247	293
68	112	38 21	18 38	28·5	37 28	18 02	28·2	36 35	17 27	27·8	35 42	16 53	27·5	34 48	16 19	27·1	33 55	15 46	26·8	248	292
69	111	38 40	17 53	27·3	37 46	17 18	27·0	36 53	16 44	26·6	35 59	16 11	26·3	35 05	15 38	26·0	34 11	15 07	25·7	249	291
70	110	38 58	17 07	26·1	38 04	16 33	25·7	37 10	16 01	25·4	36 15	15 29	25·1	35 21	14 58	24·8	34 26	14 27	24·5	250	290
71	109	39 15	16 20	24·9	38 20	15 48	24·5	37 26	15 17	24·2	36 31	14 46	23·9	35 36	14 16	23·6	34 41	13 47	23·3	251	289
72	108	39 31	15 33	23·6	38 36	15 02	23·3	37 41	14 32	23·0	36 46	14 03	22·7	35 50	13 34	22·4	34 55	13 07	22·1	252	288
73	107	39 47	14 45	22·4	38 51	14 16	22·1	37 56	13 47	21·8	37 00	13 19	21·5	36 04	12 52	21·2	35 08	12 25	20·9	253	287
74	106	40 02	13 56	21·1	39 06	13 28	20·8	38 10	13 01	20·5	37 13	12 35	20·3	36 17	12 09	20·0	35 21	11 44	19·8	254	286
75	105	40 16	13 07	19·8	39 19	12 41	19·5	38 23	12 15	19·3	37 26	11 50	19·0	36 29	11 26	18·8	35 33	11 02	18·5	255	285
76	104	40 29	12 17	18·5	39 32	11 53	18·3	38 35	11 28	18·0	37 38	11 05	17·8	36 41	10 42	17·6	35 44	10 20	17·3	256	284
77	103	40 41	11 27	17·3	39 44	11 04	17·0	38 47	10 41	16·8	37 49	10 19	16·5	36 52	9 58	16·3	35 54	9 37	16·1	257	283
78	102	40 53	10 36	16·0	39 55	10 15	15·7	38 57	9 54	15·5	38 00	9 33	15·3	37 02	9 14	15·1	36 04	8 54	14·9	258	282
79	101	41 04	9 45	14·7	40 05	9 25	14·4	39 07	9 06	14·2	38 09	8 47	14·0	37 11	8 29	13·9	36 13	8 11	13·7	259	281
80	100	41 13	8 53	13·3	40 15	8 35	13·2	39 16	8 17	13·0	38 18	8 00	12·8	37 19	7 44	12·6	36 21	7 27	12·5	260	280
81	99	41 22	8 01	12·0	40 23	7 45	11·9	39 25	7 29	11·7	38 26	7 13	11·5	37 27	6 58	11·4	36 28	6 43	11·2	261	279
82	98	41 30	7 09	10·7	40 31	6 54	10·5	39 32	6 40	10·4	38 33	6 26	10·3	37 34	6 12	10·1	36 35	5 59	10·0	262	278
83	97	41 37	6 16	9·4	40 38	6 03	9·2	39 39	5 50	9·1	38 39	5 38	9·0	37 40	5 26	8·9	36 41	5 15	8·7	263	277
84	96	41 43	5 23	8·1	40 44	5 12	7·9	39 44	5 01	7·8	38 45	4 50	7·7	37 45	4 40	7·6	36 46	4 30	7·5	264	276
85	95	41 48	4 29	6·7	40 49	4 20	6·6	39 49	4 11	6·5	38 49	4 02	6·4	37 50	3 54	6·3	36 50	3 45	6·3	265	275
86	94	41 52	3 36	5·4	40 53	3 28	5·3	39 53	3 21	5·2	38 53	3 14	5·1	37 53	3 07	5·1	36 54	3 01	5·0	266	274
87	93	41 56	2 42	4·0	40 56	2 36	4·0	39 56	2 31	3·9	38 56	2 26	3·9	37 56	2 20	3·8	36 56	2 16	3·8	267	273
88	92	41 58	1 48	2·7	40 58	1 44	2·6	39 58	1 41	2·6	38 58	1 37	2·6	37 58	1 34	2·5	36 58	1 30	2·5	268	272
89	91	42 00	0 54	1·3	41 00	0 52	1·3	40 00	0 50	1·3	39 00	0 49	1·3	38 00	0 47	1·3	37 00	0 45	1·3	269	271
90	90	42 00	0 00	0·0	41 00	0 00	0·0	40 00	0 00	0·0	39 00	0 00	0·0	38 00	0 00	0·0	37 00	0 00	0·0	270	270

N. Lat: for LHA > 180° … $Z_n = Z$
for LHA < 180° … $Z_n = 360° - Z$

S. Lat.: for LHA > 180° … $Z_n = 180° - Z$
for LHA < 180° … $Z_n = 180° + Z$

SIGHT REDUCTION TABLE

B: (–) for 90° < LHA < 270°
Dec:(–) for Lat. contrary name

Z_1: same sign as B
Z_2: (–) for F > 90°

Lat. / A		54°			55°			56°			57°			58°			59°			Lat. / A	
LHA/F		A/H	B/P	Z_1/Z_2	A/H	B/P	Z_1/Z_2	A/H	B/P	Z_1/Z_2	A/H	B/P	Z_1/Z_2	A/H	B/P	Z_1/Z_2	A/H	B/P	Z_1/Z_2	LHA	
°	°	° ′	° ′	°	° ′	° ′	°	° ′	° ′	°	° ′	° ′	°	° ′	° ′	°	° ′	° ′	°	°	°
0	180	0 00	36 00	90·0	0 00	35 00	90·0	0 00	34 00	90·0	0 00	33 00	90·0	0 00	32 00	90·0	0 00	31 00	90·0	180	360
1	179	0 35	36 00	89·2	0 34	35 00	89·2	0 34	34 00	89·2	0 33	33 00	89·2	0 32	32 00	89·2	0 31	31 00	89·1	181	359
2	178	1 11	35 59	88·4	1 09	34 59	88·4	1 07	33 59	88·3	1 05	32 59	88·3	1 04	31 59	88·3	1 02	30 59	88·3	182	358
3	177	1 46	35 58	87·6	1 43	34 58	87·5	1 41	33 58	87·5	1 38	32 58	87·5	1 35	31 58	87·5	1 33	30 58	87·4	183	357
4	176	2 21	35 56	86·8	2 18	34 56	86·7	2 14	33 56	86·7	2 11	32 56	86·6	2 07	31 56	86·6	2 04	30 56	86·6	184	356
5	175	2 56	35 54	86·0	2 52	34 54	85·9	2 48	33 54	85·9	2 43	32 54	85·8	2 39	31 54	85·8	2 34	30 54	85·7	185	355
6	174	3 31	35 51	85·1	3 26	34 51	85·1	3 21	33 51	85·0	3 16	32 51	85·0	3 11	31 52	84·9	3 05	30 52	84·9	186	354
7	173	4 06	35 48	84·3	4 00	34 48	84·3	3 54	33 48	84·2	3 48	32 48	84·1	3 42	31 48	84·1	3 36	30 49	84·0	187	353
8	172	4 42	35 44	83·5	4 35	34 44	83·4	4 28	33 44	83·4	4 21	32 45	83·3	4 14	31 45	83·2	4 07	30 45	83·1	188	352
9	171	5 17	35 40	82·7	5 09	34 40	82·6	5 01	33 40	82·5	4 53	32 41	82·4	4 45	31 41	82·3	4 37	30 41	82·3	189	351
10	170	5 51	35 35	81·9	5 43	34 35	81·8	5 34	33 36	81·7	5 26	32 36	81·6	5 17	31 36	81·5	5 08	30 37	81·4	190	350
11	169	6 26	35 30	81·1	6 17	34 30	81·0	6 08	33 31	80·8	5 58	32 31	80·7	5 48	31 31	80·6	5 38	30 32	80·5	191	349
12	168	7 01	35 24	80·2	6 51	34 24	80·1	6 41	33 25	80·0	6 30	32 25	79·9	6 20	31 26	79·8	6 09	30 27	79·7	192	348
13	167	7 36	35 18	79·4	7 25	34 18	79·3	7 14	33 19	79·2	7 02	32 19	79·0	6 51	31 20	78·9	6 39	30 21	78·8	193	347
14	166	8 11	35 11	78·6	7 59	34 12	78·5	7 46	33 12	78·3	7 34	32 13	78·2	7 22	31 14	78·1	7 09	30 15	77·9	194	346
15	165	8 45	35 04	77·8	8 32	34 04	77·6	8 19	33 05	77·5	8 06	32 06	77·3	7 53	31 07	77·2	7 40	30 08	77·1	195	345
16	164	9 19	34 56	76·9	9 06	33 57	76·8	8 52	32 58	76·6	8 38	31 58	76·5	8 24	31 00	76·3	8 10	30 01	76·2	196	344
17	163	9 54	34 47	76·1	9 39	33 48	75·9	9 25	32 49	75·8	9 10	31 50	75·6	8 55	30 52	75·5	8 40	29 53	75·3	197	343
18	162	10 28	34 39	75·3	10 13	33 40	75·1	9 57	32 41	74·9	9 41	31 42	74·8	9 25	30 43	74·6	9 09	29 45	74·4	198	342
19	161	11 02	34 29	74·4	10 46	33 30	74·2	10 29	32 32	74·1	10 13	31 33	73·9	9 56	30 35	73·7	9 39	29 36	73·6	199	341
20	160	11 36	34 19	73·6	11 19	33 21	73·4	11 02	32 22	73·2	10 44	31 24	73·0	10 27	30 25	72·8	10 09	29 27	72·7	200	340
21	159	12 10	34 09	72·7	11 52	33 10	72·5	11 34	32 12	72·3	11 15	31 14	72·2	10 57	30 15	72·0	10 38	29 17	71·8	201	339
22	158	12 43	33 58	71·9	12 24	33 00	71·7	12 06	32 01	71·5	11 46	31 03	71·3	11 27	30 05	71·1	11 07	29 07	70·9	202	338
23	157	13 17	33 46	71·0	12 57	32 48	70·8	12 37	31 50	70·6	12 17	30 52	70·4	11 57	29 54	70·2	11 37	28 57	70·0	203	337
24	156	13 50	33 34	70·2	13 29	32 36	70·0	13 09	31 38	69·7	12 48	30 41	69·5	12 27	29 43	69·3	12 06	28 46	69·1	204	336
25	155	14 23	33 22	69·3	14 02	32 24	69·1	13 40	31 26	68·9	13 18	30 29	68·6	12 56	29 31	68·4	12 34	28 34	68·2	205	335
26	154	14 56	33 09	68·5	14 34	32 11	68·2	14 11	31 14	68·0	13 49	30 16	67·8	13 26	29 19	67·5	13 03	28 22	67·3	206	334
27	153	15 29	32 55	67·6	15 06	31 58	67·3	14 42	31 00	67·1	14 19	30 03	66·9	13 55	29 06	66·6	13 31	28 10	66·4	207	333
28	152	16 01	32 41	66·7	15 37	31 44	66·5	15 13	30 47	66·2	14 49	29 50	66·0	14 24	28 53	65·7	14 00	27 57	65·5	208	332
29	151	16 33	32 26	65·8	16 09	31 29	65·6	15 44	30 32	65·3	15 19	29 36	65·1	14 53	28 39	64·8	14 28	27 43	64·6	209	331
30	150	17 05	32 11	65·0	16 40	31 14	64·7	16 14	30 17	64·4	15 48	29 21	64·2	15 22	28 25	63·9	14 55	27 29	63·7	210	330
31	149	17 37	31 55	64·1	17 11	30 58	63·8	16 44	30 02	63·5	16 17	29 06	63·3	15 50	28 10	63·0	15 23	27 15	62·7	211	329
32	148	18 09	31 38	63·2	17 42	30 42	62·9	17 14	29 46	62·6	16 47	28 51	62·3	16 19	27 55	62·1	15 50	27 00	61·8	212	328
33	147	18 40	31 21	62·3	18 12	30 25	62·0	17 44	29 30	61·7	17 15	28 34	61·4	16 47	27 39	61·2	16 17	26 45	60·9	213	327
34	146	19 11	31 04	61·4	18 42	30 08	61·1	18 13	29 13	60·8	17 44	28 18	60·5	17 14	27 23	60·2	16 44	26 29	60·0	214	326
35	145	19 42	30 46	60·5	19 12	29 50	60·2	18 42	28 55	59·9	18 12	28 01	59·6	17 42	27 06	59·3	17 11	26 12	59·0	215	325
36	144	20 13	30 27	59·6	19 42	29 32	59·2	19 11	28 37	58·9	18 40	27 43	58·6	18 09	26 49	58·4	17 37	25 55	58·1	216	324
37	143	20 43	30 07	58·6	20 12	29 13	58·3	19 40	28 19	58·0	19 08	27 25	57·7	18 36	26 31	57·4	18 03	25 38	57·1	217	323
38	142	21 13	29 48	57·7	20 41	28 53	57·4	20 08	27 59	57·1	19 35	27 06	56·8	19 02	26 13	56·5	18 29	25 20	56·2	218	322
39	141	21 43	29 27	56·8	21 10	28 33	56·4	20 36	27 40	56·1	20 03	26 47	55·8	19 29	25 54	55·5	18 55	25 02	55·2	219	321
40	140	22 12	29 06	55·8	21 38	28 13	55·5	21 04	27 20	55·2	20 30	26 27	54·9	19 55	25 35	54·6	19 20	24 43	54·3	220	320
41	139	22 41	28 44	54·9	22 06	27 51	54·5	21 31	26 59	54·2	20 56	26 07	53·9	20 21	25 15	53·6	19 45	24 24	53·3	221	319
42	138	23 10	28 22	53·9	22 34	27 29	53·6	21 58	26 37	53·3	21 22	25 46	52·9	20 46	24 55	52·6	20 10	24 04	52·3	222	318
43	137	23 38	27 59	53·0	23 02	27 07	52·6	22 25	26 15	52·3	21 48	25 24	52·0	21 11	24 34	51·7	20 34	23 43	51·4	223	317
44	136	24 06	27 36	52·0	23 29	26 44	51·7	22 51	25 53	51·3	22 14	25 02	51·0	21 36	24 12	50·7	20 58	23 23	50·4	224	316
45	135	24 34	27 11	51·0	23 56	26 20	50·7	23 17	25 30	50·3	22 39	24 40	50·0	22 00	23 50	49·7	21 21	23 01	49·4	225	315

Lat. / A		54°			55°			56°			57°			58°			59°			Lat. / A	
LHA/F		A/H	B/P	Z_1/Z_2	A/H	B/P	Z_1/Z_2	A/H	B/P	Z_1/Z_2	A/H	B/P	Z_1/Z_2	A/H	B/P	Z_1/Z_2	A/H	B/P	Z_1/Z_2	LHA	
°	°	° ′	° ′	°	° ′	° ′	°	° ′	° ′	°	° ′	° ′	°	° ′	° ′	°	° ′	° ′	°	°	°
45	135	24 34	27 11	51·0	23 56	26 20	50·7	23 17	25 30	50·3	22 39	24 40	50·0	22 00	23 50	49·7	21 21	23 01	49·4	225	315
46	134	25 01	26 47	50·0	24 22	25 56	49·7	23 43	25 06	49·4	23 04	24 17	49·0	22 24	23 28	48·7	21 45	22 39	48·4	226	314
47	133	25 28	26 22	49·1	24 48	25 32	48·7	24 08	24 42	48·4	23 28	23 53	48·0	22 48	23 05	47·7	22 08	22 17	47·4	227	313
48	132	25 54	25 56	48·1	25 14	25 06	47·7	24 33	24 17	47·4	23 53	23 29	47·0	23 11	22 41	46·7	22 30	21 54	46·4	228	312
49	131	26 20	25 29	47·1	25 39	24 40	46·7	24 58	23 52	46·4	24 16	23 05	46·0	23 34	22 17	45·7	22 52	21 31	45·4	229	311
50	130	26 46	25 02	46·0	26 04	24 14	45·7	25 22	23 26	45·3	24 40	22 39	45·0	23 57	21 53	44·7	23 14	21 07	44·4	230	310
51	129	27 11	24 34	45·0	26 28	23 47	44·7	25 45	23 00	44·3	25 02	22 14	44·0	24 19	21 28	43·7	23 36	20 43	43·4	231	309
52	128	27 36	24 06	44·0	26 52	23 19	43·6	26 09	22 33	43·3	25 25	21 48	43·0	24 41	21 03	42·7	23 57	20 18	42·3	232	308
53	127	28 00	23 37	43·0	27 16	22 51	42·6	26 32	22 06	42·3	25 47	21 21	41·9	25 02	20 37	41·6	24 17	19 53	41·3	233	307
54	126	28 24	23 07	41·9	27 39	22 22	41·6	26 54	21 38	41·2	26 09	20 54	40·9	25 23	20 10	40·6	24 37	19 27	40·3	234	306
55	125	28 47	22 37	40·9	28 01	21 53	40·5	27 16	21 09	40·2	26 30	20 26	39·9	25 44	19 43	39·5	24 57	19 01	39·2	235	305
56	124	29 10	22 07	39·8	28 24	21 23	39·5	27 37	20 40	39·1	26 50	19 57	38·8	26 04	19 16	38·5	25 17	18 34	38·2	236	304
57	123	29 32	21 35	38·8	28 45	20 52	38·4	27 58	20 10	38·1	27 11	19 29	37·8	26 23	18 48	37·4	25 35	18 07	37·1	237	303
58	122	29 54	21 03	37·7	29 06	20 21	37·3	28 19	19 40	37·0	27 31	18 59	36·7	26 42	18 19	36·4	25 54	17 40	36·1	238	302
59	121	30 15	20 31	36·6	29 27	19 50	36·3	28 38	19 09	35·9	27 50	18 30	35·6	27 01	17 50	35·3	26 12	17 12	35·0	239	301
60	120	30 36	19 58	35·5	29 47	19 18	35·2	28 58	18 38	34·9	28 09	17 59	34·5	27 19	17 21	34·2	26 29	16 43	34·0	240	300
61	119	30 56	19 24	34·4	30 07	18 45	34·1	29 17	18 06	33·8	28 27	17 29	33·5	27 37	16 51	33·2	26 46	16 14	32·9	241	299
62	118	31 16	18 50	33·3	30 26	18 12	33·0	29 35	17 34	32·7	28 45	16 57	32·4	27 54	16 21	32·1	27 03	15 45	31·8	242	298
63	117	31 35	18 15	32·2	30 44	17 38	31·9	29 53	17 02	31·6	29 02	16 26	31·3	28 10	15 50	31·0	27 19	15 15	30·7	243	297
64	116	31 53	17 40	31·1	31 02	17 04	30·8	30 10	16 28	30·5	29 19	15 53	30·2	28 27	15 19	29·9	27 35	14 45	29·6	244	296
65	115	32 11	17 04	30·0	31 19	16 29	29·7	30 27	15 55	29·4	29 35	15 21	29·1	28 42	14 48	28·8	27 50	14 15	28·5	245	295
66	114	32 29	16 28	28·8	31 36	15 54	28·5	30 43	15 20	28·2	29 50	14 48	28·0	28 57	14 16	27·7	28 04	13 44	27·4	246	294
67	113	32 45	15 51	27·7	31 52	15 18	27·4	30 59	14 46	27·1	30 05	14 14	26·8	29 12	13 43	26·6	28 18	13 13	26·3	247	293
68	112	33 01	15 14	26·5	32 08	14 42	26·3	31 14	14 11	26·0	30 20	13 40	25·7	29 26	13 10	25·5	28 31	12 41	25·2	248	292
69	111	33 17	14 36	25·4	32 23	14 05	25·1	31 28	13 35	24·8	30 34	13 06	24·6	29 39	12 37	24·4	28 44	12 09	24·1	249	291
70	110	33 32	13 57	24·2	32 37	13 28	24·0	31 42	12 59	23·7	30 47	12 31	23·5	29 52	12 04	23·2	28 57	11 37	23·0	250	290
71	109	33 46	13 18	23·1	32 51	12 51	22·8	31 55	12 23	22·6	31 00	11 56	22·3	30 04	11 30	22·1	29 09	11 04	21·9	251	289
72	108	33 59	12 39	21·9	33 04	12 13	21·6	32 08	11 46	21·4	31 12	11 21	21·2	30 16	10 56	21·0	29 20	10 31	20·8	252	288
73	107	34 12	12 00	20·7	33 16	11 34	20·5	32 20	11 09	20·2	31 23	10 45	20·0	30 27	10 21	19·8	29 30	9 58	19·6	253	287
74	106	34 24	11 19	19·5	33 28	10 55	19·3	32 31	10 32	19·1	31 34	10 09	18·9	30 37	9 46	18·7	29 41	9 24	18·5	254	286
75	105	34 36	10 39	18·3	33 39	10 16	18·1	32 42	9 54	17·9	31 44	9 32	17·7	30 47	9 11	17·5	29 50	8 50	17·4	255	285
76	104	34 46	9 58	17·1	33 49	9 37	16·9	32 52	9 16	16·7	31 54	8 56	16·6	30 57	8 36	16·4	29 59	8 16	16·2	256	284
77	103	34 56	9 17	15·9	33 59	8 57	15·7	33 01	8 38	15·6	32 03	8 19	15·4	31 05	8 00	15·2	30 07	7 42	15·1	257	283
78	102	35 06	8 35	14·7	34 08	8 17	14·5	33 10	7 59	14·4	32 11	7 41	14·2	31 13	7 24	14·1	30 15	7 07	13·9	258	282
79	101	35 14	7 54	13·5	34 16	7 37	13·3	33 18	7 20	13·2	32 19	7 04	13·0	31 21	6 48	12·9	30 22	6 32	12·8	259	281
80	100	35 22	7 11	12·3	34 24	6 56	12·1	33 25	6 41	12·0	32 26	6 26	11·9	31 27	6 12	11·7	30 29	5 57	11·6	260	280
81	99	35 29	6 29	11·1	34 30	6 15	10·9	33 32	6 01	10·8	32 33	5 48	10·7	31 34	5 35	10·6	30 35	5 22	10·5	261	279
82	98	35 36	5 46	9·9	34 37	5 34	9·7	33 37	5 22	9·6	32 38	5 10	9·5	31 39	4 58	9·4	30 40	4 47	9·3	262	278
83	97	35 41	5 04	8·6	34 42	4 53	8·5	33 43	4 42	8·4	32 43	4 32	8·3	31 44	4 21	8·2	30 45	4 11	8·2	263	277
84	96	35 46	4 21	7·4	34 47	4 11	7·3	33 47	4 02	7·2	32 48	3 53	7·1	31 48	3 44	7·1	30 49	3 36	7·0	264	276
85	95	35 51	3 37	6·2	34 51	3 30	6·1	33 51	3 22	6·0	32 52	3 14	6·0	31 52	3 07	5·9	30 52	3 00	5·8	265	275
86	94	35 54	2 54	4·9	34 54	2 48	4·9	33 54	2 42	4·8	32 55	2 36	4·8	31 55	2 30	4·7	30 55	2 24	4·7	266	274
87	93	35 57	2 11	3·7	34 57	2 06	3·7	33 57	2 01	3·6	32 57	1 57	3·6	31 57	1 52	3·5	30 57	1 48	3·5	267	273
88	92	35 58	1 27	2·5	34 59	1 24	2·4	33 59	1 21	2·4	32 59	1 18	2·4	31 59	1 15	2·4	30 59	1 12	2·3	268	272
89	91	36 00	0 44	1·2	35 00	0 42	1·2	34 00	0 40	1·2	33 00	0 39	1·2	32 00	0 37	1·2	31 00	0 36	1·2	269	271
90	90	36 00	0 00	0·0	35 00	0 00	0·0	34 00	0 00	0·0	33 00	0 00	0·0	32 00	0 00	0·0	31 00	0 00	0·0	270	270

N. Lat: for LHA > 180° … $Z_n = Z$
for LHA < 180° … $Z_n = 360° - Z$

S. Lat.: for LHA > 180° … $Z_n = 180° - Z$
for LHA < 180° … $Z_n = 180° + Z$

SIGHT REDUCTION TABLE

B: (−) for 90° < LHA < 270°
Dec:(−) for Lat. contrary name

Z_1: same sign as B
Z_2: (−) for F > 90°

Lat. / A	60°			61°			62°			63°			64°			65°			Lat. / A
LHA/F	A/H	B/P	Z_1/Z_2	A/H	B/P	Z_1/Z_2	A/H	B/P	Z_1/Z_2	A/H	B/P	Z_1/Z_2	A/H	B/P	Z_1/Z_2	A/H	B/P	Z_1/Z_2	LHA
° °	° ′	° ′	°	° ′	° ′	°	° ′	° ′	°	° ′	° ′	°	° ′	° ′	°	° ′	° ′	°	° °
0 180	0 00	30 00	90·0	0 00	29 00	90·0	0 00	28 00	90·0	0 00	27 00	90·0	0 00	26 00	90·0	0 00	25 00	90·0	180 360
1 179	0 30	30 00	89·1	0 29	29 00	89·1	0 28	28 00	89·1	0 27	27 00	89·1	0 26	26 00	89·1	0 25	25 00	89·1	181 359
2 178	1 00	29 59	88·3	0 58	28 59	88·3	0 56	27 59	88·2	0 54	26 59	88·2	0 53	25 59	88·2	0 51	24 59	88·2	182 358
3 177	1 30	29 58	87·4	1 27	28 58	87·4	1 24	27 58	87·4	1 22	26 58	87·3	1 19	25 58	87·3	1 16	24 58	87·3	183 357
4 176	2 00	29 56	86·5	1 56	28 56	86·5	1 53	27 57	86·5	1 49	26 57	86·4	1 45	25 57	86·4	1 41	24 57	86·4	184 356
5 175	2 30	29 54	85·7	2 25	28 54	85·6	2 21	27 55	85·6	2 16	26 55	85·5	2 11	25 55	85·5	2 07	24 55	85·5	185 355
6 174	3 00	29 52	84·8	2 54	28 52	84·7	2 49	27 52	84·7	2 43	26 52	84·6	2 38	25 53	84·6	2 32	24 53	84·6	186 354
7 173	3 30	29 49	83·9	3 23	28 49	83·9	3 17	27 49	83·8	3 10	26 50	83·8	3 04	25 50	83·7	2 57	24 50	83·7	187 353
8 172	3 59	29 45	83·1	3 52	28 46	83·0	3 45	27 46	82·9	3 37	26 46	82·9	3 30	25 47	82·8	3 22	24 47	82·7	188 352
9 171	4 29	29 42	82·2	4 21	28 42	82·1	4 13	27 42	82·0	4 04	26 43	82·0	3 56	25 43	81·9	3 47	24 44	81·8	189 351
10 170	4 59	29 37	81·3	4 50	28 38	81·2	4 41	27 38	81·2	4 31	26 39	81·1	4 22	25 39	81·0	4 13	24 40	80·9	190 350
11 169	5 28	29 33	80·4	5 18	28 33	80·4	5 08	27 34	80·3	4 58	26 34	80·2	4 48	25 35	80·1	4 38	24 36	80·0	191 349
12 168	5 58	29 27	79·6	5 47	28 28	79·5	5 36	27 29	79·4	5 25	26 29	79·3	5 14	25 30	79·2	5 02	24 31	79·1	192 348
13 167	6 27	29 22	78·7	6 16	28 22	78·6	6 04	27 23	78·5	5 52	26 24	78·4	5 40	25 25	78·3	5 27	24 26	78·2	193 347
14 166	6 57	29 15	77·8	6 44	28 16	77·7	6 31	27 17	77·6	6 18	26 18	77·5	6 05	25 20	77·4	5 52	24 21	77·3	194 346
15 165	7 26	29 09	76·9	7 13	28 10	76·8	6 59	27 11	76·7	6 45	26 12	76·6	6 31	25 14	76·5	6 17	24 15	76·4	195 345
16 164	7 55	29 02	76·1	7 41	28 03	75·9	7 26	27 04	75·8	7 11	26 06	75·7	6 56	25 07	75·5	6 41	24 09	75·4	196 344
17 163	8 24	28 54	75·2	8 09	27 56	75·0	7 53	26 57	74·9	7 38	25 59	74·8	7 22	25 00	74·6	7 06	24 02	74·5	197 343
18 162	8 53	28 46	74·3	8 37	27 48	74·1	8 20	26 50	74·0	8 04	25 51	73·9	7 47	24 53	73·7	7 30	23 55	73·6	198 342
19 161	9 22	28 38	73·4	9 05	27 40	73·2	8 48	26 41	73·1	8 30	25 43	72·9	8 12	24 45	72·8	7 55	23 48	72·7	199 341
20 160	9 51	28 29	72·5	9 33	27 31	72·3	9 14	26 33	72·2	8 56	25 35	72·0	8 37	24 37	71·9	8 19	23 40	71·7	200 340
21 159	10 19	28 19	71·6	10 00	27 22	71·4	9 41	26 24	71·3	9 22	25 26	71·1	9 02	24 29	71·0	8 43	23 32	70·8	201 339
22 158	10 48	28 10	70·7	10 28	27 12	70·5	10 08	26 15	70·4	9 48	25 17	70·2	9 27	24 20	70·0	9 07	23 23	69·9	202 338
23 157	11 16	27 59	69·8	10 55	27 02	69·6	10 34	26 05	69·5	10 13	25 08	69·3	9 52	24 11	69·1	9 30	23 14	69·0	203 337
24 156	11 44	27 49	68·9	11 22	26 51	68·7	11 00	25 54	68·5	10 38	24 58	68·4	10 16	24 01	68·2	9 54	23 04	68·0	204 336
25 155	12 12	27 37	68·0	11 49	26 40	67·8	11 27	25 44	67·6	11 04	24 47	67·4	10 41	23 51	67·3	10 17	22 55	67·1	205 335
26 154	12 40	27 26	67·1	12 16	26 29	66·9	11 53	25 33	66·7	11 29	24 36	66·5	11 05	23 40	66·3	10 41	22 44	66·2	206 334
27 153	13 07	27 13	66·2	12 43	26 17	66·0	12 18	25 21	65·8	11 54	24 25	65·6	11 29	23 29	65·4	11 04	22 34	65·2	207 333
28 152	13 35	27 01	65·3	13 09	26 05	65·1	12 44	25 09	64·9	12 18	24 13	64·7	11 53	23 18	64·5	11 27	22 23	64·3	208 332
29 151	14 02	26 48	64·4	13 36	25 52	64·1	13 09	24 56	63·9	12 43	24 01	63·7	12 16	23 06	63·5	11 49	22 11	63·3	209 331
30 150	14 29	26 34	63·4	14 02	25 39	63·2	13 35	24 43	63·0	13 07	23 49	62·8	12 40	22 54	62·6	12 12	21 59	62·4	210 330
31 149	14 55	26 20	62·5	14 28	25 25	62·3	14 00	24 30	62·1	13 31	23 36	61·8	13 03	22 41	61·6	12 34	21 47	61·4	211 329
32 148	15 22	26 05	61·6	14 53	25 11	61·3	14 24	24 16	61·1	13 55	23 22	60·9	13 26	22 28	60·7	12 56	21 35	60·5	212 328
33 147	15 48	25 50	60·6	15 19	24 56	60·4	14 49	24 02	60·2	14 19	23 08	59·9	13 49	22 15	59·7	13 18	21 22	59·5	213 327
34 146	16 14	25 35	59·7	15 44	24 41	59·5	15 13	23 47	59·2	14 42	22 54	59·0	14 11	22 01	58·8	13 40	21 08	58·6	214 326
35 145	16 40	25 19	58·8	16 09	24 25	58·5	15 37	23 32	58·3	15 06	22 39	58·0	14 34	21 47	57·8	14 02	20 54	57·6	215 325
36 144	17 05	25 02	57·8	16 33	24 09	57·6	16 01	23 17	57·3	15 29	22 24	57·1	14 56	21 32	56·9	14 23	20 40	56·6	216 324
37 143	17 31	24 45	56·9	16 58	23 53	56·6	16 25	23 00	56·4	15 51	22 09	56·1	15 18	21 17	55·9	14 44	20 26	55·7	217 323
38 142	17 56	24 28	55·9	17 22	23 36	55·7	16 48	22 44	55·4	16 14	21 53	55·2	15 39	21 01	54·9	15 05	20 11	54·7	218 322
39 141	18 20	24 10	55·0	17 46	23 18	54·7	17 11	22 27	54·4	16 36	21 36	54·2	16 01	20 46	54·0	15 25	19 55	53·7	219 321
40 140	18 45	23 52	54·0	18 09	23 00	53·7	17 34	22 10	53·5	16 58	21 19	53·2	16 22	20 29	53·0	15 46	19 39	52·7	220 320
41 139	19 09	23 33	53·0	18 33	22 42	52·8	17 56	21 52	52·5	17 20	21 02	52·2	16 43	20 13	52·0	16 06	19 23	51·8	221 319
42 138	19 33	23 13	52·1	18 56	22 23	51·8	18 19	21 34	51·5	17 41	20 44	51·3	17 03	19 55	51·0	16 26	19 07	50·8	222 318
43 137	19 56	22 54	51·1	19 18	22 04	50·8	18 40	21 15	50·5	18 02	20 26	50·3	17 24	19 38	50·0	16 45	18 50	49·8	223 317
44 136	20 19	22 33	50·1	19 41	21 44	49·8	19 02	20 56	49·5	18 23	20 08	49·3	17 44	19 20	49·0	17 04	18 33	48·8	224 316
45 135	20 42	22 12	49·1	20 03	21 24	48·8	19 23	20 36	48·6	18 43	19 49	48·3	18 03	19 02	48·1	17 23	18 15	47·8	225 315

Lat. / A		60°			61°			62°			63°			64°			65°			Lat. / A	
LHA/F		A/H	B/P	Z_1/Z_2	A/H	B/P	Z_1/Z_2	A/H	B/P	Z_1/Z_2	A/H	B/P	Z_1/Z_2	A/H	B/P	Z_1/Z_2	A/H	B/P	Z_1/Z_2	LHA	
°	°	° ′	° ′	°	° ′	° ′	°	° ′	° ′	°	° ′	° ′	°	° ′	° ′	°	° ′	° ′	°	°	°
45	135	20 42	22 12	49·1	20 03	21 24	48·8	19 23	20 36	48·6	18 43	19 49	48·3	18 03	19 02	48·1	17 23	18 15	47·8	225	315
46	134	21 05	21 51	48·1	20 25	21 04	47·8	19 44	20 16	47·6	19 04	19 29	47·3	18 23	18 43	47·1	17 42	17 57	46·8	226	314
47	133	21 27	21 30	47·1	20 46	20 43	46·8	20 05	19 56	46·6	19 24	19 10	46·3	18 42	18 24	46·1	18 00	17 39	45·8	227	313
48	132	21 49	21 07	46·1	21 07	20 21	45·8	20 25	19 35	45·6	19 43	18 50	45·3	19 01	18 04	45·1	18 18	17 20	44·8	228	312
49	131	22 10	20 45	45·1	21 28	19 59	44·8	20 45	19 14	44·6	20 02	18 29	44·3	19 19	17 45	44·0	18 36	17 01	43·8	229	311
50	130	22 31	20 22	44·1	21 48	19 37	43·8	21 05	18 52	43·5	20 21	18 08	43·3	19 37	17 24	43·0	18 53	16 41	42·8	230	310
51	129	22 52	19 58	43·1	22 08	19 14	42·8	21 24	18 30	42·5	20 40	17 47	42·3	19 55	17 04	42·0	19 10	16 21	41·8	231	309
52	128	23 12	19 34	42·1	22 28	18 51	41·8	21 43	18 08	41·5	20 58	17 25	41·2	20 13	16 43	41·0	19 27	16 01	40·8	232	308
53	127	23 32	19 10	41·0	22 47	18 27	40·7	22 01	17 45	40·5	21 15	17 03	40·2	20 30	16 21	40·0	19 44	15 41	39·7	233	307
54	126	23 52	18 45	40·0	23 06	18 03	39·7	22 19	17 21	39·4	21 33	16 40	39·2	20 46	16 00	39·0	20 00	15 20	38·7	234	306
55	125	24 11	18 19	39·0	23 24	17 38	38·7	22 37	16 58	38·4	21 50	16 17	38·2	21 03	15 38	37·9	20 15	14 58	37·7	235	305
56	124	24 29	17 54	37·9	23 42	17 13	37·6	22 54	16 34	37·4	22 07	15 54	37·1	21 19	15 15	36·9	20 31	14 37	36·7	236	304
57	123	24 48	17 27	36·9	23 59	16 48	36·6	23 11	16 09	36·3	22 23	15 31	36·1	21 34	14 53	35·8	20 46	14 15	35·6	237	303
58	122	25 05	17 01	35·8	24 17	16 22	35·5	23 28	15 44	35·3	22 39	15 07	35·0	21 49	14 29	34·8	21 00	13 53	34·6	238	302
59	121	25 23	16 34	34·8	24 33	15 56	34·5	23 44	15 19	34·2	22 54	14 42	34·0	22 04	14 06	33·8	21 14	13 30	33·5	239	301
60	120	25 40	16 06	33·7	24 50	15 29	33·4	23 59	14 53	33·2	23 09	14 18	32·9	22 19	13 42	32·7	21 28	13 07	32·5	240	300
61	119	25 56	15 38	32·6	25 05	15 03	32·4	24 15	14 27	32·1	23 24	13 53	31·9	22 33	13 18	31·7	21 42	12 44	31·5	241	299
62	118	26 12	15 10	31·5	25 21	14 35	31·3	24 29	14 01	31·1	23 38	13 27	30·8	22 46	12 54	30·6	21 55	12 21	30·4	242	298
63	117	26 27	14 41	30·5	25 36	14 08	30·2	24 44	13 34	30·0	23 52	13 01	29·8	22 59	12 29	29·5	22 07	11 57	29·3	243	297
64	116	26 42	14 12	29·4	25 50	13 39	29·1	24 57	13 07	28·9	24 05	12 35	28·7	23 12	12 04	28·5	22 19	11 33	28·3	244	296
65	115	26 57	13 43	28·3	26 04	13 11	28·1	25 11	12 40	27·8	24 18	12 09	27·6	23 25	11 39	27·4	22 31	11 09	27·2	245	295
66	114	27 11	13 13	27·2	26 17	12 42	27·0	25 24	12 12	26·8	24 30	11 43	26·6	23 36	11 13	26·4	22 43	10 44	26·2	246	294
67	113	27 24	12 43	26·1	26 30	12 13	25·9	25 36	11 44	25·7	24 42	11 16	25·5	23 48	10 47	25·3	22 54	10 20	25·1	247	293
68	112	27 37	12 12	25·0	26 43	11 44	24·8	25 48	11 16	24·6	24 54	10 48	24·4	23 59	10 21	24·2	23 04	9 55	24·0	248	292
69	111	27 50	11 41	23·9	26 55	11 14	23·7	26 00	10 47	23·5	25 05	10 21	23·3	24 09	9 55	23·1	23 14	9 29	23·0	249	291
70	110	28 01	11 10	22·8	27 06	10 44	22·6	26 11	10 18	22·4	25 15	9 53	22·2	24 20	9 28	22·0	23 24	9 04	21·9	250	290
71	109	28 13	10 39	21·7	27 17	10 14	21·5	26 21	9 49	21·3	25 25	9 25	21·1	24 29	9 01	21·0	23 33	8 38	20·8	251	289
72	108	28 24	10 07	20·6	27 27	9 43	20·4	26 31	9 20	20·2	25 35	8 57	20·0	24 38	8 34	19·9	23 42	8 12	19·7	252	288
73	107	28 34	9 35	19·4	27 37	9 12	19·3	26 41	8 50	19·1	25 44	8 28	18·9	24 47	8 07	18·8	23 50	7 46	18·6	253	287
74	106	28 44	9 03	18·3	27 47	8 41	18·2	26 50	8 20	18·0	25 52	8 00	17·8	24 55	7 39	17·7	23 58	7 19	17·6	254	286
75	105	28 53	8 30	17·2	27 55	8 10	17·0	26 58	7 50	16·9	26 01	7 31	16·7	25 03	7 12	16·6	24 06	6 53	16·5	255	285
76	104	29 01	7 57	16·1	28 04	7 38	15·9	27 06	7 20	15·8	26 08	7 02	15·6	25 10	6 44	15·5	24 13	6 26	15·4	256	284
77	103	29 09	7 24	14·9	28 11	7 06	14·8	27 13	6 49	14·7	26 15	6 32	14·5	25 17	6 16	14·4	24 19	5 59	14·3	257	283
78	102	29 17	6 51	13·8	28 18	6 34	13·7	27 20	6 19	13·5	26 22	6 03	13·4	25 23	5 47	13·3	24 25	5 32	13·2	258	282
79	101	29 24	6 17	12·7	28 25	6 02	12·5	27 27	5 48	12·4	26 28	5 33	12·3	25 29	5 19	12·2	24 31	5 05	12·1	259	281
80	100	29 30	5 44	11·5	28 31	5 30	11·4	27 32	5 17	11·3	26 33	5 03	11·2	25 35	4 50	11·1	24 36	4 38	11·0	260	280
81	99	29 36	5 10	10·4	28 37	4 57	10·3	27 38	4 45	10·2	26 38	4 33	10·1	25 39	4 22	10·0	24 40	4 10	9·9	261	279
82	98	29 41	4 36	9·2	28 41	4 25	9·1	27 42	4 14	9·0	26 43	4 03	9·0	25 44	3 53	8·9	24 44	3 43	8·8	262	278
83	97	29 45	4 01	8·1	28 46	3 52	8·0	27 46	3 42	7·9	26 47	3 33	7·8	25 48	3 24	7·8	24 48	3 15	7·7	263	277
84	96	29 49	3 27	6·9	28 50	3 19	6·9	27 50	3 11	6·8	26 50	3 03	6·7	25 51	2 55	6·7	24 51	2 47	6·6	264	276
85	95	29 52	2 53	5·8	28 53	2 46	5·7	27 53	2 39	5·7	26 53	2 33	5·6	25 54	2 26	5·6	24 54	2 20	5·5	265	275
86	94	29 55	2 18	4·6	28 55	2 13	4·6	27 56	2 07	4·5	26 56	2 02	4·5	25 56	1 57	4·4	24 56	1 52	4·4	266	274
87	93	29 57	1 44	3·5	28 57	1 40	3·4	27 57	1 36	3·4	26 58	1 32	3·4	25 58	1 28	3·3	24 58	1 24	3·3	267	273
88	92	29 59	1 09	2·3	28 59	1 06	2·3	27 59	1 04	2·3	26 59	1 01	2·2	25 59	0 59	2·2	24 59	0 56	2·2	268	272
89	91	30 00	0 35	1·2	29 00	0 33	1·1	28 00	0 32	1·1	27 00	0 31	1·1	26 00	0 29	1·1	25 00	0 28	1·1	269	271
90	90	30 00	0 00	0·0	29 00	0 00	0·0	28 00	0 00	0·0	27 00	0 00	0·0	26 00	0 00	0·0	25 00	0 00	0·0	270	270

N. Lat: for LHA > 180° … $Z_n = Z$
for LHA < 180° … $Z_n = 360° - Z$

S. Lat.: for LHA > 180° … $Z_n = 180° - Z$
for LHA < 180° … $Z_n = 180° + Z$

SIGHT REDUCTION TABLE

B: (−) for 90° < LHA < 270°
Dec:(−) for Lat. contrary name

Z_1: same sign as B
Z_2: (−) for F > 90°

Lat. / A		66°			67°			68°			69°			70°			71°			Lat. / A	
LHA/F		A/H	B/P	Z_1/Z_2	A/H	B/P	Z_1/Z_2	A/H	B/P	Z_1/Z_2	A/H	B/P	Z_1/Z_2	A/H	B/P	Z_1/Z_2	A/H	B/P	Z_1/Z_2	LHA	
°	°	° ′	° ′	°	° ′	° ′	°	° ′	° ′	°	° ′	° ′	°	° ′	° ′	°	° ′	° ′	°	°	°
0	180	0 00	24 00	90·0	0 00	23 00	90·0	0 00	22 00	90·0	0 00	21 00	90·0	0 00	20 00	90·0	0 00	19 00	90·0	180	360
1	179	0 24	24 00	89·1	0 23	23 00	89·1	0 22	22 00	89·1	0 22	21 00	89·1	0 21	20 00	89·1	0 20	19 00	89·1	181	359
2	178	0 49	23 59	88·2	0 47	22 59	88·2	0 45	21 59	88·1	0 43	20 59	88·1	0 41	19 59	88·1	0 39	18 59	88·1	182	358
3	177	1 13	23 58	87·3	1 10	22 58	87·2	1 07	21 58	87·2	1 04	20 58	87·2	1 02	19 58	87·2	0 59	18 59	87·2	183	357
4	176	1 38	23 57	86·3	1 34	22 57	86·3	1 30	21 57	86·3	1 26	20 57	86·3	1 22	19 57	86·2	1 18	18 57	86·2	184	356
5	175	2 02	23 55	85·4	1 57	22 55	85·4	1 52	21 55	85·4	1 47	20 56	85·3	1 42	19 56	85·3	1 38	18 56	85·3	185	355
6	174	2 26	23 53	84·5	2 20	22 53	84·5	2 15	21 53	84·4	2 09	20 54	84·4	2 03	19 54	84·4	1 57	18 54	84·3	186	354
7	173	2 50	23 50	83·6	2 44	22 51	83·6	2 37	21 51	83·5	2 30	20 51	83·5	2 23	19 52	83·4	2 16	18 52	83·4	187	353
8	172	3 15	23 48	82·7	3 07	22 48	82·6	2 59	21 48	82·6	2 52	20 49	82·5	2 44	19 49	82·5	2 36	18 50	82·4	188	352
9	171	3 39	23 44	81·8	3 30	22 45	81·7	3 22	21 45	81·6	3 13	20 46	81·6	3 04	19 46	81·5	2 55	18 47	81·5	189	351
10	170	4 03	23 41	80·8	3 53	22 41	80·8	3 44	21 42	80·7	3 34	20 42	80·7	3 24	19 43	80·6	3 14	18 44	80·5	190	350
11	169	4 27	23 36	79·9	4 17	22 37	79·9	4 06	21 38	79·8	3 55	20 39	79·7	3 45	19 40	79·6	3 34	18 41	79·6	191	349
12	168	4 51	23 32	79·0	4 40	22 33	78·9	4 28	21 34	78·9	4 16	20 35	78·8	4 05	19 36	78·7	3 53	18 37	78·6	192	348
13	167	5 15	23 27	78·1	5 03	22 28	78·0	4 50	21 29	77·9	4 37	20 30	77·8	4 25	19 32	77·8	4 12	18 33	77·7	193	347
14	166	5 39	23 22	77·2	5 25	22 23	77·1	5 12	21 24	77·0	4 58	20 26	76·9	4 45	19 27	76·8	4 31	18 28	76·7	194	346
15	165	6 03	23 16	76·2	5 48	22 18	76·1	5 34	21 19	76·0	5 19	20 21	76·0	5 05	19 22	75·9	4 50	18 24	75·8	195	345
16	164	6 26	23 10	75·3	6 11	22 12	75·2	5 56	21 13	75·1	5 40	20 15	75·0	5 25	19 17	74·9	5 09	18 19	74·8	196	344
17	163	6 50	23 04	74·4	6 34	22 06	74·3	6 17	21 08	74·2	6 01	20 09	74·1	5 44	19 11	74·0	5 28	18 14	73·9	197	343
18	162	7 13	22 57	73·5	6 56	21 59	73·3	6 39	21 01	73·2	6 21	20 03	73·1	6 04	19 06	73·0	5 46	18 08	72·9	198	342
19	161	7 37	22 50	72·5	7 19	21 52	72·4	7 00	20 54	72·3	6 42	19 57	72·2	6 24	18 59	72·1	6 05	18 02	72·0	199	341
20	160	8 00	22 42	71·6	7 41	21 45	71·5	7 22	20 47	71·4	7 02	19 50	71·2	6 43	18 53	71·1	6 24	17 56	71·0	200	340
21	159	8 23	22 34	70·7	8 03	21 37	70·5	7 43	20 40	70·4	7 23	19 43	70·3	7 02	18 46	70·2	6 42	17 49	70·1	201	339
22	158	8 46	22 26	69·7	8 25	21 29	69·6	8 04	20 32	69·5	7 43	19 35	69·3	7 22	18 39	69·2	7 00	17 42	69·1	202	338
23	157	9 09	22 17	68·8	8 47	21 21	68·7	8 25	20 24	68·5	8 03	19 28	68·4	7 41	18 31	68·3	7 19	17 35	68·1	203	337
24	156	9 31	22 08	67·9	9 09	21 12	67·7	8 46	20 16	67·6	8 23	19 19	67·4	8 00	18 24	67·3	7 37	17 28	67·2	204	336
25	155	9 54	21 58	66·9	9 30	21 03	66·8	9 07	20 07	66·6	8 43	19 11	66·5	8 19	18 15	66·3	7 55	17 20	66·2	205	335
26	154	10 16	21 49	66·0	9 52	20 53	65·8	9 27	19 57	65·7	9 02	19 02	65·5	8 37	18 07	65·4	8 12	17 12	65·2	206	334
27	153	10 38	21 38	65·0	10 13	20 43	64·9	9 48	19 48	64·7	9 22	18 53	64·6	8 56	17 58	64·4	8 30	17 03	64·3	207	333
28	152	11 00	21 28	64·1	10 34	20 33	63·9	10 08	19 38	63·8	9 41	18 43	63·6	9 14	17 49	63·5	8 48	16 55	63·3	208	332
29	151	11 22	21 17	63·1	10 55	20 22	63·0	10 28	19 28	62·8	10 00	18 34	62·6	9 33	17 39	62·5	9 05	16 46	62·3	209	331
30	150	11 44	21 05	62·2	11 16	20 11	62·0	10 48	19 17	61·8	10 19	18 23	61·7	9 51	17 30	61·5	9 22	16 36	61·4	210	330
31	149	12 06	20 53	61·2	11 37	20 00	61·1	11 07	19 06	60·9	10 38	18 13	60·7	10 09	17 20	60·5	9 39	16 27	60·4	211	329
32	148	12 27	20 41	60·3	11 57	19 48	60·1	11 27	18 55	59·9	10 57	18 02	59·7	10 27	17 09	59·6	9 56	16 17	59·4	212	328
33	147	12 48	20 29	59·3	12 17	19 36	59·1	11 46	18 43	58·9	11 15	17 51	58·8	10 44	16 58	58·6	10 13	16 06	58·4	213	327
34	146	13 09	20 16	58·4	12 37	19 23	58·2	12 06	18 31	58·0	11 34	17 39	57·8	11 02	16 47	57·6	10 29	15 56	57·5	214	326
35	145	13 29	20 02	57·4	12 57	19 10	57·2	12 24	18 19	57·0	11 52	17 27	56·8	11 19	16 36	56·7	10 46	15 45	56·5	215	325
36	144	13 50	19 49	56·4	13 17	18 57	56·2	12 43	18 06	56·0	12 10	17 15	55·9	11 36	16 24	55·7	11 02	15 34	55·5	216	324
37	143	14 10	19 34	55·5	13 36	18 44	55·3	13 02	17 53	55·1	12 27	17 03	54·9	11 53	16 12	54·7	11 18	15 23	54·5	217	323
38	142	14 30	19 20	54·5	13 55	18 30	54·3	13 20	17 40	54·1	12 45	16 50	53·9	12 09	16 00	53·7	11 34	15 11	53·5	218	322
39	141	14 50	19 05	53·5	14 14	18 15	53·3	13 38	17 26	53·1	13 02	16 37	52·9	12 26	15 48	52·7	11 49	14 59	52·6	219	321
40	140	15 09	18 50	52·5	14 33	18 01	52·3	13 56	17 12	52·1	13 19	16 23	51·9	12 42	15 35	51·7	12 05	14 47	51·6	220	320
41	139	15 29	18 34	51·5	14 51	17 46	51·3	14 14	16 57	51·1	13 36	16 09	50·9	12 58	15 22	50·8	12 20	14 34	50·6	221	319
42	138	15 48	18 18	50·6	15 09	17 30	50·3	14 31	16 43	50·1	13 52	15 55	49·9	13 14	15 08	49·8	12 35	14 21	49·6	222	318
43	137	16 06	18 02	49·6	15 27	17 15	49·4	14 48	16 28	49·2	14 09	15 41	49·0	13 29	14 54	48·8	12 50	14 08	48·6	223	317
44	136	16 25	17 46	48·6	15 45	16 59	48·4	15 05	16 12	48·2	14 25	15 26	48·0	13 45	14 40	47·8	13 04	13 55	47·6	224	316
45	135	16 43	17 29	47·6	16 02	16 42	47·4	15 22	15 57	47·2	14 41	15 11	47·0	14 00	14 26	46·8	13 19	13 41	46·6	225	315

Lat. / A		66°			67°			68°			69°			70°			71°			Lat. / A	
LHA/F		A/H	B/P	Z_1/Z_2	A/H	B/P	Z_1/Z_2	A/H	B/P	Z_1/Z_2	A/H	B/P	Z_1/Z_2	A/H	B/P	Z_1/Z_2	A/H	B/P	Z_1/Z_2	LHA	
°	°	° ′	° ′	°	° ′	° ′	°	° ′	° ′	°	° ′	° ′	°	° ′	° ′	°	° ′	° ′	°	°	°
45	135	16 43	17 29	47·6	16 02	16 42	47·4	15 22	15 57	47·2	14 41	15 11	47·0	14 00	14 26	46·8	13 19	13 41	46·6	225	315
46	134	17 01	17 11	46·6	16 19	16 26	46·4	15 38	15 41	46·2	14 56	14 56	46·0	14 15	14 11	45·8	13 33	13 27	45·6	226	314
47	133	17 18	16 53	45·6	16 36	16 09	45·4	15 54	15 24	45·2	15 12	14 40	45·0	14 29	13 56	44·8	13 46	13 13	44·6	227	313
48	132	17 36	16 35	44·6	16 53	15 51	44·4	16 10	15 08	44·2	15 27	14 24	44·0	14 43	13 41	43·8	14 00	12 58	43·6	228	312
49	131	17 53	16 17	43·6	17 09	15 34	43·4	16 25	14 51	43·2	15 42	14 08	43·0	14 58	13 26	42·8	14 13	12 44	42·6	229	311
50	130	18 09	15 58	42·6	17 25	15 16	42·4	16 41	14 33	42·1	15 56	13 52	41·9	15 11	13 10	41·8	14 27	12 29	41·6	230	310
51	129	18 26	15 39	41·6	17 41	14 57	41·3	16 56	14 16	41·1	16 10	13 35	40·9	15 25	12 54	40·8	14 39	12 14	40·6	231	309
52	128	18 42	15 20	40·5	17 56	14 39	40·3	17 10	13 58	40·1	16 24	13 18	39·9	15 38	12 38	39·7	14 52	11 58	39·6	232	308
53	127	18 57	15 00	39·5	18 11	14 20	39·3	17 24	13 40	39·1	16 38	13 00	38·9	15 51	12 21	38·7	15 04	11 42	38·6	233	307
54	126	19 13	14 40	38·5	18 26	14 01	38·3	17 39	13 22	38·1	16 51	12 43	37·9	16 04	12 05	37·7	15 16	11 26	37·5	234	306
55	125	19 28	14 20	37·5	18 40	13 41	37·3	17 52	13 03	37·1	17 04	12 25	36·9	16 16	11 48	36·7	15 28	11 10	36·5	235	305
56	124	19 42	13 59	36·4	18 54	13 21	36·2	18 06	12 44	36·0	17 17	12 07	35·8	16 28	11 30	35·7	15 40	10 54	35·5	236	304
57	123	19 57	13 38	35·4	19 08	13 01	35·2	18 19	12 25	35·0	17 29	11 49	34·8	16 40	11 13	34·6	15 51	10 37	34·5	237	303
58	122	20 11	13 17	34·4	19 21	12 41	34·2	18 31	12 05	34·0	17 42	11 30	33·8	16 52	10 55	33·6	16 02	10 20	33·5	238	302
59	121	20 24	12 55	33·3	19 34	12 20	33·1	18 44	11 45	32·9	17 53	11 11	32·8	17 03	10 37	32·6	16 12	10 03	32·4	239	301
60	120	20 37	12 33	32·3	19 47	11 59	32·1	18 56	11 25	31·9	18 05	10 52	31·7	17 14	10 19	31·6	16 23	9 46	31·4	240	300
61	119	20 50	12 11	31·2	19 59	11 38	31·1	19 08	11 05	30·9	18 16	10 33	30·7	17 24	10 00	30·5	16 33	9 29	30·4	241	299
62	118	21 03	11 48	30·2	20 11	11 16	30·0	19 19	10 44	29·8	18 27	10 13	29·7	17 35	9 42	29·5	16 42	9 11	29·4	242	298
63	117	21 15	11 26	29·2	20 22	10 54	29·0	19 30	10 24	28·8	18 37	9 53	28·6	17 45	9 23	28·5	16 52	8 53	28·3	243	297
64	116	21 27	11 03	28·1	20 34	10 32	27·9	19 41	10 03	27·7	18 47	9 33	27·6	17 54	9 04	27·4	17 01	8 35	27·3	244	296
65	115	21 38	10 39	27·0	20 44	10 10	26·9	19 51	9 41	26·7	18 57	9 13	26·5	18 03	8 45	26·4	17 10	8 17	26·3	245	295
66	114	21 49	10 16	26·0	20 55	9 48	25·8	20 01	9 20	25·7	19 07	8 52	25·5	18 12	8 25	25·4	17 18	7 58	25·2	246	294
67	113	21 59	9 52	24·9	21 05	9 25	24·8	20 10	8 58	24·6	19 16	8 32	24·5	18 21	8 06	24·3	17 26	7 40	24·2	247	293
68	112	22 09	9 28	23·9	21 14	9 02	23·7	20 19	8 36	23·5	19 24	8 11	23·4	18 29	7 46	23·3	17 34	7 21	23·1	248	292
69	111	22 19	9 04	22·8	21 24	8 39	22·6	20 28	8 14	22·5	19 33	7 50	22·4	18 37	7 26	22·2	17 42	7 02	22·1	249	291
70	110	22 28	8 39	21·7	21 32	8 16	21·6	20 37	7 52	21·4	19 41	7 29	21·3	18 45	7 06	21·2	17 49	6 43	21·1	250	290
71	109	22 37	8 15	20·7	21 41	7 52	20·5	20 45	7 30	20·4	19 48	7 07	20·2	18 52	6 45	20·1	17 56	6 24	20·0	251	289
72	108	22 45	7 50	19·6	21 49	7 28	19·4	20 52	7 07	19·3	19 56	6 46	19·2	18 59	6 25	19·1	18 02	6 04	19·0	252	288
73	107	22 53	7 25	18·5	21 56	7 04	18·4	21 00	6 44	18·2	20 03	6 24	18·1	19 05	6 04	18·0	18 08	5 45	17·9	253	287
74	106	23 01	7 00	17·4	22 04	6 40	17·3	21 06	6 21	17·2	20 09	6 02	17·1	19 12	5 44	17·0	18 14	5 25	16·9	254	286
75	105	23 08	6 34	16·3	22 10	6 16	16·2	21 13	5 58	16·1	20 15	5 40	16·0	19 17	5 23	15·9	18 20	5 06	15·8	255	285
76	104	23 15	6 09	15·3	22 17	5 52	15·2	21 19	5 35	15·1	20 21	5 18	15·0	19 23	5 02	14·9	18 25	4 46	14·8	256	284
77	103	23 21	5 43	14·2	22 23	5 27	14·1	21 24	5 12	14·0	20 26	4 56	13·9	19 28	4 41	13·8	18 30	4 26	13·7	257	283
78	102	23 27	5 17	13·1	22 28	5 03	13·0	21 30	4 48	12·9	20 31	4 34	12·8	19 33	4 20	12·7	18 34	4 06	12·7	258	282
79	101	23 32	4 51	12·0	22 33	4 38	11·9	21 35	4 24	11·8	20 36	4 11	11·8	19 37	3 58	11·7	18 38	3 46	11·6	259	281
80	100	23 37	4 25	10·9	22 38	4 13	10·8	21 39	4 01	10·8	20 40	3 49	10·7	19 41	3 37	10·6	18 42	3 25	10·6	260	280
81	99	23 41	3 59	9·8	22 42	3 48	9·8	21 43	3 37	9·7	20 44	3 26	9·6	19 45	3 16	9·6	18 45	3 05	9·5	261	279
82	98	23 45	3 33	8·7	22 46	3 23	8·7	21 46	3 13	8·6	20 47	3 03	8·6	19 48	2 54	8·5	18 48	2 45	8·5	262	278
83	97	23 49	3 06	7·7	22 49	2 58	7·6	21 50	2 49	7·5	20 50	2 41	7·5	19 51	2 32	7·4	18 51	2 24	7·4	263	277
84	96	23 52	2 40	6·6	22 52	2 32	6·5	21 52	2 25	6·5	20 53	2 18	6·4	19 53	2 11	6·4	18 54	2 04	6·3	264	276
85	95	23 54	2 13	5·5	22 54	2 07	5·4	21 55	2 01	5·4	20 55	1 55	5·4	19 55	1 49	5·3	18 55	1 43	5·3	265	275
86	94	23 56	1 47	4·4	22 56	1 42	4·3	21 57	1 37	4·3	20 57	1 32	4·3	19 57	1 27	4·3	18 57	1 23	4·2	266	274
87	93	23 58	1 20	3·3	22 58	1 16	3·3	21 58	1 13	3·2	20 58	1 09	3·2	19 58	1 05	3·2	18 58	1 02	3·2	267	273
88	92	23 59	0 53	2·2	22 59	0 51	2·2	21 59	0 48	2·2	20 59	0 46	2·1	19 59	0 44	2·1	18 59	0 41	2·1	268	272
89	91	24 00	0 27	1·1	23 00	0 25	1·1	22 00	0 24	1·1	21 00	0 23	1·1	20 00	0 22	1·1	19 00	0 21	1·1	269	271
90	90	24 00	0 00	0·0	23 00	0 00	0·0	22 00	0 00	0·0	21 00	0 00	0·0	20 00	0 00	0·0	19 00	0 00	0·0	270	270

N. Lat: for LHA > 180° … $Z_n = Z$
for LHA < 180° … $Z_n = 360° - Z$

S. Lat.: for LHA > 180° … $Z_n = 180° - Z$
for LHA < 180° … $Z_n = 180° + Z$

SIGHT REDUCTION TABLE

B: (−) for 90° < LHA < 270°
Dec:(−) for Lat. contrary name

Z$_1$: same sign as B
Z$_2$: (−) for F > 90°

Lat. / A		72°			73°			74°			75°			76°			77°			Lat. / A	
LHA/F		A/H	B/P	Z$_1$/Z$_2$	A/H	B/P	Z$_1$/Z$_2$	A/H	B/P	Z$_1$/Z$_2$	A/H	B/P	Z$_1$/Z$_2$	A/H	B/P	Z$_1$/Z$_2$	A/H	B/P	Z$_1$/Z$_2$	LHA	
°	°	° ′	° ′	°	° ′	° ′	°	° ′	° ′	°	° ′	° ′	°	° ′	° ′	°	° ′	° ′	°	°	°
0	180	0 00	18 00	90·0	0 00	17 00	90·0	0 00	16 00	90·0	0 00	15 00	90·0	0 00	14 00	90·0	0 00	13 00	90·0	180	360
1	179	0 19	18 00	89·0	0 18	17 00	89·0	0 17	16 00	89·0	0 16	15 00	89·0	0 15	14 00	89·0	0 13	13 00	89·0	181	359
2	178	0 37	17 59	88·1	0 35	16 59	88·1	0 33	15 59	88·1	0 31	14 59	88·1	0 29	14 00	88·1	0 27	13 00	88·1	182	358
3	177	0 56	17 59	87·1	0 53	16 59	87·1	0 50	15 59	87·1	0 47	14 59	87·1	0 44	13 59	87·1	0 40	12 59	87·1	183	357
4	176	1 14	17 58	86·2	1 10	16 58	86·2	1 06	15 58	86·2	1 02	14 58	86·1	0 58	13 58	86·1	0 54	12 58	86·1	184	356
5	175	1 33	17 56	85·2	1 28	16 56	85·2	1 23	15 57	85·2	1 18	14 57	85·2	1 12	13 57	85·1	1 07	12 57	85·1	185	355
6	174	1 51	17 54	84·3	1 45	16 55	84·3	1 39	15 55	84·2	1 33	14 55	84·2	1 27	13 56	84·2	1 21	12 56	84·2	186	354
7	173	2 09	17 52	83·3	2 03	16 53	83·3	1 56	15 53	83·3	1 48	14 54	83·2	1 41	13 54	83·2	1 34	12 54	83·2	187	353
8	172	2 28	17 50	82·4	2 20	16 51	82·3	2 12	15 51	82·3	2 04	14 52	82·3	1 56	13 52	82·2	1 48	12 53	82·2	188	352
9	171	2 46	17 48	81·4	2 37	16 48	81·4	2 28	15 49	81·3	2 19	14 49	81·3	2 10	13 50	81·3	2 01	12 51	81·2	189	351
10	170	3 05	17 45	80·5	2 55	16 45	80·4	2 45	15 46	80·4	2 35	14 47	80·3	2 24	13 48	80·3	2 14	12 49	80·3	190	350
11	169	3 23	17 41	79·5	3 12	16 42	79·5	3 01	15 43	79·4	2 50	14 44	79·4	2 39	13 45	79·3	2 28	12 46	79·3	191	349
12	168	3 41	17 38	78·6	3 29	16 39	78·5	3 17	15 40	78·5	3 05	14 41	78·4	2 53	13 42	78·3	2 41	12 44	78·3	192	348
13	167	3 59	17 34	77·6	3 46	16 35	77·5	3 33	15 37	77·5	3 20	14 38	77·4	3 07	13 39	77·4	2 54	12 41	77·3	193	347
14	166	4 17	17 30	76·7	4 03	16 31	76·6	3 49	15 33	76·5	3 35	14 34	76·5	3 21	13 36	76·4	3 07	12 38	76·3	194	346
15	165	4 35	17 25	75·7	4 20	16 27	75·6	4 05	15 29	75·6	3 50	14 31	75·5	3 35	13 32	75·4	3 20	12 34	75·4	195	345
16	164	4 53	17 21	74·7	4 37	16 23	74·7	4 21	15 25	74·6	4 05	14 27	74·5	3 49	13 29	74·5	3 33	12 31	74·4	196	344
17	163	5 11	17 16	73·8	4 54	16 18	73·7	4 37	15 20	73·6	4 20	14 22	73·5	4 03	13 25	73·5	3 46	12 27	73·4	197	343
18	162	5 29	17 10	72·8	5 11	16 13	72·7	4 53	15 15	72·7	4 35	14 18	72·6	4 17	13 20	72·5	3 59	12 23	72·4	198	342
19	161	5 46	17 05	71·9	5 28	16 07	71·8	5 09	15 10	71·7	4 50	14 13	71·6	4 31	13 16	71·5	4 12	12 19	71·5	199	341
20	160	6 04	16 59	70·9	5 44	16 02	70·8	5 25	15 05	70·7	5 05	14 08	70·6	4 45	13 11	70·5	4 25	12 14	70·5	200	340
21	159	6 21	16 52	69·9	6 01	15 56	69·8	5 40	14 59	69·7	5 19	14 03	69·7	4 58	13 06	69·6	4 37	12 10	69·5	201	339
22	158	6 39	16 46	69·0	6 17	15 50	68·9	5 56	14 53	68·8	5 34	13 57	68·7	5 12	13 01	68·6	4 50	12 05	68·5	202	338
23	157	6 56	16 39	68·0	6 34	15 43	67·9	6 11	14 47	67·8	5 48	13 51	67·7	5 25	12 56	67·6	5 03	12 00	67·5	203	337
24	156	7 13	16 32	67·1	6 50	15 36	66·9	6 26	14 41	66·8	6 03	13 45	66·7	5 39	12 50	66·6	5 15	11 55	66·5	204	336
25	155	7 30	16 25	66·1	7 06	15 29	66·0	6 41	14 34	65·9	6 17	13 39	65·8	5 52	12 44	65·7	5 27	11 49	65·6	205	335
26	154	7 47	16 17	65·1	7 22	15 22	65·0	6 56	14 27	64·9	6 31	13 32	64·8	6 05	12 38	64·7	5 40	11 43	64·6	206	334
27	153	8 04	16 09	64·1	7 38	15 14	64·0	7 11	14 20	63·9	6 45	13 26	63·8	6 18	12 32	63·7	5 52	11 37	63·6	207	333
28	152	8 20	16 00	63·2	7 53	15 06	63·0	7 26	14 12	62·9	6 59	13 19	62·8	6 31	12 25	62·7	6 04	11 31	62·6	208	332
29	151	8 37	15 52	62·2	8 09	14 58	62·1	7 41	14 05	61·9	7 13	13 11	61·8	6 44	12 18	61·7	6 16	11 25	61·6	209	331
30	150	8 53	15 43	61·2	8 24	14 50	61·1	7 55	13 57	61·0	7 26	13 04	60·9	6 57	12 11	60·7	6 27	11 18	60·6	210	330
31	149	9 09	15 34	60·3	8 40	14 41	60·1	8 10	13 49	60·0	7 40	12 56	59·9	7 09	12 04	59·8	6 39	11 12	59·7	211	329
32	148	9 25	15 24	59·3	8 55	14 32	59·1	8 24	13 40	59·0	7 53	12 48	58·9	7 22	11 56	58·8	6 51	11 05	58·7	212	328
33	147	9 41	15 15	58·3	9 10	14 23	58·2	8 38	13 31	58·0	8 06	12 40	57·9	7 34	11 49	57·8	7 02	10 57	57·7	213	327
34	146	9 57	15 05	57·3	9 25	14 13	57·2	8 52	13 22	57·0	8 19	12 31	56·9	7 46	11 41	56·8	7 14	10 50	56·7	214	326
35	145	10 13	14 54	56·3	9 39	14 04	56·2	9 06	13 13	56·1	8 32	12 23	55·9	7 59	11 33	55·8	7 25	10 43	55·7	215	325
36	144	10 28	14 44	55·4	9 54	13 54	55·2	9 19	13 04	55·1	8 45	12 14	54·9	8 11	11 24	54·8	7 36	10 35	54·7	216	324
37	143	10 43	14 33	54·4	10 08	13 43	54·2	9 33	12 54	54·1	8 58	12 05	53·9	8 22	11 16	53·8	7 47	10 27	53·7	217	323
38	142	10 58	14 22	53·4	10 22	13 33	53·2	9 46	12 44	53·1	9 10	11 55	53·0	8 34	11 07	52·8	7 58	10 19	52·7	218	322
39	141	11 13	14 10	52·4	10 36	13 22	52·2	9 59	12 34	52·1	9 22	11 46	52·0	8 45	10 58	51·8	8 08	10 10	51·7	219	321
40	140	11 27	13 59	51·4	10 50	13 11	51·3	10 12	12 23	51·1	9 35	11 36	51·0	8 57	10 49	50·8	8 19	10 02	50·7	220	320
41	139	11 42	13 47	50·4	11 04	13 00	50·3	10 25	12 13	50·1	9 47	11 26	50·0	9 08	10 39	49·9	8 29	9 53	49·7	221	319
42	138	11 56	13 34	49·4	11 17	12 48	49·3	10 38	12 02	49·1	9 58	11 16	49·0	9 19	10 30	48·9	8 39	9 44	48·7	222	318
43	137	12 10	13 22	48·4	11 30	12 36	48·3	10 50	11 51	48·1	10 10	11 05	48·0	9 30	10 20	47·9	8 49	9 35	47·7	223	317
44	136	12 24	13 09	47·4	11 43	12 24	47·3	11 02	11 39	47·1	10 21	10 55	47·0	9 40	10 10	46·9	8 59	9 26	46·7	224	316
45	135	12 37	12 56	46·4	11 56	12 12	46·3	11 14	11 28	46·1	10 33	10 44	46·0	9 51	10 00	45·9	9 09	9 16	45·7	225	315

Lat. / A		72°			73°			74°			75°			76°			77°			Lat. / A	
LHA/F		A/H	B/P	Z_1/Z_2	A/H	B/P	Z_1/Z_2	A/H	B/P	Z_1/Z_2	A/H	B/P	Z_1/Z_2	A/H	B/P	Z_1/Z_2	A/H	B/P	Z_1/Z_2	LHA	
°	°	° ′	° ′	°	° ′	° ′	°	° ′	° ′	°	° ′	° ′	°	° ′	° ′	°	° ′	° ′	°	°	°
45	135	12 37	12 56	46·4	11 56	12 12	46·3	11 14	11 28	46·1	10 33	10 44	46·0	9 51	10 00	45·9	9 09	9 16	45·7	225	315
46	134	12 51	12 43	45·4	12 08	11 59	45·3	11 26	11 16	45·1	10 44	10 33	45·0	10 01	9 50	44·9	9 19	9 07	44·7	226	314
47	133	13 04	12 30	44·4	12 21	11 47	44·3	11 38	11 04	44·1	10 55	10 21	44·0	10 11	9 39	43·9	9 28	8 57	43·7	227	313
48	132	13 17	12 16	43·4	12 33	11 34	43·3	11 49	10 52	43·1	11 05	10 10	43·0	10 21	9 28	42·9	9 37	8 47	42·7	228	312
49	131	13 29	12 02	42·4	12 45	11 21	42·3	12 00	10 39	42·1	11 16	9 58	42·0	10 31	9 17	41·9	9 46	8 37	41·7	229	311
50	130	13 42	11 48	41·4	12 57	11 07	41·3	12 11	10 27	41·1	11 26	9 46	41·0	10 41	9 06	40·9	9 55	8 26	40·7	230	310
51	129	13 54	11 33	40·4	13 08	10 53	40·3	12 22	10 14	40·1	11 36	9 34	40·0	10 50	8 55	39·8	10 04	8 16	39·7	231	309
52	128	14 06	11 19	39·4	13 19	10 40	39·2	12 33	10 01	39·1	11 46	9 22	39·0	10 59	8 44	38·8	10 13	8 05	38·7	232	308
53	127	14 17	11 04	38·4	13 30	10 26	38·2	12 43	9 47	38·1	11 56	9 10	38·0	11 08	8 32	37·8	10 21	7 55	37·7	233	307
54	126	14 29	10 49	37·4	13 41	10 11	37·2	12 53	9 34	37·1	12 05	8 57	36·9	11 17	8 20	36·8	10 29	7 44	36·7	234	306
55	125	14 40	10 33	36·4	13 51	9 57	36·2	13 03	9 20	36·1	12 14	8 44	35·9	11 26	8 08	35·8	10 37	7 33	35·7	235	305
56	124	14 51	10 18	35·3	14 02	9 42	35·2	13 13	9 07	35·1	12 23	8 31	34·9	11 34	7 56	34·8	10 45	7 21	34·7	236	304
57	123	15 01	10 02	34·3	14 12	9 27	34·2	13 22	8 53	34·0	12 32	8 18	33·9	11 42	7 44	33·8	10 52	7 10	33·7	237	303
58	122	15 12	9 46	33·3	14 21	9 12	33·2	13 31	8 38	33·0	12 41	8 05	32·9	11 50	7 32	32·8	11 00	6 58	32·7	238	302
59	121	15 22	9 30	32·3	14 31	8 57	32·1	13 40	8 24	32·0	12 49	7 51	31·9	11 58	7 19	31·8	11 07	6 47	31·7	239	301
60	120	15 31	9 14	31·3	14 40	8 41	31·1	13 49	8 10	31·0	12 57	7 38	30·9	12 06	7 06	30·8	11 14	6 35	30·6	240	300
61	119	15 41	8 57	30·2	14 49	8 26	30·1	13 57	7 55	30·0	13 05	7 24	29·8	12 13	6 54	29·7	11 21	6 23	29·6	241	299
62	118	15 50	8 40	29·2	14 58	8 10	29·1	14 05	7 40	28·9	13 13	7 10	28·8	12 20	6 41	28·7	11 27	6 11	28·6	242	298
63	117	15 59	8 23	28·2	15 06	7 54	28·0	14 13	7 25	27·9	13 20	6 56	27·8	12 27	6 27	27·7	11 34	5 59	27·6	243	297
64	116	16 08	8 06	27·2	15 14	7 38	27·0	14 21	7 10	26·9	13 27	6 42	26·8	12 34	6 14	26·7	11 40	5 47	26·6	244	296
65	115	16 16	7 49	26·1	15 22	7 22	26·0	14 28	6 55	25·9	13 34	6 28	25·8	12 40	6 01	25·7	11 46	5 34	25·6	245	295
66	114	16 24	7 32	25·1	15 29	7 05	25·0	14 35	6 39	24·9	13 41	6 13	24·7	12 46	5 47	24·6	11 52	5 22	24·6	246	294
67	113	16 32	7 14	24·1	15 37	6 49	23·9	14 42	6 24	23·8	13 47	5 59	23·7	12 52	5 34	23·6	11 57	5 09	23·5	247	293
68	112	16 39	6 56	23·0	15 44	6 32	22·9	14 48	6 08	22·8	13 53	5 44	22·7	12 58	5 20	22·6	12 02	4 57	22·5	248	292
69	111	16 46	6 38	22·0	15 50	6 15	21·9	14 55	5 52	21·8	13 59	5 29	21·7	13 03	5 06	21·6	12 07	4 44	21·5	249	291
70	110	16 53	6 20	20·9	15 57	5 58	20·8	15 01	5 36	20·7	14 05	5 14	20·6	13 08	4 52	20·6	12 12	4 31	20·5	250	290
71	109	16 59	6 02	19·9	16 03	5 41	19·8	15 06	5 20	19·7	14 10	4 59	19·6	13 13	4 38	19·5	12 17	4 18	19·5	251	289
72	108	17 05	5 44	18·9	16 09	5 24	18·8	15 12	5 04	18·7	14 15	4 44	18·6	13 18	4 24	18·5	12 21	4 05	18·4	252	288
73	107	17 11	5 26	17·8	16 14	5 06	17·7	15 17	4 48	17·6	14 20	4 29	17·6	13 23	4 10	17·5	12 25	3 52	17·4	253	287
74	106	17 17	5 07	16·8	16 19	4 49	16·7	15 22	4 31	16·6	14 24	4 13	16·5	13 27	3 56	16·5	12 29	3 38	16·4	254	286
75	105	17 22	4 48	15·7	16 24	4 31	15·7	15 26	4 15	15·6	14 29	3 58	15·5	13 31	3 42	15·4	12 33	3 25	15·4	255	285
76	104	17 27	4 30	14·7	16 29	4 14	14·6	15 31	3 58	14·5	14 33	3 43	14·5	13 35	3 27	14·4	12 36	3 12	14·4	256	284
77	103	17 31	4 11	13·6	16 33	3 56	13·6	15 35	3 41	13·5	14 36	3 27	13·4	13 38	3 13	13·4	12 40	2 58	13·3	257	283
78	102	17 36	3 52	12·6	16 37	3 38	12·5	15 38	3 25	12·5	14 40	3 11	12·4	13 41	2 58	12·4	12 43	2 45	12·3	258	282
79	101	17 39	3 33	11·6	16 41	3 20	11·5	15 42	3 08	11·4	14 43	2 56	11·4	13 44	2 43	11·3	12 45	2 31	11·3	259	281
80	100	17 43	3 14	10·5	16 44	3 02	10·4	15 45	2 51	10·4	14 46	2 40	10·3	13 47	2 29	10·3	12 48	2 18	10·3	260	280
81	99	17 46	2 55	9·5	16 47	2 44	9·4	15 48	2 34	9·4	14 49	2 24	9·3	13 49	2 14	9·3	12 50	2 04	9·2	261	279
82	98	17 49	2 35	8·4	16 50	2 26	8·4	15 50	2 17	8·3	14 51	2 08	8·3	13 52	1 59	8·2	12 52	1 50	8·2	262	278
83	97	17 52	2 16	7·4	16 52	2 08	7·3	15 53	2 00	7·3	14 53	1 52	7·2	13 54	1 44	7·2	12 54	1 37	7·2	263	277
84	96	17 54	1 57	6·3	16 54	1 50	6·3	15 55	1 43	6·2	14 55	1 36	6·2	13 55	1 30	6·2	12 56	1 23	6·2	264	276
85	95	17 56	1 37	5·3	16 56	1 32	5·2	15 56	1 26	5·2	14 56	1 20	5·2	13 57	1 15	5·2	12 57	1 09	5·1	265	275
86	94	17 57	1 18	4·2	16 57	1 13	4·2	15 58	1 09	4·2	14 58	1 04	4·1	13 58	1 00	4·1	12 58	0 55	4·1	266	274
87	93	17 58	0 58	3·2	16 59	0 55	3·1	15 59	0 52	3·1	14 59	0 48	3·1	13 59	0 45	3·1	12 59	0 42	3·1	267	273
88	92	17 59	0 39	2·1	16 59	0 37	2·1	15 59	0 34	2·1	14 59	0 32	2·1	13 59	0 30	2·1	13 00	0 28	2·1	268	272
89	91	18 00	0 19	1·1	17 00	0 18	1·0	16 00	0 17	1·0	15 00	0 16	1·0	14 00	0 15	1·0	13 00	0 14	1·0	269	271
90	90	18 00	0 00	0·0	17 00	0 00	0·0	16 00	0 00	0·0	15 00	0 00	0·0	14 00	0 00	0·0	13 00	0 00	0·0	270	270

N. Lat: for LHA > 180° … Z_n = Z
for LHA < 180° … Z_n = 360° − Z

S. Lat.: for LHA > 180° … Z_n = 180° − Z
for LHA < 180° … Z_n = 180° + Z

SIGHT REDUCTION TABLE

B: (−) for 90° < LHA < 270°
Dec:(−) for Lat. contrary name

Z_1: same sign as B
Z_2: (−) for F > 90°

Lat. / A		78°			79°			80°			81°			82°			83°			Lat. / A	
LHA/F		A/H	B/P	Z_1/Z_2	A/H	B/P	Z_1/Z_2	A/H	B/P	Z_1/Z_2	A/H	B/P	Z_1/Z_2	A/H	B/P	Z_1/Z_2	A/H	B/P	Z_1/Z_2	LHA	
°	°	° ′	° ′	°	° ′	° ′	°	° ′	° ′	°	° ′	° ′	°	° ′	° ′	°	° ′	° ′	°	°	°
0	180	0 00	12 00	90·0	0 00	11 00	90·0	0 00	10 00	90·0	0 00	9 00	90·0	0 00	8 00	90·0	0 00	7 00	90·0	180	360
1	179	0 12	12 00	89·0	0 11	11 00	89·0	0 10	10 00	89·0	0 09	9 00	89·0	0 08	8 00	89·0	0 07	7 00	89·0	181	359
2	178	0 25	12 00	88·0	0 23	11 00	88·0	0 21	10 00	88·0	0 19	9 00	88·0	0 17	8 00	88·0	0 15	7 00	88·0	182	358
3	177	0 37	11 59	87·1	0 34	10 59	87·1	0 31	9 59	87·0	0 28	8 59	87·0	0 25	7 59	87·0	0 22	6 59	87·0	183	357
4	176	0 50	11 58	86·1	0 46	10 58	86·1	0 42	9 59	86·1	0 38	8 59	86·0	0 33	7 59	86·0	0 29	6 59	86·0	184	356
5	175	1 02	11 57	85·1	0 57	10 58	85·1	0 52	9 58	85·1	0 47	8 58	85·1	0 42	7 58	85·0	0 37	6 58	85·0	185	355
6	174	1 15	11 56	84·1	1 09	10 56	84·1	1 02	9 57	84·1	0 56	8 57	84·1	0 50	7 57	84·1	0 44	6 58	84·0	186	354
7	173	1 27	11 55	83·2	1 20	10 55	83·1	1 13	9 56	83·1	1 06	8 56	83·1	0 58	7 56	83·1	0 51	6 57	83·1	187	353
8	172	1 39	11 53	82·2	1 31	10 54	82·1	1 23	9 54	82·1	1 15	8 55	82·1	1 07	7 55	82·1	0 58	6 56	82·1	188	352
9	171	1 52	11 51	81·2	1 43	10 52	81·2	1 33	9 53	81·1	1 24	8 53	81·1	1 15	7 54	81·1	1 06	6 55	81·1	189	351
10	170	2 04	11 49	80·2	1 54	10 50	80·2	1 44	9 51	80·1	1 33	8 52	80·1	1 23	7 53	80·1	1 13	6 54	80·1	190	350
11	169	2 16	11 47	79·2	2 05	10 48	79·2	1 54	9 49	79·2	1 43	8 50	79·1	1 31	7 51	79·1	1 20	6 52	79·1	191	349
12	168	2 29	11 45	78·3	2 16	10 46	78·2	2 04	9 47	78·2	1 52	8 48	78·1	1 39	7 50	78·1	1 27	6 51	78·1	192	348
13	167	2 41	11 42	77·3	2 28	10 43	77·2	2 14	9 45	77·2	2 01	8 46	77·2	1 48	7 48	77·1	1 34	6 49	77·1	193	347
14	166	2 53	11 39	76·3	2 39	10 41	76·2	2 24	9 43	76·2	2 10	8 44	76·2	1 56	7 46	76·1	1 41	6 48	76·1	194	346
15	165	3 05	11 36	75·3	2 50	10 38	75·3	2 35	9 40	75·2	2 19	8 42	75·2	2 04	7 44	75·1	1 48	6 46	75·1	195	345
16	164	3 17	11 33	74·3	3 01	10 35	74·3	2 45	9 37	74·2	2 28	8 39	74·2	2 12	7 42	74·1	1 56	6 44	74·1	196	344
17	163	3 29	11 29	73·4	3 12	10 32	73·3	2 55	9 34	73·2	2 37	8 37	73·2	2 20	7 39	73·2	2 03	6 42	73·1	197	343
18	162	3 41	11 26	72·4	3 23	10 28	72·3	3 05	9 31	72·3	2 46	8 34	72·2	2 28	7 37	72·2	2 09	6 40	72·1	198	342
19	161	3 53	11 22	71·4	3 34	10 25	71·3	3 14	9 28	71·3	2 55	8 31	71·2	2 36	7 34	71·2	2 16	6 37	71·1	199	341
20	160	4 05	11 18	70·4	3 45	10 21	70·3	3 24	9 24	70·3	3 04	8 28	70·2	2 44	7 31	70·2	2 23	6 35	70·1	200	340
21	159	4 16	11 13	69·4	3 55	10 17	69·4	3 34	9 21	69·3	3 13	8 25	69·2	2 52	7 28	69·2	2 30	6 32	69·1	201	339
22	158	4 28	11 09	68·4	4 06	10 13	68·4	3 44	9 17	68·3	3 22	8 21	68·2	2 59	7 25	68·2	2 37	6 30	68·1	202	338
23	157	4 40	11 04	67·5	4 17	10 09	67·4	3 53	9 13	67·3	3 30	8 18	67·3	3 07	7 22	67·2	2 44	6 27	67·2	203	337
24	156	4 51	10 59	66·5	4 27	10 04	66·4	4 03	9 09	66·3	3 39	8 14	66·3	3 15	7 19	66·2	2 50	6 24	66·2	204	336
25	155	5 02	10 54	65·5	4 38	9 59	65·4	4 13	9 05	65·3	3 47	8 10	65·3	3 22	7 16	65·2	2 57	6 21	65·2	205	335
26	154	5 14	10 49	64·5	4 48	9 55	64·4	4 22	9 00	64·3	3 56	8 06	64·3	3 30	7 12	64·2	3 04	6 18	64·2	206	334
27	153	5 25	10 43	63·5	4 58	9 50	63·4	4 31	8 56	63·4	4 04	8 02	63·3	3 37	7 08	63·2	3 10	6 15	63·2	207	333
28	152	5 36	10 38	62·5	5 08	9 44	62·4	4 41	8 51	62·4	4 13	7 58	62·3	3 45	7 04	62·2	3 17	6 11	62·2	208	332
29	151	5 47	10 32	61·5	5 18	9 39	61·4	4 50	8 46	61·4	4 21	7 53	61·3	3 52	7 00	61·2	3 23	6 08	61·2	209	331
30	150	5 58	10 26	60·5	5 28	9 33	60·5	4 59	8 41	60·4	4 29	7 49	60·3	3 59	6 56	60·2	3 30	6 04	60·2	210	330
31	149	6 09	10 20	59·6	5 38	9 28	59·5	5 08	8 36	59·4	4 37	7 44	59·3	4 07	6 52	59·2	3 36	6 00	59·2	211	329
32	148	6 20	10 13	58·6	5 48	9 22	58·5	5 17	8 30	58·4	4 45	7 39	58·3	4 14	6 48	58·3	3 42	5 57	58·2	212	328
33	147	6 30	10 06	57·6	5 58	9 16	57·5	5 26	8 25	57·4	4 53	7 34	57·3	4 21	6 43	57·3	3 48	5 53	57·2	213	327
34	146	6 41	10 00	56·6	6 08	9 09	56·5	5 34	8 19	56·4	5 01	7 29	56·3	4 28	6 39	56·3	3 54	5 49	56·2	214	326
35	145	6 51	9 53	55·6	6 17	9 03	55·5	5 43	8 13	55·4	5 09	7 24	55·3	4 35	6 34	55·3	4 00	5 45	55·2	215	325
36	144	7 01	9 45	54·6	6 26	8 56	54·5	5 51	8 07	54·4	5 17	7 18	54·3	4 42	6 29	54·3	4 06	5 40	54·2	216	324
37	143	7 11	9 38	53·6	6 36	8 49	53·5	6 00	8 01	53·4	5 24	7 13	53·3	4 48	6 24	53·3	4 12	5 36	53·2	217	323
38	142	7 21	9 31	52·6	6 45	8 43	52·5	6 08	7 55	52·4	5 32	7 07	52·3	4 55	6 19	52·3	4 18	5 32	52·2	218	322
39	141	7 31	9 23	51·6	6 54	8 35	51·5	6 16	7 48	51·4	5 39	7 01	51·3	5 01	6 14	51·3	4 24	5 27	51·2	219	321
40	140	7 41	9 15	50·6	7 03	8 28	50·5	6 25	7 42	50·4	5 46	6 55	50·3	5 08	6 09	50·3	4 30	5 22	50·2	220	320
41	139	7 50	9 07	49·6	7 11	8 21	49·5	6 32	7 35	49·4	5 53	6 49	49·4	5 14	6 03	49·3	4 35	5 18	49·2	221	319
42	138	8 00	8 59	48·6	7 20	8 13	48·5	6 40	7 28	48·4	6 01	6 43	48·4	5 21	5 58	48·3	4 41	5 13	48·2	222	318
43	137	8 09	8 50	47·6	7 29	8 05	47·5	6 48	7 21	47·4	6 07	6 36	47·4	5 27	5 52	47·3	4 46	5 08	47·2	223	317
44	136	8 18	8 42	46·6	7 37	7 58	46·5	6 56	7 14	46·4	6 14	6 30	46·4	5 33	5 46	46·3	4 51	5 03	46·2	224	316
45	135	8 27	8 33	45·6	7 45	7 50	45·5	7 03	7 06	45·4	6 21	6 23	45·4	5 39	5 41	45·3	4 57	4 58	45·2	225	315

Lat. / A		78°			79°			80°			81°			82°			83°			Lat. / A	
LHA/F		A/H	B/P	Z_1/Z_2	A/H	B/P	Z_1/Z_2	A/H	B/P	Z_1/Z_2	A/H	B/P	Z_1/Z_2	A/H	B/P	Z_1/Z_2	A/H	B/P	Z_1/Z_2	LHA	
°	°	° ′	° ′	°	° ′	° ′	°	° ′	° ′	°	° ′	° ′	°	° ′	° ′	°	° ′	° ′	°	°	°
45	135	8 27	8 33	45·6	7 45	7 50	45·5	7 03	7 06	45·4	6 21	6 23	45·4	5 39	5 41	45·3	4 57	4 58	45·2	225	315
46	134	8 36	8 24	44·6	7 53	7 41	44·5	7 11	6 59	44·4	6 28	6 17	44·4	5 45	5 35	44·3	5 02	4 53	44·2	226	314
47	133	8 45	8 15	43·6	8 01	7 33	43·5	7 18	6 51	43·4	6 34	6 10	43·4	5 51	5 28	43·3	5 07	4 47	43·2	227	313
48	132	8 53	8 06	42·6	8 09	7 25	42·5	7 25	6 44	42·4	6 41	6 03	42·4	5 56	5 22	42·3	5 12	4 42	42·2	228	312
49	131	9 02	7 56	41·6	8 17	7 16	41·5	7 32	6 36	41·4	6 47	5 56	41·4	6 02	5 16	41·3	5 17	4 36	41·2	229	311
50	130	9 10	7 47	40·6	8 24	7 07	40·5	7 39	6 28	40·4	6 53	5 49	40·3	6 07	5 10	40·3	5 21	4 31	40·2	230	310
51	129	9 18	7 37	39·6	8 32	6 58	39·5	7 45	6 20	39·4	6 59	5 42	39·3	6 13	5 03	39·3	5 26	4 25	39·2	231	309
52	128	9 26	7 27	38·6	8 39	6 49	38·5	7 52	6 12	38·4	7 05	5 34	38·3	6 18	4 57	38·3	5 31	4 19	38·2	232	308
53	127	9 33	7 17	37·6	8 46	6 40	37·5	7 58	6 03	37·4	7 11	5 27	37·3	6 23	4 50	37·3	5 35	4 14	37·2	233	307
54	126	9 41	7 07	36·6	8 53	6 31	36·5	8 05	5 55	36·4	7 16	5 19	36·3	6 28	4 43	36·3	5 39	4 08	36·2	234	306
55	125	9 48	6 57	35·6	9 00	6 22	35·5	8 11	5 47	35·4	7 22	5 11	35·3	6 33	4 37	35·3	5 44	4 02	35·2	235	305
56	124	9 56	6 47	34·6	9 06	6 12	34·5	8 17	5 38	34·4	7 27	5 04	34·3	6 38	4 30	34·3	5 48	3 56	34·2	236	304
57	123	10 03	6 36	33·6	9 13	6 03	33·5	8 22	5 29	33·4	7 32	4 56	33·3	6 42	4 23	33·3	5 52	3 50	33·2	237	303
58	122	10 09	6 26	32·6	9 19	5 53	32·5	8 28	5 20	32·4	7 37	4 48	32·3	6 47	4 16	32·3	5 56	3 43	32·2	238	302
59	121	10 16	6 15	31·6	9 25	5 43	31·5	8 34	5 11	31·4	7 42	4 40	31·3	6 51	4 08	31·2	6 00	3 37	31·2	239	301
60	120	10 22	6 04	30·6	9 31	5 33	30·5	8 39	5 02	30·4	7 47	4 32	30·3	6 55	4 01	30·2	6 04	3 31	30·2	240	300
61	119	10 29	5 53	29·5	9 36	5 23	29·5	8 44	4 53	29·4	7 52	4 23	29·3	6 59	3 54	29·2	6 07	3 24	29·2	241	299
62	118	10 35	5 42	28·5	9 42	5 13	28·4	8 49	4 44	28·4	7 56	4 15	28·3	7 04	3 46	28·2	6 11	3 18	28·2	242	298
63	117	10 41	5 31	27·5	9 47	5 03	27·4	8 54	4 35	27·4	8 01	4 07	27·3	7 07	3 39	27·2	6 14	3 11	27·2	243	297
64	116	10 46	5 19	26·5	9 52	4 52	26·4	8 59	4 25	26·3	8 05	3 58	26·3	7 11	3 32	26·2	6 17	3 05	26·2	244	296
65	115	10 52	5 08	25·5	9 57	4 42	25·4	9 03	4 16	25·3	8 09	3 50	25·3	7 15	3 24	25·2	6 20	2 58	25·2	245	295
66	114	10 57	4 56	24·5	10 02	4 31	24·4	9 08	4 06	24·3	8 13	3 41	24·3	7 18	3 16	24·2	6 24	2 52	24·2	246	294
67	113	11 02	4 45	23·5	10 07	4 21	23·4	9 12	3 56	23·3	8 17	3 32	23·3	7 22	3 09	23·2	6 26	2 45	23·2	247	293
68	112	11 07	4 33	22·4	10 11	4 10	22·4	9 16	3 47	22·3	8 20	3 24	22·2	7 25	3 01	22·2	6 29	2 38	22·1	248	292
69	111	11 12	4 21	21·4	10 16	3 59	21·4	9 20	3 37	21·3	8 24	3 15	21·2	7 28	2 53	21·2	6 32	2 31	21·1	249	291
70	110	11 16	4 09	20·4	10 20	3 48	20·3	9 23	3 27	20·3	8 27	3 06	20·2	7 31	2 45	20·2	6 35	2 24	20·1	250	290
71	109	11 20	3 58	19·4	10 24	3 37	19·3	9 27	3 17	19·3	8 30	2 57	19·2	7 34	2 37	19·2	6 37	2 17	19·1	251	289
72	108	11 24	3 45	18·4	10 27	3 26	18·3	9 30	3 07	18·3	8 33	2 48	18·2	7 36	2 29	18·2	6 39	2 10	18·1	252	288
73	107	11 28	3 33	17·4	10 31	3 15	17·3	9 34	2 57	17·2	8 36	2 39	17·2	7 39	2 21	17·2	6 42	2 03	17·1	253	287
74	106	11 32	3 21	16·3	10 34	3 04	16·3	9 37	2 47	16·2	8 39	2 30	16·2	7 41	2 13	16·1	6 44	1 56	16·1	254	286
75	105	11 35	3 09	15·3	10 37	2 53	15·3	9 39	2 37	15·2	8 41	2 21	15·2	7 44	2 05	15·1	6 46	1 49	15·1	255	285
76	104	11 38	2 57	14·3	10 40	2 42	14·3	9 42	2 27	14·2	8 44	2 12	14·2	7 46	1 57	14·1	6 47	1 42	14·1	256	284
77	103	11 41	2 44	13·3	10 43	2 30	13·2	9 44	2 16	13·2	8 46	2 02	13·2	7 48	1 49	13·1	6 49	1 35	13·1	257	283
78	102	11 44	2 32	12·3	10 45	2 19	12·2	9 47	2 06	12·2	8 48	1 53	12·1	7 49	1 40	12·1	6 51	1 28	12·1	258	282
79	101	11 47	2 19	11·2	10 48	2 07	11·2	9 49	1 56	11·2	8 50	1 44	11·1	7 51	1 32	11·1	6 52	1 21	11·1	259	281
80	100	11 49	2 07	10·2	10 50	1 56	10·2	9 51	1 45	10·2	8 52	1 35	10·1	7 53	1 24	10·1	6 54	1 13	10·1	260	280
81	99	11 51	1 54	9·2	10 52	1 45	9·2	9 53	1 35	9·1	8 53	1 25	9·1	7 54	1 16	9·1	6 55	1 06	9·1	261	279
82	98	11 53	1 42	8·2	10 53	1 33	8·1	9 54	1 24	8·1	8 55	1 16	8·1	7 55	1 07	8·1	6 56	0 59	8·1	262	278
83	97	11 55	1 29	7·2	10 55	1 21	7·1	9 55	1 14	7·1	8 56	1 06	7·1	7 56	0 59	7·1	6 57	0 51	7·1	263	277
84	96	11 56	1 16	6·1	10 56	1 10	6·1	9 57	1 03	6·1	8 57	0 57	6·1	7 57	0 50	6·1	6 58	0 44	6·0	264	276
85	95	11 57	1 04	5·1	10 57	0 58	5·1	9 58	0 53	5·1	8 58	0 47	5·1	7 58	0 42	5·0	6 58	0 37	5·0	265	275
86	94	11 58	0 51	4·1	10 58	0 47	4·1	9 59	0 42	4·1	8 59	0 38	4·0	7 59	0 34	4·0	6 59	0 29	4·0	266	274
87	93	11 59	0 38	3·1	10 59	0 35	3·1	9 59	0 32	3·0	8 59	0 28	3·0	7 59	0 25	3·0	6 59	0 22	3·0	267	273
88	92	12 00	0 26	2·0	11 00	0 23	2·0	10 00	0 21	2·0	9 00	0 19	2·0	8 00	0 17	2·0	7 00	0 15	2·0	268	272
89	91	12 00	0 13	1·0	11 00	0 12	1·0	10 00	0 11	1·0	9 00	0 10	1·0	8 00	0 08	1·0	7 00	0 07	1·0	269	271
90	90	12 00	0 00	0·0	11 00	0 00	0·0	10 00	0 00	0·0	9 00	0 00	0·0	8 00	0 00	0·0	7 00	0 00	0·0	270	270

N. Lat: for LHA > 180° … $Z_n = Z$
for LHA < 180° … $Z_n = 360° - Z$

S. Lat.: for LHA > 180° … $Z_n = 180° - Z$
for LHA < 180° … $Z_n = 180° + Z$

SIGHT REDUCTION TABLE

B: (−) for 90° < LHA < 270°
Dec:(−) for Lat. contrary name

Z_1: same sign as B
Z_2: (−) for F > 90°

Lat. / A		84°			85°			86°			87°			88°			89°			Lat. / A	
LHA/F		A/H	B/P	Z_1/Z_2	A/H	B/P	Z_1/Z_2	A/H	B/P	Z_1/Z_2	A/H	B/P	Z_1/Z_2	A/H	B/P	Z_1/Z_2	A/H	B/P	Z_1/Z_2	LHA	
°	°	° ′	° ′	°	° ′	° ′	°	° ′	° ′	°	° ′	° ′	°	° ′	° ′	°	° ′	° ′	°	°	°
0	180	0 00	6 00	90·0	0 00	5 00	90·0	0 00	4 00	90·0	0 00	3 00	90·0	0 00	2 00	90·0	0 00	1 00	90·0	180	360
1	179	0 06	6 00	89·0	0 05	5 00	89·0	0 04	4 00	89·0	0 03	3 00	89·0	0 02	2 00	89·0	0 01	1 00	89·0	181	359
2	178	0 13	6 00	88·0	0 10	5 00	88·0	0 08	4 00	88·0	0 06	3 00	88·0	0 04	2 00	88·0	0 02	1 00	88·0	182	358
3	177	0 19	6 00	87·0	0 16	5 00	87·0	0 13	4 00	87·0	0 09	3 00	87·0	0 06	2 00	87·0	0 03	1 00	87·0	183	357
4	176	0 25	5 59	86·0	0 21	4 59	86·0	0 17	3 59	86·0	0 13	3 00	86·0	0 08	2 00	86·0	0 04	1 00	86·0	184	356
5	175	0 31	5 59	85·0	0 26	4 59	85·0	0 21	3 59	85·0	0 16	2 59	85·0	0 10	2 00	85·0	0 05	1 00	85·0	185	355
6	174	0 38	5 58	84·0	0 31	4 58	84·0	0 25	3 59	84·0	0 19	2 59	84·0	0 13	1 59	84·0	0 06	1 00	84·0	186	354
7	173	0 44	5 57	83·0	0 37	4 58	83·0	0 29	3 58	83·0	0 22	2 59	83·0	0 15	1 59	83·0	0 07	1 00	83·0	187	353
8	172	0 50	5 57	82·0	0 42	4 57	82·0	0 33	3 58	82·0	0 25	2 58	82·0	0 17	1 59	82·0	0 08	0 59	82·0	188	352
9	171	0 56	5 56	81·0	0 47	4 56	81·0	0 38	3 57	81·0	0 28	2 58	81·0	0 19	1 59	81·0	0 09	0 59	81·0	189	351
10	170	1 02	5 55	80·1	0 52	4 55	80·0	0 42	3 56	80·0	0 31	2 57	80·0	0 21	1 58	80·0	0 10	0 59	80·0	190	350
11	169	1 09	5 53	79·1	0 57	4 55	79·0	0 46	3 56	79·0	0 34	2 57	79·0	0 23	1 58	79·0	0 11	0 59	79·0	191	349
12	168	1 15	5 52	78·1	1 02	4 53	78·0	0 50	3 55	78·0	0 37	2 56	78·0	0 25	1 57	78·0	0 12	0 59	78·0	192	348
13	167	1 21	5 51	77·1	1 07	4 52	77·0	0 54	3 54	77·0	0 40	2 55	77·0	0 27	1 57	77·0	0 13	0 58	77·0	193	347
14	166	1 27	5 49	76·1	1 12	4 51	76·1	0 58	3 53	76·0	0 44	2 55	76·0	0 29	1 56	76·0	0 15	0 58	76·0	194	346
15	165	1 33	5 48	75·1	1 18	4 50	75·1	1 02	3 52	75·0	0 47	2 54	75·0	0 31	1 56	75·0	0 16	0 58	75·0	195	345
16	164	1 39	5 46	74·1	1 23	4 48	74·1	1 06	3 51	74·0	0 50	2 53	74·0	0 33	1 55	74·0	0 17	0 58	74·0	196	344
17	163	1 45	5 44	73·1	1 28	4 47	73·1	1 10	3 50	73·0	0 53	2 52	73·0	0 35	1 55	73·0	0 18	0 57	73·0	197	343
18	162	1 51	5 42	72·1	1 33	4 45	72·1	1 14	3 48	72·0	0 56	2 51	72·0	0 37	1 54	72·0	0 19	0 57	72·0	198	342
19	161	1 57	5 41	71·1	1 38	4 44	71·1	1 18	3 47	71·0	0 59	2 50	71·0	0 39	1 53	71·0	0 20	0 57	71·0	199	341
20	160	2 03	5 38	70·1	1 42	4 42	70·1	1 22	3 46	70·0	1 02	2 49	70·0	0 41	1 53	70·0	0 21	0 56	70·0	200	340
21	159	2 09	5 36	69·1	1 47	4 40	69·1	1 26	3 44	69·0	1 04	2 48	69·0	0 43	1 52	69·0	0 22	0 56	69·0	201	339
22	158	2 15	5 34	68·1	1 52	4 38	68·1	1 30	3 43	68·0	1 07	2 47	68·0	0 45	1 51	68·0	0 22	0 56	68·0	202	338
23	157	2 20	5 32	67·1	1 57	4 36	67·1	1 34	3 41	67·1	1 10	2 46	67·0	0 47	1 50	67·0	0 23	0 55	67·0	203	337
24	156	2 26	5 29	66·1	2 02	4 34	66·1	1 38	3 39	66·1	1 13	2 44	66·0	0 49	1 50	66·0	0 24	0 55	66·0	204	336
25	155	2 32	5 26	65·1	2 07	4 32	65·1	1 41	3 38	65·1	1 16	2 43	65·0	0 51	1 49	65·0	0 25	0 54	65·0	205	335
26	154	2 38	5 24	64·1	2 11	4 30	64·1	1 45	3 36	64·1	1 19	2 42	64·0	0 53	1 48	64·0	0 26	0 54	64·0	206	334
27	153	2 43	5 21	63·1	2 16	4 27	63·1	1 49	3 34	63·1	1 22	2 40	63·0	0 54	1 47	63·0	0 27	0 53	63·0	207	333
28	152	2 49	5 18	62·1	2 21	4 25	62·1	1 53	3 32	62·1	1 24	2 39	62·0	0 56	1 46	62·0	0 28	0 53	62·0	208	332
29	151	2 54	5 15	61·1	2 25	4 23	61·1	1 56	3 30	61·1	1 27	2 37	61·0	0 58	1 45	61·0	0 29	0 52	61·0	209	331
30	150	3 00	5 12	60·1	2 30	4 20	60·1	2 00	3 28	60·1	1 30	2 36	60·0	1 00	1 44	60·0	0 30	0 52	60·0	210	330
31	149	3 05	5 09	59·1	2 34	4 17	59·1	2 04	3 26	59·1	1 33	2 34	59·0	1 02	1 43	59·0	0 31	0 51	59·0	211	329
32	148	3 11	5 06	58·1	2 39	4 15	58·1	2 07	3 24	58·1	1 35	2 33	58·0	1 04	1 42	58·0	0 32	0 51	58·0	212	328
33	147	3 16	5 02	57·1	2 43	4 12	57·1	2 11	3 21	57·1	1 38	2 31	57·0	1 05	1 41	57·0	0 33	0 50	57·0	213	327
34	146	3 21	4 59	56·1	2 48	4 09	56·1	2 14	3 19	56·1	1 41	2 29	56·0	1 07	1 39	56·0	0 34	0 50	56·0	214	326
35	145	3 26	4 55	55·1	2 52	4 06	55·1	2 18	3 17	55·1	1 43	2 27	55·0	1 09	1 38	55·0	0 34	0 49	55·0	215	325
36	144	3 31	4 52	54·1	2 56	4 03	54·1	2 21	3 14	54·1	1 46	2 26	54·0	1 11	1 37	54·0	0 35	0 49	54·0	216	324
37	143	3 36	4 48	53·2	3 00	4 00	53·1	2 24	3 12	53·1	1 48	2 24	53·0	1 12	1 36	53·0	0 36	0 48	53·0	217	323
38	142	3 41	4 44	52·2	3 05	3 57	52·1	2 28	3 09	52·1	1 51	2 22	52·0	1 14	1 35	52·0	0 37	0 47	52·0	218	322
39	141	3 46	4 40	51·2	3 09	3 53	51·1	2 31	3 07	51·1	1 53	2 20	51·0	1 16	1 33	51·0	0 38	0 47	51·0	219	321
40	140	3 51	4 36	50·2	3 13	3 50	50·1	2 34	3 04	50·1	1 56	2 18	50·0	1 17	1 32	50·0	0 39	0 46	50·0	220	320
41	139	3 56	4 32	49·2	3 17	3 47	49·1	2 37	3 01	49·1	1 58	2 16	49·0	1 19	1 31	49·0	0 39	0 45	49·0	221	319
42	138	4 01	4 28	48·2	3 21	3 43	48·1	2 41	2 58	48·1	2 00	2 14	48·0	1 20	1 29	48·0	0 40	0 45	48·0	222	318
43	137	4 05	4 24	47·2	3 24	3 40	47·1	2 44	2 56	47·1	2 03	2 12	47·0	1 22	1 28	47·0	0 41	0 44	47·0	223	317
44	136	4 10	4 19	46·2	3 28	3 36	46·1	2 47	2 53	46·1	2 05	2 10	46·0	1 23	1 26	46·0	0 42	0 43	46·0	224	316
45	135	4 14	4 15	45·2	3 32	3 32	45·1	2 50	2 50	45·1	2 07	2 07	45·0	1 25	1 25	45·0	0 42	0 42	45·0	225	315

Lat. / A		84°			85°			86°			87°			88°			89°			Lat. / A	
LHA/F		A/H	B/P	Z_1/Z_2	A/H	B/P	Z_1/Z_2	A/H	B/P	Z_1/Z_2	A/H	B/P	Z_1/Z_2	A/H	B/P	Z_1/Z_2	A/H	B/P	Z_1/Z_2	LHA	
°	°	° ′	° ′	°	° ′	° ′	°	° ′	° ′	°	° ′	° ′	°	° ′	° ′	°	° ′	° ′	°	°	°
45	135	4 14	4 15	45·2	3 32	3 32	45·1	2 50	2 50	45·1	2 07	2 07	45·0	1 25	1 25	45·0	0 42	0 42	45·0	225	315
46	134	4 19	4 11	44·2	3 36	3 29	44·1	2 53	2 47	44·1	2 09	2 05	44·0	1 26	1 23	44·0	0 43	0 42	44·0	226	314
47	133	4 23	4 06	43·2	3 39	3 25	43·1	2 55	2 44	43·1	2 12	2 03	43·0	1 28	1 22	43·0	0 44	0 41	43·0	227	313
48	132	4 27	4 01	42·2	3 43	3 21	42·1	2 58	2 41	42·1	2 14	2 01	42·0	1 29	1 20	42·0	0 45	0 40	42·0	228	312
49	131	4 31	3 57	41·2	3 46	3 17	41·1	3 01	2 38	41·1	2 16	1 58	41·0	1 31	1 19	41·0	0 45	0 39	41·0	229	311
50	130	4 36	3 52	40·2	3 50	3 13	40·1	3 04	2 34	40·1	2 18	1 56	40·0	1 32	1 17	40·0	0 46	0 39	40·0	230	310
51	129	4 40	3 47	39·2	3 53	3 09	39·1	3 06	2 31	39·1	2 20	1 53	39·0	1 33	1 16	39·0	0 47	0 38	39·0	231	309
52	128	4 43	3 42	38·2	3 56	3 05	38·1	3 09	2 28	38·1	2 22	1 51	38·0	1 35	1 14	38·0	0 47	0 37	38·0	232	308
53	127	4 47	3 37	37·2	3 59	3 01	37·1	3 12	2 25	37·1	2 24	1 48	37·0	1 36	1 12	37·0	0 48	0 36	37·0	233	307
54	126	4 51	3 32	36·1	4 03	2 57	36·1	3 14	2 21	36·1	2 26	1 46	36·0	1 37	1 11	36·0	0 49	0 35	36·0	234	306
55	125	4 55	3 27	35·1	4 06	2 52	35·1	3 17	2 18	35·1	2 27	1 43	35·0	1 38	1 09	35·0	0 49	0 34	35·0	235	305
56	124	4 58	3 22	34·1	4 09	2 48	34·1	3 19	2 14	34·1	2 29	1 41	34·0	1 39	1 07	34·0	0 50	0 34	34·0	236	304
57	123	5 02	3 17	33·1	4 12	2 44	33·1	3 21	2 11	33·1	2 31	1 38	33·0	1 41	1 05	33·0	0 50	0 33	33·0	237	303
58	122	5 05	3 11	32·1	4 14	2 39	32·1	3 23	2 07	32·1	2 33	1 35	32·0	1 42	1 04	32·0	0 51	0 32	32·0	238	302
59	121	5 08	3 06	31·1	4 17	2 35	31·1	3 26	2 04	31·1	2 34	1 33	31·0	1 43	1 02	31·0	0 51	0 31	31·0	239	301
60	120	5 12	3 00	30·1	4 20	2 30	30·1	3 28	2 00	30·1	2 36	1 30	30·0	1 44	1 00	30·0	0 52	0 30	30·0	240	300
61	119	5 15	2 55	29·1	4 22	2 26	29·1	3 30	1 56	29·1	2 37	1 27	29·0	1 45	0 58	29·0	0 52	0 29	29·0	241	299
62	118	5 18	2 49	28·1	4 25	2 21	28·1	3 32	1 53	28·1	2 39	1 25	28·0	1 46	0 56	28·0	0 53	0 28	28·0	242	298
63	117	5 21	2 44	27·1	4 27	2 16	27·1	3 34	1 49	27·1	2 40	1 22	27·0	1 47	0 54	27·0	0 53	0 27	27·0	243	297
64	116	5 23	2 38	26·1	4 30	2 12	26·1	3 36	1 45	26·1	2 42	1 19	26·0	1 48	0 53	26·0	0 54	0 26	26·0	244	296
65	115	5 26	2 33	25·1	4 32	2 07	25·1	3 37	1 42	25·1	2 43	1 16	25·0	1 49	0 51	25·0	0 54	0 25	25·0	245	295
66	114	5 29	2 27	24·1	4 34	2 02	24·1	3 39	1 38	24·1	2 44	1 13	24·0	1 50	0 49	24·0	0 55	0 24	24·0	246	294
67	113	5 31	2 21	23·1	4 36	1 57	23·1	3 41	1 34	23·1	2 46	1 10	23·0	1 50	0 47	23·0	0 55	0 23	23·0	247	293
68	112	5 34	2 15	22·1	4 38	1 53	22·1	3 42	1 30	22·0	2 47	1 07	22·0	1 51	0 45	22·0	0 56	0 22	22·0	248	292
69	111	5 36	2 09	21·1	4 40	1 48	21·1	3 44	1 26	21·0	2 48	1 05	21·0	1 52	0 43	21·0	0 56	0 22	21·0	249	291
70	110	5 38	2 04	20·1	4 42	1 43	20·1	3 46	1 22	20·0	2 49	1 02	20·0	1 53	0 41	20·0	0 56	0 21	20·0	250	290
71	109	5 40	1 58	19·1	4 44	1 38	19·1	3 47	1 18	19·0	2 50	0 59	19·0	1 53	0 39	19·0	0 57	0 20	19·0	251	289
72	108	5 42	1 52	18·1	4 45	1 33	18·1	3 48	1 14	18·0	2 51	0 56	18·0	1 54	0 37	18·0	0 57	0 19	18·0	252	288
73	107	5 44	1 46	17·1	4 47	1 28	17·1	3 49	1 10	17·0	2 52	0 53	17·0	1 55	0 35	17·0	0 57	0 18	17·0	253	287
74	106	5 46	1 40	16·1	4 48	1 23	16·1	3 51	1 06	16·0	2 53	0 50	16·0	1 55	0 33	16·0	0 58	0 17	16·0	254	286
75	105	5 48	1 33	15·1	4 50	1 18	15·1	3 52	1 02	15·0	2 54	0 47	15·0	1 56	0 31	15·0	0 58	0 16	15·0	255	285
76	104	5 49	1 27	14·1	4 51	1 13	14·1	3 53	0 58	14·0	2 55	0 44	14·0	1 56	0 29	14·0	0 58	0 15	14·0	256	284
77	103	5 51	1 21	13·1	4 52	1 08	13·0	3 54	0 54	13·0	2 55	0 41	13·0	1 57	0 27	13·0	0 58	0 13	13·0	257	283
78	102	5 52	1 15	12·1	4 53	1 03	12·0	3 55	0 50	12·0	2 56	0 37	12·0	1 57	0 25	12·0	0 59	0 12	12·0	258	282
79	101	5 53	1 09	11·1	4 54	0 57	11·0	3 56	0 46	11·0	2 57	0 34	11·0	1 58	0 23	11·0	0 59	0 11	11·0	259	281
80	100	5 55	1 03	10·1	4 55	0 52	10·0	3 56	0 42	10·0	2 57	0 31	10·0	1 58	0 21	10·0	0 59	0 10	10·0	260	280
81	99	5 56	0 57	9·0	4 56	0 47	9·0	3 57	0 38	9·0	2 58	0 28	9·0	1 59	0 19	9·0	0 59	0 09	9·0	261	279
82	98	5 56	0 50	8·0	4 57	0 42	8·0	3 58	0 33	8·0	2 58	0 25	8·0	1 59	0 17	8·0	0 59	0 08	8·0	262	278
83	97	5 57	0 44	7·0	4 58	0 37	7·0	3 58	0 29	7·0	2 59	0 22	7·0	1 59	0 15	7·0	1 00	0 07	7·0	263	277
84	96	5 58	0 38	6·0	4 58	0 31	6·0	3 59	0 25	6·0	2 59	0 19	6·0	1 59	0 13	6·0	1 00	0 06	6·0	264	276
85	95	5 59	0 31	5·0	4 59	0 26	5·0	3 59	0 21	5·0	2 59	0 16	5·0	2 00	0 10	5·0	1 00	0 05	5·0	265	275
86	94	5 59	0 25	4·0	4 59	0 21	4·0	3 59	0 17	4·0	3 00	0 13	4·0	2 00	0 08	4·0	1 00	0 04	4·0	266	274
87	93	6 00	0 19	3·0	5 00	0 16	3·0	4 00	0 13	3·0	3 00	0 09	3·0	2 00	0 06	3·0	1 00	0 03	3·0	267	273
88	92	6 00	0 13	2·0	5 00	0 10	2·0	4 00	0 08	2·0	3 00	0 06	2·0	2 00	0 04	2·0	1 00	0 02	2·0	268	272
89	91	6 00	0 06	1·0	5 00	0 05	1·0	4 00	0 04	1·0	3 00	0 03	1·0	2 00	0 02	1·0	1 00	0 01	1·0	269	271
90	90	6 00	0 00	0·0	5 00	0 00	0·0	4 00	0 00	0·0	3 00	0 00	0·0	2 00	0 00	0·0	1 00	0 00	0·0	270	270

N. Lat: for LHA > 180° … $Z_n = Z$
for LHA < 180° … $Z_n = 360° - Z$

S. Lat.: for LHA > 180° … $Z_n = 180° - Z$
for LHA < 180° … $Z_n = 180° + Z$

AUXILIARY TABLE

Sign of $corr_1$ for F′. *Reverse* sign if $F > 90°$. ↓

Sign for $corr_2$ for A′. ↓

F′ + −	1 59	2 58	3 57	4 56	5 55	6 54	7 53	8 52	9 51	10 50	11 49	12 48	13 47	14 46	15 45	16 44	17 43	18 42	19 41	20 40	21 39	22 38	23 37	24 36	25 35	26 34	27 33	28 32	29 31	□ 30	− + A′
P°	′	′	′	′	′	′	′	′	′	′	′	′	′	′	′	′	′	′	′	′	′	′	′	′	′	′	′	′	′	′	Z_2°
1	0	0	0	0	0	0	0	0	0	0	0	0	0	0	0	0	0	0	0	0	0	0	0	0	0	0	0	0	1	1	89
2	0	0	0	0	0	0	0	0	0	0	0	0	0	0	1	1	1	1	1	1	1	1	1	1	1	1	1	1	1	1	88
3	0	0	0	0	0	0	0	0	0	1	1	1	1	1	1	1	1	1	1	1	1	1	1	1	1	1	1	1	2	2	87
4	0	0	0	0	0	0	0	1	1	1	1	1	1	1	1	1	1	1	1	1	1	2	2	2	2	2	2	2	2	2	86
5	0	0	0	0	0	1	1	1	1	1	1	1	1	1	1	1	1	2	2	2	2	2	2	2	2	2	2	2	3	3	85
6	0	0	0	0	1	1	1	1	1	1	1	1	1	1	2	2	2	2	2	2	2	2	2	3	3	3	3	3	3	3	84
7	0	0	0	0	1	1	1	1	1	1	1	1	2	2	2	2	2	2	2	2	3	3	3	3	3	3	3	3	4	4	83
8	0	0	0	1	1	1	1	1	1	1	2	2	2	2	2	2	2	3	3	3	3	3	3	3	3	4	4	3	4	4	82
9	0	0	0	1	1	1	1	1	1	2	2	2	2	2	2	3	3	3	3	3	3	3	4	4	4	4	4	4	4	4	81
10	0	0	1	1	1	1	1	1	2	2	2	2	2	2	3	3	3	3	3	3	4	4	4	4	4	5	5	5	5	5	80
11	0	0	1	1	1	1	1	2	2	2	2	2	2	3	3	3	3	3	4	4	4	4	4	5	5	5	5	5	6	6	79
12	0	0	1	1	1	1	1	2	2	2	2	2	3	3	3	3	4	4	4	4	4	5	5	5	5	5	6	6	6	6	78
13	0	0	1	1	1	1	2	2	2	2	2	3	3	3	3	4	4	4	4	4	5	5	5	5	6	6	6	6	7	7	77
14	0	0	1	1	1	1	2	2	2	2	3	3	3	3	4	4	4	4	5	5	5	5	6	6	6	6	7	7	7	7	76
15	0	1	1	1	1	2	2	2	2	3	3	3	3	4	4	4	4	5	5	5	5	6	6	6	6	7	7	7	8	8	75
16	0	1	1	1	1	2	2	2	2	3	3	3	4	4	4	4	5	5	5	6	6	6	6	7	7	7	7	8	8	8	74
17	0	1	1	1	1	2	2	2	3	3	3	4	4	4	4	5	5	5	6	6	6	6	7	7	7	8	8	8	8	9	73
18	0	1	1	1	2	2	2	2	3	3	3	4	4	4	5	5	5	6	6	6	6	7	7	7	8	8	8	9	9	9	72
19	0	1	1	1	2	2	2	3	3	3	4	4	4	5	5	5	6	6	6	7	7	7	7	8	8	8	9	9	9	10	71
20	0	1	1	1	2	2	2	3	3	3	4	4	4	5	5	5	6	6	6	7	7	8	8	8	9	9	9	10	10	10	70
21	0	1	1	1	2	2	3	3	3	4	4	4	5	5	5	6	6	6	7	7	8	8	8	9	9	9	10	10	10	11	69
22	0	1	1	1	2	2	3	3	3	4	4	4	5	5	6	6	6	7	7	7	8	8	9	9	9	10	10	10	11	11	68
23	0	1	1	2	2	2	3	3	4	4	4	5	5	5	6	6	7	7	7	8	8	9	9	9	10	10	11	11	11	12	67
24	0	1	1	2	2	2	3	3	4	4	4	5	5	6	6	7	7	7	8	8	9	9	9	10	10	11	11	11	12	12	66
25	0	1	1	2	2	3	3	3	4	4	5	5	5	6	6	7	7	8	8	8	9	9	10	10	11	11	11	12	12	13	65
26	0	1	1	2	2	3	3	4	4	4	5	5	6	6	7	7	7	8	8	9	9	10	10	11	11	11	12	12	13	13	64
27	0	1	1	2	2	3	3	4	4	5	5	5	6	6	7	7	8	8	9	9	10	10	10	11	11	12	12	13	13	14	63
28	0	1	1	2	2	3	3	4	4	5	5	6	6	7	7	8	8	8	9	9	10	10	11	11	12	12	13	13	14	14	62
29	0	1	1	2	2	3	3	4	4	5	5	6	6	7	7	8	8	9	9	10	10	11	11	12	12	13	13	14	14	15	61
30	0	1	1	2	2	3	3	4	4	5	5	6	6	7	7	8	8	9	9	10	10	11	11	12	12	13	13	14	14	15	60
31	1	1	2	2	3	3	4	4	5	5	6	6	7	7	8	8	9	9	10	10	11	11	12	12	13	13	14	14	15	15	59
32	1	1	2	2	3	3	4	4	5	5	6	6	7	7	8	8	9	10	10	11	11	12	12	13	13	14	14	15	15	16	58
33	1	1	2	2	3	3	4	4	5	5	6	7	7	8	8	9	9	10	10	11	11	12	13	13	14	14	15	15	16	16	57
34	1	1	2	2	3	3	4	4	5	6	6	7	7	8	8	9	10	10	11	11	12	12	13	13	14	15	15	16	16	17	56
35	1	1	2	2	3	3	4	5	5	6	6	7	7	8	9	9	10	10	11	11	12	13	13	14	14	15	15	16	17	17	55
36	1	1	2	2	3	4	4	5	5	6	6	7	8	8	9	9	10	11	11	12	12	13	14	14	15	15	16	16	17	18	54
37	1	1	2	2	3	4	4	5	5	6	7	7	8	8	9	10	10	11	11	12	13	13	14	14	15	16	16	17	17	18	53
38	1	1	2	2	3	4	4	5	6	6	7	7	8	9	9	10	10	11	12	12	13	14	14	15	15	16	17	17	18	18	52
39	1	1	2	3	3	4	4	5	6	6	7	8	8	9	9	10	11	11	12	13	13	14	14	15	16	16	17	18	18	19	51
40	1	1	2	3	3	4	4	5	6	6	7	8	8	9	10	10	11	12	12	13	13	14	15	15	16	17	17	18	19	19	50

F′ +	1	2	3	4	5	6	7	8	9	10	11	12	13	14	15	16	17	18	19	20	21	22	23	24	25	26	27	28	29	□	− A′
F′ −	59	58	57	56	55	54	53	52	51	50	49	48	47	46	45	44	43	42	41	40	39	38	37	36	35	34	33	32	31	30	+ A′
P°	′	′	′	′	′	′	′	′	′	′	′	′	′	′	′	′	′	′	′	′	′	′	′	′	′	′	′	′	′	′	Z_2°
41	1	1	2	3	3	4	5	5	6	7	7	8	9	9	10	10	11	12	12	13	14	14	15	16	16	17	18	18	19	20	49
42	1	1	2	3	3	4	5	5	6	7	7	8	9	9	10	11	11	12	13	13	14	15	15	16	17	17	18	19	19	20	48
43	1	1	2	3	3	4	5	5	6	7	8	8	9	10	10	11	12	12	13	14	14	15	16	16	17	18	18	19	20	20	47
44	1	1	2	3	3	4	5	6	6	7	8	8	9	10	10	11	12	13	13	14	15	15	16	17	17	18	19	19	20	21	46
45	1	1	2	3	4	4	5	6	6	7	8	8	9	10	11	11	12	13	13	14	15	16	16	17	18	18	19	20	21	21	45
46	1	1	2	3	4	4	5	6	6	7	8	9	9	10	11	12	12	13	14	14	15	16	17	17	18	19	19	20	21	22	44
47	1	1	2	3	4	4	5	6	7	7	8	9	10	10	11	12	12	13	14	15	15	16	17	18	18	19	20	20	21	22	43
48	1	1	2	3	4	4	5	6	7	7	8	9	10	10	11	12	13	13	14	15	16	16	17	18	19	19	20	21	22	22	42
49	1	2	2	3	4	5	5	6	7	8	8	9	10	11	11	12	13	14	14	15	16	17	17	18	19	20	20	21	22	23	41
50	1	2	2	3	4	5	5	6	7	8	8	9	10	11	11	12	13	14	15	15	16	17	18	18	19	20	21	21	22	23	40
51	1	2	2	3	4	5	5	6	7	8	9	9	10	11	12	12	13	14	15	16	16	17	18	19	19	20	21	22	23	23	39
52	1	2	2	3	4	5	6	6	7	8	9	9	10	11	12	13	13	14	15	16	17	17	18	19	20	20	21	22	23	24	38
53	1	2	2	3	4	5	6	6	7	8	9	10	10	11	12	13	14	14	15	16	17	18	18	19	20	21	22	22	23	24	37
54	1	2	2	3	4	5	6	6	7	8	9	10	11	11	12	13	14	15	15	16	17	18	19	19	20	21	22	23	23	24	36
55	1	2	2	3	4	5	6	7	7	8	9	10	11	11	12	13	14	15	16	16	17	18	19	20	20	21	22	23	24	25	35
56	1	2	2	3	4	5	6	7	7	8	9	10	11	12	12	13	14	15	16	17	17	18	19	20	21	22	22	23	24	25	34
57	1	2	3	3	4	5	6	7	8	8	9	10	11	12	13	13	14	15	16	17	18	18	19	20	21	22	23	23	24	25	33
58	1	2	3	3	4	5	6	7	8	8	9	10	11	12	13	14	14	15	16	17	18	19	20	20	21	22	23	24	25	25	32
59	1	2	3	3	4	5	6	7	8	9	9	10	11	12	13	14	15	15	16	17	18	19	20	21	21	22	23	24	25	26	31
60	1	2	3	3	4	5	6	7	8	9	10	10	11	12	13	14	15	16	16	17	18	19	20	21	22	23	23	24	25	26	30
61	1	2	3	3	4	5	6	7	8	9	10	10	11	12	13	14	15	16	17	17	18	19	20	21	22	23	24	24	25	26	29
62	1	2	3	4	4	5	6	7	8	9	10	11	11	12	13	14	15	16	17	18	19	19	20	21	22	23	24	25	26	26	28
63	1	2	3	4	4	5	6	7	8	9	10	11	12	12	13	14	15	16	17	18	19	20	20	21	22	23	24	25	26	27	27
64	1	2	3	4	4	5	6	7	8	9	10	11	12	13	13	14	15	16	17	18	19	20	21	22	22	23	24	25	26	27	26
65	1	2	3	4	5	5	6	7	8	9	10	11	12	13	14	15	15	16	17	18	19	20	21	22	23	24	24	25	26	27	25
66	1	2	3	4	5	5	6	7	8	9	10	11	12	13	14	15	16	16	17	18	19	20	21	22	23	24	25	26	26	27	24
67	1	2	3	4	5	6	6	7	8	9	10	11	12	13	14	15	16	17	17	18	19	20	21	22	23	24	25	26	27	28	23
68	1	2	3	4	5	6	6	7	8	9	10	11	12	13	14	15	16	17	18	19	19	20	21	22	23	24	25	26	27	28	22
69	1	2	3	4	5	6	7	7	8	9	10	11	12	13	14	15	16	17	18	19	20	21	21	22	23	24	25	26	27	28	21
70	1	2	3	4	5	6	7	8	8	9	10	11	12	13	14	15	16	17	18	19	20	21	22	23	23	24	25	26	27	28	20
71	1	2	3	4	5	6	7	8	9	9	10	11	12	13	14	15	16	17	18	19	20	21	22	23	24	25	26	26	27	28	19
72	1	2	3	4	5	6	7	8	9	10	10	11	12	13	14	15	16	17	18	19	20	21	22	23	24	25	26	27	28	29	18
73	1	2	3	4	5	6	7	8	9	10	11	11	12	13	14	15	16	17	18	19	20	21	22	23	24	25	26	27	28	29	17
74	1	2	3	4	5	6	7	8	9	10	11	12	12	13	14	15	16	17	18	19	20	21	22	23	24	25	26	27	28	29	16
75	1	2	3	4	5	6	7	8	9	10	11	12	13	14	14	15	16	17	18	19	20	21	22	23	24	25	26	27	28	29	15
76	1	2	3	4	5	6	7	8	9	10	11	12	13	14	15	16	16	17	18	19	20	21	22	23	24	25	26	27	28	29	14
77	1	2	3	4	5	6	7	8	9	10	11	12	13	14	15	16	17	18	19	19	20	21	22	23	24	25	26	27	28	29	13
78	1	2	3	4	5	6	7	8	9	10	11	12	13	14	15	16	17	18	19	20	21	22	22	23	24	25	26	27	28	29	12
79	1	2	3	4	5	6	7	8	9	10	11	12	13	14	15	16	17	18	19	20	21	22	23	24	25	26	27	27	28	29	11
80	1	2	3	4	5	6	7	8	9	10	11	12	13	14	15	16	17	18	19	20	21	22	23	24	25	26	27	28	29	30	10

For P > 80°, use 80°

For $Z_2 < 10°$, use 10°

USE OF CONCISE SIGHT REDUCTION TABLES (continued)

4. *Example.* (b) Required the altitude and azimuth of *Vega* on 2017 July 29 at UT 04^{h} 50^{m} from the estimated position 152° west, 15° south.

1. Assumed latitude	$Lat =$	15° S		
From the almanac	$GHA =$	100° 09′		
Assumed longitude		152° 09′ W		
Local hour angle	$LHA =$	308		
2. Reduction table, 1st entry				
$(Lat, LHA) = (15, 308)$	$A =$	49 34	$A° = 50$, $A' = 34$	
	$B =$	+66 29	$Z_1 = +71{\cdot}7$,	$LHA > 270°$
3. From the almanac	$Dec =$	−38 48		*Lat* and *Dec* contrary
Sum = $B + Dec$	$F =$	+27 41	$F° = 28$, $F' = 41$	
4. Reduction table, 2nd entry				
$(A°, F°) = (50, 28)$	$H =$	17 34	$P° = 37$	
			$Z_2 = 67{\cdot}8, Z_2° = 68$	
5. Auxiliary table, 1st entry				
$(F', P°) = (41, 37)$	$corr_1 =$	−11		$F < 90°$, $F' > 29'$
Sum		17 23		
6. Auxiliary table, 2nd entry				
$(A', Z_2°) = (34, 68)$	$corr_2 =$	+10		$A' > 30'$
7. Sum = computed altitude	$H_C =$	+17° 33′		$F > 0°$
8. Azimuth, first component	$Z_1 =$	+71·7		same sign as B
second component	$Z_2 =$	+67·8		$F < 90°$, $F > 0°$
Sum = azimuth angle	$Z =$	139·5		
True azimuth	$Z_n =$	040°		S *Lat*, $LHA > 180°$

5. *Form for use with the Concise Sight Reduction Tables.* The form on the following page lays out the procedure explained on pages 284-285. Each step is shown, with notes and rules to ensure accuracy, rather than speed, throughout the calculation. The form is mainly intended for the calculation of star positions. It therefore includes the formation of the Greenwich hour of Aries (*GHA* Aries), and thus the Greenwich hour angle of the star (*GHA*) from its tabular sidereal hour angle (*SHA*). These calculations, included in step 1 of the form, can easily be replaced by the interpolation of *GHA* and *Dec* for the Sun, Moon or planets.

The form may be freely copied; however, acknowledgement of the source is requested.

Date & UT of observation h m s	**Body**	**Estimated Latitude & Longitude** ° ′ ° ′

Step	**Calculate Altitude & Azimuth**		**Summary of Rules & Notes**
Assumed latitude	*Lat* = °		Nearest estimated latitude, integral number of degrees.
Assumed longitude	*Long* = ° ′		Choose *Long* so that *LHA* has integral number of degrees.
1. From the almanac:	*Dec* = ° ′		Record the *Dec* for use in Step 3.
GHA Aries h	= ° ′		Needed if using *SHA*. Tabular value.
Increment m s	= ° ′		for minutes and seconds of time.
SHA	*SHA* = ° ′		
$GHA = GHA\ Aries + SHA$	*GHA* = ° ′		Remove multiples of 360°.
Assumed longitude	*Long* = ° ′		West longitudes are negative.
$LHA = GHA + Long$	*LHA* = °		Remove multiples of 360°.
2. Reduction table, 1st entry			
$(Lat, LHA) = (\ \ °,\ \ °)$	*A* = ° ′	$A°$ = °	nearest whole degree of *A*.
record *A*, *B* and Z_1.		A' = ′	minutes part of *A*.
	B = ° ′		*B* is minus if $90° < LHA < 270°$.
		Z_1 = °	Z_1 has the same sign as *B*.
3. From step 1	*Dec* = ° ′		*Dec* is minus if contrary to *Lat*.
$F = B + Dec$	*F* = ° ′		Regard *F* as positive until step 7.
		$F°$ = °	nearest whole degree of *F*.
		F' = ′	minutes part of *F*.
4. Reduction table, 2nd entry			
$(A°, F°) = (\ \ °,\ \ °)$	*H* = ° ′	$P°$ = °	nearest whole degree of *P*.
record *H*, *P* and Z_2.		Z_2 = °	
5. Auxiliary table, 1st entry $(F', P°) = (\ \ ′,\ \ °)$ record $corr_1$	$corr_1$ = ′		$corr_1$ is minus if $F < 90°$ & $F' > 29'$, or if $F > 90°$ & $F' < 30'$.
6. Auxiliary table, 2nd entry $(A', Z_2°) = (\ \ ′,\ \ °)$ record $corr_2$	$corr_2$ = ′		$Z_2°$ nearest whole degree of Z_2. $corr_2$ is minus if $A' < 30'$.
7. Calculated altitude = $H_C = H + corr_1 + corr_2$	H_C = ° ′		H_C is minus if *F* is negative, and object is below the horizon.
8. Azimuth, 1st component	Z_1 = °		Z_1 has the same sign as *B*.
2nd component	Z_2 = °		Z_2 is minus if $F > 90°$. If *F* is negative, $Z_2 = 180° - Z_2$
$Z = Z_1 + Z_2$	*Z* = °		Ignore the sign of *Z*.
			N *Lat*: If $LHA > 180°$, $Z_n = Z$, or if $LHA < 180°$, $Z_n = 360° - Z$,
			S *Lat*: If $LHA > 180°$, $Z_n = 180° - Z$, or if $LHA < 180°$, $Z_n = 180° + Z$.
True azimuth	Z_n = °		©HMNAO

For use with *The Nautical Almanac's* Concise Sight Reduction Tables pages 284-318.

POLAR PHENOMENA

EXPLANATION

1. *Introduction.* The graphs on pages 322-325 give data concerning the rising and setting of the Sun and Moon and the duration of civil twilight for high latitudes. Graphs are given instead of tables for high latitudes because they give a clearer picture of the phenomena and of the attainable accuracy in any given case. In the regions of the graph that are difficult to read accurately, the phenomenon itself is generally uncertain.

2. *Semiduration of sunlight.* The graphs for the semiduration of sunlight (page 322) give for latitudes north of N 65° the number of hours from sunrise to meridian passage or from meridian passage to sunset. There is continuous daylight in an area marked "Sun above horizon", and no direct sunlight in an area marked "Sun below horizon". The figures near the top indicate, for several convenient dates, the local mean times of meridian passage; with the aid of the intermediate dots the LMT on any given day may be obtained to the nearest minute. The LMT of sunrise may be found by subtracting the semiduration from the time of meridian passage, and the time of sunset by adding. The equation of time is given by subtracting the time of meridian passage from noon.

Examples. (a) Estimate the time of sunrise and sunset on 2017 March 10 at latitude N 77°. The semiduration of sunlight (page 322) is about $5^{h}00^{m}$. The time of meridian passage is $12^{h}10^{m}$, and hence the LMT of sunrise is $07^{h}10^{m}$, and of sunset $17^{h}10^{m}$. (b) Estimate the dates, for the first half of 2017, when the Sun is continuously below and above the horizon at latitude N 80°. The semiduration of sunlight graph (page 322) indicates the Sun is continuously below the horizon until about February 21, and is continuously above the horizon after April 14.

3. *Duration of civil twilight.* The graphs for the duration of twilight (page 322) give the interval from the beginning of morning civil twilight (Sun 6° below the horizon) to the time of sunrise or from the time of sunset to the end of evening civil twilight. In a region marked "No twilight or sunlight" the Sun is continuously below the horizon by more than 6°. In a region marked "Continuous twilight or sunlight" the Sun never goes lower than 6° below the horizon.

Adjacent to a region marked "No twilight or sunlight" is a region in which the Sun is continuously below the horizon, but so near to the horizon during a portion of the day that there is twilight. This area is the shaded region. The value given by the graph in this shaded region is the interval from the beginning of morning twilight to meridian passage of the Sun, or from meridian passage to the end of evening twilight, the total duration of twilight being twice the value given by the graph. The border between this shaded region and the remainder of the graph indicates that the Sun only just rises at meridian passage at the date and latitude shown. The remainder of the graph gives the total duration of civil twilight.

Examples. (a) Estimate the time of the beginning of morning civil twilight at latitude N 77° on 2017 March 10. The duration of twilight (page 322) is about $1^{h}35^{m}$. Applying this to the time of sunrise, $07^{h}10^{m}$, found in the preceding example, the beginning of morning civil twilight is $05^{h}35^{m}$ LMT. (b) Estimate, for the first half of 2017, the limiting dates of civil twilight and sunlight at latitude N 80°. The graphs (page 322) indicate there is no sunlight or twilight till about February 5, there is twilight but no sunlight from February 5 until February 21, sunlight and twilight till March 31, continuous twilight or sunlight till April 14, and then continuous sunlight. (c) Estimate the time of the beginning and end of civil twilight on 2017 February 14 at latitude N 80°. The graph (page 322) indicates there is no direct sunlight at this date and latitude, but three hours of twilight before and after meridian passage. Thus civil twilight begins at about 09^{h} and ends at about 15^{h} LMT.

4. *Semiduration of moonlight* The graphs, for each month, for the semiduration of moonlight give for the Moon the same data as the graphs for the semiduration of sunlight give for the Sun. The scale near the top gives the LMT of meridian passage. In addition, the phase symbols are placed on the graphs to show the day on which each phase occurs. Since the times of meridian passage and the semiduration change more rapidly from day to day for the Moon than for the Sun, special care will be required in reading the graphs accurately.

For most purposes, in these high latitudes a rough idea of the time of moonrise or moonset is all that is required and this may be obtained by a glance at the graph.

Example. Estimate the moon phase and the time of moonrise and moonset on 2017 January 20 at latitude N 74°. The phase is found from pages 323-325 to be near last quarter, and the Moon crosses the meridian at 06^h LMT. The semiduration of moonlight taken for the time of meridian passage is 4 hours, giving moonrise at 02^h LMT on January 20 and moonset at 10^h on January 20.

If greater accuracy is required, it is necessary to read the graph for the UT of each phenomenon at the desired meridian. The dates indicated on the graph are for 00^h UT, and intermediate values of the UT may be located by estimation.

Example. Required to improve the results obtained in the preceding example, assuming the observer to be in longitude W 90° (6^h) west.

The values found previously were:

			d h				d h	
Time of meridian passage	2017	Jan.	20 06	LMT	=	Jan.	20 12	UT
Semiduration of moonlight			4					
Time of moonrise		Jan.	20 02	LMT	=	Jan.	20 08	UT
Time of moonset		Jan.	20 10	LMT	=	Jan.	20 16	UT

Returning to the graphs (pages 323-325) with these three values of the UT, the following results are obtained:

			d h m				d h m	
Time of meridian passage	2017	Jan.	20 06 10	LMT	=	Jan.	20 12 10	UT
Semiduration for moonrise			03 50					
Time of moonrise		Jan.	20 02 20	LMT	=	Jan.	20 08 20	UT
Semiduration for moonset			03 30					
Time of moonset		Jan.	20 09 40	LMT	=	Jan.	20 15 40	UT

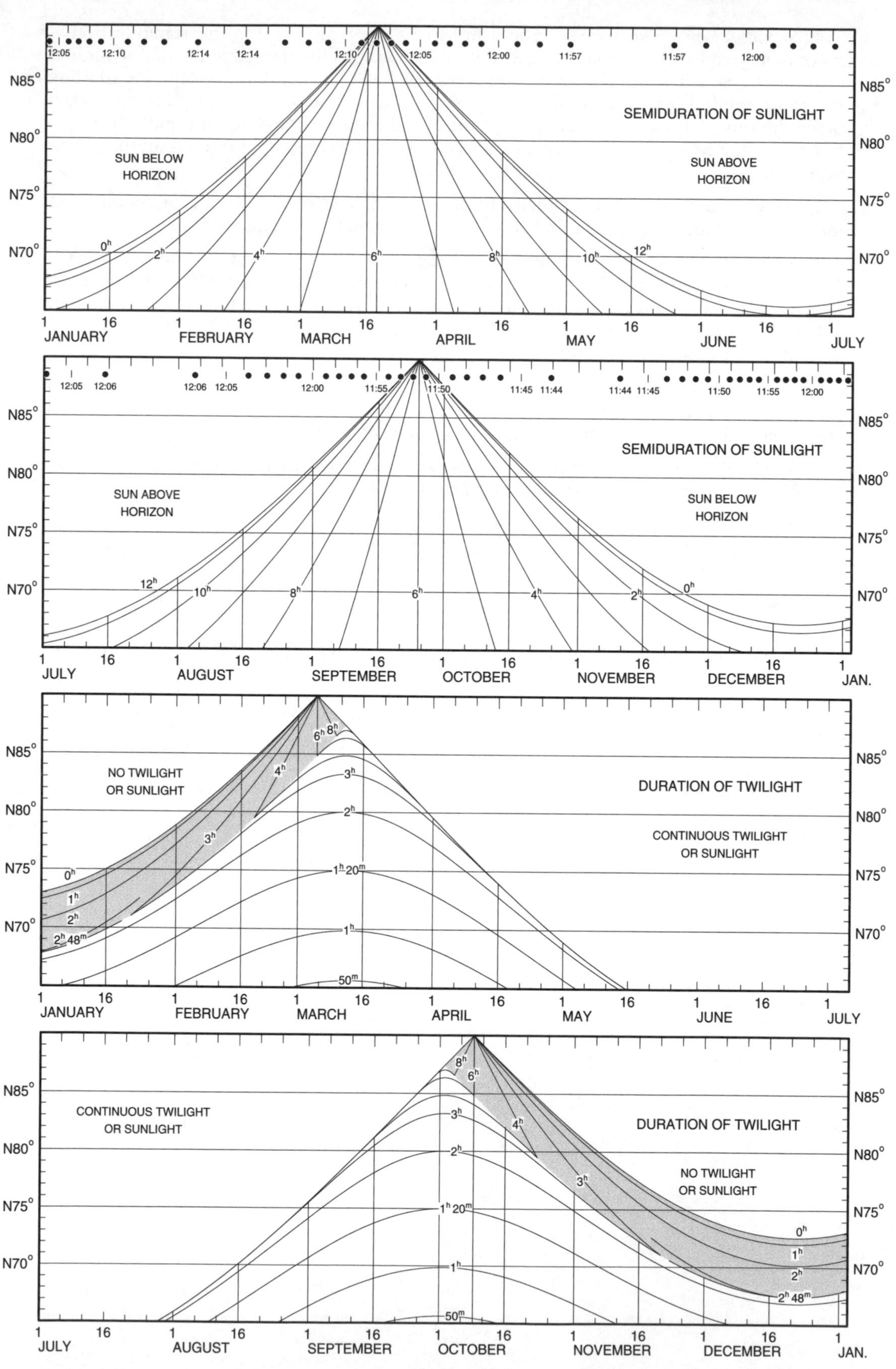

SEMIDURATION OF SUNLIGHT
SUN BELOW HORIZON
SUN ABOVE HORIZON
12:05 12:10 12:14 12:14 12:10 12:05 12:00 11:57 11:57 12:00
N85° N80° N75° N70°
0h 2h 4h 6h 8h 10h 12h
JANUARY FEBRUARY MARCH APRIL MAY JUNE JULY
SEMIDURATION OF SUNLIGHT
SUN ABOVE HORIZON
SUN BELOW HORIZON
12:05 12:06 12:06 12:05 12:00 11:55 11:50 11:45 11:44 11:44 11:45 11:50 11:55 12:00
12h 10h 8h 6h 4h 2h 0h
JULY AUGUST SEPTEMBER OCTOBER NOVEMBER DECEMBER JAN.
DURATION OF TWILIGHT
NO TWILIGHT OR SUNLIGHT
CONTINUOUS TWILIGHT OR SUNLIGHT
0h 1h 2h 2h 48m 3h 4h 6h 8h 1h 20m 50m
JANUARY FEBRUARY MARCH APRIL MAY JUNE JULY
DURATION OF TWILIGHT
CONTINUOUS TWILIGHT OR SUNLIGHT
NO TWILIGHT OR SUNLIGHT
JULY AUGUST SEPTEMBER OCTOBER NOVEMBER DECEMBER JAN.

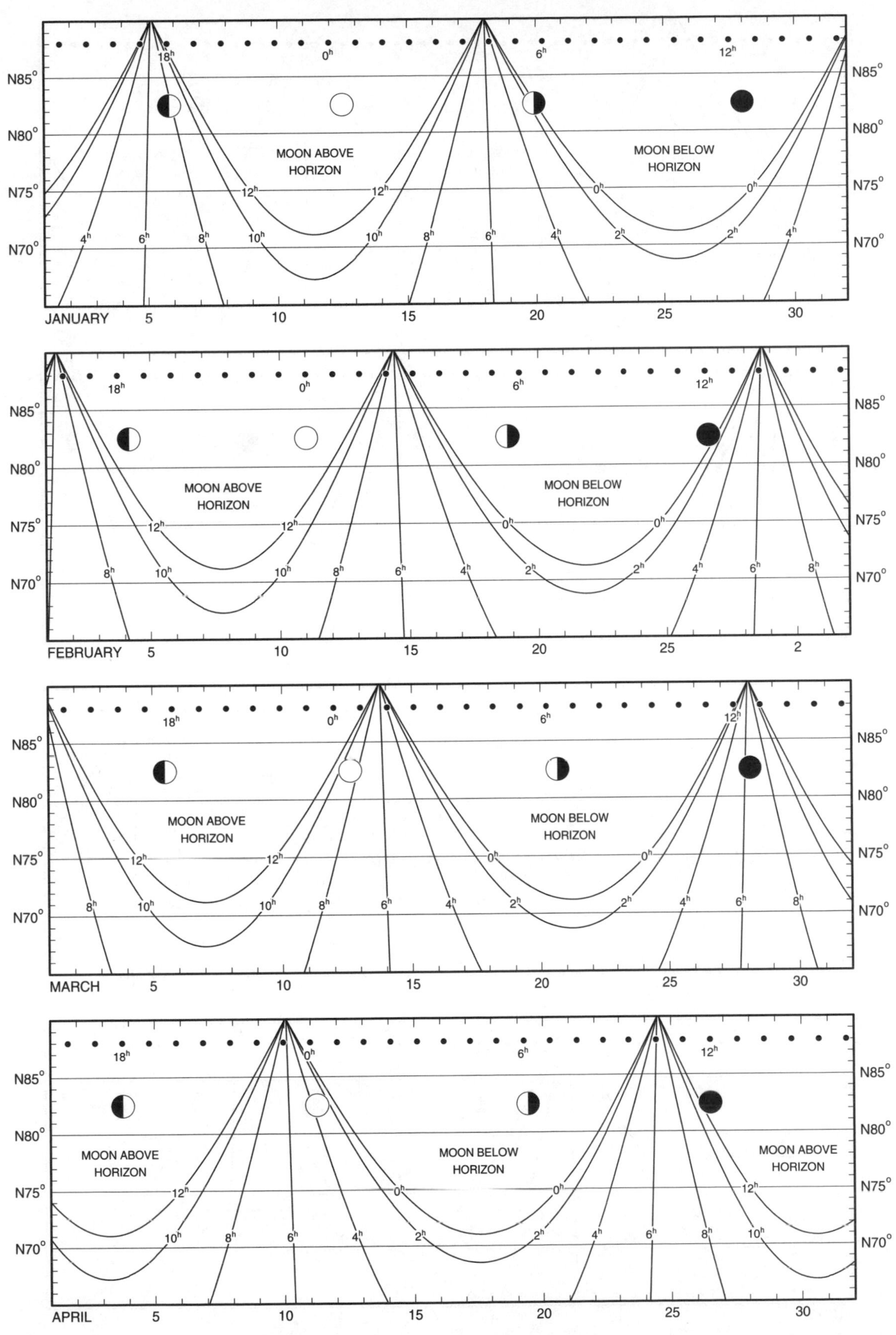

18h
0h
6h
12h
N85°
N80°
N75°
N70°
MOON ABOVE HORIZON
MOON BELOW HORIZON
12h
10h
8h
6h
4h
2h
0h
JANUARY 5 10 15 20 25 30
FEBRUARY 5 10 15 20 25 2
MARCH 5 10 15 20 25 30
APRIL 5 10 15 20 25 30

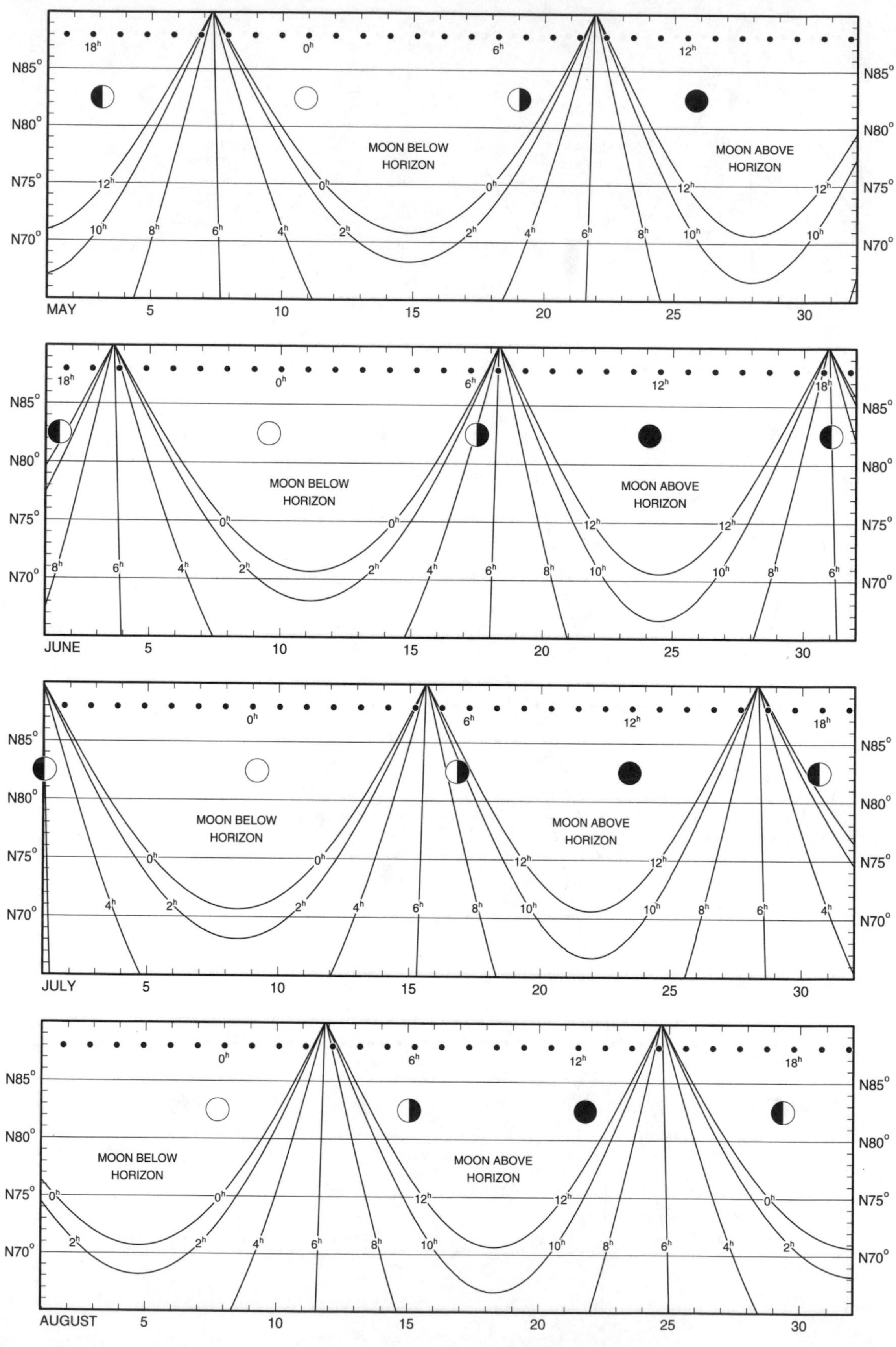
MAY
JUNE
JULY
AUGUST
MOON BELOW HORIZON
MOON ABOVE HORIZON
N85°
N80°
N75°
N70°
5
10
15
20
25
30
0h
2h
4h
6h
8h
10h
12h
18h

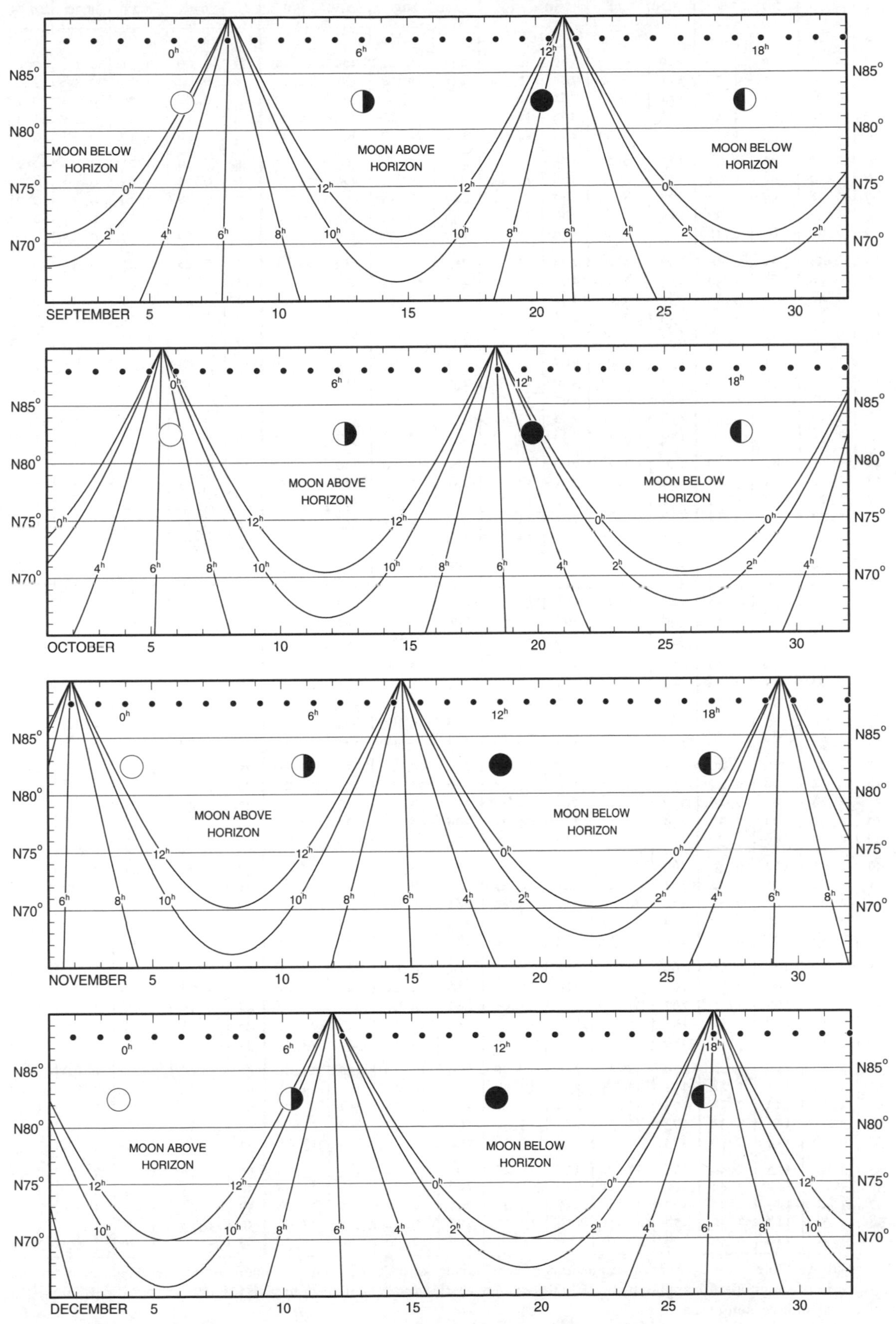
N85°
N80°
N75°
N70°
MOON BELOW HORIZON
MOON ABOVE HORIZON
MOON BELOW HORIZON
0h
6h
12h
18h
0h
2h
4h
6h
8h
10h
12h
SEPTEMBER 5
10
15
20
25
30
MOON ABOVE HORIZON
MOON BELOW HORIZON
OCTOBER 5
10
15
20
25
30
MOON ABOVE HORIZON
MOON BELOW HORIZON
NOVEMBER 5
10
15
20
25
30
MOON ABOVE HORIZON
MOON BELOW HORIZON
DECEMBER 5
10
15
20
25
30

CONVERSION OF ARC TO TIME

0°–59°		60°–119°		120°–179°		180°–239°		240°–299°		300°–359°			0′.00	0′.25	0′.50	0′.75
°	h m	°	h m	°	h m	°	h m	°	h m	°	h m	′	m s	m s	m s	m s
0	0 00	**60**	4 00	**120**	8 00	**180**	12 00	**240**	16 00	**300**	20 00	**0**	0 00	0 01	0 02	0 03
1	0 04	**61**	4 04	**121**	8 04	**181**	12 04	**241**	16 04	**301**	20 04	**1**	0 04	0 05	0 06	0 07
2	0 08	**62**	4 08	**122**	8 08	**182**	12 08	**242**	16 08	**302**	20 08	**2**	0 08	0 09	0 10	0 11
3	0 12	**63**	4 12	**123**	8 12	**183**	12 12	**243**	16 12	**303**	20 12	**3**	0 12	0 13	0 14	0 15
4	0 16	**64**	4 16	**124**	8 16	**184**	12 16	**244**	16 16	**304**	20 16	**4**	0 16	0 17	0 18	0 19
5	0 20	**65**	4 20	**125**	8 20	**185**	12 20	**245**	16 20	**305**	20 20	**5**	0 20	0 21	0 22	0 23
6	0 24	**66**	4 24	**126**	8 24	**186**	12 24	**246**	16 24	**306**	20 24	**6**	0 24	0 25	0 26	0 27
7	0 28	**67**	4 28	**127**	8 28	**187**	12 28	**247**	16 28	**307**	20 28	**7**	0 28	0 29	0 30	0 31
8	0 32	**68**	4 32	**128**	8 32	**188**	12 32	**248**	16 32	**308**	20 32	**8**	0 32	0 33	0 34	0 35
9	0 36	**69**	4 36	**129**	8 36	**189**	12 36	**249**	16 36	**309**	20 36	**9**	0 36	0 37	0 38	0 39
10	0 40	**70**	4 40	**130**	8 40	**190**	12 40	**250**	16 40	**310**	20 40	**10**	0 40	0 41	0 42	0 43
11	0 44	**71**	4 44	**131**	8 44	**191**	12 44	**251**	16 44	**311**	20 44	**11**	0 44	0 45	0 46	0 47
12	0 48	**72**	4 48	**132**	8 48	**192**	12 48	**252**	16 48	**312**	20 48	**12**	0 48	0 49	0 50	0 51
13	0 52	**73**	4 52	**133**	8 52	**193**	12 52	**253**	16 52	**313**	20 52	**13**	0 52	0 53	0 54	0 55
14	0 56	**74**	4 56	**134**	8 56	**194**	12 56	**254**	16 56	**314**	20 56	**14**	0 56	0 57	0 58	0 59
15	1 00	**75**	5 00	**135**	9 00	**195**	13 00	**255**	17 00	**315**	21 00	**15**	1 00	1 01	1 02	1 03
16	1 04	**76**	5 04	**136**	9 04	**196**	13 04	**256**	17 04	**316**	21 04	**16**	1 04	1 05	1 06	1 07
17	1 08	**77**	5 08	**137**	9 08	**197**	13 08	**257**	17 08	**317**	21 08	**17**	1 08	1 09	1 10	1 11
18	1 12	**78**	5 12	**138**	9 12	**198**	13 12	**258**	17 12	**318**	21 12	**18**	1 12	1 13	1 14	1 15
19	1 16	**79**	5 16	**139**	9 16	**199**	13 16	**259**	17 16	**319**	21 16	**19**	1 16	1 17	1 18	1 19
20	1 20	**80**	5 20	**140**	9 20	**200**	13 20	**260**	17 20	**320**	21 20	**20**	1 20	1 21	1 22	1 23
21	1 24	**81**	5 24	**141**	9 24	**201**	13 24	**261**	17 24	**321**	21 24	**21**	1 24	1 25	1 26	1 27
22	1 28	**82**	5 28	**142**	9 28	**202**	13 28	**262**	17 28	**322**	21 28	**22**	1 28	1 29	1 30	1 31
23	1 32	**83**	5 32	**143**	9 32	**203**	13 32	**263**	17 32	**323**	21 32	**23**	1 32	1 33	1 34	1 35
24	1 36	**84**	5 36	**144**	9 36	**204**	13 36	**264**	17 36	**324**	21 36	**24**	1 36	1 37	1 38	1 39
25	1 40	**85**	5 40	**145**	9 40	**205**	13 40	**265**	17 40	**325**	21 40	**25**	1 40	1 41	1 42	1 43
26	1 44	**86**	5 44	**146**	9 44	**206**	13 44	**266**	17 44	**326**	21 44	**26**	1 44	1 45	1 46	1 47
27	1 48	**87**	5 48	**147**	9 48	**207**	13 48	**267**	17 48	**327**	21 48	**27**	1 48	1 49	1 50	1 51
28	1 52	**88**	5 52	**148**	9 52	**208**	13 52	**268**	17 52	**328**	21 52	**28**	1 52	1 53	1 54	1 55
29	1 56	**89**	5 56	**149**	9 56	**209**	13 56	**269**	17 56	**329**	21 56	**29**	1 56	1 57	1 58	1 59
30	2 00	**90**	6 00	**150**	10 00	**210**	14 00	**270**	18 00	**330**	22 00	**30**	2 00	2 01	2 02	2 03
31	2 04	**91**	6 04	**151**	10 04	**211**	14 04	**271**	18 04	**331**	22 04	**31**	2 04	2 05	2 06	2 07
32	2 08	**92**	6 08	**152**	10 08	**212**	14 08	**272**	18 08	**332**	22 08	**32**	2 08	2 09	2 10	2 11
33	2 12	**93**	6 12	**153**	10 12	**213**	14 12	**273**	18 12	**333**	22 12	**33**	2 12	2 13	2 14	2 15
34	2 16	**94**	6 16	**154**	10 16	**214**	14 16	**274**	18 16	**334**	22 16	**34**	2 16	2 17	2 18	2 19
35	2 20	**95**	6 20	**155**	10 20	**215**	14 20	**275**	18 20	**335**	22 20	**35**	2 20	2 21	2 22	2 23
36	2 24	**96**	6 24	**156**	10 24	**216**	14 24	**276**	18 24	**336**	22 24	**36**	2 24	2 25	2 26	2 27
37	2 28	**97**	6 28	**157**	10 28	**217**	14 28	**277**	18 28	**337**	22 28	**37**	2 28	2 29	2 30	2 31
38	2 32	**98**	6 32	**158**	10 32	**218**	14 32	**278**	18 32	**338**	22 32	**38**	2 32	2 33	2 34	2 35
39	2 36	**99**	6 36	**159**	10 36	**219**	14 36	**279**	18 36	**339**	22 36	**39**	2 36	2 37	2 38	2 39
40	2 40	**100**	6 40	**160**	10 40	**220**	14 40	**280**	18 40	**340**	22 40	**40**	2 40	2 41	2 42	2 43
41	2 44	**101**	6 44	**161**	10 44	**221**	14 44	**281**	18 44	**341**	22 44	**41**	2 44	2 45	2 46	2 47
42	2 48	**102**	6 48	**162**	10 48	**222**	14 48	**282**	18 48	**342**	22 48	**42**	2 48	2 49	2 50	2 51
43	2 52	**103**	6 52	**163**	10 52	**223**	14 52	**283**	18 52	**343**	22 52	**43**	2 52	2 53	2 54	2 55
44	2 56	**104**	6 56	**164**	10 56	**224**	14 56	**284**	18 56	**344**	22 56	**44**	2 56	2 57	2 58	2 59
45	3 00	**105**	7 00	**165**	11 00	**225**	15 00	**285**	19 00	**345**	23 00	**45**	3 00	3 01	3 02	3 03
46	3 04	**106**	7 04	**166**	11 04	**226**	15 04	**286**	19 04	**346**	23 04	**46**	3 04	3 05	3 06	3 07
47	3 08	**107**	7 08	**167**	11 08	**227**	15 08	**287**	19 08	**347**	23 08	**47**	3 08	3 09	3 10	3 11
48	3 12	**108**	7 12	**168**	11 12	**228**	15 12	**288**	19 12	**348**	23 12	**48**	3 12	3 13	3 14	3 15
49	3 16	**109**	7 16	**169**	11 16	**229**	15 16	**289**	19 16	**349**	23 16	**49**	3 16	3 17	3 18	3 19
50	3 20	**110**	7 20	**170**	11 20	**230**	15 20	**290**	19 20	**350**	23 20	**50**	3 20	3 21	3 22	3 23
51	3 24	**111**	7 24	**171**	11 24	**231**	15 24	**291**	19 24	**351**	23 24	**51**	3 24	3 25	3 26	3 27
52	3 28	**112**	7 28	**172**	11 28	**232**	15 28	**292**	19 28	**352**	23 28	**52**	3 28	3 29	3 30	3 31
53	3 32	**113**	7 32	**173**	11 32	**233**	15 32	**293**	19 32	**353**	23 32	**53**	3 32	3 33	3 34	3 35
54	3 36	**114**	7 36	**174**	11 36	**234**	15 36	**294**	19 36	**354**	23 36	**54**	3 36	3 37	3 38	3 39
55	3 40	**115**	7 40	**175**	11 40	**235**	15 40	**295**	19 40	**355**	23 40	**55**	3 40	3 41	3 42	3 43
56	3 44	**116**	7 44	**176**	11 44	**236**	15 44	**296**	19 44	**356**	23 44	**56**	3 44	3 45	3 46	3 47
57	3 48	**117**	7 48	**177**	11 48	**237**	15 48	**297**	19 48	**357**	23 48	**57**	3 48	3 49	3 50	3 51
58	3 52	**118**	7 52	**178**	11 52	**238**	15 52	**298**	19 52	**358**	23 52	**58**	3 52	3 53	3 54	3 55
59	3 56	**119**	7 56	**179**	11 56	**239**	15 56	**299**	19 56	**359**	23 56	**59**	3 56	3 57	3 58	3 59

The above table is for converting expressions in arc to their equivalent in time; its main use in this Almanac is for the conversion of longitude for application to LMT (*added* if *west*, *subtracted* if *east*) to give UT or vice versa, particularly in the case of sunrise, sunset, etc.

m 0	SUN PLANETS	ARIES	MOON	v or d	Corrⁿ	v or d	Corrⁿ	v or d	Corrⁿ
s	° ′	° ′	° ′	′	′	′	′	′	′
00	0 00·0	0 00·0	0 00·0	0·0	0·0	6·0	0·1	12·0	0·1
01	0 00·3	0 00·3	0 00·2	0·1	0·0	6·1	0·1	12·1	0·1
02	0 00·5	0 00·5	0 00·5	0·2	0·0	6·2	0·1	12·2	0·1
03	0 00·8	0 00·8	0 00·7	0·3	0·0	6·3	0·1	12·3	0·1
04	0 01·0	0 01·0	0 01·0	0·4	0·0	6·4	0·1	12·4	0·1
05	0 01·3	0 01·3	0 01·2	0·5	0·0	6·5	0·1	12·5	0·1
06	0 01·5	0 01·5	0 01·4	0·6	0·0	6·6	0·1	12·6	0·1
07	0 01·8	0 01·8	0 01·7	0·7	0·0	6·7	0·1	12·7	0·1
08	0 02·0	0 02·0	0 01·9	0·8	0·0	6·8	0·1	12·8	0·1
09	0 02·3	0 02·3	0 02·1	0·9	0·0	6·9	0·1	12·9	0·1
10	0 02·5	0 02·5	0 02·4	1·0	0·0	7·0	0·1	13·0	0·1
11	0 02·8	0 02·8	0 02·6	1·1	0·0	7·1	0·1	13·1	0·1
12	0 03·0	0 03·0	0 02·9	1·2	0·0	7·2	0·1	13·2	0·1
13	0 03·3	0 03·3	0 03·1	1·3	0·0	7·3	0·1	13·3	0·1
14	0 03·5	0 03·5	0 03·3	1·4	0·0	7·4	0·1	13·4	0·1
15	0 03·8	0 03·8	0 03·6	1·5	0·0	7·5	0·1	13·5	0·1
16	0 04·0	0 04·0	0 03·8	1·6	0·0	7·6	0·1	13·6	0·1
17	0 04·3	0 04·3	0 04·1	1·7	0·0	7·7	0·1	13·7	0·1
18	0 04·5	0 04·5	0 04·3	1·8	0·0	7·8	0·1	13·8	0·1
19	0 04·8	0 04·8	0 04·5	1·9	0·0	7·9	0·1	13·9	0·1
20	0 05·0	0 05·0	0 04·8	2·0	0·0	8·0	0·1	14·0	0·1
21	0 05·3	0 05·3	0 05·0	2·1	0·0	8·1	0·1	14·1	0·1
22	0 05·5	0 05·5	0 05·2	2·2	0·0	8·2	0·1	14·2	0·1
23	0 05·8	0 05·8	0 05·5	2·3	0·0	8·3	0·1	14·3	0·1
24	0 06·0	0 06·0	0 05·7	2·4	0·0	8·4	0·1	14·4	0·1
25	0 06·3	0 06·3	0 06·0	2·5	0·0	8·5	0·1	14·5	0·1
26	0 06·5	0 06·5	0 06·2	2·6	0·0	8·6	0·1	14·6	0·1
27	0 06·8	0 06·8	0 06·4	2·7	0·0	8·7	0·1	14·7	0·1
28	0 07·0	0 07·0	0 06·7	2·8	0·0	8·8	0·1	14·8	0·1
29	0 07·3	0 07·3	0 06·9	2·9	0·0	8·9	0·1	14·9	0·1
30	0 07·5	0 07·5	0 07·2	3·0	0·0	9·0	0·1	15·0	0·1
31	0 07·8	0 07·8	0 07·4	3·1	0·0	9·1	0·1	15·1	0·1
32	0 08·0	0 08·0	0 07·6	3·2	0·0	9·2	0·1	15·2	0·1
33	0 08·3	0 08·3	0 07·9	3·3	0·0	9·3	0·1	15·3	0·1
34	0 08·5	0 08·5	0 08·1	3·4	0·0	9·4	0·1	15·4	0·1
35	0 08·8	0 08·8	0 08·4	3·5	0·0	9·5	0·1	15·5	0·1
36	0 09·0	0 09·0	0 08·6	3·6	0·0	9·6	0·1	15·6	0·1
37	0 09·3	0 09·3	0 08·8	3·7	0·0	9·7	0·1	15·7	0·1
38	0 09·5	0 09·5	0 09·1	3·8	0·0	9·8	0·1	15·8	0·1
39	0 09·8	0 09·8	0 09·3	3·9	0·0	9·9	0·1	15·9	0·1
40	0 10·0	0 10·0	0 09·5	4·0	0·0	10·0	0·1	16·0	0·1
41	0 10·3	0 10·3	0 09·8	4·1	0·0	10·1	0·1	16·1	0·1
42	0 10·5	0 10·5	0 10·0	4·2	0·0	10·2	0·1	16·2	0·1
43	0 10·8	0 10·8	0 10·3	4·3	0·0	10·3	0·1	16·3	0·1
44	0 11·0	0 11·0	0 10·5	4·4	0·0	10·4	0·1	16·4	0·1
45	0 11·3	0 11·3	0 10·7	4·5	0·0	10·5	0·1	16·5	0·1
46	0 11·5	0 11·5	0 11·0	4·6	0·0	10·6	0·1	16·6	0·1
47	0 11·8	0 11·8	0 11·2	4·7	0·0	10·7	0·1	16·7	0·1
48	0 12·0	0 12·0	0 11·5	4·8	0·0	10·8	0·1	16·8	0·1
49	0 12·3	0 12·3	0 11·7	4·9	0·0	10·9	0·1	16·9	0·1
50	0 12·5	0 12·5	0 11·9	5·0	0·0	11·0	0·1	17·0	0·1
51	0 12·8	0 12·8	0 12·2	5·1	0·0	11·1	0·1	17·1	0·1
52	0 13·0	0 13·0	0 12·4	5·2	0·0	11·2	0·1	17·2	0·1
53	0 13·3	0 13·3	0 12·6	5·3	0·0	11·3	0·1	17·3	0·1
54	0 13·5	0 13·5	0 12·9	5·4	0·0	11·4	0·1	17·4	0·1
55	0 13·8	0 13·8	0 13·1	5·5	0·0	11·5	0·1	17·5	0·1
56	0 14·0	0 14·0	0 13·4	5·6	0·0	11·6	0·1	17·6	0·1
57	0 14·3	0 14·3	0 13·6	5·7	0·0	11·7	0·1	17·7	0·1
58	0 14·5	0 14·5	0 13·8	5·8	0·0	11·8	0·1	17·8	0·1
59	0 14·8	0 14·8	0 14·1	5·9	0·0	11·9	0·1	17·9	0·1
60	0 15·0	0 15·0	0 14·3	6·0	0·1	12·0	0·1	18·0	0·2

m 1	SUN PLANETS	ARIES	MOON	v or d	Corrⁿ	v or d	Corrⁿ	v or d	Corrⁿ
s	° ′	° ′	° ′	′	′	′	′	′	′
00	0 15·0	0 15·0	0 14·3	0·0	0·0	6·0	0·2	12·0	0·3
01	0 15·3	0 15·3	0 14·6	0·1	0·0	6·1	0·2	12·1	0·3
02	0 15·5	0 15·5	0 14·8	0·2	0·0	6·2	0·2	12·2	0·3
03	0 15·8	0 15·8	0 15·0	0·3	0·0	6·3	0·2	12·3	0·3
04	0 16·0	0 16·0	0 15·3	0·4	0·0	6·4	0·2	12·4	0·3
05	0 16·3	0 16·3	0 15·5	0·5	0·0	6·5	0·2	12·5	0·3
06	0 16·5	0 16·5	0 15·7	0·6	0·0	6·6	0·2	12·6	0·3
07	0 16·8	0 16·8	0 16·0	0·7	0·0	6·7	0·2	12·7	0·3
08	0 17·0	0 17·0	0 16·2	0·8	0·0	6·8	0·2	12·8	0·3
09	0 17·3	0 17·3	0 16·5	0·9	0·0	6·9	0·2	12·9	0·3
10	0 17·5	0 17·5	0 16·7	1·0	0·0	7·0	0·2	13·0	0·3
11	0 17·8	0 17·8	0 16·9	1·1	0·0	7·1	0·2	13·1	0·3
12	0 18·0	0 18·0	0 17·2	1·2	0·0	7·2	0·2	13·2	0·3
13	0 18·3	0 18·3	0 17·4	1·3	0·0	7·3	0·2	13·3	0·3
14	0 18·5	0 18·6	0 17·7	1·4	0·0	7·4	0·2	13·4	0·3
15	0 18·8	0 18·8	0 17·9	1·5	0·0	7·5	0·2	13·5	0·3
16	0 19·0	0 19·1	0 18·1	1·6	0·0	7·6	0·2	13·6	0·3
17	0 19·3	0 19·3	0 18·4	1·7	0·0	7·7	0·2	13·7	0·3
18	0 19·5	0 19·6	0 18·6	1·8	0·0	7·8	0·2	13·8	0·3
19	0 19·8	0 19·8	0 18·9	1·9	0·0	7·9	0·2	13·9	0·3
20	0 20·0	0 20·1	0 19·1	2·0	0·1	8·0	0·2	14·0	0·4
21	0 20·3	0 20·3	0 19·3	2·1	0·1	8·1	0·2	14·1	0·4
22	0 20·5	0 20·6	0 19·6	2·2	0·1	8·2	0·2	14·2	0·4
23	0 20·8	0 20·8	0 19·8	2·3	0·1	8·3	0·2	14·3	0·4
24	0 21·0	0 21·1	0 20·0	2·4	0·1	8·4	0·2	14·4	0·4
25	0 21·3	0 21·3	0 20·3	2·5	0·1	8·5	0·2	14·5	0·4
26	0 21·5	0 21·6	0 20·5	2·6	0·1	8·6	0·2	14·6	0·4
27	0 21·8	0 21·8	0 20·8	2·7	0·1	8·7	0·2	14·7	0·4
28	0 22·0	0 22·1	0 21·0	2·8	0·1	8·8	0·2	14·8	0·4
29	0 22·3	0 22·3	0 21·2	2·9	0·1	8·9	0·2	14·9	0·4
30	0 22·5	0 22·6	0 21·5	3·0	0·1	9·0	0·2	15·0	0·4
31	0 22·8	0 22·8	0 21·7	3·1	0·1	9·1	0·2	15·1	0·4
32	0 23·0	0 23·1	0 22·0	3·2	0·1	9·2	0·2	15·2	0·4
33	0 23·3	0 23·3	0 22·2	3·3	0·1	9·3	0·2	15·3	0·4
34	0 23·5	0 23·6	0 22·4	3·4	0·1	9·4	0·2	15·4	0·4
35	0 23·8	0 23·8	0 22·7	3·5	0·1	9·5	0·2	15·5	0·4
36	0 24·0	0 24·1	0 22·9	3·6	0·1	9·6	0·2	15·6	0·4
37	0 24·3	0 24·3	0 23·1	3·7	0·1	9·7	0·2	15·7	0·4
38	0 24·5	0 24·6	0 23·4	3·8	0·1	9·8	0·2	15·8	0·4
39	0 24·8	0 24·8	0 23·6	3·9	0·1	9·9	0·2	15·9	0·4
40	0 25·0	0 25·1	0 23·9	4·0	0·1	10·0	0·3	16·0	0·4
41	0 25·3	0 25·3	0 24·1	4·1	0·1	10·1	0·3	16·1	0·4
42	0 25·5	0 25·6	0 24·3	4·2	0·1	10·2	0·3	16·2	0·4
43	0 25·8	0 25·8	0 24·6	4·3	0·1	10·3	0·3	16·3	0·4
44	0 26·0	0 26·1	0 24·8	4·4	0·1	10·4	0·3	16·4	0·4
45	0 26·3	0 26·3	0 25·1	4·5	0·1	10·5	0·3	16·5	0·4
46	0 26·5	0 26·6	0 25·3	4·6	0·1	10·6	0·3	16·6	0·4
47	0 26·8	0 26·8	0 25·5	4·7	0·1	10·7	0·3	16·7	0·4
48	0 27·0	0 27·1	0 25·8	4·8	0·1	10·8	0·3	16·8	0·4
49	0 27·3	0 27·3	0 26·0	4·9	0·1	10·9	0·3	16·9	0·4
50	0 27·5	0 27·6	0 26·2	5·0	0·1	11·0	0·3	17·0	0·4
51	0 27·8	0 27·8	0 26·5	5·1	0·1	11·1	0·3	17·1	0·4
52	0 28·0	0 28·1	0 26·7	5·2	0·1	11·2	0·3	17·2	0·4
53	0 28·3	0 28·3	0 27·0	5·3	0·1	11·3	0·3	17·3	0·4
54	0 28·5	0 28·6	0 27·2	5·4	0·1	11·4	0·3	17·4	0·4
55	0 28·8	0 28·8	0 27·4	5·5	0·1	11·5	0·3	17·5	0·4
56	0 29·0	0 29·1	0 27·7	5·6	0·1	11·6	0·3	17·6	0·4
57	0 29·3	0 29·3	0 27·9	5·7	0·1	11·7	0·3	17·7	0·4
58	0 29·5	0 29·6	0 28·2	5·8	0·1	11·8	0·3	17·8	0·4
59	0 29·8	0 29·8	0 28·4	5·9	0·1	11·9	0·3	17·9	0·4
60	0 30·0	0 30·1	0 28·6	6·0	0·2	12·0	0·3	18·0	0·5

2m	SUN PLANETS	ARIES	MOON	v or d	Corrⁿ	v or d	Corrⁿ	v or d	Corrⁿ
s	° ′	° ′	° ′	′	′	′	′	′	′
00	0 30·0	0 30·1	0 28·6	0·0	0·0	6·0	0·3	12·0	0·5
01	0 30·3	0 30·3	0 28·9	0·1	0·0	6·1	0·3	12·1	0·5
02	0 30·5	0 30·6	0 29·1	0·2	0·0	6·2	0·3	12·2	0·5
03	0 30·8	0 30·8	0 29·3	0·3	0·0	6·3	0·3	12·3	0·5
04	0 31·0	0 31·1	0 29·6	0·4	0·0	6·4	0·3	12·4	0·5
05	0 31·3	0 31·3	0 29·8	0·5	0·0	6·5	0·3	12·5	0·5
06	0 31·5	0 31·6	0 30·1	0·6	0·0	6·6	0·3	12·6	0·5
07	0 31·8	0 31·8	0 30·3	0·7	0·0	6·7	0·3	12·7	0·5
08	0 32·0	0 32·1	0 30·5	0·8	0·0	6·8	0·3	12·8	0·5
09	0 32·3	0 32·3	0 30·8	0·9	0·0	6·9	0·3	12·9	0·5
10	0 32·5	0 32·6	0 31·0	1·0	0·0	7·0	0·3	13·0	0·5
11	0 32·8	0 32·8	0 31·3	1·1	0·0	7·1	0·3	13·1	0·5
12	0 33·0	0 33·1	0 31·5	1·2	0·1	7·2	0·3	13·2	0·6
13	0 33·3	0 33·3	0 31·7	1·3	0·1	7·3	0·3	13·3	0·6
14	0 33·5	0 33·6	0 32·0	1·4	0·1	7·4	0·3	13·4	0·6
15	0 33·8	0 33·8	0 32·2	1·5	0·1	7·5	0·3	13·5	0·6
16	0 34·0	0 34·1	0 32·5	1·6	0·1	7·6	0·3	13·6	0·6
17	0 34·3	0 34·3	0 32·7	1·7	0·1	7·7	0·3	13·7	0·6
18	0 34·5	0 34·6	0 32·9	1·8	0·1	7·8	0·3	13·8	0·6
19	0 34·8	0 34·8	0 33·2	1·9	0·1	7·9	0·3	13·9	0·6
20	0 35·0	0 35·1	0 33·4	2·0	0·1	8·0	0·3	14·0	0·6
21	0 35·3	0 35·3	0 33·6	2·1	0·1	8·1	0·3	14·1	0·6
22	0 35·5	0 35·6	0 33·9	2·2	0·1	8·2	0·3	14·2	0·6
23	0 35·8	0 35·8	0 34·1	2·3	0·1	8·3	0·3	14·3	0·6
24	0 36·0	0 36·1	0 34·4	2·4	0·1	8·4	0·4	14·4	0·6
25	0 36·3	0 36·3	0 34·6	2·5	0·1	8·5	0·4	14·5	0·6
26	0 36·5	0 36·6	0 34·8	2·6	0·1	8·6	0·4	14·6	0·6
27	0 36·8	0 36·9	0 35·1	2·7	0·1	8·7	0·4	14·7	0·6
28	0 37·0	0 37·1	0 35·3	2·8	0·1	8·8	0·4	14·8	0·6
29	0 37·3	0 37·4	0 35·6	2·9	0·1	8·9	0·4	14·9	0·6
30	0 37·5	0 37·6	0 35·8	3·0	0·1	9·0	0·4	15·0	0·6
31	0 37·8	0 37·9	0 36·0	3·1	0·1	9·1	0·4	15·1	0·6
32	0 38·0	0 38·1	0 36·3	3·2	0·1	9·2	0·4	15·2	0·6
33	0 38·3	0 38·4	0 36·5	3·3	0·1	9·3	0·4	15·3	0·6
34	0 38·5	0 38·6	0 36·7	3·4	0·1	9·4	0·4	15·4	0·6
35	0 38·8	0 38·9	0 37·0	3·5	0·1	9·5	0·4	15·5	0·6
36	0 39·0	0 39·1	0 37·2	3·6	0·2	9·6	0·4	15·6	0·7
37	0 39·3	0 39·4	0 37·5	3·7	0·2	9·7	0·4	15·7	0·7
38	0 39·5	0 39·6	0 37·7	3·8	0·2	9·8	0·4	15·8	0·7
39	0 39·8	0 39·9	0 37·9	3·9	0·2	9·9	0·4	15·9	0·7
40	0 40·0	0 40·1	0 38·2	4·0	0·2	10·0	0·4	16·0	0·7
41	0 40·3	0 40·4	0 38·4	4·1	0·2	10·1	0·4	16·1	0·7
42	0 40·5	0 40·6	0 38·7	4·2	0·2	10·2	0·4	16·2	0·7
43	0 40·8	0 40·9	0 38·9	4·3	0·2	10·3	0·4	16·3	0·7
44	0 41·0	0 41·1	0 39·1	4·4	0·2	10·4	0·4	16·4	0·7
45	0 41·3	0 41·4	0 39·4	4·5	0·2	10·5	0·4	16·5	0·7
46	0 41·5	0 41·6	0 39·6	4·6	0·2	10·6	0·4	16·6	0·7
47	0 41·8	0 41·9	0 39·8	4·7	0·2	10·7	0·4	16·7	0·7
48	0 42·0	0 42·1	0 40·1	4·8	0·2	10·8	0·5	16·8	0·7
49	0 42·3	0 42·4	0 40·3	4·9	0·2	10·9	0·5	16·9	0·7
50	0 42·5	0 42·6	0 40·6	5·0	0·2	11·0	0·5	17·0	0·7
51	0 42·8	0 42·9	0 40·8	5·1	0·2	11·1	0·5	17·1	0·7
52	0 43·0	0 43·1	0 41·0	5·2	0·2	11·2	0·5	17·2	0·7
53	0 43·3	0 43·4	0 41·3	5·3	0·2	11·3	0·5	17·3	0·7
54	0 43·5	0 43·6	0 41·5	5·4	0·2	11·4	0·5	17·4	0·7
55	0 43·8	0 43·9	0 41·8	5·5	0·2	11·5	0·5	17·5	0·7
56	0 44·0	0 44·1	0 42·0	5·6	0·2	11·6	0·5	17·6	0·7
57	0 44·3	0 44·4	0 42·2	5·7	0·2	11·7	0·5	17·7	0·7
58	0 44·5	0 44·6	0 42·5	5·8	0·2	11·8	0·5	17·8	0·7
59	0 44·8	0 44·9	0 42·7	5·9	0·2	11·9	0·5	17·9	0·7
60	0 45·0	0 45·1	0 43·0	6·0	0·3	12·0	0·5	18·0	0·8

3m	SUN PLANETS	ARIES	MOON	v or d	Corrⁿ	v or d	Corrⁿ	v or d	Corrⁿ
s	° ′	° ′	° ′	′	′	′	′	′	′
00	0 45·0	0 45·1	0 43·0	0·0	0·0	6·0	0·4	12·0	0·7
01	0 45·3	0 45·4	0 43·2	0·1	0·0	6·1	0·4	12·1	0·7
02	0 45·5	0 45·6	0 43·4	0·2	0·0	6·2	0·4	12·2	0·7
03	0 45·8	0 45·9	0 43·7	0·3	0·0	6·3	0·4	12·3	0·7
04	0 46·0	0 46·1	0 43·9	0·4	0·0	6·4	0·4	12·4	0·7
05	0 46·3	0 46·4	0 44·1	0·5	0·0	6·5	0·4	12·5	0·7
06	0 46·5	0 46·6	0 44·4	0·6	0·0	6·6	0·4	12·6	0·7
07	0 46·8	0 46·9	0 44·6	0·7	0·0	6·7	0·4	12·7	0·7
08	0 47·0	0 47·1	0 44·9	0·8	0·0	6·8	0·4	12·8	0·7
09	0 47·3	0 47·4	0 45·1	0·9	0·1	6·9	0·4	12·9	0·8
10	0 47·5	0 47·6	0 45·3	1·0	0·1	7·0	0·4	13·0	0·8
11	0 47·8	0 47·9	0 45·6	1·1	0·1	7·1	0·4	13·1	0·8
12	0 48·0	0 48·1	0 45·8	1·2	0·1	7·2	0·4	13·2	0·8
13	0 48·3	0 48·4	0 46·1	1·3	0·1	7·3	0·4	13·3	0·8
14	0 48·5	0 48·6	0 46·3	1·4	0·1	7·4	0·4	13·4	0·8
15	0 48·8	0 48·9	0 46·5	1·5	0·1	7·5	0·4	13·5	0·8
16	0 49·0	0 49·1	0 46·8	1·6	0·1	7·6	0·4	13·6	0·8
17	0 49·3	0 49·4	0 47·0	1·7	0·1	7·7	0·4	13·7	0·8
18	0 49·5	0 49·6	0 47·2	1·8	0·1	7·8	0·5	13·8	0·8
19	0 49·8	0 49·9	0 47·5	1·9	0·1	7·9	0·5	13·9	0·8
20	0 50·0	0 50·1	0 47·7	2·0	0·1	8·0	0·5	14·0	0·8
21	0 50·3	0 50·4	0 48·0	2·1	0·1	8·1	0·5	14·1	0·8
22	0 50·5	0 50·6	0 48·2	2·2	0·1	8·2	0·5	14·2	0·8
23	0 50·8	0 50·9	0 48·4	2·3	0·1	8·3	0·5	14·3	0·8
24	0 51·0	0 51·1	0 48·7	2·4	0·1	8·4	0·5	14·4	0·8
25	0 51·3	0 51·4	0 48·9	2·5	0·1	8·5	0·5	14·5	0·8
26	0 51·5	0 51·6	0 49·2	2·6	0·2	8·6	0·5	14·6	0·9
27	0 51·8	0 51·9	0 49·4	2·7	0·2	8·7	0·5	14·7	0·9
28	0 52·0	0 52·1	0 49·6	2·8	0·2	8·8	0·5	14·8	0·9
29	0 52·3	0 52·4	0 49·9	2·9	0·2	8·9	0·5	14·9	0·9
30	0 52·5	0 52·6	0 50·1	3·0	0·2	9·0	0·5	15·0	0·9
31	0 52·8	0 52·9	0 50·3	3·1	0·2	9·1	0·5	15·1	0·9
32	0 53·0	0 53·1	0 50·6	3·2	0·2	9·2	0·5	15·2	0·9
33	0 53·3	0 53·4	0 50·8	3·3	0·2	9·3	0·5	15·3	0·9
34	0 53·5	0 53·6	0 51·1	3·4	0·2	9·4	0·5	15·4	0·9
35	0 53·8	0 53·9	0 51·3	3·5	0·2	9·5	0·6	15·5	0·9
36	0 54·0	0 54·1	0 51·5	3·6	0·2	9·6	0·6	15·6	0·9
37	0 54·3	0 54·4	0 51·8	3·7	0·2	9·7	0·6	15·7	0·9
38	0 54·5	0 54·6	0 52·0	3·8	0·2	9·8	0·6	15·8	0·9
39	0 54·8	0 54·9	0 52·3	3·9	0·2	9·9	0·6	15·9	0·9
40	0 55·0	0 55·2	0 52·5	4·0	0·2	10·0	0·6	16·0	0·9
41	0 55·3	0 55·4	0 52·7	4·1	0·2	10·1	0·6	16·1	0·9
42	0 55·5	0 55·7	0 53·0	4·2	0·2	10·2	0·6	16·2	0·9
43	0 55·8	0 55·9	0 53·2	4·3	0·3	10·3	0·6	16·3	1·0
44	0 56·0	0 56·2	0 53·4	4·4	0·3	10·4	0·6	16·4	1·0
45	0 56·3	0 56·4	0 53·7	4·5	0·3	10·5	0·6	16·5	1·0
46	0 56·5	0 56·7	0 53·9	4·6	0·3	10·6	0·6	16·6	1·0
47	0 56·8	0 56·9	0 54·2	4·7	0·3	10·7	0·6	16·7	1·0
48	0 57·0	0 57·2	0 54·4	4·8	0·3	10·8	0·6	16·8	1·0
49	0 57·3	0 57·4	0 54·6	4·9	0·3	10·9	0·6	16·9	1·0
50	0 57·5	0 57·7	0 54·9	5·0	0·3	11·0	0·6	17·0	1·0
51	0 57·8	0 57·9	0 55·1	5·1	0·3	11·1	0·6	17·1	1·0
52	0 58·0	0 58·2	0 55·4	5·2	0·3	11·2	0·7	17·2	1·0
53	0 58·3	0 58·4	0 55·6	5·3	0·3	11·3	0·7	17·3	1·0
54	0 58·5	0 58·7	0 55·8	5·4	0·3	11·4	0·7	17·4	1·0
55	0 58·8	0 58·9	0 56·1	5·5	0·3	11·5	0·7	17·5	1·0
56	0 59·0	0 59·2	0 56·3	5·6	0·3	11·6	0·7	17·6	1·0
57	0 59·3	0 59·4	0 56·6	5·7	0·3	11·7	0·7	17·7	1·0
58	0 59·5	0 59·7	0 56·8	5·8	0·3	11·8	0·7	17·8	1·0
59	0 59·8	0 59·9	0 57·0	5·9	0·3	11·9	0·7	17·9	1·0
60	1 00·0	1 00·2	0 57·3	6·0	0·4	12·0	0·7	18·0	1·1

m 4 s	SUN PLANETS ° ′	ARIES ° ′	MOON ° ′	v or d ′	Corrⁿ ′	v or d ′	Corrⁿ ′	v or d ′	Corrⁿ ′
00	1 00·0	1 00·2	0 57·3	0·0	0·0	6·0	0·5	12·0	0·9
01	1 00·3	1 00·4	0 57·5	0·1	0·0	6·1	0·5	12·1	0·9
02	1 00·5	1 00·7	0 57·7	0·2	0·0	6·2	0·5	12·2	0·9
03	1 00·8	1 00·9	0 58·0	0·3	0·0	6·3	0·5	12·3	0·9
04	1 01·0	1 01·2	0 58·2	0·4	0·0	6·4	0·5	12·4	0·9
05	1 01·3	1 01·4	0 58·5	0·5	0·0	6·5	0·5	12·5	0·9
06	1 01·5	1 01·7	0 58·7	0·6	0·0	6·6	0·5	12·6	0·9
07	1 01·8	1 01·9	0 58·9	0·7	0·1	6·7	0·5	12·7	1·0
08	1 02·0	1 02·2	0 59·2	0·8	0·1	6·8	0·5	12·8	1·0
09	1 02·3	1 02·4	0 59·4	0·9	0·1	6·9	0·5	12·9	1·0
10	1 02·5	1 02·7	0 59·7	1·0	0·1	7·0	0·5	13·0	1·0
11	1 02·8	1 02·9	0 59·9	1·1	0·1	7·1	0·5	13·1	1·0
12	1 03·0	1 03·2	1 00·1	1·2	0·1	7·2	0·5	13·2	1·0
13	1 03·3	1 03·4	1 00·4	1·3	0·1	7·3	0·5	13·3	1·0
14	1 03·5	1 03·7	1 00·6	1·4	0·1	7·4	0·6	13·4	1·0
15	1 03·8	1 03·9	1 00·8	1·5	0·1	7·5	0·6	13·5	1·0
16	1 04·0	1 04·2	1 01·1	1·6	0·1	7·6	0·6	13·6	1·0
17	1 04·3	1 04·4	1 01·3	1·7	0·1	7·7	0·6	13·7	1·0
18	1 04·5	1 04·7	1 01·6	1·8	0·1	7·8	0·6	13·8	1·0
19	1 04·8	1 04·9	1 01·8	1·9	0·1	7·9	0·6	13·9	1·0
20	1 05·0	1 05·2	1 02·0	2·0	0·2	8·0	0·6	14·0	1·1
21	1 05·3	1 05·4	1 02·3	2·1	0·2	8·1	0·6	14·1	1·1
22	1 05·5	1 05·7	1 02·5	2·2	0·2	8·2	0·6	14·2	1·1
23	1 05·8	1 05·9	1 02·8	2·3	0·2	8·3	0·6	14·3	1·1
24	1 06·0	1 06·2	1 03·0	2·4	0·2	8·4	0·6	14·4	1·1
25	1 06·3	1 06·4	1 03·2	2·5	0·2	8·5	0·6	14·5	1·1
26	1 06·5	1 06·7	1 03·5	2·6	0·2	8·6	0·6	14·6	1·1
27	1 06·8	1 06·9	1 03·7	2·7	0·2	8·7	0·7	14·7	1·1
28	1 07·0	1 07·2	1 03·9	2·8	0·2	8·8	0·7	14·8	1·1
29	1 07·3	1 07·4	1 04·2	2·9	0·2	8·9	0·7	14·9	1·1
30	1 07·5	1 07·7	1 04·4	3·0	0·2	9·0	0·7	15·0	1·1
31	1 07·8	1 07·9	1 04·7	3·1	0·2	9·1	0·7	15·1	1·1
32	1 08·0	1 08·2	1 04·9	3·2	0·2	9·2	0·7	15·2	1·1
33	1 08·3	1 08·4	1 05·1	3·3	0·2	9·3	0·7	15·3	1·1
34	1 08·5	1 08·7	1 05·4	3·4	0·3	9·4	0·7	15·4	1·2
35	1 08·8	1 08·9	1 05·6	3·5	0·3	9·5	0·7	15·5	1·2
36	1 09·0	1 09·2	1 05·9	3·6	0·3	9·6	0·7	15·6	1·2
37	1 09·3	1 09·4	1 06·1	3·7	0·3	9·7	0·7	15·7	1·2
38	1 09·5	1 09·7	1 06·3	3·8	0·3	9·8	0·7	15·8	1·2
39	1 09·8	1 09·9	1 06·6	3·9	0·3	9·9	0·7	15·9	1·2
40	1 10·0	1 10·2	1 06·8	4·0	0·3	10·0	0·8	16·0	1·2
41	1 10·3	1 10·4	1 07·0	4·1	0·3	10·1	0·8	16·1	1·2
42	1 10·5	1 10·7	1 07·3	4·2	0·3	10·2	0·8	16·2	1·2
43	1 10·8	1 10·9	1 07·5	4·3	0·3	10·3	0·8	16·3	1·2
44	1 11·0	1 11·2	1 07·8	4·4	0·3	10·4	0·8	16·4	1·2
45	1 11·3	1 11·4	1 08·0	4·5	0·3	10·5	0·8	16·5	1·2
46	1 11·5	1 11·7	1 08·2	4·6	0·3	10·6	0·8	16·6	1·2
47	1 11·8	1 11·9	1 08·5	4·7	0·4	10·7	0·8	16·7	1·3
48	1 12·0	1 12·2	1 08·7	4·8	0·4	10·8	0·8	16·8	1·3
49	1 12·3	1 12·4	1 09·0	4·9	0·4	10·9	0·8	16·9	1·3
50	1 12·5	1 12·7	1 09·2	5·0	0·4	11·0	0·8	17·0	1·3
51	1 12·8	1 12·9	1 09·4	5·1	0·4	11·1	0·8	17·1	1·3
52	1 13·0	1 13·2	1 09·7	5·2	0·4	11·2	0·8	17·2	1·3
53	1 13·3	1 13·5	1 09·9	5·3	0·4	11·3	0·8	17·3	1·3
54	1 13·5	1 13·7	1 10·2	5·4	0·4	11·4	0·9	17·4	1·3
55	1 13·8	1 14·0	1 10·4	5·5	0·4	11·5	0·9	17·5	1·3
56	1 14·0	1 14·2	1 10·6	5·6	0·4	11·6	0·9	17·6	1·3
57	1 14·3	1 14·5	1 10·9	5·7	0·4	11·7	0·9	17·7	1·3
58	1 14·5	1 14·7	1 11·1	5·8	0·4	11·8	0·9	17·8	1·3
59	1 14·8	1 15·0	1 11·3	5·9	0·4	11·9	0·9	17·9	1·3
60	1 15·0	1 15·2	1 11·6	6·0	0·5	12·0	0·9	18·0	1·4

m 5 s	SUN PLANETS ° ′	ARIES ° ′	MOON ° ′	v or d ′	Corrⁿ ′	v or d ′	Corrⁿ ′	v or d ′	Corrⁿ ′
00	1 15·0	1 15·2	1 11·6	0·0	0·0	6·0	0·6	12·0	1·1
01	1 15·3	1 15·5	1 11·8	0·1	0·0	6·1	0·6	12·1	1·1
02	1 15·5	1 15·7	1 12·1	0·2	0·0	6·2	0·6	12·2	1·1
03	1 15·8	1 16·0	1 12·3	0·3	0·0	6·3	0·6	12·3	1·1
04	1 16·0	1 16·2	1 12·5	0·4	0·0	6·4	0·6	12·4	1·1
05	1 16·3	1 16·5	1 12·8	0·5	0·0	6·5	0·6	12·5	1·1
06	1 16·5	1 16·7	1 13·0	0·6	0·1	6·6	0·6	12·6	1·2
07	1 16·8	1 17·0	1 13·3	0·7	0·1	6·7	0·6	12·7	1·2
08	1 17·0	1 17·2	1 13·5	0·8	0·1	6·8	0·6	12·8	1·2
09	1 17·3	1 17·5	1 13·7	0·9	0·1	6·9	0·6	12·9	1·2
10	1 17·5	1 17·7	1 14·0	1·0	0·1	7·0	0·6	13·0	1·2
11	1 17·8	1 18·0	1 14·2	1·1	0·1	7·1	0·7	13·1	1·2
12	1 18·0	1 18·2	1 14·4	1·2	0·1	7·2	0·7	13·2	1·2
13	1 18·3	1 18·5	1 14·7	1·3	0·1	7·3	0·7	13·3	1·2
14	1 18·5	1 18·7	1 14·9	1·4	0·1	7·4	0·7	13·4	1·2
15	1 18·8	1 19·0	1 15·2	1·5	0·1	7·5	0·7	13·5	1·2
16	1 19·0	1 19·2	1 15·4	1·6	0·1	7·6	0·7	13·6	1·2
17	1 19·3	1 19·5	1 15·6	1·7	0·2	7·7	0·7	13·7	1·3
18	1 19·5	1 19·7	1 15·9	1·8	0·2	7·8	0·7	13·8	1·3
19	1 19·8	1 20·0	1 16·1	1·9	0·2	7·9	0·7	13·9	1·3
20	1 20·0	1 20·2	1 16·4	2·0	0·2	8·0	0·7	14·0	1·3
21	1 20·3	1 20·5	1 16·6	2·1	0·2	8·1	0·7	14·1	1·3
22	1 20·5	1 20·7	1 16·8	2·2	0·2	8·2	0·8	14·2	1·3
23	1 20·8	1 21·0	1 17·1	2·3	0·2	8·3	0·8	14·3	1·3
24	1 21·0	1 21·2	1 17·3	2·4	0·2	8·4	0·8	14·4	1·3
25	1 21·3	1 21·5	1 17·5	2·5	0·2	8·5	0·8	14·5	1·3
26	1 21·5	1 21·7	1 17·8	2·6	0·2	8·6	0·8	14·6	1·3
27	1 21·8	1 22·0	1 18·0	2·7	0·2	8·7	0·8	14·7	1·3
28	1 22·0	1 22·2	1 18·3	2·8	0·3	8·8	0·8	14·8	1·4
29	1 22·3	1 22·5	1 18·5	2·9	0·3	8·9	0·8	14·9	1·4
30	1 22·5	1 22·7	1 18·7	3·0	0·3	9·0	0·8	15·0	1·4
31	1 22·8	1 23·0	1 19·0	3·1	0·3	9·1	0·8	15·1	1·4
32	1 23·0	1 23·2	1 19·2	3·2	0·3	9·2	0·8	15·2	1·4
33	1 23·3	1 23·5	1 19·5	3·3	0·3	9·3	0·9	15·3	1·4
34	1 23·5	1 23·7	1 19·7	3·4	0·3	9·4	0·9	15·4	1·4
35	1 23·8	1 24·0	1 19·9	3·5	0·3	9·5	0·9	15·5	1·4
36	1 24·0	1 24·2	1 20·2	3·6	0·3	9·6	0·9	15·6	1·4
37	1 24·3	1 24·5	1 20·4	3·7	0·3	9·7	0·9	15·7	1·4
38	1 24·5	1 24·7	1 20·7	3·8	0·3	9·8	0·9	15·8	1·4
39	1 24·8	1 25·0	1 20·9	3·9	0·4	9·9	0·9	15·9	1·5
40	1 25·0	1 25·2	1 21·1	4·0	0·4	10·0	0·9	16·0	1·5
41	1 25·3	1 25·5	1 21·4	4·1	0·4	10·1	0·9	16·1	1·5
42	1 25·5	1 25·7	1 21·6	4·2	0·4	10·2	0·9	16·2	1·5
43	1 25·8	1 26·0	1 21·8	4·3	0·4	10·3	0·9	16·3	1·5
44	1 26·0	1 26·2	1 22·1	4·4	0·4	10·4	1·0	16·4	1·5
45	1 26·3	1 26·5	1 22·3	4·5	0·4	10·5	1·0	16·5	1·5
46	1 26·5	1 26·7	1 22·6	4·6	0·4	10·6	1·0	16·6	1·5
47	1 26·8	1 27·0	1 22·8	4·7	0·4	10·7	1·0	16·7	1·5
48	1 27·0	1 27·2	1 23·0	4·8	0·4	10·8	1·0	16·8	1·5
49	1 27·3	1 27·5	1 23·3	4·9	0·4	10·9	1·0	16·9	1·5
50	1 27·5	1 27·7	1 23·5	5·0	0·5	11·0	1·0	17·0	1·6
51	1 27·8	1 28·0	1 23·8	5·1	0·5	11·1	1·0	17·1	1·6
52	1 28·0	1 28·2	1 24·0	5·2	0·5	11·2	1·0	17·2	1·6
53	1 28·3	1 28·5	1 24·2	5·3	0·5	11·3	1·0	17·3	1·6
54	1 28·5	1 28·7	1 24·5	5·4	0·5	11·4	1·0	17·4	1·6
55	1 28·8	1 29·0	1 24·7	5·5	0·5	11·5	1·1	17·5	1·6
56	1 29·0	1 29·2	1 24·9	5·6	0·5	11·6	1·1	17·6	1·6
57	1 29·3	1 29·5	1 25·2	5·7	0·5	11·7	1·1	17·7	1·6
58	1 29·5	1 29·7	1 25·4	5·8	0·5	11·8	1·1	17·8	1·6
59	1 29·8	1 30·0	1 25·7	5·9	0·5	11·9	1·1	17·9	1·6
60	1 30·0	1 30·2	1 25·9	6·0	0·6	12·0	1·1	18·0	1·7

6^m	SUN PLANETS	ARIES	MOON	v or d	Corr^n	v or d	Corr^n	v or d	Corr^n
s	° ′	° ′	° ′	′	′	′	′	′	′
00	1 30·0	1 30·2	1 25·9	0·0	0·0	6·0	0·7	12·0	1·3
01	1 30·3	1 30·5	1 26·1	0·1	0·0	6·1	0·7	12·1	1·3
02	1 30·5	1 30·7	1 26·4	0·2	0·0	6·2	0·7	12·2	1·3
03	1 30·8	1 31·0	1 26·6	0·3	0·0	6·3	0·7	12·3	1·3
04	1 31·0	1 31·2	1 26·9	0·4	0·0	6·4	0·7	12·4	1·3
05	1 31·3	1 31·5	1 27·1	0·5	0·1	6·5	0·7	12·5	1·4
06	1 31·5	1 31·8	1 27·3	0·6	0·1	6·6	0·7	12·6	1·4
07	1 31·8	1 32·0	1 27·6	0·7	0·1	6·7	0·7	12·7	1·4
08	1 32·0	1 32·3	1 27·8	0·8	0·1	6·8	0·7	12·8	1·4
09	1 32·3	1 32·5	1 28·0	0·9	0·1	6·9	0·7	12·9	1·4
10	1 32·5	1 32·8	1 28·3	1·0	0·1	7·0	0·8	13·0	1·4
11	1 32·8	1 33·0	1 28·5	1·1	0·1	7·1	0·8	13·1	1·4
12	1 33·0	1 33·3	1 28·8	1·2	0·1	7·2	0·8	13·2	1·4
13	1 33·3	1 33·5	1 29·0	1·3	0·1	7·3	0·8	13·3	1·4
14	1 33·5	1 33·8	1 29·2	1·4	0·2	7·4	0·8	13·4	1·5
15	1 33·8	1 34·0	1 29·5	1·5	0·2	7·5	0·8	13·5	1·5
16	1 34·0	1 34·3	1 29·7	1·6	0·2	7·6	0·8	13·6	1·5
17	1 34·3	1 34·5	1 30·0	1·7	0·2	7·7	0·8	13·7	1·5
18	1 34·5	1 34·8	1 30·2	1·8	0·2	7·8	0·8	13·8	1·5
19	1 34·8	1 35·0	1 30·4	1·9	0·2	7·9	0·9	13·9	1·5
20	1 35·0	1 35·3	1 30·7	2·0	0·2	8·0	0·9	14·0	1·5
21	1 35·3	1 35·5	1 30·9	2·1	0·2	8·1	0·9	14·1	1·5
22	1 35·5	1 35·8	1 31·1	2·2	0·2	8·2	0·9	14·2	1·5
23	1 35·8	1 36·0	1 31·4	2·3	0·2	8·3	0·9	14·3	1·5
24	1 36·0	1 36·3	1 31·6	2·4	0·3	8·4	0·9	14·4	1·6
25	1 36·3	1 36·5	1 31·9	2·5	0·3	8·5	0·9	14·5	1·6
26	1 36·5	1 36·8	1 32·1	2·6	0·3	8·6	0·9	14·6	1·6
27	1 36·8	1 37·0	1 32·3	2·7	0·3	8·7	0·9	14·7	1·6
28	1 37·0	1 37·3	1 32·6	2·8	0·3	8·8	1·0	14·8	1·6
29	1 37·3	1 37·5	1 32·8	2·9	0·3	8·9	1·0	14·9	1·6
30	1 37·5	1 37·8	1 33·1	3·0	0·3	9·0	1·0	15·0	1·6
31	1 37·8	1 38·0	1 33·3	3·1	0·3	9·1	1·0	15·1	1·6
32	1 38·0	1 38·3	1 33·5	3·2	0·3	9·2	1·0	15·2	1·6
33	1 38·3	1 38·5	1 33·8	3·3	0·4	9·3	1·0	15·3	1·7
34	1 38·5	1 38·8	1 34·0	3·4	0·4	9·4	1·0	15·4	1·7
35	1 38·8	1 39·0	1 34·3	3·5	0·4	9·5	1·0	15·5	1·7
36	1 39·0	1 39·3	1 34·5	3·6	0·4	9·6	1·0	15·6	1·7
37	1 39·3	1 39·5	1 34·7	3·7	0·4	9·7	1·1	15·7	1·7
38	1 39·5	1 39·8	1 35·0	3·8	0·4	9·8	1·1	15·8	1·7
39	1 39·8	1 40·0	1 35·2	3·9	0·4	9·9	1·1	15·9	1·7
40	1 40·0	1 40·3	1 35·4	4·0	0·4	10·0	1·1	16·0	1·7
41	1 40·3	1 40·5	1 35·7	4·1	0·4	10·1	1·1	16·1	1·7
42	1 40·5	1 40·8	1 35·9	4·2	0·5	10·2	1·1	16·2	1·8
43	1 40·8	1 41·0	1 36·2	4·3	0·5	10·3	1·1	16·3	1·8
44	1 41·0	1 41·3	1 36·4	4·4	0·5	10·4	1·1	16·4	1·8
45	1 41·3	1 41·5	1 36·6	4·5	0·5	10·5	1·1	16·5	1·8
46	1 41·5	1 41·8	1 36·9	4·6	0·5	10·6	1·1	16·6	1·8
47	1 41·8	1 42·0	1 37·1	4·7	0·5	10·7	1·2	16·7	1·8
48	1 42·0	1 42·3	1 37·4	4·8	0·5	10·8	1·2	16·8	1·8
49	1 42·3	1 42·5	1 37·6	4·9	0·5	10·9	1·2	16·9	1·8
50	1 42·5	1 42·8	1 37·8	5·0	0·5	11·0	1·2	17·0	1·8
51	1 42·8	1 43·0	1 38·1	5·1	0·6	11·1	1·2	17·1	1·9
52	1 43·0	1 43·3	1 38·3	5·2	0·6	11·2	1·2	17·2	1·9
53	1 43·3	1 43·5	1 38·5	5·3	0·6	11·3	1·2	17·3	1·9
54	1 43·5	1 43·8	1 38·8	5·4	0·6	11·4	1·2	17·4	1·9
55	1 43·8	1 44·0	1 39·0	5·5	0·6	11·5	1·2	17·5	1·9
56	1 44·0	1 44·3	1 39·3	5·6	0·6	11·6	1·3	17·6	1·9
57	1 44·3	1 44·5	1 39·5	5·7	0·6	11·7	1·3	17·7	1·9
58	1 44·5	1 44·8	1 39·7	5·8	0·6	11·8	1·3	17·8	1·9
59	1 44·8	1 45·0	1 40·0	5·9	0·6	11·9	1·3	17·9	1·9
60	1 45·0	1 45·3	1 40·2	6·0	0·7	12·0	1·3	18·0	2·0

7^m	SUN PLANETS	ARIES	MOON	v or d	Corr^n	v or d	Corr^n	v or d	Corr^n
s	° ′	° ′	° ′	′	′	′	′	′	′
00	1 45·0	1 45·3	1 40·2	0·0	0·0	6·0	0·8	12·0	1·5
01	1 45·3	1 45·5	1 40·5	0·1	0·0	6·1	0·8	12·1	1·5
02	1 45·5	1 45·8	1 40·7	0·2	0·0	6·2	0·8	12·2	1·5
03	1 45·8	1 46·0	1 40·9	0·3	0·0	6·3	0·8	12·3	1·5
04	1 46·0	1 46·3	1 41·2	0·4	0·1	6·4	0·8	12·4	1·6
05	1 46·3	1 46·5	1 41·4	0·5	0·1	6·5	0·8	12·5	1·6
06	1 46·5	1 46·8	1 41·6	0·6	0·1	6·6	0·8	12·6	1·6
07	1 46·8	1 47·0	1 41·9	0·7	0·1	6·7	0·8	12·7	1·6
08	1 47·0	1 47·3	1 42·1	0·8	0·1	6·8	0·9	12·8	1·6
09	1 47·3	1 47·5	1 42·4	0·9	0·1	6·9	0·9	12·9	1·6
10	1 47·5	1 47·8	1 42·6	1·0	0·1	7·0	0·9	13·0	1·6
11	1 47·8	1 48·0	1 42·8	1·1	0·1	7·1	0·9	13·1	1·6
12	1 48·0	1 48·3	1 43·1	1·2	0·2	7·2	0·9	13·2	1·7
13	1 48·3	1 48·5	1 43·3	1·3	0·2	7·3	0·9	13·3	1·7
14	1 48·5	1 48·8	1 43·6	1·4	0·2	7·4	0·9	13·4	1·7
15	1 48·8	1 49·0	1 43·8	1·5	0·2	7·5	0·9	13·5	1·7
16	1 49·0	1 49·3	1 44·0	1·6	0·2	7·6	1·0	13·6	1·7
17	1 49·3	1 49·5	1 44·3	1·7	0·2	7·7	1·0	13·7	1·7
18	1 49·5	1 49·8	1 44·5	1·8	0·2	7·8	1·0	13·8	1·7
19	1 49·8	1 50·1	1 44·8	1·9	0·2	7·9	1·0	13·9	1·7
20	1 50·0	1 50·3	1 45·0	2·0	0·3	8·0	1·0	14·0	1·8
21	1 50·3	1 50·6	1 45·2	2·1	0·3	8·1	1·0	14·1	1·8
22	1 50·5	1 50·8	1 45·5	2·2	0·3	8·2	1·0	14·2	1·8
23	1 50·8	1 51·1	1 45·7	2·3	0·3	8·3	1·0	14·3	1·8
24	1 51·0	1 51·3	1 45·9	2·4	0·3	8·4	1·1	14·4	1·8
25	1 51·3	1 51·6	1 46·2	2·5	0·3	8·5	1·1	14·5	1·8
26	1 51·5	1 51·8	1 46·4	2·6	0·3	8·6	1·1	14·6	1·8
27	1 51·8	1 52·1	1 46·7	2·7	0·3	8·7	1·1	14·7	1·8
28	1 52·0	1 52·3	1 46·9	2·8	0·4	8·8	1·1	14·8	1·9
29	1 52·3	1 52·6	1 47·1	2·9	0·4	8·9	1·1	14·9	1·9
30	1 52·5	1 52·8	1 47·4	3·0	0·4	9·0	1·1	15·0	1·9
31	1 52·8	1 53·1	1 47·6	3·1	0·4	9·1	1·1	15·1	1·9
32	1 53·0	1 53·3	1 47·9	3·2	0·4	9·2	1·2	15·2	1·9
33	1 53·3	1 53·6	1 48·1	3·3	0·4	9·3	1·2	15·3	1·9
34	1 53·5	1 53·8	1 48·3	3·4	0·4	9·4	1·2	15·4	1·9
35	1 53·8	1 54·1	1 48·6	3·5	0·4	9·5	1·2	15·5	1·9
36	1 54·0	1 54·3	1 48·8	3·6	0·5	9·6	1·2	15·6	2·0
37	1 54·3	1 54·6	1 49·0	3·7	0·5	9·7	1·2	15·7	2·0
38	1 54·5	1 54·8	1 49·3	3·8	0·5	9·8	1·2	15·8	2·0
39	1 54·8	1 55·1	1 49·5	3·9	0·5	9·9	1·2	15·9	2·0
40	1 55·0	1 55·3	1 49·8	4·0	0·5	10·0	1·3	16·0	2·0
41	1 55·3	1 55·6	1 50·0	4·1	0·5	10·1	1·3	16·1	2·0
42	1 55·5	1 55·8	1 50·2	4·2	0·5	10·2	1·3	16·2	2·0
43	1 55·8	1 56·1	1 50·5	4·3	0·5	10·3	1·3	16·3	2·0
44	1 56·0	1 56·3	1 50·7	4·4	0·6	10·4	1·3	16·4	2·1
45	1 56·3	1 56·6	1 51·0	4·5	0·6	10·5	1·3	16·5	2·1
46	1 56·5	1 56·8	1 51·2	4·6	0·6	10·6	1·3	16·6	2·1
47	1 56·8	1 57·1	1 51·4	4·7	0·6	10·7	1·3	16·7	2·1
48	1 57·0	1 57·3	1 51·7	4·8	0·6	10·8	1·4	16·8	2·1
49	1 57·3	1 57·6	1 51·9	4·9	0·6	10·9	1·4	16·9	2·1
50	1 57·5	1 57·8	1 52·1	5·0	0·6	11·0	1·4	17·0	2·1
51	1 57·8	1 58·1	1 52·4	5·1	0·6	11·1	1·4	17·1	2·1
52	1 58·0	1 58·3	1 52·6	5·2	0·7	11·2	1·4	17·2	2·2
53	1 58·3	1 58·6	1 52·9	5·3	0·7	11·3	1·4	17·3	2·2
54	1 58·5	1 58·8	1 53·1	5·4	0·7	11·4	1·4	17·4	2·2
55	1 58·8	1 59·1	1 53·3	5·5	0·7	11·5	1·4	17·5	2·2
56	1 59·0	1 59·3	1 53·6	5·6	0·7	11·6	1·5	17·6	2·2
57	1 59·3	1 59·6	1 53·8	5·7	0·7	11·7	1·5	17·7	2·2
58	1 59·5	1 59·8	1 54·1	5·8	0·7	11·8	1·5	17·8	2·2
59	1 59·8	2 00·1	1 54·3	5·9	0·7	11·9	1·5	17·9	2·2
60	2 00·0	2 00·3	1 54·5	6·0	0·8	12·0	1·5	18·0	2·3

m 8 (s)	SUN PLANETS (° ′)	ARIES (° ′)	MOON (° ′)	v or d (′)	Corrⁿ (′)	v or d (′)	Corrⁿ (′)	v or d (′)	Corrⁿ (′)
00	2 00·0	2 00·3	1 54·5	0·0	0·0	6·0	0·9	12·0	1·7
01	2 00·3	2 00·6	1 54·8	0·1	0·0	6·1	0·9	12·1	1·7
02	2 00·5	2 00·8	1 55·0	0·2	0·0	6·2	0·9	12·2	1·7
03	2 00·8	2 01·1	1 55·2	0·3	0·0	6·3	0·9	12·3	1·7
04	2 01·0	2 01·3	1 55·5	0·4	0·1	6·4	0·9	12·4	1·8
05	2 01·3	2 01·6	1 55·7	0·5	0·1	6·5	0·9	12·5	1·8
06	2 01·5	2 01·8	1 56·0	0·6	0·1	6·6	0·9	12·6	1·8
07	2 01·8	2 02·1	1 56·2	0·7	0·1	6·7	0·9	12·7	1·8
08	2 02·0	2 02·3	1 56·4	0·8	0·1	6·8	1·0	12·8	1·8
09	2 02·3	2 02·6	1 56·7	0·9	0·1	6·9	1·0	12·9	1·8
10	2 02·5	2 02·8	1 56·9	1·0	0·1	7·0	1·0	13·0	1·8
11	2 02·8	2 03·1	1 57·2	1·1	0·2	7·1	1·0	13·1	1·9
12	2 03·0	2 03·3	1 57·4	1·2	0·2	7·2	1·0	13·2	1·9
13	2 03·3	2 03·6	1 57·6	1·3	0·2	7·3	1·0	13·3	1·9
14	2 03·5	2 03·8	1 57·9	1·4	0·2	7·4	1·0	13·4	1·9
15	2 03·8	2 04·1	1 58·1	1·5	0·2	7·5	1·1	13·5	1·9
16	2 04·0	2 04·3	1 58·4	1·6	0·2	7·6	1·1	13·6	1·9
17	2 04·3	2 04·6	1 58·6	1·7	0·2	7·7	1·1	13·7	1·9
18	2 04·5	2 04·8	1 58·8	1·8	0·3	7·8	1·1	13·8	2·0
19	2 04·8	2 05·1	1 59·1	1·9	0·3	7·9	1·1	13·9	2·0
20	2 05·0	2 05·3	1 59·3	2·0	0·3	8·0	1·1	14·0	2·0
21	2 05·3	2 05·6	1 59·5	2·1	0·3	8·1	1·1	14·1	2·0
22	2 05·5	2 05·8	1 59·8	2·2	0·3	8·2	1·2	14·2	2·0
23	2 05·8	2 06·1	2 00·0	2·3	0·3	8·3	1·2	14·3	2·0
24	2 06·0	2 06·3	2 00·3	2·4	0·3	8·4	1·2	14·4	2·0
25	2 06·3	2 06·6	2 00·5	2·5	0·4	8·5	1·2	14·5	2·1
26	2 06·5	2 06·8	2 00·7	2·6	0·4	8·6	1·2	14·6	2·1
27	2 06·8	2 07·1	2 01·0	2·7	0·4	8·7	1·2	14·7	2·1
28	2 07·0	2 07·3	2 01·2	2·8	0·4	8·8	1·2	14·8	2·1
29	2 07·3	2 07·6	2 01·5	2·9	0·4	8·9	1·3	14·9	2·1
30	2 07·5	2 07·8	2 01·7	3·0	0·4	9·0	1·3	15·0	2·1
31	2 07·8	2 08·1	2 01·9	3·1	0·4	9·1	1·3	15·1	2·1
32	2 08·0	2 08·4	2 02·2	3·2	0·5	9·2	1·3	15·2	2·2
33	2 08·3	2 08·6	2 02·4	3·3	0·5	9·3	1·3	15·3	2·2
34	2 08·5	2 08·9	2 02·6	3·4	0·5	9·4	1·3	15·4	2·2
35	2 08·8	2 09·1	2 02·9	3·5	0·5	9·5	1·3	15·5	2·2
36	2 09·0	2 09·4	2 03·1	3·6	0·5	9·6	1·4	15·6	2·2
37	2 09·3	2 09·6	2 03·4	3·7	0·5	9·7	1·4	15·7	2·2
38	2 09·5	2 09·9	2 03·6	3·8	0·5	9·8	1·4	15·8	2·2
39	2 09·8	2 10·1	2 03·8	3·9	0·6	9·9	1·4	15·9	2·3
40	2 10·0	2 10·4	2 04·1	4·0	0·6	10·0	1·4	16·0	2·3
41	2 10·3	2 10·6	2 04·3	4·1	0·6	10·1	1·4	16·1	2·3
42	2 10·5	2 10·9	2 04·6	4·2	0·6	10·2	1·4	16·2	2·3
43	2 10·8	2 11·1	2 04·8	4·3	0·6	10·3	1·5	16·3	2·3
44	2 11·0	2 11·4	2 05·0	4·4	0·6	10·4	1·5	16·4	2·3
45	2 11·3	2 11·6	2 05·3	4·5	0·6	10·5	1·5	16·5	2·3
46	2 11·5	2 11·9	2 05·5	4·6	0·7	10·6	1·5	16·6	2·4
47	2 11·8	2 12·1	2 05·7	4·7	0·7	10·7	1·5	16·7	2·4
48	2 12·0	2 12·4	2 06·0	4·8	0·7	10·8	1·5	16·8	2·4
49	2 12·3	2 12·6	2 06·2	4·9	0·7	10·9	1·5	16·9	2·4
50	2 12·5	2 12·9	2 06·5	5·0	0·7	11·0	1·6	17·0	2·4
51	2 12·8	2 13·1	2 06·7	5·1	0·7	11·1	1·6	17·1	2·4
52	2 13·0	2 13·4	2 06·9	5·2	0·7	11·2	1·6	17·2	2·4
53	2 13·3	2 13·6	2 07·2	5·3	0·8	11·3	1·6	17·3	2·5
54	2 13·5	2 13·9	2 07·4	5·4	0·8	11·4	1·6	17·4	2·5
55	2 13·8	2 14·1	2 07·7	5·5	0·8	11·5	1·6	17·5	2·5
56	2 14·0	2 14·4	2 07·9	5·6	0·8	11·6	1·6	17·6	2·5
57	2 14·3	2 14·6	2 08·1	5·7	0·8	11·7	1·7	17·7	2·5
58	2 14·5	2 14·9	2 08·4	5·8	0·8	11·8	1·7	17·8	2·5
59	2 14·8	2 15·1	2 08·6	5·9	0·8	11·9	1·7	17·9	2·5
60	2 15·0	2 15·4	2 08·9	6·0	0·9	12·0	1·7	18·0	2·6

m 9 (s)	SUN PLANETS (° ′)	ARIES (° ′)	MOON (° ′)	v or d (′)	Corrⁿ (′)	v or d (′)	Corrⁿ (′)	v or d (′)	Corrⁿ (′)
00	2 15·0	2 15·4	2 08·9	0·0	0·0	6·0	1·0	12·0	1·9
01	2 15·3	2 15·6	2 09·1	0·1	0·0	6·1	1·0	12·1	1·9
02	2 15·5	2 15·9	2 09·3	0·2	0·0	6·2	1·0	12·2	1·9
03	2 15·8	2 16·1	2 09·6	0·3	0·0	6·3	1·0	12·3	1·9
04	2 16·0	2 16·4	2 09·8	0·4	0·1	6·4	1·0	12·4	2·0
05	2 16·3	2 16·6	2 10·0	0·5	0·1	6·5	1·0	12·5	2·0
06	2 16·5	2 16·9	2 10·3	0·6	0·1	6·6	1·0	12·6	2·0
07	2 16·8	2 17·1	2 10·5	0·7	0·1	6·7	1·1	12·7	2·0
08	2 17·0	2 17·4	2 10·8	0·8	0·1	6·8	1·1	12·8	2·0
09	2 17·3	2 17·6	2 11·0	0·9	0·1	6·9	1·1	12·9	2·0
10	2 17·5	2 17·9	2 11·2	1·0	0·2	7·0	1·1	13·0	2·1
11	2 17·8	2 18·1	2 11·5	1·1	0·2	7·1	1·1	13·1	2·1
12	2 18·0	2 18·4	2 11·7	1·2	0·2	7·2	1·1	13·2	2·1
13	2 18·3	2 18·6	2 12·0	1·3	0·2	7·3	1·2	13·3	2·1
14	2 18·5	2 18·9	2 12·2	1·4	0·2	7·4	1·2	13·4	2·1
15	2 18·8	2 19·1	2 12·4	1·5	0·2	7·5	1·2	13·5	2·1
16	2 19·0	2 19·4	2 12·7	1·6	0·3	7·6	1·2	13·6	2·2
17	2 19·3	2 19·6	2 12·9	1·7	0·3	7·7	1·2	13·7	2·2
18	2 19·5	2 19·9	2 13·1	1·8	0·3	7·8	1·2	13·8	2·2
19	2 19·8	2 20·1	2 13·4	1·9	0·3	7·9	1·3	13·9	2·2
20	2 20·0	2 20·4	2 13·6	2·0	0·3	8·0	1·3	14·0	2·2
21	2 20·3	2 20·6	2 13·9	2·1	0·3	8·1	1·3	14·1	2·2
22	2 20·5	2 20·9	2 14·1	2·2	0·3	8·2	1·3	14·2	2·2
23	2 20·8	2 21·1	2 14·3	2·3	0·4	8·3	1·3	14·3	2·3
24	2 21·0	2 21·4	2 14·6	2·4	0·4	8·4	1·3	14·4	2·3
25	2 21·3	2 21·6	2 14·8	2·5	0·4	8·5	1·3	14·5	2·3
26	2 21·5	2 21·9	2 15·1	2·6	0·4	8·6	1·4	14·6	2·3
27	2 21·8	2 22·1	2 15·3	2·7	0·4	8·7	1·4	14·7	2·3
28	2 22·0	2 22·4	2 15·5	2·8	0·4	8·8	1·4	14·8	2·3
29	2 22·3	2 22·6	2 15·8	2·9	0·5	8·9	1·4	14·9	2·4
30	2 22·5	2 22·9	2 16·0	3·0	0·5	9·0	1·4	15·0	2·4
31	2 22·8	2 23·1	2 16·2	3·1	0·5	9·1	1·4	15·1	2·4
32	2 23·0	2 23·4	2 16·5	3·2	0·5	9·2	1·5	15·2	2·4
33	2 23·3	2 23·6	2 16·7	3·3	0·5	9·3	1·5	15·3	2·4
34	2 23·5	2 23·9	2 17·0	3·4	0·5	9·4	1·5	15·4	2·4
35	2 23·8	2 24·1	2 17·2	3·5	0·6	9·5	1·5	15·5	2·5
36	2 24·0	2 24·4	2 17·4	3·6	0·6	9·6	1·5	15·6	2·5
37	2 24·3	2 24·6	2 17·7	3·7	0·6	9·7	1·5	15·7	2·5
38	2 24·5	2 24·9	2 17·9	3·8	0·6	9·8	1·6	15·8	2·5
39	2 24·8	2 25·1	2 18·2	3·9	0·6	9·9	1·6	15·9	2·5
40	2 25·0	2 25·4	2 18·4	4·0	0·6	10·0	1·6	16·0	2·5
41	2 25·3	2 25·6	2 18·6	4·1	0·6	10·1	1·6	16·1	2·5
42	2 25·5	2 25·9	2 18·9	4·2	0·7	10·2	1·6	16·2	2·6
43	2 25·8	2 26·1	2 19·1	4·3	0·7	10·3	1·6	16·3	2·6
44	2 26·0	2 26·4	2 19·3	4·4	0·7	10·4	1·6	16·4	2·6
45	2 26·3	2 26·7	2 19·6	4·5	0·7	10·5	1·7	16·5	2·6
46	2 26·5	2 26·9	2 19·8	4·6	0·7	10·6	1·7	16·6	2·6
47	2 26·8	2 27·2	2 20·1	4·7	0·7	10·7	1·7	16·7	2·6
48	2 27·0	2 27·4	2 20·3	4·8	0·8	10·8	1·7	16·8	2·7
49	2 27·3	2 27·7	2 20·5	4·9	0·8	10·9	1·7	16·9	2·7
50	2 27·5	2 27·9	2 20·8	5·0	0·8	11·0	1·7	17·0	2·7
51	2 27·8	2 28·2	2 21·0	5·1	0·8	11·1	1·8	17·1	2·7
52	2 28·0	2 28·4	2 21·3	5·2	0·8	11·2	1·8	17·2	2·7
53	2 28·3	2 28·7	2 21·5	5·3	0·8	11·3	1·8	17·3	2·7
54	2 28·5	2 28·9	2 21·7	5·4	0·9	11·4	1·8	17·4	2·8
55	2 28·8	2 29·2	2 22·0	5·5	0·9	11·5	1·8	17·5	2·8
56	2 29·0	2 29·4	2 22·2	5·6	0·9	11·6	1·8	17·6	2·8
57	2 29·3	2 29·7	2 22·5	5·7	0·9	11·7	1·9	17·7	2·8
58	2 29·5	2 29·9	2 22·7	5·8	0·9	11·8	1·9	17·8	2·8
59	2 29·8	2 30·2	2 22·9	5·9	0·9	11·9	1·9	17·9	2·8
60	2 30·0	2 30·4	2 23·2	6·0	1·0	12·0	1·9	18·0	2·9

10m s	SUN PLANETS ° ′	ARIES ° ′	MOON ° ′	v or d ′	Corrⁿ ′	v or d ′	Corrⁿ ′	v or d ′	Corrⁿ ′
00	2 30·0	2 30·4	2 23·2	0·0	0·0	6·0	1·1	12·0	2·1
01	2 30·3	2 30·7	2 23·4	0·1	0·0	6·1	1·1	12·1	2·1
02	2 30·5	2 30·9	2 23·6	0·2	0·0	6·2	1·1	12·2	2·1
03	2 30·8	2 31·2	2 23·9	0·3	0·1	6·3	1·1	12·3	2·2
04	2 31·0	2 31·4	2 24·1	0·4	0·1	6·4	1·1	12·4	2·2
05	2 31·3	2 31·7	2 24·4	0·5	0·1	6·5	1·1	12·5	2·2
06	2 31·5	2 31·9	2 24·6	0·6	0·1	6·6	1·2	12·6	2·2
07	2 31·8	2 32·2	2 24·8	0·7	0·1	6·7	1·2	12·7	2·2
08	2 32·0	2 32·4	2 25·1	0·8	0·1	6·8	1·2	12·8	2·2
09	2 32·3	2 32·7	2 25·3	0·9	0·2	6·9	1·2	12·9	2·3
10	2 32·5	2 32·9	2 25·6	1·0	0·2	7·0	1·2	13·0	2·3
11	2 32·8	2 33·2	2 25·8	1·1	0·2	7·1	1·2	13·1	2·3
12	2 33·0	2 33·4	2 26·0	1·2	0·2	7·2	1·3	13·2	2·3
13	2 33·3	2 33·7	2 26·3	1·3	0·2	7·3	1·3	13·3	2·3
14	2 33·5	2 33·9	2 26·5	1·4	0·2	7·4	1·3	13·4	2·3
15	2 33·8	2 34·2	2 26·7	1·5	0·3	7·5	1·3	13·5	2·4
16	2 34·0	2 34·4	2 27·0	1·6	0·3	7·6	1·3	13·6	2·4
17	2 34·3	2 34·7	2 27·2	1·7	0·3	7·7	1·3	13·7	2·4
18	2 34·5	2 34·9	2 27·5	1·8	0·3	7·8	1·4	13·8	2·4
19	2 34·8	2 35·2	2 27·7	1·9	0·3	7·9	1·4	13·9	2·4
20	2 35·0	2 35·4	2 27·9	2·0	0·4	8·0	1·4	14·0	2·5
21	2 35·3	2 35·7	2 28·2	2·1	0·4	8·1	1·4	14·1	2·5
22	2 35·5	2 35·9	2 28·4	2·2	0·4	8·2	1·4	14·2	2·5
23	2 35·8	2 36·2	2 28·7	2·3	0·4	8·3	1·5	14·3	2·5
24	2 36·0	2 36·4	2 28·9	2·4	0·4	8·4	1·5	14·4	2·5
25	2 36·3	2 36·7	2 29·1	2·5	0·4	8·5	1·5	14·5	2·5
26	2 36·5	2 36·9	2 29·4	2·6	0·5	8·6	1·5	14·6	2·6
27	2 36·8	2 37·2	2 29·6	2·7	0·5	8·7	1·5	14·7	2·6
28	2 37·0	2 37·4	2 29·8	2·8	0·5	8·8	1·5	14·8	2·6
29	2 37·3	2 37·7	2 30·1	2·9	0·5	8·9	1·6	14·9	2·6
30	2 37·5	2 37·9	2 30·3	3·0	0·5	9·0	1·6	15·0	2·6
31	2 37·8	2 38·2	2 30·6	3·1	0·5	9·1	1·6	15·1	2·6
32	2 38·0	2 38·4	2 30·8	3·2	0·6	9·2	1·6	15·2	2·7
33	2 38·3	2 38·7	2 31·0	3·3	0·6	9·3	1·6	15·3	2·7
34	2 38·5	2 38·9	2 31·3	3·4	0·6	9·4	1·6	15·4	2·7
35	2 38·8	2 39·2	2 31·5	3·5	0·6	9·5	1·7	15·5	2·7
36	2 39·0	2 39·4	2 31·8	3·6	0·6	9·6	1·7	15·6	2·7
37	2 39·3	2 39·7	2 32·0	3·7	0·6	9·7	1·7	15·7	2·7
38	2 39·5	2 39·9	2 32·2	3·8	0·7	9·8	1·7	15·8	2·8
39	2 39·8	2 40·2	2 32·5	3·9	0·7	9·9	1·7	15·9	2·8
40	2 40·0	2 40·4	2 32·7	4·0	0·7	10·0	1·8	16·0	2·8
41	2 40·3	2 40·7	2 32·9	4·1	0·7	10·1	1·8	16·1	2·8
42	2 40·5	2 40·9	2 33·2	4·2	0·7	10·2	1·8	16·2	2·8
43	2 40·8	2 41·2	2 33·4	4·3	0·8	10·3	1·8	16·3	2·9
44	2 41·0	2 41·4	2 33·7	4·4	0·8	10·4	1·8	16·4	2·9
45	2 41·3	2 41·7	2 33·9	4·5	0·8	10·5	1·8	16·5	2·9
46	2 41·5	2 41·9	2 34·1	4·6	0·8	10·6	1·9	16·6	2·9
47	2 41·8	2 42·2	2 34·4	4·7	0·8	10·7	1·9	16·7	2·9
48	2 42·0	2 42·4	2 34·6	4·8	0·8	10·8	1·9	16·8	2·9
49	2 42·3	2 42·7	2 34·9	4·9	0·9	10·9	1·9	16·9	3·0
50	2 42·5	2 42·9	2 35·1	5·0	0·9	11·0	1·9	17·0	3·0
51	2 42·8	2 43·2	2 35·3	5·1	0·9	11·1	1·9	17·1	3·0
52	2 43·0	2 43·4	2 35·6	5·2	0·9	11·2	2·0	17·2	3·0
53	2 43·3	2 43·7	2 35·8	5·3	0·9	11·3	2·0	17·3	3·0
54	2 43·5	2 43·9	2 36·1	5·4	0·9	11·4	2·0	17·4	3·0
55	2 43·8	2 44·2	2 36·3	5·5	1·0	11·5	2·0	17·5	3·1
56	2 44·0	2 44·4	2 36·5	5·6	1·0	11·6	2·0	17·6	3·1
57	2 44·3	2 44·7	2 36·8	5·7	1·0	11·7	2·0	17·7	3·1
58	2 44·5	2 45·0	2 37·0	5·8	1·0	11·8	2·1	17·8	3·1
59	2 44·8	2 45·2	2 37·2	5·9	1·0	11·9	2·1	17·9	3·1
60	2 45·0	2 45·5	2 37·5	6·0	1·1	12·0	2·1	18·0	3·2

11m s	SUN PLANETS ° ′	ARIES ° ′	MOON ° ′	v or d ′	Corrⁿ ′	v or d ′	Corrⁿ ′	v or d ′	Corrⁿ ′
00	2 45·0	2 45·5	2 37·5	0·0	0·0	6·0	1·2	12·0	2·3
01	2 45·3	2 45·7	2 37·7	0·1	0·0	6·1	1·2	12·1	2·3
02	2 45·5	2 46·0	2 38·0	0·2	0·0	6·2	1·2	12·2	2·3
03	2 45·8	2 46·2	2 38·2	0·3	0·1	6·3	1·2	12·3	2·4
04	2 46·0	2 46·5	2 38·4	0·4	0·1	6·4	1·2	12·4	2·4
05	2 46·3	2 46·7	2 38·7	0·5	0·1	6·5	1·2	12·5	2·4
06	2 46·5	2 47·0	2 38·9	0·6	0·1	6·6	1·3	12·6	2·4
07	2 46·8	2 47·2	2 39·2	0·7	0·1	6·7	1·3	12·7	2·4
08	2 47·0	2 47·5	2 39·4	0·8	0·2	6·8	1·3	12·8	2·5
09	2 47·3	2 47·7	2 39·6	0·9	0·2	6·9	1·3	12·9	2·5
10	2 47·5	2 48·0	2 39·9	1·0	0·2	7·0	1·3	13·0	2·5
11	2 47·8	2 48·2	2 40·1	1·1	0·2	7·1	1·4	13·1	2·5
12	2 48·0	2 48·5	2 40·3	1·2	0·2	7·2	1·4	13·2	2·5
13	2 48·3	2 48·7	2 40·6	1·3	0·2	7·3	1·4	13·3	2·5
14	2 48·5	2 49·0	2 40·8	1·4	0·3	7·4	1·4	13·4	2·6
15	2 48·8	2 49·2	2 41·1	1·5	0·3	7·5	1·4	13·5	2·6
16	2 49·0	2 49·5	2 41·3	1·6	0·3	7·6	1·5	13·6	2·6
17	2 49·3	2 49·7	2 41·5	1·7	0·3	7·7	1·5	13·7	2·6
18	2 49·5	2 50·0	2 41·8	1·8	0·3	7·8	1·5	13·8	2·6
19	2 49·8	2 50·2	2 42·0	1·9	0·4	7·9	1·5	13·9	2·7
20	2 50·0	2 50·5	2 42·3	2·0	0·4	8·0	1·5	14·0	2·7
21	2 50·3	2 50·7	2 42·5	2·1	0·4	8·1	1·6	14·1	2·7
22	2 50·5	2 51·0	2 42·7	2·2	0·4	8·2	1·6	14·2	2·7
23	2 50·8	2 51·2	2 43·0	2·3	0·4	8·3	1·6	14·3	2·7
24	2 51·0	2 51·5	2 43·2	2·4	0·5	8·4	1·6	14·4	2·8
25	2 51·3	2 51·7	2 43·4	2·5	0·5	8·5	1·6	14·5	2·8
26	2 51·5	2 52·0	2 43·7	2·6	0·5	8·6	1·6	14·6	2·8
27	2 51·8	2 52·2	2 43·9	2·7	0·5	8·7	1·7	14·7	2·8
28	2 52·0	2 52·5	2 44·2	2·8	0·5	8·8	1·7	14·8	2·8
29	2 52·3	2 52·7	2 44·4	2·9	0·6	8·9	1·7	14·9	2·9
30	2 52·5	2 53·0	2 44·6	3·0	0·6	9·0	1·7	15·0	2·9
31	2 52·8	2 53·2	2 44·9	3·1	0·6	9·1	1·7	15·1	2·9
32	2 53·0	2 53·5	2 45·1	3·2	0·6	9·2	1·8	15·2	2·9
33	2 53·3	2 53·7	2 45·4	3·3	0·6	9·3	1·8	15·3	2·9
34	2 53·5	2 54·0	2 45·6	3·4	0·7	9·4	1·8	15·4	3·0
35	2 53·8	2 54·2	2 45·8	3·5	0·7	9·5	1·8	15·5	3·0
36	2 54·0	2 54·5	2 46·1	3·6	0·7	9·6	1·8	15·6	3·0
37	2 54·3	2 54·7	2 46·3	3·7	0·7	9·7	1·9	15·7	3·0
38	2 54·5	2 55·0	2 46·6	3·8	0·7	9·8	1·9	15·8	3·0
39	2 54·8	2 55·2	2 46·8	3·9	0·7	9·9	1·9	15·9	3·0
40	2 55·0	2 55·5	2 47·0	4·0	0·8	10·0	1·9	16·0	3·1
41	2 55·3	2 55·7	2 47·3	4·1	0·8	10·1	1·9	16·1	3·1
42	2 55·5	2 56·0	2 47·5	4·2	0·8	10·2	2·0	16·2	3·1
43	2 55·8	2 56·2	2 47·7	4·3	0·8	10·3	2·0	16·3	3·1
44	2 56·0	2 56·5	2 48·0	4·4	0·8	10·4	2·0	16·4	3·1
45	2 56·3	2 56·7	2 48·2	4·5	0·9	10·5	2·0	16·5	3·2
46	2 56·5	2 57·0	2 48·5	4·6	0·9	10·6	2·0	16·6	3·2
47	2 56·8	2 57·2	2 48·7	4·7	0·9	10·7	2·1	16·7	3·2
48	2 57·0	2 57·5	2 48·9	4·8	0·9	10·8	2·1	16·8	3·2
49	2 57·3	2 57·7	2 49·2	4·9	0·9	10·9	2·1	16·9	3·2
50	2 57·5	2 58·0	2 49·4	5·0	1·0	11·0	2·1	17·0	3·3
51	2 57·8	2 58·2	2 49·7	5·1	1·0	11·1	2·1	17·1	3·3
52	2 58·0	2 58·5	2 49·9	5·2	1·0	11·2	2·1	17·2	3·3
53	2 58·3	2 58·7	2 50·1	5·3	1·0	11·3	2·2	17·3	3·3
54	2 58·5	2 59·0	2 50·4	5·4	1·0	11·4	2·2	17·4	3·3
55	2 58·8	2 59·2	2 50·6	5·5	1·1	11·5	2·2	17·5	3·4
56	2 59·0	2 59·5	2 50·8	5·6	1·1	11·6	2·2	17·6	3·4
57	2 59·3	2 59·7	2 51·1	5·7	1·1	11·7	2·2	17·7	3·4
58	2 59·5	3 00·0	2 51·3	5·8	1·1	11·8	2·3	17·8	3·4
59	2 59·8	3 00·2	2 51·6	5·9	1·1	11·9	2·3	17·9	3·4
60	3 00·0	3 00·5	2 51·8	6·0	1·2	12·0	2·3	18·0	3·5

12ᵐ	SUN PLANETS	ARIES	MOON	v or d	Corrⁿ	v or d	Corrⁿ	v or d	Corrⁿ
s	° ′	° ′	° ′	′	′	′	′	′	′
00	3 00·0	3 00·5	2 51·8	0·0	0·0	6·0	1·3	12·0	2·5
01	3 00·3	3 00·7	2 52·0	0·1	0·0	6·1	1·3	12·1	2·5
02	3 00·5	3 01·0	2 52·3	0·2	0·0	6·2	1·3	12·2	2·5
03	3 00·8	3 01·2	2 52·5	0·3	0·1	6·3	1·3	12·3	2·6
04	3 01·0	3 01·5	2 52·8	0·4	0·1	6·4	1·3	12·4	2·6
05	3 01·3	3 01·7	2 53·0	0·5	0·1	6·5	1·4	12·5	2·6
06	3 01·5	3 02·0	2 53·2	0·6	0·1	6·6	1·4	12·6	2·6
07	3 01·8	3 02·2	2 53·5	0·7	0·1	6·7	1·4	12·7	2·6
08	3 02·0	3 02·5	2 53·7	0·8	0·2	6·8	1·4	12·8	2·7
09	3 02·3	3 02·7	2 53·9	0·9	0·2	6·9	1·4	12·9	2·7
10	3 02·5	3 03·0	2 54·2	1·0	0·2	7·0	1·5	13·0	2·7
11	3 02·8	3 03·3	2 54·4	1·1	0·2	7·1	1·5	13·1	2·7
12	3 03·0	3 03·5	2 54·7	1·2	0·3	7·2	1·5	13·2	2·8
13	3 03·3	3 03·8	2 54·9	1·3	0·3	7·3	1·5	13·3	2·8
14	3 03·5	3 04·0	2 55·1	1·4	0·3	7·4	1·5	13·4	2·8
15	3 03·8	3 04·3	2 55·4	1·5	0·3	7·5	1·6	13·5	2·8
16	3 04·0	3 04·5	2 55·6	1·6	0·3	7·6	1·6	13·6	2·8
17	3 04·3	3 04·8	2 55·9	1·7	0·4	7·7	1·6	13·7	2·9
18	3 04·5	3 05·0	2 56·1	1·8	0·4	7·8	1·6	13·8	2·9
19	3 04·8	3 05·3	2 56·3	1·9	0·4	7·9	1·6	13·9	2·9
20	3 05·0	3 05·5	2 56·6	2·0	0·4	8·0	1·7	14·0	2·9
21	3 05·3	3 05·8	2 56·8	2·1	0·4	8·1	1·7	14·1	2·9
22	3 05·5	3 06·0	2 57·0	2·2	0·5	8·2	1·7	14·2	3·0
23	3 05·8	3 06·3	2 57·3	2·3	0·5	8·3	1·7	14·3	3·0
24	3 06·0	3 06·5	2 57·5	2·4	0·5	8·4	1·8	14·4	3·0
25	3 06·3	3 06·8	2 57·8	2·5	0·5	8·5	1·8	14·5	3·0
26	3 06·5	3 07·0	2 58·0	2·6	0·5	8·6	1·8	14·6	3·0
27	3 06·8	3 07·3	2 58·2	2·7	0·6	8·7	1·8	14·7	3·1
28	3 07·0	3 07·5	2 58·5	2·8	0·6	8·8	1·8	14·8	3·1
29	3 07·3	3 07·8	2 58·7	2·9	0·6	8·9	1·9	14·9	3·1
30	3 07·5	3 08·0	2 59·0	3·0	0·6	9·0	1·9	15·0	3·1
31	3 07·8	3 08·3	2 59·2	3·1	0·6	9·1	1·9	15·1	3·1
32	3 08·0	3 08·5	2 59·4	3·2	0·7	9·2	1·9	15·2	3·2
33	3 08·3	3 08·8	2 59·7	3·3	0·7	9·3	1·9	15·3	3·2
34	3 08·5	3 09·0	2 59·9	3·4	0·7	9·4	2·0	15·4	3·2
35	3 08·8	3 09·3	3 00·2	3·5	0·7	9·5	2·0	15·5	3·2
36	3 09·0	3 09·5	3 00·4	3·6	0·8	9·6	2·0	15·6	3·3
37	3 09·3	3 09·8	3 00·6	3·7	0·8	9·7	2·0	15·7	3·3
38	3 09·5	3 10·0	3 00·9	3·8	0·8	9·8	2·0	15·8	3·3
39	3 09·8	3 10·3	3 01·1	3·9	0·8	9·9	2·1	15·9	3·3
40	3 10·0	3 10·5	3 01·3	4·0	0·8	10·0	2·1	16·0	3·3
41	3 10·3	3 10·8	3 01·6	4·1	0·9	10·1	2·1	16·1	3·4
42	3 10·5	3 11·0	3 01·8	4·2	0·9	10·2	2·1	16·2	3·4
43	3 10·8	3 11·3	3 02·1	4·3	0·9	10·3	2·1	16·3	3·4
44	3 11·0	3 11·5	3 02·3	4·4	0·9	10·4	2·2	16·4	3·4
45	3 11·3	3 11·8	3 02·5	4·5	0·9	10·5	2·2	16·5	3·4
46	3 11·5	3 12·0	3 02·8	4·6	1·0	10·6	2·2	16·6	3·5
47	3 11·8	3 12·3	3 03·0	4·7	1·0	10·7	2·2	16·7	3·5
48	3 12·0	3 12·5	3 03·3	4·8	1·0	10·8	2·3	16·8	3·5
49	3 12·3	3 12·8	3 03·5	4·9	1·0	10·9	2·3	16·9	3·5
50	3 12·5	3 13·0	3 03·7	5·0	1·0	11·0	2·3	17·0	3·5
51	3 12·8	3 13·3	3 04·0	5·1	1·1	11·1	2·3	17·1	3·6
52	3 13·0	3 13·5	3 04·2	5·2	1·1	11·2	2·3	17·2	3·6
53	3 13·3	3 13·8	3 04·4	5·3	1·1	11·3	2·4	17·3	3·6
54	3 13·5	3 14·0	3 04·7	5·4	1·1	11·4	2·4	17·4	3·6
55	3 13·8	3 14·3	3 04·9	5·5	1·1	11·5	2·4	17·5	3·6
56	3 14·0	3 14·5	3 05·2	5·6	1·2	11·6	2·4	17·6	3·7
57	3 14·3	3 14·8	3 05·4	5·7	1·2	11·7	2·4	17·7	3·7
58	3 14·5	3 15·0	3 05·6	5·8	1·2	11·8	2·5	17·8	3·7
59	3 14·8	3 15·3	3 05·9	5·9	1·2	11·9	2·5	17·9	3·7
60	3 15·0	3 15·5	3 06·1	6·0	1·3	12·0	2·5	18·0	3·8

13ᵐ	SUN PLANETS	ARIES	MOON	v or d	Corrⁿ	v or d	Corrⁿ	v or d	Corrⁿ
s	° ′	° ′	° ′	′	′	′	′	′	′
00	3 15·0	3 15·5	3 06·1	0·0	0·0	6·0	1·4	12·0	2·7
01	3 15·3	3 15·8	3 06·4	0·1	0·0	6·1	1·4	12·1	2·7
02	3 15·5	3 16·0	3 06·6	0·2	0·0	6·2	1·4	12·2	2·7
03	3 15·8	3 16·3	3 06·8	0·3	0·1	6·3	1·4	12·3	2·8
04	3 16·0	3 16·5	3 07·1	0·4	0·1	6·4	1·4	12·4	2·8
05	3 16·3	3 16·8	3 07·3	0·5	0·1	6·5	1·5	12·5	2·8
06	3 16·5	3 17·0	3 07·5	0·6	0·1	6·6	1·5	12·6	2·8
07	3 16·8	3 17·3	3 07·8	0·7	0·2	6·7	1·5	12·7	2·9
08	3 17·0	3 17·5	3 08·0	0·8	0·2	6·8	1·5	12·8	2·9
09	3 17·3	3 17·8	3 08·3	0·9	0·2	6·9	1·6	12·9	2·9
10	3 17·5	3 18·0	3 08·5	1·0	0·2	7·0	1·6	13·0	2·9
11	3 17·8	3 18·3	3 08·7	1·1	0·2	7·1	1·6	13·1	2·9
12	3 18·0	3 18·5	3 09·0	1·2	0·3	7·2	1·6	13·2	3·0
13	3 18·3	3 18·8	3 09·2	1·3	0·3	7·3	1·6	13·3	3·0
14	3 18·5	3 19·0	3 09·5	1·4	0·3	7·4	1·7	13·4	3·0
15	3 18·8	3 19·3	3 09·7	1·5	0·3	7·5	1·7	13·5	3·0
16	3 19·0	3 19·5	3 09·9	1·6	0·4	7·6	1·7	13·6	3·1
17	3 19·3	3 19·8	3 10·2	1·7	0·4	7·7	1·7	13·7	3·1
18	3 19·5	3 20·0	3 10·4	1·8	0·4	7·8	1·8	13·8	3·1
19	3 19·8	3 20·3	3 10·7	1·9	0·4	7·9	1·8	13·9	3·1
20	3 20·0	3 20·5	3 10·9	2·0	0·5	8·0	1·8	14·0	3·2
21	3 20·3	3 20·8	3 11·1	2·1	0·5	8·1	1·8	14·1	3·2
22	3 20·5	3 21·0	3 11·4	2·2	0·5	8·2	1·8	14·2	3·2
23	3 20·8	3 21·3	3 11·6	2·3	0·5	8·3	1·9	14·3	3·2
24	3 21·0	3 21·6	3 11·8	2·4	0·5	8·4	1·9	14·4	3·2
25	3 21·3	3 21·8	3 12·1	2·5	0·6	8·5	1·9	14·5	3·3
26	3 21·5	3 22·1	3 12·3	2·6	0·6	8·6	1·9	14·6	3·3
27	3 21·8	3 22·3	3 12·6	2·7	0·6	8·7	2·0	14·7	3·3
28	3 22·0	3 22·6	3 12·8	2·8	0·6	8·8	2·0	14·8	3·3
29	3 22·3	3 22·8	3 13·0	2·9	0·7	8·9	2·0	14·9	3·4
30	3 22·5	3 23·1	3 13·3	3·0	0·7	9·0	2·0	15·0	3·4
31	3 22·8	3 23·3	3 13·5	3·1	0·7	9·1	2·0	15·1	3·4
32	3 23·0	3 23·6	3 13·8	3·2	0·7	9·2	2·1	15·2	3·4
33	3 23·3	3 23·8	3 14·0	3·3	0·7	9·3	2·1	15·3	3·4
34	3 23·5	3 24·1	3 14·2	3·4	0·8	9·4	2·1	15·4	3·5
35	3 23·8	3 24·3	3 14·5	3·5	0·8	9·5	2·1	15·5	3·5
36	3 24·0	3 24·6	3 14·7	3·6	0·8	9·6	2·2	15·6	3·5
37	3 24·3	3 24·8	3 14·9	3·7	0·8	9·7	2·2	15·7	3·5
38	3 24·5	3 25·1	3 15·2	3·8	0·9	9·8	2·2	15·8	3·6
39	3 24·8	3 25·3	3 15·4	3·9	0·9	9·9	2·2	15·9	3·6
40	3 25·0	3 25·6	3 15·7	4·0	0·9	10·0	2·3	16·0	3·6
41	3 25·3	3 25·8	3 15·9	4·1	0·9	10·1	2·3	16·1	3·6
42	3 25·5	3 26·1	3 16·1	4·2	0·9	10·2	2·3	16·2	3·6
43	3 25·8	3 26·3	3 16·4	4·3	1·0	10·3	2·3	16·3	3·7
44	3 26·0	3 26·6	3 16·6	4·4	1·0	10·4	2·3	16·4	3·7
45	3 26·3	3 26·8	3 16·9	4·5	1·0	10·5	2·4	16·5	3·7
46	3 26·5	3 27·1	3 17·1	4·6	1·0	10·6	2·4	16·6	3·7
47	3 26·8	3 27·3	3 17·3	4·7	1·1	10·7	2·4	16·7	3·8
48	3 27·0	3 27·6	3 17·6	4·8	1·1	10·8	2·4	16·8	3·8
49	3 27·3	3 27·8	3 17·8	4·9	1·1	10·9	2·5	16·9	3·8
50	3 27·5	3 28·1	3 18·0	5·0	1·1	11·0	2·5	17·0	3·8
51	3 27·8	3 28·3	3 18·3	5·1	1·1	11·1	2·5	17·1	3·8
52	3 28·0	3 28·6	3 18·5	5·2	1·2	11·2	2·5	17·2	3·9
53	3 28·3	3 28·8	3 18·8	5·3	1·2	11·3	2·5	17·3	3·9
54	3 28·5	3 29·1	3 19·0	5·4	1·2	11·4	2·6	17·4	3·9
55	3 28·8	3 29·3	3 19·2	5·5	1·2	11·5	2·6	17·5	3·9
56	3 29·0	3 29·6	3 19·5	5·6	1·3	11·6	2·6	17·6	4·0
57	3 29·3	3 29·8	3 19·7	5·7	1·3	11·7	2·6	17·7	4·0
58	3 29·5	3 30·1	3 20·0	5·8	1·3	11·8	2·7	17·8	4·0
59	3 29·8	3 30·3	3 20·2	5·9	1·3	11·9	2·7	17·9	4·0
60	3 30·0	3 30·6	3 20·4	6·0	1·4	12·0	2·7	18·0	4·1

m 14	SUN PLANETS	ARIES	MOON	v or d	Corrⁿ	v or d	Corrⁿ	v or d	Corrⁿ
s	° ′	° ′	° ′	′	′	′	′	′	′
00	3 30·0	3 30·6	3 20·4	0·0	0·0	6·0	1·5	12·0	2·9
01	3 30·3	3 30·8	3 20·7	0·1	0·0	6·1	1·5	12·1	2·9
02	3 30·5	3 31·1	3 20·9	0·2	0·0	6·2	1·5	12·2	2·9
03	3 30·8	3 31·3	3 21·1	0·3	0·1	6·3	1·5	12·3	3·0
04	3 31·0	3 31·6	3 21·4	0·4	0·1	6·4	1·5	12·4	3·0
05	3 31·3	3 31·8	3 21·6	0·5	0·1	6·5	1·6	12·5	3·0
06	3 31·5	3 32·1	3 21·9	0·6	0·1	6·6	1·6	12·6	3·0
07	3 31·8	3 32·3	3 22·1	0·7	0·2	6·7	1·6	12·7	3·1
08	3 32·0	3 32·6	3 22·3	0·8	0·2	6·8	1·6	12·8	3·1
09	3 32·3	3 32·8	3 22·6	0·9	0·2	6·9	1·7	12·9	3·1
10	3 32·5	3 33·1	3 22·8	1·0	0·2	7·0	1·7	13·0	3·1
11	3 32·8	3 33·3	3 23·1	1·1	0·3	7·1	1·7	13·1	3·2
12	3 33·0	3 33·6	3 23·3	1·2	0·3	7·2	1·7	13·2	3·2
13	3 33·3	3 33·8	3 23·5	1·3	0·3	7·3	1·8	13·3	3·2
14	3 33·5	3 34·1	3 23·8	1·4	0·3	7·4	1·8	13·4	3·2
15	3 33·8	3 34·3	3 24·0	1·5	0·4	7·5	1·8	13·5	3·3
16	3 34·0	3 34·6	3 24·3	1·6	0·4	7·6	1·8	13·6	3·3
17	3 34·3	3 34·8	3 24·5	1·7	0·4	7·7	1·9	13·7	3·3
18	3 34·5	3 35·1	3 24·7	1·8	0·4	7·8	1·9	13·8	3·3
19	3 34·8	3 35·3	3 25·0	1·9	0·5	7·9	1·9	13·9	3·4
20	3 35·0	3 35·6	3 25·2	2·0	0·5	8·0	1·9	14·0	3·4
21	3 35·3	3 35·8	3 25·4	2·1	0·5	8·1	2·0	14·1	3·4
22	3 35·5	3 36·1	3 25·7	2·2	0·5	8·2	2·0	14·2	3·4
23	3 35·8	3 36·3	3 25·9	2·3	0·6	8·3	2·0	14·3	3·5
24	3 36·0	3 36·6	3 26·2	2·4	0·6	8·4	2·0	14·4	3·5
25	3 36·3	3 36·8	3 26·4	2·5	0·6	8·5	2·1	14·5	3·5
26	3 36·5	3 37·1	3 26·6	2·6	0·6	8·6	2·1	14·6	3·5
27	3 36·8	3 37·3	3 26·9	2·7	0·7	8·7	2·1	14·7	3·6
28	3 37·0	3 37·6	3 27·1	2·8	0·7	8·8	2·1	14·8	3·6
29	3 37·3	3 37·8	3 27·4	2·9	0·7	8·9	2·2	14·9	3·6
30	3 37·5	3 38·1	3 27·6	3·0	0·7	9·0	2·2	15·0	3·6
31	3 37·8	3 38·3	3 27·8	3·1	0·7	9·1	2·2	15·1	3·6
32	3 38·0	3 38·6	3 28·1	3·2	0·8	9·2	2·2	15·2	3·7
33	3 38·3	3 38·8	3 28·3	3·3	0·8	9·3	2·2	15·3	3·7
34	3 38·5	3 39·1	3 28·5	3·4	0·8	9·4	2·3	15·4	3·7
35	3 38·8	3 39·3	3 28·8	3·5	0·8	9·5	2·3	15·5	3·7
36	3 39·0	3 39·6	3 29·0	3·6	0·9	9·6	2·3	15·6	3·8
37	3 39·3	3 39·9	3 29·3	3·7	0·9	9·7	2·3	15·7	3·8
38	3 39·5	3 40·1	3 29·5	3·8	0·9	9·8	2·4	15·8	3·8
39	3 39·8	3 40·4	3 29·7	3·9	0·9	9·9	2·4	15·9	3·8
40	3 40·0	3 40·6	3 30·0	4·0	1·0	10·0	2·4	16·0	3·9
41	3 40·3	3 40·9	3 30·2	4·1	1·0	10·1	2·4	16·1	3·9
42	3 40·5	3 41·1	3 30·5	4·2	1·0	10·2	2·5	16·2	3·9
43	3 40·8	3 41·4	3 30·7	4·3	1·0	10·3	2·5	16·3	3·9
44	3 41·0	3 41·6	3 30·9	4·4	1·1	10·4	2·5	16·4	4·0
45	3 41·3	3 41·9	3 31·2	4·5	1·1	10·5	2·5	16·5	4·0
46	3 41·5	3 42·1	3 31·4	4·6	1·1	10·6	2·6	16·6	4·0
47	3 41·8	3 42·4	3 31·6	4·7	1·1	10·7	2·6	16·7	4·0
48	3 42·0	3 42·6	3 31·9	4·8	1·2	10·8	2·6	16·8	4·1
49	3 42·3	3 42·9	3 32·1	4·9	1·2	10·9	2·6	16·9	4·1
50	3 42·5	3 43·1	3 32·4	5·0	1·2	11·0	2·7	17·0	4·1
51	3 42·8	3 43·4	3 32·6	5·1	1·2	11·1	2·7	17·1	4·1
52	3 43·0	3 43·6	3 32·8	5·2	1·3	11·2	2·7	17·2	4·2
53	3 43·3	3 43·9	3 33·1	5·3	1·3	11·3	2·7	17·3	4·2
54	3 43·5	3 44·1	3 33·3	5·4	1·3	11·4	2·8	17·4	4·2
55	3 43·8	3 44·4	3 33·6	5·5	1·3	11·5	2·8	17·5	4·2
56	3 44·0	3 44·6	3 33·8	5·6	1·4	11·6	2·8	17·6	4·3
57	3 44·3	3 44·9	3 34·0	5·7	1·4	11·7	2·8	17·7	4·3
58	3 44·5	3 45·1	3 34·3	5·8	1·4	11·8	2·9	17·8	4·3
59	3 44·8	3 45·4	3 34·5	5·9	1·4	11·9	2·9	17·9	4·3
60	3 45·0	3 45·6	3 34·8	6·0	1·5	12·0	2·9	18·0	4·4

m 15	SUN PLANETS	ARIES	MOON	v or d	Corrⁿ	v or d	Corrⁿ	v or d	Corrⁿ
s	° ′	° ′	° ′	′	′	′	′	′	′
00	3 45·0	3 45·6	3 34·8	0·0	0·0	6·0	1·6	12·0	3·1
01	3 45·3	3 45·9	3 35·0	0·1	0·0	6·1	1·6	12·1	3·1
02	3 45·5	3 46·1	3 35·2	0·2	0·1	6·2	1·6	12·2	3·2
03	3 45·8	3 46·4	3 35·5	0·3	0·1	6·3	1·6	12·3	3·2
04	3 46·0	3 46·6	3 35·7	0·4	0·1	6·4	1·7	12·4	3·2
05	3 46·3	3 46·9	3 35·9	0·5	0·1	6·5	1·7	12·5	3·2
06	3 46·5	3 47·1	3 36·2	0·6	0·2	6·6	1·7	12·6	3·3
07	3 46·8	3 47·4	3 36·4	0·7	0·2	6·7	1·7	12·7	3·3
08	3 47·0	3 47·6	3 36·7	0·8	0·2	6·8	1·8	12·8	3·3
09	3 47·3	3 47·9	3 36·9	0·9	0·2	6·9	1·8	12·9	3·3
10	3 47·5	3 48·1	3 37·1	1·0	0·3	7·0	1·8	13·0	3·4
11	3 47·8	3 48·4	3 37·4	1·1	0·3	7·1	1·8	13·1	3·4
12	3 48·0	3 48·6	3 37·6	1·2	0·3	7·2	1·9	13·2	3·4
13	3 48·3	3 48·9	3 37·9	1·3	0·3	7·3	1·9	13·3	3·4
14	3 48·5	3 49·1	3 38·1	1·4	0·4	7·4	1·9	13·4	3·5
15	3 48·8	3 49·4	3 38·3	1·5	0·4	7·5	1·9	13·5	3·5
16	3 49·0	3 49·6	3 38·6	1·6	0·4	7·6	2·0	13·6	3·5
17	3 49·3	3 49·9	3 38·8	1·7	0·4	7·7	2·0	13·7	3·5
18	3 49·5	3 50·1	3 39·0	1·8	0·5	7·8	2·0	13·8	3·6
19	3 49·8	3 50·4	3 39·3	1·9	0·5	7·9	2·0	13·9	3·6
20	3 50·0	3 50·6	3 39·5	2·0	0·5	8·0	2·1	14·0	3·6
21	3 50·3	3 50·9	3 39·8	2·1	0·5	8·1	2·1	14·1	3·6
22	3 50·5	3 51·1	3 40·0	2·2	0·6	8·2	2·1	14·2	3·7
23	3 50·8	3 51·4	3 40·2	2·3	0·6	8·3	2·1	14·3	3·7
24	3 51·0	3 51·6	3 40·5	2·4	0·6	8·4	2·2	14·4	3·7
25	3 51·3	3 51·9	3 40·7	2·5	0·6	8·5	2·2	14·5	3·7
26	3 51·5	3 52·1	3 41·0	2·6	0·7	8·6	2·2	14·6	3·8
27	3 51·8	3 52·4	3 41·2	2·7	0·7	8·7	2·2	14·7	3·8
28	3 52·0	3 52·6	3 41·4	2·8	0·7	8·8	2·3	14·8	3·8
29	3 52·3	3 52·9	3 41·7	2·9	0·7	8·9	2·3	14·9	3·8
30	3 52·5	3 53·1	3 41·9	3·0	0·8	9·0	2·3	15·0	3·9
31	3 52·8	3 53·4	3 42·1	3·1	0·8	9·1	2·4	15·1	3·9
32	3 53·0	3 53·6	3 42·4	3·2	0·8	9·2	2·4	15·2	3·9
33	3 53·3	3 53·9	3 42·6	3·3	0·9	9·3	2·4	15·3	4·0
34	3 53·5	3 54·1	3 42·9	3·4	0·9	9·4	2·4	15·4	4·0
35	3 53·8	3 54·4	3 43·1	3·5	0·9	9·5	2·5	15·5	4·0
36	3 54·0	3 54·6	3 43·3	3·6	0·9	9·6	2·5	15·6	4·0
37	3 54·3	3 54·9	3 43·6	3·7	1·0	9·7	2·5	15·7	4·1
38	3 54·5	3 55·1	3 43·8	3·8	1·0	9·8	2·5	15·8	4·1
39	3 54·8	3 55·4	3 44·1	3·9	1·0	9·9	2·6	15·9	4·1
40	3 55·0	3 55·6	3 44·3	4·0	1·0	10·0	2·6	16·0	4·1
41	3 55·3	3 55·9	3 44·5	4·1	1·1	10·1	2·6	16·1	4·2
42	3 55·5	3 56·1	3 44·8	4·2	1·1	10·2	2·6	16·2	4·2
43	3 55·8	3 56·4	3 45·0	4·3	1·1	10·3	2·7	16·3	4·2
44	3 56·0	3 56·6	3 45·2	4·4	1·1	10·4	2·7	16·4	4·2
45	3 56·3	3 56·9	3 45·5	4·5	1·2	10·5	2·7	16·5	4·3
46	3 56·5	3 57·1	3 45·7	4·6	1·2	10·6	2·7	16·6	4·3
47	3 56·8	3 57·4	3 46·0	4·7	1·2	10·7	2·8	16·7	4·3
48	3 57·0	3 57·6	3 46·2	4·8	1·2	10·8	2·8	16·8	4·3
49	3 57·3	3 57·9	3 46·4	4·9	1·3	10·9	2·8	16·9	4·4
50	3 57·5	3 58·2	3 46·7	5·0	1·3	11·0	2·8	17·0	4·4
51	3 57·8	3 58·4	3 46·9	5·1	1·3	11·1	2·9	17·1	4·4
52	3 58·0	3 58·7	3 47·2	5·2	1·3	11·2	2·9	17·2	4·4
53	3 58·3	3 58·9	3 47·4	5·3	1·4	11·3	2·9	17·3	4·5
54	3 58·5	3 59·2	3 47·6	5·4	1·4	11·4	2·9	17·4	4·5
55	3 58·8	3 59·4	3 47·9	5·5	1·4	11·5	3·0	17·5	4·5
56	3 59·0	3 59·7	3 48·1	5·6	1·4	11·6	3·0	17·6	4·5
57	3 59·3	3 59·9	3 48·4	5·7	1·5	11·7	3·0	17·7	4·6
58	3 59·5	4 00·2	3 48·6	5·8	1·5	11·8	3·0	17·8	4·6
59	3 59·8	4 00·4	3 48·8	5·9	1·5	11·9	3·1	17·9	4·6
60	4 00·0	4 00·7	3 49·1	6·0	1·6	12·0	3·1	18·0	4·7

16m s	SUN PLANETS ° ′	ARIES ° ′	MOON ° ′	v or d ′	Corrⁿ ′	v or d ′	Corrⁿ ′	v or d ′	Corrⁿ ′
00	4 00·0	4 00·7	3 49·1	0·0	0·0	6·0	1·7	12·0	3·3
01	4 00·3	4 00·9	3 49·3	0·1	0·0	6·1	1·7	12·1	3·3
02	4 00·5	4 01·2	3 49·5	0·2	0·1	6·2	1·7	12·2	3·4
03	4 00·8	4 01·4	3 49·8	0·3	0·1	6·3	1·7	12·3	3·4
04	4 01·0	4 01·7	3 50·0	0·4	0·1	6·4	1·8	12·4	3·4
05	4 01·3	4 01·9	3 50·3	0·5	0·1	6·5	1·8	12·5	3·4
06	4 01·5	4 02·2	3 50·5	0·6	0·2	6·6	1·8	12·6	3·5
07	4 01·8	4 02·4	3 50·7	0·7	0·2	6·7	1·8	12·7	3·5
08	4 02·0	4 02·7	3 51·0	0·8	0·2	6·8	1·9	12·8	3·5
09	4 02·3	4 02·9	3 51·2	0·9	0·2	6·9	1·9	12·9	3·5
10	4 02·5	4 03·2	3 51·5	1·0	0·3	7·0	1·9	13·0	3·6
11	4 02·8	4 03·4	3 51·7	1·1	0·3	7·1	2·0	13·1	3·6
12	4 03·0	4 03·7	3 51·9	1·2	0·3	7·2	2·0	13·2	3·6
13	4 03·3	4 03·9	3 52·2	1·3	0·4	7·3	2·0	13·3	3·7
14	4 03·5	4 04·2	3 52·4	1·4	0·4	7·4	2·0	13·4	3·7
15	4 03·8	4 04·4	3 52·6	1·5	0·4	7·5	2·1	13·5	3·7
16	4 04·0	4 04·7	3 52·9	1·6	0·4	7·6	2·1	13·6	3·7
17	4 04·3	4 04·9	3 53·1	1·7	0·5	7·7	2·1	13·7	3·8
18	4 04·5	4 05·2	3 53·4	1·8	0·5	7·8	2·1	13·8	3·8
19	4 04·8	4 05·4	3 53·6	1·9	0·5	7·9	2·2	13·9	3·8
20	4 05·0	4 05·7	3 53·8	2·0	0·6	8·0	2·2	14·0	3·9
21	4 05·3	4 05·9	3 54·1	2·1	0·6	8·1	2·2	14·1	3·9
22	4 05·5	4 06·2	3 54·3	2·2	0·6	8·2	2·3	14·2	3·9
23	4 05·8	4 06·4	3 54·6	2·3	0·6	8·3	2·3	14·3	3·9
24	4 06·0	4 06·7	3 54·8	2·4	0·7	8·4	2·3	14·4	4·0
25	4 06·3	4 06·9	3 55·0	2·5	0·7	8·5	2·3	14·5	4·0
26	4 06·5	4 07·2	3 55·3	2·6	0·7	8·6	2·4	14·6	4·0
27	4 06·8	4 07·4	3 55·5	2·7	0·7	8·7	2·4	14·7	4·0
28	4 07·0	4 07·7	3 55·7	2·8	0·8	8·8	2·4	14·8	4·1
29	4 07·3	4 07·9	3 56·0	2·9	0·8	8·9	2·4	14·9	4·1
30	4 07·5	4 08·2	3 56·2	3·0	0·8	9·0	2·5	15·0	4·1
31	4 07·8	4 08·4	3 56·5	3·1	0·9	9·1	2·5	15·1	4·2
32	4 08·0	4 08·7	3 56·7	3·2	0·9	9·2	2·5	15·2	4·2
33	4 08·3	4 08·9	3 56·9	3·3	0·9	9·3	2·6	15·3	4·2
34	4 08·5	4 09·2	3 57·2	3·4	0·9	9·4	2·6	15·4	4·2
35	4 08·8	4 09·4	3 57·4	3·5	1·0	9·5	2·6	15·5	4·3
36	4 09·0	4 09·7	3 57·7	3·6	1·0	9·6	2·6	15·6	4·3
37	4 09·3	4 09·9	3 57·9	3·7	1·0	9·7	2·7	15·7	4·3
38	4 09·5	4 10·2	3 58·1	3·8	1·0	9·8	2·7	15·8	4·3
39	4 09·8	4 10·4	3 58·4	3·9	1·1	9·9	2·7	15·9	4·4
40	4 10·0	4 10·7	3 58·6	4·0	1·1	10·0	2·8	16·0	4·4
41	4 10·3	4 10·9	3 58·8	4·1	1·1	10·1	2·8	16·1	4·4
42	4 10·5	4 11·2	3 59·1	4·2	1·2	10·2	2·8	16·2	4·5
43	4 10·8	4 11·4	3 59·3	4·3	1·2	10·3	2·8	16·3	4·5
44	4 11·0	4 11·7	3 59·6	4·4	1·2	10·4	2·9	16·4	4·5
45	4 11·3	4 11·9	3 59·8	4·5	1·2	10·5	2·9	16·5	4·5
46	4 11·5	4 12·2	4 00·0	4·6	1·3	10·6	2·9	16·6	4·6
47	4 11·8	4 12·4	4 00·3	4·7	1·3	10·7	2·9	16·7	4·6
48	4 12·0	4 12·7	4 00·5	4·8	1·3	10·8	3·0	16·8	4·6
49	4 12·3	4 12·9	4 00·8	4·9	1·3	10·9	3·0	16·9	4·6
50	4 12·5	4 13·2	4 01·0	5·0	1·4	11·0	3·0	17·0	4·7
51	4 12·8	4 13·4	4 01·2	5·1	1·4	11·1	3·1	17·1	4·7
52	4 13·0	4 13·7	4 01·5	5·2	1·4	11·2	3·1	17·2	4·7
53	4 13·3	4 13·9	4 01·7	5·3	1·5	11·3	3·1	17·3	4·8
54	4 13·5	4 14·2	4 02·0	5·4	1·5	11·4	3·1	17·4	4·8
55	4 13·8	4 14·4	4 02·2	5·5	1·5	11·5	3·2	17·5	4·8
56	4 14·0	4 14·7	4 02·4	5·6	1·5	11·6	3·2	17·6	4·8
57	4 14·3	4 14·9	4 02·7	5·7	1·6	11·7	3·2	17·7	4·9
58	4 14·5	4 15·2	4 02·9	5·8	1·6	11·8	3·2	17·8	4·9
59	4 14·8	4 15·4	4 03·1	5·9	1·6	11·9	3·3	17·9	4·9
60	4 15·0	4 15·7	4 03·4	6·0	1·7	12·0	3·3	18·0	5·0

17m s	SUN PLANETS ° ′	ARIES ° ′	MOON ° ′	v or d ′	Corrⁿ ′	v or d ′	Corrⁿ ′	v or d ′	Corrⁿ ′
00	4 15·0	4 15·7	4 03·4	0·0	0·0	6·0	1·8	12·0	3·5
01	4 15·3	4 15·9	4 03·6	0·1	0·0	6·1	1·8	12·1	3·5
02	4 15·5	4 16·2	4 03·9	0·2	0·1	6·2	1·8	12·2	3·6
03	4 15·8	4 16·5	4 04·1	0·3	0·1	6·3	1·8	12·3	3·6
04	4 16·0	4 16·7	4 04·3	0·4	0·1	6·4	1·9	12·4	3·6
05	4 16·3	4 17·0	4 04·6	0·5	0·1	6·5	1·9	12·5	3·6
06	4 16·5	4 17·2	4 04·8	0·6	0·2	6·6	1·9	12·6	3·7
07	4 16·8	4 17·5	4 05·1	0·7	0·2	6·7	2·0	12·7	3·7
08	4 17·0	4 17·7	4 05·3	0·8	0·2	6·8	2·0	12·8	3·7
09	4 17·3	4 18·0	4 05·5	0·9	0·3	6·9	2·0	12·9	3·8
10	4 17·5	4 18·2	4 05·8	1·0	0·3	7·0	2·0	13·0	3·8
11	4 17·8	4 18·5	4 06·0	1·1	0·3	7·1	2·1	13·1	3·8
12	4 18·0	4 18·7	4 06·2	1·2	0·4	7·2	2·1	13·2	3·9
13	4 18·3	4 19·0	4 06·5	1·3	0·4	7·3	2·1	13·3	3·9
14	4 18·5	4 19·2	4 06·7	1·4	0·4	7·4	2·2	13·4	3·9
15	4 18·8	4 19·5	4 07·0	1·5	0·4	7·5	2·2	13·5	3·9
16	4 19·0	4 19·7	4 07·2	1·6	0·5	7·6	2·2	13·6	4·0
17	4 19·3	4 20·0	4 07·4	1·7	0·5	7·7	2·2	13·7	4·0
18	4 19·5	4 20·2	4 07·7	1·8	0·5	7·8	2·3	13·8	4·0
19	4 19·8	4 20·5	4 07·9	1·9	0·6	7·9	2·3	13·9	4·1
20	4 20·0	4 20·7	4 08·2	2·0	0·6	8·0	2·3	14·0	4·1
21	4 20·3	4 21·0	4 08·4	2·1	0·6	8·1	2·4	14·1	4·1
22	4 20·5	4 21·2	4 08·6	2·2	0·6	8·2	2·4	14·2	4·1
23	4 20·8	4 21·5	4 08·9	2·3	0·7	8·3	2·4	14·3	4·2
24	4 21·0	4 21·7	4 09·1	2·4	0·7	8·4	2·5	14·4	4·2
25	4 21·3	4 22·0	4 09·3	2·5	0·7	8·5	2·5	14·5	4·2
26	4 21·5	4 22·2	4 09·6	2·6	0·8	8·6	2·5	14·6	4·3
27	4 21·8	4 22·5	4 09·8	2·7	0·8	8·7	2·5	14·7	4·3
28	4 22·0	4 22·7	4 10·1	2·8	0·8	8·8	2·6	14·8	4·3
29	4 22·3	4 23·0	4 10·3	2·9	0·8	8·9	2·6	14·9	4·3
30	4 22·5	4 23·2	4 10·5	3·0	0·9	9·0	2·6	15·0	4·4
31	4 22·8	4 23·5	4 10·8	3·1	0·9	9·1	2·7	15·1	4·4
32	4 23·0	4 23·7	4 11·0	3·2	0·9	9·2	2·7	15·2	4·4
33	4 23·3	4 24·0	4 11·3	3·3	1·0	9·3	2·7	15·3	4·5
34	4 23·5	4 24·2	4 11·5	3·4	1·0	9·4	2·7	15·4	4·5
35	4 23·8	4 24·5	4 11·7	3·5	1·0	9·5	2·8	15·5	4·5
36	4 24·0	4 24·7	4 12·0	3·6	1·1	9·6	2·8	15·6	4·6
37	4 24·3	4 25·0	4 12·2	3·7	1·1	9·7	2·8	15·7	4·6
38	4 24·5	4 25·2	4 12·5	3·8	1·1	9·8	2·9	15·8	4·6
39	4 24·8	4 25·5	4 12·7	3·9	1·1	9·9	2·9	15·9	4·6
40	4 25·0	4 25·7	4 12·9	4·0	1·2	10·0	2·9	16·0	4·7
41	4 25·3	4 26·0	4 13·2	4·1	1·2	10·1	2·9	16·1	4·7
42	4 25·5	4 26·2	4 13·4	4·2	1·2	10·2	3·0	16·2	4·7
43	4 25·8	4 26·5	4 13·6	4·3	1·3	10·3	3·0	16·3	4·8
44	4 26·0	4 26·7	4 13·9	4·4	1·3	10·4	3·0	16·4	4·8
45	4 26·3	4 27·0	4 14·1	4·5	1·3	10·5	3·1	16·5	4·8
46	4 26·5	4 27·2	4 14·4	4·6	1·3	10·6	3·1	16·6	4·8
47	4 26·8	4 27·5	4 14·6	4·7	1·4	10·7	3·1	16·7	4·9
48	4 27·0	4 27·7	4 14·8	4·8	1·4	10·8	3·2	16·8	4·9
49	4 27·3	4 28·0	4 15·1	4·9	1·4	10·9	3·2	16·9	4·9
50	4 27·5	4 28·2	4 15·3	5·0	1·5	11·0	3·2	17·0	5·0
51	4 27·8	4 28·5	4 15·6	5·1	1·5	11·1	3·2	17·1	5·0
52	4 28·0	4 28·7	4 15·8	5·2	1·5	11·2	3·3	17·2	5·0
53	4 28·3	4 29·0	4 16·0	5·3	1·5	11·3	3·3	17·3	5·0
54	4 28·5	4 29·2	4 16·3	5·4	1·6	11·4	3·3	17·4	5·1
55	4 28·8	4 29·5	4 16·5	5·5	1·6	11·5	3·4	17·5	5·1
56	4 29·0	4 29·7	4 16·7	5·6	1·6	11·6	3·4	17·6	5·1
57	4 29·3	4 30·0	4 17·0	5·7	1·7	11·7	3·4	17·7	5·2
58	4 29·5	4 30·2	4 17·2	5·8	1·7	11·8	3·4	17·8	5·2
59	4 29·8	4 30·5	4 17·5	5·9	1·7	11·9	3·5	17·9	5·2
60	4 30·0	4 30·7	4 17·7	6·0	1·8	12·0	3·5	18·0	5·3

m 18	SUN PLANETS	ARIES	MOON	v or d	Corrn	v or d	Corrn	v or d	Corrn
s	° ′	° ′	° ′	′	′	′	′	′	′
00	4 30·0	4 30·7	4 17·7	0·0	0·0	6·0	1·9	12·0	3·7
01	4 30·3	4 31·0	4 17·9	0·1	0·0	6·1	1·9	12·1	3·7
02	4 30·5	4 31·2	4 18·2	0·2	0·1	6·2	1·9	12·2	3·8
03	4 30·8	4 31·5	4 18·4	0·3	0·1	6·3	1·9	12·3	3·8
04	4 31·0	4 31·7	4 18·7	0·4	0·1	6·4	2·0	12·4	3·8
05	4 31·3	4 32·0	4 18·9	0·5	0·2	6·5	2·0	12·5	3·9
06	4 31·5	4 32·2	4 19·1	0·6	0·2	6·6	2·0	12·6	3·9
07	4 31·8	4 32·5	4 19·4	0·7	0·2	6·7	2·1	12·7	3·9
08	4 32·0	4 32·7	4 19·6	0·8	0·2	6·8	2·1	12·8	3·9
09	4 32·3	4 33·0	4 19·8	0·9	0·3	6·9	2·1	12·9	4·0
10	4 32·5	4 33·2	4 20·1	1·0	0·3	7·0	2·2	13·0	4·0
11	4 32·8	4 33·5	4 20·3	1·1	0·3	7·1	2·2	13·1	4·0
12	4 33·0	4 33·7	4 20·6	1·2	0·4	7·2	2·2	13·2	4·1
13	4 33·3	4 34·0	4 20·8	1·3	0·4	7·3	2·3	13·3	4·1
14	4 33·5	4 34·2	4 21·0	1·4	0·4	7·4	2·3	13·4	4·1
15	4 33·8	4 34·5	4 21·3	1·5	0·5	7·5	2·3	13·5	4·2
16	4 34·0	4 34·8	4 21·5	1·6	0·5	7·6	2·3	13·6	4·2
17	4 34·3	4 35·0	4 21·8	1·7	0·5	7·7	2·4	13·7	4·2
18	4 34·5	4 35·3	4 22·0	1·8	0·6	7·8	2·4	13·8	4·3
19	4 34·8	4 35·5	4 22·2	1·9	0·6	7·9	2·4	13·9	4·3
20	4 35·0	4 35·8	4 22·5	2·0	0·6	8·0	2·5	14·0	4·3
21	4 35·3	4 36·0	4 22·7	2·1	0·6	8·1	2·5	14·1	4·3
22	4 35·5	4 36·3	4 22·9	2·2	0·7	8·2	2·5	14·2	4·4
23	4 35·8	4 36·5	4 23·2	2·3	0·7	8·3	2·6	14·3	4·4
24	4 36·0	4 36·8	4 23·4	2·4	0·7	8·4	2·6	14·4	4·4
25	4 36·3	4 37·0	4 23·7	2·5	0·8	8·5	2·6	14·5	4·5
26	4 36·5	4 37·3	4 23·9	2·6	0·8	8·6	2·7	14·6	4·5
27	4 36·8	4 37·5	4 24·1	2·7	0·8	8·7	2·7	14·7	4·5
28	4 37·0	4 37·8	4 24·4	2·8	0·9	8·8	2·7	14·8	4·6
29	4 37·3	4 38·0	4 24·6	2·9	0·9	8·9	2·7	14·9	4·6
30	4 37·5	4 38·3	4 24·9	3·0	0·9	9·0	2·8	15·0	4·6
31	4 37·8	4 38·5	4 25·1	3·1	1·0	9·1	2·8	15·1	4·7
32	4 38·0	4 38·8	4 25·3	3·2	1·0	9·2	2·8	15·2	4·7
33	4 38·3	4 39·0	4 25·6	3·3	1·0	9·3	2·9	15·3	4·7
34	4 38·5	4 39·3	4 25·8	3·4	1·0	9·4	2·9	15·4	4·7
35	4 38·8	4 39·5	4 26·1	3·5	1·1	9·5	2·9	15·5	4·8
36	4 39·0	4 39·8	4 26·3	3·6	1·1	9·6	3·0	15·6	4·8
37	4 39·3	4 40·0	4 26·5	3·7	1·1	9·7	3·0	15·7	4·8
38	4 39·5	4 40·3	4 26·8	3·8	1·2	9·8	3·0	15·8	4·9
39	4 39·8	4 40·5	4 27·0	3·9	1·2	9·9	3·1	15·9	4·9
40	4 40·0	4 40·8	4 27·2	4·0	1·2	10·0	3·1	16·0	4·9
41	4 40·3	4 41·0	4 27·5	4·1	1·3	10·1	3·1	16·1	5·0
42	4 40·5	4 41·3	4 27·7	4·2	1·3	10·2	3·1	16·2	5·0
43	4 40·8	4 41·5	4 28·0	4·3	1·3	10·3	3·2	16·3	5·0
44	4 41·0	4 41·8	4 28·2	4·4	1·4	10·4	3·2	16·4	5·1
45	4 41·3	4 42·0	4 28·4	4·5	1·4	10·5	3·2	16·5	5·1
46	4 41·5	4 42·3	4 28·7	4·6	1·4	10·6	3·3	16·6	5·1
47	4 41·8	4 42·5	4 28·9	4·7	1·4	10·7	3·3	16·7	5·1
48	4 42·0	4 42·8	4 29·2	4·8	1·5	10·8	3·3	16·8	5·2
49	4 42·3	4 43·0	4 29·4	4·9	1·5	10·9	3·4	16·9	5·2
50	4 42·5	4 43·3	4 29·6	5·0	1·5	11·0	3·4	17·0	5·2
51	4 42·8	4 43·5	4 29·9	5·1	1·6	11·1	3·4	17·1	5·3
52	4 43·0	4 43·8	4 30·1	5·2	1·6	11·2	3·5	17·2	5·3
53	4 43·3	4 44·0	4 30·3	5·3	1·6	11·3	3·5	17·3	5·3
54	4 43·5	4 44·3	4 30·6	5·4	1·7	11·4	3·5	17·4	5·4
55	4 43·8	4 44·5	4 30·8	5·5	1·7	11·5	3·5	17·5	5·4
56	4 44·0	4 44·8	4 31·1	5·6	1·7	11·6	3·6	17·6	5·4
57	4 44·3	4 45·0	4 31·3	5·7	1·8	11·7	3·6	17·7	5·5
58	4 44·5	4 45·3	4 31·5	5·8	1·8	11·8	3·6	17·8	5·5
59	4 44·8	4 45·5	4 31·8	5·9	1·8	11·9	3·7	17·9	5·5
60	4 45·0	4 45·8	4 32·0	6·0	1·9	12·0	3·7	18·0	5·6

m 19	SUN PLANETS	ARIES	MOON	v or d	Corrn	v or d	Corrn	v or d	Corrn
s	° ′	° ′	° ′	′	′	′	′	′	′
00	4 45·0	4 45·8	4 32·0	0·0	0·0	6·0	2·0	12·0	3·9
01	4 45·3	4 46·0	4 32·3	0·1	0·0	6·1	2·0	12·1	3·9
02	4 45·5	4 46·3	4 32·5	0·2	0·1	6·2	2·0	12·2	4·0
03	4 45·8	4 46·5	4 32·7	0·3	0·1	6·3	2·0	12·3	4·0
04	4 46·0	4 46·8	4 33·0	0·4	0·1	6·4	2·1	12·4	4·0
05	4 46·3	4 47·0	4 33·2	0·5	0·2	6·5	2·1	12·5	4·1
06	4 46·5	4 47·3	4 33·4	0·6	0·2	6·6	2·1	12·6	4·1
07	4 46·8	4 47·5	4 33·7	0·7	0·2	6·7	2·2	12·7	4·1
08	4 47·0	4 47·8	4 33·9	0·8	0·3	6·8	2·2	12·8	4·2
09	4 47·3	4 48·0	4 34·2	0·9	0·3	6·9	2·2	12·9	4·2
10	4 47·5	4 48·3	4 34·4	1·0	0·3	7·0	2·3	13·0	4·2
11	4 47·8	4 48·5	4 34·6	1·1	0·4	7·1	2·3	13·1	4·3
12	4 48·0	4 48·8	4 34·9	1·2	0·4	7·2	2·3	13·2	4·3
13	4 48·3	4 49·0	4 35·1	1·3	0·4	7·3	2·4	13·3	4·3
14	4 48·5	4 49·3	4 35·4	1·4	0·5	7·4	2·4	13·4	4·4
15	4 48·8	4 49·5	4 35·6	1·5	0·5	7·5	2·4	13·5	4·4
16	4 49·0	4 49·8	4 35·8	1·6	0·5	7·6	2·5	13·6	4·4
17	4 49·3	4 50·0	4 36·1	1·7	0·6	7·7	2·5	13·7	4·5
18	4 49·5	4 50·3	4 36·3	1·8	0·6	7·8	2·5	13·8	4·5
19	4 49·8	4 50·5	4 36·6	1·9	0·6	7·9	2·6	13·9	4·5
20	4 50·0	4 50·8	4 36·8	2·0	0·7	8·0	2·6	14·0	4·6
21	4 50·3	4 51·0	4 37·0	2·1	0·7	8·1	2·6	14·1	4·6
22	4 50·5	4 51·3	4 37·3	2·2	0·7	8·2	2·7	14·2	4·6
23	4 50·8	4 51·5	4 37·5	2·3	0·7	8·3	2·7	14·3	4·6
24	4 51·0	4 51·8	4 37·7	2·4	0·8	8·4	2·7	14·4	4·7
25	4 51·3	4 52·0	4 38·0	2·5	0·8	8·5	2·8	14·5	4·7
26	4 51·5	4 52·3	4 38·2	2·6	0·8	8·6	2·8	14·6	4·7
27	4 51·8	4 52·5	4 38·5	2·7	0·9	8·7	2·8	14·7	4·8
28	4 52·0	4 52·8	4 38·7	2·8	0·9	8·8	2·9	14·8	4·8
29	4 52·3	4 53·1	4 38·9	2·9	0·9	8·9	2·9	14·9	4·8
30	4 52·5	4 53·3	4 39·2	3·0	1·0	9·0	2·9	15·0	4·9
31	4 52·8	4 53·6	4 39·4	3·1	1·0	9·1	3·0	15·1	4·9
32	4 53·0	4 53·8	4 39·7	3·2	1·0	9·2	3·0	15·2	4·9
33	4 53·3	4 54·1	4 39·9	3·3	1·1	9·3	3·0	15·3	5·0
34	4 53·5	4 54·3	4 40·1	3·4	1·1	9·4	3·1	15·4	5·0
35	4 53·8	4 54·6	4 40·4	3·5	1·1	9·5	3·1	15·5	5·0
36	4 54·0	4 54·8	4 40·6	3·6	1·2	9·6	3·1	15·6	5·1
37	4 54·3	4 55·1	4 40·8	3·7	1·2	9·7	3·2	15·7	5·1
38	4 54·5	4 55·3	4 41·1	3·8	1·2	9·8	3·2	15·8	5·1
39	4 54·8	4 55·6	4 41·3	3·9	1·3	9·9	3·2	15·9	5·2
40	4 55·0	4 55·8	4 41·6	4·0	1·3	10·0	3·3	16·0	5·2
41	4 55·3	4 56·1	4 41·8	4·1	1·3	10·1	3·3	16·1	5·2
42	4 55·5	4 56·3	4 42·0	4·2	1·4	10·2	3·3	16·2	5·3
43	4 55·8	4 56·6	4 42·3	4·3	1·4	10·3	3·3	16·3	5·3
44	4 56·0	4 56·8	4 42·5	4·4	1·4	10·4	3·4	16·4	5·3
45	4 56·3	4 57·1	4 42·8	4·5	1·5	10·5	3·4	16·5	5·4
46	4 56·5	4 57·3	4 43·0	4·6	1·5	10·6	3·4	16·6	5·4
47	4 56·8	4 57·6	4 43·2	4·7	1·5	10·7	3·5	16·7	5·4
48	4 57·0	4 57·8	4 43·5	4·8	1·6	10·8	3·5	16·8	5·5
49	4 57·3	4 58·1	4 43·7	4·9	1·6	10·9	3·5	16·9	5·5
50	4 57·5	4 58·3	4 43·9	5·0	1·6	11·0	3·6	17·0	5·5
51	4 57·8	4 58·6	4 44·2	5·1	1·7	11·1	3·6	17·1	5·6
52	4 58·0	4 58·8	4 44·4	5·2	1·7	11·2	3·6	17·2	5·6
53	4 58·3	4 59·1	4 44·7	5·3	1·7	11·3	3·7	17·3	5·6
54	4 58·5	4 59·3	4 44·9	5·4	1·8	11·4	3·7	17·4	5·7
55	4 58·8	4 59·6	4 45·1	5·5	1·8	11·5	3·7	17·5	5·7
56	4 59·0	4 59·8	4 45·4	5·6	1·8	11·6	3·8	17·6	5·7
57	4 59·3	5 00·1	4 45·6	5·7	1·9	11·7	3·8	17·7	5·8
58	4 59·5	5 00·3	4 45·9	5·8	1·9	11·8	3·8	17·8	5·8
59	4 59·8	5 00·6	4 46·1	5·9	1·9	11·9	3·9	17·9	5·8
60	5 00·0	5 00·8	4 46·3	6·0	2·0	12·0	3·9	18·0	5·9

20m	SUN PLANETS	ARIES	MOON	v or d	Corrn	v or d	Corrn	v or d	Corrn
s	° ′	° ′	° ′	′	′	′	′	′	′
00	5 00·0	5 00·8	4 46·3	0·0	0·0	6·0	2·1	12·0	4·1
01	5 00·3	5 01·1	4 46·6	0·1	0·0	6·1	2·1	12·1	4·1
02	5 00·5	5 01·3	4 46·8	0·2	0·1	6·2	2·1	12·2	4·2
03	5 00·8	5 01·6	4 47·0	0·3	0·1	6·3	2·2	12·3	4·2
04	5 01·0	5 01·8	4 47·3	0·4	0·1	6·4	2·2	12·4	4·2
05	5 01·3	5 02·1	4 47·5	0·5	0·2	6·5	2·2	12·5	4·3
06	5 01·5	5 02·3	4 47·8	0·6	0·2	6·6	2·3	12·6	4·3
07	5 01·8	5 02·6	4 48·0	0·7	0·2	6·7	2·3	12·7	4·3
08	5 02·0	5 02·8	4 48·2	0·8	0·3	6·8	2·3	12·8	4·4
09	5 02·3	5 03·1	4 48·5	0·9	0·3	6·9	2·4	12·9	4·4
10	5 02·5	5 03·3	4 48·7	1·0	0·3	7·0	2·4	13·0	4·4
11	5 02·8	5 03·6	4 49·0	1·1	0·4	7·1	2·4	13·1	4·5
12	5 03·0	5 03·8	4 49·2	1·2	0·4	7·2	2·5	13·2	4·5
13	5 03·3	5 04·1	4 49·4	1·3	0·4	7·3	2·5	13·3	4·5
14	5 03·5	5 04·3	4 49·7	1·4	0·5	7·4	2·5	13·4	4·6
15	5 03·8	5 04·6	4 49·9	1·5	0·5	7·5	2·6	13·5	4·6
16	5 04·0	5 04·8	4 50·2	1·6	0·5	7·6	2·6	13·6	4·6
17	5 04·3	5 05·1	4 50·4	1·7	0·6	7·7	2·6	13·7	4·7
18	5 04·5	5 05·3	4 50·6	1·8	0·6	7·8	2·7	13·8	4·7
19	5 04·8	5 05·6	4 50·9	1·9	0·6	7·9	2·7	13·9	4·7
20	5 05·0	5 05·8	4 51·1	2·0	0·7	8·0	2·7	14·0	4·8
21	5 05·3	5 06·1	4 51·3	2·1	0·7	8·1	2·8	14·1	4·8
22	5 05·5	5 06·3	4 51·6	2·2	0·8	8·2	2·8	14·2	4·9
23	5 05·8	5 06·6	4 51·8	2·3	0·8	8·3	2·8	14·3	4·9
24	5 06·0	5 06·8	4 52·1	2·4	0·8	8·4	2·9	14·4	4·9
25	5 06·3	5 07·1	4 52·3	2·5	0·9	8·5	2·9	14·5	5·0
26	5 06·5	5 07·3	4 52·5	2·6	0·9	8·6	2·9	14·6	5·0
27	5 06·8	5 07·6	4 52·8	2·7	0·9	8·7	3·0	14·7	5·0
28	5 07·0	5 07·8	4 53·0	2·8	1·0	8·8	3·0	14·8	5·1
29	5 07·3	5 08·1	4 53·3	2·9	1·0	8·9	3·0	14·9	5·1
30	5 07·5	5 08·3	4 53·5	3·0	1·0	9·0	3·1	15·0	5·1
31	5 07·8	5 08·6	4 53·7	3·1	1·1	9·1	3·1	15·1	5·2
32	5 08·0	5 08·8	4 54·0	3·2	1·1	9·2	3·1	15·2	5·2
33	5 08·3	5 09·1	4 54·2	3·3	1·1	9·3	3·2	15·3	5·2
34	5 08·5	5 09·3	4 54·4	3·4	1·2	9·4	3·2	15·4	5·3
35	5 08·8	5 09·6	4 54·7	3·5	1·2	9·5	3·2	15·5	5·3
36	5 09·0	5 09·8	4 54·9	3·6	1·2	9·6	3·3	15·6	5·3
37	5 09·3	5 10·1	4 55·2	3·7	1·3	9·7	3·3	15·7	5·4
38	5 09·5	5 10·3	4 55·4	3·8	1·3	9·8	3·3	15·8	5·4
39	5 09·8	5 10·6	4 55·6	3·9	1·3	9·9	3·4	15·9	5·4
40	5 10·0	5 10·8	4 55·9	4·0	1·4	10·0	3·4	16·0	5·5
41	5 10·3	5 11·1	4 56·1	4·1	1·4	10·1	3·5	16·1	5·5
42	5 10·5	5 11·4	4 56·4	4·2	1·4	10·2	3·5	16·2	5·5
43	5 10·8	5 11·6	4 56·6	4·3	1·5	10·3	3·5	16·3	5·6
44	5 11·0	5 11·9	4 56·8	4·4	1·5	10·4	3·6	16·4	5·6
45	5 11·3	5 12·1	4 57·1	4·5	1·5	10·5	3·6	16·5	5·6
46	5 11·5	5 12·4	4 57·3	4·6	1·6	10·6	3·6	16·6	5·7
47	5 11·8	5 12·6	4 57·5	4·7	1·6	10·7	3·7	16·7	5·7
48	5 12·0	5 12·9	4 57·8	4·8	1·6	10·8	3·7	16·8	5·7
49	5 12·3	5 13·1	4 58·0	4·9	1·7	10·9	3·7	16·9	5·8
50	5 12·5	5 13·4	4 58·3	5·0	1·7	11·0	3·8	17·0	5·8
51	5 12·8	5 13·6	4 58·5	5·1	1·7	11·1	3·8	17·1	5·8
52	5 13·0	5 13·9	4 58·7	5·2	1·8	11·2	3·8	17·2	5·9
53	5 13·3	5 14·1	4 59·0	5·3	1·8	11·3	3·9	17·3	5·9
54	5 13·5	5 14·4	4 59·2	5·4	1·8	11·4	3·9	17·4	5·9
55	5 13·8	5 14·6	4 59·5	5·5	1·9	11·5	3·9	17·5	6·0
56	5 14·0	5 14·9	4 59·7	5·6	1·9	11·6	4·0	17·6	6·0
57	5 14·3	5 15·1	4 59·9	5·7	1·9	11·7	4·0	17·7	6·0
58	5 14·5	5 15·4	5 00·2	5·8	2·0	11·8	4·0	17·8	6·1
59	5 14·8	5 15·6	5 00·4	5·9	2·0	11·9	4·1	17·9	6·1
60	5 15·0	5 15·9	5 00·7	6·0	2·1	12·0	4·1	18·0	6·2

21m	SUN PLANETS	ARIES	MOON	v or d	Corrn	v or d	Corrn	v or d	Corrn
s	° ′	° ′	° ′	′	′	′	′	′	′
00	5 15·0	5 15·9	5 00·7	0·0	0·0	6·0	2·2	12·0	4·3
01	5 15·3	5 16·1	5 00·9	0·1	0·0	6·1	2·2	12·1	4·3
02	5 15·5	5 16·4	5 01·1	0·2	0·1	6·2	2·2	12·2	4·4
03	5 15·8	5 16·6	5 01·4	0·3	0·1	6·3	2·3	12·3	4·4
04	5 16·0	5 16·9	5 01·6	0·4	0·1	6·4	2·3	12·4	4·4
05	5 16·3	5 17·1	5 01·8	0·5	0·2	6·5	2·3	12·5	4·5
06	5 16·5	5 17·4	5 02·1	0·6	0·2	6·6	2·4	12·6	4·5
07	5 16·8	5 17·6	5 02·3	0·7	0·3	6·7	2·4	12·7	4·6
08	5 17·0	5 17·9	5 02·6	0·8	0·3	6·8	2·4	12·8	4·6
09	5 17·3	5 18·1	5 02·8	0·9	0·3	6·9	2·5	12·9	4·6
10	5 17·5	5 18·4	5 03·0	1·0	0·4	7·0	2·5	13·0	4·7
11	5 17·8	5 18·6	5 03·3	1·1	0·4	7·1	2·5	13·1	4·7
12	5 18·0	5 18·9	5 03·5	1·2	0·4	7·2	2·6	13·2	4·7
13	5 18·3	5 19·1	5 03·8	1·3	0·5	7·3	2·6	13·3	4·8
14	5 18·5	5 19·4	5 04·0	1·4	0·5	7·4	2·7	13·4	4·8
15	5 18·8	5 19·6	5 04·2	1·5	0·5	7·5	2·7	13·5	4·8
16	5 19·0	5 19·9	5 04·5	1·6	0·6	7·6	2·7	13·6	4·9
17	5 19·3	5 20·1	5 04·7	1·7	0·6	7·7	2·8	13·7	4·9
18	5 19·5	5 20·4	5 04·9	1·8	0·6	7·8	2·8	13·8	4·9
19	5 19·8	5 20·6	5 05·2	1·9	0·7	7·9	2·8	13·9	5·0
20	5 20·0	5 20·9	5 05·4	2·0	0·7	8·0	2·9	14·0	5·0
21	5 20·3	5 21·1	5 05·7	2·1	0·8	8·1	2·9	14·1	5·1
22	5 20·5	5 21·4	5 05·9	2·2	0·8	8·2	2·9	14·2	5·1
23	5 20·8	5 21·6	5 06·1	2·3	0·8	8·3	3·0	14·3	5·1
24	5 21·0	5 21·9	5 06·4	2·4	0·9	8·4	3·0	14·4	5·2
25	5 21·3	5 22·1	5 06·6	2·5	0·9	8·5	3·0	14·5	5·2
26	5 21·5	5 22·4	5 06·9	2·6	0·9	8·6	3·1	14·6	5·2
27	5 21·8	5 22·6	5 07·1	2·7	1·0	8·7	3·1	14·7	5·3
28	5 22·0	5 22·9	5 07·3	2·8	1·0	8·8	3·2	14·8	5·3
29	5 22·3	5 23·1	5 07·6	2·9	1·0	8·9	3·2	14·9	5·3
30	5 22·5	5 23·4	5 07·8	3·0	1·1	9·0	3·2	15·0	5·4
31	5 22·8	5 23·6	5 08·0	3·1	1·1	9·1	3·3	15·1	5·4
32	5 23·0	5 23·9	5 08·3	3·2	1·1	9·2	3·3	15·2	5·4
33	5 23·3	5 24·1	5 08·5	3·3	1·2	9·3	3·3	15·3	5·5
34	5 23·5	5 24·4	5 08·8	3·4	1·2	9·4	3·4	15·4	5·5
35	5 23·8	5 24·6	5 09·0	3·5	1·3	9·5	3·4	15·5	5·6
36	5 24·0	5 24·9	5 09·2	3·6	1·3	9·6	3·4	15·6	5·6
37	5 24·3	5 25·1	5 09·5	3·7	1·3	9·7	3·5	15·7	5·6
38	5 24·5	5 25·4	5 09·7	3·8	1·4	9·8	3·5	15·8	5·7
39	5 24·8	5 25·6	5 10·0	3·9	1·4	9·9	3·5	15·9	5·7
40	5 25·0	5 25·9	5 10·2	4·0	1·4	10·0	3·6	16·0	5·7
41	5 25·3	5 26·1	5 10·4	4·1	1·5	10·1	3·6	16·1	5·8
42	5 25·5	5 26·4	5 10·7	4·2	1·5	10·2	3·7	16·2	5·8
43	5 25·8	5 26·6	5 10·9	4·3	1·5	10·3	3·7	16·3	5·8
44	5 26·0	5 26·9	5 11·1	4·4	1·6	10·4	3·7	16·4	5·9
45	5 26·3	5 27·1	5 11·4	4·5	1·6	10·5	3·8	16·5	5·9
46	5 26·5	5 27·4	5 11·6	4·6	1·6	10·6	3·8	16·6	5·9
47	5 26·8	5 27·6	5 11·9	4·7	1·7	10·7	3·8	16·7	6·0
48	5 27·0	5 27·9	5 12·1	4·8	1·7	10·8	3·9	16·8	6·0
49	5 27·3	5 28·1	5 12·3	4·9	1·8	10·9	3·9	16·9	6·1
50	5 27·5	5 28·4	5 12·6	5·0	1·8	11·0	3·9	17·0	6·1
51	5 27·8	5 28·6	5 12·8	5·1	1·8	11·1	4·0	17·1	6·1
52	5 28·0	5 28·9	5 13·1	5·2	1·9	11·2	4·0	17·2	6·2
53	5 28·3	5 29·1	5 13·3	5·3	1·9	11·3	4·0	17·3	6·2
54	5 28·5	5 29·4	5 13·5	5·4	1·9	11·4	4·1	17·4	6·2
55	5 28·8	5 29·7	5 13·8	5·5	2·0	11·5	4·1	17·5	6·3
56	5 29·0	5 29·9	5 14·0	5·6	2·0	11·6	4·2	17·6	6·3
57	5 29·3	5 30·2	5 14·3	5·7	2·0	11·7	4·2	17·7	6·3
58	5 29·5	5 30·4	5 14·5	5·8	2·1	11·8	4·2	17·8	6·4
59	5 29·8	5 30·7	5 14·7	5·9	2·1	11·9	4·3	17·9	6·4
60	5 30·0	5 30·9	5 15·0	6·0	2·2	12·0	4·3	18·0	6·5

22^m s	SUN PLANETS ° ′	ARIES ° ′	MOON ° ′	v or d ′	Corr^n ′	v or d ′	Corr^n ′	v or d ′	Corr^n ′
00	5 30·0	5 30·9	5 15·0	0·0	0·0	6·0	2·3	12·0	4·5
01	5 30·3	5 31·2	5 15·2	0·1	0·0	6·1	2·3	12·1	4·5
02	5 30·5	5 31·4	5 15·4	0·2	0·1	6·2	2·3	12·2	4·6
03	5 30·8	5 31·7	5 15·7	0·3	0·1	6·3	2·4	12·3	4·6
04	5 31·0	5 31·9	5 15·9	0·4	0·2	6·4	2·4	12·4	4·7
05	5 31·3	5 32·2	5 16·2	0·5	0·2	6·5	2·4	12·5	4·7
06	5 31·5	5 32·4	5 16·4	0·6	0·2	6·6	2·5	12·6	4·7
07	5 31·8	5 32·7	5 16·6	0·7	0·3	6·7	2·5	12·7	4·8
08	5 32·0	5 32·9	5 16·9	0·8	0·3	6·8	2·6	12·8	4·8
09	5 32·3	5 33·2	5 17·1	0·9	0·3	6·9	2·6	12·9	4·8
10	5 32·5	5 33·4	5 17·4	1·0	0·4	7·0	2·6	13·0	4·9
11	5 32·8	5 33·7	5 17·6	1·1	0·4	7·1	2·7	13·1	4·9
12	5 33·0	5 33·9	5 17·8	1·2	0·5	7·2	2·7	13·2	5·0
13	5 33·3	5 34·2	5 18·1	1·3	0·5	7·3	2·7	13·3	5·0
14	5 33·5	5 34·4	5 18·3	1·4	0·5	7·4	2·8	13·4	5·0
15	5 33·8	5 34·7	5 18·5	1·5	0·6	7·5	2·8	13·5	5·1
16	5 34·0	5 34·9	5 18·8	1·6	0·6	7·6	2·9	13·6	5·1
17	5 34·3	5 35·2	5 19·0	1·7	0·6	7·7	2·9	13·7	5·1
18	5 34·5	5 35·4	5 19·3	1·8	0·7	7·8	2·9	13·8	5·2
19	5 34·8	5 35·7	5 19·5	1·9	0·7	7·9	3·0	13·9	5·2
20	5 35·0	5 35·9	5 19·7	2·0	0·8	8·0	3·0	14·0	5·3
21	5 35·3	5 36·2	5 20·0	2·1	0·8	8·1	3·0	14·1	5·3
22	5 35·5	5 36·4	5 20·2	2·2	0·8	8·2	3·1	14·2	5·3
23	5 35·8	5 36·7	5 20·5	2·3	0·9	8·3	3·1	14·3	5·4
24	5 36·0	5 36·9	5 20·7	2·4	0·9	8·4	3·2	14·4	5·4
25	5 36·3	5 37·2	5 20·9	2·5	0·9	8·5	3·2	14·5	5·4
26	5 36·5	5 37·4	5 21·2	2·6	1·0	8·6	3·2	14·6	5·5
27	5 36·8	5 37·7	5 21·4	2·7	1·0	8·7	3·3	14·7	5·5
28	5 37·0	5 37·9	5 21·6	2·8	1·0	8·8	3·3	14·8	5·6
29	5 37·3	5 38·2	5 21·9	2·9	1·1	8·9	3·3	14·9	5·6
30	5 37·5	5 38·4	5 22·1	3·0	1·1	9·0	3·4	15·0	5·6
31	5 37·8	5 38·7	5 22·4	3·1	1·2	9·1	3·4	15·1	5·7
32	5 38·0	5 38·9	5 22·6	3·2	1·2	9·2	3·5	15·2	5·7
33	5 38·3	5 39·2	5 22·8	3·3	1·2	9·3	3·5	15·3	5·7
34	5 38·5	5 39·4	5 23·1	3·4	1·3	9·4	3·5	15·4	5·8
35	5 38·8	5 39·7	5 23·3	3·5	1·3	9·5	3·6	15·5	5·8
36	5 39·0	5 39·9	5 23·6	3·6	1·4	9·6	3·6	15·6	5·9
37	5 39·3	5 40·2	5 23·8	3·7	1·4	9·7	3·6	15·7	5·9
38	5 39·5	5 40·4	5 24·0	3·8	1·4	9·8	3·7	15·8	5·9
39	5 39·8	5 40·7	5 24·3	3·9	1·5	9·9	3·7	15·9	6·0
40	5 40·0	5 40·9	5 24·5	4·0	1·5	10·0	3·8	16·0	6·0
41	5 40·3	5 41·2	5 24·7	4·1	1·5	10·1	3·8	16·1	6·0
42	5 40·5	5 41·4	5 25·0	4·2	1·6	10·2	3·8	16·2	6·1
43	5 40·8	5 41·7	5 25·2	4·3	1·6	10·3	3·9	16·3	6·1
44	5 41·0	5 41·9	5 25·5	4·4	1·7	10·4	3·9	16·4	6·1
45	5 41·3	5 42·2	5 25·7	4·5	1·7	10·5	3·9	16·5	6·2
46	5 41·5	5 42·4	5 25·9	4·6	1·7	10·6	4·0	16·6	6·2
47	5 41·8	5 42·7	5 26·2	4·7	1·8	10·7	4·0	16·7	6·3
48	5 42·0	5 42·9	5 26·4	4·8	1·8	10·8	4·1	16·8	6·3
49	5 42·3	5 43·2	5 26·7	4·9	1·8	10·9	4·1	16·9	6·3
50	5 42·5	5 43·4	5 26·9	5·0	1·9	11·0	4·1	17·0	6·4
51	5 42·8	5 43·7	5 27·1	5·1	1·9	11·1	4·2	17·1	6·4
52	5 43·0	5 43·9	5 27·4	5·2	2·0	11·2	4·2	17·2	6·5
53	5 43·3	5 44·2	5 27·6	5·3	2·0	11·3	4·2	17·3	6·5
54	5 43·5	5 44·4	5 27·9	5·4	2·0	11·4	4·3	17·4	6·5
55	5 43·8	5 44·7	5 28·1	5·5	2·1	11·5	4·3	17·5	6·6
56	5 44·0	5 44·9	5 28·3	5·6	2·1	11·6	4·4	17·6	6·6
57	5 44·3	5 45·2	5 28·6	5·7	2·1	11·7	4·4	17·7	6·6
58	5 44·5	5 45·4	5 28·8	5·8	2·2	11·8	4·4	17·8	6·7
59	5 44·8	5 45·7	5 29·0	5·9	2·2	11·9	4·5	17·9	6·7
60	5 45·0	5 45·9	5 29·3	6·0	2·3	12·0	4·5	18·0	6·8

23^m s	SUN PLANETS ° ′	ARIES ° ′	MOON ° ′	v or d ′	Corr^n ′	v or d ′	Corr^n ′	v or d ′	Corr^n ′
00	5 45·0	5 45·9	5 29·3	0·0	0·0	6·0	2·4	12·0	4·7
01	5 45·3	5 46·2	5 29·5	0·1	0·0	6·1	2·4	12·1	4·7
02	5 45·5	5 46·4	5 29·8	0·2	0·1	6·2	2·4	12·2	4·8
03	5 45·8	5 46·7	5 30·0	0·3	0·1	6·3	2·5	12·3	4·8
04	5 46·0	5 46·9	5 30·2	0·4	0·2	6·4	2·5	12·4	4·9
05	5 46·3	5 47·2	5 30·5	0·5	0·2	6·5	2·5	12·5	4·9
06	5 46·5	5 47·4	5 30·7	0·6	0·2	6·6	2·6	12·6	4·9
07	5 46·8	5 47·7	5 31·0	0·7	0·3	6·7	2·6	12·7	5·0
08	5 47·0	5 48·0	5 31·2	0·8	0·3	6·8	2·7	12·8	5·0
09	5 47·3	5 48·2	5 31·4	0·9	0·4	6·9	2·7	12·9	5·1
10	5 47·5	5 48·5	5 31·7	1·0	0·4	7·0	2·7	13·0	5·1
11	5 47·8	5 48·7	5 31·9	1·1	0·4	7·1	2·8	13·1	5·1
12	5 48·0	5 49·0	5 32·1	1·2	0·5	7·2	2·8	13·2	5·2
13	5 48·3	5 49·2	5 32·4	1·3	0·5	7·3	2·9	13·3	5·2
14	5 48·5	5 49·5	5 32·6	1·4	0·5	7·4	2·9	13·4	5·2
15	5 48·8	5 49·7	5 32·9	1·5	0·6	7·5	2·9	13·5	5·3
16	5 49·0	5 50·0	5 33·1	1·6	0·6	7·6	3·0	13·6	5·3
17	5 49·3	5 50·2	5 33·3	1·7	0·7	7·7	3·0	13·7	5·4
18	5 49·5	5 50·5	5 33·6	1·8	0·7	7·8	3·1	13·8	5·4
19	5 49·8	5 50·7	5 33·8	1·9	0·7	7·9	3·1	13·9	5·4
20	5 50·0	5 51·0	5 34·1	2·0	0·8	8·0	3·1	14·0	5·5
21	5 50·3	5 51·2	5 34·3	2·1	0·8	8·1	3·2	14·1	5·5
22	5 50·5	5 51·5	5 34·5	2·2	0·9	8·2	3·2	14·2	5·6
23	5 50·8	5 51·7	5 34·8	2·3	0·9	8·3	3·3	14·3	5·6
24	5 51·0	5 52·0	5 35·0	2·4	0·9	8·4	3·3	14·4	5·6
25	5 51·3	5 52·2	5 35·2	2·5	1·0	8·5	3·3	14·5	5·7
26	5 51·5	5 52·5	5 35·5	2·6	1·0	8·6	3·4	14·6	5·7
27	5 51·8	5 52·7	5 35·7	2·7	1·1	8·7	3·4	14·7	5·8
28	5 52·0	5 53·0	5 36·0	2·8	1·1	8·8	3·4	14·8	5·8
29	5 52·3	5 53·2	5 36·2	2·9	1·1	8·9	3·5	14·9	5·8
30	5 52·5	5 53·5	5 36·4	3·0	1·2	9·0	3·5	15·0	5·9
31	5 52·8	5 53·7	5 36·7	3·1	1·2	9·1	3·6	15·1	5·9
32	5 53·0	5 54·0	5 36·9	3·2	1·3	9·2	3·6	15·2	6·0
33	5 53·3	5 54·2	5 37·2	3·3	1·3	9·3	3·6	15·3	6·0
34	5 53·5	5 54·5	5 37·4	3·4	1·3	9·4	3·7	15·4	6·0
35	5 53·8	5 54·7	5 37·6	3·5	1·4	9·5	3·7	15·5	6·1
36	5 54·0	5 55·0	5 37·9	3·6	1·4	9·6	3·8	15·6	6·1
37	5 54·3	5 55·2	5 38·1	3·7	1·4	9·7	3·8	15·7	6·1
38	5 54·5	5 55·5	5 38·4	3·8	1·5	9·8	3·8	15·8	6·2
39	5 54·8	5 55·7	5 38·6	3·9	1·5	9·9	3·9	15·9	6·2
40	5 55·0	5 56·0	5 38·8	4·0	1·6	10·0	3·9	16·0	6·3
41	5 55·3	5 56·2	5 39·1	4·1	1·6	10·1	4·0	16·1	6·3
42	5 55·5	5 56·5	5 39·3	4·2	1·6	10·2	4·0	16·2	6·3
43	5 55·8	5 56·7	5 39·5	4·3	1·7	10·3	4·0	16·3	6·4
44	5 56·0	5 57·0	5 39·8	4·4	1·7	10·4	4·1	16·4	6·4
45	5 56·3	5 57·2	5 40·0	4·5	1·8	10·5	4·1	16·5	6·5
46	5 56·5	5 57·5	5 40·3	4·6	1·8	10·6	4·2	16·6	6·5
47	5 56·8	5 57·7	5 40·5	4·7	1·8	10·7	4·2	16·7	6·5
48	5 57·0	5 58·0	5 40·7	4·8	1·9	10·8	4·2	16·8	6·6
49	5 57·3	5 58·2	5 41·0	4·9	1·9	10·9	4·3	16·9	6·6
50	5 57·5	5 58·5	5 41·2	5·0	2·0	11·0	4·3	17·0	6·7
51	5 57·8	5 58·7	5 41·5	5·1	2·0	11·1	4·3	17·1	6·7
52	5 58·0	5 59·0	5 41·7	5·2	2·0	11·2	4·4	17·2	6·7
53	5 58·3	5 59·2	5 41·9	5·3	2·1	11·3	4·4	17·3	6·8
54	5 58·5	5 59·5	5 42·2	5·4	2·1	11·4	4·5	17·4	6·8
55	5 58·8	5 59·7	5 42·4	5·5	2·2	11·5	4·5	17·5	6·9
56	5 59·0	6 00·0	5 42·6	5·6	2·2	11·6	4·5	17·6	6·9
57	5 59·3	6 00·2	5 42·9	5·7	2·2	11·7	4·6	17·7	6·9
58	5 59·5	6 00·5	5 43·1	5·8	2·3	11·8	4·6	17·8	7·0
59	5 59·8	6 00·7	5 43·4	5·9	2·3	11·9	4·7	17·9	7·0
60	6 00·0	6 01·0	5 43·6	6·0	2·4	12·0	4·7	18·0	7·1

^{m} 24	SUN PLANETS	ARIES	MOON	v or d	Corr^{n}	v or d	Corr^{n}	v or d	Corr^{n}
s	° ′	° ′	° ′	′	′	′	′	′	′
00	6 00·0	6 01·0	5 43·6	0·0	0·0	6·0	2·5	12·0	4·9
01	6 00·3	6 01·2	5 43·8	0·1	0·0	6·1	2·5	12·1	4·9
02	6 00·5	6 01·5	5 44·1	0·2	0·1	6·2	2·5	12·2	5·0
03	6 00·8	6 01·7	5 44·3	0·3	0·1	6·3	2·6	12·3	5·0
04	6 01·0	6 02·0	5 44·6	0·4	0·2	6·4	2·6	12·4	5·1
05	6 01·3	6 02·2	5 44·8	0·5	0·2	6·5	2·7	12·5	5·1
06	6 01·5	6 02·5	5 45·0	0·6	0·2	6·6	2·7	12·6	5·1
07	6 01·8	6 02·7	5 45·3	0·7	0·3	6·7	2·7	12·7	5·2
08	6 02·0	6 03·0	5 45·5	0·8	0·3	6·8	2·8	12·8	5·2
09	6 02·3	6 03·2	5 45·7	0·9	0·4	6·9	2·8	12·9	5·3
10	6 02·5	6 03·5	5 46·0	1·0	0·4	7·0	2·9	13·0	5·3
11	6 02·8	6 03·7	5 46·2	1·1	0·4	7·1	2·9	13·1	5·3
12	6 03·0	6 04·0	5 46·5	1·2	0·5	7·2	2·9	13·2	5·4
13	6 03·3	6 04·2	5 46·7	1·3	0·5	7·3	3·0	13·3	5·4
14	6 03·5	6 04·5	5 46·9	1·4	0·6	7·4	3·0	13·4	5·5
15	6 03·8	6 04·7	5 47·2	1·5	0·6	7·5	3·1	13·5	5·5
16	6 04·0	6 05·0	5 47·4	1·6	0·7	7·6	3·1	13·6	5·6
17	6 04·3	6 05·2	5 47·7	1·7	0·7	7·7	3·1	13·7	5·6
18	6 04·5	6 05·5	5 47·9	1·8	0·7	7·8	3·2	13·8	5·6
19	6 04·8	6 05·7	5 48·1	1·9	0·8	7·9	3·2	13·9	5·7
20	6 05·0	6 06·0	5 48·4	2·0	0·8	8·0	3·3	14·0	5·7
21	6 05·3	6 06·3	5 48·6	2·1	0·9	8·1	3·3	14·1	5·8
22	6 05·5	6 06·5	5 48·8	2·2	0·9	8·2	3·3	14·2	5·8
23	6 05·8	6 06·8	5 49·1	2·3	0·9	8·3	3·4	14·3	5·8
24	6 06·0	6 07·0	5 49·3	2·4	1·0	8·4	3·4	14·4	5·9
25	6 06·3	6 07·3	5 49·6	2·5	1·0	8·5	3·5	14·5	5·9
26	6 06·5	6 07·5	5 49·8	2·6	1·1	8·6	3·5	14·6	6·0
27	6 06·8	6 07·8	5 50·0	2·7	1·1	8·7	3·6	14·7	6·0
28	6 07·0	6 08·0	5 50·3	2·8	1·1	8·8	3·6	14·8	6·0
29	6 07·3	6 08·3	5 50·5	2·9	1·2	8·9	3·6	14·9	6·1
30	6 07·5	6 08·5	5 50·8	3·0	1·2	9·0	3·7	15·0	6·1
31	6 07·8	6 08·8	5 51·0	3·1	1·3	9·1	3·7	15·1	6·2
32	6 08·0	6 09·0	5 51·2	3·2	1·3	9·2	3·8	15·2	6·2
33	6 08·3	6 09·3	5 51·5	3·3	1·3	9·3	3·8	15·3	6·2
34	6 08·5	6 09·5	5 51·7	3·4	1·4	9·4	3·8	15·4	6·3
35	6 08·8	6 09·8	5 52·0	3·5	1·4	9·5	3·9	15·5	6·3
36	6 09·0	6 10·0	5 52·2	3·6	1·5	9·6	3·9	15·6	6·4
37	6 09·3	6 10·3	5 52·4	3·7	1·5	9·7	4·0	15·7	6·4
38	6 09·5	6 10·5	5 52·7	3·8	1·6	9·8	4·0	15·8	6·5
39	6 09·8	6 10·8	5 52·9	3·9	1·6	9·9	4·0	15·9	6·5
40	6 10·0	6 11·0	5 53·1	4·0	1·6	10·0	4·1	16·0	6·5
41	6 10·3	6 11·3	5 53·4	4·1	1·7	10·1	4·1	16·1	6·6
42	6 10·5	6 11·5	5 53·6	4·2	1·7	10·2	4·2	16·2	6·6
43	6 10·8	6 11·8	5 53·9	4·3	1·8	10·3	4·2	16·3	6·7
44	6 11·0	6 12·0	5 54·1	4·4	1·8	10·4	4·2	16·4	6·7
45	6 11·3	6 12·3	5 54·3	4·5	1·8	10·5	4·3	16·5	6·7
46	6 11·5	6 12·5	5 54·6	4·6	1·9	10·6	4·3	16·6	6·8
47	6 11·8	6 12·8	5 54·8	4·7	1·9	10·7	4·4	16·7	6·8
48	6 12·0	6 13·0	5 55·1	4·8	2·0	10·8	4·4	16·8	6·9
49	6 12·3	6 13·3	5 55·3	4·9	2·0	10·9	4·5	16·9	6·9
50	6 12·5	6 13·5	5 55·5	5·0	2·0	11·0	4·5	17·0	6·9
51	6 12·8	6 13·8	5 55·8	5·1	2·1	11·1	4·5	17·1	7·0
52	6 13·0	6 14·0	5 56·0	5·2	2·1	11·2	4·6	17·2	7·0
53	6 13·3	6 14·3	5 56·2	5·3	2·2	11·3	4·6	17·3	7·1
54	6 13·5	6 14·5	5 56·5	5·4	2·2	11·4	4·7	17·4	7·1
55	6 13·8	6 14·8	5 56·7	5·5	2·2	11·5	4·7	17·5	7·1
56	6 14·0	6 15·0	5 57·0	5·6	2·3	11·6	4·7	17·6	7·2
57	6 14·3	6 15·3	5 57·2	5·7	2·3	11·7	4·8	17·7	7·2
58	6 14·5	6 15·5	5 57·4	5·8	2·4	11·8	4·8	17·8	7·3
59	6 14·8	6 15·8	5 57·7	5·9	2·4	11·9	4·9	17·9	7·3
60	6 15·0	6 16·0	5 57·9	6·0	2·5	12·0	4·9	18·0	7·4

^{m} 25	SUN PLANETS	ARIES	MOON	v or d	Corr^{n}	v or d	Corr^{n}	v or d	Corr^{n}
s	° ′	° ′	° ′	′	′	′	′	′	′
00	6 15·0	6 16·0	5 57·9	0·0	0·0	6·0	2·6	12·0	5·1
01	6 15·3	6 16·3	5 58·2	0·1	0·0	6·1	2·6	12·1	5·1
02	6 15·5	6 16·5	5 58·4	0·2	0·1	6·2	2·6	12·2	5·2
03	6 15·8	6 16·8	5 58·6	0·3	0·1	6·3	2·7	12·3	5·2
04	6 16·0	6 17·0	5 58·9	0·4	0·2	6·4	2·7	12·4	5·3
05	6 16·3	6 17·3	5 59·1	0·5	0·2	6·5	2·8	12·5	5·3
06	6 16·5	6 17·5	5 59·3	0·6	0·3	6·6	2·8	12·6	5·4
07	6 16·8	6 17·8	5 59·6	0·7	0·3	6·7	2·8	12·7	5·4
08	6 17·0	6 18·0	5 59·8	0·8	0·3	6·8	2·9	12·8	5·4
09	6 17·3	6 18·3	6 00·1	0·9	0·4	6·9	2·9	12·9	5·5
10	6 17·5	6 18·5	6 00·3	1·0	0·4	7·0	3·0	13·0	5·5
11	6 17·8	6 18·8	6 00·5	1·1	0·5	7·1	3·0	13·1	5·6
12	6 18·0	6 19·0	6 00·8	1·2	0·5	7·2	3·1	13·2	5·6
13	6 18·3	6 19·3	6 01·0	1·3	0·6	7·3	3·1	13·3	5·7
14	6 18·5	6 19·5	6 01·3	1·4	0·6	7·4	3·1	13·4	5·7
15	6 18·8	6 19·8	6 01·5	1·5	0·6	7·5	3·2	13·5	5·7
16	6 19·0	6 20·0	6 01·7	1·6	0·7	7·6	3·2	13·6	5·8
17	6 19·3	6 20·3	6 02·0	1·7	0·7	7·7	3·3	13·7	5·8
18	6 19·5	6 20·5	6 02·2	1·8	0·8	7·8	3·3	13·8	5·9
19	6 19·8	6 20·8	6 02·5	1·9	0·8	7·9	3·4	13·9	5·9
20	6 20·0	6 21·0	6 02·7	2·0	0·9	8·0	3·4	14·0	6·0
21	6 20·3	6 21·3	6 02·9	2·1	0·9	8·1	3·4	14·1	6·0
22	6 20·5	6 21·5	6 03·2	2·2	0·9	8·2	3·5	14·2	6·0
23	6 20·8	6 21·8	6 03·4	2·3	1·0	8·3	3·5	14·3	6·1
24	6 21·0	6 22·0	6 03·6	2·4	1·0	8·4	3·6	14·4	6·1
25	6 21·3	6 22·3	6 03·9	2·5	1·1	8·5	3·6	14·5	6·2
26	6 21·5	6 22·5	6 04·1	2·6	1·1	8·6	3·7	14·6	6·2
27	6 21·8	6 22·8	6 04·4	2·7	1·1	8·7	3·7	14·7	6·2
28	6 22·0	6 23·0	6 04·6	2·8	1·2	8·8	3·7	14·8	6·3
29	6 22·3	6 23·3	6 04·8	2·9	1·2	8·9	3·8	14·9	6·3
30	6 22·5	6 23·5	6 05·1	3·0	1·3	9·0	3·8	15·0	6·4
31	6 22·8	6 23·8	6 05·3	3·1	1·3	9·1	3·9	15·1	6·4
32	6 23·0	6 24·0	6 05·6	3·2	1·4	9·2	3·9	15·2	6·5
33	6 23·3	6 24·3	6 05·8	3·3	1·4	9·3	4·0	15·3	6·5
34	6 23·5	6 24·5	6 06·0	3·4	1·4	9·4	4·0	15·4	6·5
35	6 23·8	6 24·8	6 06·3	3·5	1·5	9·5	4·0	15·5	6·6
36	6 24·0	6 25·1	6 06·5	3·6	1·5	9·6	4·1	15·6	6·6
37	6 24·3	6 25·3	6 06·7	3·7	1·6	9·7	4·1	15·7	6·7
38	6 24·5	6 25·6	6 07·0	3·8	1·6	9·8	4·2	15·8	6·7
39	6 24·8	6 25·8	6 07·2	3·9	1·7	9·9	4·2	15·9	6·8
40	6 25·0	6 26·1	6 07·5	4·0	1·7	10·0	4·3	16·0	6·8
41	6 25·3	6 26·3	6 07·7	4·1	1·7	10·1	4·3	16·1	6·8
42	6 25·5	6 26·6	6 07·9	4·2	1·8	10·2	4·3	16·2	6·9
43	6 25·8	6 26·8	6 08·2	4·3	1·8	10·3	4·4	16·3	6·9
44	6 26·0	6 27·1	6 08·4	4·4	1·9	10·4	4·4	16·4	7·0
45	6 26·3	6 27·3	6 08·7	4·5	1·9	10·5	4·5	16·5	7·0
46	6 26·5	6 27·6	6 08·9	4·6	2·0	10·6	4·5	16·6	7·1
47	6 26·8	6 27·8	6 09·1	4·7	2·0	10·7	4·5	16·7	7·1
48	6 27·0	6 28·1	6 09·4	4·8	2·0	10·8	4·6	16·8	7·1
49	6 27·3	6 28·3	6 09·6	4·9	2·1	10·9	4·6	16·9	7·2
50	6 27·5	6 28·6	6 09·8	5·0	2·1	11·0	4·7	17·0	7·2
51	6 27·8	6 28·8	6 10·1	5·1	2·2	11·1	4·7	17·1	7·3
52	6 28·0	6 29·1	6 10·3	5·2	2·2	11·2	4·8	17·2	7·3
53	6 28·3	6 29·3	6 10·6	5·3	2·3	11·3	4·8	17·3	7·4
54	6 28·5	6 29·6	6 10·8	5·4	2·3	11·4	4·8	17·4	7·4
55	6 28·8	6 29·8	6 11·0	5·5	2·3	11·5	4·9	17·5	7·4
56	6 29·0	6 30·1	6 11·3	5·6	2·4	11·6	4·9	17·6	7·5
57	6 29·3	6 30·3	6 11·5	5·7	2·4	11·7	5·0	17·7	7·5
58	6 29·5	6 30·6	6 11·8	5·8	2·5	11·8	5·0	17·8	7·6
59	6 29·8	6 30·8	6 12·0	5·9	2·5	11·9	5·1	17·9	7·6
60	6 30·0	6 31·1	6 12·2	6·0	2·6	12·0	5·1	18·0	7·7

m 26	SUN PLANETS	ARIES	MOON	v or d	Corrn	v or d	Corrn	v or d	Corrn
s	° ′	° ′	° ′	′	′	′	′	′	′
00	6 30·0	6 31·1	6 12·2	0·0	0·0	6·0	2·7	12·0	5·3
01	6 30·3	6 31·3	6 12·5	0·1	0·0	6·1	2·7	12·1	5·3
02	6 30·5	6 31·6	6 12·7	0·2	0·1	6·2	2·7	12·2	5·4
03	6 30·8	6 31·8	6 12·9	0·3	0·1	6·3	2·8	12·3	5·4
04	6 31·0	6 32·1	6 13·2	0·4	0·2	6·4	2·8	12·4	5·5
05	6 31·3	6 32·3	6 13·4	0·5	0·2	6·5	2·9	12·5	5·5
06	6 31·5	6 32·6	6 13·7	0·6	0·3	6·6	2·9	12·6	5·6
07	6 31·8	6 32·8	6 13·9	0·7	0·3	6·7	3·0	12·7	5·6
08	6 32·0	6 33·1	6 14·1	0·8	0·4	6·8	3·0	12·8	5·7
09	6 32·3	6 33·3	6 14·4	0·9	0·4	6·9	3·0	12·9	5·7
10	6 32·5	6 33·6	6 14·6	1·0	0·4	7·0	3·1	13·0	5·7
11	6 32·8	6 33·8	6 14·9	1·1	0·5	7·1	3·1	13·1	5·8
12	6 33·0	6 34·1	6 15·1	1·2	0·5	7·2	3·2	13·2	5·8
13	6 33·3	6 34·3	6 15·3	1·3	0·6	7·3	3·2	13·3	5·9
14	6 33·5	6 34·6	6 15·6	1·4	0·6	7·4	3·3	13·4	5·9
15	6 33·8	6 34·8	6 15·8	1·5	0·7	7·5	3·3	13·5	6·0
16	6 34·0	6 35·1	6 16·1	1·6	0·7	7·6	3·4	13·6	6·0
17	6 34·3	6 35·3	6 16·3	1·7	0·8	7·7	3·4	13·7	6·1
18	6 34·5	6 35·6	6 16·5	1·8	0·8	7·8	3·4	13·8	6·1
19	6 34·8	6 35·8	6 16·8	1·9	0·8	7·9	3·5	13·9	6·1
20	6 35·0	6 36·1	6 17·0	2·0	0·9	8·0	3·5	14·0	6·2
21	6 35·3	6 36·3	6 17·2	2·1	0·9	8·1	3·6	14·1	6·2
22	6 35·5	6 36·6	6 17·5	2·2	1·0	8·2	3·6	14·2	6·3
23	6 35·8	6 36·8	6 17·7	2·3	1·0	8·3	3·7	14·3	6·3
24	6 36·0	6 37·1	6 18·0	2·4	1·1	8·4	3·7	14·4	6·4
25	6 36·3	6 37·3	6 18·2	2·5	1·1	8·5	3·8	14·5	6·4
26	6 36·5	6 37·6	6 18·4	2·6	1·1	8·6	3·8	14·6	6·4
27	6 36·8	6 37·8	6 18·7	2·7	1·2	8·7	3·8	14·7	6·5
28	6 37·0	6 38·1	6 18·9	2·8	1·2	8·8	3·9	14·8	6·5
29	6 37·3	6 38·3	6 19·2	2·9	1·3	8·9	3·9	14·9	6·6
30	6 37·5	6 38·6	6 19·4	3·0	1·3	9·0	4·0	15·0	6·6
31	6 37·8	6 38·8	6 19·6	3·1	1·4	9·1	4·0	15·1	6·7
32	6 38·0	6 39·1	6 19·9	3·2	1·4	9·2	4·1	15·2	6·7
33	6 38·3	6 39·3	6 20·1	3·3	1·5	9·3	4·1	15·3	6·8
34	6 38·5	6 39·6	6 20·3	3·4	1·5	9·4	4·2	15·4	6·8
35	6 38·8	6 39·8	6 20·6	3·5	1·5	9·5	4·2	15·5	6·8
36	6 39·0	6 40·1	6 20·8	3·6	1·6	9·6	4·2	15·6	6·9
37	6 39·3	6 40·3	6 21·1	3·7	1·6	9·7	4·3	15·7	6·9
38	6 39·5	6 40·6	6 21·3	3·8	1·7	9·8	4·3	15·8	7·0
39	6 39·8	6 40·8	6 21·5	3·9	1·7	9·9	4·4	15·9	7·0
40	6 40·0	6 41·1	6 21·8	4·0	1·8	10·0	4·4	16·0	7·1
41	6 40·3	6 41·3	6 22·0	4·1	1·8	10·1	4·5	16·1	7·1
42	6 40·5	6 41·6	6 22·3	4·2	1·9	10·2	4·5	16·2	7·2
43	6 40·8	6 41·8	6 22·5	4·3	1·9	10·3	4·5	16·3	7·2
44	6 41·0	6 42·1	6 22·7	4·4	1·9	10·4	4·6	16·4	7·2
45	6 41·3	6 42·3	6 23·0	4·5	2·0	10·5	4·6	16·5	7·3
46	6 41·5	6 42·6	6 23·2	4·6	2·0	10·6	4·7	16·6	7·3
47	6 41·8	6 42·8	6 23·4	4·7	2·1	10·7	4·7	16·7	7·4
48	6 42·0	6 43·1	6 23·7	4·8	2·1	10·8	4·8	16·8	7·4
49	6 42·3	6 43·4	6 23·9	4·9	2·2	10·9	4·8	16·9	7·5
50	6 42·5	6 43·6	6 24·2	5·0	2·2	11·0	4·9	17·0	7·5
51	6 42·8	6 43·9	6 24·4	5·1	2·3	11·1	4·9	17·1	7·6
52	6 43·0	6 44·1	6 24·6	5·2	2·3	11·2	4·9	17·2	7·6
53	6 43·3	6 44·4	6 24·9	5·3	2·3	11·3	5·0	17·3	7·6
54	6 43·5	6 44·6	6 25·1	5·4	2·4	11·4	5·0	17·4	7·7
55	6 43·8	6 44·9	6 25·4	5·5	2·4	11·5	5·1	17·5	7·7
56	6 44·0	6 45·1	6 25·6	5·6	2·5	11·6	5·1	17·6	7·8
57	6 44·3	6 45·4	6 25·8	5·7	2·5	11·7	5·2	17·7	7·8
58	6 44·5	6 45·6	6 26·1	5·8	2·6	11·8	5·2	17·8	7·9
59	6 44·8	6 45·9	6 26·3	5·9	2·6	11·9	5·3	17·9	7·9
60	6 45·0	6 46·1	6 26·6	6·0	2·7	12·0	5·3	18·0	8·0

m 27	SUN PLANETS	ARIES	MOON	v or d	Corrn	v or d	Corrn	v or d	Corrn
s	° ′	° ′	° ′	′	′	′	′	′	′
00	6 45·0	6 46·1	6 26·6	0·0	0·0	6·0	2·8	12·0	5·5
01	6 45·3	6 46·4	6 26·8	0·1	0·0	6·1	2·8	12·1	5·5
02	6 45·5	6 46·6	6 27·0	0·2	0·1	6·2	2·8	12·2	5·6
03	6 45·8	6 46·9	6 27·3	0·3	0·1	6·3	2·9	12·3	5·6
04	6 46·0	6 47·1	6 27·5	0·4	0·2	6·4	2·9	12·4	5·7
05	6 46·3	6 47·4	6 27·7	0·5	0·2	6·5	3·0	12·5	5·7
06	6 46·5	6 47·6	6 28·0	0·6	0·3	6·6	3·0	12·6	5·8
07	6 46·8	6 47·9	6 28·2	0·7	0·3	6·7	3·1	12·7	5·8
08	6 47·0	6 48·1	6 28·5	0·8	0·4	6·8	3·1	12·8	5·9
09	6 47·3	6 48·4	6 28·7	0·9	0·4	6·9	3·2	12·9	5·9
10	6 47·5	6 48·6	6 28·9	1·0	0·5	7·0	3·2	13·0	6·0
11	6 47·8	6 48·9	6 29·2	1·1	0·5	7·1	3·3	13·1	6·0
12	6 48·0	6 49·1	6 29·4	1·2	0·6	7·2	3·3	13·2	6·1
13	6 48·3	6 49·4	6 29·7	1·3	0·6	7·3	3·3	13·3	6·1
14	6 48·5	6 49·6	6 29·9	1·4	0·6	7·4	3·4	13·4	6·1
15	6 48·8	6 49·9	6 30·1	1·5	0·7	7·5	3·4	13·5	6·2
16	6 49·0	6 50·1	6 30·4	1·6	0·7	7·6	3·5	13·6	6·2
17	6 49·3	6 50·4	6 30·6	1·7	0·8	7·7	3·5	13·7	6·3
18	6 49·5	6 50·6	6 30·8	1·8	0·8	7·8	3·6	13·8	6·3
19	6 49·8	6 50·9	6 31·1	1·9	0·9	7·9	3·6	13·9	6·4
20	6 50·0	6 51·1	6 31·3	2·0	0·9	8·0	3·7	14·0	6·4
21	6 50·3	6 51·4	6 31·6	2·1	1·0	8·1	3·7	14·1	6·5
22	6 50·5	6 51·6	6 31·8	2·2	1·0	8·2	3·8	14·2	6·5
23	6 50·8	6 51·9	6 32·0	2·3	1·1	8·3	3·8	14·3	6·6
24	6 51·0	6 52·1	6 32·3	2·4	1·1	8·4	3·9	14·4	6·6
25	6 51·3	6 52·4	6 32·5	2·5	1·1	8·5	3·9	14·5	6·6
26	6 51·5	6 52·6	6 32·8	2·6	1·2	8·6	3·9	14·6	6·7
27	6 51·8	6 52·9	6 33·0	2·7	1·2	8·7	4·0	14·7	6·7
28	6 52·0	6 53·1	6 33·2	2·8	1·3	8·8	4·0	14·8	6·8
29	6 52·3	6 53·4	6 33·5	2·9	1·3	8·9	4·1	14·9	6·8
30	6 52·5	6 53·6	6 33·7	3·0	1·4	9·0	4·1	15·0	6·9
31	6 52·8	6 53·9	6 33·9	3·1	1·4	9·1	4·2	15·1	6·9
32	6 53·0	6 54·1	6 34·2	3·2	1·5	9·2	4·2	15·2	7·0
33	6 53·3	6 54·4	6 34·4	3·3	1·5	9·3	4·3	15·3	7·0
34	6 53·5	6 54·6	6 34·7	3·4	1·6	9·4	4·3	15·4	7·1
35	6 53·8	6 54·9	6 34·9	3·5	1·6	9·5	4·4	15·5	7·1
36	6 54·0	6 55·1	6 35·1	3·6	1·7	9·6	4·4	15·6	7·2
37	6 54·3	6 55·4	6 35·4	3·7	1·7	9·7	4·4	15·7	7·2
38	6 54·5	6 55·6	6 35·6	3·8	1·7	9·8	4·5	15·8	7·2
39	6 54·8	6 55·9	6 35·9	3·9	1·8	9·9	4·5	15·9	7·3
40	6 55·0	6 56·1	6 36·1	4·0	1·8	10·0	4·6	16·0	7·3
41	6 55·3	6 56·4	6 36·3	4·1	1·9	10·1	4·6	16·1	7·4
42	6 55·5	6 56·6	6 36·6	4·2	1·9	10·2	4·7	16·2	7·4
43	6 55·8	6 56·9	6 36·8	4·3	2·0	10·3	4·7	16·3	7·5
44	6 56·0	6 57·1	6 37·0	4·4	2·0	10·4	4·8	16·4	7·5
45	6 56·3	6 57·4	6 37·3	4·5	2·1	10·5	4·8	16·5	7·6
46	6 56·5	6 57·6	6 37·5	4·6	2·1	10·6	4·9	16·6	7·6
47	6 56·8	6 57·9	6 37·8	4·7	2·2	10·7	4·9	16·7	7·7
48	6 57·0	6 58·1	6 38·0	4·8	2·2	10·8	5·0	16·8	7·7
49	6 57·3	6 58·4	6 38·2	4·9	2·2	10·9	5·0	16·9	7·7
50	6 57·5	6 58·6	6 38·5	5·0	2·3	11·0	5·0	17·0	7·8
51	6 57·8	6 58·9	6 38·7	5·1	2·3	11·1	5·1	17·1	7·8
52	6 58·0	6 59·1	6 39·0	5·2	2·4	11·2	5·1	17·2	7·9
53	6 58·3	6 59·4	6 39·2	5·3	2·4	11·3	5·2	17·3	7·9
54	6 58·5	6 59·6	6 39·4	5·4	2·5	11·4	5·2	17·4	8·0
55	6 58·8	6 59·9	6 39·7	5·5	2·5	11·5	5·3	17·5	8·0
56	6 59·0	7 00·1	6 39·9	5·6	2·6	11·6	5·3	17·6	8·1
57	6 59·3	7 00·4	6 40·2	5·7	2·6	11·7	5·4	17·7	8·1
58	6 59·5	7 00·6	6 40·4	5·8	2·7	11·8	5·4	17·8	8·2
59	6 59·8	7 00·9	6 40·6	5·9	2·7	11·9	5·5	17·9	8·2
60	7 00·0	7 01·1	6 40·9	6·0	2·8	12·0	5·5	18·0	8·3

28^{m}	SUN PLANETS	ARIES	MOON	v or d	Corr^{n}	v or d	Corr^{n}	v or d	Corr^{n}
s	° ′	° ′	° ′	′	′	′	′	′	′
00	7 00·0	7 01·1	6 40·9	0·0	0·0	6·0	2·9	12·0	5·7
01	7 00·3	7 01·4	6 41·1	0·1	0·0	6·1	2·9	12·1	5·7
02	7 00·5	7 01·7	6 41·3	0·2	0·1	6·2	2·9	12·2	5·8
03	7 00·8	7 01·9	6 41·6	0·3	0·1	6·3	3·0	12·3	5·8
04	7 01·0	7 02·2	6 41·8	0·4	0·2	6·4	3·0	12·4	5·9
05	7 01·3	7 02·4	6 42·1	0·5	0·2	6·5	3·1	12·5	5·9
06	7 01·5	7 02·7	6 42·3	0·6	0·3	6·6	3·1	12·6	6·0
07	7 01·8	7 02·9	6 42·5	0·7	0·3	6·7	3·2	12·7	6·0
08	7 02·0	7 03·2	6 42·8	0·8	0·4	6·8	3·2	12·8	6·1
09	7 02·3	7 03·4	6 43·0	0·9	0·4	6·9	3·3	12·9	6·1
10	7 02·5	7 03·7	6 43·3	1·0	0·5	7·0	3·3	13·0	6·2
11	7 02·8	7 03·9	6 43·5	1·1	0·5	7·1	3·4	13·1	6·2
12	7 03·0	7 04·2	6 43·7	1·2	0·6	7·2	3·4	13·2	6·3
13	7 03·3	7 04·4	6 44·0	1·3	0·6	7·3	3·5	13·3	6·3
14	7 03·5	7 04·7	6 44·2	1·4	0·7	7·4	3·5	13·4	6·4
15	7 03·8	7 04·9	6 44·4	1·5	0·7	7·5	3·6	13·5	6·4
16	7 04·0	7 05·2	6 44·7	1·6	0·8	7·6	3·6	13·6	6·5
17	7 04·3	7 05·4	6 44·9	1·7	0·8	7·7	3·7	13·7	6·5
18	7 04·5	7 05·7	6 45·2	1·8	0·9	7·8	3·7	13·8	6·6
19	7 04·8	7 05·9	6 45·4	1·9	0·9	7·9	3·8	13·9	6·6
20	7 05·0	7 06·2	6 45·6	2·0	1·0	8·0	3·8	14·0	6·7
21	7 05·3	7 06·4	6 45·9	2·1	1·0	8·1	3·8	14·1	6·7
22	7 05·5	7 06·7	6 46·1	2·2	1·0	8·2	3·9	14·2	6·7
23	7 05·8	7 06·9	6 46·4	2·3	1·1	8·3	3·9	14·3	6·8
24	7 06·0	7 07·2	6 46·6	2·4	1·1	8·4	4·0	14·4	6·8
25	7 06·3	7 07·4	6 46·8	2·5	1·2	8·5	4·0	14·5	6·9
26	7 06·5	7 07·7	6 47·1	2·6	1·2	8·6	4·1	14·6	6·9
27	7 06·8	7 07·9	6 47·3	2·7	1·3	8·7	4·1	14·7	7·0
28	7 07·0	7 08·2	6 47·5	2·8	1·3	8·8	4·2	14·8	7·0
29	7 07·3	7 08·4	6 47·8	2·9	1·4	8·9	4·2	14·9	7·1
30	7 07·5	7 08·7	6 48·0	3·0	1·4	9·0	4·3	15·0	7·1
31	7 07·8	7 08·9	6 48·3	3·1	1·5	9·1	4·3	15·1	7·2
32	7 08·0	7 09·2	6 48·5	3·2	1·5	9·2	4·4	15·2	7·2
33	7 08·3	7 09·4	6 48·7	3·3	1·6	9·3	4·4	15·3	7·3
34	7 08·5	7 09·7	6 49·0	3·4	1·6	9·4	4·5	15·4	7·3
35	7 08·8	7 09·9	6 49·2	3·5	1·7	9·5	4·5	15·5	7·4
36	7 09·0	7 10·2	6 49·5	3·6	1·7	9·6	4·6	15·6	7·4
37	7 09·3	7 10·4	6 49·7	3·7	1·8	9·7	4·6	15·7	7·5
38	7 09·5	7 10·7	6 49·9	3·8	1·8	9·8	4·7	15·8	7·5
39	7 09·8	7 10·9	6 50·2	3·9	1·9	9·9	4·7	15·9	7·6
40	7 10·0	7 11·2	6 50·4	4·0	1·9	10·0	4·8	16·0	7·6
41	7 10·3	7 11·4	6 50·6	4·1	1·9	10·1	4·8	16·1	7·6
42	7 10·5	7 11·7	6 50·9	4·2	2·0	10·2	4·8	16·2	7·7
43	7 10·8	7 11·9	6 51·1	4·3	2·0	10·3	4·9	16·3	7·7
44	7 11·0	7 12·2	6 51·4	4·4	2·1	10·4	4·9	16·4	7·8
45	7 11·3	7 12·4	6 51·6	4·5	2·1	10·5	5·0	16·5	7·8
46	7 11·5	7 12·7	6 51·8	4·6	2·2	10·6	5·0	16·6	7·9
47	7 11·8	7 12·9	6 52·1	4·7	2·2	10·7	5·1	16·7	7·9
48	7 12·0	7 13·2	6 52·3	4·8	2·3	10·8	5·1	16·8	8·0
49	7 12·3	7 13·4	6 52·6	4·9	2·3	10·9	5·2	16·9	8·0
50	7 12·5	7 13·7	6 52·8	5·0	2·4	11·0	5·2	17·0	8·1
51	7 12·8	7 13·9	6 53·0	5·1	2·4	11·1	5·3	17·1	8·1
52	7 13·0	7 14·2	6 53·3	5·2	2·5	11·2	5·3	17·2	8·2
53	7 13·3	7 14·4	6 53·5	5·3	2·5	11·3	5·4	17·3	8·2
54	7 13·5	7 14·7	6 53·8	5·4	2·6	11·4	5·4	17·4	8·3
55	7 13·8	7 14·9	6 54·0	5·5	2·6	11·5	5·5	17·5	8·3
56	7 14·0	7 15·2	6 54·2	5·6	2·7	11·6	5·5	17·6	8·4
57	7 14·3	7 15·4	6 54·5	5·7	2·7	11·7	5·6	17·7	8·4
58	7 14·5	7 15·7	6 54·7	5·8	2·8	11·8	5·6	17·8	8·5
59	7 14·8	7 15·9	6 54·9	5·9	2·8	11·9	5·7	17·9	8·5
60	7 15·0	7 16·2	6 55·2	6·0	2·9	12·0	5·7	18·0	8·6

29^{m}	SUN PLANETS	ARIES	MOON	v or d	Corr^{n}	v or d	Corr^{n}	v or d	Corr^{n}
s	° ′	° ′	° ′	′	′	′	′	′	′
00	7 15·0	7 16·2	6 55·2	0·0	0·0	6·0	3·0	12·0	5·9
01	7 15·3	7 16·4	6 55·4	0·1	0·0	6·1	3·0	12·1	5·9
02	7 15·5	7 16·7	6 55·7	0·2	0·1	6·2	3·0	12·2	6·0
03	7 15·8	7 16·9	6 55·9	0·3	0·1	6·3	3·1	12·3	6·0
04	7 16·0	7 17·2	6 56·1	0·4	0·2	6·4	3·1	12·4	6·1
05	7 16·3	7 17·4	6 56·4	0·5	0·2	6·5	3·2	12·5	6·1
06	7 16·5	7 17·7	6 56·6	0·6	0·3	6·6	3·2	12·6	6·2
07	7 16·8	7 17·9	6 56·9	0·7	0·3	6·7	3·3	12·7	6·2
08	7 17·0	7 18·2	6 57·1	0·8	0·4	6·8	3·3	12·8	6·3
09	7 17·3	7 18·4	6 57·3	0·9	0·4	6·9	3·4	12·9	6·3
10	7 17·5	7 18·7	6 57·6	1·0	0·5	7·0	3·4	13·0	6·4
11	7 17·8	7 18·9	6 57·8	1·1	0·5	7·1	3·5	13·1	6·4
12	7 18·0	7 19·2	6 58·0	1·2	0·6	7·2	3·5	13·2	6·5
13	7 18·3	7 19·4	6 58·3	1·3	0·6	7·3	3·6	13·3	6·5
14	7 18·5	7 19·7	6 58·5	1·4	0·7	7·4	3·6	13·4	6·6
15	7 18·8	7 20·0	6 58·8	1·5	0·7	7·5	3·7	13·5	6·6
16	7 19·0	7 20·2	6 59·0	1·6	0·8	7·6	3·7	13·6	6·7
17	7 19·3	7 20·5	6 59·2	1·7	0·8	7·7	3·8	13·7	6·7
18	7 19·5	7 20·7	6 59·5	1·8	0·9	7·8	3·8	13·8	6·8
19	7 19·8	7 21·0	6 59·7	1·9	0·9	7·9	3·9	13·9	6·8
20	7 20·0	7 21·2	7 00·0	2·0	1·0	8·0	3·9	14·0	6·9
21	7 20·3	7 21·5	7 00·2	2·1	1·0	8·1	4·0	14·1	6·9
22	7 20·5	7 21·7	7 00·4	2·2	1·1	8·2	4·0	14·2	7·0
23	7 20·8	7 22·0	7 00·7	2·3	1·1	8·3	4·1	14·3	7·0
24	7 21·0	7 22·2	7 00·9	2·4	1·2	8·4	4·1	14·4	7·1
25	7 21·3	7 22·5	7 01·1	2·5	1·2	8·5	4·2	14·5	7·1
26	7 21·5	7 22·7	7 01·4	2·6	1·3	8·6	4·2	14·6	7·2
27	7 21·8	7 23·0	7 01·6	2·7	1·3	8·7	4·3	14·7	7·2
28	7 22·0	7 23·2	7 01·9	2·8	1·4	8·8	4·3	14·8	7·3
29	7 22·3	7 23·5	7 02·1	2·9	1·4	8·9	4·4	14·9	7·3
30	7 22·5	7 23·7	7 02·3	3·0	1·5	9·0	4·4	15·0	7·4
31	7 22·8	7 24·0	7 02·6	3·1	1·5	9·1	4·5	15·1	7·4
32	7 23·0	7 24·2	7 02·8	3·2	1·6	9·2	4·5	15·2	7·5
33	7 23·3	7 24·5	7 03·1	3·3	1·6	9·3	4·6	15·3	7·5
34	7 23·5	7 24·7	7 03·3	3·4	1·7	9·4	4·6	15·4	7·6
35	7 23·8	7 25·0	7 03·5	3·5	1·7	9·5	4·7	15·5	7·6
36	7 24·0	7 25·2	7 03·8	3·6	1·8	9·6	4·7	15·6	7·7
37	7 24·3	7 25·5	7 04·0	3·7	1·8	9·7	4·8	15·7	7·7
38	7 24·5	7 25·7	7 04·3	3·8	1·9	9·8	4·8	15·8	7·8
39	7 24·8	7 26·0	7 04·5	3·9	1·9	9·9	4·9	15·9	7·8
40	7 25·0	7 26·2	7 04·7	4·0	2·0	10·0	4·9	16·0	7·9
41	7 25·3	7 26·5	7 05·0	4·1	2·0	10·1	5·0	16·1	7·9
42	7 25·5	7 26·7	7 05·2	4·2	2·1	10·2	5·0	16·2	8·0
43	7 25·8	7 27·0	7 05·4	4·3	2·1	10·3	5·1	16·3	8·0
44	7 26·0	7 27·2	7 05·7	4·4	2·2	10·4	5·1	16·4	8·1
45	7 26·3	7 27·5	7 05·9	4·5	2·2	10·5	5·2	16·5	8·1
46	7 26·5	7 27·7	7 06·2	4·6	2·3	10·6	5·2	16·6	8·2
47	7 26·8	7 28·0	7 06·4	4·7	2·3	10·7	5·3	16·7	8·2
48	7 27·0	7 28·2	7 06·6	4·8	2·4	10·8	5·3	16·8	8·3
49	7 27·3	7 28·5	7 06·9	4·9	2·4	10·9	5·4	16·9	8·3
50	7 27·5	7 28·7	7 07·1	5·0	2·5	11·0	5·4	17·0	8·4
51	7 27·8	7 29·0	7 07·4	5·1	2·5	11·1	5·5	17·1	8·4
52	7 28·0	7 29·2	7 07·6	5·2	2·6	11·2	5·5	17·2	8·5
53	7 28·3	7 29·5	7 07·8	5·3	2·6	11·3	5·6	17·3	8·5
54	7 28·5	7 29·7	7 08·1	5·4	2·7	11·4	5·6	17·4	8·6
55	7 28·8	7 30·0	7 08·3	5·5	2·7	11·5	5·7	17·5	8·6
56	7 29·0	7 30·2	7 08·5	5·6	2·8	11·6	5·7	17·6	8·7
57	7 29·3	7 30·5	7 08·8	5·7	2·8	11·7	5·8	17·7	8·7
58	7 29·5	7 30·7	7 09·0	5·8	2·9	11·8	5·8	17·8	8·8
59	7 29·8	7 31·0	7 09·3	5·9	2·9	11·9	5·9	17·9	8·8
60	7 30·0	7 31·2	7 09·5	6·0	3·0	12·0	5·9	18·0	8·9

30m s	SUN PLANETS ° ′	ARIES ° ′	MOON ° ′	v or d ′	Corrn ′	v or d ′	Corrn ′	v or d ′	Corrn ′
00	7 30·0	7 31·2	7 09·5	0·0	0·0	6·0	3·1	12·0	6·1
01	7 30·3	7 31·5	7 09·7	0·1	0·1	6·1	3·1	12·1	6·2
02	7 30·5	7 31·7	7 10·0	0·2	0·1	6·2	3·2	12·2	6·2
03	7 30·8	7 32·0	7 10·2	0·3	0·2	6·3	3·2	12·3	6·3
04	7 31·0	7 32·2	7 10·5	0·4	0·2	6·4	3·3	12·4	6·3
05	7 31·3	7 32·5	7 10·7	0·5	0·3	6·5	3·3	12·5	6·4
06	7 31·5	7 32·7	7 10·9	0·6	0·3	6·6	3·4	12·6	6·4
07	7 31·8	7 33·0	7 11·2	0·7	0·4	6·7	3·4	12·7	6·5
08	7 32·0	7 33·2	7 11·4	0·8	0·4	6·8	3·5	12·8	6·5
09	7 32·3	7 33·5	7 11·6	0·9	0·5	6·9	3·5	12·9	6·6
10	7 32·5	7 33·7	7 11·9	1·0	0·5	7·0	3·6	13·0	6·6
11	7 32·8	7 34·0	7 12·1	1·1	0·6	7·1	3·6	13·1	6·7
12	7 33·0	7 34·2	7 12·4	1·2	0·6	7·2	3·7	13·2	6·7
13	7 33·3	7 34·5	7 12·6	1·3	0·7	7·3	3·7	13·3	6·8
14	7 33·5	7 34·7	7 12·8	1·4	0·7	7·4	3·8	13·4	6·8
15	7 33·8	7 35·0	7 13·1	1·5	0·8	7·5	3·8	13·5	6·9
16	7 34·0	7 35·2	7 13·3	1·6	0·8	7·6	3·9	13·6	6·9
17	7 34·3	7 35·5	7 13·6	1·7	0·9	7·7	3·9	13·7	7·0
18	7 34·5	7 35·7	7 13·8	1·8	0·9	7·8	4·0	13·8	7·0
19	7 34·8	7 36·0	7 14·0	1·9	1·0	7·9	4·0	13·9	7·1
20	7 35·0	7 36·2	7 14·3	2·0	1·0	8·0	4·1	14·0	7·1
21	7 35·3	7 36·5	7 14·5	2·1	1·1	8·1	4·1	14·1	7·2
22	7 35·5	7 36·7	7 14·7	2·2	1·1	8·2	4·2	14·2	7·2
23	7 35·8	7 37·0	7 15·0	2·3	1·2	8·3	4·2	14·3	7·3
24	7 36·0	7 37·2	7 15·2	2·4	1·2	8·4	4·3	14·4	7·3
25	7 36·3	7 37·5	7 15·5	2·5	1·3	8·5	4·3	14·5	7·4
26	7 36·5	7 37·7	7 15·7	2·6	1·3	8·6	4·4	14·6	7·4
27	7 36·8	7 38·0	7 15·9	2·7	1·4	8·7	4·4	14·7	7·5
28	7 37·0	7 38·3	7 16·2	2·8	1·4	8·8	4·5	14·8	7·5
29	7 37·3	7 38·5	7 16·4	2·9	1·5	8·9	4·5	14·9	7·6
30	7 37·5	7 38·8	7 16·7	3·0	1·5	9·0	4·6	15·0	7·6
31	7 37·8	7 39·0	7 16·9	3·1	1·6	9·1	4·6	15·1	7·7
32	7 38·0	7 39·3	7 17·1	3·2	1·6	9·2	4·7	15·2	7·7
33	7 38·3	7 39·5	7 17·4	3·3	1·7	9·3	4·7	15·3	7·8
34	7 38·5	7 39·8	7 17·6	3·4	1·7	9·4	4·8	15·4	7·8
35	7 38·8	7 40·0	7 17·9	3·5	1·8	9·5	4·8	15·5	7·9
36	7 39·0	7 40·3	7 18·1	3·6	1·8	9·6	4·9	15·6	7·9
37	7 39·3	7 40·5	7 18·3	3·7	1·9	9·7	4·9	15·7	8·0
38	7 39·5	7 40·8	7 18·6	3·8	1·9	9·8	5·0	15·8	8·0
39	7 39·8	7 41·0	7 18·8	3·9	2·0	9·9	5·0	15·9	8·1
40	7 40·0	7 41·3	7 19·0	4·0	2·0	10·0	5·1	16·0	8·1
41	7 40·3	7 41·5	7 19·3	4·1	2·1	10·1	5·1	16·1	8·2
42	7 40·5	7 41·8	7 19·5	4·2	2·1	10·2	5·2	16·2	8·2
43	7 40·8	7 42·0	7 19·8	4·3	2·2	10·3	5·2	16·3	8·3
44	7 41·0	7 42·3	7 20·0	4·4	2·2	10·4	5·3	16·4	8·3
45	7 41·3	7 42·5	7 20·2	4·5	2·3	10·5	5·3	16·5	8·4
46	7 41·5	7 42·8	7 20·5	4·6	2·3	10·6	5·4	16·6	8·4
47	7 41·8	7 43·0	7 20·7	4·7	2·4	10·7	5·4	16·7	8·5
48	7 42·0	7 43·3	7 21·0	4·8	2·4	10·8	5·5	16·8	8·5
49	7 42·3	7 43·5	7 21·2	4·9	2·5	10·9	5·5	16·9	8·6
50	7 42·5	7 43·8	7 21·4	5·0	2·5	11·0	5·6	17·0	8·6
51	7 42·8	7 44·0	7 21·7	5·1	2·6	11·1	5·6	17·1	8·7
52	7 43·0	7 44·3	7 21·9	5·2	2·6	11·2	5·7	17·2	8·7
53	7 43·3	7 44·5	7 22·1	5·3	2·7	11·3	5·7	17·3	8·8
54	7 43·5	7 44·8	7 22·4	5·4	2·7	11·4	5·8	17·4	8·8
55	7 43·8	7 45·0	7 22·6	5·5	2·8	11·5	5·8	17·5	8·9
56	7 44·0	7 45·3	7 22·9	5·6	2·8	11·6	5·9	17·6	8·9
57	7 44·3	7 45·5	7 23·1	5·7	2·9	11·7	5·9	17·7	9·0
58	7 44·5	7 45·8	7 23·3	5·8	2·9	11·8	6·0	17·8	9·0
59	7 44·8	7 46·0	7 23·6	5·9	3·0	11·9	6·0	17·9	9·1
60	7 45·0	7 46·3	7 23·8	6·0	3·1	12·0	6·1	18·0	9·2

31m s	SUN PLANETS ° ′	ARIES ° ′	MOON ° ′	v or d ′	Corrn ′	v or d ′	Corrn ′	v or d ′	Corrn ′
00	7 45·0	7 46·3	7 23·8	0·0	0·0	6·0	3·2	12·0	6·3
01	7 45·3	7 46·5	7 24·1	0·1	0·1	6·1	3·2	12·1	6·4
02	7 45·5	7 46·8	7 24·3	0·2	0·1	6·2	3·3	12·2	6·4
03	7 45·8	7 47·0	7 24·5	0·3	0·2	6·3	3·3	12·3	6·5
04	7 46·0	7 47·3	7 24·8	0·4	0·2	6·4	3·4	12·4	6·5
05	7 46·3	7 47·5	7 25·0	0·5	0·3	6·5	3·4	12·5	6·6
06	7 46·5	7 47·8	7 25·2	0·6	0·3	6·6	3·5	12·6	6·6
07	7 46·8	7 48·0	7 25·5	0·7	0·4	6·7	3·5	12·7	6·7
08	7 47·0	7 48·3	7 25·7	0·8	0·4	6·8	3·6	12·8	6·7
09	7 47·3	7 48·5	7 26·0	0·9	0·5	6·9	3·6	12·9	6·8
10	7 47·5	7 48·8	7 26·2	1·0	0·5	7·0	3·7	13·0	6·8
11	7 47·8	7 49·0	7 26·4	1·1	0·6	7·1	3·7	13·1	6·9
12	7 48·0	7 49·3	7 26·7	1·2	0·6	7·2	3·8	13·2	6·9
13	7 48·3	7 49·5	7 26·9	1·3	0·7	7·3	3·8	13·3	7·0
14	7 48·5	7 49·8	7 27·2	1·4	0·7	7·4	3·9	13·4	7·0
15	7 48·8	7 50·0	7 27·4	1·5	0·8	7·5	3·9	13·5	7·1
16	7 49·0	7 50·3	7 27·6	1·6	0·8	7·6	4·0	13·6	7·1
17	7 49·3	7 50·5	7 27·9	1·7	0·9	7·7	4·0	13·7	7·2
18	7 49·5	7 50·8	7 28·1	1·8	0·9	7·8	4·1	13·8	7·2
19	7 49·8	7 51·0	7 28·4	1·9	1·0	7·9	4·1	13·9	7·3
20	7 50·0	7 51·3	7 28·6	2·0	1·1	8·0	4·2	14·0	7·4
21	7 50·3	7 51·5	7 28·8	2·1	1·1	8·1	4·3	14·1	7·4
22	7 50·5	7 51·8	7 29·1	2·2	1·2	8·2	4·3	14·2	7·5
23	7 50·8	7 52·0	7 29·3	2·3	1·2	8·3	4·4	14·3	7·5
24	7 51·0	7 52·3	7 29·5	2·4	1·3	8·4	4·4	14·4	7·6
25	7 51·3	7 52·5	7 29·8	2·5	1·3	8·5	4·5	14·5	7·6
26	7 51·5	7 52·8	7 30·0	2·6	1·4	8·6	4·5	14·6	7·7
27	7 51·8	7 53·0	7 30·3	2·7	1·4	8·7	4·6	14·7	7·7
28	7 52·0	7 53·3	7 30·5	2·8	1·5	8·8	4·6	14·8	7·8
29	7 52·3	7 53·5	7 30·7	2·9	1·5	8·9	4·7	14·9	7·8
30	7 52·5	7 53·8	7 31·0	3·0	1·6	9·0	4·7	15·0	7·9
31	7 52·8	7 54·0	7 31·2	3·1	1·6	9·1	4·8	15·1	7·9
32	7 53·0	7 54·3	7 31·5	3·2	1·7	9·2	4·8	15·2	8·0
33	7 53·3	7 54·5	7 31·7	3·3	1·7	9·3	4·9	15·3	8·0
34	7 53·5	7 54·8	7 31·9	3·4	1·8	9·4	4·9	15·4	8·1
35	7 53·8	7 55·0	7 32·2	3·5	1·8	9·5	5·0	15·5	8·1
36	7 54·0	7 55·3	7 32·4	3·6	1·9	9·6	5·0	15·6	8·2
37	7 54·3	7 55·5	7 32·6	3·7	1·9	9·7	5·1	15·7	8·2
38	7 54·5	7 55·8	7 32·9	3·8	2·0	9·8	5·1	15·8	8·3
39	7 54·8	7 56·0	7 33·1	3·9	2·0	9·9	5·2	15·9	8·3
40	7 55·0	7 56·3	7 33·4	4·0	2·1	10·0	5·3	16·0	8·4
41	7 55·3	7 56·6	7 33·6	4·1	2·2	10·1	5·3	16·1	8·5
42	7 55·5	7 56·8	7 33·8	4·2	2·2	10·2	5·4	16·2	8·5
43	7 55·8	7 57·1	7 34·1	4·3	2·3	10·3	5·4	16·3	8·6
44	7 56·0	7 57·3	7 34·3	4·4	2·3	10·4	5·5	16·4	8·6
45	7 56·3	7 57·6	7 34·6	4·5	2·4	10·5	5·5	16·5	8·7
46	7 56·5	7 57·8	7 34·8	4·6	2·4	10·6	5·6	16·6	8·7
47	7 56·8	7 58·1	7 35·0	4·7	2·5	10·7	5·6	16·7	8·8
48	7 57·0	7 58·3	7 35·3	4·8	2·5	10·8	5·7	16·8	8·8
49	7 57·3	7 58·6	7 35·5	4·9	2·6	10·9	5·7	16·9	8·9
50	7 57·5	7 58·8	7 35·7	5·0	2·6	11·0	5·8	17·0	8·9
51	7 57·8	7 59·1	7 36·0	5·1	2·7	11·1	5·8	17·1	9·0
52	7 58·0	7 59·3	7 36·2	5·2	2·7	11·2	5·9	17·2	9·0
53	7 58·3	7 59·6	7 36·5	5·3	2·8	11·3	5·9	17·3	9·1
54	7 58·5	7 59·8	7 36·7	5·4	2·8	11·4	6·0	17·4	9·1
55	7 58·8	8 00·1	7 36·9	5·5	2·9	11·5	6·0	17·5	9·2
56	7 59·0	8 00·3	7 37·2	5·6	2·9	11·6	6·1	17·6	9·2
57	7 59·3	8 00·6	7 37·4	5·7	3·0	11·7	6·1	17·7	9·3
58	7 59·5	8 00·8	7 37·7	5·8	3·0	11·8	6·2	17·8	9·3
59	7 59·8	8 01·1	7 37·9	5·9	3·1	11·9	6·2	17·9	9·4
60	8 00·0	8 01·3	7 38·1	6·0	3·2	12·0	6·3	18·0	9·5

32m	SUN PLANETS	ARIES	MOON	v or d	Corrn	v or d	Corrn	v or d	Corrn
s	° ′	° ′	° ′	′	′	′	′	′	′
00	8 00·0	8 01·3	7 38·1	0·0	0·0	6·0	3·3	12·0	6·5
01	8 00·3	8 01·6	7 38·4	0·1	0·1	6·1	3·3	12·1	6·6
02	8 00·5	8 01·8	7 38·6	0·2	0·1	6·2	3·4	12·2	6·6
03	8 00·8	8 02·1	7 38·8	0·3	0·2	6·3	3·4	12·3	6·7
04	8 01·0	8 02·3	7 39·1	0·4	0·2	6·4	3·5	12·4	6·7
05	8 01·3	8 02·6	7 39·3	0·5	0·3	6·5	3·5	12·5	6·8
06	8 01·5	8 02·8	7 39·6	0·6	0·3	6·6	3·6	12·6	6·8
07	8 01·8	8 03·1	7 39·8	0·7	0·4	6·7	3·6	12·7	6·9
08	8 02·0	8 03·3	7 40·0	0·8	0·4	6·8	3·7	12·8	6·9
09	8 02·3	8 03·6	7 40·3	0·9	0·5	6·9	3·7	12·9	7·0
10	8 02·5	8 03·8	7 40·5	1·0	0·5	7·0	3·8	13·0	7·0
11	8 02·8	8 04·1	7 40·8	1·1	0·6	7·1	3·8	13·1	7·1
12	8 03·0	8 04·3	7 41·0	1·2	0·7	7·2	3·9	13·2	7·2
13	8 03·3	8 04·6	7 41·2	1·3	0·7	7·3	4·0	13·3	7·2
14	8 03·5	8 04·8	7 41·5	1·4	0·8	7·4	4·0	13·4	7·3
15	8 03·8	8 05·1	7 41·7	1·5	0·8	7·5	4·1	13·5	7·3
16	8 04·0	8 05·3	7 42·0	1·6	0·9	7·6	4·1	13·6	7·4
17	8 04·3	8 05·6	7 42·2	1·7	0·9	7·7	4·2	13·7	7·4
18	8 04·5	8 05·8	7 42·4	1·8	1·0	7·8	4·2	13·8	7·5
19	8 04·8	8 06·1	7 42·7	1·9	1·0	7·9	4·3	13·9	7·5
20	8 05·0	8 06·3	7 42·9	2·0	1·1	8·0	4·3	14·0	7·6
21	8 05·3	8 06·6	7 43·1	2·1	1·1	8·1	4·4	14·1	7·6
22	8 05·5	8 06·8	7 43·4	2·2	1·2	8·2	4·4	14·2	7·7
23	8 05·8	8 07·1	7 43·6	2·3	1·2	8·3	4·5	14·3	7·7
24	8 06·0	8 07·3	7 43·9	2·4	1·3	8·4	4·6	14·4	7·8
25	8 06·3	8 07·6	7 44·1	2·5	1·4	8·5	4·6	14·5	7·9
26	8 06·5	8 07·8	7 44·3	2·6	1·4	8·6	4·7	14·6	7·9
27	8 06·8	8 00 1	7 44·6	2·7	1·5	8·7	4·7	14·7	8·0
28	8 07·0	8 08·3	7 44·8	2·8	1·5	8·8	4·8	14·8	8·0
29	8 07·3	8 08·6	7 45·1	2·9	1·6	8·9	4·8	14·9	8·1
30	8 07·5	8 08·8	7 45·3	3·0	1·6	9·0	4·9	15·0	8·1
31	8 07·8	8 09·1	7 45·5	3·1	1·7	9·1	4·9	15·1	8·2
32	8 08·0	8 09·3	7 45·8	3·2	1·7	9·2	5·0	15·2	8·2
33	8 08·3	8 09·6	7 46·0	3·3	1·8	9·3	5·0	15·3	8·3
34	8 08·5	8 09·8	7 46·2	3·4	1·8	9·4	5·1	15·4	8·3
35	8 08·8	8 10·1	7 46·5	3·5	1·9	9·5	5·1	15·5	8·4
36	8 09·0	8 10·3	7 46·7	3·6	2·0	9·6	5·2	15·6	8·5
37	8 09·3	8 10·6	7 47·0	3·7	2·0	9·7	5·3	15·7	8·5
38	8 09·5	8 10·8	7 47·2	3·8	2·1	9·8	5·3	15·8	8·6
39	8 09·8	8 11·1	7 47·4	3·9	2·1	9·9	5·4	15·9	8·6
40	8 10·0	8 11·3	7 47·7	4·0	2·2	10·0	5·4	16·0	8·7
41	8 10·3	8 11·6	7 47·9	4·1	2·2	10·1	5·5	16·1	8·7
42	8 10·5	8 11·8	7 48·2	4·2	2·3	10·2	5·5	16·2	8·8
43	8 10·8	8 12·1	7 48·4	4·3	2·3	10·3	5·6	16·3	8·8
44	8 11·0	8 12·3	7 48·6	4·4	2·4	10·4	5·6	16·4	8·9
45	8 11·3	8 12·6	7 48·9	4·5	2·4	10·5	5·7	16·5	8·9
46	8 11·5	8 12·8	7 49·1	4·6	2·5	10·6	5·7	16·6	9·0
47	8 11·8	8 13·1	7 49·3	4·7	2·5	10·7	5·8	16·7	9·0
48	8 12·0	8 13·3	7 49·6	4·8	2·6	10·8	5·9	16·8	9·1
49	8 12·3	8 13·6	7 49·8	4·9	2·7	10·9	5·9	16·9	9·2
50	8 12·5	8 13·8	7 50·1	5·0	2·7	11·0	6·0	17·0	9·2
51	8 12·8	8 14·1	7 50·3	5·1	2·8	11·1	6·0	17·1	9·3
52	8 13·0	8 14·3	7 50·5	5·2	2·8	11·2	6·1	17·2	9·3
53	8 13·3	8 14·6	7 50·8	5·3	2·9	11·3	6·1	17·3	9·4
54	8 13·5	8 14·9	7 51·0	5·4	2·9	11·4	6·2	17·4	9·4
55	8 13·8	8 15·1	7 51·3	5·5	3·0	11·5	6·2	17·5	9·5
56	8 14·0	8 15·4	7 51·5	5·6	3·0	11·6	6·3	17·6	9·5
57	8 14·3	8 15·6	7 51·7	5·7	3·1	11·7	6·3	17·7	9·6
58	8 14·5	8 15·9	7 52·0	5·8	3·1	11·8	6·4	17·8	9·6
59	8 14·8	8 16·1	7 52·2	5·9	3·2	11·9	6·4	17·9	9·7
60	8 15·0	8 16·4	7 52·5	6·0	3·3	12·0	6·5	18·0	9·8

33m	SUN PLANETS	ARIES	MOON	v or d	Corrn	v or d	Corrn	v or d	Corrn
s	° ′	° ′	° ′	′	′	′	′	′	′
00	8 15·0	8 16·4	7 52·5	0·0	0·0	6·0	3·4	12·0	6·7
01	8 15·3	8 16·6	7 52·7	0·1	0·1	6·1	3·4	12·1	6·8
02	8 15·5	8 16·9	7 52·9	0·2	0·1	6·2	3·5	12·2	6·8
03	8 15·8	8 17·1	7 53·2	0·3	0·2	6·3	3·5	12·3	6·9
04	8 16·0	8 17·4	7 53·4	0·4	0·2	6·4	3·6	12·4	6·9
05	8 16·3	8 17·6	7 53·6	0·5	0·3	6·5	3·6	12·5	7·0
06	8 16·5	8 17·9	7 53·9	0·6	0·3	6·6	3·7	12·6	7·0
07	8 16·8	8 18·1	7 54·1	0·7	0·4	6·7	3·7	12·7	7·1
08	8 17·0	8 18·4	7 54·4	0·8	0·4	6·8	3·8	12·8	7·1
09	8 17·3	8 18·6	7 54·6	0·9	0·5	6·9	3·9	12·9	7·2
10	8 17·5	8 18·9	7 54·8	1·0	0·6	7·0	3·9	13·0	7·3
11	8 17·8	8 19·1	7 55·1	1·1	0·6	7·1	4·0	13·1	7·3
12	8 18·0	8 19·4	7 55·3	1·2	0·7	7·2	4·0	13·2	7·4
13	8 18·3	8 19·6	7 55·6	1·3	0·7	7·3	4·1	13·3	7·4
14	8 18·5	8 19·9	7 55·8	1·4	0·8	7·4	4·1	13·4	7·5
15	8 18·8	8 20·1	7 56·0	1·5	0·8	7·5	4·2	13·5	7·5
16	8 19·0	8 20·4	7 56·3	1·6	0·9	7·6	4·2	13·6	7·6
17	8 19·3	8 20·6	7 56·5	1·7	0·9	7·7	4·3	13·7	7·6
18	8 19·5	8 20·9	7 56·7	1·8	1·0	7·8	4·4	13·8	7·7
19	8 19·8	8 21·1	7 57·0	1·9	1·1	7·9	4·4	13·9	7·8
20	8 20·0	8 21·4	7 57·2	2·0	1·1	8·0	4·5	14·0	7·8
21	8 20·3	8 21·6	7 57·5	2·1	1·2	8·1	4·5	14·1	7·9
22	8 20·5	8 21·9	7 57·7	2·2	1·2	8·2	4·6	14·2	7·9
23	8 20·8	8 22·1	7 57·9	2·3	1·3	8·3	4·6	14·3	8·0
24	8 21·0	8 22·4	7 58·2	2·4	1·3	8·4	4·7	14·4	8·0
25	8 21·3	8 22·6	7 58·4	2·5	1·4	8·5	4·7	14·5	8·1
26	8 21·5	8 22·9	7 58·7	2·6	1·5	8·6	4·8	14·6	8·2
27	8 21·8	8 23·1	7 58·9	2·7	1·5	8·7	4·9	14·7	8·2
28	8 22·0	0 23·4	7 59·1	2·8	1·6	8·8	4·9	14·8	8·3
29	8 22·3	8 23·6	7 59·4	2·9	1·6	8·9	5·0	14·9	8·3
30	8 22·5	8 23·9	7 59·6	3·0	1·7	9·0	5·0	15·0	8·4
31	8 22·8	8 24·1	7 59·8	3·1	1·7	9·1	5·1	15·1	8·4
32	8 23·0	8 24·4	8 00·1	3·2	1·8	9·2	5·1	15·2	8·5
33	8 23·3	8 24·6	8 00·3	3·3	1·8	9·3	5·2	15·3	8·5
34	8 23·5	8 24·9	8 00·6	3·4	1·9	9·4	5·2	15·4	8·6
35	8 23·8	8 25·1	8 00·8	3·5	2·0	9·5	5·3	15·5	8·7
36	8 24·0	8 25·4	8 01·0	3·6	2·0	9·6	5·4	15·6	8·7
37	8 24·3	8 25·6	8 01·3	3·7	2·1	9·7	5·4	15·7	8·8
38	8 24·5	8 25·9	8 01·5	3·8	2·1	9·8	5·5	15·8	8·8
39	8 24·8	8 26·1	8 01·8	3·9	2·2	9·9	5·5	15·9	8·9
40	8 25·0	8 26·4	8 02·0	4·0	2·2	10·0	5·6	16·0	8·9
41	8 25·3	8 26·6	8 02·2	4·1	2·3	10·1	5·6	16·1	9·0
42	8 25·5	8 26·9	8 02·5	4·2	2·3	10·2	5·7	16·2	9·0
43	8 25·8	8 27·1	8 02·7	4·3	2·4	10·3	5·8	16·3	9·1
44	8 26·0	8 27·4	8 02·9	4·4	2·5	10·4	5·8	16·4	9·2
45	8 26·3	8 27·6	8 03·2	4·5	2·5	10·5	5·9	16·5	9·2
46	8 26·5	8 27·9	8 03·4	4·6	2·6	10·6	5·9	16·6	9·3
47	8 26·8	8 28·1	8 03·7	4·7	2·6	10·7	6·0	16·7	9·3
48	8 27·0	8 28·4	8 03·9	4·8	2·7	10·8	6·0	16·8	9·4
49	8 27·3	8 28·6	8 04·1	4·9	2·7	10·9	6·1	16·9	9·4
50	8 27·5	8 28·9	8 04·4	5·0	2·8	11·0	6·1	17·0	9·5
51	8 27·8	8 29·1	8 04·6	5·1	2·8	11·1	6·2	17·1	9·5
52	8 28·0	8 29·4	8 04·9	5·2	2·9	11·2	6·3	17·2	9·6
53	8 28·3	8 29·6	8 05·1	5·3	3·0	11·3	6·3	17·3	9·7
54	8 28·5	8 29·9	8 05·3	5·4	3·0	11·4	6·4	17·4	9·7
55	8 28·8	8 30·1	8 05·6	5·5	3·1	11·5	6·4	17·5	9·8
56	8 29·0	8 30·4	8 05·8	5·6	3·1	11·6	6·5	17·6	9·8
57	8 29·3	8 30·6	8 06·1	5·7	3·2	11·7	6·5	17·7	9·9
58	8 29·5	8 30·9	8 06·3	5·8	3·2	11·8	6·6	17·8	9·9
59	8 29·8	8 31·1	8 06·5	5·9	3·3	11·9	6·6	17·9	10·0
60	8 30·0	8 31·4	8 06·8	6·0	3·4	12·0	6·7	18·0	10·1

m 34	SUN PLANETS	ARIES	MOON	v or d	Corrⁿ	v or d	Corrⁿ	v or d	Corrⁿ
s	° ′	° ′	° ′	′	′	′	′	′	′
00	8 30·0	8 31·4	8 06·8	0·0	0·0	6·0	3·5	12·0	6·9
01	8 30·3	8 31·6	8 07·0	0·1	0·1	6·1	3·5	12·1	7·0
02	8 30·5	8 31·9	8 07·2	0·2	0·1	6·2	3·6	12·2	7·0
03	8 30·8	8 32·1	8 07·5	0·3	0·2	6·3	3·6	12·3	7·1
04	8 31·0	8 32·4	8 07·7	0·4	0·2	6·4	3·7	12·4	7·1
05	8 31·3	8 32·6	8 08·0	0·5	0·3	6·5	3·7	12·5	7·2
06	8 31·5	8 32·9	8 08·2	0·6	0·3	6·6	3·8	12·6	7·2
07	8 31·8	8 33·2	8 08·4	0·7	0·4	6·7	3·9	12·7	7·3
08	8 32·0	8 33·4	8 08·7	0·8	0·5	6·8	3·9	12·8	7·4
09	8 32·3	8 33·7	8 08·9	0·9	0·5	6·9	4·0	12·9	7·4
10	8 32·5	8 33·9	8 09·2	1·0	0·6	7·0	4·0	13·0	7·5
11	8 32·8	8 34·2	8 09·4	1·1	0·6	7·1	4·1	13·1	7·5
12	8 33·0	8 34·4	8 09·6	1·2	0·7	7·2	4·1	13·2	7·6
13	8 33·3	8 34·7	8 09·9	1·3	0·7	7·3	4·2	13·3	7·6
14	8 33·5	8 34·9	8 10·1	1·4	0·8	7·4	4·3	13·4	7·7
15	8 33·8	8 35·2	8 10·3	1·5	0·9	7·5	4·3	13·5	7·8
16	8 34·0	8 35·4	8 10·6	1·6	0·9	7·6	4·4	13·6	7·8
17	8 34·3	8 35·7	8 10·8	1·7	1·0	7·7	4·4	13·7	7·9
18	8 34·5	8 35·9	8 11·1	1·8	1·0	7·8	4·5	13·8	7·9
19	8 34·8	8 36·2	8 11·3	1·9	1·1	7·9	4·5	13·9	8·0
20	8 35·0	8 36·4	8 11·5	2·0	1·2	8·0	4·6	14·0	8·1
21	8 35·3	8 36·7	8 11·8	2·1	1·2	8·1	4·7	14·1	8·1
22	8 35·5	8 36·9	8 12·0	2·2	1·3	8·2	4·7	14·2	8·2
23	8 35·8	8 37·2	8 12·3	2·3	1·3	8·3	4·8	14·3	8·2
24	8 36·0	8 37·4	8 12·5	2·4	1·4	8·4	4·8	14·4	8·3
25	8 36·3	8 37·7	8 12·7	2·5	1·4	8·5	4·9	14·5	8·3
26	8 36·5	8 37·9	8 13·0	2·6	1·5	8·6	4·9	14·6	8·4
27	8 36·8	8 38·2	8 13·2	2·7	1·6	8·7	5·0	14·7	8·5
28	8 37·0	8 38·4	8 13·4	2·8	1·6	8·8	5·1	14·8	8·5
29	8 37·3	8 38·7	8 13·7	2·9	1·7	8·9	5·1	14·9	8·6
30	8 37·5	8 38·9	8 13·9	3·0	1·7	9·0	5·2	15·0	8·6
31	8 37·8	8 39·2	8 14·2	3·1	1·8	9·1	5·2	15·1	8·7
32	8 38·0	8 39·4	8 14·4	3·2	1·8	9·2	5·3	15·2	8·7
33	8 38·3	8 39·7	8 14·6	3·3	1·9	9·3	5·3	15·3	8·8
34	8 38·5	8 39·9	8 14·9	3·4	2·0	9·4	5·4	15·4	8·9
35	8 38·8	8 40·2	8 15·1	3·5	2·0	9·5	5·5	15·5	8·9
36	8 39·0	8 40·4	8 15·4	3·6	2·1	9·6	5·5	15·6	9·0
37	8 39·3	8 40·7	8 15·6	3·7	2·1	9·7	5·6	15·7	9·0
38	8 39·5	8 40·9	8 15·8	3·8	2·2	9·8	5·6	15·8	9·1
39	8 39·8	8 41·2	8 16·1	3·9	2·2	9·9	5·7	15·9	9·1
40	8 40·0	8 41·4	8 16·3	4·0	2·3	10·0	5·8	16·0	9·2
41	8 40·3	8 41·7	8 16·5	4·1	2·4	10·1	5·8	16·1	9·3
42	8 40·5	8 41·9	8 16·8	4·2	2·4	10·2	5·9	16·2	9·3
43	8 40·8	8 42·2	8 17·0	4·3	2·5	10·3	5·9	16·3	9·4
44	8 41·0	8 42·4	8 17·3	4·4	2·5	10·4	6·0	16·4	9·4
45	8 41·3	8 42·7	8 17·5	4·5	2·6	10·5	6·0	16·5	9·5
46	8 41·5	8 42·9	8 17·7	4·6	2·6	10·6	6·1	16·6	9·5
47	8 41·8	8 43·2	8 18·0	4·7	2·7	10·7	6·2	16·7	9·6
48	8 42·0	8 43·4	8 18·2	4·8	2·8	10·8	6·2	16·8	9·7
49	8 42·3	8 43·7	8 18·5	4·9	2·8	10·9	6·3	16·9	9·7
50	8 42·5	8 43·9	8 18·7	5·0	2·9	11·0	6·3	17·0	9·8
51	8 42·8	8 44·2	8 18·9	5·1	2·9	11·1	6·4	17·1	9·8
52	8 43·0	8 44·4	8 19·2	5·2	3·0	11·2	6·4	17·2	9·9
53	8 43·3	8 44·7	8 19·4	5·3	3·0	11·3	6·5	17·3	9·9
54	8 43·5	8 44·9	8 19·7	5·4	3·1	11·4	6·6	17·4	10·0
55	8 43·8	8 45·2	8 19·9	5·5	3·2	11·5	6·6	17·5	10·1
56	8 44·0	8 45·4	8 20·1	5·6	3·2	11·6	6·7	17·6	10·1
57	8 44·3	8 45·7	8 20·4	5·7	3·3	11·7	6·7	17·7	10·2
58	8 44·5	8 45·9	8 20·6	5·8	3·3	11·8	6·8	17·8	10·2
59	8 44·8	8 46·2	8 20·8	5·9	3·4	11·9	6·8	17·9	10·3
60	8 45·0	8 46·4	8 21·1	6·0	3·5	12·0	6·9	18·0	10·4

m 35	SUN PLANETS	ARIES	MOON	v or d	Corrⁿ	v or d	Corrⁿ	v or d	Corrⁿ
s	° ′	° ′	° ′	′	′	′	′	′	′
00	8 45·0	8 46·4	8 21·1	0·0	0·0	6·0	3·6	12·0	7·1
01	8 45·3	8 46·7	8 21·3	0·1	0·1	6·1	3·6	12·1	7·2
02	8 45·5	8 46·9	8 21·6	0·2	0·1	6·2	3·7	12·2	7·2
03	8 45·8	8 47·2	8 21·8	0·3	0·2	6·3	3·7	12·3	7·3
04	8 46·0	8 47·4	8 22·0	0·4	0·2	6·4	3·8	12·4	7·3
05	8 46·3	8 47·7	8 22·3	0·5	0·3	6·5	3·8	12·5	7·4
06	8 46·5	8 47·9	8 22·5	0·6	0·4	6·6	3·9	12·6	7·5
07	8 46·8	8 48·2	8 22·8	0·7	0·4	6·7	4·0	12·7	7·5
08	8 47·0	8 48·4	8 23·0	0·8	0·5	6·8	4·0	12·8	7·6
09	8 47·3	8 48·7	8 23·2	0·9	0·5	6·9	4·1	12·9	7·6
10	8 47·5	8 48·9	8 23·5	1·0	0·6	7·0	4·1	13·0	7·7
11	8 47·8	8 49·2	8 23·7	1·1	0·7	7·1	4·2	13·1	7·8
12	8 48·0	8 49·4	8 23·9	1·2	0·7	7·2	4·3	13·2	7·8
13	8 48·3	8 49·7	8 24·2	1·3	0·8	7·3	4·3	13·3	7·9
14	8 48·5	8 49·9	8 24·4	1·4	0·8	7·4	4·4	13·4	7·9
15	8 48·8	8 50·2	8 24·7	1·5	0·9	7·5	4·4	13·5	8·0
16	8 49·0	8 50·4	8 24·9	1·6	0·9	7·6	4·5	13·6	8·0
17	8 49·3	8 50·7	8 25·1	1·7	1·0	7·7	4·6	13·7	8·1
18	8 49·5	8 50·9	8 25·4	1·8	1·1	7·8	4·6	13·8	8·2
19	8 49·8	8 51·2	8 25·6	1·9	1·1	7·9	4·7	13·9	8·2
20	8 50·0	8 51·5	8 25·9	2·0	1·2	8·0	4·7	14·0	8·3
21	8 50·3	8 51·7	8 26·1	2·1	1·2	8·1	4·8	14·1	8·3
22	8 50·5	8 52·0	8 26·3	2·2	1·3	8·2	4·9	14·2	8·4
23	8 50·8	8 52·2	8 26·6	2·3	1·4	8·3	4·9	14·3	8·5
24	8 51·0	8 52·5	8 26·8	2·4	1·4	8·4	5·0	14·4	8·5
25	8 51·3	8 52·7	8 27·0	2·5	1·5	8·5	5·0	14·5	8·6
26	8 51·5	8 53·0	8 27·3	2·6	1·5	8·6	5·1	14·6	8·6
27	8 51·8	8 53·2	8 27·5	2·7	1·6	8·7	5·1	14·7	8·7
28	8 52·0	8 53·5	8 27·8	2·8	1·7	8·8	5·2	14·8	8·8
29	8 52·3	8 53·7	8 28·0	2·9	1·7	8·9	5·3	14·9	8·8
30	8 52·5	8 54·0	8 28·2	3·0	1·8	9·0	5·3	15·0	8·9
31	8 52·8	8 54·2	8 28·5	3·1	1·8	9·1	5·4	15·1	8·9
32	8 53·0	8 54·5	8 28·7	3·2	1·9	9·2	5·4	15·2	9·0
33	8 53·3	8 54·7	8 29·0	3·3	2·0	9·3	5·5	15·3	9·1
34	8 53·5	8 55·0	8 29·2	3·4	2·0	9·4	5·6	15·4	9·1
35	8 53·8	8 55·2	8 29·4	3·5	2·1	9·5	5·6	15·5	9·2
36	8 54·0	8 55·5	8 29·7	3·6	2·1	9·6	5·7	15·6	9·2
37	8 54·3	8 55·7	8 29·9	3·7	2·2	9·7	5·7	15·7	9·3
38	8 54·5	8 56·0	8 30·2	3·8	2·2	9·8	5·8	15·8	9·3
39	8 54·8	8 56·2	8 30·4	3·9	2·3	9·9	5·9	15·9	9·4
40	8 55·0	8 56·5	8 30·6	4·0	2·4	10·0	5·9	16·0	9·5
41	8 55·3	8 56·7	8 30·9	4·1	2·4	10·1	6·0	16·1	9·5
42	8 55·5	8 57·0	8 31·1	4·2	2·5	10·2	6·0	16·2	9·6
43	8 55·8	8 57·2	8 31·3	4·3	2·5	10·3	6·1	16·3	9·6
44	8 56·0	8 57·5	8 31·6	4·4	2·6	10·4	6·2	16·4	9·7
45	8 56·3	8 57·7	8 31·8	4·5	2·7	10·5	6·2	16·5	9·8
46	8 56·5	8 58·0	8 32·1	4·6	2·7	10·6	6·3	16·6	9·8
47	8 56·8	8 58·2	8 32·3	4·7	2·8	10·7	6·3	16·7	9·9
48	8 57·0	8 58·5	8 32·5	4·8	2·8	10·8	6·4	16·8	9·9
49	8 57·3	8 58·7	8 32·8	4·9	2·9	10·9	6·4	16·9	10·0
50	8 57·5	8 59·0	8 33·0	5·0	3·0	11·0	6·5	17·0	10·1
51	8 57·8	8 59·2	8 33·3	5·1	3·0	11·1	6·6	17·1	10·1
52	8 58·0	8 59·5	8 33·5	5·2	3·1	11·2	6·6	17·2	10·2
53	8 58·3	8 59·7	8 33·7	5·3	3·1	11·3	6·7	17·3	10·2
54	8 58·5	9 00·0	8 34·0	5·4	3·2	11·4	6·7	17·4	10·3
55	8 58·8	9 00·2	8 34·2	5·5	3·3	11·5	6·8	17·5	10·4
56	8 59·0	9 00·5	8 34·4	5·6	3·3	11·6	6·9	17·6	10·4
57	8 59·3	9 00·7	8 34·7	5·7	3·4	11·7	6·9	17·7	10·5
58	8 59·5	9 01·0	8 34·9	5·8	3·4	11·8	7·0	17·8	10·5
59	8 59·8	9 01·2	8 35·2	5·9	3·5	11·9	7·0	17·9	10·6
60	9 00·0	9 01·5	8 35·4	6·0	3·6	12·0	7·1	18·0	10·7

36m	SUN PLANETS	ARIES	MOON	v or d	Corrn	v or d	Corrn	v or d	Corrn
s	° ′	° ′	° ′	′	′	′	′	′	′
00	9 00·0	9 01·5	8 35·4	0·0	0·0	6·0	3·7	12·0	7·3
01	9 00·3	9 01·7	8 35·6	0·1	0·1	6·1	3·7	12·1	7·4
02	9 00·5	9 02·0	8 35·9	0·2	0·1	6·2	3·8	12·2	7·4
03	9 00·8	9 02·2	8 36·1	0·3	0·2	6·3	3·8	12·3	7·5
04	9 01·0	9 02·5	8 36·4	0·4	0·2	6·4	3·9	12·4	7·5
05	9 01·3	9 02·7	8 36·6	0·5	0·3	6·5	4·0	12·5	7·6
06	9 01·5	9 03·0	8 36·8	0·6	0·4	6·6	4·0	12·6	7·7
07	9 01·8	9 03·2	8 37·1	0·7	0·4	6·7	4·1	12·7	7·7
08	9 02·0	9 03·5	8 37·3	0·8	0·5	6·8	4·1	12·8	7·8
09	9 02·3	9 03·7	8 37·5	0·9	0·5	6·9	4·2	12·9	7·8
10	9 02·5	9 04·0	8 37·8	1·0	0·6	7·0	4·3	13·0	7·9
11	9 02·8	9 04·2	8 38·0	1·1	0·7	7·1	4·3	13·1	8·0
12	9 03·0	9 04·5	8 38·3	1·2	0·7	7·2	4·4	13·2	8·0
13	9 03·3	9 04·7	8 38·5	1·3	0·8	7·3	4·4	13·3	8·1
14	9 03·5	9 05·0	8 38·7	1·4	0·9	7·4	4·5	13·4	8·2
15	9 03·8	9 05·2	8 39·0	1·5	0·9	7·5	4·6	13·5	8·2
16	9 04·0	9 05·5	8 39·2	1·6	1·0	7·6	4·6	13·6	8·3
17	9 04·3	9 05·7	8 39·5	1·7	1·0	7·7	4·7	13·7	8·3
18	9 04·5	9 06·0	8 39·7	1·8	1·1	7·8	4·7	13·8	8·4
19	9 04·8	9 06·2	8 39·9	1·9	1·2	7·9	4·8	13·9	8·5
20	9 05·0	9 06·5	8 40·2	2·0	1·2	8·0	4·9	14·0	8·5
21	9 05·3	9 06·7	8 40·4	2·1	1·3	8·1	4·9	14·1	8·6
22	9 05·5	9 07·0	8 40·6	2·2	1·3	8·2	5·0	14·2	8·6
23	9 05·8	9 07·2	8 40·9	2·3	1·4	8·3	5·0	14·3	8·7
24	9 06·0	9 07·5	8 41·1	2·4	1·5	8·4	5·1	14·4	8·8
25	9 06·3	9 07·7	8 41·4	2·5	1·5	8·5	5·2	14·5	8·8
26	9 06·5	9 08·0	8 41·6	2·6	1·6	8·6	5·2	14·6	8·9
27	9 06·8	9 08·2	8 41·8	2·7	1·6	8·7	5·3	14·7	8·9
28	9 07·0	9 08·5	8 42·1	2·8	1·7	8·8	5·4	14·8	9·0
29	9 07·3	9 08·7	8 42·3	2·9	1·8	8·9	5·4	14·9	9·1
30	9 07·5	9 09·0	8 42·6	3·0	1·8	9·0	5·5	15·0	9·1
31	9 07·8	9 09·2	8 42·8	3·1	1·9	9·1	5·5	15·1	9·2
32	9 08·0	9 09·5	8 43·0	3·2	1·9	9·2	5·6	15·2	9·2
33	9 08·3	9 09·8	8 43·3	3·3	2·0	9·3	5·7	15·3	9·3
34	9 08·5	9 10·0	8 43·5	3·4	2·1	9·4	5·7	15·4	9·4
35	9 08·8	9 10·3	8 43·8	3·5	2·1	9·5	5·8	15·5	9·4
36	9 09·0	9 10·5	8 44·0	3·6	2·2	9·6	5·8	15·6	9·5
37	9 09·3	9 10·8	8 44·2	3·7	2·3	9·7	5·9	15·7	9·6
38	9 09·5	9 11·0	8 44·5	3·8	2·3	9·8	6·0	15·8	9·6
39	9 09·8	9 11·3	8 44·7	3·9	2·4	9·9	6·0	15·9	9·7
40	9 10·0	9 11·5	8 44·9	4·0	2·4	10·0	6·1	16·0	9·7
41	9 10·3	9 11·8	8 45·2	4·1	2·5	10·1	6·1	16·1	9·8
42	9 10·5	9 12·0	8 45·4	4·2	2·6	10·2	6·2	16·2	9·9
43	9 10·8	9 12·3	8 45·7	4·3	2·6	10·3	6·3	16·3	9·9
44	9 11·0	9 12·5	8 45·9	4·4	2·7	10·4	6·3	16·4	10·0
45	9 11·3	9 12·8	8 46·1	4·5	2·7	10·5	6·4	16·5	10·0
46	9 11·5	9 13·0	8 46·4	4·6	2·8	10·6	6·4	16·6	10·1
47	9 11·8	9 13·3	8 46·6	4·7	2·9	10·7	6·5	16·7	10·2
48	9 12·0	9 13·5	8 46·9	4·8	2·9	10·8	6·6	16·8	10·2
49	9 12·3	9 13·8	8 47·1	4·9	3·0	10·9	6·6	16·9	10·3
50	9 12·5	9 14·0	8 47·3	5·0	3·0	11·0	6·7	17·0	10·3
51	9 12·8	9 14·3	8 47·6	5·1	3·1	11·1	6·8	17·1	10·4
52	9 13·0	9 14·5	8 47·8	5·2	3·2	11·2	6·8	17·2	10·5
53	9 13·3	9 14·8	8 48·0	5·3	3·2	11·3	6·9	17·3	10·5
54	9 13·5	9 15·0	8 48·3	5·4	3·3	11·4	6·9	17·4	10·6
55	9 13·8	9 15·3	8 48·5	5·5	3·3	11·5	7·0	17·5	10·6
56	9 14·0	9 15·5	8 48·8	5·6	3·4	11·6	7·1	17·6	10·7
57	9 14·3	9 15·8	8 49·0	5·7	3·5	11·7	7·1	17·7	10·8
58	9 14·5	9 16·0	8 49·2	5·8	3·5	11·8	7·2	17·8	10·8
59	9 14·8	9 16·3	8 49·5	5·9	3·6	11·9	7·2	17·9	10·9
60	9 15·0	9 16·5	8 49·7	6·0	3·7	12·0	7·3	18·0	11·0

37m	SUN PLANETS	ARIES	MOON	v or d	Corrn	v or d	Corrn	v or d	Corrn
s	° ′	° ′	° ′	′	′	′	′	′	′
00	9 15·0	9 16·5	8 49·7	0·0	0·0	6·0	3·8	12·0	7·5
01	9 15·3	9 16·8	8 50·0	0·1	0·1	6·1	3·8	12·1	7·6
02	9 15·5	9 17·0	8 50·2	0·2	0·1	6·2	3·9	12·2	7·6
03	9 15·8	9 17·3	8 50·4	0·3	0·2	6·3	3·9	12·3	7·7
04	9 16·0	9 17·5	8 50·7	0·4	0·3	6·4	4·0	12·4	7·8
05	9 16·3	9 17·8	8 50·9	0·5	0·3	6·5	4·1	12·5	7·8
06	9 16·5	9 18·0	8 51·1	0·6	0·4	6·6	4·1	12·6	7·9
07	9 16·8	9 18·3	8 51·4	0·7	0·4	6·7	4·2	12·7	7·9
08	9 17·0	9 18·5	8 51·6	0·8	0·5	6·8	4·3	12·8	8·0
09	9 17·3	9 18·8	8 51·9	0·9	0·6	6·9	4·3	12·9	8·1
10	9 17·5	9 19·0	8 52·1	1·0	0·6	7·0	4·4	13·0	8·1
11	9 17·8	9 19·3	8 52·3	1·1	0·7	7·1	4·4	13·1	8·2
12	9 18·0	9 19·5	8 52·6	1·2	0·8	7·2	4·5	13·2	8·3
13	9 18·3	9 19·8	8 52·8	1·3	0·8	7·3	4·6	13·3	8·3
14	9 18·5	9 20·0	8 53·1	1·4	0·9	7·4	4·6	13·4	8·4
15	9 18·8	9 20·3	8 53·3	1·5	0·9	7·5	4·7	13·5	8·4
16	9 19·0	9 20·5	8 53·5	1·6	1·0	7·6	4·8	13·6	8·5
17	9 19·3	9 20·8	8 53·8	1·7	1·1	7·7	4·8	13·7	8·6
18	9 19·5	9 21·0	8 54·0	1·8	1·1	7·8	4·9	13·8	8·6
19	9 19·8	9 21·3	8 54·3	1·9	1·2	7·9	4·9	13·9	8·7
20	9 20·0	9 21·5	8 54·5	2·0	1·3	8·0	5·0	14·0	8·8
21	9 20·3	9 21·8	8 54·7	2·1	1·3	8·1	5·1	14·1	8·8
22	9 20·5	9 22·0	8 55·0	2·2	1·4	8·2	5·1	14·2	8·9
23	9 20·8	9 22·3	8 55·2	2·3	1·4	8·3	5·2	14·3	8·9
24	9 21·0	9 22·5	8 55·4	2·4	1·5	8·4	5·3	14·4	9·0
25	9 21·3	9 22·8	8 55·7	2·5	1·6	8·5	5·3	14·5	9·1
26	9 21·5	9 23·0	8 55·9	2·6	1·6	8·6	5·4	14·6	9·1
27	9 21·8	9 23·3	8 56·2	2·7	1·7	8·7	5·4	14·7	9·2
28	9 22·0	9 23·5	8 56·4	2·8	1·8	8·8	5·5	14·8	9·3
29	9 22·3	9 23·8	8 56·6	2·9	1·8	8·9	5·6	14·9	9·3
30	9 22·5	9 24·0	8 56·9	3·0	1·9	9·0	5·6	15·0	9·4
31	9 22·8	9 24·3	8 57·1	3·1	1·9	9·1	5·7	15·1	9·4
32	9 23·0	9 24·5	8 57·4	3·2	2·0	9·2	5·8	15·2	9·5
33	9 23·3	9 24·8	8 57·6	3·3	2·1	9·3	5·8	15·3	9·6
34	9 23·5	9 25·0	8 57·8	3·4	2·1	9·4	5·9	15·4	9·6
35	9 23·8	9 25·3	8 58·1	3·5	2·2	9·5	5·9	15·5	9·7
36	9 24·0	9 25·5	8 58·3	3·6	2·3	9·6	6·0	15·6	9·8
37	9 24·3	9 25·8	8 58·5	3·7	2·3	9·7	6·1	15·7	9·8
38	9 24·5	9 26·0	8 58·8	3·8	2·4	9·8	6·1	15·8	9·9
39	9 24·8	9 26·3	8 59·0	3·9	2·4	9·9	6·2	15·9	9·9
40	9 25·0	9 26·5	8 59·3	4·0	2·5	10·0	6·3	16·0	10·0
41	9 25·3	9 26·8	8 59·5	4·1	2·6	10·1	6·3	16·1	10·1
42	9 25·5	9 27·0	8 59·7	4·2	2·6	10·2	6·4	16·2	10·1
43	9 25·8	9 27·3	9 00·0	4·3	2·7	10·3	6·4	16·3	10·2
44	9 26·0	9 27·5	9 00·2	4·4	2·8	10·4	6·5	16·4	10·3
45	9 26·3	9 27·8	9 00·5	4·5	2·8	10·5	6·6	16·5	10·3
46	9 26·5	9 28·1	9 00·7	4·6	2·9	10·6	6·6	16·6	10·4
47	9 26·8	9 28·3	9 00·9	4·7	2·9	10·7	6·7	16·7	10·4
48	9 27·0	9 28·6	9 01·2	4·8	3·0	10·8	6·8	16·8	10·5
49	9 27·3	9 28·8	9 01·4	4·9	3·1	10·9	6·8	16·9	10·6
50	9 27·5	9 29·1	9 01·6	5·0	3·1	11·0	6·9	17·0	10·6
51	9 27·8	9 29·3	9 01·9	5·1	3·2	11·1	6·9	17·1	10·7
52	9 28·0	9 29·6	9 02·1	5·2	3·3	11·2	7·0	17·2	10·8
53	9 28·3	9 29·8	9 02·4	5·3	3·3	11·3	7·1	17·3	10·8
54	9 28·5	9 30·1	9 02·6	5·4	3·4	11·4	7·1	17·4	10·9
55	9 28·8	9 30·3	9 02·8	5·5	3·4	11·5	7·2	17·5	10·9
56	9 29·0	9 30·6	9 03·1	5·6	3·5	11·6	7·3	17·6	11·0
57	9 29·3	9 30·8	9 03·3	5·7	3·6	11·7	7·3	17·7	11·1
58	9 29·5	9 31·1	9 03·6	5·8	3·6	11·8	7·4	17·8	11·1
59	9 29·8	9 31·3	9 03·8	5·9	3·7	11·9	7·4	17·9	11·2
60	9 30·0	9 31·6	9 04·0	6·0	3·8	12·0	7·5	18·0	11·3

38m	SUN PLANETS	ARIES	MOON	v or d	Corrn	v or d	Corrn	v or d	Corrn
s	° ′	° ′	° ′	′	′	′	′	′	′
00	9 30·0	9 31·6	9 04·0	0·0	0·0	6·0	3·9	12·0	7·7
01	9 30·3	9 31·8	9 04·3	0·1	0·1	6·1	3·9	12·1	7·8
02	9 30·5	9 32·1	9 04·5	0·2	0·1	6·2	4·0	12·2	7·8
03	9 30·8	9 32·3	9 04·7	0·3	0·2	6·3	4·0	12·3	7·9
04	9 31·0	9 32·6	9 05·0	0·4	0·3	6·4	4·1	12·4	8·0
05	9 31·3	9 32·8	9 05·2	0·5	0·3	6·5	4·2	12·5	8·0
06	9 31·5	9 33·1	9 05·5	0·6	0·4	6·6	4·2	12·6	8·1
07	9 31·8	9 33·3	9 05·7	0·7	0·4	6·7	4·3	12·7	8·1
08	9 32·0	9 33·6	9 05·9	0·8	0·5	6·8	4·4	12·8	8·2
09	9 32·3	9 33·8	9 06·2	0·9	0·6	6·9	4·4	12·9	8·3
10	9 32·5	9 34·1	9 06·4	1·0	0·6	7·0	4·5	13·0	8·3
11	9 32·8	9 34·3	9 06·7	1·1	0·7	7·1	4·6	13·1	8·4
12	9 33·0	9 34·6	9 06·9	1·2	0·8	7·2	4·6	13·2	8·5
13	9 33·3	9 34·8	9 07·1	1·3	0·8	7·3	4·7	13·3	8·5
14	9 33·5	9 35·1	9 07·4	1·4	0·9	7·4	4·7	13·4	8·6
15	9 33·8	9 35·3	9 07·6	1·5	1·0	7·5	4·8	13·5	8·7
16	9 34·0	9 35·6	9 07·9	1·6	1·0	7·6	4·9	13·6	8·7
17	9 34·3	9 35·8	9 08·1	1·7	1·1	7·7	4·9	13·7	8·8
18	9 34·5	9 36·1	9 08·3	1·8	1·2	7·8	5·0	13·8	8·9
19	9 34·8	9 36·3	9 08·6	1·9	1·2	7·9	5·1	13·9	8·9
20	9 35·0	9 36·6	9 08·8	2·0	1·3	8·0	5·1	14·0	9·0
21	9 35·3	9 36·8	9 09·0	2·1	1·3	8·1	5·2	14·1	9·0
22	9 35·5	9 37·1	9 09·3	2·2	1·4	8·2	5·3	14·2	9·1
23	9 35·8	9 37·3	9 09·5	2·3	1·5	8·3	5·3	14·3	9·2
24	9 36·0	9 37·6	9 09·8	2·4	1·5	8·4	5·4	14·4	9·2
25	9 36·3	9 37·8	9 10·0	2·5	1·6	8·5	5·5	14·5	9·3
26	9 36·5	9 38·1	9 10·2	2·6	1·7	8·6	5·5	14·6	9·4
27	9 36·8	9 38·3	9 10·5	2·7	1·7	8·7	5·6	14·7	9·4
28	9 37·0	9 38·6	9 10·7	2·8	1·8	8·8	5·6	14·8	9·5
29	9 37·3	9 38·8	9 11·0	2·9	1·9	8·9	5·7	14·9	9·6
30	9 37·5	9 39·1	9 11·2	3·0	1·9	9·0	5·8	15·0	9·6
31	9 37·8	9 39·3	9 11·4	3·1	2·0	9·1	5·8	15·1	9·7
32	9 38·0	9 39·6	9 11·7	3·2	2·1	9·2	5·9	15·2	9·8
33	9 38·3	9 39·8	9 11·9	3·3	2·1	9·3	6·0	15·3	9·8
34	9 38·5	9 40·1	9 12·1	3·4	2·2	9·4	6·0	15·4	9·9
35	9 38·8	9 40·3	9 12·4	3·5	2·2	9·5	6·1	15·5	9·9
36	9 39·0	9 40·6	9 12·6	3·6	2·3	9·6	6·2	15·6	10·0
37	9 39·3	9 40·8	9 12·9	3·7	2·4	9·7	6·2	15·7	10·1
38	9 39·5	9 41·1	9 13·1	3·8	2·4	9·8	6·3	15·8	10·1
39	9 39·8	9 41·3	9 13·3	3·9	2·5	9·9	6·4	15·9	10·2
40	9 40·0	9 41·6	9 13·6	4·0	2·6	10·0	6·4	16·0	10·3
41	9 40·3	9 41·8	9 13·8	4·1	2·6	10·1	6·5	16·1	10·3
42	9 40·5	9 42·1	9 14·1	4·2	2·7	10·2	6·5	16·2	10·4
43	9 40·8	9 42·3	9 14·3	4·3	2·8	10·3	6·6	16·3	10·5
44	9 41·0	9 42·6	9 14·5	4·4	2·8	10·4	6·7	16·4	10·5
45	9 41·3	9 42·8	9 14·8	4·5	2·9	10·5	6·7	16·5	10·6
46	9 41·5	9 43·1	9 15·0	4·6	3·0	10·6	6·8	16·6	10·7
47	9 41·8	9 43·3	9 15·2	4·7	3·0	10·7	6·9	16·7	10·7
48	9 42·0	9 43·6	9 15·5	4·8	3·1	10·8	6·9	16·8	10·8
49	9 42·3	9 43·8	9 15·7	4·9	3·1	10·9	7·0	16·9	10·8
50	9 42·5	9 44·1	9 16·0	5·0	3·2	11·0	7·1	17·0	10·9
51	9 42·8	9 44·3	9 16·2	5·1	3·3	11·1	7·1	17·1	11·0
52	9 43·0	9 44·6	9 16·4	5·2	3·3	11·2	7·2	17·2	11·0
53	9 43·3	9 44·8	9 16·7	5·3	3·4	11·3	7·3	17·3	11·1
54	9 43·5	9 45·1	9 16·9	5·4	3·5	11·4	7·3	17·4	11·2
55	9 43·8	9 45·3	9 17·2	5·5	3·5	11·5	7·4	17·5	11·2
56	9 44·0	9 45·6	9 17·4	5·6	3·6	11·6	7·4	17·6	11·3
57	9 44·3	9 45·8	9 17·6	5·7	3·7	11·7	7·5	17·7	11·4
58	9 44·5	9 46·1	9 17·9	5·8	3·7	11·8	7·6	17·8	11·4
59	9 44·8	9 46·4	9 18·1	5·9	3·8	11·9	7·6	17·9	11·5
60	9 45·0	9 46·6	9 18·4	6·0	3·9	12·0	7·7	18·0	11·6

39m	SUN PLANETS	ARIES	MOON	v or d	Corrn	v or d	Corrn	v or d	Corrn
s	° ′	° ′	° ′	′	′	′	′	′	′
00	9 45·0	9 46·6	9 18·4	0·0	0·0	6·0	4·0	12·0	7·9
01	9 45·3	9 46·9	9 18·6	0·1	0·1	6·1	4·0	12·1	8·0
02	9 45·5	9 47·1	9 18·8	0·2	0·1	6·2	4·1	12·2	8·0
03	9 45·8	9 47·4	9 19·1	0·3	0·2	6·3	4·1	12·3	8·1
04	9 46·0	9 47·6	9 19·3	0·4	0·3	6·4	4·2	12·4	8·2
05	9 46·3	9 47·9	9 19·5	0·5	0·3	6·5	4·3	12·5	8·2
06	9 46·5	9 48·1	9 19·8	0·6	0·4	6·6	4·3	12·6	8·3
07	9 46·8	9 48·4	9 20·0	0·7	0·5	6·7	4·4	12·7	8·4
08	9 47·0	9 48·6	9 20·3	0·8	0·5	6·8	4·5	12·8	8·4
09	9 47·3	9 48·9	9 20·5	0·9	0·6	6·9	4·5	12·9	8·5
10	9 47·5	9 49·1	9 20·7	1·0	0·7	7·0	4·6	13·0	8·6
11	9 47·8	9 49·4	9 21·0	1·1	0·7	7·1	4·7	13·1	8·6
12	9 48·0	9 49·6	9 21·2	1·2	0·8	7·2	4·7	13·2	8·7
13	9 48·3	9 49·9	9 21·5	1·3	0·9	7·3	4·8	13·3	8·8
14	9 48·5	9 50·1	9 21·7	1·4	0·9	7·4	4·9	13·4	8·8
15	9 48·8	9 50·4	9 21·9	1·5	1·0	7·5	4·9	13·5	8·9
16	9 49·0	9 50·6	9 22·2	1·6	1·1	7·6	5·0	13·6	9·0
17	9 49·3	9 50·9	9 22·4	1·7	1·1	7·7	5·1	13·7	9·0
18	9 49·5	9 51·1	9 22·6	1·8	1·2	7·8	5·1	13·8	9·1
19	9 49·8	9 51·4	9 22·9	1·9	1·3	7·9	5·2	13·9	9·2
20	9 50·0	9 51·6	9 23·1	2·0	1·3	8·0	5·3	14·0	9·2
21	9 50·3	9 51·9	9 23·4	2·1	1·4	8·1	5·3	14·1	9·3
22	9 50·5	9 52·1	9 23·6	2·2	1·4	8·2	5·4	14·2	9·3
23	9 50·8	9 52·4	9 23·8	2·3	1·5	8·3	5·5	14·3	9·4
24	9 51·0	9 52·6	9 24·1	2·4	1·6	8·4	5·5	14·4	9·5
25	9 51·3	9 52·9	9 24·3	2·5	1·6	8·5	5·6	14·5	9·5
26	9 51·5	9 53·1	9 24·6	2·6	1·7	8·6	5·7	14·6	9·6
27	9 51·8	9 53·4	9 24·8	2·7	1·8	8·7	5·7	14·7	9·7
28	9 52·0	9 53·6	9 25·0	2·8	1·8	8·8	5·8	14·8	9·7
29	9 52·3	9 53·9	9 25·3	2·9	1·9	8·9	5·9	14·9	9·8
30	9 52·5	9 54·1	9 25·5	3·0	2·0	9·0	5·9	15·0	9·9
31	9 52·8	9 54·4	9 25·7	3·1	2·0	9·1	6·0	15·1	9·9
32	9 53·0	9 54·6	9 26·0	3·2	2·1	9·2	6·1	15·2	10·0
33	9 53·3	9 54·9	9 26·2	3·3	2·2	9·3	6·1	15·3	10·1
34	9 53·5	9 55·1	9 26·5	3·4	2·2	9·4	6·2	15·4	10·1
35	9 53·8	9 55·4	9 26·7	3·5	2·3	9·5	6·3	15·5	10·2
36	9 54·0	9 55·6	9 26·9	3·6	2·4	9·6	6·3	15·6	10·3
37	9 54·3	9 55·9	9 27·2	3·7	2·4	9·7	6·4	15·7	10·3
38	9 54·5	9 56·1	9 27·4	3·8	2·5	9·8	6·5	15·8	10·4
39	9 54·8	9 56·4	9 27·7	3·9	2·6	9·9	6·5	15·9	10·5
40	9 55·0	9 56·6	9 27·9	4·0	2·6	10·0	6·6	16·0	10·5
41	9 55·3	9 56·9	9 28·1	4·1	2·7	10·1	6·6	16·1	10·6
42	9 55·5	9 57·1	9 28·4	4·2	2·8	10·2	6·7	16·2	10·7
43	9 55·8	9 57·4	9 28·6	4·3	2·8	10·3	6·8	16·3	10·7
44	9 56·0	9 57·6	9 28·8	4·4	2·9	10·4	6·8	16·4	10·8
45	9 56·3	9 57·9	9 29·1	4·5	3·0	10·5	6·9	16·5	10·9
46	9 56·5	9 58·1	9 29·3	4·6	3·0	10·6	7·0	16·6	10·9
47	9 56·8	9 58·4	9 29·6	4·7	3·1	10·7	7·0	16·7	11·0
48	9 57·0	9 58·6	9 29·8	4·8	3·2	10·8	7·1	16·8	11·1
49	9 57·3	9 58·9	9 30·0	4·9	3·2	10·9	7·2	16·9	11·1
50	9 57·5	9 59·1	9 30·3	5·0	3·3	11·0	7·2	17·0	11·2
51	9 57·8	9 59·4	9 30·5	5·1	3·4	11·1	7·3	17·1	11·3
52	9 58·0	9 59·6	9 30·8	5·2	3·4	11·2	7·4	17·2	11·3
53	9 58·3	9 59·9	9 31·0	5·3	3·5	11·3	7·4	17·3	11·4
54	9 58·5	10 00·1	9 31·2	5·4	3·6	11·4	7·5	17·4	11·5
55	9 58·8	10 00·4	9 31·5	5·5	3·6	11·5	7·6	17·5	11·5
56	9 59·0	10 00·6	9 31·7	5·6	3·7	11·6	7·6	17·6	11·6
57	9 59·3	10 00·9	9 32·0	5·7	3·8	11·7	7·7	17·7	11·7
58	9 59·5	10 01·1	9 32·2	5·8	3·8	11·8	7·8	17·8	11·7
59	9 59·8	10 01·4	9 32·4	5·9	3·9	11·9	7·8	17·9	11·8
60	10 00·0	10 01·6	9 32·7	6·0	4·0	12·0	7·9	18·0	11·9

40^m	SUN PLANETS	ARIES	MOON	v or d	Corr^n	v or d	Corr^n	v or d	Corr^n
s	° ′	° ′	° ′	′	′	′	′	′	′
00	10 00·0	10 01·6	9 32·7	0·0	0·0	6·0	4·1	12·0	8·1
01	10 00·3	10 01·9	9 32·9	0·1	0·1	6·1	4·1	12·1	8·2
02	10 00·5	10 02·1	9 33·1	0·2	0·1	6·2	4·2	12·2	8·2
03	10 00·8	10 02·4	9 33·4	0·3	0·2	6·3	4·3	12·3	8·3
04	10 01·0	10 02·6	9 33·6	0·4	0·3	6·4	4·3	12·4	8·4
05	10 01·3	10 02·9	9 33·9	0·5	0·3	6·5	4·4	12·5	8·4
06	10 01·5	10 03·1	9 34·1	0·6	0·4	6·6	4·5	12·6	8·5
07	10 01·8	10 03·4	9 34·3	0·7	0·5	6·7	4·5	12·7	8·6
08	10 02·0	10 03·6	9 34·6	0·8	0·5	6·8	4·6	12·8	8·6
09	10 02·3	10 03·9	9 34·8	0·9	0·6	6·9	4·7	12·9	8·7
10	10 02·5	10 04·1	9 35·1	1·0	0·7	7·0	4·7	13·0	8·8
11	10 02·8	10 04·4	9 35·3	1·1	0·7	7·1	4·8	13·1	8·8
12	10 03·0	10 04·7	9 35·5	1·2	0·8	7·2	4·9	13·2	8·9
13	10 03·3	10 04·9	9 35·8	1·3	0·9	7·3	4·9	13·3	9·0
14	10 03·5	10 05·2	9 36·0	1·4	0·9	7·4	5·0	13·4	9·0
15	10 03·8	10 05·4	9 36·2	1·5	1·0	7·5	5·1	13·5	9·1
16	10 04·0	10 05·7	9 36·5	1·6	1·1	7·6	5·1	13·6	9·2
17	10 04·3	10 05·9	9 36·7	1·7	1·1	7·7	5·2	13·7	9·2
18	10 04·5	10 06·2	9 37·0	1·8	1·2	7·8	5·3	13·8	9·3
19	10 04·8	10 06·4	9 37·2	1·9	1·3	7·9	5·3	13·9	9·4
20	10 05·0	10 06·7	9 37·4	2·0	1·4	8·0	5·4	14·0	9·5
21	10 05·3	10 06·9	9 37·7	2·1	1·4	8·1	5·5	14·1	9·5
22	10 05·5	10 07·2	9 37·9	2·2	1·5	8·2	5·5	14·2	9·6
23	10 05·8	10 07·4	9 38·2	2·3	1·6	8·3	5·6	14·3	9·7
24	10 06·0	10 07·7	9 38·4	2·4	1·6	8·4	5·7	14·4	9·7
25	10 06·3	10 07·9	9 38·6	2·5	1·7	8·5	5·7	14·5	9·8
26	10 06·5	10 08·2	9 38·9	2·6	1·8	8·6	5·8	14·6	9·9
27	10 06·8	10 08·4	9 39·1	2·7	1·8	8·7	5·9	14·7	9·9
28	10 07·0	10 08·7	9 39·3	2·8	1·9	8·8	5·9	14·8	10·0
29	10 07·3	10 08·9	9 39·6	2·9	2·0	8·9	6·0	14·9	10·1
30	10 07·5	10 09·2	9 39·8	3·0	2·0	9·0	6·1	15·0	10·1
31	10 07·8	10 09·4	9 40·1	3·1	2·1	9·1	6·1	15·1	10·2
32	10 08·0	10 09·7	9 40·3	3·2	2·2	9·2	6·2	15·2	10·3
33	10 08·3	10 09·9	9 40·5	3·3	2·2	9·3	6·3	15·3	10·3
34	10 08·5	10 10·2	9 40·8	3·4	2·3	9·4	6·3	15·4	10·4
35	10 08·8	10 10·4	9 41·0	3·5	2·4	9·5	6·4	15·5	10·5
36	10 09·0	10 10·7	9 41·3	3·6	2·4	9·6	6·5	15·6	10·5
37	10 09·3	10 10·9	9 41·5	3·7	2·5	9·7	6·5	15·7	10·6
38	10 09·5	10 11·2	9 41·7	3·8	2·6	9·8	6·6	15·8	10·7
39	10 09·8	10 11·4	9 42·0	3·9	2·6	9·9	6·7	15·9	10·7
40	10 10·0	10 11·7	9 42·2	4·0	2·7	10·0	6·8	16·0	10·8
41	10 10·3	10 11·9	9 42·4	4·1	2·8	10·1	6·8	16·1	10·9
42	10 10·5	10 12·2	9 42·7	4·2	2·8	10·2	6·9	16·2	10·9
43	10 10·8	10 12·4	9 42·9	4·3	2·9	10·3	7·0	16·3	11·0
44	10 11·0	10 12·7	9 43·2	4·4	3·0	10·4	7·0	16·4	11·1
45	10 11·3	10 12·9	9 43·4	4·5	3·0	10·5	7·1	16·5	11·1
46	10 11·5	10 13·2	9 43·6	4·6	3·1	10·6	7·2	16·6	11·2
47	10 11·8	10 13·4	9 43·9	4·7	3·2	10·7	7·2	16·7	11·3
48	10 12·0	10 13·7	9 44·1	4·8	3·2	10·8	7·3	16·8	11·3
49	10 12·3	10 13·9	9 44·4	4·9	3·3	10·9	7·4	16·9	11·4
50	10 12·5	10 14·2	9 44·6	5·0	3·4	11·0	7·4	17·0	11·5
51	10 12·8	10 14·4	9 44·8	5·1	3·4	11·1	7·5	17·1	11·5
52	10 13·0	10 14·7	9 45·1	5·2	3·5	11·2	7·6	17·2	11·6
53	10 13·3	10 14·9	9 45·3	5·3	3·6	11·3	7·6	17·3	11·7
54	10 13·5	10 15·2	9 45·6	5·4	3·6	11·4	7·7	17·4	11·7
55	10 13·8	10 15·4	9 45·8	5·5	3·7	11·5	7·8	17·5	11·8
56	10 14·0	10 15·7	9 46·0	5·6	3·8	11·6	7·8	17·6	11·9
57	10 14·3	10 15·9	9 46·3	5·7	3·8	11·7	7·9	17·7	11·9
58	10 14·5	10 16·2	9 46·5	5·8	3·9	11·8	8·0	17·8	12·0
59	10 14·8	10 16·4	9 46·7	5·9	4·0	11·9	8·0	17·9	12·1
60	10 15·0	10 16·7	9 47·0	6·0	4·1	12·0	8·1	18·0	12·2

41^m	SUN PLANETS	ARIES	MOON	v or d	Corr^n	v or d	Corr^n	v or d	Corr^n
s	° ′	° ′	° ′	′	′	′	′	′	′
00	10 15·0	10 16·7	9 47·0	0·0	0·0	6·0	4·2	12·0	8·3
01	10 15·3	10 16·9	9 47·2	0·1	0·1	6·1	4·2	12·1	8·4
02	10 15·5	10 17·2	9 47·5	0·2	0·1	6·2	4·3	12·2	8·4
03	10 15·8	10 17·4	9 47·7	0·3	0·2	6·3	4·4	12·3	8·5
04	10 16·0	10 17·7	9 47·9	0·4	0·3	6·4	4·4	12·4	8·6
05	10 16·3	10 17·9	9 48·2	0·5	0·3	6·5	4·5	12·5	8·6
06	10 16·5	10 18·2	9 48·4	0·6	0·4	6·6	4·6	12·6	8·7
07	10 16·8	10 18·4	9 48·7	0·7	0·5	6·7	4·6	12·7	8·8
08	10 17·0	10 18·7	9 48·9	0·8	0·6	6·8	4·7	12·8	8·9
09	10 17·3	10 18·9	9 49·1	0·9	0·6	6·9	4·8	12·9	8·9
10	10 17·5	10 19·2	9 49·4	1·0	0·7	7·0	4·8	13·0	9·0
11	10 17·8	10 19·4	9 49·6	1·1	0·8	7·1	4·9	13·1	9·1
12	10 18·0	10 19·7	9 49·8	1·2	0·8	7·2	5·0	13·2	9·1
13	10 18·3	10 19·9	9 50·1	1·3	0·9	7·3	5·0	13·3	9·2
14	10 18·5	10 20·2	9 50·3	1·4	1·0	7·4	5·1	13·4	9·3
15	10 18·8	10 20·4	9 50·6	1·5	1·0	7·5	5·2	13·5	9·3
16	10 19·0	10 20·7	9 50·8	1·6	1·1	7·6	5·3	13·6	9·4
17	10 19·3	10 20·9	9 51·0	1·7	1·2	7·7	5·3	13·7	9·5
18	10 19·5	10 21·2	9 51·3	1·8	1·2	7·8	5·4	13·8	9·5
19	10 19·8	10 21·4	9 51·5	1·9	1·3	7·9	5·5	13·9	9·6
20	10 20·0	10 21·7	9 51·8	2·0	1·4	8·0	5·5	14·0	9·7
21	10 20·3	10 21·9	9 52·0	2·1	1·5	8·1	5·6	14·1	9·8
22	10 20·5	10 22·2	9 52·2	2·2	1·5	8·2	5·7	14·2	9·8
23	10 20·8	10 22·4	9 52·5	2·3	1·6	8·3	5·7	14·3	9·9
24	10 21·0	10 22·7	9 52·7	2·4	1·7	8·4	5·8	14·4	10·0
25	10 21·3	10 23·0	9 52·9	2·5	1·7	8·5	5·9	14·5	10·0
26	10 21·5	10 23·2	9 53·2	2·6	1·8	8·6	5·9	14·6	10·1
27	10 21·8	10 23·5	9 53·4	2·7	1·9	8·7	6·0	14·7	10·2
28	10 22·0	10 23·7	9 53·7	2·8	1·9	8·8	6·1	14·8	10·2
29	10 22·3	10 24·0	9 53·9	2·9	2·0	8·9	6·2	14·9	10·3
30	10 22·5	10 24·2	9 54·1	3·0	2·1	9·0	6·2	15·0	10·4
31	10 22·8	10 24·5	9 54·4	3·1	2·1	9·1	6·3	15·1	10·4
32	10 23·0	10 24·7	9 54·6	3·2	2·2	9·2	6·4	15·2	10·5
33	10 23·3	10 25·0	9 54·9	3·3	2·3	9·3	6·4	15·3	10·6
34	10 23·5	10 25·2	9 55·1	3·4	2·4	9·4	6·5	15·4	10·7
35	10 23·8	10 25·5	9 55·3	3·5	2·4	9·5	6·6	15·5	10·7
36	10 24·0	10 25·7	9 55·6	3·6	2·5	9·6	6·6	15·6	10·8
37	10 24·3	10 26·0	9 55·8	3·7	2·6	9·7	6·7	15·7	10·9
38	10 24·5	10 26·2	9 56·1	3·8	2·6	9·8	6·8	15·8	10·9
39	10 24·8	10 26·5	9 56·3	3·9	2·7	9·9	6·8	15·9	11·0
40	10 25·0	10 26·7	9 56·5	4·0	2·8	10·0	6·9	16·0	11·1
41	10 25·3	10 27·0	9 56·8	4·1	2·8	10·1	7·0	16·1	11·1
42	10 25·5	10 27·2	9 57·0	4·2	2·9	10·2	7·1	16·2	11·2
43	10 25·8	10 27·5	9 57·2	4·3	3·0	10·3	7·1	16·3	11·3
44	10 26·0	10 27·7	9 57·5	4·4	3·0	10·4	7·2	16·4	11·3
45	10 26·3	10 28·0	9 57·7	4·5	3·1	10·5	7·3	16·5	11·4
46	10 26·5	10 28·2	9 58·0	4·6	3·2	10·6	7·3	16·6	11·5
47	10 26·8	10 28·5	9 58·2	4·7	3·3	10·7	7·4	16·7	11·6
48	10 27·0	10 28·7	9 58·4	4·8	3·3	10·8	7·5	16·8	11·6
49	10 27·3	10 29·0	9 58·7	4·9	3·4	10·9	7·5	16·9	11·7
50	10 27·5	10 29·2	9 58·9	5·0	3·5	11·0	7·6	17·0	11·8
51	10 27·8	10 29·5	9 59·2	5·1	3·5	11·1	7·7	17·1	11·8
52	10 28·0	10 29·7	9 59·4	5·2	3·6	11·2	7·7	17·2	11·9
53	10 28·3	10 30·0	9 59·6	5·3	3·7	11·3	7·8	17·3	12·0
54	10 28·5	10 30·2	9 59·9	5·4	3·7	11·4	7·9	17·4	12·0
55	10 28·8	10 30·5	10 00·1	5·5	3·8	11·5	8·0	17·5	12·1
56	10 29·0	10 30·7	10 00·3	5·6	3·9	11·6	8·0	17·6	12·2
57	10 29·3	10 31·0	10 00·6	5·7	3·9	11·7	8·1	17·7	12·2
58	10 29·5	10 31·2	10 00·8	5·8	4·0	11·8	8·2	17·8	12·3
59	10 29·8	10 31·5	10 01·1	5·9	4·1	11·9	8·2	17·9	12·4
60	10 30·0	10 31·7	10 01·3	6·0	4·2	12·0	8·3	18·0	12·5

42^{m} s	SUN PLANETS ° ′	ARIES ° ′	MOON ° ′	v or d ′	Corr^{n} ′	v or d ′	Corr^{n} ′	v or d ′	Corr^{n} ′
00	10 30·0	10 31·7	10 01·3	0·0	0·0	6·0	4·3	12·0	8·5
01	10 30·3	10 32·0	10 01·5	0·1	0·1	6·1	4·3	12·1	8·6
02	10 30·5	10 32·2	10 01·8	0·2	0·1	6·2	4·4	12·2	8·6
03	10 30·8	10 32·5	10 02·0	0·3	0·2	6·3	4·5	12·3	8·7
04	10 31·0	10 32·7	10 02·3	0·4	0·3	6·4	4·5	12·4	8·8
05	10 31·3	10 33·0	10 02·5	0·5	0·4	6·5	4·6	12·5	8·9
06	10 31·5	10 33·2	10 02·7	0·6	0·4	6·6	4·7	12·6	8·9
07	10 31·8	10 33·5	10 03·0	0·7	0·5	6·7	4·7	12·7	9·0
08	10 32·0	10 33·7	10 03·2	0·8	0·6	6·8	4·8	12·8	9·1
09	10 32·3	10 34·0	10 03·4	0·9	0·6	6·9	4·9	12·9	9·1
10	10 32·5	10 34·2	10 03·7	1·0	0·7	7·0	5·0	13·0	9·2
11	10 32·8	10 34·5	10 03·9	1·1	0·8	7·1	5·0	13·1	9·3
12	10 33·0	10 34·7	10 04·2	1·2	0·9	7·2	5·1	13·2	9·4
13	10 33·3	10 35·0	10 04·4	1·3	0·9	7·3	5·2	13·3	9·4
14	10 33·5	10 35·2	10 04·6	1·4	1·0	7·4	5·2	13·4	9·5
15	10 33·8	10 35·5	10 04·9	1·5	1·1	7·5	5·3	13·5	9·6
16	10 34·0	10 35·7	10 05·1	1·6	1·1	7·6	5·4	13·6	9·6
17	10 34·3	10 36·0	10 05·4	1·7	1·2	7·7	5·5	13·7	9·7
18	10 34·5	10 36·2	10 05·6	1·8	1·3	7·8	5·5	13·8	9·8
19	10 34·8	10 36·5	10 05·8	1·9	1·3	7·9	5·6	13·9	9·8
20	10 35·0	10 36·7	10 06·1	2·0	1·4	8·0	5·7	14·0	9·9
21	10 35·3	10 37·0	10 06·3	2·1	1·5	8·1	5·7	14·1	10·0
22	10 35·5	10 37·2	10 06·5	2·2	1·6	8·2	5·8	14·2	10·1
23	10 35·8	10 37·5	10 06·8	2·3	1·6	8·3	5·9	14·3	10·1
24	10 36·0	10 37·7	10 07·0	2·4	1·7	8·4	6·0	14·4	10·2
25	10 36·3	10 38·0	10 07·3	2·5	1·8	8·5	6·0	14·5	10·3
26	10 36·5	10 38·2	10 07·5	2·6	1·8	8·6	6·1	14·6	10·3
27	10 36·8	10 38·5	10 07·7	2·7	1·9	8·7	6·2	14·7	10·4
28	10 37·0	10 38·7	10 08·0	2·8	2·0	8·8	6·2	14·8	10·5
29	10 37·3	10 39·0	10 08·2	2·9	2·1	8·9	6·3	14·9	10·6
30	10 37·5	10 39·2	10 08·5	3·0	2·1	9·0	6·4	15·0	10·6
31	10 37·8	10 39·5	10 08·7	3·1	2·2	9·1	6·4	15·1	10·7
32	10 38·0	10 39·7	10 08·9	3·2	2·3	9·2	6·5	15·2	10·8
33	10 38·3	10 40·0	10 09·2	3·3	2·3	9·3	6·6	15·3	10·8
34	10 38·5	10 40·2	10 09·4	3·4	2·4	9·4	6·7	15·4	10·9
35	10 38·8	10 40·5	10 09·7	3·5	2·5	9·5	6·7	15·5	11·0
36	10 39·0	10 40·7	10 09·9	3·6	2·6	9·6	6·8	15·6	11·1
37	10 39·3	10 41·0	10 10·1	3·7	2·6	9·7	6·9	15·7	11·1
38	10 39·5	10 41·3	10 10·4	3·8	2·7	9·8	6·9	15·8	11·2
39	10 39·8	10 41·5	10 10·6	3·9	2·8	9·9	7·0	15·9	11·3
40	10 40·0	10 41·8	10 10·8	4·0	2·8	10·0	7·1	16·0	11·3
41	10 40·3	10 42·0	10 11·1	4·1	2·9	10·1	7·2	16·1	11·4
42	10 40·5	10 42·3	10 11·3	4·2	3·0	10·2	7·2	16·2	11·5
43	10 40·8	10 42·5	10 11·6	4·3	3·0	10·3	7·3	16·3	11·5
44	10 41·0	10 42·8	10 11·8	4·4	3·1	10·4	7·4	16·4	11·6
45	10 41·3	10 43·0	10 12·0	4·5	3·2	10·5	7·4	16·5	11·7
46	10 41·5	10 43·3	10 12·3	4·6	3·3	10·6	7·5	16·6	11·8
47	10 41·8	10 43·5	10 12·5	4·7	3·3	10·7	7·6	16·7	11·8
48	10 42·0	10 43·8	10 12·8	4·8	3·4	10·8	7·7	16·8	11·9
49	10 42·3	10 44·0	10 13·0	4·9	3·5	10·9	7·7	16·9	12·0
50	10 42·5	10 44·3	10 13·2	5·0	3·5	11·0	7·8	17·0	12·0
51	10 42·8	10 44·5	10 13·5	5·1	3·6	11·1	7·9	17·1	12·1
52	10 43·0	10 44·8	10 13·7	5·2	3·7	11·2	7·9	17·2	12·2
53	10 43·3	10 45·0	10 13·9	5·3	3·8	11·3	8·0	17·3	12·3
54	10 43·5	10 45·3	10 14·2	5·4	3·8	11·4	8·1	17·4	12·3
55	10 43·8	10 45·5	10 14·4	5·5	3·9	11·5	8·1	17·5	12·4
56	10 44·0	10 45·8	10 14·7	5·6	4·0	11·6	8·2	17·6	12·5
57	10 44·3	10 46·0	10 14·9	5·7	4·0	11·7	8·3	17·7	12·5
58	10 44·5	10 46·3	10 15·1	5·8	4·1	11·8	8·4	17·8	12·6
59	10 44·8	10 46·5	10 15·4	5·9	4·2	11·9	8·4	17·9	12·7
60	10 45·0	10 46·8	10 15·6	6·0	4·3	12·0	8·5	18·0	12·8

43^{m} s	SUN PLANETS ° ′	ARIES ° ′	MOON ° ′	v or d ′	Corr^{n} ′	v or d ′	Corr^{n} ′	v or d ′	Corr^{n} ′
00	10 45·0	10 46·8	10 15·6	0·0	0·0	6·0	4·4	12·0	8·7
01	10 45·3	10 47·0	10 15·9	0·1	0·1	6·1	4·4	12·1	8·8
02	10 45·5	10 47·3	10 16·1	0·2	0·1	6·2	4·5	12·2	8·8
03	10 45·8	10 47·5	10 16·3	0·3	0·2	6·3	4·6	12·3	8·9
04	10 46·0	10 47·8	10 16·6	0·4	0·3	6·4	4·6	12·4	9·0
05	10 46·3	10 48·0	10 16·8	0·5	0·4	6·5	4·7	12·5	9·1
06	10 46·5	10 48·3	10 17·0	0·6	0·4	6·6	4·8	12·6	9·1
07	10 46·8	10 48·5	10 17·3	0·7	0·5	6·7	4·9	12·7	9·2
08	10 47·0	10 48·8	10 17·5	0·8	0·6	6·8	4·9	12·8	9·3
09	10 47·3	10 49·0	10 17·8	0·9	0·7	6·9	5·0	12·9	9·4
10	10 47·5	10 49·3	10 18·0	1·0	0·7	7·0	5·1	13·0	9·4
11	10 47·8	10 49·5	10 18·2	1·1	0·8	7·1	5·1	13·1	9·5
12	10 48·0	10 49·8	10 18·5	1·2	0·9	7·2	5·2	13·2	9·6
13	10 48·3	10 50·0	10 18·7	1·3	0·9	7·3	5·3	13·3	9·6
14	10 48·5	10 50·3	10 19·0	1·4	1·0	7·4	5·4	13·4	9·7
15	10 48·8	10 50·5	10 19·2	1·5	1·1	7·5	5·4	13·5	9·8
16	10 49·0	10 50·8	10 19·4	1·6	1·2	7·6	5·5	13·6	9·9
17	10 49·3	10 51·0	10 19·7	1·7	1·2	7·7	5·6	13·7	9·9
18	10 49·5	10 51·3	10 19·9	1·8	1·3	7·8	5·7	13·8	10·0
19	10 49·8	10 51·5	10 20·2	1·9	1·4	7·9	5·7	13·9	10·1
20	10 50·0	10 51·8	10 20·4	2·0	1·5	8·0	5·8	14·0	10·2
21	10 50·3	10 52·0	10 20·6	2·1	1·5	8·1	5·9	14·1	10·2
22	10 50·5	10 52·3	10 20·9	2·2	1·6	8·2	5·9	14·2	10·3
23	10 50·8	10 52·5	10 21·1	2·3	1·7	8·3	6·0	14·3	10·4
24	10 51·0	10 52·8	10 21·3	2·4	1·7	8·4	6·1	14·4	10·4
25	10 51·3	10 53·0	10 21·6	2·5	1·8	8·5	6·2	14·5	10·5
26	10 51·5	10 53·3	10 21·8	2·6	1·9	8·6	6·2	14·6	10·6
27	10 51·8	10 53·5	10 22·1	2·7	2·0	8·7	6·3	14·7	10·7
28	10 52·0	10 53·8	10 22·3	2·8	2·0	8·8	6·4	14·8	10·7
29	10 52·3	10 54·0	10 22·5	2·9	2·1	8·9	6·5	14·9	10·8
30	10 52·5	10 54·3	10 22·8	3·0	2·2	9·0	6·5	15·0	10·9
31	10 52·8	10 54·5	10 23·0	3·1	2·2	9·1	6·6	15·1	10·9
32	10 53·0	10 54·8	10 23·3	3·2	2·3	9·2	6·7	15·2	11·0
33	10 53·3	10 55·0	10 23·5	3·3	2·4	9·3	6·7	15·3	11·1
34	10 53·5	10 55·3	10 23·7	3·4	2·5	9·4	6·8	15·4	11·2
35	10 53·8	10 55·5	10 24·0	3·5	2·5	9·5	6·9	15·5	11·2
36	10 54·0	10 55·8	10 24·2	3·6	2·6	9·6	7·0	15·6	11·3
37	10 54·3	10 56·0	10 24·4	3·7	2·7	9·7	7·0	15·7	11·4
38	10 54·5	10 56·3	10 24·7	3·8	2·8	9·8	7·1	15·8	11·5
39	10 54·8	10 56·5	10 24·9	3·9	2·8	9·9	7·2	15·9	11·5
40	10 55·0	10 56·8	10 25·2	4·0	2·9	10·0	7·3	16·0	11·6
41	10 55·3	10 57·0	10 25·4	4·1	3·0	10·1	7·3	16·1	11·7
42	10 55·5	10 57·3	10 25·6	4·2	3·0	10·2	7·4	16·2	11·7
43	10 55·8	10 57·5	10 25·9	4·3	3·1	10·3	7·5	16·3	11·8
44	10 56·0	10 57·8	10 26·1	4·4	3·2	10·4	7·5	16·4	11·9
45	10 56·3	10 58·0	10 26·4	4·5	3·3	10·5	7·6	16·5	12·0
46	10 56·5	10 58·3	10 26·6	4·6	3·3	10·6	7·7	16·6	12·0
47	10 56·8	10 58·5	10 26·8	4·7	3·4	10·7	7·8	16·7	12·1
48	10 57·0	10 58·8	10 27·1	4·8	3·5	10·8	7·8	16·8	12·2
49	10 57·3	10 59·0	10 27·3	4·9	3·6	10·9	7·9	16·9	12·3
50	10 57·5	10 59·3	10 27·5	5·0	3·6	11·0	8·0	17·0	12·3
51	10 57·8	10 59·6	10 27·8	5·1	3·7	11·1	8·0	17·1	12·4
52	10 58·0	10 59·8	10 28·0	5·2	3·8	11·2	8·1	17·2	12·5
53	10 58·3	11 00·1	10 28·3	5·3	3·8	11·3	8·2	17·3	12·5
54	10 58·5	11 00·3	10 28·5	5·4	3·9	11·4	8·3	17·4	12·6
55	10 58·8	11 00·6	10 28·7	5·5	4·0	11·5	8·3	17·5	12·7
56	10 59·0	11 00·8	10 29·0	5·6	4·1	11·6	8·4	17·6	12·8
57	10 59·3	11 01·1	10 29·2	5·7	4·1	11·7	8·5	17·7	12·8
58	10 59·5	11 01·3	10 29·5	5·8	4·2	11·8	8·6	17·8	12·9
59	10 59·8	11 01·6	10 29·7	5·9	4·3	11·9	8·6	17·9	13·0
60	11 00·0	11 01·8	10 29·9	6·0	4·4	12·0	8·7	18·0	13·1

44m s	SUN PLANETS ° ′	ARIES ° ′	MOON ° ′	v or d ′	Corrⁿ ′	v or d ′	Corrⁿ ′	v or d ′	Corrⁿ ′
00	11 00·0	11 01·8	10 29·9	0·0	0·0	6·0	4·5	12·0	8·9
01	11 00·3	11 02·1	10 30·2	0·1	0·1	6·1	4·5	12·1	9·0
02	11 00·5	11 02·3	10 30·4	0·2	0·1	6·2	4·6	12·2	9·0
03	11 00·8	11 02·6	10 30·6	0·3	0·2	6·3	4·7	12·3	9·1
04	11 01·0	11 02·8	10 30·9	0·4	0·3	6·4	4·7	12·4	9·2
05	11 01·3	11 03·1	10 31·1	0·5	0·4	6·5	4·8	12·5	9·3
06	11 01·5	11 03·3	10 31·4	0·6	0·4	6·6	4·9	12·6	9·3
07	11 01·8	11 03·6	10 31·6	0·7	0·5	6·7	5·0	12·7	9·4
08	11 02·0	11 03·8	10 31·8	0·8	0·6	6·8	5·0	12·8	9·5
09	11 02·3	11 04·1	10 32·1	0·9	0·7	6·9	5·1	12·9	9·6
10	11 02·5	11 04·3	10 32·3	1·0	0·7	7·0	5·2	13·0	9·6
11	11 02·8	11 04·6	10 32·6	1·1	0·8	7·1	5·3	13·1	9·7
12	11 03·0	11 04·8	10 32·8	1·2	0·9	7·2	5·3	13·2	9·8
13	11 03·3	11 05·1	10 33·0	1·3	1·0	7·3	5·4	13·3	9·9
14	11 03·5	11 05·3	10 33·3	1·4	1·0	7·4	5·5	13·4	9·9
15	11 03·8	11 05·6	10 33·5	1·5	1·1	7·5	5·6	13·5	10·0
16	11 04·0	11 05·8	10 33·8	1·6	1·2	7·6	5·6	13·6	10·1
17	11 04·3	11 06·1	10 34·0	1·7	1·3	7·7	5·7	13·7	10·2
18	11 04·5	11 06·3	10 34·2	1·8	1·3	7·8	5·8	13·8	10·2
19	11 04·8	11 06·6	10 34·5	1·9	1·4	7·9	5·9	13·9	10·3
20	11 05·0	11 06·8	10 34·7	2·0	1·5	8·0	5·9	14·0	10·4
21	11 05·3	11 07·1	10 34·9	2·1	1·6	8·1	6·0	14·1	10·5
22	11 05·5	11 07·3	10 35·2	2·2	1·6	8·2	6·1	14·2	10·5
23	11 05·8	11 07·6	10 35·4	2·3	1·7	8·3	6·2	14·3	10·6
24	11 06·0	11 07·8	10 35·7	2·4	1·8	8·4	6·2	14·4	10·7
25	11 06·3	11 08·1	10 35·9	2·5	1·9	8·5	6·3	14·5	10·8
26	11 06·5	11 08·3	10 36·1	2·6	1·9	8·6	6·4	14·6	10·8
27	11 06·8	11 08·6	10 36·4	2·7	2·0	8·7	6·5	14·7	10·9
28	11 07·0	11 08·8	10 36·6	2·8	2·1	8·8	6·5	14·8	11·0
29	11 07·3	11 09·1	10 36·9	2·9	2·2	8·9	6·6	14·9	11·1
30	11 07·5	11 09·3	10 37·1	3·0	2·2	9·0	6·7	15·0	11·1
31	11 07·8	11 09·6	10 37·3	3·1	2·3	9·1	6·7	15·1	11·2
32	11 08·0	11 09·8	10 37·6	3·2	2·4	9·2	6·8	15·2	11·3
33	11 08·3	11 10·1	10 37·8	3·3	2·4	9·3	6·9	15·3	11·3
34	11 08·5	11 10·3	10 38·0	3·4	2·5	9·4	7·0	15·4	11·4
35	11 08·8	11 10·6	10 38·3	3·5	2·6	9·5	7·0	15·5	11·5
36	11 09·0	11 10·8	10 38·5	3·6	2·7	9·6	7·1	15·6	11·6
37	11 09·3	11 11·1	10 38·8	3·7	2·7	9·7	7·2	15·7	11·6
38	11 09·5	11 11·3	10 39·0	3·8	2·8	9·8	7·3	15·8	11·7
39	11 09·8	11 11·6	10 39·2	3·9	2·9	9·9	7·3	15·9	11·8
40	11 10·0	11 11·8	10 39·5	4·0	3·0	10·0	7·4	16·0	11·9
41	11 10·3	11 12·1	10 39·7	4·1	3·0	10·1	7·5	16·1	11·9
42	11 10·5	11 12·3	10 40·0	4·2	3·1	10·2	7·6	16·2	12·0
43	11 10·8	11 12·6	10 40·2	4·3	3·2	10·3	7·6	16·3	12·1
44	11 11·0	11 12·8	10 40·4	4·4	3·3	10·4	7·7	16·4	12·2
45	11 11·3	11 13·1	10 40·7	4·5	3·3	10·5	7·8	16·5	12·2
46	11 11·5	11 13·3	10 40·9	4·6	3·4	10·6	7·9	16·6	12·3
47	11 11·8	11 13·6	10 41·1	4·7	3·5	10·7	7·9	16·7	12·4
48	11 12·0	11 13·8	10 41·4	4·8	3·6	10·8	8·0	16·8	12·5
49	11 12·3	11 14·1	10 41·6	4·9	3·6	10·9	8·1	16·9	12·5
50	11 12·5	11 14·3	10 41·9	5·0	3·7	11·0	8·2	17·0	12·6
51	11 12·8	11 14·6	10 42·1	5·1	3·8	11·1	8·2	17·1	12·7
52	11 13·0	11 14·8	10 42·3	5·2	3·9	11·2	8·3	17·2	12·8
53	11 13·3	11 15·1	10 42·6	5·3	3·9	11·3	8·4	17·3	12·8
54	11 13·5	11 15·3	10 42·8	5·4	4·0	11·4	8·5	17·4	12·9
55	11 13·8	11 15·6	10 43·1	5·5	4·1	11·5	8·5	17·5	13·0
56	11 14·0	11 15·8	10 43·3	5·6	4·2	11·6	8·6	17·6	13·1
57	11 14·3	11 16·1	10 43·5	5·7	4·2	11·7	8·7	17·7	13·1
58	11 14·5	11 16·3	10 43·8	5·8	4·3	11·8	8·8	17·8	13·2
59	11 14·8	11 16·6	10 44·0	5·9	4·4	11·9	8·8	17·9	13·3
60	11 15·0	11 16·8	10 44·3	6·0	4·5	12·0	8·9	18·0	13·4

45m s	SUN PLANETS ° ′	ARIES ° ′	MOON ° ′	v or d ′	Corrⁿ ′	v or d ′	Corrⁿ ′	v or d ′	Corrⁿ ′
00	11 15·0	11 16·8	10 44·3	0·0	0·0	6·0	4·6	12·0	9·1
01	11 15·3	11 17·1	10 44·5	0·1	0·1	6·1	4·6	12·1	9·2
02	11 15·5	11 17·3	10 44·7	0·2	0·2	6·2	4·7	12·2	9·3
03	11 15·8	11 17·6	10 45·0	0·3	0·2	6·3	4·8	12·3	9·3
04	11 16·0	11 17·9	10 45·2	0·4	0·3	6·4	4·9	12·4	9·4
05	11 16·3	11 18·1	10 45·4	0·5	0·4	6·5	4·9	12·5	9·5
06	11 16·5	11 18·4	10 45·7	0·6	0·5	6·6	5·0	12·6	9·6
07	11 16·8	11 18·6	10 45·9	0·7	0·5	6·7	5·1	12·7	9·6
08	11 17·0	11 18·9	10 46·2	0·8	0·6	6·8	5·2	12·8	9·7
09	11 17·3	11 19·1	10 46·4	0·9	0·7	6·9	5·2	12·9	9·8
10	11 17·5	11 19·4	10 46·6	1·0	0·8	7·0	5·3	13·0	9·9
11	11 17·8	11 19·6	10 46·9	1·1	0·8	7·1	5·4	13·1	9·9
12	11 18·0	11 19·9	10 47·1	1·2	0·9	7·2	5·5	13·2	10·0
13	11 18·3	11 20·1	10 47·4	1·3	1·0	7·3	5·5	13·3	10·1
14	11 18·5	11 20·4	10 47·6	1·4	1·1	7·4	5·6	13·4	10·2
15	11 18·8	11 20·6	10 47·8	1·5	1·1	7·5	5·7	13·5	10·2
16	11 19·0	11 20·9	10 48·1	1·6	1·2	7·6	5·8	13·6	10·3
17	11 19·3	11 21·1	10 48·3	1·7	1·3	7·7	5·8	13·7	10·4
18	11 19·5	11 21·4	10 48·5	1·8	1·4	7·8	5·9	13·8	10·5
19	11 19·8	11 21·6	10 48·8	1·9	1·4	7·9	6·0	13·9	10·5
20	11 20·0	11 21·9	10 49·0	2·0	1·5	8·0	6·1	14·0	10·6
21	11 20·3	11 22·1	10 49·3	2·1	1·6	8·1	6·1	14·1	10·7
22	11 20·5	11 22·4	10 49·5	2·2	1·7	8·2	6·2	14·2	10·8
23	11 20·8	11 22·6	10 49·7	2·3	1·7	8·3	6·3	14·3	10·8
24	11 21·0	11 22·9	10 50·0	2·4	1·8	8·4	6·4	14·4	10·9
25	11 21·3	11 23·1	10 50·2	2·5	1·9	8·5	6·4	14·5	11·0
26	11 21·5	11 23·4	10 50·5	2·6	2·0	8·6	6·5	14·6	11·1
27	11 21·8	11 23·6	10 50·7	2·7	2·0	8·7	6·6	14·7	11·1
28	11 22·0	11 23·9	10 50·9	2·8	2·1	8·8	6·7	14·8	11·2
29	11 22·3	11 24·1	10 51·2	2·9	2·2	8·9	6·7	14·9	11·3
30	11 22·5	11 24·4	10 51·4	3·0	2·3	9·0	6·8	15·0	11·4
31	11 22·8	11 24·6	10 51·6	3·1	2·4	9·1	6·9	15·1	11·5
32	11 23·0	11 24·9	10 51·9	3·2	2·4	9·2	7·0	15·2	11·5
33	11 23·3	11 25·1	10 52·1	3·3	2·5	9·3	7·1	15·3	11·6
34	11 23·5	11 25·4	10 52·4	3·4	2·6	9·4	7·1	15·4	11·7
35	11 23·8	11 25·6	10 52·6	3·5	2·7	9·5	7·2	15·5	11·8
36	11 24·0	11 25·9	10 52·8	3·6	2·7	9·6	7·3	15·6	11·8
37	11 24·3	11 26·1	10 53·1	3·7	2·8	9·7	7·4	15·7	11·9
38	11 24·5	11 26·4	10 53·3	3·8	2·9	9·8	7·4	15·8	12·0
39	11 24·8	11 26·6	10 53·6	3·9	3·0	9·9	7·5	15·9	12·1
40	11 25·0	11 26·9	10 53·8	4·0	3·0	10·0	7·6	16·0	12·1
41	11 25·3	11 27·1	10 54·0	4·1	3·1	10·1	7·7	16·1	12·2
42	11 25·5	11 27·4	10 54·3	4·2	3·2	10·2	7·7	16·2	12·3
43	11 25·8	11 27·6	10 54·5	4·3	3·3	10·3	7·8	16·3	12·4
44	11 26·0	11 27·9	10 54·7	4·4	3·3	10·4	7·9	16·4	12·4
45	11 26·3	11 28·1	10 55·0	4·5	3·4	10·5	8·0	16·5	12·5
46	11 26·5	11 28·4	10 55·2	4·6	3·5	10·6	8·0	16·6	12·6
47	11 26·8	11 28·6	10 55·5	4·7	3·6	10·7	8·1	16·7	12·7
48	11 27·0	11 28·9	10 55·7	4·8	3·6	10·8	8·2	16·8	12·7
49	11 27·3	11 29·1	10 55·9	4·9	3·7	10·9	8·3	16·9	12·8
50	11 27·5	11 29·4	10 56·2	5·0	3·8	11·0	8·3	17·0	12·9
51	11 27·8	11 29·6	10 56·4	5·1	3·9	11·1	8·4	17·1	13·0
52	11 28·0	11 29·9	10 56·7	5·2	3·9	11·2	8·5	17·2	13·0
53	11 28·3	11 30·1	10 56·9	5·3	4·0	11·3	8·6	17·3	13·1
54	11 28·5	11 30·4	10 57·1	5·4	4·1	11·4	8·6	17·4	13·2
55	11 28·8	11 30·6	10 57·4	5·5	4·2	11·5	8·7	17·5	13·3
56	11 29·0	11 30·9	10 57·6	5·6	4·2	11·6	8·8	17·6	13·3
57	11 29·3	11 31·1	10 57·9	5·7	4·3	11·7	8·9	17·7	13·4
58	11 29·5	11 31·4	10 58·1	5·8	4·4	11·8	8·9	17·8	13·5
59	11 29·8	11 31·6	10 58·3	5·9	4·5	11·9	9·0	17·9	13·6
60	11 30·0	11 31·9	10 58·6	6·0	4·6	12·0	9·1	18·0	13·7

46m s	SUN PLANETS ° ′	ARIES ° ′	MOON ° ′	v or d ′	Corrⁿ ′	v or d ′	Corrⁿ ′	v or d ′	Corrⁿ ′
00	11 30·0	11 31·9	10 58·6	0·0	0·0	6·0	4·7	12·0	9·3
01	11 30·3	11 32·1	10 58·8	0·1	0·1	6·1	4·7	12·1	9·4
02	11 30·5	11 32·4	10 59·0	0·2	0·2	6·2	4·8	12·2	9·5
03	11 30·8	11 32·6	10 59·3	0·3	0·2	6·3	4·9	12·3	9·5
04	11 31·0	11 32·9	10 59·5	0·4	0·3	6·4	5·0	12·4	9·6
05	11 31·3	11 33·1	10 59·8	0·5	0·4	6·5	5·0	12·5	9·7
06	11 31·5	11 33·4	11 00·0	0·6	0·5	6·6	5·1	12·6	9·8
07	11 31·8	11 33·6	11 00·2	0·7	0·5	6·7	5·2	12·7	9·8
08	11 32·0	11 33·9	11 00·5	0·8	0·6	6·8	5·3	12·8	9·9
09	11 32·3	11 34·1	11 00·7	0·9	0·7	6·9	5·3	12·9	10·0
10	11 32·5	11 34·4	11 01·0	1·0	0·8	7·0	5·4	13·0	10·1
11	11 32·8	11 34·6	11 01·2	1·1	0·9	7·1	5·5	13·1	10·2
12	11 33·0	11 34·9	11 01·4	1·2	0·9	7·2	5·6	13·2	10·2
13	11 33·3	11 35·1	11 01·7	1·3	1·0	7·3	5·7	13·3	10·3
14	11 33·5	11 35·4	11 01·9	1·4	1·1	7·4	5·7	13·4	10·4
15	11 33·8	11 35·6	11 02·1	1·5	1·2	7·5	5·8	13·5	10·5
16	11 34·0	11 35·9	11 02·4	1·6	1·2	7·6	5·9	13·6	10·5
17	11 34·3	11 36·2	11 02·6	1·7	1·3	7·7	6·0	13·7	10·6
18	11 34·5	11 36·4	11 02·9	1·8	1·4	7·8	6·0	13·8	10·7
19	11 34·8	11 36·7	11 03·1	1·9	1·5	7·9	6·1	13·9	10·8
20	11 35·0	11 36·9	11 03·3	2·0	1·6	8·0	6·2	14·0	10·9
21	11 35·3	11 37·2	11 03·6	2·1	1·6	8·1	6·3	14·1	10·9
22	11 35·5	11 37·4	11 03·8	2·2	1·7	8·2	6·4	14·2	11·0
23	11 35·8	11 37·7	11 04·1	2·3	1·8	8·3	6·4	14·3	11·1
24	11 36·0	11 37·9	11 04·3	2·4	1·9	8·4	6·5	14·4	11·2
25	11 36·3	11 38·2	11 04·5	2·5	1·9	8·5	6·6	14·5	11·2
26	11 36·5	11 38·4	11 04·8	2·6	2·0	8·6	6·7	14·6	11·3
27	11 36·8	11 38·7	11 05·0	2·7	2·1	8·7	6·7	14·7	11·4
28	11 37·0	11 38·9	11 05·2	2·8	2·2	8·8	6·8	14·8	11·5
29	11 37·3	11 39·2	11 05·5	2·9	2·2	8·9	6·9	14·9	11·5
30	11 37·5	11 39·4	11 05·7	3·0	2·3	9·0	7·0	15·0	11·6
31	11 37·8	11 39·7	11 06·0	3·1	2·4	9·1	7·1	15·1	11·7
32	11 38·0	11 39·9	11 06·2	3·2	2·5	9·2	7·1	15·2	11·8
33	11 38·3	11 40·2	11 06·4	3·3	2·6	9·3	7·2	15·3	11·9
34	11 38·5	11 40·4	11 06·7	3·4	2·6	9·4	7·3	15·4	11·9
35	11 38·8	11 40·7	11 06·9	3·5	2·7	9·5	7·4	15·5	12·0
36	11 39·0	11 40·9	11 07·2	3·6	2·8	9·6	7·4	15·6	12·1
37	11 39·3	11 41·2	11 07·4	3·7	2·9	9·7	7·5	15·7	12·2
38	11 39·5	11 41·4	11 07·6	3·8	2·9	9·8	7·6	15·8	12·2
39	11 39·8	11 41·7	11 07·9	3·9	3·0	9·9	7·7	15·9	12·3
40	11 40·0	11 41·9	11 08·1	4·0	3·1	10·0	7·8	16·0	12·4
41	11 40·3	11 42·2	11 08·3	4·1	3·2	10·1	7·8	16·1	12·5
42	11 40·5	11 42·4	11 08·6	4·2	3·3	10·2	7·9	16·2	12·6
43	11 40·8	11 42·7	11 08·8	4·3	3·3	10·3	8·0	16·3	12·6
44	11 41·0	11 42·9	11 09·1	4·4	3·4	10·4	8·1	16·4	12·7
45	11 41·3	11 43·2	11 09·3	4·5	3·5	10·5	8·1	16·5	12·8
46	11 41·5	11 43·4	11 09·5	4·6	3·6	10·6	8·2	16·6	12·9
47	11 41·8	11 43·7	11 09·8	4·7	3·6	10·7	8·3	16·7	12·9
48	11 42·0	11 43·9	11 10·0	4·8	3·7	10·8	8·4	16·8	13·0
49	11 42·3	11 44·2	11 10·3	4·9	3·8	10·9	8·4	16·9	13·1
50	11 42·5	11 44·4	11 10·5	5·0	3·9	11·0	8·5	17·0	13·2
51	11 42·8	11 44·7	11 10·7	5·1	4·0	11·1	8·6	17·1	13·3
52	11 43·0	11 44·9	11 11·0	5·2	4·0	11·2	8·7	17·2	13·3
53	11 43·3	11 45·2	11 11·2	5·3	4·1	11·3	8·8	17·3	13·4
54	11 43·5	11 45·4	11 11·5	5·4	4·2	11·4	8·8	17·4	13·5
55	11 43·8	11 45·7	11 11·7	5·5	4·3	11·5	8·9	17·5	13·6
56	11 44·0	11 45·9	11 11·9	5·6	4·3	11·6	9·0	17·6	13·6
57	11 44·3	11 46·2	11 12·2	5·7	4·4	11·7	9·1	17·7	13·7
58	11 44·5	11 46·4	11 12·4	5·8	4·5	11·8	9·1	17·8	13·8
59	11 44·8	11 46·7	11 12·6	5·9	4·6	11·9	9·2	17·9	13·9
60	11 45·0	11 46·9	11 12·9	6·0	4·7	12·0	9·3	18·0	14·0

47m s	SUN PLANETS ° ′	ARIES ° ′	MOON ° ′	v or d ′	Corrⁿ ′	v or d ′	Corrⁿ ′	v or d ′	Corrⁿ ′
00	11 45·0	11 46·9	11 12·9	0·0	0·0	6·0	4·8	12·0	9·5
01	11 45·3	11 47·2	11 13·1	0·1	0·1	6·1	4·8	12·1	9·6
02	11 45·5	11 47·4	11 13·4	0·2	0·2	6·2	4·9	12·2	9·7
03	11 45·8	11 47·7	11 13·6	0·3	0·2	6·3	5·0	12·3	9·7
04	11 46·0	11 47·9	11 13·8	0·4	0·3	6·4	5·1	12·4	9·8
05	11 46·3	11 48·2	11 14·1	0·5	0·4	6·5	5·1	12·5	9·9
06	11 46·5	11 48·4	11 14·3	0·6	0·5	6·6	5·2	12·6	10·0
07	11 46·8	11 48·7	11 14·6	0·7	0·6	6·7	5·3	12·7	10·1
08	11 47·0	11 48·9	11 14·8	0·8	0·6	6·8	5·4	12·8	10·1
09	11 47·3	11 49·2	11 15·0	0·9	0·7	6·9	5·5	12·9	10·2
10	11 47·5	11 49·4	11 15·3	1·0	0·8	7·0	5·5	13·0	10·3
11	11 47·8	11 49·7	11 15·5	1·1	0·9	7·1	5·6	13·1	10·4
12	11 48·0	11 49·9	11 15·7	1·2	1·0	7·2	5·7	13·2	10·5
13	11 48·3	11 50·2	11 16·0	1·3	1·0	7·3	5·8	13·3	10·5
14	11 48·5	11 50·4	11 16·2	1·4	1·1	7·4	5·9	13·4	10·6
15	11 48·8	11 50·7	11 16·5	1·5	1·2	7·5	5·9	13·5	10·7
16	11 49·0	11 50·9	11 16·7	1·6	1·3	7·6	6·0	13·6	10·8
17	11 49·3	11 51·2	11 16·9	1·7	1·3	7·7	6·1	13·7	10·8
18	11 49·5	11 51·4	11 17·2	1·8	1·4	7·8	6·2	13·8	10·9
19	11 49·8	11 51·7	11 17·4	1·9	1·5	7·9	6·3	13·9	11·0
20	11 50·0	11 51·9	11 17·7	2·0	1·6	8·0	6·3	14·0	11·1
21	11 50·3	11 52·2	11 17·9	2·1	1·7	8·1	6·4	14·1	11·2
22	11 50·5	11 52·4	11 18·1	2·2	1·7	8·2	6·5	14·2	11·2
23	11 50·8	11 52·7	11 18·4	2·3	1·8	8·3	6·6	14·3	11·3
24	11 51·0	11 52·9	11 18·6	2·4	1·9	8·4	6·7	14·4	11·4
25	11 51·3	11 53·2	11 18·8	2·5	2·0	8·5	6·7	14·5	11·5
26	11 51·5	11 53·4	11 19·1	2·6	2·1	8·6	6·8	14·6	11·6
27	11 51·8	11 53·7	11 19·3	2·7	2·1	8·7	6·9	14·7	11·6
28	11 52·0	11 53·9	11 19·6	2·8	2·2	8·8	7·0	14·8	11·7
29	11 52·3	11 54·2	11 19·8	2·9	2·3	8·9	7·0	14·9	11·8
30	11 52·5	11 54·5	11 20·0	3·0	2·4	9·0	7·1	15·0	11·9
31	11 52·8	11 54·7	11 20·3	3·1	2·5	9·1	7·2	15·1	12·0
32	11 53·0	11 55·0	11 20·5	3·2	2·5	9·2	7·3	15·2	12·0
33	11 53·3	11 55·2	11 20·8	3·3	2·6	9·3	7·4	15·3	12·1
34	11 53·5	11 55·5	11 21·0	3·4	2·7	9·4	7·4	15·4	12·2
35	11 53·8	11 55·7	11 21·2	3·5	2·8	9·5	7·5	15·5	12·3
36	11 54·0	11 56·0	11 21·5	3·6	2·9	9·6	7·6	15·6	12·4
37	11 54·3	11 56·2	11 21·7	3·7	2·9	9·7	7·7	15·7	12·4
38	11 54·5	11 56·5	11 22·0	3·8	3·0	9·8	7·8	15·8	12·5
39	11 54·8	11 56·7	11 22·2	3·9	3·1	9·9	7·8	15·9	12·6
40	11 55·0	11 57·0	11 22·4	4·0	3·2	10·0	7·9	16·0	12·7
41	11 55·3	11 57·2	11 22·7	4·1	3·2	10·1	8·0	16·1	12·7
42	11 55·5	11 57·5	11 22·9	4·2	3·3	10·2	8·1	16·2	12·8
43	11 55·8	11 57·7	11 23·1	4·3	3·4	10·3	8·2	16·3	12·9
44	11 56·0	11 58·0	11 23·4	4·4	3·5	10·4	8·2	16·4	13·0
45	11 56·3	11 58·2	11 23·6	4·5	3·6	10·5	8·3	16·5	13·1
46	11 56·5	11 58·5	11 23·9	4·6	3·6	10·6	8·4	16·6	13·1
47	11 56·8	11 58·7	11 24·1	4·7	3·7	10·7	8·5	16·7	13·2
48	11 57·0	11 59·0	11 24·3	4·8	3·8	10·8	8·6	16·8	13·3
49	11 57·3	11 59·2	11 24·6	4·9	3·9	10·9	8·6	16·9	13·4
50	11 57·5	11 59·5	11 24·8	5·0	4·0	11·0	8·7	17·0	13·5
51	11 57·8	11 59·7	11 25·1	5·1	4·0	11·1	8·8	17·1	13·5
52	11 58·0	12 00·0	11 25·3	5·2	4·1	11·2	8·9	17·2	13·6
53	11 58·3	12 00·2	11 25·5	5·3	4·2	11·3	8·9	17·3	13·7
54	11 58·5	12 00·5	11 25·8	5·4	4·3	11·4	9·0	17·4	13·8
55	11 58·8	12 00·7	11 26·0	5·5	4·4	11·5	9·1	17·5	13·9
56	11 59·0	12 01·0	11 26·2	5·6	4·4	11·6	9·2	17·6	13·9
57	11 59·3	12 01·2	11 26·5	5·7	4·5	11·7	9·3	17·7	14·0
58	11 59·5	12 01·5	11 26·7	5·8	4·6	11·8	9·3	17·8	14·1
59	11 59·8	12 01·7	11 27·0	5·9	4·7	11·9	9·4	17·9	14·2
60	12 00·0	12 02·0	11 27·2	6·0	4·8	12·0	9·5	18·0	14·3

48^{m}	SUN PLANETS	ARIES	MOON	v or d	Corr^{n}	v or d	Corr^{n}	v or d	Corr^{n}
s	° ′	° ′	° ′	′	′	′	′	′	′
00	12 00·0	12 02·0	11 27·2	0·0	0·0	6·0	4·9	12·0	9·7
01	12 00·3	12 02·2	11 27·4	0·1	0·1	6·1	4·9	12·1	9·8
02	12 00·5	12 02·5	11 27·7	0·2	0·2	6·2	5·0	12·2	9·9
03	12 00·8	12 02·7	11 27·9	0·3	0·2	6·3	5·1	12·3	9·9
04	12 01·0	12 03·0	11 28·2	0·4	0·3	6·4	5·2	12·4	10·0
05	12 01·3	12 03·2	11 28·4	0·5	0·4	6·5	5·3	12·5	10·1
06	12 01·5	12 03·5	11 28·6	0·6	0·5	6·6	5·3	12·6	10·2
07	12 01·8	12 03·7	11 28·9	0·7	0·6	6·7	5·4	12·7	10·3
08	12 02·0	12 04·0	11 29·1	0·8	0·6	6·8	5·5	12·8	10·3
09	12 02·3	12 04·2	11 29·3	0·9	0·7	6·9	5·6	12·9	10·4
10	12 02·5	12 04·5	11 29·6	1·0	0·8	7·0	5·7	13·0	10·5
11	12 02·8	12 04·7	11 29·8	1·1	0·9	7·1	5·7	13·1	10·6
12	12 03·0	12 05·0	11 30·1	1·2	1·0	7·2	5·8	13·2	10·7
13	12 03·3	12 05·2	11 30·3	1·3	1·1	7·3	5·9	13·3	10·8
14	12 03·5	12 05·5	11 30·5	1·4	1·1	7·4	6·0	13·4	10·8
15	12 03·8	12 05·7	11 30·8	1·5	1·2	7·5	6·1	13·5	10·9
16	12 04·0	12 06·0	11 31·0	1·6	1·3	7·6	6·1	13·6	11·0
17	12 04·3	12 06·2	11 31·3	1·7	1·4	7·7	6·2	13·7	11·1
18	12 04·5	12 06·5	11 31·5	1·8	1·5	7·8	6·3	13·8	11·2
19	12 04·8	12 06·7	11 31·7	1·9	1·5	7·9	6·4	13·9	11·2
20	12 05·0	12 07·0	11 32·0	2·0	1·6	8·0	6·5	14·0	11·3
21	12 05·3	12 07·2	11 32·2	2·1	1·7	8·1	6·5	14·1	11·4
22	12 05·5	12 07·5	11 32·4	2·2	1·8	8·2	6·6	14·2	11·5
23	12 05·8	12 07·7	11 32·7	2·3	1·9	8·3	6·7	14·3	11·6
24	12 06·0	12 08·0	11 32·9	2·4	1·9	8·4	6·8	14·4	11·6
25	12 06·3	12 08·2	11 33·2	2·5	2·0	8·5	6·9	14·5	11·7
26	12 06·5	12 08·5	11 33·4	2·6	2·1	8·6	7·0	14·6	11·8
27	12 06·8	12 08·7	11 33·6	2·7	2·2	8·7	7·0	14·7	11·9
28	12 07·0	12 09·0	11 33·9	2·8	2·3	8·8	7·1	14·8	12·0
29	12 07·3	12 09·2	11 34·1	2·9	2·3	8·9	7·2	14·9	12·0
30	12 07·5	12 09·5	11 34·4	3·0	2·4	9·0	7·3	15·0	12·1
31	12 07·8	12 09·7	11 34·6	3·1	2·5	9·1	7·4	15·1	12·2
32	12 08·0	12 10·0	11 34·8	3·2	2·6	9·2	7·4	15·2	12·3
33	12 08·3	12 10·2	11 35·1	3·3	2·7	9·3	7·5	15·3	12·4
34	12 08·5	12 10·5	11 35·3	3·4	2·7	9·4	7·6	15·4	12·4
35	12 08·8	12 10·7	11 35·6	3·5	2·8	9·5	7·7	15·5	12·5
36	12 09·0	12 11·0	11 35·8	3·6	2·9	9·6	7·8	15·6	12·6
37	12 09·3	12 11·2	11 36·0	3·7	3·0	9·7	7·8	15·7	12·7
38	12 09·5	12 11·5	11 36·3	3·8	3·1	9·8	7·9	15·8	12·8
39	12 09·8	12 11·7	11 36·5	3·9	3·2	9·9	8·0	15·9	12·9
40	12 10·0	12 12·0	11 36·7	4·0	3·2	10·0	8·1	16·0	12·9
41	12 10·3	12 12·2	11 37·0	4·1	3·3	10·1	8·2	16·1	13·0
42	12 10·5	12 12·5	11 37·2	4·2	3·4	10·2	8·2	16·2	13·1
43	12 10·8	12 12·8	11 37·5	4·3	3·5	10·3	8·3	16·3	13·2
44	12 11·0	12 13·0	11 37·7	4·4	3·6	10·4	8·4	16·4	13·3
45	12 11·3	12 13·3	11 37·9	4·5	3·6	10·5	8·5	16·5	13·3
46	12 11·5	12 13·5	11 38·2	4·6	3·7	10·6	8·6	16·6	13·4
47	12 11·8	12 13·8	11 38·4	4·7	3·8	10·7	8·6	16·7	13·5
48	12 12·0	12 14·0	11 38·7	4·8	3·9	10·8	8·7	16·8	13·6
49	12 12·3	12 14·3	11 38·9	4·9	4·0	10·9	8·8	16·9	13·7
50	12 12·5	12 14·5	11 39·1	5·0	4·0	11·0	8·9	17·0	13·7
51	12 12·8	12 14·8	11 39·4	5·1	4·1	11·1	9·0	17·1	13·8
52	12 13·0	12 15·0	11 39·6	5·2	4·2	11·2	9·1	17·2	13·9
53	12 13·3	12 15·3	11 39·8	5·3	4·3	11·3	9·1	17·3	14·0
54	12 13·5	12 15·5	11 40·1	5·4	4·4	11·4	9·2	17·4	14·1
55	12 13·8	12 15·8	11 40·3	5·5	4·4	11·5	9·3	17·5	14·1
56	12 14·0	12 16·0	11 40·6	5·6	4·5	11·6	9·4	17·6	14·2
57	12 14·3	12 16·3	11 40·8	5·7	4·6	11·7	9·5	17·7	14·3
58	12 14·5	12 16·5	11 41·0	5·8	4·7	11·8	9·5	17·8	14·4
59	12 14·8	12 16·8	11 41·3	5·9	4·8	11·9	9·6	17·9	14·5
60	12 15·0	12 17·0	11 41·5	6·0	4·9	12·0	9·7	18·0	14·6

49^{m}	SUN PLANETS	ARIES	MOON	v or d	Corr^{n}	v or d	Corr^{n}	v or d	Corr^{n}
s	° ′	° ′	° ′	′	′	′	′	′	′
00	12 15·0	12 17·0	11 41·5	0·0	0·0	6·0	5·0	12·0	9·9
01	12 15·3	12 17·3	11 41·8	0·1	0·1	6·1	5·0	12·1	10·0
02	12 15·5	12 17·5	11 42·0	0·2	0·2	6·2	5·1	12·2	10·1
03	12 15·8	12 17·8	11 42·2	0·3	0·2	6·3	5·2	12·3	10·1
04	12 16·0	12 18·0	11 42·5	0·4	0·3	6·4	5·3	12·4	10·2
05	12 16·3	12 18·3	11 42·7	0·5	0·4	6·5	5·4	12·5	10·3
06	12 16·5	12 18·5	11 42·9	0·6	0·5	6·6	5·4	12·6	10·4
07	12 16·8	12 18·8	11 43·2	0·7	0·6	6·7	5·5	12·7	10·5
08	12 17·0	12 19·0	11 43·4	0·8	0·7	6·8	5·6	12·8	10·6
09	12 17·3	12 19·3	11 43·7	0·9	0·7	6·9	5·7	12·9	10·6
10	12 17·5	12 19·5	11 43·9	1·0	0·8	7·0	5·8	13·0	10·7
11	12 17·8	12 19·8	11 44·1	1·1	0·9	7·1	5·9	13·1	10·8
12	12 18·0	12 20·0	11 44·4	1·2	1·0	7·2	5·9	13·2	10·9
13	12 18·3	12 20·3	11 44·6	1·3	1·1	7·3	6·0	13·3	11·0
14	12 18·5	12 20·5	11 44·9	1·4	1·2	7·4	6·1	13·4	11·1
15	12 18·8	12 20·8	11 45·1	1·5	1·2	7·5	6·2	13·5	11·1
16	12 19·0	12 21·0	11 45·3	1·6	1·3	7·6	6·3	13·6	11·2
17	12 19·3	12 21·3	11 45·6	1·7	1·4	7·7	6·4	13·7	11·3
18	12 19·5	12 21·5	11 45·8	1·8	1·5	7·8	6·4	13·8	11·4
19	12 19·8	12 21·8	11 46·1	1·9	1·6	7·9	6·5	13·9	11·5
20	12 20·0	12 22·0	11 46·3	2·0	1·7	8·0	6·6	14·0	11·6
21	12 20·3	12 22·3	11 46·5	2·1	1·7	8·1	6·7	14·1	11·6
22	12 20·5	12 22·5	11 46·8	2·2	1·8	8·2	6·8	14·2	11·7
23	12 20·8	12 22·8	11 47·0	2·3	1·9	8·3	6·8	14·3	11·8
24	12 21·0	12 23·0	11 47·2	2·4	2·0	8·4	6·9	14·4	11·9
25	12 21·3	12 23·3	11 47·5	2·5	2·1	8·5	7·0	14·5	12·0
26	12 21·5	12 23·5	11 47·7	2·6	2·1	8·6	7·1	14·6	12·0
27	12 21·8	12 23·8	11 48·0	2·7	2·2	8·7	7·2	14·7	12·1
28	12 22·0	12 24·0	11 48·2	2·8	2·3	8·8	7·3	14·8	12·2
29	12 22·3	12 24·3	11 48·4	2·9	2·4	8·9	7·3	14·9	12·3
30	12 22·5	12 24·5	11 48·7	3·0	2·5	9·0	7·4	15·0	12·4
31	12 22·8	12 24·8	11 48·9	3·1	2·6	9·1	7·5	15·1	12·5
32	12 23·0	12 25·0	11 49·2	3·2	2·6	9·2	7·6	15·2	12·5
33	12 23·3	12 25·3	11 49·4	3·3	2·7	9·3	7·7	15·3	12·6
34	12 23·5	12 25·5	11 49·6	3·4	2·8	9·4	7·8	15·4	12·7
35	12 23·8	12 25·8	11 49·9	3·5	2·9	9·5	7·8	15·5	12·8
36	12 24·0	12 26·0	11 50·1	3·6	3·0	9·6	7·9	15·6	12·9
37	12 24·3	12 26·3	11 50·3	3·7	3·1	9·7	8·0	15·7	13·0
38	12 24·5	12 26·5	11 50·6	3·8	3·1	9·8	8·1	15·8	13·0
39	12 24·8	12 26·8	11 50·8	3·9	3·2	9·9	8·2	15·9	13·1
40	12 25·0	12 27·0	11 51·1	4·0	3·3	10·0	8·3	16·0	13·2
41	12 25·3	12 27·3	11 51·3	4·1	3·4	10·1	8·3	16·1	13·3
42	12 25·5	12 27·5	11 51·5	4·2	3·5	10·2	8·4	16·2	13·4
43	12 25·8	12 27·8	11 51·8	4·3	3·5	10·3	8·5	16·3	13·4
44	12 26·0	12 28·0	11 52·0	4·4	3·6	10·4	8·6	16·4	13·5
45	12 26·3	12 28·3	11 52·3	4·5	3·7	10·5	8·7	16·5	13·6
46	12 26·5	12 28·5	11 52·5	4·6	3·8	10·6	8·7	16·6	13·7
47	12 26·8	12 28·8	11 52·7	4·7	3·9	10·7	8·8	16·7	13·8
48	12 27·0	12 29·0	11 53·0	4·8	4·0	10·8	8·9	16·8	13·9
49	12 27·3	12 29·3	11 53·2	4·9	4·0	10·9	9·0	16·9	13·9
50	12 27·5	12 29·5	11 53·4	5·0	4·1	11·0	9·1	17·0	14·0
51	12 27·8	12 29·8	11 53·7	5·1	4·2	11·1	9·2	17·1	14·1
52	12 28·0	12 30·0	11 53·9	5·2	4·3	11·2	9·2	17·2	14·2
53	12 28·3	12 30·3	11 54·2	5·3	4·4	11·3	9·3	17·3	14·3
54	12 28·5	12 30·5	11 54·4	5·4	4·5	11·4	9·4	17·4	14·4
55	12 28·8	12 30·8	11 54·6	5·5	4·5	11·5	9·5	17·5	14·4
56	12 29·0	12 31·1	11 54·9	5·6	4·6	11·6	9·6	17·6	14·5
57	12 29·3	12 31·3	11 55·1	5·7	4·7	11·7	9·7	17·7	14·6
58	12 29·5	12 31·6	11 55·4	5·8	4·8	11·8	9·7	17·8	14·7
59	12 29·8	12 31·8	11 55·6	5·9	4·9	11·9	9·8	17·9	14·8
60	12 30·0	12 32·1	11 55·8	6·0	5·0	12·0	9·9	18·0	14·9

50m s	SUN PLANETS ° ′	ARIES ° ′	MOON ° ′	v or d ′	Corrn ′	v or d ′	Corrn ′	v or d ′	Corrn ′
00	12 30·0	12 32·1	11 55·8	0·0	0·0	6·0	5·1	12·0	10·1
01	12 30·3	12 32·3	11 56·1	0·1	0·1	6·1	5·1	12·1	10·2
02	12 30·5	12 32·6	11 56·3	0·2	0·2	6·2	5·2	12·2	10·3
03	12 30·8	12 32·8	11 56·5	0·3	0·3	6·3	5·3	12·3	10·4
04	12 31·0	12 33·1	11 56·8	0·4	0·3	6·4	5·4	12·4	10·4
05	12 31·3	12 33·3	11 57·0	0·5	0·4	6·5	5·5	12·5	10·5
06	12 31·5	12 33·6	11 57·3	0·6	0·5	6·6	5·6	12·6	10·6
07	12 31·8	12 33·8	11 57·5	0·7	0·6	6·7	5·6	12·7	10·7
08	12 32·0	12 34·1	11 57·7	0·8	0·7	6·8	5·7	12·8	10·8
09	12 32·3	12 34·3	11 58·0	0·9	0·8	6·9	5·8	12·9	10·9
10	12 32·5	12 34·6	11 58·2	1·0	0·8	7·0	5·9	13·0	10·9
11	12 32·8	12 34·8	11 58·5	1·1	0·9	7·1	6·0	13·1	11·0
12	12 33·0	12 35·1	11 58·7	1·2	1·0	7·2	6·1	13·2	11·1
13	12 33·3	12 35·3	11 58·9	1·3	1·1	7·3	6·1	13·3	11·2
14	12 33·5	12 35·6	11 59·2	1·4	1·2	7·4	6·2	13·4	11·3
15	12 33·8	12 35·8	11 59·4	1·5	1·3	7·5	6·3	13·5	11·4
16	12 34·0	12 36·1	11 59·7	1·6	1·3	7·6	6·4	13·6	11·4
17	12 34·3	12 36·3	11 59·9	1·7	1·4	7·7	6·5	13·7	11·5
18	12 34·5	12 36·6	12 00·1	1·8	1·5	7·8	6·6	13·8	11·6
19	12 34·8	12 36·8	12 00·4	1·9	1·6	7·9	6·6	13·9	11·7
20	12 35·0	12 37·1	12 00·6	2·0	1·7	8·0	6·7	14·0	11·8
21	12 35·3	12 37·3	12 00·8	2·1	1·8	8·1	6·8	14·1	11·9
22	12 35·5	12 37·6	12 01·1	2·2	1·9	8·2	6·9	14·2	12·0
23	12 35·8	12 37·8	12 01·3	2·3	1·9	8·3	7·0	14·3	12·0
24	12 36·0	12 38·1	12 01·6	2·4	2·0	8·4	7·1	14·4	12·1
25	12 36·3	12 38·3	12 01·8	2·5	2·1	8·5	7·2	14·5	12·2
26	12 36·5	12 38·6	12 02·0	2·6	2·2	8·6	7·2	14·6	12·3
27	12 36·8	12 38·8	12 02·3	2·7	2·3	8·7	7·3	14·7	12·4
28	12 37·0	12 39·1	12 02·5	2·8	2·4	8·8	7·4	14·8	12·5
29	12 37·3	12 39·3	12 02·8	2·9	2·4	8·9	7·5	14·9	12·5
30	12 37·5	12 39·6	12 03·0	3·0	2·5	9·0	7·6	15·0	12·6
31	12 37·8	12 39·8	12 03·2	3·1	2·6	9·1	7·7	15·1	12·7
32	12 38·0	12 40·1	12 03·5	3·2	2·7	9·2	7·7	15·2	12·8
33	12 38·3	12 40·3	12 03·7	3·3	2·8	9·3	7·8	15·3	12·9
34	12 38·5	12 40·6	12 03·9	3·4	2·9	9·4	7·9	15·4	13·0
35	12 38·8	12 40·8	12 04·2	3·5	2·9	9·5	8·0	15·5	13·0
36	12 39·0	12 41·1	12 04·4	3·6	3·0	9·6	8·1	15·6	13·1
37	12 39·3	12 41·3	12 04·7	3·7	3·1	9·7	8·2	15·7	13·2
38	12 39·5	12 41·6	12 04·9	3·8	3·2	9·8	8·2	15·8	13·3
39	12 39·8	12 41·8	12 05·1	3·9	3·3	9·9	8·3	15·9	13·4
40	12 40·0	12 42·1	12 05·4	4·0	3·4	10·0	8·4	16·0	13·5
41	12 40·3	12 42·3	12 05·6	4·1	3·5	10·1	8·5	16·1	13·6
42	12 40·5	12 42·6	12 05·9	4·2	3·5	10·2	8·6	16·2	13·6
43	12 40·8	12 42·8	12 06·1	4·3	3·6	10·3	8·7	16·3	13·7
44	12 41·0	12 43·1	12 06·3	4·4	3·7	10·4	8·8	16·4	13·8
45	12 41·3	12 43·3	12 06·6	4·5	3·8	10·5	8·8	16·5	13·9
46	12 41·5	12 43·6	12 06·8	4·6	3·9	10·6	8·9	16·6	14·0
47	12 41·8	12 43·8	12 07·0	4·7	4·0	10·7	9·0	16·7	14·1
48	12 42·0	12 44·1	12 07·3	4·8	4·0	10·8	9·1	16·8	14·1
49	12 42·3	12 44·3	12 07·5	4·9	4·1	10·9	9·2	16·9	14·2
50	12 42·5	12 44·6	12 07·8	5·0	4·2	11·0	9·3	17·0	14·3
51	12 42·8	12 44·8	12 08·0	5·1	4·3	11·1	9·3	17·1	14·4
52	12 43·0	12 45·1	12 08·2	5·2	4·4	11·2	9·4	17·2	14·5
53	12 43·3	12 45·3	12 08·5	5·3	4·5	11·3	9·5	17·3	14·6
54	12 43·5	12 45·6	12 08·7	5·4	4·5	11·4	9·6	17·4	14·6
55	12 43·8	12 45·8	12 09·0	5·5	4·6	11·5	9·7	17·5	14·7
56	12 44·0	12 46·1	12 09·2	5·6	4·7	11·6	9·8	17·6	14·8
57	12 44·3	12 46·3	12 09·4	5·7	4·8	11·7	9·8	17·7	14·9
58	12 44·5	12 46·6	12 09·7	5·8	4·9	11·8	9·9	17·8	15·0
59	12 44·8	12 46·8	12 09·9	5·9	5·0	11·9	10·0	17·9	15·1
60	12 45·0	12 47·1	12 10·2	6·0	5·1	12·0	10·1	18·0	15·2

51m s	SUN PLANETS ° ′	ARIES ° ′	MOON ° ′	v or d ′	Corrn ′	v or d ′	Corrn ′	v or d ′	Corrn ′
00	12 45·0	12 47·1	12 10·2	0·0	0·0	6·0	5·2	12·0	10·3
01	12 45·3	12 47·3	12 10·4	0·1	0·1	6·1	5·2	12·1	10·4
02	12 45·5	12 47·6	12 10·6	0·2	0·2	6·2	5·3	12·2	10·5
03	12 45·8	12 47·8	12 10·9	0·3	0·3	6·3	5·4	12·3	10·6
04	12 46·0	12 48·1	12 11·1	0·4	0·3	6·4	5·5	12·4	10·6
05	12 46·3	12 48·3	12 11·3	0·5	0·4	6·5	5·6	12·5	10·7
06	12 46·5	12 48·6	12 11·6	0·6	0·5	6·6	5·7	12·6	10·8
07	12 46·8	12 48·8	12 11·8	0·7	0·6	6·7	5·8	12·7	10·9
08	12 47·0	12 49·1	12 12·1	0·8	0·7	6·8	5·8	12·8	11·0
09	12 47·3	12 49·4	12 12·3	0·9	0·8	6·9	5·9	12·9	11·1
10	12 47·5	12 49·6	12 12·5	1·0	0·9	7·0	6·0	13·0	11·2
11	12 47·8	12 49·9	12 12·8	1·1	0·9	7·1	6·1	13·1	11·2
12	12 48·0	12 50·1	12 13·0	1·2	1·0	7·2	6·2	13·2	11·3
13	12 48·3	12 50·4	12 13·3	1·3	1·1	7·3	6·3	13·3	11·4
14	12 48·5	12 50·6	12 13·5	1·4	1·2	7·4	6·4	13·4	11·5
15	12 48·8	12 50·9	12 13·7	1·5	1·3	7·5	6·4	13·5	11·6
16	12 49·0	12 51·1	12 14·0	1·6	1·4	7·6	6·5	13·6	11·7
17	12 49·3	12 51·4	12 14·2	1·7	1·5	7·7	6·6	13·7	11·8
18	12 49·5	12 51·6	12 14·4	1·8	1·5	7·8	6·7	13·8	11·8
19	12 49·8	12 51·9	12 14·7	1·9	1·6	7·9	6·8	13·9	11·9
20	12 50·0	12 52·1	12 14·9	2·0	1·7	8·0	6·9	14·0	12·0
21	12 50·3	12 52·4	12 15·2	2·1	1·8	8·1	7·0	14·1	12·1
22	12 50·5	12 52·6	12 15·4	2·2	1·9	8·2	7·0	14·2	12·2
23	12 50·8	12 52·9	12 15·6	2·3	2·0	8·3	7·1	14·3	12·3
24	12 51·0	12 53·1	12 15·9	2·4	2·1	8·4	7·2	14·4	12·4
25	12 51·3	12 53·4	12 16·1	2·5	2·1	8·5	7·3	14·5	12·4
26	12 51·5	12 53·6	12 16·4	2·6	2·2	8·6	7·4	14·6	12·5
27	12 51·8	12 53·9	12 16·6	2·7	2·3	8·7	7·5	14·7	12·6
28	12 52·0	12 54·1	12 16·8	2·8	2·4	8·8	7·6	14·8	12·7
29	12 52·3	12 54·4	12 17·1	2·9	2·5	8·9	7·6	14·9	12·8
30	12 52·5	12 54·6	12 17·3	3·0	2·6	9·0	7·7	15·0	12·9
31	12 52·8	12 54·9	12 17·5	3·1	2·7	9·1	7·8	15·1	13·0
32	12 53·0	12 55·1	12 17·8	3·2	2·7	9·2	7·9	15·2	13·0
33	12 53·3	12 55·4	12 18·0	3·3	2·8	9·3	8·0	15·3	13·1
34	12 53·5	12 55·6	12 18·3	3·4	2·9	9·4	8·1	15·4	13·2
35	12 53·8	12 55·9	12 18·5	3·5	3·0	9·5	8·2	15·5	13·3
36	12 54·0	12 56·1	12 18·7	3·6	3·1	9·6	8·2	15·6	13·4
37	12 54·3	12 56·4	12 19·0	3·7	3·2	9·7	8·3	15·7	13·5
38	12 54·5	12 56·6	12 19·2	3·8	3·3	9·8	8·4	15·8	13·6
39	12 54·8	12 56·9	12 19·5	3·9	3·3	9·9	8·5	15·9	13·6
40	12 55·0	12 57·1	12 19·7	4·0	3·4	10·0	8·6	16·0	13·7
41	12 55·3	12 57·4	12 19·9	4·1	3·5	10·1	8·7	16·1	13·8
42	12 55·5	12 57·6	12 20·2	4·2	3·6	10·2	8·8	16·2	13·9
43	12 55·8	12 57·9	12 20·4	4·3	3·7	10·3	8·8	16·3	14·0
44	12 56·0	12 58·1	12 20·6	4·4	3·8	10·4	8·9	16·4	14·1
45	12 56·3	12 58·4	12 20·9	4·5	3·9	10·5	9·0	16·5	14·2
46	12 56·5	12 58·6	12 21·1	4·6	3·9	10·6	9·1	16·6	14·2
47	12 56·8	12 58·9	12 21·4	4·7	4·0	10·7	9·2	16·7	14·3
48	12 57·0	12 59·1	12 21·6	4·8	4·1	10·8	9·3	16·8	14·4
49	12 57·3	12 59·4	12 21·8	4·9	4·2	10·9	9·4	16·9	14·5
50	12 57·5	12 59·6	12 22·1	5·0	4·3	11·0	9·4	17·0	14·6
51	12 57·8	12 59·9	12 22·3	5·1	4·4	11·1	9·5	17·1	14·7
52	12 58·0	13 00·1	12 22·6	5·2	4·5	11·2	9·6	17·2	14·8
53	12 58·3	13 00·4	12 22·8	5·3	4·5	11·3	9·7	17·3	14·8
54	12 58·5	13 00·6	12 23·0	5·4	4·6	11·4	9·8	17·4	14·9
55	12 58·8	13 00·9	12 23·3	5·5	4·7	11·5	9·9	17·5	15·0
56	12 59·0	13 01·1	12 23·5	5·6	4·8	11·6	10·0	17·6	15·1
57	12 59·3	13 01·4	12 23·8	5·7	4·9	11·7	10·0	17·7	15·2
58	12 59·5	13 01·6	12 24·0	5·8	5·0	11·8	10·1	17·8	15·3
59	12 59·8	13 01·9	12 24·2	5·9	5·1	11·9	10·2	17·9	15·4
60	13 00·0	13 02·1	12 24·5	6·0	5·2	12·0	10·3	18·0	15·5

52ᵐ s	SUN PLANETS ° ′	ARIES ° ′	MOON ° ′	v or d ′	Corrⁿ ′	v or d ′	Corrⁿ ′	v or d ′	Corrⁿ ′
00	13 00·0	13 02·1	12 24·5	0·0	0·0	6·0	5·3	12·0	10·5
01	13 00·3	13 02·4	12 24·7	0·1	0·1	6·1	5·3	12·1	10·6
02	13 00·5	13 02·6	12 24·9	0·2	0·2	6·2	5·4	12·2	10·7
03	13 00·8	13 02·9	12 25·2	0·3	0·3	6·3	5·5	12·3	10·8
04	13 01·0	13 03·1	12 25·4	0·4	0·4	6·4	5·6	12·4	10·9
05	13 01·3	13 03·4	12 25·7	0·5	0·4	6·5	5·7	12·5	10·9
06	13 01·5	13 03·6	12 25·9	0·6	0·5	6·6	5·8	12·6	11·0
07	13 01·8	13 03·9	12 26·1	0·7	0·6	6·7	5·9	12·7	11·1
08	13 02·0	13 04·1	12 26·4	0·8	0·7	6·8	6·0	12·8	11·2
09	13 02·3	13 04·4	12 26·6	0·9	0·8	6·9	6·0	12·9	11·3
10	13 02·5	13 04·6	12 26·9	1·0	0·9	7·0	6·1	13·0	11·4
11	13 02·8	13 04·9	12 27·1	1·1	1·0	7·1	6·2	13·1	11·5
12	13 03·0	13 05·1	12 27·3	1·2	1·1	7·2	6·3	13·2	11·6
13	13 03·3	13 05·4	12 27·6	1·3	1·1	7·3	6·4	13·3	11·6
14	13 03·5	13 05·6	12 27·8	1·4	1·2	7·4	6·5	13·4	11·7
15	13 03·8	13 05·9	12 28·0	1·5	1·3	7·5	6·6	13·5	11·8
16	13 04·0	13 06·1	12 28·3	1·6	1·4	7·6	6·7	13·6	11·9
17	13 04·3	13 06·4	12 28·5	1·7	1·5	7·7	6·7	13·7	12·0
18	13 04·5	13 06·6	12 28·8	1·8	1·6	7·8	6·8	13·8	12·1
19	13 04·8	13 06·9	12 29·0	1·9	1·7	7·9	6·9	13·9	12·2
20	13 05·0	13 07·1	12 29·2	2·0	1·8	8·0	7·0	14·0	12·3
21	13 05·3	13 07·4	12 29·5	2·1	1·8	8·1	7·1	14·1	12·3
22	13 05·5	13 07·7	12 29·7	2·2	1·9	8·2	7·2	14·2	12·4
23	13 05·8	13 07·9	12 30·0	2·3	2·0	8·3	7·3	14·3	12·5
24	13 06·0	13 08·2	12 30·2	2·4	2·1	8·4	7·4	14·4	12·6
25	13 06·3	13 08·4	12 30·4	2·5	2·2	8·5	7·4	14·5	12·7
26	13 06·5	13 08·7	12 30·7	2·6	2·3	8·6	7·5	14·6	12·8
27	13 06·8	13 08·9	12 30·9	2·7	2·4	8·7	7·6	14·7	12·9
28	13 07·0	13 09·2	12 31·1	2·8	2·5	8·8	7·7	14·8	13·0
29	13 07·3	13 09·4	12 31·4	2·9	2·5	8·9	7·8	14·9	13·0
30	13 07·5	13 09·7	12 31·6	3·0	2·6	9·0	7·9	15·0	13·1
31	13 07·8	13 09·9	12 31·9	3·1	2·7	9·1	8·0	15·1	13·2
32	13 08·0	13 10·2	12 32·1	3·2	2·8	9·2	8·0	15·2	13·3
33	13 08·3	13 10·4	12 32·3	3·3	2·9	9·3	8·1	15·3	13·4
34	13 08·5	13 10·7	12 32·6	3·4	3·0	9·4	8·2	15·4	13·5
35	13 08·8	13 10·9	12 32·8	3·5	3·1	9·5	8·3	15·5	13·6
36	13 09·0	13 11·2	12 33·1	3·6	3·2	9·6	8·4	15·6	13·7
37	13 09·3	13 11·4	12 33·3	3·7	3·2	9·7	8·5	15·7	13·7
38	13 09·5	13 11·7	12 33·5	3·8	3·3	9·8	8·6	15·8	13·8
39	13 09·8	13 11·9	12 33·8	3·9	3·4	9·9	8·7	15·9	13·9
40	13 10·0	13 12·2	12 34·0	4·0	3·5	10·0	8·8	16·0	14·0
41	13 10·3	13 12·4	12 34·2	4·1	3·6	10·1	8·8	16·1	14·1
42	13 10·5	13 12·7	12 34·5	4·2	3·7	10·2	8·9	16·2	14·2
43	13 10·8	13 12·9	12 34·7	4·3	3·8	10·3	9·0	16·3	14·3
44	13 11·0	13 13·2	12 35·0	4·4	3·9	10·4	9·1	16·4	14·3
45	13 11·3	13 13·4	12 35·2	4·5	3·9	10·5	9·2	16·5	14·4
46	13 11·5	13 13·7	12 35·4	4·6	4·0	10·6	9·3	16·6	14·5
47	13 11·8	13 13·9	12 35·7	4·7	4·1	10·7	9·4	16·7	14·6
48	13 12·0	13 14·2	12 35·9	4·8	4·2	10·8	9·5	16·8	14·7
49	13 12·3	13 14·4	12 36·2	4·9	4·3	10·9	9·5	16·9	14·8
50	13 12·5	13 14·7	12 36·4	5·0	4·4	11·0	9·6	17·0	14·9
51	13 12·8	13 14·9	12 36·6	5·1	4·5	11·1	9·7	17·1	15·0
52	13 13·0	13 15·2	12 36·9	5·2	4·6	11·2	9·8	17·2	15·1
53	13 13·3	13 15·4	12 37·1	5·3	4·6	11·3	9·9	17·3	15·1
54	13 13·5	13 15·7	12 37·4	5·4	4·7	11·4	10·0	17·4	15·2
55	13 13·8	13 15·9	12 37·6	5·5	4·8	11·5	10·1	17·5	15·3
56	13 14·0	13 16·2	12 37·8	5·6	4·9	11·6	10·2	17·6	15·4
57	13 14·3	13 16·4	12 38·1	5·7	5·0	11·7	10·2	17·7	15·5
58	13 14·5	13 16·7	12 38·3	5·8	5·1	11·8	10·3	17·8	15·6
59	13 14·8	13 16·9	12 38·5	5·9	5·2	11·9	10·4	17·9	15·7
60	13 15·0	13 17·2	12 38·8	6·0	5·3	12·0	10·5	18·0	15·8

53ᵐ s	SUN PLANETS ° ′	ARIES ° ′	MOON ° ′	v or d ′	Corrⁿ ′	v or d ′	Corrⁿ ′	v or d ′	Corrⁿ ′
00	13 15·0	13 17·2	12 38·8	0·0	0·0	6·0	5·4	12·0	10·7
01	13 15·3	13 17·4	12 39·0	0·1	0·1	6·1	5·4	12·1	10·8
02	13 15·5	13 17·7	12 39·3	0·2	0·2	6·2	5·5	12·2	10·9
03	13 15·8	13 17·9	12 39·5	0·3	0·3	6·3	5·6	12·3	11·0
04	13 16·0	13 18·2	12 39·7	0·4	0·4	6·4	5·7	12·4	11·1
05	13 16·3	13 18·4	12 40·0	0·5	0·4	6·5	5·8	12·5	11·1
06	13 16·5	13 18·7	12 40·2	0·6	0·5	6·6	5·9	12·6	11·2
07	13 16·8	13 18·9	12 40·5	0·7	0·6	6·7	6·0	12·7	11·3
08	13 17·0	13 19·2	12 40·7	0·8	0·7	6·8	6·1	12·8	11·4
09	13 17·3	13 19·4	12 40·9	0·9	0·8	6·9	6·2	12·9	11·5
10	13 17·5	13 19·7	12 41·2	1·0	0·9	7·0	6·2	13·0	11·6
11	13 17·8	13 19·9	12 41·4	1·1	1·0	7·1	6·3	13·1	11·7
12	13 18·0	13 20·2	12 41·6	1·2	1·1	7·2	6·4	13·2	11·8
13	13 18·3	13 20·4	12 41·9	1·3	1·2	7·3	6·5	13·3	11·9
14	13 18·5	13 20·7	12 42·1	1·4	1·2	7·4	6·6	13·4	11·9
15	13 18·8	13 20·9	12 42·4	1·5	1·3	7·5	6·7	13·5	12·0
16	13 19·0	13 21·2	12 42·6	1·6	1·4	7·6	6·8	13·6	12·1
17	13 19·3	13 21·4	12 42·8	1·7	1·5	7·7	6·9	13·7	12·2
18	13 19·5	13 21·7	12 43·1	1·8	1·6	7·8	7·0	13·8	12·3
19	13 19·8	13 21·9	12 43·3	1·9	1·7	7·9	7·0	13·9	12·4
20	13 20·0	13 22·2	12 43·6	2·0	1·8	8·0	7·1	14·0	12·5
21	13 20·3	13 22·4	12 43·8	2·1	1·9	8·1	7·2	14·1	12·6
22	13 20·5	13 22·7	12 44·0	2·2	2·0	8·2	7·3	14·2	12·7
23	13 20·8	13 22·9	12 44·3	2·3	2·1	8·3	7·4	14·3	12·8
24	13 21·0	13 23·2	12 44·5	2·4	2·1	8·4	7·5	14·4	12·8
25	13 21·3	13 23·4	12 44·7	2·5	2·2	8·5	7·6	14·5	12·9
26	13 21·5	13 23·7	12 45·0	2·6	2·3	8·6	7·7	14·6	13·0
27	13 21·8	13 23·9	12 45·2	2·7	2·4	8·7	7·8	14·7	13·1
28	13 22·0	13 24·2	12 45·5	2·8	2·5	8·8	7·8	14·8	13·2
29	13 22·3	13 24·4	12 45·7	2·9	2·6	8·9	7·9	14·9	13·3
30	13 22·5	13 24·7	12 45·9	3·0	2·7	9·0	8·0	15·0	13·4
31	13 22·8	13 24·9	12 46·2	3·1	2·8	9·1	8·1	15·1	13·5
32	13 23·0	13 25·2	12 46·4	3·2	2·9	9·2	8·2	15·2	13·6
33	13 23·3	13 25·4	12 46·7	3·3	2·9	9·3	8·3	15·3	13·6
34	13 23·5	13 25·7	12 46·9	3·4	3·0	9·4	8·4	15·4	13·7
35	13 23·8	13 26·0	12 47·1	3·5	3·1	9·5	8·5	15·5	13·8
36	13 24·0	13 26·2	12 47·4	3·6	3·2	9·6	8·6	15·6	13·9
37	13 24·3	13 26·5	12 47·6	3·7	3·3	9·7	8·6	15·7	14·0
38	13 24·5	13 26·7	12 47·9	3·8	3·4	9·8	8·7	15·8	14·1
39	13 24·8	13 27·0	12 48·1	3·9	3·5	9·9	8·8	15·9	14·2
40	13 25·0	13 27·2	12 48·3	4·0	3·6	10·0	8·9	16·0	14·3
41	13 25·3	13 27·5	12 48·6	4·1	3·7	10·1	9·0	16·1	14·4
42	13 25·5	13 27·7	12 48·8	4·2	3·7	10·2	9·1	16·2	14·4
43	13 25·8	13 28·0	12 49·0	4·3	3·8	10·3	9·2	16·3	14·5
44	13 26·0	13 28·2	12 49·3	4·4	3·9	10·4	9·3	16·4	14·6
45	13 26·3	13 28·5	12 49·5	4·5	4·0	10·5	9·4	16·5	14·7
46	13 26·5	13 28·7	12 49·8	4·6	4·1	10·6	9·5	16·6	14·8
47	13 26·8	13 29·0	12 50·0	4·7	4·2	10·7	9·5	16·7	14·9
48	13 27·0	13 29·2	12 50·2	4·8	4·3	10·8	9·6	16·8	15·0
49	13 27·3	13 29·5	12 50·5	4·9	4·4	10·9	9·7	16·9	15·1
50	13 27·5	13 29·7	12 50·7	5·0	4·5	11·0	9·8	17·0	15·2
51	13 27·8	13 30·0	12 51·0	5·1	4·5	11·1	9·9	17·1	15·2
52	13 28·0	13 30·2	12 51·2	5·2	4·6	11·2	10·0	17·2	15·3
53	13 28·3	13 30·5	12 51·4	5·3	4·7	11·3	10·1	17·3	15·4
54	13 28·5	13 30·7	12 51·7	5·4	4·8	11·4	10·2	17·4	15·5
55	13 28·8	13 31·0	12 51·9	5·5	4·9	11·5	10·3	17·5	15·6
56	13 29·0	13 31·2	12 52·1	5·6	5·0	11·6	10·3	17·6	15·7
57	13 29·3	13 31·5	12 52·4	5·7	5·1	11·7	10·4	17·7	15·8
58	13 29·5	13 31·7	12 52·6	5·8	5·2	11·8	10·5	17·8	15·9
59	13 29·8	13 32·0	12 52·9	5·9	5·3	11·9	10·6	17·9	16·0
60	13 30·0	13 32·2	12 53·1	6·0	5·4	12·0	10·7	18·0	16·1

54^m	SUN PLANETS	ARIES	MOON	v or d	Corr^n	v or d	Corr^n	v or d	Corr^n
s	° ′	° ′	° ′	′	′	′	′	′	′
00	13 30·0	13 32·2	12 53·1	0·0	0·0	6·0	5·5	12·0	10·9
01	13 30·3	13 32·5	12 53·3	0·1	0·1	6·1	5·5	12·1	11·0
02	13 30·5	13 32·7	12 53·6	0·2	0·2	6·2	5·6	12·2	11·1
03	13 30·8	13 33·0	12 53·8	0·3	0·3	6·3	5·7	12·3	11·2
04	13 31·0	13 33·2	12 54·1	0·4	0·4	6·4	5·8	12·4	11·3
05	13 31·3	13 33·5	12 54·3	0·5	0·5	6·5	5·9	12·5	11·4
06	13 31·5	13 33·7	12 54·5	0·6	0·5	6·6	6·0	12·6	11·4
07	13 31·8	13 34·0	12 54·8	0·7	0·6	6·7	6·1	12·7	11·5
08	13 32·0	13 34·2	12 55·0	0·8	0·7	6·8	6·2	12·8	11·6
09	13 32·3	13 34·5	12 55·2	0·9	0·8	6·9	6·3	12·9	11·7
10	13 32·5	13 34·7	12 55·5	1·0	0·9	7·0	6·4	13·0	11·8
11	13 32·8	13 35·0	12 55·7	1·1	1·0	7·1	6·4	13·1	11·9
12	13 33·0	13 35·2	12 56·0	1·2	1·1	7·2	6·5	13·2	12·0
13	13 33·3	13 35·5	12 56·2	1·3	1·2	7·3	6·6	13·3	12·1
14	13 33·5	13 35·7	12 56·4	1·4	1·3	7·4	6·7	13·4	12·2
15	13 33·8	13 36·0	12 56·7	1·5	1·4	7·5	6·8	13·5	12·3
16	13 34·0	13 36·2	12 56·9	1·6	1·5	7·6	6·9	13·6	12·4
17	13 34·3	13 36·5	12 57·2	1·7	1·5	7·7	7·0	13·7	12·4
18	13 34·5	13 36·7	12 57·4	1·8	1·6	7·8	7·1	13·8	12·5
19	13 34·8	13 37·0	12 57·6	1·9	1·7	7·9	7·2	13·9	12·6
20	13 35·0	13 37·2	12 57·9	2·0	1·8	8·0	7·3	14·0	12·7
21	13 35·3	13 37·5	12 58·1	2·1	1·9	8·1	7·4	14·1	12·8
22	13 35·5	13 37·7	12 58·3	2·2	2·0	8·2	7·4	14·2	12·9
23	13 35·8	13 38·0	12 58·6	2·3	2·1	8·3	7·5	14·3	13·0
24	13 36·0	13 38·2	12 58·8	2·4	2·2	8·4	7·6	14·4	13·1
25	13 36·3	13 38·5	12 59·1	2·5	2·3	8·5	7·7	14·5	13·2
26	13 36·5	13 38·7	12 59·3	2·6	2·4	8·6	7·8	14·6	13·3
27	13 36·8	13 39·0	12 59·5	2·7	2·5	8·7	7·9	14·7	13·4
28	13 37·0	13 39·2	12 59·8	2·8	2·5	8·8	8·0	14·8	13·4
29	13 37·3	13 39·5	13 00·0	2·9	2·6	8·9	8·1	14·9	13·5
30	13 37·5	13 39·7	13 00·3	3·0	2·7	9·0	8·2	15·0	13·6
31	13 37·8	13 40·0	13 00·5	3·1	2·8	9·1	8·3	15·1	13·7
32	13 38·0	13 40·2	13 00·7	3·2	2·9	9·2	8·4	15·2	13·8
33	13 38·3	13 40·5	13 01·0	3·3	3·0	9·3	8·4	15·3	13·9
34	13 38·5	13 40·7	13 01·2	3·4	3·1	9·4	8·5	15·4	14·0
35	13 38·8	13 41·0	13 01·5	3·5	3·2	9·5	8·6	15·5	14·1
36	13 39·0	13 41·2	13 01·7	3·6	3·3	9·6	8·7	15·6	14·2
37	13 39·3	13 41·5	13 01·9	3·7	3·4	9·7	8·8	15·7	14·3
38	13 39·5	13 41·7	13 02·2	3·8	3·5	9·8	8·9	15·8	14·4
39	13 39·8	13 42·0	13 02·4	3·9	3·5	9·9	9·0	15·9	14·4
40	13 40·0	13 42·2	13 02·6	4·0	3·6	10·0	9·1	16·0	14·5
41	13 40·3	13 42·5	13 02·9	4·1	3·7	10·1	9·2	16·1	14·6
42	13 40·5	13 42·7	13 03·1	4·2	3·8	10·2	9·3	16·2	14·7
43	13 40·8	13 43·0	13 03·4	4·3	3·9	10·3	9·4	16·3	14·8
44	13 41·0	13 43·2	13 03·6	4·4	4·0	10·4	9·4	16·4	14·9
45	13 41·3	13 43·5	13 03·8	4·5	4·1	10·5	9·5	16·5	15·0
46	13 41·5	13 43·7	13 04·1	4·6	4·2	10·6	9·6	16·6	15·1
47	13 41·8	13 44·0	13 04·3	4·7	4·3	10·7	9·7	16·7	15·2
48	13 42·0	13 44·3	13 04·6	4·8	4·4	10·8	9·8	16·8	15·3
49	13 42·3	13 44·5	13 04·8	4·9	4·5	10·9	9·9	16·9	15·4
50	13 42·5	13 44·8	13 05·0	5·0	4·5	11·0	10·0	17·0	15·4
51	13 42·8	13 45·0	13 05·3	5·1	4·6	11·1	10·1	17·1	15·5
52	13 43·0	13 45·3	13 05·5	5·2	4·7	11·2	10·2	17·2	15·6
53	13 43·3	13 45·5	13 05·7	5·3	4·8	11·3	10·3	17·3	15·7
54	13 43·5	13 45·8	13 06·0	5·4	4·9	11·4	10·4	17·4	15·8
55	13 43·8	13 46·0	13 06·2	5·5	5·0	11·5	10·4	17·5	15·9
56	13 44·0	13 46·3	13 06·5	5·6	5·1	11·6	10·5	17·6	16·0
57	13 44·3	13 46·5	13 06·7	5·7	5·2	11·7	10·6	17·7	16·1
58	13 44·5	13 46·8	13 06·9	5·8	5·3	11·8	10·7	17·8	16·2
59	13 44·8	13 47·0	13 07·2	5·9	5·4	11·9	10·8	17·9	16·3
60	13 45·0	13 47·3	13 07·4	6·0	5·5	12·0	10·9	18·0	16·4

55^m	SUN PLANETS	ARIES	MOON	v or d	Corr^n	v or d	Corr^n	v or d	Corr^n
s	° ′	° ′	° ′	′	′	′	′	′	′
00	13 45·0	13 47·3	13 07·4	0·0	0·0	6·0	5·6	12·0	11·1
01	13 45·3	13 47·5	13 07·7	0·1	0·1	6·1	5·6	12·1	11·2
02	13 45·5	13 47·8	13 07·9	0·2	0·2	6·2	5·7	12·2	11·3
03	13 45·8	13 48·0	13 08·1	0·3	0·3	6·3	5·8	12·3	11·4
04	13 46·0	13 48·3	13 08·4	0·4	0·4	6·4	5·9	12·4	11·5
05	13 46·3	13 48·5	13 08·6	0·5	0·5	6·5	6·0	12·5	11·6
06	13 46·5	13 48·8	13 08·8	0·6	0·6	6·6	6·1	12·6	11·7
07	13 46·8	13 49·0	13 09·1	0·7	0·6	6·7	6·2	12·7	11·7
08	13 47·0	13 49·3	13 09·3	0·8	0·7	6·8	6·3	12·8	11·8
09	13 47·3	13 49·5	13 09·6	0·9	0·8	6·9	6·4	12·9	11·9
10	13 47·5	13 49·8	13 09·8	1·0	0·9	7·0	6·5	13·0	12·0
11	13 47·8	13 50·0	13 10·0	1·1	1·0	7·1	6·6	13·1	12·1
12	13 48·0	13 50·3	13 10·3	1·2	1·1	7·2	6·7	13·2	12·2
13	13 48·3	13 50·5	13 10·5	1·3	1·2	7·3	6·8	13·3	12·3
14	13 48·5	13 50·8	13 10·8	1·4	1·3	7·4	6·8	13·4	12·4
15	13 48·8	13 51·0	13 11·0	1·5	1·4	7·5	6·9	13·5	12·5
16	13 49·0	13 51·3	13 11·2	1·6	1·5	7·6	7·0	13·6	12·6
17	13 49·3	13 51·5	13 11·5	1·7	1·6	7·7	7·1	13·7	12·7
18	13 49·5	13 51·8	13 11·7	1·8	1·7	7·8	7·2	13·8	12·8
19	13 49·8	13 52·0	13 12·0	1·9	1·8	7·9	7·3	13·9	12·9
20	13 50·0	13 52·3	13 12·2	2·0	1·9	8·0	7·4	14·0	13·0
21	13 50·3	13 52·5	13 12·4	2·1	1·9	8·1	7·5	14·1	13·0
22	13 50·5	13 52·8	13 12·7	2·2	2·0	8·2	7·6	14·2	13·1
23	13 50·8	13 53·0	13 12·9	2·3	2·1	8·3	7·7	14·3	13·2
24	13 51·0	13 53·3	13 13·1	2·4	2·2	8·4	7·8	14·4	13·3
25	13 51·3	13 53·5	13 13·4	2·5	2·3	8·5	7·9	14·5	13·4
26	13 51·5	13 53·8	13 13·6	2·6	2·4	8·6	8·0	14·6	13·5
27	13 51·8	13 54·0	13 13·9	2·7	2·5	8·7	8·0	14·7	13·6
28	13 52·0	13 54·3	13 14·1	2·8	2·6	8·8	8·1	14·8	13·7
29	13 52·3	13 54·5	13 14·3	2·9	2·7	8·9	8·2	14·9	13·8
30	13 52·5	13 54·8	13 14·6	3·0	2·8	9·0	8·3	15·0	13·9
31	13 52·8	13 55·0	13 14·8	3·1	2·9	9·1	8·4	15·1	14·0
32	13 53·0	13 55·3	13 15·1	3·2	3·0	9·2	8·5	15·2	14·1
33	13 53·3	13 55·5	13 15·3	3·3	3·1	9·3	8·6	15·3	14·2
34	13 53·5	13 55·8	13 15·5	3·4	3·1	9·4	8·7	15·4	14·2
35	13 53·8	13 56·0	13 15·8	3·5	3·2	9·5	8·8	15·5	14·3
36	13 54·0	13 56·3	13 16·0	3·6	3·3	9·6	8·9	15·6	14·4
37	13 54·3	13 56·5	13 16·2	3·7	3·4	9·7	9·0	15·7	14·5
38	13 54·5	13 56·8	13 16·5	3·8	3·5	9·8	9·1	15·8	14·6
39	13 54·8	13 57·0	13 16·7	3·9	3·6	9·9	9·2	15·9	14·7
40	13 55·0	13 57·3	13 17·0	4·0	3·7	10·0	9·3	16·0	14·8
41	13 55·3	13 57·5	13 17·2	4·1	3·8	10·1	9·3	16·1	14·9
42	13 55·5	13 57·8	13 17·4	4·2	3·9	10·2	9·4	16·2	15·0
43	13 55·8	13 58·0	13 17·7	4·3	4·0	10·3	9·5	16·3	15·1
44	13 56·0	13 58·3	13 17·9	4·4	4·1	10·4	9·6	16·4	15·2
45	13 56·3	13 58·5	13 18·2	4·5	4·2	10·5	9·7	16·5	15·3
46	13 56·5	13 58·8	13 18·4	4·6	4·3	10·6	9·8	16·6	15·4
47	13 56·8	13 59·0	13 18·6	4·7	4·3	10·7	9·9	16·7	15·4
48	13 57·0	13 59·3	13 18·9	4·8	4·4	10·8	10·0	16·8	15·5
49	13 57·3	13 59·5	13 19·1	4·9	4·5	10·9	10·1	16·9	15·6
50	13 57·5	13 59·8	13 19·3	5·0	4·6	11·0	10·2	17·0	15·7
51	13 57·8	14 00·0	13 19·6	5·1	4·7	11·1	10·3	17·1	15·8
52	13 58·0	14 00·3	13 19·8	5·2	4·8	11·2	10·4	17·2	15·9
53	13 58·3	14 00·5	13 20·1	5·3	4·9	11·3	10·5	17·3	16·0
54	13 58·5	14 00·8	13 20·3	5·4	5·0	11·4	10·5	17·4	16·1
55	13 58·8	14 01·0	13 20·5	5·5	5·1	11·5	10·6	17·5	16·2
56	13 59·0	14 01·3	13 20·8	5·6	5·2	11·6	10·7	17·6	16·3
57	13 59·3	14 01·5	13 21·0	5·7	5·3	11·7	10·8	17·7	16·4
58	13 59·5	14 01·8	13 21·3	5·8	5·4	11·8	10·9	17·8	16·5
59	13 59·8	14 02·0	13 21·5	5·9	5·5	11·9	11·0	17·9	16·6
60	14 00·0	14 02·3	13 21·7	6·0	5·6	12·0	11·1	18·0	16·7

56m	SUN PLANETS	ARIES	MOON	v or d	Corrⁿ	v or d	Corrⁿ	v or d	Corrⁿ
s	° ′	° ′	° ′	′	′	′	′	′	′
00	14 00·0	14 02·3	13 21·7	0·0	0·0	6·0	5·7	12·0	11·3
01	14 00·3	14 02·6	13 22·0	0·1	0·1	6·1	5·7	12·1	11·4
02	14 00·5	14 02·8	13 22·2	0·2	0·2	6·2	5·8	12·2	11·5
03	14 00·8	14 03·1	13 22·4	0·3	0·3	6·3	5·9	12·3	11·6
04	14 01·0	14 03·3	13 22·7	0·4	0·4	6·4	6·0	12·4	11·7
05	14 01·3	14 03·6	13 22·9	0·5	0·5	6·5	6·1	12·5	11·8
06	14 01·5	14 03·8	13 23·2	0·6	0·6	6·6	6·2	12·6	11·9
07	14 01·8	14 04·1	13 23·4	0·7	0·7	6·7	6·3	12·7	12·0
08	14 02·0	14 04·3	13 23·6	0·8	0·8	6·8	6·4	12·8	12·1
09	14 02·3	14 04·6	13 23·9	0·9	0·8	6·9	6·5	12·9	12·1
10	14 02·5	14 04·8	13 24·1	1·0	0·9	7·0	6·6	13·0	12·2
11	14 02·8	14 05·1	13 24·4	1·1	1·0	7·1	6·7	13·1	12·3
12	14 03·0	14 05·3	13 24·6	1·2	1·1	7·2	6·8	13·2	12·4
13	14 03·3	14 05·6	13 24·8	1·3	1·2	7·3	6·9	13·3	12·5
14	14 03·5	14 05·8	13 25·1	1·4	1·3	7·4	7·0	13·4	12·6
15	14 03·8	14 06·1	13 25·3	1·5	1·4	7·5	7·1	13·5	12·7
16	14 04·0	14 06·3	13 25·6	1·6	1·5	7·6	7·2	13·6	12·8
17	14 04·3	14 06·6	13 25·8	1·7	1·6	7·7	7·3	13·7	12·9
18	14 04·5	14 06·8	13 26·0	1·8	1·7	7·8	7·3	13·8	13·0
19	14 04·8	14 07·1	13 26·3	1·9	1·8	7·9	7·4	13·9	13·1
20	14 05·0	14 07·3	13 26·5	2·0	1·9	8·0	7·5	14·0	13·2
21	14 05·3	14 07·6	13 26·7	2·1	2·0	8·1	7·6	14·1	13·3
22	14 05·5	14 07·8	13 27·0	2·2	2·1	8·2	7·7	14·2	13·4
23	14 05·8	14 08·1	13 27·2	2·3	2·2	8·3	7·8	14·3	13·5
24	14 06·0	14 08·3	13 27·5	2·4	2·3	8·4	7·9	14·4	13·6
25	14 06·3	14 08·6	13 27·7	2·5	2·4	8·5	8·0	14·5	13·7
26	14 06·5	14 08·8	13 27·9	2·6	2·4	8·6	8·1	14·6	13·7
27	14 06·8	14 09·1	13 28·2	2·7	2·5	8·7	8·2	14·7	13·8
28	14 07·0	14 09·3	13 28·4	2·8	2·6	8·8	8·3	14·8	13·9
29	14 07·3	14 09·6	13 28·7	2·9	2·7	8·9	8·4	14·9	14·0
30	14 07·5	14 09·8	13 28·9	3·0	2·8	9·0	8·5	15·0	14·1
31	14 07·8	14 10·1	13 29·1	3·1	2·9	9·1	8·6	15·1	14·2
32	14 08·0	14 10·3	13 29·4	3·2	3·0	9·2	8·7	15·2	14·3
33	14 08·3	14 10·6	13 29·6	3·3	3·1	9·3	8·8	15·3	14·4
34	14 08·5	14 10·8	13 29·8	3·4	3·2	9·4	8·9	15·4	14·5
35	14 08·8	14 11·1	13 30·1	3·5	3·3	9·5	8·9	15·5	14·6
36	14 09·0	14 11·3	13 30·3	3·6	3·4	9·6	9·0	15·6	14·7
37	14 09·3	14 11·6	13 30·6	3·7	3·5	9·7	9·1	15·7	14·8
38	14 09·5	14 11·8	13 30·8	3·8	3·6	9·8	9·2	15·8	14·9
39	14 09·8	14 12·1	13 31·0	3·9	3·7	9·9	9·3	15·9	15·0
40	14 10·0	14 12·3	13 31·3	4·0	3·8	10·0	9·4	16·0	15·1
41	14 10·3	14 12·6	13 31·5	4·1	3·9	10·1	9·5	16·1	15·2
42	14 10·5	14 12·8	13 31·8	4·2	4·0	10·2	9·6	16·2	15·3
43	14 10·8	14 13·1	13 32·0	4·3	4·0	10·3	9·7	16·3	15·3
44	14 11·0	14 13·3	13 32·2	4·4	4·1	10·4	9·8	16·4	15·4
45	14 11·3	14 13·6	13 32·5	4·5	4·2	10·5	9·9	16·5	15·5
46	14 11·5	14 13·8	13 32·7	4·6	4·3	10·6	10·0	16·6	15·6
47	14 11·8	14 14·1	13 32·9	4·7	4·4	10·7	10·1	16·7	15·7
48	14 12·0	14 14·3	13 33·2	4·8	4·5	10·8	10·2	16·8	15·8
49	14 12·3	14 14·6	13 33·4	4·9	4·6	10·9	10·3	16·9	15·9
50	14 12·5	14 14·8	13 33·7	5·0	4·7	11·0	10·4	17·0	16·0
51	14 12·8	14 15·1	13 33·9	5·1	4·8	11·1	10·5	17·1	16·1
52	14 13·0	14 15·3	13 34·1	5·2	4·9	11·2	10·5	17·2	16·2
53	14 13·3	14 15·6	13 34·4	5·3	5·0	11·3	10·6	17·3	16·3
54	14 13·5	14 15·8	13 34·6	5·4	5·1	11·4	10·7	17·4	16·4
55	14 13·8	14 16·1	13 34·9	5·5	5·2	11·5	10·8	17·5	16·5
56	14 14·0	14 16·3	13 35·1	5·6	5·3	11·6	10·9	17·6	16·6
57	14 14·3	14 16·6	13 35·3	5·7	5·4	11·7	11·0	17·7	16·7
58	14 14·5	14 16·8	13 35·6	5·8	5·5	11·8	11·1	17·8	16·8
59	14 14·8	14 17·1	13 35·8	5·9	5·6	11·9	11·2	17·9	16·9
60	14 15·0	14 17·3	13 36·1	6·0	5·7	12·0	11·3	18·0	17·0

57m	SUN PLANETS	ARIES	MOON	v or d	Corrⁿ	v or d	Corrⁿ	v or d	Corrⁿ
s	° ′	° ′	° ′	′	′	′	′	′	′
00	14 15·0	14 17·3	13 36·1	0·0	0·0	6·0	5·8	12·0	11·5
01	14 15·3	14 17·6	13 36·3	0·1	0·1	6·1	5·8	12·1	11·6
02	14 15·5	14 17·8	13 36·5	0·2	0·2	6·2	5·9	12·2	11·7
03	14 15·8	14 18·1	13 36·8	0·3	0·3	6·3	6·0	12·3	11·8
04	14 16·0	14 18·3	13 37·0	0·4	0·4	6·4	6·1	12·4	11·9
05	14 16·3	14 18·6	13 37·2	0·5	0·5	6·5	6·2	12·5	12·0
06	14 16·5	14 18·8	13 37·5	0·6	0·6	6·6	6·3	12·6	12·1
07	14 16·8	14 19·1	13 37·7	0·7	0·7	6·7	6·4	12·7	12·2
08	14 17·0	14 19·3	13 38·0	0·8	0·8	6·8	6·5	12·8	12·3
09	14 17·3	14 19·6	13 38·2	0·9	0·9	6·9	6·6	12·9	12·4
10	14 17·5	14 19·8	13 38·4	1·0	1·0	7·0	6·7	13·0	12·5
11	14 17·8	14 20·1	13 38·7	1·1	1·1	7·1	6·8	13·1	12·6
12	14 18·0	14 20·3	13 38·9	1·2	1·2	7·2	6·9	13·2	12·7
13	14 18·3	14 20·6	13 39·2	1·3	1·2	7·3	7·0	13·3	12·7
14	14 18·5	14 20·9	13 39·4	1·4	1·3	7·4	7·1	13·4	12·8
15	14 18·8	14 21·1	13 39·6	1·5	1·4	7·5	7·2	13·5	12·9
16	14 19·0	14 21·4	13 39·9	1·6	1·5	7·6	7·3	13·6	13·0
17	14 19·3	14 21·6	13 40·1	1·7	1·6	7·7	7·4	13·7	13·1
18	14 19·5	14 21·9	13 40·3	1·8	1·7	7·8	7·5	13·8	13·2
19	14 19·8	14 22·1	13 40·6	1·9	1·8	7·9	7·6	13·9	13·3
20	14 20·0	14 22·4	13 40·8	2·0	1·9	8·0	7·7	14·0	13·4
21	14 20·3	14 22·6	13 41·1	2·1	2·0	8·1	7·8	14·1	13·5
22	14 20·5	14 22·9	13 41·3	2·2	2·1	8·2	7·9	14·2	13·6
23	14 20·8	14 23·1	13 41·5	2·3	2·2	8·3	8·0	14·3	13·7
24	14 21·0	14 23·4	13 41·8	2·4	2·3	8·4	8·1	14·4	13·8
25	14 21·3	14 23·6	13 42·0	2·5	2·4	8·5	8·1	14·5	13·9
26	14 21·5	14 23·9	13 42·3	2·6	2·5	8·6	8·2	14·6	14·0
27	14 21·8	14 24·1	13 42·5	2·7	2·6	8·7	8·3	14·7	14·1
28	14 22·0	14 24·4	13 42·7	2·8	2·7	8·8	8·4	14·8	14·2
29	14 22·3	14 24·6	13 43·0	2·9	2·8	8·9	8·5	14·9	14·3
30	14 22·5	14 24·9	13 43·2	3·0	2·9	9·0	8·6	15·0	14·4
31	14 22·8	14 25·1	13 43·4	3·1	3·0	9·1	8·7	15·1	14·5
32	14 23·0	14 25·4	13 43·7	3·2	3·1	9·2	8·8	15·2	14·6
33	14 23·3	14 25·6	13 43·9	3·3	3·2	9·3	8·9	15·3	14·7
34	14 23·5	14 25·9	13 44·2	3·4	3·3	9·4	9·0	15·4	14·8
35	14 23·8	14 26·1	13 44·4	3·5	3·4	9·5	9·1	15·5	14·9
36	14 24·0	14 26·4	13 44·6	3·6	3·5	9·6	9·2	15·6	15·0
37	14 24·3	14 26·6	13 44·9	3·7	3·5	9·7	9·3	15·7	15·0
38	14 24·5	14 26·9	13 45·1	3·8	3·6	9·8	9·4	15·8	15·1
39	14 24·8	14 27·1	13 45·4	3·9	3·7	9·9	9·5	15·9	15·2
40	14 25·0	14 27·4	13 45·6	4·0	3·8	10·0	9·6	16·0	15·3
41	14 25·3	14 27·6	13 45·8	4·1	3·9	10·1	9·7	16·1	15·4
42	14 25·5	14 27·9	13 46·1	4·2	4·0	10·2	9·8	16·2	15·5
43	14 25·8	14 28·1	13 46·3	4·3	4·1	10·3	9·9	16·3	15·6
44	14 26·0	14 28·4	13 46·5	4·4	4·2	10·4	10·0	16·4	15·7
45	14 26·3	14 28·6	13 46·8	4·5	4·3	10·5	10·1	16·5	15·8
46	14 26·5	14 28·9	13 47·0	4·6	4·4	10·6	10·2	16·6	15·9
47	14 26·8	14 29·1	13 47·3	4·7	4·5	10·7	10·3	16·7	16·0
48	14 27·0	14 29·4	13 47·5	4·8	4·6	10·8	10·4	16·8	16·1
49	14 27·3	14 29·6	13 47·7	4·9	4·7	10·9	10·4	16·9	16·2
50	14 27·5	14 29·9	13 48·0	5·0	4·8	11·0	10·5	17·0	16·3
51	14 27·8	14 30·1	13 48·2	5·1	4·9	11·1	10·6	17·1	16·4
52	14 28·0	14 30·4	13 48·5	5·2	5·0	11·2	10·7	17·2	16·5
53	14 28·3	14 30·6	13 48·7	5·3	5·1	11·3	10·8	17·3	16·6
54	14 28·5	14 30·9	13 48·9	5·4	5·2	11·4	10·9	17·4	16·7
55	14 28·8	14 31·1	13 49·2	5·5	5·3	11·5	11·0	17·5	16·8
56	14 29·0	14 31·4	13 49·4	5·6	5·4	11·6	11·1	17·6	16·9
57	14 29·3	14 31·6	13 49·7	5·7	5·5	11·7	11·2	17·7	17·0
58	14 29·5	14 31·9	13 49·9	5·8	5·6	11·8	11·3	17·8	17·1
59	14 29·8	14 32·1	13 50·1	5·9	5·7	11·9	11·4	17·9	17·2
60	14 30·0	14 32·4	13 50·4	6·0	5·8	12·0	11·5	18·0	17·3

58m s	SUN PLANETS ° ′	ARIES ° ′	MOON ° ′	v or d ′	Corrn ′	v or d ′	Corrn ′	v or d ′	Corrn ′
00	14 30·0	14 32·4	13 50·4	0·0	0·0	6·0	5·9	12·0	11·7
01	14 30·3	14 32·6	13 50·6	0·1	0·1	6·1	5·9	12·1	11·8
02	14 30·5	14 32·9	13 50·8	0·2	0·2	6·2	6·0	12·2	11·9
03	14 30·8	14 33·1	13 51·1	0·3	0·3	6·3	6·1	12·3	12·0
04	14 31·0	14 33·4	13 51·3	0·4	0·4	6·4	6·2	12·4	12·1
05	14 31·3	14 33·6	13 51·6	0·5	0·5	6·5	6·3	12·5	12·2
06	14 31·5	14 33·9	13 51·8	0·6	0·6	6·6	6·4	12·6	12·3
07	14 31·8	14 34·1	13 52·0	0·7	0·7	6·7	6·5	12·7	12·4
08	14 32·0	14 34·4	13 52·3	0·8	0·8	6·8	6·6	12·8	12·5
09	14 32·3	14 34·6	13 52·5	0·9	0·9	6·9	6·7	12·9	12·6
10	14 32·5	14 34·9	13 52·8	1·0	1·0	7·0	6·8	13·0	12·7
11	14 32·8	14 35·1	13 53·0	1·1	1·1	7·1	6·9	13·1	12·8
12	14 33·0	14 35·4	13 53·2	1·2	1·2	7·2	7·0	13·2	12·9
13	14 33·3	14 35·6	13 53·5	1·3	1·3	7·3	7·1	13·3	13·0
14	14 33·5	14 35·9	13 53·7	1·4	1·4	7·4	7·2	13·4	13·1
15	14 33·8	14 36·1	13 53·9	1·5	1·5	7·5	7·3	13·5	13·2
16	14 34·0	14 36·4	13 54·2	1·6	1·6	7·6	7·4	13·6	13·3
17	14 34·3	14 36·6	13 54·4	1·7	1·7	7·7	7·5	13·7	13·4
18	14 34·5	14 36·9	13 54·7	1·8	1·8	7·8	7·6	13·8	13·5
19	14 34·8	14 37·1	13 54·9	1·9	1·9	7·9	7·7	13·9	13·6
20	14 35·0	14 37·4	13 55·1	2·0	2·0	8·0	7·8	14·0	13·7
21	14 35·3	14 37·6	13 55·4	2·1	2·0	8·1	7·9	14·1	13·7
22	14 35·5	14 37·9	13 55·6	2·2	2·1	8·2	8·0	14·2	13·8
23	14 35·8	14 38·1	13 55·9	2·3	2·2	8·3	8·1	14·3	13·9
24	14 36·0	14 38·4	13 56·1	2·4	2·3	8·4	8·2	14·4	14·0
25	14 36·3	14 38·6	13 56·3	2·5	2·4	8·5	8·3	14·5	14·1
26	14 36·5	14 38·9	13 56·6	2·6	2·5	8·6	8·4	14·6	14·2
27	14 36·8	14 39·2	13 56·8	2·7	2·6	8·7	8·5	14·7	14·3
28	14 37·0	14 39·4	13 57·0	2·8	2·7	8·8	8·6	14·8	14·4
29	14 37·3	14 39·7	13 57·3	2·9	2·8	8·9	8·7	14·9	14·5
30	14 37·5	14 39·9	13 57·5	3·0	2·9	9·0	8·8	15·0	14·6
31	14 37·8	14 40·2	13 57·8	3·1	3·0	9·1	8·9	15·1	14·7
32	14 38·0	14 40·4	13 58·0	3·2	3·1	9·2	9·0	15·2	14·8
33	14 38·3	14 40·7	13 58·2	3·3	3·2	9·3	9·1	15·3	14·9
34	14 38·5	14 40·9	13 58·5	3·4	3·3	9·4	9·2	15·4	15·0
35	14 38·8	14 41·2	13 58·7	3·5	3·4	9·5	9·3	15·5	15·1
36	14 39·0	14 41·4	13 59·0	3·6	3·5	9·6	9·4	15·6	15·2
37	14 39·3	14 41·7	13 59·2	3·7	3·6	9·7	9·5	15·7	15·3
38	14 39·5	14 41·9	13 59·4	3·8	3·7	9·8	9·6	15·8	15·4
39	14 39·8	14 42·2	13 59·7	3·9	3·8	9·9	9·7	15·9	15·5
40	14 40·0	14 42·4	13 59·9	4·0	3·9	10·0	9·8	16·0	15·6
41	14 40·3	14 42·7	14 00·1	4·1	4·0	10·1	9·8	16·1	15·7
42	14 40·5	14 42·9	14 00·4	4·2	4·1	10·2	9·9	16·2	15·8
43	14 40·8	14 43·2	14 00·6	4·3	4·2	10·3	10·0	16·3	15·9
44	14 41·0	14 43·4	14 00·9	4·4	4·3	10·4	10·1	16·4	16·0
45	14 41·3	14 43·7	14 01·1	4·5	4·4	10·5	10·2	16·5	16·1
46	14 41·5	14 43·9	14 01·3	4·6	4·5	10·6	10·3	16·6	16·2
47	14 41·8	14 44·2	14 01·6	4·7	4·6	10·7	10·4	16·7	16·3
48	14 42·0	14 44·4	14 01·8	4·8	4·7	10·8	10·5	16·8	16·4
49	14 42·3	14 44·7	14 02·1	4·9	4·8	10·9	10·6	16·9	16·5
50	14 42·5	14 44·9	14 02·3	5·0	4·9	11·0	10·7	17·0	16·6
51	14 42·8	14 45·2	14 02·5	5·1	5·0	11·1	10·8	17·1	16·7
52	14 43·0	14 45·4	14 02·8	5·2	5·1	11·2	10·9	17·2	16·8
53	14 43·3	14 45·7	14 03·0	5·3	5·2	11·3	11·0	17·3	16·9
54	14 43·5	14 45·9	14 03·3	5·4	5·3	11·4	11·1	17·4	17·0
55	14 43·8	14 46·2	14 03·5	5·5	5·4	11·5	11·2	17·5	17·1
56	14 44·0	14 46·4	14 03·7	5·6	5·5	11·6	11·3	17·6	17·2
57	14 44·3	14 46·7	14 04·0	5·7	5·6	11·7	11·4	17·7	17·3
58	14 44·5	14 46·9	14 04·2	5·8	5·7	11·8	11·5	17·8	17·4
59	14 44·8	14 47·2	14 04·4	5·9	5·8	11·9	11·6	17·9	17·5
60	14 45·0	14 47·4	14 04·7	6·0	5·9	12·0	11·7	18·0	17·6

59m s	SUN PLANETS ° ′	ARIES ° ′	MOON ° ′	v or d ′	Corrn ′	v or d ′	Corrn ′	v or d ′	Corrn ′
00	14 45·0	14 47·4	14 04·7	0·0	0·0	6·0	6·0	12·0	11·9
01	14 45·3	14 47·7	14 04·9	0·1	0·1	6·1	6·0	12·1	12·0
02	14 45·5	14 47·9	14 05·2	0·2	0·2	6·2	6·1	12·2	12·1
03	14 45·8	14 48·2	14 05·4	0·3	0·3	6·3	6·2	12·3	12·2
04	14 46·0	14 48·4	14 05·6	0·4	0·4	6·4	6·3	12·4	12·3
05	14 46·3	14 48·7	14 05·9	0·5	0·5	6·5	6·4	12·5	12·4
06	14 46·5	14 48·9	14 06·1	0·6	0·6	6·6	6·5	12·6	12·5
07	14 46·8	14 49·2	14 06·4	0·7	0·7	6·7	6·6	12·7	12·6
08	14 47·0	14 49·4	14 06·6	0·8	0·8	6·8	6·7	12·8	12·7
09	14 47·3	14 49·7	14 06·8	0·9	0·9	6·9	6·8	12·9	12·8
10	14 47·5	14 49·9	14 07·1	1·0	1·0	7·0	6·9	13·0	12·9
11	14 47·8	14 50·2	14 07·3	1·1	1·1	7·1	7·0	13·1	13·0
12	14 48·0	14 50·4	14 07·5	1·2	1·2	7·2	7·1	13·2	13·1
13	14 48·3	14 50·7	14 07·8	1·3	1·3	7·3	7·2	13·3	13·2
14	14 48·5	14 50·9	14 08·0	1·4	1·4	7·4	7·3	13·4	13·3
15	14 48·8	14 51·2	14 08·3	1·5	1·5	7·5	7·4	13·5	13·4
16	14 49·0	14 51·4	14 08·5	1·6	1·6	7·6	7·5	13·6	13·5
17	14 49·3	14 51·7	14 08·7	1·7	1·7	7·7	7·6	13·7	13·6
18	14 49·5	14 51·9	14 09·0	1·8	1·8	7·8	7·7	13·8	13·7
19	14 49·8	14 52·2	14 09·2	1·9	1·9	7·9	7·8	13·9	13·8
20	14 50·0	14 52·4	14 09·5	2·0	2·0	8·0	7·9	14·0	13·9
21	14 50·3	14 52·7	14 09·7	2·1	2·1	8·1	8·0	14·1	14·0
22	14 50·5	14 52·9	14 09·9	2·2	2·2	8·2	8·1	14·2	14·1
23	14 50·8	14 53·2	14 10·2	2·3	2·3	8·3	8·2	14·3	14·2
24	14 51·0	14 53·4	14 10·4	2·4	2·4	8·4	8·3	14·4	14·3
25	14 51·3	14 53·7	14 10·6	2·5	2·5	8·5	8·4	14·5	14·4
26	14 51·5	14 53·9	14 10·9	2·6	2·6	8·6	8·5	14·6	14·5
27	14 51·8	14 54·2	14 11·1	2·7	2·7	8·7	8·6	14·7	14·6
28	14 52·0	14 54·4	14 11·4	2·8	2·8	8·8	8·7	14·8	14·7
29	14 52·3	14 54·7	14 11·6	2·9	2·9	8·9	8·8	14·9	14·8
30	14 52·5	14 54·9	14 11·8	3·0	3·0	9·0	8·9	15·0	14·9
31	14 52·8	14 55·2	14 12·1	3·1	3·1	9·1	9·0	15·1	15·0
32	14 53·0	14 55·4	14 12·3	3·2	3·2	9·2	9·1	15·2	15·1
33	14 53·3	14 55·7	14 12·6	3·3	3·3	9·3	9·2	15·3	15·2
34	14 53·5	14 55·9	14 12·8	3·4	3·4	9·4	9·3	15·4	15·3
35	14 53·8	14 56·2	14 13·0	3·5	3·5	9·5	9·4	15·5	15·4
36	14 54·0	14 56·4	14 13·3	3·6	3·6	9·6	9·5	15·6	15·5
37	14 54·3	14 56·7	14 13·5	3·7	3·7	9·7	9·6	15·7	15·6
38	14 54·5	14 56·9	14 13·8	3·8	3·8	9·8	9·7	15·8	15·7
39	14 54·8	14 57·2	14 14·0	3·9	3·9	9·9	9·8	15·9	15·8
40	14 55·0	14 57·5	14 14·2	4·0	4·0	10·0	9·9	16·0	15·9
41	14 55·3	14 57·7	14 14·5	4·1	4·1	10·1	10·0	16·1	16·0
42	14 55·5	14 58·0	14 14·7	4·2	4·2	10·2	10·1	16·2	16·1
43	14 55·8	14 58·2	14 14·9	4·3	4·3	10·3	10·2	16·3	16·2
44	14 56·0	14 58·5	14 15·2	4·4	4·4	10·4	10·3	16·4	16·3
45	14 56·3	14 58·7	14 15·4	4·5	4·5	10·5	10·4	16·5	16·4
46	14 56·5	14 59·0	14 15·7	4·6	4·6	10·6	10·5	16·6	16·5
47	14 56·8	14 59·2	14 15·9	4·7	4·7	10·7	10·6	16·7	16·6
48	14 57·0	14 59·5	14 16·1	4·8	4·8	10·8	10·7	16·8	16·7
49	14 57·3	14 59·7	14 16·4	4·9	4·9	10·9	10·8	16·9	16·8
50	14 57·5	15 00·0	14 16·6	5·0	5·0	11·0	10·9	17·0	16·9
51	14 57·8	15 00·2	14 16·9	5·1	5·1	11·1	11·0	17·1	17·0
52	14 58·0	15 00·5	14 17·1	5·2	5·2	11·2	11·1	17·2	17·1
53	14 58·3	15 00·7	14 17·3	5·3	5·3	11·3	11·2	17·3	17·2
54	14 58·5	15 01·0	14 17·6	5·4	5·4	11·4	11·3	17·4	17·3
55	14 58·8	15 01·2	14 17·8	5·5	5·5	11·5	11·4	17·5	17·4
56	14 59·0	15 01·5	14 18·0	5·6	5·6	11·6	11·5	17·6	17·5
57	14 59·3	15 01·7	14 18·3	5·7	5·7	11·7	11·6	17·7	17·6
58	14 59·5	15 02·0	14 18·5	5·8	5·8	11·8	11·7	17·8	17·7
59	14 59·8	15 02·2	14 18·8	5·9	5·9	11·9	11·8	17·9	17·8
60	15 00·0	15 02·5	14 19·0	6·0	6·0	12·0	11·9	18·0	17·9

TABLES FOR INTERPOLATING SUNRISE, MOONRISE, ETC.

TABLE I—FOR LATITUDE

Tabular Interval			Difference between the times for consecutive latitudes															
10°	5°	2°	5^m	10^m	15^m	20^m	25^m	30^m	35^m	40^m	45^m	50^m	55^m	60^m	1^h05^m	1^h10^m	1^h15^m	1^h20^m
° ′	° ′	° ′	m	m	m	m	m	m	m	m	m	m	m	m	h m	h m	h m	h m
0 30	**0 15**	**0 06**	0	0	1	1	1	1	1	2	2	2	2	2	0 02	0 02	0 02	0 02
1 00	**0 30**	**0 12**	0	1	1	2	2	3	3	3	4	4	4	5	05	05	05	05
1 30	**0 45**	**0 18**	1	1	2	3	3	4	4	5	5	6	7	7	07	07	07	07
2 00	**1 00**	**0 24**	1	2	3	4	5	5	6	7	7	8	9	10	10	10	10	10
2 30	**1 15**	**0 30**	1	2	4	5	6	7	8	9	9	10	11	12	12	13	13	13
3 00	**1 30**	**0 36**	1	3	4	6	7	8	9	10	11	12	13	14	0 15	0 15	0 16	0 16
3 30	**1 45**	**0 42**	2	3	5	7	8	10	11	12	13	14	16	17	18	18	19	19
4 00	**2 00**	**0 48**	2	4	6	8	9	11	13	14	15	16	18	19	20	21	22	22
4 30	**2 15**	**0 54**	2	4	7	9	11	13	15	16	18	19	21	22	23	24	25	26
5 00	**2 30**	**1 00**	2	5	7	10	12	14	16	18	20	22	23	25	26	27	28	29
5 30	**2 45**	**1 06**	3	5	8	11	13	16	18	20	22	24	26	28	0 29	0 30	0 31	0 32
6 00	**3 00**	**1 12**	3	6	9	12	14	17	20	22	24	26	29	31	32	33	34	36
6 30	**3 15**	**1 18**	3	6	10	13	16	19	22	24	26	29	31	34	36	37	38	40
7 00	**3 30**	**1 24**	3	7	10	14	17	20	23	26	29	31	34	37	39	41	42	44
7 30	**3 45**	**1 30**	4	7	11	15	18	22	25	28	31	34	37	40	43	44	46	48
8 00	**4 00**	**1 36**	4	8	12	16	20	23	27	30	34	37	41	44	0 47	0 48	0 51	0 53
8 30	**4 15**	**1 42**	4	8	13	17	21	25	29	33	36	40	44	48	0 51	0 53	0 56	0 58
9 00	**4 30**	**1 48**	4	9	13	18	22	27	31	35	39	43	47	52	0 55	0 58	1 01	1 04
9 30	**4 45**	**1 54**	5	9	14	19	24	28	33	38	42	47	51	56	1 00	1 04	1 08	1 12
10 00	**5 00**	**2 00**	5	10	15	20	25	30	35	40	45	50	55	60	1 05	1 10	1 15	1 20

Table I is for interpolating the LMT of sunrise, twilight, moonrise, etc., for latitude. It is to be entered, in the appropriate column on the left, with the difference between true latitude and the nearest tabular latitude which is *less* than the true latitude; and with the argument at the top which is the nearest value of the difference between the times for the tabular latitude and the next higher one; the correction so obtained is applied to the time for the tabular latitude; the sign of the correction can be seen by inspection. It is to be noted that the interpolation is not linear, so that when using this table it is essential to take out the tabular phenomenon for the latitude *less* than the true latitude.

TABLE II—FOR LONGITUDE

Long. East or West	Difference between the times for given date and preceding date (for east longitude) or for given date and following date (for west longitude)																	
	10^m	20^m	30^m	40^m	50^m	60^m	1^h+10^m	20^m	30^m	1^h+40^m	50^m	60^m	2^h10^m	2^h20^m	2^h30^m	2^h40^m	2^h50^m	3^h00^m
°	m	m	m	m	m	m	m	m	m	m	m	m	h m	h m	h m	h m	h m	h m
0	0	0	0	0	0	0	0	0	0	0	0	0	0 00	0 00	0 00	0 00	0 00	0 00
10	0	1	1	1	1	2	2	2	2	3	3	3	04	04	04	04	05	05
20	1	1	2	2	3	3	4	4	5	6	6	7	07	08	08	09	09	10
30	1	2	2	3	4	5	6	7	7	8	9	10	11	12	12	13	14	15
40	1	2	3	4	6	7	8	9	10	11	12	13	14	16	17	18	19	20
50	1	3	4	6	7	8	10	11	12	14	15	17	0 18	0 19	0 21	0 22	0 24	0 25
60	2	3	5	7	8	10	12	13	15	17	18	20	22	23	25	27	28	30
70	2	4	6	8	10	12	14	16	17	19	21	23	25	27	29	31	33	35
80	2	4	7	9	11	13	16	18	20	22	24	27	29	31	33	36	38	40
90	2	5	7	10	12	15	17	20	22	25	27	30	32	35	37	40	42	45
100	3	6	8	11	14	17	19	22	25	28	31	33	0 36	0 39	0 42	0 44	0 47	0 50
110	3	6	9	12	15	18	21	24	27	31	34	37	40	43	46	49	0 52	0 55
120	3	7	10	13	17	20	23	27	30	33	37	40	43	47	50	53	0 57	1 00
130	4	7	11	14	18	22	25	29	32	36	40	43	47	51	54	0 58	1 01	1 05
140	4	8	12	16	19	23	27	31	35	39	43	47	51	54	0 58	1 02	1 06	1 10
150	4	8	13	17	21	25	29	33	38	42	46	50	0 54	0 58	1 03	1 07	1 11	1 15
160	4	9	13	18	22	27	31	36	40	44	49	53	0 58	1 02	1 07	1 11	1 16	1 20
170	5	9	14	19	24	28	33	38	42	47	52	57	1 01	1 06	1 11	1 16	1 20	1 25
180	5	10	15	20	25	30	35	40	45	50	55	60	1 05	1 10	1 15	1 20	1 25	1 30

Table II is for interpolating the LMT of moonrise, moonset and the Moon's meridian passage for longitude. It is entered with longitude and with the difference between the times for the given date and for the preceding date (in east longitudes) or following date (in west longitudes). The correction is normally *added* for west longitudes and *subtracted* for east longitudes, but if, as occasionally happens, the times become earlier each day instead of later, the signs of the corrections must be reversed.

INDEX TO SELECTED STARS, 2017

Name	No	Mag	SHA °	Dec °
Acamar	**7**	3·2	315	S 40
Achernar	**5**	0·5	335	S 57
Acrux	**30**	1·3	173	S 63
Adhara	**19**	1·5	255	S 29
Aldebaran	**10**	0·9	291	N 17
Alioth	**32**	1·8	166	N 56
Alkaid	**34**	1·9	153	N 49
Al Na'ir	**55**	1·7	28	S 47
Alnilam	**15**	1·7	276	S 1
Alphard	**25**	2·0	218	S 9
Alphecca	**41**	2·2	126	N 27
Alpheratz	**1**	2·1	358	N 29
Altair	**51**	0·8	62	N 9
Ankaa	**2**	2·4	353	S 42
Antares	**42**	1·0	112	S 26
Arcturus	**37**	0·0	146	N 19
Atria	**43**	1·9	107	S 69
Avior	**22**	1·9	234	S 60
Bellatrix	**13**	1·6	278	N 6
Betelgeuse	**16**	Var.*	271	N 7
Canopus	**17**	−0·7	264	S 53
Capella	**12**	0·1	281	N 46
Deneb	**53**	1·3	49	N 45
Denebola	**28**	2·1	183	N 14
Diphda	**4**	2·0	349	S 18
Dubhe	**27**	1·8	194	N 62
Elnath	**14**	1·7	278	N 29
Eltanin	**47**	2·2	91	N 51
Enif	**54**	2·4	34	N 10
Fomalhaut	**56**	1·2	15	S 30
Gacrux	**31**	1·6	172	S 57
Gienah	**29**	2·6	176	S 18
Hadar	**35**	0·6	149	S 60
Hamal	**6**	2·0	328	N 24
Kaus Australis	**48**	1·9	84	S 34
Kochab	**40**	2·1	137	N 74
Markab	**57**	2·5	14	N 15
Menkar	**8**	2·5	314	N 4
Menkent	**36**	2·1	148	S 36
Miaplacidus	**24**	1·7	222	S 70
Mirfak	**9**	1·8	309	N 50
Nunki	**50**	2·0	76	S 26
Peacock	**52**	1·9	53	S 57
Pollux	**21**	1·1	243	N 28
Procyon	**20**	0·4	245	N 5
Rasalhague	**46**	2·1	96	N 13
Regulus	**26**	1·4	208	N 12
Rigel	**11**	0·1	281	S 8
Rigil Kentaurus	**38**	−0·3	140	S 61
Sabik	**44**	2·4	102	S 16
Schedar	**3**	2·2	350	N 57
Shaula	**45**	1·6	96	S 37
Sirius	**18**	−1·5	259	S 17
Spica	**33**	1·0	158	S 11
Suhail	**23**	2·2	223	S 44
Vega	**49**	0·0	81	N 39
Zubenelgenubi	**39**	2·8	137	S 16

No	Name	Mag	SHA °	Dec °
1	*Alpheratz*	2·1	358	N 29
2	*Ankaa*	2·4	353	S 42
3	*Schedar*	2·2	350	N 57
4	*Diphda*	2·0	349	S 18
5	*Achernar*	0·5	335	S 57
6	*Hamal*	2·0	328	N 24
7	*Acamar*	3·2	315	S 40
8	*Menkar*	2·5	314	N 4
9	*Mirfak*	1·8	309	N 50
10	*Aldebaran*	0·9	291	N 17
11	*Rigel*	0·1	281	S 8
12	*Capella*	0·1	281	N 46
13	*Bellatrix*	1·6	278	N 6
14	*Elnath*	1·7	278	N 29
15	*Alnilam*	1·7	276	S 1
16	*Betelgeuse*	Var.*	271	N 7
17	*Canopus*	−0·7	264	S 53
18	*Sirius*	−1·5	259	S 17
19	*Adhara*	1·5	255	S 29
20	*Procyon*	0·4	245	N 5
21	*Pollux*	1·1	243	N 28
22	*Avior*	1·9	234	S 60
23	*Suhail*	2·2	223	S 44
24	*Miaplacidus*	1·7	222	S 70
25	*Alphard*	2·0	218	S 9
26	*Regulus*	1·4	208	N 12
27	*Dubhe*	1·8	194	N 62
28	*Denebola*	2·1	183	N 14
29	*Gienah*	2·6	176	S 18
30	*Acrux*	1·3	173	S 63
31	*Gacrux*	1·6	172	S 57
32	*Alioth*	1·8	166	N 56
33	*Spica*	1·0	158	S 11
34	*Alkaid*	1·9	153	N 49
35	*Hadar*	0·6	149	S 60
36	*Menkent*	2·1	148	S 36
37	*Arcturus*	0·0	146	N 19
38	*Rigil Kentaurus*	−0·3	140	S 61
39	*Zubenelgenubi*	2·8	137	S 16
40	*Kochab*	2·1	137	N 74
41	*Alphecca*	2·2	126	N 27
42	*Antares*	1·0	112	S 26
43	*Atria*	1·9	107	S 69
44	*Sabik*	2·4	102	S 16
45	*Shaula*	1·6	96	S 37
46	*Rasalhague*	2·1	96	N 13
47	*Eltanin*	2·2	91	N 51
48	*Kaus Australis*	1·9	84	S 34
49	*Vega*	0·0	81	N 39
50	*Nunki*	2·0	76	S 26
51	*Altair*	0·8	62	N 9
52	*Peacock*	1·9	53	S 57
53	*Deneb*	1·3	49	N 45
54	*Enif*	2·4	34	N 10
55	*Al Na'ir*	1·7	28	S 47
56	*Fomalhaut*	1·2	15	S 30
57	*Markab*	2·5	14	N 15

*0·1 — 1·2

ALTITUDE CORRECTION TABLES 0°–35°— MOON

App. Alt.	0°–4° Corrⁿ	5°–9° Corrⁿ	10°–14° Corrⁿ	15°–19° Corrⁿ	20°–24° Corrⁿ	25°–29° Corrⁿ	30°–34° Corrⁿ	App. Alt.
′	° ′	° ′	° ′	° ′	° ′	° ′	° ′	′
00	0 34·5	5 58·2	10 62·1	15 62·8	20 62·2	25 60·8	30 58·9	00
10	36·5	58·5	62·2	62·8	62·2	60·8	58·8	10
20	38·3	58·7	62·2	62·8	62·1	60·7	58·8	20
30	40·0	58·9	62·3	62·8	62·1	60·7	58·7	30
40	41·5	59·1	62·3	62·8	62·0	60·6	58·6	40
50	42·9	59·3	62·4	62·7	62·0	60·6	58·5	50
00	1 44·2	6 59·5	11 62·4	16 62·7	21 62·0	26 60·5	31 58·5	00
10	45·4	59·7	62·4	62·7	61·9	60·4	58·4	10
20	46·5	59·9	62·5	62·7	61·9	60·4	58·3	20
30	47·5	60·0	62·5	62·7	61·9	60·3	58·2	30
40	48·4	60·2	62·5	62·7	61·8	60·3	58·2	40
50	49·3	60·3	62·6	62·7	61·8	60·2	58·1	50
00	2 50·1	7 60·5	12 62·6	17 62·7	22 61·7	27 60·1	32 58·0	00
10	50·8	60·6	62·6	62·6	61·7	60·1	57·9	10
20	51·5	60·7	62·6	62·6	61·6	60·0	57·8	20
30	52·2	60·9	62·7	62·6	61·6	59·9	57·8	30
40	52·8	61·0	62·7	62·6	61·6	59·9	57·7	40
50	53·4	61·1	62·7	62·6	61·5	59·8	57·6	50
00	3 53·9	8 61·2	13 62·7	18 62·5	23 61·5	28 59·7	33 57·5	00
10	54·4	61·3	62·7	62·5	61·4	59·7	57·4	10
20	54·9	61·4	62·7	62·5	61·4	59·6	57·4	20
30	55·3	61·5	62·8	62·5	61·3	59·5	57·3	30
40	55·7	61·6	62·8	62·4	61·3	59·5	57·2	40
50	56·1	61·6	62·8	62·4	61·2	59·4	57·1	50
00	4 56·4	9 61·7	14 62·8	19 62·4	24 61·2	29 59·3	34 57·0	00
10	56·8	61·8	62·8	62·4	61·1	59·3	56·9	10
20	57·1	61·9	62·8	62·3	61·1	59·2	56·9	20
30	57·4	61·9	62·8	62·3	61·0	59·1	56·8	30
40	57·7	62·0	62·8	62·3	61·0	59·1	56·7	40
50	58·0	62·1	62·8	62·2	60·9	59·0	56·6	50

HP	L	U	L	U	L	U	L	U	L	U	L	U	L	U	HP
′	′	′	′	′	′	′	′	′	′	′	′	′	′	′	′
54·0	0·3	0·9	0·3	0·9	0·4	1·0	0·5	1·1	0·6	1·2	0·7	1·3	0·9	1·5	54·0
54·3	0·7	1·1	0·7	1·2	0·8	1·2	0·8	1·3	0·9	1·4	1·1	1·5	1·2	1·7	54·3
54·6	1·1	1·4	1·1	1·4	1·1	1·4	1·2	1·5	1·3	1·6	1·4	1·7	1·5	1·8	54·6
54·9	1·4	1·6	1·5	1·6	1·5	1·6	1·6	1·7	1·6	1·8	1·8	1·9	1·9	2·0	54·9
55·2	1·8	1·8	1·8	1·8	1·9	1·8	1·9	1·9	2·0	2·0	2·1	2·1	2·2	2·2	55·2
55·5	2·2	2·0	2·2	2·0	2·3	2·1	2·3	2·1	2·4	2·2	2·4	2·3	2·5	2·4	55·5
55·8	2·6	2·2	2·6	2·2	2·6	2·3	2·7	2·3	2·7	2·4	2·8	2·4	2·9	2·5	55·8
56·1	3·0	2·4	3·0	2·5	3·0	2·5	3·0	2·5	3·1	2·6	3·1	2·6	3·2	2·7	56·1
56·4	3·3	2·7	3·4	2·7	3·4	2·7	3·4	2·7	3·4	2·8	3·5	2·8	3·5	2·9	56·4
56·7	3·7	2·9	3·7	2·9	3·8	2·9	3·8	2·9	3·8	3·0	3·8	3·0	3·9	3·0	56·7
57·0	4·1	3·1	4·1	3·1	4·1	3·1	4·1	3·1	4·2	3·2	4·2	3·2	4·2	3·2	57·0
57·3	4·5	3·3	4·5	3·3	4·5	3·3	4·5	3·3	4·5	3·3	4·5	3·4	4·6	3·4	57·3
57·6	4·9	3·5	4·9	3·5	4·9	3·5	4·9	3·5	4·9	3·5	4·9	3·5	4·9	3·6	57·6
57·9	5·3	3·8	5·3	3·8	5·2	3·8	5·2	3·7	5·2	3·7	5·2	3·7	5·2	3·7	57·9
58·2	5·6	4·0	5·6	4·0	5·6	4·0	5·6	4·0	5·6	3·9	5·6	3·9	5·6	3·9	58·2
58·5	6·0	4·2	6·0	4·2	6·0	4·2	6·0	4·2	6·0	4·1	5·9	4·1	5·9	4·1	58·5
58·8	6·4	4·4	6·4	4·4	6·4	4·4	6·3	4·4	6·3	4·3	6·3	4·3	6·2	4·2	58·8
59·1	6·8	4·6	6·8	4·6	6·7	4·6	6·7	4·6	6·7	4·5	6·6	4·5	6·6	4·4	59·1
59·4	7·2	4·8	7·1	4·8	7·1	4·8	7·1	4·8	7·0	4·7	7·0	4·7	6·9	4·6	59·4
59·7	7·5	5·1	7·5	5·0	7·5	5·0	7·5	5·0	7·4	4·9	7·3	4·8	7·2	4·8	59·7
60·0	7·9	5·3	7·9	5·3	7·9	5·2	7·8	5·2	7·8	5·1	7·7	5·0	7·6	4·9	60·0
60·3	8·3	5·5	8·3	5·5	8·2	5·4	8·2	5·4	8·1	5·3	8·0	5·2	7·9	5·1	60·3
60·6	8·7	5·7	8·7	5·7	8·6	5·7	8·6	5·6	8·5	5·5	8·4	5·4	8·2	5·3	60·6
60·9	9·1	5·9	9·0	5·9	9·0	5·9	8·9	5·8	8·8	5·7	8·7	5·6	8·6	5·4	60·9
61·2	9·5	6·2	9·4	6·1	9·4	6·1	9·3	6·0	9·2	5·9	9·1	5·8	8·9	5·6	61·2
61·5	9·8	6·4	9·8	6·3	9·7	6·3	9·7	6·2	9·5	6·1	9·4	5·9	9·2	5·8	61·5

DIP

Ht. of Eye	Corrⁿ	Ht. of Eye	Ht. of Eye	Corrⁿ	Ht. of Eye
m		ft.	m		ft.
2·4		8·0	9·5		31·5
	−2′·8			−5′·5	
2·6		8·6	9·9		32·7
	−2·9			−5·6	
2·8		9·2	10·3		33·9
	−3·0			−5·7	
3·0		9·8	10·6		35·1
	−3·1			−5·8	
3·2		10·5	11·0		36·3
	−3·2			−5·9	
3·4		11·2	11·4		37·6
	−3·3			−6·0	
3·6		11·9	11·8		38·9
	−3·4			−6·1	
3·8		12·6	12·2		40·1
	−3·5			−6·2	
4·0		13·3	12·6		41·5
	−3·6			−6·3	
4·3		14·1	13·0		42·8
	−3·7			−6·4	
4·5		14·9	13·4		44·2
	−3·8			−6·5	
4·7		15·7	13·8		45·5
	−3·9			−6·6	
5·0		16·5	14·2		46·9
	−4·0			−6·7	
5·2		17·4	14·7		48·4
	−4·1			−6·8	
5·5		18·3	15·1		49·8
	−4·2			−6·9	
5·8		19·1	15·5		51·3
	−4·3			−7·0	
6·1		20·1	16·0		52·8
	−4·4			−7·1	
6·3		21·0	16·5		54·3
	−4·5			−7·2	
6·6		22·0	16·9		55·8
	−4·6			−7·3	
6·9		22·9	17·4		57·4
	−4·7			−7·4	
7·2		23·9	17·9		58·9
	−4·8			−7·5	
7·5		24·9	18·4		60·5
	−4·9			−7·6	
7·9		26·0	18·8		62·1
	−5·0			−7·7	
8·2		27·1	19·3		63·8
	−5·1			−7·8	
8·5		28·1	19·8		65·4
	−5·2			−7·9	
8·8		29·2	20·4		67·1
	−5·3			−8·0	
9·2		30·4	20·9		68·8
	−5·4			−8·1	
9·5		31·5	21·4		70·5

MOON CORRECTION TABLE

The correction is in two parts; the first correction is taken from the upper part of the table with argument apparent altitude, and the second from the lower part, with argument HP, in the same column as that from which the first correction was taken. Separate corrections are given in the lower part for lower (L) and upper(U) limbs. All corrections are to be **added** to apparent altitude, *but 30′ is to be subtracted from the altitude of the upper limb.*

For corrections for pressure and temperature see page A4.

For bubble sextant observations ignore dip, take the mean of upper and lower limb corrections and subtract 15′ from the altitude.

App. Alt. = Apparent altitude = Sextant altitude corrected for index error and dip.

ALTITUDE CORRECTION TABLES 35°–90°— MOON

App. Alt.	35°–39° Corr^n	40°–44° Corr^n	45°–49° Corr^n	50°–54° Corr^n	55°–59° Corr^n	60°–64° Corr^n	65°–69° Corr^n	70°–74° Corr^n	75°–79° Corr^n	80°–84° Corr^n	85°–89° Corr^n	App. Alt.
′	° ′	° ′	° ′	° ′	° ′	° ′	° ′	° ′	° ′	° ′	° ′	′
00	**35** 56.5	**40** 53.7	**45** 50.5	**50** 46.9	**55** 43.1	**60** 38.9	**65** 34.6	**70** 30.0	**75** 25.3	**80** 20.5	**85** 15.6	**00**
10	56.4	53.6	50.4	46.8	42.9	38.8	34.4	29.9	25.2	20.4	15.5	**10**
20	56.3	53.5	50.2	46.7	42.8	38.7	34.3	29.7	25.0	20.2	15.3	**20**
30	56.2	53.4	50.1	46.5	42.7	38.5	34.1	29.6	24.9	20.0	15.1	**30**
40	56.2	53.3	50.0	46.4	42.5	38.4	34.0	29.4	24.7	19.9	15.0	**40**
50	56.1	53.2	49.9	46.3	42.4	38.2	33.8	29.3	24.5	19.7	14.8	**50**
00	**36** 56.0	**41** 53.1	**46** 49.8	**51** 46.2	**56** 42.3	**61** 38.1	**66** 33.7	**71** 29.1	**76** 24.4	**81** 19.6	**86** 14.6	**00**
10	55.9	53.0	49.7	46.0	42.1	37.9	33.5	29.0	24.2	19.4	14.5	**10**
20	55.8	52.9	49.5	45.9	42.0	37.8	33.4	28.8	24.1	19.2	14.3	**20**
30	55.7	52.8	49.4	45.8	41.9	37.7	33.2	28.7	23.9	19.1	14.2	**30**
40	55.6	52.6	49.3	45.7	41.7	37.5	33.1	28.5	23.8	18.9	14.0	**40**
50	55.5	52.5	49.2	45.5	41.6	37.4	32.9	28.3	23.6	18.7	13.8	**50**
00	**37** 55.4	**42** 52.4	**47** 49.1	**52** 45.4	**57** 41.4	**62** 37.2	**67** 32.8	**72** 28.2	**77** 23.4	**82** 18.6	**87** 13.7	**00**
10	55.3	52.3	49.0	45.3	41.3	37.1	32.6	28.0	23.3	18.4	13.5	**10**
20	55.2	52.2	48.8	45.2	41.2	36.9	32.5	27.9	23.1	18.2	13.3	**20**
30	55.1	52.1	48.7	45.0	41.0	36.8	32.3	27.7	22.9	18.1	13.2	**30**
40	55.0	52.0	48.6	44.9	40.9	36.6	32.2	27.6	22.8	17.9	13.0	**40**
50	55.0	51.9	48.5	44.8	40.8	36.5	32.0	27.4	22.6	17.8	12.8	**50**
00	**38** 54.9	**43** 51.8	**48** 48.4	**53** 44.6	**58** 40.6	**63** 36.4	**68** 31.9	**73** 27.2	**78** 22.5	**83** 17.6	**88** 12.7	**00**
10	54.8	51.7	48.3	44.5	40.5	36.2	31.7	27.1	22.3	17.4	12.5	**10**
20	54.7	51.6	48.1	44.4	40.3	36.1	31.6	26.9	22.1	17.3	12.3	**20**
30	54.6	51.5	48.0	44.2	40.2	35.9	31.4	26.8	22.0	17.1	12.2	**30**
40	54.5	51.4	47.9	44.1	40.1	35.8	31.3	26.6	21.8	16.9	12.0	**40**
50	54.4	51.2	47.8	44.0	39.9	35.6	31.1	26.5	21.7	16.8	11.8	**50**
00	**39** 54.3	**44** 51.1	**49** 47.7	**54** 43.9	**59** 39.8	**64** 35.5	**69** 31.0	**74** 26.3	**79** 21.5	**84** 16.6	**89** 11.7	**00**
10	54.2	51.0	47.5	43.7	39.6	35.3	30.8	26.1	21.3	16.4	11.5	**10**
20	54.1	50.9	47.4	43.6	39.5	35.2	30.7	26.0	21.2	16.3	11.4	**20**
30	54.0	50.8	47.3	43.5	39.4	35.0	30.5	25.8	21.0	16.1	11.2	**30**
40	53.9	50.7	47.2	43.3	39.2	34.9	30.4	25.7	20.9	16.0	11.0	**40**
50	53.8	50.6	47.0	43.2	39.1	34.7	30.2	25.5	20.7	15.8	10.9	**50**

HP	L U	L U	L U	L U	L U	L U	L U	L U	L U	L U	L U	HP
′	′ ′	′ ′	′ ′	′ ′	′ ′	′ ′	′ ′	′ ′	′ ′	′ ′	′ ′	′
54.0	1.1 1.7	1.3 1.9	1.5 2.1	1.7 2.4	2.0 2.6	2.3 2.9	2.6 3.2	2.9 3.5	3.2 3.8	3.5 4.1	3.8 4.5	**54.0**
54.3	1.4 1.8	1.6 2.0	1.8 2.2	2.0 2.5	2.2 2.7	2.5 3.0	2.8 3.2	3.1 3.5	3.3 3.8	3.6 4.1	3.9 4.4	**54.3**
54.6	1.7 2.0	1.9 2.2	2.1 2.4	2.3 2.6	2.5 2.8	2.7 3.0	3.0 3.3	3.2 3.5	3.5 3.8	3.8 4.0	4.0 4.3	**54.6**
54.9	2.0 2.2	2.2 2.3	2.3 2.5	2.5 2.7	2.7 2.9	2.9 3.1	3.2 3.3	3.4 3.5	3.6 3.8	3.9 4.0	4.1 4.3	**54.9**
55.2	2.3 2.3	2.5 2.4	2.6 2.6	2.8 2.8	3.0 2.9	3.2 3.1	3.4 3.3	3.6 3.5	3.8 3.7	4.0 4.0	4.2 4.2	**55.2**
55.5	2.7 2.5	2.8 2.6	2.9 2.7	3.1 2.9	3.2 3.0	3.4 3.2	3.6 3.4	3.7 3.5	3.9 3.7	4.1 3.9	4.3 4.1	**55.5**
55.8	3.0 2.6	3.1 2.7	3.2 2.8	3.3 3.0	3.5 3.1	3.6 3.3	3.8 3.4	3.9 3.6	4.1 3.7	4.2 3.9	4.4 4.0	**55.8**
56.1	3.3 2.8	3.4 2.9	3.5 3.0	3.6 3.1	3.7 3.2	3.8 3.3	4.0 3.4	4.1 3.6	4.2 3.7	4.4 3.8	4.5 4.0	**56.1**
56.4	3.6 2.9	3.7 3.0	3.8 3.1	3.9 3.2	3.9 3.3	4.0 3.4	4.1 3.5	4.3 3.6	4.4 3.7	4.5 3.8	4.6 3.9	**56.4**
56.7	3.9 3.1	4.0 3.1	4.1 3.2	4.1 3.3	4.2 3.3	4.3 3.4	4.3 3.5	4.4 3.6	4.5 3.7	4.6 3.8	4.7 3.8	**56.7**
57.0	4.3 3.2	4.3 3.3	4.3 3.3	4.4 3.4	4.4 3.4	4.5 3.5	4.5 3.5	4.6 3.6	4.7 3.6	4.7 3.7	4.8 3.8	**57.0**
57.3	4.6 3.4	4.6 3.4	4.6 3.4	4.6 3.5	4.7 3.5	4.7 3.5	4.7 3.6	4.8 3.6	4.8 3.6	4.8 3.7	4.9 3.7	**57.3**
57.6	4.9 3.6	4.9 3.6	4.9 3.6	4.9 3.6	4.9 3.6	4.9 3.6	4.9 3.6	4.9 3.6	5.0 3.6	5.0 3.6	5.0 3.6	**57.6**
57.9	5.2 3.7	5.2 3.7	5.2 3.7	5.2 3.7	5.2 3.7	5.1 3.6	5.1 3.6	5.1 3.6	5.1 3.6	5.1 3.6	5.1 3.6	**57.9**
58.2	5.5 3.9	5.5 3.8	5.5 3.8	5.4 3.8	5.4 3.7	5.4 3.7	5.3 3.7	5.3 3.6	5.2 3.6	5.2 3.5	5.2 3.5	**58.2**
58.5	5.9 4.0	5.8 4.0	5.8 3.9	5.7 3.9	5.6 3.8	5.6 3.8	5.5 3.7	5.5 3.6	5.4 3.6	5.3 3.5	5.3 3.4	**58.5**
58.8	6.2 4.2	6.1 4.1	6.0 4.1	6.0 4.0	5.9 3.9	5.8 3.8	5.7 3.7	5.6 3.6	5.5 3.5	5.4 3.5	5.3 3.4	**58.8**
59.1	6.5 4.3	6.4 4.3	6.3 4.2	6.2 4.1	6.1 4.0	6.0 3.9	5.9 3.8	5.8 3.6	5.7 3.5	5.6 3.4	5.4 3.3	**59.1**
59.4	6.8 4.5	6.7 4.4	6.6 4.3	6.5 4.2	6.4 4.1	6.2 3.9	6.1 3.8	6.0 3.7	5.8 3.5	5.7 3.4	5.5 3.2	**59.4**
59.7	7.1 4.7	7.0 4.5	6.9 4.4	6.8 4.3	6.6 4.1	6.5 4.0	6.3 3.8	6.1 3.7	6.0 3.5	5.8 3.3	5.6 3.2	**59.7**
60.0	7.5 4.8	7.3 4.7	7.2 4.5	7.0 4.4	6.9 4.2	6.7 4.0	6.5 3.9	6.3 3.7	6.1 3.5	5.9 3.3	5.7 3.1	**60.0**
60.3	7.8 5.0	7.6 4.8	7.5 4.7	7.3 4.5	7.1 4.3	6.9 4.1	6.7 3.9	6.5 3.7	6.3 3.5	6.0 3.2	5.8 3.0	**60.3**
60.6	8.1 5.1	7.9 5.0	7.7 4.8	7.6 4.6	7.3 4.4	7.1 4.2	6.9 3.9	6.7 3.7	6.4 3.4	6.2 3.2	5.9 2.9	**60.6**
60.9	8.4 5.3	8.2 5.1	8.0 4.9	7.8 4.7	7.6 4.5	7.3 4.2	7.1 4.0	6.8 3.7	6.6 3.4	6.3 3.2	6.0 2.9	**60.9**
61.2	8.7 5.4	8.5 5.2	8.3 5.0	8.1 4.8	7.8 4.5	7.6 4.3	7.3 4.0	7.0 3.7	6.7 3.4	6.4 3.1	6.1 2.8	**61.2**
61.5	9.1 5.6	8.8 5.4	8.6 5.1	8.3 4.9	8.1 4.6	7.8 4.3	7.5 4.0	7.2 3.7	6.9 3.4	6.5 3.1	6.2 2.7	**61.5**